The Total Spectrum of Technology

Personal Trainer®

Eliminate Grading Homework!

Instructors consistently cite reading the text and completing graded homework assignments as a key to student success in accounting; however, finding time to grade homework is difficult. Personal Trainer solves this time problem by allowing professors to assign textbook exercises and problems. Personal Trainer will grade the homework and then post the grade into a full-blown gradebook, all real time! Personal Trainer is an Internet-based homework tutor where students can complete the textbook homework assignments, receive hints, submit their answers and then receive immediate feedback on their answers. Access certificates for WebTutor™ Advantage with Personal Trainer® can be bundled with the textbook or sold separately. For more information, including a demo, visit http://webtutor.swlearning.com.

Xtra!

This online resource provides lecture enhancement resources and access to games and quizzes so that students can test their understanding of the content. Packaged FREE with a new text, students receive an online access code to receive Xtra! reinforcement in accounting!

Accounting

Concepts & Applications

edition 9

W. Steve Albrecht
PhD, CPA, CIA, CFE
Brigham Young University

James D. Stice
PhD
Brigham Young University

Earl K. Stice
PhD
Brigham Young University

Monte R. Swain
PhD, CPA, CMA
Brigham Young University

THOMSON
SOUTH-WESTERN

Australia · Canada · Mexico · Singapore · Spain · United Kingdom · United States

THOMSON

™

SOUTH-WESTERN

Accounting: Concepts and Applications, 9e
W. Steve Albrecht, James D. Stice, Earl K. Stice, and Monte R. Swain

VP/Editorial Director:
Jack W. Calhoun

VP/Editor-in-Chief:
George Werthman

Executive Editor:
Sharon Oblinger

Developmental Editor:
Carol Bennett

Marketing Manager:
Heather MacMaster

Senior Production Editor:
Kara ZumBahlen

Media Developmental Editor:
Sally Nieman

Media Production Editor:
Kelly Reid

Manufacturing Coordinator:
Doug Wilke

Production House/Composition:
Litten Editing and Production, Inc. and
GGS Information Services

Printer:
Quebecor World, Versailles, KY

Senior Design Project Manager:
Michelle Kunkler

Cover and Internal Designer:
Imbue Design/Kim Torbeck
Cincinnati, OH

Cover Image:
© Farida Zaman/Stock Illustration Source

Photo Researcher:
Stuart Kunkler

For permission to use material from this
text or product, contact us by
Tel (800) 730-2214
Fax (800) 730-2215
http://www.thomsonrights.com

For more information
contact South-Western,
5191 Natorp Boulevard,
Mason, Ohio 45040.
Or you can visit our Internet site at:
http://www.swlearning.com

W. Steve Albrecht

W. Steve Albrecht is the Associate Dean of the Marriott School of Management and Arthur Andersen Professor at Brigham Young University. Dr. Albrecht, a certified public accountant, certified internal auditor, and certified fraud examiner, came to BYU in 1977 after teaching at Stanford and at the University of Illinois. Earlier, he worked as a staff accountant for Deloitte & Touche. Prior to becoming associate dean of the Marriott School, Dr. Albrecht served for eight years as the director of the School of Accountancy and Information Systems at BYU. During that time, BYU's undergraduate and graduate accounting programs were ranked 2nd and 3rd in the United States.

Dr. Albrecht received a bachelor's degree in accounting from Brigham Young University and his MBA and PhD degrees from the University of Wisconsin at Madison. He is past President of the American Accounting Association and the Association of Certified Fraud Examiners. He was a former member of the Board of Regents of the Institute of Internal Auditors and the Board of Directors of the Utah Association of CPAs. He was also president of the Accounting Program Leadership Group (chairs of accounting departments and programs) and served on the task force of the American Institute of CPAs that wrote the fraud auditing standard. He was a member of the Committee of Sponsoring Organizations (COSO) from 1997-2000, is past president of Beta Alpha Psi, the national accounting honors fraternity. He is also a member of the AICPA Council and chairs their Pre-Certification Executive Education Committee.

Dr. Albrecht has done extensive research on business fraud. His research has resulted in the publication of over eighty articles in professional journals. He is the author or co-author of over 20 books or monographs, several of which are on fraud. His financial and principles of accounting textbooks are in their 9th editions. In 2000, he completed a major study (Accounting Education: Charting the Course through a Perilous Future) on the future of accounting education in the United States. He is a frequent speaker on the topics of fraud examination, accounting education, and personal financial planning.

Dr. Albrecht has received numerous awards and honors, including BYU's highest faculty honor, the Karl G. Maeser Distinguished Faculty Lecturer Award for superior scholarship and teaching. He has also received the BYU School of Management's Outstanding Faculty Award, the BYU Outstanding Researcher Award, and was recognized, as part of Utah's Centennial Celebration, as one of 131 Utahans who have made outstanding contributions or brought unusual recognition to the state. He has been recognized by Beta Alpha Psi, the Federation of Schools of Accountancy, and the AICPA as Educator of the Year. He has also received awards for outstanding teaching at Stanford University, the University of Illinois, and the University of Wisconsin. In 1997, 2001, and 2002, he was chosen as one of the 100 most influential accounting professionals in the United States by *Accounting Today* magazine. In 1998, he received the *Cressey Award* from the Association of Certified Fraud Examiners, the highest award given for a lifetime of achievement in fraud detection and deterrence. (Past winners were Jane Bryant Quinn of *Newsweek* magazine and Rudolph Giuliani, past United States Attorney for the Southern District of New York and mayor of New York City.) In 2002, in honor of his contribution in fighting fraud, the Association of Certified Fraud Examiners named one of the buildings at their headquarters after Dr. Albrecht. And in 2001, in recognition of his contributions to BYU and to academia, an anonymous donor endowed the W. Steve Albrecht Professorship in Accounting.

Dr. Albrecht has consulted with numerous organizations, including a variety of Fortune 500 companies, major financial institutions, the United Nations, FBI, and other organizations, and he has been an expert witness in some of the largest fraud cases in America. He currently serves on the audit committees and boards of directors of three public and two private companies.

Dr. Albrecht is married to the former LeAnn Christiansen, and they have six children and six grandchildren.

James D. Stice

James D. Stice is the Distinguished Teaching Professor in the Marriott School of Management at Brigham Young University. He is currently the Director of the Marriott School's MBA Program. He holds bachelor's and master's degrees from BYU and a PhD from the University of Washington, all in accounting. Professor Stice has been on the faculty at BYU since 1988. During that time, he has been selected by graduating accounting students as "Teacher of the Year" on numerous occasions, he was selected by his peers in the Marriott School at BYU to receive the "Outstanding Teaching Award" in 1995, and in 1999 he was selected by the University to receive its highest teaching award, the Maeser Excellence in Teaching Award. Professor Stice is also a visiting professor for INSEAD's MBA Program in France. Professor Stice has published articles in *The Journal of Accounting Research, The Accounting Review, Decision Sciences, Issues in Accounting Education, The CPA Journal*, and other academic and professional journals. In addition to this textbook, he has published two other textbooks: *Financial Accounting: Reporting and Analysis*, and *Intermediate Accounting*. In addition to his teaching and research, Dr. Stice has been involved in executive education for such companies as IBM, Bank of America, and Ernst & Young and currently serves on the board of directors of Nutraceutical Corporation. Dr. Stice and his wife, Kaye, have seven children: Crystal, J.D., Ashley, Whitney, Kara, Skyler, and Cierra.

Earl K. Stice

Earl K. Stice is the PricewaterhouseCoopers Professor of Accounting in the School of Accountancy and Information Systems at Brigham Young University where he has been on the faculty since 1998. He holds bachelor's and master's degrees from Brigham Young University and a PhD from Cornell University. Dr. Stice has taught at Rice University, the University of Arizona, Cornell University, and the Hong Kong University of Science and Technology (HKUST). He won the Phi Beta Kappa teaching award at Rice University and was twice selected at HKUST as one of the ten best lecturers on campus. Dr. Stice has also taught in a variety of executive education and corporate training programs in the United States, Hong Kong, China, and South Africa, and he is currently on the executive MBA faculty of the China Europe International Business School in Shanghai. He has published papers in the *Journal of Financial and Quantitative Analysis, The Accounting Review, Review of Accounting Studies*, and *Issues in Accounting Education*, and his research on stock splits has been cited in *Business Week, Money*, and *Forbes*. Dr. Stice has presented his research results at seminars in the United States, Finland, Taiwan, Australia,

and Hong Kong. He is co-author of *Intermediate Accounting, 15th edition* and *Financial Accounting: Reporting and Analysis, 6th Edition*. Dr. Stice and his wife, Ramona, are the parents of seven children: Derrald, Han, Ryan Marie, Lorien, Lily, Taraz, and Kamila.

Monte R. Swain

Dr. Swain received his PhD in managerial accounting and information systems from Michigan State University. His dissertation, which examined the impact of information load on capital budgeting decision processes, was awarded an Institute of Management Accountants Dissertation Grant. At BYU, Dr. Swain has received the Teaching Excellence Award for Management Skills in 1994, 1995, and 1997; the Marriott School of Management Outstanding Teacher in 1999; and was selected as the Deloitte & Touche Research Fellow in 2001. His research area includes the development and use of computer programs that capture and analyze the interaction of human decision processes and computerized information systems. Additionally, he uses the events-driven business solutions to study the incorporation of activity-based costing, the Balanced Scorecard, and the Theory of Constraints in management information systems. He has published numerous papers in leading academic and practitioner journals, sits on the editorial board for two academic journals, and is a coauthor on a management accounting textbook. Dr. Swain has spent significant time working with or researching organizations such as IBM, Clorox, Deere and Company, the Church of Jesus Christ of Latter-Day Saints, and Habitat for Humanity. He is a Certified Public Accountant and a Certified Management Accountant. Dr. Swain took an academic leave from BYU from July 1999 to July 2000 to serve as the Chief Financial Officer for Authorize.Net (payment-processing service for e-commerce), a wholly owned subsidiary of InfoSpace, Inc. He currently serves as the Associate Director of the School of Accountancy and Information Systems where he is the Deloitte & Touche Professor of Accounting. He and his wife, Shannon, have seven children.

Contents

Thank you for adopting *Accounting: Concepts and Applications, 9e.* Our newest edition provides a perfect balance of procedural and conceptual coverage which gives students a realistic view of how accounting is used by leading companies across the nation. We understand students enter the introductory accounting course with a variety of career goals and learning styles. Balancing the needs of the accounting major and non-accounting major has become increasingly difficult. Our unique text organization, student-oriented pedagogy and innovative technology are designed to better address every student's needs regardless of their career ambitions. We continue to make the text more flexible with each edition; splitting the chapters into basic and expanded material and making it easier for you to select a perfect balance of material essential to your course objectives.

We are confident that *Accounting: Concepts and Applications, 9e* will better prepare your students to make more informed business decisions regardless of their chosen career path.

W. Steve Albrecht
James D. Stice
Earl K. Stice
Monte R. Swain

new features

If you're one of our many loyal adopters, we suggest you review the NEW features we've added to this edition.

If this is the first time you've used this text, you'll want to review everything that makes your decision worthwhile.

New to the Ninth Edition

▶ **INTRODUCTION TO FINANCIAL STATEMENT ANALYSIS – Chapter 5**
Having financial statement numbers is not enough to answer the questions that financial statement users want answered. Chapter 5's innovative and comprehensive objectives are to present financial statement analysis as both a diagnosis—identifying where a firm has problems, and as a prognosis—predicting how a firm will perform in the future.

▶ **MANAGING INVENTORY AND SERVICE COSTS – Chapter 21**
This NEW chapter introduces techniques such as just-in-time (JIT) and other inventory systems that are used to manage inventory in manufacturing, service, and merchandising organizations.

▶ **THE SARBANES-OXLEY ACT OF 2002** has been incorporated throughout the text and the end-of-chapter material. Real-world discussions of companies, such as ARTHUR ANDERSEN, ENRON, WORLDCOM, and TYCO provide the background and reasons for this congressional act and how it impacts financial reporting.

▶ **EARNINGS MANAGEMENT** – In Chapter 6, an expanded discussion on Earnings Management presents the reasons, good and bad, for managing reported earnings.

▶ **CONSOLIDATED FINANCIAL STATEMENTS** – An introduction to Consolidated Financial Statements in Chapter 13 provides the basics for understanding this topic. A simple example shows how consolidation works.

▶ **PRACTICE EXERCISES** – Approximately 20 brief exercises per chapter have been added, perfect for in-class coverage or as an assignment.

▶ **JUDGMENT CALLS** –You Decide! These new and unique end-of-chapter exercises make the student the decision-maker, reinforcing critical thinking and analytical skills.

▶ **PERSONAL TRAINER® 3.0** – Students can complete exercises and problems online and receive immediate feedback with Personal Trainer. Students' results flow directly into your gradebook.

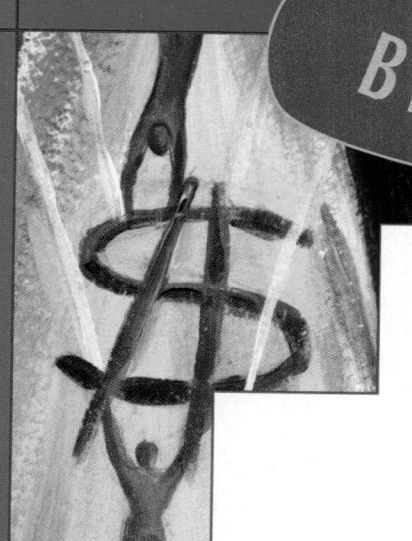

Meeting Individual Student Abilities and Learning Styles

Tailor Material to Your Students

Expanded Material found at the end of most chapters gives you the flexibility to tailor the text to meet the needs and abilities of all students.

Visual Learners

WebTutor™ Advantage for WebCT™ and Blackboard®, Xtra!, and the textbook Web site provide interactive and media reinforcement for all students, especially visual learners.

Learning Levels

End-of-Chapter Materials offer a large number of easy, medium, and difficult problems. Your best students can move on to more difficult problems while struggling learners get plenty of opportunity to build confidence before attacking more challenging problems.

Problem-Solving Help

Now you can give students who need extra problem-solving help valuable guidance without providing the answers. Each chapter includes a review problem with a fully illustrated solution. Check Figures for selected problems are included in the text.

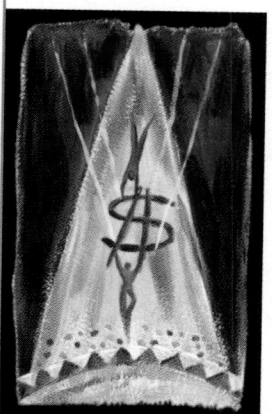

Comprehensive Problems

Three comprehensive problems, integrating multiple issues and methods, are found throughout the text. These problems provide an opportunity to challenge students and bring their knowledge full circle.

Head Start

NEW! Approximately 20 brief practice exercises per chapter are perfect to use for starting class or as a pre-lecture assignment.

IS A BALANCING ACT...

S atisfying Different Student Majors

Preparing Future CEOs with CEO

Competency **E**nhancement **O**pportunities are found at the end of all chapters and include problems that develop analysis, communication, and decision-making—skills encouraged by the AICPA and the Accounting Education Change Commission. International Cases, Ethics Cases, Writing Assignments, Debates, Cumulative Spreadsheets, and Internet Search exercises provide interesting, unique and challenging assignments.

Appealing to All Students

Each chapter is written to simplify difficult concepts and promote understanding. *Accounting: Concepts and Applications, 9e* holds their interest by focusing on current real-world situations and actual companies.

Organized Around Business Activities

The organization of the text, consistent with business activities and cycles, gives students a more accurate framework for understanding accounting and business.

B alancing Work vs. Time

Eliminate Grading Homework!

Personal Trainer® 3.0 lets students complete their assigned homework from the text. The results instantaneously flow into your online gradebook. This tool frees up your time by taking away the important, but time consuming chore of grading homework from you!

Personal Tutoring Tools for Students

Our WebTutor™ Advantage for Blackboard® or WebCT™ contains many tools that act as a tutor to your student when you can't be there to help them. Some of these include an illustrative Exercise Demo, an animation with audio of all steps to solving a problem, and visual E-Lectures with audio review of more difficult concepts of the chapter. WebTutor Advantage also automatically includes Personal Trainer (described above). Best of all, these tools are all textbook specific and already created for you!

P.A.S.S. Accounting Software

P.A.S.S. for *Accounting: Concepts and Applications, 9e* is another time saver for you because it includes an inspector CD-ROM letting you grade selected problems from the text with a few mouse clicks!

TECHNOLOGY AND

WebTutor™ Advantage on WebCT™ with Personal Trainer® 3.0
WebTutor™ Advantage on Blackboard® with Personal Trainer® 3.0

WebTutor™ Advantage provides you with the most robust and pedagogically advanced content for either the WebCT™ or Blackboard® course management platform.

WebTutor Advantage includes engaging videos and E-Lectures, plus fascinating quizzes, games, and more.

▶ **NEW Video Cases** Each two- to five-minute video covers a key accounting concept as it is played out in a real-world company or situation. Accompanying the video is a summary and some suggested critical-thinking questions for students to answer.

▶ **E-Lectures** Each chapter includes one or two visual lectures with audio presentations that review major topics.

▶ **Exercise Demos** These step-by-step Flash presentations walk the student through an illustrative problem.

▶ **Quizzes** Students make great strides with continuous reinforcement, now they can select from a variety of quizzes per chapter: pretests, multiple choice and true-false.

▶ **QuizBowl** Popular with students, this engaging Jeopardy®-like game with sound effects allows them to review key accounting concepts.

▶ **Test Your Knowledge** game provides additional reinforcement of accounting concepts and key terms in a fun, interactive format.

▶ **Accounting Cycle Review** Students get a firm grasp on the key concepts of the accounting cycle by applying what they've learned to realistic situations and problems.

▶ **Spanish Dictionary** This timely resource defines common accounting terms in Spanish.

Personal Trainer® 3.0

Specifically designed to ease the time-consuming task of grading homework, Personal Trainer lets students complete their assigned homework from the text or practice on unassigned homework online. The results are instantaneously entered into your online gradebook.

Features of New 3.0 Personal Trainer:

▶ **Enhanced Questions** The latest version now includes exercises and problems. Students get help entering their answers in the proper format and they can spell check their answers.

▶ **Enhanced Instructor Capabilities** The flexible gradebook can display and download any combination of student work, chapters, or activities. Capture grades on demand or set a particular time for grades to be automatically captured. Assign questions as "required" or "excluded," so students cannot access selected questions.

▶ **Enhanced Hints** Students get up to three hints from the text, PowerPoint slides, exhibits, spreadsheets, images and more for each problem. Plus instructors can add an additional hint.

▶ **Enhanced Look-and-Feel** Fast, reliable, dependable and even easier to use, Version 3.0 sports a fresh, new graphic design.

ELECTRONIC SOLUTIONS

Xtra!

Available as an optional, free bundle item with a new textbook, Xtra! gives students FREE access to the following set of online learning tools:

▶ **E-Lectures** Brief E-Lectures review more difficult concepts from the chapter.

▶ **Topical Quizzes** Measure a student's "test readiness" on the concepts in the chapter.

▶ **Multiple Choice Quizzing** Additional quizzes help students review chapter concepts and prepare for exams.

▶ **Crosswords** The Crossword Puzzles are a fun way students can review their understanding of key terms and concepts.

▶ **Business Environment articles** Real world vignettes, adapted from financial newspapers and business publications, which illustrate concepts in the chapter.

P.A.S.S.

Our best-selling computerized accounting software, prepared by Dale Klooster and Warren Allen, *Power Accounting System Software* (formerly General Ledger Software) shows students the effects that accounting entries have on financial

statements. P.A.S.S. is also available with our selection of comprehensive practice sets.

▶ **Text Icon** Each problem that can be completed with P.A.S.S. is marked with an icon in the text.

Excel Spreadsheet Templates

Excel templates are provided for solving selected end-of-chapter exercises and problems, which are identified with the spreadsheet icon.

Spreadsheet

Product Support Web Site — http://albrecht.swlearning.com

The Albrecht/Stice/Stice/Swain web site provides a variety of instructor and student resources. You'll find text-specific and other related resources organized by chapter and topic.

The Product Support Site includes a wide variety of materials for extra studying and review.

▶ **Learning Objectives**

▶ **PowerPoint® Presentations** Reviews each chapter's major topics.

▶ **Check Figures** Enables students to see if their entries are correct.

▶ **Internet Applications** These activities from the text allow students to apply chapter concepts and improve their online research skills.

▶ **Crosswords** This fun, interactive tool gives students a great way to review and understand the key terms from each chapter.

▶ **Quizzes** Interactive quizzes in both true-false and multiple-choice formats provide students with immediate feedback after submitting their answers.

▶ **Instructor Resources** Available to download are the Instructor's Manual, Solutions Manual, PowerPoint Presentations, Excel Spreadsheets with Solutions, Business Environment Articles, and Check Figures.

Instructor Supplements

When it comes to supporting instructors, South-Western is unsurpassed. *Accounting: Concepts and Applications, 9e*, continues the tradition with powerful printed materials along with the latest integrated classroom technology!

▶ **WebTutor Advantage with Personal Trainer** Robust content for online course management systems on WebCT and Blackboard.

▶ **Solutions Manual** This manual provides the answers to all end-of-chapter materials in the text, suggested answers to Stop and Think included.

▶ **Instructor's Manual** Contains a wide range of writing exercises, group learning activities, demonstration problems, and accounting scenarios.

▶ **Instructor's Resource CD-ROM** This convenient resource includes PowerPoint® Presentations, Instructor's Manual, Test Bank, ExamView, Solutions Manual, Excel Application Templates and Solutions, all on one CD-ROM.

▶ **Test Bank** Includes more than 700 true-false questions, multiple-choice questions, and problems, plus multiple-choice quizzes for each chapter. The Test Bank is also included in the ExamView Pro® Testing Software on the instructor's CD-ROM.

▶ **ExamView Pro® Testing Software** Lets you easily customize exams, practice tests, and tutorials and deliver them over a network, on the Internet, or in printed form.

▶ **Instructor PowerPoint® Presentations** Each presentation found at the Web site enhances lectures and simplifies class preparation.

▶ **Instructor Spreadsheet Template Solutions** Provide the completed solution for the exercises and problems marked with an icon in the text. These are available to download at http://albrecht.swlearning.com.

▶ **Solutions Transparencies** Acetate transparencies of exercise and problem solutions.

▶ **Teaching Transparencies** Acetates of the PowerPoint® Presentation Slides.

▶ **P.A.S.S. Inspector CD-ROM** The Inspector CD-ROM allows instructors to grade students' work.

▶ **Product Support Web Site (http://albrecht.swlearning.com)** Our text-specific web site provides a variety of instructor resources that are password protected. You'll find text-specific and other related resources organized by chapter and topic. Many are also available on the Instructor's Resource CD-ROM.

Student Supplements

Accounting: Concepts and Applications, 9e, offers a broad range of supplements in both printed form and in easy-to-use, affordable technologies. We've designed our entire supplement package around the comments instructors have provided, making this supplement package the best in the business!

▶ **Study Guide** Prepared by the authors, the study guide includes learning objectives, detailed chapter summaries, discussions of topics that typically cause problems for the students and suggestions for overcoming those problems and tests for self-assessment.

▶ **Working Papers for Exercises and Problems** Forms for solving end-of-chapter problems are perforated for easy removal and use.

▶ **Personal Trainer 3.0** Students can complete textbook end-of-chapter exercises and problems online and receive immediate feedback with Personal Trainer! Additionally, student results instantaneously flow into your gradebook!

▶ **P.A.S.S.** Use P.A.S.S. (Power Accounting Software System®) to complete selected end-of-chapter problems. This user-friendly software helps students learn how to use accounting software.

▶ **Spreadsheet Templates** Each spreadsheet template problem is marked with an icon in the text. Templates are available at http://albrecht.swlearning.com.

▶ **Xtra!** Gives students free access to E-Lectures, Topical Quizzes, Crosswords, and quizzing.

▶ **Product Support Web Site (http://albrecht.swlearning.com)** Our Web site provides a variety of student resources, including quizzing and lecture reviews. You'll find text-specific content and other related resources organized by chapter and topic.

Acknowledgements

The ninth edition of *Accounting: Concepts and Applications* reflects many comments from colleagues and students, all of which are deeply appreciated. In particular we wish to thank the following:

Survey Participants:

Afshad J. Irani
University of New Hampshire

Mack Tennyson
College of Charleston

Alexandra L. Anna
Colorado College

Robert W. Rouse
College of Charleston

Robert L. Vogel
College of Eastern Utah

Cindy M. Navaroli
Chaffey College

John C. Corless
CSU-Sacramento

Constance M. Cooper
University of Cincinnati

Jacqueline C. Richards
Mesa College

Paul Buck
Plymouth State College

Jeffery R. Cowan
Fullerton College

Rosalie C. Hallbauer
Florida International University

Roger A. Gee
San Diego Mesa College

Robert I. Sanner
Central Community College-Grand Island

Jill E. Whitley
University of Sioux Falls

Willaim H. Svihla
ISU School of Business

Cathy L. Miller
University of Michigan-Flint

Larry P. Hegstad
Pacific Lutheran University

Paul Buck
Plymouth State College

Hal Ranck
Franklin & Marshall College

Reviewers:

Susan Anders
St. Bonaventure University

Becky Kerr
University of South Carolina

Susan Hamlen
University of Buffalo

Progyan Basu
University of Georgia

In addition, we would like to thank the following content providers and verifiers for their professional services and consideration in providing a more concise, higher-quality product.

Content Providers:

Michael Blue
Bloomburg University

Joseph E. Dowd
Eastern Washington University

Sharie Dow
Dow Publishing

Jason Fink
University of Phoenix

Peggy Hussey
Colorado Springs, CO

Marcella Combs
Summerfield, FL

Jeff Ritter
St. Norberts College

David Cottrell
Brigham Young University

Verifiers:

Jason Fink
University of Phoenix

James Emig
Villanova University

Samuel L. Tiras
University of Buffalo

Dave O'Dell
McPherson College

Special Consideration and thanks from the Authors:

John Gammon
Brigham Young University

Cameron Pratt
Brigham Young University

Brad Tingey
Brigham Young University

W. Steve Albrecht

James D. Stice

Earl K. Stice

Monte R. Swain

Part

1

Financial Reporting and the Accounting Cycle

c h a p t e r

1

Accounting Information: Users and Uses

After studying this chapter, you should be able to:

Learning Objectives

1 Describe the purpose of accounting and explain its role in business and society.

2 Identify the primary users of accounting information.

3 Describe the environment of accounting, including the effects of generally accepted accounting principles, international business, ethical considerations, and technology.

4 Analyze the reasons for studying accounting.

chapter 1

In 1913, a young CPA named Arthur Andersen partnered with a gentleman named Clarence Delaney to form the public accounting firm of ANDERSON, DELANEY & CO. At the time there were only about 2,200 CPAs in the United States, and at the age of 23, Mr. Andersen was one of the youngest. Mr. Delaney later left the firm, and in 1918 it was renamed ARTHUR ANDERSEN.

In 1914, a railroad company executive asked Mr. Andersen to provide an opinion on the railroad company's financial statements. Mr. Andersen knew that the company's financial statements were inaccurate and that profits were artificially inflated. Mr. Andersen replied to the executive that "there was not enough money in the city of Chicago to make me approve the bad bookkeeping." Since the value of public accounting was based on the trust investors could have in a public accounting firm, Mr. Andersen knew that his firm's reputation for honesty and integrity was not for sale.

The company continued to grow and in 1989 became ANDERSEN WORLDWIDE. By 2001, Andersen had operations in 84 countries around the world and over 85,000 employees. Revenues for 2002 were $9.3 billion. Some of the companies whose financial statements were audited by Andersen include BANK ONE, COLGATE-PALMOLIVE, COSTCO WHOLESALE, DELTA AIRLINES, FEDEX CORP., HERSHEY FOODS, HILTON HOTELS, MERCK, NEWELL RUBBERMAID, ORACLE CORP., and SARA LEE.

On August 31, 2002, Arthur Anderson closed its doors and ceased to be an auditor of the financial statements of companies whose stock was traded on stock exchanges. How did this dramatic "about face" occur? In a word—Enron. Arthur Anderson was the external auditor for a Texas-based energy company named ENRON. Enron was formed in July of 1985 from a merger of HOUSTON NATURAL GAS and INTERNORTH. Enron was originally an interstate natural gas pipeline company. In 1989, Enron began trading natural gas commodities, and in 1999 ENRONONLINE, the first global commodity trading Web site, was launched.

To make its financial statements appear as though the company was performing better than it actually was,

Enron officials created several companies, established partnerships with those companies, and then used those partnerships to hide hundreds of millions of dollars in debt. Andersen officials knew about these companies and approved the accounting for the transactions. While the details of the accounting for these transactions are far beyond the scope of this accounting class, suffice it to say that it was complicated.

FYI:

It turns out that a whole lot of companies knew about Enron's partnership arrangements including GE CAPITAL, J.P. MORGAN CAPITAL, MERRILL LYNCH, and MORGAN STANLEY.

When the SEC began investigating the accounting for these partnerships, Arthur Andersen undertook a series of events that led to its eventual demise. Company officials ordered that documents relating to the Enron audit be shredded, and Andersen attorneys asked that certain internal correspondence with Enron officers that had not yet been made public be changed to hide the firm's knowledge of certain transactions. Investigation by the SEC into charges of obstruction of justice by Andersen officials led to the firm closing its doors in August of 2002.

FYI:

Following Andersen's demise, another accounting scandal involving the firm erupted onto the front page of the world news. WORLDCOM, a telecommunications giant, had artificially inflated profits by over $9 billion. Arthur Andersen was the auditor for WorldCom. And as if that wasn't enough, Andersen was also the auditor for TYCO, a company that was involved in manipulating its accounting to artificially inflate profits.

n this textbook, you will begin your study of accounting. You will learn to speak and understand accounting, "the language of business." Without an understanding of accounting, business investments, taxes, and money management will be like a foreign language to you. In brief,

an understanding of accounting facilitates the interpretation of financial information, which allows for better economic decisions.

The major objectives of this text are to provide you with a basic understanding of the language of accounting and with the ability to interpret and use

Caution

Don't be too concerned with all the new and unfamiliar terms you see in the first chapter of the book. Learning a "new language" takes time. Be patient. Before too long, you will be speaking the "language of business" (accounting) quite fluently.

financial information prepared using accounting techniques and procedures. With the knowledge you obtain from this exposure to accounting, you will be able to "read" the financial statements of companies, understand the information that is being conveyed, and use accounting information to make good business decisions. Also, through discussion of the business environment in which accounting is used, you will increase your understanding of general business concepts such as corporations, leases, annuities, leverage, derivatives (the financial kind, not the calculus kind), and so forth.

You will become convinced that accounting is not "bean counting." Time after time you will see that accountants must exercise judgment about how to best summarize and report the results of business transactions. This judgment was at the heart of the Enron, WorldCom, and Tyco scandals. As a result, you will gain a respect for the complexity of accounting and develop a healthy skepticism about the precision of any financial reports you see.

Finally, you will see the power of accounting. Financial statements are not just paper reports that get filed away and forgotten. As an example, the misleading financial statement numbers associated with Enron, WorldCom, and Tyco resulted in tens of thousands of employees being laid off and investors losing billions of dollars. You will see that financial statement numbers, and, indirectly, the accountants who prepare them, determine who receives loans and who doesn't, which companies attract investors and which don't, which managers receive salary bonuses and which don't, and which companies are praised in the financial press and which aren't.

So, let's get started.

What's the Purpose of Accounting?

1 Describe the purpose of accounting and explain its role in business and society.

bookkeeping The preservation of a systematic, quantitative record of an activity.

Imagine a long distance telephone company with no system in place to document who calls whom and how long they talk. Or a manager of a 300-unit apartment complex who has forgotten to write down which tenants have and have not paid this month's rent. Or an accounting professor who, the day before final grades are due, loses the only copy of the disk containing the spreadsheet of all the homework, quiz, and exam scores. Each of these scenarios illustrates a problem with bookkeeping, the least glamorous aspect of accounting. **Bookkeeping** is the preservation of a systematic, quantitative record of an activity. Bookkeeping systems can be very primitive—cutting notches in a stick to tally how many sheep you have or moving beads on a string to track the score in a billiards game. But the importance of routine bookkeeping cannot be overstated; without bookkeeping, business is impossible.

To evaluate the importance of bookkeeping records, we'll use a thought experiment. Suppose that sometime during the night, every copy of every novel ever written were to disappear. Could life proceed normally the next day? While the cultural loss would be incalculable, the normal activities of the next day would not be noticeably affected. What if television were suddenly gone when we woke up? While we might wander around wondering what to do with our time, life would go on. But what if we woke up tomorrow morning to find the bookkeeping records of all businesses worldwide destroyed during the night? Businesses that rely on up-to-the-minute customer account information, such as banks, simply could not open their doors. Retailers would have to insist on cash purchases, since no credit records could be verified. Manufacturers would have to do a quick count of existing inventories of raw materials and components to find out whether they could keep their production lines running. Suppliers would have to call all their customers, if they could remember who they were, to renegotiate purchase orders. Attorneys would find themselves in endless arguments about their fees because they would have no record of billable hours. Routine and dry as bookkeeping may seem, the world simply could not function for one day without it.

Rudimentary bookkeeping is ancient, probably predating both language and money. The modern system of double-entry bookkeeping still in use today (described in Chapter 3) was developed in the 1300s–1400s in Italy by the merchants in the trading and banking centers of Florence, Venice, and Genoa. The key development in accounting in the last 500 years has been the use of the bookkeeping data, not just to keep track of things, but to evaluate the performance and health of a business.

This use of bookkeeping data as an evaluation tool may seem obvious to you, but it is a step that is often not taken. Let's consider a bookkeeping system with which most of us are familiar—a checking account. Your checking account involves (or should involve) careful recording of the dates and amounts of all checks written and all deposits made, the maintenance of a running account total, and reconciliations with the monthly bank statement. Now, assume that you have a perfect checking account bookkeeping system. Will the system answer the following questions?

- Are you spending more for groceries this year than you did last year?
- What proportion of your monthly expenditures are fixed, meaning that you can't change them except through a drastic change in lifestyle?
- You plan to study abroad next year; will you be able to save enough between now and then to pay for it?

In order to answer these kinds of evaluation questions, each check must be analyzed to determine the type of expenditure, your checks must then be coded by type of expenditure, the data must be boiled down into summary reports, and past data must be used to forecast future patterns. How many of us use our checking account data like this? Not many. We do the bookkeeping (usually), but we don't structure the information to be used for evaluation.

In summary, an **accounting system** is used by a business to (1) analyze transactions, (2) handle routine bookkeeping tasks, and (3) structure information so it can be used to evaluate the performance and health of the business. Exhibit 1 illustrates the three functions of the accounting system.

Accounting is formally defined as a system for providing "quantitative information, primarily financial in nature, about economic entities that is intended to be useful in making economic decisions."[1] The key components of this definition are:

- *Quantitative.* Accounting relates to numbers. This is a strength because numbers can be easily tabulated and summarized. It is a weakness because some important business events,

accounting system The procedures and processes used by a business to analyze transactions, handle routine bookkeeping tasks, and structure information so it can be used to evaluate the performance and health of the business.

accounting A system for providing quantitative, financial information about economic entities that is useful for making sound economic decisions. Accounting is often called the "language of business" because it provides the means of recording and communicating business activities and the results of those activities.

Exhibit 1: Functions of an Accounting System

Analysis	Bookkeeping	Evaluation
Analyze business events to determine if information should be captured by the accounting system	Day-to-day keeping track of things	Use summary information to evaluate the financial health and performance of the business

1 Statement of the Accounting Principles Board No. 4, "Basic Concepts and Accounting Principles Underlying Financial Statements of Business Enterprises," New York: American Institute of Certified Public Accountants, 1970, par. 40.

such as a toxic waste spill and the associated lawsuits and countersuits, cannot be easily described by one or two numbers.

- *Financial.* The health and performance of a business are affected by and reflected in many dimensions—financial, personal relationships, community and environmental impact, and public image. Accounting focuses on just the financial dimension.
- *Useful.* The practice of accounting is supported by a long tradition of theory. U.S. accounting rules have a theoretical conceptual framework. Some people actually make a living as accounting theorists. However, in spite of its theoretical beauty, accounting exists only because it is useful.
- *Decisions.* Although accounting is the structured reporting of what has already occurred, this past information can only be useful if it impacts decisions about the future.

Making good decisions is critical for success in any business enterprise. When an important decision must be made, it is essential to use a rational decision-making process. The process is basically the same no matter how complex the issue. First, the issue or question must be clearly identified. Next, the facts surrounding the situation must be gathered and analyzed. Then, several alternative courses of action should be identified and considered before a decision is finally reached. This decision-making process is summarized in Exhibit 2.

One must be careful to make a distinction between a good decision and a good outcome. Often, many factors outside the control of the decision maker affect the outcome of a decision. The decision-making process does not guarantee a certain result; it only ensures that a good decision is made. To illustrate this process, let's consider an example. It's Friday afternoon, the sun is shining, your homework is done, and you have the rest of the afternoon and evening ahead of you. What to do? You check the movie listings in the newspaper to see if there are any new movies you haven't seen, you call several of your friends to see what they are doing, and you review your list of "things you always wanted to organize around your apartment but never had the time." With this information, you decide that you could either (1) go to the new Tom Hanks movie with a group of friends or (2) go over to your friend's house and watch TV. (Spending time at home organizing your sock drawer on a Friday night is out of the question.) You decide to go to the movies. You get to the movie theater, buy your ticket, your popcorn, and your drink, then select a seat. The lights dim, the movie starts, and the only empty seat left in the theater is right in front of you. It turns out you have the best seat in the house—until Shaquille O'Neal (7′1″, 315 pounds) comes in and sits in that seat. Good decision, bad outcome.

The four steps of the decision-making process lead to the best decision under the circumstances, but the outcome always has an element of chance. Part of business is learning how to protect yourself against bad outcomes. The first step in achieving a favorable outcome begins with making a good decision.

Accounting plays a vital role in the decision-making process. An accounting system provides information in a form that can be used to make knowledgeable financial decisions. The information supplied by accounting is in the form of quantitative data, primarily financial in nature, and relates to specific economic entities. An economic entity may be an individual, a business enterprise, or a nonprofit organization. A **business**, such as a grocery store or a car dealership, is operated with the objective of making a profit for its owners. The goal of

business An organization operated with the objective of making a profit from the sale of goods or services.

Exhibit 2: The Decision-Making Process

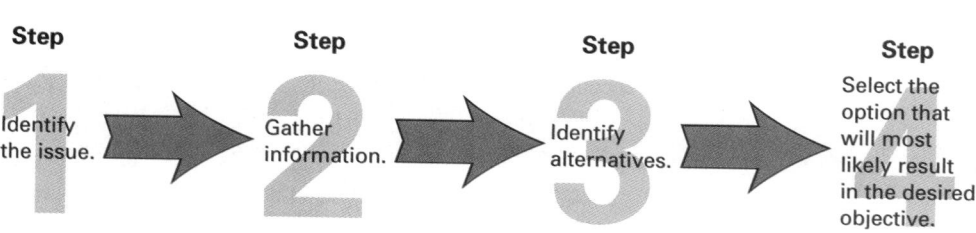

Step 1 Identify the issue.

Step 2 Gather information.

Step 3 Identify alternatives.

Step 4 Select the option that will most likely result in the desired objective.

nonprofit organization An entity without a profit objective, oriented toward providing services efficiently and effectively.

a **nonprofit organization**, such as a city government or a university, is to provide services in an effective and efficient manner. Every entity, regardless of its size or purpose, must have a way to keep track of its economic activities and to measure how well it is accomplishing its goals. Accounting provides the means for tracking activities and measuring results.

Without accounting information, many important financial decisions would be made blindly. Investors, for example, would have no way to distinguish between a profitable company and one that is on the verge of failure; bankers could not evaluate the riskiness of potential loans; corporate managers would have no basis for controlling costs, setting prices, or investing the company's resources; and governments would have no basis for taxing income. No list of examples could fully represent the pervasive use of accounting information throughout our economic, social, and political institutions. When accounting information is used effectively as a basis for making economic decisions, limited resources are more likely to be allocated efficiently. From a broad perspective, the result is a healthier economy and a higher standard of living.

The value of accounting information can also be illustrated on a personal level. Since very few of us will ever make more money than we can spend, we each will be making choices as to what to do with our limited incomes. For example, assume you have a job that results in take-home pay of $2,000 per month. What do you do with the money? If you are making monthly payments on a home and/or an automobile, you previously made choices to use part of your monthly income for these two items. How about a trip around the world, season tickets for your favorite basketball team, or a new home entertainment system? You could spend your money on these items, but that might not be the best use of your income. After all, you haven't eaten yet. Routine expenditures for food, clothing, and utilities must be made. How much money will you need for these and other everyday expenditures? By collecting financial information relating to prior months' inflows and outflows of cash, you will be able to approximate how much money you will need for this month. This process—called *budgeting* (discussed later)—is often used by individuals (and businesses) to ensure that monthly income is used in the best manner possible. While it is true that budgeting is not necessary, budgeting is part of good decision making.

The Relationship of Accounting to Business

Business is the general term applied to the activities involved in the production and distribution of goods and services. Accounting is used to record and report the financial effects of business activities. Thus, as mentioned earlier, accounting is often called the "language of business." It provides the means of recording and communicating the successes and failures of business organizations.

All business enterprises have some activities in common. As shown in Exhibit 3, one common activity is the acquisition of monetary resources. These resources, often referred to as "capital," come from three sources: (1) investors (owners), (2) creditors (lenders), and (3) the business itself in the form of earnings that have been retained. Once resources are obtained, they are used to buy land, buildings, and equipment; to purchase materials and supplies; to pay employees; and to meet any other operating expenses involved in the production and marketing of goods or services. When the product or service is sold, additional monetary resources (revenues) are generated. These resources can be used to pay loans, to pay taxes, and to buy new materials, equipment, and other items needed to continue the operations of the business. In addition, some of the resources may be distributed to owners as a return on their investment. MICROSOFT, for example, uses the earnings from its operations to fund research and development and to purchase other companies. The developed (or purchased) products can then be sold at a profit under the Microsoft name. This produces more funds that can then be used to purchase more companies or develop more products. Microsoft does not distribute many of its resources back to its owners. Owners receive a return on their investment primarily through the growth in value of the stock.

Exhibit 3: Activities Common to Business Organizations

Accountants play two roles with regard to these activities. First, they measure and communicate (report) the results of these activities—in other words, accountants keep score. In order to measure these results as accurately as possible, accountants follow a fairly standard set of procedures, usually referred to as the **accounting cycle**. The cycle includes several steps, which involve analyzing, recording, classifying, summarizing, and reporting the transactions of a business. These steps are explained in detail in Chapters 3 and 4. Second, accountants advise managers on how to structure these activities so as to achieve the goals of the business—be those goals to generate a profit, to minimize costs, to provide efficient services, etc.

accounting cycle The procedure for analyzing, recording, classifying, summarizing, and reporting the transactions of a business.

TO SUMMARIZE: Accounting is a service activity designed to accumulate, measure, and communicate financial information about economic entities—businesses and nonprofit organizations. Its purpose is to provide information used to make informed decisions about how to best use available resources. Accounting is often called the "language of business" because it provides the means of recording and communicating business activities and the results of those activities.

Who Uses Accounting Information?

2 Identify the primary users of accounting information.

management accounting The area of accounting concerned with providing internal financial reports to assist management in making decisions.

The accounting system generates output in the form of financial reports. As shown in Exhibit 4, there are two major categories of reports: internal and external. Internal reports are used by those who direct the day-to-day operations of a business enterprise. These individuals are collectively referred to as "management," and the related area of accounting is called **management accounting**. Management accounting focuses on the information needed for planning, implementing plans, and controlling costs. Managers and executives who work inside a company have access to specialized management accounting information that is not available to outsiders. For example, the management of MCDONALD'S CORPORATION has detailed management accounting data on exactly how much it costs to produce each item on the menu. Further, if BURGER KING or WENDY'S starts a local burger price war in, say, Missouri, McDonald's managers can request daily sales summaries for each store in the area to measure the impact.

Other examples of decisions made using management accounting information are whether to produce a product internally or purchase it from an outside supplier, what prices to charge, and which costs seem excessive. Consider those companies that produce computers. Most computers are shipped with an operating system already installed. Approximately 85% of computers have MICROSOFT's Windows pre-installed. The computer makers must decide whether to develop their own operating system or pay Microsoft a licensing fee to use Windows. Most computer manufacturers have determined it is cost effective to license from Microsoft. Companies such as SEARS and RADIO SHACK often use products produced by outside suppliers rather than manufacture the products themselves. The products are then labeled with the "Kenmore" or "Realistic" brand names and sold to customers. These are just two examples of decisions that must be made by management given available financial information.

annual report A document that summarizes the results of operations and financial status of a company for the past year and outlines plans for the future.

External financial reports, included in the firm's **annual report**, are used by individuals and organizations that have an economic interest in the business but are not part of its management. Information is provided to these "external users" in the form of general-purpose

Exhibit 4: Output of the Accounting Cycle

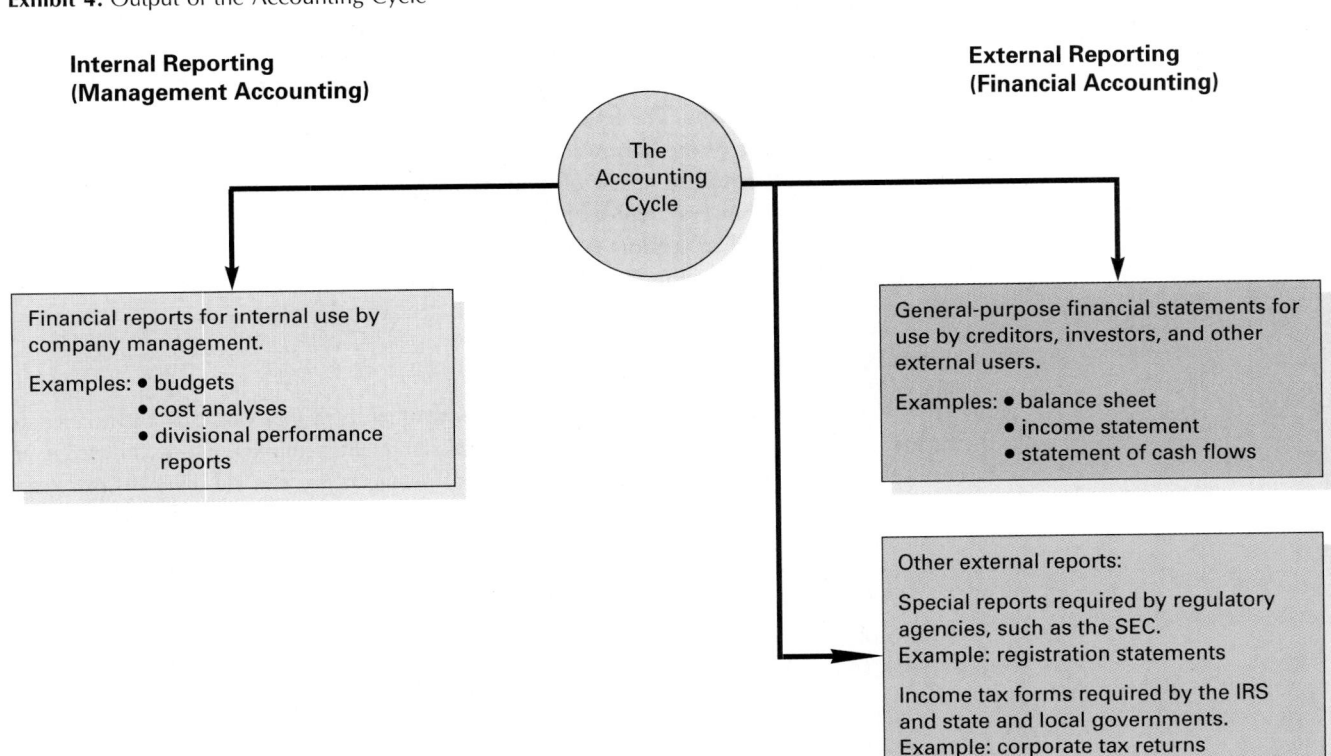

Internal Reporting
(Management Accounting)

The Accounting Cycle

External Reporting
(Financial Accounting)

Financial reports for internal use by company management.

Examples: • budgets
• cost analyses
• divisional performance reports

General-purpose financial statements for use by creditors, investors, and other external users.

Examples: • balance sheet
• income statement
• statement of cash flows

Other external reports:

Special reports required by regulatory agencies, such as the SEC.
Example: registration statements

Income tax forms required by the IRS and state and local governments.
Example: corporate tax returns

financial statements Reports such as the balance sheet, income statement, and statement of cash flows, which summarize the financial status and results of operations of a business entity.

financial accounting The area of accounting concerned with reporting financial information to interested external parties.

financial statements and special reports required by government agencies. The general-purpose information provided by **financial accounting** is summarized in the three primary financial statements: balance sheet, income statement, and statement of cash flows (more formally introduced in Chapter 2).

- The *balance sheet* reports the resources of a company (the assets), the company's obligations (the liabilities), and the owners' equity, which represents the difference between what is owned (assets) and what is owed (liabilities).
- The *income statement* reports the amount of net income earned by a company during a period, with annual and quarterly income statements being the most common. Net income is the excess of a company's revenues over its expenses; if the expenses are more than the revenues, then the company has suffered a loss for the period. The income statement represents the accountant's best effort at measuring the economic performance of a company.
- The *statement of cash flows* reports the amount of cash collected and paid out by a company in the following three types of activities: operating, investing, and financing. The types of activities in each of these three categories will be explained in Chapter 2. The statement of cash flows is the most objective of the financial statements because, as you will see in subsequent chapters, it involves a minimum of accounting estimates and judgments.

Examples of external users of the information contained in these three financial statements, along with other available information, are described in the following paragraphs.

Lenders

Lenders (creditors) are interested in one thing—being repaid, with interest. If you were to approach a bank for a large loan, the bank would ask you for the following types of information in order to evaluate whether you would be able to repay the loan:

- A listing of your assets and liabilities
- Payroll stubs, tax returns, and other evidence of your income
- Details about any monthly payments (car, rent, credit cards, etc.) you are obligated to make
- Copies of recent bank statements to document the flow of cash into and out of your account

In essence, the bank would be asking you for a balance sheet, an income statement, and a statement of cash flows. Similarly, banks use companies' financial statements in making decisions about commercial loans. The financial statements are useful because they help the lender predict the future ability of the borrower to repay the loan.

In the case of Microsoft, a review of its balance sheet indicates that the company has no formal lenders. It does, however, report a balance in its "accounts payable" account. This amount represents amounts owed to vendors from whom Microsoft has purchased on credit. Considering Microsoft's reputation, this "lending" is very low risk.

Investors

Investors want information to help them estimate how much cash they can expect to receive in the future if they invest in a business now. Financial statements, coupled with a knowledge of business plans, market forecasts, and the character of management, can aid investors in assessing these future cash flows. Many companies have broad ownership with a few individuals owning a large portion of the company's stock. At Microsoft, Bill Gates owns 621,749,668 shares (11.6% of total shares outstanding) and Steve Ballmer, Microsoft's chief executive officer, owns 235,484,037 shares (4.4%).

Obviously, millions of Americans invest in McDonald's, Microsoft, CISCO SYSTEMS, and GENERAL ELECTRIC without ever seeing the financial statements of these companies. Investors can feel justifiably safe in doing this because large companies are followed by armies of financial analysts who would quickly blow the whistle if they found information suggesting that investors in these companies were at serious risk. But what about investing in a smaller company, one that the financial press doesn't follow, or in a local family business that is seeking outside investors for the first time? In cases such as these, investing without looking at the financial statements is like jumping off the high dive without looking first to see if there is any water in the pool.

Management

In addition to using management accounting information available only to those within the firm, managers of a company can use the general financial accounting information that is also made available to outsiders. Company goals are often stated in terms of financial accounting numbers, such as a target of sales growth in excess of 5%. Also, reported "net income" is frequently used in calculating management bonuses. Finally, managers of a company can analyze the general-purpose financial statements (using the techniques introduced in Chapter 5) in order to pinpoint areas of weakness about which more detailed management accounting information can be sought. Microsoft uses internally produced accounting reports to evaluate such things as the profitability of product lines, the success of international operations, and the performance of product and management teams.

Other Users of Financial Information

There are many other external users of financial information, including suppliers, customers, employees, competitors, government agencies, and the press. These are described below.

Suppliers and Customers

In some settings, suppliers and customers are interested in the long-run staying power of a company. On the supplier side, if BOEING receives an order from an airline for 30 new 747s over the next 10 years, Boeing wants to know whether the airline will be around in the future to take delivery of and pay for the planes. On the customer side, a homeowner who has foundation repair work done wants to know whether the company making the repairs will be around long enough to honor its 50-year guarantee. Financial statements provide information that suppliers and customers can use to assess the long-run prospects of a company. Each version of a software release has a limited life, and part of Microsoft's success has been its ability to provide product upgrades. Microsoft's customers can use financial information to help them ascertain the company's ability to survive and have the resources to fix glitches and provide upgrades as the technology improves.

Employees

Employees are interested in financial accounting information for a variety of reasons. As mentioned earlier, financial statement data are used in determining employee bonuses. In addition, financial accounting information can help an employee evaluate the likelihood that the employer will be able to fulfill its long-run promises, such as pensions and retiree health-care benefits. Financial statements are also important in contract negotiations between labor and management.

Competitors

If you were a manager at PEPSICO, would you be interested in knowing the relative profitability of COCA-COLA's operations in the United States, Brazil, Japan, and France? Of course you would, because that information could help you identify strategic opportunities for marketing pushes where potential profits are high or where your competitor is weak. Microsoft can use the information in financial statements to track its competitors and identify new opportunities to grow and use its market share in operating systems to increase its revenues in other software ventures. For example, Microsoft's recent antitrust troubles relate, in large part, to its competition with NETSCAPE, an Internet-browser alternative to Microsoft's Explorer. In 1997 (the last year that Netscape provided publicly available financial information), Netscape lost over $115 million on sales of almost $534 million. During that same period, Microsoft was earning a profit of almost $3.5 billion on sales of almost $12 billion.

Government Agencies

Federal and state government agencies make frequent use of financial accounting information. For example, to make sure that investors have sufficient information to make informed investment decisions, the Securities and Exchange Commission monitors the financial accounting disclosures of companies (both U.S. and foreign) whose stocks trade on U.S. stock exchanges. The International Trade Commission uses financial accounting information to determine whether the importation of Ecuadorian roses or Chinese textiles is harming U.S. companies through unfair trade practices. The Justice Department uses financial statement data to evaluate whether companies (such as Microsoft) are earning excess monopolistic profits. In Microsoft's case, from 2000 to 2002, it reported profits of $0.32 on every dollar of sales. During that same period, General Electric, one of America's most admired companies, generated profits of $0.10 on every dollar of sales.

The Press

Financial statements are a great place for a reporter to find background information to flesh out a story about a company. For example, a story about Microsoft can be enhanced by using the sales data shown in its annual report. In addition, a surprising accounting announcement, such as a large drop in reported profits, is a trigger for an investigative reporter to write about what is going on in a company. When the Justice Department proposed the breakup of Microsoft, *The Wall Street Journal* reported analysts' estimates of the value of the company's various parts based on past revenue figures. For example, one analyst estimated that Microsoft's consumer business would be worth 50 times its revenue.[2]

In summary, who uses financial accounting information? Everyone does, or at least everyone should. External financial reports come within the area of accounting referred to as financial accounting. Most of the data needed to prepare both internal and external reports is provided by the same accounting system. A major difference between management and financial accounting is the types of financial reports prepared. Internal reports are tailored to meet the needs of management and may vary considerably among businesses. General-purpose financial statements and other external reports, however, follow certain standards or guidelines and are thus more uniform among companies. The first fourteen chapters of *Accounting: Concepts and Applications* focus on financial accounting, specifically on the primary financial statements (discussed and illustrated in Chapter 2). The remaining chapters, 15 through 24, focus on management accounting.

TO SUMMARIZE: Two major categories of reports are generated by the accounting cycle: internal and external. Management accounting focuses on providing reports for internal use by management to assist in making operating decisions and in planning and controlling a company's activities. Financial accounting provides information to meet the needs of external users. General-purpose financial statements are used by investors, creditors, and other external parties who are interested in a company's activities and results.

---

2 Gregory Zuckerman, "Figuring Worth of a Split-Up, Microsoft Leaves Analysts Scattered All Over Map," *The Wall Street Journal*, May 2, 2000, p. C1.

Within What Kind of Environment Does Accounting Operate?

3 Describe the environment of accounting, including the effects of generally accepted accounting principles, international business, ethical considerations, and technology.

Accounting functions in a dynamic environment. Changes in technology as well as economic and political factors can significantly influence accounting practice. For example, the downfall of Enron and WorldCom and the resulting demise of Arthur Andersen have significantly changed the way accounting is done. As a result of these scandals, the U.S. government has taken a more active role in the development of accounting rules and oversight of the accounting industry. Four particularly important factors that influence the environment in which accounting operates are the development of "generally accepted accounting principles" (GAAP), international business, ethical considerations, and technology.

The Significance and Development of Accounting Standards

Imagine a company that compensates a key employee in the following ways:

- Paying a cash salary of $80,000.
- Giving a new car with a value of $30,000.
- Offering the option to become, a year from now, a 10% owner of the company in exchange for an investment of $200,000.

If the company does well in the coming year, the company will increase in value, the $200,000 price tag for 10% ownership will look like a great deal, and the employee will exercise the option. If the company does poorly, it will decline in value, the $200,000 price will be too high, and the employee will throw the option away and forget the whole thing. Assume the company then sells the ownership option to interested outside investors for $25,000.

The accounting question is how to summarize in one number the company's compensation cost associated with this employee. We would probably all agree to include the $110,000 ($80,000 + $30,000) compensation cost from the cash salary and the new car. What about the option? Both of the following arguments could be put forward:

1. If the employee were to buy the option from the company, just like any other outside investor, the employee would have to pay $25,000. Therefore, giving the option to the employee is just like paying him or her $25,000 cash. The $25,000 value of the option should be added to compensation cost.
2. The option doesn't cost the company a thing. In fact, the option merely increases the probability that the employee will invest $200,000 in the company in the future. The option doesn't add a penny to compensation cost.

So, which argument is right? Should each company decide for itself whether to include the $25,000 option value as part of compensation cost, or should there be an overall accounting standard followed by all companies? And if there is a standard, who sets it?[3]

There are many situations in business, such as the option compensation case just described, in which reasonable people can disagree about how certain items should be handled for accounting purposes. And, since financial accounting information is designed to be used by people outside a company, it is important that outsiders understand the rules and assumptions used by the company in constructing its financial statements. This would be extremely difficult and costly for outsiders to find out if every company formulated its own set of accounting rules. Accordingly, in most countries in the world there exists a committee or board that establishes the accounting rules for that country.

---

3 The answer to this surprisingly controversial question of the accounting for option compensation is given in Chapter 9. Just to show how influential accounting can be, this exact issue was debated on the floor of the U.S. Senate.

The Financial Accounting Standards Board

Financial Accounting Standards Board (FASB) The private organization responsible for establishing the standards for financial accounting and reporting in the United States.

In the United States, accounting standards are set by the **Financial Accounting Standards Board (FASB)**. The FASB is based in Norwalk, Connecticut, and its seven full-time members are selected from a variety of backgrounds—professional accounting, business, government, and academia. The FASB receives about one-third of its $20 million annual operating budget through donations from the accounting profession and from businesses. The remaining two-thirds is generated through sales of publications and other services (e.g., a CD-ROM version of all the existing accounting standards). An important thing to note about the FASB is that it is not a government agency; the FASB is a private body established and supported by the joint efforts of the U.S. business community, financial analysts, and practicing accountants. Because the FASB is not a government agency, it has no legal power to enforce the accounting standards it sets. The FASB gets its authority to establish rules from the Securities and Exchange Commission (discussed later).

The FASB maintains its influence as the accounting standard setter for the United States (and the most influential accounting body in the world) by carefully protecting its prestige and reputation for setting good standards. In doing so, the FASB must walk a fine line between constant improvement of accounting practices to provide more full and fair information for external users and practical constraints on financial disclosure to appease businesses that are reluctant to disclose too much information to outsiders. To balance these opposing forces, the FASB seeks consensus by requesting written comments and sponsoring public hearings on all its proposed standards. The end result of this public process is a set of accounting rules that are

generally accepted accounting principles (GAAP) Authoritative guidelines that define accounting practice at a particular time.

described as being **generally accepted accounting principles (GAAP)**. Without general acceptance by the business community, FASB standards would merely be theoretical essays by a powerless body, and the FASB would be disbanded. This may sound overly dramatic, but the FASB was created in 1973 to replace the previously existing accounting standards body (the Accounting Principles Board or APB), which had lost credibility with the business community because it was seen as being completely controlled by accountants.

STOP & THINK

Why is it important for the FASB to remain completely independent?

As you study this text, you will be intrigued by the interesting conceptual issues the FASB must wrestle with in setting accounting standards. The FASB has deliberated over the correct way to compute motion picture profits, the appropriate treatment of the cost of dismantling a nuclear power plant, the best approach for reflecting the impact of changes in foreign currency exchange rates, and the proper accounting for complex financial instruments such as commodity futures and interest rate swaps. And since U.S. companies are always suspicious that any change in the accounting rules will make them look worse on paper, almost all FASB decisions are made in the midst of controversy.

Other Organizations

In addition to the FASB, several other organizations affect accounting standards and are important in other ways to the practice of accounting. Some of these organizations are discussed below.

Securities and Exchange Commission

Securities and Exchange Commission (SEC) The government body responsible for regulating the financial reporting practices of most publicly owned corporations in connection with the buying and selling of stocks and bonds.

In response to the Stock Market Crash of 1929, Congress created the **Securities and Exchange Commission (SEC)** to regulate U.S. stock exchanges. Part of the job of the SEC is to make sure that investors are provided with full and fair information about publicly-traded companies. The SEC is not charged with protecting investors from losing money; instead, the SEC seeks to create a fair information environment in which investors can buy and sell stocks without fear that companies are hiding or manipulating financial data.

As part of its regulatory role, the SEC has received from Congress specific legal authority to establish accounting standards for companies soliciting investment funds from the American public. Generally, the SEC refrains from exercising this authority and allows the FASB to set U.S. accounting standards. However, as a result of the accounting scandals of the early 2000s, the SEC was given more responsibility and authority to monitor financial reporting. Congress provided this additional authority with the Sarbanes-Oxley Act. This Act created, among other things, a Public Company Accounting Oversight Board. The Act also required the SEC to implement many changes to the way corporations are governed.

While the FASB is charged with creating the rules that dictate financial reporting practices, the SEC is always looming in the background, legally authorized to take over the setting of U.S. accounting standards should the FASB lose its credibility with the public.

American Institute of Certified Public Accountants

The label "CPA" has two different uses—there are individuals who are CPAs and there are CPA firms. A **certified public accountant (CPA)** is someone who has taken a minimum number of college-level accounting classes, has passed the CPA exam administered by the **American Institute of Certified Public Accountants (AICPA)**, and has met other requirements set by his or her state. In essence, the CPA label guarantees that the person has received substantial accounting training. Not all CPAs work as accountants, however. CPAs work in law firms, as business consultants, as corporate managers, for the government, and even some as accounting professors.

The second use of the label "CPA" is in association with a CPA firm. A CPA firm is a company that performs accounting services, just as a law firm performs legal services. Obviously, a CPA firm employs a large number of accountants, not all of whom have received the training necessary to be certified public accountants. CPA firms also employ attorneys, information technology specialists, experts in finance, and other business specialists. CPA firms help companies establish accounting systems, formulate business plans, redesign their operating procedures, and just about anything else you can think of. A good way to think of a CPA firm is as a freelance business-advising firm with a particular strength in accounting issues.

CPA firms are also hired to perform independent audits of the financial statements of a company. The important role of the independent audit in ensuring the reliability of the financial statements is discussed in Chapter 6.

Internal Revenue Service

Imagine that you have a contract to design a computerized accounting system for a local business. Your fee is $100,000, which will be paid in full when the job is finished. By the end of the year, you have collected nothing, but you estimate that you have completed 80% of the work on the contract.

If you are asked by a potential business partner how much money you have earned during the past year, what will you say? To say that you made $0, the amount you've collected on the contract, significantly understates the value of the work you have completed. If the 80% estimate is a fair reflection of the work you've done, it would seem reasonable for you to report to the potential partner that you've earned $80,000 ($100,000 × 0.80) during the year. And, as you'll see later in the text, this is exactly what you would report according to financial accounting rules.

Now, if you are asked by the **Internal Revenue Service (IRS)** to state your income for the year, how much should you report? You don't have much leeway in the matter, because the IRS has very specific rules about what is considered taxable income. Assume that IRS rules state that you must pay income tax on the $80,000 income from the estimated amount of the contract that you have completed. Two practical problems would arise:

1. You don't have the money to pay the tax. You won't be able to pay the tax until the job is completed and you have collected your entire fee.
2. You could have endless arguments with the IRS about the completion percentage. The IRS could send an agent to dispute your estimate. The whole thing might end up in Tax Court.

---

certified public accountant (CPA) A special designation given to an accountant who has passed a national uniform examination and has met other certifying requirements.

American Institute of Certified Public Accountants (AICPA) The national organization of CPAs in the United States.

FYI:

Other tasks accountants perform are planning for acquisitions and mergers, measuring efficiency improvements from new technology, managing quality, and developing accounting software.

FYI:

Other accounting-related certifications also exist. Examples include the Certified Management Accountant (CMA), Certified Internal Auditor (CIA), and the Certified Fraud Examiner (CFE).

Internal Revenue Service (IRS) A government agency that prescribes the rules and regulations that govern the collection of tax revenues in the United States.

This example illustrates that what works for financial accounting purposes does not necessarily work for income tax purposes. Financial accounting reports are designed to provide information about the economic performance and health of a company. Tax rules are designed to tax income when the tax can be paid and to provide concrete rules to minimize inefficient arguing between taxpayers and the IRS. Accordingly, the IRS rules would probably allow you to report $0 income and delay paying income tax until you have actually collected the cash and could thus pay the tax.

The implication of this separation between financial accounting and tax accounting is that companies must maintain two sets of books—one set from which the financial statements can be prepared and the other set to comply with income tax regulations. There is nothing shady or underhanded about this. Financial accounting and tax accounting involve different sets of rules because they are designed for different purposes.

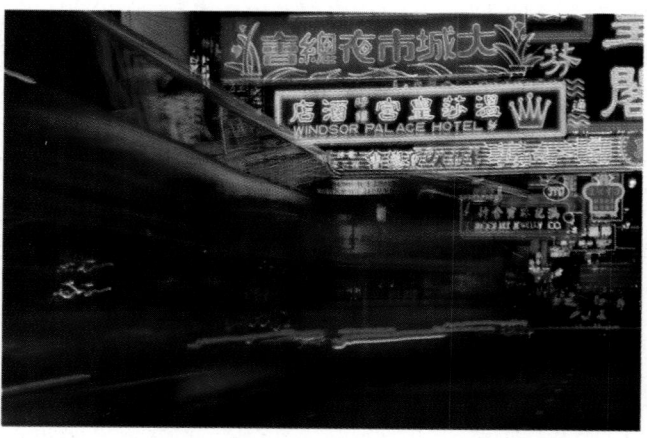

© 2003 Getty Images

Because of the expansion of international business, consumers are familiar with products from other countries, such as Hong Kong.

International Accounting Standards Board (IASB)
The committee formed in 1973 to develop worldwide accounting standards.

International Business

One of the significant environmental changes in recent years has been the expansion of business activity on a worldwide basis. As consumers, we are familiar with the wide array of products from other countries, such as electronics from Japan and clothing made in China. On the other hand, many U.S. companies have operating divisions in foreign countries. Other American companies are located totally within the United States but have extensive transactions with foreign companies. The economic environment of today's business is truly based on a global economy. As an example, in 2001 almost 60% of IBM's sales were to individuals and companies located outside the United States.

Accounting practices among countries vary widely. Attempts are being made to make those practices more consistent among countries. In an attempt to harmonize conflicting national standards, the **International Accounting Standards Board (IASB)** was formed in 1973 to develop worldwide accounting standards. The IASB includes representatives from the eight major accounting standard-setting boards around the world including the United States. Like the FASB, the IASB develops proposals, circulates them among interested organizations, receives feedback, and then issues a final pronouncement.

The accounting standards produced by the IASB are referred to as International Financial Reporting Standards (IFRS's). IFRS's are envisioned to be a set of standards that can be used by all companies regardless of where they are based. In the extreme, IAS could supplement or even replace standards set by national standard setters such as the FASB. IASB standards are gaining increasing acceptance throughout the world. For example, in November 2002, the IASB Web site listed 224 companies around the world that prepare financial statements using IFRS's. Of these companies, 66 are located in Germany and 54 are located in Switzerland. Thus far, however, the SEC has not recognized IASB standards and has barred foreign companies from listing their shares on U.S. stock exchanges unless those companies agree to provide financial statements in accordance with U.S. accounting rules (or at least provide a reconciliation between IASB GAAP and U.S. GAAP). Disclosure requirements in the United States are the strictest in the world, and foreign companies are reluctant to submit to the SEC requirement. The SEC is not alone in being reluctant to adopt IASB standards. As of December 2002, there were 67 stock exchanges in 52 countries around the world that allow the use of IFRS's, but many of those exchanges (including the New York Stock Exchange) allow the use of IFRS's only if the resulting financial statements are then recon-

FYI:

Since international accounting standards often differ from GAAP, foreign companies may be required to adjust their books to be listed on the New York Stock Exchange. For example, when Germany's DAIMLER-BENZ (makers of Mercedes Benz) became a NYSE-listed company in 1994, its GAAP-adjusted books showed a loss of $748 million, whereas its German standard books reported earnings of $636 million. Note: Daimler-Benz subsequently merged with CHRYSLER to become DAIMLERCHRYSLER.

Do You Have What It Takes? There are many opportunities in the field of accounting. The Bureau of Labor Statistics forecasts that the demand for accounting graduates will increase 10 to 20 percent over the next decade. Accounting graduates use their education to obtain jobs in public accounting, for federal, state and local governments (including the Internal Revenue Service), and in commercial banking. In addition to becoming accountants, many accounting students use their undergraduate accounting education as a stepping-stone to law school or investment banking or to obtain other graduate degrees (like an MBA).

Many accounting students who go on to become accountants pursue the CPA designation. To be a CPA, specific requirements must be met. First, CPAs are required to have a formal education. For example, although individual state laws vary, as of January 10, 2003, 39 states (including the District of Columbia) require students to have completed 150 hours of college education to become CPAs. In addition, seven other states have enacted legislation that will require 150 hours at some future date. Currently, only California, Colorado, Delaware, New Hampshire, and Vermont have not enacted the 150-hour requirement. Next, aspiring CPAs must pass an examination based on the skills obtained from their education. This ensures that accountants are competent to perform independent services for the community. In addition to the examination, field experience requirements must be met to satisfy state licensing laws for CPAs.

If you are interested in someday working in a business environment, a degree in accounting can help you understand business issues, analyze accounting information, and make business decisions.

ciled to the home country's GAAP. This conflict will be interesting to watch in the coming years: Will the SEC maintain a hard line and ultimately force U.S. accounting rules on the rest of the world? Or will the IASB standards gain increasing acceptance and become the worldwide standard? We'll see.

At numerous points throughout this text, we will point out certain international applications of accounting as well as some differences that might exist in accounting rules between the United States and other countries. In addition, each chapter includes a case in the end-of-chapter material dealing with an international accounting issue.

STOP & THINK

Why is it so difficult to make international accounting standards consistent?

Ethics in Accounting

Another environmental factor affecting accounting, and business in general, is the growing concern over ethics. This concern has been a focus of the accounting scandals of the early 2000s. Enron, WorldCom, and Tyco (to name a few) each resulted from upper management's falsifying financial reports (with the help of the company's internal accountants) and external auditors not detecting those falsifications. Accounting rules and the resulting information are designed to capture and reflect the underlying performance of a company. When management is tempted to use accounting numbers to misrepresent a company's performance, accountants (both inside and outside the company) are perceived by the public as being responsible for ensuring that the misrepresentation does not occur. The public's confidence in the accounting profession was weakened when these scandals came to light with the common denominator being that accounting information was used to mislead the public.

As mentioned previously, the SEC has taken action to see that public confidence in the accounting profession is restored. In addition, other organizations (like the Auditing Standards

Board) have taken measures to increase the public's confidence in the role of accountants and auditors and to restore the image of the accounting professional as being ethical and competent.

This concern over ethics and the accounting profession was highlighted in an almost prophetic speech given by then chairman of the SEC, Arthur Levitt, in September 1998 and was reinforced in 2001 with the business failures of Enron and WorldCom. In his speech, entitled "The Number's Game," Chairman Levitt identified several major accounting techniques that he believed were being used to undermine the integrity of financial reporting. As you will find, accounting involves significant judgment. Chairman Levitt expressed concern that this accounting judgment was giving way to pressure to "meet the numbers." In other words, Wall Street's expectations about a company, rather than the company's actual business performance, were driving the reported accounting numbers.

In his speech, Chairman Levitt mentioned the standards of objectivity, integrity, and judgment in reporting accounting numbers. These standards are an integral part of the public accounting profession's Code of Professional Conduct and form the foundation upon which audited financial statements are compiled and interpreted.

The ethical dilemmas facing businesses and their accountants often revolve around pressures placed on companies by investors, creditors, and potential investors and creditors. As Chairman Levitt mentioned, these pressures can sometimes cause company officials to become involved in "accounting hocus-pocus." Because accounting involves judgment, the reported accounting numbers can differ significantly depending on the assumptions made by those preparing the financial statements. As a simple example of how this can occur, consider again the case of Microsoft. When a customer buys a Microsoft product, part of the purchase price relates to promised customer service and future product upgrades. So the question is this: How much of the sales price should Microsoft report as a "sale" on the date of the sale, and how much relates to future services to be provided? As you can imagine, that is a difficult question to answer, and any answer will involve an estimate.

To quote again from Chairman Levitt's speech, accounting principles "allow for flexibility to adapt to changing circumstances." It is this flexibility that creates many of the ethical dilemmas faced by accountants. As businesses come under pressure to report favorable performance, accountants may also come under pressure to "flex" the rules just a little too far.

Fortunately, the public accounting profession is guided by a Code of Professional Conduct. Many other accounting organizations also have codes of conduct to provide guidance for their members.

Don't let yourself naively think that ethical dilemmas in business are rare. Such issues arise quite frequently. To help prepare you to enter the business world and to recognize and deal with ethical issues, we have included at least one ethics case at the end of each chapter. Ethics is an important topic that should be considered carefully, with the ultimate goal of improving individual and collective behavior in society.

Technology

Few developments have changed the way business is conducted as much as computers have. Computer technology allows businesses to do things that 20 years ago were unimaginable. Consider being able to use your desktop computer to track the status of a package shipped from Los Angeles to New York. Companies such as UPS and FEDEX incorporate this type of technology as an integral part of their business. Financial institutions use computer technology to wire billions of dollars each day to locations around the world.

So how have computers changed the way accounting is done? That question can be addressed on several levels. First, computer technology allows companies to easily gather vast amounts of information about individual transactions. For example, information relating to the customer, the salesperson, the product being sold, and the method of payment can be easily gathered for each transaction using computer technology. Prior to today's technology, the cost of gathering this information was prohibitive.

Second, computer technology allows large amounts of data to be compiled quickly and accurately, thereby significantly reducing the likelihood of errors. As you will soon discover, a large part of the mechanics of accounting involves moving numbers to and from various accounting records as well as adding and subtracting a lot of figures. Computers have made this process virtually invisible. What once occupied a large part of an accountant's time can now be done in an instant.

network exercises

Microsoft

Access Microsoft's Web site at **http://www.microsoft.com**. Identify the different kinds of information found on Microsoft's home page, e.g., marketing, product information, etc. Can you find any financial information?

Third, in the precomputer world of limited analytical capacity, it was essential for lenders and investors to receive condensed summaries of a company's financial activities. Now, lenders and investors have the ability to receive and process gigabytes of information, so why should the report of Microsoft's financial performance be restricted to three short financial statements? Why can't Microsoft provide access to much more detailed information online? In fact, why can't Microsoft allow investors to directly tap into its own internal accounting database? Information technology has made this type of information acquisition and analysis possible; the question accountants face now is how much information companies should be required to make available to outsiders. Ten years ago, the only way you could get a copy of Microsoft's financial statements was to call or write to receive paper copies in the mail. Now you can download those summary financial statements from Microsoft's Web site. How will you get financial information 10 years from now? No one knows, but the rapid advances in information technology guarantee that it will be different from anything we are familiar with now.

Finally, and most importantly, although technology has changed the way certain aspects of accounting are carried out, on a fundamental level the mechanics of accounting are still the same as they were 500 years ago. People are still required to analyze complex business transactions and input the results of that analysis into the computer. Technology has not replaced judgment.

So if you are asking "Why do I need to understand accounting—can't computers just do it?"—the answer is a resounding "No!" You need to know what the computer is doing if you are to understand and interpret the information resulting from the accounting process. You need to understand that since judgment was required when the various pieces of information were put into the accounting systems, judgment will be required to appropriately use that information. We have included numerous end-of-chapter opportunities for you to experience how technology helps in the accounting process. These opportunities will illustrate the important role that technology can play in the accounting process as well as emphasize the critical role that the accountant plays as well.

TO SUMMARIZE: Accounting functions in a dynamic environment. Generally accepted accounting principles (GAAP) have developed over time. The primary standard-setting body for the private sector is the Financial Accounting Standards Board (FASB). The accounting environment includes business activity that is conducted on an international basis. Consequently, accounting practices often must be modified to reflect the accounting standards of different countries. Attempts are being made to establish comparable international accounting practices. There is increasing concern in society over ethics. High standards of ethical conduct are important, especially for accountants who assume a special responsibility to the public. CPAs have adopted standards of conduct that contain principles and rules as guidelines for the performance of accounting services. Technology has changed the way accounting information is collected, analyzed, and used. The use of computers in the accounting process has increased significantly, and although they allow more information to be gathered and used, computers have not replaced the accountant nor eliminated the need for qualified decision makers.

Step one in succeeding in an accounting class is to stay current with your studies and with your assignments. Many of the concepts in accounting are new, and some time is required between the introduction of a new concept and the mastery of that concept. Some students try to "cram" all their accounting study into a short period of time right before an exam, and they almost always find, through sad experience, that the cramming strategy doesn't work in accounting. Some of you may be skeptical of this advice because you have successfully used the cramming strategy in other courses. For you, we suggest the following experiment: pair up with a classmate, with one of you studying your accounting on a regular basis and the other waiting until two days before the first exam to start studying. We guarantee that the "crammer" will have a humbling experience on that first exam whereas the regular studier will have reasonable success. We also strongly suggest that if you try this experiment, you take the role of the regular studier and let your friend be the crammer.

Our second suggestion is that you spend much of your study time working problems rather than passively reading through this book (as interesting as it may be). One of the authors remembers, with some pain, his first exam in a college chemistry course. He had attended class every day, he enjoyed the lectures, and he felt that he almost always understood what the professor was saying. He had looked through the homework problems, and they made sense to him. However, during the first exam he found to his dismay that the exam didn't ask how well he liked the lectures or whether the homework problems made sense to him when he glanced over them. Instead, the exam involved actually putting pencil to paper and solving problem after problem. The forlorn author spent about half of the exam time trying to calculate what he would have to get on subsequent exams in order to pass the class; his score on the exam was 55%. In order to avoid a similar fate, please remember that accounting exams are also heavily weighted toward the working out of problems, and the only way to properly prepare is to practice working out lots of problems.

Third, realize that many of the concepts in accounting build on one another. As a result, missing class or skipping a couple of homework assignments can be catastrophic. An initial

So, Why Should I Study Accounting?

4 Analyze the reasons for studying accounting.

You may still be asking, "But why do I need to study accounting?" Even if you have no desire to be an accountant, at some point in your life you will need financial information to make certain decisions, such as whether to buy or lease an automobile, how to budget your monthly income, where to invest your savings, or how to finance your (or your child's) college education. You can make each of these decisions without using financial information and then hope everything turns out okay, but that would be bad decision making. As noted in the discussion of Exhibit 3, a good decision does not guarantee a good outcome, but a bad decision guarantees one of two things—a bad outcome or a lucky outcome. And you cannot count on lucky outcomes time after time. On a personal level, each of us needs to understand how to collect and use accounting information.

Odds are that each of you will have the responsibility of providing some form of income for yourself and your family. Would you prefer to work for a company that is doing well and has a promising future or one that is on the brink of bankruptcy? Of course we all want to work for companies that are doing well. But how would you know? Accounting information will allow you to evaluate your employer's short- and long-term potential.

When you graduate and secure employment, it is almost certain that accounting information will play some role in your job. Whether your responsibilities include sales (where you will need information about product availability and costs), production (where you will need information regarding the costs of materials, labor, and overhead), quality control (where you will concept must be understood before a subsequent concept can be attempted. For example, imagine trying to learn to do algebra after having skipped the lessons on addition and subtraction. Similarly, jumping into Chapter 6 in this book is a difficult feat if you don't understand the material covered in Chapter 3.

The fourth step in having a good experience in your accounting class is to make sure you understand the big picture. We have included learning objectives to cover each major point in the chapter. The introductions associated with each learning objective should help you understand WHY you are studying the issue in addition to HOW to do accounting. In most cases, when you understand the "why" of something, you find it much easier to grasp the "how."

Fifth, use the real-world examples we include in the text to solidify your understanding of the learning points of the text. The beauty of accounting is that it is an applied art, and you can understand accounting concepts by considering how they would be used in the businesses you observe every day. In addition to using numerous real companies to illustrate points, we will provide some continuity by using one real company throughout the textbook as a continuing illustration.

Microsoft's 2002 Form 10-K is included in Appendix A at the back of this textbook and will be referred to often in illustrating different accounting concepts.

Finally, if you need help, don't delay in finding it. Your instructor is a valuable resource and you should take advantage of his or her office hours. (*Note:* Instructors love students who come in with written lists of specific questions. On the other hand, instructors get frustrated with students who view office hours as a time for the instructor to repeat, for an audience of one, a lecture that the student missed.) In addition, many students find that accounting study groups are beneficial. A well-organized study group is an example of the classic economic concept of specialization and trade; group members can rotate in taking the lead in studying difficult concepts and then explaining them to the rest of the group. And last, but certainly not least, we have prepared a variety of study helps to accompany this book. To see what resources are available, access the Web site for this text at **http:// albrecht.swlearning.com**.

Good luck, and enjoy the ride!

need information relating to variances between expected and actual production), or human resources (where you will need information relating to the costs of employees), you will use accounting information. The more you know about where accounting information comes from, how it is accumulated, and how it is best used, the better you will be able to perform your job.

Everyone is affected by accounting information. Saying you don't need to know accounting doesn't change the fact that you are affected by accounting information. Ignoring the value of that information simply puts you at a disadvantage. Those who recognize the value of accounting information and learn how to use it to make better decisions will have a competitive advantage over those who don't. It's as simple as that.

FYI:

The AICPA provides a Web site that introduces students to career opportunities in accounting. The Web site is **http://www .startheregoplaces.com**.

review of learning objectives

▌ **Describe the purpose of accounting and explain its role in business and society.** Accounting is a service activity designed to assist individuals and organizations in deciding how to allocate scarce resources and reach their financial objectives. It is used to accumulate, measure, and communicate economic data about organizations and to assist in the decision-making process.

2 **Identify the primary users of accounting information.** The primary users of accounting information are lenders, investors, management, and other interested individuals and organizations. Management accounting deals primarily with the internal accounting functions of planning, implementing, and control. Financial accounting is concerned with reporting business activities and results to external parties. The objectives of both areas of accounting are measurement and communication of information for decision-making purposes.

3 **Describe the environment of accounting, including the effects of generally accepted accounting principles, international business, ethical considerations, and technology.** Accounting functions in a dynamic environment. The principles of accounting have evolved over time to meet the changing demands of the business environment. They are therefore not absolute. Only if they prove useful do they become generally accepted. Accounting principles provide comparable data for external users and need to be applied with judgment.

Since the 1930s, several organizations have been involved in the development of accounting principles in the United States. The American Institute of Certified Public Accountants (AICPA), the Securities and Exchange Commission (SEC), and the Financial Accounting Standards Board (FASB) are among the most prominent. The FASB is currently the primary standard-setting body for accounting principles in the private sector.

Accounting is practiced in an international environment. Accounting procedures in the United States sometimes must be modified to accommodate foreign operations. Attempts are being made to establish consistent and comparable accounting practices throughout the world, primarily through the efforts of the International Accounting Standards Board (IASB).

Ethical considerations affect society and are particularly important for accountants, who have a special responsibility to the public. CPAs have adopted standards of conduct to guide them in the performance of their duties.

Technology has changed the way accounting information is accumulated and analyzed. What once occupied a large part of an accountant's time is now done quickly by computers, thereby freeing the accountant to be involved in more productive tasks. But computer technology has not removed the accountant from the decision-making process. Accounting judgment is still essential.

4 **Analyze the reasons for studying accounting.** Knowing how to use accounting information will help individuals make better decisions in their personal life as well as in their employment. Whatever the job, it is likely that accounting information plays a part. Knowing where information comes from, how it is accumulated, and how it is best used will result in better decision making.

key terms & concepts

accounting, 5
accounting cycle, 8
accounting system, 5
American Institute of Certified Public Accountants (AICPA), 15
annual report, 9
bookkeeping, 4
business, 6

certified public accountant (CPA), 15
financial accounting, 10
Financial Accounting Standards Board (FASB), 14
financial statements, 10
generally accepted accounting principles (GAAP), 14
Internal Revenue Service (IRS), 15

International Accounting Standards Board (IASB), 16
management accounting, 9
nonprofit organization, 7
Securities and Exchange Commission (SEC), 14

discussion questions

1. What are the three functions of an accounting system?
2. What are the essential elements in decision making, and how does accounting fit into the process?
3. What types of personal decisions have required you to use accounting information?
4. What does the term *business* mean to you?
5. Why is accounting often referred to as the "language of business"?
6. In what ways are the needs of internal and external users of accounting information the same? In what ways are they different?

7. What are generally accepted accounting principles (GAAP)? Who currently develops and issues GAAP? What is the purpose of GAAP?
8. Why is it important for financial statements and other external reports to be based on generally accepted accounting principles?
9. What are the respective roles of the Securities and Exchange Commission (SEC) and the Internal Revenue Service (IRS) in the setting of accounting standards?
10. For you as a potential investor, what is the problem with different countries having different accounting standards?

For you as the president of a multinational company, what is the problem with different countries having different accounting standards?
11. Ethical considerations affect all society. Why are ethical considerations especially important for accountants?
12. Given significant technological advances, can we expect to see less demand for accountants and accounting-type services?
13. Other than that it is a requirement for your major or that your mom or dad is making you, why should you study accounting?

e x e r c i s e s

Exercise 1-1

The Role and Importance of Accounting

Assume that you are applying for a part-time job as an accounting clerk in a retail clothing establishment. During the interview, the store manager asks how you expect to contribute to the business. How would you respond?

Exercise 1-2

Bookkeeping Is Everywhere

Describe how bookkeeping is applied in each of the following settings:

a. Your college English class.
b. The National Basketball Association.
c. A hospital emergency room.
d. Jury selection for a major murder trial.
e. Four college roommates on a weekend skiing trip.

Exercise 1-3

Accounting Information and Decision Making

You are the owner of Automated Systems, Inc., which sells APPLE computers and related data processing equipment. You are currently trying to decide whether to continue selling the Apple computer line or to distribute the Windows-based computers instead. What information do you need to consider in order to determine how successful your business is or will be? What information would help you decide whether to sell the Apple or the Windows-based personal computer line? Use your imagination and general knowledge of business activity.

Exercise 1-4

Users of Financial Information

Why might each of the following individuals or groups be interested in a firm's financial statements? (a) The current stockholders of the firm; (b) the creditors of the firm; (c) the management of the firm; (d) the prospective stockholders of the firm; (e) the Internal Revenue Service (IRS); (f) the SEC; (g) the firm's major labor union.

Exercise 1-5

Structuring Information for Use in Evaluation

You work in a small convenience store. The store is very low-tech; you ring up the sales on an old-style cash register that merely records the amount of the sale. The store owner uses this cash register tape at the end of each day to verify that the correct amount of cash is in the cash register drawer.

In addition to verifying the cash amount, how else could the information on the cash register tape be used to evaluate the store's operation? What additional bookkeeping procedures would be necessary to make these additional uses possible?

Exercise 1-6

Investing in the Stock Market

Assume your grandparents have just given you $20,000 on the condition that you invest the money in the stock market. As you contemplate making your investment choices, what accounting information do you want to help identify companies that will have high future rates of return?

Exercise 1-7

Allocation of Limited Resources

Assume you are a small business owner trying to increase your company's profits. How can accounting information help you efficiently allocate your limited resources to maximize your business profit?

Exercise 1-8

Management versus Financial Accounting

This chapter discusses two areas of accounting: management and financial accounting. Contrast management and financial accounting with respect to the following:

- Overall purpose
- Type of financial reports used (i.e., external, internal, or both)
- Users of the information

Also, in what ways are these two fields of accounting similar?

Exercise 1-9

The Role of the SEC

It is not often that the federal government has allowed the private sector to govern itself, but that is exactly what has happened with the field of accounting. The SEC has delegated the responsibility of rule making to the FASB, a group of seven individuals who are hired full-time to discuss issues, research areas of interest, and determine what GAAP is and will be. What are the advantages of allowing the private sector to determine accounting standards? Identify any advantages that the SEC might gain if it established the rules that govern the practice of accounting.

Exercise 1-10

Why Two Sets of Books?

This past year you were married. This coming April you will be faced with preparing your first tax return since mom and dad said "you are now on your own." As you review the IRS regulations, you notice several differences from what you learned in your accounting class. It appears that businesses must keep two sets of books: one for the IRS and one in accordance with GAAP. Why aren't GAAP and IRS rules the same?

Exercise 1-11

International

Differences in Accounting across Borders

In the United States, accounting for inventory is a difficult issue. Inventory is comprised of those items either purchased or manufactured to be resold at a profit. Numerous methods are available to account for inventory for financial reporting purposes. A very commonly used method—called LIFO (last-in, first-out)—minimizes a company's tax obligation. In the United Kingdom, however, LIFO is not permitted for tax purposes and thus is not used very often for financial reporting. In Turkey, the use of LIFO is severely restricted, and in Russia, LIFO is a foreign term. Only in Germany, where the tax laws have been modified to allow the use of LIFO, is LIFO being adopted. Different accounting methods are available for numerous other issues in accounting. Identify some major problems associated with comparing the financial statements of companies from different countries.

Exercise 1-12

Ethics in Accounting

The text has pointed out that ethics is an important topic, especially for CPAs. Derek Bok, former law professor and president of Harvard University, has suggested that colleges and universities have a special opportunity and obligation to train students to be more thoughtful and perceptive about moral and ethical issues. Other individuals have concluded that it is not possible to "teach" ethics. What do you think? Can ethics be taught? If you agree that colleges and universities can teach ethics, how might the ethical dimensions of accounting be presented to students?

Exercise 1-13

Career Opportunities in Accounting

You are scheduled to graduate from college with a degree in accounting, and your mother would like to know what you plan to do with the rest of your life. She assumes that your only option is to be a bookkeeper like Bob Cratchit in the story *A Christmas Carol.* What can you tell Mom regarding the options available to you with your degree in accounting?

Exercise 1-14

Why Do I Need to Know Accounting?

One of your college friends recently graduated from school with a major in music (specifically piano). He has told you that he is going to start his own piano instructional business. He plans to operate the business from home. You ask him how he is going to account for his business, and his reply is, "I graduated in music, not accounting. I am going to teach music, not number crunching. I didn't need accounting in college and I don't need it now!" Is your friend right? What financial information might he find useful in operating his business?

Exercise 1-15

Challenges to the Accounting Profession

As the business world continues to change the way in which business is conducted, accountants are faced with the challenge of accounting for these changes. Who, for example, could have anticipated the risks associated with asbestos? Or the decline of communism? Or the increasingly litigious environment in the United States? Each of these events, and many more, has influenced business—which has, in turn, influenced accounting. From your general understanding of accounting and the current business environment, what are some of the challenges you see facing the accounting profession?

 d i s c u s s i o n   c a s e s

Case 1-1

To Lend or Not To Lend—That Is the Question

Sam Love is vice president and chief lending officer of the Meeker First National Bank. Recently, Bill McCarthy, a new farmer, moved to town. Sam has not dealt with Bill previously and knows little about the Mountain Meadow Ranch that Bill operates. Bill would like to borrow $100,000 to purchase some equipment and yearling steers for his ranch. What information does Sam need to help make the lending decision? What type of information should Bill collect and analyze before even requesting the loan?

Case 1-2

Information Needs to Remain Competitive

In 2002, INTEL virtually owned the microprocessor industry with a market share of 83%. Its nearest competition was ADVANCED MICRO DEVICES (AMD) with a market share of 16%. What type of information, accounting or otherwise, do you think the management of AMD may want and need as they try to compete with Intel and other companies?

Case 1-3

International

International Happenings

July 1, 1997, marked a historic date as Hong Kong reverted to political and economic control by mainland China. The Stock Exchange of Hong Kong offers the opportunity to invest in both local Hong Kong companies and in "red-chip offerings," which are stocks of companies that are listed in Hong Kong but controlled by mainland China interests. As an international investor, what accounting information might be helpful as you consider investing in the Hong Kong stock market? For which variables in this situation is accounting information unlikely to be very helpful?

Case 1-4

Is Better Accounting the Solution to All of Life's Problems?

Your friend has just completed an introductory accounting course. She has heard that you are now taking accounting, and she has come to give you the benefit of her experience. You discover that your friend is enamored with the field of accounting, and she now believes that most business problems can be easily solved through better accounting. In fact, your friend believes that most government, social, and spiritual problems can also be solved by a better application of good accounting principles. Given what you have read in Chapter 1, do you agree with your friend? Explain.

Case 1-5

We Don't Have Time for Good Accounting!

Your sister and her business partner have just launched their own software company. They have developed software that compresses and packages email text and voice messages, allowing email and phone messages to be safely transmitted over a wireless network even while flying in a commercial airliner. Orders for the software have been pouring in, and your sister and her business partner estimate that they will make at least $10 million within the next three months. You suggest to your sister that she hire an accountant and begin to set up an accounting system within her new company. Your sister replies that accounting systems are for old-fashioned companies such as GENERAL MOTORS and PROCTER & GAMBLE; she wants to focus her time on hiring new software developers and on working on ideas for her company's next generation of software products. Is your sister correct? Explain.

Case 1-6

Is the Proposed Electricity Rate Increase Fair?

The governor of your state has just appointed you to the state's public utility rate commission. Your job is to set fair prices for the electricity and natural gas sold to residents of the state by a select number of public utilities. The state's primary electric utility has just proposed a 5.3% rate increase. How should you use accounting information to evaluate this proposed rate hike?

j udgment calls

Judgment 1-1

You Decide: How much education is necessary for an accountant?

You are at your family reunion when some relatives start asking you about your studies and plans after school. Upon learning your intentions to be an accountant, everyone was alarmed that it took five to six years to get a master's degree in accounting. Your uncle says, "All you have to do is go to a computer store and pick up a copy of QuickBooks. Computers do everything these days. The computer will do all the work and you can collect a paycheck!" Is five to six years too much time and effort to prepare to be an accountant, or is it necessary?

Judgment 1-2

You Decide: Should the Emerging Issues Task Force be allowed to have members of large corporations sit on their committee and vote on accounting issues that are facing today's companies, or should it be left to the accounting firms?

That is what happened with J.P. MORGAN at a June 2002 meeting of the EITF (Emerging Issues Task Force), an extension of the FASB. J.P. Morgan blocked a vote that would have barred companies from recognizing immediate profits or losses upon entering an energy-trading contract, a move that is critical to the financial statements of J.P. Morgan and others in its industry.

Competency Enhancement Opportunities

▶ **Analyzing Real Company Information**
▶ **International Case**
▶ **Ethics Case**
▶ **Writing Assignment**

▶ **The Debate**
▶ **Internet Search**

The following additional assignments provide opportunities for students to develop critical thinking, ethical perspectives, oral and written communication skills, experience with electronic research, and teamwork through group and business activities.

▷ *Analyzing Real Company Information*

Analyzing 1-1 (Microsoft)

In Appendix A at the back of this text is MICROSOFT's Form 10-K for the year ended June 30, 2002. Review the Form 10-K and identify its major areas. How many pages of the Form 10-K are devoted to a narrative of the prior three years' performance? How many pages focus on explaining technical accounting and business-related issues and procedures? In your opinion, given your limited knowledge of accounting, what is the most interesting part of the Form 10-K? What is the least interesting?

Analyzing 1-2 (General Motors)

Below is a condensed listing of the assets and liabilities of GENERAL MOTORS as of December 31, 2002. All amounts are in millions of U.S. dollars.

Assets		Liabilities	
Cash	$ 21,449	Payables	$229,392
Loans receivable	150,362	Pensions	22,762
Inventories	9,967	Other retiree benefits	38,187
Property & equipment	37,973	Other liabilities	72,793
Other assets	151,031		
Total assets	$370,782	Total liabilities	$363,134

1. Among its assets, General Motors lists more than $150 billion in loans receivable. This represents loans that General Motors has made and expects to collect in the future. This is exactly the kind of asset reported among the assets of banks. Given what you know about General Motors' business, how do you think the company acquired these loans receivable?
2. The difference between the reported amount of General Motors' assets and liabilities is $7.648 billion ($370.782 − $363.134). What does this difference represent?

▷ *International Case*

Should the SEC Choose the FASB or the IASB?

The SEC has received from Congress the legal authority to set accounting standards in the United States. Historically, the SEC has allowed the FASB to set those standards. In addition, the SEC has refused to allow foreign companies to seek investment funds in the United States unless they agree to provide U.S. investors with financial statements prepared using FASB rules.

International

The number of foreign companies seeking to list their shares on U.S. stock exchanges is increasing. Even more would likely sell stock to the American public if the SEC were to agree to accept financial statements prepared according to usually less stringent IASB standards.

Why do you think the SEC has so far insisted on financial statements prepared using FASB rules? Do you agree with its policy? Explain.

▶ *Ethics Case*

Disagreement with the Boss

You recently graduated with your degree in accounting and have accepted an entry-level accounting position with BigTec, Inc. One of your first responsibilities is to review expense reports submitted by various executives. The expense reports include such items as receipts for taking clients to dinner and hotel receipts for business travel. In conducting this review, you note that your boss has submitted for reimbursement several items that are clearly outside the established guidelines of the corporation. In questioning your boss about the items, he told you to process the items and not worry about them. What would you do?

▶ *Writing Assignments*

The Language of Business

Accounting is known as the "language of business." Prepare a one- to two-page paper explaining why all business students should have some accounting education. Also include a discussion of how accounting applies to at least five different types of businesses, such as a grocery store, a university, or a movie theater.

Visiting an Accounting Professional

Select a field of accounting you are interested in. Visit a professional who works in that area and discuss the career opportunities available in that specific accounting field. After the visit, prepare a one- to two-page paper summarizing what you learned from your discussion with the accounting professional.

▶ *The Debate*

Insulate the FASB

As mentioned in the text, the FASB conducts public hearings concerning any new accounting standards that it is considering. In addition, the FASB invites interested parties (businesses, trade groups, user groups, accounting professors) to send in written comments on proposed standards. This "due process" system occasionally exposes the FASB to intense lobbying pressure for and against proposed standards. For example, when the FASB was deliberating over the proper accounting for option compensation (see the example in the chapter), some companies, upset at the FASB's proposed approach, appealed to Congress to pass a bill outlawing the FASB's standard. Can the FASB establish good accounting standards in such a heated, public environment?

Divide your group into two teams.

• One team represents the "Open Door Policy." Prepare a two-minute oral argument supporting the continuation of the FASB's policy of adopting accounting standards only after public debate.

- The other team represents the "Insulate the FASB Movement." Prepare a two-minute oral argument outlining why it is impossible for the FASB to design conceptually correct accounting standards while being bombarded with the complaints and threats of self-interested companies and lobbyists.

▶ *Internet Search*

The Financial Accounting Standards Board

The FASB's Web address is **http://www.fasb.org**. Sometimes Web addresses change; so if this address is out of commission, access the Web site for this textbook (**http://albrecht.swlearning .com**) for an updated link.

Once you have gained access to the site, answer the following questions.

1. What is the mission of the FASB?
2. How many FASB statements are there? When was the most recent statement issued?
3. When was the first statement issued, and what is it about? What other statements are related to Statement No. 1?
4. In what ways are the following three types of FASB pronouncements different: (1) Statements of Financial Accounting Standards (SFAS), (2) Interpretations of SFAS, and (3) Statements of Financial Accounting Concepts?

c h a p t e r

2

Financial Statements: An Overview

After studying this chapter, you should be able to:

Learning Objectives

1 Understand the basic elements, uses, and limitations of the balance sheet.

2 Understand the basic elements and uses of the income statement.

3 Understand the categories and uses of the statement of cash flows and see how the primary financial statements tie together.

4 Recognize the need for financial statement notes and identify the types of information included in the notes.

5 Describe the purpose of an audit report and the incentives the auditor has to perform a good audit.

6 Explain the fundamental concepts and assumptions that underlie financial accounting.

chapter 2

In addition to founding the brokerage firm of MERRILL LYNCH, in 1926 Charles Merrill was instrumental in the consolidation of several grocery store chains in the western United States to form one big holding company called SAFEWAY. In 1955, control of Safeway passed to Robert Magowan, Merrill's son-in-law. Under Magowan's leadership, Safeway expanded to become the second largest supermarket chain in the United States. Shortly after Magowan retired in 1971, Safeway passed THE GREAT ATLANTIC AND PACIFIC TEA COMPANY (A&P) to become the largest supermarket chain.

During the 1970s, Safeway became too cautious and conservative (in the view of many). It was whispered that Safeway would become the A&P of the West—a fallen giant no longer willing to make the bold moves that had created its success in the first place. In 1980, Robert Magowan's 37-year-old son, Peter (who had started out in Safeway as a teenager bagging groceries), became chairman of the board of directors. As he assumed leadership of Safeway, Magowan faced a host of problems: an overall decrease in the size of the grocery market due to an increased tendency by Americans to eat at fast-food restaurants; union contracts that resulted in higher labor costs for Safeway than many of its competitors; high corporate overhead; and stores that were too small and too close together. As a result of these problems, between 1976 and 1980 Safeway lost market share in 9 of the 14 major markets in which it operated. As one executive put it, "[Losing market share] in the food business [is] a hell of an indicator you're not giving the customer what he wants." By 1981, Safeway's financial performance had hit disappointing lows.

Under Peter Magowan's leadership, Safeway eliminated 2,000 office and warehouse jobs and embarked upon an impressive program of new construction and remodeling. During much of the early 1980s, Safeway spent more on capital expenditures than any other U.S. company, averaging nearly $600 million per year. In November 1986, Safeway was acquired by KOHLBERG, KRAVIS, ROBERTS & CO. (KKR) for $5.3 billion in what was then the second-largest leveraged buyout (LBO) of all time. In an LBO, a group of private investors, sometimes joined by company managers, supplies only a small amount of the money needed to buy an entire corporation. The bulk of the purchase price is provided by banks and other lenders, with the assets of the acquired company serving as collateral for the loans. As an indication of how leveraged the Safeway buyout was, the KKR investors put only $130 million of their own money into the $5.3 billion deal.

So, how is Safeway doing today? In the 2003 Fortune 500 survey, Safeway, with 2002 sales of $32.4 billion, ranks as the third-largest food and drug chain in the United States, behind KROGER ($51.8 billion in sales) and ALBERTSON'S ($35.9 billion in sales).[1] In fact, Safeway's 2002 sales increased 2.0% to reach this peak. Sales volume isn't the only financial measure that can be used to evaluate a company. For example, Safeway reported a net loss in 2002 of ($828) million, compared to the net income reported by Kroger ($1.2 billion) and Albertson's ($485 million). Also, Safeway's cash income ("cash from operations") was $1,938 million.

to adequately answer the question of how Safeway is doing today, one must have a working knowledge of financial statements. In this chapter, you will learn that the financial statements are summary reports that show how a business is doing and where its successes and failures lie. The financial statements covered in this chapter are the same as those used every day by millions of business owners, investors, and creditors to evaluate how well or poorly organizations are doing.

Hopefully, you will come away from this chapter convinced that the purpose of accounting is not to fill out dull reports that are then filed away in dusty cabinets, but rather to prepare summary financial performance measures to be used as the basis for thousands of economic decisions every day.

---

1 In 1999, Albertson's merged with AMERICAN STORES to form what was, at the time, the largest supermarket chain in the United States. Coincidentally, American Stores traces its roots back to the Skaggs family, whose stores also formed the backbone of the original Safeway chain organized by Charles Merrill in 1926.

The Financial Statements

primary financial statements The balance sheet, income statement, and statement of cash flows, used by external groups to assess a company's economic standing.

balance sheet (statement of financial position) The financial statement that reports a company's assets, liabilities, and owners' equity at a particular date.

income statement (statement of earnings) The financial statement that reports the amount of net income earned by a company during a period.

statement of cash flows The financial statement that reports the amount of cash collected and paid out by a company during a period of time.

The job of a mortgage loan officer is to evaluate each mortgage applicant to determine the likelihood that he or she will repay the mortgage loan. A key piece of evidence in each applicant's file is the financial information included as part of the loan application. A loan officer can use this information to evaluate whether an applicant will generate enough income to make the monthly mortgage payments and continue to make the required payments on other obligations. In fact, it is difficult to imagine how a mortgage loan officer could make an informed decision without this financial information.

Gaining access to an applicant's financial information clearly helps the mortgage lender make a better loan decision, but the applicant also benefits from making these financial disclosures. If no financial disclosures were provided, lenders would be forced to make loan decisions in the absence of reliable financial information about applicants. With greater uncertainty about applicants' ability to repay loans, a lender's risk would increase, causing the lender to raise the interest rate charged on loans. Thus, disclosure of financial information allows a lender to make better lending decisions and also allows an applicant to reduce the lender's uncertainty, leading to a lower interest rate on the loan.

The financial statements prepared by companies yield the same benefits as do the financial disclosures provided by mortgage applicants. Financial statement information provides potential lenders and investors with a reliable basis for evaluating the past performance and future prospects of a company. Because financial statements are used by so many different groups (investors, creditors, managers, etc.), they are sometimes called *general-purpose financial statements*. The three **primary financial statements** are the balance sheet, the income statement, and the statement of cash flows. These statements provide answers to the following questions:

1. What is the company's current financial status?
2. What were the company's operating results for the period?
3. How did the company obtain and use cash during the period?

The **balance sheet** (or **statement of financial position**) reports the resources of a company (assets), the company's obligations (liabilities), and the difference between what is owned (assets) and what is owed (liabilities), called owners' equity. The **income statement** (or **statement of earnings**) reports the amount of net income earned by a company during a period, with annual and quarterly income statements being the most common. (Net income is discussed later in the chapter.) The income statement represents the accountant's best effort at measuring the economic performance of a company. The **statement of cash flows** reports the amount of cash collected and paid out by a company in the following three types of activities: operating, investing, and financing. As an illustration, the 2002 financial statements from MICROSOFT are reproduced in Appendix A at the end of the book. The Microsoft statements are referred to throughout this chapter and the rest of the book.

The Balance Sheet

⌐ Understand the basic elements, uses, and limitations of the balance sheet.

In the movie *The Princess Bride*, the hero, Wesley, was "mostly dead all day" until being revived by a miracle pill. Wesley was immediately challenged to come up with a plan to stop the imminent marriage of his true love, Buttercup, to the evil Prince Humperdinck. In formulating his plan, Wesley's first question to his conspirators was "What are our liabilities?" followed by "What are our assets?" In essence, the recently revived hero was saying, "Let me see a balance sheet." Similarly, the first questions asked about any business by potential investors and creditors are "What are the resources of the business?" and "What are its existing obligations?" The balance sheet answers these questions.

The three categories of the balance sheet—assets, liabilities, and owners' equity—are each explained on the following page.

Assets

assets Economic resources that are owned or controlled by a company.

Assets are economic resources that are owned or controlled[2] by a company. Exhibit 1 contains a list of common assets along with a brief explanation of each asset. To be summarized and aggregated on a balance sheet, each asset must be assigned a dollar amount. A balance sheet wouldn't be very useful with the following asset listing: one bank account, two warehouses full of goods, three trucks, and four customers who owe us money. As emphasized throughout this text, the monetary measurement and valuation of assets is an area in which accountants must exercise considerable professional judgment.

FYI:

The insurmountable difficulties in valuing some assets can cause important economic assets to be excluded from a company's balance sheet. For example, how does one put a monetary value on the worldwide reputation of Coca-Cola or on the genius and leadership of Bill Gates? These assets, though incredibly valuable, are not listed in the balance sheets of THE COCA-COLA COMPANY or of Microsoft.

Liabilities

liabilities Obligations to pay cash, transfer other assets, or provide services to someone else.

Liabilities are obligations to pay cash, transfer other assets, or provide services to someone else. Your personal liabilities might include unpaid phone bills, the remaining balance on an automobile loan, or an obligation to complete work for which you have already been paid. Exhibit 2 includes a listing of some of the more common liabilities. Like assets, liabilities must be measured in monetary amounts. And, as with assets, quantifying the amount of a liability can require extensive judgment. As one example, consider the difficulties faced by a company to quantify its obligation to clean up a particular toxic waste site when the cleanup will take years to complete; the exact extent of the environmental damage at the site is still in dispute; and legal responsibility for the toxic mess is still debated in the courts. Properly valuing a company's liabilities is one of the biggest (if not *the* biggest) challenges that an accountant faces.

Exhibit 1: Common Assets

Common Assets		
Asset	**Definition**	**Example**
Cash	Coins, currency, checks.	The amount in a company's checking account.
Accounts Receivable	Money owed to a company that sold goods or services to a customer on credit.	If you have a balance on your credit card, the credit card company classifies the amount you owe them as an accounts receivable.
Inventory	Items that are purchased or manufactured by a company and are resold.	The items you see on the shelves in WAL-MART are considered by Wal-Mart as inventory.
Buildings	Structures used in the operations of a business.	To continue the previous example, the store itself is classified by Wal-Mart as a building.
Patents	An exclusive right granted by the federal government to manufacture and sell an invention.	The chips in your computer are patented and use patented technology.

2 An example of an asset that a company technically does not own, but does economically control, is a building that the company uses under a long-term, noncancelable lease agreement.

Exhibit 2: Common Liabilities

Common Liabilities

Liability	Definition	Example
Accounts Payable	Money owed as a result of the purchase of goods and services on credit.	The amount owed by a company for inventory that was purchased on credit and has not been paid for yet.
Taxes Payable	Money owed to federal and state governments resulting from the application of tax laws.	Corporate income tax owed but not yet paid; employment taxes owed but not yet paid.
Mortgage Payable	Money owed relating to the purchase of property.	The loan associated with the purchase of a home or building would be called a Mortgage Payable.
Unearned Revenue	When customers pay for service or product in advance, the company owes service or product (not money) to the customer.	If you pay for a 12-month magazine subscription, the publishing company owes you magazines.

Owners' Equity

owners' equity The ownership interest in the net assets of an entity; equals total assets minus total liabilities.

net assets The owners' equity of a business; equal to total assets minus total liabilities.

The remaining claim against the assets of a business, after the liabilities have been deducted, is **owners' equity**. Thus, owners' equity is a residual amount; it represents the **net assets** (total assets minus total liabilities) available after all obligations have been satisfied. Exhibit 3 contains a listing of common sources of owners' equity. Obviously, if there are no liabilities (an unlikely situation, except at the start of a business), then the total assets are exactly equal to the owners' claims against those assets—the owners' equity.

In order to get a business started, investors transfer resources, usually cash, to the business in return for part ownership. Ownership of a company can be restricted to one person (a sole proprietorship), to a small group (a partnership), or to a diffuse group of owners who often don't even know one another (a corporation). When owners initially invest money in a cor-

Exhibit 3: Sources of Owners' Equity

Sources of Owners' Equity

Owners' Equity	Definition	Example
Paid-In Capital	The amount given by shareholders to obtain shares of stock from a company.	A company sell shares of stock to the public. The amount the company receives is Paid-In Capital.
Retained Earnings	Earnings that are retained in the business.	A company reports net income for the year of $100,000 and reinvests the entire amount in the business.

stockholders (shareholders) The owners of a corporation.

stockholders' equity The owners' equity section of a corporate balance sheet.

dividends Distributions to the owners (stockholders) of a corporation.

retained earnings The amount of accumulated earnings of the business that have not been distributed to owners.

capital stock The portion of a corporation's owners' equity contributed by owners in exchange for shares of stock.

accounting equation An algebraic equation that expresses the relationship between assets (resources), liabilities (obligations), and owners' equity (net assets, or the residual interest in a business after all liabilities have been met): Assets = Liabilities + Owners' Equity.

double-entry accounting A system of recording transactions in a way that maintains the equality of the accounting equation.

poration, they receive evidence of their ownership in the form of shares of stock, represented by stock certificates. These shares of stock may then be privately traded among existing owners of the corporation, privately sold to new owners, or traded publicly on an organized stock exchange such as the New York Stock Exchange (NYSE) (where SAFEWAY's shares are traded) or the NASDAQ exchange (where Microsoft's shares are traded). The owners of a corporation are called **stockholders** or **shareholders**, and the owners' equity section of a corporate balance sheet is sometimes referred to as **stockholders' equity**.

Owners' equity is increased when owners make additional investments in a business or when the business generates profits that are retained in the business. Since business profits belong to the owners, retaining the profits in the business is equivalent to giving the profits to the owners and then having them immediately reinvest that amount back into the business.

Owners' equity is decreased when the owners take back part of their investment. If the business is a corporation, distributions to the owners (stockholders) are called **dividends**. Owners' equity can also be decreased if operations generate a loss instead of a profit. In the extreme, very poor performance can result in the loss of all the assets originally invested by the owners. For a corporation, the amount of accumulated earnings of the business that have not been distributed to owners is called **retained earnings**. The portion of owners' equity contributed by owners in exchange for shares of stock is called **capital stock**. The amount of retained earnings plus the amount of capital stock equals the corporation's total owners' equity.

Accounting Equation

The balance sheet presents information based on the basic **accounting equation**:

$$\text{Assets} = \text{Liabilities} + \text{Owners' Equity}$$

In fact, the name *balance sheet* comes from the fact that a proper balance sheet must always balance—total assets must equal the total of liabilities and owners' equity. The accounting equation is not some miraculous coincidence; it is true by definition. Liabilities and owners' equity are just the methods used to finance the purchase of assets; that is, they are the claims (creditors' claims and owners' claims) against the assets. So, another way to view the accounting equation is that the total amount of the assets is equal to the total amount of financing needed to buy the assets. The total resources, therefore, equal the claims against those resources. This is illustrated in Exhibit 4.

The accounting equation is presented here merely to give you a glimpse of **double-entry accounting**. Chapter 3 gives an in-depth discussion of the equation elements and the mechanics of double-entry accounting.

The Format of a Balance Sheet

A simple balance sheet, adapted from Microsoft's 2002 balance sheet reproduced in Appendix A at the end of the book, is shown in Exhibit 5.

Note that a balance sheet is presented for a particular date because it reports a company's financial position at a point in time. The balance sheet in Exhibit 5 presents Microsoft's financial position as of June 30, 2002.

As illustrated, the balance sheet is divided into the three major sections we have described: assets, liabilities, and owners' equity. The asset section identifies the types of assets owned by Microsoft (cash, for example) and the monetary amounts associated with those assets. The liability section defines the extent and nature of Microsoft's debts (income taxes not yet paid, for example).

Remember that the balance sheet is not merely a report to be prepared and forgotten; it is a summary of important information that is useful to investors and creditors. For example, if you were a banker, would you give a loan to Microsoft based on the information from

Exhibit 4: Elements of the Accounting Equation

STOP & THINK

Actually, the Microsoft balance sheet is quite unusual. Very few companies have the large amount of cash ($38 billion) and low amount of long-term debt ($0) that Microsoft has. Is it good for a company to have so much cash?

the June 30, 2002, balance sheet? Of course you would, because you see that Microsoft already has enough cash on hand ($38 billion) to be able to pay off all existing liabilities ($15.5 billion) two times over. Based on the balance sheet information, you can see that any loan to Microsoft could be easily repaid.

Owners' equity completes the balance sheet. This section identifies the portion of Microsoft's resources that were contributed by owners, either in exchange for shares of stock or as undistributed earnings since Microsoft's inception. Together with liabilities, owners' equity indicates how a company is financed

Exhibit 5: Simplified Balance Sheet for Microsoft

Microsoft Corporation
Balance Sheet
June 30, 2002
(amounts in millions)

Assets		Liabilities	
Cash and short-term		Accounts payable	$ 1,208
investments	$38,652	Accrued compensation	1,145
Accounts receivable	5,129	Income taxes payable	2,022
Other current assets	4,795	Short-term unearned revenue	5,920
Property, plant, and		Other current liabilities	2,449
equipment	2,268	Long-term unearned revenue	1,823
Equity and other investments	14,191	Long-term loans	0
Other assets	2,611	Other liabilities	899
		Total liabilities	$15,466
		Owners' Equity	
		Capital stock	$31,647
		Retained earnings	20,533
		Total liabilities and	
Total assets	$67,646	owners' equity	$67,646

(whether by borrowing or by owner contributions and operating profits). You can see that Microsoft has been financed primarily through owner investment. Almost 40% of this owner investment ($20.5 billion) has been in the form of retained earnings.

Classified and Comparative Balance Sheets

Imagine that two people each owe you $10,000. You ask to see the balance sheets of each. Borrower A has assets of $10,000 in the form of cash. Borrower B has assets of $10,000 in the form of undeveloped land. If you need to collect the loan in the next two weeks, which of the two borrowers is more likely to be able to pay you back? Borrower A is more likely to be able to repay you quickly because the assets of A are more *liquid*, meaning that they are in the form of cash or can be easily converted into cash. Assets such as undeveloped land are said to be *illiquid* in that it takes time and effort to convert them into cash. This illustration shows that not all assets are the same. For some purposes, it is very important to distinguish between current assets, which are generally more liquid, and long-term assets. A balance sheet that distinguishes between current and long-term assets is called a **classified balance sheet**.

To illustrate a classified balance sheet, we consider the balance sheet for Safeway, the supermarket chain described in the opening scenario of this chapter. In Exhibit 6, Safeway's assets are classified as current, or short-term, and long-term.

Current assets include cash and other assets that are expected to be converted to cash within a year. Current assets generally are listed in decreasing order of **liquidity**; cash is listed first, followed by the other current assets, such as accounts receivable. **Long-term assets**, such as land, buildings, and equipment, are those that a company needs in order to operate its business over an extended period of time.

Like assets, liabilities usually are classified as either **current liabilities** (obligations expected to be paid within a year) or **long-term liabilities**. Accounts payable, for example, usually would be paid within 30 to 60 days, whereas a mortgage may remain on the books for 20 to 30 years before it is fully paid.

Safeway's balance sheet in Exhibit 6 includes financial information for both the current year and the preceding year. Most companies prepare such **comparative financial statements** so that readers can identify any significant changes in particular items. For example, notice that Safeway's total assets decreased by $1,415.3 million ($17,462.6 − $16,047.3) from 2001 to 2002. In addition, notice that Safeway's total liabilities increased by $846.8 million. A decrease in total assets coupled with an increase in total liabilities often indicates a company having trouble. The fact that the company reported an $828 million loss confirms that the company is going through tough times.

Limitations of a Balance Sheet

Although the balance sheet is useful in showing the financial status of a company, it does have some limitations. The primary limitation of the balance sheet is that it does not reflect the current value or worth of a company. Refer back to the balance sheet numbers for Microsoft in Exhibit 5. If the balance sheet were perfect, meaning that it included all economic assets reported at their current market values, then the amount of owners' equity would be equal to the market value of the company. In the case of Microsoft, the value of the company would be $52.180 billion, which is the amount of assets that would remain after all the liabilities were repaid. The actual market value of Microsoft on January 6, 2003, however, was $294 billion. How could the balance sheet be so wrong?

The discrepancy between recorded balance sheet value and actual market value is the result of the following two factors:

1. Accountants record many assets at their purchase cost, not at their current market value. **Market value** is the price that would have to be paid to buy the same asset today. For example, if land was obtained ten years ago, it would still be reported on the balance sheet at its original cost, even though its market value may have increased dramatically.

Caution

Don't worry about fully understanding all the items in Safeway's classified balance sheet, such as the "Property under capital leases" and the "Accumulated other comprehensive loss." If there was nothing else to learn, this book would be much shorter and this accounting class would last only two weeks.

classified balance sheet A balance sheet in which assets and liabilities are subdivided into current and long-term categories.

current assets Cash and other assets that can be easily converted to cash within a year.

liquidity The ability of a company to pay its debts in the short run.

long-term assets Assets that a company needs in order to operate its business over an extended period of time.

current liabilities Liabilities expected to be satisfied within a year or the current operating cycle, whichever is longer.

long-term liabilities Liabilities that are not expected to be satisfied within a year.

comparative financial statements Financial statements in which data for two or more years are shown together.

market value The value of a company as measured by the number of shares of stock outstanding multiplied by the current market price of the stock; the current value of a business.

Exhibit 6: Classified Balance Sheets for Safeway

Safeway, Inc.
Comparative Balance Sheet
December 31, 2002 and December 31, 2001
(amounts in millions)

	2002	2001
ASSETS		
Current assets:		
Cash and equivalents	$ 73.7	$ 65.7
Receivables	413.1	373.0
Merchandise inventories, net of LIFO reserve of $65.1 and $82.6	2,493.0	2,354.7
Prepaid expenses and other current assets	226.0	264.1
Assets held for sale	1,053.3	2,437.3
Total current assets	$ 4,259.1	$ 5,494.8
Property:		
Land	$ 1,257.5	$ 1,146.7
Buildings	3,438.7	3,121.5
Leasehold improvements	2,310.9	2,116.9
Fixtures and equipment	4,839.2	4,481.5
Property under capital leases	552.4	404.0
	$12,398.7	$11,270.6
Less accumulated depreciation and amortization	(4,388.5)	(3,853.9)
Total property, net	$ 8,010.2	$ 7,416.7
Goodwill	2,846.2	3,616.0
Prepaid pension costs	535.2	531.3
Investments in unconsolidated affiliates	208.3	242.2
Other assets	188.3	161.6
Total assets	$16,047.3	$17,462.6
LIABILITIES AND STOCKHOLDERS' EQUITY		
Current liabilities:		
Current maturities of notes and debentures	$ 780.3	$ 639.1
Current obligations under capital leases	25.2	37.2
Accounts payable	1,715.4	1,858.5
Accrued salaries and wages	374.9	365.1
Other accrued liabilities	687.2	796.6
Liabilities of operations held for sale	353.3	400.4
Total current liabilities	$ 3,936.3	$ 4,096.9
Long-term debt:		
Notes and debentures	7,009.2	6,236.8
Obligations under capital leases	512.3	358.4
Total long-term debt	$ 7,521.5	$ 6,595.2
Deferred income taxes	577.9	473.7
Accrued claims and other liabilities	384.1	407.2
Total liabilities	$12,419.8	$11,573.0
Commitments and contingencies		
Stockholders' equity:		
Common stock: par value $0.01 per share; 1,500 shares authorized; 573.0 and 570.8 shares outstanding	$ 5.7	$ 5.7
Additional paid-in capital	3,307.2	3,267.1
Accumulated other comprehensive loss	(68.3)	(79.3)
Retained earnings	4,287.6	5,115.7
	$ 7,532.2	$ 8,309.2
Less: Treasury stock at cost; 132.0 and 82.7 shares	(3,904.7)	(2,419.6)
Total stockholders' equity	$ 3,627.5	$ 5,889.6
Total liabilities and stockholders' equity	$16,047.3	$17,462.6

2. Not all economic assets are included in the balance sheet. For example, important economic assets of Microsoft are its proven track record of successful products, the genius of Bill Gates, and a strong, established position in the marketplace (ask NOVELL, WORDPERFECT, LOTUS, and NETSCAPE what it is like to compete against Microsoft). These intangible factors are all very valuable economic assets. In fact, they are by far the most valuable assets Microsoft has. Nevertheless, these important economic assets are outside the normal accounting process.

book value The value of a company as measured by the amount of owners' equity; that is, assets less liabilities.

Because the balance sheet can underreport the value of some long-term assets, and not report other important economic assets, the accounting **book value** of a company (measured by the amount of owners' equity) is usually less than the company's market value, measured by the market price per share times the number of shares of stock. This is illustrated in Exhibit 7 using data for the ten largest companies (in terms of market value) in the United States.

Despite its deficiencies, the balance sheet is a useful source of information regarding the financial position of a business. A lender would never loan a company money without knowing what assets the company has and what other loans the company is already obligated to repay. An investor shouldn't pay money in exchange for ownership in a company without knowing something about the company's existing resources and obligations. When a balance sheet is classified, and when comparative data are provided, the balance sheet provides an informative picture of a company's financial position.

TO SUMMARIZE: The balance sheet provides a summary of the financial position of a company at a particular date. It helps external users assess the financial relationship between assets (resources) and liabilities and owners' equity (claims against those resources). Assets and liabilities are usually classified as either current or long-term and are presented in descending order of liquidity. For a corporation, owners' equity consists of directly invested funds as well as retained earnings. Classified and comparative balance sheets provide useful information for readers of financial statements. Because not all economic assets are included on the balance sheet, the book value as shown in the balance sheet is usually less than the market value of the company.

Exhibit 7: Book Value and Market Value for the Ten Largest U.S. Firms

Rank	Company	Book Value*	Market Value*†
1	General Electric	$54,824	$401,499
2	Microsoft	47,289	331,520
3	ExxonMobil	73,161	295,762
4	Wal-Mart Stores	35,102	277,543
5	Pfizer	18,293	251,155
6	Citigroup	81,200	251,112
7	Intel	35,830	207,592
8	Johnson & Johnson	24,233	196,235
9	American Intl. Group	52,150	195,309
10	International Business Machines	23,614	183,314

*Accounting book value and market value are in millions of dollars.
†On page 37 we noted that Microsoft's market value was $294 billion on January 6, 2003. In this exhibit, Microsoft's value is listed as $331.5 billion as of April 15, 2002.

Source: Fortune 500 listing, 2002. Market values are as of April 15, 2002. Accounting book values are for the end of the immediately preceding fiscal year.

The Income Statement

2 Understand the basic elements and uses of the income statement.

Almost every day, *The Wall Street Journal* includes articles detailing the income forecasts of many publicly-traded companies. The stock prices of companies go up or down depending on whether information disclosed about a company has a positive or negative impact on the firm's expected earnings. For example, on January 8, 2003, the following events occurred:

- CISCO SYSTEMS' stock price rose $0.40 per share on news that IBM would start selling the company's storage-networking switches. Because those additional sales would increase Cisco's revenues and net income, the market reacted positively.
- ABBOT LABORATORIES' stock price fell by $1.83 when the company announced that "it will offer its new rheumatoid-arthritis drug Humira to senior citizens who don't have prescription drug coverage." While this announcement will certainly benefit senior citizens, it will reduce the company's income and revenue and, as a result, the market reacted negatively.

As companies provide additional information about revenue and income numbers, it is apparent that investors find these accounting numbers useful in evaluating the health and performance of a business.

Net income is reported in the income statement. The income statement shows the results of a company's operations for a period of time (a month, a quarter, or a year). The income statement summarizes the revenues generated and the costs incurred (expenses) to generate those revenues. The "bottom line" of an income statement is net income (or net loss), the difference between revenues and expenses. To help you understand an income statement, we must first define its elements—revenues, expenses, and net income (or net loss).

Revenues

revenue Increase in a company's resources from the sale of goods or services.

Revenue is the amount of assets created through business operations. Think of revenue as another way for a company to acquire assets. In the same way that assets can be acquired by borrowing or by owners' investment, assets can also be acquired by providing a product or service for which customers are willing to pay. Manufacturing and merchandising companies receive revenues from the sale of merchandise. For example, Safeway's revenue is the cash that customers pay in exchange for groceries. A service enterprise generates revenues from the fees it charges for the services it performs. For example, a portion of the sales price of Microsoft software is not payment for the software itself, but instead is an advance payment for the customer support service that Microsoft promises. Companies might also earn revenues from other activities, such as charging interest or collecting rent. When goods are sold or services performed, the resulting revenue is in the form of cash or accounts receivable (a promise from the buyer to pay for the goods or services by a specified date in the future). Revenues thus generally represent an increase in total assets. These new assets are not tied to any liability obligation; therefore, the assets belong to the owners and thus represent an increase in owners' equity.

Expenses

expenses Costs incurred in the normal course of business to generate revenues.

Expenses are the amount of assets consumed through business operations. Expenses are the costs incurred in normal business operations to generate revenues. Employee salaries and utilities used during a period are two common examples of expenses. For Safeway, the primary expense is the wholesale cost of the groceries that it sells to its customers at retail. Just as revenues represent an increase in assets and equity, expenses generally represent a decrease in assets and in equity.

In considering revenues and expenses, remember that not all inflows of assets are revenues; nor are all outflows of assets considered to be expenses. For example, cash may be received by borrowing from a bank, which is an increase in a liability, not a revenue. Similarly, cash may be paid for supplies, which is an exchange of one asset for another asset, not an expense. The details of properly identifying revenues and expenses will be discussed further in Chapter 3.

Net Income (or Net Loss)

net income (net loss) An overall measure of the performance of a company; equal to revenues minus expenses for the period.

Net income, sometimes called earnings or profit, is an overall measure of the performance of a company. Net income reflects the company's accomplishments (revenues) in relation to its efforts (expenses) during a particular period of time. If revenues exceed expenses, the result is called net income (revenues − expenses = net income). If expenses exceed revenues, the difference is called **net loss**. Because net income results in an increase in resources from operations, owners' equity is also increased; a net loss decreases owners' equity. Exhibit 8 lists the ten U.S. companies with the highest net incomes in 2001.

It is important to note the difference between revenues and net income. Both concepts represent an increase in the net assets (assets − liabilities) of a firm. However, revenues represent total resource increases; expenses are subtracted from revenues to derive net income or net loss. Thus, whereas revenue is a "gross" concept, income (or loss) is a "net" concept.

It is also important to note the difference between revenues and assets. Revenues are one activity of a company that generates assets. For example, selling a product (which is revenue) results in an asset (either cash or an Accounts Receivable). Assets can also be generated by other activities. For example, borrowing money from a bank would not be considered a revenue-generating activity, but it would result in an asset—cash. To summarize, activities involving revenue result in assets, but assets can result from many different activities.

The Format of an Income Statement

Comparative income statements for Safeway are presented in Exhibit 9. In contrast to the balance sheet, which is "as of" a particular date, the income statement refers to the "year ended." Remember, the income statement covers a period of time; the balance sheet is a report at a point in time. The multi-step format illustrated here highlights several profit measurements including gross profit, operating income, and net income.

The income statement usually shows two main categories, revenues and expenses, although several subcategories may also be presented (as illustrated). Revenues are listed first. Typical operating expenses for most businesses are employee salaries, utilities, and advertising. For Safeway, as with any retail firm, the largest expense is for cost of goods sold. The difference

network **exercises**

Fortune

At its Web site (**http://www.fortune.com**), *Fortune* magazine provides selected stories from current issues as well as summaries of its famous lists: the Fortune 500 (largest companies in the United States) and the Global 500 (largest companies in the world).

Net Work:

1. Search the Fortune 500 Top Performers to find out which U.S. company has the most assets.

2. Search the Global 500 Top Performers and identify which company employs more people than any other company in the world.

Exhibit 8: Top Ten U.S. Companies, Ranked by Net Income

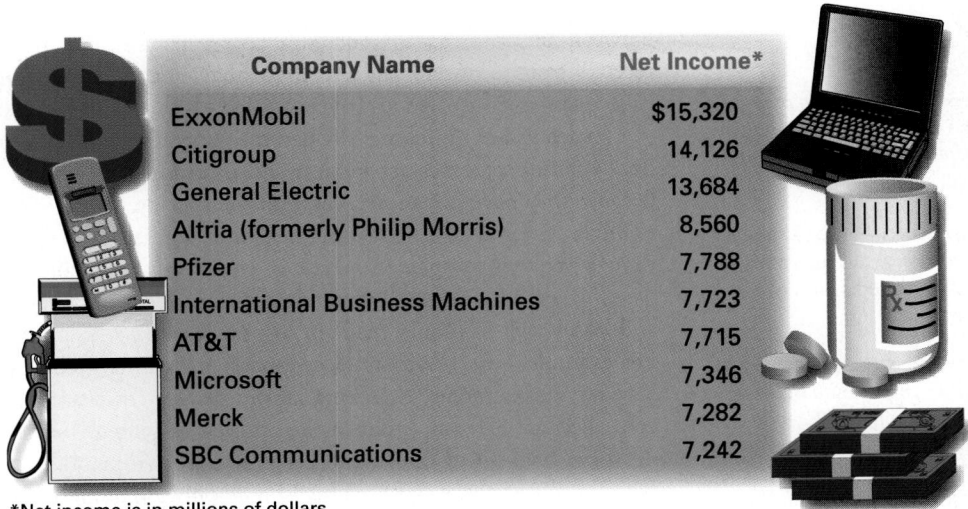

Company Name	Net Income*
ExxonMobil	$15,320
Citigroup	14,126
General Electric	13,684
Altria (formerly Philip Morris)	8,560
Pfizer	7,788
International Business Machines	7,723
AT&T	7,715
Microsoft	7,346
Merck	7,282
SBC Communications	7,242

*Net income is in millions of dollars.

Source: Fortune 500 listing, 2002.

Exhibit 9: Adapted Comparative Income Statements for Safeway

Safeway, Inc.
Comparative Income Statement
For Years Ended December 31, 2002 and December 31, 2001
(amounts in millions)

	2002	2001
Sales	$ 32,399.2	$ 31,797.0
Cost of goods sold	(22,302.8)	(21,947.4)
Gross profit	$ 10,096.4	$ 9,849.6
Operating and administrative expense	(7,718.9)	(7,212.9)
Impairment charge	(704.2)	0
Goodwill amortization	0	(101.0)
Operating profit	$ 1,673.3	$ 2,535.7
Interest expense	(368.6)	(366.1)
Other income (loss), net	15.5	(46.9)
Income from continuing operations before income taxes and cumulative effect of accounting change	$ 1,320.2	$ 2,122.7
Income taxes	(751.7)	(836.0)
Income from continuing operations before cumulative effect of accounting change	$ 568.5	$ 1,286.7
Discontinued operations:		
Loss from operations of Dominick's (including goodwill impairment charge of $583.8 and loss on disposal of $201.3 in 2002) (Note N)	$ (787.9)	$ (27.7)
Income tax benefit (expense)	91.3	(5.1)
Loss on discontinued operations	$ (696.6)	$ (32.8)
(Loss) income before cumulative effect of accounting change	$ (128.1)	$ 1,253.9
Cumulative effect of accounting change	(700.0)	0
Net (loss) income	$ (828.1)	$ 1,253.9
BASIC (LOSS) EARNINGS PER SHARE:	$(1.77)	$2.49

gross profit (gross margin)
The excess of net sales revenue over the cost of goods sold.

gains (losses) Money made or lost on activities outside the normal operation of a company.

earnings (loss) per share (EPS) The amount of net income (earnings) related to each share of stock; computed by dividing net income by the number of shares of stock outstanding during the period.

between sales and cost of goods sold represents the difference between the retail price Safeway receives from a grocery sale and the wholesale cost of the groceries that are sold. This difference (sales − cost of goods sold) is called **gross profit** or **gross margin**.

Expenses are sometimes divided into operating and nonoperating categories. The primary nonoperating expenses are interest and income taxes. These expenses are called nonoperating because they have no connection with the specific nature of the operation of the business. For example, Safeway and Microsoft deal with interest and income taxes in a similar way, even though the two companies operate in completely different industries.

Two other items that frequently appear in the income statement are **gains** and **losses**. Gains and losses refer to money made or lost on activities outside the normal business of a company. For example, when Safeway receives cash for selling groceries, it is called revenue. But when Safeway makes money by selling an old delivery truck, the amount is called a gain, not revenue, because Safeway is not in the business of selling trucks.

One final bit of information required on the income statements of corporations is **earnings (loss) per share (EPS)**. This EPS amount is computed by dividing the net income (earnings or loss) for the current period by the number of shares of stock outstanding during the period. Earnings per share information tells the owner of a single share of stock how much of

FYI:

Recently, companies have been providing an additional measure of income—comprehensive income. The wealth of a company is affected in a variety of ways that have nothing to do with the business operations of the company. **Comprehensive income** is the number used to reflect an overall measure of the change in a company's wealth during the period. The most common examples of items included in comprehensive income include changes in foreign currency exchange rates, changes in the value of certain investment securities, and changes in the value of certain derivative financial instruments. Each of these items is affected by market conditions, affects a company's reported assets and liabilities yet cannot be influenced in any large degree by the company. Therefore, they are reported as part of a firm's comprehensive income.

comprehensive income
A measure of the overall change in a company's wealth during a period; consists of net income plus changes in wealth resulting from changes in investment values and exchange rates.

statement of retained earnings A report that shows the changes in retained earnings during a period of time.

the net income for the year belongs to him or her. Often two EPS figures are disclosed—basic and diluted. Basic EPS is based on historical transactions and involves dividing net income by actual shares outstanding during the period. Diluted EPS is a bit more complicated and involves estimating what EPS would be if certain stock transactions had occurred. The most common difference between basic and diluted EPS is to compute what EPS would have been if outstanding stock options would have been exercised.

Like the balance sheet, the income statement usually shows the comparative results for two or more periods, allowing investors and creditors to evaluate how profitable an enterprise has been during the current period as compared with earlier periods. For example, examination of Safeway's comparative income statements in Exhibit 9 shows that net income in 2002 was over $2 billion lower ($1,253.9 + $828.1) than in 2001. Further analysis of the income statement is introduced in Chapter 5 and reinforced throughout the text. (For another illustration of a comparative income statement, see the income statement for Microsoft in Appendix A at the back of the book.)

The Statement of Retained Earnings

In addition to an income statement, corporations sometimes prepare a **statement of retained earnings**. This statement identifies changes in retained earnings from one accounting period to the next. Exhibit 10 illustrates the statement of retained earnings for Safeway. The statement shows a beginning retained earnings balance, the net income for the period, a deduction for any dividends paid (which were $0 for Safeway), and an ending retained earnings balance.

Note how the accounting equation is affected by the elements reported in the statement of retained earnings. Net income results in an increase in net assets and a corresponding increase in Retained Earnings, which increases Owners' Equity.

$$(\uparrow) \text{ Assets} = \text{Liabilities} + \text{Owners' Equity } (\uparrow)$$

Capital Stock   Retained Earnings ($\uparrow$)

Dividends reduce net assets (e.g., cash) and similarly reduce Retained Earnings, which reduces Owners' Equity.

$$(\downarrow) \text{ Assets} = \text{Liabilities} + \text{Owners' Equity } (\downarrow)$$

Capital Stock   Retained Earnings ($\downarrow$)

Exhibit 10: Illustrated Statement of Retained Earnings for Safeway

Safeway, Inc.
Illustrated Statement of Retained Earnings
For the Year Ended December 31, 2002
(in millions)

Retained earnings, January 1, 2002	$5,115.7
Less net loss for the year	(828.1)
	$4,287.6
Less dividends	0
Retained earnings, December 31, 2002	$4,287.6

It is worth taking a moment to review just what exactly Retained Earnings is and what Retained Earnings isn't. Retained Earnings are the earnings of a business that have been retained in the business (hence, the name Retained Earnings). The earnings that have not been retained in the business have been distributed to owners in the form of a dividend. The earnings that have been retained have been reinvested back into the business to become inventory and equipment and to pay down debt. To see where a company has reinvested the earnings it has retained would require you to examine the assets on the firm's balance sheet. Odds are that many of those assets will have been provided by the earnings that have been reinvested in the business.

Now, what isn't Retained Earnings? Retained Earnings is not cash. Some of the earnings that have been retained in a business may be retained in the form of cash, but it is more likely that the cash has been used to purchase other assets or to pay off liabilities. Students often make the mistake of assuming that if a company has Retained Earnings, the company has cash. That is not true. To determine how much cash a company has, you would examine the balance in the company's cash account—not the balance in the company's retained earnings account.

Corporations sometimes present a *statement of stockholders' equity* instead of a statement of retained earnings. The statement of stockholders' equity, illustrated for Microsoft in Appendix A at the back of the book, is more detailed and includes changes in capital stock as well as changes in retained earnings.

TO SUMMARIZE: The income statement provides a measure of the success of an enterprise over a specified period of time. The income statement shows the major sources of revenues generated and the expenses associated with those revenues. The difference between those revenues and expenses is net income or net loss. Gains and losses refer to money made or lost on activities outside the normal activities of a business. The income statements of corporations must also include earnings per share figures. Comprehensive income includes net income as well as other wealth changes resulting from changes in investment values and exchange rates. Like balance sheets, income statements are usually prepared on a comparative basis. A statement of retained earnings or statement of stockholders' equity is often provided by corporations in their annual reports to shareholders.

The Statement of Cash Flows

3 Understand the categories and uses of the statement of cash flows and see how the primary financial statements tie together.

Net income is the single best measure of a company's economic performance. However, anyone who has paid rent or college tuition knows that bills must be paid with cash, not with "economic performance." Accordingly, in addition to net income, investors and creditors also desire to know how much actual cash a company's operations generate during a period and how that cash is used. The statement of cash flows shows the cash inflows (receipts) and cash outflows (payments) of an entity during a period of time. As shown in Exhibit 11, companies receive cash primarily by selling goods or providing services, by selling other assets, by borrowing, and by receiving cash from investments by owners. Companies use cash to pay current operating expenses such as wages, utilities, and taxes; to purchase additional buildings, land, and otherwise expand operations; to repay loans; and to pay their owners a return on the investments that have been made.

In the statement of cash flows, individual cash flow items are classified according to three main activities: operating, investing, and financing.

Operating Activities

operating activities Activities that are part of the day-to-day business of a company.

Operating activities are those activities that are part of the day-to-day business of a company. Cash receipts from selling goods or from providing services are the major operating cash inflow. Major operating cash outflows include payments to purchase inventory and to pay wages, taxes, interest, utilities, rent, and similar expenses.

Exhibit 11: Cash Flows

Investing Activities

investing activities Activities associated with buying and selling long-term assets.

The primary **investing activities** are the purchase and sale of land, buildings, and equipment. You can think of investing activities as those activities associated with buying and selling long-term assets.

Financing Activities

financing activities Activities whereby cash is obtained from or repaid to owners and creditors.

Financing activities are those activities whereby cash is obtained from or repaid to owners and creditors. For example, cash received from owners' investments, cash proceeds from a loan, or cash payments to repay loans would all be classified under financing activities.

Conceptually, the statement of cash flows is the easiest to prepare of the three primary financial statements. Imagine examining every check and deposit slip you have written in the past year and sorting them into three piles—operating, investing, and financing. You would have to exercise some judgment in deciding which pile some items go into (for example, is the payment of interest an operating or a financing activity?). But overall, the three-way categorization of cash flows is not that difficult. In essence, this is all that is involved in the preparation of a statement of cash flows. As you will see in Chapter 14, however, actual preparation of a statement of cash flows can sometimes be challenging. The reason for this is that traditional accounting systems are designed to streamline the computation of net income. So, instead of preparing the statement of cash flows directly from the raw cash flow data, the process is as shown in Exhibit 12. The raw cash flow data are transformed into revenue and expense data using the accounting adjustments, assumptions, and estimates that you will learn about in this text. Then, to prepare the statement of cash flows, all of those adjustments must be undone to get back to the raw cash flow data. Challenging, but by the time we get to Chapter 14, you will be ready for it.

Exhibit 12: Cash Flow to Net Income to Cash Flow

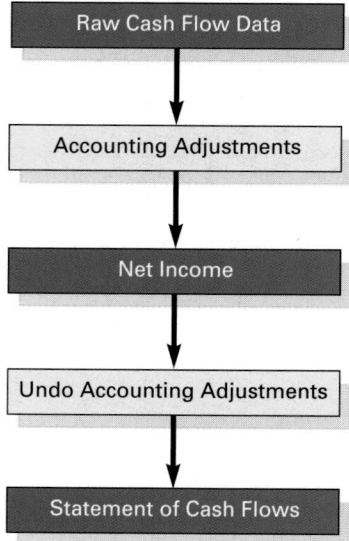

Exhibit 13 contains the statement of cash flows for Safeway for 2002. As with balance sheets and income statements, companies usually provide comparative statements of cash flows. However, we have elected not to show comparative statements of cash flows in order to keep the Safeway illustration simple. (The Microsoft financial statements in Appendix A provide comparative statements of cash flows.)

How can Safeway report such a large loss on the income statement and yet be generating almost $2 billion in cash flow from operating activities? The simple answer is that Safeway reported a large number of noncash expenses on its 2002 income statement. This issue gets at the heart of accrual accounting which is introduced in Chapter 4. The details relating to the statement of cash flows will be explored in Chapter 14.

TO SUMMARIZE: The statement of cash flows is one of the three primary financial statements. It shows the significant cash inflows (receipts) and cash outflows (payments) of a company for a period of time. These cash flows are classified according to operating, investing, and financing activities. The statement of cash flows is discussed and illustrated in Chapter 14.

How the Financial Statements Tie Together

Although we have introduced the primary financial statements as if they were independent of one another, they are interrelated and tie together. In accounting language, they "articulate." **Articulation** refers to the relationship between an operating statement (the income statement or the statement of cash flows) and comparative balance sheets, whereby an item on the operating statement helps explain the change in an item on the balance sheet from one period to the next.

articulation The interrelationships among the financial statements.

Exhibit 14 shows how the financial statements tie together. Note that the beginning amount of cash from the 2001 balance sheet is added to the net increase or decrease in cash (from the statement of cash flows) to derive the cash balance as reported on the 2002 balance sheet. Similarly, the retained earnings balance as reported on the 2002 balance sheet comes from the beginning retained earnings balance (2001 balance sheet) plus net income for the period (from the income statement) less dividends paid. As you study financial state-

Exhibit 13: Statement of Cash Flows for Safeway, Inc.

Safeway Inc. and Subsidiaries
Consolidated Statements of Cash Flows
For Year Ended December 28, 2002*

CASH FLOWS FROM OPERATING ACTIVITIES

Cash collected from customers	$ 32,359.1
Cash paid for	
Inventory	(22,420.6)
Operating and administrative expenses	(6,879.2)
Interest	(440.6)
Taxes	(680.6)
NET CASH FLOWS FROM OPERATING ACTIVITIES	1,938.1

CASH FLOWS FROM INVESTING ACTIVITIES

Cash paid for property additions	(1,370.5)
Proceeds from sale of property	89.3
Other	(31.9)
NET CASH FLOWS USED BY INVESTING ACTIVITIES	(1,313.1)

CASH FLOWS FROM FINANCING ACTIVITIES

Additions to short-term borrowings	1.4
Payments on short-term borrowings	(0.9)
Additions to long-term borrowings	2,919.3
Payments on long-term borrowing	(2,034.1)
Purchase of treasury stock	(1,502.6)
Other	(0.1)
NET CASH FLOWS USED BY FINANCING ACTIVITIES	(617.0)
INCREASE IN CASH FOR THE PERIOD	$ 8.0

*Adapted.

ments, these relationships will become clearer and you will understand the concept of articulation better.

Notes to the Financial Statements

4 Recognize the need for financial statement notes and identify the types of information included in the notes.

notes to the financial statements Explanatory information considered an integral part of the financial statements.

The three primary financial statements contain a lot of information. Still, three summary reports cannot possibly tell financial statement users everything they want to know about a company. Additional information is given in the **notes to the financial statements**. In fact, in a typical annual report, the notes go on for 15 pages or more, whereas the primary financial statements fill only 3 pages. The notes tell about the assumptions and methods used in preparing the financial statements and also give more detail about specific items.

The financial statement notes are of the following four general types:

1. Summary of significant accounting policies.
2. Additional information about the summary totals found in the financial statements.
3. Disclosure of important information that is not recognized in the financial statements.
4. Supplementary information required by the Financial Accounting Standards Board (FASB) or the Securities and Exchange Commission (SEC).

Exhibit 14: How the Financial Statements Tie Together

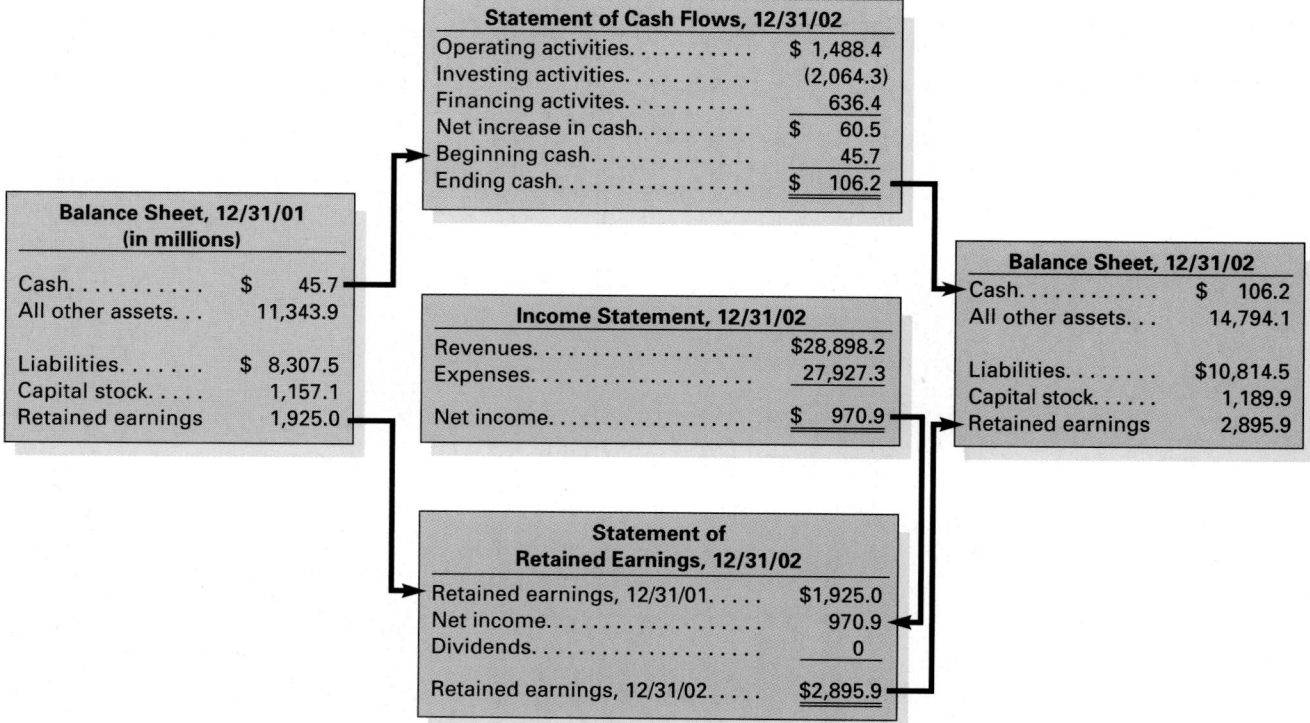

FYI:

In its 1920 annual report, IBM included zero pages of notes (and the dollar amounts were carried out to the penny). In 1966, there were four pages of notes (and dollar amounts were rounded to the nearest dollar). In 2001, IBM's annual report included 30 pages of notes (and dollar amounts were rounded to the nearest million).

Summary of Significant Accounting Policies

As mentioned earlier, accounting involves making assumptions, estimates, and judgments. In addition, in some settings, there is more than one acceptable method of accounting for certain items. For example, there are a variety of acceptable ways of estimating how much a building depreciates (wears out) in a year. In order for financial statement users to be able to properly interpret the three primary financial statements, they must know what procedures were used in preparing those statements. This information about accounting policies and practices is given in the financial statement notes.

Additional Information about Summary Totals

For a large company, such as MICROSOFT or SAFEWAY, one summary number in the financial statements represents literally thousands of individual items. For example, the $6.237 billion in long-term notes and debentures included in Safeway's 2001 balance sheet (see Exhibit 6) represents loans comprised of mortgages, senior secured debentures, senior subordinated debentures, commercial paper, short-term unsecured bank borrowings, an unsecured bank credit agreement, and more. The balance sheet includes only one number, with the details in the notes.

Disclosure of Information Not Recognized

One way to report financial information is to boil down all the estimates and judgments into one number and then report that one number in the financial statements. This is called *recognition*. The key assumptions and estimates are then described in a note to the financial statements. Another approach is to skip the financial statements and just rely on the note to convey

How to Get Your Own Copy of Microsoft's Financial Statements Microsoft's Form 10-K, containing the 2002 financial statements, is reproduced at the end of this text. Is this secret information, available only to owners of this book? No. Anyone can get a copy of the most recent Form 10-K or annual report of Microsoft or any other public corporation in the United States. Any of the following methods will work:

- Become an investor in Microsoft by buying shares of stock in the company. As a Microsoft investor, you are entitled to receive a copy of the annual report each year. In fact, according to U.S. government regulations, Microsoft is required to send a copy of the annual report to all of its investors within three months of the end of Microsoft's fiscal year on June 30.
- Call, write, fax, or e-mail Microsoft's Investor Relations department. The phone numbers and addresses are available on the Microsoft Web site at **http://www.microsoft.com**. For promotional purposes, companies are happy to mail their annual report to anyone who asks.
- Download a copy of the annual report from Microsoft's Web site at **http://www.microsoft.com**. On the Web sites of most companies (Microsoft included), the annual report is not easy to find. You have to skirt past games, promotional material, and lots of nonfinancial information, but the annual report is usually there somewhere.
- Download a copy of the annual report including the Form 10-K (and lots of other information) from the U.S. government archives at **http://sec.gov/edgar.shtml**. These government filings are pure text documents (no pictures) and are made available through the EDGAR (Electronic Data Gathering, Analysis, and Retrieval) system.

Now that you know how to get your own copy of the Microsoft annual report or Form 10-K, make sure you study the rest of this book to learn how to use the report.

the information to users. This is called *disclosure.* Disclosure is the accepted way to convey information to users when the information is too uncertain to be recognized. For example, in July 1988, Safeway suffered a fire in one of its warehouses in Richmond, California. As of February 1, 2002, there were still 2,100 unsettled personal injury lawsuits against Safeway stemming from the fire and 290 lawsuits relating to property damage resulting from the fire. It is impossible to summarize the complexity of the potential outcome of these lawsuits in one financial statement number; so, Safeway describes the situation, in some detail, in the notes to the financial statements. The related note from Safeway's annual report is included in Exhibit 15.

Supplementary Information

The FASB and SEC both require supplementary information that must be reported in the financial statement notes. For example, the FASB requires the disclosure of quarterly financial information and of business segment information. A sample of this type of disclosure can be seen in Microsoft's Form 10-K in Appendix A. In the notes to its financial statements, Microsoft reports that over 25% of its 2002 net income was generated outside of the United States.

TO SUMMARIZE: The notes to the financial statements contain additional information not included in the financial statements themselves. The notes explain the company's accounting assumptions and practices, provide details of financial statement summary numbers and additional disclosure about complex events, and report supplementary information required by the SEC or the FASB.

Exhibit 15: Safeway's Note Disclosure

NOTE L: COMMITMENTS AND CONTINGENCIES

LEGAL MATTERS In July 1988, there was a major fire at the Company's dry grocery warehouse in Richmond, California. Through February 1, 2002, in excess of 126,000 claims for personal injury and property damage arising from the fire have been settled for an aggregate amount of approximately $125 million. The Company's loss as a result of the fire damage to its property and settlement of the above claims was substantially covered by insurance.

As of February 1, 2002, there were still pending approximately 2,100 claims against the Company for personal injury (including punitive damages), and approximately 290 separate active claims for property damage, arising from the smoke, ash and embers generated by the fire. A substantial percentage of these claims have been asserted in lawsuits against the Company filed in the Superior Court for Alameda County, California. There can be no assurance that the pending claims will be settled or otherwise disposed of for amounts and on terms comparable to those settled to date. Safeway continues to believe that coverage under its insurance policy will be sufficient and available for resolution of all remaining personal injury and property damage claims arising out of the fire.

The External Audit

5 Describe the purpose of an audit report and the incentives the auditor has to perform a good audit.

Refer back to the opening scenario for this chapter. Following the November 1986 leveraged buyout by KOHLBERG, KRAVIS, ROBERTS & CO. (KKR), SAFEWAY decided to again issue shares to the public. In April 1990, Safeway issued shares at a price of $11.25 per share. The $11.25 price implied that the market value of KKR's initial investment had risen from $130 million to $731 million. The $11.25 price was determined by investment bankers and potential investors after examining the financial statements of Safeway. Now, consider the following questions:

- Who controlled the preparation of the Safeway financial statements used by investors in arriving at the $11.25 price? The owners and managers of Safeway, led by KKR.
- Did KKR have any incentive to bias the reported financial statement numbers? Absolutely. The better the numbers, the higher the stock offering price and the more money raised by KKR.
- Since KKR had control of the preparation of the financial statements and stood to benefit substantially if those statements looked overly favorable, how could the financial statements be trusted? Good question.

This situation illustrates a general truth: the owners and managers of a company have an incentive to report the most favorable results possible. Poor reported financial performance can make it harder to get loans, can lower the amount that managers receive as salary bonuses, and can lower the stock price when shares are issued to the public. With these incentives to stretch the truth, the financial statements would not be reliable unless they were reviewed by an external party.

audit report A report issued by an independent CPA that expresses an opinion about whether the financial statements fairly present a company's financial position, operating results, and cash flows in accordance with generally accepted accounting principles.

To provide this external review, a company's financial statements are often audited by an independent certified public accountant (CPA). A CPA firm issues an **audit report** that expresses an opinion about whether the statements fairly present a company's financial position, operating results, and cash flows in accordance with generally accepted accounting principles. Note that the financial statements are the responsibility of a company's management and not of the CPA. Although not all company records have to be audited, audits are needed for many purposes. For example, a banker may not make a loan without first receiving audited financial statements from a prospective borrower. As another example, most securities cannot be sold to

FYI:

Notice that MICROSOFT's audit report is dated July 18, 2002. This means that it took less than three weeks (from the end of the fiscal year on June 30) for the completion of the audit. Obviously, much audit work was conducted during the year to make this happen.

the general public until they are registered with the SEC. Audited financial statements are required for this registration process.

Though an audit report does not guarantee accuracy, it does provide added assurance that the financial statements are not misleading since they have been examined by an independent professional. However, the CPA cannot examine every transaction upon which the summary figures in the financial statements are based. The accuracy of the statements must remain the responsibility of the company's management. An example of a typical audit report is found in Appendix A in Microsoft's 2002 Form 10-K. Microsoft's financial statements were audited by DELOITTE & TOUCHE LLP, one of the large international audit firms.

One final question: Who hires and pays Deloitte & Touche to do the audit of Microsoft's financial statements? Microsoft does. At first glance, this situation appears to be similar to allowing students in an accounting class to choose and pay the graders of the examinations. However, two economic factors combine to allow us to trust the quality of the audit, even though the auditor was hired by the company being audited:

- *Reputation.* Deloitte & Touche, as one of the large accounting firms, has a reputation for doing high-quality audits (as do almost all independent auditors in the United States). It would be very reluctant to risk this reputation by signing off on a questionable set of financial statements.
- *Lawsuits.* Auditors are sued all the time, even when they conduct a perfect audit. Investors who lose money claim that they lost the money by relying on bogus financial statements that were certified by an external auditor. If even honest auditors get sued, then an auditor who intentionally approves a false set of financial statements is at great risk of losing a big lawsuit.

The business scandals of the early 2000s have reinforced the important role that auditors play in ensuring the integrity of financial statements. We will discuss the role of auditing and auditors in much greater detail in Chapter 6.

TO SUMMARIZE: An audit report is issued by an independent CPA firm attesting to the conformity of a set of financial statements with generally accepted accounting principles. CPA firms have an economic incentive to perform credible audits in order to preserve their reputations and to avoid lawsuits.

Fundamental Concepts and Assumptions

6 Explain the fundamental concepts and assumptions that underlie financial accounting.

accounting model The basic accounting assumptions, concepts, principles, and procedures that determine the manner of recording, measuring, and reporting a company's transactions.

Certain fundamental concepts and assumptions underlie financial accounting practice and the resulting financial statements. These ideas are so fundamental to any economic activity that they usually are taken for granted in conducting business. Nevertheless, it is important to be aware of them because these assumptions, together with certain basic concepts and procedures, determine the rules and set the boundaries of accounting practice. They indicate which events will be accounted for and in what manner. In total, they provide the essential characteristics of the traditional **accounting model**.

This section will describe the separate entity concept, the assumption of arm's-length transactions, the cost principle, the monetary measurement concept, and the going concern assumption. The concept of double-entry accounting was already introduced on page 35 as the basis for the accounting equation. As noted, this concept will be explained in much more detail in Chapter 3. Additional concepts and assumptions will be covered in later chapters. Remember that accounting is the language of business, and it takes time to learn a new language. The terms and concepts we introduce here will become much more familiar as your study continues.

The Separate Entity Concept

entity An organizational unit (a person, partnership, or corporation) for which accounting records are kept and about which accounting reports are prepared.

Because business involves the exchange of goods or services between entities, it follows that accounting records should be kept for those entities. For accounting purposes, an **entity** is defined as the organizational unit for which accounting records are maintained—for example, IBM CORPORATION. It is a focal point for identifying, measuring, and communicating accounting data. Furthermore, the entity is considered to be separate from its individual owners.

We are all engaged in a variety of economic activities. For example, John Scott works for a large corporation, owns some real estate, is president of the local Little League baseball organization, and manages the family estate on behalf of his brothers and sister. The **separate entity concept** is the idea that, when John Scott is called upon to report the financial activities of the local Little League, he must make sure not to include any of his personal or family financial activities in the results. Similarly, the accounting records of a small business must be kept separate from the personal finances of the owner.

separate entity concept The idea that the activities of an entity are to be separated from those of the individual owners.

Applying the separate entity concept to large corporations can also be difficult. Large corporations, such as GENERAL ELECTRIC and IBM, own networks of subsidiaries (and those subsidiaries own subsidiaries) with complex business ties among the members of the group. A key part of the accounting process for such an organization is carefully defining what is part of General Electric and what is not. For example, one difficult accounting issue (covered in advanced accounting courses) is deciding how much of another company General Electric must own (20%? 45%? 51%? 100%?) before that other company is considered part of the General Electric reporting entity.

The Assumption of Arm's-Length Transactions

transactions Exchange of goods or services between entities (whether individuals, businesses, or other organizations), as well as other events having an economic impact on a business.

Accounting is based on the recording of economic transactions. Viewed broadly, **transactions** include not only exchanges of economic resources between separate entities, but also events that have an economic impact on a business independently. The borrowing and lending of money and the sale and purchase of goods or services are examples of the former. The loss in value of equipment due to obsolescence or fire is an example of the latter. Collectively, transactions provide the data that are included in accounting records and reports.

arm's-length transactions Business dealings between independent and rational parties who are looking out for their own interests.

Accounting for economic transactions enables us to measure the success of an entity. However, the data for a transaction will not accurately represent that transaction if any bias is involved. Therefore, unless there is evidence to the contrary, accountants assume **arm's-length transactions**. That is, they make the assumption that both parties—for example, a buyer and a seller—are rational and free to act independently; each trying to make the best deal possible in establishing the terms of the transaction.

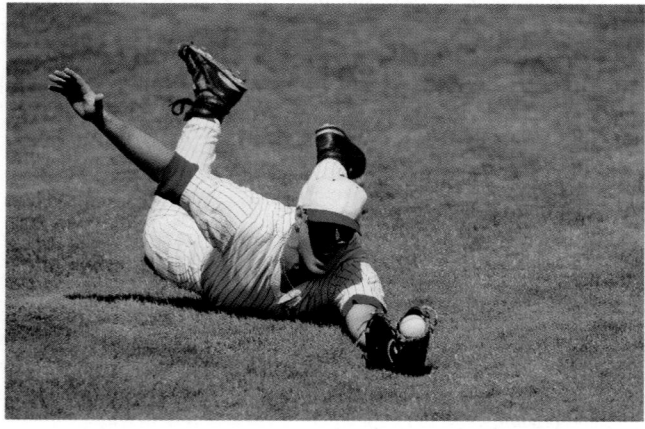

© 2003 Getty Images

Major league baseball salary disputes are frequently in the news. The lack of arm's-length transactions may contribute to some of the friction between players and owners.

To illustrate, assume you are preparing a personal balance sheet and want to list the value of your minivan. You bought the three-year-old minivan for $5,000. Of course, you should list the minivan on your balance sheet at the $5,000 price you paid for it. That should be a good reflection of the value of the vehicle. But, what if you bought the minivan from your brother (who gave you a good deal) and the real market value of the minivan is $11,000? The problem here is that the $5,000 price negotiated between you and your brother is not a market price. Market prices can be thought of as prices negotiated between two strangers who are both competing to get the best deal possible. Thus, a necessary assumption for financial statements to be informative is that the reported financial results come from arm's-length transactions. Without this assumption, the numbers in the financial statements (like the $5,000 for the minivan you bought from your brother) do not reflect true values.

An illustration of the accounting problems that can arise from the lack of arm's-length transactions is provided by the labor problems of major league baseball. The team owners and the players are always arguing about the profitability of the teams. The players do not believe the numbers in the owners' financial statements; many important transactions reported are between the baseball teams and other businesses controlled by the owners, such as television stations. Since the revenues received in these deals (between the baseball teams and related businesses) are not from arm's-length transactions, the players question whether the full value of the deals is reflected in the owners' financial reports.

Caution

When reading accounting reports, remember that many reported values are historical costs, reflecting exchange prices at various transaction dates.

The Cost Principle

historical cost The dollar amount originally exchanged in an arm's-length transaction; an amount assumed to reflect the fair market value of an item at the transaction date.

cost principle The idea that transactions are recorded at their historical costs or exchange prices at the transaction date.

To further ensure objective measurements, accountants record transactions at **historical cost**, the amount originally paid or received for goods and services in arm's-length transactions. The historical cost is assumed to represent the fair market value of the item at the date of the transaction because it reflects the actual use of resources by independent parties. In accounting, this convention of recording transactions at cost is often referred to as the **cost principle**.

The historical cost figure may be modified in the future to reflect new information. While historical cost is a reliable number in that it results from an arm's-length transaction, it may not always provide information that is as relevant as financial statement users would like. For example, the cost of an investment in another company purchased 10 years ago might bear no relation to its current value. In those instances where the market value of an asset is readily determinable, that figure will be included in the financial statements. To continue the example, if an investment purchased 10 years ago consists of stock ownership that is traded on the New York Stock Exchange, then the current market value of that investment may be disclosed in addition to the investment's original historical cost.

The Monetary Measurement Concept

monetary measurement The idea that money, as the common medium of exchange, is the accounting unit of measurement, and that only economic activities measurable in monetary terms are included in the accounting model.

Accountants do not record all the activities of economic entities. They record only those that can be measured in monetary terms. Thus, the concept of **monetary measurement** becomes another important characteristic of the accounting model. For example, employee morale cannot be measured directly in monetary terms and is not reported in the accounting records. Wages paid or owed, however, are quantifiable in terms of money and are reported. In accounting, all transactions are recorded in monetary amounts, whether or not cash is involved. In the United States, the dollar is the unit of exchange and is thus the measuring unit for accounting purposes.

As noted earlier in discussing the limitations of a balance sheet, the listed values may not be the same as actual market values for two reasons. The first is due to the cost principle. Because of such factors as inflation (an increase in the general price level of goods and services), the recorded amount of an item may be quite different from the amount required at a later time to buy or replace the item. The second reason results from the monetary measurement concept. Not all economic assets are recorded, because they are too difficult or impossible to measure in monetary amounts.

The Going Concern Assumption

going concern assumption The idea that an accounting entity will have a continuing existence for the foreseeable future.

The SAFEWAY balance sheet in Exhibit 6 was prepared under the assumption that Safeway would continue in business for the foreseeable future. This is called the **going concern assumption**. Without this assumption, preparation of the balance sheet would be much more difficult. For example, the $2.6 billion inventory for Safeway in 2001 is reported at the cost originally paid to purchase the inventory. This is a reasonable figure because, in the normal course of business, Safeway can expect to sell the inventory for this amount, plus some profit. But if it were assumed that Safeway would go out of business tomorrow, the inventory would suddenly be worth a lot less. Imagine the low prices you could get on Safeway merchandise if it had to conduct a one-day, going-out-of-business sale! The going concern assumption allows the accountant to record assets at what they are worth to a company in normal use, rather than what they would sell for in a liquidation sale.

TO SUMMARIZE: In conducting economic activities, entities enter into transactions that form the basis of accounting records. An accounting model has been developed for recording, measuring, and reporting an entity's transactions. This model is founded on certain fundamental concepts and several important assumptions, principles, and procedures. First, the organizational unit being accounted for is a separate entity. The entity may be small or large, but it is the organizational unit for which accounting records are kept and financial reports prepared. Second, the transactions are assumed to be arm's-length. Third, transactions are recorded at historical cost. Fourth, transactions must be measurable in monetary amounts. Fifth, the accounting entity is assumed to be a going concern.

review of learning objectives

1 Understand the basic elements, uses, and limitations of the balance sheet. The balance sheet provides a summary of the financial position of a company at a particular date. It lists a company's assets, liabilities, and owners' equity. Assets and liabilities are usually classified as either current or long-term. For a corporation, owners' equity consists of directly invested funds as well as retained earnings.

2 Understand the basic elements and uses of the income statement. The income statement shows the major sources of revenues generated and the expenses associated with those revenues. The difference between revenues and expenses is net income or net loss. The income statements of corporations must also include earnings per share.

3 Understand the categories and uses of the statement of cash flows and see how the primary financial statements tie together. The statement of cash flows shows the significant cash inflows (receipts) and cash outflows (payments) of a company for a period of time. These cash flows are classified according to operating, investing, and financing activities. The three financial statements are not independent of one another. They tie together—or articulate—from period to period. The statement of cash flows explains the cash balance on the balance sheet. The income statement reflects changes in the retained earnings balance on the balance sheet.

4 Recognize the need for financial statement notes and identify the types of information included in the notes.

The notes to the financial statements contain additional information not included in the financial statements themselves. The notes explain the company's accounting assumptions and practices, provide details of financial statement summary numbers and additional disclosure about complex events, and report supplementary information required by the SEC and the FASB.

5 Describe the purpose of an audit report and the incentives the auditor has to perform a good audit. An audit report is issued by an independent CPA firm attesting to the conformity of a set of financial statements with generally accepted accounting principles. CPA firms have an economic incentive to perform credible audits in order to preserve their reputations and to avoid lawsuits.

6 Explain the fundamental concepts and assumptions that underlie financial accounting. Certain fundamental concepts underlie the practice of accounting. First, a business must be accounted for as an economic entity separate from the personal affairs of the owners and separate from other businesses. Second, the transactions are assumed to be arm's-length, so that the negotiated prices reflect true market values at the dates of the transactions. Third, transactions are recorded at historical cost. Fourth, only those transactions and events that can be measured in monetary terms are reported. Fifth, the accounting entity is assumed to be a going concern.

key terms & concepts

accounting equation, 35	double-entry accounting, 35	monetary measurement, 53
accounting model, 51	earnings (loss) per share (EPS), 42	net assets, 34
arm's-length transactions, 52	entity, 52	net income (net loss), 41
articulation, 46	expenses, 40	notes to the financial statements, 47
assets, 33	financing activities, 45	operating activities, 44
audit report, 50	gains (losses), 42	owners' equity, 34
balance sheet (statement of financial position), 32	going concern assumption, 53	primary financial statements, 32
	gross profit (gross margin), 42	retained earnings, 35
book value, 39	historical cost, 53	revenue, 40
capital stock, 35	income statement (statement of earnings), 32	separate entity concept, 52
classified balance sheet, 37		statement of cash flows, 32
comparative financial statements, 37	investing activities, 45	statement of retained earnings, 43
comprehensive income, 43	liabilities, 33	stockholders (shareholders), 35
cost principle, 53	liquidity, 37	stockholders' equity, 35
current assets, 37	long-term assets, 37	transactions, 52
current liabilities, 37	long-term liabilities, 37	
dividends, 35	market value, 37	

review problem

The Income Statement and the Balance Sheet

Shirley Baum manages The Copy Shop. She has come to you for help in preparing an income statement and a balance sheet for the year ended December 31, 2006. Several amounts, determined as of December 31, 2006, are presented below. No dividends were paid this year.

Capital stock (10,000 shares outstanding)	$ 40,000	Mortgage payable	$72,000
Retained earnings (12/31/05)	12,400	Accounts payable	6,000
Advertising expense	2,000	Land	24,000
Cash	17,000	Supplies	2,000
Rent expense	2,400	Salary expense	20,000
Building (net)	100,000	Revenues	42,000
Interest expense	700	Other expenses	1,300
		Accounts receivable	3,000

Required:

1. Prepare an income statement for the year ended December 31, 2006, including EPS.
2. Determine the amount of retained earnings at December 31, 2006.
3. Prepare a classified balance sheet as of December 31, 2006.

Solution

1. Income Statement

The first step in solving this problem is to separate the balance sheet items from the income statement items. Asset, liability, and owners' equity items reflect the company's financial position and appear on the balance sheet; revenues and expenses are reported on the income statement.

Balance Sheet Items

Capital stock
Retained earnings
Cash
Building (net)
Mortgage payable
Accounts payable
Land
Supplies
Accounts receivable

Income Statement Items

Advertising expense
Rent expense
Interest expense
Salary expense
Revenues
Other expenses

After the items have been separated, the income statement and the balance sheet may be prepared using a proper format.

The Copy Shop
Income Statement
For the Year Ended December 31, 2006

Revenues		$42,000
Expenses:		
Advertising expense	$ 2,000	
Rent expense	2,400	
Interest expense	700	
Salary expense	20,000	
Other expenses	1,300	26,400
Net income		$15,600

EPS = $15,600 ÷ 10,000 shares = $1.56

2. Retained Earnings

The amount of Retained Earnings at December 31, 2006, may be calculated as follows:

Retained earnings (12/31/05)	$12,400
Add: Net income for year	15,600
Subtract: Dividends for year	0
Retained earnings (12/31/06)	$28,000

Since no dividends were paid during 2006, the ending balance in Retained Earnings is simply the beginning balance plus net income for the year.

3. Balance Sheet

The Copy Shop
Balance Sheet
December 31, 2006

Assets			Liabilities and Owners' Equity		
Current assets:			**Current liabilities:**		
Cash	$ 17,000		Accounts payable . .	$ 6,000	
Accounts receivable . .	3,000				
Supplies	2,000	$ 22,000	**Long-term liabilities:**		
			Mortgage payable . .	72,000	
Long-term assets:			Total liabilities		$ 78,000
Land	$ 24,000				
Building (net)	100,000	124,000	**Owners' equity:**		
			Capital stock	$40,000	
			Retained earnings . .	28,000*	68,000
			Total liabilities and		
Total assets		$146,000	owners' equity		$146,000

*See item 2 for calculation.

discussion questions

1. As an external user of financial statements, perhaps an investor or creditor, what type of accounting information do you need?
2. What is the major purpose of:
   a. A balance sheet?
   b. An income statement?
   c. A statement of cash flows?
3. Assume you want to invest in the stock market, and your friends tell you about a company's stock that is "guaranteed" to have an annual growth rate of 150%. Should you trust your friends and invest immediately, or should you research the company's financial statements before investing? Explain.
4. Why are classified and comparative financial statements generally presented in annual reports to shareholders?
5. Why are owners' equity and liabilities considered the "sources" of assets?
6. Owners' equity is not cash; it is not a liability; and it generally is not equal to the current worth of a business. What is the nature of owners' equity?
7. What are the limitations of the balance sheet? Why is it important to be aware of them when evaluating a company's growth potential?
8. Some people feel that the income statement is more important than the balance sheet. Do you agree? Why or why not?

9. How might an investor be misled by looking only at the "bottom line" (the net income or EPS number) on an income statement?
10. Why is it important to classify cash flows according to operating, investing, and financing activities?
11. You are thinking of investing in one of two companies. In one annual report, the auditor's opinion states that the financial statements were prepared in accordance with generally accepted accounting principles. The other makes no such claim. How important is that to you? Explain.
12. Some people think that auditors are responsible for ensuring the accuracy of financial statements. Are they correct? Why or why not?
13. What are the four general types of financial statement notes typically included in annual reports to stockholders?
14. Explain why each of the following is important in accounting:
    a. The separate entity concept
    b. The assumption of arm's-length transactions
    c. The cost principle
    d. The monetary measurement concept
    e. The going concern assumption

practice exercises

Practice 2-1	**Total Assets** Using the following information, compute total assets.

Equipment	$ 9,000
Accounts payable	1,100
Capital stock	1,750
Cash	400
Loan payable	10,000
Wages payable	250
Accounts receivable	700
Retained earnings	1,000
Inventory	4,000

Practice 2-2	**Total Liabilities** Refer to the data in Practice 2-1. Compute total liabilities.

Practice 2-3	**Total Owners' Equity** Refer to the data in Practice 2-1. Compute total owners' equity.

Practice 2-4	**The Accounting Equation** For the following four cases, use the accounting equation to compute the missing quantity.

	Assets	Liabilities	Owners' Equity
Case A	$10,000	$ 4,000	A
Case B	8,000	B	$3,500
Case C	C	5,500	7,000
Case D	13,000	15,000	D

Practice 2-5	**Balance Sheet** Using the data in Practice 2-1, prepare a balance sheet.

Practice 2-6	**Current Assets** Using the following information, compute total current assets.

Land	$ 9,000
Machinery	1,100
Accounts payable	1,750
Cash	400
Buildings	10,000
Accounts receivable	950
Retained earnings	1,000
Inventory	4,000

Practice 2-7	**Current Liabilities** Using the following information, compute total current liabilities.

Inventory	$ 9,000
Loan payable (due in 14 months)	1,100
Capital stock	1,750
Cash	400
Mortgage payable (due in 30 years)	10,000
Loan payable (due in 6 months)	250
Accounts payable	700
Retained earnings	5,000

Practice 2-8

Book Value and Market Value of Equity

For the following four cases, compute (1) the book value of equity and (2) the market value of equity.

	Assets	Liabilities	Number of Shares of Stock Outstanding	Market Price per Share
Case A	$ 10,000	$ 4,000	1,000	$15
Case B	8,000	7,000	500	10
Case C	13,500	5,500	300	20
Case D	100,000	150,000	1,000	7

Practice 2-9

Total Revenues

Using the following information, compute total revenues. *Caution:* Not all of the items listed should be included in the computation of total revenues.

Cost of goods sold	$ 9,000	Wages payable	$ 250
Interest revenue	1,100	Accounts receivable	700
Advertising expense	1,750	Retained earnings	1,000
Cash	400	Consulting revenue	4,000
Sales	10,000		

Practice 2-10

Total Expenses

Using the data in Practice 2-9, compute total expenses. *Caution:* Not all of the items listed should be included in the computation of total expenses.

Practice 2-11

Computation of Net Income

For the following four cases, compute net income (or net loss). *Caution:* Not all of the items listed should be included in the computation of net income.

	Case A	Case B	Case C	Case D
Cost of goods sold	$ 60,000	$ 30,000	$60,000	$110,000
Interest expense	18,000	47,000	25,000	31,000
Cash	3,000	4,500	2,100	6,000
Retained earnings	50,000	15,000	31,000	70,000
Sales	100,000	150,000	70,000	200,000
Accounts payable	12,000	20,000	5,000	38,000
Rent revenue	5,000	1,000	12,000	10,000
Machinery	175,000	60,000	50,000	185,000

Practice 2-12

Income Statement

Using the following information, prepare an income statement.

Cost of goods sold	$ 6,000
Interest expense	1,100
Wage expense	750
Cash	400
Sales	10,000
Accounts payable	250
Accounts receivable	700
Retained earnings	1,000
Income tax expense	1,200

Practice 2-13

Computation of Ending Retained Earnings

For the following four cases, compute the ending amount of retained earnings. *Caution:* Not all of the items listed should be included in the computation of ending retained earnings.

	Case A	Case B	Case C	Case D
Capital stock	$ 60,000	$ 30,000	$60,000	$110,000
Long-term loan payable	18,000	47,000	25,000	31,000
Dividends	3,000	4,500	2,100	6,000
Retained earnings (beginning)	50,000	15,000	31,000	70,000
Inventory	100,000	150,000	70,000	200,000
Cash	12,000	20,000	5,000	38,000
Net income (loss)	5,000	1,000	12,000	(10,000)
Machinery	175,000	60,000	50,000	185,000

Practice 2-14

Expanded Accounting Equation

For the following four cases, use the expanded accounting equation to compute the missing quantity.

	Assets	Liabilities	Capital Stock	Retained Earnings
Case A	$20,000	$ 8,000	A	$ 3,500
Case B	16,000	B	$ 5,000	2,000
Case C	C	11,000	14,000	32,000
Case D	46,000	30,000	20,000	D

Practice 2-15

Computing Cash from Operating Activities

Using the following data, compute cash flow from operating activities.

Cash Inflow (Outflow)

a.	Cash received from sale of a building	$ 5,600
b.	Cash paid for interest	(450)
c.	Cash paid to repay a loan	(1,000)
d.	Cash collected from customers	10,000
e.	Cash paid for dividends	(780)
f.	Cash paid for income taxes	(1,320)
g.	Cash received upon the issuance of new shares of stock	3,000
h.	Cash received from tenants renting part of a building	600
i.	Cash paid to purchase land	(12,000)

Practice 2-16 **Computing Cash from Investing Activities**
Refer to the information in Practice 2-15. Use that information to compute cash flow from investing activities.

Practice 2-17 **Computing Cash from Financing Activities**
Refer to the information in Practice 2-15. Use that information to compute cash flow from financing activities.

Practice 2-18 **Preparing a Statement of Cash Flows**
Refer to the information in Practice 2-15. Use that information to prepare a complete statement of cash flows. The beginning cash balance for the year was $2,000.

Practice 2-19 **Financial Statement Articulation**
For the following four cases, use the property of financial statement articulation to compute the missing amounts.

	Case A	Case B	Case C	Case D
Dividends	$ 4,000	$ 6,000	$ 1,500	G
Cash, beginning	16,000	C	5,000	$ 20,000
Retained earnings, ending	A	11,000	14,000	32,000
Net increase (decrease) in cash	7,500	4,000	E	(8,700)
Net income (loss)	26,000	30,000	F	(14,000)
Retained earnings, beginning	40,000	D	20,000	60,000
Cash, ending	B	15,000	2,200	H

e xercises

Exercise 2-1 **Classification of Financial Statement Elements**
Indicate for each of the following items whether it would appear on a balance sheet (BS) or an income statement (IS). If a balance sheet item, is it an asset (A), a liability (L), or an owners' equity item (OE)?

1. Accounts Payable
2. Sales Revenue
3. Accounts Receivable
4. Advertising Expense
5. Cash
6. Supplies
7. Consulting Revenue
8. Land
9. Capital Stock
10. Rent Expense
11. Equipment
12. Interest Receivable
13. Mortgage Payable
14. Notes Payable
15. Buildings
16. Salaries & Wages Expense
17. Retained Earnings
18. Utilities Expense

Exercise 2-2

Accounting Equation
Compute the missing amounts for companies A, B, and C.

	A	B	C
Cash	$45,000	$ 4,500	$18,000
Accounts receivable	10,000	10,000	14,000
Land and buildings	75,000	?	50,000
Accounts payable	?	12,000	28,000
Mortgage payable	60,000	17,000	22,000
Owners' equity	45,000	15,000	?

Exercise 2-3

Spreadsheet

Comprehensive Accounting Equation
Assuming no additional investments by or distributions to owners, compute the missing amounts for companies X, Y, and Z.

	X	Y	Z
Assets: January 1, 2006	$360	$?	$230
Liabilities: January 1, 2006	280	460	?
Owners' equity: January 1, 2006	?	620	150
Assets: December 31, 2006	380	?	310
Liabilities: December 31, 2006	?	520	90
Owners' equity: December 31, 2006	?	720	?
Revenues in 2006	80	?	400
Expenses in 2006	100	116	?

Exercise 2-4

Computing Elements of Owners' Equity
From the information provided, determine:

1. The amount of retained earnings at December 31.
2. The amount of revenues for the period.

Totals	January 1	December 31
Current assets	$ 10,000	$ 15,000
All other assets	190,000	180,000
Liabilities	65,000	45,000
Capital stock	60,000	?
Retained earnings	75,000	?

Additional data:
Expenses for the period were $75,000.
Dividends paid were $11,500.
Capital stock increased by $10,000 during the period.

Exercise 2-5

Balance Sheet Relationships
Correct the following balance sheet.

Canfield Corporation
Balance Sheet
December 31, 2006

Assets		Liabilities and Owners' Equity	
Cash	$ 55,000	Buildings	$325,000
Accounts payable	65,000	Accounts receivable	75,000
Interest receivable	20,000	Mortgage payable	150,000
Capital stock	200,000	Sales revenue	350,000
Rent expense	60,000	Equipment	85,000
Retained earnings	145,000	Utilities expense	5,000
		Total liabilities and	
Total assets	$545,000	owners' equity	$990,000

Exercise 2-6

Spreadsheet

Balance Sheet Preparation

From the following data, prepare a classified balance sheet for Simon Company at December 31, 2006.

Accounts payable	$ 62,500
Accounts receivable	123,000
Buildings	418,500
Owners' equity, 1/1/06	210,000
Cash	179,750
Distributions to owners during 2006	21,750
Supplies	3,750
Land	130,000
Mortgage payable	479,500
Net income for 2006	124,750
Owners' equity, 12/31/06	?

Exercise 2-7

Income Statement Computations

Following are the operating data for an advertising firm for the year ended December 31, 2006.

Revenues	$175,000
Supplies expense	45,000
Salaries expense	70,000
Rent expense	1,500
Administrative expense	6,000
Income taxes (30% of income before taxes)	?

For 2006, determine:

1. Income before taxes.
2. Income taxes.
3. Net income.
4. Earnings per share (EPS), assuming there are 15,000 shares of stock outstanding.

Exercise 2-8

Income Statement Preparation

The following selected information is taken from the records of Beckstrom Corporation.

(continued)

Accounts payable	$ 35,000
Accounts receivable	65,000
Advertising expense	15,000
Cash	19,500
Supplies expense	46,000
Rent expense	10,000
Utilities expense	3,000
Income taxes (30% of income before taxes)	?
Miscellaneous expense	4,400
Owners' equity	140,000
Salaries expense	61,000
Fees (revenues)	384,000

1. Prepare an income statement for the year ended December 31, 2006. (Assume that 7,500 shares of stock are outstanding.)
2. Explain what the EPS ratio tells the reader about Beckstrom Corporation.

Exercise 2-9

Cash Flow Computations

From the following selected data, compute:

1. Net cash flow provided (used) by operating activities.
2. Net cash flow provided (used) by investing activities.
3. Net cash flow provided (used) by financing activities.
4. Net increase (decrease) in cash during the year.
5. The cash balance at the end of the year.

Cash receipts from:	
Customers	$270,000
Investments by owners	54,000
Sale of building	90,000
Proceeds from bank loan	60,000
Cash payments for:	
Wages	$ 82,000
Utilities	3,000
Advertising	4,000
Rent	36,000
Taxes	67,000
Dividends	20,000
Repayment of principal on loan	40,000
Purchase of land	106,000
Cash balance at beginning of year	$386,000

Exercise 2-10

Income and Retained Earnings Relationships

Assume that retained earnings increased by $240,000 from December 31, 2005, to December 31, 2006, for Miller Corporation. During the year, a cash dividend of $140,000 was paid.

1. Compute the net income for the year.
2. Assume that the revenues for the year were $920,000. Compute the expenses incurred for the year.

Exercise 2-11

Retained Earnings Computations

During 2006, Edgemont Corporation had revenues of $230,000 and expenses, including income taxes, of $190,000. On December 31, 2005, Edgemont had assets of $350,000, liabilities of $80,000, and capital stock of $210,000. Edgemont paid a cash dividend of $25,000 in 2006. No additional stock was issued. Compute the retained earnings on December 31, 2005, and 2006.

Exercise 2-12

Preparation of Income Statement and Retained Earnings Statement

Prepare an income statement and a statement of retained earnings for Big Sky Corporation for the year ended June 30, 2006, based on the following information:

Capital stock (1,500 shares @ $100)		$150,000
Retained earnings, July 1, 2005		76,800
Dividends		6,500
Ski rental revenue		77,900
Expenses:		
Rent expense	$ 6,000	
Salaries expense	38,600	
Utilities expense	2,400	
Advertising expense	7,500	
Miscellaneous expense	7,700	
Income taxes	2,100	64,300

Exercise 2-13

Articulation: Relationships between a Balance Sheet and an Income Statement

The total assets and liabilities of Roloflex Company at January 1 and December 31, 2006, are presented below.

	January 1	December 31
Assets	$76,000	$112,000
Liabilities	26,000	28,800

Determine the amount of net income or loss for 2006, applying each of the following assumptions concerning the additional issuance of stock and dividends paid by the firm. Each case is independent of the others.

1. Dividends of $10,800 were paid and no additional stock was issued during the year.
2. Additional stock of $4,800 was issued and no dividends were paid during the year.
3. Additional stock of $62,000 was issued and dividends of $15,600 were paid during the year.

Exercise 2-14

Cash Flow Classifications

For each of the following items, indicate whether it would be classified and reported under the operating activities (OA), investing activities (IA), or financing activities (FA) section of a statement of cash flows:

a. Cash receipts from selling merchandise
b. Cash payments for wages and salaries
c. Cash proceeds from sale of stock
d. Cash purchase of equipment
e. Cash dividends paid
f. Cash received from bank loan
g. Cash payments for inventory
h. Cash receipts from services rendered
i. Cash payments for taxes
j. Cash proceeds from sale of property no longer needed as expansion site

Exercise 2-15

Notes to Financial Statements

Refer to MICROSOFT's Form 10-K in Appendix A at the end of the book. How important are the notes to financial statements? What are the major types of notes that Microsoft includes in its Form 10-K?

Exercise 2-16

The Cost Principle

On January 1, 2006, Save-More Construction Company paid $150,000 in cash for a parcel of land to be used as the site of a new office building. During March, the company petitioned the city council to rezone the area for professional office buildings. The city council refused, preferring to maintain the area as a residential zone. After nine months of negotiation, Save-More Construction convinced the council to rezone the property for commercial use, thus raising its value to $200,000.

For accounting purposes, what value should be used to record the transaction on January 1, 2006? At what value would the property be reported at year-end, after the city council rezoning? Explain why accountants use historical costs to record transactions.

Exercise 2-17

The Monetary Measurement Concept

Many successful companies, such as FORD MOTOR COMPANY, EXXONMOBIL, and MARRIOTT CORPORATION, readily acknowledge the importance and value of their employees. In fact, the employees of a company are often viewed as the most valued asset of the company. Yet in the asset section of the balance sheets of these companies there is no mention of the asset Employees. What is the reason for this oversight and apparent inconsistency?

Exercise 2-18

The Going Concern Assumption

Assume that you open an auto repair business. You purchase a building and buy new equipment. What difference does the going concern assumption make with regard to how you would account for these assets?

problems

Problem 2-1

Balance Sheet Classifications and Relationships

August Corporation has the following balance sheet elements as of December 31, 2006.

Land	$105,000	Mortgage payable	$250,000
Cash	?	Capital stock	315,000
Building	168,000	Retained earnings	92,000
Accounts payable	155,000	Supplies	41,000
Notes payable (short-term)	117,000	Accounts receivable	134,000
Equipment	420,000		

Required:

Compute the total amount of:

1. Current assets.
2. Long-term assets.
3. Current liabilities.
4. Long-term liabilities.
5. Stockholders' equity.

Problem 2-2

P.A.S.S.
*Power Accounting
System Software*

Preparation of a Classified Balance Sheet

Following are the December 31, 2006, account balances for Siraco Company.

Cash	$ 1,950
Accounts receivable	2,500
Supplies	1,800
Equipment	11,275

Accounts payable	$ 3,450
Wages payable	250
Dividends paid	1,500
Capital stock	775
Retained earnings, January 1, 2006	12,000
Revenues	10,000
Miscellaneous expense	1,550
Supplies expense	3,700
Wages expense	2,200

Required:
1. Prepare a classified balance sheet as of December 31, 2006.
2. **Interpretive Question:** On the basis of its 2006 earnings, was this company's decision to pay dividends of $1,500 a sound one?

Problem 2-3

Balance Sheet Preparation with a Missing Element
The following data are available for Schubert Products Inc., as of December 31, 2006.

Cash	$ 7,500
Accounts payable	24,000
Capital stock	42,000
Accounts receivable	20,000
Building	49,500
Supplies	2,000
Retained earnings	?
Land	20,000

Required:
1. Prepare a balance sheet for Schubert Products Inc.
2. Determine the amount of retained earnings at December 31, 2006.
3. **Interpretive Question:** In what way is a balance sheet a depiction of the basic accounting equation?

Problem 2-4

Income Statement Preparation
Listed below are the results of Rulon Candies' operations for 2005 and 2006. (Assume 4,000 shares of outstanding stock for both years.)

	2006	2005
Sales	$300,000	$350,000
Utilities expenses	15,000	8,500
Employee salaries	115,000	110,000
Advertising expenses	10,000	20,000
Income tax expense	9,000	36,500
Interest expense	25,000	15,000
Cost of goods sold	115,000	85,000
Interest revenue	10,000	10,000

Required:
1. Prepare a comparative income statement for Rulon Candies, Inc., for the years ended December 31, 2006, and 2005. Be sure to include figures for gross margin, operating income, income before taxes, net income, and earnings per share.
2. **Interpretive Question:** What advice would you give Rulon Candies, Inc., to improve its profitability for the year 2007?

Problem 2-5

P.A.S.S.
Power Accounting
System Software

Income Statement Preparation

The following information is taken from the records of Hill, Dunn, & Associates for the year ended December 31, 2006.

Income taxes	$ 10,800
Service revenues	150,000
Rent expense	5,500
Salaries expense	35,000
Miscellaneous expense	380
Utilities expense	1,230
Administrative expense	12,300

Required:

Prepare an income statement for Hill, Dunn, & Associates for the year ended December 31, 2006. (Assume that 4,000 shares of stock are outstanding.)

Problem 2-6

Expanded Accounting Equation

At the end of 2006, Spencer Systems, Inc., had a fire that destroyed the majority of its accounting records. Spencer Systems, Inc., was able to gather the following financial information for 2006.

a. Retained earnings was changed only as a result of net income and a $25,000 dividend payment to Spencer's investors.

b. All other account changes for the year are listed below. The amount of change for each account is shown as a net increase or decrease.

	Increase or (Decrease)
Cash	$ 12,500
Interest receivable	(7,500)
Inventory	50,000
Accounts receivable	(11,750)
Building	157,500
Accounts payable	22,500
Mortgage payable	137,500
Wages payable	(35,250)
Capital stock	26,250

Required:

Using the accounting equation, compute Spencer's net income for 2006.

Problem 2-7

Income Statement Preparation

Precision Corporation has been a leading supplier of magnetic storage disks for three years. Following are the results of Precision's operations for 2006.

Sales revenue	$68,000
Advertising expense	1,530
Income taxes	4,360
Delivery expense	480
Packaging expense	355
Salaries expense	18,350
Supplies expense	8,410
EPS = $3.45	

Required:
1. Prepare an income statement for the year ended December 31, 2006.
2. How many shares of stock were outstanding?

Problem 2-8

Statement of Cash Flows

Southwestern Rentals, Inc., rents equipment to customers ranging from homeowners to large construction companies. The financial information shown below was gathered from its accounting records for 2006. Assume any increase or decrease in the balances from 1/1/06 to 12/31/06 resulted from either receiving or paying cash in the transaction. For example, during 2006 the balance on loans for land holdings increased $150,000 because the company received $150,000 in cash by taking out an additional loan on the land.

Items	Balance as of 1/1/06	Balance as of 12/31/06
Cash	$ 20,000	$ 50,000
Cash receipts from customers	—	600,000
Loans on land holdings	100,000	250,000
Cash distributions to owners	—	150,000
Loan on building	100,000	70,000
Investments in securities	850,000	1,050,000
Cash payments for other expenses	—	50,000
Cash payments for taxes	—	55,000
Cash payments for operating expenses	—	135,000
Cash payments for wages and salaries	—	100,000

Required:
1. Prepare a statement of cash flows for Southwestern Rentals, Inc., for the year ended December 31, 2006.
2. **Interpretive Question:** Does Southwestern Rentals, Inc., appear to be in good shape from a cash flow standpoint? What other information would help you analyze the situation?

Problem 2-9

Spreadsheet

Statement of Cash Flows

The cash account for Esplin Enterprises shows the following for the year ended December 31, 2006.

Beginning cash balance	$?
Cash receipts during year from:	
Services	2,214,000
Investments by owners	93,000
Sale of land	194,000
Cash payments during year for:	
Operating expenses	1,735,000
Taxes	207,000
Purchase of building	352,000
Distributions to owners	68,000
Ending cash balance	815,000

Required:
Prepare a statement of cash flows for Esplin Enterprises for the year ended December 31, 2006.

Problem 2-10

Net Income

A summary of the operations of Streuling Company for the year ended May 31, 2006, is shown below.

Advertising expense	$ 2,760
Supplies expense	37,820
Rent expense	1,500
Salaries expense	18,150
Miscellaneous expense	4,170
Dividends	12,400
Retained earnings (6/1/05)	156,540
Income taxes	21,180
Consulting fees (revenues)	115,100
Administrative expense	7,250

Required:

1. Determine the net income for the year by preparing an income statement. (Assume that 3,000 shares of stock are outstanding.)
2. **Interpretive Question:** Assuming an operating loss for the year, is it a good idea for Streuling to still pay its shareholders dividends?

Problem 2-11

Net Income and Statement of Retained Earnings

A summary of the operations of Stellenbach Company for the year ended May 31, 2006, is shown below.

Advertising expense	$ 2,760
Supplies expense	37,820
Rent expense	1,500
Salaries expense	18,150
Miscellaneous expense	4,170
Dividends	12,400
Retained earnings (6/1/05)	156,540
Income taxes	21,180
Consulting fees (revenues)	115,100
Administrative expense	7,250

Required:

1. Determine the net income for the year by preparing an income statement. (There are 2,000 shares of stock outstanding.)
2. Prepare a statement of retained earnings for the year ended May 31, 2006.
3. Prepare a statement of retained earnings assuming that Stellenbach had a net loss for the year of $25,000.
4. **Interpretive Question:** Assuming a loss as in (3), is it a good idea for Stellenbach to still pay its shareholders dividends?

Problem 2-12

Spreadsheet

Comprehensive Financial Statement Preparation

The following information was obtained from the records of Wilcox, Inc., as of December 31, 2006.

Land	$ 42,500
Buildings	197,550
Salaries expense	125,350
Utilities expense	5,250

Accounts payable	$ 38,050
Revenues	389,950
Supplies	72,500
Retained earnings (1/1/06)	311,000
Capital stock (2,000 shares outstanding)	65,000
Accounts receivable	90,000
Supplies expense	110,600
Cash	?
Notes payable (long-term)	63,800
Rent expense	21,200
Dividends in 2006	95,500
Other expenses	11,250
Income taxes	35,000

Required:
1. Prepare an income statement for the year ended December 31, 2006.
2. Prepare a classified balance sheet as of December 31, 2006.
3. **Interpretive Question:** Why is the balance in Retained Earnings so large as compared with the balance in Capital Stock?

Problem 2-13

Elements of Comparative Financial Statements
The following report is supplied by Smith Brothers Company.

Smith Brothers Company
Comparative Balance Sheets
As of December 31, 2006 and 2005

Assets	2006	2005	Liabilities and Owners' Equity	2006	2005
Cash	$13,000	$15,000	Accounts payable	$ 5,000	$ 4,000
Accounts receivable ..	18,000	11,000	Salaries and commissions		
Notes receivable	11,000	10,000	payable	8,000	8,000
Land	38,000	38,000	Notes payable	25,000	27,000
			Capital stock	20,000	20,000
			Retained earnings	22,000	15,000
			Total liabilities and		
Total assets	$80,000	$74,000	owners' equity	$80,000	$74,000

Operating expenses for the year included utilities of $4,500, salaries and commissions of $44,800, and miscellaneous expenses of $1,500. Income taxes for the year were $3,000, and the company paid dividends of $5,000.

Required:
1. Compute the total expenses, including taxes, incurred in 2006.
2. Compute the net income or net loss for 2006.
3. Compute the total revenue for 2006.
4. **Interpretive Question:** Why are comparative financial statements generally of more value to users than statements for a single period?

d iscussion cases

Case 2-1

Creditor and Investor Information Needs

Ink Spot is a small company that has been in business for two years. Wilford Smith, the president of the company, has decided that it is time to expand. He needs $10,000 to purchase additional equipment and to pay for increased operating expenses. Wilford can either apply for a loan at First City Bank, or he can issue more stock (1,000 shares are outstanding) to new investors. Assuming that you are the loan officer at First City Bank, what information would you request from Ink Spot before deciding whether to make the loan? As a potential investor in Ink Spot, what information would you need to make a good investment decision?

Case 2-2

Analyzing Trends and Key Financial Relationships

An investor may choose from several investment opportunities: the stocks of different companies; rental property or other real estate; or savings accounts, money market certificates, and similar financial instruments. When considering an investment in the stock of a particular company, comparative financial data presented in the annual report to stockholders help an investor identify key relationships and trends. As an illustration, comparative operating results for Prime Properties, Inc., from its 2006 annual report are provided. (Dollars are presented in thousands except for earnings per share.)

	Year Ended December 31		
	2006	**2005**	**2004**
Revenues:			
Property management fees	$ 58,742	$ 63,902	$ 66,204
Appraisal fees	55,641	60,945	62,320
Total revenues	$114,383	$124,847	$128,524
Expenses:			
Selling and advertising	$ 64,371	$ 75,403	$ 80,478
Administrative expenses	30,671	31,115	31,618
Other expenses	9,265	9,540	9,446
Interest expense	2,047	1,468	26
Total expenses	$106,354	$117,526	$121,568
Income before taxes	$ 8,029	$ 7,321	$ 6,956
Income taxes	2,409	2,196	2,087
Net income	$ 5,620	$ 5,125	$ 4,869
Earnings per share*	$2.25	$2.05	$1.95

*2.5 million shares outstanding

What trends are indicated by the comparative income statement data for Prime Properties, Inc.? Which of these trends would be of concern to a potential investor? What additional information would an investor need in order to make a decision about whether to invest in this company?

Case 2-3

How Many Accounting Equations Are There?

You have recently completed Chapter 2 in your introductory accounting course and have been enthusiastically explaining the accounting equation to all of your friends. One of your friends reports that he took accounting last year and that actually there isn't just one accounting equation. For example, he says that in addition to the equation Assets = Liabilities + Owners' Equity, there are also the equations Revenues = Assets, Net Income = Cash from Operating

Activities, and Retained Earnings = Cash. Comment on these three additional accounting "equations" listed by your friend.

Case 2-4

Can Financial Statement Information Be Used to Successfully Pick Stocks?

For most companies, the only reliable source of information about the company's performance is found in the company's financial statements. However, for the 15,000 publicly-traded companies in the United States (those whose ownership shares can be bought and sold on a stock exchange), there is much information generated by business reporters and financial analysts to supplement the financial statements. In addition, ownership shares of these publicly-traded companies are bought and sold by investors, large and small, every day. For these publicly-traded companies, can the financial statements be used to pick winning and losing stocks, that is, those stocks that will go up in value and those that will decline in value in the future? Explain.

Case 2-5

Who Audits American Companies?

Your sister is a biochemist, but she prides herself on keeping a close eye on the business news. It is her opinion that the U.S. federal government should increase the amount that it pays to the auditors of the financial statements of U.S. companies. She is convinced that taxpayers would support this increase, even if it means increased income taxes. She thinks that increased government audit fees will attract more qualified auditors and will result in a dramatic rise in the reliability of the financial statements released by U.S. companies. This increased reliability will help U.S. companies compete in the global market place. Comment on your sister's opinion.

Case 2-6

Accounting for the Proper Entity

You have been hired to prepare the financial reports for White River Building Supply, a proprietorship owned by Bill Masters. Upon encountering several payments made from the company bank account to a nearby university, you contact Bill Masters to find out how to classify these payments. Masters explains that those checks were written to pay his daughter's tuition and to purchase her textbooks and miscellaneous supplies. He then tells you to include the payments with other expenses of the business. "This way," he explains, "I can deduct the payments on my tax return. Why not, since it all comes out of the same pocket?" How would you respond to Masters?

judgment calls

Judgment 2-1

You Decide: What is the most important number in the financial statements—net income or EPS?

You were talking with some of your friends, who are finance majors, and they said that the most important number in the financial statements is the earnings per share figure on the income statement. One friend said, "EPS is the only number Wall Street cares about!" Some of your fellow students in accounting believe, however, that net income and the income statement are much more important than a single EPS figure.

Judgment 2-2

You Decide: Is the cash flow statement necessary?

You were at dinner with some family and friends when one of them started talking about the long hours he has been putting in at work—a local waste management company. He said that cash flows have been bad and he has been staying up late trying to figure out the problem. When asked about the condition of his statement of cash flows, he said, "We don't have one of those statements to assess cash flows, we just use EBITDA (earnings before interest, taxes, depreciation, and amortization). Besides, everything I need to know is in either the balance sheet or income statement." Is a statement of cash flows necessary, or is the information it contains redundant of the balance sheet and income statement?

Judgment 2-3

You Decide: Should Wall Street place so much importance on the EPS figure or not?

Recently, your mom came to you with questions about some of her investments. A year ago, she made an investment in 10 companies that are traded on the S&P 500. She tried to pick enough different companies to "diversify" her portfolio. Last week, one of her companies came out with "lower than expected EPS." In the two days following the news, the stock price dropped almost 30%! She wanted to know why so many people cared about one number. How do you respond?

Judgment 2-4

You Decide: Are the footnotes to the financial statements necessary?

Do the notes to the financial statements add value to investors, or have they evolved from tradition? You were listening to talk radio on your way home from work a couple weeks ago when you heard someone say, "Everything you need to know about a company should be either in the balance sheet, income statement, or statement of cash flows. If you can't find it in there, it is not worth knowing! Besides that, the footnotes are too complex to understand!" Do you agree with this assumption?

Competency Enhancement Opportunities

- ▶ **Analyzing Real Company Information**
- ▶ **International Case**
- ▶ **Ethics Case**
- ▶ **Writing Assignment**
- ▶ **The Debate**
- ▶ **Cumulative Spreadsheet Project**
- ▶ **Internet Search**

The following additional assignments provide opportunities for students to develop critical thinking, ethical perspectives, oral and written communication skills, experience with electronic research, and teamwork through group and business activities.

Analyzing Real Company Information

Analyzing 2-1 (Microsoft)

The 2002 Form 10-K for MICROSOFT is included in Appendix A. Locate that Form 10-K and answer the following questions:

1. Locate Microsoft's 2002 balance sheet. What percentage of its total assets consists of cash and short-term investments? How much long-term debt does Microsoft have?
2. Find Microsoft's 2002 income statement. Have revenues increased or decreased over the last three years? Is the rate of increase rising?
3. Find Microsoft's statement of stockholders' equity. Did Microsoft pay a dividend in 2002? Did Microsoft buy or sell any stock in 2002?
4. Review Microsoft's statement of cash flows. What activity generates most of Microsoft's cash? What is Microsoft doing with all its money—buying back its own stock, investing in other companies, or something else?

Analyzing 2-2 (Safeway)

At the start of this chapter you learned a little about SAFEWAY and its history. Now let's take a look at the company's financial performance in recent years. Refer back to Safeway's income statement (on page 42), the balance sheet (on page 38), and the statement of cash flows (on page 47).

Based on information contained in these financial statements, answer the following questions:

1. As a percentage of total assets, did current assets increase or decrease from 2001 to 2002? What was the primary reason for the change?
2. Divide gross profit by sales for 2001 and 2002. For which year is the gross profit percentage higher? What does that change represent?
3. In 2002, did Safeway generate enough cash from operations to fund all of its investing activities? Looking at the financing activities section of the statement of cash flows, would you predict that long-term debt on the balance sheet went up or down in 2002?

▶ *International Case*

International

Diageo

DIAGEO is a United Kingdom (UK) consumer products firm, best known in the United States for the following brand names: Smirnoff, Johnnie Walker, J&B, Gordon's, Guinness, Pillsbury, Häagen-Dazs, and Burger King. Diageo's 2002 balance sheet is shown below.

Diageo
Consolidated Balance Sheet
30 June 2002
(in millions of pounds)

Fixed assets		
Intangible assets		5,434
Tangible assets		2,545
Investment in associates		2,899
Other investments		284
		11,162
Current assets		
Stocks	2,316	
Debtors—due within one year	2,209	
Debtors—due after one year	1,210	
Cash at bank and liquid resources	1,596	
	7,331	
Creditors—due within one year		
Borrowings	(3,718)	
Other creditors	(3,645)	
	(7,363)	
Net current (liabilities)/assets		(32)
Total assets less current liabilities		11,130
Creditors—due after one year		
Borrowings	(3,711)	
Other creditors	(49)	
		(3,760)
Provisions for liabilities and charges		(814)
		6,556

(continued)

Capital and reserves

Called-up share capital		930
Share premium account	1,324	
Revaluation reserve	129	
Capital redemption reserve	3,012	
Profit and loss account	606	
Reserves attributable to equity shareholders		5,071
Shareholders' funds		6,001
Minority interests		
Equity	184	
Non-equity	371	
		555
		6,556

1. Can you identify any major differences between Microsoft's and Diageo's balance sheets in terms of the order in which major categories are displayed?
2. What is Diageo's total assets? Is it as easy to determine as Microsoft's total assets?
3. Take a look at the following list of accounts and identify, given your knowledge of assets, liabilities, and owners' equity, what the American equivalent of those accounts might be (you might want to reference Microsoft's balance sheet for comparison):
   - Stocks
   - Debtors
   - Called-up share capital
   - Profit and loss account

▶ *Ethics Case*

Violating a Covenant

Often banks will require a company that borrows money to agree to certain restrictions on its activities in order to protect the lending institution. These restrictions are called "debt covenants." An example of a common debt covenant is requiring a company to maintain its current ratio (which is current assets ÷ current liabilities) at a certain level, say, 2.0.

Your boss has just come to you and asked, "How can you make our current ratio higher?" You know that the company has a line of credit with a local bank that requires the company to maintain its current ratio at 1.5. You also know that the company was dangerously close to violating this covenant during the previous quarter. The end of the fiscal period is next week, and some action must be taken to increase the current ratio. If the covenant is violated, the lending agreement allows the bank to significantly modify the terms of the debt (in the bank's favor) and also gives the bank a seat on the company's board of directors. Management would prefer not to have the bank involved in the day-to-day affairs of the business, nor do they want to alter the terms of the lending agreement.

Identify ways in which the current ratio can be increased. Would any of the alternatives you identify be good for the business, e.g., selling equipment might raise the current ratio but would that be good for the business? Should a company engage in these types of transactions?

▶ *Writing Assignment*

The Most Important Financial Statement

As you have discovered, there are three primary financial statements—balance sheet, income statement, and statement of cash flows. In no more than two pages, answer the following question: If you could have access to only one of the primary financial statements, which would it be and why? As you provide support for the financial statement of your choice, also provide reasons as to why you would not pick the other two statements.

▶ *The Debate*

Save the Notes

As pointed out in the chapter, IBM's annual report in 1920 included zero pages of notes to the financial statements. In 2001, the notes had grown to 30 pages. While the number of financial statements has remained constant, the number of notes to the financial statements continues to grow.

Divide your group into two teams and prepare two-minute presentations representing the following points of view.

- The first team represents "Kill the Notes." You are to take the position that financial statements providing information relating to a firm's current asset and liability position, a summary of its operations, and its cash inflows and outflows are all that is needed to make good resource allocation decisions. The three primary financial statements are all that need to be provided to current and potential investors and creditors. In other words, the notes do not add value to the financial reports.
- The other team represents "Save the Notes." You are to argue that the notes represent essential information that must be used when interpreting the data contained in the financial statements themselves.

▶ *Cumulative Spreadsheet Project*

Starting with this chapter, each chapter in this text will include a spreadsheet assignment based on the financial information of a fictitious company named Handyman. The first assignments are simple—in this chapter you are asked to do little more than set up financial statement formats and input some numbers. In succeeding chapters, the spreadsheets will get more complex so that by the end of the course you will have constructed a spreadsheet that allows you to forecast operating cash flow for five years in the future and adjust your forecast depending on the operating parameters that you think are most reasonable.

So, let's get started with the first spreadsheet assignment.

1. The following numbers are for Handyman Company for 2006:

Short-Term Loans Payable	$ 10	Long-Term Debt	$207
Interest Expense	9	Income Tax Expense	4
Paid-In Capital	50	Retained Earnings (as of 1/1/06)	31
Cash	10	Receivables	27
Dividends	0	Sales	700
Accumulated Depreciation	9	Accounts Payable	74
Inventory	153	Property, Plant, & Equipment	199
Cost of Goods Sold	519	Other Operating Expenses	160

Your assignment is to create a spreadsheet containing a balance sheet and an income statement for Handyman Company.

2. Handyman is wondering what its balance sheet and income statement would have looked like if the following numbers were changed as indicated:

	CHANGE	
	From	To
Sales	700	730
Cost of Goods Sold	519	550
Other Operating Expenses	160	165

Create a second spreadsheet with the numbers changed as indicated. *Note:* After making these changes, your balance sheet may no longer balance. Assume that any discrepancy is eliminated by increasing or decreasing Short-Term Loans Payable as much as necessary.

▶ *Internet Search*

Microsoft

While you have a copy of MICROSOFT's Form 10-K in Appendix A, let's go see what its most current financial statements look like. Access Microsoft's Web site at **http://www.microsoft .com**. Sometimes addresses change, so if this Microsoft address doesn't work, access the Web site for this textbook (**http://albrecht.swlearning.com**) for an updated link to Microsoft.

Once you have accessed Microsoft's Web site, answer the following questions (you may have to search a bit to answer some of these questions):

1. When was Micro-Soft founded? (That's right, the company's name originally had a hyphen.)
2. Make your way to the shareholder information and locate the company's most recent income statement. Detail the steps you had to take to find this financial statement.
3. How has the company done since its 2002 financial statements were issued? Are sales still increasing? Are profits still on the rise?
4. Microsoft was one of the first companies to provide an income statement in multiple languages. Take a look at Microsoft's income statement based on accounting principles accepted in the United Kingdom. Do you recognize any of the terms? Now look at the German version of the income statement. Even though you probably don't speak German, can you guess what the German word is for "revenues"?

The Mechanics of Accounting

After studying this chapter, you should be able to:

Learning Objectives

1 Understand the process of transforming transaction data into useful accounting information.

2 Analyze transactions and determine how those transactions affect the accounting equation (step one of the accounting cycle).

3 Record the effects of transactions using journal entries (step two of the accounting cycle).

4 Summarize the resulting journal entries through posting and prepare a trial balance (step three of the accounting cycle).

5 Describe how technology has affected the first three steps of the accounting cycle.

Ray Kroc, a 51-year-old milkshake machine distributor, first visited the McDonald brothers' drive-in (in San Bernardino, California) in July of 1954 because he wanted to know why a single "hamburger stand" needed 10 milkshake machines. That first day, Kroc spent the lunch rush hour watching the incredible volume of business the small drive-in was able to handle. By the time he left town, Kroc had received a personal briefing on the "McDonald's Speedee System" from Dick and Mac McDonald and had secured the rights to duplicate the system throughout the United States.

In his first outlet in Chicago, Ray Kroc soon discovered that duplicating the McDonald's system involved more than just signing a licensing agreement. Kroc's french fries, for example, were mushy, even though he closely copied the McDonald brothers' process. Feverish detective work finally revealed that Dick and Mac McDonald had been storing their potatoes in an outside bin before turning them into french fries. This aging process allowed some of the natural sugars in the potatoes to turn into starch, resulting in fries that would cook all the way through without burning. Further research revealed the optimal temperature for the cooking oil, the best type of potato to use, and how to make frozen french fries that taste as good as fresh. The end product, the MCDONALD'S french fry, was instrumental in establishing the McDonald's reputation for consistent quality.

As the number of McDonald's locations expanded (to over 31,000 at the end of 2002), so did the menu. Originally, the McDonald's menu contained just 15-cent hamburgers, 12-cent french fries, 20-cent milkshakes, cheeseburgers, three flavors of soft drinks, milk, coffee, potato chips, and pie. The first addition to this menu was the Filet-O-Fish sandwich in the early 1960s. The Big Mac started in Pittsburgh in 1967, and the Egg McMuffin debuted in Santa Barbara in 1971. Not all of the McDonald's menu innovations caught on—the McLean Deluxe (a low-fat hamburger held together with a seaweed-based filler) and the Hula-burger, one of Ray Kroc's personal favorites (a cheese-burger with a big slice of pineapple), are among the items that are no longer offered.

The essence of McDonald's business seems fairly simple: revenues come from selling Big Macs, Happy Meals, Chicken McNuggets, etc.; operating costs include the costs of the raw materials to produce the food items, labor costs, building rentals, income taxes, and so forth. But the magnitude of McDonald's operations in terms of volume (sales average over $111 million per day) as well as geography (McDonald's has locations in 121 countries throughout the world) makes compiling this information a challenge. In order to prepare its year-end financial reports, McDonald's must accumulate financial information from its various locations throughout the world, summarize that information according to U.S. accounting standards, and make the report available to the public in less than four weeks. In fact, McDonald's annual report for the period ended December 31, 2002, was finished on January 23, 2003.

With the number of transactions that occur on a daily basis, the accounting for McDonald's would be impossible were it not for a systematic method for analyzing these transactions and collecting and recording transaction-related information. What is the process by which McDonald's and other entities transform raw transaction data into useful information? Certainly, shareholders and others would not understand how McDonald's has performed if the company merely published volumes of raw transaction data. How are millions of transactions summarized and eventually reported in the primary financial statements? This transformation process is referred to as the **accounting cycle**.

accounting cycle The procedure for analyzing, recording, summarizing, and reporting the transactions of a business.

---

n the first two chapters, we provided an overview of accounting. We discussed the environment of accounting and its objectives, some basic concepts and assumptions of accounting, and the primary financial statements. Now we begin our study of the "accounting cycle." This simply means that we will examine the procedures for analyzing, recording, summarizing, and reporting the transactions of a business. In this chapter, we describe the first three steps in the cycle. The remaining step (preparing reports for external users) is explained in Chapter 4.

How Can We Collect All This Information?

❚ Understand the process of transforming transaction data into useful accounting information.

Suppose you were asked, "What was the total cost, to the nearest dollar, of your college education last year?" To answer this question would require that you (1) gather information (in the form of receipts, credit card statements, and canceled checks) for all your expenditures, (2) analyze that information to determine which outflows relate to your college education, and (3) summarize those outflows into one number—the cost of your college education. Once you have answered that question, answer this one, "How much did you spend on food last year?" Again you would have to go through the same process of collecting data, analyzing the information to identify those expenditures relating to food, and then summarizing those expenditures into one number. From these two examples you can see that, without a method for gathering and organizing day-to-day financial data, answers to seemingly routine questions can get quite complex.

Now you may be thinking, "Doesn't my checkbook allow me to easily answer these questions?" Your check register would certainly help, but it is limited in that it tracks only the transactions that go through your checking account. It does not track the cash in your pocket, in your savings accounts, or in other investment accounts. So, if any of your expenditures for food were made with cash, your check register would understate the amount you spent for food. In addition, you would still have to review each check and determine to what it related. Your check register provides good information for calculating exactly how much money you have in your checking account at any point in time, but it does not contain all the information necessary to determine exactly how your money was spent.

Now consider the dilemma for businesses. They typically have far more transactions than you, and the kinds of transactions are more varied. Businesses buy and sell goods or services; borrow and invest money; pay wages to employees; purchase land, buildings, and equipment; distribute earnings to owners; and pay taxes to the government. These activities are referred to as "exchange transactions" because the entity is actually trading (exchanging) one thing for another. A college bookstore, for example, exchanges textbooks for cash. **Business documents**, such as a sales invoice, a purchase order, or a check stub, are often used (1) to confirm that an arm's-length transaction has occurred, (2) to establish the amounts to be recorded, and (3) to facilitate the analysis of business events.

© 2003 Ghislain & Marie David DeLossy/Getty Images

Businesses, such as a college bookstore, have many exchange transactions in which they trade one thing for another—like textbooks for cash.

business documents
Records of transactions used as the basis for recording accounting entries; include invoices, check stubs, receipts, and similar business papers.

To determine how well an entity is managing its resources, the results of transactions must be analyzed. The accounting cycle makes the analysis possible by recording and summarizing an entity's transactions and preparing reports that present the summary results. Exhibit 1 shows the sequence of the accounting cycle. Later, we will discuss these general categories and the specific steps of the cycle.

Keeping track of a company's transactions requires a system of accounting that is tailor-made to the needs of that particular enterprise. Obviously, the accounting system of a large multinational corporation with millions of business transactions each day will be much more complex than the system needed by a small Internet start-up company. The more complex and detailed the accounting system, the more likely it is to be automated. Historically, of course, all accounting systems had to be maintained by hand. The image of the accountant with green eyeshade and quill pen, sitting on a high stool, meticulously maintaining the accounting records,

Exhibit 1: Sequence of the Accounting Cycle

Exchange Transactions
(Businesses enter into exchange transactions
signaling the beginning of the accounting cycle)

Step 1 — **Analyze transactions.**

Step 2 — **Record the effects of transactions.**

Step 3 — **Summarize the effects of transactions.**
1. Posting journal entries.
2. Preparing a trial balance.

Step 4 — **Prepare reports.**
1. Adjusting entries.
2. Preparing financial statements.
3. Closing the books.

reflects those early manual systems. Today, few accounting systems are completely manual. Even small companies generally use some type of inexpensive accounting software. Such software helps reduce the number of routine clerical functions and improves the accuracy and timeliness of the accounting records.

Although a computer-based system is faster and requires less labor than a manual system, the steps in the process are basically the same for both: transactions are recorded on source documents; they are then analyzed, journalized, and posted to the accounts; and the resulting information is summarized, reported, and used for evaluation purposes. The difference lies in who (or what) does the work. With a computer-based system, the software transforms the recorded data, summarizes the data into categories, and prepares the financial statements and other reports. Nevertheless, human judgment is still essential in analyzing and recording transactions, especially those of a nonroutine nature.

Because a manual accounting system is easier to understand, we will use a manual system for the examples in this text. As you begin studying the steps in the accounting cycle, it is important that you understand the accounting equation and double-entry accounting more fully. This concept was briefly introduced in Chapter 2. You will recall that the accounting model is built on this basic equation. You now need to learn how to use the equation in accounting for the transactions of a business.

TO SUMMARIZE: Businesses enter into exchange transactions. Evidence of these transactions is provided by business documents. Accounting is designed to accumulate and report in summary form the results of a company's transactions, therefore transforming the financial data into useful information for decision making.

How Do Transactions Affect the Accounting Equation?

2 Analyze transactions and determine how those transactions affect the accounting equation (step one of the accounting cycle).

Suppose you are the keeper of the archives at MCDONALD'S assigned to protect the secret ingredient mix for the Big Mac special sauce. You came to work this morning only to hear that BURGER KING has cracked the secret ingredient recipe and plans to come out with a Big Mac clone at half the price. How would this event be reflected in the financial statements?

Often, the most difficult aspect of accounting is determining which events are to be reflected in the accounting records and which are not. In this example, the proliferation of Big Mac clones could have a serious impact on the future of the firm. However, as discussed in Chapter 2, events that cannot be measured in monetary terms will not be reflected in the financial statements. It would be virtually impossible to reliably quantify the impact that Big Mac clones could have on the future profitability of McDonald's, and thus, that information would not be reflected in the financial statements.

Now you may be saying to yourself, "We have an obligation to inform financial statement users about this attack on the Big Mac." We would all agree that this information should be shared, but the financial statements are not the place to do it. As you review MICROSOFT'S Form 10-K (in Appendix A), you'll notice that the financial statements are only one part of the information provided to users. Information relating to the competitive environment, product development, and marketing and sales efforts is included in the annual report, but not as part of the accounting information.

After quantifying an event's monetary impact, the event must be analyzed to determine if an arm's-length transaction has occurred. Accounting is concerned primarily with reflecting the effects of transactions between two independent entities. So a mining company's oil strike on the North Slope of Alaska would not be reflected in the financial statements until that oil is sold. Likewise, signing a promising young financial analyst directly out of college for a salary of $80,000 per year involves an exchange of promises. No accounting entry would be made until the analyst actually worked and received a paycheck.

Transactions between independent parties must be analyzed to determine their effect on the accounting equation. This analysis is often what separates an accountant from a bookkeeper. While many transactions are routine, some business events are quite complex and require a comprehensive analysis to determine how the event should be reflected in the financial statements. Consider the following examples:

- An employee works for one year, earning a base salary of $60,000. In addition, if the employee stays with the company for at least five years, the company promises to make a contribution to the employee's pension fund equal to 15% of salary. Approximately 60% of employees who start with the company stay for five years. Also, by working for one year, the employee earns 15 extra vacation days. Those vacation days can be saved and used any time in the future. How do we record compensation cost associated with this employee for the year?
- A company buys a building. In addition to paying $20,000 cash, the company agrees to pay $10,000 per year for the next 10 years. The company will also pay a $2,000 property

network **exercises**

McDonald's and Burger King

Access MCDONALD'S Web site (**http://www.mcdonalds.com**) and compare it to BURGER KING's (**http://www.burgerking.com**).

Net Work:

1. In your opinion, which Web site is easier to navigate?

2. How easy is it to find information on, for example, nutrition?

3. Which site provides easier access to the company's financial information?

tax bill associated with the building from last year. As part of the purchase, the company gave the former owners of the building 500 shares of stock. Finally, the building will require $23,000 worth of repairs and renovations before it can be used. How much should be recorded as the cost of the building?

As these examples illustrate, transactions can become quite complex and the accounting for these types of transactions reflects that complexity. The good news is that the transaction analysis framework introduced in this chapter allows you to break complex transactions into manageable pieces and also provides a self-checking mechanism to ensure that you haven't forgotten anything. Once a transaction is properly analyzed and the affected accounts identified (along with the direction of those effects), the remainder of the accounting cycle can proceed without much difficulty.

The Accounting Equation

So let's begin our analysis of transactions by first reviewing some of the basics. Recall that the fundamental accounting equation is:

Assets	=	**Liabilities**	+	**Owners' Equity**
[Resources]		[A method of financing resources that requires repayment]*		[A method of financing resources that does not require repayment and represents ownership in the business]

Because the accounting equation is an equality, it must always remain in balance. To see how this balance is maintained when accounting for business transactions, consider the following activities:

Business Activity (Transaction)	**Effect in Terms of the Accounting Equation**
1. Investment of $50,000 by owners	Increase asset (Cash), increase owners' equity (Capital Stock): A ↑ $50,000 = OE ↑ $50,000
2. Borrowed $25,000 from bank	Increase asset (Cash), increase liability (Notes Payable): A ↑ $25,000 = L ↑ $25,000
3. Purchased $14,000 worth of inventory on credit. The inventory is to be resold at a later date.	Increase asset (Inventory), increase liability (Accounts Payable): A ↑ $14,000 = L ↑ $14,000
4. Purchased equipment costing $15,000 for cash	Decrease asset (Cash), increase asset (Equipment): A ↓ $15,000 = A ↑ $15,000

For each of the transactions, the terms in parentheses are the specific accounts affected by the transactions, as will be explained in the next section.

In each case, the equation remains in balance because an identical amount is added to both sides, subtracted from both sides, or added to and subtracted from the same side of the equation. Following each transaction, we can ensure that the accounting equation balances. Note how the following spreadsheet keeps track of the equality of the accounting equation:

---

*Not all liabilities represent a method of financing assets. In some cases, liabilities arise during the course of business that are not associated with the financing of assets. For example, an obligation to clean up a toxic waste spill is not associated with an asset but still represents a liability. Still, the majority of liabilities are incurred to finance assets.

TRANSACTION #	ASSETS		LIABILITIES		OWNERS' EQUITY
Beginning Balance	$ 0	=	$ 0	+	$ 0
1	+50,000				+50,000
Subtotal	$50,000	=	$ 0	+	$50,000
2	+25,000		+25,000		
Subtotal	$75,000	=	$25,000	+	$50,000
3	+14,000		+14,000		
Subtotal	$89,000	=	$39,000	+	$50,000
4	+15,000 −15,000				
Total	$89,000	=	$39,000	+	$50,000

Using Accounts to Categorize Transactions

In Chapter 2, the balance sheet and the income statement were introduced as two of the three primary financial statements, the third being the statement of cash flows. We learned that the elements of the balance sheet are assets, liabilities, and owners' equity; the elements of the income statement are revenues and expenses. Now we must learn how each of these elements is composed of many different accounts.

account An accounting record in which the results of transactions are accumulated; shows increases, decreases, and a balance.

An **account** is a specific accounting record that provides an efficient way to categorize transactions. Thus, we may designate asset accounts, liability accounts, and owners' equity accounts. Examples of asset accounts are Cash, Inventory, and Equipment. Liability accounts include Accounts Payable and Notes Payable. The equity accounts for a corporation are Capital Stock and Retained Earnings. You can think of an individual account as a summary of every transaction affecting a certain item (such as cash); the summary may be recorded on one page of a book, or in one computer file, or in one column of a spreadsheet (seen as follows).

Transaction #	ASSETS				LIABILITIES			OWNERS' EQUITY
	Cash	Inventory	Equipment		Accounts Payable	Notes Payable		Capital Stock
Beginning Balance	$ 0	$ 0	$ 0	=	$ 0	$ 0	+	$ 0
1	+50,000							+50,000
Subtotal	$50,000	$ 0	$ 0	=	$ 0	$ 0	+	$50,000
2	+25,000					+25,000		
Subtotal	$75,000	$ 0	$ 0	=	$ 0	$25,000	+	$50,000
3		+14,000			+14,000			
Subtotal	$75,000	$14,000	$ 0	=	$14,000	$25,000	+	$50,000
4	−15,000		+15,000					
Total	$60,000	$14,000	$15,000	=	$14,000	$25,000	+	$50,000

Do Accountants Record the Most Important Events? Are all important economic events captured in a company's accounting records? No. In fact, the majority of events that affect the value of a company may fall outside the scope of traditional financial reporting. Consider the following selection of business events reported on the front page of *The Wall Street Journal* (Business and Finance column) on a typical day (Friday, April 4, 2003):

- A Chinese medical official apologized for "poor coordination" in informing the public about SARS, which investigators believe began its spread from the southern province of Guangdong.
- US AIRWAYS' traffic dropped 16% in March as bookings suffered from the war in Iraq. The decline prompted the carrier to trim its April schedule by 5%.
- SUMITOMO MITSUI warned that it expects to post a net loss of $3.93 billion for its latest fiscal year due to accelerated bad-loan write-offs and losses from stock holdings.
- More guilty pleas were announced by prosecutors in the probe into accounting irregularities at HEALTHSOUTH, which is emerging as a prototype for the federal strategy against corporate fraud under Sarbanes-Oxley. Ex-CEO Richard Scrushy fired back at the government for the first time.
- ALTRIA'S PHILIP MORRIS unit must find another solution for averting a court-ordered $12 billion bond after an Illinois Senate panel rejected a bond cap.

All of these events had impacts on the values of companies. For example, US Airways' announcement caused the value of the company to decrease, and yet none of these value-relevant events would have been recorded in the accounting records of any company anywhere in the world.

Accounting academics have long been dismayed by the weak connection between a company's reported accounting numbers and the company's market value. In a famous paper, Professor Baruch Lev summarized this issue as follows:

The correlation between earnings and stock returns is very low, sometimes negligible. . . . [T]he possibility that the fault lies with the low quality . . . of reported earnings looms large.

The challenge to accountants is to figure out how to bring more business events into the accounting model in order to increase the relevance of the financial statements. The risk of doing nothing to improve accounting is that potential investors and creditors will increasingly turn their backs on the financial statements when they can get more current, comprehensive, and relevant information merely by using an Internet search engine.

Source: Baruch Lev, "On the Usefulness of Earnings and Earnings Research: Lessons and Directions from Two Decades of Empirical Research," *Journal of Accounting Research*, Supplement 1989, p. 153.

Using the previous transactions, we can easily see how the accounting equation can be expanded to include specific accounts under the headings of assets, liabilities, and owners' equity. We can also see that after each transaction, the equality of the accounting equation can be determined simply by adding up the balances of all the asset accounts and comparing the total to the sum of all the liability and owners' equity accounts.

Now suppose that a company has 200 accounts and 10,000 transactions each month—this spreadsheet would quickly get very big. Today, computers help in compiling this massive amount of data. Five hundred years ago, when double-entry accounting was formalized, all the adding and subtracting was done by hand. You can imagine the difficulties of tracking multiple accounts, involving hundreds of transactions, using the spreadsheet method described above while doing all the computations by hand. Mixing "+" and "−" in one column would provide ample opportunity to make mistakes.

This problem was solved by separating the "+" and the "−" for each account into separate columns, totaling each column, and then computing the difference between the columns

T-account A simplified depiction of an account in the form of a letter T.

to arrive at an ending balance. The simplest, most fundamental format is the configuration of the letter T. This is called a **T-account**. Note that a T-account is an abbreviated representation of an actual account (illustrated later) and is used as a teaching and learning tool. The following are examples of T-accounts, representing the transactions described previously.

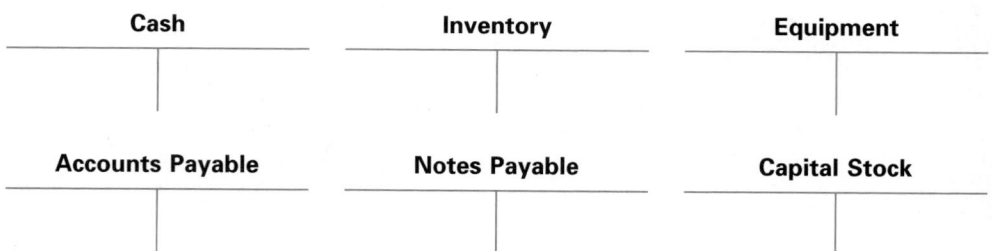

The account title (Cash, for example) appears at the top of the T-account. Transaction amounts may be recorded on both the left side and the right side of the T-account. Instead of using the terms left and right to indicate which side of a T-account is affected, terms unique to accounting were developed. **Debit** is used to indicate the left side of a T-account, and **credit** is used to indicate the right side of a T-account. Debit means left, credit means right—nothing more, nothing less.

debit An entry on the left side of a T-account.

credit An entry on the right side of a T-account.

Besides representing the left and right sides of an account, the terms *debit* (abbreviated DR) and *credit* (abbreviated CR) take on additional meaning when coupled with a specific account. By convention, for asset accounts, debits refer to increases and credits to decreases. For example, to increase the cash account, we debit it; to decrease the cash account, we credit it. Since we expect the total increases in the cash account to be greater than the decreases, the cash account will usually have a debit balance after accounting for all transactions. Thus, we can make this generalization—asset accounts will have debit balances. The opposite relationship is true of liability and owners' equity accounts; they are decreased by *debits* and increased by *credits*. As a result, liability and owners' equity accounts will typically have credit balances. The effect of this system is shown here, with an increase indicated by (+) and a decrease by (−).

Assets		=	Liabilities		+	Owners' Equity	
DR	CR		DR	CR		DR	CR
(+)	(−)		(−)	(+)		(−)	(+)

In addition to assets equaling liabilities and owners' equity, debits also equal credits. If you fully grasp the meaning of these two equalities, you are well on your way to mastering the mechanics of accounting. Debits and credits allow us to take a shortcut to ensure that the accounting equation balances. If, for every transaction, debits equal credits, then the accounting equation will balance.

To understand why this happens, keep in mind three basic facts regarding double-entry accounting:

1. Debits are always entered on the left side of an account and credits on the right side.
2. For every transaction, there must be at least one debit and one credit.
3. Debits must always equal credits for each transaction.

Now notice what this means for one of the business transactions shown earlier (page 85): investment by owners. An asset account (Cash) is debited; it is increased. An owners' equity account (Capital Stock) is credited; it is also increased. There is both a debit and a credit for the transaction, and we have increased accounts on both sides of the equation by an equal amount, thus keeping the accounting equation in balance.

Be careful not to let the general, nonaccounting meanings of the words *credit* and *debit* confuse you. In general conversation, credit has an association with plus and debit with minus. But on the asset side of the accounting equation, where debit means increase and credit means decrease, this association can lead you astray. In accounting, debit simply means left and credit simply means right. To make sure you understand the relationship between debits and credits, the various accounts, and the accounting equation, let us examine further the transactions listed on page 85.

Business Activity (Transaction)	Effect in Terms of the Accounting Equation					
	Assets		=	**Liabilities**	+	**Owners' Equity**
1. Investment by owners	Cash DR (+)					Capital Stock CR (+)
2. Borrowed money from bank	Cash DR (+)			Notes Payable CR (+)		
3. Purchased inventory on credit	Inventory DR (+)			Accounts Payable CR (+)		
4. Purchased equipment for cash	Equipment DR (+)	Cash CR (−)				

Note that every time an account is debited, other accounts have to be credited for the same amount. This is the major characteristic of the double-entry accounting system: *the debits must always equal the credits.* This important characteristic creates a practical advantage: the opportunity for "self-checking." If debits do not equal credits, an error has been made in analyzing and recording the entity's activities.

Before proceeding any further, let's stop for a moment and review the relationship between the various types of accounts and debits and credits. It is in your best interest not to go on until you understand these relationships.

Account Type		Debit or Credit?	Ending Balance
Asset	Increase results in	Debit	Debit
	Decrease results in	Credit	
Liability	Increase results in	Credit	Credit
	Decrease results in	Debit	
Owners' Equity	Increase results in	Credit	Credit
	Decrease results in	Debit	

Expanding the Accounting Equation to Include Revenues, Expenses, and Dividends

At this point, we must bring revenues and expenses into the picture. Obviously, they are part of every ongoing business. Revenues provide resource inflows; they are increases in resources from the sale of goods or services. Expenses represent resource outflows; they are costs incurred in generating revenues. Note that revenues are not synonymous with cash or other assets, but are a way of describing where the assets came from. For example, cash received from the sale of a product would be considered revenue. Cash received by borrowing from the bank would not be revenue, but an increase in a liability. By the same token, expenses are a way of describing how an asset has been used. Thus, cash paid for interest on a loan is an expense, but cash paid to buy a building represents the exchange of one asset for another.

Caution

We stated previously that owners' equity accounts will have credit balances. However, expenses, a component of Retained Earnings, will almost always have debit balances. Since revenues will usually exceed expenses, the net effect on Retained Earnings will result in a credit balance.

How do revenues and expenses fit into the accounting equation? Remember that revenues minus expenses equals net income; and net income is a major source of change in owners' equity from one accounting period to the next. Revenues and expenses, then, may be thought of as *temporary* subdivisions of owners' equity. Revenues increase owners' equity and so, like all owners' equity accounts, are increased by credits. Expenses reduce owners' equity and are therefore increased by debits. As will be explained in Chapter 4, all revenue and expense accounts are "closed" into the retained earnings account at the end of the accounting cycle.

dividends Distributions to the owners (stockholders) of a corporation.

One other temporary account affects owners' equity. It is the account that shows distributions of earnings to owners. For a corporation, this account is called **Dividends**. Since dividends reflect payments to the owners, therefore reducing owners' equity, the dividends account is increased by a debit and decreased by a credit. The dividends account, like revenues and expenses, is also "closed" into the retained earnings account.

Just a warning here: students who have trouble grasping debits and credits usually get hung up on the revenue and expense accounts. Remember that revenues and expenses are subcategories of Retained Earnings. When you credit a revenue account, you are essentially increasing Retained Earnings. When you debit an expense account, you are increasing the amount of expense, which in turn reduces Retained Earnings.

Using the corporate form of business as an example, the accounting equation may be expanded to include revenues, expenses, and dividends, as shown in Exhibit 2.

Keep in mind that in actual business practice, when a manual accounting system is used, the T-account is an integral feature of a more formal and complete account. Exhibit 3 is an example of such an account. Note that in addition to the debits and credits in the T-account portion (drawn in heavy lines in this example), the account has a title, Cash; an account number, 101; and columns for a transaction date, an explanation of the transaction, a posting reference (a cross-reference to other accounting records), and a balance.

Why Should I Understand the Mechanics of Accounting?

If computers now take care of all the routine accounting functions, why does a businessperson need to know anything about debits, credits, journals, posting, T-accounts, and trial balances? Good question. First of all, even though computers now do most of the dirty work, the essence of double-entry accounting is unchanged from the days of quill pens and handwritten ledgers. Thus, understanding the process explained in this chapter is still relevant to a computer-based accounting system. In addition, with or without computers, the use of debits, credits, and T-accounts still provides an efficient and widely used shorthand method of analyzing transactions. At a minimum, all businesspeople should be familiar enough with the language of accounting to understand, for example, why a credit balance in Cash or a debit balance in Retained Earnings is something unusual enough to merit investigation. Finally, an understanding of the

Exhibit 2: Expanded Accounting Equation

Exhibit 3: Typical Account

ACCOUNT: Cash					ACCOUNT NO. 101
Date	Explanation	Post. Ref.	Debits	Credits	Balance

accounting cycle—analyzing, recording, summarizing, and preparing—gives one insight into how information flows within an organization. And great advantages accrue to those who understand information flow.

TO SUMMARIZE: Regardless of the size or complexity of a business, or the manner in which the records are maintained (manual or automated system), the steps of the accounting cycle are the same. The entire process is based on double-entry accounting and the basic accounting equation. Accounts accumulate the results of transactions.

Debits are always entered on the left side of an account, and credits are always entered on the right side. Debits increase asset, expense, and dividend accounts and decrease liability, owners' equity, and revenue accounts. Credits decrease asset, expense, and dividend accounts and increase liability, owners' equity, and revenue accounts. Revenues increase owners' equity, whereas expenses and dividends decrease owners' equity. Therefore, under a double-entry system of accounting, it is always possible to check the accounting records to see that Assets = Liabilities + Owners' Equity and debits equal credits.

How Do We Record the Effects of Transactions?

3 Record the effects of transactions using journal entries (step two of the accounting cycle).

journal An accounting record in which transactions are first entered; provides a chronological record of all business activities.

With our knowledge of the different types of accounts (assets, liabilities, and owners' equity) and the use of the terms *debit* and *credit* (debit means left and credit means right), we are now ready to actually record the effects of transactions.

The second step in the accounting cycle is to record the results of transactions in a **journal**. Known as "books of original entry," journals provide a chronological record of all entity transactions. They show the dates of the transactions, the amounts involved, and the particular accounts affected by the transactions. Sometimes a detailed description of the transaction is also included.

This chronological recording of transactions provides a company with a complete record of its activities. If amounts were recorded directly in the accounts, it would be difficult, if not impossible, for a company to trace a transaction that occurred, say, six months previously.

Smaller companies, such as a locally owned pizza restaurant, may use only one book of original entry, called a "general journal," to record all transactions. Larger companies having thousands of transactions each year may use special journals (for example, a cash receipts journal) as well as a general journal.

journalizing Recording transactions in a journal.

journal entry A recording of a transaction where debits equal credits; usually includes a date and an explanation of the transaction.

A specific format is used in **journalizing** (recording) transactions in a general journal. The debit entry is listed first; the credit entry is listed second and is indented to the right. Normally, the date and a brief explanation of the transaction are considered essential parts of the **journal entry**. (In the text, we often ignore dates and explanations to simplify the examples.) Dollar signs usually are omitted. Unless otherwise noted, this format will be used whenever a journal entry is presented.

> **General Journal Entry Format**
> Date   Debit Entry   xx
>   Credit Entry   xx
>   *Explanation.*

Exhibit 4 is a partial page from a general journal, showing typical journal entries. Study this exhibit carefully because the entire accounting cycle is based on journal entries. If journal entries are incorrect, the resulting financial information will be inaccurate.

To give you additional exposure to analyzing transactions and recording journal entries, we are going to start our own business. Rather than spend the summer flipping burgers at the local hamburger house, you decide that you want to have an outdoor job—one that allows you to enjoy the summer sun, engage in rigorous physical activity, and sharpen your skills as an entrepreneur. You are going to start your own landscaping business. This business will involve mowing lawns, pulling weeds, trimming and planting shrubs, and so forth. We will use your new business to illustrate the journal entries used to record some common transactions of a business enterprise.[1] These transactions fit into the following four general categories: acquiring

---

1 Normally, a small business like this one would be started as a sole proprietorship or as a partnership. We assume a corporation here to show a complete set of transactions.

Exhibit 4: General Journal

	JOURNAL			Page 1
Date	**Description**	**Post. Ref.**	**Debits**	**Credits**
2006 July 1	Cash		2,000	
	Capital Stock			2,000
	Issued 200 shares of capital stock at $10 per share.			
5	Truck		800	
	Cash			800
	Purchased a used truck.			
5	Equipment		250	
	Accounts Payable			250
	Purchased a lawnmower on account.			
5	Supplies		180	
	Cash			180
	Purchased supplies for cash.			

cash, acquiring other assets, selling goods or providing services, and collecting cash and paying obligations. Obviously, we cannot present all possible transactions in this chapter. In studying the illustrations, strive to understand the conceptual basis of transaction analysis rather than memorizing specific journal entries. Pay particular attention to the dual effect of each transaction on the company in terms of the basic accounting equation (that is, its impact on assets and on liabilities and owners' equity). Remember that business activity involves revenues, expenses, and distributions to owners as well, and that these accounts eventually increase or decrease owners' equity (the retained earnings account for a corporation).

Acquiring Cash, Either from Owners or by Borrowing

Your first task in starting this business is to acquire cash, either through owners' investments or by borrowing. Your parents indicate that they will match any funds that you are going to put into your business. You have $1,000 in savings, and coupled with your parents' matching funds, you decide to issue 200 shares of stock.

Example I
The following transaction illustrates investments by owners:

assets (+)	Cash	2,000
owners' equity (+)	Capital Stock	2,000
	Issued 200 shares of capital stock at $10 per share.	

This transaction increases cash as a result of capital stock being issued to investors, or stockholders. The cash account is debited, and the capital stock account is credited. The economic impact of this situation may be summarized as follows:

	ASSETS					=	LIABILITIES		+	OWNERS' EQUITY
Transaction #	**Cash**	**Inventory**	**Equipment**	**Supplies**	**Truck**		**Accounts Payable**	**Notes Payable**		**Capital Stock**
Beginning Balance	$ 0	$0	$0	$0	$0	=	$0	$0	+	$ 0
Invested money in the business	2,000	–	–	–	–		–	–		2,000
Subtotal	$2,000	$0	$0	$0	$0	=	$0	$0	+	$2,000

Example 2

Suppose that in addition to coming up with the money yourself or from your parents, you went to a bank and convinced the loan officer to lend you the money. The journal entry for such a transaction would be:

assets (+)
liabilities (+)

Cash 2,000
    Notes Payable 2,000
      Borrowed $2,000 from First National Bank, signing a
      12-month note at 12% interest.

Here, the cash account is debited, and the notes payable account is credited. The accounting equation captures the economic impact of borrowing the money as follows:

	ASSETS					=	LIABILITIES		+	OWNERS' EQUITY
Transaction #	**Cash**	**Inventory**	**Equipment**	**Supplies**	**Truck**		**Accounts Payable**	**Notes Payable**		**Capital Stock**
Beginning Balance	$ 0	$0	$0	$0	$0	=	$0	$ 0	+	$ 0
Invested money in the business	2,000	–	–	–	–		–	–		2,000
Borrowed money from a bank	2,000	–	–	–	–		–	2,000		–
Subtotal	$4,000	$0	$0	$0	$0	=	$0	$2,000	+	$2,000

Acquiring Other Assets

Now that you have obtained the funds necessary to start your business, either from owner investment or by borrowing, you can use that money to acquire other assets needed to operate the business. Such assets include supplies (such as fertilizer), inventory (perhaps shrubs that you will plant), and equipment (for example, a lawnmower and a truck for hauling). These assets may be purchased with cash or on credit. Credit purchases require payment after a period of time, for example, 30 days. Normally, interest expense is incurred when assets are bought on a time-payment plan that extends beyond two or three months. (To keep our examples simple here, we will not include interest expense. We will show how to account for interest on page 101, where we discuss the payment of obligations.) Examples of transactions involving the acquisition of noncash assets follow.

Example I

The first thing you need is a lawnmower and some form of transportation. You find an old 1988 pickup truck for sale for $800, and you buy it paying cash.

assets (+)	Truck	800
assets (−)	Cash	800
	Purchased a used truck.	

The accounting equation shows:

	ASSETS					=	LIABILITIES		+	OWNERS' EQUITY
Transaction #	Cash	Inventory	Equipment	Supplies	Truck		Accounts Payable	Notes Payable		Capital Stock
Beginning Balance	$ 0	$0	$0	$0	$ 0	=	$0	$ 0	+	$ 0
Invested money in the business	2,000	–	–	–	–		–	–		2,000
Borrowed money from a bank	2,000	–	–	–	–		–	2,000		–
Purchased a truck paying cash	−800	–	–	–	800		–	–		–
Subtotal	$3,200	$0	$0	$0	$800	=	$0	$2,000	+	$2,000

Next, you drive to the local Sears store and purchase a Craftsman lawnmower and gas can for $250. Instead of paying for the mower with cash, you open a charge account, which will allow you to pay for the mower in 30 days with no interest charge. (If you wait and pay beyond this 30-day grace period, an interest charge will apply.) The journal entry to record this purchase is:

assets (+)	Equipment	250
liabilities (+)	Accounts Payable	250
	Purchased a lawnmower and gas can on account.	

The accounting equation is shown at the top of the following page. When you pay for the mower, cash will be reduced, and the liability, Accounts Payable, will also be reduced, thus keeping the equation in balance.

	ASSETS					=	LIABILITIES		+	OWNERS' EQUITY
Transaction #	Cash	Inventory	Equipment	Supplies	Truck		Accounts Payable	Notes Payable		Capital Stock
Beginning Balance	$ 0	$0	$ 0	$0	$ 0	=	$ 0	$ 0	+	$ 0
Invested money in the business	2,000	–	–	–	–		–	–		2,000
Borrowed money from a bank	2,000	–	–	–	–		–	2,000		–
Purchased a truck paying cash	–800	–	–	–	800		–			
Purchased a mower on account	–	–	250	–	–		250	–		–
Subtotal	$3,200	$0	$250	$0	$800	=	$250	$2,000	+	$2,000

Example 2

Off you go to the neighborhood Home Depot store to purchase fertilizer, gloves, a rake, a shovel, and other assorted supplies. The total cost is $180, which you pay in cash; an increase in one asset (supplies) results in a decrease in another asset (cash).

assets (+)	Supplies 180
assets (−)	Cash 180
	Purchased supplies for cash.

The accounting equation shows:

	ASSETS					=	LIABILITIES		+	OWNERS' EQUITY
Transaction #	Cash	Inventory	Equipment	Supplies	Truck		Accounts Payable	Notes Payable		Capital Stock
Beginning Balance	$ 0	$0	$ 0	$ 0	$ 0	=	$ 0	$ 0	+	$ 0
Invested money in the business	2,000	–	–	–	–		–	–		2,000
Borrowed money from a bank	2,000	–	–	–	–		–	2,000		–
Purchased a truck paying cash	–800	–	–	–	800		–	–		–
Purchased a mower on account	–	–	250	–	–		250	–		–
Purchased supplies for cash	–180	–	–	180	–		–	–		–
Subtotal	$3,020	$0	$250	$180	$800	=	$250	$2,000	+	$2,000

Example 3

On your way home from the hardware store, you drive past a greenhouse and notice a big sign advertising a "50% off" sale on shrubs. Since you anticipate that planting shrubs will be part of your business, you stop and purchase for cash $150 worth of shrubs as inventory. You plan to make money in two ways with the shrubs: (1) revenue from the labor associated with planting them and (2) a profit on selling the shrubs for more than you paid. (This is fair; after all, you are saving your client the time and trouble of having to go to the greenhouse.)

assets (+)	Inventory	150
assets (−)	Cash	150
	Purchased inventory for cash.	

The accounting equation shows:

	ASSETS					=	LIABILITIES		+	OWNERS' EQUITY
Transaction #	Cash	Inventory	Equipment	Supplies	Truck		Accounts Payable	Notes Payable		Capital Stock
Beginning Balance	$ 0	$ 0	$ 0	$ 0	$ 0	=	$ 0	$ 0	+	$ 0
Invested money in the business	2,000	–	–	–	–		–	–		2,000
Borrowed money from a bank	2,000	–	–	–	–		–	2,000		–
Purchased a truck paying cash	−800	–	–	–	800		–	–		–
Purchased a mower on account	–	–	250	–	–		250	–		–
Purchased supplies for cash	−180	–	–	180	–		–	–		–
Purchased inventory for cash	−150	150	–	–	–		–	–		–
Subtotal	$2,870	$150	$250	$180	$800	=	$250	$2,000	+	$2,000

Selling Goods or Providing Services

Now that you have your lawnmower, your transportation, your supplies, and your inventory, it is time to go to work. The next category of common transactions involves the sale of services or merchandise. Revenues are generated and expenses incurred during this process. Sometimes services and merchandise are sold for cash; at other times, they are sold on credit (on account), and a receivable is established for collection at a later date. Therefore, revenues indicate the source not only of cash but of other assets as well, all of which are received in exchange for the merchandise or services provided. Similarly, expenses may be incurred and paid for immediately by cash, or they may be incurred on credit—that is, they may be "charged," with a cash payment to be made at a later date. Illustrative transactions follow. Note the effect of revenues and expenses on owners' equity is indicated in brackets for each transaction.

Example 1

As soon as people find out that you are in the lawn care and landscaping business, your phone begins ringing off the hook. Although most of your clients pay you immediately when you perform the service, some prefer to pay you once a month. As a result, a portion of your revenues is received immediately in cash, while the balance becomes receivables. The journal entry to record your first week's revenue for lawn care services is:

assets (+)
assets (+)
revenues (+) [equity (+)]

Cash 270	
Accounts Receivable 80	
Lawn Care Revenue	350
To record revenue for lawn care services.	

As the journal entry illustrates, more than two accounts can be involved in recording a transaction. This type of entry is called a **compound journal entry**.

compound journal entry
A journal entry that involves more than one debit or more than one credit or both.

Because revenues increase owners' equity, the accounting equation shows:

Assets	=	Liabilities	+	Owners' Equity (Revenues)
(increase $350)		(no change)		(increase $350)

The detailed effect of this transaction and of each of the following transactions is summarized in Exhibit 5 on page 102.

Example 2

One of your customers asks if you will plant some shrubs in her backyard. You mention that you have some shrubs and describe them to her; she is thrilled that you have just the shrubs she wants, thereby saving her a trip to the greenhouse. You use one-half of your inventory of shrubs in this customer's yard, and it takes you three hours to complete the job. She pays you in cash. In this instance, we are dealing with two different types of revenue—profit from the sale of the shrubs and revenue from your labor. Let's deal with each type of revenue separately.

Sale of Shrubs.   Sales, whether made on account or for cash, require entries that reflect not only the sale, but also the cost of the inventory sold. The "cost of goods sold" is an expense and, as such, is offset with the sales revenue to determine the profitability of sales transactions. The special procedures for handling inventory are described in Chapter 8. It is sufficient here to show an example of the impact of the transaction on the accounting equation.

In this example, you charged your customer $90 for one-half of the shrubs you purchased earlier.

assets (+)
revenues (+) [equity (+)]

Cash 90	
Sales Revenue	90
Sold inventory for cash.	

expenses (+) [equity (−)]
assets (−)

Cost of Goods Sold	75
Inventory	75
To record the cost of inventory sold and to reduce inventory	
for its cost.	

In this example, inventory costing you $75 is being sold for $90. The effect on the accounting equation for each transaction is:

STOP & THINK

Could the two journal entries relating to the sale of inventory be combined into one journal entry?

Sales on Account

Assets	=	Liabilities	+	Owners' Equity (Revenues)
(increase $90)		(no change)		(increase $90)

Cost of Goods Sold

Assets	=	Liabilities	+	Owners' Equity (Expenses)
(decrease $75)		(no change)		(decrease $75)

Labor for Planting. In addition to making a profit on the sale of the shrubs, you also generated revenue planting them. The journal entry to record this revenue is:

assets (+)
revenues (+) [equity (+)]

Cash	45
Landscaping Revenue	45
To record revenue for landscaping services.	

The effect of the transaction on the accounting equation is:

Assets	=	Liabilities	+	Owners' Equity (Revenues)
(increase $45)		(no change)		(increase $45)

Example 3

In addition to expenses relating to the sale of inventory, other expenses are also incurred in operating a business. Examples include gas for your lawnmower and your truck and the wages you agreed to pay your little brother for working for you (Mom said you had to let him help). The following journal entries illustrate how these expenses would be accounted for:

expenses (+) [equity (−)]
assets (−)

Gasoline Expense	50
Cash	50
Paid cash for gas for the truck and the mower.	

expenses (+) [equity (−)]
assets (−)

Wages Expense	60
Cash	60
Paid wages expense.	

The effect on the accounting equation of the gasoline expense is:

Assets	=	Liabilities	+	Owners' Equity (Expenses)
(decrease $50)		(no change)		(decrease $50)

The entry for Wages Expense affects the equation in the same manner, the only difference being the amount, $60.

Collecting Cash and Paying Obligations

Obviously, once merchandise or services are sold on account, the receivables must be collected. The cash received is generally used to meet daily operating expenses and to pay other obligations. Excess cash can be reinvested in the business or distributed to the owners as a return on their investment.

Example 1

The collection of accounts receivable is an important aspect of most businesses. Receivables are created when you allow certain customers to pay for your services at a later date. When receivables are collected, that asset is reduced and cash is increased, as shown here.

assets (+)
assets (−)

Cash	80
Accounts Receivable	80
Collected $80 of receivables.	

The effect of collecting the receivables on the accounting equation is:

Assets	=	Liabilities	+	Owners' Equity
(increase $80;		(no change)		(no change)
decrease $80)				

Note that no revenue is involved here. Revenue is recorded when the original sales transaction creates the accounts receivable. The cash collection on account merely involves exchanging one asset for another.

Example 2

Remember that lawnmower and gas can you purchased on account? Well, now you have to pay for them. The entry to record the payment of obligations with cash is:

liabilities (−)
assets (−)

Accounts Payable	250
Cash	250
Paid $250 for the lawnmower and gas can previously purchased.	

After payment of accounts payable, the accounting equation shows:

Assets	=	Liabilities	+	Owners' Equity
(decrease $250)		(decrease $250)		(no change)

Remember that two parties are always involved in exchange transactions. What one buys, the other sells. When sales are on credit, the seller will record a receivable and the buyer will record a payable. The two accounts are inversely related. The seller of merchandise records a receivable and a sale, and simultaneously records an expense for the cost of goods sold and a reduction of inventory (as in Example 2 on page 98). The buyer records the receipt of the merchandise and, at the same time, records an obligation to pay the seller at some future time. When payment is made, the buyer reduces Accounts Payable and Cash (as in this example), whereas the seller increases Cash and reduces Accounts Receivable (as in Example 1 above).

Example 3

On page 94, we showed the entry required when cash was borrowed from the bank. In that entry, you borrowed $2,000 to be paid over 12 months. Suppose you are required to make monthly loan payments of $178 with a portion of each payment being attributed to interest and a portion to reducing the liability—just like a mortgage on a house. As the following compound journal entry shows, a note payable or similar obligation requires an entry for payment, as well as for the interest due. Note that "interest" is the amount charged for using money, as will be more fully explained in later chapters.

liabilities (−)
expenses (+) [equity (−)]
  assets (−)

Notes Payable	158	
Interest Expense	20	
Cash		178
Paid first monthly payment on note with interest		
($2,000 × 0.12 × 1/12).		

Analysis of this transaction reveals that assets have decreased for two reasons. First, a portion of a liability has been paid with cash. Second, interest expense at 12% for one month on the note payable has been paid. This relationship will generally be present in most long-term and some short-term liability transactions. Since the interest charge is an expense and decreases owners' equity, the impact of the entry on the accounting equation is:

STOP & THINK

Why are dividends NOT considered to be an expense?

Assets	=	Liabilities	+	Owners' Equity (Expenses)
(decrease $178)		(decrease $158)		(decrease $20)

Example 4

Recall that you obtained financing in two ways to start your business—investors (you, Mom, and Dad) and the bank. In the previous journal entry, we illustrated how the bank receives a return on its investment. Well, Mom and Dad would like a return as well. Corporations that are profitable generally pay dividends to their stockholders. "Dividends" represent a distribution to the stockholders of part of the earnings of a company. The following entry illustrates the payment of a cash dividend:

dividends (+) [equity (−)]
  assets (−)

Dividends	50	
Cash		50
Paid a $50 cash dividend.		

As noted earlier, dividends, like revenues and expenses, affect owners' equity. Unlike revenues and expenses, dividends are a distribution of profits and, therefore, are not considered in determining net income. Because dividends reduce the retained earnings accumulated by a corporation, they decrease owners' equity. The payment of a $50 dividend affects the accounting equation as follows:

Assets	=	Liabilities	+	Owners' Equity (Dividends)
(decrease $50)		(no change)		(decrease $50)

See Exhibit 5 for a summary of the transactions shown in this chapter and their effect on the accounting equation.

A Note on Journal Entries

When preparing a journal entry, a systematic method may be used in analyzing every transaction. A journal entry involves a three-step process:

Exhibit 5: Summary of Transactions

		ASSETS					=	LIABILITIES	
	Cash	Accounts Receivable	Inventory	Equipment	Supplies	Truck		Accounts Payable	Notes Payable
Balance	$2,870	–	$150	$250	$180	$800	=	$250	$2,000
Revenue from lawn care	270	80	–	–	–	–		–	–
Sold inventory for cash	90	–	–75	–	–	–		–	–
Revenue from landscaping	45	–	–	–	–	–		–	–
Paid for gasoline	–50	–	–	–	–	–		–	–
Paid wages	–60	–	–	–	–	–		–	–
Collected receivables	80	–80	–	–	–	–		–	–
Paid accounts payable	–250	–	–	–	–	–		–250	–
Paid loan payment	–178	–	–	–	–	–		–	–158
Paid dividend	–50	–	–	–	–	–		–	–
Total	$2,767	$ 0	$ 75	$250	$180	$800	=	$ 0	$1,842

1. Identify which accounts are involved.
2. For each account, determine if it is increased or decreased.
3. For each account, determine by how much it has changed.

The answer to step 1 tells you if the accounts involved are asset, liability, or owners' equity accounts. The answer to step 2, when considered in light of your answer to step 1, tells you if the accounts involved are to be debited or credited. Consider the instance where $25,000 is borrowed from a bank. The two accounts involved are Cash and Notes Payable. Cash increased, and since Cash is an asset and assets increase with debits, then Cash must be debited. Notes Payable increased (we owe more money), and since Notes Payable is a liability and liabilities increase with credits, then Notes Payable must be credited. The answer to step 3 completes the journal entry. Cash is debited for $25,000, and Notes Payable is credited for $25,000.

This three-step process will always work, even for complex transactions. Consider the case where inventory costing $60,000 is sold on account for $75,000. Using the three-step process results in the following:

1. *Step 1:* What accounts are involved?
   - Accounts Receivable (an asset), Inventory (an asset), Cost of Goods Sold (an expense—part of owners' equity), and Sales Revenue (a revenue account—part of owners' equity).

2. *Step 2:* Did the accounts increase or decrease?
   - Accounts Receivable increased (customers owe us more money). Since Accounts Receivable is an asset, it is increased with a debit.

+	OWNERS' EQUITY								
		Retained Earnings							
	Capital Stock	Lawn Care Revenue	Sales Revenue	Landscaping Revenue	Cost of Goods Sold*	Gasoline Expense*	Wages Expense*	Interest Expense*	Dividends*
+	$2,000	–	–	–	–	–	–	–	–
	–	350	–	–	–	–	–	–	–
	–	–	90	–	–75	–	–	–	–
	–	–	–	45	–	–	–	–	–
	–	–	–	–	–	–50	–	–	–
	–	–	–	–	–	–	–60	–	–
	–	–	–	–	–	–	–	–	–
	–	–	–	–	–	–	–	–	–
	–	–	–	–	–	–	–	–20	–
	–	–	–	–	–	–	–	–	–50
+	$2,000	$350	$90	$45	–$75	–$50	–$60	–$20	–$50

*Recall that an increase in these accounts actually decreases owners' equity, hence the – (minus sign).

- Inventory decreased (we don't have it anymore). Since Inventory is an asset, it is decreased with a credit.
- Cost of Goods Sold increased (an expense causing owners' equity to decrease). Since owners' equity decreases with a debit, Cost of Goods Sold must be debited.
- Sales Revenue increased (a revenue causing owners' equity to increase). Since owners' equity increases with a credit, Sales Revenue must be credited.

3. *Step 3:* By how much did each account change?
   - The answer to step 3 results in the following journal entries:

Accounts Receivable	75,000	
Sales Revenue		75,000
Cost of Goods Sold	60,000	
Inventory		60,000

TO SUMMARIZE: Journal entries are used to summarize the effects of business transactions. Journal entries are prepared or analyzed by answering three questions: (1) What accounts are involved? (2) Did those accounts increase or decrease? (3) By how much did each account change? By correctly answering these three questions, transactions will be properly accounted for, and the accounting equation will always balance.

Posting Journal Entries and Preparing a Trial Balance

4 Summarize the resulting journal entries through posting and prepare a trial balance (step three of the accounting cycle).

posting The process of transferring amounts from the journal to the ledger.

ledger A book of accounts in which data from transactions recorded in journals are posted and thereby summarized.

chart of accounts A systematic listing of all accounts used by a company.

Caution

Common mistakes when manually posting include posting a debit to the credit side of an account, transposing numbers (e.g., a 45 magically becomes a 54), and posting to the wrong account (e.g., Supplies instead of Inventory). The lesson—be very careful or mistakes will creep into your work. Thankfully, posting is a task done almost exclusively by computers these days.

Once transactions have been analyzed and recorded in a journal, it is necessary to classify and group all similar items. This is accomplished by the bookkeeping procedure of **posting** all the journal entries to appropriate accounts. As indicated earlier, accounts are records of like items. They show transaction dates, increases and decreases, and balances. For example, all increases and decreases in cash arising from transactions recorded in the journal are accumulated in one account called Cash. Similarly, all sales transactions are grouped together in the sales revenue account.

Posting is no more than sorting all journal entry amounts by account and copying those amounts to the appropriate account. No analysis is needed; all the necessary analysis is performed when the transaction is first recorded in the journal.

All accounts are maintained in an accounting record called the "general ledger." A **ledger** is a "book of accounts." Exhibit 6 shows how the three cash transactions in the general journal would be posted to the cash account in the general ledger, with arrows depicting the posting procedures. Observe that a number has been inserted in the "posting reference" column in both books. This number serves as a cross-reference between the general journal and the accounts in the general ledger. In the journal, it identifies the account to which the journal entry has been posted. In the ledger, it identifies the page on which the entry appears in the general journal. For example, the GJ1 notation in the cash account for the July 1 entry means that the $2,000 has been posted from page 1 of the general journal. As you will discover, these posting references are useful in tracking down mistakes. With a computer system, the software automatically generates these posting references.

A particular company will have as many (or as few) accounts as it needs to provide a reasonable classification of its transactions. The list of accounts used by a company is known as its **chart of accounts**. The normal order of a chart of accounts is assets (current and long-term), then liabilities (current and long-term), followed by owners' equity, sales, and expenses. Exhibit 7 on page 106 shows some accounts that might appear in a typical company's chart of accounts.

Determining Account Balances

At the end of an accounting period, the accounts in the general ledger are reviewed to determine each account's balance. Asset, expense, and dividend accounts normally have debit balances; liability, owners' equity, and revenue accounts normally have credit balances. In other words, the balance is normally on the side that increases the account.

To illustrate how to determine an account balance, consider the following T-account depicting all the cash transactions from our landscaping business (with dates being added). The beginning cash account balance plus all Cash debit entries, less total credits to Cash, equals the ending balance in the cash account.

Cash

Beg. Bal.	0		
7/1	2,000		
7/1	2,000	7/5	800
7/9	270	7/5	180
7/14	90	7/7	150
7/14	45	7/18	50
7/30	80	7/23	60
		7/31	250
		7/31	178
		7/31	50
	4,485		(1,718)
	(1,718)		
End. Bal.	2,767		

Exhibit 6: Posting to the General Ledger

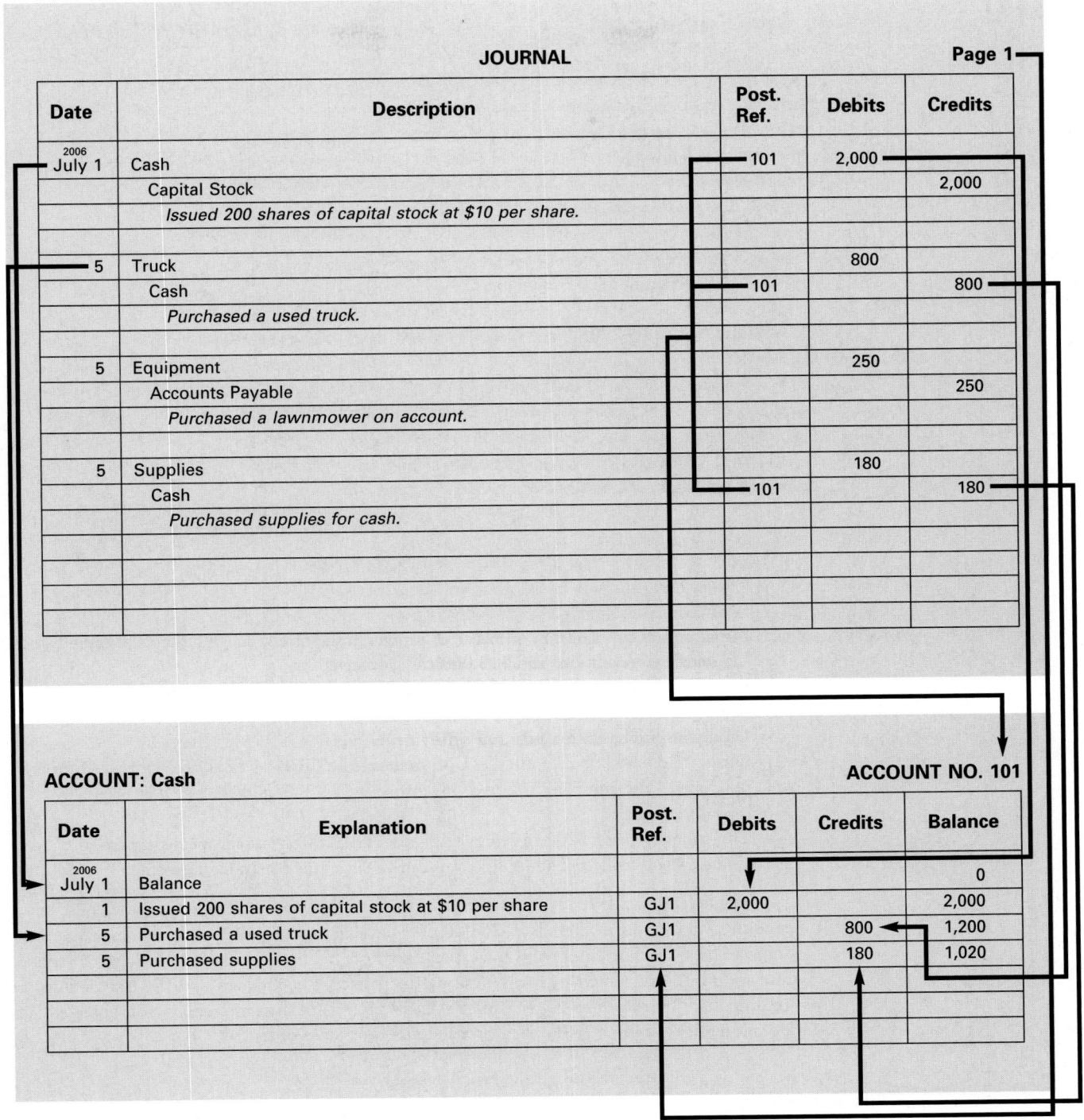

Illustration of the First Three Steps in the Accounting Cycle

We have introduced the first three steps in the accounting cycle. A simple illustration will help reinforce what you have learned about the relationship of assets, liabilities, and owners' equity, as well as revenues, expenses, and dividends, and the mechanics of double-entry accounting. Katherine Kohler established the Double K Corporation in 2006. The following transactions occurred.

Exhibit 7: Chart of Accounts for a Typical Company

Assets (100–199)	Owners' Equity (300–399)
Current Assets (100–150):	301 Capital Stock
101 Cash	330 Retained Earnings
103 Notes Receivable	
105 Accounts Receivable	**Sales (400–499)**
107 Inventory	
108 Supplies	400 Sales Revenue
Long-Term Assets (151–199):	**Expenses (500–599)**
151 Land	
152 Buildings	500 Cost of Goods Sold
154 Office Furniture or Equipment	501 Sales Salaries and Commissions
	523 Rent Expense
Liabilities (200–299)	525 Travel Expense
	528 Advertising Expense
Current Liabilities (200–219):	551 Officers' Salaries
201 Notes Payable	553 Administrative Salaries
202 Accounts Payable	570 Payroll Taxes
203 Salaries Payable	571 Office Supplies Expense
204 Interest Payable	573 Utilities Expense
206 Income Taxes Payable	578 Office Equipment Rent Expense
	579 Accounting and Legal Fees
Long-Term Liabilities (220–239):	
222 Mortgage Payable	

a. Initial capital contribution of $20,000, for which she received 1,000 shares of capital stock.
b. Double K Corporation paid $10,000 cash for inventory.
c. Borrowed $20,000 from a bank to buy some land, signing a long-term note with the bank.
d. Land was purchased for $25,000 cash.
e. During the year 2006, Double K Corporation sold 20%, or $2,000, of the inventory purchased. The company sold that inventory for $3,200, and the sale was originally made on credit.
f. The company paid $200 in selling expenses and $100 in miscellaneous expenses.
g. The company collected the full amount of the account receivable in cash.

The inventory purchases are verified by invoices showing the actual items purchased, dates, amounts, and so forth. There is a $20,000 note payable to the bank. Other business documents indicate the sale of inventory and the expenses incurred. Through analysis of these transactions and supporting documents (step 1), the pertinent facts are obtained and the transactions are recorded in a journal (step 2). The journal entries to record the transactions of Double K Corporation are as follows. (Note that letters are used in place of dates.)

Business Transaction	Account Category and Direction	Journal Entries	Debits	Credits
Issued stock	assets (+)	(a) Cash	20,000	
	owners' equity (+)	(a) Capital Stock		20,000
		Issued 1,000 shares of capital stock for $20,000.		

(continued)

Business Transaction	Account Category and Direction	Journal Entries	Debits	Credits
Purchased inventory	assets (+)	(b) Inventory	10,000	
	assets (−)	(b) Cash		10,000
		Purchased $10,000 of inventory for cash.		
Borrowed money	assets (+)	(c) Cash	20,000	
	liabilities (+)	(c) Notes Payable		20,000
		Borrowed $20,000 from a bank.		
Purchased land	assets (+)	(d) Land	25,000	
	assets (−)	(d) Cash		25,000
		Purchased land for cash.		
Sold inventory	assets (+)	(e) Accounts Receivable	3,200	
	revenues (+)	(e) Sales Revenue		3,200
		Sold inventory for $3,200 on account.		
	expenses (+)	(e) Cost of Goods Sold	2,000	
	assets (−)	(e) Inventory		2,000
		To record the cost of goods or inventory sold.		
Paid expenses	expenses (+)	(f) Selling Expenses	200	
	expenses (+)	(f) Miscellaneous Expenses	100	
	assets (−)	(f) Cash		300
		Paid selling and miscellaneous expenses.		
Collected cash	assets (+)	(g) Cash	3,200	
	assets (−)	(g) Accounts Receivable		3,200
		Collected accounts receivable.		

Next, the transactions are posted to the ledger accounts (step 3, part 1). T-accounts are used to illustrate this process, with the letters (a) through (g) showing the cross-references to the journal entries. A balance is shown for the end of the period. (Where only one transaction is involved, the amount of the transaction is also the account balance.)

	Cash				Accounts Receivable				Inventory				Land	
(a)	20,000	(b)	10,000	(e)	3,200	(g)	3,200	(b)	10,000	(e)	2,000	(d)	25,000	
(c)	20,000	(d)	25,000	Bal.	0			Bal.	8,000					
(g)	3,200	(f)	300											
Bal.	7,900													

	Notes Payable				Capital Stock				Sales Revenue	
		(c)	20,000			(a)	20,000			(e)	3,200

	Cost of Goods Sold				Selling Expenses				Miscellaneous Expenses	
(e)	2,000			(f)	200			(f)	100	

trial balance A listing of all account balances; provides a means of testing whether total debits equal total credits for all accounts.

The effect of these transactions can also be visualized using a spreadsheet format as shown in Exhibit 8.

After the account balances have been determined, a trial balance is usually prepared (step 3, part 2). A **trial balance** lists each account with its debit or credit balance, as shown in Exhibit 9. By adding all the debit balances and all the credit balances, the accountant can see whether total debits equal total credits. Even if the trial balance does show total debits equal to total credits, there may be errors. A transaction may have been omitted completely, or it may

Exhibit 8: Effects of Business Transactions on the Accounting Equation

Transaction #	ASSETS				=	LIABILITIES	+	OWNERS' EQUITY				
	Cash	Inventory	Land	Accounts Receivable		Notes Payable		Capital Stock	Retained Earnings			
Beginning Balance	$ 0	$ 0	$ 0	$ 0	=	$ 0	+	$ 0	Sales Revenue	Cost of Goods Sold*	Selling Expenses*	Misc. Expenses*
a	20,000	–	–	–		–		20,000	–	–	–	–
b	–10,000	10,000	–	–		–		0	–	–	–	–
c	20,000	–	–	–		20,000		–	–	–	–	–
d	–25,000	–	25,000	–		–		–	–	–	–	–
e	–	–2,000	–	3,200		–		–	3,200	–2,000	–	–
f	–300	–	–	–		–		–	–	–	–200	–100
g	3,200	–	–	–3,200		–		–	–	–	–	–
Total	$ 7,900	$ 8,000	$25,000	$ 0	=	$20,000	+	$20,000	$3,200	–$2,000	–$200	–$100

*Recall that an increase in these accounts actually decreases owners' equity, hence the – (minus sign).

Exhibit 9: Trial Balance

Double K Corporation
Trial Balance
December 31, 2006

	Debits	Credits
Cash	$ 7,900	
Accounts Receivable	0	
Inventory	8,000	
Land	25,000	
Notes Payable		$20,000
Capital Stock		20,000
Sales Revenue		3,200
Cost of Goods Sold	2,000	
Selling Expenses	200	
Miscellaneous Expenses	100	
Totals	$43,200	$43,200

have been recorded incorrectly or posted to the wrong account. These types of errors will not be discovered by preparing a trial balance; additional analysis would be required. In this case, total debits equal total credits. Thus, the accounting equation is in balance. The balances are taken from each ledger account.

Students frequently mistake a trial balance and the balance sheet for one another. In fact, they are very different reports. A trial balance is strictly an internal document used to summarize all of the account balances (assets, liabilities, owners' equity, revenues, expenses, and dividends) in a company's accounting system. Few people outside a company's accounting department ever see the trial balance; most businesspeople never see a real trial balance during their entire business career. The balance sheet, on the other hand, is a summary document that is frequently provided to interested parties both inside and outside a company.

From the data in the trial balance, an income statement and a balance sheet can be prepared. Exhibit 10 shows these two financial statements for Double K Corporation. Notice that there is no retained earnings account in the trial balance but there is one on the balance sheet. The reason for this is that all the income statement accounts such as Revenue, Cost of Goods Sold, and expenses are eventually accumulated into Retained Earnings. That is, earnings are reflected on the income statement. The business then decides the amount of those earnings to be retained. Those earnings that are to be retained are then disclosed on the balance sheet.

Also, the statement of cash flows can be prepared by categorizing the items in the cash account as operating, investing, or financing, as shown in Exhibit 11.

Three final notes: First, the preparation of financial statements is rarely so simple. In reality, the procedure also involves the adjustment of some ledger accounts, which need to be brought current before they can be included in the balance sheet or the income statement. In Chapter 4, we will explain how accounts are adjusted (step 4, part 1) so that the financial statements will accurately reflect the current financial position and operating results of an enterprise.

Second, net income does not usually equal the ending retained earnings balance. Only in the first year of a company's operations would this be the case. Double K Corporation began operations in 2006 and paid no dividends during the year; so, its $900 net income on the income statement equals the retained earnings figure on the balance sheet. In future years, the

Exhibit 10: Income Statement and Balance Sheet

Double K Corporation
Income Statement
For the Year Ended December 31, 2006

Sales revenue		$3,200
Expenses:		
Cost of goods sold	$2,000	
Selling expenses	200	
Miscellaneous expenses	100	2,300
Net income		$ 900
EPS ($900 ÷ 1,000 shares)		$ 0.90

Double K Corporation
Balance Sheet
December 31, 2006

Assets		Liabilities and Owners' Equity	
Cash	$ 7,900	Notes payable	$20,000
Inventory	8,000	Capital stock (1,000 shares)	20,000
Land	25,000	Retained earnings	900*
		Total liabilities and	
Total assets	$40,900	owners' equity	$40,900

*Beginning retained earnings + net income − dividends.

figures would be different, since retained earnings is an accumulation of earnings from past years adjusted for dividends and other special items.

Finally, with many businesses having hundreds or even thousands of transactions every day, it is impractical and inefficient to use only one journal. Instead, they group transactions into

Exhibit 11: Statement of Cash Flows

Double K Corporation
Statement of Cash Flows
For the Year Ended December 31, 2006

Operating activities:		
Collections from customers	$ 3,200	
Purchase of inventory	(10,000)	
Paid expenses	(300)	$ (7,100)
Investing activities:		
Purchased land		(25,000)
Financing activities:		
Issued stock	$20,000	
Borrowed from bank	20,000	40,000
Net increase in cash		$ 7,900
Beginning cash balance		0
Ending cash balance		$ 7,900

similar classes and use a *special journal* for each. These special journals can be maintained on paper or in a computerized system; the basic principles are the same. In this text's Interactive Study Center (Expanded Material) at **http://albrecht.swlearning.com**, we explain and illustrate how special journals are used to simplify the accounting for repetitive transactions.

> **TO SUMMARIZE:** Once journal entries have been made and posted to the related accounts, account balances are computed by summing the debit and credit entries in each account. A trial balance is prepared by listing each account along with its balance. An income statement and a balance sheet can be prepared from this trial balance. A statement of cash flows is prepared by analyzing the inflows and outflows of cash as detailed in the cash account.

Where Do Computers Fit In All This?

5 Describe how technology has affected the first three steps of the accounting cycle.

Students often ask, "Do I really need to know the difference between a debit and a credit? Haven't computers taken care of that?" Computers have greatly facilitated a business's ability to quickly process huge amounts of information without making mathematical errors. Most computers can make millions of calculations per second and produce more documents in 10 minutes than a person could in an entire week. The time spent posting journal entries and summarizing accounts into a trial balance has been greatly reduced as a result of computers.

But computers still can't think. That's your job. Walk up to a computer terminal and show it a sales invoice and the computer will just sit there and wait. Wait for what? For the answers to three questions: (1) What accounts are involved? (2) Did those accounts increase or decrease? (3) By how much did each account change?

Let's consider how the best-selling money management software package, Quicken®, has changed the accounting process. Quicken works a lot like a check register. For each check, you indicate the date, the check number, the payee, and the amount. Quicken then prompts you to indicate the nature of the expenditure by selecting from a list of accounts. For example, if the expenditure relates to your purchase of groceries, you would select the account "Food." Thus, all your transactions relating to "Food" will be grouped together, allowing you to quickly determine all food expenditures.

Now let's review what Quicken has done. First of all, since you indicated the transaction involved a check, Quicken knows that cash decreased. Quicken is programmed to know that when cash decreases, it involves a credit to the cash account. Quicken also has been programmed to know that debits have to equal credits, and since Cash was credited, the program knows that something was debited. Since you indicated "Food" (an expense) was the other account, Quicken debits that account, causing your expense account to increase (we now know that expenses increase with debits). Instead of telling Quicken which accounts to debit and credit, you are required to identify the accounts (question 1) and indicate if they increased or decreased (question 2). Quicken is able to determine, based on the answer to these two questions, which accounts were debited and which accounts were credited.

So has Quicken fundamentally changed the accounting process? No. It has increased the accuracy and speed with which the posting process is done, as well as the speed with which a variety of reports can be prepared. Quicken has also eliminated the need for the user to specify debit or credit. Because computers are so fast, the two-step process of identifying accounts and the direction of their change can be done as quickly as you can say "credit Cash." So why don't accountants get rid of these 500-year-old terms, debit and credit? The reason is that all accountants are familiar with and comfortable using these terms. When someone says "credit Cash," accountants everywhere know exactly what that means. Thus, debit and credit provide a useful shorthand method of communication.

It should be noted that computers also bring with them several disadvantages. The acronym "GIGO" (garbage in, garbage out) refers to the problems that result when data are entered incorrectly. If you tell the computer the wrong account or wrong amount, all the related accounts and reports will be wrong. If bookkeepers or accountants had been doing the posting, they might have caught an unrealistic figure or account and corrected the mistake at its source; computers accept data without question.

A related problem has to do with fixing an error once it has been identified. Unlike someone familiar with the accounting process, a computer cannot grasp the double-entry nature of accounting and realize that, for example, an incorrect amount may be posted to two accounts, not just one. As an example, suppose a customer calls and notifies you of an error in her account—a sale to her was incorrectly recorded as $100 instead of $10. You can correct the customer's account by making a $90 adjustment to Accounts Receivable, but Sales would need to be adjusted by $90 as well. A computer couldn't extrapolate this and would end up overlooking this Sales adjustment.

The computer has enhanced step 3 of the accounting cycle—summarizing. In fact, only in the smallest of businesses will you find the posting of journal entries and the preparation of a trial balance being done by hand. But in every business, from the largest to the smallest, you will find accountants still actively involved in analyzing transactions and turning those transactions into journal entries and eventually into useful accounting reports.

TO SUMMARIZE: The computer has changed certain aspects of the accounting cycle. The posting process has been substantially improved through the use of computers. In addition, computers have made the preparation of reports and statements easier. But computers have not replaced the need to analyze transactions and determine their effect on the accounting equation.

review of learning objectives

1 **Understand the process of transforming transaction data into useful accounting information.** The objective of the accounting process is to gather and transform transaction data into useful information that measures and communicates the results of business activity. The accounting system used to keep track of the many financial activities of a business should be tailor-made for that business and may be a manual or an automated system, depending on the organization's needs.

2 **Analyze transactions and determine how those transactions affect the accounting equation (step one of the accounting cycle).** The procedures for processing accounting data are based on double-entry accounting and the fundamental accounting equation: Assets = Liabilities + Owners' Equity. Revenues increase retained earnings, whereas expenses and dividends decrease retained earnings. Thus, these accounts have a direct impact on the amount of owners' equity. In terms of the increase/decrease relationship of accounts, assets, expenses, and dividends are increased by debits; liabilities, owners' equity, and revenues are increased by credits. The double-entry system of accounting ensures that the accounting equation will always balance because debit entries require equal credit entries; that is, total debits must always equal total credits when transactions are properly recorded.

3 **Record the effects of transactions using journal entries (step two of the accounting cycle).** The effects of business events are recorded in the accounting system using journal entries. Journal entries detail the accounts involved in a transaction, whether the accounts increased or decreased, and the amount by which each account is affected. Each journal entry requires an equal amount of debits and credits. This equality ensures that the accounting equation will always be in balance.

4 **Summarize the resulting journal entries through posting and prepare a trial balance (step three of the accounting cycle).** Once journal entries are made, they are posted to individual accounts. The posting process involves simply copying each debit and credit from a journal entry into the associated account. A trial balance can be prepared to ensure that debits equal credits and that the accounting equation is in balance. From the trial balance, the primary financial statements can be prepared.

 Describe how technology has affected the first three steps of the accounting cycle. Computers have changed the speed at which journal entries are processed through the accounting system. In most accounting systems, the posting process is done using computers. Computers ensure that no errors are made in transferring amounts from the journal entries to the accounts. Computers are also able to determine account balances and prepare reports quickly. Accountants are still required for the analysis and input of information into the accounting system.

key terms & concepts

account, 86
accounting cycle, 81
business documents, 82
chart of accounts, 104
compound journal entry, 98

credit, 88
debit, 88
dividends, 90
journal, 92
journal entry, 92

journalizing, 92
ledger, 104
posting, 104
T-account, 88
trial balance, 108

 # review problem

The First Three Steps in the Accounting Cycle

Journal entries are given below for January 2006, the first month of operation for the Svendsen Service Company.

Jan. 2	Cash	40,000	
	Capital Stock		40,000
	Issued capital stock for cash.		
2	Insurance Expense	500	
	Cash		500
	Purchased a one-month insurance policy.		
2	Rent Expense	750	
	Cash		750
	Paid rent for the month of January.		
3	Shop Equipment	8,000	
	Cash		8,000
	Purchased shop equipment for cash.		
4	Supplies	3,000	
	Accounts Payable		3,000
	Purchased shop supplies on account.		
5	Automotive Equipment	11,500	
	Cash		3,500
	Notes Payable		8,000
	Purchased a truck. Paid $3,500 cash and issued a 30-day note for the balance.		

(continued)

Jan. 8	Cash	1,750	
	Service and Repair Revenue		1,750
	Received cash for repairs.		
9	Advertising Expense	300	
	Cash		300
	Paid cash for radio spot announcements.		
12	Automotive Expense	200	
	Cash		200
	Paid gas, oil, and service costs on the truck.		
14	Accounts Payable	3,000	
	Cash		3,000
	Paid $3,000 on account.		
16	Accounts Receivable	1,200	
	Service and Repair Revenue		1,200
	Repaired truck for Acme Drilling Company on account.		
18	Telephone Expense	75	
	Cash		75
	Paid for installation and telephone service for one month.		
19	Automotive Expense	180	
	Cash		180
	Paid for minor repairs on the truck.		
20	Cash	1,000	
	Notes Receivable	1,450	
	Service and Repair Revenue		2,450
	Collected $1,000 cash from Jones for truck repairs;		
	accepted a 60-day note for the balance.		
24	Repairs and Maintenance Expense	150	
	Cash		150
	Paid cleaning and painting expenses on the building.		
25	Cash	1,500	
	Service and Repair Revenue		1,500
	Received cash for repairs and services from Hamilton, Inc.		
27	Supplies	2,500	
	Cash		2,500
	Purchased shop supplies.		
29	Office Equipment	1,250	
	Cash		1,250
	Purchased a computer.		
30	Cash	1,200	
	Accounts Receivable		1,200
	Collected receivables from Acme Drilling Company.		
31	Utilities Expense	900	
	Cash		900
	Paid the monthly utility bill.		
31	Automotive Expense	350	
	Cash		350
	Paid for gas, oil, and servicing of the truck.		

Required:

Set up T-accounts, post all journal entries to the accounts, balance the accounts, and prepare a trial balance.

Solution

The first step in solving this problem is to set up T-accounts for each item; then post all journal entries to the appropriate ledger accounts, as shown. Once the amounts are properly posted, account balances can be determined.

Cash			
1/2	40,000	1/2	500
1/8	1,750	1/2	750
1/20	1,000	1/3	8,000
1/25	1,500	1/5	3,500
1/30	1,200	1/9	300
		1/12	200
		1/14	3,000
		1/18	75
		1/19	180
		1/24	150
		1/27	2,500
		1/29	1,250
		1/31	900
		1/31	350
Bal.	23,795		

Notes Receivable			
1/20	1,450		

Accounts Receivable			
1/16	1,200	1/30	1,200
Bal.	0		

Supplies			
1/4	3,000		
1/27	2,500		
Bal.	5,500		

Shop Equipment			
1/3	8,000		

Automotive Equipment			
1/5	11,500		

Office Equipment			
1/29	1,250		

Notes Payable			
		1/5	8,000

Accounts Payable			
1/14	3,000	1/4	3,000
		Bal.	0

Capital Stock			
		1/2	40,000

Service and Repair Revenue			
		1/8	1,750
		1/16	1,200
		1/20	2,450
		1/25	1,500
		Bal.	6,900

Insurance Expense			
1/2	500		

Rent Expense			
1/2	750		

Advertising Expense			
1/9	300		

Automotive Expense			
1/12	200		
1/19	180		
1/31	350		
Bal.	730		

Telephone Expense			
1/18	75		

Repairs and Maintenance Expense			
1/24	150		

Utilities Expense			
1/31	900		

The final step is to prepare a trial balance to see whether total debits equal total credits for all accounts. List all the accounts with balances; then enter the balance in each account.

(continued)

Svendsen Service Company
Trial Balance
January 31, 2006

	Debits	Credits
Cash	$23,795	
Accounts Receivable	0	
Notes Receivable	1,450	
Supplies	5,500	
Shop Equipment	8,000	
Automotive Equipment	11,500	
Office Equipment	1,250	
Accounts Payable		$ 0
Notes Payable		8,000
Capital Stock		40,000
Service and Repair Revenue		6,900
Insurance Expense	500	
Rent Expense	750	
Advertising Expense	300	
Automotive Expense	730	
Telephone Expense	75	
Repairs and Maintenance Expense	150	
Utilities Expense	900	
Totals	$54,900	$54,900

discussion questions

1. What is the basic objective of the accounting cycle?
2. Explain the first three steps in the accounting cycle.
3. What are the advantages of a computer-based accounting system? Does such a system eliminate the need for human judgment? Explain.
4. In a double-entry system of accounting, why must total debits always equal total credits?
5. Explain the increase/decrease, debit/credit relationship of asset, liability, and owners' equity accounts.
6. How are revenues, expenses, and dividends related to the basic accounting equation?
7. In what ways are dividend and expense accounts similar, and in what ways are they different?
8. How does understanding the mechanics of accounting help a businessperson who has no intention of practicing accounting?
9. Distinguish between a journal and a ledger.
10. Assume that Company A buys $1,500 of merchandise from Company B for cash. The merchandise originally cost Company B $1,000. What entries should the buyer and seller make, and what is the relationship of the accounts for this transaction?

11. Indicate how each of the following transactions affects the accounting equation.
    a. Purchase of supplies on account.
    b. Payment of wages.
    c. Cash sales of goods for more than their cost.
    d. Payment of monthly utility bills.
    e. Purchase of a building with a down payment of cash plus a mortgage.
    f. Cash investment by a stockholder.
    g. Payment of a cash dividend.
    h. Sale of goods on account for more than their cost.
    i. Sale of land at less than its cost.
12. What is a chart of accounts? What is its purpose?
13. If a trial balance appears to be correct (debits equal credits), does that guarantee complete accuracy in the accounting records? Explain.
14. What is the difference between a trial balance and a balance sheet?
15. Have computers eliminated the need to analyze transactions? Explain.

practice exercises

For Practice 3-1 through 3-5, do the following for each transaction:

a. List the accounts impacted by the transaction.
b. For each account, indicate whether the transaction increased or decreased the account.
c. For each account, indicate how much the transaction increased or decreased the account.
d. Compute the impact of the transaction on total assets, total liabilities, and total owners' equity.

Practice 3-1

Impact of a Transaction
The company borrowed $125,000 in cash from Far West Bank.

Practice 3-2

Impact of a Transaction
The company used $45,000 in cash to purchase land on the west side of Hatu Lake.

Practice 3-3

Impact of a Transaction
The company used $30,000 in cash to repay a portion of its bank loan (see Practice 3-1). For simplicity, assume that there is no interest on the loan.

Practice 3-4

Impact of a Transaction
The company received $75,000 in cash as an additional investment by the stockholders (owners) of the company.

Practice 3-5

Impact of a Transaction
The company purchased a building for $100,000. The company paid $10,000 of the purchase price in cash and signed a mortgage contract obligating it to pay the remaining $90,000 over the next 10 years.

Practice 3-6

Computing Ending Account Balances
Refer to Practices 3-1 through 3-5. Construct a spreadsheet similar to the one shown on page 108. Enter each transaction into the spreadsheet and compute the ending balance in each account.

Practice 3-7

Understanding Debits
Below is a list of accounts. For each account, indicate whether a *debit* increases or decreases the account balance.

	Account	DEBIT Increases or Decreases?
0.	Cash	Increases
1.	Accounts Payable	
2.	Capital Stock	
3.	Land	
4.	Inventory	
5.	Loan Payable	
6.	Mortgage Payable	
7.	Building	

Practice 3-8

Understanding Credits

Below is a list of accounts. For each account, indicate whether a *credit* increases or decreases the account balance.

	Account	CREDIT Increases or Decreases?
0.	Cash	Decreases
1.	Accounts Receivable	
2.	Capital Stock	
3.	Equipment	
4.	Inventory	
5.	Accounts Payable	
6.	Building	
7.	Notes Payable	

Practice 3-9

Understanding Debits, Credits, and Retained Earnings

Below is a list of accounts and whether the account is being debited or credited. For each item, indicate whether the account balance will be increased or decreased.

	Account	Debit or Credit	ACCOUNT BALANCE Increased or Decreased?
0.	Salary Expense	Debit	Increased
1.	Sales Revenue	Credit	
2.	Retained Earnings	Debit	
3.	Insurance Expense	Credit	
4.	Dividends	Credit	
5.	Interest Revenue	Debit	
6.	Advertising Expense	Debit	
7.	Rent Revenue	Credit	

Practice 3-10

Understanding Retained Earnings

Below is a list of accounts with corresponding balances. Using these accounts, along with the fact that the beginning balance in Retained Earnings is $1,000, compute the ending balance in Retained Earnings. *Note:* Not all of the listed account balances enter into the calculation of Retained Earnings.

	Account	Account Balance
a.	Insurance Expense	$1,300
b.	Cash	750
c.	Sales Revenue	4,000
d.	Advertising Expense	2,300
e.	Accounts Payable	1,500
f.	Dividends	450
g.	Interest Revenue	200

Practice 3-11

Journal Entries

Refer to Practice 3-1. Make the journal entry necessary to record the transaction.

Practice 3-12	**Journal Entries** Refer to Practice 3-2. Make the journal entry necessary to record the transaction.
Practice 3-13	**Journal Entries** Refer to Practice 3-3. Make the journal entry necessary to record the transaction.
Practice 3-14	**Journal Entries** Refer to Practice 3-4. Make the journal entry necessary to record the transaction.
Practice 3-15	**Journal Entries** Refer to Practice 3-5. Make the journal entry necessary to record the transaction.

Practice 3-16

Posting

Refer to the journal entries made in Practice 3-11 through Practice 3-15. Construct a T-account representing each account impacted by those five transactions. Post all of the journal entries to these T-accounts. Compute the ending balance in each account. Assume that the beginning balance in each T-account is zero.

Practice 3-17

Journal Entries with Revenues, Expenses, and Dividends

Make the journal entries necessary to record the following eight transactions.

a. Purchased inventory on account for $130,000.
b. Sold goods for $100,000 cash. The goods originally cost $65,000.
c. Paid $27,000 cash for employee wages.
d. Paid $12,500 cash for advertising.
e. Sold goods for $25,000 cash and $60,000 on account (a total of $85,000). The goods originally cost $57,000.
f. Collected cash of $47,000 from the $60,000 receivable on account; the remaining $13,000 is expected to be collected later.
g. Paid cash of $55,000 on the $130,000 payable on account; the remaining $75,000 is expected to be paid later.
h. Paid cash dividends of $8,500.

Practice 3-18

Posting with Revenues, Expenses, and Dividends

Refer to the journal entries made in Practice 3-17. Construct a T-account representing each account impacted by those eight transactions. Post all of the journal entries to these T-accounts. Compute the ending balance in each account. Assume that the beginning balance in each T-account is zero.

Practice 3-19

Preparing a Trial Balance

Refer to the T-accounts constructed in Practice 3-16 and Practice 3-18. Using the ending balances in those T-accounts, construct a trial balance. *Note:* The only account that is common to these two sets of T-accounts is the cash account; add the two cash account balances together to get the total balance.

Practice 3-20

Using a Trial Balance to Prepare an Income Statement

Using the trial balance given at the top of the next page, prepare an income statement.

	Debit	Credit
Cash	$ 68,000	
Accounts Receivable	126,000	
Inventory	216,000	
Land	90,000	
Building	200,000	
Accounts Payable		$ 150,000
Loan Payable		270,000
Capital Stock		250,000
Dividends	17,000	
Sales Revenue		370,000
Cost of Goods Sold	244,000	
Utilities Expense	54,000	
Rental Expense	25,000	
Totals	$1,040,000	$1,040,000

Practice 3-21

Using a Trial Balance to Prepare a Balance Sheet
Using the trial balance given in Practice 3-20, prepare a balance sheet. *Note:* The ending retained earnings balance is equal to the beginning balance (which is assumed to be $0) plus the amount of net income less the amount of dividends.

Practice 3-22

Preparing a Statement of Cash Flows
Refer to the transactions described in Practice 3-1 through Practice 3-5 as well as to the eight transactions in Practice 3-17. Using all of these transactions, prepare a statement of cash flows. *Note:* For the building purchase described in Practice 3-5, the portion of the purchase financed with the mortgage ($90,000) is considered to be a noncash transaction; accordingly, the only portion of the transaction that impacts the statement of cash flows is the $10,000 cash down payment.

e x e r c i s e s

Exercise 3-1

Basic Accounting Equation
The fundamental accounting equation can be applied to your personal finances. For each of the following transactions, show how the accounting equation would be kept in balance. Example: Paid for semester's tuition (decrease assets: cash account; decrease owners' equity: expense account increases).

1. Took out a school loan for college.
2. Paid this month's rent.
3. Sold your old computer for cash at what it cost to buy it.
4. Received week's paycheck from part-time job.
5. Received interest on savings account.
6. Paid monthly payment on car loan (part of the payment is principal; the remainder is interest).

Exercise 3-2

Accounting Elements: Increase/Decrease, Debit/Credit Relationships
The text describes the following accounting elements: assets, liabilities, owners' equity, capital stock, retained earnings, revenues, expenses, and dividends. Which of these elements are increased by a debit entry, and which are increased by a credit entry? Give a transaction for each item that would result in a net increase in its balance.

Exercise 3-3

Expanded Accounting Equation

Payless Department Store had the following transactions during the year:

1. Purchased inventory on account.
2. Sold merchandise for cash, assuming a profit on the sale.
3. Borrowed money from a bank.
4. Purchased land, making cash down payment and issuing a note for the balance.
5. Issued stock for cash.
6. Paid salaries for the year.
7. Paid a vendor for inventory purchased on account.
8. Sold a building for cash and notes receivable at no gain or loss.
9. Paid cash dividends to stockholders.
10. Paid utilities.

Using the following column headings, identify the accounts involved and indicate the net effect of each transaction on the accounting equation (+ increase; − decrease; 0 no effect). Transaction 1 has been completed as an example.

Transaction	Assets	=	Liabilities	+	Owners' Equity
1	+		+		0
	(Inventory)		(Accounts Payable)		

Exercise 3-4

Classification of Accounts

For each of the accounts listed, indicate whether it is an asset (A), a liability (L), or an owners' equity (OE) account. If it is an account that affects owners' equity, indicate whether it is a revenue (R) or expense (E) account.

1. Cash
2. Sales
3. Accounts Receivable
4. Cost of Goods Sold
5. Insurance Expense
6. Capital Stock
7. Mortgage Payable
8. Salaries and Wages Expense
9. Retained Earnings
10. Salaries Payable
11. Accounts Payable
12. Interest Revenue
13. Inventory
14. Interest Receivable
15. Notes Payable
16. Equipment
17. Office Supplies
18. Utilities Expense
19. Interest Payable
20. Rent Expense

Exercise 3-5

Normal Account Balances

For each account listed in Exercise 3-4, indicate whether it would normally have a debit (DR) balance or a credit (CR) balance.

Exercise 3-6

Journalizing Transactions

Record each of the following transactions in Gagon's general journal. (Omit explanations.)

1. Issued capital stock for $75,000 cash.
2. Borrowed $35,000 from a bank. Signed a note to secure the debt.
3. Paid salaries and rent of $45,500 and $3,600, respectively.
4. Purchased inventory from a supplier on credit for $4,500.
5. Paid the supplier for the inventory purchased in (4) above.
6. Sold inventory that cost $850 for $1,350 on credit.
7. Collected $1,350 from customers on transaction (6) above.

Exercise 3-7

Journalizing Transactions

Silva Company had the following transactions:

1. Purchased a new building, paying $20,000 cash and issuing a note for $50,000.
2. Purchased $15,000 of inventory on account.
3. Sold inventory costing $5,000 for $6,000 on account.

(continued)

4. Paid for inventory purchased on account (item 2).
5. Issued capital stock for $25,000.
6. Collected $4,500 of accounts receivable.
7. Paid utility bills totaling $360.
8. Sold old building for $27,000, receiving $10,000 cash and a $17,000 note (no gain or loss on the sale).
9. Paid $2,000 cash dividends to stockholders.

Record the above transactions in general journal format. (Omit explanations.)

Exercise 3-8

Spreadsheet

Journal Entries

During July 2006, Woodbury, Inc., completed the following transactions. Prepare the journal entry for each transaction.

July 2   Received $400,000 for 8,000 shares of capital stock.
      4   Purchased $80,000 of equipment, with 75% down and 25% on a note payable.
      5   Paid utilities of $3,500 in cash.
      9   Sold equipment for $12,500 cash (no gain or loss).
    13   Purchased $300,000 of inventory, paying 40% down and 60% on credit.
    14   Paid $7,500 cash insurance premium for July.
    18   Sold inventory costing $45,000 for $62,000 to customers on account to be paid at a later date.
    20   Collected $4,000 from accounts receivable.
    24   Sold inventory costing $36,000 for $55,000 to customers for cash.
    27   Paid property taxes of $1,400.
    30   Paid $180,000 of accounts payable for inventory purchased on July 13.

Exercise 3-9

Posting Journal Entries

Post the journal entries prepared in Exercise 3-8 to T-accounts, and determine the final balance for each account. (Assume all beginning account balances are zero.)

Exercise 3-10

Spreadsheet

Challenging Journal Entries

The accountant for Han Company is considering how to journalize the following transactions:

a. The employees of Han Company earned $105,000. The employees received $90,000 in cash and were promised that they will receive the remaining $15,000 as a pension payment on the date that they retire.
b. On August 1, 2006, Han Company paid $1,800 cash for one year of rent on a building it is using. This one year of rent is scheduled to be in effect for the 12 months starting on August 1, 2006.

1. What journal entry should be made on the books of Han Company to record the employee compensation information in (a)?
2. Describe any assumptions necessary in making the employee compensation journal entry in (1).
3. Make the necessary journal entry on Han Company's books on August 1 to record the payment for the building rent described in (b).
4. Consider the journal entry made in (3). Is any adjustment to Han's books necessary as of December 31, 2006, as a consequence of the rent journal entry made on August 1?

Exercise 3-11

Journal Entries

The following transactions are for the Burdette Construction Company:

a. The firm bought equipment for $49,000 on credit.
b. The firm purchased land for $500,000, $190,000 of which was paid in cash and a note payable signed for the balance.

c. The firm paid $33,000 it owed to its suppliers.
d. The firm arranged for a $125,000 line of credit (the right to borrow funds as needed) from the bank. No funds have yet been borrowed.
e. The firm sold some of its products for $29,000—$14,000 for cash, the remainder on account.
f. Cost of sales in (e) are $17,000.
g. The firm borrowed $78,000 on its line of credit.
h. The firm issued a $7,500 cash dividend to its stockholders.
i. An investor invested an additional $50,000 in the company in exchange for additional capital stock.
j. One of the primary investors borrowed $75,000 from a bank. The loan is a personal loan.
k. The firm repaid $13,000 of its line of credit.
l. The firm received a $500 deposit from a customer for a product to be sold and delivered to that customer next month.

Analyze and record the transactions as journal entries. (Omit explanations.)

Exercise 3-12

Analysis of Journal Entries

The following journal entries are from the books of Kara Elizabeth Company:

a.	Buildings	90,000	
	Cash		35,000
	Mortgage Payable		55,000
b.	Cash	25,000	
	Capital Stock		25,000
c.	Cash	40,000	
	Loan Payable		40,000
d.	Salary Expense	12,000	
	Cash		12,000
e.	Inventory	12,500	
	Accounts Payable		12,500
f.	Accounts Receivable	84,000	
	Sales		84,000
	Cost of Goods Sold	51,000	
	Inventory		51,000
g.	Cash	62,000	
	Accounts Receivable		62,000
h.	Accounts Payable	38,000	
	Cash		38,000

For each of the journal entries, prepare an explanation of the business event that is being represented.

Exercise 3-13

Journalizing and Posting Transactions

Given the following T-accounts, describe the transaction that took place on each specified date during July:

Cash				Accounts Receivable				Inventory			
7/5	9,500	7/1	3,420	7/14	18,000	7/5	9,500	7/10	20,000	7/14	15,000
7/28	8,000	7/23	2,000			7/28	8,000	Bal.	5,000		
		7/25	5,000	Bal.	500						
		7/30	5,500								
Bal.	1,580										

(continued)

Equipment			Land			Accounts Payable		
7/30	1,500		7/30	4,000		7/25	5,000	7/10 20,000
								Bal. 15,000

Sales Revenue			Cost of Goods Sold			Rent Expense		
		7/14 18,000	7/14	15,000		7/23	2,000	

Advertising Expense		
7/1	3,420	

Exercise 3-14

Trial Balance

The account balances from the ledger of Sakamoto, Inc., as of July 31, 2006, are listed here in alphabetical order. The balance for Retained Earnings has been omitted. Prepare a trial balance, and insert the missing amount for Retained Earnings.

Accounts Payable	$ 9,600		Land	$27,000
Accounts Receivable	4,200		Miscellaneous Expenses	1,950
Buildings	41,000		Mortgage Payable (due 2009)	28,000
Capital Stock	12,000		Rent Expense	3,500
Cash	23,900		Retained Earnings	?
Equipment	19,500		Salary Expense	14,000
Fees Earned	43,000		Supplies	350
Insurance Expense	4,350		Utilities Expense	850

Exercise 3-15

Trial Balance

Assume you work in the accounting department at Marshall, Inc. Your boss has asked you to prepare a trial balance as of November 30, 2006, using the following account balances from the company's ledger. Prepare the trial balance and insert the missing amount for Cost of Goods Sold.

Accounts Payable	$ 55,000		Notes Payable	$250,000
Accounts Receivable	25,000		Notes Receivable	20,000
Advertising Expense	5,000		Other Expenses	1,000
Buildings	150,000		Property Tax Expense	1,500
Capital Stock	173,000		Rent Expense	7,500
Cash	35,000		Retained Earnings	40,000
Cost of Goods Sold	?		Salaries Expense	155,000
Equipment	55,000		Salaries Payable	2,000
Inventory	200,000		Sales Revenue	375,000
Land	125,000		Short-Term Investments	15,000
Mortgage Payable	95,000		Utilities Expense	7,000

Exercise 3-16

Relationships of the Expanded Accounting Equation

Skibbe, Inc., had the following information reported. From these data, determine the amount of:

1. Capital stock at December 31, 2005.
2. Retained earnings at December 31, 2006.
3. Revenues for the year 2006.

	December 31, 2005	December 31, 2006
Total assets	$125,000	$150,000
Total liabilities	30,000	35,000
Capital stock	?	25,000
Retained earnings	75,000	?
Revenues for 2006		?
Expenses for 2006		102,500
Dividends paid during 2006		2,500

Exercise 3-17

Journal Entry to Correct an Error

Legolas Company paid $5,000 cash for executive salaries. When the journal entry to record this $5,000 payment was made, the payment was mistakenly added to the cost of land purchased by Legolas. The $5,000 should have been recorded as salary expense. Make the journal entry necessary to correct this error.

 roblems

Problem 3-1

P.A.S.S.
Power Accounting
System Software

Journal Entries and Trial Balance

As of January 1, 2006, Gammon Corporation had the following balances in its general ledger:

	Debits	Credits
Cash	$ 63,000	
Accounts Receivable	47,000	
Inventory	184,000	
Office Building	416,000	
Accounts Payable		$ 33,000
Mortgage Payable		360,000
Notes Payable		137,000
Capital Stock		115,000
Retained Earnings		65,000
Totals	$710,000	$710,000

Gammon had the following transactions during 2006. All expenses were paid in cash, unless otherwise stated.

a. Collected $42,000 of receivables.
b. Accounts Payable as of January 1, 2006, were paid off.
c. Purchased inventory for $70,000 cash.
d. Paid utilities of $12,600.
e. Sold $370,000 of merchandise, 90% for cash and 10% for credit. The Cost of Goods Sold was $197,000.
f. Paid $50,000 mortgage payment, of which $30,000 represents interest expense.
g. Paid salaries expense of $120,000.
h. Paid installment of $10,000 on note.

Required:
1. Prepare journal entries to record each listed transaction. (Omit explanations.)

(continued)

2. Set up T-accounts with the proper account balances at January 1, 2006, post the journal entries to the T-accounts, and prepare a trial balance for Gammon Corporation at December 31, 2006.
3. **Interpretive Question:** If the debit and credit columns of the trial balance are in balance, does this mean that no errors have been made in journalizing the transactions? Explain.

Problem 3-2

P.A.S.S.
Power Accounting
System Software

Journalizing and Posting

Assume you are interviewing for a part-time accounting job at Spilker & Associates, Inc., and the interviewer gives you the following list of company transactions in September 2006.

Sept. 1 Received $150,000 for capital stock issued.
2 Paid $20,000 cash to employees for wages earned in September 2006.
4 Purchased $75,000 of running shoes and clothing on account for resale.
5 Paid utilities of $1,800 for September 2006.
9 Paid $1,500 cash for September's insurance premium.
11 Sold inventory of running shoes and clothing costing $35,000 for $70,000, with $20,000 received in cash and the remaining balance on credit.
15 Purchased $2,500 of supplies on account.
21 Received $25,000 from customers as payments on their accounts.
25 Paid $75,000 of accounts payable.

Using this list, you have been asked to do the following in the interview:

Required:
1. Journalize each of the transactions for September. (Omit explanations.)
2. Set up T-accounts, and post each of the journal entries made in (1).
3. **Interpretive Question:** If the business owners wanted to know at any given time how much cash the company had, where would you tell the owners to look? Why?

Problem 3-3

Journal Entries from Ledger Analysis

T-accounts for RAM Technology, Inc., are shown below.

	Cash				Accounts Receivable				Inventory		
(a)	100,000	(b)	45,000	(e)	30,000	(i)	15,000	(d)	35,000	(e)	30,000
(c)	50,000	(d)	5,000								
(e)	25,000	(f)	20,000								
(i)	15,000	(g)	53,500								
		(h)	30,000								

	Building			Accounts Payable				Mortgage Payable		
(b)	150,000		(h)	30,000	(d)	30,000			(b)	105,000

	Notes Payable				Capital Stock			Sales Revenue	
(g)	50,000	(c)	50,000			(a)	100,000		(e)	55,000

	Cost of Goods Sold			Interest Expense			Wages Expense	
(e)	30,000		(g)	3,500		(f)	20,000	

Required:
1. Analyze these accounts and detail the appropriate journal entries that must have been made by RAM Technology, Inc. (Omit explanations.)
2. Determine the amount of net income/loss from the account information.

Problem 3-4

P.A.S.S.
*Power Accounting
System Software*

Journalizing and Posting Transactions

Anna Regina, owner of Anna's Beauty Supply, completed the following business transactions during March 2006.

Mar. 1   Purchased $26,500 of inventory on credit.
    4   Collected $2,500 from customers as payments on their accounts.
    5   Purchased equipment for $1,500 cash.
    6   Sold inventory that cost $15,000 to customers on account for $20,000.
   10   Paid rent for March, $525.
   15   Paid utilities for March, $50.
   17   Paid a $150 monthly salary to the part-time helper.
   20   Collected $16,500 from customers as payments on their accounts.
   22   Paid $26,500 cash on account payable. (See March 1 entry.)
   25   Paid property taxes for March of $600.
   28   Sold inventory that cost $10,000 to customers for $15,000 cash.

Required:

1. For each transaction, give the entry to record it in the company's general journal. (Omit explanations.)
2. Set up T-accounts, and post the journal entries to their appropriate accounts.

Problem 3-5

Spreadsheet

P.A.S.S.
*Power Accounting
System Software*

Unifying Concepts: Compound Journal Entries, Posting, Trial Balance

J&W Merchandise Company had the following transactions during 2006.

a. Sam Jeakins began business by investing the following assets, receiving capital stock in exchange:

Cash	$ 20,000
Inventory	37,000
Land	25,500
Building	160,000
Equipment	12,500*
Totals	$255,000

*A note of $5,000 on the equipment was assumed by the company.

b. Sold merchandise that cost $30,000 for $45,000; $15,000 cash was received immediately, and the other $30,000 will be collected in 30 days.
c. Paid off the note of $5,000 plus $300 interest.
d. Purchased merchandise costing $12,000, paying $2,000 cash and issuing a note for $10,000.
e. Exchanged $2,000 cash and $8,000 in capital stock for office equipment costing $10,000.
f. Purchased a truck for $15,000 with $3,000 down and a one-year note for the balance.

Required:

1. Journalize the transactions. (Omit explanations.)
2. Post the journal entries using T-accounts for each account.
3. Prepare a trial balance at December 31, 2006.

Problem 3-6

Unifying Concepts: T-Accounts, Trial Balance, and Income Statement

The following list is a selection of transactions from Trafalga, Inc.'s business activities during 2006, the first year of operations.

a. Received $50,000 cash for capital stock.
b. Paid $5,000 cash for equipment.
c. Purchased inventory costing $18,000 on account.

(continued)

P.A.S.S.
*Power Accounting
System Software*

d. Sold $25,000 of merchandise to customers on account. Cost of goods sold was $15,000.
e. Signed a note with a bank for a $10,000 loan.
f. Collected $9,500 cash from customers who had purchased merchandise on account.
g. Purchased land, $10,000, and a building, $60,000, for $15,000 cash and a 30-year mortgage of $55,000.
h. Made a first payment of $2,750 on the mortgage principal plus $2,750 in interest.
i. Paid $12,000 of accounts payable.
j. Purchased $1,500 of supplies on account.
k. Paid $2,500 of accounts payable.
l. Paid $7,500 in wages earned during the year.
m. Received $10,000 cash and $3,000 of notes in settlement of customers' accounts.
n. Received $3,250 in payment of a note receivable of $3,000 plus interest of $250.
o. Paid $600 cash for a utility bill.
p. Sold excess land for its cost of $3,000.
q. Received $1,500 in rent for an unused part of a building.
r. Paid off $10,000 note, plus interest of $1,200.

Required:
1. Set up T-accounts, and appropriately record the debits and credits for each transaction directly in the T-accounts. Leave room for a number of entries in the cash account.
2. Prepare a trial balance.
3. Prepare an income statement for the period. (Ignore income taxes and the EPS computation.)

Problem 3-7

Transaction Analysis and Journal Entries

Browne Motors, Inc., entered into the following transactions during the month of June:

a. Purchased a total of eight new cars and trucks from Jerry's Motors, Inc., for a total of $105,600, one-half of which was paid in cash. The balance is due within 45 days. The total cost of the vehicles to Jerry's Motors was $91,000.
b. Purchased $3,300 of supplies on account from White Supply Company. The cost of the supplies to White Supply Company was $2,400.
c. Paid $720 to Mountain Electric for the monthly utility bill.
d. Sold a truck to Dave's Delivery, Inc. A $2,800 down payment was received with the balance of $14,500 due within 30 days. The cost of the delivery truck to Browne Motors was $13,200.
e. Paid $4,950 to Steve's Automotive for repair work on cars for the current month.
f. Sold one of the new cars purchased from Jerry's Motors to the town mayor, Rachel Mecham. The sales price was $16,250, and was paid by Mecham upon delivery of the car. The cost of the particular car sold to Mecham was $11,800.
g. Borrowed $25,000 from a local bank to be repaid in one year with 12% interest.

Required:
1. For each of the transactions, make the proper journal entry on the books of Browne Motors. (Omit explanations.)
2. For each of the transactions, make the proper journal entry on the books of the other party to the transaction, for example, (a) Jerry's Motors, Inc., (b) White Supply Company. (Omit explanations.)
3. **Interpretive Question:** Why do some of the journal entries for Browne Motors and other companies involved appear to be "mirror images" of each other?

Problem 3-8

Correcting a Trial Balance

The following trial balance was prepared by a new employee.

Trial Balance
Alden Company, Inc.
For the Year Ended November 30, 2006

	Credits	Debits
Cash	$ 18,250	
Mortgage Payable		$ 78,900
Advertising Expense	9,600	
Capital Stock		102,000
Equipment	36,900	
Notes Payable		187,350
Inventory	148,000	
Wages Expense	87,150	
Notes Receivable	5,000	
Accounts Payable		19,750
Accounts Receivable		5,300
Rent Expense		8,750
Wages Payable	9,000	
Furniture		15,000
Other Expenses	2,950	
Sales Revenue		235,600
Buildings	104,700	
Cost of Goods Sold	113,050	
Property Tax Expense		1,300
Land		87,850
Retained Earnings		14,400
Utilities Expense	3,200	
Totals	$537,800	$756,200

Required:

Prepare the corrected company trial balance. (Assume all accounts have "normal" balances and the recorded amounts are correct.)

P.A.S.S.
Power Accounting
System Software

Problem 3-9

Unifying Concepts: Journal Entries, T-Accounts, Trial Balance

Jethro Company, a retailer, had the following account balances as of April 30, 2006:

Cash	$ 5,050	
Accounts Receivable	2,450	
Inventory	8,000	
Land	13,000	
Building	12,000	
Furniture	2,000	
Notes Payable		$12,500
Accounts Payable		6,000
Capital Stock		15,000
Retained Earnings		9,000
Totals	$42,500	$42,500

During May, the company completed the following transactions.

May 3   Paid one-half of 4/30/06 accounts payable.
   4   Purchased inventory on account, $5,000.

(continued)

May 6   Collected all of 4/30/06 accounts receivable.

7   Sold inventory costing $3,850 for $3,000 cash and $2,000 on account.

8   Sold one-half of the land for $6,500, receiving $4,000 cash plus a note for $2,500.

15   Paid installment of $2,500 on notes payable (entire amount reduces the liability account).

21   Issued additional capital stock for $1,000 cash.

23   Sold inventory costing $2,000 for $3,750 cash.

25   Paid salaries of $1,000.

26   Paid rent of $250.

29   Purchased desk for $250 cash.

Required:

1. Prepare the journal entry for each transaction.
2. Set up T-accounts with the proper account balances at April 30, 2006, and post the entries to the T-accounts.
3. Prepare a trial balance as of May 31, 2006.

Problem 3-10

Spreadsheet

P.A.S.S.
Power Accounting
System Software

Unifying Concepts: First Steps in the Accounting Cycle

The following balances were taken from the general ledger of Benson Company on January 1, 2006:

	Debits	Credits
Cash	$13,500	
Short-Term Investments	10,000	
Accounts Receivable	12,500	
Inventory	15,000	
Land	25,000	
Buildings	75,000	
Equipment	20,000	
Notes Payable		$17,500
Accounts Payable		12,500
Salaries and Wages Payable		2,500
Mortgage Payable		37,500
Capital Stock (7,000 shares outstanding)		70,000
Retained Earnings		31,000

During 2006, the company completed the following transactions:

a. Purchased inventory for $110,000 on credit.
b. Issued an additional $25,000 of capital stock (2,500 shares) for cash.
c. Paid property taxes of $4,500 for the year 2006.
d. Paid advertising and other selling expenses of $8,000.
e. Paid utilities expense of $6,500 for 2006.
f. Paid the salaries and wages owed for 2005. Paid additional salaries and wages of $18,000 during 2006.
g. Sold merchandise costing $105,000 for $175,000. Of total sales, $45,000 were cash sales and $130,000 were credit sales.
h. Paid off notes of $17,500 plus interest of $1,600.
i. On November 1, 2006, received a loan of $10,000 from the bank.
j. On December 30, 2006, made annual mortgage payment of $2,500 and paid interest of $3,700.
k. Collected receivables for the year of $140,000.

l. Paid off accounts payable of $112,500.

m. Received dividends and interest of $1,400 on short-term investments during 2006. (Record as Miscellaneous Revenue.)

n. Purchased additional short-term investments of $15,000 during 2006. (*Note:* Short-term investments are current assets.)

o. Paid 2006 corporate income taxes of $11,600.

p. Paid cash dividends of $7,600.

Required:

1. Journalize the 2006 transactions. (Omit explanations.)

2. Set up T-accounts with the proper account balances at January 1, 2006, and post the journal entries to the T-accounts.

3. Determine the account balances, and prepare a trial balance at December 31, 2006.

4. Prepare an income statement and a balance sheet. (Remember that the dividends account and all revenue and expense accounts are temporary retained earnings accounts.)

5. **Interpretive Question:** Why are revenue and expense accounts used at all?

d iscussion cases

Case 3-1

How Does Microsoft (and Other Companies) Do It?

MICROSOFT's revenues exceeded $28 billion in 2002. These revenues were generated by millions of transactions all over the world—in the United States, Canada, Europe, South America, and Asia. What is the process used by Microsoft to transform this tremendous amount of transaction data into summarized information reported to the general public in the form of financial statements?

Case 3-2

Advantages and Disadvantages of a Computerized Accounting System

Your soon-to-be father-in-law owns a small retail store. He has manually kept his business accounting records for over 20 years, but he is currently thinking about switching to a computerized accounting system. What advice would you give him about the advantages and the disadvantages of using a computerized accounting system?

Case 3-3

When Is a Debit a Debit?

Your new roommate, Susan, is confused. She has just received a notice from her bank indicating that her account has been debited for the cost of new checks. This has reduced her cash account. Susan just learned in her introductory accounting class that debiting Cash increases the account. She wonders why the bank has reduced her account by debiting it. How can you help Susan understand this situation?

Case 3-4

Understanding the Mechanics of Accounting

As the CFO (chief financial officer) of Rollins Engineering Company, you are looking for someone to fill the position of office manager. Part of the job description is to maintain the company's accounting records. This means that the office manager must be able to journalize transactions, post them to the ledger accounts, and prepare monthly trial balances. You have just interviewed the first applicant, Jay McMahon, who claims that he has studied accounting. As an initial check on his understanding of the basic mechanics of accounting, you give Jay a list of accounts randomly ordered and with assumed balances and ask him to prepare a trial balance. Jay prepares the following.

(continued)

Trial Balance

	Debits	Credits
Accounts Payable		$ 4,500
Salaries Expense		175,000
Consulting Revenues	$269,000	
Cash	82,100	
Utilities Expense	12,000	
Accounts Receivable		44,000
Supplies	11,000	
Rent Expense	30,000	
Capital Stock		77,000
Supplies Expense	33,000	
Office Equipment	15,000	
Retained Earnings		24,000
Other Expenses	6,400	
Salaries Payable	34,000	
Totals	$492,500	$324,500

Based solely on your assessment of Jay McMahon's understanding of accounting, would you hire him as office manager? Explain. Prepare a corrected trial balance that you can use as a basis for your discussion with Jay and future applicants. Explain how the basic accounting equation and the system of double-entry accounting provide a check on the accounting records.

Case 3-5

Exercising Accounting Judgment

You have recently started business as an accounting consultant. Companies come to you when they face difficult decisions about how to make certain journal entries. You are currently working on the following two problems, which are independent of one another.

a. Baggins Company sells hamburgers for $1.00 each. The cost of the materials used to make each hamburger is 30 cents. Baggins has a compensation plan in which its employees are paid in the form of cash and hamburgers. During 2006, Baggins paid cash salaries of $500,000 and also issued certificates to employees entitling them to 200,000 free hamburgers. The certificates are not redeemable until 2007. What journal entry or entries should Baggins make in 2006 to record this employee compensation information?

b. Radagast Company purchased a building for $100,000 cash on January 1, 2006. Because of poor business decisions, as of December 31, 2006, the building is worthless. Make all journal entries necessary in 2006 in connection with this building.

 udgment calls

Judgment 3-1

You Decide: Is understanding the accounting cycle essential to being a good accountant, or is it a waste of time?

John, a family friend who didn't go to college, was talking to you about his job, as bookkeeper, at a local bookstore. "It is no longer necessary to learn the accounting cycle to be a good accountant," he said. "Computers do most of the work anyway. Unless you work in a small family-owned business, it doesn't make any sense to learn the correct method for posting debits and credits. If you just understand the financial statements, you will be ok!" Do you agree or disagree? Explain.

Judgment 3-2

You Decide: If you major in accounting, will you enjoy a rewarding career, or will the field be extinct in 20 years?

I thought an accounting degree would give me the solid, fundamental understanding of business I was looking for but some of my friends seem to think that accountants won't have jobs a few years from now. They argue that as computers become smarter and more powerful, they will develop enough capacities to make good business decisions. They say I am making a mistake by majoring in a field that will not be around in 20 years. What do you think?

Competency Enhancement Opportunities

▶ **Analyzing Real Company Information**
▶ **International Case**
▶ **Ethics Case**
▶ **Writing Assignment**

▶ **The Debate**
▶ **Cumulative Spreadsheet Project**
▶ **Internet Search**

The following additional assignments provide opportunities for students to develop critical thinking, ethical perspectives, oral and written communication skills, experience with electronic research, and teamwork through group and business activities.

▶ *Analyzing Real Company Information*

Analyzing 3-1 (Microsoft)

The 2002 Form 10-K for MICROSOFT is included in Appendix A. Locate that Form 10-K and consider the following questions:

1. Find Microsoft's 2002 income statement. Assume that research and development expenditures were paid in cash. What journal entry did Microsoft make in 2002 to record research and development?
2. Find Microsoft's 2002 cash flow statement. What journal entry did Microsoft make in 2002 to record the issuance of common stock?
3. Again, looking at the cash flow statement—what journal entry did Microsoft make in 2002 to record the purchase of property and equipment?
4. Using information from the cash flow statement, re-create the journal entry Microsoft made in 2002 to record the purchase of investments. Using the beginning and ending balances from the balance sheet, comment on the change in the balance of the equity and other investments account between the beginning of 2002 and the end of 2002.

Analyzing 3-2 (McDonald's)

A brief history of the origin of the MCDONALD'S CORPORATION is given at the start of this chapter. The following questions are adapted from information appearing in McDonald's 2002 annual report.

1. In 2002, total sales at all McDonald's stores worldwide were $41.5 billion. There were 31,108 McDonald's stores operating in 2002. *Estimate* how many customers per day visit an average McDonald's store.

(continued)

2. For the stores owned by the McDonald's Corporation (as opposed to those owned by franchisees), total sales in 2002 were $11.5 billion, and total cost of food and packaging was $3.917 billion. What journal entries would McDonald's make to record a $10 sale and to record the cost of food and packaging associated with the $10 sale?
3. McDonald's reported payment of cash dividends of $297.4 million in 2002. What journal entry was required?
4. McDonald's reported that the total income tax it owed for 2002 was $670.0 million. However, only $572.2 million in cash was paid for taxes during the year. What compound journal entry did McDonald's make to record its income tax expense for the year?

▶ *International Case*

International

Shanghai Petrochemical Company Limited

In July 1993, SHANGHAI PETROCHEMICAL COMPANY LIMITED became the first company organized under the laws of the People's Republic of China to publicly issue its shares on the worldwide market. Shanghai Petrochemical's shares now trade on the stock exchanges in Shanghai, Hong Kong, and New York. The following questions are adapted from information appearing in Shanghai Petrochemical's 1995 annual report.

1. In 1995, Shanghai Petrochemical reported sales of 11.835 billion renminbi (US$ 1 = 8.33 RMB) and cost of sales of RMB 9.016 billion. Make the necessary journal entries, using renminbi as the currency.
2. In 1995, Shanghai Petrochemical declared cash dividends of RMB 851.5 million. However, cash paid for dividends during the year was only RMB 818.8 million. Make the necessary compound journal entry to record the declaration and payment of cash dividends for the year.
3. In China, a 17% value added tax (VAT) is added to the invoiced value of all sales. This VAT is collected by the seller from the buyer and then held to be forwarded to the government. What journal entry would Shanghai Petrochemical make to record the sale, on account, of crude oil with an invoice sales value of $100 and a cost of $70?

▶ *Ethics Case*

Should You Go the Extra Mile?

You work in a small convenience store. The store is very low-tech; you ring up the sales on an old-style cash register that merely records the amount of the sale. The store owner uses this cash register tape at the end of each day to verify that the correct amount of cash is in the cash register drawer. On a day-to-day basis, no other financial information is collected about store operations.

Since you started studying accounting, you have become a bit uneasy about your job because you see many ways that store operations could be improved through the gathering and use of financial information. Even though you are not an expert, you are quite certain that you could help the store owner set up an improved information system. However, you also know that this will take extra effort on your part, with no real possibility of receiving an increase in pay.

Should you say anything to the store owner, or should you just keep quiet and save yourself the trouble?

▷ *Writing Assignment*

Accounting Is Everywhere!
Financial accounting information is frequently used in newspaper and magazine articles to provide background data on companies. Prepare a one-page report on the use of financial accounting data by the press. Proceed as follows:

1. Scan the articles in a recent copy of one of the popular business periodicals (such as *The Wall Street Journal, Forbes, Fortune,* or *Business Week*) for examples of the use of financial accounting data.
2. Identify and describe three interesting examples:

   - Detail the nature of the accounting data used.
   - Outline the point that the writer is trying to make by using the particular accounting data.

▷ *The Debate*

Are Computers the Hero or the Villain?
As explained in the body of the chapter, computers have revolutionized the accounting process. In addition to taking over the mundane jobs of posting and report formatting, computers have also changed the way we think about information. When accounting was done by hand, it was not possible to match individual sales with specific products, specific customers, the exact time of day of the sale, the income level of the customer, the customer's favorite TV shows and magazines, and the like. In short, computers have made it possible to use the raw financial data to track much more than just revenues and expenses. How far should the use of computers go?

Divide your group into two teams.

- One team represents the computer technology group, "To Infinity, and Beyond!" Prepare a two-minute oral presentation supporting the notion that firms have a right to use their computer database systems to gather as much information about customers as possible, and even to sell that information to other firms. Now is the Information Age, and computers have made it possible to easily buy and sell information just like any other commodity.
- The other team represents "Right to Privacy." Prepare a two-minute oral presentation arguing that firms have no right to maintain databases containing individual customer information. A company's information system should relate to that company's products and processes, and customers have the right to interact with the firm anonymously.

▷ *Cumulative Spreadsheet Project*
This spreadsheet assignment is a continuation of the spreadsheet assignment given in Chapter 2. If you completed that spreadsheet, you have a head start on this one.

Determine the impact of each of the following transactions on total assets, total liabilities, and total owners' equity. Treat each transaction independently, meaning that before determining the impact of each new transaction, you should reset the financial statement values to their original amounts. Each of the hypothetical transactions is assumed to occur on the last day of the year.

a. Collected $20 cash from customer receivables.
b. Purchased $30 in inventory on account.

(continued)

c. Purchased $100 in property, plant, and equipment. The entire amount of the purchase was financed with a mortgage. Principal repayment for the mortgage is due in 10 years.
d. Purchased $100 in property, plant, and equipment. The entire amount of the purchase was financed with new stockholder investment.
e. Borrowed $20 with a short-term loan payable. The $20 was paid out as a dividend to stockholders.
f. Received $20 as an investment from stockholders. The $20 was paid out as a dividend to stockholders.

▶ *Internet Search*

McDonald's

Access MCDONALD'S Web site at **http://www.mcdonalds.com**. Sometimes Web addresses change, so if this McDonald's address doesn't work, access the Web site for this textbook (**http://albrecht.swlearning.com**) for an updated link to McDonald's.

Once you've gained access to McDonald's Web site, answer the following questions:

1. Which has more calories—two hamburgers or one Big Mac?
2. How much money do you need to purchase a McDonald's franchise in the United States? What else is required to purchase a franchise?
3. Sometimes it isn't easy to find a company's financial statements in its Web site. Describe what you had to do to find a copy of McDonald's most recent annual report.
4. What information is contained in McDonald's most recent financial press release?

chapter

4

Completing the Accounting Cycle

After studying this chapter, you should be able to:

Learning Objectives

1 Describe how accrual accounting allows for timely reporting and a better measure of a company's economic performance.

2 Explain the need for adjusting entries and make adjusting entries for unrecorded receivables, unrecorded liabilities, prepaid expenses, and unearned revenues.

3 Explain the preparation of the financial statements, the explanatory notes, and the audit report.

4 Complete the closing process in the accounting cycle.

5 Understand how all the steps in the accounting cycle fit together.

eXpanded ▲ ▲ *Material*

6 Make adjusting entries for prepaid expenses and unearned revenues when the original cash amounts are recorded as expenses and revenues.

GENERAL MOTORS, the brainchild of William Durant, was formed through the acquisition of a number of preexisting car makers. BUICK and OLDSMOBILE were acquired in 1908; CADILLAC and PONTIAC (originally called OAKLAND) were added in 1909. With so many acquisitions in those early years, General Motors' financing was quickly depleted, and Durant lost control of his company. With Durant fighting to regain the reins of General Motors, the company was in such turmoil that, at one point, CHEVROLET MOTOR COMPANY (another Durant creation) owned a majority of GM stock. After many deals, Durant found himself back in charge in 1916, and Chevrolet became a subsidiary of GM in 1918.

Following the end of World War I, an economic slowdown stretched Durant's financial resources past the breaking point, and in 1920 he lost control of General Motors for good. Pierre S. du Pont, a GM investor since 1914, became the company's new president. Du Pont brought to General Motors the financial resources and business connections associated with his own family's chemical empire. He was also instrumental in instituting the du Pont style of management and control. Implemented at General Motors by Alfred P. Sloan (who later went on to head GM until 1956), this system emphasized decentralized decision making; evaluations of managers of autonomous divisions were based on reaching specific financial goals. This "DuPont" system of evaluation is discussed later in Chapter 5.

Under Sloan's leadership, General Motors became the dominant car maker in the world, a position it still holds. In addition to implementing the DuPont system of evaluation and control, Sloan also formalized the caste system among GM's different automobile lines. For example, Chevrolets were targeted at the lower-income end of the market, while Cadillacs were aimed at the higher end. Sloan was also instrumental in creating the annual ritual of the "car model year" to encourage owners of older models to trade them in on new cars with the latest innovations.

Although General Motors' global market share has declined with stiff competition from Japanese, European (including DAIMLERCHRYSLER), and domestic (FORD) competitors, General Motors still sells more cars and trucks than any other company in the world. In 2002, GM sold 8.5 million vehicles, nearly 15% of the worldwide total. GM also remains one of the largest private employers in the United States, ranking fifth behind WAL-MART in the 2003 Fortune 500 listing (see Exhibit 1).

In addition to being the most prolific car maker in the world, General Motors has the unenviable distinction of having posted, at the time, the world record largest annual net loss. In 1992, GM reported a loss for the year of $23.5 billion. This record loss followed losses of $2.0 billion in 1990 and $4.5 billion in 1991.

How was General Motors able to stay in business while reporting these huge losses? During the same period it was reporting large losses on its income statement, GM was reporting healthy cash from operations on its cash flow statement. In fact, in 1992 (the year of the record loss), GM's positive cash from operations was

Exhibit 1: U.S. Companies with the Most Employees, 2003

Rank	Company	500 Revenues Rank	2002 Number of Employees
1	Wal-Mart Stores	1	1,300,000
2	McDonald's	124	413,000
3	United Parcel Service	3	360,000
4	Ford Motor	4	350,321
5	General Motors	2	350,000
6	International Business Machines	8	315,889
7	General Electric	5	315,000
8	Target	25	306,000
9	Home Depot	13	300,000
10	Kroger	18	289,000

Source: 2003 Fortune 500 listing available at http://www.fortune.com.

FYI:

In 2002, AOL Time Warner established a new standard for losses by reporting a loss of $98.7 billion. This large loss related primarily to the write-off of goodwill associated with the acquisition of other companies.

$9.8 billion. This strong cash flow enabled GM to continue normal operations, pay its suppliers, repay its loans, and maintain investor confidence even while reporting significant losses.

Where did these losses come from if they weren't the result of a shortfall in cash from operations? The losses came from business expenses that General Motors had incurred as part of its operations but which had not yet been paid in cash. For example, the record $23.5 billion loss was primarily due to recording the large business expense from postretirement medical benefits that have been promised to GM employees. General Motors won't actually have to make the cash payments related to these benefits until the employees retire in the future. The benefits have already been earned, however, so they should be reported as a cost of business now. The art of accounting involves recording all business expenses—both those that are paid in cash and those that involve promises of payment in the future. As GM's $23.5 billion loss illustrates, those promises of future payment can really add up.

s the General Motors scenario illustrates, adjustments (to the original transaction data recorded in the accounts) usually are needed so that the financial statements will accurately reflect a company's economic performance during the period and its economic condition as of the end of the period. This is a part of completing the accounting cycle. In addition, certain accounts must be "closed" at the end of an accounting period to prepare the records for a new accounting cycle. The nature of year-end adjustments and the remaining steps in the accounting cycle are discussed in this chapter.

Accrual Accounting

1 Describe how accrual accounting allows for timely reporting and a better measure of a company's economic performance.

In 2005, two brothers sign a contract for a consulting project. The total contract price is $20,000. The brothers do most of the consulting work in 2005 and finish the job in 2006. They receive a $2,000 cash payment from the contract in 2005 and receive the remaining $18,000 cash in 2006. On December 31, 2005, the brothers prepare a 2005 income statement to use in applying for a bank loan. What amount of revenue should the brothers report for 2005?

This example illustrates why accounting is much more than merely tabulating cash receipts and cash payments. A proper measure of the brothers' economic performance in 2005 requires estimating the value of the work completed in 2005; to report 2005 revenue as only the $2,000 cash received grossly understates the actual economic output produced during the year. In addition, the need for the year-end income statement means that the brothers can't wait until after the final contract payment is received before preparing a summary of their activities; the bank wants the income statement now.

Accrual accounting is the process of adjusting original transaction data into refined measures of a firm's past economic performance and current economic condition. As the following sections explain, this accrual process is necessary because a business requires periodic, timely financial reports and accrual information better measures a firm's performance than do cash flow data.

The difficulty in using accrual accounting to generate a performance measure is represented in Exhibit 2. Each horizontal bar in the exhibit represents a business deal such as the production and sale of a car, the delivery of legal services for a specific lawsuit, or the development, delivery, and support of a piece of software. Some deals last less than a day from start to finish, such as when a barber provides a haircut in exchange for cash. The obligations and responsibilities associated with other deals can stretch on for years. For example, when you buy a GENERAL MOTORS car, the deal is not done from your standpoint until four or five years later after you have received all of the GM warranty services promised to you. And, from GM's standpoint, the deal is not done until 40 or 50 years later after GM has paid the assembly-line workers all of the pension benefits they earned through the labor hours spent assembling your car. Even though the economic loose ends of some business deals extend for years, financial statement users still require periodic reports about a company's operating performance. As you can see in Exhibit 2, the beginning and the end of a year are arbitrary breaks in the life of an ongoing business. The job of accountants is to consider all business deals that were at least partially completed during a year and to measure the profit associated with those deals. This profit is then reported as net income for the year. As you can see, accrual accounting is much more than mere "bean counting."

Periodic Reporting

All businesses, large or small, periodically issue their financial statements so that users can make sound economic decisions. Current owners, prospective investors, bankers, and others need up-to-date reports in order to compare and judge a company's financial position and operating results on a continuing, timely basis. They need to know the financial position of a company (from the balance sheet), the relative success or failure of current operations (from the income statement), and the nature and extent of cash flows (from the statement of cash flows).

The financial picture of a company—its success or failure in meeting its economic objectives—cannot really be complete until the "life" of a business is over. However, managers, owners, and creditors cannot wait 10, 20, or 100 years to receive an exact accounting of a business. In order to provide timely accounting information, the **time-period concept** divides the life of an enterprise into distinct and relatively short (generally 12 months or less) accounting periods. The 12-month accounting period is referred to as the **fiscal year**. When an entity closes its books on December 31, its reports are based on a **calendar year**.

Most large corporations, and even many small companies, issue a report to stockholders as of a fiscal year-end. Also, most corporations prepare reports on a quarterly basis as well. Companies whose shares are publicly traded are required by the SEC to file quarterly financial reports. As noted in Chapters 1 and 2, this annual report includes the primary financial statements (balance sheet, income statement, and statement of cash flows) and other financial data, such as a management discussion and analysis of operations. Other financial reports are prepared more frequently, perhaps quarterly or monthly. Indeed, some reports, such as sales reports for use by management, may be prepared on a daily basis.

time-period concept The idea that the life of a business is divided into distinct and relatively short time periods so that accounting information can be timely.

fiscal year An entity's reporting year, covering a 12-month accounting period.

calendar year An entity's reporting year, covering 12 months and ending on December 31.

Exhibit 2: The Problem of Income Measurement

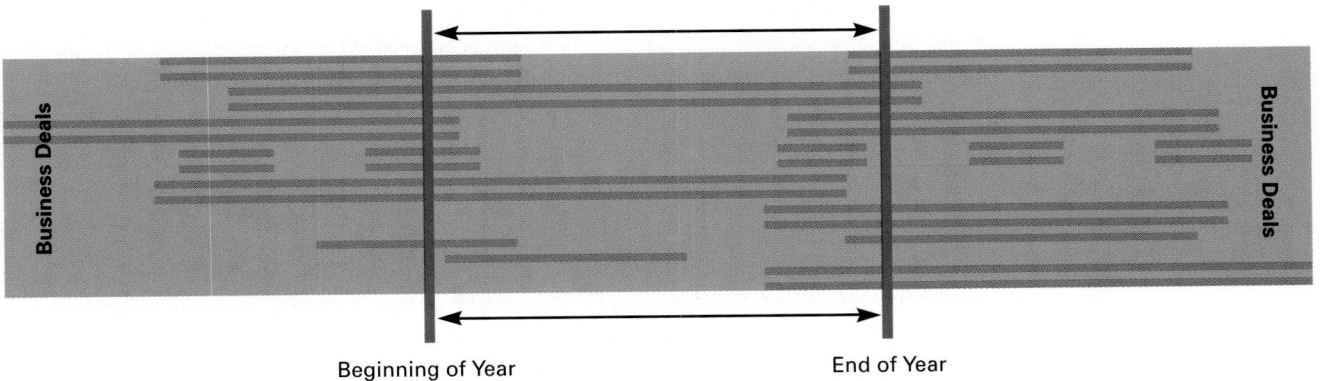

Beginning of Year   End of Year

Although periodic reporting is vital to a firm's success, the frequency of reporting forces accountants to use some data that are based on judgments and estimates. As you will see, the shorter the reporting period (for example, a month instead of a year), the less exact are the measurements of assets and liabilities and the recognition of revenues and expenses. Ideally, accounting judgments are made carefully and estimates are based on reliable evidence, but the limitations of accounting reports should be understood and kept in mind.

Accrual- versus Cash-Basis Accounting

accrual-basis accounting A system of accounting in which revenues and expenses are recorded as they are earned and incurred, not necessarily when cash is received or paid.

Closely related to the time-period concept is the concept of **accrual-basis accounting**. This important characteristic of the traditional accounting model simply means that revenues are recognized (recorded) when earned without regard for when cash is received; expenses are recorded as incurred without regard for when they are paid. Accrual accounting requires that revenues and expenses be assigned to their proper accounting periods, which do not necessarily coincide with the periods in which cash is received or paid.

Revenue Recognition

revenue recognition principle The idea that revenues should be recorded when (1) the earnings process has been substantially completed and (2) cash has either been collected or collectibility is reasonably assured.

How do we assign revenues to particular periods? First, we must determine when revenues have actually been earned. The **revenue recognition principle** states that revenues are recorded when two main criteria have been met.

1. The earnings process is substantially complete; generally, a sale has been made or services have been performed.
2. Cash has been collected or collectibility is reasonably assured.

These two criteria ensure that both parties to the transaction have fulfilled their commitment or are formally obligated to do so. In simple terms, satisfying the first criterion demonstrates that the seller has done something; satisfying the second criterion demonstrates that the buyer has done something. The seller generally records sales revenue when goods are shipped or when services are performed. When this occurs, the seller has completed his or her part of the transaction. The seller assumes, when shipment is made or services performed, that the buyer has given a valid promise to pay (if this promise is not implied, then the seller probably will not ship). The promise to pay, or the actual payment, would complete the buyer's part of the transaction. If, for example, General Motors sold and shipped $800 million of cars in 2006, but will not receive the cash proceeds until 2007, the $800 million would still be recognized as revenue in 2006, when it is earned and a promise of payment is received. Both of the revenue recognition principle criteria have been met. On the other hand, if General Motors is paid in 2006 for cars to be shipped in 2007, it would not record those payments as revenues until the cars are actually shipped. Referring back to the example that began this section, the two brothers would recognize as consulting revenue the amount associated with the proportion of the job that was completed in 2005. For example, if an objective estimate indicated that 80% of the consulting project was completed in 2005, then it would be appropriate for the brothers to recognize $16,000 ($20,000 × 0.8) as revenue in 2005—assuming that they felt they had received a valid promise that they would be paid for the consulting work.

The Matching Principle

matching principle The concept that all costs and expenses incurred in generating revenues must be recognized in the same reporting period as the related revenues.

Once a company determines which revenues should be recognized during a period, how does it identify the expenses incurred? The **matching principle** requires that all costs and expenses incurred to generate revenues must be recognized in the same accounting period as the related revenues. The cost of the merchandise sold, for example, should be matched to the revenue derived from the sale of that merchandise during the period. Expenses that cannot be matched with revenues are assigned to the accounting period in which they are incurred. For example, the exact amount of electricity used to make an automobile generally cannot be determined, but since the amount used for a month or a year is known, that amount can be matched to the revenues earned during the same period.

As shown in Exhibit 3, this process of matching expenses with recognized revenues determines the amount of net income reported on the income statement. Net income is the most widely used indicator of how well a company has performed during a period. The subject of income determination, including revenue recognition and expense matching, is discussed more completely in Chapters 7, 8, and 9.

To illustrate the difference between cash- and accrual-basis accounting, and to demonstrate why accrual-basis accounting provides a more meaningful measure of income, assume that Karas Brothers billed clients $50,500 for consulting services in 2006. By December 31, Karas had received $22,000, with the $28,500 balance expected in 2007. During 2006, Karas paid $21,900 for various expenses. At December 31, Karas still owed $11,200 for additional expenses incurred. These expenses will be paid during January 2007. How much income should Karas Brothers report for 2006? The answer depends on whether cash-basis or accrual-basis accounting is used. As shown below, with cash-basis accounting, reported income would be $100. With accrual-basis accounting, reported income would be $17,400.

cash-basis accounting A system of accounting in which transactions are recorded and revenues and expenses are recognized only when cash is received or paid.

Karas Brothers
Reported Income for 2006

Cash-Basis Accounting		**Accrual-Basis Accounting**	
Cash receipts	$22,000	Revenues earned	$50,500
Cash disbursements	21,900	Expenses incurred	33,100
Income	$ 100	Income	$17,400

Caution

Although accrual-basis net income is the measure of Karas Brothers' economic performance for the year, the cash flow information is useful in evaluating the need to obtain short-term loans, the ability to repay existing loans, and the like. The statement of cash flows is an essential companion to the accrual-basis income statement.

How do we explain this $17,300 difference? Under **cash-basis accounting**, Karas Brothers would report only $22,000 in revenue, the total amount of cash received during 2006. Similarly, the company would report only $21,900 of expenses (the amount actually paid) during 2006. The additional $11,200 of expenses incurred but not yet paid would not be reported. Using accrual-basis accounting, however, Karas earned $50,500 in revenues, which is the total increase in resources for the period (an increase of $22,000 in cash plus $28,500 in receivables). Similarly, Karas incurred a total of $33,100 in expenses, which should be matched with revenues earned to produce a realistic income measurement. The combined result of increasing revenues by $28,500 while increasing expenses by only $11,200 creates the $17,300 difference in net income ($28,500 − $11,200 = $17,300).

Exhibit 3: Determining Accrual Income

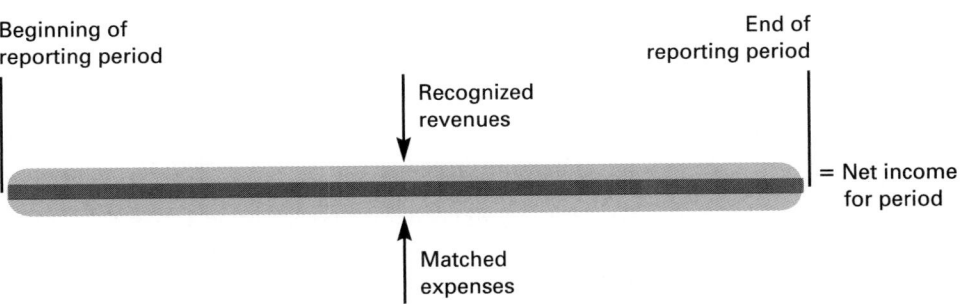

Recognized Revenues − Matched Expenses = Net Income for Period

As this example shows, accrual-basis accounting provides a more accurate picture of a company's profitability. It matches earned revenues with the expenses incurred to generate those revenues. This helps investors, creditors, and others to better assess the operating results of a company and make more informed judgments concerning its profitability and earnings potential. Accrual-basis accounting is required by generally accepted accounting principles (GAAP).

TO SUMMARIZE: Users of accounting information need timely, periodic financial reports to make decisions. The revenue recognition and matching principles provide guidelines for assigning the appropriate amounts of revenues and expenses to each period under accrual accounting. Accrual-basis accounting provides a better measure of net income than does cash-basis accounting; it is therefore required by GAAP in reporting the results of company operations.

Adjusting Entries

2 Explain the need for adjusting entries and make adjusting entries for unrecorded receivables, unrecorded liabilities, prepaid expenses, and unearned revenues.

adjusting entries Entries required at the end of each accounting period to recognize, on an accrual basis, revenues and expenses for the period and to report proper amounts for asset, liability, and owners' equity accounts.

As discussed in Chapter 3, transactions generally are recorded in a journal in chronological order and then posted to the ledger accounts. The entries are based on the best information available at the time. Although the majority of accounts are up-to-date at the end of an accounting period and their balances can be included in the financial statements, some accounts require adjustment to reflect current circumstances. In general, these accounts are not updated throughout the period because it is impractical or inconvenient to make such entries on a daily or weekly basis. At the end of each accounting period, in order to report all asset, liability, and owners' equity amounts properly and to recognize all revenues and expenses for the period on an accrual basis, accountants are required to make any necessary adjustments prior to preparing the financial statements. The entries that reflect these adjustments are called **adjusting entries**.

One difficulty with adjusting entries is that the need for an adjustment is not signaled by a specific event such as the receipt of a bill or the receipt of cash from a customer. Rather, adjusting entries are recorded on the basis of an analysis of the circumstances at the close of each accounting period. This analysis involves just two steps:

1. Determine whether the amounts recorded for all assets and liabilities are correct. If not, debit or credit the appropriate asset or liability account. In short, fix the balance sheet.
2. Determine what revenue or expense adjustments are required as a result of the changes in recorded amounts of assets and liabilities indicated in step 1. Debit or credit the appropriate revenue or expense account. In short, fix the income statement.

It should be noted that these two steps are interrelated and may be reversed. That is, revenue and expense adjustments may be considered first to fix the income statement, indicating which asset and liability accounts need adjustment to fix the balance sheet. As you will see, each adjusting entry involves at least one income statement account and one balance sheet account. T-accounts are helpful in analyzing adjusting entries and will be used in the illustrations that follow.

The areas most commonly requiring analysis to see whether adjusting entries are needed are:

1. Unrecorded receivables
2. Unrecorded liabilities
3. Prepaid expenses
4. Unearned revenues

As we illustrate and discuss adjusting entries, remember that the basic purpose of adjustments is to make account balances current in order to report all asset, liability, and owners' equity amounts properly and to recognize all revenues and expenses for the period on an accrual basis. This is done so that the income statement and the balance sheet will reflect the proper operating results and financial position, respectively, at the end of the accounting period.

Unrecorded Receivables

unrecorded receivables
Revenues earned during a period that have not been recorded by the end of that period.

In accordance with the revenue recognition principle of accrual accounting, revenues should be recorded when earned, regardless of when the cash is received. If revenue is earned but not yet collected in cash, a receivable exists. To ensure that all receivables are properly reported on the balance sheet in the correct amounts, an analysis should be made at the end of each accounting period to see whether there are any revenues that have been earned but have not yet been collected or recorded. These **unrecorded receivables** are earned and represent amounts that are receivable in the future; therefore, they should be recognized as assets.

To illustrate, we will pick up with the landscaping business we started in Chapter 3. Recall that we mow lawns, pull weeds, plant shrubs, and perform other related services. We are able to provide these services year round because we live in a region with a very mild climate. Our company reports on a calendar-year basis and has determined the following on December 31, 2006:

> On November 1, we entered into a year-long contract with an apartment complex to provide general landscaping services each week and bill the customer every three months. The terms of the contract state that we will earn $400 per month. As of December 31, Lawn Care Revenue of $800 ($400 for November and $400 for December) has not been recorded and will not be received until the end of January 2007. No entry has been made with regard to the contract.

As of year-end, no asset has been recorded, but an $800 receivable exists ($400 × 2), because two months' worth of revenue has been earned. To record this receivable, we must debit (increase) the asset Accounts Receivable for $800. With the debit, we have accomplished step 1 by fixing the balance sheet with regard to this transaction. Step 2 requires that we use the other half of the adjusting entry, the credit of $800, to fix the income statement. We know that the credit must be to a revenue or an expense account, and the nature of the transaction suggests that we should credit Lawn Care Revenue for $800. The adjusting entry is:

Dec. 31	Accounts Receivable	800	
	Lawn Care Revenue		800
	To record earned revenue not yet received.		

Adjusting entries are recorded in the general journal and are posted to the accounts in the general ledger in the same manner as other journal entries. Again note that each adjusting entry must involve at least one balance sheet account and at least one income statement account.

After this adjusting entry has been journalized and posted, the receivable will appear as an asset on the balance sheet, and the lawn care revenue is reported on the income statement. Through the adjusting entry, the asset (receivable) accounts are properly stated and revenues are appropriately reported.

Unrecorded Liabilities

unrecorded liabilities
Expenses incurred during a period that have not been recorded by the end of that period.

Just as assets are created from revenues being earned before they are collected or recorded, liabilities can be created by expenses being incurred prior to being paid or recorded. These expenses, along with their corresponding liabilities, should be recorded when incurred, no matter when they are paid. Thus, adjusting entries are required at the end of an accounting period to recognize any **unrecorded liabilities** in the proper period and to record the corresponding expenses. As the expense is recorded (increased by a debit), the offsetting liability is also recorded (increased by a credit), showing the entity's obligation to pay for the expense. If such adjustments are not made, the net income measurement for the period will not reflect all appropriate expenses and the corresponding liabilities will be understated on the balance sheet.

FYI:

Most companies don't have to be reminded to search out unrecorded assets and revenues and recognize them. On the other hand, unrecorded liabilities and expenses are things companies would rather forget. Auditors must take care to ensure that all unrecorded liabilities and expenses are properly reported.

To illustrate, we will assume that on December 31, 2006, our landscaping company has determined the following:

1. Your brother has worked for the company since its inception. He is paid every two weeks. The next payday is on Friday, January 5, 2007. On that day, your brother will be paid $700, the amount he earns every two weeks. Since December 31 falls halfway through the pay period, one-half of his wages should be allocated to 2006.
2. Recall from Chapter 3 that one of our options for financing our company was to borrow money from a bank. We borrowed $2,000 with the promise that on the first of every month we would make a $178 payment—a portion of that payment being attributed to interest[1] and a portion to principal.

Our next payment is due on January 1, 2007, but the interest expense associated with that payment should be attributed to the period in which the money was actually used—December 2006. Assume that interest of $20 must be recognized on December 31, 2006.

To represent its current financial position and earnings, our landscaping company must record the impact of these events in the accounts, even though cash transactions have not yet occurred. The wages will not be paid until 2007. Under accrual-basis accounting, however, these costs are expenses of 2006 and should be recognized on this year's income statement, with the corresponding liability shown on the balance sheet as of the end of the year. To fix the balance sheet, Wages Payable must be credited (increased) for $350; recognition of this liability ensures that the balance sheet properly reports this liability, which was created during 2006 and exists as of the end of the year. The debit of this adjusting entry is to Wages Expense, resulting in the proper inclusion of this expense in the 2006 income statement. The adjusting journal entry is as follows:

Dec. 31	Wages Expense	350	
	Wages Payable		350
	To record obligation for wages.		

The liability for the interest for the month of December is recorded by a credit (increase) to Interest Payable; this fixes the balance sheet. The debit of the adjusting entry is to Interest Expense, which properly includes this expense on the 2006 income statement. The adjusting entry is:

Dec. 31	Interest Expense	20	
	Interest Payable		20
	To record interest incurred.		

Caution

A liability is not recorded for the total amount of interest that will have to be paid over the entire life of the loan. If we repay the loan on December 31, the future interest will not have to be paid, but the interest for the month of December that has passed will still be due.

The wages expense and interest expense would be shown on the income statement for the year ended December 31, and the liabilities (wages payable and interest payable) would be shown on the balance sheet as of December 31. Because of the adjusting entries, both the income statement and the balance sheet will more accurately reflect the financial situation of our landscaping company.

---

1 As noted in Chapter 3, *interest* is the cost of using money. The amount borrowed or lent is the *principal*. The *interest rate* is an annual rate stated as a percentage. The *period of time* involved may be stated in terms of a year. For example, if interest is to be paid for 3 months, time is 3/12, or 1/4 of a year. If interest is to be paid for 90 days, time is 90/365 of a year. Thus, the formula for computing interest is Interest = Principal × Interest Rate × Time (fraction of a year).

Prepaid Expenses

prepaid expenses Payments made in advance for items normally charged to expense.

Payments that a company makes in advance for items normally charged to expense are known as **prepaid expenses**. An example would be the payment of an insurance premium for three years. Theoretically, every resource acquisition is an asset, at least temporarily. Thus, the entry to record an advance payment should be a debit to an asset account (Prepaid Expenses) and a credit to Cash, showing the exchange of cash for another asset.

Caution

Prepaid Expenses is a tricky name for an asset. Assets are reported in the balance sheet. Don't make the mistake of including Prepaid Expenses with the expenses on the income statement.

An expense is the using up of an asset. For example, when supplies are purchased, they are recorded as assets; when they are used, their cost is transferred to an expense account. The purpose of making adjusting entries for prepaid expenses is to show the complete or partial consumption of an asset. If the original entry is to an asset account, the adjusting entry reduces the asset to an amount that reflects its remaining future benefit and at the same time recognizes the actual expense incurred for the period.

For the unrecorded assets and liabilities discussed earlier, there was no original entry; the adjusting entry was the first time these items were recorded in the accounting records. For prepaid expenses, this is not the case. Because cash has already been paid (in the case of prepaid expenses), an original entry has been made to record the cash transaction. Therefore, the amount of the adjusting entry is the difference between what the updated balance should be and the amount of the original entry already recorded.

To illustrate adjustments for Prepaid Expenses, we will assume the following about our landscaping company:

1. On November 1, 2006, we purchased a six-month insurance policy on our old truck, paying a $600 premium.
2. On December 15, 2006, we purchased several months' worth of supplies (fertilizer, weed killer, etc.) at a total cost of $350. At year-end, $225 worth of supplies were still on hand.

For the prepaid insurance, we record the payment of $600 on November 1 as follows:

Nov. 1	Prepaid Insurance	600	
	Cash		600
	Paid a six-month insurance premium in advance.		

This entry shows that one asset (Cash) has been exchanged for another asset (Prepaid Insurance). Over the next six months we will use the auto insurance and the asset, Prepaid Insurance, will slowly be used up. As the asset is used, its cost is recorded as an expense.

At year-end, only those assets that still offer future benefits to the company should be reported on the balance sheet. Thus, an adjustment is required to reduce the prepaid insurance account to reflect the fact that only four months of prepaid insurance remain. See the following time line.

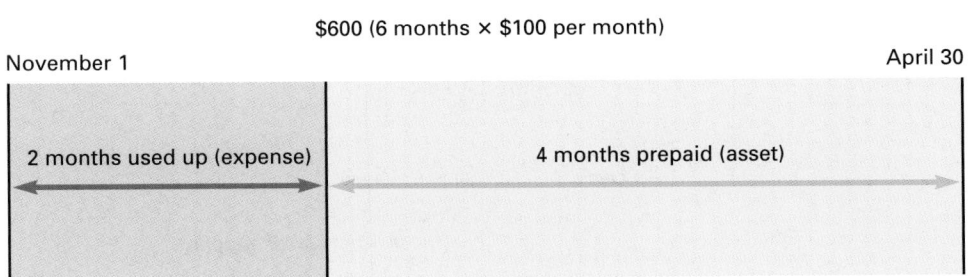

$600 (6 months × $100 per month)

November 1 — April 30

2 months used up (expense) — 4 months prepaid (asset)

December 31

The adjusting journal entry to bring the original amounts to their updated balances at year-end is:

Dec. 31	Insurance Expense	200	
	Prepaid Insurance		200
	To record insurance expense for two months:		
	2 × $100 = $200.		

When the adjusting entry is journalized and posted, the proper amount of insurance expense ($200) will be shown as an expense on the income statement and the proper amount of prepaid insurance ($400) will be carried forward to the next period as an asset on the balance sheet. This is illustrated in the following T-accounts:

	Prepaid Insurance	**Cash**	**Insurance Expense**
Original entry (11/1/06)	600	600	
Adjusting entry (12/31/06)	200		200
Updated balances (12/31/06)	400		200
	To balance sheet		To income statement

Caution

The terms *supplies* and *inventory* are often confused. Supplies include such items as paper, pencils, and soap that might be used in an office or a warehouse. Inventory includes only those items held for resale to customers or for direct use in the manufacture of products.

When supplies are consumed in the normal course of business, the asset account (Supplies on Hand) must be adjusted and the used up portion charged as an operating expense (Supplies Expense) on the income statement. Thus, the adjustment for supplies is handled the same way as for any other prepaid asset.

We initially recorded $350 of supplies as an asset:

Dec. 15	Supplies on Hand	350	
	Cash		350
	Purchased supplies.		

At year-end, an adjustment must be made to recognize that only $225 worth of supplies remains. This also implies that $125 ($350 − $225) of the supplies have been used and should be charged to expense. The entries are summarized in the following T-accounts:

	Supplies on Hand	**Cash**	**Supplies Expense**
Original entry (12/15/06)	350	350	
Adjusting entry (12/31/06)	125		125
Updated balances (12/31/06)	225		125
	To balance sheet		To income statement

The adjusting entry is:

Dec. 31	Supplies Expense	125	
	Supplies on Hand		125
	To record the use of supplies.		

Unearned Revenues

unearned revenues Cash amounts received before they have been earned.

Amounts received before the actual earning of revenues are known as **unearned revenues**. They arise when customers pay in advance of the receipt of goods or services. Because the company has received cash but has not yet given the customer the purchased goods or services, the unearned revenues are in fact liabilities. That is, the company must provide something in return for the amounts received. For example, a building contractor may require a deposit before proceeding on construction of a house. Upon receipt of the deposit, the contractor has unearned revenue, a liability. The contractor must construct the house to earn the revenue. If the house is not built, the contractor will be obligated to repay the deposit.

To illustrate the adjustments for unearned revenues, we will assume the following about our landscaping company:

> On December 1, a client pays you $225 for three months of landscaping services to be provided for the period beginning December 1, 2006, and ending February 29, 2007. This client is going to Hawaii for an extended vacation and would like you to take care of the grounds in her absence.

Typically, the original entry to record unearned revenue involves a debit to Cash and a credit to a liability account. In our example of landscaping revenue received three months in advance, the liability account would be Unearned Revenue, as shown on the next page.

> **Caution**
>
> Unearned Revenue is a tricky name for a liability. Liabilities are reported in the balance sheet. Don't make the mistake of including Unearned Revenue with the revenues on the income statement.

The deposit received by a building contractor prior to the construction of a house is classified as unearned revenue.

© 2003 Getty Images

Dec. 1	Cash	225	
	Unearned Revenue		225
	Received three months' revenue in advance:		
	$75 × 3 = $225.		

The credit to the liability account, Unearned Revenue, is logically correct; until we provide the landscaping service, the revenue received in advance is unearned and is thus an obligation (liability).

The next step is to compute the updated balances at year-end. As illustrated with the following time line, on December 31, two months' services (2 × $75 = $150) are still unearned and should be shown as a liability, Unearned Revenue, on the balance sheet. At the same time, $75, or one month's services, has been earned (1 × $75 = $75) and should be reported as Landscaping Revenue on the income statement.

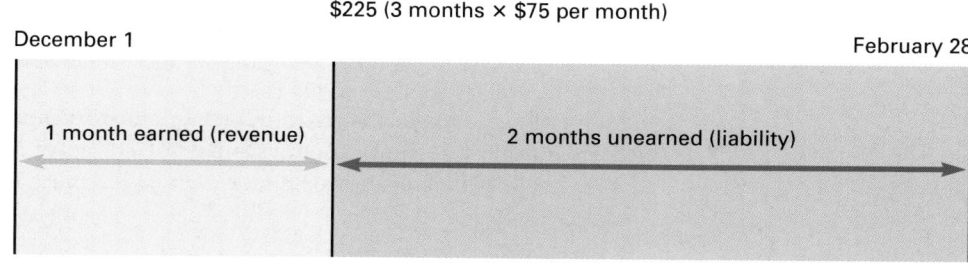

Step 1 of the adjusting entry is to fix the balance sheet. The reported liability of $225 is too much since some of the unearned revenue has been earned. The remaining obligation is $150 (2 × $75), so the liability must be reduced (debited) by $75 ($225 − $150). The second half of the adjusting entry is used to correct the income statement. The $75 credit is made to Landscaping Revenue, reflecting the fact that one month's revenue has now been earned. The appropriate adjusting entry is:

Dec. 31	Unearned Revenue	75	
	Landscaping Revenue		75
	To record landscaping revenue for one month:		
	$75 × 1 month = $75.		

These results are illustrated in the following T-accounts:

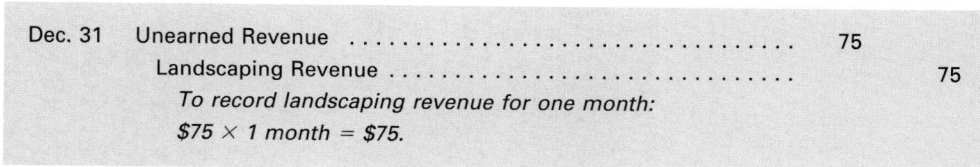

After the adjusting entry has been made on December 31, our accounts show $225 of cash received. Of this amount, $75 has been earned (1 month's service × $75) and would be reported as Landscaping Revenue on the income statement; $150 will not be earned until the next reporting period and would be shown as a liability on the balance sheet.

network
exercises

United Airlines

Airlines have a large amount of unearned revenue because customers pay for their tickets before the airlines provide the travel service. Visit the Web site of UNITED AIRLINES: **http://www.ual.com**

Net Work:

1. What title is given to Unearned Revenue for an airline?

2. What liability was reported for Unearned Revenue in the most recent annual report?

We should emphasize two characteristics of adjusting entries. First, adjusting entries made at the end of an accounting period *do not involve cash.* Cash has either changed hands prior to the end of the period (as is the case with prepaid expenses or unearned revenues), or cash will change hands in a future period (as is the case with many unrecorded receivables and unrecorded liabilities). It is precisely because cash is *not* changing hands on the last day of the accounting period that most adjusting entries must be made.

Second, each adjusting entry involves a balance sheet account and an income statement account. In each case requiring adjustment, we are either generating an asset, using up an asset, recording an incurred but unrecorded expense, or recording revenue that has yet to be earned. Knowing that each adjusting entry has at least one balance sheet and one income statement account makes the adjustment process a little easier. Once you have determined that an adjusting entry involves a certain balance sheet account, you can then focus on identifying the corresponding income statement account that requires adjustment.

The 2002 financial statements for GENERAL MOTORS offer several illustrations of the potential impact of failing to make adjusting entries. GM reports that, as of December 31, 2002, it had unearned revenue totaling $10.496 billion. If GM had failed to make the adjustment necessary to record this unearned revenue, total revenue for 2002 would have been overstated by $10.496 billion, or 5.6%. In addition, GM reported that its total warranty liability as of December 31, 2002 , was $8.856 billion. This warranty liability falls in the category of unrecorded liabilities that are not reported in the financial statements unless an appropriate adjusting entry is made. Finally, GM also reported a $32.685 billion asset related to future tax deductions; this asset would remain unrecorded unless a special adjusting entry were made at the end of the year to reflect the future tax benefits of events that had occurred in 2002 and preceding years.

TO SUMMARIZE: To present financial statements that accurately report the financial position and the results of operations on an accrual basis for specific periods of time, adjusting entries must be made. The four main categories of adjustments are unrecorded receivables, unrecorded liabilities, prepaid expenses, and unearned revenues. In analyzing accounts at the end of an accounting cycle, adjusting entries are made in order to recognize all earned revenues and all incurred expenses and to report the proper balances in the asset, liability, and owners' equity accounts. This requires a two-step analysis: (1) determine what adjustments are necessary to ensure that all asset and liability amounts have been properly recorded, and (2) determine which revenues or expenses must be adjusted to correspond with the changes in assets and liabilities recorded in step 1. With unrecorded receivables and unrecorded liabilities, there is no original entry. With prepaid expenses, the original entry includes a credit to Cash and a debit to an asset account. With unearned revenues, the original entry includes a debit to Cash and a credit to a liability account.

Preparing Financial Statements

3 Explain the preparation of the financial statements, the explanatory notes, and the audit report.

Once all transactions have been analyzed, journalized, and posted and all adjusting entries have been made, the accounts can be summarized and presented in the form of financial statements. Financial statements can be prepared directly from the data in the adjusted ledger accounts. The data must be organized into appropriate sections and categories so as to present them as simply and clearly as possible. The following process describes how the financial statements are prepared from the information taken from the trial balance:

1. Identify all revenues and expenses—these account balances are used to prepare the income statement.

2. Compute net income—subtract expenses from revenues.
3. Compute the ending retained earnings balance—this process was described in Chapter 2 and is illustrated here. Retained Earnings from the previous period is the starting point. Net income (computed in step 2) is added to the beginning retained earnings balance, and dividends for the period are subtracted.
4. Prepare a balance sheet using the balance sheet accounts from the trial balance and the modified retained earnings balance computed from step 3.

Caution

Students often make the mistake of using the beginning retained earnings balance on the end-of-year balance sheet. As we shall see in the next section, the ending retained earnings balance is arrived at when the books are closed for the year.

Note: No account on the trial balance shows up on both the income statement and the balance sheet.

Once the financial statements are prepared, explanatory notes are written. These notes clarify the methods and assumptions used in preparing the statements. In addition, the auditor must review the financial statements to make sure they are accurate, reasonable, and in accordance with generally accepted accounting principles. Finally, the financial statements are distributed to external users who analyze them in order to learn more about the financial condition of the company.

Financial Statement Preparation

To illustrate the preparation of financial statements from adjusted ledger accounts, a simplified adjusted trial balance for GENERAL MOTORS as of December 31, 2002, is provided in Exhibit 4.

Exhibit 4: Simplified Adjusted Trial Balance

General Motors Corporation Simplified Adjusted Trial Balance December 31, 2002 (in millions)		
	Debits	**Credits**
Cash	$ 21,449	
Investments	16,825	
Receivables	150,362	
Inventories	9,967	
Property and Equipment	72,784	
Intangible Assets	17,954	
Deferred Taxes	41,649	
Other Assets	39,792	
Accounts Payable		$ 27,452
Notes and Loans Payable		201,940
Pensions and Other Retirement Benefits		60,949
Accrued Expenses and Other Liabilities		72,793
Capital Stock and Other		23,449
Accumulated Other Comprehensive Loss	25,832	
Retained Earnings		9,463
Dividends	1,168	
Net Sales and Revenues		186,763
Cost of Sales and Other Expenses	153,155	
Selling, General and Administrative Expenses	23,624	
Interest Expense	7,715	
Income Tax Expense	533	
Totals	$582,809	$582,809

From these data, an income statement and a balance sheet may be prepared for General Motors, as shown below in Exhibits 5 and 6.

Exhibit 5: Income Statement

General Motors Corporation Statement of Income For the Year Ended December 31, 2002 (in millions)		
Net sales and revenues		$186,763
Cost of sales and other expenses	$153,155	
Selling, general and administrative expenses	23,624	
Total operating expenses		176,779
Operating income		$ 9,984
Interest expense	$ 7,715	
Income tax expense	533	
Total other expenses		8,248
Net income		$ 1,736

Exhibit 6: Balance Sheet

General Motors Corporation Balance Sheet December 31, 2002 (in millions)		
Assets		
Cash	$ 21,449	
Investments	16,825	
Receivables	150,362	
Inventories	9,967	
Total current assets		$198,603
Property and equipment	$ 72,784	
Intangible assets	17,954	
Deferred taxes	41,649	
Other assets	39,792	
Total long-term assets		172,179
Total assets		$370,782
Liabilities and Owners' Equity		
Accounts payable	$ 27,452	
Accrued expenses and other liabilities	72,793	
Total current liabilities		$100,245
Notes and loans payable		201,940
Pensions and other retirement benefits		60,949
Total liabilities		$363,134
Owners' equity		
Capital stock and other	$ 23,449	
Accumulated other comprehensive loss	(25,832)	
Retained earnings	10,031	
Total owners' equity		7,648
Total liabilities and owners' equity		$370,782

Note: This balance sheet is not an exact replica of General Motors' actual balance sheet due to simplifying modifications for this exhibit.

The ending retained earnings balance for General Motors for 2002 ($10,031), as reported on the balance sheet, is computed as follows:

Beginning retained earnings balance . . . . (from the adjusted trial balance)	$ 9,463
Add: Net income for the period . . . . (from the income statement)	1,736
Subtract: Dividends for the period . . . . (from the adjusted trial balance)	(1,168)
Ending retained earnings balance	$10,031

This follows the computation of retained earnings discussed in Chapter 2.

A statement of cash flows is not shown here. To prepare a statement of cash flows, we need more detailed information about the nature of the cash receipts and cash disbursements during the year. The preparation of a statement of cash flows will be illustrated in Chapter 14.

The Notes

As discussed in Chapter 2, the notes to the financial statements tell about the assumptions and methods used in preparing the financial statements and also give more detail about specific items. A sample of the kind of information that appears in the notes for General Motors' financial statements is illustrated in Exhibit 7. The first two notes, on revenue recognition and credit losses, illustrate how financial statement notes can summarize the accounting policies and assumptions that underlie the financial statements. The third note, on the debt associated with GM's financing subsidiary (GMAC), provides detailed information about a summary number that was reported in the financial statements. The fourth note, on GM's labor force, provides information that is deemed to be important to financial statement users, such as future labor costs, but that does not directly affect any of the reported historical financial statement numbers.

The financial statement notes serve to augment the summarized, numerical information contained in the financial statements. To highlight the importance of the notes, many financial statements have the following message printed at the bottom: "The notes are an integral part of these financial statements."

The Audit

As mentioned in Chapter 2, an independent audit, by CPAs from outside the company, is often conducted to ensure that the financial statements have been prepared in conformity with generally accepted accounting principles. With respect to the financial statements of General Motors, the audit procedures conducted by the external auditor, DELOITTE & TOUCHE, would probably include the following checks.

Review of Adjustments

As you learned in the first part of this chapter, adjusting entries usually require more analysis, and more judgment, than do the regular journal entries recorded throughout the year. As part of the audit, the auditor will review these adjusting entries.

When conducting the audit of the financial statements, auditors are concerned that accounts are properly adjusted. Auditors are able to focus their efforts as illustrated in Exhibit 8. Companies will make sure that assets are not UNDERstated and that liabilities are not OVERstated. Auditors will make special effort to ensure that assets are not OVERstated and that liabilities are not UNDERstated.

Exhibit 7: General Motors: Notes to the Financial Statements

General Motors Corporation
Notes to the Financial Statements (partial list)
For the Year Ended December 31, 2002

Revenue Recognition: Sales generally are recorded when products are shipped . . . to independent dealers.

Allowance for Credit Losses: The allowance for credit losses generally is established by GMAC during the period in which receivables are acquired and is maintained at a level considered appropriate by management based on historical and other factors that affect collectibility. These factors include the historical trends of repossessions, charge-offs, recoveries, and credit losses; the careful monitoring of portfolio credit quality, including the impact of acquisitions; and current and projected economic and market conditions. Different assumptions or changes in economic circumstances could result in changes to the allowance for credit losses.

Debt: Long-term debt and loans payable were as follows (dollars in millions):

	Weighted-Average Interest Rate		December 31,	
	2002	**2001**	**2002**	**2001**
Long-term debt and loans payable				
Payable within one year:				
Current portion of long-term debt	2.7%	2.5%	$ 624	$ 64
Commercial paper	—	2.7%	—	129
All other	5.7%	3.1%	892	2,209
Total loans payable			$ 1,516	$ 2,402
Payable beyond one year	6.0%	6.6%	16,625	10,720
Unamortized discount			(22)	(27)
Mark to market adjustment			48	33
Total long-term debt and loans payable			$18,167	$13,128

Labor Force: GM, on a worldwide basis, has a concentration of its labor supply in employees working under union collective bargaining agreements, a significant number of which will expire in 2003.

Exhibit 8: How Auditors Spend Their Time

	Too much recorded	**Too little recorded**
Assets	Auditors must critically scrutinize each recorded amount to ensure it does not overstate the asset's value.	Little worry for the auditor—companies themselves will work hard to make sure that assets are *not* understated.
Liabilities	Little worry for the auditor—companies themselves will work hard to make sure that liabilities are *not* overstated.	Auditors must search for unrecorded liabilities as a company might not work as hard in an effort to increase its own liabilities.

Sample of Selected Accounts

For a number of accounts, the auditor undertakes a sampling process to see whether the items reported in the balance sheet actually exist. For example, General Motors reports an ending cash and equivalents balance of $21,449,000,000. The auditor will ask to see bank statements and will probably call the bank(s) to verify the existence of the cash. For inventory, the auditor will ask to physically see the inventory and will conduct a spot check to see whether the company inventory records match what is actually in the warehouse.

Review of Accounting Systems

The auditor will also evaluate General Motors' accounting systems. If a company has a good accounting system, with all transactions being recorded in an efficient, orderly way, then the auditor has greater reason to be confident that the financial statements are reliable. On the other hand, if the company's accounting system is haphazard, with many missing documents and unexplained discrepancies, then the auditor must do more detailed work to verify the financial statements.

If the auditor finds that the financial statements have been prepared in conformance with generally accepted accounting principles, then the auditor provides a report to that effect. This report is attached and distributed as part of the financial statements. The audit report is discussed in more detail in Chapter 6.

Using a Work Sheet

work sheet A tool used by accountants to facilitate the preparation of financial statements.

A **work sheet** is a tool used by accountants to facilitate the preparation of financial statements. Unlike the financial statements, work sheets are for internal use only; they are not distributed to "outsiders." Although the use of work sheets is optional, most accountants find them helpful for organizing large quantities of data. Many work sheets are now prepared on electronic spreadsheets, using a software package such as Lotus 1-2-3, Excel, or Quattro Pro. Using a work sheet to assist in the preparation of financial statements is explained in detail in this text's Interactive Study Center at **http://albrecht.swlearning.com**.

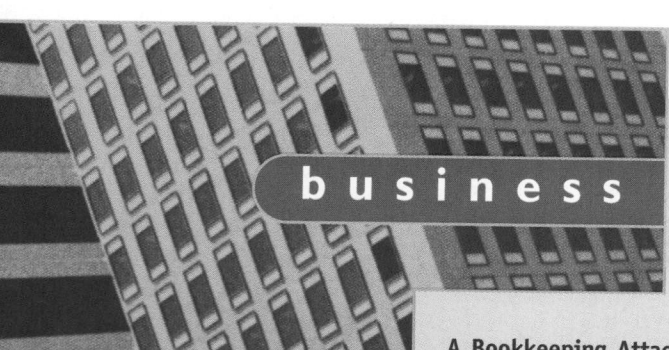

business environment

A Bookkeeping Attack Starts a War Tom Clancy typed the first draft of his first novel, *The Hunt for Red October*, on an IBM Selectric typewriter while still holding down his full-time job as an insurance agent. The book was published in October 1984, and sales took off when it became known that the book was President Ronald Reagan's favorite. To date, Clancy has published a total of over 20 novels, and the stories have been so popular that Clancy now commands a record $25 million advance per book.

In *The Hunt for Red October*, Jack Ryan, who was trained as a historian, is a part-time analyst for the CIA. By the sixth novel in the series, *Debt of Honor*, a well-earned reputation for being a "good man in a storm" has landed Ryan, against his wishes, in the position of serving as the president's National Security Adviser. Jack Ryan's abilities are tested as an international crisis is touched off when a group of Japanese businessmen gain control of their government and determine that the only way to save the Japanese economy is through neutralization of U.S. power in the Pacific.

The first act of war against the United States is an attack not on a military target but instead on the bookkeeping system used by U.S. stock exchanges. A computer virus, injected

TO SUMMARIZE: The adjusted trial balance provides the raw material for the preparation of the balance sheet and the income statement. The notes to the financial statements provide further information about the methods and assumptions used in preparing the financial statements as well as further detail about certain financial statement items. The audit is conducted by a CPA from outside the company who reviews the adjusting entries, performs tests to check the balances of selected accounts, and reviews the condition of the accounting systems.

Closing the Books

4 Complete the closing process in the accounting cycle.

We have almost reached the end of the accounting cycle. Thus far, the accounting cycle has included analyzing documents, journalizing transactions, posting to the ledger accounts, determining account balances, preparing a trial balance, making adjusting entries, and preparing the financial statements. Just two additional steps are needed: (1) journalizing and posting closing entries and (2) preparing a post-closing trial balance.

Real and Nominal Accounts

real accounts Accounts that are not closed to a zero balance at the end of each accounting period; permanent accounts appearing on the balance sheet.

To explain the closing process, we must first define two new terms. Certain accounts are referred to as **real accounts**. These accounts report the cumulative increases and decreases in certain account balances from the date the company was organized. Real accounts (assets, liabilities, and owners' equity) appear on the balance sheet and are permanent; they are not closed to a zero balance at the end of each accounting period. Balances existing in real accounts at the end of a period are carried forward to the next period.

nominal accounts Accounts that are closed to a zero balance at the end of each accounting period; temporary accounts generally appearing on the income statement.

Other accounts are known as **nominal accounts**. These accounts (revenues, expenses, and dividends) are temporary; they are really just subcategories of Retained Earnings and are reduced to a zero balance through the closing process at the end of each accounting period. Thus, nominal accounts begin with a zero balance at the start of each accounting cycle. Transactions throughout the period (generally a year) are journalized and posted to the nominal accounts.

into the program used to record trades on all the major U.S. stock exchanges, is activated at noon on Friday. The records of all trades made after that time are eliminated with this result:

No trading house, institution, or private investor could know what it had bought or sold, to or from whom, or for how much, and none could therefore know how much money was available for other trades, or for that matter, to purchase groceries over the weekend. (Tom Clancy, Debt of Honor, p. 312)

The uncertainty created by the destruction of the stock exchange bookkeeping records threatens to throw the U.S. economy into a tailspin and distract U.S. policy makers from other moves being made by Japan in the Pacific. Jack Ryan saves the world as we know it and restores the U.S. economy to sound footing by . . . well, it wouldn't be fair to say—you'll have to read the book. Suffice it to say that a key part of the restoration plan is the repair of the stock exchange bookkeeping system.

These are used to accumulate and classify all revenue and expense items, and also dividends, for that period. At the end of the accounting period, adjustments are made, the income statement is prepared, and the balances in the temporary accounts are then closed to Retained Earnings, a permanent account. These closing entries bring the income statement accounts back to a zero balance, which makes the accounts ready for a new accounting period. In addition, the closing entries transfer the net income or loss for the accounting period to Retained Earnings and reduce Retained Earnings for any dividends. Without closing entries, revenue and expense balances would extend from period to period, making it difficult to isolate the operating results of each accounting period.

> **FYI:**
>
> In a proprietorship or a partnership, the nominal accounts are closed to the owners' permanent capital accounts instead of to Retained Earnings.

Closing Entries

The actual mechanics of the closing process are not complicated. Revenue accounts normally have credit balances and are closed by being debited; expense accounts generally have debit balances and are closed by being credited. The difference between total revenues and total expenses represents the net income (or net loss) of the entity. For a corporation, net income is credited to Retained Earnings because income increases owners' equity. A net loss would be debited to Retained Earnings because a loss decreases owners' equity.

To illustrate the closing process, we will again refer to GENERAL MOTORS' financial information as discussed earlier on pages 152–155. The closing journal entry is:

Dec. 31	Net Sales and Revenues	186,763	
	Cost of Sales and Other Expenses		153,155
	Selling, General and Administrative Expenses		23,624
	Interest Expense		7,715
	Income Tax Expense		533
	Retained Earnings		1,736
	To close revenues and expenses to Retained Earnings.		

closing entries Entries that reduce all nominal, or temporary, accounts to a zero balance at the end of each accounting period, transferring their preclosing balances to a permanent balance sheet account.

Closing entries must be posted to the appropriate ledger accounts. Once posted, all nominal accounts will have a zero balance; that is, they will be "closed."

The dividends account is also a nominal (temporary) account that must be closed at the end of the accounting period. However, dividends are not expenses and will not be reported on an income statement; they are distributions to stockholders of part of a corporation's earnings. Thus, dividends reduce retained earnings. When dividends are declared by the board of directors of a corporation, the amount that will be paid is debited to Dividends and credited to a liability account, Dividends Payable, or to Cash if paid immediately. Because Dividends is a temporary account, it must be closed to Retained Earnings at the end of the accounting period. The dividends account is closed by crediting it and by debiting Retained Earnings, thereby reducing owners' equity, as illustrated below for General Motors.

> **Caution**
>
> Don't close real accounts! Consider the negative implications of eliminating all your asset accounts at the end of the year. Nominal accounts are closed because they are just temporary subaccounts of Retained Earnings.

Dec. 31	Retained Earnings	1,168	
	Dividends		1,168
	To close Dividends to Retained Earnings.		

The books are now ready for a new accounting cycle. The closing process for the revenues, expenses, and dividends of a corporation is shown schematically in Exhibit 9.

Exhibit 9: The Closing Process

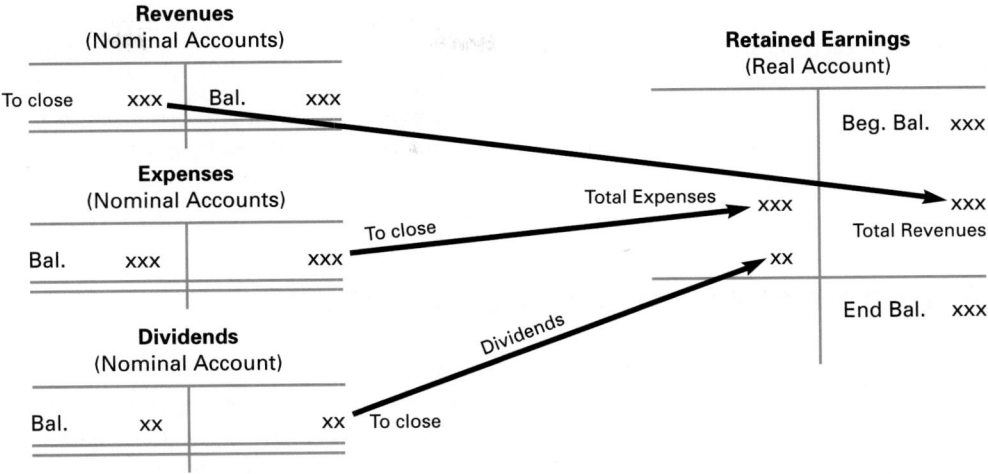

Preparing a Post-Closing Trial Balance

post-closing trial balance
A listing of all real account balances after the closing process has been completed; provides a means of testing whether total debits equal total credits for all real accounts prior to beginning a new accounting cycle.

An optional last step in the accounting cycle is to balance the accounts and to prepare a **post-closing trial balance**. The accounts are to be balanced—debits and credits added and a balance determined—only after the closing entries have been recorded and posted in the general ledger. The information for the post-closing trial balance is then taken from the ledger. The nominal accounts will not be shown since they have been closed and thus have zero balances. Only the real accounts will have current balances. This step is designed to provide some assurance that the previous steps in the cycle have been performed properly, prior to the start of a new accounting period. Exhibit 10 illustrates a post-closing trial balance for General Motors Corporation.

Exhibit 10: Post-Closing Trial Balance

General Motors Corporation Post-Closing Trial Balance December 31, 2002 (in millions)	Debits	Credits
Cash	$ 21,449	
Investments	16,825	
Receivables	150,362	
Inventories	9,967	
Property and Equipment	72,784	
Intangible Assets	17,954	
Deferred Taxes	41,649	
Other Assets	39,792	
Accounts Payable		$ 27,452
Notes and Loans Payable		201,940
Pensions and Other Retirement Benefits		60,949
Accrued Expenses and Other Liabilities		72,793
Capital Stock and Other		23,449
Accumulated Other Comprehensive Loss	25,832	
Retained Earnings		10,031
Totals	$396,614	$396,614

> **TO SUMMARIZE:** As part of the closing process, all nominal (temporary) accounts are closed to a zero balance. All real (permanent) accounts (balance sheet accounts for assets, liabilities, and owners' equity) are carried forward to the new reporting period. All nominal accounts (revenues, expenses, and dividends) are closed to Retained Earnings. Revenue accounts are closed by being debited; expense accounts are closed by being credited. Dividends also must be closed to Retained Earnings by being credited. A post-closing trial balance may be prepared to provide some assurance that the previous steps in the cycle have been performed properly.

A Summary of the Accounting Cycle

5 Understand how all the steps in the accounting cycle fit together.

We have now completed our discussion of the steps in the accounting cycle. By way of review, Exhibit 11 lists the sequence of the accounting cycle (presented earlier in Chapter 3). Many of the steps, such as analyzing transactions, occur continuously. Other steps, such as preparing the financial statements, generally occur only once during the cycle.

The financial statements that result from the accounting cycle provide useful information to investors, creditors, and other external users. These statements are included in the annual reports provided to stockholders. As illustrated earlier in the chapter, once the financial state-

Exhibit 11: Sequence of the Accounting Cycle

Exchange Transactions
(Businesses enter into exchange transactions signaling the beginning of the accounting cycle)

Step 1 Analyze transactions.

Step 2 Record the effects of transactions.

Step 3 Summarize the effects of transactions.
1. Posting journal entries.
2. Preparing a trial balance.

Step 4 Prepare reports.
1. Adjusting entries.
2. Preparing financial statements.
3. Closing the books.

Material

ments are made available to users, they can then be analyzed and compared to the financial statements of similar firms to detect strengths and weaknesses.

eXpanded *Material*

Earlier in the chapter, the adjusting entries for prepaid expenses were made assuming that the prepayments were initially recorded as assets. Alternatively, the prepayments can be initially recorded as expenses; the correct amounts of assets and expenses can still be achieved through an appropriate year-end adjusting entry. Similarly, cash receipts in advance are sometimes initially recorded as revenues instead of as liabilities. Again, although not conceptually correct, it is done in the normal course of bookkeeping; any necessary adjustments can be made at year-end.

Adjusting Entries: Original Entries to Expense or Revenue

6 Make adjusting entries for prepaid expenses and unearned revenues when the original cash amounts are recorded as expenses and revenues.

To illustrate the necessary adjusting process when expense prepayments are debited to an expense account, we will use the prepaid insurance example for the landscaping company that was illustrated earlier:

> On November 1, 2006, the landscaping company purchased a six-month insurance policy on its old truck, paying a $600 premium.

Assume that the $600 insurance prepayment was initially recorded as follows:

Nov. 1	Insurance Expense	600	
	Cash		600
	Paid six months' insurance in advance:		
	6 × $100 = $600.		

Notice that the debit is to Insurance Expense instead of Prepaid Insurance (as illustrated earlier). In order to fix the balance sheet at December 31, the asset Prepaid Insurance must be debited (increased) for $400 (4 × $100) to reflect the fact that four months of prepaid insurance still remain. The entire $400 is debited to Prepaid Insurance because, with the original debit to Insurance Expense, the existing balance in Prepaid Insurance is $0. The credit half of the adjusting entry is used to fix the income statement. The $400 credit is to Insurance Expense, representing the fact that too much insurance expense was initially recorded and some is being removed. The appropriate adjusting entry is as follows:

Dec. 31	Prepaid Insurance	400	
	Insurance Expense		400
	To record prepaid insurance for four months:		
	4 × $100 = $400.		

Although this adjusting entry is different from the one shown previously, the net effect of the original and adjusting entries is exactly the same, as illustrated at the top of the next page.

Original debit to Insurance Expense:

	Prepaid Insurance		Cash		Insurance Expense	
Original entry (11/1/06)				600	600	
Adjusting entry (12/31/06)	400					400
Updated balances (12/31/06)	400				200	
	To balance sheet				To income statement	

Original debit to Prepaid Insurance (illustrated earlier on page 148):

	Prepaid Insurance		Cash		Insurance Expense	
Original entry (11/1/06)	600			600		
Adjusting entry (12/31/06)		200			200	
Updated balances (12/31/06)	400				200	
	To balance sheet				To income statement	

STOP & THINK

Why would a company debit an insurance prepayment to Insurance Expense rather than adopting a more theoretically sound policy of debiting Prepaid Insurance?

Whether the initial debit for a prepaid expense is to a prepaid asset or to an expense, the key thing to remember in constructing the necessary adjusting entry is to first fix the balance sheet; the other half of the adjusting entry is used to fix the income statement.

To illustrate the necessary adjusting process when revenue received in advance is initially credited to a revenue account, we will use the unearned revenue example for our landscaping company that was illustrated earlier:

On December 1, a client pays $225 for landscaping services to be provided over the period December 1, 2006, to February 29, 2007.

Assume that the $225 cash received for services was initially recorded as follows:

Dec. 1	Cash	225	
	Landscaping Revenue		225
	Received three months' revenue in advance:		
	$75 × 3 = $225.		

On December 31, an adjusting entry must be made to reflect the fact that two months' worth of this revenue is still unearned and represents a liability. This adjustment is made through a credit (increase) to Unearned Revenue of $150 ($75 × 2), thereby fixing the balance sheet. The corresponding debit is used to fix the income statement. A debit to Landscaping Revenue represents a decrease in revenue because some of the revenue originally recorded on December 1 has not yet been earned. The necessary adjusting entry is as follows:

Dec. 31	Landscaping Revenue	150	
	Unearned Revenue		150
	To record unearned revenue for two months:		
	$75 × 2 = $150.		

The sequence of entries differs when the original credit is to Landscaping Revenue rather than Unearned Revenue, but the end result is the same. Compare the ending balances in the following T-accounts:

Original credit to Landscaping Revenue:

	Unearned Revenue		Cash		Landscaping Revenue	
Original entry (12/1/06)			225			225
Adjusting entry (12/31/06)		150			150	
Updated balances (12/31/06)		150				75
		To balance sheet				To income statement

Original credit to Unearned Revenue (illustrated earlier on page 150):

	Unearned Revenue		Cash		Landscaping Revenue	
Original entry (12/1/06)		225	225			
Adjusting entry (12/31/06)	75					75
Updated balances (12/31/06)		150				75
		To balance sheet				To income statement

TO SUMMARIZE: Prepayments are sometimes initially recorded as expenses instead of as prepaid expenses (assets); cash receipts for revenue in advance are sometimes initially recorded as revenues instead of as unearned revenues (liabilities). This requires an adjusting process that differs somewhat from that illustrated earlier in the chapter. No matter which approach is used, however, the resulting amounts reported in the balance sheet and the income statement are the same if the adjusting entries are made correctly.

review of learning objectives

1 Describe how accrual accounting allows for timely reporting and a better measure of a company's economic performance. Accounting information is needed on a timely basis for decision-making purposes. This requires that the total life of a business be divided into accounting periods, generally a year or less, for which reports are prepared. Some of the data presented in the periodic reports must be tentative because dividing a company's life into relatively short reporting periods requires that allocations and estimates be made.

The necessity for periodic reporting further requires that accrual accounting be used to provide accurate statements of financial position and results of operations for an accounting period. Accrual-basis accounting means that revenues are recognized as they are earned, not necessarily when cash is received; expenses are recognized as they are incurred, not necessarily when cash is paid. Accrual-basis accounting provides a more accurate picture of a company's financial position and operating results than does cash-basis accounting. The cash flow statement is also very important in analyzing financial position.

2 Explain the need for adjusting entries and make adjusting entries for unrecorded receivables, unrecorded liabilities, prepaid expenses, and unearned revenues. At the end of an accounting period, there are potentially many important events that have as yet not been recorded. Some important events occur outside the normal accounting process, while other events occur slowly over time. An important part of the accounting process is to review the financial condition and operating activities of the company for the period to make sure that all assets, liabilities, revenues, and expenses have been recorded. These year-end adjustments are called adjusting entries and may be classified under four headings: unrecorded receivables, unrecorded liabilities, prepaid expenses, and unearned revenues. The analysis process involved in making an adjusting entry involves two steps. First, determine whether an asset or liability has been recorded for the proper amount and, if not, correct it (fix the balance sheet). Second, determine what revenue or expense adjustment is needed because of the asset or liability adjustment just made (fix the income statement).

3 **Explain the preparation of the financial statements, the explanatory notes, and the audit report.** After the adjusting entries have been posted to the accounts, an adjusted trial balance is prepared. This adjusted trial balance provides the raw data for the preparation of the balance sheet and the income statement; preparation of the statement of cash flows requires more detailed information about cash receipts and cash disbursements. The notes to the financial statements provide further information about the methods and assumptions used in preparing the financial statements as well as further detail about certain financial statement items. The audit is conducted by a CPA from outside the company who reviews the adjusting entries, performs tests to check the balances of selected accounts, and reviews the condition of the accounting systems.

4 **Complete the closing process in the accounting cycle.** Once adjusting entries have been journalized and posted to the accounts and the financial statements have been prepared, the accounting records should be made ready for the next accounting cycle. This is accomplished by journalizing and posting closing entries for all nominal (temporary) accounts. Revenue accounts are closed by being debited; expense accounts and the dividends account are closed by being credited. Revenues, expenses, and dividends are closed to Retained Earnings.

5 **Understand how all the steps in the accounting cycle fit together.** The accounting cycle consists of specific steps to analyze, record, classify, summarize, and report the exchange transactions of economic entities. By way of review, Exhibit 11 identifies the steps in the accounting cycle.

6 **Make adjusting entries for prepaid expenses and unearned revenues when the original cash amounts are recorded as expenses and revenues.** Prepayments are sometimes initially recorded as expenses instead of as prepaid expenses (assets); cash receipts for revenue in advance are sometimes initially recorded as revenues instead of as unearned revenues (liabilities). However, the concepts governing the adjusting process are the same: use the first part of the adjusting entry to fix the balance sheet and the second part to fix the income statement. The end result (the updated balances reported on the balance sheet and income statement, respectively) is the same regardless of which approach is used, assuming that adjusting entries are made correctly.

key terms & concepts

accrual-basis accounting, 142
adjusting entries, 144
calendar year, 141
cash-basis accounting, 143
closing entries, 158
fiscal year, 141

matching principle, 142
nominal accounts, 157
post-closing trial balance, 159
prepaid expenses, 147
real accounts, 157
revenue recognition principle, 142

time-period concept, 141
unearned revenues, 149
unrecorded liabilities, 145
unrecorded receivables, 145
work sheet, 156

review problem

The Accounting Cycle

This review problem provides a useful summary of the entire accounting cycle. The following post-closing trial balance is for Sports Haven Company as of December 31, 2005.

Sports Haven Company
Post-Closing Trial Balance
December 31, 2005

	Debits	Credits
Cash	$17,500	
Accounts Receivable	17,000	
Inventory	28,800	
Supplies on Hand	1,200	
Prepaid Building Rental	24,000	
Accounts Payable		$18,000
Capital Stock (3,600 shares outstanding)		54,000
Retained Earnings		16,500
Totals	$88,500	$88,500

Following is a summary of the company's transactions for 2006.

a. At the beginning of 2006, the company issued 1,500 new shares of stock at $20 per share.
b. Total inventory purchases were $49,500; all purchases were made on credit and are recorded in the inventory account.
c. Total sales were $125,000; $102,900 were on credit, the rest were for cash. The cost of goods sold was $47,500; the inventory account is reduced at the time of each sale.
d. In December, a customer paid $3,500 cash in advance for merchandise that was temporarily out of stock. The advance payments received from customers are initially recorded as liabilities. The $3,500 is not included in the sales figures in (c) above.
e. The company paid $66,500 on accounts payable during the year.
f. The company collected $102,000 of accounts receivable during the year.
g. The company purchased $600 of supplies for cash during 2006, debiting Supplies on Hand.
h. The company paid $850 for advertising during the year, debiting Prepaid Advertising.
i. Total salaries paid during the year were $45,000.
j. The company paid $650 during the year for utilities.
k. Dividends of $7,500 were paid to stockholders in December.

On December 31, 2006, the company's accountant gathers the following information to adjust the accounts:

l. As of December 31, salaries of $750 had been earned by employees but will not be paid until January 3, 2007.
m. A count at December 31 shows $800 of supplies still on hand.
n. The prepaid advertising paid during 2006 includes $400 paid on December 1, 2006, for a series of radio advertisements to be broadcast throughout December 2006 and January 2007. The balance in the account, $450, represents advertisements that were broadcast during 2006.
o. On December 31, 2005, the company rented an office building for two years and paid $24,000 in cash (the full rental fee for 2006 and 2007). The payment was recorded with a debit to Prepaid Building Rental. No entries have been made for building rent in 2006.
p. On December 20, 2006, a bill for $150 was received for utilities. No entry was made to record the receipt of the bill, which is to be paid on January 4, 2007.
q. As of December 31, 2006, the merchandise paid for in advance [transaction (d)] was still out of stock. The company expects to receive the merchandise and fill the order by January 15, 2007.
r. The company's income is taxed at a rate of 15%.

Required:

1. Make entries in the general journal to record each of the transactions [items (a) through (k)].
2. Using T-accounts to represent the general ledger accounts, post the transactions recorded in the general journal. Enter the beginning balances in the accounts that appear in the December 31, 2005, post-closing trial balance before posting 2006 transactions. When all transactions have been posted to the T-accounts, determine the balance for each account.
3. Prepare a trial balance as of December 31, 2006.
4. Record adjusting entries [items (l) through (r)] in the general journal; post these entries to the general ledger (T-accounts).
5. Prepare an income statement and balance sheet for 2006.
6. Record closing entries [label (s) and (t)] in the general journal; post these entries to the general ledger (T-accounts).
7. Prepare a post-closing trial balance.

Solution

1. Following are the journal entries to record the transactions for the year. Several of these are summary entries representing numerous individual transactions.

(a)	Cash	30,000
	Capital Stock	30,000

The company issued additional shares of stock, so Capital Stock must be credited to reflect the increase in owners' equity. Since the company received cash of $30,000 (1,500 shares at $20 per share), Cash is also increased.

(b)	Inventory	49,500
	Accounts Payable	49,500

The company purchased $49,500 of goods on credit. Inventory is increased (debited) for this amount. Accounts Payable is credited to show the increase in liabilities.

(c)	Accounts Receivable	102,900
	Cash	22,100
	Sales Revenue	125,000

Total sales were $125,000, so Sales Revenue must be increased (credited) by that amount. Of this amount, $102,900 were on credit, and $22,100 were cash sales. We increase the asset accounts, Accounts Receivable and Cash, by debiting them.

(c)	Cost of Goods Sold	47,500
	Inventory	47,500

The cost of the merchandise sold during the year was $47,500. Cost of Goods Sold (expense) must be increased (debited) by this amount. Since the goods were sold, Inventory (asset) must be reduced by a credit of $47,500.

(d)	Cash	3,500
	Unearned Sales Revenue	3,500

Cash is debited (increased) by the amount received from the customer. The company recorded the advance payments for merchandise by crediting a liability account, Unearned Sales Revenue.

(e)	Accounts Payable	66,500
	Cash	66,500

The company's payments on its accounts reduce the amount of its obligation to creditors, so Accounts Payable (liability) is debited to decrease it by the amount paid. Cash must also be decreased (credited).

(f) Cash 102,000
    Accounts Receivable 102,000

Since the company has collected some of its receivables from customers, Accounts Receivable is credited to show a decrease. Cash is increased (debited).

(g) Supplies on Hand 600
    Cash 600

The company purchased $600 of supplies. By debiting Supplies on Hand, an increase is shown in that asset account. Cash must be credited to show a decrease.

(h) Prepaid Advertising 850
    Cash 850

The company purchased $850 of advertising and chose to initially debit an asset account, Prepaid Advertising. Since cash was paid, it must be reduced by a credit.

(i) Salaries Expense 45,000
    Cash 45,000

(j) Utilities Expense 650
    Cash 650

For transactions (i) and (j), an expense account must be debited to show that expenses have been incurred. Cash must be credited (reduced).

(k) Dividends 7,500
    Cash 7,500

Dividends must be debited to show a decrease in owners' equity resulting from a distribution of earnings. Cash must be reduced by a credit.

2. T-accounts with the beginning balances and journal entries posted are shown here. (Note that accounts with more than one entry must be "balanced" by drawing a rule and entering the debit or credit balance below it.)

Cash				**Accounts Receivable**				**Inventory**			
Beg.		(e)	66,500	Beg.		(f)	102,000	Beg.		(c)	47,500
bal.	17,500	(g)	600	bal.	17,000			bal.	28,800		
(a)	30,000	(h)	850	(c)	102,900			(b)	49,500		
(c)	22,100	(i)	45,000	Updated				Updated			
(d)	3,500	(j)	650	bal.	17,900			bal.	30,800		
(f)	102,000	(k)	7,500								
Updated											
bal.	54,000										

Supplies on Hand				**Prepaid Building Rental**				**Prepaid Advertising**			
Beg.				Beg.				(h)	850		
bal.	1,200			bal.	24,000						
(g)	600										
Updated											
bal.	1,800										

Accounts Payable		
(e) 66,500	Beg. bal.	18,000
	(b)	49,500
	Updated bal.	1,000

Unearned Sales Revenue		
	(d)	3,500

Capital Stock		
	Beg. bal.	54,000
	(a)	30,000
	Updated bal.	84,000

Retained Earnings		
	Beg. bal.	16,500

Dividends	
(k) 7,500	

Sales Revenue		
	(c)	125,000

Cost of Goods Sold	
(c) 47,500	

Salaries Expense	
(i) 45,000	

Utilities Expense	
(j) 650	

3. The balance of each account is entered in a trial balance. Each column in the trial balance is totaled to determine that total debits equal total credits.

Sports Haven Company
Trial Balance
December 31, 2006

	Debits	Credits
Cash	$ 54,000	
Accounts Receivable	17,900	
Inventory	30,800	
Supplies on Hand	1,800	
Prepaid Building Rental	24,000	
Prepaid Advertising	850	
Accounts Payable		$ 1,000
Unearned Sales Revenue		3,500
Capital Stock		84,000
Retained Earnings		16,500
Dividends	7,500	
Sales Revenue		125,000
Cost of Goods Sold	47,500	
Salaries Expense	45,000	
Utilities Expense	650	
Totals	$230,000	$230,000

4. The adjusting entries for Sports Haven Company are presented in journal form and explained. Updated T-accounts are provided showing the posting of the adjusting entries.

(l)	Salaries Expense	750	
	Salaries Payable		750

As of December 31, there is an unrecorded liability and expense of $750 for salaries owed to employees. Because the salaries were earned in 2006, the liability and related expense must be recorded in 2006.

(m) Supplies Expense 1,000
       Supplies on Hand   1,000

Supplies on Hand (asset) has a debit balance before adjustment of $1,800 [beginning balance of $1,200 plus $600 of supplies purchased during the year, transaction (g)]. Since $800 of supplies are on hand at the end of the year, Supplies on Hand should be reduced (credited) by $1,000. Supplies Expense must be debited to show that $1,000 of supplies were used during the period.

(n) Advertising Expense 650
       Prepaid Advertising   650

Prepaid Advertising has a debit balance before adjustment of $850, the total amount paid for advertising during the year [transaction (h)]. This amount includes $400 that was paid for radio advertising throughout December 2006 and January 2007. Only that portion that applies to 2007 should be shown as Prepaid Advertising, $200 ($400 ÷ 2 months), since it is not an expense of the current year. The remainder, $650, is advertising expense for the period. Thus, the asset account, Prepaid Advertising, must be credited for $650, and Advertising Expense must be increased by a debit of $650.

(o) Building Rent Expense 12,000
       Prepaid Building Rental   12,000

The original entry at the end of 2005 was a debit to the asset account, Prepaid Building Rental, and a credit to Cash. An adjusting entry is needed to record rent expense of $12,000 for 2006 ($24,000 ÷ 2 years). The expense account must be debited and the asset account must be reduced by a credit. The remaining $12,000 in Prepaid Building Rental reflects the portion of the total payment for building rent expense in 2007.

(p) Utilities Expense 150
       Utilities Payable   150

As of December 31, 2006, there is an unrecorded liability and expense of $150 for utilities. Because the expense was incurred in 2006, an adjusting entry is needed to record the liability and related expense.

(q) No entry required.

The original entry to record the advance payment from a customer was made by crediting a liability [transaction (d)]. As of December 31, no revenue has been earned. The company still has an obligation to deliver goods or refund the advanced payment. Therefore, no adjustment is required, since the liability is already properly recorded.

(r) Income Tax Expense 2,595
       Income Taxes Payable   2,595

The remaining adjustment is for income taxes. The difference between total revenues and total expenses is the amount of income before taxes, $17,300. This amount is multiplied by the applicable tax rate of 15% to determine income taxes for the period. The expense account is debited to show the income taxes incurred for the year and the liability account is credited to show the obligation to the government.

Cash			
Beg.		(e)	66,500
bal.	17,500	(g)	600
(a)	30,000	(h)	850
(c)	22,100	(i)	45,000
(d)	3,500	(j)	650
(f)	102,000	(k)	7,500
Updated			
bal.	54,000		

Accounts Receivable			
Beg.		(f)	102,000
bal.	17,000		
(c)	102,900		
Updated			
bal.	17,900		

Inventory			
Beg.		(c)	47,500
bal.	28,800		
(b)	49,500		
Updated			
bal.	30,800		

Supplies on Hand			
Beg.		(m)	1,000
bal.	1,200		
(g)	600		
Updated			
bal.	800		

Prepaid Building Rental			
Beg.		(o)	12,000
bal.	24,000		
Updated			
bal.	12,000		

Prepaid Advertising			
(h)	850	(n)	650
Updated			
bal.	200		

Accounts Payable			
(e)	66,500	Beg.	
		bal.	18,000
		(b)	49,500
		Updated	
		bal.	1,000

Salaries Payable		
	(l)	750

Utilities Payable		
	(p)	150

Income Taxes Payable		
	(r)	2,595

Unearned Sales Revenue		
	(d)	3,500

Capital Stock			
		Beg.	
		bal.	54,000
		(a)	30,000
		Updated	
		bal.	84,000

Retained Earnings		
	Beg.	
	bal.	16,500

Dividends		
(k)	7,500	

Sales Revenue		
	(c)	125,000

Cost of Goods Sold	
(c)	47,500

Salaries Expense	
(i)	45,000
(l)	750
Updated	
bal.	45,750

Utilities Expense	
(j)	650
(p)	150
Updated	
bal.	800

Advertising Expense	
(n)	650

Supplies Expense	
(m)	1,000

Building Rent Expense	
(o)	12,000

Income Tax Expense	
(r)	2,595

5. Data for the financial statements may be taken from the adjusted ledger accounts and reported as follows:

Sports Haven Company
Income Statement
For the Year Ended December 31, 2006

Sales revenue	$125,000	
Less cost of goods sold	47,500	
Gross profit		$77,500
Less operating expenses:		
Salaries expense	$ 45,750	
Utilities expense	800	
Advertising expense	650	
Supplies expense	1,000	
Building rent expense	12,000	60,200
Income before income taxes		$17,300
Income tax expense		2,595
Net income		$14,705

Earnings per share:
$14,705 ÷ 5,100 shares = $2.88 (rounded)

Sports Haven Company
Balance Sheet
December 31, 2006

Assets

Cash	$54,000	
Accounts receivable	17,900	
Inventory	30,800	
Supplies on hand	800	
Prepaid building rental	12,000	
Prepaid advertising	200	
Total assets		$115,700

Liabilities and Owners' Equity

Liabilities:		
Accounts payable	$ 1,000	
Salaries payable	750	
Utilities payable	150	
Income taxes payable	2,595	
Unearned sales revenue	3,500	
Total liabilities		$ 7,995
Owners' equity:		
Capital stock (5,100 shares outstanding)	$84,000	
Retained earnings	23,705*	
Total owners' equity		107,705
Total liabilities and owners' equity		$115,700

*Note that in preparing the balance sheet, net income must be added to the beginning balance in Retained Earnings and dividends must be subtracted ($16,500 + $14,705 − $7,500 = $23,705).

6. The next step is to record the closing entries in the general journal and then post those entries to the general ledger (T-accounts). T-accounts are shown with all previous entries and the closing entries [items (s) and (t)] posted.

   The first entry is to close the revenue account and each of the expense accounts. Sales Revenue has a credit balance; it is debited to reduce the balance to zero. The expense accounts are closed by crediting them. The difference in total revenues and total expenses is $14,705 (net income for the period). Net income represents an increase in retained earnings. All of this is captured in the single, compound closing entry (s), as follows:

(s)	Sales Revenue	125,000	
	Cost of Goods Sold		47,500
	Salaries Expense		45,750
	Utilities Expense		800
	Advertising Expense		650
	Supplies Expense		1,000
	Building Rent Expense		12,000
	Income Tax Expense		2,595
	Retained Earnings		14,705

Second, Dividends, a nominal account, must also be closed to Retained Earnings.

(t)	Retained Earnings	7,500	
	Dividends		7,500

Cash

Beg.		(e)	66,500
bal.	17,500	(g)	600
(a)	30,000	(h)	850
(c)	22,100	(i)	45,000
(d)	3,500	(j)	650
(f)	102,000	(k)	7,500
Updated			
Bal.	54,000		

Accounts Receivable

Beg.		(f)	102,000
bal.	17,000		
(c)	102,900		
Updated			
bal.	17,900		

Inventory

Beg.		(c)	47,500
bal.	28,800		
(b)	49,500		
Updated			
bal.	30,800		

Supplies on Hand

Beg.		(m)	1,000
bal.	1,200		
(g)	600		
Updated			
bal.	800		

Prepaid Building Rental

Beg.		(o)	12,000
bal.	24,000		
Updated			
bal.	12,000		

Prepaid Advertising

(h)	850	(n)	650
Updated			
bal.	200		

Accounts Payable

(e)	66,500	Beg.	
		bal.	18,000
		(b)	49,500
		Updated	
		bal.	1,000

Salaries Payable

		(l)	750

Utilities Payable

		(p)	150

Income Taxes Payable

		(r)	2,595

Unearned Sales Revenue

		(d)	3,500

Capital Stock

		Beg.	
		bal.	54,000
		(a)	30,000
		Updated	
		bal.	84,000

Retained Earnings			**Dividends**			**Sales Revenue**		
(t)	7,500	Beg.	(k)	7,500	(t) 7,500	(s)	125,000	(c) 125,000
		bal. 16,500						
		(s) 14,705						
		Updated						
		bal. 23,705						

Cost of Goods Sold			**Salaries Expense**			**Utilities Expense**		
(c)	47,500	(s) 47,500	(i)	45,000	(s) 45,750	(j)	650	(s) 800
			(l)	750		(p)	150	

Advertising Expense			**Supplies Expense**			**Building Rent Expense**		
(n)	650	(s) 650	(m)	1,000	(s) 1,000	(o)	12,000	(s) 12,000

Income Tax Expense		
(r)	2,595	(s) 2,595

7. The final (optional) step in the accounting cycle is to prepare a post-closing trial balance. This procedure is a check on the accuracy of the closing process. It is a listing of all ledger account balances at year-end. Note that only real accounts appear because all nominal accounts have been closed to a zero balance in preparation for the next accounting cycle.

Sports Haven Company
Post-Closing Trial Balance
December 31, 2006

	Debits	Credits
Cash	$ 54,000	
Accounts Receivable	17,900	
Inventory	30,800	
Supplies on Hand	800	
Prepaid Building Rental	12,000	
Prepaid Advertising	200	
Accounts Payable		$ 1,000
Salaries Payable		750
Utilities Payable		150
Income Taxes Payable		2,595
Unearned Sales Revenue		3,500
Capital Stock		84,000
Retained Earnings		23,705
Totals	$115,700	$115,700

discussion questions

1. Why are financial reports prepared on a periodic basis?
2. Distinguish between reporting on a calendar-year and on a fiscal-year basis.
3. When are revenues generally recognized (recorded)?
4. What is the matching principle?
5. Explain why accrual-basis accounting is more appropriate than cash-basis accounting for most businesses.
6. Why are accrual-based financial statements considered somewhat tentative?
7. Why are adjusting entries necessary?
8. Since there are usually no source documents for adjusting entries, how does the accountant know when to make adjusting entries and for what amounts?
9. The analysis process for preparing adjusting entries involves two basic steps. Identify the two steps and explain why both are necessary.
10. Why are supplies not considered inventory? What type of account is Supplies on Hand?
11. Cash is not one of the accounts increased or decreased in an adjusting entry. Why?

12. Which are prepared first: the year-end financial statements or the general journal adjusting entries? Explain.
13. Of what value are the notes to the financial statements and the audit report, both of which are usually included in the annual report to shareholders?
14. Distinguish between real and nominal accounts.
15. What is the purpose of closing entries?
16. What is the purpose of the post-closing trial balance? Explain where the information for the post-closing trial balance comes from.

17. Explain why there are alternative ways of recording certain transactions, either as assets or expenses, or as liabilities or revenues.

practice exercises

Practice 4-1

Periodic Reporting
Which one of the following statements is true with respect to periodic reporting?

a. All companies in the United States are required to have a fiscal year that ends on December 31.
b. The issuance of frequent periodic financial reports reduces the need for accountants to make estimates and judgments.
c. In the United States, only large businesses (those with total assets in excess of $650 million) prepare periodic financial statements.
d. Some financial reports may be prepared on a daily basis.
e. The Securities and Exchange Commission (SEC) requires all publicly-traded companies in the United States to file monthly financial statements.

Practice 4-2

Revenue Recognition
In which one of the following situations should revenue be recognized?

a. The earnings process has begun and cash collectibility is reasonably assured.
b. The earnings process has begun and cash has been collected.
c. The earnings process is substantially complete and cash collectibility is not yet reasonably assured.
d. The earnings process will soon begin and cash has been collected.
e. The earnings process is substantially complete and cash collectibility is reasonably assured.

Practice 4-3

Matching
Select the one phrase below that best completes the following statement: According to the matching principle, . . .

a. The amount of cash collected should be matched and recognized in the same period as the related revenue.
b. Expenses should be matched and recognized in the same period as the related revenue.
c. The amount of cash collected should be matched and recognized in the same period as the related expense.
d. Revenue should be matched and recognized in the same period as the related cash collection.
e. Expenses should be matched and recognized in the same period as the related shareholder investment.

Practice 4-4

Cash-Basis Accounting
A lawn care company started business on January 1, 2006. The company billed clients $100,000 for lawn care services completed in 2006. By December 31, the company had received $82,000 cash from the customers, with the $18,000 balance expected to be collected in 2007. During 2006, the company paid $71,000 cash for various expenses. At December 31, the company still owed $43,000 for additional expenses incurred which have not yet been paid in cash. These expenses will be paid during January 2007. How much income should the company report for 2006? *Note:* The company computes income using cash-basis accounting.

Practice 4-5

Accrual-Basis Accounting
Refer to Practice 4-4. Compute income for 2006 assuming that the company uses accrual-basis accounting.

Practice 4-6

Unrecorded Receivable: Original Entry
Greg operates a sizeable newspaper delivery service. On the last day of each month, Greg receives a statement from the newspaper publisher detailing how much money Greg earned that month from delivering papers. On the 10th day of the following month, Greg receives the cash for the preceding month's deliveries. On December 10, Greg received $12,300 cash for deliveries made in November. Make the journal entry necessary on Greg's books on December 10 to record the receipt of this cash, assuming that Greg did not make any adjusting entry as of the end of November.

Practice 4-7

Unrecorded Receivable: Adjusting Entry
Refer to Practice 4-6. On December 31, Greg received a statement from the newspaper publisher notifying him that he had earned $13,700 for his December deliveries. Because December 31 is the end of Greg's fiscal year, he makes adjusting entries at that time. (1) Make the adjusting journal entry necessary on Greg's books on December 31 to record the $13,700 in delivery revenue earned during December and (2) make the journal entry necessary on Greg's books on January 10 to record the receipt of the $13,700 in cash. *Note:* When making the January 10 entry, don't forget the adjusting entry that was made on December 31.

Practice 4-8

Unrecorded Liability: Original Entry
On May 1, the company borrowed $60,000 from Far West Bank. The loan is for five years and bears an annual interest rate of 8%. Interest on the loan is to be paid in cash each year on April 30; the $60,000 loan amount is to be repaid in full after five years. Make the journal entry necessary on the company's books to record the receipt of this loan on May 1.

Practice 4-9

Unrecorded Liability: Adjusting Entry
Refer to Practice 4-8. (1) Make the adjusting entry necessary on the company's books with respect to this loan on December 31. (2) Make the journal entry necessary on the company's books on the following April 30 to record payment of interest for the first year of the loan. *Note:* When making this April 30 entry, don't forget the adjusting entry that was made on December 31.

Practice 4-10

Prepaid Expense: Original Entry
On August 1, the company paid $72,000 cash for a four-year insurance policy. The policy went into effect on August 1. Make the journal entry necessary on the company's books to record the payment for the insurance on August 1.

Practice 4-11

Prepaid Expense: Adjusting Entry
Refer to Practice 4-10. (1) Make the adjusting entry necessary on the company's books on December 31 with respect to this insurance policy and (2) compute the ending balance in the prepaid insurance account; assume that the balance as of the beginning of the year was $0.

Practice 4-12

Unearned Revenue: Original Entry
The company provides security services to its clients. On March 1, the company received $180,000 cash for a two-year security contract. The contract went into effect on March 1. Make the journal entry necessary on the company's books to record the receipt of the payment for the contract on March 1.

Practice 4-13

Unearned Revenue: Adjusting Entry
Refer to Practice 4-12. (1) Make the adjusting entry necessary on the company's books on December 31 with respect to this security contract and (2) compute the ending balance in the unearned security revenue account; assume that the balance as of the beginning of the year was $0.

Practice 4-14

Wages Payable: Adjusting Entry and Subsequent Payment
The company pays its employees at the end of the day Friday for work done during that five-day work week. Total wages for a week are $24,000. In the current year, December 31 occurred on a Tuesday. (1) Make the adjusting entry necessary on the company's books on December 31 with respect to unpaid employee wages and (2) make the journal entry necessary on Friday, January 3, of the following year to record the cash payment of wages for the week. Ignore the new year's holiday season and assume that employees worked each of the five days. *Note:* When making the January 3 entry, don't forget the adjusting entry that was made on December 31.

Practice 4-15

Supplies: Original Purchase and Adjusting Entry
On January 1, the company had office supplies costing $2,300. On March 23, the company bought additional office supplies costing $7,800; the company paid cash. On December 31, a physical count of office supplies revealed that supplies costing $3,000 remained. (1) Make the journal entry necessary on the company's books on March 23 to record the purchase of office supplies and (2) make the adjusting entry necessary on December 31 with respect to office supplies.

Practice 4-16

Preparing an Adjusted Trial Balance
Before any adjusting entries were made, the company prepared the following trial balance as of December 31:

	Debit	Credit
Cash	$ 68,000	
Notes Receivable	126,000	
Prepaid Rent	216,000	
Building	290,000	
Accounts Payable		$ 150,000
Unearned Fee Revenue		270,000
Capital Stock		150,000
Retained Earnings		100,000
Dividends	17,000	
Fee Revenue		370,000
Wages Expense	244,000	
Utilities Expense	79,000	
Totals	$1,040,000	$1,040,000

In order to make the adjusting entries, the following information has been assembled:

a. The notes receivable were issued on June 1. The annual interest rate on the notes is 12%. Interest is to be received each year on May 31; accordingly, no interest has been received.

b. The unearned fee revenue represents cash received in advance on February 1. This $270,000 relates to a three-year contract which began on February 1. It is expected that the fees will be earned evenly over the three-year contract period. As of December 31, no revenue had yet been recognized on this contract.

c. The prepaid rent represents cash paid in advance on October 1. This $216,000 relates to a five-year rental agreement that began on October 1. As of December 31, no expense had yet been recognized in association with this rental agreement.

d. As of December 31, unpaid (and unrecorded) wages totaled $22,000.

(1) Prepare the necessary adjusting journal entries and (2) prepare an adjusted trial balance.

Practice 4-17

Using an Adjusted Trial Balance to Prepare an Income Statement
Refer to Practice 4-16. Using the adjusted trial balance prepared in part (2), prepare an income statement for the year.

Practice 4-18

Using an Adjusted Trial Balance to Prepare a Balance Sheet
Refer to Practice 4-16. Using the adjusted trial balance prepared in part (2), prepare a balance sheet as of the end of the year. *Note:* The ending retained earnings balance is equal to the beginning balance plus the amount of net income less the amount of dividends.

Practice 4-19

Adjusting Entries and the Audit
Consider the auditor's review of a company's adjusting entries. For which one of the following would a concerned auditor be required to make a search of items not included in the accounting records?

a. Overstated assets
b. Overstated liabilities
c. Understated assets
d. Understated liabilities

Practice 4-20

Closing Entries: Revenues
At the top of the next page is a list of accounts with corresponding ending balances.

(continued)

	Account	Account Balance
a.	Prepaid Insurance	$1,300
b.	Cash	750
c.	Sales Revenue	4,000
d.	Retained Earnings	2,300
e.	Accounts Payable	1,500
f.	Capital Stock	450
g.	Interest Revenue	200

Prepare one summary entry to close those accounts that should be closed at the end of the year.

Practice 4-21

Closing Entries: Expenses
Below is a list of accounts with corresponding ending balances.

	Account	Account Balance
a.	Insurance Expense	$1,300
b.	Cash	750
c.	Accounts Receivable	4,000
d.	Cost of Goods Sold	2,300
e.	Interest Payable	1,500
f.	Building	450
g.	Interest Receivable	200

Prepare one summary entry to close those accounts that should be closed at the end of the year.

Practice 4-22

Closing Entries: Everything
Below is a list of accounts with corresponding ending balances.

	Account	Account Balance
a.	Inventory	$1,300
b.	Dividends	750
c.	Sales Revenue	5,000
d.	Wages Expense	2,500
e.	Cash	1,500
f.	Cost of Goods Sold	2,450
g.	Rent Revenue	400
h.	Retained Earnings (beginning)	1,000

(1) Prepare all entries necessary to close those accounts that should be closed at the end of the year and (2) compute the ending balance in the retained earnings account.

Practice 4-23

Post-Closing Trial Balance
Refer to Practice 4-16. Prepare a post-closing trial balance. For this exercise, ignore the adjustments described in Practice 4-16; just use the reported trial balance.

e x e r c i s e s

Exercise 4-1

Reporting Income: Cash versus Accrual Accounting

On December 31, 2006, Matt Morgan completed the first year of operations for his new computer retail store. The following data were obtained from the company's accounting records:

Sales to customers	$197,000
Collections from customers	145,000
Interest earned and received on savings accounts	2,500
Cost of goods sold	98,500
Amounts paid to suppliers for inventory	103,000
Wages owed to employees at year-end	3,500
Wages paid to employees	40,000
Utility bill owed: to be paid next month	1,100
Interest due at 12/31 on loan to be paid in March of next year	1,200
Amount paid for one and one-half years' rent, beginning Jan. 1, 2006	17,500
Income taxes owed at year-end	4,000

1. How much net income (loss) should Matt report for the year ended December 31, 2006, according to (a) cash-basis accounting and (b) accrual-basis accounting?
2. Which basis of accounting provides the better measure of operating results for Matt?

Exercise 4-2

Reporting Income: Cash versus Accrual Accounting

On December 31, Brian Silvaggi completed the first year of operations for his new business. The following data are available from the company's accounting records:

Sales to customers	$145,000
Collections from customers	125,000
Interest earned and received on savings accounts	1,500
Amount paid for one and one-half years' rent	3,600
Utility bill owed: to be paid next month	960
Cost of goods sold	80,000
Amount paid to suppliers for materials	83,000
Wages paid to employees	47,500
Wages owed to employees at year-end	1,200
Interest due at 12/31 on a loan to be paid the middle of next year	800

1. How much net income (loss) should Brian report for the year ended December 31 according to (a) cash-basis accounting and (b) accrual-basis accounting?
2. Which basis of accounting provides the better measure of operating results for Brian?

Exercise 4-3

Classifying Account Balances

For each of the following accounts, indicate whether it would be found in the income statement or in the balance sheet.

1. Cash
2. Inventory
3. Salaries Expense
4. Prepaid Salaries
5. Retained Earnings
6. Office Supplies Expense
7. Accounts Receivable
8. Cost of Goods Sold
9. Maintenance Expense
10. Interest Receivable
11. Capital Stock
12. Accounts Payable
13. Buildings
14. Mortgage Payable
15. Interest Expense
16. Accounts Payable
17. Notes Receivable
18. Office Supplies
19. Sales Revenue
20. Insurance Expense
21. Machinery
22. Land
23. Salaries Payable
24. Prepaid Insurance
25. Notes Payable
26. Dividends

Exercise 4-4

Classifications of Accounts Requiring Adjusting Entries

For each type of adjustment listed, indicate whether it is an unrecorded receivable, an unrecorded liability, an unearned revenue, or a prepaid expense at December 31, 2006.

1. Property taxes that are for the year 2006, but are not to be paid until 2007.
2. Rent revenue earned during 2006, but not collected until 2007.
3. Salaries earned by employees in December 2006, but not to be paid until January 5, 2007.
4. A payment received from a customer in December 2006 for services that will not be performed until February 2007.
5. An insurance premium paid on December 29, 2006, for the period January 1, 2007, to December 31, 2007.
6. Gasoline charged on a credit card during December 2006. The bill will not be received until January 15, 2007.
7. Interest on a certificate of deposit held during 2006. The interest will not be received until January 7, 2007.
8. A deposit received on December 15, 2006, for rental of storage space. The rental period is from January 1, 2007, to December 31, 2007.

Exercise 4-5

Adjusting Entries: Prepaid Expenses and Unearned Revenues

Boswell Group is a professional corporation providing management consulting services. The company initially debits assets in recording prepaid expenses and credits liabilities in recording unearned revenues. Give the entry that Boswell would use to record each of the following transactions on the date it occurred. Prepare the adjusting entries needed on December 31, 2006.

1. On July 1, 2006, the company paid a three-year premium of $7,200 on an insurance policy that is effective July 1, 2006, and expires June 30, 2009.
2. On February 1, 2006, Boswell paid its property taxes for the year February 1, 2006, to January 31, 2007. The tax bill was $1,800.
3. On May 1, 2006, the company paid $180 for a three-year subscription to an advertising journal. The subscription starts May 1, 2006, and expires April 30, 2009.
4. Boswell received $1,800 on September 15, 2006, in return for which the company agreed to provide consulting services for 18 months beginning immediately.
5. Boswell rented part of its office space to Bristle Brush Company. Bristle paid $1,200 on November 1, 2006, for the next six months' rent.
6. Boswell loaned $100,000 to a client. On November 1, the client paid $24,000, which represents two years' interest in advance (November 1, 2006, through October 31, 2008).

Exercise 4-6

Adjusting Entries: Prepaid Expenses and Unearned Revenues

Erickson Group provides computer network consulting services. The company initially debits assets in recording prepaid expenses and credits liabilities in recording unearned revenues. Give the appropriate entry that Erickson would use to record each of the following transactions on the date it occurred. Prepare the adjusting entries needed on December 31, 2006. (Round all numbers to the nearest dollar.)

1. On March 15, 2006, Erickson received $35,000 for a contract to provide consulting services for 18 months beginning immediately.
2. On April 1, 2006, the company paid $350 for a two-year subscription to a computer networking journal. The subscription starts April 1, 2006, and expires March 31, 2008.
3. On May 1, 2006, Erickson paid $4,500 in property taxes for the year May 1, 2006, to April 30, 2007.
4. Erickson rented part of its office building to Boss Graphics, LLC. Boss paid $1,900 on August 1, 2006, for the next six months' rent.
5. On September 1, 2006, the company paid a two-year premium of $20,000 on an insurance policy that is effective September 1, 2006, and expires August 31, 2008.
6. Erickson loaned $250,000 to a client. On October 1, 2006, the client paid $21,000 for interest in advance (October 1, 2006, to September 30, 2007).

Exercise 4-7

Spreadsheet

Adjusting Entries

Shop Rite Services is ready to prepare its financial statements for the year ended December 31, 2006. The following information can be determined by analyzing the accounts:

1. On August 1, 2006, Shop Rite received a $4,800 payment in advance for rental of office space. The rental period is for one year beginning on the date payment was received. Shop Rite recorded the receipt as unearned rent.
2. On March 1, 2006, Shop Rite paid its insurance agent $3,000 for the premium due on a 24-month corporate policy. Shop Rite recorded the payment as prepaid insurance.
3. Shop Rite pays its employee wages the middle of each month. The monthly payroll (ignoring payroll taxes) is $22,000.
4. Shop Rite received a note from a customer on June 1, 2006, as payment for services. The amount of the note is $1,000 with interest at 12%. The note and interest will be paid on June 1, 2008.
5. On December 20, 2006, Shop Rite received a $2,500 check for services. The transaction was recorded as unearned revenue. By year-end, Shop Rite had completed three-fourths of the contracted services. The rest of the services won't be completed until at least the middle of January 2007.
6. On September 1, Shop Rite purchased $500 worth of supplies. At December 31, 2006, one-fourth of the supplies had been used. Shop Rite initially recorded the purchase of supplies as an asset.

Where appropriate, prepare adjusting journal entries at December 31, 2006, for each of these items.

Exercise 4-8

Adjusting Entries

Consider the following two independent situations:

1. On June 1, Brown Company received $4,800 cash for a two-year subscription to its monthly magazine. The term of the subscription begins on June 1. Make the entry to record the receipt of the subscription on June 1. Also make the necessary adjusting entry at December 31. The company uses an account called Unearned Subscription Revenue.
2. Clark Company pays its employees every Friday for a five-day workweek. Salaries of $200,000 are earned equally throughout the week. December 31 of the current year is a Tuesday.
   a. Make the adjusting entry at December 31.
   b. Make the entry to pay the week's salaries on Friday, January 3, of the next year. Assume that all employees are paid for New Year's Day.

Exercise 4-9

Adjusting Entries

Consider the following items for Williams Company:

1. On July 1 of the current year, Williams Company borrowed $300,000 at 9% interest. As of December 31, no interest expense has been recognized.
2. On September 1 of the current year, Williams Company rented to another company some excess space in one of its buildings. Williams Company received $24,000 cash on September 1. The rental period extends for six months, starting on September 1. Williams Company credited the account Unearned Rent Revenue upon receipt of the rent paid in advance.
3. At the beginning of the year, Williams Company had $750 of supplies on hand. During the year, another $3,900 of supplies were purchased for cash and recorded in the asset account Office Supplies. At the end of the year, Williams Company determined that $980 of supplies remained on hand.
4. On February 1 of the current year, Williams Company loaned Botts Company $125,000 at 8% interest. The loan amount, plus accrued interest, will be repaid in one year.

For each of the items, make the appropriate adjusting journal entry, if any, necessary in Williams Company's books as of December 31.

Exercise 4-10

Spreadsheet

Adjusting Entries

Davis Company opened a Web page design business on January 1 of the current year. The following information relates to Davis Company's operations during the current year:

1. On February 1, Davis Company rented a new office. Before moving in, it prepaid a year's rent of $24,000 cash.
2. On March 31, Davis Company borrowed $50,000 from a local bank at 15%. The loan is to be repaid, with interest, after one year. As of December 31, no interest payments had yet been made.
3. Davis Company bills some of its customers in advance for its design services. During the year, Davis received $60,000 cash in advance from its customers. As of December 31, Davis's accountant determined that 40% of that amount had not yet been earned.
4. On June 15, Davis Company purchased $1,400 of supplies for cash. On September 14, Davis made another cash purchase of $1,100. As of December 31, Davis's accountant determined that $1,700 of supplies had been used during the year.
5. Before closing its books, Davis Company found a bill for $800 from a free-lance programmer who had done work for the company in November. Davis had not yet recorded anything in its books with respect to this bill. Davis plans to pay the bill in January of next year.

For each of the items, make the initial entry, where appropriate, to record the transaction and, if necessary, the adjusting entry at December 31.

Exercise 4-11

Adjusting Entries

Lane Enterprises disclosed the following information on December 31, 2006 (before any adjusting entries were made):

1. In June, Lane purchased an insurance premium for $36,000 for the 18 months beginning July 1, 2006.
2. On November 1, Lane received $9,000 from Jimmy Fillmore for six months of rent beginning on November 1.
3. On February 1, Lane borrowed $60,000 at 8% interest. Lane has not recognized any interest expense this year.
4. On October 1, Lane loaned Ashley Royal $20,000 at 10% interest. No interest revenue has been collected or recorded.

For each item listed, prepare the necessary adjusting entries to be made on December 31, 2006.

Exercise 4-12

Adjusting Entries

Consider the following information related to the Timmy Thompson Company:

1. At the beginning of the year, the company had $460 in supplies on hand. During the year, the company purchased $5,300 in supplies. At the end of the year, the company had $1,320 in supplies on hand.
2. The company pays its employees on the 15th of each month. The monthly payroll (ignoring payroll taxes) is $19,000.
3. On November 1, the company received a $10,000 check for services. The transaction was recorded as unearned revenue. By year-end, the Timmy Thompson Company had completed one-fourth of the required work related to this service. Timmy expects to complete the rest of the work within the first two months of the next year.
4. On December 15, Timmy paid $4,800 for factory rental related to January of the next year.

For each item listed, prepare the necessary adjusting entries to be made on December 31.

Exercise 4-13

Adjusting Entries

Consider the following information related to Pendleton Consulting:

1. On October 1, 2006, Pendleton Consulting entered into an agreement to provide consulting services for six months to Soelberg Company. Soelberg agreed to pay Pendleton $750 for each month of service. Payment will be made at the end of the contract (March 31, 2007).
2. On April 30, Pendleton borrowed $40,000 from a local bank at 12%. The loan is to be repaid, with interest, after one year. As of December 31, no interest expense had been recognized.
3. On February 25, Pendleton paid $36,000 for 12 months of rent beginning on March 1. On February 25, Pendleton made a journal entry debiting Prepaid Rent Expense.
4. At the beginning of 2006, Pendleton had $825 in supplies on hand. During 2006, Pendleton purchased $7,290 in supplies. On December 31, 2006, Pendleton had $1,035 in supplies on hand.

For each item listed, prepare the necessary adjusting entries to be made on December 31, 2006.

Exercise 4-14

Analysis of Accounts

Answer the following questions:

1. If office supplies on hand amounted to $4,000 at the beginning of the period and total purchases of office supplies during the period amounted to $22,000, determine the ending balance of office supplies on hand if office supplies expense for the period amounted to $20,000.
2. If beginning and ending accounts receivable were $10,000 and $12,000, respectively, and total sales made on account for the period amounted to $52,000, determine the amount of cash collections from customers on account for the period.
3. Assume all rent revenues are received in advance and accounted for as unearned rent, and beginning and ending balances of unearned rent are $3,000 and $2,500, respectively. If total rent revenue for the period amounts to $15,000, determine the amount of rent collections in advance for the period.

Exercise 4-15

Real and Nominal Accounts

Classify each of the following accounts as either a real account (R) or a nominal account (N):

1. Cash
2. Sales Revenue
3. Accounts Receivable
4. Cost of Goods Sold
5. Prepaid Insurance
6. Capital Stock
7. Retained Earnings
8. Insurance Expense
9. Salaries Payable
10. Interest Expense
11. Insurance Premiums Payable
12. Salaries Expense
13. Accounts Payable
14. Prepaid Salaries
15. Utilities Expense
16. Notes Payable
17. Inventory
18. Property Tax Expense
19. Rent Expense
20. Interest Payable
21. Income Taxes Payable
22. Dividends
23. Buildings
24. Office Supplies
25. Income Tax Expense

Exercise 4-16

Closing Entry

The income statement for Roberts Enterprises for the year ended June 30, 2006, is provided.

(continued)

Roberts Enterprises
Income Statement
For the Year Ended June 30, 2006

Sales revenue	$ 263,000
Cost of goods sold	(148,000)
Selling and general expenses	(21,300)
Income before income taxes	$ 93,700
Income tax expense	(33,000)
Net income	$ 60,700

1. Prepare a journal entry to close the accounts to Retained Earnings.
2. What problem may arise in closing the accounts if the information from the income statement is used?

Exercise 4-17

Closing Entry

Revenue and expense accounts of Rushford Publishing Company for November 30, 2006, are given as follows. Prepare a compound journal entry that will close the revenue and expense accounts to the retained earnings account.

	Debits	Credits
Sales Revenue		$250,500
Cost of Goods Sold	$124,500	
Salaries Expense	35,000	
Interest Expense	1,000	
Rent Expense	9,300	
Insurance Expense	1,700	
Property Tax Expense	800	
Supplies Expense	1,000	
Advertising Expense	10,000	

Exercise 4-18

Closing Entries

Johstoneaux, Inc. reports the following numbers for 2006:

Johstoneaux, Inc.
Income Statement
For the Year Ended December 31, 2006

Sales	$ 420,300
Cost of goods sold	(230,000)
Insurance expense	(3,000)
Selling and administrative expenses	(90,000)
Income before taxes	$ 97,300
Income tax expense	(30,100)
Net income	$ 67,200

Prepare journal entries to close the revenue and expense accounts to the retained earnings account.

Exercise 4-19

Closing Entries

The following information relates to the Wycherly Company:

Wycherly Company Income Statement For the Year Ended December 31, 2006	
Sales revenue	$ 906,000
Interest revenue	23,000
Net revenue	$ 929,000
Cost of goods sold	(450,000)
Selling and administrative expenses	(140,000)
Income before taxes	$ 339,000
Income tax expense	(135,600)
Net income	$ 203,400

Prepare journal entries to close the revenue and expense accounts to the retained earnings account.

Exercise 4-20

Closing Dividends and Preparing a Post-Closing Trial Balance

A listing of account balances taken from the adjusted ledger account balances of The Miners' Guild shows the following:

Cash	$ 45,160	Salaries Payable	$ 18,000
Accounts Receivable	112,960	Taxes Payable	48,800
Inventory	156,720	Unearned Rent	30,400
Prepaid Insurance	13,040	Mortgage Payable	180,000
Land	272,000	Capital Stock	88,000
Accounts Payable	57,280	Dividends	40,000
Notes Payable	80,000	Retained Earnings	137,400

All revenue and expense accounts have been closed to Retained Earnings. Dividends has not yet been closed.

Prepare (1) the closing entry for Dividends and (2) a post-closing trial balance for December 31, 2006.

Exercise 4-21

Closing Dividends and Preparing a Post-Closing Trial Balance

Below is a listing of account balances taken from the adjusted ledger account balances of Goldsmith Corporation.

Cash	$25,500	Income Taxes Payable	$ 4,000
Accounts Receivable	24,000	Mortgage Payable	55,000
Inventory	60,000	Notes Payable	27,500
Prepaid Advertising	5,500	Unearned Rent	2,500
Building	95,000	Capital Stock	95,500
Land	35,000	Dividends	15,500
Accounts Payable	20,000	Retained Earnings	51,000
Wages Payable	5,000		

All revenues and expense accounts have been closed to Retained Earnings. Dividends has not yet been closed.

(continued)

Prepare (1) the closing entry for Dividends and (2) a post-closing trial balance for December 31, 2006.

Exercise 4-22

Adjusting Entries

The trial balance of Carol Company shows the following balances, among others, on December 31, 2006, the end of its first fiscal year:

Rent Revenue	$ 52,100
Office Supplies Expense	8,300
Mortgage Payable	220,000

Inspection of the company's records reveals that:

1. Rent revenue of $3,250 is unearned at December 31, 2006.
2. Interest of $9,600 on the mortgage is payable semiannually on March 1 and September 1.
3. Office supplies of $750 are on hand on December 31. When purchases of office supplies were made during the year, they were charged to the office supplies expense account.

Given this information, prepare journal entries to adjust the books as of December 31, 2006.

problems

Problem 4-1

Cash- and Accrual-Basis Accounting

In the course of your examination of the books and records of Karen Company, you find the following data:

Salaries earned by employees in 2006	$ 61,000
Salaries paid in 2006	53,000
Total sales revenue in 2006	927,000
Cash collected from sales in 2006	952,000
Utilities expense incurred in 2006	7,500
Utility bills paid in 2006	6,300
Cost of goods sold in 2006	602,000
Cash paid on purchases in 2006	613,000
Inventory at December 31, 2006	416,000
Tax assessment for 2006	6,210
Taxes paid in 2006	5,930
Rent expense for 2006	36,000
Rent paid in 2006	41,000

Required:
1. Compute Karen's net income for 2006 using cash-basis accounting.
2. Compute Karen's net income for 2006 using accrual-basis accounting.
3. **Interpretive Question:** Why is accrual-basis accounting normally used? Can you see any opportunities for improperly reporting income under cash-basis accounting? Explain.

Problem 4-2

Spreadsheet

Adjusting Entries

The information presented below is for Sun Marketing, Inc.

a. Salaries for the period December 26, 2006, through December 31, 2006, amounted to $14,240 and have not been recorded or paid. (Ignore payroll taxes.)

b. Interest of $6,000 is payable for three months on a 15%, $160,000 loan and has not been recorded.

c. Rent of $24,000 was paid for six months in advance on December 1 and debited to Prepaid Rent.

d. Rent of $82,000 was credited to an unearned revenue account when received. Of this amount, $33,400 is still unearned at year-end.

e. The expired portion of an insurance policy is $1,000. Prepaid Insurance was originally debited.

f. Interest revenue of $300 from a $2,000 note has been earned but not collected or recorded.

Required:

Prepare the adjusting entries that should be made on December 31, 2006. (Omit explanations.)

Problem 4-3

Adjusting Entries

The information presented below is for Susan's Sweet Shop.

a. Interest of $9,600 is payable for September 2006 through December 2006 on a 9%, $320,000 loan and has not been recorded.

b. Rent of $93,500 was credited to an unearned revenue account when received. Of this amount, $42,250 is still unearned at year-end.

c. Interest revenue of $9,450 from a $105,000 note has been earned but not collected or recorded.

d. The expired portion of an insurance policy is $4,960. Prepaid Insurance was originally debited.

e. Rent of $30,000 was paid for six months in advance on November 15, 2006, and debited to Prepaid Rent.

f. Salaries for the period December 26, 2006, to December 31, 2006, amounted to $15,300 and have not been recorded or paid. (Ignore payroll taxes.)

Required:

Prepare the adjusting entries that should be made on December 31, 2006. (Omit explanations.)

Problem 4-4

Year-End Analysis of Accounts

An analysis of cash records and account balances of Wells, Inc., for 2006 is as follows:

	Account Balances Jan. 1, 2006	Account Balances Dec. 31, 2006	Cash Received or Paid in 2006
Wages Payable	$2,600	$3,000	
Unearned Rent	4,500	5,000	
Prepaid Insurance	100	120	
Paid for wages			$29,600
Received for rent			12,000
Paid for insurance			720

Required:

Determine the amounts that should be included on the 2006 income statement for (1) wages expense, (2) rent revenue, and (3) insurance expense.

Problem 4-5

Year-End Analysis of Accounts

An analysis of cash records and account balances of Computer Networking, Inc., for 2006 is as follows:

	Account Balances Jan. 1, 2006	Account Balances Dec. 31, 2006	Cash Received or Paid in 2006
Salaries Payable	$10,750	$12,750	
Unearned Rent	23,250	26,500	
Prepaid Insurance	2,000	3,100	
Paid for salaries			$125,000
Received for rent			64,250
Paid for insurance			12,600

Required:

Determine the amounts that should be included on the 2006 income statement for (1) salaries expense, (2) rent revenue, and (3) insurance expense.

Problem 4-6

Account Classifications and Debit-Credit Relationships

Using the format provided, for each account identify (1) whether the account is a balance sheet (B/S) or an income statement (I/S) account; (2) whether it is an asset (A), a liability (L), an owners' equity (OE), a revenue (R), or an expense (E) account; (3) whether the account is a real or a nominal account; (4) whether the account will be "closed" or left "open" at year-end; and (5) whether the account normally has a debit or a credit balance. The following example is provided:

Account Title	(1) B/S or I/S	(2) A, L, OE, R, E	(3) Real or Nominal	(4) Closed or Open	(5) Debit/ Credit
Cash	B/S	A	Real	Open	Debit

1. Accounts Receivable
2. Accounts Payable
3. Prepaid Insurance
4. Mortgage Payable
5. Rent Expense
6. Sales Revenue
7. Cost of Goods Sold
8. Dividends
9. Capital Stock
10. Inventory
11. Retained Earnings
12. Prepaid Rent
13. Supplies on Hand
14. Utilities Expense
15. Income Taxes Payable
16. Interest Revenue
17. Notes Payable
18. Income Tax Expense
19. Wages Payable
20. Unearned Rent Revenue
21. Land
22. Unearned Consulting Fees
23. Interest Receivable
24. Consulting Fees

Problem 4-7

Closing Entries

The income statement for Joe's Asphalt, Inc., for the year ended December 31, 2006, is as follows:

Joe's Asphalt, Inc.
Income Statement
For the Year Ended December 31, 2006

Sales revenue		$904,000
Less expenses:		
Cost of goods sold	$726,000	
Salaries expense	144,000	
Interest expense	10,500	
Office supplies expense	7,640	
Insurance expense	9,860	
Property tax expense	22,400	
Total expenses		920,400
Net loss		$(16,400)

Required:

Dividends of $36,000 were paid on December 30, 2006.

1. Give the entry required on December 31, 2006, to properly close the income statement accounts.
2. Give the entry required to close the dividends account at December 31, 2006.

Problem 4-8

P.A.S.S.
Power Accounting System Software

Closing Entries

The income statement for Quality Plumbing, Inc., for the year ended December 31, 2006, is as follows:

Quality Plumbing, Inc.
Income Statement
For the Year Ended December 31, 2006

Sales revenue		$623,400
Less expenses:		
Cost of goods sold	$447,000	
Wages expense	98,350	
Utilities expense	1,720	
Insurance expense	2,790	
Property tax expense	2,110	
Rent expense	26,000	
Advertising expense	9,830	
Interest expense	4,300	
Total expenses		592,100
Net income		$ 31,300

Dividends of $23,200 were paid on December 30, 2006.

Required:
1. Give the entry required on December 31, 2006, to properly close the income statement accounts.
2. Give the entry required to close the dividends account at December 31, 2006.

Problem 4-9

Spreadsheet

P.A.S.S.
Power Accounting
System Software

Unifying Concepts: Adjusting and Closing Entries

The unadjusted and adjusted trial balances of White Company as of December 31, 2006, are presented below.

White Company
Trial Balance
December 31, 2006

	Unadjusted		Adjusted	
	Debits	Credits	Debits	Credits
Cash	$ 21,250		$ 21,250	
Accounts Receivable	11,250		11,250	
Supplies on Hand	5,195		3,895	
Prepaid Rent	17,545		7,545	
Prepaid Insurance	1,985		1,100	
Buildings (net)	95,000		95,000	
Land	45,720		45,720	
Accounts Payable		$ 9,350		$ 9,350
Wages Payable				5,700
Income Taxes Payable				580
Interest Payable		450		1,050
Notes Payable		65,000		65,000
Capital Stock		84,320		84,320
Consulting Fees Earned		142,380		142,380
Wages Expense	92,335		98,035	
Rent Expense			10,000	
Interest Expense	3,500		4,100	
Insurance Expense	585		1,470	
Supplies Expenses	4,365		5,665	
Income Tax Expense	2,770		3,350	
Totals	$301,500	$301,500	$308,380	$308,380

Required:

1. Prepare the journal entries that are required to adjust the accounts at December 31, 2006.
2. Prepare the journal entry that is required to close the accounts at December 31, 2006.

Problem 4-10

P.A.S.S.
Power Accounting
System Software

Unifying Concepts: Analysis of Accounts

The bookkeeper for Davey James Company accidentally pressed the wrong computer key and erased the amount of Retained Earnings. You have been asked to analyze the following data and provide some key numbers for the board of directors meeting, which is to take place in 30 minutes. With the exception of Retained Earnings, the following account balances are available at December 31, 2006.

Cash	$ 61,000	Accounts Receivable	$ 49,000
Furniture (net)	40,000	Inventory	160,000
Accounts Payable	120,000	Notes Payable	250,000
Land	260,000	Supplies on Hand	10,000
Buildings (net)	240,000	Capital Stock	300,000
Sales Revenue	415,000	Dividends	20,000
Salaries Expense	50,000	Retained Earnings	?
Cost of Goods Sold	220,000		

Required:
1. Compute the amount of total assets at December 31, 2006.
2. Compute the amount of net income for the year ended December 31, 2006.
3. After all closing entries are made, what is the amount of Retained Earnings at December 31, 2006?
4. What was the beginning Retained Earnings balance at January 1, 2006?

Problem 4-11

P.A.S.S.
Power Accounting
System Software

Unifying Concepts: Analysis and Correction of Errors
At the end of November 2006, the general ledger of Porridge Milling Company showed the following amounts:

Assets	$64,250
Liabilities	28,800
Owners' Equity	62,000

The company's bookkeeper is new on the job and does not have much accounting experience. Because the bookkeeper has made numerous errors, total assets do not equal liabilities plus owners' equity. The following is a list of errors made.

a. Inventory that cost $42,000 was sold, but the entry to record cost of goods sold was not made.
b. Credit sales of $12,100 were posted to the general ledger as $21,100. The accounts receivable were posted correctly.
c. Inventory of $12,500 was purchased on account and received before the end of November, but no entry to record the purchase was made until December.
d. November salaries payable of $5,000 were not recorded until paid in December.
e. Common stock was issued for $18,500 and credited to Accounts Payable.
f. Inventory purchased for $31,050 was incorrectly posted to the asset account as $13,500. No error was made in the liability account.

Required:
Determine the correct balances of assets, liabilities, and owners' equity at the end of November.

Problem 4-12

Spreadsheet

P.A.S.S.
Power Accounting
System Software

Unifying Concepts: The Accounting Cycle
The post-closing trial balance of Anderson Company at December 31, 2005, is shown here.

Anderson Company
Post-Closing Trial Balance
December 31, 2005

	Debits	Credits
Cash	$ 15,000	
Accounts Receivable	20,000	
Inventory	30,000	
Land	150,000	
Accounts Payable		$ 25,000
Notes Payable		35,000
Capital Stock		125,000
Retained Earnings		30,000
Totals	$215,000	$215,000

During 2006, Anderson Company had the following transactions:

a. Inventory purchases were $80,000, all on credit (debit Inventory).
b. An additional $10,000 of capital stock was issued for cash.

(continued)

   c. Merchandise that cost $100,000 was sold for $180,000; $100,000 were credit sales and the balance were cash sales. (Debit Cost of Goods Sold and credit Inventory for sale of merchandise.)

   d. The notes were paid, including $7,000 interest.

   e. $105,000 was collected from customers.

   f. $95,000 was paid to reduce accounts payable.

   g. Salaries expense was $30,000, all paid in cash.

   h. A $10,000 cash dividend was declared and paid.

Required:

1. Prepare journal entries to record each of the 2006 transactions.
2. Set up T-accounts with the proper balances at January 1, 2006, and post the journal entries to the T-accounts.
3. Prepare an income statement for the year ended December 31, 2006, and a balance sheet as of that date. Also prepare a statement of retained earnings.
4. Prepare the entries necessary to close the nominal accounts, including Dividends.
5. Post the closing entries to the ledger accounts [label (i) and (j)] and prepare a post-closing trial balance at December 31, 2006.

d iscussion cases

Case 4-1

Using Financial Statements for Investment Decisions

Several doctors are considering the purchase of a small real estate business as an investment. Because you have some training in the mechanics of the accounting cycle, they have hired you to review the real estate company's accounting records and to prepare a balance sheet and an income statement for their use. In analyzing various business documents, you verify the following data.

The account balances at the beginning of the current year were as follows:

Cash in Bank	$ 7,800
Notes Receivable (from Current Owner)	10,000
Supplies on Hand	750
Prepaid Office Rent	4,500
Accounts Payable	450
Owners' Equity	22,600

During the current year, the following summarized transactions took place:

   a. The owner paid $1,200 to the business to cover the interest on the note receivable ($10,000 × 0.12 × 1 year). Nothing was paid on the principal.

   b. Real estate commissions earned during the year totaled $45,500. Of this amount, $1,000 has not been received by year-end.

   c. The company purchased $500 of supplies during the year. A count at year-end shows $300 worth still on hand.

   d. The $4,500 paid for office rental was for 18 months, beginning in January of this year.

   e. Utilities paid during the year amounted to $1,500.

   f. During the year, $400 of accounts payable were paid; the balance in Accounts Payable at year-end is $300, with the adjustment being debited to Miscellaneous Office Expense.

   g. The owner paid himself $1,500 a month as a salary and paid a part-time secretary $2,400 for the year. (Ignore payroll taxes.)

On the basis of the above data, prepare a balance sheet and an income statement for the real estate business. Does the business appear profitable? Does the balance sheet raise any questions or concerns? What other information might the doctors want to consider in making this investment decision?

Case 4-2

Accounting and Ethical Issues Involving the Closing Process

Silva and Wanita Rodriques are the owners of Year-Round Landscape, Inc., a small landscape and yard service business in southern California. The business is three years old and has grown significantly, especially during the past year. To sustain this growth, Year-Round Landscape must expand operations.

In the past, the Rodriques have been able to secure funds for the business from personal resources. Now those resources are exhausted, and the Rodriques are seeking a loan from a local bank.

To satisfy bank requirements, Year-Round Landscape, Inc., must provide a set of financial statements, including comparative income statements showing the growth in earnings over the past three years. In analyzing the records, Silva notices that the nominal accounts have not yet been closed for this year. Furthermore, Silva is aware of a major contract that is to be signed on January 3, only three days after the December 31 year-end for the business. Silva suggests that the closing process be delayed one week so that this major contract can be included in this year's operating results. Silva estimates that this contract will increase current year earnings by 20%.

What accounting issues are involved in this case? What are the ethical issues?

Case 4-3

Wrestling with Your Conscience and GAAP

You are the controller for South Valley Industries. Your assistant has just completed the financial statements for the current year and has given them to you for review. A copy of the statements also has been given to the president of the company. The income statement reports a net income for the year of $50,000 and earnings per share of $2.50.

In reviewing the statements, you realize the assistant neglected to record adjusting entries. After making the necessary adjustments, the company shows a net loss of $10,000. The difference is due to an unusually large amount of unrecorded expenses at year-end. You realize that these expenses are not likely to be found by the independent auditors.

You wonder if it would be better to delay the recording of the expenses until the first part of the subsequent year in order to avoid reporting a net loss on the income statement for the current year. A significant increase in revenues is expected in the coming year, and the expenses in question could be "absorbed" by the higher revenues.

What issues are involved in this case? What course of action would you take?

Case 4-4

Making Sure Operating Results Are Accurate

Dian Karen and Kathy Gillen are considering forming a company to purchase a small business that specializes in interior decoration services. The business records show a modest profit over each of the past five years (approximately $5,000 net income per year). However, the past year's operating results appear to be much better, as shown by the unaudited income statement.

(continued)

Fashion Design, Inc.
Income Statement
For the Year Ended December 31, 2006

Revenues:		
Consulting revenues	$51,000	
Commissions on furnishings sold	18,000	
Total revenues		$69,000
Expenses:		
Advertising expense	$ 1,200	
Rent expense	4,800	
Salaries expense	36,000	
Supplies expense	500	
Utilities expense	1,800	
Other expenses	1,500	45,800
Income before taxes		$23,200
Income taxes (estimated at 25%)		5,800
Net income		$17,400

EPS: $17,400 ÷ 1,000 shares = $17.40 per share

In an attempt to verify what appears to be unusually high net income for 2006, Karen and Gillen hire a CPA to audit the records. The CPA discovers the following:

a. The company pays salaries on the 1st and 15th of each month. Salaries amounting to $2,500 have been earned by employees by December 31 but will not be paid until January 1. No adjusting entry has been made.

b. Of the $18,000 in commissions received by December 31, 30% will not be earned until completion of a job in mid-February of 2007. All commissions received have been recorded as revenues.

c. A $10,000 payment was received on November 1 for a consulting assignment that is only one-half earned at December 31. The total amount was credited to Consulting Revenues when received.

d. The rent is $400 per month and must be paid in advance on a one-year lease. A check for $4,800 was given to the landlord on March 1, 2006, and recorded as rent expense on that date.

According to the CPA, except for these data, the income statement appears to accurately reflect the operating results of Fashion Design, Inc.

Answer the following questions:

1. Do the 2006 operating results offer encouragement to Karen and Gillen as potential investors? Explain.

2. What adjustments (if any) are required to make the income statement more accurately reflect the results of operations for the year?

3. What is the impact on the balance sheet (if any) of the data discovered by the CPA?

judgment calls

Judgment 4-1

You Decide: Should deferred compensation packages be disclosed in the footnotes to the financial statements, or should they be recorded as liabilities?

Recently, corporate accounting scandals have brought about an increased scrutiny of executive compensation. Companies are being criticized for their role in accounting for stock options, inflated salaries, and personal loans to executives. However, there is one hidden treasure that should not be overlooked: deferred compensation packages for executives. These are retirement packages that will allow executives to set aside, pretax, up to 100% of their cash compensation, earning as much as a 10% return. For many companies, these deferred compensation packages represent corporate liabilities that are not in the financial statements or even disclosed in the notes. How should they be reported and/or disclosed, if at all?

Judgment 4-2

You Decide: Should intellectual properties be recorded as assets on the balance sheet or disclosed in the notes to the financial statements?

Intellectual property refers to creations of the mind. Examples include inventions, symbols, names, images, logos, and designs used in commerce. For example, the annual reports for a mutual fund company will often list all fund managers with their associated professional credentials, academic history, and honors they have received. This provides useful information to the investors and helps individuals realize the value of good fund managers. Is there a way to "quantify" this type of information so that it can appear in the balance sheet as an asset to the firm?

Judgment 4-3

You Decide: Can wages payable be deferred to make the financial statements look better?

It is early December and you have just been hired as an accountant for a local computer hardware store. Business is expanding due to the increased number of sales reps your boss just hired. Your boss is excited about expanding the business into other nearby communities, but will need a loan from the bank to do so. He has hired you to clean up the books and get the company's financial information ready so he can present it to the bank's loan officer after the first of the year. On December 30, your boss asks you not to record the sales force's wages for the month of December because he won't be able to pay them until mid-January. He wants the financial statements to be in good shape when he visits the loan officer. What should you do?

Competency Enhancement Opportunities

▶ **Analyzing Real Company Information**
▶ **International Case**
▶ **Ethics Case**
▶ **Writing Assignment**

▶ **The Debate**
▶ **Cumulative Spreadsheet Project**
▶ **Internet Search**

The following additional assignments provide opportunities for students to develop critical thinking, ethical perspectives, oral and written communication skills, experience with electronic research, and teamwork through group and business activities.

▷ *Analyzing Real Company Information*

Analyzing 4-1 (Microsoft)

Using MICROSOFT's 2002 Form 10-K contained in Appendix A, answer the following questions:

1. Microsoft discloses that as of June 30, 2002, the company had received cash of $5.920 billion that had not been earned as of that date and had been classified as short-term unearned revenue. In addition, Microsoft reported $1.823 billion of long-term unearned revenue. Accordingly, the company made an adjusting entry to recognize the unearned revenue. Provide the adjusting entry that was made by Microsoft.
2. Read the note related to Microsoft's unearned revenue and determine what this amount relates to—volume licensing programs, undelivered elements, operating systems, and so forth.

Analyzing 4-2 (Home Depot)

Selected financial statement information for HOME DEPOT is given in the table below. Using this information, answer the following questions.

(all numbers in millions)
Retained Earnings balance—01/30/2000 $7,941 million

	Net Income	Dividends
For year ended January 28, 2001	$2,581	$371
For year ended February 3, 2002	3,044	396
For year ended February 2, 2003	3,644	492

1. Compute Home Depot's Retained Earnings balance at the end of each year.
2. Divide dividends into net income for each year. The result is termed the "dividend payout ratio." Did Home Depot's dividend payout ratio increase or decrease over time?

Analyzing 4-3 (Campbell Soup)

Information from the 2002 income statement for CAMPBELL SOUP COMPANY is shown below.

(in millions, except per-share amounts)	2002	2001	2000
Net Sales	$6,133	$5,771	$5,626
Costs and expenses			
Cost of products sold	3,443	3,132	3,088
Marketing and selling expenses	1,069	886	801
Administrative expenses	421	372	319
Research and development expenses	77	63	64
Other expenses	139	124	89
Total costs and expenses	5,149	4,577	4,361
Earnings Before Interest and Taxes	$ 984	$1,194	$1,265
Interest expense	(190)	(219)	(198)
Interest income	4	12	10
Earnings before taxes	798	987	1,077
Taxes on earnings	273	338	363
Net Earnings	$ 525	$ 649	$ 714

Using the information from the income statement, perform the following:

1. Prepare the entries made by Campbell to close the revenue and expense accounts to Retained Earnings.
2. Campbell Soup paid dividends of $258 million in 2002. Provide the entry made to close the dividends account to Retained Earnings.
3. If the beginning balance in Campbell's Retained Earnings was $4,651 million, what would the ending balance be after the above closing entries have been posted?

▶ *International Case*

International

Exchange Rate Adjustments

Given the international economy in which many firms operate, it is not unusual for companies to have transactions with companies in foreign countries. Relatedly, it is becoming common for some of those transactions to be denominated in a foreign currency. That is, if a company in the United States makes a purchase from a company in Japan, it is possible that the U.S. company will have to pay Japanese yen when the invoice comes due.

For example, suppose American, Inc., purchased inventory from Japan, Inc., on December 15, 2005. Japan, Inc., expects to receive 1,000,000 Japanese yen in 30 days. To record a journal entry for this purchase, you would need to know what 1,000,000 yen are worth today. Suppose that on December 15, 2005, one yen is worth $0.07 (this is called an exchange rate). What journal entry would be made on American, Inc.'s books?

Since exchange rates change every day, the amount of U.S. dollars to be paid on January 15, 2006, will likely be different than the originally recorded $70,000. In addition, to correctly state the liability on December 31, 2005, an adjustment will be required. Suppose that at year-end, one Japanese yen is worth $0.08. What adjusting entry would be made to reflect this change in exchange rates as of December 31, 2005? (*Hint:* The accounts being adjusted with this journal entry will be the accounts payable account and an exchange gain or loss.)

When the invoice is paid on January 15, 2006, it is likely that the number of U.S. dollars required to purchase 1,000,000 Japanese yen will again have changed. Suppose exchange rates have increased to $0.09. Provide the journal entry to pay the invoice.

▶ *Ethics Case*

Do Two Wrongs Make a Right?

Jex Varner, chief financial officer of Wyndam, Inc., is involved in a meeting with the firm's newly hired external auditors, Ernst & Price. The external auditors have noted several adjusting entries that they believe should be reflected in the current period's financial statements. Specifically, there are questions regarding $400,000 of cash that has been received (and recorded as revenue) but not yet earned. The auditors feel that this amount should be recognized as a liability.

Jex counters that the firm's policy has always been to recognize revenue when the cash is received. He states that $350,000 of cash was received in December of last year, earned in January, and no adjustment was made. To be consistent, he continues, he doesn't believe any adjustments should be made this year.

As a member of the external auditing team, do you agree with Jex's reasoning? If you think that an adjustment needs to be made, what journal entry would you propose? What should be done about the $350,000 that has been earned this year even though the cash was received last year?

▷ *Writing Assignment*

Are Adjusting Entries More Trouble Than They Are Worth?

You are taking an introductory accounting class. You think that making regular journal entries is not too difficult, but making adjusting entries is still a bit of a mystery. You have found that your answers to homework questions on adjusting entries are incorrect at least half the time. You mentioned your difficulties to the other members of your study group, and they all agreed—adjusting entries are brutal. As you and your study colleagues shared your frustration with adjusting entries, the following consensus formed: adjusting entries are more trouble than they are worth. You were selected by your study group to pass this sentiment along to your accounting instructor. She agreed that adjusting entries can be difficult, but she insisted that they are worth the effort. She has now given you the following writing assignment: write a one-page paper describing the value of adjusting entries.

▷ *The Debate*

No More Debits and Credits!

Some accounting academics and professionals argue that debits and credits are relics from the 15th century. Advocates of this position feel that computer spreadsheets and accounting software packages have made debits and credits obsolete, and accountants should no longer have to be constrained by the use of these terms. For example, most popular computer financial software packages (like Intuit's Quicken and Microsoft's Money) allow users to create balance sheets and statements of cash flows without ever learning the terms *debit* and *credit*.

Divide your group into two teams.

- One team is to prepare a five-minute oral presentation explaining why the use of the terms *debit* and *credit* is still useful.
- The second team is to prepare a five-minute presentation explaining why current computer technology allows us to do away with the terms *debit* and *credit*.

▷ *Cumulative Spreadsheet Project*

This spreadsheet assignment is a continuation of the spreadsheet assignments given in earlier chapters. If you completed those spreadsheets, you have a head start on this one.

1. Refer back to the balance sheet and income statement created using the financial statement numbers for Handyman Company for 2006 [given in part (1) of the Cumulative Spreadsheet Project assignment in Chapter 2]. With these historical numbers for 2006 as a starting point, Handyman wishes to prepare a forecasted balance sheet and a forecasted income statement for 2007. In preparing the forecasted financial statements for 2007, consider the following additional information:
    a. Sales in 2007 are expected to increase by 40% over 2006 sales of $700.
    b. In the forecasted balance sheet for 2007, cash, receivables, inventory, and accounts payable will all increase at the same rate as sales (40%) relative to 2006. These increases occur because, with the planned 40% increase in the volume of business and no plans to significantly change its methods of operation, Handyman will probably also experience a 40% increase in the levels of its current operating assets and liabilities.
    c. In 2007, Handyman expects to acquire new property, plant, and equipment costing $80.
    d. Accumulated depreciation is the cumulative amount of depreciation expense that Handyman has reported over its years in business. Thus, the forecasted amount of

accumulated depreciation for 2007 can be computed as accumulated depreciation as of the end of 2006 plus the forecasted depreciation expense for 2007.

e. New short-term loans payable will be acquired in an amount sufficient to make Handyman's current ratio (current assets divided by current liabilities) in 2007 exactly equal to 2.0.

f. No new long-term debt will be acquired in 2007.

g. No cash dividends will be paid in 2007. Remember that the amount of retained earnings at the end of any year is the beginning retained earnings amount plus net income minus dividends.

h. In this exercise, the forecasted amount of paid-in capital is the "plug" figure. In other words, the forecasted balance in paid-in capital at the end of 2007 is the amount necessary to make the forecasted balance sheet balance such that forecasted total assets equal forecasted total liabilities. A key reason for preparing forecasted financial statements is to identify in advance whether any additional financing will be required.

i. The $160 in operating expenses reported in 2006 breaks down as follows: $5 depreciation expense, $155 other operating expenses.

j. In the forecasted income statement for 2007, cost of goods sold and other operating expenses will both increase at the same rate as sales (40%) relative to 2006. This is another way of saying that the amount of these expenses, relative to the amount of sales, will probably stay about the same year to year unless Handyman plans to significantly change the way it does business.

k. The amount of Handyman's depreciation expense is determined by how much property, plant, and equipment the company has. In 2006, Handyman had $5 of depreciation expense on $199 of property, plant, and equipment, meaning that depreciation was equal to 2.5% ($5/$199) of the amount of property, plant, and equipment. It is expected that the same relationship will hold in 2007.

l. Interest expense depends on how much interest-bearing debt a company has. In 2006, Handyman reported interest expense of $9 on long-term debt of $207. (*Note:* To simplify this exercise, we will ignore interest expense on the short-term loan payable.) Because Handyman is expected to have the same amount of long-term debt in 2007, our best guess is that interest expense will remain the same.

m. Income tax expense is determined by how much pretax income a company has. And, the most reasonable assumption to make is that a company's tax rate, equal to income tax expense divided by pretax income, will stay constant from year to year. Handyman's income tax rate in 2006 was 33% ($4/$12).

2. Repeat (1) assuming that forecasted sales growth in 2007 is 20% instead of 40%. Clearly state any assumptions that you make.

▷ *Internet Search*

General Motors

We began this chapter with an introduction to GENERAL MOTORS; we will end this chapter with a look at its Web site. Access GM's Web site at **http://www.gm.com**. Sometimes Web addresses change, so if this address doesn't work, access the Web site for this textbook (**http://albrecht .swlearning.com**) for an updated link to GM.

Once you have located the company's Web site, answer the following questions:

1. Locate GM's financial statements. Write down the path you took to get to the statements. In your opinion, is GM's Web site easy to navigate relative to others you have accessed?

(continued)

2. Locate GM's statement of stockholders' equity for the most recent year. In the column associated with Retained Earnings, determine what factors caused retained earnings to change for the most recent year.

3. Access the company's note information relating to accounting estimates. Since these estimates result in most adjusting entries, identify who makes these estimates and, as a result, who is responsible for making the adjusting entries.

4. As pointed out in the chapter, revenue is recognized when it is earned and a promise of payment has been received. Using the note relating to revenue recognition, identify when GM recognizes revenue for its various segments within the firm.

c h a p t e r

5

Introduction to Financial Statement Analysis

After studying this chapter, you should be able to:

Learning Objectives

1 Explain the purpose of financial statement analysis.

2 Understand the relationships between financial statement numbers and use ratios in analyzing and describing a company's performance.

3 Use common-size financial statements to perform comparison of financial statements across years and between companies.

4 Understand the DuPont framework and how return on equity can be decomposed into its profitability, efficiency, and leverage components.

5 Use cash flow information to evaluate cash flow ratios.

6 Understand the limitations of financial statement analysis.

In 1987, IBM was the most valuable company in the world, worth an estimated $105.8 billion. By the end of 1992, IBM had an estimated value of $28.8 billion. This decline in value can be traced to a strategic error made by IBM in the early 1980s. Prior to 1981, IBM was the major player in the computer market and was the primary provider of computers for government, universities, and businesses. At this time, believe it or not, virtually no computers were available at an affordable price for individuals. Then, in 1981, IBM introduced its personal computer (IBM PC), and it quickly established the standard by which other PCs would be measured. However, IBM elected to leave the software development for PCs to other companies. Instead of developing its own disk operating system (DOS), IBM elected to use a DOS developed by a small company located in Seattle—MICROSOFT.[1]

Microsoft was founded in 1975 by Bill Gates and Paul Allen.[2] When they founded Microsoft, Gates and Allen envisioned that computers would eventually find their way into everyday life (contrary to IBM's prediction in the 1950s when one IBM executive forecast the total worldwide demand for computers to be about five). While IBM's performance floundered in the mid- and late-1980s, Microsoft demonstrated an amazing ability to become a major player in practically every aspect of the computer software market—from operating systems to the Internet to networks to spreadsheets and word processors.

With Microsoft's many accomplishments comes the question: "Just how successful is the company?" The answer to that question depends on how you define "success." Measured in terms of number of employees, Microsoft has grown from just 32 employees in 1981 when IBM elected to use Microsoft's DOS to 50,500 as of the June 30, 2002, fiscal year. In terms of social impact, Microsoft and its employees donate millions of dollars each year to such charitable causes as Special Olympics, Boys and Girls Clubs, and the United Negro College Fund. Microsoft also supports elementary and high schools throughout the country in their efforts to incorporate technology into the curriculum, and the company has established scholarship programs to encourage minorities and women to pursue careers in computer science and related technical fields. In addition, Bill Gates and his wife Melinda have started a foundation dedicated primarily to health and education. Thus far they have contributed several billion dollars to their foundation.

FYI:

In fact, many people are of the opinion that Microsoft has succeeded too well. Several of Microsoft's competitors allege that Microsoft is involved in monopolistic practices that stifle competition.

In terms of stock price, Microsoft's per-share stock price (adjusted for stock splits) has gone from $0.10 in 1986 to almost $26 in April of 2003 (see Exhibit 1). But as the graph illustrates, Microsoft's stock price is down from its historic high of over $58 per share in 1999. An analysis of Microsoft's financial statements reveals some of the reasons for the declining stock price. That is the topic of this chapter—an introduction to financial statement analysis. With some basic analysis tools (called ratios), we will be able to conduct some fundamental analysis of a company's financial statements. Our analysis will provide us with insights as to a company's performance and will help us identify areas of concern. Keep in mind that this is merely an introduction to financial statement analysis. There are entire textbooks devoted to the analysis of financial statements. Our objective here is to expose you to some of the basic tools to help you start to understand what financial statements can tell us about the operations of a business. To illustrate the analysis techniques introduced in this chapter, we will reference the financial statement of Microsoft included in Appendix A.

---

1 The decision to have another company develop the software for its personal computer was not IBM's only strategic error. At the same time, IBM decided to use another company's microprocessors—the "brains" of the computer. As a result, another successful company was born—INTEL. IBM lost the opportunity to dominate the software market as well as the computer chip market. By September 2003, Microsoft, Intel, and IBM had market values exceeding $317 billion, $187 billion, and $158 billion, respectively.

2 Everybody knows Bill Gates, but few people know about Paul Allen. Allen was Microsoft's head of research and new product development until 1983 when a serious illness caused him to leave the company. He now spends much of his time investing in technology companies and watching the Seattle Seahawks, a professional football team, and the Portland Trailblazers, a professional basketball team, both of which he owns.

Exhibit 1: History of Microsoft's Stock Price per Share

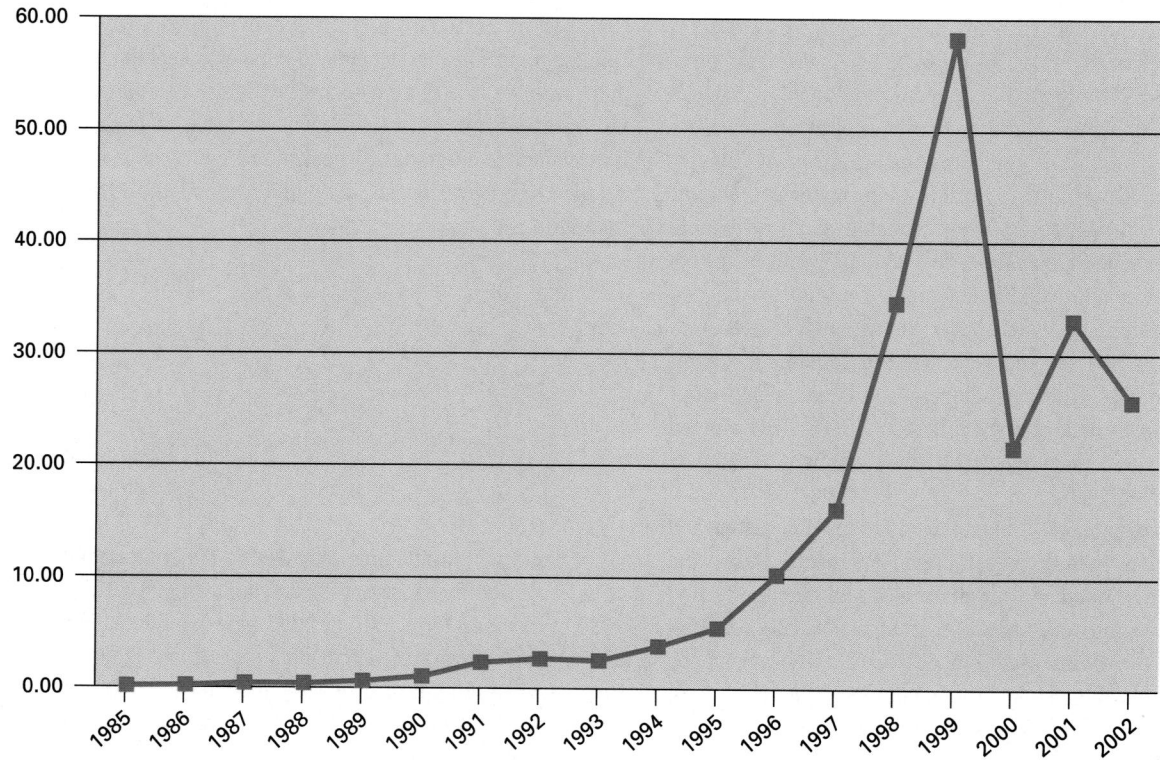

The Need for Financial Statement Analysis

I Explain the purpose of financial statement analysis.

Consider the following questions related to financial statement information for MICROSOFT in 2002:

- Microsoft's net income in 2002 was $7.829 billion. That seems like a lot, but does it represent a large amount for a company the size of Microsoft?
- Total assets for Microsoft at the end of 2002 were $67.646 billion. Given the volume of business that Microsoft does, is this amount of assets too much, too little, or just right?
- By the end of 2002, Microsoft's liabilities totaled $15.466 billion. Is this level of debt too much for Microsoft?

The important point to recognize is that just having the financial statement numbers is not enough to answer the questions that financial statement users want answered. Without further analysis, the raw numbers themselves don't tell much of a story.

financial statement analysis The examination of both the relationships among financial statement numbers and the trends in those numbers over time.

Financial statement analysis involves the examination of both the relationships among financial statement numbers and the trends in those numbers over time. One purpose of financial statement analysis is to use the past performance of a company to predict how it will do in the future. Another purpose is to evaluate the performance of a company with an eye toward identifying problem areas. In sum, financial statement analysis is both diagnosis—identifying where a firm has problems—and prognosis—predicting how a firm will perform in the future.

financial ratios Relationships between financial statement amounts.

Relationships between financial statement amounts are called **financial ratios**. Net income divided by sales, for example, is a financial ratio called return on sales, which tells you how many pennies of profit a company makes on each dollar of sales. The return on sales for Microsoft is 27.6%, meaning that Microsoft makes 28 cents' worth of profit for every dollar of product sold. There are hundreds of different financial ratios, each shedding light on a different aspect of the health of a company.

Exhibit 2 illustrates how financial statement analysis fits into the decision cycle of a company's management. Notice that the preparation of the financial statements is just the starting point of the process. After the statements are prepared, they are analyzed using techniques akin to those to be introduced in this chapter. Analysis of the summary information in the financial statements usually doesn't provide detailed answers to management's questions, but it does identify areas in which further data should be gathered. Decisions are then made and implemented, and the accounting system captures the results of these decisions so that a new set of financial statements can be prepared. The process then repeats itself.

For external users of financial statements, such as investors and creditors, financial statement analysis plays the same role in the decision-making process. Whereas management uses the analysis to help in making operating, investing, and financing decisions, investors and creditors analyze financial statements to decide whether to invest in, or loan money to, a company.

In analyzing a company's financial statements, merely computing a list of financial ratios is not enough. Most pieces of information are meaningful only when they can be compared with some benchmark. For example, knowing that Microsoft's return on sales in 2002 was 27.6% tells you a little, but you can evaluate the ratio value much better if you know that Microsoft's return on sales was 29.0% and 41.0% in 2001 and 2000, respectively. In short, the usefulness of financial ratios is greatly enhanced when they are compared with past values and with values for other firms in the same industry.

TO SUMMARIZE: Financial statement analysis is used to predict a company's future profitability and cash flows from its past performance and to evaluate the performance of a company with an eye toward identifying problem areas. The informativeness of financial ratios is greatly enhanced when they are compared with past values and with values for other firms in the same industry.

Exhibit 2: The Need for Financial Statement Analysis

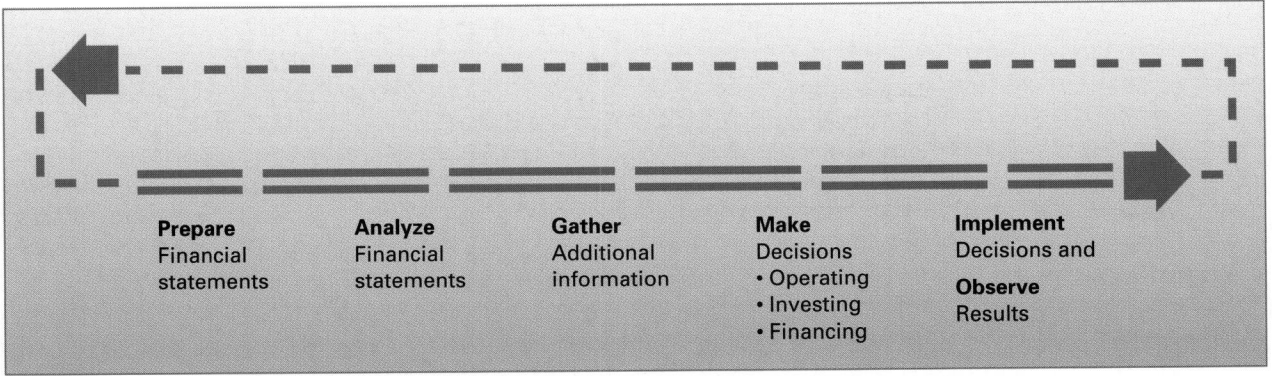

Prepare Financial statements | Analyze Financial statements | Gather Additional information | Make Decisions • Operating • Investing • Financing | Implement Decisions and Observe Results

Market Efficiency: Can Financial Statement Analysis Help You Win in the Stock Market? An efficient market is one in which information is reflected rapidly in prices. For example, if the real estate market in a city is efficient, then news of an impending layoff at a major employer in the city should result quickly in lower housing prices because of an anticipated decrease in demand. The major stock exchanges in the United States often are considered to be efficient markets in the sense that information about specific companies or about the economy in general is reflected almost immediately in stock prices. One implication of market efficiency is that because current stock prices reflect all available information, future movements in stock prices should be unpredictable.

It seems clear that capital markets in the United States are efficient in a general sense, but accumulated evidence suggests the existence of a number of puzzling "anomalies" in the form of predictability in the pattern of stock returns. For example, prices tend to continue to drift upward for weeks or months after favorable earnings news is released. In addition, prices continue to climb for at least a year after a stock split is announced.

Widely Used Financial Ratios

2 Understand the relationships between financial statement numbers and use ratios in analyzing and describing a company's performance.

Before diving into a comprehensive treatment of financial ratio analysis, we'll first get our feet wet with the most widely used ratios. Familiarity with financial ratios will allow you to hold your own in most casual business conversations and will enable you to understand most ratios used in the popular business press. Data from Microsoft's 2002 financial statements will be used to illustrate the ratio calculations. The data are displayed in Exhibit 3.

Debt Ratio

debt ratio A measure of leverage, computed by dividing total liabilities by total assets.

Comparing the amount of liabilities with the amount of assets indicates the extent to which a company has borrowed money to leverage the owners' investments and increase the size of the company. One frequently used measure of leverage is the **debt ratio**, computed as total liabilities divided by total assets. An intuitive interpretation of the debt ratio is that it represents the proportion of borrowed funds used to acquire the company's assets. For Microsoft, the debt ratio is computed as shown on the following page.

Exhibit 3: Selected Financial Data for Microsoft for 2002

Current assets	$ 48,576*
Total assets	67,646
Current liabilities	12,744
Total liabilities	15,466
Stockholders' equity	52,180
Sales	28,365
Net income	7,829
Market value of shares	293,137

*All numbers are in millions of dollars.

From an accounting standpoint, market efficiency relates to the usefulness of so-called "fundamental analysis." Fundamental analysis is the practice of using financial data to calculate the underlying value of a firm and using this underlying value to identify over- and underpriced stocks. The notion of fundamental analysis is in conflict with market efficiency, because the analysis works only if current stock prices do not fully reflect all available accounting information. For this reason, fundamental analysis frequently has been regarded with skepticism by academics. However, some research has suggested that accounting data may be useful in predicting future stock returns. Ou and Penman and Holthausen and Larcker demonstrate that financial ratios derived from publicly available financial statements can be used to successfully forecast stock returns for the coming year. So contrary to what is expected of an efficient stock market, it looks like you can use publicly available accounting data to make money in the U.S. stock market.

Sources: Jane A. Ou and Stephen H. Penman, "Financial Statement Analysis and the Prediction of Stock Returns," *Journal of Accounting and Economics* (November 1989): 295.

Robert W. Holthausen and David F. Larcker, "The Prediction of Stock Returns Using Financial Statement Information," *Journal of Accounting and Economics* (June 1992): 373.

$$\text{Debt Ratio: } \frac{\text{Total Liabilities}}{\text{Total Assets}} = \frac{\$15,466}{\$67,646} = 22.9\%$$

Caution

The debt ratio is often confused with the debt-to-equity ratio and the asset-to-equity ratio. Each of these ratios is a measure of a company's leverage. However, each is computed slightly differently. Make sure when discussing a leverage ratio, it is understood which one is being used.

In other words, Microsoft borrowed 22.9% of the money it needed to buy its assets.

Is 22.9% a good or bad debt ratio, or is it impossible to tell? If you are a banker thinking of lending money to Microsoft, you want Microsoft to have a low debt ratio because a smaller amount of other liabilities increases your chances of being repaid. If you are a Microsoft stockholder, you want a higher debt ratio because you want the company to add borrowed funds to your investment dollars to expand the business. Thus, there is some happy middle ground where the debt ratio is not too high for creditors but not too low for investors. The general rule of thumb across all industries is that debt ratios should be around 50%, but this benchmark varies widely from one industry to the next. By comparison, APPLE COMPUTER's 2002 debt ratio was 35.0%.

Current Ratio

liquidity A company's ability to pay its debts in the short run.

current ratio A measure of the liquidity of a business; equal to current assets divided by current liabilities.

An important concern about any company is its **liquidity**, or ability to pay its debts in the short run. If a firm can't meet its obligations in the short run, it may not survive to enjoy the long run. The most commonly used measure of liquidity is the **current ratio**, which is a comparison of current assets (cash, receivables, and inventory) with current liabilities. Current ratio is computed by dividing total current assets by total current liabilities. For Microsoft, the current ratio is computed as follows:

$$\text{Current Ratio: } \frac{\text{Current Assets}}{\text{Current Liabilities}} = \frac{\$48,576}{\$12,744} = 3.812$$

Historically, the rule of thumb has been that a current ratio below 2 suggests the possibility of liquidity problems. However, advances in information technology have enabled companies to be much more effective in minimizing the need to hold cash, inventories, and other

Exhibit 4: Current Ratios for Selected U.S. Companies

	2002
Coca-Cola	1.00
Delta Air Lines	0.60
Dow Chemical	1.32
McDonald's	0.71
Wal-Mart	0.93

current assets. As a result, current ratios for successful companies these days are frequently less than 1. Current ratios for selected U.S. companies are shown in Exhibit 4.

Return on Sales

return on sales A measure of the amount of profit earned per dollar of sales, computed by dividing net income by sales.

As mentioned earlier, Microsoft makes 27.6 cents of profit on each dollar of sales. This ratio is called **return on sales** and, using Microsoft's numbers, is computed as follows:

$$\text{Return on Sales:} \quad \frac{\text{Net Income}}{\text{Sales}} = \frac{\$7,829}{\$28,365} = 27.6\%$$

As with all ratios, the return-on-sales value for Microsoft must be evaluated in light of the appropriate industry. For example, the 2001 return on sales for Microsoft was 29%. At the other end of the spectrum, return on sales in the supermarket industry is frequently between 1% and 2%. These values, because they come from outside Microsoft's industry, do not really provide a useful benchmark against which Microsoft's return on sales can be compared. A better comparison for Microsoft is the 2002 return-on-sales value for Apple Computer, which was 1.1%. So, it appears that return on sales for Microsoft was substantially above the industry average in 2002; why this happened will be examined later in the chapter.

Asset Turnover

asset turnover A measure of company efficiency, computed by dividing sales by total assets.

Microsoft's balance sheet reveals total assets of $67.646 billion. Are those assets being used efficiently? A financial ratio that gives an overall measure of company efficiency is called **asset turnover** and is computed as follows:

$$\text{Asset Turnover:} \quad \frac{\text{Sales}}{\text{Total Assets}} = \frac{\$28,365}{\$67,646} = 0.42$$

Microsoft's asset turnover ratio of 0.42 means that for each dollar of assets Microsoft is able to generate $0.42 in sales. The higher the asset turnover ratio, the more efficient the company is at using its assets to generate sales. In evaluating Microsoft's asset turnover, note that asset turnover for Apple Computer in 2002 was 0.91, indicating that Microsoft was less efficient than its competitor at using its assets to generate sales.

Caution

The computed asset turnover ratio can be misleading, as discussed in the concluding section of this chapter, because not all economic assets are recorded as assets on the balance sheet. Thus, the denominator of the ratio can be understated, sometimes very significantly.

Return on Equity

What investors really want to know is not how many pennies of profit are earned on a dollar of sales or what the current ratio is—they want to know how much

return on equity A measure of the amount of profit earned per dollar of investment, computed by dividing net income by equity.

profit they earn for each dollar they invest. This amount, called **return on equity**, is the overall measure of the performance of a company. Return on equity for Microsoft is computed as follows:

$$\text{Return on Equity: } \frac{\text{Net Income}}{\text{Stockholders' Equity}} = \frac{\$7,829}{\$52,180} = 15.0\%$$

Microsoft's return on equity of 15% means that 15 cents of profit were earned for each dollar of stockholder investment in 2002. By comparison, Apple Computer's return on equity in 2002 was 1.6%. Good companies typically have return on equity values between 15% and 25%. Return on equity is the fundamental measure of overall company performance and forms the basis of the DuPont framework discussed later on.

Price-Earnings Ratio

price-earnings ratio A measure of growth potential, earnings stability, and management capabilities; computed by dividing market value of a company by net income.

If a company earned $100 this year, how much should I pay to buy that company? If I expect the company to make more in the future, I'd be willing to pay a higher price than if I expected the company to make less. Also, I'd probably be willing to pay a bit more for a stable company than for one that experiences wild swings in earnings. The relationship between the market value of a company and that company's current earnings is measured by the **price-earnings ratio**, or PE ratio, and is computed by dividing the market value of the shares outstanding by the company's net income.[3] Microsoft's PE ratio at the end of 2002 was:

$$\text{PE Ratio: } \frac{\text{Market Value of Shares}}{\text{Net Income}} = \frac{\$293,137}{\$7,829} = 37.4$$

In the United States, PE ratios typically range between 5 and 30. High PE ratios are associated with firms for which strong growth is predicted in the future. YAHOO, for example, has one of the highest PE ratios in the world, but it is not found on the list of companies with high net income. The reason Yahoo is valued so highly is that it is expected to continue to grow so rapidly in the future that its current income is small compared with what investors are expecting in the future. This expected future growth is reflected in Yahoo's PE ratio of 113. Sample PE ratios for several companies as of May 14, 2003, are included in Exhibit 5.

A summary of the financial ratios discussed in this section is presented in Exhibit 6.

Note that the PE ratio is different from the other ratios in that it is not the ratio of two financial statement numbers. Instead, the PE ratio is a comparison of a financial statement number to a market value number. The large majority

network exercises

PE Ratios

Net Work:

To see what each company's latest PE ratio is, go to **http://finance.yahoo.com** and enter the stock symbol for each company in Exhibit 5. A chart for each company will provide interesting financial information about the company's stock price performance.

Exhibit 5: Sample PE Ratios for Several U.S. Companies

Company Name	Stock Symbol	PE Ratio
Yahoo!	Yhoo	112.9
Wal-Mart	wmt	29.8
Berkshire Hathaway	brka	22.2
Home Depot	hd	19.2
Sears	s	6.1

3 The PE ratio can be equivalently computed using per share amounts: PR ratio = Market price per share/Earnings per share.

Exhibit 6: Summary of Selected Financial Ratios

1. Debt ratio	$\dfrac{\text{Total liabilities}}{\text{Total assets}}$	Percentage of funds needed to purchase assets that were obtained through borrowing.
2. Current ratio	$\dfrac{\text{Current assets}}{\text{Current liabilities}}$	Measure of liquidity; number of times current assets could cover current liabilities.
3. Return on sales	$\dfrac{\text{Net income}}{\text{Sales}}$	Number of pennies earned during the year on each dollar of sales.
4. Asset turnover	$\dfrac{\text{Sales}}{\text{Total assets}}$	Number of dollars of sales during the year generated by each dollar of assets.
5. Return on equity (ROE)	$\dfrac{\text{Net income}}{\text{Stockholders' equity}}$	Number of pennies earned during the year on each dollar invested.
6. Price-earnings ratio (PE)	$\dfrac{\text{Market value of shares}}{\text{Net income}}$	Amount investors are willing to pay for each dollar of earnings; indication of growth potential.

of financial ratios, however, are (1) a comparison of two amounts found in the same financial statement (such as return on sales, which compares two income statement amounts) or (2) a comparison of two amounts from different financial statements (such as asset turnover, which compares an income statement and a balance sheet amount). These two types of ratios are illustrated in Exhibit 7.

In looking at Exhibit 7, you might justifiably conclude that the cash flow statement is completely ignored when computing financial ratios. Unfortunately, that is often true. Relative to the other two primary financial statements, the statement of cash flows is relatively new (the balance sheet and the income statement have been a part of accounting since its invention—the statement of cash flows has only been required since 1988). As a result, ratios involving balance sheet and income statement accounts have been in existence for decades. Given the newness of the statement of cash flows, standardized ratios are still developing. The ENRON accounting scandal has highlighted the usefulness of ratios involving cash flow information (see Judgment 5-1 in the end-of-chapter material). To make sure you don't fall victim to the oversight of ignoring cash flow ratios, we include a special section on cash flow ratios later in this chapter.

TO SUMMARIZE: Financial ratios result from the relationship between two financial statement numbers. Some of the most common financial ratios are the debt ratio, the current ratio, the return on sales, asset turnover, return on equity, and price-earnings ratio. Each of these ratios provides information about a company's past performance.

Exhibit 7: Financial Ratios and the Relationships among the Financial Statements

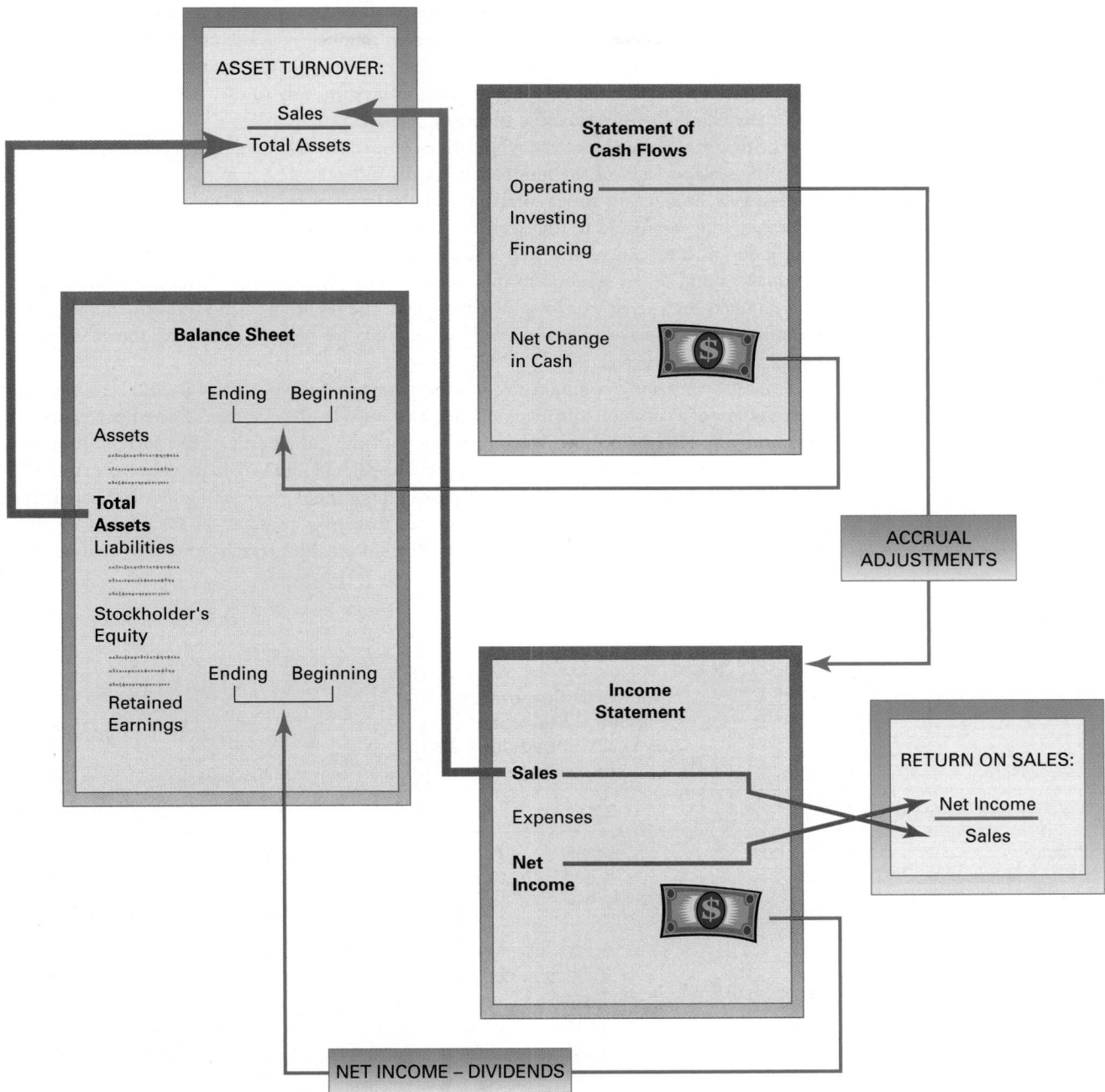

Common-Size Financial Statements

3 Use common-size financial statements to perform comparison of financial statements across years and between companies.

common-size financial statements Financial statements achieved by dividing all financial statement numbers by total sales for the year.

Financial statement analysis is sometimes wrongly viewed as just the computation of a bunch of financial ratios—divide every financial statement number by every other number. This shotgun approach usually fails to lead to any concrete conclusions. This section explains the use of common-size financial statements that are easy to prepare, easy to use, and should be the first step in any comprehensive financial statement analysis.

The first problem encountered when using comparative data to analyze financial statements is that the scale, or size, of the numbers is usually different. If a firm has more sales this year than last year, it is now a larger company and the levels of expenses and assets this year can't be meaningfully compared to the levels last year. In addition, if a company is of medium size in its industry, how can its financial statements be compared with those of the larger firms? The quickest and easiest solution to this comparability problem is to divide all financial statement numbers for a given year by sales for the year. The resulting financial statements are called **common-size financial statements**, with all amounts for a given year being shown as a percentage of sales for that year.

Exhibit 8 contains a common-size income statement for Microsoft for 2002. To illustrate the usefulness of a common-size income statement, consider the question of whether Microsoft's gross profit in 2002 is too low. In comparison with the gross profit of $21,841 in 2001, the $23,174 gross profit for 2002 looks pretty good. But sales in 2002 are higher than sales in 2001, so the absolute levels of gross profit in the two years cannot be meaningfully compared. But looking at the common-size information, we see that gross profit is 86.3% of sales in 2001 compared with 81.7% in 2002. The common-size information reveals something that was not

Exhibit 8: Common-Size Income Statement for Microsoft

Year Ended June 30	2000	%	2001	%	2002	%
Microsoft Corporation Income Statement For Years Ended June 30 (in millions)						
Revenue	22,956	100.0%	25,296	100.0%	28,365	100.0%
Cost of revenue	3,002	13.1%	3,455	13.7%	5,191	18.3%
Gross profit on sales	19,954	86.9%	21,841	86.3%	23,174	81.7%
Operating expenses:						
Research and development	3,772	16.4%	4,379	17.3%	4,307	15.2%
Sales and marketing	4,126	18.0%	4,885	19.3%	5,407	19.1%
General and administrative	1,050	4.6%	857	3.4%	1,550	5.5%
Total operating expenses	8,948	39.0%	10,121	40.0%	11,264	39.7%*
Operating income	11,006	47.9%	11,720	46.3%	11,910	42.0%
Losses on equity investees and other	−57	−0.2%	−159	−0.6%	−92	−0.3%
Investment income/(loss)	3,326	14.5%	−36	−0.1%	−305	−1.1%
Income before income taxes	14,275	62.2%	11,525	45.6%	11,513	40.6%
Provision for income taxes	4,854	21.1%	3,804	15.0%	3,684	13.0%
Income before accounting change	9,421	41.0%*	7,721	30.5%*	7,829	27.6%
Cumulative effect of accounting change (net of income taxes of $185)	—		−375	−1.5%	—	
Net income	9,421	41.0%	7,346	29.0%	7,829	27.6%

*Note: Because of rounding, the percentages don't always add up exactly. This is a minor arithmetic problem that shouldn't get in the way of the analysis.

Caution

Notice in Exhibit 8 that the results for 2002, the most recent year reported, are shown in the far right column. This is the way Microsoft reports in its annual report. However, most companies choose to report the most recent information in the far left column.

FYI:

The SEC requires publicly-traded companies to provide three years of income statements and two years of balance sheets when providing financial reports to the public.

FYI:

A common-size balance sheet can also be prepared using total assets to standardize each amount instead of using total sales, in which case the asset percentages are a good indication of the company's asset mix.

apparent in the raw numbers—in 2001 an item selling for $1 yielded an average gross profit of 86.3¢; in 2002 an item selling for $1 yielded an average gross profit of just 81.7¢. Microsoft made less gross profit from each dollar of sales in 2002 than in 2001. The news is even worse because the 2002 gross profit represents a continuation of the decline from the 86.9% gross profit percentage in 2000.

Each item on the income statement can be analyzed in the same way. In 2002, income before income taxes was 40.6% of sales compared with 45.6% in 2001. Operating expenses as a percentage of sales remained relatively constant from 2001 to 2002 (40.0% vs. 39.7%) indicating the difference in operating income related almost exclusively to an increase in the cost of revenue percentage from 13.7% to 18.3%. With a common-size income statement, each of the income statement items can be examined in this way, yielding much more information than just looking at the raw income statement numbers.

At this point, you should be saying to yourself: "Yes, but what is the exact explanation for Microsoft's drop in gross profit percentage since 2002? And why did regular operating expenses increase? And what is this large 'other operating expense'?" These questions illustrate the usefulness and the limitations of financial statement analysis. Our quick analysis of Microsoft's income statement has pointed out the major areas in which Microsoft has experienced significant income statement change in the past two years. But the only way to find out *why* these financial statement numbers changed is to gather information from outside the financial statements—ask management, read press releases, talk to financial analysts who follow the firm, read industry newsletters, and dig into the notes to the financial statements. In short, financial statement analysis usually doesn't tell you the final answers, but it does suggest which questions you should be asking and where you should look to find the answers.

A common-size balance sheet also expresses each amount as a percentage of sales for the year. As an illustration, a comparative balance sheet for Microsoft with each item expressed in both dollar amounts and percentages is shown in Exhibit 9.

The most informative section of the common-size balance sheet is the asset section, which can be used to determine how efficiently a company is using its assets. For example, looking at total assets for Microsoft in 2001 and 2002, you see the company's total assets were $67,646 in 2002. Did Microsoft manage its assets more efficiently in 2002 than in 2001 when total assets were $58,830? Comparing the raw numbers can't give a clear answer because Microsoft's level of sales is different in the two years. The common-size balance sheet indicates that each dollar of sales in 2001 required assets in place of $2.326, whereas each dollar of sales in 2002 required assets of $2.385. So in which of the two years was Microsoft more efficient at using its assets to generate sales? Microsoft was more efficient in 2001, when each dollar of sales required a lower level of assets.

Common-size financial statements are not a sophisticated analytical tool, and they don't constitute a complete analysis. However, they are the easiest, most intuitive, and fastest tool available, and they should be included in the initial stages of any comprehensive analysis of financial statements.

TO SUMMARIZE: Common-size financial statements are computed by dividing all financial statement amounts for a given year by sales for that year. A common-size income statement reveals the number of pennies of each expense for each dollar of sales. The asset section of a common-size balance sheet tells how many pennies of each asset are needed to generate each dollar of sales.

Exhibit 9: Common-Size Balance Sheet for Microsoft

30-Jun	2001		2002	
Assets				
Current assets:				
Cash and equivalents	3,922	15.5%	3,016	10.6%
Short-term investments	27,678	109.4%	35,636	125.6%
Total cash and short-term investments	31,600	124.9%	38,652	136.3%*
Accounts receivable, net	3,671	14.5%	5,129	18.1%
Inventories	83	0.3%	673	2.4%
Deferred income taxes	1,522	6.0%	2,112	7.4%
Other	2,334	9.2%	2,010	7.1%
Total current assets	39,210	155.0%*	48,576	171.3%
Property and equipment, net	2,309	9.1%	2,268	8.0%
Equity and other investments	14,361	56.8%	14,191	50.0%
Goodwill	1,511	6.0%	1,426	5.0%
Intangible assets, net	401	1.6%	243	0.9%
Other long-term assets	1,038	4.1%	942	3.3%
Total assets	58,830	232.6%	67,646	238.5%
Liabilities and stockholders' equity				
Current liabilities:				
Accounts payable	1,188	4.7%	1,208	4.3%
Accrued compensation	742	2.9%	1,145	4.0%
Income taxes	1,468	5.8%	2,022	7.1%
Short-term unearned revenue	4,395	17.4%	5,920	20.9%
Other	1,461	5.8%	2,449	8.6%
Total current liabilities	9,254	36.6%	12,744	44.9%
Long-term unearned revenue	1,219	4.8%	1,823	6.4%
Deferred income taxes	409	1.6%	398	1.4%
Other long-term liabilities	659	2.6%	501	1.8%
Total liabilities	11,541	45.6%	15,466	54.5%
Stockholders' equity:				
Common stock and paid-in capital	28,390	112.2%	31,647	111.6%
Retained earnings, including accumulated other comprehensive income of $587 and $583	18,899	74.7%	20,533	72.4%
Total stockholders' equity	47,289	186.9%	52,180	184.0%
Total liabilities and stockholders' equity	58,830	232.6%*	67,646	238.5%

*Note: Because of rounding, the percentages don't always add up exactly. This is a minor arithmetic problem that shouldn't get in the way of the analysis.

DuPont Framework

4 Understand the DuPont framework and how return on equity can be decomposed into its profitability, efficiency, and leverage components.

As discussed earlier, return on equity (net income ÷ equity) is the single measure that summarizes the financial health of a company. Return on equity can be interpreted as the number of cents of net income an investor earns in one year by investing one dollar in the company. As a very rough rule of thumb, return on equity (ROE) consistently above 15% is a sign of a company in good health; ROE consistently below 15% is a sign of trouble. Return on equity for Microsoft for the years 2002 and 2001 is computed at the top of the next page.

	2002	2001
Net income	$7,829	$7,346
Stockholders' equity	$52,180	$47,289
Return on equity	15.0%	15.5%

What can we say about Microsoft's overall performance in 2002? It was OK relative to the rough ROE benchmark of 15%, but it was down slightly when compared to the ROE of 2001. But how do we pin down the exact reason or reasons for any change in a company's ROE? The answer is the focus of this section.

The **DuPont framework** (named after a system of ratio analysis developed 70 years ago at DuPont by F. Donaldson Brown) provides a systematic approach to identifying general factors causing ROE to deviate from normal. The DuPont system also provides a framework for computation of financial ratios to yield a more in-depth analysis of a company's areas of strength and weakness. The insight behind the DuPont framework is that ROE can be decomposed into three components as shown in Exhibit 10.

For each of the three ROE components—profitability, efficiency, and leverage—there is one ratio that summarizes a company's performance in that area. These ratios are as follows:

- **Return on sales** is computed as net income divided by sales and is interpreted as the number of pennies in profit generated from each dollar of sales.
- **Asset turnover** is computed as sales divided by assets and is interpreted as the number of dollars in sales generated by each dollar of assets.
- **Assets-to-equity ratio** is computed as assets divided by equity and is interpreted as the number of dollars of assets acquired for each dollar invested by stockholders.

The DuPont analysis of Microsoft's ROE for 2002 and 2001 is as follows:

$$\text{Return on Equity} = \underset{\text{Profitability}}{\frac{\text{Net Income}}{\text{Sales}}} \times \underset{\text{Efficiency}}{\frac{\text{Sales}}{\text{Assets}}} \times \underset{\text{Leverage}}{\frac{\text{Assets}}{\text{Equity}}}$$

2002	15.0%	=	$\frac{\$7,829}{\$28,365}$	×	$\frac{\$28,365}{\$67,646}$	×	$\frac{\$67,646}{\$52,180}$	
		=	27.6%	×	0.42	×	1.30	
2001	15.5%	=	$\frac{\$7,346}{\$25,296}$	×	$\frac{\$25,296}{\$58,830}$	×	$\frac{\$58,830}{\$47,289}$	
		=	29.0%	×	0.43	×	1.24	

Exhibit 10: Analysis of ROE Using the DuPont Framework

$$\begin{aligned} \text{Return on Equity} &= \text{Profitability} \times \text{Efficiency} \times \text{Leverage} \\ &= \text{Return on Sales} \times \text{Asset Turnover} \times \text{Assets-to-Equity Ratio} \\ &= \frac{\text{Net Income}}{\text{Sales}} \times \frac{\text{Sales}}{\text{Assets}} \times \frac{\text{Assets}}{\text{Equity}} \end{aligned}$$

Profitability = The company's ability to generate net income per dollar of sales
Efficiency = The ability of the company to generate sales through the use of assets
Leverage = The degree to which a company uses borrowed funds instead of invested funds

DuPont framework A systematic approach for breaking down return on equity into three ratios: return on sales, asset turnover, and assets-to-equity ratio.

assets-to-equity ratio A measure of the number of dollars of assets a company is able to acquire using each dollar of equity; calculated by dividing assets by equity.

The results of the DuPont analysis suggest that Microsoft's ROE was lower in 2002 for the following reasons:

1. In 2002, each sale was less profitable than in 2001: each dollar of sales produced 27.6¢ of profit in 2002, compared to 29.0¢ in 2001.
2. In 2002, assets were used less efficiently to generate sales: each dollar of assets generated $0.42 in sales in 2002 compared to $0.43 in sales in 2001.

In 2002, Microsoft was slightly more effective at leveraging stockholders' investment. Through the use of liabilties, Microsoft was able to turn each dollar of invested funds in 2002 into $1.30 of assets, more than the $1.24 in assets in 2001.

The DuPont analysis allows a financial statement user to begin to answer the question of "Why?" Why did a company's return on equity increase (or decrease) during a period? What has been the trend over time in each of the three areas of profitability, efficiency, and leverage? Answers to these questions will allow the user to begin to focus attention on those areas of the business that have experienced changes as reflected in the ratios.

This preliminary DuPont analysis is only the beginning of a proper ratio analysis. If a DuPont analysis suggests problems in any of the three ROE components, additional ratios in each area can shed more light on the exact nature of the problem.

One of the insights behind the DuPont framework is that overall company performance is a function of both the profitability of each sale, measured by return on sales, and the ability to use assets to generate sales, measured by asset turnover. For example, comparing Microsoft and Apple indicates that Microsoft is better than Apple Computer in terms of profitability (return on sales) but is worse in terms of efficiency (asset turnover).

network exercises

Microsoft Corporation

Net Work:

Go to **http://www.microsoft.com** and locate the company's most recent set of financial statements. Using these financial statements, compute each component of the DuPont framework and determine how Microsoft has performed since this text was published.

Profitability Ratios

When the DuPont calculations indicate that a company has a profitability problem, then a common-size income statement can be used to identify which expenses are causing the problem. Referring back to the common-size income statement in Exhibit 8, cost of goods sold as a percentage of sales was higher in 2002 than in 2001 (18.3% vs. 13.7%). This negative development was offset by slightly lower 2002 operating expenses (39.7% vs. 40.0%). To summarize, the return on sales indicates overall whether a firm has a problem with the profitability of each dollar of sales; the common-size income statement can be used to pinpoint exactly which expenses are causing the problem.

Efficiency Ratios

The asset turnover ratio suggests that Microsoft was less efficient at using its assets to generate sales in 2002 than it was in 2001. But which assets were causing this decreased efficiency? One way to get a quick indication is to review the common-size balance sheet in Exhibit 9, whose numbers indicate that in 2002 Microsoft had a much higher amount of cash and short-term investments as a percentage of sales (136.3%) than in 2001 (124.9%), suggesting that Microsoft was not using a large part of the company's assets in an income-producing fashion.

In addition to the common-size balance sheet, specific financial ratios have been developed to indicate whether a firm is holding too much or too little of a particular asset These additional ratios will be introduced as we proceed through the text. For example, ratios relating to accounts receivable will be introduced in Chapter 7, ratios relating to inventory will be discussed in Chapter 8, and so on.

Leverage Ratios

leverage Borrowing that allows a company to purchase more assets than its stockholders are able to pay for through their own investment.

Leverage ratios are an indication of the extent to which a company is using other people's money to purchase assets. **Leverage** is borrowing that allows a company to purchase more assets than its stockholders are able to pay for through their own investment. The assets-to-equity ratios for Microsoft for 2001 and 2002 indicate that leverage was higher in 2002 (1.24 in 2001; 1.30 in 2002). Higher leverage increases return on equity through the following chain of events:

- More borrowing means that more assets can be purchased without any additional equity investment by stockholders.
- More assets mean that more sales can be generated.
- More sales mean that net income should increase.

STOP & THINK

Company Z has an asset-to-equity ratio of 2.5. Can you compute what its debt ratio would be?

Investors generally prefer high leverage in order to increase the size of their company without increasing their investment, but lenders prefer low leverage to increase the safety of their debt. The field of corporate finance deals with how to optimally balance these opposing tendencies and choose the perfect capital structure for a firm. As mentioned earlier, a general rule of thumb is that large U.S. companies borrow about half of the funds they use to purchase assets. There are specific ratios that allow financial statement users to analyze the leverage of a firm. Those ratios will be introduced in the chapters on debt (Chapter 11) and equity (Chapter 12).

Exhibit 11 show the DuPont framework ratios for a number of familiar companies for 2002.

Note that while WAL-MART does not have the highest return on sales, it does have the highest return on equity. The reason becomes readily apparent by looking at the components of return on equity. Wal-Mart has the highest asset turnover of the companies included in the list as well as having the highest asset-to-equity ratio. Wal-Mart's efficiency and leverage combine to make for a high return on equity.

network **exercises**

Wal-Mart

Let us see how Wal-Mart has performed in recent years. Locate Wal-Mart's most recent financial statement at **http://www.walmart.com**.

Net Work:

1. Compute return on equity for Wal-Mart for its most recent year.

2. How does that number compare to the company's performance in 2002?

Remember, the preparation of financial statements by the accountant is not the end of the process but just the beginning. The statements are then analyzed by investors, creditors, and management to detect signs of existing deficiencies in performance and to predict how the firm will perform in the future. The Business Environment feature on page 206 explains how financial statement analysis may even be useful in predicting future returns on shares of stock. As repeated throughout this section, proper interpretation of a ratio depends on comparing the ratio value to the value for the same firm in the previous year and to values for other firms in the same industry. Finally, ratio analysis doesn't reveal the answers to a company's problems, but it does highlight areas in which further information should be gathered to find those answers.

Exhibit 11: DuPont Framework Ratios for Selected U.S. Companies

	ROE	Return on Sales	Asset Turnover	Assets-to-Equity Ratio
Disney	5.3%	4.9%	0.5	2.1
Wal-Mart	20.4%	3.3%	2.6	2.4
Home Depot	18.5%	6.3%	1.9	1.5
Federal Express	9.5%	2.9%	1.5	2.1
Southwest Airlines	5.5%	4.4%	0.6	2.0

Information for financial analysis comes from many sources. Electronic media offer a wealth of information that can be timelier than print sources of financial information.

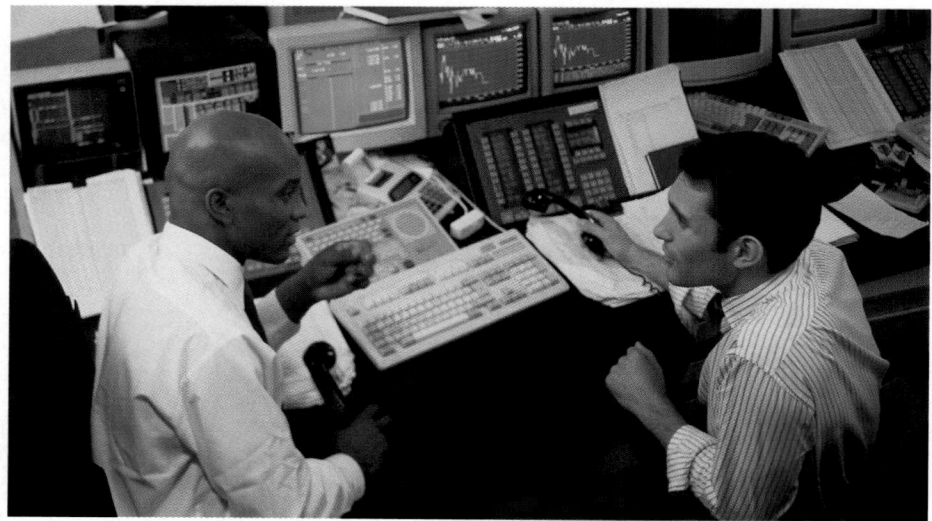

© 2003 Getty Images

TO SUMMARIZE: The DuPont framework decomposes return on equity (ROE) into three areas:

- **Profitability.** Return on sales is computed as net income divided by sales and is interpreted as the number of pennies in profit generated from each dollar of sales.

- **Efficiency.** Asset turnover is computed as sales divided by assets and is interpreted as the number of dollars in sales generated by each dollar of assets.

- **Leverage.** Assets-to-equity ratio is computed as assets divided by equity and is interpreted as the number of dollars of assets a company is able to acquire using each dollar invested by stockholders.

Cash Flow Ratios

5 Use cash flow information to evaluate cash flow ratios.

The requirement that companies provide a cash flow statement is very recent (since 1988), especially when you remember that double-entry accounting itself is over 500 years old. Because the cash flow statement is relatively new, it often fails to get the emphasis it deserves as one of the three primary financial statements. Most of the age-old tools of financial statement analysis, such as the DuPont framework, do not incorporate cash flow data. Accordingly, information from the cash flow statement is not yet ingrained in the analytical tradition, but it will be. In fact, one way to impress others that you are a modern, well-trained, future-looking professional is to become proficient in analyzing cash flow data.

Usefulness of Cash Flow Ratios

Analysis of cash flow information is especially important in those situations in which net income does not give an accurate picture of the economic performance of a company. Three such situations are discussed briefly below.

Large Noncash Expenses

When a company reports large noncash expenses, such as write-offs and depreciation, earnings may give a gloomier picture of current operations than is warranted. In fact, a company may report record losses in the same years it is reporting positive cash flow from operations. In such cases, cash flow from operations is a better indicator of whether the company can continue to honor its commitments to creditors, customers, employees, and investors in the near term. Don't misunderstand this to mean that a reported loss is nothing to worry about so long as cash flow is positive: the positive cash flow indicates that business can continue for the time being, but the reported loss may hint at looming problems in the future. As an example, consider the case of AOL TIME WARNER. In 2002, the company reported the largest net loss in the history of American business—$98.7 billion. However, much of that loss related to the impairment of certain assets—a noncash expenditure for the year. For 2002, AOL Time Warner reported a positive cash flow from operations of $7 billion.

Rapid Growth

Cash flow analysis is also a valuable tool for evaluating rapidly growing companies that use large amounts of cash to expand inventory. In addition, cash collections on growing accounts receivable often lag behind the need to pay creditors. In these cases, reported earnings may be positive but operations are actually consuming rather than generating cash. For example, PIXAR, the company that has produced such films as *Toy Story* and *Monsters, Inc.*, experienced revenue growth in 2002 of 77%. The company reported record net income in 2002 of $90 million. However, cash flow from operations was a negative $4.5 million. The message: For high-growth companies, positive earnings are no guarantee that sufficient cash flows are there to service current needs.

Window Dressing Time

Cash flow analysis offers important insights into companies that are striving to present a stellar financial record. Accrual accounting involves making assumptions in order to adjust raw cash flow data into a better measure of economic performance—net income. For companies entering phases in which it's critical that reported earnings look good, accounting assumptions and adjustments can be stretched—sometimes to the breaking point. Such phases include the period just before a company applies for a large loan, just before an initial public offering of stock (when founding entrepreneurs cash in all those years of struggle and sweat), and just before a company is being bought out by another company. In these cases, cash flow from operations, which is not impacted by accrual assumptions, provides an excellent reality check for reported earnings.

To illustrate the computation of selected cash flow ratios, the data in Exhibit 12 from Microsoft's 2002 and 2001 financial statements are used.

Cash Flow to Net Income

Perhaps the most important cash flow relationship is that between cash from operations and reported net income. The **cash flow-to-net income ratio** reflects the extent to which accrual accounting assumptions and adjustments have been included in computing net income. For

FYI:

Although net income may sometimes paint a misleading picture of a company's performance, in most cases net income is the single best measure of a firm's economic performance.

cash flow-to-net income ratio A ratio that reflects the extent to which accrual accounting assumptions and adjustments have been included in computing net income.

Exhibit 12: Selected Cash Flow Data for Microsoft for 2002 and 2001*

	2002	2001
Net income	$ 7,829	$ 7,346
Cash from operations	14,509	13,422
Cash paid for capital expenditures	770	1,103

*All amounts are in millions of dollars.

Microsoft, computation of the cash flow-to-net income ratio (in millions of dollars) is as follows:

	2002	2001
Cash from operations	$14,509	$13,422
Net income	$7,829	$7,346
Cash flow-to-net income ratio	1.85	1.83

STOP & THINK

Can you think of some accrual accounting adjustments that might cause a difference between net income and cash from operations?

In general, the cash flow-to-net income ratio will have a value greater than one because of significant noncash expenses (such as depreciation) that reduce reported net income but have no impact on cash flow. For a given company, the cash flow-to-net income ratio should remain fairly stable from year to year. A significant change in the ratio indicates that accounting assumptions were instrumental in reducing reported net income.

Cash Flow Adequacy

cash flow adequacy ratio
Cash from operations divided by expenditures for fixed asset additions and acquisitions of new businesses.

A "cash cow" is a business that is generating enough cash from operations to completely pay for all new plant and equipment purchases with cash left over to repay loans or distribute to investors. The **cash flow adequacy ratio**, computed as cash from operations divided by expenditures for fixed asset additions and acquisitions of new businesses, indicates whether a business is a cash cow. Computation of the cash flow adequacy ratio for Microsoft is as follows:

	2002	2001
Cash from operations	$14,509	$13,422
Cash paid for capital expenditures	$770	$1,103
Cash flow adequacy ratio	18.84	12.17

FYI:

Cash paid for dividends is sometimes added to the denominator of the cash flow adequacy ratio. With this formulation, the ratio indicates whether operating cash flow is sufficient to pay for both capital additions and regular dividends to stockholders.

The calculations indicate that in 2002 and in 2001 Microsoft's cash from operations was sufficient to pay for its capital expansion with something left over. This means that Microsoft could pay for its expansion without incurring any new debt or seeking funds from investors. It would be fair to say that Microsoft could be considered a cash cow. 2002 cash flow ratios for a group of companies are presented in Exhibit 13.

FEDERAL EXPRESS reports cash flow from operations as being more than three times its reported net income. In addition, three of the companies in the list—WAL-MART, HOME DEPOT, and Federal Express—each generated enough cash flow from operations in 2002 to more than pay for all their capital expenditures for the year.

Remember that cash flow ratios fall outside many financial statement analysis models because the cash flow statement hasn't been around long enough to work its way into traditional models. Rebel against tradition and don't forget cash flow!

TO SUMMARIZE: Because the statement of cash flows is a relatively recent requirement, time-tested ratios using information from that statement are still developing. Cash flow ratios are useful in that they can identify instances where accrual basis accounting measures are not providing a complete picture. The ratio of cash flow to net income highlights when there are significant differences between cash from operations and net income. The cash flow adequacy ratio demonstrates a company's ability to finance its capital expansion through cash from operations.

Exhibit 13: 2002 Cash Flow Ratios for Selected U.S. Companies

	Cash Flow/ Net Income	Cash Flow Adequacy Ratio
Disney	1.8	0.6
Wal-Mart	1.6	1.3
Home Depot	1.3	1.7
Federal Express	3.1	1.3
Southwest Airlines	2.2	0.9

Potential Pitfalls

6 Understand the limitations of financial statement analysis.

Financial statement analysis, as emphasized previously, usually does *not* give answers but instead points in directions where further investigation is needed. This section discusses several reasons why we must be careful not to place too much weight on an analysis of financial statement numbers themselves.

Financial Statements Don't Contain All Information

Accountants, including the authors, should be forgiven for mistakenly thinking that all knowledge in the universe can be summarized in numerical form in financial statements. Accountants love numbers, they love things that balance, and they love condensing and summarizing the complexity of business—in short, accountants love financial statements. Businesspeople don't have this emotional relationship with financial statements and therefore should be able to take a more detached view. Businesspeople should remember that financial statements represent just one part of the information spectrum. Microsoft's financial statements, for example, tell nothing about the morale of Microsoft's employees, about new products being developed in Microsoft's research laboratories, or about the strategic plans of Microsoft's competitors. In addition, as discussed in Chapter 2, many valuable economic assets, such as the value of a company's own homegrown reputation, brand recognition, and customer loyalty, are not recognized in financial statements. The danger in financial statement analysis is that, in computing dozens of ratios and comparing common-size financial statements across years and among competitors, we can forget there is lots of decision-relevant information to be found *outside* financial statements. Don't let the attractiveness of the apparent precision of financial statement numbers distract you from searching for all relevant information, no matter how imprecise and nonquantitative.

Lack of Comparability

Ratio analysis is most meaningful when ratios can be benchmarked to comparable values for the same company in prior years and to ratio values for other companies in the same industry. A problem arises when reported financial statement numbers that seem to be comparable are actually measurements of different things. For example, the income statement of DUPONT (the actual company, not the analysis technique) lists depreciation expense separately and includes advertising expense as part of selling, general, and administrative expense. In contrast, DuPont's competitor DOW CHEMICAL does not list depreciation expense separately but does report a separate line for advertising expense. This classification difference makes it more difficult to compare the income statements of the two companies.

Another benchmarking difficulty arises because many large U.S. companies are **conglomerates**, meaning that they are composed of divisions operating in different industries, sometimes quite unrelated to one another. Throughout this chapter APPLE COMPUTER, for

conglomerates A company comprised of a number of divisions with those divisions often operating in different industries.

example, was used as a benchmark competitor for MICROSOFT, but in addition to operating in the software industry, Apple is also heavily involved in the computer hardware business. Thus, a true benchmark firm for Microsoft would be to use (if available) only the results for the software segment of Apple Computer.

Finally, comparison difficulties arise because all companies don't use the same accounting practices. In this text, you'll learn that companies can choose different methods of computing depreciation expense, cost of goods sold, and bad debt expense. Some companies report leased assets as part of property, plant, and equipment in the balance sheet, and some companies don't report leased assets anywhere at all on the balance sheet. In future chapters, you will learn more about these accounting differences.

Search for the Smoking Gun

Financial case studies are very useful and fun because they allow students to discover key business insights for themselves in the context of real situations. When analyzing a case, one feels a bit like Sherlock Holmes scouring financial statements to see whether a company's problems are caused by poor inventory management, short-sighted tax planning, or growing difficulties collecting receivables. This detective mentality can be counterproductive, however, because not every company you analyze is going to be a candidate for a Harvard Business School case that illustrates one particular management principle. For example, not every company suffering from poor profitability has one stupendous flaw that will leap out at you as you do your ratio analysis. If you focus too much on trying to "solve" the case and find the smoking gun, you may overlook indications of a collection of less spectacular problems.

Anchoring, Adjustment, and Timeliness

Financial statements are based on historical data. A large part of the value of this historical data lies in its ability to indicate how a company will perform in the future. The danger in performing ratio analysis on several years of past data is that we might then tend to focus on the company's past performance and ignore current year information. All of the analysis performed in this chapter using historical data for Microsoft for 2002 and before may tell us less about Microsoft's operating position than the news that Microsoft and the U.S. Department of Justice had reached an agreement on a three-year-old antitrust dispute. The careful analyst must balance what he or she learns from an analysis of historical financial statement data with more current data available from different sources.

TO SUMMARIZE: One must use care when analyzing financial statements. The financial statements summarize the financial performance of a company, but there is more to a company and its future than just the information contained in the financial statements. In addition, care must be taken to ensure that when comparing financial statement information across time or across companies at the same point in time, that similar accounting practices have been used. Finally, financial statement analysis is a study of the past to give users a glimpse into the future. Care must be taken to ensure that current information is included when analyzing past data.

review of learning objectives

1 Explain the purpose of financial statement analysis. The entire reason for having financial statements is to use them. Financial statement analysis is used (1) to predict a company's future profitability and cash flows from its past performance and (2) to evaluate the performance of a company with an eye toward identifying problem areas. The informativeness of financial ratios is greatly enhanced when they are compared with past values and with values for other firms in the same industry.

2 Understand the relationships between financial statement numbers and use ratios in analyzing and describing a company's performance. Financial ratios are often used in a business context to describe various characteristics of companies. Six of the most commonly used ratios are:

- **Debt ratio:** Percentage of company funding that is borrowed.
- **Current ratio:** Indication of a company's ability to pay its short-term debts.
- **Return on sales:** Pennies in profit on each dollar of sales.
- **Asset turnover:** Measure of efficiency; number of sales dollars generated by each dollar of assets.
- **Return on equity:** Pennies in profit for each dollar invested by stockholders.
- **Price-earnings ratio:** Number of dollars an investor must pay to "buy" the future rights to each dollar of current earnings.

3 Use common-size financial statements to perform comparison of financial statements across years and between companies. Common-size financial statements are the easiest, most intuitive, and fastest tool available for starting an analysis of a company's financial statements. A common-size income statement reveals the number of pennies of each expense for each dollar of sales. The asset section of a common-size balance sheet tells how many pennies of each asset are needed to generate each dollar of sales.

4 Understand the DuPont framework and how return on equity can be decomposed into its profitability, efficiency, and leverage components. The DuPont framework decomposes return on equity (ROE) into three areas:

- **Profitability:** Return on sales is computed as net income divided by sales and is interpreted as the number of pennies in profit generated from each dollar of sales.
- **Efficiency:** Asset turnover is computed as sales divided by assets and is interpreted as the number of dollars in sales generated by each dollar of assets.
- **Leverage:** Assets-to-equity ratio is computed as assets divided by equity and is interpreted as the number of dollars of assets a company is able to acquire using each dollar invested by stockholders.

If a company has a profitability problem, the common-size income statement is the best tool for detecting which expenses are responsible. Financial ratios for detailed analysis of a company's efficiency and leverage have been developed—a number of them are summarized in Exhibit 6.

Margin is the profitability of each dollar in sales and asset turnover is the degree to which assets are used to generate sales. Companies with a low margin can still earn an acceptable level of return on assets if they have a high asset turnover.

5 Use cash flow information to evaluate cash flow ratios. Cash flow ratios are particularly useful when net income is impacted by large noncash expenses, when rapid growth causes cash from operations to be much less than reported net income, and when company management has a strong incentive to bias reported net income in order to get a loan or issue shares at a favorable price.

6 Understand the limitations of financial statement analysis. Financial statement analysis usually does not provide answers but only points out areas in which more information should be gathered. We must be careful not to base a decision solely on an analysis of financial statement numbers because

- financial statements don't contain all the relevant information;
- financial statements sometimes can't be properly compared among companies because of differences in classification, industry mix, and accounting methods;
- most sets of financial statements will not reveal a smoking gun that, if fixed, will solve all of a company's problems; and
- focusing on historical financial statement data may cause us to overlook important current information.

key terms & concepts

review problem

Financial Statement Analysis

The comparative income statements and balance sheets for Montana Corporation for the years ending December 31, 2006 and 2005, are given here.

Montana Corporation
Income Statements
For the Years Ended December 31, 2006 and 2005

	2006	2005
Net sales	$600,000	$575,000
Cost of goods sold	500,000	460,000
Gross margin	$100,000	$115,000
Expenses:		
Selling and administrative expenses	$ 66,000	$ 60,000
Interest expense	4,000	3,000
Total expenses	$ 70,000	$ 63,000
Income before taxes	$ 30,000	$ 52,000
Income taxes	12,000	21,000
Net income	$ 18,000	$ 31,000
Earnings per share	$1.80	$3.10

Montana Corporation
Balance Sheets
December 31, 2006 and 2005

	2006	2005
Assets		
Current assets:		
Cash	$ 11,000	$ 13,000
Accounts receivable (net)	92,000	77,000
Inventory	103,000	92,000
Prepaid expenses	6,000	5,000
Total current assets	$212,000	$187,000

(continued)

	2006	2005
Property, plant, and equipment:		
Land and building	$ 61,000	$ 59,000
Machinery and equipment	172,000	156,000
Total property, plant, and equipment	$233,000	$215,000
Less accumulated depreciation	113,000	102,000
Net property, plant, and equipment	$120,000	$113,000
Other assets	$ 8,000	$ 7,000
Total assets	$340,000	$307,000

Liabilities and Stockholders' Equity

	2006	2005
Current liabilities:		
Accounts payable	$ 66,000	$ 55,000
Notes payable	—	23,000
Dividends payable	2,000	—
Income taxes payable	3,000	5,000
Total current liabilities	$ 71,000	$ 83,000
Long-term debt	75,000	42,000
Total liabilities	$146,000	$125,000
Stockholders' equity:		
Common stock ($1 par)	$ 10,000	$ 10,000
Paid-in capital in excess of par	16,000	16,000
Retained earnings	168,000	156,000
Total stockholders' equity	$194,000	$182,000
Total liabilities and stockholders' equity ...	$340,000	$307,000

Additional information:	
Dividends declared in 2006	$6,000
Market price per share, December 31, 2006 ...	$14.50
Cash Flow Information:	
Cash from operations for 2006	$11,000
Cash paid for capital expenditures for 2006 ...	$19,000

Required:

Prepare a comprehensive financial statement analysis of Montana Corporation for 2006. Note that though financial statement analysts usually compare data from two or more years, we are more concerned here with the methods of analysis than the results, so we will use only one year, 2006.

Solution

1. Key Relationships

The computation of the four key ratios for 2006 provides the analyst with an overall view of the company's performance and gives an indication of how well management performed with respect to operations, asset turnover, and debt-equity management.

Computation of Key Ratios (2006)

Operating Performance		**Asset Turnover**		**Debt-Equity Management**		**Return on Stockholders' Equity**
$\dfrac{\text{Net Income}}{\text{Net Sales}}$	$\times$	$\dfrac{\text{Net Sales}}{\text{Average Total Assets}}$	$\times$	$\dfrac{\text{Average Total Assets}}{\text{Average Stockholders' Equity}}$	$=$	$\dfrac{\text{Net Income}}{\text{Average Stockholders' Equity}}$
$\dfrac{\$18,000}{\$600,000}$	$\times$	$\dfrac{\$600,000}{\$323,500}$	$\times$	$\dfrac{\$323,500}{\$188,000}$	$=$	$\dfrac{\$18,000}{\$188,000}$
3.00%	$\times$	1.85 times	$\times$	1.72 times	$=$	9.57%*

*The factors do not multiply to the product because of rounding.

2. Analysis of Operating Performance

Operating performance is measured by means of vertical and horizontal analyses of the income statement.

Vertical analysis of the income statement: When the income statement is analyzed vertically, net sales is set at 100 percent, and each expense and net income are shown as percentages of net sales.

Montana Corporation
Vertical Analysis of Income Statement
For the Year Ended December 31, 2006

Net sales	$600,000	100.0%
Cost of goods sold	500,000	83.3
Gross margin	$100,000	16.7%
Expenses:		
Selling and administrative expenses	$ 66,000	11.0%
Interest expense	4,000	0.7
Total expenses	$ 70,000	11.7%
Income before taxes	$ 30,000	5.0%
Income taxes	12,000	2.0
Net income	$ 18,000	3.0%

3. Analysis of Asset Turnover and Utilization

Asset turnover and utilization are analyzed by performing vertical analysis of the balance sheet.

Montana Corporation
Vertical Analysis of the Balance Sheet (as a % of sales)
December 31, 2006

Assets		
Current assets:		
Cash	$ 11,000	1.8%
Accounts receivable (net)	92,000	15.3
Inventory	103,000	17.2
Prepaid expenses	6,000	1.0
Total current assets	$212,000	35.3%
Property, plant, and equipment:		
Land and building	$ 61,000	10.2%
Machinery and equipment	172,000	28.7
Total property, plant, and equipment	$233,000	38.8%*
Less accumulated depreciation	113,000	18.8
Net property, plant, and equipment	$120,000	20.0%
Other assets	$ 8,000	1.3%
Total assets	$340,000	56.7%

Liabilities and Stockholders' Equity		
Current liabilities:		
Accounts payable	$ 66,000	11.0%
Dividends payable	2,000	0.3
Income taxes payable	3,000	0.5
Total current liabilities	$ 71,000	11.8%
Long-term debt	75,000	12.5
Total liabilities	146,000	24.3%
Stockholders' equity	194,000	32.3
Total liabilities and stockholders' equity	$340,000	56.7%*

*Note: Because of rounding, the percentages don't always add up exactly.

4. **Common Ratios**

  a. Debt Ratio

  $$\frac{\text{Total Liabilities}}{\text{Total Assets}} = \frac{\$146,000}{\$340,000} = 42.9\%$$

  b. Current Ratio:

  $$\frac{\text{Current Assets}}{\text{Current Liabilities}} = \frac{\$212,000}{\$71,000} = 2.99$$

  c. Return on Sales

  $$\frac{\text{Net Income}}{\text{Net Sales}} = \frac{\$18,000}{\$600,000} = 0.03$$

  d. Asset Turnover Ratio:

  $$\frac{\text{Net Sales}}{\text{Average Total Assets}} = \frac{\$600,000}{\dfrac{\$340,000 + \$307,000}{2}} = \frac{\$600,000}{\$323,500} = 1.85$$

  e. Return on Stockholders' Equity

  $$\frac{\text{Net Income}}{\text{Average Stockholders' Equity}} = \frac{\$18,000}{\dfrac{\$194,000 + \$182,000}{2}} = \frac{\$18,000}{\$188,000} = 9.6\%$$

  f. Price-earnings Ratio

  $$\frac{\text{Market Price Per Share}}{\text{Earnings Per Share}} = \frac{\$14.50}{\$1.80} = 8.1$$

discussion questions

1. Financial statement analysis can be used to identify a company's weak areas so that management can work toward improvement. Can financial statement analysis be used for any other purpose? Explain.
2. "An analysis of a company's financial ratios reveals the underlying reasons for the company's problems." Do you agree or disagree? Explain.
3. What benchmarks can be used to add meaning to a computed financial ratio value?
4. What characteristic of a company does current ratio measure?
5. Company A has a return on sales of 6%. Is this a high value for return on sales?
6. How does the price-earnings ratio differ from most other financial ratios?
7. What is a common-size financial statement? What are its advantages?
8. What other types of information should be gathered if an analysis of common-size financial statements suggests that a company has problems?

9. What is the most informative section of the common-size balance sheet? Explain.
10. What is the purpose of the DuPont framework?
11. Identify the three ROE components represented in the DuPont framework and tell what ratio summarizes a company's performance in each area.
12. What further analysis can be done if the DuPont calculations suggest that a company has a profitability problem?
13. Why are cash flow ratios often excluded from financial analysis models?
14. Why is it especially important to look at cash flow data when examining a firm that is preparing to make an application for a large loan?
15. What does it mean when the value of a company's cash flow adequacy ratio is less than one?
16. What factors can reduce comparability among financial statements?
17. What is the danger in focusing a financial analysis solely on the data found in the historical financial statements?

practice exercises

Practice 5-1

What Is a Financial Ratio?
Choose the letter of the correct answer. A financial ratio is a

a. key source of external financing for most publicly-traded companies.
b. relationship between financial statement amounts.
c. stockbroker who performs financial statement analysis.
d. trend in a number over time.
e. complete set of the three primary financial statements.

Practice 5-2

Usefulness of Financial Ratios
Choose the letter of the correct answer. The usefulness of financial ratios is greatly enhanced when the values are

a. computed by the SEC.
b. compared to values for companies in different industries.
c. compared to past values of the same ratio.
d. compared to the retained earnings balance.
e. included in the body of the statement of cash flows.

Practice 5-3

Financial Ratios Defined
Write the formula for computing each of the following financial ratios.

a. Debt ratio
b. Current ratio
c. Return on sales
d. Asset turnover
e. Return on equity
f. Price-earnings ratio

Practice 5-4

Debt Ratio
Using the following data, compute the debt ratio.

Accounts Payable	$ 1,800
Accounts Receivable	5,475
Building	40,000
Cash	1,125
Capital Stock	20,000
Inventory	3,400
Land	10,000
Long-Term Notes Payable	27,000
Market Value of Equity	90,000
Net Income	7,000
Retained Earnings (ending)	5,000
Sales	100,000
Short-Term Notes Payable	2,300
Stockholders' Equity	25,000
Unearned Revenue	3,900

Practice 5-5

Current Ratio
Refer to the data in Practice 5-4. Compute the current ratio.

Practice 5-6	**Return on Sales** Refer to the data in Practice 5-4. Compute return on sales.
Practice 5-7	**Asset Turnover** Refer to the data in Practice 5-4. Compute asset turnover.
Practice 5-8	**Return on Equity** Refer to the data in Practice 5-4. Compute return on equity.
Practice 5-9	**Price-Earnings Ratio** Refer to the data in Practice 5-4. Compute the price-earnings ratio.

Practice 5-10

Common-Size Income Statement

Using the following data, prepare a common-size income statement.

Sales		$75,000
Cost of goods sold		40,000
Gross profit		$35,000
Operating expenses:		
Sales and marketing	$3,000	
General and administrative	8,000	
Total operating expenses		11,000
Operating income		$24,000
Interest expense		4,000
Income before income taxes		$20,000
Income tax expense		3,500
Net income		$16,500

Practice 5-11

Comparative Common-Size Income Statements

Using the following data, (1) prepare comparative common-size income statements for Years 1 and 2 and (2) briefly outline why return on sales is lower in Year 2 (1.8%) compared to Year 1 (7.0%).

	Year 2	Year 1
Sales	$100,000	$80,000
Cost of goods sold	70,000	50,000
Gross profit	$ 30,000	$30,000
Operating expenses	25,000	20,000
Operating income	$ 5,000	$10,000
Interest expense	2,000	2,000
Income before income taxes	$ 3,000	$ 8,000
Income tax expense	1,200	2,400
Net income	$ 1,800	$ 5,600

Practice 5-12

Common-Size Balance Sheet

Using the following data, prepare a common-size balance sheet. Sales for the year were $60,000.

(continued)

Assets

Current assets:

Cash	$3,600	
Accounts receivable	8,500	
Inventory	7,000	
Total current assets		$19,100
Property, plant, and equipment (net)		25,000
Goodwill		6,400
Total assets		$50,500

Liabilities and stockholders' equity

Current liabilities:

Accounts payable	$4,000	
Unearned revenue	6,500	
Total current liabilities		$10,500
Long-term debt		15,000
Total liabilities		$25,500
Capital stock		15,000
Retained earnings		10,000
Total liabilities and stockholders' equity		$50,500

Practice 5-13

Common-Size Balance Sheet Standardized Using Total Assets

Refer to the data in Practice 5-12. Prepare a common-size balance sheet using total assets to standardize each amount instead of using total sales.

Practice 5-14

Comparative Common-Size Balance Sheets

Using the following data, (1) prepare comparative common-size balance sheets for Years 1 and 2 (standardized by sales) and (2) briefly outline any significant changes from Year 1 to Year 2. Sales for Year 1 were $80,000, and sales for Year 2 were $100,000.

	Year 2	Year 1
Assets		
Cash	$ 4,000	$ 3,200
Accounts receivable	8,000	6,400
Inventory	17,000	15,000
Property, plant, and equipment (net)	25,000	25,000
Total assets	$54,000	$49,600
Liabilities and stockholders' equity		
Accounts payable	$ 9,000	$ 7,200
Long-term debt	20,000	20,000
Total liabilities	$29,000	$27,200
Capital stock	15,000	15,000
Retained earnings	10,000	7,400
Total liabilities and stockholders' equity	$54,000	$49,600

Practice 5-15

DuPont Framework Defined

(1) List the three ratios that combine to form the DuPont framework. Also list the formulas used to compute each ratio. (2) Give a brief intuitive explanation of the interpretation of the values of each of the three ratios.

Practice 5-16

Computation of Return on Equity Using the DuPont Framework

Using the following DuPont framework ratios, compute return on equity for Year 1, Year 2, and Year 3.

	Year 3	Year 2	Year 1
Return on sales	25.9%	23.4%	22.5%
Asset turnover	0.71	0.67	0.60
Asset-to-equity ratio	1.52	1.45	1.20

Practice 5-17

Analysis of Return on Equity Using the DuPont Framework
Refer to the data in Practice 5-16. Briefly explain why the company's return on equity increased from Year 1 to Year 3.

Practice 5-18

DuPont Framework Computations
Using the following data, compute return on equity, return on sales, asset turnover, and the assets-to-equity ratio.

Total assets	$100,000
Interest expense	$2,000
Total stockholders' equity	$40,000
Sales	$250,000
Net income	$13,000
Total liabilities	$60,000
Market value of equity	$83,000
Current ratio	1.87

Practice 5-19

DuPont Framework Computations
Using the following data, compute return on equity, return on sales, asset turnover, and the assets-to-equity ratio.

Sales	$450,000
Cash flow from operating activities	$12,000
Net income	$20,000
Total assets	$300,000
Total liabilities	$120,000
Price-earnings ratio	17.4

Practice 5-20

DuPont Framework Intuition Test
Return on equity can be computed by dividing net income by stockholders' equity. It can also be computed by multiplying return on sales, asset turnover, and the assets-to-equity ratio. Using the definitions of the various ratios, show why both of these approaches yield the same answer.

Practice 5-21

When Operating Cash Flow Information Is Particularly Valuable
Which one of the following is *not* a situation in which cash flow data can provide a better picture of a company's economic performance than does net income?

a. A company preparing for an initial public offering.
b. A company experiencing rapid growth.
c. A company reporting large noncash expenses.
d. A company with high asset turnover.
e. A company preparing to apply for a large loan.

Practice 5-22

Cash Flow-To-Net Income Ratio
Using the following data, compute the cash flow-to-net income ratio.

(continued)

Total revenues	$190,000
Cash expenses	84,000
Noncash expenses	60,000
Cash paid for capital expenditures	110,000
Cash from operations	95,000

Practice 5-23

Cash Flow Adequacy Ratio
Refer to the data in Practice 5-22. Compute the cash flow adequacy ratio.

Practice 5-24

Potential Pitfalls of Financial Statement Analysis
Which one of the following statements is true with respect to financial statement analysis?

a. All aspects of a business can be summarized neatly into the three primary financial statements.
b. Comparing the financial statements of different companies is relatively easy because all companies are required to use the same financial statement formats and classifications.
c. Every company examined using financial statement analysis will be found to have at least one prominent flaw.
d. Analysts should use only historical ratio analysis, rather than information about current events, in deciding how to rate a company's future prospects.
e. Financial statement analysis usually does not give answers but instead points in directions where further investigation is needed.

e x e r c i s e s

Exercise 5-1

Spreadsheet

Computation of Ratios
The balance sheet for Tony Corporation is as follows:

Tony Corporation
Balance Sheet
December 31, 2006

Assets
Current assets:

Cash	$ 11,000
Accounts receivable	18,000
Total current assets	$ 29,000
Long-term investments	25,000
Property, plant, and equipment	55,000
Total assets	$109,000

Liabilities and stockholders' equity
Current liabilities:

Accounts payable	$ 15,000
Salaries payable	5,000
Total current liabilities	$ 20,000
Long-term liabilities	17,500
Total liabilities	$ 37,500

Stockholders' equity:

Paid-in capital	$ 50,000
Retained earnings	21,500
Total stockholders' equity	$ 71,500
Total liabilities and stockholders' equity	$109,000

In addition, the following information for 2006 has been assembled:

Sales	$265,000
Net income	33,000
Market value at December 31, 2006	150,000

Compute the following ratios:

1. Debt ratio
2. Current ratio
3. Return on sales
4. Asset turnover
5. Return on equity
6. Price-earnings ratio

Exercise 5-2

Ratios and Computing Missing Values

The balance sheet for Magily Company is as follows:

Magily Company
Balance Sheet
December 31, 2006

Assets
Current assets:

Cash	$	(a)
Accounts receivable		50,000
Total current assets	$	(b)
Long-term investments		40,000
Property, plant, and equipment		100,000
Total assets	$	(c)

Liabilities and stockholders' equity
Current liabilities:

Accounts payable	$	30,000
Income taxes payable		(d)
Total current liabilities	$	40,000
Long-term liabilities		(e)
Total liabilities	$	(f)
Stockholders' equity:		
Paid-in capital	$	(g)
Retained earnings		35,000
Total stockholders' equity	$	(h)
Total liabilities and stockholders' equity	$	(i)

In addition, the following information for 2006 has been assembled:

Debt ratio	60%
Current ratio	1.5

Compute the missing values (a) through (i).

Exercise 5-3

Computations Using Ratios

The following information for Chong Lai Company for 2006 has been assembled:

(continued)

Market value at December 31, 2006	$600,000
Total liabilities	$100,000
Debt ratio	40%
Return on sales	10%
Asset turnover	2.0

Compute the following:

1. Total assets
2. Sales
3. Net income
4. Price-earnings ratio

Exercise 5-4

Common-Size Income Statement

Comparative income statements for Long Pond Company for 2006 and 2005 are given below.

	2006	2005
Sales	$ 800,000	$ 450,000
Cost of goods sold	(510,000)	(240,000)
Gross profit on sales	$ 290,000	$ 210,000
Selling and general expenses	(100,000)	(80,000)
Operating income	$ 190,000	$ 130,000
Interest expense	(40,000)	(30,000)
Income before income tax	$ 150,000	$ 100,000
Income tax expense	(45,000)	(30,000)
Net income	$ 105,000	$ 70,000

1. Prepare common-size income statements for Long Pond Company for 2006 and 2005.
2. Return on sales for Long Pond is lower in 2006 than in 2005. What expense or expenses are causing this lower profitability?

Exercise 5-5

Common-Size Balance Sheet

The following data are taken from the comparative balance sheet prepared for Warren Road Company:

	2006	2005
Cash	$ 34,000	$ 25,000
Accounts receivable	43,000	40,000
Inventories	68,000	30,000
Property, plant, and equipment	91,000	55,000
Total assets	$236,000	$150,000

Sales for 2006 were $1,000,000. Sales for 2005 were $800,000.

1. Prepare the asset section of a common-size balance sheet for Warren Road Company for 2006 and 2005.
2. Overall, Warren Road is less efficient at using its assets to generate sales in 2006 than in 2005. What asset or assets are responsible for this decreased efficiency?

Exercise 5-6

Common-Size Balance Sheet

The following data are taken from the comparative balance sheet prepared for Elison Company:

	2006	2005
Cash	$ 68,000	$ 50,000
Accounts receivable	86,000	80,000
Inventory	136,000	60,000
Property, plant, and equipment	182,000	110,000
Total assets	$472,000	$300,000

Sales for 2006 were $2,000,000. Sales for 2005 were $1,600,000.

1. Prepare the asset section of a common-size balance sheet for Elison Company for 2006 and 2005.
2. Overall, Elison is less efficient at using its assets to generate sales in 2006 than in 2005. What asset or assets are responsible for this decreased efficiency?

Exercise 5-7

Common-Size Income Statement

Comparative income statements for Callister Company for 2006 and 2005 are given below.

	2006	2005
Sales	$1,600,000	$900,000
Cost of goods sold	1,020,000	480,000
Gross profit	$ 580,000	$420,000
Selling and administrative expenses	200,000	160,000
Operating income	$ 380,000	$260,000
Interest expense	80,000	60,000
Income before taxes	$ 300,000	$200,000
Income tax expense	90,000	60,000
Net income	$ 210,000	$140,000

1. Prepare common-size income statements for Callister Company for 2006 and 2005.
2. The profit margin for Callister is lower in 2006 than in 2005. What expense or expenses are causing this lower profitability?

Exercise 5-8

Spreadsheet

Income Statement Analysis

You have obtained the following data for Jamie Elli Company:

Sales	$170,000
Gross profit (as a percentage of sales)	25%
Return on sales	5%
Operating expenses (as a percentage of sales)	10%

Based on the above data, determine the following:

1. Cost of goods sold
2. Net income
3. Operating expenses
4. Income taxes (assume there are no other expenses or revenues)

Exercise 5-9

Income Statement and Balance Sheet Analysis

Answer each of the following independent questions:

1. Nicholas Toy Company had a net income for the year ended December 31, 2006, of $72,000. Its total assets at December 31, 2006, were $1,860,000. Its total stockholders' equity at December 31, 2006, was $910,000. Calculate Nicholas Toy's return on equity.

(continued)

2. On January 1, 2006, Andrew's Bookstore had current assets of $293,000 and current liabilities of $185,000. By the end of the year, its current assets had increased to $324,000 and its current liabilities to $296,000. Did the current ratio change during the year? If so, by how much?

3. The total liabilities and stockholders' equity of Ryan James Corporation is $750,000. Its current assets equal 40% of total assets and the current ratio is 1.5. Further, the ratio of stockholders' equity to total liabilities is 3 to 1. Determine (a) the amount of current liabilities and (b) the debt ratio.

Exercise 5-10

DuPont Framework

The following information is for Calle Concordia Company:

	2006	2005	2004
Current assets	$ 30,000	$ 25,000	$ 35,000
Total assets	100,000	80,000	90,000
Current liabilities	20,000	15,000	15,000
Total liabilities	45,000	40,000	50,000
Stockholders' equity	55,000	40,000	40,000
Sales	400,000	300,000	300,000
Net income	20,000	10,000	5,000

For the years 2004, 2005, and 2006, compute:

1. Return on equity
2. Return on sales
3. Asset turnover
4. Assets-to-equity ratio

Exercise 5-11

DuPont Framework

The numbers below are for Iffy Company and Model Company for the year 2006:

	Iffy	Model
Cash	$ 120	$ 900
Accounts receivable	600	4,500
Inventory	480	6,000
Property, plant, and equipment	3,440	15,000
Total liabilities	3,190	18,150
Stockholders' equity	1,450	8,250
Sales	10,000	75,000
Cost of goods sold	9,200	66,750
Wage expense	700	5,250
Net income	100	3,000

1. Compute return on equity, return on sales, asset turnover, and the assets-to-equity ratio for both Iffy and Model.
2. Briefly explain why Iffy's return on equity is lower than Model's.

Exercise 5-12

DuPont Framework

The numbers for Question Company and Standard Company for the year 2006 are as follows:

	Question	Standard
Cash	$ 60	$ 300
Accounts receivable	600	4,000
Inventory	1,400	3,650
Property, plant, and equipment	1,000	8,650
Total liabilities	2,448	13,280
Stockholders' equity	612	3,320
Sales	10,000	50,000
Cost of goods sold	7,350	36,750
Wage expense	700	3,500
Other expenses	1,900	8,500
Net income	50	1,250

1. Compute return on equity, return on sales, asset turnover, and the assets-to-equity ratio for both Question and Standard.
2. Briefly explain why Question's return on equity is lower than Standard's.

Exercise 5-13

DuPont Framework

The following information is for Ina Company:

	2006	2005	2004
Total assets	$200,000	$160,000	$180,000
Total liabilities	90,000	80,000	100,000
Stockholders' equity	110,000	80,000	80,000
Sales	800,000	600,000	600,000
Net income	40,000	20,000	10,000

For the years 2004, 2005, and 2006, compute:

1. Return on equity
2. Profit margin
3. Asset turnover
4. Assets-to-equity ratio

Exercise 5-14

DuPont Framework for Analyzing Financial Statements

The income statement and balance sheet for Rollins Company are provided below. Using the DuPont framework, compute the profit margin, asset turnover, assets-to-equity ratio, and resulting return on equity for the year 2006.

Rollins Company
Income Statement
For the Year Ended December 31, 2006

Revenue from services		$151,920
Operating expenses:		
Insurance expense	$ 5,480	
Rent expense	500	
Office supplies expense	2,960	
Salaries expense	55,000	63,940
Net income		$ 87,980

(continued)

Rollins Company
Balance Sheet
December 31, 2006

Assets		Liabilities and Owners' Equity	
Cash	$ 22,000	Accounts payable	$ 54,800
Accounts receivable	40,000	Capital stock	50,000
Notes receivable	12,800	Retained earnings	150,000
Machinery	180,000	Total liabilities	
Total assets	$254,800	and owners' equity	$254,800

Exercise 5-15

DuPont Framework for Analyzing Financial Statements

Using the income statement and balance sheet for Jacobson and Sons Company, compute the three components of return on equity—profitability, efficiency, and leverage—based on the DuPont framework, for the year 2006.

Jacobson and Sons Co.
Income Statement
For the Year Ended December 31, 2006

Revenues		$265,000
Expenses:		
Supplies expense	$138,600	
Salaries expense	26,700	
Utilities expense	6,500	
Rent expense	17,100	
Other expenses	8,700	197,600
Net income		$ 67,400

Jacobson and Sons Co.
Balance Sheet
December 31, 2006

Assets		Liabilities and Owners' Equity	
Cash	$ 38,900	Accounts payable	$ 17,100
Accounts receivable	31,000	Notes payable	17,200
Supplies	46,300	Capital stock	30,000
Land	25,000	Retained earnings	173,600
Buildings	96,700	Total liabilities	
Total assets	$237,900	and owners' equity	$237,900

Exercise 5-16

DuPont Framework

DuPont framework data for four industries are presented below.

	Assets-to Equity Ratio	Asset Turnover	Return on Sales
Retail jewelry stores	1.578	1.529	0.050
Retail grocery stores	1.832	5.556	0.014
Electric service companies	2.592	0.498	0.069
Legal services firms	1.708	3.534	0.083

For the four industries, compute:

1. Return on assets
2. Return on equity

Exercise 5-17

Financial Statement Analysis

You have obtained the following data for the Jacob Company for the year ended December 31, 2006. (Some income statement items are missing.)

Cost of goods sold	$485,000
General and administrative expenses	80,000
Interest expense	8,500
Net income	12,000
Sales	790,000
Tax expense	8,000

Answer each of the following questions:

1. What is the total gross profit?
2. What is the amount of operating income?
3. What is the amount of other operating expenses (in addition to general and administrative expenses)?
4. What is the gross profit percentage (that is, gross profit as a percentage of sales)?
5. If the return on assets is 4%, what are the total assets?
6. If the return on stockholders' equity is 8%, what is the stockholders' equity?
7. What is the return on sales?
8. What is the income tax rate? (Tax Expense/Income before Taxes)

Exercise 5-18

Cash Flow Ratios

Below are data extracted from the financial statements for Choi Hung Company.

Choi Hung Company Selected Financial Statement Data For the Years Ended December 31, 2006 and 2005		
	2006	**2005**
Net income	$32,000	$ 68,850
Cash from operating activities	25,500	155,030
Cash paid for purchase of fixed assets	35,000	178,000
Cash paid for interest	27,000	23,000
Cash paid for income taxes	20,000	40,430

Compute the following for both 2005 and 2006:

1. Cash flow-to-net income ratio
2. Cash flow adequacy ratio

 p roblems

Problem 5-1

Computing and Using Common Ratios

The following information is for the year 2006 for Millard Company and Grantsville Company, which are in the same industry:

(continued)

	Millard	Grantsville
Current assets	$20,000	$75,000
Long-term assets	$40,000	$140,000
Current liabilities	$8,000	$60,000
Long-term liabilities	$15,000	$110,000
Sales	$200,000	$850,000
Net income	$4,000	$10,000
Market price per share	$15	$50
Number of shares outstanding	6,000 shares	3,000 shares

Required:
Compute the following:

1. Current ratio
2. Debt ratio
3. Return on sales

4. Asset turnover
5. Return on equity
6. Price-earnings ratio

Problem 5-2

Financial Ratios
The following information for High Flying Company is provided:

Current assets	$145,000
Long-term assets	$750,000
Current liabilities	$75,000
Long-term liabilities	$300,000
Owners' equity	$520,000
Sales for year	$1,425,000
Net income for year	$105,000
Average market price per share	$145.00
Average number of shares outstanding	10,000

Required:
1. Compute the current ratio, debt ratio, return on sales, return on equity, asset turnover, and price-earnings ratio.
2. **Interpretive Question:** What do these ratios show for High Flying Company?

Problem 5-3

Working Backwards Using Common Ratios
The following information for Steven Benjamin Company for 2006 has been assembled:

Price-earnings ratio	39.0
Stockholders' equity	$150,000
Debt ratio	80%
Net income	$41,000
Asset turnover	0.75
Current liabilities	$135,000
Long-term assets	$280,000

Required:
Compute the following:

1. Return on equity
2. Total assets
3. Sales

4. Return on sales
5. Current ratio
6. Total market value of shares

Problem 5-4

P.A.S.S.
*Power Accounting
System Software*

Common-Size Income Statement

Operations for Gordo Company for 2005 and 2006 are summarized below.

	2006	2005
Net sales	$480,000	$440,000
Cost of goods sold	350,000	240,000
Gross profit on sales	$130,000	$200,000
Selling and general expenses	100,000	120,000
Operating income	$ 30,000	$ 80,000
Interest expense	35,000	30,000
Income (loss) before income tax	$ (5,000)	$ 50,000
Income tax (refund)	2,000	20,000
Net income (loss)	$ (3,000)	$ 30,000

Required:

1. Prepare common-size income statements for 2006 and 2005.
2. What caused Gordo's profitability to decline so dramatically in 2006?

Problem 5-5

P.A.S.S.
*Power Accounting
System Software*

Common-Size Financial Statements

Below are financial statement data for Wong Shek Company for the years 2005 and 2006.

Wong Shek Company Financial Statements For 2005 and 2006		
	2006	2005
Cash	$ 14	$ 10
Receivables	35	27
Inventory	230	153
Property, plant, and equipment	221	190
Total assets	$ 500	$ 380
Accounts payable	$ 106	$ 74
Long-term debt	217	217
Total liabilities	$ 323	$ 291
Paid-in capital	$ 113	$ 50
Retained earnings	64	39
Total liabilities and equity	$ 500	$ 380
Sales	$1,000	$ 700
Cost of goods sold	(700)	(500)
Gross profit	$ 300	$ 200
Operating expenses	(240)	(160)
Operating profit	$ 60	$ 40
Interest expense	(22)	(22)
Income before taxes	$ 38	$ 18
Income tax expense	(13)	(6)
Net income	$ 25	$ 12

Required:

1. Prepare common-size financial statements for Wong Shek for 2005 and 2006.
2. Did Wong Shek do better or worse in 2006 compared with 2005? Explain your answer.

Problem 5-6

Spreadsheet

Common-Size Financial Statements

The comparative income statements and balance sheets for Clarksville Corporation for the years 2004, 2005, and 2006 are given below.

Clarksville Corporation
Comparative Income Statements
For the Years Ended December 31

	2006	2005	2004
Net sales	$5,700,000	$6,600,000	$3,800,000
Cost of goods sold	4,000,000	4,800,000	2,520,000
Gross profit on sales	$1,700,000	$1,800,000	$1,280,000
Selling expense	$1,120,000	$1,200,000	$ 960,000
General expense	400,000	440,000	400,000
Total operating expenses	$1,520,000	$1,640,000	$1,360,000
Operating income (loss)	$ 180,000	$ 160,000	$ (80,000)
Other revenue (expense)	80,000	130,000	160,000
Income before taxes	$ 260,000	$ 290,000	$ 80,000
Income tax	80,000	85,000	20,000
Net income	$ 180,000	$ 205,000	$ 60,000

Clarksville Corporation
Comparative Balance Sheets
December 31

	2006	2005	2004
Assets:			
Current assets	$ 855,000	$ 955,500	$ 673,500
Land, building, and equipment	1,275,000	1,075,000	925,000
Intangible assets	100,000	100,000	100,000
Other assets	48,000	60,500	61,500
Total assets	$2,278,000	$2,191,000	$1,760,000
Liabilities:			
Current liabilities	$ 410,000	$ 501,000	$ 130,000
Long-term liabilities	400,000	600,000	400,000
Total liabilities	$ 810,000	$1,101,000	$ 530,000
Stockholders' equity:			
Paid-in capital	$1,100,000	$ 800,000	$1,000,000
Retained earnings	368,000	290,000	230,000
Total stockholders' equity	$1,468,000	$1,090,000	$1,230,000
Total liabilities and stockholders' equity	$2,278,000	$2,191,000	$1,760,000

Required:

1. Prepare common-size income statements and balance sheets for Clarksville Corporation for the years 2004, 2005, and 2006.
2. Summarize any trends you see in Clarksville's numbers from 2004 to 2006.

Problem 5-7

DuPont Analysis

Financial information (in thousands of dollars) relating to three different companies follows.

	Company A	Company B	Company C
Net sales	$ 60,000	$28,000	$21,000
Net income	9,600	1,850	360
Total assets	155,400	21,500	3,200
Total equity	61,000	11,300	1,690

Required:

1. Compute the following ratios:
   a. Return on sales
   b. Asset turnover
   c. Assets-to-equity ratio
   d. Return on equity
2. **Interpretive Question:** Assume the three companies are (a) a large department store, (b) a large supermarket, and (c) a large electric utility. Based on the above information, identify each company. Explain your answer.

Problem 5-8

Spreadsheet

DuPont Analysis

Refer to the financial statement information in Problem 5-6 for Clarksville Corporation.

Required:

For the years 2004, 2005, and 2006, compute the following ratios:

1. Return on sales
2. Asset turnover
3. Assets-to-equity ratio
4. Return on equity

Problem 5-9

Ratio Analysis

The following financial data are taken from the records of Emily Kate Company.

Emily Kate Company
Comparative Balance Sheet
December 31

	2006	2005
Assets:		
Cash	$ 45,000	$ 29,000
Accounts receivable	5,000	9,000
Inventory	255,000	225,000
Property, plant, and equipment	49,000	49,000
Total assets	$354,000	$312,000
Liabilities and stockholders' equity:		
Current liabilities	$ 44,000	$ 27,000
Noncurrent liabilities	180,000	165,000
Stockholders' equity	130,000	120,000
Total liabilities and stockholders' equity	$354,000	$312,000

(continued)

Emily Kate Company
Comparative Income Statement
For the Years Ended December 31

	2006	2005
Sales	$580,000	$410,000
Cost of goods sold	245,000	185,000
Gross margin on sales	$335,000	$225,000
Operating expenses	145,000	133,000
Interest expense	12,000	9,000
Income tax expense	56,000	35,000
Net income	$122,000	$ 48,000

Required:
1. Compute the following ratios for 2005 and 2006:
   a. Current ratio
   b. Debt ratio
   c. Asset turnover
   d. Return on sales
   e. Return on equity
2. Have the firm's performance and financial position improved from 2005 to 2006? Explain.

Problem 5-10

Ratio Analysis
The following data are taken from the records of John Spencer Corporation.

John Spencer Corporation
Comparative Balance Sheet
December 31

	2006	2005
Assets:		
Cash	$ 4,000	$ 6,000
Accounts receivable	16,000	14,000
Inventory	40,000	20,000
Property, plant, and equipment	100,000	100,000
Other assets	16,000	20,000
Total assets	$176,000	$160,000
Liabilities and stockholders' equity:		
Current liabilities	$ 44,000	$ 50,000
Long-term liabilities	24,000	10,000
Paid-in capital	60,000	60,000
Retained earnings	48,000	40,000
Total liabilities and stockholders' equity	$176,000	$160,000

John Spencer Corporation
Comparative Income Statement
For the Years Ended December 31

	2006	2005
Sales	$530,000	$448,000
Cost of goods sold	372,000	338,000
Gross margin on sales	$158,000	$110,000
Operating expense	102,000	68,000
Operating income	$ 56,000	$ 42,000
Interest expense	4,000	2,000
Income before taxes	$ 52,000	$ 40,000
Income taxes	13,000	12,000
Net income	$ 39,000	$ 28,000

Required:
1. Compute the following ratios for 2005 and 2006:
   a. Current ratio
   b. Debt ratio
   c. Asset turnover
   d. Return on sales
   e. Return on equity
2. Have the firm's performance and financial position improved from 2005 to 2006? Explain.

Problem 5-11

Cash Flow Analysis
Below are data extracted from the financial statements for Ping Shek Company.

Ping Shek Company
Selected Financial Statement Data
For the Years Ended December 31, 2006 and 2005
(in millions of dollars)

	2006	2005
Total assets	84,000	70,000
Stockholders' equity	22,000	20,000
Sales	$88,000	$74,000
Net income	7,200	4,800
Cash from operations	9,600	13,000
Cash paid for capital expenditures	8,900	6,600
Cash paid for acquisitions	2,500	200
Cash paid for interest	1,500	1,100
Cash paid for income taxes	4,100	4,000

Required:
1. Compute the following for 2005 and 2006:
   a. Return on sales   c. Cash flow-to-net income ratio
   b. Return on equity   d. Cash flow adequacy ratio
2. In which year did Ping Shek Company perform better: 2005 or 2006? Explain your answer.

discussion cases

Case 5-1

Analyzing Earnings

Roger Donahoe owns two businesses: a drug store and a retail department store.

	Drug Store	Department Store
Net sales	$1,050,000	$670,000
Cost of goods sold	1,000,000	600,000
Average total assets	50,000	200,000
Other expenses	39,500	36,500

Which business is more profitable? Which business is more efficient? Overall, which business would you consider to be a more attractive investment?

Case 5-2

Can a Ratio Be Too Good?

Tony Christopher is analyzing the financial statements of Shaycole Company and has computed the following ratios:

	Shaycole	Industry Comparison
Current ratio	4.7	1.9
Asset turnover	1.8 times	1.4 times
Debt ratio	0.317	0.564

Andy Martinez, Tony's colleague, tells Tony that Shaycole looks great. Andy points out that, although Shaycole's ratios deviate significantly from the industry norms, all the deviations suggest that Shaycole is doing better than other firms in its industry. Is Andy right?

Case 5-3

Evaluating Alternative Investments

Judy Snow is considering investing $10,000 and wishes to know which of two companies offers the better alternative.

The Hoffman Company earned net income of $63,000 last year on average total assets of $280,000 and average stockholders' equity of $210,000. The company's shares are selling for $100 per share; 6,300 shares of common stock are outstanding.

The McMahon Company earned $24,375 last year on average total assets of $125,000 and average stockholders' equity of $100,000. The company's common shares are selling for $78 per share; 2,500 shares are outstanding.

Which stock should Judy buy?

judgment calls

Judgment 5-1

You Decide: Could we see Enron coming?

Sherron Watkins, the whistle-blower at ENRON, made the following statement at a conference that one of the authors attended: "If anyone would have been watching the cash flows of

Enron, they could have figured out that there were problems." While traditional ratios don't reveal the problems, the following ratio provides some interesting results when looked at on a quarterly basis:

$$\frac{\text{Net Income from Operations} - \text{Cash Flows from Operations}}{\text{Net Income from Operations}}$$

During the period 1998 and 2001, this ratio revealed the following:

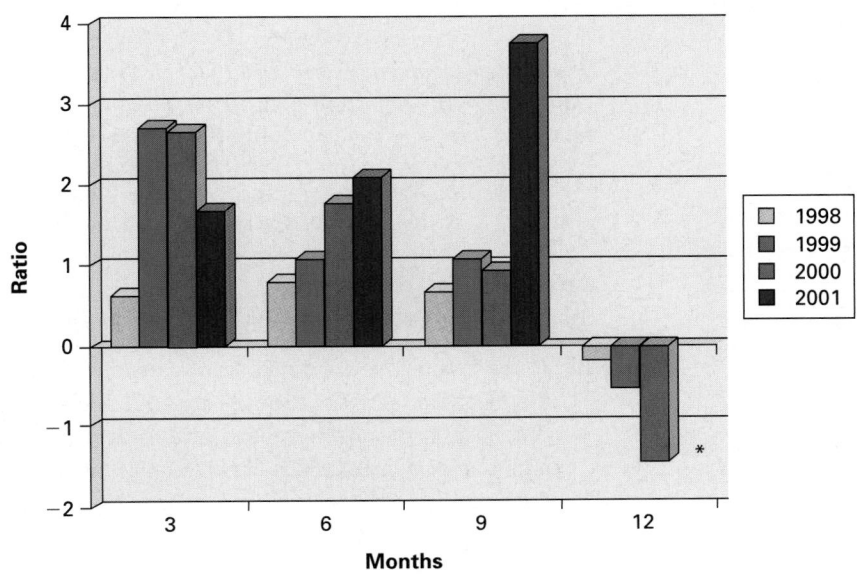

*Note: The Enron fraud was discovered in the 4th quarter of 2001. As a result, comparable 12-month numbers are not available.

Does this ratio look normal or as expected for a nonfraud committing company? What would you expect this ratio to look like? Why do the yearly results look so different than the quarterly results?

Judgment 5-2

You Decide: Ratios and debt covenants

XYZ Company has some leases on buildings that are structured so they do not have to be reported on the balance sheet as assets and liabilities (synthetic leases). However, as a term of the agreement, the lessor—a financial institution—requires that the company maintain an amount of cash in its institution so that the buildings could be purchased if the company misses some restrictive covenant agreements (i.e., certain ratio requirements, such as a current ratio of 2:1, etc.). The total amount of cash required to be held by the bank is $60 million. So far, XYZ has been including the $60 million in its cash account when calculating its current ratio. Your auditor has suggested that since the $60 million is restricted for a certain purpose, it should be reported as a long-term investment rather than as cash. Reclassifying the $60 million from cash to long-term investments would throw all kinds of ratios in default and you definitely don't want to do it. What is the appropriate accounting?

C o m p e t e n c y   E n h a n c e m e n t   O p p o r t u n i t i e s

▶ **Analyzing Real Company Information**   ▶ **The Debate**
▶ **International Case**   ▶ **Cumulative Spreadsheet Project**
▶ **Ethics Case**   ▶ **Internet Search**
▶ **Writing Assignment**

The following additional assignments provide opportunities for students to develop critical thinking, ethical perspectives, oral and written communication skills, experience with electronic research, and teamwork through group and business activities.

▷ *Analyzing Real Company Information*

Analyzing 5-1 (Microsoft)

Using MICROSOFT's 2002 Form 10-K contained in Appendix A, answer the following questions:

1. In the chapter, we computed ratio values for Microsoft for the fiscal year 2002. Compute the following ratios for Microsoft for 2001 and compare those results to the 2002 results contained in the chapter—debt ratio, current ratio, return on sales, asset turnover, and return on equity. For which of these ratios did Microsoft improve from 2001 to 2002?
2. Examine Microsoft's common-size balance sheet on page 214. Microsoft's short-term investments and equity and long-term investments represent what percentage of sales? What percentage of total assets do these two line items represent? Why do you think Microsoft has so much money tied up in investments?

Analyzing 5-2 (DuPont)

In this chapter, you were introduced to the DuPont framework. Let us take a moment and apply that framework to the DUPONT COMPANY. DuPont is a company made up of many business segments and has the challenge of how to manage the diverse set of businesses operating under the control of the DuPont management team. In its 2002 annual report, DuPont described its business segments as follows:

> The company's reporting segments include five market- and technology-focused growth platforms, Textiles & Interiors, which is targeted for separation from the company, and Pharmaceuticals. The growth platforms are Agriculture & Nutrition; Coatings & Color Technologies; Electronic & Communication Technologies; Performance Materials; and Safety & Protection. The company reports results of its nonaligned businesses and embryonic businesses as Other.

Summary segment results for 2002 are as follows:

2002	Agriculture & Nutrition	Coatings & Color Technologies	Electronic & Communication Technologies	Performance Materials	Pharmaceuticals	Safety & Protection	Textiles & Interiors
Total segment sales	$4,510	$5,026	$2,540	$4,868	$ —	$3,483	$6,279
After-tax operating income (loss)(2)	443	483	217	476	329	490	72
Segment net assets	5,963	3,235	2,190	3,254	118	1,942	5,598

1. Using segment after-tax operating income as a substitute for total company net income, tell which segment has the highest return on sales? The lowest?
2. Which segment has the highest asset turnover? The lowest?

Analyzing 5-3 (The Walt Disney Company)

Information from the 2002 financial statements of THE WALT DISNEY COMPANY is listed below. This information reports Disney's performance, by geographic area.

	United States	Europe	Rest of the world
Sales	$ 9,858.8	$1,552.1	$701.2
Operating income	1,745.8	464.1	323.2
Identifiable assets	13,437.5	1,060.2	108.1

1. Disney divides its worldwide operations into three geographic areas: the United States, Europe, and the rest of the world. Which of these three has the best 2002 profitability as measured by return on sales?
2. Which of Disney's three geographic areas has the best overall asset efficiency in 2002 as measured by asset turnover?
3. Discuss why return on equity cannot be computed for each geographic area.

International Case

Which Is the Stronger Partner in the Merger?

International

In May 1998, DAIMLER-BENZ and CHRYSLER announced their intention to merge. Daimler-Benz was the largest industrial company in Europe, and Chrysler was Number 3 of the Big Three automakers in the United States. The merger resulted in DAIMLERCHRYSLER becoming (at the time) the second largest automobile company in the world with 2000 sales exceeding $150 billion (GENERAL MOTORS reported sales in 2000 of $160 billion).

An interesting question is, "At the time of the merger, which of the two companies was the stronger?" Below are summary data for the two companies, both overall and for their respective automotive divisions.

	Daimler-Benz		Chrysler	
	Overall	Automotive	Overall	Automotive
Sales	DM 124,050	DM 91,632	$61,147	$58,662
Net income	8,042	3,501	2,805	4,238
Total assets	137,099	46,955	60,418	44,483

The amounts are in millions of Deutsche marks for Daimler-Benz and millions of U.S. dollars for Chrysler.

For the automotive segment information, net income is the operating income for the segment and total assets are the assets that are identifiable with the segment.

1. Compute the following for both companies for overall results and automotive division results:
   a. Return on sales
   b. Asset turnover

(continued)

2. In comparing the ratios calculated in (1), why don't you have to make adjustments for currency differences?

3. Which company had more worldwide automotive sales in 1997? *Note:* Don't forget the currency difference.

▷ *Ethics Case*

Does the Bonus Plan Reward the Right Thing?

Roaring Springs Booksellers is an Internet book company. Customers choose their purchases from an online catalog and make their orders online. Roaring Springs then assembles the books from its warehouse inventory, packs the order, and ships it to the customer within three working days. The rapid turnaround time on orders requires Roaring Springs to have a large warehouse staff; wage expense averages almost 20% of sales.

Each member of Roaring Springs's top management team receives an annual bonus equal to 1% of his or her salary for every 0.1% that Roaring Springs's return on sales exceeds 5.0%. For example, if return on sales is 5.3%, each top manager would receive a bonus of 3% of salary. Historically, return on sales for Roaring Springs has ranged between 4.5% and 5.5%.

The management of Roaring Springs has come up with a plan to dramatically increase return on sales, perhaps to as high as 6.5% to 7.0%. The plan is to acquire a sophisticated, computerized packing machine that can receive customer order information, mechanically assemble the books for each order, box the order, print an address label, and route the box to the correct loading dock for pickup by the delivery service. Acquisition of this machine will allow Roaring Springs to lay off 100 warehouse employees, resulting in a significant savings in wage expense. Top management intends to acquire the machine by using new investment capital from stockholders and thus avoid an increase in interest expense. Because the depreciation expense on the new machine will be much less than the savings in reduced wage expense, return on sales will increase.

All the top managers of Roaring Springs are excited about the new plan because it could increase their bonuses to as much as 20% of salary. As assistant to the chief financial officer of Roaring Springs, you have been asked to prepare a briefing for the board of directors explaining exactly how this new packing machine will increase return on sales. As part of your preparation, you decide to examine the impact of the machine acquisition on the other two components of the DuPont framework—efficiency and leverage. You find that even with the projected increase in return on sales, the decrease in asset turnover and in the assets-to-equity ratio will cause total return on equity to decline from its current level of 18% to around 14%.

Your presentation is scheduled for the next board of directors meeting in two weeks. What should you do?

▷ *Writing Assignment*

Who Should Get a Holiday Loan?

You are head of the loan department at Wilshire National Bank and have been approached by two firms in the retail toy business. Each firm is requesting a nine-month term loan to purchase inventory for the holiday season. You must make your recommendations to the loan committee and have gathered the following data in order to make your analysis. Fun Toy Company was organized in early 2005. The first year of operations was fairly successful, as the firm earned net income of $45,000. Total sales for the year were $600,000, and total assets at year-end December 31, 2005, were $350,000. A condensed balance sheet at September 30, 2006, follows. The firm is requesting a $100,000 loan.

Assets:		Liabilities and stockholders' equity:	
Cash	$ 60,000	Accounts payable	$ 70,000
Accounts receivable	65,000	Note payable, due 10/5/06	100,000
Inventory	125,000	Stockholders' equity	240,000
Prepaid expenses	5,000		
Furniture and fixtures	155,000	Total liabilities and	
Total assets	$410,000	stockholders' equity	$410,000

The Toy Store, the other firm, has been in business for many years. The firm's net income was $100,000 on total sales of $2,000,000 in the most recent fiscal year. A balance sheet as of September 30, 2006, is given below. The firm is seeking a $200,000 loan.

Assets:		Liabilities and stockholders' equity:	
Cash	$ 60,000	Accounts payable	$ 350,000
Accounts receivable	100,000	Current bank loan payable	150,000
Inventory	400,000	Long-term debt	400,000
Supplies	10,000	Stockholders' equity	500,000
Prepaid expenses	5,000		
Property, plant, and			
equipment	825,000	Total liabilities and	
Total assets	$1,400,000	stockholders' equity	$1,400,000

Write a one-page memo to the loan committee containing your recommendation about making loans to Fun Toy Company and to The Toy Store. You should use selected financial ratios in making your recommendation. Remember, your memo is only one page, so you can't just present a list of every possible ratio computation. Build your recommendation around a few key numbers.

▶ *The Debate*

Standardizing Ratios

Up to this point in the text, you have been introduced to numerous ratios—current ratio, profit margin, return on equity, and so forth. The DuPont framework introduced in this chapter provides a meaningful way of using ratios to compare a company's performance both across time and across companies. Using ratios for comparison purposes could be facilitated by standardizing certain ratios and requiring all companies to compute a specified set of ratios in exactly the same way. For example, when computing a debt-to-equity ratio, should debt include all liabilities or only long-term liabilities? Having a specified definition of what should be included in the debt number and what should be included in the equity number might facilitate comparison.

Divide your group into two teams and defend the following positions:

- Team 1 represents "Standardize the Ratios." The FASB (or some other group) should establish standards for computing ratios. All firms would be required to compute certain ratios and include them with other financial statement information. In addition, definitions should be provided that specify what account balances are to be included in the numerator and denominator of each ratio.
- Team 2 represents "Freedom of Ratios." Ratios should be neither defined nor required by standard setters. Different financial statement users use the information for different purposes and in different ways. Requiring ratios for all companies may result in inappropriate comparisons being made.

▷ *Cumulative Spreadsheet Project*

The balance sheet and income statement created for Handyman Company in the spreadsheet assignment in Chapter 2 will be used for ratio computations and analysis in this chapter.

1. Refer back to the financial statement numbers for Handyman Company for 2006 [given in part (1) of the cumulative spreadsheet project assignment in Chapter 2]. Using the balance sheet and income statement created with those numbers, do the following:
   a. Create common-size financial statements.
   b. Create spreadsheet cell formulas to compute and display values for the following ratios:
      i. Current ratio
      ii. Debt ratio
      iii. Asset turnover
      iv. Return on sales
      v. Return on equity

2. Change the financial statement numbers used in (1) by following the instructions given in part (2) of the cumulative spreadsheet project assignment in Chapter 2. This should also change the common-size percentages and the ratio values.

3. From the differences in the common-size financial statements and in the computed ratio values between parts (1) and (2), which set of financial statements represents a stronger company? Explain your answer.

▷ *Internet Search*

Dupont

To find out a little more about DUPONT, access DuPont's Web site at **http://www.dupont.com**. Sometimes Web addresses change, so if this address doesn't work, access the Web site for this textbook (**http://albrecht.swlearning.com**) for an updated link.

Once you've gained access to the site, answer the following questions:

1. Who is the current chief executive officer (CEO) of DuPont? How long has he or she been the CEO?

2. The DuPont organization includes a wide range of diverse types of businesses. How many employees does DuPont have? In how many countries does DuPont operate? How many manufacturing facilities does DuPont operate? What fraction of DuPont's business is done outside the United States?

3. DuPont has a number of well-known products. The company's Web site offers further information on some of those products. When did DuPont's polymer chemists invent nylon? In addition to bulletproof vests, what else is Kevlar used for?

4. DuPont reports a corporate commitment to moving toward zero emissions, zero employee injuries, and zero material waste. What progress does it report in its effort to reduce air carcinogenic emissions?

c h a p t e r

6

Ensuring the Integrity of Financial Information

Learning Objectives

After studying this chapter, you should be able to:

1 Identify the types of problems that can appear in financial statements.

2 Describe the safeguards employed within a firm to ensure that financial statements are free from problems.

3 Understand the concept of earnings management and why it occurs.

4 Understand the major parts of the Sarbanes-Oxley Act and how it impacts financial reporting.

5 Describe the role of auditors and how their presence affects the integrity of financial statements.

6 Explain the role of the Securities and Exchange Commission in adding credibility to financial statements.

chapter 6

Until 2002, WORLDCOM, a telecom giant, appeared to be one of the greatest corporate success stories ever. In 1983, a group of partners led by former basketball coach Bernard Ebbers sketched out their idea for a long distance telephone company on a napkin in a coffee shop in Hattiesburg, Mississippi. Soon after, their company LDDS (Long Distance Discount Service) began providing service as a long distance reseller. For 15 years, it grew quickly through acquisitions and mergers. Bernard Ebbers was named CEO in 1985, and the company sold shares of stock to the public in August 1989. Its $40 billion merger with MCI in 1998 was the largest corporate merger in history at the time.

The company was a favorite with investors and Wall Street analysts. The stock reached a peak of $64.51 per share in June 1999. At that time, CEO Bernard Ebbers was listed by *Forbes Magazine* as one of the richest men in the United States. Michael Jordan, the famous professional basketball player and most popular athlete in the world, provided commercial endorsements for WorldCom.

In October 1999, WorldCom attempted to purchase SPRINT in a stock buyout for $129 billion in stock and debt. The deal was vetoed by the Department of Justice. Even without the Sprint merger, by 1999, WorldCom owned a third of all U.S. data cables, which handled over 50% of all U.S. Internet traffic and e-mails worldwide, owned the 2nd largest long distance operator, MCI, and had over 20 million customers.

At the same time, however, the success of the company began to unravel with the accumulation of debt and expenses, the fall of the stock market, and drops in long distance rates and revenue. While it would take nearly two years for the extent of these problems to become public, in the end, WorldCom disclosed massive financial statement fraud and filed for Chapter 11 bankruptcy. In 2002, WorldCom became a horror story that involved the largest accounting fraud ever reported, SEC investigations, the resignation of CEO Bernard Ebbers, a $101.9 billion dollar bankruptcy, and a stock that was worth less than a payphone call.

While there were several different types of financial statement frauds committed by WorldCom, by far the largest was the manipulation of expenses and assets. In a court filing in New York in November 2002, the Securities and Exchange Commission (SEC) said that WorldCom admitted that it concealed over $9 billion in expenses, all of which was converted into false profits.

As you learned in earlier chapters, expenditures should be classified as assets and listed on the balance sheet if they have future value, such as expenditures for buildings or equipment. If expenditures are for current operating costs such as salaries or rent, however, you learned that they should be expensed as incurred and reported as expenses on the income statement.

In simple terms, instead of expensing costs that had been incurred, the company was capitalizing those costs and putting them on the balance sheet. These expenditures should have been subtracted from revenues on the income statement and reported as expenses when incurred. The result was that reported expenses were lower than they should have been on the income statement and reported assets and owners' equity were higher than they should have been on the balance sheet. Essentially, what WorldCom was doing was the equivalent of buying paper clips and recording them as buildings.

This hiding of expenses by accounting for them as assets and pushing operating costs into the future gave the appearance of high profits. This apparent profitability pleased investors who pushed the stock up to a high of $64.51 in June 1999. Reported profits in 2001 alone were $1.38 billion when in reality the company was experiencing and should have reported a loss.

The simple WorldCom fraud was discovered when some obscure tips provided to the company's internal auditors were pursued by Cynthia Cooper, Gene Morse, and Glyn Smith, all internal auditors working for the company. At the same time, the SEC started an investigation into WorldCom's profitability, wondering how WorldCom could be so profitable at the same time other telecom companies were losing money. The following sequence of events details WorldCom's quick downfall:

- June 20, 2002—The internal auditors explained the financial statement frauds to the company's audit committee.
- June 25, 2002—WorldCom publicly announced that it had inflated profits by over $3.8 billion for the previous five quarters (a number that would grow to over $9 billion).
- June 26, 2002—Several civil suits were filed against the company and its auditors, and trading in the company's stock was halted.
- July 21, 2002—The company declared bankruptcy. The fraud eventually cost over 17,000 people their jobs.

At a subsequent hearing, David Myers, an accountant with WorldCom, stated: "I was instructed on a quarterly basis by Scott Sullivan, chief financial officer, to ensure that entries were made to falsify WorldCom's books to reduce WorldCom's reported actual costs and therefore to increase WorldCom's reported earnings." He said that Scott Sullivan and he would ". . . work backward, picking the earnings numbers that they knew Wall Street analysts expected to see, and then force WorldCom's financials to match those numbers." While these shenanigans worked for a time, in the end, WorldCom's total market value (number of shares of stock times stock price) went from a high of about $120 billion to almost nothing and several individuals were indicted for fraud.

FYI:

On April 14, 2002, WorldCom announced that it was changing its name to MCI—the company it purchased in 1998.

n Chapters 1 and 2, you were introduced to financial accounting and shown the outputs (financial statements) of the financial reporting process. You learned that the balance sheet, income statement, and statement of cash flows are reports used by organizations to summarize their financial results for various users. In Chapters 3 and 4, the accounting cycle, the method of entering and processing financial transaction information in the accounting records, was described. You learned that transaction data are captured by journal entries, journal entry data are summarized in accounts and ledgers, ledger information is summarized on trial balances, and trial balance information provides the basis for the balance sheet, income statement, and statement of cash flows. In Chapter 5, you learned how financial statement information is used by comparing ratios over time for the same company or by comparing ratios across companies at the same point in time.

In Chapters 1 through 5, the assumption was made that the financial reporting process always works the way it should and that the resulting financial statements are accurate. In reality, however, because of unintentional errors, as well as intentional deception or fraud (such as in the WorldCom case), the resulting financial statements sometimes contain errors or omissions that can mislead investors, creditors, and other users.

In this chapter, we show how financial statements might be manipulated, and we discuss the safeguards built into the financial reporting system to prevent these abuses. We also examine the role that auditors play in ensuring that the financial statements fairly represent the financial performance of the firm.

The Types of Problems That Can Occur

▌ Identify the types of problems that can appear in financial statements.

Obviously, most businesses do not engage in massive frauds like those that occurred at WORLDCOM. Financial deception does not come about mainly for two reasons: (1) the vast majority of business managers are honest, possess integrity, and would not be associated with fraudulent activity, and (2) safeguards have been built into the accounting system to prevent and detect activities that are inconsistent with the objectives of a business. These safeguards attempt to eliminate problems from being introduced into the financial statements. However, during the past few years, there have been numerous financial statement frauds disclosed at companies such as ENRON, WORLDCOM, ADELPHIA, GLOBAL CROSSING, XEROX, QUEST, WASTE MANAGEMENT, CENDANT, ANICOM, HOMESTORE, SUNBEAM, TYCO, and others.

Before proceeding further, we need to make an important distinction regarding these problems. Problems in the financial statements can result for several different reasons.

1. *Errors*—result when unintentional mistakes are made in recording transactions, posting transactions, summarizing accounts, and so forth. Errors are *not intentional* and when detected are immediately corrected. Errors can result from sloppy accounting, misinformation, miscalculations, and other factors.

2. *Disagreements*—result when different people arrive at different conclusions based on the same set of facts. Because accounting involves judgment and estimates, opportunities for honest disagreements in judgment abound. These disagreements often come about because of the different incentives that motivate those involved with producing the financial statements. An example of a disagreement might be differing views about what percentage of reported receivables will be collected or how long equipment and other assets will last.
3. *Frauds*—result from intentional errors. Fraudulent financial reporting occurs when management chooses to intentionally manipulate the financial statements to serve their own purposes, such as meeting Wall Street's earnings forecasts as was the case with WorldCom.

An accounting system should be designed to significantly reduce the possibility that problems, in whatever form, will make their way into financial statements.

Types of Errors in the Reporting Process

Errors, and other problems, can occur in most stages of the accounting cycle. We will first describe the kinds of errors that can occur and then identify controls to minimize these errors.

Errors in Transactions and Journal Entries

Transactions, such as selling products or services, paying salaries, buying inventory, and paying taxes, are entered into the accounting records through journal entries. For example, if $5,000 is paid to an attorney for legal services, the following journal entry is made:

Legal Expense	5,000	
Cash		5,000
Paid an attorney $5,000 for legal services.		

An invoice from the law firm should support this entry. Errors could be introduced into the financial reporting process if (1) the invoice from the law firm was lost and the legal expense was not entered into the accounting records, (2) the amount entered into the accounting records was incorrect, or (3) the accounts involved were incorrectly identified.

Errors in Accounts and Ledgers

Even when journal entries properly summarize legitimate transactions, errors and misstatements can be introduced into the financial records because journal entry data are not summarized appropriately or accurately in the ledgers. Using the previous example of paying an attorney $5,000, errors could occur at the posting stage of the accounting cycle if the legal expense is entered in the wrong account in the ledger or if an incorrect amount is posted to the correct account. Posting the correct amount to the wrong expense account would result in the correct total for all expenses, but individual expense account balances would be incorrect.

A more severe error occurs at the ledger stage if amounts that should be included in asset or liability accounts are improperly included in expense or revenue accounts, or vice versa. Examples include (1) recording insurance expense as prepaid insurance (an asset), (2) recording purchases of goods for resale as inventory (an asset) when they should be reported as cost of goods sold (an expense), (3) recording money received from customers as revenue when it should be recorded as unearned revenue (a liability), or (4) not reporting supplies used as an expense.

Disagreements in Judgment

Many think that the accounting profession involves exactness and precision and that the accountant simply records the facts, totals the numbers, and presents unbiased results. Nothing could be further from the truth. Accountants are constantly making judgments and estimates regarding the past and the future. Let's return to the landscaping business that we introduced in Chapters 3 and 4 to illustrate some of the judgments involved in the accounting process.

As your lawn care and landscaping business has become more and more successful, you have been able to obtain bigger and better jobs. Recently, you signed a contract to provide all the landscaping for a new condominium complex currently under construction. The terms of the contract call for payment of one-half of the contract amount up front and the remaining one-half upon completion. You begin working on the condominium landscaping in early December, but it looks as though you will not finish until well into January. To prepare financial statements at the end of the year, how much of the condominium contract should you report as revenue? Well, that depends on how close to completion the job is. If you are 25% complete, it makes sense to report 25% of the contract amount as revenue. If you are 75% complete, report 75% of the contract amount as revenue. The hard part is determining how much of the job has been completed.

Suppose you contact two landscapers (friendly competitors) and ask them to provide you with an estimate of how complete the landscaping job is at year-end. Would it be possible for these two people to arrive at different conclusions regarding the percentage of completion? Which one would be right? Different people can look at the same set of facts and arrive at different conclusions. They're not wrong, just different. In this case, the different estimates would result in different financial statement numbers. These different numbers could make the difference between your company showing a profit or reporting a loss.

Consider another example. Most of your customers pay promptly, but some take a little longer to pay. A few customers discontinue their lawn care service and never pay for some of the services they received. Your problem is that when you provide a service for a customer, you do not know if that customer will be a "prompt payer," a "slow payer," or a "no payer." Recognizing that a certain percentage of your customers will be "no payers," should you record a receivable (and a revenue) for the full amount of every sale? As you will learn in Chapter 7, most businesses recognize that a certain percentage of receivables will be uncollectible. How should you arrive at the amount of your receivables that won't be collected? Is it possible that

business environment

Manipulation of Journal Entries Adam F.* graduated in accounting from a large university. Upon graduation, he accepted a job with one of the "Big 4" CPA firms. He worked there for three years, during which time he became a CPA and served as the in-charge auditor on a number of audit engagements.

After three years, he left the CPA firm to accept a job as controller in a small bank. Along with two other individuals, he invested in a farm implement dealership. Unfortunately, business wasn't as good as expected, and the dealership lost large sums of money. To keep the business afloat, Adam began embezzling money from the bank. At first, he stole small amounts. As the business's cash needs became greater, he increased the amounts until he was stealing more than $15,000 per month. He concealed his frauds by creating journal entries debiting Advertising Expense and crediting Cash, as shown:

Advertising Expense	15,000	
Cash		15,000
Paid monthly advertising cost.		

your estimate will be slightly off? Could different people legitimately arrive at different estimates? Of course. These different estimates will then affect the results reported in the financial statements.

Fraudulent Financial Reporting

As mentioned previously, fraudulent financial reporting is intentional. To illustrate, consider the journal entry made previously related to legal expense. Assume that a company's accountant embezzles $5,000 and prepares the following journal entry to conceal the fraud:

Legal Expense	5,000	
Cash		5,000
Paid an attorney $5,000 for legal services.		

The accountant could prepare the journal entry without supporting documentation (e.g., an invoice) or create a fictitious invoice from a phantom law firm.

Unless someone is watching closely, the theft may go undetected. Because the accountant made a fictitious entry to Legal Expense, the accounting records appear to be correct, and the accounting equation still balances. Cash, an asset, is stolen, and the recognition of an expense results in owners' equity being reduced by the same amount.

$$\text{Assets} \quad = \text{Liabilities} + \quad \text{Owners' Equity}$$
$$\text{(decreased by \$5,000)} \qquad\qquad \text{(decreased by \$5,000)}$$

In addition, sometimes amounts for which there are no legitimate transactions are added or deducted directly from financial statement balances. Examples are listing sales that don't exist (as was the case with WASTE MANAGEMENT, the trash disposal company, which was making false entries to record revenues and receivables that overstated income by as much as 35% in 1996 and a total of $1.7 billion from 1992–1997); not recording sales returns or

Adam's fraud went undetected until he became greedy and expanded his methods of embezzling. He was caught when a customer of the bank twice made interest payments of $10,000. Adam took the second $10,000 payment and deposited it in his own account at the bank. The customer, realizing the error, notified the bank. The search for the missing $10,000 revealed Adam's thefts.

As a result of his fraud, Adam was sentenced to four years in prison and entered into a restitution agreement to repay the bank. The IRS also informed Adam that his embezzled funds were taxable, and since he hadn't paid timely taxes, he owed fines, penalties, interest, and taxes totaling nearly $100,000.

When released from jail, Adam will probably spend the rest of his life paying back the bank and the IRS the $250,000 he now owes.

*All Business Environments in this chapter are real cases. In some instances, such as here, the names have been changed.

Source: This case is from the video *The Red Flags of Fraud*, The Association of Certified Fraud Examiners, Austin, Texas.

STOP & THINK

Before reading about the safeguards designed to minimize the types of problems we have just discussed, can you think of things that could be done to ensure that errors, disagreements in judgment, and fraudulent financial reporting do not occur?

uncollectible receivables (as was the case with the vacuum maker, REGINA, which did not record the return of over 40,000 vacuums); and not recording various expenses, understating liabilities, and overstating assets such as inventory or receivables (as was the case with PHAR-MOR, which overstated its assets by shipping products back and forth between stores when inventory was counted). Sometimes these types of mistatements are unintentional, but in many cases they are intentional.

TO SUMMARIZE: The accounting cycle and resulting financial reports of most organizations are accurate and can be relied on. Nevertheless, unintentional errors, disagreements in judgment, and fraudulent financial reporting can occur in the accounting process, thereby producing erroneous financial reports.

Safeguards Designed to Minimize Problems

2 Describe the safeguards employed within a firm to ensure that financial statements are free from problems.

Accounting is a language just as is English. In the same way that a falsehood can be written in English, a misleading story can be expressed by financial statements. By far, the vast majority of financial statements are as accurate as possible, and the preparers are honest. FEDERAL EXPRESS, the shipping company, for example, requires that its executives annually sign off on a code of ethics that gives assurances in writing that they have no conflicts of interest or know of no improprieties. The company's policy requires that any employee involved in any kind of dishonesty be immediately terminated and prosecuted. According to FedEx's policy, ". . . magnitude is not the issue. It doesn't matter if the impropriety involves a thousand or a million dollars, our company will not tolerate anything that is done unethically or inappropriately." Most organizations prepare accounting records and financial reports with integrity, and in most cases, preparers are even conservative when judgments and estimates are required. To help ensure that financial reports are accurate and to prevent problems such as those that occurred at WORLDCOM, several safeguards have been built into the financial reporting structure of most organizations in the United States. As a future user of accounting information, you should be aware of these safeguards and the reasons for their existence.

internal control structure
Safeguards in the form of policies and procedures established to provide management with reasonable assurance that the objectives of an entity will be achieved.

Most organizations build controls into their organization and financial reporting processes so that abuses are difficult. These safeguards, called the **internal control structure**, are internal to the organization preparing the financial statements. The American Institute of Certified Public Accountants (AICPA) has defined *internal control* as "the policies and procedures established to provide reasonable assurance that specific entity objectives will be achieved."[1] These internal controls protect investors and creditors and even help management in their efforts to run their organizations as effectively and efficiently as possible. When you encounter an organization or financial statements that do not have these controls and safeguards, you should exercise extreme care. Most companies have the following five concerns in mind when they are designing internal controls:

1. To provide accurate accounting records and financial statements containing reliable data for business decisions.
2. To safeguard assets and records. Most companies think of their assets as including their financial assets (such as cash or property), their employees, their confidential information, and their reputation and image.
3. To effectively and efficiently run their operations, without duplication of effort or waste.

1 AU Section 319, par. 06, Codification of Statements on Auditing Standards, CCH Inc., 1994, p. 98.

4. To follow management policies.
5. To comply with the Foreign Corrupt Practices Act, which requires companies to maintain proper record-keeping systems and controls.

The responsibility for establishing and maintaining the internal control structure belongs to a company's management. Until several years ago, this responsibility was only implied; there was no formal legal requirement. However, in the wake of illegal political campaign contributions, business frauds, and numerous illegal payments to foreign officials in exchange for business favors, in 1977, Congress passed the **Foreign Corrupt Practices Act (FCPA)**. As a result of this legislation, all companies whose stock is publicly traded are required by law to keep records that represent the firm's transactions accurately and fairly. In addition, they must maintain adequate systems of internal accounting control. Following the rash of reported financial statement frauds in 2001 and 2002, Congress passed the **Sarbanes-Oxley Act** (known as the corporate responsibility act) in 2002. This far-sweeping corporate reform act requires, among other things, that every company's annual report contain an "internal control report," which must (1) state the responsibility of management for establishing and maintaining an adequate internal control structure and procedures for financial reporting and (2) contain an assessment of the effectiveness of the internal control structure. (This act, by the way, requires that the CEO and CFO of every public company prepare and sign a statement to accompany their financial statements that certifies the "appropriateness of the financial statements and disclosures contained in the report.")

A company's internal control structure can be divided into five basic categories: (1) the control environment, (2) risk assessment, (3) control activities, (4) information and communication, and (5) monitoring. In this chapter, we will only briefly cover the control environment and control activities (sometimes called control procedures), as well as the need for monitoring (the areas of risk assessment and information and communication are left to courses covering the details of auditing). We will also discuss elements of accounting systems that are important from a control perspective.

The Control Environment

The **control environment** consists of the actions, policies, and procedures that reflect the overall attitudes of top management, the directors, and the owners about control and its importance to the company. In a strong control environment, management believes control is important and makes sure that everyone responds conscientiously to the control policies and procedures. Some of the key components of the control environment that relate to financial reporting are described below.

Management Philosophy and Operating Style

Does management set a good example by following controls? Do they stress the importance of controls to other employees? What is their management style? Are they, for example, risk averse or apt to take risks, dominated by one or two individuals or open to input from others, realistic or unrealistic about goals?

An example of a company with a poor management philosophy and operating style was ENRON. As you learned earlier in this book, Enron was a company that falsified its financial statements by hiding debt and other undesirable elements of the financial statements in off-balance sheet entities known as special purpose entities. Enron's environment became extremely competitive and compromising to the point where lower-level managers, who saw that top management was manipulating the books, participated in dishonest actions that enriched themselves at the cost of the company. In Enron's case, management was extremely dominant and dishonest; there were no clear lines of responsibility, budgets were unrealistic, and the company had no system of organizational checks and balances in place. Management's dishonest actions led to a climate of moral decay that filtered throughout the organization, resulting in widespread abuse.

Foreign Corrupt Practices Act (FCPA) Legislation requiring any company that has publicly traded stock to maintain records that accurately and fairly represent the company's transactions; additionally, requires any publicly-traded company to have an adequate system of internal accounting controls.

Sarbanes-Oxley Act A law passed by Congress in 2002 that gives the SEC significant oversight responsibility and control over companies issuing financial statements and their external auditors. The Act creates a Public Company Accounting Oversight Board with broad powers and authority to regulate the public accounting profession.

control environment The actions, policies, and procedures that reflect the overall attitudes of top management, the directors, and the owners about control and its importance to the entity.

organizational structure
Lines of authority and responsibility.

Organizational Structure

Does the **organizational structure** identify clear lines of authority and responsibility? Is the organizational structure so complex that dishonest transactions can be concealed?

An example of a complex organizational structure that was used to conceal a large fraud is the ESM COMPANY in Ohio. ESM was a brokerage business that bought and sold government securities. Over a period of seven years, the officers of the company funneled cash to themselves until the company owed approximately $300 million more in payables than it had in receivables. This net payable was concealed by setting up related entities and reporting a fictitious receivable from one of those companies in ESM Company's financial statements. If anyone had investigated the receivable, he or she would have found that the related company from which it was supposedly collectible was bankrupt.

Audit Committee

audit committee Members of a company's board of directors who are responsible for dealing with the external and internal auditors.

Every major company has a board of directors. A good control environment would suggest that a subset of these directors should form an **audit committee**. Generally, the audit committee should be comprised of outside directors (members of the board who are not officers of the company). The internal and external auditors would then be accountable to this audit committee. Under the Sarbanes-Oxley Act, members of the audit committee must be financially literate. The audit committee must be directly responsible for the appointment, compensation, and oversight of the work of the external auditor and must have the authority to engage independent legal counsel or other advisors if it suspects any wrongdoing.

External auditors who suspect wrongdoing in financial reporting should forward those concerns to the audit committee.

The Accounting System

accounting system The set of manual and computerized procedures and controls that provide for identifying relevant transactions or events, preparing accurate source documents, entering data into the accounting records accurately, processing transactions precisely, updating master files properly, and generating correct documents and reports.

The purpose of a company's accounting system is to identify, assemble, classify, analyze, record, and report the entity's transactions and to maintain accountability for assets. To be effective, the **accounting system** should contain adequate controls to ensure that seven control objectives are met.

1. *Validity.* Only valid transactions are recorded. If fictitious sales are recorded, for example, reported revenues will be too high, and the integrity of the financial statements will be lost.
2. *Authorization.* All transactions are properly authorized. If, for example, any employee could authorize purchases, a company might make duplicate purchases of the same items or purchase unneeded items.
3. *Completeness.* All legitimate transactions are recorded and the records are complete. If, for example, all liabilities are not recorded, a company will report a more favorable financial condition than actually exists.
4. *Classification.* All transactions are properly classified. For example, the current portion of long-term debt should be classified as a current liability. Incorrect classification would result in incorrect liability subtotals that would affect such ratios as the current ratio.
5. *Timeliness.* All transactions are recorded in the proper time period. A company might try to make its revenues and income look better than they are, for example, by recording early January sales in December.
6. *Valuation.* All transactions are properly valued. For example, if a receivable is uncollectible, it should not be classified as a current asset.
7. *Posting and summarization.* All transactions are properly included in subsidiary records and correctly summarized. Errors could occur, for example, if an accounts receivable entry was posted to the accounts payable account.

Control Activities (Procedures)

control activities (procedures) Policies and procedures used by management to meet their objectives; generally divided into adequate segregation of duties, proper procedures for authorization of transactions and activities, adequate documents and records, physical control over assets and records, and independent checks on performance.

Control activities or **control procedures** are those policies and procedures, in addition to the control environment and accounting system, that management has adopted to provide reasonable assurance that the company's established objectives will be met and that financial reports are accurate. Generally, control activities fall into five categories: adequate segregation of duties, proper procedures for authorization, adequate documents and records, physical control over assets and records, and independent checks on performance.

Adequate Segregation of Duties

segregation of duties A strategy to provide an internal check on performance through separation of authorization of transactions from custody of related assets, separation of operational responsibilities from record-keeping responsibilities, and separation of custody of assets from accounting personnel.

A good internal control system should provide for the appropriate **segregation of duties**. This means that no one department or individual should be responsible for handling all phases of a transaction. In some small businesses, this segregation is not possible because the limited number of employees prevents division of all the different functions. Nevertheless, there are three functions that should be performed by separate departments or by different people.

1. *Authorization.* Authorizing and approving the execution of transactions; for example, approving the sale of a building or land.
2. *Record keeping.* Recording the transactions in the accounting journals.
3. *Custody of assets.* Having physical possession of or control over the assets involved in transactions, including operational responsibility; for example, having the key to the safe in which cash or investment securities are kept or, more generally, having control over the production function.

By separating the responsibilities for these duties, a company realizes the efficiency derived from specialization and also reduces the errors, both intentional and unintentional, that might otherwise occur.

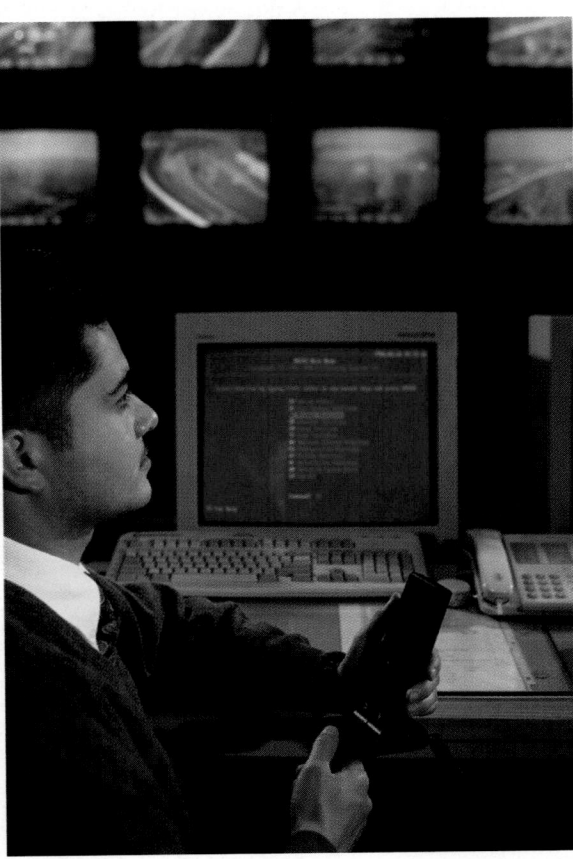

© Royalty-Free/CORBIS

Many companies use physical safeguards, such as surveillance cameras, to protect their resources.

Proper Procedures for Authorization

A strong system of internal control requires proper authorization for every transaction. In the typical corporate organization, this authorization originates with the stockholders who elect a board of directors. It is then delegated from the board of directors to upper-level management and eventually throughout the organization. While the board of directors and upper-level management possess a fairly general power of authorization, a clerk usually has limited authority. Thus, the board would authorize dividends, a general change in policies, or a merger; a clerk would be restricted to authorizing credit or a specific cash transaction. Only certain people should be authorized to enter data into accounting records and prepare accounting reports.

As an example of journal entries and misstated financial statements that were not authorized, consider the following example:

> In one of the large financial statement frauds that was disclosed in 2002, the CFO instructed the chief accountant to increase earnings by $105 million. The chief accountant was skeptical about the purpose of these instructions, but he did not challenge them. The mechanics were left to the chief accountant to carry out. The chief accountant created a spreadsheet containing seven pages of improper journal entries, 105 in total, that he determined were necessary to carry out the CFO's instructions. These types of fictitious and unauthorized journal entries were made over a five-year period.

Adequate Documents and Records

A key to good controls is an adequate system of documentation and records. As explained in Chapter 3, documents are the physical, objective evidence of accounting transactions. Their existence allows management to review any transaction for appropriate authorization. Documents are also the means by which information is communicated throughout an organization. In short, adequate documentation provides evidence that the recording and summarizing functions that lead to financial reports are being performed properly. A well-designed document has several characteristics: (1) it is easily interpreted and understood, (2) it has been designed with all possible uses in mind, (3) it has been prenumbered for easy identification and tracking, and (4) it is formatted so that it can be handled quickly and efficiently. Documents can be actual pieces of paper or information in a computer database.

Physical Control Over Assets and Records

physical safeguards Physical precautions used to protect assets and records, such as locks on doors, fireproof vaults, password verification, and security guards.

Some of the most crucial policies and procedures involve the use of adequate **physical safeguards** to protect resources. For example, a bank would not allow significant amounts of money to be transported in an ordinary car. Similarly, a company should not leave its valuable assets unprotected. Examples of physical safeguards are fireproof vaults for the storage of classified information, currency, and marketable securities; and guards, fences, and remote control cameras for the protection of equipment, materials, and merchandise. Records and documents are also important resources and must be protected. Re-creating lost or destroyed records can be costly and time-consuming, so companies make backup copies of records.

Independent Checks on Performance

independent checks Procedures for continual internal verification of other controls.

Having **independent checks** on performance is a valuable control technique. Independent checks incorporate reviews of functions, as well as the internal checks created from a proper segregation of duties.

There are many ways to independently check performance. Using independent reviewers, such as auditors, is one of the most common. In addition, mandatory vacations, where another employee performs the vacationing person's duties, periodic rotations or transfers, or merely having someone independent of the accounting records reconcile the bank statement are all types of independent checks.

TO SUMMARIZE: Most organizations have an internal control system that, among other things, helps ensure integrity in financial reports. The various elements of control that relate to financial reporting are summarized as follows:

Control Environment	Accounting System	Control Procedures
1. Management philosophy and operating style.	1. Valid transactions.	1. Segregation of duties.
2. Organizational structure.	2. Properly authorized transactions.	2. Proper procedures for authorization.
3. Audit committee.	3. Completeness.	3. Adequate documents and records.
	4. Proper classification.	4. Physical control over assets and records.
	5. Proper timing.	5. Independent checks on performance.
	6. Proper valuation.	
	7. Correct summarization.	

Public companies are required to include in their annual report a statement signed by management that describes and accepts responsibility for the internal controls of the company. The statement shown in Exhibit 1 was included in the 2002 annual report of IBM CORPORATION.

Reasons for Earnings Management

3 Understand the concept of earnings management and why it occurs.

Accountants, using the concepts of accrual accounting and the accounting standards that have been issued, add information value by using estimates and assumptions to convert the raw cash flow data into accrual data. However, the same flexibility that allows accountants to use pro-

Exhibit 1: IBM Corporation's 2002 Management Letter

Report of Management

Responsibility for the integrity and objectivity of the financial information presented in this Annual Report rests with IBM management. The accompanying financial statements have been prepared in conformity with generally accepted accounting principles, applying certain estimates and judgments as required.

IBM maintains an effective internal control structure. It consists, in part, of organizational arrangements with clearly defined lines of responsibility and delegation of authority, and comprehensive systems and control procedures. We believe this structure provides reasonable assurance that transactions are executed in accordance with management authorization, and that they are appropriately recorded in order to permit preparation of financial statements in conformity with generally accepted accounting principles and to adequately safeguard, verify and maintain accountability of assets. An important element of the control environment is an ongoing internal audit program.

To assure the effective administration of internal controls, we carefully select and train our employees, develop and disseminate written policies and procedures, provide appropriate communication channels, and foster an environment conducive to the effective functioning of controls. We believe that it is essential for the company to conduct its business affairs in accordance with the highest ethical standards, as set forth in the IBM Business Conduct Guidelines. These guidelines, translated into numerous languages, are distributed to employees throughout the world, and reemphasized through internal programs to assure that they are understood and followed.

PricewaterhouseCoopers LLP, independent accountants, is retained to examine IBM's financial statements. Its accompanying report is based on an examination conducted in accordance with generally accepted auditing standards, including a review of the internal control structure and tests of accounting procedures and records.

The Audit Committee of the Board of Directors is composed solely of outside directors, and is responsible for recommending to the Board the independent accounting firm to be retained for the coming year, subject to stockholder approval. The Audit Committee meets periodically and privately with the independent accountants, with the company's internal auditors, as well as with IBM management, to review accounting, auditing, internal control structure and financial reporting matters.

Samuel J. Palmisano
Chairman of the Board,
President and Chief Executive Officer

John R. Joyce
Senior Vice President
Chief Financial Officer

---

fessional judgment to produce financial statements that accurately portray a company's financial condition also allows desperate managers to manipulate the reported numbers.

This section describes four reasons for managing reported earnings. These aren't necessarily good reasons. However, they do reflect the forces that are often spoken of as pushing managers to manipulate reported earnings. These four reasons are as follows:

- Meet internal targets.
- Meet external expectations.
- Income smoothing.
- Window dressing for an IPO or a loan.

Meet Internal Targets

internal earnings targets
Financial goals established within a company.

Internal earnings targets are an important tool in motivating managers to increase sales efforts, control costs, and use resources more efficiently. But as with any performance measurement tool, it is a fact of life that the person being evaluated will have a tendency to forget the economic factors underlying the measurement and instead focus on the measured number itself.

Meet External Expectations

A wide variety of external stakeholders have an interest in the financial performance of a company. For example, employees and customers want a company to do well so that it can survive for the long run and make good on its long-term pension and warranty obligations. Suppliers want assurance that they will receive payment and, more importantly, that the purchasing company will be a reliable purchaser for many years into the future. For these stakeholders, signs of financial weakness, such as the reporting of negative earnings, are very bad news indeed. Accordingly, we shouldn't be surprised that in some companies when the initial computations reveal that a company will report a net loss, the company's accountants are asked to go back to the accrual judgments and estimates to see if just a few more dollars of earnings can be squeezed in order to get earnings to be positive.

Income Smoothing

Examine the time series of earnings for Company A and Company B shown in Exhibit 2. For Company A, the amount of earnings increases steadily for each year from Year 1 through Year 10. For Company B, the earnings series is like a roller coaster ride. Companies A and B have the same earnings in Year 1 and the same earnings in Year 10, and they also have the same total earnings over the 10-year period included in the graph. At the end of Year 10, if you were asked which company you would prefer to loan money to or to invest in, you would almost certainly choose Company A. The earnings stream of Company A gives you a sense of stability, reliability, and reduced risk.

Now, imagine yourself as the chief executive officer of Company B. You know that through aggressive accounting assumptions, you can strategically defer or accelerate the recognition of some revenues and expenses and smooth your reported earnings stream to be exactly like that shown for Company A. Would you be tempted to so? Of course you would. The practice of

Exhibit 2: Income Smoothing

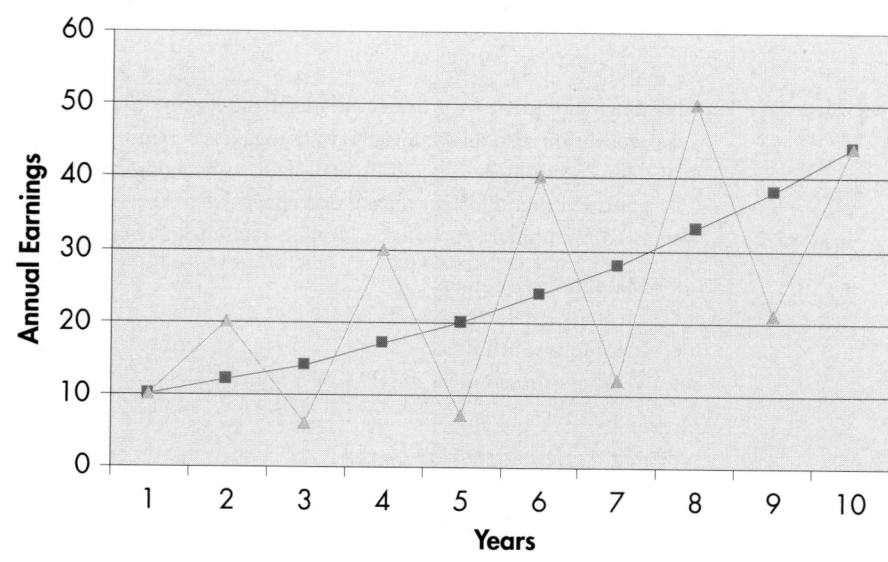

Time Series of Earnings for Companies A and B

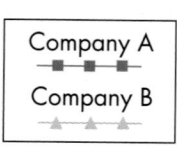

income smoothing The practice of carefully timing the recognition of revenues and expenses to even out the amount of reported earnings from one year to the next.

carefully timing the recognition of revenues and expenses to even out the amount of reported earnings from one year to the next is called **income smoothing**. By making a company appear to be less volatile, income smoothing can make it easier for a company to obtain a loan on favorable terms and to attract investors.

Window Dressing for an IPO or a Loan

For companies entering phases where it is critical that reported earnings look good, accounting assumptions can be stretched—sometimes to the breaking point. Such phases include just before making a large loan application or just before the initial public offering (IPO) of stock. Many studies have demonstrated the tendency of managers in U.S. companies to boost their reported earnings using accounting assumptions in the period before an IPO.

With all of the incentives to manage earnings, it isn't surprising that managers occasionally do use the flexibility inherent in accrual accounting to actually manage earnings. And the more accounting training one has, the easier it is to see ways in which accounting judgments and estimates can be used to "enhance" the reported numbers. In fact, there have been nationwide seminars on exactly how to effectively manage earnings. One popular seminar sponsored by the National Center for Continuing Education in 2001 was titled, "How to Manage Earnings in Conformance with GAAP." The target audience for the two-day seminar was described as CFOs, CPAs, controllers, auditors, bankers, analysts, and securities attorneys.

The Earnings Management Continuum

Not all earnings management schemes are created equal. The continuum in Exhibit 3 illustrates that earnings management can range from savvy timing of transactions to outright fraud. The discussion in this section discusses each activity on the earnings management continuum. Keep in mind that in most companies, earnings management, if it is practiced at all, does not extend beyond the savvy transaction timing found at the left end of the continuum in Exhibit 3. However, because of the importance, and economic significance, of the catastrophic reporting failures that are sometimes associated with companies that engage in more elaborate earnings management, the entire continuum is discussed here.

Strategic Matching

As mentioned in the earlier discussion of income smoothing, through awareness of the benefits of consistently meeting earnings targets or of reporting a stable income stream, a company can make extra efforts to ensure that certain key transactions are completed quickly, or delayed, in order for them to be recognized in the most advantageous quarter.

Change in Methods or Estimates with Full Disclosure

Companies frequently change accounting estimates respecting bad debts, return on pension funds, depreciation lives, and so forth. Although such changes are a routine part of adjusting

Exhibit 3: The Earnings Management Continuum

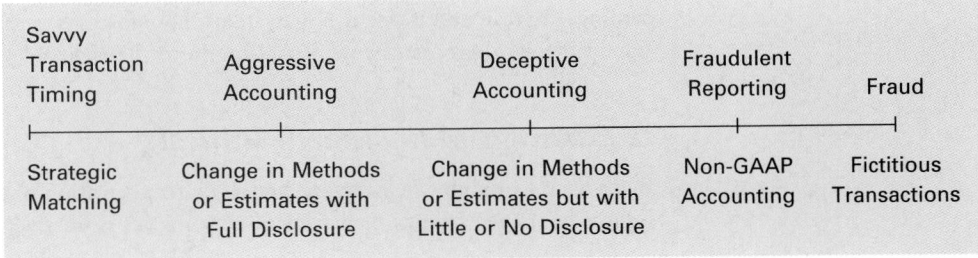

accounting estimates to reflect the most current information available, they can be used to manage the amount of reported earnings. Because the impact of such changes is fully disclosed, any earnings management motivation could be detected by financial statement users willing to do a little detective work.

Change in Methods or Estimates with Little or No Disclosure

In contrast to the accounting changes referred to in the preceding paragraph, other accounting changes are sometimes made without full disclosure. For example, in 1999 XEROX reported that the company changed the estimated interest rate used in recording sales-type leases without describing the change in the notes to the financial statements. While one might debate whether the new estimated interest rate was more appropriate, what is certain is that failing to disclose the impact of the change resulted in financial statement users being misled. These users evaluated the reported earnings of Xerox under the incorrect assumption that the results were compiled using a consistent set of accounting methods and estimates and could therefore be meaningfully compared to prior-year results. As indicated by the label in Exhibit 3, this constitutes deceptive accounting.

Non-GAAP Accounting

Toward the right end of the earnings management continuum lies the earnings management tool that can be politely called "non-GAAP accounting." A more descriptive label in many cases is "fraudulent reporting," although non-GAAP accounting can also be the result of inadvertent errors. For example, a brief description of some of ENRON's accounting practices was given in Chapter 1. It is clear that some (though certainly not all) of these accounting practices were established for the express purpose of hiding information from financial statement users. In so doing, Enron violated the spirit of the accounting standards. In some cases, Enron also violated the letter of the standards by using some accounting practices that were not allowed under GAAP.

Fictitious Transactions

As mentioned previously in this chapter, REGINA did not record the return of over 40,000 vacuums. In fact, the company rented secret warehouses in which to store returned merchandise in order to avoid recording the returns. This is an example of outright fraud, which is the deceptive concealment of transactions (like the sales returns) or the creation of fictitious transactions.

The five items displayed in Exhibit 3 also mirror the progression in earnings management strategies followed by individual companies. These activities start small and legitimate and really reflect nothing more than the strategic timing of transactions to smooth reported results. In the face of operating results that fall short of targets, a company might make some cosmetic changes in accounting estimates in order to meet earnings expectations, but would fully disclose these changes to avoid deceiving serious financial statement users. If operating results are far short of expectations, an increasingly desperate management might cross the line into deceptive accounting by making accounting changes that are not disclosed or by violating GAAP completely. Finally, when the gap between expected results and actual results is so great that it cannot be closed by any accounting assumption, a manager who is still fixated on making the target number must resort to out-and-out fraud by inventing transactions and customers. The key thing to remember is that the forces encouraging managers and accountants to manage earnings are real, and if one is not aware of those forces it is easy to gradually slip from the left side of the earnings management continuum to the right side.

Is Earnings Management Ethical?

Refer back to Exhibit 3. Everyone agrees that the creation of fictitious transactions, at the far right side of the earnings management continuum, is unethical. But there the universal agreement ends with respect to what is and is not ethical. For example, managers and their auditors frequently disagree about what constitutes fraudulent, non-GAAP reporting. In the WORLD-COM example mentioned earlier, the company's CFO vigorously defended the capitalization, rather than the expensing, of the disputed $3.8 billion in local phone access charges. The CFO reiterated this defense, based on his understanding of the appropriate accounting standards, in a multi-day series of meetings with the external auditor and the audit committee. In the view of the CFO, this "fraudulent reporting" was both ethical and in conformity with GAAP. And as one moves even further to the left on the earnings management continuum, disagreement about whether a certain act is or is not ethical increases. For example, when a company makes an accounting change, how can a bright line be drawn between sufficient and deceptive disclosure? And who is to judge whether the strategic timing of gains and losses by a company is unethical or just prudent business practice?

GAAP oval A diagram that represents the flexibility a manager has, within GAAP, to report one earnings number from among many possibilities based on different methods and assumptions.

Exhibit 4 contains a figure called the **GAAP oval**. This oval represents the flexibility a manager has, within GAAP, to report one earnings number from among many possibilities based on different methods and assumptions. Clearly, reporting a number corresponding with points D or E, which are both outside the GAAP oval, is unethical. The difficult ethical question is whether the manager has a responsibility to try to report an earnings number exactly in the middle of the possible range, such as point B in Exhibit 4. Or does the manager have a responsibility to report the most conservative, worst-case number, like point A in the exhibit? Is it wrong for the manager to try to use accounting flexibility to report an earnings number corresponding with point C, which is the highest possible earnings number that is still in conformity with GAAP? And what cost is there, in terms of credibility, for a manager who makes a conservative set of accounting assumptions one year, perhaps when overall operating performance is good, and an aggressive set of assumptions the next year, perhaps to try to hide lackluster operating performance? Finally, note also that the boundary of the oval is fuzzy, so it sometimes is not clear whether a certain set of computations is or is not in conformity with GAAP.

Of course, whether a manager actually does manage earnings, and whether he or she crosses the line and violates GAAP to do so, is partially a function of the fear (and costs) of getting caught and of the general ethical culture of the company. But it is also a function of the personal ethics of the manager, and the manager's ability to recognize that fraudulent and deceptive financial reporting is part of a continuum that

Exhibit 4: The GAAP Oval

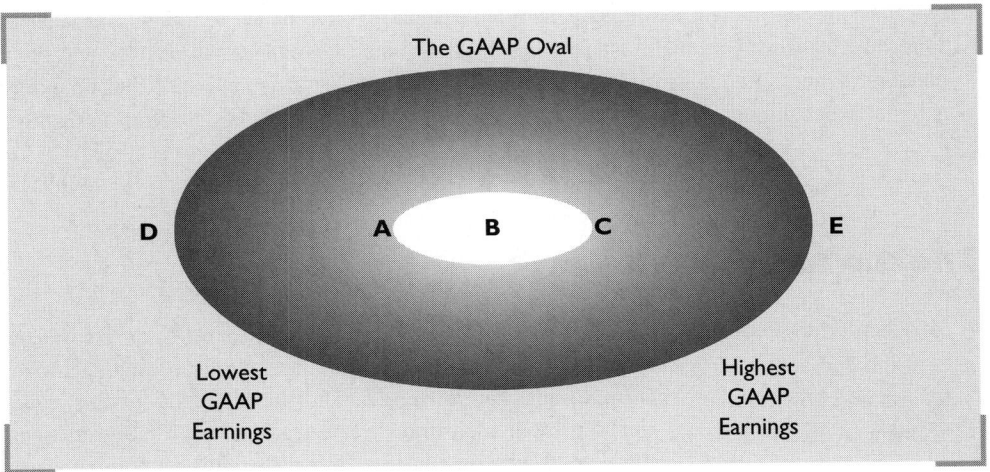

starts with innocent window dressing but can end with full-scale fraud. There is no neon sign giving a final warning saying, "Beware, don't cross this line!" Thus, each individual must be constantly aware of where he or she is with respect to the earnings management continuum in Exhibit 3 and the GAAP oval in Exhibit 4. Boards of directors and financial statement preparers should also be aware that, as a group, managers are notoriously overoptimistic about the future business prospects of their companies. Therefore, a company policy of having a consistently conservative approach to accounting is a good counterbalance to managers who might try to justify optimistic accounting assumptions on the basis of a business turnaround that is "just around the corner."

Personal Ethics

Personal ethics is not a topic one typically expects to study in a financial accounting course. However, the large number of accounting scandals in 2001 and 2002 demonstrated that personal ethics and financial reporting are inextricably connected. The GAAP oval in Exhibit 4 illustrates that there is a range of earnings numbers a company can report for a year and still be in strict conformity with GAAP. Thus, earnings management can and does occur without any violation of the accounting rules. If one takes a strictly legalistic view of the world, then it is clear that managers should manage earnings, when they have concluded that the potential costs in terms of lost credibility are outweighed by the financial reporting benefits, because earnings can be managed without violating any rules.

A contrasting view is that the practice of financial accounting is not a matter of simply applying a list of rules to a set of objective facts. Management intent often enters into the decision of how to report a particular item. For example, land is reported as a long-term asset in the balance sheet unless management intends to sell the land within one year of the balance sheet date. In the context of earnings management, an important consideration is whether savvy transaction timing or changes in accounting methods or estimates are done to better communicate the economic performance of the business to financial statement users or whether the earnings management techniques are used with the intent to deceive. And if earnings management is done to deceive, who is management trying to deceive? If management is trying to deceive potential investors, lenders, regulatory authorities, employees, or other company stakeholders, then managing earnings poses a real risk of lost credibility in the future. And there is one final important item to consider—most of us believe that intentionally trying to deceive others is wrong, no matter what the economic consequences.

TO SUMMARIZE: Because accounting earnings is a function of management's estimates and assumptions, management can influence earnings. There are several reasons that management might manage earnings including pressure to meet internal earnings targets, pressure to meet external expectations, smoothing income, and preparing to receive a loan or to offer stock to the public. Earnings management can take the form of outright fraud or, more commonly, earnings management results from the careful application of rules and the careful timing of transactions. It is important that financial statement users recognize the pressures that can influence the reported earnings figures.

The Sarbanes-Oxley Act

4 Understand the major parts of the Sarbanes-Oxley Act and how it impacts financial reporting.

The Sarbanes-Oxley Act that was passed by Congress in 2002 was by far the most comprehensive legislation ever affecting the accuracy of financial reports. Because of its significance, it is important that you understand the highlights of this legislation. The effects of this legislation can be divided into three categories: the establishment of independent oversight of auditors, constraints on auditors, and constraints on company management.

FYI:

Who are Sarbanes and Oxley? Paul Sarbanes is a Democratic senator from Maryland, and Michael Oxley is a Republican member of the House of Representatives from Ohio. These two gentlemen co-sponsored this sweeping reform.

Public Company Accounting Oversight Board (PCAOB) Board of five full-time members established by the Sarbanes-Oxley Act to oversee the accounting and auditing profession.

Public Company Oversight Board

Sarbanes-Oxley required the establishment of a **Public Company Accounting Oversight Board (PCAOB)**, with five full-time members, to oversee the accounting and auditing profession. This board is required to:

- Register all public accounting firms that provide audits for public companies.
- Establish standards relating to the preparation of audit reports for public companies.
- Conduct inspections (reviews) of accounting firms.
- Conduct investigations and disciplinary proceedings and impose appropriate sanctions on pubic accounting firms whose performance is inadequate.
- Enforce compliance with the Sarbanes-Oxley Act.

Constraints on Auditors

To ensure that external auditors remain independent, Sarbanes-Oxley requires the following:

- Accounting firms who audit public companies are prohibited from providing any non-audit services to their clients, including: (1) bookkeeping or other services related to the accounting records or financial statements, (2) financial information systems design and implementation, (3) appraisal or valuation services, (4) actuarial services, (5) internal audit outsourcing services, (6) management functions or human resources, (7) broker or dealer, investment adviser or investment banking services, (8) legal services and expert services unrelated to the audit, and (9) any other service that the Board determines is impermissible.
- Requires that audit partners on engagements be rotated off the audit every five years.
- Requires that auditors report to the audit committee rather than the CFO or other members of the company's management.

Constraints on Management

Restoring public confidence in the financial reporting process will require that management ensure financial statement users of the steps taken to provide quality financial information. To that end, Sarbanes-Oxley requires management to do the following:

- The CEO and CFO of each public company are required to prepare a statement to accompany the audit report to certify to the appropriateness of the financial statements and disclosures. As discussed earlier, management is still required to provide an assessment of internal controls in each annual report.
- All public companies are required to develop and enforce an officer code of ethics.
- Loans to executive officers and directors are prohibited.
- Support a much stronger audit committee in each public company. The audit committee is a subset of the board of directors and consists only of individuals who are not part of the management team of the company.

Only time will tell how effective this law is in preventing and deterring financial statement misstatements. One thing is for sure, however, and that is that because of this legislation, public companies are taking their financial reporting responsibilities much more seriously than ever before.

TO SUMMARIZE: Because of the rash of financial statement frauds, the Sarbanes-Oxley Act of 2002 provided sweeping legislative reforms that increased the responsibilities of public companies and their auditors in ensuring that financial reports are accurate.

The Role of Auditors in the Accounting Process

5 Describe the role of auditors and how their presence affects the integrity of financial statements.

Someone needs to check and make sure that the accounting system is running as designed and that the resulting financial statements fairly present the financial performance of the company. Auditors are that "someone." Auditors provide management (and stockholders) with some assurance that the internal control system is functioning properly and that the financial statements fairly represent the financial performance of the firm. Two types of auditors are typically employed by management—internal and external auditors.

Internal Auditors

internal auditors An independent group of experts (in controls, accounting, and operations) who monitor operating results and financial records, evaluate internal controls, assist with increasing the efficiency and effectiveness of operations, and detect fraud.

Most large organizations have a staff of **internal auditors**, an independent group of experts in controls, accounting, and operations. This group's major purpose is to monitor operating results and financial records, evaluate internal controls, assist with increasing the efficiency and effectiveness of operations, and even detect fraud. The internal audit staffs in some large organizations include over 100 individuals. The audit manager reports directly to the president (or other high-level executive officer) and to the audit committee of the board of directors. By performing independent evaluations of an organization's internal controls, the internal auditors are helping preserve integrity in the reporting process. Employees who know that internal auditors are reviewing operations and reports are less likely to manipulate records. Even if they do, their actions may be revealed by the work of the internal auditors.

Internal auditors' responsibilities vary considerably, depending upon the organization. Some internal audit staffs consist of only one or two employees who spend most of their time performing reviews of financial records or internal controls. Other organizations may have a large number of auditors who search for and investigate fraud, work to improve operational efficiency and effectiveness, and make sure their organization is complying with various laws and regulations.

external auditors Independent CPAs who are retained by organizations to perform audits of financial statements.

generally accepted auditing standards (GAAS) Auditing standards developed by the AICPA.

Organizations that have a competent group of internal auditors generally have fewer financial reporting problems than do organizations that don't have internal auditors. An example of an industry that generally did not have effective internal audit staffs is the savings and loan industry, where many companies went bankrupt during the late 1980s. In many of those companies, managers who were committing fraud did not want internal auditors, who would have made it more difficult for management to manipulate financial statements. As you learned at the beginning of this chapter, it was the internal auditors who detected and investigated the financial statement fraud at WORLDCOM.

External Auditors

FYI:

As of February 2002, four international public accounting firms—the "Big 4": ERNST & YOUNG, PRICEWATERHOUSECOOPERS, DELOITTE & TOUCHE, and KPMG—were responsible for auditing the majority of the Fortune 500 companies, as well as most other large, publicly-traded companies in the United States. Until 2001, there were five but as you learned in Chapter 1, ARTHUR ANDERSEN's involvement in WASTE MANAGEMENT, ENRON, and WORLDCOM dealt a one-two-three knock-out punch that put Arthur Andersen out of business.

Probably the greatest safeguard in the financial reporting system in the United States is the requirement that firms have external audits. **External auditors** examine an organization's financial statements to determine if they are prepared and presented in accordance with generally accepted accounting principles and are free from material (significant) misstatement. External audits are performed by certified public accounting (CPA) firms. CPA audits are required by the Securities and Exchange Commission and the major stock exchanges for all companies whose stock is publicly traded. Even companies that are not public, however, often employ CPAs to perform audits of their financial statements. Banks and other lenders usually require audits, and audits can instill confidence in users of financial reports. In conducting audits, CPAs are required by **generally accepted auditing standards (GAAS)** to provide reasonable assurance that significant fraud or misstatement is not present in financial statements. Because CPAs cannot audit every transaction of an organization, and because detecting collusive management deception is sometimes impossible, it is not possible for auditors to guarantee that financial statements are "correct." Instead, they can only provide reasonable assurance that financial statements are "presented fairly." Even with audits, there are still a few occasions when major financial statement fraud is not detected. As we have already discussed in this chapter, the Sarbanes-Oxley Act of 2002 made major reforms in the way CPAs must conduct their audits, who they report to, and what their penalties are for not conducting proper audits.

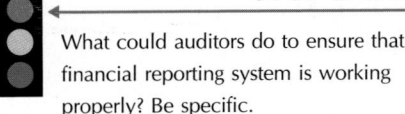

STOP & THINK

What could auditors do to ensure that the financial reporting system is working properly? Be specific.

CPA audits of financial statements have become very important in the United States because of the enormous size of many corporations. Because the stockholders, who own corporations, are usually different individuals from a company's management, audits provide comfort to these owners/investors that management is carrying out its stewardship function appropriately.

What Do Auditors Do?

While management has the primary responsibility of ensuring that the internal control system is functioning properly, internal auditors provide an independent assessment of how well the controls are working. External auditors usually study the internal control system to see if they can rely on it as they perform their audits. After all, if the internal control system is functioning correctly, it increases the likelihood that the resulting financial information is reliable. Often the external auditors will rely on the assessment of the internal controls made by the internal auditors.

Caution

Auditors are responsible for evaluating the assumptions and estimates of management as well as testing the internal control system. The auditors do not make the assumptions and estimates, nor are they responsible for designing the internal control system.

Auditors gain confidence in the quality of the reporting process using several different processes: interviews, observation, sampling, confirmation, and analytical procedures. Several of these processes are used by both internal and external auditors, while some are used primarily by external auditors. Exhibit 5 provides a summary of these procedures and indicates who uses them most often. A brief discussion of each process then follows.

Interviews

Auditors *interview* employees to ensure that procedures are understood, proper documentation is being made, and proper authorization is being obtained. Through interviews, auditors identify potential weaknesses in the control system that will be examined using testing procedures.

Observation

Observation is done to verify compliance with procedures and to ensure that accounting records agree with physical records. For example, auditors in a bank will count the cash in a vault to ensure that recorded amounts agree with the actual cash on hand. Auditors will also verify the existence of inventory by doing a physical count of product. In addition to using observation to verify the existence of assets, auditors will also use observation to ensure that employees are complying with proper procedures.

Exhibit 5: Audit Processes Used by Auditors

	Internal Auditors	External Auditors
Interviews	X	X
Observation	X	X
Sampling	X	X
Confirmation	—	X
Analytical procedures	—	X

Sampling

As mentioned previously, auditors cannot examine every transaction. Typically, they will select a *sample of transactions* for analysis. Based on the results of their analysis of the sample, they may conclude that the internal control procedures are being complied with, resulting in reliable financial information. Auditors may also conclude from the results that the internal control system is not reliable, resulting in further testing being required.

Confirmation

Used primarily by external auditors, *confirmations* are used to verify the balances in accounts that result from transactions with outsiders. For example, customers are often contacted and asked to verify account balances. Banks are contacted to verify loan amounts, lines of credit, and other account balances. This procedure ensures that the balances listed on the financial statements do, in fact, exist.

Analytical Procedures

Analytical procedures are used to provide guidance to external auditors as they attempt to identify areas that may deserve attention. Analytical procedures involve the use of such techniques as comparative ratio analysis (the same ratio analysis we have discussed in Chapter 5). By comparing the results of ratio analysis from one period to the next, auditors may be able to identify areas where additional investigation may be appropriate.

At the completion of an audit, the auditors issue a report that accompanies the financial statements and describes to readers, in very general terms, what was done by the audit firm and whether accounting rules were followed; the report also indicates an opinion as to whether the financial statements and the accompanying notes fairly represent the financial condition of the firm.

As an example of an auditors' report, MICROSOFT's 2002 independent auditors' report, taken from the company's 2002 financial statements, is included in Exhibit 6.

Are Auditors Independent?

Auditors are hired by *management* to make sure that the financial statements prepared by *management* fairly represent the financial performance of the company. Since management is paying the auditors, is there a danger that the auditors may not be independent? Is there a possibility that auditors will go along with whatever management says because management is paying them? That possibility exists, but there are a number of factors that work as a counterbalance.

First, recall from our discussion of the internal control structure that the Foreign Corrupt Practices and Sarbanes-Oxley acts require companies to maintain an adequate system of internal controls. If management knowingly violate this law, they can go to jail (a number of top managers have) and would be subject to personal fines. In addition, the company is subject to corporate fines. Thus, management would be taking a big risk if they interfere with the auditors.

Second, external auditors have a responsibility to financial statement users to ensure that financial statements are fairly presented. The legal system in the United States provides auditors with financial incentives to remain independent. As an example, the auditors in the PHARMOR financial statement fraud case were sued by plaintiffs for over $1 billion. A jury held the audit firm liable, and that firm settled with the plaintiffs for a lesser, though undisclosed (but not insignificant), amount. Thus, external auditors are taking a big risk if they allow their independence and integrity to be compromised.

Third, auditors have a reputation to protect. The reason auditors are hired at all is because the investing public believes they provide an independent check on the reliability and integrity of the financial information. If an audit firm were no longer perceived in this manner, companies would cease to employ it. CPA firms obtain audit clients based on the quality of their reputation. Would they sell that reputation to the highest bidder? That would be very short-sighted indeed.

Exhibit 6: Microsoft's 2002 Independent Auditors' Report

INDEPENDENT AUDITORS' REPORT

To the Board of Directors and Stockholders of Microsoft Corporation:

We have audited the accompanying consolidated balance sheets of Microsoft Corporation and subsidiaries (the Company) as of June 30, 2001 and 2002, and the related consolidated statements of income, cash flows, and stockholders' equity for each of the three years in the period ended June 30, 2002. These financial statements are the responsibility of the Company's management. Our responsibility is to express an opinion on these financial statements based on our audits.

We conducted our audits in accordance with auditing standards generally accepted in the United States of America. Those standards require that we plan and perform the audit to obtain reasonable assurance about whether the financial statements are free of material misstatement. An audit includes examining, on a test basis, evidence supporting the amounts and disclosures in the financial statements. An audit also includes assessing the accounting principles used and significant estimates made by management, as well as evaluating the overall financial statement presentation. We believe that our audits provide a reasonable basis for our opinion.

In our opinion, such consolidated financial statements present fairly, in all material respects, the financial position of Microsoft Corporation and subsidiaries as of June 30, 2001 and 2002, and the results of their operations and their cash flows for each of the three years in the period ended June 30, 2002 in conformity with accounting principles generally accepted in the United States of America.

As described in Note 2 to the financial statements, the Company adopted Statement of Financial Accounting Standards No. 133, *Accounting for Derivative Instruments and Hedging Activities*, effective July 1, 2000, and Statement of Financial Accounting Standards No. 142, *Goodwill and Other Intangible Assets*, effective July 1, 2001.

DELOITTE & TOUCHE LLP
Deloitte & Touche LLP
Seattle, Washington

July 18, 2002

Knowing the incentives that influence auditors to provide fair and reliable financial information, we can now begin to see how the issues relating to disagreements in judgment can work themselves out. On the one hand, we have a management team that has an incentive to provide financial statement information that portrays the company in the most favorable position possible. On the other hand, we have auditors who are responsible to ensure that the information being provided is unbiased and fair. If auditors don't live up to their charge, they can end up paying to litigants much more than they ever received in audit fees.

The Securities and Exchange Commission (SEC) and the new Public Company Accounting Oversight Board are working with public accounting firms to ensure that independence remains a keystone of the auditing profession.

If management is allowed to paint an overly optimistic picture of the firm's performance by using estimates that bias the financial reports, the audit firm will pay (via litigation) if those estimates prove to be materially wrong in the future. To protect itself, the audit firm would actually prefer that management use conservative estimates, but management will not always go along with the auditors in this regard. It is this tension, resulting from differing incentives, that provides financial statement users with information that, taken as a whole, fairly represents the financial performance of a business.

FYI:

This give and take between the auditors and management typically results in financial statements that fairly reflect the financial performance of a business. For example, in 2001, of 7,421 audits conducted for firms listed on the New York, American, and NASDAQ stock exchanges, only 26 involved significant issues on which auditors and management could not reach agreement on disclosure.

TO SUMMARIZE: Auditors provide a check and balance to ensure that the financial statements fairly reflect the financial performance of a business. Most large organizations have internal auditors whose role it is to ensure integrity in the financial records and to evaluate and encourage adherence to the organization's internal controls. Internal auditors are a very effective deterrent to fraud by employees and to the overriding of controls by management. Integrity in the financial reporting process is ensured with independent audits of financial statements by external certified public accountants. Such independent financial statement audits are required for all public companies, and often by creditors and other users. While audits can't "guarantee" accuracy in the financial statements, they do add credibility.

The Securities and Exchange Commission

6 Explain the role of the Securities and Exchange Commission in adding credibility to financial statements.

Securities and Exchange Commission (SEC) The government body responsible for regulating the financial reporting practices of most publicly owned corporations in connection with the buying and selling of stocks and bonds.

In addition to the role of independent internal and external auditors, the U.S. government plays a role in ensuring the integrity of financial information. The **Securities and Exchange Commission (SEC)** is responsible for ensuring that investors, creditors, and other financial statement users are provided with reliable information upon which to make investment decisions.

The SEC is an agency of the federal government. The SEC was organized in the 1930s because of financial reporting and stock market abuses. One such abuse was price manipulation. It was not uncommon in the 1920s for stockbrokers or dealers to indulge in "wash sales" or "matched orders," in which successive buy and sell orders created a false impression of stock activity and forced prices up. This maneuver allowed those involved to reap huge profits before the price fell back to its true market level. Outright deceit by issuing false and misleading financial statements was another improper practice. The objective of these manipulative procedures was to make profits at the expense of unwary investors.

One classic example of a major fraud that may have contributed to the formation of the SEC is the Ivar Kreugar case. During the 1920s, the most widely held securities in the United States, and perhaps the world, were the stocks and bonds of KREUGAR & TOLL, INC., a Swedish match company. These securities were popular because they paid high dividends (over 20% annually) and were sold in small denominations, making them attractive to both large and small investors. Ivar Kreugar, known as the "Match King," became wealthy and famous as a financial genius, building his business into a multibillion-dollar international enterprise. In fact, Kreugar defrauded millions of investors by personally creating false and misleading financial statements. Instead of being paid out of profits, the dividends were paid out of capital that was raised by selling securities to unsuspecting investors. Eventually, the giant pyramid collapsed, Kreugar committed suicide, and Kreugar & Toll, Inc., went bankrupt. On the day Kreugar died, his company's stock was selling for $5 a share. Within weeks, it was selling for five cents a share. The American public was outraged, and some have speculated that this major fraud was instrumental in causing Congress to enact securities legislation to prevent such deception from happening again.

FYI:

The first chairman of the SEC was Joseph P. Kennedy, father of the late President John F. Kennedy.

The Securities Act of 1933 requires most companies planning to issue new debt or stock securities to the public to submit a registration statement to the SEC for approval. The SEC examines these statements for completeness and adequacy before permitting companies to sell securities through securities exchanges. The Securities Exchange Act of 1934 requires all public companies to file detailed periodic reports with the SEC.

The SEC requires a considerable amount of information to be included in these filings. Among other things, a company must submit financial statements that have been audited by CPAs and that contain an opinion issued by those CPAs.

Of the many reports required by the SEC, the following have the most direct impact on financial reporting:

- *Registration statements.* These include various forms that must be filed and approved before a company can sell securities through the securities exchanges.
- *Form 10-K.* This report must be filed annually for all publicly held companies. The report contains extensive financial information, including audited financial statements by independent CPAs. The 10-K also requires additional disclosure beyond that typically provided in the audited financial statements. Examples of additional information include the executive compensation of top management and the details of property, plant, and equipment transactions.
- *Form 10-Q.* This report must be filed quarterly for all publicly held companies. It contains certain financial information and requires a CPA's involvement.

Because the SEC has statutory power to mandate any reporting requirement it feels is needed, it has considerable influence in setting generally accepted accounting principles and disclosure requirements for financial statements. Generally, the SEC accepts the accounting pronouncements of the Financial Accounting Standards Board and other bodies such as the AICPA. In addition, the SEC has the power to establish rules for any CPA associated with audited financial statements submitted to the commission.

The SEC is given broad enforcement powers under the 1934 Act. If the rules of operation for stock exchanges prove to be ineffectual in implementing the requirements of the SEC, the SEC can alter or supplement them. The SEC can suspend trading of a company's stock for not more than 10 days (a series of orders has enabled the SEC to suspend trading for extended periods, however) and can suspend all trading on any exchange for up to 90 days. If substantive hearings show that the issuer failed to comply with the requirements of the securities laws, the SEC can "de-list" any security. Brokers and dealers can be prevented, either temporarily or permanently, from working in the securities market, and investigations can be initiated, if deemed necessary, to determine violations of any of the Acts or rules administered by the SEC.

The Effect of the 1934 Act on Independent Accountants

Accountants are involved in the preparation and review of a major portion of the reports and statements required by the 1934 Act. Accountants also can be censured, and their work is subject to approval by the SEC. The financial statements in the annual report to stockholders and in the 10-K report must be audited. In addition, accountants consult and assist in the preparation of the quarterly 10-Q reports and the other periodic reports.

More recently, the Sarbanes-Oxley Act has strengthened the authority of the SEC to monitor financial reporting. Under the Act, the SEC is given more resources and authority, has oversight for the new Public Company Accounting Oversight Board, has more control over auditors and reporting companies, and, in general, has a greater responsibility to protect investors and creditors who rely on financial reports.

TO SUMMARIZE: The Securities and Exchange Commission is an agency of the federal government whose purpose is to assist investors in public companies by regulating stock and bond markets and by requiring certain disclosures. Although the SEC has statutory authority to establish accounting principles, it basically accepts pronouncements of the FASB and AICPA as authoritative. Common reports required by the SEC are registration statements and Forms 10-K and 10-Q. Because the SEC can suspend trading and even de-list securities, it is a powerful organization that significantly influences financial reporting in the United States.

review of learning objectives

1 **Identify the types of problems that can appear in financial statements.** Three types of problems can affect financial statements: (1) Errors involve unintentional mistakes that can enter the accounting system at the transaction and journal entry stage or when journal entries are posted to accounts. These errors, when detected, are immediately fixed. (2) Disagreements in judgment occur because of the differing incentives of those associated with the financial statements. While management may have an incentive to present an optimistic view of the company's performance, auditors have an incentive to ensure full disclosure of all relevant issues. These differing incentives typically result in financial statements that fairly reflect the financial performance of the company. (3) Fraudulent financial reporting involves intentional misrepresentations in the financial statements. Safeguards are built into the accounting and reporting system to minimize the possibility that these problems will be reflected in the financial statements.

2 **Describe the safeguards employed within a firm to ensure that financial statements are free from problems.** Internal controls are safeguards built into an organization that help to protect assets and increase reliability of the accounting records. The three basic internal control structure categories are (1) the control environment, (2) the accounting systems, and (3) the control procedures. The five types of control procedures are (1) segregation of duties, (2) procedures for authorizations, (3) documents and records, (4) physical safeguards, and (5) independent checks. The control environment is comprised of such things as management's philosophy and operating style, the organizational structure, and the audit committee.

3 **Understand the concept of earnings management and why it occurs.** Earnings management occurs when judgment in financial reporting and in structuring transactions is used to alter financial reports to influence the perceptions of stakeholders about the underlying economic performance of the company and/or to influence outcomes that depend on reported accounting numbers. The practice of earnings management may potentially affect the transparency of the underlying economic reality of a company's financial performance or position to such an extent that decisions with respect to the allocation of resources may change in the absence of such a practice.

4 **Understand the major parts of the Sarbanes-Oxley Act and how it impacts financial reporting.** The Sarbanes-Oxley Act is the most significant and far-sweeping legislation ever passed by Congress. The Act provides for a Public Company Accounting Oversight Board that will regulate and monitor both auditors and officers of public companies.

5 **Describe the role of auditors and how their presence affects the integrity of financial statements.** Most large organizations have internal auditors who are "independent" internal control experts. They examine the various functions and divisions of the business to evaluate internal controls, operating efficiency and effectiveness, and compliance with laws and company policy. Internal auditors usually report to top management or the board of directors and increase the reliability of financial statements by ensuring that internal controls function as they should.

External audits are required of most public companies by the Securities and Exchange Commission. By conducting audits of financial statements according to generally accepted auditing standards put into effect by the AICPA, external audits provide "reasonable assurance" that financial statements are presented fairly and are not materially misstated. External audits must be performed by CPAs who are licensed by the individual states in which they practice.

6 **Explain the role of the Securities and Exchange Commission in adding credibility to financial statements.** The SEC is the agency of the federal government charged with the responsibility of assisting investors by making sure they are provided with reliable information upon which to make investment decisions. The SEC was organized in the 1930s and requires certain periodic reports such as the Forms 10-Q and 10-K of companies that sell stock publicly in the United States. It adds credibility to financial statements by requiring independent audits, reviewing financial statements itself, and sanctioning firms that violate its standards.

key terms & concepts

accounting system, 262
audit committee, 262
control activities (procedures), 262
control environment, 261
external auditors, 272
Foreign Corrupt Practices Act (FCPA), 261
GAAP oval, 269

generally accepted auditing standards (GAAS), 272
income smoothing, 267
independent checks, 264
internal auditors, 272
internal control structure, 260
internal earnings target, 265
organizational structure, 262

physical safeguards, 264
Public Company Accounting Oversight Board (PCAOB), 271
Sarbanes-Oxley Act, 261
Securities and Exchange Commission (SEC), 276
segregation of duties, 263

discussion questions

1. How can a person tell whether an entry to an expense account is payment for a legitimate expenditure or a means of concealing a theft of cash?
2. How would it be possible to overstate revenues? What effect would an overstatement of revenues have on total assets?
3. What is the Foreign Corrupt Practices Act, and how is it important to financial reporting?
4. What are the major elements of a system of internal controls?
5. Identify five different types of control procedures.
6. What are the four factors that might motivate a manager to attempt to manage earnings?
7. (a) What is the purpose of internal earnings targets? (b) What is the risk associated with internal earnings targets?
8. What is meant by the term *income smoothing*?
9. What are the five labels in the earnings management continuum (see Exhibit 3), and what general types of actions are associated with each of the labels?
10. Is there anything wrong with using a different accounting estimate this year compared to last year, as long as both estimates fall within a generally accepted range for your industry?
11. Refer to the GAAP oval in Exhibit 4. (a) In what important way is point E different from point C? (b) In what important way is point A different from point C?

12. The Sarbanes-Oxley Act established the Public Company Accounting Oversight Board. Identify the duties of that board.
13. What constraints were placed on auditors as a result of the Sarbanes-Oxley Act?
14. As a result of the Sarbanes-Oxley Act, public companies are required to make changes in the way they do business. What practice does Sarbanes-Oxley forbid?
15. How do internal auditors add to the credibility of financial statements?
16. What is the purpose of a financial statement audit by CPAs?
17. Do you believe that outside auditors (CPAs) who examine the financial statements of a company, while being paid by that company, can be truly independent?
18. The SEC requires companies to register with it when they sell stocks or bonds and also requires periodic reporting thereafter. Which of these reports, the initial registration statements or the subsequent periodic reports, do you believe would be scrutinized more closely by the SEC?
19. What do you suspect is the relationship between the FASB and the SEC?

e xercises

Exercise 6-1

Accounting Errors—Transaction Errors

How would the following errors affect the account balances and the basic accounting equation, *Assets = Liabilities + Owners' Equity*? How do the misstatements affect income?

a. The purchase of a truck is recorded as an expense instead of an asset.
b. A cash payment on accounts receivable is received but not recorded.
c. Fictitious sales on account are recorded.
d. A clerk misreads a handwritten invoice for repairs and records it as $1,500 instead of $1,800.
e. Payment is received on December 31 for the next three months' rent and is recorded as revenue.

Exercise 6-2

Spreadsheet

Errors in Financial Statements

The following financial statements are available for SHERWOOD REAL ESTATE COMPANY:

Balance Sheet

Assets		Liabilities		
Cash	$ 1,300	Accounts payable	$ 100,000	
Receivable from sale		Mortgage payable	6,000,000	
of real estate	5,000,000	Total liabilities		$ 6,100,000
Interest receivable*	180,000			
Real estate properties	6,000,000	**Stockholders' Equity**		
		Capital stock	$ 10,000	
		Retained earnings	5,071,300	
		Total stockholders' equity		5,081,300
		Total liabilities and stock-		
Total assets	$11,181,300	holders' equity		$11,181,300

*Interest Receivable applies to Receivable from sale of real estate.

Income Statement

Gain on sale of real estate	$3,200,000
Interest income*	180,000
Total revenues	$3,380,000
Expenses	1,200,000
Net income	$2,180,000

*Interest Income applies to Receivable from sale of real estate.

Sherwood Company is using these financial statements to entice investors to buy stock in the company. However, a recent FBI investigation revealed that the sale of real estate was a fabricated transaction with a fictitious company that was recorded to make the financial statements look better. The sales price was $5,000,000 with a zero cash down payment and a $5,000,000 receivable. Prepare financial statements for Sherwood Company showing what its total assets, liabilities, stockholders' equity, and income really are with the sale of real estate removed.

Exercise 6-3

Appropriateness of Accounting Rules

In the early 1990s, the top executive of a large oil refining company (based in New York) was convicted of financial statement fraud. One of the issues in the case involved the way the company accounted for its oil inventories. In particular, the company would purchase crude oil from exploration companies and then process the oil into finished oil products, such as jet fuel, diesel fuel, and so forth. Because there was a ready market for these finished products, as soon as the company purchased the crude oil, it would value its oil inventory at the selling prices of the finished products less the cost to refine the oil. Although the case involved fraud, the type of accounting used was also questioned because it allowed the company to recognize profit before the actual sale (and even refining) of the oil. Nevertheless, one of the large CPA firms attested to the use of this method. If you were the judge in this case, would you be critical of this accounting practice?

Exercise 6-4

Internal Control Procedures

As an auditor, you have discovered the following problems with the accounting system control procedures of Jefferson Retailers. For each of the following occurrences, tell which of the five internal control procedures was lacking. Also, recommend how the company should change its procedures to avoid the problem in the future.

a. Jefferson Retailers' losses due to bad debts have increased dramatically over the past year. In an effort to increase sales, the managers of certain stores have allowed large credit sales to occur without review or approval.
b. An accountant hid his theft of $200 from the company's bank account by changing the monthly reconciliation. He knew the manipulation would not be discovered.
c. Steve Meyer works in the storeroom. He maintains the inventory records, counts the inventory, and has unlimited access to the storeroom. He occasionally steals items of inventory and hides the theft by including the value of the stolen goods in his inventory count.
d. Receiving reports are sometimes filled out days after shipments have arrived.

Exercise 6-5

Internal Auditing—Staffing Internal Audits

A manufacturing corporation recently reassigned one of its accounting managers to the internal audit department. He had successfully directed the western-area accounting office, and the corporation thought his skills would be valuable to the internal audit department. The director of the internal audit division knew of this individual's experience in the western-area accounting office and assigned him to audit that same office.

Should the internal auditor be assigned to audit the same office in which he recently worked? What problems could arise in this situation?

Exercise 6-6

Internal Auditing

Which of the following is not applicable to the internal audit function?

a. Deter or catch employee fraud.
b. Issue an opinion for investors regarding the reliability of the financial statements.
c. Be guided by its own set of professional standards.
d. Help to ensure that the accounting function is performed correctly and that the financial statements are prepared accurately.

Exercise 6-7

Internal Auditing—External Auditor's Reliance on Internal Auditors

North, CPA, is planning an audit of the financial statements of General Company. In determining the nature, timing, and extent of the auditing procedures, North is considering General's internal audit function, which is staffed by Tyler.

1. In what ways may Tyler's work be relevant to North?
2. What factors should North consider, and what inquiries should North make in deciding whether to rely on Tyler's work?

Exercise 6-8

Ensuring the Integrity of Financial Reporting

Three college seniors with majors in accounting are discussing alternative career plans. All three want to enter careers that will help to ensure the integrity of financial reporting. The first wants to become an internal auditor. She believes that by ensuring appropriate internal controls within a company, the financial statements will be reliable. The second wants to go to work in public accounting and perform external audits of companies. He believes that external auditors are independent and can make sure that financial statements are correct. The third student believes that neither choice will be adding much value to the integrity of financial statements because, in both cases, the auditors will be receiving their pay (either directly or indirectly) from the companies they audit. He believes the only way to make a real difference is to work for the Securities and Exchange Commission, using the "arm of government regulation" to force companies to issue appropriate financial statements and then punishing them (through jail sentences and large fines) when their financial statements are misleading. In your opinion, which of these three students will make the largest contribution toward ensuring integrity in the financial statements?

Exercise 6-9

External Auditors—Purpose of an Audit

What is the purpose of external auditors providing an opinion on a company's financial statements?

Exercise 6-10

Auditing Financial Statements

The Utah Lakers professional basketball team has recently decided to sell stock and become a public company. In determining what it must do to file a registration statement with the SEC, the company realizes that it needs to have an audit opinion to accompany its financial statements. The company has recently approached two accounting students at a major university and asked them to "audit" its financial statements to be submitted to the SEC. Should the two accounting students accept the work and perform the audit?

Exercise 6-11

Securities and Exchange Commission—Authority to Set Accounting Standards

Which organization—the Securities and Exchange Commission, the American Institute of Certified Public Accountants, or the Financial Accounting Standards Board—has federal government authority to set accounting standards and reporting requirements? Some people have argued that all accounting rule making should be done by the federal government. Do you agree? Why or why not?

Exercise 6-12

Securities and Exchange Commission—Role of the SEC

Describe the role of the Securities and Exchange Commission and its influence on the practice of auditing.

Exercise 6-13

Securities and Exchange Commission—Information Needed for Investing

As an investor you are considering buying stock in a relatively new company. American Shipping, Ltd., has been in existence for 10 years and is now about to go public. The first stock offering will be listed on the New York Stock Exchange next week.

1. What kind of information would you like to know before investing in the company? Where can you find this information?
2. How does the SEC protect the securities market from companies that are fraudulent or in poor financial condition?
3. Besides stock market investors, what other parties might be interested in knowing financial data about companies?

Exercise 6-14

Auditing Negligence

A few years ago, the officers of PHAR-MOR, a discount retail chain, were convicted of issuing fraudulent financial statements. It was learned at the trial that the company overstated its inventory by moving inventory from store to store and counting the same inventory several times. For example, a case of Coca-Cola would be counted at one store and then moved to another store and counted again. In a separate civil trial, Phar-Mor's auditors were accused of performing negligent audits because they didn't catch these inventory movements. Do you believe that the external auditors were negligent in this case?

Exercise 6-15

Securities and Exchange Commission

Many people have argued that the purpose of the SEC is to protect investors. Some believe that the best way to do this is by preventing weak companies from issuing stock. Others say that the SEC should require full disclosure and then let the buyer beware. Which do you think is more appropriate: a preventive role or a disclosure role?

discussion cases

Case 6-1

Auditing a Company

Jerry Stillwell, the owner of a small company, asked Jones, a CPA, to conduct an audit of the company's financial statements. Stillwell told Jones that the audit needed to be completed in time to submit audited financial statements to a bank as part of a loan application. Jones immediately accepted the assignment and agreed to provide an auditor's report within two weeks.

Because Jones was busy, he hired two accounting students to perform the audit. After two hours of instruction, he sent them off to conduct the audit. Jones told the students not to spend time reviewing the internal controls, but instead to concentrate on proving the mathematical accuracy of the ledgers and other financial records.

The students followed Jones's instructions, and after 10 days, they provided the financial statements, which did not include notes. Jones reviewed the statements and prepared an auditor's report. The report did not refer to generally accepted accounting principles and contained no mention of any qualifications or disclosures. Briefly describe the problems with this audit.

Case 6-2

Auditing Practice

A few years ago, the owners of an electronics wholesale company committed massive fraud by overstating revenues on the financial statements. They recorded three large fictitious sales near the end of the year to the retailers SILO, CIRCUIT CITY, and WAL-MART. The three transactions overstated revenues, receivables, and income by nearly $20 million. As part of the audit procedures, the external auditors sent requests for confirmation to the three stores to ensure that they did, in fact, owe the electronics company $20 million. In the meantime, the owners of the electronics company rented mailboxes in the cities where the three "customers" were headquartered, using names very similar to those of the three "customers." The requests for confirmation were sent to the mailboxes. The owners completed the confirmations and sent them back to the auditors, confirming the $20 million in receivables. With respect to the fraud, answer the following two questions:

1. What journal entries would the fraud perpetrators have entered into the financial records to overstate revenues?
2. Should the external auditors be held liable for not catching the fraud?

Case 6-3

Income Smoothing and an IPO

You are an analyst for an investment fund that invests in initial public offerings (IPOs). You are looking at the financial statements of two companies, Clark Company and Durfee Company, that plan to go public soon. Net income for the past three years for the two companies has been as follows (in thousands):

Year	Clark Net Income	Durfee Net Income
2005	$10,000	$17,000
2006	14,000	1,000
2007	20,000	26,000

If both companies issue the same number of shares and if the initial share prices are the same, which of the two companies appears to be a more attractive investment? Explain your reasoning. Also, what alternate sources of data would you look at to find out if the reported earnings amounts accurately portray the business performance of these two companies over the past three years?

Case 6-4

If It Isn't Fraud, Then It's Ethical

Cruella DeVil is the chief financial officer (CFO) of a local publicly-traded company. Cruella was recently invited to speak to accounting students at the local university. One of the students asked Cruella whether she thought earnings management was ethical. Cruella laughed and responded that her view was that anything that was not explicitly prohibited by the accounting standards or by government regulations was ethical. What do you think of Cruella's opinion?

Case 6-5

GAAP Is a Point, Not an Oval!

You are the chief financial officer (CFO) of Lorien Company, which is publicly traded. At the annual shareholders' meeting, you have been asked to discuss the company's recent reported results. As part of your presentation, you illustrated the minimum and maximum values for net income that could have been reported by Lorien using a range of accounting assumptions used by other companies in your industry. Your statement prompted a cry of outrage from one of the shareholders present at the meeting. This shareholder accused you of being an unprincipled liar. This shareholder stated that any suggestion that there is a range of possible net income values for a given company in a given year indicates an overly liberal approach to financial reporting. This shareholder has moved that your employment contract be immediately terminated because of an apparent lack of moral character. The shareholder's arguments have been persuasive to a large number of people present at the meeting. What can you say to defend yourself?

ⓙudgment calls

Judgment 6-1

You Decide: Which is more important—having a good system of internal controls or hiring honest employees?

Is an internal control structure really necessary? Your uncle doesn't seem to think so. He works for a regional employment staffing service and recently commented, "As long as a company hires hard-working, honest people, fraud and abusive financial reporting cases will be almost nonexistent. People with integrity will always make the right choice. In the last six months, we haven't placed anyone for employment who has been fired or let go for fraudulent activity!" A friend argues, however, that anyone presented with the right pressures can commit fraud and that opportunities must be eliminated through an effective internal control structure. Who do you agree with?

Judgment 6-2

You Decide: Can auditors rely on client personnel to assist them with their audit?

Should external auditors do all audit procedures themselves, or should the relationship between the auditor and the client be more friendly? You have just graduated from college and are now working as an auditor for a public accounting firm. Your first client is a major shipping company on the west coast that specializes in sending goods to China. As part of your first assignment, you are asked to count the number of metal containers in the storage warehouse and also verify their contents. As you begin, the warehouse manager (and long-time friend of the firm) comes to you and says, "Don't worry about looking inside the containers. Our guys did that last week and we are running low on time." What should you do?

Competency Enhancement Opportunities

▶ **Analyzing Real Company Information**
▶ **International Case**
▶ **Ethics Case**
▶ **Writing Assignment**

▶ **The Debate**
▶ **Cumulative Spreadsheet Project**
▶ **Internet Search**

The following additional assignments provide opportunities for students to develop critical thinking, ethical perspectives, oral and written communication skills, experience with electronic research, and teamwork through group and business activities.

▶ *Analyzing Real Company Information*

Analyzing 6-1 (Microsoft)

The 2002 Form 10-K for MICROSOFT is included in Appendix A. Locate that Form 10-K and consider the following questions:

1. With respect to the report of the external auditors to "the Board of Directors and Stockholders of Microsoft Corporation":
   a. Who is Microsoft's external auditor?
   b. How long after the end of Microsoft's fiscal year did the external auditor complete the audit?
2. With respect to the report of management concerning the financial statements:
   a. Who is responsible for the financial statements?
   b. After reading the paragraph on internal control, indicate whether you agree or disagree with the following statement: "The purpose of an internal control system is to ensure that all transactions are always recorded and that all assets are always completely safeguarded."
   c. After looking at the description of the members of the audit committee, do you think that Bill Gates is a member of that committee?

Analyzing 6-2 (Circle K)

At one time, CIRCLE K was the second-largest convenience store chain in the United States (behind 7-ELEVEN). At its peak, Circle K, based in Phoenix, Arizona, operated 4,685 stores in 32 states. Circle K's rapid expansion was financed through long-term borrowing. Interest on this large debt, combined with increased price competition from convenience stores operated by oil companies, squeezed the profits of Circle K. For the fiscal year ended April 30, 1990, Circle K reported a loss of $773 million. In May 1990, Circle K filed for Chapter 11 bankruptcy protection. Subsequently, Circle K was taken over by TOSCO, a large independent oil company.

1. In the fiscal year ended April 30, 1989, Circle K experienced significant financial difficulty. Reported profits were down 74.5% from the year before. In the president's letter to the shareholders, Circle K explained that 1989 was a "disappointing" year and that management was seeking some outside company to come in and buy out the Circle K shareholders. How do you think all this bad news was reflected in the auditor's report accompanying the financial statements dated April 30, 1989?

2. As mentioned, Circle K reported a loss of $773 million for the year ended April 30, 1990. Just a week after the end of the fiscal year, the CEO was fired. One week after that, Circle K declared bankruptcy. The audit report was completed approximately two months later. How do you think the news of the bankruptcy was reflected in the auditor's report accompanying the financial statements dated April 30, 1990?

▶ *International Case*

International

Do the Financial Statements Give a True and Fair View?

SWIRE PACIFIC, LTD., based in Hong Kong, is one of the largest companies in the world. The primary operations of the company are in the region of Hong Kong, China, and Taiwan where it has operated for over 125 years. Swire operates CATHAY PACIFIC AIRWAYS and has extensive real estate holdings in Hong Kong. The 2002 auditor's report (prepared by PRICEWATERHOUSE-COOPERS) for Swire Pacific, dated March 6, 2003, read as follows (in part):

> An audit includes examination, on a test basis, of evidence relevant to the amounts and disclosures in the accounts. It also includes an assessment of the significant estimates and judgments made by the directors in the preparation of the accounts, and of whether the accounting policies are appropriate to the circumstances of the Company and the group consistently applied and adequately disclosed. . . .
>
> In our opinion the accounts give a true and fair view of the state of affairs of the company and of the group as at 31st December 2002. . . .

Although the concept of a "true and fair view" is not part of the auditor's terminology in the United States, it is used by auditors all over the world and is also discussed as part of International Accounting Standards (IAS). The "true and fair view" concept states that an auditor must make sure that the financial statements give an honest representation of the economic status of the company, even if the company violates generally accepted accounting principles in order to do so.

1. Review the opinion language in the auditor's report for MICROSOFT (see Appendix A). Does the audit report state unconditionally that Microsoft's financial statements are a fair representation of the economic status of the company?

2. Auditors in the United States concentrate on performing audits to ensure that financial statements are prepared in accordance with generally accepted accounting principles. What

economic and legal realities in the United States would make it difficult for U.S. auditors to apply the "true and fair view" concept?

▷ *Ethics Case*

Blowing the Whistle on Former Partners

On St. Patrick's Day in 1992, CHAMBERS DEVELOPMENT COMPANY, one of the largest landfill and waste management firms in the United States, announced that it had been engaging in improper accounting for years. Wall Street fear (over what this announcement implied about the company's track record of steady earnings growth) sent Chambers' stock price plunging by 62% in one day.

The improper accounting by Chambers had been discovered in the course of the external audit. The auditors found that $362 million in expenses had not been reported since Chambers first became a public company in 1985. If this amount of additional expense had been reported, it would have completely wiped out all the profit reported by Chambers since it first went public. The difficult part of this situation was that a large number of the financial staff working for Chambers were former partners in the audit firm performing the audit. These accountants had first worked as independent external auditors at Chambers, then were hired by Chambers, and subsequently were audited by their old partners.

What ethical and economic issues did the auditors of Chambers Development Company face as they considered whether to blow the whistle on their former partners?

▷ *Writing Assignment*

External Auditors

Visit or call a local CPA firm (or the local office of a multi-office CPA firm). Ask about career opportunities, the size of the firm's staff, who some of its major clients are, and other facts about the firm. Then, write a one-page summary of your visit.

▷ *The Debate*

Who Needs Internal Control?

An internal control system is intended to ensure that all transactions are properly approved and recorded, that assets and records are safeguarded, and that operations run efficiently. As with any other system in a business, an internal control system costs money to operate.

Divide your group into two teams.

- One team represents the "Hire Honest and Smart" group. Prepare a two-minute oral presentation supporting the notion that if a company would focus on hiring only honest and smart employees, it would not need to spend money designing and operating an internal control system. Most of the functions of internal control are to prevent employees from stealing and to make it difficult for inept employees to commit costly mistakes.

- The other team represents the "No Trust" group. Prepare a two-minute oral presentation arguing that a company must set up a careful internal control system because, given the right opportunity and motive, any employee can turn into a thief. In addition, a company cannot rely on the good intentions of employees to keep the business running smoothly. Instead, top management must design systems that will keep things running smoothly in spite of the mistakes of employees.

▷ *Cumulative Spreadsheet Project*

This spreadsheet assignment is a continuation of the spreadsheet assignment given in Chapter 2. If you completed that spreadsheet, you have a head start on this one.

1. Refer back to the financial statement numbers for Handyman Company for 2006 [given in part (1) of the Cumulative Spreadsheet Project assignment in Chapter 2]. Using the balance sheet and income statement created with those numbers, create spreadsheet cell formulas to compute and display values for the following ratios:
   a. Current ratio
   b. Debt ratio
   c. Asset turnover
   d. Return on equity

2. To observe the impact that errors and fraudulent transactions can have on the financial statements, determine what the ratios computed in (1) would have been if (1) each of the following transactions was recorded as described and (2) the transaction was recorded correctly. Treat each transaction independently, meaning that before determining the impact of each new transaction you should reset the financial statement values to their original amounts. Each of the hypothetical transactions is assumed to occur on the last day of the year.
   a. Created receivables by creating fictitious sales of $140 all on account.
   b. Purchased $80 of inventory on account but incorrectly increased the property, plant, and equipment account instead of increasing Inventory.
   c. Borrowed $60 with a short-term payable. The liability was incorrectly recorded as Long-Term Debt.
   d. An inventory purchase on account in the amount of $90 was not recorded until the next year.

▷ *Internet Search*

MCI (formerly WorldCom)

Access the Web site of MCI at **http://www.mci.com**. Sometimes Web addresses change, so if this address doesn't work, access the Web site for this textbook (**http://albrecht.swlearning .com**) for an updated link.

Once you've gained access to the site, answer the following questions:

1. How many individuals does MCI employ around the world, and in how many countries?
2. Who assumed the position of CEO of the company following the accounting scandals that occurred in 2002?
3. Locate the company's April 14, 2003, press release (look in "press release archives"). At the same time the company announced its name change, it also made another announcement related to a court filing. What was that announcement?

As a recently hired accountant for a small business, SMC, Inc., you are provided with last year's balance sheet, income statement, and post-closing trial balance to familiarize yourself with the business.

SMC, Inc.
Balance Sheet
December 31, 2006

Assets

Cash	$34,500	
Accounts receivable	25,000	
Inventory	10,000	
Supplies	200	
Total assets		$69,700

Liabilities and Stockholders' Equity

Liabilities:

Accounts payable	$12,000	
Salaries payable	1,000	
Income taxes payable	3,675	
Total liabilities		$16,675
Stockholders' equity:		
Capital stock (10,000 shares outstanding)	$25,000	
Retained earnings	28,025	
Total stockholders' equity		53,025
Total liabilities and stockholders' equity		$69,700

SMC, Inc.
Income Statement
For the Year Ended December 31, 2006

Sales revenue	$110,000	
Rent revenue	1,000	
Total revenues		$111,000
Less cost of goods sold		60,000
Gross margin		$ 51,000
Less operating expenses:		
Supplies expense	$ 400	
Salaries expense	22,000	
Miscellaneous expense	4,100	26,500
Income before taxes		$ 24,500
Less income taxes		3,675
Net income		$ 20,825
Earnings per share ($20,825 ÷ 10,000 shares)		$ 2.08

SMC, Inc.
Post-Closing Trial Balance
December 31, 2006

	Debits	Credits
Cash	$34,500	
Accounts Receivable	25,000	
Inventory	10,000	
Supplies	200	
Accounts Payable		$12,000
Salaries Payable		1,000
Income Taxes Payable		3,675
Capital Stock		25,000
Retained Earnings		28,025
Totals	$69,700	$69,700

You are also given the following information that summarizes the business activity for the current year, 2007.

a. Issued 5,000 additional shares of capital stock for $10,000 cash.
b. Borrowed $5,000 on January 2, 2007, from Downtown Bank as a long-term loan. Interest for the year is $500, payable on January 2, 2008.
c. Paid $3,600 cash on November 1 to lease a truck for one year.
d. Received $1,200 on November 1 from a tenant for six months' rent.
e. Paid $600 on October 1 for a one-year insurance policy.
f. Purchased $500 of supplies for cash.
g. Purchased inventory for $100,000 on account.
h. Sold inventory for $150,000 on account; cost of the merchandise sold was $80,000.
i. Collected $120,000 cash from customers' accounts receivable.
j. Paid $70,000 cash for inventories purchased during the year.
k. Paid $25,000 for sales reps' salaries, including $1,000 owed at the beginning of 2007.
l. No dividends were paid during the year.
m. The income taxes payable for the year were paid. Income taxes are based on a 15% corporate tax rate.
n. For adjusting entries, all prepaid expenses are initially recorded as assets, and all unearned revenues are initially recorded as liabilities.
o. At year-end, $150 worth of supplies are on hand.
p. At year-end, an additional $5,000 of sales salaries are owed, but have not yet been paid.

You are asked to do the following:

1. Journalize the transactions for the current year, 2007, using the accounts listed on the financial statements and other appropriate accounts (you may omit explanations).
2. Set up T-accounts and enter the beginning balances from the December 31, 2006, post-closing trial balance for SMC. Post all current year journal entries to the T-accounts.
3. Journalize and post any necessary adjusting entries at the end of 2007. (*Hint:* Items b, c, d, e, m, o, and p require adjustment.)
4. After the adjusting entries are posted, prepare a trial balance, a balance sheet, and an income statement for 2007. (*Hint:* Income before income taxes should equal $39,600.)
5. Journalize and post closing entries for 2007 and prepare a post-closing trial balance.
6. Using the DuPont framework, compute the return on equity for SMC for 2006 and 2007.
7. **Interpretive Question:** What is your overall assessment of the financial health of SMC, Inc.?

Part

2

Operating Activities

c h a p t e r

7

Selling a Product or a Service

After studying this chapter, you should be able to:

Learning Objectives

1 Understand the three basic types of business activities: operating, investing, and financing.

2 Use the two revenue recognition criteria to decide when the revenue from a sale or service should be recorded in the accounting records.

3 Properly account for the collection of cash and describe the business controls necessary to safeguard cash.

4 Record the losses resulting from credit customers who do not pay their bills.

5 Evaluate a company's management of its receivables by computing and analyzing appropriate financial ratios.

6 Match revenues and expenses by estimating and recording future warranty and service costs associated with a sale.

7 Reconcile a checking account.

8 Account for the impact of changing exchange rates on the value of accounts receivable denominated in foreign currencies.

chapter 7

Jerry Yang was born in Taiwan in 1968. His father died when he was just two, so Jerry and his brother were raised by their mother, an English professor at a university in Taipei. Jerry's mother moved the family to San Jose, California, in 1978. In spite of what he calls a "very short attention span," Jerry was an excellent student—he was valedictorian of his high school class, and he completed his bachelor's and master's degrees in electrical engineering at Stanford University in a total of just four years.[1]

David Filo was born in Wisconsin in 1966. He describes his parents as "hippie wannabes," who moved their family to Moss Bluff, Louisiana, to join a commune. David eventually left the commune to attend Tulane University where he studied computer engineering. David then went to Stanford as a graduate student, working part-time as a teaching assistant. As luck would have it, one of his students was Jerry Yang. Jerry and David's friendship was strengthened when they both went on a six-month academic exchange program to Japan in 1992.

In 1993, Jerry and David were supposed to be working on their Ph.D. theses in computer-aided design at Stanford. Instead, they found themselves spending more and more research time surfing through the incredible amount of information available on the newly created "World Wide Web." Their first project was to write software that scanned the Web for NBA player statistics. The first Web site that Jerry designed was dedicated to another of his sports passions—sumo wrestling.

Jerry and David quickly learned that the key to surfing the vast quantities of information on the Web was to be able to organize the information. They compiled a list of their favorite Web sites, which they e-mailed to friends and posted on the Web under the title "Jerry's Guide to the World Wide Web." This title was a bit unwieldy, so they came up with the shorthand title "YAHOO!" Jerry and David liked the irreverent, lively tone of the name; they then went back and developed a "formal" title to fit the Yahoo! acronym: Yet Another Hierarchical Officious Oracle.

By 1994, thousands were using Yahoo! to access information on the Web. In fact, the demand was so great that Jerry and David were spending 20-plus hours a day on their "hobby." In addition, the resources of the Stanford computer network were being taxed by Yahoo! users, and university officials asked Jerry and David to find an-

other computer to host their service. Interest in hosting the Yahoo! service was high, and representatives from MCI WORLDCOM, AOL, and NETSCAPE visited Jerry and David in their disheveled 10-by-10-foot work space in a trailer on the Stanford campus. Jerry and David accepted Netscape's offer of help, and the Yahoo! service moved over to the Netscape computer network in 1995.

FYI:

Jonathan Swift coined the word *yahoo* in his book *Gulliver's Travels*. The "yahoos" were savage humans who lived in a land where horses were the dominant species. Swift, a noted satirist, used the term *yahoo* to illustrate how easy it is to justify committing atrocities against people once they are categorized with an unfavorable label.

In March 1995, Jerry and David were finally convinced that their Web search hobby could actually be turned into a business. They accepted a $4 million investment from SEQUOIA, a **venture capital firm**. Realizing that they lacked business expertise, they chose Tim Koogle, another Stanford graduate who was running a $400 million high-tech equipment company, to join them in running their company. In essence, Jerry and David hired Koogle to be their boss. In Yahoo!'s organizational hierarchy, Koogle bears the title of chief executive officer (CEO), and Jerry and David are officially titled the "Chief Yahoos." This team has turned Yahoo! into the most recognized name among Internet companies. In January of 2000, the company was worth over $100 billion. Then the "Internet bubble" burst. The year 2000 saw many Internet companies fall by the wayside and those that remained had market value a fraction of what they once were. For example, Yahoo!'s value in May of 2003 was approximately $15 billion.

So what happened to Internet companies? Investors were afraid of missing out on the next "Microsoft." As a result, the value of many high-tech companies was based on rumors, beta versions, and vaporware. Once investors realized the outlandish prices being paid for these

venture capital firm A company that provides needed cash to companies in return for an ownership interest.

1 The Yahoo! background material was obtained from the following sources: Beverly Schuch, "Yang and Filo: Chief Yahoos!" *CNN Pinnacle*, November 14, 1999, Transcript #99111400V39; and Brent Schlender, "How a Virtuoso Plays the Web," *Fortune*, March 6, 2000, p. F-79.

tech companies, they began focusing on the basics of a business—revenues and profits. Many Internet companies never posted a profit—Yahoo! did not report its first profitable year until 1999. Once investors began expecting companies to post profits and generate cash, many Internet companies went out of business—the "bubble" burst.

So, how does Yahoo! make money? Throughout its history, Yahoo! has generated almost all of its revenue through the sale of advertising space on its Web pages. For example, in 2002, 68% of Yahoo!'s $953 million in revenue was generated through advertising. Yahoo! has various methods of advertising and is very specific in its annual report as to how revenue is recognized for each of its revenue sources. For example, "The Company recognizes marketing services revenues related to banner advertisements as 'impressions' are delivered by the Company. 'Impressions' are defined as the number of times that an advertisement appears in pages viewed by users of the Yahoo! network." Another source of advertising revenue is text-link advertisements and revenues from that source are "recognized as the net amount earned in the period in which the 'click-throughs' occur. 'Click-throughs' are defined as the number of times a user clicks on an advertisement or search result." As you can see, companies are very careful when it comes to the recognition of revenue—and for good reason. The recent accounting scandals coupled with the bursting of the Internet bubble have placed a renewed emphasis on "when should revenue be recognized?"

or Internet companies such as Yahoo!, investors are extremely interested in the amount of revenue reported in the income statement. In fact, in the gold rush of e-commerce, investors are more concerned about how much e-business a company is doing than about whether the company is able to generate immediate profits. The amount of revenue reported by an Internet company is a key indicator of how large the company is in the Internet economy. For example, as of 2002, AMAZON.COM had never reported a profit (revenue minus expenses) in its history; the company lost $149 million in 2002 alone. Yet, because of the $3.9 billion in revenue it reported in 2002, Amazon.com is viewed as a major player in the Internet economy. As a result, Amazon.com had a market value of $12 billion in May 2003.

Exhibit 1 illustrates how the stock of both Yahoo! and Amazon.com has performed since 1998. The Internet boom peaked in January of 2000 and in one year both companies had lost significant market value. The bright side is that both of these companies are still in existence. Many Internet companies are gone.

The amount of revenue reported by traditional companies, such as GENERAL MOTORS, WAL-MART, and GENERAL ELECTRIC, is also of interest to investors because increased revenues almost always lead to increased profits. Consequently, there is sometimes great pressure on companies to report as much revenue as possible. To balance this pressure, accounting rules have been established to govern exactly when it is appropriate for a company to report the revenue from a transaction in the income statement. These accounting rules are not just conceptual toys for accountants; investor concern about whether MICROSTRATEGY, a software company, was correctly applying the accounting rules associated with revenue caused the company's stock price to drop from $333 per share on March 10, 2000, to $22.25 per share just 10 weeks later.[2]

In this chapter, you will study the accounting rules governing the proper recognition of revenue. You will also learn how to account for cash collections and how to handle customer accounts that are uncollectible. Selling goods and services, collecting the cash, and handling customer accounts are fundamental to the operation of any business. Accordingly, properly recording these activities is fundamental to the practice of accounting.

2 Michael Schroeder, "SEC Widens MicroStrategy Investigation," *The Wall Street Journal*, May 24, 2000, p. C1.

Exhibit 1: Stock Performance for Yahoo! and Amazon.com

Major Activities of a Business

❚ Understand the three basic types of business activities: operating, investing, and financing.

In the first six chapters, you were introduced to the accounting environment, the basic financial statements, and the accounting cycle (the way business transactions are entered into the accounting records). That material was necessary for you to understand some basic terminology and procedures used in accounting. Accounting has often been called the language of business. By studying the first six chapters, you should now be somewhat familiar with this new business language.

With the basics behind us, it is now time to use accounting to understand how businesses work, how the various activities of business are accounted for, and how businesses report their operating results to investors. The activities of most businesses can be divided into three groups:

- Operating activities
- Investing activities
- Financing activities

operating activities Transactions and events that involve selling products or services and incurring the necessary expenses associated with the primary activities of the business.

Operating activities involve selling products or services, buying inventory for resale, and incurring and paying for necessary expenses associated with the primary activities of the business. The operating activities of a motel, for example, would include renting rooms (the selling activity); buying soap, shampoo, and other supplies to operate the motel; and incurring and paying for electricity, heat, water, cleaning, television and telephone service, and salaries and taxes of workers. The operating activities of a grocery store would include buying produce, meats, canned goods, and other items for resale; selling products to customers; and incurring and paying for expenses associated with the store's operations such as utilities, salaries, and taxes. The operating activities of YAHOO! include selling advertising space on the company's Web pages, paying employees to maintain the Yahoo! system and to develop new software, and paying to advertise the Yahoo! brand name on TV and in magazines. It is easy to identify operating activities because they are always associated with the primary purpose of a business.

In this chapter we cover the operating activities for selling products and services, the recognition of revenues from those sales, accounting for cash, and problems associated with collecting receivables arising from sales. In Chapter 8 we examine the purchase of inventory for resale to customers and the necessary accounting procedures. In Chapter 9 we conclude our discussion of operating activities by considering other operating expenses and how revenues and expenses are combined to compute the net income of a business. Incurring and paying for operating expenses such as employee compensation, insurance, advertising, research and development, and income taxes are also covered in Chapter 9.

© 2003 Getty Images

A motel deals with operating activities on a daily basis when renting rooms, buying supplies, and paying utility expenses.

investing activities Transactions and events that involve the purchase and sale of property, plant, equipment, and other assets not generally held for resale.

financing activities Transactions and events whereby resources are obtained from, or repaid to, owners (equity financing) and creditors (debt financing).

Investing activities involve the purchase of assets for use in the business. The assets purchased as part of investing activities include property, plant, and equipment, as well as financial assets such as investments in stocks and bonds of other companies. Investing activities are distinguishable from operating activities because they occur less frequently and the amounts involved in each transaction are usually quite large. For example, while most businesses buy and sell inventory or services to customers on a daily basis (operating activities), only rarely do they buy and sell buildings, equipment, and stocks and bonds of other companies. It is important to note that buying inventory for resale is an operating activity, not an investing activity. Investing activities are covered in Chapters 10 and 13.

Financing activities involve raising money to finance a business by means other than operations. In addition to earning money through profitable operations, there are two other ways to fund a business: (1) money can be borrowed from creditors (debt financing), or (2) money can be raised by selling stock or ownership interests in the business to investors (equity financing). Debt financing is the subject of Chapter 11, while equity financing will be discussed in Chapter 12.

Once you have studied Chapters 7 through 13, you will have a good understanding of how businesses operate, invest, and are financed. That knowledge should be helpful in the future if you own your own business, invest in companies as a stockholder, work for a financial institution (or other lender of funds), or work in any position where a knowledge of business is essential.

After studying the operating, investing, and financing activities of a business, you will be ready to combine your knowledge of how businesses operate with the basic accounting knowledge you gained from Chapters 1 through 6. To do this, we will study in detail the statement of cash flows, which is structured around the three activities of a business (Chapter 14). You will discover that preparation of a statement of cash flows requires a sound understanding of the balance sheet and the income statement, as well as a good grasp of how the activities of a business tie together. Exhibit 2 provides a graphical road map of the business and reporting activities that will be discussed in the subsequent eight chapters.

Although Chapters 7 through 13 are organized around business activities, it is important to understand how these activities relate to the basic financial statements. To help you understand these relationships, at the beginning of each of the next seven chapters, we present basic financial statements that highlight the accounts that will be covered in that chapter. As you can see in Exhibit 3, Cash, Accounts Receivable, and Warranty Liability on the balance sheet; Sales, Bad Debt Expense, and Warranty Expense on the income statement; and Receipts from Customers on the statement of cash flows are covered in Chapter 7.

TO SUMMARIZE: Activities of a business can be divided into (1) operating activities, (2) investing activities, and (3) financing activities. Operating activities involve selling products or services, buying inventory for resale, and incurring and paying for necessary expenses associated with the primary activities of a business. Investing activities include purchasing assets for use in the business and making investments in such items as stocks and bonds. Financing activities include raising money to finance a business by means other than operations.

Exhibit 2: Major Activities of a Business

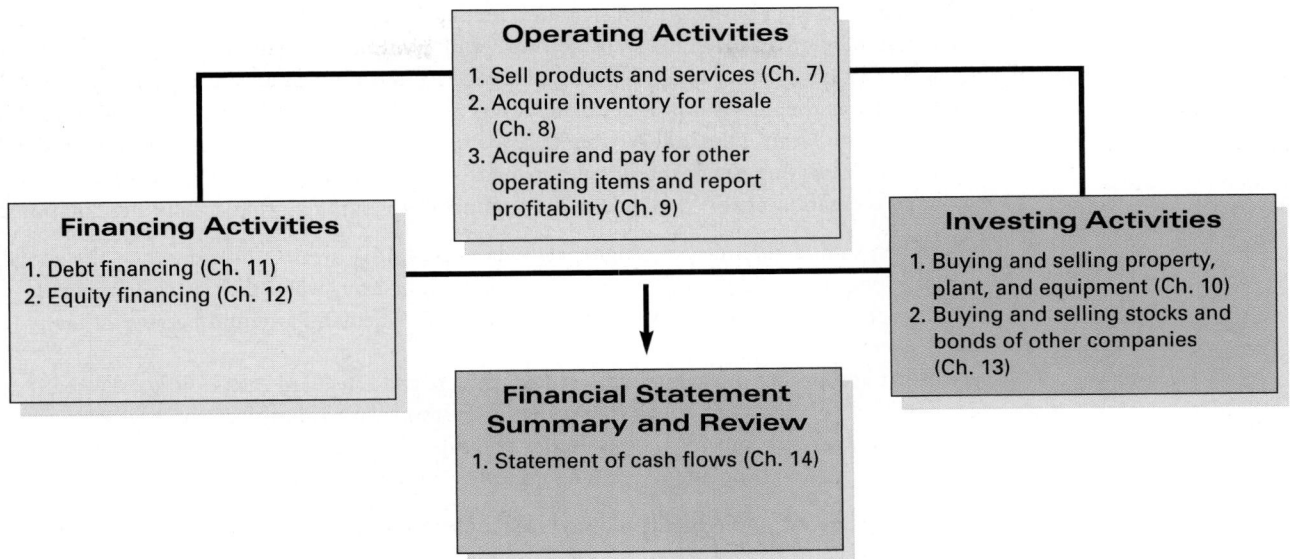

Exhibit 3: Financial Statement Items Covered in This Chapter

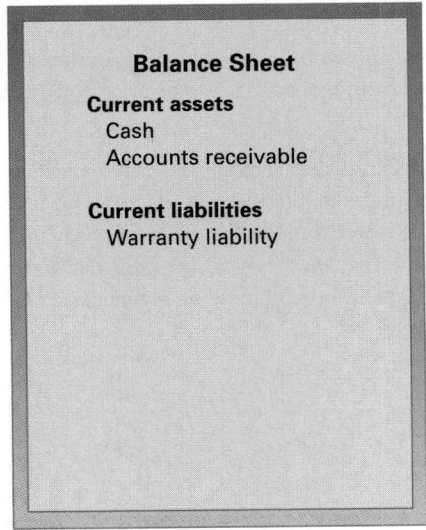

Balance Sheet

Current assets
Cash
Accounts receivable

Current liabilities
Warranty liability

Statement of Cash Flows

Operating activities
Receipts from
customers

Income Statement

Revenue
Sales of goods
and services

Expenses
Bad debt expense
Warranty expense

Recognizing Revenue

2 Use the two revenue recognition criteria to decide when the revenue from a sale or service should be recorded in the accounting records.

The operations of a business revolve around the sale of a product or a service. MCDONALD'S sells fast food; MICROSOFT sells software and continuing customer support; BANK OF AMERICA loans money and sells financial services; YAHOO! sells advertising space on its Web pages. Just as the sale of a product or service is at the heart of any business, proper recording of the revenue from sales and services is fundamental to the practice of accounting. A simple time line illustrating the business issues involved with a sale is given in Exhibit 4.

Consideration of this time line raises a number of very interesting accounting questions:

- When should revenue be recognized—when the initial order is placed, when the good or service is provided, when the cash is collected, or later, when there is no longer any chance that the customer will return the product or demand a refund because of faulty service?
- What accounting procedures are used to manage and safeguard cash as it is collected?
- How do you account for bad debts, that is, customers who don't pay their bills?
- How do you account for the possibility that sales this year may obligate you to make warranty repairs and provide continuing customer service for many years to come?

The following sections will address these accounting issues, beginning with the important question of when to recognize revenue.

When Should Revenue Be Recognized?

revenue recognition The process of recording revenue in the accounting records; occurs after (1) the work has been substantially completed and (2) cash collection is reasonably assured.

Revenue recognition is the phrase that accountants use to refer to the recording of a sale through a journal entry in the formal accounting records. Revenue is usually recognized when two important criteria have been met:

1. The work has been substantially completed (the company has done something), and
2. Cash, or a valid promise of future payment, has been received (the company has received something in return).

As a practical matter, most companies record sales when goods are shipped to customers. Credit sales are recognized as revenues before cash is collected, and revenue from services is usually recognized when the service is performed, not necessarily when cash is received.

To illustrate, we will assume that on a typical business day Farm Land Products sells 30 sacks of fertilizer for cash and 20 sacks on credit, all at $10 per sack. Given these data, the $500 of revenue is recorded as follows:

Exhibit 4: Time Line of Business Issues Involved with a Sale

| **ACCEPT** | **DELIVER** | **COLLECT** | **ACCEPT** | **STRUGGLE** | **PROVIDE** |
| an order | a product or a service | cash | returned products | with nonpaying customers | continuing service |

Cash	300
Accounts Receivable	200
Sales Revenue	500

Sold 30 sacks of fertilizer for cash and 20 sacks on credit.

FYI:

In the majority of companies, the most frequent types of journal entries are those to record sales, cash collections, purchases, and payments to suppliers. Because such transactions are so frequent, most firms maintain four separate special journals: (1) the sales journal, (2) the purchases journal, (3) the cash receipts journal, and (4) the cash disbursements journal. These journals are discussed in detail in this text's Interactive Study Center at **http://albrecht .swlearning.com**.

Although the debit entries are made to different accounts, the credit entry for the full amount is to a revenue account. Thus, accrual-basis accounting requires the recognition of $500 in revenue instead of the $300 that would be recognized if the focus were merely on cash collection.

This example is a simple illustration of how sales are recorded and revenue is recognized. In reality, sales transactions are usually more complex, involving such things as uncertainty about exactly when the transaction is actually completed and whether a valid promise of payment has actually been received from the customer. These difficulties are compounded by the fact that companies often have an understandable desire to report revenue as soon as possible in order to enhance their reported performance and make it easier to get loans or attract investors. The discussion below will further examine the two revenue recognition criteria (work done and cash collectible) to see how accountants apply these rules to ensure that reported revenue fairly reflects the economic performance of a business.

Application of the Revenue Recognition Criteria

The Farm Land example was used to illustrate a straightforward case of revenue recognition at the time a sale is made. The Farm Land customers bought $500 worth of fertilizer, paying $300 cash and promising to pay $200 later; the $500 of revenue was recognized immediately. But what if the terms of the sale had also required Farm Land to deliver the fertilizer to the customers at no extra charge? In this case, proper application of the "work done" revenue recognition criterion would require that the revenue not be recorded until actual delivery had taken place. Alternatively, assume that the fertilizer sale was accompanied by a guarantee that, within 30 days, customers could return the unused portion of fertilizer for a full refund. If very few customers ever seek a refund, revenue should still be recognized at the time of sale. But, for example, if over 70% of fertilizer customers later seek refunds, the "cash collectible" revenue recognition criterion suggests that no revenue should be recognized until the completion of the 30-day return period; Farm Land then becomes reasonably assured of the amount of cash it will collect from the $500 in sales. This situation illustrates the need for accountants to exercise professional judgment and account for the economic reality of a transaction instead of blindly relying on technical legal rules about whether a sale has taken place. Other examples of the application of the revenue recognition criteria are given below.

network exercises

Yahoo!

You have probably accessed Yahoo!'s Web site (**http://www.yahoo.com**) hundreds of times, but you were always on your way to somewhere else. This time, stop to find out something about Yahoo! itself.

Net Work:

1. Access Yahoo!'s company press release file to find out how much revenue Yahoo! reported in the most recent fiscal year.

2. Use Yahoo!'s stock quote search engine to find out Yahoo!'s current market value (ticker symbol: YHOO).

3. Comment on the relationship between reported revenue and current market value.

Yahoo!

As mentioned in the opening scenario of this chapter, Yahoo! derives most of its revenue from the sale of banner advertising space on its Web pages. As mentioned, Yahoo! recognizes advertising revenue as the impressions occur. This revenue recognition practice makes sense if Yahoo! is reasonably certain of collecting payment for these impressions because Yahoo! has completed its work of providing the impressions. Yahoo! often guarantees an advertiser a minimum number of impressions. To the extent that the minimum guaranteed impressions are not met as of the date the financial statements are prepared, Yahoo! delays recognizing the advertising revenue until the guaranteed number of impressions is reached.

Microsoft

The nature of the computer software industry presents several sticky revenue recognition issues. The installation of software and the promise of software upgrades require software companies to consider when the earnings process is substantially complete. Are the revenue recognition criteria satisfied at the point of sale, when the software is installed, or after promised upgrades are delivered? Microsoft recognizes a portion (about 80% for the Office XP software) of the software price as revenue immediately upon delivery of the software to you. The rest of the software price is recognized as revenue gradually over time as the technical support service is provided.

Boeing

BOEING recognizes revenue from commercial aircraft sales at the time the aircraft is delivered to the airline. For example, in 2002 Boeing recognized revenue from the delivery of 371 commercial aircraft, including 223 737s. In contrast, many of Boeing's government contracts require years of work before any product is delivered. If Boeing did not recognize any revenue during this extended production period, its economic activity for that period would be understated. Thus, the accounting rules allow Boeing to recognize revenue piecemeal as it reaches "scheduled performance milestones." This type of "proportional performance" technique is commonly used to recognize revenue from transactions that extend over a long time period, such as for highway construction projects or season tickets for a professional sports team.

Rent-A-Center

RENT-A-CENTER operates 2,542 rent-to-own stores in the United States under both its own name and the name "ColorTyme." Customers rent furniture, VCRs, and other consumer goods under an agreement giving them ownership of the item if they continue to make their payments for the entire rental period. Rent-to-own stores attract customers who cannot afford the outright purchase of consumer goods and who anticipate difficulty in receiving credit through normal channels. Thus, a big concern for Rent-A-Center is collecting the full amount of cash due under a rental contract. In fact, Rent-A-Center states that only about 25% of its customers complete the full term of their agreement. With such a high likelihood of customers stopping payments on their rental agreements, Rent-A-Center recognizes revenue from a specific contract only gradually as the cash is actually collected.

Cendant

Discount-club retailers, such as SAM'S CLUB, are an increasing presence in the market. In 2002, for example, Sam's Club locations had total sales of $31.7 billion. The revenue recognition issue with these clubs is when to recognize the revenue from the up-front membership fees. In 1998, a dispute about the accounting for membership fees exploded in the face of CENDANT, which markets consumer goods and travel services to its members. Cendant had been recognizing its membership fees evenly over the 12-month membership period. However, the Securities and Exchange Commission ruled that, because members can cancel at any time and get their money back, Cendant should not recognize any revenue until the end of the membership period. The change caused Cendant to revise its reported 1997 results from a net income of $55.4 million to a net loss of $217.2 million. The uproar over this change caused the company's market value to plummet by $20 billion.

As mentioned initially, the accounting for most sales transactions is straightforward—the revenue is recognized when the sale is made. However, as illustrated by the examples in this section, when the "work" associated with a sale extends over a significant period of time, or when cash collectibility is in doubt, the accountant must use professional judgment in applying the revenue recognition criteria to determine the proper time to record the sale.

Many colleges and universities prepare financial statements that are released to the public. When do you think a college or university should recognize revenue from student tuition?

Properly recognizing revenue is made more difficult by the fact that companies often have an understandable desire to report revenue as soon as possible. For example, for a company that is applying for a large loan or making an initial public offering of stock, it is critical that reported revenue, and thus reported net income, be as high as possible. In addition, company managers are often scrambling to make revenue or profit targets. In many cases, the managers' bonuses depend on whether these targets are met. Accordingly, managers often have great interest in making sure that revenue is recognized this year rather than waiting until next year. Receivables and revenue continue to be ripe areas for abuse or outright fraud because the associated accounting journal entry is so temptingly easy to make: debit Accounts Receivable and credit Revenue.

TO SUMMARIZE: Revenue is recognized when the work is done and when cash collectibility is reasonably assured. The entries to record revenue from the sale of merchandise or from the performance of a service involve debits to Cash or Accounts Receivable and credits to Sales Revenue or Service Revenue.

Cash Collection

3 Properly account for the collection of cash and describe the business controls necessary to safeguard cash.

Recall the Farm Land Products example in which fertilizer was sold, partially for cash and partially on credit. Farm Land recorded the sales as follows:

Cash	300	
Accounts Receivable	200	
Sales Revenue		500
Sold 30 sacks of fertilizer for cash and 20 sacks on credit.		

Subsequent collection of the $200 accounts receivable is recorded as follows:

Cash	200	
Accounts Receivable		200
Collected cash for $200 credit sale.		

Note that Sales Revenue is not credited again when the cash is collected; the revenue was already recognized when the sale was made.

The following T-accounts show that the net result of these two transactions is an increase in Cash and Sales Revenue of $500.

	Cash		Accounts Receivable		Sales Revenue	
Original sale	300		200			500
Collection of account	200			200		
Final balances	500		0			500
	To balance sheet					To income statement

These two entries illustrate simple sales and collection transactions. Many companies, however, offer sales discounts and must deal with merchandise returns. The accounting for discounts and returns is explained on the following page.

Sales Discounts

sales discount A reduction in the selling price that is allowed if payment is received within a specified period.

In many sales transactions, the buyer is given a discount if the bill is paid promptly. Such incentives to pay quickly are called **sales discounts**, or cash discounts, and the discount terms are typically expressed in abbreviated form. For example, 2/10, n/30 means that a buyer will receive a 2% discount from the selling price if payment is made within 10 days of the date of purchase, but that the full amount must be paid within 30 days or it will be considered past due. (Other common terms are 1/10, n/30 and 2/10, EOM. The latter means that a 2% discount is granted if payment is made within 10 days after the date of sale; otherwise the balance is due at the end of the month.) A 2% discount is a strong incentive for a customer to pay within 10 days because it is equivalent to paying an annual interest rate of about 36% to wait and pay after the discount period.[3] In fact, if the amount owed is substantial, most firms will borrow money, if necessary, to take advantage of a sales discount. The interest rate they will have to pay a lending institution to borrow the money is considerably less than the effective interest rate of missing the sales discount.

If an account receivable is paid within a specified discount period, the entry to record the receipt of cash is different from the cash receipt entry shown earlier. Thus, if the $200 in Farm Land credit sales were made with discount terms of 2/10, n/30, and if the customers paid within the discount period, the entry to record the receipt of cash is:

Cash	196	
Sales Discounts ($200 × 0.02)	4	
Accounts Receivable		200
Collected cash within the discount period for $200 credit sale.		

contra account An account that is offset or deducted from another account.

Sales Discounts is a **contra account** (specifically, a contra-revenue account), which means that it is deducted from sales revenue on the income statement. This account is included with other revenue accounts in the general ledger, but unlike other revenue accounts, it has a debit balance rather than a credit balance.

Sales Returns and Allowances

Customers often return merchandise, either because the item is defective or for a variety of other reasons. Most companies generally accept merchandise returns in order to maintain good customer relations. When merchandise is returned, the company must make an entry to reduce revenues and to reduce either Cash (a cash refund) or Accounts Receivable (an adjustment to the customer's account). A similar entry is required when the sales price is reduced because the merchandise was defective or damaged during shipment to the customer.

To illustrate the type of entry needed, we will assume that before any payments on account are made, Farm Land customers return goods costing $150; $100 in returns were made by cash customers, and $50 in returns were made by credit customers. The entry to record the return of merchandise is:

Sales Returns and Allowances	150	
Cash		100
Accounts Receivable		50
Received $150 of returned merchandise; $100 from		
cash customers and $50 from credit customers.		

---

3 This is calculated by computing an annual interest rate for the period that the money is "sacrificed." With terms 2/10, n/30, a buyer who pays on the 10th day instead of the 30th "sacrifices" the money for 20 days. Since 2% is earned in 20 days, and there are just over 18 periods of 20 days in a year, earnings would be 18 × 2%, or approximately 36% annual interest.

sales returns and allowances A contra-revenue account in which the return of, or allowance for reduction in the price of, merchandise previously sold is recorded.

The credit customers will be sent a credit memorandum for the return, stating that credit has been granted and that the balance of their accounts (in total) is now $150 ($200 original credit purchase − $50 returns). Like Sales Discounts, **Sales Returns and Allowances** is a contra account that is deducted from sales revenue on the income statement. The income statement presentation for the revenue accounts, assuming payment within the discount period on the $150 balance in Accounts Receivable, is as follows:

Income Statement	
Sales revenue	$ 500
Less: Sales discounts*	(3)
Less: Sales returns and allowances	(150)
Net sales revenue	$347

*($200 − $50) × 0.02 = $3

Note that when merchandise is returned, sales discounts for the subsequent payment are granted only on the selling price of the merchandise not returned.

It might seem that the use of contra accounts (Sales Discounts and Sales Returns and Allowances) involves extra steps that would not be necessary if discounts and returns of merchandise were deducted directly from Sales Revenue. Although such direct deductions would have the same final effect on net income, the contra accounts separate initial sales from all returns, allowances, and discounts. This permits a company's management to analyze the extent to which customers are returning merchandise, receiving allowances, and taking advantage of discounts. If management find that excessive amounts of merchandise are being returned, they may decide that the company's sales returns policy is too liberal or that the quality of its merchandise needs improvement.

A company's total recorded sales, before any discounts or returns and allowances, are referred to as **gross sales**. When sales discounts or sales returns and allowances are deducted from gross sales, the resulting amount is referred to as **net sales**.

gross sales Total recorded sales before deducting any sales discounts or sales returns and allowances.

net sales Gross sales less sales discounts and sales returns and allowances.

cash Coins, currency, money orders, checks, and funds on deposit with financial institutions; the most liquid of assets.

Control of Cash

Cash includes coins, currency, money orders and checks (made payable or endorsed to the company), and money on deposit with banks or savings institutions that are available for use to satisfy the company's obligations. All the various transactions involving these forms of cash are usually summarized and reported under a single balance sheet account, Cash.

Because it is the easiest asset to spend if it is stolen, cash is a tempting target and must be carefully safeguarded. Several control procedures have been developed to help management monitor and protect cash. In Chapter 6, internal controls for cash and other assets were discussed. Because cash is particularly vulnerable to loss or misuse, however, we will discuss three important controls that are an integral part of accounting for cash.

One of the most important controls is that the handling of cash be separated from the recording of cash. The purpose of this separation of duties is that it becomes more difficult for theft or errors to occur when two or more people are involved. If the cash records are maintained by an employee who also has access to the cash itself, cash can be stolen or "borrowed," and the employee can cover up the shortage by falsifying the accounting records.

A second cash control practice is to require that all cash receipts be deposited daily in bank accounts. This disciplined, rigid process ensures that personal responsibility for the handling of cash is focused on the individual assigned to make the regular deposit. In addition, this process prevents the accumulation of a large amount of cash—even the most trusted employee can be tempted by a large cash hoard.

FYI:

In its balance sheet (see Appendix A), MICROSOFT follows the common practice of combining cash and short-term investments (bonds and U.S. Treasury securities) for the total Cash amount.

FYI:

Consider the case of an employee who both receives payments and keeps the books. He or she could pocket a cash payment from one customer and not record the receipt until payment is received from a second customer. The second customer's payment could be recorded when a third customer pays, and so on. This type of delayed recording of payments is called *lapping*; it allows an employee to use company money for extended periods of time.

A third cash control practice is to require that all cash expenditures (except those paid out of a miscellaneous petty cash fund) be made with prenumbered checks. As we all know from managing our personal finances, payments made with pocket cash are quickly forgotten and easily concealed. In contrast, payments made by check are well documented, both in our personal check registers and by our bank.

In addition to safeguarding cash, a business must ensure that cash is wisely managed. In fact, many businesses establish elaborate control and budgeting procedures for monitoring cash balances and estimating future cash needs. Companies also try to keep only minimum balances in no-interest or low-interest checking accounts; other cash is kept in more high-yielding investments such as certificates of deposit.

TO SUMMARIZE: The amount of cash collected from customers can be reduced because of sales discounts and sales returns and allowances. On the income statement, sales discounts and sales returns and allowances are subtracted from gross sales to arrive at net sales. Cash is a tempting target for fraud or theft, so companies must carefully monitor and control the way cash is handled and accounted for. Common controls include (1) separation of duties in handling and accounting for cash, (2) daily deposits of all cash receipts, and (3) payment of all expenditures by prenumbered checks.

Accounting for Credit Customers Who Don't Pay

4 Record the losses resulting from credit customers who do not pay their bills.

receivables Claims for money, goods, or services.

accounts receivable A current asset representing money due for services performed or merchandise sold on credit.

FYI:

Credit card sales can be viewed as a way for a business to reap the benefit of increased credit sales without having to set up a bookkeeping and collection service for accounts receivable. The credit card company screens customers based on their creditworthiness, sends out the bills, collects the cash, and bears the cost of any uncollectible accounts. A business that accepts credit card sales pays a fee ranging from 1 to 5% of credit card sales.

The term **receivables** refers to a company's claims for money, goods, or services. Receivables are created through various types of transactions, the two most common being the sale of merchandise or services on credit and the lending of money. On a personal level, we are all familiar with credit. Because credit is so readily available, we can buy such items as cars, refrigerators, and big-screen TVs, even when we cannot afford to pay cash for them. Major retail companies such as SEARS, oil companies such as SHELL, and credit card companies such as VISA, MASTERCARD, and AMERICAN EXPRESS have made credit available to almost every person in the United States. We live in a credit world—not only on the individual level, but also at the wholesale and manufacturing business levels.

In business, credit sales give rise to the most common type of receivables: accounts receivable. **Accounts receivable** are the amounts owed to a business by its credit customers and are usually collected in cash within 10 to 60 days. Accounts receivable result from agreements between a company and its credit customers; a more formal contract, including interest on the unpaid balance, is called a note receivable. Other receivables may result from loans to officers or employees of a company, for example. To identify and maintain the distinction between these receivables, businesses establish a separate general ledger account for each classification. If the amount of a receivable is material, it is separately identified on the balance sheet. Receivables that are to be converted to cash within a year (or the normal operating cycle) are classified as current assets and listed on the balance sheet below Cash. In this section of the chapter, we discuss the accounting issues associated with credit customers who don't pay.

When companies sell goods and services on credit (as most do), there are usually some customers who do not pay for the merchandise they purchase; these are referred to as **bad debts**. In fact, most businesses expect a small percentage of their receivables to be uncollectible. If a firm tries too hard to eliminate the

FYI:

Sometimes companies need cash prior to the due dates of their receivables. Often, in these circumstances, such companies will sell or "factor" their accounts receivables to financing or factoring companies. To learn more about how companies account for the "factoring" of receivables, visit this text's Interactive Study Center at **http://albrecht .swlearning.com**.

possibility of losses from nonpaying customers, it usually makes its credit policy so restrictive that valuable sales are lost. On the other hand, if a firm extends credit too easily, the total cost of maintaining the accounts receivable system may exceed the benefit gained from attracting customers by allowing them to buy on credit (due to the number of accounts to track and uncollectible receivables to try to collect). Because of this dilemma, most firms carefully monitor their credit sales and accounts receivable to ensure that their policies are neither too restrictive nor too liberal.

When an account receivable becomes uncollectible, a firm incurs a bad debt loss. This loss is recognized as a cost of doing business, so it is classified as a selling expense. There are two ways to account for losses from uncollectible accounts: the direct write-off method and the allowance method.

Direct Write-Off Method

bad debt An uncollectible account receivable.

direct write-off method The recording of actual losses from uncollectible accounts as expenses during the period in which accounts receivable are determined to be uncollectible.

With the **direct write-off method**, an uncollectible account is recognized as an expense at the time it is determined to be uncollectible. For example, assume that during the year 2006, Farm Land Products had total credit sales of $300,000. Of this amount, $250,000 was subsequently collected in cash during the year, leaving a year-end balance in Accounts Receivable of $50,000 ($300,000 − $250,000). The summary journal entries to record this information are:

Accounts Receivable	300,000	
Sales Revenue		300,000
To record total credit sales for the year.		
Cash	250,000	
Accounts Receivable		250,000
To record total cash collections for the year.		

Assume that one credit customer, Jake Palmer, has an account balance of $1,500 that remains unpaid for several months in 2007. If, after receiving several past-due notices, Palmer still does not pay, Farm Land will probably turn the account over to an attorney or a collection agency. Then, if collection attempts fail, the company may decide that the Palmer account will not be collected and write it off as a loss. The entry to record the expense under the direct write-off method is:

Bad Debt Expense	1,500	
Accounts Receivable		1,500
To write off the uncollectible account of Jake Palmer.		

bad debt expense An account that represents the portion of the current period's credit sales that are estimated to be uncollectible.

Bad Debt Expense is usually considered a selling expense on the income statement. Although the direct write-off method is objective (the account is written off at the time it proves to be uncollectible), it most likely would violate the matching principle, which requires that all costs and expenses incurred in generating revenues be identified with those revenues period by period. With the direct write-off method, sales made near the end of one accounting period may not be recognized as uncollectible until the next period. In this example, the revenue from the sale to Jake Palmer is recognized in 2006, but the expense from the bad debt is not recognized until 2007. As a result, expenses are understated in 2006 and overstated in 2007. This makes the direct write-off method unacceptable from a theoretical point of view. The direct write-off method is allowable only if bad debts involve small, insignificant amounts.

Overstating Receivables One of the easiest ways to overstate income is to overstate receivables. For example, Michael Weinstein, former chairman and CEO of COATED SALES, INC., orchestrated a financial fraud scheme that ultimately cost investors close to $100 million. Coated Sales, Inc., was a New Jersey company that manufactured textiles coated with special chemicals, used for making such products as yacht sails, bullet-proof vests, conveyor belts, and parachutes. The company was best known for supplying the fabric used in the sails of the America's Cup-winning yacht *Stars and Stripes*.

Coated Sales was started as the second career of millionaire entrepreneur Michael Weinstein, who had "retired" in his 30s and sold the discount drug store chain he had built. Looking for a new business, he became interested in textiles through a friend. The proposition was simple: take unfinished textiles, known as gray goods, and finish them with specialized coatings or treatments. The company's earnings, though minuscule at first, began to double and even triple every year—sometimes every six months.

The fraud was instigated by inflating Coated's sales and earnings through the creation of phony invoices purporting to show sales of goods. Coated officials "prebilled" invoices to customers so they could obtain payment for goods before they were shipped. Coated then began sending out false invoices to customers, recording receivables, and obtaining funds for sales that never occurred. To prevent the customers from denying the sales, the company involved the customers in the racket. For example, Robert Solomon of GLOBE SPORTS PRODUCTS paid the fictitious bills and would then receive the money back from Weinstein. Due to the inflated sales and receivables, the value of Coated's stock rose from $1.50 per share in its initial public offering to over $12 per share in 1987. From 1984 to 1987, sales allegedly rose from $9.9 million to over $90 million.

In addition, Weinstein inflated accounts receivable by billing fictitious customers. He used the inflated accounts receivable account to secure large bank loans. For example, BANC-BOSTON FINANCIAL COMPANY loaned Coated $45 million, based on the supposed existence of $51 million in accounts receivable that served as collateral for the loan.

Coated's auditor, KPMG PEAT MARWICK, withdrew because of its suspicions. Within days, Coated Sales' stock value tumbled from $8 to $2 a share. Shortly thereafter, the corporation's credit dried up, forcing it to declare bankruptcy.

Source: Graham Button, "Homeless Jailbird," *Forbes*, August 17, 1992, p. 13.

The Allowance Method

allowance method The recording of estimated losses due to uncollectible accounts as expenses during the period in which the sales occurred.

The **allowance method** satisfies the matching principle because it accounts for uncollectibles during the same period in which the sales occurred. With this method, a firm uses its experience (or industry averages) to estimate the amount of receivables arising from this year's credit sales that will ultimately become uncollectible. That estimate is recorded as bad debt expense in the period of sale. Although the use of estimates may result in a somewhat imprecise expense figure, this is generally thought to be a less serious problem than the direct write-off method's failure to match bad debt expenses with the sales that caused them. In addition, with experience, these estimates tend to be quite accurate.

To illustrate the allowance method, assume that Farm Land Products estimates that the bad debts created by its $300,000 in credit sales in 2006 will ultimately total $4,500. Note that this is a statistical estimate—on average, bad debts will be $4,500, but Farm Land does not yet know exactly which customers will be the ones who will fail to pay. The entry to record this estimated bad debt expense for 2006 is:

Bad Debt Expense	4,500	
Allowance for Bad Debts		4,500
To record the estimated bad debt expense for the current year.		

allowance for bad debts
A contra account, deducted from Accounts Receivable, that shows the estimated losses from uncollectible accounts.

Bad Debt Expense is a selling expense on the income statement, and **Allowance for Bad Debts** is a contra account to Accounts Receivable on the balance sheet. An allowance account is used because the company does not yet know which receivables will not be collected. Later on, for example, in 2007, as actual losses are recognized, the balance in Allowance for Bad Debts is reduced. For example, if in 2007 Jake Palmer's receivable for $1,500 is specifically identified as being uncollectible, the entry is:

Allowance for Bad Debts	1,500	
Accounts Receivable		1,500
To write off the uncollectible account of Jake Palmer.		

Note that the write-off entry in 2007 does not affect net income in 2007. Instead, the net income in 2006, when the credit sale to Jake Palmer was originally made, already reflects the estimated bad debt expense. Think of this entry as follows: The $1,500 Jake Palmer account has been shown to be bad, so it is "thrown away" via a credit to Accounts Receivable. In addition, Allowance for Bad Debts, which is a general estimate of the amount of bad accounts, is reduced by $1,500 because the bad Palmer account has been specifically identified and eliminated. In one entry, the amounts in Accounts Receivable and Allowance for Bad Debts have been reduced. Assume that the balance in Accounts Receivable was $50,000 and the balance in Allowance for Bad Debts was $4,500 before the Palmer account was written off. The net amount in Accounts Receivable after the $1,500 write-off is exactly the same as it was before the entry, as shown here.

Before Write-Off Entry		**After Write-Off Entry**	
Accounts receivable	$50,000	Accounts receivable ($50,000 − $1,500)	$48,500
Less allowance for bad debts	4,500	Less allowance for bad debts ($4,500 − $1,500)	3,000
Net balance	$45,500	Net balance	$45,500

net realizable value of accounts receivable The net amount that would be received if all receivables considered collectible were collected; equal to total accounts receivable less the allowance for bad debts.

The net balance of $45,500 reflects the estimated **net realizable value of accounts receivable**, that is, the amount of receivables the company actually expects to collect.

The following T-account shows the kinds of entries that are made to Allowance for Bad Debts:

Allowance for Bad Debts

Actual write-offs of uncollectible accounts	Estimates of uncollectible accounts

Occasionally, a customer whose account has been written off as uncollectible later pays the outstanding balance. When this happens, the company reverses the entry that was used to write off the account and then recognizes the payment. For example, if Jake Palmer pays the $1,500 after his account has already been written off, the entries to correct the accounting records are:

Accounts Receivable	1,500	
Allowance for Bad Debts		1,500
To reinstate the balance previously written off as uncollectible.		

Cash	1,500
Accounts Receivable	1,500
Received payment in full of previously written-off accounts receivable.	

FYI:

Banks often recover loan amounts that were previously written off as uncollectible. For example, for the three-year period ending in 2002, CITICORP managed to collect a total of $3.887 billion in loans that had been written off in prior years.

Because customers sometimes pay their balances after their accounts are written off, it is important for a company to have good control over both the cash collection procedures and the accounting for accounts receivable. Otherwise, such payments as the previously written-off $1,500 could be pocketed by the employee who receives the cash, and it would never be missed. This is one reason that most companies separate the handling of cash from the recording of cash transactions in the accounts.

Because the amount recorded in Bad Debt Expense affects both the reported net realizable value of the receivables and net income, companies must be careful to use good estimation procedures. These estimates can focus on an examination of either the total number of credit sales during the period or the outstanding receivables at year-end to determine their collectibility.

Estimating Uncollectible Accounts Receivable as a Percentage of Credit Sales

One method of estimating bad debt expense is to estimate uncollectible receivables as a percentage of credit sales for the period. If a company uses this method, the amount of uncollectibles will be a straight percentage of the current year's credit sales. That percentage will be a projection based on experience in prior years, modified for any changes expected for the current period. For example, in the Farm Land example, credit sales for the year of $300,000 are expected to generate bad debts of $4,500, indicating that 1.5% of all credit sales are expected to be uncollectible ($4,500/$300,000 = 1.5%). Farm Land would evaluate the percentage each year, in light of its continued experience, to see whether the same percentage still seems reasonable. In addition, if economic conditions have changed for Farm Land's customers (such as the onset of a recession making it more likely that debts will remain uncollected), the percentage would be adjusted.

When this percentage of sales method is used, the existing balance (if there is one) in Allowance for Bad Debts does not affect the amount computed and is not included in the adjusting entry to record bad debt expense. The 1.5% of the current year's sales that is estimated to be uncollectible is calculated and entered separately, and then added to the existing balance. For example, if the existing credit balance is $2,000, the $4,500 will be added, making the new credit balance $6,500. The rationale for not considering the existing $2,000 balance in Allowance for Bad Debts is that it relates to previous periods' sales and reflects the company's estimate (as of the beginning of the year) of prior years' accounts receivable that are expected to be uncollectible.

STOP & THINK

Should a company work to reduce its bad debt expense to zero? Explain.

In determining the percentage of credit sales that will be uncollectible, a company must estimate the total amount of loss on the basis of experience or industry averages. Obviously, a company that has been in business for several years should be able to make more accurate estimates than a new company. Many established companies use a three- or five-year average as the basis for estimating losses from uncollectible accounts.

Estimating Uncollectible Accounts Receivable as a Percentage of Total Receivables

Another way to estimate uncollectible receivables is to use a percentage of total receivables. Using this method, the amount of uncollectibles is a percentage of the total receivables balance at the end of the period. Assume that Farm Land decides to use this method and determines that

12% of the $50,000 in the year-end Accounts Receivable will ultimately be uncollectible. Accordingly, the credit balance in Allowance for Bad Debts should be $6,000 ($50,000 × 0.12). If there is no existing balance in Allowance for Bad Debts representing the estimate of bad accounts left over from prior years, then an entry for $6,000 is made. If the account has an existing balance, however, only the net amount needed to bring the credit balance to $6,000 is added. For example, an existing credit balance of $2,000 in Allowance for Bad Debts results in the following adjusting entry:

Bad Debt Expense	4,000	
Allowance for Bad Debts		4,000
To adjust the allowance account to the desired balance		
($6,000 − $2,000 = $4,000).		

In all cases, the ending balance in Allowance for Bad Debts should be the amount of total receivables estimated to be uncollectible.

In estimating bad debt expense, the percentage of sales method focuses on an estimation based directly on the level of the current year's credit sales. With the percentage of total receivables method, the focus is on estimating total bad debts existing at the end of the period; this number is compared to the leftover bad debts from prior years, and the difference is bad debt expense, the new bad debts created in the current period. These two techniques are merely alternative estimation approaches. In practice, as a check, a company would probably use both procedures to ensure that they yield roughly consistent results.

Aging Accounts Receivable.   In the example just given, the correct amount of the ending Allowance for Bad Debts balance was computed by applying the estimated uncollectible percentage (12%) to the entire Accounts Receivable balance ($50,000). In a more refined method of estimating the appropriate ending balance in Allowance for Bad Debts, a company bases its calculations on how long its receivables have been outstanding. With this procedure, called **aging accounts receivable**, each receivable is categorized according to age, such as current, 1–30 days past due, 31–60 days past due, 61–90 days past due, 91–120 days past due, and over 120 days past due. Once the receivables in each age classification are totaled, each total is multiplied by an appropriate uncollectible percentage (as determined by experience), recognizing that the older the receivable, the less likely the company is to collect. Exhibit 5 shows how Farm Land could use an aging accounts receivable analysis to estimate the amount of its $50,000 ending balance in Accounts Receivable that will ultimately be uncollectible.

aging accounts receivable
The process of categorizing each account receivable by the number of days it has been outstanding.

The allowance for bad debts estimate obtained using the aging method is $5,897. If the existing credit balance in Allowance for Bad Debts is $2,000, the required adjusting entry is:

Bad Debt Expense	3,897	
Allowance for Bad Debts		3,897
To adjust the allowance account to the desired ending		
balance ($5,897 − $2,000 = $3,897).		

Caution

The aging method is merely a more refined technique for estimating the desired balance in Allowance for Bad Debts.

The aging of accounts receivable is probably the most accurate method of estimating uncollectible accounts. It also enables a company to identify its problem customers. Companies that base their estimates of uncollectible accounts on credit sales or total outstanding receivables also often age their receivables as a way of monitoring the individual accounts receivable balances.

Exhibit 5: Aging Accounts Receivable

Customer	Balance	Current	Days Past Due				
			1–30	31–60	61–90	91–120	Over 120
A. Adams	$10,000	$10,000					
R. Bartholomew	6,500			$ 5,000			$1,500
F. Christiansen	6,250	5,000	$1,250				
G. Dover	7,260			7,260			
M. Ellis	4,000	4,000					
G. Erkland	2,250				$2,250		
R. Fisher	1,500		500			$1,000	
J. Palmer	1,500		1,500				
E. Zeigler	10,740	4,000	6,740				
Totals	$50,000	$23,000	$9,990	$12,260	$2,250	$1,000	$1,500

Estimate of Losses from Uncollectible Accounts

Age	Balance	Percentage Estimated to Be Uncollectible	Amount
Current	$23,000	1.5	$ 345
1–30 days past due	9,990	4.0	400
31–60 days past due	12,260	20.0	2,452
61–90 days past due	2,250	40.0	900
91–120 days past due	1,000	60.0	600
Over 120 days past due	1,500	80.0	1,200
Totals	$50,000		$5,897*

*Receivables that are likely to be uncollectible.

Real-World Illustration of Accounting for Bad Debts

The application of bad debt accounting is illustrated using the financial statements of YAHOO! for 2000–2002. As shown in Exhibit 6, Yahoo! reported accounts receivable at the end of 2002 of $137.5 million and a bad debt allowance for bad debts of $23.8 million. In other words, credit customers owed Yahoo! $137.5 million as of the end of 2002; however, Yahoo!'s best estimate was that $23.8 million of this amount would never be collected. This bad debt allowance amounted to 17.4% of the Accounts Receivable balance, down from 22.6% in 2001 but up from 14.6% in 2000. For a company operating in a stable economic environment with little change in the nature of its credit customers, this percentage would be expected to be about the

Exhibit 6: Bad Debt Expense for Yahoo!

Year	Ending Accounts Receivable	Ending Bad Debt Allowance	Bad Debt Allowance as a Percentage of Accounts Receivable
2000	$105,998*	$15,437	14.6%
2001	88,643	19,995	22.6%
2002	137,464	23,852	17.4%

*Dollar amounts are in millions.

same from year to year. In the case of Yahoo!, operating in the volatile Internet economy, it appears that there has been some variation in the collectibility of accounts receivable from one year to the next.

TO SUMMARIZE: Accounts receivable arise from credit sales to customers. Even though companies monitor their customers carefully, there are usually some who do not pay for the merchandise they purchase. There are two ways of accounting for losses from uncollectible receivables: the direct write-off method and the allowance method. The allowance method is generally accepted in practice because it is consistent with the matching principle. Two ways of estimating losses from uncollectible receivables are (1) as a percentage of credit sales and (2) as some fraction of total outstanding receivables. A common method for applying the latter technique uses an aging accounts receivable analysis.

Assessing How Well Companies Manage Their Receivables

5 Evaluate a company's management of its receivables by computing and analyzing appropriate financial ratios.

As you recall from the DuPont framework explained in Chapter 5, an important element of overall company performance is the efficient use of assets. With regard to accounts receivable, inefficient use means that too much cash is tied up in the form of receivables. A company that collects its receivables on a timely basis has cash to pay its bills. Companies that do not do a good job of collecting receivables are often cash poor, paying interest on short-term loans to cover their cash shortage or losing interest that could be earned by investing cash.

There are several methods of evaluating how well an organization is managing its accounts receivable. The most common method involves computing two ratios, accounts receivable turnover and average collection period. The **accounts receivable turnover** ratio is an attempt to determine how many times during the year a company is "turning over" or collecting its receivables. It is a measure of how many times old receivables are collected and replaced by new receivables. Accounts receivable turnover is calculated as follows:

accounts receivable turnover A measure used to indicate how fast a company collects its receivables; computed by dividing sales by average accounts receivable.

$$\text{Accounts Receivable Turnover} = \frac{\text{Sales Revenue}}{\text{Average Accounts Receivable}}$$

Notice that the numerator of this ratio is sales revenue, not credit sales. Conceptually, one might consider comparing the level of accounts receivable to the amount of credit sales instead of total sales. However, companies rarely, if ever, disclose how much of their sales are credit sales. For this ratio, you can think of cash sales as credit sales with a very short collection time (0 days). Also note that the denominator uses average accounts receivable instead of the ending balance. This recognizes that sales are generated throughout the year; the average Accounts Receivable balance is an approximation of the amount that prevailed during the year. If the Accounts Receivable balance is relatively unchanged during the year, then using the ending balance is acceptable and common. The following are the accounts receivable turnover ratios for two well-known companies for 2002:

Wal-Mart $\dfrac{\$224.524 \text{ billion}}{\$2.054 \text{ billion}} = 109.3$ times

Boeing $\dfrac{\$54.069 \text{ billion}}{\$5.082 \text{ billion}} = 10.6$ times

From this analysis, you can see that WAL-MART turns its receivables over much more often than does BOEING. This is not surprising given the different nature of the two businesses. Wal-Mart sells primarily to retail customers for cash. Remember, from Wal-Mart's standpoint, a credit card sale is the same as a cash sale since Wal-Mart receives its money instantly; it is the credit card company that must worry about collecting the receivable. Boeing, on the other hand, sells to airlines and governments that have established business credit relationships with Boeing. Thus, the nature of its business dictates that Boeing has a much larger fraction of its sales tied up in the form of accounts receivable than does Wal-Mart.

Accounts receivable turnover can then be converted into the number of days it takes to collect receivables by computing a ratio called **average collection period**. This ratio is computed by dividing 365 (or the number of days in a year) by the accounts receivable turnover as follows:

average collection period
A measure of the average number of days it takes to collect a credit sale; computed by dividing 365 days by the accounts receivable turnover.

$$\text{Average Collection Period} = \frac{365}{\text{Accounts Receivable Turnover}}$$

Computing this ratio for both Wal-Mart and Boeing shows that it takes Wal-Mart only 3.3 days (365 ÷ 109.3) on average to collect its receivables, while Boeing takes an average of 34.4 days (365 ÷ 10.6).

Consider what might happen to Boeing's average collection period during an economic recession. During a recession, purchasers are often strapped for cash and try to delay paying on their accounts for as long as possible. Boeing might be faced with airlines that still want to buy airplanes but wish to stretch out the payment period. The result would be a rise in Boeing's average collection period; more of Boeing's resources would be tied up in the form of accounts receivable. In turn, Boeing would have to increase its borrowing in order to pay its own bills since it would be collecting less cash from its slow-paying customers. Proper receivables management involves balancing the desire to extend credit in order to increase sales with the need to collect the cash quickly in order to pay off your own bills.

TO SUMMARIZE: Careful management of accounts receivable is a balance between extending credit to increase your sales and collecting cash quickly to reduce your need to borrow. Two ratios commonly used in monitoring the level of receivables are accounts receivable turnover and average collection period. The level of these ratios is determined by how well a company manages its receivables, as well as by what kind of business the company is in.

Recording Warranty and Service Costs Associated with a Sale

6 Match revenues and expenses by estimating and recording future warranty and service costs associated with a sale.

Let's return to the Farm Land example in which 50 sacks of fertilizer were sold for $500. Assume that as part of each sale, Farm Land offers to send a customer service representative to the home or place of business of any purchaser who wants more detailed instructions on how to apply the fertilizer. Historical experience suggests that the buyer of one fertilizer sack in 10 will request a visit from a Farm Land representative, and the material and labor cost of each visit averages $35. So, with 50 sacks of fertilizer sold, Farm Land has obligated itself to provide, on average, $175 in future customer service [(50 ÷ 10) × $35]. Proper matching requires that this $175 expense be estimated and recognized in the same period in which the associated sale is recognized. Otherwise, if the company waited to record customer service expense until the actual visits are requested, this period's sales revenue would be reported in the same income statement with customer service expense arising from last period's sales. The accountant is giving up some precision because the service expense must be estimated in advance. This sacrifice in precision is worth the benefit of being able to better match revenues and expenses.

The entry to recognize Farm Land's estimated service expense from the sale of 50 sacks of fertilizer is as follows:

Customer Service Expense	175	
Estimated Liability for Service		175
Estimated customer service costs on sales [(50 ÷ 10) × $35].		

The credit entry, Estimated Liability for Service, is a liability. When actual expenses are incurred in providing the customer service, the liability is eliminated with the following type of entry:

Estimated Liability for Service	145	
Wages Payable (to service employees)		100
Supplies		45
Actual customer service costs incurred.		

This entry shows that supplies and labor were required to honor the service agreements. This procedure results in the service expense being recognized at the time of sale, not necessarily when the actual service occurs.

After these two journal entries are made, the remaining balance in Estimated Liability for Service will be $30, shown as follows:

Estimated Liability for Service

Estimate at time of sale		175
Actual service costs incurred	145	
Remaining balance		30

The $30 balance represents the estimated amount of service that still must be provided in the future resulting from the sale of the 50 sacks of fertilizer. If actual experience suggests that the estimated service cost is too high, a lower estimate would be made in connection with subsequent fertilizer sales. If estimated liability for service is too low, a higher estimate is made for subsequent sales. The important point is that the accountant would not try to go back and "fix" an estimate that later proves to be inexact; the accountant merely monitors the relationship between the estimated and actual service costs in order to adjust future estimates accordingly.

The accounting just shown for estimated service costs is the same procedure used for estimated warranty costs. For example, GENERAL MOTORS promises automobile buyers that it will fix, at no charge to the buyer, certain mechanical problems for a certain period of time. GM estimates and records this warranty expense at the time the automobile sales are made. At the end of 2002, GM reported an existing liability for warranty costs of $8.9 billion. This amount is what GM estimates it will have to spend on warranty repairs in 2003 (and later years) on cars sold in 2002 (and earlier).

TO SUMMARIZE: In addition to bad debt expense, there are other costs that must be estimated and recognized at the time a sale is made in order to ensure the proper matching of revenues and expenses. If a company makes promises about future warranty repairs or continued customer service as part of the sale, the value of these promises should be estimated and recorded as an expense at the time of the sale.

e**X**panded *Material*

Thus far the chapter has covered the main topics associated with selling goods or services, collecting the proceeds from those sales, and estimating and recording bad debt expense and service expense. The expanded material will cover two additional topics. First, an important tool of cash control, the bank reconciliation, will be explained. Second, the financial statement implications of making sales denominated in foreign currencies will be illustrated.

Reconciling the Bank Account

7 Reconcile a checking account.

NSF (not sufficient funds) check A check that is not honored by a bank because of insufficient cash in the check writer's account.

With the exception of small amounts of petty cash kept for miscellaneous purposes, most cash is kept in various bank accounts. Generally, only a few employees are authorized to sign checks, and they must have their signatures on file with the bank.

Each month the business receives a bank statement that shows the cash balance at the beginning of the period, the deposits, the amounts of the checks processed, and the cash balance at the end of the period. With the statement, the bank includes all of that month's canceled checks (or at least a listing of the checks), as well as debit and credit memos [for example, an explanation of charges for **NSF (not sufficient funds) checks** and service fees]. From a bank's perspective, customers' deposits are liabilities; hence, debit memos reduce the company's cash balance, and credit memos increase the balance.

The July bank statement for one of Hunt Company's accounts is presented in Exhibit 7. This statement shows all activity in the cash account as recorded by the bank and includes four bank adjustments to Hunt's balance—a bank service charge of $7 (the bank's monthly fee), $60 of interest paid by First Security Bank on Hunt's average balance, a $425 transfer into another account, and a $3,200 direct deposit made by a customer who regularly deposits payments directly to Hunt's bank account. Other adjustments that are commonly made by a bank to a company's account include:

1. *NSF (not sufficient funds).* This is the cancellation of a prior deposit that could not be collected because of insufficient funds in the check writer's (payer's) account. When a check is received and deposited in the payee's account, the check is assumed to represent funds that will be collected from the payer's bank. When a bank refuses to honor a check because of insufficient funds in the account on which it was written, the check is returned to the payee's bank and is marked "NSF." The amount of the check, which was originally recorded as a deposit (addition) to the payee's account, is deducted from the account when the check is returned unpaid.
2. *MS (miscellaneous).* Other adjustments made by a bank.
3. *ATM (automated teller machine) transactions.* These are deposits and withdrawals made by the depositor at automated teller machines.
4. *Withdrawals for credit card transactions paid directly from accounts.* These types of cards, called debit cards, are like using plastic checks. Instead of the card holder getting a bill or statement, the amount charged is deducted from the card holder's bank balance.

It is unusual for the ending balance on the bank statement to equal the amount of cash recorded in a company's cash account. The most common reasons for differences are:

1. *Time period differences.* The time period of the bank statement does not coincide with the timing of the company's postings to the cash account.
2. *Deposits in transit.* These are deposits that have not been processed by the bank as of the bank statement date, usually because they were made at or near the end of the month.
3. *Outstanding checks.* These are checks that have been written and deducted from a company's cash account but have not cleared or been deducted by the bank as of the bank statement date.
4. *Bank debits.* These are deductions made by the bank that have not yet been recorded by the company. The most common are monthly service charges, NSF checks, and bank transfers out of the account.
5. *Bank credits.* These are additions made by the bank to a company's account before they are recorded by the company. The most common source is interest paid by the bank on the account balance.
6. *Accounting errors.* These are numerical errors made by either the company or the bank. The most common is transposition of numbers.

bank reconciliation The process of systematically comparing the cash balance as reported by the bank with the cash balance on the company's books and explaining any differences.

The process of determining the reasons for the differences between the bank balance and the company's cash account balance is called a **bank reconciliation**. This usually results in

Exhibit 7: July Bank Statement for Hunt Company

First Security Bank
Helena, Montana 59601

Statement of Account

HUNT COMPANY
1900 S. PARK LANE
HELENA, MT 59601

Account Number 325-78126

Date of Statement JULY 31, 2006

Check Number	Checks and Withdrawals	Deposits and Additions	Date	Balance
			6/30	13,000
620	140		7/01	12,860
621	250	1,500	7/03	14,110
622	860		7/05	13,250
623	210		7/08	13,040
		2,140	7/09	15,180
624	205		7/10	14,975
626	310		7/14	14,665
	425 T		7/15	14,240
		3,200 D	7/18	17,440
628	765		7/19	16,675
629	4,825		7/22	11,850
630	420		7/24	11,430
632	326	1,600	7/25	12,704
		2,100	7/26	14,804
633	210		7/29	14,594
635	225		7/31	14,369
	7 SC	60 I	7/31	14,422
	9,178	**10,600**		**14,422**
	TOTAL CHECKS AND WITHDRAWALS	TOTAL DEPOSITS AND ADDITIONS		BALANCE

NSF = Not Sufficient Funds   D = Direct Deposit   I = Interest   T = Transfer Out of Account
SC = Service Charge   MS = Miscellaneous   ATM = Automated Teller Machine Transaction

adjusting both the bank statement and the book (cash account) balances. If the balances were not reconciled (if the cash balance were left as is), the figure used on the financial statements would probably be incorrect, and external users would not have accurate information for decision making. More importantly, the bank reconciliation can serve as an independent check to ensure that the cash is being accounted for correctly within the company.

We will use Hunt Company's bank account to illustrate a bank reconciliation. The statement shown in Exhibit 7 indicates an ending balance of $14,422 for the month of July. After arranging the month's canceled checks in numerical order and examining the bank statement, Hunt's accountant notes the following:

1. A deposit of $3,100 on July 31 was not shown on the bank statement. (It was in transit at the end of the month.)
2. Checks No. 625 for $326, No. 631 for $426, and No. 634 for $185 are outstanding. Check No. 627 was voided at the time it was written.
3. The bank's service charge for the month is $7.

4. A direct deposit of $3,200 was made by Joy Company, a regular customer.
5. A transfer of $425 was made out of Hunt's account into the account of Martin Custodial Service for payment owed.
6. The bank paid interest of $60 on Hunt's average balance.
7. Check No. 630 for Thelma Jones's wages was recorded in the accounting records as $240 instead of the correct amount, $420.
8. The cash account in the general ledger shows a balance on July 31 of $13,937.

The bank reconciliation is shown in Exhibit 8. Since the bank and book balances now agree, the $16,585 adjusted cash balance is the amount that will be reported on the financial statements. If the adjusted book and bank balances had not agreed, the accountant would have had to search for errors in bookkeeping or in the bank's figures. When the balances finally agree, any necessary adjustments are made to the cash account to bring it to the correct balance. The entries to correct the balance include debits to Cash for all reconciling additions to the book balance and credits to Cash for all reconciling deductions from the book balance. Additions and deductions from the bank balance do not require adjustments to the company's books; the deposits in transit and the outstanding checks have already been recorded by the company, and, of course, bank errors are corrected by notifying the bank and having the bank make corrections. The adjustments required to correct Hunt's cash account are:

Cash	3,260	
Accounts Receivable		3,200
Interest Revenue		60
To record the additions due to the July bank reconciliation		
(a $3,200 deposit made by Joy Company and $60 interest).		
Custodial Expense	425	
Miscellaneous Expense	7	
Wages Expense	180	
Cash		612
To record the deductions due to the July bank reconciliation		
(service charge, $7; a $180 recording error, check No. 630;		
bank transfer of $425 to Martin Custodial Service).		

Exhibit 8: July Bank Reconciliation for Hunt Company

Hunt Company
Bank Reconciliation
July 31, 2006

Balance per bank statement		$14,422	Balance per books		$13,937
Additions to bank balance:			*Additions to book balance:*		
Deposit in transit		3,100	Direct deposit	$3,200	
Total		$17,522	Interest	60	3,260
			Total		$17,197
Deductions from bank balance:			*Deductions from book balance:*		
Outstanding checks: 625	$326		Service charge	$ 7	
631	426		Bank transfer	425	
634	185	(937)	Error in recording check No. 630		
			(for Jones's wages)	180	(612)
Adjusted bank balance		**$16,585**	**Adjusted book balance**		**$16,585**

TO SUMMARIZE: Because most payments are made by check, companies need to reconcile monthly bank statements with the cash balance reported on the company's books. This reconciliation process involves determining rea- sons for the differences and bringing the book and bank balances into agreement. Adjusting entries are then made for additions to and deductions from the book balance.

Foreign Currency Transactions

8 Account for the impact of changing exchange rates on the value of accounts receivable denominated in foreign currencies.

All of the sales illustrated to this point in the text have been denominated in U.S. dollars. However, many U.S. companies do a large portion of their business in foreign countries. For example, 26% of MICROSOFT's sales in 2002 were denominated in currencies other than the U.S. dollar. So, what would Microsoft have to do to record a software sale denominated in Japanese yen or British pounds? This section answers that question.

When a U.S. company sells a good or provides a service to a party in a foreign country, the transaction amount is frequently denominated in U.S. dollars. The U.S. dollar is a relatively stable currency, and buyers from Azerbaijan to Zimbabwe are often eager to avoid the uncertainty associated with payments denominated in their local currencies. For example, no matter where they are located, buyers and sellers of crude oil almost always write the contract price in terms of U.S. dollars. A U.S. company accounts for a sales contract with a foreign buyer with the sales price denominated in U.S. dollars in the way illustrated previously in this chapter; no new accounting issues are raised. However, if a U.S. company enters into a transaction in which the price is denominated in a foreign currency, the U.S. company must use special accounting procedures to recognize the change in the value of the transaction as foreign currency exchange rates fluctuate. For example, if Microsoft makes a sale with a price of 100,000 Indonesian rupiah, Microsoft knows that it will eventually collect 100,000 rupiah, but Microsoft does not know what those rupiah will be worth, in U.S. dollar terms, until the actual rupiah payment is received. Such a transaction is called a **foreign currency transaction**; the accounting for these transactions is demonstrated in the following section.

foreign currency transaction A sale in which the price is denominated in a currency other than the currency of the seller's home country.

Foreign Currency Transaction Example

To illustrate the accounting for a sale denominated in a foreign currency, assume that American Company sold goods with a price of 20,000,000 Korean won on March 23 to one of its Korean customers. Payment in Korean won is due July 12. American Company prepares quarterly financial statements on June 30. The following exchange rates apply:

	U.S. Dollar Value of One Korean Won	Event
April 23	$0.0010	Sale
June 30	0.0007	Financial statements prepared
July 12	0.0008	Payment received on account

On April 23, each Korean won is worth one-tenth of one U.S. cent. In other words, it takes 1,000 Korean won (1/0.0010) to buy one U.S. dollar. At this exchange rate, the 20,000,000-Korean-won contract is worth $20,000 (20,000,000 × $0.0010).

On April 23, American Company records the sale and the account receivable in its books as follows:

Accounts Receivable (fc)	20,000	
Sales Revenue		20,000

Note that this journal entry is exactly the same as those illustrated earlier in the chapter. The (fc) indicates that the Accounts Receivable asset is denominated in a foreign currency and, thus, subject to exchange rate fluctuations. Because the financial statements of American Company are reported in U.S. dollars, all transaction amounts must be converted into their U.S. dollar equivalents when they are entered into the formal accounting system.

On June 30, American Company prepares its quarterly financial statements. Because the 20,000,000-Korean-won contract price has not yet been collected in cash, American Company still has a receivable denominated in Korean won and must reflect the effect of the change in the exchange rate on the U.S. dollar value of that receivable. In this case the Korean won has decreased in value and is worth only $0.0007 on June 30. If American Company had to settle the contract on June 30, it would receive only $14,000 (20,000,000 × $0.0007). Thus, American Company must recognize an exchange loss of $6,000, or 20,000,000 × ($0.0010 − $0.0007). On July 12, American Company receives payment from its Korean customer. In the interim the value of the Korean won has increased slightly to $0.0008. When the receivable is collected, the 20,000,000 Korean won are worth $16,000 (20,000,000 × $0.0008), so now American Company has experienced a gain relative to its position on June 30. The effects of the fluctuation in the value of the Korean won can be summarized as follows:

> **FYI:**
>
> The wide fluctuations in exchange rates in this illustration are unusual, but not unprecedented. For example, as part of the Asian financial crisis of 1997, the number of Korean won needed to purchase one U.S. dollar increased from 917.77 on October 23, 1997, to 1,952.68 on December 23, 1997.

	U.S. Dollar Value of the Receivable	Gain or Loss
April 23	$20,000	Not applicable
June 30	14,000	$6,000 loss
July 12	16,000	$2,000 gain

This information would be reported in American Company's three primary financial statements in the second quarter (ending June 30) and the third quarter (beginning July 1) as follows:

Second Quarter:

Income Statement		Balance Sheet		Statement of Cash Flows	
Sales revenue	$20,000	Accounts receivable	$14,000	Cash collected from customers	$ 0
Foreign exchange loss	(6,000)				

Third Quarter:

Income Statement		Balance Sheet		Statement of Cash Flows	
Sales revenue	$ 0	Cash	$16,000	Cash collected from customers	$16,000
Foreign exchange gain	2,000	Accounts receivable	0		

The net result of the sale in the second quarter, the collection of cash in the third quarter, and the changing exchange rates in between is to record a sale of $20,000, the collection of cash of $16,000, and a net exchange loss of $4,000 (a $6,000 loss in the second quarter and a $2,000 gain in the third quarter). The important point to note is that the sale is measured at the exchange rate on the date of sale and that any fluctuations between the sale date and the settlement date are recognized as exchange gains or losses.

What could American Company have done in the previous example to reduce its exposure to the risk associated with changing exchange rates? The easiest thing would have been to denominate the transaction in U.S. dollars. Then the risk of exchange rate changes would have fallen on the Korean company. Secondly, American Company could have locked in the price of Korean won by entering into a forward contract with a foreign currency broker. A forward contract is an example of a derivative contract. Derivatives are becoming more and more commonplace in today's business environment, and in Chapter 13 we examine derivatives and their uses and risks.

> **TO SUMMARIZE:** When a U.S. company makes a sale that is denominated in a foreign currency, the sale is called a foreign currency transaction. The sale is measured at the exchange rate on the date of sale, and any fluctuations between the sale date and the settlement date are recognized as exchange gains or losses.

review of learning objectives

1 **Understand the three basic types of business activities: operating, investing, and financing.** The three major types of business activities are: (1) operating activities, (2) investing activities, and (3) financing activities. Operating activities include selling products or services, buying inventory for resale, and incurring and paying for necessary expenses associated with the primary activities of a business. Investing activities include purchasing property, plant, and equipment for use in the business or purchasing investments, such as stocks and bonds of other companies. Financing activities include raising money by means other than operations to finance a business. The two common financing activities are borrowing (debt financing) and selling ownership or equity interests (equity financing) in the company.

2 **Use the two revenue recognition criteria to decide when the revenue from a sale or service should be recorded in the accounting records.** Revenue is recognized when the work is done and when cash collectibility is reasonably assured. The entries to record revenue from the sale of merchandise or from the performance of a service involve debits to Cash or Accounts Receivable and credits to Sales Revenue or Service Revenue. In general, revenues are recognized at the time of a sale. If cash is collected before a service is provided or a product is delivered, however, then revenue should not be recognized until the promised action has been completed. Revenue for long-term contracts is recognized in proportion to the amount of the contract completed.

3 **Properly account for the collection of cash and describe the business controls necessary to safeguard cash.** The amount of cash collected from customers can be reduced because of sales discounts and sales returns and allowances. Sales discounts are reductions in the payments required of customers who pay their accounts quickly. Sales returns and allowances are payment reductions granted to dissatisfied customers. On an income statement, sales discounts and sales returns and allowances are subtracted from gross sales to arrive at net sales. Cash is a tempting target for fraud or theft, so companies must carefully monitor and control the way cash is handled and accounted for. Common controls include (1) separation of duties in the handling of and accounting for cash, (2) daily deposits of all cash receipts, and (3) payment of all expenditures by prenumbered checks.

4 **Record the losses resulting from credit customers who do not pay their bills.** Accounts receivable balances are generally collected from 10 to 60 days after the date of sale. There are two ways to account for losses from uncollectible receivables: the direct write-off method and the allowance method. Only the allowance method is generally acceptable because it matches expenses with revenues. Losses from uncollectible receivables can be estimated (1) as a percentage of total credit sales for the period or (2) as a percentage of total outstanding receivables. One technique for estimating uncollectible receivables as a percentage of total receivables is to perform an aging of accounts receivable.

5 **Evaluate a company's management of its receivables by computing and analyzing appropriate financial ratios.** Careful management of accounts receivable is a balance between extending credit to increase sales and collecting cash quickly to reduce the need to borrow. Two ratios commonly used in monitoring the level of receivables are accounts receivable turnover and average collection period. The level of these ratios is determined by how well a company manages its receivables, as well as by what kind of business the company is in.

6 **Match revenues and expenses by estimating and recording future warranty and service costs associated with a sale.** If a company makes promises about future warranty repairs or continued customer service as part of a sale, the value of these promises is estimated and recorded as an expense at the time of the sale. If experience suggests that the original estimate was in error, adjustments are made to the estimates made in relation to subsequent sales; however, no attempt is made to go back and "fix" the original estimates.

7 **Reconcile a checking account.** Most cash is kept in bank accounts, which are reconciled each month. Bank reconciliations adjust the bank and book balances so that they are the same correct amount. Differences arise between the book and bank balances because the company knows about some cash transactions before the bank does (such as deposits in transit and outstanding checks) and because the bank knows about some cash transactions before the company does (such as bank service charges).

8 **Account for the impact of changing exchange rates on the value of accounts receivable denominated in foreign currencies.** U.S. companies transact large amounts of business with foreign parties. When the transaction is denominated in U.S. dollars, no new accounting issues are introduced. However, when a U.S. company enters into a transaction in which the price is denominated in a foreign currency, the U.S. company must use special accounting procedures to recognize the change in the value of the transaction as foreign currency exchange rates fluctuate. The sale is measured at the exchange rate on the date of sale, and any fluctuations between the sale date and the settlement date are recognized as exchange gains or losses.

k ey terms & concepts

accounts receivable, 304
accounts receivable turnover, 311
aging accounts receivable, 309
allowance for bad debts, 307
allowance method, 306
average collection period, 312
bad debt, 304
bad debt expense, 305
cash, 303
contra account, 302
direct write-off method, 305

financing activities, 296
gross sales, 303
investing activities, 296
net realizable value of accounts
    receivable, 307
net sales, 303
operating activities, 295
receivables, 304
revenue recognition, 298
sales discounts, 302
sales returns and allowances, 303

venture capital firm, 293

bank reconciliation, 314
foreign currency transaction, 317
NSF (not sufficient funds) checks,
    314

r eview problem

Accounting for Receivables and Warranty Obligations

Douglas Company sells furniture. Approximately 10% of its sales are cash; the remainder are on credit. During the year ended December 31, 2006, the company had net credit sales of $2,200,000. As of December 31, 2006, total accounts receivable were $800,000, and Allowance for Bad Debts had a debit balance of $1,100 prior to adjustment. In the past, approximately 1% of credit sales have proved to be uncollectible. An aging analysis of the individual accounts receivable revealed that $32,000 of the Accounts Receivable balance appeared to be uncollectible.

The largest credit sale during the year occurred on December 4, 2006, for $72,000 to Aaron Company. Terms of the sale were 2/10, n/30. On December 13, Aaron Company paid $60,000 of the receivable balance and took advantage of the 2% discount. The remaining $12,000 was still outstanding on March 31, 2007, when Douglas Company learned that Aaron Company had declared bankruptcy. Douglas wrote the receivable off as uncollectible.

On December 31, 2006, Douglas Company estimated that it would cost $11,000 in labor and various expenditures to service the furniture it had sold (under 90-day warranty agreements) during the last three months of 2006. During January 2007, the company spent $430 in labor and $600 for supplies to perform service on defective furniture that was sold during the year 2006.

Required:
Prepare the following journal entries:

1. The sale of $72,000 of furniture on December 4, 2006, to Aaron Company on credit.
2. The collection of $58,800 from Aaron Company on December 13, 2006, assuming the company allows the discount on partial payment.
3. Record Bad Debt Expense on December 31, 2006, using the percentage of credit sales method.
4. Record Bad Debt Expense on December 31, 2006, using the aging of receivables method.
5. Record estimated warranty expense on December 31, 2006.
6. Record actual expenditures to service defective furniture under the warranty agreements on January 31, 2007.
7. Write off the balance of the Aaron Company receivable as uncollectible, March 31, 2007.

Solution
The journal entries would be recorded as follows:

1. Dec. 4, 2006	Accounts Receivable	72,000	
	Sales Revenue		72,000
	Sold $72,000 of furniture to Aaron Company on credit.		

2. Dec. 13, 2006	Cash	58,800	
	Sales Discounts	1,200	
	Accounts Receivable		60,000
	Collected $58,800 from Aaron Company on December 4 sale and recognized the 2% discount taken (0.02 × $60,000 = $1,200).		

3. Dec. 31, 2006	Bad Debt Expense	22,000	
	Allowance for Bad Debts		22,000
	Recorded bad debt expense as 1% of credit sales of $2,200,000 ($2,200,000 × 0.01 = $22,000).		

Note: When using the percentage of credit sales method to estimate bad debt expense, the existing balance in the allowance for bad debts account is ignored.

4. Dec. 31, 2006	Bad Debt Expense	33,100	
	Allowance for Bad Debts		33,100
	Recorded bad debt expense using the aging of accounts receivable method ($32,000 + $1,100 debit balance).		

Note: When using the percentage of total receivables method (e.g., by aging receivables) to estimate bad debt expense, the existing balance in Allowance for Bad Debts must be taken into consideration so that the new balance is the amount of receivables not expected to be collected.

5. Dec. 31, 2006	Customer Service Expense	11,000	
	Estimated Liability for Service		11,000
	Estimated customer service (warranty) costs on furniture sold during the last three months of 2006. (The warranty period is 90 days.)		

6. Jan. 31, 2007 Estimated Liability for Service   1,030

        Wages Payable (to service employees)   430

        Supplies   600

        Actual customer service costs incurred.

7. March 31, 2007 Allowance for Bad Debts   12,000

        Accounts Receivable   12,000

        Wrote off the balance in the Aaron Company
        account as uncollectible.

d iscussion questions

1. What are the three types of basic business activities?
2. Why is the purchase of inventory for resale to customers classified as an operating activity rather than an investing activity?
3. When should revenues be recognized and reported?
4. Why do you think misstatement of revenues (e.g., recognizing revenues before they are earned) is one of the most common ways to manipulate financial statements?
5. Why is it important to have separate sales returns and allowances and sales discounts accounts? Wouldn't it be much easier to directly reduce the sales revenue account for these adjustments?
6. Why do companies usually have more controls for cash than for other assets?
7. What are three generally practiced controls for cash, and what is the purpose of each control?
8. Why do most companies tolerate having a small percentage of uncollectible accounts receivable?
9. Why does the accounting profession require the use of the allowance method of accounting for losses due to bad debts rather than the direct write-off method?
10. With the allowance method, why is the net balance, or net realizable value, of Accounts Receivable the same after the write-off of a receivable as it was prior to the write-off of the uncollectible account?
11. Why is the "aging" of accounts receivable usually more accurate than basing the estimate on total receivables?
12. Why is it important to monitor operating ratios such as accounts receivable turnover?
13. Why must the customer service expense (warranty) sometimes be recorded in the period prior to when the actual customer services will be performed?

14. What are the major reasons that the balance of a bank statement is usually different from the cash book balance (Cash per the general ledger)?
15. Why don't the additions and deductions from the bank balance on a bank reconciliation require adjustment by the company?
16. Do all transactions by U.S. companies with foreign parties require special accounting procedures by the U.S. companies? Explain.

p ractice exercises

Practice 7-1 **Classifying Major Business Activities**

Classify each of the following business activities as an operating, investing, or financing activity.

a. Acquiring inventory for resale.
b. Buying and selling stocks and bonds of other companies.
c. Selling shares of stock to investors for cash.
d. Selling products or services.
e. Buying property, plant, or equipment.
f. Acquiring and paying for other operating items.
g. Selling property, plant, or equipment.
h. Borrowing cash from creditors.

Practice 7-2

Revenue Recognition

In which one of the following situations should revenue be recognized?

a. The earnings process has begun and cash collectibility is reasonably assured.
b. The earnings process has begun and cash has been collected.
c. The earnings process is substantially complete and cash collectibility is not yet reasonably assured.
d. The earnings process will soon begin and cash has been collected.
e. The earnings process is substantially complete and cash collectibility is reasonably assured.

Practice 7-3

Revenue Recognition

Make the journal entry necessary to record the sale of 40 books at $15 per book. Twenty-five of the books were sold for cash, and 15 were sold on credit.

Practice 7-4

Cash Collection

Refer to the data in Practice 7-3. Make the journal entry necessary when the company receives payment for the 15 books sold on credit.

Practice 7-5

Sales Discounts

Refer to the data in Practice 7-3. Assume that all of the books were sold to a single customer and that the terms of the credit sale were 2/10, n/30. Make the journal entry necessary to record the receipt of the cash payment assuming that (1) the customer paid the balance on the account five days after the purchase and (2) the customer paid the balance on the account 20 days after the purchase.

Practice 7-6

Sales Returns and Allowances

Refer to the data in Practice 7-3. Assume a customer found that 10 of the books were misprinted and returned the 10 books for a refund. Prepare the journal entry necessary in the records of the selling company to record the receipt of the returned books assuming that (1) the books were returned by a cash customer and (2) the books were returned by a credit customer.

Practice 7-7

Computing Net Sales

Using the following data, compute net sales.

Sales discounts	$ 50,000
Accounts receivable, ending	125,000
Gross sales	2,500,000
Inventory, ending	200,000
Sales returns and allowances	75,000

Practice 7-8

Control of Cash

Which one of the following is *not* an important control associated with cash?

a. All cash expenditures must be made with prenumbered checks.
b. The cash balance must never fall below the sum of inventory and accounts receivable.
c. All cash receipts must be deposited daily.
d. The handling of cash must be separated from the recording of cash.

Practice 7-9

The Direct Write-Off Method

The company has an accounts receivable balance of $5,000,000 at the end of the year. The company decides that $120,000 of those accounts receivable are uncollectible because the customers associated with those accounts had filed for bankruptcy protection during the year. Using the direct write-off method of accounting for bad debt expense, make the journal entry necessary to record bad debt expense for the year.

Practice 7-10

The Allowance Method

The company had credit sales of $2,500,000 during the year, its first year of business. The company has estimated that $50,000 of these sales on account will ultimately be uncollectible. In addition, a year-end review of accounts identified that of the $200,000 in accounts outstanding as of the end of the year, $43,000 were worthless because the business customers associated with those accounts had gone bankrupt. Using the allowance method of accounting for bad debt expense, make the journal entries necessary to record (1) bad debt expense for the year and (2) the write-off of uncollectible accounts at the end of the year.

Practice 7-11

Computing Net Accounts Receivable

Refer to the data in Practice 7-10. Taking into account the allowance for bad debts established at the end of the year, compute the net realizable value of accounts receivable (1) before the write-off of uncollectible accounts and (2) after the write-off of uncollectible accounts.

Practice 7-12

Collecting an Account Previously Written Off

Refer to the data in Practice 7-10. Assume that one customer, whose account had previously been written off, returned from exile in the Bahamas and paid his account of $7,000. Make the journal entry or entries necessary to record the receipt of this payment.

Practice 7-13

**Estimating Uncollectible Accounts Receivable as a
Percentage of Credit Sales**

The company had an Accounts Receivable balance of $60,000 and an Allowance for Bad Debts balance of $2,500 (credit) at the end of the year (before any adjusting entry). Credit sales for the year totaled $600,000. The accountant determined that 1% of this year's credit sales will ultimately be uncollectible. Make the journal entry necessary to record bad debt expense for the year.

Practice 7-14

**Estimating Uncollectible Accounts Receivable as a
Percentage of Total Receivables**

The company had an Accounts Receivable balance of $60,000 and an Allowance for Bad Debts balance of $2,500 (credit) at the end of the year (before any adjusting entry). Credit sales for the year totaled $600,000. The accountant determined that 15% of the ending accounts receivable will ultimately be uncollectible. Make the journal entry necessary to record bad debt expense for the year.

Practice 7-15

**Estimating Uncollectible Accounts Receivable Using
Aging Accounts Receivable**

The company reports the following aging accounts receivable data:

Customer	Balance	Current	1–30	31–60	61–90	91–120	Over 120
T. Gardner	$ 3,750	$ 2,250	$1,500				
J. Gammon	4,000	1,000		$2,500		$ 500	
M. Orser	2,000		2,000				
K. Saxton	1,000			750	$250		
K. Welch	4,000						$4,000
R. Beckstrom	10,900	8,000	2,900				
B. Roberts	3,900			3,900			
L. Wilcox	5,850	5,200			650		
J. Gagon	1,500					1,500	
A. Wycherly	1,750		1,750				
Totals	$38,650	$16,450	$8,150	$7,150	$900	$2,000	$4,000

In addition, the company provides the following estimates for accounts that will ultimately be uncollectible:

Age	Percentage Estimated to Be Uncollectible
Current	1.75%
1–30 days past due	6
31–60 days past due	15
61–90 days past due	35
91–120 days past due	65
Over 120 days past due	90

Using this information, make the journal entry necessary to record bad debt expense. Assume that (1) the balance in the allowance for bad debts account (before adjustment) is $2,000 (credit) and (2) the balance in the allowance for bad debts account (before adjustment) is $3,600 (debit).

Practice 7-16

Evaluating Quality of Accounts Receivable

The company reports the following data for the past three years:

Year	Ending Accounts Receivable	Ending Allowance for Bad Debts
Year 3	$60,450	$10,360
Year 2	50,250	7,690
Year 1	43,200	4,400

Compute the allowance for bad debts as a percentage of accounts receivable and evaluate the quality of accounts receivable over the three-year period.

Practice 7-17

Accounts Receivable Turnover

Using the following data, calculate the company's accounts receivable turnover.

Accounts receivable balance, December 31	$ 35,000
Inventory balance, December 31	42,000
Sales revenue	350,000
Cost of goods sold	200,000
Accounts receivable balance, January 1	25,000

Practice 7-18

Average Collection Period

Refer to the data in Practice 7-17. Calculate the company's average collection period.

Practice 7-19

Warranty Expense

The company has determined, based on past experience, that 15% of all tires sold will need repairs within the warranty period. When customers request a tire repair under the warranty agreement, each visit costs an average of $20 in parts and labor. The company sold 600 tires during the year. Make the journal entry necessary to record warranty expense for the year.

Practice 7-20

Repairs under Warranty

Refer to the data in Practice 7-19. Assume that during the following year, 20 customers bring in 80 tires for warranty repairs. The labor and supplies associated with these repairs were $900 and $350, respectively. Make the journal entry necessary to record the performance of these warranty services.

Practice 7-21

Bank Reconciliation

The company received a bank statement at the end of the month. The statement contained the following:

Ending balance	$24,000
Bank service charge for the month	165
Interest earned and added by the bank to the account balance	90

In comparing the bank statement to its own cash records, the company found the following:

Deposits made but not yet recorded by the bank	$10,800
Checks written and mailed but not yet recorded by the bank	19,500

Before making any adjustments suggested by the bank statement, the cash balance according to the books is $15,375. What is the correct cash balance as of the end of the month? Verify this amount by reconciling the bank statement with the cash balance on the books.

Practice 7-22

Journal Entries from a Bank Reconciliation

Refer to Practice 7-21. Make all journal entries necessary on the company's books to adjust the reported cash balance in response to the receipt of the bank statement.

Practice 7-23

Journal Entry to Record a Foreign Currency Transaction

On November 6 of Year 1, the company provided services (on account) to a client located in Thailand. The contract price is 100,000 Thai baht. On November 6, the exchange rate was 50 baht for one U.S. dollar. On December 31, the exchange rate was 40 baht for one U.S. dollar. The company received payment on the account on March 23 of Year 2. On that date, the exchange rate was 100 baht for one U.S. dollar. Make the journal entry necessary on November 6 to record the performance of the service.

Practice 7-24

Computation of Foreign Exchange Gains and Losses

Refer to Practice 7-23. Compute the foreign exchange gain or loss that should be reported in (1) Year 1 and (2) Year 2.

e xercises

Exercise 7-1

Recognizing Revenue

Supposedly, there is an over 200-year wait to buy GREEN BAY PACKERS season football tickets. The fiscal year-end (when they close their books) for the Green Bay Packers is March 30 of each year. If the Packers sell their season football tickets in February for the coming football season, when should the revenue from those ticket sales be recognized?

Exercise 7-2

Recognizing Revenue

James Dee Company cleans the outside walls of buildings. The average job generates revenue of $800,000 and takes about two weeks to complete. Customers are required to pay for a job within 30 days after its completion. James Dee Company guarantees its work for five years—

if the building walls get dirty within five years, James Dee will clean them again at no charge. James Dee is considering recognizing revenue using one of the following methods:

a. Recognize revenue when James Dee signs the contract to do the job.
b. Recognize revenue when James Dee begins the work.
c. Recognize revenue immediately after the completion of the job.
d. Recognize revenue 30 days after the completion of the job when the cash is collected.
e. Wait until the five-year guarantee period is over before recognizing any revenue.

Which revenue recognition option would you recommend to James Dee? Explain your answer.

Exercise 7-3

Recognizing Revenue—Long-Term Construction Projects
In the year 2002, Salt Lake City, Utah, hosted the Winter Olympics. To get ready for the Olympics, most of the major roads and highways in and around Salt Lake City were renovated. It took over three years to complete the highway projects, and WASATCH CONSTRUCTORS, the construction company performing the work, didn't want to wait until the work was completed to recognize revenue. How should the revenue on these highway construction projects have been recognized?

Exercise 7-4

Revenue Recognition
Yummy, Inc., is a franchiser that offers for sale an exclusive franchise agreement for $30,000. Under the terms of the agreement, the purchaser of a franchise receives a variety of services associated with the construction of a Yummy Submarine and Yogurt Shop, access to various product supply services, and continuing management advice and assistance once the retail unit is up and running. The contract calls for the franchise purchaser to make cash payments of $10,000 per year for three years to Yummy, Inc.

How should Yummy, Inc., account for the sale of a franchise contract? Specifically, when should the revenue and receivable be recognized?

Exercise 7-5

Control of Cash
Molly Maloney is an employee of Marshall Company, a small manufacturing concern. Her responsibilities include opening the daily mail, depositing the cash and checks received into the bank, and making the accounting entries to record the receipt of cash and the reduction of receivables. Explain how Maloney might be able to misuse some of Marshall's cash receipts. As a consultant, what control procedures would you recommend?

Exercise 7-6

P.A.S.S.
Power Accounting
System Software

Recording Sales Transactions
On June 24, 2006, Doxey Company sold merchandise to Nathan Ray for $40,000 with terms 2/10, n/30. On June 30, Ray paid $19,600 on his account and was allowed a discount for the timely payment. On July 20, Ray paid $12,000 on his account and returned $8,000 of merchandise, claiming that it did not meet contract terms.

Record the necessary journal entries for Doxey Company on June 24, June 30, and July 20.

Exercise 7-7

Recording Sales Transactions
Lee Company sold merchandise on account to Peart Company for $16,000 on June 3, 2006, with terms 2/10, n/30. On June 7, 2006, Lee Company received $650 of returned merchandise from Peart Company and issued a credit memorandum for the appropriate amount. Lee Company received payment for the balance of the bill on June 21, 2006.

Record the necessary journal entries for Lee Company on June 3, June 7, and June 21.

Exercise 7-8

Estimating Bad Debts
The trial balance of Stardust Company at the end of its 2006 fiscal year included the following account balances:

(continued)

Account	
Accounts receivable	$48,900
Allowance for bad debts	2,500 (debit balance)

The company has *not yet* recorded any bad debt expense for 2006.

Determine the amount of bad debt expense to be recognized by Stardust Company for 2006, assuming the following independent situations:

1. An aging accounts receivable analysis indicates that probable uncollectible accounts receivable at year-end amount to $4,500.
2. Company policy is to maintain a provision for uncollectible accounts receivable equal to 3% of outstanding accounts receivable.
3. Company policy is to estimate uncollectible accounts receivable as equal to 0.5% of the previous year's annual sales, which were $200,000.

Exercise 7-9

Spreadsheet

Accounting for Bad Debts

The following data were associated with the accounts receivable and uncollectible accounts of Julia Jay, Inc., during 2006:

a. The opening credit balance in Allowance for Bad Debts was $600,000 at January 1, 2006.
b. During 2006, the company realized that specific accounts receivable totaling $630,000 had gone bad and had been written off.
c. An account receivable of $35,000 was collected during 2006. This account had previously been written off as a bad debt in 2005.
d. The company decided that Allowance for Bad Debts would be $650,000 at the end of 2006.

1. Prepare journal entries to show how these events would be recognized in the accounting system using:
   a. The direct write-off method.
   b. The allowance method.
2. Discuss the advantages and disadvantages of each method with respect to the matching principle.

Exercise 7-10

Accounting for Uncollectible Accounts Receivable

Dodge Company had the following information relating to its accounts receivable at December 31, 2005, and for the year ended December 31, 2006:

Accounts receivable balance at 12/31/05	$ 900,000
Allowance for bad debts at 12/31/05 (credit balance)	50,000
Gross sales during 2006 (all credit)	5,000,000
Collections from customers during 2006	4,500,000
Accounts written off as uncollectible during 2006	60,000
Estimated uncollectible receivables at 12/31/06	110,000

Dodge Company uses the percentage of receivables method to estimate bad debt expense.

1. At December 31, 2006, what is the balance of Dodge Company's Allowance for Bad Debts? What is the bad debt expense for 2006?
2. At December 31, 2006, what is the balance of Dodge Company's gross accounts receivable?

Exercise 7-11

Aging of Accounts Receivable

Madariaga Company's accounts receivable reveal the following balances:

Age of Accounts	Receivable Balance
Current	$840,000
1–30 days past due	405,000
31–60 days past due	95,000
61–90 days past due	60,000
91–120 days past due	11,000

The credit balance in Allowance for Bad Debts is now $38,000. After a thorough analysis of its collection history, the company estimates that the following percentages of receivables will eventually prove uncollectible:

Current	0.5%
1–30 days past due	3.5
31–60 days past due	15.0
61–90 days past due	55.0
91–120 days past due	94.0

Prepare an aging schedule for the accounts receivable, and give the journal entry for recording the necessary change in the allowance for bad debts account.

Exercise 7-12

Spreadsheet

Aging of Accounts Receivable

The following aging of accounts receivable is for Harry Company at the end of its first year of business:

Aging of Accounts Receivable December 31, 2006					
	Overall	Less Than 30 Days	31 to 60 Days	61 to 90 Days	Over 90 Days
Ken Nelson	$ 10,000	$ 8,000		$1,000	$1,000
Elaine Anderson	40,000	31,000	$ 4,000		5,000
Bryan Crist	12,000	3,000	4,000	2,000	3,000
Renee Warner	60,000	50,000	10,000		
Nelson Hsia	16,000	10,000	6,000		
Stella Valerio	25,000	20,000		5,000	
Totals	$163,000	$122,000	$24,000	$8,000	$9,000

Harry Company has collected the following bad debt information from a consultant familiar with Harry's industry:

Age of Account	Percentage Ultimately Uncollectible
Less than 30 days	2%
31–60 days	10
61–90 days	30
Over 90 days	75

(continued)

1. Compute the appropriate Allowance for Bad Debts as of December 31, 2006.
2. Make the journal entry required to record this allowance. Remember that, since this is Harry's first year of operations, the allowance account at the beginning of the year was $0.
3. What is Harry's net accounts receivable balance as of December 31, 2006?

Exercise 7-13

Direct Write-Off versus Allowance Method

The vice president for Tres Corporation provides you with the following list of accounts receivable written off in the current year. (These accounts were recognized as bad debt expense at the time they were written off; i.e., the company was using the direct write-off method.)

Date	Customer	Amount
March 30	Rasmussen Company	$12,000
July 31	Dodge Company	7,500
September 30	Larsen Company	10,000
December 31	Peterson Company	12,000

Tres Corporation's sales are all on a n/30 credit basis. Sales for the current year total $3,600,000, and analysis has indicated that uncollectible receivable losses historically approximate 1.5% of sales.

1. Do you agree or disagree with Tres Corporation's policy concerning recognition of bad debt expense? Why or why not?
2. If Tres were to use the percentage of sales method for recording bad debt expense, by how much would income before income taxes change for the current year?

Exercise 7-14

Accounting for Uncollectible Receivables—Percentage of Sales Method

The trial balance of Marchant's Sporting House, Inc., shows a $150,000 outstanding balance in Accounts Receivable at the end of 2005. During 2006, 80% of the total credit sales of $3,500,000 was collected, and no receivables were written off as uncollectible. The company estimated that 2.0% of the credit sales would be uncollectible. During 2007, the account of Prior Sybrowsky, who owed $4,200, was judged to be uncollectible and was written off. At the end of 2007, the amount previously written off was collected in full from Mr. Sybrowsky.

Prepare the necessary journal entries for recording all the preceding transactions relating to uncollectibles on the books of Marchant's Sporting House, Inc.

Exercise 7-15

Comparing the Percentage of Sales and the Percentage of Receivables Methods

Keefer Company uses the percentage of sales method for computing bad debt expense. As of January 1, 2006, the balance of Allowance for Bad Debts was $200,000. Write-offs of uncollectible accounts during 2006 totaled $240,000. Reported bad debt expense for 2006 was $320,000, computed using the percentage of sales method.

Keith & Harding, the auditors of Keefer's financial statements, compiled an aging accounts receivable analysis of Keefer's accounts at the end of 2006. This analysis has led Keith & Harding to estimate that, of the accounts receivable Keefer has as of the end of 2006, $700,000 will ultimately prove to be uncollectible.

Given their analysis, Keith & Harding, the auditors, think that Keefer should make an adjustment to its 2006 financial statements. What adjusting journal entry should Keith & Harding suggest?

Exercise 7-16

Ratio Analysis

The following are summary financial data for Parker Enterprises, Inc., and Boulder, Inc., for three recent years:

	Year 3	Year 2	Year 1
Net sales (in millions):			
Parker Enterprises, Inc.	$ 3,700	$ 3,875	$ 3,882
Boulder, Inc.	17,825	16,549	15,242
Net accounts receivable (in millions):			
Parker Enterprises, Inc.	1,400	1,800	1,725
Boulder, Inc.	5,525	5,800	6,205

1. Using the above data, compute the accounts receivable turnover and average collection period for each company for years 2 and 3.
2. Which company appears to have the better credit management policy?

Exercise 7-17

Assessing How Well Companies Manage Their Receivables

Assume that Hickory Company has the following data related to its accounts receivable:

	2005	2006
Net sales	$1,425,000	$1,650,000
Net receivables:		
Beginning of year	375,000	333,500
End of year	420,000	375,000

Use these data to compute accounts receivable turnover ratios and average collection periods for 2005 and 2006. Based on your analysis, is Hickory Company managing its receivables better or worse in 2006 than it did in 2005?

Exercise 7-18

Measuring Accounts Receivable Quality

The following accounts receivable information is for Katelyn Company:

	2006	2005	2004
Accounts receivable	$600,000	$520,000	$420,000
Allowance for bad debts	36,000	35,000	33,000

Did the creditworthiness of Katelyn's customers increase or decrease between 2004 and 2006? Explain.

Exercise 7-19

Accounting for Warranties

Rick Procter, president of Sharp Television Stores, has been concerned recently about declining sales due to increased competition in the area. Rick has noticed that many of the national stores selling television sets and appliances have been placing heavy emphasis on warranties in their marketing programs. In an effort to revitalize sales, Rick has decided to offer free service and repairs for one year as a warranty on his television sets. Based on experience, Rick believes that first-year service and repair costs on the television sets will be approximately 5% of sales. The first month of operations following the initiation of Rick's new marketing plan showed significant increases in sales of TV sets. Total sales of TV sets for the first three months under the warranty plan were $10,000, $8,000, and $12,000, respectively.

1. Assuming that Rick prepares adjusting entries and financial statements for his own use at the end of each month, prepare the appropriate entry to recognize customer service (warranty) expense for each of these first three months.

(continued)

2. Prepare the appropriate entry to record services provided to repair sets under warranty in the second month, assuming that the following costs were incurred: labor (paid in cash), $550; supplies, $330.

Exercise 7-20

Accounting for Warranties

Sumsion Auto sells used cars and trucks. During 2006, it sold 62 cars and trucks for a total of $1,640,000. Sumsion provides a 24-month, 24,000-mile warranty on the used cars and trucks sold. Sumsion estimates that it will cost $30,000 in labor and $18,000 in parts to service (during the following year) the cars and trucks sold in 2006.

In January 2007, Karla Jeanne brought her truck in for warranty repairs. Sumsion Auto fixed the truck under its warranty agreement. It cost Sumsion $550 in labor and $340 in parts to fix Karla Jeanne's truck. Prepare the journal entries to record (1) Sumsion Auto's estimated customer service liability as of December 31, 2006, and (2) the costs incurred in repairing the truck in January 2007.

Exercise 7-21

Preparing a Bank Reconciliation

Prepare a bank reconciliation for Eugene Company at January 31, 2006, using the information shown.

1. Cash per the accounting records at January 31 amounted to $145,604; the bank statement on this same date showed a balance of $129,004.
2. The canceled checks returned by the bank included a check written by the LeRoy Company for $3,528 that had been deducted from Eugene's account in error.
3. Deposits in transit as of January 31, 2006, amounted to $21,856.
4. The following amounts were adjustments to Eugene Company's account on the bank statement:
   a. Service charges of $52.
   b. An NSF check of $2,800.
   c. Interest earned on the account, $80.
5. Checks written by Eugene Company that have not yet cleared the bank include four checks totaling $11,556.

Exercise 7-22

Spreadsheet

Preparing a Bank Reconciliation

The records of Denna Corporation show the following bank statement information for December:

a. Bank balance, December 31, 2006, $87,450
b. Service charges for December, $50
c. Rent collected by bank, $1,000
d. Note receivable collected by bank (including $300 interest), $2,300
e. December check returned marked NSF (check was a payment of an account receivable), $200
f. Bank erroneously reduced Denna's account for a check written by Dunna Company, $1,000
g. Cash account balance, December 31, 2006, $81,200
h. Outstanding checks, $9,200
i. Deposits in transit, $5,000

1. Prepare a bank reconciliation for December.
2. Prepare the entry to correct the cash account as of December 31, 2006.

Exercise 7-23

Reconciling Book and Bank Balances

Jensen Company has just received the September 30, 2006, bank statement summarized in the following schedule:

	Charges	Deposits	Balance
Balance, September 1			$ 5,100
Deposits recorded during September		$27,000	32,100
Checks cleared during September	$27,300		4,800
NSF check, J. J. Jones	50		4,750
Bank service charges	10		4,740
Balance, September 30			4,740

Cash on hand (recorded on Jensen's books but not deposited) on September 1 and September 30 amounted to $200. There were no deposits in transit or checks outstanding at September 1, 2006. The cash account for September reflected the following:

Cash

Sept. 1 Balance	5,300	Sept. Checks	28,000
Sept. Deposits	29,500		

Answer the following questions. (*Hint:* It may be helpful to prepare a complete bank reconciliation.)

1. What is the ending balance per the cash account before adjustments?
2. What adjustments should be added to the depositor's books?
3. What is the total amount of the deductions from the depositor's books?
4. What is the total amount to be added to the bank's balance?
5. What is the total amount to be deducted from the bank's balance?

Exercise 7-24

Foreign Currency Transaction

Rabona Slice, a U.S. company, sold 100,000 cases of tropical fruit to Ben Thanh Market, a Vietnamese firm, for 2.5 billion Vietnamese dong. The sale was made on November 17, 2006, when one U.S. dollar equaled 14,000 dong. Payment of 2.5 billion Vietnamese dong was due to Rabona Slice on January 16, 2007. At December 31, 2006, one U.S. dollar equaled 15,000 dong, and on January 16, 2007, one U.S. dollar equaled 15,600 dong.

1. What will be the value of the accounts receivable on December 31, 2006, in Vietnamese dong?
2. What will be the value of the accounts receivable on December 31, 2006, in U.S. dollars?
3. Will Rabona Slice recognize an exchange gain or loss at December 31, 2006? Explain.
4. Will Rabona Slice recognize an exchange gain or loss on January 16, 2007? Explain.
5. In connection with this sale, what amount will Rabona Slice report as Sales Revenue in its income statement for 2006?
6. In connection with this sale, what amount will Rabona Slice report as Cash Collected from Customers in its statement of cash flows for 2007?

Exercise 7-25

Foreign Currency Transaction

American, Inc., sells one widget to Japanese Company at an agreed-upon price of 1,000,000 yen. On the day of the sale, one yen is equal to $0.01. American, Inc., maintains its accounting records in U.S. dollars. Therefore, the amount in yen must be converted to U.S. dollars.

1. Provide the journal entry that would be made by American, Inc., on the day of the sale, assuming Japanese Company pays for the widget on the day of the sale.
2. Most sales are on account, meaning that payment will not be received for 30 days or even longer. What issues will arise for American, Inc., if the sale is made with payment due in 30 days? (*Hint:* What might happen to the value of the yen in relation to the dollar during the 30-day period?)
3. Suppose that 30 days from the date of the sale the value of one yen is equal to $0.008. What journal entry would be made when the 1,000,000 yen are received by American, Inc.?

r o b l e m s

Problem 7-1

Recognizing Revenue

Brad Company sells ships. Each ship sells for over $25 million. Brad never starts building a ship until it receives a specific order from a customer. Brad usually takes about four years to build a ship. After construction is completed and during the first three years the customer uses the ship, Brad agrees to repair anything on the ship free of charge. The customers pay for the ships over a period of 10 years after the date of delivery.

Brad Company is considering the following alternatives for recognizing revenue from its sale of ships:

a. Recognize revenue when Brad receives the order to do the job.
b. Recognize revenue when Brad begins the work.
c. Recognize revenue proportionately during the four-year construction period.
d. Recognize revenue immediately after the customer takes possession of the ship.
e. Wait until the three-year guarantee period is over before recognizing any revenue.
f. Wait until the 10-year payment period is over before recognizing any revenue.

Required:
1. Which of the methods, (a) through (f), should Brad use to recognize revenue? Support your answer.
2. **Interpretive Question:** A member of Congress has introduced a bill that would require the SEC to crack down on lenient revenue recognition practices by shipbuilding companies. This bill would require Brad Company to use method (f) above. The "logic" behind the congressperson's bill is that no revenue should ever be recognized until the complete amount of cash is in hand. You have been hired as a lobbyist by Brad Company to speak against this bill. What arguments would you use on Capitol Hill to sway representatives to vote against this bill?

Problem 7-2

Recognizing Revenue

The Ho Man Tin Tennis Club sells lifetime memberships for $20,000 each. A lifetime membership entitles a person to unlimited access to the club's tennis courts, weight room, exercise equipment, and swimming pool. Once a lifetime membership fee is paid, it is not refundable for any reason.

Judy Chan and her partners are the owners of Ho Man Tin Tennis Club. In order to overcome a cash shortage, they intend to seek investment funds from new partners. Judy and her partners are meeting with their accountant to provide information for preparation of financial statements. They are considering when they should recognize revenue from the sale of lifetime memberships.

Required:
Answer the following questions:

1. When should the lifetime membership fees be recognized as revenue? Remember, they are nonrefundable.
2. **Interpretive Question:** What incentives would Judy and her partners have for recognizing the entire amount of the lifetime membership fee as revenue at the time it is collected? Since the entire amount will ultimately be recognized anyway, what difference does the timing make?

Problem 7-3

P.A.S.S.
Power Accounting System Software

Sales Transactions

Company R and Company S entered into the following transactions:

a. Company R sold merchandise to Company S for $40,000, terms 2/10, n/30.
b. Prior to payment, Company S returned $3,000 of the merchandise for credit.

c. Company S paid Company R in full within the discount period.

d. Company S paid Company R in full after the discount period. [Assume that transaction (c) did not occur.]

Required:

Prepare journal entries to record the transactions for Company R (the seller).

Problem 7-4

Cash Fraud

Mac Faber was the controller of the Lewiston National Bank. In his position of controller, he was in charge of all accounting functions. He wrote cashier's checks for the bank and reconciled the bank statement. He alone could approve exceptions to credit limits for bank customers, and even the internal auditors reported to him. Unknown to the bank, Mac had recently divorced and was supporting two households. In addition, many of his personal investments had soured, including a major farm implement dealership that had lost $40,000 in the last year. Several months after Mac had left the bank for another job, it was discovered that a vendor had paid twice and that the second payment had been deposited in Mac's personal account. Because Mac was not there to cover his tracks (as he had been on previous occasions), an investigation ensued. It was determined that Mac had used his position in the bank to steal $117,000 over a period of two years. Mac was prosecuted and sentenced to 30 months in a federal penitentiary.

Required:

1. What internal control weaknesses allowed Mac to perpetrate the fraud?
2. What motivated Mac to perpetrate the fraud?

Problem 7-5

Analysis of Allowance for Bad Debts

Boulder View Corporation accounts for uncollectible accounts receivable using the allowance method.

As of December 31, 2005, the credit balance in Allowance for Bad Debts was $130,000. During 2006, credit sales totaled $10,000,000, $90,000 of accounts receivable were written off as uncollectible, and recoveries of accounts previously written off amounted to $15,000. An aging of accounts receivable at December 31, 2006, showed the following:

Classification of Receivable	Accounts Receivable Balance as of December 31, 2006	Percentage Estimated Uncollectible
Current	$1,140,000	2%
1–30 days past due	600,000	10
31–60 days past due	400,000	23
Over 60 days past due	120,000	75
	$2,260,000	

Required:

1. Prepare the journal entry to record bad debt expense for 2006, assuming bad debts are estimated using the aging of receivables method.
2. Record journal entries to account for the actual write-off of $90,000 uncollectible accounts receivable and the collection of $15,000 in receivables that had previously been written off.

Problem 7-6

Spreadsheet

Accounting for Accounts Receivable

Assume that Neo Company had the following balances in its receivable accounts on December 31, 2005:

Accounts receivable	$460,000
Allowance for bad debts	12,400 (credit balance)

(continued)

P.A.S.S.
Power Accounting
System Software

Transactions during 2006 were as follows:

Gross credit sales	$1,750,000
Collections of accounts receivable ($1,660,000 less cash discounts of $25,000)	1,635,000
Sales returns and allowances (from credit sales)	12,000
Accounts receivable written off as uncollectible	7,000
Balance in Allowance for Bad Debts on December 31, 2006 (based on percent of total accounts receivable)	13,500

Required:

1. Prepare entries for the 2006 transactions.
2. What amount will Neo Company report for:
   a. Net sales in its 2006 income statement?
   b. Total accounts receivable on its balance sheet of December 31, 2006?

Problem 7-7

Analysis of Receivables

Juniper Company was formed in 1996. Sales have increased on the average of 5% per year during its first 10 years of existence, with total sales for 2005 amounting to $400,000. Since incorporation, Juniper Company has used the allowance method to account for uncollectible accounts receivable.

On January 1, 2006, the company's Allowance for Bad Debts had a credit balance of $5,000. During 2006, accounts totaling $3,500 were written off as uncollectible.

Required:

1. What does the January 1, 2006, credit balance of $5,000 in Allowance for Bad Debts represent?
2. Since Juniper Company wrote off $3,500 in uncollectible accounts receivable during 2006, was the prior year's estimate of uncollectible accounts receivable overstated?
3. Prepare journal entries to record:
   a. The $3,500 write-off of receivables during 2006.
   b. Juniper Company's 2006 bad debt expense, assuming an aging of the December 31, 2006, accounts receivable indicates that potential uncollectible accounts at year-end total $9,000.

Problem 7-8

P.A.S.S.
Power Accounting
System Software

Computing and Recording Bad Debt Expense

During 2006, Wishbone Corporation had a total of $5,000,000 in sales, of which 80% were on credit. At year-end, the Accounts Receivable balance showed a total of $2,300,000, which had been aged as follows:

Age	Amount
Current	$1,900,000
1–30 days past due	200,000
31–60 days past due	100,000
61–90 days past due	70,000
Over 90 days past due	30,000
	$2,300,000

Prepare the journal entry required at year-end to record the bad debt expense under each of the following independent conditions. Assume, where applicable, that Allowance for Bad Debts had a credit balance of $5,500 immediately before these adjustments.

Required:

1. Use the direct write-off method. (Assume that $60,000 of accounts are determined to be uncollectible and are written off in a single year-end entry.)
2. Based on experience, uncollectible accounts existing at year-end are estimated to be 3% of total accounts receivable.
3. Based on experience, uncollectible accounts are estimated to be the sum of:

   1% of current accounts receivable
   6% of accounts 1–30 days past due
   10% of accounts 31–60 days past due
   20% of accounts 61–90 days past due
   30% of accounts over 90 days past due

Problem 7-9

P.A.S.S.
Power Accounting System Software

Unifying Concepts: Aging of Accounts Receivable and Uncollectible Accounts

Asburry Company has found that, historically, 0.5% of its current accounts receivable, 2% of accounts 1 to 30 days past due, 3.5% of accounts 31 to 60 days past due, 7% of accounts 61 to 90 days past due, and 10% of accounts over 90 days past due are uncollectible. The following schedule shows an aging of the accounts receivable as of December 31, 2006:

	Days Past Due				
	Current	**1–30**	**31–60**	**61–90**	**Over 90**
Balance	$91,200	$19,700	$8,200	$1,700	$390

The balances at December 31, 2006, in selected accounts are as follows. (Assume that the allowance method is used.)

Sales revenue	$250,032
Sales returns	2,523
Allowance for bad debts	460 (credit balance)

Required:

1. Given these data, make the necessary adjusting entry (or entries) for uncollectible accounts receivable on December 31, 2006, on Asburry's books.
2. On February 14, 2007, Sara Spar, a customer, informed Asburry Company that she was going bankrupt and would not be able to pay her account of $73. Make the appropriate entry (or entries).
3. On June 29, 2007, Sara Spar was able to pay the amount she owed in full. Make the appropriate entry (or entries).
4. Assume that Allowance for Bad Debts at December 31, 2006, had a debit balance of $460 instead of a credit balance of $460. Make the necessary adjusting journal entry that would be needed on December 31, 2006.

Problem 7-10

Estimating Uncollectible Accounts

Ulysis Corporation makes and sells clothing to fashion stores throughout the country. On December 31, 2006, before adjusting entries were made, it had the following account balances on its books:

Accounts receivable	$ 2,320,000
Sales revenue, 2006 (60% were credit sales)	16,000,000
Allowance for bad debts (credit balance)	4,000

(continued)

Required:

1. Make the appropriate adjusting entry on December 31, 2006, to record the allowance for bad debts if uncollectible accounts receivable are estimated to be 3% of accounts receivable.
2. Make the appropriate adjusting entry on December 31, 2006, to record the allowance for bad debts if uncollectible accounts receivable are estimated on the basis of an aging of accounts receivable; the aging schedule reveals the following:

	Balance of Accounts Receivable	Percent Estimated to Become Uncollectible
Current	$1,200,000	0.5%
1–30 days past due	800,000	1
31–60 days past due	200,000	4
61–90 days past due	80,000	20
Over 90 days past due	40,000	30

3. Now assume that on March 3, 2007, it was determined that a $64,000 account receivable from Petite Corners is uncollectible. Record the bad debt, assuming:
   a. The direct write-off method is used.
   b. The allowance method is used.
4. Further assume that on June 4, 2007, Petite Corners paid this previously written-off debt of $64,000. Record the payment, assuming:
   a. The direct write-off method had been used on March 3 to record the bad debt.
   b. The allowance method had been used on March 3 to record the bad debt.
5. **Interpretive Question:** Which method of accounting for bad debts, direct write-off or allowance, is generally used? Why?

Problem 7-11

The Aging Method

The following aging of accounts receivable is for Coby Company at the end of 2006:

Aging of Accounts Receivable December 31, 2006					
	Overall	Less Than 30 Days	31 to 60 Days	61 to 90 Days	Over 90 Days
Travis Campbell	$ 50,000	$ 40,000	$ 5,000	$ 2,000	$ 3,000
Linda Reed	35,000	31,000	4,000		
Jack Riding	110,000	100,000	10,000		
Joy Riddle	20,000	3,000	10,000	4,000	3,000
Afzal Shah	90,000	60,000	21,000	4,000	5,000
Edna Ramos	80,000	60,000	16,000		4,000
Totals	$385,000	$294,000	$66,000	$10,000	$15,000

Coby Company had a credit balance of $20,000 in its allowance for bad debts account at the beginning of 2006. Write-offs for the year totaled $16,500. Coby Company makes only one adjusting entry to record bad debt expense at the end of the year. Historically, Coby Company has experienced the following with respect to the collection of its accounts receivable:

Age of Account	Percentage Ultimately Uncollectible
Less than 30 days	1%
31–60 days	5
61–90 days	30
Over 90 days	90

Required:
1. Compute the appropriate balance of allowance for bad debts as of December 31, 2006.
2. Make the journal entry required to record this allowance for bad debts balance. Remember that the allowance account already has an existing balance.
3. What is Coby's net accounts receivable balance as of December 31, 2006?

Problem 7-12

Analysis of Accounts Receivable Quantity and Quality
The following accounts receivable information is for MaScare Company:

	2006	2005	2004
Accounts receivable	$100,000	$ 30,000	$ 50,000
Allowance for bad debts	4,000	2,000	3,000
Sales revenue	210,000	180,000	170,000

Required:
1. With the big increase in Allowance for Bad Debts in 2006, MaScare Company is concerned that the creditworthiness of its customers declined from 2005 to 2006. Is there any support for this view in the accounts receivable data? Explain.
2. **Interpretive Question:** Is there any cause for alarm in the accounts receivable data for 2006? Explain.

Problem 7-13

Spreadsheet

P.A.S.S.
Power Accounting System Software

Preparing a Bank Reconciliation
Milton Company has just received the following monthly bank statement for June 2006.

Date	Checks	Deposits	Balance
June 01			$25,000
June 02	$ 150		24,850
June 03		$ 6,000	30,850
June 04	750		30,100
June 05	1,500		28,600
June 07	8,050		20,550
June 09		8,000	28,550
June 10	3,660		24,890
June 11	2,690		22,200

(continued)

Date	Checks	Deposits	Balance
June 12		$ 9,000	$31,200
June 13	$ 550		30,650
June 17	7,500		23,150
June 20		5,500	28,650
June 21	650		28,000
June 22	700		27,300
June 23		4,140[†]	31,440
June 25	1,000		30,440
June 30	50*		30,390
Totals	$27,250	$32,640	

*Bank service charge.
[†]Note collected, including $140 interest.

Data from the cash account of Milton Company for June are as follows:

June 1 balance $20,440

Checks written:

June 1	$ 1,500
4	8,500
6	2,690
8	550
9	7,500
12	650
19	700
22	1,000
26	1,300
27	1,360
	$25,750

Deposits:

June 2	$ 6,000
5	8,000
10	9,000
18	5,500
30	6,000
	$34,500

At the end of May, Milton had three checks outstanding for a total of $4,560. All three checks were processed by the bank during June. There were no deposits outstanding at the end of May. It was discovered during the reconciliation process that a check for $8,050, written on June 4 for supplies, was improperly recorded on the books as $8,500.

Required:
1. Determine the amount of deposits in transit at the end of June.
2. Determine the amount of outstanding checks at the end of June.
3. Prepare a June bank reconciliation.
4. Prepare the journal entries to correct the cash account.
5. **Interpretive Question:** Why is it important that the cash account be reconciled on a timely basis?

Problem 7-14

Determining Where the Cash Went

Kim Lee, the bookkeeper for Briton Company, had never missed a day's work for the past 10 years until last week. Since that time, he has not been located. You now suspect that Kim may have embezzled money from the company. The following bank reconciliation, prepared by Kim last month, is available to help you determine if a theft occurred:

Briton Company
Bank Reconciliation for August 2006
Prepared by Kim Lee

Balance per bank statement ...	$192,056	Balance per books	$169,598
Additions to bank balance:		*Additions to book balance:*	
Deposits in transit	8,000	Note collected by bank	250
		Interest earned	600
Deductions from bank balance:		*Deductions from book balance:*	
Outstanding checks:		NSF check	(1,800)
#201	(19,200)	Bank service charges	(48)
#204	(5,000)		
#205	(4,058)		
#295	(195)		
#565	(1,920)		
#567	(615)		
#568	(468)		
Adjusted bank balance	**$168,600**	**Adjusted book balance**	**$168,600**

In examining the bank reconciliation, you decide to review canceled checks returned by the bank. You find that check stubs for check nos. 201, 204, 205, and 295 indicate that these checks were supposedly voided when written. All other bank reconciliation data have been verified as correct.

Required:
1. Compute the amount suspected stolen by Kim.
2. **Interpretive Question:** Describe how Kim accounted for the stolen money. What would have prevented the theft?

Problem 7-15

P.A.S.S.
Power Accounting System Software

Accounting for a Foreign Currency Transaction
On December 19, 2006, Mr. Kitty Company performed services for Cartour Company. The contracted price for the services was 20,000 euros, to be paid on March 23, 2007. On December 19, 2006, one euro equaled $0.94. On December 31, 2006, one euro equaled $0.98, and on March 23, 2007, one euro equaled $0.91. Mr. Kitty is a U.S. company.

Required:
1. Make the journal entry on Mr. Kitty's books to record the provision of services on December 19, 2006.
2. Make the necessary adjusting entry on Mr. Kitty's books on December 31 to adjust the account receivable to its appropriate U.S. dollar value.
3. Make the journal entry on Mr. Kitty's books to record the collection of the 20,000 euros on March 23.
4. **Interpretive Question:** Why would Mr. Kitty, a U.S. company, agree to denominate the contract in euros instead of in U.S. dollars?

d iscussion cases

Case 7-1

ZZZZ Best and Fictitious Receivables
ZZZZ BEST was a Los Angeles-based company specializing in carpet cleaning and insurance restoration. Prior to allegations of fraud and its declaration of bankruptcy in 1988, ZZZZ Best

was touted as one of the hottest stocks on Wall Street. In 1987, after only six years in business, the company had a market valuation exceeding $211 million, giving its "genius" president a paper fortune of $109 million. Lawsuits, however, alleged that the company was nothing more than a massive fraud scheme that fooled major banks, two CPA firms, an investment banker, and a prestigious law firm.

ZZZZ Best was started as a carpet-cleaning business by Barry Minkow, a 15-year-old high school student, in 1981. Although ZZZZ Best had impressive growth as a carpet-cleaning business, the growth was not nearly fast enough for the impatient Minkow. In 1985, ZZZZ Best announced that it was expanding into the insurance restoration business, restoring buildings that had been damaged by fire, floods, and other disasters. During 1985 and 1986, ZZZZ Best reported undertaking several large insurance restoration projects. The company reported high profits from these restoration jobs. A public stock offering in 1986 stated that 86% of ZZZZ Best Corporation's business was in the insurance restoration area.

Based on the company's high growth and reported income in 1987, a spokesperson for a large brokerage house was quoted in *Business Week* as saying that "Barry Minkow is a great manager and ZZZZ Best is a great company." He recommended that his clients buy ZZZZ Best stock. That same year, the Association of Collegiate Entrepreneurs and the Young Entrepreneurs' Organization placed Minkow on their list of the top 100 young entrepreneurs in America; and the mayor of Los Angeles honored Minkow with a commendation that said that he had "set a fine entrepreneurial example of obtaining the status of a millionaire at the age of 18."

Unfortunately, ZZZZ Best's insurance business, its impressive growth, and its high reported income were totally fictitious. In fact, the company never once made a legitimate profit. Barry Minkow himself later said that he was a "fraudster" who convincingly deceived almost everyone involved with the company. Through the use of widespread collusion among company officials, Minkow was even able to hide the fraud from ZZZZ Best's external auditor. For example, when ZZZZ Best reported an $8.2 million contract to restore a building in San Diego, the external auditor demanded to see the building; this was difficult since neither the building nor the job existed. However, officials of ZZZZ Best gained access to a construction site and led the auditor through a tour of an unfinished building in San Diego to show that the "restoration" work was ongoing. The situation became very complicated for ZZZZ Best when the auditor later asked to see the finished job. ZZZZ Best had to spend $1 million to lease the building and hire contractors to finish six of the eight floors in 10 days. The auditor was led on another tour and wrote a memo saying, "Job looks very good." The auditor was subsequently faulted for looking only at what ZZZZ Best officials chose to show, without making independent inquiries.

Minkow's house of cards finally came crashing down as it became apparent to banks, suppliers, investors, and the auditors that the increasing difficulty ZZZZ Best was having with paying its bills was entirely inconsistent with a company reporting so much revenue and profit. In January 1988, a federal grand jury in Los Angeles returned a 57-count indictment, charging 11 individuals—including ZZZZ Best founder and president, Barry Minkow—with engaging in a massive fraud scheme. Minkow was later convicted and sentenced to 25 years in a federal penitentiary in Colorado.

ZZZZ Best grossly inflated its operating results by reporting bogus revenue and receivables. What factors prevent a company from continuing to report fraudulent results indefinitely? What could the auditor have done to uncover the ZZZZ Best fraud?

Source: This description is based on articles in *The Wall Street Journal, Forbes,* and investigative proceedings of the U.S. House of Representatives, Subcommittee on Energy and Commerce hearings: *The Wall Street Journal,* July 7, 1987, p. 1; July 9, 1987, p. 1; August 23, 1988, p. 1; U.S. House of Representatives, Subcommittee on Oversight and Investigation of the Committee on Energy and Commerce, January 27, 1988; U.S. House of Representatives, Subcommittee on Oversight and Investigation of the Committee on Energy and Commerce, February 1, 1988; Daniel Akst, "How Barry Minkow Fooled the Auditors," *Forbes,* October 2, 1989, p. 126.

Case 7-2

Recognizing Revenue

HealthCare, Inc.,* operates a number of medical testing facilities around the United States. Drug manufacturers, such as MERCK and BRISTOL-MYERS SQUIBB, contract with Health-Care for testing of their newly developed drugs and other medical treatments. HealthCare advertises, gets patients, and then administers the drugs or other experimental treatments, under a doctor's care, to determine their effectiveness. The Food and Drug Administration requires such human testing before allowing drugs to be prescribed by doctors and sold by pharmacists. A typical contract might read as follows:

> HealthCare, Inc., will administer the new drug, "Lexitol," to 50 patients, once a week for 10 weeks, to determine its effectiveness in treating male baldness. Merck will pay HealthCare, Inc., $100 per patient visit, to be billed at the conclusion of the test period. The total amount of the contract is $50,000 (50 patients × 10 visits × $100 per visit).

Given these kinds of contracts, when should HealthCare recognize revenue—when contracts are signed, when patient visits take place, when drug manufacturers are billed, or when cash is collected?

*The name of the actual company has been changed.

Case 7-3

Credit Policy Review

The president, vice president, and sales manager of Moorer Corporation were discussing the company's present credit policy. The sales manager suggested that potential sales were being lost to competitors because of Moorer Corporation's tight restrictions on granting credit to consumers. He stated that if credit policies were loosened, the current year's estimated credit sales of $3,000,000 could be increased by at least 20% next year with an increase in uncollectible accounts receivable of only $10,000 over this year's amount of $37,500. He argued that because the company's cost of sales is only 25% of revenues, the company would certainly come out ahead.

The vice president, however, suggested that a better alternative to easier credit terms would be to accept consumer credit cards such as VISA or MASTERCARD. She argued that this alternative could increase sales by 40%. The credit card finance charges to Moorer Corporation would be 4% of the additional sales.

At this point, the president interrupted by saying that he wasn't at all sure that increasing credit sales of any kind was a good thing. In fact, he suggested that the $37,500 of uncollectible accounts receivable was altogether too high. He wondered whether the company should discontinue offering sales on account.

With the information given, determine whether Moorer Corporation would be better off under the sales manager's proposal or the vice president's proposal. Also, address the president's suggestion that credit sales of all types be abolished.

udgment calls

Judgment 7-1

You Decide: Which method is better—the direct write-off method or the allowance method?

Your father-in-law has asked you to help him with some basic accounting duties dealing with a local irrigation company of which he is president. The company has issued shares of stock allowing shareholders the right to use a specified amount of water every week from a water canal that passes through town. Your main duties would consist of billing and collecting yearly dues from the shareholders and maintaining the books with a canned software system. There are less than 60 shareholders in the company. Should you write off receivables from customers when it is determined they will not pay, or should you estimate the percentage of receivables that will be uncollectible and establish an allowance? Your father-in-law does not want an allowance because he believes all customers will pay. What should you do?

Judgment 7-2

You Decide: Can pre-billing customers increase revenues?
For the past year, you have been working as an accountant for a local Internet Service Provider. Business is growing steadily with the holiday season just around the corner. The company hopes to reach more customers next year through additional advertising. In order to do so, it will need a loan from the bank. You overheard your boss say that if revenues increase 5% by year-end, the company will be in good enough shape to receive the loan. Your boss asks you to send out invoices to a handful of customers charging them for a service that won't be provided until the next year and to recognize the billings as revenue. He says they will eventually receive the service but it is more important to recognize the sale now. What should you do?

Judgment 7-3

You Decide: Can a company overestimate bad debts in good years and then use lower estimates when times are bad?
The company you work for has been highly profitable this year. Your boss tells you to overestimate the allowance for doubtful accounts. He says the income statement can handle the charge this year and the excess reserve can be used to increase earnings in future years. Is his proposal acceptable?

Competency Enhancement Opportunities

▶ **Analyzing Real Company Information**
▶ **International Case**
▶ **Ethics Case**
▶ **Writing Assignment**

▶ **The Debate**
▶ **Cumulative Spreadsheet Project**
▶ **Internet Search**

The following additional assignments provide opportunities for students to develop critical thinking, ethical perspectives, oral and written communication skills, experience with electronic research, and teamwork through group and business activities.

▶ *Analyzing Real Company Information*

Analyzing 7-1 (Microsoft)
The 2002 Form 10-K for MICROSOFT is included in Appendix A. Locate that Form 10-K and consider the following questions:

1. Provide the summary journal entry that Microsoft would have made to record its revenue for the fiscal year ended June 30, 2002 (assume all sales were on account).
2. Given Microsoft's beginning and ending balances in accounts receivable, along with your journal entry from part (1), estimate the amount of cash collected from customers during the year.
3. Notice that Microsoft has an unearned revenue account. The balance in that account increased from 2001 to 2002. Provide the summary journal entry that was made to record that increase.
4. Locate Microsoft's note on revenue recognition. What is Microsoft's revenue recognition policy?

Analyzing 7-2 (Bank of America)

BANK OF AMERICA is one of the oldest banks in America, as well as one of the largest. Founded in the late 1800s, Bank of America has grown from a strictly California-based bank to one with operations in over 20 states. Information from Bank of America's annual report follows. (Amounts are in millions.)

	2002	2001
Bad debt expense	$3,697	$4,287
Write-off of uncollectible accounts	4,460	4,844
Allowance for bad debts (year-end)	6,851	6,875

Using this information, answer the following questions:

1. Provide the journal entry made by Bank of America to record bad debt expense for 2002.
2. Provide the journal entry made by Bank of America to record the write-off of actual bad debts during 2002.
3. Estimate the amount of bad debts previously written off that Bank of America recovered in 2002.

Analyzing 7-3 (Microsoft and IBM)

Information from comparative income statements and balance sheets for MICROSOFT and IBM is given below. (Amounts are in millions.)

	Microsoft		IBM	
	2002	**2001**	**2002**	**2001**
Sales	$28,363	$25,296	$81,186	$83,067
Accounts receivable	5,129	3,671	9,915	9,101

Use this information to answer the following questions:

1. Without doing any computations, which company do you think has the lowest average collection period?
2. Compute Microsoft's average collection period for 2002.
3. Compute IBM's average collection period for 2002.

▷ *International Case*

International

Samsung

The economic downturn in South Korea in late 1997 focused world attention on what had heretofore been viewed as one of the world's economic powerhouses. Symptomatic of the economic collapse was the freefall in Korea's currency, the won, which declined in value from 845 won per U.S. dollar on December 31, 1996, to 1,695 won per dollar on December 31, 1997.

When Korea's economy soured, many sought to blame the economy's unusual structure, which concentrates a large fraction of the economic activity in the hands of just a few companies, called *chaebol*. Chaebol are large Korean conglomerates (groups of loosely connected firms with central ownership) that are usually centered around a family-owned parent company. The growth of the chaebol in the years since the Korean War has been aided by government nurturing—it is said that the chaebol have received government assistance in getting loans and obtaining trading licenses, for example.

In Korea there are now four super-chaebol—HYUNDAI, SAMSUNG, DAEWOO, and LUCKY GOLDSTAR. Collectively, these four conglomerates account for between 40 and 45% of South Korea's gross national product.

Samsung, one of the four super-chaebol, was founded in 1938 in Taegu, Korea. The company had humble beginnings; its original products included fruit, dried seafood, flour, and noodles, and its original exports were squid and apples. Now, Samsung has a worldwide presence in electronics, machinery, automobiles, chemicals, and financial services. To illustrate the size of Samsung's operations, it is estimated that one out of every five televisions or monitors in the world was made by Samsung.

The following information is from Samsung's 1997 annual report. All numbers are in trillions of Korean won.

	1997	1996
Net sales	91.519	74.641
Accounts receivable	10.064	6.233

1. Did Samsung's sales increase in 1997, relative to 1996, in terms of U.S. dollars? Explain. What exchange rate information would allow you to make a more accurate calculation?
2. Compute Samsung's average collection period for both 1996 and 1997. Instead of using the average accounts receivable balance, use the end-of-year balance.
3. Comment on the change in the average collection period from 1996 to 1997, especially in light of the economic conditions in Korea in 1997.
4. What do you think happened to Samsung's accounts payable balance in 1997, relative to 1996? Explain.

▶ *Ethics Case*

Changing Our Estimates in Order to Meet Analysts' Expectations

John Verner is the controller for BioMedic, Inc., a biotechnology company. John is finishing his preparation of the preliminary financial statements for a meeting of the board of directors scheduled for later in the day. At the board's prior meeting, members discussed the need to report earnings of at least $1.32 per share. It was not mentioned specifically at the meeting, but everyone on the board knows that financial analysts have forecast that BioMedic will report earnings per share (EPS) of $1.32; failure to meet analysts' expectations could hurt BioMedic's chances of going forward with its planned initial public offering (IPO) later this year.

Unfortunately for John and the company, the preliminary EPS figure is coming up short. John knows that the board will take a serious look at the estimates and assumptions made in preparing the income statement. In anticipation of the board's review, John has identified the following two issues:

1. In the past, bad debt expense has been computed using the percentage of sales method. The percentage used has varied between 3 and 3.5%. This year, John assumed a rate of 3%. If he were to modify his estimate of bad debt expense to 2.5% of sales, income would increase by $700,000.
2. BioMedic, Inc., offers a warranty on many of the products it sells. Like bad debt expense, warranty expense is computed as a percentage of sales. John is considering modifying his estimate of warranty expense from 1.4% of sales down to 1.1%. This modification would result in a $420,000 increase in net income.

These two changes, considered together, would result in BioMedic being able to report EPS of $1.33 per share, thereby allowing the company to publicly announce that it had exceeded analysts' expectations. Without these changes, BioMedic will report EPS of $1.21 per share.

What issues should John consider before he makes the changes to the income statement? Would John be doing something wrong by making these changes? Would John be breaking the law?

▶ *Writing Assignment*

Revenue Recognition for Health Clubs

The health fitness business has become increasingly popular as the sedentary lifestyle of most Americans has caused a large percentage of the population to feel, and be, out of shape. Health clubs have popped up all over, and with these clubs come some interesting accounting issues. Members typically sign up for one year and pay an up-front fee, followed by a monthly payment. The up-front fee covers, among other things, a health assessment by a club expert as well as a customized training program. For the monthly fee, members get the use of the facilities. The big accounting question is: How should the up-front fee be accounted for? Can the entire amount of the up-front fee be recognized at the beginning of the contract, or should it be recognized over the course of the year? Prepare a one-page paper explaining your point of view.

▶ *The Debate*

Bad Debt Expense: Relevance versus Reliability

When it comes to recognizing bad debt expense, the allowance method is used because it complies with the matching principle (e.g., expenses are matched with revenues in the period in which those revenues are earned). However, the allowance method requires estimation, and the estimates may not be reliable. An alternative is to use the direct write-off method. Under the direct write-off method, when a receivable is deemed worthless it is written off, and the bad debt expense is recognized at that time. This method requires no estimates and is thus more reliable.

Divide your group into two teams.

- One team represents "The Direct Write-Off Method." Prepare a two-minute oral argument supporting the use of this method.
- The other team represents "The Allowance Method." Prepare a two-minute presentation supporting your position.

▶ *Cumulative Spreadsheet Project*

This spreadsheet assignment is a continuation of the spreadsheet assignments given in earlier chapters. If you completed those spreadsheets, you have a head start on this one. If needed, review the spreadsheet assignment for Chapter 4 to refresh your memory on how to construct forecasted financial statements.

1. Handyman wishes to prepare a forecasted balance sheet and income statement for 2007. Use the original financial statement numbers for 2006 [given in part (1) of the Cumulative Spreadsheet Project assignment in Chapter 2] as the basis for the forecast, along with the following additional information:
    a. Sales in 2007 are expected to increase by 40% over 2006 sales of $700.

(continued)

b. In 2007, Handyman expects to acquire new property, plant, and equipment costing $80.
c. The $160 in other operating expenses reported in 2006 includes $5 of depreciation expense.
d. No new long-term debt will be acquired in 2007.
e. No cash dividends will be paid in 2007.
f. New short-term loans payable will be acquired in an amount sufficient to make Handyman's current ratio in 2007 exactly equal to 2.0.

Note: These statements were constructed as part of the spreadsheet assignment in Chapter 4; you can use that spreadsheet as a starting point if you have completed that assignment.

For this exercise, the current assets are expected to behave as follows:

i. Cash and inventory will increase at the same rate as sales.
ii. The forecasted amount of accounts receivable in 2007 is determined using the forecasted value for the average collection period. For simplicity, do the computations using the end-of-period accounts receivable balance instead of the average balance. The average collection period for 2007 is expected to be 14.08 days.

Clearly state any additional assumptions that you make.

2. Repeat (1), with the following change in assumptions:
   a. Average collection period is expected to be 9.06 days.
   b. Average collection period is expected to be 20.00 days.
3. Comment on the differences in the forecasted values of accounts receivable in 2007 under each of the following assumptions about the average collection period: 14.08 days, 9.06 days, and 20.00 days. Under which assumption will Handyman's forecasted cash flow from operating activities be higher? Explain.

▶ *Internet Search*

Yahoo!

YAHOO! is one of the best-known Internet brand names in the world. Access Yahoo!'s Web site at **http://www.yahoo.com** and answer the following questions. Sometimes Web addresses change, so if this address doesn't work, access the Web site for this textbook (**http://albrecht .swlearning.com**) for an updated link.

1. On its home page, Yahoo! has a link to information about job openings at the company. Use that link to find out what kind of benefits Yahoo! offers its employees.
2. Look at the current job openings at Yahoo! and identify one opening in the general field of finance.
3. Yahoo! is proud of the proliferation of "local Yahoos!" based in foreign countries. List the Asian countries in which a local Yahoo! is currently in operation.
4. Search the Yahoo! press release archive to find the most recent announcement about quarterly financial results. What was Yahoo!'s reported total revenue in the most recent quarter?

c h a p t e r

8

Inventory

After studying this chapter, you should be able to:

SEARS, ROEBUCK & COMPANY began as the result of an inventory mistake. In 1886, a shipment of gold watches was mistakenly sent to a jeweler in Redwood Falls, Minnesota. When the jeweler refused to accept delivery of the unwanted watches, they were purchased by an enterprising railroad agent who saw an opportunity to make some money. Richard Sears sold all of those watches, ordered more, and started the R. W. SEARS WATCH COMPANY. The next year, Sears moved his operation to Chicago, where he found a partner in watchmaker Alvah Roebuck, and in 1893 they incorporated under the name "Sears, Roebuck & Co."

The company's initial growth was fueled by mail-order sales to farmers. Sears bought goods in volume from manufacturers. Then, taking advantage of cheap parcel post and rural free delivery (RFD) rates, Sears shipped the goods directly to the customers, thereby bypassing the profit markups of the chain of middlemen usually standing between manufacturers and farmers. Sales growth was partially driven by the persuasive advertising copy written by Richard Sears for the famous Sears catalog. In fact, his product descriptions have been politely called "fanciful." But the company compensated by backing its products with an unconditional money-back guarantee for dissatisfied customers.

The next wave of growth at Sears began in 1925 when the first Sears retail store was opened in Chicago. The shift from mail-order catalog sales to retail outlet sales paralleled the rise in popularity of the automobile in the United States. The automobile made it practical for rural customers to shop in the city. Reflecting the importance of the automobile, Sears pioneered the provision of free parking lots next to its stores. In the post–World War II boom, Sears' sales skyrocketed, leaving chief rival MONTGOMERY WARD far behind.

The 1980s was a decade of diversification at Sears. Actually, the diversification had begun in 1931 when Sears started selling ALLSTATE auto insurance, first by mail and then from its retail locations. In the 1980s, Sears acquired DEAN WITTER, a financial services firm, and COLDWELL BANKER, a real estate firm. In addition, Sears launched the Discover® credit card and backed Prodigy®, the first widespread online service (a joint project with IBM and CBS).

In the early 1990s, the diversified Sears empire began to show increasing weakness, culminating in a reported loss of almost $2.3 billion in 1992. The company's management responded by going back to the basics of retail marketing. The financial services operations (including the Discover card) and the real estate operations (along with the famous Sears Tower in Chicago) were sold. Sears focused on clothing sales in its mall-based stores and appliance and automotive product sales in its off-the-mall stores. In addition, Sears returned to emphasizing its in-house Sears credit card. In 2002, credit card receivables represented over 50% of Sears' total assets, and Sears' credit card customers had over $294 billion in unused lines of credit.

Sears is continuing to leverage one of its biggest assets—its in-house brand names such as Kenmore and Craftsman. In fact, sales of Sears appliances and tools make up two-thirds of the company's annual revenue. Currently, Sears is the leader in appliance sales and outsells the next 12 competitors combined. Sears has also streamlined its purchasing, cut 30% of its dealer network, and is keeping more popular fashions in stock in its clothing department. In an attempt to overhaul its clothing lines, Sears recently bought the well-known catalog and Internet retailer, LAND'S END, in June 2002. This streamlining has resulted in higher inventory turnover. As a result of these changes and others, Sears' stock price has risen from $15 per share in 1992 to almost $60 per share in June of 2002.[1]

ike Sears, every business has products or services that it sells. Some companies, usually referred to as diversified companies or conglomerates, sell many unrelated products and services, just as Sears did in the 1980s. Other companies focus on a core set of products or services, as Sears did in the 1990s.

In Chapter 7, the focus was on revenues and receivables arising from the sale of products and services. In this chapter, the focus is on accounting for the products and services that are sold. Exhibit 1 shows how the financial statements are affected by the material covered in this chapter. The inventory and accounts payable accounts on the balance sheet,

1 This description is based on the Sears Company History at **http://www.sears.com**; "Sears, Roebuck and Co.," *International Directory of Company Histories*, Vol. 18 (Detroit: St. James Press, 1997), pp. 475–479.

Exhibit 1: Financial Statement Items Covered in This Chapter

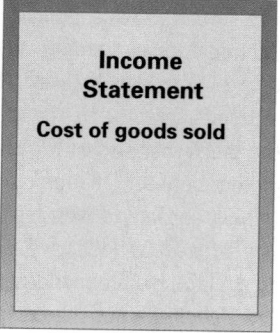

cost of goods sold on the income statement, and payments for inventory on the statement of cash flows are discussed in this chapter.

Traditionally, companies have been divided into two groups: service companies and product companies. Companies such as hotels, cable TV networks, banks, carpet cleaners, and firms of lawyers, accountants, or engineers sell services. In contrast, supermarkets, steel mills, and book stores sell products. Because the practice of accounting evolved in a business environment dominated by manufacturing and merchandising firms, the accounting for service companies is significantly less developed than the accounting for companies that sell products. In this chapter we discuss traditional accounting for product companies, emphasizing cost of goods sold and inventory. In Chapter 9 we will discuss operating expenses that are common to both service and product firms. Further discussion of the developing area of accounting for service companies is included in Chapter 17 in the management accounting section of *Accounting: Concepts and Applications*.

Inventory accounting is considerably more complex for manufacturing firms than for merchandising firms. In a retail or wholesale business, the cost of goods sold is simply the costs incurred in pur-

STOP & THINK

The clear separation between product and service companies is disappearing. For example, does MICROSOFT sell a product or a service? What about MCDONALD'S—product or service?

chasing the merchandise sold during the period; inventory is simply the cost of products purchased and not yet sold. Manufacturing firms, however, produce the goods they sell, so inventory and cost of goods sold must include all manufacturing costs of the products produced and sold. Because it is much easier to understand the concept of inventory and cost of goods sold in the context of retail and wholesale firms, manufacturing firms will not be considered in detail in this chapter. The details of inventory accounting for manufacturing firms will be covered in Chapter 16 in the management accounting section of *Accounting: Concepts and Applications*.

Fifty years ago, inventory was arguably the most important asset on the balance sheet. However, changes in the economy have led to a decrease in the relative importance of inventory. For example, as illustrated in Exhibit 2, inventory for the 50 largest companies in the United States declined steadily

Exhibit 2: How Much Inventory Do Companies Have?

Inventory Levels for the 50 Largest Companies, 1979–2001

Source: Standard and Poor's COMPUSTAT.

from over 15% of total assets in 1979 to 5.74% of total assets in 2001. This trend is a result of two factors: more efficient management of inventory because of improved information technology and a decrease in the prominence of old-style, smokestack industries that carried large inventories. Companies in the growth industries of services, technology, and information often have little or no inventory.

Inventory and Cost of Goods Sold

I Identify what items and costs should be included in inventory and cost of goods sold.

inventory Goods held for resale.

cost of goods sold The costs incurred to purchase or manufacture the merchandise sold during a period.

Inventory is the name given to goods that are either manufactured or purchased for resale in the normal course of business. A car dealer's inventory is comprised of automobiles; a grocery store's inventory consists of vegetables, meats, dairy products, canned goods, and bakery items; SEARS' inventory is composed of shirts, Kenmore appliances, DieHard® batteries, and more. Like other items of value, such as cash or equipment, inventory is classified as an asset and reported on the balance sheet. When products are sold, they are no longer assets. The costs to purchase or manufacture the products must be removed from the asset classification (inventory) on the balance sheet and reported on the income statement as an expense—**cost of goods sold**.

The time line in Exhibit 3 illustrates the business issues involved with inventory. The accounting questions associated with the items in the time line are as follows:

- When is inventory considered to have been purchased—when it is ordered, shipped, received, or paid for?
- Similarly, when is the inventory considered to have been sold?
- Which of the costs associated with the "value added" process are considered to be part of the cost of inventory, and which are simply business expenses for that period?
- How should total inventory cost be divided between the inventory that was sold (cost of goods sold) and the inventory that remains (ending inventory)?

These questions are addressed in the following sections of the chapter.

What Is Inventory?

In a merchandising firm, either wholesale or retail, inventory is composed of the items that have been purchased in order to be resold. In a supermarket, milk is inventory, a shopping cart is

Exhibit 3: Time Line of Business Issues Involved with Inventory

BUY	ADD	SELL	COMPUTE	
raw materials or goods for resale	value	finished inventory	ending inventory	cost of goods sold

not. In a manufacturing company, there are three different types of inventory: raw materials, work in process, and finished goods.

Raw Materials

raw materials Materials purchased for use in manufacturing products.

Raw materials are goods acquired in a relatively undeveloped state that will eventually compose a major part of the finished product. If you are making bicycles, one of the raw materials is tubular steel. For a computer assembler, raw materials inventory is composed of plastic, wires, and INTEL Pentium® chips.

Work In Process

work in process Partially completed units in production.

Work in process consists of partially finished products. When you take a tour of a manufacturing plant, you are seeing work-in-process inventory.

Finished Goods

finished goods Manufactured products ready for sale.

Finished goods are the completed products waiting for sale. A completed car rolling off the automobile assembly line is part of finished goods inventory.

What Costs Are Included in Inventory Cost?

Inventory cost consists of all costs involved in buying the inventory and preparing it for sale. In the case of raw materials or goods acquired for resale by a merchandising firm, cost includes the purchase price, freight, and receiving and storage costs.

manufacturing overhead The indirect manufacturing costs associated with producing inventory.

The cost of work-in-process inventory is the sum of the costs of the raw materials, the production labor, and some share of the **manufacturing overhead** required to keep the factory running. The cost of an item in finished goods inventory is the total of the materials, labor, and overhead costs used in the production process for that item. As you can imagine, accumulating these costs and calculating a cost per unit is quite a demanding task. The cost of a finished automobile includes the cost of the steel and rubber; the salaries and wages of assembly workers, inspectors, and testers; the factory insurance; the workers' pension benefits; and much more. This costing process is a key part of management accounting and is covered in Chapter 17 in the management accounting section of *Accounting: Concepts and Applications.*

The costs just described are all costs expended in order to get inventory produced and ready to sell. These costs are appropriately included in inventory costs. Those costs incurred in the sales effort itself are *not* inventory costs, but instead should be reported as operating expenses in the period in which they are incurred. For example, the costs of maintaining the finished goods warehouse or the retail showroom are period expenses. Salespersons' salaries are period expenses, as is the cost of advertising (a more detailed discussion of advertising is included in Chapter 9). In addition, general nonfactory administrative costs are also period expenses. Examples are the costs of the corporate headquarters and the company president's salary.

Who Owns the Inventory?

As a general rule, goods should be included in the inventory of the business holding legal title. So, a merchandising firm is considered to have purchased inventory once it has legal title to the inventory. Similarly, the inventory is considered to be sold when legal title passes to the customer. In most cases, this "legal title" rule is easy to apply—if you go into a business and look around, it is probably safe to assume that the inventory you see belongs to that business. In the case of goods in transit and goods on consignment, however, this "legal title" rule can be rather difficult to apply.

Goods in Transit

FOB (free-on-board) destination A business term meaning that the seller of merchandise bears the shipping costs and maintains ownership until the merchandise is delivered to the buyer.

FOB (free-on-board) shipping point A business term meaning that the buyer of merchandise bears the shipping costs and acquires ownership at the point of shipment.

consignment An arrangement whereby merchandise owned by one party, the consignor, is sold by another party, the consignee, usually on a commission basis.

When goods are being shipped from the seller to the buyer, who owns the inventory that is on a truck or railroad car—the seller or the buyer? If the seller pays for the shipping costs, the arrangement is known as **FOB (free-on-board) destination**, and the seller owns the merchandise from the time it is shipped until it is delivered to the buyer. If the buyer pays the shipping costs, the arrangement is known as **FOB (free-on-board) shipping point**, and the buyer owns the merchandise during transit. Thus, in determining which items should be counted and included in the inventory balance for a period, a company must note the amount of merchandise in transit and the terms under which it is being shipped. In all cases, merchandise should be included in the inventory of the party who owns it; for goods in transit, this is generally the party who is paying the shipping costs. The impact of shipping terms on the ownership of goods in transit is summarized in Exhibit 4.

Goods on Consignment

Sometimes the inventory a firm stocks in its warehouse has not actually been purchased from suppliers. With a **consignment** arrangement, suppliers (the consignors) provide inventory for resale while retaining ownership of the inventory until it is sold. The firm selling the merchandise (the consignee) merely stocks and sells the merchandise for the supplier/owner and receives a commission on any sales as payment for services rendered. Through a consignment arrangement, the manufacturer enables dealers to acquire a broad sample of inventory without incurring the purchase and finance charges required to actually buy the inventory. It is extremely important that goods being held on consignment not be included in the inventory of the firm holding the goods for sale even though they are physically on that firm's premises. It is equally important that the supplier/owner properly include all such goods in its records even though the inventory is not on its premises.

Auditing goods in transit and consigned inventory presents the auditor with a special set of problems. Inventory that is on the premises may not belong to the company because the goods are held on consignment. On the other hand, goods that are in transit in trucks and boats scattered around the world may belong to the company and should be included in the inventory count.

Exhibit 4: Ownership Transfer for Goods in Transit

An example of a company that successfully uses consignment sales as part of its business strategy is INTERNATIONAL AIRLINE SUPPORT GROUP, INC. This company is a leading distributor of aircraft spare parts for large jet airplanes. The company uses consignments because, as stated in its annual report, this arrangement allows it "to obtain parts inventory on a favorable basis without committing its capital to purchasing inventory."

Ending Inventory and Cost of Goods Sold

cost of goods available for sale The cost of all merchandise available for sale during the period; equal to the sum of beginning inventory and net purchases.

Inventory purchased or manufactured during the period is added to beginning inventory, and the total cost of this inventory is called the **cost of goods available for sale**. At the end of an accounting period, total cost of goods available for sale must be allocated between inventory still remaining (to be reported in the balance sheet as an asset) and inventory sold during the period (to be reported in the income statement as an expense, Cost of Goods Sold).

This cost allocation process is extremely important because the more cost that is said to remain in ending inventory, the less cost is reported as cost of goods sold in the income statement. This is why accurately determining who owns the inventory is such a big issue. Making a mistake with inventory ownership will result in misstating both the income statement and the balance sheet. For this reason, accountants must be careful of inventory errors because they directly affect reported net income. The impact of inventory errors is illustrated later in the chapter.

The cost allocation process also involves a significant amount of accounting judgment. Identical inventory items are usually purchased at varying prices throughout the year, so to calculate the amount of ending inventory and cost of goods sold, the accountant must determine which items (the low cost or high cost) remain and which were sold. Again, this decision can directly affect the amount of reported cost of goods sold and net income. The use of inventory cost flow assumptions is discussed later in the chapter.

TO SUMMARIZE: Inventory is composed of goods held for sale in the normal course of business. Cost of goods sold is the cost of inventory sold during the period. For a manufacturing firm, the three types of inventory are raw materials, work in process, and finished goods. All costs incurred in producing and getting inventory ready to sell should be added to inventory cost. The costs associated with the selling effort itself are operating expenses of the period. Inventory should be recorded on the books of the company holding legal title. At the end of an accounting period, the total cost of goods available for sale during the period must be allocated between ending inventory and cost of goods sold.

Accounting for Inventory Purchases and Sales

2 Account for inventory purchases and sales using both a perpetual and a periodic inventory system.

To begin a more detailed study of inventory accounting, we must first establish a solid understanding of the journal entries used to record inventory transactions. The accounting procedures for recording purchases and sales using both a periodic and a perpetual inventory system are detailed in this section.

Overview of Perpetual and Periodic Systems

Some businesses track changes in inventory levels on a continuous basis, recording each individual purchase and sale to maintain a running total of the inventory balance. This is called a perpetual inventory system. Other businesses rely on quarterly or yearly inventory counts to reveal which inventory items have been sold. This is called a periodic inventory system.

perpetual inventory system A system of accounting for inventory in which detailed records of the number of units and the cost of each purchase and sales transaction are prepared throughout the accounting period.

Perpetual

You own a discount appliance superstore. Your biggest-selling items are washers, dryers, refrigerators, microwaves, and dishwashers. You advertise your weekly sale items on local TV stations, and your sales volume is quite heavy. You have 50 salespeople who work independently of one another. You have found that customers get very upset if they come to buy an advertised item and you have run out. In this business environment, would it make sense to keep a running total of the quantity remaining of each inventory item and update it each time a sale is made? Yes, the benefit of having current information on each inventory item would make it worthwhile to spend a little extra time to update the inventory records when a sale is made.

This appliance store would probably use a **perpetual inventory system**. With a perpetual system, inventory records are updated whenever a purchase or a sale is made. In this way, the inventory records at any given time reflect how many of each inventory item should be in the warehouse or out on the store shelves. A perpetual system is most often used when each individual inventory item has a relatively high value or when there are large costs to running out of or overstocking specific items.

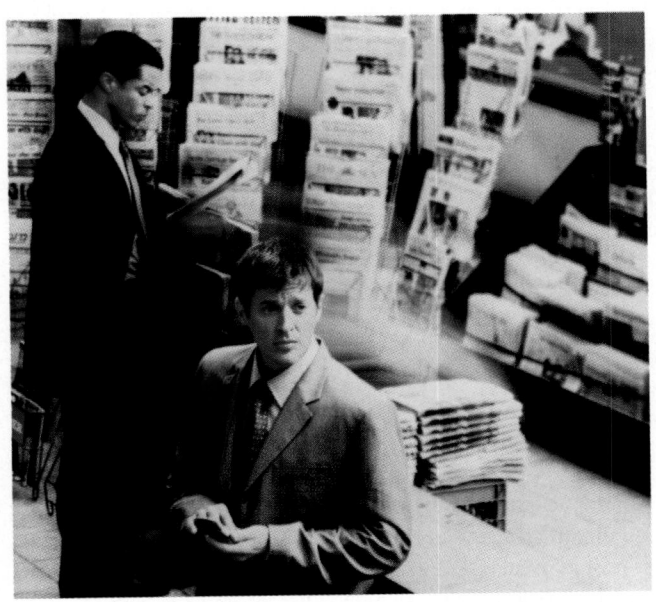

© 2003 Getty Images

A newsstand will wait until the end of the day to count inventory by comparing what items it started with to what is left. This is an example of a periodic inventory system.

Periodic

You operate a newsstand in a busy metropolitan subway station. Almost all of your sales occur during the morning and the evening rush hours. You sell a diverse array of items—newspapers, magazines, pens, snacks, and other odds and ends. During rush hour, your business is a fast-paced pressure cooker; the longer you take with one customer, the more chance that the busy commuters waiting in line for service will tire of waiting and you will lose sales. In this business environment, would it make sense to make each customer wait while you meticulously check off on an inventory sheet exactly which items were sold? No, the delay caused by this detailed bookkeeping would cause you to lose customers. It makes more sense to wait until the end of the day, count up what inventory you still have left, compare that to what you started with, and use those numbers to deduce how many of each inventory item you sold during the day.

This subway newsstand scenario is an example of a situation where a **periodic inventory system** is appropriate. With a periodic system, inventory records are not updated when a sale is made; only the dollar amount of the sale is recorded. Periodic systems are most often used when inventory is composed of a large number of diverse items, each with a relatively low value.

periodic inventory system
A system of accounting for inventory in which cost of goods sold is determined and inventory is adjusted at the end of the accounting period, not when merchandise is purchased or sold.

Impact of Information Technology

Over the past 25 years, advances in information technology have lowered the cost of maintaining a perpetual inventory system. As a result, more businesses have adopted perpetual systems so that they can more closely track inventory levels. The most visible manifestation of this trend is in supermarkets. Twenty years ago, the checkout clerk rang up the price of each item on a cash register. After the customers walked out of the store with their groceries, the store knew the total amount of the sale but did not know which individual items had been sold. This was a periodic inventory system. Now, with laser scanning equipment tied into the supermarket's computer system, most supermarkets operate under a perpetual system. The store manager knows exactly what you bought and exactly how many of each item should still be left on the store shelves.

STOP & THINK

If you buy your groceries with a credit card or a bank debit card, what kind of information can the supermarket accumulate about you?

Perpetual and Periodic Journal Entries

The following transactions for Grantsville Clothing Store will be used to illustrate the differences in bookkeeping procedures between a business using a perpetual inventory system and one using a periodic inventory system:

a. Purchased on account: 1,000 shirts at a cost of $10 each for a total of $10,000.
b. Purchased on account: 300 pairs of pants at a cost of $18 each for a total of $5,400.
c. Paid cash for separate shipping costs on the shirts purchased in (a), $970. The supplier of the pants purchased in (b) included the shipping costs in the $18 purchase price.
d. Returned 30 of the shirts (costing $300) to the supplier because they were stained.
e. Paid for the shirt purchase. A 2% discount was given on the $9,700 bill [(1,000 purchased − 30 returned) × $10] because of payment within the 10-day discount period (payment terms were 2/10, n/30).
f. Paid $5,400 for the pants purchase. No discount was allowed because payment was made after the discount period.
g. Sold on account: 600 shirts at a price of $25 each for a total of $15,000.
h. Sold on account: 200 pairs of pants at a price of $40 each for a total of $8,000.
i. Accepted return of 50 shirts by dissatisfied customers.

The journal entries for the perpetual inventory system should seem familiar to you—a perpetual system has been assumed in all earlier chapters of the text. A perpetual system was assumed because it is logical and is the system all companies would choose if there were no cost to updating the inventory records each time a sale or purchase is made. As mentioned, a periodic inventory system is sometimes a practical necessity.

Purchases

With a perpetual system, all purchases are added (debited) directly to Inventory. With a periodic system, the inventory balance is only updated using an inventory count at the end of the period; inventory purchases during the period are recorded in a temporary holding account called Purchases. As will be illustrated later, at the end of the period, the balance in Purchases is closed to Inventory in connection with the computation of cost of goods sold.

Entries (a) and (b) to record the shirt and pants purchases are given below.

		Perpetual			**Periodic**		
a.	Inventory	10,000		Purchases	10,000	
	Accounts Payable		10,000	Accounts Payable		10,000
b.	Inventory	5,400		Purchases	5,400	
	Accounts Payable		5,400	Accounts Payable		5,400

Transportation Costs

The cost of transporting the inventory is an additional inventory cost. Sometimes, as with the pants in the Grantsville Clothing example, the shipping cost is already included in the purchase price, so a separate entry to record the transportation costs is not needed. When a separate payment is made for transportation costs, it is recorded as follows:

		Perpetual			**Periodic**		
c.	Inventory	970		Freight In	970	
	Cash		970	Cash		970

With a perpetual inventory system, transportation costs are added directly to the inventory balance. With a periodic inventory system, another temporary holding account, Freight In, is created, and transportation costs are accumulated in this account during the period. Like the purchases account, Freight In is closed to Inventory at the end of the period in connection with the computation of cost of goods sold.

Purchase Returns

With a perpetual system, the return of unsatisfactory merchandise to the supplier results in a decrease in Inventory. In addition, since no payment will have to be made for the returned merchandise, Accounts Payable is reduced by the same amount. With a periodic system, the amount of the returned merchandise is recorded in yet another temporary holding account called Purchase Returns. Purchase Returns is a contra account to Purchases and is also closed to Inventory as part of the computation of cost of goods sold.

		Perpetual			**Periodic**		
d.	Accounts Payable	300		Accounts Payable	300	
	Inventory		300	Purchase Returns		300

If the returned merchandise had already been paid for, the supplier would most likely return the purchase price. In this case, the debit would be to Cash instead of to Accounts Payable.

Purchase Discounts

As discussed in Chapter 7, sellers sometimes offer inducements for credit customers to pay quickly. In this example, Grantsville Clothing takes advantage of purchase discounts to save money on the payment for the shirts. The amount of the purchase discount is $194 ($9,700 × 0.02), so the total payment for the shirts is $9,506 ($9,700 − $194). The amount recorded for inventory should reflect the actual amount paid to purchase the inventory. With a perpetual inventory system, this is shown by subtracting the purchase discount amount from the inventory account. With a periodic inventory system, another holding account is created to accumulate purchase discounts taken during the period.

Perpetual			Periodic		
e. Accounts Payable	9,700		Accounts Payable	9,700	
Inventory		194	Purchase Discounts		194
Cash		9,506	Cash		9,506
f. Accounts Payable	5,400		Accounts Payable	5,400	
Cash		5,400	Cash		5,400

FYI:

In practice, this same inventory adjustment information (e.g., Freight In, Purchase Returns, etc.) would be maintained in supplemental records under a perpetual inventory system. Such information is useful to management in evaluating company purchasing practices.

Note that the payment for the pants is made after the discount period, so the full amount must be paid. Since this transaction had no impact on Inventory, the entry is the same for both the perpetual and the periodic system.

In terms of journal entries, you should recognize that the difference between a perpetual and a periodic inventory system is that all adjustments to inventory under a perpetual system are entered directly in the inventory account; with a periodic system, all inventory adjustments are accumulated in an array of temporary holding accounts: Purchases, Freight In, Purchase Returns, and Purchase Discounts.

Sales

The sales of shirts and pants would be recorded as follows:

Perpetual			Periodic		
g. Accounts Receivable	15,000		Accounts Receivable	15,000	
Sales (600 × $25)		15,000	Sales		15,000
Cost of Goods Sold	6,000				
Inventory (600 × $10)		6,000			
h. Accounts Receivable	8,000		Accounts Receivable	8,000	
Sales (200 × $40)		8,000	Sales		8,000
Cost of Goods Sold	3,600				
Inventory (200 × $18)		3,600			

These entries reflect the primary difference between a perpetual and a periodic inventory system—with a periodic system, no attempt is made to recognize cost of goods sold on a transaction-by-transaction basis. In fact, with a periodic system, Grantsville Clothing would not even know how many shirts and how many pairs of pants had been sold. Instead, only total sales of $23,000 ($15,000 + $8,000) would be known.

For simplicity, we have recorded the cost of goods sold for the shirts as $10 each. The actual cost per shirt, after adjusting for freight in and purchase discounts, is $10.80, computed as follows:

Total purchase price (1,000 shirts)	$10,000
Plus: Freight in	970
Less: Purchase returns (30 shirts)	(300)
Less: Purchase discounts	(194)
Total cost of shirts (970 shirts)	$10,476

Total cost $10,476 ÷ 970 shirts = $10.80 per shirt

In practice, it is unlikely that a firm using a perpetual inventory system would bother to adjust unit costs for the effects of freight cost and purchase discounts on an ongoing basis. The cost of doing these calculations could easily outweigh any resulting improvement in the quality of cost information.

Sales Returns

As discussed in Chapter 7, dissatisfied customers sometimes return their purchases. The journal entries to record the return of 50 shirts are as follows:

	Perpetual			Periodic		
i.	Sales Returns (50 × $25)	1,250		Sales Returns	1,250	
	Accounts Receivable		1,250	Accounts Receivable		1,250
	Inventory (50 × $10)	500				
	Cost of Goods Sold		500			

STOP & THINK

Should the returned inventory be recorded at its original cost of $10 per shirt?

Under the perpetual system, not only are the sales for the returned items canceled, but the cost of the returned inventory is also removed from Cost of Goods Sold and restored to the inventory account.

Closing Entries

After all of the journal entries are posted to the ledger, the T-accounts for Inventory and Cost of Goods Sold, under a perpetual system, would appear as follows:

	Inventory				Cost of Goods Sold		
(a)	10,000	(d)	300	(g)	6,000	(i)	500
(b)	5,400	(e)	194	(h)	3,600		
(c)	970	(g)	6,000				
(i)	500	(h)	3,600				
Bal.	6,776			Bal.	9,100		

These numbers, after being verified by a physical count of the inventory (as described in the next section), would be reported in the financial statements—the $6,776 of Inventory in the balance sheet and the $9,100 of Cost of Goods Sold in the income statement.

Review the journal entries (a) through (i) under the periodic inventory system and notice that none of the amounts have been entered in either Inventory or Cost of Goods Sold. As a result, both of these accounts will have zero balances at year-end. Actually, the inventory account would have the same balance it had at the beginning of the period, which, in this example, we will assume to be zero.

With a periodic inventory system, the correct balances are recorded in Inventory and Cost of Goods Sold through a series of closing entries. Two entries are made:

1. Transfer all the temporary holding accounts to the inventory account balance. At this point, the inventory account balance is equal to the cost of goods available for sale (beginning inventory plus the net cost of purchases for the period).
2. Reduce Inventory by the amount of Cost of Goods Sold. At this point, the inventory account balance is equal to the ending inventory amount, and the appropriate cost of goods sold amount is also recognized.

To illustrate, the information for Grantsville Clothing will be used. The entry to transfer all the temporary holding accounts to the inventory account is as follows:

```
Inventory ............................................... 15,876
Purchase Returns ......................................     300
Purchase Discounts ....................................     194
   Freight In ..........................................          970
   Purchases ..........................................          15,400
      Closing of temporary inventory accounts for periodic system.
```

net purchases The net cost of inventory purchased during a period, after adding the cost of freight in and subtracting returns and discounts.

The inventory debit of $15,876 is the amount of **net purchases** for the period. Notice that, after this entry has been posted, the balances in all the temporary holding accounts will have been reduced to zero. As mentioned, after the addition of net purchases, the inventory account balance represents cost of goods available for sale (the sum of beginning inventory and net purchases). Remember that, in this example, beginning inventory is assumed to be zero.

The second closing entry involves the adjustment of Inventory to its appropriate ending balance and the creation of the cost of goods sold account. This cost of goods sold account would be closed when other nominal accounts (e.g., Sales Salaries, Interest Expense, etc.) are closed. If the year-end physical count indicates that the ending inventory balance should be $6,776, the appropriate entry is as follows:

```
Cost of Goods Sold ..................................... 9,100
   Inventory ($15,876 − $6,776) .......................          9,100
      Adjustment of inventory account to appropriate ending balance.
```

In this example, the values for both ending inventory ($6,776) and cost of goods sold ($9,100) are the same with either a perpetual or a periodic inventory system. So, what is the practical difference between the two systems? One difference is that a perpetual system can tell you the inventory balance and the cumulative cost of goods sold at any time during the period. With a periodic system, on the other hand, you must wait until the inventory is counted at the end of the period to compute the amount of inventory or cost of goods sold. Another difference is that, with a perpetual system, you can compare the inventory records to the amount of inventory actually on hand and thus determine whether any inventory has been lost or stolen. As described in the next section, this comparison is not possible with a periodic system.

> **TO SUMMARIZE:** With a perpetual inventory system, the amount of inventory and cost of goods sold for the period are tracked on an ongoing basis. With a periodic inventory system, inventory and cost of goods sold are computed using an end-of-period inventory count. With a periodic system, inventory-related items are recorded in temporary holding accounts that are transferred to the inventory account at the end of the period.

Counting Inventory and Calculating Cost of Goods Sold

3 Calculate cost of goods sold using the results of an inventory count and understand the impact of errors in ending inventory on reported cost of goods sold.

Regular physical counts of the existing inventory are essential to maintaining reliable inventory accounting records. With a perpetual system, the physical count can be compared to the recorded inventory balance to see whether any inventory has been lost or stolen. With a periodic system, a physical count is the only way to get the information necessary to compute cost of goods sold.

Taking a Physical Count of Inventory

No matter which inventory system a company is using, periodic physical counts are a necessary and important part of accounting for inventory. With a perpetual inventory system, the physical count either confirms that the amount entered in the accounting records is accurate or highlights shortages and clerical errors. If, for example, employees have been stealing inventory, the theft will show up as a difference between the balance in the inventory account and the amount physically counted.

A physical count of inventory involves two steps:

1. *Quantity count.* In most companies, physically counting all inventory is a time-consuming activity. Because sales transactions and merchandise deliveries can complicate matters, inventory is usually counted on holidays or after the close of business on the inventory day. Special care must be taken to ensure that all inventory owned, wherever its location, is counted and that inventory on hand but not owned (consignment inventory) is not counted.

2. *Inventory costing.* When the physical count has been completed, each type of merchandise is assigned a unit cost. The quantity of each type of merchandise is multiplied by its unit cost to determine the dollar value of the inventory. These amounts are then added to obtain the total ending inventory for the business. This is the amount reported as Inventory on the balance sheet. The ending balance in the inventory account may have to be adjusted for any shortages discovered.

To illustrate the impact of a physical inventory count on the accounting records for both a periodic and a perpetual system, we will refer back to the Grantsville Clothing Store example used earlier. Assume that a physical count, combined with inventory costing analysis, suggests that the correct amount for ending inventory is $5,950. This information can be combined with previous information from the accounting system as follows:

	Periodic System	Perpetual System
Beginning inventory	$ 0	$ 0
Plus: Net purchases	15,876	15,876
Cost of goods available for sale	$15,876	$15,876
Less: Ending inventory	5,950	6,776 (from inventory system)
Cost of goods sold	$ 9,926	$ 9,100 (from inventory system)
Goods lost or stolen	unknown	826 ($6,776 − $5,950)
Total cost of goods sold, lost, or stolen	$ 9,926	$ 9,926

Recall that, in this example, the beginning inventory is assumed to be zero. The amount of net purchases is a combination of the items affecting the amount paid for inventory purchases during the period: purchase price, freight in, purchase returns, and purchase discounts. The $15,876 amount for net purchases was computed earlier in connection with the closing entry for the periodic system.

This cost of goods sold computation highlights the key difference between a periodic and a perpetual inventory system. With a periodic system, the company does not know what ending inventory *should be* when the inventory count is performed. The best the company can do is count the inventory and assume that the difference between the cost of goods available for sale and the cost of goods still remaining (ending inventory) must represent the cost of goods that were sold. Actually, a business using a periodic system has no way of knowing whether these goods were sold, lost, stolen, or spoiled—all it knows for sure is that the goods are gone.

With a perpetual system, the accounting records themselves yield the cost of goods sold during the period, as well as the amount of inventory that should be found when the physical count is made. In the Grantsville Clothing example, the predicted ending inventory is $6,776 (from the T-account shown earlier); the actual ending inventory, according to the physical count, is only $5,950. The difference of $826 ($6,776 − $5,950) represents inventory lost, stolen, or spoiled during the period. This amount is called inventory shrinkage. The adjusting entry needed to record this **inventory shrinkage** is as follows:

Inventory Shrinkage	826	
Inventory ($6,776 − $5,950)		826
Adjustment of perpetual inventory balance to reflect inventory shrinkage.		

For internal management purposes, the amount of inventory shrinkage would be tracked from one period to the next to detect whether the amount of "shrinkage" for any given period is unusually high. For external reporting purposes, the shrinkage amount would probably be combined with normal cost of goods sold, and the title "Cost of Goods Sold" would be given to the total. Notice that if this practice is followed, reported cost of goods sold would be the same under both a perpetual and a periodic inventory system. The difference is that, with a perpetual system, company management knows how much of the goods was actually sold and how much represents inventory shrinkage.

With a periodic inventory system, no journal entry for inventory shrinkage is made because the amount of shrinkage is unknown. Instead, the ending inventory amount derived from the physical count is used to make the second periodic inventory closing entry (refer back to the previous section). Using the $5,950 ending inventory amount, the appropriate periodic inventory closing entry is:

Cost of Goods Sold	9,926	
Inventory ($15,876 − $5,950)		9,926
Adjustment of inventory account to appropriate ending balance.		

The Income Effect of an Error in Ending Inventory

As shown in the previous section, the results of the physical inventory count directly affect the computation of cost of goods sold with a periodic system and inventory shrinkage with a perpetual system. Errors in the inventory count will cause the amount of cost of goods sold or inventory shrinkage to be misstated. To illustrate, assume that the correct inventory count for Grantsville Clothing is $5,950 but that the ending inventory value is mistakenly computed to be $6,450. The impact of this $500 ($6,450 − $5,950) inventory overstatement is as follows:

	Periodic System	Perpetual System
Beginning inventory	$ 0	$ 0
Plus: Net purchases	15,876	15,876
Cost of goods available for sale	$15,876	$15,876
Less: Ending inventory	6,450	6,776 (from inventory system)
Cost of goods sold	$ 9,426	$ 9,100 (from inventory system)
Goods lost or stolen	unknown	326 ($6,776 − $6,450)
Total cost of goods sold, lost, or stolen	$ 9,426	$ 9,426

The $500 inventory overstatement reduces the reported cost of goods sold, lost, or stolen by $500, from $9,926 (computed earlier) to $9,426. This is because if we mistakenly think that we have more inventory remaining, then we will also mistakenly think that we must have sold less. Conversely, if the physical count understates ending inventory, total cost of goods sold will be overstated.

Since an inventory overstatement decreases reported cost of goods sold, it will also increase reported gross margin and net income. For this reason, the managers of a firm that is having difficulty meeting profit targets are sometimes tempted to "mistakenly" overstate ending inventory. Because of this temptation, auditors must take care to review a company's inventory counting process and also to physically observe a sample of the actual inventory. Many new accounting graduates who are hired by public accounting firms spend a portion of their first year on the job checking the inventory counts done by clients. The benefits of this exposure are twofold: (1) these new auditors get an opportunity to see what a business actually does, and (2) the inventory count provides assurance that the inventory amount stated on the financial statements is accurate.

TO SUMMARIZE: A physical inventory count is necessary to ensure that inventory records match the actual existing inventory. If a perpetual system is used, an inventory count can be used to compute the amount of inventory shrinkage during the period. An error in the reported ending inventory amount can have a significant effect on reported cost of goods sold, gross margin, and net income. For example, overstatement of ending inventory results in understatement of cost of goods sold and overstatement of net income.

Inventory Cost Flow Assumptions

4 Apply the four inventory cost flow alternatives: specific identification, FIFO, LIFO, and average cost.

FIFO (first in, first out) An inventory cost flow assumption whereby the first goods purchased are assumed to be the first goods sold so that the ending inventory consists of the most recently purchased goods.

LIFO (last in, first out) An inventory cost flow assumption whereby the last goods purchased are assumed to be the first goods sold so that the ending inventory consists of the first goods purchased.

average cost An inventory cost flow assumption whereby cost of goods sold and the cost of ending inventory are determined by using an average cost of all merchandise available for sale during the period.

Consider the following transactions for the Ramona Rice Company for the year 2006.

Mar. 23 Purchased 10 kilos of rice, $4 per kilo.
Nov. 17 Purchased 10 kilos of rice, $9 per kilo.
Dec. 31 Sold 10 kilos of rice, $10 per kilo.

The surprisingly difficult question to answer with this simple example is "How much money did Ramona make in 2006?" As you can see, it depends on which rice was sold on December 31. There are three possibilities:

	Case #1 Sold Old Rice	Case #2 Sold New Rice	Case #3 Sold Mixed Rice
Sales ($10 × 10 kilos)	$100	$100	$100
Cost of goods sold (10 kilos)	40	90	65
Gross margin	$ 60	$ 10	$ 35

In Case #1, it is assumed that the 10 kilos of rice sold on December 31 were the old ones, purchased on March 23 for $4 per kilo. Accountants call this a **FIFO (first in, first out)** assumption. In Case #2, it is assumed that the company sold the new rice, purchased on November 17 for $9 per kilo. Accountants call this a **LIFO (last in, first out)** assumption. In Case #3, it is assumed that all the rice is mixed together, so the cost per kilo is the average cost of all the rice available for sale, or $6.50 per kilo [($40 + $90) ÷ 20 kilos]. Accountants call this an **average cost** assumption.

The point of the Ramona Rice example is this: in most cases, there is no feasible way to track exactly which units were sold. Accordingly, in order to compute cost of goods sold, the accountant must make an assumption. Note that this is not a case of tricky accountants trying to manipulate the reported numbers; instead, this is a case in which income simply cannot be computed unless the accountant uses his or her judgment and makes an assumption.

All three of the assumptions described in the example—FIFO, LIFO, and average cost—are acceptable under U.S. accounting rules. An interesting question is whether a company would randomly choose one of the three acceptable methods, or whether the choice would be made more strategically. For example, if Ramona Rice were preparing financial statements to be used to support a bank loan application, which assumption would you suggest that the company make? On the other hand, if Ramona were completing its income tax return, which assumption would be the best? This topic of strategic accounting choice will be discussed later in this chapter.

In the following sections, we will examine in more detail the different cost flow assumptions used by companies to determine inventories and cost of goods sold.

Specific Identification Inventory Cost Flow

specific identification A method of valuing inventory and determining cost of goods sold whereby the actual costs of specific inventory items are assigned to them.

An alternative to the assumptions just described is to specifically identify the cost of each particular unit that is sold. This approach, called **specific identification**, is often used by automobile dealers and other businesses that sell a limited number of units at a high price. To illustrate the specific identification inventory costing method, we will consider the September 2006 records of Nephi Company, which sells one type of bicycle.

Sept. 1 Beginning inventory consisted of 10 bicycles costing $200 each.
3 Purchased 8 bicycles costing $250 each.
18 Purchased 16 bicycles costing $300 each.
20 Purchased 10 bicycles costing $320 each.
25 Sold 28 bicycles, $400 each.

These inventory records show that during September the company had 44 bicycles (10 from beginning inventory and 34 that were purchased during the month) that it could have sold. However, only 28 bicycles were sold, leaving 16 on hand at the end of September. Using the specific identification method of inventory costing requires that the individual costs of the actual units sold be charged against revenue as cost of goods sold. To compute cost of goods sold and ending inventory amounts with this alternative, a company must know which units were actually sold and what the unit cost of each was.

Suppose that of the 28 bicycles sold by Nephi on September 25, 8 came from the beginning inventory, 4 came from the September 3 purchase, and 16 came from the September 18 purchase. With this information, cost of goods sold and ending inventory are computed as follows:

	Bicycles	Costs
Beginning inventory	10	$ 2,000
Net purchases	34	10,000
Goods available for sale	44	$12,000
Ending inventory	16	4,600
Cost of goods sold	28	$ 7,400

The cost of ending inventory is the total of the individual costs of the bicycles still on hand at the end of the month, or:

2 bicycles from beginning inventory, $200 each	$ 400
4 bicycles purchased on September 3, $250 each	1,000
0 bicycles purchased on September 18, $300 each	0
10 bicycles purchased on September 20, $320 each	3,200
Total ending inventory (16 units)	$4,600

Similarly, the cost of goods sold is the total of the costs of the specific bicycles sold, or:

8 bicycles from beginning inventory, $200 each	**$1,600**
4 bicycles purchased on September 3, $250 each	1,000
16 bicycles purchased on September 18, $300 each	4,800
0 bicycles purchased on September 20, $320 each	0
Total cost of goods sold (28 units)	**$7,400**

For many companies, it is impractical, if not impossible, to keep track of specific units. In that case, an assumption must be made as to which units were sold during the period and which are still in inventory, as illustrated earlier in the Ramona Rice example.

It is very important to remember that the accounting rules do not require that the assumed flow of goods for costing purposes match the actual physical movement of goods purchased and sold. In some cases, the assumed cost flow may be similar to the physical flow, but firms are not required to match the assumed accounting cost flow to the physical flow. A grocery store, for example, usually tries to sell the oldest units first to minimize spoilage. Thus, the physical flow of goods would reflect a FIFO pattern, but the grocery store could use a FIFO, LIFO, or average cost assumption in determining the ending inventory and cost of goods sold numbers to be reported in the financial statements. On the other hand, a company that stockpiles coal must first sell the coal purchased last since it is on top of the pile. That company might use the LIFO cost assumption, which reflects physical flow, or it might use one of the other alternatives.

In the next few sections, we will illustrate the FIFO, LIFO, and average inventory costing methods. The bicycle inventory data for Nephi Company will again be used in illustrating the different inventory cost flows.

FIFO Cost Flow Assumption

With FIFO, it is assumed that the oldest units are sold and the newest units remain in inventory. Using the FIFO inventory cost flow assumption, the ending inventory and cost of goods sold for Nephi Company are:

	Bicycles	**Costs**
Beginning inventory	10	$ 2,000
Net purchases	34	10,000
Goods available for sale	44	$12,000
Ending inventory	16	5,000
Cost of goods sold	28	$ 7,000

The $7,000 cost of goods sold and $5,000 cost of ending inventory are determined as follows:

FIFO cost of goods sold (oldest 28 units):

10 bicycles from beginning inventory, $200 each	$2,000
8 bicycles purchased on September 3, $250 each	2,000
10 bicycles purchased on September 18, $300 each	3,000
Total FIFO cost of goods sold	$7,000

FIFO ending inventory (newest 16 units):

6 bicycles purchased on September 18, $300 each	$1,800
10 bicycles purchased on September 20, $320 each	3,200
Total FIFO ending inventory	$5,000

LIFO Cost Flow Assumption

LIFO is the opposite of FIFO. With LIFO, the cost of the most recent units purchased is transferred to cost of goods sold. When prices are rising, as they are in the Nephi Company example, LIFO provides higher cost of goods sold, and hence lower net income, than FIFO. This is because the newest (high-priced) goods are assumed to have been sold. Using the LIFO inventory cost flow assumption, the ending inventory and cost of goods sold for Nephi Company are:

	Bicycles	Costs
Beginning inventory	10	$ 2,000
Net purchases	34	10,000
Goods available for sale	44	$12,000
Ending inventory	16	3,500
Cost of goods sold	28	$ 8,500

The $8,500 cost of goods sold and $3,500 cost of ending inventory are determined as follows:

LIFO cost of goods sold (newest 28 units):
10 bicycles purchased on September 20, $320 each	$3,200
16 bicycles purchased on September 18, $300 each	4,800
2 bicycles purchased on September 3, $250 each	500
Total LIFO cost of goods sold	$8,500

LIFO ending inventory (oldest 16 units):
10 bicycles from beginning inventory, $200 each	$2,000
6 bicycles purchased on September 3, $250 each	1,500
Total LIFO ending inventory	$3,500

Average Cost Flow Assumption

With average costing, an average cost must be computed for all the inventory available for sale during the period. The average unit cost for Nephi Company during September is computed as follows:

	Bicycles	Costs
Beginning inventory	10	$ 2,000
Net purchases	34	10,000
Goods available for sale	44	$12,000

$12,000 ÷ 44 units = $272.73 per unit

With the average cost assumption, cost of goods sold is computed by multiplying the number of units sold by the average cost per unit. Similarly, the cost of ending inventory is computed by multiplying the number of units in ending inventory by the average cost per unit. These calculations are as follows:

Average Cost of Goods Sold: 28 Units × $272.73 per Unit = $7,636 (rounded)

Average Ending Inventory: 16 Units × $272.73 per Unit = $4,364 (rounded)

This information can be shown as follows:

	Bicycles	Costs
Beginning inventory	10	$ 2,000
Net purchases	34	10,000
Goods available for sale	44	$12,000
Ending inventory	16	4,364
Cost of goods sold	28	$ 7,636

A Comparison of All Inventory Costing Methods

The cost of goods sold and ending inventory amounts we have calculated using the three cost flow assumptions are summarized along with the resultant gross margins as follows:

	FIFO	LIFO	Average
Sales revenue (28 × $400)	$11,200	$11,200	$11,200
Cost of goods sold	7,000	8,500	7,636
Gross margin	$ 4,200	$ 2,700	$ 3,564
Ending inventory	$ 5,000	$ 3,500	$ 4,364

Note that the net result of each of the inventory cost flow assumptions is to allocate the total cost of goods available for sale of $12,000 between cost of goods sold and ending inventory.

Conceptual Comparison

From a conceptual standpoint, LIFO gives a better reflection of cost of goods sold in the income statement than does FIFO because the most recent goods ("last in"), with the most recent costs, are assumed to have been sold. Thus, LIFO cost of goods sold matches current revenues with current costs. Average cost is somewhere between LIFO and FIFO. On the balance sheet, however, FIFO gives a better measure of inventory value because, with the FIFO assumption, the "first in" units are sold and the remaining units are the newest ones with the most recent costs. In summary, LIFO gives a conceptually better measure of income, but FIFO gives a conceptually better measure of inventory value on the balance sheet.

Financial Statement Impact Comparison

As illustrated in the Nephi Company example, in times of rising inventory prices (the most common situation in the majority of industries today), cost of goods sold is highest with LIFO and lowest with FIFO. As a result, gross margin, net income, and ending inventory are lowest with LIFO and highest with FIFO. With the impact on the reported financial statement numbers being so uniformly bad, you may be wondering why any company would ever voluntarily choose to use LIFO (during times of inflation). It might further surprise you to learn that, since 1974, hundreds of U.S. companies have voluntarily switched from FIFO to LIFO and that over half of the large companies in the United States currently use LIFO in accounting for at least some of their inventories.

The attractiveness of LIFO can be explained with one word—TAXES. If a company uses LIFO in a time of rising prices, reported cost of goods sold is higher, reported taxable income is lower, and cash paid for income taxes is lower. In fact, LIFO was invented in the 1930s in the United States for the sole

STOP & THINK

Over the entire life of a company—from its beginning with zero inventory until its final closeout when the last inventory item is sold—is aggregate cost of goods sold more, less, or the same as aggregate purchases? How is this relationship affected by the inventory cost flow assumption used?

purpose of allowing companies to lower their income tax payments. In most instances where accounting alternatives exist, firms are allowed to use one accounting method for tax purposes and another for financial reporting. In 1939, however, when the Internal Revenue Service (IRS) approved the use of LIFO, it ruled that firms may use LIFO for tax purposes only if they also use LIFO for financial reporting purposes. Therefore, companies must choose between reporting higher profits and paying higher taxes with FIFO or reporting lower profits and paying lower taxes with LIFO.

TO SUMMARIZE: Some companies can use specific identification as a method of valuing inventory and determining cost of goods sold. In most cases, however, an accountant must make an inventory cost flow assumption in order to compute cost of goods sold and ending inventory. With FIFO (first in, first out), it is assumed that the oldest inventory units are sold first. With LIFO (last in, first out), it is assumed that the newest units are sold first. With the average cost assumption, the total goods available for sale are used to compute an average cost per unit for the period; this average cost is then used in calculating cost of goods sold and ending inventory. LIFO produces a better matching of current revenues and current expenses in the income statement; FIFO yields a balance sheet inventory value that is closer to the current value of the inventory. The primary practical attraction of LIFO is that it lowers income tax payments.

Assessing How Well Companies Manage Their Inventories

5 Use financial ratios to evaluate a company's inventory level.

Money tied up in the form of inventories cannot be used for other purposes. Therefore, companies try hard to minimize the necessary investment in inventories while at the same time assuring that they have enough inventory on hand to meet customer demand. In recent years a method of inventory management called just-in-time (JIT) inventory has become popular. JIT, which will be described in Chapter 21 of *Accounting: Concepts and Applications*, is an inventory management method that attempts to have exactly enough inventory arrive just in time for sale. Its purpose is to minimize the amount of money needed to purchase and hold inventory.

Evaluating the Level of Inventory

Two widely used measurements of how effectively a company is managing its inventory are the inventory turnover ratio and number of days' sales in inventory. **Inventory turnover** provides a measure of how many times a company turns over, or replenishes, its inventory during a year. The calculation is similar to the accounts receivable turnover discussed in Chapter 7. It is calculated by dividing cost of goods sold by average inventory as follows:

inventory turnover A measure of the efficiency with which inventory is managed; computed by dividing cost of goods sold by average inventory for a period.

$$\text{Inventory Turnover} = \frac{\text{Cost of Goods Sold}}{\text{Average Inventory}}$$

The average inventory amount is the average of the beginning and ending inventory balances. The inventory turnover ratios for SEARS, SAFEWAY, and CATERPILLAR for 2002 are as follows (dollar amounts are in billions):

	Sears	Safeway	Caterpillar
Cost of goods sold	$25.646	$22.303	$14.709
Beginning inventory	4.912	2.355	2.925
Ending inventory	5.115	2.493	2.763
Average inventory	5.014	2.424	2.844
Inventory turnover	5.11	9.20	5.17

number of days' sales in inventory An alternative measure of how well inventory is being managed; computed by dividing 365 days by the inventory turnover ratio.

From this analysis, you can see that Safeway, the supermarket, turns its inventory over more frequently than Sears, the department store, and Caterpillar, the equipment dealer. This result is what we would have predicted given that the companies are in different businesses and have different types of inventory.

Inventory turnover can also be converted into the **number of days' sales in inventory**. This ratio is computed by dividing 365, or the number of days in a year, by the inventory turnover, as follows:

$$\frac{\text{Number of Days'}}{\text{Sales in Inventory}} = \frac{365}{\text{Inventory Turnover}}$$

Computing this ratio for Sears, Safeway, and Caterpillar yields the following:

Caution

Sometimes these two inventory ratios are computed using ending inventory rather than average inventory. This is appropriate if the inventory balance does not change much from the beginning to the end of the year.

	Number of Days' Sales in Inventory
Sears	71.4 days
Safeway	39.7 days
Caterpillar	70.6 days

Individuals analyzing how effective a company's inventory management is would compare these ratios with those of other firms in the same industry and with comparable ratios for the same firm in previous years.

network exercises

Safeway and Kroger

In addition to SAFEWAY, another large supermarket chain is KROGER, based in Cincinnati. Access Kroger's Web site at **http://kroger.com**.

Net Work:

1. Is Kroger's inventory turnover higher or lower than Safeway's?

2. Does Kroger use LIFO or FIFO?

Impact of the Inventory Cost Flow Assumption

As mentioned previously, in times of rising prices, the use of LIFO results in higher cost of goods sold and lower inventory values. All three of the companies in the ratio illustration above use LIFO. Each company includes supplemental disclosures in the financial statement notes that allow users to compute what reported inventory and cost of goods sold would have been if the company had used FIFO. To illustrate the impact that the choice of inventory cost flow assumption can have on the reported numbers, consider the following comparison for Caterpillar for 2002:

	Reported LIFO Numbers	**Numbers if Using FIFO**
Cost of goods sold	$14.709	$14.341
Average inventory	2.844	4.794
Inventory turnover	5.17	2.99
Number of days' sales in inventory	70.6 days	122.1 days

The difference in cost of goods sold for 2002 is not great because inflation was relatively low in that year. However, the difference in the reported average inventory balance reflects the cumulative effect of inflation for the many years since Caterpillar first started using LIFO. The impact on the ratio values is dramatic. Of course, the difference between LIFO and FIFO is not as great for most companies as shown here for Caterpillar, but the general point is that the choice of inventory cost flow assumption can affect the conclusions drawn about the financial statements—if the financial statement user is not careful.

Number of Days' Purchases in Accounts Payable

In Chapter 7, we introduced the average collection period ratio. In this chapter we have discussed the computation of the number of days' sales in inventory. Taken together, these two ratios indicate the length of a firm's operating cycle. The two ratios measure the amount of time it takes, on average, from the point when inventory is purchased to the point when cash is collected from the customer who purchased the inventory. For example, Sears' 331-day operating cycle for 2002 is depicted below.

Is Sears' operating cycle too long, too short, or just right? That is difficult to tell without information from prior years and from competitors. But by including one additional ratio in the analysis, we can learn more about how Sears is managing its operating cash flow. The number of days' purchases in accounts payable reveals the average length of time that elapses between the purchase of inventory on account and the cash payment for that inventory. The **number of days' purchases in accounts payable** is computed by dividing total inventory purchases by average accounts payable and then dividing the result into 365 days:

> **number of days' purchases in accounts payable** A measure of how well operating cash flow is being managed; computed by dividing total inventory purchases by average accounts payable and then dividing 365 days by the result.

$$\frac{\text{Number of Days' Purchases}}{\text{in Accounts Payable}} = \frac{365\ \text{Days}}{\text{Purchases/Average Accounts Payable}}$$

The amount of inventory purchased during a year is computed by combining cost of goods sold with the change in the inventory balance for the year. If inventory increased during the year, then inventory purchases are equal to cost of goods sold plus the increase in the inventory balance. Similarly, if inventory decreased during the year, inventory purchases are equal to cost of goods sold minus the decrease in the inventory balance.

The number of days' purchases in accounts payable indicates how long a company takes to pay its suppliers. For example, Sears' number of days' purchases in accounts payable for 2002 is computed as follows (dollar figures are in millions):

Cost of goods sold for 2002	$25,646
Add increase in inventory during 2002	203
Inventory purchases during 2002	$25,849
Average accounts payable during 2002	$ 7,331

$$\frac{\text{Number of Days' Purchases}}{\text{in Accounts Payable}} = \frac{365\ \text{Days}}{\$25,849/\$7,331}$$

$$= 104\ \text{days}$$

Number of Days'
Sales in Inventory

Average Collection Period

71 days

260 days

——————————331 days——————————

104 days

227 days

Number of Days'
Purchases in
Accounts Payable

External Financing
Needed

Caution

This computation of the number of days' purchases in accounts payable assumes that only inventory purchases on account are included in accounts payable. It is likely that the accounts payable balance also includes such items as supplies purchased on account. Nevertheless, the purchase of inventory is typically the most significant element of accounts payable.

Sears must pay its suppliers in 104 days but must wait for 331 days before receiving the cash from its customers. Sears must finance the remaining 227 days (331 days − 104 days) of its operating cycle with bank loans or additional stockholder investment or by charging interest to those using its credit card debt. Sears is famous for using the last option—charging customers for the use of credit. In 2002 alone, Sears reported revenue from its credit card activities of over $5.6 billion.

These calculations illustrate that proper management of the sales/collection cycle, coupled with prudent financing of inventory purchases on account, can reduce a company's reliance on external financing.

TO SUMMARIZE: Proper inventory management seeks a balance between keeping a lower inventory level to avoid tying up excess resources and maintaining a sufficient inventory balance to ensure smooth business operation. Companies assess how well their inventory is being managed by using two ratios: (1) inventory turnover and (2) number of days' sales in inventory. A company's choice of inventory cost flow assumption can significantly affect the values of these inventory ratios; intelligent ratio analysis requires considering possible accounting differences among companies. Comparison of the average collection period, number of days' sales in inventory, and number of days' purchases in accounts payable reveals how much of a company's operating cycle it must finance through external financing.

Thus far we have defined inventory and cost of goods sold; we have described the perpetual and periodic inventory systems, three inventory cost flow assumptions, and the use of financial ratios to evaluate a company's management of its inventory. These topics are all sufficient for a basic understanding of the nature of inventory and cost of goods sold, as well as the most common ways of accounting for inventory. The four topics that will be discussed in the expanded material are (1) the impact of more complicated inventory errors, (2) complications that arise in using LIFO and average cost with a perpetual inventory system, (3) reporting inventory at amounts below cost, and (4) a method for estimating inventory without taking a physical count.

Further Coverage of Inventory Errors

6 Analyze the impact of inventory errors on reported cost of goods sold.

Incorrect amounts for inventory on the balance sheet and cost of goods sold on the income statement can result from errors in counting inventories, recording inventory transactions, or both. The effect of an error in the end-of-period inventory count was discussed earlier in the chapter. To examine the effects of other types of inventory errors, we will assume that Richfield Company had the following inventory records for 2006:

Inventory balance, January 1, 2006	$ 8,000
Purchases through December 30, 2006	20,000
Inventory balance, December 30, 2006	12,000

We will further assume that on December 31 the company purchased and received another $1,000 of inventory. The following comparison shows the kinds of inventory situations that might result:

The $1,000 of merchandise purchased on December 31 was	Incorrect* not recorded as a purchase and not counted as inventory	Incorrect recorded as a purchase but not counted as inventory	Incorrect not recorded as a purchase but counted as inventory	Correct recorded as a purchase and counted as inventory
Beginning inventory	$ 8,000 (OK)**	$ 8,000 (OK)	$ 8,000 (OK)	$ 8,000 (OK)
Net purchases	20,000 (↓)	21,000 (OK)	20,000 (↓)	21,000 (OK)
Cost of goods available for sale	$28,000 (↓)	$29,000 (OK)	$28,000 (↓)	$29,000 (OK)
Ending inventory	12,000 (↓)	12,000 (↓)	13,000 (OK)	13,000 (OK)
Cost of goods sold	$16,000 (OK)	$17,000 (↑)	$15,000 (↓)	$16,000 (OK)

*This calculation produces the correct cost of goods sold but by an incorrect route—the errors in purchases and ending inventory offset each other.
**For the amount, ↓ indicates it is too low, ↑ means it is too high, and OK means it is correct.

In these calculations, the beginning inventory plus purchases equals the cost of goods that were "available for sale." In other words, everything that "could be sold" must have either been on hand at the beginning of the period (beginning inventory) or purchased during the period (net purchases). Then, ending inventory (what wasn't sold) was subtracted from the cost of goods available for sale. The result is the cost of goods that were sold. Everything on hand (available) had to be either sold or left in ending inventory. From this example, you can see how inventory and cost of goods sold can be misstated by the improper recording of inventory purchases or counting of inventory.

Similar errors can occur when inventory is sold. If a sale is recorded but the merchandise remains in the warehouse and is counted in the ending inventory, cost of goods sold will be understated, whereas gross margin and net income will be overstated. If a sale is not recorded but inventory is shipped and not counted in the ending inventory, gross margin and net income will be understated, and cost of goods sold will be overstated.

To illustrate these potential inventory errors, we will again consider the data of Richfield Company. Note that sales figures have been added and the ending inventory and the 2006 purchases now correctly include the $1,000 purchase of merchandise made on December 31, 2006.

Sales revenue through December 30, 2006 (200% of cost)	$32,000
Inventory balance, January 1, 2006	8,000
Net purchases during 2006	21,000
Inventory balance, December 31, 2006	13,000

In addition, assume that on December 31, inventory that cost $1,000 was sold for $2,000. The merchandise was delivered to the buyer on December 31. The following analysis shows the kinds of situations that might result:

	Incorrect	**Incorrect**	**Incorrect**	**Correct**
The $2,000 sale on December 31 was	not recorded and the merchandise was counted as inventory	recorded and the merchandise was counted as inventory	not recorded and the merchandise was excluded from inventory	recorded and the merchandise was excluded from inventory
Sales revenue	$32,000 (↓)*	$34,000 (OK)	$32,000 (↓)	$34,000 (OK)
Cost of goods sold:				
Beginning inventory	$ 8,000 (OK)	$ 8,000 (OK)	$ 8,000 (OK)	$ 8,000 (OK)
Net purchases	21,000 (OK)	21,000 (OK)	21,000 (OK)	21,000 (OK)
Cost of goods available for sale	$29,000 (OK)	$29,000 (OK)	$29,000 (OK)	$29,000 (OK)
Ending inventory	13,000 (↑)	13,000 (↑)	12,000 (OK)	12,000 (OK)
Cost of goods sold	$16,000 (↓)	$16,000 (↓)	$17,000 (OK)	$17,000 (OK)
Gross margin	$16,000 (↓)	$18,000 (↑)	$15,000 (↓)	$17,000 (OK)

*For the amount, ↓ indicates it is too low, ↑ means it is too high, and OK means it is correct.

To reduce the possibility of these types of inventory cutoff errors, most businesses close their warehouses at year-end while they count inventory. If they are retailers, they will probably count inventory after hours. During the inventory counting period, businesses do not accept or ship merchandise, nor do they enter purchase or sales transactions in their accounting records.

As explained, an error in inventory results in cost of goods sold being overstated or understated. This error has the opposite effect on gross margin and, hence, on net income. For example, if at the end of the accounting period $2,000 of inventory is not counted, cost of goods sold will be $2,000 higher than it should be, and gross margin and net income will be understated by $2,000. Such inventory errors affect gross margin and net income not only in the current year but in the following year as well. A recording delay resulting in an understatement of purchases in one year, for example, results in an overstatement in the next year.

To illustrate how inventory errors affect gross margin and net income, let us first assume the following correct data for Salina Corporation:

	2005		**2006**	
Sales revenue		$50,000		$40,000
Cost of goods sold:				
Beginning inventory	$10,000		$ 5,000	
Net purchases	20,000		25,000	
Cost of goods available for sale	$30,000		$30,000	
Ending inventory	5,000		10,000	
Cost of goods sold		25,000		20,000
Gross margin		$25,000		$20,000
Operating expenses		10,000		10,000
Net income		$15,000		$10,000

Now suppose that ending inventory in 2005 was overstated; that is, instead of the correct amount of $5,000, the count erroneously showed $7,000 of inventory on hand. The following analysis shows the effect of the error on net income in both 2005 and 2006:

	2005	2006
Sales revenue	$50,000	$40,000
Cost of goods sold:		
Beginning inventory	$10,000	$ 7,000 (↑)
Net purchases	20,000	25,000
Cost of goods available for sale	$30,000	$32,000 (↑)
Ending inventory	7,000 (↑)*	10,000
Cost of goods sold	23,000 (↓)	22,000 (↑)
Gross margin	$27,000 (↑)	$18,000 (↓)
Operating expenses	10,000	10,000
Net income	$17,000 (↑)	$ 8,000 (↓)

*For the amount, ↑ means it is too high, ↓ means it is too low.

When the amount of ending inventory is overstated (as it was in 2005), both gross margin and net income are overstated by the same amount ($2,000 in 2005). If the ending inventory amount had been understated, net income and gross margin would also have been understated, again by the same amount.

Since the ending inventory in 2005 becomes the beginning inventory in 2006, the net income and gross margin for 2006 are also misstated. In 2006, however, beginning inventory is overstated, so gross margin and net income are understated, again by $2,000. Thus, the errors in the two years offset or counterbalance each other, and if the count taken at the end of 2006 is correct, income in subsequent years will not be affected by this error.

> **TO SUMMARIZE:** Inventory errors can have a significant effect on cost of goods sold, gross margin, and net income. In addition, a misstatement of an ending inventory balance affects net income, both in the current year and in the next year. Errors in beginning and ending inventory have the opposite effect on cost of goods sold, gross margin, and net income. Errors in inventory correct themselves after two years if the physical count at the end of the second year shows the correct amount of ending inventory for that period.

Complications of the Perpetual Method with LIFO and Average Cost

7 Describe the complications that arise when LIFO or average cost is used with a perpetual inventory system.

In the Nephi Company bicycle example used earlier in the chapter, the simplifying assumption was made that all 28 bicycles were sold at the end of the month. In essence, this is the assumption made when a periodic inventory system is used—goods are assumed to be sold at the end of the period because the exact time when particular goods are sold is not recorded. Computation of average cost and LIFO under a perpetual system is complicated because the average cost of units available for sale changes every time a purchase is made, and the identification of the "last in" units also changes with every purchase.

These perpetual system complications are illustrated below using the same Nephi Company example used earlier, but now assuming that sales occurred at different times during the month.

Sept. 1   Beginning inventory consisted of 10 bicycles costing $200 each.
     3   Purchased 8 bicycles costing $250 each.
     5   Sold 12 bicycles, $400 each.
   18   Purchased 16 bicycles costing $300 each.
   20   Purchased 10 bicycles costing $320 each.
   25   Sold 16 bicycles, $400 each.

When a perpetual system is used and sales occur during the period, the identification of the "last in" units must be evaluated at the time of each individual sale, as follows:

September 5 sale of 12 bicycles, identification of "last in" units:

8 bicycles purchased on September 3, $250 each	$2,000	
4 bicycles in beginning inventory, $200 each	800	
		$2,800

September 25 sale of 16 bicycles, identification of "last in" units:

10 bicycles purchased on September 20, $320 each	$3,200	
6 bicycles purchased on September 18, $300 each	1,800	
		5,000
Total perpetual LIFO cost of goods sold		$7,800

This $7,800 amount for LIFO cost of goods sold under a perpetual inventory system compares to the $8,500 LIFO cost of goods sold computed earlier in the chapter assuming a periodic inventory system. Again, the difference arises because the "last in" units are identified at the end of the period with a periodic system; with a perpetual system, the "last in" units are identified at the time of each individual sale.

A similar difference arises with the average cost method because, with a perpetual system, a new average cost per unit must be determined at the time each individual sale is made. This process is illustrated as follows:

September 5 sale of 12 bicycles, determination of average cost:

10 bicycles in beginning inventory, $200 each	$2,000	
8 bicycles purchased on September 3, $250 each	2,000	
Total cost of goods available for sale on September 5		$4,000

Average cost on September 5: $4,000 ÷ 18 bicycles = $222.22 per bicycle
September 5 cost of goods sold:
  12 bicycles × $222.22 per bicycle = $2,667 (rounded)

September 25 sale of 16 bicycles, determination of average cost:

6 (18 − 12) bicycles; remaining cost ($4,000 − $2,667)	$1,333	
16 bicycles purchased on September 18, $300 each	4,800	
10 bicycles purchased on September 20, $320 each	3,200	
Total cost of goods available for sale on September 25		$9,333

Average cost on September 25: $9,333 ÷ 32 bicycles = $291.66 per bicycle
September 25 cost of goods sold:
  16 bicycles × $291.66 per bicycle = $4,667 (rounded)
Total cost of goods sold: $2,667 + $4,667 = $7,334

This $7,334 cost of goods sold under the perpetual average method compares with $7,636 cost of goods sold under the periodic average method. Again, the difference is that one overall average cost for all goods available for sale during the period is used with a periodic system; with a perpetual system, a new average cost is computed at the time of each sale.

By the way, no complications arise in using FIFO with a perpetual system. This is because, no matter when sales occur, the "first in" units are always the same ones. So, FIFO periodic and FIFO perpetual yield the same numbers for cost of goods sold and ending inventory.

Because of the complications associated with computing perpetual LIFO and perpetual average cost, many businesses that use average cost or LIFO for financial reporting purposes use a simple FIFO assumption in maintaining their day-to-day perpetual inventory records. The perpetual FIFO records are then converted to periodic average cost or LIFO for the financial reports.

> **TO SUMMARIZE:** Using the average cost and LIFO inventory cost flow assumptions with a perpetual inventory system leads to some complications. These complications arise because the identity of the "last in" units changes with each new inventory purchase, as does the average cost of units purchased up to that point.

Reporting Inventory at Amounts below Cost

8 Apply the lower-of-cost-or-market method of accounting for inventory.

All the inventory costing alternatives we have discussed in this chapter have one thing in common: they report inventory at cost. Occasionally, however, it becomes necessary to report inventory at an amount that is less than cost. This happens when the future value of the inventory is in doubt—when it is damaged, used, or obsolete, or when it can be replaced new at a price that is less than its original cost.

Inventory Valued at Net Realizable Value

net realizable value The selling price of an item less reasonable selling costs.

When inventory is damaged, used, or obsolete, it should be reported at no more than its **net realizable value**. This is the amount the inventory can be sold for, minus any selling costs. Suppose, for example, that an automobile dealer has a demonstrator car that originally cost $18,000 and now can be sold for only $16,000. The car should be reported at its net realizable value. If a commission of $500 must be paid to sell the car, the net realizable value is $15,500, or $2,500 less than cost. This loss is calculated as follows:

Cost		$18,000
Estimated selling price	$16,000	
Less selling commission	500	15,500
Loss		$ 2,500

To achieve a good matching of revenues and expenses, a company must recognize this estimated loss as soon as it is determined that an economic loss has occurred (even before the car is sold). The journal entry required to recognize the loss and reduce the inventory amount of the car is:

Loss on Write-Down of Inventory (Expense)	2,500	
Inventory		2,500
To write down inventory to its net realizable value.		

By writing down inventory to its net realizable value, a company recognizes a loss when it happens and shows no profit or loss when the inventory is finally sold. Using net realizable values means that assets are not being reported at amounts that exceed their future economic benefits.

Inventory Valued at Lower of Cost or Market

lower-of-cost-or-market (LCM) rule A basis for valuing inventory at the lower of original cost or current market value.

Inventory must also be written down to an amount below cost if it can be replaced new at a price that is less than its original cost. In the electronics industry, for instance, the costs of computers and compact disc players have fallen dramatically in recent years. When goods remaining in ending inventory can be replaced with identical goods at a lower cost, the lower unit cost must be used in valuing the inventory (provided that the replacement cost is not higher than net realizable value or lower than net realizable value minus a normal profit). This is known as the **lower-of-cost-or-market (LCM) rule**. (In a sense, a more precise name would be the lower-of-actual-or-replacement-cost rule.)

ceiling The maximum market amount at which inventory can be carried on the books; equal to net realizable value.

The **ceiling**, or maximum market amount at which inventory can be carried on the books, is equivalent to net realizable value, which is the selling price less estimated selling costs. The ceiling is imposed because it makes no sense to value an inventory item above the amount that can be realized upon sale. For example, assume that a company purchased an inventory item for $10 and expected to sell it for $14. If the selling costs of the item amounted to $3, the ceiling or net realizable value would be $11 ($14 − $3).

floor The minimum market amount at which inventory can be carried on the books; equal to net realizable value minus a normal profit.

The **floor** is defined as the net realizable value minus a normal profit. Thus, if the inventory item costing $10 had a normal profit margin of 20%, or $2, the floor would be $9 (net realizable value of $11 less normal profit of $2). This is the lowest amount at which inventory should be carried in order to prevent showing losses in one period and large profits in subsequent periods.

In applying this LCM rule, you can follow certain basic guidelines:

1. Define market value as:
   a. replacement cost, if it falls between the ceiling and the floor.
   b. the floor, if the replacement cost is less than the floor.
   c. the ceiling, if the replacement cost is higher than the ceiling.
   (As a practical matter, when replacement cost, ceiling, and floor are compared, market is always the middle value.)
2. Compare the defined market value with the original cost and choose the lower amount.

The following chart gives four separate examples of the application of the LCM rule; the resulting LCM amount is highlighted in each case.

| | | | | Market | |
| | | | | | |
Item	Number of Items in Inventory	Original Cost (LIFO, FIFO, etc.)	Replacement Cost	Net Realizable Value (Ceiling)	Net Realizable Value Minus Normal Profit (Floor)
A	10	$17	$16	$15	$10
B	8	21	18	23	16
C	30	26	21	31	22
D	20	19	16	34	25

The LCM rule can be applied in one of three ways: (1) by computing cost and market figures for each item in inventory and using the lower of the two amounts in each case, (2) by computing cost and market figures for the total inventory and then applying the LCM rule to that total, or (3) by applying the LCM rule to categories of inventory. For a clothing store, categories of inventory might be all shirts, all pants, all suits, or all dresses.

To illustrate, we will use the above data to show how the LCM rule would be applied to each inventory item separately and to total inventory. (The third method is similar to the second, except that it may involve several totals, one for each category of inventory.)

Item	Number of Items in Inventory	Original Cost	Market Value	LCM for Individual Items
A	10	$17 × 10 units = $ 170	$15 × 10 units = $ 150	$ 150
B	8	$21 × 8 units = 168	$18 × 8 units = 144	144
C	30	$26 × 30 units = 780	$22 × 30 units = 660	660
D	20	$19 × 20 units = 380	$25 × 20 units = 500	380
		$1,498	$1,454	$1,334

————— $44 —————
————— $164 —————

Using the first method, applying the LCM rule to individual items, inventory is valued at $1,334, a write-down of $164 from the original cost. With the second method, using total inventory, the lower of total cost ($1,498) or total market value ($1,454) is used for a write-down of $44. The write-down is smaller when total inventory is used because the increase in market value of $120 in item D offsets decreases in items A, B, and C. In practice, each of the three methods is acceptable, but once a method has been selected, it should be followed consistently.

The journal entry to write down the inventory to the lower of cost or market applying the LCM rule to individual items is:

Loss on Write-Down of Inventory (Expense)	164	
Inventory		164
To write down inventory to lower of cost or market.		

The amount of this entry would have been $44 if the LCM rule had been applied to total inventory.

The LCM rule has gained wide acceptance because it reports inventory on the balance sheet at amounts that are consistent with future economic benefits. With this method, losses are recognized when they occur, not necessarily when a sale is made.

> **TO SUMMARIZE:** The recorded amount of inventory should be written down (1) when it is damaged, used, or obsolete and (2) when it can be replaced (purchased new) at an amount that is less than its original cost. In the first case, inventory is reported at its net realizable value, an amount that allows a company to break even when the inventory is sold. In the second case, inventory is written down to the lower of cost or market. When using the lower-of-cost-or-market rule, market is defined as falling between the ceiling and floor. Ceiling is defined as the net realizable value; floor is net realizable value minus a normal profit margin. In no case should inventory be reported at an amount that exceeds the ceiling or is less than the floor. These reporting alternatives are attempts to show assets at amounts that reflect realistic future economic benefits.

Method of Estimating Inventories

9 Explain the gross margin method of estimating inventories.

We have assumed that the number of inventory units on hand is known by a physical count that takes place at the end of each accounting period. For the periodic inventory method, this physical count is the only way to determine how much inventory is on hand at the end of a period. For the perpetual inventory method, the physical count verifies the quantity on hand or indicates the amount of inventory shrinkage or theft. There are times, however, when a company needs to know the dollar amount of ending inventory, but a physical count is either impossible or impractical. For example, many firms prepare quarterly, or even monthly, financial statements, but it is too expensive and time-consuming to count the inventory at the end of each period. In such cases, if the perpetual inventory method is being used, the balance in the inventory account is usually assumed to be correct. With the periodic inventory method, however, some estimate of the inventory balance must be made. A common method of estimating the dollar amount of ending inventory is the gross margin method.

gross margin method A procedure for estimating the amount of ending inventory; the historical relationship of cost of goods sold to sales revenue is used in computing ending inventory.

The Gross Margin Method

With the **gross margin method**, a firm uses available information about the dollar amounts of beginning inventory and purchases, and the historical gross margin percentage to estimate the dollar amounts of cost of goods sold and ending inventory.

To illustrate, we will assume the following data for Payson Brick Company:

Net sales revenue, January 1 to March 31 . . . . $100,000
Inventory balance, January 1 15,000
Net purchases, January 1 to March 31 65,000
Gross margin percentage (historically determined percentage of net sales) 40%

With this information, the dollar amount of inventory on hand on March 31 is estimated as follows:

	Dollars	Percentage of Sales
Net sales revenue	$100,000	100%
Cost of goods sold:		
Beginning inventory $15,000		
Net purchases 65,000		
Total cost of goods available for sale $80,000		
Ending inventory ($80,000 − $60,000) . . . . . 20,000 (3)*		
Cost of goods sold ($100,000 − $40,000)	60,000 (2)*	60%
Gross margin ($100,000 × 0.40)	$ 40,000 (1)*	40%

*The numbers indicate the order of calculation.

In this example, gross margin is first determined by calculating 40% of sales (step 1). Next, cost of goods sold is found by subtracting gross margin from sales (step 2). Finally, the dollar amount of ending inventory is obtained by subtracting cost of goods sold from total cost of goods available for sale (step 3). Obviously, the gross margin method of estimating cost of goods sold and ending inventory assumes that the historical gross margin percentage is appropriate for the current period. This assumption is a realistic one in many fields of business. In cases where the gross margin percentage has changed, this method should be used with caution.

The gross margin method of estimating ending inventories is also useful when a fire or other calamity destroys a company's inventory. In these cases, the dollar amount of inventory lost must be determined before insurance claims can be made. The dollar amounts of sales, purchases, and beginning inventory can be obtained from prior years' financial statements and from customers, suppliers, and other sources. Then the gross margin method can be used to estimate the dollar amount of inventory lost.

TO SUMMARIZE: The gross margin method is a common technique for estimating the dollar amount of inventory. The historical gross margin percentage is used in conjunction with sales to estimate cost of goods sold. This estimated cost of goods sold amount is subtracted from cost of goods available for sale to yield an estimate of ending inventory.

review of learning objectives

Identify what items and costs should be included in inventory and cost of goods sold. Inventory is composed of goods held for sale in the normal course of business.

Cost of goods sold is the cost of inventory sold during the period. For a manufacturing firm, the three types of inventory are raw materials, work in process, and finished goods.

All costs incurred in producing and getting inventory ready to sell should be added to inventory cost. The costs associated with the selling effort itself are operating expenses of the period. Inventory should be recorded on the books of the company holding legal title. Goods in transit belong to the company paying for the shipping. Goods on consignment belong to the supplier/owner, not to the business holding the inventory for possible sale. At the end of an accounting period, the total cost of goods available for sale during the period must be allocated between ending inventory and cost of goods sold.

2 **Account for inventory purchases and sales using both a perpetual and a periodic inventory system.** With a perpetual inventory system, the inventory account is adjusted for every sale or purchase transaction. Discounts on purchases, returns of merchandise, and the cost of transporting goods intended for resale into the firm are also adjustments made directly to the inventory account. With a periodic inventory system, inventory-related items are recorded in temporary holding accounts that are closed to Inventory at the end of the period. The closing entries for a periodic system involve closing Purchases, Freight In, Purchase Returns, and Purchase Discounts to Inventory, and then adjusting the inventory account balance to reflect the appropriate amount given the results of the ending inventory physical count.

3 **Calculate cost of goods sold using the results of an inventory count and understand the impact of errors in ending inventory on reported cost of goods sold.** Obtaining an accurate inventory amount involves counting the physical units and then properly computing the cost of those units. Special care must be taken in dealing with goods in transit and consigned goods. When a perpetual inventory system is used, the ending inventory count provides an opportunity to compute inventory shrinkage. When ending inventory is not correctly counted, both cost of goods sold and net income will be reported incorrectly. For example, an overstatement in ending inventory leads to an overstatement in reported net income.

4 **Apply the four inventory cost flow alternatives: specific identification, FIFO, LIFO, and average cost.** The four major costing methods used in accounting for inventories are specific identification, FIFO, LIFO, and average cost. Each of these may result in different dollar amounts of ending inventory, cost of goods sold, gross margin, and net income. A firm may choose any costing alternative without regard to the way goods physically flow through that firm. With FIFO, the oldest units are assumed to be sold first; with LIFO, the newest units are assumed to be sold first. LIFO matches current revenues and current expenses in the income statement; FIFO results in current values being reported in

the balance sheet. During an inflationary period, LIFO provides the lowest reported income and, therefore, lower taxes.

5 **Use financial ratios to evaluate a company's inventory level.** Companies assess how well their inventory is being managed by using two ratios: (1) inventory turnover and (2) number of days' sales in inventory. Inventory turnover is computed as cost of goods sold divided by average inventory; it tells how many times during the period the company turned over, or replenished, its inventory. The number of days' sales in inventory is computed by dividing 365 by the inventory turnover value. A company's choice of inventory cost flow assumption can significantly affect the values of these inventory ratios. The sum of the average collection period and the number of days' sales in inventory is the length of time between the purchase of inventory and the collection of cash from the sale of that inventory. Comparing this sum to the number of days' purchases in accounts payable reveals how much of a company's operating cycle it must finance through external financing.

eXpanded *Material*

6 **Analyze the impact of inventory errors on reported cost of goods sold.** Inventory errors can have a significant effect on reported cost of goods sold, gross margin, and net income. In addition, a misstatement of an ending inventory balance affects net income, both in the current year and in the next year. Errors in beginning and ending inventory have the opposite effect on cost of goods sold, gross margin, and net income. Errors in inventory correct themselves after two years if the physical count at the end of the second year shows the correct amount of ending inventory for that period.

7 **Describe the complications that arise when LIFO or average cost is used with a perpetual inventory system.** Using the average cost and LIFO inventory cost flow assumptions with a perpetual inventory system leads to some complications. These complications arise because the identity of the "last in" units changes with each new inventory purchase, as does the average cost of units purchased up to that point.

8 **Apply the lower-of-cost-or-market method of accounting for inventory.** Sometimes inventory must be reported at amounts below cost. This occurs (1) when inventory is damaged, used, or obsolete, or (2) when the replacement cost drops below the original inventory cost. In the first case, inventory is valued at a net realizable value; in the second, it is valued at the lower of cost or market. When lower-of-cost-or-market valuation is used, market is defined as the replacement cost of the inventory; in no case can the value be greater than the item's net realizable value (the ceiling) or less than net realizable value minus a normal profit (the floor).

9 **Explain the gross margin method of estimating inventories.** Although most firms take a physical count of inventory at the end of each year, they sometimes need to estimate the value of inventory prior to year-end. The gross margin method is a common technique for estimating the dollar amount of inventory. The historical gross margin percentage is used in conjunction with sales to estimate cost of goods sold. This estimated cost of goods sold amount is subtracted from cost of goods available for sale to yield an estimate of ending inventory.

key terms & concepts

average cost, 365
consignment, 355
cost of goods available for sale, 356
cost of goods sold, 353
FIFO (first in, first out), 365
finished goods, 354
FOB (free-on-board) destination, 355
FOB (free-on-board) shipping point, 355
inventory, 353
inventory shrinkage, 364
inventory turnover, 370

LIFO (last in, first out), 365
manufacturing overhead, 354
net purchases, 362
number of days' purchases in accounts payable, 372
number of days' sales in inventory, 371
periodic inventory system, 358
perpetual inventory system, 357
raw materials, 354
specific identification, 366
work in process, 354

ceiling, 379
floor, 379
gross margin method, 380
lower-of-cost-or-market (LCM) rule, 378
net realizable value, 378

review problems

Inventory Cost Flow Alternatives

Lehi Wholesale Distributors buys printers from manufacturers and sells them to office supply stores. During January 2006, its periodic inventory records showed the following:

Jan. 1 Beginning inventory consisted of 26 printers at $200 each.
    10 Purchased 10 printers at $220 each.
    15 Purchased 20 printers at $250 each.
    28 Purchased 9 printers at $270 each.
    31 Sold 37 printers.

Required:
Calculate ending inventory and cost of goods sold, using:

1. FIFO inventory.
2. LIFO inventory.
3. Average cost.

Solution
When computing ending inventory and cost of goods sold, it is usually easiest to get an overview first. The following calculations are helpful:

Beginning inventory, 26 units at $200 each	$ 5,200
Purchases: 10 units at $220	$ 2,200
20 units at $250	5,000
9 units at $270	2,430
Total purchases (39 units)	$ 9,630
Cost of goods available for sale (65 units)	$14,830
Less ending inventory (28 units)	?
Cost of goods sold (37 units)	?

Given a beginning inventory, only ending inventory and cost of goods sold will vary with the different inventory costing alternatives. Because ending inventory and cost of goods sold are complementary numbers whose sum must equal total goods available for sale, you can calculate only one of the two missing numbers in each case and then compute the other by subtracting the first number from goods available for sale. Thus, in the calculations that follow, we will always calculate ending inventory first.

1. FIFO Inventory

Since we know that 28 units are left in ending inventory, we look for the last 28 units purchased because the first units purchased would all be sold. The last 28 units purchased were:

9 units at $270 each on January 28 =	$2,430
19 units at $250 each on January 15 =	4,750
Ending inventory	$7,180

Ending inventory is $7,180, and cost of goods sold is $7,650 ($14,830 − $7,180).

2. LIFO Inventory

The first 28 units available would be considered the ending inventory (since the last ones purchased are the first ones sold). The first 28 units available were:

Beginning inventory: 26 units at $200 =	$5,200
January 10 purchase: 2 units at $220 =	440
Ending inventory	$5,640

Thus,

Cost of goods available for sale	$14,830
Ending inventory	5,640
Cost of goods sold	$ 9,190

3. Average Cost

The total cost of goods available for sale is divided by total units available for sale to get a weighted average cost:

$$\frac{\text{Cost of Goods Available for Sale}}{\text{Units Available for Sale}} = \frac{\$14,830}{65} = \$228.15 \text{ per Unit}$$

Cost of goods available for sale	$14,830
Less ending inventory (28 units at $228.15)	6,388
Cost of goods sold (37 units at $228.15)	$ 8,442

Note: With the average cost alternative, the computed amounts may vary slightly due to rounding.

Perpetual Inventory Cost Flow Alternatives

Using the above example, we assume Lehi Wholesale Distributors buys printers from manufacturers and sells them to office supply stores. During January 2006, its inventory records showed the following:

Jan. 1   Beginning inventory consisted of 26 printers at $200 each.
     10   Purchased 10 printers at $220 each.
     12   Sold 15 printers.
     15   Purchased 20 printers at $250 each.
     17   Sold 14 printers.
     19   Sold 8 printers.
     28   Purchased 9 printers at $270 each.

Required:
Calculate ending inventory and cost of goods sold, using:

1. Perpetual FIFO inventory.
2. Perpetual LIFO inventory.
3. Perpetual average cost.

Solution

When computing ending inventory and cost of goods sold, it is usually easiest to get an overview first. The following calculations are helpful:

Beginning inventory, 26 units at $200 each	$ 5,200
Purchases: 10 units at $220	$ 2,200
20 units at $250	5,000
9 units at $270	2,430
Total purchases (39 units)	$ 9,630
Cost of goods available for sale (65 units)	$14,830
Less ending inventory (28 units)	?
Cost of goods sold (37 units)	?

Given a beginning inventory, only ending inventory and cost of goods sold will vary with the different inventory costing alternatives. Because ending inventory and cost of goods sold are complementary numbers whose sum must equal total goods available for sale, you can calculate only one of the two missing numbers in each case, and then compute the other by subtracting the first number from goods available for sale. Thus, in the calculations that follow, we will always calculate ending inventory first.

1. Perpetual FIFO Inventory

With this alternative, records must be maintained throughout the period, as shown. The final calculation is:

Cost of goods available for sale	$14,830
Ending inventory [(19 × $250) + (9 × $270)]	7,180
Cost of goods sold	$ 7,650

PERPETUAL FIFO CALCULATIONS

	Purchased			Sold			Remaining		
Date	Number of Units	Unit Cost	Total Cost	Number of Units	Unit Cost	Total Cost	Number of Units	Unit Cost	Total Cost
Beginning inventory							26	$200	$5,200
January 10	10	$220	$2,200				36	26 at $200	$7,400
								10 at $220	
12				15	15 at $200	$3,000	21	11 at $200	$4,400
								10 at $220	
15	20	$250	5,000				41	11 at $200	$9,400
								10 at $220	
								20 at $250	
17				14	11 at $200	2,860	27	7 at $220	$6,540
					3 at $220			20 at $250	
19				8	7 at $220	1,790	19	19 at $250	$4,750
					1 at $250				
28	9	$270	2,430	—			28	19 at $250	$7,180
								9 at $270	
Totals	39		$9,630	37		$7,650			

2. Perpetual LIFO Inventory

With this alternative, as shown below, the calculation is:

Cost of goods available for sale $14,830
Ending inventory 6,230
Cost of goods sold . . . . $ 8,600

PERPETUAL LIFO CALCULATIONS

	Purchased			Sold			Remaining		
Date	Number of Units	Unit Cost	Total Cost	Number of Units	Unit Cost	Total Cost	Number of Units	Unit Cost	Total Cost
Beginning inventory							26	$200	$5,200
January 10	10	$220	$2,200				36	26 at $200	$7,400
								10 at $220	
12				15	10 at $220	$3,200	21	21 at $200	$4,200
					5 at $200				
15	20	$250	5,000				41	21 at $200	$9,200
								20 at $250	
17				14	14 at $250	3,500	27	21 at $200	$5,700
								6 at $250	
19				8	6 at $250	1,900	19	19 at $200	$3,800
					2 at $200				
28	9	$270	2,430	—			28	19 at $200	$6,230
								9 at $270	
Totals	39		$9,630	37		$8,600			

3. Perpetual Average Cost

With this alternative, a new average cost of inventory items must be calculated each time a purchase is made, as shown in the following table:

Cost of goods available for sale	$14,830
Ending inventory	6,748
Cost of goods sold	$ 8,082

PERPETUAL AVERAGE COST CALCULATIONS

	Purchased	Sold	Remaining	Computations
Beginning inventory			26 units at $200.00 = $5,200	
January 10	10 units at $220 = $2,200		36 units at $205.56 = $7,400	$5,200 + $2,200 = $7,400; $7,400 ÷ 36 = $205.56
12		15 units at $205.56 = $3,083	21 units at $205.56 = $4,317	
15	20 units at $250 = $5,000		41 units at $227.24 = $9,317	$4,317 + $5,000 = $9,317; $9,317 ÷ 41 = $227.24
17		14 units at $227.24 = $3,181	27 units at $227.24 = $6,135	
19		8 units at $227.24 = $1,818	19 units at $227.24 = $4,318	
28	9 units at $270 = $2,430		28 units at $241.00 = $6,748	$4,318 + $2,430 = $6,748; $6,748 ÷ 28 = $241.00

discussion questions

1. In wholesale and retail companies, inventory is composed of the items that have been purchased for resale. What types of inventory does a manufacturing firm have?
2. What comprises the cost of inventory?
3. Why is it more difficult to account for the inventory of a manufacturing firm than for that of a merchandising firm?
4. Who owns merchandise during shipment under the terms FOB shipping point?
5. When is the cost of inventory transferred from an asset to an expense?
6. Which inventory method (perpetual or periodic) provides better control over a firm's inventory?
7. Is the accounting for purchase discounts and purchase returns the same with the perpetual and the periodic inventory methods? If not, what are the differences?
8. Are the costs of transporting inventory into and out of a firm treated the same way? If not, what are the differences?
9. Why is it usually important to take advantage of purchase discounts?
10. Why are the closing entries for inventory under a periodic system more complicated than those for a perpetual system?
11. Why is it necessary to physically count inventory when the perpetual inventory method is being used?
12. What adjusting entries to Inventory are required when the perpetual inventory method is used?
13. What is the effect on net income when goods held on consignment are included in the ending inventory balance?
14. Explain the difference between cost flow and the movement of goods.
15. Which inventory cost flow alternative results in paying the least amount of taxes when prices are rising?
16. Would a firm ever be prohibited from using one inventory costing alternative for tax purposes and another for financial reporting purposes?
17. Why is it necessary to know which inventory cost flow alternative is being used before the financial performances of different firms can be compared?
18. What can the inventory turnover ratio tell us?

19. Is net income under- or overstated when purchased merchandise is counted and included in the inventory balance but not recorded as a purchase?
20. Is net income under- or overstated if inventory is sold and shipped but not recorded as a sale?

21. Why do the LIFO and average cost inventory cost flow assumptions result in different inventory numbers for the perpetual and periodic inventory methods?
22. When should inventory be valued at its net realizable value?
23. When should inventory be valued at the lower of cost or market?
24. When firms cannot count their inventory, how do they determine how much inventory is on hand for the financial statements?

practice exercises

Practice 8-1

Inventory Identification
Which one of the following is *not* an example of inventory?

a. Cranes at a construction site
b. Books on the shelves of a bookstore
c. Apples in a supermarket
d. Screws to be used in assembling tables at a carpentry shop
e. Computer software for sale at a computer store

Practice 8-2

Costs Included in Inventory
Which one of the following costs is *not* included in inventory?

a. Salaries paid to assembly workers
b. Direct materials used in assembly
c. Salary paid to the company president
d. Rent paid for use of the company factory
e. Salary paid to the factory supervisor

Practice 8-3

Goods in Transit
Collin Wholesale sold $2,500 inventory to Jennifer Company on December 27, year 1, with shipping terms of FOB destination. The inventory arrived on January 2, year 2. Which company owns the inventory at year-end (December 31, year 1)?

Practice 8-4

Computing Cost of Goods Sold
Using the following data, compute cost of goods sold.

Inventory, December 31	$ 45,000
Inventory, January 1	52,000
Cash, December 31	10,000
Purchases during the year	255,000
Sales during the year	480,000

Practice 8-5

Perpetual and Periodic Inventory Systems
For each of the following businesses, indicate whether the business would be more likely to use a perpetual or a periodic inventory system.

a. Automobile dealer
b. Summer snow-cone stand
c. Supermarket
d. Large appliance retailer
e. Newsstand
f. Discount clothing retailer

Practice 8-6

Inventory Purchases

The company purchased (on account) 250 tables to be resold to customers. The cost of each table was $100. Make the journal entry to record this transaction under (1) a perpetual inventory system and (2) a periodic inventory system.

Practice 8-7

Transportation Costs

The company incurred $690 in shipping costs related to the inventory purchases in Practice 8-6. The company paid for the shipping costs in cash. Make the journal entry necessary to record this transaction under (1) a perpetual inventory system and (2) a periodic inventory system.

Practice 8-8

Purchase Returns

The company returned 20 of the tables purchased in Practice 8-6 because of defects in assembly. Make the journal entry necessary to record this return under (1) a perpetual inventory system and (2) a periodic inventory system.

Practice 8-9

Purchase Discounts

The company paid for the tables purchased in Practice 8-6 (less the tables returned in Practice 8-8). Because the company paid within 10 days, it received a 2% discount on the purchase. Make the journal entry necessary to record this transaction under (1) a perpetual inventory system and (2) a periodic inventory system.

Practice 8-10

Sales

The company sold 50 tables on account for $160 each. Make the journal entry or entries necessary to record this transaction under (1) a perpetual inventory system and (2) a periodic inventory system. Don't forget the impact of the 2% discount described in Practice 8-9 and the transportation costs mentioned in Practice 8-7.

Practice 8-11

Sales Returns

A dissatisfied customer returned eight of the tables that were sold in Practice 8-10. Make the journal entry or entries necessary to record this transaction under (1) a perpetual inventory system and (2) a periodic inventory system.

Practice 8-12

Closing Inventory Entries for a Periodic System

Refer to the data in Practice 8-6 through Practice 8-11. Assume the beginning balance in the inventory account was $0 for the periodic inventory system. A physical count of the inventory at the end of the period shows the ending balance of inventory is $18,830. Prepare the necessary entries for a periodic inventory system (1) to close the temporary accounts to the inventory account and (2) to adjust the inventory account to the appropriate ending balance.

Practice 8-13

Inventory Shrinkage

The company's perpetual inventory records show that the ending inventory balance should be $182,000. However, a physical count of the inventory reveals the true ending balance of inventory to be $178,500. Prepare the journal entry necessary to record inventory shrinkage for the period.

Practice 8-14

Computing Cost of Goods Sold with a Periodic System

The company uses a periodic inventory system. Beginning inventory was $6,000. Net purchases (including freight in, purchase returns, and purchase discounts) were $23,000. The physical count of inventory at the end of the year revealed ending inventory to be $7,500. Compute cost of goods sold.

Practice 8-15

Errors in Ending Inventory

The company uses a periodic inventory system and *overstated* its ending inventory by $20,000. How will this inventory error affect reported net income for the company?

Practice 8-16

Specific Identification Inventory Cost Flow

The company reports the following activity during October related to its inventory of cameras:

Oct. 1   Beginning inventory consisted of 8 cameras costing $100 each.
3   Purchased 12 cameras costing $110 each.
14   Purchased 7 cameras costing $115 each.
20   Purchased 15 cameras costing $125 each.
29   Sold 26 cameras for $150 each.

The 26 cameras sold on October 29 consisted of the following: 4 cameras from the beginning inventory, 5 cameras purchased on October 3, 3 cameras purchased on October 14, and 14 cameras purchased on October 20. Determine (1) the cost of goods sold for the month and (2) the ending inventory balance for October 31 using the specific identification cost flow assumption.

Practice 8-17

FIFO Cost Flow Assumption

Refer to the data in Practice 8-16. Determine (1) the cost of goods sold for the month and (2) the ending inventory balance for October 31 using the FIFO cost flow assumption.

Practice 8-18

LIFO Cost Flow Assumption

Refer to the data in Practice 8-16. Determine (1) the cost of goods sold for the month and (2) the ending inventory balance for October 31 using the LIFO cost flow assumption.

Practice 8-19

Average Cost Flow Assumption

Refer to the data in Practice 8-16. Determine (1) the cost of goods sold for the month and (2) the ending inventory balance for October 31 using the average cost flow assumption. Round unit costs to the nearest tenth of a cent.

Practice 8-20

Inventory Turnover

Using the following data, compute inventory turnover.

Inventory, December 31, year 1	$ 45,000
Cost of goods sold	295,000
Sales	429,000
Inventory, January 1, year 1	51,000

Practice 8-21

Number of Days' Sales in Inventory

Refer to the data in Practice 8-20. Compute number of days' sales in inventory.

Practice 8-22

Number of Days' Purchases in Accounts Payable

Using the following data, compute number of days' purchases in accounts payable.

Accounts payable, December 31, year 1	$ 52,000
Cost of goods sold	358,000
Accounts payable, January 1, year 1	46,000
Purchases	364,000

Practice 8-23

Inventory Errors—Multiple Years

At the beginning of year 1, the company's inventory level was stated correctly. At the end of year 1, inventory was *understated* by $2,000. At the end of year 2, inventory was *overstated* by $450. Reported net income was $3,000 in year 1 and $3,000 in year 2. Compute the correct amount of net income in year 1.

Practice 8-24

Inventory Errors—Multiple Years

Refer to Practice 8-23. Compute the correct amount of net income in year 2.

Practice 8-25

LIFO and a Perpetual Inventory System

The company reported the following inventory data for the year:

	Units	Cost per Unit
Beginning inventory	300	$17.50
Purchases:		
July 15	900	18.00
October 11	1,200	18.25

Units remaining at year-end: 300

Sales occurred as follows:

	Units Sold
January 16	200
July 23	600
November 1	1,300
Total	2,100

Compute (1) cost of goods sold and (2) ending inventory making a LIFO cost flow assumption. The company uses a *perpetual* inventory system.

Practice 8-26

Average Cost and a Perpetual Inventory System

Refer to Practice 8-25. Compute (1) cost of goods sold and (2) ending inventory making an average cost assumption. The company uses a *perpetual* inventory system.

Practice 8-27

Lower of Cost or Market

The following information pertains to the company's ending inventory:

	Original Cost	Net Realizable Value	Replacement Cost	Normal Profit
Item A	$ 560	$ 650	$ 600	$100
Item B	700	740	550	150
Item C	1,180	1,150	1,120	300

Apply lower-of-cost-or-market accounting to each inventory item individually. What total amount should be reported as inventory in the balance sheet?

Practice 8-28

Recording an Inventory Write-Down

The company started business at the beginning of year 1. The company applies the lower-of-cost-or-market (LCM) rule to its inventory as a whole. Inventory cost and market value as of the end of year 1 were as follows:

(continued)

	Cost	Market Value
Year 1	$1,200	$900

The market value number already includes consideration of the replacement cost, the ceiling, and the floor. Make the journal entry necessary to record the LCM adjustment at the end of year 1.

Practice 8-29

Estimating Inventory

On August 17, the company's inventory was destroyed in a hurricane-related flood. For insurance purposes, the company must reliably estimate the amount of inventory on hand on August 17. The company uses a periodic inventory system. The following data have been assembled:

Inventory, January 1	$1,000,000
Purchases, January 1–August 17	3,700,000
Sales, January 1–August 17	5,000,000
Historical gross profit percentages:	
Last year	65%
Two years ago	70%

Estimate the company's inventory as of August 17 using (1) last year's gross profit percentage and (2) the gross profit percentage from two years ago.

e xercises

Exercise 8-1

Goods on Consignment

Company A has consignment arrangements with Supplier B and with Customer C. In particular, Supplier B ships some of its goods to Company A on consignment, and Company A ships some of its goods to Customer C on consignment. At the end of 2006, Company A's accounting records showed:

Goods on consignment from Supplier B	$ 8,000
Goods on consignment with Customer C	10,000

1. If a physical count of inventory reveals that $30,000 of goods are on hand, what amount of ending inventory should be reported?
2. If the amount of the beginning inventory for the year was $27,000 and purchases during the year were $59,000, then what is the cost of goods sold for the year? (Assume the ending inventory from question 1.)
3. If, instead of these facts, Company A had only $4,000 of goods on consignment with Customer C, but had $10,000 of consigned goods from Supplier B, and physical goods on hand totaled $36,000, what would the correct amount of the ending inventory be?
4. With respect to question 3, if beginning inventory totaled $24,000 and the cost of goods sold was $47,500, what were the purchases?

Exercise 8-2

Recording Sales Transactions—Perpetual Inventory Method

On June 24, 2006, Hansen Company sold merchandise to Jill Selby for $80,000 with terms 2/10, n/30. On June 30, Selby paid $39,200, receiving the cash discount on her payment, and returned $16,000 of merchandise, claiming that it did not meet contract terms.

Assuming that Hansen uses the perpetual inventory method, record the necessary journal entries on June 24 and June 30. The cost of merchandise to Hansen Company is 70% of its selling price.

Exercise 8-3

Spreadsheet

Perpetual Inventory Method

Orser Furniture purchases and sells dining room furniture. Its management uses the perpetual method of inventory accounting. Journalize the following transactions that occurred during October 2006:

Oct. 2 Purchased on account $27,000 of inventory with payment terms 2/10, n/30, and paid $650 in cash to have it shipped from the vendor's warehouse to the Orser showroom.

5 Sold inventory costing $4,900 for $8,250 on account.

10 Paid $13,950 on account (from October 2 purchase).

14 Returned two damaged tables purchased on October 2 (costing $550 each) to the vendor.

19 Received payment of $4,560 from customers.

20 Paid the balance of the account from October 2 purchase.

22 Sold inventory costing $3,800 for $5,200 on account.

24 A customer returned a dining room set that she decided didn't match her home. She paid $3,250 for it, and its cost to Orser was $1,800.

Assuming the balance in the inventory account is $12,000 on October 1, and no other transactions relating to inventory occurred during the month, what is the inventory balance at the end of October?

Exercise 8-4

Adjusting Inventory (Perpetual Method)

Deer Company's perpetual inventory records show an inventory balance of $120,000. Deer Company's records also show cost of goods sold totaling $240,000. A physical count of inventory on December 31, 2006, showed $92,000 of ending inventory.

Adjust the inventory records assuming that the perpetual inventory method is used.

Exercise 8-5

Recording Sales Transactions—Periodic Inventory Method

On June 24, 2006, Mowen Company sold merchandise to Jack Simpson for $80,000 with terms 2/10, n/30. On June 30, Simpson paid $39,200, receiving the cash discount on his payment, and returned $16,000 of merchandise, claiming that it did not meet contract terms.

Assuming that Mowen Company uses the periodic inventory method, record the necessary journal entries on June 24 and June 30.

Exercise 8-6

Adjusting Inventory and Closing Entries (Periodic Method)

As of December 31, 2006, Deer Company had the following account balances:

Inventory (beginning)	$120,000
Purchases	220,000
Purchase returns	4,000

A physical count of inventory on December 31, 2006, showed $92,000 of ending inventory. Prepare the closing entries that are needed to adjust the inventory records and close the related purchases accounts, assuming that the periodic inventory method is used.

Exercise 8-7

Cost of Goods Sold Calculation

The accounts of Berrett Company have the following balances for 2006:

Purchases	$520,000
Inventory, January 1, 2006	80,000
Purchase returns	15,280
Purchase discounts	1,760
Freight in	24,800
Freight out (selling expense)	4,800
Cash	8,000

(continued)

The inventory count on December 31, 2006, is $96,000. Using the information given, compute the cost of goods sold for Berrett Company for 2006.

Exercise 8-8

Spreadsheet

Cost of Goods Sold Calculations

Complete the Cost of Goods Sold section for the income statements of the following five companies:

	Able Company	Baker Company	Carter Company	Delmont Company	Eureka Company
Beginning inventory	$16,000	$24,800	_____	_____	$19,200
Purchases	26,500	_____	$43,000	$89,500	_____
Purchase returns	_____	1,000	1,800	200	2,200
Cost of goods available for sale . .	42,100	_____	58,300	_____	81,500
Ending inventory	_____	22,200	15,200	28,800	_____
Cost of goods sold	33,400	67,200	_____	93,400	68,400

Exercise 8-9

P.A.S.S.
Power Accounting System Software

Journalizing Inventory Transactions

Gardner Machinery uses the periodic method of inventory accounting.

1. Journalize the following transactions relating to the company's purchases in 2006:

Jan. 24 Purchased $12,000 of inventory on credit, terms 2/10, n/30.
    30 Paid $11,760 to pay off the debt from the January 24 purchase.
Mar. 14 Purchased $165,000 of inventory on credit, terms 2/10, n/30. Paid $650 in cash for transportation.
Apr. 1 Returned defective machinery worth $35,000 from the March 14 purchase to manufacturer.
    13 Paid $130,000 to pay off the debt from the March 14 purchase.

2. Assuming these were the only purchases in 2006, compute the cost of goods sold. Beginning inventory was $18,500 and ending inventory was $25,750.

Exercise 8-10

Adjusting Inventory Records for Physical Counts

Spartacas, Inc., which uses the perpetual inventory method, recently had an agency count its inventory of frozen chickens. The agency left the following inventory sheet:

Type of Merchandise	Date Purchased	Quantity on Hand	Unit Cost	Inventory Amount
Chicken grade A	2/12/06	30	$5.00	(a)
Chicken grade B	2/18/06	16	(b)	$54.40
Chicken grade C	2/08/06	(c)	$2.50	$60.00
Chicken grade D	2/15/06	46	(d)	$52.90

Complete the inventory calculations for Spartacas (items a–d) and provide the journal entry necessary to adjust ending inventory, if necessary. The balance in Inventory before the physical count was $305.05.

Exercise 8-11

Specific Identification Method

E's Diamond Shop is computing its inventory and cost of goods sold for November 2006. At the beginning of the month, these items were in stock:

	Quantity	Cost	Total
Ring A	8	$600	$ 4,800
Ring A	10	650	6,500
Ring B	5	300	1,500
Ring B	6	350	2,100
Ring B	3	450	1,350
Ring C	7	200	1,400
Ring C	8	250	2,000
			$19,650

During the month, the shop purchased four type A rings at $600, two type B rings at $450, and five type C rings at $300 and made the following sales:

Ring Type		Quantity Sold	Price	Cost
A	....	2	$1,000	$600
A	....	3	1,050	600
A	....	1	1,200	650
B	....	2	850	450
B	....	2	800	350
C	....	4	450	200
C	....	3	500	250
C	....	1	550	250

Because of the high cost per item, E's uses specific identification inventory costing.

1. Calculate the cost of goods sold and ending inventory balances for November.
2. Calculate the gross margin for the month.

Exercise 8-12

Inventory Costing Methods

For each of the descriptions listed below, identify the inventory costing method to which it applies. The costing methods are: average cost, LIFO, and FIFO.

1. The value of ending inventory does not include the cost of the most recently acquired goods.
2. In a period of rising prices, cost of goods sold is highest.
3. In a period of rising prices, ending inventory is highest.
4. Ending inventory is between the levels of the other two methods.
5. The balance of the inventory account may be unrealistic because inventory on hand is valued at old prices.

Exercise 8-13

FIFO and LIFO Inventory Costing

Jefferson's Jewelry Store is computing its inventory and cost of goods sold for November 2006. At the beginning of the month, the following jewelry items were in stock (rings were purchased in the order listed):

(continued)

	Quantity	Cost	Total
Ring A	8	$600	$ 4,800
Ring A	10	650	6,500
Ring B	5	300	1,500
Ring B	6	350	2,100
Ring B	3	450	1,350
Ring C	7	200	1,400
Ring C	8	250	2,000
			$19,650

During the month, the following rings were purchased: four type A rings at $600, two type B rings at $450, and five type C rings at $300. Also during the month, these sales were made:

Ring Type		Quantity Sold	Price
A		2	$1,000
A		3	1,050
A		1	1,200
B		2	850
B		2	800
C		4	450
C		3	500
C		1	550

Jefferson's uses the periodic inventory method. Calculate the cost of goods sold and ending inventory balances for November using FIFO and LIFO.

Exercise 8-14

FIFO, LIFO, and Average Cost Calculations (Periodic Inventory Method)
The following transactions took place with respect to Model J computers in Osmond's Computer Store during November 2006:

Nov.	1	Beginning inventory	50 computers at $1,100
	5	Purchase of Model J computers	12 computers at $1,250
	11	Purchase of Model J computers	17 computers at $1,300
	24	Purchase of Model J computers	13 computers at $1,450
	30	Sale of Model J computers	42 computers at $2,500

Assuming the periodic inventory method, compute cost of goods sold and ending inventory using the following inventory costing alternatives: (a) FIFO, (b) LIFO, and (c) average cost.

Exercise 8-15

Inventory Ratios
The following data are available for 2006, regarding the inventory of two companies:

	Atkins Computers	Burbank Electronics
Beginning inventory	$ 40,000	$ 80,000
Ending inventory	48,000	95,000
Cost of goods sold	690,000	910,000

Compute inventory turnover and number of days' sales in inventory for both companies. Which company is handling its inventory more efficiently?

Exercise 8-16

Analysis of the Operating Cycle

The following information was taken from the records of Dallen Company for the year 2007:

Sales	$600,000
Beginning inventory	$114,000
Ending inventory	$87,000
Beginning accounts receivable	$68,000
Average collection period	44 days
Beginning accounts payable	$36,000
Ending accounts payable	$42,000
Gross profit percentage	37%

1. Compute the number of days' sales in inventory.
2. Compute the ending balance in Accounts Receivable.
3. Compute the number of days' purchases in accounts payable.
4. How many days elapse, on average, between the time Dallen must pay its suppliers for inventory purchases and the time Dallen collects cash from its customers for the sale of that same purchased inventory?
5. Repeat the computations in (1), (2), (3), and (4) using the end-of-year balance sheet balances rather than the average balances.

Exercise 8-17

Inventory Errors

As the accountant for Mt. Pleasant Enterprises, you are in the process of preparing the income statement for the year ended December 31, 2006. In doing so, you have noticed that merchandise costing $2,000 was sold for $4,000 on December 31.

Before the effects of the $4,000 sale were taken into account, the relevant income statement figures were:

Sales revenue	$80,000
Beginning inventory	18,000
Purchases	44,000
Ending inventory	13,000

1. Prepare a partial income statement through gross margin under each of the following three assumptions:
   a. The sale is recorded in the 2006 accounting record; the inventory is included in the ending physical inventory count.
   b. The sale is recorded in 2006; the inventory is not included in ending inventory.
   c. The sale is not recorded in the 2006 accounting records; the merchandise is not included in the ending inventory count.
2. Under the given circumstances, which of the three assumptions is correct?
3. Which assumption overstates gross margin (and therefore net income)?

Exercise 8-18

Spreadsheet

FIFO, LIFO, and Average Cost Calculations (Perpetual Inventory Method)

The July 2006 inventory records of Mario's Bookstore showed the following:

July	1	Beginning inventory	28,000 at $2.00 = $56,000
	5	Sold	4,000
	13	Purchased	6,000 at $2.25 = 13,500
	17	Sold	3,000
	25	Purchased	8,000 at $2.50 = 20,000
	27	Sold	5,000
			$89,500

(continued)

1. Using the perpetual inventory method, compute the ending inventory and cost of goods sold balances with (a) FIFO, (b) LIFO, and (c) average cost. Compute unit costs to the nearest cent.
2. Which of the three alternatives is best? Why?

Exercise 8-19

Lower of Cost or Market

Prepare the necessary journal entries to account for the purchases and year-end adjustments of the inventory of Payson Manufacturing Company. All purchases are made on account. Payson uses the periodic inventory method.

1. Purchased 50 standard widgets for $8 each to sell at $14 per unit.
2. Purchased 15 deluxe widgets at $20 each to sell for $30 per unit.
3. At the end of the year, the standard widgets could be purchased for $9 and are selling for $15.
4. At the end of the year, the deluxe widgets could be purchased for $10 and are selling for $16 per unit. Selling costs are $4 per unit, and normal profit is $6 per unit. Inventory is 15 units.
5. At the end of the second year, standard widgets could be purchased for $6 and are selling for $8. Selling costs are $1 per widget, and normal profit is $2 per widget. Inventory is 50 units.
6. At the end of the second year, the deluxe widgets could be purchased for $9 and are selling for $20. Selling costs and normal profit remain as in (4). Inventory is 15 units.

Exercise 8-20

Lower of Cost or Market

Broderick Company sells lumber. Inventory cost data per 1,000 board feet of lumber for the Broderick Company are as follows:

Item	Plywood	Oak	Pine	Redwood
Quantity on hand	25	20	43	12
Original cost	$600	$2,000	$800	$1,400
Current replacement cost	600	1,800	700	1,800
Net realizable value	500	1,900	800	1,600
Net realizable value minus normal profit	400	1,850	600	1,300

1. By what amount, if any, should each item (considered separately) be written down?
2. Make the appropriate journal entry (or entries):
   a. Assuming that each inventory item is considered separately.
   b. Assuming that LCM is applied to total inventory.

Exercise 8-21

Gross Margin Method of Estimating Inventory

Jason Company needs to estimate the inventory balance for its quarterly financial statements. The periodic inventory method is used. Records show that quarterly sales totaled $400,000, beginning inventory was $80,000, and net purchases totaled $280,000; the historical gross margin percentage has averaged approximately 40%.

1. What is the approximate amount of ending inventory?
2. If a physical count shows only $100,000 in inventory, what could be the explanation for the difference?

Exercise 8-22

Estimating Inventory Amounts

Erin's Boutique was recently destroyed by fire. For insurance purposes, she must determine the value of the destroyed inventory. She knows the following information about her 2006 operations before the fire occurred:

Beginning inventory	$ 5,750
Net purchases	58,000
Sales	91,300
Profit margin	35%

Estimate the cost of Erin's destroyed inventory.

Exercise 8-23

Estimating Inventory

Ted Smyth manages an electronics store. He suspects that some employees are stealing items from inventory. Determine the cost of the missing inventory. The following information is available from the accounting records:

Beginning inventory	$ 300,000
Sales	2,000,000
Net purchases	1,600,000
Actual ending inventory	450,000
Historical profit margin	30%

 p r o b l e m s

Problem 8-1

What Should Be Included in Inventory?

Demetrius is trying to compute the inventory balance for the December 31, 2005, financial statements of his automotive parts shop. He has computed a tentative balance of $52,600 but suspects that several adjustments still need to be made. In particular, he believes that the following could affect his inventory balance:

a. A shipment of goods that cost $3,000 was received on December 28, 2005. It was properly recorded as a purchase in 2005 but not counted with the ending inventory.
b. Another shipment of goods (FOB destination) was received on January 2, 2006, and cost $800. It was properly recorded as a purchase in 2006 but was counted with 2005's ending inventory.
c. A $2,800 shipment of goods to a customer on January 3 was recorded as a sale in 2006 but was not included in the December 31, 2005, ending inventory balance. The goods cost $2,000.
d. The company had goods costing $6,000 on consignment with a customer, and $5,000 of merchandise was on consignment from a vendor. Neither amount was included in the $52,600 figure.
e. The following amounts represent merchandise that was in transit on December 31, 2005, and recorded as purchases and sales in 2005 but not included in the December 31 inventory.
   1. Ordered by Demetrius, $1,800, FOB destination.
   2. Ordered by Demetrius, $600, FOB shipping point.
   3. Sold by Demetrius, cost $4,000, FOB shipping point.
   4. Sold by Demetrius, cost $4,600, FOB destination.

Required:
1. Determine the correct amount of ending inventory at December 31, 2005.
2. Assuming net purchases (before any adjustment, if any) totaled $86,400 and beginning inventory (January 1, 2005) totaled $31,600, determine the cost of goods sold in 2005.

Problem 8-2

P.A.S.S.
Power Accounting System Software

Perpetual and Periodic Journal Entries

The following transactions for Goodmonth Tire Company occurred during the month of March 2006:

a. Purchased 500 automobile tires on account at a cost of $40 each for a total of $20,000.
b. Purchased 300 truck tires on account at a cost of $80 each for a total of $24,000.
c. Returned 12 automobile tires to the supplier because they were defective.
d. Paid for the automobile tires.
e. Paid for half the truck tires.
f. Paid the remaining balance owed on the truck tires.
g. Sold on account 400 automobile tires at a price of $90 each for a total of $36,000.
h. Sold on account 200 truck tires at a price of $150 each for a total of $30,000.
i. Accepted return of 7 automobile tires from dissatisfied customers.

(continued)

Required:
1. Prepare journal entries to account for the above transactions assuming a periodic inventory system.
2. Prepare journal entries to account for the above transactions assuming a perpetual inventory system.
3. Assume that inventory levels at the beginning of March (before these transactions) were 100 automobile tires that cost $40 each and 70 truck tires that cost $80 each. Also, assume that a physical count of inventory at the end of March revealed that 184 automobile tires and 164 truck tires were on hand. Given these inventory amounts, prepare the closing entries to account for inventory and related accounts as of the end of March.

Problem 8-3

*S*preadsheet

Income Statement Calculations

Criddle Company has gross sales of 175% of cost of goods sold. It has also provided the following information for the calendar year 2006:

Inventory balance, January 1, 2006	$ 25,000
Total cost of goods available for sale	75,000
Sales returns	3,250
Purchase returns	1,250
Freight in	500
Sales (net of returns)	101,750
Operating expenses	6,750

Using the available information, compute the following. (Ignore income taxes.)

Required:
1. Gross sales for 2006.
2. Net purchases and gross purchases for 2006.
3. Cost of goods sold for 2006.
4. Inventory balance at December 31, 2006.
5. Gross margin for 2006.
6. Net income for 2006.

Problem 8-4

Income Statement Calculations

	Company A	Company B	Company C	Company D
Sales revenue	$2,000	(4) _____	$480	$1,310
Beginning inventory	200	76	0	600
Purchases	(1) _____	423	480	249
Purchase returns	(20)	(19)	(0)	(8) _____
Ending inventory	300	110	(6) _____	195
Cost of goods sold	1,200	370	(7) _____	(9) _____
Gross margin	(2) _____	(5) _____	155	(10) _____
Operating expenses	108	22	34	129
Net income	(3) _____	107	121	546

Required:
Complete the income statement calculations by filling in all missing numbers.

Problem 8-5

Inventory Cost Flow Alternatives

Stocks, Inc., sells weight-lifting equipment. The sales and inventory records of the company for January through March 2006 were as follows:

	Weight Sets	Unit Cost	Total Cost
Beginning inventory, Jan. 1	460	$30	$13,800
Purchase, Jan. 16	110	32	3,520
Sale, Jan. 25 ($45 per set)	216		
Purchase, Feb. 16	105	36	3,780
Sale, Feb. 27 ($40 per set)	307		
Purchase, March 10	150	28	4,200
Sale, March 30 ($50 per set)	190		

Required:

1. Determine the amounts for ending inventory, cost of goods sold, and gross margin under the following costing alternatives. Use the periodic inventory method, which means that all sales are assumed to occur at the end of the period no matter when they actually occurred. Round amounts to the nearest dollar.
   a. FIFO
   b. LIFO
   c. Average cost
2. **Interpretive Question:** Which alternative results in the highest gross margin? Why?

Problem 8-6

Periodic Inventory Cost Flow Method

Pippin Wholesale buys peaches from farmers and sells them to canneries. During May 2006, Pippin's inventory records showed the following:

			Cases	Price
May	1	Beginning inventory	4,250	$ 9.50
	4	Purchase	1,350	10.00
	9	Sale	920	18.45
	13	Purchase	980	10.50
	19	Sale	1,320	18.45
	26	Purchase	1,830	11.00
	30	Sale	2,050	18.45

Pippin Wholesale uses the periodic inventory method to account for its inventory, which means that all sales are assumed to occur at the end of the period no matter when they actually occurred.

Required:

Calculate the cost of goods sold and ending inventory using the following cost flow alternatives. (Calculate unit costs to the nearest cent.)

1. FIFO
2. LIFO
3. Average cost

Problem 8-7

Calculating and Interpreting Inventory Ratios

Captain Geech Boating Company sells fishing boats to fishermen. Its beginning and ending inventories for 2006 are $462 million and $653 million, respectively. It had cost of goods sold of $1,578 million for the year ended December 31, 2006. Merchant Marine Company also sells fishing boats. Its beginning and ending inventories for the year 2006 are $120 million and $90 million, respectively. It had cost of goods sold of $1,100 million for the year ended December 31, 2006.

(continued)

Required:

1. Calculate the inventory turnover and number of days' sales in inventory for the two companies.
2. **Interpretive Question:** Are the results of these ratios what you expected? Which company is managing its inventory more efficiently?

Problem 8-8

The Effect of Inventory Errors

The accountant for Steele Company reported the following accounting treatments for several purchase transactions (FOB shipping point) that took place near December 31, 2006, the company's year-end:

Date Inventory Was Shipped	Was the Purchase Recorded in the Books on or before December 31, 2006?	Amount	Was the Inventory Counted and Included in Inventory Balance on December 31, 2006?
2006:			
December 26	Yes	$1,100	Yes
December 29	Yes	800	No
December 31	No	1,800	Yes
2007:			
January 1	No	300	Yes
January 1	Yes	3,000	No
January 1	No	600	No

Required:

1. If Steele Company's records reported purchases and ending inventory balances of $80,800 and $29,800, respectively, for 2006, what would the proper amounts in these accounts have been?
2. What would be the correct amount of cost of goods sold for 2006, if the beginning inventory balance on January 1, 2006, was $20,200?
3. By how much would cost of goods sold be over- or understated if the corrections in question (1) were not made?

Problem 8-9

Correction of Inventory Errors

The annual reported income for Salazar Company for the years 2003–2006 is shown here. However, a review of the inventory records reveals inventory misstatements.

	2003	2004	2005	2006
Reported net income	$30,000	$40,000	$35,000	$45,000
Inventory overstatement, end of year		3,000		2,000
Inventory understatement, end of year	4,000		1,000	

Required:

Using the data provided, calculate the correct net income for each year.

Problem 8-10

The Effect of Inventory Errors

You have been hired as the accountant for Tracy Company, which uses the periodic inventory method. In reviewing the firm's records, you have noted what you think are several accounting errors made during the current year, 2006. These potential mistakes are listed as follows:

a. A $43,000 purchase of merchandise was properly recorded in the purchases account, but the related accounts payable account was credited for only $2,000.
b. A $3,500 shipment of merchandise received just before the end of the year was properly recorded in the purchases account but was not physically counted in the inventory and, hence, was excluded from the ending inventory balance.
c. A $6,700 purchase of merchandise was erroneously recorded as a $7,600 purchase.
d. A $500 purchase of merchandise was not recorded either as a purchase or as an account payable.
e. During the year, $1,200 of defective merchandise was sent back to a supplier. The original purchase had been recorded, but the merchandise return entry was not recorded.
f. During the physical inventory count, inventory that cost $400 was counted twice.

Required:
1. If the previous accountant had tentatively computed the 2006 gross margin to be $10,000, what would be the correct gross margin for the year?
2. If these mistakes are not corrected, by how much will the 2007 net income be in error?

Problem 8-11

Unifying Concepts: Inventory Cost Flow Alternatives

Stan's Wholesale buys canned tomatoes from canneries and sells them to retail markets. During August 2006, Stan's inventory records showed the following:

			Cases	Price
Aug.	1	Beginning inventory	4,100	$10.50
	4	Purchase	1,500	11.00
	9	Sale	950	19.95
	13	Purchase	1,000	11.00
	19	Sale	1,450	19.95
	26	Purchase	1,700	11.50
	30	Sale	1,900	19.95

Even though it requires more computational effort, Stan's uses the perpetual inventory method because management feels that the advantage of always having current knowledge of inventory levels justifies the extra cost.

Required:
Calculate the cost of goods sold and ending inventory using the following cost flow alternatives. (Calculate unit costs to the nearest cent.)

1. FIFO
2. LIFO
3. Average cost

Problem 8-12

Perpetual Inventory Cost Flow Alternatives

Pump-It, Inc., sells weight-lifting equipment. The sales and inventory records of the company for January through March 2006 were as follows:

(continued)

Spreadsheet

	Weight Sets	Unit Cost	Total Cost
Beginning inventory, Jan. 1	460	$30	$13,800
Purchase, Jan. 16	110	32	3,520
Sale, Jan. 25 ($45 per set)	216		
Purchase, Feb. 16	105	36	3,780
Sale, Feb. 27 ($40 per set)	307		
Purchase, March 10	150	28	4,200
Sale, March 30 ($50 per set)	190		

Required:

1. Determine the amounts for ending inventory, cost of goods sold, and gross margin under the following costing alternatives. Use the perpetual inventory method. Round amounts to the nearest dollar.
   a. FIFO
   b. LIFO
   c. Average cost (calculate unit costs to the nearest cent)
2. **Interpretive Question:** Which alternative results in the highest gross margin? Why?

Problem 8-13

Unifying Concepts: Inventory Estimation Method

Hawkes Clothing Store has the following information available:

	Cost	Selling Price	Other
Purchases during March 2006	$135,000	$200,000	
Inventory balance March 1, 2006	70,000	62,000	
Sales during March		230,000	
Average gross margin rate for the last three years			35%

Required:

1. On the basis of this information, estimate the cost of inventory on hand at March 31, 2006, using the gross margin method. Round to the nearest whole percent.
2. How accurate do you think this method is?

d iscussion cases

Case 8-1

Why Use a Perpetual System?

You are a consultant for the ABC Consulting Company. You have been hired by Eddie's Electronics, a company that owns 25 electronics stores selling radios, televisions, compact disc players, stereos, and other electronic equipment. Since the company began business 10 years ago, it has been using a periodic inventory system. However, Mark Eddie just returned from a seminar where some of his competitors told him he should be using the perpetual inventory method. Mr. Eddie is not sure he should believe his competitors. He wants you to advise him about his inventory choices and make a recommendation about the inventory method he should use.

Case 8-2

Should We Reduce Inventory?

It has now been two years since you advised Mr. Eddie to switch to the perpetual inventory method. He is very happy with the additional information he has about inventory levels and theft. He has hired you for advice once again. This time, Mr. Eddie has been to an inventory management seminar where he heard that most companies have too much money tied up in inventory. He wonders if his company could be much more profitable if it reduced its inventory levels. What would you tell him?

judgment call

Judgment 8-1

You Decide: Should inventory be recorded at cost or fair market value?
You recently ran into Bill Autograph, a friend from high school who has been really busy getting his sports collectible/memorabilia business off the ground. When he heard you were an accountant, he became very interested and wanted you to clarify something. One concept he seemed particularly confused about was the fact that when inventory is purchased, it is recorded on the books at cost but the books are not adjusted for subsequent increases in the value of the inventory. This concept is of particular importance to Bill because he often buys collectibles that will increase in value depending on how successful a particular player or team becomes. Can he record increases in the value of his sports memorabilia inventory?

Competency Enhancement Opportunities

▶ **Analyzing Real Company Information**
▶ **International Case**
▶ **Ethics Case**
▶ **Writing Assignment**

▶ **The Debate**
▶ **Cumulative Spreadsheet Project**
▶ **Internet Search**

The following additional assignments provide opportunities for students to develop critical thinking, ethical perspectives, oral and written communication skills, experience with electronic research, and teamwork through group and business activities.

▷ *Analyzing Real Company Information*

Analyzing 8-1 (Microsoft)
Using MICROSOFT's 2002 Form 10-K in Appendix A, answer the following questions:

1. What type of items compose Microsoft's inventory?
2. Review Microsoft's balance sheet to determine the amount of inventory on hand on June 30, 2002. Does this mean Microsoft has absolutely no inventory? Where would Microsoft's inventory probably be disclosed?
3. Review the management's discussion note disclosure on operating expenses, specifically the discussion relating to cost of revenue. Does this discussion help explain what might make up some of Microsoft's inventory?

Analyzing 8-2 (General Electric)
Selected financial statement information relating to inventories for GENERAL ELECTRIC (GE) is given on the following page.

December 31 (in millions)	2002	2001
Cost of goods sold	35,951	32,419
Inventory—FIFO valuation	9,645	8,971
Inventory—LIFO valuation	9,039	8,295

1. Compute GE's number of days' sales in inventory for 2002 using (a) the FIFO valuation for inventory and (b) the LIFO valuation for inventory. Are the differences significant enough to concern you?
2. Suppose that GE purchases its inventory with the terms "net 30 days." That is, GE's creditors expect payment in 30 days. Is GE going to have a cash flow problem?

Analyzing 8-3 (La-Z-Boy and McDonald's)

The following information is taken from the 2002 financial statements of LA-Z-BOY, INC., maker of recliners and other home furnishings, and the 2002 financial statements of MCDONALD'S, maker of the Big Mac® and other fast foods.

	La-Z-Boy	McDonald's
Cost of goods sold	$1,647.33*	$3,917.40*
Beginning inventory	257.89	105.50
Ending inventory	208.66	111.70

*Amounts in millions.

1. Before you do any computations, forecast which of the two companies will have a lower number of days' sales in inventory.
2. Compute each company's number of days' sales in inventory. Was your forecast in (1) correct?
3. How can these two very successful companies have number of days' sales in inventory that are so different?

▷ *International Case*

International

Why No LIFO?

The LIFO method of accounting for inventory is primarily a U.S. invention. Many countries around the world will not allow LIFO to be used, and other countries discourage its use. For example, the International Accounting Standards Board calls LIFO an undesirable but "allowable" method. In the United Kingdom, LIFO is allowable under corporate law but is unacceptable under professional accounting standards.

Why do you think other countries have such an unfavorable opinion of LIFO? Think about these issues: In periods of rising prices, does the amount shown on the balance sheet relating to inventory reflect current cost? If a company's inventory on the balance sheet reflected costs from years past, what would happen to the income statement if those inventory costs were suddenly moved to Cost of Goods Sold? Would the result reflect a firm's actual performance?

▷ *Ethics Case*

Shipping Bricks

In 1989 the U.S. Department of Justice Criminal Division discovered a massive inventory fraud that was being conducted by managers at MINISCRIBE CORPORATION. MiniScribe manufactured and sold computer disk drives. The fraud included placing bricks in disk drive boxes, shipping those boxes to customers, and recording a sale when the box was shipped. MiniScribe managers also knowingly shipped defective drives and recorded sales even though they knew those drives would be returned.

What would be the effect on the income statement and the balance sheet of shipping bricks and recording those shipments as sales? (*Hint:* Think about the journal entry that would have been made by MiniScribe accountants when a box of bricks was shipped to customers who were expecting disk drives.) Would company officials be able to fool financial statement users for a long time using this type of deception? What could financial statement users have looked for to detect this type of fraud?

▶ *Writing Assignment*

Estimating Inventory

Jon Johnson, an accountant with a local CPA firm, has just completed an inventory count for Mom & Pop's Groceries. Mom and Pop provide audited financial statements to their bank annually, and part of that audit requires an inventory count. Don Squire, a partner with the CPA firm, has also conducted an analysis to estimate this period's ending inventory. Don used the gross margin method, a method whereby the prior period's gross margin percentage is used to infer this period's percentage, to estimate ending inventory. In addition, the store is equipped with cash registers that scan each product as it is sold and, as a result, provide a perpetual inventory record.

These three inventory analysis methods have resulted in three very different answers, which are summarized in the following table:

Method	Inventory Value
Inventory count	$ 98,500
Gross margin analysis	119,750
Point-of-sale scanners	111,500

In evaluating the results, Jon and Don are curious as to why the three methods result in such large differences. Since the inventory count reports actual inventory on hand, they begin to wonder if Mom and Pop have an inventory theft problem. Write a short memo explaining why the other two methods, gross margin analysis and point-of-sale scanners, can result in significantly different answers without there being a theft problem.

▶ *The Debate*

One Method for All

As you know, we have periodic and perpetual inventory methods, along with LIFO, FIFO, and average cost variations of each. How can we compare the financial statements of different companies if they are using different inventory methods? This debate focuses on the question of whether financial statement users would be better able to compare information if all companies used the same inventory method.

Divide your group into two teams and prepare a five-minute presentation defending the following positions:

- One team represents "What's Good for One Is Good for All." To make financial statements comparable, all companies should be required to use the same inventory method. Which one?

Rather than fight over the pros and cons of LIFO and FIFO, a compromise position would be to require all firms to use perpetual average cost. With the availability of computers, the computational problems associated with this method no longer exist. The resulting information would then allow more comparability across firms.

- The other team represents "It's OK to Be Different." Firms are different. One size does not fit all, and one inventory method is not appropriate for all firms. Firms should be allowed to use the inventory method(s) that are best suited for their unique operations.

▶ *Cumulative Spreadsheet Project*

This spreadsheet assignment is a continuation of the spreadsheet assignments given in earlier chapters. If you completed those spreadsheets, you have a head start on this one. If needed, review the spreadsheet assignment for Chapter 4 to refresh your memory on how to construct forecasted financial statements.

1. Handyman wishes to prepare a forecasted balance sheet and income statement for 2007. Use the original financial statement numbers for 2006 [given in part (1) of the Cumulative Spreadsheet Project assignment in Chapter 2] as the basis for the forecast, along with the following additional information:
   a. Sales in 2007 are expected to increase by 40% over 2006 sales of $700.
   b. Cash will increase at the same rate as sales.
   c. The forecasted amount of accounts receivable in 2007 is determined using the forecasted value for the average collection period. For simplicity, do the computations using the end-of-period accounts receivable balance instead of the average balance. The average collection period for 2007 is expected to be 14.08 days.
   d. In 2007, Handyman expects to acquire new property, plant, and equipment costing $80.
   e. The $160 in operating expenses reported in 2006 breaks down as follows: $5 depreciation expense, $155 other operating expenses.
   f. No new long-term debt will be acquired in 2007.
   g. No cash dividends will be paid in 2007.
   h. New short-term loans payable will be acquired in an amount sufficient to make Handyman's current ratio in 2007 exactly equal to 2.0.

   Note: These statements were constructed as part of the spreadsheet assignment in Chapter 7; you can use that spreadsheet as a starting point if you have completed that assignment. *Clearly state any additional assumptions that you make.*

   For this exercise, add the following additional assumptions:
   i. The forecasted amount of inventory in 2007 is determined using the forecasted value for the number of days' sales in inventory (computed using the end-of-period inventory balance). The number of days' sales in inventory for 2007 is expected to be 107.6 days.
   ii. The forecasted amount of accounts payable in 2007 is determined using the forecasted value for the number of days' purchases in accounts payable (computed using the end-of-period accounts payable balance). The number of days' purchases in accounts payable for 2007 is expected to be 48.34 days.

2. Repeat (1), with the following changes in assumptions:
   a. Number of days' sales in inventory is expected to be 66.2 days.
   b. Number of days' sales in inventory is expected to be 150.0 days.

3. Comment on the differences in the forecasted values of cash from operating activities in 2007 under each of the following assumptions about the number of days' sales in inventory: 107.6 days, 66.2 days, and 150.0 days.

4. Is there any impact on the forecasted level of accounts payable when the number of days' sales in inventory is changed? Why or why not?

5. What happens to the forecasted level of short-term loans payable when the number of days' sales in inventory is reduced to 66.2 days? Explain.

▷ *Internet Search*

Sears

We began this chapter with a discussion of SEARS, ROEBUCK & COMPANY. Access its Web site at **http://www.sears.com**. Sometimes Web addresses change, so if this address doesn't work, access the Web site for this textbook (**http://albrecht.swlearning.com**) for an updated link.

Once you have located the company's Web site, answer the following questions:

1. Locate the portion of the Web site dedicated to Sears' history. Can you find information about Sears' beginnings (similar to the narrative at the beginning of this chapter)? In what year did Sears issue its first large general catalog?

2. Locate Sears' balance sheet. Have inventories, as a percentage of total assets, increased or decreased over the time period presented?

3. Compute Sears' number of days' sales in inventory. Is it increasing or decreasing over the time period presented?

4. Locate Sears' note information relating to inventory. Which inventory methods does Sears employ?

chapter

9

Completing the Operating Cycle

After studying this chapter, you should be able to:

Learning Objectives

1 Account for the various components of employee compensation expense.

2 Compute income tax expense, including appropriate consideration of deferred tax items.

3 Distinguish between contingent items that should be recognized in the financial statements and those that should be merely disclosed in the financial statement notes.

4 Understand when an expenditure should be recorded as an asset and when it should be recorded as an expense.

5 Prepare an income statement summarizing operating activities as well as other revenues and expenses, extraordinary items, and earnings per share.

Before 1850, the primary use for petroleum was as a medicine. Known variously as Seneca oil, American oil, and rock oil, a mixture of water and petroleum was reportedly good for rheumatism, chronic cough, ague, toothache, corns, neuralgia, urinary disorders, indigestion, and liver ailments. The oil was collected by wringing out woolen blankets that had been thrown onto the surfaces of ponds that had been fouled by seeping oil. Oil was also a nuisance by-product of drilling wells in search of underground salt brine deposits.

Gradually, additional properties of oil were discovered. It was found that oil could serve as a lubricant for the machinery that was becoming more common as the Industrial Revolution progressed. In addition, distilled oil was found to burn well in the household lamps that had traditionally burned vegetable oil or sperm whale oil. As the demand for petroleum increased, the search for oil began in earnest. A group of investors hired Edwin L. Drake to drill for oil in northwestern Pennsylvania, where oil had long been found in springs and wells. In late August 1859, Drake struck oil at a depth of 69½ feet, creating an oil well that yielded 25 barrels per day. This discovery touched off an oil rush in western Pennsylvania, and the opportunities to get rich were soon fanned by the increased demand for lubricating oil associated with the North's war production during the Civil War.

FYI:

The oil boom did not hit Texas until 1901 when a well on Spindletop Hill, south of Beaumont, Texas, began to gush 100,000 barrels of oil a day.

In those early days, Cleveland, Ohio, was the center of oil refining, and one of the earliest players in the refining business was John D. Rockefeller. Rockefeller had started his business career in Cleveland as a bookkeeper(!) in 1855. By saving his earnings, he acquired some investment capital, and, with a partner, he put up $4,000 to begin a refinery in Cleveland in 1862. Rockefeller's aggressive business tactics aroused controversy almost from the beginning. In particular, Rockefeller was accused of negotiating favorable freight rates with the railroads hauling his oil whereas his competitors were required to pay the stated rates. In 1872, Rockefeller was able to persuade a large number of his Cleveland refining competitors to sell out to him by convincing them that he had arranged such a favorable deal with the railroads that competing head-to-head with him would be impossible.

Rockefeller was eager to expand the business interests of his STANDARD OIL COMPANY OF OHIO into other areas, but the incorporation laws in existence at the time made it difficult for corporations to merge. Therefore, Rockefeller created a "trust," which was basically a corporation of corporations. The stockholders of each corporation transferred their shares to the care of the nine trustees of the STANDARD OIL TRUST; in exchange, the stockholders received trust certificates. Thereafter, the nine trustees ran the businesses and the stockholders received the dividends. When the Ohio Supreme Court ruled this trust illegal in 1892, lawyers for Standard Oil sought another business structure that would preserve the essence of the trust. They found the answer in the incorporation laws of the state of New Jersey, which allowed the formation of a holding company that would own shares of various corporations, duplicating the function of the central trust. In 1899, legal ownership of the companies controlled by Rockefeller was transferred to a holding company called the STANDARD OIL COMPANY OF NEW JERSEY.

FYI:

John D. Rockefeller used some of his Standard Oil profits to found the University of Chicago in 1891.

In the early 1890s, the spirit of reform spread over the United States. Many people felt that Big Business was too powerful and must be reined in by the federal government. President Theodore Roosevelt set the tone by proclaiming himself a "trustbuster," and his administration vigorously pursued an antitrust case against Standard Oil. In 1911, the U.S. Supreme Court mandated the breakup of the Standard Oil Company into 34 smaller companies. Many of those companies are still very well known, as evidenced by the partial list contained in Exhibit 1.

FYI:

The federal antitrust case against MICROSOFT was compared to the Standard Oil case of 1911, with Bill Gates playing the role of a modern-day Rockefeller.

Exhibit 1: Companies Descended from the Original Standard Oil

Ashland*	
ChevronTexaco	Chevron* merged with Texaco in 2001
ConocoPhillips	Conoco* merged with Phillips in 2002
ExxonMobil	Exxon* merged with Mobil in 1999
Amoco*	Merged with BP (British Petroleum)
Atlantic Richfield*	Merged with BP
Pennzoil*-Quaker State	Merged with Royal Dutch/Shell

*Originally part of Standard Oil.

The largest piece of the dismembered Standard Oil Trust was the Standard Oil Company of New Jersey, which changed its named to EXXON in 1972. Exxon now operates in over 100 countries, exploring for oil, producing petrochemical products, and transporting oil and natural gas. In many places, the company is known as ESSO, representing the initials "SO" for Standard Oil. On December 1, 1998, Exxon (the former Standard Oil Company of New Jersey) announced an agreement to merge with MOBIL (the former STANDARD OIL COMPANY OF NEW YORK), thus reuniting these two pieces of the vast empire built by John D. Rockefeller. The formal joining of the two companies was completed on November 30, 1999, creating EXXONMOBIL.[1] To illustrate the size of ExxonMobil's operations, the company had worldwide proved oil reserves of 11.8 billion barrels and proved natural gas reserves of 55.7 trillion cubic feet as of December 31, 2002.

ⓘ n Chapters 7 and 8, we discussed the accounting for sales and the cost of inventory sold. For firms that sell a product, the cost of the inventory sold typically represents the largest expense. For example, cost of goods sold was the largest expense category for EXXONMOBIL in 2002, totaling 44% of sales. For WAL-MART, cost of goods sold was 78% of sales in 2002. Although cost of goods sold represents a significant expense for those companies such as ExxonMobil and Wal-Mart that manufacture and/or sell a product, it is certainly not the only expense. And for those companies that sell a service, other expenses such as employee compensation or advertising can be far more significant than cost of goods sold.

In this chapter, we discuss a number of these other significant operating issues. We will begin with a discussion of two significant operating expenses that are incurred by almost every firm: employee compensation and income taxes. We also discuss the accounting for the costs associated with contingencies, which are items that are not fully resolved at the time the financial statements are prepared. Two common examples of contingencies are lawsuits and environmental cleanup obligations. Also in this chapter we discuss how one determines whether a cost should be recorded as an asset (capitalized) or recorded as an expense. The expense versus capitalize issue has arisen many times over the years as accountants have wrestled with how to account for advertising costs, research costs, and others.

The financial statement items covered in this chapter are illustrated in Exhibit 2. Various operating items affecting the income statement are covered in the chapter. The two most significant are employee compensation and income taxes. The bal-

---

1 Information for this description was obtained from Daniel J. Boorstin, *The Americans: The Democratic Experience* (New York: Random House, 1973) and Ida M. Tarbell, *The History of the Standard Oil Company* (New York: MacMillan Company, 1904).

Exhibit 2: Financial Statement Items Covered in This Chapter

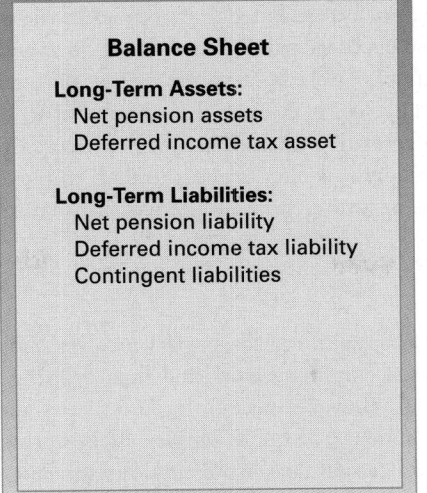

Balance Sheet

Long-Term Assets:
Net pension assets
Deferred income tax asset

Long-Term Liabilities:
Net pension liability
Deferred income tax liability
Contingent liabilities

Statement of Cash Flows

Operating:
Cash Paid for:
Employee Compensation
Research and Development
Advertising
Income Taxes

Income Statement

Employee Compensation Expense
Research and Development Expense
Advertising Expense

Losses/Gains on Contingent Items

Income Tax Expense

ance sheet items discussed are pension liabilities, deferred income tax liabilities, and contingent liabilities. The accounting aspects of these balance sheet items are intriguing in that both the pension and deferred tax items are sometimes reported as assets rather than liabilities. In addition, contingent liabilities are frequently not reported on the balance sheet at all. The details of all these topics, and more, are discussed in this chapter.

Employee Compensation

| Account for the various components of employee compensation expense.

Often, one of the largest operating expenses of a business is the salaries and wages of its employees. But the cost of employees is not simply the expense associated with the current period's wages. As the following time line illustrates, issues associated with employee compensation can extend long after the employee has retired.

Employee Compensation Event Line

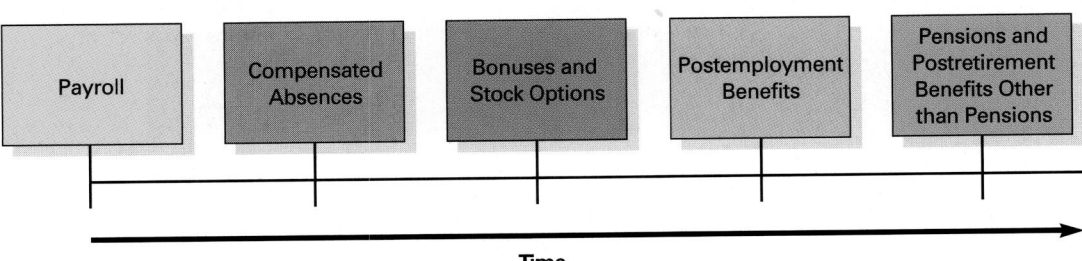

Payroll   Compensated Absences   Bonuses and Stock Options   Postemployment Benefits   Pensions and Postretirement Benefits Other than Pensions

Time

Payroll relates to the salaries and wages earned by employees for work done in the current period. Wages are paid anywhere from weekly to monthly, depending on the company. Compensated absences exist when an employer agrees to pay workers for sick days or vacation days. These obligations must be estimated and accrued in the period that the employee earns those days off. Many employees are paid bonuses based on some measure of performance (such as income or sales volume). Those bonuses are often paid quarterly or annually. One way to provide bonuses to employees is through the granting of stock options. In some cases, employees may earn what are termed "postemployment benefits," which kick in if an employee is laid off or terminated. Finally, firms offer benefits to their employees upon retirement. We will discuss each of these items in further detail in the sections that follow.

Payroll

In its simplest form, accounting for payroll involves debiting Salaries Expense and crediting Salaries Payable when employees work and then debiting Salaries Payable and crediting Cash when wages are paid. However, accounting for salaries and related payroll taxes is never quite that simple and can, in fact, be quite complex. This is primarily because every business is legally required to withhold certain taxes from employees' salaries and wages.

Social Security (FICA) taxes Federal Insurance Distributions Act taxes imposed on the employee and the employer; used mainly to provide retirement benefits.

Very few people receive their full salary as take-home pay. For example, an employee who earns $30,000 a year probably takes home between $20,000 and $25,000. The remainder is withheld by the employer to pay the employee's federal and state income taxes, **Social Security (FICA) taxes**,[2] and any voluntary or contractual withholdings that the employee has authorized (such as union dues, medical insurance premiums, and charitable contributions). Thus, the accounting entry to record the expense for an employee's monthly salary (computed as 1/12 of $30,000) might be:

Salaries Expense	2,500	
FICA Taxes Payable, Employees		191
Federal Withholding Taxes Payable		400
State Withholding Taxes Payable		200
Salaries Payable		1,709
To record Mary Perrico's salary for July.		

All the credit amounts (which are arbitrary in this example) are liabilities that must be paid by the employer to the federal and state governments and to the employee. It should be noted that these withholdings do not represent an additional expense to the employer because the employee actually pays them. The employer merely serves as an agent for the governments for collecting and paying these withheld amounts.

In addition to remitting employees' income and FICA taxes, companies must also pay certain payroll-related taxes, such as the employer's portion of the FICA tax (an amount equal to the employee's portion) and state and federal unemployment taxes. The payroll-related taxes paid by employers are expenses to the company and are included in operating expenses on the income statement. An entry to record the company's share of payroll taxes relating to Mary Perrico's employment (again using arbitrary amounts) would be:

---

2 Congress has split FICA taxes into two parts—Social Security and Medicare. For the purposes of this chapter, we will combine the two.

Payroll Tax Expense	279	
FICA Taxes Payable, Employer		191
Federal Unemployment Taxes Payable		18
State Unemployment Taxes Payable		70
To record employer payroll tax liabilities associated with		
Mary Perrico's salary for July.		

The different liabilities recorded in the preceding two entries for payroll would be eliminated as payments are made. The entries to account for the payments are:

FICA Taxes Payable	382	
Federal Withholding Taxes Payable	400	
Federal Unemployment Taxes Payable	18	
Cash		800
Paid July withholdings and payroll taxes to federal government.		
State Withholding Taxes Payable	200	
State Unemployment Taxes Payable	70	
Cash		270
Paid July withholdings and payroll taxes to state government.		
Salaries Payable	1,709	
Cash		1,709
Paid July salary to Mary Perrico.		

As these entries show, three checks are written for payroll-related expenses: one to the federal government, one to the state, and one to the employee.

One further point about salaries and wages needs to be made. The period of time covered by the payroll may not coincide with the last day of the year for financial reporting. Thus, if the reporting year ends on Wednesday, December 31, and the salaries and wages for that week will be paid Monday, January 5 of the following year, then the company must show the salaries and wages earned from Monday through Wednesday (December 29, 30, and 31) as a liability on the December 31 balance sheet. To accomplish this, the company would record an end-of-year adjusting entry to record the salaries and wages earned for those three days.

Compensated Absences

Suppose that you work for a business that provides each employee one day of sick leave for each full month of employment. When should that sick day (or compensated absence) be accounted for? When it is taken by the employee? When it is earned by the employee? And how much of an accrual should be associated with the compensated absences?

The matching principle requires that the expense associated with the compensated absence be accounted for in the period in which it is earned by the employee. Some of the conceptual issues associated with accounting for compensated absences are similar to those addressed in accounting for bad debts. In the case of bad debts, if we waited until we were sure a customer wasn't going to pay, then we could be certain about our bad debt expense. But we may not find out that we are not going to be paid until several periods later, and as a result, the bad debt expense would be reflected in the wrong accounting period. So instead of waiting until accounts are dishonored, we estimate the expense for each period. The same is true with compensated absences. Although we could wait until those sick days are taken and then know exactly what they will cost, it may be years before we know. Rather than wait, we estimate instead. For example, if you earn both $100 a day and one sick day per month, then it makes sense for your employer to recognize an expense (and accrue a liability) of $100 per month related to your sick pay. This would be done with the following journal entry:

Salaries Expense	100	
Sick Days Payable		100
To recognize accrued sick pay.		

When you take that sick day (and let's not forget that the government will take its share of your sick pay also), the journal entry would be:

Sick Days Payable	100	
Various Taxes Payable		20
Cash		80
To record payment of sick day net of FICA, federal, and state taxes.		

Now suppose that you don't take your sick day until next year. Assume also that you received a $10 raise per day. This makes our estimate of $100 incorrect, so we will fix that estimate in the period in which you take the sick day. The journal entry in this instance would be:

Sick Days Payable	100	
Salaries Expense	10	
Various Taxes Payable		22
Cash		88
To record payment of sick day net of FICA, federal, and state taxes.		

The same procedures would apply when accounting for accrued vacation pay or other types of compensated absences.

Bonuses

bonus Additional compensation, beyond the regular compensation, that is paid to employees if certain objectives are achieved.

Many companies offer employee **bonus** plans that allow employees to receive additional compensation should certain objectives be achieved. These bonus plans sometimes apply to all employees although more often they are restricted to members of top management. In many instances, the terms of the bonus plan are defined using financial statement numbers. For example, in its 2002 proxy statement filed with the Securities and Exchange Commission (SEC), EXXONMOBIL disclosed that it paid $4.65 million in bonuses to its top six executives. ExxonMobil's chief executive officer (CEO), Lee R. Raymond, received the lion's share of that bonus amount at $2.16 million (this on top of his regular annual compensation of $3.25 million).

The purpose of an earnings-based bonus plan is to encourage managers to work harder and smarter to improve the performance of the company. However, such a plan also increases the incentive of managers to manipulate reported earnings. In fact, one of the factors looked at by auditors in evaluating the risk of financial statement fraud in a company is whether the company has an earnings-based management bonus plan.

Stock Options

employee stock options
Rights given to employees to purchase shares of stock of a company at a predetermined price.

Employee stock options have become an increasingly popular way to compensate top executives. Under a stock option plan, managers are given the option of purchasing shares of the company's stock in the future at a price that is specified today. For example, in 2002, Lee Raymond, CEO of ExxonMobil, was granted 1,050,000 options, each allowing him to buy one share of ExxonMobil stock in the future for $37.12, which was the market value of ExxonMobil shares on the date the options were granted. Raymond will make money from these options if he is able to improve the performance of ExxonMobil and increase its stock price. If, for example, the company's stock price were to increase to $50.00 per share, these 1,050,000 options, allowing Raymond to buy ExxonMobil shares at the fixed price of $37.12, would be worth $13,524,000 [1,050,000 × ($50.00 − $37.12)]. Stock options are an attractive way to compensate top management because the options pay off only if the managers are able to increase the value of the company, which is exactly what the owners of the company (the stockholders) desire.

There has been significant debate in the United States about how to compute the compensation expense associated with employee stock options. The debate centers around the issue of what the value of an option is. Two methods for valuing employee options for accounting purposes are described below.

Intrinsic Value Method

The "intrinsic value" of an option is the value it has if it must be exercised immediately. For example, if a company's stock price is $50 and it issues an option allowing an employee to buy a share of stock for $50, the option has no "intrinsic value" because the employee would be just as well off purchasing the company's stock in the market for $50, just as anyone not holding an option could do.

Fair Value Method

The "fair value" of an option stems from the possibility that the employee may want to exercise the option in the future if the company's stock price goes up. For example, even if an option exercise price of $50 is equal to the stock price on the date the option is granted to an employee, there is a chance that the stock price may increase during the life of the option. This means that an option with no "intrinsic value" can still have substantial economic value because the employee holding the option may be able to buy the stock at less than its market value some time in the future. Exact computation of the fair value of options involves complex formulas derived using stochastic calculus, but commercially available software packages make option valuation no more difficult than using a spreadsheet.

The fair value method, with its theoretically correct emphasis on estimating the actual value of the options granted to employees, is backed by the FASB. However, the vast majority of U.S. corporations opposed the FASB's attempt in 1994 to require recognition of a stock option compensation expense. The reason for this opposition was simple: recognition of a stock option compensation expense would reduce reported earnings. The surprising vigor of the opposition to the fair value method caused the FASB to reluctantly allow the use of the intrinsic value method while encouraging the use of the fair value method.

The accounting scandals of 2001–2002 have prompted the FASB to revisit the issue of accounting for stock options. The same vigor that was shown by companies and politicians in 1994 seems to have resurfaced but this time in favor of the fair value method. As this book goes to press, the FASB is planning to issue a new accounting standard in the fall of 2003 that will eliminate the intrinsic value method as an accounting option for stock-based compensation.

Like most U.S. companies, ExxonMobil used the intrinsic value method in 2002 (the company announced in its 2002 annual report that effective January 1, 2003, it would use the fair value method to account for stock-based

FYI:

MICROSOFT reports that if it had used the fair value method instead of the intrinsic value method in 2002, its reported net income would have decreased by almost $2.5 billion.

compensation). In 2002, ExxonMobil reported that if the fair value method had been used to account for stock options, income for the year would have been reduced by $161 million, or 1.4% of net income.

Postemployment Benefits

postemployment benefits
Benefits paid to employees who have been laid off or terminated.

Postemployment benefits are perhaps the least common of the topics covered in this section on employee compensation. **Postemployment benefits** are those benefits that are incurred after an employee has ceased to work for an employer but before that employee retires. A common example is a company-provided severance package for employees who have been laid off. This severance package might include salary for a certain time period, retraining costs, education costs, and the like. Accounting standards require that the amount of the postemployment cost be estimated and accrued in the period in which the employee is actually terminated. For example, suppose a company decides to close a segment of its operations, thereby laying off a certain percentage of its labor force. The company must estimate the costs associated with the benefits offered to those laid-off employees and would record the following journal entry when the employees are actually terminated:

Salaries Expense	XXX	
Benefits Payable		XXX
To record postemployment benefits for laid-off employees.		

When the benefits are paid, a journal entry would be made to reduce the payable and to record the cash outflow.

business environment

What Goes into Pensions? A pension is an agreement between an employer and the employees that the employees will receive a certain sum of money upon retirement. That money may be paid in a single sum or over several years. In addition, employers often offer other postretirement benefits such as medical and life insurance. Consider how difficult it can be to account for these items.

Let's assume that you are 25 years old when you start working for your current employer. Your employer's pension plan states that upon retirement you will receive medical and life insurance benefits in addition to a monthly pension check. The pension will be a percentage, commonly 2%, of your average annual salary over the last five years of your employment multiplied by the number of years of employment. What factors need to be considered in determining the employer's future liability?

As you can imagine, estimating these various factors involves some enormous assumptions. Plus, once the estimates have been made, the fact that those expenditures will not be made for 40 years (assuming you retire when you turn 65) must be factored in.

As if that isn't enough, the employer must do this computation for every employee. In the case of large companies, such as EXXONMOBIL with 92,500 employees, the computations are staggering. Fortunately, businesses have help in the form of actuaries. Actuaries make their living predicting the future.

Pensions

pension An agreement between an employer and employees that provides for benefits upon retirement.

A **pension** is cash compensation received by an employee after that employee has retired. Two primary types of pension plans exist. A **defined contribution plan** requires the company to place a certain amount of money into a pension fund each year on behalf of the employees. Then, after the employees retire, they receive the money contributed to the pension fund plus the earnings on those contributions. With a **defined benefit plan**, on the other hand, the company promises the employees a certain monthly cash amount after they retire, based on factors such as number of years worked by the employee, employee's highest salary, and so forth.

defined contribution plan A pension plan under which the employer contributes a defined amount to the pension fund; after retirement, the employees receive the amount contributed plus whatever it has earned.

The accounting for a defined contribution plan is quite simple—a company merely reports pension expense equal to the amount of cash it is required to contribute to its employees' pension fund during the year. Normally, no balance sheet liability is reported in connection with a defined contribution plan because, once the company has made the required contribution to the pension fund, it has no remaining obligation to the employees.

defined benefit plan A pension plan under which the employer defines the amount that retiring employees will receive and contributes enough to the pension fund to pay that amount.

The accounting issues associated with defined benefit plans are much more complex because the ultimate amount that a company will have to pay into its employees' pension fund depends on how long the employees work before retiring, what their highest salaries are, how long the employees live after they retire, and how well the investments in the pension fund perform. The accounting concept underlying this complexity, however, is still the same basic idea of matching: the income statement this year should contain all expenses related to generating revenue this year, whether those expenses are paid in cash this year (like cash wages) or are not expected to be paid for many years (like pension benefits).

 STOP & THINK

Who bears the risks associated with a defined contribution plan—the employer or the employee? Which party bears the risks associated with a defined benefit plan?

They estimate birth and death rates, trends in inflation, health-care costs, salaries, and other relevant information. There are about 14,000 actuaries in the United States, compared to over 1.1 million accountants.

So, if you start thinking that accounting is difficult and you become uncomfortable with all the assumptions and estimates, remember that it could be worse: you could be studying to be an actuary!

Postretirement Benefit	Factors to Consider
Medical insurance	What will health-care costs be in the future?
	How long will you live to enjoy those health insurance benefits?
	(The longer you live, the greater the cost.)
Life insurance	What will insurance premiums be for the remainder of your employment?
Pension check	How long will you work?
	What will your average annual salary be in your last five years of employment?
	How long will you or your spouse live after you retire?

Pension-Related Items in the Financial Statements

Each of the major balance sheet and income statement items related to pension accounting is briefly introduced below.

- *Pension fund.* When a company has a defined benefit pension plan, it is required by U.S. federal law to establish a separate pension fund to ensure that employees receive the defined benefits promised under the plan. The pension fund is basically a large investment fund of stocks and bonds. The company still owns these pension fund assets, but it cannot use them for any purpose except to pay pension benefits to employees.
- *Pension obligation.* The promise to make defined benefit pension payments to employees represents a liability to the company making the promise. The amount of this liability is quite difficult to estimate because it depends on future salary increases, employee turnover, employee life span, and so forth. The estimation of the liability is done by professionals called actuaries. These are the same individuals who provide the computations that life insurance companies use in setting premiums.
- *Net pension asset or liability.* One possible way to present the pension information on a balance sheet is to list the pension plan assets among the long-term assets and the pension liability as a long-term liability. However, the accounting standards stipulate that these two items be offset against one another and a single net amount be shown as either a net pension asset or a net pension liability.
- *Pension-related interest cost.* The estimated pension obligation represents an amount owed by a company to its employees. Accordingly, a pension-related interest cost is recognized each year; the amount of this interest cost is the increase in the pension obligation resulting from interest on the unpaid pension obligation.
- *Service cost.* The amount of a company's pension obligation increases each year as employees work and earn more pension benefits. This increase in the pension obligation is an expense associated with work done during the year and is called the pension service cost.
- *Return on pension fund assets.* The cost of a company's pension plan is partially offset by the return that the company earns on the assets in its pension fund.
- *Pension expense.* Just as pension liabilities and assets are offset against one another to arrive at a single net liability or asset to be reported on the balance sheet, the three components of pension expense (interest cost, service cost, and return on pension fund assets) are netted against one another to yield a single number that is reported on the income statement.

Illustration from ExxonMobil's Financial Statements

In the notes to its 2002 financial statements, ExxonMobil discloses the following about its pension benefit obligation and its pension fund. All numbers are in millions of dollars.

	U.S. Plans	Non-U.S. Plans	Total
Pension benefit obligation	$9,139	$13,543	$22,682
Pension fund assets	4,616	6,735	11,351
Net pension liability	$4,523	$ 6,808	$11,331

Note that ExxonMobil has separated its pension plans into those covering employees in the United States and those covering employees located outside the United States. This is a useful separation because the laws governing the maintenance of pension plans vary from country to country; U.S. laws are generally viewed as giving more protection to the rights of the employees covered by pension plans than foreign laws do. Also note that ExxonMobil's pension plans are "underfunded," meaning that the market value of the assets in the pension funds is less than the estimated pension liability. ExxonMobil also provides the following information about its pension expense in 2002. Again, all of the numbers are in millions.

	U.S. Plans	Non-U.S. Plans	Total
Service cost	$ 224	$ 257	$ 481
Interest cost	577	621	1,198
Less: Expected return on fund assets	(501)	(561)	(1,062)
Other miscellaneous items	170	208	378
Net pension expense	$ 470	$ 525	$ 995

Caution

The *expected*, not the actual, return on the pension fund assets is subtracted in computing pension expense. The accounting for the difference between expected and actual return involves deferring gains and losses, corridor amounts, and other complexities best left for an intermediate accounting course.

Note the significant reduction in reported pension expense caused by the expected return on pension fund assets; without the return on the pension fund, ExxonMobil's pension expense would be more than twice as high.

Postretirement Benefits Other Than Pensions

In addition to pension benefits, employers often offer employees other benefits after their retirement. For example, ExxonMobil promises its employees that it will continue to cover them with health-care and life insurance plans after retirement. These types of plans are typically less formal than pension plans and often are not backed by assets accumulated in a separate fund. For example, ExxonMobil has only a $345 million separate fund set up to cover its estimated $3.5 billion obligation to cover the health-care needs of employees.

The accounting rules require companies to currently recognize the expense and long-term liability associated with the postretirement benefits that are earned in the current year, in keeping with the normal practice of matching expenses to the period in which they are initially incurred. The actual accounting is complex but similar to that required for pensions. The potential liabilities for these future payments can be quite significant for many firms. GENERAL MOTORS has the largest postretirement benefit plan in the United States, with a nonpension postretirement obligation totaling $57.229 billion as of December 31, 2002.

As illustrated in this section, compensation expense includes much more than just wages and salaries. Companies presumably have calculated that the value of the services provided by employees justifies the additional compensation cost beyond salaries and wages. The fact that employees earn benefits in one year that they do not receive until later, sometimes many years later, necessitates careful accounting to ensure that compensation expense is reported in the year in which it is earned.

network exercises

ING

ING's Web site, **http://www.ing-usa.com/ us/tools_calcs/index.html**, features a set of retirement and investment calculators to help in financial planning. How much money do you need to save per month in order to accumulate $1 million by the time you are 65?

TO SUMMARIZE: Employee compensation is not limited to just the current period's payroll. The cost of employees also includes compensated absences, bonuses, stock options, postemployment benefits, pensions, and other postretirement benefits. Most companies account for employee stock options using the intrinsic value method, meaning that, typically, no compensation expense is recognized. A pension obligation is reported on the balance sheet as the difference between the obligation and the amount in an associated pension fund. Pension expense is the sum of interest cost and service cost, less the expected return on the pension fund assets.

Taxes

2 Compute income tax expense, including appropriate consideration of deferred tax items.

In addition to the payroll taxes described in the previous section, companies are responsible for paying several other taxes to federal, state, and/or local governments, including sales taxes, property taxes, and income taxes. The accounting for these taxes is described next.

Sales Taxes

Most states and some cities charge a sales tax on retail transactions. These taxes are paid by customers to the seller, who in turn forwards them to the state or city. Sales taxes collected from customers represent a current liability until remitted to the appropriate governmental agency. For example, assume that a sporting goods store in Denver prices a pair of skis at $200 and that the combination of state and city sales tax is 6.5%. When the store sells the skis, it collects $213 and records the transaction as follows:

Cash	213	
Sales Revenue		200
Sales Tax Payable		13
Sold a pair of skis for $200. Collected $213, including 6.5% sales tax.		

sales tax payable Money collected from customers for sales taxes that must be remitted to local governments and other taxing authorities.

The sales revenue is properly recorded at $200, and the $13 is recorded as **Sales Tax Payable**, a liability. Then, on a regular basis, a sales tax return is completed and filed with the state or city tax commission, and sales taxes collected are paid to those agencies. Note that the collection of the sales tax from customers creates a liability to the state but does not result in the recognition of revenue when collected or an expense when paid to the state. The company acts as an agent of the state in collecting the sales tax and recognizes a liability only until the collected amount is remitted to the state.

Property Taxes

Property taxes are usually assessed by county or city governments on land, buildings, and other company assets. The period covered by the assessment of property taxes is often from July 1 of one year to June 30 of the next year. If a property taxpayer is on a calendar-year financial reporting basis (or on a fiscal-year basis ending on a day other than June 30), the property tax assessment year and the company's financial reporting year will not coincide. Therefore, when the company prepares its financial statements at calendar-year end, it must report a prepaid tax asset (if taxes are paid at the beginning of the tax year) or a property tax liability (if taxes are paid at the end of the tax year) for the taxes associated with the first portion of the assessment year. To illustrate, assume that Yokum Company pays its property taxes of $3,600 on June 30, 2005, for the period July 1, 2005, to June 30, 2006. If the company is on a calendar-year basis and records the prepayment as an asset, then the adjusting entry at December 31, 2005, would be:

Property Tax Expense	1,800	
Prepaid Property Taxes		1,800
To record property tax expense for six months.		

The prepaid property taxes account balance of $1,800 would be shown on Yokum's balance sheet at December 31, 2005, as a current asset. On June 30, 2006, property tax expense would be recognized for the period January 1, 2006, through June 30, 2006, with the following entry:

Property Tax Expense	1,800	
Prepaid Property Taxes		1,800
To record property tax expense for the property assessment period January 1–June 30, 2006.		

Income Taxes

Corporations pay income taxes just as individuals do. This corporate income tax is usually reported as the final expense on the income statement. For example, in 2002, three lines from EXXONMOBIL's income statement relating to taxes were as follows, with all numbers in millions:

	2002	2001	2000
Income before income taxes	$17,510	$23,970	$26,881
Income taxes	6,499	8,967	11,075
Income from continuing operations	$11,011	$15,003	$15,806

The $6.499 billion in income tax expense reported by ExxonMobil in 2002 is not necessarily equal to the amount of cash paid for income taxes during the year. In fact, ExxonMobil paid $6.106 billion for income taxes in 2002. Reported income tax expense may differ from the actual amount of cash paid for taxes for two reasons. First, like many other expenses, income taxes are not necessarily paid in cash in the year in which they are incurred. The important point to remember is that reported income tax expense reflects the amount of income taxes attributable to income earned during the year, whether the tax was actually paid in cash during the year or not.

The second reason reported income tax expense may differ from the actual amount of cash paid for taxes is that income tax expense is based on reported financial accounting income, whereas the amount of cash paid for income taxes is dictated by the applicable government tax law. The $6.499 billion income tax expense reported by ExxonMobil in 2002 reflects the total estimated amount of income tax the company expects will eventually be paid based on the income reported in the current year's income statement. However, because the income computed using the tax rules is almost always different from the income computed using financial accounting standards, some of this tax may not have to be paid for several years. In addition, tax rules may require income tax to be paid on income before the financial accounting standards consider that income to be "earned." These differences in tax law income and financial accounting income give rise to deferred income tax items, which are discussed in this section.

Corporations in the United States compute two different income numbers—financial income for reporting to stockholders and taxable income for reporting to the Internal Revenue Service (IRS). The existence of these two "sets of books" seems unethical to some, illegal to others. However, the difference between the stockholders' need for information and the government's need for efficient revenue collection makes the computation of the two different income numbers essential. The different purposes of these reporting systems were summarized by the U.S. Supreme Court in the *Thor Power Tool* case (1979):

> The primary goal of financial accounting is to provide useful information to management, shareholders, creditors, and others properly interested; the major responsibility of the accountant is to protect these parties from being misled. The primary goal of the income tax system, in contrast, is the equitable collection of revenue.

In summary, U.S. corporations compute income in two different ways, and rightly so. Nevertheless, the existence of these two different numbers that can each be called "income before taxes" makes it surprisingly difficult to define what is meant by "income tax expense."

Deferred Tax Example

Assume that you invest $1,000 by buying shares in a mutual fund on January 1. Also assume that the income tax rate is 40%. According to the tax law, any economic gain you experience through an increase in the value of your mutual fund shares is not taxed until you actually sell your shares. The rationale behind this tax rule is that until you sell your shares, you don't have the cash to pay any tax. Now, assume further that the economy does well and that the value of your mutual fund shares increases to $1,600 by December 31. You decide to prepare partial financial statements to summarize your holdings and the performance of your shares during the year. These financial statements are as follows:

Balance Sheet		Income Statement	
Assets:		Revenues:	
Mutual Fund Shares	$1,600	Gain on Mutual Fund Investment	$600

A moment's consideration reveals that this balance sheet and income statement are misleading. Yes, it is true that your shares are now worth $1,600, but if and when you liquidate the shares, you will have to pay income tax of $240 [($1,600 − $1,000) × 0.40]. Thus, you are overstating your economic position by only reporting the $1,600 in mutual fund shares; you should also report that a liability of $240 exists in relation to these shares. Similarly, it is misleading to report the $600 gain on your income statement without also reporting that, at some future time, you will have to pay $240 in income tax on that gain. A more accurate set of financial statements would appear as follows:

Balance Sheet		Income Statement	
Assets:		Revenues:	
Mutual Fund Shares	$1,600	Gain on Mutual Fund Investment	$600
Liabilities:		Expenses:	
Deferred Income Tax Liability	$ 240	Income Tax Expense	$240

The appropriate journal entry to recognize income tax expense in this case is as follows:

```
Income Tax Expense ........................................  240
    Deferred Income Tax Liability ...............................      240
```

Note that the deferred income tax liability is not a legal liability because, as far as the IRS is concerned, you do not currently owe any tax on the increase in the value of your mutual fund. Nevertheless, the deferred tax liability is an economic liability that should be reported now because it reflects an obligation that will have to be paid in the future as a result of an event (the increase in the value of the mutual fund shares) that occurred this year.

Now, what if the mutual fund shares had decreased in value from $1,000 to $400? Consider whether the following set of financial statements would accurately reflect your economic position and performance:

Balance Sheet		Income Statement	
Assets:		Revenues:	
Mutual Fund Shares	$400	Loss on Mutual Fund Investment	$600

Again, these financial statements are somewhat misleading because they ignore the future tax implications of the change in the value of the mutual fund shares. In this case, when the shares are sold, you will realize a taxable loss of $600. If you have other investment income, that loss can be used to reduce your total taxable income by $600, which will save you $240 ($600 $\times$ 0.40) in income taxes. Thus, in a real sense, this loss on the mutual funds is not all bad because it will provide you with a $240 reduction in income taxes in the year in which you sell the shares. This reduction in taxes is an asset, a deferred income tax asset, because it represents a probable future economic benefit that has arisen from an event (the drop in the value of the mutual fund shares) that occurred this year. Similarly, the income statement effect of this future savings in taxes is to soften the blow of the reported $600 loss. The loss that occurred this year will result in an income tax benefit in the future, so the benefit is reported on this year's income statement, as follows:

Balance Sheet		Income Statement	
Assets:		Expenses:	
Mutual Fund Shares	$400	Loss on Mutual Fund Investment	$ 600
		Less: Income Tax Benefit	(240)
Deferred Income Tax Asset	$240		
		Net Loss	$ 360

The journal entry to recognize the income tax "expense" is as follows:

Deferred Income Tax Asset	240	
Income Tax Expense		240

Notice that Income Tax Expense is credited, or reduced, in this entry. If there are other income taxes for the year, this credit will result in a reduction in reported income tax expense. If there are no other income taxes, then the credit amount will be reported on the income statement as an addition to income under the title "income tax benefit."

As this simple mutual fund example illustrates, the amount of income tax expense reported on a company's income statement is not necessarily the same as the amount of income tax the company must pay on taxable income generated during the year. There are literally hundreds of accounting areas in which income is taxed by the taxing authorities in a different year than the year in which the income is reported to the financial statement users in the income statement. The details of deferred income tax accounting are among the most complicated issues covered in intermediate accounting courses.

FYI:

The value of the deferred tax asset depends on your having other investment income in the future against which the loss on the mutual fund shares can be offset. Thus, accounting for deferred tax assets is complicated by the fact that one must make an assumption about the likelihood that a company will have enough taxable income in the future to be able to take advantage of the deferred tax benefit.

TO SUMMARIZE: The amount of sales tax collected is reported as a liability until the funds are forwarded to the appropriate government agency. When property taxes are paid in advance, the amount is reported as a prepaid asset until the time period covered by the property tax has expired. Reported income tax expense is not merely the amount of income tax that a company legally owes for a given year. Because of differences between financial accounting rules and income tax rules, revenues and expense can enter into the computation of income in different years for financial accounting purposes and for income tax purposes. Proper accounting for deferred income taxes ensures that reported income tax expense for a year represents all of the income tax consequences arising from transactions undertaken during the year.

Contingencies

3 Distinguish between contingent items that should be recognized in the financial statements and those that should be merely disclosed in the financial statement notes.

contingency Circumstances involving potential losses or gains that will not be resolved until some future event occurs.

By its very nature, business is full of uncertainty. As discussed in relation to employee compensation and taxes, proper recording of an expense in the current period frequently requires making estimates about what will occur in future periods. Sometimes the very existence of an asset or liability depends on the occurrence, or nonoccurrence, of a future event. For example, whether a company will have to make a payment as a result of a lawsuit arising from events occurring this year depends on a judge or jury ruling that may not be known for several years. In accounting terms, a **contingency** is an uncertain circumstance involving a potential gain or loss that will not be resolved until some future event occurs. In this section, we discuss the conceptual issues associated with contingencies and the accounting for events for which the outcome is uncertain.

If you were a financial statement user, would you want to be informed of events known to management that might have an adverse effect on the company's future? Consider as an example a lawsuit filed against a company. Because litigation can take years, how should that company account for the possibility of a loss? Would you want the company to wait until the lawsuit is resolved before informing financial statement users of the litigation? Of course not. You would want to know about the lawsuit if the outcome could potentially materially affect the operations of the company. But would you want to know about every lawsuit filed against the company? Probably not.

Accounting standard-setters have addressed this issue and determined that the proper disclosure for a contingency depends upon the assessed outcome. The first thing to note is that accounting standard-setters determined that accounting for contingent gains is, in most cases, inappropriate. Contingent gains are typically not accounted for until the future event relating to the contingent gain resolves itself. Contingent liabilities are to be accounted for differently depending on an assessment of the likely outcome of the contingency. Exhibit 3 contains the relevant terms, definitions, and proper accounting for contingent liabilities.

If you think about it, this probability spectrum makes a great deal of sense. For example, if it is likely that your company will lose a lawsuit in which it is the defendant, then it would be appropriate to account for that outcome now by recognizing a loss and establishing a payable. If the likelihood of your company losing the case is slight, then it makes sense to do nothing. And if you are unsure of the outcome, then disclosure in the notes seems appropriate.

The problem in implementing these terms relates to assessing the likelihood of an outcome. Who is to say if your company will lose a lawsuit? The company must obtain objective assessments as to the possible outcome of future events. In the case of litigation, the company would ask its attorneys about the possible outcome. The firm auditing the company might use its own

Exhibit 3: Accounting for Contingent Liabilities

Term	Definition	Accounting
Probable	The future event is likely to occur.	Estimate the amount of the contingency and make the appropriate journal entry; provide detailed disclosure in the notes.
Reasonably possible	The chance of the future event occurring is more than remote but less than likely.	Provide detailed disclosure of the possible liability in the notes.
Remote	The chance of the future event occurring is slight.	No disclosure required.

STOP & THINK

Why might a company hesitate to assess the likelihood of losing an ongoing lawsuit as being probable? If you were the attorney for the plaintiff, how could you use the resulting information from the financial statements?

attorneys to assess the possible outcome. In any case, companies are required to make objective assessments as to the likely outcome of contingent events and then account for those events based on that assessment.

MICROSOFT's 2002 Form 10-K (see Appendix A) contains the company's disclosure relating to contingencies. At the time, the company was being investigated by the Justice Department for potential monopolistic practices. Note that the initial judgment of the District Court was that Microsoft should be broken up into two companies. Microsoft appealed the judgment and, as detailed in the note, negotiated settlements with a number of states and has ongoing settlement talks with other states. Contrast Microsoft's disclosure with the 2002 disclosure provided by PHILIP MORRIS, the tobacco company, (now a subsidiary of ALTRIA GROUP) relating to its involvement in ongoing tobacco litigation. The company provides over seven pages of disclosure relating to its potential tobacco-related liability.

Environmental Liabilities

environmental liabilities
Obligations incurred because of damage done to the environment.

Environmental liabilities have gained increasing attention of late because of their potential magnitude. **Environmental liabilities** are obligations incurred because of damage done by companies to the environment. Common environmental liabilities include cleanup costs associated with oil spills, toxic waste dumps, or air pollution. These liabilities are usually brought to the company's attention as a result of fines or penalties imposed by the federal government or when damage that is caused by the company is recognized. Although the accounting and disclosures associated with environmental liabilities fall under the guidelines for contingencies discussed in the previous section, environmental liabilities present a unique problem.

In the case of a lawsuit, one can typically make a reasonable estimate as to the upper bound of the potential settlement. For example, if your company is being sued for $4 million, it is unlikely that any potential settlement will be higher than that amount. In the case of environmental liabilities, it is often very difficult to estimate the cost of environmental cleanup. Thus, while the company may deem it probable that a liability exists, estimating that liability can be difficult. Recall that the contingency standard requires a liability to be recorded on the company's books if it is probable and estimable. If a potential liability is possible and estimable, the standards require note disclosure.

What about the situation where a potential liability is probable but cannot be estimated with much accuracy, as is often the case with environmental liabilities? Obviously, if a company cannot estimate a probable obligation, it makes sense to provide extensive note disclosure. Most companies will estimate at least a minimum amount and provide note disclosure as to the possibility of additional costs. As an illustration, EXXONMOBIL disclosed the information in Exhibit 4 in its 1991 and 2002 annual reports in connection with lawsuits filed as a result of the *Exxon Valdez* oil spill. Note that in 1991, the company sounds quite optimistic that it has settled the bulk of the claims related to the oil spill and that any further claims "will not have a materially adverse effect" upon the company. This optimistic disclosure is particularly interesting in light of the $4 billion adverse judgment discussed in the 2002 disclosure.

TO SUMMARIZE: Contingent liabilities depend on some future event to determine if a liability actually exists. Companies are required to assess the likelihood of certain future events occurring and then, based on that assessment, provide appropriate disclosure. If the company deems the future event to be likely, the journal entries are made and the liability is accrued. If the future event is deemed reasonably possible, note disclosure is required. For those events considered remote, no disclosure is required. Environmental liabilities represent a case where a liability exists but measurement is difficult. A minimum liability is typically established along with extensive note disclosure.

Exhibit 4: ExxonMobil—1991 and 2002 Disclosures Concerning *Exxon Valdez* Oil Spill

Disclosure in 1991

On March 24, 1989, the Exxon Valdez, a tanker owned by Exxon Shipping Company, a subsidiary of Exxon Corporation, ran aground on Bligh Reef in Prince William Sound off the port of Valdez, Alaska, and released approximately 260,000 barrels of crude oil. More than 315 lawsuits, including class actions, have been brought in various courts against Exxon Corporation and certain of its subsidiaries.

On October 8, 1991, the United States District Court for the District of Alaska approved a civil agreement and consent decree. . . . These agreements provided for guilty pleas to certain misdemeanors, the dismissal of all felony charges and the remaining misdemeanor charges by the United States, and the release of all civil claims against Exxon . . . by the United States and the state of Alaska. The agreements also released all claims related to or arising from the oil spill by Exxon. . . .

Payments under the plea agreement totaled $125 million—$25 million in fines and $100 million in payments to the United States and Alaska for restoration projects in Alaska. Payments under the civil agreement and consent decree will total $900 million over a ten-year period. The civil agreement also provides for the possible payment, between September 1, 2002, and September 1, 2006, of up to $100 million for substantial loss or decline in populations, habitats, or species in areas affected by the oil spill which could not have been reasonably anticipated on September 25, 1991.

The remaining cost to the corporation from the Valdez accident is difficult to predict and cannot be determined at this time. It is believed the final outcome, net of reserves already provided, will not have a materially adverse effect upon the corporation's operations or financial condition.

Disclosure in 2002

A number of lawsuits, including class actions, were brought in various courts against Exxon Mobil Corporation and certain of its subsidiaries relating to the accidental release of crude oil from the tanker Exxon Valdez in 1989. The vast majority of the claims have been resolved leaving a few compensatory damages cases to be resolved. All of the punitive damage claims were consolidated in the civil trial that began in May 1994.

In that trial, on September 24, 1996, the United States District Court for the District of Alaska entered a judgment in the amount of $5 billion in punitive damages to a class composed of all persons and entities who asserted claims for punitive damages from the corporation as a result of the Exxon Valdez grounding. ExxonMobil appealed the judgment. On November 7, 2001, the United States Court of Appeals for the Ninth Circuit vacated the punitive damage award as being excessive under the Constitution and remanded the case to the District Court for it to determine the amount of the punitive damage award consistent with the Ninth Circuit's holding. On December 6, 2002, the District Court reduced the punitive damages award from $5 billion to $4 billion. This case will return to the Ninth Circuit for its determination. The corporation has posted a $4.8 billion letter of credit.

The ultimate cost to ExxonMobil from the lawsuits arising from the Exxon Valdez grounding is not possible to predict and may not be resolved for a number of years.

Capitalize versus Expense

4 Understand when an expenditure should be recorded as an asset and when it should be recorded as an expense.

To this point in the text, we have assumed that the decision of expensing a cost to the income statement or capitalizing an expenditure and placing it on the balance sheet as an asset is an easy one. In reality, that decision is often difficult and one that makes accounting judgment critical. For example, should a building that cost $1 million and is expected to benefit 20 future periods be capitalized and placed on the balance sheet? The answer is pretty clear—of course. What about office supplies that are used this period? Will they benefit future periods? No, and as a result, the costs of those supplies should be expensed. What about research and development costs? Should they be capitalized as an asset or expensed to the income statement? Now you see the problem. Sometimes it is difficult to determine whether an expenditure will benefit the future. Exhibit 5 provides an expense/asset continuum that demonstrates the difficulty of the decision to capitalize or expense a cost.

The endpoints of the continuum are easy. The decision starts to get fuzzy, though, once you leave the endpoints. Do repairs and maintenance benefit future periods (and therefore need to be capitalized), or are they necessary expenditures just to keep a machine running (and should be expensed)? To illustrate the issues involved in deciding whether an expenditure should be capitalized or expensed, two specific areas will be discussed—research and development (R&D) and advertising.

Research and Development

Research is an activity undertaken to discover new knowledge that will be useful in developing new products, services, or processes. Development involves the application of research findings to develop a plan or design for new or improved products and processes. EXXONMOBIL reports that, from 2000 through 2002, it spent an average of $600 million per year on R&D activities.

Because of the uncertainty surrounding the future economic benefit of R&D activities, the FASB decided in 1974 that research and development expenditures should be expensed in the period incurred. Among the arguments for expensing R&D costs is the frequent inability to find a definite causal relationship between the expenditures and future revenues. Sometimes very large expenditures do not generate any future revenue, while relatively small expenditures lead to significant discoveries that generate large revenues. The FASB found it difficult to establish criteria that would distinguish between those R&D expenditures that would most likely benefit future periods and those that would not.

In summary, the FASB concluded that R&D expenditures are undertaken to benefit future periods, but that it is impractical to identify which R&D expenditures actually do provide future economic benefit. Accordingly, all R&D costs are to be recorded as expenses in the year they are incurred. This rule leads to a systematic overstatement of R&D expenses and a systematic understatement of R&D assets. The rule was roundly criticized in 1974 as the FASB prepared to release it. The FASB received many comments predicting that if firms were required to expense all R&D costs, they would be forced to significantly cut back on research expenditures to avoid hurting reported earnings. This, according to

STOP & THINK

Would you expect that a rule requiring all firms to expense R&D outlays would cause R&D expenditures to decrease? Why or why not?

FYI:

The International Accounting Standards Board (IASB) has established an R&D accounting rule that many think is superior to the FASB rule. The IASB rule requires research costs to be expensed and development costs to be capitalized. Research costs are defined as those R&D costs incurred before technological feasibility has been established.

Exhibit 5: Expense/Asset Continuum

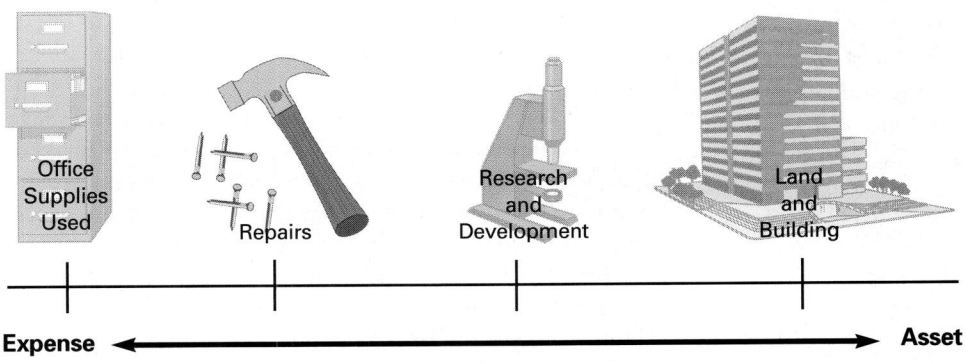

these comment letters, would cripple the U.S. economy. And the U.S. economy did indeed suffer in the mid-1970s, and R&D expenditures did decrease, but these occurrences may have had more to do with skyrocketing oil prices and double-digit inflation than with the R&D accounting rule passed by the FASB.

Advertising

Every year in the two weeks of hype preceding the Super Bowl, we hear about the incredible number of media people covering the event and about how much money advertisers are paying for a 30-second spot during the broadcast. We also hear a little bit about the football teams. With advertising costs running in excess of $2 million for 30 seconds, one has to believe that the advertisers expect some future economic benefit from the advertising. So, should advertising costs be capitalized or expensed?

For accounting purposes, the general presumption is that advertising costs should be expensed because of the uncertainty of the future benefits. However, in selected cases in which the future benefits are more certain, advertising costs should be capitalized. This type of advertising involves targeted advertising to customers who have purchased products in the past. Such advertising is also characterized by the ability to estimate how many customers will respond favorably. For example, SEARS discloses in the notes to its 2002 financial statements that it expenses newspaper, television, and radio advertising costs but capitalizes the cost of specialty catalogs and other direct response advertising. As of December 31, 2002, Sears reported an "advertising asset" of $58 million in its balance sheet. Of course, this is a rather small amount compared to the $1.80 billion in advertising that Sears expensed during 2002.

As these discussions of R&D and advertising illustrate, capitalize-or-expense decisions can be quite difficult from a conceptual standpoint. The general rule of thumb is that, when there is significant uncertainty about whether an expenditure should be capitalized or expensed, expense it. This approach is in line with the traditional conservatism of accounting, but be aware that it can result in a significant understatement of the economic assets of a company.

TO SUMMARIZE: Conceptually, a cost should be recorded as an asset whenever it has a probable future economic benefit. In practice, it is frequently quite difficult to tell when a cost should be recorded as an asset (capitalized) and when it should be recorded as an expense. In some areas, such as research and development (R&D) and advertising, specific accounting rules have been developed to create more uniformity about which costs should be expensed and which should be capitalized.

Summarizing Operations on an Income Statement

5 Prepare an income statement summarizing operating activities as well as other revenues and expenses, extraordinary items, and earnings per share.

Having now completed our discussion of operating revenues and expenses (in Chapters 7, 8, and thus far in 9), you are ready to examine an income statement, such as the one in Exhibit 6, and see how operating results are communicated to investors and creditors. The numbers in the income statement do not relate to any previous examples; they are shown here for illustrative purposes only.

This income statement shows that with net sales revenue of $2,475,000, P & L Company had net income of $385,000. The income statement classifies and accounts for the other $2,090,000 ($2,475,000 − $385,000). Sales revenue, cost of goods sold, and operating expenses (which are separated into selling expenses and general and administrative expenses on the income statement) have already been explained. It is important to note that operating income of $726,000 shows how much P & L Company earned from carrying on its major operations. These items constitute the major ongoing components of the income statement. Items shown at the bottom of the income statement are not part of the main operations of the business or are unusual and nonrecurring in nature.

Exhibit 6: Sample Income Statement

P & L Company
Income Statement
For the Year Ended December 31, 2006

Revenues:			
Gross sales revenue		$2,500,000	
Less: Sales returns		(12,000)	
Less: Sales discounts		(13,000)	
Net sales revenue			$2,475,000
Cost of goods sold			1,086,000
Gross margin			$1,389,000
Operating expenses:			
Selling expenses:			
Sales salaries expense	$200,000		
Sales commissions expense	60,000		
Advertising expense	45,000		
Delivery expense	14,000		
Total selling expenses		$ 319,000	
General and administrative expenses:			
Administrative salaries expense	$278,000		
Rent expense, office equipment	36,000		
Property tax expense	22,000		
Miscellaneous expenses	8,000		
Total general and administrative expenses		344,000	
Total operating expenses			663,000
Operating income			$ 726,000
Other revenues and expenses:			
Dividend revenue		$ 5,000	
Gain on sale of land		4,000	
Interest expense		(85,000)	
Net other revenues and expenses			(76,000)
Income from operations before income taxes			$ 650,000
Income taxes on operations (30%)			195,000
Income before extraordinary item			$ 455,000
Extraordinary item:			
Flood loss		$ (100,000)	
Income tax effect (30%)		30,000	(70,000)
Net income			$ 385,000
Earnings per share (100,000 shares outstanding):			
Income before extraordinary item			$4.55
Extraordinary loss			(0.70)
Net income			$3.85

other revenues and expenses Items incurred or earned from activities that are outside of, or peripheral to, the normal operations of a firm.

Other Revenues and Expenses

Other revenues and expenses are those items incurred or earned from activities outside of, or peripheral to, the normal operations of a firm. For example, a manufacturing company that receives dividends from its investments in the stock of another firm would show those dividend revenues as "Other Revenues and Expenses." This way, investors can see how much of a firm's income is from its major operating activity and how much is from peripheral activities, such as investing in other companies. The most common items reported in this section are interest and investment revenues and expenses. The other revenues and expenses category also includes gains and losses from the sale of assets other than inventory, such as land and buildings.

Extraordinary Items

extraordinary items Non-operating gains and losses that are unusual in nature, infrequent in occurrence, and material in amount.

The **extraordinary items** section of an income statement is reserved for reporting special non-operating gains and losses. This category is restrictive and includes only those items that are (1) unusual in nature, (2) infrequent in occurrence, and (3) material in amount. They are separated from other revenues and expenses so that readers can identify them as onetime, or nonrecurring, events. Extraordinary items are rare but can include losses or gains from floods, fires, earthquakes, and so on. For example, in 1980 when Mount St. Helens erupted in Washington, mudslides and flooding adversely affected much of the WEYERHAEUSER COMPANY's timberlands. Weyerhaeuser reported an extraordinary loss of $66.7 million in 1980 to cover standing timber, buildings, equipment, and other damaged items. Interestingly enough, the attack on the World Trade Center in September of 2001 was not accounted for as an extraordinary item. Accounting standard-setters determined that the economic effects of the World Trade Center attack were so pervasive as to make it impossible to separate the direct costs stemming from the attack from the economic costs (including lost revenue) created by the transformation of the economic landscape created by the attack.

If a firm has an extraordinary loss, its taxes are lower than they would be on the basis of ordinary operations. P & L Company, for example, actually paid only $165,000 ($195,000 based on operations less a $30,000 tax benefit from the extraordinary loss) in taxes. On the other hand, if a firm has an extraordinary gain, its taxes are increased. Therefore, to ensure that the full effect of the gain or loss is presented, extraordinary items are always shown together with their tax effects so that a net-of-tax amount can be seen. Thus, income tax expense may appear in two places on the income statement: below operating income before income taxes and in the extraordinary items section.

© 2003 Getty Images

The 1980 eruption of Mount St. Helens caused WEYER-HAEUSER COMPANY to report an extraordinary loss of $66.7 million. However, it's not likely Weyerhaeuser will have to worry about that extraordinary event happening again anytime soon!

earnings per share (EPS) The amount of net income (earnings) related to each share of stock; computed by dividing net income by the number of shares of stock outstanding during the period.

Earnings per Share

As noted in Chapter 2, a company is required to show **earnings per share (EPS)** on the income statement. If extraordinary items are included on the income statement, a firm will report EPS figures on income before extraordinary items, on extraordinary items, and on net income. Earnings per share is calculated by dividing a firm's net income by the number of shares of stock outstanding during the period. Exhibit 6 assumes that 100,000 shares of stock are outstanding. Earnings-per-share amounts are important because they allow potential investors to compare the profitability of all firms, whether large or small. Thus, the performance of a company earning $200 million and having 200,000 shares of stock outstanding can be compared with a company earning $60,000 and with 30,000 shares outstanding.

Income statements will often report two EPS figures—basic and diluted. The basic earnings per share figure is based on historical information. The diluted earnings per share number considers stock transactions that might occur in the future, the most common example being the exercise of stock options. Consider the following simplified example.

Burt Company reported net income for the year 2006 of $300,000. As of January 1, Burt had 100,000 shares of stock outstanding; those shares of stock were outstanding throughout the year. In addition, as of January 1, Burt had stock options outstanding that allowed certain executives to receive 50,000 shares of stock *for free* at a time of their choosing. As of December 31, the executives had not yet exercised the options.

basic earnings per share
An earnings per share figure that divides net income by the number of shares of stock outstanding.

diluted earnings per share
An earnings per share figure that considers the effect on net income and shares outstanding of events that will likely occur in the future, such as the exercising of favorable stock options.

Burt Company will compute two EPS numbers for 2006. The **basic earnings per share** is a straightforward computation based on Burt's reported net income and number of shares outstanding during the year. In this case, basic EPS is $3.00 per share ($300,000 net income/ 100,000 shares outstanding). Burt also computes **diluted earnings per share**. The diluted EPS number can be thought of as the earnings per share that would have been earned by each owner of one share *if* the holders of favorable contracts, such as the stock options in the case of Burt Company, had decided to exercise their rights at the beginning of the year. The diluted EPS number is really a future-oriented number; it gives the shareholders an indication of what their earnings per share next year might be if existing contracts, such as the options in this case, are exercised and new shares are issued. In this case, the diluted EPS is $2.00 per share [$300,000/ (100,000 shares + 50,000 potential shares)]. Options are just one example of contracts that can "dilute" the earnings per share of existing shareholders; another example is bonds (basically corporate IOUs) that can be converted into shares of stock. Bonds are discussed in Chapter 11.

Differing Income Statement Formats

The income statement featured in Exhibit 6 demonstrates detailed disclosure of a company's operations. Most companies do not provide that level of detail. The information contained in income statements varies from company to company. For example, MICROSOFT (see Appendix A) summarizes the results of its operations in 20 lines. IBM, on the other hand, provides detailed revenue and cost figures on the face of its income statements for each of its five operating segments (hardware sales, services, software, maintenance, and rentals). FORD MOTOR COMPANY provides detail in its income statements as to the operations of its two very different lines of business—automotive and financial services. Keep in mind that the format of the income statement will vary across companies but the information contained in the income statement is the same—revenues and expenses.

TO SUMMARIZE: The results of operating activities are summarized and reported on an income statement. On an income statement, cost of goods sold is subtracted from net sales to arrive at gross margin, or the amount a company marks up its inventory. Operating expenses are then subtracted from gross margin to arrive at operating income. Nonoperating items, such as other revenues and expenses, extraordinary items, and earnings per share, are reported on the income statement below operating income.

review of learning objectives

Account for the various components of employee compensation expense. Total employee compensation can involve some or all of the following:

- *Payroll.* Companies serve as the agents of federal, state, and local governments in withholding necessary taxes from employees' wages and salaries. These withholdings are then periodically forwarded to the appropriate government unit.
- *Compensated absences.* The value of vacation and sick days earned this year should be reported as an expense this year even though the actual vacation or sick days are not expected to be used until a future year.
- *Bonuses.* Employee bonuses, especially those for top management, are frequently based on reported accounting numbers such as net income. This creates some incentive for managers to manipulate reported earnings in order to boost their own bonuses.
- *Stock options.* The receipt of stock options gives managers an incentive to take value-enhancing actions that will increase their company's stock price. The intrinsic

value method of accounting for stock options assumes that options have potential value only on the day that they are granted; this method almost always results in no reported compensation expense. A more theoretically satisfying accounting method is the fair value method, which results in reported compensation expense being equal to the estimated value of the options granted. The FASB encourages use of the fair value method, but almost all companies continue to use the intrinsic value method.

- *Postemployment benefits.* When a company makes a decision to terminate employees as part of a restructuring, an expense equal to the expected value of the employee severance benefits is reported in the year in which the termination decision is made.

- *Pensions.* The difference between the pension obligation liability and the market value of the pension fund assets is reported as a net asset or liability in the balance sheet. Net pension expense is composed of interest cost and service cost, which are offset by the expected return on the pension fund assets.

- *Postretirement benefits other than pensions.* Companies are required to report an annual expense equal to the value of retiree benefits such as health care and life insurance that were earned during the year. These benefit plans are not structured as formally as pension plans.

2 **Compute income tax expense, including appropriate consideration of deferred tax items.** Sales taxes collected are reported as a liability until the funds are forwarded to the appropriate government agency. When property taxes are paid in advance, the amount is reported as a prepaid asset until the time period covered by the property tax has expired. With respect to income tax, corporations in the United States compute two different income numbers—financial income for reporting to stockholders and taxable income for reporting to the IRS. For income tax purposes, some income is not taxed until after it has already been reported as financial accounting income in a previous year. In this case, a deferred income tax liability is recognized in the year when the income is first reported in the income statement to reflect that the income will be taxed in a subsequent year. Similarly, some income tax deductions are not allowed for income tax purposes until after they have been reported as a financial accounting expense in a prior year. These items represent potentially valuable future deductions and are recorded as deferred income tax assets.

3 **Distinguish between contingent items that should be recognized in the financial statements and those that should be merely disclosed in the financial statement notes.** A contingent item is one for which the existence of a liability or asset depends on the outcome of uncertain future events. An example is litigation. A company must make an assessment as to the likely outcome and then account for the event accordingly. An event that is "probable" will be recognized on the financial statements. An event for which the outcome is reasonably possible will be disclosed in the notes to the financial statements, and an event considered remote is not disclosed.

Environmental liabilities represent another difficulty for businesses. These liabilities result when firms damage the environment. The difficulty with these liabilities is determining an amount. Typically, estimates are made along with extensive note disclosure.

4 **Understand when an expenditure should be recorded as an asset and when it should be recorded as an expense.** Many expenditures fall into a gray area where it isn't certain whether they should be expensed immediately or capitalized as assets. Specific practices have arisen with respect to many of these difficult-to-classify expenditures. For research and development expenditures, all regular R&D costs are expensed as incurred. For advertising expenditures, most advertising costs are expensed immediately. However, the cost of targeted advertising for which customer response can be reasonably estimated is capitalized.

5 **Prepare an income statement summarizing operating activities as well as other revenues and expenses, extraordinary items, and earnings per share.** The income statement is the means of reporting net income. Its major sections are revenues, cost of goods sold, operating expenses, operating income, other revenues and expenses, extraordinary items, net income, and earnings per share.

In addition to cost of goods sold expense, businesses incur many other operating expenses. With accrual accounting these are reported on the income statement as they are incurred, not when they are paid. Interest and other nonoperating revenues and expenses are classified separately below operating income. The income statement is not complete until all extraordinary items and earnings-per-share amounts have been included.

key terms & concepts

review problem

The Income Statement

From the following information prepare an income statement for Southern Corporation for the year ended December 31, 2006. Assume that there are 200,000 shares of stock outstanding.

Sales Returns	$ 50,000
Sales Discounts	70,000
Gross Sales Revenue	9,000,000
Flood Loss	80,000
Income Taxes on Operations	500,000
Administrative Salaries Expense	360,000
Sales Salaries Expense	800,000
Rent Expense (General and Administrative)	32,000
Utilities Expense (General and Administrative)	4,000
Supplies Expense (General and Administrative)	16,000
Delivery Expense (Selling)	6,300
Payroll Tax Expense (Selling)	6,000
Automobile Expense (General and Administrative)	3,800
Insurance Expense (General and Administrative)	34,000
Advertising Expense (Selling)	398,000
Interest Revenue	6,000
Interest Expense	92,000
Insurance Expense (Selling)	7,000
Entertainment Expense (Selling)	7,200
Miscellaneous Selling Expenses	15,000
Miscellaneous General and Administrative Expenses	10,800
Cost of Goods Sold	5,950,000
Tax rate applicable to flood loss	30%

Solution

The first step in preparing an income statement is classifying items, as follows:

Revenue Accounts	
Sales Returns	$ 50,000
Sales Discounts	70,000
Gross Sales Revenue	9,000,000

Cost of Goods Sold Accounts	
Cost of Goods Sold	$5,950,000

Selling Expense Accounts

Sales Salaries Expense	$800,000
Delivery Expense	6,300
Payroll Tax Expense	6,000
Advertising Expense	398,000
Insurance Expense	7,000
Entertainment Expense	7,200
Miscellaneous Selling Expenses	15,000

General and Administrative Expense Accounts

Administrative Salaries Expense	$360,000
Rent Expense	32,000
Utilities Expense	4,000
Supplies Expense	16,000
Automobile Expense	3,800
Insurance Expense	34,000
Miscellaneous General and Administrative Expenses	10,800

Other Revenue and Expense Accounts

Interest Revenue	$ 6,000
Interest Expense	92,000

Miscellaneous Accounts

Income Taxes on Operations	$500,000

Extraordinary Item Accounts

Flood Loss	$80,000
Tax rate	30%

Once the accounts are classified, the income statement is prepared by including the accounts in the following format:

	Net Sales Revenue (Gross Sales Revenue − Sales Returns − Sales Discounts)
−	Cost of Goods Sold
=	Gross Margin
−	Selling Expenses
−	General and Administrative Expenses
=	Operating Income
+/−	Other Revenues and Expenses (add Net Revenues, subtract Net Expenses)
=	Income before Income Taxes
−	Income Taxes on Operations
=	Income before Extraordinary Items
+/−	Extraordinary Items (add Extraordinary Gains, subtract Extraordinary Losses, net of applicable taxes)
=	Net Income

After net income has been computed, earnings per share is calculated and added to the bottom of the statement. It is important that the proper heading be included.

Southern Corporation
Income Statement
For the Year Ended December 31, 2006

Revenues:			
Gross sales revenue	$9,000,000		
Less: Sales returns	(50,000)		
Less: Sales discounts	(70,000)		
Net sales revenue		$8,880,000	
Cost of goods sold		5,950,000	
Gross margin		$2,930,000	
Operating expenses:			
Selling expenses:			
Sales salaries expense	$800,000		
Delivery expense	6,300		
Payroll tax expense	6,000		
Advertising expense	398,000		
Insurance expense	7,000		
Entertainment expense	7,200		
Miscellaneous expenses	15,000		
Total selling expenses		$1,239,500	
General and administrative expenses:			
Administrative salaries expense	$360,000		
Rent expense	32,000		
Utilities expense	4,000		
Supplies expense	16,000		
Automobile expense	3,800		
Insurance expense	34,000		
Miscellaneous expenses	10,800		
Total general and administrative expenses		460,600	
Total operating expenses			1,700,100
Operating income			$1,229,900
Other revenues and expenses:			
Interest revenue		$ 6,000	
Interest expense		(92,000)	
Net other revenues and expenses			(86,000)
Income from operations before income taxes			$1,143,900
Income taxes on operations			500,000
Income before extraordinary item			$ 643,900
Extraordinary item:			
Flood loss		$ (80,000)	
Income tax effect (30%)		24,000	(56,000)
Net income			$ 587,900
Earnings per share:			
Before extraordinary items	$ 3.22 ($643,900 ÷ 200,000 shares)		
Extraordinary loss	(0.28) ($ 56,000 ÷ 200,000 shares)		
Net income	$ 2.94 ($587,900 ÷ 200,000 shares)		

discussion questions

1. Why is the accounting for payroll-related liabilities more complicated than the accounting for other current liabilities?
2. If the period of time covered by a company's payroll does not coincide with the last day of the year for financial reporting, how is accounting for the payroll affected by this situation?
3. What is a compensated absence?
4. What danger is there in basing a manager's bonus on reported net income?
5. What is the primary difference between the intrinsic value method and the fair value method of accounting for stock-based compensation plans? Which method does the FASB recommend?
6. What additional disclosure is required of companies that use the intrinsic value method?
7. Severance benefits resulting from a company restructuring are reported as an expense in the period that the restructuring decision is made rather than when the benefits are actually paid. Why?
8. What is the difference between a defined contribution pension plan and a defined benefit pension plan?
9. How is a company's pension obligation reported in its balance sheet?
10. List and briefly discuss the three components of pension expense discussed in the chapter.
11. In what ways do postretirement health-care and life insurance benefit plans differ from postretirement pension plans?
12. Why is an end-of-year adjusting entry for property taxes often necessary?
13. In your opinion, what is the primary objective of determining pretax financial accounting income? How does this objective differ from the objectives of determining taxable income as defined by the IRS?
14. When and how does a company record the amount owed to the government for income taxes for a given year?
15. What causes deferred income taxes?
16. What is the difference between a "contingent liability" and a "liability"?
17. Escalating environmental liabilities are a major concern of companies today. How does a company know when to record such liabilities?
18. Currently MICROSOFT spends a tremendous amount of money on research and development costs to continuously develop new products. How are such R&D costs accounted for?
19. XYZ Corporation pays for advertising costs all the time. Sometimes the company records these payments as assets, and sometimes it records them as expenses. Why would XYZ use different accounting treatments?
20. What types of items would be included on an income statement as "other revenues and expenses"?
21. More than ever before, tremendous attention is being paid to a company's earnings-per-share number. Why do you think investors and creditors pay so much attention to earnings per share?

practice exercises

Practice 9-1

Salaries Expense Calculation

Using the following data, compute salaries expense.

State Withholding Taxes Payable	$ 5,200
FICA Taxes Payable, Employer	4,973
Salaries Payable	44,427
Federal Unemployment Taxes Payable	468
Federal Withholding Taxes Payable	10,400
State Unemployment Taxes Payable	1,820
FICA Taxes Payable, Employees	4,973

Practice 9-2

Salaries Expense Journal Entry

Refer to the data in Practice 9-1. Make the journal entry necessary to record salaries expense for the period.

Practice 9-3

Payroll Tax Expense Calculation
Refer to the data in Practice 9-1. Compute payroll tax expense.

Practice 9-4

Payroll Tax Expense Journal Entry
Refer to the data in Practice 9-1. Make the journal entry necessary to record payroll tax expense for the period.

Practice 9-5

Salaries and Payroll Tax Payments
Refer to the data in Practice 9-1. Make the journal entries necessary to record the payment of the payable accounts related to salaries expense and payroll tax expense to (1) the federal government, (2) the state government, and (3) the employees.

Practice 9-6

Accruing Compensated Absences
Assume an employee earns $150 per day and accrues one sick day each month. Make the journal entry necessary at the end of the quarter to record the accrual of the sick days during the quarter.

Practice 9-7

Using Compensated Absences
The employee mentioned in Practice 9-6 used one sick day. For simplicity, combine the various taxes into one account called "Various Taxes Payable." The effective tax rate for all of the various taxes is 20%. Make the journal entry necessary to record the use of the sick day.

Practice 9-8

Accounting for Employee Stock Options
Which one of the following statements correctly describes the intrinsic value and the fair value methods of accounting for employee stock options?

a. The intrinsic value method requires an estimate of the actual value of the options whereas the fair value method uses the value of the options if they are exercised immediately.
b. Companies are required to use the intrinsic value method and barred from using the fair value method.
c. Companies are required to use the fair value method and barred from using the intrinsic value method.
d. Companies using the fair value method must disclose what their net income would have been if they had used the intrinsic value method.
e. The fair value method requires an estimate of the actual value of the options whereas the intrinsic value method uses the value of the options if they are exercised immediately.

Practice 9-9

Postemployment Benefits
Because of a drop in demand for its products, the company found it necessary to lay off 200 employees. The employment contract grants termination benefits worth an estimated $5,000 to each employee. Make the journal entry necessary to record the termination of the employees.

Practice 9-10

Pension Terminology
Identify which one of the following terms correctly matches the following definition: The amount a company's pension obligation increases as a result of employees working and earning more benefits.

a. Pension fund
b. Pension-related interest cost
c. Service cost
d. Pension expense
e. Return on pension fund

Practice 9-11

Net Pension Asset/Liability

Companies A, B, and C report the following information:

	A	B	C
Pension benefit obligation	$3,920	$9,230	$1,302
Service cost	235	500	150
Pension fund assets	2,004	11,023	1,350
Expected return on pension fund assets	200	1,000	120

For each of the companies, determine the amount of the net pension asset/liability. Be sure to specify whether the amount is an asset or a liability.

Practice 9-12

Pension Expense

Using the following numbers, compute pension expense.

Expected return on fund assets	$ 305
Pension benefit obligation	2,000
Service cost	285
Interest cost	190
Pension fund assets	3,000

Practice 9-13

Sales Tax

The company sold merchandise for $448; this price does *not* include sales tax. The state sales tax rate is 6.25%. Make the journal entry necessary to record this transaction.

Practice 9-14

Property Taxes

The company paid $7,200 in advance for one year of property taxes on September 24. The property taxes are for the one-year period beginning October 1. Make the journal entries necessary to record (1) the payment of the property taxes and (2) the year-end adjusting entry on December 31.

Practice 9-15

Income Tax Expense

Which one of the following statements correctly describes income tax expense?

a. The amount of cash paid for income taxes during the year.
b. The amount of income tax owed as of the end of the year.
c. The amount of cash that will be paid for income taxes next year.
d. The amount of income taxes attributable to the income earned during the year.
e. The amount of income taxes payable as reported in a company's income tax return.

Practice 9-16

Deferred Tax Liability

The company invested $2,500 in a mutual fund on April 1. By December 31, the value of the mutual fund had increased to $3,100, and the company did *not* sell any portion of the mutual fund during the year. The company's income tax rate is 35%. Prepare the journal entry necessary to record the deferred income tax liability.

Practice 9-17

Deferred Tax Assets

The company invested $3,000 in a mutual fund on August 1. By December 31, the value of the mutual fund had declined to $2,200, and the company did *not* sell any portion of the mutual fund during the year. The company's income tax rate is 25%. Prepare the journal entry necessary to record the deferred income tax asset.

Practice 9-18

Contingent Liabilities

Which one of the following correctly describes the circumstances in which a contingent liability should be recognized as a liability in the financial statements?

a. The chance of the future event occurring is remote.
b. The chance of the future event occurring is possible.
c. The chance of the future event occurring is probable.
d. The chance of the future event occurring is slight.
e. The chance of the future event occurring is more likely than not.

Practice 9-19

Capitalize versus Expense

Which one of the following statements is correct?

a. When there is significant uncertainty about whether an expenditure should be capitalized or expensed, capitalize it.
b. When there is significant uncertainty about whether an expenditure should be capitalized or expensed, expense it.
c. Generally, advertising costs are capitalized because it is easy for firms to trace advertising dollars spent to revenue generated from such advertisements.
d. Expenditures made for equipment and buildings should be expensed in the period of the purchase.
e. Research and development expenditures are typically capitalized in the period in which they are incurred.

Practice 9-20

Income Statement Classification

Using the following data, prepare a classified income statement. The income tax rate on all items is 25%. (*Hint:* Net income is $52,050.)

Advertising expense	$ 4,000
Sales returns	5,000
Cost of goods sold	80,000
Dividend revenue	2,000
Gain on sale of equipment	1,000
Interest expense	5,000
Rent expense	3,600
Sales discounts	10,000
Salaries expense	11,000
Gross sales	215,000
Tornado loss	30,000

Practice 9-21

Earnings per Share

The company had 100,000 shares of stock outstanding throughout the year. In addition, as of January 1 the company had issued stock options that allowed employees to receive 40,000 shares of stock for free at a time of their choosing in the future. As of the end of the year, none of the options had been exercised. Net income for the year was $200,000. Compute (1) basic earnings per share and (2) diluted earnings per share.

x e r c i s e s

Exercise 9-1

Payroll Accounting

Stockbridge Stores, Inc., has three employees, Frank Wall, Mary Jones, and Susan Wright. Summaries of their 2006 salaries and withholdings are as follows:

(*continued*)

Employee	Gross Salaries	Federal Income Taxes Withheld	State Income Taxes Withheld	FICA Taxes Withheld
Frank Wall	$54,000	$6,500	$2,500	$4,131
Mary Jones	39,000	4,800	1,900	2,984
Susan Wright	34,000	4,250	1,500	2,601

1. Prepare the summary entry for salaries paid to the employees for the year 2006.
2. Assume that, in addition to FICA taxes, the employer has incurred $192 for federal unemployment taxes and $720 for state unemployment taxes. Prepare the summary journal entry to record the payroll tax liability for 2006, assuming no taxes have yet been paid.
3. **Interpretive Question:** What other types of items are frequently withheld from employees' paychecks in addition to income taxes and FICA taxes?

Exercise 9-2

Spreadsheet

Bonus Computation and Journal Entry

Rulon Wilcox is the president of Wilcox Company, and his brother, Harry Wilcox, is the vice president. Their compensation package includes bonuses of 4% for Rulon Wilcox and 3% for Harry Wilcox of net income that exceeds $250,000. Net income for the year 2006 has just been computed to be $885,000.

1. Compute the amount of bonuses to be paid to Rulon and Harry Wilcox.
2. Prepare the journal entries to record the accrual and payment of the bonuses. Summarize all withholding taxes related to the bonuses in an account called Various Taxes Payable. Taxes payable on the bonuses total $9,800 for Rulon and $7,620 for Harry.

Exercise 9-3

Stock Options: Intrinsic and Fair Value Methods

On January 1, 2006, the Magily Company established a stock option plan for its senior employees. A total of 60,000 options were granted that permit employees to purchase 60,000 shares of stock at $48 per share. Each option had a fair value of $11 on the date the options were granted. The market price for Magily stock on January 1, 2006, was $50. The employees are required to remain with Magily Company for the entire year of 2006 in order to be able to exercise these options.

Compute the total amount of compensation expense to be associated with these options under the:

1. fair value method.
2. intrinsic value method.

Exercise 9-4

Stock Options: Required Disclosure

Refer to the information in Exercise 9-3. Magily's income for 2006, before subtracting any compensation expense associated with the stock option plan, is $500,000.

Prepare the required supplemental disclosure for 2006 assuming that Magily decides to use the intrinsic value method.

Exercise 9-5

Pensions on the Balance Sheet

Pension plan information for Rabona Company is as follows:

December 31, 2006
Pension obligation liability $3,000,000
December 31, 2006
Pension fund assets 3,150,000
During 2006
Total pension expense 200,000

How will this information be reported on Rabona's balance sheet as of December 31, 2006?

Exercise 9-6

Computing Pension Expense

Chanelle Company reports the following pension information for 2006:

Pension-related interest cost for the year	$ 65,000
Pension fund assets, end of year	895,000
Pension obligation liability, end of year	930,000
Pension service cost for the year	90,000
Return on pension fund assets for the year	115,000

1. What pension amount would Chanelle report on its balance sheet as of the end of the year?
2. Compute the amount to be reported on the income statement as pension expense for the year.

Exercise 9-7

Pension Computations

The following pension information is for three different companies. For each company, compute the missing amount or amounts.

	Company 1	Company 2	Company 3
Pension fund assets	$100,000	$75,000	$ (e)
Pension obligation liability	(a)	80,000	100,000
Net pension asset (liability)	20,000	(c)	(25,000)
Pension-related interest cost	$ 10,000	$ (d)	$ 20,000
Service cost	8,000	6,000	23,000
Return on pension plan assets	5,000	8,000	(f)
Pension expense	(b)	10,000	35,000

Exercise 9-8

Accounting for Property Taxes

In June 2005, Jensen Company received a bill from the county government for property taxes on its land and buildings for the period July 1, 2005, through June 30, 2006. The amount of the tax bill is $15,300, and payment is due August 1, 2005. Jensen Company uses the calendar year for financial reporting purposes.

1. Prepare the journal entries to record payment of the property taxes on August 1, 2005.
2. Prepare the adjusting entry for property taxes on December 31, 2005.

Exercise 9-9

Deferred Income Taxes

Yosef Company began operating on January 1, 2006. At the end of the first year of operations, Yosef reported $750,000 income before income taxes on its income statement but only $660,000 taxable income on its tax return. This difference arose because $90,000 in income earned during 2006 was not yet taxable according to the income tax regulations. The tax rate is 35%.

1. Compute the amount of income tax that Yosef legally owes for taxable income generated during 2006.
2. Compute the amount of income tax expense to be reported on Yosef's income statement for 2006.
3. State whether Yosef has a deferred income tax asset or a deferred income tax liability as of the end of 2006. What is the amount of the asset or liability?

Exercise 9-10

Deferred Income Taxes

Boatogooso Company began operating on January 1, 2006. At the end of the first year of operations, Boatogooso reported $500,000 income before income taxes on its income statement but taxable income of $600,000 on its tax return. This difference arose because $100,000 in expenses incurred during 2006 were not yet deductible for income tax purposes according to the income tax regulations. The tax rate is 40%.

1. Compute the amount of income tax that Boatogooso legally owes for taxable income generated during 2006.
2. Compute the amount of income tax expense to be reported on Boatogooso's income statement for 2006.
3. State whether Boatogooso has a deferred income tax asset or a deferred income tax liability as of the end of 2006. What is the amount of the asset or liability?

Exercise 9-11

Contingent Liabilities

Rayn Company is involved in the following legal matters:

a. A customer is suing Rayn for allegedly selling a faulty and dangerous product. Rayn's attorneys believe that there is a 40% chance of Rayn's losing the suit.
b. A federal agency has accused Rayn of violating numerous employee safety laws. The company faces significant fines if found guilty. Rayn's attorneys feel that the company has complied with all applicable laws, and they therefore place the probability of incurring the fines at less than 10%.
c. Rayn has been named in a gender discrimination lawsuit. In the past, Rayn has systematically promoted its male employees at a faster rate than it has promoted its female employees. Rayn's attorneys judge the probability that Rayn will lose this lawsuit at more than 90%.

For each item, determine the appropriate accounting treatment.

Exercise 9-12

Classifying Expenditures as Assets or Expenses

Determining whether an expenditure should be expensed or capitalized is often difficult. Consider each of the following independent situations and indicate whether you would recommend that the cost be expensed or capitalized as an asset. Explain your answer.

1. Splash.com has spent $1.5 million for a 30-second advertisement to be aired during the Super Bowl. The ad introduces the company's new Web-based product, and the company expects the ad to increase sales for at least 18 months.
2. Chromosome.com has spent $8 million on research related to genetic diseases. The company expects this research to lead to substantial revenues, beginning in the next year.
3. Catalog.com is an online catalog sales company. Catalog.com has just spent $5 million designing a targeted advertising campaign that will encourage regular customers of the company's online catalog service to buy new products.
4. Food.com is an online seller of groceries. The company just spent $4 million building a new warehouse. The warehouse is expected to be useful for the next 15 years.

Exercise 9-13

Spreadsheet

Preparing an Income Statement

Hoopes Company is preparing financial statements for the calendar year 2006. The following totals for each account have been verified as correct:

Office Supplies on Hand	$ 600
Insurance Expense	240
Gross Sales Revenue	12,000
Cost of Goods Sold	6,440
Sales Returns	400
Interest Expense	200
Accounts Payable	240
Accounts Receivable	520
Extraordinary Loss	2,160
Selling Expenses	720
Office Supplies Used	160
Cash	600
Revenue from Investments	560
Number of shares of capital stock	180

Prepare an income statement. Assume a 30% income tax rate on both income from operations and extraordinary items. Include EPS numbers.

Exercise 9-14

P.A.S.S.
Power Accounting
System Software

Unifying Concepts: The Income Statement

Use the following information to prepare an income statement for Fairchild Corporation for the year ended December 31, 2006. You should show separate classifications for revenues, cost of goods sold, gross margin, selling expenses, general and administrative expenses, operating income, other revenues and expenses, income before income taxes, income taxes, and net income. (*Hint:* Net income is $27,276.)

Sales Returns	$ 4,280
Income Taxes	26,000
Interest Revenue	2,400
Office Supplies Expense (General and Administrative)	400
Utilities Expense (General and Administrative)	3,980
Office Salaries Expense (General and Administrative)	12,064
Miscellaneous Selling Expenses	460
Insurance Expense (Selling)	1,160
Advertising Expense	6,922
Sales Salaries Expense	40,088
Sales Discounts	3,644
Interest Expense	1,170
Miscellaneous General and Administrative Expenses	620
Insurance Expense (General and Administrative)	600
Payroll Tax Expense (General and Administrative)	3,600
Store Supplies Expense (Selling)	800
Delivery Expense (Selling)	2,198
Inventory, January 1, 2006	79,400
Sales Revenue	395,472
Cost of Goods Sold	262,610
Purchases	230,560
Purchases Discounts	3,050
Inventory, December 31, 2006	44,300
Average number of shares of stock outstanding	10,000

roblems

Problem 9-1

P.A.S.S.
Power Accounting
System Software

Payroll Accounting

Orange County Bank has three employees, Albert Myers, Juan Moreno, and Michi Endo. During January 2006, these three employees earned $6,000, $4,200, and $4,000, respectively. The following table summarizes the required withholding rates on each individual's income for the month of January:

Employee	Federal Income Tax Withholdings	State Income Tax Withholdings	FICA Tax
Albert Myers	33%	3%	7.65%
Juan Moreno	28	4	7.65
Michi Endo	28	5	7.65

You are also informed that the bank is subject to the following unemployment tax rates on the salaries earned by the employees during January 2006:

(continued)

Federal unemployment tax	. . . .	0.8%
State unemployment tax	. . . .	3.0%

Required:
1. Prepare the journal entry to record salaries payable for the month of January.
2. Prepare the journal entry to record payment of the January salaries to employees.
3. Prepare the journal entry to record the bank's payroll taxes for the month of January.

Problem 9-2

Determining Payroll Costs

Orson Nutrition pays its salespeople a base salary of $1,000 per month plus a commission. Each salesperson starts with a commission of 1% of total gross sales for the month. The commission is increased thereafter according to seniority and productivity, up to a maximum of 5%. Orson has five salespeople with gross sales for the month of March and commission rates as follows:

	Commission Rate	Gross Sales
JD	4.5%	$100,000
Derrald	5.0	120,000
Cierra	2.5	80,000
Hannah	3.0	50,000
Skyler	1.0	200,000

The FICA tax rate is 7.65%. In addition, state and federal income taxes of 20% are withheld from each employee.

Required:
1. Compute Orson's total payroll expense (base salary plus commissions) for the month.
2. Compute the total amount of cash paid to employees for compensation for the month.
3. **Interpretive Question:** Briefly outline the advantages and disadvantages of having *no* income taxes withheld, but instead relying on individual taxpayers to pay the entire amount of their income tax at the end of the year when they file their tax return.

Problem 9-3

Stock Options

On January 1, 2006, Tiger Man Company established a stock option plan for its senior employees. A total of 400,000 options were granted that permit employees to purchase 400,000 shares of stock at $20 per share. Each option had a fair value of $5 on the grant date. The market price for Tiger Man stock on January 1, 2006, was $20. The employees are required to remain with Tiger Man for three years (2006, 2007, and 2008) in order to be able to exercise these options. Tiger Man's net income for 2006, before including any consideration of compensation expense, is $675,000.

Required:
1. Compute the compensation expense associated with these options for 2006 under the fair value method. Note that the period of time that the employees must work to be able to exercise the options is three years.
2. Repeat (1) using the intrinsic value method.
3. Prepare any supplemental disclosures needed if Tiger Man uses the intrinsic value method.
4. **Interpretive Question:** You are a Tiger Man stockholder. What objections might you have to Tiger Man's employee stock option plan?

Problem 9-4

Accounting for Pensions

The following information is available from John Gammon Company relating to its defined benefit pension plan:

Balances as of January 1, 2006:

Pension obligation liability	$4,300
Pension fund assets	3,800

Activity for 2006:

Service cost	$ 550
Contributions to pension fund	240
Benefit payments to retirees	200
Return on plan assets	340
Pension-related interest cost	344

Required:

1. Compute the amount of pension expense to be reported on the income statement for 2006.
2. Determine the net pension amount to be reported on the balance sheet at the end of the year. *Note:* The benefit payments to retirees are made out of the pension fund assets. These payments reduce both the amount in the pension fund and the amount of the remaining pension obligation.
3. **Interpretive Question:** You are an employee of John Gammon Company and have just received the above information as part of the company's annual report to the employees on the status of the pension plan. Does anything in this information cause you concern? Explain.

Problem 9-5

Accounting for Pensions

Kiev Company reported the following information relating to its pension plan for the years 2004 through 2007:

	Year-End Obligation	Year-End Plan Assets	Interest Cost	Service Cost	Return on Assets
2004	$522,500	$469,000	—	—	—
2005	581,250	505,050	$52,250	$61,500	$62,750
2006	643,000	549,700	58,125	65,625	71,650
2007	681,500	615,600	64,300	37,900	68,500

Required:

1. Compute the amount of pension expense to be reported on the income statement for each of the years 2005 through 2007.
2. Determine the net pension amount to be reported on the balance sheet at the end of each year 2004 through 2007. Clearly indicate whether the amount is an asset or a liability.
3. Each year, the amount of the pension obligation is increased by the interest cost and the service cost. The pension obligation is reduced by the amount of pension benefits paid. Compute the amount of pension benefits paid in each of the years 2005 through 2007.
4. Each year, the amount in the pension fund is increased by contributions to the fund and by the return earned on the fund assets. The pension fund amount is reduced by the amount of pension benefits paid. Compute the amount of contributions to the pension fund in each of the years 2005 through 2007.

Problem 9-6

Life Cycle of a Deferred Tax Item

Black Kitty Company recorded certain revenues of $10,000 and $20,000 on its books in 2004 and 2005, respectively. However, these revenues were not subject to income taxation until 2006.

(continued)

Company records reveal pretax financial accounting income and taxable income for the three-year period as follows:

	Financial Income	Taxable Income
2004	$44,000	$34,000
2005	38,000	18,000
2006	21,000	51,000

Assume Black Kitty's tax rate is 40% for all periods.

Required:

1. Determine the amount of income tax that will be *paid* each year from 2004 through 2006.
2. Determine the amount of income tax expense that will be reported on the income statement each year from 2004 through 2006.
3. Compute the amount of deferred tax liability that would be reported on the balance sheet at the end of each year.
4. **Interpretive Question:** Why would the IRS allow Black Kitty to defer payment of taxes on some of the revenue earned in 2004 and 2005?

Problem 9-7

Spreadsheet

P.A.S.S.
Power Accounting System Software

Unifying Concepts: The Income Statement

From the following information, prepare an income statement for Moriancumer, Inc., for the year ended December 31, 2006. (*Hint:* Net income is $98,500.) Assume that there are 15,000 shares of capital stock outstanding.

Gross Sales Revenue	$4,230,000
Income Taxes	99,000
Cost of Goods Sold	3,116,000
Sales Salaries Expense	350,000
Rent Expense (Selling)	16,000
Payroll Tax Expense (Selling)	4,900
Entertainment Expense (Selling)	1,500
Miscellaneous Selling Expenses	6,300
Miscellaneous General and Administrative Expenses	5,400
Automobile Expense (Selling)	3,500
Insurance Expense (General and Administrative)	700
Interest Expense	39,000
Interest Revenue	2,000
Sales Returns	8,000
Advertising and Promotion Expense	204,000
Insurance Expense (Selling)	17,000
Delivery Expense (Selling)	3,100
Office Supplies Expense (General and Administrative)	8,000
Utilities Expense (General and Administrative)	1,100
Administrative Salaries Expense	200,000
Fire Loss (net of tax)	50,000

Problem 9-8

Income Statement Analysis

The following table represents portions of the income statements of Brinkerhoff Company for the years 2004–2006:

Spreadsheet

	2006	2005	2004
Gross sales revenue	$42,000	$ (9)	$25,800
Sales discounts	0	100	100
Sales returns	0	200	700
Net sales revenue	42,000	(10)	(1)
Beginning inventory	(15)	8,000	(2)
Purchases	24,800	(11)	15,000
Purchases discounts	700	300	500
Freight-in	(16)	0	500
Cost of goods available for sale	29,000	25,000	(3)
Ending inventory	3,800	(12)	(4)
Cost of goods sold	(17)	(13)	(5)
Gross margin	(18)	14,000	(6)
Selling expenses	4,000	(14)	(7)
General and administrative expenses	(19)	3,200	3,000
Income before income taxes	9,000	8,000	4,000
Income taxes	4,500	4,000	(8)
Net income	(20)	4,000	2,000

Required:

Fill in the missing numbers. Assume that gross margin is 40% of net sales revenue.

discussion cases

Case 9-1

Recording Liabilities and the Effect on Bonuses

John Flowers, president of Marquette Company, is paid a salary plus a bonus equal to 10% of pretax income. The company has just computed its pretax income to be $3.4 million. Based on this income, Flowers expects to receive a bonus of $340,000. However, the company has just been told by outside experts that it may have an environmental liability of $2.1 million and that, based on new actuarial estimates, the recorded amount of postretirement benefits is too low by $1.2 million. The experts recommend that both of these liabilities be recorded, which would reduce income to $100,000 and Flowers's bonus to $10,000. Flowers believes he does not need to record the adjustments for the following reasons: the environmental liability is not certain, the amount of the potential liability can't be accurately estimated, and "actuarial estimates" are always changing. Is Flowers violating GAAP if he refuses to allow the company to adjust pretax income, or is the decision to not record the adjustments acceptable because of the uncertainty of the liabilities and the amounts?

Case 9-2

Questioning the Accounting for Pensions, Research, and Income Taxes

Tatia Wilks, the president of Lewbacca Company, is concerned about the low earnings that Lewbacca is scheduled to report this year. She called the company's accounting staff into her office to question them about the accounting treatment of several items. She raised the following points:

a. Why do we have to report an expense this year associated with our pension plan? Our company is new, and none of our employees is within even 15 years of retirement. Accordingly, the pension plan won't cost us anything for at least 15 years.

(continued)

b. Research to find new products and improve our old products is one of our key competitive advantages. However, you tell me that all of the money we spend on research is reported as an expense this year. This is silly because the results of our research comprise our biggest economic asset.

c. We have an excellent staff of tax planners who work hard to legally minimize the amount of income taxes we pay each year. However, I see in the notes to the financial statements that you are requiring our company to report a "deferred income tax expense" for taxes that we don't even owe yet! Why?

How would you respond to each of these points?

j udgment calls

Judgment 9-1

You Decide: Are stock options and bonus plans an appropriate incentive or a cause for corruption?

Do employee bonus plans provide incentives to work harder and achieve personal and corporate goals, or are they a catalyst for corporate corruption? For example, assume you work for a Fortune 500 company. You are the chief financial officer of the company and are in charge of the company's accounting. The company is doing well; in fact, you have just been informed that members of top management will each receive 10,000 stock options to purchase company stock if earnings meet forecasts. Your associate tells you that the options will create pressure to meet the forecasts. Is he right?

Judgment 9-2

You Decide: Should start-up costs be capitalized or expensed?

Your spouse is setting up a home-based Web design business. Her purpose for setting up the business is to earn some extra income now and, in two to three years, sell the business. Your spouse is wondering whether she can capitalize the start-up costs or whether they must be expensed. She has heard from other business owners that in order to minimize taxes, it is a lot better to expense as much as you can. With this end goal in mind, what should your spouse do?

C o m p e t e n c y E n h a n c e m e n t O p p o r t u n i t i e s

▶ **Analyzing Real Company Information**
▶ **International Case**
▶ **Ethics Case**
▶ **Writing Assignment**

▶ **The Debate**
▶ **Cumulative Spreadsheet Project**
▶ **Internet Search**

The following additional assignments provide opportunities for students to develop critical thinking, ethical perspectives, oral and written communication skills, experience with electronic research, and teamwork through group and business activities.

▶ *Analyzing Real Company Information*

Analyzing 9-1 (Microsoft)

The 2002 Form 10-K for MICROSOFT is included in Appendix A. Locate that Form 10-K and consider the following questions:

1. Find Microsoft's financial statement note on "Income taxes."
   a. Using the current tax information and the information given on income before income taxes, compute Microsoft's 2002 effective tax rate for both U.S. and international income. The effective tax rate is computed by dividing current taxes by income before income taxes.
   b. As of June 30, 2002, Microsoft had $3,508 million in deferred income tax liabilities. What was the source of most of this deferred tax liability?
2. Find Microsoft's financial statement note concerning "employee stock and savings plans."
   a. Briefly describe Microsoft's employee stock purchase plan.
   b. Microsoft also has an employee stock option plan whereby certain key employees are granted incentive stock options that allow them to buy Microsoft stock at a fixed price in the future. If Microsoft's stock price continues to rise, these options could be very valuable. Microsoft (as of December 2002) is not required to report any expense associated with the granting of these options. However, Microsoft is required to estimate the value of these options and disclose what net income would have been if this value had been recognized as an expense. How much would Microsoft's 2002 net income have decreased if the value of the incentive stock options had been recognized as an expense?

Analyzing 9-2 (General Motors)

GENERAL MOTORS has the largest set of private pension plans in the world. The company has many different pension plans covering different groups of employees. The following information was extracted from the notes to GM's 2002 financial statements. All numbers are in millions of U.S. dollars. As you can see, for reporting purposes these plans are separated into U.S. plans and non-U.S. plans.

	U.S. Plans Pension Benefits		Non-U.S. Plans Pension Benefits	
	2002	**2001**	**2002**	**2001**
Fair value of plan assets at end of year	$ 60,860	$67,322	$ 5,943	$ 6,340
Projected benefit obligation at end of year	80,114	76,383	12,129	9,950
Funded status	$(19,254)	$ (9,061)	$ (6,186)	$(3,610)

1. The projected benefit obligation is the measure of the value of the pension benefits earned by GM's employees that has not yet been paid. What is GM's total projected benefit obligation?
2. To ensure that employees will be able to collect their pension benefits, GM is required by law to set aside funds in a pension plan. What is the total value of assets in all of these pension funds?
3. Why do you think GM is required to separate its disclosure of pension plans into U.S. and non-U.S. plans?

Analyzing 9-3 (IBM)

Note P to IBM's 2002 financial statements describes how taxes affect IBM's operations. Among the information given is the following (all amounts are in millions of U.S. dollars):

For the year ended December 31:	2002	2001	2000
Income from continuing operations before income taxes:			
U.S. operations	$3,838	$ 5,644	$ 5,914
Non-U.S. operations	3,686	5,806	5,497
Total income from continuing operations before income taxes	$7,524	$11,450	$11,411

The continuing operations provision for income taxes by geographic operations is as follows:

For the year ended December 31:	2002	2001	2000
U.S. operations	$ 934	$1,543	$1,798
Non-U.S. operations	1,256	1,761	1,739
Total continuing operations provision for income taxes	$2,190	$3,304	$3,537
Provision for social security, real estate, personal property, and other taxes	$2,789	$2,730	$2,734

1. a. Compute the effective tax rate (income taxes/earnings before income taxes) for both U.S. and non-U.S. operations for 2000, 2001, and 2002.
   b. For each year 2000–2002, compute the percentage of the total tax burden that was made up of income taxes.
2. A deferred tax asset is a tax deduction that has already occurred and has been reported as a financial accounting expense but cannot be used to reduce income taxes until a future year. As of December 31, 2002, IBM reports that it has a deferred tax asset of $4.636 billion related to employee benefits. How would such a deferred tax asset arise?

▶ *International Case*

International

Hutchison Whampoa

In Hong Kong, Li Ka-shing is known as "Superman." Li's personal wealth is estimated to be in excess of $1 billion, and there is a saying in Hong Kong that for every dollar spent, five cents goes into Li's pocket. Li and his family fled from China in 1940 in order to escape the advancing Japanese army. Li dropped out of school at age 13 to support his family by selling plastic trinkets on the streets of Hong Kong. Later, he scraped together enough money to buy a company that produced plastic flowers. His big success came when he bought the real estate surrounding his factory and watched the land skyrocket in value. Today, Li continues his simple lifestyle even though the companies he controls comprise over 10% of the value of the Hong Kong stock market. When asked why his sons have much nicer houses and cars than he does, Li responded, "My sons have a rich father; I did not."

Li is chairman of HUTCHISON WHAMPOA LIMITED. Hutchison has five major business segments: property development, container port operations, retailing, telecommunications, and energy. In 2002, Hutchison Whampoa reported net income of HK$14.288 billion (equivalent to approximately US$1.832 billion).

1. Assume that one of Hutchison Whampoa's overseas subsidiaries earns income of $1,000. The income tax rate in Hong Kong is 15%. When this income of $1,000 is transferred to the parent company in Hong Kong, it will be taxed, but no income tax is owed until then. What journal entry should Hutchison Whampoa make to record the income tax consequences of this $1,000 in income?

2. In 2002, Hutchison Whampoa reported earnings per share of HK$3.35. How many shares were outstanding during the year? (*Note:* See the net income information given on the previous page.)

3. Hutchison Whampoa reports that it records as assets the costs it incurs to sign up new subscribers to its cellular phone service network. These signup costs are then systematically transferred to expense over the following three years. What is the theoretical justification for this accounting practice?

▷ *Ethics Case*

Twisting the Contingency Rules to Save the Environment

You are a member of an environmental group that is working to clean up Valley River, which runs through your town. Right now, the group is focusing on forcing Allied Industrial, a manufacturer with a large plant located on the river, to conduct its operations in a more environmentally friendly way.

The leader of your group, Frank Bowers, is a political science major at the local university. Frank discovers that Allied Industrial is involved in ongoing litigation with respect to toxic waste cleanup at 13 factory sites in other states. Frank is shocked to learn that Allied itself estimates that the total cost to clean up the toxic waste at these 13 sites could be as much as $140 million yet has not reported any liability on its balance sheet. Frank found this information buried in the notes to Allied Industrial's financial statements.

Frank is convinced that he has found a public relations tool that can be used to force Allied Industrial to clean up Valley River. He has called a press conference and plans to accuse Allied of covering up its $140 million obligation to clean up the toxic waste at the 13 sites. His primary piece of evidence is the fact that the $140 million obligation is not mentioned anywhere in Allied's primary financial statements.

You have taken a class in accounting and are somewhat troubled by Frank's interpretation of Allied's financial statement disclosures. You look at Allied's annual report and see that it does give complete disclosure about the possible obligation although it does not report the $140 million as a liability. The report also states that, in the opinion of its legal counsel, it is possible but not probable that Allied will be found liable for the $140 million toxic waste cleanup cost.

The press conference is scheduled for 3 P.M. What should you do?

▷ *Writing Assignment*

Computing the Total Compensation for a Professor

Eunice Burns is a new assistant professor of phrenology at the University of Winnemucca. Her academic year salary is $30,000. In addition, she receives a summer salary equal to two-ninths (approximately 22%) of her academic year salary. The university agrees to contribute an amount equal to 7% of Eunice's academic year salary to a pension fund. Eunice acquires legal title to these pension contributions only if she stays at the university for five years or more. Historically, approximately 60% of new assistant professors have remained with the university at least five years. The university withholds $840 per year from Eunice's salary as her contribution to medical coverage. It costs the university $3,000 per year per employee for medical coverage. Eunice has a term-life insurance policy through the university because of the favorable group rate she can get. The $300 annual cost is withheld from her salary. If she were to get the same insurance on her own, it would cost $450. The FICA tax rate is 7.65%. This amount is withheld from Eunice's pay, and in addition, the university must match this amount and pay it to the federal government. Federal income taxes totaling 15% of income are withheld from Eunice's pay. Both the FICA tax and the federal income tax withholding are applied only to Eunice's academic year salary; no amounts are withheld from her summer salary.

You have just been hired as an assistant to the chief financial officer of the university. You have been asked to compute the total cost to the university of having Eunice Burns on the faculty. Write a one-page memo to the chief financial officer of the university outlining your calculations. Be sure to explain any assumptions that you make.

▶ *The Debate*

Is Research and Development an Asset or an Expense?

According to U.S. accounting rules (FASB Statement No. 2), all research and development expenditures should be recognized as expenses in the period in which they are incurred. This accounting treatment basically assumes that any expected benefit from the R&D is so uncertain or unpredictable that the R&D benefit should not be recorded as an asset. In contrast, international accounting rules (IAS No. 9) provide for R&D expenditures to be recorded as an asset if the technological feasibility of the research project has been established.

Divide your group into two teams.

- The first team represents the "Expense All R&D!" group. Prepare a two-minute oral presentation supporting the notion that the benefit of R&D activity is so uncertain that no assets should be recorded in conjunction with R&D.
- The second team represents the "R&D is an Asset!" group. Prepare a two-minute oral presentation arguing that the whole point of R&D is to generate future economic benefit. Accordingly, R&D should be recorded as an asset.

▶ *Cumulative Spreadsheet Project*

This spreadsheet assignment is a continuation of the spreadsheet assignments given in earlier chapters. If you completed those spreadsheets, you have a head start on this one.

This assignment is based on the spreadsheet prepared in part (1) of the spreadsheet assignment for Chapter 8. Review that assignment for a summary of the assumptions made in preparing a forecasted balance sheet and income statement for 2007 for Handyman Company. Using those financial statements, complete the following two independent sensitivity exercises.

1. Handyman is involved in a class-action lawsuit in which a number of customers allege that they injured their thumbs while using hammers purchased at Handyman. These customers are seeking $50 million in compensatory and punitive damages. (*Note:* All of the numbers in Handyman's financial statements are in millions.) In making the financial statement projections for Handyman for 2007, it has been assumed that losing this lawsuit is possible, but not probable. Compute how each of the following quantities would be affected if a loss in this lawsuit becomes probable during 2007:
   a. Debt ratio (total liabilities/total assets) as of the end of 2007.
   b. Return on equity (net income/ending stockholders' equity) for 2007.

2. Ignore the lawsuit described in (1). It is expected that Handyman's total "other operating expenses" will be $217 million in 2007. Of this amount, $20 million is for expected development costs that would be capitalized if Handyman were allowed to use International Accounting Standards. Compute how the capitalization of these development costs in 2007 would affect the following quantities. (*Note:* This is a hypothetical exercise because, as a U.S. company, Handyman is not currently allowed to use International Accounting Standards in preparing its financial statements.)
   a. Debt ratio (total liabilities/total assets) as of the end of 2007.
   b. Return on equity (net income/ending stockholders' equity) for 2007.

▶ *Internet Search*

ExxonMobil

Access EXXONMOBIL's Web site at **http://www.exxonmobil.com**. Sometimes Web addresses change, so if this ExxonMobil address doesn't work, access the Web site for this textbook (**http://albrecht.swlearning.com**) for an updated link to ExxonMobil. Once you've gained access to ExxonMobil's Web site, answer the following questions:

1. Using ExxonMobil's "history" site, determine the original names of the two companies that later became Exxon and Mobil.
2. Review ExxonMobil's note disclosure relating to litigation and other contingencies. What significant legal actions are being taken against the company, and what is their status?
3. Locate ExxonMobil's note relating to income taxes. What is the company's effective tax rate (income tax expense/income before taxes)? How does it compare to the U.S. statutory rate (as of 2002) of 35%?
4. Review ExxonMobil's disclosure relating to its pension plans. Does the amount of funding the company has set aside to satisfy its pension obligation exceed the company's pension obligation?

comprehensive problem 7 – 9

Zepplin Enterprises is a small business that purchases electronic personal information managers (PIM) from manufacturers and sells them to consumers. These PIMs keep track of appointments, phone numbers, to-do lists, and the like. Zepplin conducts business via the Internet and, at this point, carries only one model of PIM, the YO-660. Zepplin provides the following trial balance as of January 1, 2006.

Zepplin Enterprises
Trial Balance
January 1, 2006

	Debits	Credits
Cash	$ 8,500	
Accounts Receivable	28,400	
Allowance for Bad Debts		$ 568
Inventory	34,855	
Prepaid Rent	1,500	
Office Supplies	1,000	
Accounts Payable		19,700
Wages Payable		3,200
Taxes Payable		4,500
Common Stock (10,000 shares)		25,000
Retained Earnings		21,287
Total	$74,255	$74,255

Zepplin uses the periodic FIFO inventory method in accounting for its inventory. The inventory of YO-660 consists of the following inventory layers:

Layer	Units	Price per Unit	Total Price
1 (oldest purchase)	60	$150	$ 9,000
2	70	155	10,850
3	65	157	10,205
4 (most recent purchase)	30	160	4,800
Total	225		$34,855

Zepplin provides the following additional relevant information:

- The company uses the percentage of receivables method in estimating bad debts; 2% of the ending receivables balance is deemed to be uncollectible.
- Zepplin conducts an actual physical count of its inventory and office supplies at the end of each month.
- Zepplin rents its warehouse, office facilities, and computer equipment. Rent on the computer equipment is paid at the beginning of each month. Rent on the warehouse and office space is paid on the 15th of each month.

- Payroll is paid on the 5th and the 20th (pay periods end on the 15th and the last day of the month).
- Taxes Payable represents payroll taxes that are due by the 5th of the following month.
- All sales and all inventory purchases are on account.

The following transactions occurred for Zepplin during January of 2006:

Jan. 1 Paid rent on the computer equipment, $1,800.

5 Recorded sales for the week, 125 units at $220 per unit. (The company uses a periodic inventory system.)

5 Paid wages payable and taxes payable from the prior period.

5 Collected $15,000 from customers on account during the week.

8 Purchased office supplies for cash, $350.

10 Received 50 YO-660s from the manufacturer at a cost of $160 per unit.

11 Paid accounts payable, $17,500.

12 Collected $27,000 from customers on account during the week.

12 Recorded sales for the week, 140 units at $220 per unit.

15 Paid monthly rent for the office and warehouse, $3,000.

15 Received 140 YO-660s from the manufacturer at a cost of $162 per unit.

18 A customer returned a YO-660 and requested a refund. A check was immediately mailed to the customer in the amount of $220.

19 Collected $38,000 from customers on account during the week.

19 Recorded sales for the week, 115 units at $220 per unit.

20 Paid the semimonthly payroll for the pay period ending on January 15. Salaries and wages total $5,300 and payroll taxes were as follows: FICA taxes payable, employee, $405; FICA taxes payable, employer, $405; state withholding taxes payable, $280; federal withholding taxes payable, $810; federal unemployment taxes payable, $50; state unemployment taxes payable, $150.

22 Received notice that a customer owing Zepplin $440 had filed bankruptcy and would be unable to pay.

23 Paid the taxes payable from the payroll on January 20.

24 Received 190 YO-660s from the manufacturer at a cost of $160 per unit.

25 Purchased office supplies for cash, $730.

25 Paid accounts payable, $39,000.

26 Collected $44,500 from customers on account during the week.

26 Recorded sales for the week, 135 units at $225 per unit.

29 Customers returned 5 YO-660s and requested refunds. Checks were immediately mailed to each customer in the amount of $220 each.

30 Received 130 YO-660s from the manufacturer at a cost of $160 per unit.

31 Collected $21,800 from customers on account.

31 Recorded sales for the partial week, 65 units at $225 per unit.

31 Accrued the semimonthly payroll for the pay period ending on January 31. Salaries and wages total $5,400 and payroll taxes were as follows: FICA taxes payable, employee, $410; FICA taxes payable, employer, $410; state withholding taxes payable, $285; federal withholding taxes payable, $820; federal unemployment taxes payable, $55; state unemployment taxes payable, $160.

Required:
1. Provide the required journal entries to record each of the above events.
2. Make the adjusting entries necessary (1) to record bad debt expense for the period and (2) to adjust inventory and office supplies. A count of inventory and office supplies revealed 160 YO-660s on hand and supplies valued at $800.
3. Prepare a trial balance as of January 31, 2006.

(continued)

4. Prepare an income statement and a balance sheet for Zepplin Enterprises.
5. Prepare a common-size income statement for Zepplin Enterprises.
6. Compute Zepplin's number of days' sales in inventory, number of days' sales in accounts receivable, and number of days' sales in accounts payable ratios. What can you conclude about the company's liquidity position based on this analysis?

Part

3

Investing and Financing Activities

chapter

10

Investments in Property, Plant, and Equipment and in Intangible Assets

Learning Objectives

After studying this chapter, you should be able to:

1 Identify the two major categories of long-term operating assets: property, plant, and equipment and intangible assets.

2 Understand the factors important in deciding whether to acquire a long-term operating asset.

3 Record the acquisition of property, plant, and equipment through a simple purchase as well as through a lease, by self-construction, and as part of the purchase of several assets at once.

4 Compute straight-line and units-of-production depreciation expense for plant and equipment.

5 Account for repairs and improvements of property, plant, and equipment.

6 Identify whether a long-term operating asset has suffered a decline in value and record the decline.

7 Record the discarding and selling of property, plant, and equipment.

8 Account for the acquisition and amortization of intangible assets and understand the special difficulties associated with accounting for intangibles.

9 Use the fixed asset turnover ratio as a measure of how efficiently a company is using its property, plant, and equipment.

eXpanded *Material*

10 Compute declining-balance and sum-of-the-years'-digits depreciation expense for plant and equipment.

11 Account for changes in depreciation estimates.

Setting the Stage

Thomas Edison received $300,000 in investment funds in 1878 in order to start his EDISON ELECTRIC LIGHT COMPANY. Today, GENERAL ELECTRIC is the direct descendant of Edison's company and, with a market value of $289 billion (as of October 2003), is the most valuable company in the world. General Electric has been a fixture in corporate America since the late 1800s and is the only one of the 12 companies in the original Dow Jones Industrial Average that is still included among the 30 companies making up the Dow today.[1]

The stated purpose of the creation of the Edison Electric Light Company was the development of an economically practical electric light bulb. After a year of experimentation, Thomas Edison discovered that carbonized bamboo would provide a long-lasting light filament that was also easy to produce. Edison quickly found that delivering electric light to people's homes required more than a light bulb, however. So, he developed an entire electricity generation and distribution system, inventing new pieces of equipment when he couldn't find what he needed. The first public electric light system was built in London, followed soon after by the Pearl Street Station system in New York City in 1882. In 1892, Edison's company merged with the THOMSON-HOUSTON ELECTRIC COMPANY [developer of alternating-current (AC) equipment that could transmit over longer distances than Edison's direct-current (DC) system], and the General Electric Company (GE) was born.

From the beginning, General Electric's strength has been research. In addition to improving the design of the light bulb (including the development in the early 1900s of gas-filled, tungsten-filament bulbs that are the model for bulbs still used today), GE was also instrumental in developing almost every familiar household appliance—the iron, washing machine, refrigerator, range, air conditioner, dishwasher, and more. In addition, GE research scientists helped create FM radio, aircraft jet engines, and nuclear-power reactors.

Today, General Electric operates in a diverse array of businesses, ranging from train locomotives to medical CT scanners to consumer financing to the NBC television network. When Jack Welch became CEO of GE in 1981, his goal was to make GE number one or number two in each market segment in which it operates, or else get out of that particular line of business. This strategy has enabled GE's success to continue—its market value has grown by an average of 21% per year over the past 19 years. In 2001, Jack Welch stepped down as CEO of General Electric and turned the company over to Jeffrey Immelt who has helped GE continue in its position as a market leader.

To support its broad array of businesses, General Electric maintains a vast quantity of long-term assets that cost almost $80 billion to acquire. In 2002 alone, GE spent an additional $13.3 billion in acquiring long-term operating assets and received $6 billion for disposing of old assets. Its long-term assets include $3.3 billion in rail cars, $8.4 billion in buildings, $22.3 billion in machinery, and $46.2 billion in "intangible" assets.

ℹ️ n Chapters 7 through 9, operating activities of a business and the assets and liabilities arising from those operations were discussed. In this and the next three chapters, investing and financing activities are covered. In this chapter, investments in long-term assets that are used in the business, such as buildings, property, land, and equipment, are discussed. In Chapter 11, long-term debt financing is covered. In Chapter 12, equity financing is discussed. Once you understand debt and equity securities, as discussed in Chapters 11 and 12, you will understand how these same securities can be purchased as investments. Therefore, in Chapter 13, investments in stocks and bonds (securities) of other companies are discussed. Exhibit 1 shows the balance sheet and income statement accounts as well as the cash flow items that will be covered in this chapter.

The two primary categories of long-term assets discussed in this chapter are (1) property, plant, and equipment and (2) intangible assets. Because property, plant, and equipment and intangible assets are essential to a business in carrying out its operating activities, they are sometimes called long-term

1 This description is based on General Electric Company History at **http://ge.com/en/company/companyinfo/at_a_glance/hist_leader.htm**; General Electric Company, *International Directory of Company Histories*, vol. 12 (Detroit: St. James Press, 1996), pp. 193–197; 1999 Annual Report of the General Electric Company.

operating assets. Unlike inventories, these **long-term operating assets** are not acquired for resale to customers but are held and used by a business to generate revenues. As illustrated by the numbers given for GENERAL ELECTRIC at the beginning of the chapter, long-term operating assets often comprise a significant portion of the total assets of a company.

long-term operating assets Assets expected to be held and used over the course of several years to facilitate operating activities.

Exhibit 1: Financial Statement Items Covered in This Chapter

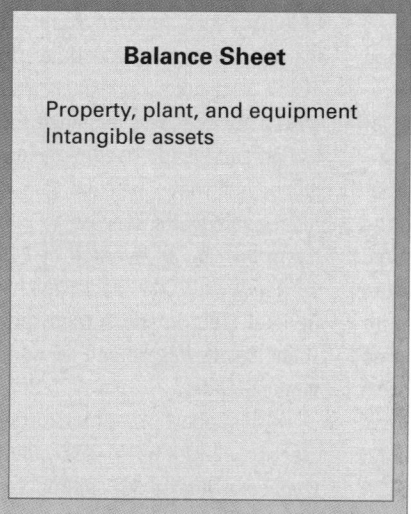

Balance Sheet

Property, plant, and equipment
Intangible assets

Statement of Cash Flows

Investing activities
    Purchase of property, plant,
      and equipment
    Proceeds from sale of property,
      plant, and equipment

Income Statement

Expenses
    Depreciation expense
    Amortization expense
    Impairment losses

Nature of Long-Term Operating Assets

I Identify the two major categories of long-term operating assets: property, plant, and equipment and intangible assets.

property, plant, and equipment Tangible, long-lived assets acquired for use in business operations; include land, buildings, machinery, equipment, and furniture.

intangible assets Long-lived assets without physical substance that are used in business, such as licenses, patents, franchises, and goodwill.

Businesses make money by selling products and services. A company needs an infrastructure of long-term operating assets in order to profitably produce and distribute these products and services. For example, GENERAL ELECTRIC needs factories in which to manufacture the locomotives and light bulbs that it sells. GE also needs patents on its unique technology to protect its competitive edge in the marketplace. A factory is an example of a long-term operating asset that is classified as property, plant, and equipment. A patent is an example of an intangible asset. **Property, plant, and equipment** refers to tangible, long-lived assets acquired for use in business operations. This category includes land, buildings, machinery, equipment, and furniture. **Intangible assets** are long-lived assets that are used in the operation of a business but do not have physical substance. In most cases, they provide their owners with competitive advantages over other firms. Typical intangible assets are patents, licenses, franchises, and goodwill. The time line in Exhibit 2 illustrates the important business issues associated with long-term operating assets.

The following section outlines the process used in deciding whether to acquire a long-term operating asset. The subsequent sections discuss the accounting issues that arise when a long-term operating asset is acquired: accounting for the acquisition of the asset, recording periodic depreciation, accounting for new costs and changes in asset value, and properly removing the asset from the books upon disposition.

Exhibit 2: Time Line of Business Issues Involved with Long-Term Operating Assets

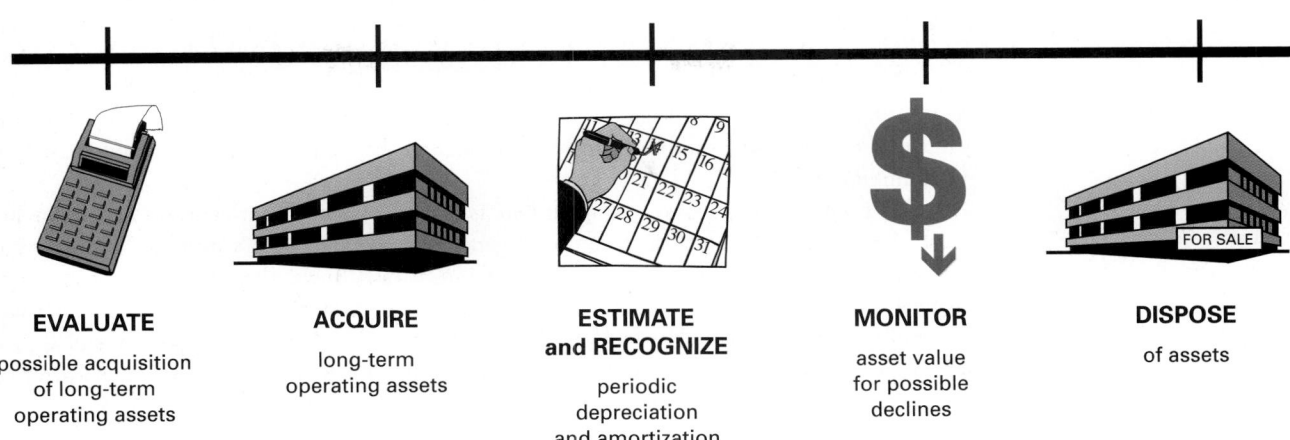

EVALUATE	**ACQUIRE**	**ESTIMATE and RECOGNIZE**	**MONITOR**	**DISPOSE**
possible acquisition of long-term operating assets	long-term operating assets	periodic depreciation and amortization	asset value for possible declines	of assets

> **TO SUMMARIZE:** Long-term operating assets provide an infrastructure in which to conduct operating activities. The category of property, plant, and equipment refers to tangible, long-lived assets such as land and equipment. Examples of intangible assets are patents and licenses.

Deciding Whether to Acquire a Long-Term Operating Asset

2 Understand the factors important in deciding whether to acquire a long-term operating asset.

capital budgeting Systematic planning for long-term investments in operating assets.

As mentioned in the previous section, long-term operating assets are acquired to be used over the course of several years. The decision to acquire a long-term asset depends on whether the future cash flows generated by the asset are expected to be large enough to justify the asset cost. The process of evaluating a long-term project is called **capital budgeting**. This process is briefly introduced here and is covered in more detail in Chapter 4 in the management accounting section of *Accounting: Concepts and Applications*.

Assume that Yosef Manufacturing makes joysticks and other computer game accessories. Yosef is considering expanding its operations by buying an additional production facility. The cost of the new factory is $100 million. Yosef expects to be able to sell the joysticks and other items made in the factory for $80 million per year. At that level of production, the annual cost of operating the factory (wages, insurance, materials, maintenance, etc.) is expected to total $65 million. The factory is expected to remain in operation for 20 years. Should Yosef buy the new factory for $100 million?

To summarize the information in the preceding paragraph, Yosef must decide whether to pay $100 million for a factory that will generate a net profit of $15 million ($80 million − $65 million) per year for 20 years. At first glance, you might think that the decision is obvious because the factory costs only $100 million but will generate $300 million in profit ($15 million × 20 years) during its 20-year life. But this analysis ignores the important fact that dollars received far in the future are not worth as much as dollars received right now. For example, if you can invest your money and earn 10%, receiving $1 today is the same as receiving $6.73 20 years from now because the $1 received today could be invested and would grow to $6.73 in 20 years. This important concept is called the **time value of money** and is essential to properly evaluating whether to acquire any long-term asset.

time value of money The concept that a dollar received now is worth more than a dollar received far in the future.

Using the time value of money calculations that will be explained in detail in Chapter 11, it can be shown that receiving the future cash flows from the factory of $15 million per year for 20 years is the same as receiving $128 million in one lump sum right now, if the prevailing interest rate is 10%. Thus, the decision to acquire the factory boils down to the following comparison: Should we pay $100 million to buy a factory now if the factory will generate future cash flows that are worth the equivalent of $128 million now? The decision is yes, because the $128 million value of the expected cash inflows is greater than the $100 million cost of the factory. On the other hand, if the factory were expected to generate only $10 million per year, then, using the computations that will be explained in Chapter 11, it can be calculated that the value of the cash flows would be only $85 million, and the factory should not be purchased for $100 million.

The important concept to remember here is that long-term operating assets have value because they are expected to help a company generate cash flows in the future. If events occur that change the expectation concerning those future cash flows, then the value of the asset changes. For example, if consumer demand for computer joysticks dries up, the value of a factory built to produce joysticks can plunge overnight even though the factory itself is still as productive as it ever was. Accounting for this type of decline in the value of a long-term operating asset is discussed later in the chapter.

> **TO SUMMARIZE:** Long-term operating assets have value because they help companies generate future cash flows. The decision to acquire a long-term operating asset involves comparing the cost of the asset to the value of the expected cash inflows, after adjusting for the time value of money. An asset's value can decline or disappear if events cause a decrease in the expected future cash flows generated by the asset.

Accounting for Acquisition of Property, Plant, and Equipment

3 Record the acquisition of property, plant, and equipment through a simple purchase as well as through a lease, by self-construction, and as part of the purchase of several assets at once.

Like all other assets, property, plant, and equipment are initially recorded at cost. The cost of an asset includes not only the purchase price but also any other costs incurred in acquiring the asset and getting it ready for its intended use. Examples of these other costs include shipping, installation, and sales taxes. The items that should be included in the acquisition cost of various types of property, plant, and equipment are outlined in Exhibit 3.

Property, plant, and equipment are usually acquired by purchase. In some cases, assets are acquired by leasing but are accounted for as assets in much the same way as purchased assets. Plant and equipment can also be constructed by a business for its own use. Also, a company can in one transaction purchase several different assets or even another entire company. The accounting for each of these types of acquisition is explained on the following pages.

Exhibit 3: Items Included in the Acquisition Cost of Property, Plant, and Equipment

Land	Purchase price, commissions, legal fees, escrow fees, surveying fees, clearing and grading costs.
Land improvements (e.g., landscaping, paving, fencing)	Cost of improvements, including expenditures for materials, labor, and overhead.
Buildings	Purchase price, commissions, reconditioning costs.
Equipment	Purchase price, taxes, freight, insurance, installation, and any expenditures incurred in preparing the asset for its intended use, e.g., reconditioning and testing costs.

Assets Acquired by Purchase

A company can purchase an asset by paying cash, incurring a liability, exchanging another asset, or by a combination of these methods. If a single asset is purchased for cash, the accounting is relatively simple. To illustrate, we assume that Wheeler Resorts, Inc., purchases a new delivery truck for $15,096 (purchase price, $15,000, less 2% discount for paying cash, plus sales tax of $396). The entry to record this purchase is:

Delivery Truck	15,096	
Cash		15,096
Purchased a delivery truck for $15,096		
($15,000 − $300 cash discount + $396 sales tax).		

In this instance, cash was paid for a single asset, the truck. An alternative would be to borrow part of the purchase price. If the company had borrowed $12,000 of the $15,096 from a bank, the entry would have been:

Delivery Truck	15,096	
Cash		3,096
Notes Payable		12,000
Purchased a delivery truck for $15,096; paid $3,096 cash		
and issued a note for $12,000 to Chemical Bank.		

The $12,000 represents the principal of the note; it does not include any interest charged by the lending institution. (The interest is recognized later as interest expense.)

When one long-term operating asset is acquired in exchange for another, the cost of the new asset is usually set equal to the market value of the asset given up in exchange.

Assets Acquired by Leasing

lease A contract that specifies the terms under which the owner of an asset (the lessor) agrees to transfer the right to use the asset to another party (the lessee).

lessee The party that is granted the right to use property under the terms of a lease.

lessor The owner of property that is leased (rented) to another party.

operating lease A simple rental agreement.

Leases are often short-term rental agreements in which one party, the **lessee**, is granted the right to use property owned by another party, the **lessor**. For example, as a student, you may decide to lease (rent) an apartment to live in while you are attending college. The owner of the apartment (lessor) will probably require you to sign a lease specifying the terms of the arrangement. The lease states the period of time in which you will live in the apartment, the amount of rent you will pay, and when each rent payment is due. When the lease expires, you will either sign a new lease or move out of the apartment, which would then be rented to someone else.

Companies enter into similar types of lease arrangements. For example, Wheeler Resorts might decide to lease a building because it needs additional office space. Assume Wheeler signs a two-year lease requiring monthly rental payments of $1,000. When the lease expires, Wheeler will either move out of the building or negotiate a new lease with the owner. Accounting for this type of rental agreement, called an **operating lease**, is straightforward. When rent is paid each month, Wheeler records the following journal entry:

Rent (or Lease) Expense	1,000	
Cash		1,000
To record monthly rent of office building.		

© 2003 Leland Bobbe/Getty Images

A college student (lessee) often rents an apartment while attending college. The apartment owner (lessor) will require the student to sign a lease stating the terms of the arrangement.

Some lease agreements, however, are not so simple. Suppose Wheeler has decided to expand its operations and wants to acquire a hotel in the Phoenix, Arizona, area. Wheeler's alternatives are to buy land and build a new hotel, purchase an existing hotel, or lease a hotel. Assume Wheeler locates a desirable piece of land, and the owner of the land agrees to build a hotel and lease the property to Wheeler. The lease agreement is noncancelable and requires Wheeler to make annual lease payments of $100,000 for 20 years. At the end of 20 years, Wheeler will become the owner of the property. Clearly, this is not a simple rental agreement, even though the transaction is called a lease by the parties involved. In reality, this transaction is a purchase of the property with the payments being spread over 20 years. The result is the same as if Wheeler had borrowed money on a 20-year mortgage and purchased the property.

Generally accepted accounting principles require that the recording of a transaction reflect its true economic nature, not its form. Instead of recognizing the individual lease payments as an expense as was done with the operating lease, Wheeler records the property as an asset and also records a liability reflecting the obligation to the lessor. The amount to be recorded is the cash amount that Wheeler would have to pay right now in order to completely pay off the obligation to make the future lease payments. This amount is called the present value of the lease payments (in the Wheeler example, the present value of 20 annual payments of $100,000) and takes into account the time value of money. As mentioned earlier, the time value concept will be explained in more detail in Chapter 11.

Continuing the example, assume that, at the beginning of the lease term, the present value of the future lease payments is $851,360. Wheeler makes the following journal entry to record the lease:

Leased Property	851,360	
Lease Liability		851,360
To record hotel acquired under a 20-year noncancelable lease.		

capital lease A leasing transaction that is recorded as a purchase by the lessee.

This type of lease is called a **capital lease** because the lessee records (capitalizes) the leased asset the same as if the asset had been acquired in an outright purchase. The asset is reported with Property, Plant, and Equipment on the lessee's balance sheet. The lessee (Wheeler Resorts) also shows the lease liability on the balance sheet as a long-term liability.

When annual lease payments are made, Wheeler will not record the payment as rent expense. Instead, the payment will be recorded as a reduction in the lease liability, with part of each payment being interest on the outstanding obligation. The difference between the total lease payments (20 years × $100,000, or $2 million) and the "cost" or present value of the property is the amount of interest that will be paid over the term of the lease. To illustrate, assume that the first payment is made one year after the lease term begins and includes interest of $85,136 and a $14,864 reduction in the liability. The payment is recorded as follows:

Lease Liability	14,864	
Interest Expense	85,136	
Cash		100,000
To record annual lease payment under capital lease.		

Accounting for payments on capital leases is discussed in more detail in Chapter 11.

Classifying Leases

As illustrated, an operating lease is accounted for as a simple rental, whereas a capital lease is accounted for as a purchase of the leased asset. Because the accounting treatment of a lease can have a major impact on the financial statements, the accounting profession has established criteria for determining whether a lease should be classified as an operating or a capital lease. If a lease is noncancelable and meets any one of the following four criteria, it is recorded as a capital lease:

1. The lease transfers ownership of the leased asset to the lessee by the end of the lease term (as in the Wheeler Resorts example).
2. The lease contains an option allowing the lessee to purchase the asset at the end of the lease term at a bargain price, essentially guaranteeing that ownership will eventually transfer to the lessee.
3. The lease term is equal to 75% or more of the estimated economic life of the asset, meaning that the lessee will use the asset for most of its economic life.
4. The present value of the lease payments at the beginning of the lease is 90% or more of the fair market value of the leased asset. Meeting this criterion means that, in agreeing to make the lease payments, the lessee is agreeing to pay almost as much as the cash price to purchase the asset outright.

If just one of the above criteria is met, then the lease agreement is classified as a capital lease and is accounted for by the lessee as a debt-financed purchase. A lease that does not meet any of the capital lease criteria is considered an operating lease. Keep in mind that these two types of leases are not alternatives for the same transaction. If the terms of the lease agreement meet any one of the capital lease criteria, the lease must be accounted for as a capital lease.

FYI:

One of the most interesting accounting manipulations involving the four lease criteria relates to the 90% threshold for the present value of the minimum lease payments. By hiring an insurance company to guarantee a portion of the lease payments, a lessee is able to exclude these payments from the present value computations, lowering the present value below the 90% threshold.

The accounting for leases has been a thorn in the side of accounting standard-setters for at least 50 years. From the beginning, the crucial issue has been how to require companies to report leased assets and lease liabilities in the balance sheet when a lease constitutes an effective transfer of ownership. The four lease criteria outlined above were issued by the FASB in 1976, with the thought that the rigidity and strictness of the criteria would result in most leases being reported on lessee companies' balance sheets as capital leases. In practice, U.S. companies have taken these four criteria as a challenge and have carefully crafted their lease agreements so that none of the criteria is satisfied, allowing the leases to continue to be accounted for as operating leases.

One of the largest leasing companies in the United States is a subsidiary of GENERAL ELECTRIC called GE CAPITAL SERVICES. GE Capital Services leases industrial equipment, factory buildings, rail cars, shipping containers, computers, medical equipment, and more. In 2002, the total original cost of assets leased by GE Capital Services to other companies was $41.6 billion.

Assets Acquired by Self-Construction

Sometimes buildings or equipment are constructed by a company for its own use. This may be done to save on construction costs, to utilize idle facilities or idle workers, or to meet a special set of technical specifications. Self-constructed assets, like purchased assets, are recorded at cost, including all expenditures incurred to build the asset and make it ready for its intended use. These costs include the materials used to build the asset, the construction labor, and some reasonable share of the general company overhead (electricity, insurance, supervisors' salaries, etc.) during the time of construction.

Another cost that is included in the cost of a self-constructed asset is the interest cost associated with money borrowed to finance the construction project. Just as the cost to rent a crane to be used to construct a building would be included in the cost of the building, the cost to "rent" money to finance the construction project should also be included in the building

Lease or Buy? Leasing is an integral part of American business. From its beginning, a major aspect of IBM's business has been the leasing, rather than the outright sale, of its equipment. Over the years, Ray Kroc's MCDONALD'S empire has made more money leasing land and buildings to franchisees than it has made selling hamburgers. In short, leasing has long been a popular method of acquiring and financing operating assets. For example, airlines such as AMER-ICAN, DELTA, SOUTHWEST, and UNITED often lease many of their airplanes. Retail chains such as WAL-MART and SAFEWAY often lease their stores.

Virtually any type of operating asset can be acquired by leasing. Companies often lease such assets as rail cars, automobiles and trucks, airplanes, and various other types of equipment, as well as real estate. There are several reasons why a company might choose to lease rather than purchase an asset. A purchase transaction often requires a significant cash outlay in the form of a down payment at the date of purchase; leasing, therefore, can be used to minimize the amount of cash paid initially to acquire the asset. For some types of assets,

---

capitalized interest Interest that is recorded as part of the cost of a self-constructed asset.

cost. Interest that is recorded as part of the cost of a self-constructed asset is called **capitalized interest**. The amount of interest that should be capitalized is that amount that could have been saved if the money used on the construction project had instead been used to repay loans.

The following illustration demonstrates the computation of the cost of a self-constructed asset. Wheeler Resorts decided to construct a new hotel using its own workers. The construction project lasted from January 1 to December 31, 2006. Building materials costs for the project were $4,500,000. Total labor costs attributable to the project were $2,500,000. Total company overhead (costs other than materials and labor) for the year was $10,000,000; of this amount, it is determined that 15% can be reasonably assigned as part of the cost of the construction project. A construction loan was negotiated with Wheeler's bank; during the year, Wheeler was able to borrow from the bank to pay for materials, labor, etc. The total amount of interest paid on this construction loan during the year was $500,000. The total cost of the self-constructed hotel is computed as follows:

Materials	$4,500,000
Labor	2,500,000
Overhead allocation ($10,000,000 × 0.15)	1,500,000
Capitalized interest	500,000
Total hotel cost	$9,000,000

The new hotel would be reported in Wheeler's balance sheet at a total cost of $9,000,000. As with other long-term operating assets, self-constructed assets are reported at the total cost necessary to get them ready for their intended use.

STOP & THINK

What is the difference between capitalized interest and regular interest?

The amount of capitalized interest reported by several large U.S. companies, relative to their total interest expense, is displayed in Exhibit 4. As you can see, General Electric capitalized only an insignificant amount of its $10.216 billion in interest during 2002. On the other hand, EXXONMOBIL capitalized more than one-half of its interest during 2002.

Acquisition of Several Assets at Once

basket purchase The purchase of two or more assets acquired together at a single price.

A **basket purchase** occurs when two or more assets are acquired together at a single price. A typical basket purchase is the purchase of a building along with the land on which the building sits. Because there are differences in the accounting for land and buildings, the purchase such as computers, leasing enables the lessee to avoid risks of obsolescence if the appropriate terms are written into the lease agreement.

Another potential advantage of leasing is that if the agreement can be recorded as an operating lease, the lessee does not have to report any related liability. This is an important consideration if a company is concerned about the effect of reporting additional debt on the balance sheet. Before criteria were established for classifying leases as operating or capital, almost all leases were treated as operating leases. Often the primary purpose of a leasing arrangement was to acquire an asset without reporting any related liability. Some companies are still using leasing for this purpose. They do so by writing the terms of a lease agreement in a manner that circumvents the generally accepted accounting capitalization criteria. The result is that some leasing transactions are reported as simple rental agreements (operating leases) when in fact they have many characteristics of a purchase transaction. Leasing and other forms of "off-balance-sheet financing" are of major concern to the accounting profession and financial statement users.

price must be allocated between the two assets on some reasonable basis. The relative fair market values of the assets are usually used to determine the respective costs to be assigned to the land and the building.

To illustrate, we will assume that Wheeler Resorts purchases a 40,000-square-foot building on 2.6 acres of land for $3,600,000. How much of the total cost should be assigned to the land and how much to the building? If an appraisal indicates that the fair market values of the land and the building are $1,000,000 and $3,000,000, respectively, the resulting allocated costs would be $900,000 and $2,700,000, calculated as follows:

Asset	Fair Market Value	Percentage of Total Value	Apportionment of Lump-Sum Cost
Land	$1,000,000	25%	0.25 × $3,600,000 = $ 900,000
Building	3,000,000	75	0.75 × $3,600,000 = 2,700,000
Total	$4,000,000	100%	$3,600,000

Exhibit 4: Magnitude of Capitalized Interest for Several Large U.S. Companies

Company	Capitalized Interest	Interest Expense**	Capitalized, as a Percentage of Total Interest
General Electric*	$ 0	$10,216	0.0%
General Motors	191	7,715	2.4
ExxonMobil	426	398	51.7
McDonald's	14	374	3.6
Disney	36	453	7.4

Note: Numbers are for 2002 and are in millions of dollars.
*Once again, GE reports it capitalized only an "insignificant" amount.
**These amounts come from the income statement, and are net of capitalized interest, which explains the high percentage for ExxonMobil.

In this case, the fair market value of the land is $1,000,000, or 25% of the total market value of the land and building. Therefore, 25% of the actual cost, or $900,000, is allocated to the land, and 75% of the actual cost, or $2,700,000, is allocated to the building. The journal entry to record this basket purchase is:

Land	900,000	
Building	2,700,000	
Cash		3,600,000
Purchased 2.6 acres of land and a 40,000-square-foot building.		

If part of the purchase price is financed by a bank, an additional credit to Notes Payable or Mortgage Payable would be included in the entry.

Sometimes one company will buy all the assets of another company. For example, in its 2002 annual report, Microsoft discloses that, in July 2002, it purchased NAVISION for $1.45 billion in stock and cash. The purchase of an entire company raises a number of accounting issues. The first, already discussed above, is how to allocate the purchase price to the various assets acquired. In general, all acquired assets are recorded on the books of the acquiring company at their fair values as of the acquisition date.

The second major accounting issue associated with the purchase of an entire company is the recording of goodwill. **Goodwill** represents all the special competitive advantages enjoyed by a company, such as a trained staff, good credit rating, reputation for superior products and services, and an established network of suppliers and customers. These factors allow an established business to earn more profits than would a new business, even though the new business might have the same type of building, the same equipment, and the same type of production processes.

When one company purchases another established business, the excess of the purchase price over the value of the identifiable net assets is assumed to represent the purchase of goodwill. The accounting for goodwill is illustrated later in the chapter.

goodwill An intangible asset that exists when a business is valued at more than the fair market value of its net assets, usually due to strategic location, reputation, good customer relations, or similar factors; equal to the excess of the purchase price over the fair market value of the net assets purchased.

TO SUMMARIZE: When property, plant, and equipment assets are purchased, they are recorded at cost, which includes all expenditures associated with acquiring and getting them ready for their intended use, such as sales tax, shipping, and installation. Sometimes assets are acquired by lease rather than purchase. A lease may be a simple short-term rental agreement, called an operating lease, or it may be substantially the same as a purchase transaction. In the latter case, called a capital lease, the party acquiring the asset (the lessee) records the asset and related liability as if the property had been purchased and financed with long-term debt. When a company constructs an asset for its own use, the recorded cost includes materials, labor, a reasonable allocation of overhead, and the cost of interest used to finance the construction. When two or more assets are acquired for a single price in a basket purchase, the relative fair market values are used to determine the respective costs.

Calculating and Recording Depreciation Expense

4 Compute straight-line and units-of-production depreciation expense for plant and equipment.

depreciation The process of cost allocation that assigns the original cost of plant and equipment to the periods benefited.

The second element in accounting for plant and equipment is the allocation of an asset's cost over its useful life. The matching principle requires that this cost be assigned to expense in the periods benefited from the use of the asset. The allocation procedure is called **depreciation**, and the allocated amount, recorded in a period-ending adjusting entry, is an expense that is deducted from revenues in order to determine income. It should be noted that the asset "plant" normally refers to buildings only; land is recorded as a separate asset and is not depreciated because it is usually assumed to have an unlimited useful life.

Accounting for depreciation is often confusing because students tend to think that depreciation expense reflects the decline in an asset's value. The concept of depreciation is nothing more than a systematic write-off of the original cost of an asset. The undepreciated cost is referred to as **book value**, which represents that portion of the original cost not yet assigned to the income statement as an expense. A company never claims that an asset's recorded book value is equal to its market value. In fact, market values of assets could increase at the same time that depreciation expense is being recorded.

To calculate depreciation expense for an asset, you need to know (1) its original cost, (2) its estimated useful life, and (3) its estimated salvage, or residual, value. **Salvage value** is the amount expected to be received when the asset is sold at the end of its useful life. When an asset is purchased, its actual life and salvage value are obviously unknown. They must be estimated as realistically as is feasible, usually on the basis of experience with similar assets. In some cases, an asset will have little or no salvage value. If the salvage value is not significant, it is usually ignored in computing depreciation.

Several methods can be used for depreciating the costs of assets for financial reporting. In the main part of this chapter, we describe two: straight-line and units-of-production. In the expanded material section of this chapter, we describe two more depreciation methods: sum-of-the-years'-digits and declining-balance.

The **straight-line depreciation method** assumes that an asset will benefit all periods equally and that the cost of the asset should be assigned on a uniform basis for all accounting periods. If an asset's benefits are thought to be related to its productive output (miles driven in an automobile, for example), the **units-of-production method** is usually appropriate.

To illustrate straight-line and units-of-production depreciation methods, we assume that Wheeler Resorts purchased a van on January 1 for transporting hotel guests to and from the airport. The following facts apply:

Acquisition cost	$24,000
Estimated salvage value	$2,000
Estimated life:	
In years	4 years
In miles driven	60,000 miles

Straight-Line Method of Depreciation

The straight-line depreciation method is the simplest depreciation method. It assumes that an asset's cost should be assigned equally to all periods benefited. The formula for calculating annual straight-line depreciation is:

$$\frac{\text{Cost} - \text{Salvage value}}{\text{Estimated useful life (years)}} = \text{Annual depreciation expense}$$

With this formula, the annual depreciation expense for the van is calculated as:

$$\frac{\$24,000 - \$2,000}{4 \text{ years}} = \$5,500 \text{ depreciation expense per year}$$

When the depreciation expense for an asset has been calculated, a schedule showing the annual depreciation expense, the total accumulated depreciation, and the asset's book value (undepreciated cost) for each year can be prepared. The depreciation schedule for the van (using straight-line depreciation) is shown in Exhibit 5.

The entry to record straight-line depreciation each year is:

Depreciation Expense	5,500	
Accumulated Depreciation, Hotel Van		5,500
To record annual depreciation for the hotel van.		

book value For a long-term operating asset, the asset's original cost less any accumulated depreciation.

salvage value The amount expected to be received when an asset is sold at the end of its useful life.

straight-line depreciation method The depreciation method in which the cost of an asset is allocated equally over the periods of an asset's estimated useful life.

units-of-production method The depreciation method in which the cost of an asset is allocated to each period on the basis of the productive output or use of the asset during the period.

Exhibit 5: Depreciation Schedule with Straight-Line Depreciation

	Annual Depreciation Expense	Accumulated Depreciation	Book Value
Acquisition date	—	—	$24,000
End of year 1	$ 5,500	$ 5,500	18,500
End of year 2	5,500	11,000	13,000
End of year 3	5,500	16,500	7,500
End of year 4	5,500	22,000	2,000
	$22,000		

FYI:

A comparison of the amounts of cost and accumulated depreciation reveals how old the plant and equipment is relative to its total expected life.

Depreciation Expense is reported on the income statement. Accumulated Depreciation is a contra-asset account that is offset against the cost of the asset on the balance sheet. Book value is equal to the asset account balance, which retains the original cost of the asset as a debit balance, minus the credit balance in the accumulated depreciation account.

At the end of the first year, the acquisition cost, accumulated depreciation, and book value of the van are presented on the balance sheet as follows:

Property, Plant, and Equipment:
Hotel van $24,000
Less: Accumulated depreciation 5,500
Book value $18,500

Similar information is provided in the annual reports of all companies with property, plant, and equipment. For example, GENERAL ELECTRIC reported the following in the notes to its 2002 financial statements:

	Original Cost (in millions)	
(December 31)	2002	2001
GE		
Land and improvements	$ 623	$ 577
Buildings, structures, and related equipment	8,398	7,281
Machinery and equipment	21,414	21,414
Leasehold costs and manufacturing plant under construction	1,964	1,960
	$32,399	$31,232
GE Capital Services		
Buildings and equipment	$ 4,731	$ 3,600
Equipment leased to others		
Aircraft	20,053	16,173
Vehicles	10,859	10,779
Railroad rolling stock	3,376	3,439
Marine shipping containers	1,611	1,618
Mobile and modular structures	1,383	1,325
Information technology equipment	1,033	1,321
Construction and manufacturing equipment	1,239	799
Scientific, medical, and other equipment	2,058	1,001
	$46,343	$40,055
	$78,742	$71,287

	Accumulated Depreciation and Amortization	
GE	$19,506	$18,433
GE Capital Services		
Buildings and equipment	1,838	1,579
Equipment leased to others	11,044	9,135
	$32,388	$29,147

Using this information, one can calculate that the property, plant, and equipment used by General Electric had been used for 60% ($19,506/$32,399) of its useful life as of the end of 2002. Similarly, the buildings and equipment used by GE CAPITAL SERVICES had been used for 39% ($1,838/$4,731) of its life, and the equipment leased by GE Capital Services to others had been used for 27% ($11,044/$41,612) of its useful life.

Units-of-Production Method of Depreciation

The units-of-production depreciation method allocates an asset's cost on the basis of use rather than time. This method is used primarily when a company expects that asset usage will vary significantly from year to year. If the asset's usage pattern is uniform from year to year, the units-of-production method will produce the same depreciation pattern as the straight-line method. Assets with varying usage patterns for which this method of depreciation may be appropriate include automobiles and other vehicles whose life is estimated in terms of number of miles driven. It is also used for certain machines whose life is estimated in terms of number of units produced or number of hours of operating life. The formula for calculating the units-of-production depreciation for the year is:

$$\frac{\text{Cost} - \text{Salvage value}}{\text{Total estimated life in units, hours, or miles}} \times \frac{\text{Number of units produced, hours used, or miles driven during the year}}{} = \text{Current year's depreciation expense}$$

To illustrate, we again consider Wheeler Resorts' van, which has an expected life of 60,000 miles. With the units-of-production method, if the van is driven 12,000 miles during the first year, the depreciation expense for that year is calculated as follows:

$$\frac{\$24,000 - \$2,000}{60,000 \text{ miles}} \times 12,000 \text{ miles} = \$4,400 \text{ depreciation expense}$$

The entry to record units-of-production depreciation at the end of the first year of the van's life is:

Depreciation Expense	4,400	
Accumulated Depreciation, Hotel Van		4,400
To record depreciation for the first year of the hotel van's life.		

The depreciation schedule for the four years is shown in Exhibit 6. This exhibit assumes that 18,000 miles were driven the second year, 21,000 the third year, and 9,000 the fourth year.

Note that part of the formulas for straight-line and units-of-production depreciation is the same. In both cases, cost − salvage value is divided by the asset's useful life. With straight-line, life is measured in years; with units-of-production, life is in miles or hours. With units-of-production, the depreciation per mile or hour must then be multiplied by the usage for the year to determine depreciation expense.

Exhibit 6: Depreciation Schedule with Units-of-Production Depreciation

	Miles Driven	Depreciation Expense	Accumulated Depreciation	Book Value
Acquisition date	—	—	—	$24,000
End of year 1	12,000	$ 4,400	$ 4,400	19,600
End of year 2	18,000	6,600	11,000	13,000
End of year 3	21,000	7,700	18,700	5,300
End of year 4	9,000	3,300	22,000	2,000
		$22,000		

What if the van lasts longer than four years or is driven for more than 60,000 miles? Once the $22,000 difference between cost and salvage value has been recorded as depreciation expense, there is no further expense to record. Thus, any additional years or miles are "free" in the sense that no depreciation expense will be recognized in connection with them. However, as other vans are purchased in the future, the initial estimates of their useful lives will be adjusted to reflect the experience with previous vans.

What if the van lasts less than four years or is driven fewer than 60,000 miles? This topic is covered later in the chapter in connection with the accounting for the disposal of property, plant, and equipment.

A Comparison of Depreciation Methods

The amount of depreciation expense will vary according to the depreciation method used by a company. Exhibit 7 compares the annual depreciation expense for Wheeler Resorts' van under the straight-line and units-of-production depreciation methods. As this schedule makes clear, the total amount of depreciation is the same regardless of which method is used.

Straight-line is by far the most commonly used depreciation method because it is the simplest to apply and makes intuitive sense. For example, in the notes to its 2002 financial statements (see Appendix A), MICROSOFT discloses that it depreciates its property, plant, and equipment using the straight-line method over useful lives ranging from 1 to 15 years.

Partial-Year Depreciation Calculations

Thus far, depreciation expense has been calculated on the basis of a full year. Businesses purchase assets at all times during the year, however, so partial-year depreciation calculations are often required. To compute depreciation expense for less than a full year, first calculate the depreciation expense for the year and then distribute it evenly over the number of months the asset is held during the year.

Exhibit 7: Comparison of Depreciation Expense Using Different Depreciation Methods

	Straight-Line Depreciation	Units-of-Production Depreciation
End of year 1	$ 5,500	$ 4,400
End of year 2	5,500	6,600
End of year 3	5,500	7,700
End of year 4	5,500	3,300
Totals	$22,000	$22,000

Exhibit 8: Partial-Year Depreciation

Method	Full-Year Depreciation	Depreciation 1st Year (6 months)	Depreciation 2nd Year (12 months)
Straight-line	$5,500	$2,750 ($5,500 × ½)	$5,500

To illustrate, assume that Wheeler Resorts purchased its $24,000 van on July 1 instead of January 1. The depreciation calculations for the first one and one-half years, using straight-line depreciation, are shown in Exhibit 8. The units-of-production method has been omitted from the exhibit; midyear purchases do not complicate the calculations with this method because it involves number of miles driven, hours flown, and so on, rather than time periods.

In practice, many companies simplify their depreciation computations by taking a full year of depreciation in the year an asset is purchased and none in the year the asset is sold, or vice versa. This is allowed because depreciation is based on estimates, and in the long run, the difference in the amounts is usually immaterial.

Units-of-Production Method with Natural Resources

natural resources Assets that are physically consumed or waste away, such as oil, minerals, gravel, and timber.

depletion The process of cost allocation that assigns the original cost of a natural resource to the periods benefited.

Another common use for the units-of-production method is with natural resources. **Natural resources** include such assets as oil wells, timber tracts, coal mines, and gravel deposits. Like all other assets, newly purchased or developed natural resources are recorded at cost. This cost must be written off as the assets are extracted or otherwise depleted. This process of writing off the cost of natural resources is called **depletion** and involves the calculation of a depletion rate for each unit of the natural resource. Conceptually, depletion is exactly the same as depreciation; with plant and equipment, the accounting process is called depreciation, whereas with natural resources it is called depletion.

To illustrate, assume that Power-T Company purchases a coal mine for $1,200,000 cash. The entry to record the purchase is:

Coal Mine	1,200,000	
Cash		1,200,000
Purchased a coal mine for $1,200,000.		

If the mine contains an estimated 200,000 tons of coal deposits (based on a geologist's estimate), the depletion expense for each ton of coal extracted and sold will be $6 ($1,200,000/200,000 tons). Here, the unit of production is the extraction of one ton of coal. If 12,000 tons of coal are mined and sold in the current year, the depletion entry is:

Depletion Expense	72,000	
Accumulated Depletion, Coal Mine		72,000
To record depletion for the year: 12,000 tons at $6 per ton.		

After the first year's depletion expense has been recorded, the coal mine is shown on the balance sheet as follows:

Coal mine	. . . .	$1,200,000
Less: Accumulated depletion	. . . .	72,000
Book value	. . . .	$1,128,000

But how do you determine the number of tons of coal in a mine? Because most natural resources cannot be counted, the amount of the resource owned is an estimate. The depletion calculation is therefore likely to be revised as new information becomes available. When an estimate is changed, a new depletion rate per unit is calculated and used to compute depletion during the remaining life of the natural resource or until another new estimate is made. Coverage of accounting for changes in estimates is included in the expanded material section of this chapter.

TO SUMMARIZE: Depreciation is the process whereby the cost of an asset is allocated over its useful life. Two common and simple methods of depreciation are straight-line and units-of-production. The straight-line and units-of-production methods allocate cost proportionately over an asset's life on the bases of time and use, respec-tively. Regardless of which method is used, depreciation is only an allocation of an asset's cost over the periods ben-efited and is not a method of valuation. Natural resources are assets, such as gravel deposits or coal mines, that are consumed or that waste away. The accounting process of depreciation for natural resources is called depletion.

Repairing and Improving Property, Plant, and Equipment

5 Account for repairs and improvements of property, plant, and equipment.

Sometime during its useful life, an asset will probably need to be repaired or improved. The accounting issue associated with these postacquisition expenditures is whether they should be immediately recognized as an expense or be added to the cost of the asset (capitalized). Re-member from the discussion in Chapter 9 that an expenditure should be capitalized if it is ex-pected to have an identifiable benefit in future periods.

Two types of expenditures can be made on existing assets. The first is ordinary expendi-tures for repairs, maintenance, and minor improvements. For example, a truck requires oil changes and periodic maintenance. Because these types of expenditures typically benefit only the period in which they are made, they are expenses of the current period.

The second type is an expenditure that lengthens an asset's useful life, increases its capac-ity, or changes its use. These expenditures are capitalized; that is, they are added to the asset's cost instead of being expensed in the current period. For example, overhauling the engine of a delivery truck involves a major expenditure to extend the useful life of the truck. To qualify for capitalization, an expenditure should meet three criteria: (1) it must be significant in amount; (2) it should benefit the company over several periods, not just during the current one; and (3) it should increase the productive life or capacity of the asset.

To illustrate the differences in accounting for capital and ordinary expenditures, assume that Wheeler Resorts also purchases a delivery truck for $42,000. This truck has an estimated useful life of eight years and a salvage value of $2,000. The straight-line depreciation is $5,000 per year [($42,000 − $2,000)/8 years]. If the company spends $1,500 each year for normal maintenance, its annual recording of these expenditures is:

Repairs and Maintenance Expense	. . . .	1,500
Cash	. . . .	1,500
Spent $1,500 for maintenance of delivery truck.		

This entry has no effect on either the recorded cost or the depreciation expense of the truck. Now suppose that at the end of the sixth year of the truck's useful life, Wheeler spends $8,000 to overhaul the engine. This expenditure will increase the truck's remaining life from two to four years, but will not change its estimated salvage value. The depreciation for the last four years will be $4,500 per year, calculated as shown below.

	Depreciation before Overhaul		Depreciation after Overhaul
Original cost	$42,000	Original cost	$42,000
Less salvage value	2,000	Accumulated depreciation	
Cost to be allocated (depreciable amount)	$40,000	(prior to overhaul)	30,000
Original life of asset	8 years	Remaining book value	$12,000
Original depreciation per year ($40,000/8)	$5,000	Capital expenditure (overhaul)	8,000
Usage before overhaul	× 6 years	New book value	$20,000
Accumulated depreciation prior to overhaul	$30,000	Less salvage value	2,000
		New depreciable amount	$18,000
		Remaining life	4 years
		New annual depreciation ($18,000/4)	$4,500

The journal entry to record the $8,000 capitalized expenditure is:

Delivery Truck	8,000	
Cash		8,000
Spent $8,000 to overhaul the engine of the $42,000 truck.		

Another example of a capital expenditure is the cost of land improvements. Certain improvements are considered permanent, such as moving earth to change the land contour. Such an expenditure would be capitalized as part of the land account. Other expenditures may have a limited life, such as those incurred in building a road, a sidewalk, or a fence. These expenditures would be capitalized in a separate land improvements account and be depreciated over their useful lives.

It is often difficult to determine whether a given expenditure should be capitalized or expensed. The two procedures produce a different net income, however, so it is extremely important that such expenditures be properly classified. When in doubt, accepted practice is to record an expenditure as an expense to ensure that the asset is not reported at an amount that exceeds its future benefit.

TO SUMMARIZE: There are two types of expenditures for existing long-term operating assets: capital and ordinary. In general, for an expenditure to be capitalized, it must (1) be significant in amount, (2) provide benefits for more than one period, and (3) increase the productive life or capacity of an asset. Ordinary expenditures merely maintain an asset's productive capacity at the level originally projected. Capital expenditures are added to the cost of an asset and thus affect future depreciation, whereas ordinary expenditures are expenses of the current period.

Recording Impairments of Asset Value

6   Identify whether a long-term operating asset has suffered a decline in value and record the decline.

impairment A decline in the value of a long-term operating asset.

As mentioned earlier, the value of a long-term asset depends on the future cash flows expected to be generated by that asset. Occasionally, events occur after the purchase of an asset that significantly reduce its value. For example, a decline in the consumer demand for high-priced athletic shoes can cause the value of a shoe-manufacturing plant to plummet. Accountants call this **impairment**. When an asset is impaired, the event should be recognized in the financial statements, both as a reduction in the reported value of the asset in the balance sheet and as a loss in the income statement. Of course, the value of long-term assets can also increase after the purchase date. In the United States, these increases are not recorded, as explained more fully later in this section.

Recording Decreases in the Value of Property, Plant, and Equipment

According to U.S. accounting rules, the value of an asset is impaired when the sum of estimated future cash flows from that asset is less than the book value of the asset. This computation ignores the time value of money. As illustrated in the example below, this is a strange impairment threshold—a more reasonable test would be to compare the book value to the fair value of the asset.

Once it has been determined that an asset is impaired, the amount of the impairment is measured as the difference between the book value of the asset and the fair value. To summarize, the existence of an impairment loss is determined using the sum of the estimated future cash flows from the asset, ignoring the time value of money. The amount of the impairment loss is measured using the fair value of the asset, which does incorporate the time value of money. The practical result of this two-step process is that an impairment loss is not recorded unless it is quite certain that the asset has suffered a permanent decline in value.

To illustrate, assume that Wheeler Resorts purchased a fitness center building five years ago for $600,000. The building has been depreciated using the straight-line method with a 20-year useful life and no residual value. Wheeler estimates that the building has a remaining useful life of 15 years, that net cash inflow from the building will be $25,000 per year, and that the fair value of the building is $230,000.

Annual depreciation for the building has been $30,000 ($600,000 ÷ 20 years). The current book value of the building is computed as follows:

Original cost	$600,000
Accumulated depreciation ($30,000 × 5 years)	150,000
Book value	$450,000

The book value of $450,000 is compared with the $375,000 ($25,000 × 15 years) sum of future cash flows (ignoring the time value of money) to determine whether the building is impaired. The sum of future cash flows is only $375,000, which is less than the $450,000 book value, so an impairment loss should be recognized. The loss is equal to the $220,000 ($450,000 − $230,000) difference between the book value of the building and its fair value. The impairment loss would be recorded as follows:

Accumulated Depreciation, Building	150,000	
Loss on Impairment of Building	220,000	
Building ($600,000 − $230,000)		370,000
Recognized $220,000 impairment loss on building.		

This journal entry basically records the asset as if it were being acquired brand new at its fair value of $230,000. The existing accumulated depreciation balance is wiped clean, and the new recorded value of the asset is its fair value of $230,000 ($600,000 − $370,000). After an impairment loss is recognized, no restoration of the loss is allowed even if the fair value of the asset later recovers.

STOP & THINK

Do you think businesses would prefer an impairment test involving only the comparison of the book value of an asset to its fair value? Explain.

The odd nature of the impairment test can be seen if the facts in the Wheeler example are changed slightly. Assume that net cash inflow from the building will be $35,000 per year and that the fair value of the building is $330,000. With these numbers, no impairment loss is recognized, even though the fair value of $330,000 is less than the book value of $450,000, because the sum of future cash flows of $525,000 ($35,000 × 15 years) exceeds the book value. Thus, in this case the asset would still be recorded at its book value of $450,000, even though its fair value is actually less. As mentioned above, the practical impact of the two-step impairment test is that no impairment losses are recorded unless the future cash flow calculations offer very strong evidence of a permanent decline in asset value. The impairment test is summarized in Exhibit 9.

AOL TIME WARNER set a world record when it recorded an impairment loss in 2002 of $99.737 billion. Over half of that amount related to a write-off of goodwill associated with the 2000 merger of AOL and TIME WARNER. This record write-off resulted in AOL Time Warner reporting a net loss for the year of $98.7 billion.

Recording Increases in the Value of Property, Plant, and Equipment

Under U.S. accounting standards, increases in the value of property, plant, and equipment are not recognized. Gains from increases in asset value are recorded only if and when the asset is sold. Thus, in the Wheeler example discussed above, if the fair value of the building rises to $800,000, the building would still be reported in the financial statements at its depreciated book value of $450,000. This is an example of the conservative bias that often exists in the accounting rules: losses are recognized when they occur, but the recognition of gains is deferred until the asset is sold.

Although increases in the value of property, plant, and equipment are not recognized in the United States, accounting rules in other countries do allow for their recognition. For example,

Exhibit 9: Impairment Test

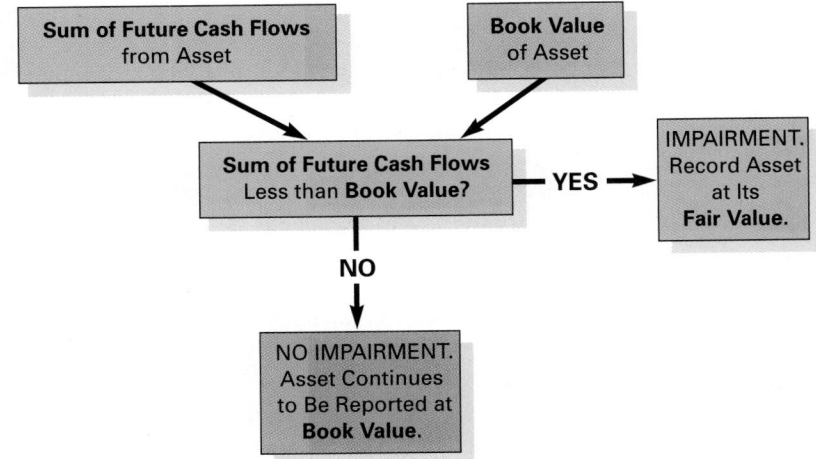

companies in Great Britain often report their long-term operating assets at their fair values. Because this upward revaluation of property, plant, and equipment is allowable under international accounting standards, it will be interesting to watch over the next decade or so to see whether sentiment grows to allow this practice in the United States as well.

TO SUMMARIZE: When an asset's value declines after it is purchased, it is said to be impaired. Recording an impairment loss is a two-step process. First, the recorded book value of the asset is compared with the sum of future cash flows expected to be generated by the asset. Second, if the book value is higher, then a loss is recognized in an amount equal to the difference between the book value of the asset and its fair value. According to U.S. accounting rules, increases in the value of property, plant, and equipment are not recognized.

Disposal of Property, Plant, and Equipment

7 Record the discarding and selling of property, plant, and equipment.

Plant and equipment eventually become worthless or are sold. When a company removes one of these assets from service, it has to eliminate the asset's cost and accumulated depreciation from the accounting records. There are basically three ways to dispose of an asset: (1) discard or scrap it, (2) sell it, or (3) exchange it for another asset.

Discarding Property, Plant, and Equipment

When an asset becomes worthless and must be scrapped, its cost and its accumulated depreciation balance should be removed from the accounting records. If the asset's total cost has been depreciated, there is no loss on the disposal. If, on the other hand, the cost is not completely depreciated, the undepreciated cost represents a loss on disposal.

To illustrate, we assume that Wheeler Resorts, Inc., purchases a computer for $15,000. The computer has a five-year life and no estimated salvage value and is depreciated on a straight-line basis. If the computer is scrapped after five full years, the entry to record the disposal is as follows:

Accumulated Depreciation, Computer	15,000	
Computer		15,000
Scrapped $15,000 computer.		

If Wheeler must pay $300 to have the computer dismantled and removed, the entry to record the disposal is:

Accumulated Depreciation, Computer	15,000	
Loss on Disposal of Computer	300	
Computer		15,000
Cash		300
Scrapped $15,000 computer and paid disposal costs of $300.		

If the computer had been scrapped after only four years of service (and after $12,000 of the original cost has been depreciated), there would have been a loss on disposal of $3,300 (including the disposal cost), and the entry would have been:

Accumulated Depreciation, Computer	12,000	
Loss on Disposal of Computer	3,300	
Computer		15,000
Cash		300
Scrapped $15,000 computer and recognized loss of $3,300		
(including $300 disposal costs).		

Don't think of the losses recognized above as "bad" or the gains as "good." A loss on disposal simply means that, given the information we now have, it appears that we didn't record enough depreciation expense in previous years. As a result, the book value of the asset is higher than the amount we can get on disposal. Similarly, a gain means that too much depreciation expense was recognized in prior years, making the book value of the asset lower than its actual disposal value.

Selling Property, Plant, and Equipment

A second way of disposing of property, plant, and equipment is to sell it. If the sales price of the asset exceeds its book value (the original cost less accumulated depreciation), there is a gain on the sale. Conversely, if the sales price is less than the book value, there is a loss.

To illustrate, we refer again to Wheeler's $15,000 computer. If the computer is sold for $600 after five full years of service, assuming no disposal costs, the entry to record the sale is:

Cash	600	
Accumulated Depreciation, Computer	15,000	
Computer		15,000
Gain on Sale of Computer		600
Sold $15,000 computer at a gain of $600.		

Because the asset was fully depreciated, its book value was zero and the $600 cash received represents a gain. If the computer had been sold for $600 after only four years of service, there would have been a loss of $2,400 on the sale, and the entry to record the sale would have been:

Cash	600	
Accumulated Depreciation, Computer	12,000	
Loss on Sale of Computer	2,400	
Computer		15,000
Sold $15,000 computer at a loss of $2,400.		

The $2,400 loss is the difference between the sales price of $600 and the book value of $3,000 ($15,000 − $12,000). The amount of a gain or loss is thus a function of two factors: (1) the amount of cash received from the sale, and (2) the book value of the asset at the date of sale. The book value can vary from the market price of the asset for two reasons: (1) the accounting for the asset is not intended to show market value in the financial statements, and (2) it is difficult to estimate salvage value and useful life at the outset of an asset's life.

Exchanging Property, Plant, and Equipment

A third way of disposing of property, plant, and equipment is to exchange it for another asset. Such exchanges occur regularly with cars, trucks, machines, and other types of large equipment.

When dissimilar assets are exchanged, such as a truck for a computer, the transaction is accounted for exactly as outlined previously: the acquired asset is recorded in the books at its fair market value, and a gain or loss may be recognized depending on the difference between this market value and the book value of the asset that was disposed of. Accounting for exchanges of similar assets can be more complicated and therefore is not discussed in this text. For a full treatment of the accounting for the exchange of similar assets, see an intermediate accounting text.

> **TO SUMMARIZE:** There are three ways of disposing of assets: (1) discarding (scrapping), (2) selling, and (3) exchanging. If a scrapped asset has not been fully depreciated, a loss equal to the undepreciated cost or book value is recognized. When an asset is sold, there is a gain if the sales price exceeds the book value and a loss if the sales price is less than the book value.

Accounting for Intangible Assets

8 Account for the acquisition and amortization of intangible assets and understand the special difficulties associated with accounting for intangibles.

patent An exclusive right granted for 20 years by the federal government to manufacture and sell an invention.

network exercises

Equity

Fortune magazine posts its Fortune 500 list on its Web site, **http://fortune.com**. The information posted includes the reported equity and market values for the 500 largest companies in the United States.

Net Work:

What are the differences between reported equity and the market value of equity for THE COCA-COLA COMPANY and for GENERAL MOTORS CORPORATION?

Intangible assets are rights and privileges that are long-lived, are not held for resale, have no physical substance, and usually provide their owner with competitive advantages over other firms. Familiar examples are **patents**, franchises, licenses, and goodwill.

The importance of intangible assets can be illustrated by considering GENERAL ELECTRIC. As mentioned in Chapter 2, if the balance sheet were perfect, the amount of owners' equity would be equal to the market value of the company. On December 31, 2002, GE's reported equity was equal to $54.824 billion. The actual market value of GE on December 31, 2002, was $401 billion. The reason for the large difference between the recorded value and the actual value is that a traditional balance sheet excludes many important intangible economic assets. Examples of GE's important intangible economic assets are its track record of successful products and its entrenched market position in the many industries in which it operates. These intangible factors are by far the most valuable assets owned by GE, but they fall outside the traditional accounting process.

As with many accounting issues, accounting for intangibles involves a trade-off between relevance and reliability. Information concerning intangible assets is relevant, but to meet the standard for recognition in the financial statements, the recorded amount for the intangible must also be reliable. The most important distinction in intangible assets for accounting purposes is between those intangible assets that are internally generated and those that are externally purchased. This distinction is important because the transfer of externally-purchased intangible assets in an arm's-length market transaction provides reliable evidence that the intangibles have probable future economic benefit. Such reliable evidence does not exist for most internally-generated intangibles. Accordingly, as discussed in Chapter 9, most costs associated with generating and maintaining internally-generated intangibles are expensed as incurred.

Keep in mind, however, that an intangible asset that is internally generated (and therefore not recorded as an asset on a company's books) is still valued by the stock market. As an illustration, consider Exhibit 10, which lists the 10 most valuable brands in the world in 2002. Each of these brands represents a valuable economic asset that has been internally generated. For example, the $69.6 billion Coca-Cola brand name has been created over the years by THE COCA-COLA COMPANY through successful business operations and relentless marketing. But because the valuation of this asset is not deemed sufficiently reliable to meet the standard for financial statement recognition, it is not included in The Coca-Cola Company's balance sheet. However, as explained below, if another company were to buy The Coca-Cola Company, an important part of recording the transaction would be allocating the total purchase price to the various economic assets acquired, including previously unrecorded intangible assets.

Exhibit 10: Ten Most Valuable Brands in the World for 2002

Rank	Brand	Brand Value (in billions)
1	Coca-Cola	$69.6
2	Microsoft	64.1
3	IBM	51.2
4	General Electric	41.3
5	Intel	30.9
6	Nokia	30.0
7	Disney	29.3
8	McDonald's	26.4
9	Marlboro	24.2
10	Mercedes	21.0

Source: Interbrand at http://www.interbrand.com.

In the future, financial reporting will move toward providing more information about internally-generated intangibles. Whether this will involve actual valuation and recognition of these intangibles in the financial statements, or simply more extensive note disclosure, remains to be seen.

A short description of some of the common types of intangible assets is given below.

Trademark

A trademark is a distinctive name, symbol, or slogan that distinguishes a product or service from similar products or services. Well-known examples include Coke, Windows, Yahoo!, and the Nike Swoosh. As shown in Exhibit 10 above, it was estimated in 2002 that the value of the Coca-Cola trademark was in excess of $69 billion. Because the Coca-Cola trademark is an internally-generated intangible asset, it is not reported in The Coca-Cola Company's balance sheet. However, the company has purchased other trademarks (such as Minute Maid), with a total cost of $2.6 billion; these are reported in The Coca-Cola Company's balance sheet.

Franchises

franchise An entity that has been licensed to sell the product of a manufacturer or to offer a particular service in a given area.

Franchise operations have become so common in everyday life that we often don't realize we are dealing with them. In fact, these days it is difficult to find a nonfranchise business in a typical shopping mall. When a business obtains a **franchise**, the recorded cost of the franchise includes any sum paid specifically for the franchise right as well as legal fees and other costs incurred in obtaining it. Although the value of a franchise at the time of its acquisition may be substantially in excess of its cost, the amount recorded should be limited to actual outlays. For example, approximately 70% of MCDONALD's locations are operated under franchise agreements. A McDonald's franchisee must contribute an initial cash amount of $175,000, which is used to buy some of the equipment and signs and also to pay the initial franchise fee. The value of a McDonald's franchise alone is much more than $175,000, but the franchisee would only record a franchise asset in his or her financial statements equal to the cost (not value) of the franchise. However, if a franchise right is included when one company purchases another company, presumably the entire value is included in the purchase price, and the fair value attributable to the franchise right is recorded as an intangible asset in the acquirer's books.

FYI:

The original Coca-Cola bottling franchise sold for $1.

Goodwill

Goodwill is the business contacts, reputation, functioning systems, staff camaraderie, and industry experience that make a business much more than just a collection of assets. As mentioned above, if these factors are the result of a contractual right or are associated with intangibles that can be bought and sold separately, then the value of the factor should be reported as a separate intangible asset. In essence, goodwill is a residual number, the value of all of the synergies of a functioning business that cannot be specifically identified with any other intangible factor. Goodwill is recognized only when it is purchased as part of the acquisition of another company. In other words, a company's own goodwill, its homegrown goodwill, is not recognized. Goodwill will be discussed more in depth later in the chapter.

Estimating the Fair Value of an Intangible

The most difficult part of recording an amount for an intangible asset is not in identifying the asset but instead is in estimating a fair value of the asset. The objective in estimating the fair value is to duplicate the price at which the intangible asset would change hands in an arm's-

Exhibit 11: Acquisition Costs of Goodwill and Other Intangible Assets

Patent	An exclusive right granted by a national government that enables an inventor to control the manufacture, sale, or use of an invention. In the United States, legal life is is 20 years from patent application date.	**COST:** Purchase price, filing and registry fees, cost of subsequent litigation to protect right. Does not include internal research and development costs.
Trademark	An exclusive right granted by a national government that permits the use of distinctive symbols, labels, and designs, e.g., McDonald's golden arches, Nike's Swoosh, Apple's computer name and logo. Legal life is virtually unlimited.	**COST:** Same as Patent.
Copyright	An exclusive right granted by a national government that permits an author to sell, license, or control his/her work. In the United States, copyrights expire 50 years after the death of the author.	**COST:** Same as Patent.
Franchise agreement	An exclusive right or privilege received by a business or individual to perform certain functions or sell certain products or services.	**COST:** Expenditures made to purchase the franchise. Legal fees and other costs incurred in obtaining the franchise.
Acquired customer list	A list or database containing customer information such as name, address, past purchases, and so forth. Companies that originally develop such a list often sell or lease it to other companies, unless prohibited by customer confidentiality agreements.	**COST:** Purchase price when acquired from another company. Costs to internally develop a customer list are expensed as incurred.
Goodwill	Miscellaneous intangible resources, factors, and conditions that allow a company to earn above-normal income with its identifiable net assets. Goodwill is recorded only when a business entity is acquired by a purchase.	**COST:** Portion of purchase price that exceeds the sum of the current market value for all identifiable net assets, both tangible and intangible.

Source: Some of these illustrations are taken from SFAS No. 141, "Business Combinations," Appendix A.

length market transaction. If there is a market for similar intangibles assets, then the best estimate of fair value is made with reference to these observable market prices.

To illustrate the accounting for the purchase of an intangible patent, assume that Wheeler Resorts, Inc., acquires, for $200,000, a patent granted seven years earlier to another firm. The entry to record the purchase of the patent is:

Patent	200,000	
Cash		200,000
Purchased patent for $200,000.		

The one exception to valuing purchased intangibles at market value involves goodwill, which arises when an entire business is purchased. Goodwill is best thought of as a residual amount, the amount of the purchase price of a business that is left over after all other tangible and intangible assets have been identified. As such, goodwill is that intangible something that makes the whole company worth more than its individual parts. In general, goodwill represents all the special advantages, not otherwise separately identifiable, enjoyed by an enterprise, such as a high credit standing, reputation for superior products and services, experience with development and distribution processes, favorable government relations, and so forth. These factors allow a business to earn above-normal income with the identifiable assets, tangible and intangible, employed in the business.

To illustrate the accounting for goodwill, assume that, in order to cater to the medicinal needs of its guests, Wheeler Resorts purchases Valley Drug Store for $400,000. At the time of purchase, the recorded assets and liabilities of Valley Drug have the following fair market values:

Inventory	$220,000
Long-term operating assets	110,000
Other assets (prepaid expenses, etc.)	10,000
Liabilities	(20,000)
Total net assets	$320,000

Note that Wheeler Resorts records these items at their fair market values on the date purchased, just as it does when purchasing individual assets.

Because Wheeler was willing to pay $400,000 for Valley Drug, there must have been other favorable, intangible factors worth approximately $80,000. These factors are called goodwill, and the entry to record the purchase of the drug store is:

Inventory	220,000	
Long-Term Operating Assets	110,000	
Other Assets	10,000	
Goodwill	80,000	
Liabilities		20,000
Cash		400,000
Purchased Valley Drug Store for $400,000.		

Amortization of Intangible Assets

amortization The process of cost allocation that assigns the original cost of an intangible asset to the periods benefited.

Like tangible assets, intangible assets are recorded at their historical costs. Unlike tangible assets, the costs associated with intangible assets are not always allocated as expenses over time. The periodic allocation to expense of an intangible asset's cost is called **amortization**. Conceptually, depreciation (with plant and equipment), depletion (with natural resources), and amortization (with intangible assets) are exactly the same thing. Straight-line amortization is generally used for intangible assets.

In accounting for an intangible asset after its acquisition, a determination first must be made as to whether the intangible asset has a finite life. If no economic, legal, or contractual factors cause the intangible to have a finite life, then its life is said to be indefinite, and the asset is not to be amortized until its life is determined to be finite. An indefinite life is one that extends beyond the foreseeable horizon. An example of an intangible asset that has an indefinite life is a broadcast license which includes an extension option that can be renewed indefinitely. If an intangible asset is determined to have a finite life, then the asset is to be amortized over its estimated life; the useful life estimate should be reviewed periodically.

To illustrate the amortization of an intangible asset, let us continue with the patent example with Wheeler Resorts, Inc., used earlier. Recall that the patent, with a legal life of 20 years, was purchased from another company after seven years. Because seven years of its 20-year legal life have already elapsed, the patent now has a legal life of only 13 years, although it may have a shorter useful life. If its useful life is assumed to be eight years, one-eighth of the $200,000 cost should be amortized each year for the next eight years. The entry each year to record the patent amortization expense is:

Amortization Expense, Patent	25,000	
Patent		25,000
To amortize one-eighth of the cost of the patent.		

Notice that in the above entry, the patent account was credited. Alternatively, a contra-asset account, such as Accumulated Amortization, could have been credited. In practice, however, crediting the intangible asset account directly is more common. This is different from the normal practice of crediting Accumulated Depreciation for buildings or equipment.

Many intangible assets that used to be amortized are no longer amortized. For example, goodwill used to be amortized over a 40-year period. Goodwill is now no longer amortized.

Impairment of Intangible Assets

While many intangible assets are not amortized, all intangible assets must be evaluated every year to determine if (1) their estimated useful life has changed and (2) the intangible asset has become impaired. Previously in this chapter the issue of asset impairment was discussed with regard to tangible assets. While the specifics of the various impairment tests associated with the different kinds of intangible assets are beyond the scope of this textbook, suffice it to say that when evaluating whether or not an intangible asset has become impaired, the objective is to ensure that the intangible assets recorded on the books of a company are not overstated. If an intangible asset is determined to be impaired, an impairment loss is recorded on the income statement and the intangible asset is reduced on the books of the company.

TO SUMMARIZE: Intangible assets are long-term rights and privileges that have no physical substance but provide competitive advantages to owners. Because it is often difficult to trace the development of specific intangible assets to specific costs, it is difficult to reliably recognize the assets in the financial statements. Intangible assets are only recognized in the financial statements if they have been purchased through an arm's-length transaction.

Common intangible assets are patents, franchises, licenses, and goodwill. Certain intangible assets are amortized over the economic life of the asset. Many intangible assets are not amortized because their value does not decline. However, all intangible assets must be analyzed to determine if impairment has occurred. If it has, then an impairment loss is recognized.

Measuring Property, Plant, and Equipment Efficiency

9 Use the fixed asset turnover ratio as a measure of how efficiently a company is using its property, plant, and equipment.

fixed asset turnover The number of dollars in sales generated by each dollar of fixed assets; computed as sales divided by property, plant, and equipment.

In this section we discuss the fixed asset turnover ratio, which uses financial statement data to give a rough indication of how efficiently a company is utilizing its property, plant, and equipment to generate sales. We also illustrate that the fixed asset turnover ratio must be interpreted carefully because, as with most other financial ratios, acceptable values for this ratio differ significantly from one industry to the next.

Evaluating the Level of Property, Plant, and Equipment

Fixed asset turnover can be used to evaluate the appropriateness of the level of a company's property, plant, and equipment. Fixed asset turnover is computed as sales divided by average property, plant, and equipment (fixed assets) and is interpreted as the number of dollars in sales generated by each dollar of fixed assets. This ratio is also often called PP&E turnover. The computation of the fixed asset turnover for GENERAL ELECTRIC is given below. All financial statement numbers are in millions.

	2002	2001
Sales	$131,698	$125,913
Property, plant, and equipment		
Beginning of year	$ 42,140	$ 40,015
End of year	47,204	42,140
Average fixed assets	$ 44,672	$ 41,078
Fixed asset turnover	2.95 times	3.07 times

The fixed asset turnover calculations suggest that GE used its fixed assets to generate sales a little less efficiently in 2002 than in 2001. In 2002, each dollar of fixed assets generated $2.95 in sales, down from $3.07 in 2001.

Industry Differences in Fixed Asset Turnover

As with all ratios, the fixed asset turnover ratio must be used carefully to ensure that erroneous conclusions are not made. For example, fixed asset turnover ratio values for two companies in different industries cannot be meaningfully compared. This point can be illustrated using the fact that General Electric is composed of two primary parts—General Electric, the manufacturing company, and GE Capital Services, the financial services firm. The fixed asset turnover ratio computed earlier was for both these parts combined. Because GE Capital Services does not use property, plant, and equipment for manufacturing but instead leases the assets to other companies in order to earn financial revenue, one would expect its fixed asset turnover ratio to be quite unlike that for a manufacturing firm. In fact, as shown below, the fixed asset turnover ratio for the manufacturing segments of General Electric was 5.96 in 2002, nearly double the ratio value for the company as a whole.

Fixed Asset Turnover Ratio **General Electric—Manufacturing Segments Only**		
	2002	2001
Sales	$79,049	$74,037
Property, plant, and equipment		
Beginning of year	$12,799	$12,199
End of year	13,743	12,799
Average fixed assets	$13,271	$12,499
Fixed asset turnover	5.96 times	5.92 times

> **TO SUMMARIZE:** The fixed asset turnover ratio can be used as a general measure of how efficiently a company is using its property, plant, and equipment. Fixed asset turnover is computed as sales divided by average property, plant, and equipment and is interpreted as the number of dollars in sales generated by each dollar of fixed assets. Standard values for this ratio differ significantly from industry to industry.

Two topics related to operational assets that are traditionally covered in introductory accounting classes were not covered in the main part of this chapter. These two topics relate to depreciation—accelerated depreciation methods and changes in depreciation estimates.

Accelerated Depreciation Methods

10 Compute declining-balance and sum-of-the-years'-digits depreciation expense for plant and equipment.

Earlier in the chapter, straight-line and units-of-production depreciation methods were discussed. Both of these methods allocate the cost of an asset evenly over its life. With straight-line depreciation, each time period during the asset's useful life is assigned an equal amount of depreciation. With units-of-production depreciation, each mile driven, hour used, or other measurement of useful life is assigned an equal amount of depreciation. Sometimes, a depreciation method that does not assign costs equally over the life of the asset is preferred. For example, if most of an asset's benefits will be realized in the earlier periods of the asset's life, the method used should assign more depreciation to the earlier years and less to the later years. Examples of these "accelerated" depreciation methods are the declining-balance and the sum-of-the-years'-digits methods. These methods are merely ways of assigning more of an asset's depreciation to earlier periods and less to later periods.

To illustrate these depreciation methods, we will again use the Wheeler Resorts example from earlier in the chapter. Assume again that Wheeler Resorts purchased a van for transporting hotel guests to and from the airport. The following facts apply:

Acquisition cost	$24,000
Estimated salvage value	$2,000
Estimated life:	
In years	4 years
In miles driven	60,000 miles

Declining-Balance Method of Depreciation

declining-balance depreciation method An accelerated depreciation method in which an asset's book value is multiplied by a constant depreciation rate (such as double the straight-line percentage, in the case of double-declining-balance).

The **declining-balance depreciation method** provides for higher depreciation charges in the earlier years of an asset's life than does the straight-line method. The declining-balance method involves multiplying a fixed rate, or percentage, by a decreasing book value. This rate is a multiple of the straight-line rate. Typically, it is twice the straight-line rate, but it also can be 175, 150, or 125% of the straight-line rate. Our depreciation of Wheeler's hotel van will illustrate the declining-balance method using a fixed rate equal to twice the straight-line rate. This method is often referred to as the double-declining-balance depreciation method.

Declining-balance depreciation differs from the other depreciation methods in two respects: (1) the initial computation ignores the asset's salvage value, and (2) a constant depreciation rate is multiplied by a decreasing book value. The salvage value is not ignored completely because the depreciation taken during the asset's life cannot reduce the asset's book value below the estimated salvage value.

The double-declining-balance (DDB) rate is twice the straight-line rate, computed as follows:

$$\frac{1}{\text{Estimated life (years)}} \times 2 = \text{DDB rate}$$

This rate is multiplied times the book value at the beginning of each year (cost − accumulated depreciation) to compute the annual depreciation expense for the year. If the 150% declining balance were being used instead, the 2 in the rate formula would be replaced by 1.5 and so on for any other percentages.

To illustrate, the depreciation calculation for the van using the 200% (or double) declining-balance method is:

Straight-line rate	4 years = 1/4 = 25%
Double the straight-line rate	25% × 2 = 50%
Annual depreciation	50% × undepreciated cost (book value)

Caution

With declining-balance depreciation, the asset is not depreciated below its salvage value, though this figure is ignored in the initial computations.

Based on this information, the formula for double-declining-balance depreciation can be expressed as (straight-line rate × 2) × (cost − accumulated depreciation) = current year's depreciation expense. The double-declining-balance depreciation for the four years is shown in Exhibit 12. As you review this exhibit, note that the book value of the van at the end of year 4 is $2,000, its salvage value.

If Wheeler had applied the declining-balance method to depreciate the hotel van on the basis of 150% of the straight-line rate, the fixed rate would have been 37.5%, computed as follows: 25% × 1.50 = 37.5%. Using the 37.5% fixed rate, the annual depreciation of the hotel van would have been as follows:

First year:	$24,000 × 37.5% = $9,000
Second year:	$24,000 − $9,000 = $15,000 × 37.5% = $5,625
Third year:	$15,000 − $5,625 = $9,375 × 37.5% = $3,516
Fourth year:	$9,375 − $3,516 = $5,859 − $2,000 salvage value = $3,859

Since a total book value of $5,859 remains at the end of year 3, the remaining book value less the estimated salvage value is expensed in year 4.

Exhibit 12: Depreciation Schedule with Double-Declining-Balance Depreciation

	Computation	Annual Depreciation Expense	Accumulated Depreciation	Book Value
Acquisition date	—	—	—	$24,000
End of year 1	$24,000 × 0.50	$12,000	$12,000	12,000
End of year 2	12,000 × 0.50	6,000	18,000	6,000
End of year 3	6,000 × 0.50	3,000	21,000	3,000
End of year 4	*	1,000	22,000	2,000
		$22,000		

*In year 4, depreciation expense cannot exceed $1,000 because the book value cannot be reduced below salvage value.

Depreciation for Income Tax Purposes

Net income reported on the financial statements prepared for stockholders, creditors, and other external users often differs from taxable income reported on income tax returns. The most common cause of differences between financial reporting and tax returns is the computation of depreciation. Depreciation for income tax purposes must be computed in accordance with federal income tax law, which specifies rules to be applied in computing tax depreciation for various categories of assets. Income tax rules are designed to achieve economic objectives, such as stimulating investment in productive assets.

The income tax depreciation system in the United States is called the Modified Accelerated Cost Recovery System (MACRS). MACRS is based on declining-balance depreciation and is designed to allow taxpayers to quickly deduct the cost of assets acquired. Allowing this accelerated depreciation deduction for income tax purposes gives companies tax benefits for investing in new productive assets. Presumably, this will spur investment, create jobs, and make voters more likely to reelect their representatives.

Sum-of-the-Years'-Digits Method of Depreciation

sum-of-the-years'-digits (SYD) depreciation method The accelerated depreciation method in which a constant balance (cost minus salvage value) is multiplied by a declining depreciation rate.

Like the declining-balance method, the **sum-of-the-years'-digits (SYD) depreciation method** provides for a proportionately higher depreciation expense in the early years of an asset's life. It is therefore appropriate for assets that provide greater benefits in their earlier years (such as trucks, machinery, and equipment) as opposed to assets that benefit all years equally (as buildings do). The formula for calculating SYD is:

$$\frac{\text{Number of years of life remaining at beginning of year}}{\text{Sum-of-the-years'-digits}} \times (\text{Cost} - \text{Salvage value}) = \text{Depreciation expense}$$

The numerator is the number of years of estimated life remaining at the beginning of the current year. The van, with a four-year life, would have four years remaining at the beginning of the first year, three at the beginning of the second, and so on. The denominator is the sum of the years of the asset's life. The sum of the years' digits for the van is 10 (4 + 3 + 2 + 1). In other words, the numerator decreases by one year each year, whereas the denominator remains the same for each year's calculation of depreciation. Also note that the asset's cost is reduced by the salvage value in computing the annual depreciation expense as is done for the straight-line method but not for the declining-balance method.

The depreciation on the van for the first two years is:

First year: 4/10 × ($24,000 − $2,000) = $8,800
Second year: 3/10 × ($24,000 − $2,000) = $6,600

The depreciation schedule for four years is shown in Exhibit 13.

Exhibit 13: Depreciation Schedule with Sum-of-the-Years'-Digits Depreciation

	Annual Depreciation Expense	Accumulated Depreciation	Book Value
Acquisition date	—	—	$24,000
End of year 1	$ 8,800	$ 8,800	15,200
End of year 2	6,600	15,400	8,600
End of year 3	4,400	19,800	4,200
End of year 4	2,200	22,000	2,000
Total	$22,000		

The entry to record the sum-of-the-years'-digits depreciation for the first year is:

Depreciation Expense	8,800	
Accumulated Depreciation, Hotel Van		8,800
To record the first year's depreciation for the hotel van.		

Subsequent years' depreciation entries would show depreciation expense of $6,600, $4,400, and $2,200.

When an asset has a long life, the computation of the denominator (the sum-of-the-years'-digits) can become quite involved. There is, however, a simple formula for determining the denominator. It is:

$$\frac{n(n + 1)}{2} \text{ where n is the life (in years) of the asset}$$

Given that the van has a useful life of four years, the formula works as follows:

$$\frac{4(5)}{2} = 10$$

As you can see, the answer is the same as if you had added the years' digits (4 + 3 + 2 + 1). If an asset has a 10-year life, the sum of the years' digits is:

$$\frac{10(11)}{2} = 55$$

The depreciation fraction in year 1 would be 10/55, in year 2, 9/55, and so on.

A Comparison of Depreciation Methods

Now that you have been introduced to the four most common depreciation methods, we can compare them both graphically and by using the Wheeler Resorts van example. Exhibit 14 compares the straight-line, sum-of-the-years'-digits, and declining-balance depreciation methods with regard to the relative amount of depreciation expense incurred in each year for an asset that has a five-year life. The units-of-production method is not illustrated because there would not be a standard pattern of cost allocation. Exhibit 15 shows the results for the Wheeler Resorts' van for all four depreciation methods.

Exhibit 14: Comparison of Depreciation Methods

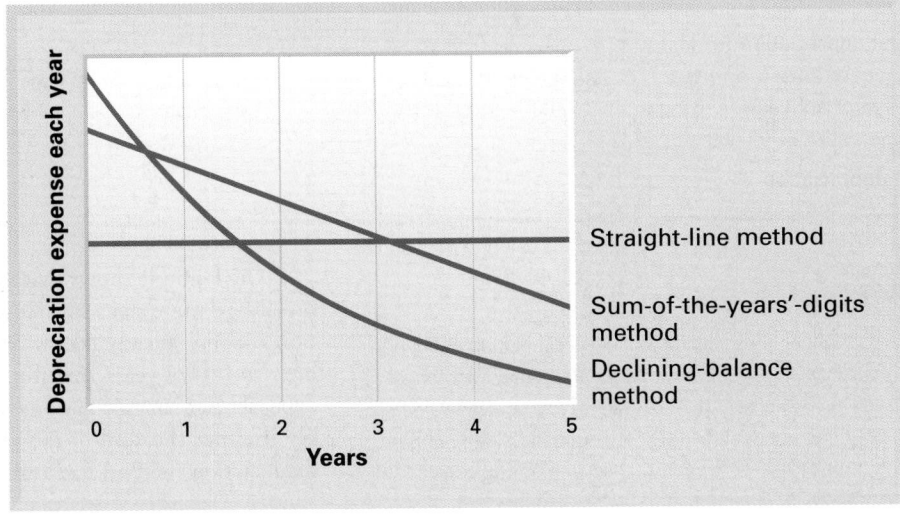

Exhibit 15: Comparison of Depreciation Expense Using Different Depreciation Methods

	Straight-Line Depreciation	Units-of-Production Depreciation	DDB Depreciation	SYD Depreciation
Year 1	$ 5,500	$ 4,400	$12,000	$ 8,800
Year 2	5,500	6,600	6,000	6,600
Year 3	5,500	7,700	3,000	4,400
Year 4	5,500	3,300	1,000	2,200
Totals	$22,000	$22,000	$22,000	$22,000

TO SUMMARIZE: Two depreciation methods that allow for more depreciation expense in the early years of an asset's life are the declining-balance and the sum-of-the-years'-digits methods. The declining-balance method involves multiplying the asset's declining book value by a fixed rate that is a multiple of the straight-line rate. Sum-of-the-years'-digits depreciation is computed by multiplying (cost − salvage value) by a declining ratio based on the number of years in the asset's estimated life.

Changes in Depreciation Estimates

ǀ ǀ Account for changes in depreciation estimates.

As mentioned earlier in the chapter, useful lives and salvage values are only estimates. Wheeler Resorts' van, for example, was assumed to have a useful life of four years and a salvage value of $2,000. In reality, the van's life and salvage value may be different from the original estimates. If, after three years, Wheeler realizes that the van will last another three years and that the salvage value will be $3,000 instead of $2,000, the accountant would need to calculate a new depreciation expense for the remaining three years. Using straight-line depreciation, the calculations would be as follows:

	Formula	Calculation	Total Depreciation
Annual depreciation for the first three years	$\dfrac{\text{Cost} - \text{Salvage value}}{\text{Estimated useful life}} = \dfrac{\text{Depreciation}}{\text{expense}}$	$\dfrac{\$24,000 - \$2,000}{4 \text{ years}} = \$5,500$	$16,500
Book value after three years	$\dfrac{\text{Cost} - \text{Accumulated}}{\text{depreciation to date}} = \text{Book value}$	$24,000 − $16,500 = $7,500	
Annual depreciation for last three years (based on new total life of six years and new salvage value of $3,000	$\dfrac{\text{Book value} - \text{Salvage value}}{\text{Remaining useful life}} = \dfrac{\text{Depreciation}}{\text{expense}}$	$\dfrac{\$7,500 - \$3,000}{3 \text{ years}} = \$1,500$	4,500
Total depreciation			$21,000

FYI:

To illustrate the uncertainty about depreciation life estimates, consider that BOEING 727 airplanes are lasting a lot longer than initially expected. The first Boeing 727 was delivered in 1963; the last was built in 1984. As of January 2001, almost 1,300 of the 1,831 727s delivered were still in service.

The example shows that a change in the estimate of useful life or salvage value does not require a modification of the depreciation expense already taken. New information affects depreciation only in future years. Exhibit 16 shows the revised depreciation expense. Similar calculations, although more complex, would apply if either the sum-of-the-years'-digits or the declining-balance depreciation method had been used.

Exhibit 16: Depreciation Schedule When There Is a Change in Estimate

	Annual Depreciation Expense	Accumulated Depreciation	Book Value
Acquisition date	—	—	$24,000
Year 1	$ 5,500	$ 5,500	18,500
Year 2	5,500	11,000	13,000
Year 3	5,500	16,500	7,500
Change			
Year 4	1,500	18,000	6,000
Year 5	1,500	19,500	4,500
Year 6	1,500	21,000	3,000
Total	$21,000		

TO SUMMARIZE: Because depreciation is only an estimate, changes in estimates of useful life or salvage value may be required as new information becomes available. When there is a change in estimate, past periods' depreciation amounts remain the same. The only change is in future years' depreciation where the remaining book value is allocated over the new life (in the case of a change in useful life), or the difference between the book value and the new salvage value is allocated over the remaining life (in the case of a change in salvage value).

review of learning objectives

1 Identify the two major categories of long-term operating assets: property, plant, and equipment and intangible assets. There are two major types of operating assets. Property, plant, and equipment are long-lived, tangible assets acquired for use in a business. This category includes land, buildings, machinery, equipment, and furniture. Intangible assets are long-lived assets used in a business, but they have no physical substance. Common intangible assets are patents, licenses, franchises, and goodwill.

2 Understand the factors important in deciding whether to acquire a long-term operating asset. The value of long-term operating assets stems from the fact that they help companies generate future cash flows. Capital budgeting is the name given to the process whereby decisions are made about acquiring long-term operating assets. Capital budgeting involves comparing the cost of the asset to the value of the expected cash inflows, after adjusting for the time value of money. The value of a long-term operating asset can disappear instantly if events lower the expectations about the future cash flows generated by the asset.

3 Record the acquisition of property, plant, and equipment through a simple purchase as well as through a lease, by self-construction, and as part of the purchase of several assets at once. Property, plant, and equipment may be acquired by purchase, lease, or self-construction. When purchased, the assets are recorded at cost, which includes all expenditures associated with acquiring them and getting them ready for their intended use. When these types of assets are leased, the lease agreement may be classified as an operating lease or as a capital lease. An operating lease results in a short-term use of the asset without recording the asset on the books of the user, the lessee. Instead, the lessee records only the rental expense paid each period. If the lease is for a longer term and meets the conditions of a capital lease, the lessee records the leased property as an asset and the related liability as if the property had been purchased and financed with long-term debt. The asset is recorded at the present value of the lease rental payments, which usually is equivalent to the current market value or the cash equivalent price. When a company constructs an asset for its own use, the recorded cost includes building materials, labor, a reasonable allocation of general administrative costs, and capitalized interest equal to the amount of interest that could have been avoided if the construction expenditures had been used to repay loans.

If two or more assets are acquired in a "basket" purchase, the relative fair market value method is used to assign costs to individual assets. If one company buys all the assets of another company, the excess of the purchase price over the aggregate fair value of the acquired net assets is recorded as goodwill, an intangible asset.

4 **Compute straight-line and units-of-production depreciation expense for plant and equipment.** Depreciation is the process of allocating the cost of plant and equipment to expense in the periods that are benefited from the use of the asset. The two most common and simple methods of depreciation are straight-line and units-of-production.

The straight-line method is the only method that results in the same amount of depreciation for each full year. The units-of-production method allocates cost over the useful life measured in units of output or usage. Both methods require salvage value to be subtracted from the original cost in computing depreciation expense.

The units-of-production method is also used with natural resources such as coal, gravel, and timber. Depletion expense for a year is computed by first computing a depletion rate by dividing the cost assigned to the natural resource by the estimated number of remaining units to be extracted. This depletion rate is multiplied by the number of units extracted for the year to arrive at the dollar amount of depletion for the year.

5 **Account for repairs and improvements of property, plant, and equipment.** Expenditures incurred for property, plant, and equipment after acquisition may be classified as either ordinary expenditures or capital expenditures. Since ordinary expenditures merely maintain an asset's productive capacity at the level originally projected, they are reported as repairs and maintenance expense and do not affect the asset's reported cost. For an expenditure to be classified as a capital expenditure, it must (1) increase the productive life or annual capacity of the asset, (2) be significant in amount, and (3) benefit the company over several periods. Because capital expenditures are added to the cost of an asset, they affect future depreciation, whereas ordinary expenditures are expenses of the current period.

6 **Identify whether a long-term operating asset has suffered a decline in value and record the decline.** Impairment is the decline in a long-term operating asset's value after it is purchased. In recording an impairment loss, the recorded book value of the asset is first compared with the sum of future cash flows to be generated by the asset. Next, if the book value is higher, a loss is recognized. The amount of the loss is the difference between the book value of the

asset and its fair value. According to U.S. accounting rules, increases in the value of property, plant, and equipment are not recognized.

7 **Record the discarding and selling of property, plant, and equipment.** Property, plant, and equipment may be disposed of by discarding, selling, or exchanging. When an asset is sold, a gain is reported if the sales price exceeds the book value, or a loss is reported if the book value exceeds the sales price.

8 **Account for the acquisition and amortization of intangible assets and understand the special difficulties associated with accounting for intangibles.** Intangible assets are rights and privileges that are long-lived, are not held for resale, have no physical substance, and usually provide competitive advantages for the owner. Common examples are patents, franchises, licenses, and goodwill. Intangible assets are recorded at the price paid for them. Some intangible assets have a limited economic life and those assets are amortized over their useful life. Other intangible assets have infinite life and, as a result, their costs are not amortized. All intangible assets must be examined periodically to determine if they have become impaired. If it is determined that an intangible asset is impaired, an impairment loss is recognized on the income statement and the amount of the asset on the balance sheet is reduced.

9 **Use the fixed asset turnover ratio as a measure of how efficiently a company is using its property, plant, and equipment.** Fixed asset turnover is computed as sales divided by average property, plant, and equipment (fixed assets) and is interpreted as the number of dollars in sales generated by each dollar of fixed assets. Fixed asset turnover ratios can be meaningfully compared only between firms in similar industries.

10 **Compute declining-balance and sum-of-the years'-digits depreciation expense for plant and equipment.** The two most common accelerated depreciation methods are declining-balance and sum-of-the-years'-digits. The declining-balance method is different from straight-line, units-of-production, and sum-of-the-years'-digits depreciation. The salvage value is ignored in the declining-balance method in the annual computation, but the book value of the asset cannot be less than the salvage value at the end of any reporting year. With declining-balance, the depreciation rate is calculated by multiplying a desired factor (such as 1.5 or 2.0) by the straight-line depreciation rate. This rate is then multiplied times the book value to determine annual depreciation expense. The declining-balance method is the basis for the MACRS income tax depreciation calculations in the United States. With sum-of-the-years'-digits depreciation, a ratio, computed by dividing the number of years of estimated life remaining at the beginning of the year by the sum of the years of the asset's life, is multiplied by the book value (cost − salvage value) of the asset to determine annual depreciation expense.

 Account for changes in depreciation estimates. Useful lives and salvage values of plant and equipment are only estimates and may need adjustment during an asset's life. Changes in estimates of useful life or salvage value do not require modification of depreciation expense already taken. Rather, only future depreciation amounts are affected by changes in estimates.

key terms & concepts

amortization, 485
basket purchase, 468
book value, 471
capital budgeting, 463
capital lease, 466
capitalized interest, 468
depletion, 475
depreciation, 470
fixed asset turnover, 487
franchise, 483
goodwill, 470
impairment, 478

intangible assets, 462
lease, 465
lessee, 465
lessor, 465
long-term operating assets, 462
natural resources, 475
operating lease, 465
patent, 482
property, plant, and equipment, 462
salvage value, 471
straight-line depreciation method, 471
time value of money, 463

units-of-production method, 471

eXpanded *Material*

declining-balance depreciation method, 488
sum-of-the-years'-digits (SYD) depreciation method, 490

review problems

Property, Plant, and Equipment

Swift Motor Lines is a trucking company that hauls crude oil in the Rocky Mountain states. It currently has 20 trucks. The following information relates to a single truck:

a. Date truck was purchased, July 1, 2003.
b. Cost of truck:

Truck	$125,000
Paint job	3,000
Sales tax	7,000

c. Estimated useful life of truck, 120,000 miles.
d. Estimated salvage value of truck, $27,000.
e. 2005 expenditures on truck:
   (1) $6,000 on new tires and regular maintenance.
   (2) On January 1, spent $44,000 to completely rework the truck's engine; increased the total life to 200,000 miles but left expected salvage value unchanged.
f. Miles driven:

2003	11,000
2004	24,000
2005 (after reworking of engine)	20,000
2006	14,000

Required:

Record journal entries to account for the following. (Use the units-of-production depreciation method.)

1. The purchase of the truck.
2. The expenditures on the truck during 2005.
3. Depreciation expense for:
    a. 2003
    b. 2004
    c. 2005
    d. 2006

Solution

1. Truck Purchase

The cost of the truck includes both the amount paid for it and all costs incurred to get it in working condition. In this case, the cost includes both the paint job and the sales tax. Thus, the entry to record the purchase is:

Truck	135,000	
Cash		135,000
Purchased truck for cash.		

2. Expenditures

The expenditure of $6,000 is an ordinary expenditure and is expensed in the current year. The engine overhaul is capitalized. The entries are:

Repairs and Maintenance Expense	6,000	
Cash		6,000
Recorded purchase of new tires and regular maintenance on truck.		

Truck	44,000	
Cash		44,000
Recorded major overhaul to truck's engine.		

3. Depreciation Expense

The formula for units-of-production depreciation on the truck is:

$$\frac{\text{Cost} - \text{Salvage value}}{\text{Total miles expected to be driven}} \times \frac{\text{Number of miles}}{\text{driven in any year}} = \text{Depreciation expense}$$

Journal entries and calculations are as follows:

a. 2003:

Depreciation Expense	9,900	
Accumulated Depreciation, Truck		9,900
Recorded depreciation expense for 2003.		

$$\frac{\$135,000 - \$27,000}{120,000 \text{ miles}} \times 11,000 \text{ miles} = \$9,900 \text{ or } \$0.90 \text{ per mile} \times 11,000 \text{ miles}$$

b. 2004:

Depreciation Expense	21,600	
Accumulated Depreciation, Truck		21,600
Recorded depreciation expense for 2004.		

$0.90 \times 24,000$ miles = $21,600

c. 2005:

Depreciation Expense	14,600	
Accumulated Depreciation, Truck		14,600
Recorded depreciation expense for 2005.		

$$\frac{\$135{,}000 - \$9{,}900 - \$21{,}600 + \$44{,}000 - \$27{,}000}{\substack{165{,}000 \text{ miles} \\ (200{,}000 - 11{,}000 - 24{,}000)}} \times 20{,}000 \text{ miles} = \$14{,}600 \text{ or } \$0.73^{*} \text{ per mile} \times 20{,}000 \text{ miles}$$

*Rounded to the nearest cent.

d. 2006:

Depreciation Expense	10,220	
Accumulated Depreciation, Truck		10,220
Recorded depreciation expense for 2006.		

$0.73 \times 14{,}000$ miles $= \$10{,}220$

Property, Plant, and Equipment

Swift Motor Lines is a trucking company that hauls crude oil in the Rocky Mountain states. It currently has 20 trucks. The following information relates to a single truck:

a. Date truck was purchased, July 1, 2003.
b. Cost of truck:

Truck	$125,000
Paint job	3,000
Sales tax	7,000

c. Estimated useful life of truck, eight years.
d. Estimated salvage value of truck, $27,000.
e. 2005 expenditures on truck:
    (1) $6,000 on new tires and regular maintenance.
    (2) On January 1, spent $44,000 to completely rework the truck's engine. As a result of the engine work, the remaining life of the truck is increased to nine years, but the expected salvage value remains the same.

Required:
Record journal entries to account for the following. (Use the sum-of-the-years'-digits depreciation method.)

1. The purchase of the truck.
2. Depreciation expense for:
    a. 2003
    b. 2004
    c. 2005
3. The expenditures on the truck during 2005.

Solution
1. Truck Purchase
The cost of the truck includes both the amount paid for it and all costs incurred to get it in working condition. In this case, the cost includes both the paint job and the sales tax. Thus, the entry to record the purchase is:

```
Truck . . . . . . . . . . . . . . . . . . . . . . . . . . . . . . . . . . . . . . . . . . . . . . .   135,000
    Cash  . . . . . . . . . . . . . . . . . . . . . . . . . . . . . . . . . . . . . . . . . . . .            135,000
        Purchased truck for cash.
```

2. Depreciation Expense

The formula for sum-of-the-years'-digits depreciation on the truck is:

$$\frac{\text{Number of years of life remaining at beginning of year}}{\text{Sum-of-the-years'-digits}} \times (\text{Cost} - \text{Salvage value}) = \text{Depreciation expense}$$

Depreciation for the three years is calculated as follows:

2003: $\dfrac{8}{36}$ × ($135,000 − $27,000) = $24,000; $24,000 × 1/2 year = $12,000

2004: $\dfrac{7.5}{36}$ × ($135,000 − $27,000) = $22,500

2005: $\dfrac{9}{45}$ × [($135,000 + $44,000) − ($12,000 + $22,500) − $27,000] = $23,500

The depreciation entries are:

a. 2003:
```
    Depreciation Expense  . . . . . . . . . . . . . . . . . . . . . . . . . . . . .   12,000
        Accumulated Depreciation, Truck . . . . . . . . . . . . . . . . . . . .            12,000
            Recorded depreciation expense for 2003.
```

b. 2004:
```
    Depreciation Expense  . . . . . . . . . . . . . . . . . . . . . . . . . . . . .   22,500
        Accumulated Depreciation, Truck . . . . . . . . . . . . . . . . . . . .            22,500
            Recorded depreciation expense for 2004.
```

c. 2005:
```
    Depreciation Expense  . . . . . . . . . . . . . . . . . . . . . . . . . . . . .   23,500
        Accumulated Depreciation, Truck . . . . . . . . . . . . . . . . . . . .            23,500
            Recorded depreciation expense for 2005.
```

3. Expenditures

The first expenditure of $6,000 is an ordinary expenditure and is expensed in the current year. The $44,000 expenditure is capitalized because it lengthens the truck's life. The entries are:

```
Repairs and Maintenance Expense . . . . . . . . . . . . . . . . . . . . . . .    6,000
    Cash . . . . . . . . . . . . . . . . . . . . . . . . . . . . . . . . . . . . . . . . . . .            6,000
        Recorded purchase of new tires and regular maintenance
        on truck.

Truck . . . . . . . . . . . . . . . . . . . . . . . . . . . . . . . . . . . . . . . . . . . . .   44,000
    Cash . . . . . . . . . . . . . . . . . . . . . . . . . . . . . . . . . . . . . . . . . . . .            44,000
        Recorded major overhaul of truck engine.
```

discussion questions

1. What are the major characteristics of property, plant, and equipment?
2. When buying a long-term asset such as a building or piece of equipment, the time value of money must be considered. With respect to time value, it is often said that the last payment (say, 20 years in the future) doesn't cost as much as the next payment today. Explain.
3. Why are expenditures other than the net purchase price included in the cost of an asset?
4. Why would a company include leased assets in the property, plant, and equipment section of its balance sheet when the assets are owned by another entity?
5. A company that borrows money to construct its own building generally should include the interest paid on the loan during the construction period in the cost of the building. Why?
6. Why are fair market values used to determine the cost of operating assets acquired in a basket purchase?
7. Companies usually depreciate assets such as buildings even though those assets may be increasing in value. Why?
8. How does the company accountant decide whether an expenditure should be capitalized or expensed?
9. If a firm is uncertain whether an expenditure will benefit one or more than one accounting period, or whether it will increase the capacity or useful life of an operational asset, most firms will expense rather than capitalize the expenditure. Why?
10. Sometimes long-term assets experience sudden dramatic decreases in value. For example, a waste dump might suddenly be constructed next to an office building. When such impairment of value occurs, should the decrease in value be recognized immediately, or should the same amount of depreciation expense be recognized as in past years?
11. Accountants in other countries sometimes write up the recorded amounts of long-term assets when their values

increase. Why are U.S. accountants reluctant to increase the recorded value of property, plant, and equipment when their value increases?
12. Why is it common to have a gain or loss on the disposal of a long-term operating asset? Is it true that if the useful life and salvage value of an asset could be known with certainty and were realized, there would never be such a gain or loss?
13. When recording the disposal of a long-term operating asset, why is it necessary to debit the accumulated depreciation of the old asset?
14. Why are intangible assets considered assets although they have no physical substance?
15. Goodwill can be recorded only when a business is purchased. Does this result in similar businesses having incomparable financial statements?
16. How is fixed asset turnover calculated, and what does the resulting ratio value mean?

17. Which of the depreciation methods discussed in this chapter will usually result in the highest net income in the early years of an asset's life?
18. How does the declining-balance method of depreciation differ from other methods of depreciation?
19. Modified accelerated cost recovery system (MACRS) depreciation is allowed by the IRS but usually is not used in financial reporting. Why do you think this is the case?
20. When changing the estimate of the useful life of an asset, should depreciation expense for all the previous years be recalculated? If not, how do you account for a change in this estimate?
21. Why is it often necessary to recalculate the depletion rate for natural resources?

practice exercises

Practice 10-1   **Long-Term Operating Assets**
Which one of the following is *not* an example of a long-term operating asset?

a. Buildings
b. Land
c. Goodwill
d. Equipment
e. Office Supplies

Practice 10-2

Decision of Long-Term Asset Acquisition
Pekka Inc. has the option to purchase a new drilling machine for $50,000 today. The company expects a net profit of $13,000 per year from using the machine, and the machine will last five years. According to the time value of money, the value today of $13,000 per year for five years is $46,862. Should the company purchase the new drilling machine?

Practice 10-3

Asset Purchased with Cash
The company used cash to purchase a stamping machine. The retail price on the machine is $20,000, but the company received a 2% discount. It also paid $1,225 in sales tax for the purchase. Make the necessary journal entry(ies) to record this transaction.

Practice 10-4

Asset Purchased Partially with Cash
Refer to the data in Practice 10-3. Assume the company borrowed $15,000 of the purchase price from a bank. Make the necessary journal entry(ies) to record this transaction.

Practice 10-5

Operating Lease
On January 1, ABC Company entered into a lease for equipment rental. The company agreed to pay $3,000 per year for six years. The present value of all six lease payments is $13,066. Assuming the company classified the lease as an operating lease, make the necessary journal entry(ies) to record the payment of the first year's rent expense for the equipment. The first lease payment is made at the end of the year.

Practice 10-6

Capital Lease Acquisition
On January 1, ABC Company entered into a lease for equipment rental. The company agreed to pay $3,000 per year for six years. The present value of all six lease payments is $13,066. Assuming the company classified the lease as a capital lease, make the necessary journal entry(ies) to record the acquisition of the equipment. The first lease payment is made at the end of the year.

Practice 10-7

Capital Lease Payments
Refer to the data in Practice 10-6. The interest included in the first lease payment is $1,307. Make the necessary journal entry(ies) to record the first $3,000 lease payment at the end of the first year.

Practice 10-8

Classifying Leases
Which one of the following characteristics of a lease would *not* cause the lease to be classified as a capital lease?

a. Lease ownership transfers to the lessee at the end of the lease.
b. The present value of the lease payments at the beginning of the lease is 90% or more of the fair market value of the leased asset.
c. The lease term is equal to 50% of the estimated economic life of the asset.
d. The lease contains a bargain purchase option.

Practice 10-9

Assets Acquired by Self-Construction
Using the following data, compute the total cost of a self-constructed office building.

Percentage of overhead attributable to construction of office building	30%
Direct materials	$1,450,000
Capitalized interest	140,000
Direct labor	860,000
Total overhead incurred during year	2,450,000

Practice 10-10

Acquisition of Several Assets at Once
The company purchased a building and the accompanying land for $710,000 cash. Independent appraisers estimated the fair market value of the building and the land to be $600,000 and 150,000, respectively. Make the necessary journal entry(ies) to record this transaction.

Practice 10-11

Straight-Line Method of Depreciation
Using the following data and the straight-line method of depreciation, compute depreciation expense, and make the necessary journal entry to record depreciation expense for the first year.

Cost of machine	$1,000,000
Estimated useful life (years)	8 years
Salvage value	$40,000
Estimated useful life (units)	1,600,000
Units produced during the first year	180,000

Practice 10-12

Units-of-Production Method of Depreciation
Refer to the data in Practice 10-11. Using the units-of-production method of depreciation, compute depreciation expense, and make the necessary journal entry to record depreciation expense for the first year.

Practice 10-13

Partial-Year Depreciation Calculations
On September 30, the company purchased a $25,000 delivery truck. The company estimates the truck will last five years and have a salvage value of $5,000 at the end of five years. Using the straight-line method of depreciation, compute the amount of depreciation in the first two years of the truck's service.

Practice 10-14

Units-of-Production Method with Natural Resources
The company purchased an oil field for $2,400,000 cash. The oil field contains an estimated 500,000 barrels of oil. During the first year of operation, the company extracts 60,000 barrels of oil. Compute the amount of depletion expense, and make the necessary journal entry(ies) to record depletion expense for the year.

Practice 10-15

Repairing and Improving Property, Plant, and Equipment
The company has a molding machine with a historical cost of $150,000 and accumulated depreciation of $110,000. On January 1, the company performed a major motor overhaul costing $24,000. The company expects the machine will last seven more years and have a salvage value of $8,000. Compute depreciation expense for the current year using the straight-line method.

Practice 10-16

Determining Asset Impairment
The company purchased a building 14 years ago for $720,000. The building has accumulated depreciation of $504,000 and a fair market value of $150,000. The company expects the building will generate a net cash inflow of $30,000 per year for the next six years. Determine whether, from an accounting point of view, the building is impaired.

Practice 10-17

Recording Decreases in the Value of Property, Plant, and Equipment
Using the information in Practice 10-16, determine the amount of impairment and record the impairment loss.

Original cost	$720,000
Accumulated depreciation	504,000
Book value	$216,000
Sum of future cash flows ($30,000 × 6 years)	$180,000

Practice 10-18

Discarding Property, Plant, and Equipment
The company scrapped a truck with a historical cost of $30,000 and accumulated depreciation of $24,000. In addition, the company had to pay $150 to discard the truck. Make the necessary journal entry(ies) to record this transaction.

Practice 10-19

Selling Property, Plant, and Equipment
The company sold a truck with a historical cost of $30,000 and accumulated depreciation of $24,000 for $7,000 cash. Make the necessary journal entry(ies) to record this transaction.

Practice 10-20

Patents
On January 1, the company purchased a 14-year-old patent from another company for $160,000. The patent has a six-year legal life remaining. Make the necessary journal entry(ies) to record amortization of the year the patent was acquired.

Practice 10-21

Goodwill
Parent Company purchased Daughter Company for $200,000. At the time of purchase, the fair market value of Daughter Company's assets and liabilities was as follows:

Inventory	$ 25,000
Property, plant, and equipment	140,000
Other assets	64,000
Liabilities	59,000

Make the necessary journal entry(ies) (on Parent's books) to record the purchase of Daughter Company.

Practice 10-22

Fixed Asset Turnover
Using the following data, compute the fixed asset turnover.

Current assets, end of year	$ 35,000
Fixed assets, end of year	180,000
Fixed assets, beginning of year	195,000
Sales during the year	595,000

Practice 10-23

Declining-Balance Method of Depreciation
Using the following data and the declining-balance method of depreciation, compute depreciation expense for the first two years.

Cost of machine	$1,000,000
Estimated useful life (years)	8 years
Salvage value	$40,000

Practice 10-24

Sum-of-the-Years'-Digits Method of Depreciation
Using the data in Practice 10-23 and the sum-of-the-years'-digits method of depreciation, compute depreciation expense for the first two years.

Practice 10-25

Changes in Depreciation Estimates
Using the information in Practice 10-11, the company computed depreciation expense of $120,000 per year. After two years, the company determined that the machine would last 10 more years (for a total of 12 years). Compute depreciation expense for the third year.

exercises

Exercise 10-1

Acquisition Decision

Johnson Company is considering acquiring a new airplane. It has looked at two financing options. The first is to lease the airplane for 10 years with lease payments of $70,000 each year. The second is to purchase the airplane, making a down payment of $250,000 and annual payments of $40,000 for 10 years. If the present value of the two financing options is the same, what other factors must be considered in deciding whether to purchase or to lease?

Exercise 10-2

Accounting for the Acquisition of a Long-Term Asset

Action Jackson Company acquired a new machine in order to expand its productive capacity. The costs associated with the machine purchase were as follows:

Purchase price	$25,000
Installation costs	750
Cost of initial testing	900
Sales tax	1,563

1. Make the journal entry to record the acquisition of the machine. Assume that all costs were paid in cash.
2. Make the journal entry to record the acquisition of the machine. Assume that Action Jackson Company signed a note payable for the $25,000 purchase price and paid the remaining costs in cash.

Exercise 10-3

Computing Asset Cost and Depreciation Expense

Antique Furniture Company decided to purchase a new furniture-polishing machine for its store in New York City. After a long search, it found the appropriate polisher in Chicago. The machine costs $75,000 and has an estimated 10-year life and no salvage value. Antique Furniture Company made the following additional expenditures with respect to this purchase:

Sales tax	$4,000
Delivery costs (FOB shipping point)	1,500
Installation costs	2,200
Painting of machine to match the decor	300

1. What is the cost of the machine to Antique Furniture Company?
2. What is the amount of the first full year's depreciation if Antique uses the straight-line method?

Exercise 10-4

Acquisition and Depreciation of Assets

Vandre Oil Company, which prepares financial statements on a calendar-year basis, purchased new drilling equipment on July 1, 2006, using check numbers 1035 and 1036. The check totals are shown here, along with a breakdown of the charges.

1035 (Payee—Oil Equipment, Inc.):

Cost of drilling equipment	$150,000
Cost of cement platform	50,000
Installation charges	26,000
Total	$226,000

1036 (Payee—Red Ball Freight):

Freight costs for drilling equipment	$ 4,000

(continued)

Assume that the estimated life of the drilling equipment is 10 years and its salvage value is $7,000.

1. Record the disbursements on July 1, 2006, assuming that no entry had been recorded for the drilling equipment.
2. Disregarding the information given about the two checks, assume that the drilling equipment was recorded at a total cost of $195,000. Calculate the depreciation expense for 2006 using the straight-line method.

Exercise 10-5

Accounting for Leased Assets

On January 1, 2006, Hartmeyer Company leased a fax machine with a laser printer from Teleproducts, Inc. The five-year lease is noncancelable and requires monthly payments of $150 at the end of each month, with the first payment due on January 31, 2006. At the end of five years, Hartmeyer will own the equipment. The present value of the lease payments at the beginning of the lease is determined to be $6,740.

1. Prepare journal entries to record:
   a. The lease agreement on January 1, 2006.
   b. The first lease payment on January 31, 2006, assuming that $68 of the $150 payment is interest.
2. Now assume that the lease expires after one year at which time a new lease can be negotiated or Hartmeyer can return the equipment to Teleproducts. Prepare any journal entries relating to the lease that would be required on January 1 and January 31, 2006.

Exercise 10-6

Interest Capitalization

Litton Company is constructing a new office building. Costs of the building are as follows:

Wages paid to construction workers	$185,000
Building materials purchased	456,000
Interest expense on construction loan	13,800
Interest expense on mortgage loan during the first year subsequent to the building's completion	22,000

Given the above costs, at what amount should the building be recorded in the accounting records?

Exercise 10-7

Accounting for the Acquisition of Assets—Basket Purchase

Sealise Corporation purchased land, a building, and equipment for a total cost of $450,000. After the purchase, the property was appraised. Fair market values were determined to be $120,000 for the land, $280,000 for the building, and $80,000 for the equipment. Given these appraisals, record the purchase of the property by Sealise Corporation.

Exercise 10-8

Depreciation Calculations

Buhler Company purchased a new car on July 1, 2005, for $20,000. The estimated life of the car was six years or 120,000 miles, and its salvage value was estimated to be $2,000. The car was driven 8,000 miles in 2005 and 23,000 miles in 2006.

1. Compute the amount of depreciation expense for 2005 and 2006 using the following methods:
   a. Straight-line.
   b. Units-of-production.
2. Which depreciation method more closely reflects the used-up service potential of the car? Explain.

Exercise 10-9

Depreciation Calculations

Denver Hardware Company has a giant paint mixer that cost $31,500 plus $400 to install. The estimated salvage value of the paint mixer at the end of its useful life in 15 years is estimated to be $1,900. Denver estimates that the machine can mix 850,000 cans of paint during its lifetime. Compute the second full year's depreciation expense, using the following methods:

1. Straight-line.
2. Units-of-production, assuming that the machine mixes 51,000 cans of paint during the second year.

Exercise 10-10

Acquisition and Improvement of Assets

Prepare entries in the books of Sanmara, Inc., to reflect the following. (Assume cash transactions.)

1. Purchased a lathing machine to be used by the firm in its production process.

Invoice price	$45,000
Cash discount taken	900
Installation costs	1,200
Sales tax on machine	1,800

2. Performed normal periodic maintenance on the lathing machine at a cost of $200.
3. Added to the lathing machine a governor costing $400, which is expected to increase the machine's useful life.

Exercise 10-11

Asset Impairment

Consider the following three independent scenarios:

	1	2	3
Original cost of asset	$1,400	$1,400	$1,400
Accumulated depreciation	400	400	400
Sum of future cash flows	1,500	1,500	900
Fair value of the asset	1,100	800	800

1. For each of the three scenarios, answer the following questions:
   a. Is the asset impaired?
   b. At what amount (net of accumulated depreciation) should the asset be reported?
2. Make the journal entry required in Scenario 3.

Exercise 10-12

Asset Impairment

In 2001, Rhode Company purchased land and a building at a cost of $800,000, of which $200,000 was allocated to the land and $600,000 was allocated to the building. As of December 31, 2005, the accounting records related to these assets were as follows:

Land	$200,000
Building	600,000
Accumulated Depreciation, Building	100,000

On January 1, 2006, it is determined that there is toxic waste under the building and the future cash flows associated with the land and building are less than the recorded total book value for those two assets. The fair value of the land and building together is now only $100,000, of which $40,000 is land and $60,000 is the building. How should this impairment in value be

(continued)

recognized? Make the entry on January 1, 2006, to record the impairment of the land and building.

Exercise 10-13

Spreadsheet

Accounting for the Disposal of Assets

Canlas Concrete Company has a truck that it wants to sell. The truck had an original cost of $80,000, was purchased four years ago, and was expected to have a useful life of eight years with no salvage value.

Using straight-line depreciation, and assuming that depreciation expense for four full years has been recorded, prepare journal entries to record the disposal of the truck under each of the following independent conditions:

1. Canlas Concrete Company sells the truck for $45,000 cash.
2. Canlas Concrete Company sells the truck for $38,000 cash.
3. The old truck is wrecked and Canlas Concrete Company hauls it to the junkyard.

Exercise 10-14

Disposal of an Asset

Honey Bee Company purchased a machine for $91,000. The machine has an estimated useful life of seven years and a salvage value of $7,000. Journalize the disposal of the machine under each of the following conditions. (Assume straight-line depreciation.)

1. Sold the machine for $72,000 cash after two years.
2. Sold the machine for $28,000 cash after five years.

Exercise 10-15

Spreadsheet

Accounting for Intangible Assets

Gaylord Research, Inc., has the following intangible assets:

Asset	Cost	Date Purchased	Expected Useful or Legal Life
Goodwill	$ 16,000	January 1, 1997	Unlimited
Patent	136,000	January 1, 1999	20 years

1. Record the amortization expense for both of these intangible assets for 2006 assuming neither of the assets is impaired.
2. Prepare the intangible assets section of the balance sheet for Gaylord Research, Inc., as of December 31, 2006.

Exercise 10-16

Intangible Assets

On January 1, 2005, Landon Company purchased a patent for $250,000 to allow it to improve its product line. On July 1, 2005, Landon Company purchased another existing business in a nearby city for a total cost of $750,000. The market value of the land, building, equipment, and other tangible assets was $550,000. The excess $200,000 was recorded as goodwill.

Assuming Landon Company amortizes patents over a 20-year period, record the following:

1. The purchase of the patent on January 1, 2005.
2. The amortization of the patent at December 31, 2005.
3. Under what conditions would goodwill be amortized on the books of Landon?

Exercise 10-17

Computing Goodwill

Stringtown Company purchased Stansbury Island Manufacturing for $1,800,000 cash. The book value and fair value of the assets of Stansbury Island as of the date of the acquisition are listed on the following page.

	Book Value	Market Value
Cash	$ 30,000	$ 30,000
Accounts receivable	300,000	300,000
Inventory	350,000	600,000
Property, plant, and equipment	500,000	900,000
Totals	$1,180,000	$1,830,000

In addition, Stansbury Island had liabilities totaling $400,000 at the time of the acquisition.

1. At what amounts will the individual assets of Stansbury Island be recorded on the books of Stringtown, the acquiring company?
2. How will Stringtown account for the liabilities of Stansbury Island?
3. How much goodwill will be recorded as part of this acquisition?

Exercise 10-18

Fixed Asset Turnover

Handy Corner Stores reported the following asset values in 2005 and 2006:

	2006	2005
Cash	$ 30,000	$ 20,000
Accounts receivable	400,000	300,000
Inventory	600,000	350,000
Land	200,000	150,000
Buildings	600,000	500,000
Equipment	300,000	200,000

In addition, Handy Corner had sales of $2,000,000 in 2006. Cost of goods sold for the year was $1,500,000.

Compute Handy Corner's fixed asset turnover ratio for 2006.

Exercise 10-19

Acquisition and Depreciation of Assets

Brough Oil Company, which prepares financial statements on a calendar-year basis, purchased new drilling equipment on July 1, 2006. A breakdown of the cost follows:

Cost of drilling equipment	$125,000
Cost of cement platform	35,000
Installation charges	22,000
Freight costs for drilling equipment	3,000
Total	$185,000

Assuming that the estimated life of the drilling equipment is 20 years and its salvage value is $10,000:

1. Record the purchase on July 1, 2006.

(continued)

2. Assume that the drilling equipment was recorded at a total cost of $140,000. Calculate the depreciation expense for 2006 using the following methods:
   a. Sum-of-the-years'-digits.
   b. Double-declining-balance.
   c. 150% declining-balance.
3. Prepare the journal entry to record the depreciation for 2006 in accordance with part (2)a.

Exercise 10-20

Acquisition and Depreciation

At the beginning of 2006, Lowham's Guest Ranch constructed a new walk-in freezer that had a useful life of 10 years. At the end of 10 years, the motor could be salvaged for $2,000. In addition to construction costs that totaled $10,000, the following costs were incurred:

Sales taxes on components	$1,250
Delivery costs	800
Installation of motor	200
Painting of both interior and exterior of freezer	100

1. What is the cost of the walk-in freezer to Lowham's Guest Ranch?
2. Compute the amount of depreciation to be taken in the first year assuming Lowham's Guest Ranch uses the
   a. Double-declining-balance method.
   b. Sum-of-the-years'-digits method.

Exercise 10-21

Depreciation Computations

Hsin-Yo Company purchases an $850,000 piece of equipment on January 2, 2004, for use in its manufacturing process. The equipment's estimated useful life is 10 years with no salvage value. Hsin-Yo uses 150% declining-balance depreciation for all its equipment.

1. Compute the depreciation expense for 2004, 2005, and 2006.
2. Compute the book value of the equipment on December 31, 2006.

Exercise 10-22

Depreciation Calculations

Letha Enterprises purchased a new van on January 1, 2005, for $35,000. The estimated life of the van was four years or 76,000 miles, and its salvage value was estimated to be $3,000. Compute the amount of depreciation expense for 2005, 2006, and 2007 using the following methods:

1. Double-declining-balance.
2. 175% declining-balance.
3. Sum-of-the-years'-digits.

Exercise 10-23

Depreciation Calculations

On January 1, 2005, MAC Corporation purchased a machine for $60,000. The machine cost $800 to deliver and $2,000 to install. At the end of 10 years, MAC expects to sell the machine for $2,000. Compute depreciation expense for 2005 and 2006 using the following methods:

1. Double-declining-balance.
2. 150% declining-balance.
3. Sum-of-the-years'-digits.

Exercise 10-24

Accounting for Natural Resources

On January 1, 2005, Castle Investment Corporation purchased a coal mine for cash, having taken into consideration the favorable tax consequences and the inevitable energy crunch in the future. Castle paid $800,000 for the mine. Shortly before the purchase, an engineer estimated that there were 80,000 tons of coal in the mine.

1. Record the purchase of the mine on January 1, 2005.
2. Record the depletion expense for 2005, assuming that 20,000 tons of coal were mined during the year.
3. Assume that on January 1, 2006, the company received a new estimate that the mine now contained 120,000 tons of coal. Record the entry (if any) to show the change in estimate.
4. Record the depletion expense for 2006, assuming that another 20,000 tons of coal were mined.

Exercise 10-25

Change in Estimated Useful Life

On January 1, 2004, Landon Excavation Company purchased a new bulldozer for $120,000. The equipment had an estimated useful life of 10 years and an estimated residual value of $10,000. On January 1, 2006, Landon determined that the bulldozer would have a total useful life of only 8 years instead of 10 years with no change in residual value. Landon uses straight-line depreciation.

Compute depreciation expense on this bulldozer for 2004, 2005, and 2006.

p roblems

Problem 10-1

P.A.S.S.
Power Accounting
System Software

Acquisition, Depreciation, and Disposal of Assets

On January 2, 2006, Scott Company purchased a building and land for $440,000. The most recent appraisal values for the building and the land are $360,000 and $120,000, respectively. The building has an estimated useful life of 20 years and a salvage value of $10,000.

Required:
1. Assuming cash transactions and straight-line depreciation, prepare journal entries to record:
   a. Purchase of the building and land on January 2, 2006.
   b. Depreciation expense on December 31, 2006.
2. Assume that after three years the property (land and building) was sold for $350,000. Prepare the journal entry to record the sale.

Problem 10-2

Purchasing Property, Plant, and Equipment

Jordon Company is considering replacing its automated stamping machine. The machine is specialized and very expensive. Jordon is considering three acquisition alternatives. The first is to lease a machine for 10 years at $1 million per year, after which time Jordon can buy the machine for $1 million. The second alternative is to pay cash for the machine at a cost of $7 million. The third alternative is to make a down payment of $3 million, followed by 10 annual payments of $550,000. The company is trying to decide which alternative to select.

Required:
1. Assuming the present value of the lease payments is $7.2 million and the present value of the 10 loan payments of $550,000 is $4.1 million, determine which alternative Jordon should choose.
2. **Interpretive Question:** Your decision in part (1) was based only on financial factors. What other qualitative issues might influence your decision?

Problem 10-3

Acquisition of an Asset

Ray's Printing Company purchased a new printing press. The invoice price was $184,250. The company paid for the press within 10 days, so it was allowed a 2% discount. The freight cost for delivering the press was $3,000. A premium of $1,200 was paid for a special insurance policy to cover the transportation of the press. The company spent $3,400 to install the press and an additional $655 in start-up costs to get the press ready for regular production.

(continued)

Required:
1. At what amount should the press be recorded as an asset?
2. What additional information must be known before the depreciation expense for the first year of operation of the new press can be computed?
3. **Interpretive Question:** What criterion is used to determine whether the start-up costs of $655 are included in the cost of the asset? Explain.

Problem 10-4

Accounting for Leased Assets

On January 2, 2006, Cameron Company contracted to lease a computer on a noncancelable basis for five years at an annual rental of $63,000, payable at the end of each year. The computer has an estimated economic life of six years. There is no bargain purchase option, and the computer will be returned to the lessor at the end of the five-year term of the lease. At the beginning of the lease, the computer has a fair market value of $240,000, and the present value of the lease payments equals $238,820.

Required:
1. Is this a capital lease or an operating lease? Explain.
2. Assuming that the lease is an operating lease, prepare the journal entries for Cameron Company for 2006.
3. Assuming that the lease is a capital lease, prepare the journal entries for Cameron Company for 2006. Assume the lease payment at the end of 2006 includes interest of $23,882.

Problem 10-5

Accounting for Leased Assets

The board of directors of Swogen Company authorized the president to lease a corporate jet to facilitate her travels to domestic and international subsidiaries of the company. After extensive investigation of the alternatives, the company agreed to lease a jet for $300,548 each year for five years, payable at the end of each year. Title to the jet will pass to Swogen Company at the end of five years with no further payments required. The lease agreement starts on January 2, 2006. The jet has an economic life of eight years. The lease contract is noncancelable and contains an interest rate of 8%, resulting in a present value of the lease payments of $1,200,000 as of January 2, 2006.

Required:
1. Does this lease contract meet the requirements to be accounted for as a capital lease? Why or why not?
2. Assuming that the lease contract is to be accounted for as a capital lease, prepare the journal entries for Swogen Company for 2006. Interest included in the first payment is $96,000.

Problem 10-6

Interest Capitalization

Jennifer Cosmetics wants to construct a new building. It has two building options, as follows:

a. Hire a contractor to do all the work. Jennifer has a bid of $850,000 from a reputable contractor to complete the project.
b. Construct the building itself by taking out a construction loan of $800,000. Using this alternative, Jennifer believes materials and labor will cost $800,000, and interest on the construction loan will be calculated as follows:

$200,000 @ 12% for 9 months
$300,000 @ 12% for 6 months
$200,000 @ 12% for 3 months
$100,000 @ 12% for 1 month

Required:
1. What will be the recorded cost of the building under each alternative?
2. Assuming the building is depreciated over a 20-year period using straight-line depreciation with no salvage value, how much is the annual depreciation expense under each alternative?

Problem 10-7

Depreciation Calculations

On January 1, Clauser Company purchased a $79,000 machine. The estimated life of the machine was four years, and the estimated salvage value was $4,000. The machine had an estimated useful life in productive output of 90,000 units. Actual output for the first two years was: year 1, 25,000 units; year 2, 18,000 units.

Required:

1. Compute the amount of depreciation expense for the first year, using each of the following methods:
    a. Straight-line.
    b. Units-of-production.
2. What was the book value of the machine at the end of the first year, assuming that straight-line depreciation was used?
3. If the machine is sold at the end of the third year for $20,000, how much should the company report as a gain or loss (assuming straight-line depreciation)?

Problem 10-8

Purchase of Multiple Assets for a Single Sum

On April 1, 2006, Mission Company paid $360,000 in cash to purchase land, a building, and equipment. The appraised fair market values of the assets were as follows: land, $90,000; building, $260,000; and equipment, $50,000. The company incurred legal fees of $3,000 to determine that it would have a clear title to the land. Before the facilities could be used, Mission had to spend $2,500 to grade and landscape the land, $4,000 to put the equipment in working order, and $15,000 to renovate the building. The equipment was then estimated to have a useful life of six years with no salvage value, and the building would have a useful life of 20 years with a net salvage value of $15,000. Both the equipment and the building are to be depreciated on a straight-line basis. The company is on a calendar-year reporting basis.

Required:

1. Allocate the single purchase price to the individual assets acquired.
2. Prepare the journal entry to acquire the land, building, and equipment.
3. Prepare the journal entry to record the title search, landscape, put the equipment in working order, and renovate the building.
4. Prepare the journal entries on December 31, 2006, to record the depreciation on the building and the equipment.

Problem 10-9

Basket Purchase and Partial-Year Depreciation

On April 1, 2006, Rosenberg Company purchased for $200,000 a tract of land on which was located a fully equipped factory. The following information was compiled regarding this purchase:

	Market Value	Seller's Book Value
Land	$ 75,000	$ 30,000
Building	100,000	75,000
Equipment	50,000	60,000
Totals	$225,000	$165,000

Required:

1. Prepare the journal entry to record the purchase of these assets.
2. Assume that the building is depreciated on a straight-line basis over a remaining life of 20 years and the equipment is depreciated on a straight-line basis over five years. Neither the building nor the equipment is expected to have any salvage value. Compute the depreciation expense for 2006 assuming the assets were placed in service immediately upon acquisition.

Problem 10-10

Acquisition, Depreciation, and Sale of an Asset
On January 2, 2004, Union Oil Company purchased a new airplane. The following costs are related to the purchase:

Airplane, base price	$112,000
Cash discount	3,000
Sales tax	4,000
Delivery charges	1,000

Required:
1. Prepare the journal entry to record the payment of these items on January 2, 2004.
2. Ignore your answer to part (1) and assume that the airplane cost $90,000 and has an expected useful life of five years or 1,500 hours. The estimated salvage value is $3,000. Using units-of-production depreciation and assuming that 300 hours are flown in 2005, calculate the amount of depreciation expense to be recorded for the second year.
3. Ignore the information in parts (1) and (2) and assume that the airplane costs $90,000, that its expected useful life is five years, and that its estimated salvage value is $5,000. The company now uses the straight-line depreciation method. On January 1, 2007, the following balances are in the related accounts:

Airplane	$90,000
Accumulated Depreciation, Airplane	51,000

Prepare the necessary journal entries to record the sale of this airplane on July 1, 2007, for $40,000.

Problem 10-11

Acquisition, Depreciation, and Sale of an Asset
On July 1, 2006, Philip Ward bought a used pickup truck at a cost of $5,300 for use in his business. On the same day, Ward had the truck painted blue and white (his company's colors) at a cost of $800. Mr. Ward estimates the life of the truck to be three years or 40,000 miles. He further estimates that the truck will have a $450 scrap value at the end of its life, but that it will also cost him $50 to transfer the truck to the junkyard.

Required:
1. Record the following journal entries:
   a. July 1, 2006: Paid all bills pertaining to the truck. (No previous entries have been recorded concerning these bills.)
   b. December 31, 2006: The depreciation expense for the year, using the straight-line method.
   c. December 31, 2007: The depreciation expense for 2007, again using the straight-line method.
   d. January 2, 2008: Sold the truck for $2,600 cash.
2. What would the depreciation expense for 2006 have been if the truck had been driven 8,000 miles and the units-of-production method of depreciation had been used?
3. **Interpretive Question:** In part (1)d, there is a loss of $650. Why did this loss occur?

Problem 10-12

Accounting for Natural Resources
On May 31, 2004, Brennan Oil Company purchased an oil well, with estimated reserves of 150,000 barrels of oil, for $1.5 million cash.

Required:
Prepare journal entries for the following:
1. Record the purchase of the oil well.
2. During 2004, 13,000 barrels of oil were extracted from the well. Record the depletion expense for 2004.

3. During 2005, 23,000 barrels of oil were extracted from the well. Record the depletion expense for 2005.

Problem 10-13

Asset Impairment

Delta Company owns plant and equipment on the island of Lagos. The cost and book value of the building are $2,800,000 and $2,400,000, respectively. Until this year, the market value of the factory was $7 million. However, a new dictator just came to power and declared martial law. As a result of the changed political status, the future cash inflows from the use of the factory are expected to be greatly reduced. Delta now believes that the output from the factory will generate cash inflows of $100,000 per year for the next 20 years. In addition, the market value of the factory building is now just $1,300,000. Delta is not sure how to account for the sudden impairment in value.

Required:
1. Explain how to decide whether an impairment loss is to be recognized.
2. Prepare the necessary journal entry, if any, to account for an impairment in the value of the factory.

Problem 10-14

P.A.S.S.
Power Accounting System Software

Accounting for Intangible Assets (Goodwill)

On January 1, 2006, Universal Company purchased the following assets and liabilities from Grand Company for $250,000:

	Book Value	Fair Market Value
Inventory	$ 40,000	$ 50,000
Building	80,000	100,000
Land	50,000	60,000
Accounts receivable	20,000	20,000
Accounts payable	(10,000)	(10,000)

Required:
Prepare a journal entry to record the purchase of Grand by Universal.

Problem 10-15

Accounting for Goodwill

On January 1, 2006, Fishing Creek Company purchased Skull Valley Technologies for $8,800,000 cash. The book value and fair value of Skull Valley's assets as of the date of the acquisition are listed below.

	Book Value	Market Value
Cash	$ 100,000	$ 100,000
Accounts receivable	500,000	500,000
Inventory	950,000	1,200,000
Property, plant, and equipment	1,500,000	1,900,000
Trademark	0	2,000,000
Totals	$3,050,000	$5,700,000

In addition, Skull Valley had liabilities totaling $4,000,000 at the time of the acquisition.

(continued)

Required:

1. At what amount will Skull Valley's trademark be recorded on the books of Fishing Creek, the acquiring company?
2. How much goodwill will be recorded as part of this acquisition?
3. **Interpretive Question:** What was Skull Valley's recorded stockholders' equity immediately before the acquisition? Under what circumstances does stockholders' equity yield a poor measure of the fair value of a company?

Problem 10-16

Fixed Asset Turnover Ratio

Waystation Company reported the following asset values in 2005 and 2006:

	2006	2005
Cash	$ 40,000	$ 30,000
Accounts receivable	500,000	400,000
Inventory	700,000	500,000
Land	300,000	200,000
Buildings	800,000	600,000
Equipment	400,000	300,000

In addition, Waystation had sales of $4,000,000 in 2006. Cost of goods sold for the year was $2,500,000.

As of the end of 2005, the fair value of Waystation's total assets was $2,500,000. Of the excess of fair value over book value, $50,000 resulted because the fair value of Waystation's inventory was greater than its recorded book value. As of the end of 2006, the fair value of Waystation's total assets was $3,500,000. As of December 31, 2006, the fair value of Waystation's inventory was $100,000 greater than the inventory's recorded book value.

Required:

1. Compute Waystation's fixed asset turnover ratio for 2006.
2. Using the fair value of fixed assets instead of the book value of fixed assets, recompute Waystation's fixed asset turnover ratio for 2006. State any assumptions that you make.
3. **Interpretive Question:** Waystation's primary competitor is Handy Corner. Handy Corner's fixed asset turnover ratio for 2006, based on publicly available information, is 2.8 times. Is Waystation more or less efficient at using its fixed assets than is Handy Corner? Explain your answer.

Problem 10-17

P.A.S.S.
Power Accounting
System Software

Depreciation Calculations

Vineyard Hardware Company has a giant paint mixer that cost $42,400 plus $600 to install. The estimated salvage value of the paint mixer at the end of its useful life in 12 years is estimated to be $3,000. Vineyard estimates that the machine can mix 650,000 cans of paint during its lifetime.

Required:

Compute the second full year's depreciation expense, using the following methods:

1. Double-declining-balance.
2. Sum-of-the-years'-digits.

Problem 10-18

P.A.S.S.
Power Accounting
System Software

Depreciation Calculations

On January 1, Top Flight Company purchased a $68,000 machine. The estimated life of the machine was five years, and the estimated salvage value was $5,000. The machine had an estimated useful life in productive output of 75,000 units. Actual output for the first two years was: year 1, 20,000 units; year 2, 15,000 units.

Required:

1. Compute the amount of depreciation expense for the first year, using each of the following methods:
   a. Straight-line.
   b. Units-of-production.
   c. Sum-of-the-years'-digits.
   d. Double-declining-balance.
2. What was the book value of the machine at the end of the first year, assuming that straight-line depreciation was used?
3. If the machine is sold at the end of the fourth year for $15,000, how much should the company report as a gain or loss (assuming straight-line depreciation)?

Problem 10-19

P.A.S.S.
Power Accounting
System Software

Financial Statement Effects of Depreciation Methods

On July 1, 2005, the consulting firm of Little, Smart, and Quick bought a new computer for $120,000 to help it service its clients more efficiently. The new computer was estimated to have a useful life of five years with an estimated salvage value of $20,000 at the end of five years. It was further estimated that the computer would be in operation about 1,500 hours in each of the five years with some variation of use from year to year. Janet Little, who manages the firm's internal operations, has asked you to help her decide which depreciation method should be selected for the new computer. The methods being considered are straight-line, double-declining-balance, and sum-of-the-years'-digits.

Required:

1. Prepare a schedule showing depreciation for 2005, 2006, and 2007 for each of the three methods being considered.
2. For each of the three methods, compute the asset book value that would be reported on the balance sheet at December 31, 2007.
3. **Interpretive Question:** Which method would maximize income for the three years (2005–2007), and which would minimize income for the same period?

Problem 10-20

Spreadsheet

P.A.S.S.
Power Accounting
System Software

Depreciation Calculations

Uffens, Inc., a firm that makes oversized boots, purchased a machine for its factory. The following data relate to the machine:

Price	$32,000
Delivery charges	$450
Installation charges	$1,650
Date purchased	May 1, 2005
Estimated useful life:	
In years	10 years
In hours of production	20,000 hours of operating time
Salvage value	$2,100

During 2005, the machine was used 3,800 hours. During 2006, the machine was used 4,000 hours.

(continued)

Required:
Determine the depreciation expense and the year-end book values for the machine for the years 2005 and 2006, assuming that:

1. The straight-line method is used.
2. The double-declining-balance method is used.
3. The units-of-production method is used.
4. The sum-of-the-years'-digits method is used.
5. **Interpretive Question:** If you were Uffens, which method would you use in order to report the highest profits in 2005 and 2006 combined?

Problem 10-21

Changes in Depreciation Estimates and Capitalization of Expenditures

Ironic Metal Products, Inc., acquired a machine on January 2, 2004, for $76,600. The useful life of the machine was estimated to be eight years with a salvage value of $4,600. Depreciation is recorded on December 31 of each year using the sum-of-the-years'-digits method.

At the beginning of 2006, the company estimated the remaining useful life of the machine to be four years and changed the estimated salvage value from $4,600 to $2,600. On January 2, 2007, major repairs on the machine cost the company $34,000. The repairs added two years to the machine's useful life and increased the salvage value to $3,000.

Required:
1. Prepare journal entries to record:
   a. The purchase of the machine.
   b. Annual depreciation expense for the years 2004 and 2005.
   c. Depreciation in 2006 under the revised estimates of useful life and salvage value.
   d. The expenditure for major repairs in 2007.
   e. Depreciation expense for 2007.
2. Compute the book value of the machine at the end of 2007.

Problem 10-22

Spreadsheet

Unifying Concepts: Accounting for Natural Resources

Forest Products, Inc., buys and develops natural resources for profit. Since 2003, it has had the following activities:

1/1/03   Purchased for $800,000 a tract of timber estimated to contain 1,600,000 board feet of lumber.
1/1/04   Purchased for $600,000 a silver mine estimated to contain 30,000 tons of silver ore.
7/1/04   Purchased for $60,000 a uranium mine estimated to contain 5,000 tons of uranium ore.
1/1/05   Purchased for $500,000 an oil well estimated to contain 100,000 barrels of oil.

Required:
1. Provide the necessary journal entries to account for the following:
   a. The purchase of these assets.
   b. The depletion expense for 2005 on all four assets, assuming that the following were extracted:
      (1) 200,000 board feet of lumber.
      (2) 5,000 tons of silver.
      (3) 1,000 tons of uranium.
      (4) 10,000 barrels of oil.
2. Assume that on January 1, 2006, after 20,000 tons of silver had been mined, engineers' estimates revealed that only 4,000 tons of silver remained. Record the depletion expense for 2006, assuming that 2,000 tons were mined.
3. Compute the book values of all four assets as of December 31, 2006, assuming that the total extracted to date is:
   a. Timber tract, 800,000 board feet.
   b. Silver mine, 22,000 tons [only 2,000 tons are left per part (2)].
   c. Uranium mine, 3,000 tons.
   d. Oil well, 80,000 barrels.

Problem 10-23

Unifying Concepts: Property, Plant, and Equipment

Smithfield Corporation owns and operates three sawmills that make lumber for building homes. The operations consist of cutting logs in the forest, hauling them to the various sawmills, sawing the lumber, and shipping it to building supply warehouses throughout the western part of the United States. To haul the logs, Smithfield has several trucks. Relevant data pertaining to one truck are:

a. Date of purchase, July 1, 2004.
b. Cost:

Truck	$60,000
Trailer	20,000
Paint job (to match company colors)	1,500
Sales tax	3,500

c. Estimated useful life of the truck, 150,000 miles.
d. Estimated salvage value, zero.
e. 2005 expenditures on truck:
   (1) Spent $5,000 on tires, oil changes, greasing, and other miscellaneous items.
   (2) Spent $22,000 to overhaul the engine and replace the transmission on January 1, 2005. This expenditure increased the life of the truck by 135,000 miles.

Required:

Record journal entries to account for:

1. The purchase of the truck.
2. The 2004 depreciation expense using units-of-production depreciation and assuming the truck was driven 45,000 miles.
3. The expenditures relating to the truck during 2005.
4. The 2005 depreciation expense using the units-of-production method and assuming the truck was driven 60,000 miles.

d iscussion cases

Case 10-1

Intangible Assets

Renford Company owns two restaurants. One, located in Tacoma, was purchased from a previous owner and the other, located in Seattle, was built by Renford Company. The restaurant was built nine years ago. The Tacoma restaurant was purchased last year and has goodwill of $550,000 on the books. As it turns out, the Seattle restaurant does twice as much business as the Tacoma restaurant and is much more profitable. The Seattle restaurant is in a prime location, and business keeps increasing each year. The Tacoma restaurant does about the same amount of business each year, and it doesn't look as if it will ever do any better. Does it make sense to you to have goodwill on the books of the less profitable restaurant? Should Renford record goodwill on the books of the Seattle restaurant, or should it write off the goodwill on the Tacoma restaurant's books?

Case 10-2

Straight-Line versus Accelerated Depreciation

Dennis Company currently depreciates its assets using the straight-line method for both tax and financial accounting. Total depreciation expense for this year will be $250,000 using straight-line depreciation. A consultant has just advised the company that it should use accelerated depreciation methods for both tax and financial accounting because "paying lower taxes is better than recognizing higher income." Using accelerated depreciation methods, total depreciation expense this year would be $400,000. The company has an effective tax rate of 40%. Do you agree with the consultant? Why or why not?

(j)udgment call

Judgment 10-1

You Decide: Should companies leasing equipment be required to record the equipment and leases as assets and liabilities on the balance sheet or as expenses on the income statement?

Current rules require that leases meeting any one of the following requirements should be classified as an asset and liability on the balance sheet:

- A transfer of ownership.
- A bargain purchase option.
- A lease term equal to 75% or more of the economic life of the asset.
- The present value of the payments are 90% or more of the fair market value of the asset at the beginning of the lease term.

However, what if a company leasing the asset decides to structure the lease so that the lease term is 73% of the economic life of the asset or the present value of the lease payments equals 88% of the fair market value of the asset? Should a company be able to use creative techniques in order to structure a lease so that it does not appear on the balance sheet?

Competency Enhancement Opportunities

▶ **Analyzing Real Company Information**
▶ **International Case**
▶ **Ethics Case**
▶ **Writing Assignment**

▶ **The Debate**
▶ **Cumulative Spreadsheet Project**
▶ **Internet Search**

The following additional assignments provide opportunities for students to develop critical thinking, ethical perspectives, oral and written communication skills, experience with electronic research, and teamwork through group and business activities.

▶ *Analyzing Real Company Information*

Analyzing 10-1 (Microsoft)
Using MICROSOFT's 2002 Form 10-K contained in Appendix A, answer the following questions:

1. As a percentage of total assets, is Microsoft's investment in property, plant, and equipment increasing or decreasing over time? Which of Microsoft's assets is increasing the fastest as a percentage of total assets? What does that indicate Microsoft is doing?

2. Reference the notes to the financial statements. Which depreciation method does Microsoft use? Estimate the average useful life of Microsoft's depreciable assets (i.e., not including land) by dividing the ending balance in the depreciable asset accounts by the depreciation expense for the year. Does the resulting estimated useful life seem reasonable?

3. Microsoft notes in its statement of cash flows that $770 million of property, plant, and equipment was purchased in 2002. Using that information along with the detailed information from the notes, compute (a) the original cost of the equipment disposed of during 2002 and (b) the accumulated depreciation associated with that equipment. (*Hint:* For property, plant, and equipment, beginning balance + purchases − disposals = ending balance; a similar calculation is used for accumulated depreciation.)

Analyzing 10-2 (FedEx)

FEDEX delivers packages around the world. To accomplish this task, FedEx has made huge investments in long-term assets.

1. Identify what you consider to be the major long-term assets of FedEx. Review the information shown below from FedEx's balance sheet (numbers are in millions) to see how well you did.

May 31	2002	2001
Property and Equipment, at Cost		
Aircraft and related equipment	$ 5,843	$ 5,313
Package handling and ground support equipment and vehicles	4,866	4,621
Computer and electronic equipment	2,816	2,637
Other	4,051	3,841
	$17,576	$16,412
Less accumulated depreciation and amortization	9,274	8,312
Net property and equipment	$ 8,302	$ 8,100

2. FedEx uses the straight-line depreciation method in depreciating most of its assets. For each major category—aircraft and related equipment, package handling and ground support equipment and vehicles (mainly trucks and buildings), and computer and electronic equipment—provide an estimate (or a range) as to what you would deem a reasonable useful life for each category.

3. Using the information above, compute the accumulated depreciation associated with the property and equipment sold during 2002 given that depreciation for the year was $1,331,000,000.

Analyzing 10-3 (U.S. Steel)

1. U.S. STEEL provides the following information in the notes to its financial statements relating to its use of the straight-line method of depreciation. Can you interpret the information contained in the note?

> *Property, plant and equipment*—U.S. Steel records depreciation on a modified straight-line or straight-line method utilizing a composite or group asset approach based upon estimated lives of assets. The modified straight-line method is utilized for domestic steel producing assets and is based upon

(continued)

production levels. The modification factors applied to straight-line calculations range from a minimum of 85% at a production level below 81% of capability, to a maximum of 105% for a 100% production level. No modification is made at the 95% production level, considered the normal long-range level.

2. U.S. Steel also provides information relating to the balances in its individual property, plant and equipment accounts, as shown below. In very general terms, how old is the company's property, plant, and equipment? Provide support for your answer.

	December 31	
(in millions)	2002	2001
Land and depletable property	$ 184	$ 193
Buildings	591	572
Machinery and equipment	9,195	9,080
Leased assets	103	105
Total	$10,073	$9,950
Less accumulated depreciation, depletion and amortization	7,095	6,866
Net	$ 2,978	$3,084

International Case

International

Swire Pacific

SWIRE PACIFIC, LTD., based in Hong Kong, is one of the largest companies in the world. The primary operations of the company are in the regions of Hong Kong, China, and Taiwan where it has operated for over 125 years. Swire operates CATHAY PACIFIC AIRWAYS and has extensive real estate holdings in Hong Kong.

Swire includes in its fixed assets those long-term assets held as investment properties. The company also notes that it revalues those assets each year for increases and decreases in fair value. During 2002, Swire reduced the value of those assets on their books by $5.161 billion in Hong Kong dollars.

1. Can you compose the journal entry made by Swire Pacific accountants to write the assets down in value? What would be the debit portion of the journal entry? (*Hint:* Although you may not know the exact answer, think about it and make an educated guess. Would the debit be to another asset account? Would it be to a liability account?)
2. Suppose that in the next year, the assets were again revalued and it was determined that a difference existed between market value and book value of only $3 billion Hong Kong dollars. How would this year's journal entry differ from the previous year's?

Ethics Case

Strategic Accounting Method Choices

You saw in Chapter 7 that a company's management selects the percentage to be used when computing bad debt expense. You noted in Chapter 8 that management is allowed to choose the method for valuing inventory. In this chapter you found that management gets to choose the method used for depreciating assets, the estimated salvage value, and the estimated useful life.

Suppose that you are involved in negotiations with the local labor union regarding wages for your company's employees. Labor leaders are asking that their members be given an average annual raise of 12%. The company president has asked you to prepare a set of financial statements that portrays the company's performance as being mediocre at best. The president also makes it clear that she does not want you to prepare fraudulent financial statements. All estimates must be within the bounds of reason.

So you come up with the following:

- Change the percentage used for estimating bad debts from 1.5% to 2%.
- Elect to use the LIFO method for valuing inventory because the prices associated with inventory have been rising.
- Change the average estimated salvage value of long-term assets from 15% to 10% of historical cost.
- Change the depreciation method from straight-line to an accelerated method.
- Change the average estimated useful life of long-term assets from 10 years to 7 years.

As you know, each of these changes will result in net income being lower. Each of these changes is also still within the bounds of reason required by the company president.

1. Would it be appropriate to make the changes described above in order to obtain favorable terms from the labor union negotiators?
2. If the above changes are made, what sort of disclosure do you think should be required?

▷ Writing Assignment

Gains Are Good, Losses Are Bad—Right?

When a long-term asset is sold for more than its book value, we record a gain. When a long-term asset is sold for less than its book value, we record a loss.

Your assignment is to write a two-page memo addressing the following questions:

1. What factors affect a long-term asset's book value?
2. What factors affect a long-term asset's fair value?
3. Should financial statement users expect an asset's book value to equal its fair value?
4. In the case of an asset sold for a loss, if we knew when we purchased the asset what we know at the point of sale, how would depreciation expense have differed if our objective was to ensure that book value equaled fair value when the asset was sold?
5. Is recognizing a loss on the sale of a long-term asset a bad thing? Is a gain good?

▷ The Debate

Depreciating an Asset with an Increasing Value

Paul Didericksen owns and operates a limousine service. He purchases luxury cars and hires drivers to transport people from place to place. Last year, Paul expanded his operations by renting out luxury vehicles on a daily basis for such events as weddings, proms, etc. One car Paul purchased for rental is a 1957 FORD Thunderbird. He paid $45,000 for the car and rents it for $250 per day.

Paul's accountant recently provided financial information indicating that the Thunderbird has a book value of $36,000. Paul questions this figure because he recently received an offer of $53,000 for the Thunderbird. Paul thinks that the car should not be depreciated because its value is increasing. In fact, Paul argues that the asset should be written up in value rather than down.

Divide your group into two teams and prepare to represent the following positions:

- The first team supports the position that the Thunderbird should be depreciated because it is used in generating revenues. You are also to provide support against writing the asset up to its fair market value.
- The second team argues that the Thunderbird should not be depreciated because its value is increasing rather than decreasing. Also, your group is to argue that the car should be written up to its fair value on the company's books.

▶ *Cumulative Spreadsheet Project*

This spreadsheet project is a continuation of the spreadsheet projects in earlier chapters. If you completed those spreadsheets, you have a head start on this one.

1. Handyman wishes to prepare a forecasted balance sheet and income statement for 2007. Use the original financial statement numbers for 2006 [given in part (1) of the Cumulative Spreadsheet Project assignment in Chapter 2] as the basis for the forecast, along with the following additional information:
    a. Sales in 2007 are expected to increase by 40% over 2006 sales of $700.
    b. Cash will increase at the same rate as sales.
    c. The forecasted amount of accounts receivable in 2007 is determined using the forecasted value for the average collection period. For simplicity, do the computations using the end-of-period accounts receivable balance instead of the average balance. The average collection period for 2007 is expected to be 14.08 days.
    d. The forecasted amount of inventory in 2007 is determined using the forecasted value for the number of days' sales in inventory (computed using the end-of-period inventory balance). The number of days' sales in inventory for 2007 is expected to be 107.6 days.
    e. The forecasted amount of accounts payable in 2007 is determined using the forecasted value for the number of days' purchases in accounts payable (computed using the end-of-period accounts payable balance). The number of days' purchases in accounts payable for 2007 is expected to be 48.34 days.
    f. The $160 in operating expenses reported in 2006 breaks down as follows: $5 depreciation expense, $155 other operating expenses.
    g. No new long-term debt will be acquired in 2007.
    h. No cash dividends will be paid in 2007.
    i. New short-term loans payable will be acquired in an amount sufficient to make Handyman's current ratio in 2007 exactly equal to 2.0.

    Note: These statements were constructed as part of the spreadsheet assignment in Chapter 8; you can use that spreadsheet as a starting point if you have completed that assignment. *Clearly state any additional assumptions that you make.*
    For this exercise, add the following additional assumptions:

    j. The forecasted amount of property, plant, and equipment (PP&E) in 2007 is determined using the forecasted value for the fixed asset turnover ratio. For simplicity, compute the fixed asset turnover ratio using the end-of-period gross PP&E balance. The fixed asset turnover ratio for 2007 is expected to be 3.518 times.
    k. In computing depreciation expense for 2007, use straight-line depreciation and assume a 30-year useful life with no residual value. Gross PP&E acquired during the year is only depreciated for half the year. In other words, depreciation expense for 2007 is the sum of two parts: (1) a full year of depreciation on the beginning balance in PP&E, assuming a 30-year life and no residual value, and (2) a half-year of depreciation on any new PP&E acquired during the year, based on the change in the gross PP&E balance.

Clearly state any additional assumptions that you make.

2. Repeat (1), with the following changes in assumptions:
   a. Fixed asset turnover ratio is expected to be 6.000 times.
   b. Fixed asset turnover ratio is expected to be 2.000 times.
3. Comment on the differences in the forecasted values of the following items in 2007 under each of the following assumptions about the fixed asset turnover ratio: 3.518 times, 6.000 times, and 2.000 times:
   a. Property, plant, and equipment.
   b. Depreciation expense.
   c. Income tax expense.
   d. Paid-in capital.
4. Return the fixed asset turnover ratio to 3.518 times. Now, repeat (1), with the following changes in assumptions:
   a. Estimated useful life is expected to be 15 years.
   b. Estimated useful life is expected to be 60 years.
5. Comment on the differences in the forecasted values of the following items in 2007 under each of the following assumptions about the estimated useful life of property, plant, and equipment: 30 years, 15 years, and 60 years.
   a. Depreciation expense.
   b. Income tax expense.

▷ *Internet Search*

General Electric

We began this chapter with a review of the history of GENERAL ELECTRIC. Let's go to GE's Web site at **http://www.ge.com** and learn a little more about the company and its financial position. Sometimes Web addresses change, so if this address doesn't work, access the Web site for this textbook (**http://albrecht.swlearning.com**) for an updated link to GE.

Once you have gained access to General Electric's Web site, answer the following questions:

1. General Electric was formed in 1892 and constructed the nation's first industrial research laboratory in 1900. Can you identify where this laboratory was located?
2. Locate the company's most recent balance sheet. What percentage of total assets does property, plant, and equipment represent for General Electric? Is that percentage increasing, decreasing, or remaining constant?
3. Access the notes to the financial statements. What depreciation method does General Electric use for most of its manufacturing plant and equipment?
4. Find the note relating specifically to property, plant, and equipment. What types of property, plant, and equipment does General Electric own? Is GE involved strictly in producing light bulbs?

c h a p t e r

11

Long-Term Debt Financing

After studying this chapter, you should be able to:

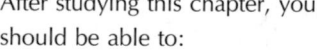

Learning Objectives

1 Use present value concepts to measure long-term liabilities.

2 Account for long-term liabilities, including notes payable and mortgages payable.

3 Account for capital lease obligations and understand the significance of operating leases being excluded from the balance sheet.

4 Account for bonds, including the original issuance, the payment of interest, and the retirement of bonds.

5 Use debt-related financial ratios to determine the degree of a company's financial leverage and its ability to repay loans.

e**X**panded ▲ ▲ *Material*

6 Amortize bond discounts and bond premiums using either the straight-line method or the effective-interest method.

In 1923, two brothers, Walt and Roy Disney, founded the DISNEY BROTHERS STUDIO as a partnership to produce animated features for film. Five years later, the Disney Brothers Studio released its first animated film with sound effects and dialogue, *Steamboat Willie*, featuring a soon-to-become-famous mouse, Mickey. Pluto was introduced to American audiences in 1930, and Goofy was created just two years later. Walt Disney earned his first Academy Award in 1932 with the release of *Flowers and Trees*, the first full-color animated film. Donald Duck appeared on the scene in 1934, and in 1937 *Snow White and the Seven Dwarfs* was released, accompanied by the first comprehensive merchandising campaign.

But Walt Disney's vision encompassed more than animated films. In 1952, Disney began designing and creating Disneyland, which opened on July 17, 1955. Beginning in the late 1950s, the television shows *Disneyland* (which ran for 29 seasons under various names) and *The Mickey Mouse Club* were also successful Disney ventures. Though Walt Disney passed away in 1966, his influence is still felt around the world. We have Walt Disney World in Florida and Disneylands in Anaheim, California; Paris; Tokyo; and one being built in Hong Kong.

FYI:

Not everything that Disney touches turns to gold. Disney opened an indoor theme park—DisneyQuest—in Chicago in June 1999 and closed the park in September 2001 citing a lack of long-range financial return potential.

Disney's company has expanded far beyond what even he could have foreseen. THE WALT DISNEY COMPANY is now involved in television and radio stations; international film distribution; home video production; live theatrical entertainment; online computer programs; interactive computer games; telephone company partnerships; cruise lines; Disney Stores; newspaper, magazine, and book publishing; Internet marketing; and the convention business. In the past decade, The Walt Disney Company has grown over 300%. How has the company financed this growth? In part through very successful operations, but these have not been enough. The company has also borrowed to finance its expansion. As of September 30, 2002, The Walt Disney Company had long-term debt totaling over $12 billion. This long-term financing includes lines of credits with U.S. banks as well as loans denominated (or made) in Japanese yen and Italian lira. The effective interest rates on Disney's loans range from 3.4 to 8.9%.[1]

network exercises

National Debt

Speaking of debt, let's take a look at our government's debt situation. To see what the national debt is to the penny, go to **http://www.publicdebt.treas.gov/opd/opd.htm**.

Net Work:

What was the national debt 100 years ago? 200 years ago?

how does the market determine the appropriate rate of interest that Disney, or any company, must pay when it borrows money? What factors affect interest rates, and how do interest rate changes influence the value of a liability? What other types of liabilities are affected by interest rates? In this chapter, we will introduce various types of long-term liabilities. We will explain a concept used in measuring the present value of an obligation due in the future. This concept—the time value of money—is useful for computing the value of bonds and notes, as in the Disney example, as well

as for computing mortgage payments and pension obligations. In the main part of this chapter, we discuss the measurement of long-term liabilities and introduce numerous types of long-term liabilities—notes, mortgages, leases, and bonds. The basic accounting procedures associated with several of these liabilities are also discussed. In the expanded material, the complexities associated with the amortization of a bond issued at a premium or discount are discussed. Exhibit 1 highlights the financial statement accounts discussed in this chapter.

1 The information for this scenario was obtained from Disney's Web site at **http://www.disney.com**.

Exhibit 1: Financial Statement Items Discussed in This Chapter

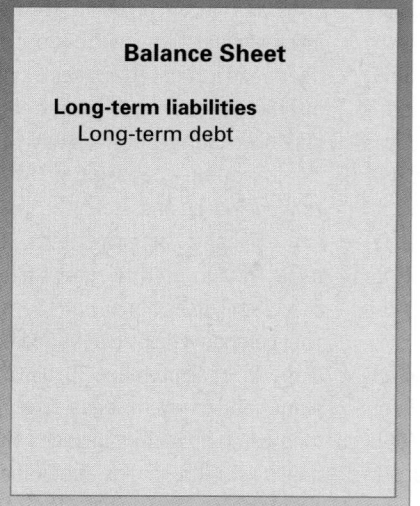

Balance Sheet

Long-term liabilities
Long-term debt

Statement of Cash Flows

Operating activities
Payments for interest

Financing activities
Proceeds from borrowing
Repayments of borrowing

Income Statement

Other revenues and expenses
Interest expense

Measuring Long-Term Liabilities

▌ Use present value concepts to measure long-term liabilities.

long-term liabilities Debts or other obligations that will not be paid within one year.

Conceptually, the value of a liability is the cash that would be required to pay the liability in full today. Because money has a time value, most people are willing to accept less money today than they would if a liability were paid in the future. Therefore, with the exception of Accounts Payable, liabilities to be paid in the future usually involve interest.

Accounting for **long-term liabilities** is complex because usually payments of interest, or in some cases principal and interest, are made periodically over the period in which the liability is outstanding. Further, in some cases the amount of the liability in a noncash transaction may not be readily apparent. The time value of money concept is used in measuring and recording these liabilities.

Present Value and Future Value Concepts

The concepts of present value and future value are used to measure the effect of time on the value of money. To illustrate, if you are to receive $100 one year from today, is it worth $100 today? Obviously not, because if you had the $100 today you could either use it now or invest it and earn interest. If the $100 isn't to be received for one year, those options are not available. The **present value of $1** is the value today of $1 to be received or paid in the future, given a specified interest rate. To determine the value today of money to be received or paid in the future, we must "discount" the future amount (reduce the amount to its present value) by an appropriate interest rate. For example, if money can earn 10% per year, $100 to be received one year from now is approximately equal to $90.91 received today.

present value of $1 The value today of $1 to be received or paid at some future date, given a specified interest rate.

Putting it another way, if $90.91 is invested today in an account that earns 10% interest for one year, the interest earned will be $9.09 ($90.91 × 10% × 1 year = $9.09). The sum of the $90.91 principal and the $9.09 interest will equal $100 at the end of one year. Thus, the present value of $100 to be received (or paid) in one year with 10% interest is $90.91. This present value relationship can be diagrammed as follows:

Present Value
(Computed)
$90.91

Future Amount
(Known)
$100

(One-Year Period @ 10%)

$90.91 is the present value of the $100 future amount.

The relationships in this diagram can be described in two ways. We have just seen that the $90.91 is the present value of $100 to be received one year from now when interest is 10%. In this example, the $100 to be received one year from now is known, and the present value of $90.91 must be computed. We are computing a present value amount from a known future value amount.

Another way to look at the relationship is on a future value basis. Future values apply when the amount today ($90.91) is known, and the future amount must be calculated. Future values are exactly the opposite of present values. Thinking in terms of future values, $100 is the future amount we can expect to receive in one year, given a present known amount of $90.91 when the interest rate is 10%. We can diagram this relationship as follows:

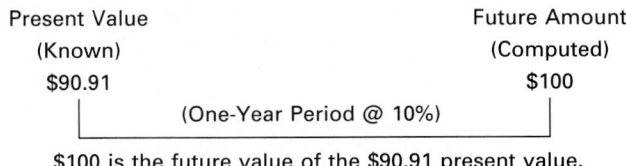

Present Value
(Known)
$90.91

Future Amount
(Computed)
$100

(One-Year Period @ 10%)

$100 is the future value of the $90.91 present value.

Present and future values can be calculated using formulas. If more than one period is involved, however, the formula is exponential, and the calculations become rather complicated. Therefore, it is more convenient to use either a present value table or a calculator that gives the present value of $1 for various numbers of periods and interest rates (see Table I, page 554) or a future value table that gives the future value of $1 for various numbers of periods and interest rates (see Table III, page 556). We will illustrate the use of both a present value table and a future value table as well as the keystrokes needed when using a standard business calculator.

Computing the Present Value of a Single Amount

To use a present value table, you simply locate the appropriate number of periods in the leftmost column and the interest rate in the row at the top of the table. The intersection of the row and column is the factor representing the present value of $1 for the number of periods and the relevant interest rate. To find the present value of an amount other than $1, multiply the factor in the table by that amount.

To illustrate the use of a present value table (Table I) to find the present value of a known future amount, assume that $10,000 is to be paid four years from today when the interest rate is 10%. What is the present value of the $10,000 payment?

Amount of payment . . . . $ 10,000
Present value factor of $1 to be paid in 4 periods
  at 10% interest (from Table I) . . . . × 0.6830
Present value of payment . . . . $ 6,830

This present value amount, $6,830, is the amount that could be paid today to satisfy the obligation that is due four years from now. As indicated, this procedure is sometimes referred to as "discounting." Thus, we say that $10,000 discounted for four years at 10% is $6,830. Stated another way, if $6,830 is invested today in an account that pays 10% interest, in four years the balance in that account will be $10,000.

Another way to compute this same amount is to use a business calculator. The keystrokes described below are for a Hewlett-Packard 10B business calculator; similar keystrokes are used with other business calculators. To compute the present value of $10,000 to be received four years from today, with a prevailing interest rate of 10%, make the following keystrokes:

Hewlett-Packard Keystrokes:

a. Always **CLEAR ALL** before doing anything else. With a Hewlett-Packard 10B, one does this by pressing the yellow key, then pressing "Input." This has the effect of clearing out any information left over from a prior computation.

b. Always set **P/YR** (payments per year) to the correct number—"1" in this case. With a Hewlett-Packard 10B, one does this by pressing "1," then pressing the yellow key, then pressing "PMT." This has the effect of telling the calculator that each year is being viewed as a separate period. As described later in this chapter, interest can be compounded over different periods, such as monthly, quarterly, daily, or even continuously. Setting **P/YR** equal to 1 means that the interest rate is compounded annually. Sometimes, the default for this amount is "12" because the calculator is set to compute monthly payments. Until you are comfortable using your calculator, your best strategy is to set this amount to "1" to avoid having the calculator doing too many mysterious things automatically.

1. 10,000   Press **FV**.
2. 4   Press **N**.
3. 10   Press **I/YR**.
4. Press **PV** for the answer of $6,830.13.

Computing the Future Value of a Single Amount

To find the future value of an amount that is known today, use a future value table. When using a future value table, simply locate the appropriate number of periods in the leftmost column and the interest rate in the row at the top of the table. The intersection of the row and column is the factor representing the future value of $1 for the number of periods and the relevant interest rate. To find the future value of an amount other than $1, multiply the factor in the table by that amount.

To illustrate the use of a future value table (Table III), we will use the same information as before, except that we will now assume that the present value of $6,830 is known, not the future amount of $10,000. Assume that we have a savings account with a current balance of $6,830 that earns interest of 10%. What will be the balance in that account in four years?

Present value in savings account	$ 6,830*
Future value factor of $1 in 4 periods at 10% interest (from Table III)	× 1.4641*
Future value	$ 10,000*

*Rounded; other calculations in chapter will also be rounded.

Hewlett-Packard Keystrokes:

a. **CLEAR ALL.**
b. Set **P/YR** to 1.

1. 6,830   Press **PV**.
2. 4   Press **N**.
3. 10   Press **I/YR**.
4. Press **FV** for the answer of $9,999.80.

When computing future values, we often use the term *compounding* to mean the frequency with which interest is added to the principal. Thus, we say that interest of 10% has been compounded once a year (annually) to arrive at a future value at the end of four years of $10,000. If the interest is added more or less frequently than once a year, the future amount will be different.

compounding period The period of time for which interest is computed.

The preceding example assumed an annual **compounding period** for interest. If the 10% interest had been compounded semiannually (twice a year) for four years, the calculation would have used a 5% (one-half of the 10%) rate for eight periods (4 years × 2 periods per year) instead of 10% for four periods. To illustrate, what is the present value of $10,000 to be paid in four years if interest of 10% is compounded semiannually?

Amount of payment	$ 10,000
Present value factor of $1 to be paid in 8 periods	
at 5% interest (from Table I)	× 0.6768
Present value of payment	$ 6,768

Thus, the present value of $10,000 to be paid in four years is $6,768 if interest is compounded semiannually. Likewise, if semiannual compounding is used to determine the future value of $6,768 in four years at 10% compounded semiannually, the result is as follows:

Present value in savings account	$ 6,768
Future value factor of $1 in 8 periods	
at 5% interest (from Table III)	× 1.4775
Future value	$ 10,000

Note that the present value ($6,768) is lower with semiannual compounding than with annual compounding ($6,830). The more frequently interest is compounded, the greater the total amount of interest deducted (in computing present values) or added (in computing future values).

For practice using semiannual compounding with a business calculator, try the following set of keystrokes:

Hewlett-Packard Keystrokes:

a. **CLEAR ALL**.
b. Set **P/YR** to 1. There is a simple way to tell the calculator to automatically compute the impact of semiannual compounding. Look in your calculator instruction book if you are interested in knowing how to do this. Alternatively, you can do some of the calculations yourself (divide the interest rate by two and double the number of periods) and use the keystrokes below.

1. 6,768   Press **PV**.
2. 8   Press **N**.
3. 5   Press **I/YR**.
4. Press **FV** for the answer of $9,999.72.

STOP & THINK

Without referencing the present value tables, answer these questions: As interest rates increase, would you expect the present value factors to increase or decrease? Why?

Because interest may also be compounded quarterly, monthly, or for some other period, you should learn the relationship of interest to the compounding period. Semiannual interest means that you double the interest periods and halve the annual interest rate; with quarterly interest, you quadruple the periods and take one-fourth of the annual interest rate. The formula for interest rate is:

$$\frac{\text{Yearly interest rate}}{\text{Compounding periods per year}} = \frac{\text{Interest rate per}}{\text{compounding period}}$$

The number of interest periods is simply the number of periods per year times the number of years. That formula is:

$$\text{Compounding periods per year} \times \text{Number of years} = \text{Number of interest periods}$$

Computing the Present Value of an Annuity

In discussing present values and future values, we have assumed only a single present value or future value with one of the amounts known and the other to be computed. With liabilities, we generally know the future amount that must be paid and would like to compute the present value of that future payment. Because this chapter focuses on liabilities, we will concentrate on present value calculations.

Many long-term liabilities involve a series of payments rather than one lump-sum payment. For example, a company might purchase equipment under an installment agreement requiring payments of $5,000 each year for five years. Determining the value today (present value) of a series of equally spaced, equal-amount payments (called an **annuity**) is more complicated than determining the present value of a single future payment. If you were to try to calculate the **present value of an annuity** by hand, you would have to discount the first payment for one period, the second payment for two periods, and so on, and then add all the present values together. Because such calculations are time-consuming, a table is generally used (see Table II, page 555). The factors in the table are the sums of the individual present values of all future payments. Based on the present value of an annuity of $1, the table provides factors for various interest rates and number of payments.

C a u t i o n

Use care when referencing the present value and future value tables. You can do all your computations correctly, but if you pull the factor from the wrong table, your answer will be wrong.

To illustrate the use of a present value of an annuity table (Table II), we will assume that $10,000 is to be paid at the end of each of the next 10 years. This series of payments is illustrated below.

If the interest rate is 12% compounded annually, Table II shows a present value factor of 5.6502. This factor means that the present value of $1 paid each year for 10 years discounted at 12% is approximately $5.65. Applying this factor to payments of $10,000 results in the following:

FYI:

The underlying mathematical formula for computing the present value of an annuity is actually an elegant simplification of a long series of present value formulas, one for each payment. Unfortunately, it is beyond the scope of this text to illustrate how this annuity formula can be derived as the difference between two infinite sums.

Amount of the annual payment	$ 10,000
Present value factor of an annuity of $1 discounted for 10 payments at 12%	× 5.6502
Present value	$ 56,502

This amount, $56,502, is the amount (present value) that could be paid today to satisfy the obligation if the interest rate is 12%.

The present value of an annuity can also be computed with a business calculator as follows:

Hewlett-Packard Keystrokes:

a. **CLEAR ALL.**
b. Set **P/YR** to 1.

(continued)

1. 10,000   Press **PMT**.
2. 10   Press **N**.
3. 12   Press **I/YR**.
4. Press **PV** for the answer of $56,502.23.

Computing Periodic Payments

With some modifications, the same calculations used to compute the present value of an annuity can be used to compute the proper amount of a periodic loan payment. For example, consider the task of computing the appropriate monthly payment on an automobile loan of $20,000 if the interest rate is 12% compounded monthly (i.e., 1% per month) and the loan period is 60 months. This problem can be viewed as follows:

In this case, we know the present value of the annuity—it is $20,000, or the amount we would have to pay today to pay off the entire loan. What we want to know is what series of 60 payments (P in the diagram) has a present value exactly equal to the $20,000 that we owe. The calculation of the payment amount can be set up as follows:

Amount of the annual payment	Payment
Present value factor of an annuity of $1	
discounted for 60 payments at 1%	× 44.9550
Present value	$ 20,000

In equation format, this can be written as follows:

$$\$20,000 = \text{Payment} \times 44.9550$$
$$\text{Payment} = \$20,000/44.9550$$
$$\text{Payment} = \$444.89$$

In other words, paying $444.89 per month for 60 months is the same as paying $20,000 right now, if the interest rate on borrowed money is 12% compounded monthly (1% per month). This payment amount can also be computed with a business calculator as follows:

Hewlett-Packard Keystrokes:

a. **CLEAR ALL**.
b. Set **P/YR** to 1.

1. 20,000   Press **PV**.
2. 60   Press **N**.
3. 1   Press **I/YR**.
4. Press **PMT** for the answer of $444.88895.

TO SUMMARIZE: Long-term liabilities are debts or other obligations that will not be paid or satisfied within one year. Present value concepts, which equate the value of money received or paid in different periods, are used to measure long-term liabilities. Although present values can be computed using formulas, it is usually more convenient to use a table, such as Table I or II on pages 554–555, or a business calculator. If a future lump-sum payment is involved, Table I can be used to determine the present value. Table II is used to compute the present value of an annuity, which is a series of equally spaced, equal-amount payments. To determine the value of an amount at some point in the future, future value tables can be used. Tables III and IV allow one to compute the future value of a lump sum or an annuity, respectively. In calculating present and fu-

ture values, you must consider the compounding period and the interest rate. For other than annual payments, the number of periods used is the number of periods per year times the number of years; the interest rate used is the annual rate divided by the number of periods per year. The same type of computations used to compute the present value of an annuity can also be used to compute the proper amount of a periodic payment, such as the monthly payment on a car loan.

Accounting for Long-Term Liabilities

2 Account for long-term liabilities, including notes payable and mortgages payable.

Now that we have explained how present value concepts are applied in measuring long-term liabilities, we are ready to discuss the accounting for those liabilities. The time line in Exhibit 2 illustrates the business events associated with long-term liabilities.

A company's first decision is to determine the type of long-term financing to use. In this chapter we will discuss four different types of financing: notes payable, mortgages payable, leasing, and bonds. There are advantages and disadvantages to each type of financing. For example, bonds (which are sold in $1,000 increments) allow a company to borrow a little bit of money from a lot of different people, whereas notes involve borrowing a lot of money from one lender (or perhaps a consortium of lenders). The benefit of a mortgage is typically a lower interest rate because the property being purchased is used as collateral on the loan, thereby providing the lender with less risk. Leases have the advantage of typically requiring a lower down payment as there are no risks associated with product obsolescence. (At the end of many leases, the asset being leased is returned to the owner.) Once the pros and cons of the various types of financing are analyzed, and the company selects an option, the accounting differs, depending upon the type of financing chosen. In this section, we will discuss the recording of long-term debt, including notes payable and mortgages payable.

Interest-Bearing Notes

To illustrate the accounting for a long-term interest-bearing note payable, assume that on January 1, 2006, Giraffe Company borrowed $10,000 from City Bank for three years at 10%

Exhibit 2: Time Line of Business Issues Involved with Long-Term Liabilities

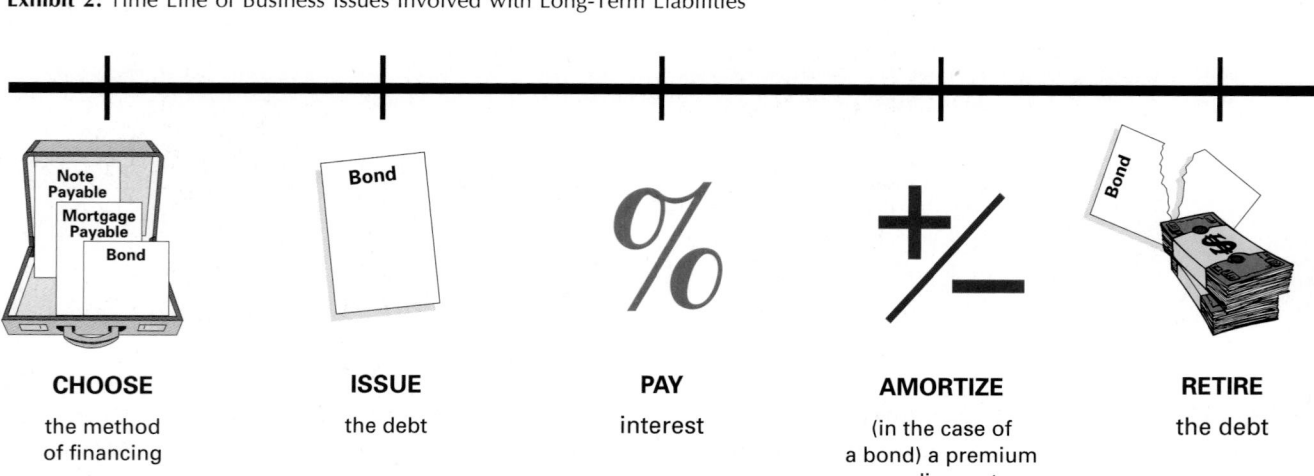

| **CHOOSE** | **ISSUE** | **PAY** | **AMORTIZE** | **RETIRE** |
| the method of financing | the debt | interest | (in the case of a bond) a premium or discount | the debt |

interest. Assume also that interest is payable annually on December 31. The entries to account for the note are:

```
2006
Jan. 1    Cash ........................................ 10,000
             Note Payable ..................................        10,000
             Borrowed $10,000 from City Bank for three years.

Dec. 31   Interest Expense ...............................  1,000
             Cash .......................................         1,000
             Made first annual interest payment
             on City Bank note ($10,000 × 0.10).

2007
Dec. 31   Interest Expense ...............................  1,000
             Cash .......................................         1,000
             Made second annual interest payment
             on City Bank note ($10,000 × 0.10).

2008
Dec. 31   Interest Expense ...............................  1,000
             Note Payable .................................. 10,000
             Cash .......................................        11,000
             Made final interest payment ($10,000 × 0.10)
             and repaid principal on City Bank note.
```

A long-term note such as this three-year note should be recorded in the books at the present value of the future cash payments to be made in connection with the note. If the market interest rate is 10%, then the present value of the cash payments on the note is computed as follows:

FYI:

As illustrated later in the chapter in the discussion of accounting for bonds, if the market rate of interest differs from the annual interest rate to be paid on a loan, then the present value of the cash payments will not be the same as the face amount of the loan. For example, if no interest payments were to be made on the note in the example given here, then the present value of the cash flows associated with the note would be just $7,513, which is the present value of the $10,000 payment to be made at the end of three years.

Present value of interest payments:
Amount of each interest payment	$ 1,000	
Table II factor for 3 payments at 10%	× 2.4869	
Present value of annuity		$ 2,487
Present value of principal payment:		
Amount of principal payment	$10,000	
Table I factor for 3 periods at 10%	× 0.7513	
Present value of single payment		7,513
Present value of interest and principal		$10,000

The total present value is the sum of the present values of the interest payments (an annuity) and the single principal payment due in three years. In this case, the present value of the cash payments on the note is exactly equal to the note's face amount of $10,000. This is because the annual interest payments of 10% are equal to the market rate of interest, or the rate of interest that lenders would insist on earning for lending money in exchange for the note.

In the notes to its 2002 financial statements, THE WALT DISNEY COMPANY reported the existence of a variety of notes payable, including notes for which the amounts to be repaid were stated in Japanese yen, South African rand, Singapore dollars, Hong Kong dollars, and U.S. dollars. These notes included various types of debt instruments including "fixed or floating rate notes, U.S. dollar or foreign currency denominated notes, redeemable notes, index linked and dual currency notes."

How Interest Rates Affect Mortgage Payments The interest rate on a mortgage is as important as the amount of the loan in determining whether a person can afford a mortgage. This is because the amount of interest paid over an extended period of time will be at least equal to, or even two or three times, the amount of the loan. The table on the next page shows the monthly payments on a $100,000, 25-year mortgage at interest rates from 7 to 14%, as well as the qualifying annual income.

The qualifying annual income is the minimum amount a person must earn to afford the payments at each interest rate.

The FEDERAL HOME LOAN MORTGAGE CORPORATION and most lending institutions recommend that the monthly payment not exceed 28% of a person's monthly gross income. If, for example, you earn $30,000 a year, you should pay no more than $700 a month on a mortgage, which would be a $100,000 mortgage at 7% or a $58,000 mortgage at 14%. For this reason, most people "shop around" for the lowest mortgage rates—and even then, many will not qualify for a loan.

To calculate the monthly payments on a smaller or larger mortgage, divide the amount by $100,000, then multiply that percentage by the figure in the table. For example, the monthly payment on a $60,000 mortgage at 9% is $503.40 [($60,000/$100,000) × $839].

Mortgages Payable

mortgage payable A written promise to pay a stated amount of money at one or more specified future dates; a mortgage is secured by the pledging of certain assets, usually real estate, as collateral.

A **mortgage payable** is similar to a note payable in that it is a written promise to pay a stated sum of money at one or more specified future dates. It differs from a note in the way it is applied. Whereas money borrowed with a note can often be used for any business purpose, mortgage money is usually related to a specific asset, typically real estate. Assets purchased with a mortgage are usually pledged as security or collateral on the loan. Individuals commonly obtain home mortgages, and companies frequently use plant mortgages. In either case, a mortgage generally requires periodic (usually monthly) payments of principal plus interest.

To illustrate the accounting for a mortgage, we will assume that McGiven Automobile Company borrows $100,000 on January 1 to purchase a new showroom and signs a mortgage agreement pledging the showroom as collateral on the loan. If the mortgage is at 8% for 30 years, and the monthly payment is $733.76, payable on January 31 with subsequent payments due at the end of each month thereafter, the entries to record the acquisition of the mortgage and the first monthly payment are:

Jan. 1	Cash	100,000	
	Mortgage Payable		100,000
	Borrowed $100,000 to purchase the automobile		
	showroom.		
Jan. 31	Mortgage Payable	67.09	
	Interest Expense	666.67	
	Cash		733.76
	Made first month's mortgage payment.		

As this entry shows, only $67.09 of the $733.76 payment is applied to reduce the mortgage; the remainder is interest ($100,000 × 0.08 × $1/_{12}$). In each successive month, the amount applied to reduce the mortgage will increase slightly until, toward the end of the 30-year mort-

$100,000, 25-Year Mortgage

Interest Rate	Monthly Payment	Total Amount Paid	Qualifying Annual Income
7%	$ 707	$212,100	$30,300
8%	772	231,600	33,086
9%	839	251,700	35,957
10%	909	272,700	38,957
11%	980	294,000	42,000
12%	1,053	315,900	45,129
13%	1,128	338,400	48,343
14%	1,204	361,200	51,600

mortgage amortization schedule A schedule that shows the breakdown between interest and principal for each payment over the life of a mortgage.

gage, almost all of the payment will be for principal. A **mortgage amortization schedule** identifies how much of each mortgage payment is interest and how much is principal reduction, as shown in Exhibit 3. Note that during the first 20 years of McGiven's $100,000, 8%, 30-year mortgage, more of each mortgage payment is for interest than for principal.

At the end of each year, a mortgage is reported on the balance sheet in two places: (1) the principal to be paid during the next year is shown as a current liability, and (2) the balance of the mortgage payable is shown as a long-term liability. Further, any accrued interest on the mortgage is reported as a current liability, and the interest expense for the year is included with other expenses on the income statement.

Exhibit 3: Mortgage Amortization Schedule ($100,000, 30-Year Mortgage at 8%)

		End-of-Year Totals		
Year	Monthly Payment	Principal Paid during Year	Interest Paid during Year	Outstanding Mortgage Balance
1	$733.76	$ 835	$7,970	$99,165
2	733.76	905	7,900	98,260
3	733.76	980	7,825	97,280
4	733.76	1,061	7,744	96,219
5	733.76	1,149	7,656	95,070
10	733.76	1,712	7,093	87,725
15	733.76	2,551	6,254	76,783
20	733.76	3,800	5,005	60,080
25	733.76	5,661	3,144	36,793
30	733.76	8,434	371	0

Total payments over life of mortgage: $264,154*
*$733.76 × 360 payments = $264,154.

TO SUMMARIZE: Long-term interest-bearing notes are obligations that will be repaid over several years. Interest on the note is computed by multiplying the outstanding balance of the note times the rate of interest. Mortgages payable are long-term liabilities that arise when companies borrow money to buy land, construct buildings, or purchase additional operating assets. Mortgages are tied to specific assets. They are amortized over a period of time and involve periodic, usually monthly, payments that include both principal and interest.

Accounting for Lease Obligations

3 Account for capital lease obligations and understand the significance of operating leases being excluded from the balance sheet.

© 2003 Getty Images

A construction company may choose to lease large equipment rather than purchase such an asset.

As discussed in Chapter 10, a company may choose to lease rather than purchase an asset. If a lease is a simple, short-term rental agreement, called an operating lease, lease payments are recorded as Rent Expense by the lessee and as Rent Revenue by the lessor. However, if the terms of a lease agreement meet specific criteria (see Chapter 10, page 467), the transaction is classified as a capital lease and is accounted for as if the asset had been purchased with long-term debt. The lessee records the leased property as an asset and recognizes a liability to the lessor.

In Chapter 10, we focused on the recording of assets acquired under capital leases, using assumed amounts for the present value. Here we will explain how the present value of a capital lease is determined. To illustrate the measurement and recording of a capital lease, we will assume that Malone Corporation leases a mainframe computer from Macro Data, Inc., on December 31, 2005. The lease requires annual payments of $10,000 for 10 years, with the first payment due on December 31, 2006.[2] The rate of interest applicable to the lease is 14% compounded annually.

Assuming the lease meets the criteria for a capital lease, Malone Corporation will record the computer and the related liability at the present value of the future lease payments. From Table II, on page 555, the factor for the present value of an annuity for 10 payments at 14% is 5.2161. This factor is multiplied by the annual lease payment to determine the present value. The entry to record the lease on Malone's books is:

2005			
Dec. 31	Leased Computer	52,161	
	Lease Liability		52,161
	Leased a computer from Macro Data, Inc., for		
	$10,000 a year for 10 years discounted at 14%		
	($10,000 × 5.2161 = $52,161).		

FYI:

Many companies structure their lease agreements so as not to meet the lease capitalization criteria. In these cases, the companies must still disclose their expected future lease payments in the notes to the financial statements.

If Malone Corporation uses a calendar year for financial reporting, the December 31, 2006, balance sheet will report the leased asset in the property, plant, and equipment section and the lease liability in the liabilities section.

---

2 Readers should be aware that the illustration of a capital lease presented here assumes that lease payments are made at the end of each year, with the present values based on an ordinary annuity. Usually, lease payments are made at the beginning of each lease period, which requires present value calculations using the concept of an annuity in advance or "annuity due." These calculations are explained in intermediate accounting texts.

A schedule of the computer lease payments is presented in Exhibit 4. Each year the lease liability account balance is multiplied by 14% to determine the amount of interest included in each of the annual $10,000 lease payments.

Note that this is the same procedure used with a mortgage when determining the amount of each payment that is applied to reduce the principal and the amount that is considered interest expense.

The remainder of the payment is a reduction in the liability. For example, the first lease payment is recorded as follows:

2006			
Dec. 31	Interest Expense	7,303	
	Lease Liability	2,697	
	Cash		10,000
	Paid annual lease payment for computer		
	($52,161 × 0.14 = $7,303; $10,000 − $7,303 = $2,697).		

Similar entries would be made in each of the remaining nine years of the lease, except that the principal payment (reduction in Lease Liability) would increase while the interest expense would decrease. Interest expense decreases over the lease term because a constant rate (14%) is applied to a decreasing principal balance.

Although the asset and liability accounts have the same balance at the beginning of the lease term, they seldom remain the same during the lease period. The asset and the liability are accounted for separately, with the asset being depreciated using one of the methods discussed in Chapter 10.

Operating Leases

When a lease is accounted for as a capital lease, the lease obligation (and an associated leased asset) will appear on the balance sheet of the company using the leased asset. If, on the other hand, a company is able to classify a lease as an operating lease according to the criteria outlined in Chapter 10, *nothing will appear on the balance sheet.* Neither the leased asset nor the lease liability will be recognized. For this reason, an operating lease is often referred to as a form of "off-balance-sheet financing"—the economic obligation associated with the financing arrangement entered into to secure the use of an asset is not reported on the balance sheet.

Exhibit 4: Schedule of Computer Lease Payments

Year	Annual Payment	Interest Expense (0.14 × Lease Liability)	Principal	Lease Liability
				$52,161
1	$10,000	(0.14 × $52,161) = $7,303	$2,697	49,464
2	10,000	(0.14 × 49,464) = 6,925	3,075	46,389
3	10,000	(0.14 × 46,389) = 6,494	3,506	42,883
4	10,000	(0.14 × 42,883) = 6,004	3,996	38,887
5	10,000	(0.14 × 38,887) = 5,444	4,556	34,331
6	10,000	(0.14 × 34,331) = 4,806	5,194	29,137
7	10,000	(0.14 × 29,137) = 4,079	5,921	23,216
8	10,000	(0.14 × 23,216) = 3,250	6,750	16,466
9	10,000	(0.14 × 16,466) = 2,305	7,695	8,771
10	10,000	(0.14 × 8,771) = 1,229*	8,771	0

*Rounded.

Because operating leases are not reported on the balance sheet, accounting rules require companies to disclose operating lease details in the financial statement notes so that financial statement users will be aware of these off-balance-sheet obligations. The information from the operating lease note from DISNEY'S 2002 financial statements is reproduced below.

> Contractual commitments, primarily broadcast programming rights and future minimum lease payments under the non-cancelable operating lease payments under the non-cancelable operating leases, totaled $16.2 billion at September 30, 2002, payable as follows:

	Broadcast Programming	Operating Leases	Total
2003	$4,198	$223	$ 4,421
2004	3,107	200	3,307
2005	2,882	173	3,055
2006	2,296	156	2,452
2007	1,128	141	1,269
Thereafter	980	715	1,695
			$16,199

Recall that the obligation to make this $16.2 billion in operating lease payments is not reported as a liability on Disney's balance sheet.

TO SUMMARIZE: A lease is a contract whereby the lessee makes periodic payments to the lessor for the use of an asset. A simple short-term rental agreement, or operating lease, involves only the recording of rent expense by the lessee and rent revenue by the lessor. A capital lease is accounted for as a debt-financed purchase of the leased asset. Both the asset and the liability are initially recorded by the lessee at the present value of the future lease payments discounted at the applicable interest rate. Subsequently, the asset is depreciated and the lease liability is written off as periodic payments are made. Part of each lease payment is interest expense, computed at a constant interest rate, and the remainder is a reduction of the principal amount of the liability. Operating leases are a form of off-balance-sheet financing because the obligation to make future operating lease payments is not recognized as a liability on the balance sheet. Companies are required to disclose the amount of their future operating lease payments in the notes to the financial statements.

The Nature of Bonds

4 Account for bonds, including the original issuance, the payment of interest, and the retirement of bonds.

bond A contract between a borrower and a lender in which the borrower promises to pay a specified rate of interest for each period the bond is outstanding and repay the principal at the maturity date.

debentures (unsecured bonds) Bonds for which no collateral has been pledged.

A **bond** is a contract between the borrowing company (issuer) and the lender (investor) in which the borrower promises to pay a specified amount of interest at the end of each period the bond is outstanding and to repay the principal at the maturity date of the bond contract. Bonds generally have maturity dates exceeding 10 years and, as a result, are another example of a long-term liability.

Types of Bonds

Bonds can be categorized on the basis of various characteristics. The following classification system considers three characteristics:

1. The extent to which bondholders are protected.
   a. **Debentures** (or **unsecured bonds**). Bonds that have no underlying assets pledged as security, or collateral, to guarantee their repayment.

secured bonds Bonds for which assets have been pledged in order to guarantee repayment.

registered bonds Bonds for which the names and addresses of the bondholders are kept on file by the issuing company.

coupon bonds Unregistered bonds for which owners receive periodic interest payments by clipping a coupon from the bond and sending it to the issuer as evidence of ownership.

term bonds Bonds that mature in one single sum at a specified future date.

serial bonds Bonds that mature in a series of installments at specified future dates.

callable bonds Bonds for which the issuer reserves the right to pay the obligation before its maturity date.

convertible bonds Bonds that can be traded for, or converted to, other securities after a specified period of time.

zero-coupon bonds Bonds issued with no promise of interest payments; only a single payment will be made.

junk bonds Bonds issued by companies in weak financial condition with large amounts of debt already outstanding; these bonds yield high rates of return because of high risk.

bond indenture A contract between a bond issuer and a bond purchaser that specifies the terms of a bond.

principal (face value or **maturity value)** The amount that will be paid on a bond at the maturity date.

bond maturity date The date at which a bond principal or face amount becomes payable.

b. **Secured bonds**. Bonds that have a pledge of company assets, such as land or buildings, as a protection for lenders. If the company fails to meet its bond obligations, the pledged assets can be sold and used to pay the bondholders. Bonds that are secured with the issuer's assets are often referred to as "mortgage bonds."

2. How the bond interest is paid.
   a. **Registered bonds**. Bonds for which the issuing company keeps a record of the names and addresses of all bondholders and pays interest only to those whose names are on file.
   b. **Coupon bonds**. Unregistered bonds for which the issuer has no record of current bondholders but instead pays interest to anyone who can show evidence of ownership. Usually, these bonds have a printed coupon for each interest payment. When a payment is due, the bondholder clips the coupon from the certificate and sends it to the issuer as evidence of bond ownership. The issuer then sends an interest payment to the bondholder.

3. How the bonds mature.
   a. **Term bonds**. Bonds that mature in one single sum on a specified future date.
   b. **Serial bonds**. Bonds that mature in a series of installments.
   c. **Callable bonds**. Term or serial bonds that the issuer can redeem at any time at a specified price.
   d. **Convertible bonds**. Term or serial bonds that can be converted to other securities, such as stocks, after a specified period, at the option of the bondholder. (The accounting for this type of bond is discussed in advanced accounting texts.)

Two other types of bonds that are often encountered are zero-coupon bonds and junk bonds. **Zero-coupon bonds** are issued with no promise of interest payments. The company issuing the bonds promises only to repay a fixed amount at the maturity date. While the idea of having to make no interest payments might be initially appealing to the issuer, remember that the present value of the bond is affected by both the single payment at the end of the bond's life and the annuity payment. If this annuity (interest) payment will not be part of the bond, potential buyers will pay much less for the bond. For this reason, zero-coupon bonds are often referred to as *deep-discount bonds*.

Junk bonds are high-risk bonds issued by companies in weak financial condition or with large amounts of debt already outstanding. These bonds typically yield returns of at least 12%, but some may return in excess of 20%. Of course, with these high returns comes greater risk.

Characteristics of Bonds

When an organization issues bonds, it usually sells them to underwriters (brokers and investment bankers), who in turn sell them to various institutions and to the public. At the time of the original sale, the company issuing the bonds chooses a trustee to represent the bondholders. In most cases, the trustee is a large bank or trust company to which the company issuing the bonds delivers a contract called a bond indenture, deed of trust, or trust indenture. The **bond indenture** specifies that in return for an investment of cash by investors, the company promises to pay a specific amount of interest (based on a specified, or stated, rate of interest) each period the bonds are outstanding and to repay the **principal** (also called **face value** or **maturity value**) of the bonds at a specified future date (the **bond maturity date**). It is the duty of the trustee to protect investors and to make sure that the bond issuer fulfills its responsibilities.

The total value of a single "bond issue" often exceeds several million dollars. A bond issue is generally divided into a number of individual bonds, which may be of varying denominations. The principal, or face value, of each bond is usually $1,000 or a multiple thereof. Note that the price of bonds is quoted as a percentage of $1,000 face value. Thus, a bond quoted at 98 is selling for $980 (98% × $1,000), and a bond quoted at 103 is selling for $1,030 (103% × $1,000). By issuing bonds in small denominations, a company increases the chances that a broad range of investors will be able to compete for the purchase of the bonds. This increased demand usually results in the bonds selling for a higher price.

In most cases, the market price of bonds is influenced by (1) the riskiness of the bonds and (2) the interest rate at which the bonds are issued. The first factor, riskiness of the bonds, is determined by general economic conditions and the financial status of the company selling the bonds, as measured by organizations (MOODY'S or STANDARD AND POOR'S, for instance) that regularly assign a rating, or a grade, to all corporate bonds.

Companies strive to earn as high a bond rating as possible because the higher the rating, the lower the interest rate they will have to pay to attract buyers. For example, using the widely cited Moody's bond rating, an Aaa bond is a bond of the highest quality with the least risk of nonpayment. As of May 2003, bonds with this rating were paying interest of approximately 6.5%. A high-risk bond, on the other hand, will have a low rating, which means the company will have to offer a higher rate of interest to attract buyers. For example, as of June 2003, the bonds of financially troubled DOLE FOOD COMPANY INC. (the fruit company) were rated B by Moody's, a rating indicating that the bonds were "highly speculative."

TO SUMMARIZE: Bonds are certificates of debt issued by companies or government agencies, guaranteeing a stated interest rate and repayment of the principal at a specified maturity date. Corporations issue bonds as a form of long-term borrowing to finance the acquisition of operating assets, such as land, buildings, and equipment. Bonds can be classified by their level of security (debentures versus secured bonds), by the way interest is paid (registered versus coupon bonds), and by the way they mature (term bonds, serial bonds, callable bonds, and convertible bonds).

Determining a Bond's Issuance Price

When a company issues bonds, it is generally promising to make two types of payments: (1) a payment of interest of a fixed amount at equal intervals (usually semiannually but sometimes quarterly or annually) over the life of the bond and (2) a single payment—the principal, or face value, of the bond—at the maturity date. For example, assume that Denver Company issues 10%, five-year bonds with a total face value of $800,000. Interest is to be paid semiannually. This information tells us that Denver Company agrees to pay $40,000 ($800,000 × 0.10 × ½ year) in interest every six months and also agrees to pay to the investors the principal amount of $800,000 at the end of five years. The following diagram reflects this agreement between Denver Company and the bond investors:

In this example, we assumed that the bonds were issued at their face value of $800,000. However, bonds are frequently issued at a price that is more or less than their face value. The

STOP & THINK

If the market rate of interest is higher than the rate of interest stated on the bonds, will the bonds sell at a price higher or lower than the face value? Think about the question this way: Is the higher rate more attractive to investors, and if it is, what would investors do as a result?

market rate (effective rate or yield rate) of interest The actual interest rate earned or paid on a bond investment.

stated rate of interest The rate of interest printed on the bond.

bond discount The difference between the face value and the sales price when bonds are sold below their face value.

bond premium The difference between the face value and the sales price when bonds are sold above their face value.

actual price at which bonds are issued is affected by the interest rate investors are seeking at the time the bonds are sold in relation to the interest rate specified by the borrower in the bond indenture. How, then, is the issuance price of bonds determined?

Essentially, present value concepts are used to measure the effect of time on the value of money. The price should equal the present value of the interest payments (an annuity) plus the present value of the bond's face value at maturity. These present values are computed using the **market rate of interest** (also called the **effective rate** or **yield rate**), which is the rate investors expect to earn on their investment. It is contrasted with the **stated rate of interest**, which is the rate printed on the bond (10% in the Denver Company example).

If the effective rate is equal to the stated rate, the bonds will sell at face value (that is, at $800,000). If the effective rate is higher than the stated rate, the bonds will sell at a **bond discount** (at less than the face value) because the investors desire a higher rate than the company is promising to pay. Likewise, if the effective rate is lower than the stated rate, the bonds will sell at a **bond premium** (at more than face value) because the company is promising to pay a higher rate than the market is paying at that time.

Consider the following scenario: If Company A is issuing bonds with a stated rate of 12% and the market rate for similar bonds is 10%, what will happen to the price of Company A's bonds? Investors, eager to receive a 12% return, will bid the price of the bonds up until the price at which the bonds sell yields a 10% return. The amount paid for the bonds over and above the maturity value is the bond premium. If Company A were issuing bonds with a stated rate of 8%, no one would buy the bonds until the price was lowered sufficiently to allow investors to earn a return of 10%. The difference between the selling price and the maturity value would be the amount of the bond discount.

We will use the Denver Company bonds example (from page 540) to explain how the price is computed in each situation.

Bonds Issued at Face Value

Denver Company has agreed to issue $800,000 bonds and pay 10% interest, compounded semiannually. Assume that the effective interest rate demanded by investors for bonds of this level of risk is also 10%. Using the effective interest rate, which happens to be the same as the stated rate, the calculation to determine the price at which the bonds will be issued is shown below. (Note that because the interest is compounded semiannually, the interest rate is halved and the five-year bond life is treated as 10 six-month periods.)

The calculation shows why the bonds sell at face value. At the effective rate, the sum of the present value of the interest payments and the payment at maturity is $800,000, which is the issuance price at the stated rate. This equality of present values will occur only when the effective rate and the stated rate are the same.

1. Semiannual interest payments . . . . $ 40,000
   Present value of an annuity of
      10 payments of $1 at 5% (Table II) . . . . × 7.7217
   Present value of interest payments $308,868

2. Maturity value of bonds $800,000
   Present value of $1 received 10 periods
      in the future discounted at 5% (Table I) . . . . × 0.6139
   Present value of principal amount 491,132*

3. Issuance price of bonds (total present value) $800,000

*Difference is due to the rounding of the present value factor.

The value of the bonds can also be computed using a business calculator as follows:

Hewlett-Packard Keystrokes:

a. **CLEAR ALL**.
b. Set **P/YR** to 1.

1. 800,000   Press **FV**.
2. 40,000   Press **PMT**.
3. 10   Press **N**.
4. 5   Press **I/YR**.
5. Press **PV** for the answer of $800,000.

Bonds Issued at a Discount

Denver Company will sell its bonds at less than the face value of $800,000 (at a discount) if the stated rate of interest is less than the effective rate that investors are seeking. To illustrate the issuance of bonds at a discount, assume that the effective rate is 12% compounded semi-annually; the stated rate remains 10% compounded semiannually. In this case, the bonds will be issued at a price of $741,124, as shown here:

1.	Semiannual interest payments	$ 40,000	
	Present value of an annuity of 10 payments of $1 at 6% (Table II)	× 7.3601	
	Present value of interest payments		$294,404
2.	Maturity value of bonds	$800,000	
	Present value of $1 received 10 periods in the future discounted at 6% (Table I)	× 0.5584	
	Present value of principal amount		446,720
3.	Issuance price of bonds (total present value)		$741,124

Denver Company will receive less than the $800,000 face value because the stated rate of interest is lower than the effective rate. In this case, there is a discount of $58,876 ($800,000 − $741,124).

The following keystrokes are used to compute the value of the bonds using a business calculator:

Caution

The most common mistake made in computing bond values is to use the stated rate of interest in calculating the present value of the cash flows. The stated rate of interest is used *only* to compute the amount of the semiannual interest payments. The present value computations are done using the current market rate (i.e., effective or yield rate) of interest.

Hewlett-Packard Keystrokes:

a. **CLEAR ALL**.
b. Set **P/YR** to 1.

1. 800,000   Press **FV**.
2. 40,000   Press **PMT**.
3. 10   Press **N**.
4. 6   Press **I/YR**.
5. Press **PV** for the answer of $741,119.30. This answer differs slightly from the value computed using the tables because of rounding.

Bonds Issued at a Premium

The Denver Company bonds will be issued for more than $800,000 (at a premium) when the stated interest rate is higher than the effective rate. Let us now assume that the effective rate is 8% compounded semiannually and that the stated rate is still 10% compounded semiannually. In this case, the bonds will be issued at $864,916, as shown here:

1. Interest payments .... $ 40,000
   Present value of an annuity of
       10 payments of $1 at 4% (Table II) .... × 8.1109
   Present value of interest payments $324,436

2. Maturity value of bonds $800,000
   Present value of $1 received 10 periods
       in the future discounted at 4% (Table I) .... × 0.6756
   Present value of principal amount 540,480

3. Issuance price of bonds (total present value) $864,916

Denver Company will receive more than the $800,000 face value when the bonds are issued because the company has agreed to pay the investors a higher rate of interest than the market rate.

The same calculation can be done using a business calculator as follows:

Hewlett-Packard Keystrokes:

a. **CLEAR ALL.**
b. Set **P/YR** to 1.

1. 800,000   Press **FV.**
2. 40,000   Press **PMT.**
3. 10   Press **N.**
4. 4   Press **I/YR.**
5. Press **PV** for the answer of $864,887.17. This answer differs slightly from the value computed using the tables because of rounding.

In all three situations, the 10% stated rate determined the amount of each interest payment. The price of the bonds was determined by discounting the $40,000 of interest payments and the $800,000 face amount at maturity by the effective rate of interest, which may vary from day to day, depending on market conditions. In essence, the issuance price depends on four factors: (1) face value of the bonds, (2) periodic interest payments (face value × stated interest rate), (3) time period, and (4) effective interest rate. Although the bond price is the exact amount that allows investors to earn the interest rate they are seeking, it also reflects the real cost of money to the borrowing company.

Now that you know how to calculate bond values, you may feel ready to move to New York City and become a Wall Street bond trader. Not so fast. There are four steps to computing bond values, as outlined below.

1. Determine the market interest rate.
2. Compute the present value of the maturity amount (using the market interest rate as the discount rate).
3. Compute the present value of the annuity of annual interest payments (using the market interest rate as the discount rate).
4. Add the quantities computed in (2) and (3).

Three of these steps—2, 3, and 4—are very straightforward. These are the steps that you have learned in this chapter. The initial step of determining the market interest rate is where the art and analysis of bond trading are brought to bear. For example, how can you tell whether a company's riskiness requires that the market interest rate on its bonds should be 7.2% or 7.3%? This is an extremely difficult determination to make, and yet it is exactly the type of decision that bond traders must make many times each day.

TO SUMMARIZE: The price at which bonds are issued is a function of the interest rate investors are seeking when the bonds are issued in relation to the interest rate the borrowing company is promising to pay. The bond's face value, or principal, and future interest payments (face value × stated interest rate) are discounted by the interest rate desired by investors (the effective, yield, or market rate) to arrive at the issuance price of the bonds. Bonds will sell at their face value if the stated interest rate is equal to the effective rate. If the effective rate is higher than the stated rate, the bonds will sell at a discount. If the effective rate is lower than the stated rate, the bonds will sell at a premium. The effective rate used to discount the payments promised by the borrower reflects the real cost of the money borrowed.

Accounting for Bonds Payable Issued at Face Value

When a company issues bonds, it must account for the issuance (sale) of the bonds, for the interest payments, and for the amortization of any bond premium or discount. Then, at or before maturity, the company must account for the bond's retirement.

The accounting for these four elements depends on the issuance price of the bonds and on the date of issuance in relation to the date on which interest is paid. In the following sections, we explain the accounting for bonds when the issue price is equal to face value. The accounting for bonds issued at a premium or at a discount is discussed in the expanded material section of the chapter. For most of this discussion, we will use the following data:

Issuing company	Central Trucking Company
Accounting year	Calendar year ending December 31
Face value of bonds issued	$100,000
Stated interest rate	12%
Effective interest rate when issued	12%
Initial date of issuance	January 1, 2006
Date of maturity	January 1, 2016
Interest payment dates	January 1 and July 1

Central Trucking Company issued $100,000 bonds with a stated interest rate of 12% on January 1, 2006. The bonds were issued at face value because 12% is the effective, or market, rate of interest for similar bonds. The journal entry to record their issuance on January 1, 2006, is as follows:

Cash	100,000	
Bonds Payable		100,000
Issued $100,000, 12%, 10-year bonds at face value.		

The entry to record the first payment of interest on July 1, 2006, is:

Bond Interest Expense	6,000	
Cash		6,000
Paid semiannual interest on the $100,000, 12%,		
10-year bonds ($100,000 × 0.12 × ½ year).		

Because Central Trucking operates on a calendar-year basis, it will need to make the following adjusting entry on December 31, 2006, to account for the interest expense between July 1 and December 31, 2006:

Bond Interest Expense	6,000	
Bond Interest Payable		6,000
To recognize expense for the six months July 1 to December 31, 2006 ($100,000 × 0.12 × ½ year).		

At the end of the accounting period (December 31, 2006), the financial statements will report the following:

Income Statement

Bond interest expense ($6,000 × 2)	$ 12,000

Balance Sheet

Current liabilities:	
Bond interest payable	$ 6,000
Long-term liabilities:	
Bonds payable (12%, due January 1, 2016)	$100,000

On January 1, 2007, when the semiannual interest is paid, the bond interest payable account is eliminated. The January 1 entry is:

Bond Interest Payable	6,000	
Cash		6,000
Paid semiannual bond interest.		

The entries to record the interest expense payments during the remaining nine years will be the same as those made during 2006 and on January 1, 2007. The only other entry required in accounting for these bonds is the recording of their retirement on January 1, 2016. That entry, assuming that all interest has been accounted for, will be:

Bonds Payable	100,000	
Cash		100,000
Retired the $100,000, 10-year, 12% bonds.		

As the preceding entries illustrate, accounting for the issuance of bonds, the payment of the interest, and the retirement of the bonds is relatively simple when the bonds are issued at face value.

Bond Retirements before Maturity

Bond issues are, by definition, an inflexible form of long-term debt. The issuing company has a set schedule of interest payments and a specified maturity date, usually at least 5 or 10 years from the issuance date. In many cases, however, a company may want to pay off (redeem) and retire its bonds before maturity. This situation might occur when interest rates fall—a company uses the money obtained by issuing new bonds at a lower interest rate to retire the older, higher-interest bonds. As a result, the company retains the money it needs for expansion or other long-range projects but pays less interest for using that money.

As noted earlier, callable bonds are issued with an early redemption provision. Although the company usually has to pay a premium (penalty) for the privilege of redeeming (calling) the bonds, the amount of the penalty will probably be less than the amount gained by paying a lower interest rate. With bonds that are not callable, the company simply purchases the bonds in the open market, as available, at the going price.

To illustrate the retirement of bonds before maturity, assume that the Central Trucking Company bonds are now selling in the bond market at 109 and are callable at 110. The company decides to take advantage of the lower interest rate (8%) by issuing new bonds and using the proceeds to pay off the outstanding bonds. Given that the bonds were issued at their face value, the penalty (the call premium) is $10,000. The entry to record the retirement of the bonds at 110 is:

Bonds Payable	100,000	
Loss on Bond Retirement	10,000	
Cash ($100,000 × 1.10)		110,000
To retire $100,000 of bonds at a call price of 110.		

In this case, the bonds were retired at a loss of $10,000. The loss is probably tolerable because the company expects to pay significantly less interest over the life of the new bond issue than it would have had to continue to pay on the old bonds. Gains and losses on the early retirement of bonds are reported on the income statement.

> **TO SUMMARIZE:** Accounting for bonds involves three steps: (1) accounting for their issuance, (2) accounting for the periodic interest payments, and (3) accounting for their retirement. When bonds are retired at maturity, there is no gain or loss because the amount paid is equal to the face value of the bonds. When bonds are retired before maturity, a gain or loss often results because the price paid to retire the bonds can be different from the carrying value of the bonds. The gain or loss on retirement of bonds is reported on the income statement.

Using Debt-Related Financial Ratios

5 Use debt-related financial ratios to determine the degree of a company's financial leverage and its ability to repay loans.

As illustrated earlier in the chapter in Exhibit 2, an important business issue associated with long-term debt is the determination of how a company wishes to obtain the money it needs to buy necessary assets. A company's leverage is the degree to which the company has borrowed the funds needed for asset acquisitions. This section describes the financial ratios that are commonly used to evaluate the level of a company's financial leverage.

Debt Ratio and Debt-to-Equity Ratio

debt ratio A measure of leverage, computed by dividing total liabilities by total assets.

The **debt ratio** measures the amount of assets supplied by lenders. It is calculated as follows:

$$\text{Debt ratio} = \frac{\text{Total liabilities}}{\text{Total assets}}$$

The computed value of the debt ratio indicates the percentage of a company's funding that has come through borrowing.

The debt ratio for DISNEY for 2002 is calculated as follows (the numbers are in millions):

$$\text{Debt ratio} = \frac{\$26,166}{\$50,045} = 52.3\%$$

Thus, 52% of Disney's assets are provided by lenders and 48% by stockholders.

The **debt-to-equity ratio** also measures the balance of funds being provided by creditors and stockholders. This ratio is calculated by dividing total liabilities by total stockholders' equity. The higher the debt-to-equity ratio, the more debt the company has. The debt-to-equity ratio for Disney is calculated as follows:

debt-to-equity ratio The number of dollars of borrowed funds for every dollar invested by owners; computed as total liabilities divided by total stockholders' equity.

$$\text{Debt-to-equity ratio} = \frac{\text{Total liabilities}}{\text{Total stockholders' equity}}$$

$$\text{Debt-to-equity ratio} = \frac{\$26,166}{\$23,879} = 1.10$$

In this case, the debt-to-equity ratio indicates that Disney's debt is about 10% higher than its equity. Note that the debt ratio and the debt-to-equity ratio both indicate the same thing—that Disney has acquired just a little bit more of its total financing from borrowing than from stockholders. It doesn't matter which of these two ratios you use to measure a company's leverage; the important thing is that you are consistent and that any ratios you use for comparison have been computed using the same formula.

Times Interest Earned Ratio

Lenders like to have an indication of the borrowing company's ability to meet the required interest payments. **Times interest earned** is the ratio of the income that is available for interest payments to the annual interest expense. Times interest earned is computed as follows:

times interest earned A measure of a borrower's ability to make required interest payments; computed as income before interest and taxes divided by annual interest expense.

$$\text{Times interest earned} = \frac{\text{Income before interest and taxes (operating profit)}}{\text{Annual interest expense}}$$

To illustrate the computation of this ratio, we will return to Disney. For year-end 2002, Disney's interest expense was $453 million, and its operating profit was $2,643 million. This results in times interest earned of 5.8 times, computed as follows:

$$\text{Times interest earned} = \frac{\$2,643}{\$453} = 5.8 \text{ times}$$

Disney's times interest earned value of 5.8 times means that its operations in 2002 generated enough profit to be able to pay Disney's interest expense for the year 5.8 times. This suggests that Disney's creditors have a substantial cushion before they need to be concerned about Disney's ability to meet its required periodic interest payments.

eXpanded *Material*

The present value techniques discussed in this chapter are useful in determining the value of obligations due at some future time. The computations and accounting are similar for interest-bearing notes, mortgages, capital leases, and bonds. However, there are certain complexities associated with these liabilities that deserve additional attention. In this section of the chapter, we discuss the procedures associated with the amortization of a bond discount or premium.

Bonds Issued at a Discount or at a Premium

6 Amortize bond discounts and bond premiums using either the straight-line method or the effective-interest method.

As we have explained, bonds may be issued at a discount or a premium because their stated interest rate may be (and often is) lower or higher than the effective rate. The two rates often differ because economic conditions in the marketplace change between the date the stated interest is set and the date the bonds are actually sold. Various factors determine this second date—for example, the time it takes to print the bonds and the investment banker's decision regarding the best time to offer the bonds. Because the cost to the company for the use of the bond money is really the effective interest rate rather than the stated rate, the discount or premium must be written off (amortized) over the period the bonds are outstanding, and the amortization is treated as an adjustment to bond interest expense.

straight-line amortization A method of systematically writing off a bond discount or premium in equal amounts each period until maturity.

effective-interest amortization A method of systematically writing off a bond premium or discount that takes into consideration the time value of money and results in an equal interest rate being used for amortization for each period.

There are two methods of amortizing bond discounts and bond premiums: straight-line amortization and effective-interest amortization. With **straight-line amortization**, a company writes off the same amount of discount or premium each period the bonds are held. For example, with a $4,000 discount on a 10-year bond, $400 is amortized each year. **Effective-interest amortization** takes the time value of money into consideration. The amount of discount or premium amortized is the difference between the interest actually incurred (based on the effective rate) and the interest actually paid (based on the stated rate). The straight-line amortization method will be used to explain the accounting for the amortization of discounts and premiums; then the effective-interest method will be explained and illustrated.

Accounting for Bonds Issued at a Discount

When bonds are issued at a discount, a contra-liability account is used to keep a separate record of the discounted amount. To illustrate, we will assume that the $100,000, 10-year, 12% bonds issued by Central Trucking on January 1, 2006, sold for $98,000. The entry to record the issuance of the bonds is:

Cash	98,000	
Discount on Bonds	2,000	
Bonds Payable		100,000
Issued $100,000, 12%, 10-year bonds at 98.		

The discount on bonds account represents the difference between the face value of the bonds and the issuance price. This discount is accounted for as additional bond interest expense over the life of the bonds. In other words, if the company receives only $98,000 when the bonds are issued and is required to pay $100,000 at maturity, the $2,000 difference is additional interest. The following analysis shows that total interest on the bonds is $122,000, comprised of the periodic interest payments ($120,000) plus the $2,000 discount.

Amount to be paid to bondholders:	
Interest paid each year for 10 years ($100,000 × 0.12 × 10)	$120,000
Face value to be paid at maturity	100,000
Total amount to be paid to bondholders	$220,000
Proceeds received from sale of bonds ($100,000 × 0.98)	98,000
Total interest expense	$122,000
Average annual interest expense ($122,000/10 years)	$ 12,200

Although the $2,000 of additional interest arising from the discount will not be paid until the bonds mature, interest accrues, or accumulates, over time. Thus, each year that the bonds are outstanding, Central Trucking will record bond interest expense for the amount paid at the stated rate ($100,000 × 0.12 = $12,000) and will also recognize a portion of the discount as bond interest expense. In recording the additional bond interest expense, the contra account Discount on Bonds is amortized or written off over the life of the bonds. Using straight-line amortization, an even amount is amortized each period. In the Central Trucking Company example, the semiannual amortization would be $100 ($2,000 discount/10 years × $1/2$). Bond amortization is recorded when interest payments are made, and the entry on July 1, 2006, is:

Bond Interest Expense	6,100	
Discount on Bonds		100
Cash		6,000
Paid semiannual interest on the $100,000, 12%, 10-year bonds		
($100,000 × 0.12 × $1/2$ year) and amortized the bond discount		
($2,000/10 years × $1/2$ year).		

As illustrated, amortization of a discount increases bond interest expense. In this case, the bond interest expense is $6,100, or the sum of the semiannual interest payment and the semiannual amortization of the bond discount. Over the 10-year life of the bonds, the bond interest expense will be increased by $2,000 (20 periods × $100), the amount of the discount. Thus, these bonds pay an effective interest rate of approximately 12.45%[3] per year ($12,200 interest/ $98,000 received on the bonds).

The adjusting entry to record the bond interest expense on December 31, 2006, is:

Bond Interest Expense	6,100	
Discount on Bonds		100
Bond Interest Payable		6,000
To recognize bond interest expense for the six months July 1 to		
December 31, 2006.		

The financial statements prepared at December 31, 2006, would report the following:

Income Statement

Bond interest expense ($6,100 × 2)	$12,200

Balance Sheet

Current liabilities:		
Bond interest payable		$ 6,000
Long-term liabilities:		
Bonds payable (12%, due January 1, 2016)	$100,000	
Less unamortized discount ($2,000 − $200)	1,800	$98,200

---

[3] Because straight-line amortization was used, this effective rate of 12.45% is only an approximation that will change slightly each period. An accurate effective rate can be calculated only if the effective-interest method of amortization is used.

The entries to account for the bond interest expense and bond discount amortization during the remaining nine years will be the same as those illustrated. And because the bond discount will be completely amortized at the end of the 10 years, the entry to record the retirement of the bonds will be the same as that for bonds issued at face value. That entry is:

Bonds Payable	100,000	
Cash		100,000
Retired the $100,000, 12%, 10-year bonds.		

Accounting for Bonds Issued at a Premium

Like discounts, premiums must be amortized over the life of the bonds. To illustrate the accounting for bonds sold at a premium, we will assume that Central Trucking was able to sell its $100,000, 12%, 10-year bonds at 103 (that is, at 103% of face value). The entry to record the issuance of these bonds on January 1, 2006, is:

Cash	103,000	
Premium on Bonds		3,000
Bonds Payable		100,000
Sold $100,000, 12%, 10-year bonds at 103.		

Premium on Bonds is added to Bonds Payable on the balance sheet and, like Discount on Bonds, is amortized using either the straight-line method or the effective-interest method. Thus, if Central Trucking uses the straight-line method, the annual amortization of the premium will be $300 ($3,000/10 years), or $150 every six months. The entry to record the first semiannual interest payment and the premium amortization of July 1, 2006, is:

Bond Interest Expense	5,850	
Premium on Bonds	150	
Cash		6,000
Paid semiannual interest on the $100,000, 12%, 10-year bonds		
($100,000 × 0.12 × ½ year) and amortized the bond premium		
($3,000/10 years × ½).		

The amortization of a premium on bonds reduces the actual bond interest expense. The following analysis shows why bond interest expense is reduced when bonds are sold at a premium:

Caution

If bonds issued at a premium or discount are retired before maturity, remember that the bond payable and any associated premium or discount would be taken off the books.

Amount to be paid to bondholders:	
[($12,000 interest × 10 years) + $100,000 face value]	$220,000
Proceeds received from sale of bonds	103,000
Total interest to be paid	$117,000
Average annual interest expense ($117,000/10 years)	$ 11,700

In this case, the annual payments of $12,000 include interest of $11,700 and $300, which represents a partial repayment (one-tenth) of the bond premium. Thus, the effective interest rate is approximately 11.36% ($11,700/$103,000), which is less than the stated rate of 12%.

The adjusting entry to record the accrual of the interest expense on December 31, 2006, is:

Bond Interest Expense	5,850	
Premium on Bonds	150	
Bond Interest Payable		6,000
To recognize bond interest expense for the six months		
July 1 to December 31, 2006.		

The financial statements prepared at December 31, 2006, would report the following:

Income Statement

Bond interest expense ($5,850 × 2)	$ 11,700

Balance Sheet

Current liabilities:		
Bond interest payable		$ 6,000
Long-term liabilities:		
Bonds payable (12%, due January 1, 2016)	$100,000	
Plus unamortized premium ($3,000 − $300)	2,700	$102,700

Effective-Interest Amortization

Companies can often justify use of the straight-line method of amortizing bond premiums and discounts on the grounds that its results are not significantly different from those of the theoretically more accurate effective-interest method. Nevertheless, because the effective-interest method considers the time value of money, it is required by generally accepted accounting principles if it leads to results that differ significantly from those obtained by the straight-line method.

The effective-interest method amortizes a varying amount each period, which is the difference between the interest actually incurred and the cash actually paid. The amount actually incurred is the changing **bond carrying value** (the face value of the bond minus the unamortized discount or plus the unamortized premium) multiplied by a constant rate, the effective-interest rate.

bond carrying value The face value of bonds minus the unamortized discount or plus the unamortized premium.

To illustrate the effective-interest method, let's continue with the Central Trucking Company example we have used previously. We will assume that the Central Trucking Company $100,000, 12%, 10-year bonds were issued on January 1, 2006, for $112,463. The bonds pay interest semiannually on January 1 and July 1, so their effective interest rate is approximately 10%[4] a year, or 5% every six months. Because the actual bond interest expense for each interest period is equal to the effective rate of 5% multiplied by the bond carrying value, the amortization (rounded to the nearest $1) for the 10 years is calculated as shown in the following table.

FYI:

Note that the table on the next page looks a lot like the mortgage amortization schedule on page 535 and the schedule of computer lease payments on page 537. The reason is that these other schedules also use the effective-interest amortization method.

---

4 The 10% rate is the rate that will discount the face value of the bonds and the semiannual interest payments to a present value that equals the issuance price of the bonds, computed as follows:

Present value of $100,000 at 5% for 20 payments	$100,000 × 0.3769 =	$ 37,690
Present value of $6,000 at 5% for 20 payments	$ 6,000 × 12.4622 =	74,773
Total present value = issuance price of the bonds		$112,463

Period	1 Cash Paid for Interest	2 Semiannual Interest Expense (0.05 × Bond Carrying Value)	3 Premium Amortization (1) − (2)	4 Carrying Value
Issuance date				$112,463
Year 1, first six months	$6,000	$5,623	$377	112,086
Year 1, second six months	6,000	5,604	396	111,690
Year 2, first six months	6,000	5,585	415	111,275
Year 2, second six months	6,000	5,564	436	110,839
Year 3, first six months	6,000	5,542	458	110,381
Year 3, second six months	6,000	5,519	481	109,900
Year 4, first six months	6,000	5,495	505	109,395
Year 4, second six months	6,000	5,470	530	108,865
Year 5, first six months	6,000	5,443	557	108,308
Year 5, second six months	6,000	5,415	585	107,723
Year 6, first six months	6,000	5,386	614	107,109
Year 6, second six months	6,000	5,355	645	106,464
Year 7, first six months	6,000	5,323	677	105,787
Year 7, second six months	6,000	5,289	711	105,076
Year 8, first six months	6,000	5,254	746	104,330
Year 8, second six months	6,000	5,217	783	103,547
Year 9, first six months	6,000	5,177	823	102,724
Year 9, second six months	6,000	5,136	864	101,860
Year 10, first six months	6,000	5,093	907	100,953
Year 10, second six months	6,000	5,047	953	100,000

In this computation, the $6,000 in column (1) is the actual cash paid each six months. Column (2) shows the interest expense for each six months, which is the amount that will be reported on the income statement. Column (3), which is the difference between columns (1) and (2), represents the amortization of the premium. Column (4) shows the carrying, or book, value of the bonds (that is, the total of the bonds payable and the unamortized bond premium), which is the amount that will be reported on the balance sheet each period. Using the effective-interest method, the bond carrying value is always equal to the present value of the bond obligation. As the carrying value decreases, while the effective rate of interest remains constant, the interest expense also decreases from one period to the next, as illustrated in column (2) of the amortization schedule.

To help you translate this table into the entries for the interest payments and premium amortization at the end of each six-month period, we have provided the semiannual journal entries for year 3.

Year 3, End of First Six Months

Bond Interest Expense	5,542	
Bond Premium	458	
Cash		6,000

To record effective-interest expense on Central Trucking Company bonds for the first six months of year 3.

Year 3, End of Second Six Months

Bond Interest Expense	5,519	
Bond Premium	481	
Bond Interest Payable		6,000

To record effective-interest expense on Central Trucking Company bonds for the second six months of year 3.

Because the straight-line method would show a constant amortization ($12,463/20 = $623.15 per six-month period) on a decreasing bond balance, the straight-line interest rate cannot be constant. When the straight-line results differ significantly from the effective-interest results, generally accepted accounting principles require use of the effective-interest method.

The effective-interest method of amortizing a bond discount is essentially the same as amortizing a bond premium. The main difference is that the bond carrying value is increasing instead of decreasing.

TO SUMMARIZE: When bonds are issued at a premium or a discount, the premium or discount must be amortized over the life of the bond. A discount or premium results when the market rate and the stated rate are different. Because of this difference, bond interest expense recognized on the income statement is not equal to the amount of cash paid for interest. The objective of amortization is to reflect the actual bond interest expense incurred over the life of the bond. Two methods of amortization are available—the straight-line method and the effective-interest method. The straight-line method amortizes an equal amount of premium or discount every period. When the effective-interest method is used, the amount of discount or premium amortized each period is equal to the market rate of interest multiplied by the bond's carrying value.

Table I: The Present Value of $1 Due in n Periods*

Period	1%	2%	3%	4%	5%	6%	7%	8%	9%	10%	12%	14%	15%	16%	18%	20%
1	.9901	.9804	.9709	.9615	.9524	.9434	.9346	.9259	.9174	.9091	.8929	.8772	.8696	.8621	.8475	.8333
2	.9803	.9612	.9426	.9246	.9070	.8900	.8734	.8573	.8417	.8264	.7972	.7695	.7561	.7432	.7182	.6944
3	.9706	.9423	.9151	.8890	.8638	.8396	.8163	.7938	.7722	.7513	.7118	.6750	.6575	.6407	.6086	.5787
4	.9610	.9238	.8885	.8548	.8227	.7921	.7629	.7350	.7084	.6830	.6355	.5921	.5718	.5523	.5158	.4823
5	.9515	.9057	.8626	.8219	.7835	.7473	.7130	.6806	.6499	.6209	.5674	.5194	.4972	.4761	.4371	.4019
6	.9420	.8880	.8375	.7903	.7462	.7050	.6663	.6302	.5963	.5645	.5066	.4556	.4323	.4104	.3704	.3349
7	.9327	.8706	.8131	.7599	.7107	.6651	.6227	.5835	.5470	.5132	.4523	.3996	.3759	.3538	.3139	.2791
8	.9235	.8535	.7894	.7307	.6768	.6274	.5820	.5403	.5019	.4665	.4039	.3506	.3269	.3050	.2660	.2326
9	.9143	.8368	.7664	.7026	.6446	.5919	.5439	.5002	.4604	.4241	.3606	.3075	.2843	.2630	.2255	.1938
10	.9053	.8203	.7441	.6756	.6139	.5584	.5083	.4632	.4224	.3855	.3220	.2697	.2472	.2267	.1911	.1615
11	.8963	.8043	.7224	.6496	.5847	.5268	.4751	.4289	.3875	.3503	.2875	.2366	.2149	.1954	.1619	.1346
12	.8874	.7885	.7014	.6246	.5568	.4970	.4440	.3971	.3555	.3186	.2567	.2076	.1869	.1685	.1372	.1122
13	.8787	.7730	.6810	.6006	.5303	.4688	.4150	.3677	.3262	.2897	.2292	.1821	.1625	.1452	.1163	.0935
14	.8700	.7579	.6611	.5775	.5051	.4423	.3878	.3405	.2992	.2633	.2046	.1597	.1413	.1252	.0985	.0779
15	.8613	.7430	.6419	.5553	.4810	.4173	.3624	.3152	.2745	.2394	.1827	.1401	.1229	.1079	.0835	.0649
16	.8528	.7284	.6232	.5339	.4581	.3936	.3387	.2919	.2519	.2176	.1631	.1229	.1069	.0930	.0708	.0541
17	.8444	.7142	.6050	.5134	.4363	.3714	.3166	.2703	.2311	.1978	.1456	.1078	.0929	.0802	.0600	.0451
18	.8360	.7002	.5874	.4936	.4155	.3503	.2959	.2502	.2120	.1799	.1300	.0946	.0808	.0691	.0508	.0376
19	.8277	.6864	.5703	.4746	.3957	.3305	.2765	.2317	.1945	.1635	.1161	.0829	.0703	.0596	.0431	.0313
20	.8195	.6730	.5537	.4564	.3769	.3118	.2584	.2145	.1784	.1486	.1037	.0728	.0611	.0514	.0365	.0261
25	.7798	.6095	.4776	.3751	.2953	.2330	.1842	.1460	.1160	.0923	.0588	.0378	.0304	.0245	.0160	.0105
30	.7419	.5521	.4120	.3083	.2314	.1741	.1314	.0994	.0754	.0573	.0334	.0196	.0151	.0116	.0070	.0042
40	.6717	.4529	.3066	.2083	.1420	.0972	.0668	.0460	.0318	.0221	.0107	.0053	.0037	.0026	.0013	.0007
50	.6080	.3715	.2281	.1407	.0872	.0543	.0339	.0213	.0134	.0085	.0035	.0014	.0009	.0006	.0003	.0001
60	.5504	.3048	.1697	.0951	.0535	.0303	.0173	.0099	.0057	.0033	.0011	.0004	.0002	.0001	†	†

*The formula used to derive the values in this table was $PV = F \dfrac{1}{(1 + i)^n}$ where PV = present value, F = future amount to be discounted, i = interest rate, and n = number of periods.
†The value of 0 to four decimal places.

Table II: The Present Value of an Annuity of $1 per Number of Payments*

Number of Payments	1%	2%	3%	4%	5%	6%	7%	8%	9%	10%	12%	14%	15%	16%	18%	20%
1	0.9901	0.9804	0.9709	0.9615	0.9524	0.9434	0.9346	0.9259	0.9174	0.9091	0.8929	0.8772	0.8596	0.8621	0.8475	0.8333
2	1.9704	1.9416	1.9135	1.8861	1.8594	1.8334	1.8080	1.7833	1.7591	1.7355	1.6901	1.6467	1.6257	1.6052	1.5656	1.5278
3	2.9410	2.8839	2.8286	2.7751	2.7232	2.6730	2.6243	2.5771	2.5313	2.4869	2.4018	2.3216	2.2832	2.2459	2.1743	2.1065
4	3.9820	3.8077	3.7171	3.6299	3.5460	3.4651	3.3872	3.3121	3.2397	3.1699	3.0373	2.9137	2.8550	2.7982	2.6901	2.5887
5	4.8884	4.7135	4.5797	4.4518	4.3295	4.2124	4.1002	3.9927	3.8897	3.7908	3.6048	3.4331	3.3522	3.2743	3.1272	2.9906
6	5.7985	5.6014	5.4172	5.2421	5.0757	4.9173	4.7665	4.6229	4.4859	4.3553	4.1114	3.8887	3.7845	3.6847	3.4976	3.3255
7	6.7282	6.4720	6.2303	6.0021	5.7864	5.5824	5.3893	5.2064	5.0330	4.8684	4.5638	4.2883	4.1604	4.0386	3.8115	3.6046
8	7.6517	7.3255	7.0197	6.7327	6.4632	6.2098	5.9713	5.7466	5.5348	5.3349	4.9676	4.6389	4.4873	4.3436	4.0776	3.8372
9	8.5660	8.1622	7.7861	7.4353	7.1078	6.8017	6.5152	6.2469	5.9952	5.7590	5.3282	4.9464	4.7716	4.6065	4.3030	4.0310
10	9.4713	8.9826	8.5302	8.1109	7.7217	7.3601	7.0236	6.7101	6.4177	6.1446	5.6502	5.2161	5.0188	4.8332	4.4941	4.1925
11	10.3676	9.7868	9.2526	8.7605	8.3064	7.8869	7.4987	7.1390	6.8052	6.4951	5.9377	5.4527	5.2337	5.0286	4.6560	4.3271
12	11.2551	10.5733	9.9540	9.3851	8.8633	8.3838	7.9427	7.5361	7.1607	6.8137	6.1944	5.6603	5.4206	5.1971	4.7932	4.4392
13	12.1337	11.3484	10.6350	9.9856	9.3936	8.8527	8.3577	7.9038	7.4869	7.1034	6.4235	5.8424	5.5831	5.3423	4.9095	4.5327
14	13.0037	12.1062	11.2961	10.5631	9.8986	9.2950	8.7455	8.2442	7.7862	7.3667	6.6282	6.0021	5.7245	5.4675	5.0081	4.6106
15	13.8651	12.8493	11.9379	11.1184	10.3797	9.7122	9.1079	8.5595	8.0607	7.6061	6.8109	6.1422	5.8474	5.5755	5.0916	4.6755
16	14.7179	13.5777	12.5611	11.6523	10.8378	10.1059	9.4466	8.8514	8.3126	7.8237	6.9740	6.2651	5.9542	5.6685	5.1624	4.7296
17	15.5623	14.2919	13.1661	12.1657	11.2741	10.4773	9.7632	9.1216	8.5436	8.0216	7.1196	6.3729	6.0472	5.7487	5.2223	4.7746
18	16.3983	14.9920	13.7535	12.6593	11.6896	10.8276	10.0591	9.3719	8.7556	8.2014	7.2497	6.4674	6.1280	5.8178	5.2732	4.8122
19	17.2260	15.6785	14.3238	13.1339	12.0853	11.1581	10.3356	9.6036	8.9501	8.3649	7.3658	6.5504	6.1982	5.8775	5.3162	4.8435
20	18.0456	16.3514	14.8775	13.5903	12.4622	11.4699	10.5940	9.8181	9.1285	8.5136	7.4694	6.6231	6.2593	5.9288	5.3527	4.8696
25	22.0232	19.5235	17.4131	15.6221	14.0939	12.7834	11.6536	10.6748	9.8226	9.0770	7.8431	6.8729	6.4641	6.0971	5.4669	4.9476
30	25.8077	22.3965	19.6004	17.2920	15.3725	13.7648	12.4090	11.2578	10.2737	9.4269	8.0552	7.0027	6.5660	6.1772	5.5168	4.9789
40	32.8347	27.3555	23.1148	19.7928	17.1591	15.0463	13.3317	11.9246	10.7574	9.7791	8.2438	7.1050	6.6418	6.2335	5.5482	4.9966
50	39.1961	31.4236	25.7298	21.4822	18.2559	15.7619	13.8007	12.2335	10.9617	9.9148	8.3045	7.1327	6.6605	6.2463	5.5641	4.9995
60	44.9550	34.7609	27.6756	22.6235	18.9293	16.1614	14.0392	12.3766	11.0480	9.9672	8.3240	7.1401	6.6651	6.2482	5.5553	4.9999

*The formula used to derive the values in this table was $PV = F\left(\dfrac{1 - \dfrac{1}{(1+i)^n}}{i}\right)$ where PV = present value, F = periodic payment to be discounted, i = interest rate, and n = number of payments.

Table III: Amount of $1 Due in *n* Periods

Period	1%	2%	3%	4%	5%	6%	7%	8%	9%	10%	12%	14%	15%	16%	18%	20%
1	1.0100	1.0200	1.0300	1.0400	1.0500	1.0600	1.0700	1.0800	1.0900	1.1000	1.1200	1.1400	1.1500	1.1600	1.1800	1.2000
2	1.0201	1.0404	1.0609	1.0816	1.1025	1.1236	1.1449	1.1664	1.1881	1.2100	1.2544	1.2996	1.3225	1.3456	1.3924	1.4400
3	1.0303	1.0612	1.0927	1.1249	1.1576	1.1910	1.2250	1.2597	1.2950	1.3310	1.4049	1.4815	1.5209	1.5609	1.6430	1.7280
4	1.0406	1.0824	1.1255	1.1699	1.2155	1.2625	1.3108	1.3605	1.4116	1.4641	1.5735	1.6890	1.7490	1.8106	1.9388	2.0736
5	1.0510	1.1041	1.1593	1.2167	1.2763	1.3382	1.4026	1.4693	1.5386	1.6105	1.7623	1.9254	2.0114	2.1003	2.2878	2.4883
6	1.0615	1.1262	1.1941	1.2653	1.3401	1.4185	1.5007	1.5869	1.6771	1.7716	1.9738	2.1950	2.3131	2.4364	2.6996	2.9860
7	1.0721	1.1487	1.2299	1.3159	1.4071	1.5036	1.6058	1.7138	1.8280	1.9487	2.2107	2.5023	2.6600	2.8262	3.1855	3.5832
8	1.0829	1.1717	1.2668	1.3686	1.4775	1.5938	1.7182	1.8509	1.9926	2.1436	2.4760	2.8526	3.0590	3.2784	3.7589	4.2998
9	1.0937	1.1951	1.3048	1.4233	1.5513	1.6895	1.8385	1.9990	2.1719	2.3579	2.7731	3.2519	3.5179	3.8030	4.4355	5.1598
10	1.1046	1.2190	1.3439	1.4802	1.6289	1.7908	1.9672	2.1589	2.3674	2.5937	3.1058	3.7072	4.0456	4.4114	5.2338	6.1917
11	1.1157	1.2434	1.3842	1.5395	1.7103	1.8983	2.1049	2.3316	2.5804	2.8531	3.4785	4.2262	4.6524	5.1173	6.1759	7.4031
12	1.1268	1.2682	1.4258	1.6010	1.7959	2.0122	2.2522	2.5182	2.8127	3.1384	3.8960	4.8179	5.3502	5.9360	7.2876	8.9161
13	1.1381	1.2936	1.4685	1.6651	1.8856	2.1329	2.4098	2.7196	3.0658	3.4523	4.3635	5.4924	6.1528	6.8858	8.5994	10.699
14	1.1495	1.3195	1.5126	1.7317	1.9799	2.2609	2.5785	2.9372	3.3417	3.7975	4.8871	6.2613	7.0757	7.9875	10.147	12.839
15	1.1610	1.3459	1.5580	1.8009	2.0789	2.3966	2.7590	3.1722	3.6425	4.1772	5.4736	7.1379	8.1371	9.2655	11.973	15.407
16	1.1726	1.3728	1.6047	1.8730	2.1829	2.5404	2.9522	3.4259	3.9703	4.5950	6.1304	8.1372	9.3576	10.748	14.129	18.488
17	1.1843	1.4002	1.6528	1.9479	2.2920	2.6928	3.1588	3.7000	4.3276	5.0545	6.8660	9.2765	10.761	12.467	16.672	22.186
18	1.1961	1.4282	1.7024	2.0258	2.4066	2.8543	3.3799	3.9960	4.7171	5.5599	7.6900	10.575	12.375	14.462	19.673	26.623
19	1.2081	1.4568	1.7535	2.1068	2.5270	3.0256	3.6165	4.3157	5.1417	6.1159	8.6128	12.055	14.231	16.776	23.214	31.948
20	1.2202	1.4859	1.8061	2.1911	2.6533	3.2071	3.8697	4.6610	5.6044	6.7275	9.6463	13.743	16.366	19.460	27.393	38.337
30	1.3478	1.8114	2.4273	3.2434	4.3219	5.7435	7.6123	10.062	13.267	17.449	29.959	50.950	66.211	85.849	143.37	237.37
40	1.4889	2.2080	3.2620	4.8010	7.0400	10.285	14.974	21.724	31.409	45.259	93.050	188.88	267.86	378.72	750.37	1469.7
50	1.6446	2.6916	4.3839	7.1067	11.467	18.420	29.457	46.901	74.357	117.39	289.00	700.23	1083.6	1670.7	3927.3	9100.4
60	1.8167	3.2810	5.8916	10.519	18.679	32.987	57.946	101.25	176.03	304.48	897.59	2595.9	4383.9	7370.1	20555.	56347.

Table IV: Amount of an Annuity of $1 per Number of Payments

Number of Payments	1%	2%	3%	4%	5%	6%	7%	8%	9%	10%	12%	14%	15%	16%	18%	20%
1	1.0000	1.0000	1.0000	1.0000	1.0000	1.0000	1.0000	1.0000	1.0000	1.0000	1.0000	1.0000	1.0000	1.0000	1.0000	1.0000
2	2.0100	2.0200	2.0300	2.0400	2.0500	2.0600	2.0700	2.0800	2.0900	2.1000	2.1200	2.1400	2.1500	2.1600	2.1800	2.2000
3	3.0301	3.0604	3.0909	3.1216	3.1525	3.1836	3.2149	3.2464	3.2781	3.3100	3.3744	3.4396	3.4725	3.5056	3.5724	3.6400
4	4.0604	4.1216	4.1836	4.2465	4.3101	4.3746	4.4399	4.5061	4.5731	4.6410	4.7793	4.9211	4.9934	5.0665	5.2154	5.3680
5	5.1010	5.2040	5.3091	5.4163	5.5256	5.6371	5.7507	5.8666	5.9847	6.1051	6.3528	6.6101	6.7424	6.8771	7.1542	7.4416
6	6.1520	6.3081	6.4684	6.6330	6.8019	6.9753	7.1533	7.3359	7.5233	7.7156	8.1152	8.5355	8.7537	8.9775	9.4420	9.9299
7	7.2135	7.4343	7.6625	7.8983	8.1420	8.3938	8.6540	8.9228	9.2004	9.4872	10.0890	10.7305	11.0668	11.4139	12.1415	12.9159
8	8.2857	8.5830	8.8923	9.2142	9.5491	9.8975	10.2598	10.6366	11.0285	11.4359	12.2997	13.2328	13.7268	14.2401	15.3270	16.4991
9	9.3685	9.7546	10.1591	10.5828	11.0266	11.4913	11.9780	12.4876	13.0210	13.5795	14.7757	16.0853	16.7858	17.5185	19.0859	20.7989
10	10.4622	10.9497	11.4639	12.0061	12.5779	13.1808	13.8164	14.4866	15.1929	15.9374	17.5487	19.3373	20.3037	21.3215	23.5213	25.9587
11	11.5668	12.1687	12.8078	13.4864	14.2068	14.9716	15.7836	16.6455	17.5603	18.5312	20.6546	23.0445	24.3493	25.7329	28.7551	32.1504
12	12.6825	13.4121	14.1920	15.0258	15.9171	16.8699	17.8885	18.9771	20.1407	21.1843	24.1331	27.2707	29.0017	30.8502	34.9311	39.5805
13	13.8093	14.6803	15.6178	16.6268	17.7130	18.8821	20.1406	21.4953	22.9534	24.5227	28.0291	32.0887	34.3519	36.7862	42.2187	48.4966
14	14.9474	15.9739	17.0863	18.2919	19.5986	21.0151	22.5505	24.2149	26.0192	27.9750	32.3926	37.5811	40.5047	43.6720	50.8180	59.1959
15	16.0969	17.2934	18.5989	20.0236	21.5786	23.2760	25.1290	27.1521	29.3609	31.7725	37.2797	43.8424	47.5804	51.6595	60.9653	72.0351
16	17.2579	18.6393	20.1569	21.8248	23.6575	25.6725	27.8881	30.3243	33.0034	35.9497	42.7535	50.9804	55.7178	60.9250	72.9390	87.4421
17	18.4304	20.0121	21.7616	23.6975	25.8404	28.2129	30.8402	33.7502	36.9737	40.5447	48.8837	59.1176	65.0751	71.6730	87.0680	105.9306
18	19.6147	21.4123	23.4144	25.6454	28.1324	30.9057	33.9990	37.4502	41.3013	45.5992	55.7497	68.3941	75.8364	84.1407	103.7403	128.1167
19	20.8190	22.8406	25.1169	27.6712	30.5390	33.7600	37.3790	41.4463	46.0185	51.1591	63.4397	78.9692	88.2118	98.6032	123.4135	154.7400
20	22.0190	24.2974	26.8704	29.7781	33.0660	36.7856	40.9955	45.7620	51.1601	57.2750	72.0524	91.0249	102.4436	115.3797	146.6280	186.6880
30	34.7849	40.5681	47.5754	56.0849	66.4388	79.0582	94.4608	113.2832	136.3075	164.4940	241.3327	356.7868	434.7451	530.3117	790.9480	1181.8816
40	48.8864	60.4020	75.4013	95.0255	120.7998	154.7620	199.6351	259.0565	337.8824	442.5926	767.0914	1342.0251	1779.0903	2360.7572	4163.2130	7343.8578
50	64.4632	84.5794	112.7969	152.6671	209.3480	290.3359	406.5289	573.7702	815.0836	1163.9085	2400.0182	4994.5213	7217.7163	10435.6488	21813.0937	45497.1908
60	81.6697	114.0515	163.0534	237.9907	353.5837	533.1282	813.5204	1253.2133	1944.7921	3034.8164	7471.6411	18535.1333	29219.9916	46057.5085	114189.6665	281732.5718

review of learning objectives

1 **Use present value concepts to measure long-term liabilities.** Obligations that will not be paid or otherwise satisfied within one year are classified on the balance sheet as long-term liabilities. Some common types of long-term liabilities are notes payable, mortgages payable, lease obligations, and pension obligations. The present value of a long-term liability is the current value, which is computed by discounting the known future amount using the current interest rate. If the present value amounts of assets or liabilities are known and a future amount is desired, then the present value must be compounded to arrive at a future amount that includes both principal and interest.

2 **Account for long-term liabilities, including notes payable and mortgages payable.** Interest-bearing notes are recorded on the books of the issuer at face value. Interest expense is incurred based on the rate of interest, the carrying value of the note, and the passage of time. Interest Expense is debited for the amount of interest incurred and Cash or Interest Payable is credited.

Mortgage liabilities are paid by a series of regular payments that include interest expense and a reduction of the principal of the mortgage note. The balance sheet liability at any given time is the present value of the remaining mortgage payments.

3 **Account for capital lease obligations and understand the significance of operating leases being excluded from the balance sheet.** A firm can acquire new assets by either purchasing or leasing them. Leasing involves periodic payments over the life of the lease. The lease is classified as an operating lease if it is short term and does not meet any of the criteria of a capital lease. If the lease meets one of the specified capital lease criteria, it is treated as a purchase and referred to as a capital lease. As such, it is recorded as both an asset and a long-term liability. The asset is depreciated and the liability is reduced as lease payments are made. Operating leases are a form of off-balance-sheet financing because the obligation to make the future operating lease payments is not recognized on the balance sheet. However, the amount of future operating lease payments is disclosed in the notes to the financial statements.

4 **Account for bonds, including the original issuance, the payment of interest, and the retirement of bonds.** Accounting for bonds by the borrowing company (the issuer)

includes three elements: accounting for their issuance, for interest payments, and for their retirement. If bonds are sold at face value, Cash is debited and Bonds Payable is credited. More often, however, bonds are sold at a premium or a discount. The bond liability is recorded at face value in the bonds payable account, and the premium or discount is recorded in a separate account and added to (in the case of a premium) or subtracted from (in the case of a discount) Bonds Payable on the balance sheet. When interest is paid, Bond Interest Expense is debited and Cash is credited. An adjustment is made to bond interest expense if the bond is sold at a premium or discount. At the date a bond matures, the borrowing company pays the face value to the investors, and the bonds are canceled. If the bonds are retired before maturity, a gain or loss will be recognized when the carrying value of the bonds differs from the amount paid to retire the bonds.

5 **Use debt-related financial ratios to determine the degree of a company's financial leverage and its ability to repay loans.** Higher leverage allows a company to expand without requiring additional stockholder investment. However, higher leverage also makes repayment of debt less certain. Both the debt ratio (total liabilities divided by total assets) and the debt-to-equity ratio (total liabilities divided by total stockholders' equity) measure the level of a company's leverage. These ratios are also sometimes computed using only interest-bearing debt instead of total liabilities. The times interest earned ratio (operating income divided by interest expense) measures how much cushion a company has in terms of being able to make its periodic interest payments.

eXpanded Material

6 **Amortize bond discounts and bond premiums using either the straight-line method or the effective-interest method.** If bonds are issued at a discount, the bond interest expense for the year is the amount of interest paid plus the bond discount amortized during that year. If the bonds are sold at a premium, the bond interest expense for the year is the interest paid minus the bond premium amortized that year. Bond premiums and discounts generally should be amortized using the effective-interest method. The straight-line method is allowed provided that the two methods produce similar results.

ey terms & concepts

annuity, 530
bond, 538
bond discount, 541
bond indenture, 539
bond maturity date, 539
bond premium, 541
callable bonds, 539
compounding period, 529
convertible bonds, 539
coupon bonds, 539
debentures (unsecured bonds), 538
debt ratio, 546
debt-to-equity ratio, 547

junk bonds, 539
long-term liabilities, 526
market rate (effective rate or yield rate) of interest, 541
mortgage amortization schedule, 535
mortgage payable, 534
present value of $1, 526
present value of an annuity, 530
principal (face value or maturity value), 539
registered bonds, 539
secured bonds, 539
serial bonds, 539

stated rate of interest, 541
term bonds, 539
times interest earned, 547
zero-coupon bonds, 539

bond carrying value, 551
effective-interest amortization, 548
straight-line amortization, 548

r eview problems

Accounting for Long-Term Liabilities

Energy Corporation had the following transactions relating to its long-term liabilities for the year:

a. Issued a $30,000, three-year, 8% note payable to White Corporation for a truck purchased on January 2. Interest is payable annually on December 31 of each year.

b. Issued $300,000 of 12%, 10-year bonds on July 1. The market rate on the date of issuance was 12%. Interest payments are made on June 30 and December 31 of each year.

c. Purchased a warehouse on December 1 by borrowing $250,000. The terms of the mortgage call for monthly payments of $2,194 for 30 years to be made at the end of each month. The interest rate on the mortgage is 10%.

Required:
Make all journal entries required during the year to account for the above liabilities. Energy Corporation reports on a calendar-year basis.

Solution

Jan. 2	Truck	30,000	
	Note Payable		30,000
	Purchased a truck by issuing a note.		
July 1	Cash	300,000	
	Bonds Payable		300,000
	Issued 12%, 10-year bonds with a face value of $300,000.		
Dec. 1	Warehouse	250,000	
	Mortgage Payable		250,000
	Purchased a warehouse by issuing a 10%, 30-year mortgage.		

(continued)

Dec. 31	Interest Expense	2,400	
	Cash		2,400
	Paid yearly interest on the 3-year, 8% note		
	($30,000 × 8% = $2,400).		
31	Bond Interest Expense	18,000	
	Cash		18,000
	Paid semiannual interest payment on 12%, 10-year		
	bonds ($300,000 × 0.12 × ⁶/₁₂ = $18,000).		
	Interest Expense	2,083	
	Mortgage Payable	111	
	Cash		2,194
	Paid first monthly payment on 30-year mortgage		
	(interest: $250,000 × 0.10 × ¹/₁₂ = $2,083;		
	reduction in principal: $2,194 − $2,083 = $111).		

Bonds Payable

Scientific Engineering Company received authorization on July 1, 2006, to issue $300,000 of 12% bonds. The maturity date of the bonds is July 1, 2026. Interest is payable on January 1 and July 1 of each year. The bonds were sold for $289,200 on July 1, 2006 (the same day as authorized). Scientific Engineering uses straight-line amortization.

Required:

1. Compute the approximate effective interest rate for the bonds.
2. Record the journal entries on:
   a. July 1, 2006.
   b. December 31, 2006.
   c. January 1, 2007.
   d. July 1, 2007.
   e. December 31, 2007.
3. Record the journal entries on July 1, 2026, for the final interest payment and the retirement of the bonds.

Solution

1. Effective Interest Rate

Because the bonds sold at a discount, the actual or effective rate of interest is higher than the stated interest rate of 12%. The effective interest rate can be approximated as follows:

Bond discount amortized per year = $10,800/20 periods = $540
Annual interest expense = ($300,000 × 12%) + $540 = $36,540
Effective interest rate = $36,540/$289,200 = 12.63%

2. Journal Entries

a.	2006		
	July 1	Cash	289,200	
		Discount on Bonds	10,800	
		Bonds Payable		300,000
		To record the sale of $300,000 of 12% bonds		
		due on July 1, 2026.		

(continued)

b. 2006

Dec. 31	Bond Interest Expense	18,270	
	Discount on Bonds		270
	Bond Interest Payable		18,000

To record semiannual bond interest expense on $300,000, 12%, 20-year bonds ($300,000 × 0.12 × ½ year) and amortize bond discount ($10,800 ÷ 20 years × ½ year).

c. 2007

Jan. 1	Bond Interest Payable	18,000	
	Cash		18,000

Paid semiannual interest on $300,000 bonds.

d. 2007

July 1	Bond Interest Expense	18,270	
	Discount on Bonds		270
	Cash		18,000

Paid semiannual interest on $300,000 bonds and amortized bond discount.

e. 2007

Dec. 31	Bond Interest Expense	18,270	
	Discount on Bonds		270
	Bond Interest Payable		18,000

To record semiannual bond interest expense on $300,000 bonds and amortize bond discount.

3. Retirement of the Bonds

2026

July 1	Bond Interest Expense	18,270	
	Discount on Bonds		270
	Bond Interest Payable		18,000

To record the bond interest expense and discount amortization up to the date of maturity.

	Bonds Payable	300,000	
	Bond Interest Payable	18,000	
	Cash		318,000

To record the payment of interest for six months and retire the bonds at maturity.

The first entry on July 1, 2026, updates the amortization of the bond discount to the retirement date and reflects the cash owed for interest for the period January 1–July 1, 2026. The second entry reflects payment for retiring the bonds plus payment of the interest owed. Alternatively, Cash could have been credited for $18,000 in the first entry. If Cash had been credited, the second entry would have included only a debit to Bonds Payable and a credit to Cash for $300,000.

d i s c u s s i o n   q u e s t i o n s

1. The higher the interest rate, the lower the present value of a future amount. Why?

2. What is an annuity?

3. When does the stated amount of a liability equal its present value?

4. What is the difference between a note payable and a mortgage payable?

5. When a mortgage payment is made, a portion of it is applied to interest, and the balance is applied to reduce the principal. How is the amount applied to reduce the principal computed?

6. If a lease is recorded as a capital lease, what is the relationship of the lease payments and the lease liability?

7. Why do companies prefer to classify leases as operating leases rather than as capital leases?

8. To whom do companies usually sell bonds?

9. What are two important characteristics that determine the issuance price of a bond?

10. Identify four different ways in which bonds can mature or be eliminated as liabilities.

11. If a bond's stated interest rate is below the market interest rate, will the bond sell at a premium or at a discount? Why?

12. If you think the market interest rate is going to drop in the near future, should you invest in bonds?

13. When do you think bonds will sell at or near face value?

14. Explain why bonds retired before maturity may result in a gain or loss to the issuing company.

15. What does the debt ratio measure?

16. From the standpoint of a lender, which is more attractive: a high times interest earned ratio or a low times interest earned ratio? Explain.

17. What type of account is Discount on Bonds?

18. Why does the amortization of a bond discount increase the book value of bonds?

19. Why is the effective-interest amortization method more theoretically appropriate than the straight-line amortization method?

20. What is the carrying value of a bond?

21. How does the carrying value of a bond affect the accounting for bonds payable under the effective-interest method?

22. If the effective rate of interest for a bond is greater than its stated rate of interest, explain why the annual bond interest expense will be different from the periodic cash interest payments to the bondholders.

practice exercises

Practice 11-1

Present Value of a Single Amount

The company will receive $20,000 in five years when the interest rate is 8%. Compute the present value of this payment.

Practice 11-2

Future Value of a Single Amount

The company invests $42,000 today in a savings account that earns 12% compounded annually. What will be the balance in the savings account seven years from today (e.g., future value)?

Practice 11-3

Interest Rate per Compounding Period

The interest rate is 16% compounded quarterly for six years. Compute the interest rate per compounding period.

Practice 11-4

Number of Interest Periods

The interest rate is 12% compounded monthly for seven years. Compute the number of interest periods.

Practice 11-5

Future Value of Single Amount Compounded Monthly

Compute the future value of $10,000 invested today at 24% interest compounded monthly for five years.

Practice 11-6

Computing the Present Value of an Annuity

The company will receive $2,500 every six months for nine years. The company's interest rate is 8% compounded semiannually. Compute the present value of this annuity payment.

Practice 11-7

Computing Periodic Payment Amount

The company borrowed $50,000 to be repaid in equal monthly installments at 12% interest over five years. Compute the periodic payment amount.

Practice 11-8

Interest-Bearing Notes

The company borrowed $20,000 at 8% interest by issuing a note payable. The terms of the note require yearly interest payments for seven years and repayment of the principal at the end of seven years. Make the necessary journal entries to record the following transactions:

1. Issuance of the note payable.
2. Payment of the first interest expense.

Practice 11-9

Mortgages Payable Issuance and First Payment

On January 1, the company borrowed $250,000 to purchase a new building and signed a mortgage agreement pledging the building as collateral on the loan. The mortgage is at 9% for 30 years, and the monthly payment is $2,012 payable on January 31 with subsequent payments due at the end of each month thereafter. Make the necessary journal entries to record the following transactions:

1. Acquisition of the mortgage.
2. January 31 (first month) payment on mortgage.

Practice 11-10

Mortgages Payable Second Payment

Refer to the data in Practice 11-9. Make the necessary journal entry(ies) to record the second month's mortgage payment on February 28. Round to the nearest penny.

Practice 11-11

Capital Lease Acquisition

The company leased a delivery truck on January 1, 2006. The lease requires annual payments of $7,500 for seven years at a 12% rate of interest payable at the end of each year. The company classifies this lease as a capital lease. Make the necessary journal entry(ies) to record the lease of this asset.

Practice 11-12

Capital Lease Payment

Refer to the data in Practice 11-11. Make the necessary journal entry(ies) to record the first lease payment on December 31, 2006. Round amounts to the nearest penny.

Practice 11-13

Types of Bonds

Which one of the following statements is false?

a. Debentures are bonds that have no underlying assets pledged as collateral to guarantee their payment.
b. Serial bonds mature in one single sum on a specified future date.
c. Callable bonds can be redeemed by the issuer at any time at a specified price.
d. Companies keep a record of the names and addresses of all registered bondholders and pay interest only to those whose names are on file.

Practice 11-14

Bonds Issued at Face Value

The company issued 10-year, $50,000 bonds with a stated rate of interest of 16%, compounded quarterly. The effective interest rate demanded by investors for bonds of this level of risk is also 16%. Calculate the issuance price of the bond (e.g., the total present value).

Practice 11-15

Bonds Issued at a Discount

The company issued five-year, $25,000 bonds with a stated rate of interest of 8%, compounded semiannually. The effective interest rate demanded by investors for bonds of this level of risk is 12%. Calculate the issuance price of the bond (e.g., the total present value).

Practice 11-16

Bonds Issued at a Premium

The company issued seven-year, $100,000 bonds with a stated rate of interest of 8%, compounded semiannually. The effective interest rate demanded by investors for bonds of this level of risk is 6%. Calculate the issuance price of the bond (e.g., the total present value).

Practice 11-17

Accounting for Bonds Payable Issued at Face Value

The company issued 10-year, $300,000 bonds with a stated rate of interest of 9%, compounded semiannually. The effective interest rate demanded by investors for bonds of this level of risk is also 9%. Since these bonds are issued at face value (i.e., the stated rate of interest is equal to the interest rate demanded by investors for bonds of this level of risk), the issuance price is also $300,000. Make the necessary journal entries for:

1. The issuance of the bonds.
2. The first interest payment.

Practice 11-18

Accounting for Retirement of Bonds Payable Issued at Face Value

Refer to the data in Practice 11-17. Assuming all interest has been accounted for, make the necessary journal entry(ies) to record the retirement of the bonds at the end of 10 years.

Practice 11-19

Bond Retirements before Maturity

The company had $450,000 in callable bonds in the open market. The company's bonds were selling in the open market at 108 and were callable at 109. The company decided to retire the bonds early. Make the necessary journal entry(ies) to record the retirement of these bonds.

Practice 11-20

Debt Ratio

Using the following information, compute the debt ratio.

Total liabilities	$247,500
Annual interest expense	5,204
Total assets	542,850
Income before interest and taxes	62,030

Practice 11-21

Debt-to-Equity Ratio

Refer to the data in Practice 11-20. Compute the debt-to-equity ratio.

Practice 11-22

Times Interest Earned Ratio

Refer to the data in Practice 11-20. Compute the times interest earned ratio.

 e x e r c i s e s

Exercise 11-1

Computing the Present Value of a Single Sum

Find the present value (rounded to the nearest dollar) of:

1. $20,000 due in 4 years at 6% compounded annually.
2. $40,000 due in 6½ years at 4% compounded semiannually.
3. $15,000 due in 5 years at 16% compounded quarterly.
4. $11,000 due in 25 years at 10% compounded semiannually.

Exercise 11-2

Computing the Future Value of a Single Sum

Compute the future value (rounded to the nearest dollar) of the following investments:

1. $15,842 invested to earn interest at 6% compounded annually for 4 years.
2. $30,920 invested to earn interest at 4% compounded semiannually for 6½ years.

3. $6,846 invested to earn interest at 16% compounded quarterly for 5 years.
4. $959 invested to earn interest at 10% compounded semiannually for 25 years.

Exercise 11-3

Computing the Present Value of an Annuity
What is the present value (rounded to the nearest dollar) of an annuity of $16,000 per year for six years if the interest rate is:

1. 12% compounded annually.
2. 14% compounded annually.

Exercise 11-4

Computing the Amount of Periodic Payments
Howard Company has just borrowed $250,000. The loan is to be repaid in regular annual payments made at the end of each year. What is the amount of each annual payment under the following sets of terms:

1. Interest rate of 8% compounded annually; repayment in four annual payments.
2. Interest rate of 7% compounded annually; repayment in eight annual payments.

Exercise 11-5

Accounting for Long-Term Note Payable
Karl Company borrowed $25,000 on a two-year, 12% note dated October 1, 2005. Interest is payable annually on October 1, 2006, and October 1, 2007, the maturity date of the note. The company prepares its financial statements on a calendar-year basis. Prepare all journal entries relating to the note for 2005, 2006, and 2007.

Exercise 11-6

Spreadsheet

Accounting for Long-Term Note Payable
Silmaril, Inc., borrowed $25,000 from First National Bank by issuing a three-year, 10% note dated July 1, 2005. Interest is payable semiannually on December 31 and June 30. The principal amount is to be repaid in full on June 30, 2008. Silmaril, Inc., reports on a calendar-year basis. Prepare all journal entries relating to the note during 2005, 2006, 2007, and 2008.

Exercise 11-7

Spreadsheet

Accounting for a Mortgage
Kohler Kleaners borrowed $50,000 on June 1, 2006, to finance the purchase of a building. The mortgage requires payments of $525 to be made at the end of every month for 12 years with the first payment being due on June 30, 2006. The interest rate on the mortgage is 8%.

1. Prepare a mortgage amortization schedule for 2006.
2. How much interest will be paid in 2006?
3. By how much will the principal amount of the mortgage be reduced by the end of 2006?

Exercise 11-8

Accounting for a Mortgage
On January 1, 2006, Paik, Inc., borrowed $75,000 to finance the purchase of machinery. The terms of the mortgage require payments to be made at the end of every month with the first payment being due on January 31, 2006. The length of the mortgage is five years, and the mortgage carries an interest rate of 24%.

1. Compute the amount of the monthly payment.
2. Prepare a mortgage amortization schedule for 2006.
3. Prepare the journal entry to be made on January 31, 2006, when the first payment is made.
4. For the remainder of the year, how will the journal entries relating to the mortgage differ from the one made on January 31?

Exercise 11-9

Lease Accounting
Temple Corporation signed a lease to use a machine for four years. The annual lease payment is $10,500 payable at the end of each year.

(continued)

1. Record the lease, assuming that the lease should be accounted for as a capital lease and the applicable interest rate is 10%. (Round to the nearest dollar.)
2. For the initial year, record the annual lease payment.

Exercise 11-10

Lease Accounting

Digital, Inc., leased computer equipment from Young Leasing Company on January 2, 2006. The terms of the lease required annual payments of $4,141 for five years beginning on December 31, 2006. The interest rate on the lease is 14%.

1. Assuming the lease qualifies as an operating lease, what journal entry would be made on January 2 to record the leased asset?
2. If the lease qualifies as an operating lease, what journal entry would be made when the first payment is made on December 31, 2006?
3. Provide the journal entry made on January 2, 2006, assuming the lease qualifies as a capital lease.
4. Provide the journal entry made on December 31, 2006, to record the first lease payment, assuming a capital lease.

Exercise 11-11

Issuance Price of Bonds

Neukoelln Company issued seven-year bonds on January 1. The face value of the bonds is $72,000. The stated interest rate on the bonds is 12%. The market rate of interest at the time of issuance was 10%. The bonds pay interest semiannually. Calculate the issuance price of the bonds.

Exercise 11-12

Issuance Price of Bonds

Neubrandenburg Company issued eight-year bonds on January 1. The face value of the bonds is $90,000. The stated interest rate on the bonds is 6%. The market rate of interest at the time of issuance was 8%. The bonds pay interest semiannually. Calculate the issuance price of the bonds.

Exercise 11-13

Accounting for Bonds Issued at Face Value

Romulus, Inc., issued $500,000 of 10%, five-year bonds at face value on July 1, 2006. Interest on the bonds is payable semiannually on December 31 and June 30.

1. Provide the journal entry to record the issuance of the bonds on July 1, 2006.
2. Provide the journal entry made on December 31, 2006, to account for these bonds.
3. On September 29, 2007, Romulus elected to retire the bonds early. The market price of the bonds on this date was $486,000. Provide the journal entries to record the early retirement.
4. Why do you think Romulus elected to retire the bonds early?

Exercise 11-14

Accounting for Bonds Issued at Face Value

Schwedt Company issued $280,000 of 9%, 10-year bonds at face value on September 1, 2006. The bonds pay interest on March 1 and September 1. Schwedt uses the calendar year for financial reporting purposes.

1. Provide the journal entry to record the bond issuance on September 1, 2006.
2. Provide the journal entry to record interest expense on December 31, 2006.
3. Provide the journal entries made during 2007 relating to the bond.
4. On February 20, 2008, Schwedt elected to retire the bond issue early. The market price on the day of retirement was $300,000. Provide the journal entries to record the bond retirement.
5. Why do you think Schwedt elected to retire the bonds early?

Exercise 11-15

Computation of Debt-Related Financial Ratios

The following information comes from the financial statements of Schwerin Company:

Long-term debt	$60,000
Total liabilities	96,000
Total stockholders' equity	60,000
Operating income	14,000
Interest expense	8,000

Compute the following ratio values:

1. Debt ratio.
2. Debt-to-equity ratio.
3. Times interest earned.

Exercise 11-16

Impact of Capitalizing the Value of Operating Leases

The following information comes from the financial statements of Karlla Peterson Company:

Total liabilities	$100,000
Total stockholders' equity	80,000

In addition, Karlla Peterson has a large number of operating leases. The payments on these operating leases total $20,000 per year for the next 15 years. The present value of the economic obligation associated with these operating leases is $150,000. Of course, because these are operating leases, this economic obligation is off the balance sheet.

Compute the following ratio values:

1. Debt ratio. *Hint:* Remember the accounting equation.
2. Debt-to-equity ratio.
3. Debt-to-equity ratio assuming that Karlla Peterson's operating leases are accounted for as capital leases.
4. Debt ratio assuming that Karlla Peterson's operating leases are accounted for as capital leases.

Exercise 11-17

Accounting for Bonds Issued at a Discount

Hawaii Equipment Company issued $300,000 of 8%, five-year bonds at 97 on June 30, 2006. Interest is payable on June 30 and December 31. The company uses the straight-line method to amortize bond premiums and discounts. The company's fiscal year is from February 1 through January 31.

Prepare all necessary journal entries to account for the bonds from the date of issuance through June 30, 2007. Also record the retirement of the bonds on June 30, 2011, assuming that all interest has been paid and that the discount has been fully amortized.

Exercise 11-18

Accounting for Bonds Issued at a Premium

Sealon Corporation issued $100,000 of 10%, 10-year bonds at 102 on April 1, 2006. Interest is payable semiannually on April 1 and October 1. Sealon Corporation uses the calendar year for financial reporting.

1. Record the necessary entries to account for these bonds on the following three dates. (Use the straight-line method to amortize the bond premium.)
   a. April 1, 2006.
   b. October 1, 2006.
   c. December 31, 2006.
2. Show how the bonds would be reported on the balance sheet of Sealon Corporation on December 31, 2006.

Exercise 11-19

Effective-Interest Calculation
Determine the *approximate* effective rate of interest for $300,000, 8%, five-year bonds issued at 95. (Assume straight-line amortization.)

Exercise 11-20

Bond Amortization Schedule
The following is a partially completed amortization schedule prepared for the Liggett Company to account for its three-year bond issue with a face value of $50,000. The schedule covers the first three semiannual interest payment dates. Amounts are rounded to the nearest dollar. Compute the missing numbers.

Year	Interest Paid	Bond Expense	Premium Amortized	Bonds Payable Carrying Value
0				$52,537
1/2	(1)	$2,627	(2)	52,164
1	$3,000	(3)	$392	(4)
1 1/2	(5)	(6)	(7)	(8)

Exercise 11-21

Accounting for Bonds
Tanner Corporation, a calendar-year firm, is authorized to issue $400,000 of 12%, 10-year bonds dated May 1, 2006, with interest payable semiannually on May 1 and November 1.

Amortization of bond premiums or discounts is recorded using the straight-line amortization method. Prepare journal entries to record the following events, assuming that the bonds are sold at 96 on May 1, 2006.

1. The bond issuance on May 1, 2006.
2. Payment of interest on November 1, 2006.
3. Adjusting entry on December 31, 2006.
4. Payment of interest on May 1, 2007.

roblems

Problem 11-1

Present and Future Value Computations

Required:
1. Determine the present value in each of the following situations:
   a. A $9,000 loan to be repaid in full at the end of five years. Interest on the loan is payable quarterly. The interest rate is 8% compounded quarterly.
   b. A six-year note for $12,000 bearing interest at an annual rate of 12%, compounded semiannually. Interest is payable semiannually.
   c. A one-year mortgage to be paid in monthly installments of $6,000. The interest rate is 12% compounded monthly.
2. Determine the future value in each of the following situations:
   a. An investment of $20,000 today to earn interest at 8% compounded semiannually to provide for a down payment on a house four years from now.
   b. An investment of $40,000 today to earn interest at 12% compounded quarterly that is designated for a charitable contribution 15 years from now when the donor retires.

Problem 11-2

Present and Future Value Computations

Required:

1. Compute the present value for each of the following situations, assuming an interest rate of 10% compounded annually. (Round amounts to the nearest dollar.)
   a. A single payment of $30,000 due on a mortgage five years from now.
   b. A series of payments of $5,000 each, due at the end of each year for five years.
   c. A five-year, 10% loan of $25,000, with interest payable annually, and the principal due in five years.
2. Compute the future value amounts (rounded to the nearest dollar) in each of the following situations:
   a. A $20,000 lump-sum investment today that will earn interest at 10% compounded annually over five years.
   b. A $5,000 lump-sum investment today that will earn interest at 8%, compounded quarterly to provide money for a child's college education 15 years from now.

Problem 11-3

Computing the Amount of Periodic Payments

Kenneth J. Nelson has just purchased a new car for $35,000. He paid $5,000 down and signed a note for the remaining $30,000. The interest rate on the note is 12% compounded monthly, or 1% per month.

Required:

1. Compute the amount of Mr. Nelson's monthly payment if he plans to pay off the $30,000 note in 30 monthly payments. Remember: The interest rate is 1% per month.
2. Repeat part (1) assuming that Mr. Nelson wishes to repay the note in 60 monthly payments.
3. Assume that Mr. Nelson decides to repay the note in 60 monthly payments. What is the balance remaining on the note immediately after he makes the 30th payment? *Hint:* Compute the present value of the remaining 30 payments.

Problem 11-4

Accounting for Notes Payable

Sweet's Candy Company needed cash for its current business operations. On January 1, 2005, the company borrowed $8,000 on a two-year, interest-bearing note from Peterson Bank at an annual interest rate of 10%. Interest is payable annually on January 1, and the note matures January 1, 2007. Sweet's Candy Company also borrowed $4,500 from Laurence National Bank on January 1, 2005, signing a three-year, 11% note due on January 1, 2008, with interest payable annually on January 1.

Required:

Prepare all journal entries relating to the two notes for 2005, 2006, 2007, and 2008. Assume that Sweet's Candy Company uses the calendar year for financial reporting. (Round all amounts to the nearest dollar.)

Problem 11-5

P.A.S.S.
Power Accounting System Software

Accounting for Notes Payable

During 2005, Schmaal Corporation had the following transactions relating to long-term liabilities:

May 1   Purchased a machine costing $600,000 from Kretschmar Corporation. Issued a three-year, interest-bearing note with interest payable on May 1 of each year. The note matures on May 1, 2008, and carries an interest rate of 7%.

July 1   Borrowed $25,000 from South-Central National Bank. The terms of the note require semiannual payments of interest on December 31 and June 30. The note matures in two years and carries an interest rate of 6%.

(continued)

Required:
1. Prepare the journal entries made on May 1 and July 1 to record the issuance of these two notes.
2. Prepare all journal entries made on December 31, 2005.
3. Prepare all journal entries made during 2006.

Problem 11-6

P.A.S.S.
Power Accounting
System Software

Accounting for a Mortgage

On November 1, 2006, Richards Company arranges with an insurance company to borrow $350,000 on a 20-year mortgage to purchase land and a building to be used in its operations. The land and the building are pledged as collateral for the loan, which has an annual interest rate of 12%, compounded monthly. The monthly payments of $3,854 are made at the end of each month, beginning on November 30, 2006.

Required:
1. Prepare the journal entry to record the purchase of the land and building, assuming that $50,000 of the purchase price is assignable to the land.
2. Prepare the journal entries on November 30 and December 31 for the monthly payments on the mortgage.
3. **Interpretive Question:** Explain generally how the remaining liability at December 31, 2006, will be reported on the company's balance sheet dated December 31, 2006.

Problem 11-7

P.A.S.S.
Power Accounting
System Software

Lease Accounting

On January 1, 2005, Linda Lou Foods, Inc., leased a tractor. The lease agreement qualifies as a capital lease and calls for payments of $7,000 per year (payable each year on January 1, starting in 2006) for eight years. The annual interest rate on the lease is 8%. Linda Lou Foods uses a calendar-year reporting period.

Required:
1. Prepare the journal entries for the following dates:
   a. January 1, 2005, to record the leasing of the tractor.
   b. December 31, 2005, to recognize the interest expense for the year 2005.
   c. January 1, 2006, to record the first lease payment.
2. Prepare the appropriate journal entries at December 31, 2006, and January 1, 2007.
3. **Interpretive Question:** Explain briefly how the leased asset is accounted for annually.

Problem 11-8

Lease Accounting

Bradshaw, Inc., leased a starship on January 2, 2006. Terms of the lease require annual payments of $63,023 per year for seven years. The interest rate on the lease is 14%, and the first payment is due on December 31, 2006.

Required:
1. Compute the present value of the lease payments.
2. Assuming the lease qualifies as a capital lease, prepare the journal entry to record the lease.
3. Prepare the journal entry to record the first lease payment on December 31, 2006, and to depreciate the leased asset. Bradshaw, Inc., uses the straight-line method for depreciating all long-term assets.
4. **Interpretive Question:** How would the leased asset, and its associated liability, be disclosed on the balance sheet prepared on December 31, 2006?

Problem 11-9

Issuance Price of Bonds

Patterson Company issued 30-year bonds on June 30. The face value of the bonds was $750,000. The stated interest rate on the bonds was 6%. The market rate of interest at the time of issuance was 4%. Patterson also issued another set of bonds on August 31. These bonds were 20-year bonds and had a face value of $556,000. The stated rate of interest on these bonds was 5%. The market rate of interest at the time these bonds were issued was 8%. Both sets of bonds pay interest semiannually.

Required:
Calculate the issuance price of these bonds.

Problem 11-10

Accounting for Bonds
On July 1, 2006, Paramount, Inc. issued $500,000, 8%, 30-year bonds with interest paid semi-annually on January 1 and July 1. The bonds were sold when the market rate of interest was 8%. On October 1, 2009, the bonds were retired when their fair market value was $495,000.

Required:
1. Demonstrate, using the present value tables, that the bonds were sold for $500,000.
2. Provide the journal entry made on July 1 to record the issuance of the bonds.
3. Provide the journal entry made on December 31, 2006, relating to interest.
4. Provide the journal entries to record the retirement of the bonds.

Problem 11-11

Accounting for Bonds
Itarare Enterprises issued $2 million, 12%, 20-year bonds on November 1, 2005. Interest payment dates are May 1 and November 1. The bonds were sold at face value.

Required:
1. Provide the journal entry to record the initial issuance of the bonds.
2. Provide the required journal entry on December 31, 2005.
3. Provide all journal entries relating to the bonds made during 2006.

Problem 11-12

Reporting Liabilities on the Balance Sheet
The following list of accounts is taken from the adjusted trial balance of Goforth Company.

Accounts Payable	$45,000
Notes Payable (due in 6 months)	24,000
Income Taxes Payable	18,000
Unearned Sales Revenue	27,500
Notes Payable (due in 2 years)	40,000
Prepaid Insurance	6,200
Accounts Receivable	53,000
Current Portion of Mortgage Payable	12,300
Mortgage Payable (due beyond 1 year)	93,000
Retained Earnings	91,400
Property Taxes Payable	8,700
Salaries & Wages Payable	15,200
Sales Tax Payable	3,100

Required:
Prepare the liabilities section of the company's balance sheet.

Problem 11-13

Reporting Liabilities on the Balance Sheet
The following amounts are shown on Plymouth Company's adjusted trial balance for the year 2006:

Accounts Payable	$ 36,000
Property Taxes Payable	6,300
Short-Term Notes Payable	44,000
Mortgage Payable (due within 1 year)	28,000
Mortgage Payable (due after 1 year)	300,000
Accrued Interest on Mortgage Payable	3,000
Lease Liability (current portion)	58,000
Lease Liability (long term)	414,000
Rent Payable	70,000
Income Taxes Payable	50,000
Federal & State Unemployment Taxes Payable	16,000

(continued)

Required:

Prepare the liabilities section of Plymouth Company's balance sheet at December 31, 2006.

Problem 11-14

Computation of Debt-Related Financial Ratios

The following information comes from the financial statements of Hart Company:

Long-term debt	$360,000
Total liabilities	460,000
Total stockholders' equity	315,000
Current assets	160,000
Earnings before income taxes	22,000
Interest expense	48,000

Required:

Compute the following ratio values. State any assumptions that you make.

1. Current ratio.
2. Debt ratio.
3. Debt-to-equity ratio.
4. Times interest earned.
5. **Interpretive Question:** You are a bank manager considering making a new $35,000 loan to Hart that would replace part of the existing long-term debt. You expect Hart to repay your loan in two years. Which of the ratios computed in parts (1) through (4) would be most useful to you in evaluating whether to make the loan to Hart?

Problem 11-15

Impact of Capitalizing the Value of Operating Leases

The following information comes from the financial statements of Travis Campbell Company:

Total liabilities	$100,000
Total stockholders' equity	80,000
Property, plant, and equipment	110,000
Sales	500,000
Earnings before income taxes	11,000
Interest expense	23,000

In addition, Travis Campbell has a large number of operating leases. The payments on these operating leases total $30,000 per year for the next 10 years. The present value of the economic obligation associated with these operating leases is $180,000. Of course, because these are operating leases, this economic obligation is off the balance sheet.

Required:

Compute the following ratio values:

1. Debt ratio. *Hint:* Remember the accounting equation.
2. Debt ratio assuming that Travis Campbell's operating leases are accounted for as capital leases.
3. Asset turnover (sales/total assets).
4. Asset turnover assuming that Travis Campbell's operating leases are accounted for as capital leases.
5. **Interpretive Question:** You are Travis Campbell's banker. You are concerned that the times interest earned ratio is not accurately reflecting the risk that Travis Campbell will not meet its fixed annual payments because most of those fixed payments are operating lease payments, not interest payments. Design an alternative ratio that will reflect the fact that, like interest payments, operating lease payments are fixed obligations that must be covered through operating profits each year. Compute the value for the ratio that you have designed.

Problem 11-16

Accounting for Bonds

Nemo Company authorized and sold $90,000 of 10%, 15-year bonds on April 1, 2006. The bonds pay interest each April 1, and Nemo's year-end is December 31.

Required:
1. Prepare journal entries to record the issuance of Nemo Company's bonds under each of the following three assumptions:
   a. Sold at 97.
   b. Sold at face value.
   c. Sold at 105.
2. Prepare adjusting entries for the bonds on December 31, 2006, under all three assumptions. (Use the straight-line amortization method.)
3. Show how the bond liabilities would appear on the December 31, 2006, balance sheet under each of the three assumptions.
4. **Interpretive Question:** What condition would cause the bonds to sell at 97? At 105?

Problem 11-17

P.A.S.S.
Power Accounting
System Software

Accounting for Bonds Issued at a Premium

On March 1, 2006, Devone Corporation issued $50,000 of 10%, five-year bonds at 118. The bonds were dated March 1, 2006, and interest is payable on March 1 and September 1. Devone records amortization using the straight-line method. Devone's financial reporting year ends on December 31.

Required:
Provide all necessary journal entries on each of the following dates:

1. March 1, 2006.
2. September 1, 2006.
3. December 31, 2006.
4. March 1, 2011.

Problem 11-18

P.A.S.S.
Power Accounting
System Software

Bonds Retired at Maturity

Stottard Company issued $450,000 of 10%, 10-year bonds on June 1, 2005, at 103. The bonds were dated June 1, and interest is payable on June 1 and December 1 of each year.

Required:
1. Record the issuance of the bonds on June 1, 2005. (Round to the nearest dollar.)
2. Record the interest payment on December 1, 2005. Stottard uses the straight-line method of amortization.
3. Record the interest accrual on December 31, 2005, including amortization.
4. Record the journal entries required on June 1, 2015, when the bonds mature.

Problem 11-19

Spreadsheet

Straight-Line versus Effective-Interest Amortization

Cyprus Corporation issued $150,000 of bonds on January 1, 2006, to raise funds to buy some special machinery. The maturity date of the bonds is January 1, 2011, with interest payable each January 1 and July 1. The stated rate of interest is 10%. When the bonds were sold, the effective rate of interest was 12%. The company's financial reporting year ends December 31.

Required:
1. Determine the price at which the bonds would be sold.
2. Prepare the amortization schedule using the effective-interest method.
3. Prepare a comparative schedule of interest expense for each year (2006–2011) for the effective-interest and straight-line methods of amortization.

(continued)

4. Record the journal entry for the last payment using the amortization schedule in part (2).
5. Record the journal entry for the retirement of the bonds.
6. **Interpretive Question:** Is the difference between the interest expense each year between the straight-line and effective-interest methods sufficient to require the use of the effective-interest method? How do you think this question would be answered in practice?

Problem 11-20

P.A.S.S.
Power Accounting System Software

Effective-Interest Amortization

Lancell Corporation issued $100,000 of three-year, 10% bonds on January 1, 2005. The bonds pay interest on January 1 and July 1 each year. The bonds were sold to yield an 8% return, compounded semiannually.

Required:
1. At what price were the bonds issued?
2. Prepare a schedule to amortize the premium or discount on the bonds using the effective-interest amortization method.
3. Use the information in the amortization schedule prepared for part (2) to record the interest payment on July 1, 2007, including the appropriate amortization of the premium or discount.
4. **Interpretive Question:** Explain why these bonds sold for more or less than face value.

Problem 11-21

Accounting for Bonds

Bell Company sold $200,000 of 10-year bonds on January 1, 2005, to Brown Corporation. The bond indenture included the following information:

Face value	$200,000
Date of bonds	January 1, 2005
Maturity date	January 1, 2015
Stated rate of interest	14%*
Effective (market) rate of interest	12%*

*Compounded semiannually

Required:
1. Prepare the journal entry to record the issuance of the bonds.
2. What is the interest expense on the Bell Company books for the years ending December 31, 2005, and December 31, 2006, using straight-line amortization?
3. Explain how the bonds would be presented on Bell's balance sheet at December 31, 2006.

Problem 11-22

Straight-Line versus Effective-Interest Amortization

Foster Corporation issued three-year bonds with a $180,000 face value on March 1, 2005, in order to pay for a new computer system. The bonds mature on March 1, 2008, with interest payable on March 1 and September 1. The contract rate of interest is 10%. (Interest is compounded semiannually.) When the bonds were sold, the effective rate of interest was 12%. The company's fiscal year ends on February 28.

Required:
1. At what price were the bonds issued based on the information presented?
2. Prepare an amortization schedule using the effective-interest method.
3. Prepare a schedule of interest expense for each year (2005–2008), comparing the annual interest expense for straight-line and effective-interest amortization.
4. Using the amortization schedule prepared in part (2), prepare the journal entry to record the interest payment on September 1, 2005.
5. Prepare the adjusting journal entry to record accrued interest on February 28, 2006.
6. Prepare the journal entry to retire the bonds on March 1, 2008, assuming all interest has been paid prior to retirement.

Problem 11-23

Bonds Retired before Maturity

Amity Construction Company issued $100,000 of 10% bonds on January 1, 2006. The maturity date of the bonds is January 1, 2016. Interest is payable January 1 and July 1. The bonds were sold at 111.4 on July 1, 2006. The company uses the straight-line method of amortizing bond premiums and discounts.

Required:

1. Make the required journal entries for each of the following dates:
   a. July 1, 2006.
   b. December 31, 2006.
   c. January 1, 2007.
   d. July 1, 2007.
2. Because of a substantial decline in the market rate of interest, Amity Construction Company purchased all the bonds on the open market at face value (100) on July 1, 2009. The following entry had just been made on that day:

Bond Interest Expense	4,400	
Premium on Bonds	600	
Cash		5,000

     Made semiannual interest payment on the bonds
     and amortized bond premium for six months.

Prepare the journal entry to record the retirement of the bonds on July 1, 2009.

Problem 11-24

Unifying Concepts: Accounting for Bonds Payable

Durham Corporation was authorized to issue $500,000 of 8%, four-year bonds, dated May 1, 2006. All the bonds were sold on that date when the effective interest rate was 10%. Interest is payable on May 1 and November 1 each year. The company follows a policy of amortizing premium or discount using the effective-interest method. The company closes its books on December 31 of each year.

Required:

1. Calculate the issuance price of the bonds.
2. Prepare an amortization schedule that covers the life of the bond.
3. Prepare journal entries at the following dates based on the information shown in the amortization schedule prepared for part (2).
   a. December 31, 2006.
   b. May 1, 2007.
   c. November 1, 2007.
   d. December 31, 2007.
4. Based on the journal entries prepared for part (3), how much interest expense related to this bond issue did the company report on its income statement for the year 2007?
5. What was the carrying value of this bond issue on the balance sheet of the company at December 31, 2007?
6. **Interpretive Question:** Explain why another company in the same industry, which issued bonds with the same amount of face value, the same date of issuance, and the same stated rate of interest, might have had an issuance price of more or less than the price you computed for the issuance of the Durham Corporation bonds.

Problem 11-25

Analysis of Bonds

Bonds with a face value of $200,000 and a stated interest rate of 12% were issued on March 1, 2006. The bonds pay interest each February 28 and August 31 and mature on March 1, 2016. The issuing company uses the calendar year for financial reporting.

(continued)

Required:
Using these data, complete the following tables for each of the conditions listed. (Show computations and assume straight-line amortization.)

1. The bonds sold at face value.
2. The bonds sold at 97.
3. The bonds sold at 103.

	Case 1	Case 2	Case 3
Cash received at issuance date	_____	_____	_____
Total cash paid to bondholders through maturity	_____	_____	_____
Income statement for 2006:			
Bond interest expense	_____	_____	_____
Balance sheet at December 31, 2006:			
Long-term liabilities:			
Bonds payable, 12%	_____	_____	_____
Unamortized discount	_____	_____	_____
Unamortized premium	_____	_____	_____
Bond carrying value	_____	_____	_____
Approximate effective interest rate*	_____	_____	_____

*Round to the nearest tenth of a percent.

d iscussion cases

Case 11-1

Present Value Concepts

Hamburg Company recently began business and purchased a large facility to make beach clothing. Hamburg Company managed to make a small profit in its initial year of operations, although it used all its cash to purchase inventory and equipment. After preparing its tax return for the year, Hamburg's managers realized that they could pay less taxes than they thought. Because IRS accelerated depreciation methods allow for higher depreciation expense than the straight-line method the company is using for financial-reporting purposes, Hamburg can claim more depreciation expense than it thought it could and can reduce taxable income by $30,000. However, Hamburg's managers know that the two depreciation methods will eventually even out because the difference is only temporary and will create a deferred income tax liability, which must be recorded on the books. The managers are very conservative, though, and would rather pay the additional taxes now than record a liability that must be paid in the future, even if they must borrow the money from a bank to pay the extra taxes. They have come to you for advice. What would you tell them?

Case 11-2

Debt and Equity Financing

Berlin Company is in a world of hurt. For the past 15 years, the company has been the exclusive toy supplier to Infants-R-Us toy stores. Unfortunately for Berlin Company, Infants-R-Us just declared bankruptcy and went out of business. Berlin is the supplier for a few local toy stores, but Infants-R-Us was by far its largest customer. Berlin's managers believe that they can save the company if they can raise enough money to develop a new product line of a popular toy, "Nano Babies." Developing the new product line will require a considerable investment, however. Berlin is trying to decide the best way to finance the investment. It has found a bank that will loan it the money at 18%, a very high rate but the only one it can get because of its precarious financial position. Berlin can also issue bonds to raise the money, but because of investors' concerns about the future viability of the company, the only kind of bonds investors will buy are high-interest junk bonds at an interest rate of 17%. Even then, there is concern that the bonds will be discounted when they are marketed. Which financing alternative would you recommend to the company? If you were an investor, would you buy Berlin Company's bonds?

j udgment calls

Judgment 11-1

You Decide: Should the following bonds be classified as debt or equity on the balance sheet?

A company has recently issued bonds that are convertible into stock at the bondholder's request. The interest rate on the bonds is ridiculously low because it is expected that most holders will exercise the conversion options! How should the bonds be reported?

Judgment 11-2

You Decide: If a young company has a negative "times interest earned" ratio, should the company be refused or given a loan by lenders?

Design Arts Inc. is a young computer game design company that has been in business for two years. The company has been working on a computer game that is scheduled for release in six months. However, it has exhausted all its financial resources and needs one last loan of $100,000 to help it meet its deadline. The company has not had any revenues up to this point but knows that once the game hits the market, it will be extremely profitable. Would you make a loan to this company?

Competency Enhancement Opportunities

▶ **Analyzing Real Company Information**
▶ **International Case**
▶ **Ethics Case**
▶ **Writing Assignment**

▶ **The Debate**
▶ **Cumulative Spreadsheet Project**
▶ **Internet Search**

The following additional assignments provide opportunities for students to develop critical thinking, ethical perspectives, oral and written communication skills, experience with electronic research, and teamwork through group and business activities.

▶ *Analyzing Real Company Information*

Analyzing 11-1 (Microsoft)

The 2002 Form 10-K for MICROSOFT is included in Appendix A. Locate that Form 10-K and consider the following questions:

1. Examine Microsoft's balance sheet as of June 30, 2002. Do you notice anything unusual in connection with Microsoft's reported long-term debt?
2. Compute Microsoft's debt ratio for 2002 and 2001. Is the ratio increasing or decreasing? Identify the primary reason for the change.

Analyzing 11-2 (IBM)

INTERNATIONAL BUSINESS MACHINES (IBM) included the following information in Note J to its 2002 financial statements:

**Long-Term Debt
At December 31, 2002
(dollars in millions)**

At December 31:	Maturities	2002	2001
U.S. dollars:			
Debentures:			
6.22%	2027	$ 500	$ 500
6.5%	2028	700	700
7.0%	2025	600	600
7.0%	2045	150	150
7.125%	2096	850	850
7.5%	2013	550	550
8.375%	2019	750	750
3.43% convertible notes	2007	328	—
Notes: 6.0% average	2003–2032	2,130	2,772
Medium-term note program: 4.0% average	2003–2018	7,113	3,620
Other: 4.9% average	2003–2009	610	828
		$14,281	$11,320
Other currencies (average interest rate at December 31, 2002, in parentheses):			
Euros (5.4%)	2003–2009	$ 2,111	$ 3,042
Japanese yen (1.0%)	2003–2015	4,976	4,749
Canadian dollars (5.8%)	2003–2011	445	441
Swiss francs (4.0%)	2003	180	151
Other (6.6%)	2003–2014	730	726
		$22,723	$20,429

1. IBM lists seven different issues of debentures. What is a debenture?
2. What is unusual about the 7.125% debentures?
3. IBM has borrowed the equivalent of $8.442 billion in the form of foreign currency loans. Why would IBM get loans denominated in foreign currencies rather than get all of its loans in U.S. dollars?
4. The average interest rates on the foreign currency loans range from a low of 1.0% for loans of Japanese yen to 5.8% for loans of Canadian dollars (and even higher for the "other" category). What factors would cause IBM to pay a higher interest rate when it borrows Canadian dollars than when it borrows Japanese yen?

Analyzing 11-3 (Citicorp)

The CITY BANK OF NEW YORK was chartered on June 16, 1812, just two days before the start of the War of 1812 between the United States and Great Britain. To get around twentieth-century bank holding laws, a holding company was organized to own the bank. This holding company took the name of CITICORP in 1974, and the bank itself is now called CITIBANK. Citibank is one of the largest banks in the United States.

On the following page are a simplified balance sheet for Citicorp as of December 31, 2002, and a schedule outlining the interest rate on Citicorp's outstanding long-term debt:

Citicorp
Balance Sheet
December 31, 2002

	(millions of dollars)
Cash	$ 17,326
Investment securities	169,513
Loans receivable	436,304
Other assets	474,047
Total	$1,097,190
Deposit liabilities	$ 430,895
Other liabilities	452,650
Long-term debt	126,927
Stockholders' equity	86,718
Total	$1,097,190

Interest Rates Prevailing on Parent and Subsidiary Loans
for Loans Outstanding on December 31, 2002

Type of Loan	Average Interest Rate
Parent Company	
Senior notes	4.99%
Subordinated notes	6.58%
Parent Company and Subsidiaries	
Senior notes	4.86%
Subordinated notes	6.72%

1. Citicorp's simplified balance sheet is representative of most banks' balance sheets. Using the information about relative sizes of assets and liabilities given in that balance sheet, write a brief description of the primary operating activity of a bank.

2. Compute Citicorp's debt ratio (total liabilities divided by total assets). Comment on whether the value seems high or low to you.

3. In its long-term debt of $126.9 billion, Citicorp has both fixed-rate loans and floating-rate (or variable-rate) loans. What is the advantage of borrowing with a fixed-rate loan? What is the advantage of borrowing with a variable-rate loan?

4. Citicorp includes the following information in its 2002 financial statement note on long-term debt: "Approximately 51% in 2002 and 71% in 2001 of subsidiary long-term debt was guaranteed by Citicorp, and of the debt not guaranteed by Citicorp, approximately 31% in 2002 and 50% in 2001 was secured by the assets of the subsidiary."

   When Citicorp guarantees the long-term debt of one of its subsidiaries, does that raise or lower the interest rate that the subsidiary must pay on the debt? Explain. Is the interest rate on a loan higher when it is secured by assets or when it is unsecured? Explain.

▷ *International Case*

British Petroleum
In May 1901, William Knox D'Arcy convinced the Shah of Persia (present-day Iran) to allow him to hunt for oil. The oil discovered in Persia in 1908 was the first commercially significant

International

amount of oil found in the Middle East. The company making the discovery called itself the ANGLO-PERSIAN OIL COMPANY, later named BRITISH PETROLEUM, or BP. Today, BP Amoco is one of the largest oil and gas exploration and refining companies in the world.

The information below comes from Note 28 (Finance debt) of British Petroleum's 2002 financial statements.

(millions of dollars)	Loans	Finance Leases
Payments due within:		
1 year	$10,002	$ 106
2 to 5 years	5,628	836
after 5 years	4,372	3,481
	$20,002	$4,423
Less finance charge	0	2,417
Net obligation	$20,002	$2,006

1. In Great Britain, a finance lease is what we in the United States would call a capital lease. According to Note 28, British Petroleum expects to make total lease payments of $4.423 billion under finance leases. However, a liability of only $2.006 billion is reported on the balance sheet. Why is there a difference between the two amounts?

2. The $4.423 billion payment amount for the finance leases reflects the total of all lease payments that will be made under the agreements. Does the $20.002 billion amount reported for loans reflect the amount of all payments that will be made under the loan agreements? Explain.

3. The future loan and finance lease payments are separated into amounts to be repaid within one year, within two to five years, and after five years. How would a financial statement user find this payment timing information to be useful?

▷ *Ethics Case*

Hiding an Obligation By Calling It a Lease

You and your partner own Miss Karma's Preschool, which provides preschool and day care services for about 100 children per day. Business is booming, and you are right in the middle of expanding your operation. Three months ago you took your financial statements to the local bank and applied for a five-year, $145,000 loan. The bank approved the loan, but it included as part of the loan agreement a condition that you would incur no other long-term liabilities during the five-year loan period. You cheerfully agreed to this condition because you didn't anticipate any further financing needs.

Two weeks ago a state government inspector came to your facility and said that your square footage was not enough for the number of children enrolled in your programs. The inspector gave you one month to find another facility, or else you would have to shut down. Luckily, you were able to find another building to use. However, the owner of the building insists on having you sign a 20-year lease. Alternatively, you can buy the building for $220,000. To buy the building, you would have to get a mortgage, which would, of course, violate the agreement on your five-year bank loan.

Your partner suggests that the lease is the way to solve all of your problems. Your partner has studied some accounting and reports that you can sign the lease but carefully construct the lease contract so that the lease will be accounted for as an operating lease. In this way, the lease obligation will not be reported as an accounting liability, the loan agreement will not be violated, and you can move to the new facility without any problem.

Is your partner right? Is it possible to avoid reporting the 20-year lease contract as an accounting liability? By signing the lease, are you violating the bank loan agreement? What do you think is the best course of action?

► *Writing Assignment*

My Contract's Bigger Than Your Contract!

You are an agent for professional athletes. One of your clients is a superstar in the NBA. Last month you negotiated a new deal for your client that pays him $22 million per year for each of the next six years. Your client was very pleased with this $132 million contract, especially because it was a bigger contract than any of the other players on his team received.

This morning, while you were relaxing in your Jacuzzi, you got an angry cellular call from your client. It seems that one of his teammates just signed a $150 million deal, paying him $15 million per year for each of the next 10 years. Your client is outraged because you guaranteed that no one on his team would be receiving a bigger contract this season. Your client has threatened to terminate his agreement with you and also to spread the word among all his friends that you are not trustworthy.

Write a one-page memo to your client explaining that the actual value of his $132 million contract is greater than the $150 million contract signed by his teammate. Your client has a marketing degree from an ACC school, so he has had some exposure to the concept of the time value of money.

► *The Debate*

Which is the Better Way to Borrow—Bank Loan or Bonds?

When a major corporation is seeking to borrow a large sum of money, it can choose to arrange a loan through a single bank (or group of banks), or it can issue bonds and essentially borrow the money from the public.

Divide your group into two teams.

- One team represents "Bank Loans." Prepare a two-minute oral presentation arguing that the best way for a major corporation to borrow money is through bank loans negotiated directly with a single bank or group of banks.
- The other team represents "Bonds." Prepare a two-minute oral presentation arguing that bonds offer the best way for a major corporation to borrow a large sum of money.

► *Cumulative Spreadsheet Project*

This spreadsheet assignment is a continuation of the spreadsheet assignments given in earlier chapters. If you completed those spreadsheets, you have a head start on this one.

1. Handyman wishes to prepare a forecasted balance sheet and income statement for 2007. Use the original financial statement numbers for 2006 [given in part (1) of the Cumulative Spreadsheet Project assignment in Chapter 2] as the basis for the forecast, along with the following additional information:
    a. Sales in 2007 are expected to increase by 40% over 2006 sales of $700.
    b. Cash will increase at the same rate as sales.

(continued)

c. The forecasted amount of accounts receivable in 2007 is determined using the forecasted value for the average collection period. For simplicity, do the computations using the end-of-period accounts receivable balance instead of the average balance. The average collection period for 2007 is expected to be 14.08 days.

d. The forecasted amount of inventory in 2007 is determined using the forecasted value for the number of days' sales in inventory (computed using the end-of-period inventory balance). The number of days' sales in inventory for 2007 is expected to be 107.6 days.

e. The forecasted amount of accounts payable in 2007 is determined using the forecasted value for the number of days' purchases in accounts payable (computed using the end-of-period accounts payable balance). The number of days' purchases in accounts payable for 2007 is expected to be 48.34 days.

f. The $160 in operating expenses reported in 2006 breaks down as follows: $5 depreciation expense, $155 other operating expenses.

g. See item (l) for the assumption concerning the amount of new long-term debt that will be acquired in 2007.

h. No cash dividends will be paid in 2007.

i. New short-term loans payable will be acquired in an amount sufficient to make Handyman's current ratio in 2007 exactly equal to 2.0.

j. The forecasted amount of property, plant, and equipment (PP&E) in 2007 is determined using the forecasted value for the fixed asset turnover ratio. For simplicity, compute the fixed asset turnover ratio using the end-of-period *gross PP&E* balance. The fixed asset turnover ratio for 2007 is expected to be 3.518 times.

k. In computing depreciation expense for 2007, use straight-line depreciation and assume a 30-year useful life with no residual value. Gross PP&E acquired during the year is depreciated for only half the year. In other words, depreciation expense for 2007 is the sum of two parts: (1) a full year of depreciation on the beginning balance in PP&E, assuming a 30-year life and no residual value and (2) a half-year of depreciation on any new PP&E acquired during the year, based on the change in the gross PP&E balance.

Note: These statements were constructed as part of the spreadsheet assignment in Chapter 10; you can use that spreadsheet as a starting point if you have completed that assignment. *Clearly state any additional assumptions that you make.*

For this exercise, add the following additional assumptions:

l. New long-term debt will be acquired (or repaid) in an amount sufficient to make Handyman's debt ratio (total liabilities divided by total assets) in 2007 exactly equal to 0.80.

m. Assume an interest rate on short-term loans payable of *6.0%* and on long-term debt of *8.0%*. Only a half-year's interest is charged on loans taken out during the year. For example, if short-term loans payable at the end of 2007 are $15 and given that short-term loans payable at the end of 2006 were $10, total short-term interest expense for 2007 would be $0.75 [($10 $\times$ 0.06) + ($5 $\times$ 0.06 $\times$ $\frac{1}{2}$)].

Clearly state any additional assumptions that you make.

2. Repeat (1), with the following changes in assumptions:
   a. The debt ratio in 2007 is exactly equal to 0.70.
   b. The debt ratio in 2007 is exactly equal to 0.90.
3. Prepare a table displaying the forecasted values of long-term debt and paid-in capital in 2007 under each of the following assumptions about the debt ratio: 0.70, 0.80, and 0.90.

The sum of these two items can be viewed as the total amount of long-term financing (both debt and equity) received from outsiders. Comment on why the total of these two items is not the same under each debt ratio assumption.

▶ *Internet Search*

Disney

The history of DISNEY was outlined at the beginning of the chapter. Access Disney's Web site at **http://www.disney.com**. Sometimes Web addresses change, so if this Disney address doesn't work, access the Web site for this textbook (**http://albrecht.swlearning.com**) for an updated link to Disney.

Once you've gained access to Disney's Web site, answer the following questions:

1. Disney's home page offers a link to a site promoting Disney's current movies. What movie is currently featured at that site?
2. Use Disney's link to its international operations in France to see if you can find the Web site for Disneyland Paris. What is the Web address? Is the site in English or in French?
3. If you wish to enroll in Disney's direct stock purchase plan, meaning that you will buy ownership shares from Disney itself rather than going through a stockbroker, what is the minimum amount you must invest?
4. According to Disney's most recent statement of cash flows, how much new borrowing did Disney do in the most recent year? How much was spent to repay loans in the most recent year?

chapter

12

Equity Financing

After studying this chapter, you should be able to:

Learning Objectives

1 Distinguish between debt and equity financing, and describe the advantages and disadvantages of organizing a business as a proprietorship or a partnership.

2 Describe the basic characteristics of a corporation and the nature of common and preferred stock.

3 Account for the issuance and repurchase of common and preferred stock.

4 Understand the factors that affect retained earnings, describe the factors determining whether a company can and should pay cash dividends, and account for cash dividends.

5 Describe the purpose of reporting comprehensive income in the equity section of the balance sheet, and prepare a statement of stockholders' equity.

eXpanded *Material*

6 Account for stock dividends and distinguish them from stock splits.

7 Explain prior-period adjustments and prepare a statement of retained earnings.

In 1882, two young newspaper reporters, Charles Dow and Edward Jones, teamed up to provide the Wall Street financial community with handwritten news bulletins. In 1889, when the staff of DOW JONES & COMPANY had grown to 50, they decided to convert the bulletin service into a daily newspaper. The first issue of *The Wall Street Journal* appeared on July 8, 1889. Clarence Barron, who operated a financial news service in Boston, was the paper's first out-of-town reporter. Barron purchased Dow Jones & Company in 1902 for $130,000, and his heirs still hold majority control of the company today.

In the 1940s, *The Wall Street Journal* began publishing more than just business news, expanding its coverage to include economics, politics, and general news. Today, *The Wall Street Journal* has a paid circulation of 1.89 million and is read by an estimated 4.9 million people every day. Dow Jones also publishes *The Wall Street Journal Europe* and *The Asian Wall Street Journal*, and each day it contributes special business pages to 23 Spanish and Portuguese language newspapers in Latin American countries. *The Wall Street Journal* is also a leader in Web-based news, with more than 679,000 paid subscribers for **http://wsj.com** as of December 31, 2002. This is particularly impressive in that the public is accustomed to getting information for free on the Web.

The Wall Street Journal is the flagship of the company, but the name "Dow Jones" is best known because of the Dow Jones Industrial Average that is cited in the news every day. "The Dow" is widely used to reflect the general health of the U.S. economy. So, what is it? Simply put, the Dow Jones Industrial Average measures the average movement of the stock prices of selected U.S. companies. The very first value of the average was 40.94 on May 26, 1896. Charles Dow computed this value by adding the share prices of 12 important companies chosen by him (GENERAL ELECTRIC was one of them) and then dividing by 12. Thus, the average price per share for these 12 companies was $40.94. Since 1928, the average has included 30 companies selected by the editors of *The Wall Street Journal*. The average is no longer computed by simply averaging share prices, but the underlying concept remains the same. Changes in the companies included in the average are rare. Nevertheless, since 1990, 11 companies have been replaced to reflect the decreasing importance of manufacturing in the U.S. economy. For example, BETHLEHEM STEEL, which had been in "The Dow" since 1928, was replaced in March 1997 by WAL-MART. In 1999, the first two NASDAQ companies were added to "The Dow"—MICROSOFT and INTEL. The 30 companies included in the average as of March 10, 2003, are listed in Exhibit 1. The 30 companies in the average are listed every day in *The Wall Street Journal*, often on page C3.[1]

DOW JONES & COMPANY is an appropriate symbol of capitalism—a corporation that has done business in and around the spiritual heart of capitalistic finance, the New York Stock Exchange, for over one hundred years. With the disintegration of the former Soviet Union and the rapid conversion of China into a "socialist market" economy, it seems that the economic battle of capitalism and communism has been won by capitalism. As the history of many of the companies profiled in earlier chapters (MICROSOFT, SEARS, YAHOO!, GENERAL ELECTRIC) illustrates, the true story of capitalism is not the story of rich "capitalists" exploiting the masses, but rather the story of unknown individuals using a free market to find outside investor financing that will turn their ideas into reality. Accounting for investor financing is the topic of this chapter.

This is the second chapter on financing activities. In the previous chapter, financing through borrowing (debt) was discussed. Another way organizations raise money to finance operations is from investments by owners. In corporations, those investments take the form of stock purchases. In proprietorships and partnerships, they take the form of capital investments in the business. Exhibit 2 shows the financial statement items that will be covered in this chapter.

1 This description is based on information obtained from Dow Jones & Company History at **http://dowjones.com**; Dow Jones & Company, *International Directory of Company Histories*, vol. 19 (Detroit: St. James Press, 1998), pp. 128–131.

Exhibit 1: The 30 Firms Included in the Dow Jones Industrial Average (as of March 10, 2003)

Altria	General Electric Co.	McDonald's Corp.
Aluminum Co. of America	General Motors Corp.	Merck & Co.
American Express Co.	Hewlett-Packard Co.	Microsoft
AT&T Corp.	Home Depot	Minnesota Mining & Manufacturing Co.
Boeing Co.	Honeywell	Procter & Gamble Co.
Caterpillar, Inc.	Intel	SBC Communications
Citigroup, Inc.	International Business Machines Corp.	United Technologies Corp.
Coca-Cola Co.	International Paper Co.	Wal-Mart Stores, Inc.
DuPont Co.	J. P. Morgan & Co.	Walt Disney Co.
Eastman Kodak Co.	Johnson & Johnson	
ExxonMobil Corp.		

Exhibit 2: Financial Statement Items Covered in This Chapter

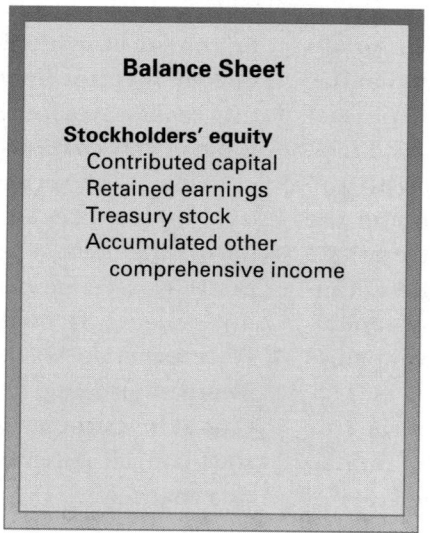

Balance Sheet

Stockholders' equity
Contributed capital
Retained earnings
Treasury stock
Accumulated other
comprehensive income

Statement of Cash Flows

Financing activities
Sale of stock
Purchase of treasury stock
Payments of dividends

Certain basic characteristics are common to all investor financing, no matter what the form of business. The first is that owner investments affect the equity accounts of the business. Second, together with the liabilities, these owners' equity accounts show the sources of the cash that was used to buy the assets. There are three primary ways to bring money into a business: borrowing (debt financing), selling owners' interests (equity financing), and earning profits (also reflected in the equity accounts through the retained earnings account).

In the first part of this chapter, we illustrate the accounting for equity financing in the context of corporations. In the expanded material section of the chapter, we discuss issues relating to stock dividends and prior-period adjustments.

Raising Equity Financing

1 Distinguish between debt and equity financing, and describe the advantages and disadvantages of organizing a business as a proprietorship or a partnership.

Most business owners do not have enough excess personal cash to establish and expand their companies. Therefore, they eventually need to look for money from outsiders, either in the form of loans or as funds contributed by investors. The business issues associated with investor financing are summarized in the time line in Exhibit 3.

The factors affecting the choice between borrowing and seeking additional investment funds are described in this section of the chapter. This section also outlines the advantages and disadvantages of organizing a business as a proprietorship or a partnership. The decision to incorporate and the process that a corporation follows in soliciting investor funds are described in the next section. The bulk of the chapter is devoted to the accounting procedures used to give a proper reporting of stockholders' equity to the investors. Of course, proper financial reporting to current and potential investors is one of the primary reasons for the existence of financial accounting.

Difference between a Loan and an Investment

Imagine that you own a small business and need $40,000 for expansion. What is the difference between borrowing the $40,000 and finding a partner who will invest the $40,000? If you borrow the money, you must guarantee to repay the $40,000 with interest. If you fail to make these payments, the lender can haul you into court and use the power of the law to force repayment. On the other hand, if your company does very well and you generate more than enough cash to repay the $40,000 plus interest, the lender does not get to share in your success. You owe the lender $40,000 plus interest and not a penny more. So, a loan is characterized by a fixed, legal obligation to repay a specified amount, whether the borrowing company performs poorly or performs well.

If you receive $40,000 in investment funds from a new partner, the partner now shares in your company's failures and successes. If business is bad and the investor is never able to recover his or her $40,000 investment—well, that's the way it goes. The law will not help the

Exhibit 3: Time Line of Business Issues Involved with Investor Financing

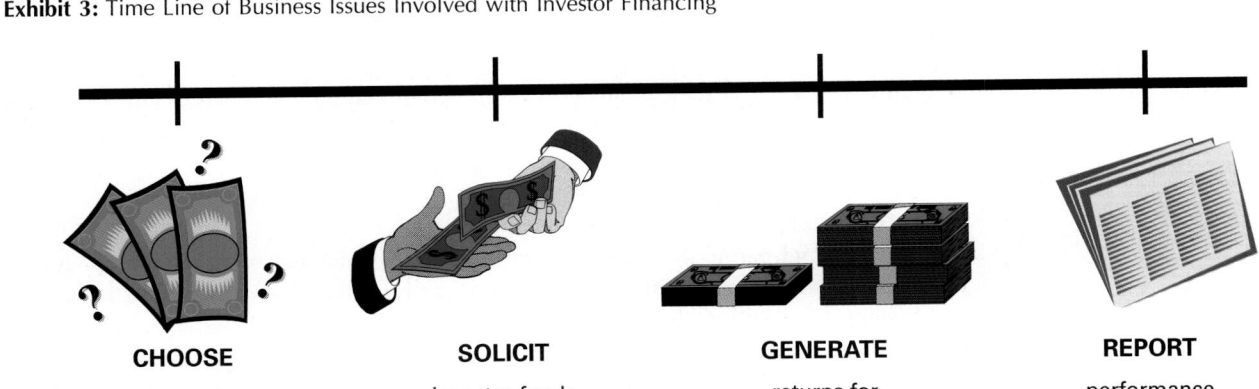

CHOOSE
form of financing

SOLICIT
investor funds

GENERATE
returns for investors

REPORT
performance to current and potential investors

investor recover the investment because the very nature of an investment is that the investor accepts the risk of losing everything. However, in exchange for accepting this risk, the investor also gets to share in the success if the company does well. For example, if you had loaned $40,000 to Bill Gates for MICROSOFT's expansion back in 1986, you would have been repaid the $40,000 plus a little interest. If you had invested that same $40,000 in Microsoft, however, your investment would have grown in value to $14.4 million by May 2003. Thus, an investment is characterized by a higher risk of losing your money, balanced by the chance of sharing in the wealth if the company does well.

Proprietorships and Partnerships

As explained in Chapter 2, a business can be organized as a proprietorship, a partnership, or a corporation. These three types of organization are merely different types of legal contracts that define the rights and responsibilities of the owner or owners of the business. The advantages and disadvantages of proprietorships and partnerships are discussed below. Corporations are discussed in the next section.

proprietorship A business owned by one person.

partnership An association of two or more individuals or organizations to carry on economic activity.

A **proprietorship** is a business owned by one person. A **partnership** is a business owned by two or more persons or entities. In most respects, proprietorships and partnerships are similar to each other but very different from corporations. Both a proprietorship and a partnership are characterized by ease of formation, limited life, and unlimited liability.

Ease of Formation

Proprietorships and partnerships can be formed with few legal formalities. When a person decides to establish a proprietorship, he or she merely acquires the necessary cash, inventory, equipment, and other assets; obtains a business license; and begins providing goods or services to customers. The same is true for a partnership, except that because two or more persons are involved, they must decide together which assets will be acquired and how business will be conducted.

Limited Life

Because proprietorships and partnerships are not legal entities that are separate and distinct from their owners, they are easily terminated. In the case of a proprietorship, the owner can decide to dissolve the business at any time. For a partnership, anything that terminates or changes the contract between the partners legally dissolves the partnership. Among the events that dissolve a partnership are

1. the death or withdrawal of a partner,
2. the bankruptcy of a partner,
3. the admission of a new partner,
4. the retirement of a partner, or
5. the completion of the project for which the partnership was formed.

The occurrence of any of these events does not necessarily mean that a partnership must cease business; rather, the existing partnership is legally terminated, and another partnership must be formed.

Unlimited Liability

Proprietorships and partnerships have unlimited liability, which means that the proprietor or partners are personally responsible for all debts of the business. If a partnership is in poor financial condition, creditors first attempt to satisfy their claims from the assets of the partnership. After those assets are exhausted, creditors may seek payment from the personal assets of the partners. In addition, because partners are responsible for one another's actions (within the scope of the partnership), creditors may seek payment for liabilities created by a departed or bankrupt partner from the personal assets of the remaining partners. This unlimited liability feature is probably the single most significant disadvantage of a proprietorship or partnership.

It can deter a wealthy person from joining a partnership for fear of losing personal assets. (For more information relating to proprietorship and partnership accounting, access this book's Web site at **http://albrecht.swlearning.com**.)

> **TO SUMMARIZE:** A loan is a fixed, legal obligation to repay a specified amount, whether the borrowing company performs poorly or performs well. With an investment, the investor risks losing the investment funds if the company performs poorly but shares in the wealth if the company does well. A proprietorship is a business owned by one person. A partnership is a business owned by two or more persons. Both types of businesses are easy to start and easy to terminate. A major disadvantage of proprietorships and partnerships is the unlimited liability of the owner or partners.

Corporations and Corporate Stock

2 Describe the basic characteristics of a corporation and the nature of common and preferred stock.

corporation A legal entity chartered by a state; ownership is represented by transferable shares of stock.

limited liability The legal protection given stockholders whereby they are responsible for the debts and obligations of a corporation only to the extent of their capital contributions.

Corporations are the dominant form of business enterprise in the United States. Established as separate legal entities, **corporations** are legally distinct from the persons responsible for their creation. In many respects, they are accorded the same rights as individuals; they can conduct business, be sued, enter into contracts, and own property. Firms are incorporated by the state in which they are organized and are subject to that state's laws and requirements.

Characteristics of a Corporation

Corporations have several characteristics that distinguish them from proprietorships and partnerships. These characteristics are discussed below.

Limited Liability

Limited liability means that in the event of corporate bankruptcy, the maximum financial loss any stockholder can sustain is his or her investment in the corporation (unless fraud can be proved). Because a corporation is a separate legal entity and is responsible for its own acts and obligations, creditors usually cannot look beyond the corporation's assets for satisfaction of their claims. This limited liability feature is probably the main reason for the phenomenal growth of the corporate form of business because it protects investors from sustaining losses beyond their investments. In most cases of bankruptcy, however, stockholders will lose most of their investment because the claims of creditors must be satisfied before stockholders receive anything.

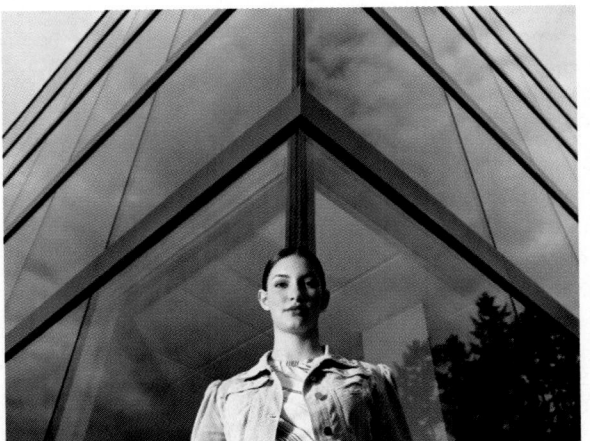

© 2003 Getty Images

Corporations are the dominant form of business in the United States. A corporation is a legal entity, and its ownership is represented by transferable shares of stock.

Easy Transferability of Ownership

Shares of stock in a corporation can be bought, sold, passed from one generation to another, or otherwise transferred without affecting the legal or economic status of the corporation. In other words, most corporations have perpetual existence—the life of the corporation continues by the transfer of shares of stock to new owners.

Ability to Raise Large Amounts of Capital

Raising large amounts of capital can be easier for a corporation than for a proprietorship or a partnership because a corporation can sell shares of its stock. The sale of shares of stock permits many investors, both large and small, to participate in ownership of the business. Some corporations actually have thousands of individual stockholders. In its 2002 annual report, DOW JONES & COMPANY reports that it has 14,571 stockholders of record. Because of this widespread ownership, large corporations are said to be publicly owned.

FYI:

There are some hybrid organizations that have characteristics of both partnerships and corporations. For example, several of the large international accounting firms are organized as limited liability partnerships (LLPs). An LLP offers the advantages of a partnership structure but also provides each partner with limited liability for the costs of lawsuits caused by the actions of his or her partners.

FYI:

An LLC (limited liability company) offers the limited liability legal protection of a corporation as well as the favorable partnership treatment for income tax purposes.

Double Taxation

Because corporations are separate legal entities, they are taxed independently of their owners. This often results in a disadvantage, however, because the portion of corporate profits that is paid out in dividends is taxed twice. First, the profits are taxed to the corporation; second, the owners, or stockholders, are taxed on their dividend income.

Close Government Regulation

Because large corporations may have thousands of stockholders, each with only a small ownership interest, the government has assumed the task of monitoring certain corporate activities. For example, the government requires that all major corporations be audited and that they issue periodic financial statements. As a result, in certain respects, major corporations often enjoy less freedom than do partnerships and proprietorships.

Starting a Corporation

Suppose that you want to start a corporation. First, you should study your state's corporate laws (usually with the aid of an attorney). Then you must apply to the appropriate state official for a charter. Your application will include the intended name of your corporation, its purpose (that is, the type of activity it will engage in), the type and amount of stock you plan to have authorized for your corporation, and, in some cases, the names and addresses of the potential stockholders. Finally, if the state approves your application, you will be issued a "charter" (also called "articles of incorporation"), giving legal status to your corporation.

Of course, one of the purposes of forming a corporation is to then sell stock in the corporation in order to obtain business financing. If the business you intend to establish will operate across state lines and if you intend to seek investment funds from the general public, then you must register your intended stock issue with the Securities and Exchange Commission in Washington, D.C. You are required to provide a **prospectus** to each potential investor; the prospectus outlines your business plan, sources of financing, significant risks, and the like. Finally, you can sell your shares to the public in what is called an "initial public offering" (IPO). You will receive the proceeds from the IPO, minus the commission charged by the investment banker sponsoring the issue.

When an investor buys stock in a corporation, he or she receives a stock certificate as evidence of ownership. For convenience, these stock certificates are frequently held by the stockbroker through whom the investor purchased the shares. The investors in a corporation are called **stockholders**, and they govern the corporation through an elected **board of directors**. In most corporations, the board of directors then chooses a management team to direct the daily affairs of the corporation. In smaller companies, the board of directors is usually made up of members of that management team.

Several types of stock can be authorized by the charter and issued by the corporation. The most familiar types are common stock and preferred stock, and the major difference between them concerns the degree to which their holders are allowed to participate in the rights of ownership of the corporation.

prospectus A report provided to potential investors that represents a company's financial statements and explains its business plan, sources of financing, and significant risks.

stockholders Individuals or organizations that own a portion (shares of stock) of a corporation.

board of directors Individuals elected by the stockholders to govern a corporation.

Common Stock

Certain basic rights are inherent in the ownership of **common stock**. These rights are as follows:

1. The right to vote in corporate matters such as the election of the board of directors or the undertaking of major actions such as the purchase of another company.
2. The preemptive right, which permits existing stockholders to purchase additional shares whenever stock is issued by the corporation. This allows common stockholders to maintain the same percentage of ownership in the company if they choose to do so.

common stock The most frequently issued class of stock; usually, it provides a voting right but is secondary to preferred stock in dividend and liquidation rights.

Investing in the Stock Market

"October," said Mark Twain, "is one of the peculiarly dangerous months to speculate in stocks. Others are July, January, September, April, November, May, March, June, December, August, and February." Despite Mark Twain's warning, stocks have always been one of the most prestigious and desired investments. These days, stock trading is easier than ever. There are scores of Internet stock trading firms that will allow you to buy and sell as many shares as you wish for less than $10 per trade. For some people, Internet stock trading has become the ultimate video game, with shooting lasers and fighting ninjas being replaced by stock price charts and the Federal Reserve Board.

This textbook won't make you an expert in picking promising stocks. In fact, you should be suspicious of any book or investment adviser claiming to have the secrets to deciphering the stock market. Here are some practical guidelines to help you avoid some of the pitfalls when deciding to buy stock:

1. Do not make hasty, emotional decisions about buying and selling stocks.
2. Do not "fall in love" with stocks so that you are no longer objective in appraising them.
3. Remember, you will seldom, if ever, buy stocks at their lowest price and sell them at their highest price.
4. There are stock market "fads," so when you buy at the height of a stock's popularity, you almost always pay too much.
5. Don't invest in stocks unless you can afford to lose the money you invest or at least have no access to it for a long time.
6. Plan to hold your stock investments for a long time. Most stock market millionaires were not speculators, and commissions on frequent sales and purchases will eat up your short-term gains.

Source: W. S. Albrecht, *Money Wise* (Salt Lake City, Utah: Deseret Book Company, 1983), pp. 134–139.

FYI:

Occasionally, a corporation will have more than one class of common stock. For example, Dow Jones & Company has common stock and Class B common stock. Each Class B share gets 10 votes in corporate matters, and most of the Class B shares are owned by the descendants of Clarence Barron.

3. The right to receive cash dividends if they are paid. As explained later, corporations do not have to pay cash dividends, and the amount received by common stockholders is sometimes limited.
4. The right to ownership of all corporate assets once obligations to everyone else have been satisfied. This means that once all loans have been repaid and the claims of the preferred stockholders have been met (as discussed below), all the excess assets belong to the common stockholders.

In essence, the common stockholders of a corporation are the true owners of the business. They delegate their decision-making authority to the board of directors, who in turn delegate authority for day-to-day operations to managers hired for that purpose. Thus, a distinguishing characteristic of business ownership as a common stockholder of a corporation is a clear separation between owning the business and operating the business.

Preferred Stock

preferred stock A class of stock that usually provides dividend and liquidation preferences over common stock.

The term "preferred stock" is somewhat misleading because it gives the impression that **preferred stock** is better than common stock. Preferred stock isn't better; it's different. A good way to think of preferred stock is that preferred stockholders give up some of the ownership rights of the common stockholders in exchange for some of the protection enjoyed by lenders.

In most cases, preferred stockholders are not allowed to vote for the corporate board of directors. In addition, preferred stockholders are usually allowed to receive only a fixed cash dividend, meaning that if the company does well, preferred stockholders do not get to share in the success. In exchange for these limitations, in the event that the corporation is liquidated,

convertible preferred stock Preferred stock that can be converted to common stock at a specified conversion rate.

preferred stockholders are entitled to receive their cash dividends and have their claims fully paid before any cash is paid to common stockholders.

Preferred stock may also include other types of privileges, the most common of which is convertibility. **Convertible preferred stock** is preferred stock that can be converted to common stock at a specified conversion rate. For example, in the notes to MICROSOFT's 1999 financial statements, Microsoft detailed the terms of 12.5 million shares of Microsoft convertible preferred stock that was sold in December 1996. Holders of those shares of preferred stock were able to exchange them for Microsoft common stock beginning in December 1999. On December 15, 1999, each preferred share was converted in 1.1273 common shares. Convertible preferred stock can be very appealing to investors. They can enjoy the dividend privileges of the preferred stock while having the option to convert to common stock if the market value of the common stock increases significantly. By issuing shares of stock with varying rights and privileges, companies can appeal to a wider range of investors.

> **TO SUMMARIZE:** A corporation is a business entity that has a legal existence separate from that of its owners; it can conduct business, own property, and enter into contracts. The five major features of a corporation are (1) limited liability for stockholders, (2) easy transferability of ownership, (3) the ability to raise large amounts of capital, (4) separate taxation, and (5) for large corporations, closer regulation by government. Common stock confers four basic rights upon its owners: (1) the right to vote in corporate matters, (2) the right to maintain proportionate ownership, (3) the right to receive cash dividends, and (4) the ownership of all excess corporate assets upon liquidation of the corporation. Preferred stock typically carries preferential claims to dividend and liquidation privileges but has no voting rights.

Accounting for Stock

3 Account for the issuance and repurchase of common and preferred stock.

In this section we focus on the accounting for the issuance of stock as well as the accounting for stock repurchases.

Issuance of Stock

par value A nominal value assigned to and printed on the face of each share of a corporation's stock.

Each share of common stock usually has a **par value** printed on the face of the stock certificate. For example, the common stock of DOW JONES & COMPANY has a $1 par value. This par value has little to do with the market value of the shares. In May 2003, each Dow Jones common share with a $1 par value was selling for about $42 per share. When par-value stock sells for a price above par, it is said to sell at a premium. In most states it is illegal to issue stock for a price below par value. If stock were issued at a discount (below par), stockholders could later be held liable to make up the difference between their investment and the par value of the shares they purchased. The par value multiplied by the total number of shares outstanding is usually equal to a company's "legal capital," and it represents the amount of the invested funds that cannot be returned to the investors as long as the corporation is in existence. This legal capital requirement was originally intended to protect a company's creditors; without it, excessive dividends could be paid, leaving nothing for creditors. The par value really was of more importance a hundred years ago and is something of a historical oddity today. These days, most states allow the sale of no-par stock.

FYI:

Most companies establish a very low par value, such as $0.10 or $1.00 per share. In fact, in 2001, 38% of the publicly-traded companies in the United States had par values of exactly $0.01.

When par-value stock is issued by a corporation, usually Cash is debited, and the appropriate stockholders' equity accounts are credited. For par-value common stock, the equity accounts credited are Common Stock, for an amount equal to the par value, and Paid-In Capital in Excess of Par, Common Stock, for the premium on the common stock.

To illustrate, we will assume that the Boston Lakers Basketball Team (a corporation) issued 1,000 shares of $1 par-value common stock for $50 per share. The entry to record the stock issuance is:

Cash (1,000 shares × $50)	50,000	
Common Stock (1,000 shares × $1 par value)		1,000
Paid-In Capital in Excess of Par,		
Common Stock (1,000 shares × $49)		49,000
Issued 1,000 shares of $1 par-value common stock at		
$50 per share.		

A similar entry would be made if the stock being issued were preferred stock. The total par value of the common and preferred stock, along with the associated amounts of paid-in capital in excess of par, constitutes a corporation's **contributed capital**.

This illustration points out two important elements in accounting for the issuance of stock: (1) the equity accounts identify the type of stock being issued (common or preferred), and (2) the proceeds from the sale of the stock are divided into the portion attributable to its par value and the portion paid in excess of par value. These distinctions are important because the owners' equity section of the balance sheet should correctly identify the specific sources of capital so that the respective rights of the various stockholders can be known.

If the stock being issued has no par value, only one credit is included in the entry. To illustrate, assume that the Lakers' stock does not have a par value and that the corporation issued 1,000 shares for $50 per share. The entry to record this stock issuance would be:

Cash	50,000	
Common Stock		50,000
Issued 1,000 shares of no-par stock at		
$50 per share.		

Although stock is usually issued for cash, other considerations may be involved. To illustrate the kinds of entries made when stock is issued for noncash considerations, we will assume that a prospective stockholder exchanged a piece of land for 5,000 shares of the Boston Lakers' $1 par-value common stock. Assuming the market value of the stock at the date of the exchange was $40 per share, the entry is:

Land (5,000 shares × $40)	200,000	
Common Stock (5,000 shares × $1)		5,000
Paid-In Capital in Excess of Par,		
Common Stock (5,000 shares × $39)		195,000
Issued 5,000 shares of $1 par-value common stock for land		
(5,000 shares × $40 per share = $200,000).		

When noncash considerations are received in payment for stock, the assets or services received should be recorded at the current market value of the stock issued. If the market value of the stock cannot be determined, the market value of the assets or services received should be used as the basis for recording the transaction.

contributed capital The portion of owners' equity contributed by investors (the owners) in exchange for shares of stock.

net*work* exercises

Buying Stock

Do you want to try your hand at buying some shares of stock? Go to **http://ameritrade.com**, the Web site for one of the leading Internet stock trading companies.

Net Work:

How much is the commission for executing one stock trade?

Accounting for Stock Repurchases

treasury stock Issued stock that has subsequently been reacquired by the corporation.

Sometimes, when a company has excess cash or needs some of its shares of stock back from investors, it may purchase some of its own outstanding stock. This repurchased stock is called **treasury stock** by accountants. There are many reasons for a firm to buy its own stock. Five of the most common are that management:

1. wants the stock for a profit-sharing, bonus, or stock-option plan for employees,
2. feels that the stock is selling for an unusually low price and is a good buy,
3. wants to stimulate trading in the company's stock,
4. wants to remove some shares from the market in order to avoid a hostile takeover, or
5. wants to increase reported earnings per share by reducing the number of shares of stock outstanding.

Many successful U.S. companies have ongoing stock repurchase plans. For example, MICROSOFT disclosed in its 2002 Form 10-K (Appendix A) that it spent $6.069 billion in 2002 to repurchase 122.8 million of its own shares. COCA-COLA spent $1.101 billion in the years 2000–2002 repurchasing its own shares. The most aggressive stock buyback program is GENERAL ELECTRIC's—a number of years ago GE announced its intention to buy back its own shares. In December 2001, GE's board of directors authorized an increase in the amount of share repurchases to $30 billion. As of the end of 2002, GE had spent a cumulative total of $26.6 billion on stock repurchases.

When a firm purchases stock of another company, the investment is included as an asset on the balance sheet. However, a corporation cannot own part of itself, so treasury stock is not considered an asset. Instead, it is a contra-equity account and is included on the balance sheet as a deduction from stockholders' equity. Think of it this way: when a corporation issues shares, its equity is increased; when the corporation buys those shares back, its equity is reduced. The reporting of treasury stock is illustrated in the stockholders' equity section of the balance sheet for General Electric in Exhibit 4.

STOP & THINK

For General Electric, the total amount invested by stockholders is $17,957 million, which is the sum of common stock at par ($669 million) and paid-in capital in excess of par (other capital of $17,288 million). And yet GE has spent $26,627 million buying back shares from stockholders. How is this possible?

Notice that the $26.627 billion spent by General Electric to buy back its own shares as of December 31, 2002, is shown as a subtraction from total share owners' equity. By the way, the "other capital" included in GE's equity section is primarily composed of paid-in capital in excess of par. Also, the "accumulated nonowner changes other than earnings" item is quite interesting and controversial, as will be explained in a later section.

Treasury stock is usually accounted for on a cost basis; that is, the stock is debited at its cost (market value) on the date of repurchase. To illustrate, we

Exhibit 4: Share Owners' Equity for General Electric

General Electric Company December 31, 2002 and 2001 Share Owners' Equity (in millions of U.S. dollars)		
	2002	**2001**
Common stock	$ 669	$ 669
Accumulated nonowner changes other than earnings	(3,177)	(4,323)
Other capital	17,288	16,693
Retained earnings	75,553	68,701
Less common stock held in treasury	(26,627)	(26,926)
Total share owners' equity	$ 63,706	$ 54,814

assume that 100 shares of the $1 par-value common stock were reacquired by the Boston Lakers for $60 per share. The entry to record the repurchase is:

Treasury Stock, Common	6,000	
Cash (100 shares × $60)		6,000
Purchased 100 shares of treasury stock at $60 per share.		

FYI:

An alternative way to account for stock repurchases is called the par-value method. This method, though not used as frequently as the cost method illustrated in this section, is the method of choice for a number of large U.S. companies including Microsoft, INTEL, and WAL-MART. The par-value method of accounting for stock repurchases is covered in intermediate accounting courses.

The effect of this entry is to reduce both total assets (Cash) and total stockholders' equity by $6,000.

When treasury stock is reissued, the treasury stock account must be credited for the original amount paid to reacquire the stock. If the treasury stock's reissuance price is greater than its cost, an additional credit must be made to an account called Paid-In Capital, Treasury Stock. Together, these credits show the net increase in total stockholders' equity. At the same time, the cash account is increased by the total amount received upon reissuance of the treasury stock.

To illustrate, we assume that 40 of the 100 shares of the treasury stock that were originally purchased for $60 per share are reissued at $80 per share. The entry to record that reissuance is:

Cash (40 shares × $80)	3,200	
Treasury Stock, Common (40 shares × $60 cost)		2,400
Paid-In Capital, Treasury Stock [40 × ($80 − $60)]		800
Reissued 40 shares of treasury stock at $80 per share.		

Caution

Do not credit a gain when treasury stock is reissued at a price greater than its cost. Gains are associated with a company's operations, not with a company buying and selling its own shares.

The company now has a balance of $3,600 in the treasury stock account (60 shares at $60 per share).

Sometimes the reissuance price of treasury stock is less than its cost. As before, the entry involves a debit to Cash for the amount received and a credit to Treasury Stock for the cost of the stock. However, because an amount less than the repurchase cost has been received, an additional debit is required. The debit is to Paid-In Capital, Treasury Stock if there is a balance in that account from previous transactions, or to Retained Earnings if there is no balance in the paid-in capital, treasury stock account.

To illustrate, we will consider two more treasury stock transactions. First, we assume that another 30 shares of treasury stock are reissued for $40 per share, $20 less than their cost. Because Paid-In Capital, Treasury Stock has a balance of $800, the entry to record this transaction is:

Cash (30 shares × $40)	1,200	
Paid-In Capital, Treasury Stock	600	
Treasury Stock, Common (30 shares × $60 cost)		1,800
Reissued 30 shares of treasury stock at $40 per share;		
original cost was $60 per share.		

Note that after this transaction is recorded, the balance in Paid-In Capital, Treasury Stock is $200 ($800 − $600).

Next, we assume that the company reissues 20 additional shares at $45 per share. The entry to record this transaction is:

Cash (20 shares × $45)	900	
Paid-In Capital, Treasury Stock	200	
Retained Earnings	100	
Treasury Stock (20 shares × $60 cost)		1,200
Reissued 20 shares of treasury stock at $45 per share;		
original cost was $60 per share.		

In this transaction, the selling price was $300 less than the cost of the treasury stock. Because the paid-in capital, treasury stock account had a balance of only $200, Retained Earnings was debited for the remaining $100.

Balance Sheet Presentation

We have discussed the ways in which stock transactions affect owners' equity accounts. We will now show how these accounts are summarized and presented on the balance sheet. The following data, with the addition of the preferred stock information in (1), summarize the stock transactions of the Boston Lakers shown earlier:

1. $40 par-value preferred stock: issued 1,000 shares at $45 per share.
2. $1 par-value common stock: issued 1,000 shares at $50 per share.
3. $1 par-value common stock: issued 5,000 shares for land with a fair market value of $200,000.
4. Treasury stock, common: purchased 100 shares at $60; reissued 40 shares at $80; reissued 30 shares at $40; reissued 20 shares at $45.

With these data, and assuming a Retained Earnings balance of $100,000, the stockholders' equity section would be as shown in Exhibit 5.

Exhibit 5: Stockholders' Equity for Boston Lakers

Boston Lakers Basketball Team **Stockholders' Equity**	
Preferred stock ($40 par value, 1,000 shares issued and outstanding)	$ 40,000
Common stock ($1 par value, 6,000 shares issued, 5,990 shares outstanding)*	6,000
Paid-in capital in excess of par, preferred stock	5,000
Paid-in capital in excess of par, common stock	244,000
Total contributed capital	$295,000
Retained earnings (to be discussed)	100,000
Total contributed capital and retained earnings	$395,000
Less treasury stock (10 shares of $1 par common at cost of $60 per share)	(600)
Total stockholders' equity	$394,400

*Treasury shares are described as being issued but not outstanding. Thus, 6,000 common shares have been issued, but only 5,990 are outstanding because 10 are held by the Boston Lakers as treasury shares.

TO SUMMARIZE: When a company issues stock, it debits Cash or a noncash account (Property, for example) and credits various stockholders' equity accounts. Shares typically are assigned a par value, which is usually small in relation to the market value of the shares. Amounts received upon issuance of shares are divided into par value and paid-in capital in excess of par. A company's own stock that is repurchased is known as treasury stock and is included in the financial statements as a contra-stockholders' equity account. Treasury stock is usually accounted for on a cost basis. The stockholders' equity section of a balance sheet contains separate accounts for each type of stock issued, amounts paid in excess of par values, treasury stock, and retained earnings.

Retained Earnings

4 Understand the factors that affect retained earnings, describe the factors determining whether a company can and should pay cash dividends, and account for cash dividends.

retained earnings The portion of a corporation's owners' equity that has been earned from profitable operations and not distributed to stockholders.

Common stockholders can invest money in a corporation in two ways. First, as described in the previous section, common stockholders can buy shares of stock. Second, when the corporation makes money, the common stockholders can allow the corporation to keep those earnings to be reinvested in the business. **Retained earnings** is the name given to the aggregate amount of corporate earnings that have been reinvested in the business. The retained earnings balance is increased each year by net income and decreased by losses, dividends, and some treasury stock transactions (as illustrated earlier).

Remember, retained earnings is not the same as cash. In fact, a company can have a large Retained Earnings balance and be without cash, or it can have a lot of cash and a very small Retained Earnings balance. For example, on December 31, 2002, DOW JONES & COMPANY had a Cash balance of $39 million but a Retained Earnings balance of $733 million. Although both Cash and Retained Earnings are usually increased when a company has earnings, they typically are increased by different amounts. This occurs for two reasons: (1) the company's net income, which increases Retained Earnings, is accrual-based, not cash-based; and (2) cash from earnings may be invested in productive assets such as inventories, used to pay off loans, or spent in any number of ways, many of which do not affect net income or retained earnings. In summary, cash is an asset; retained earnings is one source of financing (along with borrowing and direct stockholder investment) that a corporation can use to get funds to acquire assets.

dividends Distributions to the owners (stockholders) of a corporation.

cash dividend A cash distribution of earnings to stockholders.

Cash Dividends

If you had your own business and wanted to withdraw money for personal use, you would simply withdraw it from the company's checking account or cash register. In a corporation, a formal action by the board of directors is required before money can be distributed to the owners. In addition, such payments must be made on a pro rata basis. That is, each owner must receive a proportionate amount on the basis of ownership percentage. These pro rata distributions to owners are called **dividends**. When paid in the form of cash, they are called **cash dividends**. The amount of dividends an individual stockholder receives depends on the number of shares owned and on the per-share amount of the dividend.

Should a Company Pay Cash Dividends?

Note that a company does not have to pay cash dividends. Theoretically, a company that does not pay dividends should be able to reinvest its earnings in assets that will enable it to grow more rapidly than its dividend-paying competitors. This added growth will presumably be reflected in increases in the per-share price of the stock. In practice, most public companies pay regular cash dividends, but some well-known companies do not. For example, BERKSHIRE HATHAWAY has never paid cash dividends to its common stockholders.

FYI:

Fortune magazine maintains a list of the top 50 e-companies, called the Fortune e-50. A random sample of 10 of these companies indicated that only one of the 10 paid cash dividends to common stockholders in 1999. Thus, we see that high-tech, high-growth companies are not likely to pay cash dividends. By the way, the only one of the sampled e-50 companies to pay cash dividends to common stockholders was IBM, not exactly a young start-up.

So, should a corporation pay cash dividends or not? Well, the surprising answer is that no one knows the answer to that question. Ask your finance professor what he or she thinks. Although no one knows the theoretically best dividend policy, three general observations can be made:

- Stable companies pay out a large portion of their income as cash dividends.
- Growing companies (such as MICROSOFT) pay out a small portion of their income as cash dividends. They keep the funds inside the company for expansion.
- Companies are very cautious about raising dividends to a new level because once investors come to expect a certain level of dividends, they see it as very bad news if the company reduces the dividends back to the old level.

STOP & THINK

If you were a MICROSOFT shareholder, would you want to receive a high level of cash dividends, or would you prefer that Bill Gates use your share of the profits for business expansion?

Although cash dividends are the most common type of dividend, corporations can distribute other types of dividends as well. A stock dividend is a distribution of additional shares of stock to stockholders. Stock dividends will be discussed in the expanded material section of this chapter. A property dividend is a distribution of corporate assets (for example, the stock of another firm) to stockholders. Property dividends are quite rare. In this section, only the accounting for cash dividends will be discussed.

Accounting for Cash Dividends

Three important dates are associated with dividends: (1) declaration date, (2) date of record, and (3) payment date. The first is when the board of directors formally declares its intent to pay a dividend. On this **declaration date**, the company becomes legally obligated to pay the dividend. Assuming that the board of directors votes on December 15, 2006, to declare an $8,000 dividend, this liability may be recorded as follows:

declaration date The date on which a corporation's board of directors formally decides to pay a dividend to stockholders.

Dividends	8,000	
Dividends Payable		8,000
Declared dividend on December 15, 2006.		

At the end of the year, the dividends account is closed to Retained Earnings by the following entry:

Retained Earnings	8,000	
Dividends		8,000
To close Dividends to Retained Earnings.		

From this entry, you can see that a declaration of dividends reduces Retained Earnings and, eventually, the amount of cash on hand. Thus, though not considered to be an expense, dividends do reduce the amount a company could otherwise invest in productive assets.

Alternatively, a declaration of dividends can be recorded by debiting Retained Earnings directly. However, using the dividends account instead of Retained Earnings allows a company to keep separate records of dividends paid to preferred and common stockholders. Whichever method is used, the end result is the same: a decrease in Retained Earnings.

The second important dividend date is the **date of record**. Falling somewhere between the declaration date and the payment date, this is the date selected by the board of directors on which the stockholders of record are identified as those who will receive dividends. Because many corporate stocks are in flux—being bought and sold daily—it is important that the stockholders who will receive the dividends be identified. No journal entry is required on the date of record; the date of record is simply noted in the minutes of the directors' meeting and in a letter to stockholders.

date of record The date selected by a corporation's board of directors on which the stockholders of record are identified as those who will receive dividends.

dividend payment date The date on which a corporation pays dividends to its stockholders.

As you might expect, the third important date is the **dividend payment date**. This is the date on which, by order of the board of directors, dividends will be paid. The entry to record a dividend payment would typically be:

Dividends Payable	8,000	
Cash		8,000
Paid dividends declared on December 15, 2006.		

The following press release, made by FORD MOTOR COMPANY on April 9, 2003 (declaration date), identifies both the date of record and the dividend payment date:

> The Board of Directors of Ford Motor Company (NYSE: F) today declared a second quarter dividend of 10 cents per share, on the company's Class B and common stock. This is the same level of dividend paid in the first quarter of 2003. The second quarter dividend is payable on June 2, 2003 to shareholders of record on May 2, 2003.

As mentioned earlier, once a dividend-paying pattern has been established, the expectation of dividends is built into the per-share price of the stock. A reduction in the dividend usually produces a sharp drop in the price. Similarly, an increased dividend usually triggers an increase in the stock price. Dividend increases are usually considered to set a precedent, indicating that future dividends will be at this per-share amount or more. With this in mind, boards of directors are careful about increasing or decreasing dividends.

Dividend Preferences

When cash dividends are declared by a corporation that has both common and preferred stock outstanding, how the dividends are allocated to the two classes of investors depends on the rights of the preferred stockholders. These rights are identified when the stock is approved by the state. Two "dividend preferences," as they are called, are (1) current-dividend preference and (2) cumulative-dividend preference.

current-dividend preference The right of preferred stockholders to receive current dividends before common stockholders receive dividends.

Current-Dividend Preference. Preferred stock has a dividend percentage associated with it and is typically described as follows: "5% preferred, $40 par-value stock, 1,000 shares outstanding." The first figure—"5%" in this example—is a percentage of the par value and can be any amount, depending on the particular stock. So, $2 per share (0.05 × $40 par) is the amount that will be paid in dividends to preferred stockholders each year that dividends are declared. The fact that preferred stock dividends are fixed at a specific percentage of their par value makes them somewhat similar to the interest paid to bondholders. The **current-dividend preference** requires that when dividends are paid, this percentage of the preferred stock's par value be paid to preferred stockholders before common stockholders receive any dividends.

To illustrate the payment of different types of dividends, the following data from the Boston Lakers Basketball Team will be used throughout this section. (The various combinations of dividend preferences illustrated over the next few pages are summarized in Cases 1 to 4 in Exhibit 6.) As a reminder, the outstanding stock includes:

- Preferred stock: 5%, $40 par value, 1,000 shares issued and outstanding.
- Common stock: $1 par value, 6,000 shares issued, 5,990 shares outstanding.

To begin, note that, as with all preferred stock, the Lakers' 5% preferred stock has a current-dividend preference: Before any dividends can be paid to common stockholders, preferred stockholders must be paid a total of $2,000 ($40 × 0.05 × 1,000 shares). Thus, if only $1,500 of dividends are declared (Case 1), preferred stockholders will receive the entire dividend payment. If $3,000 are declared (Case 2), preferred stockholders will receive $2,000 and common stockholders, $1,000.

cumulative-dividend preference The right of preferred stockholders to receive current dividends plus all dividends in arrears before common stockholders receive any dividends.

dividends in arrears Missed dividends for past years that preferred stockholders have a right to receive under the cumulative-dividend preference if and when dividends are declared.

Cumulative-Dividend Preference.   The **cumulative-dividend preference** can be quite costly for common stockholders because it requires that preferred stockholders be paid current dividends plus all unpaid dividends from past years before common stockholders receive anything. If dividends have been paid in all previous years, then only the current 5% must be paid to preferred stockholders. But if dividends on preferred stock were not paid in full in prior years, the cumulative deficiency must be paid before common stockholders receive anything.

With respect to the cumulative feature, it is important to repeat that companies are not required to pay dividends. Any past unpaid dividends are called **dividends in arrears**. Because they do not have to be paid unless dividends are declared in the future, dividends in arrears do not represent actual liabilities and thus are not recorded in the accounts. Instead, they are reported in the notes to the financial statements.

To illustrate the distribution of dividends for cumulative preferred stock, we will assume that the Boston Lakers Basketball Team has not paid any dividends for the last two years but has declared a dividend in the current year. The Lakers must pay $6,000 in dividends to preferred stockholders before they can give anything to the common stockholders. The calculation is as follows:

Dividends in arrears, 2 years	$4,000
Current-dividend preference	
($40 × 0.05 × 1,000 shares)	2,000
Total	$6,000

Therefore, if the Lakers pay only $5,000 in dividends (Case 3), preferred stockholders will receive all the dividends, common stockholders will receive nothing, and there will still be dividends in arrears of $1,000 the next year. If $11,000 in dividends are paid (Case 4), preferred stockholders will receive $6,000, and common stockholders will receive $5,000.

The entries to record the declaration and payment of dividends in Case 4 are:

Date of Declaration		
Dividends, Preferred Stock	6,000	
Dividends, Common Stock	5,000	
Dividends Payable		11,000
Declared dividends on preferred and common stock.		

Date of Payment		
Dividends Payable	11,000	
Cash		11,000
Paid dividends on preferred and common stock.		

Exhibit 6: Dividend Preferences: Summary of Cases 1 to 4

Case	Preferred Dividend Feature	Years in Arrears	Total Dividend	Preferred Dividend	Common Dividend
1	5%, Noncumulative	Not applicable	$ 1,500	$1,500	$ 0
2	5%, Noncumulative	Not applicable	3,000	2,000	1,000
3	5%, Cumulative	2	5,000	5,000	0
4	5%, Cumulative	2	11,000	6,000	5,000

Constraints on Payment of Cash Dividends

Earlier in this section, the question was asked whether a company should pay cash dividends. A related question is: Can the company legally pay cash dividends? To illustrate, consider the following exaggerated scenario. Tricky Company obtains a corporate charter, borrows $1 million from Naïve Bank, pays out a $1 million cash dividend to the stockholders, and all the stockholders disappear to the Bahamas. Is this a legal possibility? No, it isn't, because the corporate right to declare cash dividends is regulated by state law in order to protect creditors. The right to declare cash dividends is often linked to a company's Retained Earnings balance.

In many states, a company is not allowed to pay cash dividends in an amount that would cause the retained earnings balance to be negative. Thus, if the retained earnings balance of the Boston Lakers were $8,500, the $11,000 dividend in Case 4 discussed previously could not be paid, even if the Lakers had the available cash to make the payment. The incorporation laws in many states are less restrictive and allow the payment of cash dividends in excess of the retained earnings balance if, for example, current earnings are strong or the market value of the assets is high.

Frequently, lenders do not rely on state incorporation laws to protect them from excess cash dividend payments by corporations to which they lend money. Instead, the loan contract itself includes restrictions on the payment of cash dividends during the period that the loan is outstanding. In this way, lenders are able to prevent cash that should be used to repay loans from being paid to stockholders as dividends.

Dividend Payout Ratio

dividend payout ratio A measure of the percentage of earnings paid out in dividends; computed by dividing cash dividends by net income.

A ratio of interest to stockholders is the **dividend payout ratio**. This ratio indicates the percentage of net income paid out during the year in the form of cash dividends and is computed as follows:

$$\text{Dividend payout ratio} = \frac{\text{Cash dividends}}{\text{Net income}}$$

Dividend payout ratio values for Dow Jones, Microsoft, and GENERAL ELECTRIC for 2002 are computed below. The numbers are in millions.

	Dow Jones	**Microsoft**	**General Electric**
Cash dividends	$83.65	$0.00	$7,157.00
Net income	$201.51	$9,421.00	$14,118.00
Dividend payout ratio	41.51%	0.00%	50.69%

Both Dow Jones and General Electric pay out approximately 40 to 50% of their annual income as dividends, a normal level for large U.S. corporations. Microsoft's low dividend payout ratio is indicative of a rapidly expanding company. However, things appear to be changing a little for Microsoft. In the latter part of 2002, Microsoft announced it would pay its first ever dividend on common stock.

TO SUMMARIZE: The retained earnings account reflects the total undistributed earnings of a business since incorporation. It is increased by net income and decreased by dividends, net losses, and some treasury stock transactions. The important dates associated with a cash dividend are the date of declaration, the date of record, and the payment date. Preferred stockholders can be granted a current and a cumulative preference for dividends over the rights of common stockholders. In some states, the payment of cash dividends is limited to an amount not to exceed the existing Retained Earnings balance. The dividend payout ratio (cash dividends divided by net income) reveals the percentage of net income that is paid out as cash dividends.

Other Equity Items

5 Describe the purpose of reporting comprehensive income in the equity section of the balance sheet, and prepare a statement of stockholders' equity.

In addition to the two major categories of contributed capital and retained earnings, the equity section of a balance sheet often includes a number of miscellaneous items. These items are gains or losses that bypass the income statement when they are recognized. A further discussion of these items is given below.

Equity Items That Bypass the Income Statement

Since 1980, the equity sections of U.S. balance sheets have begun to fill up with a strange collection of items, each the subject of an accounting controversy. Two of these items are summarized below.

- *Foreign currency translation adjustment.* The foreign currency translation adjustment arises from the change in the equity of foreign subsidiaries (as measured in terms of U.S. dollars) that occurs as a result of changes in foreign currency exchange rates. For example, if the Japanese yen weakens relative to the U.S. dollar, the equity of Japanese subsidiaries of U.S. firms will decrease, in dollar terms. Before 1981, these changes were recognized as losses or gains on the income statement. Multinational firms disliked this treatment because it added volatility to reported earnings. The FASB changed the accounting rule, and now these changes are reported as direct adjustments to equity on the balance sheet, insulating the income statement from this aspect of foreign currency fluctuations.

- *Unrealized gains and losses on available-for-sale securities.* As will be explained in Chapter 13, available-for-sale securities are securities that a company purchased without intending to resell them immediately but also not necessarily planning to hold them forever. When the FASB was considering requiring securities to be reported at their market values on the balance sheet, companies complained about the income volatility that would be caused by recognizing these changes as gains or losses on the income statement. The FASB made the standard more acceptable to businesses by allowing unrealized gains and losses on available-for-sale securities to bypass the income statement and go straight to the equity section of the balance sheet.

The hodgepodge of direct equity adjustments described above is conceptually unsatisfying. These adjustments have arisen on a case-by-case basis as part of the FASB's effort to establish accounting standards that are accepted by the business community. As mentioned, many businesspeople are opposed to including these categories on the income statement because, they say, the income statement would become cluttered with gains and losses from market value changes, distracting from the purpose of the income statement, which is to focus on reporting profits from the activities of the business. The compromise that allows market values in the balance sheet while keeping the income statement uncluttered is the creation of a separate category of equity called **accumulated other comprehensive income**. Accumulated other comprehensive income is composed of certain market-related gains and losses that are not included in the computation of net income. It is important to remember that accumulated other comprehensive income is not income at all, but an equity category that summarizes the changes in equity that result during the period from market-related increases and decreases in the reported values of assets and liabilities. The reporting of accumulated other comprehensive income equity is illustrated in the 2002 equity section of DOW JONES & COMPANY, shown in Exhibit 7.

A **statement of comprehensive income** provides a place, outside the regular income statement, for reporting all the unrealized gains and losses that are reported as equity adjustments. The appeal of comprehensive income is that this approach preserves the traditional income statement (calming the fears of the business community) but allows unrealized gains and losses to be reported. In essence, comprehensive income makes it possible to recognize unrealized gains and losses so that current market values can be reported on the balance sheet without having those unrealized gains and losses affect the income statement.

accumulated other comprehensive income Certain market-related gains and losses that are not included in the computation of net income; for example, foreign currency translation adjustments and unrealized gains or losses on investments.

statement of comprehensive income A statement outlining the changes in accumulated comprehensive income that arose during the period.

Exhibit 7: Equity Section for Dow Jones & Company

Dow Jones & Company's Equity Section (amounts in million of dollars)		
	2002	**2001**
Common stock, par value $1.00 per share	$ 81,405	$ 81,287
Class B common stock, convertible, par value $1.00 per share . .	20,776	20,894
	$102,181	$102,181
Additional paid-in capital	120,645	127,846
Retained earnings	732,720	614,863
Accumulated other comprehensive income:		
Unrealized gain on investments	1,565	1,128
Unrealized gain on hedging	2,059	
Foreign currency translation adjustment	266	(2,427)
Minimum pension liability, net of deferred taxes	(9,979)	
	$949,457	$843,591
Less, treasury stock	918,886	801,814
Total stockholders' equity	$ 30,571	$ 41,777

STOP & THINK

Which will have a greater impact on a company's stock price: net income of $100 million or a $100 million unrealized gain from a change in exchange rates or securities prices? Explain your answer.

The statement of comprehensive income is very new; U.S. companies have been required to present it starting December 31, 1998. Dow Jones & Company's comprehensive income presentation for 2002 is shown in Exhibit 8. Note that net income is one component in the computation of comprehensive income. For Dow Jones, 2000 was a particularly bad year, with three of the four reported elements of comprehensive income being negative.

Statement of Stockholders' Equity

statement of stockholders' equity A financial statement that reports all changes in stockholders' equity.

Companies that have numerous changes in their stockholders' equity accounts during the year usually include a **statement of stockholders' equity** (also called a statement of changes in stockholders' equity) with their financial statements. This statement reconciles the beginning and ending balances for all stockholders' equity accounts reported on the balance sheet.

An illustrative statement of stockholders' equity from the 2002 annual report of Dow Jones & Company is presented in Exhibit 9. Note the following items in the statement:

• As mentioned earlier in the chapter, Dow Jones has two classes of common stock. Class B common shares with a par value of $118,000 were converted into ordinary common shares during the year.

Exhibit 8: Statement of Comprehensive Income for Dow Jones & Company

(in thousands)	**2002**	**2001**	**2000**
Net income (loss)	$201,506	$ 98,220	$(118,962)
Unrealized gain (loss) on investments	437	(118)	(4,019)
Unrealized gain (loss) on hedging	2,059	0	2,360
Foreign currency translation adjustments	2,693	(472)	(698)
Minimum pension liability	(9,979)	3,846	0
Comprehensive income (loss)	$196,716	$101,476	$(121,319)

- Dow Jones paid a dividend during the year of $83.649 million.
- The company purchased $143 million of its own shares during the year.

The last column in the statement reflects the total beginning and ending stockholders' equity account balances and all increases and decreases. Both the individual account balances and total Stockholders' Equity at December 31, 2002, are reported on the balance sheet of Dow Jones & Company.

Exhibit 9: Statement of Stockholders' Equity for Dow Jones & Company

Consolidated Statement of Stockholders' Equity
Dow Jones & Company, Inc.
For the Year Ended December 31, 2002
(amounts in thousands of U.S. dollars)

	Common Stock	Class B Common Stock	Additional Paid-In Capital	Retained Earnings	Accumulated Other Comprehensive Income (Loss)	Treasury Stock Shares	Treasury Stock Amount	Total
Balance, December 31, 2001	$81,287	$20,894	$127,846	$614,863	$(1,299)	(17,549,237)	$(801,814)	$ 41,777
Net income—2002				201,506				$ 201,506
Unrealized gain on investments ..					437			437
Unrealized gain on hedging					2,059			2,059
Translation adjustment					2,693			2,693
Minimum pension liability, net of deferred taxes of $6,609					(9,979)			(9,979)
Comprehensive income								$ 196,716
Dividends, $1.00 per share				(83,649)				$ (83,649)
Conversion of class B common stock into common stock	118	(118)						
Sales under stock compensation plans			(5,738)			534,139	26,234	20,496
Purchase of treasury stock			(1,463)			(3,249,595)	(143,306)	(144,769)
Balance, December 31, 2002	$81,405	$20,776	$120,645	$732,720	$(6,089)	(20,264,693)	$(918,886)	$ 30,571

TO SUMMARIZE: Accumulated other comprehensive income is not income at all, but an equity category that summarizes the effect on equity of certain market-related gains and losses. Two examples of items giving rise to accumulated other comprehensive income are market fluctuations in the value of some investment securities and changes in the value of assets and liabilities held by foreign subsidiaries that are caused by exchange rate changes. A statement of stockholders' equity summarizes the changes affecting all the different categories of equity during the year.

Three topics related to equity financing need additional explanation. These topics are stock dividends, stock splits, and prior-period adjustments.

Accounting for Stock Dividends

6 Account for stock dividends and distinguish them from stock splits.

stock dividend A pro rata distribution of additional shares of stock to stockholders.

Corporations sometimes distribute additional shares of their own stock to stockholders instead of paying a cash dividend. These **stock dividends** must be distributed to each stockholder in proportion to the number of shares held. For example, if a company issues a 10% stock dividend, each stockholder will receive one additional share for every 10 shares owned.

There is considerable disagreement as to whether stockholders receive anything of value from a stock dividend. Certainly, they do not receive corporate assets, as with a cash dividend. Nor does any stockholder own a larger percentage of the corporation after the stock dividend than before, because each stockholder receives a pro rata share of the stock issued. In fact, one way to view a stock dividend is that the company has just cut the total ownership up into smaller pieces, with each stockholder owning proportionately more pieces, and nothing has really changed.

Those who argue that stock dividends have value to stockholders point out that companies frequently maintain the same level of cash dividends per share after the stock dividend as before. Accordingly, a stock dividend is an indirect method of increasing the amount of total cash dividends to be received in the future by each stockholder.

Stock dividends are also sometimes used to mollify investors and lull them into thinking that a company is maintaining its record of paying dividends when, in fact, it is not. Corporations that issue dividends each year do not want to miss a year, so for them a stock dividend can be a useful substitute for cash when poor financial circumstances make payment of cash dividends difficult. It isn't clear whether investors are actually fooled by this tactic.

To illustrate the accounting for a stock dividend and to keep the example simple, we will assume that the stockholders' equity of the Boston Lakers Basketball Team is:

Common stock ($1 par value, 10,000 shares issued and outstanding) . . . . $ 10,000
Paid-in capital in excess of par 40,000
Retained earnings 80,000
Total stockholders' equity $130,000

If a 10% stock dividend is declared and issued when the stock's current market price is $70, the entry to record the stock dividend is:

Retained Earnings (1,000 shares × $70)	70,000	
Common Stock (1,000 shares × $1 par)		1,000
Paid-In Capital in Excess of Par, Common Stock		69,000
Declared and issued a 10% common stock dividend.		

Because the dividend was 10% and there were previously 10,000 common shares outstanding, 1,000 additional shares were issued for the dividend. The accounting rules dictate that when a "small" stock dividend is issued, the market value of the newly issued shares is transferred out of Retained Earnings, just as if that same amount had been paid out in cash. If a stock dividend is relatively large, the accounting rules state that only the par value of the newly issued shares is to be transferred out of Retained Earnings. A small stock dividend is one that is less than 25%.

To illustrate the accounting for a large stock dividend, we assume the same stockholders' equity for the Boston Lakers Basketball Team, except that the stock dividend is now 30%. The entry is:

STOP & THINK

Look at the Boston Lakers example and explain how the accounting rules discourage companies from declaring small stock dividends on a regular basis.

Retained Earnings	3,000	
Common Stock (3,000 shares × $1 par)		3,000
Declared and issued a 30% common stock dividend		
(10,000 shares × 0.30 = 3,000 shares).		

The impact of the 10 and 30% stock dividends on the Boston Lakers' stockholders' equity is detailed below.

	Before Stock Dividend	With 10% Stock Dividend	With 30% Stock Dividend
Common stock, $1 par value	$ 10,000	$ 11,000	$ 13,000
Paid-in capital in excess of par	40,000	109,000	40,000
Retained earnings	80,000	10,000	77,000
Total stockholders' equity	$130,000	$130,000	$130,000

Note that a stock dividend does not change the total amount of stockholders' equity, regardless of the size of the dividend. The only effect is to reallocate some of the stockholders' equity into different categories.

Stock Splits

stock split The replacement of outstanding shares of stock with a greater number of new shares.

Many investors, particularly individuals with limited amounts to invest, will not purchase stocks with high market prices per share. For example, consider the case of BERKSHIRE HATH-AWAY, which will be spotlighted in Chapter 13 and is the holding company controlled by Warren Buffett (one of the richest people in the United States). In May 2003, the shares of Berkshire Hathaway were selling for over $74,000 per share! At that price, not many of us can own even one share. To encourage more investors to buy their stocks, companies sometimes enact a **stock split**, replacing the outstanding shares with a larger number of new shares that sell at a lower price per share. MICROSOFT, for example, has split its stock nine times in order to bring down the price per share. Because of these splits, a single original share of Microsoft stock is now the equivalent (as of May 2003) of 288 shares.

In essence, the difference between a stock dividend and a stock split is that a stock split is usually bigger. Whereas a stock dividend might increase the number of shares outstanding by 10 or 25%, a stock split is likely to increase the number of shares outstanding by 50% (3-for-2 stock split), by 100% (2-for-1 stock split), or more. Actually, there is no clear distinction between a stock split and a stock dividend. For example, there are 50% stock dividends and there are also 5-for-4 stock splits.

From an accounting standpoint, stock splits are accounted for in one of two ways. The most common way is to simply account for the stock split as if it were a large stock dividend. Thus, a 2-for-1 stock split would be accounted for as a 100% stock dividend with the par value of the newly created shares transferred from Retained Earnings. Alternatively, a stock split can be accounted for by reducing the par value of all outstanding shares. For a 2-for-1 stock split accounted for in this way, the par value is halved and the number of shares is doubled. Thus, the total par value of stock outstanding is unchanged. For example, a firm with 20,000 shares of $10 par-value common stock outstanding may reduce the par value to $5 and increase the number of shares outstanding to 40,000. No journal entry is needed to account for a stock split in this way; the company merely makes note of the fact that the par value and number of shares outstanding have changed.

TO SUMMARIZE: Stock dividends are distributions of additional stock to stockholders. Although a stock dividend does not increase a stockholder's percentage of ownership in a corporation, the additional stock may provide the expectation of increased future cash dividends. With small stock dividends, Retained Earnings is debited at the stock's market value; with large stock dividends (25% or more), Retained Earnings is debited at the stock's par value.

A stock split is also an increase in the number of shares outstanding. Generally, stock splits are authorized so that companies can attract more investors with a lower market price per share. A stock split can be accounted for as a large stock dividend or by lowering the par value of each share.

Prior-Period Adjustments

7 Explain prior-period adjustments and prepare a statement of retained earnings.

prior-period adjustments Adjustments made directly to Retained Earnings in order to correct errors in the financial statements of prior periods.

statement of retained earnings A report that shows the changes in the retained earnings account during a period of time.

In the first part of this chapter, it was shown that profits and losses, dividends, and certain treasury stock transactions affect retained earnings. In addition to these three events, there is one other type of event that affects retained earnings directly. This category includes adjustments to restate the net income of prior periods; these are called, appropriately, **prior-period adjustments**. Prior-period adjustments are relatively infrequent. In addition to some technical adjustments involving taxes and bonds, which are beyond the scope of this book, the main event that qualifies as a prior-period adjustment is the correction of an error in previous financial statements, such as an error in accounting for revenues or expenses of a previous period. In accounting for prior-period adjustments, Retained Earnings is increased or decreased directly because the net income for the years affected by the adjustments has already been closed to the retained earnings account.

Prior-period adjustments (if there are any) and dividends are usually disclosed in a **statement of retained earnings**. Exhibit 10 shows how the Boston Lakers Basketball Team might present a statement of retained earnings, using arbitrary numbers.

Exhibit 10: Statement of Retained Earnings for Boston Lakers

Boston Lakers Basketball Team Statement of Retained Earnings For the Year Ended December 31, 2006		
Retained earnings, January 1, 2006		$300,000
Prior-period adjustment:		
Deduct adjustment for 2005 inventory correction		(25,000)
Balance as restated		$275,000
Net income for 2006		50,000
Less dividends declared in 2006:		
Preferred stock	$10,000	
Common stock	12,000	(22,000)
Retained earnings, December 31, 2006		$303,000

TO SUMMARIZE: In addition to net income, dividends, and certain treasury stock transactions, retained earnings can also be either increased or decreased by prior-period adjustments, which do not occur often. Prior-period adjustments usually involve corrections of errors in previous financial statements. Prior-period adjustments are disclosed in a statement of retained earnings.

r e v i e w   o f   l e a r n i n g   o b j e c t i v e s

1 **Distinguish between debt and equity financing, and describe the advantages and disadvantages of organizing a business as a proprietorship or a partnership.** Borrowing money imposes a legal obligation to repay the amount borrowed, plus interest. Receiving investment funds does not obligate the company to repay investors. Investors stand to lose their investments if the company does poorly, but they also stand to share in the wealth if the company does well. Proprietorships are owned by one person; partnerships are owned by two or more persons or entities. Partnerships and proprietorships share three characteristics: (1) ease of formation, (2) limited life, and (3) unlimited liability.

2 **Describe the basic characteristics of a corporation and the nature of common and preferred stock.** A corporation is a business entity that is legally separate from its owners and is chartered by a state. It is independently taxed, and it can incur debts, conduct business, own property, and enter into contracts. Among the benefits of the corporate form of business are that ownership interests are easily transferred and that the liability of the owners is limited to the amount of their investment. Common stockholders are the true owners of a corporation. They have the right to vote in corporate matters and own all corporate assets that are left after the claims of others have been satisfied. Preferred stockholders are entitled to receive their full cash dividend payments before any dividends can be paid to common stockholders. Preferred stockholders are entitled to a fixed amount of the corporate assets, and that amount does not increase when the company is successful.

3 **Account for the issuance and repurchase of common and preferred stock.** Stock that is issued often has a par value associated with each share. This par value is a legal technicality and represents the minimum amount that must be invested. When stock is issued in exchange for a noncash item, the transaction is recorded at the market value of the noncash item. Repurchased stock is called treasury stock. When treasury stock is purchased by a corporation, it is accounted for at cost and deducted from total stockholders' equity as a contra-equity account.

4 **Understand the factors that affect retained earnings, describe the factors determining whether a company can and should pay cash dividends, and account for cash dividends.** Retained earnings is increased by net income and is decreased by a net loss, by dividends, and by some treasury stock transactions. Corporations usually distribute cash dividends to their owners. The three important dates in accounting for cash dividends are the declaration date, the date of record, and the payment date. Dividends are not a liability

until they are declared. If a company has common and preferred stock, the allocation of dividends between the two types of stock depends on the dividend preferences of the preferred stock. According to the incorporation laws in some states, the ability of a company to pay cash dividends can be restricted by the balance in Retained Earnings. In addition, private lending agreements sometimes constrain a company's ability to pay cash dividends. The dividend payout ratio, which is cash dividends divided by net income, reveals what percentage of a company's income it is paying out in dividends.

5 **Describe the purpose of reporting comprehensive income in the equity section of the balance sheet, and prepare a statement of stockholders' equity.** The accumulated amount of comprehensive income is reported in the equity section of the balance sheet. Comprehensive income items result from changes in market values of certain assets and liabilities. Comprehensive income is not income in the traditional sense but instead represents unrealized gains and losses that are excluded from the income statement. The statement of stockholders' equity summarizes the changes in each equity category during a year.

6 **Account for stock dividends and distinguish them from stock splits.** Stock dividends and stock splits involve dividing the ownership of the corporation into smaller pieces but giving shareholders proportionately more of these smaller pieces. Generally speaking, stock dividends are smaller than stock splits. A small stock dividend is one that is less than 25% and is accounted for by transferring the market value of the newly created shares out of Retained Earnings. With a large stock dividend, only the par value of the new shares is transferred. A stock split can be accounted for as a large stock dividend or by decreasing the par value of the shares.

7 **Explain prior-period adjustments and prepare a statement of retained earnings.** Prior-period adjustments are adjustments to restate net income of prior periods. The most common prior-period adjustments stem from past accounting errors that have been discovered in the current period. Because past periods' net income has already been closed to Retained Earnings, the corrections are made directly to the retained earnings account. Companies often include a statement of retained earnings with their financial statements. A statement of retained earnings reconciles the ending retained earnings balance with beginning retained earnings.

key terms & concepts

accumulated other comprehensive income, 602
board of directors, 590
cash dividend, 597
common stock, 590
contributed capital, 593
convertible preferred stock, 592
corporation, 589
cumulative-dividend preference, 600
current-dividend preference, 599
date of record, 598
declaration date, 598
dividend payment date, 599

dividend payout ratio, 601
dividends, 597
dividends in arrears, 600
limited liability, 589
par value, 592
partnership, 588
preferred stock, 591
proprietorship, 588
prospectus, 590
retained earnings, 597
statement of comprehensive income, 602
statement of stockholders' equity, 603

stockholders, 590
treasury stock, 594

prior-period adjustments, 607
statement of retained earnings, 607
stock dividend, 605
stock split, 606

review problem

Stockholders' Equity

Clarke Corporation was organized during 1976. At the end of 2006, the equity section of the balance sheet was:

Contributed capital:

Preferred stock (8%, $30 par, 6,000 shares authorized, 5,000 shares issued and outstanding)	$150,000
Common stock ($5 par, 50,000 shares authorized, 20,000 shares issued, 17,000 shares outstanding)	100,000
Paid-in capital in excess of par, common stock	80,000
Total contributed capital	$330,000
Retained earnings	140,000
Total contributed capital plus retained earnings	$470,000
Less treasury stock (3,000 shares of common stock at cost, $10 per share)	(30,000)
Total stockholders' equity	$440,000

During 2006, the following stockholders' equity transactions occurred in chronological sequence:

a. Issued 800 shares of common stock at $11 per share.
b. Reissued 1,200 shares of treasury stock at $12 per share.
c. Issued 300 shares of preferred stock at $33 per share.
d. Reissued 400 shares of treasury stock at $9 per share.
e. Declared and paid a dividend large enough to meet the current-dividend preference on the preferred stock and to pay the common stockholders $1.50 per share.
f. Net income for 2006 was $70,000, which included $400,000 of revenues and $330,000 of expenses.
g. Closed the dividends accounts for 2006.

Required:
1. Journalize the transactions.

(continued)

2. Set up T-accounts with beginning balances and post the journal entries to the T-accounts, adding any necessary new accounts. (Assume a beginning balance of $20,000 for the cash account.)
3. Prepare the stockholders' equity section of the balance sheet as of December 31, 2006.

Solution

1. Journalize the Transactions

a.   Cash 8,800

     Common Stock   4,000

     Paid-In Capital in Excess of Par, Common Stock   4,800

         Issued 800 shares of common stock at $11 per share.

Cash received is $11 × 800 shares; common stock is par value times the number of shares ($5 × 800); paid-in capital is the excess.

b.   Cash 14,400

     Treasury Stock   12,000

     Paid-In Capital, Treasury Stock   2,400

         Reissued 1,200 shares of treasury stock at $12 per share.

Cash is $12 × 1,200 shares; treasury stock is the cost times the number of shares sold ($10 × 1,200 shares); paid-in capital is the excess.

c.   Cash 9,900

     Preferred Stock   9,000

     Paid-In Capital in Excess of Par, Preferred Stock   900

         Issued 300 shares of preferred stock at $33 per share.

Cash is $33 × 300 shares; preferred stock is par value times the number of shares issued ($30 × 300); paid-in capital is the excess.

d.   Cash 3,600

     Paid-In Capital, Treasury Stock 400

     Treasury Stock   4,000

         Reissued 400 shares of treasury stock at $9 per share.

Cash is $9 × 400 shares; treasury stock is the cost times the number of shares sold ($10 × 400); paid-in capital is decreased for the difference. If no Paid-In Capital, Treasury Stock balance had existed, Retained Earnings would have been debited.

e.   Dividends, Preferred Stock 12,720

     Dividends, Common Stock 29,100

     Cash   41,820

         Declared and paid cash dividend.

Calculations:

Preferred Stock	Number of Shares	Par-Value Amount
Original balance	5,000	$150,000
Entry (c)	300	9,000
Total	5,300	$159,000
		× 0.08
		$ 12,720

Common Stock	Number of Shares
Original balance (excludes treasury stock)	17,000
Entry (a)	800
Entry (b)	1,200
Entry (d)	400
Total	19,400 shares
	× $1.50
	$29,100
Total preferred stock dividend	$12,720
Total common stock dividend	29,100
Total dividend	$41,820

f.	Revenues (individual revenue accounts)	400,000	
	Expenses (individual expense accounts)		330,000
	Retained Earnings		70,000
	To close net income to Retained Earnings.		
g.	Retained Earnings	41,820	
	Dividends, Preferred Stock		12,720
	Dividends, Common Stock		29,100
	To close the dividends accounts for 2006.		

2. Set up T-Accounts and Post to the Accounts

Cash

Beg.			
Bal.	20,000	(e)	41,820
(a)	8,800		
(b)	14,400		
(c)	9,900		
(d)	3,600		
Bal.	14,880		

Preferred Stock

		Beg.	
		Bal.	150,000
		(c)	9,000
		Bal.	159,000

Paid-In Capital in Excess of Par, Preferred Stock

		(c)	900
		Bal.	900

Common Stock

		Beg.	
		Bal.	100,000
		(a)	4,000
		Bal.	104,000

Paid-In Capital in Excess of Par, Common Stock

		Beg.	
		Bal.	80,000
		(a)	4,800
		Bal.	84,800

Treasury Stock

Beg.			
Bal.	30,000	(b)	12,000
		(d)	4,000
Bal.	14,000		

Paid-In Capital, Treasury Stock

(d)	400	(b)	2,400
		Bal.	2,000

Retained Earnings

		Beg.	
(g)	41,820	Bal.	140,000
		(f)	70,000
		Bal.	168,180

Dividends, Preferred Stock

(e)	12,720	(g)	12,720
Bal.	0		

Dividends, Common Stock

(e)	29,100	(g)	29,100
Bal.	0		

Revenues

		Beg.	
(f)	400,000	Bal.	400,000
		Bal.	0

Expenses

Beg.			
Bal.	330,000	(f)	330,000
Bal.	0		

3. Prepare Stockholders' Equity Section of the Balance Sheet

Clarke Corporation
Partial Balance Sheet
December 31, 2006

Stockholders' Equity

Contributed capital:

Preferred stock (8%, $30 par, 6,000 shares authorized, 5,300 shares issued and outstanding)	$159,000
Common stock ($5 par, 50,000 shares authorized, 20,800 shares issued, 19,400 outstanding)	104,000
Paid-in capital in excess of par, preferred stock	900
Paid-in capital in excess of par, common stock	84,800
Paid-in capital, treasury stock	2,000
Total contributed capital	$350,700
Retained earnings	168,180
Total contributed capital plus retained earnings	$518,880
Less treasury stock (1,400 shares of common stock at cost, $10 per share)	(14,000)
Total stockholders' equity	$504,880

Transaction	Common Stock Issued	Common Stock Authorized	Treasury Stock
Number of shares originally issued	20,000	50,000	3,000
Entry (a)	800		
Entry (b)			(1,200)
Entry (d)			(400)
Total	20,800	50,000	1,400

---

discussion questions

1. What are the primary differences between debt financing and equity financing?
2. What are the major differences between a partnership and a corporation?
3. How is a proprietorship or partnership established?
4. Does the death of a partner legally terminate a partnership? If so, does it mean that the partnership must cease operating?
5. Are partners legally liable for the actions of other partners? Explain.
6. In which type of business entity do all owners have limited liability?
7. In what way are corporate profits subject to double taxation?

8. How do common and preferred stock differ?
9. What is the purpose of having a par value for stock?
10. Why would a company repurchase its own shares of stock that it had previously issued?
11. Is treasury stock an asset? If not, why not?
12. How is treasury stock usually accounted for?
13. In what way does the stockholders' equity section of a balance sheet identify the sources of the assets?
14. What factors affect the Retained Earnings balance of a corporation?
15. Is it possible for a firm to have a large Retained Earnings balance and no cash? Explain.
16. When is a company legally barred from paying cash dividends?

17. Why should a potential common stockholder carefully examine the dividend preferences of a company's preferred stock?
18. The dividend payout ratio for Deedle Company is 40%. What does this mean?
19. What is accumulated other comprehensive income? Why was this concept adopted by accounting standard-setters?
20. Give two examples of other equity items (items that bypass the income statement and go directly to the equity section of the balance sheet).

21. Does a stock dividend have value to stockholders? Explain.
22. What is the difference between large and small stock dividends?
23. Why are prior-period adjustments entered directly into Retained Earnings instead of being reflected on the income statement?

practice exercises

Practice 12-1

Characteristics of Proprietorships and Partnerships
Which one of the following is *not* a usual characteristic of either a proprietorship or a partnership?

a. Limited size.
b. Limited life.
c. Ease of formation.
d. Unlimited liability.

Practice 12-2

Characteristics of Corporations
Which one of the following is *not* a usual characteristic of a corporation?

a. Limited liability.
b. Limited life.
c. Close government regulation.
d. Easy transferability of ownership.
e. Ability to raise large amounts of capital.

Practice 12-3

Characteristics of Common Stock and Preferred Stock
Which one of the following statements is true regarding common stock and preferred stock?

a. Preferred stockholders always have the right to vote in corporate matters.
b. Common stockholders are the true owners of the business.
c. Preferred stock is better than common stock.
d. Common stockholders receive dividends before preferred stockholders.
e. Preferred stock can never be converted into common stock.

Practice 12-4

Issuance of No-Par Common Stock
The company issued 2,500 shares of no-par common stock at $30 per share for cash. Make the necessary journal entry(ies) to record this transaction.

Practice 12-5

Issuance of Common Stock for Cash
The company issued 3,000 shares of $1 par-value common stock for $40 per share for cash. Make the necessary journal entry(ies) to record this transaction.

Practice 12-6

Issuance of Common Stock for Other Assets
The company issued 5,500 shares of $2 par-value common stock in exchange for a building. The market value of the stock at the date of the exchange was $25 per share. Make the necessary journal entry(ies) to record this transaction.

Practice 12-7

Accounting for Stock Repurchases
The company repurchased 2,000 shares of $1 par-value common stock for $36 per share from the open market. Make the necessary journal entry(ies) to record this transaction.

Practice 12-8

Accounting for Sale of Treasury Stock at Price Higher than Cost
Refer to the data in Practice 12-7. The company resells 500 shares of treasury stock for $45 per share. Make the necessary journal entry(ies) to record this transaction.

Practice 12-9

Accounting for Sale of Treasury Stock at Price Lower than Cost
Refer to the data in Practice 12-7 and Practice 12-8. The company resells 250 shares of treasury stock for $30 per share. Make the necessary journal entry(ies) to record this transaction.

Practice 12-10

Accounting for Sale of Treasury Stock at Price Lower than Cost
Refer to the data in Practice 12-7 through Practice 12-9. The paid-in capital, treasury stock account currently has a $3,000 credit balance. The company resells 1,000 shares of treasury stock for $28 per share. Make the necessary journal entry(ies) to record this transaction.

Practice 12-11

Balance Sheet Preparation
Using the following data, prepare a statement of stockholders' equity for the company.

Paid-in capital in excess of par, common stock	$492,000
Retained earnings	200,000
Common stock ($1 par value, 8,400 shares issued, 8,000 outstanding)	8,000
Treasury stock (400 shares of $1 common at cost of $45)	18,000
Preferred stock ($20 par value, 2,500 shares issued and outstanding)	50,000

Practice 12-12

Dividend Declaration Accounting
The company has the following two types of stock:

1. 2,000 shares of 10% cumulative preferred stock with a $20 par value.
2. 5,000 shares of common stock with a $1 par value.

The company declared a $21,000 cash dividend. Make the necessary journal entry(ies) to record this event.

Practice 12-13

Dividend Payment Accounting
Refer to the data in Practice 12-12. Make the necessary journal entry(ies) to record the payment of the cash dividend.

Practice 12-14

Dividend Closing Entry(ies)
Refer to the data in Practice 12-12. Make the necessary journal entry(ies) to close the dividend accounts to retained earnings at the end of the year.

Practice 12-15

Dividend Payout Ratio
Using the following data, compute the dividend payout ratio.

Cash dividends	$ 21,000
Sales	496,000
Net income	85,000

Practice 12-16

Statement of Comprehensive Income
Using the following items, compute the company's comprehensive income.

1. The company's investment in a foreign subsidiary increased by $4,000 because the Euro strengthened relative to the U.S. dollar during the year.
2. Net income for the year was $52,000.
3. Unrealized loss on investments for the year was $11,000.

Practice 12-17

Stock Dividends

The company reports the following stockholders' equity:

Common stock ($1 par value, 8,000 shares issued and outstanding)	$ 8,000
Paid-in capital in excess of par, common stock	128,000
Retained earnings	200,000

The company declares and issues a 10% stock dividend when the market price of the stock is $22. Prepare the entry to record the stock dividend.

e x e r c i s e s

Exercise 12-1

Issuance of Stock

Brockbank Corporation was organized on July 15, 2006. Record the journal entries for Brockbank to account for the following:

a. The state authorized 30,000 shares of 7% preferred stock ($20 par) and 100,000 shares of no-par common stock.
b. The company gave 6,000 shares of common stock to its attorney in return for her help in incorporating the business. Fees for this work are normally about $18,000. (*Note:* The debit is to Legal Expense.)
c. Brockbank Corporation gave 15,000 shares of common stock to an individual who contributed a building worth $50,000.
d. Brockbank Corporation issued 5,000 shares of preferred stock at $25 per share.
e. Peter Brockbank paid $70,000 cash for 30,000 shares of common stock.
f. Another individual donated a $15,000 machine and received 4,000 shares of common stock.
g. The attorney sold all her shares to her brother-in-law for $18,000.

Exercise 12-2

Spreadsheet

No-Par Stock Transactions

Harmsen Maintenance Corporation was organized in early 2006 with 60,000 shares of no-par common stock authorized. During 2006, the following transactions occurred:

a. Issued 31,000 shares of stock at $24 per share.
b. Issued another 3,900 shares of stock at $28 per share.
c. Issued 3,000 shares for a building appraised at $90,000.
d. Declared dividends of $1.50 per share.
e. Earned net income of $187,000 for the year, including $405,000 of revenues and $218,000 of expenses, and closed these accounts.
f. Closed the dividends accounts.

Given this information:

1. Journalize the transactions.
2. Present the stockholders' equity section of the balance sheet as it would appear on December 31, 2006.

Exercise 12-3

Treasury Stock Transactions

Provide the necessary journal entries to record the following:

a. Fayette Corporation was granted a charter authorizing the issuance of 100,000 shares of $16 par-value common stock.
b. The company issued 40,000 shares of common stock at $20 per share.
c. The company reacquired 2,000 shares of its own stock at $22 per share, to be held in treasury.
d. Another 2,000 shares of stock were reacquired at $24 per share.
e. Of the shares reacquired in (c), 800 were reissued for $26 per share.
f. Of the shares reacquired in (d), 1,400 were reissued for $18 per share.
g. Given the preceding transactions, what is the balance in the treasury stock account?

Exercise 12-4

Stock Issuance and Cash Dividends

Lindstrom Corporation was organized in January 2006. The state authorized 200,000 shares of no-par common stock and 75,000 shares of 8%, $24 par, preferred stock. Record the following transactions that occurred in 2006:

a. Issued 20,000 shares of common stock at $35 per share.
b. Issued 3,500 shares of preferred stock for a building appraised at $100,000.
c. Declared a cash dividend sufficient to meet the current-dividend preference on preferred stock and pay common shareholders $3.50 per share.

Exercise 12-5

Stock Issuance, Treasury Stock, and Dividends

On January 1, 2006, Abbott Corporation was granted a charter authorizing the following capital stock: common stock, $20 par, 100,000 shares; preferred stock, $10 par, 6%, 30,000 shares. Record the following 2006 transactions:

a. Issued 80,000 shares of common stock at $30 per share.
b. Issued 14,000 shares of preferred stock at $12 per share.
c. Bought back 5,000 shares of common stock at $40 per share.
d. Reissued 500 shares of treasury stock at $25 per share.
e. Declared cash dividends of $38,600 to be allocated between common and preferred stockholders. (The preferred stock, which has a current-dividend preference, is noncumulative.)
f. Paid dividends of $38,600.

Exercise 12-6

Stock Issuance, Treasury Stock, and Dividends

On January 1, 2006, Snow Company was authorized to issue 100,000 shares of common stock, par value $10 per share and 10,000 shares of 8% preferred stock, par value $20 per share. Record the following transactions for 2006:

a. Issued 70,000 shares of common stock at $25 per share.
b. Issued 8,000 shares of preferred stock at $30 per share.
c. Reacquired 5,000 shares of common stock at $20 per share.
d. Reissued 2,000 shares of treasury stock for $46,000.
e. Declared a cash dividend sufficient to meet the current-dividend preference on preferred stock and pay common shareholders $1 per share.

Exercise 12-7

Stock Transactions and Dividends

Fowler Corporation was organized in January 2006. The state authorized 150,000 shares of no-par common stock and 50,000 shares of 12%, $8 par, preferred stock. Record the following transactions that occurred in 2006:

a. Issued 28,000 shares of common stock at $32 per share.
b. Issued 15,000 shares of preferred stock for a piece of land appraised at $200,000.
c. Declared a cash dividend sufficient to meet the current-dividend preference on preferred stock and paid common shareholders $2 per share.

d. How would your answer to (c) change if the dividend declared were not sufficient to meet the current-dividend preference on preferred stock?

Exercise 12-8

Dividend Calculations

On January 1, 2006, Oldroyd Corporation had 130,000 shares of common stock issued and outstanding. During 2006, the following transactions occurred (in chronological order):

a. Oldroyd issued 10,000 new shares of common stock.
b. The company reacquired 2,000 shares of stock for use in its employee stock option plan.
c. At the end of the option period, 1,200 shares of treasury stock had been purchased by corporate officials.

Given this information, compute the following:

1. After the foregoing three transactions have occurred, what amount of dividends must Oldroyd Corporation declare in order to pay 50 cents per share? To pay $1 per share?
2. What is the dividend per share if $236,640 is paid?
3. If all 2,000 treasury shares had been purchased by corporate officials through the stock option plan, what would the dividends per share have been, again assuming $236,640 in dividends were paid? (Round to the nearest cent.)

Exercise 12-9

Dividend Calculations

Nothbaar Corporation has the following stock outstanding:

Preferred stock (7%, $24 par value, 25,000 shares)	$600,000
Common stock ($3 par value, 200,000 shares)	600,000

For the two independent cases that follow, compute the amount of dividends that would be paid to preferred and common shareholders. Assume that total dividends paid are $180,000. No dividends have been paid for the past three years.

Case A, Preferred is noncumulative.
Case B, Preferred is cumulative.

Exercise 12-10

P.A.S.S.
Power Accounting
System Software

Stock Issuance, Treasury Stock, and Dividends

During 2006, Doxey Corporation had the following transactions and related events:

Jan. 15   Issued 6,500 shares of common stock at par ($16 per share), bringing the total number of shares outstanding to 121,300.

Feb. 6   Declared a 50-cent-per-share dividend on common stock for stockholders of record on March 6.

Mar. 6   Date of record.

      8   Pedro Garcia, a prominent banker, purchased 20,000 shares of Doxey Corporation common stock from the company for $346,000.

Apr. 6   Paid dividends declared on February 6.

June 19   Reacquired 800 shares of common stock as treasury stock at a total cost of $9,350.

Sept. 6   Declared dividends of 55 cents per share to be paid to common stockholders of record on October 15, 2006.

Oct. 6   The Dow Jones Industrial Average plummeted 300 points, and Doxey's stock price fell $3 per share.

    15   Date of record.

Nov. 16   Paid dividends declared on September 6.

Dec. 15   Declared and paid a 6% cash dividend on 18,000 outstanding shares of preferred stock (par value $32).

(continued)

Given this information:

1. Prepare the journal entries for these transactions.
2. What is the total amount of dividends paid to common and preferred stockholders during 2006?

Exercise 12-11

Dividend Payout Ratio

The following numbers are for three different companies:

	A	B	C
Total assets	$2,400	$2,950	$3,500
Cash dividends	20	140	310
Total liabilities	1,300	1,540	2,640
Net income	240	330	360

For each company, compute the dividend payout ratio.

Exercise 12-12

Analysis of Stockholders' Equity

The stockholders' equity section of Kay Corporation at the end of the current year showed:

Preferred stock (6%, $40 par, 10,000 shares authorized, 6,000 shares issued and outstanding)	$?
Common stock ($6 par, 80,000 shares authorized, 53,000 issued, 52,650 shares outstanding)	318,000
Paid-in capital in excess of par, preferred stock	?
Paid-in capital in excess of par, common stock	129,000
Retained earnings	86,000
Less treasury stock (350 shares at cost)	(2,000)
Total stockholders' equity	$?

1. What is the dollar amount to be reported for preferred stock?
2. What is the average price for which common stock was issued? (Round to the nearest cent.)
3. If preferred stock was issued at an average price of $43 per share, what amount should appear in the paid-in capital in excess of par, preferred stock account?
4. What is the average cost per share of treasury stock? (Round to the nearest cent.)
5. Assuming that the preferred stock was issued for an average price of $43 per share, what is total stockholders' equity?
6. If net income for the year were $67,000 and if only dividends on preferred stock were paid, by how much would retained earnings increase?

Exercise 12-13

Spreadsheet

Preparing the Stockholders' Equity Section

The following account balances, before any closing entries, appear on the books of Spring Company as of December 31, 2006:

Retained Earnings (balance at Jan. 1, 2006)	$240,000
Dividends, Preferred Stock	15,000
Dividends, Common Stock	35,000
Common Stock ($5 par, 100,000 shares authorized, 70,000 issued and outstanding)	350,000
Paid-In Capital in Excess of Par, Common Stock	350,000
Preferred Stock (6%, $50 par, 50,000 shares authorized, 5,000 issued and outstanding)	250,000
Paid-In Capital in Excess of Par, Preferred Stock	25,000

Based on these account balances, and assuming net income for 2006 of $80,000, prepare the stockholders' equity section of the December 31, 2006, balance sheet for Spring Company.

Exercise 12-14

Comprehensive Income

The following information relates to Hicken Company:

a. Hicken Company's net income for the year was $14,000.
b. Hicken Company has an investment portfolio for long-term investment purposes. That portfolio decreased in value by $3,500 during the year.
c. Hicken Company has several foreign subsidiaries. The currencies in the countries where those subsidiaries are located increased in value (relative to the U.S. dollar) during the year. Accordingly, the computed value of the equity of those subsidiaries, in U.S. dollars, decreased by $1,800.

Compute Hicken's comprehensive income for the year.

Exercise 12-15

Other Equity Items

Red Rider Company has the following stockholders' equity section on its balance sheet as of December 31, 2006 and 2005.

Red Rider Company (in millions)		
	2006	**2005**
Stockholders' Equity		
Preferred stock	$ 2.0	$ 2.0
Common stock	32.0	32.0
Paid-in capital—various	12.4	11.2
Retained earnings	24.5	24.6
Subtotal	$ 70.9	$69.8
Accumulated foreign currency translation adjustments	5.2	4.5
Net unrealized gains on investments in certain debt and equity securities	25.6	20.0
Total stockholders' equity	$101.7	$94.3

Based on this stockholders' equity section, answer the following questions:

1. At the end of 2006, what was the total amount of equity financing provided by Red Rider's investors?
2. At the end of 2006, how much of Red Rider's earnings had not been distributed to investors?
3. What is the total amount of "other equity items" contained in the 2006 stockholders' equity section?
4. What contributed most to the increased equity from 2005 to 2006?

Exercise 12-16

Stock Dividends and Stock Splits

The stockholders' equity section of Ardvark Corporation's December 31, 2005, balance sheet included the following items:

(continued)

Common stock ($20 par, 250,000 shares authorized,	
50,000 shares issued and outstanding)	$1,000,000
Paid-in capital in excess of par, common stock	1,500,000
Retained earnings	2,000,000

Record the following transactions for 2006:

a. On March 1, Ardvark declared and issued a 25% stock dividend on common stock. The market price of the stock was $40 per share on that date.
b. On June 30, a 4-for-1 stock split was declared.
c. On September 15, a 10% stock dividend on common stock was declared and distributed. The market price of the stock was $30 per share on the dividend date.

Exercise 12-17

Stock Dividends

Allred Company has issued 90,000 shares of common stock with a par value of $5. Of the shares issued, 80,000 shares are outstanding. Allred's board of directors has decided to issue a stock dividend. The current market price of the stock is $30 per share. Provide journal entries to record the issuance of the dividend under each of the following independent circumstances:

1. The dividend is a 20% stock dividend.
2. The dividend is a 30% stock dividend.

Exercise 12-18

Stock Dividends

On July 1, 2006, Sanford Corporation's balance sheet reported the following account balances in the stockholders' equity section:

Common stock, $5 par	$150,000
Paid-in capital in excess of par, common stock	20,000
Retained earnings	180,000
Total stockholders' equity	$350,000

On August 31, 2006, Sanford's board of directors declared and issued a 10% stock dividend. The market value on August 31 is $12 per share.

1. Compare the book value per share before and after the issuance of the stock dividend.
2. Compute the new balance for all stockholders' equity accounts after the stock dividend.

Exercise 12-19

P.A.S.S.
Power Accounting System Software

Stockholders' Equity Transactions

On December 31, 2005, White Lighting Corporation's stockholders' equity section of the balance sheet showed the following:

Common stock ($10 par, 50,000 shares authorized,	
25,000 issued, and 17,000 outstanding)	$250,000
Paid-in capital in excess of par, common stock	375,000
Retained earnings	450,000
Treasury stock (8,000 shares, at cost)	(90,000)
Total stockholders' equity	$985,000

During 2006, the following transactions occurred:

a. On March 1, 2006, White Lighting purchased 5,000 shares of its stock at $20 per share.
b. On April 15, 2006, White Lighting reissued the 5,000 shares of its stock purchased in (a); the market price on that day was $30 per share.
c. On June 10, 2006, White Lighting declared and paid a 10% stock dividend. Market price of the stock was $32 per share.

d. On June 30, 2006, White Lighting declared a cash dividend of 50 cents per share. The dividend was paid on July 30. The record date was July 15.

e. On October 1, 2006, White Lighting issued 5,000 shares of new stock for $40 per share.

Prepare journal entries to record each of the above transactions.

Exercise 12-20

Statement of Retained Earnings

The stockholders' equity section of Summer Corporation's balance sheet shows the following as of the end of 2006:

Preferred stock (5%, $30 par, 10,000 shares authorized, 5,000 shares issued and outstanding)	$?
Common stock ($12 par, 50,000 shares authorized, 28,000 issued, 27,500 outstanding)	336,000
Paid-in capital in excess of par, preferred stock	?
Paid-in capital in excess of par, common stock	424,000
Retained earnings	78,000
Treasury stock (purchased at $14)	?
Total stockholders' equity	$?

Prepare a statement of retained earnings for the year ended December 31, 2006. Assume the following additional facts:

a. Retained earnings as of December 31, 2005, was $25,500.

b. Net income as of 2006 was $72,000.

c. Dividends equal to the current-dividend preference on preferred stock were declared and issued.

d. A prior-period adjustment was made to retained earnings to correct an overstatement of 2005 net income in the amount of $12,000.

e. Common stock was sold for $12.

problems

Problem 12-1

Stock Transactions and Analysis

The following selected items and amounts were taken from the balance sheet of Quale Company as of December 31, 2006:

Cash	$ 93,000
Property, plant, and equipment	850,000
Accumulated depreciation	150,000
Liabilities	50,000
Preferred stock (7%, $100 par, noncumulative, 10,000 shares authorized, 5,000 shares issued and outstanding)	500,000
Common stock ($10 par, 100,000 shares authorized, 80,000 shares issued and outstanding)	800,000
Paid-in capital in excess of par, preferred stock	1,000
Paid-in capital in excess of par, common stock	125,000
Paid-in capital, treasury stock	1,000
Retained earnings	310,000

(continued)

Required:

For each of parts (1) to (5), (a) prepare the necessary journal entry (or entries) to record each transaction, and (b) calculate the amount that would appear on the December 31, 2006, balance sheet as a consequence of this transaction only for the account given. (*Note:* In your answer to each part of this problem, consider this to be the only transaction that took place during 2006.)

1. Quale Company issued 200 shares of common stock in exchange for cash of $4,000.
   a. Entry
   b. Paid-In Capital in Excess of Par, Common Stock
2. The company issued 200 shares of preferred stock at a price of $102 per share.
   a. Entry
   b. Paid-In Capital in Excess of Par, Preferred Stock
3. The company issued 500 shares of common stock in exchange for a building. The common stock is not actively traded, but the building was recently appraised at $11,000.
   a. Entry
   b. Property, Plant, and Equipment
4. The company reacquired 1,000 shares of common stock from a stockholder for $23,000 and subsequently reissued the shares to a different investor for $21,500. (*Note:* Make two entries.)
   a. Entries
   b. Paid-In Capital, Treasury Stock
5. The board of directors declared dividends of $75,000. This amount includes the current-year dividend preference on preferred stock, with the remainder to be paid to common shareholders.
   a. Entry
   b. Retained Earnings

Problem 12-2

Stock Transactions and the Stockholders' Equity Section

The following is West Valley Company's stockholders' equity section of the balance sheet on December 31, 2005:

Preferred stock (8%, $60 par, noncumulative, 16,000 shares authorized, 8,000 shares issued and outstanding)	$480,000
Common stock ($10 par, 120,000 shares authorized, 80,000 shares issued and outstanding)	800,000
Paid-in capital in excess of par, preferred stock	130,000
Paid-in capital in excess of par, common stock	252,000
Retained earnings	330,000

Required:

1. Journalize the following 2006 transactions:
   a. Issued 2,000 preferred shares at $70 per share.
   b. Reacquired 1,000 common shares for the treasury at $13 per share.
   c. Declared and paid a $2-per-share dividend on common stock in addition to paying the required preferred dividends. (*Note:* Debit Retained Earnings directly.)
   d. Reissued 600 treasury shares at $14 per share.
   e. Reissued the remaining treasury shares at $12 per share.
   f. Earnings for the year were $92,000, including $200,000 of revenues and $108,000 of expenses.
2. Prepare the stockholders' equity section of the balance sheet for the company at December 31, 2006.

Problem 12-3

Recording Stockholders' Equity Transactions

Zina Corporation was organized during 2005. At the end of 2005, the stockholders' equity section of the balance sheet appeared as follows:

P.A.S.S.
Power Accounting
System Software

Contributed capital:

Preferred stock (5%, $30 par, 15,000 shares authorized,
  8,000 shares issued and outstanding) $240,000

Common stock ($22 par, 36,000 shares authorized, 18,000 issued,
  15,000 outstanding) 396,000

Paid-in capital in excess of par, preferred stock 56,000

  Total contributed capital $692,000

Retained earnings 244,000

Total contributed capital plus retained earnings $936,000

Less treasury stock (3,000 shares at cost of $28 per share) . . . . (84,000)

    Total stockholders' equity $852,000

During 2006, the following transactions occurred in the order given:

a. Issued 1,200 shares of common stock at $25 per share.
b. Reissued 1,600 shares of treasury stock at $30 per share.
c. Reissued 750 shares of treasury stock at $21 per share.

Required:
Record the transactions.

Problem 12-4

Spreadsheet

P.A.S.S.
Power Accounting
System Software

Stock Transactions and Stockholders' Equity Section

The balance sheet for Lakeland Corporation as of December 31, 2005, is as follows:

Assets $750,000

Liabilities $410,000

Stockholders' equity:

Preferred stock, convertible (5%, $20 par) . . . . $ 50,000

Common stock ($10 par) 150,000

Paid-in capital in excess of par, common stock 30,000

Retained earnings 116,000

    $346,000

Less treasury stock, common (500 shares at cost) . . . . (6,000)   340,000

  Total liabilities and stockholders' equity $750,000

During 2006, the following transactions were completed in the order given:

a. The company reacquired 750 shares of outstanding common stock at $7 per share.
b. The company reacquired 150 shares of common stock in settlement of an account receivable of $1,500.
c. Semiannual cash dividends of 75 cents per share on common stock and 50 cents per share on preferred stock were declared and paid.
d. Each share of preferred stock is convertible into three shares of common stock. Five hundred shares of preferred stock were converted into common stock. (*Hint:* Shares are converted at par values, and any excess reduces Retained Earnings.)
e. The 900 shares of common treasury stock acquired during 2006 were sold at $13. The remaining treasury shares were exchanged for a machine with a fair market value of $6,300.
f. The company issued 3,000 shares of common stock in exchange for land appraised at $39,000.
g. Semiannual cash dividends of 75 cents per share on common stock and 50 cents per share on preferred stock were declared and paid.
h. Closed net income of $35,000 to Retained Earnings, which included $135,000 of revenues and $100,000 of expenses.
i. Closed dividends accounts to Retained Earnings.

(continued)

Required:
1. Give the necessary journal entries to record the transactions listed.
2. Prepare the stockholders' equity section of the balance sheet as of December 31, 2006.

Problem 12-5

P.A.S.S.
*Power Accounting
System Software*

Stockholders' Equity, Dividends, and Treasury Stock

The stockholders' equity section of Nielsen Corporation's December 31, 2005, balance sheet is as follows:

Stockholders' equity:

Preferred stock (10%, $50 par, 10,000 shares authorized, 1,000 shares issued and outstanding)	$ 50,000
Common stock ($15 par, 100,000 shares authorized, 5,000 shares issued and outstanding)	75,000
Paid-in capital in excess of par, preferred stock	2,000
Paid-in capital in excess of par, common stock	25,000
Total contributed capital	$152,000
Retained earnings	102,000
Total stockholders' equity	$254,000

During 2006, Nielsen Corporation had the following transactions affecting stockholders' equity:

Jan. 20 Paid a cash dividend of $2 per share on common stock. The dividend was declared on December 15, 2005.
Aug. 15 Reacquired 1,000 shares of common stock at $20 per share.
Sept. 30 Reissued 500 shares of treasury stock at $21 per share.
Oct. 15 Declared and paid cash dividends of $3 per share on the common stock.
Nov. 1 Reissued 200 shares of treasury stock at $18 per share.
Dec. 15 Declared and paid the 10% preferred cash dividend.
    31 Closed net income of $40,000 to Retained Earnings. (Revenues were $260,000; expenses were $220,000.) Also closed the dividends accounts to Retained Earnings.

Required:
1. Journalize the transactions.
2. Prepare the stockholders' equity section of Nielsen Corporation's December 31, 2006, balance sheet.
3. **Interpretive Question:** What is the effect on earnings per share when a company purchases treasury stock?

Problem 12-6

Spreadsheet

Dividend Calculations

Salty Corporation was organized in January 2003 and issued shares of preferred and common stock as shown. As of December 31, 2006, there have been no changes in outstanding stock.

Preferred stock (8%, $10 par, 20,000 shares issued and outstanding)	$200,000
Common stock ($40 par, 10,000 shares issued and outstanding)	400,000

Required:
For each of the following independent situations, compute the amount of dividends that would be paid for each class of stock in 2005 and 2006. Assume that total dividends of $10,000 and $80,000 are paid in 2005 and 2006, respectively.

1. Preferred stock is noncumulative.
2. Preferred stock is cumulative, and no dividends are in arrears in 2005.
3. Preferred stock is cumulative, and no dividends have been paid during 2003 and 2004.

Problem 12-7

Dividend Calculations

Lowe Corporation had authorization for 80,000 shares of 8% preferred stock, par value $20 per share, and 24,000 shares of common stock, par value $120 per share, all of which are issued and outstanding. During the years beginning in 2005, Lowe Corporation maintained a policy of paying out 50% of net income in cash dividends. One-half the net income for the three years beginning in 2005 was $50,000, $280,000, and $340,000. There are no dividends in arrears for years prior to 2005.

Required:

Compute the amount of dividends paid to each class of stock for each year under the following separate cases:

1. Preferred stock is noncumulative.
2. Preferred stock is cumulative.
3. **Interpretive Question:** Why is it important that a common stockholder know about the dividend privileges of the preferred stock?

Problem 12-8

Dividend Payout Ratio

The following numbers are for three different companies:

	A	B	C
Cash	$ 50	$ 200	$ 400
Retained earnings	900	800	3,500
Cash dividends	80	0	500
Paid-in capital	1,000	2,500	2,000
Total liabilities	600	300	1,400
Sales	5,000	10,000	4,000
Net income	200	500	800

Required:

1. For each company, compute the dividend payout ratio.
2. **Interpretive Question:** Which of the three companies is most likely to be a high-growth Internet company? Which is most likely to be an old, stable company? Explain.

Problem 12-9

Preparing the Stockholders' Equity Section and Recording Dividends

In 2004, Lee Ann Adams and some college friends organized The Candy Jar, a gourmet candy company. In 2004, The Candy Jar issued 150,000 of the 300,000 authorized shares of common stock, par value $15, for $3,000,000 and all the 50,000 authorized shares of 10%, $20 par, cumulative preferred stock for $1,100,000. Combined earnings for 2004, 2005, 2006, and 2007 amounted to $1,250,000. Dividends paid in the four years were as follows: 2004— $100,000; 2005—$300,000; 2006—$0; 2007—$150,000.

Required:

1. Prepare the stockholders' equity section of the balance sheet as of December 31, 2007, for The Candy Jar.
2. Prepare the journal entry that would be necessary to record the dividends paid in 2007.

Problem 12-10

Stockholders' Equity Calculations

A computer virus destroyed important financial information pertaining to Denton Company's stockholders' equity section. Your expertise is needed to compute the missing account balances. The only information you can recover from the computer's backup system is as follows:

a. During 2006, 8,000 shares of common stock with a par value of $10 were issued when the market price per share was $22.

(continued)

b. Cash dividends of $30,000 were paid to preferred shareholders.
c. Denton Company acquired 4,000 shares of common stock at $15 to hold as treasury stock.
d. Denton Company reissued 3,000 shares of treasury stock for $18.

	December 31, 2005	December 31, 2006
Preferred stock	$ 2,000	$ 2,000
Common stock	6,000	?
Paid-in capital in excess of par, preferred stock	750	750
Paid-in capital in excess of par, common stock	1,750	?
Paid-in capital, treasury stock	0	?
Retained earnings	4,500	5,250
Treasury stock	0	(15,000)
Total stockholders' equity	15,000	?

Required:

1. Calculate the account balances for the following accounts:
   a. Common Stock
   b. Paid-In Capital in Excess of Par, Common Stock
   c. Paid-In Capital, Treasury Stock
   d. Stockholders' Equity
2. How much net income did Denton Company report for 2006?

Problem 12-11

Stock Calculations and the Stockholders' Equity Section
The following account balances appear on the books of World Corporation as of December 31, 2006:

Preferred stock (7%, $40 par, 70,000 shares authorized, 50,000 shares issued and outstanding)	$2,000,000
Common stock ($3 par, 500,000 shares authorized, 300,000 shares issued and outstanding)	900,000
Paid-in capital in excess of par, preferred stock	310,000
Paid-in capital in excess of par, common stock	490,000
Net income for 2006	130,000
Dividends paid during 2006	70,000
Retained earnings, January 1, 2006	1,360,000

Required:

1. If the preferred stock is selling at $45 per share, what is the maximum amount of cash that World Corporation can obtain by issuing additional preferred stock given the present number of authorized shares?
2. If common stock is selling for $12 per share, what is the maximum amount of cash that can be obtained by issuing additional common stock given the present number of authorized shares?
3. Given the account balances at December 31, 2006, and ignoring parts (1) and (2), prepare, in good form, the stockholders' equity section of the balance sheet.

Problem 12-12

Unifying Concepts: Stock Transactions and the Stockholders' Equity Section
Richard Corporation was founded on January 1, 2006, and entered into the following stock transactions during 2006.

a. Received authorization for 100,000 shares of $20 par-value common stock, 50,000 shares of 6% preferred stock with a par value of $5, and 50,000 shares of no-par common stock.

b. Issued 25,000 shares of the $20 par-value common stock at $24 per share.
c. Issued 10,000 shares of the preferred stock at $8 per share.
d. Issued 5,000 shares of the no-par common stock at $22 per share.
e. Reacquired 1,000 shares of the $20 par-value common stock at $25 per share.
f. Reacquired 500 shares of the no-par common stock at $20 per share.
g. Reissued 250 of the 1,000 reacquired shares of $20 par-value common stock at $23 per share.
h. Reissued all the 500 reacquired shares of no-par common stock at $23 per share.
i. Closed the $14,000 net income to Retained Earnings. Revenues and expenses for the year were $90,000 and $76,000, respectively.

Required:
1. Prepare journal entries to record the 2006 transactions in Richard Corporation's books.
2. Prepare the stockholders' equity section of Richard Corporation's balance sheet at December 31, 2006. Assume that the transactions represent all the events involving equity accounts during 2006.

Problem 12-13

Unifying Concepts: Stock Transactions, the Stockholders' Equity Section, and the Statement of Stockholders' Equity

The condensed balance sheet of IBC Corporation at December 31, 2005, is shown below.

IBC Corporation
Balance Sheet
December 31, 2005

Assets

Cash	$ 400,000
All other assets	1,042,000
	$1,442,000

Liabilities and Stockholders' Equity

Current liabilities	$ 164,000
Long-term liabilities	230,000
	$ 394,000
Contributed capital:	
Common stock ($10 par, 100,000 shares authorized, 80,000 shares outstanding)	$ 800,000
Paid-in capital in excess of par, common stock	80,000
Retained earnings	168,000
	$1,048,000
	$1,442,000

During 2006, the following transactions affected stockholders' equity:

Feb. 15 Purchased 2,000 shares of IBC outstanding common stock at $15 per share.
May 21 Sold 1,200 of the shares purchased on February 15 at $19 per share.
Sept. 15 Issued 8,000 shares of previously unissued common stock at $21 per share.
Dec. 21 Sold the remaining 800 shares of treasury stock at $22 per share.
31 Closed net income of $85,360 to Retained Earnings. Revenues were $185,360; expenses were $100,000.

Required:
1. Prepare the journal entries to record the 2006 transactions.
2. Prepare the stockholders' equity section of the balance sheet at December 31, 2006.
3. Prepare a statement of stockholders' equity for the year ended December 31, 2006.

Problem 12-14

P.A.S.S.
Power Accounting
System Software

Unifying Concepts: Stockholders' Equity

Icon Corporation was organized during 2004. At the end of 2005, the equity section of its balance sheet appeared as follows:

Contributed capital:	
Preferred stock (6%, $20 par, 10,000 shares authorized,	
5,000 shares issued and outstanding)	$100,000
Common stock ($10 par, 50,000 shares authorized,	
11,000 shares issued, 10,000 outstanding)	110,000
Paid-in capital in excess of par, preferred stock	20,000
Total contributed capital	$230,000
Retained earnings	100,000
Total contributed capital plus retained earnings	$330,000
Less treasury stock (1,000 shares of common at cost)	(12,000)
Total stockholders' equity	$318,000

During 2006, the following stockholders' equity transactions occurred (in chronological sequence):

a. Issued 500 shares of common stock at $13 per share.
b. Reissued 500 shares of treasury stock at $13 per share.
c. Issued 1,000 shares of preferred stock at $25 per share.
d. Reissued 500 shares of treasury stock at $10 per share.
e. Declared a dividend large enough to meet the current-dividend preference of the preferred stock and to pay the common stockholders $2 per share. Dividends are recorded directly in the retained earnings account.
f. Closed net income of $65,000 to Retained Earnings. Revenues were $400,000; expenses were $335,000.

Required:
1. Journalize the transactions.
2. Prepare the stockholders' equity section of the balance sheet at December 31, 2006.

Problem 12-15

Comprehensive Income

The following information relates to McMurray Company:

Sales	$30,000
Cost of goods sold	12,000
Other operating expenses	5,000
Interest expense	800
Income tax expense	6,000

In addition, the following events occurred during the year:

a. McMurray Company has an investment portfolio for long-term investment purposes. That portfolio decreased in value by $10,000 during the year.
b. McMurray Company owns a substantial amount of land. During the year, the land increased in value by $20,000.
c. McMurray Company has several foreign subsidiaries. The currencies in the countries where those subsidiaries are located declined in value (relative to the U.S. dollar) during the year. Accordingly, the computed value of the equity of those subsidiaries, in U.S. dollars, decreased by $2,600.

Required:
1. Compute McMurray's comprehensive income for the year.
2. **Interpretive Question:** Is comprehensive income a good measure of the change in a company's value during the year?

Problem 12-16

Stockholders' Equity Section with Selected "Other Information"

The stockholders' equity section of Glory Company's balance sheet was as follows as of December 31, 2006, and December 31, 2005:

Glory Company
Stockholders' Equity Sections of Balance Sheet
December 31, 2006 and 2005
(in millions)

	2006	2005
Preferred stock	$ 21.4	$ 21.4
Common stock	48.4	43.2
Paid-in capital, various types	22.6	15.3
Retained earnings	51.8	41.2
Subtotal	$144.2	$121.1
Accumulated foreign currency translation adjustments	21.4	57.3
Net unrealized gains (losses) on investments in certain debt and equity securities	(46.4)	(8.8)
Total stockholders' equity	$119.2	$169.6

Required:

Based on the stockholders' equity section for Glory Company, answer the following questions:

1. Do you believe Glory Company made a profit during the year 2006? Assuming that only net income and dividends changed the retained earnings balance from 2005 to 2006, by how much did net income exceed dividends?
2. What was the total amount of money raised during 2006 from the selling of stock? (Assume that only the selling of stock affected the contributed capital accounts.)
3. Did the market value of Glory Company's securities that affect the equity section increase or decrease in 2006? By how much?
4. **Interpretive Question:** The board of directors believes it should fire the current management of the company because total stockholders' equity decreased substantially. Do you agree? Why or why not?

Problem 12-17

P.A.S.S.
Power Accounting System Software

Recording Stockholders' Equity Transactions

The stockholders' equity section of Hathaway Corporation's December 31, 2005, balance sheet is as follows:

Contributed capital:	
Preferred stock (5%, $25 par, 2,000 shares issued and outstanding)	$ 50,000
Common stock ($30 par, 10,000 shares issued and outstanding)	300,000
Paid-in capital in excess of par, preferred stock	10,000
Paid-in capital in excess of par, common stock	100,000
Total contributed capital	$460,000
Retained earnings	340,000
Total stockholders' equity	$800,000

(continued)

During 2006, Hathaway Corporation had the following transactions:

Feb. 1 Paid a cash dividend of $3 per share on common stock. The dividend was declared December 31, 2005.

Mar. 15 Declared and issued a 19% common stock dividend. The market price of the stock on this date was $40 per share.

June 1 Reacquired 3,000 shares of common stock at $35 per share.

Sept. 1 Reissued 500 shares of treasury stock at $40 per share.

Nov. 15 Reissued 500 shares of treasury stock at $32 per share.

Required:
Record the transactions.

Problem 12-18

Dividend Transactions and Calculations

As of December 31, 2005, Nibley Corporation has 300,000 shares of $12 par-value common stock authorized, with 120,000 of these shares issued and outstanding.

Required:

1. Prepare journal entries to record the following 2006 transactions:

Jan. 1 Received authorization for 150,000 shares of 5%, cumulative preferred stock with a par value of $15.

2 Issued 14,000 shares of the preferred stock at $20 per share.

June 1 Reacquired 30% of the common stock outstanding for $25 per share.

2 Declared a cash dividend of $20,000. The date of record is June 15.

30 Paid the previously declared cash dividend of $20,000.

2. Determine the proper allocation to preferred and common stockholders of a $150,000 cash dividend declared on December 31, 2006. (This dividend is in addition to the June 2 dividend.)

3. **Interpretive Question:** Why didn't the preferred stockholders receive their current-dividend preference of $10,500 in part (2)?

Problem 12-19

Recording Dividend Transactions and Reporting Stockholders' Equity

Murtry, Inc., reported the following stockholders' equity balances in its June 30, 2005, balance sheet:

Preferred stock (6%, $100 par, cumulative; 20,000 shares authorized,	
6,000 shares issued and outstanding)	$ 600,000
Common stock ($20 par; 250,000 shares authorized,	
60,000 shares issued and outstanding)	1,200,000
Retained earnings	950,000

Required:

1. The following stockholders' equity transactions occurred (in the order presented) during the fiscal year ending June 30, 2006. Prepare the necessary journal entries to record the transactions.

   a. Murtry declared and issued a 5% dividend on common stock; the market value of the stock was $30 per share on the date of the dividend.

   b. A 50% stock dividend on common stock was declared and issued when the stock was trading at a market price of $40 per share.

   c. A cash dividend was declared at the end of the fiscal year. The common stockholders will receive 50 cents per share after the current and cumulative preference on the preferred stock is satisfied. Preferred stock dividends are one year in arrears.

2. Assuming Murtry's net income for the year ended June 30, 2006, is $310,000, prepare the stockholders' equity section of the June 30, 2006, balance sheet and a statement of stockholders' equity for the 2005–2006 fiscal year.

3. **Interpretive Question:** What is the effect on earnings per share when a company has a stock dividend or stock split?

Problem 12-20

Statement of Retained Earnings and Stockholders' Equity

The following balances appear in the accounts of Iron Corporation as of December 31, 2006:

Retained earnings, January 1, 2006	$128,000
Prior-period adjustment (tax adjustment for 2004)	(57,000)
Net income for 2006	60,000
Preferred stock (7%, $12 par, 20,000 shares authorized, 5,000 shares issued and outstanding)	60,000
Common stock ($5 par, 100,000 shares authorized, 16,000 shares issued, 200 held as treasury stock)	80,000
Paid-in capital in excess of par, preferred stock	13,400
Paid-in capital in excess of par, common stock	42,800
Treasury stock	3,600
Cash dividends (declared during 2006)	10,000

Required:

1. Prepare the statement of retained earnings for Iron Corporation as of December 31, 2006.
2. Prepare the stockholders' equity section of Iron Corporation's balance sheet as of December 31, 2006.

Problem 12-21

Statement of Retained Earnings

Jamon Corporation records show the following at December 31, 2006:

Extraordinary loss (net of tax)	$ (37,500)
Cash dividends declared during 2006	45,000
Stock dividends issued during 2006	10,000
January 1, 2006, retained earnings balance	780,000
Prior-period adjustment (net of tax)	(19,500)
Net income before extraordinary items and taxes (assume a 35% tax rate)	172,000

Required:

Prepare a 2006 statement of retained earnings.

discussion cases

Case 12-1

Does Stockholders' Equity Tell the Real Story?

Last year, Shades International (a hypothetical company) invented the famous Shades Sunglasses that are widely popular around the world and especially in Japan and the Far East. Citizens of these countries love the new-age sunglasses and are buying them as fast as they can. Shades International owns the patent but contracts out to other companies to manufacture the glasses. Shades International also leases its research and development facility, the only building it occupies. Royalties from the glasses exceeded $10 million last year and are expected to increase dramatically this year. Selected data (in millions of dollars) from Shades International's financial statements are as follows:

Patent	$ 0.3
Other assets	0.9
Total liabilities	4.5
Total stockholders' equity	(3.3)

In the next two months, Shades International will be offering stock for sale to the public. Your friend is encouraging you to buy some of the stock. You are leery about the negative stockholders' equity balance. Is Shades International worth even considering as a possible investment?

Case 12-2

To Pay or Not To Pay Dividends

Assume Lenny Company manufactures specialized computer peripheral parts such as speakers and modems. It is a new company that has been in operation for just two years. During those two years, Lenny Company's stock price has increased over 400%. Lenny Company does not pay dividends nor does the company plan to do so in the future. However, the company's stock seems to be heavily traded. Why do you think there is so much interest in buying Lenny Company's stock if stockholders do not receive dividends?

j udgment calls

Judgment 12-1

You Decide: Should partners of a business be held personally liable for the debts of the business, or should their business activities and debts be kept separate from their personal activities?
John and Jeff formed a partnership and started selling cookies based on a secret recipe they created. After one year of strong sales, Jeff left the company with $30,000 cash and was never heard of again. Now, the creditors are requesting payment from John to satisfy a loan Jeff signed. If John can't make the payments from what is left in the business, who will the bank look to for payment?

Judgment 12-2

You Decide: Should the U.S. government change the current corporate tax system from double to single taxation, or is the present system (taxing corporate profits and then dividends to shareholders) adequate?
You were recently at a family gathering when the topic of conversation turned political. Your father, a retired CEO of a regional grocery chain, commented on his dissatisfaction with the current corporate tax system. He said, "It was very frustrating to see profits of my company taxed once at the corporate level and then again when the shareholders receive dividends. Something should be done about that!" Do you agree with your father?

Judgment 12-3

You Decide: Should companies be required to pay cash dividends on their stock to shareholders, or should it be left up to the companies' discretion whether they pay dividends or reinvest those funds back in the company?
Your father asked you why his investment in a publicly-traded stock is not paying him any dividends. He said, "As far as I know, they never have. I invested in the company to get something back and so far, I haven't received anything. Shouldn't the company be looking after its shareholders?" Should all companies be required to pay dividends?

Competency Enhancement Opportunities

▶ Analyzing Real Company Information
▶ International Case
▶ Ethics Case
▶ Writing Assignment

▶ The Debate
▶ Cumulative Spreadsheet Project
▶ Internet Search

The following additional assignments provide opportunities for students to develop critical thinking, ethical perspectives, oral and written communication skills, experience with electronic research, and teamwork through group and business activities.

▶ Analyzing Real Company Information

Analyzing 12-1 (Microsoft)

The 2002 Form 10-K for MICROSOFT is included in Appendix A. Microsoft's stockholders' equity statements provide details of equity transactions of the company during the 2002 fiscal year. Locate the statements and consider the following questions:

1. What was the major reason that stockholders' equity increased for the year?
2. How much did common stockholders receive in dividends during the year? How much did preferred stockholders receive?
3. Did Microsoft issue more shares than it repurchased during the year or vice versa? How can you tell? (*Hint:* You should look in the notes to the statements to answer this question.)

Analyzing 12-2 (Wal-Mart Stores, Inc.)

WAL-MART has a simple, straightforward statement of shareholders' equity. That statement for the year 2002 is reproduced below.

Wal-Mart's Consolidated Statement of Stockholders' Equity
For the Year Ended January 31, 2002
(amounts in millions of U.S. dollars)

	Number of Shares	Common Stock	Capital in Excess of Par Value	Retained Earnings	Other Accumulated Comprehensive Income (Loss)	Total
Balance—January 31, 2001	4,470	$447	$1,411	$30,169	$ (684)	$31,343
Net income				6,671		$ 6,671
Other accumulated comprehensive income						
Foreign currency translation adjustment					(472)	(472)
Hedge accounting adjustment					(112)	(112)
Total Comprehensive Income						$ 6,087
Cash dividends ($0.28 per share)				(1,249)		(1,249)
Purchase of company stock	(24)	(2)	(62)	(1,150)		(1,214)
Stock options exercised and other	7		135			135
Balance—January 31, 2002	4,453	$445	$1,484	$34,441	$(1,268)	$35,102

(continued)

1. Based on the dividends paid during 2002, how many shares of stock were outstanding when the dividends were paid?
2. Why isn't the number of shares receiving dividends exactly the same as the number of shares outstanding on January 31 as indicated in the statement?
3. Estimate Wal-Mart's dividend payout ratio for each year. (*Hint:* You will need to estimate an earnings-per-share figure given the available data.)

▷ International Case

International

The EMI Group

The shareholders' equity section of the balance sheet of THE EMI GROUP, a company based in the United Kingdom, is reproduced below. Review this information and answer the questions below.

The EMI Group Balance Sheets at 31 March 2002	Group	
	2002 £m	2001 Restated* £m
Capital and reserves		
Called-up share capital	110.4	110.4
Share premium account	445.8	445.6
Capital redemption reserve	495.8	495.8
Other reserves	256.0	256.0
Profit and loss reserve (including goodwill previously written off)	(2,338.2)	(2,084.0)
Equity shareholders' funds	(1,030.2)	(776.2)
Minority interests (equity)	141.1	136.3
	(889.1)	(639.9)

1. What do you think the term "called-up share capital" means?
2. What do you think the term "share premium account" means?
3. What does the term "profit and loss reserve" mean?

▷ Ethics Case

Buying Your Own Shares Back

You are the chief financial officer for Esoteric, Inc., a company whose stock is publicly traded. The stock market has recently experienced an overall downturn, and the price of your company's stock has decreased by about 15%. This significantly affects the compensation of the executives of your company as their bonuses are based on the company's stock price. The bonus plan rewards company executives who take actions to increase the value of the company to shareholders. The reasoning is that if management increases the value of the company to shareholders, management should be rewarded.

As you consider ways to increase the value of the company, when the market itself is slumping, the following idea pops into your head: We will buy back our own stock. That will cause the remaining outstanding stock to increase in value, which is good for those individuals holding that stock. And it will also result in you and the other corporate executives receiving sizable bonuses.

Do you think this plan of action to increase stock price was what the designers of the compensation plan had in mind when they linked executive bonuses to company stock price? Does buying back the company's own stock add value to the company as a whole? Should the compensation plan prohibit activities like buying stock back? Consider these issues and be prepared to discuss them.

▶ *Writing Assignment*

Stock Splits versus Stock Dividends

In this chapter, you learned that we account for stock dividends differently than we account for stock splits. For stock dividends, the accounting also varies, depending on the size of the dividend. Prepare a two-page memo summarizing the following points:

1. To an investor who holds stock in a company, what is the difference between a small stock dividend, a large stock dividend, and a stock split?
2. To the accountant who must account for business transactions, what is the difference between a small stock dividend, a large stock dividend, and a stock split?
3. If you held stock in a company that was contemplating the declaration of a stock dividend or a stock split, which would you prefer?

▶ *The Debate*

Microsoft Should Share the Wealth!

Turn to MICROSOFT's Form 10-K in Appendix A and notice its cash balance. As of June 30, 2002, the company had over $38.6 billion in cash and short-term investments. It is likely that the company has a lot more cash on hand now. On January 16, 2003, the company announced a first-ever dividend of $0.16 per share. That amounts to a dividend payment of about $864 million. Should Microsoft use more of its cash to pay a bigger dividend to its common shareholders?

Divide your group into two teams.

-   The first team represents the position that "Bill Knows Best—Pay a Small Dividend." Prepare a two-minute presentation outlining the reasons why Microsoft's small-dividend policy is appropriate.
-   The second team represents the position that "A Bigger Dividend Should Be Paid." Prepare a two-minute presentation outlining reasons why Microsoft should use some of its stockpile of cash to reward common shareholders with a much larger dividend payout.

▶ *Cumulative Spreadsheet Project*

This spreadsheet assignment is a continuation of the spreadsheet assignments given in earlier chapters. If you completed those spreadsheets, you have a head start on this one.

1. Handyman wishes to prepare a forecasted balance sheet and income statement for 2007. Use the original financial statement numbers for 2006 [given in part (1) of the Cumulative Spreadsheet Project assignment in Chapter 2] as the basis for the forecast, along with the following additional information:
    a. Sales in 2007 are expected to increase by 40% over 2006 sales of $700.

(continued)

b. Cash will increase at the same rate as sales.

c. The forecasted amount of accounts receivable in 2007 is determined using the forecasted value for the average collection period. For simplicity, do the computations using the end-of-period accounts receivable balance instead of the average balance. The average collection period for 2007 is expected to be 14.08 days.

d. The forecasted amount of inventory in 2007 is determined using the forecasted value for the number of days' sales in inventory (computed using the end-of-period inventory balance). The number of days' sales in inventory for 2007 is expected to be 107.6 days.

e. The forecasted amount of accounts payable in 2007 is determined using the forecasted value for the number of days' purchases in accounts payable (computed using the end-of-period accounts payable balance). The number of days' purchases in accounts payable for 2007 is expected to be 48.34 days.

f. The $160 in operating expenses reported in 2006 breaks down as follows: $5 depreciation expense, $155 other operating expenses.

g. New long-term debt will be acquired (or repaid) in an amount sufficient to make Handyman's debt ratio (total liabilities divided by total assets) in 2007 exactly equal to 0.80.

h. No cash dividends will be paid in 2007.

i. New short-term loans payable will be acquired in an amount sufficient to make Handyman's current ratio in 2007 exactly equal to 2.0.

j. The forecasted amount of property, plant, and equipment (PP&E) in 2007 is determined using the forecasted value for the fixed asset turnover ratio. For simplicity, compute the fixed asset turnover ratio using the end-of-period *gross* PP&E balance. The fixed asset turnover ratio for 2007 is expected to be 3.518 times.

k. In computing depreciation expense for 2007, use straight-line depreciation and assume a 30-year useful life with no residual value. Gross PP&E acquired during the year is depreciated for only half the year. In other words, depreciation expense for 2007 is the sum of two parts: (1) a full year of depreciation on the beginning balance in PP&E, assuming a 30-year life and no residual value and (2) a half-year of depreciation on any new PP&E acquired during the year, based on the change in the gross PP&E balance.

l. Assume an interest rate on short-term loans payable of *6.0%* and on long-term debt of *8.0%*. Only a half-year's interest is charged on loans taken out during the year. For example, if short-term loans payable at the end of 2007 are $15 and given that short-term loans payable at the end of 2006 were $10, total short-term interest expense for 2007 would be $0.75 [($10 × 0.06) + ($5 × 0.06 × 1/2)].

Note: These statements were constructed as part of the spreadsheet assignment in Chapter 11; you can use that spreadsheet as a starting point if you have completed that assignment.

For this exercise, add the following additional assumptions:

- In addition to preparing forecasted financial statements for 2007, Handyman also wishes to prepare forecasted financial statements for 2008. All assumptions applicable to 2007 are also assumed to be applicable to 2008. Sales in 2008 are expected to be 40% higher than sales in 2007.

Clearly state any additional assumptions that you make.

2. For each forecasted year, 2007 and 2008, state whether Handyman is expected to issue new shares of stock or to repurchase shares of stock.

3. Repeat (2), with the following changes in assumptions:
   a. The debt ratio in 2007 and 2008 is exactly equal to 0.70.
   b. The debt ratio in 2007 and 2008 is exactly equal to 0.95.
4. Comment on how it is possible for a company to have negative paid-in capital.

▷ *Internet Search*

Dow Jones & Company

We began this chapter with a look at the history of DOW JONES & COMPANY. Let's continue our examination of this company using its Internet site. Access Dow Jones' site at **http://dowjones .com**. Sometimes Web addresses change, so if this address doesn't work, access the Web site for this book (**http://albrecht.swlearning.com**) for an updated link to Dow Jones & Company.

Once you have gained access to the company's Web site, answer the following questions:

1. What business publications is the company responsible for? What other services does the company provide?
2. Locate the company's most recent annual report. Which of the company's business segments is the most profitable as measured by operating income as a percentage of revenues?
3. Did the company pay a dividend in the most recent year? If so, how much per share? Compute the company's dividend payout ratio.
4. Review the note disclosure relating to the company's executive incentive plan (employee stock compensation plans). What is the objective of this plan?

chapter

13

Investments in Debt and Equity Securities

After studying this chapter, you
should be able to:

Learning Objectives

1 Understand why com-
panies invest in other
companies.

2 Understand the different classifications for securities.

3 Account for the purchase, recognition of revenue, and sale of trading
and available-for-sale securities.

4 Account for changes
in the value of securities.

5 Account for held-to-
maturity securities.

6 Account for securities
using the equity method.

7 Understand the basics
of consolidated financial
statements.

Warren Buffett, who has been called "the world's greatest investor," has lived most of his life not far from the house in which he grew up in Omaha, Nebraska.[1] He attended the Wharton School at the University of Pennsylvania (but dropped out because he thought he wasn't learning anything); received a bachelor's degree from the University of Nebraska; applied for admission to do graduate work at Harvard but was rejected; and instead earned a master's degree in economics at Columbia.

Buffett began his professional career as a stock trader and eventually created an investment fund called the Buffett Partnership, which earned a 32% average annual return over its life from 1956 to 1969. Buffett also began purchasing shares in a small textile manufacturer called BERKSHIRE HATHAWAY. His first 2,000 shares of Berkshire Hathaway stock cost $7.50 per share (plus $0.10 per share in commissions). Buffett transformed Berkshire Hathaway from a textile manufacturer into a holding company that invests in the stock of other companies. A selection of the companies controlled by Berkshire Hathaway, along with some of Berkshire Hathaway's major investments, is shown in Exhibit 1.

How has Berkshire Hathaway's stock performed under Warren Buffett's leadership? Well, on May 14, 2003, the company's stock closed at $73,710 per share! How has Warren Buffett done personally? He receives a salary of only $100,000 per year (making him the lowest paid CEO among the nation's top 200 companies). But don't

Exhibit 1: Berkshire Hathaway's Operations and Investments

Companies Owned by Berkshire Hathaway*

	Industry
GEICO	Property and casualty insurance
FlightSafety	Aviation training
See's Candy	Candy
Nebraska Furniture Mart, R.C. Willey, Star Furniture, and Jordan's Furniture	Home furnishings
Helzberg Diamonds, Borsheim's Fine Jewelry, and Ben Bridge Jeweler	Retail jewelry stores
International Dairy Queen	Fast food and dairy desserts
Fruit of the Loom	Underwear
Acme Brick Company	Bricks

Companies in Which Berkshire Hathaway Has Invested*

Company Name	Ownership Percentage
American Express Company	11.6%
The Coca-Cola Company	8.1%
The Gillette Company	9.2%
H&R Block, Inc.	8.9%
M&T Bank	7.3%
Moody's Corporation	15.7%
The Washington Post Company	17.3%
Wells Fargo & Company	3.2%

*This information is as of the end of 2002.

1 Janet Lowe, *Warren Buffett Speaks: Wit and Wisdom from the World's Greatest Investor* (New York: John Wiley & Sons, 1997).

feel sorry for Mr. Buffett. He was smart enough to purchase a large number of Berkshire Hathaway shares when the price was low. With a personal worth of approximately $35 billion, he ranks second on the list of the world's richest people.[2]

In this chapter we focus on why companies invest in other companies and how to account for those investments. When a company purchases the debt or equity securities of another company, several accounting issues are raised: how to account for the initial purchase, how to account for the receipt of dividends or interest, how to account for any subsequent changes in value of the security, and how to account for the security if it is sold or matures. The remainder of this chapter focuses on each of these issues. First, we examine how securities are classified and the different accounting implications of these classifications. We then introduce proper accounting for the purchase, receipt of revenue, sale, and valuation of securities. In the expanded material section of the chapter, we review the computations and accounting for a bond premium or discount from the point of view of the purchaser (we focused on the seller's perspective in Chapter 11). We also introduce the equity method of accounting and discuss when its application is appropriate. Exhibit 2 highlights the financial statement accounts that will be discussed in this chapter.

Why Companies Invest in Other Companies

| Understand why companies invest in other companies.

Companies invest in the debt and equity securities of other companies for a variety of reasons. A major reason is to earn a return on their excess cash. Most businesses are cyclical or seasonal; that is, their cash inflows and outflows vary significantly throughout the year. At certain times (particularly when inventories are being purchased), a company's cash supply is low. At other times (usually during or shortly after heavy selling seasons), there is excess cash on hand. A typical cash flow pattern for a retail firm is illustrated in Exhibit 3. The time line shows that the company has insufficient cash for inventory buildup for the Christmas rush, followed by large amounts of accounts receivable (from credit sales), and then an excess of cash immediately after Christmas.

When a company needs cash to meet current obligations, funds can be obtained through such means as borrowing from financial institutions or selling (factoring) accounts receivable or other assets. During those periods of time when excess cash exists, firms usually prefer to invest that money and earn a return. One possibility is to place the money in a bank and earn a fixed return. Most firms, however, are not satisfied with the low interest rates offered by financial institutions and have turned to other investment alternatives. Investing in the stocks (equity) and bonds (debt) of other companies allows a firm to earn a higher rate of return by accepting a higher degree of risk. BERKSHIRE HATHAWAY is perhaps the most famous example of a company whose sole purpose is to invest in the debt and equity securities of other companies.

Firms also invest in other companies for reasons other than to earn a return. The desire to ensure a supply of raw materials, to influence the board of directors, or to diversify its product offerings are additional reasons for a company to invest in other companies. For example, THE COCA-COLA COMPANY owns 38% of COCA-COLA ENTERPRISES and 35% of COCA-COLA AMATIL LTD. These two companies bottle many of Coke's products, and

2 If you have never had the pleasure of reading one of Warren Buffett's "Chairman's Letter to the Shareholders," you should take the opportunity now. No one writes a funnier, more insightful letter than Mr. Buffett. The company's Internet address is **http://www.berkshirehathaway.com.**

Exhibit 2: Financial Statement Items Covered in This Chapter

Balance Sheet

Current assets
Investments

Long-term investments

Stockholders' equity
Unrealized increase/decrease
in value of securities

Statement of Cash Flows

Operating activities
Purchase of trading securities
Sale of trading securities

Investing activities
Purchase of debt and equity
securities other than
trading securities
Sale of debt and equity
securities other than
trading securities

Income Statement

Other revenues and expenses
Gains and losses on sales
of securities
Unrealized gains and losses
on securities
Interest revenue
Dividend revenue

Exhibit 3: A Cash Flow Pattern

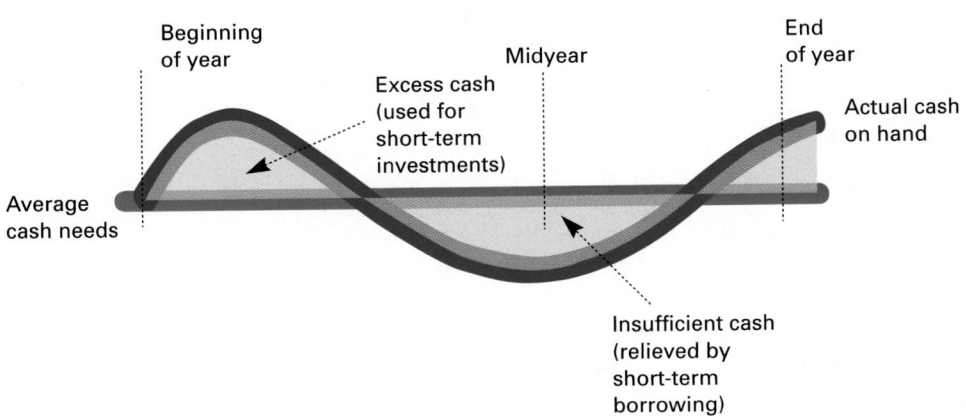

THE COCA-COLA COM-
PANY owns significant stakes
in companies that bottle its
products. Such investments
allow Coca-Cola to ensure
that its bottling facilities remain available and that its
soft-drink products consistently meet the company's
quality standards.

© 2003 Jack Andersen/Getty Images

The Coca-Cola Company maintains a significant ownership percentage to ensure that the bottling facilities remain available. As indicated in Exhibit 1, Berkshire Hathaway owns a number of companies outright and has significant investments in other companies. These
investments allow Berkshire Hathaway to significantly influence or even control the operating
decisions of the investees.

Rather than investing in the research and development required to develop a product or
an area of expertise, many companies find it cheaper to purchase all or part of another company that has already expended the effort and the time to develop the desired product or know-
how. As an example, to complement its existing software, NOVELL (a computer company
specializing in networking) purchased WordPerfect and Quattro Pro, word-processing and
spreadsheet software packages, respectively. This purchase then allowed Novell
to assemble a menu of software packages to compete with MICROSOFT's Word,
Excel, PowerPoint, and Access software packages. Novell's attempt to compete
with Microsoft failed, however, and the company eventually sold WordPerfect
to COREL.

STOP & THINK

Can you think of additional reasons why
companies would purchase interests in
other companies?

TO SUMMARIZE: Companies invest in other
companies for a variety of reasons. In most cases, the objective is to earn a return on the investment, either through
the receipt of interest or dividends, or through an increase
in the value of the investment. A firm may also invest in
other companies so that it will be able to influence their
operating decisions. In some cases, companies find it
cheaper to buy another company to gain access to its assets than to expend the resources necessary to develop the
assets on their own.

Classifying a Security

2 Understand the different classifications for securities.

debt securities Financial instruments issued by a company that carry with them a promise of interest payments and the repayment of principal.

equity securities (stock) Shares of ownership in a corporation that can change significantly in value and that provide for a return to investors in the form of dividends.

Two general types of securities are purchased by companies—debt securities and equity securities. **Debt securities** are financial instruments that carry with them the promise of interest payments and the repayment of the principal amount. Bonds are the most common type of debt security. Debt securities are issued by companies when the need for cash arises. These securities are often traded on public exchanges such as the New York Bond Exchange. Investors often prefer debt securities to equity securities because of the certainty of the income stream (interest) and the relative safety (low risk) of debt as an investment. Investors in corporate debt securities have priority over investors in equity securities, both for the yearly interest payments and for the return of principal if the issuing corporation gets into financial difficulty. Bonds issued by corporations are the most common type of debt securities (recall from Chapter 11 that bonds are typically issued in multiples of $1,000). Once the bonds are issued, ownership of the entire bond issuance, or just a portion, can change hands frequently.

Unlike bonds, **equity securities** (or **stock**), which are also traded on public exchanges, represent actual ownership interest in a corporation. The owner of equity securities is allowed to vote on such corporate matters as executive compensation policies, who will serve on the board of directors of the corporation, and who will be the outside auditor. In addition to voting, the owner of stock often receives a return on that investment in the form of a dividend. A second type of return often accumulates to the stockholder as well—appreciation in stock price. Many investors invest in a company not for the dividend but for the potential increase in stock price. High-tech companies typically do not pay dividends, instead electing to funnel their profits back into the company. Investors know that their return in high-tech companies will come in the form of an increased stock price, not a dividend. With the potential for increased stock price also comes a risk—the stock price could fall. Holders of debt securities, barring extreme financial difficulties by the issuer, will always receive the face amount of the bond upon maturity. Equity holders do not have that same promise. Stock can greatly increase in value or become worthless.

As mentioned earlier, investors can purchase both debt and equity securities with different goals in mind. Some may purchase to receive interest or dividend payments or to realize quick gains on price changes, while others may invest for more long-term reasons. Accounting standard-setters have developed different methods of accounting for investments depending on the intentions of the holder of the security. Exhibit 4 outlines the major classifications of debt and equity securities.

net*work* exercises

Berkshire Hathaway

Do you follow the stock price of individual companies? How can you get a company's stock price history? You can find the current stock price for any company that is publicly traded on the major stock exchanges at **http://finance.yahoo.com**.

Net Work:

At what price is BERKSHIRE HATHAWAY (trading symbol BRKa) currently trading?

Exhibit 4: Classifications of Debt and Equity Securities

Held-to-Maturity Securities

held-to-maturity security
A debt security purchased by an investor with the intent of holding the security until it matures.

If an investor purchases a debt security with the intent of holding the security until it matures, it is classified as a **held-to-maturity security** and is accounted for using techniques similar to those discussed in Chapter 11 for the bond issuer. The investor and the issuer record the same amounts but in a different way. With bond liabilities, the face value of the bonds is recorded in Bonds Payable, and a separate contra account is maintained for any discount or premium. Amortization of the discount or premium is then recorded in these contra accounts. With bond investments, the actual amount paid for the bonds (the cost of the asset), not the face value, is originally debited to the investment account. The amortization of any bond premium or discount is then recorded directly in the investment account. Thus, if you recall the accounting for Bonds Payable as presented in Chapter 11, you already know most of the accounting for a bond investment that is expected to be held to maturity. The procedures relating to amortizing premiums and discounts for the investors are discussed in the expanded material section of this chapter. Note that equity securities cannot be classified as held-to-maturity securities; equity securities typically do not mature.[3]

FYI:

Equity securities cannot be classified as held-to-maturity securities.

Equity Method Securities

equity method A method used to account for an investment in the stock of another company when significant influence can be imposed (presumed to exist when 20 to 50% of the outstanding voting stock is owned).

consolidated financial statements Statements that report the combined operating results, financial position, and cash flows of two or more legally separate but affiliated companies as if they were one economic entity.

In the case of equity securities, accounting standard-setters have determined that if securities are held with the objective of significantly influencing the operations of the investee, then the securities should be accounted for using the **equity method**. The equity method records changes in the value of the investment as the net assets of the investee change. The assumption underlying the equity method is that if the investor can influence the operating decisions of the investee, then any change in the net assets of the investee should be reflected on the books of the investor. In determining what constitutes significant influence, the Accounting Principles Board suggests that, unless evidence exists to the contrary, ownership of at least 20% of the outstanding common stock of a company, but less than 50%, indicates the existence of significant influence. Because accounting for a security using the equity method can get complicated, details of the equity method are presented in the expanded material section of this chapter. If ownership exceeds 50%, then a controlling interest is assumed, and the accounting becomes far more complex. The FASB is examining the issue of control and has suggested that companies look beyond ownership percentage and examine other factors that may indicate control.[4] Two factors the FASB has highlighted are (1) ownership of a large minority voting interest (approximately 40%) with no other group owning a significant interest and (2) a company's domination of the process for electing the investee's board of directors. In cases where it is determined that control exists, the parent company (the acquiring company) and the subsidiary company (the acquired company) are required to combine their financial statements into one set of statements as if they were one economic entity. Such combined statements are called **consolidated financial statements**. The preparation of consolidated financial statements is briefly covered in expanded material of this chapter.

FYI:

Debt securities cannot be classified as equity method securities.

Trading and Available-for-Sale Securities

trading securities Debt and equity securities purchased with the intent of selling them should the need for cash arise or to realize short-term gains.

In those instances where securities are not being held to maturity (in the case of debt) or to control or significantly influence an investee (in the case of equity), the Financial Accounting Standards Board has developed two other classes of securities—trading and available-for-sale. **Trading securities** are those debt and equity securities held with the intent of selling the

---

3 There are exceptions to this rule, as in the case of "mandatorily redeemable preferred stock," but the accounting for these types of securities is beyond the scope of this text.
4 Exposure Draft: Consolidated Financial Statements: Purpose and Policy (Stamford: Financial Accounting Standards Board, 1999).

available-for-sale securities
Debt and equity securities not classified as trading, held-to-maturity, or equity method securities.

securities should the need for cash arise or to realize gains arising from short-term changes in price. These types of securities are purchased simply to earn a return on excess cash. **Available-for-sale securities** are publicly traded securities that are classified as neither held-to-maturity nor trading (in the case of debt securities). In the case of equity securities, they represent securities that are not classified as trading securities or accounted for using the equity method.

Why the Different Classifications?

Why are there different classifications for debt and equity securities? Why not simply classify all securities as "investments"? The reason for the distinction lies in the different treatments of accounting for changes in market value. In the case of securities classified as held-to-maturity, changes in the securities' value between the date of purchase and the maturity date do not affect the amount to be received at maturity. That amount is fixed on the day the bonds are issued. Thus, temporary changes in the value of securities classified as held-to-maturity are not recognized on the investor's books. Similar reasoning applies to securities accounted for under the equity method. These securities are purchased, not with the intent of selling them in the future, but instead to be able to exercise influence over a corporation. Again, temporary changes in the value of these securities are not recognized on the investor's books.

Trading securities are purchased with the intent of earning a return—through interest or dividends and through short-term resale of the securities. Firms are required to recognize these two types of returns on the income statement. For example, assume that XYZ Company purchases 100 shares of ABC, Inc. stock for $5 per share. During the year, ABC pays a $1 dividend per share, and the value of the stock increases to $7 per share. XYZ will recognize, as income, $100 in dividend income as well as $200 in unrealized market gains. While the $100 in dividends was actually received, the $200 gain was not. The securities would have to have been sold in order to actually receive the $200 increase in value. Recognizing this gain, even though it was not realized through an arm's-length transaction, represents a major departure from the historical cost principle that has guided accounting for centuries. In 1994, the FASB determined that because the fair market value of many debt and equity securities can be objectively determined (via market quotes) and they can easily be sold (one phone call to a broker), it would be appropriate to include any unrealized gains or losses on changes in value of trading securities on the income statement.

> **FYI:**
>
> Many companies avoid the issue of what to include on the income statement by classifying all their investment securities as being available-for-sale. Berkshire Hathaway and MICROSOFT are examples of companies that use this classification scheme.

Changes in the value of securities classified as available-for-sale are recorded on the balance sheet. However, no gain or loss is realized on the income statement. Instead, an adjustment is made directly to a stockholders' equity account—Unrealized Increase/Decrease in Value of Available-for-Sale Securities Equity. The obvious question is "Why aren't changes in the value of these securities reflected on the income statement?" The answer lies in the intent behind holding the securities. Trading securities will probably be sold sooner rather than later. We cannot make that same assumption with available-for-sale securities. We are less certain they will be sold. Because of this uncertainty as to when the change in value will actually be realized, the FASB elected to go around the income statement in reporting changes in value relating to available-for-sale securities. Whatever the classification used, companies disclose their classification in the notes to the financial statements. For example, BERKSHIRE HATHAWAY provides the following note disclosure relating to its investments:

> Berkshire's management determines the appropriate classifications of investments in securities with fixed maturities and equity securities at the time of acquisition and re-evaluates the classifications at each balance sheet date. Berkshire's investments in fixed maturity and equity securities are primarily classified as available-for-sale, except for certain investments which are classified as held-to-maturity. Held-to-maturity investments are carried at amortized cost, reflecting Berkshire's intent and ability to hold the securities to

maturity. Available-for-sale securities are stated at fair value with net unrealized gains or losses reported as a component of accumulated other comprehensive income.

As you can see, Berkshire Hathaway classifies virtually every security as available-for-sale and is very specific as to what this classification means for the financial statements: current values go on the balance sheet, with unrealized gains and losses disclosed in stockholders' equity, while realized gains and losses are reported on the income statement.

Exhibit 5 summarizes the classification and disclosure issues relating to investments in debt and equity securities.

Exhibit 5: Classification and Disclosure of Securities

Classification of Securities	Types of Securities	Disclosed at	Reporting of Temporary Changes in Fair Value
Trading	Debt and equity	Fair value	Income statement
Available-for-sale	Debt and equity	Fair value	Stockholders' equity
Held-to-maturity	Debt	Amortized cost	Not recognized
Equity method	Equity	Cost adjusted for changes in net assets of investee	Not recognized

TO SUMMARIZE: Securities are classified depending upon the intent of management. If management's intent is to hold the investment until maturity (debt) or to influence the decisions of an investee (equity), then the held-to-maturity (debt) and equity method (equity) classifications are appropriate. If the securities are being held for other reasons, then management may classify them as either trading or available-for-sale. The importance of the classification becomes apparent when accounting for changes in value.

Accounting for Trading and Available-for-Sale Securities

3 Account for the purchase, recognition of revenue, and sale of trading and available-for-sale securities.

Four issues are associated with accounting for securities: (1) accounting for the purchase, (2) accounting for the revenue earned, (3) accounting for the sale, and (4) accounting for the changes in value. The first three issues are fairly straightforward and are presented in this section. Accounting for changes in the value of securities is discussed in the following section. The time line in Exhibit 6 on p. 648 illustrates the important business issues associated with buying and selling investment securities.

Accounting for the Purchase of Securities

Investments in securities, like all other assets, are recorded at cost when purchased. This is the case whether the security being purchased is debt or equity or whether it is being held with the intent to sell it quickly or hold it for the long term. Cost includes the market price of the security plus any extra expenditures required in making the purchase (such as a stockbroker's fee).

Following the Stock Market Stocks are sold in a variety of markets in the same way that bonds are sold. Original issues of stocks are usually sold by an investment banking group, referred to as the underwriters.

After stocks are originally sold, they are traded in the marketplace, either on the New York Stock Exchange, the American Stock Exchange, regional market exchanges, or the over-the-counter market. A selected portion of stocks traded on the New York Stock Exchange on Tuesday, March 25, 2003, is listed here as they were reported in *The Wall Street Journal* on Wednesday, March 26, 2003. The quotations show the following information for each stock: (1) 52-week high and low; (2) the name of the company; (3) the trading symbol for that company; (4) the current dividend; (5) the yield percentage in relation to the purchase price; (6) the price-earnings (PE) ratio; (7) the volume of sales for that day; (8) the high, low, and closing prices for that day; and (9) the net change from the closing price of the previous day's trading. To illustrate how to read the quotation, the information for BERKSHIRE HATHAWAY class A common stock is as follows: The 52-week high was $78,500, and the low was $59,600. Berkshire does not pay a dividend. Thus, the dividend amount and dividend yield are blank. The current price is 24 times the annual earnings. A total of 320 (the z indicates that the 320 is actual number of shares sold) shares were traded on Tuesday, March 25, 2003. The stock closed for the day at $66,800, which was $200 lower than the close on Monday, March 24, 2003.

NEW YORK STOCK EXCHANGE
COMPOSITE TRANSACTIONS
For Tuesday, March 25, 2003

YTD % CHG	52-week HI	52-week LO		STOCK (SYM)	DIV	YLD %	PE	VOL 100s	CLOSE	NET CHG
13.9	38.60	24.70		BectonDksn **BDX**	0.40	1.10	19	13189	34.97	0.05
⇑ 8.2	27.65	20.67		BedfdPrpty **BED**	2.00	7.20	13	455	27.79	0.34
−25.9	25.30	10.90	♣	Belden **BWC**	0.2	1.8	dd	3831	11.28	−0.77
−15	37.70	18.32		BellSouth **BLS**	.84f	3.8	15	60465	22	0.15
−2.4	24.52	17.75		Belo **BLC**	0.30	1.40	18	2201	20.8	0.20
−11.4	57.05	39.33	♣	Bemis **BMS**	1.12f	2.50	14	3471	43.99	0.54
8.8	35.99	14.25		BenchmkElec **BHE**	—	—	21	2422	31.18	0.55
−19.4	28.67	12.70		Benetton **BNG**	.71e	4.9	—	75	14.42	0.08
6.7	43.20	29.90		Berkley **BER** s	.40f	0.9	13	3660	42.25	−0.29
−8.2	78500	59600		**BerkHathwy A BRKA**	—	—	24	z320	66800	−200
−8.6	2620	1925		BerkHathwy B **BRKB**	—	—	—	z11940	2215	−9
−11.4	18.31	14.52	♣	BerryPete A **BRY**	0.4	2.6	11	103	15.1	0.12
25.8	53.33	16.99		BestBuy **BBY** s	—	—	17	45274	30.37	1.32
−30.2	9.18	1.60		BeverlyEnt **BEV**	—	—	dd	4198	1.99	0.04
−12.4	19.90	9.92		BigLots **BLI**	—	—	17	4513	11.59	0.37
52.8	52.05	19.90		Biovail **BVF**	g	—	—	15413	40.35	1.57
−14.2	50.50	33.20		BlackDeck **BDK**	0.48	1.30	13	10137	36.81	0.12
3.3	36.90	18.35		BlackHills **BKH**	1.20f	4.4	15	1477	27.39	−0.09

Source: *The Wall Street Journal*, March 27, 2003.

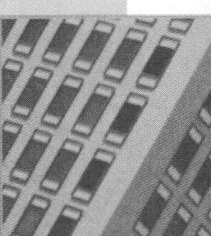

Exhibit 6: Time Line of Business Issues Associated with Buying and Selling Investment Securities

PURCHASE	EARN	CHANGES	SELL
securities	a return on securities	in the value of securities	securities

To illustrate the accounting for securities, we will use the following information throughout the chapter. On July 1, 2006, Far Side, Inc., purchased the following securities:

Security	Type	Classification	Cost (including Broker's Fees)
1	Debt	Trading	$ 5,000
2	Equity	Trading	27,500
3	Debt	Available-for-sale	17,000
4	Equity	Available-for-sale	9,200

The initial entry to record the investments is as follows:

Investment in Trading Securities	32,500	
Investment in Available-for-Sale Securities	26,200	
Cash		58,700

Though investments in securities are all recorded at cost, each of the four classifications of securities is accounted for differently subsequent to purchase. As a result, separate accounts are used to record the initial purchase. Management purchased Securities 1 and 2 with the intent of earning a return on the investment and selling the securities should the need for cash arise. Therefore, those securities are classified as "trading." Securities 3 and 4 were also purchased to earn a return on excess cash, but management has classified them as "available-for-sale." While the journal entry illustrated above combines all securities of the same classification into one account, subsidiary records will be kept for each individual security purchased.

Accounting for the Return Earned on an Investment

When a firm invests in the debt or equity of another firm with the intent of earning a return on its investment, how that return is accounted for varies depending on the classification of the investment. Recall from Chapter 11 that when debt securities are sold, a premium or discount can arise as a result of differences between the stated rate of interest and the market rate of interest. The resulting premium or discount must then be amortized over the life of the investment, thereby affecting the amount of interest expense recorded by the issuer. Theoretically, the purchaser of that debt security must also account for the difference between the purchase price and the eventual maturity value. In the discussion that follows, however, we are assuming that the time for which the investor anticipates holding debt securities classified as "trading" or as "available-for-sale" is not long enough for any amortization of premium or discount to materially affect interest expense. Amortization of premiums and discounts on debt securities is illustrated for "held-to-maturity" securities in the expanded material section of this chapter.

With this caveat in mind, the accounting for dividends and interest received on trading and available-for-sale securities becomes relatively straightforward. Cash received relating to interest and dividends is credited to Interest Revenue and Dividend Revenue, respectively. Interest earned but not yet received or dividends that have been declared but not paid are also recorded as revenue with a corresponding receivable. Continuing our example, interest and dividends received during 2006 relating to Far Side's securities investments were as follows:

FYI:

BERKSHIRE HATHAWAY reported interest, dividends, and other investment income earned of $3.1 billion during 2002.

Security	Interest	Dividends
1	$225	
2		$825
3	850	
4		644

The appropriate journal entry to record the receipt of interest and dividends is:

Cash	2,544	
Interest Revenue		1,075
Dividend Revenue		1,469

Accounting for the Sale of Securities

Suppose that Far Side sells all of its investment in Security 2 for $28,450 on October 31, 2006. As Security 2 was purchased for $27,500, the security has increased in value and that increase must be recorded. The journal entry to record the sale is:

Cash	28,450	
Investment in Trading Securities		27,500
Realized Gain on Sale of Trading Securities		950

If Security 2 had been sold for less than $27,500, a loss would have been recorded. If a broker's fee had been charged on the transaction, the fee would reduce the amount of cash received and decrease the gain recognized. If the broker's fee exceeded $950, a loss would be recorded on the books of the seller.

At the end of the accounting period, any gain or loss on the sale of securities must be included on the income statement. In the above example, the "Realized Gain on Sale of Trading Securities" would be included with Other Revenues and Expenses on the income statement. Note the term *realized*. **Realized gains and losses** indicate that an arm's-length transaction has occurred and that the securities have actually been sold. This distinction is important because in the next section we focus on accounting for unrealized gains and losses—those gains and losses that occur while a security is still being held and no arm's-length transaction has taken place.

realized gains and losses
Gains and losses resulting from the sale of securities in an arm's-length transaction.

On its statement of cash flows, BERKSHIRE HATHAWAY reported proceeds of $18,506 million from the sale of debt securities and equity securities. On its income statement, the company reported net realized gains of $637 million from the sale of securities. With this information, we can compute the historical cost of the securities sold during the period. Proceeds of $18,506 million less a gain of $637 million indicate that the cost of the securities was $17,869 million. A summary journal entry indicating the effects of these transactions for Berkshire Hathaway is as follows:

Cash	18,506	
Available-for-Sale Securities		17,869
Realized Gain on Sale of Securities		637

> **TO SUMMARIZE:** Investments in debt and equity securities are recorded at cost, which includes the fair value of the securities plus any other expenditures required to purchase the securities. When purchased, the securities are classified into one of four categories: held-to-maturity, equity method, trading, or available-for-sale securities. Revenues from securities take the form of interest, dividends, or gains or losses from selling the securities and are included under Other Revenues and Expenses on the income statement.

Accounting for Changes in the Value of Securities

4 Account for changes in the value of securities.

Investments in debt and equity securities are initially recorded at cost. If the value of a security changes after it is purchased, should that change in value be recorded on the investor's books? As stated previously in the chapter, the answer is "it depends." It depends on management's intent regarding that security. In the case of trading and available-for-sale securities, changes in market value are recorded on the books of the investor. For held-to-maturity securities and equity method securities, changes in value are not recorded unless they are considered permanent. To illustrate the accounting for changes in value of securities, we will continue the Far Side example. On December 31, 2006, the following market values were available:[5]

Security	Classification	Historical Cost	Market Value (December 31, 2006)
1	Trading	$ 5,000	$ 5,200
3	Available-for-sale	17,000	16,700
4	Available-for-sale	9,200	9,250

Changes in the Value of Trading Securities

At the end of 2006, Far Side computes the market value of its trading securities portfolio and compares it to the historical cost of the portfolio. In this instance, market value is $200 greater than historical cost. The journal entry to record this increase in value is:

Market Adjustment—Trading Securities	200	
Unrealized Gain on Trading Securities—Income		200

unrealized gains and losses Gains and losses resulting from changes in the value of securities that are still being held.

This journal entry recognizes the $200 increase in the value of the trading securities and records the unrealized gain on the income statement. **Unrealized gains and losses** indicate that

---

5 Remember that Security 2 was sold on October 31, 2006.

the securities have changed in value and are still being held. This journal entry also introduces a new account—**Market Adjustment—Trading Securities**. This account is combined with the trading securities account and reported on the balance sheet. Thus, the balance sheet will reflect the trading securities at their fair market value. Why not adjust the trading securities account directly instead of creating this market adjustment account? The reason is that the use of a valuation account, Market Adjustment—Trading Securities, allows a record of historical cost to be maintained. With this approach, a company can easily determine realized and unrealized gains. Perhaps the most important reason for keeping a record of historical cost is that, for tax purposes, only realized gains and losses are relevant. Other decisions made within a firm also rely on this historical cost information.

STOP & THINK

In Chapter 8, we were not to write inventory up if its value increased, though we were to write it down if its value declined. In Chapter 10, we were not to write property, plant, and equipment up if its value increased, though we were to write it down if its value declined. Why can we write up the value of securities if their price increases above the original cost?

Changes in the Value of Available-for-Sale Securities

A market adjustment account is also employed when adjusting available-for-sale securities to their fair market value. However, the change in value is not recorded on the income statement but is instead recorded in the account "Unrealized Increase/Decrease in Value of Available-for-Sale Securities—Equity." The "equity" used in the account title refers to the fact that this account is disclosed in the stockholders' equity section of the balance sheet, and its balance is carried forward from year to year. To illustrate, the available-for-sale portfolio of Far Side has a fair market value of $25,950 at year-end and a historical cost of $26,200. The appropriate adjustment is:

Unrealized Increase/Decrease in Value of Available-for-Sale Securities—Equity	250	
Market Adjustment—Available-for-Sale Securities		250

This journal entry adjusts the portfolio of available-for-sale securities to its fair market value at year-end and records the difference in the equity account.

Subsequent Changes in Value

Assume that no securities were bought or sold by Far Side, Inc., during 2007. At the end of 2007, its portfolio of securities had the following fair market values:

Security	Classification	Historical Cost	Market Value (December 31, 2007)
1	Trading	$ 5,000	$ 4,850
3	Available-for-sale	17,000	16,900
4	Available-for-sale	9,200	9,150

The value of the trading securities has declined to $4,850. Since the market adjustment account relating to trading securities should reflect the difference between historical cost and market, an entry is made to adjust the balance in Market Adjustment—Trading Securities from its previous $200 debit balance to the required $150 credit balance ($5,000 − $4,850). Where did this $200 debit balance come from? It came from the adjusting entry made on December 31, 2006. Remember that the market adjustment account is a real (balance sheet) account and is not closed at the end of an accounting period. Its balance carries forward from year to year. The required adjusting entry is:

Unrealized Loss on Trading Securities—Income	350	
Market Adjustment—Trading Securities		350

When this entry is posted, the Market Adjustment—Trading Securities T-account will appear as follows:

**Market Adjustment—
Trading Securities**

12/31/06	200		
		Adjustment	350
		12/31/07	150

Caution

The amount of the adjustment for the current period depends on the balance in the market adjustment account. Don't forget to factor that balance into your calculations.

The $150 credit balance will be netted against the $5,000 balance in the trading securities account and disclosed on the balance sheet as "Investment in Trading Securities (net)" for $4,850. The $350 unrealized loss will be included in the current period's net income and reported on the income statement. This adjustment procedure ensures that changes in the value of the trading securities portfolio are reflected in the period in which those changes in value occurred.

A similar procedure is employed in valuing the available-for-sale securities portfolio, except that the stockholders' equity account is used instead of the income statement account. For Far Side, the market value of the available-for-sale securities portfolio is $26,050. In comparing this to the historical cost of $26,200, a $150 credit balance in the market adjustment account is required. Take a moment and read the information again. An adjustment *to* get to a $150 credit balance is required—not an adjustment *of* $150. Given the previous credit balance in Market Adjustment—Available-for-Sale Securities of $250, the following adjusting entry is required:

Market Adjustment—Available-for-Sale Securities	100	
Unrealized Increase/Decrease in Value of Available-for-Sale Securities—Equity		100

Once this entry is posted, Market Adjustment—Available-for-Sale Securities will have the required $150 credit balance as follows:

**Market Adjustment—
Available-for-Sale Securities**

		12/31/06	250
Adjustment	100		
		12/31/07	150

When individual securities from a portfolio are sold, a realized gain or loss is recognized for the difference between the original cost of the securities and the selling price, without regard to previous adjustments made to a market adjustment account. At the end of the period, the cost of the remaining securities is compared to the fair market value of the remaining securities, and the market adjustment account is updated to account for the difference.

As mentioned earlier, BERKSHIRE HATHAWAY classifies all of its securities as available-for-sale. To determine how well Warren Buffett has managed the portfolio during the year, the financial statement reader must review both the income statement and the statement of stockholders' equity. Comparing the performance of the company's portfolio of securities for the years 2000 through 2002 results in the following (in millions):

	2000	2001	2002
Realized investment gains (from the income statement) . . .	$3,955	$ 1,363	$ 637
Unrealized appreciation of investments			
(from the statement of shareholders' equity)	4,406	(5,708)	2,859
Total portfolio performance	$8,361	$(4,345)	$3,496

TO SUMMARIZE: When the value of a trading or available-for-sale security changes, that change is reflected on the balance sheet using a market adjustment account. For trading securities, the unrealized gain or loss is reflected on the income statement for the period. For available-for-sale securities, the unrealized increase or decrease is recorded in a stockholders' equity account.

In this section of the chapter, we turn our attention to some of the complexities associated with purchasing debt and equity securities. First, we examine held-to-maturity securities and how any associated premium or discount associated with these securities is amortized. We also address the issue of purchasing a debt security between interest payment dates. The accounting issues associated with an equity security accounted for under the equity method are also presented, and the chapter concludes with a brief discussion of consolidated financial statements.

Accounting for Held-to-Maturity Securities

5 Account for held-to-maturity securities.

Held-to-maturity securities are debt securities issued by companies to raise needed funding for expansion, acquisitions, or other business reasons. Bonds (discussed in Chapter 11 from the point of view of the issuer) are by far the most common type of debt instrument that can be readily bought and sold. Because bonds represent the most common type of publicly traded debt instrument, the following discussion will focus on bonds purchased as investments to be held to maturity.

Accounting for the Initial Purchase

Bonds can be purchased at amounts either above face value (at a premium), below face value (at a discount), or at face value. Regardless of the purchase price, like all other assets, bonds are initially recorded at cost. The cost is the total amount paid to acquire the bonds; this includes the actual price paid for the bonds and any other purchasing expenditures, such as commissions or broker's fees.

To illustrate, assume that Far Side, Inc., purchased a fifth security and classified it as held-to-maturity. Security 5 consists of twenty $1,000 bonds of Chicago Company. The bonds were issued on July 1, 2006, and will mature five years from the date of issuance. The bonds will pay interest at a stated annual rate of 12%, with payments to be made semiannually on June 30 and December 31. In determining the value of the bonds, the present value of these future cash flows must be determined at the market rate on the date of the purchase. Assuming the market rate on bonds of similar risk is 16%, the purchase price of the bonds is obtained by adding the present value of $20,000 (received 10 periods in the future and discounted at 8%) to the present value of the annuity of the 10 interest payments of $1,200 each (discounted at

8%). The reason 8% is used is that interest is received semiannually; recall that in calculating present value, you must halve the interest rate (16%/2) for semiannual compounding periods. Likewise, you must double the number of years to determine the number of periods (5 years × 2 periods per year = 10 periods). The calculations are:

1. Semiannual interest payment .... $ 1,200
   Present value of an annuity of 10 payments of
   $1 at 8% (Table II, page 555) .... × 6.7101
   Present value of interest payments .... $ 8,052
2. Principal (face value) of bonds $20,000
   Present value of $1 received 10 periods in the
   future discounted at 8% (Table I, page 554) .... × 0.4632
   Present value of principal 9,264
3. Total present value of investment $17,316

In this example, 16% is the effective rate of interest because that is the amount of interest actually earned; 12% is the stated, or nominal, rate of interest on Chicago Company's bonds. Note that the 12% stated rate determines the size of the annuity payments ($20,000 × 0.12 × ¹/₂ year) but not the purchase price of the bonds; the purchase price varies according to market conditions. The 16% effective rate depends on three amounts: the purchase price, the interest payments, and the face value of the bonds. The $17,316 bond price is the amount that earns Far Side exactly 16%. The journal entry to record the acquisition is:

Investment in Held-to-Maturity Securities 17,316
    Cash 17,316

Note that the investment account is debited for the cost of the bonds with no separate amount shown for the discount of $2,684 ($20,000 − $17,316). Although the discount could be recorded in a separate contra-asset account, in practice it is more common for investors to record the asset cost in the investment account as shown.

Accounting for Bonds Purchased between Interest Dates

The preceding entry assumes that the investing company purchased the bonds on the issuance date, which was also the beginning date for the first interest period. In many cases, however, the date bonds are actually issued does not coincide with an interest date. Further, investors often acquire bonds in the "secondary market"; that is, they purchase bonds from other investors rather than from the issuing company. The secondary market for bonds includes the New York Bond Exchange. Since bonds are traded actively in this market each weekday, investors often acquire bonds between interest dates.

An investor who buys bonds between interest dates, either from the issuing company or in the secondary market, has to pay for the interest that has accrued since the last interest payment date. As explained in Chapter 11, this is necessary because whoever owns the bonds at the time interest is paid receives interest for one full interest period, usually six months, regardless of how long the bonds have been held.

To illustrate, we will assume that Far Side purchased the Chicago Company bonds in the secondary market for $17,316 on November 1, 2006. Semiannual interest of $1,200 ($20,000 × 0.12 × ¹/₂) is paid on the bonds on June 30 and December 31 of each year. On December 31, 2006, Far Side will receive $1,200 even though the bonds were purchased only two months earlier. Since the previous owner is entitled to 4 months' interest on November 1, Far Side will have to pay that individual or company the interest for the period July 1 to October 31. This is illustrated in Exhibit 7.

Exhibit 7: Investing between Interest Dates

The entry to record the investment in bonds on November 1 (between interest dates) is:

Investment in Held-to-Maturity Securities	17,316	
Bond Interest Receivable	800	
Cash		18,116
Purchased $20,000 of Chicago Company bonds for $17,316		
and paid four months' accrued interest.		

When Far Side receives $1,200 in interest on December 31, it will make the following entry:

Cash	1,200	
Interest Receivable		800
Interest Revenue		400
Received interest on Chicago Company bonds.		

Accounting for the Amortization of Bond Discounts and Premiums

Only in those rare instances when the stated interest rate of a bond is exactly equivalent to the prevailing market (or yield) rate for similar investments is a bond purchased at face value. At all other times, bonds are purchased either at a discount (below face value) or at a premium (above face value). Because the face amount of a bond is received at maturity, discounts and premiums must be written off (amortized) over the period that a bond is held.

As you learned in Chapter 11, there are two common methods of amortizing bond discounts and premiums: the straight-line method and the effective-interest method. Because straight-line amortization is simpler, it will be used first to illustrate the amortization process; then the effective-interest method will be described.

straight-line amortization
A method of systematically writing off a bond discount or premium in equal amounts each period until maturity.

Straight-Line Amortization

To illustrate the **straight-line amortization** of a bond discount, we will assume again that Far Side purchased the Chicago Company $20,000, 12%, five-year bonds for $17,316 on the issuance date, July 1, 2006. The entry to record this investment was given on page 654. Far Side will record amortization of $268.40 ($2,684/5 years $\times$ $\frac{1}{2}$) on each interest date. Thus, every six months, beginning on December 31, 2006, Far Side will make the following entry:

Cash	1,200.00	
Investment in Held-to-Maturity Securities	268.40	
Bond Interest Revenue		1,468.40
Received semiannual bond interest and amortized		
bond discount.		

At the end of five years, the investment in the held-to-maturity securities account will have a balance of $20,000.

The discount amortization is revenue earned on the bonds; when the bonds mature, Far Side will receive $20,000 (the face value) in return for an original investment of $17,316. It is this additional revenue of $2,684 that increases the return the investor actually earns from the 12% stated interest rate to the effective interest rate of 16%. The following analysis shows how this works:

Maturity value to be received	$20,000
Interest to be received ($1,200 $\times$ 10 payments)	12,000
Total amount to be received	$32,000
Investment	17,316
Total interest revenue to be earned	$14,684

Interest earned per year:

Stated amount of interest ($20,000 $\times$ 0.12)	$2,400.00	12%
Additional interest from discount ($2,684/5 years)	536.80	4%*
Total	$2,936.80	16%

*This is an approximation; with the straight-line method, the actual interest earned each year changes.

When accounting for the amortization of a bond discount, a company must be careful to amortize the discount only over the period the bonds are actually held. For example, if Far Side had purchased the Chicago Company bonds four months after the issuance date, the discount would have been amortized over a period of 56 months (4 full years plus 8 months of the first year). The amortization for the first year would then have been approximately $383.43 ($2,684 $\times$ $\frac{8}{56}$), and the amortization for each of the succeeding four years would be approximately $575.14 ($2,684 $\times$ $\frac{12}{56}$).

Accounting for the amortization of a premium on investments is essentially the opposite of accounting for a discount. Amortization of a premium decreases revenue earned, and the effect of the amortization entry is to reduce Investment in Held-to-Maturity Securities to the face value of the bonds by the maturity date.

To illustrate the amortization of a bond premium by the investor, assume that Far Side acquired the $20,000, 12%, five-year Chicago Company bonds for $21,540 on July 1, 2006, the date of issuance. The entry to record the purchase is:

Investment in Held-to-Maturity Securities	21,540	
Cash		21,540
Purchased $20,000 of Chicago Company bonds for $21,540.		

At each interest payment date, beginning December 31, 2006, Far Side will make the following entry:

Cash	1,200	
Investment in Held-to-Maturity Securities		154
Bond Interest Revenue		1,046
Received semiannual bond interest and amortized bond premium		
($1,540/5 years × ¹/₂).		

The effect of the amortization entries is to reduce the return earned on the bonds from the stated annual interest rate of 12% to the rate actually earned on the investment (approximately 10%).

Effective-Interest Amortization

effective-interest amortization A method of systematically writing off a bond premium or discount that takes into consideration the time value of money and results in an equal rate of amortization for each period.

To illustrate the computations involved in using the **effective-interest amortization** method, we will again consider Far Side's purchase of the 12%, five-year, $20,000 bonds of Chicago Company for $17,316 on the issuance date. The amount of discount amortized in each of the five years using the effective-interest method is computed as shown in Exhibit 8.

In the computation, column (2) represents the cash received at the end of each interest period; column (3) shows the amount of effective interest earned, which is the amount that will be reported on the income statement each period; column (4) is the difference between columns (3) and (2) and so represents the amortization; and column (5) shows the investment balance that will be reported on the balance sheet at the end of each period. Note that the interest rate used to compute the actual interest earned is the effective rate of 8% (16%/2) and not the stated rate of 12%. Also note that the total discount is the same as it was when the straight-line method was used, $2,684.

When bonds are purchased at a discount, the amount of amortization increases each successive period. This is so because the investment balance of the bonds increases, and a constant interest rate times an increasing balance results in an increasing amount of interest income. If

Exhibit 8: Amortization Table for Chicago Company Bonds

(1) Time Period	(2) Cash Received	(3) Interest Actually Earned (0.16 × ¹/₂ × Investment Balance)	(4) Amount of Amortization (3) − (2)	(5) Investment Balance
Acquisition date				$17,316
Year 1, first six months	$1,200	(0.08 × $17,316) = $1,385	$ 185	17,501
Year 1, second six months	1,200	(0.08 × $17,501) = 1,400	200	17,701
Year 2, first six months	1,200	(0.08 × $17,701) = 1,416	216	17,917
Year 2, second six months	1,200	(0.08 × $17,917) = 1,433	233	18,150
Year 3, first six months	1,200	(0.08 × $18,150) = 1,452	252	18,402
Year 3, second six months	1,200	(0.08 × $18,402) = 1,472	272	18,674
Year 4, first six months	1,200	(0.08 × $18,674) = 1,494	294	18,968
Year 4, second six months	1,200	(0.08 × $18,968) = 1,517	317	19,285
Year 5, first six months	1,200	(0.08 × $19,285) = 1,543	343	19,628
Year 5, second six months	1,200	(0.08 × $19,628) = 1,572*	372	20,000
			$2,684	

*Difference due to rounding.

FYI:

Note the similarities between this table and the amortization tables prepared in Chapter 11. The computations are identical—the only difference is that in Chapter 11, we were paying cash, whereas in Chapter 13, we are receiving cash.

bonds are purchased at a premium, the effective-interest amortization method will involve a constant interest rate being multiplied by a declining investment balance each period. The result will be a decline in actual interest earned each period.

Since the effective-interest amortization method takes into account the time value of money, and thus shows the true revenue earned each period (whereas the straight-line method represents only approximations), companies normally should use the effective-interest amortization method. As an exception to this rule, companies are allowed to use the straight-line method when the two methods produce amortization amounts that are not significantly different. Because that is often the case, both methods continue to be used.

Accounting for the Sale or Maturity of Bond Investments

If bonds are held until their maturity date, the accounting for the proceeds at maturity includes a debit to Cash and a credit to the investment account for the principal amount. For example, if Far Side, Inc., holds the $20,000, 12% bonds from Chicago Company to maturity, the entry to record the receipt of the bond principal on the maturity date will be:

Cash	20,000	
Investment in Held-to-Maturity Securities		20,000
Received the principal of Chicago Company bonds at maturity.		

This entry assumes, of course, that all previous receipts of interest and bond amortizations have been properly recorded.

Because held-to-maturity securities are usually traded on major exchanges, thus providing a continuous and ready market, they can be sold to other investors prior to their maturity. When these securities are sold prior to their maturity, the difference between the sales price and the investment balance is recognized as a gain or loss on the sale of the investment.

To illustrate, we will assume that Sawyer Company purchased ten $1,000, 8%, five-year bonds of REX Company. We will also assume that the bonds were originally purchased on January 1, 2006, at 101% of their face value; on January 1, 2007, Sawyer showed a balance of $10,040 for these bonds. If the bonds are sold on that day for $10,300, the entry to record the sale and recognize the gain is (assuming no sales commission):

Cash	10,300	
Gain on Sale of Bonds		260
Investment in Held-to-Maturity Securities		10,040
Sold the REX bonds for $10,300.		

If held-to-maturity securities are sold prior to their maturity date, it is important that the amortization of the bond premium or discount be recorded up to the date of sale. If the amortization of the discount or premium is not updated, the gain or loss recognized on the sale will be incorrect.

TO SUMMARIZE: Accounting for investments in held-to-maturity securities involves four steps: (1) accounting for the purchase of the securities, (2) accounting for interest received on the securities, (3) accounting for amortization of the premium or discount, and (4) account-ing for the sale or maturity of the securities. Amortization of premiums and discounts is usually accounted for by the simple straight-line amortization method or the theoretically more correct effective-interest method. The amortization adjusts the interest earned on the bonds from the stated to the effective rate. Investments in held-to-maturity securities are generally reported at cost (adjusted for premium or discount amortization), regardless of whether the current market value is less than or greater than their historical cost. When held-to-maturity securities are sold before maturity, the premium or discount must be amortized to the date of sale; a gain or loss would be reflected in the income statement for the difference between the selling price and the carrying value on the date of sale. Debt securities held until maturity result in no gain or loss on retirement because the carrying value after amortization of a premium or discount should be equal to the face value of the securities.

Accounting for Equity Investments Using the Equity Method

6 Account for securities using the equity method.

When enough of the outstanding common stock of a company is purchased by another company, the acquiring company may have the ability to significantly influence the operating decisions of the investee. If the ability to influence is present, then accounting standards require the use of the equity method in accounting for the investment. As stated previously, significant influence is presumed if a company owns between 20 and 50% of a company. Keep in mind that the percentage ownership criterion serves only as a guideline. The ability to influence is the key criterion. For example, assume that a company owns 35% of a firm that is headquartered in a foreign country whose government is undergoing a period of volatility. Some of the radical leaders in that country are calling for more internal investment and less outside interference from U.S. corporations. These leaders, if able to gain positions of power, have threatened to expropriate (take over all operations owned by U.S. companies). Even though the U.S. company meets the percentage ownership criterion, it may not be able to significantly influence the operations of the foreign subsidiary. Consider another example of a firm whose ownership is widespread, with no single shareholder owning more than 2% of the corporation. If one stockholder were able to acquire 15% of the outstanding common stock, that investor might be able to influence the decisions of the investee simply because of the size of the ownership percentage relative to that of all other stockholders. The important point is that the ability to influence is the key criterion for using the equity method of accounting.

Under the equity method, dividend payments represent a return of investment; they do not represent revenue, as they do when accounting for trading or available-for-sale securities. Revenue is recognized when the investee company has earnings. When earnings are announced, the carrying (book) value of the investment is increased because the investor owns a fixed percentage of a company that is worth more now than it was when the investment was originally made.

In accounting for investments with the equity method, the original investment is first recorded on the books at cost and is subsequently modified to reflect the investor's share of the investee's reported income, losses, and dividends. In this way, book value is increased to recognize the investor's share of earnings and decreased by the dividends received or to recognize the investor's share of losses. Temporary changes in value of investments accounted for using the equity method are not recorded.

There are two reasons why the procedures employed under the equity method are preferred over those used when accounting for trading or available-for-sale securities. First, the equity method assumes that significant influence can be exerted. Thus, the accounting procedures prevent the investing company from manipulating earnings by dictating the dividend policy of the investee. For a trading or available-for-sale security, where dividend payments are reported as revenue, an influential investor could increase its income by putting pressure on the investee to pay larger and more frequent dividends. With the equity method, dividends do not affect earnings. Second, the equity method provides more timely recognition of the investee's earnings and losses than do the procedures employed for trading or available-for-sale securities.

FYI:

Although temporary changes in the value of equity method securities are not accounted for, permanent changes are recognized.

Caution

A common mistake in accounting for equity method securities is to debit or credit the investment account for the entire amount of the investee's income or dividends. Remember, the investor accounts only for its share of the investee's income and dividends.

Illustrating the Equity Method

To illustrate the accounting for the equity method, we will use the following information: Kimball, Inc. purchases 20% (2,000 shares) of Holland Enterprises outstanding common stock (10,000 shares), paying $100 per share. Later in the year, Kimball receives a dividend of $2.50 per share; at year-end, Kimball receives Holland's income statement showing that the company earned $50,000 for the year. To ensure that you understand how the equity method differs from the accounting demonstrated earlier in the chapter, we will proceed with two scenarios: (1) Kimball is not able to exercise significant influence on Holland and, as a result, classifies the security as available-for-sale, and (2) Kimball is able to exercise significant influence and uses the equity method.

The accounting for this purchase of stock and subsequent events is shown in Exhibit 9. Column 1 shows the journal entries assuming that the Holland stock is considered an available-for-sale security. Column 2 illustrates the equity method. It is assumed that the Holland stock is selling for $102 per share at year-end.

Although accounting for the holding of equity method securities is different from the accounting for available-for-sale or trading securities, accounting for the sale of a stock investment is the same regardless of the classification. If the selling price exceeds the balance in the investment account, the difference is recognized as a gain. If the selling price is less than the recorded investment balance, the difference is recognized as a loss. To illustrate, assume that Kimball sells its 2,000 shares of Holland Enterprises stock (previously accounted for under the equity method) for $225,000 shortly after the year-end recognition of its $10,000 share of Holland's earnings. The entry to record the sale is:

FYI:

COCA-COLA, a company in which BERKSHIRE HATHAWAY owns over 8%, has a number of subsidiaries that it accounts for using the equity method. In 2002, Coca-Cola reported equity income from those subsidiaries of $384 million accounted for using the equity method.

Cash	225,000	
Investment in Equity Method Securities		205,000
Realized Gain on Sale of Investment		20,000

The $205,000 is obtained by adding Kimball's share of Holland's reported net income to the original investment cost and subtracting the dividends received from Holland ($200,000 + $10,000 − $5,000).

Exhibit 9: Accounting for Equity Securities

	(1) Available-for-Sale Security		(2) Equity Method Security	
Accounting for the initial purchase of the stock	Investment in Available-for-Sale Securities .... 200,000 Cash	200,000	Investment in Equity Method Securities .... 200,000 Cash	200,000
Payment of a $2.50 per share dividend by Holland Company	Cash .... 5,000 Dividend Revenue	5,000	Cash .... 5,000 Investment in Equity Method Securities	5,000
Announcement by Holland of net income for the year of $50,000	No entry		Investment in Equity Method Securities .... 10,000 Revenue from Investments..	10,000
Holland stock is selling at $102 per share at year-end	Market Adjustment—Available-for-Sale Securities .... 4,000 Unrealized Increase in Available-for-Sale Securities—Equity	4,000	No entry	

TO SUMMARIZE: All investments in stock are initially accounted for at cost. However, because different levels of investment provide different degrees of influence over investee companies, accounting for subsequent events relating to the investee will differ depending on the degree of influence. When the percentage of outstanding voting common stock owned is sufficient to exercise influence (as is usually true with ownership of 20 to 50%), the equity method is used. This method involves increasing the book value of the investment for earnings and decreasing it for dividends and losses.

Consolidated Financial Statements

7 Understand the basics of consolidated financial statements.

The equity method is used when an investor is able to exercise significant influence over an investee's operations. If the investor is able to control decisions made by the investee, then consolidated financial statements are appropriate. The objective with consolidated financial statements is to reflect in one set of financial statements the results of all companies owned or controlled by the parent corporation.

To show how consolidation works, a simple example of a parent company owning part or all of three other companies will be used. The income statement and balance sheet data for the four companies are given below.

		Percentage of the Parent's Ownership		
	Parent	**100% Sub1**	**80% Sub2**	**30% Sub3**
Assets				
Cash	$ 48	$ 20	$ 20	$ 20
Accounts receivable	200	80	80	80
Plant and equipment	500	100	100	100
Investment in Sub 1 ($120 × 1.00)	120			
Investment in Sub 2 ($120 × 0.80)	96			
Investment in Sub 3 ($120 × 0.30)	36			
Total assets	$ 1,000	$ 200	$ 200	$ 200
Liabilities	600	80	80	80
Equity	400	120	120	120
Total liabilities and stockholders' equity	$ 1,000	$ 200	$ 200	$ 200
Revenues				
Sales	$ 4,790	$ 2,000	$ 2,000	$ 2,000
Income from Sub 1 ($100 × 1.00)	100			
Income from Sub 2 ($100 × 0.80)	80			
Income from Sub 3 ($100 × 0.30)	30			
Expenses	(3,000)	(1,900)	(1,900)	(1,900)
Net income	$ 2,000	$ 100	$ 100	$ 100

Note that in the parent company's books, ownership of all three subsidiaries has been accounted for using the equity method. So, in each case the parent reports an investment asset equal to its share of the net assets, or equity, of the subsidiary, and investment income equal to its share of the net income of the subsidiary.

The objective of consolidation is to create financial statements for the parent and its controlled subsidiaries to report their performance as if they were one company. Operationally, this means that the individual assets, liabilities, revenues, and expenses of the parent and all subsidiaries of which it owns more than 50% are added together and included in the consolidated financial statements. Companies of which the parent owns less than 50% but more than 20% are accounted for using the equity method, as described in the preceding section. The consolidated balance sheet and income statement for the parent company and its subsidiaries are shown in Exhibit 10.

Exhibit 10: Consolidated Financial Statements

Parent Company and Subsidiaries
Consolidated Balance Sheet

Assets

Cash ($48 + $20 + $20)	$ 88
Accounts receivable ($200 + $80 + $80)	360
Plant and equipment ($500 + $100 + $100)	700
Investment in Sub 3 ($120 × 0.30)	36
Total assets	$ 1,184
Liabilities ($600 + $80 + $80)	760
Minority interest ($120 × 0.20)	24
Equity	400
Total liabilities and equities	$ 1,184

Parent Company and Subsidiaries
Consolidated Income Statement

Revenues

Sales ($4,790 + $2,000 + $2,000)	$ 8,790
Income from Sub 3 ($100 × 0.30)	30
Expenses ($3,000 + $1,900 + $1,900)	(6,800)
Minority interest income ($100 × 0.20)	(20)
Net income	$ 2,000

You should note four things concerning these consolidated results:

1. The consolidated balance sheet and income statement include *all* assets, liabilities, revenues, and expenses of the parent and the subsidiaries it controls. Thus, even though the parent owns only 80% of Sub 2, all of that subsidiary's assets, liabilities, revenues, and expenses are included in the consolidated total. An example of the intuition here is that the parent, with its 80% ownership, completely *controls* the assets of Sub 2 even though it doesn't own them completely.

2. *None* of the individual assets, liabilities, revenues, and expenses of Sub 3 are included in the consolidated financial statements because that subsidiary is not controlled by the parent. Instead, the parent's ownership of 30% of Sub 3 is accounted for using the equity method.

3. The fact that all of the assets, liabilities, revenues, and expenses of Sub 2 have been included in the consolidated total and yet the parent owns only 80% of that subsidiary is reflected in the minority interest items. In the consolidated balance sheet, **minority interest** is the amount of equity investment made by outside shareholders to consolidated subsidiaries that are not 100% owned by the parent. In the consolidated income statement, minority interest income (shown as a subtraction) reflects the amount of income belonging to outside shareholders of consolidated subsidiaries that are not 100% owned.

4. Total consolidated equity of $400 in this example is the same as total equity reported by the parent. Consolidated equity can be thought of as the amount invested by the group of shareholders who control the entire consolidated economic entity; this group of shareholders is the shareholders of the parent company. Of course, some of this equity investment, along with some funds borrowed by the parent, has been used to purchase 100% of Sub 1, 80% of Sub 2, and 30% of Sub 3. But to add portions of the equity of each of those subsidiaries in computing consolidated equity would essentially result in double counting the original investment made by the parent shareholders.

minority interest The amount of equity investment made by outside shareholders to consolidated subsidiaries that are not 100% owned by the parent.

> **TO SUMMARIZE:** Consolidated financial statements are prepared when a parent owns more than 50% of one or more subsidiaries. All of the assets, liabilities, revenues, and expenses of the parent and the majority-owned subsidiaries are added in preparing the consolidated financial statements.

review of learning objectives

1 **Understand why companies invest in other companies.** Companies invest in the debt and equity securities of other companies for a variety of reasons. The primary reason is to earn a return on invested funds. Bonds and stocks offer a higher potential return for investors than the interest rates offered by government-backed securities or savings rates offered by banks and other financial institutions. Along with the potential for higher returns comes the prospect of higher risks; the investor faces the possibility of earning little return or even losing money. Besides earning a return, companies invest in the securities of other companies for additional reasons, including establishing a long-term business relationship, ensuring an adequate supply of raw materials, ensuring a sales network for inventory, or gaining access to developed assets, such as software programs or oil reserves.

2 **Understand the different classifications for securities.** Debt and equity securities are classified according to management's intent in holding the securities. If the securities are being held for the short term with the intent to sell the securities if cash is needed, the securities are accounted for as "trading" securities. If debt securities are expected to be held until they mature, the securities are classified as "held-to-maturity." If equity securities are purchased with the intent of being able to significantly influence the operating decisions of the investee (ownership of between 20 and 50% of outstanding common stock typically reflects the ability to significantly influence), the securities are accounted for using the equity method. Debt and equity securities not classified as trading, held-to-maturity, or equity method securities are classified as "available-for-sale." The importance of these distinctions becomes clear when changes in the value of the securities are accounted for by the investor.

3 **Account for the purchase, recognition of revenue, and sale of trading and available-for-sale securities.** Investments in securities are initially recorded at cost. Cost includes the fair market value of the securities as well as broker's fees. For trading and available-for-sale securities, dividends or interest earned is recorded as revenue. For held-to-maturity securities and equity method securities, the recognition of revenue is more complex. When a security is sold, regardless of its classification, its carrying (book) value is compared to the selling price to determine any realized gain or loss on the sale. These realized gains and losses are disclosed on the income statement with Other Revenues and Expenses.

4 **Account for changes in the value of securities.** When the market value of a security changes, the classification of the security determines whether the change in value is recorded on the financial statements. With held-to-maturity securities and equity method securities, because the intent of management is to hold these types of securities for long periods of time, changes in market value are not recognized. For securities classified as trading, any unrealized gains and losses are recognized on the income statement. A market adjustment account is offset against Investment in Trading Securities to value the securities at their fair market value on the balance sheet. Available-for-sale securities are also adjusted to fair market value using a market adjustment account. However, the offset is recorded in a stockholders' equity account.

5 **Account for held-to-maturity securities.** The purchase price of a held-to-maturity security may be less than face value, resulting in a discount, or it may be more than face value, resulting in a premium. The discount or premium is amortized over the life of the bond by adjusting the cost upward if purchased at a discount and downward if purchased at a premium. Adjusting the cost of the bond up or down ensures that the recorded cost will be equal to the face value of the bond at the maturity date. This adjustment is accomplished through the amortization of the premiums and discounts, which adjusts the interest earned on the bonds from the stated to the effective rate. Bond discounts and premiums can be amortized using either the straight-line or the effective-interest method. The latter is theoretically more correct, but if the differences between the two are insignificant, either can be used.

6 **Account for securities using the equity method.** If ownership of the outstanding stock of another company gives the investor the ability to significantly influence the company (as generally happens with 20 to 50% ownership), the equity method is used to account for the investment. With the equity method, the purchase is recorded at cost. The investment balance (its book value) is decreased by dividends and losses and increased by the investor's share of the investee company's earnings.

7 **Understand the basics of consolidated financial statements.** When a company owns more than 50% of the outstanding common stock of another company, consolidated financial statements are prepared. Consolidated financial statements reflect all of the assets, liabilities, revenues, and expenses of the parent company, as well as those of the majority-owned subsidiaries. The portion of the assets, liabilities, revenues, and expenses not owned by the parent company is reflected in the financial statements under the classification of minority interest.

key terms & concepts

available-for-sale securities, 645
consolidated financial statements, 644
debt securities, 643
equity method, 644
equity securities (stock), 643
held-to-maturity security, 644

Market Adjustment—Trading
  Securities, 651
realized gains and losses, 649
trading securities, 644
unrealized gains and losses, 650

effective-interest amortization, 657
minority interest, 662
straight-line amortization, 655

review problem

Investments in Debt and Equity Securities
On January 1, 2006, Schultz, Inc., purchased the following securities:

Security	Type	Classification	Cost
1	Debt	Trading	$2,500
2	Debt	Trading	1,500
3	Equity	Trading	1,750
4	Debt	Available-for-sale	4,300
5	Equity	Available-for-sale	2,750

On March 31, one-half of Security 2 was sold for $900. During the year, interest and dividends were received as follows:

Security	Interest	Dividends
1	$200	
2	85	
3		none
4	435	
5		$200

The following fair market values are available on December 31, 2006. Schultz had no balance in its market adjustment accounts on January 1, 2006.

Security	Market Value
1	$2,400
2	950
3	1,600
4	4,250
5	2,900

Required:

Record all necessary journal entries to account for these investments during 2006.

Solution

To account for these investments, four events must be accounted for:

1. The initial purchase on January 1.
2. The sale of one-half of Security 2 on March 31.
3. The receipt of interest and dividends during the year.
4. The changes in value as of December 31.

The initial purchase

Jan. 1	Investment in Trading Securities	5,750	
	Investment in Available-for-Sale Securities	7,050	
	Cash		12,800
	To record the purchase of trading and available-for-sale securities.		

The sale of one-half of Security 2 on March 31

Mar. 31	Cash	900	
	Realized Gain on Sale of Securities		150
	Investment in Trading Securities		750
	Sold one-half of Security 2 ($750 book value) for $900.		
	Recorded the $150 realized gain ($900 − $750).		

The receipt of interest and dividends during the year

	Cash	920	
	Interest Revenue		720
	Dividend Revenue		200
	Received $720 in interest during the year and $200 in dividends.		

Note: Even if cash were not received by year-end, the interest and dividends earned would need to be recorded, with the offsetting debit to a receivable account(s).

The changes in value as of December 31, 2006

Dec. 31	Unrealized Loss on Trading Securities	50	
	Market Adjustment—Trading Securities		50
	To account for the difference between book value		
	($5,000) and fair market value ($4,950) of trading securities.		

Note: Remember that one-half of Security 2 was sold during the year.

Dec. 31	Market Adjustment—Available-for-Sale Securities	100	
	Unrealized Increase/Decrease in Value of		
	Available-for-Sale Securities—Equity		100
	To account for the difference between book value ($7,050) and		
	fair market value ($7,150) of available-for-sale securities.		

discussion questions

1. Why do firms invest in assets that are not directly related to their primary business operations?
2. Describe the risk and return trade-off of investments.
3. What are the four different classifications of debt and equity securities?
4. When will a security be classified as "trading"?
5. What types of securities can be classified as "held-to-maturity"?
6. To be classified as an equity method security, the investor must typically own at least a certain percentage of the outstanding common stock of the investee. What is that minimum percentage? That percentage of ownership represents the investor's ability to do what?
7. Identify the different types of returns an investor can realize when investing in debt and equity securities.
8. When a security is sold, what information must be known to account for that transaction?
9. What is the difference between a realized gain or loss and an unrealized gain or loss?
10. What does the account "Market Adjustment" represent?
11. How are changes in the value of trading securities accounted for on the books of the investor?
12. How are changes in the value of available-for-sale securities accounted for on the books of the investor?
13. What is the process for adjusting the value of a trading or available-for-sale security after a valuation account has been established?
14. Why aren't premiums and discounts on available-for-sale securities amortized?
15. Why aren't changes in the value of held-to-maturity and equity method securities accounted for on the books of the investor?

16. How does the accounting for changes in the value of trading and available-for-sale securities differ?

17. What future cash inflows is a company buying when it purchases a held-to-maturity security?
18. When would a company be willing to pay more than the face amount (a premium) for a held-to-maturity security?
19. Why does the amortization of a discount increase the amount of interest revenue earned on a held-to-maturity security?
20. Why must an investor purchasing held-to-maturity securities between interest payment dates pay the previous owner for accrued interest on those securities?
21. Why is the effective-interest amortization method theoretically superior to the straight-line method?
22. What is the key criterion for using the equity method of accounting for equity securities?
23. What guidelines have been provided to determine if the ability to significantly influence the decisions of an investee exists?
24. How does the equity method of accounting for securities differ from the procedures employed for a trading security?
25. Under what circumstances should consolidated financial statements be prepared?
26. What financial statement accounts are shown only in consolidated financial statements and never in the financial statements of individual companies?

practice exercises

Practice 13-1

Why Companies Invest in Other Companies
Which one of the following is *not* a primary reason companies invest in other companies?

a. To earn return on excess cash.
b. To eliminate risk in other investments.
c. To gain influence over another company.
d. To gain control over another company.

Practice 13-2

Classifying a Security
Which one of the following types of investments is *always* an example of a debt security?

a. Available-for-sale securities.
b. Trading securities.
c. Held-to-maturity securities.
d. Equity method securities.

Practice 13-3

Equity Method Securities

What is the general rule for what percentage an entity must own in another company to account for the investment using the equity method?

a. The entity should own 20 to 50% of the other company's outstanding voting stock.
b. The entity should own 5 to 10% of the other company's outstanding voting stock.
c. The entity should own 50 to 90% of the other company's outstanding voting stock.
d. The entity should own 10 to 20% of the other company's outstanding voting stock.

Practice 13-4

Disclosure of Securities

Which two of the following classifications of securities are valued at fair value on a company's balance sheet?

a. Available-for-sale securities.
b. Equity method securities.
c. Trading securities.
d. Held-to-maturity securities.

Practice 13-5

Accounting for the Purchase of Trading and Available-for-Sale Securities

The company purchased the following securities with cash:

Security	Type	Classification	Cost (including Broker's Fees)
1	Equity	Trading	$34,000
2	Equity	Available-for-sale	52,000
3	Debt	Available-for-sale	12,300
4	Debt	Trading	23,500

Make the necessary journal entry(ies) to record the purchase of these securities.

Practice 13-6

Accounting for the Return Earned on an Investment

Refer to the data in Practice 13-5. The company received the following interest and dividends from its securities investments during the year:

Security	Interest	Dividends
1		$340
2		560
3	$154	
4	305	

Make the necessary journal entry(ies) to record the receipt of interest and dividends during the year.

Practice 13-7

Accounting for the Sale of Securities

Refer to the data in Practice 13-5. Near the end of the year, the company sold Security 1 for $33,100. Make the necessary journal entry(ies) to record the sale.

Practice 13-8

Changes in Value of Trading Securities

At the end of the year, the company had the following securities (building on the data from Practice 13-5).

(continued)

Security	Classification	Historical Cost	Market Value (December 31)
2	Available-for-sale	$52,000	$52,400
3	Available-for-sale	12,300	11,500
4	Trading	23,500	24,250

Make the necessary journal entry(ies) to record the change in value of the company's trading security (Security 4).

Practice 13-9

Changes in Value of Available-for-Sale Securities
Refer to the data in Practice 13-8. Make the necessary journal entry(ies) to record the change in value of the company's available-for-sale securities.

Practice 13-10

Subsequent Changes in Value of Trading Securities
At the end of year 2, the company owned the following security (which was originally purchased for $23,500 and had a market value at the end of year 1 of $24,250).

Classification	Historical Cost	Market Value (December 31, Year 2)
Trading	$23,500	$23,150

Make the necessary journal entry(ies) to record the change in value of the security in the second year.

Practice 13-11

Computing the Value of Held-to-Maturity Securities
On January 1, 2006, the company purchased thirty $1,000 held-to-maturity bonds of another company. The bonds mature in four years from the date of issuance and pay interest at a stated annual rate of 8%, with payments to be made quarterly on March 31, June 30, September 30, and December 31. The market rate on bonds of similar risk is 12%. Compute the present value of this investment.

Practice 13-12

Accounting for the Initial Purchase of Held-to-Maturity Securities
Using the information from Practice 13-11, make the necessary journal entry to record the purchase of this held-to-maturity security.

Practice 13-13

Straight-Line Amortization of Bond Discounts
The company purchased $40,000, 10%, three-year bonds for $35,939. Interest on the bonds is payable semiannually. Using straight-line amortization of the bond discounts, make the necessary journal entry(ies) to be made at each interest payment date to record the semiannual interest payment.

Practice 13-14

Straight-Line Amortization of Bond Premiums
The company purchased $40,000, 10%, three-year bonds for $42,096.85. Interest on the bonds is payable semiannually. Using straight-line amortization of the bond premiums, make the necessary journal entry(ies) to be made at each interest payment date to record the semiannual interest payment.

Practice 13-15

Effective-Interest Amortization of Bond Premiums

Refer to the data in Practice 13-14. Using the effective-interest method of bond premium amortization, make the necessary journal entries to record the first two interest payments received on the bonds.

Practice 13-16

Accounting for the Sale of Bond Investments

Refer to the data in Practices 13-14 and 13-15. The company decided to sell the bonds for $41,000 immediately after receiving the second interest payment. Make the necessary journal entry(ies) to record the sale of these bonds.

Practice 13-17

Accounting for Investments Using the Equity Method

Manwill Company owns 40% (30,000 shares) of Hall Company's voting stock. Since Manwill has a significant interest in Hall Company, it uses the equity method of accounting for the investment. Hall Company reported the following information for the year:

1. Hall reported net income of $80,000.
2. Hall paid dividends of $20,000.
3. Hall's stock value increased from $40 to $45.

Make the necessary journal entry(ies) to record the change in value of Manwill Company's investment in Hall Company.

Practice 13-18

Consolidated Financial Statements

Parent Company owns 90% of the outstanding stock of Sub Company. At the end of the year, Sub Company reports revenues of $1,000 and expenses of $850. What will Parent Company report on its own financial statements as "Income from Sub"? On the consolidated financial statements, how much of Sub Company's revenues and expenses will be reported?

e x e r c i s e s

Exercise 13-1

Investment in Trading Securities—Journal Entries

Prepare the journal entries to account for the following investment transactions of Samuelson Company:

2005
July 1   Purchased 350 shares of Bateman Company stock at $22 per share plus a brokerage fee of $600. The Bateman stock is classified as trading.
Oct. 31   Received a cash dividend of $2.00 per share on the Bateman Company stock.
Dec. 31   At year-end, Bateman Company stock had a market price of $19 per share.

2006
Feb. 20   Sold 175 shares of the Bateman Company stock for $26 per share.
Oct. 31   Received a cash dividend of $2.20 per share on the Bateman Company stock.
Dec. 31   At year-end, Bateman Company stock had a market price of $29 per share.

Exercise 13-2

Investment in Trading Securities—Journal Entries

In June 2006, Hatch Company had no investment securities but had excess cash that would not be needed for nine months. Management decided to use this money to purchase trading securities as a short-term investment. The following transactions relate to the investments:

July 16   Purchased 4,000 shares of Eli Corporation stock. The price paid, including brokerage fees, was $41,880.

(continued)

Sept. 23 Received a cash dividend of $0.90 per share on the Eli stock.
  28 Sold 2,000 shares of Eli Corporation stock at $11 per share. Paid a selling commission of $160.
Dec. 31 The market value of Eli's stock was $11.25 per share.

Given these data, prepare the journal entries to account for Hatch's investment in Eli Corporation stock.

Exercise 13-3

Investment in Available-for-Sale Securities—Journal Entries

Wishbone Corporation made the following available-for-sale securities transactions:

Jan. 14 Purchased 2,000 shares of Clarke Corporation common stock at $31.60 per share.
Mar. 31 Received a cash dividend of $0.30 per share on the Clarke Corporation stock.
Aug. 28 Sold 800 shares of Clarke Corporation stock at $37.50 per share.
Dec. 31 The market value of the Clarke Corporation stock was $36 per share.

Prepare journal entries to record the transactions.

Exercise 13-4

Investment in Securities

In January 2004, Solitron, Inc., determined that it had excess cash on hand and decided to invest in Horner Company stock. The company intends to hold the stock for a period of three to five years, thereby making the investment an available-for-sale security. The following transactions took place in 2004, 2005, and 2006.

2004
Jan. 17 Purchased 2,750 shares of Horner Company stock for $89,500.
May 10 Received a cash dividend of $1.30 per share on Horner Company stock.
Dec. 31 The market value of the Horner Company stock was $30 per share.

2005
May 22 Purchased 750 shares of Horner Company stock at $40 per share.
July 18 Received a cash dividend of $0.90 per share on the Horner Company stock.
Dec. 31 The market value of the Horner Company stock was $42 per share.

2006
June 7 Received a cash dividend of $1 per share on the Horner Company stock.
Oct. 5 Sold the Horner Company stock at $27 per share for cash.
Dec. 31 The market value of the Horner Company stock was $25 per share.

Prepare the journal entries required to record each of these events.

Exercise 13-5

Investment in Equity Securities

During 2004, Keetch Company purchased trading securities as a short-term investment. The costs of the securities and their market values on December 31, 2006, are listed below.

Security	Cost	Market Value (December 31, 2006)
A	$130,000	$162,000
B	200,000	108,000
C	440,000	452,000

Keetch had no trading securities in the years before 2006. Before any adjustments related to these trading securities, Keetch had net income of $450,000 in 2006.

1. What is net income (ignoring income taxes) after making any necessary trading security adjustments?
2. What would net income be if the market value of Security B were $190,000?

Exercise 13-6

Investment in Debt and Equity Securities

In February 2006, Packard Corporation purchased the following securities. Prior to these purchases, Packard had no portfolio of investment securities.

Security	Type	Classification	Cost
1	Debt	Trading	$11,500
2	Equity	Trading	9,000
3	Equity	Available-for-sale	7,250
4	Debt	Available-for-sale	12,300

During 2006, Packard received $2,400 in interest and $1,800 in dividends. On December 31, 2006, Packard's portfolio of securities had the following market values:

Security	Fair Market Value
1	$12,000
2	8,750
3	7,500
4	12,500

Prepare the journal entries required to record each of these transactions.

Exercise 13-7

Spreadsheet

Investment in Debt and Equity Securities

Andrews, Inc., purchased the following securities during 2006:

Security	Type	Classification	Cost
1	Debt	Trading	$ 2,400
2	Equity	Trading	3,500
3	Debt	Available-for-sale	4,200
4	Equity	Available-for-sale	1,800
5	Debt	Held-to-maturity	11,000

During 2006, Andrews received interest of $1,400 and dividends of $600 on its investments. On September 29, 2006, Andrews sold one-half of Security 1 for $1,600. On December 31, 2006, the portfolio of securities had the following fair market values:

Security	Fair Market Value
1	$ 1,700
2	3,600
3	4,000
4	1,900
5	12,000

Andrews had no balance in its market adjustment accounts at the beginning of the year.

Prepare the journal entries required to record the purchase of the securities, the receipt of interest and dividends, the sale of securities, and the adjustments required at year-end.

Exercise 13-8

Investment in Securities—Changes in Value

Sharp, Inc., had the following portfolio of investment securities on January 1, 2006:

Security	Type	Classification	Historical Cost	Fair Market Value (1/1/06)
1	Debt	Trading	$1,000	$ 800
2	Equity	Trading	1,250	1,100
3	Debt	Trading	1,700	1,650
4	Debt	Available-for-sale	2,200	2,150
5	Debt	Held-to-maturity	1,800	1,750

Appropriate adjustments have been made in prior years. No securities were bought or sold during 2006. On December 31, 2006, Sharp's portfolio of securities had the following fair market values:

Security	Fair Market Value (12/31/06)
1	$ 650
2	1,200
3	1,700
4	2,250
5	1,850

Prepare the necessary adjusting entry(ies) on December 31, 2006.

Exercise 13-9

Investment in Securities—Changes in Value

Atlantic, Inc., held the following portfolio of securities on December 31, 2005 (the end of its first year of operations):

	Cost	Market Value (12/31/05)
Trading securities	$18,700	$17,500
Available-for-sale securities	21,350	22,000
Held-to-maturity securities	15,000	15,700

No additional securities were bought or sold during 2006. On December 31, 2006, Atlantic's securities had a fair market value of:

Trading securities	$18,250
Available-for-sale securities	22,500
Held-to-maturity securities	15,300

Prepare the entries required at the end of 2005 and 2006 to properly adjust Atlantic's portfolio of securities.

Exercise 13-10

Accounting for the Purchase of Securities

The Running Store is a chain of sporting goods stores. The Running Store is interested in using some of its excess cash to invest in securities. It decides to buy the following securities:

Security	Type	Price
Steven Company	Available-for-sale	$ 2,750
Nick, Inc.	Trading	11,040
Ryan Company	Available-for-sale	6,830
Jacob Company	Held-to-maturity	15,000

Prepare the journal entry to record the purchase of these securities.

Exercise 13-11

Accounting for the Sale of Securities

Jerrod Company owns the following securities, which it is interested in selling:

Security	Type	Cost	Market Adjustments	Market Price
Monsen Company	Available-for-sale	$ 4,000	$ 300 increase	$ 5,000
Jensen Company	Trading	7,500	1,000 decrease	5,500
Stic Company	Available-for-sale	3,200	500 increase	4,000
Larouse Company	Held-to-maturity	10,000	None	11,000

Prepare the journal entry to record the sale of these securities.

Exercise 13-12

Spreadsheet

Held-to-Maturity Security Price Determination

1. How much should an investor pay for $100,000 of debenture bonds that pay interest every six months at an annual rate of 8%, assuming that the bonds mature in 10 years and that the effective interest rate at the date of purchase is also 8%?
2. How much should an investor pay for $100,000 of debenture bonds that pay $5,000 of interest every six months, have a maturity date in 10 years, and are sold to yield 8% interest, compounded semiannually?

Exercise 13-13

Held-to-Maturity Security Price Determination

McMinville Corporation has decided to purchase bonds of La Verkin Corporation as a long-term investment. The 10-year bonds have a stated rate of interest of 12%, with interest payments being made semiannually. How much should McMinville be willing to pay for $150,000 of the bonds if:

1. A rate of return of 14% is deemed necessary to justify the investment?
2. A rate of return of 10% is considered to be an adequate return?

Exercise 13-14

Investments in Held-to-Maturity Securities

Control Group purchased thirty $1,000, 10%, 20-year bonds of Natchez Corporation on January 1, 2006, as a long-term investment. The bonds mature on January 1, 2026, and interest is payable every January 1 and July 1. Control Group's reporting year ends December 31, and the company uses the straight-line method of amortizing premiums and discounts.

Make all necessary journal entries relating to the bonds for 2006, assuming:

1. The purchase price is 104% of face value.
2. The purchase price is 94% of face value.

Exercise 13-15

Straight-Line Amortization of Premium

On their issuance date, Salina Company purchased thirty-five $1,000, 10%, six-year bonds of AF Corporation as a long-term investment for $38,285. Interest payments are made semiannually. Prepare a schedule showing the amortization of the bond premium over the six-year life of the bonds. Use the straight-line method of amortization.

Exercise 13-16

Spreadsheet

Effective-Interest Amortization of Premium

Assume the same facts as in Exercise 13-15. Prepare a schedule showing the amortization of the bond premium over the six-year life of the bonds. Use the effective-interest method of amortization. (*Hint:* The effective rate of interest earned on the bonds is 6% compounded semiannually.)

Exercise 13-17

Investments in Stock—Equity Method

On January 3, 2006, Atkinson, Inc., purchased 15,000 shares of the outstanding common stock of Norris Corporation. At the time of this transaction, Norris has 50,000 shares of common stock outstanding. The cost of the purchase (including brokerage fees) was $24 per share. During the year, Norris reported income of $16,000 and paid dividends of $6,000. On December 31, 2006, Norris' stock was valued at $28 per share.

Provide the entries necessary to record the above transactions.

Exercise 13-18

Equity Method

Foster Enterprises purchased 20% of the outstanding common stock of Novelties, Inc., on January 2, 2006, paying $150,000. During 2006, Novelties, Inc., reported net income of $20,000 and paid dividends to shareholders of $15,000. On December 31, 2006, Foster's investment in Novelties stock had a fair market value of $158,000. Assuming this is the only security owned by Foster, prepare all journal entries required by Foster in 2006 assuming:

1. The security is classified as a trading security.
2. The security is classified as an available-for-sale security.
3. The equity method is applied to the investment.

Exercise 13-19

Investments in Stock—Equity Method

During 2006, Genco Corporation purchased 10,000 shares of Wiener Company stock for $85 per share. Wiener had a total of 40,000 shares of stock outstanding.

1. Prepare journal entries for the following transactions:

   Jan. 1   Purchased 10,000 shares of common stock at $85.
   Dec. 31   Wiener Company declared and paid a $4.60-per-share dividend.
       31   Wiener Company reported net income for 2006 of $360,000.

2. On December 31, 2006, the market price of Wiener's stock was $79 per share. Show how this investment would be reported on Genco's balance sheet at December 31, 2006, assuming that this is the only stock investment owned by Genco.

Exercise 13-20

Consolidated Financial Statements—Balance Sheet

Ecotec Inc. purchased 70% of the outstanding common stock of Beatrix Co. on January 1, 2004, paying $875,000. On that day, the balance sheets of the two companies immediately after the purchase are as follows:

(in thousands)	Ecotec	Beatrix
Cash	$ 410	$ 260
Other current assets	1,875	1,240
Property, plant, & equipment	1,100	850
Investment in Beatrix	875	0
Total assets	$4,260	$2,350
Current liabilities	$1,225	$ 800
Long-term liabilities	775	300
Common stock	800	500
Retained earnings	1,460	750
Total liabilities & equities	$4,260	$2,350

1. Compute the amount that will be disclosed on the consolidated balance sheet as "Minority Interest."
2. Prepare a consolidated balance sheet as of January 1, 2004.

Exercise 13-21

Consolidated Financial Statements—Income Statement

On January 1, 2004, Exrock Inc. purchased 80% of the outstanding common stock of Udora Co. at a price of $680,000. At the end of 2004, each company prepared separate income statements, which are presented below.

(in thousands)	Exrock	Udora
Sales	$2,850	$1,115
Income from Udora	72	0
Interest revenue	352	34
	$3,274	$1,149
Cost of goods sold	1,700	620
Other operating expenses	840	417
Interest expense	115	22
Net income	$ 619	$ 90

1. Compute the amount that will be reported on the consolidated income statement as "Minority Interest Income."
2. Prepare a consolidated income statement.
3. Compare Exrock's reported net income with consolidated net income. Explain the relationship.

problems

Problem 13-1

Investment in Securities—Recording and Analysis

The following data pertain to the securities of Linford Company during 2006, the company's first year of operations:

a. Purchased 400 shares of Corporation A stock at $40 per share plus a commission of $200. This security is classified as trading.

(continued)

 b. Purchased $6,000 of Corporation B bonds. These bonds are classified as trading.

 c. Received a cash dividend of $0.50 per share on the Corporation A stock.

 d. Sold 100 shares of Corporation A stock for $46 per share.

 e. Received interest of $240 on the Corporation B bonds.

 f. Purchased 50 shares of Corporation C stock for $3,500. Classified the stock as available-for-sale.

 g. Received interest of $240 on the Corporation B bonds.

 h. Sold 150 shares of Corporation A stock for $28 per share.

 i. Received a cash dividend of $1.40 per share on the Corporation C stock.

 j. Interest receivable at year-end on the Corporation B bonds amounts to $60.

Required:

Prepare journal entries to record the preceding transactions. Post the entries to T-accounts, and determine the amount of each of the following for the year:

1. Dividend revenue.
2. Bond interest revenue.
3. Net gain or loss from selling securities.

Problem 13-2

Buying and Selling Trading Securities

Yor Company incurred the following transactions relating to the common stock of Zith Company:

July 14, 2004	Purchased 15,000 shares at $56 per share.
Sept. 4, 2005	Sold 1,500 shares at $62 per share.
Aug. 24, 2006	Sold 1,000 shares at $45 per share.

The end-of-year market prices for the shares were as follows:

Dec. 31, 2004	$53 per share
Dec. 31, 2005	$68 per share
Dec. 31, 2006	$35 per share

Yor Company classifies the Zith stock as trading securities.

Required:

1. Determine the amount of (a) realized gain or loss and (b) unrealized gain or loss to be reported on the income statement each year relating to the Zith stock.
2. How would your answer to part (1) change if the securities were classified as available-for-sale? Explain.

Problem 13-3

Trading and Available-for-Sale Securities

Lorien Technologies, Inc., purchased the following securities during 2005:

Security	Classification	Cost	Market Value (12/31/05)
A	Trading	$ 5,000	$ 4,000
B	Trading	7,000	10,000
C	Available-for-sale	10,000	8,000
D	Available-for-sale	6,000	3,500

The following transactions occurred during 2006:

a. On January 1, 2006, Lorien purchased Security E for $12,000. Security E is classified as available-for-sale.

b. On March 23, 2006, Security B was sold for $4,700.

c. On July 23, 2006, Security C was sold for $19,500.

The remaining securities had the following market values as of December 31, 2006:

Security	Market Value
A	$ 4,500
D	5,000
E	13,000

Required:

1. Determine the amount of (a) realized gain or loss and (b) unrealized gain or loss to be reported relating to Lorien's trading securities for 2006.
2. Determine the amount of (a) realized gain or loss and (b) unrealized gain or loss to be reported relating to Lorien's available-for-sale securities for 2006. Which amounts will appear on the income statement?

Problem 13-4

P.A.S.S.
Power Accounting
System Software

Investments in Trading Securities

In December 2006, the treasurer of Toth Company concluded that the company had excess cash on hand and decided to invest in Soren Corporation stock. The company intends to hold the stock for a period of 6 to 12 months and classifies the security as trading. The following transactions took place:

Jan. 1	Purchased 7,600 shares of Soren Corporation stock for $152,000.
Apr. 24	Received a cash dividend of $1.20 per share on the Soren Corporation stock.
May 5	Sold 2,000 shares of the Soren Corporation stock at $23 per share for cash.
July 21	Received a cash dividend of $1.30 per share on the Soren Corporation stock.
Aug. 9	Sold the balance of the Soren Corporation stock at $15 per share for cash.

Required:

Prepare the appropriate journal entries to record each of these transactions.

Problem 13-5

P.A.S.S.
Power Accounting
System Software

Investments in Debt and Equity Securities

Wilbur Company often invests in the debt and equity securities of other companies as short-term investments. During 2006, the following events occurred:

July 1   Wilbur purchased the securities listed here:

Security	Type	Classification	Cost
1	Debt	Trading	$41,200
2	Equity	Trading	23,940
3	Equity	Trading	51,250
4	Equity	Available-for-sale	21,300

Sept. 30	Wilbur received a cash dividend of $2,460 on Security 2.
Dec. 1	Wilbur sold Security 4 for $18,300.
31	Wilbur received interest of $4,300 on Security 1.
31	The market prices were quoted as follows: Security 1, $40,900; Security 2, $25,550; Security 3, $44,000.

Required:

1. Prepare journal entries to record the events.
2. Illustrate how these investments would be reported on the balance sheet at December 31.
3. What items and amounts would be reported on the income statement for the year?

Problem 13-6

Unifying Concepts: Short-Term Investments in Stocks and Bonds

FRC Manufacturing Company produces and sells one main product. There is significant seasonality in demand, and the unit price is quite high. As a result, during the heavy selling season, the company generates cash that is idle for a few months. The company uses this cash to acquire investments. The following transactions relate to FRC's investments during 2006:

Mar. 15 Purchased 800 shares of Lewis Corporation stock at $25 per share, plus brokerage fees of $624. This stock is classified as trading.

Apr. 1 Purchased $42,000 of 12% bonds of Martin Company. This investment is classified as available-for-sale.

June 3 Received a cash dividend of $1.80 per share on the Lewis Corporation stock.

Oct. 1 Received a semiannual interest payment of $2,520 on the Martin Company bonds.

10 Sold 600 shares of the Lewis Corporation stock at $29 per share less a $325 brokerage fee.

Dec. 31 Recorded $1,260 of interest earned on the Martin Company bonds for the period October 1, 2006, through December 31, 2006.

31 The market price of the Lewis Corporation stock was $22 per share; the market price of the Martin Company bonds was $40,320.

Required:
Prepare journal entries to record these transactions.

Problem 13-7

P.A.S.S.
Power Accounting System Software

Recording Investment Transactions

The following data pertain to the investments of Sumner Company during 2006, the company's first year of operations:

a. Purchased 200 shares of Corporation A stock at $40 per share, plus brokerage fees of $100. Classified as trading.

b. Purchased $10,000 of Corporation B bonds at face value. Classified as trading.

c. Received a cash dividend of $0.50 per share on the Corporation A stock.

d. Received interest of $600 on the Corporation B bonds.

e. Purchased 50 shares of Corporation C stock for $3,500. Classified as available-for-sale.

f. Received interest of $600 on the Corporation B bonds.

g. Sold 80 shares of Corporation A stock for $32 per share due to a significant decline in the market.

h. Received a cash dividend of $1.40 per share on the Corporation C stock.

i. Interest receivable at year-end on the Corporation B bonds amounts to $200.

j. Market value of securities at year-end: Corporation A stock, $42 per share; Corporation B bonds, $10,200; Corporation C stock, $3,450.

Required:
Enter these transactions in T-accounts, and determine each of the following for the year:

1. Dividend revenue.
2. Bond interest revenue.
3. Net gain or loss from selling securities.
4. Unrealized gain or loss from holding securities.

Problem 13-8

Investments in Available-for-Sale Securities

Lindorf Company often purchases common stocks of other companies as long-term investments. At the end of 2005, Lindorf held the common stocks listed. (Assume that Lindorf Company exercises no significant influence over these companies; that is, they are classified as available-for-sale securities.)

Corporation	Number of Shares	Cost per Share
A	2,500	$ 40
B	2,000	26
C	2,300	153
D	750	75

Additional information for 2005:

Sept. 30   Lindorf received a cash dividend of $1.15 per share on Corporation A stock.

Dec. 31   The market prices were quoted as follows:
Corporation A stock, $35; Corporation B stock, $28;
Corporation C stock, $154; Corporation D stock, $70.

Required:

1. Illustrate how these investments would be reported on the balance sheet at December 31, 2005, and prepare the adjusting entry at that date.
2. What items and amounts would be reported on the income statement for 2005?
3. Prepare the journal entry for the sale of Corporation D stock for $71 per share in 2006.
4. **Interpretive Question:** Why are losses from the write-down of available-for-sale securities not included in the current year's income, whereas similar losses for trading securities are included?

Problem 13-9

Unifying Concepts: Investments in Debt and Equity Securities

On January 1, Draxton Company had surplus cash and decided to make some long-term investments. The following transactions occurred during the year:

Jan. 1   Purchased twenty $1,000, 12% bonds of Sifco Corporation at face value. Semiannual interest payment dates are January 1 and July 1 each year. The bonds are classified as available-for-sale.

Feb. 15   Purchased 4,000 shares of Porto Corporation stock at $35 per share, plus brokerage fees of $1,500. The stock is classified as available-for-sale.

July 1   Received a semiannual interest payment on the Sifco Corporation bonds.

Sept. 30   Received an annual cash dividend of $1.50 per share on Porto Corporation stock.

Oct. 15   Sold 1,000 shares of the Porto Corporation stock at $42 per share.

Dec. 31   Adjusted the accounts to accrue interest on the Sifco Corporation bonds.

Required:

1. Prepare journal entries for these transactions.
2. The market quote for Sifco Corporation's bonds at closing on December 31 was 104. The Porto Corporation stock closed at $40 per share. Prepare a partial balance sheet showing all the necessary data for these securities. Assume that Draxton exercises no significant influence over its investees.

Problem 13-10

Investments in Equity Securities

On March 15, 2006, Boston Company acquired 5,000 shares of Richfield Corporation common stock at $45 per share as a long-term investment. Richfield has 50,000 shares of outstanding voting common stock. Boston does not own any other stocks. The following additional events occurred during the fiscal year ended December 31, 2006:

Dec. 1   Boston received a cash dividend of $2.50 per share from Richfield Corporation.

31   Richfield Corporation announced earnings for the year of $150,000.

31   Richfield common stock had a closing market price of $42 per share.

(continued)

Required:
1. What accounting method should be used to account for this investment? Why?
2. Prepare journal entries for the above transactions.
3. Prepare a partial income statement and balance sheet to show how the investments accounts would be shown on the financial statements.

Problem 13-11

Investment Portfolio

General Corporation has the following investments in equity securities at December 31, 2005 (there are no existing balances in the market adjustment account):

Company	Classification	Shares	Percentage of Shares Owned	Cost	Market Price at 12/31/05
Clarke Corporation	Trading	1,000	2%	$75	$78
Marlin Company	Available-for-sale	4,000	15	34	32
Air Products, Inc.	Available-for-sale	3,000	10	46	43

Required:
1. Prepare any adjusting entries required at December 31, 2005.
2. Illustrate how these investments would be presented on General Corporation's balance sheet at December 31, 2005. The available-for-sale securities are expected to be held for two to five years.
3. Prepare the journal entry on April 10, 2006, when General Corporation sold the Clarke Corporation investment for $72 per share.
4. Assume that General Corporation still owns its investment in Marlin Company and Air Products at December 31, 2006; the market prices on that date are $37 for Marlin and $44 for Air Products. Prepare all adjusting journal entries needed at December 31, 2006.

Problem 13-12

P.A.S.S.
Power Accounting
System Software

Investments in Held-to-Maturity Securities

Eyre Corporation purchased $45,000 of Cameron Construction Company's 8% bonds at $103\frac{1}{2}$ plus accrued interest on February 1, 2005. The bonds mature on April 1, 2012, and interest is payable on April 1 and October 1. Eyre Corporation uses the straight-line method of amortizing bond premiums and discounts.

Required:
1. Record all journal entries to account for this investment during the years 2005 and 2006, assuming that Eyre closes its books annually on December 31.
2. **Interpretive Question:** At the time these bonds were purchased (February 1, 2005), was the market rate of interest above or below 8%? Explain.

Problem 13-13

Investments in Held-to-Maturity Securities

On January 1, 2006, Eurowest Company purchased a $25,000, 12% bond at 104 as a long-term investment. The bond pays interest annually on each December 31 and matures on December 31, 2008.

Assuming straight-line amortization, answer the following questions:

Required:

1. What will be the net amount of cash received (total inflows minus total outflows) from this investment over its life?
2. How much cash will be collected each year?
3. How much premium will be amortized each year?
4. By how much will Investment in Held-to-Maturity Securities decrease each year?
5. How much revenue will be reported on the income statement each year relating to this security?

Problem 13-14

Determining the Purchase Price of Held-to-Maturity Securities and Effective-Interest Amortization

Corbett Corporation decided to purchase twenty $1,000, 10%, six-year bonds of Texas Manufacturing Company as a long-term investment on February 1, 2005. The bonds mature on February 1, 2011, and interest payments are made semiannually on February 1 and August 1.

Required:

1. How much should Corbett Corporation be willing to pay for the bonds if the current interest rate on similar bonds is 8%?
2. Prepare a schedule showing the amortization of the bond premium or discount over the remaining life of the bonds, assuming that Corbett Corporation uses the effective-interest method of amortization.
3. How much bond interest revenue would be recorded each year if the straight-line method of amortization were used? Show how these amounts differ from the annual interest recognized using the effective-interest method. (Assume a fiscal year ending July 31.)
4. **Interpretive Question:** Which of the two amortization methods is preferable? Why?

Problem 13-15

P.A.S.S.
Power Accounting System Software

Investments in Held-to-Maturity Securities

Strong Equipment Company made the following purchases of debt securities during 2006. All are classified as held-to-maturity, and all pay interest semiannually.

Purchase Date	Corp.	Face Amount	Cost	Interest Rate, %	Maturity Date	Last Interest Payment Date
10/15/06	A	$ 5,000	102	9	1/1/11	7/1/06
11/30/06	B	10,000	96	12	4/1/09	10/1/06
12/15/06	C	15,000	98	14	6/1/10	12/1/06
12/31/06	D	12,000	105	10¼	5/1/07	11/1/06

Required:

1. Prepare journal entries for the purchases.
2. Show all adjusting entries relating to the bonds on December 31, 2006, assuming that Strong Equipment Company closes its book on that date and uses the straight-line amortization method.

Problem 13-16

Long-Term Investments in Equity Securities

Century Corporation acquired 8,400 common shares of Fidelity Company on January 10, 2006, for $12 per share and acquired 15,000 common shares of Essem Corporation on January 25, 2006, for $22 per share. Fidelity has 60,000 shares of common stock outstanding, and Essem has 50,000 shares outstanding. At December 31, 2006, the following information was obtained about the operations of Fidelity and Essem:

(continued)

	Fidelity	Essem
Net income	$36,000.00	$100,000.00
Dividends paid per share	0.40	1.00
Market value per share at December 31, 2006	10.00	20.00

Assume that Century Corporation exerted significant influence over the policies of Essem Corporation, but influenced the policies of Fidelity Corporation only to a very limited extent. Century classified its investment in Fidelity as an available-for-sale security.

Required:
1. How should Century account for its investments in Essem Corporation?
2. Prepare the journal entries for each investment for the year 2006 using the method or methods you selected in part (1).

Problem 13-17

Investments in Stocks—Equity Method

On March 20, 2006, Schneider Company acquired 35,000 shares of Brenchley Industries common stock at $45 per share as a long-term investment. Brenchley has 100,000 shares of outstanding voting common stock. The following additional information is presented for the calendar year ended December 31, 2006:

Nov. 15 Schneider received a cash dividend of $1.75 per share from Brenchley Industries.
Dec. 31 Brenchley announced earnings for the year of $170,000.
    31   Brenchley Industries common stock had a closing market price of $41 per share.

Required:
1. **Interpretive Question:** What accounting method should be used by Schneider Company to account for this investment? Why?
2. Prepare journal entries for the transactions and events described.

Problem 13-18

P.A.S.S.
Power Accounting
System Software

Long-Term Investments in Stock—Available-for-Sale and Equity Method

The following activities relate to Merrill Company during the years 2005 and 2006:

2005
Feb. 15 Merrill purchased 10,000 shares of Hendershot Equipment stock for $40 per share.
Dec. 1   Merrill received an $0.80-per-share cash dividend from Hendershot Equipment.
    31   Hendershot Equipment common stock had a closing market price of $37 per share. Hendershot's 2005 net income was $120,000.

2006
July 1   Merrill sold all 10,000 shares of Hendershot Equipment stock for $42 per share.

Additional information: Hendershot Equipment had 50,000 shares of common stock outstanding on January 1, 2005.

Required:
1. Prepare journal entries to record the transactions assuming:
   a. The securities are classified as available-for-sale.
   b. The equity method is used.
2. Show the amounts that would be reported on the financial statements of Merrill Company at December 31, 2005, under each assumption.
3. **Interpretive Question:** What is the minimum number of shares of stock that Hendershot could have outstanding in order for Merrill to use the equity method?

Problem 13-19

Spreadsheet

Long-Term Investments in Equity Securities

During January 2006, Danbury, Inc., acquired 40,000 shares of Corporation A common stock for $24 per share. In addition, it purchased 5,000 shares of Corporation B preferred (nonvoting) stock for $112 per share. Corporation A has 160,000 shares of common stock outstanding, and Corporation B has 12,000 shares of nonvoting stock outstanding. Danbury anticipates holding both securities for at least five years.

The following data were obtained from operations during 2006:

	2006
Net income:	
Corporation A	$190,000
Corporation B	80,000
Dividends paid (per share):	
Corporation A	$0.60
Corporation B	2.50
Market value per share at December 31:	
Corporation A	$ 25
Corporation B	109

Required:

1. **Interpretive Question:** What method should Danbury, Inc., use in accounting for the investment in Corporation A stock? Why? What accounting method should be used in accounting for Corporation B nonvoting stock? Why?
2. Prepare the journal entries necessary to record the transactions for 2006.

Problem 13-20

Spreadsheet

Unifying Concepts: Long-Term Investments in Stocks and Bonds

On January 2, 2006, Drexello, Inc., purchased $75,000 of 10%, five-year bonds of Greasy Trucking as a held-to-maturity security at a price of $77,610 plus accrued interest. The bonds mature on November 1, 2010, and interest is payable semiannually on May 1 and November 1. Drexello uses the straight-line method of amortizing bond premiums and discounts.

In addition to the bonds, Drexello purchased 30% of the 50,000 shares of outstanding common stock of Mellon Company at $42 per share, plus brokerage fees of $450, on January 10, 2006. On December 31, 2006, Mellon announced that its net income for the year was $150,000 and paid an annual dividend of $2 per share as advised by the board of directors of Drexello. The closing market price of Mellon common stock on December 31 was $38 per share.

Required:

1. Record all the 2006 transactions relating to these two investments in general journal form.
2. Show how the long-term investments and the related revenues would be reported on the financial statements of Drexello at December 31, 2006.

Problem 13-21

Consolidated Financial Statements

Parent Company owns parts of three different subsidiaries. The balance sheets and income statements for these four companies are listed on the following page. Note that, in the financial statements of Parent Company, its ownership interest in the three subsidiaries has been accounted for using the equity method.

(continued)

		Percentage of the Parent's Ownership		
	Parent	**90% Sub 1**	**60% Sub 2**	**40% Sub 3**
Assets				
Cash	$ 48	$ 10	$ 20	$ 80
Accounts receivable	300	90	80	40
Plant and equipment	700	200	100	400
Investment in Sub 1	198			
Investment in Sub 2	72			
Investment in Sub 3	88			
Total assets	$ 1,406	$ 300	$ 200	$ 520
Liabilities	500	80	80	300
Equity	906	220	120	220
Total liabilities and stockholders' equity	$ 1,406	$ 300	$ 200	$ 520
Sales	4,790	2,000	2,000	10,000
Income from Sub 1	90			
Income from Sub 2	180			
Income from Sub 3	80			
Expenses	(3,000)	(1,900)	(1,700)	(9,800)
Net income	$ 2,140	$ 100	$ 300	$ 200

Required:
1. Prepare a consolidated balance sheet for Parent Company and its subsidiaries.
2. Prepare a consolidated income statement for Parent Company and its subsidiaries.
3. **Interpretive Question:** Return on sales is net income divided by total sales. Without doing any computations, state what would happen to consolidated return on sales if Sub 3 were consolidated rather than accounted for using the equity method. Explain.

d iscussion cases

Case 13-1

Which Investment Should We Make?

Pentron Data Corporation has a significant amount of excess cash on hand and has decided to make a long-term investment in either debt or equity securities. After a careful analysis, the investment committee has recommended to the company treasurer that Pentron purchase either one of the following two investments. The first investment involves purchasing sixty $1,000, 8% bonds issued by Andrea Company. The bonds mature in four years, pay interest semiannually, and are currently selling at 92. The second investment alternative involves purchasing 3,000 shares of Franklin Corporation common stock at $30 per share (including brokerage fees). The investment committee believes that the Franklin stock will pay an annual dividend of $3.50 per share and is likely to be salable at the end of four years for $36 per share.

Discuss the following questions:

1. If Pentron wants to earn 12% per year, should it make either investment?
2. Which of the two investments would you advise the treasurer to invest in assuming the inherent risk is approximately equal? Your decision should be based on which investment provides the more attractive return, ignoring income tax effects.

Case 13-2

Classification of Securities

Memphis Company has just purchased five securities; it intends to hold the stock until the price increases to a sufficiently high level, at which time it plans to sell the stock. In fact, it is unlikely that the company will hold the securities for more than a few months. Nevertheless, Memphis's management has decided to classify the securities as available-for-sale rather than as trading securities. Why is Memphis choosing this type of classification, and would you allow it if you were the auditor?

judgment call

Judgment 13-1

You Decide: Should the trading securities that companies own be left on the books at historical cost, or should they be adjusted annually to their current market price (as is now required by GAAP)?

When physical assets are purchased, they are recorded on the balance sheet at cost and left there until the asset is sold. For example, when land is purchased, the cost of the land is recorded on the books. If the land declines in value, no adjustment is made. The company realizes the loss in value when it sells the land at a loss. Why don't we do this for marketable securities? Why should the assets for land and securities be different?

Competency Enhancement Opportunities

▶ **Analyzing Real Company Information**
▶ **International Case**
▶ **Ethics Case**
▶ **Writing Assignment**

▶ **The Debate**
▶ **Cumulative Spreadsheet Project**
▶ **Internet Search**

The following additional assignments provide opportunities for students to develop critical thinking, ethical perspectives, oral and written communication skills, experience with electronic research, and teamwork through group and business activities.

▷ *Analyzing Real Company Information*

Analyzing 13-1 (Microsoft)

The 2002 Form 10-K for MICROSOFT is included in Appendix A. Locate that Form 10-K and consider the following questions:

1. Find Microsoft's note on accounting policies. Using the information in that note (under the heading "Financial Instruments"), determine what fraction of Microsoft's investment securities are classified as "available-for-sale."

2. In its note on "Cash and short-term investments," Microsoft lists the general types of investments that make up its $38.652 billion portfolio. Certificates of deposit are listed both as "cash and cash equivalents" and as "short-term investments." What is the difference between these two categories? *Hint:* Go back to the note you looked at to answer (1).

3. Look at Microsoft's stockholders' equity statement. Where in the equity section does Microsoft report the unrealized gains and losses from available-for-sale securities?

Analyzing 13-2 (Berkshire Hathaway)

The following note comes from the 2002 annual report of BERKSHIRE HATHAWAY:

(5) Investments in equity securities

Data with respect to investments in equity securities are shown below. Amounts are in millions.

December 31, 2002	Cost	Unrealized Gains	Fair Value
Common stock of:			
American Express Company	$1,470	$ 3,889	$ 5,359
The Coca-Cola Company	1,299	7,469	8,768
The Gillette Company	600	2,315	2,915
Wells Fargo & Company	306	2,191	2,497
Other equity securities	5,489	3,335	8,824
	$9,164	$19,199	$28,363

December 31, 2001	Cost	Unrealized Gains	Fair Value
Common stock of:			
American Express Company	$1,470	$ 3,940	$ 5,410
The Coca-Cola Company	1,299	8,131	9,430
The Gillette Company	600	2,606	3,206
Wells Fargo & Company	306	2,009	2,315
Other equity securities	4,868	3,446	8,314
	$8,543	$20,132	$28,675

Berkshire Hathaway also discloses that it classifies each of these investments as an available-for-sale security.

1. All securities included in the tables in Berkshire Hathaway's Note 5 are classified as available-for-sale. Make all journal entries that were required in 2002 to account for Berkshire Hathaway's investments in:
   a. AMERICAN EXPRESS COMPANY.
   b. Other equity securities.
2. Did the performance of Berkshire Hathaway's portfolio of equity securities have any bright spots in 2002?
3. How has Berkshire Hathaway's portfolio of equity securities performed over time?

▶ *International Case*

International

Sony

SONY CORPORATION was organized in 1946 under the name TOKYO TSUSHIN KOGYO. The name "Sony" is a combination of the Latin word *sonus* (sound) and the English word *sonny*; it was given to a small transistor radio sold by the company in the United States, starting in 1954. The radio was so popular that the entire company changed its name to Sony in 1958.

In its 2002 annual report, Sony included the note to its financial statements shown on the following page.

9. Marketable securities and securities investments and other

| | Yen in millions | | | | | | | |
| | March 31, 2001 | | | | March 31, 2002 | | | |
	Cost	Gross unrealized gains	Gross unrealized losses	Fair value	Cost	Gross unrealized gains	Gross unrealized losses	Fair value
Available-for-sale:								
Debt securities	¥883,571	¥53,264	¥ 2,396	¥ 934,439	¥1,150,630	¥41,241	¥15,930	¥1,175,941
Equity securities	45,868	32,555	8,119	70,304	58,374	30,371	7,829	80,916
Held-to-maturity								
securities	16,493	63	—	16,556	19,835	353	9	20,179
Total	¥945,932	¥85,882	¥10,515	¥1,021,299	¥1,228,839	¥71,965	¥23,768	¥1,277,036

| | Dollars in millions | | | |
| | March 31, 2002 | | | |
	Cost	Gross unrealized gains	Gross unrealized losses	Fair value
Available-for-sale:				
Debt securities	$8,651	$310	$119	$8,842
Equity securities	439	228	59	608
Held-to-maturity				
securities	149	3	—	152
Total	$9,239	$541	$178	$9,602

1. In the notes to its English-language financial statements, Sony states that those statements "conform with accounting principles generally accepted in the United States." However, Sony's official accounting records are maintained using Japanese accounting principles. Why would Sony go to the trouble of preparing a separate set of English-language financial statements using U.S. accounting principles?
2. Assuming that approximately the same available-for-sale securities were on hand in both 2001 and 2002, how well did Sony's investments perform in 2002?
3. What journal entries did Sony make during the year to record the revaluation of available-for-sale securities? Use only the total amounts (that is, don't use the separate amounts for debt and equity securities), and ignore the fact that securities were bought and sold during the year.

▷ *Ethics Case*

Is It OK to Strategically Classify Securities?

You have recently been hired as a staff assistant in the office of the chairman of the board of directors of Clefton, Inc. Because you have some background in accounting, the chairman has asked you to review the preliminary financial statements that have been prepared by the company's accounting staff. After the financial statements are approved by the chairman of the board, they will be audited by external auditors. This is the first year that Clefton has had its financial statements audited by external auditors.

In examining the financial statement note on investment securities, you notice that all of the securities that had unrealized gains for the year have been classified as trading, whereas all of the securities that had unrealized losses have been classified as available-for-sale. You realize that this has the impact of placing all the gains on the income statement and hiding all the losses in the equity section of the balance sheet. You call the chief accountant who confirms that the securities are not classified until the end of the year and that the classification depends on whether a particular security has experienced a gain or a loss during the year. The chief accountant states that this policy was adopted, with the approval of the chairman of the board, in order to maximize the reported net income of the company. The chief accountant tells you that investment security classification is based on how management intends to use those securities; therefore, management is free to classify the securities in any way it wishes.

You are uncomfortable with this investment security classification strategy. You are also dismayed that the chief accountant and the chairman of the board seem to have agreed on this scheme to maximize reported income. You are also worried about what the external auditors will do when they find out about this classification scheme. You have been asked to report to the chairman of the board this afternoon to give your summary of the status of the preliminary financial statements. What should you do?

▷ *Writing Assignment*

Why Doesn't the Gain Go on the Income Statement?

You are the controller for Chong Lai Company. You just received a very strongly worded e-mail message from the president of the company. The president has learned that a $627,000 gain on a stock investment made by the company last year will not be reported in the income statement because you have classified the security as available-for-sale. With the gain, the company would report a record profit for the year. Without the gain, profits are actually down slightly from the year before. The president wants an explanation—*now*.

It has been your policy for the past several years to routinely classify all investments as available-for-sale. Your company is not in the business of actively buying and selling stocks and bonds. Instead, all investments are made to strengthen relationships with either suppliers or major customers. As such, your practice is to buy securities and hold them for several years.

Write a one-page memo to the president explaining the rationale behind your policy of security classification.

▷ *The Debate*

Market Values Do Not Belong in the Financial Statements!

Accounting traditionalists opposed the move to report investment securities in the balance sheet at their current market value. These traditionalists complain that inclusion of market values reduces the reliability of the financial statements and introduces an unnecessary amount of variability in the reported numbers. On the other hand, supporters of reporting market values claim that market values are extremely relevant and, for investment securities traded on active markets, are reliable as well.

Divide your group into two teams.

- One team represents "Market Value." Prepare a two-minute oral presentation arguing that the market value of investment securities should be reported in the balance sheet. To do otherwise is to make the statements an out-of-date curiosity rather than a useful tool.

- The other team represents "Historical Cost." Prepare a two-minute oral presentation arguing for a return to strict historical cost in the balance sheet.

▶ *Cumulative Spreadsheet Project*

This spreadsheet assignment is a continuation of the spreadsheet assignments given in earlier chapters. If you completed those spreadsheets, you have a head start on this one.

This assignment is based on the spreadsheet prepared in part (1) of the spreadsheet assignment for Chapter 10. Review that assignment for a summary of the assumptions made in preparing a forecasted balance sheet, income statement, and statement of cash flows for 2006 for Handyman Company. Using those financial statements, complete the following exercise.

Handyman has decided that, in 2006, it will create an available-for-sale investment portfolio. Handyman plans to invest $20 million in a variety of stocks and bonds. (Recall that the numbers in the Handyman spreadsheet are in millions.) As of the end of 2005, Handyman has no investment portfolio. Adapt your spreadsheet to include this expected $20 million investment portfolio as a current asset in 2006. Ignore the possibility of any interest, dividends, gains, or losses on this portfolio. Answer the following questions:

1. With the assumptions built into your spreadsheet, where will Handyman get the $20 million in funding necessary to acquire these investment securities?
2. Where in the statement of cash flows did you put the cash outflow associated with the acquisition of these investment securities? Explain your placement.

▶ *Internet Search*

Berkshire Hathaway

The history of BERKSHIRE HATHAWAY was outlined at the beginning of this chapter. Access Berkshire Hathaway's Web site at **http://www.berkshirehathaway.com**. Sometimes Web addresses change, so if this address doesn't work, access the Web site for this textbook (**http://albrecht.swlearning.com**) for an updated link.

Once you've gained access to the site, answer the following questions:

1. Berkshire Hathaway can be described as primarily a holding company, which is a company that has no real operations of its own but instead holds ownership shares of other companies. Berkshire Hathaway's Web site offers links to a number of the subsidiaries that it holds. What are some of these subsidiaries?
2. Warren Buffett writes the best "Chairman's Letters to Shareholders" in corporate America. A historical collection of these letters is included in Berkshire Hathaway's Web site. Look at the 1994 letter and find out whom Warren Buffett quoted on the dangers of hard work.
3. Berkshire Hathaway has two classes of common stock. What does the Web site say about the difference between them?
4. Berkshire Hathaway is constantly making new investments. Search the Web site for recent news releases and identify the most recent investments.

comprehensive problem 10-13

P.A.S.S.
Power Accounting System Software

Hannah Company started business on January 1, 2006. The following transactions and events occurred in 2006 and 2007. For simplicity, information for sales, inventory purchases, collections on account, and payments on account is given in summary form at the end of each year.

2006

Jan. 1 Issued 100,000 shares of $1-par common stock to investors at $20 per share.

1 Purchased a building for $550,000. The building has a 25-year expected useful life and a $50,000 expected salvage value. Hannah uses the straight-line method of depreciation.

1 Leased equipment under a five-year lease. The five lease payments of $30,000 each are to be made on December 31 of each year. The cash price of the equipment is $113,724. This lease is accounted for as a capital lease with an implicit interest rate of 10%. The equipment has a five-year useful life and zero expected salvage value; Hannah uses straight-line depreciation with all of its equipment.

Feb. 1 Borrowed $1.5 million from Burtone Bank. The loan bears an 11% annual interest rate. Interest is to be paid each year on February 1. The principal on the loan will be repaid in four years.

Mar. 1 Purchased 40,000 shares of Larry Company for $35 per share. Hannah classifies this as an investment in trading securities. These securities are reported as a current asset.

July 15 Purchased 50,000 shares of Frances Ann Company for $21 per share. Hannah classifies this as an investment in available-for-sale securities. These securities are reported as a long-term asset.

Nov. 17 Declared a cash dividend of $0.25 per share, payable on January 15, 2007.

Dec. 31 Made the lease payment.

31 The Larry Company shares had a market value of $30 per share. The Frances Ann Company shares had a market value of $27 per share.

Summary:
a. Sales for the year (all on credit) totaled $800,000. The cost of inventory sold was $350,000.
b. Cash collections on credit sales for the year were $370,000.
c. Inventory costing $420,000 was purchased on account. (Hannah Company uses the perpetual inventory method.)
d. Payments on account totaled $400,000.

2007

Jan. 1 Issued $500,000 in bonds at par value. The bonds have a stated interest rate of 8%, payable semiannually on July 1 and January 1.

1 The estimated useful life and salvage value for the building were changed. It is now estimated that the building has a remaining life (as of January 1, 2007) of 20 years. Also, it is now estimated that the building will have no salvage value. These changes in estimate are to take effect for the year 2007 and subsequent years.

15 Paid the cash dividend declared in November 2006.

Feb. 1 Hannah Company repurchased 10,000 shares of its own common stock to be held as treasury stock. The price paid was $37 per share.

1 Paid the interest on the loan from Burtone Bank.

Apr. 10 Sold all 40,000 shares of the Larry Company stock. The shares were sold for $28 per share.

July 1 Paid the interest on the bonds.

Oct. 1   Retired the bonds that were issued on January 1. Hannah had to pay $470,000 to retire the bonds. This amount included interest that had accrued since July 1.

Nov. 20   Declared a cash dividend of $0.40 per share. The dividend applies only to outstanding shares, not to treasury shares.

Dec. 31   Made the lease payment.

31   After recording depreciation expense for the year, the building was evaluated for possible impairment. The building is expected to generate cash flows of $20,000 per year for its 19-year remaining life. The building has a current market value of $325,000.

31   The Frances Ann Company shares had a market value of $18 per share.

Summary:

a. Sales for the year (all on credit) totaled $1.7 million. The cost of inventory sold was $800,000.

b. Cash collections on credit sales for the year were $1.43 million.

c. Inventory costing $900,000 was purchased on account.

d. Payments on account totaled $880,000.

Required:

1. Prepare all journal entries to record the information for 2006. Also prepare any necessary adjusting entries.

2. Prepare a trial balance as of December 31, 2006. There is no need to show your ledger T-accounts; however, preparing and posting to T-accounts may aid in the preparation of the trial balance.

3. Prepare an income statement for the year ended December 31, 2006, and a balance sheet as of December 31, 2006.

4. Prepare all journal entries to record the information for 2007. Also prepare any necessary adjusting entries.

5. Prepare a trial balance as of December 31, 2007. (As you compute the amounts to include in the trial balance, don't forget the beginning balances left over from 2006.)

6. Prepare an income statement for the year ended December 31, 2007, and a balance sheet as of December 31, 2007.

Part

4

Other Dimensions of Financial Reporting

14 The Statement of Cash Flows

c h a p t e r

14

The Statement of Cash Flows

After studying this chapter, you should be able to:

Learning Objectives

1 Understand the purpose of a statement of cash flows.

2 Recognize the different types of information reported in the statement of cash flows.

3 Prepare a simple statement of cash flows.

4 Analyze financial statements to prepare a statement of cash flows.

5 Use information from the statement of cash flows to make decisions.

HOME DEPOT is the leading retailer in the "do-it-yourself" home handyman market. In January 2003, Home Depot had 1,532 stores in the United States, five Canadian provinces, and Mexico. With each store averaging 108,000 square feet (and an additional 24,000 square feet in the outside garden center), a lot of shelf space is filled with paint, lumber, hardware, and plumbing fixtures. If plumbing fixtures don't seem very exciting to you, consider this: Home Depot is the 33rd largest company in the United States (in terms of market value), with a 2003 market value of $53.5 billion.[1] And if lumber and hardware seem obsolete in this high-tech world, consider that, for the past 10 years, Home Depot's earnings per share (EPS) have grown an average of 24.4% per year, not too far behind the 36.0% annual growth in EPS experienced by high-flying INTEL during the same period. In fiscal 2003, Home Depot's sales reached $58.2 billion.[2]

But Home Depot's prospects weren't always so rosy. Back in 1985, when sales were only $700 million, Home Depot experienced cash flow problems, in large part due to rapid increases in the level of inventory. Part of this inventory increase was the natural result of Home Depot's expansion. But Home Depot stores were also starting to fill up with excess inventory because of lax inventory management. In 1983, the average Home Depot store contained enough inventory to support average sales for 75 days. By 1985, the number of days' sales in inventory had increased to 83 days. Combined with Home Depot's rapid growth, this inventory inefficiency caused total inventory to increase by $69 million in 1985, and this increase in inventory was instrumental in Home Depot's negative cash from operations of $43 million. Concerns about this declining profitability and negative cash flow caused Home Depot's stock value to take a dive in 1985, and the beginning of 1986 found Home Depot wondering where it would find the investors and creditors to finance its aggressive expansion plans. Exhibit 1 summarizes the differences between Home Depot's reported net income and the company's cash flow from operations for the fiscal years 1984 through 1986 as well as the company's recent performance.

Home Depot's current success is the result of an incredible operating cash flow turnaround that the company pulled off in fiscal 1987. Operating income almost tripled compared to fiscal 1986, and net income increased from $8.2 million to $23.9 million. A computerized inventory management program was instituted, and the number of days' sales in inventory dropped to 80 days. Improved profitability and more efficient management of inventory combined to transform the negative $43 million operating cash flow in fiscal 1986 into positive cash from operations of $66 million in fiscal 1987.

Exhibit 1: Home Depot's Net Income and Cash Flows from Operations

(in thousands)	Fiscal Year Ended		
	February 2, 1986	February 3, 1985	January 29, 1984
Net earnings	$ 8,219	$14,122	$ 10,261
Net cash provided by operations	(43,120)	(3,056)	(10,574)

(in thousands)	Fiscal Year Ended		
	February 2, 2003	February 3, 2002	January 28, 2001
Net earnings	$3,664,000	$3,044,000	$2,581,000
Net cash provided by operations	4,802,000	5,963,000	2,796,000

1 See the Fortune 500 listing at **http://www.fortune.com**.
2 January 30, 2003, 10-K filing of The Home Depot, Inc.

n this chapter, we will study the statement of cash flows. You will learn that this statement provides one of the earliest warning signs of cash concerns of the type experienced by Home Depot. The statement of cash flows alerts financial statement readers to increases and decreases in cash as well as to the reasons and trends for the changes.

In today's business environment, it is not enough simply to monitor earnings and earnings per share measurements. An entity's financial position and especially its inflows and outflows of cash are also critical to its financial success.

The three primary financial statements were introduced and illustrated in Chapter 2. In subsequent chapters, we examined in detail the components of the balance sheet and income statement. For our discussion of the statement of cash flows, we will first describe the purpose and general format of a statement of cash flows. We will then show how easy it is to prepare a statement of cash flows if detailed cash flow information is available. A statement of cash flows can also be prepared based on an analysis of balance sheet and income statement accounts. We will also distinguish between the direct and indirect methods of reporting operating cash flows and discuss the usefulness of the statement of cash flows. Finally, we will explain how the statement of cash flows can be used to make investment and lending decisions.

What's the Purpose of a Statement of Cash Flows?

❙ Understand the purpose of a statement of cash flows.

statement of cash flows
The financial statement that shows an entity's cash inflows (receipts) and outflows (payments) during a period of time.

The **statement of cash flows**, as its name implies, summarizes a company's cash flows for a period of time. It provides answers to such questions as, "Where did our money come from?" and "Where did our money go?" The statement of cash flows explains how a company's cash was generated during the period and how that cash was used.

You might think that the statement of cash flows is a replacement for the income statement, but the two statements have two different objectives. The income statement, as you know, measures the results of operations for a period of time. Net income is the accountant's best estimate at reflecting a company's economic performance for a period. The income statement provides details as to how the retained earnings account changes during a period and ties together, in part, the owners' equity sections of comparative balance sheets.

The statement of cash flows, on the other hand, provides details as to how the cash account changed during a period. The statement of cash flows reports the period's transactions and events in terms of their impact on cash. In Chapter 4, we compared the cash-basis and accrual-basis methods of measuring income and explained why accrual-basis income is considered a better measure of periodic income. The statement of cash flows provides important information from a cash-basis perspective that complements the income statement and balance sheet, thus providing a more complete picture of a company's operations and financial position. It is important to note that the statement of cash flows does not include any transactions or accounts that are not already reflected in the balance sheet or the income statement. Rather, the statement of cash flows simply provides information relating to the cash flow effects of those transactions.

Users of financial statements, particularly investors and creditors, need information about a company's cash flows in order to evaluate the company's ability to generate positive net cash flows in the future to meet its obligations and to pay dividends. In some cases, careful analysis of cash flows can provide early warning of impending financial problems, as was the case with HOME DEPOT.

Before moving on, it is important to reiterate that the statement of cash flows does not replace the income statement. The income statement summarizes the results of a company's operations, whereas the statement of cash flows summarizes a company's inflows and outflows of cash. Information contained in the income statement can be used to facilitate the preparation of a statement of cash flows; information in the statement of cash flows sheds some light on the company's ability to generate income in the future. The statement of cash flows and the income statement provide complementary information about different aspects of a business.

TO SUMMARIZE: The statement of cash flows, one of the three primary financial statements, provides information about the cash receipts and payments of an entity during a period. It provides important information that complements the income statement and balance sheet.

What Information Is Reported in the Statement of Cash Flows?

2 Recognize the different types of information reported in the statement of cash flows.

cash equivalents Short-term, highly liquid investments that can easily be converted into cash.

Accounting standards include specific requirements for the reporting of cash flows. The general format for a statement of cash flows, with details and dollar amounts omitted, is presented in Exhibit 2. As illustrated, the inflows and outflows of cash must be divided into three main categories: operating activities, investing activities, and financing activities. Further, the statement of cash flows is presented in a manner that reconciles the beginning and ending balances of cash and cash equivalents. **Cash equivalents** are short-term, highly liquid investments that can easily be converted into cash. Generally, only investments with maturities of three months or less qualify as cash equivalents. Examples are U.S. Treasury bills, money market funds, and commercial paper (short-term debt issued by corporations). In this chapter, as is common in practice, the term *cash* will be used to include cash and cash equivalents.

network **exercises**

U.S. Treasury Department

Speaking of cash, what is the largest denomination ever printed by the U.S. Treasury Department? Go to **http://www.ustreas.gov/topics/currency** to find out.

Major Classifications of Cash Flows

Exhibit 3 shows the three main categories of cash inflows and outflows—operating, investing, and financing. Exhibit 4 summarizes the specific activities included in each category. Beginning with operating activities, each of the cash flow categories will be explained. We will also discuss the reporting of significant noncash transactions and events.

Operating Activities

operating activities Transactions and events that enter into the determination of net income.

Operating activities include those transactions and events that enter into the determination of net income. Cash receipts from the sale of goods or services are the major cash inflows for most businesses. Other inflows are cash receipts for interest revenue, dividend revenue, and similar items. Major outflows of cash are for the purchase of inventory and for the payment of wages, taxes, interest, utilities, rent, and similar expenses. As we will explain later, the amount of cash provided by (or used in) operating activities is a key figure and should be highlighted on the statement of cash flows.

FYI:

Although cash inflows from interest and dividends logically might be classified as financing activities, the FASB has decided to classify them as operating activities, which conforms to their presentation on the income statement.

Note that our focus in analyzing operating activities is to determine cash flows from operations. An analysis is required to convert income from an accrual-basis to a cash-basis number.

To do this, we begin with the net income figure, remove all items relating to investing activities (such as depreciation and gains/losses on the sale of equipment)

Exhibit 2: General Format for a Statement of Cash Flows

Cash provided by (used in):	
Operating activities	$XXX
Investing activities	XXX
Financing activities	XXX
Net increase (decrease) in cash and cash equivalents	$XXX
Cash and cash equivalents at beginning of year	XXX
Cash and cash equivalents at end of year	$XXX

Exhibit 3: The Flow of Cash

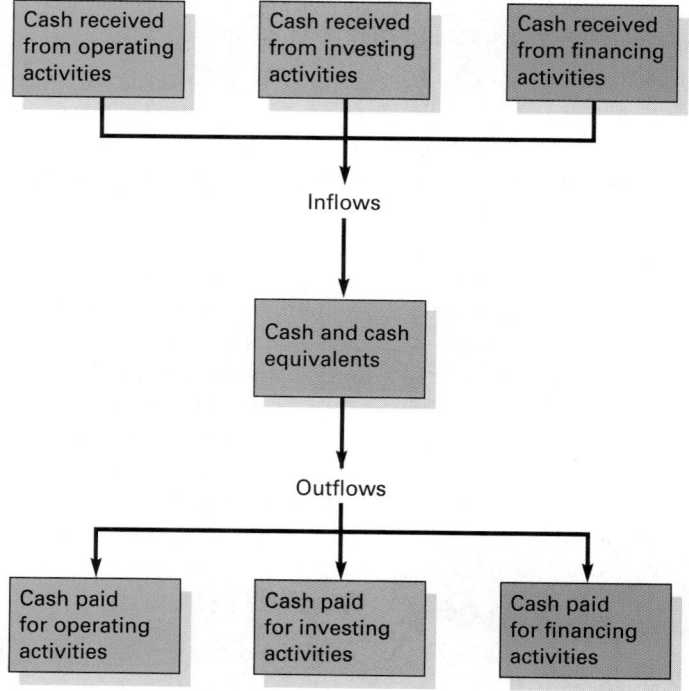

Operating activities, including the sale of goods, help determine net income and are reported on the statement of cash flows.

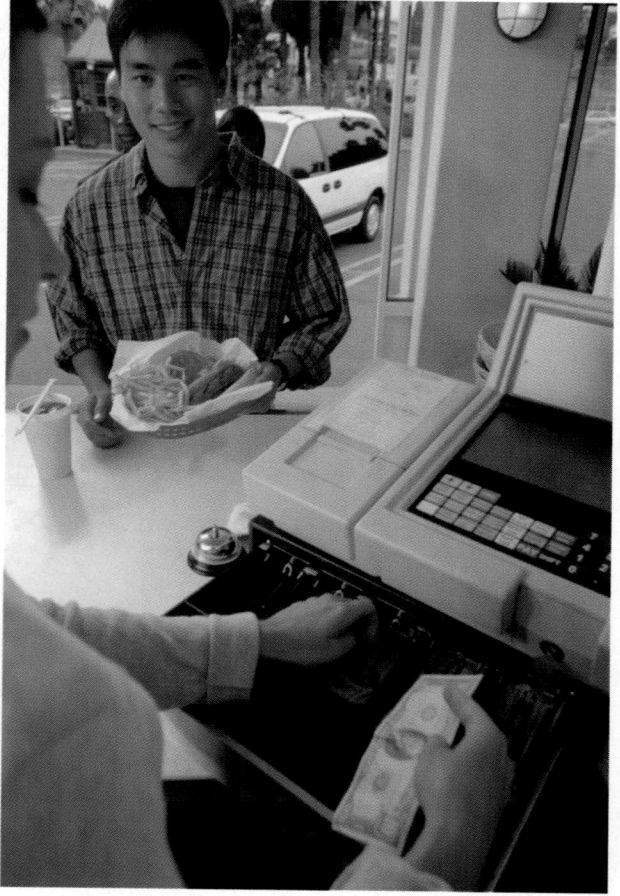

© 2003 Getty Images

Exhibit 4: Major Classifications of Cash Flows

Operating Activities
Cash receipts from:
  Sale of goods or services
  Interest revenue
  Dividend revenue
  Sale of investments in trading securities
Cash payments to:
  Suppliers for inventory purchases
  Employees for services
  Governments for taxes
  Lenders for interest expense
  Brokers for purchase of trading securities
  Others for other expenses (e.g., utilities, rent)

Investing Activities
Cash receipts from:
  Sale of property, plant, and equipment
  Sale of a business segment
  Sale of investments in securities other than trading securities
  Collection of principal on loans made to other entities
Cash payments to:
  Purchase property, plant, and equipment
  Purchase debt or equity securities of other entities (other than trading securities)
  Make loans to other entities

Financing Activities
Cash receipts from:
  Issuance of own stock
  Borrowing (e.g., bonds, notes, mortgages)
Cash payments to:
  Stockholders as dividends
  Repay principal amounts borrowed
  Repurchase an entity's own stock (treasury stock)

and financing activities (such as gains/losses on retirement of debt), and then adjust for changes in those current assets and current liabilities that involve cash and relate to operations (which are most of the current assets and current liabilities).

investing activities Transactions and events that involve the purchase and sale of securities (excluding cash equivalents), property, plant, equipment, and other assets not generally held for resale, and the making and collecting of loans.

Investing Activities

Transactions and events that involve the purchase and sale of securities (other than trading securities), property, buildings, equipment, and other assets not generally held for resale, and the making and collecting of loans are classified as **investing activities**. These activities occur regularly and result in cash inflows and outflows. They are not classified under operating activities because they relate only indirectly to the entity's central, ongoing operations, which usually involve the sale of goods or services.

The analysis of investing activities involves identifying those accounts on the balance sheet relating to investments (typically long-term asset accounts) and then explaining how those accounts changed and how those changes affected the cash flows for the period.

FYI:

The purchase and sale of trading securities is classified as an operating activity.

financing activities Transactions and events whereby resources are obtained from, or repaid to, owners (equity financing) and creditors (debt financing).

Financing Activities

Financing activities include transactions and events whereby resources are obtained from or paid to owners (equity financing) and creditors (debt financing). Dividend payments, for example, fit this definition. As noted earlier, the receipt of dividends and interest and the payment

The W. T. Grant Company's Negative Cash Flows Perhaps the most famous case highlighting the deficiencies of accrual-basis net income was that of the W. T. GRANT COMPANY. In 1906, William T. Grant opened his first 25-cent store in Lynn, Massachusetts. Twenty-two years later, stock of the W. T. Grant Company was offered for sale to the public. By 1953, the company had expanded to include over 500 stores, and the expansion continued into the 1960s. In 1969 alone, 410 new stores were opened. In 1973, the company's stock was selling at nearly 20 times earnings and peaked at $70⅝ per share. As late as September 1974, a group of banks loaned the company $600 million.

A careful analysis of W. T. Grant's financial statements, however, would have indicated that although the company was reporting profits through 1974, cash flows from operations were almost always negative from 1966 to 1975. Once the market realized the magnitude of W. T. Grant's cash flow problems, it reacted quickly. In December 1974, the company's stock was trading at $2 per share. The company closed 107 stores and laid off 7,000 employees in September 1975. On October 2, 1975, the nation's largest retailer filed for protection under Chapter 11 of the National Bankruptcy Act. Only four months later, the creditors' committee voted for liquidation, and W. T. Grant ceased to exist.

Why didn't creditors and stockholders see W. T. Grant's impending problems sooner? As the chart shows, net income and working capital provided by operations were of little help in predicting W. T. Grant's problems, but a careful analysis of the company's cash flows would have revealed the problems as much as a decade before the collapse.

How could this happen? Oddly enough, firms were not required to provide investors and creditors with information about cash flows until 1987. Prior to that time, companies prepared a statement of changes in financial position, which measured changes in current assets and current liabilities. This statement of changes in financial position provided information that, if not carefully interpreted, could lead one to believe that a buildup of inventory and receivables was as good as money in the bank (as was the case with W. T. Grant).

The requirement of a statement of cash flows eliminated many of the alternatives used by companies to detail their liquidity position. Now, under generally accepted accounting principles, companies must disclose their liquidity position in terms of cash. Had this standard been applied to W. T. Grant, the negative cash flows from operations would have been highlighted and easily detected.

FYI:

The activities are typically listed in this order: operating, investing, and financing. However, there is no requirement that they be listed in this way. MICROSOFT, for example, uses this order: operating, financing, and investing.

of interest are classified under operating activities simply because they are reported as a part of income on the income statement. The receipt or payment of the principal amount borrowed or repaid (but not the interest) is considered a financing activity.

Analyzing the cash flow effects of financing activities involves identifying those accounts relating to financing (typically long-term debt and common stock) and explaining how changes in those accounts affected the company's cash flows. Exhibit 5 summarizes the activities reflected on the statement of cash flows and indicates how the balance sheet and income statement accounts relate to the various activities.

Noncash Investing and Financing Activities

Some investing and financing activities do not affect cash. For example, equipment may be purchased with a note payable, or land may be acquired by issuing stock. These noncash transactions are not reported in the statement of cash flows. However, if a company has significant noncash financing and investing activities, they should be disclosed in a separate schedule or in a narrative explanation. The disclosures may be presented below the statement of cash flows or in the notes to the financial statements.

Financial History of the W. T. Grant Company 1966–1975

Exhibit 5: How Balance Sheet and Income Statement Accounts Relate to the Statement of Cash Flows

Cash Flow Activity	Related Balance Sheet and Income Statement Accounts	Examples	Chapters in Which Accounts Were Covered
Operating	All income statement accounts **except** those income statement items relating to:	Sales, Cost of Goods Sold, Salaries Expense, etc.	Chs. 7–9
	• Investing	Depreciation, Gains/Losses on Sale of Equipment	Ch. 10
	• Financing	Gains/Losses on Retirement of Debt	Ch. 11
	Current assets	Accounts Receivable	Ch. 7
		Inventory	Ch. 8
	Current liabilities	Accounts Payable	Ch. 8
Investing	Long-term assets	Property, Plant, and Equipment	Ch. 10
	Long-term investments	Available-for-Sale and Held-to-Maturity Securities	Ch. 13
Financing	Long-term debt	Bonds and Mortgages	Ch. 11
	Stockholders' equity (except for	Common Stock	Ch. 12
	net income in Retained Earnings)	Dividends	Ch. 12

Cash Flow Patterns

Most U.S. companies (about 60%) report positive cash flows from operations. That shouldn't come as a big surprise because companies need to generate cash from operating activities to survive in the long term. In addition, about 80% of U.S. companies report negative cash flows from investing activities. Again, this is expected as companies must expand, enhance, or replace long-term assets. Predicting whether the sign for cash from financing activities will be positive or negative is more difficult. That sign depends on whether the company is young, growing, and in need of cash, or mature, stable, and flush with cash. As a company proceeds through the normal life cycle of a business, cash from financing typically will vary between positive and negative. As an example, in fiscal 2003 Home Depot reported positive cash flows from operations ($4.8 billion), negative cash flows from investing ($2.9 billion), and negative cash flow from financing ($2,165 million).

TO SUMMARIZE: The statement of cash flows is presented in a manner that highlights three major categories of cash flows: operating activities, investing activities, and financing activities. In addition, the format of the statement should provide a reconciliation of the beginning and ending balances of cash and cash equivalents (short-term, highly liquid investments). Any significant noncash investing and financing activities should be disclosed separately, either below the statement of cash flows or in the notes to the financial statements.

Preparing a Statement of Cash Flows—A Simple Example

3 Prepare a simple statement of cash flows.

Now that we have reviewed the three types of cash flow activities disclosed on the statement of cash flows, let's start with a simple example to see how easy (conceptually) a statement of cash flows is to prepare. For this example, we will begin with the following trial balance information for Silmaril, Inc.

Silmaril, Inc.
Trial Balance
January 1, 2006

	Debit	Credit
Cash	$ 300	
Accounts Receivable	2,500	
Inventory	1,900	
Property, Plant, and Equipment	4,000	
Accumulated Depreciation		$1,200
Accounts Payable		1,700
Taxes Payable		40
Long-Term Debt		2,200
Common Stock		1,000
Retained Earnings		2,560
Totals	$8,700	$8,700

The following transactions were conducted by Silmaril, Inc., during 2006:

1. Sales on account, $13,500.
2. Collections on account, $14,000.

3. Purchased inventory on account, $7,900.
4. Cost of goods sold, $8,000.
5. Paid accounts payable, $8,100.
6. Purchased property, plant, and equipment for cash, $1,700.
7. Sold property, plant, and equipment for cash, $500 (original cost, $1,200; accumulated depreciation, $800).
8. Paid long-term debt, $200.
9. Issued stock at par value, $450.
10. Recorded depreciation expense, $500.
11. Paid interest on debt, $180.
12. Recorded interest owed (accrued) but not paid, $20.
13. Paid miscellaneous expenses (e.g., wages, supplies, etc.) for the period, $3,200.
14. Recorded tax expense for the period, $450.
15. Paid taxes during the period, $440.

With this information, we can reconstruct the journal entries made by Silmaril, Inc., during the year:

1.	Accounts Receivable	13,500	
	Sales		13,500
2.	Cash	14,000	
	Accounts Receivable		14,000
3.	Inventory	7,900	
	Accounts Payable		7,900
4.	Cost of Goods Sold	8,000	
	Inventory		8,000
5.	Accounts Payable	8,100	
	Cash		8,100
6.	Property, Plant, and Equipment	1,700	
	Cash		1,700
7.	Cash	500	
	Accumulated Depreciation	800	
	Property, Plant, and Equipment		1,200
	Gain on Sale of Equipment		100
8.	Long-Term Debt	200	
	Cash		200
9.	Cash	450	
	Common Stock		450
10.	Depreciation Expense	500	
	Accumulated Depreciation		500
11.	Interest Expense	180	
	Cash		180
12.	Interest Expense	20	
	Interest Payable		20
13.	Miscellaneous Expenses	3,200	
	Cash		3,200
14.	Tax Expense	450	
	Taxes Payable		450
15.	Taxes Payable	440	
	Cash		440

When these journal entries are posted, the following trial balance results:

Silmaril, Inc.
Trial Balance
December 31, 2006

	Debit	Credit
Cash	$ 1,430	
Accounts Receivable	2,000	
Inventory	1,800	
Property, Plant, and Equipment	4,500	
Accumulated Depreciation		$ 900
Accounts Payable		1,500
Interest Payable		20
Taxes Payable		50
Long-Term Debt		2,000
Common Stock		1,450
Retained Earnings		2,560
Sales		13,500
Gain on Sale of Equipment		100
Cost of Goods Sold	8,000	
Depreciation Expense	500	
Interest Expense	200	
Tax Expense	450	
Miscellaneous Expenses	3,200	
Totals	$22,080	$22,080

To this point, this is all a review—journalizing transactions, posting journal entries, and preparing a trial balance. From this trial balance, we can easily prepare an income statement and a balance sheet; but our objective here is to prepare a statement of cash flows. With information from the Cash T-account, we can prepare a statement of cash flows. The Cash T-account would contain the following information (journal entry reference numbers are in parentheses):

Cash

Beg. Bal.	300		
(2)	14,000	(5)	8,100
(7)	500	(6)	1,700
(9)	450	(8)	200
		(11)	180
		(13)	3,200
		(15)	440
End. Bal.	1,430		

Our task at this point is simply to categorize each cash inflow and outflow as an operating, investing, or financing activity. The inflows and outflows break down as follows:

Operating Activities:

Collections on account (2)		$ 14,000
Payments for inventory (5)	$ 8,100	
Payments for miscellaneous expenses (13)	3,200	
Payment for interest (11)	180	
Payment for taxes (15)	440	(11,920)
Cash flows from operating activities		$ 2,080

Investing Activities:

Sold equipment (7)	$ 500	
Purchased equipment (6)	(1,700)	
Cash flows from investing activities		(1,200)

Financing Activities:

Issued stock (9)	$ 450		
Paid debt (8)	(200)		
Cash flows from financing activities		250	
Net increase in cash			$ 1,130
Beginning cash balance			300
Ending cash balance			$ 1,430

As you can see, if we have access to the detailed transaction data from the Cash T-account, preparing a statement of cash flows involves determining the proper cash flow category (operating, investing, or financing) for each inflow or outflow and then properly formatting the statement. More advanced accounting software programs allow financial statement preparers to categorize each cash inflow and outflow as an operating, investing, or financing activity and to prepare a statement of cash flows with the press of a key. Once considered one of the most difficult parts of accounting, preparing a statement of cash flows has been greatly simplified as a result of computer technology.

If information is properly coded when input into a computerized accounting system, the preparation of a statement of cash flows is easy. As mentioned, the more advanced accounting software facilitates this process. But what happens if an accounting system does not classify cash transactions according to their activities? In the next section, we discuss how a statement of cash flows is prepared if one does not have ready access to detailed cash inflow and outflow information.

TO SUMMARIZE: If transactions are properly classified when input into the accounting system, the preparation of a statement of cash flows is straightforward. Cash inflows and outflows are segregated according to type of activity (operating, investing, or financing), and a statement of cash flows is prepared based on that information. As technology continues to advance, the preparation of a statement of cash flows is becoming easier.

Analyzing the Other Primary Financial Statements to Prepare a Statement of Cash Flows

4 Analyze financial statements to prepare a statement of cash flows.

If detailed cash flow information is not accessible, the preparation of a statement of cash flows is more difficult. The income statement and comparative balance sheets must be analyzed to determine how cash was generated and how cash was used by a business. How can we determine a company's cash inflows and outflows by looking at balance sheets and an income statement? The secret lies in remembering the basics of double-entry accounting: each journal entry has two parts—a debit and a credit. In the case of the cash account, every time Cash is debited, some other account is credited; every time Cash is credited, some other account is debited. If we don't have access to the details of the cash account, we can infer those details based on our knowledge of accounting and by analyzing changes in accounts other than Cash.

For example, consider the accounts receivable account. A debit to that account means what? Ninety-nine percent of the time, a debit to Accounts Receivable is associated with a sale on account. A credit to Accounts Receivable means what? Most likely, cash was collected. If we have the beginning and ending balances for the accounts receivable account (from comparative balance sheets) and sales for the period (from the income statement), we can infer the cash collected for the period. Consider the information taken from Silmaril's beginning trial balance and the year-end trial balance relating to Accounts Receivable (remember, we are assuming that the detailed journal entries are not available to us, only the resulting financial statements):

Accounts Receivable

Beg. Bal.	2,500		
Sales	13,500	Collections	?
End. Bal.	2,000		

To reconcile the accounts receivable account, we can only assume that cash collections of $14,000 occurred. With any other amount the account will not reconcile.[3] In other words, we can infer that the following journal entry must have been made:

```
Cash ..................................................  14,000
    Accounts Receivable ...................................        14,000
```

As you can see from this analysis, we don't necessarily need the detailed cash account information to prepare a statement of cash flows. We can use our knowledge of double-entry accounting to infer those details.

A similar analysis is conducted for every balance sheet account (except Cash). The analyses draw on our knowledge of the relationship between the income statement and balance sheet accounts and of what accounts are associated with operating, investing, and financing activities. Consider another example—Common Stock. First of all, we know that changes in the common stock account are considered financing activities. Second, what do we know about credits to the common stock account? They typically are associated with the issuance (sale) of stock. Debits to the common stock account? They are associated with the retirement of common stock. Assume we are given comparative balance sheet information (transactions in a company's own stock are not reflected on the income statement) relating to the common stock account of Silmaril, Inc., as follows:

Caution

Every balance sheet account (except Cash) must be analyzed to determine any cash flow effects. Then those effects must be classified by activity.

	Beginning Balance	Ending Balance
Common stock	$1,000	$1,450

What would you infer about Silmaril's cash flow activities relating to its common stock account? Without any additional information, it would be safe to assume that the company sold stock for $450. If something out of the ordinary happened in the common stock account (like the retirement of stock), that information would generally be available in the notes to the financial statements and would be used to modify the analysis.

FYI:

Buying and using PP&E would be considered common activities. Selling PP&E would be considered less common.

As an illustration of this type of complexity, consider Silmaril's property, plant, and equipment (PP&E) account. First of all, the PP&E account is associated with what type of cash flow activity? Investing. Increases in property, plant, and equipment correspond to purchases of PP&E, and decreases relate to the sale of PP&E. Because the sale of PP&E is typically an out-of-the-ordinary type of transaction, we could look at the notes to the financial statements for information relating to any sales. In the case of Silmaril, Inc., we find that equipment costing $1,200, with accumulated depreciation of $800, was sold for $500. Based on this information, and using informa-

---

3 Some of you may be thinking that Accounts Receivable can be credited when accounts are written off. This is true, and write-offs would affect our analysis. However, our purpose here is to understand the concepts. A more complicated analysis including write-offs will be covered in an intermediate accounting class.

tion from the comparative balance sheets, we can infer the purchases made during the period as follows:

Property, Plant, and Equipment

Beg. Bal.	4,000		
Purchases	?	Sold	1,200
End. Bal.	4,500		

How much PP&E was purchased during the period? The only amount that will reconcile the PP&E account is $1,700. The journal entry would have been a debit to PP&E and a credit to Cash. Again, we find that we don't need the details of the cash account to be able to infer the cash inflows and outflows for the company. Our knowledge of double-entry accounting allows us to do a little detective work and infer what went on in the cash account.

A Six-Step Process for Preparing a Statement of Cash Flows

Is there a systematic method for analyzing the income statement and comparative balance sheets to prepare a statement of cash flows? Yes, the following six-step process can be used in preparing a statement of cash flows:

1. Compute the change in the cash and cash-equivalent accounts for the period of the statement. Seldom is one handed a check figure in real life, but such is the case when preparing a statement of cash flows. The statement of cash flows is not complete until you have explained the change from the beginning balance in the cash account to the balance at year-end.

2. Convert the income statement from an accrual-basis to a cash-basis summary of operations. This is done in three steps: (1) eliminate from the income statement those expenses that do not involve cash (such **noncash items** would include depreciation expense that does not involve an outflow of cash in the current period even though income was reduced); (2) eliminate from the income statement the effects of nonoperating activity items (such items include gains and losses on the sale of long-term assets and gains and losses associated with the retirement of debt); and (3) identify those current asset and current liability accounts associated with the income statement accounts, and adjust those income statement accounts for the changes in the associated current assets and current liabilities. For example, Sales will be adjusted for the change between the beginning and ending balance in Accounts Receivable to derive the cash collections for the period. The final result will be cash flows from operating activities.

3. Analyze the long-term assets to identify the cash flow effects of investing activities. Changes in property, plant, and equipment and in long-term investments may indicate that cash has either been spent or been received.

4. Analyze the long-term debt and stockholders' equity accounts to determine the cash flow effects of any financing transactions. These transactions could be borrowing or repaying debt, issuing or buying back stock, or paying dividends.

5. Prepare a formal statement of cash flows by classifying all cash inflows and outflows according to operating, investing, and financing activities. The net cash flows provided by (used in) each of the three main activities of an entity should be highlighted. The net cash flows amount for the period is then added (subtracted) from the beginning Cash balance to report the ending Cash balance.

6. Report any significant investing or financing transactions that did not involve cash in a narrative explanation or in a separate schedule to the statement of cash flows. This would include such transactions as the purchase of land by issuing stock or the retirement of bonds by issuing stock.

noncash items Items included in the determination of net income on an accrual basis that do not affect cash; for example, depreciation and amortization.

STOP & THINK

Why must gains (losses) on the sale of equipment be subtracted (added) when computing cash flows from operations?

Caution

Make sure that the total net cash flows from the statement (the sum of net cash flows from operating, investing, and financing activities) are equal to the net increase (decrease) in cash as computed in step 1.

An Illustration of the Six-Step Process

We will illustrate this six-step process for preparing the statement of cash flows using the information from the Silmaril, Inc., example presented earlier. Remember that in this case we are assuming that we do not have access to the detailed cash flow information. Thus, we are going to have to make inferences about cash flows by examining all other balance sheet and income statement accounts other than the cash account.

Step 1. Compute the Change in the Cash and Cash-Equivalent Accounts for the Period of the Statement

Recall that Silmaril began the year with a Cash balance of $300 and ended with a Cash balance of $1,430. Thus, our objective in preparing the statement of cash flows is to explain why the cash account changed by $1,130 during the year.

Step 2. Convert the Income Statement from an Accrual Basis to a Cash Basis

From the trial balance prepared at the end of the year, we can prepare the following income statement for Silmaril, Inc.:

Sales	$13,500
Cost of goods sold	8,000
Gross margin	$ 5,500
Miscellaneous expenses	3,200
Depreciation expense	500
Income from operations	$ 1,800
Interest expense	(200)
Gain on sale of equipment	100
Income before taxes	$ 1,700
Tax expense	450
Net income	$ 1,250

Our objective at this point is to convert the income statement to cash flows from operations. Recall that this involves three steps: (1) eliminating expenses not involving cash, (2) eliminating the effects of nonoperating activities, and (3) adjusting the remaining figures from an accrual basis to a cash basis. We will use a work sheet to track the adjustments that will be made. The first two adjustments involve removing depreciation expense (because it does not involve an outflow of cash) and eliminating the gain on the sale of the equipment (because the sale of equipment is an investing activity, the effect of which will be disclosed in the investing activities section of the statement). The following work sheet reflects these adjustments:

	Income Statement	Adjustments	Cash Flows from Operations
Sales	$13,500		
Cost of goods sold	(8,000)		
Miscellaneous expenses	(3,200)		
Depreciation expense	(500)	+500 (not a cash flow item)	0
Interest expense	(200)		
Gain on sale of equipment	100	−100 (not an operating activity)	0
Tax expense	(450)		
	$ 1,250		

Note that because depreciation expense was initially subtracted to arrive at net income, our adjustment involves adding $500 back because no cash actually flowed out of the company relating to depreciation. The cash flow effect of the sale of the equipment should be reflected

Caution

When equipment is initially purchased, the cash outflow is reported as an investing activity. When the equipment is used, this use is recorded as depreciation and does not involve any cash flow even though it is reported as an expense on the income statement.

in the investing activities section of the statement of cash flows. Therefore, the effect of the gain must be removed from the operating activities section. Because the gain was initially added, we must subtract $100 as an adjustment to remove the effects of this investing activity from the operating activities section.

The adjustments now involve converting the remaining revenue and expense items from an accrual basis to a cash basis. Recall from our analysis earlier in this section that the amount of cash collected from customers differed from sales for the period. In fact, collections exceeded sales by $500 (explaining how the accounts receivable account declined by $500). An adjustment must be made to increase the accrual-basis sales figure to its cash-basis counterpart. We add $500 as illustrated below.

	Income Statement	Adjustments	Cash Flows from Operations
Sales	$13,500	+500 (decrease in accounts receivable)	$14,000
Cost of goods sold	(8,000)		
Miscellaneous expenses	(3,200)		
Depreciation expense	(500)	+500 (not a cash flow item)	0
Interest expense	(200)		
Gain on sale of equipment	100	−100 (not an operating activity)	0
Tax expense	(450)		
	$ 1,250		

Caution

Remember that Cost of Goods Sold is subtracted from Sales. Adding $100 serves to reduce the negative number, and subtracting $200 makes the cost of goods sold figure a larger negative number.

Next, we turn our attention to Cost of Goods Sold. The statement of cash flows should reflect the amount of cash paid for inventory during the period. We can compute that amount by adjusting Cost of Goods Sold to reflect the inventory used this period but purchased last period, as well as inventory that was purchased last period and paid for this period.

Because Inventory declined for the period from a beginning balance of $1,900 to an ending balance of $1,800, we must adjust Cost of Goods Sold to reflect that it includes inventory that was purchased last period and used this period (explaining how the inventory balance declined). To reduce Cost of Goods Sold, our adjustment involves adding $100. The resulting number represents the amount of inventory purchased during the year. A similar adjustment is made for the change in the balance in Accounts Payable and reflects the amount of inventory paid for during the year. What event would cause Accounts Payable to decline? Obviously, Accounts Payable would most likely decline because more was paid for this period than was purchased this period. If more was paid for this period, we are required to subtract an additional $200 to reflect the additional cash outflow. The net effect of these two adjustments is to convert the accrual-basis Cost of Goods Sold figure to the amount of inventory paid for during the year. The following T-account analysis shows the net effect of these two adjustments:

Cash		Inventory		Accounts Payable		Cost of Goods Sold	
	8,100ᶜ	1,900			1,700	8,000ᴬ	
			8,000ᴬ		7,900ᴮ		
		7,900ᴮ		8,100ᶜ			
		1,800			1,500		

ᴬCost of inventory sold during the period (from the income statement).
ᴮInventory purchased during the period [solved for based on the beginning and ending inventory balances and the cost of goods sold (A)].
ᶜInventory paid for during the period [solved for based on the beginning and ending Accounts Payable balances and the inventory purchased during the period (B)].

Updating our work sheet results in the following:

	Income Statement	Adjustments	Cash Flows from Operations
Sales	$13,500	+500 (decrease in accounts receivable)	$14,000
Cost of goods sold	(8,000)	+100 (decrease in inventory)	(8,100)
		−200 (decrease in accounts payable)	
Miscellaneous expenses	(3,200)		
Depreciation expense	(500)	+500 (not a cash flow item)	0
Interest expense	(200)		
Gain on sale of equipment	100	−100 (not an operating activity)	0
Tax expense	(450)		
	$ 1,250		

Because neither a miscellaneous expenses payable account nor a prepaid expenses account exists, we can safely assume that all the miscellaneous expenses were paid for in cash. Therefore, there would be no adjustment.

Both Interest Expense and Tax Expense require adjustments similar to that done for Accounts Payable and/or Inventory. Let's first adjust Interest Expense from an accrual basis to a cash basis. Note that Interest Payable increased from $0 at the beginning of the period to $20 at the end of the period. How would that happen? Obviously, if a payable account increases, the company owes for products and services it has purchased or used. In this case what was used is money. Interest expense for the period was $200, of which Silmaril has yet to pay $20. Thus, the cash flow related to interest must be $180—requiring an adjustment of $20.

Tax Expense is adjusted in a similar fashion. Because the amount of taxes owed increased from the beginning to the end of the period, Silmaril must have paid a lesser amount relating to taxes than is reflected on the income statement. Reviewing the T-account for Taxes Payable helps us see how that can be:

Taxes Payable

	Beg. Bal. 40
Taxes paid during the period ?	Amount related to tax expense 450
	End. Bal. 50

As you can determine, the only amount that will balance the above T-account is $440—the amount paid for taxes during the period. Because the income statement reflects expense of $450 related to taxes, yet the cash outflow was only $440, we must make an adjustment of $10. The work sheet, with these final adjustments, appears as follows:

	Income Statement	Adjustments	Cash Flows from Operations
Sales	$13,500	+500 (decrease in accounts receivable)	$14,000
Cost of goods sold	(8,000)	+100 (decrease in inventory)	(8,100)
		−200 (decrease in accounts payable)	
Miscellaneous expenses	(3,200)	+0	(3,200)
Depreciation expense	(500)	+500 (not a cash flow item)	0
Interest expense	(200)	+20 (increase in interest payable)	(180)
Gain on sale of equipment	100	−100 (not an operating activity)	0
Tax expense	(450)	+10 (increase in taxes payable)	(440)
	$ 1,250	+830 net adjustment	$ 2,080

Note that the cash flows from operations figure obtained through an analysis of the income statement accounts and current asset and current liability accounts is the same figure obtained previously when we assumed access to the detailed cash account information. We should always get the same answer when the question is the same—"What were cash flows from operations?"

The Direct and Indirect Methods. Our final task relating to cash flows from operations relates to preparing the operating activities section of the statement of cash flows. At this point, we have two alternatives—the indirect method or the direct method.

indirect method A method of reporting net cash flows from operations that involves converting accrual-basis net income to a cash basis.

The **indirect method** begins with net income as reported on the income statement and then details the adjustments made to arrive at cash flows from operations. For Silmaril, Inc., it involves beginning with the net income figure and then listing the adjustments from the work sheet. In other words, the following highlighted portions of the work sheet are used.

	Income Statement	Adjustments	Cash Flows from Operations
Sales	$13,500	+500 (decrease in accounts receivable)	$14,000
Cost of goods sold	(8,000)	+100 (decrease in inventory)	(8,100)
		−200 (decrease in accounts payable)	
Miscellaneous expenses	(3,200)	+0	(3,200)
Depreciation expense	(500)	+500 (not a cash flow item)	0
Interest expense	(200)	+20 (increase in interest payable)	(180)
Gain on sale of equipment	100	−100 (not an operating activity)	0
Tax expense	(450)	+10 (increase in taxes payable)	(440)
	$ 1,250	+830 net adjustment	$ 2,080

The operating activities section is formatted as follows:

Operating Activities:

Net income		$1,250
Add: Depreciation expense	$ 500	
Decrease in accounts receivable	500	
Decrease in inventory	100	
Increase in interest payable	20	
Increase in taxes payable	10	
Less: Gain on sale of equipment	(100)	
Decrease in accounts payable	(200)	830
Cash flows from operations		$2,080

direct method A method of reporting net cash flows from operations that shows the major classes of cash receipts and payments for a period of time.

Using the **direct method**, the operating activities section of a statement of cash flows is, in effect, a cash-basis income statement. Unlike the indirect method, the direct method does not start with net income. Instead, this method directly reports the major classes of operating cash receipts and payments of an entity during a period. This information is obtained from the last column of the work sheet as follows:

	Income Statement	Adjustments	Cash Flows from Operations
Sales	$13,500	+500 (decrease in accounts receivable)	$14,000
Cost of goods sold	(8,000)	+100 (decrease in inventory)	(8,100)
		−200 (decrease in accounts payable)	
Miscellaneous expenses	(3,200)	+0	(3,200)
Depreciation expense	(500)	+500 (not a cash flow item)	0
Interest expense	(200)	+20 (increase in interest payable)	(180)
Gain on sale of equipment	100	−100 (not an operating activity)	0
Tax expense	(450)	+10 (increase in taxes payable)	(440)
	$ 1,250	+830 net adjustment	$ 2,080

The resulting operating activities section, given below, looks a lot like the operating activities section we prepared when we had access to the detailed cash flow information.

Operating Activities:

Collections from customers		$ 14,000
Payments for inventory	$8,100	
Payments for miscellaneous expenses	3,200	
Payments for interest	180	
Payments for taxes	440	(11,920)
Cash flows from operating activities		$ 2,080

STOP & THINK

Now that you have seen both methods for preparing the operating activities section of the statement of cash flows, which method do you prefer? Which method do you think is used most often by companies?

Note that the same amount of cash flows from operating activities is derived using either the indirect method or the direct method.

Why Two Methods? You may be wondering, "Why are there two methods for preparing a statement of cash flows when both methods always result in the same answer?" Good question. Each method has advantages and disadvantages. Most companies prefer and use the indirect method because it is relatively easy to apply and reconciles the difference between net income and the net cash flows provided by operations. Many users of financial statements favor the direct method because it reports the sources of cash inflows and outflows directly without out the potentially confusing adjustments to net income. The accounting standard-setters considered the arguments for both methods, and although they preferred the clarity of the direct method, they permitted either method to be used. Because they can choose either method and already have to compute net income, approximately 95% of large U.S. corporations use the indirect method when preparing a statement of cash flows.

Some Rules of Thumb. Although all this analysis may seem complex, the guidelines below will help you as you analyze accounts and prepare a statement of cash flows.

Accounts	Direction of Change during the Period	Adjustment to Be Made
Current assets	Increase	Subtracted
Current assets	Decrease	Added
Current liabilities	Increase	Added
Current liabilities	Decrease	Subtracted

When current assets increase (decrease) during the period, the difference between the beginning and ending balances is subtracted (added) from the appropriate income statement account to arrive at cash flows for the period. As an example, if accounts receivable increase during the period, that means sales exceed collections and Sales on the income statement must be reduced to reflect the cash collected for the period. The reverse would be true when accounts receivable decrease.

In the case of current liabilities, an increase (decrease) requires that an adjustment be made to add (subtract) the difference between the beginning and ending balances. For example, when interest payable increases from the beginning to the end of the period, interest expense exceeds the cash paid during the period. Interest Expense must be reduced (by adding back) to reflect the cash paid during the period. Again, the reverse would be true if interest payable were to decrease during the period. Exhibit 6 summarizes the procedures for converting selected accounts from an accrual to a cash basis.

Caution

These guidelines will help you to understand *how* certain adjustments are made, but they will not help you understand *why* the adjustments are being made. To understand why, you must use your knowledge of accounting.

Step 3. Analyze the Long-Term Assets to Identify the Cash Flows Effect of Investing Activities

The only long-term asset account for Silmaril, Inc., is the property, plant, and equipment (PP&E) account with its associated accumulated depreciation. The balance in the PP&E account in-

Exhibit 6: Guidelines for Converting from Accrual to Cash Basis

Accrual Basis	± Adjustments Required	= Cash Basis
Net sales	+ Beginning accounts receivable* − Ending accounts receivable*	Cash receipts from customers
Other revenues (e.g., rent and interest):		
Rent revenue	+ Ending unearned rent − Beginning unearned rent	Cash received for rent
Interest revenue	+ Beginning interest receivable − Ending interest receivable	Cash received for interest
Cost of goods sold	+ Ending inventory − Beginning inventory + Beginning accounts payable − Ending accounts payable	Cash paid for inventory
Operating expenses** (e.g., insurance and wages): Insurance expense	+ Ending prepaid insurance − Beginning prepaid insurance	Cash paid for insurance
Wages expense	+ Beginning wages payable − Ending wages payable	Cash paid for wages
Income tax expense	+ Beginning income taxes payable − Ending income taxes payable	Cash paid for income taxes
		Net cash flows provided by (used in) operating activities

*Net of allowance for uncollectible accounts.
**Excluding depreciation and other noncash items.

creased by $500 during the period. What does an increase in the PP&E account indicate? Obviously, something was purchased. If we had no additional information, we would assume that PP&E was purchased by paying $500. But we do have additional information. We know that PP&E was purchased during the period by paying $1,700. With that information, we can prepare the following PP&E T-account:

Property, Plant, and Equipment

Beg. Bal.	4,000		
Purchased	1,700	Sold	?
End. Bal.	4,500		

To make the T-account balance, equipment must have been sold. What was the original cost of the equipment that was sold? It must have been $1,200 (that is the only number that will make the T-account balance). What was the accumulated depreciation associated with the sold equipment? Let's take a look at the accumulated depreciation T-account. Entries on the debit side of that account track the accumulated depreciation associated with equipment that has been sold. Entries to the credit side are associated with depreciation expense for the period. Because we know depreciation expense for the period (from the income statement), and we know the beginning and ending balances in the account (from the balance sheet), we can infer the accumulated depreciation associated with the equipment that was sold.

Accumulated Depreciation

		Beg. Bal.	1,200
Sold	?	Depreciation Expense	500
		End. Bal.	900

The accumulated depreciation associated with the equipment that was sold must have been $800. In addition, we know from the income statement that the sale resulted in a gain of $100. With this information, we can infer that the following journal entry was made relating to the sale of PP&E:

Cash	500	
Accumulated Depreciation	800	
Property, Plant, and Equipment		1,200
Gain on Sale of Equipment		100

As you can see, we can determine the amount of cash received from the sale of PP&E by monitoring the change in other related accounts on the income statement and balance sheet.

As Silmaril's only investing activity related to the PP&E account, we have analyzed all the changes in that account and are now ready to prepare the investing activities section of the statement of cash flows. Had Silmaril bought or sold available-for-sale or held-to-maturity securities during the year, we would need to analyze these accounts to determine any cash flow effects. The investing activities section of the statement of cash flows for Silmaril, Inc., would be as follows:

Investing Activities:

Proceeds from the sale of property, plant, and equipment	$ 500	
Purchased property, plant, and equipment	(1,700)	
Cash flows from investing activities		(1,200)

Step 4. Analyze the Long-Term Debt and Stockholders' Equity Accounts to Determine the Cash Flow Effects of any Financing Transactions

Consider long-term debt accounts. What would make them increase? What would make them decrease? Obviously, these debt accounts would increase when a company borrows more money (an inflow of cash) and decrease when the company pays back the debt (an outflow of cash). In the case of Silmaril, we observe that the company's long-term debt account declined from $2,200 to $2,000. Unless something unusual happened (such as additional debt was issued and then some debt was repaid), we assume that the reason for the decrease was that cash was used to reduce the liability.

In the case of stockholders' equity accounts, we examine both the common stock and retained earnings accounts for increases and decreases resulting from cash flows. The common stock account will increase as a result of the sale of stock and decrease if any stock is repurchased and retired. Because the common stock account increased by $450 during the period, we assume that the increase resulted from the sale of stock. Again, if an unusual transaction had occurred, information relating to the transaction would be available in the notes. Retained Earnings increases from the recognition of net income (an operating activity) and decreases as a result of net losses (also an operating activity) or through the payment of dividends (a financing activity). In the case of Silmaril, Inc., because no dividends are disclosed on the trial balance, the entire change in Retained Earnings results from net income; the cash flow effect has already been included in operating activities.

Exhibit 7: Analysis of Cash Flows Statement: Patterns

	CF from Operating	CF from Investing	CF from Financing	General Explanation
#1	+	+	+	Company is using cash generated from operations, from sale of assets, and from financing to build up pile of cash—very liquid company—possibly looking for acquisition.
#2	+	−	−	Company is using cash flows generated from operations to buy fixed assets and to pay down debt or pay owners.
#3	+	+	−	Company is using cash from operations and from sale of fixed assets to pay down debt or pay owners.
#4	+	−	+	Company is using cash from operations and from borrowing (or from owner investment) to expand.
#5	−	+	+	Company's operating cash flow problems are covered by sale of fixed assets, by borrowing, or by stockholder contributions.
#6	−	−	+	Company is growing rapidly, but has shortfalls in cash flows from operations and from purchase of fixed assets financed by long-term debt or new investment.
#7	−	+	−	Company is financing operating cash flow shortages and payments to creditors and/or stockholders via sale of fixed assets.
#8	−	−	−	Company is using cash reserves to finance operation shortfall and pay long-term creditors and/or investors.

Source: Michael T. Dugan, Benton E. Gup, and William D. Samson, "Teaching the Statement of Cash Flows," *Journal of Accounting Education*, Vol. 9, 1991, p. 36.

Positive cash flows from operations are necessary if a company is to succeed over the long term (patterns 1 through 4). The most common cash flow pattern is 2. Companies use cash flows from operations to purchase fixed assets or to pay down debt. Growing companies follow cash flow pattern 6. Cash is being borrowed to cover a shortage of cash from operations as well as to purchase fixed assets. Most (about 80%) of the publicly-traded companies in the United States follow patterns 2, 4, and 6.

TO SUMMARIZE: Conducting financial statement analysis using information from the statement of cash flows is more difficult than analyses using information from the income statement and the balance sheet. The primary reason is that it is common for cash flows for certain categories to be negative, thereby making interpretation difficult. Nevertheless, an analysis of the relationships among the categories on the statement of cash flows can provide insight into a company's performance.

r eview of learning objectives

1 **Understand the purpose of a statement of cash flows.** The statement of cash flows is one of the three primary financial statements presented by companies in their annual reports. Its primary purpose is to provide information about the cash receipts and payments of an entity during a period. The statement of cash flows also explains the changes in the balance sheet accounts and the cash effects of the accrual-basis amounts reported in the income statement.

2 **Recognize the different types of information reported in the statement of cash flows.** The statement of cash flows reports an entity's inflows and outflows of cash for a period of time and reconciles the beginning and ending balances of cash and cash equivalents.

The inflows and outflows of cash should be classified and reported for three main categories: operating activities, investing activities, and financing activities. Cash receipts and payments classified under operating activities generally include all items that enter into the determination of net income. Examples include receipts from the sale of goods or services and from interest, and the payments for inventory, wages, utilities, taxes, and interest.

Investing activities include the purchase and sale of certain securities (other than cash equivalents, which are included with cash), buildings and equipment, and other assets that generally are not purchased for resale by the entity. Also included are the making and collecting of loans.

Financing activities include obtaining and repaying cash from owners (equity financing) and from creditors (debt financing). Selling stock, paying cash dividends, and borrowing money, for example, are included under this category.

Significant noncash transactions involving investing and financing activities should be reported in a note or in a separate schedule to the financial statements. Because such transactions do not involve cash flows, they should not be reported in the statement of cash flows. An example would be the purchase of land by the issuance of stock.

3 **Prepare a simple statement of cash flows.** If cash inflows and outflows can be categorized according to the activity (operating, investing, or financing) when entered into the accounting system, the preparation of a statement of cash flows is straightforward. At the end of the period, inflows and outflows are divided by category and type of cash flow, e.g., collections from customers, payments for inventory, etc. A statement of cash flows then simply lists those inflows and outflows by activity.

4 **Analyze financial statements to prepare a statement of cash flows.** Often, detailed cash flow information is not available. When that happens, the statement of cash flows is prepared by analyzing comparative balance sheets and the income statement. A six-step process can be employed to assist in the analysis. First, the change in the cash balance for the period is computed. Second, the income statement is converted from an accrual basis to a cash basis. The result is cash flows from operating activities. Third, long-term assets are analyzed to determine the cash flow effects of investing activities. Fourth, long-term liabilities and stockholders' equity accounts are analyzed to determine the cash flow effects of financing activities. Fifth, a formal statement of cash flows is prepared. And sixth, significant noncash transactions are disclosed in the notes to the financial statements or in a separate schedule at the bottom of the statement of cash flows.

5 **Use information from the statement of cash flows to make decisions.** A careful analysis of the statement of cash flows will indicate shifts in a company's operating, investing, and financing policies. The statement explains the change in the cash balance during the period by identifying the inflows and outflows of cash. This helps investors and creditors observe trends related to a company's use of operating income and to its use of external sources of capital such as the issuance of stock or bonds. Used with the income statement and the balance sheet, the statement of cash flows is a valuable source of information.

key terms & concepts

cash equivalents, 697
direct method, 711
financing activities, 699

indirect method, 711
investing activities, 699
noncash items, 707

noncash transactions, 715
operating activities, 697
statement of cash flows, 696

review problems

Classifying Cash Flows

Anna Dimetros is the bookkeeper for Russia Imports, Inc. (RII), a New York City–based company. Anna has collected the following cash flow information about RII for the most current year of operations. The cash balance at the beginning of the year was $105,000.

Cash receipts:

Cash received from issuance of stock	$ 50,000
Cash received from customers	252,300
Cash received from interest at bank	4,600
Cash received from borrowing at bank	25,000
Total cash receipts	$331,900

Cash payments:

Cash paid for wages of employees	$134,600
Cash paid to stockholders as dividends	5,500
Cash paid to bank for interest	7,200
Cash paid to bank to repay earlier loan	10,000
Cash paid for taxes	23,500
Cash paid for operating expenses	128,100
Cash paid for equipment	15,000
Total cash payments	$323,900

Required:

1. From the information provided, classify the cash flows for Russia Imports, Inc., according to operating, investing, and financing activities.
2. Determine the ending cash balance.

Solution

Russia Imports, Inc.
Cash Flows
20XX

1. *Cash flows from operating activities:*		
Cash receipts from:		
Customers	$252,300	
Bank (interest)	4,600	$256,900
Cash payments to:		
Employees (wages)	$134,600	
Bank (interest)	7,200	
Government (taxes)	23,500	
Various entities (operating expenses)	128,100	293,400
Net cash flows used in operating activities		$ (36,500)

(continued)

Cash flows from investing activities:

Cash payments to:

Purchase equipment	$ (15,000)	
Net cash flows used in investing activities		$ (15,000)

Cash flows from financing activities:

Cash receipts from:

Issuance of stock	$ 50,000		
Borrowing at bank	25,000	$ 75,000	
Cash payments to:			
Stockholders (dividends)	$ (5,500)		
Repay earlier loan	(10,000)	(15,500)	
Net cash flows provided by financing activities			$ 59,500
Total net cash flows for period			$ 8,000

2. Beginning cash balance $105,000

Total net cash flows for period 8,000

Ending cash balance $113,000*

*Alternatively, beginning balance ($105,000) + receipts ($331,900) − payments ($323,900) = ending balance ($113,000).

Preparing a Statement of Cash Flows

Snow Corporation produces clock radios. Comparative income statements and balance sheets for the years ended December 31, 2006 and 2005, are presented.

Snow Corporation
Comparative Income Statements
For the Years Ended December 31, 2006 and 2005

	2006	2005
Net sales revenue	$600,000	$575,000
Cost of goods sold	500,000	460,000
Gross margin	$100,000	$115,000
Operating expenses	66,000	60,000
Operating income	$ 34,000	$ 55,000
Interest expense	4,000	3,000
Income before taxes	$ 30,000	$ 52,000
Income taxes	12,000	21,000
Net income	$ 18,000	$ 31,000

Snow Corporation
Comparative Balance Sheets
December 31, 2006 and 2005

	2006	2005
Assets		
Current assets:		
Cash and cash equivalents	$ 11,000	$ 13,000
Accounts receivable (net)	92,000	77,000
Inventory	103,000	92,000
Prepaid expenses	6,000	5,000
Total current assets	$ 212,000	$ 187,000

	2006	2005
Property, plant, and equipment:		
Land	$ 69,000	$ 66,000
Machinery and equipment	172,000	156,000
Accumulated depreciation, machinery and equipment	(113,000)	(102,000)
Total property, plant, and equipment	$ 128,000	$ 120,000
Total assets	$ 340,000	$ 307,000
Liabilities and Stockholders' Equity		
Current liabilities:		
Accounts payable	$ 66,000	$ 78,000
Dividends payable	2,000	0
Income taxes payable	3,000	5,000
Total current liabilities	$ 71,000	$ 83,000
Long-term debt	75,000	42,000
Total liabilities	$ 146,000	$ 125,000
Stockholders' equity:		
Common stock, no par	$ 26,000	$ 26,000
Retained earnings	168,000	156,000
Total stockholders' equity	$ 194,000	$ 182,000
Total liabilities and stockholders' equity	$ 340,000	$ 307,000

The following additional information is available.

a. Dividends declared during 2006 were $6,000.
b. The market price per share of stock on December 31, 2006, was $14.50.
c. Equipment worth $16,000 was acquired by the issuance of a long-term note ($10,000) and by paying cash ($6,000).
d. Land was acquired for $3,000 cash.
e. Depreciation of $11,000 was included in operating expenses for 2006.
f. There were no accruals or prepaid amounts for interest.

Required:
Analyze the data provided to prepare a statement of cash flows. Use (1) the indirect method and (2) the direct method to report cash flows from operating activities.

Solution
1. Indirect Method

Snow Corporation
Statement of Cash Flows (Indirect Method)
For the Year Ended December 31, 2006

Cash flows from operating activities:		
Net income	$ 18,000	
Add (deduct) adjustments to cash basis:		
Depreciation expense	11,000	
Increase in accounts receivable	(15,000)	
Increase in inventory	(11,000)	
Increase in prepaid expenses	(1,000)	
Decrease in accounts payable	(12,000)	
Decrease in income taxes payable	(2,000)	
Net cash flows used in operating activities		$(12,000)

(continued)

Cash flows from investing activities:
Cash payments for:

Land	$ (3,000)	
Machinery and equipment	(6,000)	
Net cash flows used in investing activities		(9,000)

Cash flows from financing activities:

Cash receipts from long-term borrowing	$ 23,000	
Cash payments for dividends	(4,000)*	
Net cash flows provided by financing activities		19,000
Net decrease in cash		$ (2,000)
Cash and cash equivalents at beginning of year		13,000
Cash and cash equivalents at end of year		$ 11,000

*Cash dividends declared ($6,000) less increase in dividends payable ($2,000)

Supplemental disclosure:
Cash payments for:

Interest	$ 4,000
Income taxes	14,000

Noncash transaction:
Equipment was purchased by issuing a long-term note for $10,000.

The statement of cash flows for Snow Corporation shows that although reported net income was positive for 2006, the net cash flows generated from operating activities were negative. Only by borrowing cash was Snow Corporation able to pay dividends and purchase land and equipment. Even then the cash account decreased by $2,000 during the period.

2. Direct Method

Snow Corporation
Statement of Cash Flows (Direct Method)
For the Year Ended December 31, 2006

Cash flows from operating activities:

Cash receipts from customers		$ 585,000
Cash payments for:		
Inventory	$523,000	
Operating expenses	56,000	
Interest expense	4,000	
Income tax expense	14,000	(597,000)
Net cash flows used in operating activities		$ (12,000)

Cash flows from investing activities:
Cash payments for:

Land	$ (3,000)	
Machinery and equipment	(6,000)	
Net cash flows used in investing activities		(9,000)

Cash flows from financing activities:

Cash receipts from long-term borrowing	$ 23,000	
Cash payments for dividends	(4,000)	
Net cash flows provided by financing activities		19,000
Net decrease in cash		$ (2,000)
Cash and cash equivalents at beginning of year		13,000
Cash and cash equivalents at end of year		$ 11,000

*Supplemental Disclosure**
Equipment was purchased by issuing a long-term note for $10,000.

*A schedule reconciling net income with net cash flow used by operating activities would also be presented, either with the statement of cash flows or in the notes to the financial statements. The information provided in the schedule is the same as the operating activities section of the statement of cash flows prepared using the indirect method (see part 1).

discussion questions

1. What is the main purpose of a statement of cash flows?
2. What are cash equivalents, and how are they treated on a statement of cash flows?
3. Distinguish among cash flows from operating, investing, and financing activities, providing examples for each type of activity.
4. How are significant noncash investing and financing transactions to be reported?
5. Describe the process of converting from accrual revenues to cash receipts.
6. Describe the six-step process that can be used to prepare a statement of cash flows by analyzing the income statement and comparative balance sheets.
7. Distinguish between the indirect and direct methods of reporting net cash flows provided by (used in) operating activities.
8. How are depreciation and similar noncash items treated on a statement of cash flows?
9. What supplemental disclosures are likely to be required in connection with a statement of cash flows?
10. How might investors and creditors use a statement of cash flows?

practice exercises

Practice 14-1

Categories of Cash Inflows and Outflows
Which one of the following is *not* one of the three main sections in the statement of cash flows for a company?

a. Earning activities.
b. Financing activities.
c. Operating activities.
d. Investing activities.

Practice 14-2

Identifying Operating Activities
Which one of the following is an example of an operating activity?

a. Cash payments to repay principal amounts borrowed.
b. Cash payments to suppliers for inventory purchases.
c. Cash receipts from sale of a business segment.
d. Cash receipts from issuance of own stock.

Practice 14-3

Identifying Investing Activities
Which one of the following is an example of an investing activity?

a. Cash payments to lenders for interest expense.
b. Cash receipts from borrowing notes.
c. Cash receipts from sale of goods or services.
d. Cash payments to purchase property, plant, and equipment.

Practice 14-4

Identifying Financing Activities
Which one of the following is an example of a financing activity?

a. Cash payments to purchase debt or equity securities of other entities (other than trading securities).
b. Cash payments to stockholders as dividend.
c. Cash receipts from dividend revenue.
d. Cash receipts from collection of principal on loans made to other entities.

Practice 14-5

Computing Net Change in Cash for the Period

The company had a beginning cash balance of $154. In addition, the company reported the following amounts of cash provided by (used in) each category of the statement of cash flows:

Operating activities	$ 2,530
Investing activities	(3,290)
Financing activities	792

Using the above information, compute the company's ending cash balance.

Practice 14-6

Computation of Cash from Operating Activities

Using the following information, compute the amount of cash provided by operating activities.

Payments for miscellaneous expenses	$1,031
Payment to stockholders as dividends	350
Payment for taxes	135
Payment for interest	43
Collections on account	4,286
Payments for inventory	2,874

Practice 14-7

Using Accounts Receivable to Compute Cash Collections

Assume all of the company's sales are on account. The accounts receivable balance at the beginning of the year was $126, and the ending balance was $183. During the year, the company had sales of $3,252. Compute the amount of cash collections on sales.

Practice 14-8

Identifying Noncash Flow Items and Non-Operating Activity Items

Using the following income statement accounts, identify the items that are noncash items and/or should not be included in the operating activities section of the statement of cash flows. (These items will be added to or subtracted from net income to compute cash flow from operating activities.)

Sales revenues	$ 23,236
Gain on sale of land	540
Cost of goods sold	(15,304)
General and administrative expenses	(2,634)
Depreciation expense	(1,785)
Interest expense	(429)
Tax expense	(1,450)

Practice 14-9

Using Inventory and Accounts Payable to Compute Cash Paid for Inventory

Using the following information and assuming that all inventory is purchased on account, compute cash paid for inventory:

Cost of goods sold	$41,468
Inventory, beginning balance	2,353
Inventory, ending balance	2,104
Accounts payable, beginning balance	3,260
Accounts payable, ending balance	3,542

Practice 14-10

Using Taxes Payable to Compute Cash Paid for Taxes

Using the following information, compute cash paid for taxes.

Income tax expense	$1,235
Taxes payable, beginning balance	133
Taxes payable, ending balance	154

Practice 14-11

Indirect Method

Using the following information, prepare the operating activities section of the statement of cash flows using the indirect method.

	Income Statement		Adjustments	Cash Flows from Operations
Sales	$ 32,840	−340	(increase in accounts receivable)	$ 32,500
Cost of goods sold	(21,352)	−103	(increase in inventory)	(21,310)
		+145	(increase in accounts payable)	
Miscellaneous expenses	(4,670)	+130	(decrease in prepaid expenses)	(4,540)
Depreciation expense	(4,503)	+4,503	(not a cash flow item)	0
Interest expense	(362)	−24	(decrease in interest payable)	(386)
Loss on sale of land	(1,030)	+1,030	(not an operating activity)	0
Income tax expense	(369)	+14	(increase in taxes payable)	(355)
	$ 554	+5,355	(net adjustment)	$ 5,909

Practice 14-12

Direct Method

Refer to the data in Practice 14-11. Prepare the operating activities section of the statement of cash flows using the direct method.

Practice 14-13

Computing Cash Paid for Property, Plant, and Equipment

The company reported the following information related to its long-term assets:

Property, plant, and equipment, beginning balance	$150,350
Property, plant, and equipment, ending balance	160,330
Accumulated depreciation, beginning balance	65,030
Accumulated depreciation, ending balance	64,260
Depreciation expense	12,295

In addition, the company disclosed that it sold equipment with a historical cost of $15,400 for $10,810.

Using this information, compute cash paid for property, plant, and equipment.

Practice 14-14

Computing Gain on Sale of Property, Plant, and Equipment

Refer to the data in Practice 14-13. Compute the realized gain on the sale of equipment.

Practice 14-15

Computing Cash from Financing Activities

Using the following information, compute the amount of cash from financing activities:

1. The company purchased $12,000 of its own common stock to be held in the treasury.
2. The company paid cash dividends of $2,350 to its stockholders.
3. The company repaid $25,000 of long-term debt.

Practice 14-16

Solving for Cash from Investing Activities

Using the following information, compute the amount of cash provided by (used in) investing activities:

Cash from operating activities	$136,190
Cash from financing activities	86,340
Beginning cash balance	12,540
Ending cash balance	13,405

Practice 14-17

Using Information from the Statement of Cash Flows to Make Decisions

Using the following information about a company, decide whether you would want to loan money to that company:

	2004	2005	2006
Net income	$ 2,045	$ 1,295	$ 2,540
Cash provided by (used in) operating activities	121	(2,023)	(6,843)
Cash provided by (used in) investing activities	(6,300)	(1,450)	(2,460)
Cash provided by (used in) financing activities	4,010	5,300	9,200

exercises

Exercise 14-1

Classification of Cash Flows

Indicate whether each of the following items would be associated with a cash inflow (I), cash outflow (O), or noncash item (N) and under which category each would be reported on a statement of cash flows: Operating Activities (OA); Investing Activities (IA); Financing Activities (FA); or not on the statement (NOS). An example is provided.

Item	Classified as	Reported under
Example: Sales Revenue	I	OA

1. Fees collected for services
2. Interest paid
3. Proceeds from sale of equipment
4. Cash (principal) received from bank on long-term note
5. Purchase of treasury stock for cash
6. Collection of loan made to company officer
7. Cash dividends paid
8. Taxes paid
9. Depreciation expense
10. Wages paid to employees
11. Cash paid for inventory purchases
12. Proceeds from sale of common stock
13. Interest received on loan to company officer
14. Purchase of land by issuing stock
15. Utility bill paid

Exercise 14-2

Classification of Cash Flows

The following items summarize certain transactions that occurred during the past year for Alta Inc. Show in which section of the statement of cash flows the information would be reported by placing an X in the appropriate column. (Assume the direct method is used to report operating cash flows.)

Transaction	Reported in Statement of Cash Flows			Not Reported in Statement of Cash Flows
	Operating	Investing	Financing	
a. Collections from customers				
b. Depreciation expense				
c. Wages and salaries paid				
d. Cash dividends paid				
e. Taxes paid				
f. Utilities paid				
g. Building purchased in exchange for stock				
h. Stock of Western Co. purchased				
i. Inventory purchased for cash				
j. Interest on Alta's note to local bank paid				
k. Interest received from a note with a customer				
l. Delivery truck sold at no gain or loss				

Exercise 14-3

Transaction Analysis

Following are the transactions of Reiner Company:

a. Sold equipment for $2,500. The original cost was $12,350; the book value is $2,100.
b. Purchased equipment costing $92,000 by paying cash of $32,000 and signing a $60,000 long-term note at 10% interest.
c. Received $7,500 of the principal and $675 in interest on a long-term note receivable.
d. Received $4,600 in cash dividends on stock held as a trading security. (Assume that the cost method is used.)
e. Purchased treasury stock for $1,900.

Complete the following:

1. Prepare journal entries for each of the transactions. (Omit explanations.)
2. For each transaction, indicate the amount of cash inflow or outflow. Then, note how each transaction would be classified on a statement of cash flows.

Exercise 14-4

Transaction Analysis

The Vikon Company had the following selected transactions during the past year:

a. Sold (issued) 1,000 shares of common stock, $10 par, for $25 per share.
b. Collected $100,000 of accounts receivable.
c. Paid dividends to current stockholders in the amount of $50,000 (assume dividends declared earlier establishing a dividends payable account).
d. Received $1,500 interest on a note receivable from a company officer.
e. Paid the annual insurance premium of $1,200.
f. Recorded depreciation expense of $5,000.

Complete the following:

1. Prepare appropriate journal entries for each of the above transactions. (Omit explanations.)
2. For each transaction, indicate the amount of cash inflow or outflow and also how each cash flow would be classified on a statement of cash flows.

Exercise 14-5

Preparing a Simple Cash Flow Statement

Assume you have access to the ledger (specifically, the detail of the cash account) for Stern Company, represented by the following T-account:

(continued)

Cash

Beg. Bal.	29,870	(2)	60,000
(1)	145,500	(3)	64,000
(4)	4,750	(5)	4,000
(6)	45,000	(7)	10,500
(8)	17,000	(9)	25,000
End. Bal.	78,620		

The transactions that are represented by posting entries (1) through (9) in the cash account are as follows:

1. Collections on account
2. Payments for wages and salaries
3. Payments for inventory
4. Proceeds from sale of equipment
5. Payments of dividends
6. Proceeds from new bank loan
7. Payments for other cash operating expenses
8. Proceeds from sale of nontrading securities
9. Payments for taxes

From these data, prepare a statement of cash flows for Stern Company for the year ended December 31, 2005.

Exercise 14-6

Determining Cash Receipts and Payments
Assuming the following data, compute:

1. Cash collected from customers.
2. Cash paid for wages and salaries.
3. Cash paid for inventory purchases.
4. Cash paid for taxes.

	Income Statement Amount for Year	Balance Sheet	
		Beg. of Year	End of Year
Sales revenue	$225,000		
Accounts receivable (net)		$20,000	$22,000
Wages and salaries expense	55,000		
Wages and salaries payable		14,000	11,000
Cost of goods sold	105,000		
Accounts payable		24,500	26,000
Inventory		34,000	28,000
Income tax expense	35,000		
Income taxes payable		15,500	18,000

Exercise 14-7

Adjustments to Cash Flows from Operations (Indirect Method)
Assume that you are using the indirect method of preparing a statement of cash flows. For each of the changes listed, indicate whether it would be added to or subtracted from net income in computing net cash flows provided by (used in) operating activities. If the change does not affect net cash flows provided by (used in) operating activities, so indicate.

1. Increase in Accounts Receivable (net)
2. Decrease in Accounts Payable
3. Increase in securities classified as cash equivalents
4. Gain on sale of equipment

5. Decrease in Inventory
6. Increase in Prepaid Insurance
7. Depreciation
8. Increase in Wages Payable
9. Decrease in Dividends Payable
10. Decrease in Interest Receivable

Exercise 14-8

Spreadsheet

Cash Flows from Operations (Direct Method)

Gordon Summoner is the proprietor of a small company. The results of operations for last year are shown, along with selected balance sheet data. From the information provided, determine the amount of net cash flows provided from operations, using the direct method.

Sales revenue	$350,000	
Cost of goods sold	260,000	
Gross margin		$90,000
Operating expenses:		
Wages expense	$ 25,000	
Utilities expense	1,200	
Rent expense	10,750	
Insurance expense	2,400	39,350
Net income		$50,650

	Beginning of Year	End of Year
Accounts receivable (net)	$33,000	$32,000
Inventory	35,000	31,000
Prepaid insurance	1,500	500
Accounts payable	12,000	17,000
Wages payable	5,000	2,500

Exercise 14-9

Cash Flows from Operations (Indirect Method)

Given the data in Exercise 14-8, show how the amount of net cash flows from operating activities would be calculated using the indirect method.

Exercise 14-10

Spreadsheet

Cash Flows Provided by Operations (Direct Method)

The following information was taken from the comparative financial statements of Imperial Corporation for the years ended December 31, 2005 and 2006:

Net income for 2006	$ 90,000
Sales revenue	500,000
Cost of goods sold	300,000
Depreciation expense for 2006	60,000
Amortization of goodwill for 2006	10,000
Interest expense on short-term debt for 2006	3,500
Dividends declared and paid in 2006	65,000

	Dec. 31, 2006	Dec. 31, 2005
Accounts receivable (net)	$30,000	$43,000
Inventory	50,000	42,000
Accounts payable	56,000	59,400

(continued)

Use the direct method to compute cash flows provided by operating activities in 2006. (*Hint:* You need to calculate cash paid for operating expenses.)

Exercise 14-11

Cash Flows Provided by Operations (Indirect Method)
Given the data in Exercise 14-10, show how the amount of cash provided by operations for 2006 is computed using the indirect method.

Spreadsheet

Exercise 14-12

Cash Flows Provided by Operations (Direct Method)
The following information was taken from the comparative financial statements of Knapp Industries, Inc., for the years ended December 31, 2005 and 2006:

Net income for 2006	$215,000
Sales revenue	800,000
Cost of goods sold	475,000
Depreciation expense for 2006	45,000
Interest expense on short-term debt for 2006	6,500
Dividends declared and paid in 2006	40,000
Utilities expense	3,600

	Dec. 31, 2006	Dec. 31, 2005
Accounts receivable (net)	$45,000	$40,000
Inventory	71,400	62,300
Accounts payable	70,000	74,100

Use the direct method to compute cash flows provided by operating activities in 2006. (*Hint:* You need to calculate cash paid for operating expenses.)

Exercise 14-13

Cash Flows Provided by Operations (Indirect Method)
Given the data in Exercise 14-12, show how the amount of cash flows provided by operations for 2006 is computed using the indirect method.

Exercise 14-14

Net Cash Flows (Indirect Method)
Given the following selected data for Milton Corporation, using the indirect method to report cash flows from operating activities, determine the net increase (decrease) in cash for the year ended December 31, 2006.

Net income	$ 95,000
Depreciation	25,000
Other operating expenses	140,000
Cost of goods sold	240,000
Sales revenue	500,000
Increase in accounts receivable (net)	10,000
Decrease in accounts payable	5,000
Decrease in inventory	3,000
Increase in prepaid assets	7,000
Increase in wages payable	15,000
Equipment purchased for cash	40,000
Increase in bonds payable	100,000
Dividends declared and paid	40,000
Decrease in dividends payable	2,000

Exercise 14-15

Net Cash Flows (Direct Method)

Based on the following information, determine the net increase (decrease) in cash for Litster Corporation for the year ended December 31, 2006. Use the direct method to report cash flows from operating activities.

Cash received from interest revenue	$ 28,000
Cash paid for dividends	90,000
Cash collected from customers	698,000
Cash paid for wages	508,000
Depreciation expense for the period	50,000
Cash received from issuance of common stock	400,000
Cash paid for retirement of bonds at par	200,000
Cash received on sale of equipment at book value	10,000
Cash paid for land	170,000

Exercise 14-16

Statement of Cash Flows (Indirect Method)

North Western Company provides the following financial information. Prepare a statement of cash flows for 2006, using the indirect method to report cash flows from operating activities.

North Western Company
Comparative Balance Sheets
December 31, 2006 and 2005

	2006	2005
Assets		
Cash and cash equivalents	$ 4,500	$ 9,000
Accounts receivable (net)	33,000	36,000
Inventory	75,000	60,000
Plant and equipment (net)	262,500	225,000
Total assets	$375,000	$330,000
Liabilities and Stockholders' Equity		
Accounts payable	$ 60,000	$ 54,000
Capital stock	225,000	217,500
Retained earnings	90,000	58,500
Total liabilities and stockholders' equity	$375,000	$330,000

North Western Company
Income Statement
For the Year Ended December 31, 2006

Sales	$412,500
Cost of goods sold	225,000
Gross margin	$187,500
Operating expenses	135,000
Net income	$ 52,500

Note: Dividends of $21,000 were declared and paid during 2006. Depreciation expense for the year was $22,500.

Exercise 14-17

Statement of Cash Flows (Direct Method)

By analyzing the information in Exercise 14-16, prepare a statement of cash flows. Use the direct method to report cash flows from operating activities.

Exercise 14-18

Cash Flow Patterns

Below are recent financial statement data for the following companies:

- AMAZON.COM
- COCA-COLA
- EXXONMOBIL
- MICROSOFT

Use the financial statement data to match each company with its numbers. All numbers are in millions.

| | Net Income | Cash Flow from | | |
		Operating Activities	Investing Activities	Financing Activities
1	$ (720)	$ (91)	$ (922)	$ 1,104
2	7,910	15,013	(10,985)	(4,779)
3	7,785	10,030	(11,191)	2,245
4	2,431	3,883	(3,421)	(471)

Consider the following information as you match the companies:

1. Start-ups have high positive financing cash flows relative to investing cash flows.
2. Companies with lots of property, plant, and equipment have cash from operations that is greater than net income because of lots of depreciation expense.
3. Old cash cows are spending money on investing but still have plenty left over for a net cash outflow from financing activities.

Exercise 14-19

Analyzing Cash Flows

Study the comparative cash flow statements for MICROSOFT in Appendix A. What observations do you have about Microsoft's cash flow position? From a liquidity standpoint, is the trend over the last few years positive or negative? Explain.

 roblems

Problem 14-1

Transaction Analysis

Klein Corporation reports the following summary data for the current year:

a. Sales revenue totaled $125,750.
b. Interest revenue for the period was $1,100.
c. Interest expense for the period was $400.
d. Cost of goods sold for the period was $78,000.
e. Operating expenses, all paid in cash (except for depreciation of $7,500), were $24,000.
f. Income tax expense for the period was $4,000.
g. Accounts receivable (net) increased by $5,000 during the period.
h. Accounts payable increased by $2,500 during the period.
i. Inventory at the beginning and end of the period was $17,500 and $12,500, respectively.
j. Cash increased during the period by $2,500.

Assume all other current asset and current liability accounts remained constant during the period.

Required:
1. Compute the amount of cash collected from customers.
2. Compute the amount of cash paid for inventory.
3. Compute the amount of cash paid for operating expenses.
4. Compute the amount of cash flows provided by (used in) operations.
5. **Interpretive Question:** What must have been the combined amount of cash flows provided by (used in) investing and financing activities?

Problem 14-2

Analysis of the Cash Account

The following information, in T-account format, is provided for the M & M Company for the year 2006:

Cash Account

Beg. Bal.	15,400	(b)	56,500
(a)	147,000	(c)	23,000
(d)	3,500	(f)	59,700
(e)	15,000	(g)	1,600
		(h)	2,400
End. Bal.	37,700		

Additional information:

a. Sales revenue for the period was $145,000. Accounts receivable (net) decreased $2,000 during the period.
b. Net purchases of $58,000 were made during 2006, all on account. Accounts payable increased $1,500 during the period.
c. The equipment account increased by $18,000 during the year.
d. One piece of equipment that cost $5,000, with a net book value of $3,000, was sold for a $500 gain.
e. The company borrowed $15,000 from its bank during the year.
f. Various operating expenses were all paid in cash, except for depreciation of $1,800. Total operating expenses were $61,500.
g. Interest expense for the year was $1,200. The interest payable account decreased by $400 during the year.
h. Income tax expense for the year was $3,600. The income taxes payable account increased by $1,200 during the year.

Required:
1. From the information given, reconstruct the journal entries that must have been made during the year (omit explanations).
2. Prepare a statement of cash flows for M & M Company for the year ended December 31, 2006.

Problem 14-3

Analyzing Cash Flows

The following information was provided by the treasurer of Surety, Inc., for the year 2006:

a. Cash sales for the year were $50,000; sales on account totaled $60,000.
b. Cost of goods sold was 50% of total sales.
c. All inventory is purchased on account.
d. Depreciation on equipment was $31,000 for the year.
e. Amortization of goodwill was $2,000.
f. Collections of accounts receivable were $38,000.
g. Payments on accounts payable for inventory equaled $39,000.
h. Rent expense paid in cash was $11,000.

(continued)

i. The company issued 20,000 shares of $10-par stock for $240,000.
j. Land valued at $106,000 was acquired by issuance of a bond with a par value of $100,000.
k. Equipment was purchased for cash at a cost of $84,000.
l. Dividends of $46,000 were declared but not yet paid.
m. The company paid $15,000 of dividends that had been declared the previous year.
n. A machine used on the assembly line was sold for $12,000. The machine had a book value of $7,000.
o. Another machine with a book value of $500 was scrapped and was reported as an ordinary loss. No cash was received on this transaction.
p. The cash account increased $191,000 during the year to a total of $274,000.

Required:
1. Compute the beginning balance in the cash account.
2. How much cash was provided by (or used in) operating activities?
3. How much cash was provided by (or used in) investing activities?
4. How much cash was provided by (or used in) financing activities?
5. Would all the above items, (a) through (p), be reported on a cash flow statement? Explain.

Problem 14-4

Cash Flows from Operations (Indirect Method)

Gardner Enterprises reported a net loss of $40,000 for the year just ended. Relevant data for the company follow.

	Beginning of Year	End of Year
Cash and cash equivalents	$ 50,000	$ 20,000
Accounts receivable (net)	80,000	65,000
Inventory	123,000	130,000
Prepaid expenses	7,500	4,500
Accounts payable	55,000	60,000
Accrued liabilities	10,000	4,000
Dividends payable	25,000	35,000
Depreciation for the year, $43,000		
Dividends declared, $35,000		

Required:
1. Using the indirect method, determine the net cash flows provided by (used in) operating activities for Gardner Enterprises.
2. **Interpretive Question:** Explain how Gardner Enterprises can pay cash dividends during a year when it reports a net loss.

Problem 14-5

Cash Flows from Operations (Direct Method)

Super Sales, Inc., shows the following information in its accounting records at year-end:

Sales revenue	$890,000
Interest revenue	12,000
Cost of goods sold	425,000
Wages expense	225,000
Depreciation expense	50,000
Other (cash) operating expenses	84,000
Dividends declared	40,000

Selected balance sheet data are as follows:

	Beginning of Year	End of Year
Accounts receivable (net)	$ 55,000	$ 78,000
Interest receivable	10,000	12,000
Inventory	225,000	220,000
Accounts payable	42,000	35,000
Wages payable	20,000	25,000
Dividends payable	35,000	40,000

Required:

1. Using the direct method, compute the net cash flows provided by (used in) operating activities for Super Sales, Inc.
2. **Interpretive Question:** Explain the main differences between the net amount of cash flows from operations and net income (loss).

Problem 14-6

Cash Flows from Operations (Indirect and Direct Methods)

The following combined income and retained earnings statement, along with selected balance sheet data, are provided for McDuffie Company:

McDuffie Company
Combined Income and Retained Earnings Statement
For the Year Ended December 31, 2006

Net sales revenue		$105,000
Other revenues		3,000*
Total revenues		$108,000
Expenses:		
Cost of goods sold	$55,000	
Selling and administrative expenses	15,200	
Depreciation expense	5,400	
Interest expense	1,200	
Total expenses		76,800
Income before taxes		$ 31,200
Income taxes		9,360
Net income		$ 21,840
Retained earnings, January 1, 2006		33,500
		$ 55,340
Dividends declared and paid		4,000
Retained earnings, December 31, 2006		$ 51,340

*Gain on sale of equipment (cost, $8,400; book value, $6,000; sales price $9,000).

	Beginning of Year	End of Year
Accounts receivable (net)	$12,300	$11,000
Inventory	16,800	18,000
Prepaid expenses	950	1,100
Accounts payable	7,200	7,000
Interest payable	750	1,000
Income taxes payable	2,200	2,500

(continued)

Required:

1. Using the indirect method, compute the net cash flows from operations for McDuffie Company for 2006.
2. Using the direct method, compute the net cash flows from operations for McDuffie Company for 2006.
3. What is the impact of dividends paid on net cash flows from operations? Explain.

Problem 14-7

Computation of Net Income from Cash Flows from Operations (Direct Method)

The following partially completed work sheet is provided for ATM Corporation, which uses the direct method in computing net cash flows from operations:

ATM Corporation
Partial Work Sheet—Cash Flows from Operations
(Direct Method)
For the Year Ended December 31, 2006

	Accrual Basis	Adjustments Debits	Adjustments Credits	Cash Basis
Net sales revenue				$150,000
Expenses:				
Cost of goods sold				$ 75,000
Depreciation				0
Loss on sale of equipment				0
Other (cash) expenses				26,000
Total expenses				$101,000
Net income (net cash flows from operations) ..				$ 49,000

Key:

1. Decrease in Accounts Receivable (net), $4,500.
2. Loss on sale of equipment, $1,500.
3. Increase in Inventory, $10,000.
4. Increase in Accounts Payable, $3,000.
5. Depreciation for the year, $8,000.
6. Decrease in Prepaid Expenses, $1,000.
7. Increase in Accrued Liabilities, $2,500.

Required:

Complete the work sheet with the key items above and compute the net income (loss) to be reported by ATM Corporation on its income statement for 2006.

Problem 14-8

Spreadsheet

Income Statement from Cash Flow Data

Jackson Corporation computed the amount of cash flows from operations using both the direct and indirect methods, as follows:

Direct method:

Collections from customers	$ 445,000
Payments to suppliers	(130,000)
Payments for operating expenses	(210,000)
Cash flows provided by operating activities	$ 105,000

Indirect method:

Net income	$ 95,000
Depreciation	20,000
Gain on sale of equipment	(7,500)
Decrease in inventory	1,000
Decrease in accounts receivable (net)	1,500
Decrease in accounts payable	(7,500)
Increase in miscellaneous accrued payable	2,500
Cash flows provided by operating activities	$ 105,000

Required:

Using the data provided, prepare an income statement for Jackson Corporation for the year 2006.

Problem 14-9

Statement of Cash Flows (Indirect Method)

JEM Company's comparative balance sheets for 2005 and 2006 are provided.

JEM Company
Comparative Balance Sheets
December 31, 2006 and 2005

	2006	2005
Assets		
Cash and cash equivalents	$ 30,500	$ 10,000
Accounts receivable (net)	64,500	51,000
Inventory	100,000	115,000
Equipment	55,000	30,000
Accumulated depreciation—equipment	(21,500)	(14,000)
Total assets	$228,500	$192,000
Liabilities and Stockholders' Equity		
Accounts payable	$ 52,500	$ 46,000
Long-term notes payable	70,000	50,000
Capital stock	60,000	60,000
Retained earnings	46,000	36,000
Total liabilities and stockholders' equity	$228,500	$192,000

(continued)

The following additional information is available:

a. Net income for the year 2006 (as reported on the income statement) was $50,000.
b. Dividends of $40,000 were declared and paid.
c. Equipment that cost $8,000 and had a book value of $1,000 was sold during the year for $2,500.

Required:

Based on the information provided, prepare a statement of cash flows for JEM Company for the year ended December 31, 2006. Use the indirect method to report cash flows from operating activities.

Problem 14-10

P.A.S.S.
Power Accounting
System Software

Statement of Cash Flows (Direct Method)

Financial statement data for Bankhead, Inc., are provided. (All numbers are shown rounded to the nearest thousand, with 000's omitted.)

Bankhead, Inc.
Income and Retained Earnings Statements
For the Year Ended December 31, 2006

Sales revenue	$1,450
Cost of goods sold	1,030
Gross margin	$ 420
Operating expenses:	
Sales and administrative expenses	$ 110
Depreciation expense	17
Other expenses	81
Total operating expenses	$ 208
Income before taxes	$ 212
Income taxes	53
Net income	$ 159
Dividends paid	25
Increase in retained earnings	$ 134

Bankhead, Inc.
Comparative Balance Sheets
December 31, 2006 and 2005

	2006	2005
Assets		
Cash and cash equivalents	$ 783	$ 612
Accounts receivable (net)	456	448
Inventory	245	980
Land	1,450	1,300
Store fixtures	255	255
Accumulated depreciation, store fixtures	(72)	(55)
Total assets	$3,117	$3,540

	2006	2005
Liabilities and Stockholders' Equity		
Liabilities:		
Accounts payable	$ 170	$ 366
Short-term notes payable	574	735
Long-term debt	824	1,024
Total liabilities	$1,568	$2,125
Stockholders' equity:		
Common stock	$ 145	$ 145
Paid-in capital in excess of par	550	550
Retained earnings	854	720
Total stockholders' equity	$1,549	$1,415
Total liabilities and stockholders' equity	$3,117	$3,540

Required:

1. Compute the net cash flows from operations using the direct method.
2. **Interpretive Question:** Comment on the difference between net income and net cash flows from operations.
3. Prepare a statement of cash flows for Bankhead, Inc., for the year ended December 31, 2006.

Problem 14-11

Statement of Cash Flows (Indirect Method)

1. Using the data from Problem 14-10, prepare a statement of cash flows. Use the indirect method to report cash flows from operating activities.
2. **Interpretive Question:** What are the main differences between a statement of cash flows prepared using the indirect method and one prepared using the direct method?

Problem 14-12

P.A.S.S.
Power Accounting System Software

Unifying Concepts: Analysis of Operating, Investing, and Financing Activities

Grant Kesler is the manager and one of three brothers who own the Rocky Mountain Auto Parts Company in Denver, Colorado. Grant is pleased that sales were up last year and that his new, small company has been able to expand and open a second store in Denver. After reviewing the balance sheet, however, Grant is concerned that Cash shows a negative balance. He can't understand how his company can show net income, based on increased sales, yet have a negative Cash position. He is concerned about what his banker is going to say when they meet next month to discuss a loan for the company to expand to a third store. Grant provides the following financial information and asks for your help.

(continued)

Rocky Mountain Auto Parts Company
Income Statement
For the Year Ended December 31, 2006

Sales		$150,000
Less cost of goods sold		63,000
Gross margin		$ 87,000
Operating expenses:		
Salary and wages	$32,000	
Depreciation	4,500	
Other operating expenses	12,400	48,900
Operating income		$ 38,100
Income taxes		8,200
Net income		$ 29,900

Rocky Mountain Auto Parts Company
Comparative Balance Sheets
As of December 31, 2006 and 2005

	2006	2005
Assets		
Current assets:		
Cash	$ (3,200)	$ 6,400
Accounts receivable (net)	3,100	2,700
Inventory	63,000	42,000
Total current assets	$ 62,900	$ 51,100
Other assets:		
Property, plant, and equipment	$ 82,300	$ 39,000
Less accumulated depreciation	(20,100)	(15,600)
Total other assets	$ 62,200	$ 23,400
Total assets	$125,100	$ 74,500

	2006	2005
Liabilities and Stockholders' Equity		
Current liabilities:		
Accounts payable	$ 6,400	$ 5,700
Wages payable	1,500	1,300
Taxes payable	1,900	2,100
Total current liabilities	$ 9,800	$ 9,100
Other liabilities:		
Notes payable	30,000	10,000
Total liabilities	$ 39,800	$ 19,100
Stockholders' equity:		
Capital stock	$ 40,000	$ 40,000
Retained earnings	45,300	15,400
Total stockholders' equity	$ 85,300	$ 55,400
Total liabilities and stockholders' equity	$125,100	$ 74,500

Required:

1. Using the direct method, compute the net cash flows from operations. Also determine net cash flows for investing and financing activities.

2. **Interpretive Question:** Is Rocky Mountain Auto Parts Company in a good liquidity position? As Mr. Kesler's banker, would you loan him more money to fund the company's expansion?

discussion cases

Case 14-1

Should We Make the Loan?

Save More, Inc., a discount department store, has applied to its bankers for a loan. Although the company has been profitable, it is short of cash. The loan application includes the following information about current assets, current liabilities, net income, depreciation expense, and dividends for the past five years. (All numbers are rounded to the nearest thousand, with the 000's omitted.)

(continued)

	Dec. 31, 2001	Dec. 31, 2002	Dec. 31, 2003	Dec. 31, 2004	Dec. 31, 2005
Cash and cash equivalents . . .	$ 5	$ 73	$ 10	$158	$ (189)
Accounts receivable (net)	403	555	516	576	654
Inventory	253	142	383	385	1,022
Accounts payable	19	17	281	253	52
Net income	454	492	467	440	481
Depreciation expense	50	50	55	60	60
Dividends paid	177	197	208	211	211

As a bank loan officer, you have been asked to review these figures in order to determine whether the bank should loan money to Save More, Inc.

1. Compute the net cash flows from operations for the last four years.
2. What caused the sudden decrease in cash flows from operations?
3. What factors would you focus on, and what additional information would you need before deciding whether to make the loan?

Case 14-2

Analyzing the Cash Position of Good Time, Inc.

The following data show the account balances of Good Time, Inc., at the beginning and end of the company's fiscal year:

	Aug. 31, 2006	Sept. 1, 2005
Debits		
Cash and cash equivalents	$ 88,200	$ 29,000
Accounts receivable (net)	15,000	13,300
Inventory	10,500	12,700
Prepaid insurance	2,800	2,000
Long-term investments (cost equals market)	3,000	8,400
Equipment	40,000	33,000
Treasury stock (at cost)	5,000	10,000
Cost of goods sold	184,000	
Operating expenses	93,500	
Income taxes	18,800	
Loss on sale of equipment	500	
Total debits	$461,300	$108,400

	Aug. 31, 2006	Sept. 1, 2005
Credits		
Accumulated depreciation—equipment	$ 9,500	$ 9,000
Accounts payable	3,500	5,600
Interest payable	500	1,000
Income taxes payable	6,000	4,000
Notes payable—long-term	8,000	12,000
Common stock	55,000	50,000
Paid-in capital in excess of par	16,000	15,000
Retained earnings	9,800*	11,800
Sales	352,000	
Gain on sale of long-term investments	1,000	
Total credits	$461,300	$108,400

*Preclosing balance

The following information concerning this year was also available:

a. All purchases and sales were on account.
b. Equipment with an original cost of $5,000 was sold for $1,500; a loss of $500 was recognized on the sale.
c. Among other items, the operating expenses included depreciation expense of $3,500; interest expense of $1,400; and insurance expense of $1,200.
d. Equipment was purchased by issuing common stock and paying the balance ($6,000) in cash.
e. Treasury stock was sold for $2,000 less than it cost; the decrease in stockholders' equity was recorded by reducing Retained Earnings.
f. No dividends were paid this year.

You are to examine Good Time's cash position by:

1. Preparing schedules showing the amount of cash collected from accounts receivable, cash paid for accounts payable, cash paid for interest, and cash paid for insurance.
2. Preparing a statement of cash flows for Good Time for the fiscal year 2006 using the direct method.
3. Identifying the major reasons why Good Time's cash and cash equivalents increased so dramatically during the year.
4. Comment on whether the dividend policy seems appropriate under the current circumstances.

Case 14-3

Analyzing Cash Flow Patterns

Paula Dalton is a security analyst for DJM, Inc. She claims that she can tell a great deal about companies by analyzing their cash flow patterns. Specifically, she looks at the negative or positive cash flow trends in the three categories on cash flow statements. Paula thinks this information is even more valuable than net income trend data from income statements. She illustrates her theory with the following patterns of cash flows for Abbott Company over the past three years.

	2006	2005	2004
Net income	−	+	+
Cash flows from:			
Operating activities	−	−	+
Investing activities	+	+	+
Financing activities	+	+	+

How do you think Paula would analyze these results? Do you agree that analyzing cash flow patterns provides superior analytical information?

j udgment calls

Judgment 14-1

You Decide: Which method is better at reporting information on the statement of cash flows—the indirect or direct method?

Your finance professor said that the indirect method is a better way to prepare the statement of cash flows because it starts with a known number—net income. However, in your accounting course, your professor teaches that the direct method gives you more information on *how* the cash is used and, therefore, contains more useful information. Which professor do you agree with?

Judgment 14-2

You Decide: Ignoring all other factors, will a company that is generating negative cash flows from operating activities be a good or bad investment?

When evaluating a company, you notice the following on its cash flow statement: negative cash flow from operating activities, negative cash from investing activities, and positive cash flow from financing activities. A fellow student commented, "I wouldn't invest in a company that cannot generate cash from its core business activities!" However, in 1985, HOME DEPOT had a very large negative cash flow from operating activities and later turned into a very large, successful company. How would you answer your friend?

Competency Enhancement Opportunities

▶ **Analyzing Real Company Information**   ▶ **The Debate**
▶ **International Case**   ▶ **Cumulative Spreadsheet Project**
▶ **Ethics Case**   ▶ **Internet Search**
▶ **Writing Assignment**

The following additional assignments provide opportunities for students to develop critical thinking, ethical perspectives, oral and written communication skills, experience with electronic research, and teamwork through group and business activities.

▷ *Analyzing Real Company Information*

Analyzing 14-1 (Microsoft)

The 2002 Form 10-K for MICROSOFT appears in Appendix A. Locate that Form 10-K and consider the following questions:

1. Does Microsoft present the three cash flow statement categories—operating, investing, and financing—in the same order as that illustrated in the chapter?
2. In 2002, Microsoft spent $10.845 billion on various investing activities. Were the cash flows from operations sufficient to pay for these investments?
3. In its 2002 operating activities section, Microsoft reports both $11.152 billion and $8.929 billion in relation to unearned revenue. Exactly what does each of these numbers represent? Compare these numbers to the corresponding numbers in 2001 and comment on the reason for such a big difference.
4. Did Microsoft pay any cash dividends to common stockholders during 2002? Did Microsoft make any payments to common stockholders during the year?

Analyzing 14-2 (The Coca-Cola Company)

The 2002 statement of cash flows for THE COCA-COLA COMPANY is given on page 746. Use the statement to answer the following questions:

1. Compute Coca-Cola's "Net cash provided by operations after reinvestment." This amount is computed by subtracting "Net cash used in investing activities" from "Net cash provided by operating activities." Interpret the results of the calculation for Coca-Cola for the period 2000–2002.
2. In its operating activities section, Coca-Cola subtracts gains on sales of assets in computing net cash provided by operating activities. Why are these gains subtracted?
3. Think of the dealings that The Coca-Cola Company has with its shareholders. The shareholders give money to the company by purchasing new shares of stock. In turn, the company returns cash to shareholders by paying cash dividends and by repurchasing shares of stock. For the three-year period 2000–2002, did The Coca-Cola Company receive more cash from its shareholders than it paid back to them, or did it pay more cash to its shareholders than it received? Show your calculations.
4. Look carefully at the statement of cash flows. Did the U.S. dollar get stronger or weaker during the three-year period 2000–2002?

(continued)

The Coca-Cola Company and Subsidiaries
Consolidated Statements of Cash Flows
For the Years Ended December 31, 2000, 2001, 2002
(in millions)

	2002	2001	2000
Operating activities:			
Net income	$ 3,050	$ 3,969	$ 2,177
Depreciation and amortization	806	803	773
Stock-based compensation expense	365	41	43
Deferred income taxes	40	56	3
Equity income or loss, net of dividends	(256)	(54)	380
Foreign currency adjustments	(76)	(60)	196
Gain on issuances of stock by equity investee	0	(91)	0
(Gains) losses on sales of assets, including bottling interests	3	(85)	(127)
Cumulative effect of accounting changes	926	10	0
Other operating charges	0	0	916
Other items	291	(17)	76
Net change in operating assets and liabilities	(407)	(462)	(852)
Net cash provided by operating activities	$ 4,742	$ 4,110	$ 3,585
Investing activities:			
Acquisitions and investments, principally trademarks and bottling companies	$ (544)	$ (651)	$ (397)
Purchases of investments and other assets	(156)	(456)	(508)
Proceeds from disposals of investments and other assets	243	455	290
Purchases of property, plant and equipment	(851)	(769)	(733)
Proceeds from disposals of property, plant and equipment	69	91	45
Other investing activities	52	142	138
Net cash used in investing activities	$(1,187)	$(1,188)	$(1,165)
Financing activities:			
Issuances of debt	$ 1,622	$ 3,011	$ 3,671
Payments of debt	(2,378)	(3,937)	(4,256)
Issuances of stock	107	164	331
Purchases of stock for treasury	(691)	(277)	(133)
Dividends	(1,987)	(1,791)	(1,685)
Net cash used in financing activities	$(3,327)	$(2,830)	$(2,072)
Effect of exchange rate changes on cash and cash equivalents	$ 32	$ (45)	$ (140)
Cash and cash equivalents:			
Net increase during the year	$ 260	$ 47	$ 208
Balance at beginning of year	1,866	1,819	1,611
Balance at end of year	$ 2,126	$ 1,866	$ 1,819

▶ *International Case*

International

GlaxoSmithKline

GLAXOSMITHKLINE, a British company, is one of the largest pharmaceutical firms in the world. The name "Glaxo" comes from the company's first major product line, baby food products that were sold with the slogan, "Builds Bonnie Babies." Growth of the company in recent years has been driven by sales of Zantac, an anti-ulcer drug.

GlaxoSmithKline's 2002 statement of cash flows is shown on the next page. Look at the statement and answer the following questions. (*Note:* Translations of British accounting terms into American English are shown in square brackets.)

1. In a U.S. statement of cash flows, cash flows are sorted into three categories. How many categories does GlaxoSmithKline use?
2. List some of the items that GlaxoSmithKline has excluded from the computation of cash from operating activities that would be included if the statement of cash flows were prepared according to U.S. standards.
3. Given your answer in (2), which is a better indication of cash from operating activities: the number reported by GlaxoSmithKline using a British classification of cash flows, or the number that would be reported using a U.S. classification? Explain your answer.
4. If you were to redo GlaxoSmithKline's statement of cash flows for 2002 using the U.S. classification scheme with just three categories, the total of these three categories would result in the same net change in cash (405) reported by GlaxoSmithKline using the British classification. Why is this?

(continued)

GlaxoSmithKline plc
Consolidated Statement of Cash Flows
31st December 2002
(in millions of £)

Reconciliation of operating profit to operating cash flows	2002 £m	2001 £m	2000 £m
Operating profit	5,551	4,734	4,729
Depreciation	764	761	735
Impairment and assets written off	288	178	136
Amortization of goodwill and intangible fixed assets	72	50	38
Loss on sale of tangible fixed assets	26	99	41
Profit on sale of equity investments	(46)	(118)	(225)
(Increase)/decrease in stocks [Inventory]	(2)	252	(16)
Increase in trade and other debtors [Accounts Receivable]	(72)	(77)	(333)
Increase in trade and other creditors [Accounts Payable]	459	601	402
Increase in pension and other provisions	256	144	70
Other	(41)	(93)	(39)
Merger transaction costs paid	—	(24)	(97)
Net cash inflow from operating activities	7,255	6,507	5,441
Cash flow statement			
Net cash inflow from operating activities	7,255	6,507	5,441
Dividends from joint ventures and associated undertakings	2	—	1
Returns on investment and servicing of finance	(237)	(191)	(322)
Taxation paid	(1,633)	(1,717)	(1,240)
Capital expenditure and financial investment	(1,120)	(1,779)	(327)
Acquisitions and disposals	(20)	(657)	66
Equity dividends paid	(2,327)	(2,325)	(2,028)
Net cash inflow/(outflow) before management of liquid resources and financing	1,920	(162)	1,591
Management of liquid resources	52	994	(223)
Financing	(1,567)	(1,444)	(546)
Increase/(decrease) in cash in the year	405	(612)	822

▶ *Ethics Case*

Manipulating the Federal Budget Deficit

Assume that you are the paymaster in charge of all U.S. Department of Defense (DOD) payroll matters. The total amount that you disburse in payroll checks in any given week is in excess of $1 billion.

Assume also that tax receipts have been lower than expected and that a federal budget deficit, and not a surplus, is now projected. Currently, Congress is struggling to reduce the projected budget deficit. It is an election year, and the members of Congress are worried that they will be stuck with a "tax and spend" label if the government runs a deficit this year. Of course, the DOD budget has been scrutinized very carefully to reduce reported expenditures as much as possible.

Yesterday, a congressional leader came to your office with a disturbing proposal. Because the federal budget numbers are reported on a cash basis, rather than on an accrual basis, expenses are reported when they are paid instead of when they are incurred. This year, the final DOD payday of the year happens to fall on the last day of the federal government's fiscal year (September 30). The congressional leader suggested that you delay issuing the payroll checks by one day. This would push the actual payment of the cash into the next fiscal year. Thus, even though the payment would be for services performed in the current fiscal year, the expense wouldn't be reported until next year. With this simple trick, the reported deficit for this year (an election year) can be reduced by $1 billion.

What should you do?

▶ *Writing Assignment*

Convincing the Old-Timers of the Need for Cash Flow Data

You are the chief accountant for Harry Monst Company. The president of the company is a former accountant who worked her way up through the management ranks over the course of 30 years. She is a great manager, but her knowledge of accounting is outdated.

Harry Monst Company has a revolving line of credit with Texas Commercial Bank. A new loan officer has just been put in charge of the Harry Monst account. The new loan officer is surprised to see that Harry Monst has not been submitting a statement of cash flows along with the rest of the financial statements that comprise the annual loan review packet. The new loan officer called you and asked for a statement of cash flows.

You were surprised when you took the completed statement of cash flows to the president for her signature. She refused to sign, stating that she had never looked at or prepared a statement of cash flows in her career and she wouldn't start now.

Write a one-page memo to the president with the objective of convincing her of the usefulness of the statement of cash flows.

▶ *The Debate*

No One Can Understand the Indirect Method!

Companies have the option of reporting cash flows from operating activities using either the direct or the indirect method. Many financial statement users think that the information provided with the direct method is easier to understand. In spite of this, more than 95% of large U.S. companies use the indirect method.

Divide your group into two teams.

- One team represents the "Direct Method." Prepare a two-minute oral presentation arguing that the direct method is just what its name implies—direct and easy to understand. The indirect method is merely an attempt by accountants to confuse financial statement users.
- The other team represents the "Indirect Method." Prepare a two-minute oral presentation arguing that the direct method may seem easy to understand, but only to unsophisticated financial statement readers. The indirect method reveals much more useful information.

▶ *Cumulative Spreadsheet Project*

This spreadsheet assignment is a continuation of the spreadsheet assignments given in earlier chapters. If you completed those spreadsheets, you have a head start on this one.

1. Handyman wishes to prepare a forecasted balance sheet, income statement, and statement of cash flows for 2007. Use the original financial statement numbers for 2006 [given in part (1) of the Cumulative Spreadsheet Project assignment in Chapter 2] as the basis for the forecast along with the following additional information:
   a. Sales in 2007 are expected to increase by 40% over 2006 sales of $700.
   b. In 2007, Handyman expects to acquire new property, plant, and equipment costing $80.
   c. The $160 in operating expenses reported in 2006 breaks down as follows: $5 depreciation expense, $155 other operating expenses.
   d. No new long-term debt will be acquired in 2007.
   e. No cash dividends will be paid in 2007.
   f. New short-term loans payable will be acquired in an amount sufficient to make Handyman's current ratio in 2007 exactly equal to 2.0.

Construction of the forecasted statement of cash flows for 2007 involves analyzing the forecasted income statement for 2007, along with the balance sheets for 2006 (actual) and 2007 (forecasted).

For this exercise, the current assets are expected to behave as follows:

   a. Cash will increase at the same rate as sales.
   b. The forecasted amount of accounts receivable in 2007 is determined using the forecasted value for the average collection period (computed using the end-of-period Accounts Receivable balance). The average collection period for 2007 is expected to be 14.08 days. This is from the *Chapter 7 spreadsheet*.
   c. The forecasted amount of inventory in 2007 is determined using the forecasted value for the number of days' sales in inventory (computed using the end-of-period Inventory balance). The number of days' sales in inventory for 2007 is expected to be 107.6 days. This is from the *Chapter 8 spreadsheet*.

d. The forecasted amount of accounts payable in 2007 is determined using the fore-casted value of the number of days' purchases in accounts payable (computed using the end-of-period Accounts Payable balance). The number of days' purchases in accounts payable for 2007 is expected to be 48.34 days. This is from the *Chapter 8 spreadsheet.*

Clearly state any additional assumptions that you make.

2. Repeat (1), with the following changes in assumptions:
   a. The average collection period is expected to be 9.06 days with days' sales in inventory remaining at 107.6 days and days' purchases in payables remaining at 48.34 days.
   b. The average collection period is expected to be 20 days with days' sales in inventory remaining at 107.6 days and days' purchases in payables remaining at 48.34 days.
   c. Days' sales in inventory are expected to be 66.2 days with the average collection period remaining at 14.08 days and days' purchases in payables remaining at 48.34 days.
   d. Days' sales in inventory are expected to be 150 days with the average collection period remaining at 14.08 days and days' purchases in payables remaining at 48.34 days.
3. Comment on the forecasted values of cash from operating activities in 2007 under each of the scenarios given in (2).

▷ *Internet Search*

Home Depot

Access HOME DEPOT's Web site at **http://www.homedepot.com**. Sometimes Web addresses change, so if this address does not work, access the Web site for this textbook (**http://albrecht .swlearning.com**) for an updated link.

Once you've gained access to the site, answer the following questions:

1. Locate Home Depot's services site and determine how many different ways Home Depot can help you finance your home improvement plans.
2. Home Depot is highly supportive of various community efforts. Use its Web site to identify the community activities that Home Depot sponsors or is associated with.
3. Home Depot's Web site also includes a number of calculators designed to help buyers determine how much of a given item they need to purchase. Access the calculator for ceramic tile and determine how many tiles you would have to purchase if the room is 10 feet by 20 feet, the surface tiles are 12 inches by 12 inches, and the border tiles are 6 inches by 6 inches.
4. Find Home Depot's most recent set of financial statements. In its statement of cash flows, does Home Depot use the direct method or the indirect method in reporting cash from operating activities?
5. In the most recent year, which is greater—Home Depot's net income or its cash flows from operating activities?
6. Did Home Depot pay any cash dividends in the most recent year?

Part

5

Foundations

chapter

15

Introduction to Management Accounting

After studying this chapter, you should be able to:

1 Understand the essential differences between management accounting and financial accounting.

2 Understand that successfully managing a company requires good information that supports effective planning, controlling, and evaluating processes.

3 Describe how the concepts of fixed and variable costs are used in C-V-P analysis in the management planning process.

4 Realize how the product cost classifications of direct materials, direct labor, and overhead are used in the management controlling process.

5 Understand the concepts of direct, indirect, and opportunity costs in the management evaluating process.

6 Understand that management accounting still continues to evolve.

7 Discuss the need for ethics in management accounting and describe the Standards of Ethical Conduct that apply to this profession.

chapter 15

You may not have heard of E. I. DU PONT DE NEMOURS AND COMPANY, but you may be familiar with its more common name, DUPONT. Some of this company's best-known brands are Teflon® (cookware), Coolmax® (athletic clothing), Lycra® (stretch fabric), Stainmaster® (carpet), Hollofil® (sleeping bags), Kevlar® (protective covering), Corian® (countertops), and Mylar® (packaging). With revenues of over $24 billion in 2002, DuPont ranks number 70 in the Fortune 500 list. DuPont operates in more than 70 countries worldwide with roughly 135 manufacturing and processing facilities. Working in these facilities are 79,000 employees; approximately one-half of them work outside the United States. In addition to its manufacturing and processing facilities, DuPont has more than 40 research and development and customer service labs in the United States and more than 35 labs in 11 other countries. This is a big company!

The DuPont company was established in 1802 near Wilmington, Delaware, by a French immigrant, Eleuthére Irénée du Pont de Nemours, to produce black blasting powder. During the 1800s, the company grew into a major family corporation. However, the start of the twentieth century brought increased competition from other companies, and DuPont fell on hard times. To deal with the crisis, three of E. I. du Pont's great-grandsons, Alfred, Coleman, and Pierre, borrowed a lot of money and purchased the firm's assets from the family in 1902. With all of this debt hanging over them, the three cousins felt great pressure to make the company profitable very quickly. In a bold and risky move, they decided to make the company even bigger by borrowing more money to purchase many of the company's suppliers of raw materials (such as charcoal, sodium nitrate, and crude glycerin) used in DuPont's explosive products. In addition, instead of wholesaling the products through traditional retailers, DuPont's new managers decided to create their own network of branch sales offices scattered across the United States. As a result of expanding the company's manufacturing operations to include mining, transportation, and retailing, most of the profits usually earned by outside companies (either by selling DuPont products to customers or by selling raw materials to DuPont) were now being earned by DuPont itself.

Diversified companies are quite common today, but DuPont's diversification was unusual at the turn of the twentieth century when most companies focused on just one business activity. Although Alfred, Coleman, and Pierre were confident that their new way of doing business was going to make them a lot of money (and they were right!), they had created a serious challenge for themselves. They knew how to run a manufacturing business, but now they were in the mining, shipping, and sales business as well. They were now operating in four different industries, each with its own way of communicating results and measuring success. The three cousins had a limited amount of time and resources to invest in developing their company. How were they going to be able to effectively plan schedules, control operations, and evaluate the profitability of each division? Essentially, Alfred, Coleman, and Pierre had an accounting problem. What would you have done if you were in their shoes in 1903? As you'll see in a moment, the cousins handled this multi-million dollar challenge with some simple arithmetic.[1]

---

1 Historical sources: A. D. Chandler, *The Invisible Hand* (Boston: HBS Press, 1977); H. T. Johnson and R. S. Kaplan, *Relevance Lost* (Boston: HBS Press, 1987); the DuPont Heritage Web site at **http://heritage.dupont.com/**.

his chapter introduces management accounting and distinguishes it from financial accounting. The key purpose of management accounting is fulfilling the competitive needs of the company. DuPont had a competitive need to manage a very large and diverse organization and so invented new accounting measurements to serve as important management tools. A company's management accounting system is used to support the management processes of planning, controlling, and evaluating. In this chapter we will use cost-volume-profit analysis to introduce the planning process, product cost classifications to introduce the controlling process, and segment analysis to introduce the evaluating process. These topics are merely introduced in this chapter; more detailed coverage is given in subsequent chapters.

Business professionals who are in a position to use management accounting data to make important decisions must take care to make the best decisions possible on behalf of the organization, its owners, its employees, the surrounding community, and the public at large. As a result, it is critical that these decision makers understand the ethics of good business and are committed to perform ethically.

In summary, this chapter has four purposes.

1. To distinguish management accounting from financial accounting.
2. To introduce the management processes of planning, controlling, and evaluating.
3. To introduce management accounting terminology in the context of several key management tools.
4. To present the need for business ethics in management accounting and describe the Institute of Management Accountant's Standards of Ethical Conduct.

Management Accounting and Financial Accounting

▌ Understand the essential differences between management accounting and financial accounting.

The differences between management accounting and financial accounting can be summarized as follows:

Source:
- Management accounting *evolves* from the best practices of managers working within their companies.
- Financial accounting is *legislated and governed* by regulatory agencies and professional institutions.

Purpose:
- Management accounting exists to serve the *competitive needs* of organizations that must constantly plan, control, and evaluate operations.
- Financial accounting exists to serve the need for organizations to *periodically report* results to outside investors and lenders.

Outcome:
- Management accounting results in both *financial and nonfinancial data* that are *proprietary* (i.e., guarded from becoming available to competitors and the general public).
- Financial accounting results in *only financial data* that are *public* and reported to investors and creditors.

Knowing a little of the history of management accounting is very useful in understanding the differences between management accounting and financial accounting. Hence, as you read further about the history of the DUPONT company, be sure to see that the "rules" of management accounting are not governed by anything other than by market forces.

Example of a Management Accounting Technique: Return on Investment (ROI)

By the time Alfred, Coleman, and Pierre du Pont had finished buying out suppliers and establishing sales offices throughout the country, they had created a giant organization. The fact that their company was big, however, is not what makes their situation interesting. There were a lot of big companies in America at that time. However, most companies at the turn of the twentieth century focused on doing *one thing well* such as making cloth, moving railway cars, producing steel, or selling goods. The du Ponts, on the other hand, were trying to combine within one company many different types of businesses: mining and shipping, raw materials and finished goods manufacturing, and retail distribution and sales.

DuPont had many employees and a complicated management organization, production processes that were expensive and complicated, divisions spread all over North and South America, and high levels of expensive inventory that needed to be manufactured and sold quickly. Each of these divisions required constant attention and additional investments in order to grow and flourish. The du Ponts knew they could make or lose money in any part of their monstrous new company. Obviously, neither they (nor their money) could be everywhere at once. They needed to make trade-off decisions. The problem was, with very diverse divisions, how could they decide which divisions should receive additional investments of time and money? They couldn't really compare the cost reports of retail stores in Denver with a black powder manufacturing factory in Delaware or with a sodium nitrate processing plant in Chile. Having all these unique business activities also made it quite difficult to relate various measures of efficiency directly to overall company profit.

The first thing the new DuPont management team did was develop extensive budgets to coordinate the flow of resources from raw materials to the final customer. Notice that the development of these budgets was not mandated by a government regulatory agency or by an accounting standard-setting body. Instead, DuPont's management team decided that they could improve their business through better budgeting, so they did it. As mentioned above, this is a key characteristic of management accounting—management accounting practices are intended to fill a company's competitive business needs.

But improved budgets alone were not enough to satisfy DuPont's need for better measurements with which to plan, control, and evaluate their far-flung operations. The company still needed a measure for comparing performance in its separate divisions with performance of the whole company. Enter the management accountant, Donaldson Brown (DuPont's chief financial officer or CFO). Mr. Brown, along with other executives at DuPont, realized that every division required an investment in assets in order to be in business. The overall goal of every business should be to effectively use its assets to make a profit. For example, an explosives plant using assets worth $10 million and earning $500,000 in profit is not performing as well as a major sales division that also creates a $500,000 profit but only requires $5 million in assets. If you had an additional $1 million to invest, which division should receive your money? The sales division is earning a 10% return ($500,000 ÷ $5,000,000) on the DuPont investment in inventory, equipment, and buildings. The explosives plant is earning only a 5% return on investment ($500,000 ÷ $10,000,000). Obviously, additional investment would first go to the sales division in order to earn a 10% return rather than a mere 5% return.

FYI:

Actually, Donaldson Brown was an electrical engineer turned accountant. Nevertheless, if a management accounting hall of fame existed, the bust of F. Donaldson Brown should grace its entrance!

return on investment (ROI) A measure of operating performance and efficiency in utilizing assets; computed in its simplest form by dividing net income by average total assets. This measure is also known as ROA (return on assets).

Although this simple formula was not really new to American business in the first part of the twentieth century, Brown took the idea of **return on investment (ROI)** and began expanding it from a simple formula into a more complex management technique that could be used in the process of managing any kind of business operation at DuPont. He demonstrated how ROI can be decomposed and used to *separately* measure how well assets are being used and how well profit is being created. Use of ROI in evaluating diverse business divisions within a company

! Caution

Don't think management accounting is not important just because it is not defined as precisely as financial accounting. Management accounting is critical to the success of businesses throughout the world.

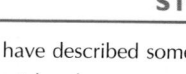

STOP & THINK

We have described some differences in financial and management accounting. Why is it important for an accounting system to provide both types of accounting information?

is explained in detail in a later chapter on monitoring performance. The ROI tool allowed the du Pont cousins to be hugely successful in managing the country's first integrated company by combining cost management with asset management and raising it to an art form! It's likely that few management accounting techniques have had as great an impact on business management as the DuPont ROI formula.

Management Accounting and Financial Accounting

The DuPont story is an example of how management accounting evolves within organizations that have a particular need for good information. This development pattern has been playing out across companies for a long time. Since the first days of the Industrial Revolution, business owners and managers have generally adopted the best accounting ideas available from other companies and then created their own new accounting system that provided a competitive edge in terms of good management information. Over time, management accounting has, quite literally, evolved within and migrated between organizations and industries in the process of satisfying individual information needs in a competitive world. In fact, a company often regards a good management accounting system as a valuable company secret—and rarely discloses its details to the public.

In contrast, financial accounting has effectively developed in the United States to provide a *common reporting platform* to the public. The purpose of financial accounting, as defined by generally accepted accounting principles (GAAP), is to satisfy the needs of outside investors, creditors, and regulators for fair and consistent reports of operations. Accordingly, all companies are required to apply the same general financial accounting rules so that outsiders can compare financial reports coming from many different companies. These financial accounting rules are established by the Financial Accounting Standards Board (FASB) and are enforced by the Securities and Exchange Commission (SEC). However, no government regulator or auditor is going to insist that a company implement a good management accounting system; the choice of how to collect and use information within a company is part of a company's competitive strategy. For example, no one forced the du Pont cousins to use the ROI formula to better manage their business; however, because the ROI evaluation framework worked well for DuPont, it was subsequently mimicked by many (but not all) of DuPont's competitors. Remember, the only reason a company does management accounting is to satisfy a competitive need, and competitive need often dictates that one organization's management accounting system will not look like another's!

TO SUMMARIZE: A good management accounting system is the product of many years of business owners and managers experimenting with methods for capturing and using information about their organization that will give them a unique competitive edge. Organizations and managers are motivated to be innovative in developing and effective in deploying these new accounting tools by the need to compete in a growing economy. In contrast, financial accounting rules are established by an authoritative body in order to enhance company-to-company comparability of financial accounting reports.

The Management Process and Management Accounting Terminology

2 Understand that successfully managing a company requires good information that supports effective planning, controlling, and evaluating processes.

Critical to the success experienced by great companies such as DUPONT is intelligent decision making by individuals supported by competitive management accounting information. Managers will always need to make choices. What should be produced? What should be sold? How should the service be delivered? What does this client need? Which supplier should be used? Who should be promoted? How should financing be obtained? Hence, as you prepare yourself to participate in the management process of an organization, you need to think carefully about how good decisions are made and how you're going to make them! Exhibit 1 illustrates the central role that decision making plays in the general management process.

Notice that the decision-making circle intersects three other circles, each representing a major management function. This intersection is meant to show that each of these functions requires decision making. The three management functions of planning, controlling, and evaluating generally follow a natural order—at least in theory. In practice, managers are often required to work with processes, customers, and employees requiring all three decision-making functions at once. For example, the manager of a campus copy center must simultaneously plan the week's work flow, control the production process by balancing the needs of student customers and faculty copy requests, and evaluate the performance of both the employees and the copy machines.

Planning

planning Outlining the activities that need to be performed for an organization to achieve its objectives.

Management **planning** involves a process of identifying problems or opportunities, identifying alternatives, evaluating alternatives, then choosing and implementing the best alternative(s). There are two basic types of planning:

1. Long-run planning, which includes:
   a. Strategic planning
   b. Capital budgeting
2. Short-run planning, which includes:
   a. Production and process prioritizing
   b. Operational budgeting (profit planning)

strategic planning Broad, long-range planning usually conducted by top management.

capital budgeting Systematic planning for long-term investments in operating assets.

Long-run planning involves making decisions with effects that extend several years into the future—usually three to five years, but sometimes longer. This includes broad-based decisions about products, markets, productive facilities, and financial resources. Long-run planning is often called strategic planning. **Strategic planning**, likely the most critical decision-making process that takes place at the executive level in any organization today, usually involves identifying an organization's mission, the goals flowing from that mission, and strategies and action steps to accomplish those goals. Successful executives, such as Bill Gates (MICROSOFT) or Warren Buffett (BERKSHIRE HATHAWAY), have always displayed great skill in studying the market, identifying customer needs, evaluating competitors' strengths and weaknesses, and defining the right investments and processes their organization needs for success. Good management accounting supports good strategic planning by providing the internal information needed by executives to evaluate and adjust their strategic plans.

With strategic planning in place (or in process), the company can then plan for the purchase and use of major assets such as buildings or equipment to help the company meet its long-range goals. For example, if part of a university's long-run strategic plan is to increase the competitive level of its football team, then the university probably should consider replacing its existing football stadium and practice facility. This type of long-run planning of the acquisition of assets is called **capital budgeting**. We will cover capital budgeting in detail in a later chapter.

Short-run planning is divided into two categories. Once the organization has made long-term resource commitments (e.g., land, buildings, equipment,

FYI:

Colleges and universities often conduct "capital" campaigns. These are fundraising campaigns targeted at generating funds for the construction of long-term assets such as academic buildings and athletic facilities.

Exhibit 1: The Management Process

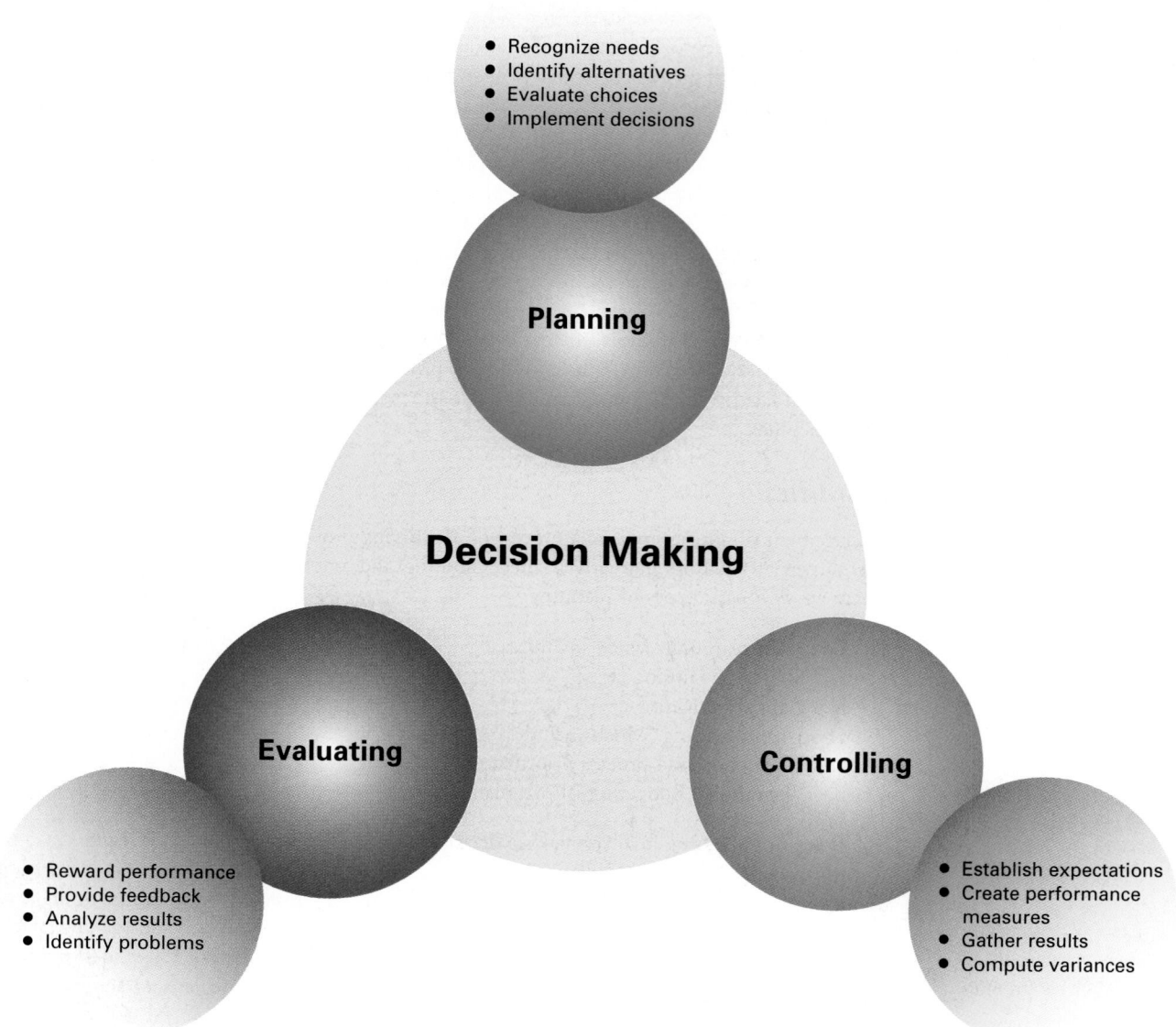

production prioritizing
Management's continual evaluation of the profitability of the various product lines and divisions within an organization so that products or divisions that are performing below expectations can be analyzed to identify problems and potential solutions.

management personnel, etc.), then managers need to determine how to best use those committed resources to maximize the return on their capital investments—a process often referred to as **production prioritizing**.[2] Did you catch the phrase "return on capital investment" in the last sentence? Sound familiar? The DuPont ROI concept is one way to establish priorities on products, service processes, or divisions that make the largest contributions to the goals of the organization. For example, you can view your study of accounting as a production process; production prioritizing involves analysis to determine how you should best spend your time in preparing for the next exam—reading the chapters, doing homework problems, studying in a group, or catching up on your sleep.

2 Production prioritizing includes the process of prioritizing what *services* will be created and delivered to the marketplace (e.g., airlines, consulting, and banking).

operational budgeting Managerial planning decisions regarding current operations and those of the immediate future (typically one year or less) that are characterized by regularity and frequency.

controlling Implementing management plans and identifying how plans compare with actual performance.

evaluating Analyzing results, rewarding performance, and identifying problems.

Once the organization has determined what to provide to the marketplace in order to maximize its goals, then managers are ready to go on to the next phase of short-run planning—**operational budgeting**. Sometimes known as profit plans, operational budgets are used by managers to establish and communicate daily, weekly, and monthly goals (also known as "standards") for the organization. Many individuals—young, middle-aged, and old—face severe personal financial problems because they fail to use even the most basic techniques of regular operational budgeting. We will discuss operational budgets in a later chapter.

Controlling

Controlling involves a process of tracking actual performance in terms of measuring costs, quality, and timeliness. These data are then used subsequently in the evaluating process to compare against the budgets previously prepared in the planning process to measure deviations from the original goals or standards. Controlling also involves the real-time, day-to-day management of all of a company's business processes. A good example of a control device is the radar gun used by major league baseball teams to measure the speed the pitcher is throwing his pitches. These measurements can be used at the end of the season in evaluating which pitchers are most valuable to the team. But these measurements can also be used by the manager during the course of a game to indicate when a pitcher is getting tired and should be replaced. The radar gun measurements are useful for evaluating individual performance after the fact but are also useful in effectively managing the team.

Evaluating

Evaluating involves analyzing results, providing feedback to managers and other employees, rewarding performance, and identifying problems. Evaluating is typically a process of comparing actual performance against expected inputs of costs, expected outputs of quality, and expected timelines. This comparison typically results in information called *variances*, which tell management how well the organization is achieving its plans. If performance is in accordance with the plan, the variances signal that operations are in control and no unusual management action is necessary. If performance is substantially different from the plan, management needs to decide how to alter operations in order to improve future performance. For example, most students in college classes are asked to evaluate their instructors near the end of the term. These evaluation results can be used by conscientious faculty members who are trying to improve their teaching, and the results can also be used by department heads in deciding which teachers should be retained or replaced.

Evaluating products and processes also takes place regularly. Managers need to assess the performance of their products or services, as well as the processes that have been put into place to create products and services. Such evaluation naturally leads to decisions that will affect future operations, including whether to enter or exit a market for a particular service or product, whether to make or buy a component, whether to sell a product before or after additional processing, and what prices to charge for services and products. The process of making these types of decisions is discussed in a later chapter on activity-based costing.

This third function in the management process, evaluating, brings us back to the point where we started, planning. The information gained through the evaluating function is used in planning for the following period. Remember that as managers *evaluate* performance in the last period, they may also be making *planning* decisions to improve operations for the next period while gathering and receiving results to *control* the current period.

TO SUMMARIZE: The essential purpose of management accounting is to support decision making that adds value to the organization. Effective decision making is the key to the management process, and it is central to the management functions of planning, controlling, and evaluating. Planning is the process of making decisions about future products and services, operations, and investments. Controlling involves tracking actual costs, quality, and timing performance within the organization. Evaluating is a process of analyzing results, computing variances, and providing feedback to assess personnel, divisions, products, and processes. The natural end result of evaluating is the identification of problems and opportunities, and from there, the next stage of planning begins.

Introduction to Cost-Volume-Profit Analysis

3 Describe how the concepts of fixed and variable costs are used in C-V-P analysis in the management planning process.

cost-volume-profit (C-V-P) analysis Techniques for determining how changes in revenues, costs, and level of activity affect the profitability of an organization.

variable costs Costs that change in total in direct proportion to changes in activity level.

This section introduces **cost-volume-profit (C-V-P) analysis**, which is a management tool primarily used in the planning process. The basic objective of C-V-P analysis is determining the volume of products or services that will be required to generate a desired profit. For example, before opening a new Thai restaurant, the would-be restaurateur should calculate how many customers a day, on average, must be served in order to pay the rent and generate a reasonable profit. If the necessary number of customers to "break even" seems unreasonably high, the business plan must be revised or abandoned. This sounds like an obvious planning exercise, but too many small business owners neglect doing even this basic analysis.

To use C-V-P analysis successfully, a manager must categorize costs as either fixed or variable costs. The concept of fixed and variable costs is fairly simple. Total **variable costs** change in *direct proportion* to changes in some particular activity level, such as production or sales volumes. One example of a variable cost is the costs of materials (such as bolts of cloth in a clothing factory), which vary proportionately with the number of units produced. Sales commissions, which vary proportionately with sales volume, are another example of a variable cost. Another way to think of a variable cost is that the cost is a set amount per unit—$3.50 per meal or $2,000 per car or $12 per book. The more meals or cars or books that are sold, the higher the total variable cost.

The cost of bolts of cloth used in a clothing factory is classified as a variable cost because it varies proportionately by the number of units produced. The more cloth used in production, the more the total amount of this cost.

fixed costs Costs that remain constant in total, regardless of activity level, at least over a certain range of activity.

Caution

In theory, distinguishing between variable and fixed costs sounds simple. If the activity, such as production volume or sales volume, increases and the cost in question increases, then it must be a variable cost. Otherwise, it is a fixed cost. In reality, however, identifying and managing variable and fixed costs can involve many complexities. Subsequent chapters, particularly the next chapter, will focus more on identifying and using variable and fixed costs in the planning process.

In contrast, **fixed costs** remain constant in total, regardless of activity level, at least over a certain range of activity. Examples of fixed costs are rent, insurance, equipment depreciation, and supervisors' salaries. Regardless of changes in sales or production output, these costs typically remain constant. For example, think back on the Thai restaurant example mentioned earlier. The rent on the restaurant location is a fixed cost because, no matter how many customers are attracted to the restaurant during the month, the monthly rent is typically still the same amount.

To demonstrate C-V-P analysis in the planning process, let's use an example involving two DUPONT products, Teflon and Kevlar. Let's assume that you as a DuPont executive need to work through which product line to prioritize for the next year. It's not simply a matter of which product line is more profitable or which is expected to return the higher ROI. The decision also involves an assessment of the risk of these two products—in this case, the risk that either or both of these products will generate a loss instead of a profit. C-V-P analysis is used to assess this risk. The fundamental question addressed by C-V-P analysis is as follows: At what sales volume will the company "break even" (i.e., profit is exactly zero) in the Kevlar product line and in the Teflon product line? Answering this question requires that you use the concept of fixed and variable costs. Assume the following estimated price and cost data for the Kevlar and Teflon product lines for the upcoming year:

	Kevlar Product Line	**Teflon Product Line**
Sales price	$50.00 per pound	$140.00 per gallon
Variable cost	$18.00 per pound	$65.00 per gallon
Total monthly fixed costs	$5,600,000	$9,600,000

Introduction to Teflon® and Kevlar®

To better understand the nature of planning, controlling, and evaluating, we work through in this chapter some typical decisions that managers at DuPont may, in fact, be working on at the moment. We will focus on two product lines at DuPont—Teflon® resins and Kevlar® fiber. These flagship products at DuPont are actually quite amazing. You may already be familiar with them. Teflon is considered the most slippery material in existence. It begins as a mixture of chemicals that are then manipulated by DuPont's engineers to produce a product that has become a familiar household name through its use as a nonstick liner for pots and pans and as a soil and stain repellant for fabrics and clothing. One of Teflon's many less-known uses is as a coating for fiberglass fabrics used in permanent structures such as the Pontiac Silverdome in Detroit, Michigan, and the Carrier Dome at Syracuse University in Syracuse, New York. Currently, Teflon has an average sales price of approximately $140 per gallon.

Kevlar is an even more interesting product. It is a specialty fabric that is extremely strong and tough—so tough that ordinary scissors will not cut through a piece of the fabric! Kevlar starts in a liquid form, is then spun to the point where the Kevlar fibers come together, and finally is heated to complete the process. It is used for boat hulls, bullet-resistant vests, cut-resistant gloves, fiber-optic cables, tennis rackets, and skis. For example, a bullet-resistant vest that is made of seven layers of Kevlar weighs only 2.5 pounds, but can stop a .38-caliber bullet shot from only 10 feet away. The average sales price for Kevlar is approximately $50 per pound. This is expensive fabric! Usually, DuPont ships Kevlar as a staple fiber (similar to cotton balls), continuous filament (essentially, a yarn), or chopped fiber.

FYI:

C-V-P analysis is often referred to as break-even analysis.

STOP & THINK

Refer back to the fixed and variable cost data for the Teflon product line. For some C-V-P analysis practice, compute the number of gallons of Teflon that DuPont must sell each month in order to break even.

Typical variable costs are the costs of the raw chemicals used to produce Kevlar and Teflon and the labor costs of the workers involved in the manufacturing process. These costs are variable because the more Kevlar or Teflon produced, the more the total amount of these costs increases. Typical fixed costs are the cost of insurance on a chemical plant, the cost of plant supervisors, and the property taxes paid on a chemical facility. These costs are fixed because, within certain limits, they are the same no matter how much Kevlar or Teflon is produced.

As you examine the assumed cost numbers for Kevlar, you can see that DuPont sells a pound of Kevlar for $32.00 more than the *variable* costs associated with making the product ($50.00 sales price per pound − $18.00 variable cost per pound). A basic objective of C-V-P analysis is to determine how many pounds of Kevlar must be sold each month to generate enough profit to pay the $5,600,000 in fixed costs associated with manufacturing that product. The computation of this "break-even" amount is as follows:

$$\frac{\$5,600,000 \text{ fixed cost}}{\$50 \text{ sales price per pound} - \$18 \text{ variable cost per pound}} = 175,000 \text{ pounds}$$

This computation means that DuPont must sell 175,000 pounds of Kevlar each month, generating a profit of $32.00 on each pound, in order to be able to pay for its fixed costs of $5,600,000 per month. If DuPont sells fewer than 175,000 pounds in a month, then the fixed costs will not be covered, and the Kevlar product line will report a loss. Remember that the fixed costs of $5,600,000 will be there no matter how many pounds of Kevlar are sold!

You can use the information from this simple C-V-P analysis to make production plans with respect to Kevlar. For example, if current production plans, in conjunction with an assessment of the market demand, indicate that DuPont will consistently sell fewer than 175,000 pounds of Kevlar per month, you will almost certainly wish to change the plans. Costs must be squeezed, new markets need to be sought, perhaps prices should be raised—in short, something has to change because the C-V-P analysis suggests that sales of less than 175,000 pounds per month will not result in profits. We will study C-V-P analysis in detail in the next chapter.

TO SUMMARIZE: By defining costs as either fixed or variable, managers can add cost-volume-profit (C-V-P) analysis to the set of tools available in the management process of planning. Fixed costs are defined as those costs that will not change in relationship to a particular activity level such as sales volume. Conversely, variable costs are those costs that change in direct proportion to sales volume. Organizations can use C-V-P analysis to determine the sales volume necessary to break even (i.e., profit equals zero). Insights gained from C-V-P computations are extremely useful in the process of planning how and which product lines to emphasize for the future.

Product and Period Costs

4 Realize how the product cost classifications of direct materials, direct labor, and overhead are used in the management controlling process.

product costs Costs associated with products or services offered.

Imagine a trip to your favorite fast-food restaurant. Now consider all of the costs incurred by that entire fast-food organization, from the president's salary down to the cost of the lettuce for the sandwiches. For management accounting purposes, we can divide these costs into two groups, product costs and period costs. Costs closely associated with the products or services offered are called **product costs**. Examples in a fast-food setting are the cost of the food, the wages of the food preparers, the salary of the store manager, and the rent on the store location. As you sit there, ready to bite into your sandwich, you can look around and see all of these costs. In this sense, they are closely associated with the product (the sandwich) and are classified as product costs. In a manufacturing company such as DUPONT, for example, product

The Steely-Eyed Business Tycoon In the nineteenth century and much of the twentieth century, management accounting, known then as cost accounting, focused strictly on cost measurement and cost management. Business owners were making a great deal of money using this information to build and expand large companies. And no one understood cost information quite like Andrew Carnegie, who controlled about 25% of the American iron and steel produc-

tion in 1899. Carnegie was obsessed with costs. One of his favorite sayings was "Watch the costs and the profits will take care of themselves." Was Carnegie's management accounting focus successful? In 1901 he sold his company, CARNEGIE STEEL, to the UNITED STATES STEEL CORPORATION for $250 million and retired. During his lifetime he gave more than $350 million to various educational, cultural, and peace institutions, many of which bear his name. Not bad for an immigrant with no formal education.

STOP & THINK

A major difference between Kelly Services and manufacturers or merchandisers is inventory. Kelly sells services. Can we put service labor into inventory? Think about this question; we'll discuss it later in the chapter on product cost flows.

period costs Costs not directly related to a product, service, or asset. These costs are charged as expenses to the income statement in the period in which they are incurred.

costs (often referred to as manufacturing costs) are all costs necessary to create finished goods ready for sale. They include all costs related to production: the factory manager's salary, depreciation and taxes on the factory building, wages of the factory workers, and the materials that go into the product. In a merchandising company such as MACY'S or SEARS, product costs are the costs incurred to purchase goods and get them ready for resale to customers. In a service company such as the UNION PACIFIC RAILROAD or KELLY SERVICES (which provides temporary employees), product costs (sometimes called cost of services) involve labor, supplies, and other costs directly related to providing services to customers.

Period costs are all costs incurred that are not closely associated with a specific product or service. In the fast-food setting we considered earlier, examples of period costs are the president's salary, advertising, and office costs incurred in the corporate headquarters. These are costs that are not associated with the sandwich that you are eating or the environment in which you are eating it. In general, the most common period costs are selling and administrative costs. Examples of selling costs are sales salaries, advertising, and delivery costs. Examples of administrative costs are salaries of the president and controller, depreciation or rent on office buildings, taxes on assets used in administration, and other office expenditures such as postage, supplies, and utilities.

The labels "product" and "period" stem from the procedure followed in reporting these costs as expenses on the income statement. For product costs, these costs are associated with specific products or services and are expensed when those products are sold. For example, if Sears sells two-thirds of the inventory it purchased during November, only the cost of the inventory sold (i.e., Cost of Goods Sold) becomes an expense on that month's income statement. The other third of the inventory cost remains an asset (i.e., Inventory) on the balance sheet. In contrast, period costs are reported as an expense *immediately* in the period in which they are incurred. So, regardless of how many products are sold during the month, the president's entire salary for November is recognized as an expense on the November monthly income statement. Thus, these costs are called period costs because they are always expensed in the period (e.g., month) in which they are incurred.

Types of Product Costs

Now let's consider how you might measure and control product and period costs in a variety of organizations. How would you measure product costs for a merchandiser? Actually, that is

Watch Your Language in Management Accounting! As good business professionals work to compete in the marketplace, a set of common management accounting terms has evolved. Remember, this is not financial accounting—it is important to understand that no official regulatory body of professionals has defined these terms. As you work in various organizations later in your career, you may find that these definitions can become a little unclear. Depending on the decision context, a particular cost can have several names. You need to understand this fact and recognize that allowing these definitions to "shift about" can be completely appropriate!

To illustrate, if you like playing card games such as bridge or canasta, you understand that it is often very important in the game to distinguish between cards of different suits—hearts, spades, clubs, or diamonds. On the other hand, for some decisions in the card game it may be more useful to concentrate on the value of the card—ace, 10, deuce, and so on. Thus, sometimes you care about the ace of hearts because of its "heartness," and at other times you are really more interested in its "aceness." Similarly, a product cost may also be a variable cost. Depending on the management setting, you may choose to categorize costs as fixed or variable versus product or period or direct or indirect.

So, in business conversations (discussions concerning costs, for example), never assume you are talking about the same concept as another individual. You always need to be sure that everyone is using the same definition of a management accounting term or concept before you let the conversation get too far.

a fairly easy question. The resources Macy's spends to acquire store inventory for resale to customers clearly are product costs. As products are sold, these inventory costs become an expense on the income statement. What about the wages and salaries of Macy's store clerks and managers? Macy's will likely categorize these costs as part of its selling and administrative expenses and treat them as a period cost on the income statement. That's not too difficult.

Now consider the same question for ERNST & YOUNG LLP, one of the largest certified public accounting (CPA) firms in the world. What are the products sold by this service firm? Ernst & Young sells the time of its tax accountants, auditors, and consultants. The salaries of these professionals represent the costs of its "product." These costs are reported as the expense "cost of services sold" in the same period in which Ernst & Young reports the corresponding service revenue. Thus, if the consulting revenue from a specific job is reported in January 2006, any product costs associated with that job which were incurred in 2005 are not expensed until January 2006. As of the end of 2005, these costs are given a label such as "consulting projects in progress" or "unbilled services" and reported as inventory on the December 2005 balance sheet. Ernst & Young also employs many other people (such as clerks, secretaries, and office managers) to support the professionals and to administer office needs. The costs of these people are not closely associated with specific consulting jobs. Accordingly, the wages and salaries of these clerks and office managers, along with costs of office rent, desk supplies, and computers, are likely treated as period costs and recognized as selling and administrative expenses on the income statement in the period in which they are incurred.

When identifying product costs for control purposes, the most challenging organization to analyze is a manufacturing business. Does DuPont purchase inventory for resale? Actually, it does purchase some inventory, such as basic chemicals. But it doesn't simply turn around and resell these basic chemicals to customers. Significant processing has to take place before these raw materials become a finished product ready for sale. DuPont must employ laborers to work with these chemicals. In addition, DuPont builds factory buildings and purchases manufactur-

direct materials Materials that become part of the product and are traceable to it.

indirect materials Materials that are necessary to a manufacturing or service business but are not directly included in or are not a significant part of the actual product.

direct labor Wages that are paid to those who physically work on direct materials to transform them into a finished product and are traceable to specific products.

indirect labor Labor that is necessary to a manufacturing or service business but is not directly related to the actual production of the manufactured or service product.

manufacturing overhead All costs incurred in the manufacturing process other than direct materials and direct labor.

ing equipment. DuPont must also employ managers and other support personnel (such as engineers and custodians) to support the line workers' efforts to convert basic chemicals into finished products. These are all product costs. Basically, any cost required to get the product manufactured and ready for sale is a product cost.

To help management analyze the manufacturing cost of its products, product costs are divided into three components: (1) direct materials, (2) direct labor, and (3) manufacturing overhead. **Direct materials** are materials that become part of the product and are traceable to it. Some materials, however, such as the glue and nails in a finished piece of furniture, are so minor and their use so difficult to trace to a specific product that they are not considered direct materials, but rather **indirect materials**. Indirect materials also include the materials and supplies used in nonproduction activities such as maintenance and custodial processes. **Direct labor** consists of the wages that are paid to those who physically work on the direct materials to transform them into a finished product. Conversely, wages and salaries paid to factory supervisors and management, maintenance staff, and factory security guards are treated as **indirect labor**. **Manufacturing overhead** includes all other costs incurred in the manufacturing process not specifically identified as direct materials or direct labor. Both indirect materials and indirect labor are included in manufacturing overhead. Exhibit 2 summarizes the relationship between product costs and period costs in various types of organizations.

Computing the Cost of Manufactured Products: How Low Can You Go?

Imagine that another company has recently introduced a new product on the market that competes directly with DuPont's Kevlar. Soon the intense competition between DuPont and the other company for customer orders starts to force down the market price of Kevlar. Now you and the rest of the DuPont management team have a problem. How low can you let the price of Kevlar drop before the company starts losing money? Answering this question requires that DuPont's accountants do a good job of measuring the costs of creating Kevlar. The following simple numbers illustrate how difficult it is to answer the straightforward question: How much does it cost to make a pound of Kevlar?

Direct materials	$16.00 per pound
Direct labor	$0.60 per pound
Manufacturing overhead:	
Variable	$1.40 per pound
Fixed	$1,500,000 per month
General corporate sales and administrative costs	$4,100,000 per month

Exhibit 2: Product Costs and Period Costs in Business Organizations

Type of Company	Product Costs	Period Costs
Service company	Costs of providing services	Selling costs Administrative costs
Merchandising company (wholesale or retail)	Costs incurred in purchasing goods from suppliers	Selling costs Administrative costs
Manufacturing company	All manufacturing costs including direct materials, direct labor, and manufacturing overhead	Selling costs Administrative costs

The $4,100,000 per month in general corporate sales and administrative costs is a period cost and, therefore, would not be included in computing the cost to make a pound of Kevlar.

The variable manufacturing overhead costs might include some utility costs (e.g., power to run the equipment) and repairs and maintenance costs that change based on production volumes (similar to the way maintenance costs of your car increase the more you drive it). From the data in the cost table above, it is clear that the variable product cost to make a pound of Kevlar is $18.00 ($16.00 + $0.60 + $1.40), as mentioned earlier in our discussion of fixed and variable costs. But it clearly isn't correct to state that a pound of Kevlar "costs" $18.00 because the Kevlar manufacturing process includes fixed manufacturing overhead costs as well. These fixed costs include factory rent, depreciation, production supervisor salaries, and so forth. So, the cost of a pound of Kevlar is at least $18.00, plus some addition for the fixed manufacturing overhead costs.

Determining the proper amount of fixed manufacturing overhead that should be assigned to, or allocated to, each unit of production is one of the most difficult tasks in the field of management accounting. For one thing, the amount of fixed manufacturing overhead per pound of Kevlar produced depends on the number of pounds that are actually produced in a month. Remember that, by definition, the fixed overhead amount of $1,500,000 per month is the same whether one pound or one million pounds are produced. If one pound is produced, the fixed overhead per unit is $1,500,000; if one million pounds are produced, the fixed overhead per pound is $1.50. With these numbers, we see that we can compute a cost per pound of Kevlar of anywhere from $19.50 ($18.00 variable + $1.50 fixed allocation) to $1,500,018 ($18.00 variable + $1,500,000 fixed allocation). Obviously, this ridiculously wide range of cost estimates is useless in helping to determine what price DuPont should charge for a pound of Kevlar. The company needs accurate, reliable estimates of production volume in order to generate useful cost computations. Assuming that DuPont expects to produce on average 300,000 pounds of Kevlar each month, the fixed manufacturing overhead cost per pound can be allocated as follows:

$$\$1,500,000 \div 300,000 \text{ pounds} = \$5.00 \text{ per pound}$$

Adding together the fixed and variable manufacturing costs per batch, the expected total manufacturing cost is $23.00 per pound of Kevlar ($18.00 variable manufacturing costs + $5.00 fixed manufacturing overhead). Assuming that this method of allocating manufacturing overhead costs to Kevlar is appropriate, you can use this measure as a benchmark to track actual production costs as they come in throughout the year.

You've probably already wondered if this simple spreading of the fixed manufacturing overhead costs evenly across the units produced might ignore some important realities in manufacturing. Some products simply require more overhead costs than do others. For example, producing a pound of Kevlar involves hazardous chemicals and careful inspection by chemical engineers trained in quality control. The existence of these hazardous chemicals necessitates the use of special handling equipment and extra insurance, and the quality control inspectors must be paid a salary commensurate with their skills. Accordingly, the production of Kevlar requires additional overhead costs that would not be required by the production of, say, Lycra® fabric. Proper management accounting involves the identification of specific activities (often called cost drivers) that create a need to spend money on fixed manufacturing overhead. A good managerial accounting system assigns a higher cost to those products that create more fixed manufacturing overhead. The computation of product costs, and the procedures involved in the allocation of fixed manufacturing overhead costs to different products, are discussed later in two chapters on product cost flows and activity-based costing, respectively.

TO SUMMARIZE: Costs are initially categorized as either product or period costs. Many period costs are classified as sales and administrative overhead and are, generally, quite difficult to associate with any of the particular products or services that the company provides to the marketplace. Examples of period costs include salaries of selling and advertising personnel and rent or depreciation costs on administrative office buildings. On the other hand, product costs are closely related to the actual process of providing specific goods and services to customers. Because the management process of controlling costs involves the effort to classify and track costs of providing specific goods and services, product costs are typically assigned to specific products or services in an effort to effectively control these costs. Product costs for manufacturing companies such as DuPont are traditionally divided into costs of direct materials, direct labor, and manufacturing overhead. Direct materials are those items that become part of the final product and are easily traceable to it. Direct labor costs are the wages of workers who are "hands on" involved in the production of the final product. Manufacturing overhead costs are essentially defined as all costs essential to the production of goods or services that cannot be categorized as direct materials and direct labor and *directly* assigned to specific goods and services. Perhaps the most challenging aspect of controlling costs for accountants is the process of *indirectly* assigning (i.e., allocating) overhead costs to specific products.

Segment Analysis

5 Understand the concepts of direct, indirect, and opportunity costs in the management evaluating process.

Managers and executives are typically paid well to make hard decisions. You may find in your future business career as a manager that the process of evaluating the performance of divisions, personnel, processes, and products is complicated as markets for particular products change based on developments in technology, new fads and trends in consumer taste, and increased pressure from new and existing competitors. Occasionally, the situation requires a serious look at the potential need to exit from a particular market or to drop a specific product line. Sometimes these decisions are motivated by the opportunity to enter a new market or add a new product line. For example, airlines are constantly evaluating whether to cut service on less-traveled routes, to increase or cut back the number of first-class seats, and so forth. The decision to drop a product line is critical because subsequently reversing the decision can be difficult or impossible. Good management accounting can do much to facilitate the process of evaluating divisions, personnel, processes, and products. Conversely, a poor understanding of some critical management accounting concepts can lead to painful, if not potentially lethal, company problems. To illustrate how accounting supports this evaluation process, we need to extend your vocabulary of key management accounting terms.

Direct and Indirect Costs

So far we have identified fixed and variable costs as a method of cost classification that provides good support to the planning process. We've also defined product and period costs and used those classifications to demonstrate the management controlling process. Now we introduce some new ways to classify costs that are useful for evaluating performance. One of these classifications is direct costs and indirect costs. **Direct costs** are costs that can be obviously and physically traced to a business unit or segment being analyzed. The unit may be a sales territory, product line, division, plant, or any other subdivision for which performance needs to be analyzed. Direct costs are often described as those costs that could be saved if the segment were to be discontinued. Typically, many types of direct costs are variable, but some direct costs are fixed. For example, if the business segment being considered is a branch sales office, the cost of inventory and labor to run the store would be direct costs that are variable, while the cost to rent the building would be a direct cost that is fixed.

Indirect costs—sometimes referred to as common costs or joint costs—are costs that are normally incurred for the benefit of several segments. Indirect costs can also be either fixed or

direct costs Costs that are specifically traceable to a unit of business or segment being analyzed.

indirect costs Costs normally incurred for the benefit of several segments within the organization; sometimes called common costs or joint costs.

variable, although these costs are nearly always fixed. Sometimes these costs are allocated in order to be assigned to a segment. For example, consider a sales manager's salary. If a segment is defined as a branch sales office and a sales manager supervises only one segment, the manager's salary is likely a direct cost of that sales office. If the manager is responsible for several segments, however, the salary would then be an indirect cost to any one of the sales offices. Total indirect costs, such as the manager's salary, normally do not change if one or more of the segments (in this case, the sales offices) are discontinued. Another example of an indirect cost may be manufacturing overhead. In most large organizations, many (but not all) types of manufacturing overhead costs are not directly identifiable with a specific product or product line. Hence, manufacturing overhead costs are typically classified as indirect costs to these products or product lines because they are incurred as a consequence of general or overall operating activities.

FYI:

Activity-based costing (ABC) is a relatively new method of cost assignment that we will fully discuss in a later chapter on activity-based costing. A major emphasis of ABC is to connect costs directly with certain activities. One result of ABC is an increase in the number of costs that can be classified as direct costs.

Costs are designated as either direct or indirect so that a business segment such as a division or product line can be evaluated on the basis of only those costs *directly* traceable or chargeable to it. Although companies sometimes allocate indirect costs among segments, such allocations often confuse the analysis of the segment's operations. By focusing only on direct costs, management can both identify segments where performance needs to be improved and recognize segments where performance is outstanding and should be rewarded.

Differential Costs and Sunk Costs

differential costs Future costs that change as a result of a decision; also called incremental or relevant costs.

sunk costs Costs, such as depreciation, that are past costs and do not change as a result of a future decision.

The difference between direct costs and indirect costs is similar to the difference between another set of cost terms—differential costs and sunk costs. The **differential costs** of a decision—sometimes called avoidable costs, incremental costs, or relevant costs—are the future costs that change as a result of that decision. In the context of making a decision as to whether to drop a product line, there is likely little difference between the terms *differential cost* and *direct cost*. (The term *differential* is also commonly applied to future *revenues* that will be affected by the decision.) **Sunk costs**, on the other hand, are past costs that cannot be changed as the result of a future decision. You should note that the definition of sunk costs is not quite the same as that of indirect costs. Indirect costs are those costs that are not affected by a *particular* decision. For example, whether DUPONT decides to continue or discontinue its Kevlar product line will likely not affect its general and administrative costs. These costs are indirect to the Kevlar product line. This does not mean that management cannot change any of DuPont's general and administrative costs. It just means that a different management decision process is required to change these costs than the process used in evaluating the feasibility of the Kevlar product line. If this sounds as though a cost could be indirect to one evaluation situation or focus and direct to another, you're right! Defining a cost as direct or indirect depends on the object of the decision. On the other hand, sunk costs are not dependent at all on any decision object. A sunk cost is exactly what it sounds like—sunk! There is nothing a company can reasonably do to change a sunk cost.

As an example of sunk costs, the costs that DuPont may have spent last year upgrading its Teflon manufacturing facilities are not relevant to the decision this year as to whether it should continue to compete in the market for performance coatings. Yet many individuals and companies make poor decisions because they fail to correctly distinguish between differential costs and sunk costs. As a personal example, assume you have season tickets to a school's basketball game. On the night of a game, a friend asks you to go to a movie with her. You have wanted to see the movie for a long time. If you decline because you have already purchased the basketball tickets and believe you must therefore go to the game, you may have made the wrong decision. The cost of the basketball tickets is a sunk cost. The only costs that are relevant to your decision are the costs associated with going to the movie, such as the ticket price and popcorn and other goodies you might buy, as well as any out-of-pocket costs you might spend at the basketball game.

Out-of-Pocket Costs and Opportunity Costs

out-of-pocket costs Costs that require an outlay of cash or other resources.

opportunity costs The benefits lost or forfeited as a result of selecting one alternative course of action over another.

At the most general level, costs can be separated into out-of-pocket costs and opportunity costs. **Out-of-pocket costs** require an outlay of cash or other resources. Many of the costs discussed thus far in this chapter could be called out-of-pocket costs (though sunk costs are never considered an out-of-pocket cost). If a company is deciding whether to accept a special order, the costs of materials needed to produce that order are out-of-pocket costs. If a fast-food restaurant is considering installing a drive-up window, the cost of construction is an out-of-pocket cost. Naïve individuals and organizations usually consider only out-of-pocket costs when making decisions. For example, an individual deciding whether to attend a movie might consider only the $9 cost of the ticket required to gain admittance. On the other hand, opportunity costs do not require an outlay of resources. Nevertheless, they are as important as out-of-pocket costs to good management decision making. **Opportunity costs** are the benefits lost or forfeited as a result of selecting one alternative course of action over another. For example, choosing to go to a movie instead of working two hours at $8 per hour has an opportunity cost of $16, as well as an out-of-pocket cost of $9 for the ticket. Installing a drive-up window at a fast-food outlet may have several opportunity costs, such as lost seating or lost parking available to customers.

STOP & THINK

Which of the following costs are typically recorded in a traditional accounting system: product costs, fixed costs, indirect costs, out-of-pocket costs, sunk costs, opportunity costs?

Segment Analysis at DuPont

Let's return once more to DuPont and have you apply these new cost concepts in the process of evaluating the Kevlar and Teflon product lines to determine if the company can continue to

business environment

Accounting and the "Shaq Impact" Opportunity costs are important in all organizations but are especially critical in situations where there are defined limits on available resources. Professional basketball teams, for example, have league-imposed salary caps that dictate the maximum total amount of salaries they can pay to team members. In the 2002/2003 season, the salary cap was $40.3 million per team. When an exceptional player, such as Shaquille O'Neal (Shaq) of the LOS ANGELES LAKERS, comes up for salary negotiations, the team's management must consider both out-of-pocket and opportunity costs when deciding whether to pay the salary requested. For example, Shaq's salary in the 2002/2003

season with the Los Angeles Lakers was close to $24 million. Before agreeing to this contract, the Lakers management had to decide whether ticket sales and TV revenues would be sufficient to meet the out-of-pocket cost of $24 million. Management also had to consider what other player(s) it could sign for $24 million per year and whether, based on the existence of the salary cap, it would be able to pay other current and prospective players enough. For example, the Lakers paid Kobe Bryant approximately $12 million for the 2002/2003 season. Paying $36 million per year to Shaq and Kobe makes it nearly impossible for the Lakers to pay other players that much money and thus is a high opportunity cost for a professional basketball team. (*Note:* The Lakers' total team salary payout for 2002/2003 was nearly $63 million. The NBA penalizes teams going over the salary cap with a hefty salary "luxury tax.")

profitably offer both products to the public. Assume that the following data represent the results of operations this last month for these two products:

Operating Statements	Kevlar	Teflon	Total
Sales revenue	$15,000,000	$14,000,000	$ 29,000,000
Variable manufacturing costs	(5,400,000)	(6,500,000)	(11,900,000)
Fixed manufacturing overhead	(1,500,000)	(3,200,000)	(4,700,000)
Sales and administrative costs	(4,100,000)	(6,400,000)	(10,500,000)
Operating profit	**$ 4,000,000**	**$ (2,100,000)**	**$ 1,900,000**

It looks as though DuPont had a tough month with the Teflon product. In fact, let's assume that the past several months show similar losses on the Teflon product line. In evaluating these results, perhaps you should consider the possibility of dropping this product line. Doing so would certainly improve overall profits for the organization, wouldn't it? Actually, we need to be careful with this analysis. The operating statements above categorize the costs in terms of product costs and period costs. Is that the right way to view these costs for this particular decision? What are the *direct* costs in this decision? Stated another way, what are the *differential* (or *avoidable*) costs of producing Teflon? If you choose to exit from the market for Teflon products, can all of the variable manufacturing costs be avoided in the future? With some effort, yes. How about fixed manufacturing overhead? These costs are going to be more difficult to handle. Fixed manufacturing overhead includes items such as supervisors' salaries and depreciation on equipment and plant facilities. Can you avoid some of these costs? Actually, perhaps some of these costs can be avoided, but many of these costs are usually unavoidable. For example, let's assume that both Kevlar and Teflon are manufactured in the same building. The depreciation on this building, a fixed manufacturing cost, is allocated to both product lines (a classic example of an indirect cost). In this case, if you choose to drop a product line, the cost related to building depreciation is simply reassigned to the remaining products. Sales and administrative costs assigned to the Teflon product line are even less likely to be avoided by a decision to exit this market. These costs often remain within the company and are the responsibility of all of the product lines.

To better support a decision process involving the possibility of dropping Teflon from DuPont's mix of products, you really need to reclassify the product and period costs above as either direct or indirect to the product line. In making this new classification, we'll assume that approximately 30% of the fixed manufacturing overhead can be avoided if Teflon is dropped (e.g., 30% of the fixed manufacturing overhead costs are salaries of personnel that can be dismissed or reassigned to other product lines). This means that 30% of the fixed manufacturing overhead is a *direct* cost to the segment.

Operating Statements	Kevlar	Teflon	Total
Sales revenue	$15,000,000	$14,000,000	$ 29,000,000
Direct costs:			
Variable manufacturing costs	(5,400,000)	(6,500,000)	(11,900,000)
Fixed manufacturing overhead (30%)	(450,000)	(960,000)	(1,410,000)
Segment profit	**$ 9,150,000**	**$ 6,540,000**	**$ 15,690,000**
Indirect costs:			
Fixed manufacturing overhead (70%)	(1,050,000)	(2,240,000)	(3,290,000)
Sales and administrative costs	(4,100,000)	(6,400,000)	(10,500,000)
Operating profit	**$ 4,000,000**	**$ (2,100,000)**	**$ 1,900,000**

What do you learn from this new analysis? Those costs that can be removed from the system by discontinuing the Teflon business segment are direct costs to the segment, and these are the only costs relevant to this decision. All other costs are actually indirect costs (also called common costs) that have been assigned by the accounting system to the Teflon segment. Should you choose to exit the market for Teflon products, these costs will remain in the company and will likely be reallocated to the remaining business segments. So what will be the financial impact of dropping the Teflon product line? The "true" performance of Teflon last month was *not* a loss, but a $6,540,000 contribution to overall company profits.

Finally, in your analysis of the profitability of these two products lines, you also need to think about the opportunity costs of producing Teflon. In other words, if you choose to leave the Teflon business, can DuPont use the Teflon assets to produce and sell another product? Whatever value that alternative product might contribute to overall company profits is an opportunity cost of producing Teflon. This is an important cost that doesn't get formally reported in most accounting systems, yet a good business manager (like you!) will need to consider these very relevant costs in some decisions. We'll talk more about opportunity cost and segment analysis in a later chapter on making decisions.

Caution

It is important to understand that opportunity costs are very important costs that are not formally tracked in the company's accounting system.

TO SUMMARIZE: Different terms are used to describe costs depending on the aspect of the management process involved—planning, controlling, or evaluating. In the evaluation of segments such as product lines or business divisions, managers need to be clear about the difference between direct and indirect costs. Direct costs are costs that are specifically traceable to a segment. Sometimes direct costs are referred to as differential costs, avoidable costs, incremental costs, or relevant costs. The direct costs of a particular segment will change based on future decisions affecting the segment. On the other hand, indirect costs, also known as common costs, are costs that are normally incurred for the benefit of several segments. Although indirect costs can be changed by some high-level management processes, decisions that specifically affect any one of the segments will not affect indirect costs that are common across all the segments. On the other hand, sunk costs are costs that cannot be changed based on *any* decisions made by management. These are costs that have already been spent (such as depreciation on a purchased building) or costs that cannot be realistically avoided (such as the property tax on the administration building). Finally, opportunity costs are measured as the benefits lost by choosing one alternative over another. Opportunity costs, though not recorded formally in most companies' accounting systems, are relevant to most decisions. These cost terms are particularly useful in the management process of evaluating the contribution of product lines or departments in an organization.

Expanding Management Accounting: Cost, Quality, and Time

6 Understand that management accounting still continues to evolve.

The DUPONT ROI (return on investment) formula is a terrific tool for managing most kinds of organizations. You realize, though, that ROI has been with us now for nearly a century. Most educated managers are fully aware of ROI and how to apply it within their particular organization. Remember that the development of management accounting is a function of the need for information and tools that provide a competitive edge. Would you expect then that the use of ROI provides managers a significant competitive edge in *today's* economy? The truth of the matter is that, in most industries, effective use of ROI and other traditional management accounting tools is still necessary, but using only these tools is probably not sufficient to successfully plan, control, and evaluate a business process. In order to be competitive, today's managers constantly need more and better information. In fact, beginning with the Japanese innovation of **just-in-time (JIT)** in the mid-twentieth century, accountants and other information providers have moved beyond just providing data on costs to include innovative methods of measuring the *quality* and the *timeliness* of products and production processes, as well as service and distribution systems. As an example, businesses today create a competitive advantage by delivering more

just-in-time (JIT) A management philosophy that emphasizes removing all waste of effort, time, and inventory costs from the organization. One obvious result of JIT is the reduction or removal of needless inventory in a production process.

cycle time The total time a product spends moving through a particular process or cycle within the organization, such as the product design cycle, the production cycle, or the order and delivery cycle.

value to customers in less **cycle time** than competitors. As a firm creates and exploits a competitive advantage in cost, quality, and time, it creates increased shareholder value. In other words, if you make your customers happy, you create more profitable financial outcomes and, in the process, make the owners (shareholders) of the business happy! As a result, new performance measures related to cost, quality, and time are being created, tracked, and monitored by firms in many modern industries and have become a hot topic for research among managers and accountants. Some examples of the new performance measures being tracked by managers

business environment

One Company's Experience with Cost, Quality, and Time Developing measures of cost, quality, and time is a highly proprietary strategic activity. Many organizations are very reluctant to disclose the specifics of their efforts to develop competitive information in these three areas. One company (a medium-sized aerospace corporation in the Pacific Northwest that chooses to remain anonymous) provides a good illustration of the process of creating cost, quality, and time strategic measures. In 1989, the executive team started work to develop new competitive information for this company. It first conducted a survey of key customers, asking about product design, quality, and reliability; the company's ability to meet delivery schedules and other commitments; pricing and perceived value; service and the capability to recover from mistakes; and the overall ease of doing business with the company.

The results were surprising. Contrary to expectations, customers weren't concerned with the company's technological innovations that management had been proud of for years. Instead, customers were concerned with cost, quality, and delivery performance. To their dismay, the executives discovered that customers were dissatisfied with the company's performance in these three areas. Some said they continued to buy from the company only because it was easy to do business with and resolved problems quickly. Clearly, the company was at risk of losing its customers to a competitor unless some changes were made!

To refocus the company on the needs of its customers, an executive staff team was formed to meet weekly to develop a new performance measurement system. The meetings turned into prolonged debates over the number and kind of measures to use. Hours of brainstorming eventually led to the following list:

Cost Measures
- Engineering cost performance
- Production efficiency
- Rework and scrap costs

Quality Measures
- Quality of supplier's products
- Manufacturing first-pass yield
- Warranty returns

Time Measures
- New-product development cycle time
- Master schedule stability
- Manufacturing cycle time
- On-time delivery

The executive team assigned the company's controller to collect performance data for each of these 10 measures and issue a monthly report. Graphs of the results were posted for employees and customers to see and became a critical part of any meeting in which management reviewed performance. Some adjustments to these measures were made based on feedback from employees and customers. Eventually, this new approach to performance measures played a crucial role in the company's overall efforts to increase its competitive position. By 1993, it achieved the following performance improvements:

- Customer-quoted delivery times were cut by 50%.
- On-time shipments rose 89%.
- Product-development cycle time fell 35%.
- Manufacturing costs as a percentage of manufacturing sales fell 10%.

Source: K. V. Ramanathan and D. S. Schaffer, "How Am I Doing?" *Journal of Accountancy*, May 1995, pp. 79–82.

FYI:

In deciding how to make trade-offs between costs, quality, and other factors, high cost doesn't always lead to high quality. Take the 30 teams in Major League Baseball, for example. In 2002, the team with the highest player payroll was the New York Yankees ($126 million). The team with the lowest player payroll was the Tampa Bay Devil Rays ($34 million). The Devil Rays ended the season with the worst record of the 30 teams with 55 wins and 106 losses. On the other hand, while the Yankees won their division, they did not make it to The World Series. You may remember that two wild card teams played in The World Series, and the Anaheim Angels won. Yet while the Angels were the best team in the world in 2002, the players were paid a "mediocre cost" of $62 million. In contrast, the third-highest paid team in 2002 was the Texas Rangers at $103 million, and they took last place in their division! It appears that the fans in Anaheim got a pretty good deal.

in the strategic areas of cost, quality, and time are displayed in Exhibit 3. We'll discuss many of these performance measures in later chapters.

The idea of extending beyond cost to also compete on quality and time is having a major impact in industries across the world. These developments present a real opportunity for today's accountants to jump in and be a part of the competitive management process! However, some accountants are frankly not paying attention to this recent shift in management information needs. These accountants continue to focus on providing cost data only. Apparently, they haven't learned their history lesson. Success and profits flow to the business that creates new views of information it can use to gain a competitive edge in the marketplace. On the other hand, some farsighted managers and accountants see this trend and are currently bringing together "balanced scorecards" that combine cost, quality, and time data to support decision making that can literally redefine customer and client service. We'll talk more about balanced scorecards and other recent innovations in management accounting in the final chapter on continuous improvement.

Exhibit 3: New Measures of Cost, Quality, and Time

Cost Measures	Quality Measures	Time Measures
Engineering cost performance	Manufacturing first-pass yield	On-time delivery
Rework and scrap costs	Warranty returns	Master schedule stability
Cost versus features/benefits delivered	Vendor supply quality	New-product development cycle time
Costs of quality	Service and support events	Manufacturing cycle time
Life cycle costs	Successful availability events	Recovery-response time
Target costs	Alignment with customer expectations	Time to market
Learning costs	Six sigma error rate	Order fulfillment cycle time
Activity costs	Waste, scrap, and rework rates	Rework and other non-value-added time

TO SUMMARIZE: In the twenty-first century, strategic performance measures of cost, quality, and time have continued to support and improve decisions that build organizations both in the profit and the not-for-profit sectors of our society. Accountants working inside of companies, if they expect to have jobs as key decision-support professionals in the twenty-first century, must provide data that encompass all three of these strategic imperatives.

The Role of Ethics in Management Accounting

7 Discuss the need for ethics in management accounting and describe the Standards of Ethical Conduct that apply to this profession.

The function of management accounting in the organization is to support competitive decision making by collecting, processing, and communicating information that helps managers plan, control, and evaluate business processes and company strategy. The top accountant in most large organizations is usually called the controller. In most organizations, professionals responsible for accounting systems and other critical decision-support data report to the controller. The controller usually reports to a vice president of finance or perhaps the chief finance officer (CFO). This individual, in turn, reports to the organization's president or chief executive

FYI:

As the importance of technology continues to grow in business society, many organizations have recently been creating a new role to manage the technology function, the chief information officer (CIO). The CIO's job is to design, implement, and manage all information systems. However, there may be a bit of conflict here. Do CIOs also handle the *accounting* information systems? Should accounting information systems now be strictly limited to financial data? Who should those involved with management accounting report to? The CIO or the controller? Organizations are grappling with these issues as they work to include this new position in their management structure.

FYI:

Those who work in management accounting can obtain a professional certificate that is much like the CPA certification. The Certificate in Management Accounting (CMA) is sponsored by the Institute of Management Accountants. Five areas of study are emphasized on the CMA exam: (1) economics and finance, (2) organizational behavior, (3) public financial accounting reporting and analysis, (4) internal management accounting reporting and analysis, and (5) decision analysis and information systems.

officer (CEO). As the chief accounting officer, the controller is ultimately responsible for what information is created to manage the organization, as well as how that information is used. This individual, as well as all others who work with him or her, are in a position of significant power. Those who manage the management accounting process have access to the organization's most important and sensitive competitive information used to make operational and strategic decisions. Hence, it is absolutely critical that these individuals conduct their work professionally and with utmost integrity. Otherwise, the consequences of unethical behavior in the practice of management accounting can ruin (and, on occasion, has ruined) individuals, companies, and communities.

Unfortunately, ethical dilemmas in both large and small organizations are not rare. As white-collar crime continues to rise, those who work in management accounting are often confronted with ethical issues on the job and need to be prepared to deal with them on a rational basis. A sampling of some of the ethical dilemmas that business professionals may be exposed to are listed in Exhibit 4. If your career path leads you to the position that involves management accounting (and most management positions in an organization do somehow involve management accounting processes), you will find that dealing with these types of ethical indiscretions is often not easy. The situation is often complicated by the fact that violators are frequently people you know and work with. Further, your role as a member of the management team requires that as far as possible you work to handle questions of ethics *within* the organization. However, some occasions may require you to involve outside authorities. The Institute of Management Accountants (IMA) is the leading professional organization in North America devoted exclusively to management accounting. Its goals are to help those working in management accounting to develop both personally and professionally, by means of education, certification, and association with other business professionals. As a respected leader within the global financial community, the IMA's ethical standards provide guidance to practitioners for maintaining the highest levels of ethical conduct. Essentially, the IMA notes that its members are ethically required to (1) be competent in their profession, (2) not disclose confidential information, (3) act with both actual and apparent integrity in all situations, and (4) maintain objectivity when communicating information to decision makers. If confronted with situations that may involve ethical conflicts, the business professional should consider the following courses of action:

Exhibit 4: Ethical Dilemmas Faced by Management Accountants

> ### Ethical internal dilemmas
> - Padding expense accounts
> - Theft in the workplace
> - Inflating profits on financial reports
> - Violating a firm's purchasing policies
> - Understating or postponing recognition of costs to achieve higher bonuses or make the financial statements look better
> - Using company assets for personal use
>
> ### Ethical issues involving third-party transactions
> - Bid rigging to give business to favored suppliers
> - Taking kickbacks on purchase contracts
> - Adjusting inspection reports to reflect higher quality of product
> - Withholding unfavorable information

(1) Discuss the problem with the immediate supervisor (only when the supervisor is involved should higher management levels be involved). (2) Confidentially use an objective advisor to help clarify the issues. (3) Resign from the organization and submit an informative report to an appropriate representative of the organization (after exhausting all levels of internal communication).[3]

Although the IMA has a formal code of ethics, there really isn't a perfect set of rules you can follow to help you resolve every conflict. Therefore, you need to be developing values and skills right now in order to prepare for future challenges. To help you, we have included at the end of each chapter at least one ethics case. Perhaps more than anything else you do, developing a commitment to and an understanding of good ethics will develop you into a great business professional and will help improve our society.

TO SUMMARIZE: Management accounting plays a key role in organizations today. The chief accountant in most organizations is the controller. This person is ultimately responsible for the quality of the management accounting used in the organization. The fact that management accounting provides a wide variety of information critical to many decisions means that those involved with creating this information will occasionally confront ethical issues inside the organization. Hence, these business professionals need to anticipate and be prepared to deal with various ethical dilemmas. The Institute of Management Accountants provides standards of ethical conduct to help guide professionals involved in management accounting processes.

In Conclusion—The Management Process

We have focused this chapter around DUPONT and the way this company uses management accounting to provide managers with information that has competitive value. To accomplish this, however, those who use management accounting must understand the types of decisions being made and how these decisions affect management of a successful organization. In particular, we've introduced a number of important accounting terms in the context of the management process of planning, controlling, and evaluating. Throughout the remainder of this text, we'll continue to organize management accounting topics around this management process.

r eview of learning objectives

1 **Understand the essential differences between management accounting and financial accounting.** Management accounting as we know it today is a product of managers and owners reacting to competitive forces. At the turn of the twentieth century, the DUPONT CORPORATION combined many management accounting innovations into a new performance evaluation model based on the return on investment (ROI) measure. Hence, the development trend of management accounting is in contrast to the legislative and regulatory forces that define financial accounting.

2 **Understand that successfully managing a company requires good information that supports effective planning, controlling, and evaluating processes.** Planning involves both long-term planning such as strategic planning and capital budgeting and short-term planning involving

---

[3] A more complete description of the IMA's "Standards of Ethical Conduct" can be viewed at the following URL: **http://www.imanet.org/ima/sec.asp?TRACKID=&CID=191&DID=323**

production and process prioritizing as well as operational budgeting. Effective control of costs in the organization requires good tracking of actual performance. Evaluating involves analyzing results, providing feedback to managers and other employees, rewarding performance, and identifying problems. Evaluating naturally leads management back to the planning process, illustrating the interrelationship of the management process.

3 **Describe how the concepts of fixed and variable costs are used in C-V-P analysis in the management planning process.** It is important to understand how accounting terminology must change to support specific management settings. In the context of cost-volume-profit (C-V-P) analysis, costs are classified as variable costs or fixed costs. Using this classification, C-V-P analysis then follows a formula approach to determine the sales volumes necessary to achieve a specified profit level.

4 **Realize how the product cost classifications of direct materials, direct labor, and overhead are used in the management controlling process.** For manufacturing firms, product costs include direct materials, direct labor, and manufacturing overhead. In a merchandising company, product costs are costs incurred to purchase goods and get them ready for resale. For service firms, product costs are costs of providing services to customers. These costs are used to determine both asset values on the balance sheet and costs of goods sold on the income statement. In contrast to product costs, period costs are used strictly to compute the selling and general administrative expenses on the income statement. The process of identifying, tracking, and controlling product costs requires an intelligent method of allocating overhead costs to goods and services.

5 **Understand the concepts of direct, indirect, and opportunity costs in the management evaluating process.** Costs can be distinguished as being direct or indirect depending on their relationship to a particular segment being evaluated. Essentially, all costs that would be eliminated if the business discontinued the segment are considered the direct costs of that particular segment. Other costs currently allocated to the segment being considered for removal that would essentially shift to other segments are indirect costs. Sunk costs are those costs in the organization that no reasonable decision of any kind can avoid. These costs are essentially irrelevant to any decisions in the organization. On the other hand, opportunity costs, which are rarely tracked in the formal accounting system, are nearly always relevant to decisions.

6 **Understand that management accounting still continues to evolve.** As competition has increased and markets have become more sophisticated, management accounting today is expanding beyond cost management to include performance measures of quality and timeliness.

7 **Discuss the need for ethics in management accounting and describe the Standards of Ethical Conduct that apply to this profession.** The process of management accounting is critical in most organizations. Therefore, those involved in this process must conduct themselves professionally at all times and be prepared to deal with ethical dilemmas. The Institute of Management Accountants (IMA) has a code of ethical conduct that establishes an expectation of competence, confidentiality, integrity, and objectivity.

k ey terms & concepts

capital budgeting, 759
controlling, 761
cost-volume-profit (C-V-P) analysis, 762
cycle time, 774
differential costs, 770
direct costs, 769
direct labor, 767
direct materials, 767

evaluating, 761
fixed costs, 763
indirect costs, 769
indirect labor, 767
indirect materials, 767
just-in-time (JIT), 773
manufacturing overhead, 767
operational budgeting, 761
opportunity costs, 771

out-of-pocket costs, 771
period costs, 765
planning, 759
product costs, 764
production prioritizing, 760
return on investment (ROI), 757
strategic planning, 759
sunk costs, 770
variable costs, 762

discussion questions

1. The chapter states that the focus of management accounting is to create information to fill a competitive need. Explain how management accounting can provide a competitive edge in business.
2. How can management accounting information help companies to be competitive and profitable?
3. What exactly did Donaldson Brown, the accountant for DuPont, develop, and why was it so revolutionary?
4. Management accounting and financial accounting provide different information for different purposes. Explain what this means and provide an example that illustrates the differences between management and financial accounting.
5. Managers need not be concerned about external financial statements. Do you agree or disagree with this statement? Explain.
6. Why is GAAP so important for external financial reporting but not for internal management reporting?
7. Identify the three management functions relating to the decision-making process. Briefly define each function.
8. How is strategic planning related to capital budgeting?
9. How do variable costs and fixed costs differ? Give an example of each.
10. Analyze your personal expenses on a variable and fixed basis. What are some of your personal fixed costs and variable costs? What would cause them to change?
11. What is C-V-P analysis used for? In the process of using C-V-P analysis, what does it mean to "break even"?
12. Explain the difference between a product cost and a period cost.
13. What are the three components of manufacturing costs? Briefly describe them.
14. How do nonmanufacturing costs and indirect costs differ?
15. What classification determines whether materials used in the production of a product are direct materials or indirect materials? Is the classification always simple to determine? What are some examples of direct materials and indirect materials used in the production of a chair?
16. What are some of the major challenges in tracking and controlling manufacturing overhead costs?
17. What is the difference between a direct cost and an indirect cost? Give an example of each in the context of teaching an accounting class at your school.
18. What is the difference between sunk costs and differential costs? Give an example of each.
19. How can out-of-pocket costs and opportunity costs be applied to your personal financial decisions?

practice exercises

Practice 15-1

Management Accounting and Financial Accounting
Which one of the following is correct?

a. Management accounting reports are usually available to the public.
b. Management accounting is legislated and governed by regulatory agencies.
c. Financial accounting focuses primarily on qualitative company data.
d. Financial accounting exists to serve the competitive needs of an organization.
e. Management accounting evolves from the best practices of managers working within their companies.

Practice 15-2

DuPont's Development of ROI (Return on Investment)
Which one of the following statements best describes the reason DuPont developed return on investment (ROI) into an important management technique?

a. A bankruptcy court trustee required DuPont to improve its management practices.
b. Antitrust legislation passed at the turn of the twentieth century required all corporations to adopt ROI.
c. DuPont was concerned about competition from low-cost foreign imports.

(continued)

d. DuPont needed a technique for comparing the operating performance of its different business divisions.
e. DuPont needed a technique for evaluating the performance of its stock market investment portfolio.

| Practice 15-3 | **Management Accounting and Financial Accounting**
Which one of the following is incorrect?

a. Management accounting is not as important as financial accounting for the competitive success of a company.
b. Governments do not require a company to implement a good management accounting system.
c. Management accounting systems evolve over time to adapt to the needs of a company.
d. Financial accounting provides a common reporting platform to the public.
e. A company often regards a good management accounting system as a valuable company secret.

| Practice 15-4 | **Primary Management Functions**
The three primary management functions are:

a. Planning, surveying, and competing.
b. Planning, evaluating, and aerating.
c. Planning, controlling, and evaluating.
d. Planning, controlling, and competing.
e. Planning, competing, and evaluating.

| Practice 15-5 | **Planning**
Which one of the following is correct?

a. Short-run planning includes capital budgeting and operational budgeting.
b. Long-run planning includes production and process prioritizing.
c. Long-run planning includes strategic planning and capital budgeting.
d. Short-run planning includes strategic planning, and production and process prioritizing.
e. Long-run planning includes capital budgeting and operational budgeting.

| Practice 15-6 | **Controlling**
Which one of the following is a correct description of "controlling" in a management accounting context?

a. Deciding on the acquisition of long-term assets
b. The real-time, day-to-day management of a company's business processes
c. Identifying a company's mission and the goals flowing from that mission
d. Prioritizing the production potential of an organization through cost-volume-profit analysis
e. Communicating daily, weekly, and monthly goals

| Practice 15-7 | **Evaluating**
Which of the following is *not* an example of evaluating?

a. Comparing actual costs and budgeted costs
b. Budgeting costs between various departments
c. Assessing the performance of products and services
d. Analyzing profitability of different products
e. Identifying problems in the production process

| Practice 15-8 | **Fixed Costs and Variable Costs**
Which of the following is an example of a variable cost?

a. Insurance premium for fire insurance on the factory building

b. The salary of the company president
c. Wood used to make custom tables
d. Rent for use of a storage warehouse
e. Depreciation on the factory building

Practice 15-9

Computing the Break-Even Point
Using the following data, compute the company's break-even point in terms of the number of units.

Sales price per unit	$	240
Variable cost per unit		165
Total monthly fixed costs		187,500

Practice 15-10

Product and Period Costs
Which one of the following is an example of a product cost for a manufacturing company?

a. Office supplies at corporate headquarters
b. Wages paid to office staff
c. Wages paid to factory workers
d. Fire insurance premium on office building
e. Commissions paid to salespeople

Practice 15-11

Types of Product Costs
Which one of the following statements is incorrect?

a. Manufacturing overhead includes all direct material and direct labor costs.
b. Indirect materials include those materials that become part of the product but cannot be traced to specific products.
c. Direct labor includes the wages paid to factory workers who do the actual assembly of a product.
d. Direct materials include those materials that become part of the product and can be traced to specific products.
e. Indirect labor includes the salaries of manufacturing supervisors.

Practice 15-12

Computing the Cost of a Manufactured Product
The company manufactures filing cabinets. The company's costs are as follows:

Direct materials	$22.30 per unit
Direct labor	$46.25 per unit
Variable manufacturing overhead	$9.34 per unit
Fixed manufacturing overhead	$1,000,000 per year
Administrative costs	$750,000 per year

In an average year, the company manufactures 40,000 units.
What is the variable cost to manufacture each filing cabinet?

Practice 15-13

Direct and Indirect Costs
Which one of the following statements best explains why companies want to distinguish between direct and indirect costs?

a. To evaluate business segments on the basis of only those costs directly traceable to each segment
b. To better determine whether a company is a large organization or a small organization
c. To determine the sales prices necessary to break even
d. To better distinguish between variable and fixed costs for each product
e. To better distinguish between materials costs and labor costs

Practice 15-14

Differential Costs and Sunk Costs
Which one of the following statements is incorrect?

a. Sunk costs should be irrelevant in decision making.
b. Differential costs are the costs a company considers when making decisions.
c. Differential costs cannot be reasonably changed by a company.
d. Sunk costs are costs made in the past that do not pertain to future decisions.
e. Differential costs are sometimes called avoidable costs.

Practice 15-15

Out-of-Pocket Costs and Opportunity Costs
Which one of the following is an example of an opportunity cost?

a. Revenue lost from sale of cakes by deciding to sell only cookies
b. Wages paid to construction workers
c. Materials used to assemble computers
d. Ordering costs related to a customer's special order of guitar strings
e. Rent paid for the use of a factory building

Practice 15-16

Expanding Management Accounting
Which one of the following statements is incorrect?

a. Management accountants can add value to an organization by giving insights related to the strategic performance measures of cost, quality, and time.
b. In today's business environment, accountants should not focus only on cost issues.
c. Management accounting is constantly evolving, so accountants need to show innovation to keep up with the many changes.
d. Although it is an old technique, the use of return on investment (ROI) analysis is still sufficient to give most companies a competitive edge over their competitors.
e. Balanced scorecards combine cost, quality, and time data.

Practice 15-17

Ethics in Management Accounting
Which one of the following statements is correct?

a. The Institute of Management Accountants has implemented a perfect set of rules to resolve every conflict.
b. The top accountant in most large organizations is usually called the controller.
c. Upon discovering an ethical dilemma in an organization, a management accountant's first responsibility is to notify outside authorities and government officials.
d. Ethical dilemmas in both large and small organizations are rare.
e. The chief executive officer (CEO) in a company typically reports to the company's chief financial officer (CFO).

e xercises

Exercise 15-1

Changes in Business Affecting Management Accounting
You are at the student union having lunch with a friend who is attending law school. In the course of your conversation, you tell your friend that, in contrast to financial accounting or tax accounting, management accounting has "competitive value" and is highly proprietary. Further, management accounting is more important in business today than ever before, and only those organizations that best control costs and improve quality are competitive. Your friend asks you two questions:

1. What do you mean by "competitive value"?
2. Why is it more important for accountants to provide useful information to management to-day than it was before?

Exercise 15-2

Characteristics of Accounting Reports

Indicate whether each of the following is characteristic of financial accounting reports, management accounting reports, or both:

1. They are used primarily by creditors and investors.
2. They aid management in identifying problems.
3. They are based on generally accepted accounting principles.
4. They are standardized across companies.
5. They provide information for decision making by management.
6. They measure performance and isolate differences between planned and actual results.
7. They are created based on competitive needs that are unique to the organization.

Exercise 15-3

Financial and Management Accounting

A friend who is thinking about majoring in accounting has asked you to distinguish between the work of financial accounting and management accounting. What is your response?

Exercise 15-4

Period Costs and Product Costs

Bright, Inc., a producer of educational toys for children, incurs the following types of costs:

a. Depreciation on the production plant
b. Depreciation on the corporate offices
c. Paper, toner, and miscellaneous supplies for the office copy machines
d. Wages of production-line employees
e. Raw materials used in the production of toys
f. Wages of the corporate headquarters' secretarial staff
g. Maintenance costs on the production equipment
h. Advertising costs
i. Shipping costs for products sold
j. Salaries of plant supervisors
k. Interest on bank loans
l. Property tax on the production plant
m. Property tax on the corporate offices
n. Commissions paid to sales personnel
o. Administrative salaries of corporate executives

Classify each cost as a period cost or a product cost. For each item classified as a product cost, indicate whether it would usually be included in direct materials, direct labor, or manufacturing overhead.

Exercise 15-5

Spreadsheet

Manufacturing Costs

Jordan Industries is a manufacturing company that produces solid oak office furniture. During the year, the following costs were incurred. The building depreciation and the utilities are allocated three-fourths to production and one-fourth to administration. The cost of furniture parts can be traced to specific production runs.

Oak wood	$ 50,000
Miscellaneous supplies (glue, saw blades, varnish, etc.)	10,000
Furniture parts (wheels, locks, etc.)	5,500
Payroll—plant manager's salary	25,000
Payroll—administrative salaries	100,000
Payroll—production-line employees' wages	45,500
Building depreciation	28,000
Maintenance—plant and equipment	5,000
Utilities	16,000
Income taxes	8,500

(continued)

1. Classify the costs into the following four categories: direct materials, direct labor, manufacturing overhead, and period costs.
2. Calculate the total amount of cost for each category.

Exercise 15-6

Manufacturing and Nonmanufacturing Costs

The Benson Manufacturing Company produces rides for amusement parks. Parts for the rides are purchased from other suppliers. Rides are then assembled in various company plants.

Recently, Benson Manufacturing hired two new employees. One will be working in an assembly plant, and the other will be working in the marketing division of the corporate offices as a sales representative.

The assembly plant employee will be paid an annual salary of $34,000, or $17.00 per hour. Her time will be charged to the individual rides that she assembles. The marketing division employee will receive an annual salary of $30,000 plus commission. He will be responsible for both advertising and selling. His salary is for advertising responsibilities, and he will be paid a commission on sales of amusement rides.

1. Should the salary of the assembly plant employee be classified as a manufacturing or a nonmanufacturing cost? Should the salary of the marketing division employee be classified as a manufacturing or a nonmanufacturing cost? How is this classification made?
2. After classifying the salaries as manufacturing or nonmanufacturing costs, determine how the salary costs will affect the cost of assembling the amusement rides. Classify the employee costs as direct, indirect, fixed, variable, product, or period. (Each cost can be classified in more than one way.)

Exercise 15-7

Performance Measurement

The president of Radkline Corporation, Karen Pinkus, has asked you, the company's controller, to advise her on whether Radkline should develop a new inventory management system. Is the decision facing Karen Pinkus an example of a strategic planning decision, a capital budgeting decision, a production prioritization decision, or an operational budgeting decision? Be sure to defend your answer.

Exercise 15-8

Cost Classifications

The following are costs associated with manufacturing firms, merchandising firms, or service firms:

a. Miscellaneous materials used in production
b. Salesperson's commission in a real estate firm
c. Administrators' salaries for a furniture wholesaler
d. Administrators' salaries for a furniture manufacturer
e. Freight costs associated with acquiring inventories for a grocery store
f. Office manager's salary in a doctor's office
g. Utilities for the corporate offices of a toy manufacturer
h. Line supervisor's salary for a clothing manufacturing firm
i. Training seminar for sales staff of a service firm
j. Fuel used in a trucking firm
k. Paper used at a printing business
l. Oil for machinery at a plastics manufacturing firm
m. Food used at a restaurant
n. Windshields used for a car manufacturer

Classify the costs as (1) product or period; (2) variable or fixed; and (3) for those that are product costs, as direct materials, direct labor, or manufacturing overhead. Write "not applicable (N/A)" if a category doesn't apply.

Exercise 15-9

Cost Classifications

The following are costs associated with manufacturing firms, merchandising firms, or service firms:

a. Legal services for an accounting firm
b. Car leases for company management
c. Oil used to service manufacturing equipment
d. Office supplies for a grocery store
e. Entertainment expense for clients
f. Travel expenses for doctors in a medical firm
g. Plastic used in making computers
h. Collection costs of accounts receivable
i. Electricity to run saws at a lumber yard
j. Food for a company banquet
k. Advertising expense
l. Continuing education for a doctor
m. Commissions paid to salespersons
n. Depreciation on sports equipment by a professional football team
o. Calculators used by office employees
p. Fuel used in baggage transporters at an airport
q. Toll charges incurred because of business travel
r. Fuel used in manufacturing equipment

Classify the costs as (1) product or period; (2) variable or fixed; and (3) for those that are product costs, as direct materials, direct labor, or manufacturing overhead. Write "not applicable (N/A)" if a category doesn't apply.

Exercise 15-10

C-V-P Analysis

Tyrell, Inc., located in Sacramento, California, manufactures high-end baby chairs. The firm's cost accountant, Lisa, has been assigned by the CEO to determine how many baby chairs Tyrell, Inc., needs to make to break even. She is given the following data:

Baby chair sales price	$ 15
Variable cost per baby chair	7
Production worker salary	1,600

Determine how many baby chairs Tyrell, Inc., needs to make to break even.

Exercise 15-11

Spreadsheet

C-V-P Analysis

The DALLAS MAVERICKS basketball team has hired you as its new accountant. On your first day on the job, Mavericks' owner, Mark Cuban, comes to you and asks, "How many tickets must we sell to pay for Michael Finley's salary?" He then hands you a sheet of paper with the following information:

Michael Finley's salary	$12,000,000
Average ticket price	80
Printing cost of one ticket	1

1. Prepare your response to Mark's question.
2. How many tickets would the Mavericks have to sell to pay for the entire Mavericks team if the total team salary (including Finley) is $80,000,000?

Exercise 15-12

C-V-P Analysis

In the text you used accounting data on DUPONT's Kevlar product line to compute the number of pounds sold of Kevlar in order for DuPont to break even on this product line. Similar data on DuPont's Teflon product line are provided on the following page.

(continued)

Wholesale price	$145.00 per gallon
Variable cost	$60.30 per gallon
Total monthly fixed costs	$9,630,000

1. How many gallons of Teflon does DuPont need to sell each month in order to break even?
2. Assume that DuPont is considering a significant change to the Teflon production process. As a result of this change, variable costs would increase to $64.60, but monthly fixed costs would be reduced to $8,100,000. Recompute the number of gallons that need to be sold each month in order to break even if these changes are made. What would you recommend to DuPont?

Exercise 15-13

*S*preadsheet

Product Costing

In the text you used accounting data on DuPont's Kevlar product line to determine the total manufacturing cost to produce a pound of Kevlar. Similar data on DuPont's Teflon product line are provided below.

Direct materials	$60.00 per gallon
Direct labor	$1.80 per gallon
Manufacturing overhead:	
Variable	$3.20 per gallon
Fixed	$3,200,000 per month
General corporate sales and administrative costs	$6,400,000 per month

Following the same costing procedure as was used with the Kevlar product line, and assuming that DuPont expects to produce 100,000 gallons in the next month, what appears to be the total manufacturing cost per gallon of Teflon?

Exercise 15-14

Product Costing

BatsRUs, Inc., has created a unique line of aluminum baseball bats that, while illegal for league use, are designed to nearly double the average length of a batted ball. They are a great "hit" in the personal and family use market. Recently, a new competitor, Awesome Bats, Inc., has introduced a competing bat to the market. Suddenly, BatsRUs is experiencing severe market pressure to significantly lower its normal market price of $175. The problem is that management is not very confident about the actual production cost per bat. With some effort, the following data have been developed for management to use in setting a new market price and, more importantly, beginning an effort to better control costs.

Standard Variable Costs to Produce One Batch of 10 Bats (600 batches are typically produced each week)

	Average Cost per Pound	Average Pounds per Batch	Total Costs
Direct materials	$ 3	16	$ 48
	Average Rate per Hour	**Average Hours per Batch**	
Direct labor	$15	2	30
Variable manufacturing overhead	20	2	40
Total variable costs			$118

Standard Weekly Fixed Costs

Manufacturing overhead	$240,000
Sales and administrative costs	180,000
Total fixed costs	$420,000

1. What appears to be the average cost for BatsRUs to manufacture a single baseball bat?
2. Do you have any questions or concerns about how the data are being used to determine the cost of manufacturing a baseball bat at BatsRUs?

Exercise 15-15

Product Costing and C-V-P Analysis

Wakefield, Inc., offers a CPA review course in cities throughout the eastern United States. Wakefield hires local CPAs to do the teaching. Each instructor is paid $120 an hour to teach the course; a course consists of 12 weeks of instruction with sessions taking place four evenings a week for two hours at each session. The other instruction costs to Wakefield are to pay for hotel conference rooms to host the course. Generally, Wakefield pays the hotel $625 per evening to rent a conference room. Also, tuition for the course includes all course materials, which cost the company $180 for each student.

1. What is the product cost of providing one evening of instruction for all students?
2. What is the product cost of training a student over the entire course (there are 75 students in this particular course)?
3. Assuming that Wakefield charges each student $1,200 for the course, how many students would be required to break even on this course?

Exercise 15-16

Spreadsheet

Segment Analysis

You are the accountant for the largest manufacturer of sheet steel. The company's hottest product is the RX-6, which provides most of the firm's revenue. Management is considering dropping the RX-5 product line, which hasn't turned a profit for two consecutive years. The CFO comes to you and asks what you would do given the following data:

Operating Statements	RX-6	RX-5	Total
Batches produced and sold	200	240	
Sales revenue	$30,000	$ 43,200	$ 73,200
Direct materials	(2,000)	(8,400)	(10,400)
Direct labor	(4,000)	(7,680)	(11,680)
Variable manufacturing overhead	(1,000)	(4,800)	(5,800)
Fixed manufacturing overhead	(2,000)	(17,400)	(19,400)
Sales and administrative costs	(2,000)	(6,000)	(8,000)
Operating profit	$19,000	$ (1,080)	$ 17,920

Note: Approximately 20% of the fixed manufacturing overhead is directly related to (i.e., created within) each segment.

1. Distinguish between direct and indirect costs and find the segment profit for each product.
2. Determine the gain or loss that the firm would incur if it dropped the RX-5 product line. What figure would you provide the CFO?
3. Explain your recommendation to continue or discontinue product line RX-5.

Exercise 15-17

Opportunity Costs

Dave is employed by a company that currently pays him $65,000 per year. He owns a new car that he bought for cash of $32,500. Dave is thinking about returning to school to obtain a law degree. Tuition for the school he wants to attend is $28,000 per year, books average $1,350 per year, and room and board average $12,550 per year.

Determine the total sunk cost and the total opportunity cost for Dave if he decides to go back to law school for three years.

Exercise 15-18

Segment Analysis and Opportunity Costs

The text used accounting data to perform a segment analysis of DUPONT's Teflon product line. Assume that sales of Kevlar have dropped significantly. DuPont reported the following

(continued)

results for this product line for the past month and expects this sales pattern to continue into the future.

Operating Statements	Kevlar
Sales revenue	$ 7,500,000
Variable manufacturing costs	(2,700,000)
Fixed manufacturing overhead	(1,500,000)
Sales and administrative costs	(4,100,000)
Operating profit	$ (800,000)

1. Assume that approximately 30% of the fixed manufacturing overhead can be avoided if Kevlar is dropped. In order to determine the "true performance" of the Kevlar product line, what is its incremental segment profit or loss?
2. If DuPont were to drop the Kevlar product line and use the available resources to produce another product that provided an incremental profit of $3,500,000, what is the economic profit or loss of the Kevlar product line?

discussion cases

Case 15-1

Developing Management Accounting Information (DuPont)

The story of E. I. DU PONT DE NEMOURS AND COMPANY detailed at the beginning of this chapter provides key insights into the development of management accounting. In particular, we see how the structure of a business affects the kinds of information required for planning, controlling, and evaluating purposes. Consider the decision to expand and diversify the company by acquiring its suppliers and creating its own network of sales offices. What were the potential risks to DUPONT of this decision? What accounting information would have been required to determine if the decision to diversify was successful? Does the traditional accounting system designed to produce external financial reports provide the required information in an easily obtainable fashion?

Case 15-2

Supporting the Management Process (IBM)

INTERNATIONAL BUSINESS MACHINES CORPORATION (IBM) has faced challenges this last decade due to increased competition in the home-consumer segment of the personal computer (PC) market. When IBM introduced the PC in the early 1980s, it was a huge success. Over time, however, the PC market grew immensely, and competition began to rise.

Although the PC was initially marketed toward businesses, a home-consumer market emerged as well. In 1995, IBM, under the direction of then-CEO Louis Gerstner, set up a home-consumer PC division to augment its business PC division. IBM hoped that with the two divisions, each employing its own design, manufacturing, and marketing personnel, it could better focus on the needs of its various customers and increase total sales.

IBM's consumer division quickly developed PCs that had high customer appeal. In early 1996, the division released its "Aptiva" PC in a sleek, dark gray color. The model was equipped with many high-tech features. Also, IBM's reputation for quality allowed the consumer division to charge a higher price for the PCs. (In December 1996, IBM PCs sold for an average of $1,880, whereas other companies charged as little as $1,300 to $1,400.)

Initially, the manufacturing department in IBM's consumer division could not keep up with consumer demand. Soon, however, IBM began losing market share to companies such as DELL, COMPAQ, and GATEWAY. These companies discovered that consumers prefer low price to the extra "frills" that IBM offers in its computers. Furthermore, IBM found that many consumers were no longer willing to pay higher prices for IBM's reputation. IBM, the company that originally created and dominated the PC market, began losing market share in the PC business very fast. IBM's PC division lost almost $1 billion in 1998. In 1999, IBM reduced its PC workforce from 10,000 to approximately 9,000 employees and cut its losses down to $360 million. In early 2000, IBM unveiled a new line of sleek, stylish machines that it branded as the NetVista line of products. With these and a number of other changes in place, business finally began growing in the second half of 2000. By the fourth quarter of 2000, IBM regained enough market share to be listed as No. 5 for PC shipments in the United States.

1. Did IBM make a good decision in setting up its consumer division? How so?
2. Analyze IBM's decisions and actions involving the consumer division. Try to categorize these decisions and actions following the threefold management process of planning, controlling, and evaluating.

3. Based on the threefold management process of planning, controlling, and evaluating, where do you think IBM was weakest in its decision-making practice with respect to the consumer division? Where do you think it was strongest?
4. If you were Sam Palmisano (IBM's current CEO), what information would you want from your accountants in order to effectively plan, control, and evaluate the decision to either shut down or continue to operate a division?

Source: Raju Narisetti, "IBM to Revamp Struggling Home-PC Business," *The Wall Street Journal*, October 14, 1997; Lisa Smith, "IBM's Personal Computer Unit Makes Turnaround," *The Herald-Sun*, March 22, 2001.

judgment calls

Judgment 15-1

You Decide: When allocating costs, if you don't know where costs should be allocated, should you take time to figure out if the costs relate to materials or labor, or should you allocate all the costs as manufacturing overhead?

It is your first day on the job at a bicycle manufacturing company. Your first job is to determine the cost of a new line of bikes. After reviewing all the cost information, your boss says, "If you don't know how to allocate a cost, just put it in manufacturing overhead. Whether it is a direct or indirect material, it will end up in the same place." Do you agree with your boss? Why or why not?

Judgment 15-2

You Decide: Should sunk costs be considered in a planning decision or ignored?

You currently work part time at a flower shop. You split your time between keeping the books and making deliveries. The van you use to make these deliveries has been in and out of the repair shop over the past two months. In addition to the engine, the transmission was just replaced. The mechanic said that the van is old enough to require constant repair. Your boss isn't too happy about all this repair work and was heard saying, "I would like to get a new van, but I can't afford it. I have invested too much money in the one we have now!" What should you tell your boss?

Competency Enhancement Opportunities

▶ **Analyzing Real Company Information**
▶ **International Case**
▶ **Ethics Case**
▶ **Writing Assignment**

▶ **The Debate**
▶ **Internet Search**

The following additional assignments provide opportunities for students to develop critical thinking, ethical perspectives, oral and written communication skills, experience with electronic research, and teamwork through group and business activities.

Analyzing Real Company Information

Analyzing 15-1 (Microsoft)

1. Bill Gates is the chairman of the Board for MICROSOFT, and Steve Ballmer is the CEO. Together, they are committed to investing heavily in the future. In 2002, Microsoft spent $4.3 billion on research and development for the products of tomorrow, probably more than any company in the world. Since 1997, Microsoft has increased its R&D spending by nearly 225%! R&D is currently more than 27% of its current operating expenses. Microsoft clearly spends a lot of money on R&D. What are the potential advantages and disadvantages of this cost commitment to R&D?

2. A large part of Microsoft's R&D expenditures is for outside software developers who contract with Microsoft to work on specific projects. What factors does Microsoft need to consider in deciding to assign a research project to an outside contractor rather than to its internal software development staff?

Analyzing 15-2 (DuPont)

As described in the chapter, the challenge facing DUPONT in the early twentieth century was how to manage the diverse set of businesses operating under the control of the DuPont management team. This diversity still exists today. In its 2002 annual report, DuPont notes that its strategic business units (operating segments) are organized by product line. For purposes of financial reporting, these have been aggregated into eight reportable segments: Agriculture & Nutrition, Coatings & Color Technologies, Electronic & Communication Technologies, Performance Materials, Pharmaceuticals, Safety & Protection, Textiles & Interiors, and Other.

Summary segment results for 2002 for six of these eight segments are as follows (dollars in millions):

	Agriculture & Nutrition	Coatings & Color Technologies	Electronic & Communication Technologies	Performance Materials	Safety & Protection	Textiles & Interiors
Total revenue	$4,510	$5,026	$2,540	$4,868	$3,438	$6,279
After-tax operating income	443	483	217	476	490	72
Identifiable assets at December 31, 2002	5,963	3,235	2,190	3,254	1,942	5,598

1. Which segment has the highest return on investment? The lowest?
2. How could the segment with the lowest return on investment improve its financial performance?

International Case

International

Toyota

TOYOTA MOTOR CORPORATION was the company that originally defined and implemented the just-in-time (JIT) management technique mentioned in this chapter. Toyota was started in 1918 by Sakichi Toyoda as the TOYOTA SPINNING AND WEAVING COMPANY; in fact, a subsidiary of Toyota still makes spinning and weaving equipment today. By 1995, Toyota was the third-largest motor vehicle producer in the world, manufacturing 4,512,076 vehicles (behind GENERAL MOTORS at 7,997,794 and FORD at 6,401,495). In January 1997, Toyota made its 100 millionth vehicle. Despite a difficult world economy since 2000, Toyota has continued to prosper. In 2002, consolidated net income rose 29%, to 1,094 billion yen ($8,207 million). In the 2002 annual report, Fujio Cho, president of Toyota, noted three main factors behind his company's strong financial performance in 2002. First, Toyota sold more vehicles than ever in North America, reaching 1.78 million units. Second, efforts to reduce costs through partnership with suppliers began to generate tangible results. Finally, a favorable foreign exchange rate contributed to financial performance.

1. Toyota attributes its 29% increase in net income to three factors: growth in sales volume, cost savings, and the weakening of the yen (which makes its cars cheaper in North America). Consider conducting a performance evaluation on the following people, and decide which of the three factors should be considered in the evaluation of:
    a. an assembly-line worker
    b. a factory manager
    c. a sales manager
    d. the company president

2. In relation to its cost savings, Toyota reports that the savings stem from improvements in engineering design, improvements in manufacturing processes, and improved logistics. Consider conducting a performance evaluation on the following people, and decide which (and why!) of the three cost savings factors should be considered in the evaluation of:
    a. an assembly-line worker
    b. a factory manager
    c. a purchasing manager
    d. the company president

▶ *Ethics Case*

Whom to Tell about Medicare Overbilling

Professor Mary Allen is sitting in her office one day when Mark Sullivan, an accounting graduate from five years ago, knocks on her door. Mark had been an exceptionally good student and had started with the CPA firm Peat & Price upon graduation. After three years with that firm, he joined MiniCare Health Company as the chief accountant and is now serving as its controller. Mark asks if he can talk with Professor Allen in confidence and then tells her that he has a problem: "Two years ago, I started working for MiniCare. Not long after I was promoted to controller, I noticed that the officers of the company were doing things that I didn't think were right. They have overbilled Medicare on several occasions, and senior management executives are misusing their positions by taking company perks that are against the company code of ethics. I have talked to my superior, the financial vice president, and he has, in essence, told me to mind my own business—that accountants are to report results and assist management, not question them."

Mark informs Professor Allen that he is making $110,000 a year, far more than he could earn in another company at this stage in his career. He asks for her advice. What should Professor Allen recommend that he do? Should Mark quit his job? Should he talk to someone else? If so, who? Should he go public with his information?

▶ *Writing Assignment*

Sunk Costs: They May Be Sunk, but They Aren't Forgotten

You are the manager of the tire manufacturing subdivision of Uniyear Diversified Products. Last year, you were successful in convincing corporate executives that your division needed to purchase a new warehouse facility costing $40 million to house raw materials. You argued at the time that you could be much more productive if delays in getting materials from suppliers could be eliminated.

During the past 18 months, your company has worked hard to adopt JIT inventory and total quality control. You have successfully placed online terminals at key supplier locations, and the lag time in getting the raw materials you need has dropped from an average of four weeks to six hours.

Your problem now is that you no longer need the $40 million warehouse. It is a sunk cost. However, you are afraid that if you reveal that fact to the corporate executives, they will penalize or even fire you for being so shortsighted.

Draft a one-page memo to the president of Uniyear Diversified Products that explains why the $40 million warehouse is no longer needed. Remember that the memo has two purposes: to inform the president that the warehouse is no longer needed and to do so in a way that doesn't cost you your job.

▷ *The Debate*

When Should You Surrender?

You are a partner in a CPA firm. For over 15 years, you conducted the audit of XYZ Corporation. Three years ago, however, the company went bankrupt. To your surprise, a class-action lawsuit was filed against your firm for $5 million, alleging that you failed to warn stockholders that the company was in financial difficulty. Your audit fee for XYZ Corporation was only $15,000 per year. Thus far you have spent $957,000 on legal fees and expert witness costs. Your attorney has worked out a settlement that would involve you paying the plaintiffs $750,000. You believe your defense is excellent, that the quality of your audits of XYZ Corporation was high, and that you will win the lawsuit. However, you also believe that it will cost another $900,000 in legal fees to successfully defend the case. Should you settle?

Divide your group into two teams.

- One team represents the "Fight to the Death" group. Prepare a two-minute oral presentation supporting the notion that you should not pay a penny to settle the lawsuit when you know that you did nothing wrong. You believe that the best long-run business strategy is to vigorously fight every lawsuit in order to discourage future suits.
- The other team represents the "Cut Our Losses" group. Prepare a two-minute oral presentation arguing that the past litigation costs are sunk and that the only reasonable comparison is between the cost of settling now and the cost of continuing the lawsuit.

▷ *Internet Search*

DuPont

Access DUPONT's Web site at **http://www.dupont.com**. Sometimes Web addresses change, so if this DuPont address doesn't work, access the Web site for this textbook (**http://albrecht .swlearning.com**) for an updated link to DuPont.

Once you've gained access to DuPont's Web site, answer the following questions:

1. Click on the "DuPont Overview" tab. Who is the current chief executive officer (CEO) of DuPont? How long has he or she been with the company? What is his or her background (e.g., legal, accounting, engineering, etc.)?
2. As mentioned in the chapter, the DuPont organization includes many diverse types of businesses. DuPont also has a strong commitment to diversity among its employees, including

the members of its Board of Directors. Click on the "DuPont Overview" tab. What is the current state of diversity within DuPont's outside directors?

3. The history of DuPont, and some of its well-known products, is summarized in the chapter. DuPont's Web site offers further information. Click on the "Consumer Solutions" tab. How does CoolMax® work? How does Kevlar® compare to steel?

4. DuPont reports a corporate commitment to community outreach. Click on the "Social Commitment" tab. What are the three focus areas of DuPont's community outreach?

chapter

16

Analyzing Cost-Volume-Profit Relationships

Learning Objectives

After studying this chapter, you should be able to:

1 Understand the key factors involved in cost-volume-profit (C-V-P) analysis and why it is such an important tool in management decision making.

2 Explain and analyze the basic cost behavior patterns—variable, fixed, stepped, and mixed.

3 Analyze mixed costs using the scattergraph and high-low methods.

4 Perform C-V-P analyses, and describe the effects potential changes in C-V-P variables have on company profitability.

5 Visualize C-V-P relationships using graphs.

6 Identify the limiting assumptions of C-V-P analysis, and explain the issues of quality and time relative to C-V-P analysis decisions.

e**X**panded
▲ ▲ *Material*

7 Analyze mixed costs using the least squares method.

8 Explain the effects of sales mix on profitability.

9 Describe how fixed and variable costs differ in manufacturing, service, merchandising, and e-commerce organizations, and illustrate these differences with the operating leverage concept.

chapter 16

If you've ever watched an international-caliber soccer match, you know that goals are scarce. Each goal requires extensive work, patient play, and many attempts. This same approach seems to apply to the business of professional soccer in the United States where MAJOR LEAGUE SOCCER (MLS) completed its seventh season in the United States in 2002. The year 2002 was a banner year for U.S. soccer with the men's national soccer team reaching new heights by finally cracking the Top 10 of the FIFA World Rankings and competing in the quarterfinals of the World Cup in Korea/Japan (after taking last place at the previous World Cup tournament). This followed on the momentum generated by the U.S. women's team, which won the World Cup in 1999 and placed third in the world in 2003. Nevertheless, MLS has so far been unable to score financially in America where sports fans continue to prefer attending basketball, football, and even baseball games to watching the most popular sport in the (rest of the) world.

Professional soccer has been launched several times in the United States amid much fanfare, but so far each attempt has failed. The last failure, that of the NORTH AMERICAN SOCCER LEAGUE (NASL)—which brought Pelé, Cruyff, Best, and Beckenbauer to the United States in the early 1970s—was especially painful because, with the big names, professional soccer looked so promising. One of the major reasons previous efforts failed is that fixed costs were too high for the small number of fans and meager TV revenues. Each attempt ended up with the team owners losing money. To better manage player salaries, which are a significant part of the fixed costs of running a soccer team, the MLS set up an unusual single-entity structure in 1996, under which the league owns all the teams as well as all player contracts, and investors buy operating rights rather than setting up franchises. The purpose of this structure is to eliminate the financial disparities between large and small markets and to control player salaries and other fixed costs. This approach has successfully kept players' salaries low; so low in fact that a number of players have filed class action lawsuits arguing the MLS structure is holding down salaries in violation of U.S. antitrust laws.

Despite these efforts to contain the fixed cost of players' salaries, MLS teams continue to lose millions of dollars, largely due to their inability to generate enough revenue from ticket sales alone to cover another significant fixed cost, the cost of the leases on the stadiums in which they play their games. And while the cost of these lease payments is high, the larger problem is that soccer teams forced to rent their facilities are only able to keep the revenue from ticket sales and are generally cut off from the all-important ancillary revenue that accompanies each game—revenue from concessions, parking, merchandise, stadium signage and naming rights, and luxury boxes.

The situation faced currently by Nick Sakiewicz, general manager of the METROSTARS in New Jersey, is pretty typical of the rest of the league. New Jersey has long been a hotbed of soccer in America, from producing three of the greatest American players of all-time (Tab Ramos, John Harkes, and Tony Meola) to being home to the winningest high school soccer coach in U.S. history (Gene Chyzowych of Columbia High School). Nonetheless, the MetroStars can't seem to break even financially. Part of this shortfall stems from the $1.5 million annual rent the MetroStars must pay to use Giants Stadium at the Meadowlands. Worse, the Meadowlands stadium is also used by two NFL teams (the GIANTS and the JETS), the New Jersey State Fair, and multiple concerts, which means that the MetroStars can only play one or two home games each month in June and July. With most of the home games being played in April and May, average attendance is not as high as it could be (attendance in 2002 averaged just 19,000 per game). Hence, the team loses millions of dollars every year.

General Manager Nick Sakiewicz is convinced that a new stadium is crucial to the MetroStars' financial success. At an estimated cost of $152 million, Sakiewicz wants to build a roofed, 25,000-seat stadium in Harrison City (also in New Jersey) to be located in a vast complex that would include residential housing, retail space, and a shopping center. And although he believes that more people would buy a ticket to come see the MetroStars play in their own stadium, what makes the construction proposal most attractive is the ancillary revenue that would finally belong to the team because it would own the stadium. It is estimated that a crowd of 20,000 can generate an extra $100,000 in profit from concessions, parking, and so forth. Sakiewicz believes strongly that those kinds of numbers will move his soccer team beyond the break-even point and into profitability.[1]

---

1 John McLaughlin, *Sky*, October 1997, pp. 27-32; Ridge Mahoney, "Homes of Their Own," July 30, 2001, **http://www.si.com**; Chris Isidore, "New Homes Get Old Quickly," July 27, 2001, **http://www.cnnmoney.com**; and the homepage for the MetroStars, **http://www.metrostars.com**.

n the previous chapter, we discussed different ways to categorize costs, and we briefly illustrated how you can use these cost categories to make management decisions. We also emphasized the fact that management accounting is defined as all accounting information that is useful in planning, controlling, and evaluating an organization. Some costs, such as direct materials and direct labor costs in a manufacturing firm, increase in direct proportion to the number of products or services produced. These are called variable costs. Other costs, such as factory rent, remain the same no matter what the level of production is. These are called fixed costs. We used these definitions of variable costs and fixed costs in the previous chapter to introduce you to **cost-volume-profit (C-V-P) analysis**, a critical tool in the management process. C-V-P analysis is used to make important planning decisions concerning appropriate levels of production and spending. C-V-P analysis allows a manager to answer the very important question: How much do I need to sell in order to earn a profit?

In this chapter, you will further explore the C-V-P analysis tool to analyze relationships between variable costs, fixed costs, and revenues. You will learn that successful managers must think carefully about **cost behavior**—how costs change in relation to changes in activity levels, such as the number of patients in a hospital or the pounds of ore processed in a copper smelter. An understanding of how costs behave in relation to levels of activity helps managers predict the effects of their plans on future performance. In addition, because the C-V-P analysis technique is applicable to all types of firms, we will discuss the behavior of costs in manufacturing, merchandising, service, and e-commerce firms.

You will also use the knowledge of cost behavior patterns to analyze the kinds of problems facing organizations such as the MetroStars' lack of profitability as described in the opening scenario. As you work through this chapter making calculations that will determine how profits will change in relation to changes in sales volume, fixed costs, and variable costs, be sure to think about how these calculations reflect the process of managing actual organizations. For instance, because of decreased air travel in the wake of the 9/11 attacks, the airline industry has struggled to be profitable in light of the heavy fixed costs of owning and operating commercial aircraft. Many owners of retail outlets in a mall breathe a sigh of relief each month on the day when enough profit has been generated to allow them to pay the monthly fixed cost of the lease payment to the mall. The owner of a baseball team will look out over a half-filled stadium on game day and worry that the ticket sales may not have been enough to cover the costs of paying the players and running the stadium. Every business owner must carefully plan how he or she is going to generate enough money to cover the fixed costs of the business. Those who have a clear idea of exactly how many airline seats, or pairs of pants, or hot dogs must be sold to break even will be in a better position to create and maintain profitability in the organization.

We believe that the best way to appreciate the importance of good management information is to begin by using that data to make significant management planning decisions. Accordingly, this chapter will give you lots of opportunities to practice. Also note that although we will focus primarily on examining the financial implications of cost-volume-profit analysis decisions, we will also pay attention to the effects these decisions have on quality and time issues as well.

cost-volume-profit (C-V-P) analysis Techniques for determining how changes in revenues, costs, and level of activity affect the profitability of an organization.

cost behavior The way a cost is affected by changes in activity levels.

Understanding Why C-V-P Analysis Is Important

I Understand the key factors involved in cost-volume-profit (C-V-P) analysis and why it is such an important tool in management decision making.

Management must make many critical operating decisions that affect a firm's profitability. With respect to planning, management is often interested in the impact a particular action will have on profitability. C-V-P analysis can help managers assess that impact. The following are examples of questions that can be answered with C-V-P analysis:

- When planning whether or not to open a scuba shop in the mall, how many customers will need to be served each month in order to break even and be able to pay the monthly store rental fee?

- How will the profits of a bookstore be affected if the store raises its prices by 10%, resulting in a reduction of 2% in the number of books sold?
- How many carpets must a fledgling entrepreneur clean in a month in order to generate a net profit of $3,000 each month?
- By how much will the profits of a discount electronics store change if a $100,000 advertising campaign increases the number of computers sold by 13%?
- How will the profits of a fast-food restaurant change if the restaurant stops selling milk shakes and instead focuses on raising the volume of soft drink sales by 25%?

It should be clear to you from these examples that C-V-P analysis involves studying the interrelationships among revenues, costs, levels of activity, and profits. However, quality of products and services and speed of production and delivery must also be considered as managers use C-V-P analysis to determine product prices, the mix of products, market strategy, appropriate sales commissions, advertising budgets, production schedules, and a host of other important planning decisions. Although C-V-P analysis is most useful for planning, it can also be used to assist with controlling decisions (e.g., are the costs too high for the level of sales?) and evaluating decisions (e.g., should we reward employees for holding costs down or be concerned that sales growth has slowed?). In fact, a lot of what is done in management accounting involves some aspect of C-V-P analysis because of the tremendous potential it has to help management increase the profitability and effectiveness of an organization. For this reason, as you use this chapter to learn the mechanics of C-V-P analysis, be sure to see how important it is to be able to understand and manage costs. As you study C-V-P analysis, you will gain a better understanding of basic cost behavior patterns. And once you understand these cost behavior patterns and how to work with them, you can use them to make effective planning, controlling, and evaluating decisions.

TO SUMMARIZE: C-V-P analysis is a very important concept in management accounting. Key factors involved in C-V-P analysis include (1) the revenues derived from the sales prices charged for goods and services, (2) the fixed and variable costs, (3) the sales volume, (4) the mix of products, (5) the speed and quality of production, and (6) the resulting profits. Understanding the interrelationships of the key variables in C-V-P analysis can assist you in planning and in making critical control and evaluation decisions.

Basic Cost Behavior Patterns

2 Explain and analyze the basic cost behavior patterns—variable, fixed, stepped, and mixed.

The two basic cost behavior patterns—variable and fixed—were introduced in the previous chapter. Other cost behavior patterns, such as mixed costs, are variations of these two. Mixed costs exhibit characteristics of both variable and fixed costs. In this section, we will review both variable and fixed costs and examine the reality of how these costs often look in many organizations. We will also introduce stepped costs and mixed costs.

A quick example of what we're talking about may be helpful before we dive into all the details of working with cost behavior. A cost may be classified as either fixed or variable by the way it reacts to changes in level of activity. Think of a doughnut shop such as KRISPY KREME or WINCHELL'S. Activity in the shop may be measured in terms of the volume of doughnuts sold, the number of customers served, the number of hours the shop is open, the number of employees, or the total square feet of the serving area, and so forth. Get the point? There are a lot of ways to measure activity in this organization. There are also a lot of different kinds of costs. The first task is to identify the costs and activities where we intend to focus our management effort. Let's say that we are initially interested in understanding how the number of doughnuts sold impacts costs and profits. Which costs will change, and which costs will not change, as we expect to sell more or less doughnuts? This is the starting point of C-V-P analysis. It seems logical that as more doughnuts are sold, the cost of doughnut ingredients will increase. This is a variable cost. On the other hand, we probably wouldn't expect the cost of property taxes to increase as more doughnuts are sold. This is a fixed cost. However, there are costs that have both variable and fixed components. For instance, the electricity costs to run the doughnut shop will increase as we sell more doughnuts because of the cost of the power to make the additional doughnuts. However, even if we don't sell any doughnuts, we will have to pay the utility costs of just keeping the shop open. Utility costs are a mixed cost. The cost of a supervisor's salary isn't normally going to increase as we sell more doughnuts *until* we have so many customers that we need to hire an additional supervisor to help with the higher volume. At this point, the fixed cost of salaries will *jump* to a new level. This is an example of a stepped cost.

Overall, once we have defined the activity, measurements of changes in activity level can be used to determine cost behavior patterns.

Measuring Level of Activity

Before we can manage an organization, we need to identify exactly what it is that we intend to manage. In other words, what is the activity upon which we intend to focus our planning, controlling, and evaluating efforts? In the doughnut shop example, it makes sense for management to focus on increasing the number of doughnuts sold; management efforts can reasonably be expected to influence the number of doughnuts sold. Activity is often measured in terms of output, input, or a combination of the two. Some of the most common activity bases used are number of units sold and number of units produced in manufacturing firms, number of units sold in merchandising firms, and number of contract hours paid for or billed in service firms. We will generally use production volume or sales volume as the activity basis in this chapter to demonstrate the use of C-V-P analysis.

Note that just because a cost doesn't vary with a particular activity base (e.g., total units sold) does not mean it could never be considered as a variable cost. For example, the total cost of wages for a doughnut shop may not vary with the amount of sales volume (the clerks get paid the same whether they sell a lot of doughnuts or just a few), but total wages would vary based on the number of hours per week that the store is open. So, if another type of activity other than sales volume is more relevant in determining changes in the variable costs being planned, the C-V-P analysis should be based on that activity. It all comes down to an issue of "focus." Where do you believe you can best focus your management attention in order to plan for and control costs and profits—on store hours, doughnuts sold, or customers served? There is some subjectivity in this focus decision. Nevertheless, managers must be careful to understand the various activity bases within their company so that they can properly plan for and control costs. We will discuss a number of alternative activity bases in a later chapter on managing inventory.

Manufacturing and merchandising companies with a single product generally measure volume of activity in terms of output, for example, number of cars, television sets, or desks produced. However, many companies produce or sell several different products (refrigerators, toasters, and irons, for example), and a simple total of all the products manufactured or sold during a given period may not provide a good measure of activity. This is particularly true for manufacturing firms. For example, GENERAL ELECTRIC manufactures a wide variety of products, ranging from light bulbs to locomotives. It obviously takes more effort (and consequently costs more) to produce a locomotive than a light bulb; accordingly, it wouldn't make any sense to state that total production for a given day was 1,000,001—1,000,000 light bulbs and 1 locomotive. In multiproduct situations, these manufacturing firms usually use input measures, such as direct labor hours worked, machine time used, or the time needed to set up a job, as the activity base. Such specific input measures are often more useful than general output measures.

Variable Costs

variable costs Costs that change in total in direct proportion to changes in activity level.

Total **variable costs** change in direct proportion to changes in activity level. Examples are costs of direct materials, which vary proportionately with the number of units produced, and sales commissions, which vary proportionately with the sales volume. For instance, as an automobile manufacturer, you might define the activity of focus as the number of cars produced. If engines, tires, axles, and steering wheels are purchased from suppliers, the related costs would be variable because the total cost of steering wheels, for example, would vary proportionately with the number of cars produced. If no cars are produced, there are no steering wheel costs; if 1,000 cars are manufactured during a period, the total cost for steering wheels and other purchased parts is 1,000 times the unit cost of each item. As more cars are produced, the total cost of each item increases. The unit cost, however, remains constant. For example, if an auto company pays $150 per steering wheel, the total cost of steering wheels for 200 cars is $30,000; for 500 cars, it is $75,000. At both levels of activity, however, the unit cost is still $150. This relationship between variable costs and level of activity is shown graphically in Exhibit 1, which relates the number of cars produced to the total cost of the steering wheels used in production.

STOP & THINK

In a manufacturing plant, are direct labor costs variable or fixed? Does your answer change if the direct labor employees belong to a powerful union?

In addition to sales commissions and materials, many other costs (such as labor) have a variable cost behavior pattern. For example, if it takes four hours of labor to assemble a frame and each hour costs $25, a unit labor cost of $100 per frame is a variable cost; the total labor cost would be $100 times the number of frames produced.

Curvilinear Variable Costs

curvilinear costs Variable costs that do not vary in direct proportion to changes in activity level but vary at decreasing or increasing rates due to economies of scale, productivity changes, and so on.

Our definition of the variable cost behavior pattern specifies that variable costs have a linear relationship to the level of activity; that is, when the level of activity increases, total variable costs rise at a directly proportional rate. For example, if the level of activity doubles, the total variable costs will also double; this is called a linear relationship. The reality is that, in practice, a truly linear relationship usually does not exist. Overall, many variable costs are actually **curvilinear costs** when considered over many activity levels. That is, these curvilinear costs actually vary at increasing or decreasing rates across large changes in the activity level. To illustrate, think about a manufacturer that makes a very specialized "premium natural" ice cream that is handmade. Now consider Exhibit 2. The top diagram is a graph that shows the cost of raw materials (for example, milk, sugar, and other ingredients) purchased from suppliers to make ice cream. Because the ice cream maker gets a bigger price discount as it purchases higher volumes of raw materials, the variable cost of these materials is not linear but curvilinear. That is, the cost increases at a decreasing rate.

FYI:

If you've had an introductory class in economics, you have likely been introduced to the term *economies of scale*. The cost of milk that becomes cheaper as production volume increases (top graph in Exhibit 2) is a cost that displays economies of scale. On the other hand, the direct labor costs to produce ice cream that become more costly as production increases (bottom graph in Exhibit 2) represent costs with *diseconomies* of scale.

On the other hand, the manager of the ice cream production process faces an understandable labor challenge—it is difficult to find people who can make ice cream efficiently. Plans to increase the production volume of the operation mean that the manager will have to hire more individuals for the ice cream production crew. As the manager scrambles to satisfy her labor needs, she will

Exhibit 1: An Example of Variable Costs

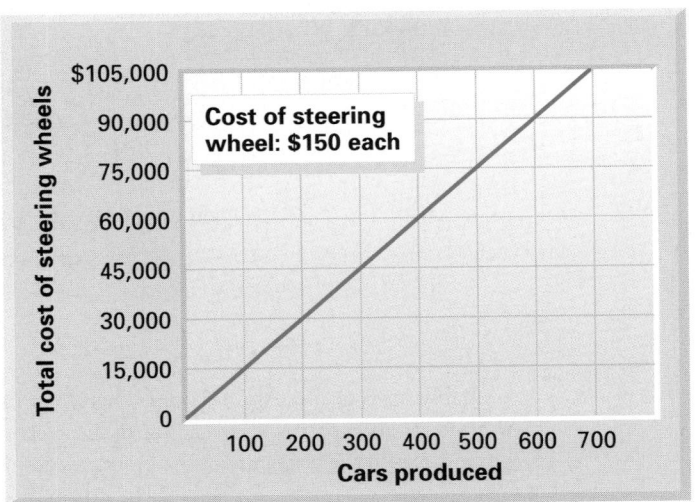

Exhibit 2: Curvilinear Variable Costs

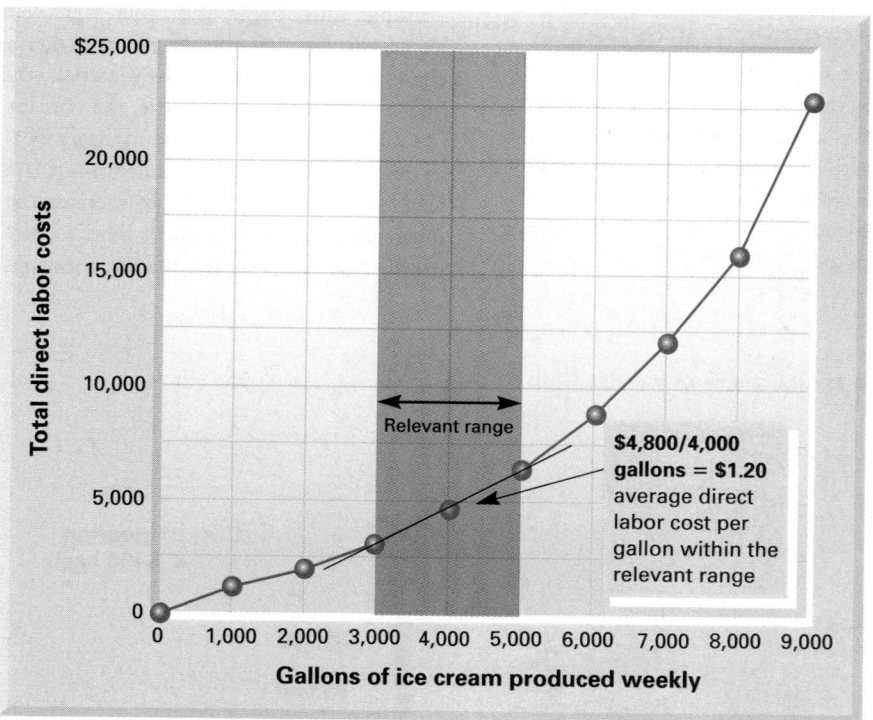

probably have to increase the wages she offers in order to attract more employees. As a result, the direct labor cost of each gallon of ice cream will increase as planned production volumes go up because the wage rate of the workers goes up. Thus, this curvilinear variable cost increases at an *increasing* rate, as depicted in the bottom graph in Exhibit 2. If you've ever had a class in economics, then this concept of curvilinear costs is familiar to you. The fact that most variable costs are curved instead of linear is an economic fact of most organizations. However, when doing C-V-P analysis, we assume that costs are *linear*. This is a potentially limiting assumption of C-V-P work; but, as you'll see in the next section, it is an appropriate assumption for most managers.

Relevant Range and the Linearity of Variable Costs

relevant range The range of operating level, or volume of activity, over which the relationship between total costs (variable plus fixed) and activity level is approximately linear.

While this is never exactly true, it is usually safe to assume that variable costs are *approximately* linear within a certain range of production, called the **relevant range**. To illustrate the relevant range concept, let's return to our ice cream manufacturing business. Realistically, the production manager does not expect to vary weekly production volume outside the range of 3,000 to 5,000 gallons of ice cream. As displayed in Exhibit 2 for both milk material cost and direct labor cost, a linear segment within the relevant range of weekly production can effectively approximate the curvilinear cost relationship of producing between 3,000 and 5,000 gallons of ice cream. By assuming a linear (rather than a curvilinear) relationship, the variable costs of milk and direct labor are estimated at $1.55 and $1.20, respectively, per gallon of ice cream using the costs in the midpoint of the relevant range (weekly production of 4,000 gallons of ice cream).

Caution

The relevant range concept is particularly difficult to apply when using C-V-P analysis in companies in very high growth situations, such as high-tech start-ups. If a company's sales are increasing by 60% each quarter, for example, it is unlikely to remain in the same "relevant range" from quarter to quarter; so careful analysis of variable and fixed costs must be repeated on a regular basis.

Relevant range is an important concept. If activity increases or decreases significantly, cost relationships will probably change. If production volume soars, for example, such factors as overtime work and bulk-purchase discounts may cause direct labor and materials costs per unit to change. That is why we say that the definition of variable costs—costs that are constant per unit of activity—is applicable only within relevant ranges. The important point to remember is that whenever we define a particular variable cost, we are assuming that the cost is within the relevant range of activity.

Fixed Costs

fixed costs Costs that remain constant in total, regardless of activity level, at least over a certain range of activity.

Fixed costs remain constant in total, regardless of activity level, at least within the relevant range of activity. Examples include property taxes, insurance, executives' salaries, plant depreciation, and rent. Because total fixed costs remain constant as activity increases, the fixed cost per unit (total fixed cost ÷ level of activity) decreases. Similarly, as the level of activity decreases, the fixed cost per unit increases. This is in contrast to variable costs, where the costs per unit are assumed to remain constant through changes in the level of activity within the relevant range.

Caution

While total variable costs increase as production increases, the per-unit variable cost is constant across activity levels within the relevant range. In contrast, while total fixed costs are constant over the relevant range, the per-unit fixed cost changes with increases or decreases in production. Many introductory students of management accounting become confused and forget that per-unit variable costs are *fixed* and per-unit fixed costs will *vary* over the relevant range!

Before we go any further, it is a good idea for us to remind ourselves why identifying fixed and variable costs is important. Remember that this chapter is about managing the relationships among costs, volume, and profit. In the previous chapter, we briefly introduced the concept of C-V-P and break-even analysis. In the C-V-P formula below (which we introduced in the previous chapter), you can see that calculating what a company needs to do to "break even" and start making a profit requires a clear measure of total fixed costs and variable costs per unit:

$$\frac{\text{Total fixed costs}}{(\text{Sales price per unit} - \text{Variable cost per unit})} = \text{Break-even sales (in units)}$$

In an actual company, the fixed and variable costs are very challenging to identify. That is why it is important that you understand the nature of cost behavior and how to classify costs as either fixed or variable. Once we've completed our discussion of cost behavior, we'll be ready to spend some time on this very useful C-V-P formula later in this chapter.

Fixed Costs Are Shifting Over the past few decades, fixed costs have increased as a percentage of total costs for many manufacturing companies, primarily due to the increase in factory automation. As a machine replaces each manual job, costs change from variable labor costs to fixed depreciation or rental charges. It is important to note that many service companies have much higher ratios of fixed-to-variable costs than do manufacturing companies. The costs of providing services in companies such as banks, consulting agencies, and airlines typically do not vary much depending on the volume of banking transactions, consulting hours, or passengers carried. Perhaps more significantly, e-commerce organizations often have even fewer variable costs than service organizations do! Once the technology has been put in place to run an e-commerce business, there is typically very little additional cost of technology based on usage (within the relevant range). Personnel costs in e-commerce organizations, such as engineering personnel, marketing teams, and executive personnel, also do not change much based on the volume of customer use of the organization's technology.

As fixed costs in manufacturing organizations increase, and the economy continues to shift more and more to service and e-commerce organizations, this fixed cost emphasis has a significant effect on the decision-making process. When costs are fixed, management's ability to influence costs with activity-level decisions is limited. With variable costs, management has more flexibility to change activity levels and thereby increase or decrease total operating cost structures. This trend of replacing variable costs with fixed costs has an important impact on the cost structure of an organization that is captured in the concept of operating leverage, which is discussed in the expanded material section of this chapter.

FYI:

Have you ever wondered why you always wait so long and why there are so many patients at one time in a dentist's office? Think about the nature of the dentist's costs. Most costs are fixed—dentists' salaries, rent or depreciation, and so forth. When costs are mostly fixed, seeing a high volume of patients is important to cover the fixed costs. Then, once fixed costs are covered, almost all additional patient revenue becomes profit. Thus, by squeezing in only a few additional patients, dentists can increase their profits substantially.

stepped costs Costs that change in total in a stair-step fashion (in large amounts) with changes in volume of activity.

Stepped Fixed Costs

Let's continue with our example of the ice cream manufacturer. The top graph in Exhibit 3 shows the relationship between the production line supervisor cost and the total number of gallons of ice cream produced. In this case, until weekly ice cream production reaches 1,000 gallons a week, the manufacturing manager is able to oversee all line workers. At 1,000 gallons a week production, however, the manager expects to hire a production line supervisor at $500 per week to provide more supervision of the workers. Further, the manager expects that she'll need to hire an additional supervisor each time weekly production is increased another 2,000 gallons. Although the production line supervisor cost is changing as the scale of ice cream production changes, we still consider this cost to be fixed *within the relevant range.* Hence, as shown in the top graph in Exhibit 3, within a relevant range of activity of between 3,000 and 5,000 gallons of ice cream, the total fixed manufacturing supervisor cost of $1,000 does not change. On the other hand, the per-unit supervisor cost will drop considerably as production increases. For example, when the fixed supervisor cost is $1,000 and 3,000 gallons of ice cream are being produced, the supervisor cost per gallon of ice cream is $0.33 ($1,000 ÷ 3,000 gallons). With production of 4,000 gallons, however, this fixed cost is only $0.25 ($1,000 ÷ 4,000 gallons) per gallon.

As you can see in Exhibit 3, the fixed cost of the production line supervision "steps up" as the volume of ice cream production increases. **Stepped costs** are costs that change in total in a stair-step fashion with changes in volume of activity. Another example of a stepped cost might be the labor charges for the maintenance of the tools and machinery in a small manufacturing plant. One maintenance worker can handle the upkeep of all the equipment during normal

Exhibit 3: Stepped Fixed Costs

STOP & THINK

If the "steps" in a stepped cost are wide compared to the relevant range (in other words, the costs essentially are unchanged within the relevant range), the costs are usually treated as fixed. This would be the case with the production line supervisor costs in Exhibit 3. On the other hand, how would you treat a stepped cost with very narrow steps as is displayed in the bottom graph in Exhibit 3?

mixed costs Costs that contain both variable and fixed cost components.

levels of activity. However, when there is a significant increase in activity, a second worker must be hired, and the maintenance cost approximately doubles.

Mixed Costs

Mixed costs, like curvilinear costs and stepped costs, are variations of the basic fixed and variable cost behavior patterns. Specifically, mixed costs are costs that contain both variable and fixed components. An example is rent that is based on a fixed fee plus a percentage of total sales. Thus, the rental terms for an automobile dealer's showroom might include a flat payment of $4,000 per month plus 1% of each month's sales. The 1% of sales is the variable portion, and the $4,000 is the fixed cost. The total rent, therefore, would be considered a mixed cost and could be diagrammed as shown in Exhibit 4. As this exhibit shows, the cost of renting the showroom increases as sales increase. The total rent is $4,000 when there are no sales; $6,000 when sales are $200,000 [$4,000 + (0.01 × $200,000)]; and $8,000 when sales are $400,000 [$4,000 + (0.01 × $400,000)]. This increase is directly due to the variable cost element, which increases in total as activity level (car sales) increases.

One of the important challenges in using C-V-P analysis in the planning process is the need to effectively separate mixed costs into their fixed and variable cost components. Over

Exhibit 4: An Example of a Mixed Cost

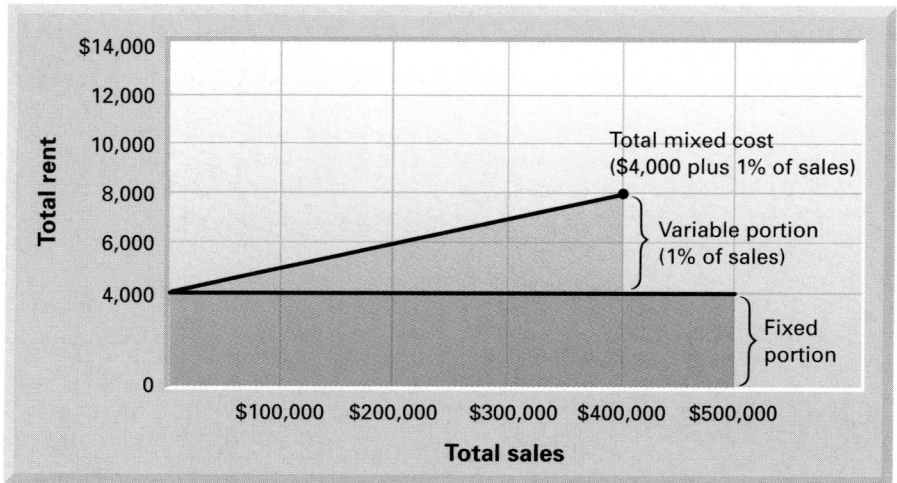

the years several management accounting techniques have been developed by organizations for this purpose. We will explore these mixed cost analysis methods in the next section of this chapter.

TO SUMMARIZE: Cost behavior is the way a cost changes in response to changes in activity level. There are two basic cost behavior patterns, variable and fixed. Total variable costs change in direct proportion to changes in the level of activity over the relevant range; therefore, variable costs are constant per unit over this range. In analyzing variable costs, we generally assume a linear relationship between total costs and the level of activity within the relevant range; outside of this range, variable costs are usually curvilinear. On the other hand, total fixed costs do not change over the relevant range; therefore, fixed costs decrease per unit as the level of activity increases within the relevant range. Stepped costs increase with the level of activity but not smoothly. If the steps are wide in relation to the relevant range, these costs can be treated as fixed; if the steps are narrow, they can be treated as variable. Mixed costs have both a fixed and a variable component. An increase in a mixed cost with a rising level of activity is due entirely to the variable cost element.

Analysis of Mixed Costs

3 Analyze mixed costs using the scattergraph and high-low methods.

With an understanding of the different types of cost behavior, we can discuss how to identify and separate mixed costs into variable and fixed components. This separation is essential because we have to clearly classify all costs as fixed or variable before doing C-V-P analysis. When it comes to mixed costs, remember that the fixed portion represents the cost necessary to maintain a service (such as a telephone) or a facility (such as a building), and the variable portion covers actual use. Recall the example of the automobile showroom's rental cost, part of which was a flat monthly fee and part a percentage of sales. Other common mixed costs are such overhead costs as electricity and repairs.

The most accurate way to separate the actual fixed and variable components of mixed costs is to analyze each invoice. An electricity bill, for example, may include a flat monthly service charge that would be classified as a fixed cost. Additional variable costs are those based on the amount of electricity actually used during the month. This approach could be very time consuming, however, and may not be cost effective (that is, it would cost more to do the analysis than the detailed information is worth). An alternative approach is to analyze the historical trend in past costs as the level of activity has changed as the basis for classifying costs as fixed or variable. There are several methods of doing this. In this section, we will introduce you to two methods: the scattergraph method and the high-low method. In the expanded material, we introduce least squares analysis, a more sophisticated method for analyzing mixed costs.

The Scattergraph, or Visual-Fit, Method

scattergraph (visual-fit) method A method of segregating the fixed and variable components of a mixed cost by plotting on a graph total costs at several activity levels and drawing a regression line through the points.

regression line On a scattergraph, the straight line that most closely expresses the relationship between the variables.

variable cost rate The change in cost divided by the change in activity; the slope of the regression line.

Probably the simplest method of separating mixed costs into their variable and fixed components is the **scattergraph** (or **visual-fit**) **method**. Essentially, we're talking here about simply *looking* at a trend of mixed cost points over time and learning how to "see" the fixed and variable cost components. To do this, the total mixed cost for each level of activity is plotted on a graph, and a straight line (called the **regression line**) is visually fitted through the points. The idea is to position the line through the set of plotted data points in a way that minimizes the average distance between all the data points and the fitted regression line. With the regression line inserted into the graph, the fixed portion of the mixed cost is estimated to be the amount on the cost (vertical) axis at the point where it is intercepted by the regression line. The variable cost per unit (referred to as the **variable cost rate**) is equal to the slope of the regression line, which is simply the change in cost divided by the change in activity.

Caution

When making these cost graphs, remember that the dollars go on the vertical axis and the level of activity goes on the horizontal axis.

To illustrate the scattergraph method, let's use the example of electricity costs for an automobile manufacturer. In the analysis and calculations that follow, all costs are assumed to fall within the relevant range of activity. In this example, we use direct labor hours as a measure of the activity level.

Exhibit 5 shows a scattergraph on which electricity costs and direct labor hours have been plotted. The regression line has been visually fitted to minimize the distance between data points. It appears that the total fixed portion of electricity cost is about $40,000 per month, which is where the regression line intersects the cost axis. The variable cost rate is approximately $4.29 per direct labor hour, which is the slope of the regression line. To calculate the slope, we use the following formula and the data points of zero and 7,000 direct labor hours, respectively.

$$\text{Variable cost rate} = \frac{\text{Change in (electricity) cost}}{\text{Change in activity (direct labor hours)}}$$

$$X = \frac{\$70,000 - \$40,000}{7,000 - 0}$$

$$X = \frac{\$30,000}{7,000}$$

$$X = \$4.29 \text{ (rounded)}$$

Caution

Once the regression line has been fitted through the data points, the scattergraph method does not depend any longer on the *data points* to estimate fixed and variable costs. Cost estimations are entirely based on *points along the regression line*. For instance, notice that in this case we used the points 0 and 7,000 along the visually fitted regression line. However, we could have used any two points on the regression line (such as 2,000 direct labor hours and 10,000 direct labor hours) to calculate the variable costs per direct labor hour.

Obviously, the scattergraph method has some limitations as a cost estimation tool. Perhaps the most critical limitation is that how the user fits the regression line through the data points is entirely subjective. Consider Exhibit 5 once more. If you were the one fitting the regression line to these data points, would you have set the line exactly where it is in this graph? Hopefully, your line would have been quite close to the current line. Still, it probably wouldn't have been exactly the same, resulting in some small differences in your own estimations of fixed and variable costs. Hence, the scattergraph method is a classic "quick and dirty" management accounting technique. Yet, although the scattergraph

Exhibit 5: Total Electricity Costs

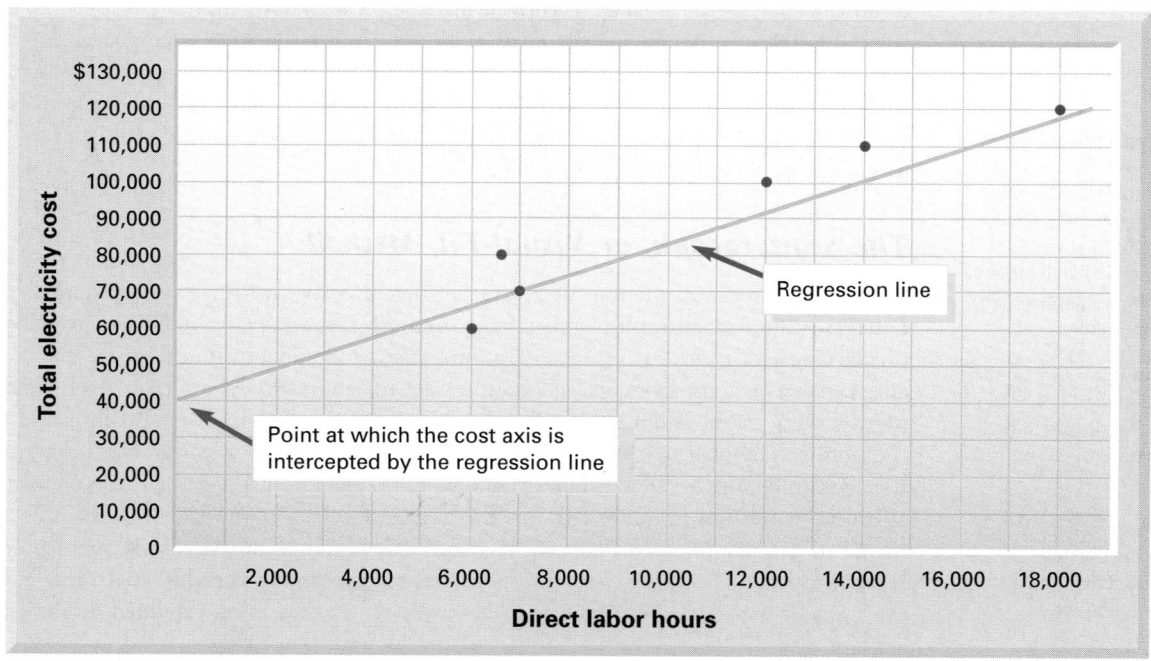

provides only subjective estimates of the fixed and variable portions of mixed costs, it can be an extremely useful tool to describe and discuss cost behavior in the planning process. It is also useful for thinking about how to control operating costs. For instance, it shows at a glance any trends and abrupt changes in cost behavior patterns. As such, it can be used as a preliminary step before using more sophisticated methods of cost evaluation.

The High-Low Method

high-low method A method of segregating the fixed and variable components of a mixed cost by analyzing the costs at the highest and the lowest activity levels within a relevant range.

A second approach to identifying fixed and variables costs is the **high-low method**, which analyzes mixed costs on the basis of total costs incurred at both the highest and the lowest levels of activity. To illustrate this method, we refer again to the electricity costs of the automobile manufacturer. This time, however, we will focus on the following table of reported electricity costs and direct labor hours worked. (The numbers in this table correspond exactly to the points plotted in the scattergragh in Exhibit 5.)

Month	Direct Labor Hours Worked	Total Electricity Cost
January	7,000	$ 70,000
February	6,000	60,000
March	12,000	100,000
April	6,600	80,000
May	18,000	120,000
June	14,000	110,000

Although these two columns of figures do not visually show trends as clearly as the scattergraph does, they do suggest that as the activity level (direct labor hours) increases, total electricity costs increase. Given this relationship, the high-low method can be used to determine the fixed and variable portions of the electricity cost as follows:

1. Identify the highest and lowest activity levels (18,000 hours in May and 6,000 hours in February). As you can see, these two months also represent the highest and lowest levels of electricity costs, or $120,000 and $60,000, respectively (although this may not always be the case).
2. Determine the differences between the high and low points.

	Total Electricity Cost	Direct Labor Hours
High point (May)	$120,000	18,000
Low point (February)	60,000	6,000
Difference	$ 60,000	12,000

3. Calculate the variable cost rate (variable cost per unit). The formula is the same as the one used to compute the slope of the regression line in the scattergraph method. The results are different, of course, because the scattergraph method is based on a regression line that is plotted, as much as possible, using all the data points, whereas the high-low method uses only the highest and lowest data points.

$$\text{Variable cost rate} = \frac{\text{Change in costs}}{\text{Change in activity}}$$

$$= \frac{\$60,000}{12,000}$$

$$= \$5 \text{ per direct labor hour}$$

4. Determine fixed costs based on the variable cost rate ($5 in this case). The formula for this computation is:

Fixed costs = Total costs − Variable costs

At the high level of activity, the calculation is as follows:

$X = \$120,000 - (18,000 \times \$5)$
$X = \$120,000 - \$90,000$
$X = \$30,000$

You get the same result if you calculate fixed costs at the low level of activity as follows:

$X = \$60,000 - (6,000 \times \$5)$
$X = \$60,000 - \$30,000$
$X = \$30,000$

Caution

Once you have selected the high and low activity levels to use in the high-low method, don't use any other activity levels or costs than these two data points to calculate the fixed costs.

In summary, using the high-low method of analyzing mixed costs, the variable portion of the total electricity cost is estimated to be $5 per direct labor hour, and the fixed portion is $30,000 per month. This means that $30,000 appears to be the amount the company pays each month just to have electricity available, and $5 is the average additional electricity cost for each hour of direct labor worked.

A Comparison of the Scattergraph and High-Low Methods

As we have illustrated, the scattergraph and high-low methods may produce different results.

Method	Variable Cost Rate	Fixed Cost
Scattergraph	$4.29	$40,000
High-low	5.00	30,000

Both methods are useful for a quick approximation. The scattergraph method takes all the data into account. Therefore, this method tends to be more accurate, although it is somewhat subjective and inconsistent because different people might draw the line through the points differently. On the other hand, anyone using the high-low method will consistently get the same results. However, because only two data points are used, the high-low method may not be representative of the costs incurred at all levels of activity. It is important that you realize that the math used in the high-low method essentially plots the regression line through the two most extreme points in a scattergraph. To understand what we mean, look at the scattergraph of the electricity cost data in Exhibit 5. Notice that the low point lies below the scattergraph regression line and the high point lies above the scattergraph regression line. Now, if you were to draw a straight line through the high and low points, that line would not be the same line created using the scattergraph (visual-fit) method, and may not necessarily represent all six data points plotted. Nevertheless, you can use either method or both methods to predict future costs. If, for example, management wants to know how much electricity will cost next month with 10,000 direct labor hours budgeted, the following calculations would be made:

Method	Formula	Estimated Cost
Scattergraph	$40,000 + 10,000($4.29) =	$82,900
High-low	$30,000 + 10,000($5.00) =	$80,000

As you can see, the total estimated costs resulting from these two methods, in this case, are reasonably close to each other (although this may not necessarily be the case with sets of actual cost and activity data in some real-life companies).

TO SUMMARIZE: Two common techniques for analyzing mixed costs are the scattergraph and high-low methods. The scattergraph method involves visually fitting a straight line (the regression line) through data points plotted on a graph, then noting where the line intercepts the cost axis (the fixed cost) and calculating the slope of the line (the variable cost rate). With the high-low method, the high and the low levels of activity are used to calculate first the variable cost rate and then the fixed cost component.

Methods of C-V-P Analysis

4 Perform C-V-P analyses, and describe the effects potential changes in C-V-P variables have on company profitability.

Now that you have a better understanding of cost behaviors and can separate mixed costs into their fixed and variable cost elements, you are ready to use your knowledge of cost behaviors to make planning decisions. The previous chapter provided a quick introduction to C-V-P analysis in the process of planning and analyzing decisions to prioritize Kevlar versus Teflon products at DUPONT. However, in order to effectively use this valuable tool, we need a more detailed discussion and lots of practice.

If you haven't done so already, now is a good time to think of an actual business organization that is familiar to you, perhaps one by which you've been employed or are now employed. Think about the product or service this organization creates and the costs and processes it uses. Now, as you study the C-V-P analysis method below, be sure to consider how this tool

business environment

Managing an Airline in the Post-9/11 Economy Is Not Easy. Prior to the terrorist tragedies in 2001, CONTINENTAL AIRLINES was posting an incredible string of consecutive profitable quarters. Since filing for bankruptcy protection in 1995, Continental reported 24 straight quarters of profit, even when most of the other major U.S. airlines reported losses. This all changed, of course, on September 11, 2001. Since then, Continental, the fifth largest airline in the United States, has struggled very hard just to stay alive. Both 2001 and 2002 resulted in significant operating losses for Continental, as was the case with many of its competitors. Continental, however, appears to be weathering the storm better than most other airlines. In 2002, three of the top seven U.S.-based international carriers filed bankruptcy. By the end of the first quarter in 2003, TWA no longer existed, and UNITED and US AIRWAYS were still struggling in bankruptcy. In contrast, Continental Airlines again earned a coveted spot on Fortune's list of the 100 Best Companies to Work For—the only airline to do so and the fifth consecutive year for it to make the list. More importantly, in March 2002, Continental posted its first profitable month since 9/11, and Gordon Bethune, chairman and CEO, predicted that his company would be able to break even in 2004. This progress is significant in that the Air Transport Association (ATA) forecasts that the overall airline industry will lose $7 billion in 2003.

How has Continental's management team carried this company through a disastrous period of time for the airline industry? For one thing, Continental Airlines' management carefully analyzed its costs, divided those costs into fixed and variable components, and made several decisions to reduce fixed costs. For example, Continental grounded planes and slashed excess capacity. The airline eliminated 12,000 jobs in 2002 and planned to cut another 1,200 jobs, including 25% of top management, in 2003. All of this helped reduce Continental's jet cost per available seat mile by 3.8%, which is a significant percentage in an industry defined by extremely thin profit margins.

With better control of its fixed costs, Continental Airlines is again becoming profitable, and becoming profitable more quickly than most of its competitors. Because of these cut costs, Continental Airlines' passengers pay lower fares than on other airlines and receive better service. These lower fares and better service enable Continental to fill more seats than its competitors. Because its costs are low, it is profitable. Fixed costs are now a smaller percentage of total costs at Continental Airlines than at almost all other airlines.

Sources: Adapted from PR Newswire, "Continental Airlines Reports First Quarter Loss; Carrier Profitable for Month of March, the First Profitable Month Since 9/11," April 15, 2002; Continental Airlines 2002 Annual Report; "Continental Air CEO Now Sees Break-Even Results for 2004," *The Wall Street Journal,* March 19, 2003.

would be used in your own organization to plan and manage costs and activities in order to obtain desired results.

Contribution Margin

contribution margin The difference between total sales and variable costs; the portion of sales revenue available to cover fixed costs and provide a profit.

In order to effectively use C-V-P analysis, we first need to spend some time working with the concept of contribution margin. **Contribution margin** is equal to sales revenue less variable costs; it is the amount of revenue that remains to cover fixed costs and provide a profit for an organization. For example, the contribution margin from the sale of one order of French fries by a fast-food restaurant is the selling price less the variables costs (potatoes, salt, container, cooking oil, wages of the cook) of producing the fries. Any contribution margin generated by the sale of an order of French fries can be used to pay the fixed costs of the fast-food outlet, such as the monthly rent, the insurance, the supervisor's salary, and so forth. Contribution margin is one of the most important management accounting concepts you will learn because many operating decisions are made on the basis of how contribution margin will be affected. A company may decide, for example, to advertise one product more than others because that product has a higher contribution margin.

© 2003 Getty Images

The contribution margin generated by the sale of an order of French fries can be used to pay fixed costs such as rent, insurance, and salaries. Now you know why you often hear that ever popular question "Would you like fries with that?" at fast-food restaurants.

The Contribution Margin Income Statement

To illustrate the concept of contribution margin, let's use the following format of a contribution margin income statement. The statement data for Jewels Corporation, a producer of high-quality baseball gloves, follow.[2]

Jewels Corporation
Contribution Margin Income Statement
For the Month Ended November 30, 2006

	Total	Per Unit
Sales revenue (1,000 gloves)	$200,000	$200
Less variable costs	110,000	110
Contribution margin	$ 90,000	$ 90
Less fixed costs	63,000	
Profit*	$ 27,000	

*In this chapter, "profit" means pretax income; the terms *income* and *profit* are interchangeable.

per-unit contribution margin The excess of the sales price of one unit over its variable costs.

FYI:

French fries and soft drinks are good examples of products with a high contribution margin. A $2 order of French fries might have a contribution margin in excess of $1.50. That's why fast-food employees are told to specifically ask customers if they want fries and a drink with their order!

As this income statement shows, for internal decision-making purposes, Jewels Corporation computes its contribution margin on a per-unit (glove) and total-dollar basis. During November, Jewels' **per-unit contribution margin** is $90; the total contribution margin at a sales volume of 1,000 baseball gloves is $90,000.

The per-unit contribution margin tells us that $90 is available from each glove sold to cover fixed costs and provide a profit. By showing the $63,000 of fixed costs separately, this income statement also tells us that Jewels must generate sufficient contribution margin to cover these costs before a profit can be earned. With $200,000 of sales revenue, the contribution margin ($90,000) is sufficient to cover the fixed costs and provide a profit of $27,000.

2 In this example, we assume that there is only one model of baseball glove, which sells for $200.

This type of contribution margin income statement is particularly useful as a planning tool. The statement helps a company to project profits at any level of activity within the relevant range. For example, if Jewels Corporation forecasts sales of 1,200 baseball gloves next month, the company can prepare a forecasted (or pro-forma) income statement (in contribution margin format) as follows:

Jewels Corporation
Pro-Forma Contribution Margin Income Statement
For the Month Ended December 31, 2006

Sales revenue (1,200 gloves × $200)	$240,000
Less variable costs (1,200 gloves × $110)	132,000
Contribution margin	$108,000
Less fixed costs	63,000
Profit	$ 45,000

Notice that with an increase in sales of 200 baseball gloves, the contribution margin increases $18,000 ($108,000 − $90,000). You can confirm this by multiplying the per-unit contribution margin by the increase in volume ($90 per unit × 200 gloves = $18,000). Because we assume that the increase in volume is still within the relevant range of activity (which is a *very* important assumption!), the fixed costs remain at $63,000, and profit increases by the $18,000 increase in contribution margin. The critical thing you should see here is that once the fixed costs are covered, each subsequent dollar in contribution margin goes straight to profit! In other words, when Jewels Corporation hits its break-even point (which is the point where all fixed costs are covered), each additional glove sold will generate $90 in profit.

Notice the importance of accurately determining cost behavior when forecasting profit levels. If one ignores cost behavior, then the $27,000 profit generated by November sales of 1,000 gloves may lead to the conclusion that each glove creates $27 ($27,000 profit/1,000 gloves) in profit. With this *incorrect* information, the forecasted level of profit for December sales of 1,200 gloves is $32,400 ($27 per glove × 1,200 gloves). This forecast differs significantly from the $45,000 profit forecast above that stems from a *correct* consideration of the behavior (fixed or variable) of Jewels Corporation's costs.

The Contribution Margin Ratio

contribution margin ratio
The percentage of net sales revenue left after variable costs are deducted; the contribution margin divided by net sales revenue.

Knowing the **contribution margin ratio**, which is the percentage of sales revenue left after variable costs are deducted, will help you compare the profitability of various products. For example, if product A has a 60% contribution margin ratio and the contribution margin ratio of product B is only 20%, the company should emphasize product A, assuming that other factors are equal. As a concrete example, in a supermarket the prepared foods (baked goods, squeezed juices, ready-to-eat barbecued chicken) have high contribution margin ratios whereas the staples such as milk and eggs have lower contribution margin ratios.

To illustrate the calculation of contribution margin ratios, let's look again at the initial Jewels Corporation example. The ratio is computed as follows:

	Total	Per Unit	Ratio (Percentage)
Sales revenue (1,000 gloves)	$200,000	$200	100%
Less variable costs	110,000	110	55
Contribution margin	$ 90,000	$ 90	45%
Less fixed costs	63,000		
Profit	$ 27,000		

The contribution margin ratio is 45% of sales revenue ($90 ÷ $200), which means that for every $1.00 increase in sales revenue, the contribution margin increases by $0.45 (45% of $1.00). If fixed costs are already covered, profit will also increase by $0.45 for every $1.00 increase in sales. As you can see, there is another ratio presented in these calculations—the variable cost ratio. These two ratios are complements of each other. Hence, the variable cost ratio ($110 ÷ $200 = 55%) plus the contribution margin ratio (45%) will always equal 100%. This is important because whether we're describing contribution margin ratios or variable cost ratios, we are really talking about the same basic issue—the relationship of variable costs to sales revenue.

With contribution margin or variable cost ratios, it is easy to analyze the impact of changes in sales on the contribution margin. For example, if you estimate that Jewels' sales will increase by $20,000, you can apply the contribution margin ratio of 45% or the variable cost ratio of 55% and estimate that the contribution margin will increase by $9,000, which is equal to $20,000 × 0.45 or $20,000 × (1 − 0.55). The higher the contribution margin ratio, the larger the share of each additional dollar of sales that goes toward covering fixed costs and increasing profit.

The C-V-P Equation

As you can see, contribution margin calculations will be very useful to you when analyzing cost-volume-profit relationships in the management planning process. Doing C-V-P analysis using contribution margin calculations is a straightforward process. C-V-P analysis does require some simple algebra; here is where you reap the benefits of paying attention during your eighth grade math class.

We began this chapter with the assumption that all costs can be described as either fixed or variable. To highlight the important idea that C-V-P analysis depends on dividing costs into fixed and variable behavior patterns, we will develop the C-V-P equation as follows:[3]

1. Because all costs can be classified as either variable or fixed, we can express the calculation of profit with the following basic formula:

    Sales revenue − Variable costs − Fixed costs = Profit

2. We can specify the formula more precisely by expressing the equation in units:

    (Sales price × Units) − (Variable cost × Units) − Fixed costs = Profit

3. Or, we can express the equation using ratios:

    Sales revenue − (Variable cost ratio × Sales revenue) − Fixed costs = Profit

These equations are quick and useful methods for examining the financial aspects of C-V-P analysis problems. To illustrate, see if you can use the C-V-P equation based on units and the data from the Jewels Corporation example to determine profit assuming that sales of 1,200 baseball gloves are expected.

(Sales price × Units) − (Variable cost × Units) − Fixed costs = Profit
($200 × 1,200) − ($110 × 1,200) − $63,000 = Profit
$240,000 − $132,000 − $63,000 = Profit
$45,000 = Profit

Alternatively, you could calculate Jewels' profits using the equation based on ratios.

---

3 Granted, fixed and variable costs often get "mixed together" and can be difficult (and sometimes impossible) to separate. The fact that C-V-P analysis is based on an assumption that all costs can be divided clearly into fixed and variable is one of the limitations of this technique.

$$\text{Sales revenue} - (\text{Variable cost ratio} \times \text{Sales revenue}) - \text{Fixed costs} = \text{Profit}$$
$$\$240{,}000 - [(\$110 \div \$200) \times \$240{,}000] - \$63{,}000 = \text{Profit}$$
$$\$240{,}000 - (0.55 \times \$240{,}000) - \$63{,}000 = \text{Profit}$$
$$\$240{,}000 - \$132{,}000 - \$63{,}000 = \text{Profit}$$
$$\$45{,}000 = \text{Profit}$$

Note that we calculated the same profit of $45,000 using both formula approaches. This result is no surprise because these are simply alternative routes to the same destination. Both methods are commonly used in business, depending on the data available for the analysis. So, although there may appear to be many alternative ways to write the C-V-P formula, there is really only one formula, and it is not hard to remember:

$$\text{Sales revenue} - \text{Variable costs} - \text{Fixed costs} = \text{Profit}$$

Once you understand this fact, C-V-P analysis using the equation approach is basic math; you merely insert the known elements into the formula and solve for the one unknown element.

Break-Even Point

break-even point The amount of sales at which total costs of the number of units sold equal total revenues; the point at which there is no profit or loss.

In many cases, as a manager you will want to know how many units need to be sold to break even. The **break-even point** is defined as the volume of activity at which total revenues equal total costs, or where profit is zero. The break-even point may also be thought of as the volume of activity at which the contribution margin equals the fixed costs.

Although the goal of business planning is to make a profit, not just to break even, knowing the break-even point can be useful in assessing the risk of selling a new product, setting sales goals and commission rates, deciding on marketing and advertising strategies, and other similar operating decisions. Because the break-even point is, by definition, that activity level at which no profit or loss is earned, the basic C-V-P equation can be modified to calculate the break-even point as follows:

$$\text{Sales revenue} - \text{Variable costs} - \text{Fixed costs} = \$0$$

As you can see, to compute the break-even point, all that you need to do is simply set income equal to zero and then solve for the unknown—such as the number of units to be sold or the total revenues to be achieved.

Let's again use the Jewels Corporation example. How many units must Jewels sell to break even? (Note that we will use "X" to represent the unknown element, in this case, the number of baseball gloves.)

$$(\text{Sales price} \times \text{Units}) - (\text{Variable cost} \times \text{Units}) - \text{Fixed costs} = \$0$$
$$[\text{Sales price} \times (X)] - [\text{Variable cost} \times (X)] - \text{Fixed costs} = \$0$$
$$\$200X - \$110X - \$63{,}000 = \$0$$
$$\$90X = \$63{,}000$$
$$X = \$63{,}000 \div \$90 = 700 \text{ units (baseball gloves)}$$

In this case, if Jewels sells 700 baseball gloves, the company will generate enough revenues to cover its variable and fixed costs, earning zero profit [($200 × 700) − ($110 × 700) − $63,000 = $0]. Once you understand the basic C-V-P formula, you just set it up and solve for whatever unknown you're interested in planning. Think you've got it? Then try this one as a check on yourself: Assuming that Jewels can sell only 600 baseball gloves, what price per glove would the company have to use in order to break even?[4]

---

4 $(\text{Sales price} \times \text{Units}) - (\text{Variable cost} \times \text{Units}) - \text{Fixed costs} = \$0$
$[(X) \times \text{Units}] - (\text{Variable cost} \times \text{Units}) - \text{Fixed costs} = \$0$
$[(X) \times 600] - (\$110 \times 600) - \$63{,}000 = \$0$
$600X - \$66{,}000 - \$63{,}000 = \$0$
$600X = \$129{,}000$
$X = \$215 \text{ (new baseball glove price)}$

Determining Sales Volume to Achieve Target Income

Another way we can use C-V-P analysis in the planning process is to determine what level of activity is necessary to reach a target level of income. Instead of setting profit at $0 to do a break-even analysis, we can just as easily set income in the formula at the targeted level and then use the formula to plan or predict what fixed costs, variable costs, sales prices, and sales volumes are needed to achieve the target level of income. **Target income** is usually defined as the amount of income that will enable management to reach its objectives—paying dividends, meeting analysts' predictions, purchasing a new plant and equipment, or paying off existing loans. Target income can be expressed as either a percentage of revenues or as a fixed amount.

target income A profit level desired by management.

To illustrate target income, suppose that we want to know how many baseball gloves must be sold by Jewels Corporation to achieve a target income of $36,000, assuming no changes in per-unit variable costs or total fixed costs. The calculation is as follows:

(Sales price × Units) − (Variable cost × Units) − Fixed costs = Target income

$$\$200X - \$110X - \$63,000 = \$36,000$$
$$\$90X = \$99,000$$
$$X = 1,100 \text{ units (baseball gloves)}$$

Thus, we can see that if Jewels sells 1,100 baseball gloves at a contribution margin of $90 each, and assuming that fixed costs are $63,000, the company will earn a pretax profit of $36,000 [($90 × 1,100 units) − $63,000 = $36,000].

A fixed dollar amount of income, such as the $36,000 that would be earned by selling 1,100 baseball gloves, is probably the most typical way of expressing a target income goal for many companies. However, because investors often evaluate companies partially on the basis of the **return on sales revenue** (or simply "return on sales"), management may want to state its goal as a percentage return as opposed to a fixed amount of income. For example, if Jewels Corporation set a target income of a 20% return on sales, the computation would be:

return on sales revenue A measure of operating performance; computed by dividing net income by total sales revenue. Similar to profit margin.

Sales revenue − Variable costs − Fixed costs = 0.20 × Sales revenue

$$\$200X - \$110X - \$63,000 = 0.2(\$200X)$$
$$\$200X - \$110X - \$63,000 = \$40X$$
$$\$200X - \$110X - \$40X = \$63,000$$
$$\$50X = \$63,000$$
$$X = \$63,000 \div \$50 = 1,260 \text{ gloves}$$

As we can see in this calculation, Jewels Corporation can earn a 20% return on sales by selling 1,260 baseball gloves.

Short-Cut Formulas for C-V-P Analysis

Notice that in the C-V-P analysis examples that we've worked through so far, the basic C-V-P equation remains constant. That's what makes this formula so powerful. Once you're comfortable with it, you can use it to manage any number of factors in planning for profits. However, you may remember from your brief introduction to C-V-P analysis in the previous chapter and from our C-V-P formula example on page 801 that we calculated break-even sales in units directly using the following formula.

$$\frac{\text{Total fixed costs}}{(\text{Sales price per unit} - \text{Variable cost per unit})} = \text{Break-even sales (in units)}$$

This formula is a "short-cut" version of the C-V-P formulas above. You can see that it is simply the last step in the C-V-P calculation above for Jewels' break-even point of 700 baseball gloves. So, if you understand the basic C-V-P equation, you can simply skip to the last step of the calculation. There are short cuts for computing the level of sales for both break-even volume and target income volume. The short-cut formula for both the break-even volume and the target income volume in units is:

$$\frac{\text{Fixed costs} + \text{Target income}}{\text{Contribution margin per unit}^5}$$

Note that if you use this formula to determine the break-even volume, then you will assume that target income is $0, giving you:

$$\frac{\text{Fixed costs}}{\text{Contribution margin per unit}}$$

Plugging in the numbers for Jewels Corporation, the results are the same as shown earlier. As you can see, the short-cut calculation for both the break-even volume and the target income volume is really the same formula. For target sales:

$$\frac{\$63,000 + \$36,000}{\$90} = 1,100 \text{ units}$$

For the break-even volume:

$$\frac{\$63,000 + \$0}{\$90} = 700 \text{ units}$$

Always remember, though, that short cuts are useful, but they should not be applied until you fully understand the basic C-V-P relationships. In addition, managing some aspects of the C-V-P relationships can be tricky when you use short cuts. So if you ever get confused in solving a C-V-P analysis problem, just put the problem back in the original C-V-P equation:

$$\text{Sales revenue} - \text{Variable costs} - \text{Fixed costs} = \text{Target income}$$

Computation in Dollar Amounts versus Units

Before we finish with C-V-P equations, you should note that a variable cost ratio is sometimes used instead of a per-unit variable cost. In such cases, the basic C-V-P equation is modified as follows:

$$\text{Sales revenue} - (\text{Variable cost ratio} \times \text{Sales}) - \text{Fixed costs} = \text{Profit}$$

Because the variable costs are stated as a percentage of sales dollars rather than on a per-unit basis, this approach expresses activity in terms of sales dollars, not units. This is still the same basic C-V-P equation, but setting up the equation using the variable cost ratio will result in a break-even point in dollars instead of units. For example, the break-even point for Jewels Corporation would then be expressed as $140,000 in sales revenue ($200 per unit × 700 units) instead of 700 units as previously illustrated. This may be verified using the preceding equation and a 55% variable cost ratio as follows:

$$\text{Sales revenue} - (0.55)\text{Sales revenue} - \$63,000 = \$0$$
$$(0.45)\text{Sales revenue} = \$63,000$$
$$\text{Sales revenue} = \$140,000$$

The short-cut formula for break-even volume and target income volume in sales dollars is:

$$\frac{\text{Fixed costs} + \text{Target income}}{\text{Contribution margin ratio}}$$

(Remember the following: Contribution margin ratio = 1 − Variable cost ratio.)

---

5 Remember that per-unit contribution margin is the sales price per unit less the variable cost per unit.

IBM Gets on the Internet Wave In 1998, if you wanted an IBM desktop personal computer (PC), you had to walk into a store to make the purchase. In hindsight, this was a strange way to sell computers for a company that believed itself to be at the forefront of the e-business revolution. And in hindsight, this sales approach, being both slow and expensive, clearly didn't work. The PC division for IBM lost $986 million in 1998 and was bracing itself for similar losses in 1999. Market analysts were pushing IBM to sell its PC division based in Research Triangle Park in North Carolina. Finally, in the last quarter of 1999, IBM officials announced that it would yank its entire line of home desktop PCs from retail stores in the United States and sell the machines almost exclusively over the Internet. IBM also launched a $20 million advertising campaign (TV and direct mail flyers) to back up the move.

IBM's decision to sell over the Internet was driven largely by cut-throat pricing of components and systems by its major competitors and suppliers, the overhead costs of selling through dealers, and the inability to distinguish its product from dozens of competitor PCs sitting next to it on the retail shelf. In 2000, IBM followed the Internet decision by cutting $1.1 billion in annual manufacturing and distribution expenses. These cost savings were achieved largely by three means. First, IBM changed the way the PCs are built and redesigned the PC product to use as many industry standard parts as possible. Second, by building PCs to order (i.e., only building PCs when an order was placed), IBM was able to significantly reduce the amount of inventory it had to keep on hand. Third, IBM told its suppliers that it wanted 95% of its components ready on demand in well-stocked mini-warehouses near IBM manufacturing facilities. "The whole object is to not own the parts for very long," said Adalio Sanchez, general manager of manufacturing and operations for the PC division.

The change to IBM's PC business started to pay off as costs were reduced and shipments increased using the new ShopIBM Web site. Losses in the PC division were cut to $360 million in 1999 and $148 million in 2000. In 2001, after four straight years of losing money, the PC division was back in the black with a pretax profit of $99 million by the middle of the year. In a business today where prices on desktop PCs are typically in the $800 range, if IBM is $10 or $20 higher than the price of a DELL or COMPAQ PC, it can lose the sale. Clearly, controlling costs and managing sales is becoming more and more important in the very competitive PC market.

Sources: Ed Scannell, "IBM to Go Online with Home PC Sales," *InfoWorld Daily News*, October 19, 1999; Lisa Smith, "IBM's Personal Computer Unit Makes Turnaround," *The Herald-Sun*, March 22, 2001.

Caution

If you want to use C-V-P analysis to calculate the necessary sales volume in terms of *dollars*, the per-unit variable cost is *not* used. Rather, use the variable cost *ratio* times sales to determine total variable costs. Many students make the mistake of multiplying the per-unit variable cost times sales instead of the variable cost ratio times sales to get total variable costs.

Measuring the Effect of Potential Changes in C-V-P Variables

The basic techniques of C-V-P analysis that you have worked with in this chapter are used almost daily by organizations in the management processes of planning, controlling, and evaluating. As a result of understanding C-V-P analysis, you will be adept at evaluating the effects on profitability of the following common changes in C-V-P variables: (1) the amount of fixed costs, (2) the variable cost rate, (3) the sales price, (4) the sales volume or the number of units sold, and (5) combinations of these variables.

Changes in Fixed Costs

Many factors, such as an increase in property taxes or an increase in management's salaries, for example, will cause an increase in fixed costs. (Recall also from the opening scenario for this chapter that building a new facility such as a stadium can also increase fixed costs.) If all other factors remain constant, an increase in fixed costs always increases the number of units needed to break even. Obviously, the number of units needed to reach a target income will also increase. To illustrate, let's return again to the Jewels Corporation and assume that we need to analyze the effect on profits if fixed costs increase from $63,000 to $81,000. How many more baseball gloves must be sold to maintain Jewels' income goal of $36,000?

$$\text{Sales revenue} - \text{Variable costs} - \text{Fixed costs} = \text{Target income}$$
$$\$200X - \$110X - \$81,000 = \$36,000$$
$$\$90X = \$117,000$$
$$X = 1,300 \text{ gloves}$$

Because of the added fixed costs, Jewels must now sell 1,300 baseball gloves, instead of 1,100, to earn a target income of $36,000. The computations are quite simple. In fact, you may have found them unnecessary, realizing that if fixed costs increase by $18,000 ($81,000 − $63,000), and if the unit contribution margin remains $90 per glove, 200 additional gloves ($18,000 ÷ $90) will have to be sold in order to reach the $36,000 target income (1,100 + 200 = 1,300 gloves).

Changes in the Variable Cost Rate

Like an increase in fixed costs, an increase in the variable cost rate also increases the number of units needed to break even or to reach target income levels, when all other factors remain constant. Suppose that the variable cost rate increased from $110 per baseball glove to $130 per glove because of higher wages for factory personnel, increased costs of direct materials, or other factors. How does this cost increase affect the number of gloves needed to reach the target income, assuming that fixed costs are again $63,000?

$$\text{Sales revenue} - \text{Variable costs} - \text{Fixed costs} = \text{Target income}$$
$$\$200X - \$130X - \$63,000 = \$36,000$$
$$\$70X = \$99,000$$
$$X = 1,415 \text{ gloves*}$$

*Technically, if the C-V-P analysis results in a fractional answer, you should always round the answer *up* to the next digit. In this case, if you round the calculated answer of 1,414.29 to 1,414 gloves, you won't quite achieve the target income of $36,000.

The increase in the variable cost rate reduces the unit contribution margin (from $90 to $70), which means that more gloves must be sold to maintain the same target income. With a unit contribution margin of $90, the company would make a $36,000 target income by selling 1,100 baseball gloves; with a unit contribution margin of only $70, an additional 315 (1,415 − 1,100) gloves must be sold to earn at least a $36,000 target income.

Changes in Sales Price

If all other variables remain constant, an increase in the sales price decreases the sales volume needed to reach a target income. This is because an increase in sales price increases the contribution margin per baseball glove, thereby decreasing the number of gloves that must be sold to earn the same amount of target income.

To illustrate, assume that the demand for baseball gloves is overwhelming and that Jewels cannot produce gloves fast enough. Hence, we make a decision to increase the price from $200 to $230 per glove. As a result of the price increase, the number of gloves that must be sold to reach the target income of $36,000 decreases:

$$\text{Sales revenue} - \text{Variable costs} - \text{Fixed costs} = \text{Target income}$$
$$\$230X - \$110X - \$63,000 = \$36,000$$
$$\$120X = \$99,000$$
$$X = 825 \text{ gloves}$$

With the sales price increase of $30 per glove, the contribution margin also increases $30 per glove to $120; and with a $120 contribution margin per glove, only 825 gloves need to be sold to reach the $36,000 target income. Obviously, a decrease in the sales price would have the opposite effect; it would increase the number of units needed to reach the target income.

Changes in Sales Volume

As you have seen, the sales volume (the number of gloves to be sold) for the target income has varied with each change in one of the other variables. When other variables remain constant, an increase in the sales volume will result in an increase in income. Very simply, the more gloves sold, the higher the income (as long as the contribution margin is positive!). The degree of change in profits resulting from volume change depends on the size of the unit contribution margin. To be specific, the change in income will be equal to the change in sales volume units multiplied by the contribution margin per unit. So, when the unit contribution margin is high, a slight change in volume results in a dramatic change in profit. With a lower unit contribution margin, the change in profit is less.

Simultaneous Changes in Several Variables

Thus far, we have examined changes in only one variable at a time. However, in your work in actual business organizations, you will find that individual changes are quite rare. More often, a decision will affect several variables, all at the same time. For example, should Jewels Corporation increase fixed advertising costs by $20,000 and reduce the sales price by 10% if the result would be to increase sales volume by 500 units? The impact on the target income from these proposed changes is as follows:

Initial Data		Proposed Changes
Sales price per glove	$200	$180 ($200 × 90%)
Variable costs per glove	$110	$110
Fixed costs	$63,000	$83,000 ($63,000 + $20,000)
Target income	$36,000	X
Sales volume	1,100 gloves	1,600 gloves (1,100 + 500)

Computations and Result:

$$\text{Sales revenue} - \text{Variable costs} - \text{Fixed costs} = \text{Target income}$$
$$(\$180 \times 1,600) - (\$110 \times 1,600) - \$83,000 = X$$
$$\$288,000 - \$176,000 - \$83,000 = X$$
$$\$29,000 = X \text{ (target income)}$$

The analysis shows that target income would drop by $7,000 ($36,000 − $29,000) as a result of these changes. So, our decision should be to *not* implement the proposed changes.

Consider another possible decision: Should Jewels automate part of its production, thereby reducing (by $10) variable costs to $100 per unit and increasing (by $5,000) fixed costs to $68,000? The computation is as follows:

$$\text{Sales revenue} - \text{Variable costs} - \text{Fixed costs} = \text{Target income}$$
$$(\$200 \times 1,100) - (\$100 \times 1,100) - \$68,000 = X$$
$$\$220,000 - \$110,000 - \$68,000 = X$$
$$\$42,000 = X \text{ (target income)}$$

This analysis shows that implementing these proposed changes would be beneficial because they would increase target income by $6,000 ($42,000 − $36,000). Obviously, this is true only if the assumptions can be relied on—that is, if fixed costs will rise by no more than $5,000 and unit variable costs will decrease by a full $10.

Consider another example. Suppose Jewels Corporation could use part of the excess capacity of its operating facilities to make baseball bats. These bats would sell for $90 per unit, increase fixed costs by $40,000, and have a variable cost per unit of $45. Jewels wants to add this new product line only if it can increase income by $25,000. How many baseball bats must Jewels sell to reach this target income? The computation follows:

Caution

Remember, any change that affects the number of units sold changes both the total sales revenue *and* total variable costs.

$$\text{Sales revenue} - \text{Variable costs} - \text{Fixed costs} = \text{Target income}$$
$$\$90X - \$45X - \$40,000 = \$25,000$$
$$\$45X = \$65,000$$
$$X = 1,445 \text{ baseball bats (rounded up)}$$

Now that we have completed the C-V-P calculations, we must determine whether the company can produce and sell 1,445 baseball bats. If that sales goal seems attainable, the facilities should be used to make the bats. Don't forget that making C-V-P calculations is the easy part of managing an organization. It takes an excellent manager to successfully implement the results of a C-V-P analysis into a real business process.

business environment

Breaking Even in the Hotel Industry An international hotel chain undertook a project to increase the effectiveness of decision making of its properties in Europe, the Middle East, and Africa. In 1996, company executives wanted to improve the financial planning and control decisions of the hotel management teams. The Europe, Middle East, Africa division was responsible at that time for approximately 240 hotels. Essentially, the executives aimed to encourage a greater use of basic managerial accounting techniques such as budgeting models and C-V-P analysis in order to improve the profitability of individual hotels.

It was clear to the company that understanding how hotel costs behaved is absolutely key to making good decisions that affect market share analysis, annual budget preparation and monitoring of results, sales volume and business mix decisions, pricing policies, and cost management. In order to identify the fixed and variable costs in the hotels, the company first worked with individual hotel management teams within its organization who were intimately familiar with how costs behaved based on changes in sales volumes (i.e., hotel rooms rented). Initially, the company had these individuals determine from their own experience which costs were fixed, variable, or semi-variable (i.e., mixed) costs with respect to changes in sales volume. Scattergraph and statistical analyses were then used to estimate the fixed and variable proportions of the mixed costs—again related to sales volume—and allocate these costs to the main fixed and variable groups.

Computer spreadsheets were then used to assess key "what if" questions. For instance, "What is the likely effect on profit of a 3% shortfall in room revenue?". . . or . . . "How will profit change if a 5% growth in total sales volume occurs?" This alerts managers to the critical areas of profitability and indicates which revenue and cost areas require greater attention for a given decision. It also enables management to gain an overall indication of "profit stability" or "profit instability'" in relation to changes in revenue and cost of particular hotel properties. Knowledge of break-even levels and profit-and-loss implications of different business scenarios are relevant if managers are to make informed decisions which ensure survival, optimize profits, and limit risk, giving rise to a feeling of "being more in control" when making decisions.

In 1995, the year before the new management focus on C-V-P analysis commenced, the average operating profit margin in the Europe, Middle East, Africa division was 35%. In 1998, the average operating profit margin was 39%. Although the hotel executives do not believe that the new focus on C-V-P tools is the only reason for this improvement, it has played a positive role in significantly adding to shareholder value.

Source: Ian C. Graham and Peter J. Harris, "Development of a Profit Planning Framework in an International Hotel Chain: A Case Study," *International Journal of Contemporary Hospitality Management*, 1999 (Issue 5), pp. 198–204.

TO SUMMARIZE: The contribution margin is sales revenue less variable costs and is the amount of revenue left to cover fixed costs and provide a profit. The contribution margin can be expressed in total dollars, on a per-unit basis, or on a percentage basis. Because fixed costs remain constant within a relevant range, once fixed costs have been covered, income increases by the amount of the per-unit contribution margin for every additional unit sold. This relationship is used in C-V-P analysis. The basic C-V-P equation is:

$$\text{Sales revenue} - \text{Variable costs} - \text{Fixed costs} = \text{Target income}$$

Using this equation, you as a manager can work to plan, control, and evaluate the costs, prices, and sales output of the organization. The effects of changes in costs, prices, and volume on profitability may be determined by C-V-P analysis. Changes in individual variables or simultaneous changes in several variables can be analyzed with this technique.

Using Graphs to "See" C-V-P Relationships

5 Visualize C-V-P relationships using graphs.

Earlier in this chapter, we talked about using scattergraph methods as a way to analyze cost behavior. Recall that once we have plotted the history of costs on a graph and visually fitted a regression line through the data, we can then essentially "see" how the cost can be separated into its fixed and variable cost components. Now, by simply adding a line to the cost chart to represent revenue, we can graphically work with cost-volume-profit relationships. In fact, using graphs may be the most effective way to manage and communicate C-V-P information. This graphical approach allows you to visually examine cost and revenue data over a range of activity rather than at a single volume. Sometimes, though, reading precise information from a graph can be difficult. Hence, when analyzing specific proposals in the future, you will typically combine the C-V-P equations discussed in the preceding section with the graphs discussed in this section.

On a C-V-P graph, volume or activity level usually is shown on the horizontal axis, and total dollars of sales and costs are shown on the vertical axis. Lines are then drawn to represent total fixed costs, total costs, and total revenues. Exhibit 6 shows a C-V-P graph for Jewels Corporation.

Remember that fixed and variable cost relationships are valid only for the relevant range of activity (the screened area on the graph in Exhibit 6). In this case, fixed costs are $63,000, and variable costs are $110 per glove over the range of activity between 400 and 1,200 gloves sold. Total costs are $118,000 at 500 gloves [$63,000 + ($110 × 500 gloves)], $129,000 at 600 gloves [$63,000 + ($110 × 600 gloves)], and so on. Similarly, total revenues are $100,000 at 500 gloves ($200 × 500 gloves), $120,000 at 600 gloves, and so forth. The break-even point, the point at which total revenues equal total costs, is 700 gloves, or $140,000 in sales.

As shown in Exhibit 7, we can use the graphic format to isolate such items of interest as total variable costs, total fixed costs, the area in which losses occur, the area in which profits will be realized, and the break-even point. Because C-V-P graphs illustrate a wide range of activity, this tool can help in quickly determining approximately how much profit or loss will be realized at various levels of sales.

The Profit Graph

profit graph A graph that shows how profits vary with changes in volume.

With a few adjustments to a standard C-V-P graph, we can create what is called a **profit graph**, which plots only profits and losses and omits costs and revenues. A profit graph is another useful way to visualize how decisions regarding costs and revenues will impact profit. Exhibit 8 shows a profit graph for Jewels Corporation based on the same underlying data used in Exhibit 6.

Exhibit 6: A Cost-Volume-Profit Graph

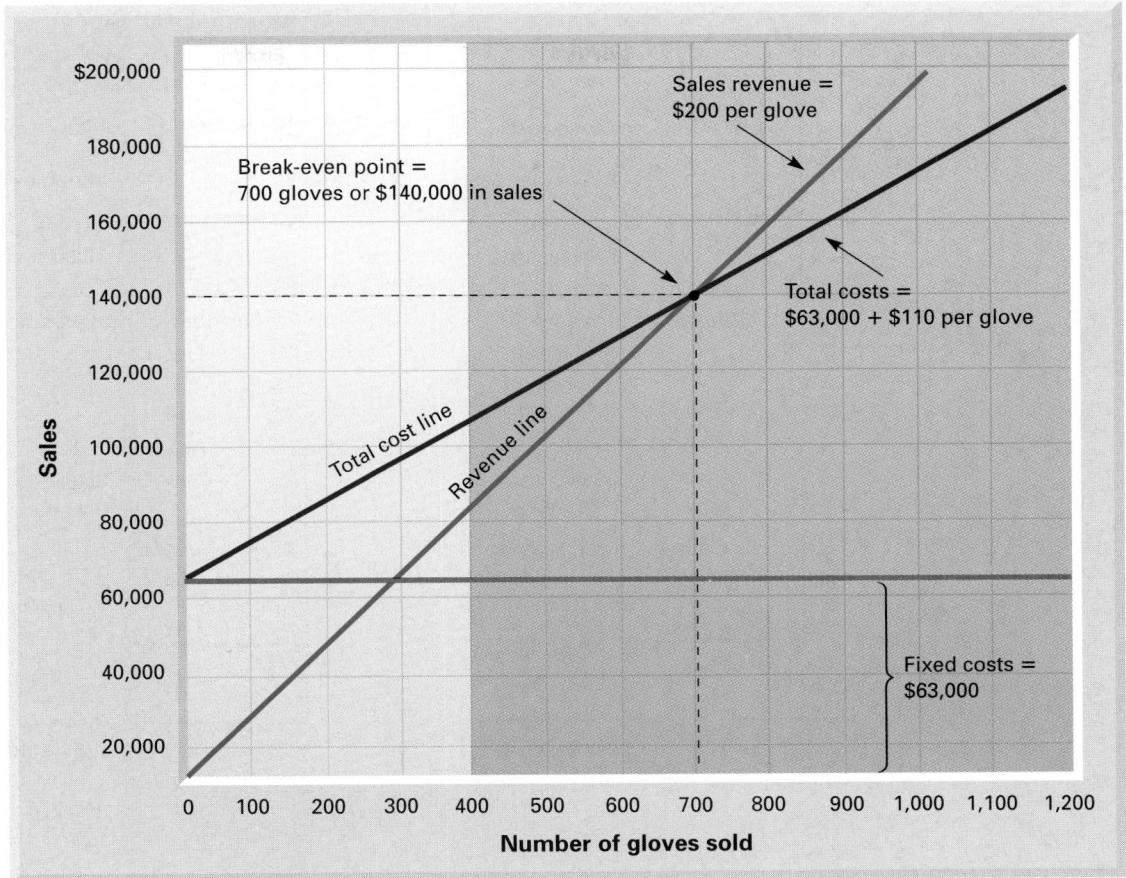

Notice that, though the horizontal axis of the profit graph is the same as those of the previous graphs, the vertical axis represents only profits and losses. As long as the contribution margin is positive, the maximum amount of losses that can occur is at a zero level of sales. With no sales, total losses will be the amount of the fixed costs. With the axes properly labeled, we can draw the profit line as follows:

1. Locate the loss for zero sales volume on the vertical axis. This is the total fixed cost, or negative $63,000 in this case.
2. Locate the profit or loss at another sales volume. For example, at sales of 700 gloves, profits are zero [$140,000 − ($63,000 + $77,000)], or at sales of 1,000 gloves, profits are $27,000 [$200,000 − ($63,000 + $110,000)].
3. After the two profit or loss points have been identified, draw a line through them back to the vertical axis.

Because of how simple it is to create, the profit graph is widely used for comparing competing projects. It has the disadvantage, however, of not showing specifically how revenues and costs vary with changes in sales volume.

A Comparison of C-V-P Graphs with C-V-P Equations

C-V-P graphs are very useful in understanding contribution margin income statements and C-V-P equations. To illustrate this point, let's again explore the question of what volume of

Exhibit 7: Cost-Volume-Profit Graphs

Exhibit 8: Profit Graph for Jewels Corporation

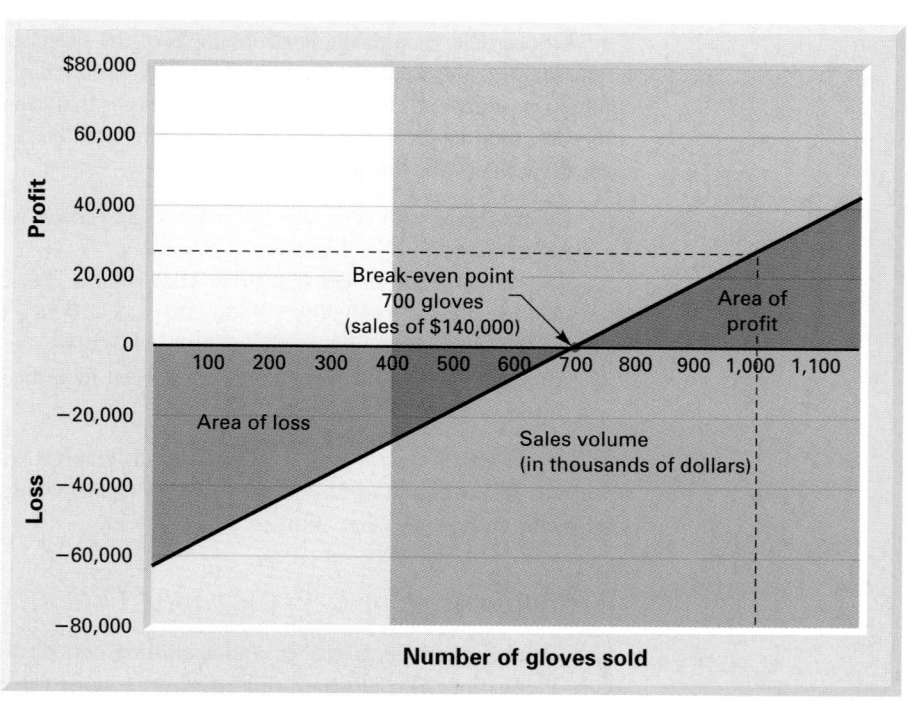

activity Jewels Corporation needs to reach a target income of $36,000. This was illustrated earlier with the equation approach, but it is repeated here to show that the graph approach will produce the same quantitative results. As you can see in Exhibit 9, Jewels Corporation must sell 1,100 baseball gloves to reach a target income of $36,000.

Exhibit 9: Comparison of C-V-P Equation with C-V-P Graph

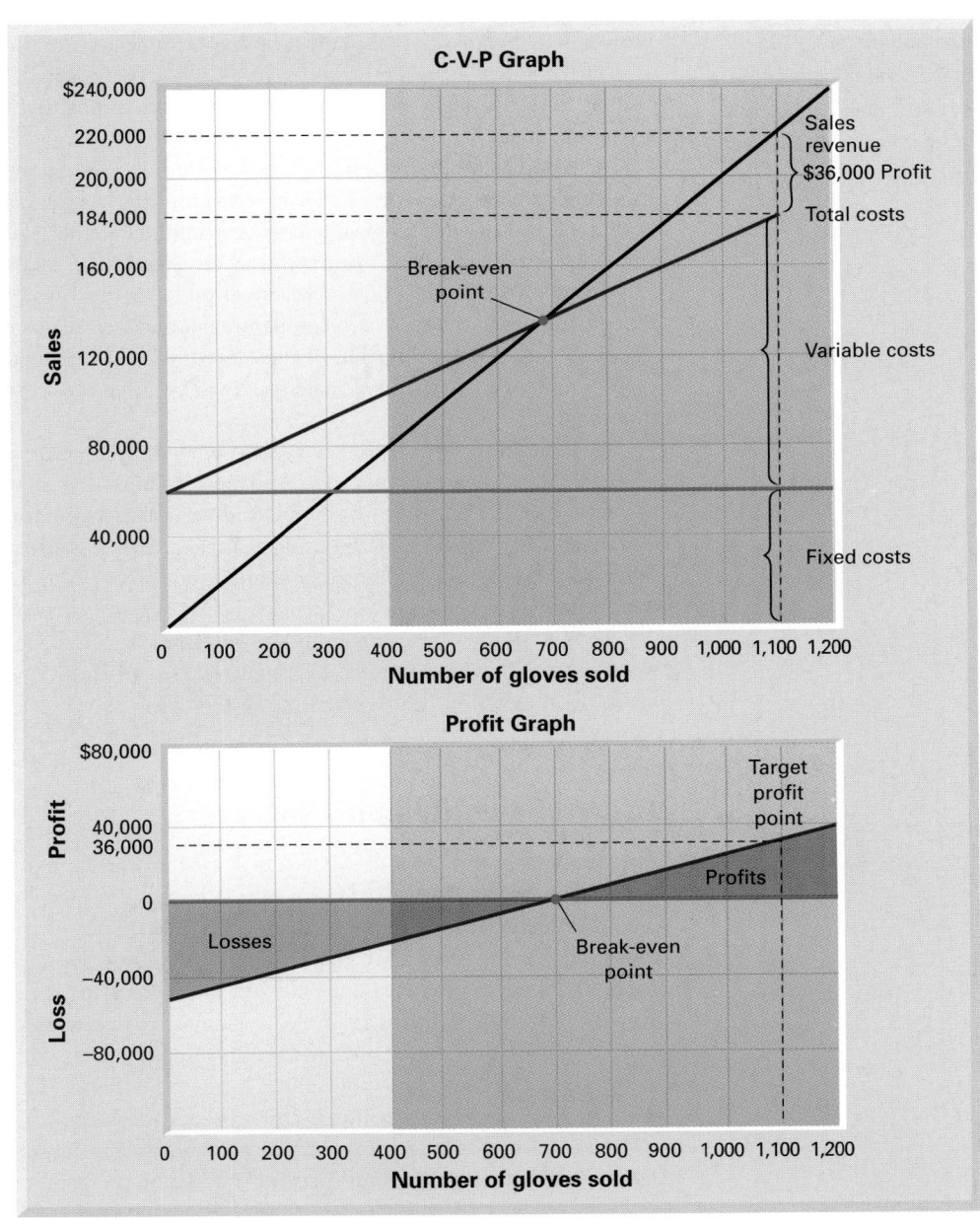

C-V-P Equation

(Sales price × Units) − (Variable costs × Units) − Fixed costs = Profit

$$\$200X - \$110X - \$63,000 = \$36,000$$
$$\$90X = \$99,000$$
$$X = 1,100 \text{ gloves}$$

TO SUMMARIZE: The financial effects on cost-volume-profit decisions can be examined by using either equations or graphs. These methods of analysis can be used to calculate the break-even point, which occurs at the point where total revenues equal total fixed costs plus total variable costs. These methods can also be used to project a target profit level, with profit being equal to the excess of revenues over total costs. The graphic approaches are useful because they highlight cost-volume-profit relationships over wide ranges of activity. The most common graphic approach involves plotting fixed costs as a horizontal line with variable costs representing the distance between the fixed costs and total costs line. A profit graph, which shows only profit or loss and volume, is much simpler, but it does not show how costs vary with changes in sales volume. Regardless of the approach, all variations of C-V-P analysis are based on the same calculations and on the same underlying concept of fixed and variable costs.

Limiting Assumptions of C-V-P Analysis

6 Identify the limiting assumptions of C-V-P analysis, and explain the issues of quality and time relative to C-V-P analysis decisions.

C-V-P analysis is an extremely useful tool to assist in making short-term operating decisions. However, C-V-P analysis has some limiting assumptions that must not be overlooked.

The first key assumption underlying C-V-P analysis is that the behavior of revenues and costs is linear throughout the relevant range. This means that C-V-P analysis is valid only for a relevant range.

A second assumption is that all costs, including mixed costs, can be accurately divided into fixed and variable categories. As we have seen in this chapter, some costs have characteristics of both fixed and variable costs. These costs sometimes are not easily classified into their fixed and variable components, which limits the accuracy of C-V-P analysis.

For companies with more than one product, a third major assumption in C-V-P analysis is required—that the mix of a company's products does not change over the relevant range. The sales mix is the proportion of the total units sold (or the total dollar sales) represented by each of a company's products. Sales mix will be discussed in the expanded material section of this chapter.

In addition to these three key assumptions, there are other limiting assumptions implicit in C-V-P analysis. For example, C-V-P analysis assumes that efficiency and productivity are held constant, that the prices of materials and other product components are constant, and that revenues and costs can be analyzed using a single activity base, such as volume. A related and very significant assumption, and one that clearly is not always valid, is that volume is the only, or even the primary, driver of costs. As discussed below, delivery time and quality can also impact costs.

Because of the limiting assumptions just described, a manager must use reasonable caution when making decisions using C-V-P analysis. Nevertheless, C-V-P analysis does provide a good model for predicting future operating results when specific relationships are defined and recognized.

Issues of Quality and Time

The emphasis in this chapter has been primarily on costs and profits and how they change when changes in variable costs, fixed costs, sales prices, and sales volume are made. Remember, however, that financial results are just one of several elements of performance that a manager must consider. Good managers are equally interested in how these changes will affect the quality of goods and services produced and sold and the speed at which products and services can be delivered to customers. If, for example, reducing fixed costs means that goods will be produced more slowly or that the quality of manufactured products will be reduced, then a decision to reduce fixed costs may be a poor one. On the other hand, if a company can automate a function using robotics instead of high-cost workers, for example, it may be possible to simultaneously reduce total costs, increase quality and consistency, and improve speed of production. To determine whether quality and speed of production are good or bad, a management team may need to compare its results with those of other firms, a process called *benchmarking*, which will be introduced in a later chapter.

TO SUMMARIZE: C-V-P analysis is based on three critical and limiting assumptions: (1) that the behavior of revenues and costs is linear throughout the relevant range, (2) that all costs can be categorized as either fixed or variable, and (3) that the sales mix does not change. When considering how changes in variable costs, fixed costs, sales prices, sales volume, and sales mix will affect profits, it is important to also consider how these changes will affect the quality of goods and services and the speed at which products and services can be delivered to customers. Decisions that increase quality, reduce costs, and speed up production are valuable changes and should be made; decisions that have a negative effect on one or more of these variables must be carefully analyzed and trade-offs considered.

Thus far, we have covered various types of costs, simple methods of analyzing mixed costs, and the basics of C-V-P analysis. In this expanded section, we cover an additional, more advanced method of analyzing mixed costs—least squares analysis. We also cover the effect of the sales mix on profitability and use the concept of operating leverage to explore differences in cost structures among manufacturing, merchandising, service, and e-commerce organizations.

Analysis of Mixed Costs—The Least Squares Method

7 Analyze mixed costs using the least squares method.

least squares method A method of segregating the fixed and variable portions of a mixed cost; the regression line, a line of averages, is statistically fitted through all cost points.

Earlier, we described two common methods for analyzing mixed costs: the scattergraph and high-low methods. These methods are relatively easy to use and provide useful estimates of the fixed and variable components of mixed costs. A more sophisticated method for analyzing mixed costs is the **least squares method**, which is the most accurate method of using a specific set of data to determine the fixed and variable portions of a mixed cost. Like the scattergraph, the least squares method fits a straight line through all points on a graph. However, instead of visually fitting the regression line through the cost points, it uses statistical analysis to guarantee that the line is the best possible fit for the applicable costs. As a result, the least squares method provides a better analysis because it isn't based on a subjective regression line like scattergraphs and because it uses all the cost data points rather than just the high and low data points as with the high-low method.

The formula for the least squares method is based on the equation for a straight line:

$$Y = a + bX$$

You probably recognize this classic equation from previous math classes you may have had. When this equation is used to do cost analysis, Y represents the total predicted cost; a represents the intercept and the fixed cost (if in the relevant range); b represents the variable cost rate or the slope of the line; and X represents the activity level being considered. Using cost and activity level data, this method involves the use of simultaneous equations to find the values of a and b. Once computed, these values can be combined with the projected activity level X to predict or estimate the total future cost Y. For example, if the values of a and b are computed to be $200 and $5, respectively, then for an estimated activity level of 100 direct labor hours, we can predict that:

$$Y \text{ (total predicted cost)} = \$200 + \$5(100 \text{ hours})$$
$$Y = \$200 + \$500$$
$$Y = \$700$$

You should understand that the regression line is basically a line of averages. Therefore, the *actual* total cost for 100 direct labor hours might be somewhat different from the *predicted* cost of $700. The method of least squares, however, attempts to minimize the differences between predicted and actual costs. Once a regression line has been fitted to historical data, the fixed and variable costs represented by the line can be used to predict the level of future costs.

Calculating the estimates of *a* (the intercept, or the total fixed cost) and *b* (the slope, or variable cost rate) requires solving the following two simultaneous equations:

$$1.\ \Sigma XY = a\Sigma X + b\Sigma X^2$$
$$2.\ \Sigma Y = na + b\Sigma X$$

where

a = fixed cost
b = variable cost rate
n = number of observations
Σ = summation sign (which means the sum of all historical data indicated by the sign)
X = activity level, or independent variable
Y = total (predicted) mixed cost, or dependent variable

Actually, solving these equations is easy with a calculator or computer, but difficult and tedious by hand. Initially solving these equations by hand may be useful to you in learning exactly how these equations work. However, as a manager working with cost estimations, you are going to have computers available to analyze large amounts of data very quickly. Hence, we will focus on describing and interpreting the typical output from a computerized application of least squares analysis. We will leave it to math classes to illustrate the manual calculations of the least squares method.

To illustrate the concept of least squares, let's return once more to the electricity cost data used earlier in this chapter to work with the scattergraph and high-low methods. Note that the historical data that we are using for this example are given for only six months; thus, the resulting regression equation will likely be less accurate than it would be with more data (say, 12 or 18 months of data).

Month	Direct Labor Hours Worked	Total Electricity Cost
January	7,000	$ 70,000
February	6,000	60,000
March	12,000	100,000
April	6,600	80,000
May	18,000	120,000
June	14,000	110,000

Using these data, the following output, shown in Exhibit 10, can be generated in just a matter of minutes using the "data analysis" tool in Excel®, a Microsoft database software program.[6] Now compare the least squares output with the results from our earlier work using the scattergraph and high-low methods:

	Fixed Costs	Variable Cost per Direct Labor Hour
Scattergraph method	$40,000 per month	$4.29 per direct labor hour
High-low method	30,000 per month	5.00 per direct labor hour
Least squares analysis	40,402 per month	4.68 per direct labor hour

6 There are literally hundreds of software programs that can be used to run regressions or least squares analysis.

Exhibit 10: Output of Least Squares Analysis Application

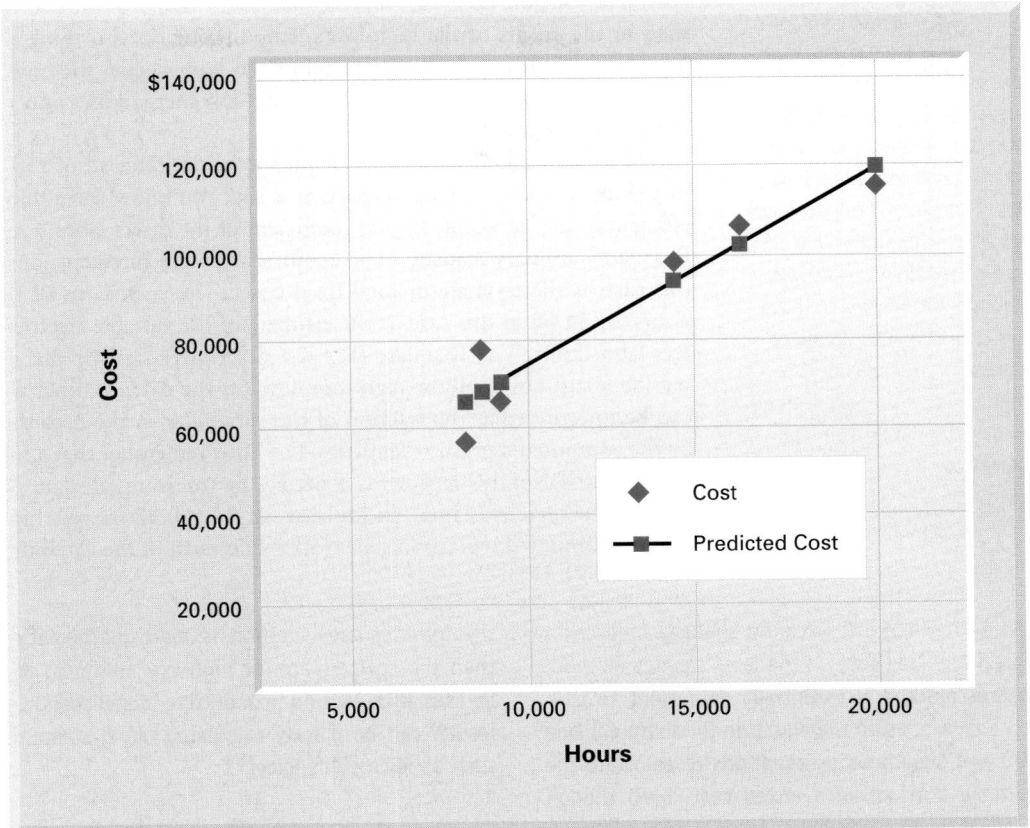

Month	Hours	Cost
January	7,000	$ 70,000
February	6,000	60,000
March	12,000	100,000
April	6,600	80,000
May	18,000	120,000
June	14,000	110,000

Summary Output

Regression Statistics

Multiple R	0.962
R square	0.926
Adjusted R square	0.907
Standard error	7207.705
Observations	6

	Coefficients	Standard Error	t Stat	P-value	Lower 95%	Upper 95%
Intercept	$40,402.03	$7,613.10	$5.31	0.0061	$19,264.63	$61,539.43
Hours	$ 4.68	$ 0.66	$7.05	0.0021	$ 2.84	$ 6.52

FYI:

An R² of more than 0.9 is actually not very common in practice. It is often quite rare to identify a *single* cost driver that explains most of the variance of important costs in an organization. Typically, organizations find that there are many things that affect a particular cost (e.g., headcount, floor space, operating hours, etc.), which requires that cost analysis be based on multiple cost drivers. The least squares analysis method we have discussed here is also known as simple or single linear regression. *Multiple* linear regression, a technique you may have learned about in a statistics class, uses a similar approach to identify the impact of several activities on changes in a specific cost.

You can see that the least squares analysis results in fixed costs estimated at $40,402 and the variable cost rate estimated to be $4.68 per direct labor hour. As you can see, the results are more similar to the results of the scattergraph method than to the results of the high-low method. Why do you think this is the case? The reason is that both the scattergraph and least squares methods are essentially using all of the historical data while the high-low method uses only two data points (February and May).

We won't take time in this chapter to understand all of the output shown in Exhibit 10; what is most important is that you know three things: (1) the coefficient of the intercept, (2) the coefficient of the direct labor hours, and (3) the R square summary statistic. The coefficient of the intercept, or $40,402.03 in this case, is the estimate of total fixed costs. The coefficient of the direct labor hours, or $4.68 in this case, is the estimate of the variable electricity cost per direct labor hour. The R square (R^2) is a descriptive statistic that provides information about how well the regression line fits the data; in other words, R square can be interpreted as the fraction of the variability in the data that is explained by the computed regression statistics. For now, remember that a higher R^2 is better, and an R^2 of 1.0 represents a perfect fit (meaning all data points were exactly on the regression line). In this case, an R^2 of 0.926 is very high and suggests that the computed regression statistics explain most of the variability in the data.[7]

TO SUMMARIZE: A more sophisticated technique for analyzing mixed costs is the least squares method. The least squares method is essentially equivalent to simple regression analysis, using the equation for a straight line ($Y = a + bX$) and simultaneous equations to calculate the fixed and variable portions of a mixed cost. Even though the least squares method is more mathematically correct than the scattergraph or high-low methods, it still should be used with caution in analyzing mixed costs. Least squares results can be quickly calculated using computer programs such as Microsoft's Excel®.

Sales Mix

8 Explain the effects of sales mix on profitability.

sales mix The relative proportion of total units sold (or total sales dollars) that is represented by each of a company's products.

Earlier in this chapter, we described some important limiting assumptions of C-V-P analysis. As a manager using C-V-P, you need to be aware of what this tool can and cannot do. One important issue is that C-V-P analysis must be adjusted when a company starts changing the mix of products that it sells. **Sales mix** is the proportion of the total units represented by each of a company's products. To keep our discussions simple, in previous sections of the chapter we used examples of companies with only one product. Many companies have more than one product, however, so you need to understand how sales mix issues are resolved. To illustrate how a change in sales mix can affect a company's C-V-P relationships, let's assume that Multi-Product, Inc., sells three different products. Following are the monthly revenues and costs for each type of product:

	Product A		Product B		Product C		Total	
	Amount	Percent	Amount	Percent	Amount	Percent	Amount	Percent
Sales revenue	$25,000	100%	$45,000	100.00%	$30,000	100%	$100,000	100%
Less variable costs	20,000	80	30,000	66.67	21,000	70	71,000	71
Contribution margin	$ 5,000	20%	$15,000	33.33%	$ 9,000	30%	$ 29,000	29%
Sales mix	25%		45%		30%		100%	

---

[7] The adjusted R^2 of 0.907 is a more conservative estimate of the variance explained in the data and is preferred to the R^2 statistic in some circumstances.

FYI:

A computer can make sales mix and other C-V-P analysis computations easier to do. Using simulation or other programs, you can quickly calculate the financial effects of changes in the sales of one product or simultaneous changes in sales of several products.

Total sales are $100,000, which in this example includes $25,000 in sales of Product A, $45,000 of Product B, and $30,000 of Product C. Therefore, the sales mix is 25% Product A ($25,000 ÷ $100,000), 45% Product B ($45,000 ÷ $100,000), and 30% Product C ($30,000 ÷ $100,000). With this sales mix, the average variable cost ratio is 71%, which is determined by dividing total variable costs of $71,000 by total sales of $100,000. If Multi-Product, Inc., had fixed costs of $17,400 and desired a target income of $40,000, the necessary sales volume (in dollars) would be:

$$\text{Sales revenue} - (0.71)\text{Sales revenue} - \$17,400 = \$40,000$$
$$(0.29)\text{Sales revenue} = \$57,400$$
$$\text{Sales revenue} = \$57,400 \div 0.29$$
$$\text{Sales revenue} = \$197,932 \text{ (rounded up)}$$

Alternatively, you could calculate the average contribution margin ratio by subtracting the total variable costs from total sales and dividing the result (total contribution margin of $29,000) by total sales of $100,000. The company could then divide the average contribution margin ratio (29%) into fixed costs plus target income ($17,400 + $40,000). This revised, more compact formula is simply a restatement of the preceding equation.

$$\frac{\text{Fixed costs} + \text{Target income}}{\text{Average contribution margin ratio}} = \frac{\$57,400}{0.29} = \$197,932 \text{ (rounded up)}$$

Remember, though, that $197,932 in sales will achieve the target income only if the average variable cost and contribution margin ratios, and therefore the sales mix, do not change. In order for you to better understand this fact, assume that the total sales revenue and the sales price of each product remain the same but that the sales mix changes as follows:

	Product A		Product B		Product C		Total	
	Amount	Percent	Amount	Percent	Amount	Percent	Amount	Percent
Sales revenue	$50,000	100%	$30,000	100.00%	$20,000	100%	$100,000	100%
Less variable costs	40,000	80	20,000	66.67	14,000	70	74,000	74
Contribution margin	$10,000	20%	$10,000	33.33%	$ 6,000	30%	$ 26,000	26%
Sales mix	50%		30%		20%		100%	

As you can see in this example, the variable cost and contribution margin ratios for each product remain the same, but the sales mix changes. Product A now comprises 50% of total sales instead of 25%. Because Product A has a lower contribution margin ratio than Products B and C, the average contribution margin ratio decreases from 29 to 26% (stated another way, the average variable cost ratio increases from 71% to 74%). Now think about how this change in the sales mix would affect profit and the volume of sales revenue needed to break even. Would you expect the necessary sales volume to increase or decrease?

Let's use the more compact formula based on the average contribution margin ratio to calculate the new sales volume. When we run the new C-V-P calculation, the sales volume needed to generate $40,000 of target income increases to $220,770, computed as follows:

STOP & THINK

Before moving on, can you calculate the necessary sales volume of $220,770 in the second sales mix example using the familiar C-V-P equation: Sales revenue − Variable costs − Fixed costs = Target income?

$$\frac{\text{Fixed costs} + \text{Target income}}{\text{Average contribution margin ratio}} = \frac{\$57,400}{0.26} = \$220,770 \text{ (rounded up)}$$

The important thing that we've learned from these sales mix calculations is that one sensible profit-maximizing strategy for management would be to maintain as large a contribution margin as possible on all products and then

STOP & THINK

Would maximizing the sales of the highest contribution margin products still be the best profit-maximizing strategy if the company experienced production constraints such that producing more of the highest contribution margin products severely limited the quality or production speed of other products?

to emphasize those products with the largest individual contribution margins. In the remaining chapters of this text, we discuss procedures that management can use to control costs and, hence, maintain high contribution margins. The second part of this strategy—emphasizing the products with the highest contribution margin ratios—is a marketing function. Multi-Product, Inc., for example, should promote Product B more aggressively than Product A. With other factors being equal, a company should spend more advertising dollars and pay higher sales commissions on its products with higher contribution margin ratios. In fact, instead of paying commissions based on total sales, a good strategy would be to base sales commissions on the total contribution margin generated. This way, the mix of products that maximizes the sales staff's commissions will be the mix that provides the company with the greatest overall profit.

> **TO SUMMARIZE:** Sales mix is the proportion of the total units sold represented by each of a company's products. Changes in sales mix can affect profits because not all products have the same contribution margin. Other things being equal, to maximize profits, management should put greater emphasis on the sale of products with higher contribution margin ratios.

Cost Structure in Different Types of Organizations

9 Describe how fixed and variable costs differ in manufacturing, service, merchandising, and e-commerce organizations, and illustrate these differences with the operating leverage concept.

operating leverage The extent to which fixed costs are part of a company's cost structure; the higher the proportion of fixed costs to variable costs, the faster income increases or decreases with changes in sales volume.

Now that we have nearly completed this chapter, we have developed a lot of insight into how to think about and manage costs in the process of making profit-planning decisions. This chapter is actually a lot about the strategy—the strategy of how a company works with its specific types of costs and activities to create a profit. Overall, we now basically understand how cost-volume-profit relationships and contribution margins highlight the different effects that variable and fixed costs have on profitability. As we close this chapter, an important management issue to be understood has to do with the amount of fixed costs a company has in its cost structure. The amount of fixed costs an organization commits itself to often has a lot to do with its type of business, e.g., merchandising, manufacturing, or service. In addition, the arrival of e-commerce into the economy is having an impact on cost structures of organizations. We'll talk more about differences between merchandising, manufacturing, service, and e-commerce companies throughout the remaining chapters in this textbook. For now, we'll simply illustrate the differences among these organizations by applying the concept of **operating leverage** to illustrate how a company can manage risk (in terms of profits) by the way it organizes its cost structure—in other words, how much the company is committed to using fixed costs versus variable costs to do business.

Imagine that you have worked with two of your college friends to design a new computer software game that you expect to market to college campuses across the nation. You and your partners have identified three ways to approach the market. First, you can take on the role of the merchant by contracting with a software manufacturing company to handle all the production of the packaged software. You can then concentrate on the sales and marketing of their new game. This approach won't require an expensive production facility, but the reality is that you will have to pay a high price per unit to the company that handles the production of the packaged software. In the second approach, you can take on the role of manufacturer by setting up your own production facilities. In this case, because all of your effort will be dedicated to producing the game, you will need to wholesale the software product to another merchant company that will then resell the product to the actual customers. Finally, you can "virtually" sell the game to other college students by contracting with an e-commerce company that will host your software download site for a significant fixed fee per month. In any case, regardless of whether you and your partners will wholesale the game to another merchant or retail the game directly to the college student market, you have determined that you can sell the game for $100. The costs of each of these methods of structuring your business are as follows:

Business Structure	Variable Cost per Unit to Manufacture or to Purchase from a Manufacturer	Fixed Cost per Year for the Merchandising, Manufacturing, or E-Commerce Facility
Traditional retail merchant	$80	$100,000
Manufacturer	25	375,000
E-commerce merchant	0	500,000

Caution

Don't confuse the concept of operating leverage with the concept of financial leverage, though there is a lot of similarity in these concepts. While both concepts focus on risk and the sensitivity of profit to changes in sales volume, financial leverage has to do with the use of debt versus equity to provide financing for a company. In general, the financial leverage (and risk) of a company increases as management chooses to use debt, rather than equity, to raise funds for the company. Similarly, the operating leverage (and risk) of a company increases as management chooses to emphasize fixed cost, rather than variable cost, to create or obtain the product for sale to the marketplace.

STOP & THINK

Think about the level of operating leverage you would expect to find in a service organization such as a consulting company or a law firm. Would these kinds of organizations typically have high or low levels of operating leverage?

As you can see, one of the issues that you must decide when selecting your company's business structure is whether you and your partners want to commit to high fixed costs in order to have low variable costs, or vice versa. This trade-off of fixed versus variable costs is what we mean when we talk about operating leverage. As total fixed costs increase and variable costs per unit decrease, the operating leverage of the organization increases. In the example above, the operating leverage of your company will be very high if you choose to structure your company as an e-commerce merchant. So, the question you should be asking yourself is whether it is good or bad to have high operating leverage? The answer is that it depends on whether the company is operating above or below the break-even point.

The C-V-P graphs in Exhibit 11 show us the impact of operating leverage for these three types of companies. The break-even point (which is the same for all three companies) is at a sales volume of 5,000 games sold each year. At this point, all three companies would generate the same level of profit—nothing. As sales move above or below the break-even point, however, there are significant differences in profit (i.e., the distance between the revenue line and the total costs line) between the company structures. If sales are below the break-even point, then structuring the company as an e-commerce merchant will generate a lot of losses. If the company can sell more than 5,000 games per year, however, then the e-commerce merchant structure will generate the most profit per year. Essentially, operating leverage is a measure of risk. With high levels of operating leverage, the company is at risk of losing a lot of money if sales go down. But business risk often has an upside. In the case of operating leverage, the risk of loss is balanced by the potential for large gains in income as sales go up. So your decision on how to structure your company partly depends on the impact on operating leverage and on how much risk you are willing to accept.

TO SUMMARIZE: The relationship between fixed and variable costs differs across different types of organizations. Generally, traditional merchandising companies have relatively low levels of fixed costs and high levels of variable costs. On the other hand, manufacturing companies often have higher levels of fixed costs and lower levels of variable costs. The emergence of e-commerce in this economy has resulted in some companies that are even more extremely committed to fixed costs with little or no variable product costs. These cost structure differences are important and are illustrated in the concept of operating leverage. Operating leverage relates to the amount of fixed costs a company has in its cost structure. When sales are expected to increase, high operating leverage results in higher income, and vice versa.

Exhibit 11: "Seeing" Operating Leverages

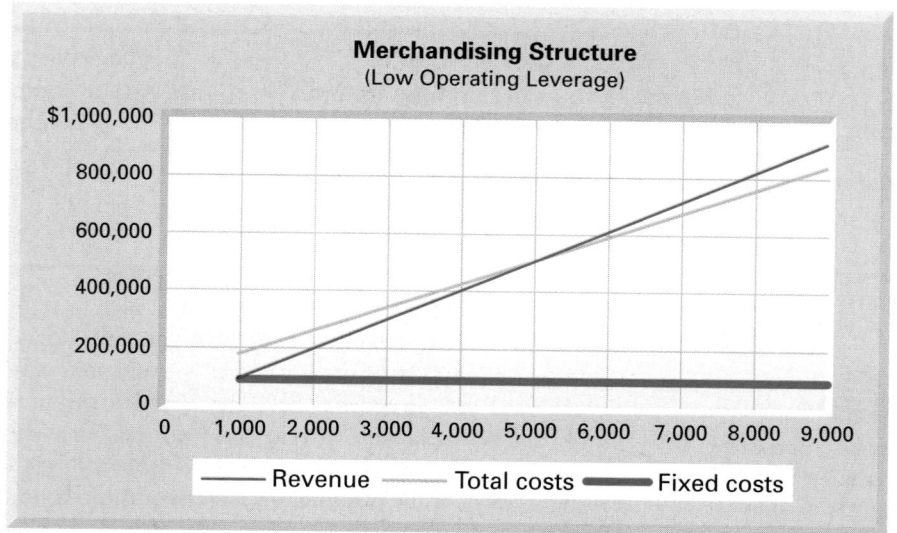

			Sales in Units	Revenue	Total Variable Costs	Contribution Margin	Total Fixed Costs	Operating Income
Price per unit	$	100	3,000	$300,000	$(240,000)	$ 60,000	$(100,000)	$(40,000)
Variable cost per unit		80	5,000	500,000	(400,000)	100,000	(100,000)	—
Total fixed costs		100,000	7,000	700,000	(560,000)	140,000	(100,000)	40,000

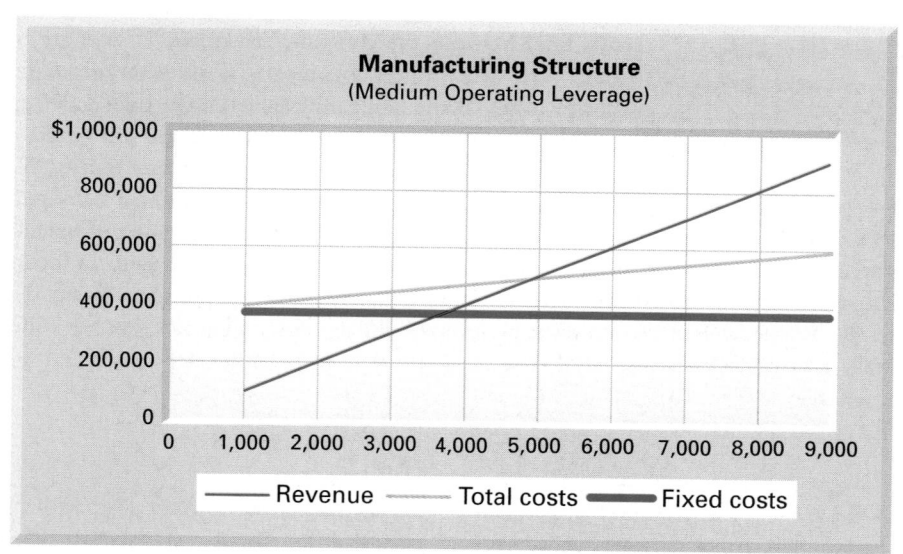

			Sales in Units	Revenue	Total Variable Costs	Contribution Margin	Total Fixed Costs	Operating Income
Price per unit	$	100	3,000	$300,000	$ (75,000)	$225,000	$(375,000)	$(150,000)
Variable cost per unit		25	5,000	500,000	(125,000)	375,000	(375,000)	—
Total fixed costs		375,000	7,000	700,000	(175,000)	525,000	(375,000)	150,000

Exhibit 11: (Concluded)

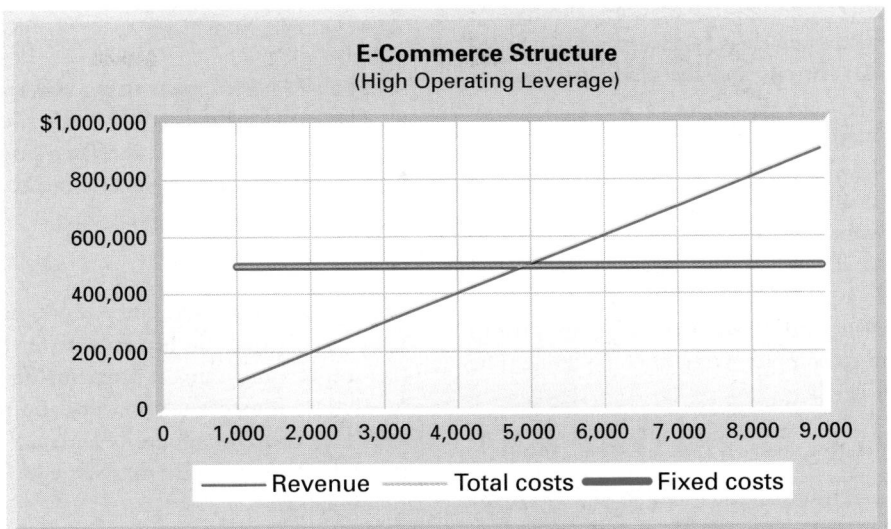

		Sales in Units	Revenue	Total Variable Costs	Contribution Margin	Total Fixed Costs	Operating Income
Price per unit	$ 100	3,000	$300,000	$ —	$300,000	$(500,000)	$(200,000)
Variable cost per unit	0	5,000	500,000	—	500,000	(500,000)	—
Total fixed costs	500,000	7,000	700,000	—	700,000	(500,000)	200,000

review of learning objectives

1 **Understand the key factors involved in cost-volume-profit (C-V-P) analysis and why it is such an important tool in management decision making.** C-V-P analysis is a very important management concept. It is a technique you will use as a manager to understand how profits may be expected to vary in relation to changes in key variables: sales price and volume, variable costs, fixed costs, and mix of products. C-V-P analysis is a particularly useful tool for planning and making operating decisions. It can provide data to stimulate increased sales efforts or cost reduction programs; assist in production scheduling or marketing strategy; and help establish company policies, for example, the appropriate product mix or the fixed cost structure of a company. In order to be effective as a manager, you will need a comprehensive understanding and ability to use C-V-P analysis.

2 **Explain and analyze the basic cost behavior patterns—variable, fixed, mixed, and stepped.** Understanding cost behavior patterns can assist you in making key operating decisions. The two basic cost behavior patterns are variable and

fixed. Costs that vary in total in direct proportion to changes in the level of activity are variable costs. Therefore, per-unit variable costs remain constant. Generally, we assume that there is a linear relationship between variable costs and level of activity within the relevant range; for other ranges, variable costs are curvilinear. Costs that do not change in total with changes in activity level (within the relevant range) are fixed costs; thus, per-unit fixed costs decrease as level of activity increases. Costs that contain both fixed and variable components are mixed costs. Stepped costs increase in total in a stair-step fashion with the level of activity. If the steps are wide, the cost is treated as a fixed cost for analysis purposes; if the steps are narrow, the cost is approximated as a variable cost.

3 **Analyze mixed costs using the scattergraph and high-low methods.** Before mixed costs can be analyzed and used in decision making, they must be divided into their fixed and variable components. The scattergraph and high-low methods are commonly used to analyze mixed costs. The scattergraph method involves visually plotting a straight line (the regression line) through points on a graph of cost data at various activity levels. With the high-low method, the highest and lowest levels of activity and their associated costs are used to calculate the variable cost rate and the total fixed costs.

4 **Perform C-V-P analyses, and describe the effects potential changes in C-V-P variables have on company profitability.** C-V-P analysis is based on the computation of contribution margin, which is sales revenue less variable costs. Contribution margin is the amount available to cover fixed costs and then provide a profit. C-V-P analysis is commonly used to assess break-even points (where contribution margin equals fixed costs) and to compute target income levels. The basic C-V-P equation is:

Sales revenue − Variable costs − Fixed costs = Profit

The C-V-P equation will be especially useful to you as a manager in assessing how profits can be expected to change when costs or sales revenue change. Increases in fixed or variable costs result in a larger number of sales being required to break even and reach target income levels. Increases in sales price result in a decreased number of sales being required to break even and reach target income levels.

5 **Visualize C-V-P relationships using graphs.** C-V-P graphs and profit graphs are effective methods for visualizing the effect of impacts on key variables in the C-V-P equation. In addition, the graphic approach effectively allows managers to simultaneously analyze several different activity levels.

6 **Identify the limiting assumptions of C-V-P analysis, and explain the issues of quality and time relative to C-V-P analysis decisions.** C-V-P analysis has several limiting assumptions, including the following: (1) cost and revenue behavior patterns are linear and remain constant over the relevant range, (2) all costs can be categorized as either fixed or variable, and (3) the sales mix of products is constant over the relevant range. When making changes in costs, revenues, and volume, remember to consider the impact on the quality of products or services and the speed at which those products and services can be delivered to customers. Changes that result in decreased costs that also decrease product or service quality or that slow down the delivery of products or services may not be good decisions.

7 **Analyze mixed costs using the least squares method.** The least squares method uses a simple regression analysis to identify the variable and fixed portions of mixed costs. The formula for the least squares method is based on the following equation for a straight line:

$$Y = a + bX$$

where a is total fixed cost and b is per-unit variable cost. Least square calculations can be easily performed using basic computer software programs or programmed calculators. One output of least square analysis calculations is the R^2 statistic, which measures the amount of variance in the cost that is explained by changes in the activity level (depicted by X in the equation above).

8 **Explain the effects of sales mix on profitability.** Sales mix is the proportion of total units sold represented by each of a company's products. Because all products do not have the same contribution margin ratios, changes in the sales mix of products sold can significantly affect total profits. When you are working as a manager to maximize profits, it is best to maintain as large a contribution margin as possible on all products and then emphasize those products with the largest individual contribution margin ratios.

9 **Describe how fixed and variable costs differ in manufacturing, service, merchandising, and e-commerce organizations, and illustrate these differences with the operating leverage concept.** The trade-off between fixed costs and variable costs is often related to whether a company is structured as a manufacturing, merchandising, or service firm. The advent of e-commerce has created the potential for companies to have very high levels of fixed costs and very low levels of variable costs. The impact of the fixed cost/variable cost relationship on profits is captured in the concept of operating leverage. Operating leverage is a measure of the extent to which a company's costs are fixed rather than variable. Companies with higher fixed costs and lower per-unit variable costs will experience higher operating leverage and, therefore, a tendency for profits to increase at a faster rate when sales increase. Hence, a company with high operating leverage will be more profitable in good times but have higher losses in bad times.

 ey terms & concepts

r eview problems

Variable and Fixed Costs Analyses

Blade Corporation manufactures two types of inline skates—a basic model and a racing model. During the year 2006, Blade accumulated the following summary information about its two products:

	Racing Model	Basic Model
Selling price	$130	$65
Number of units manufactured and sold	14,000	9,000

	Racing Model		Basic Model	
	Units	**Costs**	**Units**	**Costs**
January	1,200	$ 112,000	800	$ 39,600
February	900	91,000	600	30,000
March	800	76,400	450	25,800
April	1,400	124,800	900	36,900
May	950	92,650	1,000	47,000
June	1,600	146,800	1,200	57,300
July	1,400	134,600	1,300	60,600
August	1,700	154,500	650	32,195
September	1,550	140,200	850	44,250
October	1,500	134,500	500	27,000
November	600	62,500	350	20,700
December	400	44,000	400	22,000
Totals	14,000	$1,313,950	9,000	$443,345

Required:
1. Use the high-low method to estimate the variable and fixed production costs of both the racing model and the basic model skates.
2. All selling costs are fixed, and they total $200,000 for the racing model and $80,000 for the basic model. Prepare a contribution margin income statement for each model at sales of 10,000 racing and 10,000 basic skates.

Solution
1. Variable and Fixed Costs
The high-low method involves finding the variable and fixed costs at the high and low levels of production. In this case:

	Racing Model	Basic Model
High-production month	1,700 (Aug.)	1,300 (July)
Low-production month	400 (Dec.)	350 (Nov.)
Difference	1,300	950
Total production costs of high month	$154,500	$60,600
Total production costs of low month	44,000	20,700
Difference	$110,500	$39,900

Once the differences are known, the change in units (production) is divided into the change in costs to determine the variable cost rate.

$$\frac{\text{Change in costs}}{\text{Change in units}} = \text{Variable cost rate}$$

$$\text{Racing model: } \frac{\$110,500}{1,300} = \$85$$

$$\text{Basic model: } \frac{\$39,900}{950} = \$42$$

Because total variable costs equal unit variable cost times number of units produced, and total costs equal total variable costs plus total fixed costs, fixed costs can now be calculated.

$$\text{Total costs} - (\text{Variable cost per unit} \times \text{Number of units}) = \text{Total fixed costs}$$

	Racing Model	Basic Model
High production level (X) =	$154,500 - $85(1,700)	$60,600 - $42(1,300)
	$X = \$154,500 - \$144,500$	$X = \$60,600 - \$54,600$
	$X = \$10,000$	$X = \$6,000$
Low production level (X) =	$44,000 - $85(400)	$20,700 - $42(350)
	$X = \$44,000 - \$34,000$	$X = \$20,700 - \$14,700$
	$X = \$10,000$	$X = \$6,000$

Thus, we have the following:

	Racing Model	Basic Model
Variable cost rate	$ 85	$ 42
Total fixed costs	10,000	6,000

2. Contribution Margin Income Statements

Blade Corporation
Contribution Margin Income Statements
For the Year Ended December 31, 2006

	Racing Model	Basic Model
Sales revenue (at 10,000 units)	$1,300,000	$ 650,000
Less variable cost of goods sold*	(850,000)	(420,000)
Contribution margin	$ 450,000	$ 230,000
Less fixed cost of goods sold	(10,000)	(6,000)
Less fixed selling costs	(200,000)	(80,000)
Income	$ 240,000	$ 144,000

*$85 per unit for racing model; $42 per unit for basic model.

Assessing the Effects of Changes in Costs, Prices, and Volume on Profitability

K&D Company plans the following for the coming year:

Sales volume	100,000 units
Sales price	$2.50 per unit
Variable costs	$1.30 per unit
Fixed costs	$60,000

Required:

1. Determine K&D's target income.
2. Compute what the target income would be under each of the following independent assumptions:
   a. The sales volume increases 20%.
   b. The sales price decreases 20%.
   c. Variable costs increase 20%.
   d. Fixed costs decrease 20%.

Solution

1. Target Income

Basic C-V-P equation: Sales revenue − Variable costs − Fixed costs = Target income

$$\text{(Units sold} \times \text{Sales price)} - \text{(Units sold} \times \text{Variable unit cost)} - \text{Fixed costs} = \text{Target income}$$
$$(100{,}000 \times \$2.50) - (100{,}000 \times \$1.30) - \$60{,}000 = X$$
$$\$250{,}000 - \$130{,}000 - \$60{,}000 = X$$
$$\$60{,}000 = X$$

This answer can be validated by dividing fixed costs by the per-unit contribution margin to find the break-even point and then multiplying the excess units to be sold above the break-even point by the per-unit contribution margin of $1.20 ($2.50 − $1.30).

$$\frac{\text{Fixed costs}}{\text{Per-unit contribution margin}} = \text{Break-even point}$$

$$\frac{\$60{,}000}{\$1.20} = 50{,}000 \text{ units}$$

Units sold	100,000
Less break-even point (units)	50,000
Excess	50,000
Per-unit contribution margin	× $1.20
Target income	$60,000

2a. The sales volume increases 20%.

$$(100{,}000 \times 1.2 \times \$2.50) - (100{,}000 \times 1.2 \times \$1.30) - \$60{,}000 = X$$
$$\$300{,}000 - \$156{,}000 - \$60{,}000 = X$$
$$\$84{,}000 = X$$

In this case, the contribution margin does not change. Therefore, the answer can be validated by multiplying the units to be sold in excess of the break-even point by the per-unit contribution margin of $1.20 to find the target income.

Units sold	120,000
Less break-even point (units)	50,000
Excess	70,000
Per-unit contribution margin	× $1.20
Target income	$84,000

2b. The sales price decreases 20%.

$$(100,000 \times \$2.50 \times 0.8) - (100,000 \times \$1.30) - \$60,000 = X$$
$$\$200,000 - \$130,000 - \$60,000 = X$$
$$\$10,000 = X$$

In this case, the contribution margin changes. Therefore, the answer can be validated by dividing fixed costs by the new per-unit contribution margin of $0.70 ($2.00 − $1.30) to find the new break-even point and then multiplying the units to be sold in excess of the break-even point by the new per-unit contribution margin.

$$\frac{\$60,000 \text{ (fixed costs)}}{\$0.70 \text{ (new per-unit contribution margin)}} = 85,715 \text{ units (new break-even point, rounded up)}$$

Units sold	100,000
Less break-even point (units)	85,715
Excess	14,285
Per-unit contribution margin	× $0.70
Target income	$10,000 (rounded)

2c. Variable costs increase 20%.

$$(100,000 \times \$2.50) - (100,000 \times \$1.30 \times 1.2) - \$60,000 = X$$
$$\$250,000 - \$156,000 - \$60,000 = X$$
$$\$34,000 = X$$

In this case, the contribution margin changes. Therefore, the answer can be validated by dividing fixed costs by the new per-unit contribution margin of $0.94 ($2.50 − $1.56) to find the new break-even point and then multiplying the units to be sold in excess of the break-even point by the new per-unit contribution margin.

$$\frac{\$60,000 \text{ (fixed costs)}}{\$0.94 \text{ (new per-unit contribution margin)}} = 63,830 \text{ units (new break-even point, rounded up)}$$

Units sold	100,000
Less break-even point (units)	63,830
Excess	36,170
Per-unit contribution margin	× $0.94
Target income	$34,000 (rounded)

2d. Fixed costs decrease 20%.

$$(100,000 \times \$2.50) - (100,000 \times \$1.30) - (\$60,000 \times 0.8) = X$$
$$\$250,000 - \$130,000 - \$48,000 = X$$
$$\$72,000 = X$$

In this case, the contribution margin does not change, but fixed costs, and hence the break-even point, do. Therefore, the answer can be validated by dividing the per-unit contribution margin of $1.20 into the new fixed costs to find the break-even point and then multiplying the units to be sold in excess of the break-even point by the per-unit contribution margin.

$$\frac{\$48,000 \text{ (new fixed costs)}}{\$1.20 \text{ (per-unit contribution margin)}} = 40,000 \text{ units (new break-even point)}$$

Units sold	100,000
Less break-even point (units)	40,000
Excess	60,000
Per-unit contribution margin	× $1.20
Target income	$72,000

discussion questions

1. Explain how understanding cost behavior patterns can assist management.
2. Discuss how level of activity is measured in manufacturing, merchandising, and service firms.
3. What is meant by the linearity assumption, and why is it made? Relate this assumption to the relevant-range concept.
4. What factors in the current economy seem to have caused the shift from variable to fixed cost patterns?
5. How should stepped costs be treated in the planning process?
6. Why must all mixed costs be segregated into their fixed and variable components?
7. What is the major weakness of the scattergraph, or visual-fit, method of analyzing mixed costs?
8. What is the major limitation of the high-low method of analyzing mixed costs?
9. What is the basic C-V-P equation? What is a more detailed version of this equation?
10. What is the contribution margin, and why is it important for managers to know the contribution margins of their products?
11. How much will profits increase for every unit sold over the break-even point?
12. What is the major advantage of using C-V-P graphs?
13. When other factors are constant, what is the effect on profits of an increase in fixed costs? Of a decrease in variable costs?
14. What are the limiting assumptions of C-V-P analysis?
15. How do the issues of quality and time relate to C-V-P analysis decisions?

16. How does the method of least squares differ from the scattergraph method?
17. What effect is a change in the sales mix likely to have on a firm's overall contribution margin ratio?

practice exercises

Practice 16-1

Measuring Level of Activity
Which one of the following is *not* an activity base used by a company?

a. Number of defects per hour in an assembly plant
b. Number of units sold for a merchandising firm
c. Number of units produced for a manufacturing firm
d. Number of client hours billed for an accounting firm
e. Number of hours a retail store is open

Practice 16-2

Variable Costs
Which one of the following would *not* be a variable cost for a construction company?

a. Cost of trusses used to construct a roof for a house
b. Cost of windows to be installed in a house
c. Salary paid to overall project supervisor
d. Cost of drywall to be installed in house
e. Cost of exterior house paint

Practice 16-3

Linearity of Variable Costs within the Relevant Range
The company has assembled the following data about its variable costs:

(continued)

Level of Activity	Total Variable Cost
1,000 units	$ 25,000
2,000 units	46,000
3,000 units	69,000
4,000 units	92,000
5,000 units	100,000

The company is currently producing 3,300 units. According to these data, what is the relevant range over which the company can assume that the variable cost per unit is constant?

Practice 16-4

Fixed Costs

If the level of activity increases during the month, does the fixed cost per unit increase, decrease, or remain constant?

Practice 16-5

Break-Even Computation

The company reports the following items.

Direct materials per unit	$ 2.50
Direct labor per unit	4.60
Variable overhead per unit	2.10
Monthly rent	1,900.00
Monthly depreciation	650.00
Other monthly fixed costs	2,680.00
Sales price per unit	14.25

Using the above information, compute the company's monthly break-even point (in units).

Practice 16-6

Stepped Fixed Costs

The company pays $3,000 per month to each of its four production supervisors. Each supervisor can handle the workload associated with up to 2,400 units of production per month; the current level of production is 9,000 units. If the company increases its level of production to 12,800 units per month, how much will the company pay, in total, for the salaries of the necessary production supervisors?

Practice 16-7

Mixed Costs

The company's president receives a $100,000 base salary and a bonus of 0.5% of sales for the year. How much will the president earn at a sales level of $2,750,000 for the year?

Practice 16-8

Scattergraph Method

Which one of the following statements is incorrect?

a. The scattergraph method can be somewhat subjective depending on where one visually places the regression line.
b. The scattergraph method is the most accurate method of analyzing mixed costs.
c. When graphing mixed costs, the dollars go on the vertical axis, and the level of activity goes on the horizontal axis.
d. Regression lines attempt to minimize the average distance between all the data points and the fitted regression line.
e. The slope of the regression line is equal to the variable cost per unit of activity.

Practice 16-9

Using the High-Low Method to Estimate the Variable Cost Rate

The company reports the following utility costs for different levels of activity during the first half of the year:

Month	Machine Hours	Total Utility Costs
January	470	$14,000
February	410	12,500
March	520	14,400
April	500	14,450
May	550	15,350
June	535	15,100

Using the high-low method, estimate the variable cost rate.

Practice 16-10

Using the High-Low Method to Estimate Fixed Costs
Refer to the data in Practice 16-9. Using the high-low method, estimate the fixed costs per month based on the variable cost rate (computed in Practice 16-9).

Practice 16-11

Contribution Margin Income Statement
The company sells desks for $550 each. The variable cost per desk is $385. The company's monthly fixed costs are $72,000. Prepare a contribution margin income statement for a month in which the company sells 500 desks.

Practice 16-12

Contribution Margin Ratio and Variable Cost Ratio
Refer to the data in Practice 16-11. Compute the contribution margin ratio and the variable cost ratio.

Practice 16-13

The C-V-P Equation
The company sells lawnmowers for $895 each. The variable cost per lawnmower is $520. The company's monthly fixed costs are $84,500. Using the C-V-P equation, compute the amount of profit the company will have for a month in which the company sells 375 lawnmowers.

Practice 16-14

Break-Even Units
The company sells shovels for $27.75 each. The variable cost per shovel is $14.25. The company's monthly fixed costs are $2,538. Compute the number of shovels the company must sell to break even.

Practice 16-15

Determining Sales Volume to Achieve Target Income
Refer to the data in Practice 16-14. How many shovels must the company sell to achieve a profit of $10,000?

Practice 16-16

Determining Sales Volume to Achieve Target Return on Sales
The company sells pianos for $7,000 each. The variable cost per piano is $5,500. The company has fixed costs per month of $45,000. Compute the number of units the company must sell in a month to achieve a 15% return on sales.

Practice 16-17

Break-Even Sales Revenue
The company has a variable cost ratio of 65% and monthly fixed costs of $91,000. What is the company's break-even point in terms of sales dollars?

Practice 16-18

C-V-P Analysis with Simultaneous Changes in Several Variables
The company currently sells 50,000 feet of cable each month for $3.50 per foot. The variable cost of the cable is $1.10 per foot, and monthly fixed costs are $75,000. The company is considering whether to raise the sales price for the cable to $4.00 per foot. The marketing team has determined that such an increase in sales price will discourage some customers from purchasing

(continued)

the cable, so the company will be able to sell only 40,000 feet of cable per month. Calculate the profit for the company under both of the following scenarios:

1. 50,000 feet of cable at $3.50 per foot.
2. 40,000 feet of cable at $4.00 per foot.

In terms of profit maximization, should the company raise the price per foot?

Practice 16-19

C-V-P Analysis with Simultaneous Changes in Several Variables
Refer to the data in Practice 16-18. The company is considering whether to change its production process to reduce the variable cost per foot to $0.90 by raising fixed costs per month to $83,000. This change will have no impact on selling price ($3.50) or sales volume (50,000 feet). In terms of profit maximization, should the company change its production process?

Practice 16-20

Interpreting a C-V-P Graph

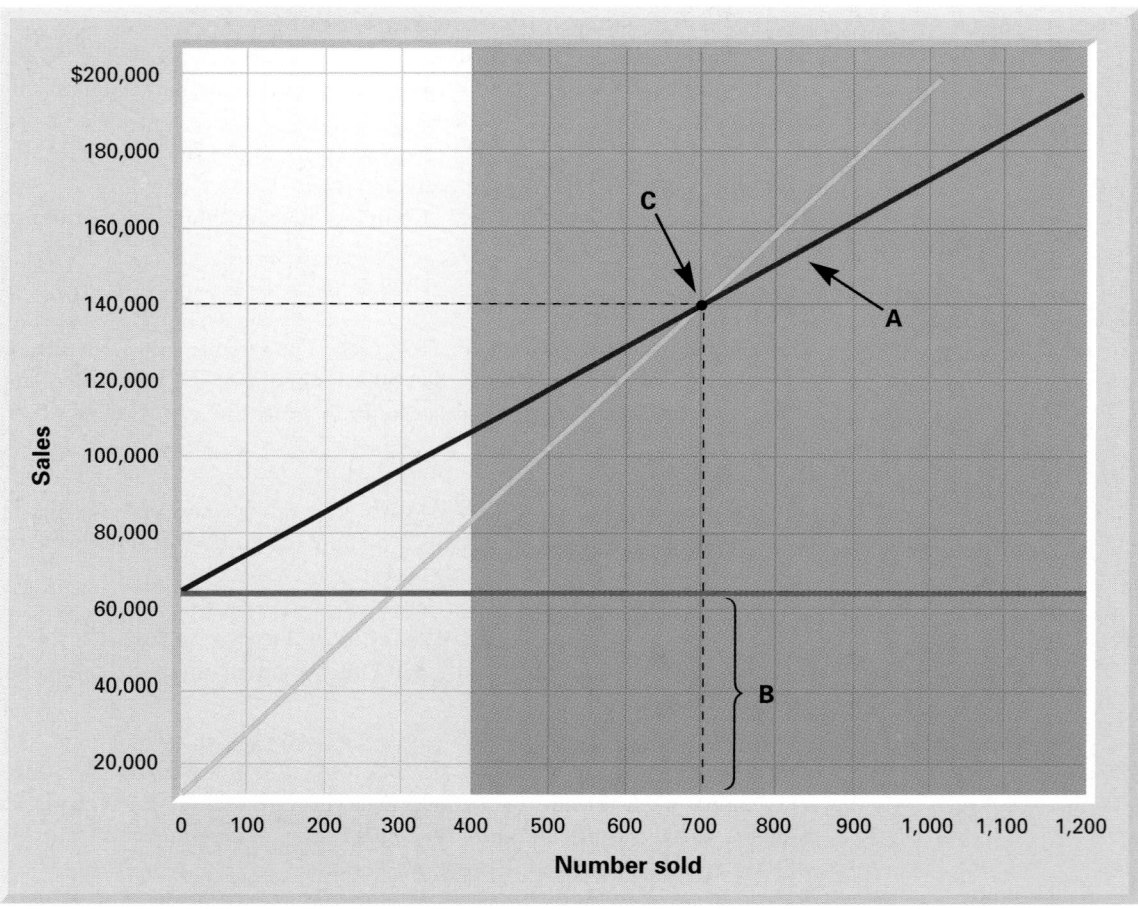

Look at the given C-V-P graph. Which one of the following sets of labels correctly labels items A, B, and C in the C-V-P graph?

a. A: Total cost line; B: Fixed costs; C: Break-even point
b. A: Revenue line; B: Variable costs; C: Fixed costs
c. A: Fixed cost line; B: Break-even point; C: Fixed costs
d. A: Revenue line; B: Break-even point; C: Fixed costs
e. A: Total cost line; B: Break-even point; C: Fixed costs

Practice 16-21 **Interpreting a Profit Graph**

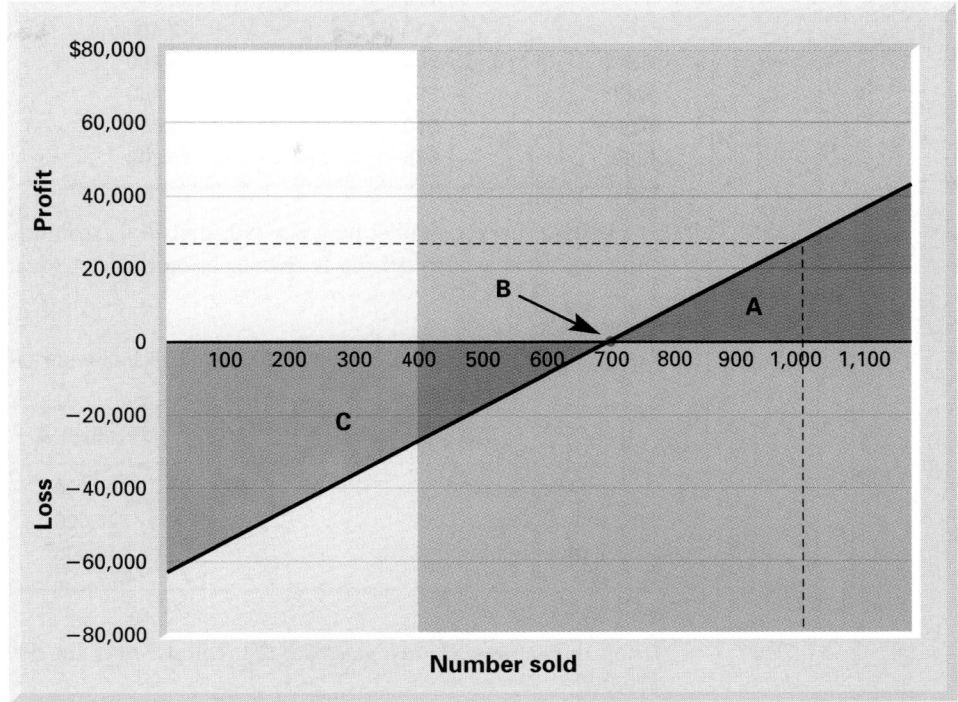

Look at the given profit graph. Which one of the following sets of labels correctly labels items A, B, and C in the profit graph?

a. A: Area of loss; B: Break-even point; C: Area of profit
b. A: Area of loss; B: Area of profit; C: Break-even point
c. A: Break-even point; B: Area of loss; C: Area of profit
d. A: Area of profit; B: Break-even point; C: Area of loss
e. A: Area of profit; B: Area of loss; C: Break-even point

Practice 16-22 **Limiting Assumptions of C-V-P Analysis**

Which one of the following is *not* an assumption of C-V-P analysis?

a. Fixed costs are always greater than variable costs.
b. All costs can be divided into fixed and variable categories.
c. C-V-P analysis is valid only for a relevant range.
d. The mix of a company's products does not change over the relevant range.

Practice 16-23 **Least-Squares Method**

The company reports the following costs at different levels of activity for the first half of the year.

(continued)

Month	Machine Hours	Total Utility Costs
January	470	$14,000
February	410	12,500
March	520	14,400
April	500	14,450
May	550	15,350
June	535	15,700

Using Excel (or another program with statistical capabilities), estimate the company's fixed costs and variable costs per machine hour using the least-squares method.

Practice 16-24

Sales Mix

The company has fixed costs of $21,500 and the following sales mix.

	Product A	Product B	Product C
Sales revenue	$35,000	$70,000	$45,000
Less variable costs	20,000	50,000	36,000
Contribution margin	$15,000	$20,000	$ 9,000

Using this same sales mix, calculate the required sales (in dollars) to earn a target income of $25,000.

Practice 16-25

Cost Structure

If you experience much higher sales than expected this year, which kind of operating leverage would you like to have in your company for profit maximization?

a. High operating leverage
b. Low operating leverage
c. Medium operating leverage
d. Operating leverage does not affect profitability.

e x e r c i s e s

Exercise 16-1

Variable and Fixed Costs Over the Relevant Range

Cook Corporation manufactures plastic garbage cans. In a typical year, the firm produces between 40,000 and 50,000 cans. At this level of production, fixed costs are $10,000 and variable costs are $2 per can.

1. Graph the cost of producing cans, with cost as the vertical axis and production output as the horizontal axis.
2. Indicate on the graph the relevant range of the $10,000 in fixed costs, and explain the significance of the relevant range.
3. What would total production costs be if 46,000 cans were produced?

Exercise 16-2

Fixed Costs—The Relevant Range

Sabrina Company manufactures large leisure boats. The following schedule shows total fixed costs at various levels of boat production:

Units Produced	Total Fixed Costs
0–100	$150,000
101–400	250,000
401–900	400,000

1. What is the fixed cost per unit when 75 boats are produced?
2. What is the fixed cost per unit when 300 boats are produced?
3. What is the fixed cost per unit when 750 boats are produced?
4. Plot total fixed costs on a graph similar to that shown in Exhibit 3.

Exercise 16-3

Scattergraph Method of Analyzing Mixed Costs
Wyoming Company makes windmills. The company has the following total costs at the given levels of windmill production:

Units Produced	Total Costs
20	$16,000
30	22,000
40	20,000
50	28,000

1. Use the scattergraph method to estimate the fixed and variable elements of Wyoming's total costs.
2. Compute the total cost of making 44 windmills, assuming that total fixed costs are $10,000 and that the variable cost rate computed in part (1) does not change.

Exercise 16-4

Scattergraph Method of Analyzing Mixed Costs
Given the following mixed costs at various levels of production, complete the requirements.

Month	Units Produced	Mixed Costs
January	2	$24.00
February	3	28.00
March	1	21.00
April	5	30.00
May	4	25.00

1. Plot the data on a scattergraph, and visually fit a straight line through the points.
2. Based on your graph, estimate the monthly fixed cost and the variable cost per unit produced.
3. Compute the total cost of producing eight units in a month, assuming that the same relevant range applies.
4. **Interpretive Question:** Why is it so important to be able to determine the components of a mixed cost?

Exercise 16-5

Scattergraph Method and High-Low Method of Analyzing Mixed Costs
Sailmaster makes boats and has the following costs and production levels for the last eight quarters:

(continued)

Quarter	Boats Produced	Total Costs
1	108	$101,250
2	128	168,750
3	185	189,000
4	245	200,145
5	311	276,200
6	352	255,250
7	389	305,700
8	428	376,500

1. Plot the data on a scattergraph, and visually fit a straight line through the points.
2. Based on your graph, estimate the quarterly fixed cost and the variable cost per unit produced.
3. Use the high-low method to compute the variable and fixed elements of Sailmaster's total costs, and then draw a straight line through the high and low data points on the scattergraph.
4. Compute the total cost of making 500 boats using first the scattergraph results and then using the high-low method results.
5. Comment on the differences between these two methods. Which method appears to most accurately represent the actual variable and fixed costs for Sailmaster?

Exercise 16-6

High-Low Method of Analyzing Mixed Costs

The *Stamford Times* has determined that the annual printing of 750,000 newspapers costs 11 cents per copy. If production were to be increased to 1,000,000 copies per year, the per-unit cost would drop to 9 cents per copy.

1. Using the high-low method, determine the total fixed and variable costs of printing 750,000 newspapers.
2. Using the fixed and variable costs you determined in part (1), what would be the total cost of producing 900,000 copies?

Exercise 16-7

Contribution Margin Calculations

Jerry Stone owns and operates a small beach shop in a mall on Sanibel Island, Florida. For the last six months, Jerry has had a display of sunglasses in the front window. Largely because of the display, Jerry has sold 100 pairs of sunglasses per month at an average cost of $26 and selling price of $50. The sales volume has doubled since the display was put in the window. One-fourth of Jerry's storage space is occupied by 190 ice coolers. The coolers have not been selling as well as Jerry hoped, but he is convinced that a front window display of coolers would increase sales by 50%. The coolers cost Jerry a total of $2,280 and have been selling at a rate of 100 per month at $28 each.

1. Assuming that cost of goods sold is the only variable cost, compute the contribution margin per unit for sunglasses and ice coolers.
2. Compute the total contribution margins for both sunglasses and ice coolers assuming window displays and no window displays for both items.
3. What are the economic costs associated with keeping the sunglass display in the store window?
4. What are the economic costs associated with replacing the sunglass display with an ice cooler display?

Exercise 16-8

Spreadsheet

Contribution Margin Income Statement

The following data apply to Gordon Company for 2006:

Sales revenue (10 units at $25 each)	$250
Variable selling expenses	45
Variable administrative expenses	25
Fixed selling expenses	30

Fixed administrative expenses	$ 15
Direct labor	50
Direct materials	60
Fixed manufacturing overhead	5
Variable manufacturing overhead	3

1. Prepare a contribution margin income statement. Assume there were no beginning or ending inventories in 2006.
2. How much would Gordon Company have lost if only five units had been sold during 2006?

Exercise 16-9

Analysis of a Contribution Margin Income Statement

Fill in the missing amounts for the following three cases:

	Case I	Case II	Case III
Sales revenue	$50,000	$60,000	$ (7)
Variable cost of goods sold:			
Direct materials	$12,500	$ (4)	$20,000
Direct labor	(1)	15,000	20,000
Variable selling and administrative costs	3,500	(5)	10,000
Contribution margin	$ (2)	$20,000	$ (8)
Gross margin	20,000	30,000	40,000
Fixed selling and administrative costs*	5,500	10,000	(9)
Rent expense on office building	(3)	5,000	2,000
Depreciation expense on delivery trucks	5,000	2,500	8,000
Profit	$ 4,000	$ (6)	$ 0

*Except rent and depreciation.

Exercise 16-10

Analysis of the Contribution Margin

Dr. Hughes and Dr. Hawkins, owners of the Spanish Fork Care Clinic, have $150,000 of fixed costs per year. They receive 20,000 patient visits in a year, charging each patient an average of $20 per visit; variable costs average $2 per visit (needles, medicines, and so on).

1. What is the contribution margin per patient visit?
2. What is the total contribution margin per year?
3. What is the total pretax profit for a year?
4. Drs. Hughes and Hawkins can bring in another doctor at a salary of $100,000 per year. If this new doctor can handle 5,000 patient visits per year, should the new doctor be hired? (Assume no additional fixed costs will be incurred.)

Exercise 16-11

Contribution Margin Analysis

Compute the missing amounts for the following independent cases. (Assume zero beginning and ending inventories.)

	Case I	Case II	Case III
Sales volume (units)	24,000	(5)	16,000
Sales price per unit	$10	$8	(9)
Variable costs (total)	(1)	$200,000	$100,000
Contribution margin (total)	(2)	(6)	$60,000
Contribution margin per unit (rounded)	$4	$3	(10)
Fixed costs (total)	(3)	(7)	(11)
Fixed costs per unit (rounded)	(4)	$2	(12)
Profit	$20,000	(8)	$40,000

Exercise 16-12

Spreadsheet

Break-Even Point and Target Income

Detienne Company manufactures and sells one product for $20 per unit. The unit contribution margin is 40% of the sales price, and fixed costs total $80,000.

1. Using the equation approach, compute:
   a. The break-even point in sales dollars and units.
   b. The sales volume (in units) needed to generate a profit of $40,000.
   c. The break-even point (in units) if variable costs increase to 80% of the sales price and fixed costs increase to $100,000.
2. See if you can recompute the solutions to 1(a), 1(b), and 1(c) in *one equation step* using either the contribution margin ratio or the contribution margin dollars per unit.

Exercise 16-13

Break-Even Point and Target Income

Steven Newman, Inc., estimates 2006 costs to be as follows:

Direct materials	$5 per unit
Direct labor	$8 per unit
Variable manufacturing overhead	$3 per unit
Variable selling and administrative expenses	$2 per unit
Fixed expenses	$80,000

1. Assuming that Newman will sell 55,000 units, what sales price per unit will be needed to achieve a $75,000 profit?
2. Assuming that Newman decides to sell its product for $23 per unit, determine the break-even sales volume in dollars and units.
3. Assuming that Newman decides to sell its product for $23 per unit, determine the number of units it must sell to generate a $100,000 profit.

Exercise 16-14

Break-Even Point—Graphic Analysis

Using the graph below, answer the following questions:

1. Copy the graph and identify (label) fixed costs, variable costs, total revenues, the total cost line, and the break-even point.
2. Determine the break-even point in both sales dollars and volume.
3. Suppose that as a manager you forecast sales volume at 7,000 units. At this level of sales, what would be your total fixed costs, approximate variable costs, and profit (or loss)?
4. At a sales volume of 3,000 units, what would be the level of fixed costs, variable costs, and approximate profit (or loss)?

Exercise 16-15

The Profit Graph
Using the graph below, answer the following questions:

1. What is the break-even point in sales volume (in units)?
2. Approximately what volume of sales (in units) must this company have to generate an income of $300?
3. How much are the fixed costs?

Exercise 16-16

Graphing Revenues and Costs
Montana Company manufactures chocolate candy. Its manufacturing costs are as follows:

Annual fixed costs $15,000
Variable costs . . . . $2 per box of candy

1. Plot variable costs, fixed costs, and total costs on a graph for activity levels of 0 to 30,000 boxes of candy.
2. Plot a revenue line on the graph, assuming that Montana sells the chocolates for $5 a box.

Exercise 16-17

C-V-P Analysis
The Last Outpost is a tourist stop in a western resort community. Kerry Yost, the owner of the shop, sells hand-woven blankets for an average price of $30 per blanket. Kerry buys the blankets from weavers at an average cost of $21. In addition, he has selling expenses of $3 per blanket. Kerry rents the building for $300 per month and pays one employee a fixed salary of $500 per month.

1. Determine the number of blankets Kerry must sell to break even.
2. Determine the number of blankets Kerry must sell to generate a profit of $1,000 per month.
3. Assume that Kerry can produce and sell his own blankets at a total variable cost of $16 per blanket, but that he would need to hire one additional employee at a monthly salary of $600.
   a. Determine the number of blankets Kerry must sell to break even.
   b. Determine the number of blankets Kerry must sell to generate a profit of $1,000 per month.

Exercise 16-18

C-V-P Analysis—Changes in Variables
Tracy, Inc., estimates that next year's results will be:

Sales revenue (75,000 units) . . . . $ 900,000
Less variable costs . . . . (375,000)
Less fixed costs . . . . (300,000)
Profit . . . . $ 225,000

Recompute profit, assuming each of the following independent conditions:

1. A 9% increase in the contribution margin.
2. An 8% increase in the sales volume.
3. A 4% decrease in the sales volume.

(continued)

4. A 6% increase in variable costs per unit.
5. A 5% decrease in fixed costs.
6. A 5% increase in fixed costs.
7. A 12% increase in the sales volume and a 6% increase in fixed costs.

Exercise 16-19

C-V-P Analysis—Changes in Variables
Modern Fun Corporation sells electronic games. Its three salespersons are currently being paid fixed salaries of $30,000 each; however, the sales manager has suggested that it might be more profitable to pay the salespersons on a straight commission basis. He has suggested a commission of 15% of sales. Current data for Modern Fun Corporation are as follows:

Sales volume . . . . 15,000 units
Sales price . . . . $40 per unit
Variable costs . . . . $29 per unit
Fixed costs $140,000

1. Assuming that Modern Fun Corporation has a target income of $50,000 for next year, which alternative is more attractive?
2. The sales manager believes that by switching to a commission basis, sales will increase 20%. If that is the case, which alternative is more attractive? (Assume that sales are expected to remain at 15,000 units under the fixed salary alternative.)

Exercise 16-20

Mixed Costs—Least Squares Analysis
Given the following mixed costs at various levels of production, complete the requirements.

Month	Units Produced	Mixed Costs
January	8	$30
February	12	36
March	4	22
April	20	44
May	8	26

1. Using the least squares method (either the equation approach or a software package), calculate the monthly fixed and variable components of the mixed costs.
2. Using the estimates from part (1), compute the total cost of producing 16 units in a month.
3. Describe a major advantage and a major disadvantage of the least squares method.

Exercise 16-21

Sales Mix
Klein Brothers sells products X and Y. Because of the nature of the products, Klein sells two units of product X for each unit of product Y. Relevant information about the products is as follows:

	X	Y
Sales price per unit	$10	$30
Variable cost per unit	8	18

1. Assuming that Klein's fixed costs total $140,000, compute Klein's break-even point in sales dollars.

2. Assuming that Klein sells one unit of product X for each unit of product Y, and fixed costs remain at $140,000, compute Klein's break-even point in sales dollars.

3. Explain any differences in your answers to parts (1) and (2).

Exercise 16-22

C-V-P Analysis

Mower Manufacturing's income statement for January 2006 is given below.

Sales (25,000 units × $25)	$625,000
Less variable costs	468,750
Contribution margin	$156,250
Less fixed costs	125,000
Profit	$ 31,250

1. Calculate the company's break-even point in sales dollars and units.

2. The company is contemplating the purchase of new production equipment that would reduce variable costs per unit to $16.25. However, fixed costs would increase to $175,000 per month. Assuming sales of 26,000 units next month, prepare an income statement for both the current and the proposed production methods. Calculate the break-even point (in dollars and units) for the new production method.

3. Comment on the difference (if any) in the break-even point for the new production method. What explains the difference in income at sales of 26,000 units between the two production methods?

Exercise 16-23

Operating Leverage

Ludlam Company and Kassandra Company both make school desks. They have the same production capacity, but Ludlam is more automated than Kassandra. At an output of 2,500 desks per year, the two companies have the following costs:

	Ludlam	Kassandra
Fixed costs	$137,500	$ 37,500
Variable costs at $20 per desk	50,000	
Variable costs at $60 per desk		150,000
Total cost	$187,500	$187,500
Unit cost (2,500 desks)	$ 75	$ 75

Assuming that both companies sell desks for $100 each and that there are no other costs or expenses for the two firms, complete the following:

1. Which company will lose the least money if production and sales fall to 1,000 desks per year?

2. What would be each company's profit or loss at production and sales levels of 1,000 desks per year?

3. What would be each company's profit or loss at production and sales levels of 4,000 desks per year?

p roblems

Problem 16-1

Graphing Revenues and Costs

Cloward and Hawkins, CPAs, took in $350,000 of gross revenues this year. Besides themselves, they have two professional staff (one manager and one senior) and a full-time secretary. Fixed operating expenses for the office were $50,000 last year. This year the volume of activity is up

5%, and fixed operating expenses are still $50,000. Total variable operating costs, except for bonuses, average $5 per billable hour. The billable time for all professionals is as follows:

Partners: 3,000 hours at $75/hour
Manager: 1,800 hours at $40/hour
Senior: 2,120 hours at $25/hour

Salaries for the professional staff are $40,000 and $28,000, respectively; the secretary is paid $18,000. The partners each draw salaries of $60,000; plus they share a 5% bonus based on gross revenues. The manager is given a 2% bonus, also based on gross revenues.

Required:
1. Plot the data on a graph clearly showing (a) fixed costs, (b) variable costs, (c) total costs, and (d) total revenues.
2. How much profit did the CPA firm make this year (after partners' salaries)?

Problem 16-2

High-Low and Scattergraph Methods of Analysis
Woodfield Company makes bed linens. During the first six months of 2006, Woodfield had the following production costs:

Month	Units Produced	Total Costs
January	10,000	$ 68,000
February	20,000	100,000
March	15,000	90,000
April	8,000	52,000
May	17,000	94,000
June	12,000	74,000

Required:
1. Use the high-low method to compute the monthly fixed cost and the variable cost rate.
2. Plot the costs on a scattergraph.
3. **Interpretive Question:** Based on your scattergraph, do you think the fixed costs and the variable cost rate determined in part (1) are accurate? Why?

Problem 16-3

Contribution Margin Income Statement
Early in 2007, Lili H Company (a retailing firm) sent the following income statement to its stockholders:

Lili H Company
Income Statement
For the Year Ended December 31, 2006

Sales revenue (2,000 units)	$240,000	
Less cost of goods sold (variable)	160,000	
Gross margin		$80,000
Operating expenses:		
Selling	$ 24,000	
Administrative	16,000	
Depreciation (fixed)	4,000	
Insurance (fixed)	200	
Utilities ($80 fixed and $120 variable)	200	44,400
Profit		$35,600

Required:

1. Prepare a contribution margin income statement. (Assume that the fixed components of the selling and administrative expenses are $12,000 and $8,000, respectively.)
2. **Interpretive Question:** Why is a contribution margin income statement helpful to management?
3. **Interpretive Question:** How would the analysis in part (1) be different if the depreciation expense was considered a stepped cost with wide steps compared to the relevant range?

Problem 16-4

Contribution Margin Income Statement

Susan Young is an attorney for a small law firm in Arizona. She is also a part-time inventor and an avid golfer. One day Susan's golf foursome included a man named Henry Jones, a manufacturer of Christmas ornaments. Henry explained to Susan that he manufactures an ornament everyone loves, but stores will not carry the ornaments because they are very fragile and often break during shipping. Susan told Henry about a plastic box she had developed recently that would protect such fragile items during shipping. After crash testing the plastic box, Henry offered Susan a contract to purchase 100,000 of the boxes for $2.20 each. Susan is convinced that the box has many applications and that she can obtain future orders. Production of the plastic boxes will take one year. Estimated costs for the first year are as follows:

Lease payments on building	$800 per month
Lease payments on machine	$2,200 per month
Cost to retool machine	$10,000
Depreciation on machine	$9,600
Direct materials	$0.70 per box
Direct labor	$0.30 per box
Indirect materials and other manufacturing overhead	$10,000
Interest on loan	$2,500
Administrative salaries	$15,000

Required:

1. Using the information provided, determine Susan's contribution margin and projected profit at a sales level of 100,000 boxes.
2. If Susan's salary as an attorney is $44,500, determine how many boxes Susan must sell to earn profits equal to her salary.

Problem 16-5

Functional and Contribution Margin Income Statements

Bassically Jammin', Inc. (BJI) is a retail outlet for customized bass guitars. The average cost of a bass guitar to the company is $1,000. BJI includes a markup of 50% of cost in the sales price. In 2006, BJI sold 380 bass guitars and finished the year with the same amount of inventory it had at the beginning of the year. Additional operating costs for the year were as follows:

Selling expenses:

Advertising (fixed)	$ 700 per month
Commissions (mixed)	3,000 per month plus 2% of sales
Depreciation (fixed)	400 per month
Utilities (fixed)	125 per month
Freight on delivery (variable)	20 per bass guitar

Administrative expenses:

Salaries (fixed)	$4,200 per month
Depreciation (fixed)	330 per month
Utilities (fixed)	200 per month
Clerical (variable)	12 per sale

Required:

1. Prepare a traditional income statement using the functional approach.
2. Prepare an income statement using the contribution margin format.
3. **Interpretive Question:** Which statement is more useful for decision making? Why?

Problem 16-6

Contribution Margin and Functional Income Statements

The following information is available for Dabney Company for 2006:

Sales revenue (at $20 per unit)	$151,200
Fixed manufacturing costs	24,000
Variable manufacturing costs (at $8 per unit)	60,480
Fixed selling expenses	70,000
Variable selling expenses (at $2 per unit)	15,120

Required:
1. Prepare a contribution margin income statement.
2. Prepare a functional income statement.
3. Calculate the number of units sold.
4. Calculate the contribution margin per unit.
5. **Interpretive Question:** Why is a knowledge of the contribution margin more useful than a knowledge of the markup per unit when management has to make a decision about profitability?

Problem 16-7

Unifying Concepts: High-Low Method, Contribution Margins, and Analysis

Press Publishing Corporation has two major magazines: *Star Life* and *Weekly News*. During 2006, *Star Life* sold 3 million copies at $1.00 each, and *Weekly News* sold 2.1 million copies at $1.10 each. Press Publishing accumulated the following cost information:

	Star Life		Weekly News	
Month	**Copies Produced**	**Manufacturing Cost**	**Copies Produced**	**Manufacturing Cost**
January	400,000	$170,000	300,000	$170,000
February	300,000	150,000	150,000	105,000
March	400,000	180,000	130,000	100,000
April	200,000	120,000	120,000	90,000
May	250,000	140,000	200,000	130,000
June	200,000	125,000	250,000	150,000
July	240,000	130,000	150,000	110,000
August	200,000	130,000	200,000	135,000
September	180,000	110,000	150,000	105,000
October	230,000	130,000	150,000	108,000
November	200,000	125,000	150,000	115,000
December	200,000	126,000	150,000	112,500

Required:
1. Use the high-low method to estimate the per-unit variable and total fixed manufacturing costs of each magazine. (Round the variable cost rate to three decimal places.)
2. If all selling expenses are fixed and they total $500,000 for *Star Life* and $400,000 for *Weekly News*, prepare contribution margin income statements for the two magazines at sales of 3 million copies each.
3. Which magazine is more profitable at sales of 2 million copies?
4. **Interpretive Question:** If the same total dollar amount spent on either magazine will result in the same number of new subscriptions, which magazine should be advertised?

Problem 16-8

Contribution Margin Analysis

Clearview Company is a manufacturer of glass vases. The following information pertains to Clearview's 2006 sales:

Sales price per unit	$	32
Variable costs per unit		24
Total fixed costs		500,000

Required:
1. Determine Clearview Company's per-unit contribution margin and contribution margin ratio.
2. Using the per-unit contribution margin and the contribution margin ratio, compute:
   a. The break-even point in sales dollars and units.
   b. The sales volume (in dollars and units) needed to generate a target income of $75,000.
3. Using the equation approach of C-V-P analysis, compute:
   a. The break-even point in sales dollars and units.
   b. The sales volume (in dollars and units) needed to generate a 15% return on sales.

Problem 16-9

Break-Even Analysis

Jane Tamlyn paid $225 to rent a carnival booth for four days. She has to decide whether to sell doughnuts or popcorn. Doughnuts cost $1.80 per dozen and can be sold for $3.60 per dozen. Popcorn will require a $113 rental fee for the popcorn maker and $0.08 per bag of popcorn for the popcorn, butter, salt, and bags; a bag of popcorn could sell for $0.45.

Required:
1. Compute the break-even point in dozens of doughnuts if Jane decides to sell doughnuts exclusively and the break-even point in bags of popcorn if she decides to sell popcorn exclusively.
2. Jane estimates that she can sell either 75 doughnuts or 45 bags of popcorn every hour the carnival is open (10 hours a day for four days). Which product should she sell?
3. Jane can sell back to the baker at half cost any doughnuts she fails to sell at the carnival. Unused popcorn must be thrown away. If Jane sells only 70% of her original estimate, which product should she sell? (Assume that she bought or produced just enough to satisfy the demands she originally estimated.)

Problem 16-10

C-V-P Graphic Analysis

Using the graph below, complete the requirements.

Required:
1. Determine the following:
   a. The break-even point in sales dollars and volume.
   b. The sales price per unit.
   c. Total fixed costs.
   d. Total variable costs at the break-even point.
   e. The variable cost per unit.
   f. The unit contribution margin.
2. What volume of sales must the company generate to reach a target income of $7,500?

Problem 16-11

Spreadsheet

Contribution Margin Analysis—Changes in Variables

SMC, Inc., is a producer of hand-held electronic games. Its 2006 income statement was as follows:

SMC, Inc. Contribution Margin Income Statement For the Year Ended December 31, 2006		
	Total	**Per Unit**
Sales revenue (150,000 games)	$5,250,000	$35
Less variable costs	3,750,000	25
Contribution margin	$1,500,000	$10
Less fixed costs	900,000	
Profit	$ 600,000	

In preparing its budget for 2007, SMC is evaluating the effects of changes in costs, prices, and volume on profit.

Required:

1. Evaluate the following independent cases, and determine SMC's 2007 budgeted profit or loss in each case. (Assume that 2006 figures apply unless stated otherwise.)
   a. Fixed costs increase $150,000.
   b. Fixed costs decrease $100,000.
   c. Variable costs increase $3 per unit.
   d. Variable costs decrease $4 per unit.
   e. Sales price increases $5 per unit.
   f. Sales price decreases $5 per unit.
   g. Sales volume increases 25,000 units.
   h. Sales volume decreases 15,000 units.
   i. Sales price decreases $4 per unit, sales volume increases 40,000 units, and variable costs decrease by $2.50 per unit.
   j. Fixed costs decrease by $100,000, and variable costs increase $4 per unit.
   k. Sales volume increases 30,000 units, with a decrease in sales price of $2 per unit. Variable costs drop $1.50 per unit, and fixed costs increase $50,000.
2. What sales volume in units would be needed to realize $1,000,000 in profit if SMC reduces its price to $30?

Problem 16-12

Income Statement and Break-Even Analysis

Zimmerman Company records the following costs associated with the production and sale of a steel slingshot:

Selling expenses:

Fixed	$6,500
Variable	$0.50 per unit sold

Administrative expenses:

Fixed	$4,500
Variable	$0.25 per unit sold

Manufacturing costs:

Fixed	$15,500
Variable	$7.50 per unit produced

Required:

Assume that in 2006 the beginning and ending inventories were the same. Also assume that 2006 sales were 11,000 units at $11.50 per slingshot.

1. Prepare a contribution margin income statement.
2. Determine the break-even point in sales dollars.
3. **Interpretive Question:** Zimmerman believes that sales volume could be improved 20% if an additional commission of $0.50 per unit were paid to the salespeople. Zimmerman also believes, however, that the same percentage increase could be achieved through an increase of $3,000 in annual advertising expense. Which action, if either, should Zimmerman take? Why?

Problem 16-13

C-V-P Analysis—Changes in Variables

Wonder T Manufacturing Company produces lanterns. The firm has not been as profitable as expected in the past three years. As a result, it has excess capacity that could be used to produce an additional 20,000 lanterns per year. However, any production above that amount would require a capital investment of $100,000. Operating results for the previous year are shown here. Assume that there is never any ending inventory.

Sales revenue (31,250 lanterns × $40)		$1,250,000
Variable costs (31,250 lanterns × $25)	$781,250	
Fixed costs	400,000	1,181,250
Profit		$ 68,750

Required:

Respond to the following independent proposals, and support your recommendations:

1. The production manager believes that profits could be increased through the purchase of more automated production machinery, which would increase fixed costs by $100,000 and reduce the variable costs by $2.00 per lantern. Is she correct if sales are to remain at 31,250 lanterns annually?
2. The sales manager believes that a 10% discount on the sales price would increase the sales volume to 40,000 units annually. If he is correct, would this action increase or decrease profits?
3. Would the implementation of both proposals be worthwhile?
4. The sales manager believes that an increase in sales commissions could improve the sales volume. In particular, he suggests that an increase of $2.50 per lantern would increase the sales volume 30%. If he is correct, would this action increase profits?
5. The accountant suggests another alternative: Reduce administrative salaries by $15,000 so that prices can be reduced by $0.50 per unit. She believes that this action would increase the volume to 35,000 units annually. If she is correct, would this action increase profits?
6. The corporate executives finally decide to spend an additional $42,000 on advertising to bring the sales volume up to 34,050 units. If the increased advertising can bring in these extra sales, is this a good decision?

Problem 16-14

C-V-P Analysis—Return on Sales

The federal government recently placed a ceiling on the selling price of sheet metal produced by MOB Company. In 2006, MOB was limited to charging a price that would earn a 20% return on gross sales. On the basis of this restriction, MOB had the following results for 2006:

Sales revenue (1,150,000 feet at $2.00 per foot)		$2,300,000
Variable costs (1,150,000 feet × $1.40)	$1,610,000	
Fixed costs	230,000	1,840,000
Profit		$ 460,000

In 2007, MOB predicted that the sales volume would decrease to 900,000 feet of sheet metal. With this level of sales, however, the company anticipated no changes in the levels of fixed and variable costs.

Required:

1. Determine MOB's profit for 2007 if all forecasts are realized. Compute both the dollar amount of profit and the percentage return on sales.

(continued)

2. MOB plans to petition the government for a price increase so that the 2006 rate of return on sales (20%) can be maintained. What sales price should the company request, based on 2007 projections? (Round to the nearest cent.)
3. How much profit (in dollars) will MOB earn in 2007 if this sales price, as determined in part (2), is approved?
4. **Interpretive Question:** What other factors must be considered by MOB and the government?

Problem 16-15

Unifying Concepts: C-V-P Analysis and Changes in Variables
The 2006 pro-forma income statement for Grover Company is as follows (ignore taxes):

Grover Company
Pro-Forma Income Statement
For the Year Ended December 31, 2006

Sales (50,000 units)		$450,000
Cost of goods sold:		
Direct materials	$ 35,000	
Direct labor	60,000	
Variable manufacturing overhead	14,000	
Fixed manufacturing overhead	5,000	
Total cost of goods sold		114,000
Gross margin		$336,000
Selling expenses:		
Variable	$ 45,000	
Fixed	102,000	
Administrative expenses:		
Variable	15,000	
Fixed	75,000	
Total selling and administrative expenses		237,000
Profit		$ 99,000

Required:
1. Compute how many units must be sold to break even.
2. Compute the increase (decrease) in profit under the following independent situations:
   a. Sales increase 25%.
   b. Fixed selling and administrative expenses decrease 5%.
   c. Contribution margin decreases 20%.
3. Compute sales in units and dollars at the break-even point if fixed costs increase from $182,000 to $224,800.
4. Compute the number of units that must be sold if expected profit is $1 million.

Problem 16-16

Least Squares Methods
This problem uses the same data for Press Publishing Corporation as displayed in Problem 16-7.

Required:
Use the least squares method to estimate the per-unit variable and total fixed manufacturing costs of the *Star Life* and *Weekly News* magazines. (Round the variable cost rate to three decimal places.)

Problem 16-17

Spreadsheet

Unifying Concepts: High-Low, Scattergraph, and Least Squares Methods
You have been hired as a consultant for Jones Inc. The company manufactures high-density compact disks and sells them to a wide variety of business clients. Management is eager to learn more about the company's cost behavior. You have been provided the following data. Assume all production falls within the relevant range.

Month	Machine Hours	Utility Costs
January	290	$10,700
February	280	10,400
March	320	11,600
April	340	12,100
May	350	12,400
June	290	10,750
July	300	10,800
August	300	10,900
September	310	11,200
October	340	12,200
November	290	10,600
December	310	11,000

Required:
1. Using the high-low method, compute the variable and fixed elements of Jones' utility costs.
2. Plot the information on a scattergraph. Based on your graph, determine the unit variable cost and monthly fixed costs.
3. Using the least squares method (either the equation approach or a software package), calculate the variable and fixed cost components. Determine the cost formula.
4. **Interpretive Question:** Why are the variable cost per unit and fixed costs different for each of these methods of analysis? Which method is the most accurate for determining variable and fixed cost components?

Problem 16-18

Sales Mix
Mike's Ice Cream Company produces and sells ice cream in three sizes: quart, half-gallon, and gallon. Relevant information for each of the sizes is as follows:

	Quart	Half-Gallon	Gallon
Average sales price	$1.00	$1.85	$3.60
Less variable cost	0.80	1.40	2.40
Unit contribution margin	$0.20	$0.45	$1.20
Sales mix (% of sales)	15%	60%	25%

Mike anticipates sales of $500,000 and fixed costs of $120,000 in 2006.

Required:
1. Determine the break-even sales volume in units and dollars for 2006.
2. Determine Mike's 2006 projected profit.
3. Assume that Mike's sales mix changes to 10% quarts, 40% half-gallons, and 50% gallons. Determine Mike's break-even sales volume in units and dollars.

Problem 16-19

Unifying Concepts: Break-Even Point and Operating Leverage
The summary data are provided on the following page for Spencer Mercantile Corporation and James Service, Inc. During the year for which these data are reported, Spencer sold 50,000 units and James sold 100,000 units.

(continued)

(000's omitted)	Spencer Mercantile Corporation	James Service, Inc.
Sales revenue	$1,040	$2,100
Less variable costs	520	630
Contribution margin	$ 520	$1,470
Less fixed costs	200	600
Income	$ 320	$ 870

Required:

1. Determine the break-even point for Spencer and James in both sales dollars and units.
2. **Interpretive Question:** Which company has a higher operating leverage? Why?
3. **Interpretive Question:** Based on your analysis of the cost structures of Spencer and James, which company's cost structure is better? What factors are important to consider in answering such a question?

discussion cases

Case 16-1

Colorado Outdoors Federation

The Colorado Outdoors Federation sponsors an annual banquet. This year the guest speaker is a noted wildlife photographer and lecturer. In planning for the event, the group's treasurer has determined the following costs:

Rental of meeting facility	$250
Honorarium for speaker	800
Tickets and advertising	300
Cost of dinner (per person)	20
Door prizes	500

Last year, tickets were sold at $20 per person, and 350 people attended the banquet. This year the planning committee is hoping for an attendance of 450 at a price of $25 each.

1. a. At $25 per person, how many people must attend the banquet for the Federation to break even?
   b. How much profit (loss) will occur if 450 people attend?
2. Should the Federation increase its advertising costs by $200 and its door prizes by $300 if it can expect 550 people to attend the banquet?
3. If the Federation maintains its original expected costs but reduces the price per ticket from $25 to $22, it can expect 500 people to attend the banquet. Should the Federation reduce the price of its tickets to $22 per person?

Case 16-2

Entertainment Enterprises

Entertainment Enterprises, a firm that sells magazine subscriptions, is experiencing increased competition from a number of companies. The president, Betty Kincher, has asked you, the controller, to prepare an income statement that will highlight the fixed and variable costs; this will provide more useful information for planning and control purposes. Sales revenues are $25 per subscription. An analysis of company costs for the past six months reveals the following:

Administrative salaries	$10,000 per month
Advertising expense	$2,000 per month
Cost of goods sold	$12.50 per subscription
Rent expense	$5,000 per month
Sales commissions	15% of sales

In addition, the company makes most sales contacts through an extensive telephone network. Consequently, the telephone expense is significant and has both fixed and variable components. Relevant data concerning the telephone expense for the past six months follow:

Month	Unit Sales	Telephone Expense
July	4,000	$10,200
August	5,000	12,300
September	3,500	9,150
October	4,500	11,250
November	5,200	12,720
December	5,500	13,350

Prepare a management report for the president that:

1. Computes the fixed and variable portions of the telephone expense using the high-low method. (*Note:* A scattergraph may be used to visually check your answer.)

2. Presents a budgeted (pro-forma) contribution margin income statement for Entertainment Enterprises for the next six months (January through June), assuming that it expects to sell 30,000 subscriptions at a price of $25 each.

3. Explains how the information provided in part (2) might help the president make better management decisions.

judgment calls

Judgment 16-1

You Decide: Should the management of a company consider fixed costs in the decision-making process, or should they ignore fixed costs and base their decision on what makes the most business sense?

Recently, the board of directors for a television manufacturing company was considering a change in products from TVs to computers. The board claims, after performing a C-V-P analysis of a new computer manufacturing plant facility, that the computer industry is more profitable and would increase the bottom line immediately. However, just six months earlier, the company built a state-of-the-art television manufacturing plant. The overhead costs on the television plant represent a sizable portion of the company's fixed costs. If the board voted to begin computer manufacturing, a new plant would need to be constructed. What should the board do?

Judgment 16-2

You Decide: Should companies have large amounts of inventory on hand for customers, or should companies keep inventory at a minimum to free up cash for other parts of the business?

Your uncle, Tim, started a very successful "home improvement" business 10 years ago. He wanted to create a place where people could go to get anything they needed to complete their "do-it-yourself" home building projects. Coupled with excellent service, Tim believes that he can gain and retain customers by having a large assortment of inventory from which to choose. In addition, he can obtain significant purchase discounts by buying the inventory in large bulk. You argue that maintaining amounts of inventory requires significant commitments to fixed warehousing and other costs that could be avoided by setting up an e-commerce Web site and taking customer orders that are then acquired and delivered one customer at a time. Although this approach will increase the overall variable costs as a result of not receiving bulk discounts on the smaller individual orders, you are able to demonstrate with C-V-P analysis that there is less risk in your approach to selling home improvement products. Your uncle strongly argues that, "Having the inventory on hand for your customers is the key to success. If I don't have what they are looking for, they will just go down the street to HOME DEPOT! I have got to have inventory in the stores. There is no other way!"

Competency Enhancement Opportunities

▶ **Analyzing Real Company Information**
▶ **International Case**
▶ **Ethics Case**
▶ **Writing Assignment**

▶ **The Debate**
▶ **Internet Search**

The following additional assignments provide opportunities for students to develop critical thinking, ethical perspectives, oral and written communication skills, experience with electronic research, and teamwork through group and business activities.

▶ *Analyzing Real Company Information*

Analyzing 16-1 (Microsoft)

Annual revenues, as well as sales and marketing expenses, for the 1991–2002 years are provided below for MICROSOFT CORPORATION:

Microsoft Corporation (millions)		
Year	Sales and Marketing Expenses	Annual Revenue
1991	$ 490	$ 1,847
1992	758	2,777
1993	1,086	3,786
1994	1,135	4,714
1995	1,564	6,075
1996	2,185	9,050
1997	2,411	11,936
1998	2,887	15,262
1999	3,238	19,747
2000	4,126	22,956
2001	4,885	25,296
2002	5,407	28,365

1. Operating output data, such as the number of software products sold each year, are not provided in Microsoft's Form 10-K. However, while it is a little odd to use revenues to predict marketing expense (instead of the other way around), it seems sensible that changes in revenues can serve as an approximate measure of changes in the number of products sold by Microsoft. Use the high-low method to analyze the data above to determine if there is a relationship between revenues and sales and marketing expenses. (*Hint:* Don't round off the value you calculate for variable costs per revenue dollar.) What appears to be the amount of fixed costs in these expenses? Does this fixed cost amount make sense? (*Note:* Remember that the data are in millions of dollars!)

2. Using your calculator (or some computer software program such as Microsoft Excel®), compute a regression analysis on the data above. What do you learn from the analysis? The Management's Discussion in Microsoft's 2002 Form 10-K generally uses the following language to describe changes to sales and marketing expenses: "Sales and marketing expenses increased due to higher relative headcount-related costs, higher marketing and sales expenses associated with MSN (Microsoft's popular portal destination on the Web), the Microsoft Agility advertising campaign, and other new sales initiatives." Does this statement provide any help in understanding the analysis? (*Hint:* When setting up to perform the regression, remember that the revenue is the X variable and the sales and marketing expense is the Y variable.)

Analyzing 16-2 (Star Video)

It is likely that a number of grocery stores in your town have video rental departments. Generally, however, grocery stores do not focus much management attention on their small video rental businesses. The main purpose of having a video department is to encourage more customers to come into the store and purchase groceries! Nevertheless, a grocery store cannot simply buy a large selection of videotapes, corner off a section of floor space, and start renting tapes. Successfully managing a rental business requires being aware of an unimaginably large number of video titles. Obviously, new movies are constantly being released, while old movies gradually lose their appeal and are eventually scrapped. Further, large-scale video rental chains such as BLOCKBUSTER constantly track shifting consumer tastes for certain titles and movie categories. These consumer preferences differ based on demographic data like geographic location, average age, ethnicity, average income, etc. A grocery store really can't manage all these data without losing focus on its main business. Hence, most grocery stores contract out their video rental business to a large-scale video management company. These management companies can purchase huge quantities of tapes, maintain large distribution warehouses, and track demographic data that allow them to manage and move specific inventories to the appropriate grocery store locations. In 1992, one such video management company, Star Video (not its real name), was managing 86 stores representing three supermarket chains in five states—Arizona, California, Montana, Washington, and Wyoming. Total revenue in 1992 for Star Video was $3.6 million. Star Video made all the inventory investments and handled all management activities involved in providing video rentals at each of the 86 stores. Video rental revenue was then split between Star Video and each grocery store, with Star Video keeping the lion's share. Stores liked this arrangement because they made most of their money on grocery sales to customers who came to rent videotapes. Star Video needed to carefully manage revenue and costs at each store in order to stay profitable. Following are the data for six stores located in Washington:

Store Name	Monthly Revenue	Monthly Operating Expenses
Moses Lake	$ 6,408	$ 3,295
W. Kennewick	4,264	2,289
Pasco	4,038	2,270
S. Kennewick	3,692	2,142
E. Wenatchee	1,395	1,316
Richland	2,104	1,516
Total	$21,901	$12,828

Use the high-low method to analyze the operating expenses at these six stores. Determine if operating expenses are related to store revenue. What appear to be the fixed costs of operating each store? Create a graph and plot these costs using revenue on the horizontal axis and operating expenses on the vertical axis. Does the scattergraph agree or disagree with the results of your high-low analysis?

▶ *International Case*

International

The Paper Company

The GHANATA GROUP OF COMPANIES (GGC) is a locally owned and controlled company in Ghana, West Africa. One of its principal operating divisions, THE PAPER COMPANY, is one of Africa's most modern and largest manufacturers/distributors of paper products. For both operating and reporting purposes, The Paper Company is organized into product lines: scholastic, envelope, and stationery. During the 1980s, the economy in Ghana was stagnant. The country faced severe economic problems as a result of unfavorable trade terms with other countries. The official exchange rate of U.S. $1.00 to the local currency, the *cedi*, was about 39.00 as of the end of 1984. (The unofficial rate, e.g., the black market rate, was at least five times worse!) As a result of the economy, it became very difficult for GGC to secure direct materials for its divisions. If a division could secure direct materials, it could sell almost everything it produced. Hence, in terms of being able to predict sales volumes, there was a great deal of risk for GGC divisions. The 1985 budgeted operating data for the three departments in The Paper Company were as follows:

The Paper Company 1985 Budgeted Operations Data (*Cedi* 000's)	Scholastic	Envelope	Stationery
Budgeted sales	$ 1,785,000	$ 984,000	$ 3,334,050
Budgeted variable costs	(410,550)	(442,800)	(2,200,473)
Contribution margin	$ 1,374,450	$ 541,200	$ 1,133,577
Budgeted fixed costs	(1,267,350)	(482,160)	(933,534)
Income	$ 107,100	$ 59,040	$ 200,043

Using these operating data, create C-V-P graphs for each department. (*Note:* Since you don't have per-unit prices and costs, you may assume that the product sales price for each department is $1 per unit, and then plot your graphs at 0, 2 million, and 4 million units.) Given the high-risk business environment in Ghana at this time, which department presents the highest risk to GGC? The lowest risk? Be sure to explain your answer in terms of operating leverage. You may also want to consider each department's break-even point compared to budgeted (expected) operations.

Source: A. Oppong, "The Paper Company," *The Journal of Accounting Case Research*, Vol. 3, No. 2 (1996), pp. 80–88. Permission to use has been granted by Captus Press, Inc. and the Accounting Education Resource Centre of The University of Lethbridge. [Journal Subscription: Captus Press, Inc., York University Campus, 4700 Keele Street, North York, Ontario, M3J 1P3, by calling (416) 736-5537, or by fax at (416) 736-5793, E-mail: info@captus.com, Internet: **http://www.captus.com**]

▶ *Ethics Case*

Pickmore International

Joan Hildabrand is analyzing some cost data for her boss, Ross Cumings. The data relate to a special sales order that Pickmore International is considering from a large customer in Singapore. The following data are applicable to the product being ordered:

Normal unit sales price	$49.95
Variable unit manufacturing costs	10.50
Variable unit selling and administrative expenses	18.25

The customer is requesting that the sales order be accepted on the following terms:

a. The unit sales price would equal the unit contribution margin plus 10%.
b. Freight would be paid by the customer.
c. Pickmore International would pay a $5,000 "facilitating payment" to a "friend of the customer" to get the product through customs more quickly.

In considering the order, Ross has indicated to Joan that this is a very important customer. Furthermore, this work would help some employees earn a little extra Christmas money with overtime.

1. What are the accounting and ethical issues involved in this case?
2. Should Joan recommend acceptance of the sales terms proposed for this special order?

▶ *Writing Assignment*

Issues of Quality and Time on C-V-P Analysis Decisions

This chapter described how to analyze whether the difference between sales price and variable costs, as well as the volume of sales, is sufficient to pay for all fixed costs in an organization and provide a sufficient profit. A number of methods have been presented for analyzing these costs, volume, and price relationships. These methods all focus on *quantitative* issues that affect how a company manages its resources to maximize overall profits. However, there are a number of *qualitative* issues involving quality and time that should also affect decisions about what sales prices to set, how to manage fixed and variable costs, and which products should be emphasized within the organization. One way to trade off fixed costs for variable costs is to consider making large fixed cost investments in technology that result in automated production, merchandising, and service processes. These kinds of investments allow some variable costs, such as direct labor, to be reduced. Managing this cost trade-off often has strong implications on the quality of the product or service, as well as the timeliness with which it can be delivered. Both of these qualitative issues eventually affect the quantitative issues of costs, volume, and price. Go to your library and find an article describing one organization's effort to invest in automation or other technologies in order to reduce costs. Determine what quality and time issues are affected by the investment. Write a one- to two-page memo describing what you found.

▶ *The Debate*

Which Cost Analysis Method Is Better?

Many costs within an organization are mixed costs, combining elements of both fixed and variable costs. Separating these types of costs into their fixed and variable cost components is necessary before C-V-P analysis work can be done. Two potential cost analysis methods are the scattergraph (visual-fit) approach and the high-low approach. Each of these methods has both disadvantages and advantages compared to the other.

Divide your group into two teams and prepare a two-minute oral argument supporting your assigned position.

- One team represents "The scattergraph (visual-fit) method is superior!" Explain why this method should be used for determining the variable and fixed cost components in a mixed cost.
- The other team represents "High-low; the way to go!" Explain why this method should be used for determining the variable and fixed cost components in a mixed cost.

▶ *Internet Search*

Applied Ethics Resources on WWW

We have discussed ethical issues for accountants in this text and have included an ethics case at the end of each chapter. Obviously, ethical issues are of concern to accountants and all other business professionals. There are a number of good resources on the Internet for those interested in further exploring ethical issues in business (hopefully, we're all interested in this topic!). One of the better sites is Applied Ethics Resources on WWW Centre at **http://www.ethicsweb.ca/resources/**. Sometimes Web addresses change, so if this address doesn't work, access the Web site for this textbook (**http://albrecht.swlearning.com**) for an updated link.

Go to this site and explore the materials regarding applied ethics resources on the World Wide Web. Find a publication that discusses either business or professional ethics. Write a short paragraph that describes exactly where you found the article and give a brief summary.

chapter

17

Product Cost Flows and Business Organizations

After studying this chapter, you should be able to:

Learning Objectives

1 Understand the difficulty, yet importance, of having accurate product cost information.

2 Explain the flow of goods and services in a manufacturing organization and follow the corresponding accumulation of product costs in the accounting system.

3 Understand the process of accounting for overhead.

4 Create a Cost of Goods Manufactured schedule and understand how it is used to calculate cost of goods sold.

5 Explain the flow of goods and services in a merchandising organization and follow the corresponding accumulation of product costs in the accounting system.

6 Explain the flow of goods and services in a service organization and follow the corresponding accumulation of product costs in the accounting system.

7 Understand the impact of e-business on product costing.

8 Use the FIFO method to do process costing.

Before 1810, American business was basically made up of a loose collection of independent contractors, each focused on doing just one thing.[1] As you can imagine, the wheels of commerce turned rather slowly. However, these small businesses were fairly easy to manage. They had few employees and simple processes. Cost accounting, if it existed at all, was not a difficult procedure. For example, if the wainwright wanted to know how much it cost to build a wagon for a customer, he simply added up the costs of buying lumber products from the sawmill, leather products from the tanner, and iron products from the blacksmith. He then set the price of the wagon high enough to compensate him for the time he spent assembling the materials.

The Industrial Revolution came to the United States with the mechanized, integrated cotton textile factories of New England. In 1814, at a cotton mill established by the American industrialist Francis Cabot Lowell in Waltham, Massachusetts, all the steps of an industrial process were combined under one roof for the first time. Instead of contracting with a dozen different little family-owned businesses to card, spin, and sew raw material into cloth, Lowell brought raw cotton fiber into a heavily equipped factory staffed with workers who were organized by specialty. In one massive facility, Lowell could take raw materials and create a finished product ready for sale. This was "big business," and like all business innovations before and since, Lowell's integrated production facility substantially complicated the accounting process. In order to run this textile mill, Lowell and his managers needed a reporting system that would provide the information to plan, control, and evaluate work they themselves could not personally oversee. History shows that the managers of these early textile mills developed a remarkably good accounting system that tracked inventory, payroll, and production work.

Shortly after the textile manufacturing industry was launched, the advent of railroads presented some of the most complex administrative problems of the nineteenth century. On May 10, 1869, the UNION PACIFIC RAILROAD from the East and the CENTRAL PACIFIC RAILROAD from the West were joined at Promontory Point, Utah. Railroad companies soon grew to sizes that dwarfed the scale of the largest textile factories, and the names of railroad tycoons like J. P. Morgan and Edward Henry Harriman became famous (or infamous, depending on your perspective). Managing these huge administrative entities required special record-keeping systems that captured enormous numbers of daily transactions and summarized essential information for frequent internal reports to management. The challenge for railroads was that employees and processes were literally spread all over the map! Senior managers needed some means of assessing the performance of station managers at terminals and yards across the country. Management accounting expanded as "costs per ton-mile" (the average cost to move a ton of material one mile) and "operating ratio" (a ratio of operating expenses to revenues) began providing competitive information to indicate how the performance of various station managers would affect the railroad's total financial performance. These performance measures were used to delegate responsibilities and to control and evaluate the business from a distance, facilitating the spread of the railroads.

The last quarter of the nineteenth century brought an incredible outpouring of inexpensive, mass-produced goods and services for consumers, leading to the emergence of the mass merchandising industry composed of wholesalers and retailers. In addition to making many diverse items available for purchase from a single source, these wholesalers and retailers provided other critical services, including distribution, delivery, and extension of credit. Companies such as R. H. MACY & COMPANY, INC., in New York City and SEARS, ROEBUCK & COMPANY in Chicago were achieving tremendous financial success by focusing on a very important idea: move the inventory! The success of the mass merchant hinged on **inventory turnover**, called "**stockturns.**" By selling goods faster than smaller local merchants, large-scale wholesalers and retailers could charge lower prices and still realize tremendous profit. Up to this point, big business in America had focused almost exclusively on costs. But wholesalers and retailers introduced a new concept to management accounting. By controlling and evaluating the use of assets (in this case, inventory), merchandisers helped management accounting grow to include the process management technique of asset management (also known as capital management). As is described in the opening scenario for the chapter on managing inventory, this is a strategy that has been perfected in our day by WAL-MART.

inventory turnover (stockturns) The number of times the inventory in an organization "turns over" during a period of time. It is often easier to think of inventory turnover as the number of times a dollar invested in inventory is sold during a period of time. Inventory turnover is computed as cost of goods sold divided by average inventory value.

---

1 Historical sources: A. D. Chandler, *The Invisible Hand* (Boston: HBS Press, 1977); H. T. Johnson and R. S. Kaplan, *Relevance Lost* (Boston: HBS Press, 1987).

management accounting is the result of the efforts of many individuals and organizations to create information that has a competitive value in the marketplace. To really understand management accounting, you need to grasp how **manufacturing, merchandising,** and **service organizations** do business. Management accounting historically began with a focus on planning, controlling, and evaluating costs. Cost accounting continues to be a central facet of management accounting. In fact, understanding cost flows is a useful way to understand how a business is structured or organized. And although accurately determining the costs of products and services is difficult, it is one of the most important aspects of management accounting and provides one of the most useful pieces of information for business decision makers. Without accurate cost information, it is difficult to set appropriate prices, evaluate performance, reward employees, or make production decisions. It is even difficult to know whether a company should be competing in a specific market.

In this chapter, you will learn how goods and services flow in manufacturing, merchandising, and service companies and how product costs incurred in these organizations are tracked and accumulated. In subsequent chapters you will learn how to use product costs to manage and control manufacturing, merchandising, and service companies.

manufacturing organizations Organizations that focus on using labor and/or machinery to convert raw materials into marketable products.

merchandising organizations Organizations that focus on procuring tangible products, then distributing them to customers. These customers may include individuals or other business organizations such as manufacturing organizations.

service organizations Organizations that focus on delivery of marketable services, such as legal advice or education, to individuals or other organizations.

Why Having Accurate Product Costs Is so Difficult, Yet Important

1 Understand the difficulty, yet importance, of having accurate product cost information.

Managers need accurate product cost information to plan for the future, to control current operations, and to evaluate past performance. They also need accurate product cost information so that they can deliver high-quality products to customers at the lowest price and at the fastest speed. For most companies, accurately determining product costs is a surprisingly difficult challenge. Regardless of the difficulty, however, having accurate product cost information is critical for a business. Without knowledge of accurate product costs, managers could easily over- or underprice products and make other poor decisions.

What if, for example, TOYOTA sells its 2003 Camry SE V-6 for $23,265 (its intended sales price), but the actual cost of producing the car is $26,000? How long could Toyota stay in business losing $2,735 ($26,000 − $23,265) per car? In this case, buyers will probably rush to buy Camrys because they will likely be priced much lower than other comparable cars (assuming Toyota's competitors have more accurate cost information and have priced their cars to cover their total manufacturing costs). Not only will Toyota lose money on every car it sells, but the more cars Toyota sells, the greater its losses will be.

On the other hand, what if Toyota attempts to sell its Camry SE for $23,265, not realizing that its cost of making the car is actually only $15,000? If the accurate cost is only $15,000, other manufacturers, such as FORD, may sell their cars for much less than Toyota (assuming Ford has a better cost accounting system); sales of Camrys will dwindle. If Toyota mistakenly believes its costs are higher than $15,000, say, $22,500, it will not lower prices to the point where the company can compete with Ford and other manufacturers. The competitors that better understand their own costs will probably reduce prices, leaving Toyota behind in the market. With lower sales, Toyota may again lose money because it can't sell enough cars to cover its fixed operating expenses. As you can see, having accurate product cost information helps managers in many ways, including making planning, controlling, and evaluating decisions such as the following:

network **exercises**

Toyota

Access TOYOTA's Web site at **http://www .toyota.com**. The base price for the 2003 Camry SE V-6 4 cylinder is $23,265.

Net Work:

1. How much does the price increase if options package #1, a CD autochanger, a simulated maple dash, and a V.I.P. Plus security system are added?

2. How do these features affect Toyota's manufacturing costs?

1. As part of the *planning* process, a company can determine whether it can or should compete in certain markets. It is possible that prices of competitors in some markets are already lower than the manufacturing costs would be for a new company trying to enter the market. For example, before starting a new airline, you should calculate whether the prevailing prices on the routes you intend to serve are high enough to cover the costs of the aircraft, air crew, ground crew, airport gate rental charges, regulatory approvals, ticketing system, and so forth.

2. When *controlling* operations, a company can analyze the relationship between production levels and costs and determine whether to increase, decrease, or stop production of certain products. For example, some MAJOR LEAGUE BASEBALL teams (the OAKLAND ATHLETICS are the prime example) have determined that some types of players (big-time free agents, glamorous closing relief pitchers, and highly-touted high school players are some examples) just cost too much to allow the team to make a profit with such players on the payroll.[2]

3. In the *evaluation* process, a company can compare actual costs against budgeted costs (a management accounting process known as variance analysis that we'll discuss later in a chapter on making decisions) and identify both progress and problems for subsequent management action. For example, when President Reagan initially proposed the construction of the International Space Station in 1984, the estimated cost was $8 billion. Recent estimates on the ultimate total cost of the project run as high as $90 billion, prompting some rather unfavorable "evaluation" of NASA.

Having accurate product cost information also allows a company to identify and eliminate costly, complicated processes so that higher-quality, lower-priced products and services can be delivered to customers in increasingly shorter **cycle times**. Accurate cost information allows management to determine the appropriate level at which to operate, to assess the long-term profitability of various products, and to manage the costs of production activities.

Overhead: The Problem in Determining Accurate Product Costs

You have learned in a previous chapter that costs of manufacturing products can be broken down into three elements: (1) direct materials, (2) direct labor, and (3) manufacturing overhead. Direct materials include the cost of raw materials that are used directly in the manufacture of products. Direct materials are kept in the raw materials warehouse until used and include such things as rubber used in making tires, steel used to make cars, wood used to make tables, and plastic used to make eyeglasses. Direct labor includes the wages and other payroll-related expenses of factory employees who work directly on products. Direct labor includes the cost of wages and benefits for assembly-line workers, but it does not include the wages and benefits of the factory custodians or the factory controller because, even though they work in the factory, they don't work directly on making products. Manufacturing overhead includes all manufacturing costs that are not classified as direct materials or direct labor. This includes miscellaneous materials used in production, such as glue or nails; wages for the factory supervisor, controller, and custodians who work in the factory, but not directly on products; and other manufacturing costs such as utilities, depreciation of manufacturing facilities, insurance, and property taxes.

Although it is usually easy to assign direct materials and direct labor costs to specific products, it is extremely difficult to assign manufacturing costs, such as rent or the custodian's salary, to specific manufactured products. Most manufacturing overhead costs are not related to the flow of production. For example, think about the cost of driving your car (if you have one) from your house or apartment to the nearest supermarket and back. It is unlikely that your tires will

cycle times The total time a product spends moving through a particular process or cycle within the organization, such as the product design cycle, the production cycle, or the order and delivery cycle.

Caution

Product costs are only one element management must consider when establishing prices for its products. Pricing is a complex issue, and management usually looks to its own strategy and to the market to set prices (also considering competitors' prices, market's ability to pay, and so forth). It would be wrong to assume that management uses only its product cost information to set prices.

---

2 M. Lewis, *Moneyball* (New York: W. W. Norton & Company, 2003).

The Commercialization of the Internet Who invented the Internet? The Internet began at the U.S. Department of Defense in the late 1950s at the direction of President Dwight D. Eisenhower. At the time of the Cold War and the Soviet Union's successful launch of *Sputnik*, the Eisenhower administration felt the need for a network of computers between major U.S. cities so that the Department of Defense could easily connect with them. Soon major universities began to tap into the network. The timeline below shows the network's origins and growth.

Fifteen servers

First cross-country connection installed by AT&T.

Four servers

Number of Internet users estimated to be 2,000.

First e-mail management program written.

Domain Name System (DNS) introduced; 1,000 servers.

10,000 servers

Domain name "business.com" is sold for $7.5 million. Originally purchased for $150,000 in 1997.

Over 80,000 Internet security incidents (less than 4,000 in 1998)

1954 1965 1970 1971 1972 **1973** 1973 **1983** 1984 1987 **1991** **1992** 1999 **2000** 2002

USSR launches *Sputnik*, first artificial earth satellite. In response, the following year, the United States forms the Advanced Research Projects Agency (ARPA) within the Department of Defense to establish U.S. lead in science and technology applicable to the military.

Desktop workstations come into being; 113 servers.

1 million servers

1 billion searchable Web pages

Commercialization of the Internet begins.

First international connection made between United States and England.

Source: Robert Hobbes, *Hobbes' Internet Timeline.* http://www.zakon.org/robert/internet/timeline/.

wear out or that you will need an engine overhaul or an oil change on this short trip. However, over the life of the car, you will spend substantial amounts of money on maintenance and repair costs. An extremely difficult accounting issue is computing how much of the overhead maintenance and repair cost should be included in the calculation of the cost of your short trip to the store and back. And this cost information is essential as you decide whether it is better to use your car or sell your car and ride a bicycle.

Companies face the same problem. They have insurance and tax bills that are part of manufacturing overhead costs that must be paid only once or twice a year. Utility costs, like heating and air conditioning in the plant, vary from month to month, sometimes significantly. The oc-

As early as 1988, pressure to commercialize the Internet began when businesses saw its potential as a means of communication and a way to create new marketplaces. Before the Internet could become commercial property, however, Congress had to enact new laws. A few years passed before the Internet was successfully commercialized. Then businesses jumped onto the "backbone" that the government had established and have since created a World Wide Web that enables businesses and consumers to enjoy the technology of the Internet that has been termed the "Technological Revolution" in business.

Like the Industrial Revolution, the Technological Revolution started with individuals who had a unique vision that eventually profited millions of people. For example, Barry Shein, a college dropout, created the first ISP (Internet service provider)

in 1989. Barry's idea stemmed from the "withdrawal" he felt when he no longer had Internet access after leaving his university. Soon after, giants such as AMERICA ONLINE (AOL), PRODIGY, and COMPUSERVE began reaping the benefits of Barry's "withdrawal" symptoms. E-commerce on the Internet as we know it today is the result of the vision and efforts of many individuals such as Barry Shein. Without them, the explosive growth in e-commerce shown in the following graph would not have occurred. As a result, managers need to clearly understand the impact of e-commerce on business and accounting.

Source: John Thomson, Jr., *Privatization of the New Communication Channel: Computer Networks and the Internet,* © 2000. **http://www.sit.wisc.edu/%7Ejcthomsonjr/j561/.**

Worldwide E-commerce Projected Sales Revenue Growth

Legend: Rest of world, Asia Pacific, Western Europe, North America

y-axis: $U.S. billions ($8,000 / 6,000 / 4,000 / 2,000 / 0)
x-axis: Year (2000, 2001, 2002, 2003, 2004)

Source: Data from Forrester Research, Inc., 2000. Data are located at http://www.forrester.com/ER/Research/Brief/0,1317,9229,00.html.

casional repairs and maintenance on equipment are difficult to predict and to budget for accurately. Nevertheless, most management accountants are required by their organizations to relate these "lumpy" costs back to the volume of production output. In addition, accurate product costing is even more difficult because the actual amount of all manufacturing overhead costs isn't known until the end of the period, long after some products have been completed and even sold.

Management accountants must find some artificial (but hopefully logical) and fair way to assign or "allocate" manufacturing overhead costs to products produced. This "artificial allocation," if done poorly, can result in inaccurate product costs and can lead to serious problems when making planning, controlling, and evaluating decisions.

activity-based costing (ABC) A method of attributing costs to products based on first assigning costs of resources to activities and then costs of activities to products or other cost objects.

FYI:

The very nature of the grocery business—selling perishable and dated products—makes inventory cost management crucial. One grocery food chain, HANNAFORD BROS., has implemented a new inventory management system that allows for quick and efficient communication between store managers and has saved several hundreds of thousands of dollars in paper reports, giving the company an important competitive advantage.

Source: Cisco Systems Retail Case Studies at **http://www.cisco.com**.

New Methods of Cost Accumulation

Many researchers and manufacturers have spent more time trying to determine ways to provide accurate product cost information than they have spent on any other management accounting topic. The result has been the introduction of several new product costing methods including **activity-based costing (ABC)**. Advocates maintain that ABC can provide management with a more accurate assignment of overhead to products and, therefore, a better understanding of profitability. Because of these changes in management accounting and cost accumulation systems, many business organizations are currently in a state of transition. Companies such as DELUXE CORPORATION (the world's largest printer of bank checks as well as a provider of electronic products and services to financial institutions) have completely restructured strategies and operations based on new cost accounting systems.[3] Other companies have been slower to change and still use conventional cost accumulation systems. As a result, some companies struggle to compete effectively in their markets.

In view of the transitional state of accounting for product costs, we will cover both conventional product costing systems (in this chapter) and new cost accumulation systems (in later chapters). You need to understand both types of systems in order to facilitate organizational transitions to more competitive costing systems during your career. In the remainder of this chapter, we describe the conventional accumulation of product costs. The ABC concept will be defined and discussed in a later chapter.

By integrating technology such as robotics into the production process, companies can reduce costs, improve quality, and increase productivity. However, technology also leads to significant changes in the types of costs companies must now manage.

© Romilly Lockyer/2003 Getty Images

TO SUMMARIZE: While it is difficult to exactly measure a product's true cost, having accurate product cost information is extremely important. Without accurate costs, management can easily overprice or underprice products and make bad business decisions. Although it is usually easy to allocate direct material and direct labor costs to specific products, manufacturing overhead costs make accurate product costing difficult. New methods of cost accumulation, though challenging to implement, offer significant potential benefits to manufacturing, merchandising, and service companies. Hence, in order to be competitive in today's economy, management needs accurate product cost information in order to plan for the future, control current operations, and evaluate past performance.

3 P. B. B. Turney, *Deluxe Corporation: A Strategic Need for Activity-Based Costing* (Charlottesville, Va.: University of Virginia Darden School Foundation, 1999).

The Flow of Goods and Costs in a Manufacturing Firm

2 Explain the flow of goods and services in a manufacturing organization and follow the corresponding accumulation of product costs in the accounting system.

It should be clear to you at this point that management accounting provides information with competitive value that supports management efforts to plan, control, and evaluate the organization's performance in providing goods and services to the world. In addition, you know that organizations compete on the basis of costs, quality, and timeliness, and that management accounting needs to provide information regarding all three of these performance characteristics. As you read in the opening of this chapter, however, management accounting had its beginnings in tracking and reporting costs. Today, one of the best ways to understand how an organization works to provide goods and services is to "follow the money"; in other words, observe how costs flow through the organization. We'll use cost flows to introduce you to manufacturing, merchandising, and service organizations. For a long time, manufacturing was the basis of the U.S. economy. Today, relative to other industries, manufacturing is much smaller. Nevertheless, management accounting systems were originally built to support the manufacturing process, so we'll start there.

Consider the layout for a simple, hypothetical manufacturing company shown in Exhibit 1. This floor plan is for a manufacturer of furniture, Broyman Furniture Company. The floor plan

Exhibit 1: Broyman Furniture Company (A Manufacturing Firm's Layout)

shows a building that is partitioned into two sections. The administrative offices include office space for various vice presidents, the sales staff, the president, and the word-processing staff. The manufacturing facility encompasses the offices of the vice president of manufacturing, the plant manager, and the controller; the raw materials and finished goods warehouses; and the factory floor, where production takes place.

The manufacturing process for Broyman is quite straightforward. When purchased, raw materials are delivered to the **raw materials inventory** warehouse where they are stored until requisitioned for production. When requisitioned, raw materials are moved out onto the factory floor for the actual manufacturing process; there all material is referred to as **work-in-process inventory** until the process is completed. The factory floor includes three different manufacturing departments: cutting, machining, and finishing. Whereas some furniture products require work in all three areas, others may require work in only one or two areas. On the factory floor, factory employees combine materials with their labor to produce finished products. The finished products are then moved into the **finished goods inventory** warehouse and stored until sold.

Although the movement of goods through this simple factory is straightforward, tracking the costs of goods manufactured (the product costs) is not always so simple. You remember from the chapter that introduced management accounting that product costs include all costs necessary to create the product: essentially, the costs of all people and processes within Broyman's manufacturing facility. On the other hand, the costs of people and processes in Broyman's administrative offices, which are not associated with the production of furniture, are period costs. The basic idea that defines product costs is that these are the costs that can be associated with specific products. Certainly, the costs of the raw materials and the wages of factory employees who work on the factory floor are manufacturing costs that can be traced to specific products. But what about the salaries of the vice president of manufacturing, the plant manager, and the individuals working in the administrative offices? Should any part of their salaries be included in product costs? What about the utility bills to heat and light the building, the depreciation or rent on the building, the cost of the parking lot, the cost of paper towels for the washrooms, and other miscellaneous expenditures? Should any part of these expenses be included in manufacturing costs?

Because the individuals working in the administrative offices perform administrative and selling duties, rather than manufacturing functions, their salaries should probably not be classified as product costs. Likewise, the costs to pay for electricity, heat, and other expenses for the administrative offices are probably not manufacturing costs. However, the vice president of manufacturing and the plant manager perform functions related to manufacturing, so their salaries should probably be included as product costs. Although these employees perform administrative functions within the manufacturing facility, the work they perform cannot easily be identified with or assigned to specific products, unlike the factory employees who work directly on the products. Similarly, the heat, power, and depreciation related to the manufacturing facility should be included as manufacturing costs but cannot be easily traced to specific products. What about the costs of delivering purchased raw materials to the plant or the delivery of finished goods to customers? Should these delivery costs be classified as manufacturing, administrative, or selling expenses?

As you can see, accurately determining the costs of manufactured products can be challenging, even in a simple firm with one product and one location. When the "real world" introduces the complexities of multiple products being produced, changing prices and labor rates, multiple manufacturing locations (perhaps some international locations), and individuals performing multiple functions, etc., it becomes very challenging to accurately determine product costs. Essentially, in order to accurately measure product costs, management accountants must be able to:

1. Determine which costs relate to manufacturing and which relate to administrative and selling functions.

---

raw materials inventory
The inventory of raw materials that have not yet begun the production process.

work-in-process inventory
Inventory that is partly completed in the production process, but not yet ready for sale to customers.

finished goods inventory
Inventory that has completed the production process and is ready for sale to customers.

FYI:

In 2001, U.S. domestic companies created $8.7 trillion in products and services (known as gross domestic product or GDP). When we break this number down by industries, manufacturers (including mining and construction) created $2 trillion, merchandisers created another $1.6 trillion, and service companies (including transportation and finance companies) created $5.1 trillion. As you can see, service industries created more output than the other two industries combined! Perhaps more importantly, service industries grew nearly 90% during the prior 10-year period, while manufacturers and merchandisers grew approximately 60% during the same time.

Source: U.S. Department of Commerce, Bureau of Economic Analysis, 2002, **http://www.bea.gov**.

2. Accurately identify and measure all costs associated with manufacturing.
3. Determine appropriate ways to assign costs incurred to the individual products manufactured.

These issues are discussed in the following section.

The Product Costing System

Most accounting systems that track costs of producing and providing goods and services are based on a few key procedures.

- First, identify the product or project that needs cost measurement and track this project through the production process.[4]
- Second, specifically trace the direct costs (costs of direct materials and direct labor) to each product or project.
- Finally, allocate an appropriate amount of overhead costs to each product or project.

job order costing A method of product costing whereby each job, product, or batch of products is costed separately.

This accounting approach is traditionally called **job order costing**. As we discuss the mechanics of this product costing system, keep in mind the overall procedure—identify the product or service (the "job"), trace the direct costs, and allocate the overhead. Also be sure to remember the big picture. In other words, why are we doing this? Product and service cost information is used to plan future operations (e.g., at what level of production should we operate?), to control current operations (e.g., are our costs too high?), and to evaluate performance (e.g., were our costs and performance last period good or bad?). This information is used by management to support continuous decisions about costs, quality, and time.

In our example, we will track product costs as we follow an order for a mahogany table that is manufactured by Broyman Furniture Company. The production of the table is a custom job requiring two operations: machining (preparing the mahogany) and finishing (assembling, staining, and packaging the table). (You will recall that there were three manufacturing areas in Exhibit 1. This table does not require work in the cutting department.)

Exhibit 2 shows that the mahogany table costs $393.50 to make. This amount includes $135 of direct materials, $134 of direct labor, and $124.50 of manufacturing overhead (which includes supervisor and production staff salaries, insurance, utilities, depreciation on plant and machinery, and so on). Looking at the cost summary in Exhibit 2, we can see that the hourly wage rate for direct labor is $10 per hour in machining and $12 per hour in finishing; the manufacturing overhead rate is $11 per machine hour in machining and $13 per direct labor hour in finishing. The **manufacturing overhead rate** is an estimate of the overhead that will be incurred for each unit (in this case, allocated on the basis of machine and direct labor hours). In this example, the company incurs an average of $11 of overhead for every hour the machine is run in the machining department. Thus, each table that requires the use of the machine is allocated a portion of the overhead costs. The use of different manufacturing overhead rates is common. Each department will allocate manufacturing overhead to products on the basis of the most meaningful activity in that department. (Remember the challenge discussed earlier of accurately estimating and allocating manufacturing overhead to products.) The machining department is more automated, so activity is tied more closely to machine hours; the finishing department requires more handwork, so activity is tied more closely to direct labor hours. With these "finished costs" in mind, let's talk about how Broyman Furniture Company actually created these data on the mahogany table. But first, take a brief look at Exhibit 3 on page 877. In this rather complicated-looking exhibit you can literally "see" how the costs follow the

manufacturing overhead rate The rate at which manufacturing overhead is assigned to products; equals estimated manufacturing overhead for the period divided by the number of units of the activity base being used.

---

4 In some organizations, it is not reasonable or possible to specifically track the product being produced. For example, a lumber mill that continuously processes timber into planks may not specifically track individual products. Instead, the mill would track the total production costs expended for a particular period of time (e.g., a day), then assign those costs to the total amount of timber processed during that same period of time. This management accounting approach is called process costing and will be discussed in the expanded material section of this chapter.

computer) that serves as the basis for the accounting records. The storeroom manager sends the requisition information to the accounting department, where the unit cost is entered and the total cost calculated. The accounting entry made to record the transfer of mahogany from storage to machining is provided below. In addition, the finishing department requisitioned some packaging material to prepare mahogany tables for shipping.

Work-in-Process Inventory	100	
Raw Materials Inventory		100
Issued 50 board feet of mahogany to production at $2 per foot.		
Work-in-Process Inventory	35	
Raw Materials Inventory		35
Issued packaging material to production.		

The mahogany and packaging material were used directly in the production and shipping preparation of the table; the cost is assigned as direct materials for this particular job. Because the amount of direct materials used varies proportionately with the level of production, direct materials are almost always variable costs. Indirect materials and supplies used in production (classified as manufacturing overhead costs), such as glue, nails, and varnish, are ordered from the storeroom in the same manner. Although some inexpensive materials, such as glue, are used directly in the manufactured products and others are used to support production, it is generally not cost-beneficial to trace such miscellaneous items to a particular job. These miscellaneous items are treated as indirect materials costs and recorded in the manufacturing overhead account (explained later in the chapter). Manufacturing overhead consists of numerous expenditures such as indirect labor, indirect materials, utilities, rent, and the like. The sum of these

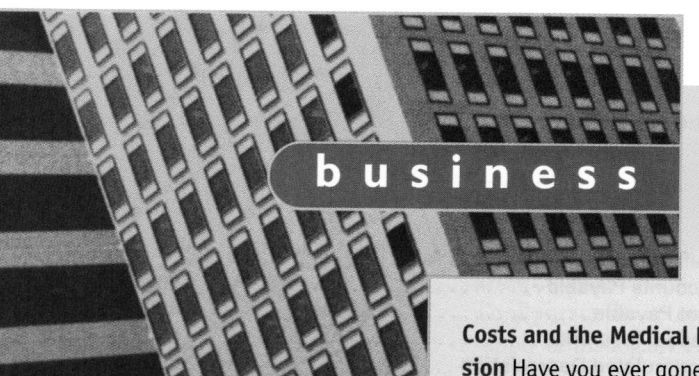

business environment

Costs and the Medical Profession Have you ever gone to the doctor's office, spent 20 minutes in the waiting room, then another 20 minutes in the examination room before the doctor comes in? When she finally comes in, she examines you for 10 minutes and then sends you on your way, charging you $85 for the visit. No wonder medical doctors make so much money—or do they? Does the doctor put your $85 right in her pocket?

What costs must your $85 cover? Unfortunately, you must help the doctor pay for office medical supplies, rent on the office, utilities, salaries of nurses and office personnel,

fees charged by hospitals to use their facilities, and costs of training seminars to remain current in her field. While these costs are expensive, perhaps the most rapidly rising cost is for malpractice insurance. As an example, in many communities in the United States, the cost of obstetrical malpractice insurance is so high that some doctors will no longer deliver babies.

Where does the doctor get the money to cover these costs? By charging you $85 for your visit. Medicine is a business. The doctor is pricing patient visits to cover all costs incurred in providing that service. Costs must be covered and we, the consumers, must pay for them. The next time you visit the doctor, take a look around the waiting room, enjoy those pictures, and read those magazines. After all, you paid for them!

various expenditures provides the balance in the manufacturing overhead account. The following entry records the sum of all the requisitions for indirect materials for the period:

Manufacturing Overhead (indirect materials)	15,000	
Raw Materials Inventory		15,000
Issued miscellaneous materials and supplies to the production floor.		

At the end of a period, the amount of materials and supplies that remain on hand in the raw materials warehouse is shown on the balance sheet as Raw Materials Inventory.

Direct Labor Costs

The method of charging direct labor costs to production jobs is similar to that for direct materials costs. Most factories have a time clock where employees punch in and record their hourly activities. These time clocks often allow workers to identify specific jobs worked on. When the time clocks do not capture specific job information, the information is noted by making entries in the computer or on manual time tickets. The product costs, shown in Exhibit 2, reveal that machining employees worked on the mahogany table for 8 hours. Because the wage rate was $10 per hour in machining, the total direct labor cost in machining was $80 ($10 per hour $\times$ 8 hours). Similar calculations provide the entry to record the direct labor costs in the finishing department. The entries to record all the direct labor costs (ignoring payroll taxes and benefits) for the mahogany table are:

Work-in-Process Inventory	80	
Wages Payable		80
To record the machining department's direct labor costs.		
Work-in-Process Inventory	54	
Wages Payable		54
To record the finishing department's direct labor costs.		

Remember that within certain limits, direct labor costs vary proportionately with the number of products made and, thus, are typically considered variable costs.

Like materials, labor costs can be either direct or indirect. Indirect labor costs include the wages of employees who perform functions not related to a specific job, such as maintenance and custodial. Usually, these employees still punch time clocks, but their wages become part of the indirect labor costs that are included in manufacturing overhead, as discussed in the next section. The following entry records the sum of all indirect labor for the period:

Manufacturing Overhead (indirect labor)	20,000	
Wages Payable		20,000
To record indirect labor costs.		

Manufacturing Overhead Costs

In contrast to direct materials and direct labor, manufacturing overhead (the third type of product cost) involves more complex accounting procedures and estimation problems. As we've discussed earlier, usually direct materials and direct labor can be readily assigned to specific jobs or products. However, manufacturing overhead costs are difficult to trace directly to the production of a single item and must often be estimated in advance of their incurrence. By definition, most manufacturing overhead costs benefit all products made in a department or a company during a period. The depreciation on equipment and the wages paid for maintenance in the machining department, for example, ensure the smooth operation of the entire department for the period; however, these costs cannot be traced directly to individual items produced during the period. Some manufacturing overhead costs, such as property taxes and repairs, are not known until the end of an accounting period. However, managers need current product cost information (for pricing similar jobs, estimating costs for next year, and so forth), so each job is assigned a share of *estimated* (i.e., budgeted) manufacturing overhead costs. In accounting terminology, manufacturing overhead costs are applied to (or absorbed by) jobs or products. Overall, knowing how to set up and handle the accounting for overhead costs at Broyman Company is a tricky business, which we'll talk further about later in this chapter.

STOP & THINK

In our example, the company makes a mahogany table using two operations: machining and finishing. When making a real table, how many separate operations do you think would be necessary? Can you envision how complicated it is to track product costs in a "real-world" production setting?

For now, as *actual* manufacturing overhead costs for Broyman are incurred, the management accounting system needs to recognize and record the costs. During the current production period, these costs include $1,200 for repairs to equipment, $6,450 for monthly rent allocated to the production facility, $850 for liability insurance, and $2,900 in depreciation of manufacturing equipment. The total of these costs is debited to Manufacturing Overhead, and the individual amounts are credited to their respective accounts, as shown here.

Manufacturing Overhead	11,400	
Accounts Payable		1,200
Rent Payable		6,450
Prepaid Insurance		850
Accumulated Depreciation		2,900
To record actual manufacturing overhead costs.		

Caution

Many students will make the mistake of debiting manufacturing overhead costs to an expense account. Although these costs eventually do become an expense, first they are debited to Manufacturing Overhead, then allocated to Work-in-Process Inventory, then transferred to Finished Goods Inventory, and finally expensed in Cost of Goods Sold.

predetermined overhead rate A rate at which estimated manufacturing overhead costs are assigned to products throughout the year; equals total estimated manufacturing overhead costs divided by a suitable allocation base, such as number of units produced, direct labor hours, direct materials used, or direct labor costs.

In addition to recording the actual costs of manufacturing overhead, Broyman's accountants need to allocate overhead costs to the mahogany table in production. As you can see in Exhibit 2, the Broyman management accountants follow a traditional approach of assigning manufacturing overhead costs by taking the expected annual costs of overhead for each department and dividing this estimated amount by the selected activity base (in this case, machine hours for the machining department and direct labor hours for the finishing department). Estimated overhead costs typically come from the company's annual budgets. Selection of the activity base is the result of experience and analysis. The result is an allocation rate for each department that is used to uniformly assign a "fair share" of manufacturing overhead costs to production volume throughout the year. This allocation rate is called the **predetermined overhead rate**. In this case, Broyman's accountants allocate to the mahogany table $66 based on activity in the machining department ($11 predetermined overhead rate × 6 machine hours) and $58.50 based on activity in the finishing department ($13 rate × 4.5 direct labor hours). The entries to record these allocations are:

Work-in-Process Inventory	66.00	
Manufacturing Overhead		66.00
To apply manufacturing overhead from the machining department.		
Work-in-Process Inventory	58.50	
Manufacturing Overhead		58.50
To apply manufacturing overhead from the finishing department.		

Notice in Exhibit 3 that as *actual* overhead costs are incurred (as with indirect materials and indirect labor), the manufacturing overhead account is debited. As overhead costs are *applied* to products, the manufacturing overhead account is credited. This relationship is better illustrated and discussed later in this chapter.

Transferring the Costs of Completed Jobs and Computing Unit Costs

While a job is in process, the costs of direct materials, direct labor, and manufacturing overhead are accounted for separately. When the job is completed, however, these costs (in total) are transferred from Work-in-Process Inventory to Finished Goods Inventory. In the Broyman Furniture Company example, the total cost assigned to the mahogany table is $393.50, as illustrated in Exhibit 2. The entry to transfer the completed cost of the table to Finished Goods Inventory is:

Finished Goods Inventory	393.50	
Work-in-Process Inventory		393.50
To record the completion of the mahogany table.		

It's important that you now take a moment to compare Exhibits 1 and 3. Can you see that how the flow of costs through the accounts in Exhibit 3 closely resembles how the product is created and moves through the manufacturing facility in Exhibit 1? The product costs assigned to the table literally follow that table as it moves through the factory floor (and through the work-in-process inventory account) until the table is completed and moves into the finished goods warehouse (and into the finished goods inventory account). Once completed, cost data for the mahogany table are used in pricing similar jobs, estimating costs for the next year, and measuring income. Note that this process would be no different if, instead of a single table, Broyman were to identify and cost an entire batch of mahogany tables. In this case, at the completion of the job, the unit cost of each table is computed by adding the direct materials, direct labor, and manufacturing overhead costs for the batch and dividing the total by the number of tables produced in the batch (i.e., the job).

Transferring the Costs of Products That Are Sold

When a product is sold, the costs assigned to it are transferred to Cost of Goods Sold. For example, when the mahogany table, which cost $393.50 to make, is shipped to a customer, the table is loaded from the warehouse onto the truck, and the cost of the table is transferred from Finished Goods Inventory to Cost of Goods Sold, using the following entry:

Cost of Goods Sold	393.50	
Finished Goods Inventory		393.50
To record the cost of goods sold for the mahogany table.		

STOP & THINK

Compare Exhibit 1 with Exhibit 3. Try to identify the physical location (from Exhibit 1) with each type of accounting cost in Exhibit 3.

With this entry, costs have been traced all the way through the production cycle and expensed onto the income statement. Once again, inspect Exhibit 3 and be sure that you can clearly see how all the costs flow through the manufacturing process for Broyman. Note that direct labor, when incurred, and raw materials, when used, are debited directly to Work-in-Process Inventory. Actual manufacturing overhead costs, on the other hand, are entered first as debits to Manufacturing Overhead and then are allocated to Work-in-Process Inventory by crediting Manufacturing Overhead. Be careful to note that in Exhibit 3, entry 1 is for mahogany that will be used on several jobs; entries 3, 5, and 6 are actual manufacturing costs incurred for the entire accounting period in which the table was manufactured. Entries 2, 4, 7, 8, and 9 are entries specifically associated with the mahogany table in our example. At the end of the period, the company will usually have three inventory balances: Raw Materials Inventory, Work-in-Process Inventory, and Finished Goods Inventory.

TO SUMMARIZE: In traditional job order cost accounting systems for manufacturing organizations where a specific product can be identified, all direct labor, direct materials, and manufacturing overhead costs are accumulated for each unit or batch (generally referred to as a job). Because the exact amount of manufacturing overhead cannot be determined until the accounting period is completed, an estimated amount of manufacturing overhead is applied to jobs. To estimate the amount of manufacturing overhead to be applied to a job, a predetermined overhead rate is calculated for each department involved in production, using an appropriate measure of activity. This rate is multiplied by the actual quantity of the activity used to complete the job. Total costs for completed jobs are then transferred from Work-in-Process Inventory to Finished Goods Inventory. When manufactured goods are sold, costs are transferred from Finished Goods Inventory to Cost of Goods Sold.

Accounting For Overhead

3 Understand the process of accounting for overhead.

In the Broyman Company example of producing a mahogany table and tracking its production costs, you can see that accounting for manufacturing overhead costs is not the same process as accounting for direct materials and direct labor costs. Because manufacturing overhead costs generally do not coincide with the flow of production, a few extra steps are required to handle the accounting. These steps are:

1. Before the year begins, budget the *estimated* manufacturing overhead, estimate the allocation activity, and establish the predetermined overhead rate.
2. During the year, as costs are incurred, record *actual* manufacturing overhead as debits to the manufacturing overhead account.
3. During the year, as activity takes place, record *applied* manufacturing overhead as credits to the manufacturing overhead account and debits to the work-in-process account.
4. At the end of the year, compare *actual* and *applied* overhead balances and close out the difference in the manufacturing overhead account.

Estimated Manufacturing Overhead

As you can see, the list above includes three difference classifications of manufacturing overhead costs—estimated, actual, and applied. It is *critical* that you understand the differences among these numbers. **Estimated manufacturing overhead** is the amount of overhead costs that management has budgeted for the upcoming production period. The predetermined overhead rate is created by dividing estimated manufacturing overhead by the estimate of the expected level of activity (e.g., direct labor hours) to be used to allocate overhead during the year.

estimated manufacturing overhead Budgeted manufacturing overhead costs that are used to establish the predetermined overhead rate.

To illustrate the use of estimated manufacturing overhead to create the predetermined overhead rate for the machining department at Broyman Company, assume that at the beginning of the year the accountants and production personnel estimated that 24,500 machine hours would be used on the factory floor. Budgeted (estimated) overhead costs for the machining department are shown below. Note that these costs have been separated into fixed and variable components.

Variable manufacturing overhead:

Indirect labor	$ 45,000	
Indirect materials	15,000	
Repairs	7,500	$ 67,500

Fixed manufacturing overhead:		
Rent	$105,000	
Depreciation	85,000	
Insurance	12,000	202,000
Total expected manufacturing overhead cost		
for the year (machining department)		$269,500

Using these data, the accountants then computed the predetermined overhead rate in the machining department to be $11 per machine hour, as follows:

$$\frac{\text{Total estimated manufacturing overhead cost for the year}}{\text{Total estimated machine hours}} = \frac{\$269,500}{24,500} = \$11 \text{ per machine hour in machining department}$$

Similar calculations were used to calculate the predetermined overhead rate of $13 per direct labor hour in the finishing department.

Actual Manufacturing Overhead

After studying financial accounting, some students have a difficult time with the accounting for actual manufacturing overhead. For example, in financial accounting, we accounted for salaries by debiting Salaries Expense and crediting Salaries Payable, which is the correct entry when the salaries are for sales or other nonmanufacturing personnel. However, as you saw in tracking production costs for Broyman's mahogany table, when the wages are related to manufacturing, the debit is to Work-in-Process Inventory for direct labor and to Manufacturing Overhead for indirect labor. Thus, in management accounting, it is important to determine first whether salaries are for manufacturing or for nonmanufacturing personnel. Then, for manufacturing personnel, it must be determined whether the individuals worked directly on the product (Work-in-Process Inventory) or indirectly on the product (Manufacturing Overhead). The same is true for other costs such as depreciation and rent. If these costs relate to manufacturing, they are debited to Manufacturing Overhead; costs not related to manufacturing are debited to Depreciation Expense, Rent Expense, and so forth. The manufacturing costs will eventually become expenses when the products are sold (Cost of Goods Sold).

Applied Manufacturing Overhead

It is important to understand that the debit side of the manufacturing overhead account is used to record actual overhead expenses. Conversely, the credit side of this account is used to record applied manufacturing overhead that is simultaneously debited to the work-in-process inventory account, as illustrated in Exhibit 4. In essence, this entry transfers the overhead cost from the temporary holding account called Manufacturing Overhead to the asset account called Work-in-Process Inventory.

Actual costs, including actual manufacturing overhead costs, are needed for accurate reporting of annual income and for computing a company's income tax liability at the end of the

Exhibit 4: Recording Costs in the Manufacturing Overhead Account

Manufacturing Overhead

Actual manufacturing overhead costs are entered as debits on a regular basis as they are incurred.	Applied overhead costs are entered as credits as production takes place; costs are applied to Work-in-Process on the basis of a predetermined overhead rate.

year. However, the management process of controlling and evaluating costs and setting prices cannot wait until the end of the year. Hence, while both actual and applied manufacturing overhead costs are accounted for constantly throughout the year, actual overhead costs are too sporadic to be effectively used for pricing and costing decisions that take place continuously. For this reason, predetermined overhead rates are used to apply overhead throughout the year.

Disposition of Over- and Underapplied Manufacturing Overhead

If the beginning-of-the-year estimates of both manufacturing overhead costs *and* the activity basis (e.g., machine hours) are perfect, then at the end of the year the accountants at the Broyman Company will have applied as much overhead to Work-in-Process as was actually incurred, and the ending balance in the manufacturing overhead account will be $0 (this rarely happens). Typically, though, the ending balance in the manufacturing overhead account is not very large. Nevertheless, the manufacturing overhead account is a temporary account that must be closed out at the end of the year. Handling any balance left in Manufacturing Overhead is the process of disposing of over- and underapplied manufacturing overhead.

Note in Exhibit 3 that a total of $46,400 in actual costs have been debited to the manufacturing overhead account. To illustrate the accounting for the difference between actual and applied manufacturing overhead costs, we will assume that these costs represent the total actual manufacturing overhead for March 2006. Further, including the work done on the mahogany table in our example, the machining department at Broyman used a total of 1,600 machine hours and applied $17,600 to Work-in-Process Inventory, and the finishing department employed 1,250 direct labor hours and applied $16,250. Finally, the cutting department (using a similar overhead allocation procedure) applied $11,800. At the end of March, the manufacturing overhead account would appear as follows.

Manufacturing Overhead

(Actual costs)	(Applied costs)
20,000	17,600 applied in machining department
15,000	16,250 applied in finishing department
11,400	11,800 applied in cutting department
46,400	45,650
750 balance (underapplied)	

STOP & THINK

What would it mean if the debit (actual overhead) and credit (applied overhead) amounts in the manufacturing overhead account were vastly different?

overapplied manufacturing overhead The excess of applied manufacturing overhead (based on a predetermined application rate) over the actual manufacturing overhead costs for a period.

underapplied manufacturing overhead The excess of actual manufacturing overhead costs over the applied overhead costs for a period (based on a predetermined application rate).

A comparison of the debit and credit sides of the manufacturing overhead account shows that actual manufacturing overhead costs incurred were $750 higher than applied costs (which indicates that overhead was underapplied for the month). This difference is usually ignored until year-end because management is concerned with immediate decisions, for which current estimates are adequate. At year-end, however, this difference must be accounted for, not only to balance the books, but also to show actual costs in measuring income.

If, at the end of the year, total actual manufacturing overhead is less than the amount applied, the account will have a credit balance. This result is referred to as **overapplied manufacturing overhead**. Conversely, if applied manufacturing overhead is less than actual costs, the account will have a debit balance representing **underapplied manufacturing overhead**.

Which is better to have at the end of the year—under- or overapplied overhead? If overhead is underapplied, then the total cost of jobs will be understated. If a company were to price its products in the future based on this understated cost, the company could lose money because it might not cover its actual manufacturing overhead costs. On the other hand, overapplied manufacturing overhead indicates that jobs were overcharged for overhead and costs were overstated. If future pricing decisions were made based on these overstated costs, the company would soon find customers looking elsewhere for more reasonably priced products. Neither under- nor overapplied overhead is desirable. A company's objective is to attempt to anticipate overhead costs and accurately charge those costs to the various jobs.

There are two methods of treating over- and underapplied manufacturing overhead in the accounting system:

1. Close over- or underapplied manufacturing overhead directly to Cost of Goods Sold.
2. Allocate over- or underapplied manufacturing overhead to Work-in-Process Inventory, Finished Goods Inventory, and Costs of Goods Sold on the basis of the ending balances in these three accounts.

The first method is easier and more commonly used, especially if the over- or underapplied amount is small, because it requires only a single entry to correct the amount of manufacturing overhead applied. Let's assume that at year-end, when total actual and applied manufacturing overhead have been recorded, manufacturing overhead for Broyman was overapplied by $1,900. The entry to assign this overapplied manufacturing overhead to Cost of Goods Sold would be:

Manufacturing Overhead	1,900	
Cost of Goods Sold		1,900

     *To recognize the excess of applied manufacturing
     overhead costs over actual manufacturing overhead.*

*Note: The entries for *underapplied* manufacturing overhead would be opposite from what is shown above—debit Cost of Goods Sold and credit Manufacturing Overhead.

This entry will decrease the cost of goods sold account for the year by $1,900 and will close out the manufacturing overhead account. Companies that have very small or zero inventory balances would normally charge any over- or underapplied overhead to Cost of Goods Sold.

The second method is more accurate because, theoretically, any difference between applied and actual manufacturing overhead should be allocated proportionately to all items in production during the period. The items in production include those produced and sold (Cost of Goods Sold), those produced and not sold (Finished Goods Inventory), and those still being produced (Work-in-Process Inventory). If the estimate had been accurate, manufacturing overhead costs would have been allocated proportionately to all products. Therefore, those products actually sold should not be burdened with, or relieved of, the entire amount of the estimation error. This alternative is more complicated, however, and requires detailed calculations and several journal entries, so it will not be illustrated here. When differences between actual and applied overhead are small, this more accurate method is usually not worth the extra effort.

TO SUMMARIZE: Actual manufacturing overhead costs are accumulated and debited to Manufacturing Overhead throughout the year. Applied (or estimated) manufacturing overhead costs are assigned to jobs on the basis of a predetermined overhead rate. These costs are credited to Manufacturing Overhead and debited to Work-in-Process Inventory. Any difference between actual and applied manufacturing overhead at the end of the period must be accounted for in order to properly measure income. When total actual manufacturing overhead exceeds total applied overhead, the excess is referred to as underapplied manufacturing overhead. When total applied overhead exceeds total actual overhead, the excess is referred to as overapplied manufacturing overhead. The easiest and most commonly used method of eliminating over- or underapplied manufacturing overhead is to transfer it directly to Cost of Goods Sold. In some cases, the over- or underapplied manufacturing overhead is allocated among Work-in-Process Inventory, Finished Goods Inventory, and Cost of Goods Sold to arrive at a more accurate assignment of costs.

The Cost of Goods Manufactured Schedule

4 Create a Cost of Goods Manufactured schedule and understand how it is used to calculate cost of goods sold.

Cost of Goods Manufactured schedule A schedule supporting the income statement that summarizes the total cost of goods manufactured and transferred out of the work-in-process inventory account during a period. These costs include direct materials, direct labor, and applied manufacturing overhead.

In this section we will examine a single report, the Cost of Goods Manufactured schedule, that summarizes the cost flows in a manufacturing organization during a given period. We will also see how this cost information is used to then compute cost of goods sold.

Be sure that you review Exhibit 3 and see again how manufacturing costs (materials, labor, and overhead) are accumulated in the work-in-process inventory account, then flow to Finished Goods Inventory, and finally to the cost of goods sold account. These cost flows are summarized on a **Cost of Goods Manufactured schedule**, which supports the cost of goods sold calculation on the income statement.

The purpose of the Cost of Goods Manufactured schedule is to report the total costs that have been incurred to manufacture goods during a period. In our example, Exhibit 5 shows the Cost of Goods Manufactured schedule for Broyman Furniture Company. You will note that the numbers used in Exhibit 5 cannot be specifically traced back to Exhibit 3. This is because the costs flowing through the accounts in Exhibit 3 are focused on the cost associated with the manufacture of a single table. Conversely, the costs in Exhibit 5 are for an entire year. The important thing for you to focus on in Exhibit 5 is the format for summarizing and reporting manufacturing cost flows. Note how the calculation for raw materials used in production is actually based on using the raw materials inventory account to calculate (or "plug") the number that flows into the work-in-process account as shown below.

Raw Materials Inventory

Beginning Balance	50,000		
Purchases	270,000	*290,000* ←	Transferred to Work-in-Process
Ending Balance	30,000		

Plug this

Exhibit 5: Cost of Goods Manufactured Schedule

Broyman Furniture Company
Cost of Goods Manufactured Schedule
For the Year Ended December 31, 2006

Raw materials:		
Beginning raw materials inventory	$ 50,000	
Add: Raw materials purchased	270,000	
Total raw materials available	$320,000	
Less: Ending raw materials inventory	30,000	
Raw materials used in production		$290,000
Direct labor		300,000
Manufacturing overhead:		
Indirect labor	$ 20,000	
Utilities	7,000	
Rent	72,000	
Depreciation	30,000	
Indirect materials	15,000	
Insurance	24,000	
Total actual manufacturing overhead	$168,000	
Add: Overapplied manufacturing overhead	6,000	
Applied manufacturing overhead		174,000
Total manufacturing costs		$764,000
Add: Beginning work-in-process inventory		90,000
Less: Ending work-in-process inventory		(80,000)
Cost of goods manufactured		$774,000

The Cost of Goods Manufactured schedule provides the calculations that support the flow of costs for a manufacturing firm. In our example, the schedule shows that materials costing $290,000 were combined with direct labor costs of $300,000 and *applied* manufacturing overhead costs of $174,000 to transfer $764,000 of manufacturing costs to Work-in-Process Inventory. This $764,000 amount of total manufacturing costs represents the new manufacturing costs incurred during the period and is a good representation of the level of production activity carried out during the period. The $764,000 was then adjusted for the beginning and ending work-in-process inventories to determine the $774,000 cost of goods manufactured for the period. The amount of cost of goods manufactured represents the total cost of items for which production was completed during the period; this cost includes some costs incurred in prior periods (from beginning work-in-process inventory) and most costs incurred during this period. Effectively, cost of goods manufactured represents the flow of costs out of the work-in-process account as shown below.

Work-in-Process Inventory

Beginning Balance	90,000		
Direct Materials Costs	290,000		
Direct Labor Costs	300,000		
Applied Manuf. Overhead Costs	174,000	*774,000*	Transferred to Finished Goods
Ending Balance	80,000		

Plug this

Note that the cost of goods manufactured number of $774,000 is based on *applied* manufacturing overhead costs (not actual overhead costs). However, the actual manufacturing overhead costs are reported in the Cost of Goods Manufactured schedule in Exhibit 5. The reason for this is to provide useful information for purposes of management planning, control, and evaluation. Overapplied manufacturing overhead is then *added* to the actual overhead costs in order to adjust these costs to applied manufacturing overhead for the calculation of cost of goods manufactured.

Knowing the total cost of goods manufactured makes it easy to determine the total cost of goods sold. The cost of goods manufactured amount is added to beginning finished goods inventory (assume $60,000) and adjusted for any over- or underapplied manufacturing overhead (assume $6,000 overapplied) to arrive at cost of goods available for sale of $828,000. The ending finished goods inventory (assume $40,000) is then subtracted to determine the cost of goods sold ($788,000). This calculation of cost of goods sold is shown below.

Cost of Goods Sold

Beginning finished goods inventory	$ 60,000
Add: Cost of goods manufactured	774,000
Cost of goods available for sale	$834,000
Less: Ending finished goods inventory	(40,000)
Unadjusted cost of goods sold	$794,000
Less: Overapplied manufacturing overhead	(6,000)
Adjusted cost of goods sold	$788,000

This calculation can also be shown using the finished goods inventory and cost of goods sold accounts as shown below.

Finished Goods Inventory

Beginning Balance	60,000		
Cost of Goods Manufactured	774,000	*794,000*	Transferred to Cost of Goods Sold
Ending Balance	40,000		

Plug this

Cost of Goods Sold

Cost of Goods Sold			
Unadjusted Cost of Goods Sold	794,000*	6,000	Overapplied Manuf. Overhead Costs
Adjusted Cost of Goods Sold	788,000		

Caution

Remember that over- or underapplied overhead is usually charged to the cost of goods sold account. Thus, in the cost of goods sold calculation, underapplied overhead is added to, and overapplied overhead is subtracted from, the costs transferred from the finished goods inventory account. However, when actual overhead costs are reported in the Cost of Goods Manufactured schedule, the underapplied overhead is *subtracted* from, and overapplied overhead is *added* to, the actual overhead costs in order to adjust these costs to *applied* overhead for the calculation of cost of goods manufactured.

*Cost of Goods Sold	794,000	
Finished Goods Inventory		794,000
Sale of inventory valued using the applied		
manufacturing overhead rate.		

Total cost of goods manufactured should include only those costs that have gone through the work-in-process inventory account during the period. Thus, as shown both in Exhibit 3 and Exhibit 5, applied (rather than actual) overhead costs are included in the Cost of Goods Manufactured schedule. As illustrated, the cost of goods sold account is then adjusted for the amount of over- or underapplied overhead. Cost of goods sold, while an important number for reporting on the income statement for investors and creditors, is not particularly useful for management purposes. Much more detailed information that is useful for planning, controlling, and evaluating manufacturing activities is provided in the Cost of Goods Manufactured schedule.

TO SUMMARIZE: The costs of direct materials, direct labor, and applied overhead used during the period are summarized on a Cost of Goods Manufactured schedule in order to provide information useful for planning, controlling, and evaluating these costs. The cost of goods manufactured is added to the beginning finished goods inventory to determine cost of goods available for sale. Ending finished goods inventory is then subtracted from this number to compute unadjusted cost of goods sold. Cost of goods sold is then adjusted for over- or underapplied manufacturing overhead costs. Cost of goods sold is a summary number that is audited and used in the financial statements, but is not very useful for internal management decision making. For decision making, managers examine more detailed manufacturing costs in the Cost of Goods Manufactured schedule.

The Flow of Goods and Costs in a Merchandising Firm

5 Explain the flow of goods and services in a merchandising organization and follow the corresponding accumulation of product costs in the accounting system.

Retailing is the most visible component of our economic system. Nevertheless, we probably fail to appreciate that what happens over that last three feet of counter in the store is the culmination of the efforts of a great industrial machine and the related mass distribution system. Similar to the concept of an ecosystem in nature, manufacturers, wholesalers, and retailers are linked together in an economic system called a **channel**. If retailers cannot move goods and services the last three feet into the hands of those who will use them, the whole distribution system of manufacturing, wholesaling, and retailing falls apart.

channel The distribution line that a product travels from the original manufacturer to the eventual end-user customer. The channel is typically composed of a manufacturer, a wholesaler, a retailer, and the end-user customer.

The Distribution Channel

Exhibit 6 illustrates the channel system that typically interrelates manufacturers, wholesalers, and retailers. We've discussed manufacturing operations (the starting point of the channel) and the related management accounting systems. In order to understand the full cycle of business, we now discuss the process of distributing goods to customers. As you can see in Exhibit 6, the existence of wholesale middlemen in the distribution channel does not prevent retailers from occasionally dealing directly with manufacturers. For example, WAL-MART is noted for its

Exhibit 6: A Typical Channel of Distribution

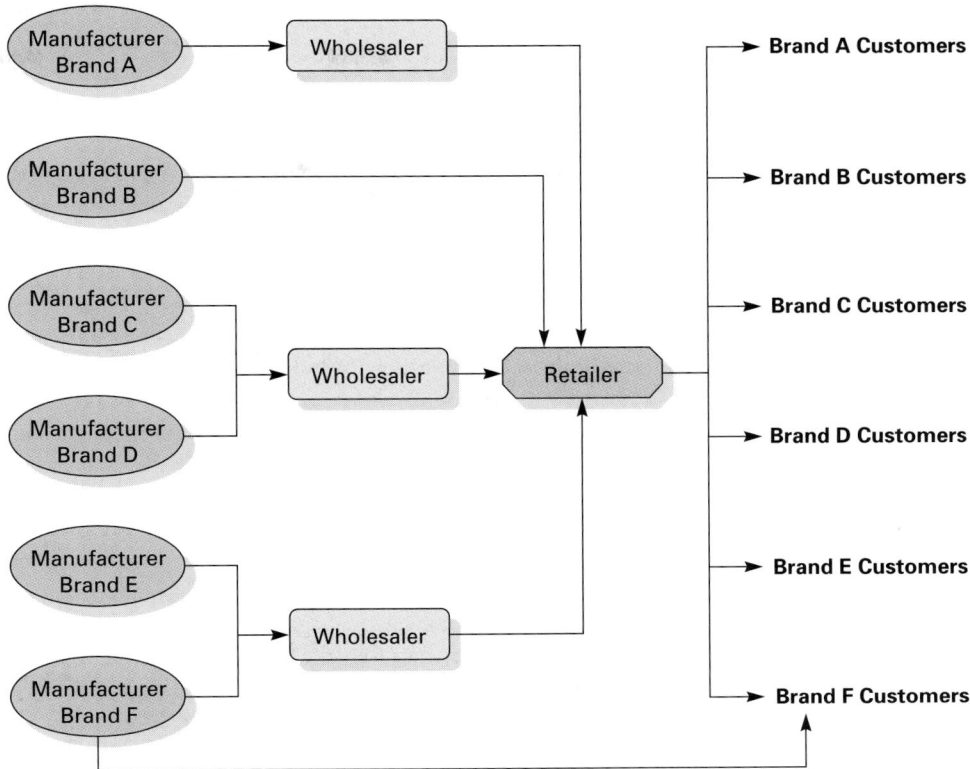

ability to use technology to make direct contact with manufacturers to obtain a significant number of its inventory items. Similarly, some manufacturers may handle some (or even all) of their distribution to retailers. HONDA and FORD, as an example, work directly with their car dealerships and bypass the wholesalers to distribute their products directly to retailers. Finally, a limited number of manufacturers, particularly small manufacturers, have direct relationships with the ultimate end-user customers of their products. They do this by setting up the well-known factory outlet store or by allowing customers to order directly from them; these direct sales are increasingly being done through the Web. A good example of this particular distribution approach is DELL COMPUTER CORPORATION. Dell is one of several large personal computer manufacturers in the United States that take orders directly from end-user customers, build computers to customer specifications, and then ship the finished computers directly to the customers.

Some people argue that the presence of middlemen simply adds to the cost of getting products from manufacturers to consumers. In some cases, this is true. The furniture store probably adds to the consumer's cost of buying a rocking chair from our example manufacturer, the Broyman Furniture Company. But the reality is that most customers cannot buy directly from furniture manufacturers. Further, Broyman may not be interested in (nor equipped for) dealing directly with its many customers! Similarly, many retailers (such as your local grocery store) are not in a position to deal directly with the manufacturers of the items they sell to the public. In addition, wholesalers may be able to provide the retailer such things as next-day delivery, unlimited returns, expert advice on merchandise selection, and customized product mix. If the cost of using a wholesaler is less than the cost to the retailers of providing these services for themselves, then the use of a middleman makes good economic sense. Hence, in providing important options, services, and convenience, wholesalers and retailers can actually add to the efficiency of the distribution system and decrease costs for the ultimate consumer. Management accountants help merchandising companies carefully manage the costs of obtaining and distributing inventory. If costs become too high, then the merchant's customers may either go to a competitor to obtain the goods or skip over the middleman to negotiate directly with the supplier.

Inventory Flow in the Distribution Channel

Spend a few minutes studying Exhibit 7. This exhibit shows the basic layout of a typical wholesaler's operation and a retailer's operation. Although the layouts of operations vary for both retailers and wholesalers, this exhibit will help us visualize the process of moving inventory from manufacturers into the hands of the ultimate end-user.

Wholesalers

wholesalers Top-tier merchants who typically deal directly with the original manufacturers to distribute products to retailers.

Let's begin with wholesalers. **Wholesalers** generally work within a particular industry (e.g., vegetable produce, running shoes, or calculators) to secure distribution contracts with a few key manufacturers. They receive goods in huge bulk shipments that they then break down for smaller shipments to retailers. This is a lot of inventory to manage, and a lot of money is at risk. Obviously, wholesalers will not make a profit unless there is a difference between the price at which they buy goods from manufacturers and the price at which they sell goods to retailers. However, the wholesaling process is much more involved than simply managing the cost of buying and selling goods. Quality and timeliness are also important performance measures that are critical to successful wholesale management. Not only must wholesalers negotiate profitable contracts with manufacturers, but they must then handle the **logistics** of transporting those goods long distances to multiple retail locations. This requires wholesalers to work closely with large transportation companies to both receive and ship out goods as quickly and inexpensively as possible. To help control transportation costs and make the process as timely as possible, wholesalers often locate their distribution centers near large transit hubs such as train yards, shipping docks, airports, and major freeways. Usually, these distribution centers are very large buildings with little advertisement of their business to passersby. If you happen to live or travel near a large transit hub, see if you can spot these giant distribution warehouses, typically surrounded by lots of trucks, trains, or ships.

logistics The management process involved in obtaining, managing, and transporting inventory and other assets in organizations.

Retailers

retailers Second-tier merchants who typically purchase products from wholesalers to distribute to end-user customers. Many large retailers, however, often bypass wholesalers to purchase products directly from the original manufacturers.

The business process for retailers is probably quite familiar to you. Most **retailers** place orders with and receive shipments from wholesalers. As shown in the floor plan in Exhibit 7, many retailers have a receiving dock and a breakdown area used to prepare goods for display on their sales floor. Some retailers also keep a stock room for holding excess inventory. However, the cost of holding inventory in today's competitive environment is causing retailers to demand that wholesalers provide smaller and more frequent shipments. As a result, many retailers are able to avoid having a stock room. Inventory in these companies can then be moved directly from the breakdown area onto the sales floor.

Like wholesalers, retailers invest a lot of money in their inventory. Also similar to wholesalers, the big risk in the retailing business is having money tied up in inventory that is not selling. Obviously, having inventory is important to a retailer's business, but holding on to inventory for too long usually results in a significant opportunity cost. For example, as long as a shoe retailer has its money currently invested in a large inventory of running shoes, it is unable to use that money to purchase basketball shoes. These opportunity costs become particularly painful when the retailer is unable to sell its inventory of running shoes during the running season and, as a result, lacks the money to purchase basketball shoe inventory in time for the basketball season. This is why management accountants in the merchandising business are so focused on measuring stockturns. The faster you can turn your stock (i.e., sell your inventory), the sooner you have the money available to purchase more inventory to sell. Obviously, retailers are just as concerned as wholesalers with the cost and timeliness involved in managing inventory. Further, given the demanding nature of today's informed consumer, management accountants must

Exhibit 7: A Comparison of the Floor Plans for a Wholesaler and a Retailer

Wholesaler's Floor Plan

Inventory is delivered

Receiving Dock	Receiving Dock	Receiving Dock
	Breakdown Area	
	Pick and Package Area	
Shipping Dock	Shipping Dock	Shipping Dock

Inventory is delivered

Inventory is delivered

Inventory is shipped

Retailer's Floor Plan

Inventory is delivered

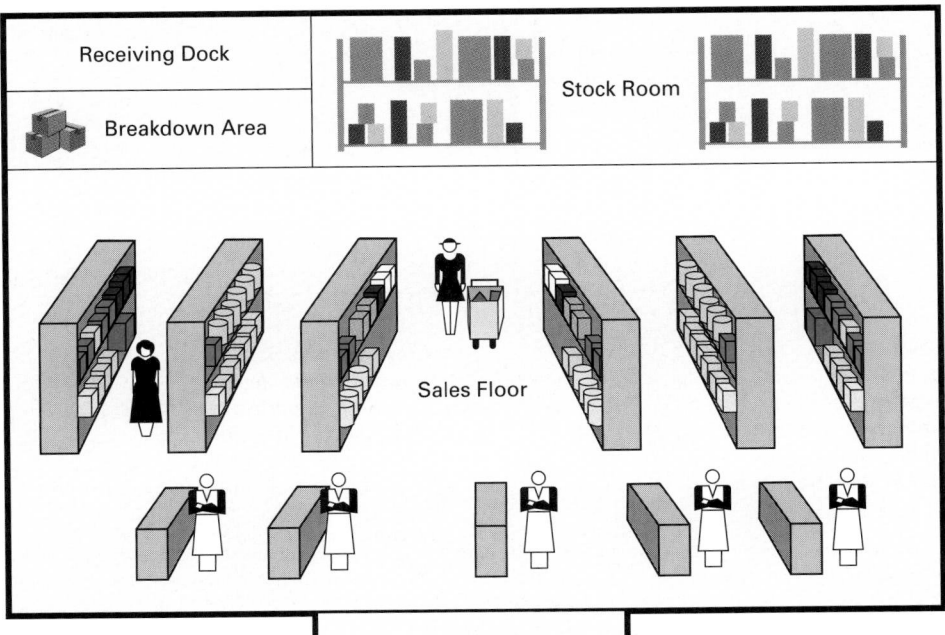

also provide retail managers with information on inventory quality. We'll talk more about the opportunity costs of holding inventory too long in a later chapter on monitoring performance.

Product Cost Accumulation in Merchandising Organizations

The bulk of this chapter so far has focused on manufacturing companies and how management accountants accumulate costs for these organizations. Although both merchandising and service organizations borrow much of their management accounting from the manufacturing industry, there are some important differences, as outlined below.

Inventory Flow and the Income Statement

In contrast to accounting for manufacturing businesses, the flow of costs through the merchandising accounting system is relatively simple. Examine Exhibit 8 and compare it to Exhibit 3 on page 877. Notice how simple the flow of inventory costs is in Exhibit 8. Essentially, accounting for inventory in merchandising organizations is a fairly straightforward process. There are no raw materials inventory, manufacturing overhead, or work-in-process inventory accounts. Merchandise inventory, by definition, is essentially complete and ready for sale when purchased. Hence, the cost of pur-

Exhibit 8: Flow of Product Costs in a Merchant's Cost Accounting System

Journal entries:

1 Merchandise Inventory   xxxx
      Accounts Payable   xxxx
      Purchased inventory for sale.
2 Merchandise Inventory   xx
      Accounts Payable   xx
      Incurred freight in costs on purchased inventory.*

3 Cost of Goods Sold   xxx
      Merchandise Inventory   xxx
      Sold inventory to customers.
4 Merchandise Inventory   xx
      Cost of Goods Sold   xx
      Inventory is returned by customers.

*Note: Freight in is considered part of the purchase cost and should be added to inventory, eventually to be split between Cost of Goods Sold and the ending balance in Merchandise Inventory as goods are sold. In practice, the entire cost of freight in for a period is often simply debited directly to Cost of Goods Sold.

chased inventory is debited to Merchandise Inventory throughout the year as it is acquired.[6] Conceptually, the inventory costs for a merchant should also include all costs required to purchase the inventory, transport it to the merchant's place of business, and prepare it for sale (unpacking, displaying, etc.). Hence, the inventory cost should include the purchase price, shipping costs (freight in), insurance while in transit, administrative costs incurred by the merchant related to purchasing and handling activities, and storage costs prior to sale. In practice, though, most of these overhead-related costs, other than freight in costs, are difficult to allocate to specific inventory items. As a result, overhead costs related to merchandise inventory are often expensed as a period cost and included in Selling and General Administrative Expenses.

As inventory is sold, the cost of inventory is credited from Merchandise Inventory and debited to Cost of Goods Sold. When customers return merchandise that can be resold, Cost of Goods Sold is credited and the inventory account is debited (if the returned merchandise cannot be resold, then nothing happens in either of these particular accounts).

Tracking inventory costs in a merchant's accounting system may appear to be a fairly easy conceptual process. However, developing useful information on merchandise inventory for managers who need to plan, control, and evaluate inventory and inventory costs is a bit more involved. Managing merchandise inventory is a significant topic we'll reserve for a later chapter.

TO SUMMARIZE: Merchants are interconnected with manufacturers in a distribution channel that basically involves manufacturers selling to large-scale wholesalers, who then sell to retailers, who then sell to the end-user customer. Managing the movement (i.e., logistics) of inventory across the distribution channel is a critical business activity. Because wholesalers and retailers generally do not have to deal with raw materials or work in process, the process of accounting for inventory in a merchandising business is not nearly as complicated as it is in a manufacturing business. However, *managing* inventory costs (discussed in a later chapter on managing inventory) is both complicated and critical for a merchant.

The Flow of Services and Costs in Service Companies

6 Explain the flow of goods and services in a service organization and follow the corresponding accumulation of product costs in the accounting system.

So far in this chapter we have defined and discussed the nature of manufacturing and merchandising businesses and identified examples of companies in each type of business. The third type of business is service. What is a service business? Frankly, this is a rather difficult question. Simply stated, the service industry in the United States generally comprises all businesses that cannot be classified as merchandising or manufacturing (this assumes that we classify organizations that convert natural resources into useful products, such as farming or mining, as manufacturers). This is obviously a simple definition, but it is not very useful for us. It is important to more precisely define the service industry because nonmerchandising/nonmanufacturing businesses are the largest and fastest-growing sector in our economy. Hence, it is more likely that your career will involve working with service businesses than any other business type. For our purposes, we'll define a service business as follows:

A service business is any organization whose main economic activity involves producing a nonphysical product that provides value to a customer.

6 Recall that this method of continuously debiting and crediting Merchandise Inventory as inventory is purchased and sold (and debiting Cost of Goods Sold as inventory is sold) is called the *perpetual* inventory method of accounting. The alternative to the perpetual method is the *periodic* inventory method. There are several more accounts involved with the periodic inventory method, including Purchases, Purchase Discounts, and Purchase Returns. A significant difference between the perpetual and periodic inventory methods is that the periodic inventory method adjusts Merchandise Inventory *only at the end* of each period when cost of goods sold is calculated for the income statement.

The definition sounds pretty academic, but it needs to cover a lot of conceptual ground. As you'll see in the list in Exhibit 9, there is a lot of variety in the specific types of organizations that are neither merchandising nor manufacturing. As you study Exhibit 9, try to apply our definition of a service business to each of these categories and see if the definition fits.

Caution

When trying to decide whether a company is in the service business, consider the following old joke:

A plumber is called out to fix a clogged pipe. The plumber examines the situation for a few seconds, then pulls out a hammer and taps on the offending pipe. The problem is solved. However, the customer is a bit upset upon receiving the bill for $100.17. "All you did was tap on the pipe. I demand an itemized bill!" the customer complains. So, the plumber sends the following itemized bill:

Tapping on pipe	$ 0.17
Knowing where to tap	100.00
Total	$100.17

Remember that expertise is a significant component of most service companies.

Comparing Service and Manufacturing Business Activities

Service companies actually share more similarities with manufacturing companies than with merchandising companies. In this section, we will discuss the similarities of and the differences between service and manufacturing firms.

Similarities between Service and Manufacturing Firms

As you now understand, merchants purchase goods from manufacturers in finished condition. As a result, inventory in merchandising companies requires little, if any, conversion cost before being sold to customers. Inventory costs used to determine cost of goods sold on the merchant's income statement are relatively easy to determine. On the other hand, like manufacturers, most service companies perform a significant number of activities to prepare their service products for sale and delivery to their customers. Typically, a lot of direct labor and overhead is involved in a service business. Hence, the management process in service organizations shares a number of similarities with the process of managing a manufacturing business.

Most service companies engage in a very real production activity. However, what they provide is not nearly as tangible as the product provided by manufacturers. Yes, an architect or engineer does provide a tangible set of drawings or blueprints. But what is really being sold is the knowledge and customized advice that is represented by the drawings.

Service companies essentially build a product (the service) and deliver it to the customer (versus a merchant that resells a product built by another company). Consider the organizational effort required for a CPA firm to provide an audit service to a client. This organization is depicted in Exhibit 10. As you can see, there is direct labor (the auditing staff) involved in this audit that is supported by a complex system of supervisors, supplies, equipment, capital as-

---

Exhibit 9: Categories of Service Businesses

- Accounting/legal
- Architectural/engineering
- Communications (e.g., television, radio, etc.)
- Banking/financial (including insurance, investment brokers, consulting, etc.)
- Health care
- Software/systems integration (e.g., programming, installation, service, consulting, etc.)
- Marketing/advertising
- Public utilities
- Research and development
- Transportation
- Entertainment
- Education and training (not including state-owned schools and universities)

Source: Adapted from O. B. Martinson, *Cost Accounting in the Service Industry: A Critical Assessment* (Montvale, N.J.: Institute of Management Accountants, 1989).

Exhibit 10: The Service Process at a CPA Firm

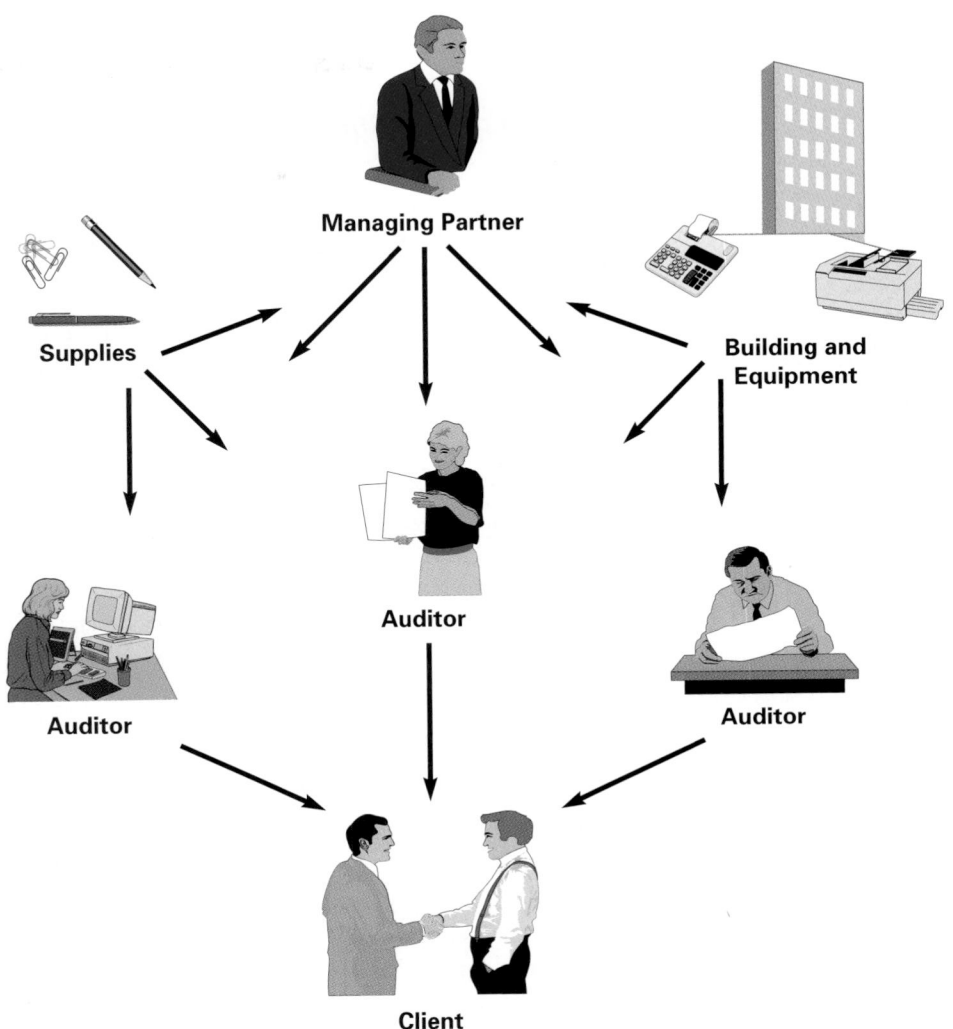

sets, computer network and databases, and so forth. This support system essentially forms the overhead costs of the audit product, and these overhead costs will need to be appropriately allocated as part of the product cost of the audit. You can see, then, that there are many similarities between the process of manufacturing and service companies.

Differences between Service and Manufacturing Firms

Some service organizations do sound as though they are really in the manufacturing business. Notwithstanding, there are some important differences between most service and manufacturing businesses that affect the information provided by management accountants. Whereas manufacturers are dependent on merchants to distribute their products to the final customers, most service businesses deal directly with the end-user customer. Also, there is probably a lot more customization in the service process than in the manufacturing process. Hence, most service businesses use a job order approach rather than a process approach to cost accounting. Additionally, very little raw material is involved in the process of converting labor or capital equipment into a service product. Note, though, that items such as paper and syringes are sometimes included as part of the delivered service, but these items are not the main focus of what the customer is paying to receive. As a result, raw material inventories are typically insignificant or nonexistent in a service business. Similarly, it is often difficult to store a finished service in anticipation of a later sale to customers, making finished goods inventories insignificant or nonexistent. At the close of a reporting period, however, most service companies will be in the process of completing a service for delivery to a customer. This indicates that work-in-process inventories exist and may be significant for many service organizations. (We will discuss work-in-process inventories further below.)

Product Cost Accumulation in Service Organizations

FYI:

Over the past 100 years, costs for raw materials in manufacturing firms have averaged nearly 50% of total product costs.

As you now understand, there are a number of accounting similarities between manufacturing and service organizations. One important similarity is that both manufacturing and service organizations use a significant amount of direct labor in producing their products. In addition, large amounts of overhead costs typically are allocated to individual products. Similar to many manufacturers, service businesses often allocate overhead on the basis of direct labor hours. One important difference is that manufacturers must also manage large amounts of raw materials costs, while the materials included in the services sold by service companies are typically limited to insignificant amounts of supplies used in the service process.

"Inventory" Flow and the Income Statement in Service Companies

Exhibit 11 summarizes the flow of costs for a service company. Comparing Exhibit 11 to Exhibits 3 and 8 illustrates that accounting for service cost flows can be more complicated than accounting for merchandise inventory cost flows, but is quite similar to accounting for manufacturing cost flows. Materials (e.g., supplies), labor, and overhead costs are all involved in, and should be assigned to, the process of creating and delivering a service product to the customer.

The overhead for service firms can involve nearly any kind of management costs—service firms generally do not distinguish between manufacturing and administrative overhead costs. Allocating overhead to service activities generally involves factoring an overhead rate into the billing rate used to charge customers. Think about all the services you buy and use. Often, some type of a billing rate per hour or per event is used to determine the price you pay for the service. For example, accountants, lawyers, consultants, computer programmers, and automotive repair shops often charge by the hour. When you get the bill, you understand that the huge rate per hour does not represent solely the wage or salary of the professional who provided the service to you. This rate has been enhanced (sometimes significantly!) in order to cover all the overhead and supplies costs necessary to support the work done by the service professional. Similarly, doctors, trainers, entertainers, and transportation companies usually charge by event. You understand that the doctor isn't paid the full $175 charge when he or she gives you a physical exam. Much of that amount goes to pay for the costs of staff, equipment, and building occupancy necessary to support the actual service provided by your doctor.

Assigning overhead costs to a service event follows a pattern very similar to that for manufacturing firms. Total overhead for the service organization is estimated for a period of time, generally a year. This estimated overhead is then divided by an appropriate activity measure. For an accountant, this activity measure may be billable hours. The measure for a bank could be the number of teller transactions or number of accounts. For a cable TV company, it could be the average number of accounts expected for the year or the total billable months of service. The activity measure for an electric company might be the expected number of kilowatts produced during the next year. Other examples of possible overhead rate calculations for several types of service companies are shown below.

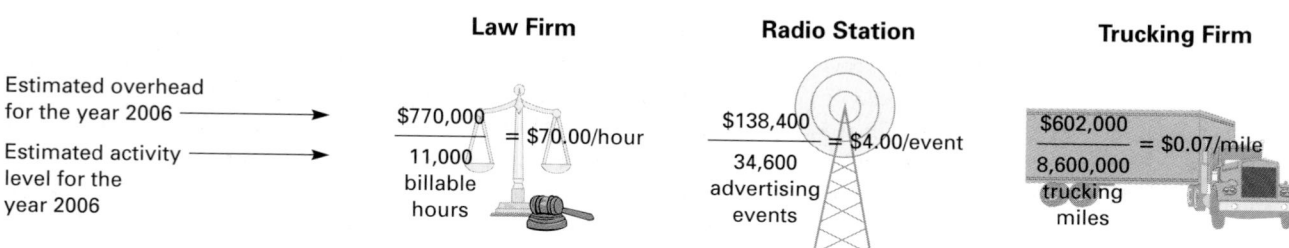

Exhibit 11: Summary of Service Cost Flows

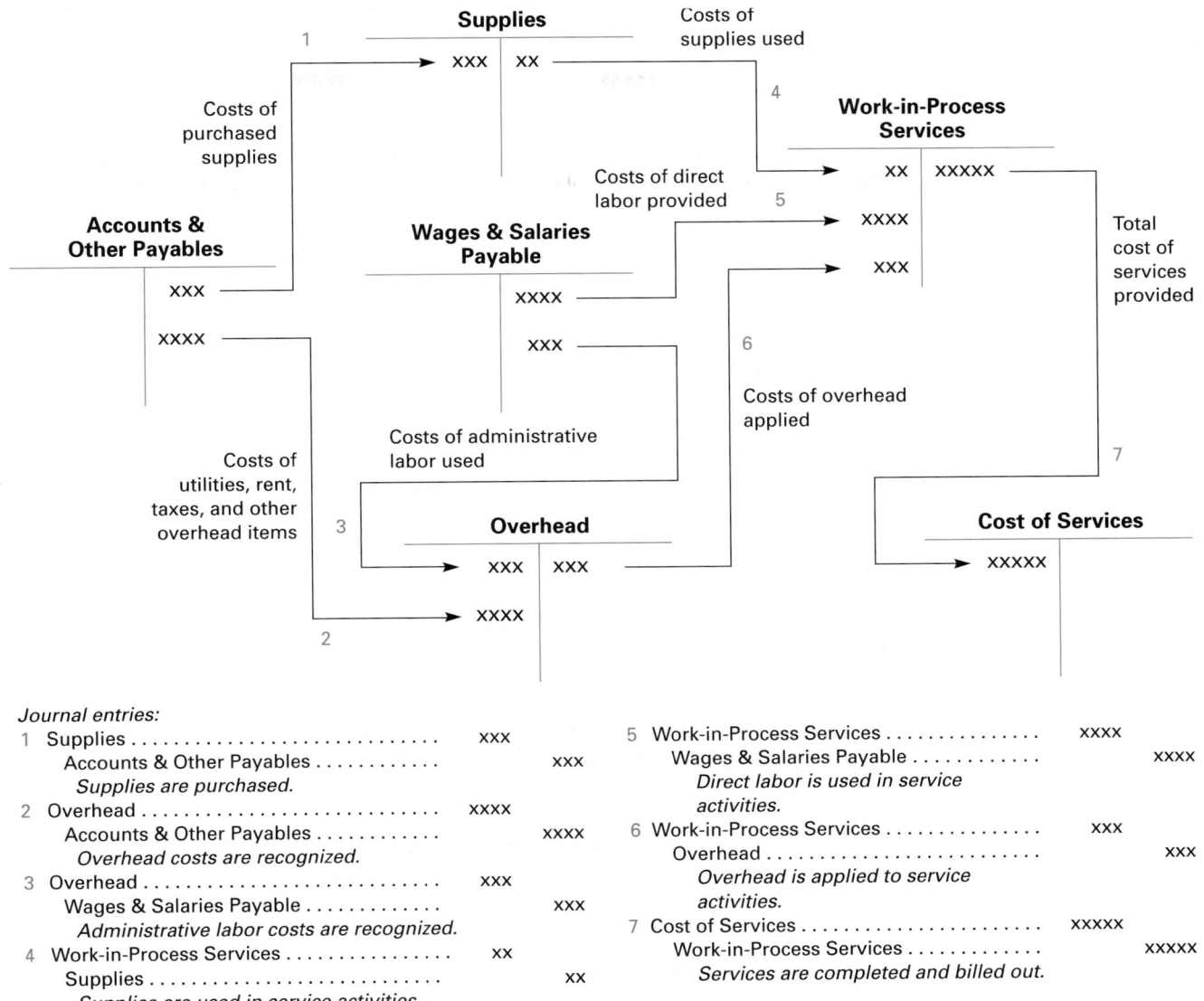

Journal entries:

1 Supplies   xxx
       Accounts & Other Payables   xxx
       Supplies are purchased.
2 Overhead   xxxx
       Accounts & Other Payables   xxxx
       Overhead costs are recognized.
3 Overhead   xxx
       Wages & Salaries Payable   xxx
       Administrative labor costs are recognized.
4 Work-in-Process Services   xx
       Supplies   xx
       Supplies are used in service activities.

5 Work-in-Process Services   xxxx
       Wages & Salaries Payable   xxxx
       *Direct labor is used in service
       activities.*
6 Work-in-Process Services   xxx
       Overhead   xxx
       *Overhead is applied to service
       activities.*
7 Cost of Services   xxxxx
       Work-in-Process Services   xxxxx
       Services are completed and billed out.

The selection of the activity base that is used to allocate overhead is a very important management decision because any particular activity base could have a significant impact on how much cost is assigned to one product versus another. For example, suppose that the academic advisement center at your college is trying to determine what it costs to provide advisement services to a specific student each semester. What are some possible activity bases this department might use to allocate the costs of the office equipment, supervisor salary, and other overhead items? Would your choice of a base have an effect on which students are then identified as "high-cost-to-serve" students?

With a predetermined overhead rate, service companies are able to allocate overhead costs to service events as they occur. This method of allocating overhead helps managers control overhead costs, establish prices for services provided, and measure profit on each service event or contract. The overhead account for a service company is used in much the same manner as in a manufacturing firm. As actual overhead costs are incurred, they are debited to the overhead account rather than being debited to an expense account. Then, as the appropriate overhead activities actually take place (e.g., consulting hours, teller transactions, and kilowatts), overhead costs are allocated to Work-in-Process Services (more about this account in the next section). As services are actually billed, these overhead costs are combined with the direct labor costs of the service professionals (if any) and any incidental costs of supplies are debited to Cost of Services (an account very similar to the cost of goods sold account used by manufacturers and merchants). At the end of the year (or any other time period relevant to the company), the total actual overhead costs are compared to the total allocated overhead costs to determine an over- or underapplied overhead amount. If overhead is overapplied, there will be a credit balance in the service company's overhead account. This balance means that too much overhead cost was allocated to the cost of service activities. The overapplied costs are removed (and the overhead account is closed) with the following entry:

Overhead	xxx	
Cost of Services		xxx

If overhead is underapplied, then there will be a debit balance in the overhead account, and Cost of Services is adjusted (increased) by closing the overhead account with the following entry:

Cost of Services	xxx	
Overhead		xxx

Similar to manufacturing firms, the service company may choose to apportion the over- or underapplied overhead amount between Cost of Services and Work-in-Process Services. The question you might be asking at this point is, "Why would a service organization have a work-in-process inventory account?" Good question! We'll talk about this account next.

Who Has Work-in-Process Inventory?

In manufacturing companies, accounting for work-in-process inventory is a significant part of the product cost accounting effort. Costs of resources used in the process of creating a product are attached to that product. Typically, at the end of an income period (e.g., a month, a quarter, or a year), a number of products are still in process. A significant amount of costs can be tied up in these in-process products. GAAP requires that these costs be capitalized (identified as assets) and assigned to the balance sheet until the products are actually sold. Only at the time that goods are sold and revenue is recognized are the related costs charged to the income statement. The basic underlying accounting concept behind this approach is the all-important matching principle.

The logic for identifying work-in-process inventory as a balance sheet asset applies to both manufacturing and service businesses. Service companies typically earn revenue as the service is provided to the customer. At the end of an accounting period, however, significant effort and resources may have been invested in a service product that is not yet completed for the customer. As a result, revenue is not yet earned, and the costs invested at this point should not be recognized as expenses. In other words, until they actually complete the project and bill it to the client, service companies have work in process.

The following are some examples of work in process that are likely to exist at the end of an accounting period for various types of service companies:[7]

- Accounting/legal—An audit that will take three months to complete is in its initial stage.
- Architectural/engineering—The blueprints for a large construction project are only partially completed.
- Banking/financial—The fieldwork has been completed and the lending documents are being finalized for a large loan that will be closed next month.

---

7 O. B. Martinson, *Cost Accounting in the Service Industry: A Critical Assessment* (Montvale, N.J.: Institute of Management Accountants, 1989), pp. 47–48.

- Marketing/advertising—Three weeks of effort have been expended on the development of a new advertising campaign that will not be ready for presentation to the client for another three weeks.
- Transportation—A large shipment of coal is being held in a midwestern freight yard en route to its shipping point on the East Coast.

In each of these examples, resources have been invested in creating a service that the customer has not yet received. As a result, work in process exists and should be recognized on the balance sheet. As you can see in Exhibit 11, as supplies and labor costs are directly invested in the process of creating a service for customers, these amounts are debited to Work-in-Process Services. As overhead costs such as utilities, rent, taxes, and support staff salaries are incurred, these costs are debited to the overhead account and are subsequently allocated to Work-in-Process Services using an overhead rate. When the service is completed and delivered to the customer, then the revenue earning process is complete and the service costs are transferred out of Work-in-Process Services and into Cost of Services.[8]

TO SUMMARIZE: Essentially, a service business is any organization whose main economic activity involves producing a nonphysical product that provides value to a customer. Because service companies generally create the service they provide, they have some similarities with manufacturing companies in both the management and the accounting processes, including the need to manage and account for work in process. A major difference between service and manufacturing operations is that raw materials typically are not a significant component of a service company's product. Costs flow through a service firm in a manner very similar to a manufacturing firm. Costs of supplies (usually insignificant in size) and direct labor (usually significant in size) accumulate in an account called Work-in-Process Services. This account performs much the same function as a work-in-process inventory account in a manufacturing firm. In addition, overhead must often be applied to Work-in-Process Services as service activities take place. The process of applying overhead is typically done using a predetermined overhead application rate.

The Effect of E-Business

7 Understand the impact of e-business on product costing.

Before we conclude the main part of this chapter, we should say a little about the impact of e-business on business organizations and the product costing process.[9] First of all, it is important to understand that e-business is not a separate new industry like manufacturing, merchandising, or service. Rather, e-business provides new platforms for conducting business *within* the current industries in the economy.

You have probably had some experience in shopping on the Internet. Most organizations today have an Internet site. Often all you have to do is open your Internet browser and add a ".com" to the end of the name of your favorite company, and you can be doing business with that company in no time. Obviously, a lot of business is being transacted on the Internet. However, the lion's share of Internet business is *not* taking place with individual consumers like most of us. To help you understand this point, we need to distinguish between two kinds of e-business. One kind is conducted between companies and consumers (or end-users). This sort of business is often referred to as business-to-consumer (or "B2C"). When you shop at WALMART.COM or NORDSTROMS.COM, you're engaged in B2C e-business. B2C e-business in the United

---

8 Some fairly large long-term service contracts are sometimes designed to allow the provider to bill and receive partial payments as the contract is completed. In these cases, as the revenue process is partially completed, some service costs can be transferred out of Work-in-Process Services and into Cost of Services. Learning about this type of accounting, called percentage-of-completion accounting, is reserved for more advanced accounting courses.

9 Some of the material in this section is based on information presented in S. M. Glover, S. W. Liddle, and D. F. Prawitt, *eBusiness: Principles & Strategies for Accountants*, 2nd ed. (Upper Saddle River, N.J.: Prentice Hall, 2002).

The Birth of an e-Business Jeffrey P. Bezos quit his lucrative job with a New York investment firm and moved his family to Seattle, Washington, to start a new company in a new industry. A short time later, on July 16, 1995, AMAZON.COM, the largest e-tailer in the world in 2001, opened its Web doors. After having 300 of his friends and family members test the site, Jeff asked them to tell everyone they knew about Amazon.com. Within 30 days, with no press or traditional advertising, Amazon.com had sold books in all 50 states and 45 countries—an instant Web success! How did this all begin?

Amazon.com began as a bookseller over the Internet that offered competitive prices, accessibility, and extreme convenience. It was readily apparent to Bezos, as his book-selling Web site grew exceptionally fast, that Amazon.com could become the "Earth's Biggest Store." In 1998, Amazon.com offered its first product other than books—music CDs. From there, Amazon.com has expanded into videos, DVD movies, toys, hardware, greeting cards, electronics, software, home improvement products, auctions, and more. How does Amazon.com manage this huge distribution channel?

With more than 2 million unique visitors a month currently, Amazon.com has established a highly automated system that prides itself on discovering and satisfying customer needs. In addition, the Amazon system must maintain a critical relationship with manufacturers and suppliers. One glitch in the system could spell disaster for the company and its end-users (us!). The life of an order begins well before a customer hits the "Buy it" button on the site. Management must forecast consumer needs, arrange to be able to ship merchandise from suppliers on demand, maintain a precise calculation of inventory available from its suppliers, and meet customer demands quickly and effectively. One of the original strengths of Amazon's business model was that it rarely held inventory (recently, Amazon expanded its business operations significantly by building some large distribution warehouses that do hold inventory). Instead, in many cases Amazon has direct connections to its suppliers that allow customer orders to be shipped directly from supplier to customer. Computers track most of this complicated distribution channel, but it is the knowledge of management that ultimately provides the success that Amazon.com enjoys.

Source: J. C. Ramo, "1999 Person of the Year," *Time*, December 27, 1999.

FYI:

Many people originally predicted that the Internet would significantly change how goods and services are sold. The reality is that, in the first quarter of 2003, only 1.5% of consumer retail sales takes place on the Internet. In other words, the Internet is not creating a lot of new sales. Nevertheless, 1.5% of retail sales in the first quarter of 2003 represents nearly $14 billion! More importantly, the percentage of Internet retail sales has doubled since the first quarter of 2001.

Source: U.S. Department of Commerce News, May 23, 2003.

States amounted to 71 billion in 2001 and is expected to continue growing at a significant rate in the future. In addition, business also takes place between businesses, such as the purchase of raw materials, consulting, outsourcing of services, and important partnerships or joint ventures where companies work together to provide goods and services to the public. When this work is managed with Internet-type technology, it is referred to as a business-to-business process (or "B2B"). This aspect of e-business is, frankly, huge. B2B e-business amounted to $995 billion in 2001 and is growing very fast![10]

As manufacturers, merchants, and service providers move more and more of their business onto the Internet, they expect to enjoy a number of significant benefits, including expanded sales opportunities; improved communications, customer service, and loyalty; and better management of human resources and supply channels. Perhaps most relevant to this chapter is the fact that companies expect to lower their costs of business using Internet technology. For example, bank transactions involving a teller cost an average of $1.07 per transaction. On the other hand, ATM transactions cost just $0.39. However, when you log on to your bank at its ".com" Internet site, an online banking transaction costs only $0.01! As another example, IBM bought $13 billion worth of goods and services

---

10 U.S. Census Bureau, 2001 E-commerce Multi-Sector Report (March 19, 2003).

over the Internet in 1999, saving more than $270 million in procurement costs. Further, SOUTHWEST AIRLINES saved $80 million in 2000 in commissions and reservation-system fees by Web-enabling its reservation and ticketing processes. E-billing, the delivery of routine bills online, can save as much as 60% per bill in handling costs. Hence, cost savings in running a billing process at a large utility could be as much as $50 million per year when an e-billing process is implemented. WAL-MART has achieved tremendous improvements in the costs, quality, and timing of goods purchased from wholesalers through the use of inventory management systems that have direct Internet-based connections to its suppliers. Even hiring costs can be reduced, as evidenced by the fact that IBM has installed Internet software that has cut the cost of hiring temporary workers by $3 million annually.

E-business can have tremendous impacts on product costs. Specifically, costs of raw materials are reduced as organizations use the Internet to find and demand better pricing and save significant costs in the process of ordering and managing raw material inventories. Costs of direct labor can also be better managed by using the Internet to identify, hire, and train the organization's workforce. In some cases, direct service labor, such as bank tellers, are redeployed to new assignments in the organization as Internet technology becomes the means of interacting with clients and customers. Perhaps most significantly, companies are making significant changes in the structure of their organizations, which can greatly affect the costs of overhead. At many companies, overhead costs are much higher than the costs of raw materials/supplies and direct labor combined, so finding new ways to handle the management and logistics of a company can have immediate and important impacts on costs. The example of IBM using the Internet to change the way it obtains goods and services (and temporary employees) demonstrates the savings that can result.

TO SUMMARIZE: E-business and Internet technology are dramatically changing all types of business organizations, including manufacturing, merchandising, and service organizations. As these companies make adjustments in both their organizational structure and in the way they connect to and do business with suppliers and customers within their distribution channel, there have been (and will continue to be) significant changes and improvements in the costs, quality, and timeliness of goods and services. These changes are affecting the process of both business-to-consumer (B2C) and business-to-business (B2B) operations.

In the first part of the chapter we illustrated product costing using the job order costing method. This method is commonly used in both manufacturing and service organizations. In this expanded material section, we discuss how companies, predominantly manufacturers, use process costing when it is difficult to specifically identify unique products or jobs during the manufacturing process.

The Process Costing System

8 Use the FIFO method to do process costing.

All the product costing methods described so far in this chapter assume that the accountant is able to specifically identify the job (i.e., the product or service) being produced for customers.

By identifying each specific job, the accountant is then able to specifically track a job as it moves through the work-in-process inventory and into the finished goods inventory. While it is in the production process, the accountant assigns the actual direct materials and direct labor costs, as well as allocates a specific amount of overhead costs, that are required to produce a particular job. This cost accounting method is often referred to as job order costing. Some manufacturing companies cannot use job order costing because they cannot specifically identify each job (product) being produced. Examples of such companies include manufacturers of bricks, lumber, paint, soft drinks, and newspapers and most food processing plants. These companies manufacture large volumes of product using a series of uniform processes. For these companies, **process costing** is the appropriate product cost accounting method. Because these companies can't focus on costing a particular job, they focus on costing the amount of work done for a particular *period of time*. We'll talk more about this concept of work done in a particular time period below. For now, remember that for process costing to be appropriate, two general conditions typically exist:

1. The activities performed in each process center are identical for all units.
2. The units produced as a result of passing through the process centers are basically the same.

Steps in Process Costing

A firm whose products and processes meet the preceding conditions would employ process costing using five steps:

1. Identify units that went into the process and identify where those units are at the end of the processing time. Determine the amount of "work done" (equivalent units of production) during the processing time period.
2. Determine the amount of production costs that went into the process and compute the product costs per unit for the processing time period.
3. Compute the total cost of units completed and transferred out (cost of goods manufactured) during the processing time period.
4. Compute the total cost of units remaining in process (ending work-in-process inventory) at the end of the processing time period.
5. Prepare the production cost report.

Step 1. Compute Equivalent Units of Production

The first step in process costing is to track the flow of units and compute the **equivalent units of production**. The concept of equivalent units of production essentially means to calculate the amount of work actually done during any particular period of time in terms of units of output. It's really a very simple concept. For example, let's assume that you are being paid by the hour to hand paint porcelain figurines for a small local art shop. It's an arduous process, taking several hours to paint a single figurine. On average, you can do only three or four figurines per day. At the end of your first day on the job, you have painted three figurines and have another one nearly complete. If your boss were to ask you how much work you did for the day, are you going to reply that you painted only three figurines? Of course not! Instead, you'll likely tell her that you completely painted three figurines and that you have another one nearly done (let's say it is 90% done). So, did you paint four figurines? Not really. The amount of work done on your first day is 3.9 figurines (three whole units plus 90% of a fourth unit), right? In other words, you did 3.9 equivalent units of production. The work that you have done includes one unit in ending work-in-process inventory (the figurine that is 90% done).

The more interesting measure of equivalent units of production is what happens on your second day on the job. When you come back to the shop the next day, the first thing you will do is work on that day's beginning work-in-process inventory, which is the figurine that is 90% done from the day before.[11] Let's assume that you then start and complete three more figurines.

---

11 This is the reason we call this particular method of process costing the FIFO (first in, first out) method. It is based on the assumption that all beginning work-in-process inventory is completed before any new units are started.

(left margin, vertical) e**X**panded *Material*

*(left margin definitions)*

process costing A method of product costing whereby costs are accumulated by process or work centers and averaged over all products manufactured in a center or department during a particular production period. There are two methods of process costing: The FIFO method separately tracks the costs of beginning work-in-process units and the costs of units started in the current production period. The weighted-average method (not discussed in this text) averages together the costs of beginning work-in-process units and the costs of units started in the current production period.

equivalent units of production A method used in a process costing system to measure the production output during a period. Equivalent units of production essentially measures the "work done" by the center or department in terms of units of output.

Before it's time to go home, you are able to start one more figurine and get it about 30% done. Now how do you answer the boss's question about how much work was done on your second day? You completed a total of four figurines (the figurine that was work-in-process when you came to work plus three more that were both started and completed this same day), but to say that you did the work of four figurines isn't quite accurate, is it? To be accurate, you completed 10% of one figurine, 100% of three figurines, and 30% of a final figurine that is still work-in-process. In other words, the work done for the day was 3.4 figurines, computed as follows:

	Physical Units	Percent Completed (i.e., "work done")	Equivalent Units of Production
Beginning work-in-process	1	× 10%	= 0.1
Started and completed	3	× 100%	= 3.0
Ending work-in-process	1	× 30%	= 0.3
Total equivalent units of production			**3.4**

With this example of equivalent units of production in mind, let's now use an example that's more representative of manufacturers that follow the process costing approach to accounting for product costs. Exhibit 12 shows how products and costs move through the two process centers (mixing and bagging) of the Allied Cement Company. For now, we will focus on the process costing for the mixing center at Allied Cement. Production units at Allied are measured in pounds of finished cement. When the mixing machines are shut down at the end of a production period (let's assume a production period at Allied is one month), not all pounds of cement started the last day of the month in the mixing center will have been completed. In fact, as at most manufacturers, units are usually in process at both the beginning and the end of a period. Were it not for these beginning and ending work-in-process inventories, the number of units actually produced in the mixing center for the period could be determined merely by counting all pounds of cement that were transferred out of the mixing center and into the bagging center. However, as you saw in our earlier example of hand painting figurines, the amount of work actually done in the mixing center for the period also includes how much work was done in the beginning and ending work-in-process inventories.

With this in mind, look at the report below on equivalent units of production for the mixing center.

Step 1: Compute equivalent units of production.

	Physical Units (pounds)	Direct Materials Costs		Conversion Costs	
		Percent Done	Equivalent Units	Percent Done	Equivalent Units
Beginning work-in-process	4,000	× 0%	= 0	× 80%	= 3,200
Started and completed	44,000	× 100%	= 44,000	× 100%	= 44,000
Ending work-in-process	2,000	× 100%	= 2,000	× 60%	= 1,200
Equivalent units of production			**46,000**		**48,400**
Transferred out (to Bagging)	48,000				

The "Physical Units" column reports that the mixing center had 4,000 pounds of cement in beginning work-in-process when the month started. The department finished mixing these 4,000 pounds and mixed an additional 44,000 pounds before the end of the month, allowing the mixing center to transfer a total of 48,000 pounds to the bagging center. At the end of the month, 2,000 pounds of cement remained in ending work-in-process.

Exhibit 12: The Flow of Products and Costs through Process Centers

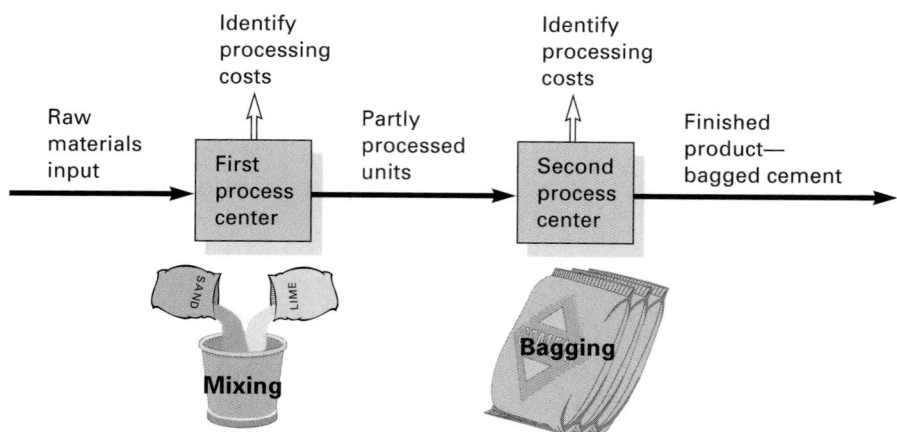

FYI:

In the FIFO approach to process costing, the total *physical* units "started" always equal total units "started and completed" plus total units in "ending work-in-process." Similarly, the total *physical* units "transferred out" always equal total units "started and completed" plus total units in "beginning work-in-process."

conversion costs The costs of converting raw materials to finished products; include direct labor and manufacturing overhead costs.

Now look at the "Equivalent Units" column for the Direct Materials Costs. In this case, all of the materials necessary to mix a pound of cement are put in place at the beginning of the mixing process. In other words, when the month began, the 4,000 pounds of cement in beginning work-in-process were already 100% complete in terms of materials. Similarly, at the end of the month, the 2,000 pounds of cement in ending work-in-process were 100% complete in terms of materials. As a result, the equivalent units of production (i.e., "work done") to be used when accounting for costs of direct materials for Allied is simply the number of pounds of cement *started* into production during the production period, or 100% of units started and completed plus 100% of units in ending work-in-process (and 0% of units in beginning work-in-process).[12]

Finally, look at the "Equivalent Units" column under "Conversion Costs." **Conversion costs** is the term we use to describe all product costs necessary to "convert" raw materials into finished goods. Hence, conversion costs include all costs of direct labor and manufacturing overhead.[13] In this example, at the beginning of the month, the beginning work-in-process inventory was 20% complete in terms of costs of direct labor and manufacturing overhead. As a result, the first work done in the mixing center for the current production period was to finish the remaining 80% of the effort required to complete these 4,000 pounds of cement. In other words, the mixing center did 3,200 equivalent units of production (4,000 × 80%) on beginning work-in-process. At the end of the month, there were 2,000 pounds in ending work-in-process that were 60% complete in terms of direct labor and manufacturing overhead costs, which means that the mixing center did 1,200 equivalent units of production (2,000 × 60%) on ending work-in-process. When combined with the work done on units started and completed, the mixing center's "work done" in terms of direct labor and manufacturing overhead was 48,400 equivalent units (3,200 + 44,000 + 1,200).

Step 2. Compute the Product Costs per Unit

With Step 1 completed, we know how much work was done in terms of production output for the mixing center. Now, to compute the product cost per unit, we need to determine how

---

12 When computing equivalent units in this chapter, we will always assume that direct materials are all added at the beginning of the process. However, this assumption is not always the case in actual companies.

13 Because we assume in this example that costs of manufacturing overhead are being allocated on the basis of direct labor, we can combine the equivalent units calculation for direct labor and for manufacturing overhead costs into one calculation for conversion costs. This is the assumption that we will follow for all subsequent equivalent units calculations in this chapter.

much was spent on production. For the mixing center, we will assume that the beginning work-in-process of 4,000 pounds includes $800 in direct materials and $1,200 in direct labor and manufacturing overhead (i.e., conversion costs). Further, Allied spent $9,660 for direct materials and $70,180 for conversion costs in the current production period. Computing the product costs per unit (pound) for the mixing department is then a simple matter of dividing the product costs by the appropriate equivalent units of production, reported as follows:

Step 2: Compute the product costs per unit.			
	Total Costs	**Equivalent Units**	**Cost per Unit**
Beginning work-in-process			
Direct materials costs	$ 800	× 4,000	= $0.20
Conversion costs	1,200	× 800	= 1.50
Total	$ 2,000		**$1.70**
Current period			
Direct materials costs	$ 9,660	× 46,000	= $0.21
Conversion costs	70,180	× 48,400	= 1.45
Total	$79,840		**$1.66**

Caution

When using beginning work-in-process in the calculation of equivalent units of production for the current production period, remember to use the percentage *yet to be done*. In other words, the "work done" in the current period on *beginning* work-in-process is:

$$\text{Number of physical units in inventory} \times (1 - \text{Percent completed})$$

The "work done" on *ending* work-in-process for the current period is:

$$\text{Number of physical units in inventory} \times \text{Percent completed}$$

As you can see in the report above on product costs per unit, Allied spent $0.21 per pound for direct materials in the mixing center in the current production period. This cost is based on dividing the total equivalent units of 46,000 for work done on direct materials into the total direct materials costs of $9,660. Bearing in mind that beginning work-in-process came from the previous production period, Allied can compare the current direct materials cost to the direct materials cost in the previous production period, which was $0.20 per pound. This cost is obtained by dividing the costs of direct materials in beginning work-in-process by the equivalent units in beginning work-in-process (remember that when the day begins, all 4,000 pounds in inventory are 100% done with respect to direct materials). The current-period conversion cost per unit is $1.45, based on dividing the total equivalent units of 48,400 for work done in terms of direct labor and manufacturing overhead into the total conversion costs of $70,180. Again, Allied's management can check their efforts to control conversion costs by comparing the current-period costs with the previous period's cost of $1.50 per pound, which is calculated by dividing conversion costs in beginning work-in-process by the work already done in beginning work-in-process when the month begins (800 equivalent pounds = 4,000 physical pounds × 20% "work done").

Step 3. Compute the Costs Transferred Out

Allied has spent a total of $79,840 in the current production period in the mixing center. In addition, when the production period began, there was work-in-process inventory in the mixing center that had a total value of $2,000. Hence, as you can see in the report above on product costs per unit, the mixing center needs to account for $81,840. Assuming that there has been no waste or pilferage in the mixing process, at the end of the production period all costs have either been transferred out to the bagging center or remain in ending work-in-process. To compute the costs transferred out to the bagging center, the mixing center needs to account for the costs of completing the cement in beginning work-in-process, as well as the cement that was started and completed in the current period. The following report shows the costs transferred out:

Step 3: Compute the costs transferred out.

	Cost per Unit		Equivalent Units		
Beginning work-in-process					
Initial direct materials costs					$ 800
Initial conversion costs					1,200
Costs to complete materials	$0.21	×	0	=	0
Costs to complete conversion	$1.45	×	3,200	=	4,640
Total					$ 6,640
Started and completed	$1.66	×	44,000	=	73,040
Total costs transferred out					**$79,680**

As you can see in the above report, the mixing center did not need to add any more direct materials costs to complete the beginning work-in-process. However, there were 3,200 equivalent units of work in terms of direct labor and manufacturing overhead that needed to be completed in the current period before the 4,000 pounds of cement in beginning work-in-process could be transferred out to the bagging center. Hence, the mixing department spent $4,640 in conversion costs ($1.45 per unit × 3,200 equivalent units) to complete the mixing on beginning work-in-process. When added to the initial beginning work-in-process costs of $2,000 ($800 + $1,200), the first 4,000 pounds of cement transferred to the bagging center carried total production costs of $6,640.

Of the total 48,000 pounds transferred to the bagging center, 44,000 pounds were started and completed in the current production period. At a total cost per unit of $1.66 ($0.21 per unit for direct materials + $1.45 per unit for direct labor and manufacturing overhead), the mixing department spent $73,040 to mix the remaining units transferred out of its operations in the current production period.

Step 4. Compute Costs of Ending Work-in-Process Inventory

The fourth step in the mixing center's process costing effort is to determine the costs of the 2,000 pounds of cement remaining in work-in-process inventory at the end of the current production period. These calculations are reported below.

Step 4: Compute costs of ending work-in-process inventory.

	Cost per Unit		Equivalent Units		
Costs for direct materials	$0.21	×	2,000	=	$ 420
Conversion costs	$1.45	×	1,200	=	1,740
Cost of ending work-in-process					**$2,160**

Because all 2,000 pounds are 100% complete in terms of direct materials, this inventory represents $420 ($0.21 per unit × 2,000 pounds × 100%) in direct materials costs. On the other hand, because these 2,000 pounds are only 60% complete in terms of direct labor and manufacturing overhead, there are $1,740 ($1.45 per unit × 2,000 pounds × 60%) in conversion costs residing in ending work-in-process inventory. In total, ending work-in-process contains $2,160 ($420 + $1,740) in product costs.

Step 5. Prepare the Production Cost Report

All the data calculated so far are combined into the **production cost report** for the mixing center. This report is shown in Exhibit 13. As you can see, this report includes a large number of calculations. However, we've carefully worked through all the calculations in this report together, so you should feel fairly comfortable understanding how it all fits together. (You'll feel

production cost report A document that compiles all the costs of a manufacturing center for a particular production period. The information on this report is used to control and evaluate production costs, as well as transfer costs and units of output from one manufacturing center to another.

Exhibit 13: A Production Cost Report

Allied Cement Company
Mixing Center
Production Cost Report
For the Month of October 2006

Equivalent Units of Production

	Physical Units (pounds)	Direct Materials Costs		Conversion Costs	
		Percent Done	Equivalent Units	Percent Done	Equivalent Units
Beginning work-in-process	4,000	× 0%	= 0	× 80%	= 3,200
Started and completed	44,000	× 100%	= 44,000	× 100%	= 44,000
Ending work-in-process	2,000	× 100%	= 2,000	× 60%	= 1,200
Equivalent units of production			**46,000**		**48,400**
Transferred out.	48,000				

Product Costs Per Unit

	Total Costs	Equivalent Units	Cost per Unit
Beginning work-in-process			
Direct materials costs.	$ 800	÷ 4,000	= $0.20
Conversion costs	1,200	÷ 800	= 1.50
Total	$ 2,000		**$1.70**
Current period			
Direct materials costs.	$ 9,660	÷ 46,000	= $0.21
Conversion costs	70,180	÷ 48,400	= 1.45
Total	$79,840		**$1.66**
TOTAL DOLLARS IN	**$81,840** ←		

Costs Transferred Out

	Cost per Unit	Equivalent Units	
Beginning work-in-process			
Initial direct materials costs			$ 800
Initial conversion costs.			1,200
Costs to complete materials	$0.21	× 0	= 0
Costs to complete conversion.	$1.45	× 3,200	= 4,640
Total			$ 6,640
Started and completed	$1.66	× 44,000	= 73,040
Total costs transferred out			**$79,680**

Costs of Ending Work-in-Process

	Cost per Unit	Equivalent Units	
Costs for direct materials.	$0.21	× 2,000	= $ 420
Conversion costs.	$1.45	× 1,200	= 1,740
Cost of ending work-in-process			$ 2,160
TOTAL DOLLARS OUT.			**$81,840** ←

more comfortable once you've worked through the review problem at the end of this chapter and a few homework problems!) Remember that the report is composed of four overall steps, each of which should make sense to you.

When a lot of calculations are involved, as in the production cost report in Exhibit 13, a good check figure can be a wonderful tool! Notice in Exhibit 13 that the arrows point to a very good check figure—$81,840. This amount represents the total dollars that have gone into the mixing center in the current period ($2,000 in beginning work-in-process + $79,840 in current production costs), as well as the total dollars that have come out of the mixing process ($79,680 transferred out + $2,160 in ending work-in-process). If the production cost report can balance out to this check figure, you have good (though not perfect) assurance that the calculations have been done correctly.

> **TO SUMMARIZE:** Process costing involves five steps: (1) determine the amount of "work done" (equivalents units of production) during the processing time period, (2) compute the product costs per unit by dividing total costs by "work done," (3) compute the total cost of units completed and transferred out, (4) compute the total cost of units in ending work-in-process inventory, and (5) prepare the production cost report. With process costing, both units and costs must be transferred from one process center to the next until the final unit cost is accumulated at the end of the total production process. The production cost report provides a method of accounting for the flow of units and costs between process centers.

review of learning objectives

1 **Understand the difficulty, yet importance, of having accurate product cost information.** It is usually easy to associate direct materials and direct labor costs with specific products. However, it is very difficult, and often even arbitrary, to assign overhead costs to specific products. Hence, it is difficult to accurately determine the cost of products because overhead costs have to be estimated before being incurred; they often cannot be easily assigned to units produced; and they are often "lumpy"—that is, overhead costs typically do not follow the same even flow pattern of production and service output as followed by direct materials and direct labor. Regardless of the difficulty, however, having accurate product cost information is critical for management to make good planning, controlling, and evaluation decisions.

2 **Explain the flow of goods and services in a manufacturing organization and follow the corresponding accumulation of product costs in the accounting system.** In a manufacturing firm, employees work with raw materials to make finished goods to be sold to customers. When purchased, raw materials are stored in a raw materials warehouse as raw materials inventory; as they are manufactured, goods move through the factory floor as work-in-process inventory; when completed, goods are stored in a finished goods warehouse as finished goods inventory. The costs of direct materials and direct labor (factory employees who work directly in

production) are combined with manufacturing overhead costs as goods are being produced to make up the cost of finished goods. The process of tracing manufacturing costs to specific goods typically follows an accounting method traditionally known as job order costing. When a manufacturing firm purchases materials, the costs are recorded in a raw materials inventory account. As direct materials are used, costs are removed from this account and debited to Work-in-Process Inventory. Direct labor and manufacturing overhead costs are also debited to Work-in-Process Inventory. As units are completed, the costs in Work-in-Process Inventory are transferred to Finished Goods Inventory. When the units are sold, the costs are transferred to Cost of Goods Sold. Whereas direct materials and direct labor costs assigned to products are actual costs, manufacturing overhead is transferred to Work-in-Process Inventory and assigned to products on the basis of some predetermined overhead rate.

3 **Understand the process of accounting for overhead.** *Estimated* manufacturing overhead costs for a period are determined at the beginning of the period and combined with an estimated level of activity (such as direct labor hours) to create the predetermined overhead rate that is used to allocate overhead costs to products as they are produced. As *actual* manufacturing overhead costs are incurred, they are debited to Manufacturing Overhead. This account is credited (and

Work-in-Process Inventory is debited) as overhead costs are applied to specific jobs on the basis of the predetermined rate. At the end of the period, if total *applied* manufacturing overhead costs are larger (smaller) than total *actual* manufacturing overhead costs, the manufacturing overhead account will have a credit (debit) balance, indicating that manufacturing overhead costs were overapplied (underapplied). The debit or credit balance in the manufacturing overhead account is either closed directly to Cost of Goods Sold or allocated among Cost of Goods Sold, Finished Goods Inventory, and Work-in-Process Inventory.

4 **Create a Cost of Goods Manufactured schedule and understand how it is used to calculate cost of goods sold.** The computation of cost of goods sold can be quite complex for manufacturing organizations because the computation involves combining information about materials, labor, and overhead costs, as well as adjusting for beginning and ending inventory balances in raw materials, work-in-process, and finished goods. The Cost of Goods Manufactured schedule is used as an important input into the calculation of cost of goods sold. More importantly, the Cost of Goods Manufactured schedule is used as an important management tool for planning, controlling, and evaluating manufacturing costs.

5 **Explain the flow of goods and services in a merchandising organization and follow the corresponding accumulation of product costs in the accounting system.** Manufacturers sell to large-scale wholesalers, who then sell to retailers, who then sell to the end-user customers. These interconnected business relationships are called a distribution channel. Within this system, wholesalers and retailers are the merchants who are most concerned with effectively managing the costs involved in the inventory movement along the distribution channel. Because merchants basically purchase inventory in a finished state, the process of accounting for inventory in a merchandising business is not nearly as complicated as it is in a manufacturing business. As inventory is purchased, it is essentially ready for resale. Although there is often some effort expended to make some final preparations of the inventory for the customer, merchants will rarely assign additional costs of materials, labor, and overhead to specific products. Hence, inventory is debited to the merchandise inventory account as it is purchased. These costs are then directly transferred to the cost of goods sold account as merchandise is sold. In contrast to manufacturing (and service) organizations, there is little need for merchants to involve the complexities of tracking labor and overhead costs into a work-in-process account.

6 **Explain the flow of goods and services in a service organization and follow the corresponding accumulation of product costs in the accounting system.** Essentially, a service business is any organization whose main economic activity involves producing a nonphysical product that provides value to a customer. As service industries have deregulated in the last few decades, increased competition has forced these companies to develop better cost management systems. There are a number of similarities between accounting for service organizations and accounting for manufacturing organizations. Although most service firms do not need to manage large investments in raw materials, some firms do have large investments in partially completed service projects and contracts. Partially completed service jobs require management accounting that is very similar to the process of accounting for work-in-process in manufacturing firms. Supplies, direct labor, and overhead costs accumulate in an account called Work-in-Process Services. This account performs much the same function as Work-in-Process Inventory in a manufacturing firm. In addition, as service activities take place, overhead is applied to Work-in-Process Services using a predetermined overhead application rate. When the firm has completed and delivered the contracted service, the relevant costs are transferred from Work-in-Process Services to Cost of Services (an account similar to the cost of goods sold account used by manufacturing and merchandising firms).

7 **Understand the impact of e-business on product costing.** As a result of the growth of e-business being conducted on the Internet, accountants and managers are experiencing tremendous change in the way business is conducted across all types of organizations (manufacturing, merchandising, and service). These changes in business processes are also dramatically changing the size of (and the process of managing) all three types of product costs, i.e., direct materials, direct labor, and overhead.

8 **Use the FIFO method to do process costing.** Process costing involves five steps: (1) Identify units that went into the process and identify where those units are at the end of the processing time. Determine the amount of "work done" (equivalent units of production) during the processing time period. (2) Determine the amount of production costs that went into the process and compute the product costs per unit for the processing time period. (3) Compute the total cost of units completed and transferred out (cost of goods manufactured) during the processing time period. (4) Compute the total cost of units that remain in process (ending work-in-process inventory) at the end of the processing time period. (5) Prepare the production cost report. The production cost report provides unit cost data that are used to cost inventory as it transfers from one process center to the next and to cost the ending work-in-process inventory of each process center.

k ey terms & concepts

activity-based costing (ABC), 872
channel, 888
Cost of Goods Manufactured
    schedule, 886
cycle times, 869
estimated manufacturing overhead,
    882
finished goods inventory, 874
inventory turnover (stockturns), 867
job order costing, 875
logistics, 900

manufacturing organizations, 868
manufacturing overhead rate, 875
merchandising organizations, 868
overapplied manufacturing overhead,
    884
predetermined overhead rate, 880
raw materials inventory, 874
retailers, 890
service organizations, 868
underapplied manufacturing overhead,
    884

wholesalers, 890
work-in-process inventory, 874

conversion costs, 904
equivalent units of production, 902
process costing, 902
production cost report, 906

r eview problems

Job Order Costing

Salem Manufacturing Company applies manufacturing overhead costs on the basis of direct materials costs. The year 2006 estimates are:

Direct materials costs	$300,000
Manufacturing overhead	180,000

For every dollar of direct materials costs, 60 cents of overhead is applied ($180,000 ÷ $300,000 = $0.60).

Following are the Salem Manufacturing Company transactions for 2006 (entries rounded to the nearest dollar):

a. Purchased materials for cash, $500,000.
b. Issued $400,000 of materials to production (80% direct, 20% indirect).
c. Incurred direct labor costs of $250,000.
d. Incurred indirect labor costs of $70,000.
e. Incurred costs for administrative and sales salaries of $70,000 and $60,000, respectively.
f. Incurred manufacturing overhead costs: property taxes on manufacturing plant, $6,000; plant utilities, $14,000; insurance on plant and equipment, $3,000. (Assume these expenses have not yet been paid.)
g. Recorded depreciation on manufacturing plant and equipment of $18,000 and $6,000, respectively.
h. Applied manufacturing overhead.
i. Transferred 65% of Work-in-Process Inventory to Finished Goods Inventory. Beginning Work-in-Process Inventory was $13,000.
j. Sold 90% of finished goods on account at a markup of 60% of cost. There was no beginning inventory of finished goods.
k. Closed the balance in Manufacturing Overhead to Cost of Goods Sold.

Required:

Prepare a journal entry for each transaction.

Solution

a.	Raw Materials Inventory	500,000	
	Cash		500,000
	Purchased raw materials.		

b. Manufacturing Overhead 80,000
      Work-in-Process Inventory 320,000
         Raw Materials Inventory 400,000
            Issued materials to production.

c. Work-in-Process Inventory 250,000
      Wages Payable (or Cash) 250,000
         Incurred direct labor costs.

d. Manufacturing Overhead 70,000
      Wages Payable (or Cash) 70,000
         Incurred indirect labor costs.

e. Salaries Expense, Administrative 70,000
   Salaries Expense, Sales 60,000
      Salaries Payable (or Cash) 130,000
         Incurred sales and administrative salaries expense.

f. Manufacturing Overhead 23,000
      Property Taxes Payable 6,000
      Utilities Payable 14,000
      Insurance Payable 3,000
         Incurred manufacturing overhead costs.

g. Manufacturing Overhead 24,000
      Accumulated Depreciation—Plant 18,000
      Accumulated Depreciation—Equipment 6,000
         Recorded depreciation on plant and equipment.

h. Work-in-Process Inventory 192,000
      Manufacturing Overhead 192,000*
         Applied manufacturing overhead to Work-in-Process Inventory.

*The predetermined overhead rate is equal to estimated total manufacturing overhead divided by
estimated direct materials costs ($180,000 ÷ $300,000), or 60% of direct materials costs. In this case,
$192,000 ($320,000 × 0.60) is applied because direct materials costs were $320,000 ($400,000 × 0.80).

i. Finished Goods Inventory 503,750
      Work-in-Process Inventory 503,750*
         *Transferred Work-in-Process Inventory to
         Finished Goods Inventory (0.65 × $775,000).*

*The amount transferred is determined as follows:

Work-in-Process Inventory

Beginning Balance	13,000		
(b)	320,000		
(c)	250,000		
(h)	192,000		
	775,000	(i)	503,750
Ending Balance	271,250		

j. Accounts Receivable 725,400
      Sales 725,400*
   Cost of Goods Sold 453,375*
      Finished Goods Inventory 453,375
         Sold 90% of Finished Goods Inventory.

*Because Finished Goods Inventory is $503,750 (i), Cost of Goods Sold is $453,375 ($503,750 × 0.90).
Because Finished Goods Inventory is marked up 60%, Sales are $725,400 ($453,375 × 1.6).

k. Cost of Goods Sold   5,000

    Manufacturing Overhead 5,000*

    Closed underapplied manufacturing overhead.

*The amount of underapplied manufacturing overhead is determined as follows:

Manufacturing Overhead

Actual Overhead	(b)	80,000	(h)	192,000	Applied Overhead
	(d)	70,000			
	(f)	23,000			
	(g)	24,000			
	Balance	5,000			

Accounting for Overhead in a Service Business

Columbus & Hercules, a public accounting firm, is computing the overhead rates to use when billing customers and bidding on jobs. Columbus & Hercules provides the following estimates relating to overhead costs for the year 2006:

Utilities	$ 12,000
Rent	30,000
Equipment depreciation	22,000
Office supplies	20,000
Support staff salaries	120,000
Total estimated overhead costs	$204,000

In addition, Columbus & Hercules offers the following annual estimates (based on a 50-week work year) regarding the salaries and estimated hours associated with the professionals employed by the firm:

Position	Total Estimated Salaries	Total Estimated Billable Hours
Partners (2 × $100,000)	$200,000	4,400
Managers (3 × $70,000)	210,000	6,600
Seniors (6 × $50,000)	300,000	13,200
Staff auditors (10 × $25,000)	250,000	22,000

Columbus & Hercules computes a chargeable hourly rate for each position that is the sum of the following: (1) each position's hourly rate (based on salary), (2) an overhead rate, and (3) a markup of 20% of (1) and (2). The overhead rate allocates estimated overhead costs to each position, then relates the allocated costs to the hours expected to be worked by each position. Travel and materials costs are directly traceable and billed to each job.

Columbus & Hercules has no client projects in process on January 1, 2006. During January of 2006, Columbus & Hercules worked on several auditing and accounting jobs and incurred the following costs:

Jan. 1   Paid rent for January, $2,500.

4   Purchased office supplies on account, $1,200.

9   Paid $4,500 for payables from last year.

15   Paid office support salaries, $5,000.

15   Paid biweekly salaries of professionals: partners, $8,000; managers, $8,400; seniors, $12,000; staff, $10,000.

15   Applied overhead costs based on billable hours: partners, 170 hours; managers, 270 hours; seniors, 500 hours; staff, 900 hours.

18   Used office supplies totaling $800 to prepare client materials.

Jan. 21   Purchased office supplies on account, $1,100.

    25   Received and paid invoice from office supply store for purchase on January 4.

    27   Billed clients for the following jobs using the computed hourly rate for each position:

	Job #1	Job #2
Partner	90 hours	80 hours
Manager	150 hours	140 hours
Senior	320 hours	200 hours
Staff	560 hours	400 hours

    27   Transferred costs from Work-in-Process Services to Cost of Services based on information from January 27.

    31   Estimated utility costs for the month of January to be $1,000.

    31   Paid office support salaries, $5,400.

    31   Recognized depreciation of office equipment, $1,900.

    31   Paid biweekly salaries of professionals: partners, $8,000; managers, $8,400; seniors, $12,000; staff, $10,000.

    31   Applied overhead costs based on billable hours: partners, 180 hours; managers, 280 hours; seniors, 525 hours; staff, 950 hours.

Required:

1. Compute the billing rate to be used for each position.
2. Provide the journal entries made by Columbus & Hercules for January.
3. Compute the ending balance in Work-in-Process Services.
4. Compute the ending balance in Overhead.

Solution

1. Billing rate

Overhead allocation rate: $204,000 ÷ $960,000 = $0.2125 per dollar of salary.

Position	Estimated Salaries	Preliminary Rate	Allocated Overhead	Billable Hours	Overhead Rate per Hour
Partner	$200,000	$0.2125	$ 42,500	4,400	$9.66
Manager	210,000	0.2125	44,625	6,600	6.76
Senior	300,000	0.2125	63,750	13,200	4.83
Staff	250,000	0.2125	53,125	22,000	2.41
Total	$960,000		$204,000		

Billable Rate for Each Position				
Position	Hourly Rate (1)	Overhead Rate (2)	Markup [(1) + (2)] × 0.20 = (3)	Billable Rate (1) + (2) + (3)
Partner	$45.45[1]	$9.66	$11.02	$66.13
Manager	31.82[2]	6.76	7.72	46.30
Senior	22.73[3]	4.83	5.51	33.07
Staff	11.36[4]	2.41	2.75	16.52

[1]$200,000 ÷ 4,400 hours = $45.45 per hour
[2]$210,000 ÷ 6,600 hours = $31.82 per hour
[3]$300,000 ÷ 13,200 hours = $22.73 per hour
[4]$250,000 ÷ 22,000 hours = $11.36 per hour

2. Journal entries

Jan. 1	Overhead	2,500	
	Cash		2,500
	Paid rent for the month of January.		

4	Office Supplies	1,200	
	Accounts Payable		1,200
	Purchased office supplies on account.		

9	Accounts Payable	4,500	
	Cash		4,500
	Paid accounts payable from prior period.		

15	Overhead	5,000	
	Cash		5,000
	Paid office support salaries.		

15	Work-in-Process Services	38,400	
	Cash		38,400
	Paid salaries of professionals.		

Partners	$ 8,000
Managers	8,400
Seniors	12,000
Staff	10,000
Total	$38,400

15	Work-in-Process Services	8,051	
	Overhead		8,051
	Allocated overhead based on billable hours.		

Partners—170 hours $\times$ \$9.66	$1,642
Managers—270 hours $\times$ \$6.76	1,825
Seniors—500 hours $\times$ \$4.83	2,415
Staff—900 hours $\times$ \$2.41	2,169
Total	$8,051

18	Work-in-Process Services	800	
	Office Supplies		800
	Used office supplies on behalf of clients.		

21	Office Supplies	1,100	
	Accounts Payable		1,100
	Purchased office supplies on account.		

25	Accounts Payable	1,200	
	Cash		1,200
	Paid for supplies purchased on January 4.		

27	Accounts Receivable	57,724	
	Service Revenue		57,724
	Billed clients for Jobs #1 and #2.		

Partners—170 hours $\times$ \$66.13	$11,242
Managers—290 hours $\times$ \$46.30	13,427
Seniors—520 hours $\times$ \$33.07	17,196
Staff—960 hours $\times$ \$16.52	15,859
Total	$57,724

27	Cost of Services	48,107	
	Work-in-Process Services		48,107
	Transferred completed work in process to cost of services;		
	comprised of each position's hourly rate and overhead rate.		

Partners—170 hours $\times$ (\$45.45 + \$9.66)	$ 9,369
Managers—290 hours $\times$ (\$31.82 + \$6.76)	11,188
Seniors—520 hours $\times$ (\$22.73 + \$4.83)	14,331
Staff—960 hours $\times$ (\$11.36 + \$2.41)	13,219
Total	$48,107

Jan. 31	Overhead	. . . .	1,000	
	Utilities Payable	. . . .		1,000
	To record estimated utilities expense for the month.			

31	Overhead	. . . .	5,400	
	Cash	. . . .		5,400
	Paid office support salaries.			

31	Overhead	. . . .	1,900	
	Accumulated Depreciation—Office Equipment	. . . .		1,900
	To record depreciation expense for the month.			

31	Work-in-Process Services	. . . .	38,400	
	Cash	. . . .		38,400
	Paid salaries of professionals.			

Partners	$ 8,000	
Managers	8,400	
Seniors	12,000	
Staff	10,000	
Total	$38,400	

31	Work-in-Process Services	. . . .	8,458	
	Overhead	. . . .		8,458
	Allocated overhead based on billable hours.			

Partners—180 hours × $9.66	$1,739	
Managers—280 hours × $6.76	1,893	
Seniors—525 hours × $4.83	2,536	
Staff—950 hours × $2.41	2,290	
Total	$8,458	

3. Ending balance in Work-in-Process Services

Work-in-Process Services

1/15	38,400	1/27	48,107
1/15	8,051		
1/18	800		
1/31	38,400		
1/31	8,458		
End. bal.	46,002		

4. Ending balance in Overhead

Overhead

1/1	2,500	1/15	8,051
1/15	5,000	1/31	8,458
1/31	1,000		
1/31	5,400		
1/31	1,900		
		End. bal. (overapplied)	709

Process Costing

Cleveland Enterprises produces flour in a continuous manufacturing process. The flour is mixed in one step and transferred to the finished goods department. At the beginning of September,

Cleveland had 1,600 bags of flour in process (100% complete as to materials and 20% complete as to processing) that held $2,800 in costs of direct materials and $800 in conversion costs. During September, 20,000 bags of flour were placed into production, and by the end of the month, only 2,000 bags of flour remained in process (100% complete as to materials and 30% complete as to processing). Production costs for September are as follows:

Direct materials	$36,000
Conversion costs	47,712

Required:

1. Prepare the production cost report for September.
2. Prepare the journal entries required to record the production of flour and the transfer of the finished bags to finished goods inventory. Assume that the processing costs are 75% direct labor and 25% manufacturing overhead.

Solution

1. Production cost report

Cleveland Enterprises
Production Cost Report
For the Month of September

EQUIVALENT UNITS OF PRODUCTION

	Physical Units	Direct Materials Costs Percent Done	Equivalent Units	Conversion Costs Percent Done	Equivalent Units
Beginning work-in-process	1,600	0%	0	80%	1,280
Started and completed	18,000	100%	18,000	100%	18,000
Ending work-in-process	2,000	100%	2,000	30%	600
Equivalent units of production			20,000		19,880
Transferred out	19,600				

PRODUCT COSTS PER UNIT

	Total Costs	Equivalent Units	Cost per Unit
Beginning work-in-process			
Direct materials costs	$ 2,800	1,600	$1.75
Conversion costs	800	320	2.50
Total	$ 3,600		$4.25
Current period			
Direct materials costs	$36,000	20,000	$1.80
Conversion costs	47,712	19,880	2.40
Total	$83,712		$4.20
TOTAL DOLLARS IN	$87,312		

COSTS TRANSFERRED OUT

	Cost per Unit	Equivalent Units	
Beginning work-in-process			
Initial direct materials costs			$ 2,800
Initial conversion costs			800
Costs to complete materials	$1.80	0	0
Costs to complete conversion	$2.40	1,280	3,072
Total			$ 6,672
Started and completed	$4.20	18,000	75,600
Total costs transferred out			$82,272

COSTS OF ENDING WORK-IN-PROCESS

	Cost per Unit	Equivalent Units	
Costs for direct materials	$1.80	2,000	$ 3,600
Conversion costs	$2.40	600	1,440
Cost of ending work-in-process			**$ 5,040**
TOTAL DOLLARS OUT			**$87,312**

2. Journal entries

Work-in-Process Inventory	36,000	
Direct Materials Inventory		36,000

Transferred direct materials to work-in-process inventory.

Work-in-Process Inventory	47,712	
Wages Payable		35,784
Manufacturing Overhead		11,928

To record the department's payroll costs and applied manufacturing overhead ($47,712 × 75% = $35,784; $47,712 × 25% = $11,928).

Finished Goods Inventory	82,272	
Work-in-Process Inventory		82,272

Transferred finished goods to the finished goods inventory.

discussion questions

1. Why do managers need accurate product cost information?
2. For financial reporting, which costs are usually included as product costs in a manufacturing company?
3. Why should a firm know how much it costs to produce its goods and services?
4. Describe some possible resources that organizations can use to help in the effort to improve quality while also reducing product costs.
5. Why is it difficult to track the costs of manufactured products?
6. What is the difference in the accounting treatment for direct materials and indirect materials?
7. Why are actual manufacturing overhead costs not assigned directly to products as they are incurred?
8. What is the normal flow of costs in a job order costing system?
9. What are some common bases for applying manufacturing overhead costs to products?
10. Why might Manufacturing Overhead be referred to as a "clearing account"?
11. How does a firm dispose of over- or underapplied overhead costs?
12. Cost of goods manufactured represents the costs being transferred out of the work-in-process account into the finished goods inventory account. Does the cost of goods manufactured calculation include actual manufacturing overhead costs or applied manufacturing overhead costs? Why does the Cost of Goods Manufactured schedule include both actual and applied manufacturing overhead costs?

13. What is the difference between a manufacturing company and a merchandising company? Between a merchandising company and a service company?
14. What does a distribution channel consist of?
15. What is a service organization?
16. Name three ways in which the service industry differs from the manufacturing industry.
17. What is the principal "product cost" for a service company?
18. Which three costs go into the work-in-process services account for a service company? How does this account differ between service and manufacturing firms?
19. What similarities and differences exist among the costs of merchandising, manufacturing, and service firms?
20. Should managers concentrate only on the costs of production (e.g., the cost of goods sold), or should they also consider other costs and factors?

21. What is the major difference between job order costing and process costing?
22. What two conditions generally exist for process costing to be appropriate?

23. What are the five steps involved in employing process costing?

24. What is meant by the term "equivalent units of production"?

practice exercises

Practice 17-1

Importance of Accurately Identifying Product Costs
Which one of the following statements is *false?*

a. A company wishing to enter a new market may decide not to enter the market because the prices charged by potential competitors are too low to allow the company to cover its costs.
b. Because gathering accurate cost data is so difficult, the benefits rarely outweigh the costs.
c. Having accurate cost information helps companies identify and eliminate costly processes or products.
d. Comparing budgeted costs with actual costs helps companies identify progress and problems of current projects.

Practice 17-2

Manufacturing Overhead Components
Which one of the following is *not* an example of manufacturing overhead?

a. Tires used in the assembly of cars
b. Production supervisor's salary
c. Utilities for production plant
d. Staples used in assembling furniture
e. Insurance on assembly equipment

Practice 17-3

Cost Flow Sequence
Which one of the following sequences is the *correct* sequence for the flow of costs through a production process?

a. Raw materials inventory, work-in-process inventory, cost of goods sold, finished goods inventory
b. Raw materials inventory, cost of goods sold, work-in-process inventory, finished goods inventory
c. Raw materials inventory, work-in-process inventory, finished goods inventory, cost of goods sold
d. Cost of goods sold, raw materials inventory, work-in-process inventory, finished goods inventory
e. Raw materials inventory, finished goods inventory, cost of goods sold, work-in-process inventory

Practice 17-4

Purchasing Raw Materials
The company purchased plastic costing $20,000 and sheet metal costing $75,000. The company paid cash. Both of these materials are used in the production process. Make the necessary journal entry or entries to record these transactions.

Practice 17-5

Direct Materials
The company transferred plastic costing $4,000 and sheet metal costing $22,000 to the factory floor to be used as direct materials in production. Make the necessary journal entry or entries to record these transactions.

Practice 17-6

Indirect Materials
The company transferred plastic costing $1,400 and sheet metal costing $3,000 to the factory floor to be used in general maintenance projects. Because these materials will not be used in the production process itself, they are classified as indirect materials. Make the necessary journal entry or entries to record these transactions.

Practice 17-7

Direct Labor

Two workers worked six hours each to build a custom entertainment center. Each worker earns $12 per hour. Make the necessary journal entry to record this transaction. *Note:* The wages have not yet been paid in cash.

Practice 17-8

Indirect Labor

The company paid $4,500 to its production supervisor for her April salary. Make the necessary journal entry to record this transaction.

Practice 17-9

Recording Actual Manufacturing Overhead

The cost of certain overhead items for the month was as follows:

Rent for production facility	$3,900
Insurance premium for the month	2,250
Monthly depreciation on equipment	4,750
Repairs on equipment	5,200

Payment for these items was as follows:

a. The company is required to pay for one year's rent in advance. The total for one year is $46,800; this amount was paid three months ago. The $3,900 amount represents the rent applicable for this month.
b. The company is required to pay for six months' insurance in advance. The total for six months is $13,500; this amount was paid two months ago. The $2,250 amount represents the insurance applicable for this month.
c. Depreciation is recognized on a straight-line basis.
d. The repairs were performed in the current month. The company will pay for the repairs next month.

Make the necessary journal entries to record these items.

Practice 17-10

Applying Manufacturing Overhead

The company used 150 direct labor hours to complete a certain job. The company applies manufacturing overhead based on direct labor hours at a rate of $5.75 per hour. Make the necessary journal entry to record the application of manufacturing overhead to this job.

Practice 17-11

Transferring the Cost of Completed Jobs

The total cost allocated to a job was $563. The company transferred this job to its finished goods warehouse. Make the necessary journal entry to record this transaction.

Practice 17-12

Transferring the Costs of Products That Are Sold

Refer to the data in Practice 17-11. The company sold for $1,000 the inventory produced in this job. Make the journal entry to record this transaction. The sale was on account. The company uses a perpetual inventory system.

Practice 17-13

Calculating Predetermined Overhead Rates

The company reports the following information from the budget for the coming year:

Estimated total amount of manufacturing overhead	$1,600,000
Average wage for production employees	$13.50
Estimated direct labors hours	250,000
Estimated machine hours	145,000

The company allocates manufacturing overhead based on direct labor hours. Compute the company's predetermined overhead rate.

Practice 17-14

Over- and Underapplied Manufacturing Overhead
The company incurred $32,056 in manufacturing overhead and applied $32,537. The company uses the most common and simple method of handling differences between actual and applied overhead. Make the necessary journal entry to dispose of the difference.

Practice 17-15

Computing Cost of Goods Manufactured
Using the following information, compute cost of goods manufactured, which is the cost of inventory transferred to Finished Goods Inventory.

Work-in-process inventory, beginning balance	$124,500
Work-in-process inventory, ending balance	130,240
Direct materials costs	340,700
Direct labor costs	369,080
Actual manufacturing overhead costs	284,200
Applied manufacturing overhead costs	284,200

Practice 17-16

Cost of Goods Manufactured Schedule
Using the following information, prepare a cost of goods manufactured schedule.

Work-in-process inventory, beginning balance	$160,000
Work-in-process inventory, ending balance	180,000
Raw materials inventory, beginning balance	100,000
Raw materials inventory, ending balance	60,000
Raw materials purchased	540,000
Direct labor cost	600,000
Depreciation on factory building	100,000
Indirect labor	150,000
Other manufacturing overhead costs	86,000
Applied manufacturing overhead costs	330,000

Practice 17-17

Computing Cost of Goods Sold
Using the following information, compute cost of goods sold. Make sure to consider all necessary adjustments.

Finished goods inventory, beginning balance	$120,000
Finished goods inventory, ending balance	130,000
Cost of goods manufactured	340,000
Actual manufacturing overhead costs	160,000
Applied manufacturing overhead costs	175,000

Note: The $340,000 amount of cost of goods manufactured includes the $175,000 in applied manufacturing overhead.

Practice 17-18

The Flow of Goods and Costs in Merchandising Companies
Which one of the following is *not* an example of a way in which middlemen, such as wholesalers, add value?

a. Some manufacturers are not set up to deal with a large number of retail customers.
b. Wholesalers can provide retailers with inventory management services such as fast delivery, easy returns, and enhanced product mix.
c. Wholesalers are given special tax incentives by most state and local governments.
d. Wholesalers can efficiently break down large manufacturer product shipments into the small amounts needed by individual retailers.
e. Customers benefit from the diversity of products available in one retail location rather than going directly to a manufacturer for each product.

Practice 17-19

The Flow of Services and Costs in Service Companies
Which one of the following statements is *false?*

a. Service companies use predetermined overhead rates.
b. Service firms generally do not distinguish between manufacturing and administrative overhead costs.
c. Regarding the accounting for cost of "goods" sold, service companies are more similar to merchants than to manufacturers.
d. Service companies use work-in-process inventory accounts to accumulate costs such as direct labor and manufacturing overhead.
e. A service business is any organization whose main economic activity involves producing a nonphysical product.

Practice 17-20

Units Started and Completed
At the beginning of the month, the company had 35 units that were 45% complete in inventory. At the end of the month, the company had 50 units that were 80% complete in inventory. During the month, the company completed and transferred 1,200 units out of inventory. Compute the number of units started and completed during the month.

Practice 17-21

Equivalent Units of Production
Given the following information, compute the equivalent units of production.

	Physical Units	Percent Complete
Beginning work-in-process	25	20%
Started and completed	430	100
Ending work-in-process	35	40

Practice 17-22

Product Costs per Unit
Using the following information, compute the total product costs per unit for both beginning work-in-process inventory and for current period production.

	Total Costs	Equivalent Units
Beginning work-in-process direct materials costs	$ 2,840	5,400
Current period direct materials costs	7,400	13,300
Beginning work-in-process conversion costs	3,200	2,100
Current period conversion costs	21,700	14,000

Practice 17-23

Costs Transferred out of Work-in-Process Inventory
The company spent a total of $102,340 in the current period in one of its production centers. In addition, when the production period began, there was work-in-process inventory in the production center that had a total value of $3,820. If the costs of the inventory at the end of the period are $4,190, what are the total costs of the inventory transferred out of the production center?

Practice 17-24

Costs of Ending Work-in-Process Inventory
The company spent a total of $309,203 in the current period in one of its production centers. In addition, when the production period began, there was work-in-process inventory in

the production center that had a total value of $18,802. If the total costs of the inventory transferred out of the production center are $311,214, what are the costs of the inventory at the end of the period?

e x e r c i s e s

Exercise 17-1

Manufacturing Costs
Springville Manufacturing Company uses a job order costing system. For Job #151, the production manager requisitioned $1,200 of direct materials and used 40 hours of direct labor at $18 per hour. Manufacturing overhead is applied on the basis of direct labor hours, using a predetermined overhead rate. At the beginning of the year, $800,000 of manufacturing overhead costs were estimated based on a forecast of 200,000 direct labor hours. Prepare a summary of the costs for Job #151. (*Note:* You have to calculate the predetermined overhead rate.)

Exercise 17-2

Manufacturing Costs
The Make-It-Right Company manufactures special wheelchairs for handicapped athletes. The company uses a job order costing system. Partial data for a particular job include:

Direct materials	$450
Direct labor	375
Manufacturing overhead	?
Total cost	$?

The company allocates manufacturing overhead on the basis of direct labor hours. The estimated total manufacturing costs for the year are $750,000, and the total estimated direct labor hours are 150,000. Factory workers are paid $15 per hour.

1. Compute the predetermined manufacturing overhead rate.
2. What is the allocated manufacturing overhead cost and the total cost of the above referenced job?

Exercise 17-3

Predetermined Manufacturing Overhead Rates
Memphis Corporation uses a job order costing system. Thus, management must establish a predetermined overhead rate for applying manufacturing overhead. During the past three years, the following data have been accumulated:

	2004	**2005**	**2006**
Direct labor hours	40,000	52,000	65,000
Machine hours	80,000	65,000	45,000
Direct materials costs	$400,000	$250,000	$390,000
Total budgeted manufacturing overhead	$80,000	$65,000	$45,000

1. What would the predetermined overhead rate be for each of the three years, if based on (a) direct labor hours, (b) machine hours, and (c) direct materials costs?
2. **Interpretive Question:** Which allocation basis would you recommend be used in the future for applying manufacturing overhead? Why?

Exercise 17-4

Predetermined Manufacturing Overhead Rates
East Lake Corporation uses a job order costing system and applies manufacturing overhead using a predetermined overhead rate. The following data are available for the past two years.

Spreadsheet

	2005	2006
Direct labor hours	104,000	130,000
Direct materials costs	$500,000	$780,000
Machine hours	100,000	70,000
Total budgeted manufacturing overhead	$130,000	$90,000

1. Compute the predetermined overhead rate for each of the two years, based on (a) direct labor hours, (b) direct materials costs, and (c) machine hours.
2. **Interpretive Question:** Which allocation basis would you recommend for applying manufacturing overhead? Why?

Exercise 17-5

Work-in-Process Analysis in a Manufacturing Organization

Matt Jones, a recently hired internal auditor, is currently auditing the work-in-process inventory account. Matt has forgotten some basic cost accounting concepts and asks for your assistance. Identify the four types of transactions or events that affect the work-in-process inventory account in a manufacturing organization. Prepare and explain a sample journal entry for each type of transaction.

Exercise 17-6

Flow of Manufacturing Costs

Post the following cost data to the appropriate T-accounts to trace the flow of costs from the time they are incurred until the product is completed and sold. (Assume that purchases and expenses are credited to Cash or Accounts Payable.)

a.	Direct materials purchased	$ 60,000
b.	Direct materials used	50,000
c.	Indirect materials purchased	9,000
d.	Indirect materials used	7,000
e.	Wages payable, direct	60,000
f.	Wages payable, indirect	12,000
g.	Selling and administrative expenses	32,000
h.	Actual manufacturing overhead costs other than indirect materials and indirect labor	25,000
i.	Manufacturing overhead applied	40,000
j.	Work-in-process completed	120,000
k.	Finished goods sold	135,000

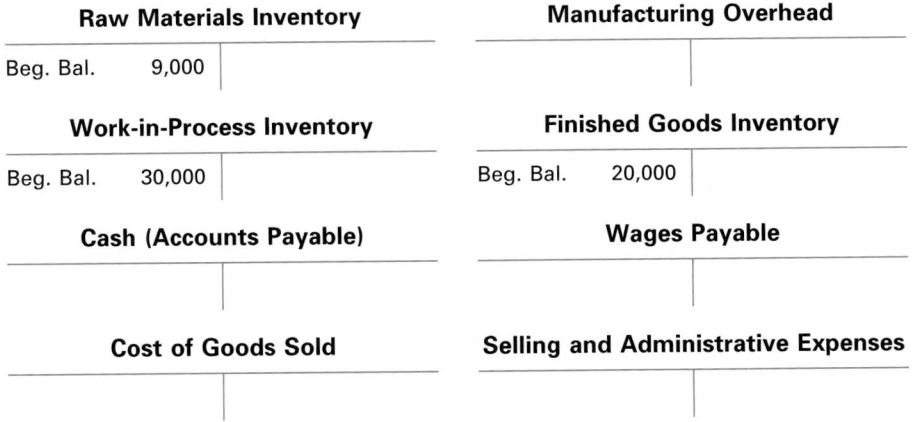

Raw Materials Inventory

Beg. Bal. 9,000

Manufacturing Overhead

Work-in-Process Inventory

Beg. Bal. 30,000

Finished Goods Inventory

Beg. Bal. 20,000

Cash (Accounts Payable)

Wages Payable

Cost of Goods Sold

Selling and Administrative Expenses

Exercise 17-7

Applying Manufacturing Overhead

Keith Company has four manufacturing subsidiaries: W, X, Y, and Z. Each subsidiary keeps a separate set of accounting records. Manufacturing cost forecasts for 2006 for each subsidiary are:

(continued)

924 | **Part 5** | **E O C** | Foundations

	Subsidiaries			
	W	**X**	**Y**	**Z**
Materials to be used (lbs.)	40,000	40,000	30,000	26,250
Direct labor hours	15,000	20,000	12,500	20,000
Direct labor costs	$6,000	$5,000	$1,875	$3,500
Machine hours	12,500	7,500	4,750	20,000
Manufacturing overhead	$30,000	$25,000	$10,000	$50,000

The predetermined overhead rates for each subsidiary are based on the following:

Subsidiary W: Machine hours
Subsidiary X: Direct labor costs
Subsidiary Y: Materials to be used
Subsidiary Z: Direct labor hours

1. Compute the predetermined overhead rate to be used in 2006 by each subsidiary.
2. If Subsidiary X actually had $4,000 of direct labor costs and $18,750 of manufacturing overhead, will overhead be over- or underapplied and by how much?
3. If Subsidiary Y used 33,000 pounds of materials in 2006, what will be the applied manufacturing overhead?
4. **Interpretive Question:** Identify the two most commonly used methods to dispose of under- or overapplied manufacturing overhead. What is the major advantage of each method?

Exercise 17-8

Applying Manufacturing Overhead

Valtec Company has three manufacturing divisions: A, B, and C. Each division has its own job order costing system and forecasts the following manufacturing costs for the year 2006:

	Division		
	A	**B**	**C**
Materials to be used (lbs.)	120,000	100,000	80,000
Direct labor hours	45,000	60,000	25,000
Machine hours	40,000	25,000	15,000
Total budgeted manufacturing overhead	$50,000	$70,000	$45,000

The predetermined overhead rates for each division are based on the following:

Division A: Machine hours
Division B: Materials to be used
Division C: Direct labor hours

1. Compute the predetermined overhead rate to be used in 2006 by each division.
2. If Division A actually had 37,000 machine hours and $49,000 of manufacturing overhead, will overhead be over- or underapplied and by how much?
3. If Division B used 95,000 pounds of materials in 2006, what will be the applied manufacturing overhead?
4. **Interpretive Question:** Of the two commonly used methods to dispose of over- or underapplied manufacturing overhead, which method would you recommend and why?

Exercise 17-9

Assigning Manufacturing Costs to Jobs

Farrer Manufacturing Company uses a job order costing system. All relevant information for Jobs #203 and #204, which were completed during May, is provided here. No other jobs were in process during the month of May.

Spreadsheet

	Job #203	Job #204
Direct materials cost	$10,000	$13,000
Direct labor cost	$7,800	$10,800
Direct labor hours on job	800	1,400
Units produced	1,000	1,750

A predetermined overhead rate of $12 per direct labor hour is used to apply manufacturing overhead costs to jobs. Actual manufacturing overhead for the month of May totaled $25,000. All completed products are delivered to customers immediately after completion, so costs are transferred directly to Cost of Goods Sold without going through Finished Goods Inventory.

1. How much manufacturing overhead will be assigned to each job completed during May?
2. Compute the total cost of each job.
3. Compute the unit cost for each job.
4. Compute the over- or underapplied manufacturing overhead for May.
5. Prepare the journal entries to transfer the cost of direct materials, direct labor, and manufacturing overhead to Work-in-Process Inventory and to transfer the cost of completed jobs to Cost of Goods Sold. (Omit explanations.)
6. **Interpretive Question:** How would the company have computed its predetermined overhead rate of $12 per direct labor hour? Explain.

Exercise 17-10

Assigning Manufacturing Costs to Jobs

Remington Company uses predetermined overhead rates in assigning manufacturing overhead costs to jobs. The rates are based on machine hours in the machining department and on direct labor hours in the assembly department. Estimated costs, machine hours, and direct labor hours for the year in each department are:

	Machining	Assembly
Direct labor cost	$64,000	$100,000
Manufacturing overhead	$90,000	$50,000
Direct labor hours	12,000	32,000
Machine hours	18,000	2,500

During the month of April, Job #402X had the following data for 50 completed units of product:

	Machining	Assembly
Direct materials cost	$400	$700
Direct labor cost	$650	$2,300
Direct labor hours	120	740
Machine hours	900	80

1. What predetermined overhead rates would be used by the company in assigning manufacturing overhead costs to Job #402X in machining and in assembly? (*Note:* You should round all rates you calculate to two decimal places.)
2. Using the overhead rates you calculated in part (1), how much manufacturing overhead is applied to Job #402X?
3. What is the unit cost for Job #402X? (Round the unit cost to two decimal places.)

Exercise 17-11

Analyzing Manufacturing Costs

The following T-accounts represent inventory costs as of December 31, 2006:

(continued)

Raw Materials Inventory			Finished Goods Inventory		
Bal. 12/31/05	70,000	200,000	Bal. 12/31/05	39,500	336,500
	175,000			350,000	
Bal. 12/31/06	45,000		Bal. 12/31/06	53,000	

Work-in-Process Inventory			Manufacturing Overhead		
Bal. 12/31/05	12,500	350,000		24,500	124,500
	200,000			26,000	
	124,500			30,000	
	86,000			36,000	
Bal. 12/31/06	73,000				

1. Determine the direct labor costs for 2006.
2. Determine the cost of goods manufactured for 2006.
3. Determine the cost of goods sold for 2006.
4. Compute over- or underapplied manufacturing overhead for 2006.
5. Determine actual indirect manufacturing costs for 2006.

Exercise 17-12

Total Manufacturing Costs and Cost of Goods Manufactured
The following information is for Kiev Derrald Company:

Manufacturing overhead (actual)	$100,000
Ending raw materials inventory	12,000
Manufacturing overhead (applied)	95,000
Beginning work-in-process inventory	55,000
Ending work-in-process inventory	47,000
Beginning raw materials inventory	10,000
Direct labor costs	60,000
Raw materials purchases	40,000

1. Compute total manufacturing costs.
2. Compute cost of goods manufactured.

Exercise 17-13

Total Manufacturing Costs, Cost of Goods Manufactured, and Cost of Goods Sold
The following information is for MTC Harry Company:

Beginning raw materials inventory	$ 25,000
Raw materials *used* in production as direct materials	110,000
Ending raw materials inventory	40,000
Manufacturing overhead (actual)	300,000
Beginning work-in-process inventory	150,000
Ending work-in-process inventory	180,000
Direct labor costs	95,000
Beginning finished goods inventory	71,000
Ending finished goods inventory	86,000
Underapplied manufacturing overhead	19,000

1. Compute total manufacturing costs.
2. Compute cost of goods manufactured.
3. Compute cost of goods sold.

Exercise 17-14

Service Cost Flows

Xavier & Associates Law Firm estimated its total overhead costs for 2006 to be $1.8 million. It allocates overhead based on direct labor hours. Xavier employs a total of 11 attorneys, each working an average of 2,000 hours per year. The average annual salary for Xavier attorneys is $140,000, or approximately $70 per hour. Xavier attorneys worked a total of 23 hours and used $150 of supplies in doing work for Mr. Bailey, one of Xavier's clients.

1. What is Xavier's overhead rate?
2. Prepare the journal entry to record the overhead for the Bailey job.
3. Prepare the journal entry to record the cost of supplies for the Bailey job.
4. Prepare the journal entry to record the cost of labor for the Bailey job.

Exercise 17-15

Service Cost Flows

Pierce Engineers incurred (but has not yet paid) the following costs in 2006:

Use of supplies for clients	$ 3,500
Utilities	8,000
Property taxes	12,000
Engineers' salaries	100,000
Support staff salaries	35,000
Applied overhead	50,000

Prepare the journal entries to account for the costs given. Close the overhead account to Cost of Services.

Exercise 17-16

Predetermined Service Overhead Rates

The following data are available for Haul-It-Away Truckers:

	2005	2006
Budgeted direct labor hours	135,000	140,000
Planned number of moving jobs	300	310
Total miles to be driven	450,000	597,000
Total budgeted overhead	$900,000	$1,200,000

1. Compute the predetermined overhead rate for each of the two years, if based on (a) direct labor hours, (b) number of moving jobs, and (c) total miles driven.
2. **Interpretive Question:** Which allocation basis would you recommend for applying overhead? Why?

Exercise 17-17

Applying Overhead

Gammonomics Schools teaches private accounting courses. It applies overhead based on instructor hours. The following information was forecasted for 2006:

Direct labor	$270,000
Property tax on equipment	$2,700
Supplies	$9,000
Rent	$18,000
Support staff salaries	$120,000
Instructor hours	16,000

1. Calculate the predetermined overhead rate for 2006.
2. If Gammonomics actually had 18,000 instructor hours and spent $150,000 on overhead, will overhead be under- or overapplied for 2006? By how much?

Exercise 17-18

Service Costs

The following information is available for a particular consulting contract performed by Newland Business Consultants in 2006:

Consulting labor costs	$4,000
Supplies	500
Overhead	?
Total cost	$?

Newland applies overhead on the basis of client consulting hours. The estimated total overhead costs for 2006 are $6.2 million, and the estimated total consulting hours are 150,000. Newland pays its consultants $40 per hour.

1. Compute the predetermined overhead rate.
2. What are the allocated overhead cost and the total cost of this particular contract?

Exercise 17-19

Equivalent Units—Process Costing

Assume that you are the owner and sole employee of a lube, oil, and filter service business that you run out of your home. Currently, you are running a spring special on a "super maintenance service" on cars. The maintenance service you offer is quite comprehensive and includes (among other things) changing the oil, rotating the tires, topping off all fluids, and washing and waxing each car. It takes about one to two hours to complete a car. With the great price you're offering on this service, you immediately find yourself with about five days of customer order backlog. To catch up, you decide to spend the next week working solely on the "super maintenance service." Further, you want to track your output to see if you can improve the amount of maintenance work you do each of the next five days.

When you come to work the following Monday, you have one car that is about 70% complete. At the end of the week, the results are as follows:

	Total Cars Completed Each Day	End-of-Day Car in Process
Monday	5	50% complete
Tuesday	5	80% complete
Wednesday	7	10% complete
Thursday	6	80% complete
Friday	7	10% complete

How much work did you get done each day? In other words, how many equivalent units of production did you have each day?

Exercise 17-20

Equivalent Units and Unit Costs—Process Costing

A large factory that manufactures wooden furniture has several assembly lines. One of the assembly lines is dedicated to assembly of wooden kitchen chairs. All raw materials necessary to complete each chair are requisitioned from the raw materials warehouse at the time each chair starts production on the assembly line. The following data relate to one week of production:

Beginning Work-in-Process
40 chairs; 80% complete; $350 in direct materials costs; $320 in conversion costs

Ending Work-in-Process
60 chairs; 40% complete

Current Week
550 chairs started and completed; $4,880 requisitioned from raw materials warehouse, $5,820 incurred in conversion costs

1. Compute the equivalent units of production for both direct materials and conversion costs for the week.
2. Compute the total production cost per chair for the week on the assembly line.
3. How does this week's production cost on the assembly line compare to last week's production cost?

Exercise 17-21

Spreadsheet

Equivalent Units and Unit Costs—Process Costing

Heidi Corporation began producing quick-drying paper cement in June 2006 (i.e., there was no beginning work-in-process inventory on June 1). The manufacturing process involves only one step. In June, the costs were $4,000 for direct materials and $3,108 for conversion costs. During the month, 3,200 pounds of direct materials were placed in production. At the end of June, 600 pounds of direct materials were still being processed and were 40% complete. Assume that all direct materials are added at the beginning of production.

1. Compute the number of equivalent units of output in terms of materials costs and labor and overhead (conversion) costs for June, assuming FIFO cost flow.
2. Determine the total cost of goods transferred to Finished Goods Inventory and the total cost of Work-in-Process Inventory at the end of June.

problems

Problem 17-1

Job Order Costing in a Manufacturing Organization—Journal Entries

Following are transactions for Montigo Manufacturing Company. Assume that the company has no beginning work-in-process inventory.

1. Montigo purchased $600,000 of raw materials, paying 10% down, with the remainder to be paid in 10 days.
2. The production manager requisitioned $260,000 of materials (90% for direct use and the remainder for indirect purposes).
3. The liability incurred in (1) was paid in full.
4. 24,000 hours of direct labor and 2,000 hours of indirect labor were incurred. (Assume an average hourly wage rate of $9 for both direct and indirect labor.)
5. The following salaries were paid:

Factory supervisor (a product cost)	$80,000
Administrative executives	70,000
Sales personnel	90,000

6. Rent and utilities for the building of $30,000 and $7,000, respectively, were paid. Three-fourths of these expenses are applicable to manufacturing and the remainder to administration.
7. Depreciation on factory equipment was $15,000.
8. Advertising costs for the year totaled $15,000.
9. Manufacturing overhead is applied at a rate of $6.90 per direct labor hour.
10. All but $35,000 of Work-in-Process Inventory was completed and transferred to Finished Goods Inventory.

(continued)

11. The sales price of finished goods that were sold was 130% of manufacturing costs. Assume a perpetual inventory system and that all finished goods were sold.
12. Close over- or underapplied overhead directly to cost of goods sold.

Required:
Prepare journal entries for the transactions.

Problem 17-2

Accounting For Manufacturing Transactions—Journal Entries

Payson Company uses a job order costing system. The following is a *partial* list of the company's accounts. (*Note:* Additional accounts may be needed.)

Cash
Manufacturing Overhead
Sales
Cost of Goods Sold
Sales Commissions Expense
Administrative Expenses
Accounts Receivable
Commissions Payable

Required:
1. Prepare journal entries for each of the following transactions (omit explanations).
2. Prepare T-accounts and post the journal entries to the T-accounts. Transaction (a) has been completed as an example.
   a. Raw materials previously purchased on account were paid for in cash, $700.

Cash			**Accounts Payable**	
(a)	700	(a)	700	

   b. Raw materials were purchased for $1,500 on account.
   c. Direct labor costs of $3,000 were recorded.
   d. Direct materials costing $1,100 were issued directly to production.
   e. Depreciation of $1,500 on manufacturing equipment was recorded. (Assume this is a product cost.)
   f. Property taxes payable of $2,600 were recorded, half to manufacturing and half to administration.
   g. Manufacturing overhead costs of $400 were applied to a job in process.
   h. Materials previously purchased on account were paid for in cash, $1,500.
   i. Sales commissions of $240 were recorded.
   j. Goods costing $2,700 were transferred from Work-in-Process Inventory to Finished Goods Inventory.
   k. Finished goods costing $2,300 were sold for $3,200 on credit, and the cost of goods sold was recorded.

Problem 17-3

Manufacturing Cost Flows

Lehi Corporation uses a job order costing system in its manufacturing operation. For the year 2006, Lehi's predetermined overhead rate was 75% of direct labor costs. For September 2006, the company incurred the following costs:

Purchased raw materials on account	$ 70,000
Issued raw materials to manufacturing process	65,000
Incurred direct labor costs ($10 per hour × 7,500 hrs.)	75,000
Actual manufacturing overhead costs	52,300
Cost of goods completed and sold	211,250

The company's inventories at the beginning of September 2006 were as follows:

Raw materials	$12,000
Work-in-process	57,500

The costs of all completed orders are transferred directly from Work-in-Process Inventory to Cost of Goods Sold.

Required:
1. Compute the following amounts.
   a. Work-in-Process Inventory balance at the end of September 2006.
   b. Over- or underapplied manufacturing overhead for the month of September.
2. Prepare journal entries to reflect the flow of costs into and out of Work-in-Process Inventory during September (omit explanations).

Problem 17-4

Using T-Accounts: Cost Flows in a Job Order Manufacturing Organization

High Country Furniture Company manufactures custom furniture only and uses a job order costing system to accumulate costs. Actual direct materials and direct labor costs are accumulated for each job, but a predetermined overhead rate is used to apply manufacturing overhead costs to individual jobs. Manufacturing overhead is applied on the basis of direct labor hours. In computing a predetermined overhead rate, the controller estimated that manufacturing overhead costs for 2006 would be $80,000 and direct labor hours would be 20,000. The following information is available for the year 2006:

a. Direct materials purchased, $22,000.
b. Direct materials used in production, $19,500.
c. Wages and salaries paid for the year: direct labor (18,000 hours), $117,000; indirect labor, $12,000; sales and administrative salaries, $21,000.
d. Depreciation on machinery and equipment, $9,000.
e. Rent and utilities for building (75% factory), $16,000.
f. Miscellaneous manufacturing overhead, $51,500.
g. Advertising costs, $12,000.
h. Manufacturing overhead is applied to Work-in-Process Inventory.
i. Eighty percent of Work-in-Process Inventory was completed and transferred to Finished Goods Inventory.

Required:
1. Compute the predetermined overhead rate at which manufacturing overhead costs will be applied to jobs.
2. Set up T-accounts and post the transactions.
3. Compute the under- or overapplied manufacturing overhead. Prepare a journal entry to close Manufacturing Overhead and transfer the balance to Cost of Goods Sold.

Problem 17-5

Applying Manufacturing Overhead

Swenson Corporation has four independent manufacturing divisions. The following data apply to the divisions for the year ended December 31, 2006:

	A	B	C	D
Direct materials costs	$240,000	$280,000	$160,000	$130,000
Direct labor hours	80,000	60,000	48,000	28,000
Direct labor costs	$220,000	$130,000	$140,000	$84,000
Actual manufacturing overhead	$146,900	$205,400	$140,000	$33,000
Machine hours worked	40,000	12,000	28,000	16,000
Number of units produced	200,000	4,000	30,000	10,000
Predetermined overhead rate	80% of direct labor costs	65% of direct materials costs	$3.30 per direct labor hour	$2.10 per machine hour

(continued)

Required:

1. For each of the four divisions, calculate:
   a. Applied manufacturing overhead.
   b. Over- or underapplied manufacturing overhead.
   c. Cost of goods manufactured, assuming no work-in-process inventories.
   d. Average cost per unit produced.
2. **Interpretive Question:** How would you recommend that the over- or underapplied manufacturing overhead be disposed of in each division? Why?

Problem 17-6

Applying Manufacturing Overhead

Openshaw Manufacturing Company made the following estimates at the beginning of the year:

	Department G	Department H
Direct labor costs	$219,000	$166,980
Manufacturing overhead	$86,700	$153,340
Machine hours	17,000	12,500
Direct labor hours	30,000	22,000

Manufacturing overhead is applied on the basis of machine hours in Department G and on the basis of direct labor hours in Department H. During the year, the following two jobs were completed (there were no jobs in process at the beginning or end of the year):

Job #29

	Department G	Department H
Direct materials used	$16,000	$9,200
Direct labor costs	$18,250	$14,420
Direct labor hours	2,500	1,900
Machine hours	1,410	1,080

Job #30

	Department G	Department H
Direct materials used	$17,500	$8,100
Direct labor costs	$19,710	$13,920
Direct labor hours	2,700	1,800
Machine hours	1,530	1,020

Required:

1. Compute the predetermined overhead rate for each department.
2. Determine the amount of manufacturing overhead to be applied to each job.
3. Determine the total cost of each job.
4. Given that the actual manufacturing overhead costs for the year in Departments G and H were $88,200 and $152,500, respectively; that the actual machine hours in Department G were 18,100; and that the direct labor hours in Department H were 21,600; compute the amount of over- or underapplied manufacturing overhead.
5. **Interpretive Question:** Why is the predetermined overhead rate based on estimated rather than actual information?

Problem 17-7

Unifying Concepts: Job Order Costing, Cost Flows, Journal Entries, and Predetermined Overhead Rates

Brooks Manufacturing Company applies manufacturing overhead on the basis of direct materials costs. The estimates for 2006 were:

Direct materials costs	$250,000
Manufacturing overhead	75,000

Following are the transactions of Brooks Manufacturing Company for 2006:

a. Raw materials purchased on account, $275,000 (80% for direct use and 20% for indirect use).
b. Raw materials issued to production, 80% for direct use and 20% for indirect use, for a total of $175,000.
c. Direct labor costs, $250,000.
d. Indirect labor costs, $25,000.
e. Administrative and sales salaries, $70,000 and $45,000, respectively.
f. Utilities, $10,500; plant depreciation, $20,000; maintenance, $7,500; miscellaneous administrative expenses, $2,000. (These costs are allocated on the basis of plant floor space—administrative facilities, 1,000 square feet; manufacturing, 5,000 square feet; sales facilities, 2,000 square feet.)
g. Manufacturing equipment depreciation, $6,000.
h. Additional raw materials issued to production for direct use, $125,000.
i. Manufacturing overhead is applied.
j. Recorded factory foreman's salary, $27,000.
k. Ninety percent of existing Work-in-Process Inventory is transferred to Finished Goods Inventory. (Work-in-Process beginning inventory was $15,000.)
l. All finished goods are sold. (Assume no beginning inventory. Sales are marked up 40% of cost.)
m. Over- or underapplied manufacturing overhead is closed to Cost of Goods Sold.

Required:
1. Prepare a journal entry for each of the transactions and show the T-accounts for Manufacturing Overhead and Work-in-Process Inventory.
2. What is the ending balance in the cost of goods sold account?
3. **Interpretive Question:** Comparing actual manufacturing overhead with estimates for 2006, what would you recommend that Brooks Manufacturing Company estimate for manufacturing overhead costs in 2007?

Problem 17-8

Unifying Concepts: Job Order Costing

Jones Custom Furniture Manufacturing, Inc., made the following estimates at the beginning of the year, 2006:

Budgeted direct labor costs	$300,000
Budgeted direct labor hours	20,000
Budgeted manufacturing overhead	$520,000

Jones applies manufacturing overhead to specific job orders on the basis of direct labor hours. During the month of January, the following transactions occurred for Job #345, an order for 10 custom oak chairs, manufactured in the first week of January 2006:

Jan. 3 Requisitioned direct materials (lumber, fabric, paint), $876; put into production on Job #345.

(continued)

Jan. 3   Requisitioned indirect materials (glue, staples, sandpaper, and equipment grease), $154, for use in manufacturing the 10 chairs for Job #345, as well as other subsequent jobs.

    7   Processed time card for Employee #214; 25 direct labor hours attributed to Job #345 at wage rate of $15 per hour.

    7   Applied manufacturing overhead at the predetermined rate to Job #345, based on the actual direct labor hours.

    7   Processed the manufacturing supervisor's weekly salary of $1,000. (This salary is considered indirect labor because the supervisor oversees all jobs in process and does not account for her time on a job-by-job basis.)

    7   Job #345 was completed and transferred to the finished goods warehouse to await shipment to the customer.

    9   The 10 oak chairs (Job #345) were shipped to the customer. The sales invoice reflects a sales price of $3,000 on account.

In addition to Job #345, Jones completed 47 other job orders in January and had 7 others in process at month-end. The following information summarizes additional manufacturing transactions for Jones for the month of January (not relating to Job #345):

a. Raw materials purchased on account, $102,675.
b. Requisitioned raw materials to specific job orders, $90,430; 80% direct materials and the remainder indirect materials not directly attributable to any one specific job.
c. Incurred and paid direct labor wages totaled, $24,600; an average of $15 per hour for 1,640 total direct labor hours for January.
d. Applied manufacturing overhead at the predetermined rate to all jobs in progress on the basis of the actual direct labor hours incurred by job.
e. Incurred and paid supervisor salaries and other indirect manufacturing labor (e.g., maintenance labor) totaled $7,000.
f. Incurred and paid the following costs associated with the manufacturing process and facility:

Factory rent	$ 7,600
Factory utilities	2,700
Insurance	1,200
Miscellaneous	1,900
	$13,400

g. Recorded depreciation of manufacturing equipment for the month, $5,500.
h. The cost of the 47 jobs completed during the month totaled $125,446.
i. Shipped all completed jobs to customers by month-end at a total sales price of $200,714 on account.
j. Incurred and paid selling and administrative costs (e.g., administrative salaries, sales commissions, office supplies, office rent, etc.), $46,514.

Required:

1. a. Calculate Jones' predetermined overhead rate for the year 2006.
   b. Prepare journal entries for the first seven transactions (relating to Job #345). Omit explanations.
   c. Determine the total cost of manufacturing each of the 10 oak chairs.
   d. Determine the total gross margin earned on all 10 oak chairs.
2. Prepare the journal entries for transactions (a)–(j). Omit explanations.
3. Close Manufacturing Overhead to Cost of Goods Sold (include all transactions noted for Job #345).
4. Calculate Jones' total gross margin for January, including Job #345.
5. Calculate Jones' total operating income for January.
6. Determine the ending January balances in Raw Materials Inventory, Work-in-Process Inventory, and Finished Goods Inventory (assume no beginning balances).

Problem 17-9

Cost of Goods Manufactured

The following data apply to Newton Company and Alexander Company (two independent companies):

	Newton Company	Alexander Company
Raw materials inventory, January 1, 2006	$ 1	$ 4,000
Raw materials purchased	21,000	4
Raw materials inventory, December 31, 2006	6,000	3,000
Manufacturing overhead (actual)	8,000	5
Manufacturing overhead (applied)	2	16,000
Selling and administrative expenses	14,000	25,000
Work-in-process inventory, January 1, 2006	3	20,000
Work-in-process inventory, December 31, 2006	16,000	22,000
Direct (raw) materials used in production	15,000	6
Direct labor costs	25,000	30,000
Cost of goods manufactured	49,000	55,000
Overapplied (or underapplied) manufacturing overhead	(2,000)	4,000

Required:

Fill in the unknowns for the two cases. (*Hint:* Indirect materials are not used in either company.)

Problem 17-10

Cost of Goods Manufactured Schedule

(*Note:* This problem is a continuation of Problem 17-7.) Brooks Manufacturing Company's journal entries and T-accounts for Manufacturing Overhead and Work-in-Process Inventory were completed in Problem 17-7. Assume that Brooks had the following beginning inventory amounts:

Raw materials inventory	$80,000
Work-in-process inventory	15,000
Finished goods inventory	0

Required:

Prepare a Cost of Goods Manufactured schedule for 2006 for Brooks Manufacturing Company. Assume all beginning and ending raw materials amounts include only direct materials.

Problem 17-11

Cost of Goods Manufactured Schedule

Delta Manufacturing Company applies manufacturing overhead to jobs on the basis of machine hours. The 2006 estimates of manufacturing overhead and machine hours were:

Manufacturing overhead	$1,825,000
Machine hours	365,000

Delta had the following transactions for October 2006:

a. Raw materials of $420,000 were purchased on account.

b. Raw materials of $400,000 were issued to production; 90% were direct materials, and the balance was indirect materials.

c. Direct labor costs incurred, $300,000.

d. Indirect labor costs incurred, $55,000.

e. Selling, general, and administrative expenses incurred, $150,000.

f. Manufacturing overhead costs incurred:

(continued)

Plant depreciation (factory)	$25,000
Equipment depreciation (factory)	14,000
Utilities (factory)	7,000
Factory maintenance	9,000
Factory taxes and insurance	5,000
Miscellaneous manufacturing overhead	6,000

g. Machine hours for the month, 30,400.

h. Eighty-five percent of Work-in-Process Inventory was transferred to Finished Goods Inventory. Assume that beginning Work-in-Process Inventory amounted to $95,000.

i. *All* finished goods are sold for cash at a 20% markup over costs of production. (There is no beginning or ending finished goods inventory.)

j. Over- or underapplied manufacturing overhead is charged to Cost of Goods Sold, and the overhead account is closed.

Required:

1. Prepare journal entries to reflect the flow of costs incurred during October.

2. Assuming that beginning raw materials inventory was $16,000 and beginning work-in-process inventory was $95,000, prepare a Cost of Goods Manufactured schedule for October 2006.

Problem 17-12

Analysis of Manufacturing Cost Flows

The following T-accounts represent manufacturing cost flows for Kanton Manufacturing Company for the year 2006.

Direct Materials Inventory

1/1	70,000	250,000
	210,000	
12/31	30,000	

Work-in-Process Inventory

1/1	80,000	700,000
	250,000	
	310,000	
	140,000	
12/31	80,000	

Finished Goods Inventory

1/1	90,000	740,000
	700,000	
12/31	50,000	

Manufacturing Overhead

	30,000	140,000
	22,000	
	16,000	
	38,000	
	40,000	

Required:

1. Compute the following amounts for 2006:
   a. Direct labor cost.
   b. Cost of goods manufactured.
   c. Cost of goods sold.
   d. Actual manufacturing overhead costs.

2. Prepare a Cost of Goods Manufactured schedule for 2006.

3. Prepare a cost of goods sold schedule for 2006.

4. **Interpretive Question:** Explain how the over- or underapplied manufacturing overhead is usually accounted for.

Problem 17-13

Computing Overhead Rates and Client Billing in a Service Firm

Sutherland Estimating Company employs three professional estimators, each having a different specialty. John Spencer specializes in structural estimating; Steve Ray, electrical estimating; and

Dave Eugene, mechanical estimating. The firm expects to incur the following operating costs for 2006; travel and materials costs are billed separately to clients.

Office salaries and wages	$ 54,000
Office supplies	30,000
Utilities and telephone	23,100
Depreciation	24,300
Taxes and insurance	15,450
Miscellaneous expenses	3,150
Total estimated costs for 2006	$150,000

The salaries and billable hours of the three estimators are expected to be as follows:

	Expected Salary	Expected Hours
Spencer	$ 90,000	1,900
Ray	72,000	2,000
Eugene	63,000	1,850
Total	$225,000	5,750

Required:
1. Compute the overhead cost rate that should be used for each of the estimators (based on the expected hours to be billed, with overhead cost rates varying in proportion to each estimator's compensation) to ensure that the total expected operating costs for 2006 will be recovered from clients. (*Hint:* Allocate total estimated overhead costs to each estimator based on relative salaries, then relate the allocated costs to the hours expected to be worked by each estimator.)
2. Using the overhead cost rates determined in part (1), determine the costs associated with the firm's work for Landslide Company with the following estimating services and related costs: Spencer, 150 hours; Ray, 60 hours; Eugene, 15 hours; transportation and supplies costs, $2,400.

Problem 17-14

Service Costing—Journal Entries
Following are transactions for Andersen Custodial, Inc. Assume the company's beginning work-in-process services account balance is zero.

a. Purchased supplies costing $5,000 for cash.
b. Received and immediately paid a utility bill, $800.
c. Used supplies costing $3,000 in doing work for a customer.
d. Incurred and paid 3,000 hours of direct labor and 1,500 hours of indirect labor. The average hourly wage rate for both direct and indirect labor is $7.
e. Made monthly rent payment, $2,000.
f. Applied overhead at $4.50 per direct labor hour.
g. Andersen bills its customers at a rate of $20 per direct labor hour. All work in process was moved to Cost of Services.
h. Closed all under- or overapplied overhead to Cost of Services.

Required:
Prepare the journal entries for the above transactions.

Problem 17-15

Service Costing—Journal Entries
Blake Accounting Services has the following transactions. Its beginning work-in-process services account balance is zero.

a. Purchased supplies costing $11,000 on account.
b. Paid property tax, $20,000.

(continued)

c. Paid rent, $2,000; and utilities, $700.
d. Paid support staff salaries, $35,000.
e. Used supplies costing $9,000.
f. Paid direct labor salaries, $50,000. Average rate was $10 per hour.
g. Applied overhead at $11.50 per direct labor hour.
h. Transferred $100,000 from Work-in-Process to Cost of Services and billed customers for 4,500 hours of work. Blake bills its customers $40 per direct labor hour.
i. Closed under- or overapplied overhead to Cost of Services.

Required:
1. Prepare the journal entries for the above transactions.
2. Determine the ending balance in the work-in-process services account.

Problem 17-16

Service Cost Flows

Allee Company had the following balances at the beginning of 2006:

	Debit	Credit
Accounts receivable	$44,000	
Supplies	10,000	
Work-in-process services	30,000	
Accounts payable (related to supplies)		$ 7,000
Salaries and wages payable		70,000
Utilities payable		2,400
Rent payable		3,000

Allee estimates that its total 2006 overhead will amount to $400,000. It allocates overhead based on direct labor hours. Allee estimates that its total 2006 direct labor hours will be 100,000 hours. Because it produces monthly financial statements, Allee makes adjusting entries at the end of each month. However, over- or underapplied overhead is not closed to Cost of Services until the end of the year.

During January 2006, Allee had the following transactions:

Jan. 1 Paid rent. Allee has a three-year, $162,000 lease. Rent is payable on the first of each month.
3 Paid for all supplies purchased in 2005.
4 Paid all utilities payable from 2005.
7 Purchased supplies, $1,200.
10 Paid all salaries and wages payable from 2005. $46,000 was for direct labor; $24,000 was for indirect labor.
12 Used supplies, $900.
19 Collected $30,000 from a customer for services performed and billed in December 2005.
27 Used supplies, $2,600.
31 Paid all employees for January labor. Total direct labor costs for the month of January were $50,000, direct labor hours, 8,000. Indirect labor costs were $30,000.
31 Applied overhead for the month.
31 Estimated its January utility expenses to be $2,000.
31 Completed and billed jobs costing $80,000. The company billed customers $140,000.

Required:
1. Prepare all journal entries necessary for the month of January.
2. What is the balance in the work-in-process services account at the end of January?
3. Compute the balance in the overhead account on January 31.

Problem 17-17

FIFO Cost Flow—Process Costing

The cleaning division of Rulon Corn Company had the following data for January 2006:

	Tons	Percentage Completed	Direct Materials Costs	Conversion Costs
Beginning work-in-process inventory . .	600	80%	$ 12,750	$ 1,800
Units started in production	39,900	—		
Costs added this month			897,750	189,072
Ending work-in-process inventory	900	30%		
Units completed during month				
and transferred to packing	39,600	—		

Required:

1. Using the FIFO cost flow method, compute the per-ton cost of corn processed by the cleaning division in this period (all materials are in place at the beginning of the process).
2. Compute the cost of the 39,000 tons of corn that were started and completed during January.
3. Compute the cost of the ending work-in-process inventory.

Problem 17-18

FIFO Cost Flow—Process Costing

Western Oil Company has three process centers: drilling, processing, and distributing. During September 2006, the processing department had the following operating data:

	Barrels	Percentage Completed	Direct Materials Costs	Conversion Costs
Beginning work-in-process inventory	4,000	60%	$ 2,200	$ 4,200
Units started and completed this month . .	36,000	—		
Costs added this month			33,150	88,410
Ending work-in-process inventory	15,000	30%		
Units completed during month				
and transferred to distributing	40,000	—		

Required:

All raw materials are put in place at the beginning of the operation in the processing department. Assuming a FIFO flow of costs, compute:

1. The "work done" for September (in equivalent units of production) for direct materials and for conversion costs.
2. The September cost per barrel of oil in the processing department.
3. The cost of all oil transferred to distributing.
4. The cost of ending work-in-process inventory in the processing department.

Problem 17-19

FIFO Cost Flow—Process Costing

The assembly department of Charles Manufacturing Company reported the following data for the month of August 2006:

(continued)

	Units	Costs
Beginning inventory (75% complete)	3,000	
Units transferred from prior department	22,500	
Ending inventory (50% complete)	4,500	
Cost of beginning inventory (prior department $18,300;		
assembly materials $11,250; assembly conversion $12,375)		$ 41,925
Cost transferred in from prior department		135,000
Cost of materials used in assembly department		67,500
Conversion costs for August in assembly department		117,600
Total cost		$362,025

(*Note:* Materials used in the assembly department are added at the beginning of the assembly process.)

Required:
Prepare the production cost report for the assembly department. (*Note:* The prior department's manufacturing costs should be included in this department's production cost report.)

Problem 17-20

Spreadsheet

Equivalent Units and FIFO Cost Flow—Process Costing
Midtown Manufacturing Company has two process centers—manufacturing and assembly. The data that follow show the production and cost results for the manufacturing center for the month of July 2006:

Production data:

Units in process, July 1 (materials 50% complete,	
conversion 40% complete)	500
Units started in production	2,500
Units in process, July 31 (materials 100% complete,	
conversion 60% complete)	700

Cost data:

Units in process, July 1:	
Direct materials	$ 3,000
Conversion costs	6,400
Direct materials used in July	27,500
Conversion costs for July	73,080
Total	$109,980

(*Note:* In this problem, materials are *not* added at the beginning of the manufacturing process.)

Required:
Prepare the production cost report for the manufacturing center.

d iscussion cases

Case 17-1

Packard, Inc.
Packard, Inc., produces and sells mousetraps. The cost of a mousetrap can be broken down as follows:

Direct materials	$0.23
Direct labor	0.09
Manufacturing overhead	0.12
Cost per trap	$0.44

The traps are then sold for 120% of cost, or $0.53 each. The manufacturing overhead is applied based on direct labor costs and was computed at the beginning of the year using the following estimates:

Estimated manufacturing overhead for the period	$540,000
Estimated direct labor costs	405,000
Predetermined overhead rate (per direct labor dollar)	1.33

For the first six months of the year, overhead costs of $272,000 were actually incurred. For that same time period, actual direct labor costs were $204,000. However, during the year several changes in the production process were made. As a result, by the midpoint of the year, expected manufacturing overhead costs have been significantly reduced below the original estimate of $540,000. Hence, for the last six months of the year, overhead costs are expected to be $225,000, and direct labor costs are expected to be $202,500.

1. What changes (if any) should be made in the predetermined manufacturing overhead rate for Packard, Inc.?
2. Assuming that per-unit direct materials and direct labor costs will remain the same for the last six months of the year, determine the new cost of a single mousetrap.
3. Because the cost of producing mousetraps dropped during the second half of the year, Packard can reduce the price of its traps and still earn its 20% markup on cost. Should the company reduce the price of its mousetraps? What factors would affect your decision?

Case 17-2

US MacDonald Corporation

You work for US MacDonald Corporation (USMC), an airplane manufacturer. USMC makes airplanes for commercial airlines, such as UNITED, AMERICAN, and DELTA, and for the U.S. AIR FORCE. Many parts are common to all planes made by USMC. The market for commercial planes is extremely competitive with GENERAL DYNAMICS, LOCKHEED, and European manufacturer AIRBUS often bidding lower than USMC. However, USMC's contract with the Air Force allows it to bill them at cost plus a 9% profit.

Times have been tough lately for USMC. In fact, if you can't find a way to increase profits, the company may have to lay off 5,000 employees.

A colleague has just presented you with an idea that he believes will increase profits. He suggests that instead of using direct labor hours to allocate overhead costs among airplanes, you should allocate costs on the basis of the number of each type of airplane made. Because you make far more, smaller, less expensive planes for the Air Force, more of the overhead costs will be allocated to those planes. This action will not only decrease your cost per unit on commercial planes (allowing you to be competitive in that market), but will also increase your profits on Air Force planes because the cost per plane will be higher.

You are not sure about your colleague's suggested action. You do know that your allocation base of direct labor hours is quite arbitrary and probably does not correspond well to the way overhead costs are consumed.

1. What is an appropriate allocation basis? Would adopting the suggestion be ethical?
2. Would you change your mind if you learned that competitors were allocating overhead on the basis of number of each type of plane made?
3. Is your action appropriate, from both a business and an ethical point of view, if direct labor hours is not an accurate allocation base?

Case 17-3

The Distribution Channel

You have just been hired as a branch manager for Perkins Retailers, a chain of office-supply stores in the Midwest. Perkins often purchases inventory items from Walker Wholesalers, a local distributor. However, Perkins also has the option of purchasing directly from various manufacturers, all of whom ensure prompt delivery. A comparative price list is as follows:

Lined paper:	
Gates Paper Manufacturers	$ 0.25
Walker Wholesalers	0.35
Steno chairs:	
Sturdychairs Manufacturers	$27.80
Walker Wholesalers	30.00
Desk lamps:	
Illumination Manufacturers	$ 7.60
Walker Wholesalers	11.25
Day planners:	
Olsen Manufacturers	$12.50
Walker Wholesalers	15.40

While examining past purchase invoices, you are perplexed to discover that despite the significantly higher prices, the previous branch manager had made most of his purchases from Walker Wholesalers.

1. Why might the previous branch manager have purchased from Walker Wholesalers when purchasing directly from the manufacturers is less expensive?
2. Why do wholesalers need to charge higher prices than manufacturers? Are they justified from the customers' point of view?
3. Will you, the new branch manager, always purchase from the manufacturers? Why or why not?

Case 17-4

Service Cost Flows

The CPA firm you work for has just been hired by Phillips Attorneys at Law to perform an audit. In the process of the audit, you notice that Phillips' accountant has been inconsistent in accounting for the company president's salary. You notice that sometimes he has accounted for the company president's salary as follows:

Overhead	20,000	
Salaries and Wages Payable		20,000
To record the company president's salary.		

Other times, the accountant has debited Salaries and Wages Expense instead of Overhead. When you confront the accountant about the inconsistency, he gets somewhat defensive and says that it doesn't matter which method is used because both methods result in an expense, and net income will be the same either way.

1. Assuming that the company president's tasks are exclusively administrative, do you agree with the accountant? Why or why not?
2. Which journal entry is correct? Why?

 j u d g m e n t c a l l s

Judgment 17-1

You Decide: With advancements in the Internet and e-commerce, will retailers be important to the future success of businesses, or will their services be eliminated in order to decrease costs?

Companies such as AMAZON.COM and EBAY eliminated retailers altogether and have changed the way their customers shop. Amazon.com and Ebay have no physical store locations. Customers order their products over the Internet and pay shipping to have goods delivered to any location they choose. Amazon.com and Ebay are able to pass the extra savings on to the consumer in the form of lower prices. Will retailers be completely eliminated in 15 years? What do you think?

Judgment 17-2

You Decide: Should the costs associated with an uncompleted consulting project be classified as a work-in-process asset on the balance sheet, or should the cost be expensed on the income statement as a part of doing business?

Your marketing company has been working on a consulting project for a client. Your team has worked on the project for two months, and it is now year-end. The project will be completed by February of the next year, and the client has not yet been billed. For the financial statements, how should the project be classified?

C o m p e t e n c y E n h a n c e m e n t O p p o r t u n i t i e s

▶ **Analyzing Real Company Information**
▶ **International Case**
▶ **Ethics Case**
▶ **Writing Assignment**

▶ **The Debate**
▶ **Internet Search**

The following additional assignments provide opportunities for students to develop critical thinking, ethical perspectives, oral and written communication skills, experience with electronic research, and teamwork through group and business activities.

▶ *Analyzing Real Company Information*

Analyzing 17-1 (Microsoft)

1. Is MICROSOFT a service business, a manufacturing business, or a merchandising business? Explain.

2. Microsoft's 2002 income statement (Appendix A) lists research and development expense of $4,379 billion for the year. The notes to the financial statements say that "research and development costs are expensed as incurred" in accordance with generally accepted accounting principles. Do you think that Microsoft treats R&D costs any differently in its internal accounting reports? Explain.

3. In its management's discussion and analysis (Appendix A), Microsoft describes four primary segments that it uses to categorize its product revenue. What are these segments, and what are some of the familiar products or services within these revenue segments?

Analyzing 17-2 (Pump, Inc.)

Acquiring management accounting data on real companies can be a challenge because this information is generally highly proprietary and of significant competitive value. The cost data below are for a medium-size family-owned pump manufacturing business located in the Mid-west. (This business chooses to remain anonymous in order to keep its competitors from using these data to compete against it.) We'll refer to this company simply as Pump, Inc.

Pump, Inc., had reorganized much of its production into manufacturing "cells": self-supervising work centers that produce complete products. The cell program was initiated because of a strategic decision (with no management accounting data to support it) to improve customer service. The financial impact of the program was unclear; the operational causes and the financial effects were murky. As a result, the management team at Pump, Inc., was having a difficult time evaluating the effects of its strategic decision to change *most* of the company to manufacturing cells. (Some of the production process continued to be organized as a typical production line, similar to what is demonstrated in the chapter.) The current year's cost data are presented below in the standard format typically used by the management accountant for Pump, Inc.

Typical Cost Data Format

Cost Category	Cost	Percent of Cost
Direct materials	$433,966	54.55%
Direct labor	96,990	12.19
Manufacturing overhead	264,583	33.26
Total costs	$795,539	100.00%

The management team, however, had a difficult time using the cost data in the typical format to effectively control and evaluate its reorganization decision. The management accountant was asked to reformat the data to make them more useful for the management team. After some analysis, the accountant decided to provide more detail by breaking down Manufacturing Overhead into subcategories organized by function: Indirect Materials, Indirect Labor, Factory Support, Occupancy Costs, and Non-Factory Support. The accountant also realized that she could divide all costs into two additional categories: People Costs (represent costs for wages and salaries) and Purchased Costs (represent costs for materials, supplies, and services acquired from outside agencies). The new report format is presented on the following page.

(continued)

New Cost Data Format

Cost Category	People Costs	Purchased Costs	Total Cost
Direct materials		$433,966	$433,966
Indirect materials		9,460	9,460
Direct labor	$ 96,990		96,990
Indirect labor (production line supervision)	29,100		29,100
Factory support (material handling, equipment depreciation, utilities, expediting, engineering, etc.)	80,953	71,310	152,263
Occupancy costs (rents, taxes, maintenance, etc.)	15,180	32,550	47,730
Non-factory support (cost accounting, personnel, etc.)	23,390	2,640	26,030
Total costs	$245,613	$549,926	$795,539

Source: Adapted from J. S. McGroarty and C. T. Horngren, "Functional Costing for Better Teamwork and Decision Support," *Journal of Cost Management*, Winter 1993, pp. 24–36. Reprinted with permission.

Consider the two reports on cost data for Pump, Inc.

1. Do you think the new report format provides any additional information value for controlling and evaluating the decision to change most of the production process into manufacturing cells?
2. What costs do you think the management team at Pump, Inc., should pay careful attention to in its effort to better control costs in the production plant?
3. Most importantly, if you were on the management team at Pump, Inc., what *additional* data would you like to see the management accountant provide?

International Case

International

Management Accounting in France

France has a well-developed set of financial accounting rules, as embodied in the *Plan Comptable Général (PCG)*. The French PCG is comparable to U.S. GAAP. You may not have realized it, but the cost accounting for manufacturers we have studied in this chapter has a very clear connection to the way financial accounting is reported. Exhibit 1 in the text visibly demonstrates the difference between the production process and the administration process in a manufacturing organization. U.S. cost accounting makes a clear functional distinction between costs related to the production process (e.g., direct materials, direct labor, and manufacturing overhead) versus the administration process (e.g., selling costs and general administration costs). Further, Exhibit 3 demonstrates that the flow of direct materials costs and direct labor costs through the accounting system, as well as the allocation of manufacturing overhead costs, allows U.S. companies to determine product costs and easily compute cost of goods sold for financial reporting purposes. However, cost accounting (*comptabilité analytique*) in France is explicitly decoupled from financial accounting, as defined by the PCG. What this means is that the chart of accounts French companies use for cost accounting is completely different from the chart of accounts used for financial accounting. The reason is not necessarily because French companies perform cost accounting differently from U.S. companies, but that the nature of French financial accounting is quite different from financial accounting in the United States. The PCG requires financial accounting reports in France to organize and report costs by their inherent nature (materials, labor, depreciation, etc.). Costs are not assigned to products or to departments. Hence, one wouldn't expect to see a French company report Cost of Goods Sold or Selling and General Administrative Expense.

Think about this for a moment. If costs are not being assigned to products, departments, or operations within the organization, how does the organization perform the management processes of planning, controlling, and evaluating? Actually, French companies do not have a tradition of using costs to manage their companies. In fact, the traditional phrase used in France to describe the techniques and practices of planning, control, and evaluation has been *contrôle de gestion*, literally, "management control." The absence of the word *comptabilité* (accounting) in this phrase is significant: it indicates that accounting numbers play a limited role in managerial reporting systems in France. Only very recently has the phrase *comptabilité de gestion* become more common. French business has had a long tradition of being led by engineers, not by accountants and financiers. Even today some 50% of managing directors in France are engineers by profession or training.

Costs are not being used as the main tool for managing companies in France. Given that a large number of the management executives of French companies have engineering backgrounds, how do French companies handle the management processes of planning, controlling, and evaluating (e.g., what kinds of numbers and reports might you expect to find in a French company)? Would you expect that French companies reconcile their *comptabilité analytique* systems with their financial accounting systems, as U.S. companies typically do?

Source: Reprinted from A. Roberts, "Management Accounting in France," *Management Accounting (UK)*, March 1995, pp. 44–46, by permission of the publisher Academic Press Limited, London.

▷ *Ethics Case*

State Home Builders Inc.

You have recently been hired as an accountant for the largest residential construction company in the state. Your primary responsibility is to track costs for each home being constructed. Tracking the costs for direct materials and direct labor is relatively straightforward. Materials requisitioned for each home site are carefully tracked, and the construction workers are very careful about assigning their time to the homes they work on.

Accounting for manufacturing overhead costs, on the other hand, presents quite a problem. In the past, overhead has been allocated on the basis of direct labor hours. As a result, because larger houses require more workers, those houses have been allocated a larger share of the overhead.

Your company was recently selected by the state to build a number of low-income housing complexes. The state has agreed to an arrangement whereby it will pay your costs plus a 10% profit. Construction of these low-income housing units will be relatively simple and will not require a great deal of materials or labor, compared to the average house the company builds.

At a meeting following the granting of the construction contract by the state, the production foreman proposes the following idea:

> Since the state has agreed to pay our costs plus 10%, the higher the costs on the project, the more money we make. What we need to do is to funnel as much of our costs as possible to this low-income housing project. Now I don't want anyone to think I am proposing something unethical. I am not saying that we should charge the state for fictitious costs. What I am saying is that we should allocate as much overhead as possible to the low-income project. Therefore, I propose that we allocate overhead on a per-house basis with each house, regardless of size, being allocated the same amount of overhead.

(continued)

You have analyzed the activities that drive overhead costs and have found that bigger houses, in addition to requiring more direct materials and direct labor, require more inspections, more supervision, etc. You can see that most in attendance at the meeting are being persuaded by the production foreman's idea. You slowly raise your hand. It takes about 10 seconds before all the voices quiet. You look around the table and see 10 of your colleagues staring at you. You open your mouth and. . .

1. What would you do in this situation? Is the overhead allocation method being proposed by the production foreman illegal? Is it unethical?
2. Suppose you argue that overhead should continue to be allocated on the basis of direct labor hours. After hearing your points, the group votes to go with the production foreman and allocate the overhead on a per-house basis. What would you do next?

▷ *Writing Assignment*

Trends in Product Cost Relationships

The ratios among the three types of product costs have changed quite a bit over the last 150 years of business. Generally, costs of direct materials have consistently formed approximately 50% of total product costs for manufacturing firms. However, the ratio of direct labor costs has been decreasing with an offsetting increase in the ratio of manufacturing overhead costs. What kinds of costing challenges does this shift from direct costs to manufacturing overhead costs pose for a manufacturing company? What factors do you think have contributed to this trend? Do you think that the advent of e-business will significantly affect the amount or ratio of direct labor costs in manufacturing products? If so, how? Write a one- to two-page paper on this topic.

▷ *The Debate*

When Does a Direct Materials Cost Turn into an Indirect Cost (e.g., Manufacturing Overhead)?

Consider your automobile. What costs would be considered direct materials? What costs would be considered indirect materials? Are the fender panels direct or indirect materials? Are the rivets that connect the fender to the frame direct or indirect materials? Are the headlights direct or indirect materials? Are the screws that hold the headlights in place direct or indirect materials? In light of the intense price competition that takes place in the automobile industry, these are important cost questions: direct materials are assigned to a specific automobile (or automobile model), while indirect materials are gathered together in the pool of manufacturing overhead costs and generally allocated across all types of automobiles in the manufacturing plant.

Divide your group into two teams.

- One team represents: "Rivets and screws should be treated as direct costs." Prepare a two-minute oral argument supporting this view. Be careful that you don't make too many quick assumptions. Tracking direct materials costs to specific product units or product lines can be a very expensive process in a complex manufacturing organization.
- The other team represents: "Rivets and screws should be treated as indirect costs." Prepare a two-minute oral argument supporting this view. You must be careful that you don't make too many quick assumptions. Before you say that rivets and screws are indirect because their costs are small, consider that the bigger automakers spend tens of millions of dollars each year on rivets and screws.

▶ *Internet Search*

Wal-Mart

Access WAL-MART's customer Web site at **http://www.walmart.com**. Sometimes Web addresses change, so if this address doesn't work, access the Web site for this textbook (**http://albrecht .swlearning.com**) for an updated link.

Once you've gained access to the site, answer the following questions.

1. Use Wal-Mart's Store Finder to find the store nearest you (look at the bottom of its homepage).
2. What is the current price on a hardback version of J. K. Rowling's *Harry Potter and the Order of the Phoenix* (a popular children's book)?

Now access Wal-Mart's corporate Web site at **http://www.walmartstores.com** (you could also click on the "Wal-Mart Stores Info" link at the bottom of the customer Web site). Again, if this Web address should change, access the Web site for this textbook (**http://albrecht .swlearning.com**) for an updated link.

Once you've gained access to this site, answer the following questions:

3. In order to be a Wal-Mart supplier you would need to adhere to certain "Supplier Standards." Although these standards are very detailed, what are the seven general areas of supplier standards?
4. Wal-Mart's first non-U.S. store opened in December 1991. Where? How many Wal-Mart stores are operating outside of the United States? Which countries, other than the United States, now have Wal-Mart stores?

Part

6

Planning

chapter

18

Capital Investment Decisions

After studying this chapter, you should be able to:

Learning Objectives

1 Understand the importance of capital budgeting and the concepts underlying strategic and capital investment decisions.

2 Describe and use two nondiscounted capital budgeting techniques: the payback method and the unadjusted rate of return method.

3 Describe and use two discounted capital budgeting techniques: the net present value method and the internal rate of return method.

4 Understand the need for evaluating qualitative factors in strategic and capital investment decisions.

5 Use sensitivity analysis to assess the potential effects of uncertainty in capital budgeting.

6 Explain how to use capital budgeting techniques in ranking capital investment projects.

7 Explain how income taxes affect capital budgeting decisions.

FEDERAL EXPRESS CORPORATION (FEDEX) is the largest air-freight company in the world. Fred Smith, founder of Federal Express, came up with his initial overnight-delivery idea as he was writing a term paper in 1965 as a Yale undergraduate. Smith's Yale professor was unimpressed with the idea and gave the paper a "C" grade. After serving two tours of duty in Vietnam as a Marine, Smith returned to the United States and began assembling the pieces to implement his idea. In 1971, Smith was optimistic about obtaining the contract to ship canceled checks around the country; he named his company "Federal Express" because the contract would have been with the Federal Reserve System. That contract never came to be, and Smith focused his attention on shipping small, time-sensitive packages through his hub-and-spoke air system centered in Memphis, Tennessee. The inaugural night of service was March 12, 1973, but only six packages arrived at the 10,000-per-hour package handling system in Memphis. After further marketing in an expanded set of cities, a second start was attempted on April 17, 1973. That night, Federal Express handled 186 packages, and daily volume has climbed steadily ever since. In 2003, FedEx Corporation delivered 5.3 million shipments per day.

For FedEx and other firms in the air-freight industry, the most important investment is the airplanes that haul the freight. Indeed, making good airplane acquisition decisions is critical to the success of FedEx and its competitors. Although FedEx is profitable and expanding, questions have been raised about whether the company has made the right kind of airplane investment decisions. In early 1998, the Federal Aviation Administration (FAA) began public hearings to question the structural safety of scores of FedEx's aircraft. The FAA contended that the maximum allowed weight limit of these 727s should be cut from 8,000 pounds per modular cargo container to 3,000 pounds, which would significantly increase the per-pound cost of shipping cargo and reduce FedEx's profitability.

For years, the air-freight industry has relied heavily on the practice of converting retired passenger planes into cargo freighters. The safety questions raised by the FAA involve how cargo doors were installed and other structural changes made when the aircraft were modified. Safety concerns range from the stability of cargo doors to the ability of aircraft to survive a strong downward gust. FAA research has shown that under combinations of certain extreme conditions, the floor beams of 727s might fail, causing the aircraft to suddenly break apart in a massive midair convulsion. [Those who have seen the Tom Hanks movie *Cast Away* are familiar with this scenario.]

FedEx countered that the probability of the combination of conditions that would cause such an accident is highly remote. The FAA said it didn't want to wait until after an accident had occurred to raise safety issues about the 727s. In the end, the FAA compromised and only required FedEx to reduce its modular cargo container weights to 4,800 pounds in the 120 FedEx BOEING 727s in question. While FedEx was fighting the FAA claims and allegations, the company must have wondered if it made the right kind of investment decision by acquiring and converting the 727s. At a minimum, the questions raised about the safety of FedEx's operations represented a public relations nightmare for FedEx.

Sources: Douglas A. Blackmon, "FedEx Faults Claims by FAA over Aircraft," *The Wall Street Journal*, Wednesday, February 18, 1998, p. A3; Paul Richfield, "FAA Issues Final Ruling on 727 Freighters," *The Wall Street Journal*, January 11, 1999, p. B2; Robert A. Sigafoos, *Absolutely Positively Overnight!: The Unofficial History of Federal Express* (Memphis: St. Lukes Press, 1988).

how do FedEx and other companies decide which types of equipment to buy and what other capital investments to make? In this chapter, we examine that part of planning called **capital budgeting,** the systematic planning for long-term investments in operating assets (primarily property, plant, equipment, intangible assets, and natural resources). Capital budgeting techniques are also important in planning for a company's investments in people and information. For example, the most important decisions a university makes are not about where or when to build buildings but instead are about whom to hire for the university's faculty.

Capital budgeting differs from the types of planning already discussed in that it is more permanent and less retractable. A decision to increase inventory levels, for example, can be reversed within a relatively short time by cutting back on future purchases or by lowering prices to increase sales. Even

capital budgeting Systematic planning for long-term investments in operating assets.

a nonroutine decision to purchase, rather than make or deliver internally, a component or service can generally be changed without too much disruption to operations. On the other hand, a capital investment decision to purchase 120 Model 727 freight aircraft at several million dollars each requires a long-term commitment of resources, a commitment that will probably be difficult and very expensive to change at a later date. Because of its long-term consequences, capital budgeting is an important part of a company's strategic plan. Strategic planning involves establishing the overall direction of a company's activities. Strategic planning is discussed in the next chapter.

Because capital budgeting involves long-range planning, the time value of money must be consid-

ered. But before we begin to explain how capital budgeting provides management with information for evaluating long-term investments in operating assets, we must introduce some basic concepts.

Conceptual Basis of Capital Budgeting

1 Understand the importance of capital budgeting and the concepts underlying strategic and capital investment decisions.

capital The total amount of money or other resources owned or used to acquire future income or benefits.

The primary objective of a business is to generate a profit for its owners. Profitable businesses can be based on a low-cost strategy (such as WAL-MART), a customer service strategy (such as FEDEX), a product-branding strategy (such as COCA-COLA), and a variety of other business strategies. No matter what a company's underlying strategy, it must make long-term investment decisions in buildings, equipment, information technology, personnel, and so forth. Capital budgeting is the process of determining whether the future sales, cost savings, quality improvements, and other future benefits stemming from these strategic investment decisions are sufficient to justify the significant up-front costs associated with those decisions. In short, capital budgeting involves a comparison of the magnitude of up-front costs to the magnitude of estimated future multi-year benefits.

The term **capital** may be defined broadly as any form of material wealth. As used in business, it is more specifically defined as the total amount of money or other resources owned or used by an individual or a company to acquire future income or benefits.

Thus, capital is something to be invested with the expectation that it will be recovered along with a profit, and capital budgeting is the planning for that investment. From a quantitative viewpoint, the success of an investment depends on the amount of net future cash inflows (or future cash savings) in relation to the cost (current cash outlays) of the investment. Ignoring the time value of money for the moment, if a company invests $10,000 and receives only $10,000 in the future, there has been only a return of the investment but no profit. However, if $15,000 is received in the future, there is not only a return of the original investment but also an additional return, or profit, of $5,000. Other things being equal, investors obviously wish to receive the greatest future benefits for the least investment cost.

Importance of Capital Investment Decisions in Planning

Three aspects of capital investment decisions are critical to long-run profitability:

1. *Large initial outlay.* Decisions to invest in assets such as land, buildings, and equipment usually require large outlays of capital. Unless a reasonable return is received on such significant investments, the overall profitability of a firm will suffer.

2. *Potential long-term impact on earnings.* Long-term investments, by definition, extend over several years. Thus, poor capital budgeting, resulting in bad investment decisions, is likely to have an adverse effect on earnings over a long period.

3. *Difficult to reverse course.* Long-term investments in land, buildings, and specialized equipment are much less liquid than other investments. Investments in stocks and bonds, for example, can usually be terminated by sale through regularly established markets at almost any time; operating assets may not be so readily disposed of.

Each of these three factors can be seen in the FedEx scenario described at the beginning of the chapter. FedEx had expended millions of dollars on the 120 BOEING 727s that the FAA was concerned about. The efficient, or inefficient, use of this portion of FedEx's fleet would have implications for FedEx's reported earnings for many years; many 727s have now been in use for over 30 years. Finally, once FedEx had committed itself to using these converted 727 freighters, it was extremely costly to overhaul or retire the planes in response to the FAA concerns.

Uses of Capital Budgeting: Screening and Ranking

Clearly, all long-term investment decisions are important. The larger the investment, however, the more critical is the need to budget for that expenditure. And the longer the time period, the more difficult it is to assess future outcomes and to plan accordingly. Following are some typical business situations that lend themselves to analysis with capital budgeting techniques:

1. A machine breaks down. Should the manager have the machine repaired or replaced?
2. Should a pharmaceutical company hire a renowned research scientist and commit to supporting this scientist and her staff for the next 10 years?
3. Should a company add to its manufacturing facility or build a new, larger factory?
4. Should a professional sports team sign a long-term guaranteed contract for $252 million with a key player?
5. Should Company A purchase Company B and, if so, on what terms?

Situations such as these require careful consideration of all factors, qualitative as well as quantitative, and it is just as important for nonprofit organizations to make sound strategic and capital investment decisions as for-profit organizations. Thus, the concepts and techniques discussed in this chapter are applicable to all types of organizations—companies, governmental agencies, school districts, hospitals, city governments, and so forth.

Capital budgeting analysis can help by answering two basic questions. First, does the investment make sense? That is, does it meet a minimum standard of financial acceptability? This is the **screening** function of capital budgeting. Second, is an investment the best among available acceptable alternatives? We determine this by ranking the alternatives. Before we discuss the screening and **ranking** of investment alternatives, we will briefly review the time value of money concept.

screening Determining whether a capital investment meets a minimum standard of financial acceptability.

ranking The ordering of acceptable investment alternatives from most to least desirable.

interest The payment (cost) for the use of money.

The Time Value of Money

Like other commodities, money has value because it is a scarce resource. Therefore, a payment is generally required for its use. This payment is called **interest**. Because the time value of money is widely recognized, few people would consider hiding money under a mattress or otherwise keeping large amounts of idle cash; they realize that there is a significant opportunity cost in doing so. Money left idle will not earn interest, nor will it earn the potentially higher returns that can be obtained from investments in corporate stocks and bonds or real estate, for example.

Because money has value over time, the timing of expected cash flows is important in investment decisions. This is the essence of capital budgeting—comparing the cost of an investment with the expected future net cash inflows to decide whether, given the risks and available alternatives, the project should be undertaken. An investment made today will not generate cash inflows until the future, either periodically over a number of years or in a lump sum several years hence. Thus, for the comparison of cash flows to be accurate, all amounts should be stated at their value at one point in time, generally the present; this means that all future cash flows should be stated in terms of their present values. This mathematical process of adjusting future cash flows to their present values is called discounting.

The choice of the correct interest rate, or discount rate, to use in doing time value of money computations is extremely important. In fact, this is one of the topics emphasized in the field of finance. Generally speaking, managers use relatively high discount rates when evaluating projects or investments that involve a high degree of risk; an expectation of a high rate of return is necessary to entice a rational manager into undertaking a very risky project. In addition, a manager must consider what it will cost to obtain the funds to finance the project. We will return later to the problem of selecting a discount rate for making capital investment decisions.

In the remainder of this chapter and in the end-of-chapter exercises and problems, we will assume that you understand the concepts of present value and the underlying notion of the time value of money. If you do not, or if you want to refresh your memory, you might want to review the appendix to this chapter.

Caution

If you are using a business calculator, you might note that a more precise calculation of the present value of $100,000 to be received one year from now, if the interest rate is 10%, is $90,909.09. The $90,910 amount results from using present value tables. In this chapter, calculations using both present value tables and business calculators will be illustrated.

Discounting Cash Flows

Because of the time value of money, a difference in the timing of cash flows can make one investment more attractive than another, even if both involve the same total amount of money. To illustrate, we assume that project A will produce $100,000 at the end of one year and that project B will return $50,000 at the end of each year for two years. Both projects will generate a total of $100,000. However, by using present value computations (reviewed in the chapter appendix) and assuming a discount (interest) rate of 10% per year, you will see that the discounted cash flows from project A are $90,910 and from project B are $86,775. In other words, if the appropriate discount rate is 10%, receiving $90,910 right now is the same as receiving $100,000 one year from now. Similarly, receiving

Project A

Project B

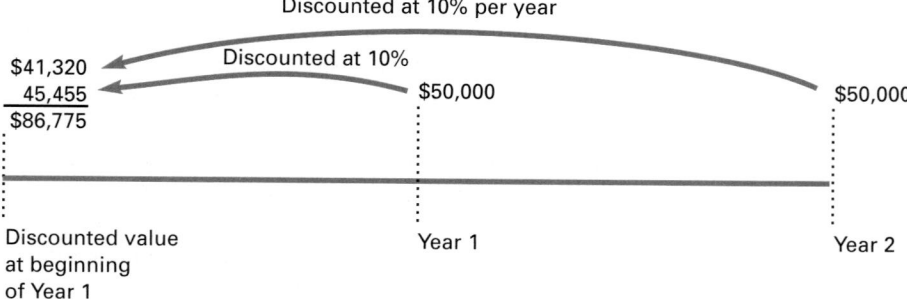

$86,775 right now is the same as receiving $50,000 at the end of each year for the next two years. The difference in the present values of these two projects with the same total cash flows arises because with project A, the cash is received sooner. Cash received sooner is worth more because it can be put to productive use—invested, used to pay off loans, and so forth. If all other factors—that is, any qualitative considerations—are the same, an investor would be $4,135 (in today's dollars) better off by investing in project A.

As the analysis on the previous page shows, discounted cash flows reflect the time value of money and should be considered in capital budgeting. The determination of net income in accordance with GAAP is based, as you know, on accrual concepts that recognize income when it is earned, not when cash is actually received. Thus, accounting net income doesn't necessarily coincide with cash flows. For short-term investments, this approach does not significantly affect the results. Ignoring the time value of money can be misleading, however, for evaluating long-term projects.

To be able to compare cash outflows and inflows, you need a solid understanding of the discounting of cash flows. In the following paragraphs, we provide some definitions and examples.

Cash Outflows

cash outflows The initial cost and other expected outlays associated with an investment.

Cash outflows include the initial cost of an investment plus any other expected future cash outlays associated with the investment. For example, suppose that a company purchases a drill press for $8,000 cash less a trade-in allowance of $500 for its old press. With maintenance expenses of $400 at the end of each year for the 5-year life of the press, and assuming a 12% discount rate, the present value of the cash outflows for the investment is computed as follows:

	Time Period	Cash Outflows	Present Value Factor	Present Value of Cash Outflows
Initial cash outlay	Today	$7,500	1.0000	$7,500
Future cash outlays	Years 1–5	400	3.6048*	1,442
Total present value of cash outflows				$8,942

*From Table II, 5 years at 12%.

The $7,500 is invested immediately, so it is already stated at its present value. The $400 series of equal payments (an annuity) is to be extended over five years, so it must be discounted to its present value equivalent.

Maintenance expense is only one category of future cash outflows. Another is manufacturing overhead costs—such as heat, electricity, and rent—that may be incurred as a consequence of an investment. In addition, income taxes are expenses that must be considered in almost all capital budgeting decisions made by businesses. For simplicity, income taxes are ignored in the first part of this chapter; the impact of income taxes on capital budgeting decisions is explained in the expanded material section of the chapter. In brief, all current or expected cash outlays (expressed in terms of present values) should be considered as cash outflows in evaluating investments.

Note that some expenses, although deducted from revenues in arriving at accounting net income, do not involve actual cash disbursements and so should not be considered outflows in capital budgeting. It would obviously be wrong, for example, to include depreciation expense as an outflow, since no cash flow is directly involved.

cash inflows Any current or expected revenues or savings directly associated with an investment.

Cash Inflows

Cash inflows include all current and expected future revenues or savings directly associated with an investment. For example, rent receipts, installment payments, and other revenues represent cash inflows. Returning to our earlier example, we now assume that the drill press is expected to generate annual revenues of $2,500 for five years, after which it can be sold as scrap for $750. The present value of the cash inflows for the investment is computed as follows:

	Time Period	Cash Outflows	Present Value Factor	Present Value of Cash Outflows
Revenues	Years 1–5	$2,500	3.6048*	$9,012
Salvage value	Year 5	750	0.5674**	426
Total present value of cash inflows				$9,438

*From Table II, 5 years at 12%.
**From Table I, 5 years at 12%.

These revenues may be shown "net"—that is, reduced by any direct expenses, such as those for maintenance or materials and supplies. Thus, the net annual cash inflows from the drill press would be $2,100 per year ($2,500 − $400 maintenance expense).

Less obvious cash inflows are represented by the present value of the savings to be derived from an investment that reduces costs. In brief, the present value of all cash that is likely to be received or saved as a result of an investment should be included as cash inflows.

> **TO SUMMARIZE:** Certain long-term investment decisions require significant capital outlays. Proper planning for these decisions is critical to long-run profitability. Capital budgeting techniques are designed to help in analyzing the quantitative factors relating to these decisions. Essentially, capital budgeting involves a comparison of the current and expected cash outflows and inflows in order to decide whether, given the risks and available alternatives, an investment should be made. To make comparisons more meaningful, all future cash flows should be discounted to the present.

Nondiscounted Capital Budgeting Techniques

2 Describe and use two nondiscounted capital budgeting techniques: the payback method and the unadjusted rate of return method.

discounted cash flow methods Capital budgeting techniques that take into account the time value of money by comparing discounted cash flows.

The four most commonly used capital budgeting techniques are (1) the payback method, (2) the unadjusted rate of return method, (3) the net present value method, and (4) the internal rate of return method. We will discuss the first two methods in this section and the latter two in the next section.

We have chosen the sequence of our discussion to parallel the pattern of most companies as they grow larger and become more sophisticated in the way that they make investment decisions. That is, companies generally first use the payback method or the unadjusted rate of return method because these techniques are relatively simple. Both of these techniques have a serious weakness, however, in that they ignore the time value of money. As a result, most companies eventually turn to either the net present value method or the internal rate of return method, both of which are more theoretically correct approaches to capital budgeting. The last two techniques are referred to as **discounted cash flow methods** because they use a discount rate in comparing the cash flows of investments.

Payback Method

payback method A capital budgeting technique that determines the amount of time it takes the net cash inflows of an investment to repay the investment cost.

The **payback method** is widely used in business because it is simple to apply and it provides a preliminary screening of investment opportunities. It can also be used as a crude measure of a project's risk. Basically, this method is used to determine the length of time it will take the net cash inflows of an investment to equal the cash outlay. The payback period may be a particularly important consideration for companies in a tight credit position. Assuming that the payback period is to be computed in years (any time frame can be applied) and that equal cash flows are generated for each period, the formula for a project's payback period is:

$$\frac{\text{Investment cost}}{\text{Annual net cash inflows}} = \text{Payback period}$$

To illustrate the payback method, we will consider Kristi Felt's decision to purchase a personal computer, printer, and software for typing and printing essays and term papers for other students. A reasonably good PC, printer, and appropriate software will cost Kristi a total of $1,500. She can borrow the $1,500 from her parents, who require no interest but need to be repaid at the end of 18 months. Kristi expects to make $100 per month after paying for supplies and other related expenses. The payback period (in months) may be computed as follows:

$$\frac{\$1,500}{\$100} = 15 \text{ months}$$

Since Kristi would generate sufficient cash to recover the investment in 15 months, she could repay her parents within the agreed period of time (assuming she spends none of the money).

This is one of the strengths of the payback method: It can be used to determine whether an investment fits within an acceptable period for the use of funds. For example, a company's cash position may lead it to establish a rule of thumb that no investment with a payback period exceeding three years will be accepted. In such a situation, a manager may be obliged to select an investment alternative with a slightly lower rate of return but a shorter payback period.

The payback method has several weaknesses, however. One is that it measures the time needed to recover the initial outlay but does not consider the investment's profitability. Investments obviously are made in order to earn an acceptable return, not just to recover their costs. In our example, Kristi is not solely interested in recovering the $1,500 in the shortest time possible. Her purpose in buying the equipment is to earn some extra money. Assuming that the equipment will last for more than 15 months, Kristi not only will recover her initial investment, but will also generate subsequent earnings (at least $100 per month). Although the payback method may provide some clues about the advisability of investments, it does not directly measure profitability.

To clarify this last point and show why the payback method must be used with care, consider a manager's decision to purchase one of two machines. Machine A costs $5,500 and is expected to generate $1,000 of net cash inflows annually. Machine B costs $3,500 and will produce $800 of net cash inflows annually. The payback period for machine A is 5.5 years ($5,500 ÷ $1,000); for machine B, the payback period is 4.4 years ($3,500 ÷ $800). Other things being equal, the payback method would indicate that the manager should purchase machine B because it would result in a shorter payback period. That is, its original cost would be recovered in a shorter time. However, if machine B were expected to last less than 4.4 years, such an investment would be unwise. The machine would not last long enough to recover its original cost, let alone generate any earnings.

Now suppose that both machines were estimated to have a 7-year life. Which machine would be the better investment? What if the estimated lifetimes of both machines were more than 10 years? To answer these questions, we would have to use one of the discounted cash flow methods (to be discussed later) in conjunction with the payback period.

unadjusted rate of return method A capital budgeting technique in which a rate of return is calculated by dividing the increase in the average annual net income a project will generate by the initial investment cost.

This example highlights the other major weakness of the payback method: It does not take into account the time value of money. As a result, incorrect investment decisions may result unless the payback period is relatively short.

Unadjusted Rate of Return Method

Another commonly used capital budgeting technique is the **unadjusted rate of return method**. Also referred to as the simple rate of return method or the accounting rate of return method, the unadjusted rate of return is computed as follows:

$$\frac{\text{Increase in future average net income}}{\text{Initial investment cost}} = \text{Unadjusted rate of return}$$

To illustrate the unadjusted rate of return method, consider the following situation. Seal Right Company manufactures cans for fruits, vegetables, and other farm produce. Management wants to add a new, larger can size to the product line in order to take advantage of a potential demand for food storage items in the western states. This new can is expected to increase the company's annual revenues by an average of $51,500 a year for 10 years. The additional machinery needed to manufacture the can will cost $215,000. Assuming that there are no other expenses, the new can will increase annual net income by $30,000 each year; this $30,000 is computed as the difference between the $51,500 increase in revenues and the $21,500 ($215,000 ÷ 10 years) increase in annual depreciation. The unadjusted rate of return (or accounting rate of return) on the investment is $30,000 ÷ $215,000 = 14% (rounded).

Unlike the payback method, the unadjusted rate of return method attempts to measure the profitability of an investment. A company compares the unadjusted rate of return with a preselected rate that it considers acceptable. Management invests only in projects with accounting rates of return that are equal to or greater than the established standard. Thus, if Seal Right's standard acceptance rate is less than or equal to 14%, the project would be acceptable. In the business world, any investment that provides a positive return (increases net income and EPS) is said to be **accretive**.

The main weakness of the unadjusted rate of return method is that, like the payback method, it does not consider the time value of money. The computation uses average future net income rather than expected future earnings discounted to the present. A second problem is that this method counts the initial investment cost twice. This occurs because depreciation is a component in the computation of the average net income added by a project.

The problem of double counting can be eliminated by using refined models of the unadjusted rate of return method. The more serious problem—the omission of the time value of money—cannot be corrected. And because this omission can produce misleading results and incorrect long-term investment decisions, the unadjusted rate of return method must be used with extreme care.

TO SUMMARIZE: The payback method measures the time required to recover the initial cost of an investment from future net cash inflows (investment cost divided by annual net cash inflows). It may be useful as a preliminary screen of investment projects. The unadjusted rate of return method provides a measure of the profitability of an investment (increases in future average net income divided by the cost of the investment). If the resulting return is greater than the company's minimum standard of acceptability, the project is acceptable quantitatively. Because the payback and the unadjusted rate of return methods do not consider the time value of money, they should be used only in conjunction with one of the discounted cash flow methods.

Discounted Capital Budgeting Techniques

3 Describe and use two discounted capital budgeting techniques: the net present value method and the internal rate of return method.

Two widely used capital budgeting techniques recognize the time value of money—the net present value method and the internal rate of return method. Both methods apply discounted cash flow principles in determining the acceptability of an investment. The net present value method uses a standard discount rate to restate all cash flows in terms of present values and then makes comparisons. The internal rate of return method calculates the investment's "true" discounted rate of return and compares it with the firm's "hurdle" rate. Thus, an appropriate discount rate is extremely important in capital budgeting. Before explaining each of the two methods, we first discuss how to select an appropriate discount rate.

Selecting a Discount Rate

cost of capital The average cost of a firm's debt and equity capital; equals the rate of return that a company must earn in order to satisfy the demands of its owners and creditors.

An excellent starting point for computing the correct discount rate is a company's cost of capital. The **cost of capital** is basically an average cost of a firm's debt (primarily bank loans and bonds) and its equity (primarily common and preferred stock and retained earnings). These costs are measured in terms of effective interest rates on bank loans and bonds and the rate of return expected to be earned by the company's stockholders. In essence, then, the cost of capital is the rate a company must earn in order to satisfy its owners and creditors.

The computation of the cost of capital is complex and beyond the scope of this book. However, the following example should help you understand the concept. Assume that 30% of a company's total capital is debt, 20% is equity from the issuance of stock, and 50% is equity from retained earnings. Upon analysis, the company has determined that the cost of its debt capital is 10%, and the cost of its equity capital is 22% from stock and 16% from retained earnings. (*Note:* The cost of equity capital from the issuance of new shares is considered to be higher because of the commissions, registration fees, and so forth, associated with the issuance of new shares.) The firm's cost of capital would be determined as follows:

Type	Cost of Capital	×	Weight	=	Average Cost of Capital
Debt (bonds)	10%	×	30%	=	3.0%
Equity (stocks)	22	×	20	=	4.4
Equity (retained earnings)	16	×	50	=	8.0
Total cost of capital			100%		15.4%

 STOP & THINK

Assume you were trying to decide whether to purchase or lease an automobile and you wanted to use the net present value method to determine which alternative to choose. What factors would you consider in determining the rate at which to discount the future cash outflows (i.e., what factors would determine your personal cost of capital)?

The weighting procedure may seem fairly simple. As you will learn in more advanced courses, however, it is not always easy to calculate the costs of the different types of capital. This is because the necessary information is often not readily available or absolutely verifiable. For example, debt costs must be adjusted to an after-tax basis, and equity costs include some subjective elements, such as the opportunity cost of retained earnings. Although you now have a general understanding of the cost of capital, you will need further study in finance courses in order to be able to confidently use this concept.

As mentioned above, the cost of capital is a starting point in identifying an appropriate discount rate. The riskiness of a project should also be considered in choosing the appropriate discount rate. For example, the cost of capital computed earlier is 15.4%. If the company were considering a very risky project, a higher discount rate would be used because high-risk projects must yield higher-than-average returns in order to compensate for the increased probability of no returns at all. The techniques of correctly computing risk-adjusted discount rates are beyond the scope of this text; however, remember that the selection of the right discount rate is critical in the execution of a useful capital budgeting analysis.

Net Present Value Method

net present value method
A capital budgeting technique that uses discounted cash flows to compare the present values of an investment's expected cash inflows and outflows.

The **net present value method** compares all expected cash inflows associated with an investment with the current and future cash outflows. All cash flows are discounted to their present values, giving recognition to the time value of money. For this reason, the net present value method is superior to both the payback method and the unadjusted rate of return method.

In general, the net present value method involves the following five steps:

1. *Estimate* the amount and timing of all cash flows associated with the investment.
2. *Evaluate* the riskiness of the cash flows in order to determine the appropriate discount rate to use in the present value calculations.
3. *Compute* the present values of all the expected cash inflows and outflows of the investment. (Note that most present value calculations assume end-of-year inflows and outflows.)
4. *Subtract* the total present value of the cash outflows from the total present value of the cash inflows. The difference is the investment's net present value.
5. *Decide* whether to undertake the investment. If the net present value of the investment is positive, or at least zero, the project is acceptable from a financial standpoint.

Steps 1 and 2, the estimation of the amount and timing of the cash flows and the selection of an appropriate discount rate, are the most difficult steps in evaluating a long-term investment. These steps are where business judgment, experience, and careful analysis of details separate companies that make good long-term investment decisions from those that make bad long-term investment decisions. Implementation of steps 1 and 2 is a topic for more advanced finance and accounting courses as well as being the object of much on-the-job training for young managers. For the illustrations in this chapter, the cash flows and the discount rate will be given so that we can focus on the calculations and decision process in steps 3, 4, and 5.

The following case illustrates the net present value method. The fleet manager of MBK Company is thinking of replacing an old truck before it begins to need major repairs. Because the company has limited funds and cannot spend more than $18,000, the manager is considering a small, fuel-efficient pickup truck that is presently selling for that amount. The truck would save the company $5,625 a year in gas and other expenses. The truck's estimated useful life is four years, and the expected salvage value is $1,800. The company uses a 10% discount rate. What is this investment's net present value? Should the truck be purchased?

Because the cash flows and the discount rate are given, we are assuming that steps 1 and 2 have already been completed. Step 3 of the net present value method is to use the predetermined discount rate to state all cash flows at their present values (rounded to the nearest dollar in this example).

Cash inflows:

	Annual cash savings	× Discount factor	= Present value
	$5,625	× 3.1699*	= $17,831
	Salvage value	× Discount factor	= Present value
	$1,800	× 0.6830**	= $1,229

Cash outflows:

	Initial cost	× Discount factor	= Present value
	$18,000	× 1.0000	= $18,000

*From Table II, 4 years at 10%.
**From Table I, 4 years at 10%.

net present value The difference between the present values of an investment's expected cash inflows and outflows.

Step 4 is to compute the **net present value**, that is, the difference between the present values of cash inflows and outflows.

Present value of inflows:

Cash savings	$17,831
Salvage value	1,229
Total	$19,060

Less present value of outflows:

Cost of truck	18,000
Net present value	$ 1,060

FYI:

Another way to think of the $1,060 net present value is that on the day the company decides to buy the truck, the market value of the company immediately increases by $1,060. This increase stems from the fact that the company has embarked on a course that involves exchanging cash flows with a present value of $18,000 for cash flows with a present value of $19,060. When viewed this way, it is obvious that a company should want to engage in as many positive net present value projects as possible.

The analysis in step 4 shows that investing in the truck would produce a positive net present value. In other words, after adjusting for the time value of money, purchasing the truck is like paying $18,000 in exchange for a stream of cash flows that is worth $19,060. Clearly, this is something that you would want to do. Thus, from a quantitative standpoint, it seems that the truck should be purchased. Exhibit 1 illustrates the process just described.

A common misinterpretation of the $1,060 net present value is that the acquisition of the truck will generate a net profit of just $1,060. Actually, because a 10% discount rate was used in evaluating the truck, the $1,060 net present value means that the investment in the truck will yield a net value gain of $1,060 OVER AND ABOVE the 10% minimum required rate of return. Similarly, a computed net present value of $0 does not mean that an investment just barely breaks even; instead, a $0 net present value means that the investment yields a return exactly equal to the discount rate used in evaluating the investment.

Before the company decides whether to purchase the truck, however, management must consider other factors. For example, a policy of support for U.S. car manufacturers or a lack of certain safety features on the pickup might dictate a particular course of action. Qualitative factors are discussed in greater detail later in the chapter.

Exhibit 1: Computing Net Present Value

	Present Time	Year 1	Year 2	Year 3	Year 4
Cost	$18,000				
Savings		$5,625	$5,625	$5,625	$5,625
Salvage value					1,800

	Time Period	Cash Flows	Present Value Factor	Present Value of Cash Flows
Present value of cash inflows:				
Savings	Years 1–4	$ 5,625	3.1699*	$17,831
Salvage value	Year 4	1,800	0.6830**	1,229
				$19,060
Present value of cash outflows:				
Cost	Today	(18,000)	1.0000	18,000
Net present value				$ 1,060

*From Table II, 4 years at 10%.
**From Table I, 4 years at 10%.

© 2003 Getty Images

Managers must sometimes make least-cost decisions to fulfill certain imposed requirements at the lowest possible cost. For example, government regulations may require a company to purchase pollution-control equipment.

least-cost decision A decision to undertake the project with the smallest negative net present value.

STOP & THINK

Over your lifetime, you will make many personal, long-term investments such as buying automobiles and buying a home. Are the capital budgeting techniques we have discussed in this chapter relevant to these personal decisions? Since you probably won't be earning a return on your automobile and home investments, what type of capital budgeting decisions are these?

FYI:

This pollution control example is somewhat misleading. Many companies have found that the effort to control emissions or reduce waste actually improves overall efficiency, turning environmental initiatives into positive net present value business projects.

Source: Martha Hamilton, "Generating Profit from the Waste Up," *The Washington Post*, April 12, 1995, p. F01.

Least-Cost Decisions

The net present value method generally assumes that an investment must be justified by cash savings or increased revenues. Sometimes, however, funds must be used to purchase assets regardless of whether they can be justified financially. Such situations arise, for example, when (1) government regulations require a firm to purchase safety or pollution-control equipment, (2) personnel contracts stipulate the establishment of retirement funds, or (3) a company is required to invest in cafeteria or recreational facilities, either to comply with a labor union contract or because management is persuaded that morale considerations warrant it.

Such situations may seem to be beyond help from capital budgeting. However, the net present value method may assist managers in making a **least-cost decision**—a decision that satisfies certain requirements at the lowest possible cost to the firm. The two major differences between least-cost decisions and all other capital budgeting decisions are:

1. Least-cost decisions are limited to alternatives that fulfill certain imposed requirements.
2. None of the alternatives may produce a positive net present value.

To illustrate, we will assume that New England Steel Company has been told by the Environmental Protection Agency to install a pollution-control device. One alternative would cost $1,000,000 immediately but would not add to operating costs. It would last for 10 years. A second alternative is a device that costs $200,000 immediately but would add $125,000 to annual operating costs. Like the first device, it would last 10 years. Which device should be purchased? The firm uses a 12% discount rate.

The first alternative involves no future cash inflows or outflows. Its outlay cost in net present value terms is its initial cash outlay of $1,000,000. The second alternative has an initial cost of $200,000 plus future cash outflows of $125,000 per year for the next 10 years. Therefore, its outlay cost in net present value terms would be:

Annual cash outflows	×	Discount factor	=	Present value
$125,000	×	5.6502*	=	$706,275
Initial cost				200,000
Outlay cost at net present value				$906,275

*From Table II, 10 years at 12%.

If the company had a choice between installing and not installing, neither alternative would be acceptable because both net present values are negative. However, one of the alternatives must be accepted. Because a cost of $906,275 is less than a cost of $1,000,000, the second alternative should be chosen to minimize costs.

Internal Rate of Return Method

The **internal rate of return method**, also known as the time-adjusted rate of return method or the discounted rate of return method, is similar to the net present value approach in that it emphasizes the profitability of investments and takes into account the time value of money. As a discounted cash flow method, it is superior to either the payback method or the unadjusted rate of return method. Some managers consider the internal rate of return method more diffi-

Investing for a Cleaner World
Businesses have traditionally used capital budgeting to guide them on making wise investments in property, plant, and equipment that will earn a return. However, in recent years, investments in environmental cleanup activities have become extremely common. Companies today face a climate with increasingly significant environmental concerns. Environmental costs have soared, in some cases to billion of dollars each year. Fines and penalties for violation of environmental regulations are substantial. And, due to new sentencing guidelines, strict liability for environmental losses has been imposed on directors and officers of companies. There is currently a myriad of environmental laws forcing companies to spend huge amounts of money to comply with these laws and to clean up environmental damage. Some of the most costly laws are the Clean Air Act, the Clean Water Act, the Resource Conservation and Recovery Act of 1976, the Comprehensive Environmental Response, the Compensation and Liability Act of 1980 (known as Superfund), and the Superfund Amendments Reauthorization Act of 1986 (SARA). The impact of these laws on capital investment decisions can be substantial. For example, under SARA, purchasers of real property are usually financially liable for environmental cleanup costs even if the property was contaminated before it was purchased.

Environmental concerns impact several stages of the capital budgeting decision. First, capital budgeting decision makers must expand traditional company boundaries to consider all entities affected by environmental degradation. Even though a project may be profitable from the firm's perspective, if it pollutes the environment, cleanup liability may make the investment a real loser. Second, environmental laws, current conditions, and trends can significantly affect the feasibility of an investment. Third, in deciding whether an investment is profitable, environmental costs and benefits, as well as environmental risk, must be considered. Finally, once an investment in a capital asset is made, attention must be given to environmental events such as accidents or increased regulation, which might affect the continued viability of the investment.

Source: Devaun Kite, "Capital Budgeting: Integrating Environmental Impact," *Journal of Cost Management*, Summer 1995, Vol. 9, No. 2, pp. 11–14.

internal rate of return method A capital budgeting technique that uses discounted cash flows to find the "true" discount rate of an investment; this true rate produces a net present value of zero.

internal rate of return The "true" discount rate that will produce a net present value of zero when applied to the cash flows of investment inventory goods held for resale.

cult than the net present value method because the computations can be challenging. Some managers, however, prefer to analyze investment alternatives in terms of comparative rates of return rather than net present values.

The **internal rate of return** is defined as the "true" discount rate that an investment yields. For example, assume that your parents have $100,000 that they are considering investing in one of two ways—in a mutual fund containing the stocks of large U.S. companies or in your college education. They learn that the mutual fund investment will yield an average return of 12%. They estimate the increased value of your lifetime annual earnings stemming from your college education and calculate that, after adjusting for the time value of money, the investment in your college education will yield an average return of, say, 20% per year. The 20% number is the internal rate of return generated by an investment in your education; because this return is higher than the return your parents can earn on a mutual fund, they would naturally invest the $100,000 in your future.

Mathematically, the internal rate of return is the discount rate that yields a net present value of zero when applied to the cash flows of an investment—both inflows and outflows.

When using present value tables, the internal rate of return method involves three steps.

1. Calculate the present value factor by dividing the investment cost by the annual net cash inflows.
2. Using applicable present value tables and the life of the investment, find the present value factor closest to the number derived in step 1.
3. Using interpolation, if necessary, find the exact internal rate of return represented by the present value factor in step 1.

Caution

Of course, as mentioned earlier, there may be QUALITATIVE considerations that would cause your parents to invest in your education even if the MONETARY return were expected to be lower than what they could earn in the stock market.

To help you understand this concept, we will again refer to MBK Company's plan to purchase a new truck. For the purpose of this explanation, however, we will ignore the truck's salvage value; later, we will show how to incorporate salvage value into the calculation. The calculations for the MBK example are as follows:

1. Calculate the present value factor with the following formula:

$$\frac{\text{Investment cost}}{\text{Annual net cash inflows}} = \text{Present value factor}$$

$$\frac{\$18,000}{\$5,625} = 3.2000$$

(Note that this is also the formula for calculating the payback period.)

2. In Present Value Table II, find the applicable row for the life of the investment. By moving across the table, you can find the present value factor closest to the number derived in step 1. In our example, the investment's life is known to be 4 years, so find row 4 and move across the row until you come to the factor 3.2397. This is the factor for 9%. The next factor, 3.1699, represents 10%. Since the factor is between these two numbers, the truck purchase yields between a 9 and 10% return.

interpolation A method of determining the internal rate of return when the factor for that rate lies between the factors given in the present value table.

3. If necessary, use **interpolation** to find the exact internal rate of return. Interpolation is most easily visualized by setting up a table as follows:

	Rate of Return (Discount Rate)	Present Value Factors	
		High and True Factors	High and Low Factors
High factor*	9%	3.2397	3.2397
True factor		3.2000	
Low factor	10		3.1699
Differences	1%	0.0397	0.0698

*Note that the high factor is associated with the low rate and that the low factor is associated with the high rate.

The number 0.0397 is the difference between the high factor and the true factor determined in step 1. The number 0.0698 is the difference between the high factor and the low factor. One percent is the difference between the discount rates for the high and the low factors. To find the approximate rate of return in this example, you would make the following calculation:

$$\text{Internal rate of return} = 0.09 + \left(0.01 \times \frac{0.0397}{0.0698}\right) = 0.0957 \text{ or } 9.6\% \text{ (rounded)}$$

What we are doing is adding the proportion $0.0397 \div 0.0698$ of the 1% difference to the low rate to get the true rate. The result, 9.6%, means that if the annual savings of $5,625 were discounted at 9.6%, the net present value of the investment would be zero. (Note that there may be slight differences due to rounding.)

The purpose of interpolation is to determine the "true" rate of interest indicated by the present value factor. Although the factor's true rate of interest is fairly easy to roughly estimate, interpolation produces a more precise estimate.

Computation of internal rates of return is one area in which knowledge of how to use a standard business calculator really pays off. For example, the internal rate of return in the MBK example could be computed using the following keystrokes with a Hewlett-Packard business calculator:

Caution

For you mathematicians, it is necessary to note that this interpolation process only approximates the internal rate of return. This is because the formulas generating the present value factors are nonlinear.

> **Hewlett-Packard Keystrokes:**
>
> 1. −18,000: Press **PV** (you must enter the cash outflow as a NEGATIVE number)
> 2. 5,625: Press **PMT** (this is the annual cash inflow)
> 3. 4: Press **N** (number of years)
> 4. Press **I/YR** for the answer = 9.5642274%

Using the Internal Rate of Return

hurdle rate The minimum rate of return that an investment must provide in order to be acceptable.

To determine the value of an investment, management must compare the project's internal rate of return with the company's usual discount rate, often called the **hurdle rate**, or the rate that must be cleared for a project to be acceptable. If the internal rate is higher than or equal to the company's hurdle rate, the project is acceptable. If the internal rate is lower than the hurdle rate, the project is usually rejected. As with any of the capital budgeting techniques, even if the investment is acceptable from an internal rate of return standpoint, qualitative factors must still be considered before a final decision can be made.

FYI:

A calculator actually computes the internal rate of return using a repeated interpolation process; most business calculators take a couple of seconds to come up with the final answer.

The Problem of Uneven Cash Flows

In the truck example, annual cash flows were the same because salvage value was ignored. However, when salvage value is considered, the investment will have uneven cash flows. When this occurs, an annuity table cannot be used. Each cash flow has to be discounted back at an assumed discount rate until the net present value of all the cash flows discounted at this rate approximates zero. The rate that results after a trial-and-error process is the internal rate of return. A simplified example of this method is shown on page 967. Although this can be a tedious procedure, it is facilitated by using a business calculator. For example, computing the internal rate of return of the MBK truck purchase, including consideration of the $1,800 salvage value cash inflow at the end of four years, would be done as follows using a Hewlett-Packard business calculator:

> **Hewlett-Packard Keystrokes:**
>
> 1. −18,000: Press **PV**
> 2. 5,625: Press **PMT**
> 3. 4: Press **N** (number of years)
> 4. 1,800: Press **FV** (this is a single amount occurring at the end of the period of time indicated in step 3)
> 5. Press **I/YR** for the answer = 12.5774719%

Note that the internal rate of return is higher (12.6% vs. 9.6%) when the additional cash inflow from the salvage value is considered.

In addition to using present value tables and business calculators, net present values and internal rates of return can also be calculated using Excel spreadsheet functions. These calculations are illustrated in the appendix to this chapter.

TO SUMMARIZE: The net present value method is a capital budgeting technique that takes into consideration the time value of money by discounting future cash flows to their present values. By comparing the discounted net cash inflows and outflows, this method derives a net present value figure. If the net present value is zero or positive, the project is acceptable from a quantitative stand-point. The discount rate used is the minimum rate of interest that a company will accept. The net present value method also may be used in making least-cost decisions. The internal rate of return is a capital budgeting technique that utilizes discounted cash flows. It derives the "true" rate of return for an investment by comparing the cost of the project with the amounts to be returned. This produces a present value factor that is associated with the internal rate of return for the project. Often, the rate must be derived by interpolation and, if uneven cash flows are involved, by trial and error or business calculator.

Comparative Example of Capital Budgeting Techniques

To solidify your understanding of the capital budgeting techniques introduced thus far in this chapter, we present the example of Will's Pit Stop, a small service station that sells gasoline on a self-service basis as its only source of revenue. Because one wall of the enclosed station area is vacant, the manager has decided to install one or two food vending machines. A sales representative has suggested that a freezer for ice cream and other dairy items would do well. The freezer would cost $42,045. It has an estimated useful life of 10 years, with an expected salvage value of $4,000. The sales representative is confident that the freezer will generate revenues of $15,000 a year on goods that cost $7,600. The freezer will need $8,000 of servicing during its fifth year of operation. The increase in Will's average yearly net income if the freezer is purchased is estimated to be $3,500. Note that the difference between annual net cash inflows of $7,400 ($15,000 − $7,600) and the estimated average net income of $3,500 is due to non-cash expenses, such as depreciation, which are deducted on the income statement.

The manager of the station has come to you for advice, indicating that the firm's hurdle rate is 12%—Will's estimated cost of capital. Compute the payback period, the unadjusted rate of return, the net present value, and the internal rate of return of the project. Then give your recommendations. Note that companies generally do not analyze an investment with all these techniques. They are all used here for illustrative purposes.

1. *Payback period:*

$$\frac{\$50,045 \text{ (investment cost)*}}{\$7,400 \text{ (annual net cash inflows)}} = 6.76 \text{ years}$$

*$42,045 initial investment + $8,000 servicing cost after 5 years.

Note that the salvage value is not considered here because it is received in the tenth year.

2. *Unadjusted rate of return:*

$$\frac{\$3,500 \text{ (increase in future average annual net income)}}{\$42,045 \text{ (initial investment cost)}} = 8.3\%$$

3. *Net present value:*

	Time Period	Cash Flows	Present Value Factor	Present Value of Cash Flows
Present value of cash inflows:				
Net revenues ($15,000 − $7,600) ..	Years 1–10	$ 7,400	5.6502*	$41,811
Salvage value	Year 10	4,000	0.3220**	1,288
Total cash inflows				$43,099
Present value of cash outflows:				
Initial cost	Today	$42,045	1.0000	$42,045
Servicing cost	Year 5	8,000	0.5674***	4,539
Total cash outflows				$46,584
Net present value				$ (3,485)

*From Table II, 10 years at 12%.
**From Table I, 10 years at 12%.
***From Table I, 5 years at 12%.

4. *Internal rate of return:*

Since the cash flows are uneven due to the servicing cost and the salvage value, a trial-and-error process is required in computing the internal rate of return. From the net present value method, we can see that the 12% rate is too high. A 10% rate is selected for trial, and the net present value at that rate is calculated.

	Time Period	Cash Flows	Present Value Factor	Present Value of Cash Flows
Present value of cash inflows:				
Net revenues ($15,000 − $7,600) ..	Years 1–10	$ 7,400	6.1446*	$45,470
Salvage value	Year 10	4,000	0.3855**	1,542
Total cash inflows				$47,012
Present value of cash outflows:				
Initial cost	Today	$42,045	1.0000	$42,045
Servicing cost	Year 5	8,000	0.6209***	4,967
Total cash outflows				$47,012
Net present value				$ 0

*From Table II, 10 years at 10%.
**From Table I, 10 years at 10%.
***From Table I, 5 years at 10%.

At 10%, the net present value is zero. Therefore, 10% is the internal rate of return.

On the basis of the foregoing information, you should recommend rejection. The payback period is well within the life of the investment; however, it is not short enough to warrant any special consideration. The unadjusted rate of return is only 8.3%, and the internal, or adjusted, rate of return of 10% is well under Will's hurdle rate, which means that the project's net present value is negative. Therefore, on the basis of the quantitative results, the manager should look for an opportunity that is more attractive financially. However, if the 10% rate is close enough to the 12% hurdle rate, perhaps qualitative factors, such as the probability that the additional customers attracted by the freezer items will also buy gas, might make the project acceptable.

Qualitative Factors in Strategic and Capital Investment Decisions

4 Understand the need for evaluating qualitative factors in strategic and capital investment decisions.

In explaining the fundamental concepts of capital budgeting, we have focused on the financial (quantitative) aspects of analyzing investment alternatives. However, a discussion of capital budgeting is incomplete without mentioning factors that cannot be reduced to numbers. These qualitative factors are often of overriding importance in strategic and capital investment decisions. Here, we consider three types of qualitative factors: (1) an investment's effect on the *quality* of products and services offered, (2) an investment's effect on the *time* with which products and services can be produced and delivered to customers, and (3) other qualitative factors. Thus far in the chapter, we have made the determination of whether a capital investment decision is a good one solely on the basis of its financial return, computed using one of four methods. If the financial return was positive, our conclusion was to invest; if the financial return was negative, we recommended that the project not be undertaken. However, throughout the management accounting chapters of this book, we have focused on three aspects of decision making: cost, quality, and time.

Quality and time considerations can sometimes dictate that a capital investment should be made even if the financial returns don't justify the expenditure. For example, if buying a new machine will help the company produce higher quality products or deliver those products to its

FYI:

In today's world economy, most companies have to be competitive on a cost basis. What makes good companies even better is their attention to quality and time (speed of delivery of products and services) considerations—the same factors that are important in capital investment decisions.

customers faster, the machine may be a good investment. Companies know that their competitors are doing everything possible to speed up delivery and increase quality. Thus, even if a company has a cost of capital of 12%, and an investment will return only 8%, if buying a machine will allow the company to deliver products or services faster than competitors, the purchase may be a good one. Likewise, if buying a machine will mean fewer defects, higher quality, and more satisfied customers, the purchase may be a good one. Companies must always be continuously improving in order to keep up with or surpass their competition. Unfortunately, capital investments often are long-term decisions that make continuous improvement difficult. Thus, even if a company has not completely recovered its investment in a capital project, recognizing that competitors have better or more efficient equipment may motivate a company to abandon an investment (a machine that works fine, for example) and make a costlier new investment that will allow the company to remain competitive. The impact of quality and time on capital budgeting decisions cannot be underestimated. In fact, because of the need to continuously improve, companies are always looking for shorter and shorter capital investment opportunities so that they are more flexible, such as leasing or renting equipment and other operating assets where possible.

In addition to quality and time, there are a number of other qualitative factors that must be considered when making capital budgeting decisions. Consider, for example, consumer safety. In one lawsuit, a major U.S. automobile manufacturer was cited for producing cars that were not as safe as they should have been. The company was essentially accused of comparing the present value of the legal and other costs that might result from the unsafe condition of the cars with the cash savings from manufacturing the cars more cheaply, and of choosing the less expensive route. The question was then posed: What is the value of a life? This situation provides a dramatic illustration of the need to include qualitative factors in capital investment decisions.

Other qualitative factors include such matters as (1) government regulations, (2) pollution control and environmental protection, (3) worker safety, (4) company image and prestige,

business environment

Ethics in Capital Investment Decisions In 1990, after making substantial investments in two plants in Thailand and one in China, HUNTSMAN CHEMICAL CORPORATION (HCC) abruptly sold out its business interests when unethical practices were encountered. After winning a major bid in competition with worldwide firms, HCC was virtually guaranteed a significant profit on a $40 million investment. It became clear, however, that business practices involving bribes, payoffs, inflated invoices, and the like were going to be a part of the deal. As soon as Jon Huntsman, founder, chairman, and CEO of HCC, became aware of these unethical prac-

tices, he called his managers home and refused to participate further in the projects. HCC sold all its interests and walked away from the deal. When asked about this situation, Mr. Huntsman was quoted as saying, "We simply refuse to carry out negotiations based on factors other than competitiveness, quality, and productivity."

Although the quantitative factors led HCC to become involved in a major capital investment project, other factors caused the company to withdraw. As noted in the text, qualitative factors often override purely quantitative results.

Source: Adapted from "The Heart of the Deal," *Wharton Alumni Magazine* (Summer 1991), pp. 8–14.

(5) preferences of owners and management, and (6) the general welfare of the community in which the company operates. The business environment on the previous page provides a specific example of one company that combined strategic objectives with humanitarian motives in making a major capital investment decision. Many more examples could be mentioned, but the point is that numbers alone do not control the investment decisions of a good manager. Quality, time, and other qualitative, as well as quantitative, factors should all be considered in reaching long-term investment decisions.

> **TO SUMMARIZE:** In making capital budgeting decisions, the effects of a decision on the quality of and the time with which products can be delivered to customers must be considered. In addition, other qualitative factors such as litigation effects, government regulations, environmental impact, worker safety, company image, preferences of owners, and welfare of community must also be considered.

In the previous sections of the chapter, we have explained the importance of capital budgeting and the concepts underlying strategic and capital investment decisions, including the time value of money. We have also described and illustrated the four most commonly used capital budgeting techniques. Finally, we have discussed briefly the need for evaluating qualitative factors in any investment decision. In the expanded material, we explain how to use sensitivity analysis in dealing with uncertainty in capital budgeting decisions and the concept of "capital rationing," which is the process of ranking capital investment projects. We also discuss the impact of taxes on capital budgeting decisions.

Dealing with Uncertainty in Strategic and Capital Investment Decisions

5 Use sensitivity analysis to assess the potential effects of uncertainty in capital budgeting.

sensitivity analysis A method of assessing the reasonableness of a decision that was based upon estimates; involves calculating how far reality can differ from an estimate without invalidating the decision.

Throughout this chapter, we have applied capital budgeting techniques as though the future were certain. That is, we have assumed perfect knowledge of expected cash flows, the useful lives of assets, salvage values, and so forth. Actually, the future is almost always uncertain, and the applicable numbers are estimates. By using "sensitivity analysis," we can evaluate, at least to some extent, the degree to which an error in a particular estimate is likely to invalidate the decision reached. Essentially, **sensitivity analysis** is a method of examining the effect of changes in an estimate on the results of the calculations. We use sensitivity analysis to determine whether the conclusions still seem reasonable under modified circumstances.

To illustrate this approach, we will consider the following situation. An asset can be purchased for $100,000; it is expected to provide $20,000 of annual net cash inflows. It has a 10-year life and an expected salvage value of $10,000. The hurdle rate is 8%. We can use either of the discounted cash flow techniques to assess this investment opportunity. For illustrative purposes, we use both.

Net present value method:

Discounted expected cash inflows ($20,000 × 6.7101*)	$134,202
Discounted disposal value ($10,000 × 0.4632**)	4,632
Net cash inflows	$138,834
Net cash outflows	100,000
Net present value	$ 38,834

*From Table II, 10 years at 8%.
**From Table I, 10 years at 8%.

Internal rate of return method:

$$\frac{\text{Investment cost (\$100,000} - \text{\$4,632)}}{\text{Annual net cash inflows}} = \frac{\$95,368}{\$20,000} = 4.7684 \text{ present value factor}$$

For 10 years, the internal rate of return is between 16 and 18%.

The net present value is greater than zero, and the internal rate of return is considerably more than the minimum acceptable rate of 8%. Therefore, from a quantitative standpoint, we should accept this investment opportunity. But what about the uncertainties? What if $20,000 is not received each year? What if the asset does not last 10 years? What if the disposal value is less than $10,000? Sensitivity analysis enables us to evaluate the potential effect of each of these uncertainties.

If Expected Cash Flows Are Uncertain

To assess the amount of error we can tolerate in expected cash flows, we need to determine the break-even amount of net cash flow—that is, the annual cash flow that would earn the minimum rate of 8%. We accomplish this by determining the discounted net cost of the investment and dividing that amount by the present value factor for the minimum acceptable interest rate (8%) for 10 years.

Computations:

Initial cost	$100,000
Discounted disposal value	4,632
Net cost of investment	$ 95,368

$95,368 ÷ 6.7101 (present value factor of 8%) = $14,213 cash flow return in order to break even.

We could then assess how likely it is that this project will generate annual cash flows of at least $14,213. Any amount above that, of course, would be acceptable with an 8% hurdle rate.

If Useful Life Is Uncertain

To assess the amount of error we can tolerate in the estimate that the asset will have a useful life of 10 years, we take the discounted net cost of the investment and divide it by the expected cash flows. This produces a present value factor of 4.7684. Looking under 8% interest in Table II, we find that this factor falls between 6 and 7 years. Thus, assuming that the $20,000 estimate of cash inflows is reliable, the asset does not have to last a full 10 years for the investment to be acceptable. In fact, only 7 years are necessary.

Computations:

$$\frac{\text{Net cost of investment}}{\text{Annual net cash inflows}} = \frac{\$95,368}{\$20,000} = 4.7684 \text{ at } 8\%$$

$$= \text{Between 6 and 7 years of useful life in order to break even}$$

If Disposal Value Is Uncertain

Usually, the disposal value is an insignificant factor in the investment decision. However, to see if it would make a difference in the acceptability of a project, we can assume it is zero. In our example, if the asset has a zero disposal value, the investment cost of $100,000 divided by $20,000 annual net cash inflows equals a 5.0 present value factor. For an assumed 10-year life, the return is between 15 and 16%, which is clearly acceptable according to our 8% hurdle rate.[1]

---

1 In this example, we looked at the uncertainty of each variable separately. Using computer simulation, uncertainty in all variables could have been examined simultaneously.

Computations:

$$\frac{\text{Initial investment cost}}{\text{Annual net cash inflows}} = \frac{\$100,000}{\$20,000} = 5.0 \text{ for 10 years}$$

$$= 15 \text{ to } 16\% \text{ return}$$

TO SUMMARIZE: Capital budgeting decisions always involve estimates of future amounts, and estimates involve uncertainty. To evaluate the potential effect of this uncertainty, we can use sensitivity analysis, which shows how far reality can deviate from the estimate without invalidating an investment decision.

Capital Rationing

6 Explain how to use capital budgeting techniques in ranking capital investment projects.

Thus far, we have dealt exclusively with the screening function of capital budgeting—that is, determining whether an investment meets a minimum standard of acceptability. In many cases, however, a company has not one but several investment opportunities, all of which offer returns in excess of the company's hurdle rate. Since a company's resources are limited, some projects should be given priority. The ranking function of capital budgeting enables management to select the most profitable investments first. Projects should not be ranked, however, until the screening process is completed.

Another factor to consider in ranking projects is whether particular projects are compatible, complementary, or mutually exclusive. We assume mutually exclusive projects in this section on ranking, that is, that each project is independent and adds neither an advantage nor a disadvantage to other projects. Certainly, there are situations where the acceptance of one project adds value, directly or indirectly, to another project and might therefore alter a ranking consideration. These factors, like the qualitative factors that we discussed earlier, may significantly influence the strategy involved in a capital investment decision.

capital rationing Allocating limited resources among ranked acceptable investments.

The objective of ranking is to help a company use limited resources to the best advantage by investing only in the projects that offer the highest return. The process of allocating limited resources based on the ranking of projects is called **capital rationing**. Either the internal rate of return method or the net present value method may be used in ranking investments.

Ranking by the Internal Rate of Return Method

If the internal rate of return method is used, investments that pass the screening test are ranked in the order of their internal rate of return, from highest to lowest. This method is simple, requires no additional computations, and is widely used.

To illustrate the process, we will assume the following situation. Sundance Enterprises is considering six capital investment projects. Management requires a minimum return of 15% on its investments. The six projects are first screened, then ranked by their internal rates of return, as shown below.

Project	Expected Rate of Return	Screening Decision	Ranking Decision
A	10%	Reject	—
B	18	Accept	3
C	12	Reject	—
D	22	Accept	1
E	20	Accept	2
F	16	Accept	4

From a quantitative standpoint, Sundance should invest in all four of the projects that passed the screening test. If resources are limited, however, capital must be rationed. In this situation, the ranking process indicates that limited resources would be allocated to project D first, then to projects E, B, and F, respectively. This conclusion ignores the additional complications of the investments having different lives. It also does not consider differences in the size of the initial investment.

Ranking by the Net Present Value Method

If the net present value method is used for ranking investments, additional computations are necessary because the net present value of one investment usually cannot be directly compared with that of another. Only projects that require the same amount of investment are comparable. For example, you cannot readily compare an investment of $10,000 that produces a $2,000 net present value (project A) with a $20,000 investment that also results in a $2,000 net present value (project B), although project A certainly seems more desirable. To rank such projects, we need to compute a **profitability index**.

profitability index The present value of net cash inflows divided by the cost of an investment.

$$\frac{\text{Present value of net cash inflows}}{\text{Investment cost}} = \text{Profitability index}$$

Projects can then be ranked from highest to lowest in terms of their respective profitability indexes. The project with the highest profitability index should obviously be undertaken first; other projects will be undertaken according to the amount of resources available for investment.

To illustrate the ranking of projects using the net present value method, we will use the example in the preceding paragraph. The amount of the investment and its net present value are added to arrive at the present value of net cash inflows. Then, present value is divided by the investment cost to calculate a profitability index and respective ranking.

	Project A	Project B
Present value of net cash inflows	$12,000 (a)	$22,000 (a)
Investment cost	10,000 (b)	20,000 (b)
Net present value	$ 2,000	$ 2,000
Profitability index (a ÷ b)	1.20	1.10
Rank	1	2

Note that the profitability index must be 1.0 or greater for a project to be acceptable; this means that the net present value is at least zero.

Exhibit 2 summarizes the rules for making screening and ranking decisions using the net present value (with a profitability index) and the internal rate of return methods. Note that each technique leads management to the same screening decision. However, the methods may produce different rankings. In selecting between the two for the purposes of ranking, the profitability index is preferred because it considers directly the amount invested in each project, which results in the selection of the most profitable alternative.

TO SUMMARIZE: The screening function determines if projects are acceptable; the ranking function enables management to select the most profitable investment first and thus use limited resources to the best advantage. Ranking may be accomplished by the internal rate of return or by the net present value method.

Exhibit 2: Capital Budgeting Decision Rules

Selected Capital Budgeting Techniques	Decision Rules	
	Screening	Ranking
Net present value method (NPV) using the profitability index (PI)	If PI > 1, invest If PI = 1, indifferent If PI < 1, don't invest	For two projects, a and b; If PI$_a$ > PI$_b$, pick a, etc.
Internal rate of return (IRR)	If IRR > CC*, invest If IRR = CC, indifferent If IRR < CC, don't invest	For two projects, a and b; If IRR$_a$ > IRR$_b$, pick a, etc.

*CC = cost of capital, or hurdle rate.

Income Tax Considerations in Capital Budgeting Decisions

7 Explain how income taxes affect capital budgeting decisions.

To keep the concepts simple, when considering capital budgeting decisions thus far in the chapter, we ignored the effects of income taxes on capital budgeting decisions. Unfortunately, ignoring tax effects is not very realistic because capital budgeting decisions can be significantly affected by tax considerations. As an example of the income tax effects, the net cash inflows from the profits stemming from a project are reduced because those profits are taxed. On the other hand, any losses stemming from a project will generate tax savings. And the depreciation of the cost of an investment also generates tax deductions, leading to cash savings. Such tax effects can be so significant that the net present value of the cash flows changes from positive to negative, or vice versa.

To illustrate these income tax effects, we will use the Will's Pit Stop example discussed earlier. Recall that the gas station owner was considering installing a freezer for ice cream and other dairy products. The cost of the freezer was $42,045. It was expected to have a salvage value of $4,000 at the end of its 10-year useful life and to generate revenues of $15,000 per year on goods that cost $7,600. Thus, the cash flow was expected to be $7,400 ($15,000 − $7,600). At the end of the fifth year, the freezer would need $8,000 of repairs and servicing. Based on this information, the management of Will's Pit Stop decided not to buy the freezer because, at a hurdle rate of 12%, the net present value was negative. Furthermore, the internal rate of return was only 10%.

In making this decision, management neglected to consider the income tax effects. Here, we will incorporate the tax effects of the investment, based on the following initial assumptions: (1) Will's Pit Stop is a corporation with an effective tax rate of 25%, and (2) the hurdle rate of 12% is an after-tax rate. Assumption (2) means that the calculation of the cost of capital reflects the after-tax cost of interest expense, which is a deduction in computing a corporation's tax liability.

To compute the present values of the cash inflows and outflows, we must first convert them to after-tax amounts. This conversion is accomplished as follows:

1. Income on the freezer before taxes was $7,400 ($15,000 revenues − $7,600 cost of goods sold). This $7,400 represents the before-tax net cash inflow from the freezer. At a 25% tax rate, the after-tax net cash inflow is $5,550 ($7,400 × 0.25 = $1,850; $7,400 − $1,850 = $5,550). In other words, the company keeps 75% (1.00 less the tax rate of 25%) of the before-tax net cash inflow from the freezer ($7,400 × 0.75 = $5,550).

2. The U.S. income tax regulations allow a company to reduce its income tax liability by expensing some of the cost of tangible personal property immediately in the year of

FYI:

In 2003, the annual cap on the amount an individual could elect to expense under Section 179 was $25,000.

acquisition. The tax people call this the "Section 179 expensing election." If Will's Pit Stop elects to expense $10,000 of the cost of the freezer, this amount is deducted from the original cost in computing the depreciation base. The tax savings from taking this deduction in the year of acquisition is $2,500 ($10,000 × 0.25 tax rate).

3. Although the freezer has an estimated useful life of 10 years, the modified accelerated cost recovery system (MACRS), which is the depreciation method used for income tax purposes in the United States, would allow Will's Pit Stop to write the freezer off over a 7-year period on an accelerated basis (using the double-declining-balance method). Accordingly, under MACRS Will's Pit Stop will use the 7-year period to deduct the $32,045 ($42,045 − $10,000) in cost that remains after the Section 179 election discussed in item 2. The depreciation deduction for each year will be as follows:

Year	Pretax Depreciation Deduction
1	$ 4,578 ($32,045 on a double-declining-balance basis for ½ year)
2	7,848 [($32,045 − $4,578) ÷ 7 × 2]
3	5,605 [($27,467 − $7,848) ÷ 7 × 2]
4	4,004 [($19,619 − $5,605) ÷ 7 × 2]
5	2,860 [($14,014 − $4,004) ÷ 7 × 2]
6	2,860 [straight-line: ($10,010 − $2,860) ÷ 2½ years]
7	2,860 (straight-line)
8	1,430 (straight-line for ½ year)
	$32,045

Caution

Under MACRS, a half year of depreciation is deducted in the first and last year of the asset's life. In addition, estimated salvage values are ignored in the computations.

Note that the company shifts to the straight-line method in Year 6 in order to deduct as much depreciation as possible in that year and thereafter. As shown in Exhibit 3, at a 25% tax rate, the MACRS deduction will save the company $1,145 in taxes in the first year in addition to the $2,500 saved by expensing the first $10,000 of the freezer's cost under Section 179.

4. Under MACRS, the entire cost of the freezer will have been written off in the first eight years of its life. If the freezer is sold at the end of 10 years at its $4,000 estimated salvage value, there will be a $4,000 gain on the sale. This gain will be taxable as ordinary income at 25% (assuming no change in tax rates), so the after-tax cash inflow will be only $3,000 ($4,000 × 0.75).

5. The estimated repairs and servicing cost of $8,000 at the end of Year 5 is an expense deduction from the company's income for that year. Therefore, the net cost of this expense to the company is only $6,000 ($8,000 × 0.75).

These adjusted cash flows can now be used to compute the net present value of the cash inflows and outflows that would result if the freezer were purchased. The present values of these cash flows are presented in Exhibit 3 at three different hurdle rates: 8, 10, and 12%.

Three different rates are used to illustrate that the net present value decreases as the hurdle rate increases from 8 to 12%. In other words, as the rate of return increases, the present value of the cash inflows decreases in relation to the present value of the cash outflows, eventually changing the net present value from positive to negative. The point at which the present values of the inflows and outflows are equal reflects the expected internal rate of return. If the expected return is less than the company's hurdle rate, it is unlikely that the company will acquire the asset unless there are compensating qualitative factors.

Exhibit 3 shows that the tax effects on cash inflows and outflows, given a tax rate of 25%, reduce the rate of return on Will's Pit Stop's proposed freezer from a pretax 10% calculated earlier in the chapter to just over 8%. This occurs because taxes reduce the present value of the

Exhibit 3: Income Tax Effects of Capital Budgeting

Will's Pit Stop
Net Present Value of Cash Inflows and Outflows (25% Tax Rate)

Type of Cash Flow	Period	After-Tax Cash Flow	8% Present Value	8% Amount*	10% Present Value	10% Amount*	12% Present Value	12% Amount*
Inflows:								
Revenue less cost of goods sold (net of tax): ($15,000 − $7,600) × 0.75 ...	Years 1–10	$ 5,550	6.7101	$37,241	6.1446	$34,103	5.6502	$31,359
MACRS expensing ($10,000 × 0.25)	Year 1	2,500	0.9259**	2,315	0.9091	2,273	0.8929	2,232
MACRS [($42,045 − $10,000): $32,045 at 7-year, 200%]:								
$4,578 × 0.25 ...	Year 1	$ 1,145	0.9259	$ 1,060	0.9091	$ 1,041	0.8929	$ 1,022
7,848 × 0.25 ...	2	1,962	0.8573	1,682	0.8264	1,621	0.7972	1,564
5,605 × 0.25 ...	3	1,401	0.7938	1,112	0.7513	1,053	0.7118	997
4,004 × 0.25 ...	4	1,001	0.7350	736	0.6830	684	0.6355	636
2,860 × 0.25 ...	5	715	0.6806	487	0.6209	444	0.5674	406
2,860 × 0.25 ...	6	715	0.6302	451	0.5645	404	0.5066	362
2,860 × 0.25 ...	7	715	0.5835	417	0.5132	367	0.4523	323
1,430 × 0.25 ...	8	357	0.5403	193	0.4665	167	0.4039	144
				$ 6,138		$ 5,781		$ 5,454
Salvage value ($4,000 × 0.75)...	End of Year 10	3,000	0.4632	$ 1,390	0.3855	$ 1,157	0.3220	$ 966
Total cash inflows ...				$47,084		$43,314		$40,011
Outflows:								
Initial freezer cost...	Today	42,045	1.0000	$42,045	1.0000	$42,045	1.0000	$42,045
Repairs and servicing cost ($8,000 × 0.75).	End of Year 5	6,000	0.6806	4,084	0.6209	3,725	0.5674	3,404
Total cash outflows ...				$46,129		$45,770		$45,449
Excess cash inflow (outflow)...				$ 955		$ (2,456)		$ (5,438)

*After-tax cash flow × present value.
**Note that this is the present value of the cash flow discounted for 1 year.

cash inflows more than they reduce the present value of the cash outflows. (Remember the initial cost is already at its present value.) If the tax rate were at the U.S. federal corporate rate of 35%, which is the rate that would be applicable to almost all large U.S. corporations, the internal rate of return would decrease even further. This is because the negative effect of the increased tax expense on gross margin is greater than the positive effect of the increased tax savings from expensing the first $10,000 of the freezer's cost and from the tax effects of the annual depreciation deduction and the deduction for repairs. In general, income taxes reduce the internal rate of return—and the higher the tax rate, the greater the reduction.

For the company to justify purchasing the freezer in the face of a 12% hurdle rate, the company would have to increase its gross margin significantly (increase sales volume with the same freezer capacity). You should also keep in mind that when the net present value at a selected hurdle rate is at or near zero, important qualitative factors not incorporated into the calculations of net present value will be the primary determinants of whether the asset is acquired.

TO SUMMARIZE: The cash inflows and outflows of capital budgeting decisions must be converted to after-tax amounts before the present values are computed in order to obtain a realistic measure of net present value. Income taxes cause after-tax amounts of both cash revenues and cash expenses to be less than their before-tax amounts. Depreciation is a noncash expense, but because depreciation can be deducted in the computation of taxable income, depreciation results in a cash inflow in the form of income tax savings.

Appendix: The Time Value of Money

Present Value and Future Value Concepts

The concepts of present value and future value are used to measure the effect of time on the value of money. To illustrate, if you are to receive $100 one year from today, is it worth $100 today? Obviously not, because if you had the $100 today you could either use it now or invest it and earn interest. If the $100 isn't to be received for one year, those options are not available. The present value of $1 is the value today of $1 to be received or paid in the future, given a specified interest rate. To determine the value today of money to be received or paid in the future, we must "discount" the future amount (reduce the amount to its present value) by an appropriate interest rate. For example, if money can earn 10% per year, $100 to be received one year from now is approximately equal to $90.91 received today.

Putting it another way, if $90.91 is invested today in an account that earns 10% interest for one year, the interest earned will be $9.09 ($90.91 × 10% × 1 year = $9.09). The sum of the $90.91 principal plus $9.09 interest would equal $100 at the end of one year. Thus, the present value of $100 to be received (or paid) in one year with 10% interest is $90.91. This present value relationship can be diagramed as follows:

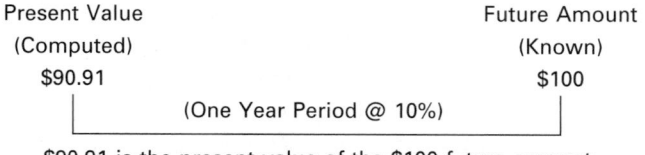

Present Value (Computed) $90.91 — (One Year Period @ 10%) — Future Amount (Known) $100

$90.91 is the present value of the $100 future amount.

The relationships in this diagram can be described in two ways. We have just looked at the relationship by recognizing that the $90.91 is the present value of $100 to be received one year from now when interest is 10%. In this example, the $100 to be received one year from now is known, and the present value of $90.91 must be computed. We are computing a present value amount from a known future value amount.

Another way to look at the relationship is on a future value basis. Future values apply when the amount today ($90.91) is known, and the future amount must be calculated. Future values are exactly the opposite of present values. Thinking in terms of future values, $100 is the future amount we can expect to receive in one year, given a present known amount of $90.91 when the interest rate is 10%. We can diagram this relationship as follows:

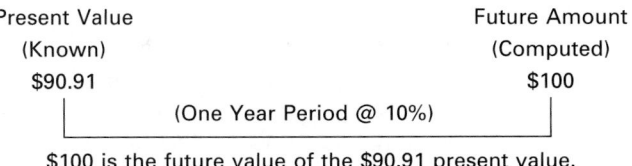

Present Value	Future Amount
(Known)	(Computed)
$90.91	$100

(One Year Period @ 10%)

$100 is the future value of the $90.91 present value.

Present and future values can be calculated using formulas. However, if more than one period is involved, the calculations become rather complicated. Therefore, it is more convenient to use either a present value table or a calculator that gives the present value of $1 for various numbers of periods and interest rates (see Table I, page 983) or a future value table that gives the future value of $1 for various numbers of periods and interest rates (see Table III, page 985). We will illustrate the use of both a present value table and a future value table.

Present Value Table

To use a present value table, you simply locate the appropriate number of periods in the left-most column and the interest rate in the row at the top of the table. The intersection of the row and column is the factor representing the present value of $1 for the number of periods and the relevant interest rate. To find the present value of an amount other than $1, multiply the factor in the table by that amount.

To illustrate the use of a present value table (Table I) to find the present value of a known future amount, assume that $10,000 is to be paid four years from today when the interest rate is 10%. What is the present value of the $10,000 payment?

Amount of payment	$10,000
Present value factor of $1 to be paid in 4 periods	
at 10% interest (from Table I)	×0.6830
Present value of payment	$ 6,830

This present value amount, $6,830, is the amount that could be paid today to satisfy the obligation that is due four years from now. As indicated, this procedure is sometimes referred to as "discounting." Thus, we say that $10,000 discounted for four years at 10% is $6,830. Stated another way, if $6,830 is invested today in an account that pays 10% interest, in four years the balance in that account would be $10,000.

The same present value computed in the previous example can be obtained using a business calculator. The necessary keystrokes are illustrated below. *Note:* The exact sequences of keystrokes illustrated are for a Hewlett-Packard business calculator; the keystrokes for other business calculators are similar if not exactly the same.

Hewlett-Packard Keystrokes for Present Value of a Single Payment:

1. 10,000: Press **FV** (this is the amount of the future payment)
2. 4: Press **N** (number of years)
3. 10: Press **I** (interest rate)
4. Press **PV** for the answer = $6,830.13455 = $6,830 (rounded)

Future Value Table

To find the future value of an amount that is known today, you use a future value table. When using a future value table, you simply locate the appropriate number of periods in the leftmost column and the interest rate in the row at the top of the table. The intersection of the row and column is the factor representing the future value of $1 for the number of periods and the relevant interest rate. To find the future value of an amount other than $1, multiply the factor in the table by that amount.

To illustrate the use of a future value table (Table III), we will use the same information that was presented before, except that we will now assume that the present value of $6,830 is known, not the future amount of $10,000. Assume that we have a savings account with a current balance of $6,830 that earns interest of 10%. What will be the balance in that account in four years?

Present value in savings account	$ 6,830
Future value factor of $1 in 4 periods	
at 10% interest (from Table III)	×1.4641
Future value	$10,000*

*Rounded

Hewlett-Packard Keystrokes for Future Value of a Single Payment:

1. 6,830: Press **PV** (this is the amount of the current payment)
2. 4: Press **N** (number of years)
3. 10: Press **I** (interest rate)
4. Press **FV** for the answer = $9,999.80300 = $10,000 (rounded)

When computing future values, we often use the term *compounding* to mean the frequency with which interest is added to the principal. Thus, we say that interest of 10% has been compounded once a year (annually) to arrive at a future value at the end of four years of $10,000. If the interest is added more or less frequently than once a year, the future amount will be different.

The preceding example assumed an annual compounding period for interest. If the 10% interest had been compounded semiannually (twice a year) for four years, the calculation would have involved using a 5% (one-half of the 10%) rate for 8 periods (4 years × 2 periods per year) instead of 10% for 4 periods. To illustrate, what is the present value of $10,000 to be paid in four years if interest of 10% is compounded semiannually?

Amount of payment	$10,000
Present value factor of $1 to be paid in 8 periods	
at 5% interest (from Table I)	×0.6768
Present value of payment	$ 6,768

Thus, the present value of $10,000 to be paid in four years is $6,768 if interest is compounded semiannually. Likewise, if semiannual compounding is used to determine the future value of $6,768 in four years at 10% compounded semiannually, the result is as follows:

Present value in savings account	$ 6,768
Future value factor of $1 in 8 periods	
at 5% interest (from Table III)	×1.4775
Future value	$10,000*

*Rounded

Note that the present value ($6,768) is lower with semiannual compounding than with annual compounding ($6,830). The more frequently interest is compounded, the greater the total amount of interest deducted (in computing present values) or added (in computing future values).

Hewlett-Packard Keystrokes for Present Value of a Single Payment:

1. 10,000: Press **FV** (this is the amount of the future payment)
2. 8: Press **N** (number of semiannual periods)
3. 5: Press **I** (interest rate per semiannual period)
4. Press **PV** for the answer = $6,768.39362 = $6,768 (rounded)

Hewlett-Packard Keystrokes for Future Value of a Single Payment:

1. 6,768: Press **PV** (this is the amount of the current payment)
2. 8: Press **N** (number of semiannual periods)
3. 5: Press **I** (interest rate per semiannual period)
4. Press **FV** for the answer = $9,999.41844 = $10,000 (rounded)

Since interest may also be compounded quarterly, monthly, daily, or for some other period, you should learn the relationship of interest to the compounding period. Semiannual interest means that you double the interest periods and halve the annual interest rate; with quarterly interest you quadruple the periods and take one-fourth of the annual interest rate. The formula for interest rate is:

$$\frac{\text{Yearly interest rate}}{\text{Compounding periods per year}} = \text{Interest rate per compounding period}$$

The number of interest periods is simply the number of periods per year times the number of years. That formula is:

$$\frac{\text{Compounding}}{\text{periods per year}} \times \frac{\text{Number}}{\text{of years}} = \frac{\text{Number of}}{\text{interest periods}}$$

The Present Value of an Annuity

In discussing present values and future values, we have assumed only a single present value or future value with one of the amounts known and the other to be computed. With liabilities, we generally know the future amount that must be paid and would like to compute the present value of that future payment.

Many long-term liabilities involve a series of payments rather than one lump-sum payment. For example, a company might purchase equipment under an installment agreement requiring payments of $5,000 each year for five years. Determining the value today (present value) of a series of equally spaced, equal amount payments (called annuities) is more complicated than determining the present value of a single future payment. If you were to try to calculate the present value of an annuity by hand, you would have to discount the first payment for one period, the second payment for two periods, and so on, and then add all the present values together. Because such calculations are time-consuming, a table is generally used (see Table II, page 984). The factors in the table are the sums of the individual present values of all future payments. Based on the present value of an annuity of $1, the table provides factors for various interest rates and payments.

To illustrate the use of a present value of an annuity table (Table II), we will assume that $10,000 is to be paid at the end of each of the next 10 years. If the interest rate is 12% compounded annually, Table II shows a present value factor of 5.6502. This factor means that the present value of $1 paid each year for 10 years discounted at 12% is approximately $5.65. Applying this factor to payments of $10,000 results in the following:

Amount of the annual payment	$10,000
Present value factor of an annuity of $1 discounted for 10 payments at 12%	×5.6502
Present value	$56,502

This amount, $56,502, is the amount (present value) that could be paid today to satisfy the obligation if interest is 12%.

Hewlett-Packard Keystrokes for Present Value of an Annuity:

1. 10,000: Press **PMT** (this is the amount of the annual payments)
2. 10: Press **N** (number of payments)
3. 12: Press **I** (interest rate)
4. Press **PV** for the answer = $56,502.23028 = $56,502 (rounded)

Using Excel Spreadsheets for Time Value of Money Calculations

Because of the widespread use of laptop computers, many people now use functions available in Excel spreadsheets to do time value of money calculations. Three of those functions—PV, NPV, and IRR—are introduced in this section.

The following example will be used to illustrate the use of all three Excel functions.

Initial cost of machine	$10,000
Net annual cash inflows from the machine	$3,000
Salvage value at the end of the machine's useful life	$1,000
Useful life	5 years
Appropriate discount rate	12%

For simplicity, income taxes will be ignored.

PV Excel Function

If you push the "Insert Function," or f_x button, in Excel, you can scan the menu of "Financial" functions and find the PV function. The function arguments for the PV function are as follows:

Rate   The discount rate, which is 12% in this example.

Nper   The number of periods, which is five years in this example.

Pmt   The regular annuity (or periodic, equal cash flow) amount. In this case, the annuity is $3,000.

Fv   The amount of any single cash flow to occur in the future. In this case, the salvage value is a single cash flow at the end of five years of $1,000.

Type   Indication of whether the cash flows occur at the beginning or the end of the periods. In the examples shown in this chapter, we have always assumed that cash flows occur at the end of the periods; this is indicated by leaving this field blank or by inserting a zero. If the cash flows occur at the beginning of the period, this is indicated by entering a one in this field. In this case, we will enter a zero to indicate that the cash flows occur at the end of the periods.

The completed set of Excel function arguments appears as follows:

Rate	.12
Nper	5
Pmt	3000
Fv	1000
Type	0

With these inputs, the value of the function is ($11,381.76). Note that Excel is designed such that the function returns a negative number. This can easily be remedied by placing a minus sign in front of the function. This calculation indicates that the net present value, or NPV, of this project is positive because the initial cost of the machine is just $10,000. Thus, the NPV is $1,381.76 ($11,381.76 − $10,000.00). This computation will be confirmed in an alternate way using the NPV Excel function.

NPV Excel Function

The annual cash flow information regarding the machine can be entered into a spreadsheet in the following format:

This format, rather than emphasizing the cash flows that come from each source (initial cost, annual cash inflows, or salvage value), instead emphasizes the net annual cash inflow or outflow from all sources. An advantage of presenting the cash flows in this fashion is that it allows for the use of the NPV function in Excel. If you push the "Insert Function," or f_x button, in Excel, you can scan the menu of "Financial" functions and find the NPV function. The function arguments for the NPV function are as follows:

Rate   The discount rate, which is 12% in this example.

Value1   The range of spreadsheet cells containing the net annual cash flows. In this case, that range is C5:G5. This function requires that all cash flows occur at the end of the periods. Note that the initial outflow of $10,000 is not included in the C5:G5 range of cells because that outflow occurs at the beginning, not the end, of the first year.

The completed set of Excel function arguments appears as follows:

Rate	.12
Value1	C5:G5

With these inputs, the value of the function is $11,381.76. Computation of the NPV of the project requires subtracting the initial cost of $10,000 from the present value of these net annual cash flows. Again, as computed previously, the NPV is $1,381.76.

IRR Excel Function

Another advantage of presenting the total net cash flows by year as shown in the preceding section is that it allows for the use of the IRR function in Excel. If you push the "Insert Function," or f_x button, in Excel, you can scan the menu of "Financial" functions and find the IRR function. The function arguments for the IRR function are as follows:

Values The range of spreadsheet cells containing the net annual cash flows. In this case, that range is B5:G5. In contrast to the NPV function, the IRR function requires that the first cash flow included in the function occur immediately.

Guess An initial estimate of the IRR. Because the IRR calculation involves an iterative interpolation process, the mathematical algorithm has to have a starting place. It is almost always safe to leave this field blank; if the field is blank, Excel uses 10% as the initial estimate.

The completed set of Excel function arguments appears as follows:

Caution

The NPV function assumes that the first cash flow included in the function occurs at the end of the first year. The IRR function assumes that the first cash flow occurs immediately.

Values	B5:G5
Guess	.10

With these inputs, the value of the IRR function is 17.23%. We expected an IRR greater than 12% because our previous computations demonstrated that the NPV (using a 12% discount rate) is greater than zero.

Table I: The Present Value of $1 Due in _n_ Periods*

Period	1%	2%	3%	4%	5%	6%	7%	8%	9%	10%	12%	14%	15%	16%	18%	20%
1	.9901	.9804	.9709	.9615	.9524	.9434	.9346	.9259	.9174	.9091	.8929	.8772	.8696	.8621	.8475	.8333
2	.9803	.9612	.9426	.9246	.9070	.8900	.8734	.8573	.8417	.8264	.7972	.7695	.7561	.7432	.7182	.6944
3	.9706	.9423	.9151	.8890	.8638	.8396	.8163	.7938	.7722	.7513	.7118	.6750	.6575	.6407	.6086	.5787
4	.9610	.9238	.8885	.8548	.8227	.7921	.7629	.7350	.7084	.6830	.6355	.5921	.5718	.5523	.5158	.4823
5	.9515	.9057	.8626	.8219	.7835	.7473	.7130	.6806	.6499	.6209	.5674	.5194	.4972	.4761	.4371	.4019
6	.9420	.8880	.8375	.7903	.7462	.7050	.6663	.6302	.5963	.5645	.5066	.4556	.4323	.4104	.3704	.3349
7	.9327	.8706	.8131	.7599	.7107	.6651	.6227	.5835	.5470	.5132	.4523	.3996	.3759	.3538	.3139	.2791
8	.9235	.8535	.7894	.7307	.6768	.6274	.5820	.5403	.5019	.4665	.4039	.3506	.3269	.3050	.2660	.2326
9	.9143	.8368	.7664	.7026	.6446	.5919	.5439	.5002	.4604	.4241	.3606	.3075	.2843	.2630	.2255	.1938
10	.9053	.8203	.7441	.6756	.6139	.5584	.5083	.4632	.4224	.3855	.3220	.2697	.2472	.2267	.1911	.1615
11	.8963	.8043	.7224	.6496	.5847	.5268	.4751	.4289	.3875	.3503	.2875	.2366	.2149	.1954	.1619	.1346
12	.8874	.7885	.7014	.6246	.5568	.4970	.4440	.3971	.3555	.3186	.2567	.2076	.1869	.1685	.1372	.1122
13	.8787	.7730	.6810	.6006	.5303	.4688	.4150	.3677	.3262	.2897	.2292	.1821	.1625	.1452	.1163	.0935
14	.8700	.7579	.6611	.5775	.5051	.4423	.3878	.3405	.2992	.2633	.2046	.1597	.1413	.1252	.0985	.0779
15	.8613	.7430	.6419	.5553	.4810	.4173	.3624	.3152	.2745	.2394	.1827	.1401	.1229	.1079	.0835	.0649
16	.8528	.7284	.6232	.5339	.4581	.3936	.3387	.2919	.2519	.2176	.1631	.1229	.1069	.0930	.0708	.0541
17	.8444	.7142	.6050	.5134	.4363	.3714	.3166	.2703	.2311	.1978	.1456	.1078	.0929	.0802	.0600	.0451
18	.8360	.7002	.5874	.4936	.4155	.3503	.2959	.2502	.2120	.1799	.1300	.0946	.0808	.0691	.0508	.0376
19	.8277	.6864	.5703	.4746	.3957	.3305	.2765	.2317	.1945	.1635	.1161	.0829	.0703	.0596	.0431	.0313
20	.8195	.6730	.5537	.4564	.3769	.3118	.2584	.2145	.1784	.1486	.1037	.0728	.0611	.0514	.0365	.0261
25	.7798	.6095	.4476	.3751	.2953	.2330	.1842	.1460	.1160	.0923	.0588	.0378	.0304	.0245	.0160	.0105
30	.7419	.5521	.4120	.3083	.2314	.1741	.1314	.0994	.0754	.0573	.0334	.0196	.0151	.0116	.0070	.0042
40	.6717	.4529	.3066	.2083	.1420	.0972	.0668	.0460	.0318	.0221	.0107	.0053	.0037	.0026	.0013	.0007
50	.6080	.3715	.2281	.1407	.0872	.0543	.0339	.0213	.0134	.0085	.0035	.0014	.0009	.0006	.0003	.0001
60	.5504	.3048	.1697	.0951	.0535	.0303	.0173	.0099	.0057	.0033	.0011	.0004	.0002	.0001	†	†

*The formula used to derive the values in this table was $PV = F \dfrac{1}{(1 + i)^n}$ where PV = present value, F = future amount to be discounted, _i_ = interest rate, and _n_ = number of periods.

†The value of 0 to four decimal places.

Table II: The Present Value of an Annuity of $1 per Number of Payments*

Number of Payments	1%	2%	3%	4%	5%	6%	7%	8%	9%	10%	12%	14%	15%	16%	18%	20%
1	0.9901	0.9804	0.9709	0.9615	0.9524	0.9434	0.9346	0.9259	0.9174	0.9091	0.8929	0.8772	0.8596	0.8621	0.8475	0.8333
2	1.9704	1.9416	1.9135	1.8861	1.8594	1.8334	1.8080	1.7833	1.7591	1.7355	1.6901	1.6467	1.6257	1.6052	1.5656	1.5278
3	2.9410	2.8839	2.8286	2.7751	2.7232	2.6730	2.6243	2.5771	2.5313	2.4869	2.4018	2.3216	2.2832	2.2459	2.1743	2.1065
4	3.9820	3.8077	3.7171	3.6299	3.5460	3.4651	3.3872	3.3121	3.2397	3.1699	3.0373	2.9137	2.8550	2.7982	2.6901	2.5887
5	4.8884	4.7135	4.5797	4.4518	4.3295	4.2124	4.1002	3.9927	3.8897	3.7908	3.6048	3.4331	3.3522	3.2743	3.1272	2.9906
6	5.7985	5.6014	5.4172	5.2421	5.0757	4.9173	4.7665	4.6229	4.4859	4.3553	4.1114	3.8887	3.7845	3.6847	3.4976	3.3255
7	6.7282	6.4720	6.2303	6.0021	5.7864	5.5824	5.3893	5.2064	5.0330	4.8684	4.5638	4.2883	4.1604	4.0386	3.8115	3.6046
8	7.6517	7.3255	7.0197	6.7327	6.4632	6.2098	5.9713	5.7466	5.5348	5.3349	4.9676	4.6389	4.4873	4.3436	4.0776	3.8372
9	8.5660	8.1622	7.7861	7.4353	7.1078	6.8017	6.5152	6.2469	5.9952	5.7590	5.3282	4.9464	4.7716	4.6065	4.3030	4.0310
10	9.4713	8.9826	8.5302	8.1109	7.7217	7.3601	7.0236	6.7101	6.4177	6.1446	5.6502	5.2161	5.0188	4.8332	4.4941	4.1925
11	10.3676	9.7868	9.2526	8.7605	8.3064	7.8869	7.4987	7.1390	6.8052	6.4951	5.9377	5.4527	5.2337	5.0286	4.6560	4.3271
12	11.2551	10.5733	9.9540	9.3851	8.8633	8.3838	7.9427	7.5361	7.1607	6.8137	6.1944	5.6603	5.4206	5.1971	4.7932	4.4392
13	12.1337	11.3484	10.6350	9.9856	9.3936	8.8527	8.3577	7.9038	7.4869	7.1034	6.4235	5.8424	5.5831	5.3423	4.9095	4.5327
14	13.0037	12.1062	11.2961	10.5631	9.8986	9.2950	8.7455	8.2442	7.7862	7.3667	6.6282	6.0021	5.7245	5.4675	5.0081	4.6106
15	13.8651	12.8493	11.9379	11.1184	10.3797	9.7122	9.1079	8.5595	8.0607	7.6061	6.8109	6.1422	5.8474	5.5755	5.0916	4.6755
16	14.7179	13.5777	12.5611	11.6523	10.8378	10.1059	9.4466	8.8514	8.3126	7.8237	6.9740	6.2651	5.9542	5.6685	5.1624	4.7296
17	15.5623	14.2919	13.1661	12.1657	11.2741	10.4773	9.7632	9.1216	8.5436	8.0216	7.1196	6.3729	6.0472	5.7487	5.2223	4.7746
18	16.3983	14.9920	13.7535	12.6593	11.6896	10.8276	10.0591	9.3719	8.7556	8.2014	7.2497	6.4674	6.1280	5.8178	5.2732	4.8122
19	17.2260	15.6785	14.3238	13.1339	12.0853	11.1581	10.3356	9.6036	8.9501	8.3649	7.3658	6.5504	6.1982	5.8775	5.3162	4.8435
20	18.0456	16.3514	14.8775	13.5903	12.4622	11.4699	10.5940	9.8181	9.1285	8.5136	7.4694	6.6231	6.2593	5.9288	5.3527	4.8696
25	22.0232	19.5235	17.4131	15.6221	14.0939	12.7834	11.6536	10.6748	9.8226	9.0770	7.8431	6.8729	6.4641	6.0971	5.4669	4.9476
30	25.8077	22.3965	19.6004	17.2920	15.3725	13.7648	12.4090	11.2578	10.2737	9.4269	8.0552	7.0027	6.5660	6.1772	5.5168	4.9789
40	32.8347	27.3555	23.1148	19.7928	17.1591	15.0463	13.3317	11.9246	10.7574	9.7791	8.2438	7.1050	6.6418	6.2335	5.5482	4.9966
50	39.1961	31.4236	25.7298	21.4822	18.2559	15.7619	13.8007	12.2335	10.9617	9.9148	8.3045	7.1327	6.6605	6.2463	5.5641	4.9995
60	44.9550	34.7609	27.6756	22.6235	18.9293	16.1614	14.0392	12.3766	11.0480	9.9672	8.3240	7.1401	6.6651	6.2482	5.5553	4.9999

*The formula used to derive the values in this table was $PV = F \left(\dfrac{1 - \dfrac{1}{(1 + i)^n}}{i} \right)$ where PV = present value, F = periodic payment to be discounted, i = interest rate, and n = number of payments.

Table III: Amount of $1 Due in n Periods

Period	1%	2%	3%	4%	5%	6%	7%	8%	9%	10%	12%	14%	15%	16%	18%	20%
1	1.0100	1.0200	1.0300	1.0400	1.0500	1.0600	1.0700	1.0800	1.0900	1.1000	1.1200	1.1400	1.1500	1.1600	1.1800	1.2000
2	1.0201	1.0404	1.0609	1.0816	1.1025	1.1236	1.1449	1.1664	1.1881	1.2100	1.2544	1.2996	1.3225	1.3456	1.3924	1.4400
3	1.0303	1.0612	1.0927	1.1249	1.1576	1.1910	1.2250	1.2597	1.2950	1.3310	1.4049	1.4815	1.5209	1.5609	1.6430	1.7280
4	1.0406	1.0824	1.1255	1.1699	1.2155	1.2625	1.3108	1.3605	1.4116	1.4641	1.5735	1.6890	1.7490	1.8106	1.9388	2.0736
5	1.0510	1.1041	1.1593	1.2167	1.2763	1.3382	1.4026	1.4693	1.5386	1.6105	1.7623	1.9254	2.0114	2.1003	2.2878	2.4883
6	1.0615	1.1262	1.1941	1.2653	1.3401	1.4185	1.5007	1.5869	1.6771	1.7716	1.9738	2.1950	2.3131	2.4364	2.6996	2.9860
7	1.0721	1.1487	1.2299	1.3159	1.4071	1.5036	1.6058	1.7138	1.8280	1.9487	2.2107	2.5023	2.6600	2.8262	3.1855	3.5832
8	1.0829	1.1717	1.2668	1.3686	1.4775	1.5938	1.7182	1.8509	1.9926	2.1436	2.4760	2.8526	3.0590	3.2784	3.7589	4.2998
9	1.0937	1.1951	1.3048	1.4233	1.5513	1.6895	1.8385	1.9990	2.1719	2.3579	2.7731	3.2519	3.5179	3.8030	4.4355	5.1598
10	1.1046	1.2190	1.3439	1.4802	1.6289	1.7908	1.9672	2.1589	2.3674	2.5937	3.1058	3.7072	4.0456	4.4114	5.2338	6.1917
11	1.1157	1.2434	1.3842	1.5395	1.7103	1.8983	2.1049	2.3316	2.5804	2.8531	3.4785	4.2262	4.6524	5.1173	6.1759	7.4031
12	1.1268	1.2682	1.4258	1.6010	1.7959	2.0122	2.2522	2.5182	2.8127	3.1384	3.8960	4.8179	5.3502	5.9360	7.2876	8.9161
13	1.1381	1.2936	1.4685	1.6651	1.8856	2.1329	2.4098	2.7196	3.0658	3.4523	4.3635	5.4924	6.1528	6.8858	8.5994	10.699
14	1.1495	1.3195	1.5126	1.7317	1.9799	2.2609	2.5785	2.9372	3.3417	3.7975	4.8871	6.2613	7.0757	7.9875	10.147	12.839
15	1.1610	1.3459	1.5580	1.8009	2.0789	2.3966	2.7590	3.1722	3.6425	4.1772	5.4736	7.1379	8.1371	9.2655	11.973	15.407
16	1.1726	1.3728	1.6047	1.8730	2.1829	2.5404	2.9522	3.4259	3.9703	4.5950	6.1304	8.1372	9.3576	10.748	14.129	18.488
17	1.1843	1.4002	1.6528	1.9479	2.2920	2.6928	3.1588	3.7000	4.3276	5.0545	6.8660	9.2765	10.761	12.467	16.672	22.186
18	1.1961	1.4282	1.7024	2.0258	2.4066	2.8543	3.3799	3.9960	4.7171	5.5599	7.6900	10.575	12.375	14.462	19.673	26.623
19	1.2081	1.4568	1.7535	2.1068	2.5270	3.0256	3.6165	4.3157	5.1417	6.1159	8.6128	12.055	14.231	16.776	23.214	31.948
20	1.2202	1.4859	1.8061	2.1911	2.6533	3.2071	3.8697	4.6610	5.6044	6.7275	9.6463	13.743	16.366	19.460	27.393	38.337
30	1.3478	1.8114	2.4273	3.2434	4.3219	5.7435	7.6123	10.062	13.267	17.449	29.959	50.950	66.211	85.849	143.37	237.37
40	1.4889	2.2080	3.2620	4.8010	7.0400	10.285	14.974	21.724	31.409	45.259	93.050	188.88	267.86	378.72	750.37	1469.7
50	1.6446	2.6916	4.3839	7.1067	11.467	18.420	29.457	46.901	74.357	117.39	289.00	700.23	1083.6	1670.7	3927.3	9100.4
60	1.8167	3.2810	5.8916	10.519	18.679	32.987	57.946	101.25	176.03	304.48	897.59	2595.9	4383.9	7370.1	20555.	56347.

Table IV: Amount of an Annuity of $1 per Number of Payments

Number of Payments	1%	2%	3%	4%	5%	6%	7%	8%	9%	10%	12%	14%	15%	16%	18%	20%
1	1.0000	1.0000	1.0000	1.0000	1.0000	1.0000	1.0000	1.0000	1.0000	1.0000	1.0000	1.0000	1.0000	1.0000	1.0000	1.0000
2	2.0100	2.0200	2.0300	2.0400	2.0500	2.0600	2.0700	2.0800	2.0900	2.1000	2.1200	2.1400	2.1500	2.1600	2.1800	2.2000
3	3.0301	3.0604	3.0909	3.1216	3.1525	3.1836	3.2149	3.2464	3.2781	3.3100	3.3744	3.4396	3.4725	3.5056	3.5724	3.6400
4	4.0604	4.1216	4.1836	4.2465	4.3101	4.3746	4.4399	4.5061	4.5731	4.6410	4.7793	4.9211	4.9934	5.0665	5.2154	5.3680
5	5.1010	5.2040	5.3091	5.4163	5.5256	5.6371	5.7507	5.8666	5.9847	6.1051	6.3528	6.6101	6.7424	6.8771	7.1542	7.4416
6	6.1520	6.3081	6.4684	6.6330	6.8019	6.9753	7.1533	7.3359	7.5233	7.7156	8.1152	8.5355	8.7537	8.9775	9.4420	9.9299
7	7.2135	7.4343	7.6625	7.8983	8.1420	8.3938	8.6540	8.9228	9.2004	9.4872	10.8090	10.7305	11.0668	11.4139	12.1415	12.9159
8	8.2857	8.5830	8.8923	9.2142	9.5491	9.8975	10.2598	10.6366	11.0285	11.4359	12.2997	13.2328	13.7268	14.2401	15.3270	16.4991
9	9.3685	9.7546	10.1591	10.5828	11.0266	11.4913	11.9780	12.4876	13.0210	13.5795	14.7757	16.0853	16.7858	17.5185	19.0859	20.7989
10	10.4622	10.9497	11.4639	12.0061	12.5779	13.1808	13.8164	14.4866	15.1929	15.9374	17.5487	19.3373	20.3037	21.3215	23.5213	25.9587
11	11.5668	12.1687	12.8078	13.4864	14.2068	14.9716	15.7836	16.6455	17.5603	18.5312	20.6546	23.0445	24.3493	25.7329	28.7551	32.1504
12	12.6825	13.4121	14.1920	15.0258	15.9171	16.8699	17.8885	18.9771	20.1407	21.3843	24.1331	27.2707	29.0017	30.8502	34.9311	39.5805
13	13.8093	14.6803	15.6178	16.6268	17.7130	18.8821	20.1406	21.4953	22.9534	24.5227	28.0291	32.0887	34.3519	36.7862	42.2187	48.4966
14	14.9474	15.9739	17.0863	18.2919	19.5986	21.0151	22.5505	24.2149	26.0192	27.9750	32.3926	37.5811	40.5047	43.6720	50.8180	59.1959
15	16.0969	17.2934	18.5989	20.0236	21.5786	23.2760	25.1290	27.1521	29.3609	31.7725	37.2797	43.8424	47.5804	51.6595	60.9653	72.0351
16	17.2579	18.6393	20.1569	21.8245	23.6575	25.6725	27.8881	30.3243	33.0034	35.9497	42.7535	50.9804	55.7178	60.9250	72.9390	87.4421
17	18.4304	20.0121	21.7616	23.6975	25.8404	28.2129	30.8402	33.7502	36.9737	40.5447	48.8837	59.1176	65.0751	71.6730	87.0680	105.9306
18	19.6147	21.4123	23.4144	25.6454	28.1324	30.9057	33.9990	37.4502	41.3013	45.5992	55.7497	68.3941	75.8364	84.1407	103.7403	128.1167
19	20.8190	22.8406	25.1169	27.6712	30.5390	33.7600	37.3790	41.4463	46.0185	51.1591	63.4397	78.9692	88.2118	98.6032	123.4135	154.7400
20	22.0190	24.2974	26.8704	29.7781	33.0660	36.7856	40.9955	45.7620	51.1601	57.2750	72.0524	91.0249	102.4436	115.3797	146.6280	186.6880
30	34.7849	40.5681	47.5754	56.0849	66.4388	79.0582	94.4608	113.2832	136.3075	164.4940	241.3327	356.7868	434.7451	530.3117	790.9480	1181.8816
40	48.8864	60.4020	75.4013	95.0255	120.7998	154.7620	199.6351	259.0565	337.8824	442.5926	767.0914	1342.0251	1779.0903	2360.7572	4163.2130	7343.8578
50	64.4632	84.5794	112.7969	152.6671	209.3480	290.3359	406.5289	573.7702	815.0836	1163.9085	2400.0182	4994.5213	7217.7163	10435.6488	21813.0937	45497.1908
60	81.6697	114.0515	163.0534	237.9907	353.5837	533.1282	813.5204	1253.2133	1944.7921	3034.8164	7471.6411	18535.1333	29219.9916	46057.5085	114189.6665	281732.5718

review of learning objectives

1 **Understand the importance of capital budgeting and the concepts underlying strategic and capital investment decisions.** Strategic planning, especially as related to capital investment decisions, is critical to the success of organizations. The systematic planning for long-term investments in operating assets is known as capital budgeting. Long-term investments are usually large and represent commitments that are difficult to change, so capital budgeting is crucial to the long-run profitability of a company.

2 **Describe and use two nondiscounted capital budgeting techniques: the payback method and the unadjusted rate of return method.** Several capital budgeting techniques have been developed to assist in the decision-making process. The payback and unadjusted rate of return methods are commonly used in business because they are simple to apply. However, they generally should be used together with the discounted cash flow methods—net present value and internal rate of return—which are theoretically more correct because they consider the time value of money.

3 **Describe and use two discounted capital budgeting techniques: the net present value method and the internal rate of return method.** The net present value method uses a predetermined discount rate to state all the cash flows of an investment in present value terms. This rate is a company's cost of capital. The discounted cash inflows and outflows are then compared, and if the result is positive, or at least zero, the project is acceptable from a quantitative standpoint.

The internal rate of return method determines the "true" rate of return on an investment. This is the discount rate at which a project would have a net present value of zero. The internal rate is compared with the company's hurdle rate. If the internal rate is higher than or equal to the hurdle rate, the project is acceptable from a quantitative standpoint.

4 **Understand the need for evaluating qualitative factors in strategic and capital investment decisions.** Qualitative factors—such as the effect of an investment on quality and time, consumer and worker safety, and environmental and civic responsibility—are important considerations in capital investment decisions and may override the conclusions suggested by quantitative data.

5 **Use sensitivity analysis to assess the potential effects of uncertainty in capital budgeting.** Sensitivity analysis is used to assess the potential effect of uncertainty with regard to capital budgeting. It enables management to examine how the results of the calculations would vary if certain estimates were to change and thereby to gauge how reasonable the decision is.

6 **Explain how to use capital budgeting techniques in ranking capital investment projects.** Capital budgeting deals with both the screening and the ranking of projects. Investments must first be screened to determine which are acceptable. They must then be ranked to ensure that a company's limited funds are invested in the projects that will earn the greatest rate of return and otherwise accomplish the company's overall objectives.

7 **Explain how income taxes affect capital budgeting decisions.** The cash inflows and outflows of capital budgeting decisions must be converted to after-tax amounts before the present values are computed in order to obtain realistic measures of net present values. Cash inflows and outflows are converted to after-tax amounts by taking into account such tax provisions as expense deductions for repairs and depreciation, the estimated gain on disposal of the asset at the end of its useful life, and annual operating revenues and expenses.

key terms & concepts

capital, 952
capital budgeting, 951
cash inflows, 956
cash outflows, 955
cost of capital, 959
discounted cash flow methods, 956
hurdle rate, 965
interest, 953
internal rate of return, 963

internal rate of return method, 962
interpolation, 964
least-cost decision, 962
net present value, 961
net present value method, 960
payback method, 957
ranking, 953
screening, 953
unadjusted rate of return method, 958

capital rationing, 971
profitability index, 972
sensitivity analysis, 969

review problem

Capital Budgeting

High Flying Company has an opportunity to make an investment that will yield $1,000 net cash inflow per year for the next 10 years. The investment will cost $6,000 and will have no salvage value. After cost reductions and depreciation related to the new investment, the future average annual net income will increase $800.

Required:
Compute the following:

1. The payback period.
2. The unadjusted rate of return.
3. The net present value. (Use a 10% discount rate.)
4. The internal rate of return. (The hurdle rate is 10%.)

Solution
1. The Payback Period
To compute the payback period, divide the investment cost by the annual net cash inflows.

$$\frac{\text{Investment cost}}{\text{Annual net cash inflows}} = \frac{\$6,000}{\$1,000} = 6 \text{ years}$$

2. The Unadjusted Rate of Return
To compute the unadjusted rate of return, divide the increase in future average annual net income by the initial investment cost.

$$\frac{\text{Increase in future average annual net income}}{\text{Initial investment cost}} = \frac{\$800}{\$6,000} = 13.3\%$$

3. The Net Present Value
To compute the net present value, first state in present value terms all expected cash outflows and inflows.

Present value of 10 annual payments of $1,000 discounted at 10%	$6,145
Present value of payment of $6,000 now	6,000
Net present value of project (present value of cash inflows minus present value of cash outflow)	$ 145

Since this investment's net present value is greater than zero, it is acceptable from a quantitative standpoint.

4. The Internal Rate of Return
To compute the internal rate of return, first compute the present value factor, as follows:

$$\frac{\text{Investment cost}}{\text{Annual net cash inflows}} = \frac{\$6,000}{\$1,000} = 6.0000$$

Next, use this present value factor to find the investment's internal rate of return in a present value table. Using Table II, find the row for 10 years, the life of the investment. Move across the row until you find the present value factor closest to 6.0000, which is 6.1446. This is the factor for 10%. Since 6.0000 is between 6.1446 and 5.6502, the investment's internal rate of return is between 10 and 12%. Next, use interpolation to find a more exact internal rate of return.

	Rate of Return	Present Value Factors	
High factor	10%	6.1446	6.1446
True factor		6.0000	0.0000
Low factor	12		5.6502
Differences	2%	0.1446	0.4944

The number 0.1446 is the difference between the high factor and the true factor. The number 0.4944 is the difference between the high factor and the low factor. The difference between the high rate and the low rate is 2%. The proportion 0.1446 ÷ 0.4944 of this 2% difference must be added to the low rate to give the true internal rate of return.

$$\text{True internal rate of return} = 0.10 + \left(0.02 \times \frac{0.1446}{0.4944}\right) = 10.58\%$$

The internal rate of return could also be computed using the following keystrokes with a Hewlett-Packard business calculator:

Hewlett-Packard Keystrokes:

1. −6,000: Press **PV** (you must enter the cash outflow as a NEGATIVE number)
2. 1,000: Press **PMT** (this is the annual cash inflow)
3. 10: Press **N** (number of years)
4. Press **I/YR** for the answer = 10.56%

Note that the answer obtained using table interpolation (10.58%) is very close to the actual internal rate of return of 10.56%.

Next, this internal rate of return is compared with the hurdle rate. Since it is greater, the investment is acceptable quantitatively. Note that this is the same decision reached by calculating the net present value.

d iscussion questions

1. Define *capital budgeting*. Give two examples of long-term investment decisions that require capital budgeting.
2. Why do long-term capital investment decisions often have a significant effect on a company's profitability?
3. Why is the time value of money so important in capital budgeting decisions?
4. If the time value of money is so important, why isn't the timing of cash flows emphasized in the accounting cycle?
5. How is depreciation expense treated when the discounted cash flow methods are used? Why?
6. How are cost savings and increased revenues related in capital budgeting?
7. Identify four capital budgeting methods, and explain why some are considered better than others.
8. Why is the payback method inferior to the discounted cash flow methods? When is the payback method helpful?

9. What is the major weakness of the unadjusted rate of return method?
10. Does a net present value of zero indicate that a project should be rejected? Explain.
11. As the desired rate of return increases, does the net present value of a project increase? Explain.
12. Under what circumstances might a project with a negative net present value be accepted?
13. What discount rate yields a net present value of zero? How is it determined?
14. What is a company's hurdle rate? How is it used?
15. How do quality and time considerations affect capital budgeting decisions?
16. Identify several qualitative factors, other than quality and time considerations, that may affect strategic and capital investment decisions. Why are qualitative factors important?

17. How can we deal with uncertainties involved in capital budgeting?

18. Distinguish between the screening and ranking functions of capital budgeting.
19. Of what value is a profitability index in capital budgeting?
20. How do income taxes influence capital budgeting decisions?

p r a c t i c e e x e r c i s e s

Practice 18-1

Capital Investment Decisions in Planning

Which one of the following is *not* a reason why a company should carefully plan its capital investment decisions?

a. Capital investments usually require a large initial outlay of capital.
b. Capital investments are usually tied to management bonus plans.
c. Capital investment decisions affect earnings over a long period of time.
d. Capital investments are less liquid, so poor investment decisions are difficult to reverse.

Practice 18-2

Screening, Ranking, and Discounting

Which one of the following statements is correct?

a. Screening is the process of finding the best among available acceptable alternatives.
b. Ranking is the process of determining whether an investment meets a minimum standard of financial acceptability.
c. For the comparison of cash flows to be accurate, all amounts should be stated at their value at the point in time when the cash flow occurs.
d. Cash received sooner is worth more than cash received later.
e. Generally speaking, managers use relatively low discount rates when evaluating investments that involve a high degree of risk.

Practice 18-3

Discounting Cash Outflows

The company is deciding whether to invest in a certain capital investment. The investment requires an initial outlay of $65,000 and annual payments of $7,500 made at the end of the year for four years. The company's discount rate is 14%. What is the present value of cash outflows related to this investment?

Practice 18-4

Discounting Cash Inflows

Refer to the data in Practice 18-3. The company expects the new investment will generate revenues of $22,500 per year for the four years of the investment's life. At the end of the four years, the company expects the investment to have a salvage value of $20,750. What is the present value of cash inflows related to this investment? Should the company make this investment?

Practice 18-5

Payback Method

The company paid $50,000 cash for a capital investment. The company expects the investment to generate net cash inflows of $8,400 per year. What is the payback period of this investment?

Practice 18-6

Unadjusted Rate of Return Method

Refer to the data in Practice 18-5. What is the unadjusted rate of return on the investment? *Note:* The investment is expected to have a useful life of 10 years, and the company uses straight-line depreciation with zero salvage value.

Practice 18-7

Cost of Capital

Twenty percent of a company's total capital is debt, 35% is from the issuance of stock, and 45% is equity from retained earnings. The company has determined that the cost of its debt capital is 8% and the cost of its equity capital is 20% from stock and 15% from retained earnings. Compute the company's average cost of capital.

Practice 18-8

Net Present Value Method

Which one of the following investment opportunities would be rejected by a company that accepts all projects with net present values greater than zero?

    a. Present value of inflows = $35,740; present value of outflows = $32,023.
    b. Present value of inflows = $452,800; present value of outflows = $450,020.
    c. Present value of inflows = $1,003,840; present value of outflows = $1,003,810.
    d. Present value of inflows = $125,114; present value of outflows = $125,843.
    e. Present value of inflows = $85,084; present value of outflows = $82,000.

Practice 18-9

Least-Cost Decisions

The company is required to install a new piece of safety equipment. The company has two alternatives for the equipment. One alternative would cost $260,000 immediately but would not add to operating costs over the 5-year life of the equipment. The second alternative costs $75,000 immediately but would add $45,000 to annual operating costs for five years. The company uses an 8% discount rate. Which alternative should the company purchase?

Practice 18-10

Calculating Internal Rate of Return

The company is considering a 7-year investment. The initial cost of the investment is $45,638. The investment will yield net cash inflows of $10,000 per year. What is the internal rate of return for this investment?

Practice 18-11

Internal Rate of Return Interpolation

The company is considering whether to invest in a project with an initial cost of $538,000 that will provide annual net cash inflows of $82,500 for 10 years. Use interpolation to estimate the internal rate of return.

Practice 18-12

Uneven Cash Flows and Internal Rate of Return

The company is considering whether to invest in a piece of equipment that requires an investment of $250,000 today. The project will provide net cash flows of $50,000 per year for eight years, and it will have a salvage value of $51,509 at the end of eight years. Calculate the internal rate of return. (*Hint:* The IRR is greater than 10%.)

Practice 18-13

Qualitative Factors in Strategic and Capital Investment Decisions

Which one of the following is an important qualitative factor to consider when making strategic and capital investment decisions?

    a. Company image and prestige.
    b. Pollution control and environmental protection.
    c. Government regulation.
    d. Worker safety.
    e. All of the above are examples of important qualitative factors.

Practice 18-14

Uncertain Expected Cash Flows

The company is considering an investment that costs $785,000 today and has a salvage value in 10 years of $137,714, but the company is not sure how much net annual cash inflow will be provided by the investment. The company has a discount rate of 7%. Compute the net amount of annual cash inflow required to break even.

Practice 18-15

Uncertain Useful Life

The company is considering an investment that costs $430,000 today and will provide $72,000 each year in net cash inflow, but the company is not sure how long the investment will last. The company has a discount rate of 10%. Compute the number of years of useful life required for this investment to break even.

Practice 18-16

Ranking by the Internal Rate of Return Method

The company is considering eight capital investment projects. The company has a minimum required internal rate of return of 13%. Screen and rank the eight capital investment projects using the internal rate of return.

Project		Expected Rate of Return
S		14%
T		24
U		20
V		10
W		17
X		9
Y		12
Z		18

Practice 18-17

Profitability Index

The company is considering a project with a present value of net cash inflows of $1,340,000 and an initial investment cost of $973,000. What is the profitability index of this investment?

Practice 18-18

Ranking Using the Profitability Index

Screen and rank the following projects using the profitability index.

	Project J	Project K	Project L	Project M
Present value of net cash inflows ...	$1,000,000	$500,000	$1,250,000	$250,000
Investment cost	950,000	430,000	1,280,000	205,000

Practice 18-19

Income Tax Considerations in Capital Budgeting Decisions

The company has decided to invest in some equipment that costs $50,000 today and will generate cash inflows of $20,000 per year for the 5-year life of the equipment. At the end of the five years, the equipment will have no salvage value. The company will depreciate the equipment using straight-line depreciation. The company's tax rate is 30%, and its discount rate is 10%. Compute the net present value of this investment.

Practice 18-20

Capital Budgeting, MACRS, and Section 179

Refer to the data in Practice 18-19. Assume that the company elects to deduct $10,000 of the cost of the equipment immediately as a Section 179 expensing election. The remaining cost of $40,000 is deducted according to the MACRS schedule for 5-year property. The MACRS percentages (incorporating the half-year convention) are as follows:

Year 1	0.2000
Year 2	0.3200
Year 3	0.1920
Year 4	0.1152
Year 5	0.1152
Year 6	0.0576

Compute the net present value of the investment. As before, the tax rate is 30%, and the discount rate is 10%.

e xercises

Note: Unless otherwise indicated, the exercises and problems assume that all payments are made or received at the end of the year.

Exercise 18-1

Present Values

Consider each part independently.

1. Super-Fix Company would like to move its auto repair shop to a downtown location in order to attract more customers. What is the maximum Super-Fix should pay to purchase a building at the new location, assuming that the company needs to earn 12%? The new building will last 40 years. Super-Fix estimates that moving to the new location will result in a $10,000 increase in annual income.
2. If Audrey Ostler buys a new small automobile that costs $14,000 and provides annual gasoline savings of $1,200, how long must she own the car before the savings justify its cost? Assume an 8% cost of capital.

Exercise 18-2

Time Value of Money

Your late, rich uncle left you $250,000. The executor of the estate has asked if you would rather receive the full amount now or $30,000 a year for the next 40 years.

Which of these options would you take, assuming that your desired rate of return is:

1. 10%?
2. 12%?

Exercise 18-3

Payback Method

The manager of Simple Company must choose between two investments. Project A costs $50,000 and promises cash savings of $10,000 a year over a useful life of 10 years. Project B costs $60,000, and the estimated cash savings are $11,000 per year over a useful life of 11 years. Using the payback method, determine which project the manager should choose.

Exercise 18-4

Unadjusted Rate of Return Method

Um Good, Inc., a candy maker, is thinking of purchasing a new machine. A marketing firm has estimated that the new machine could increase revenues by $30,000 a year for the next five years. The expenses directly relating to the machine total $60,000 ($12,000 × 5 years). The initial purchase cost would be $80,000. What is the unadjusted rate of return?

Exercise 18-5

Net Present Value Method

The Carroll Broom Company is thinking of purchasing a new automatic straw-binding machine. The company president, Joan Carroll, has determined that such a machine would save the company $10,000 per year in labor costs. The machine would cost $46,500 and would have a useful life of 10 years and a scrap value of $500. The machine would require servicing after five years at a cost of $1,000. Carroll uses a discount rate of 16%. Compute the net present value. From a quantitative standpoint, should the machine be purchased?

Exercise 18-6

Least-Cost Decision

The local fire department has determined the Sleep-Eazy Mattress Company is not in full compliance with local fire regulations. To comply, Sleep-Eazy has two alternatives: It may install an automatic sprinkler system, or it may hire a fire safety expert to make weekly fire safety checks. The automatic sprinkler system will cost $125,000, including installation charges, and will last for 10 years. It will have no salvage value. The entire system is virtually maintenance-free. The fire safety expert's fee is $14,000 per year. The cost of capital is 10%. Which alternative should Sleep-Eazy Mattress Company choose? Why?

Exercise 18-7

Internal Rate of Return

Juan Gonzales, the president of Nogalis Corporation, is trying to decide whether he should buy a new machine that will improve production efficiency. The machine will increase cash inflows $5,000 a year for five years. It will cost $18,000, and there will be no salvage value. What is the internal rate of return?

Exercise 18-8

Cost of Capital

Daphney Corporation has raised $200,000 in equity financing through the issuance of shares. Stockholders expect to earn an average of 20% per year on their equity investment in Daphney. In addition, the corporation has issued $100,000 of 10% bonds. The corporation has also accumulated $25,000 in earnings that have been retained in the company. Investors expect to earn about 16% on the earnings that are retained in the company. Using the weighting procedure discussed in the chapter, calculate Daphney Corporation's cost of capital. (Ignore taxes in calculating the cost of debt.)

Exercise 18-9

Net Present Value and Internal Rate of Return

A real estate investment requires an initial outlay of $150,000 in cash. The investment will return a single sum cash payment of $606,796 after 10 years. The rate of return required on projects as risky as this one is 18%.

1. What is the net present value of this real estate investment?
2. What is the internal rate of return of this real estate investment?
3. Is this an attractive investment?

Exercise 18-10

Net Present Value and Internal Rate of Return

A retired person has $700,000 in a retirement account. An insurance company is offering to give the retired person an annuity of $61,029 at the end of each year for the next 20 years in exchange for the $700,000. The retired person requires a rate of return of 8% on investments; this is the rate currently being earned in the retirement account.

1. What is the net present value of this exchange?
2. What is the internal rate of return implied in this exchange?
3. Should the retired person accept the exchange offered by the insurance company?

Exercise 18-11

Quality and Time Factors

Tucker Yard Service Company is contemplating purchasing a new riding lawnmower for its business. One particular model has special features that enhance the cutting and the collecting of the mowed grass, but that mower is quite expensive. Another model is more basic and costs $1,000 less. The payback period on the more expensive model is estimated to be 3.5 years and on the less expensive model 2.5 years. The "bumper-to-bumper" warranties are two years and one year, respectively. From these limited data, what factors should Tucker consider in making this decision?

Exercise 18-12

Qualitative Considerations

The Upscale Department Store has been plagued with shoplifting. The president, Hector Conrad, has suggested that the store hire a security force to "frisk" all customers as they leave the store. It is estimated that annual shoplifting losses are $100,000. Expenses associated with the security force are estimated to be $50,000 annually. Before Mr. Conrad makes his final decision, what other factors might he consider?

Exercise 18-13

Sensitivity Analysis

You have accumulated $10,500 in a savings account that pays 10% interest. You are offered the opportunity to buy 30 ounces of gold at $350 per ounce. The price of gold is expected to rise to $700 per ounce by the end of 10 years. You realize, however, that this is only an estimate.

To what price would gold have to rise in order to earn a 10% return? (Note that the future value factor for $10,500 at 10% at the end of 10 years is 2.5937.)

Exercise 18-14

Screening Function

Your company's cost of capital was determined to be 12%. Several investment alternatives are being considered, and the discounted cash flows have given the following results:

Net present value:

1. A new machine was analyzed, and a net present value of zero resulted.
2. A new product line was analyzed, and a negative net present value of $60 resulted.
3. An investment was being considered. The analysis yielded a net present value of $250.

Internal rate of return:

1. A plant expansion project promised a yield of 12%.
2. An investment in additional transport trucks would yield an internal rate of return of 10%.
3. The addition of another assembly line would add cash flows that would give an internal rate of return of 16%.

Determine which projects should be accepted as investment opportunities and which should be rejected.

Exercise 18-15

Ranking Projects

Using net present value (NPV) analysis, a manager can select those projects that will maximize the present value of future cash flows. NPV analysis is a powerful tool; however, surveys of current practice indicate that the internal rate of return (IRR) method enjoys considerable popularity among decision makers. What would account for IRR's appeal? What are the drawbacks to using only the IRR method to rank projects?

Exercise 18-16

Profitability Index

California Company is trying to determine the relative profitability of two alternative investments. Investment A requires an initial cash outlay of $10,000 and has a net present value of $500. Investment B requires an initial cash outlay of $2,000 and has a net present value of $150. Compute the profitability index of each investment. Which alternative is more profitable?

Exercise 18-17

$preadsheet

Income Tax Effects

Kade Corporation is considering purchasing a new piece of equipment. The equipment will cost $135,000 and is expected to have a useful life of five years. The gross cash flow savings is estimated to be $50,000 per year. The company elects not to take the expense deduction and will depreciate the full cost of the asset for tax purposes under MACRS using a 5-year recovery period and the straight-line method. The company is in the 40% tax bracket (including federal, state, and local taxes).

1. Compute the after-tax cash flow savings on the asset.
2. Compute the after-tax internal rate of return that will equate the present value of the savings with the net outlay cost.

problems

Problem 18-1

Spreadsheet

Net Present Value Method

A fast-food establishment is thinking of buying a new cooking grill and refrigeration unit. The costs of these new machines are $12,500 and $9,000, respectively. The installation costs of the new equipment will run about $800. It is estimated that 10% more customers can be served with the new equipment, which would mean an additional annual net cash flow of approximately $4,500. The salvage value of the old grill and refrigeration unit is estimated to be $1,000. The firm's cost of capital is 12%. The equipment should last 10 years, at a minimum.

Required:
Using the net present value method, should the company purchase the new equipment? (Ignore income tax effects.)

Problem 18-2

Net Present Value Method—Uneven Cash Flows

Southside Junk Yard needs to buy a car smasher. The machine would add the following revenues to the business over the next three years:

Year 1 Cash savings = $30,000
Year 2 Cash savings plus additional scrap sales = $40,000
Year 3 Cash savings plus additional scrap sales = $55,000

The initial cost of the machine is $100,000. At the end of three years, its salvage value is estimated at $20,000. The firm has a cost of capital of 12%.

Required:
Using the net present value method, determine whether the company should purchase the machine. (Ignore income tax effects.)

Problem 18-3

Internal Rate of Return

You have been offered the opportunity to purchase a franchise of Sunshine Juice Stores. You will have to pay $155,625 for the initial investment in the store and its equipment, plus $30,000 per year for the lease payments and the franchise fee. The franchise contract obligates you for 10 years. Operating costs for each year will be $125,000, and the expected revenue is $180,000 a year. Your hurdle rate is 10%. Ignore income taxes.

Required:
1. Does this investment yield a satisfactory rate of return?
2. What qualitative factors might be considered?

Problem 18-4

Internal Rate of Return and Hurdle Rate

Nina Roberts has the opportunity to invest in a timber forest. She would have to invest $100,000. Revenues of $20,000 per year are projected for 20 years. However, these revenues will not begin coming in for five years because the timber must be seasoned before cutting and selling can begin. Ms. Roberts's hurdle rate is 10%. Ignore income taxes.

Required:
1. Calculate the internal rate of return, and determine whether or not Ms. Roberts should make the investment.
2. If Ms. Roberts has to borrow the $100,000 necessary for the investment from her bank at 12% interest, should she make the investment?
3. **Interpretive Question:** Why is it important for Ms. Roberts to determine her cost of capital before making this investment decision?

Problem 18-5

Spreadsheet

Payback, Net Present Value, and Internal Rate of Return Methods

Nucore Company is thinking of purchasing a new candy-wrapping machine at a cost of $370,000. The machine should save the company approximately $70,000 in operating costs per year over its estimated useful life of 10 years. The salvage value at the end of 10 years is expected to be $15,000. (Ignore income tax effects.)

Required:
1. What is the machine's payback period?
2. Compute the net present value of the machine if the cost of capital is 12%.
3. What is the expected internal rate of return for this machine?

Problem 18-6

Internal Rate of Return

The manager of Soft & Creamy Ice Cream is thinking of buying a new soft ice cream machine. The machine will cost $13,500 and will last 10 years. Soft ice cream sales are expected to generate $3,000 in income per year.

Required:
What is the internal rate of return on this project?

Problem 18-7

Choosing among Alternatives

Tom Thurlow wants to buy a boat but is short of cash. Two alternatives are available: Tom can accept $2,000 per year from his brother for partial ownership in the boat, or he can earn money by renting the boat to others. Rental income would be $2,500 per year. Under either alternative, the boat will last eight years. If Tom rents the boat out, he will have to pay $3,000 to overhaul the engine at the end of the fourth year.

Required:
Which alternative should Tom select, assuming that the cost of capital is 12% and that only quantitative considerations are involved?

Problem 18-8

Lease-or-Buy Decision

A small sales company is committed to supplying three sales representatives with new cars. The company has two alternatives. It can either buy the three cars and sell them after two years, or it can lease the cars for two years. The company uses a 16% discount rate. The information for each alternative is as follows:

Alternative 1: Buy

Cost	$36,000
Annual service costs	3,000
Anticipated repairs during the 1st year	700
Anticipated repairs during the 2nd year	1,500
Salvage value at the end of 2 years	10,000

Alternative 2: Lease
To lease the cars, the company would simply pay $20,000 a year for the two years.

Required:
Assuming the lease is paid at the end of each year, determine the better alternative.

Problem 18-9

Spreadsheet

Rent-or-Purchase Decision

As one aspect of its business, New Lawn Company currently rents a ditch-digging machine for an average of $48 per job. A used machine is available for $995 but would cost $498 to repair. The machine, if purchased, would cost $800 a year to maintain and in two years would need a new chain costing $394. The used digger has a useful life of four years with no salvage value.

(continued)

Required:
If the company averages 30 jobs a year and has a cost of capital of 10%, which alternative is more profitable?

Problem 18-10

Sell-or-Rent Decision

Clarence Gleason has inherited an apartment complex. He is now faced with the decision of whether to sell or to rent the property. A real estate adviser believes that Clarence should rent the property, because he could receive $65,000 per year for 10 years and then could sell the property for $400,000. A development company has offered Clarence $300,000 down and promises to pay $50,000 per year for the next 15 years. The land has a remaining mortgage of $130,000. If Clarence sells the complex, he will have to pay that sum now. If he rents the property, he will have to pay $20,000 per year for 10 years. The cost of capital is 16%.

Required:
1. Calculate the net present value of each alternative.
2. **Interpretive Question:** Discuss the qualitative factors that might affect the decision to sell or rent.

Problem 18-11

Unifying Concepts: Net Present Value and Internal Rate of Return Methods

Julie Kowalis, an investment analyst, wants to know if her investments during the past four years have earned at least a 12% return. Four years ago, she had the following investments:

a. She purchased a small building for $50,000 and rented space in it. She received rental income of $8,000 for each of the four years and then sold the building this year for $55,000.
b. She purchased a small refreshment stand near the city park for $25,000. Annual income from the stand was $5,000 for each of the four years. She sold the stand for $20,000 this year.
c. She purchased an antique car for $5,000 four years ago. She sold it this year to a collector for $7,000.

Required:
1. Using the net present value method, determine whether or not each investment earned at least 12%.
2. Did the investments as a whole earn at least 12%? Explain.

Problem 18-12

Sensitivity Analysis

Falcon Manufacturing is a leading manufacturer of airframe components for small aircraft. Heidi Saxton, Falcon's operations manager, has submitted a request for a new piece of production equipment. Using the new machine, the company will be able to reduce expenses for both maintenance and labor. Data on the project are as follows:

Initial investment	$80,000
Useful life	10 years
Salvage value of old machine	$1,500
Annual cash savings	$15,000
Salvage value of new machine	$10,000
Maintenance overhaul (Year 5)	$7,600
Cost of capital	12%

Assume all cash flows occur at the end of each year. (Ignore income tax effects.)

Required:

1. Using the above data, calculate the net present value of the investment. From a strictly quantitative standpoint, should the machine be purchased?
2. Suppose that Heidi receives another analysis that increases the cost of capital estimate to 14% and the new machine's salvage value to $17,000. Would the purchase still make sense?
3. Falcon's CEO, Kevin Davis, is responsible for approving all capital investment projects. Having spent his entire career dealing with one estimate after another, Kevin has asked you to consider two specific changes:
   a. Reduce annual cash inflows by 10%.
   b. Cut in half the estimated salvage value of new equipment.
   Using the original problem data, calculate the net present value using the CEO's two changes.

Problem 18-13

Net Present Value Used to Rank Alternatives

Taglioni's Pizza Company has to choose a new delivery car from among three alternatives. Assume that gasoline costs $1.30 per gallon and that the firm's cost of capital is 12%. The car will be driven 12,000 miles per year.

	Car 1	Car 2	Car 3
Cost	$12,000	$4,000	$8,000
Mileage per gallon	40	8	12
Useful life	5 years	5 years	5 years
Salvage value	$2,000	$500	$1,000

Required:

1. Which car should the company purchase?
2. How would your answer change if the price of gasoline increased to $2 per gallon?

Problem 18-14

Screening and Ranking Alternatives

Sunshine Corporation is considering several long-term investments. Management wants to accept the two best projects, given the following data:

	Project				
	A	B	C	D	E
Present value of net cash inflows	$24,000	$44,000	$15,000	$30,000	$50,000
Investment cost	20,000	40,000	16,000	24,000	41,000

Required:

1. Determine the net present value and the profitability index for each project.
2. Which projects are acceptable using the profitability index as a screening tool?
3. What would be the ranking of the acceptable projects according to the profitability indexes?
4. **Interpretive Question:** What additional information would be needed to screen and rank the projects using the internal rate of return method? What are the decision rules using the IRR method for screening and ranking capital budgeting projects?

Problem 18-15

Unifying Concepts: Comparing the Internal Rate of Return and the Net Present Value Methods

Get Rich Corporation has to choose between two investment opportunities. Investment A requires an immediate cash outlay of $100,000 and provides after-tax income of $20,000 per year for 10 years. Investment B requires an immediate cash outlay of $1,000 and generates after-tax income of $350 per year for five years.

(continued)

Required:

1. Using a cost of capital of 12%, calculate the net present value of each investment, and determine which one Get Rich should select.
2. Calculate the internal rate of return of each investment. On the basis of this method, which investment should Get Rich select?
3. **Interpretive Question:** How do you account for the difference in rankings? Under the circumstances, which method would you rely on for your decision?

Problem 18-16

Unifying Concepts: Payback and Internal Rate of Return

The management of Kitchen Shop is thinking of buying a new drill press to aid in adapting parts for different machines. The press is expected to save Kitchen Shop $8,000 per year in costs. However, Kitchen Shop has an old punch machine that isn't worth anything on the market and that will probably last indefinitely. The new press will last 12 years and will cost $41,595. (Ignore income tax effects.)

Required:

1. Compute the payback period of the new machine.
2. Compute the internal rate of return.
3. **Interpretive Question:** What uncertainties are involved in this decision? Discuss how they might be dealt with.

Problem 18-17

Unifying Concepts: Capital Rationing Using the Payback and Net Present Value Methods

Dino Corporation is trying to decide which of five investment opportunities it should undertake. The company's cost of capital is 16%. Owing to a cash shortage, the company has a policy that it will not undertake any investment unless it has a payback period of less than three years. The company is unwilling to undertake more than two investment projects. The following data apply to the alternatives:

Investment	Initial Cost	Expected Returns
A	$100,000	$30,000 per year for 5 years
B	50,000	25,000 per year for 6 years
C	30,000	8,000 per year for 10 years
D	20,000	7,000 per year for 6 years
E	10,000	3,500 per year for 3 years

Required:

1. Using the payback method, screen out any investment project that fails to meet the company's payback period requirement.
2. Using the net present value method, determine which of the remaining projects the company should undertake, keeping in mind the capital rationing constraint.
3. **Interpretive Question:** What advantages do you see in using the payback method together with other capital budgeting methods?

Problem 18-18

Income Tax Effects

Sylvania Manufacturing Company is considering the purchase of new equipment to perform operations currently being performed on less efficient equipment. The purchase price is $142,000 delivered and installed. The company elects to expense $10,000 of the purchase price in the first year. A company engineer estimates that the new equipment will save $28,000 in labor and other direct costs annually. The new equipment will have an estimated life of 10 years and zero salvage value at the end of the 10 years. The equipment will be depreciated over 10 years on the optional straight-line basis for income tax purposes, after taking the

$10,000 expense election in the first year. The existing equipment has a book value of $4,000, a remaining economic life of five years, and can be disposed of now for $4,000. The company's average tax rate is 40% (including federal, state, and local taxes), and its after-tax cost of capital is 12%.

Required:
1. Should the new equipment be purchased?
2. What would the decision be if the cost of capital were 10%?
3. **Interpretive Question:** Assuming that the net present value of an investment in new equipment is so small that you are indifferent about whether to make the purchase or keep the old equipment, what other factors would you consider in making the decision?

d iscussion cases

Case 18-1

Should We Purchase That New Copier?

Campus Print Shop is thinking of purchasing a new, modern copier that automatically collates pages. The machine would cost $22,000 cash. A service contract on the machine, considered a must because of its complexity, would be an additional $200 per month. The machine is expected to last eight years and have a resale value of $4,000. By purchasing the new machine, Campus would save $450 per month in labor costs and $100 per month in materials costs due to increased efficiency. Other operating costs are expected to remain the same. The old copier would be sold for its scrap value of $1,000. Campus requires a return of 14% on its capital investments.

1. As a consultant to Campus, compute:
   a. The payback period.
   b. The unadjusted rate of return.
   c. The net present value.
   d. The internal rate of return.
2. On the basis of these computations and any qualitative considerations, would you recommend that Campus purchase the new copier?

Case 18-2

Cost and Qualitative Factors in Capital Investment Decisions

Yoshika Landscaping is contemplating purchasing a new ditch-digging machine that promises savings of $5,600 per year for 10 years. The machine costs $21,970, and no salvage value is expected. The company's cost of capital is 12%. You have been asked to advise Yoshika relative to this capital investment decision. As part of your analysis, compute:

1. The payback period.
2. The unadjusted rate of return.
3. The net present value.
4. The internal rate of return.

What factors besides your quantitative analysis should be considered in making this decision?

j udgment calls

Judgment 18-1

You Decide: Which measurement is the most important when making a capital budgeting decision, net present value or improved customer satisfaction?

Your company is considering purchasing a server to host the company Web site, which customers use to place their orders.

When deciding on this new capital investment, you realize that the net present value of the purchase is negative, meaning the future cash flows associated with the server will not replace the initial investment. However, an important qualitative factor that should be considered with the purchase of a new server is the improved customer service and satisfaction that will be achieved as a result of the purchase. What should you do?

Judgment 18-2

You Decide: Should a project be accepted or rejected if the project has an internal rate of return that is less than the company's hurdle rate?

You are the CFO for an automobile manufacturer. The board of directors is considering expanding the current product line to include sports utility vehicles. As you look at the new product line's internal rate of return, it is 12% and the company's overall discount rate is 15%. Should the new line be added to the company's existing lines? The board wants your input before they make a decision. What factors should you consider?

Competency Enhancement Opportunities

▶ **Analyzing Real Company Information**
▶ **International Case**
▶ **Ethics Case**
▶ **Writing Assignment**

▶ **The Debate**
▶ **Internet Search**

The following additional assignments provide opportunities for students to develop critical thinking, ethical perspectives, oral and written communication skills, experience with electronic research, and teamwork through group and business activities.

▶ ## Analyzing Real Company Information

Analyzing 18-1 (Microsoft)

The 2002 Form 10-K for MICROSOFT is included in Appendix A. The section of the Form 10-K relating to management's discussion and analysis provides detail as to factors that might affect Microsoft's future and, as a result, the company's long-term decisions. Review the financial statements and the "Management Discussion and Analysis" section, and answer the following questions:

1. Microsoft has no long-term debt. Does that mean its cost of capital is zero? Explain.
2. Microsoft specifically states that the company "does not provide forecasts of future financial performance." If that is the case, how can it make any capital budgeting decisions?

Analyzing 18-2 (The Boeing Company)

As you probably know, BOEING builds airplanes. While most famous for the big 747, Boeing is continually developing newer models. Over the past several years, Boeing has been developing the 737 and 777 families of airplanes. In 1996, Boeing formed a joint venture with GENERAL ELECTRIC to develop planes that can fly over 6,000 miles without refueling.

1. What factors must Boeing consider when making the decision to produce a new family of airplanes like the 777? What would be the expected cash inflows, and what would be the expected cash outflows? Categorize the outflows into two types: one-time outflows and annual outflows.
2. The costs of developing a new family of airplanes are enormous. Why would Boeing agree to incur these costs when it is able to continue producing older model planes like the 747 and the 767? Frame this discussion in terms of a capital budgeting decision. That is, evaluate the opportunities in terms of cash inflows and cash outflows.

International

▶ *International Case*

DaimlerChrysler

DAIMLERCHRYSLER discloses the following information relating to its long-term debt in its 2002 annual report:

- 6.3% notes/bonds
- 2.6% commercial paper
- 5.3% liabilities to financial institutions

FORD MOTOR COMPANY also provides information relating to its debt in the notes to its annual report. That information is given below.

- Secured indebtedness, 7.6%
- Unsecured senior indebtedness—notes and bank debt, 4.8%
- Unsecured subordinated indebtedness—notes, 9.4%

1. Assume that each company's debt is distributed equally across the various categories. Compute an average cost interest rate for each company.
2. If your answer from part (1) represented each firm's cost of capital, what would it tell you about the kinds of projects that DaimlerChrysler can undertake as compared to Ford?

▶ *Ethics Case*

Wheeler, Nevada

The city council of Wheeler, Nevada, is faced with an important decision: whether or not to re-zone a parcel of property and allow ChemStor, Inc., to purchase the land and build a chemical waste storage facility on the property. Several factors enter into the decision.

a. The property is currently zoned for agricultural use and is surrounded by ranching operations in a rural community.
b. Several ranchers have joined together and offered to buy the property from the city over a 40-year period. In return for an agreed-upon interest rate of one point below prime, they will donate 20 acres of the land for a city park.
c. ChemStor has offered to pay cash for the land. Company management also points out that the facility will create about 25 new jobs for local residents and generate close to $100,000 a year in increased property taxes for the city.
d. ChemStor, a New Jersey-based company, learned of this property from its controller, who is a brother-in-law to one of the Wheeler City council members. ChemStor has offered a "finder's fee" for locating a waste storage site. The finder's fee would be split between the controller and the brother-in-law.

Identify the ethical and other issues involved in this capital investment decision.

▶ *Writing Assignment*

Lease versus Buy

You are fresh out of college, have your first real job, and just received your first big paycheck. You decide you need some wheels. Off you go to the car dealer. You carefully review the various makes and models of cars, determine the price range you can afford, and select "YOUR FIRST CAR." You thought that was the hard part. Now you need to decide on financing. The sales-person says you can either borrow money to purchase the vehicle or you can lease the car.

What factors should you consider in making this capital budgeting decision? Identify those factors that should enter into the lease versus buy decision. Prepare a short memo discussing the pros and cons of leasing versus buying and identifying the cash inflows and outflows associated with each option.

▷ *The Debate*

The Time Value of Money

The text discusses two general types of capital budgeting techniques: nondiscounted and discounted. The nondiscounted methods involve comparing the outflows of cash to the inflows. These methods do not take into account the time value of money. The discounted capital budgeting techniques factor in the evaluation of the time value of money.

Divide your group into two teams.

- Team 1 is to take the position that the nondiscounted methods provide the best means of evaluating capital budgeting alternatives. Prepare a short presentation that identifies the advantages of using the nondiscounted methods and discusses the disadvantages of the discounted capital budgeting techniques.
- Team 2 is to take the position that the discounted methods are preferred. Prepare a short presentation in support of the various methods that incorporate into their analysis the time value of money.

▷ *Internet Search*

Federal Express

We began this chapter with a look at FEDERAL EXPRESS. Let's continue our examination of this company using its Internet site. Access Federal Express's site at **http://www.fedex.com**. Sometimes Web addresses change, so if this address doesn't work, access the Web site for this book at **http://albrecht.swlearning.com** for an updated link to Federal Express.

Once you have gained access to the company's Web site, answer the following questions:

1. Find the portion of the Web site containing information about the early history of FedEx Express. Why was Memphis, Tennessee, chosen as the company headquarters?
2. Find the portion of the Web site containing "FedEx Express Facts." How many aircraft does FedEx have in its worldwide fleet?
3. Find FedEx's most recent annual report. Does the company lease any of its aircraft or equipment? (*Hint:* Look in the notes to the financial statements.) What factors would the company have considered when determining whether to lease or buy its aircraft and equipment?

comprehensive problem 15-18

Imagine that one of your parents has traveled across the country to visit you at college. As the two of you have dinner together at one of your favorite restaurants, the discussion turns to your accounting class. You begin describing some of the new ideas and techniques you have been learning lately. Suddenly, your parent wants to talk about the family business. As the discussion goes on, it becomes clear that your parent is expecting you to provide some specific ideas about how to improve the management process in the family business using current accounting methods. You certainly want to impress your parent with all the detailed knowledge that you have gained since beginning your course work in accounting. However, you are also concerned that you may describe something incorrectly or say something misleading. One day you expect to inherit the family business, and you would hate to say anything during dinner that might later cause problems in the company!

Required:

You need to respond to your parent using insights gained from the first four chapters of management accounting. Further, answering your parent's questions will require you to carefully construct your remarks in light of the exact nature of the family business. Hence, we will assume three separate types of businesses for your family:

1. Computer manufacturing plant
2. Neighborhood grocery store
3. Large architectural firm

Listed below are a number of topics from the first four chapters of management accounting. Briefly describe in three sentences or less how each topic may relate to the family business.

1. Direct materials costs
2. Direct labor costs
3. Overhead costs
4. Direct materials inventory
5. Work-in-process inventory
6. Finished goods inventory
7. Job order costing
8. Process costing*
9. Cost behavior
10. Break-even analysis
11. Capital budgeting
12. Net present value
13. Internal rate of return

*Relates to expanded material.

c h a p t e r

19

Operational Budgeting

After studying this chapter, you should be able to:

Learning Objectives

1 Describe the importance of personal budgeting.

2 Identify the purposes of budgeting for organizations.

3 Explain the budgeting process and its behavioral implications in organizations.

4 Construct an operating budget and its components for manufacturing firms.

5 Compare the operating budget for a manufacturing firm to that of a merchandising or service firm.

6 Create the cash budget.

7 Prepare pro-forma financial statements.

8 Distinguish between static and flexible budgets.

Every organization needs to budget. Budgets help allocate resources effectively so that the organization can accomplish its mission. Consider how the federal government budgets, for example. The arrival of the president's budget on Capitol Hill signals the beginning of the annual budget process in Congress—a process that can last more than eight months and require the passage of scores of bills and resolutions.[1] Congress drafts a budget resolution—a spending plan that defines in broad terms how much the government will take in through taxes and other receipts and spend on all government accounts during the coming fiscal year. The House and Senate Budget Committees each draft their own version, bring the drafts to their respective chambers for approval, iron out differences in conference, and return the resulting version to their chambers for adoption. Discretionary spending is allocated to the Appropriations Committees in both chambers. Throughout the budget process, Congress passes authorization bills that set the maximum amounts that may be spent in specific fiscal years for individual discretionary programs, as well as goals for those programs. The budget resolution serves as a blueprint for congressional spending decisions. It sets the total levels for budget authority, outlays, incoming revenues, direct-loan obligations, and loan guarantee commitments, as well as the public debt ceiling for the upcoming fiscal year.

For example, the 2004 federal budget is broken down as follows:

Spending Category	Amount*	Percentage of Total
Social Security	$ 478 billion	21.8%
Other human resources (training, health, etc.)	697	31.8
Defense	376	17.2
Medicare	245	11.2
Interest on debt	161	7.4
Other functions (science, justice, etc.)	118	5.4
Physical resources (energy, commerce, etc.)	115	5.3
Total	$2,190 billion	100.0%

*Amounts reflect estimates provided in fiscal year 2004. Available at **http://www.whitehouse.gov/omb/budget**.

As you can see, a significant portion of the budget goes to pay interest on the national debt. However, given that between $200 and $300 billion in budget deficits are predicted in each of the six years beginning with 2003 (see Exhibit 1 on the next page), you can probably expect this cost to grow.

Budgeting probably consumes more congressional time than any other single activity. Even though you may argue that Congress and the president have not been as fiscally responsible as they could have been, you should be comforted that the budgeting process instills some discipline in their spending habits and provides a sense of order for governmental expenditures and management of programs.

Exhibit 1 demonstrates the expectations of the 2003 administration. However, these numbers are only estimates, and many economic factors can influence the amount of taxes collected (i.e., receipts) by the government. It is important to point out that it is difficult to make changes to spending (i.e., outlays) on committed government programs like Social Security. On the other hand, economic downturns create smaller tax bases that *immediately* result in less revenue receipts for the federal government. It's not easy to maintain a balanced federal government budget!

1 Further information on the federal budget process can be obtained from **http://www.house.gov/rules/budget_pro.htm**.

Exhibit 1: U.S. Federal Government Estimated Annual Budget*

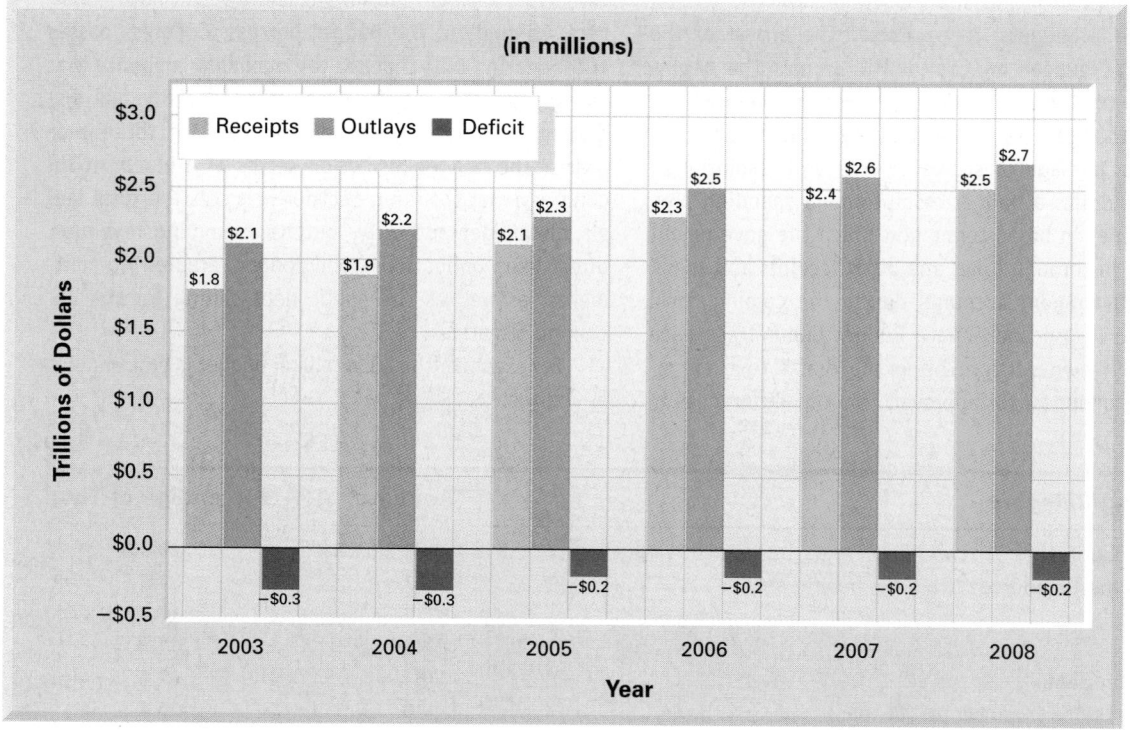

*Amounts reflect estimates provided in fiscal year 2004. Available at **http://www.whitehouse.gov/omb/budget**.

a **budget** is a quantitative expression of a plan of action that shows how a firm, an organization (such as the government in the opening scenario), or an individual will acquire and use resources over a specified period of time. For a firm, implicit in most budgets is management's expectation of earning sufficient profit to provide a reasonable return on investment. The budget identifies and allocates resources necessary to effectively and efficiently carry out the mission of the organization. Al-

though budgeting may sound to you like an unappealing activity (maybe you have tried budgeting your personal expenditures), successful budgeting is absolutely critical to the success of a business. In this chapter, we will briefly touch on personal budgeting and then cover budgeting for manufacturing, merchandising, and service firms.

budget A quantitative expression of a plan of action that shows how a firm or an organization will acquire and use resources over some specified period of time.

Purposes of Budgeting

1 Describe the importance of personal budgeting.

Whether we're talking about an individual, a family, or a large organization, the overall purpose of a budget is to clearly establish a plan so that performance in relation to a goal can be carefully monitored. Thus, budgeting has a twofold purpose. The first purpose is to allow individuals or companies to develop a plan to meet a specified goal. The second purpose is to allow ongoing comparison between actual results and the plan in order to better control operations or activities. To illustrate, let us assume that Dick Cotton earns $3,600 a month (and takes home only $2,390 after taxes) and has prepared a budget of his income and expenses.

The budget in Exhibit 2 contains an important warning that spending is exceeding earnings. The commitment of $1,700 to fixed expenses leaves only $690 to cover all of Dick's necessary expenditures for utilities, food, clothing, and the like. Because Dick cannot cover these expenditures using his **disposable income** of $690 a month, he must revise his plans; perhaps he could ask for a raise, get a second job or a new job that pays more, or decrease his spending. This simple illustration shows that budgeting is extremely important. Unless Dick takes corrective action, he will soon join the growing number of individuals declaring bankruptcy.

disposable income Income left after withholdings and fixed expenses have been subtracted from gross salary; the amount left to cover variable expenditures.

In addition, someday Dick will want to retire. Currently, Dick's budget does not provide for any savings or investments. With all the planning tools available today, such as tax-sheltered retirement plans, investments, annuities, and so forth, an individual who plans and budgets well can prepare adequately for the future. Unfortunately, at his present rate, Dick will not be one of these individuals.

Indeed, the penalty for not budgeting is severe. Individuals who budget successfully typically find that they can purchase those things that they feel they really want to have. In fact, budgeting does not really limit spending. The only real difference between individuals who budget and those who don't is that those who budget will spend money how, where, and when they want to, and those who do not budget often feel like they never have enough money to purchase those things that they really need.

Are you wondering which category you fall into—those who successfully budget or those who don't? Review these characteristics of good personal budgeters and see how you compare.

- Understand debt and interest
- Disciplined
- Flexible
- Organized
- Good communicator (especially important if married)
- Proactive
- Goal-driven

Exhibit 2: Monthly Budget for Dick Cotton

Gross salary		$ 3,600
Withholdings:		
Federal income taxes	$ 600	
State income taxes	180	
FICA taxes	270	
Other withholdings	160	(1,210)
Net take-home pay		$ 2,390
Fixed expenses:		
House mortgage	$1,100	
Car payment	350	
Insurance	250	(1,700)
Disposable income		$ 690
Utilities	$ 200	
Food	400	
Clothing	100	
Entertainment	100	
Miscellaneous	200	(1,000)
Net surplus (deficit)		$ (310)

$$\left[\begin{array}{l}\text{TO SUMMARIZE: It is just as important for individuals to create and follow a budget as it is for organizations. Individuals who budget are able to plan their} \quad \text{spending and are better prepared for the future. Those who budget typically are goal oriented, organized, proactive, and disciplined.}\end{array}\right]$$

Types and Purposes of Budgeting

2 Identify the purposes of budgeting for organizations.

As you learned in the earlier chapter when we introduced management accounting, budgeting is part of the management planning process, a process that involves identifying problems or opportunities, identifying alternative solutions, evaluating those alternatives, then choosing and implementing the best alternatives. There are two basic types of planning: (1) long-run planning, which includes strategic planning and capital budgeting, and (2) short-run planning, which includes production and process prioritizing and operational budgeting or profit planning. Long-run planning involves making decisions where the effects will extend several years into the future. Long-run planning includes broad-based decisions about products, markets, productive facilities, and financial resources. This type of planning is often referred to as strategic planning. Strategic planning takes place at the executive level in an organization and involves identifying the organization's mission, the goals flowing from that mission, and the strategies and actions that will be taken to accomplish those goals. With strategic planning in place, the company can then plan for the purchase and use of major assets such as buildings or equipment to help the company meet its long-range goals. This type of planning, which you studied in the previous chapter, is called capital budgeting.

To further review, short-run planning is divided into two categories. Once the organization has made long-term commitments to capital structure (land, buildings, equipment, management personnel, etc.), then managers need to determine how to best use those committed resources to maximize the return on their capital investments—a process often referred to as production prioritizing. We'll discuss production prioritizing decisions in a later chapter on making decisions.

Once the organization has determined what to produce or otherwise provide to the marketplace in order to maximize its goals, managers are ready to go to the next phase of short-run planning—operational budgeting. Sometimes known as profit plans, operational budgets are used by managers to establish and communicate daily, weekly, and monthly goals for the organization. Failure to carefully perform strategic planning, capital budgeting, or budgeting for operations can have adverse consequences for organizations, even to the point of causing bankruptcy. The list of companies that have failed in recent years as a result of poor planning and execution is getting longer each day. Casualties of poor planning include such common names as K-MART, ADELPHIA, US AIRWAYS, EXIDE TECHNOLOGIES (the world's largest maker of car batteries), POLAROID, CONVERSE, CONSECO, and UAL (the parent of UNITED AIRLINES). (Some of these companies were done under by unethical behavior as well.) In 2002, the 186 companies that filed for bankruptcy had combined total assets equal to $368 billion, over $100 billion greater than the 2001 mark of $259 billion.[2] In this chapter, our focus is on creating a "profit plan" in order to better control operations companies both large and small.

The **master budget** is the most detailed and most heavily used budget in an organization. As the name implies, this budget depicts the organization's goals and plans for revenues, pro-

FYI:

While budgeting is very helpful for decision making, organizations are often required to prepare detailed budgets before bankers will loan money or before a company can issue stock or debt for sale to the public. When companies declare bankruptcy and are taken over by court-ordered trustees, one of the trustee's first steps is to prepare detailed budgets. These budgets help to determine whether the company should cease operations and liquidate (known as a Chapter 7 bankruptcy), or whether the trustee should ask the court to give the company time to work through its financial problems so that it can fully or partially repay its debts (known as a Chapter 11 bankruptcy).

master budget A network of many separate schedules and budgets that together constitute the overall operating and financing plan for the coming period.

2 "U.S. Bankruptcies Break Records," *BBC News*, December 30, 2002, **http://news.bbc.co.uk/1/hi/business/2616135.stm**.

duction, expenses, and cash for the next period. Essentially, the same advantages that individuals experience with personal budgeting also exist for organizations that follow a master budget. Specifically, there are six major reasons why a master budget is important to an organization's success. As you review this list, think about your own personal budget and how these budgeting objectives relate to you.

1. *Planning and setting objectives.* The preparation of a master budget forces managers to consider explicitly where the firm is going and how it is going to get there. By budgeting, an organization, such as the U.S. government as described in the opening scenario, will be better prepared to decide where its scarce resources will be spent.

2. *Communication and coordination.* Budgets improve communication between the various management levels of a business, helping managers plan activities that focus the organization on its strategy and goals, as well as enhance the smooth functioning of the enterprise in general. In both families and business organizations, it is usually not the lack of money that causes problems but the lack of communication about money. Couples and organizations that budget adequately find that their budgets are a great coordination tool when a critical resource (such as money) is in short supply!

3. *Authorization.* Once budgets are approved by top management, they provide authorization for investing, spending, ordering, producing, and borrowing by lower-level managers and employees. At most major companies, IBM for example, the budget becomes the law. If something is budgeted, it can be purchased. If not budgeted, the purchase cannot be made without careful consideration and approval from a high level of management. (This is one area where many personal budgets fail.)

4. *Motivation.* Budgets help motivate people. By providing a clear set of quantified objectives, budgets can help guide people to focus on important activities that need to be accomplished. The motivational aspect of budgets can be quite strong.

5. *Conflict resolution.* In most organizations, everyone usually wants additional resources. Budgeting forces up-front planning, which helps resolve conflicts over how limited resources will be allocated among an organization's various parts. (Remember the conflicting objectives of the government in the opening scenario?) Similarly, when a couple or a family prepares a budget together, the budget can help them resolve conflicting priorities by providing a way for them to plan when important purchases can be made (either now or sometime later in the future).

6. *Evaluation.* Budgets provide quantitative measures of expectations and objectives. These objectives later serve as performance measures (or benchmarks) against which the performance of managers and others in a firm can be evaluated.

In recent years, a number of concerns have been expressed about operational budgeting and the way firms budget. Some companies have found that their business environment is changing so rapidly that once the process is finally finished, the budget has little to do with the realities they face. In some companies, managers use budgets to analyze detailed spending without recognizing the bigger picture, such as the fact that the company is losing customers or that a new product is selling far below expectations. In other companies, traditional budgets have undermined the long-term growth potential of companies by motivating managers to focus exclusively on short-term financial numbers. The following are some of the problems with traditional budgeting that have led to revisions in the way companies budget:

• Departments and business units tend to create budgets based on how much they spent in previous years.

• Once budgets are set, resource allocations are too inflexible and are unable to adapt to change.

• In many companies, managers who have been evaluated and compensated according to how well they met their budget numbers feel powerless to act on new opportunities that are not already factored into the master budget.

- Often budgeting timelines do not match new product schedules, which makes it difficult to budget and measure performance on a long-term (e.g., three-year) development project using annual or quarterly budgets.
- Frequently, because of fast-paced business changes, a budget is outdated before it is even completed!

A high-level manager of a large company summed up the shortcomings of traditional budgets with this comment: "Trying to figure out how much fax paper you will need next November and what that will cost is like forecasting the weather." Recognizing such concerns but also realizing that a well-conceived strategy and supporting budgets are essential to effective growth, in recent years some organizations have spent large sums of money to make their budgeting more relevant and timely to what they do. Effective and timely budgets, aided by developments in technology, can help companies overcome the weaknesses in traditional budgeting. As noted earlier, however, the faster an industry moves, and the faster a company shifts its priorities, the more often plans must be adjusted and budgets changed.

Recent developments in software have made the budgeting process much more useful and relevant. Using enterprise-wide software systems, such as that developed by ORACLE, SAP, and PEOPLESOFT, companies can now integrate their budgeting process into their accounting systems, get immediate feedback about how they are doing, and use the feedback to make timely changes in their budgeting process. With developments in technology, companies can now measure results almost instantly. CISCO and DELL COMPUTER, for example, can receive immediate information about how they are doing (compared to processes that used to take several months) and can use these data to make real-time decisions on resource allocations and forecasts about profit margins and growth rates of different products. With such timely information, organizations can now both predict revenues and costs and measure them on a timely basis. Because companies can make real-time changes in their budgets, projections are much more accurate, and the budgeting process is much more meaningful. FUJITSU, for example, uses a monthly, rolling forecast, which is part of its enterprise planning software, that allows financial managers to make corrective budget changes on a timely basis.

network exercises

Congressional Budget Office

The best-known budget in the United States is the budget of the federal government. The Congressional Budget Office (CBO) offers a monthly update on the level of government receipts and outlays relative to budgeted levels.

Net Work:

Go to the CBO's Web site at **http://www .cbo.gov** to get a budget review for the most recent month.

TO SUMMARIZE: Budgeting in most organizations is based on that organization's strategic plan. Using the strategic plan to guide decisions, organizations perform two types of budgeting: capital budgeting and operations budgeting. The operating budget has several purposes: (1) assist in planning and setting objectives, (2) facilitate communication and coordinate activities, (3) authorize expenditures and actions, (4) motivate employees, (5) assist in resolving conflicts, and (6) provide a vehicle for performance measurement.

The Budgeting Process

3 Explain the budgeting process and its behavioral implications in organizations.

budget committee A management group responsible for establishing budgeting policy and for coordinating the preparation of budgets.

Budgeting is such an important activity that the top executives of most companies coordinate and participate in the process. Large firms usually establish a **budget committee**, which includes among its members the vice presidents for sales, production, purchasing, and finance and the controller or chief financial officer. These executives work to implement the organization's strategy by coordinating the preparation of a detailed budget in their areas of responsibility and then together oversee the integration of a comprehensive master budget for the firm. Two important issues faced by executives in the budgeting process are:

1. Behavioral considerations, and
2. Involvement in preparing the budget.

Behavioral Considerations

Research has shown that several behavioral factors determine how successful the budgeting process will be. First, the process must have the support of top management. Without a clear indication from top management that the budgeting process is important to the organization, managers will not be motivated to devote the time necessary to formulate an effective and efficient budget.

Second, managers and other employees are more motivated to achieve budget goals that they understand and helped design. For this process to work, managers must feel that their opinions are respected and given full consideration. In addition, this communication and participation process should remain open throughout the year. When internal or external circumstances change, all parties involved should discuss the necessary budget adjustments. Generally, the most effective (though not necessarily the most *efficient*) companies are those that involve employees in the decision-making process. However, as you'll see in the next section, involving a lot of employees adds significant time and cost to the budgeting process.

Third, deviations (also known as variances) from the budget must be addressed by managers in a positive and constructive manner. Identifying deviations from the plan is simply a way to focus management's attention on areas needing improvement. Unfortunately, some managers treat these deviations as an opportunity to find fault and assign blame to lower-level managers. The result is usually a loss of motivation, accompanied by such dysfunctional behavior as interdepartmental bickering, defensive attitudes, and overall unethical behavior. One output of such behavior is **budgetary slack** in the budget system; that is, intentionally creating an easy budget target that a manager is certain he or she can meet.

budgetary slack The process of inflating a department's budget request for resource inputs (e.g., materials, labor, time, etc.) or deflating the department's budget commitment to output (products, services, etc.) so that the department manager can more easily achieve the budget.

Obviously, all these behaviors waste an organization's resources and do not contribute to meeting its strategic and operational goals. A more useful reaction to deviations is to focus on the action to be taken. As one CEO stated, "I never made a dime for the company by assessing blame or firing a manager. If I can provide help to a manager to solve a problem, though, we can see the benefit." In administering the budget process, it is extremely important that top management not use the budget as a "club" or "whipping stick."

Involvement in Preparing the Budget: Top-Down versus Bottom-Up

A firm-wide operating budget could be prepared by top management, distributed to the major segments of the firm, and then further spread out to each lower-level segment manager. This is the top-down approach. Its proponents argue that only top management knows the strategic direction of the firm and is aware of all the external factors influencing its operations. Further, since top management involves only a few people who have risen to positions where they should no longer have special interests to protect, they are in the best position to *efficiently* coordinate the competing needs of the segments.

participative budgeting A bottom-up approach to budgeting that involves the full cooperation and participation of managers at all levels of the organization.

The alternative is the bottom-up approach, also known as **participative budgeting**. Essentially, each division manager in a bottom-up approach prepares a budget request for his or her segment. These requests are combined and reviewed as they move up the organization hierarchy, with adjustments being made to coordinate the needs and goals of individual units with the overall organization. Proponents of this approach contend that segment managers have the best information on the products or services they provide, the customers they serve, and the technology that is emerging; they are, therefore, in the best position to identify segment needs and to weigh alternative courses of action. More importantly, as mentioned earlier, managers who have a role in setting segment goals are more motivated to achieve these goals. It is also good training for managers to develop their planning skills in preparation for promotions to positions of greater authority. Naturally, the organization also benefits when its managers are proficient in planning. However, the bottom-up approach is very costly and time-intensive when compared to the top-down approach. In order to achieve personal goals, participants may also engage in political maneuvering that creates budgetary slack and other problems in the budgeting system.

Because both top-down and bottom-up are legitimate approaches, most organizations use some combination of the two. The budget committee members know the strategic direction of the firm and the important external factors that affect it, so they prepare a set of planning guidelines that are communicated to lower-level managers. These guidelines include such things as a forecast of key economic variables and their potential impact on the firm, plans for introducing and advertising new products, and some broad sales targets and resource allocations. With these guidelines in mind, lower-level managers prepare their individual budgets. These budgets are always reviewed to be sure they are consistent with the objectives of other segments and of the company as a whole. The budget committee understands that, from a behavioral point of view, any changes to a manager's budget should be made with great care. This is not to suggest that changes should not be made, only that reasons for those changes should be substantial and should be discussed with the managers involved.

The blending of these two approaches will vary among organizations. A smaller organization with few management levels will rely more on the top-down approach than a larger organization. Top management in smaller organizations tends to be more knowledgeable about and more involved in the operating details.

> **TO SUMMARIZE:** The behavioral factors that contribute to the success of the budgeting process include the support of top management, the participation of all managers in the budgeting process, and the need to address deviations from the budget in a positive and constructive manner. With the top-down approach, top management prepares the entire budget. With bottom-up budgeting, each segment manager makes budget requests. Most firms use a combination of the two approaches.

The Master Budget

4 Construct an operating budget and its components for manufacturing firms.

The master budget is an integrated group of detailed budgets that together constitute the overall operating and financing plans for a specific time period. In a manufacturing firm, the master budget begins with a forecast of sales; is followed by detailed budgets for the production, selling, administrative, and financial activities; and culminates in a set of pro-forma (or budgeted) financial statements. The flow of the preparation of the individual budgets within this master budget network is shown in Exhibit 3. Notice that the budgeting process is based on the long-term strategic and short-term operational plans established by top management in the organization. Also note how the capital budgeting process fits into the master budget. The final items forming the financial budget include the capital expenditures budget (or the capital budget), the cash budget, and the budgeted or pro-forma financial statements. Preparing the cash budget and the pro-forma statements is discussed in the expanded material. (You have already studied capital budgeting in the previous chapter.)

STOP & THINK

Review Exhibit 3 carefully because we will follow these budget schedules in sequence in the next sections of this chapter. Consider each budget and think for a moment about how it feeds into the subsequent budget.

To help explain these steps, we will illustrate the budgeting process in a manufacturing firm using an integrated example of budgets for the Sunbird Boat Company, a manufacturer of small fishing boats. Because it is important that you understand the budgeting process, you should work through the calculations of each budget schedule. Be sure to keep in mind that this formalized budgeting activity forces management to make many important decisions that guide a company toward its goals—decisions involving scheduling, pricing, borrowing, investing, and cost control.

Budgeting for Operations in a Manufacturing Firm

Our first illustration of the budgeting process is for Sunbird Boat Company, a manufacturing company that makes fishing boats. The boats are made of fiberglass and wood. To help us move

Exhibit 3: The Master Budget

through this example more quickly, we will assume that Sunbird only makes one type of boat—a 15-foot fishing boat. Exhibit 4 contains Sunbird's actual balance sheet for 2005. This is our beginning point for creating Sunbird's 2006 operational budget. In explaining the budgeting for Sunbird Boat Company, we will begin with the sales budget and then discuss each budget identified in Exhibit 3.

Exhibit 4: Sunbird Boat Company 2005 Balance Sheet

Sunbird Boat Company
Balance Sheet (Actual)
December 31, 2005

Assets

Current assets:

Cash	$ 135,000	
Accounts receivable	56,000	
Direct materials inventory[1]	7,980	
Finished goods inventory[2]	83,520	$ 282,500

Long-term assets:

Land	$ 234,305	
Building and equipment	1,500,000	
Less accumulated depreciation	(120,000)	1,614,305
Total assets		$1,896,805

Liabilities & Stockholders' Equity

Current liabilities:

Accounts payable[3]	$ 9,000	
Income taxes payable[3]	96,000	$ 105,000

Stockholders' equity:

Common stock, $5 par	$1,000,000	
Paid-in capital in excess of par	250,000	
Retained earnings	541,805	1,791,805
Total liabilities & stockholders' equity		$1,896,805

[1]Composed of 588 board feet of lumber and 420 square feet of fiberglass.
[2]Composed of 18 finished boats.
[3]Expected to be paid in the first quarter of 2006.

Sales Budget

sales budget A schedule of projected sales over the budget period.

The first step in developing a master budget is to prepare a **sales budget**. As shown in Exhibit 3, all the other budgets are developed from this budget. Projecting accurate sales is very difficult, however, because sales are a function of both uncontrollable external variables (customer tastes and economic conditions, for example) and controllable internal variables (such as price, sales effort, and advertising expenditures).

Uncontrollable external factors driving sales include the following:

- The business environment, which includes current government policies and law, the status of the economy, demographics (characteristics of the population such as age, wealth, family status, etc.), and the state of technology.
- Customer needs and tastes with respect to the product or service being analyzed and other substitute products.
- Intensity of the competition and possible barriers to market entry (barriers can include technology copyrights, government contracts, reputation, or large sales volumes that provide economies of scale).
- Seasonal cycles creating abrupt changes in sales demand due to holidays or weather patterns.
- Unexpected events such as terrorist acts, droughts, hurricanes, and earthquakes.

Analysis of external variables is accomplished through research and sales forecasting techniques. These techniques may be as simple as having the sales staff ask major customers about their buying plans for the next year or as sophisticated as statistical market research techniques. Some firms use quantitative forecasting models—these range from simple growth rate trends derived from the past year's sales to complex forecasting models that attempt to measure the influence of many economic and industry variables. Data used to drive these analyses are obtained from a variety of sources.

Controllable internal variables include the following four factors (sometimes known as the "4 P's" of the marketing mix):

- Product design in order to establish its function and appeal to customers.
- Pricing of the product, which can be used to brand the product as a luxury or a common good.
- Promotion of the product in order to target the product to specific groups in the market.
- Placement of the product, which involves the logistics of how the product will be made available and distributed to customers.

The marketing research on uncontrollable external variables is complicated. However, analyzing the influence of controllable internal variables is also a very difficult management process because these variables affect and are affected by the external variables. In fact, many or all of these factors must be considered when performing cost-volume-profit (C-V-P) analysis—the subject of an earlier chapter on cost-volume-profit analysis.

For purposes of this illustration, we will not go further into the details about the development of data for the sales budget. This is an important topic for your coursework in marketing and strategy. At this point, let's assume that Sunbird Boat Company has projected 2006 sales to be 100 boats. The anticipated sales price for each boat is $10,000.

Most organizations divide their yearly sales budget into monthly, weekly, or even daily budgets in order to plan production schedules and cash flows more precisely. For our illustration, we will assume that Sunbird Boat Company projects its boat sales on a quarterly basis, as shown in Schedule 1. However, whether the budget is on a quarterly or a daily basis, the concepts we're going to talk about are the same.

Schedule 1

Schedule 1 **Sunbird Boat Company** **2006 Sales Budget**					
	Q1	**Q2**	**Q3**	**Q4**	**Total**
Sales volume	24 boats	28 boats	30 boats	18 boats	100 boats
Price	×$ 10,000	×$ 10,000	×$ 10,000	×$ 10,000	×$ 10,000
Revenue earned	$240,000	$280,000	$300,000	$180,000	$1,000,000
Received in current quarter	× 80%	× 80%	× 80%	× 80%	
Current revenue collected	$192,000	$224,000	$240,000	$144,000	$ 800,000
Prior revenue collected*	56,000	48,000	56,000	60,000	220,000
Collections from customers	$248,000	$272,000	$296,000	$204,000	$1,020,000

*Prior revenue collected in Q1 (Quarter 1) represents the accounts receivable balance from the 2005 balance sheet. Prior revenue collected in Q2 through Q4 represents the revenue not collected in the prior quarter (i.e., revenue earned in prior quarter times 20%).

As you can see in Schedule 1, the sales budget that we are creating for Sunbird is computing two important numbers. First, we can assume that the marketing department for Sunbird has effectively researched all the relevant variables in order to predict the number of boats that will be sold each quarter. These numbers are used to determine the budgeted sales revenue that Sunbird expects to recognize. However, remember that this revenue still needs to be collected because at least some boats are sold on account. Based on past experience, Sunbird is able to collect approximately 80% of revenue from customers in the quarter in which the sale took place, with the remaining 20% collected in the following quarter. Happily, in this example, Sunbird doesn't expect to have any uncollectible accounts. Using this information, Sunbird also budgets the level of cash collections from customers for each quarter. Take a moment to study Schedule 1 in order to understand exactly how Sunbird is computing cash collections.

production budget A schedule of production requirements for the budget period.

Production Budget

The second detailed budget (Schedule 2) covers production, the number of units to be produced during the period. Factors to be considered in preparing this **production budget** are projected sales volume for the period, the desired amount of ending inventory, and the amount of inventory already on hand in the beginning inventory.

Ending inventory is an important figure because management wants enough units on hand to meet customer demands, but not so many that unnecessary costs will be incurred because of excessive inventory. Inventory management is an important management process that we'll discuss in a later chapter. For our work in this chapter, the desired ending inventory for any period will be expressed as a percentage of the following period's expected sales volume. Let's assume that Sunbird Boat Company has determined that its desired ending inventory for each quarter should be approximately 50% of projected sales for the next quarter. The fourth quarter's ending inventory is 13 15-foot boats, which is 50% of the next quarter's (first quarter of 2007) expected sales.

The production budget (Schedule 2) supplies information needed for all manufacturing cost budgets. Only after production quantities are known can management determine the amount of direct materials, direct labor, and manufacturing overhead needed during the period. As you study Schedule 2, be sure to note how the expected inventory of boats leads to the result that budgeted production levels are different from the budgeted levels of sales volumes.

STOP & THINK

Sunbird plans to keep its inventory level of boats at 50% of next quarter's sales. That is a lot of inventory! Why do you think that Sunbird follows this kind of an inventory policy?

STOP & THINK

Some companies work very hard to reduce or remove inventory from their organization. You'll learn in a later chapter on activity-based costing that this management technique is called a just-in-time or JIT inventory method. Think carefully about Sunbird's production budget (Schedule 2). Would this budget be needed if Sunbird had a JIT inventory system?

Schedule 2

Schedule 2 Sunbird Boat Company 2006 Production Budget					
	Q1	**Q2**	**Q3**	**Q4**	**Total**
Sales volume (Schedule 1)	24 boats	28 boats	30 boats	18 boats	100 boats
Desired ending inventory[1]	14 boats	15 boats	9 boats	13 boats	13 boats
Total boats needed	38 boats	43 boats	39 boats	31 boats	113 boats
Less beginning inventory[2]	(18 boats)	(14 boats)	(15 boats)	(9 boats)	(18 boats)
Total boats to produce	20 boats	29 boats	24 boats	22 boats	95 boats

[1]Sunbird desires to have ending boat inventory equal to 50% of the expected sales volume for the following quarter. Sunbird's marketing department forecasts sales of 26 boats during the first quarter of 2007.
[2]Sunbird's beginning finished goods inventory for 2006 is 18 boats. Beginning inventory for Q2 through Q4 is equal to the ending inventory for the prior quarter.

direct materials budget A schedule of direct materials to be used during the budget period and direct materials to be purchased during that period.

Caution

Note that the entries in the Total column do not always equal the sum of the four quarters. For example, the beginning inventory balance in Schedule 2 is the same for the year as it is for the first quarter. Similarly, the ending inventory balance is the same for the year as it is for the fourth quarter. Be sure to watch for similar patterns in subsequent budget schedules.

Direct Materials Budget

The next detailed budget to be prepared is the **direct materials budget** (Schedule 3). Based on the engineering department's estimates of the materials required to make a boat, this budget helps management schedule purchases from suppliers. Sunbird's engineers estimate that the amounts of wood and fiberglass needed per boat are as follows:

	15-Foot Boat
Direct materials requirements:	
Wood	70 board feet
Fiberglass	50 square feet

Sunbird's purchasing agent has been able to purchase wood at $10 per board foot and fiberglass at $5 per square foot. The purchasing agent expects that these prices will continue to be available to Sunbird through 2006.

Schedule 3

Schedule 3
Sunbird Boat Company
2006 Direct Materials Budget

Wood	Q1	Q2	Q3	Q4	Total
Production volume (Schedule 2)	20 boats	29 boats	24 boats	22 boats	95 boats
Standard feet per boat	× 70 feet	× 70 feet	× 70 feet	× 70 feet	× 70 feet
Wood needed in production	1,400 feet	2,030 feet	1,680 feet	1,540 feet	6,650 feet
Desired ending inventory¹	609 feet	504 feet	462 feet	546 feet	546 feet
Total wood needed	2,009 feet	2,534 feet	2,142 feet	2,086 feet	7,196 feet
Less beginning inventory²	(588) feet	(609) feet	(504) feet	(462) feet	(588) feet
Total wood to purchase	1,421 feet	1,925 feet	1,638 feet	1,624 feet	6,608 feet
Standard purchase price	× $10	× $10	× $10	× $10	× $10
Wood purchases	$14,210	$19,250	$16,380	$16,240	$66,080

Fiberglass	Q1	Q2	Q3	Q4	Total
Production volume (Schedule 2)	20 boats	29 boats	24 boats	22 boats	95 boats
Standard feet per boat	× 50 feet	× 50 feet	× 50 feet	× 50 feet	× 50 feet
Fiberglass needed in production	1,000 feet	1,450 feet	1,200 feet	1,100 feet	4,750 feet
Desired ending inventory¹	435 feet	360 feet	330 feet	390 feet	390 feet
Total fiberglass needed	1,435 feet	1,810 feet	1,530 feet	1,490 feet	5,140 feet
Less beginning inventory²	(420) feet	(435) feet	(360) feet	(330) feet	(420) feet
Total fiberglass to purchase	1,015 feet	1,375 feet	1,170 feet	1,160 feet	4,720 feet
Standard purchase price	× $5	× $5	× $5	× $5	× $5
Fiberglass purchases	$ 5,075	$ 6,875	$ 5,850	$ 5,800	$23,600
Total materials purchases	$19,285	$26,125	$22,230	$22,040	$89,680
Paid in current quarter	× 75%	× 75%	× 75%	× 75%	× 75%
Current purchase payments	$14,464	$19,594	$16,673	$16,530	$67,260
Prior purchase payments³	9,000	4,821	6,531	5,558	25,910
Payments to suppliers	$23,464	$24,415	$23,204	$22,088	$93,170

¹Sunbird desires to have ending raw materials inventory equal to 30% of the materials needed to support production volume for the following quarter. Sunbird's production volume for the first quarter of 2007 is expected to be 26 boats.
²Sunbird's beginning raw materials inventory for 2006 is 588 board feet of wood and 420 square feet of fiberglass. Beginning inventory for Q2 through Q4 is equal to the ending inventory for the prior quarter.
³Prior purchase payments in Q1 represent the accounts payable balance from the 2005 balance sheet. Prior purchase payments in Q2 through Q4 represent the purchases not paid for in the prior quarter (i.e., total materials purchases in prior quarter times 25%).

Based on these requirements for materials, the direct materials budget for Sunbird Boat Company for 2006 is shown in Schedule 3. Note that the materials needed are based on expected quarterly production and on the desired quarterly ending inventories. Then, similar to the approach used in the production schedule, the materials needed are adjusted for the beginning inventory expected for each quarter. Like the production budget, the direct materials budget depends on the desired level of ending inventory. If management does not maintain sufficient materials inventory levels, costly work stoppages can occur; if inventories are excessive, inventory investment and storage costs may be unduly high. Based on how long it takes Sunbird to receive wood and fiberglass from its suppliers, Sunbird's management has decided to maintain a supply of about 30% of the next quarter's production requirements for wood and fiberglass.

Finally, as is typical in most supplier relationships, Sunbird does not pay for raw materials at the time of the purchase, which means that Sunbird maintains an accounts payable balance. Sunbird's policy is to pay for 75% of its raw materials purchases in the current quarter, and the remaining 25% in the subsequent quarter. This payment policy is used to adjust the total purchases in Schedule 3 to compute the cash payments made to suppliers in each quarter (similar to the approach used to compute cash payments received from customers in the sales budget in Schedule 1).

Direct Labor Budget

direct labor budget A schedule of direct labor requirements for the budget period.

The fourth budget in the master budget is the **direct labor budget** (Schedule 4). The direct labor budget for Sunbird Boat Company is based on an average hourly wage rate of $15 per hour for production workers and 80 labor hours to make a 15-foot boat. In our example, the $15 per-hour wage rate includes fringe benefits (i.e., the cost of sick leave, vacation pay, insurance, etc.) and payroll taxes.[3] We will assume in our example that Sunbird's budgeted labor costs for each quarter are all paid in that same quarter. Hence, there is no need to adjust the labor costs in order to budget for labor cash payments each quarter.

Schedule 4

Schedule 4
Sunbird Boat Company
2006 Direct Labor Budget

	Q1	Q2	Q3	Q4	Total
Production volume (Schedule 2)	20 boats	29 boats	24 boats	22 boats	95 boats
Standard hours per boat	× 80 hours	× 80 hours	× 80 hours	× 80 hours	× 80 hours
Budgeted labor hours	1,600 hours	2,320 hours	1,920 hours	1,760 hours	7,600 hours
Standard wage rate per hour[1]	× $15	× $15	× $15	× $15	× $15
Direct labor cost[2]	$24,000	$34,800	$28,800	$26,400	$114,000

[1]Includes fringe benefits and payroll taxes.
[2]These costs are all paid in the quarter incurred.

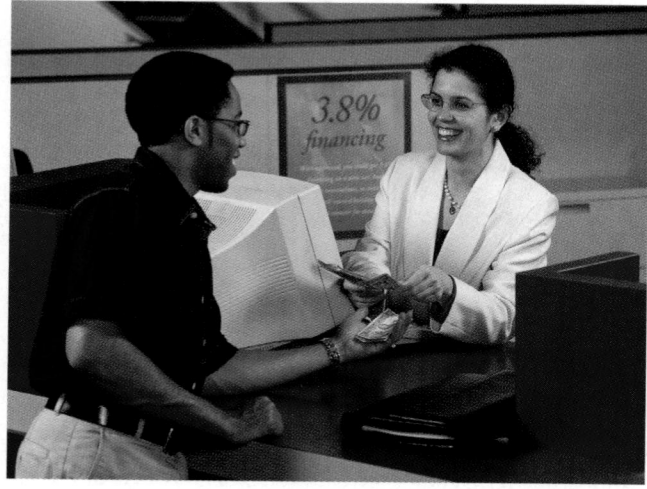

© 2003 Getty Images

Banks have replaced many of their full-time customer representatives with part-time employees. From management's perspective, the use of part-time workers makes direct labor budgeting easier.

Management must plan so that sufficient (but not excessive) labor is always available.[4] Otherwise, the company is likely to suffer the high cost of frequent hiring, firing, layoffs, and overtime work. Probably even more important than the high cost of employee turnover, however, is the feeling of demoralization among employees that such events can cause. If employees lack job security, they usually behave in ways that maximize their own personal short-run benefits (e.g., they may slow down production, thus creating the need for more employment or overtime work).

The recent trend in many companies has been to keep a relatively small full-time staff and hire an increasing number of part-time or temporary employees. Not only are these employees much easier to hire and terminate, but the company does not have to pay retirement and other benefits for them. Banks, for example, have replaced many of their full-time customer representatives with part-time employees. As a result of

3 The inclusion of fringe benefits and payroll taxes into the standard wage rate per hour is a significant decision in the budgeting process. Companies may also choose to include in the standard wage rate some measure of expected overtime pay. Other companies do not include some or all of these costs into the standard wage rate, but add them to the overhead application rate. This has the effect of spreading these costs evenly across all production output. However, including these costs into overhead will enhance the impact of inventory changes on the income statement due to absorption costing (a topic that we'll discuss in a chapter on managing inventory).

4 Just how variable labor costs are has aroused significant controversy in the management accounting literature. Some researchers argue that employees cannot easily be hired or terminated and, therefore, labor should be a fixed cost. Other researchers argue that labor is constantly hired and terminated—just read business newspapers where announcements of employee layoffs are printed every day. One thing is certain, though—labor costs are a very large component of the product cost that management strives to be able to control.

the smaller full-time workforce, companies that provide temporary workers are increasing in both size and number. From management's perspective, both part-time and temporary workers increase workforce flexibility and make direct labor budgeting easier. Unfortunately, these same trends probably mean less stable and secure careers for more and more workers unless, of course, part-time employment agencies take over the role of providing job security, retirement, and other benefits.

Manufacturing Overhead Budget

manufacturing overhead budget A schedule of production costs other than those for direct labor and direct materials.

The **manufacturing overhead budget** (Schedule 5) includes all production costs other than those for direct materials and direct labor. As noted in earlier chapters, manufacturing overhead is a major element of total manufacturing costs in many organizations. Hence, organizations that are able to effectively plan and control these costs have a significant advantage in the marketplace.

Schedule 5

Schedule 5
Sunbird Boat Company
2006 Manufacturing Overhead (MOH) Budget

Variable MOH costs		Q1	Q2	Q3	Q4	Total
Total labor hours (Schedule 4)		1,600 hours	2,320 hours	1,920 hours	1,760 hours	7,600 hours
Variable MOH rates per hour:						
Indirect materials	$ 1.50	$ 2,400	$ 3,480	$ 2,880	$ 2,640	$ 11,400
Indirect labor	5.50	8,800	12,760	10,560	9,680	41,800
Utilities	1.00	1,600	2,320	1,920	1,760	7,600
Total variable MOH costs	$ 8.00	$12,800	$18,560	$15,360	$14,080	$ 60,800
Fixed MOH costs per quarter						
Property taxes	$ 760	$ 760	$ 760	$ 760	$ 760	$ 3,040
Insurance	900	900	900	900	900	3,600
Depreciation—plant	16,500	16,500	16,500	16,500	16,500	66,000
Supervisors' salaries	22,500	22,500	22,500	22,500	22,500	90,000
Total fixed MOH costs	$40,660	$40,660	$40,660	$40,660	$40,660	$162,640
Total MOH costs		$53,460	$59,220	$56,020	$54,740	$223,440
Less depreciation		(16,500)	(16,500)	(16,500)	(16,500)	(66,000)
Total MOH payments*		$36,960	$42,720	$39,520	$38,240	$157,440

*Because depreciation does not represent a cash payment, these costs are removed to determine cash payments made each quarter for manufacturing overhead costs. All other manufacturing overhead costs are paid for in the quarter incurred.

In preparing this budget, Sunbird's accounting department first estimates the annual variable and fixed manufacturing overhead costs, as shown in the first column of Schedule 5. As you can see, the estimated variable manufacturing overhead costs are based on a cost per direct labor hour. In our example, we are assuming that volume of direct labor hours is a good predictor of variable manufacturing overhead costs for Sunbird, and that Sunbird uses direct labor hours to allocate these costs to each quarter. These variable cost rates per hour have been estimated previously by Sunbird's accountants. These rates are then multiplied by the number of direct labor hours estimated for each quarter (from Schedule 4) to figure the budgeted variable manufacturing overhead cost for boats for that quarter.[5] Total fixed costs are simply allocated evenly across the four quarters.

5 In an earlier chapter on product cost flows, we typically used direct labor hours to assign manufacturing overhead costs. This is actually a very simplistic approach to managing these important costs. The basic approach is for the total variable cost of each item to be allocated among the four quarters on the basis of some appropriate activity or cost driver. In a later chapter, we'll talk about an important technique called activity-based costing that is used by some organizations to carefully manage all overhead costs. We use direct labor hours here because using various cost drivers would unnecessarily complicate our examples.

Caution

Remember that the budgets being discussed in this chapter are for only one level of expected sales. If the level of sales changes, the budgeted variable costs will also change. This means that all the direct materials and direct labor budgets will change, as will some of the manufacturing overhead and selling and administrative expense budgets. This issue of changing levels of sales or operations is covered in the expanded material section of the chapter under the topic of flexible budgeting.

budgeted product cost sheet A schedule of all of the product costs (i.e., the costs of direct materials, direct labor, and manufacturing overhead) used to create a single product.

Schedule 6

To be sure that you understand how the variable manufacturing overhead cost rates are used to create Schedule 5, assume that total indirect materials costs for 2006 were estimated to be $11,400. Dividing that number by 7,600 direct labor hours (the total labor hours from Schedule 4) yields a rate of $1.50 per hour. Multiplying the $1.50 rate by 1,600 direct labor hours produces $2,400 to be assigned to the first quarter as the budgeted cost of indirect materials. With 2,320 direct labor hours in the second quarter, the cost for that quarter is $3,480. The calculation is the same for the remaining quarters, as well as for other variable overhead items.

The final computation on the manufacturing overhead budget is to determine the budgeted cash payments for these costs to be made each quarter. We assume that Sunbird stays current with these costs and makes payments as the costs are used in production. However, depreciation does not represent an actual cash outflow. Hence, these costs are removed from the budgeted manufacturing overhead costs to determine the payments expected to be made each quarter related to manufacturing overhead.

Budgeted Product Cost Sheet

The **budgeted product cost sheet** (Schedule 6) accumulates all the budgeted product costs (direct materials, direct labor, and manufacturing overhead) to estimate the total production cost of building each boat. The product cost sheet is useful to help us understand that the operational budget serves two different management purposes. First, by comparing actual sales and costs, the master budget data can be used as the basis for controlling costs and evaluating the performance of the managers responsible for those costs. (You'll clearly see how this control process works when we study variance analysis in the next chapter.)

Schedule 6
Sunbird Boat Company
2006 Budgeted Product Cost Sheet

		Total
Direct materials cost per boat (Schedule 3):		
Wood (70 board feet @ $10 per foot)	$700	
Fiberglass (50 board feet @ $5 per foot)	250	$ 950
Direct labor cost per boat (Schedule 4): 80 hours x $15 per hour		1,200
Variable MOH cost per boat (Schedule 5): 80 hours x $8 per hour		640
Total variable cost per boat		$2,790
Total Fixed MOH (Schedule 5)	$162,640	
Divided by production volume (Schedule 2)	÷ 95 boats	
Fixed MOH cost allocated per boat*		1,712
Total production cost per boat		$4,502

*Note that the production costs per boat for Sunbird will actually vary from quarter to quarter because of the change in fixed MOH costs per boat due to changes in quarterly production volume. To avoid these artificial changes in quarterly budgeted boat production costs, Sunbird creates the budgeted product cost sheet on an annual basis only.

Second, these budgets are used in product costing. As you will recall from a previous chapter, the manufacturing overhead costs that flow through Work-in-Process Inventory to Finished Goods Inventory (and eventually to Cost of Goods Sold) are standardized costs that are *applied* based on predetermined overhead rates. Accountants then track the difference between actual overhead costs and applied overhead costs (the over- or underapplied manufacturing overhead amount you studied in the earlier chapter on product cost flows) in order to determine if overhead resources are being efficiently used.[6] In our example, this predetermined overhead rate

---

6 In fact, as you will learn in the next chapter on monitoring performance, we can use similar standardized costs of direct materials and direct labor to track and control how efficiently direct materials and direct labor are used to produce goods and services.

that Sunbird will use during the year to apply overhead costs to products being manufactured is calculated by dividing estimated annual direct labor hours (from Schedule 4) into estimated annual *total* manufacturing overhead (from Schedule 5). The rate is then computed as $223,440 ÷ 7,600 hours = $29.40 per hour.

Using the direct materials, direct labor, and manufacturing overhead budgets (the three elements of a product's cost), we are able to compute Sunbird's budgeted cost of making its 15-foot boats. As you can see in Schedule 6, these costs are largely based on data from the budgets we have been preparing. This information is then used to measure budgeted cost of goods sold for the pro-forma income statement that we will study in the expanded material section of this chapter.

Selling and Administrative Expense Budget

The **selling and administrative expense budget** (Schedule 7) includes planned expenditures for all areas other than production. The costs of supplies used by the office staff, the salaries of the sales manager and company president, and the depreciation of administrative office buildings (*not* production facilities) all belong in this category. Because this budget covers several areas, it is usually quite large and may be supported by individual budgets for specific departments within the selling and administrative functions.

The selling and administrative expense budget for Sunbird is prepared in a manner similar to the manufacturing overhead budget. Total selling and administrative expenses are estimated for the year, with each expense then being distributed among the four quarters. As shown in Schedule 7, fixed expenses are assigned equally to each quarter, whereas variable expenses are allocated according to the number of boats to be sold. Variable delivery expenses, for example, are allocated to quarters by first determining the delivery expense rate [$50,000 estimated delivery expenses ÷ 100 boats expected to be sold during the year (from Schedule 1) = $500 per boat]. This rate is multiplied by the number of boats sold in a quarter to determine the delivery expenses allocated to that quarter. Because Sunbird expects to sell 24 boats in the first quarter at a rate of $500 per boat, the amount of delivery expense budgeted for that quarter is $12,000 ($500 × 24 boats). Sales commissions are allocated to each quarter in the same way.

Schedule 7

Schedule 7
Sunbird Boat Company
2006 Selling and Administrative (S&A) Expense Budget

Variable S&A expenses		Q1	Q2	Q3	Q4	Total
Sales volume (Schedule 1)		24 boats	28 boats	30 boats	18 boats	100 boats
Variable expense per boat sold:						
Delivery expense	$ 500	$ 12,000	$ 14,000	$ 15,000	$ 9,000	$ 50,000
Sales commissions	1,600	38,400	44,800	48,000	28,800	160,000
Total variable S&A expenses	$ 2,100	$ 50,400	$ 58,800	$ 63,000	$ 37,800	$210,000
Fixed S&A expenses per quarter						
Executives' salaries	$35,000	$ 35,000	$ 35,000	$ 35,000	$ 35,000	$140,000
Depreciation expense	8,000	8,000	8,000	8,000	8,000	32,000
Advertising expense	20,000	20,000	20,000	20,000	20,000	80,000
Miscellaneous expenses	2,500	2,500	2,500	2,500	2,500	10,000
Total fixed S&A expenses	$65,500	$ 65,500	$ 65,500	$ 65,500	$ 65,500	$262,000
Total S&A expenses		$115,900	$124,300	$128,500	$103,300	$472,000
Less depreciation		(8,000)	(8,000)	(8,000)	(8,000)	(32,000)
Total S&A payments*		$107,900	$116,300	$120,500	$ 95,300	$440,000

*Because depreciation does not represent a cash payment, these expenses are removed to determine cash payments made each quarter for selling and administrative expenses. All other selling and administrative expenses are paid for in the quarter incurred.

Similar to our approach with the manufacturing overhead budget (Schedule 5), depreciation expense is eliminated from the budgeted selling and administrative expense to determine the expected quarterly cash payments for these expenses.

Although the selling and administrative expense budget in Schedule 7 looks reasonably simple, it is often more complex in actual practice than it appears here. Traditionally, these types of costs have not been a focus of management accounting control efforts. However, selling and administrative costs have become proportionately larger for many organizations and now receive substantial management attention. Hence, rather than classifying these costs based on their function (salaries, depreciation, etc.), we often see in practice that these budgets are divided into multiple categories that may emphasize how costs are related to important management emphases such as research and development (R&D), product or service design, marketing, distribution, and customer service.

Caution

Variable expenses in the sales and administrative expense budget are typically based on the volume of *sales*, not on the volume of production.

TO SUMMARIZE: The operating budget, an important part of the master budget, consists of detailed budgets for sales revenue, production costs, and selling and administrative expenses. The detailed schedules that make up the operating budget are prepared in a logical sequence, as shown in Exhibit 3. The sales budget is largely determined by marketing research. The production budget is based on the expected volume of sales for each period and the desired ending inventory of finished goods and is adjusted for the expected beginning inventory of finished goods. The direct materials budget is based on the expected volume of production for each period and the desired ending inventory of direct materials and is similarly adjusted for the expected beginning inventory of direct materials. The direct labor budget is also based on the expected volume of production. The manufacturing overhead budget is divided into its variable and fixed cost components, with the variable cost component based on some activity driver (such as direct labor hours), which is in turn based on production volume. Data from the direct materials, direct labor, and manufacturing overhead budgets are then used to create a budgeted product cost sheet. Finally, the selling and administrative expense budget, like the manufacturing overhead budget, is divided into its variable and fixed cost components, with the variable costs determined based on sales (not production) volume.

Budgeting in Merchandising and Service Firms

5 Compare the operating budget for a manufacturing firm to that of a merchandising or service firm.

We have worked through the operating budget process for a manufacturing firm, Sunbird Boat Company, a manufacturer of small fishing boats. We will now compare this integrated budget with budgets for merchandising firms (retail and wholesale) by describing the operating budget process for Wind River Boat Company, a company that buys its boats for resale from other manufacturers rather than making the boats itself. Then we will illustrate budgeting in service firms by illustrating the operating budget process for a small motel, the Boulder View Inn.

As we examine a merchandise company and a service company, you will see similarities in the budgeting process for manufacturing businesses. Basically, the budgeting process involves budgeting (or forecasting) revenues and cash that will be generated by those revenues and budgeting expenses that will be incurred and cash that will be expended. Managers are always interested in how much revenues and expenses they will have during each budgeted period and how much cash and other assets and liabilities they will have at the end of each budgeted period.

Budgeting for Operations in a Merchandising Firm

As we discussed previously in a chapter on product cost flows, organizations that purchase the products they resell are often referred to as merchandising companies; these include retailers that sell directly to consumers and wholesale distributors that buy products from manufacturers or other suppliers and sell to retailers. Well-known retail companies include WAL-MART, SEARS, and KMART. Retail companies such as Wal-Mart buy many of the products they sell directly from manufacturers (e.g., COCA-COLA, NABISCO, WRIGLEY, etc.); however, they also buy from wholesalers who either buy from domestic manufacturers or import their products from other countries.

Because merchandising companies buy products (rather than make them), their budgeting process is less complicated than the budgeting done by manufacturing companies. For example, if Sunbird Boat Company were a merchandising firm rather than a manufacturing firm, the company would prepare a purchases budget, rather than a production budget, for boats. However, the format of the merchant's purchases budget would be *very* similar to the format of the manufacturer's production budget (see, for example, Schedule 2 for Sunbird Boat Company). By combining expected sales with desired ending inventory, and subtracting the beginning inventory expected to be on hand, the merchant will arrive at the number of boats to be purchased (rather than produced) for the period.

Exhibit 5 compares the master budgeting process for a merchandising firm with that for a manufacturing firm (from Exhibit 3).

Looking at Exhibit 5, you can see that in merchandising companies, the purchases budget replaces four budgets (production budget, direct materials budget, direct labor budget, and manufacturing overhead budget) used by manufacturing firms.

Because the sales budget and the selling and administrative expense budget are similar to those prepared for manufacturing firms, we will not discuss them again. To illustrate budgeting in a merchandising company, we will assume that Wind River Boat Company is a retail company that buys boats from manufacturers and sells them to consumers.

Purchases Budget

purchases budget A schedule of projected purchases over the budget period.

Assuming the same level of sales as we did for Sunbird, the **purchases budget** for Wind River Boat Company is shown in Schedule 8.

You can see from Schedule 8 that Wind River Boat Company pays its suppliers $8,000 for each 15-foot boat. (If you compare this cost with the total manufacturing cost for Sunbird Boat Company, you will see that it is higher. This is because manufacturing companies also need to make a profit.) In Schedule 8, we have assumed the same beginning and ending inventory policy we used in Schedule 2 for Sunbird, the manufacturing company.

Schedule 8

Schedule 8 Wind River Boat Company 2006 Purchases Budget					
15-Foot Boats	**Q1**	**Q2**	**Q3**	**Q4**	**Total**
Sales volume (Schedule 1)	24 boats	28 boats	30 boats	18 boats	100 boats
Desired ending inventory[1]	14 boats	15 boats	9 boats	13 boats	13 boats
Total boats needed	38 boats	43 boats	39 boats	31 boats	113 boats
Less beginning inventory[2]	(18 boats)	(14 boats)	(15 boats)	(9 boats)	(18 boats)
Total boats to purchase	20 boats	29 boats	24 boats	22 boats	95 boats
Cost per boat	×$ 8,000	×$ 8,000	×$ 8,000	×$ 8,000	×$ 8,000
Boat purchases	$160,000	$232,000	$192,000	$176,000	$760,000
Paid in current quarter	× 75%	× 75%	× 75%	× 75%	× 75%
Current purchase payments	$120,000	$174,000	$144,000	$132,000	$570,000
Prior purchase payments[3]	9,000	40,000	58,000	48,000	155,000
Payments to suppliers	$129,000	$214,000	$202,000	$180,000	$725,000

[1]Wind River desires to have ending boat inventory equal to 50% of the expected sales volume for the following quarter. Wind River's marketing department forecasts sales of 26 boats during the first quarter of 2007.
[2]Wind River's beginning finished goods inventory for 2006 is 18 boats. Beginning inventory for Q2 through Q4 is equal to the ending inventory for the prior quarter.
[3]Prior purchase payments in Q1 represent the accounts payable balance from the 2005 balance sheet. Prior purchase payments in Q2 through Q4 represent the purchases not paid for in the prior quarter (i.e., total boat purchases in prior quarter times 25%).

Exhibit 5: A Comparison of the Master Budgets for a Manufacturing and a Merchandising Firm

MANUFACTURING FIRM

MERCHANDISING FIRM

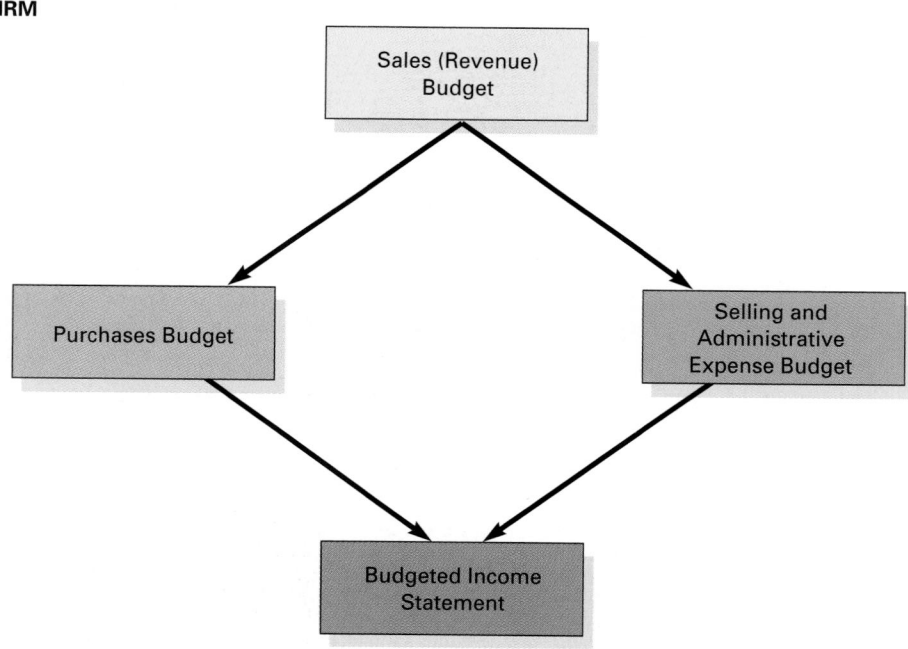

Budgeting for Operations in a Service Firm

Each year, a larger and larger percentage of businesses in the United States is service companies. Service companies differ from manufacturing and merchandising companies in that they provide services to customers instead of products. Examples of service organizations are law, accounting, and engineering firms; doctors and dentists; hotels and motels; hunting and fishing guide services; automotive, home, and appliance repair services; and Internet providers. Budgeting for service firms is similar to budgeting for manufacturing firms. As was the case with both manufacturing and merchandising companies, the budgeting process for service firms begins with a sales budget (sometimes called a revenue budget). Exhibit 6 compares the operating budgeting process for a service firm with a manufacturing firm. You can see that the service firm does not require a production budget. If you compare Schedule 1 and Schedule 2 for Sunbird Boat Company, you can see that the production budget starts with the sales volume and makes adjustments to it based on expected beginning and ending inventories of finished goods. Service firms sell intangible products (for example, physician appointments, car repairs, room rentals, monthly Internet access) that can't be inventoried. Therefore, the sales volume determined in the revenue budget is the "production" for the operating period.

Revenue Budget

To illustrate the budgeting process in service firms, we will use the example of Boulder View Inn, a small motel that has 12 rooms to rent each night. Boulder View Inn is located adjacent to a national park in southern Utah, and its business is highly seasonal, with April through December being busy (peak period) and January through March being very slow. Boulder View Inn rents its rooms for an average rate of $155 per night during the peak period and $85 per night during the slow period. Guests who stay at the hotel either pay cash or use credit cards, such as VISA, MASTERCARD, AMERICAN EXPRESS, or DISCOVER. The motel has a direct link with its bank that immediately deposits credit card receipts in Boulder View Inn's bank account after charging a 4 to 5% discount fee, which covers the bank's costs as well as fees charged by the credit card companies. Historically, Boulder View Inn has found that because most customers use credit cards to pay for their rooms, it pays an average of $4 per room per night to the credit card companies to cover the discount fee. Based on past experience, occupancy rates for the coming year are expected to be as follows:

January–March	25%
April–June	90%
July–September	80%
October–December	60%

revenue budget A service entity's budget that identifies how much revenue (and often cash) will be generated during a period.

Using these data, the **revenue budget** for Boulder View Inn is shown in Schedule 9.

Schedule 9

Schedule 9 Boulder View Inn 2006 Revenue Budget					
	Q1	**Q2**	**Q3**	**Q4**	**Total**
Number of rooms	12 rooms	12 rooms	12 rooms	12 rooms	
Number of days in quarter	× 90 days	× 91 days	× 92 days	× 92 days	
Potential rental volume	1,080 rentals	1,092 rentals	1,104 rentals	1,104 rentals	
Occupancy rate	× 25%	× 90%	× 80%	× 60%	
Rented rooms[1]	270 rentals	983 rentals	883 rentals	662 rentals	2,798 **rentals**
Room rate	× $85	× $155	× $155	× $155	
Revenue[2]	$22,950	$152,365	$136,865	$102,610	$414,790

[1]These calculations are rounded to the nearest whole unit.
[2]These revenues are all collected in the quarter earned.

Exhibit 6: A Comparison of the Master Budgets for a Manufacturing and a Service Firm

MANUFACTURING FIRM

SERVICE FIRM

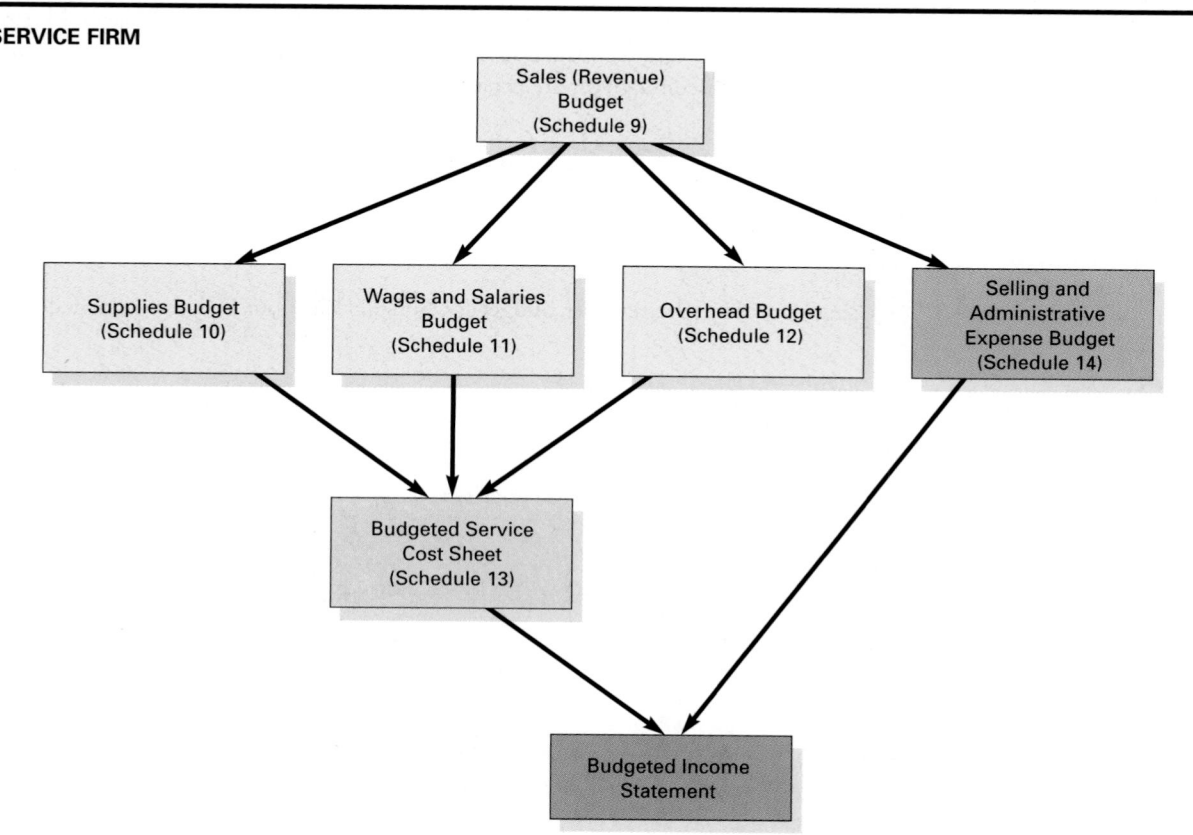

This budget shows that Boulder View Inn will generate gross revenues of $414,790 during the next year. Because Boulder View Inn collects cash or its equivalent (credit cards) from each guest, the revenue earned is expected to be collected each quarter. Remember that the revenue budget also establishes the expected "production," or number of rooms expected to be rented each quarter. Hence, you can see from the revenue budget that Boulder View Inn expects to rent 2,798 rooms next year. And as you can see in Exhibit 6, this volume will be used to determine the subsequent supplies, wages and salaries, overhead, and selling and administrative expense budgets.

The revenue budget for Boulder View Inn would be similar for other types of service firms, except that instead of a per-room revenue, the revenue would be based on per patient visit (for doctors and dentists), per contract (for engineers, accountants, and lawyers), or per subscription (for Internet providers). Service companies that do not collect cash, but rather bill clients on a periodic basis (such as lawyers and accountants), would also need to extend the revenue budget to determine when the cash generated from revenues will be collected.

Supplies Budget

supplies budget The budget, prepared by service entities, that identifies projected supplies expenses over the budget period.

Most service businesses need supplies to operate. For a restaurant, supplies include the food used in preparing meals, cleaning materials, and the paper goods needed for menus and customer invoices. For a medical doctor, supplies might include needles, tape, and bandages, as well as office supplies. For Boulder View Inn, supplies include soap and shampoo for the guest rooms, as well as doughnuts, cereal, juice, and milk for the continental breakfast. The **supplies budget** for Boulder View Inn is shown in Schedule 10.

Schedule 10

		Q1	Q2	Q3	Q4	Total
Schedule 10 Boulder View Inn 2006 Supplies Budget						
Total rental days (Schedule 9)		270 rooms	983 rooms	883 rooms	662 rooms	2,798 rooms
Supplies needed per room:						
Bathroom supplies cost	$1.20	$ 324.00	$1,179.60	$1,059.60	$ 794.40	$ 3,357.60
Laundry supplies cost	0.50	135.00	491.50	441.50	331.00	1,399.00
Breakfast supplies cost	7.50	2,025.00	7,372.50	6,622.50	4,965.00	20,985.00
Total supplies cost per room*	$9.20	$2,484.00	$9,043.60	$8,123.60	$6,090.40	$25,741.60

*Because the level of supplies is immaterial, the supplies cost each quarter is essentially paid in cash in each quarter.

Wages and Salaries Budget

wages and salaries budget The budget, prepared by service entities, that identifies projected labor costs involved directly in providing the service over the budget period.

The **wages and salaries budget** is reserved for labor costs involved directly in providing the service (similar to direct labor in a manufacturing firm). Administrative labor costs are not included in this budget; they are part of the selling and administrative expense budget. For a law firm, the wages and salaries budget would include salaries of lawyers; but not of paralegals, photocopy personnel, computer specialists, or office secretaries—these personnel costs would all be part of the selling and administrative expense budget. For Boulder View Inn, the only labor cost included in this budget is the $15 per room that is paid for cleaning the rooms. Schedule 11 is the wages and salaries budget for Boulder View Inn.

Overhead Budget

service overhead budget The budget, prepared by service entities, that identifies projected costs associated with providing the service.

As was the case with manufacturing firms, the **service overhead budget** includes all the costs associated with providing the product, or service, in this case. The overhead budget does not include selling and administrative costs not directly associated with providing the service. For Boulder View Inn, overhead includes utilities, depreciation, TV and telephone service, and

Schedule 11

Schedule 11 Boulder View Inn 2006 Wages and Salaries Budget	Q1	Q2	Q3	Q4	Total
Total rental days (Schedule 9)	270 rooms	983 rooms	883 rooms	662 rooms	2,798 rooms
Cleaning fee[1]	× $15	× $15	× $15	× $15	× $15
Total wages[2]	$4,050	$14,745	$13,245	$9,930	$41,970

[1]Includes fringe benefits and payroll taxes.
[2]These costs are all paid in the quarter incurred.

miscellaneous expenses. In the case of this particular service provider, all overhead costs are fixed. In other words, regardless of whether or not a room is rented, these overhead costs are incurred. Schedule 12 is the overhead budget for Boulder View Inn.

Schedule 12

Schedule 12 Boulder View Inn 2006 Overhead Budget	Q1	Q2	Q3	Q4	Total
Utilities	$3,000	$3,000	$3,000	$3,000	$12,000
Depreciation expense	5,000	5,000	5,000	5,000	20,000
TV and telephone	1,200	1,200	1,200	1,200	4,800
Miscellaneous costs	600	600	600	600	2,400
Total overhead costs	$9,800	$9,800	$9,800	$9,800	$39,200
Less depreciation	(5,000)	(5,000)	(5,000)	(5,000)	(20,000)
Total overhead payments*	$4,800	$4,800	$4,800	$4,800	$19,200

*Because depreciation does not represent a cash payment, these costs are removed to determine cash payments made each quarter for overhead costs. All other overhead costs are paid for in the quarter incurred.

The depreciation in Schedule 12 is calculated by dividing the motel cost of $500,000 by its 25-year life to arrive at $20,000 per year (and further divided into quarterly costs of $5,000). The utilities include heat, lights, sewer, and garbage removal.

Budgeted Service Cost Sheet

budgeted service cost sheet A schedule of all of the service costs (i.e., the costs of supplies, wages and salaries, and overhead) used to provide a single service event.

The **budgeted service cost sheet** (Schedule 13) is similar to the budgeted product cost sheet for manufacturing firms. This schedule accumulates all the budgeted service costs (supplies, wages and salaries, and overhead) to estimate the total service cost of providing a room to rent at Boulder View Inn. Based on the three service-related budgets (supplies, wages and salaries, and overhead), we know it costs Boulder View Inn approximately $24.20 in variable costs to provide the services needed to rent one room for one night. Because Boulder View Inn expects to rent 2,798 rooms during the year, the overhead cost assigned to each room rental (all of which is fixed) is $14.01 ($39,200 ÷ 2,798 rooms). The calculation of these service costs is shown in Schedule 13.

Selling and Administrative Expense Budget

As was the case for Sunbird Boat Company, the selling and administrative expense budget for Boulder View Inn includes planned expenditures for all selling and administrative expenses. As in manufacturing companies, the selling and administrative expense budget for a service firm

Schedule 13

Schedule 13
Boulder View Inn
2006 Budgeted Service Cost Sheet

		Total
Annual supplies cost (Schedule 10)	$25,741.60	
Annual wage cost (Schedule 11)	41,970.00	
Total annual variable service costs	$67,711.60	
Annual volume of rental rooms	÷ 2,798 rooms	
Total variable cost per rental		$24.20
Annual fixed overhead costs (Schedule 12)	$39,200.00	
Annual volume of rental rooms	÷ 2,798 rooms	
Fixed MOH cost allocated per rental*		14.01
Total service cost per room rental		$38.21

*Note that the service costs per room rental for Boulder View Inn will actually vary from quarter to quarter because of the change in fixed overhead costs per rental due to changes in occupancy rate each quarter.

can be quite large and is sometimes supported by individual budgets for specific elements included in this budget. The selling and administrative expense budget for Boulder View Inn would be as shown in Schedule 14.

Schedule 14

Schedule 14
Boulder View Inn
2006 Selling and Administrative (S&A) Expense Budget

Variable S&A expenses	Q1	Q2	Q3	Q4	Total
Total rental days (Schedule 9)	270 rooms	983 rooms	883 rooms	662 rooms	2,798 rooms
Average credit card discount fee	× $4	× $4	× $4	× $4	× $4
Total variable S&A expenses	$ 1,080	$ 3,932	$ 3,532	$ 2,648	$11,192
Fixed S&A expenses per quarter					
Manager's salary	$ 7,500	$ 7,500	$ 7,500	$ 7,500	$30,000
Depreciation expense	1,200	1,200	1,200	1,200	4,800
Advertising expense	800	800	800	800	3,200
Miscellaneous expenses	500	500	500	500	2,000
Total fixed S&A expenses	$10,000	$10,000	$10,000	$10,000	$40,000
Total S&A expenses	$11,080	$13,932	×$13,532	×$12,648	×$51,192
Less depreciation	(1,200)	(1,200)	(1,200)	(1,200)	(4,800)
Total S&A payments*	$ 9,880	$12,732	$12,332	$11,448	$46,392

*Because depreciation does not represent a cash payment, these expenses are removed to determine cash payments made each quarter for selling and administrative expenses. All other selling and administrative expenses are paid for in the quarter incurred.

This selling and administration expense budget shows that Boulder View Inn's total selling and administrative expense for the year is budgeted to be $51,192. The selling and administrative expenses include credit card charges, the manager's salary, miscellaneous expenses around the office, and advertising expense (which includes yellow page directory advertisement and Internet listings). This budget also includes the depreciation expense on the cottage provided by Boulder View to the manager who must be available at the inn on a 24-hour, 7-days-a-week basis.

Wall Street Is Unforgiving of Companies Who Don't Hit Their Mark Not only must companies forecast their revenues and earnings as part of the budgeting process, but analysts and various investment institutions forecast companies' earnings as well. And, when a company's actual earnings fall short of analysts' expectations, the company's stock price usually falls.

Security analysts are often optimistic when making earnings forecasts—particularly forecasts made months in advance of the actual report date. Nevertheless, investors often punish companies that consistently fail to meet their early forecasts.

One research project analyzed companies in the S&P 500 and found eight companies that, over eight consecutive quarters from 2000 to 2002, rarely lived up to their consensus forecasts made 60 days prior to quarterly report dates. These eight stocks had an average price decline of 39%.

Over the same 2-year period, the S&P 500 was down 42%. In contrast, the 31 S&P stocks that met or beat their 60-day-out consensus numbers for eight straight quarters had an average gain of 40%.

One of the companies that consistently missed its consensus numbers during that time was pharmaceuticals giant BRISTOL-MYERS SQUIBB. The third quarter of 2002 was representative of what happened to this New York City-based firm. In early summer 2002, security analysts, as a group, initially thought that Bristol-Myers Squibb would earn $1.34 per share for the third quarter. Eventually, the 26 analysts reporting on Bristol-Myers Squibb revised their forecast to $1.20 per share (versus $2.41 in 2001—a 50% decline). Not surprisingly, shares of Bristol were off 59% in October 2002 compared to the previous year when they traded at their 52-week high of $59.95.

The table below lists the eight companies that consistently missed their 60-day prior estimates over eight quarters ending in 2002.

	Price	Price Change	Sales ($ in millions)	Estimated 2002 EPS	Actual 2002 EPS
ALCOA	$19.57	−35%	$20,920	$ 1.15	$ 1.06
AON	20.25	−47	8,158	1.64	0.74
BRISTOL-MYERS SQUIBB	24.55	−51	18,160	1.20	1.30
DELTA AIR LINES	10.06	−58	12,379	−7.59	−9.99
DOW CHEMICAL	27.64	−14	26,554	0.98	−0.46
FLEETBOSTON FINANCIAL	19.98	−42	11,668	1.52	0.84
J.P. MORGAN CHASE	18.64	−43	27,316	1.74	0.84
UNUMPROVIDENT	19.73	−17	9,389	2.54	2.41

Source: John J. Ray, "Companies Missing the Mark" *Forbes*, September 25, 2002. **http://www.forbes.com/2002/09/25/0925sf.html**.

TO SUMMARIZE: The operating budgeting process for merchandising organizations (both retail and wholesale companies) is similar, but significantly easier, than that for manufacturing firms. The major difference is that a merchandising firm's purchases budget replaces four of a manufacturing firm's budgets—the production, direct materials, direct labor, and manufacturing overhead budgets. Otherwise, the entire master budgeting process is the same.

The operating budgets for a service company are quite similar to the operating budgets in a manufacturing company. The major difference is that a production budget is generally not required. Because services cannot usually be inventoried, the sales volume for most service firms also represents the production (i.e., service) budgeted volume. As a result, six operating budgets are prepared: the revenue budget, the supplies budget, the wages and salaries budget, the overhead budget, the budgeted service cost sheet, and the selling and administrative expense budget. The revenue budget is usually based on the expected volume of service to be performed (e.g., rooms rented, services performed, patients seen, subscriptions delivered). The expected volume of service is then used to prepare the supplies, wages and salaries, and overhead budgets. The selling and administrative expense budget includes all costs not directly related to providing the service.

The budgeting process discussed to this point allows management to plan various operating activities within the firm, such as purchasing, hiring, and overall management of the production or service process. Armed with these budgets, management is now prepared to monitor the firm's performance and compare actual results to budgeted results. If corrective action is needed, management can identify deviations from the budget early and take the appropriate steps to remedy problems. In addition to preparing the detailed operating budgets, management can combine the various budgets to arrive at financial budgets, specifically, the cash budget and the pro-forma (or budgeted) financial statements. In this section, we use the operating budgets from the Sunbird Boat Company to prepare a cash budget, as well as a pro-forma income statement, balance sheet, and statement of cash flows. The section concludes with a discussion of static and flexible budgeting and illustrates the advantages of flexible budgeting.

Cash Budget

6 Create the cash budget.

cash budget A schedule of expected cash receipts and disbursements during the budget period.

The **cash budget**, which shows expected cash receipts and disbursements during a period, summarizes much of the information discussed thus far. A detailed cash budget will point out when a company has excess cash to invest and when it has to borrow funds. This allows a firm to earn maximum interest on excess funds and to avoid the costs of unnecessary borrowing.

Typically, a cash budget is divided into four sections:

1. Cash receipts
2. Cash payments
3. Cash excess or deficiency
4. Financing

The cash receipts section summarizes all cash expected to flow into the business during the budget period. Because companies generally extend credit to their customers, most of their sales are originally recorded as accounts receivable. The collection of accounts receivable is thus a major source of cash, and its timing is an important consideration in preparing a cash budget.

As we worked through the operating budgeting process for Sunbird Boat Company, we determined the impact on cash flows of this company's management policies regarding its receivables and payables. In fact, you can see this effort illustrated clearly in Schedules 1, 3, 5, and 7.

As you can see in Schedule 1, an analysis of how Sunbird's customers pay on accounts receivable shows that total collections during 2006 are budgeted to be $1,020,000. In particular, you should note that based on Sunbird's expectation that the remaining 20% of accounts are collected in the subsequent quarter, we can assume that the entire beginning balance in

Caution

When preparing a cash budget, be careful not to include expenditures that do not require cash (e.g., depreciation expense from the manufacturing overhead and selling and administrative expense budgets).

accounts receivable is collected in the first quarter of 2006. Further, in the Sunbird example, we assumed that all proceeds from credit sales are eventually collected. Usually, however, some customers never pay, and these uncollectible accounts must be considered when analyzing estimated cash collections from accounts receivable. You should recognize that economic factors play a significant role in the timing of collections of accounts receivable. During recessionary periods, customers often drag out their payments much longer than they would in prosperous times.[7]

The cash budget for Sunbird is shown in Schedule 15. Cash receipts for Sunbird are composed solely of what the company collects from its customers, and the computation is reasonably straightforward. However, the cash payments section of this schedule is a bit more involved. You can see that the first four items come directly from the operating budgets for purchases of materials, payments for direct labor, and payments for manufacturing overhead and selling and administrative expense. In addition, there are four other payments that Sunbird has scheduled which take place outside of its day-to-day operations.

Schedule 15

Schedule 15 Sunbird Boat Company 2006 Cash Budget					
	Q1	**Q2**	**Q3**	**Q4**	**Total**
Beginning cash balance	$135,000	$140,000	$147,308	$201,284	$ 135,000
Collections from customers (Schedule 1)[1]	248,000	272,000	296,000	204,000	1,020,000
Cash available	$383,000	$412,000	$443,308	$405,284	$1,155,000
Payments:					
Direct materials (Schedule 3)[2]	$ 23,464	$ 24,415	$ 23,204	$ 22,088	$ 93,170
Direct labor (Schedule 4)	24,000	34,800	28,800	26,400	114,000
Manufacturing overhead (Schedule 5)[3]	36,960	42,720	39,520	38,240	157,440
Selling and admin. expense (Schedule 7)[3]	107,900	116,300	120,500	95,300	440,000
Income tax payment for 2005	96,000				96,000
Interest payments (10% annual rate)[4]		1,133			1,133
Dividends			30,000		30,000
Equipment purchase				100,000	100,000
Total payments	$288,324	$219,368	$242,024	$282,028	$1,031,743
Minimum cash balance desired[5]	140,000	140,000	140,000	140,000	140,000
Total cash needed	$428,324	$359,368	$382,024	$422,028	$1,171,743
Excess (deficiency)[6]	$ (45,324)	$ 52,632	$ 61,284	$ (16,743)	$ (16,743)
Financing:					
Borrowings	$ 45,324			$ 16,743	$ 62,067
Repayments of principle		$ (45,324)			(45,324)
Total financing inflows (outflows)	$ 45,324	$ (45,324)		$ 16,743	$ 16,743
Ending cash balance	$140,000	$147,308	$201,284	$140,000	$ 140,000

[1]Q1 = Beginning accounts receivable balance from balance sheet + 80% of Q1 revenue; Q2 thru Q4 = 80% of current quarter revenue + 20% of previous quarter revenue.
[2]Q1 = Beginning accounts payable balance from balance sheet + 75% of Q1 purchases; Q2 thru Q4 = 75% of current quarter purchases + 25% of previous quarter purchases.
[3]MOH and S&A depreciation is not included in the cash cost of these expenses.
[4]Interest expense for Q2 = $45,324 $\times$ 10% $\times$ $\frac{1}{4}$ year = $1,133 (rounded).
[5]Ending cash balance for each quarter must be at least $140,000. Otherwise, the company must borrow on its line of credit at the bank (interest rate is 10% annual).
[6]Due to rounding of earlier numbers on the Direct Materials Budget (Schedule 3), the deficiency in Q4 appears to be in error by $1 (actually it's not an error).

- First, Sunbird accrued at the end of 2005 a $96,000 payable for income taxes (see Sunbird's 2005 balance sheet in Exhibit 4). This bill to the IRS is expected to be paid during the first quarter of 2006.

7 Although the reality that some customers never pay off their account does complicate the cash collection budget for accounts receivable, the use of a contra account such as "Allowance for Doubtful Accounts" establishes a net balance for accounts receivable on the balance sheet that represents what is realistically expected to be collected. The "net balance" accounting is very helpful when creating a budget for cash receipts.

- Second, at the end of the first quarter, Sunbird needs to borrow $45,324 from the bank in order to maintain its desired $140,000 cash balance. At the end of the second quarter, Sunbird has enough excess cash to repay this loan and pay the interest outstanding on this loan (the interest calculation is shown as a footnote in this schedule). This is perhaps the most complicated item on the cash budget. You should be sure to work through the calculation of the loan amount in the first quarter, as well as the interest calculation in the second quarter.
- Third, Sunbird plans to declare dividends in the first quarter of 2006, which it expects to pay in the third quarter.
- Fourth, based on its capital projects plan, Sunbird is planning to make a capital expenditure of $100,000 for equipment in the final quarter of 2006. You can see how this capital expenditure decision fits into the master budget by reviewing Exhibit 3.

By combining the expected cash payments with the desired ending cash balance, Sunbird can determine its total cash need for each quarter and compare that need with the total amount of cash it expects to have available during the quarter. The final section of this budget reports the cash excess or deficiency as the difference between budgeted cash availability and cash needs. With a prospective excess of cash, management may want to look for some attractive short-term investments. A deficiency obviously means that additional short-term funds will be needed.

In addition to the timing and amounts of all projected borrowings and repayments during the period, the financing section of the cash budget is also used to estimate the amount of interest to be paid on borrowed funds. By accurately projecting these amounts and events, firms can give banks and other lending institutions advance notice of their needs. Banks appreciate, and sometimes insist, that companies plan their cash needs in advance. Because money has a time value, management always walks a tightrope between having too much or too little cash on hand.

Exhibit 7 shows how a typical company's cash balance and requirements fluctuate constantly. Most of this fluctuation is due to the varying amounts of raw materials and finished goods that are needed in the different seasons of the year. A prosperous firm could, if it desired, maintain enough cash on hand so that short-term borrowing would never be necessary, but such a policy might not be cost-beneficial. Long-term investments in productive assets usually earn considerably more than short-term cash investments; firms are generally better off maintaining lower cash balances, keeping as much capital as possible "at work" in the company's productive assets, and borrowing from time to time for short periods. For this reason, most companies obtain a line of credit from banks. A **line of credit** is a prearranged agreement whereby an organization or individual can borrow money on demand, up to a specific amount at specific rates.

line of credit An arrangement whereby a bank agrees to loan an amount of money (up to a certain limit) on demand for short periods of time, usually less than a year.

Exhibit 7: A Typical Relationship between Cash Balance and Cash Needs

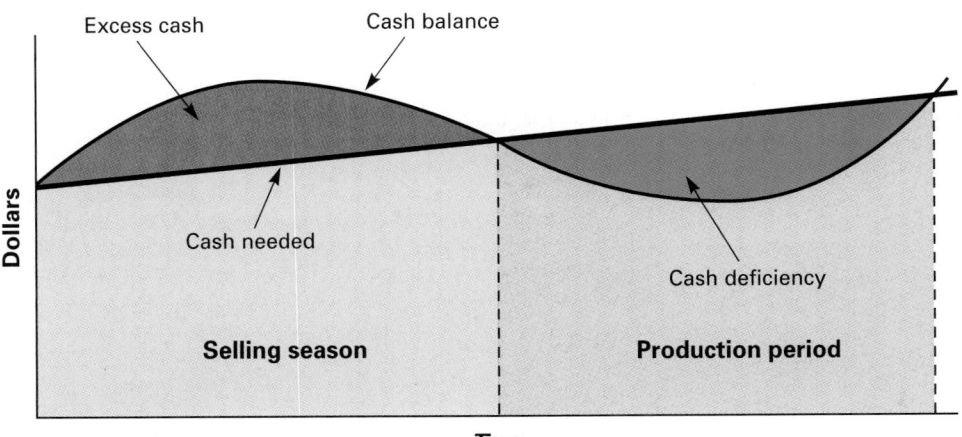

FYI:

Remember that having income does *not* mean that the organization will have cash. Revenues don't get collected immediately (which leads to accounts receivable). Expenses don't get paid immediately (which leads to accounts payable). And capital expenditures (which are not reflected on the income statement) use up a lot of cash.

With the cash budget, the company is now able to make planning decisions regarding financing. For example, Sunbird is now aware that although the cash balance will be sufficient at the end of the year, there will probably be a cash shortage in the second quarter of 2006. With this knowledge, the company can take steps to deal with the situation. One solution would be to negotiate with a bank to obtain a loan. The company might also obtain money by attempting to get customers to pay sooner, trying to negotiate with creditors for a longer repayment period, or simply reducing the desired ending cash balance (currently at $140,000). The point is, with knowledge of the coming cash shortfall, Sunbird is able to formulate a method of dealing with the problem now, rather than waiting until the company actually finds itself in a cash shortage crisis.

TO SUMMARIZE: The cash budget shows expected cash receipts and disbursements as the result of receipts from customers, payments for inventory, labor, and overhead. Cash budgets must also track expenditures for capital equipment, taxes, interest payments, and various other items. The budgets are important in that they signal when the company can expect a cash shortage, which requires outside financing using a line of credit or another similar finance tool, or a cash excess, which should be temporarily invested in income-producing assets.

Pro-Forma Financial Statements

7 Prepare pro-forma financial statements.

The pro-forma income statement (often called a budgeted income statement) projects income for the coming period and, therefore, is valuable to management in making key decisions. Such questions as how high a dividend to pay, whether to invest in a new plant, and how strenuously to bargain with unions are usually decided on the basis of projected and actual profits. Because budgeting for manufacturing firms is the most complicated, we will illustrate pro-forma financial statements using the Sunbird Boat Company example used throughout the chapter.

Perhaps the most challenging aspect of determining Sunbird's pro-forma income statement is computing cost of goods sold. To help you better understand this computation, we will carefully lay out the computation for cost of goods sold. This computation requires a careful assessment of changes in Sunbird's inventory balances. In making this computation, we will assume that Sunbird does not typically have significant work-in-process inventory at the end of a quarter. However, the company does have significant inventory in direct (or raw) materials and finished goods (as shown in Sunbird's balance sheet in Exhibit 4).

Cost of Goods Sold	2006
Direct materials purchases (Schedule 3)	$ 89,680
Direct materials beginning inventory (2005 balance sheet)	7,980
Less direct materials ending inventory (Schedule 3)[1]	(7,410)
Direct materials costs in production	$ 90,250
Direct labor costs in production (Schedule 4)	114,000
MOH costs in production (Schedule 5)	223,440
Cost of goods manufactured	$427,690
Finished goods beginning inventory (2005 balance sheet)	83,520
Less finished goods ending inventory (Schedules 2 and 6)[2]	(58,526)
Cost of goods sold	$452,684

[1](546 feet of wood × $10 purchase price) + (390 feet of fiberglass × $5 purchase price) = $7,410.
[2]13 boats × $4,502 product cost per boat = $58,526.

You will note that this computation is based on the standard calculation that we studied earlier in the chapter on product cost flows for cost of goods manufactured and cost of goods sold.

Now that we have computed the expected cost of goods sold for 2006, Sunbird is ready to compose its pro-forma income statement, which is shown in Schedule 16. In this income statement, we assume an income tax rate of 27% for Sunbird.

Schedule 16

Schedule 16 Sunbird Boat Company Pro-Forma Income Statement For the Year Ended December 31, 2006		
Sales revenue (Schedule 1)		$1,000,000
Cost of goods sold:		
Finished goods beginning inventory	$ 83,520	
Cost of goods manufactured	427,690	
Cost of goods available for sale	$511,210	
Less finished goods ending inventory	(58,526)	(452,684)
Gross margin		547,316
Selling and administrative expense (Schedule 7)		(472,000)
Operating income		$ 75,316
Interest expense (Schedule 15)		(1,133)
Income taxes (27% average tax rate)		(20,335)
Net income		$ 53,848

The final two items to be projected are the balance sheet and the statement of cash flows. These statements are presented in Schedules 17 and 18. All of the calculations necessary to complete these pro-forma financial statements have been effectively developed all along as we have worked through previous budgets. Be sure to work through each line item in these pro-forma

Schedule 17

Schedule 17 Sunbird Boat Company Pro-Forma Balance Sheet December 31, 2006		
Assets		
Current assets:		
Cash (Schedule 15)	$ 140,000	
Accounts receivable (Schedule 1)[1]	36,000	
Direct materials inventory[2]	7,410	
Finished goods inventory[2]	58,526	$ 241,936
Long-term assets:		
Land	$ 234,305	
Building and equipment (Schedule 15)[3]	1,600,000	
Less accumulated depreciation (Schedules 5 and 7)[4]	(218,000)	1,616,305
Total assets		$1,858,241
Liabilities & Stockholders' Equity		
Current liabilities:		
Accounts payable (Schedule 3)[5]	$ 5,510	
Income taxes payable (Schedule 16)	20,335	
Short-term loan payable (Schedule 15)	16,743	$ 42,588
Stockholders' equity:		
Common stock, $5 par	$1,000,000	
Paid-in capital in excess of par	250,000	
Retained earnings (Schedules 15 and 16)[6]	565,653	$1,815,653
Total liabilities & stockholders' equity		$1,858,241

[1] Q4 revenue × 20%.
[2] See the calculation for cost of goods sold in chapter text.
[3] Original account balance ($1,500,000) + equipment purchase ($100,000).
[4] Original account balance ($120,000) + MOH depreciation ($66,000) + S&A depreciation ($32,000).
[5] Q4 purchases × 25%.
[6] Original account balance ($541,805) + income ($53,848) − dividends ($30,000).

Schedule 18

Schedule 18
Sunbird Boat Company
Pro-Forma Statement of Cash Flows
For the Year Ended December 31, 2006

Cash flow from operating activities		
Net Income (Schedule 16)		$ 53,848
Adjustments:		
Depreciation (Schedules 5 and 7)	$ 98,000	
Accounts receivable decrease (Schedule 17)*	20,000	
Direct materials inventory decrease (Schedule 17)*	570	
Finished goods inventory decrease (Schedule 17)*	24,994	
Accounts payable decrease (Schedule 17)*	(3,490)	
Income taxes payable decrease (Schedule 16)*	(75,665)	64,409
Net cash provided by operating activities		$118,257
Cash flow from investing activities		
Purchase of Equipment (Schedule 15)	$(100,000)	
Net cash used in investing activities		(100,000)
Cash flow from financing activities		
Cash obtained from borrowing (Schedule 15)	$ 62,067	
Repayment of borrowed funds (Schedule 15)	(45,324)	
Payment of dividends (Schedule 15)	(30,000)	
Net cash used in financing activities		(13,257)
Net Increase in cash		$ 5,000
Beginning cash balance		135,000
Ending cash balance		$140,000

*Compare the relevant ending account balance on these schedules with the beginning account balance on Sunbird's 2005 balance sheet (Exhibit 4).

STOP & THINK

How would the three financial statements be different if we assumed Sunbird was a merchandising company instead of a manufacturing company?

statements to be sure you see which schedule is the source of the computation. (This is an excellent way to review everything you've studied in this chapter on computing budgets for manufacturing companies!)

The master budget is now complete. It is ready for use to communicate information, coordinate and authorize activities, motivate employees, and measure performance. The decisions to be made on the basis of this budget depend on the answers to such questions as:

1. Is the net income of approximately $53,848 adequate? If not, how can it be increased?
2. How does the expected financial position at the end of the year fit with long-range objectives and goals?
3. Is the projected increase in cash sufficient to meet the firm's goals?
4. Are there sufficient liquid assets to purchase needed assets?
5. How should management be rewarded if these budgets are met?
6. Who should be responsible for meeting the goals set for sales, production, and costs?

These are only a few of the questions that management needs to answer. However, these questions should give you a sense of the master budget's usefulness. In fact, it is hard to imagine how a company could be profitable in the long run without such planning.

TO SUMMARIZE: Following the preparation of the cash budget, which provides an indication of the financing activities of the business, pro-forma financial statements can be prepared. The pro-forma income statement, balance sheet, and statement of cash flows follow directly from the components of the master budget. The pro-forma balance sheet also relies heavily on beginning account balances. Once these pro-forma financial statements have been prepared, management can then determine if budgeted sales and production levels will allow the company to achieve its strategic goals. These pro-forma financial statements serve as a basis for key management decisions.

Budgeting for Long-Term Company and Shareholder Value Jack Welch, the famous CEO recently retired from GEN-ERAL ELECTRIC, described the budgeting process as "the bane of corporate America. It never should have existed. A budget is this: if you make it, you generally get a pat on the back and a few bucks. If you miss it, you get a stick in the eye—or worse." Some reports state that managers spend up to 20% of their valuable time on planning and budgeting. If the time and effort apparently outweigh the benefit, why do corporations, governments, and (for that matter) individuals continue to budget? *Because budgeting is important.* However, focusing solely on the quarterly budget can be problematic, creating a budget trap.

A "traditional" budgeting process can motivate managers to:

- Lowball the budget target.
- Do whatever it takes to "make the numbers."
- Overestimate required resources.
- Use the budgeted funds ("use it or lose it!").

Possible results from these actions are:

- Negotiating superficial budget targets.
- "Cooking the books."
- Pushing to "book orders" at year-end, despite customers' true needs.
- Budget wasting.

The increase in the pace of change across most industries, combined with an increasingly harsh and punitive investment community, has forced many companies to become focused on short-term results at the expense of long-term value. The drive to focus on short-term results leads to decision making that is focused on the quarterly budget, rather than on long-term strategy. And while maintaining a reign on the quarterly budget ap-

pears to be in the interest of the organization's health, these short-term decisions in fact can and do cut off longer-term opportunities. Short-term decisions can stifle the potential for growth because they appear to be made in a vacuum independent of what the organization is trying to achieve over time.

The Keys to Success
There are five key principles that distinguish successful organizations that are able to forecast results and allocate resources efficiently while achieving their overall long-term strategy. These organizations do the following:

- Align operational planning and budgeting for strategy execution: Bring together the often disparate processes of operations planning and budgeting to ensure they are consistent, linked together, and reflective of each others' priorities.
- Increase adaptability to change through continuous planning: Adopt a rolling forecast approach.
- Manage strategic initiatives to achieve results: Focus the organization on the key strategic initiatives, while systematically and rigorously jettisoning those initiatives and activities that are not tied to strategic goals.
- Motivate people and actions through relative performance targets: Engage everyone in the long-term success of the organization by tying individual performance targets to strategic results.
- Increase planning efficiency by reducing detail and effort: Home in on the key strategic elements and activities to focus on doing and reporting on only those aspects of the business that drive the strategy, eliminating the effort and time required to track and plan elements of the business that derail this focus.

Sources: Marshall Loeb, "Jack Welch Lets Fly on Budgets, Bonuses, and Buddy Boards," *Fortune*, May 29, 1995; Horvath & Partners Database; IMA and Balanced Scorecard Collaborative, Inc., found on the site **http://www.smartpros.com/x38510.xml**.

Static versus Flexible Budgeting

8 Distinguish between static and flexible budgets.

static budget A quantified plan that projects revenues and costs for only one level of activity.

The budgets discussed thus far in this chapter are **static budgets**; that is, they are geared to only one level of sales activity. Although such budgets help in planning, they are not very useful for controlling costs and measuring performance because the actual level of activity may differ significantly from the planned level. In the next chapter, we will compare actual results to budgets in order to control and evaluate performance. However, before we can do this, we will need to adjust budgets to make them relevant to the actual results. To be specific, we will need to recompute the budgets based on the actual sales activity. This is the process of creating a flexible budget.

A **flexible budget** is much more useful for control and performance evaluation because it is not confined to one level of activity. Flexible budgets are dynamic; that is, they can be tailored to any level of activity within the relevant range. Using flexible budgeting, a manager can look at the actual level of activity attained and then determine what costs should have been at that level.

flexible budget A quantified plan that projects revenues and costs for varying levels of activity.

Weaknesses in Static Budgeting

STOP & THINK

Suppose that a production department's budget is based on manufacturing and selling 10,000 widgets at a standard product cost of $10 per widget. The department actually produced 9,000 widgets and spent $95,000. Obviously, it didn't meet its sales goal. However, did it spend more or less than it should have? What if it had actually produced 11,000 widgets and spent $105,000?

To illustrate why a static budget is inadequate for controlling operations, let's return once more to the Sunbird Boat Company example. In particular, let's look at its budgeted product cost sheet (Schedule 6). Based on the information from that schedule, Sunbird developed the following budgeted per-unit manufacturing costs for 15-foot boats:

Direct materials	$ 950
Direct labor	1,200
Variable manufacturing overhead	640
Fixed manufacturing overhead	1,712
Total	$4,502

As you consider these numbers, you need to be very careful with the fixed manufacturing overhead. The $1,712 represents the *average* fixed manufacturing overhead cost per boat for the year. However, fixed manufacturing overhead is expected to be $40,660 each quarter (for a total of $162,640 for the year, *regardless of the number of boats actually produced.* (You can review these numbers in Schedule 5.) And if you review Schedule 2, you'll see that Sunbird's expected production will vary from quarter to quarter. What this means is that we shouldn't multiply the $1,712 with the expected volume of production in order to determine the budgeted fixed manufacturing overhead for the quarter. Fixed manufacturing overhead is actually what it says—it is fixed! In other words, if you want to predict the level of total manufacturing costs each quarter for Sunbird, you won't multiply the expected production volume by $4,502. The better way to do this is to use the following formula:

Total budgeted manufacturing costs =
Total fixed manufacturing costs + (Variable manufacturing cost per unit × Production volume)

Extending this budget formula to establish a total budgeted amount for the first quarter of 2006, Sunbird Boat Company might then prepare a static budget as follows:

Sunbird Boat Company
Budgeted Manufacturing Costs
January–March 2006

Budgeted production (boats)		20
Variable manufacturing costs per boat:		
Direct materials	$ 950	
Direct labor	1,200	
Variable manufacturing overhead	640	
Total variable manufacturing costs per boat	$2,790	
Total variable manufacturing costs ($2,790 × 20 boats)		$55,800
Total fixed manufacturing costs		40,660
Total budgeted manufacturing costs		$96,460

STOP & THINK

Consider the budget formula used to compute total budgeted manufacturing costs of $96,460 in the first quarter of 2006 for Sunbird Boat Company. Does this formula look familiar to you? If should look familiar if you studied how to analyze mixed costs using the least squares method in the earlier chapter on cost-volume-profit analysis!

This simple operating budget for the first quarter of 2006 can be quite useful to Sunbird *if* it actually produces 20 boats. Now, let's assume that Sunbird actually produced 23 boats in that first quarter. Sunbird's actual costs incurred were $63,350 for direct materials, direct labor, and variable manufacturing overhead, and $41,040 for fixed manufacturing overhead. Comparing actual results with the static budget information, the performance report for the quarter would be as follows:

Sunbird Boat Company
Static Budget Performance Report
January–March 2006

	Budgeted	Actual	Difference
Production (units)	20	23	3
Manufacturing costs:			
Variable manufacturing costs	$55,800	$ 63,350	$7,550
Fixed manufacturing overhead	40,660	41,040	380
Total actual and budgeted manufacturing costs	$96,460	$104,390	$7,930

According to this report, Sunbird has spent $7,930 more than it should have. However, something is wrong with this performance report. Producing more boats than budgeted (23 actual boats versus 20 budgeted boats) has led to more actual costs than were expected. But given the increase in production, Sunbird should have spent more in manufacturing costs (right?). The real question is, should management be punished for allowing actual costs to be $104,390 or rewarded for producing more units than budgeted? Using the static budget doesn't help us answer this question. The deficiencies of this static budget performance report can be explained as follows: A production manager is responsible for controlling two things—production (output) and costs (input); that is, he or she must try to meet budgeted production volume and control costs in the process. To measure a manager's performance, the production and cost control functions must be separated. It makes no sense to note that the total actual cost of producing 23 boats is more than the budgeted cost of producing 20 boats. It obviously should be. The manager in our example clearly has exceeded budgeted production volume, but to determine whether he or she has controlled costs adequately, we must be able to compare actual costs to budgeted costs at the same number of units of production. In other words, how much more costs *should have* been incurred given this higher level of production? Answering this question correctly *is* the process of using a flexible budget.

Using the Flexible Budget

Instead of providing budgeted costs for only a single level of production or sales activity that was predicted before the operating period began, the flexible budget effectively recomputes that static budget after the conclusion of the operation period based on the actual activity level. To make it possible to prepare budgeted costs at any possible activity level within the relevant range, per-unit variable costs and total fixed costs are budgeted at the beginning of the operating period and are then used at the end of the period to create a flexible budget that is useful in measuring and analyzing actual input and output performance. The steps in preparing a flexible operating budget are as follows:

1. Determine a relevant range over which production is expected to vary during the coming operating period.

2. Before the operating period begins, establish the budgeted per-unit variable manufacturing costs and total fixed manufacturing costs.
3. At the conclusion of the operating period, use the per-unit variable costs and total fixed costs to build a flexible budget based on actual output activity.

To illustrate the preparation of a flexible budget, let us assume that Sunbird's relevant range of production activity per quarter is between 20 and 30 boats. This is important because producing outside of this relevant range is likely to result in expected differences in per-unit variable and total fixed costs.[8] As noted earlier, the per-unit variable manufacturing costs are expected to be $2,790, while total fixed manufacturing costs are expected to be $40,660 per quarter. These budgeted costs can now be used at the conclusion of the first quarter of 2006 to prepare a flexible budget that is relevant to assess the actual costs of producing 23 boats. This performance report based on flexible budgeting for the 23 boats actually produced now makes much more sense.

Sunbird Boat Company
Flexible Budget Performance Report
January–March 2006

Actual production (units)				23
Budgeted production (units)				20
Difference				3

	Budgeted Costs	Budgeted Costs for 23 Boats	Actual Costs Incurred for 23 Boats	Difference
Variable manufacturing costs	$ 2,790 per boat	$ 64,170	$ 63,350	$ 820
Fixed manufacturing costs	40,660 in total	40,660	41,040	380
Total costs		$104,830	$104,390	$ 440

Caution

Note that the "flex" in flexible budgeting really only relates to the variable costs. Fixed costs are expected to remain fixed!

Notice that the actual variable manufacturing costs are lower than the flexible budget, which is based on how much should have been spent to produce 23 boats. Only the actual fixed manufacturing costs have exceeded the flexible budget. We are now comparing apples with apples, or actual costs of producing 23 boats with budgeted costs of producing 23 boats. Using the same activity level has revealed that total manufacturing costs actually were less than budget by $440.

Flexible budgets provide management with useful information for investigating problem areas. This flexible budget performance report shows that actual production exceeded planned production, and that the costs incurred were less than those budgeted at the attained level of activity. Assuming that the company actually needed those 23 boats, the manager appears to be doing well with cost control. Having meaningful cost comparisons as a result of using flexible budgeting is very useful for evaluating performance. We'll spend a lot of time in the next chapter to more specifically analyze cost variances for Sunbird Boat Company.

TO SUMMARIZE: The master budget described in this chapter was a static budget. A static budget is a budget that is prepared for only one level of activity. Static budgets are useful for planning purposes, but flexible budgets are much more useful for control and performance evaluation. A flexible budget can be prepared over a range of actual activity levels by multiplying the variable costs per unit of output and then adding the total budgeted fixed cost amount. Flexible budgets allow budgeted and actual costs to be compared at the same level of activity.

8 See the earlier chapter on cost-volume-profit analysis if you need to review the concept of "relevant range."

review of learning objectives

1 Describe the importance of personal budgeting. A budget is a quantitative expression of a plan of action. Individuals who budget spend money how, where, and when they want. Those who do not budget often don't have enough money to purchase those things that they really need.

2 Identify the purposes of budgeting for organizations. The master budget identifies and allocates resources necessary to carry out the mission of the organization. Based on the strategic plan, the organization prepares a capital budget and a budget for operations. The operating budget provides quantitative estimates of sales and expected costs for each activity to be performed during a specified period of time (usually, one year). The budgeting process has several purposes. Budgeting encourages planning, enhances communication and coordination, provides authorization for actions (investing, spending, borrowing, producing), helps motivate employees to perform, assists in reducing conflicts, and provides quantitative measures of expectations and objectives.

3 Explain the budgeting process and its behavioral implications in organizations. Most organizations establish a budget committee composed of several vice presidents who coordinate the preparation of detailed budgets in their areas of responsibility and oversee the preparation of the overall budget. There are significant behavioral ramifications to consider in preparing an operating budget. For the process to be successful, top management must give its full support, all members of management must actively participate in the process, and deviations from the budget must be addressed in a constructive manner. If only the top management is involved in budget preparation, it is referred to as top-down budgeting. When each segment manager prepares a budget for that segment's operations, it is called bottom-up budgeting. Most budgeting processes incorporate both approaches to some degree.

4 Construct an operating budget and its components for manufacturing firms. The operating budget, an integral part of the master budget, is an integrated group of detailed budgets that together provide overall operating plans for a specific time period. The operating budget for a manufacturing firm starts with a sales forecast, which serves as the basis for the sales budget. The sales budget is followed in sequence with detailed budgets for production, direct materials usage and purchases, direct labor, manufacturing overhead, the product cost sheet, and selling and administrative ex-

penses. These detailed budgets are usually prepared on a monthly or quarterly basis.

5 Compare the operating budget for a manufacturing firm to that of a merchandising or service firm. For operational budgeting in merchandising companies, a purchases budget replaces the production, direct materials, direct labor, and manufacturing overhead budgets used in manufacturing companies. Because service firms cannot effectively hold an inventory of finished services ready to deliver to customers, the revenue and production budgets in service firms are typically the same budget. Thereafter, operational budgeting in services firms is quite similar to that of manufacturing firms. Operational budgets provide management of manufacturing, merchandising, or service firms with a plan of action for the coming year.

6 Create the cash budget. The cash budget shows expected cash receipts and disbursements; it also signals when the company can expect a cash shortage requiring outside financing or excess cash that could be temporarily invested in income-producing assets.

7 Prepare pro-forma financial statements. Once a cash budget is prepared to project the firm's ending cash balances and borrowing and investing activities, pro-forma financial statements can be prepared. The pro-forma balance sheet relies heavily on the balances at the beginning of the period, along with components of the master budget. The pro-forma income statement and statement of cash flows are prepared primarily from the detailed budgets included in the master budget. With these pro-forma financial statements, management is able to determine if budgeted results are consistent with the firm's master plan.

8 Distinguish between static and flexible budgets. Static budgets project expected results at only one activity level. When the actual production level differs significantly from the budgeted level, it is difficult to know what costs should have been for the actual production level. Flexible budgets allow costs to be estimated for the actual activity level, which then allows actual costs to be compared to budgeted costs for the actual production level.

k **ey terms & concepts**

budget, 1008
budget committee, 1012
budgetary slack, 1013
budgeted product cost sheet, 1022
budgeted service cost sheet, 1030
direct labor budget, 1020
direct materials budget, 1018
disposable income, 1009
manufacturing overhead budget, 1021
master budget, 1010

participative budgeting, 1013
production budget, 1018
purchases budget, 1025
revenue budget, 1027
sales budget, 1016
selling and administrative expense
    budget, 1023
service overhead budget, 1029
supplies budget, 1029
wages and salaries budget, 1029

cash budget, 1033
flexible budget, 1040
line of credit, 1035
static budget, 1039

r **eview problem**

Budgeting in a Manufacturing Firm

The following information is available for the Call Company:

Expected sales (units):	
June	840
July	980
August	1,400
Selling price per unit	$15
Accounts receivable balance, June 1	$6,300
Accounts payable balance, June 1	$2,350
Desired finished goods inventory, August 31 (units)	250
Beginning finished goods inventory, June 1 (units)	270
Direct materials needed per unit	11 lbs.
Desired direct materials inventory, August 31	2,800 lbs.
Beginning direct materials inventory, June 1	2,700 lbs.
Total direct labor time per finished unit	3 hours
Direct materials cost per pound	$0.60
Direct labor cost per hour	$8

Additional information:

a. Seventy-five percent of a month's sales is collected by the month's end; the remaining 25% is collected in the following month.
b. Sixty percent of a month's purchases are paid by the month's end; the remaining 40% is paid in the following month.
c. The desired ending finished goods inventory every month is 25% of the next month's sales.
d. The desired ending direct materials inventory every month is 20% of the next month's production needs.

Required:
1. Prepare the sales budget, including cash collections, for June, July, and August (in dollars).
2. Prepare the production budget for June, July, and August (in units).
3. Prepare the direct materials budget, including cash payments, for June, July, and August (in dollars).
4. Prepare the direct labor budget for June, July, and August (in dollars).

Solution
1. Sales Budget

	June	July	August
Expected sales (units)	840	980	1,400
Selling price per unit	× $15	× $15	× $15
Revenue earned	**$12,600**	**$14,700**	**$21,000**
Percent received in current month	× 75%	× 75%	× 75%
Current revenue collected	$ 9,450	$11,025	$15,750
Prior revenue collected*	6,300	3,150	3,675
Collections from customers	**$15,750**	**$14,175**	**$19,425**

*Prior revenue collected in June represents the accounts receivable balance on June 1. Prior revenue collected in July and August represents the revenue *not* collected in the prior month (i.e., revenue earned in prior month times 25%).

2. Production Budget

	June	July	August
Expected sales (units)	840	980	1,400
Add desired ending inventory*	245	350	250
Total needed	1,085	1,330	1,650
Less beginning inventory**	(270)	(245)	(350)
Budgeted production (units)	**815**	**1,085**	**1,300**

*Desired ending inventory for June and July is equal to 25% of next month's sales. Desired ending inventory in August is given.
**Beginning inventory in June is given. Beginning inventory in July and August is based on the desired ending inventory for the previous month.

3. Direct Materials Budget

	June	July	August
Units to be produced	815	1,085	1,300
Direct materials needed per unit	× 11 lbs.	× 11 lbs.	× 11 lbs.
Total production needs	8,965 lbs.	11,935 lbs.	14,300 lbs.
Desired ending direct materials inventory*	2,387	2,860	2,800
Total pounds needed	11,352 lbs.	14,795 lbs.	17,100 lbs.
Less beginning inventory**	(2,700)	(2,387)	(2,860)
Materials to be purchased	**8,652 lbs.**	**12,408 lbs.**	**14,240 lbs.**
Standard cost per pound	× $0.60	× $0.60	× $0.60
Materials purchases (rounded)	**$ 5,191**	**$ 7,445**	**$ 8,544**
Paid in current month	× 60%	× 60%	× 60%
Current purchase payments (rounded)	$ 3,115	$ 4,467	$ 5,126
Prior purchase payments***	2,350	2,076	2,978
Payments to suppliers	**$ 5,465**	**$ 6,543**	**$ 8,104**

*Desired ending direct materials inventory for June and July is equal to 20% of next month's production needs. Desired ending direct materials inventory in August is given.
**Beginning direct materials inventory in June is given. Beginning direct materials inventory in July and August is based on the desired ending direct materials inventory for the previous month.
***Prior purchase payments in June represent the June 1 accounts payable balance. Prior purchase payments in July and August represent the purchases *not* paid for in the prior month (i.e., material purchases in prior month times 40%—rounded).

4. Direct Labor Budget

	June	July	August
Units to be produced	815	1,085	1,300
Direct labor hours per unit	× 3 hrs.	× 3 hrs.	× 3 hrs.
Total hours needed	2,445 hrs.	3,255 hrs.	3,900 hrs.
Cost per hour	× $8	× $8	× $8
Direct labor cost	**$19,560**	**$26,040**	**$31,200**

discussion questions

1. How are strategic planning, capital budgeting, and operations budgeting different?
2. What are the advantages of budgeting?
3. How does management use the operating budget?
4. Describe the advantages of the top-down approach and the bottom-up approach to budgeting.
5. Why are budgets usually prepared for one year?
6. Why does the accuracy of the entire master budget depend on a reliable sales forecast?
7. Identify the sequence of schedules used in preparing a master budget for a manufacturing firm.
8. How is the budgeting process for a merchandising firm different from the budgeting process for a manufacturing firm?

9. How is the budgeting process for a service firm similar to the budgeting process for a manufacturing firm? What are any differences?

10. Describe the four sections of a cash budget.
11. How does a cash budget differ from a pro-forma income statement?
12. How are flexible budgets useful in controlling costs?

practice exercises

Practice 19-1

Purposes of Budgeting

Which one of the following statements is *false*?

a. Budgeting facilitates communication in an organization.
b. Budgeting is best used as a management tool to punish departments that do not perform well.
c. Budgeting helps management coordinate activities of business segments.
d. Budgeting can help motivate managers and workers.
e. Budgeting can help resolve conflicts that arise regarding the use of limited resources.

Practice 19-2

Behavioral Considerations of Budgeting

Which one of the following is *not* a behavioral consideration of the budgeting process?

a. Top management must support the budgeting process.
b. All managers, and as many employees as possible, should participate in the budgeting process.
c. Deviations from the budget must be addressed by managers in a positive and constructive manner.
d. The budgeting process should remain impersonal in nature.

Practice 19-3

Top-Down versus Bottom-Up Budgeting

Which one of the following statements is *false*?

a. An advantage of top-down budgeting is that upper management knows the strategic objectives of the company.
b. An advantage of bottom-up budgeting is that segment managers have an excellent understanding of products, technology, and current customer needs.
c. An advantage of top-down budgeting is universal acceptance of the final budget from line employees.
d. An advantage of bottom-up budgeting is that lower managers who help prepare the budget are likely to support the final budget.

Practice 19-4

Master Budget

Which one of the following is *not* part of the master budget of a manufacturing firm?

a. Depreciation budget
b. Sales budget
c. Production budget
d. Direct labor budget
e. Selling and administrative expense budget

Practice 19-5

Master Budget Information Flow

Place the following schedules in chronological order from start to finish in the master budgeting process.

a. Cash budget
b. Pro-forma income statement
c. Production budget
d. Sales budget
e. Direct materials budget

Practice 19-6

Sales Budget

Is the following statement true or false?

Since external variables (such as customer tastes and economic conditions) cannot be controlled by a company, those inputs are not used when computing a sales budget. Instead, the sales budget is generated using only historical sales data and internal cost information.

Practice 19-7

Production Budget

Using the following information, compute the number of units to be produced.

Desired ending inventory (in units)	3,600
Beginning inventory (in units)	3,400
Expected sales (in units)	24,150

Practice 19-8

Direct Materials Budget

Refer to the data in Practice 19-7. Using the following additional information, compute the cost of materials to be used in the coming period. (Assume no beginning nor ending direct materials inventory.)

Wood requirement per unit	10 board feet
Aluminum requirement per unit	7.5 square feet
Cost of wood (per board foot)	$4.60
Cost of aluminum (per square foot)	$5.75

Practice 19-9	**Direct Labor Budget**

Refer to the data in Practice 19-7. Using the following additional information, compute the direct labor cost.

Direct labor hours per unit 6
Rate per direct labor hour $12

Practice 19-10	**Manufacturing Overhead Budget**

Using the following information, compute total manufacturing overhead.

Indirect labor rate . . . . $4.00 per unit
Indirect materials rate . . . . $2.50 per unit
Utilities rate . . . . $1.25 per unit
Property tax expense $29,000
Depreciation expense $133,600
Insurance expense $38,000
Supervisor salaries expense $240,300
Expected production (in units) 21,000

Practice 19-11	**Purchases Budget**

Using the following information, compute the dollar amount of total purchases to be made in the coming period.

Beginning inventory (in units) 123
Expected sales (in units) 1,240
Desired ending inventory (in units) 128
Cost per unit $685

Practice 19-12	**Master Budget for Manufacturing Firms versus Service Firms**

Which one of the following budgets do manufacturing firms and service firms have in common?

a. Direct labor budget
b. Supplies budget
c. Revenue budget
d. Production budget
e. Direct materials budget

Practice 19-13	**Revenue Budget**

The company performs tune-ups on standard diesel engines. Using the following information, compute the budgeted gross revenue for the period.

Gross revenue per tune-up $180
Tune-up capacity per day 13
Number of working days in period 76
Historical occupancy rate* 65%

*This refers to the rate at which the companies' service bays are actually occupied compared to their total capacity. It is similar to the concept of hotel room occupancy rate.

Practice 19-14	**Cash Budget**

Using the following information, determine how much external funding will be necessary during the coming period (if any).

Collections from customers	$104,300
Minimum cash balance desired	25,000
Direct labor expense	24,350
Cash balance, beginning	32,000
Manufacturing overhead expense	22,750
Income tax expense	21,680
Selling and administrative expenses	54,140
Direct materials expense	43,200

Practice 19-15

Pro-Forma Financial Statements

Which one of the following statements regarding pro-forma financial statements is *false*?

a. Most companies do not create pro-forma financial statements because of the many assumptions required.
b. The pro-forma financial statements complete the master budget for a company.
c. Pro-forma financial statements help companies make decisions regarding dividends and management bonus opportunities for the coming year.
d. Pro-forma financial statements include an income statement, a balance sheet, and a statement of cash flows.

Practice 19-16

Flexible Budgets

Using the following manufacturing costs per unit, prepare a flexible budget for the company at levels of production of 550, 600, and 650 units.

Direct materials	$6.80
Direct labor	8.90
Manufacturing overhead	5.20

Practice 19-17

Flexible Budget Performance Report

Refer to the data in Practice 19-16. Using the flexible budget created in Practice 19-16 and the following actual data, prepare a flexible budget performance report.

Actual number of units produced	650
Actual direct materials costs	$4,200
Actual direct labor costs	$5,750
Actual manufacturing overhead costs	$3,430

 exercises

Exercise 19-1

Spreadsheet

Personal Budgeting

Jennifer Swartz works as an interior decorator for Modern Fashion Corporation. Her annual salary is $36,500. Of that amount, 20% is withheld for federal income taxes, 7.15% for state taxes, 7.65% for FICA taxes, and 2% as a contribution to the United Way. Another 5% is deposited directly into a company credit union for savings. Jennifer has four monthly payments: $225 for her car, $80 for furniture, $410 for rent, and $100 to repay college loans. Jennifer's other monthly expenses are approximately:

Food expense	$250
Clothing expense	100
Entertainment expense	125
Utilities expense	80
Insurance expense	30
Gas and maintenance expenses on car	180
Miscellaneous expenses	200
Total	$965

(continued)

Prepare both a monthly budget and an annual budget for Jennifer that identifies gross salary, net take-home pay, net disposable income, and net surplus or deficit.

Exercise 19-2

Personal Budgeting

George Marcus, a recent college graduate, has been hired by Taylor Corporation at a salary of $54,000 per year. In anticipation of his salary, George purchased a $20,000 new ski boat and will pay for it at a rate of $425 per month, including interest, for five years. He also rented a condominium for $600 a month and bought a car on account for $350 a month. In addition, George figures that his other monthly expenses will be:

Food expense	$250
Clothing expense	125
Entertainment expense	250
Insurance expense	150
Gas and other car expenses	200
Utilities expense	130

1. On the assumption that George also pays income and FICA taxes of 25 and 7.65%, respectively, prepare his monthly budget.
2. George plans to save enough money for a down payment on a house. If a $20,000 down payment is needed, how long will it take him to save the needed amount? (For this exercise, ignore interest on savings, and assume that George does not have any savings at the present time.)

Exercise 19-3

Budgeting Sales Revenue and Collections

Frank's Frames mass produces and wholesales wooden picture frames at an average price of $7 per frame. Expected sales volumes over the first six months of 2006 are forecasted as follows.

January	7,900
February	8,500
March	8,200
April	9,000
May	8,800
June	8,000

Frank's Frames expects to collect 85% of its revenues in the month of the sale, with the remaining 15% collected in the following month.

1. Compute the expected balance in Accounts Receivable as of February 1, 2006. (*Hint:* It is based solely on sales in January 2006.)
2. Budget the expected monthly revenue and collections for the *five months* of February through June.

Exercise 19-4

Spreadsheet

Production Budgeting

Daytona Electric makes and sells two kinds of portable music players—a CD player and an MP3 player. The sales forecasts for these players for the next four quarters are as follows:

	CD Player	MP3 Player
First quarter	170	130
Second quarter	178	139
Third quarter	166	127
Fourth quarter	190	145
Totals	704	541

At the beginning of the first quarter, Daytona has 140 CD players and 120 MP3 players in stock. Experience has shown that Daytona must maintain an inventory equal to two-thirds of the next quarter's sales.

How many players of each type must be produced during each of the first three quarters to meet sales and inventory demands?

Exercise 19-5

Production Budgeting

James Seigel is the CEO of Seigel Monitor Company, a manufacturer of computer monitors. Seigel manufactures three types of flat panel LCD computer monitors: 15-inch, 17-inch, and 19-inch. The sales projections (in units) for 2006 and the first quarter of 2007 are:

	15-inch	17-inch	19-inch
First quarter, 2006	3,000	5,000	2,000
Second quarter, 2006	2,500	4,750	2,150
Third quarter, 2006	2,850	4,900	1,800
Fourth quarter, 2006	3,200	4,876	2,150
First quarter, 2007	2,900	5,100	2,200

Beginning inventory for 15-inch, 17-inch, and 19-inch monitors are 1,350, 1,500, and 1,275, respectively. Seigel requires that half of the next quarter's sales be maintained in inventory.

How many monitors must be manufactured for each quarter of 2006 to meet sales and inventory demand?

Exercise 19-6

Direct Materials Budgeting

Shaver Bicycle Shop assembles and sells tricycles and bicycles. The frames are purchased from one supplier and the wheels from another. The following materials are required:

Bicycles	Tricycles
One 22-inch frame, $35	One 12-inch frame, $15
Two 22-inch wheels, $10 each	Two 4-inch wheels, $10 each
	One 12-inch wheel, $7.50

Management anticipates that 150 bicycles and 160 tricycles will be assembled during the first quarter of 2006. On December 31, 2005, the following assembly parts are on hand:

22-inch frames	12
22-inch wheels	20
12-inch frames	8
4-inch wheels	24
12-inch wheels	10

Management also decides that, beginning in January, the inventory of parts on hand at the end of each month should be sufficient to make 10 bicycles and 10 tricycles.

Prepare a budget for direct materials purchases for the first quarter of 2006. (*Note:* You are not required to extend the budget to determine the budget for cash payments to suppliers.)

Exercise 19-7

Direct Materials Budgeting

Shanahan Corporation produces three types of videocassettes: VHS, S-VHS, and 8 millimeter. Shanahan purchases tape for the videocassettes from a firm in Mexico and purchases the cases from another supplier in Brazil. The following materials are required for production.

(continued)

	VHS	S-VHS	8MM
Tape	$1.75	$2.30	$3.05
Cases	2.50	2.50	2.00

Beginning inventory for Shanahan Corporation is 5,000, 7,000, and 3,500 tapes for VHS, S-VHS, and 8 MM, respectively. Management wants to have 5,000 VHS and 8 MM tapes and 2,500 S-VHS tapes in ending inventory. Projected sales for the first half of 2006 are 40,000 VHS tapes, 14,000 S-VHS tapes, and 21,000 8 MM tapes.

Shanahan's policy is to pay 80% of its accounts with suppliers by the end of each half year. The balance in accounts payable on January 1, 2006, is $55,000.

1. Prepare a budget for direct materials purchases for the first half of 2006.
2. Prepare a budget for payments to direct materials suppliers for the first half of 2006.

Exercise 19-8

Direct Labor Budgeting

Super Good Chocolate Company makes and sells two kinds of candy: chocolate peanut bars and caramel bars. The production budget for the next three months for each of the bars is as follows:

	Boxes of Chocolate Peanut Bars	Boxes of Caramel Bars
January	640	700
February	870	450
March	920	630

From experience, Super Good's management knows that it takes approximately 20 minutes to make a box of chocolate peanut bars and 30 minutes to make a box of caramel bars. Super Good pays its direct labor employees $8 per hour.

Prepare a direct labor budget for each of the two products in both hours and costs for January, February, and March.

Exercise 19-9

Direct Labor Budgeting

Sanford Shoe Company makes three shoe styles: loafers, work boots, and tennis shoes. The production budget for the next three months for each type of shoe is:

	Loafers	Work Boots	Tennis Shoes
January	2,900	5,400	3,160
February	3,100	6,000	5,400
March	2,750	6,600	4,300

From experience, Sanford's management knows that it takes 15 minutes of direct labor to make a pair of loafers, 20 minutes to make a pair of work boots, and 12 minutes to make a pair of tennis shoes. At Sanford, direct labor employees are paid $10 per hour.

Prepare a direct labor budget in both hours and costs for each of the three months.

Exercise 19-10

Production Overhead Cost Budget

Linden Nursery grows and sells potted perennial plants, as well as ornamental and fruit trees. The owner of Linden Nursery has determined that variable overhead costs are largely a function of direct labor hours spent growing and tending the plants and trees. Variable overhead costs include supervisory costs, indirect materials, and utilities (power and water) and are estimated to be $0.75, $0.40, and $0.55 per direct labor hour, respectively. Fixed overhead costs for property taxes, equipment depreciation, and night security are expected to be $1,500, $900, and $1,100, respectively, each quarter. Linden keeps a minimal staff during the winter season and then expands its workforce substantially during the gardening season. The direct labor hours budgeted for 2006 are as follows:

First quarter	1,000 hours
Second quarter	9,500
Third quarter	6,100
Fourth quarter	800

Prepare a production overhead budget for Linden Nursery.

Exercise 19-11

Budgeted Product Costs

Hard Hitting Bat Company makes two types of baseball bats: aluminum and wood. During the past several years, management has kept accurate records of costs and resource requirements and has determined that the following is needed to make the baseball bats:

Wood Bat	**Production Requirements**	**Unit Cost**
Wood	4 board feet	$ 5.50
Paint and protective finish	1 pint	8.50
Direct labor	3 hours	12.00
Manufacturing overhead	3 hours	6.75
Aluminum Bat		
Aluminum	6 pounds	$ 4.00
Paint and protective finish	½ pint	8.50
Direct labor	2½ hours	12.00
Manufacturing overhead	2½ hours	6.75

Compute the budgeted product costs for both the wood and aluminum baseball bats.

Exercise 19-12

Operational Budgeting (Service Company)

Dr. Dawn Gifford is a new dentist specializing in treating children under the age of 18. Dr. Gifford has two primary sources of revenues: (1) fees from regular dental work (checkups, cleanings, fillings, etc.) and (2) fees from specialized dental reconstructive surgery. Last year, Dr. Gifford earned an average of $75 per patient visit from regular customers and $800 per surgery. The following operating expenses were incurred last year in running the office:

Variable operating expenses:		
Dental supplies (per patient)		$ 10
Hospital surgery room rental (per surgery)		200
Annual fixed operating expenses:		
Office manager's salary		$18,000
Dental hygienist's salary		26,000
Utilities		3,600
Rental of office space		12,000
Depreciation expense on office equipment*		20,000
Liability insurance		48,000
Other expenses		9,600

*Total equipment cost, $200,000; depreciated over 10 years on a straight-line basis.

(continued)

Last year, Dr. Gifford treated an average of 200 patients per month and performed an average of eight surgeries per month. She expects to increase the number of patients serviced by 10% this coming year and the number of surgeries by two per month. She also expects the average patient fee to be $80 and the average surgical fee to be $850. Dr. Gifford expects the variable expenses to remain constant this year, but is expecting to raise the manager's salary by 5% and the hygienist's by 15%. She thinks the other expenses will stay about the same. All revenues are expected to be collected and all payable expenses are expected to be paid during the year.

Based on these data (and ignoring payroll and income taxes):

1. What was the operating profit (loss) for last year?
2. Prepare a revenue budget and an operating expense budget for this coming year.

Exercise 19-13

Cash Budgeting—Hospital

The management of West Valley Memorial Hospital needs to prepare a cash budget for July 2006. The following information is available:

a. The cash balance on July 1, 2006, is $236,000.
b. Actual services performed during May and June and projected services for July are:

	May	June	July
Cash services (bills paid by individuals as they leave the hospital)	$110,000	$ 90,000	$120,000
Credit services (bills paid by insurance companies and Medicare)	900,000	1,000,000	875,000

Credit sales are collected over a 2-month period, with 60% collected during the month the service is performed and 40% in the following month.

c. Hospital personnel plan to purchase $80,000 of supplies during July on account. Accounts payable are usually paid one-half in the month of purchase and one-half in the following month. The accounts payable balance on July 1, 2006, is $35,000.
d. Salaries and wages paid during July will be approximately $600,000. (Ignore income and other tax withholdings.)
e. Depreciation on the hospital and equipment for July will be $100,000.
f. A short-term bank loan of $80,000 (including interest) will be repaid in July.
g. All other cash expenses for July will total $56,000.

Prepare the hospital's July cash budget.

Exercise 19-14

Cash Budgeting

Medical Supplies, Inc., purchases first-aid items from large wholesalers. Medical Supplies then assembles and sells first-aid kits to businesses and contracts to maintain the first-aid kits. You have been asked to prepare a cash budget for January. The following information is provided:

a. Cash in the bank on January 1 is $33,000.
b. Actual sales for October, November, December, and projected sales for January are as follows:

	October	November	December	January
Cash	$12,000	$11,500	$ 8,200	$12,500
Credit	31,000	29,400	32,000	28,000

Payments on credit sales are received 50% in the month of sale, 31% in the month following the sale, and 15% and 4% in the second and third months, respectively, following the sale.

c. Total administrative and selling expenses (all cash) are $25,000.

d. Purchases are always paid 30 days after delivery. Purchases for October, November, and December were $28,000, $39,000, and $29,500, respectively.

e. Cash dividends of $22,000 are paid.

f. Any cash excess is used to purchase 30-day government securities, and any cash deficiency is compensated by short-term borrowing.

g. Management desires a minimum balance of $9,000 in the bank.

Prepare a cash budget for the month of January.

Exercise 19-15

Spreadsheet

Cash Budgeting (Merchandising Company)

Whitlock, Inc., buys hardware parts from various manufacturers and sells them to retail stores. Management is currently trying to prepare a cash budget for August and has the following information available:

a. The cash balance on August 1 is $25,000.

b. Actual sales for June and July and projected sales for August are as follows:

	June	July	August
Cash sales	$ 30,000	$ 45,000	$ 50,000
Credit sales	100,000	120,000	130,000

Credit sales are collected 63% during the month of sale, 26% during the month following the sale, and 11% during the second month following the sale.

c. Whitlock's actual purchases for June and July and its projected purchases for August are as follows:

	June	July	August
Cash purchases	$10,000	$20,000	$25,000
Credit purchases	40,000	50,000	60,000

All accounts payable are paid in the month following the purchase.

d. Total administrative and selling expenses (including $14,000 depreciation) for August are expected to be $105,000.

e. Whitlock expects to pay a $26,000 dividend to stockholders and to purchase, for cash, a $25,000 piece of land during August.

f. Cash on hand should never drop below $25,000.

1. Prepare Whitlock's August cash budget, assuming that the company borrows any amounts needed to meet its minimum desired balance.

2. **Interpretive Question:** What types of expenses other than depreciation would be excluded from a cash budget?

Exercise 19-16

Pro-Forma Income Statement

Gold Manufacturing, Inc., is a manufacturer of electric pencil sharpeners. The following is information regarding Gold Manufacturing for the fiscal year-end, May 31, 2006:

Beginning finished goods inventory	$ 55,000
Ending finished goods inventory	42,000
Interest expense	28,000
Selling and administrative expenses	72,000
Sales revenue	425,000
Direct materials used	52,000
Direct labor	63,000
Manufacturing overhead	32,000

Assume a tax rate of 33%. Prepare a pro-forma income statement for the year ended May 31, 2006, for Gold Manufacturing, Inc. (Note that Gold Manufacturing does not have work-in-process inventory.)

Exercise 19-17

Pro-Forma Income Statement

Silver Company has asked you to prepare a pro-forma income statement for the coming year. The following information is available:

Expected sales revenue	$1,240,000
Manufacturing costs:	
Variable cost of goods sold	625,000
Fixed overhead	125,000
Selling expenses:	
Variable expenses	140,000
Fixed expenses	45,000
Administrative expenses:	
Variable expenses	45,000
Fixed expenses	160,000
Other:	
Interest expense	28,000
Income tax rate	35%

Prepare a pro-forma contribution margin income statement for Silver Company.

Exercise 19-18

Pro-Forma Statement of Cash Flows

The accountants at Karl's Fish Hatchery are currently preparing the pro-forma statement of cash flows for May. In getting ready to prepare the statement, they have the following information available:

Dividends to be paid in May	$ 1,500
Bonds to be issued in May	8,000
Equipment to be purchased in May	15,000
Repayment of short-term loans in May	3,000
Depreciation expense during May	2,500
Expected May net income	10,000
Expected changes in current assets and	
liabilities during May:	
Accounts receivable decrease	1,200
Accounts payable decrease	1,730
Increase in inventory	2,580
Increase in income taxes payable	2,550

Prepare Karl's pro-forma statement of cash flows (using the indirect method).

Exercise 19-19

Pro-Forma Income Statement and Balance Sheet (Service Industry)
Horrock's, Inc., is a small engineering corporation that surveys land for development. The company has grown rapidly over the past few years, and management has to decide whether to hire new engineers and open new offices. To assess future growth, the company's accountant has gathered budgeted information for the coming year, 2006:

Ending common stock balance	$ 48,000
Beginning retained earnings balance	34,000
Ending accounts payable balance	6,000
Ending equipment balance	159,000
Ending accumulated depreciation balance	24,000
Ending accounts receivable balance	19,500
Ending cash balance	18,000
Interest expense	3,000
Salary expense	105,000
Other expenses (including depreciation)	37,500
Service revenue	300,000
Income tax rate	33%

Income taxes due on the coming year's net income will be paid during 2007. Dividends of $70,000 are to be declared and paid during 2006.

1. Prepare a pro-forma income statement and balance sheet for 2006 from which the company president can make expansion decisions.
2. **Interpretive Question:** On the basis of this information, is the company very profitable? How should this level of profits affect its expansion plans?

Exercise 19-20

Static versus Flexible Budgeting—Performance Reports (Service Firm)
Flannery Muffler Shop has budgeted to repair 10,000 mufflers during 2006. Each repair job takes $1^1/2$ hours, and employees are paid $12 per hour. During 2006, Flannery actually repaired 9,425 mufflers, and the salary expense amounted to $179,000.

1. Assuming a static budget, use the information to prepare a performance report for Flannery Muffler Shop for 2006.
2. Assuming a flexible budget, use the information to prepare a performance report for Flannery Muffler Shop for 2006.
3. **Interpretive Question:** The manager of the muffler shop believes he deserves a bonus because the actual wage expense ($179,000) was less than budgeted. Do you agree? Explain.

Exercise 19-21

Flexible Budgets (Service Firm)
Outdoors Unlimited operates a fishing lodge in northern Canada. The following cost information has been developed by the company's accountant:

Fixed costs:	
Salaries	$68,000
Mortgage payments	24,000
Taxes	4,000
Other	3,000
Variable costs (per guest):	
Fishing tackle	$20
Food	80
Other	16

(continued)

1. In planning for its 2006 summer season, Outdoors Unlimited does not know exactly how many guests to expect and, hence, how much to charge per guest. Prepare a flexible budget showing expected total costs at 200, 300, 400, and 500 guests.
2. Assume that Outdoors Unlimited conservatively estimates 300 guests for the year. If it wants to earn profits of $100,000 for the 300 guests, how much should it charge per guest?

p roblems

Problem 19-1

Personal Budgeting

Ben Fleming has just received a job offer of $35,000 salary per year plus overtime pay, which will amount to 10% of his salary. Ben estimates his living costs as follows:

Federal, state, and FICA taxes amount to	35% of income
Rent	$550/month
Car payment	$210/month
IRA	$1,500/year
Other savings	4% of net take-home pay
Utilities	$90/month
Gas and maintenance—automobile	$130/month
Insurance	$75/month
Food	$240/month
Entertainment	$170/month
Clothing	$80/month

Required:
1. Prepare a budget for the year. Assume Ben starts his job on January 1.
2. Is Ben's offer sufficient to meet his projected expenses?
3. Ben has always dreamed of going to Africa to photograph wildlife. The trip will cost $5,000. How long will it take Ben to save for the trip? (Ignore interest earnings, and assume that he has no savings at the present time.)

Problem 19-2

Personal Budgeting

Carol Baum is an advertising specialist for Success Advertising, Inc. Her annual salary is $37,500, of which 20% is withheld for federal income taxes, 7% for state income taxes, 7.65% for FICA taxes, and 5% for a tax-sheltered annuity. She estimates that her monthly expenses are approximately as follows:

Rent	$ 475
Automobile payment	250
Food	240
Automobile gasoline and maintenance	120
Utilities	70
Clothing	100
Entertainment	150
Miscellaneous	130
Total monthly expenses	$1,535

Required:
1. Prepare Carol's monthly budget, assuming that the car payments will continue for about three years.
2. Assume that Carol would like to accumulate savings of $12,000 in order to take an extended leave from her job. This will allow her to travel and take courses as a way of gener-

ating some fresh ideas she can use in creating new approaches to advertising. How long will it take her to save the needed amount? (Ignore interest earnings, and assume that she has no savings at the present time.)

3. **Interpretive Question:** If Carol asked you for advice on how she might reduce her expenses, what would you suggest?

Problem 19-3

Sales Revenue Budgeting (Service Firm)

Six-Peak Pools in Montana is open May through September. It has the capability of serving approximately 600 patrons each day. July is the peak month for Six-Peak Pools. With kids being in school, May and September are its slowest months. For the upcoming 2006 season, Six-Peak's management projects the following usage rates.

May	30%
June	80
July	90
August	75
September	20

The pool admission fees for Six-Peak are as follows.

Adults (12 years and up)	$5
Children (3 to 11 years)	$3
Babies (2 and under)	Free

On a typical day, 40% of the patrons are adults, 50% are children, and 10% are babies. Because Six-Peak only accepts cash and credit cards, its daily admission revenue and daily cash collections are the same.

Required:
Budget the expected monthly sales in admission fees for Six-Peak Pools.

Problem 19-4

Sales Collections

Rocky Peak Company plans on the following collection pattern on its sales:

Collected in month of sale	70%
Collected in the first month after sale	15
Collected in the second month after sale	10
Collected in the third month after sale	4
Uncollectible	1

Budgeted sales for the last six months of 2006 are shown below:

July	$ 60,000
August	70,000
September	80,000
October	90,000
November	100,000
December	85,000

Required:
1. What are the estimated total cash collections during October 2006?
2. How much of the third quarter sales (i.e., July, August, and September) are expected to be collected during the third quarter?
3. What is the expected 2006 ending balance in accounts receivable, net of allowance for doubtful accounts?

Problem 19-5

Production Budgeting

Nebo Company makes and sells two products: leather and vinyl briefcases. The sales forecasts for these briefcases for the next four quarters are as follows:

	Leather Briefcases	Vinyl Briefcases
First quarter	90	90
Second quarter	150	180
Third quarter	270	228
Fourth quarter	288	144
Total	798	642

On January 1, Nebo has a stock of 80 completed leather briefcases and 60 vinyl briefcases. Experience indicates that Nebo must maintain an inventory equal to one-half of the next quarter's sales.

Required:
1. How many leather and vinyl briefcases must be produced during each of the first three quarters to meet sales and inventory demands?
2. **Interpretive Question:** Assume Nebo is a wholesale merchandising company instead of a manufacturing company. How would the budget information provided in part (1) change?

Problem 19-6

Production and Direct Materials Budget

Chandler Manufacturing Company makes two products: widgets and gidgets. The following information is available on May 1:

a. Direct materials needed to make a widget: six units of X, three units of Y. Direct materials needed to make a gidget: two units of X, six units of Y.
b. Number of units available at beginning of May:

Direct material X	72 units
Direct material Y	43 units
Finished widgets	12
Finished gidgets	15

c. Expected sales during May:

Widgets	100
Gidgets	95

d. Desired levels of ending inventory:

Direct material X	70 units
Direct material Y	35 units
Widgets	11
Gidgets	13

e. Cost of direct materials:

Direct material X	$3 per unit
Direct material Y	$2 per unit

Chandler has a $1,300 balance in accounts payable on May 1 and expects to pay for half of its May purchases by the end of the month. All accounts are paid in full within 30 days.

Required:
Prepare a production budget and a direct materials budget for Chandler Company for the month of May.

Problem 19-7

Manufacturing Overhead Cost Budget

World-Wide Gym, Inc. makes weight lifting equipment. It designs and manufactures its own weight plates, as well as home gym sets such as workout towers, strength cages, and universal stations. Its variable manufacturing overhead (MOH) costs are determined as a result of either the pounds of weight plates or the number of gym sets manufactured. The variable MOH rates are as follows: $0.05 and $0.02 per pound of weight plates for materials handling and storage costs, respectively; and $45 and $12 per gym set for insurance and inspection work, respectively. The fixed MOH costs each month are $2,200 for property taxes, $3,200 for plant depreciation, $450 for utilities, and $17,000 for research and development.

The following monthly manufacturing volumes are expected for the second quarter of 2006:

	Pounds of Weight Plates	Number of Gym Sets
April	10,000	775
May	11,500	650
June	11,000	700
Total	32,500	2,125

Required:
Prepare a monthly manufacturing overhead budget for World-Wide Gym, Inc.

Problem 19-8

Budgeted Product Cost Sheet

Jersey Candy Company makes and sells two kinds of candy bars: chocolate almond and coconut. During the past several years, the company has kept accurate records of costs and resource requirements and has determined that the following are needed to make the candy bars:

One Box of 24 Chocolate Almond Bars	Cost
Chocolate (1¹/₂ pounds)	$3.00/pound
Almonds (1 pound)	$5.00/pound
Sugar (2 pounds)	$0.50/pound
Direct labor (20 minutes)	$9.00/hour
Manufacturing overhead (20 minutes)	$7.00/direct labor hour

One Box of 24 Coconut Bars	Cost
Chocolate (1 pound)	$3.00/pound
Coconut (1¹/₄ pounds)	$2.00/pound
Sugar (1³/₄ pounds)	$0.50/pound
Direct labor (30 minutes)	$9.00/hour
Manufacturing overhead (30 minutes)	$7.00/direct labor hour

Required:
1. Establish the budgeted product cost sheet for each type of candy bar.
2. If management wants to mark up each box of candy 30% to cover other costs and earn a profit, how much should be charged for a box of each type of candy bar?

Problem 19-9

Unifying Concepts: Sales, Cash Collections, and Purchases Budgets

The following information is available for Laura Company, a wholesale company:

Expected sales volume:

October	6,400 units
November	6,000 units
December	7,000 units
Selling price per unit	$40
Accounts receivable balance, October 1	$50,000
Desired ending inventory, December 31	1,850 units
Beginning inventory, October 1	2,000 units

Additional information:

a. Each month 75% of sales is collected by month-end; the remaining 25% is collected in the following month.
b. The desired inventory every month is 30% of the next month's sales.

Required:
1. Prepare sales budgets for October, November, and December (in dollars).
2. Prepare cash collection budgets for October, November, and December (in dollars). Assume that all sales are on credit.
3. Prepare purchases budgets for October, November, and December (in units).

Problem 19-10

Spreadsheet

Unifying Concepts: Production, Direct Materials, Direct Labor, and Manufacturing Overhead Budgets; and Budgeted Product Cost Sheets

San Antonio Furniture Company makes two products: bookshelves and rocking chairs. The following information is available for September:

a. Production requirements:

	Bookshelves	**Rocking Chairs**
Materials needed:		
Wood	100 board feet at $0.90 per foot	90 board feet at $0.90 per foot
Stain	2 gallons at $9 per gallon	3 gallons at $9 per gallon
Bolts, nuts, etc.	1 dozen at $1.50 per dozen	1½ dozen at $1.50 per dozen
Direct labor	12 hours at $8.50 per hour	10 hours at $8.50 per hour
Variable manufacturing overhead	12 hours at $4 per direct labor hour	10 hours at $4 per direct labor hour
Fixed manufacturing overhead*	$1,521 per month	

*Fixed manufacturing overhead is assigned to products using direct labor hours.

b. Levels of inventories:

	Actual Beginning Inventory	**Desired Ending Inventory**
Wood	1,100 board feet	1,000 board feet
Stain	11 gallons	12 gallons
Bolts, nuts, etc.	15 dozen	9 dozen
Finished bookshelves	3	5
Finished rocking chairs	6	7

Required:
1. Prepare the production budget, assuming that the company expects to sell 40 bookshelves and 50 rocking chairs in September.
2. Based on the production budget and the desired ending inventory level, prepare the direct materials usage and purchases budget for September. (*Note:* Direct materials purchases are paid for at the time of the purchase.)
3. Based on the production budget, prepare the direct labor budget for September.
4. Based on the production budget, prepare the manufacturing overhead budget for September.
5. Based on the operating budgets prepared above, prepare the budgeted product cost sheets for bookshelves and rocking chairs for September.

Problem 19-11

Spreadsheet

Unifying Concepts: Sales, Cash Collections, Production, Direct Materials, and Direct Labor Budgets

The following information is available for Raleigh Company:

Expected sales volume:

April	1,600 units
May	1,500 units
June	1,750 units
Selling price per unit	$12
Accounts receivable balance, April 1	$6,000
Accounts payable balance, April 1	$796
Desired finished goods inventory, June 30	200 units
Beginning finished goods inventory, April 1	210 units
Direct materials needed per unit	5 pounds
Desired direct materials inventory, June 30	550 pounds
Beginning direct materials inventory, April 1	420 pounds
Total direct labor time per finished product	2 hours
Direct materials cost per pound	$0.50
Direct labor cost per hour	$8

Additional information:

a. Each month 70% of sales are collected by month-end; the remaining 30% are collected in the following month.
b. The desired finished goods inventory every month is 20% of the next month's sales.
c. The desired direct materials inventory every month is 10% of the next month's production needs.
d. Each month 80% of direct materials purchases are paid by month-end; the remaining 20% are paid in the following month.

Required:
1. Prepare sales budgets for April, May, and June (in dollars).
2. Prepare cash collection budgets for April, May, and June (in dollars). Assume that all sales are on credit.
3. Prepare production budgets for April, May, and June (in units).
4. Prepare direct materials budgets for April, May, and June (in dollars).
5. Prepare direct labor budgets for April, May, and June (in dollars).

Problem 19-12

Budgeting for a Service Company

Riverside Country Club has 435 members at the end of 2005 (including 25 new members who joined during the year). Each member has paid a $10,000 initiation fee and pays $100 a month in dues to remain an active member of the club (new members do not pay monthly dues during the first calendar year of their membership). The club offers golf, tennis, and food and beverage services. The club is essentially run on a cash basis. Operating data for 2005 are as follows:

(continued)

Riverside Country Club
Operating Data
For the Year 2005

Revenues:		
Dues[1]	$742,000	
Guest fees[2]	6,500	
Golf revenues	455,000	
Tennis revenues	145,000	
Food and beverage	325,000	
Miscellaneous	2,500	$ 1,676,000
Expenses:		
Golf course	$395,000	
Tennis courts	170,000	
Food and bar	272,000	
Administration and maintenance[3]	515,000	
Interest on debt[4]	50,000	
Miscellaneous	27,000	(1,429,000)
Net operating profit		$ 247,000

[1]Dues (410 × $1,200 = $492,000; 25 new members × $10,000 = $250,000).
[2]Guest fees (130 × $50 = $6,500).
[3]Maintenance includes $125,000 depreciation on facilities.
[4]Interest ($500,000 × 0.10 × 1 year).

Assume the following additional facts for the year 2006:

a. There are 435 members paying dues, as well as 10 additional new members.
b. Guest fees are 110% of 2005 fees.
c. Golf revenues are 125% of 2005 revenues.
d. Tennis revenues are 90% of 2005 revenues (due to courts being closed for one month).
e. Food and beverage revenues are the same as 2005.
f. Operating expenses (golf, tennis, and food and beverage) are up 5%.
g. Administration and maintenance will increase $40,000 due to expected repairs.
h. Principal payment of $50,000 during 2006 will reduce interest expense by 10% for 2006.
i. Miscellaneous revenues will stay the same; miscellaneous expenses are expected to be $25,000.

Required:
1. Prepare an annual budget for Riverside for the year 2006.
2. **Interpretive Question:** Is Riverside in better shape financially in 2006 as compared to 2005? What areas of concern do you see?

Problem 19-13

Cash Budgeting (Manufacturing Company)
Hare Manufacturing Company makes wax for automobiles. As part of overall planning, a cash budget is prepared quarterly each year. You have been asked to assist in preparing the cash budget for the fourth quarter of the company's fiscal year. The following information is available:

a. Sales:

Third quarter (actual)	$180,000
Fourth quarter (expected)	175,000

All sales are made on account, with 70% collected in the quarter in which the sales are made and 30% collected during the following quarter.

b. Materials purchases are scheduled as follows:

Third quarter (actual)	$90,000
Fourth quarter (expected)	80,000

Materials are purchased on account and paid for at the rate of 80% in the quarter of purchase and 20% in the following quarter.

c. Direct labor and manufacturing overhead costs (including $6,000 of depreciation) are expected to be $45,000 and $21,000, respectively, during the fourth quarter.

d. Selling and administrative expenses are expected to total $27,000 during the fourth quarter, including $2,000 of depreciation.

e. Plans have been made to purchase, for cash, $15,000 of equipment during the fourth quarter.

f. The cash balance at the beginning of the quarter is $16,000. The company can borrow money in $1,000 multiples at 12% interest from a local bank. The bank assesses interest for a full quarter, both for the quarter in which the money is borrowed and for the quarter in which it is repaid. All interest is paid at the time of note repayment. Hare ran short of cash during the third quarter and had to borrow $8,000 from the bank. Hare wishes to maintain a minimum cash balance of $16,000.

Required:

Prepare a schedule showing the cash budget and financing needs of Hare Manufacturing Company for the fourth quarter.

Problem 19-14

Cash Budgeting (Merchandising Company)

Jim Henry, owner of Henry's Retail, is negotiating a $100,000, 15%, four-month loan from the Garfield County Bank, effective October 1, 2006. The bank loan officer has requested that Henry's prepare a cash budget for each of the next four months as evidence of its ability to repay the loan. The following information is available as of September 30, 2006:

Cash on hand	$ 9,000
Accounts receivable	97,500
Inventory	64,000
Accounts payable	144,500

a. The accounts payable are for September merchandise purchases and operating expenses and will all be paid in October. Sales forecasts for the next few months are October, $220,000; November, $300,000; December, $400,000; January, $200,000; February, $140,000.

b. Collections on sales are usually made at the rate of 20% during the month of the sale, 60% during the month following the sale, and 15% during the second month after the sale. Five percent of accounts receivable are written off as uncollectible. Of the $97,500 of accounts receivable at September 30, $65,000 will be collected in October, and $32,500 will be collected in November. Cost of goods sold is 55% of sales, with all purchases paid for in the month following purchase. Ending inventory should always equal the cost of the goods that will be sold during the next month. Operating expenses are $18,000 a month plus 5% of sales, all paid in the month following their incurrence.

Required:

Prepare a cash budget showing receipts and disbursements for October, November, December, and January. Also prepare supporting schedules for cash collections, purchases, and operating expenses. Assume that the loan plus interest will be paid on January 31.

Problem 19-15

Cash Budgeting

Athlete World is a sporting goods store. The following data are for use in preparing its forecast of cash needs for June:

(continued)

a. Current assets (May 31):

Cash	$22,000
Inventory	17,500
Accounts receivable	29,400
Property, plant, and equipment	90,000
Accounts payable (merchandise purchases only)	13,100

Recent and estimated future sales:

May	49,000
June	57,000
July	52,000

b. Sales are made 60% on credit and 40% for cash. All credit sales are collected in the month following the sale.

c. Athlete World's June expenses are estimated to be:

Salaries and wages expense	20% of sales
Rent expense	4% of sales
All other cash expenses	6% of sales
Depreciation expense	$600
Gross margin	40% of sales

d. Athlete World buys all its inventory from companies on the West Coast and wants to maintain an inventory level equal to one-half of the next month's sales. Payments for merchandise are made 50% during the month of purchase and 50% in the next month.

e. Other cash expenditures planned for June are:
  (1) The purchase of $8,000 of furniture.
  (2) The payment of $5,000 of dividends.

f. Athlete World desires to maintain a minimum cash balance of $10,000. The store has an arrangement with a local bank whereby it can borrow money in multiples of $1,000. Interest is charged on all loans at an annual rate of 10% and is assessed for a full quarter both in the quarter in which the money is borrowed and in the quarter in which the money is repaid. Interest is paid when the loan is repaid.

Required:
Prepare Athlete World's cash budget for June.

Problem 19-16

Unifying Concepts: The Pro-Forma Income Statement, Balance Sheet, and Statement of Cash Flows

Pun Corporation makes construction cranes. During the past few days, the company's accountants have been preparing the master budget for 2006. To date, they have gathered the following projected data:

For the Year Ended December 31, 2006:

Sales revenue	$20,254,400
Variable selling expenses	896,000
Variable administrative expenses	1,344,000
Interest expense	134,400
Cost of goods sold (variable costs only)	11,200,000
Fixed manufacturing expenses	1,568,000
Fixed administrative expenses	984,000
Fixed selling expenses	672,000

Account Balances at December 31, 2006:

Cash	$ 896,000
Accounts receivable	336,000
Land	834,400
Buildings	1,008,000
Equipment	716,800
Accumulated depreciation—equipment	179,200
Accumulated depreciation—buildings	160,000
Direct materials inventory	212,800
Finished goods inventory	235,200
Accounts payable	90,480
Common stock	1,400,000
Retained earnings	?
Paid-in capital in excess of par	80,000
Income taxes payable	400,000

Other Information:

Dividends to be declared and paid during 2006	$1,303,680
Income tax rate	30%

In addition, last year's balance sheet was as follows:

Pun Corporation
Balance Sheet
December 31, 2005

Assets

Cash		$ 379,200
Accounts receivable		90,800
Direct materials inventory		180,000
Finished goods inventory		246,400
Land		672,000
Buildings	$ 896,000	
Less accumulated depreciation	(100,000)	796,000
Equipment	$ 649,600	
Less accumulated depreciation	(120,000)	529,600
Total assets		$2,894,000

Liabilities and Stockholders' Equity

Liabilities:

Accounts payable	$ 150,000	
Income taxes payable	450,000	
Total liabilities		$ 600,000

Stockholders' Equity:

Common stock	$1,400,000	
Paid-in capital in excess of par, common stock	80,000	
Retained earnings	814,000	
Total stockholders' equity		2,294,000
Total liabilities and stockholders' equity		$2,894,000

Required:

1. Prepare a pro-forma income statement for 2006 (contribution margin approach).
2. Prepare a pro-forma balance sheet as of December 31, 2006.
3. Prepare a pro-forma statement of cash flows for 2006 (indirect method).

Problem 19-17

Pro-Forma Income Statement and Balance Sheet

Style Right Company makes hair dryers. During the past few days, its accountants have been preparing the master budget for the coming year, 2006. To date, they have gathered the following projected data:

Sales revenue (at $20 per unit)	$281,750
Variable selling expenses	17,250
Variable administrative expenses	40,250
Interest expense (not included in selling and administrative expenses)	1,725
Cost of goods sold (includes only variable costs)	103,500
Ending cash balance	30,475
Ending accounts receivable balance	47,150
Ending land balance	24,150
Ending buildings balance	71,300
Ending equipment balance	24,150
Ending accumulated depreciation—buildings balance	47,150
Ending accumulated depreciation—equipment balance	9,200
Ending direct materials inventory balance	16,100
Ending finished goods inventory balance	25,300
Ending accounts payable balance	6,900
Ending common stock balance	32,200
Retained earnings balance, January 1	64,050
Balance in paid-in capital in excess of par account	23,000
Fixed selling expenses	23,000
Fixed administrative expenses	28,750
Fixed manufacturing overhead	11,150
Income tax rate	35%

Required:
1. Prepare a pro-forma income statement (contribution margin approach) and balance sheet for the coming year. Any income taxes owed on the coming year's net income will be paid the following year.
2. By approximately how much would Style Right's profits increase if another 3,000 units were produced and sold for $20 each?

Problem 19-18

Pro-Forma Statement of Cash Flows

The accountants at Toledo Department Store are preparing the pro-forma statement of cash flows for 2006. The following information is available:

Expected net income	$70,000
Dividends to be paid	22,000
Equipment to be purchased	34,000
Expected short-term borrowing	8,000
Expected long-term borrowing	24,000
Expected depreciation expense for 2006	15,000
Expected issuance of common stock	80,000
Expected purchase of a new plant	71,000
Expected changes in current assets and liabilities during 2006:	
Increase in accounts receivable	$ 900
Increase in accounts payable	1,000
Increase in inventory	1,000
Decrease in income taxes payable	1,800

Required:
Prepare the pro-forma statement of cash flows for Toledo Department Store (indirect method).

Problem 19-19

Static versus Flexible Budgeting (Service Firm)

Wasatch Medical Clinic has three doctors on staff. The clinic's budget for 2006 is as follows:

Wasatch Medical Clinic
Budget for the Year Ended December 31, 2006

Expected number of patient visits		26,000
Average charge per patient		× $25
Total revenues		$650,000
Budgeted costs:		
Variable costs:		
Supplies for each patient ($2 × 26,000)		$ 52,000
Fixed costs:		
Utilities	$ 2,400	
Rent	9,600	
Nurses' salaries	90,000	
Malpractice insurance	150,000	
Equipment leases	25,000	
Other	30,000	
Total fixed costs		307,000
Total budgeted costs		$359,000
Expected income		$291,000
Number of doctors on staff		÷ 3
Expected income per doctor		$ 97,000

Required:

1. Is this a static or flexible budget?
2. Prepare a flexible budget showing expected income per doctor at 22,000, 26,000, 30,000, and 34,000 total patient visits.
3. **Interpretive Question:** Why does the expected income per doctor increase so dramatically as the number of patient visits increases?

Problem 19-20

Static versus Flexible Budgeting (Service Firm)

Peterson Management, Inc., is a small firm that sponsors time-management seminars in hotels throughout the country. It sponsors 20 two-day seminars during the year for a tuition fee of $200 per student. The following is a budget for a single seminar:

Peterson Management, Inc.
Budget per Seminar

Expected enrollment	40
Tuition per person	× $200
Revenue per seminar	$8,000
Variable costs:	
Catering ($25 per person)	$1,000
Books and handouts ($10 per person)	400
Fixed costs:	
Airfare	425
Hotel rental fee	600
Advertising	1,000
Other	300
Total costs	$3,725
Expected income	$4,275

(continued)

Required:

1. Bruce Peterson, owner of the company and the speaker at the seminars, would be pleased with an income of $4,275 per seminar. With 20 seminars per year, the company's annual income would be $85,500. He is concerned, however, that every seminar may not have 40 participants. Prepare a flexible budget, showing what annual income would be if 10, 20, 40, or 50 people enroll in each seminar.
2. What is the break-even point per seminar in number of participants?

d i s c u s s i o n   c a s e s

Case 19-1

West Mountain Canning Company

West Mountain Canning Company produces several food items, including certain tomato-based products. For about nine months during the year, the company is able to purchase tomatoes from various parts of the country. The tomatoes are then processed and canned for sale in grocery stores.

The processing department employs three highly skilled workers, who are paid an average of $15 per hour. Between January and March, tomatoes are not available, and the processing and canning departments are shut down. Rather than lay off these three specialists, who have excellent alternative job opportunities, the company transfers them to the shipping department, at the same $15 pay rate. The shipping department manager is not happy, however, because his five regular employees are paid only $9 per hour. His unhappiness has become particularly acute since he was told he was $9,000 over budget for wages during the January-to-March quarter (budget was $36,000; actual was $45,000). Note that the actual amount includes 1,500 hours (3 employees × 500 hours) at $15 per hour, and that each employee works 2,000 hours in a year.

The shipping department manager feels that he is being unduly penalized for two reasons: (1) $15 is too much to pay even a good shipping clerk, and (2) the three skilled workers do not work as hard as his regular employees because they know they are needed for tomato processing and will not be fired. Therefore, he has suggested to his boss that the wages in excess of the $9 he normally pays be assigned elsewhere or that he be allowed to hire his own temporary employees (if needed) during this part of the year.

Answer the following questions:

1. Does the shipping department manager have a legitimate complaint? Explain.
2. Explain how management arrived at the budgeted figure of $36,000 for shipping wages.
3. How might the quarterly figures be reported to satisfy the shipping department manager?
4. How would you recommend that the problem be solved?

Case 19-2

Tip Top Company

Tip Top Company recently hired a new hot-shot CEO. Traditionally, the budgeting process at Tip Top has been pretty relaxed, with the executive vice president for sales providing "best-guess" sales projections and the controller providing "ballpark" cost estimates. Although the budget has been due each year 30 days prior to the new fiscal year, it generally is not finalized until two or three months into the new fiscal year. One of the first actions of the new CEO is to institute a formalized top-down budgeting process, complete with fairly sophisticated sales projections and cost data based on benchmark statistics from industry competitors.

Discuss the issues involved in the new budgeting process for Tip Top Company.

Case 19-3

New Age Budgeting

Manes.com is an Internet company that searches out job listings on corporate home pages, organizes them by type of job, and lists them so that individuals seeking jobs can see the kinds of jobs that are available. The Internet site is free to all users. Manes.com hopes that by providing a job-matching service, its site will attract substantial traffic, and advertisers will be willing to pay large sums of money to advertise. The company has a $20 million investment from a venture capitalist to get started but must provide budget projections to secure additional funding. Assume you are the controller for the company. How would you go about forecasting revenues and preparing budgets and profit projections to show potential investors?

Case 19-4

Disagreements over the Value of Budgets

Tueller Enterprises is a large manufacturer of airplane parts for commercial and military aircraft. In addition to making parts, it also serves as a distributor for other, smaller manufacturers. Traditionally, the company has spent large amounts of time preparing operational budgets, only to find that they are rarely useful and often outdated. Some managers have even argued that because they are evaluated on the basis of how well they meet the budget, they have been unable to react to changing markets and take advantage of new opportunities that have become available. The managers argue that the entire budgeting process is too constraining and should be scrapped. The new controller agrees that the traditional budgeting process has been flawed but argues that with the availability of new computer technology and up-to-date performance information, budgets can now be revised more frequently and will be much more useful than in the past. The company is trying to decide what to do. Should it scrap the entire budgeting process? Or, should it work to make the budgeting process more relevant and useful?

judgment calls

Judgment 19-1

You Decide: Is budgeting a necessary tool to help a fast-growing company plan and prepare for the future, or is budgeting too complicated and subjective for a growing company?

A budget is a good tool for a company to use to determine how it will secure the necessary finances to accomplish its business goals. However, a fast-growing company does not always know how its needs will grow or change over a short time frame. In addition, often a new company has no history to use in guiding budgets and, as a result, budgeting often involves substantial guesswork.

Judgment 19-2

You Decide: Should pro-forma financial statements be prepared in a manner consistent with GAAP, or do pro-forma statements provide enough useful information to investors in their current form?

Most financial statements prepared by companies and filed with the Securities and Exchange Commission are prepared using generally accepted accounting principles. However, pro-forma financial statements are often not prepared in accordance with these standards. Many of the numbers included by companies in these "pro-forma" statements are based on assumptions that are not recognized as appropriate for SEC filings. Sometimes, companies highlight positive information and leave out information about certain costs or charges, such as stock-based compensation, interest, and taxes. The real question is whether or not investors are being misled.

Competency Enhancement Opportunities

▶ **Analyzing Real Company Information**   ▶ **The Debate**
▶ **International Case**   ▶ **Internet Search**
▶ **Ethics Case**
▶ **Writing Assignment**

The following additional assignments provide opportunities for students to develop critical thinking, ethical perspectives, oral and written communication skills, experience with electronic research, and teamwork through group and business activities.

▶ *Analyzing Real Company Information*

Analyzing 19-1 (Microsoft)

Auditors are extremely reluctant to publish any projections of future financial performance for the companies they are auditing. DELOITTE & TOUCHE LLP obviously has made no such predictions in its audit of MICROSOFT's 2002 financial performance (see the Form 10-K in Appendix A). However, the Management's Discussion and Analysis of Results of Operations and Financial Condition, in the section titled "Issues and Uncertainties," provide some hints about what executives may expect to affect future revenues. Elsewhere in the management discussion are insights useful in predicting future operating expenses, interest income, and income taxes. These discussions can be extremely useful to investors who are trying to understand what Microsoft plans to do in 2003. Essentially, these investors need to put together their own pro-forma financial statements on Microsoft for use in planning, controlling, and evaluating their investment decisions in this company.

Consider the 2002 income statement below and use the information provided in Microsoft's Management Discussion of "Issues and Uncertainties," as well as any other comments in the management's discussion that you might find useful, to prepare your own pro-forma 2003 income statement for Microsoft. Be sure to read and consider each item in the management discussion relating to Microsoft's income statement in the Form 10-K in Appendix A. You may also want to consider the 2000 and 2001 revenue and cost trends from the income statement published in this same Form 10-K. For each line item (i.e., for each revenue and cost category), briefly defend the budget number you chose to use.

	2002
Revenue	$28,365
Operating expenses:	
Cost of revenue	$ 5,191
Research and development	4,307
Sales and marketing	5,407
General and administrative	1,550
Total operating expenses	$16,455
Operating income	$11,910
Losses on equity investees	(92)
Investment income	(305)
Income before income taxes	$11,513
Provision for income taxes	3,684
Net income	$ 7,829

Analyzing 19-2 (Participative Living, Inc.)

Participative Living, Inc. (a fictitious name) is an actual charitable organization in a medium-size community in Canada. It was organized by parents of disabled adults to provide accommodation and training for severely disabled adults in the community. With the help of the Ministry of Community and Social Services, the parents eventually organized six different homes, each with two to four residents. In addition to the six homes, Participative Living also had an employment and education program that provided training and assistance for residents seeking employment or educational opportunities. Overall, the organization had eight divisions composed of six homes, the employment and education program, and an administrative program. A supervisor who reports to the Participative Living executive team staffs each division. The executive team, in turn, reports to a volunteer board of directors composed of 12 people from the community.

Participative Living is a not-for-profit organization. Hence, while surpluses and deficits are occasionally expected, each division is expected to break even each operating period. Seven of the eight divisions are established as break-even operations, with responsibility for both revenues and expenses. The main revenue source is the Ontario government, through the Ministry of Community and Social Services, which provides all funding necessary to support each home as well as the employment and education program. All costs of Participative Living's administrative division in excess of any donations from the community are allocated to its other seven divisions. The Ministry follows a procedure of disbursing operating funds for all social service agencies under its direction based on annual operating budgets submitted to the Ministry. Generally, the Ministry is not concerned about whether an individual budget item was overspent as long as the overall spending is within the approved budget. As a result, it became a common practice among agencies to transfer expenses from one budget line to another and, in the case of Participative Living, to transfer expenses from one division to another depending on which division had excess budgeted funds. As with most government organizations, the Ministry's administrative process of reviewing and approving a new home for Participative Living is often quite slow. As long as the Ministry is holding up the establishment of a proposed new home, it provides significant interest payments to Participative Living. The Ministry was making large interest payments during the first few months of Participative Living's 2000 fiscal year (which ended on March 31, 2000) while the organization waited for government approval and funding of the sixth group home.

In November 1999, Mr. Brad Dunford, the executive director of Participative Living, Inc., was reviewing the financial statements for the first seven months of the 2000 fiscal year. He was puzzled about how the agency could suddenly be $50,000 over budget in salaries and benefits when just last month the statements indicated that spending was slightly under budget.

1. As you review operating results for the last seven months at Participative Living, Inc., what problems do you foresee?
2. Consider the style of management and management accounting for this not-for-profit organization, as well as its relationship with the Ministry of Community and Social Services. What aspects of the way business is conducted here do you think have led to the current situation?

(continued)

Participative Living, Inc.
Operating Results
For the Seven Months Ended October 31, 1999

YTD	Admin. Costs	Admin. Budget	Employ. and Edu. Costs	Employ. and Edu. Budget	Group Homes Costs	Group Homes Budget	Total Actual	Total Budget*	% of Budget
Revenues:									
Ministry**	$ —	$ —	$206,315	$297,675	$521,841	$476,714	$728,156	$774,389	94.0%
Interest	20,943	—	—	—	—	—	20,943	—	0%
Donations	1,567	—	—	—	—	—	1,567	—	0%
Total revenues	$ 22,510	$ —	$206,315	$297,675	$521,841	$476,714	$750,666	$774,389	96.9%
Expenses:									
Salaries	$ 59,029	$ 61,754	$141,034	$197,386	$434,014	$327,789	$634,077	$586,929	108.0%
Occupancy costs	10,392	12,264	39	2,205	61,598	68,761	72,029	83,230	86.5%
Services, supplies, and food	4,375	7,000	3,643	14,147	16,812	35,301	24,830	56,448	44.0%
Personal needs	—	—	3,077	—	35	26,327	3,112	26,327	11.8%
New furnishing and equip.	5	350	60	2,765	6,548	19,236	6,613	22,351	29.6%
Other expenses	1,176	4,669	197	7,707	15,681	7,868	17,054	20,244	84.2%
Travel and training	436	875	1,972	8,792	1,992	4,900	4,400	14,567	30.2%
Specific reimbursements	—	—	—	—	(32,119)	(35,707)	(32,119)	(35,707)	90.0%
Allocated admin. costs	(75,417)	(86,912)	56,293	64,673	19,123	22,239	(1)	—	0.0%
Total expenses	$ (4)	$ —	$206,315	$297,675	$523,684	$476,714	$729,995	$774,389	94.3%
Net surplus (deficit)	$ 22,514	$ —	$ —	$ —	$ (1,843)	$ —	$ 20,671	$ —	N/A

*Budget columns represent the total annual budget. Note that Participative Living is now seven months into its fiscal year.
**Ministry revenues are based on actual payments made by the Ministry. Total payments limited to maximum of total annual budget approved.

Source: Adapted from M. Heisz, "Participative Living, Inc.," *Journal of Accounting Case Research* 2(3), 1995, pp. 87–91. Permission to use has been granted by Captus Press, Inc. and the Accounting Education Resource Centre of The University of Lethbridge. [Journal Subscription: Captus Press Inc., York University Campus, 4700 Keele Street, North York, Ontario, M3J1P3, by calling (416) 736-5537, or by fax at (416) 736-5793, E-mail: info@captus.com, Internet: **http://www.captus.com**]

▶ *International Case*

International

It's Not Easy Being an Accountant in Poland

The late 1980s and early 1990s were a very significant time for Eastern Europe. Several national boundaries and political ideologies, as well as the names of a few countries, changed during this period. Poland, like its neighbors, experienced tremendous upheaval in its political and economic climate during this time. In 1989, Poland changed to a non-Communist government and a free market economy. Since the end of World War II in 1945, Poland had been a centrally planned economy with government-enforced economic rules based on Marxism-Leninism. A Polish accountant's professional life during the 1945–1989 period was not very exciting. Most university-trained accountants worked in a state-owned enterprise, earning a reasonable salary. The work was not complicated, generally entailing only basic bookkeeping. Performing the accounting work essentially required simple mathematical operations. In addition, the nature of Poland's history since the fifteenth century had generally created disdain for business and profiteering in general. These traditions, coupled with the social environment engendered by a Marxist government, resulted in a serious lack of respect (sometimes bordering on distrust) for accountants, economists, and business managers from 1945 to 1989.

The failure of the Communist system in 1989 was the beginning of a new career stage for most accountants in Poland. The accounting profession suddenly became prestigious. It also became very challenging. Past accounting knowledge and skills were simply inadequate for the new economic situation, particularly for accountants moving out of state-owned enterprises and into the private sector. Business terminology, performance measures, and goals changed. Before 1989, the Communist regime promoted a view that everything a "capitalist" did was wrong and everything a Communist did was right. After the change in the political system, a lot of people began to see things in an opposite way; they expected that life in a capitalist country would be completely just and everyone would be employed with plenty of money. Obviously, life in a capitalist country is not perfect. There are problems, including injustice and unemployment. Complicating this reality, many people also carried over into the 1990s some of the prevailing pre-1989 attitudes that accountants and for-profit businesses were not trustworthy. Today Poland is making steady progress, but the accounting profession continues to face a number of challenges as attitudes and business processes are still in transition.

Assume that you have just been transferred by your U.S.-based company to an accounting or management position in the company's Poland division. Your assignment is to implement a traditional budgeting system (similar to the budget systems described in this chapter) in a large-scale manufacturing plant. Based on your understanding of Polish history and attitudes, what specific challenges would you expect to encounter in this new assignment? Do you have any ideas on how to handle these challenges?

Source: Adapted from P. Stec, "Mr. Kowalski: A Man Against All Odds," *The Journal of Accounting Case Research* 2(3), 1995, pp. 52–54. Permission to use has been granted by Captus Press, Inc. and the Accounting Education Resource Centre of The University of Lethbridge. [Journal Subscription: Captus Press Inc., York University Campus, 4700 Keele Street, North York, Ontario, M3J 1P3, by calling (416) 736-5537, or by fax at (416) 736-5793, E-mail: info@captus.com, Internet: **http://www.captus.com**]

▶ *Ethics Case*

Skipper Enterprises

You are the management accountant for Skipper Enterprises, a manufacturer of screen doors. Recently, one of the commissioned salespersons (your close personal friend) confided in you that a problem with the budgets is hurting the company's profitability.

Your friend explained that salespersons are paid a straight commission of $15 for every screen door they sell. If a salesperson meets the budgeted sales of 3,000 screen doors per year, he or she is paid an annual bonus of $5,000. Your friend stated that it is actually quite easy to reach budgeted sales of 3,000 doors by October or early November. Because there is no financial incentive to sell additional doors once the 3,000 sales level is met and the $5,000 bonus is earned, salespersons only "line up" sales for next year during the last couple of months of each year. In other words, instead of selling additional doors during November and December, they commit customers to buy during January of next year. This way, the doors count as next year's sales, ensuring that the commissioned salespersons are well on their way to meeting the sales budget for next year.

You realize the current bonus plan is causing two problems. First, valuable sales are being deferred each year because there is less incentive to sell near the end of the year. Second, customers are receiving less than optimum service because it can take as long as two months for customers to get their desired doors.

You don't know what to do with your new information.

1. Should you inform management that the sales plan is hurting company profits, or should you keep the information confidential as your friend requested?

(continued)

2. If it becomes known that you had this information and didn't come forward, you could lose your job. On the other hand, you hate to lose a good friend. What should you do?

▶ *Writing Assignment*

Preparing a Personal Budget

Most people have the ability to spend more than they make. As a student, you probably fit in that category. This writing assignment requires you to prepare a personal budget for a one-month period. Forecast your income and expenses to determine what your cash position will be at the end of the month. If you forecast a cash shortage, what actions can you take to address the problem (e.g., increase income, reduce expenses, borrow money, etc.)? If you forecast a cash surplus, what are your options for the surplus?

▶ *The Debate*

The Hatchet Has Arrived!

Assume that your local hospital has just hired a new COO (chief operating officer). Everyone in the hospital understands that the new COO was essentially hired to save the hospital. During the last five years, cost overruns have created tremendous spending deficits in the organization. The hospital is clearly headed for insolvency within three to five years if something isn't done. The new COO has a reputation as a focused manager, who is able to make difficult decisions. She doesn't waste any time proving her reputation in the new job. At the first meeting with the chief medical staff and administrators, the COO rolls out the new budget goals with the following statement:

> Everyone here knows that this hospital is in serious financial trouble, and it's not hard to understand why. After carefully reviewing cost reports for the last several years, it's obvious that there has been very little discipline in controlling costs. There are no improvement goals for cost savings, and no one is required to take responsibility when cost overruns occur. Looking at next quarter's operating budget doesn't give me much hope for improvement in this mess. Well, folks, that party is over! It's time to get to work saving this hospital. We will reconvene in one week; I expect each department head to provide a new departmental operating budget that demonstrates a reduction in costs that is equal to 5% of department revenues. Thereafter, until we turn this situation around, each new quarterly budget will reflect an additional decrease in operating costs equal to 2% of department revenues. Any questions?

There were no questions. Everyone filed out of the meeting in shocked silence. Five percent of revenues is a big number!

Divide your group into two teams and prepare a two-minute defense of your team's assigned position.

- One team represents "Support the COO!" A difficult situation requires a tough response. Defend the COO's new budget proposal. What should be the positive results in the hospital if the COO's budget instructions are fully implemented?
- The other team represents "Out with the new budget proposal!" Overreacting to a difficult situation only worsens the problem. Criticize the COO's new budget proposal. What could be the negative results in the hospital if the COO's budget instructions are fully implemented?

▶ *Internet Search*

Using the Internet to Budget Personal Finances

There are a number of terrific tools on the Internet that can be very useful to you in managing your finances. For one example, go to **http://www.financenter.com**. Sometimes Web addresses change, so if this address does not work, access the Web site for this textbook (**http://albrecht .swlearning.com**) for an updated link. Once there, select the "Consumer Tools" tab, and then select "Calculators" from the drop down menu. Finally, scroll down to the Budget area and select "How much am I spending?" You will see here that you can enter your current income and expenditures, as well as your desired expenditures.

1. Complete the information on the input form, and then hit the "get your results" button. You should now learn whether your income is sufficient to handle your expenditures (actually, you probably already knew the answer to this question). You'll also learn about the importance of creating some excess in your budget to save for the future. Print out your budget.

2. Now go back to the input form and change the numbers in order to assess what might need to change in your future personal "operations." Put together a realistic budget. Try to create a little "extra" that can be used for investment. Note how the difference affects your long-term savings. When you're satisfied, print out your new budget.

3. Now that you have a better understanding of your cash budget, work through FinanCenter's budget calculators to identify and answer another important personal finance and budgeting question for yourself. Go back to the Calculators page and select an additional budgeting function to perform. When completed, list two important insights you learned about your personal budgeting process.

Part

7

Control

c h a p t e r

20

Monitoring Performance in Cost, Profit, and Investment Centers

After studying this chapter, you should be able to:

Learning Objectives

1 Explain why control is such an important activity in the management process.

2 Describe the responsibility accounting concept and identify the three types of organizational control units.

3 Describe standard costing and the basic variance analysis model.

4 Use materials and labor cost variance analysis to explain how performance is controlled in cost centers.

5 Use revenue variance analysis to explain how performance is controlled in profit centers.

6 Use ROI and residual income analysis to explain how performance is controlled in investment centers.

e✗panded *Material*

7 Compute and interpret variable overhead cost variances.

8 Compute and interpret fixed overhead cost variances.

Before Randy Curran was appointed CEO, ICG COMMUNICATIONS was losing $34 million a month. That was in September 2000. On November 14, 2000, ICG filed for Chapter 11 bankruptcy. Chapter 11 is a plan that allows the company some time to try to work out its financial matters. Many companies never successfully emerge from Chapter 11 bankruptcy. ICG, on the other hand, is currently a prosperous company. ICG's story is about how a company gone awry can be saved through fiscal responsibility and customer focus.[1]

ICG's intial strategy was to provide the systems—networks of switches, modem banks, and fiber-optic cable—that linked people at home via their local telephone company with the high-speed fiber-optic lines that carry Internet traffic. If the Internet is a super-highway, ICG would build the entry ramps that carried traffic from the local roads—i.e., local telephone lines—onto the Internet superhighway. Because more and more people wanted to get onto the Internet, the demand for the ramps was practically unlimited in the heyday of the Internet explosion in the late 1990s. Although its intent was to dominate the ramp business, ICG became the poster child for the failed "build it and they will come" business model. However, today the company's local network presence spans more than 30 metropolitan areas including Denver, Cleveland, Dallas, Los Angeles, San Francisco, Seattle, Atlanta, New York, Boston, and Washington, D.C. Randy Curran, as the current CEO, is largely responsible for this tremendous recovery.

Curran is a stark contrast to previous CEO J. Shelby Bryan. Until Bryan left his position with ICG in 2000, he seemed to be obsessed with the spotlight, not just in trade and business publications, but in the society pages as well. Although ICG is headquartered in Colorado, Bryan lived in Manhattan where he held fund-raising parties for President Clinton and Vice President Al Gore. This fact alone raised serious concerns with ICG's investors; in fact, it led one major investor to nix an earlier investment in 1999 due in part to worry that Bryan was not keeping a close eye on the company. During this time, ICG quickly burned through $2 billion raised through Wall Street investors. While some of the money was used to build Internet ramps, part of it was used to build ICG's striking new headquarters, a tower that the architect described as "the curve of a ship's prow looking toward the mountains." One staffer remarked, "when we show people the building, it becomes clear to them why we went bankrupt."

Randy Curran faced a difficult task in carefully controlling a turnaround of ICG's financial position. He also needed to restore ICG's image. Curran said, "The relationships with our customers were . . . awful. When you do these turnarounds, you have to have strengths that you can build off of. When you turn [a company] around, you strip it back to its core and then you go from there." Curran believes strongly that ICG's core strength is its $4 billion dollar Internet ramp system, but ICG also has employees with tremendous technical capabilities. Curran stated at the time he took over the company, "Our staff is young and energetic, so the talent here is fabulous. [And] even though the customer relationships are bad, they are still great customers." ICG's customer list has included such giants as MICROSOFT, ORACLE, NETZERO, EARTHLINK, and some of the nation's major universities.

When Curran looked at a high level view of the company, he found numerous problems that needed his immediate attention. He realized that a poor-performing network would kill the business, regardless of the reported value of the network assets. He identified a large number of unprofitable markets, products and services, and customers. The reorganization involved turning $2.5 billion of debt on the balance sheet into $200 million of equity.

ICG emerged from Chapter 11 protection on October 10, 2002, and is alive and well today, although its employee head count has dropped from 3,000 to 1,000. With the conclusion of its bankruptcy plan, ICG distributed about 8 million new shares of common stock to certain creditors to pay down some debt. Upon its emergence, ICG had $205 million in short- and long-term debt and $94 million in cash. If ICG continues to thrive, its management model might serve as an outline for other tech companies on how to control and grow a successful business in the post-Internet bubble era.

1 Paul M. Sherer and Gary McWilliams, "How a Brash Provider of Internet Services Became Unplugged," *The Wall Street Journal*, November 13, 2000, p. A1; Paul M. Sherer, "ICG Files for Protection from Creditors," *The Wall Street Journal*, November 15, 2000, p. A1; John Sullivan and Tom Cross, "A New Day at ICG," *Boardwatch Magazine*, April 2002, Vol. 16, Issue 4, pp. 42–44; "ICG out of Bankruptcy," *Denver Business Journal*, October 10, 2002, **http://denver.bizjournals.com**, accessed September 5, 2003; Client Interview with ICG, **http://www.gapinter.com/ClientProfiles**, accessed September 5, 2003.

n the previous chapter, we created the master budget, which is a major planning tool for management. In this chapter, we will examine how managers and executives create and maintain an effective system of control within their organizations. Traditional control systems are initially based on using the standard cost and revenue data created in the master budget. These data are used to assess business processes throughout the year in order to identify performance in various organizational units that require management attention.

In the process of establishing effective management control within an organization, it is critical to clearly define each division's and each person's specific responsibility within the organization. Since it is often difficult to separate the performance of a unit from the performance of its managers, man-

agers are most often evaluated on how well their units perform. If managers are responsible for costs only, they are usually evaluated on how well they control costs. If they are responsible for revenues and costs, they are usually evaluated on the profitability of their units. And, if they are responsible for costs, revenues, and investments, managers are most frequently evaluated on the return their division investments generate. In the case of ICG, past CEO J. Shelby Bryan was responsible for costs, revenues, and investments. Since the company initially lost large sums of money, one may fairly question the effectiveness of cost, revenue, and asset controls at ICG prior to 2000. On the other hand, ICG's turnaround since 2000 is largely attributable to new CEO Randy Curran's fiscal responsibility and his efforts to bring ICG's operations into control.

Management Control of Personnel and Divisions

I Explain why control is such an important activity in the management process.

Today, we live in a new and different economy. At least three major developments have dramatically changed the environment in which businesses operate. First, new technology has made information inexpensive. Low-cost, high-speed digital and cable video and data transmission hardware produces information quickly and easily, and the constant churn of new software makes preparation, data, and communication tools available to individuals who previously did not have access to needed information. As technology continues to develop, constraints on acquiring the information you will want in your business career will continue to be reduced, or even be eliminated.

A second major development that has significantly affected business has been globalization. Faster methods of transportation, together with nearly instantaneous information, have allowed the world to become one giant marketplace. Consumers can now buy products from foreign firms as easily as from a local store. Organizations such as GENERAL MOTORS have to worry not only about what CHRYSLER and FORD are doing, but also about what TOYOTA, VOLKSWAGEN, and BMW are doing as well. In fact, Chrysler is not just "Chrysler" anymore. It is now a conglomeration of European, North American, and Asian manufacturers known as DAIMLERCHRYSLER. Instead of having only two major American competitors, General Motors and all other business organizations now have to compete with similar companies throughout the world. In addition, with the increased availability of inexpensive information, more is known about these competitors and about General Motors than ever before. If a GM product has deficiencies, for example, the world knows about and can act on those problems instantly. If GM or one of its units is not performing well, investors will be reluctant to invest money and GM's management may direct its resources to other operating units.

A third major change is the concentration of power in certain market investors, primarily large mutual and pension funds. Mutual funds such as FIDELITY and VANGUARD and pension funds such as CALPERS and TIAA-CREF, for example, now hold major stock positions in many companies. The influence of these major market players is so significant that if they are displeased, corporate executives will find that their positions within the company are in jeopardy. Armed with easily available and inexpensive information about investees and their competitors, large institutional investors raise the competitive bar very high and shorten the periods over which success is measured. The influence of these institutional investors, combined with the power of readily-accessible information and the intensity of global competition, means that only organizations that are truly the best will be able to survive and remain successful.

A number of business developments have occurred because of these changes. Some of the most obvious are:

- An increased pace of change in the business world
- Shorter product life cycles and shorter competitive advantages
- Demand for better, quicker, and more decisive actions by management
- The emergence of new companies, new industries, and new professional services
- Outsourcing of many company processes to specialty organizations
- Increased uncertainty that requires careful and explicit management of risk
- Increasingly complex business transactions
- Increased focus on customer service and satisfaction

To be able to react to fast-paced business changes, managers and investors must have good control of and/or good insight on business units and their managements. They must know as early as possible whether a unit's profit or market share is decreasing. They must be able to assess trends and changes in performance quickly. They must know when new competitors are getting stronger and encroaching on the business's success. They must know when supervisors and staff are performing in ways that are resulting in the organization losing ground to competitors. Only if they have accurate information about how well personnel and various organizational units are performing can managers effectively plan, control, and evaluate personnel, processes, and resources. As we have stated previously, good planning leads to good control, which leads to good evaluation. If management does not carefully plan for and control the operations in their organization, then they cannot accurately evaluate how they are doing, what needs to be improved, and where resources must be placed and withdrawn. As a result, their organizations will most likely be unsuccessful in the future. The result of faster-paced changes in today's economy must be better planning and control of fast-paced organizations. We described the planning process in the two previous chapters on capital budgeting and operational budgeting. This chapter focuses on traditional methods of establishing an effective system of management control.

TO SUMMARIZE: The business world is changing faster than ever before. These fast-paced changes require that decision makers (managers and investors) have better information and perform more timely evaluations of organizational units and the individuals responsible for the organizations. Good evaluation leads to better planning and control decisions and the better allocation of resources.

Control of Divisions and Personnel in Different Types of Operating Units

2 Describe the responsibility accounting concept and identify the three types of organizational control units.

segments Parts of an organization requiring separate reports for evaluation by management.

Most companies are made up of a number of relatively independent **segments** or subunits, sometimes called groups, divisions, or subsidiaries. As an example, Exhibit 1 shows an organizational chart for a hypothetical company that we will call International Manufacturing Corporation (IMC). IMC has three operating (subsidiary) companies: Acme Computer, Edison Automobile, and Jennifer Cosmetics. Although each of these companies has several divisions and other subsegments, only a few of those for Edison Automobile are shown. Edison has three geographic bases: the United States, the Far East, and Europe. The making and selling of automobiles in the Far East division is further broken down into the Japanese and Korean units.

Exhibit 1: An Organizational Chart

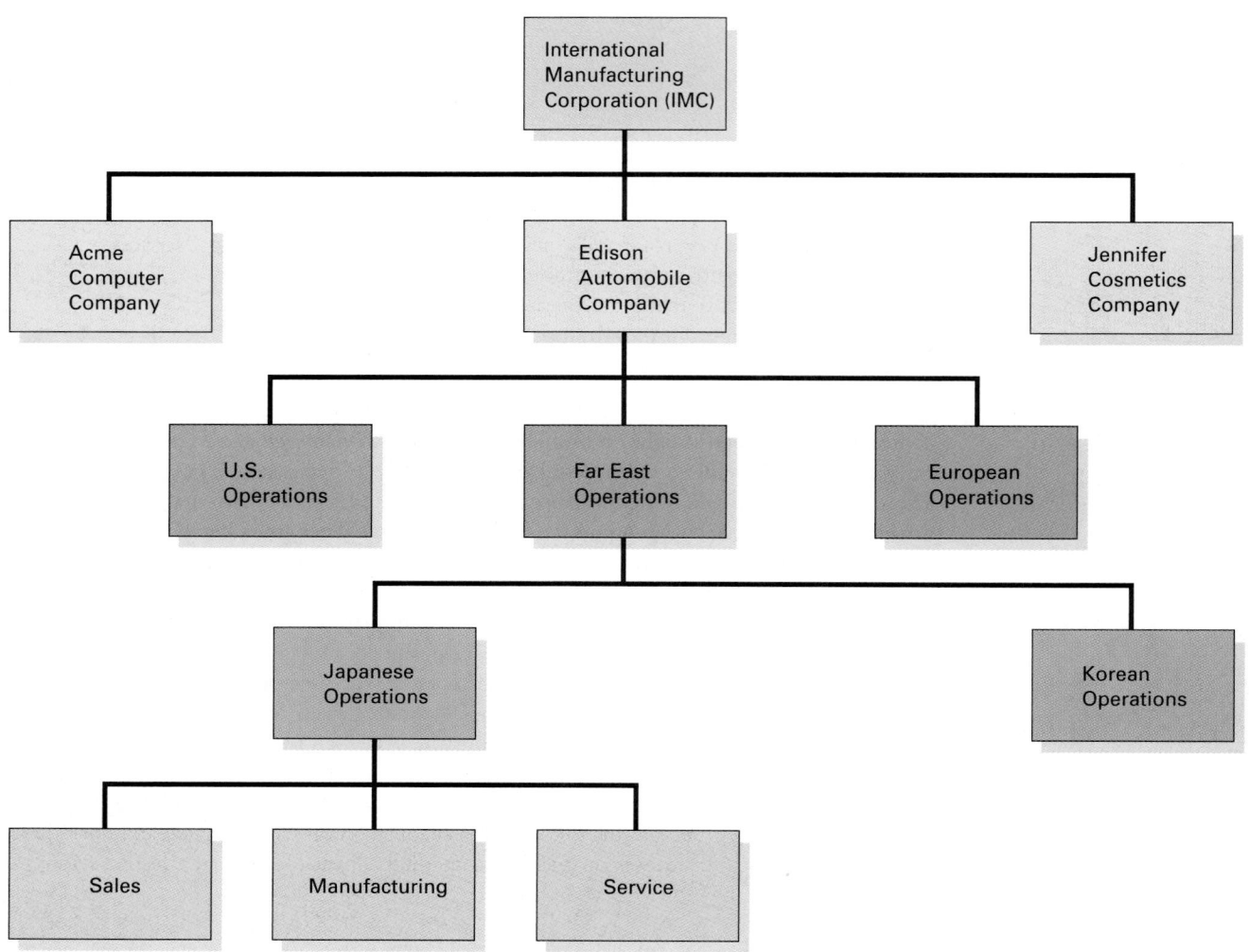

The Japanese unit is separated into its sales, manufacturing, and service functions. Edison Automobile's other geographic divisions have similar subsegments.

You will notice that IMC uses different criteria to define its segments at each level. At the highest level, product group (computers, autos, cosmetics) is used, probably because there is a significant difference in the business knowledge needed to produce and sell these products. At the middle level, segments are defined geographically because of the unique needs of each market and the distances involved. At the lowest level, each country unit is subdivided by function—sales, manufacturing, and service.

Given the organizational chart in Exhibit 1, how much autonomy should the executives of each division be granted by corporate management? If each company (Acme, Edison, and Jennifer) has its own president, vice presidents, and other officers, should these executives be allowed to operate independently of one another? If Acme, for example, is the most profitable company, should it be given more operating capital than Edison and Jennifer, or less? Should a decision for Acme to expand into hand-held computers be made by Acme's executives or by IMC's corporate officers? Within Edison Automobile, how much autonomy should each of the geographic offices have? Should a decision to double the advertising budget or offer consumer rebates in the Far East operations be made by the manager of that division, by the president of Edison Automobile, or by the CEO of IMC?

decentralized company An organization in which managers at all levels have the authority to make decisions concerning the operations for which they are responsible.

Questions such as these are difficult to answer. In fact, it would probably be difficult to find two companies that would answer them the same way. Assuming that IMC is basically a **decentralized company**, managers at all levels will have the authority to make decisions concerning the operations for which they are directly responsible. Regarding the question of rebates in the Far East, for example, the operating manager of that geographic division should probably decide whether to offer them. Likewise, the manager of the Japanese Manufacturing division should decide where to buy engine parts, and the manager of the Service division should have primary responsibility for setting the price to charge for repairing a muffler in Japan. These managers would also be held responsible for the consequences of their decisions.

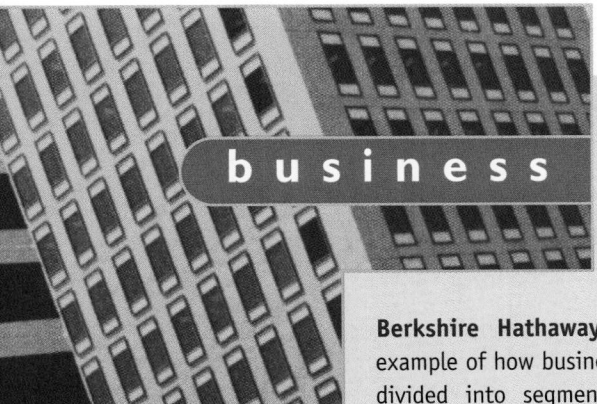

business environment

Berkshire Hathaway As an example of how businesses are divided into segments, consider BERKSHIRE HATHAWAY, INC., which is primarily owned by Warren E. Buffett, one of the richest individuals in the United States. In a 2002 SEC filing, Berkshire stated that its most important business is the property and casualty insurance business, which includes GEICO, the sixth largest auto insurer in the United States, GENERAL RE, one of the four largest reinsurers in the world, and the BERKSHIRE HATHAWAY REINSURANCE GROUP. In addition, it identified several other types of businesses, including the publication of a daily and Sunday newspaper in western New York (BUFFALO NEWS); the manufacture and sale of boxed chocolates and other confectionery products (SEE'S CANDIES); diversified manufacturing and distribution; the retail sale of home furnishings (NEBRASKA FURNITURE MART, R.C. WILLEY HOME FURNISHINGS, STAR FURNITURE COMPANY, and JORDAN'S, INC.); the manufacture, import, and distribution of footwear (H.H. BROWN SHOE COMPANY, LOWELL SHOE, INC., DEXTER SHOE COMPANY, and JUSTIN BRANDS); the retail sale of fine jewelry; the providing of training to operators of aircraft and ships throughout the world; the providing of fractional ownership programs for general aviation aircraft; the licensing and servicing of almost 6,000 DAIRY QUEEN stores; the rental of furniture and accessories; the PAMPERED CHEF, the largest direct seller of houseware products in the United States; and the manufacturing and production of face brick and concrete masonry products (ACME BUILDING BRANDS).

In addition to its own business segments, Berkshire Hathaway also owns large segments of AMERICAN EXPRESS COMPANY, THE COCA-COLA COMPANY, FEDERAL HOME LOAN MORTGAGE CORPORATION, THE GILLETTE COMPANY, THE WASHINGTON POST COMPANY, and WELLS FARGO COMPANY.

As you consider all of these different businesses that are owned or controlled by Berkshire Hathaway, can you see what they all have in common? It's difficult to see the relationship, isn't it? Actually, the one thing they have in common is that they are all considered to be good investments by Warren Buffett, who is generally believed to be one of the most astute investors in the United States. As he states in his annual report, "We are eager to hear from principals or their representatives about businesses that meet all of the following criteria:

1. Large purchases (at least $50 million of before-tax earnings),
2. Demonstrated consistent earning power (future projections are of no interest to us, nor are "turnaround" situations),
3. Businesses earning good returns on equity while employing little or no debt,
4. Management in place (we can't supply it),
5. Simple businesses (if there's lots of technology, we won't understand it),
6. An offering price (we don't want to waste our time or that of the seller by talking, even preliminarily, about a transaction when price is unknown).

Source: Berkshire Hathaway, 2002 Annual Report.

Benefits and Problems of Decentralization

To what degree should a company decentralize? BERKSHIRE HATHAWAY, for example, is very decentralized, allowing managers of its various business units to operate nearly autonomously. Clearly, a large company employing thousands of people in different geographic areas could not remain completely centralized, with top management making all the decisions. The president of IMC would not know enough about the costs and varieties of paint in Japan, for example, or have enough time to make all the operating decisions for the manufacturing subsegment of the Japanese operations of Edison Automobile. Though such decisions would never be made by the president of a large international company, they would be made at a higher level in a **centralized company** than in a decentralized one.

Currently, the trend in most companies is to decentralize. The reasons often cited for making decisions at the lowest possible level in an organization are:

1. Segment managers usually have more information about matters within their area of responsibility than do managers at higher levels.
2. Segment managers are in a better position to see current problems and to react quickly to local situations.
3. Higher-level management can spend more time on broader policy and strategic issues because the burden of daily decision making is distributed.
4. Segment managers have a greater incentive to perform well because they receive the credit (or blame) for performance resulting from their decisions.
5. Employees have greater incentives and motivation to perform well because there are more opportunities for advancement into leadership positions when a company is decentralized.
6. Managers and officers can be evaluated more easily because their responsibilities are more clearly defined.

Decentralization has its drawbacks as well. Decisions made by managers of decentralized units are sometimes not consistent with the overall objectives of the firm. For example, Edison Automobile might find it less expensive to buy computer parts for its automobiles from an outside source than from Acme Computer, or the Service division of Japanese operations may find it cheaper to buy repair parts from outsiders rather than from the Manufacturing division. Such decisions would allow the buying divisions to report lower costs, but the decisions might decrease the company's overall profitability (depending on the costs in the selling divisions that can actually be avoided).

There are two ways to prevent such problems. First, certain decisions should be centralized. For example, all decisions related to insurance coverage, which benefits the entire company, should probably be made at the corporate level. Second, a system of responsibility accounting should be established so that a manager's decisions will benefit not only the segment but also the firm as a whole. This **goal congruence**, whereby the goals of the company and all its segments are in harmony, can be achieved only if the responsibility accounting system is well designed.

Responsibility Accounting

Responsibility accounting is a system in which managers are assigned and held accountable for certain costs, revenues, and/or assets. There are two important behavioral considerations in assigning responsibilities to managers.

• First, the responsible manager should be involved in developing the plan for the unit over which the manager has control. Current research indicates that people are more motivated to achieve a goal (budget or standard) if they participate in setting it. Such participation assures that the goals will be reasonable and, more importantly, that they will be *perceived* to be reasonable by the managers.

centralized company An organization in which top management makes most of the major decisions for the entire company rather than delegating decisions to managers at lower levels.

goal congruence The selection of goals for responsibility centers that are consistent, or congruent, with those of the company as a whole.

responsibility accounting A system of evaluating performance; managers are held accountable for the costs, revenues, assets, or other elements over which they have control.

- Second, a manager should be held accountable only for those costs, revenues, or assets over which the manager has substantial control. Some costs may be generated within a segment, but control over them lies outside that unit. The manager of the Japanese Manufacturing division, for example, may be responsible for labor costs, but employee wages may be determined by a union scale controlled elsewhere. Admittedly, determining "substantial control" requires a judgment based on the circumstances, but if all relevant factors are considered, careful and fair judgments can be made.

Responsibility Accounting Reports

Regardless of the degree of autonomy given to managers at various operating levels, performance reports based on responsibility accounting are needed at all levels of the organization. At the lowest levels, these reports tell managers where corrective action must be taken to control their segments' operations. At top levels, these reports keep management informed of the activities of all segments. The reports are then used to reward past performance and set incentives for future performance.

exception reports Reports that highlight variances from, or exceptions to, the budget.

Exhibit 2 illustrates the kind of responsibility accounting reports a company might use. Note that reporting begins at the bottom and "rolls" upward, with each manager receiving information on the operations for which that manager is responsible, as well as summary information on the performance of lower-level managers. Note also that these reports are **exception reports**, meaning that variances from, or exceptions to, the budget are highlighted. In the report, unfavorable variances are labeled "U" while favorable variances are labeled "F." Such reports direct management immediately to the areas requiring their attention. Note that Exhibit 2 reports only on cost management. In this chapter, we'll also discuss reporting performance on revenue and asset management.

Responsibility Centers

In our example, the president of IMC is responsible for the entire organization and should be held accountable for the company's overall successes and failures. At lower levels, the president of Edison Automobile Company, the manager of Edison's operations in the Far East, the manager in charge of Japanese operations in Edison's Far East operations, and the manager of the Japanese Manufacturing division, for example, would be held responsible for operations within their respective units.

responsibility center An organizational unit in which a manager has control over and is held accountable for performance.

cost center An organizational unit in which a manager has control over and is held accountable for cost performance.

profit center An organizational unit in which a manager has control over and is held accountable for both cost and revenue performance.

investment center An organizational unit in which a manager has control over and is held accountable for cost, revenue, and asset performance.

Each unit is referred to as a **responsibility center**, and, depending on the operation, it may be a cost, profit, or investment center. As the name implies, a **cost center** is any organizational unit in which the manager of that unit has control only over the costs incurred. The manager of a cost center has no responsibility for revenues or assets, either because revenues are not generated in the center or because revenues and assets are under the control of someone else. The manufacturing unit of Japanese operations of IMC, for example, could be designated a cost center. A **profit center** manager, however, has responsibility for both costs and revenues. Profit centers are usually found at higher levels in an organization than are cost centers. The geographic regions (United States, Far East, and Europe, as well as various country operations within the Far East region) of Edison Automobile would probably be profit centers.

In an **investment center**, the manager is responsible for costs, revenues, and assets. This means that the manager is responsible not only for operating costs and revenues, but also for determining the amount of funds to be invested in the center's plant and equipment and for the rate of return earned on those investments. Investment centers are usually found at relatively high levels in organizations. The different companies in IMC (Acme Computer, Edison Automobile, and Jennifer Cosmetics) would probably be investment centers.

TO SUMMARIZE: Most companies are divided into segments with specific responsibilities assigned to each segment manager. In a centralized organization, top management makes most of the operating decisions; in a decentralized organization, decision-making authority is delegated down the corporate ladder to the managers most immediately responsible. It is very important in a decentralized company that the goals of the company and all its segments are in harmony. This concept is referred to as goal congruence. Regardless of the degree of decentralization, almost all companies use performance reports that show variances from budgeted amounts for each division, department, and unit. These reports pass upward through an organization so that supervisors and managers at all levels can assess the performance of the units serving under them. Decentralized companies are divided into fairly independent responsibility centers. There are three types of responsibility centers: cost, profit, and investment. Managers of responsibility centers usually have control over, and are held accountable for, the performance of the center.

Exhibit 2: Responsibility Accounting Reports for Edison Automobile Company of IMC

President, Edison Automobile	Responsibility Centers	Budgeted Costs	Actual Costs	Variance*
The president receives from each geographic area of operations a report summarizing its performance. The president can see where corrective action needs to be made by tracing the differences between budget and actual downward to their sources.	General Administration	x	x	x
	United States	x	x	x
	Far East	$58,000	$65,000	$7,000 U
	Europe	x	x	x

Far East Operations	Responsibility Centers	Budgeted Costs	Actual Costs	Variance
The manager of Far East operations receives a report from each country segment's head. These reports are then summarized and passed on to the president of Edison Automobile.	Japanese Operations	$21,000	$23,000	$2,000 U
	Korean Operations	x	x	x
	Total costs	$58,000	$65,000	$7,000 U

Japanese Operations	Responsibility Centers	Budgeted Costs	Actual Costs	Variance
The manager of Japanese operations receives from each unit a report summarizing its performance. These reports are combined and sent up to the next level, the manager of Far East operations.	Sales	x	x	x
	Manufacturing	$ 9,000	$10,200	$1,200 U
	Service	x	x	x
	Total costs	$21,000	$23,000	$2,000 U

Japanese Manufacturing Division	Variable Costs of Manufacturing	Budgeted Costs	Actual Costs	Variance
The Manufacturing division supervisor receives a performance report on the supervisor's center of responsibility. The totals from these reports are then communicated to the manager of Japanese operations, the next level of responsibility.	Direct materials	$ 2,000	$ 2,500	$ 500 U
	Direct labor	6,000	6,400	400 U
	Manufacturing overhead	1,000	1,300	300 U
	Total costs	$ 9,000	$10,200	$1,200 U

*U means unfavorable.

Standard Cost Systems

3 Describe standard costing and the basic variance analysis model.

standard cost system A cost-accumulation system in which standard costs are used as product costs instead of actual costs. The standard costs are then adjusted to actual costs when financial reports are created. This adjustment creates variances that are reported to management.

If managers are to be held responsible for the costs incurred in their centers, they must have control over those costs, have relevant information about those costs, and have a system that focuses on and supports effective cost controls. Traditionally, companies have used a *standard costing* system that isolates differences between actual and standard (or budgeted) costs to determine whether costs are too high or too low, as well as whether costs are improving (decreasing) or getting worse (increasing). This is critical information if the organization expects to be competitive. In a standard costing management system, standard costs are compared to actual costs, and variances are computed.

Service, merchandising, and manufacturing firms that use standard costing design their accounting systems to incorporate standard costs and variances. This type of system, called a **standard cost system**, is a cost-accumulation process based on costs that *should have been* incurred rather than costs that *were actually* incurred. The steps in establishing and operating a standard cost system are:

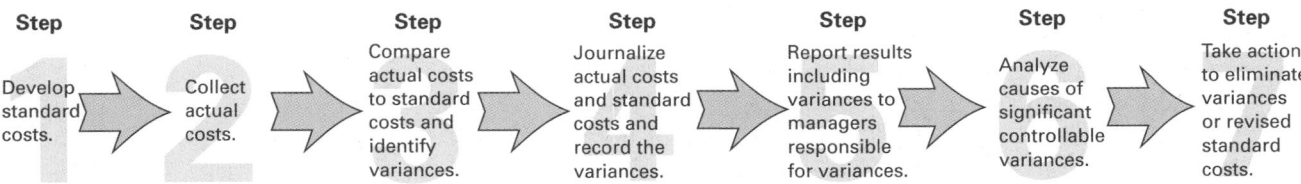

Step 1 Develop standard costs. → **Step 2** Collect actual costs. → **Step 3** Compare actual costs to standard costs and identify variances. → **Step 4** Journalize actual costs and standard costs and record the variances. → **Step 5** Report results including variances to managers responsible for variances. → **Step 6** Analyze causes of significant controllable variances. → **Step 7** Take action to eliminate variances or revised standard costs.

standard cost cards An itemization of the components of a product's standard cost.

Caution

All of the cost variances we compute in this chapter are based on Sunbird's standard cost card. Be sure to return to Exhibit 3 to review these standards as you work through the remainder of this chapter.

These steps describe a typical standard cost system. You are likely to find an extensive standard cost system in most manufacturing firms, which usually have standard costs for direct materials, direct labor, and manufacturing overhead. However, many service and merchandising firms also use a standard cost system to effectively manage critical costs in their organizations. Standard costs usually are reported on **standard cost cards**, often stored in a computer. In the previous chapter on operational budgeting, we created an operating budget for Sunbird Boat Company. A critical part of creating this budget was establishing the standard costs to produce a 15-foot fishing boat. These costs are reported in the previous chapter, although they are spread across a number of budget schedules that we created in that chapter. The management team and accountants at Sunbird Boat Company can compile all of these standard cost data into a standard cost card for 15-foot fishing boats. The standard cost card for Sunbird Boat Company is shown in Exhibit 3. We will use the data in Exhibit 3 to illustrate how variances are calculated and analyzed.

Determining Standard Costs and Identifying Variances

In a manufacturing firm, standard costs are determined on the basis of careful analysis and the experience of many people, including accountants, industrial engineers, purchasing agents, and the managers of the departments to be judged. Accountants play an important role in developing standard costs because they have the data needed to determine how costs have changed in the past in relation to levels of activity. This is not an easy task. Changes in methods of production, technology, worker efficiency, and plant layout, for example, can affect the behavior of costs. Before using standard costs to create the annual budget, past costs often have to be adjusted to take changes in operating conditions into account. These changes sometimes occur gradually and may not be easily noticeable, making it difficult for accountants to identify cost characteristics that will be useful in setting standards for the future.

Engineers are often involved in setting standard costs because of their knowledge of the most efficient way of performing each task in relation to the existing technology of the operation.

Exhibit 3: Standard Cost Card

Sunbird Boat Company **Standard Cost Card—15-Foot Fishing Boats**			
	(1) **Standard** **Quantity**	**(2)** **Standard** **Price or Rate**	**(3)** **Standard Cost** **(1) × (2)**
Inputs:			
Direct materials:			
Wood	70 feet	$10.00	$ 700.00
Fiberglass	50 feet	5.00	250.00
Direct labor	80 hours	15.00	1,200.00
Manufacturing overhead:			
Variable	80 hours	8.00	640.00
Fixed	80 hours	21.40	1,712.00
Total standard cost per boat			$4,502.00

Managers who will be judged by the standard costs should be involved in the standard-setting process; they are more likely to be motivated to meet standards if they have participated in setting the standards and have accepted them. In addition, managers' experience and judgment can be quite valuable in establishing appropriate cost standards.

variance Any deviation from standard.

management by exception The strategy of focusing attention on significant deviations from a standard.

Once management has established a standard price for each resource (direct materials, direct labor, and manufacturing overhead) and has determined the standard input quantity allowed, the standard price is multiplied by the standard quantity to arrive at a standard dollar cost for the product or service. Actual costs are then compared with these standards to calculate the **variance**, the amount by which the actual cost differs from the standard. This variance, if significant, is a signal to management that costs may be "out of control" and that corrective action should be taken to eliminate the variance. This process of using variances from a standard to isolate problem areas is called **management by exception**. It is the basis of the control function.

STOP & THINK

Is it possible for a company to have positive variances (actual costs are less than standard costs) and still have problems? Can you think of an example?

Let's review Exhibit 3 again. You can see in the third column that the standard costs to produce boats at Sunbird Boat Company are composed of both a price (or rate) and a quantity (or usage). Hence, comparing actual costs with standard costs results in two variances: a price (or rate) variance and a quantity (or usage) variance. These variances are usually computed for direct materials, direct labor, and variable manufacturing overhead.

Exhibit 4 is a general model for calculating variances for direct materials, direct labor, and variable manufacturing overhead. (It is *not* the model used to calculate variances for fixed manufacturing overhead.) Let's first consider column (1) and column (2). These two columns are used to compute the price (rate) variance, which is the difference between the actual quantity of inputs times the actual price and the actual quantity of inputs times the standard price. Another way of mathematically saying the same thing is the price variance is the difference between the actual price and the standard price, times the actual quantity. Now before you start to memorize either of these equations, think about what a price variance is signaling—that the actual price is different than the standard or expected price.[2] Essentially, if the actual price is more than the expected price, then we have an unfavorable variance. And if the actual price is

---

2 In this discussion, the terms *standard* and *expected* are often used interchangeably. Some people refer to prices and quantities as standard; others refer to them as expected because they aren't under the complete control of the company.

Exhibit 4: General Model for Variance Analysis

(1) **AQ × AP** (Actual quantity of inputs × Actual price)	(2) **AQ × SP** (Actual quantity of inputs × Standard price)	(3) **SQ × SP** (Standard quantity of inputs allowed for actual output × Standard price)
Price (rate) variance (Materials price variance) (Labor rate variance) (Manufacturing overhead spending variance)	**Quantity (usage) variance** (Materials quantity variance) (Labor efficiency variance) (Manufacturing overhead efficiency variance)	

less than the expected price, then the variance is favorable. It then makes sense to multiply the difference between these two prices by the actual quantity in order to know the total financial impact on the organization of paying a price or rate that was more or less than was expected.

Now let's consider how column (2) and column (3) are used to compute the quantity (or usage) variance. This variance is essentially an input-output analysis. It compares the actual quantity of inputs to the standard quantity of inputs allowed for actual output. The concept *quantity allowed for actual output* is important here. This concept essentially refers to the quantity that should have been used to produce the actual output and relates back to the principle of flexible budgeting that we discussed in the expanded material section of the previous chapter on operational budgeting. Unless actual production output equals budgeted production output, management can't really know how much material, labor, and overhead input should have been used during the period. Hence, at the end of the operating period, the accountant will multiply the standard quantity per unit of product by the actual volume of units produced to determine the *standard quantity allowed*. This number is then compared to the actual quantity used to determine if there is a favorable or unfavorable quantity (usage) variance. Then, in order to be able to account for this variance in the organization's accounting system (which we will discuss in the next section), we multiply this difference by the standard price per unit of input. The standard price is used so that the quantity variances will not be influenced by price changes. Hence, the quantity variance is the difference between the actual quantity and the standard quantity allowed, times the standard price.

STOP & THINK

When computing the quantity (usage) variance, do you understand why it is important to compare actual quantity of inputs to the standard quantity of inputs allowed for actual output? Is the standard quantity budgeted (determined at the beginning of the operating period) different from the standard quantity allowed for actual output (determined at the end of the operating period)? If so, what is the difference?

Evaluation of Standard Costing

Standard cost systems, such as those discussed in this chapter, have many advantages and disadvantages. The advantages include the following:

1. Standard costs are very important to the budgeting process.
2. A standard cost system is simpler to operate than a system using actual costs because the cost flows are recorded at standard.
3. The setting of standard costs requires a careful analysis of operations. Such an analysis can lead to improvements in costs and efficiencies even before the standard cost system is fully operative.
4. A standard cost system helps identify and control problem areas, which leads to increased production efficiency.
5. Standard costs provide a basis for measuring performance by assigning variances to the responsible manager.

6. A standard cost system is compatible with the principle of management by exception, which contributes to the effective utilization of management's time and effort.

The disadvantages of standard costing include the following:

1. A standard cost system is expensive and time consuming to develop.
2. It is easy to misinterpret the causes of a variance because so many factors are involved.
3. Standard costs must be changed as conditions change (e.g., as the product, the materials, or the production methods change). Sometimes these changes occur so quickly that standards become out of date before management realizes it.
4. Workers tend to view measures of efficiency with mistrust. Responsibility for significant variances may be erroneously assigned, which then leads to morale problems.
5. The setting of standards is not an exact science. Although standards are reported as specific figures, smart managers realize that these numbers should sometimes be treated as ranges of acceptable performance.
6. Random fluctuations in the differences between standards and actual results are to be expected but often are hard to distinguish from situations requiring action.
7. Standard costs are based on the simplistic cost model in which every cost has to be treated as either fixed or variable. In the real world, however, many costs do not behave according to these idealized models, which means that managers can always legitimately point to shortcomings in the variance analysis and standard costing.

Although the disadvantages noted here are real and should not be minimized, standard cost systems have generally been cost beneficial and are widely used across manufacturing, service, and even merchandising organizations. Manufacturing firms use standards and budgets for their nonmanufacturing activities, as do merchandising and service businesses. In essence, the concepts of standards and cost systems apply to all types of organizations in varying degrees.

TO SUMMARIZE: Standard cost systems are used to accumulate costs based on standards rather than actual costs. Standard costs are predetermined or budgeted costs that serve as benchmarks for judging what actual costs should be. Standard costs are usually expressed as the per-unit cost of materials, labor, and manufacturing overhead and are used by managers for planning, implementing, and controlling decisions. The total variance between actual and standard costs is made up of price (or rate) and quantity (or efficiency) variances. Standard costs are based on careful analysis by many people, including accountants, engineers, and managers. Standard costs are compared with actual costs incurred to determine variances, the amounts by which actual costs differ from standards. Significant variances alert management to specific problem areas that may require corrective action. The strategy of focusing on significant variances, called management by exception, is essential to the controlling function.

Overall, standard costs can be used in nonmanufacturing firms, as well as manufacturing firms. Standard cost systems have both advantages and disadvantages. Most advantages center on achieving greater accuracy and efficiency. Most disadvantages center on the challenges involved in setting standards and the inability to establish exact standards in a changing environment.

Controlling Performance in Cost Centers

4 Use materials and labor cost variance analysis to explain how performance is controlled in cost centers.

As we stated earlier, managers of cost centers are responsible for costs incurred. Most cost centers usually have one type of cost that is more significant than any other. In service organizations, salaries are generally the major cost. In wholesale and retail businesses, the cost of merchandise purchased for resale is often the most significant cost. In manufacturing firms, costs incurred to make products (direct materials, direct labor, and manufacturing overhead) are usually most significant. The standard cost system described in the previous section is an effective method of controlling these kinds of costs.

Direct Materials Variances

Variance analysis is an essential part of an effective standard cost system. We will first explain how direct materials variances are computed and analyzed. Then, we will explain the computation and analysis of direct labor variances. The more complex variances for manufacturing overhead will be discussed and illustrated in the expanded material section of this chapter.

To illustrate the computation of the price and quantity variances for direct materials, we will assume the following actual results for the year on the 90 fishing boats made by Sunbird Boat Company:

Direct materials purchased	
Wood	6,900 feet at $9.20 per foot
Fiberglass	4,800 feet at $5.20 per foot
Direct materials used	
Wood	6,435.0 feet
Fiberglass	4,432.5 feet
Boats produced	90

Keep in mind throughout the following discussion that the standard cost card (Exhibit 3) specifies that wood materials should cost $10 per foot, fiberglass materials should cost $5 per foot, and each boat produced should require 70 feet of wood and 50 feet of fiberglass. (Obviously, many different kinds of raw materials are required to make boats. To keep the example simple, we are assuming only two materials are used.)

Materials Price Variance

materials price variance
The extent to which the actual price varies from the standard price for the quantity of materials purchased or used; computed by multiplying the difference between the actual and standard prices by the quantity purchased or used.

The **materials price variance** reflects the extent to which the actual price varies from the standard price for the actual quantity of materials purchased or used. Although the price variance can be calculated either when materials are purchased or when they are used, it is generally best to isolate the variance at purchase and report the variance to the purchasing manager who has responsibility for controlling the purchase price. If management waits until the materials are used before calculating variances, the information needed by the purchasing managers to take corrective action is delayed.

In calculating the materials price variance, the standard price per unit of materials should reflect the final, delivered cost of materials, net of any discounts taken. For example, Sunbird Boat Company may have determined its standard materials price per foot of wood as follows:

Purchase price	$ 9.84
Freight	0.17
Handling costs	0.04
Less purchase discounts	(0.05)
Standard wood materials cost per foot	$10.00

The standard cost above assumes that the materials were purchased in certain lot sizes (for example, 100-foot quantities) and delivered a certain way (by rail, for example). Handling costs and purchase discounts have also been included.

Assume that variances are determined when materials are purchased. Based on the fact given above that 6,900 feet of wood are purchased by Sunbird during the year, the price variance for wood is computed as follows:

Materials Price Variance
(based on quantity purchased)

AQ × AP (Actual quantity of input × Actual price)	AQ × SP (Actual quantity of input × Standard price)	SQA × SP (Standard quantity allowed for actual output × Standard price)
6,900 feet × $9.20 = $63,480	6,900 feet × $10.00 = $69,000	

Materials price variance
6,900 feet × ($10.00 − $9.20) = $5,520 F

Caution

As you can see in the illustration on this page, when the actual quantity used is the basis for the materials price variance, the materials price variance and the materials quantity variance share some of the same computations, making these calculations somewhat easier. However, remember that basing the materials price variance on the actual quantity used will delay the recognition of price problems from the time that the materials are purchased until the time they are transferred to production.

This variance indicates that the company spent $5,520 less than the total standard cost for the wood purchased. Because less money was spent than the standard cost, the variance is labeled "F," meaning "favorable." If the amount expended had been more than the standard cost, the variance would have been "unfavorable," designated with a "U."

Isolating materials price variances at the time of purchase has the advantage of providing immediate information on purchasing decisions. This also allows companies to carry inventory in the accounting records at the standard cost. Some companies, however, prefer to compute materials price variances at the time the materials are transferred to Work-in-Process Inventory (i.e., when these materials are actually used in production). The facts stated above indicate that 6,435 feet were used in production. If materials price variances are computed when materials are transferred to Work-in-Process, the 6,435 feet would be used in the calculation rather than the 6,900 feet purchased. In this case, a favorable price variance of $5,148 would result, as shown below.

Materials Price Variance and Materials Quantity Variance
(based on quantity used in production)

AQ × AP (Actual quantity of input × Actual price)	AQ × SP (Actual quantity of input × Standard price)	SQA × SP (Standard quantity allowed for actual output × Standard price)
6,435 feet × $9.20 = $59,202	6,435 feet × $10.00 = $64,350	6,300 feet × $10.00 = $63,000

Materials price variance
6,435 feet × ($10.00 − $9.20) = $5,148 F

Materials quantity variance
$10.00 × (6,435 feet − 6,300 feet) = $1,350 U

materials quantity variance The extent to which the actual quantity of materials varies from the standard quantity; computed by multiplying the difference between the actual quantity of materials used and the standard quantity of materials allowed by the standard price.

Materials Quantity Variance

The standard quantity of materials should reflect the amount needed for each completed unit of product but should allow for normal waste, spoilage, and other unavoidable inefficiencies. The standard cost card indicates that 70 feet of wood is allowed for each 15-foot fishing boat produced. Because Sunbird Boat Company produced 90 of these boats last year, the standard quantity of wood allowed is 6,300 feet (70 feet × 90 boats). As already reported above, actual use of wood amounted to 6,435 feet. The computation of the **materials quantity variance** for wood is shown in the illustration above. As you can see, the company used 135 more feet of wood than expected, resulting in an unfavorable quantity variance of $1,350 (135 feet × $10 per foot).

Controlling Materials Variances

Materials price variances are usually under the control of the purchasing department. The purchasing function involves getting a variety of price quotations, buying in economic lot sizes to take advantage of quantity discounts, buying and paying on a timely basis to obtain cash discounts, and paying attention to alternative forms of delivery to minimize shipping costs. Some of these factors will be less important when there are few suppliers or when purchase contracts with suppliers are for long periods. In any case, the existence of unfavorable price variances may suggest a problem that needs correcting.

The buyer responsible for these purchases should be able to explain the variance even though the buyer may not be able to control its occurrence. This may be the case, for example, when market prices change after the standard is set, which could be the explanation for the favorable price variance. Or materials may be damaged, requiring the reorder of a small quantity on a rush basis; this usually raises the price of the materials as well as the cost of shipping, causing an unfavorable price variance. The point is that the cause of any significant variance (whether favorable or unfavorable) must be explained and steps taken to avoid such variances in the future. The purpose of variance analysis is not to browbeat employees for failing to meet impossible expectations, but rather to provide information that will help management identify ways of improving the production process.

Materials quantity variances may be caused by quality defects, poor workmanship, poor choice of materials, inexperienced workers, machines that need repair, or an inaccurate materials quantity standard. Just as the purchasing manager must explain significant price variances, generally the production manager must analyze significant quantity variances to determine their cause. If the material is of inferior quality, the purchasing manager, rather than the production manager, may be responsible for the variance. Again, the point is that the cause of the variance must be determined; only then can it be decided what action, if any, to take to prevent its recurrence. Further, production managers should constantly receive reports on these variances in order to maintain good control of costs and usage. If this is done, production managers can then take quick corrective action before many problems become significant in size. Corrective action, for example, may involve being careful to return excess materials to the storeroom rather than being careless about control in the production area, which could lead to waste or theft.

Accounting for Materials Variances

The journal entries for recording the purchase and use of materials, as well as the materials price variance (isolated at purchase) and the quantity variance (isolated when materials are used), are:

Materials Price Variance:

Direct Materials Inventory ($10.00 × 6,900 feet)	69,000	
Materials Price Variance [($10.00 − $9.20) × 6,900 feet]		5,520
Cash (or Accounts Payable) ($9.20 × 6,900 feet)		63,480

Purchased 6,900 feet of wood at $9.20 per foot and entered the materials in inventory at the standard price of $10.00 per foot.

Materials Quantity Variance:

Work-in-Process Inventory (6,300 feet × $10.00)	63,000	
Materials Quantity Variance [(6,435 feet − 6,300 feet) × $10.00]	1,350	
Direct Materials Inventory (6,435 feet × $10.00)		64,350

Transferred 6,435 feet of wood out of inventory and recorded standard usage of 6,300 feet of wood to produce 90 boats.

Note that the $63,000 debit to Work-in-Process Inventory is based on the standard amount of wood allowed for 90 boats actually produced, which is 6,300 feet (90 boats × 70 standard feet per boat).

As you can see, Materials Price Variance and Materials Quantity Variance are debited when the variances are unfavorable; they are credited when the variances are favorable. A good way to remember that unfavorable variances are debited is to think of an unfavorable variance as an expense, which is also debited. Conversely, a favorable variance, which is credited, can be considered an expense reduction or savings. The actual cost deviations from the standard costs are now recorded in variance accounts. Similar to the approach used to close over- or underapplied manufacturing overhead (discussed previously in the chapter on product cost flows), the variance accounts are usually closed and the amounts transferred to Cost of Goods Sold at the end of the period. Thus, Cost of Goods Sold as reported on the income statement is based on actual costs, while inventory accounts on the balance sheet include only the standard costs of materials. Alternatively, when variances are significant in amount, variance account balances at the end of a period should be allocated among Cost of Goods Sold, Raw Materials Inventory, Work-in-Process Inventory, and Finished Goods Inventory instead of simply transferred entirely to Cost of Goods Sold.

Now that we've worked through the accounting for variances on Sunbird's wood materials, see if you can correctly compute and account for the variances on Sunbird's fiberglass materials (base the price variance on the amount purchased). As you make the variance computations, try to understand the *meaning* of each calculation. To help you, consider the following three-step conceptual approach to variance analysis.

1. First, determine whether the variance is favorable or unfavorable.

   In the case of the wood price variance, the fact that the actual price ($9.20) is less than the standard price ($10.00) is obviously a favorable situation. And the fact that the actual quantity of wood used (6,435 feet) is more than the standard quantity allowed (6,300 feet) is clearly an unfavorable situation.

2. Next, compute the underlying difference that actually determines the variance calculation.

   What we mean here is that the "real" price variance is $0.80 (the difference between $9.20 and $10.00) and the "real" quantity variance is 135 feet (the difference between 6,435 feet and 6,300 feet).

3. Finally, calculate the financial impact of the underlying difference on the company. This is the variance that must be accounted for in the company's accounting system.

   Given a "real" price variance of $0.80 per foot that is favorable, the impact of this difference on Sunbird is a function of the number of board feet actually purchased; that is, $0.80 favorable × 6,900 feet = $5,520 F. Similarly, the financial impact on Sunbird of a "real" quantity variance of 135 feet that is unfavorable is a function of the standard price of $10 per foot; that is, 135 feet unfavorable × $10 = $1,350 U.

The correct computations and journal entries for Sunbird's fiberglass variances are provided in the footnote below.[3]

---

3 The actual fiberglass price was $5.20 and the standard price is $5.00. Hence, the price variance is unfavorable based on an underlying difference of $0.20. Because 4,800 feet of fiberglass were actually purchased, the total financial impact of the underlying unfavorable price difference is a price variance of $960 U ($0.20 × 4,800 feet).

Now turning to the quantity variance, the actual fiberglass used was 4,432.5 feet and the standard quantity allowed is 4,500 feet (50 standard feet per boat × 90 boats actually produced). Hence, the quantity variance is favorable based on the underlying difference of 67.5 feet (4,500 feet − 4,432.5 feet). Using a standard price per foot of $5, the total financial impact of the underlying favorable quantity difference is a quantity variance of $337.50 F (67.5 feet × $5).

The journal entries to account for the price and quantity variances, respectively, are:

Direct Materials Inventory ($5.00 × 4,800 feet)	24,000	
Materials Price Variance [($5.20 − $5.00) × 4,800 feet]	960	
Cash (or Accounts Payable) ($5.20 × 4,800 feet)		24,960
Work-in-Process Inventory (4,500 feet × $5.00)	22,500	
Materials Quantity Variance [(4,500 feet − 4,432.5 feet) × $5.00]		337.50
Direct Materials Inventory (4,432.5 feet × $5.00)		22,162.50

Direct Labor Variances

Typically when a standard cost system is being used in a manufacturing or service firm, a direct labor rate variance and a direct labor efficiency variance are determined for personnel directly involved in the creation of the organization's product or service. These variances are computed in a manner similar to the materials price and quantity variances.

Labor Rate Variance

labor rate variance The extent to which the actual labor rate varies from the standard rate for the quantity of labor used; computed by multiplying the difference between the actual rate and the standard rate by the quantity of labor used.

A **labor rate variance** is a price variance; it shows the difference between actual and standard wage rates. Unfavorable labor rate variances may occur when skilled workers with high hourly pay rates are placed in jobs intended for less skilled or lower-wage-rate employees. Unfavorable labor rate variances may also occur when employees work overtime at premium pay (time and a half or double time). Conversely, favorable labor rate variances occur when less skilled or lower-wage-rate employees perform duties intended for higher-paid workers.

For Sunbird Boat Company, the standard cost card (Exhibit 3) indicates that the standard direct labor rate per boat is 80 hours at $15 per hour. Actual labor used during the year to make 90 boats was 7,092 hours at an average rate of $14.50 per hour. The labor rate variance is thus $3,546 favorable, computed as follows:

Labor Rate Variance and Labor Efficiency Variance

AH × AR	AH × SR	SHA × SR
(Actual hours of input × Actual rate)	(Actual hours of input × Standard rate)	(Standard hours allowed for actual output × Standard rate)
7,092 hours × $14.50 = $102,834	7,092 hours × $15.00 = $106,380	7,200 hours × $15.00 = $108,000

Labor rate variance
7,092 hours × ($15.00 − $14.50) = $3,546 F

Labor efficiency variance
$15.00 × (7,200 hours − 7,092 hours) = $1,620 F

As this variance indicates, the $0.50 difference between the standard wage rate and actual average wage rate results in $3,546 less spent than expected for the actual number of direct labor hours used. Sunbird's management now needs to determine whether the variance should be investigated. Depending on the company's hiring policies, and the degree of authority given to the operating manager in setting wage rates and assigning workers to particular jobs, the operating manager may or may not be responsible for this labor rate variance. In general, labor rates are the responsibility of the manager who makes hiring and staffing decisions.

Labor Efficiency Variance

labor efficiency variance The extent to which the actual labor used varies from the standard quantity; computed by multiplying the difference between the actual quantity of labor used and the standard quantity of labor allowed by the standard rate.

The **labor efficiency variance** is a quantity variance. It measures the cost (or benefit) of using labor for more (or fewer) hours than prescribed by the standard. Computed in the same manner as the materials quantity variance, the labor efficiency variance computation is also illustrated in the schedule above for Sunbird Boat Company. Note that total standard hours are computed by multiplying the standard hours per boat by the actual number of boats produced (80 hours × 90 boats = 7,200 standard hours allowed). The manufacturing division used 108 less direct labor hours than the standard allowed for actual production output, which generates a favorable efficiency variance of $1,620 (108 hours × $15).

The labor efficiency variance shows how efficiently the workers performed, which is an important measure of the productivity of the department. The variances might be unfavorable for a variety of reasons, including poorly trained employees, poor-quality materials that require extra processing time, old or faulty equipment, and improper supervision of employees. Note

Caution

When computing variances, be careful not to confuse actual and standard hours and actual and standard rates. The rate variance is always the difference between the standard and actual rate multiplied by the actual hours. (To multiply it by standard hours would not tell you how much the rate increase actually cost or saved the company in total.) On the other hand, the efficiency variance is a time-based variance; therefore, it is the difference between the standard hours allowed and actual hours multiplied by the standard rate.

that the labor efficiency variance is probably the most important and closely watched manufacturing variance. It has become even more important in recent years as U.S. industries have tried to increase the efficiency of their production to match that of Japan, Korea, and other countries.

Controlling Labor Variances

Labor rate variances are normally the responsibility of either the production manager who is responsible for employees' work assignments or the individuals responsible for hiring employees. As indicated, rate variances are likely to be due to (1) certain tasks being performed by workers with different pay rates or (2) working overtime at rates higher than the normal wage rate. These variances may be manageable if care is taken in assigning workers to jobs that are consistent with their skills and pay scales. Deviations may be necessary in certain situations because of vacations, sickness, or absences of other employees. If the variances are caused by factors beyond the manager's control, he or she should not be held responsible for the unfavorable variance.

In a labor-intensive company, the labor efficiency variance is much more important than in a company that has low labor costs. Depending on the intensity of management attention on labor costs, the related variances can be separated into categories by causes so that judgments can be made about what corrective action should be taken. Some typical causes of labor inefficiency variances are absenteeism, machinery breakdowns, poor-quality materials, poor work environment, inadequate machinery, lack of employee skills on a given job, poor employee attitudes, lazy employees, and inaccurate standards. The sooner these causes can be identified, the more opportunity exists for management to effectively take corrective action. However, if management waits until labor efficiency variances are computed before taking action, the data necessary to take action may not be available until the end of each pay period when accounting reports are issued.

Accounting for Labor Variances

Because the labor rate and labor efficiency variances are both computed for a given period of time or for a given amount of production, the labor costs and variances for Sunbird Boat Company can be accounted for in a single journal entry.

Work-in-Process Inventory (7,200 hours × $15.00) 108,000	
Labor Rate Variance	
[($15.00 − $14.50) × 7,092 hours]	3,546
Labor Efficiency Variance	
[(7,200 hours − 7,092 hours) × $15.00]	1,620
Wages Payable (7,092 hours × $14.50)	102,834

To charge Work-in-Process Inventory for standard labor hours at the standard wage rate to produce 90 boats; to set up favorable labor rate and efficiency variances to reflect the use of 108 hours below standard at an average wage rate that was $0.50 below standard.

As with all production variances, labor variances are closed to Cost of Goods Sold at the end of the period or allocated among Cost of Goods Sold and the inventory accounts on the balance sheet. By closing variances into Cost of Goods Sold, actual cost of goods sold will be reported on the income statement, and Work-in-Process Inventory and Finished Goods Inventory will include only the standard costs of labor.

Satisfied Employees Are More Productive For many companies, labor costs are the highest cost. This is certainly true for service firms and may even be true for manufacturing firms. Labor rate and labor efficiency variances provide information about whether labor rates are higher than expected or standard and whether workers are performing as efficiently as expected or standard. However, there are important labor costs that are difficult to report and control using traditional labor variances. Take employee turnover, for example. Common estimates are that employee turnover costs range from $10,000 to $40,000 per person, depending on the position, while employee retention actually increases revenues. In addition, it has been estimated that a 5% increase in employee retention can result in a 10% decrease in labor costs and lead to productivity increases ranging from 25 to 65%.

Because of the high costs of employee turnover, most companies work hard to increase employee retention. The most common approach is to "buy" employee satisfaction with increased pay and benefits. However, a 1998 survey of 206 medium-to-large companies conducted by WILLIAM M. MERCER, INC., found that in organizations with high turnover, compensation was the most common reason for dissatisfaction. In companies with very low turnover, 40% of the respondents said that emotional factors (work satisfaction, good relationships with managers and other employees) were the sole reasons for their retention; only 21% attributed their retention to financial factors (satisfaction with compensation and benefits).

If these data seem conflicting, then consider the following management theory of employee motivation. Certain aspects of our job create dissatisfaction, but do not generate satisfaction. Other factors can lead to strong feelings of satisfaction with our job, but do not necessarily create dissatisfaction if the factor is absent. In other words, employees are generally unsatisfied with their jobs if the compensation is unacceptable, regardless of any other positive aspects of the job. On the other hand, if the compensation is acceptable, most employees are not necessarily satisfied. At this point, their attention turns to other factors such as feedback, recognition, opportunities for growth, etc. Evidence suggests that creating a workplace where employees feel better about themselves is extremely important. If a work environment constantly raises employees' self-esteem to a higher level than they experience elsewhere, they will want to spend more time at work and will enjoy very high job satisfaction.

Source: "Increasing Employee Satisfaction," **http://www.performance-unlimited.com/satisfy.htm**.

TO SUMMARIZE: The difference between actual and standard costs of materials for a given production level can be separated into a materials price variance and a materials quantity variance. The materials price variance can be computed when the materials are purchased or when they are used in production. The managers responsible for the variances must determine their causes and, if the variances are outside an acceptable range, take corrective action. The materials variances (price and quantity) are recorded in individual accounts when materials are acquired and used. The accounts for materials variances are generally closed into Cost of Goods Sold in order to adjust this account to actual costs; inventory accounts on the balance sheet include only standard materials costs.

The labor rate variance is the difference between the actual and the standard labor rates multiplied by the actual hours worked. The labor efficiency variance is the difference between actual and standard hours multiplied by the standard wage rate. Labor variances are usually controllable by manufacturing division managers. The labor variances (rate and efficiency) are recorded in individual accounts when labor costs are incurred. Like materials variances, labor variances are typically closed in their entirety to Cost of Goods Sold so that the work-in-process inventory and finished goods inventory accounts include only standard labor costs.

© 2003 Getty Images

A nonmanufacturing organization sometimes expresses standards in quantitative terms. For example, a hospital might have standard times for activities such as taking blood pressure readings.

Controlling Performance in Profit Centers

5 Use revenue variance analysis to explain how performance is controlled in profit centers.

As defined earlier, a profit center is an organizational unit (segment) in which a manager has responsibility for both costs and revenues. Profit centers both produce and market goods or services. For example, the U.S., Far East, and European operations of the Edison Automobile Company of IMC, illustrated in Exhibit 1 on page 1084, might be profit centers.

The Segment-Margin Income Statement

segment-margin income statement An income statement that identifies costs directly chargeable to a segment and further divides them into variable and fixed cost behavior patterns.

To evaluate the performance of profit centers and to decide how limited resources will be divided among profit centers, management needs a report that compares the revenues and costs of the profit centers being evaluated. One report that is often used is the **segment-margin income statement**, such as the one presented in Exhibit 5 for IMC on pages 1102–1103.

To keep Exhibit 5 reasonably simple, we have limited the report to only two divisions for IMC: Acme Computer and Edison Automobile. Further, we have included only the regions of Edison Automobile. You will note that it includes three geographic regions; the Far East Region has operations in two countries—Japan and Korea. As you read across, note that the segment focus becomes narrower: from divisions to geographic regions to countries within geographic regions.

Before reviewing specific aspects of this segment-margin income statement, we want to remind you of that very important management accounting principle called *responsibility accounting*. Following this principle, segment managers should be evaluated on only the items they can control or influence. As was the case with cost centers, in evaluating profit centers it is important that managers be held responsible only for the controllable costs; the costs over which they have control are usually called **direct costs**. In Exhibit 5, we apply responsibility accounting to IMC by including in each segment report only the revenues and costs controlled by that segment manager. This implies that some costs, **indirect costs**, will not be assigned to

direct costs Costs that are specifically traceable to a unit of business or segment being analyzed.

indirect costs Costs normally incurred for the benefit of several segments or activities; sometimes called common costs or joint costs.

a particular segment because the manager cannot control them. As you can observe in Exhibit 5, when we break IMC down into smaller and smaller segments, more and more costs are considered to be indirect or common. For example, the $1.5 million indirect costs listed in the IMC column are not assigned to the Acme Computer and Edison Automobile segments. These costs might include the IMC president's salary and interest on company-wide debt. As you can imagine, these costs are not controlled by Acme Computer and Edison Automobile. Therefore, these costs are not assigned to these segments.

Similarly, when Edison Automobile is broken down into smaller segments for analysis, we see an additional $200,000 of indirect costs that are not assigned to Edison Automobile's three regions. Costs such as the division manager's salary and advertising for all regions are not controlled by the region manager and so are not allocated to the regions. You will note that as we move down the organizational hierarchy, from divisions to geographic regions to countries, indirect costs increase in total; managers at the lower levels have the narrowest range of responsibility and the fewest costs to control. The manager of manufacturing in Japan, for example, will be responsible for the items ordered for that unit but not for setting the salary of the manager of Far East operations; this is the responsibility of the manager of Edison Automobile. The salary of the manager of Far East operations is thus a direct and controllable cost of Edison Automobile and is an indirect and noncontrollable cost to Japanese operations.

Caution

Many students confuse the terms *variable* and *fixed costs, controllable* and *noncontrollable costs,* and *direct* and *indirect costs.* Costs are variable if they fluctuate with activity. If they don't fluctuate with activity, costs are fixed. Costs are controllable if they can be changed by the activity manager. If they can't be changed by the activity manager, costs are noncontrollable. Costs are direct if removing the activity results in the costs being eliminated. Costs that remain after an activity is eliminated are indirect.

Interpreting Profit Center Performance Results

Given that the segment-margin income statement in Exhibit 5 was prepared in light of the principles of controllable and direct costs, how does management use the information it contains? First, the net income figure provides management with concrete information for evaluating the performance of the company as a whole. Second, the **segment margins** enable management to analyze company results by evaluating the performance of each segment.

segment margins The difference between segment revenue and direct segment costs; a measure of the segment's contribution to cover indirect fixed costs and provide profits.

We are now ready to examine the operations of IMC segments in detail. In absolute terms, Edison Automobile has a larger segment margin than Acme Computer ($2 million versus $1.8 million). U.S. operations has earned more than the Far East and European operations; the Japanese operations has a larger segment margin than the Korean operations. Absolute profits, however, often favor those segments with a larger asset base—with larger manufacturing facilities, for example. A larger facility with more manufacturing capacity should naturally have higher production and higher sales and, hence, a higher segment margin and higher income. A more equitable way to assess performance is to compare **segment-margin ratios** (segment margin divided by net sales), because ratios focus on relationships rather than absolute dollar amounts. For example, though the segment margin of European operations is larger than that of Far East operations, the latter has a higher segment-margin ratio (25% versus 18.3%).

segment-margin ratios The segment margin divided by the segment's net sales revenue; a measure of the efficiency of the segment's operating performance and, therefore, of its profitability.

In using segment-margin income statements to evaluate profit centers, it is important to review performance over several periods or months. A single period or month may not be typical of overall performance. In our example, September might have been an unusually bad profitability month for the Korean unit of Far East operations because of a slump in the Korean economy or a labor strike. In fact, the performance can be evaluated only by looking at cost and profit trends over several periods, and by comparing the results of these units with those of other similar units.

Managing Revenues in Profit Centers

Profit center managers manage their costs the same way cost center managers evaluate and manage costs. That is, they use the standard costing concepts that we have already discussed. Unlike cost center managers, however, profit center managers are also responsible for managing revenues because the segment profit they are evaluated on is a function of both costs and revenues. In the next section, we examine how variance analysis is used to manage revenues.

Exhibit 5: A Segment-Margin Income Statement

International Manufacturing Corporation (IMC)
Segment-Margin Income Statement
September 2006
(in thousands of dollars)

| | | Segments | |
| | | Acme | Edison |
	IMC	Computers	Automobile
Net sales revenue	$ 25,000	$ 15,000	$10,000
Variable costs:			
Cost of goods sold	$(16,000)	$(10,000)	$ (6,000)
Selling and administrative costs	(3,300)	(2,000)	(1,300)
Total variable costs	$(19,300)	$(12,000)	$ (7,300)
Contribution margin	$ 5,700	$ 3,000	$ 2,700
Less fixed costs controllable by segment manager	(1,900)	(1,200)	(700)
Segment margin	$ 3,800	$ 1,800	$ 2,000
Less indirect costs to segments (common costs)	(1,500)		
Net income	$ 2,300		
Segment-margin ratio	9.2%	12.0%	20.0%

Managing Revenues and Revenue Variances

A segment's actual and expected revenues may differ for several reasons including the following:

- Sales prices were higher or lower than expected → a sales price variance.
- Sales volume was higher or lower than expected → a sales volume variance.
- The company's market share was higher or lower than expected → a market share variance.
- The industry, as a whole, sold fewer products than expected → an industry volume variance.
- The mix of products sold was different than expected → a sales mix variance.[4]

Because management is interested in knowing which of these factors contributed to differences between actual and expected or standard[5] revenues, variances that help isolate these factors are calculated. To illustrate how revenue variances are calculated, let's return to our Sunbird Boat Company example. Market share, industry volume, and sales data for Sunbird's 15-foot boat line are as follows:

| | Expected (Standard) Sales Data | | | |
	Sales Price	Boat Sales	Total Market	Percent of Market
15-foot boats	$10,000	100	625 boats	16.00%

| | Actual Sales Data | | | |
	Sales Price	Boat Sales	Total Market	Percent of Market
15-foot boats	$10,500	90	480 boats	18.75%

---

4 Sales mix variance is a complex topic that we'll reserve for more advanced textbooks.
5 Again remember that the terms *standard* and *expected* are being used interchangeably in this analysis work.

International Manufacturing Corporation (IMC)
Segment-Margin Income Statement
September 2006
(in thousands of dollars)

| | Segments | | | | Segments | |
Edison Automobile	U.S. Operations	Far East Operations	European Operations	Far East Operations	Japanese Operations	Korean Operations
$10,000	$ 5,000	$ 2,000	$ 3,000	$ 2,000	$1,200	$ 800
$ (6,000)	$(2,900)	$(1,100)	$(2,000)	$(1,100)	$ (700)	$(400)
(1,300)	(700)	(300)	(300)	(300)	(170)	(130)
$ (7,300)	$(3,600)	$(1,400)	$(2,300)	$(1,400)	$ (870)	$(530)
$ 2,700	$ 1,400	$ 600	$ 700	$ 600	$ 330	$ 270
(500)	(250)	(100)	(150)	(70)	(60)	(10)
$ 2,200	$ 1,150	$ 500	$ 550	$ 530	$ 270	$ 260
(200)				(30)		
$ 2,000				$ 500		
20.0%	23.0%	25.0%	18.3%	25.0%	22.5%	32.5%

Now take a moment and study these data. In terms of Sunbird's revenue performance, what do you see? You should see both positive (favorable) and negative (unfavorable) results on sales-related issues. For instance, the sales price is higher than expected. If Sunbird can sell the same volume of boats at a higher sales price, then revenue is going to increase. This would mean that Sunbird had a favorable sales price variance. On the other hand, Sunbird actually sold fewer boats than expected, which means that it had an unfavorable sales volume variance. This sales volume variance could be explained in part due to the fact that the overall industry is selling fewer boats. This fact means that there was an unfavorable industry volume variance. However, Sunbird would have had even fewer sales but it was able to increase its share of the overall boat market (from 16% to 18.75%). Hence, Sunbird's unfavorable sales volume variance was offset by a favorable market share variance. Does this discussion of Sunbird's revenue performance make sense to you? If so, then you're getting a good feel for how variances are computed and what they signal to management. All that we need to do now is determine the total dollar value (i.e., size) of these revenue variances. The calculations for these four revenue variances are shown below.

sales price variance The difference between the actual price and the expected or standard price multiplied by the actual quantity sold; measures that part of the variance between expected and actual sales revenue that is due to differences between expected and actual prices of goods.

Sales Price Variance. The **sales price variance** indicates the impact of a different price than expected on the organization's revenues. Hence, the sales price variance is a function of the difference between the actual sales price and the expected (or standard) sales price. This difference is then multiplied by the actual quantity of goods or services sold in order to determine the financial impact of this variance on the company. Therefore, Sunbird's favorable price variance of $500 ($10,500 − $10,000) is multiplied by the 90 boats actually sold to determine a total sales price variance of $45,000 F.

sales volume variance The difference between the actual quantity and the expected quantity sold multiplied by the expected or standard price; measures that part of the variance between expected and actual sales revenue that is due to the difference between expected and actual volume of goods sold.

Sales Volume Variance. As the organization sells more or less than what was expected, this results in a **sales volume variance** that has an important and immediate effect on the organization's revenues. Sunbird has an unfavorable sales volume variance of ten boats. What is the economic impact on Sunbird of selling ten fewer boats? We need to be careful here. If you understand economics, then you understand one important factor that determines the volume of sales is the sales price (e.g., higher prices typically result in lower volumes and vice-versa).

However, there are other factors that affect the volume of sales (effort, advertising, competitors, technology, etc.). Nevertheless, in variance analysis it is important to isolate the effect of sales volume on revenues from the effect of sale prices on revenues. Therefore, similar to the approach used with materials quantity and labor efficiency variances, we multiply the underlying "real" volume variance of ten boats by the expected (or standard) sales price to calculate the financial impact on Sunbird of selling fewer boats; in other words, 10 boats × $10,000 = $100,000 U.

You can see how the calculations of the sales price variance and the sales volume variance are related in the illustration below.

Sales Price Variance and Sales Volume Variance

Actual quantity × Actual price	Actual quantity × Standard price	Expected quantity × Standard price
90 boats × $10,500 = $945,000	90 boats × $10,000 = $900,000	100 boats × $10,000 = $1,000,000

Sales price variance = $45,000 F   Sales volume variance = $100,000 U

As you work through these calculations, be sure to keep in mind that you already know which variances are favorable and unfavorable even before you make the calculations. As we discussed previously with cost variances, it's usually best to determine the nature of the variance (favorable versus unfavorable) before you calculate the actual size of the variance.

Market Share Variance.   The sales volume variance can be further analyzed by breaking it down into two underlying variances, one of which is the **market share variance**. One of the reasons that an organization has lower sales is because its share of the overall market for the goods and services it sells has declined. This probably seems like an obvious point to you, but sometimes an organization has an unfavorable sales volume even though its share of the overall market has increased! This happens when the overall market is shrinking. It is one thing to compete for sales in a growing market, and it is entirely another thing to compete in a shrinking market. The market share variance, coupled with the industry volume variance, helps the organization understand both of these important revenue performance issues. You can see in the illustration on the following page how the calculation is done for the market share variance. You can also see the underlying cause of this variance: the difference between the actual and expected market share.

market share variance The part of the sales volume variance that accounts for the difference between the actual market share of each product sold and the expected market share of each product sold.

Industry Volume Variance.   To a large extent, the organization can't individually control the size of the overall industry in which it competes for customers' business. For example, as consumer tastes change, the overall industry (or market) will shift in size. Alternative and complimentary products and services also impact the size of the market. And, these market changes generally have a very direct impact on the sales volume for each merchant in the market. The **industry volume variance** isolates the effect of the changing size of the industry from changes in the merchant's individual share of the industry's total sales. You can see from the original data for Sunbird that the overall industry has reduced in total size from 625 annual boat sales to 480. Holding all else equal (that is, Sunbird's expected market share and standard selling price), we can calculate the financial impact of the change in the industry. As you review the calculation for this variance in the illustration on the next page, you should note that we isolate the impact of industry volume on Sunbird's revenues by multiplying the change in industry volume (145 boats) by the expected market share (16%) and by the standard price ($10,000).

industry volume variance The part of the sales volume variance that accounts for the impact on sales revenue of an actual total market size that is different from the expected size.

There is one more thing to note before we finish the calculations for the market share and industry volume variances. If you inspect carefully the calculations in the earlier illustrations for the sales volume variance, market share variance, and industry volume variance, you may see that these calculations are very closely related. In fact, once you've calculated the sales volume variance, you only need to compute one more number to compute both the market share and industry volume variances. This is illustrated below.

Summarizing these variances, we see that the revenue variances for Sunbird's 15-foot boats are as follows:

Variances	Sales Price	Sales Volume	Total
15-foot boats	$ 45,000 F	$100,000 U	$ 55,000 U

Breakdown of Sales Volume Variance

	Market Share	Total Industry	Total
15-foot boats	$132,000 F	$232,000 U	$100,000 U

The sales price variance informs users whether actual sales prices were higher or lower than expected. The sales volume variance informs users whether the number of units sold was more or less than expected. The market share variance informs users whether the company's share of the total market was higher or lower than expected. Finally, the industry volume variance informs users whether the actual total market was higher or lower than expected.

Controlling Revenue Variances

Typically, sales prices are under the control of the marketing executives in the organization. These are the people who carefully establish the strategy of setting prices. On the other hand, the sales volume is largely under the control of the sales executives and sales teams in the organization. These are the people who work closely with customers to sell the product. As we've discussed above, several factors impact sales volume, including price (which is under the control of marketing) and the size of the total industry (which is very difficult to control at all).

Accounting for Revenue Variances

The nature of the sales volume variance makes accounting for revenue variances in the general ledger more challenging than the accounting for materials and labor variances. While the organization can recognize and record sales price variances throughout the reporting period, it really doesn't know if there is a sales volume variance until the end of the period. To handle this difficulty, some organizations set up a revenue control account at the beginning of the period and use it to immediately record revenues at the expected level. The control account is then used throughout the period to record actual revenue. Any remaining balance in the control account at the end of the period is equal to the difference between expected and actual revenue. This difference is used in the process of recording the revenue variances in a single entry at the end of the period as shown.

Caution

Remember that the industry volume variance and the market share variance combine to make up the sales volume variance. In other words, you either make a single accounting entry for the sales volume variance or you can make two separate entries for the industry volume variance and the market share variance. Managers who want more rather than less information for revenue management decisions will generally choose to report the two separate variances.

Industry Volume Variance		
(145 boats × 16% × $10,000)	232,000	
Market Share Variance		
(480 boats × 2.75% × $10,000)		132,000
Sales Price Variance (90 boats × $500)		45,000
Revenue Control		55,000

Use the revenue control account to establish the unfavorable industry volume variance to reflect an overall market decline of 145 boat sales; to establish the favorable market share variance to reflect a 2.75% increase; to establish the favorable sales price variance to reflect a $500 price increase.

STOP & THINK

Is it possible that a manager could be doing a poor job of managing revenues and revenue growth even though revenues were increasing from period to period?

Once the revenue variances have been established, they are immediately closed to Revenue. By closing these variances to Revenue, the expected revenues will be adjusted to actual revenues which are then reported on the income statement.

TO SUMMARIZE: Profit center managers are usually evaluated on both costs and revenues. The most common profit center measurement tool is the segment-margin income statement. This statement identifies both direct and indirect costs and charges only the direct costs to segments. Segment-margin income statements subdivide direct costs into their variable and fixed cost components. Costs in profit centers are analyzed and managed the same way they are in cost centers—using standard costing. Because profit center managers are also held responsible for revenues, a revenue variance analysis procedure is used that breaks down differences between actual and expected revenues into sales price variances and sales volume variances. Sales volume variances can be further broken down into market share variances and industry volume variances.

Evaluating Performance in Investment Centers

6 Use ROI and residual income analysis to explain how performance is controlled in investment centers.

An investment center was defined earlier as an organizational unit in which a manager has responsibility for costs, revenues, and assets. Overall, companies would be considered investment centers, as would some independent segments of decentralized companies. For example, the Acme Computer and Edison Automobile subsidiaries of IMC (see Exhibit 1) would probably both be investment centers. Officers of such segments are responsible for acquiring and managing the assets required to manufacture and market their products, as well as for managing the revenues and costs related to those products. The assets include inventory, accounts receivable, and long-term operating assets such as equipment and delivery trucks. On the other hand, Edison's Japanese operation could be considered a profit center if all asset management decisions are handled by Far East operations. Further, the Manufacturing center for Japanese operations is likely a cost center since it doesn't control sales.

In business, the distinction between profit and investment centers often becomes blurred or even nonexistent. Many companies refer to segments as profit centers when they are really investment centers. Nevertheless, because the distinction between profit and investment centers is important for defining responsibilities and determining how performance will be evaluated, we discuss them separately.

There are several methods of evaluating the performance of an investment center. When a segment operates almost as a separate company, the rate of return on invested assets and the residual income are usually measured.

Return on Investment (ROI)

return on investment (ROI) A measure of operating performance and efficiency in utilizing assets; computed in its simplest form by dividing net income by total assets.

As you will recall, we introduced management accounting in an earlier chapter by describing how the management team at DUPONT used **return on investment (ROI)** (sometimes called return on total assets[6]) to manage their company to success in the early 1900s. ROI is a measure of how much has been earned on the assets of a company; it is equal to net income divided by total assets. For example, if a company earned $1,000 on $10,000 of assets for one year, its ROI would be $1,000 \div $10,000, or 10%.

Because an investment center operates as if it were an independent company, its performance can also be evaluated using ROI. In calculating the ROI for an investment center, however, management must be sure to consider only the assets, revenues, and costs controlled by that center. In other words, assets used and costs incurred for the benefit of several investment centers should not be included in the calculation. To stress this concept, we will restate the basic ROI formula as:

$$\text{Investment center ROI} = \frac{\text{Investment center income}}{\text{Investment center average assets}}$$

Generally, when an investment center's ROI is analyzed, this formula is divided into its components—the operations performance (sometimes called profit margin) and asset turnover ratios—as follows:

$$\text{Profit margin} \times \text{Asset turnover} = \text{ROI}$$

$$\frac{\text{Net income}}{\text{Revenue}} \times \frac{\text{Revenue}}{\text{Average total assets}} = \frac{\text{Net income}}{\text{Average total assets}}$$

Net income, which is a function of costs or expenses and revenues, and revenues were considered in profit centers. The ROI formula expands the use of cost and revenue measures to

---

6 In this chapter, we will use the term *ROI* instead of *return on total assets* because it is more commonly used in management decision making. To be consistent with how we've calculated ROI in other chapters, we will use average total assets instead of ending total assets (although in actual practice, management teams in some organizations may choose to use ending total assets). Average total assets is generally computed by adding the assets balances at the beginning and end of the year, and then dividing the sum in half.

also include measures of assets. Thus, when combined with cost and revenue variance analysis, ROI is an effective tool in evaluating investment centers where management has responsibility for assets as well as profits. It is this ROI calculation that investors commonly use to evaluate companies in which they are considering investing.

Clearly, in the above calculations, we could have eliminated the two revenue figures because they cancel each other out, making ROI equal to net income divided by average total assets. However, including revenue draws attention to the important concept that ROI is a function of both operating performance and asset turnover.

The expanded formula shown above helps us identify the three ways an investment center can improve its ROI: (1) it can decrease costs to increase its **profit margin (operating performance) ratio** (net income divided by revenue), (2) it can decrease assets to increase its **asset turnover ratio** (revenue divided by average total assets), or (3) it can increase revenue with a corresponding increase in net income. An investment center requiring a major investment in assets (such as a steel mill) will necessarily have a low asset turnover and will therefore have to rely primarily on a higher operating performance to increase its return. An investment center with few operating assets (such as a grocery store) has a more rapid asset turnover and can sustain a lower profit margin ratio while still earning an attractive ROI. For example, a grocery store might make only 2 cents profit per dollar of product sold, but its asset turnover of 12 times a year makes its ROI 24%. A steel mill with an asset turnover of 2 times a year would have to earn 12 cents per dollar of sales to produce an ROI of 24%.

To illustrate the three ways of increasing ROI, we will assume that Acme Computer has revenue of $10,000,000, profit (segment) margin of $1,000,000, and average total assets of $5,000,000. The ROI is:

$$\text{Profit margin} \times \text{Asset turnover} = \text{ROI}$$

$$\frac{\$1,000,000}{\$10,000,000} \times \frac{\$10,000,000}{\$5,000,000} = \text{ROI}$$

$$10\% \times 2 = 20\%$$

The following examples show how each of the three alternatives increases ROI:

1. Increase ROI by reducing expenses by $400,000, providing a profit margin of $1,400,000:

$$\frac{\$1,400,000}{\$10,000,000} \times \frac{\$10,000,000}{\$5,000,000} = \text{ROI}$$

$$14\% \times 2 = 28\%$$

2. Increase ROI by reducing average total assets to $4,000,000:

$$\frac{\$1,000,000}{\$10,000,000} \times \frac{\$10,000,000}{\$4,000,000} = \text{ROI}$$

$$10\% \times 2.5 = 25\%$$

3. Increase ROI by increasing revenue to $12,000,000 (assume that profits increase proportionately):[7]

$$\frac{\$1,200,000}{\$12,000,000} \times \frac{\$12,000,000}{\$5,000,000} = \text{ROI}$$

$$10\% \times 2.4 = 24\%$$

---

7 As discussed earlier in the cost-volume-profit chapter, because of the concept of operating leverage, profits are likely to increase more than proportionately when revenue rises. When revenue increases 10%, fixed costs may remain the same. The result is that both the operating performance and asset turnover ratios are likely to increase when revenue goes up. We are ignoring these C-V-P considerations in order to keep the example simple.

profit margin (operating performance) ratio An overall measure of the profitability of operations during a period; computed by dividing net income by revenue.

asset turnover ratio An overall measure of how effectively assets are used during a period; computed by dividing revenue by average total assets.

Although ROI is an effective way of evaluating managers of investment centers, it has certain drawbacks. For example, assume that an investment center currently has an ROI of 22%, but the company has an overall ROI of only 16%. If a new project or investment that promises a return of 19% becomes available to the investment center manager, it might be rejected because the center's ROI would be reduced, even though the company's overall ROI would be increased.

Residual Income

residual income The amount of net income earned above a specified minimum rate of return on assets; used to evaluate investment centers.

Although ROI is widely used to evaluate investment centers, because of its drawbacks, some companies use a closely related measure called **residual income**, which is the amount of net income an investment center is able to earn above a certain minimum rate of return on assets. The formula for residual income is as follows:

Net income − (Minimum required rate of return × Average total assets) = Residual income

To illustrate, let's return to Acme Computer and calculate its residual income. Assuming that the specified minimum rate of return on assets at IMC is 15%, Acme Computer needs to earn at least $750,000 (15% × $5,000,000 average total assets) before it can report any residual income. We then compute Acme Computer's residual income as follows:

$1,000,000 segment margin − $750,000 minimum return on assets = $250,000 residual income

To further illustrate why many companies prefer to use residual income over ROI for evaluating investment center performance, assume that Acme Computer has an opportunity to invest $1,200,000 in a new project that will generate a return of 16% ($192,000 per year). If Acme Computer's manager is being evaluated on ROI, she would probably reject this investment opportunity because, as the following analysis shows, it would reduce the division's overall ROI from 20% to 19.2%.

	Without the New Investment	The New Investment	With the New Investment
Total assets	$5,000,000	$1,200,000	$6,200,000
Segment margin	$1,000,000	$ 192,000	$1,192,000
ROI	20%	16%	19.2%

On the other hand, if the manager is being evaluated on residual income (with a minimum rate of return of 15%), she would probably be more positive about the project because it increases residual income from $250,000 to $262,000.

	Without the New Investment	The New Investment	With the New Investment
Total assets	$5,000,000	$1,200,000	$6,200,000
Segment margin	$1,000,000	$ 192,000	$1,192,000
Less the minimum rate of return ...	750,000*	180,000**	930,000
Residual income	$ 250,000	$ 12,000	$ 262,000

*$5,000,000 × 15% = $750,000
**$1,200,000 × 15% = $180,000

Whether or not the investment should actually be made also depends on several other factors, including what other alternatives are or will be available. The advantage of residual income is that it encourages managers to make as much profit as possible rather than merely achieving a certain ROI; this means making investments that benefit not only their centers but also the company as a whole.

TO SUMMARIZE: Managers of investment centers are usually held responsible for costs, revenues, and assets. The most common performance measures used in investment centers are ROI and residual income. ROI is a function of both operating performance and asset turnover.

Residual income is the amount of income left over after a certain minimum rate of return has been earned on assets. Both ROI and residual income must be used with care because they can encourage managers to maximize short-run profits at the expense of long-term profitability.

Earlier in the chapter, you were introduced to standard costing as a way to evaluate performance in cost centers and were shown how standard costing can be used to compute variances for materials and labor. Information relating to these material and labor variances can be used by decision makers to evaluate the acquisition and use of these important resources. In this expanded material section, we introduce you to the variances associated with manufacturing overhead costs. While several of the computations associated with overhead variances are similar to those used for materials and labor, they are generally more complicated. As a result, interpreting the results and assigning responsibility must be done with caution.

Variable Manufacturing Overhead Variances in Cost Centers

7 Compute and interpret variable overhead cost variances.

Manufacturing overhead is the third type of product cost that must be controlled and accounted for. In this section we will cover variable overhead. Fixed overhead will be covered in the next section.

Measuring and Controlling Variable Manufacturing Overhead Costs

Variable manufacturing overhead includes such costs as indirect materials, indirect labor, utilities, and repairs and maintenance. Like direct materials and direct labor, variable manufacturing overhead is measured and controlled by establishing standard costs, measuring actual costs, analyzing variances from standard, and reporting the variances to managers so they can take necessary corrective action.

Identifying Variable Overhead Elements, Cost Drivers, and Per-Unit Costs

The first step in controlling variable manufacturing overhead is to study the behavior of each overhead cost to determine whether it is fixed, variable, or mixed. (You will recall that we analyzed cost behavior previously in the cost-volume-profit chapter.) The second step is to develop a cost driver for each variable manufacturing overhead element that relates the variable manufacturing overhead cost to specific activities or volume changes. In a later chapter, we will introduce you to new product costing methods, including activity-based costing, where multiple cost drivers are used. For simplicity in illustrating variable overhead variances, we will assume that variable manufacturing overhead costs vary with direct labor hours. However, you should be aware that, where possible, costs are assigned to activities based on cost drivers that reflect the actual usage of costs for each activity. Thus, instead of using one cost driver, such as direct labor hours, a company might identify different cost drivers for each type of variable overhead cost.

To illustrate the calculation of variable manufacturing cost variances using direct labor hours as the cost driver, we will return again to our Sunbird Boat Company example. Assume that, for Sunbird, direct labor hours worked fluctuate between 6,500 and 8,500 hours each month. At the beginning of the year, Sunbird's management team and accountants analyzed the company's cost behavior patterns over this relevant range to create an annual budget. Based on their sales budget, they also established a production budget to produce 95 15-foot boats.[8] As you recall from its standard cost card (Exhibit 3 on page 1090), Sunbird allows 80 standard direct labor hours for each 15-foot boat produced. This means that 7,600 direct labor hours (95 boats × 80 standard hours) were originally estimated to be used in the current year. These data were then used to establish standard variable manufacturing overhead rates as shown below:

	Annual Budgeted Costs		Divided by the Total Standard Direct Labor Hours Allowed		Variable Manufacturing Overhead Rate
Indirect materials	$11,400	÷	7,600 hours	=	$1.50 per hour
Indirect labor	41,800	÷	7,600 hours	=	5.50 per hour
Utilities	7,600	÷	7,600 hours	=	1.00 per hour
Variable manufacturing overhead . . .	$60,800				$8.00 per hour

Caution

Be sure you understand that in our Sunbird example overhead costs are applied on the basis of *standard direct labor hours allowed*, and not on the actual direct labor hours used. Hence, regardless of how many hours are actually used to produce a boat, variable manufacturing overhead of $640 is applied ($8.00 × 80 hours). This is the approach used by most companies that follow a standard cost accounting system.

As you can see, by summing these amounts, Sunbird developed a total standard variable manufacturing overhead rate of $8.00 per direct labor hour. Since Sunbird allows 80 standard direct labor hours for each 15-foot boat produced, it applies $640.00 to each boat produced ($8.00 × 80 hours).

Variable Manufacturing Overhead Variances

Let's now illustrate how variances are calculated for variable manufacturing overhead costs. You'll recall from our work with direct labor variances that the Sunbird Boat Company actually used 7,092 direct labor hours to produce 90 15-foot boats during the year. Given that only 90 boats were actually produced (rather than the 95 boats originally budgeted to be produced), Sunbird Boat Company should have used 7,200 direct labor hours (as calculated in the table below). Sunbird's end-of-year results, including the total variable manufacturing overhead costs actually incurred, are summarized as follows:

Caution

The 7,600 direct labor hours *budgeted* at the beginning of the year are not to be confused with the 7,200 hours *allowed for actual production* by the end of the year. Similarly, do not confuse the $60,800 variable manufacturing overhead costs *budgeted* at the beginning of the year with the $57,600 variable manufacturing overhead costs *allowed for actual production* by the end of the year.

Boats produced	90
Direct labor hours used	7,092
Standard direct labor hours for boats produced (80 hours × 90 boats)	7,200
Standard variable manufacturing overhead for boats produced (7,200 hours × $8)	$57,600
Actual variable manufacturing overhead costs incurred:	
Indirect materials	$ 9,373
Indirect labor	42,710
Utilities	8,199
Total variable manufacturing overhead costs	$60,282

8 These are the same production and sales numbers we created in the previous chapter on operational budgeting. In fact, all standard costs and budgets used in the Sunbird Boat Company example in this chapter are based on data established in the operational budgeting chapter. You're encouraged to review the previous chapter if needed to better understand these standard (or budgeted) costs.

As you can see in the table on the previous page, on the basis of 7,200 standard direct labor hours allowed to produce an actual output of 90 boats, the standard cost allowed for variable manufacturing overhead is $57,600 (7,200 hours × $8.00 per hour). The difference between the $60,282 actually incurred and the $57,600 standard cost allowed is the amount of over- or underapplied variable overhead. In this example, variable manufacturing overhead has been underapplied by $2,682 ($60,282 − $57,600). As with direct materials and direct labor, the total variable manufacturing overhead variance is separated into two major variances: spending and efficiency. The spending and efficiency variances are computed as follows:

Variable Manufacturing Overhead Variances		
Actual amount spent	**AH × SR** Actual hours of input × Standard rate	**SHA × SR** Standard hours allowed for actual output × Standard rate
$60,282	7,092 hours × $8.00 = $56,736	7,200 hours × $8.00 = $57,600
	Variable overhead spending variance $60,282 − $56,736 = $3,546 U	**Variable overhead efficiency variance** $8.00 × (7,200 hours − 7,092 hours) = $864 F

variable manufacturing overhead spending variance The difference between actual variable manufacturing overhead incurred and the amount that should have been incurred based on the actual activity used to assign overhead costs to production.

Variable Manufacturing Overhead Spending Variance. The **variable manufacturing overhead spending variance** ($3,546 U) is the difference between the actual variable manufacturing overhead costs incurred ($60,282) and the amount that should have been incurred at the actual activity level, $56,736 (7,092 direct labor hours × $8.00 standard rate).

Because manufacturing overhead contains several different cost items, it is possible to compute a spending variance for each variable overhead item. This analysis helps managers determine which costs are largely responsible for creating the variances. For Sunbird Boat Company, the analysis would be as follows:

	Actual Costs	Actual Hours of Input × Standard Rate	Spending Variance
Indirect materials	$ 9,373	7,092 hours × $1.50 = $10,638	$1,265 F
Indirect labor	42,710	7,092 hours × $5.50 = 39,006	3,704 U
Utilities	8,199	7,092 hours × $1.00 = 7,092	1,107 U
	$60,282	$56,736	$3,546 U

variable manufacturing overhead efficiency variance The difference between the standard variable manufacturing overhead for the actual activity level and standard variable manufacturing overhead for the standard activity level allowed. This variance effectively measures the efficiency of the underlying activity used to assign variable manufacturing overhead costs; it does not measure the efficiency of how variable manufacturing overhead costs are used.

Looking at the spending variance column, we see a $1,265 favorable variance for indirect materials, a $3,704 unfavorable variance for indirect labor, and a $1,107 unfavorable variance for utilities. The favorable variance for indirect materials means that less was spent than was expected for the actual hours worked, indicating either that spending is in control or that the standards are too high. The unfavorable variances indicate that spending exceeded the standard and that there may be a problem. In both cases, managers and others responsible for any significant variances (favorable or unfavorable) should be asked to explain the reasons for their existence. Of course, this example assumes that variable overhead is a function of direct labor hours. If direct labor hours is not a good cost driver of (i.e., does not influence) variable overhead costs, the variances are highly suspect.

Variable Manufacturing Overhead Efficiency Variance. The $864 favorable **variable manufacturing overhead efficiency variance** is the standard variable overhead rate times the difference between the standard and actual activity levels [$8.00 × (7,200 standard direct labor hours allowed − 7,092 actual direct labor hours)]. When direct labor hours are used as the basis for assigning manufacturing overhead, the efficiency variance simply indicates whether the standard number of hours allowed for production are more (favorable) or less (unfavorable) than the actual hours used for production. As you will recall, the same relationship was used on page 1097 in computing the direct labor efficiency variance. Hence, since Sunbird's direct labor efficiency variance is favorable ($1,620), the variable manufacturing overhead efficiency variance is also favorable ($864). Conversely, of course, an unfavorable direct labor efficiency variance would have produced an unfavorable variable manufacturing overhead efficiency variance. The only difference between the value for the direct labor efficiency variance and the variable manufacturing overhead efficiency variance is the rate used in computing each variance. What this means is that the variable manufacturing overhead efficiency variance really doesn't describe the efficiency of using variable manufacturing overhead; rather, it reports the efficiency of how the manufacturing allocation basis is being used. Since Sunbird is using direct labor hours to assign manufacturing overhead, the variable manufacturing overhead variance doesn't really provide any additional information for management beyond that already provided by the direct labor efficiency variance. As a result, the manager responsible for the control of direct labor hours should be credited for Sunbird's favorable manufacturing overhead efficiency variance because the variance is a measure of the efficiency with which direct labor is used. (Again, it is important to note that we are assuming that direct labor hours is an appropriate cost driver at Sunbird Boat Company for variable manufacturing overhead costs.)

The only reason for computing the variable manufacturing overhead efficiency variance at Sunbird Boat Company is to be able to account for over- or underapplied manufacturing overhead and close the amount to Cost of Goods Sold. We'll talk more about over- or underapplied manufacturing overhead in the next section.

> **TO SUMMARIZE:** Cost drivers that relate to individual overhead items are used to relate overhead costs to activities. Standard overhead costs are then computed for each variable overhead item to determine a standard variable rate that is used in applying variable manufacturing overhead to each unit of product. This rate is also used in the process of analyzing variable manufacturing overhead variances. The total variable manufacturing overhead variance can be segregated into two variances: spending and efficiency. The variable manufacturing overhead spending variance measures the difference between the costs actually incurred and the amount that should have been incurred at the actual activity level. The variable manufacturing overhead efficiency variance is the difference between variable manufacturing overhead costs at the actual and standard activity levels. Because the spending variance highlights the differences between actual costs incurred and standard amounts for individual manufacturing overhead items, it is generally the more useful overhead variance to analyze for control purposes. The variable manufacturing overhead efficiency variance doesn't really report on the efficiency of variable manufacturing overhead costs, but on the efficiency of the *activity used to allocate* variable manufacturing overhead costs.

Fixed Manufacturing Overhead Variances in Cost Centers

8 Compute and interpret fixed overhead cost variances.

The final product cost to account for is fixed manufacturing overhead. Fixed manufacturing overhead includes such costs as rent, insurance, depreciation, staff and supervisor salaries, and taxes. This cost is unique among the product costs. Since direct materials and direct labor are generally characterized as variable costs similar to variable manufacturing overhead, the process of "controlling" fixed manufacturing overhead is different from the other costs we've studied in this chapter. Nevertheless, fixed manufacturing overhead is a very significant cost in most organizations that requires careful management attention.

Measuring and Controlling Fixed Manufacturing Overhead Costs

Reporting on how well fixed manufacturing overhead costs are controlled is actually a fairly straightforward process. Because these costs are fixed in total, measuring variances around these costs is simply a matter of comparing the original budget with the total fixed overhead costs that were actually spent. To demonstrate, let's return once more to our Sunbird Boat Company example. Similar to the variable manufacturing overhead budget established at the beginning of the year, Sunbird's management team and accountants also created a fixed manufacturing overhead budget. Then, in order to subsequently allocate these costs to boats as they are produced during the year, Sunbird created standard fixed manufacturing overhead rates using an approach similar to that used to create standard variable manufacturing overhead rates. This process is shown below:

	Annual Budgeted Costs		Divided by the Total Standard Direct Labor Hours Allowed	Fixed Manufacturing Overhead Rate
Property taxes	$ 3,040	÷	7,600 hours	= $ 0.40 per hour
Insurance	3,600	÷	7,600 hours	= 0.47 per hour
Depreciation on the plant	66,000	÷	7,600 hours	= 8.68 per hour
Supervisors' salaries	90,000	÷	7,600 hours	= 11.84 per hour
Fixed manufacturing overhead . . .	$162,640			$21.40 per hour*

*Rounded.

As you compare this chart to the similar chart we created earlier for variable manufacturing overhead, be sure to bear in mind that we're dealing with fixed costs here. Similar to the $8.00 variable manufacturing overhead rate created earlier, the $21.40 fixed manufacturing overhead rate above will be used by Sunbird's accountants to allocate manufacturing overhead to production (again, remember that we discussed the overhead allocation process previously in an earlier chapter on product cost flows). Hence, Sunbird applies $1,712 ($21.40 × 80 hours) in fixed manufacturing overhead costs to each 15-foot boat produced. In addition, you'll remember from the previous section on variable manufacturing overhead that Sunbird uses the variable manufacturing overhead rate of $8.00 to apply $640 ($8.00 × 80 hours) to each boat produced. Sunbird also uses the $8.00 rate to measure expected variable manufacturing overhead costs based on actual production. On the other hand, Sunbird's accountants don't use the $21.40 rate to measure expected fixed manufacturing overhead costs. These costs are fixed and are expected to be $162,640, regardless of the level of boats actually produced.

Fixed Manufacturing Overhead Variances

During the year, Sunbird incurred the following costs:

Actual fixed manufacturing overhead costs incurred:

Property taxes	$ 4,015
Insurance	2,986
Depreciation on the plant	65,533
Supervisors' salaries	83,490
Total actual fixed manufacturing overhead costs	$156,024

These costs, combined with Sunbird's fixed manufacturing overhead budget and the standard fixed manufacturing overhead rate (also known as the predetermined manufacturing overhead rate), are used by Sunbird's accountants to create the two variances in this illustration:

Fixed Manufacturing Overhead Variances

Actual amount spent	Budgeted amount (used to establish the predetermined allocation rate)	**SHA × SR** Standard hours allowed for actual output × Standard rate
$156,024	$162,640; $162,640 ÷ 7,600 hours = $21.40 per hour	7,200 hours × $21.40 = $154,080

Fixed overhead budget variance
$162,640 − $156,024 = $6,616 F

Volume variance
$21.40 × (7,600 hours − 7,200 hours) = $8,560 U

---

fixed manufacturing overhead budget variance The difference between actual fixed manufacturing overhead incurred and the standard (or budgeted) fixed manufacturing overhead established at the beginning of the reporting period.

Fixed Manufacturing Overhead Budget Variance. The $6,616 favorable **fixed manufacturing overhead budget variance** is the difference between what was actually spent and the original budget. Hence, it is a simple matter to create a detailed budget variance report for each fixed overhead item. This analysis helps managers determine which costs have the biggest impact on the budget variance. For Sunbird Boat Company, the analysis would be as follows:

	Actual Costs	Budgeted Costs	Budget Variance
Property taxes	$ 4,015	$ 3,040	$ 975 U
Insurance	2,986	3,600	614 F
Depreciation on the plant	65,533	66,000	467 F
Supervisors' salaries	83,490	90,000	6,510 F
	$156,024	$162,640	$6,616 F

A quick review of the table above reveals that supervisors' salaries are the largest source of the favorable fixed manufacturing overhead budget variance. Generally, one would expect little change in fixed costs unless a decision is made by management to make a direct change to a cost item. For example, buying or selling property, changing the insurance contract, or adjusting the depreciation schedule will affect the actual fixed costs incurred. Apparently, Sunbird's management team made little change to these items. However, there was apparently a big adjustment in the salaries, perhaps due to a shift in personnel serving in management roles.

volume variance The difference between actual production output and the expected (or budgeted) production output established at the beginning of the reporting period. This difference is then converted into a dollar number by multiplying it by the standard fixed manufacturing overhead costs per unit.

Volume Variance. The $8,560 unfavorable **volume variance** shown in the illustration above is a variance unlike any other we've studied in this chapter. Every variance studied thus far has been an *input* variance; that is, it has been either a variance on how much was spent on the input (materials price, labor rate, variable overhead spending, fixed overhead budget) or a variance on how much of the input was used (materials quantity, labor efficiency, variable overhead efficiency). The volume variance is an *output* variance and measures the difference between expected and actual production volumes.

In the case of Sunbird Boat Company, you will recall that at the beginning of the year management expected to produce 95 15-foot boats. However, at the end of the year the company had only produced 90 boats. This is an unfavorable volume variance, and the amount of that variance is five boats. The problem in a standard costing system is that you can't debit or credit "five boats" into the accounting system. To record this variance requires that the difference between expected and actual output volume be changed into a dollar amount. This is done

Caution

Remember that overhead costs are applied on the basis of *standard direct labor hours allowed,* and not on the actual direct labor hours used. Sunbird will apply $1,712 in fixed manufacturing overhead to each boat produced *regardless* of how many hours are actually used to produce the boat.

FYI:

Managers who understand how to use the volume variance as a performance measure know that this dollar figure doesn't really indicate the volume of costs flowing into or out of their organization. They know that if they divide this number by the predetermined fixed manufacturing overhead rate, they can then see exactly how many units were actually produced above or below the expected level of production.

using the fixed manufacturing overhead rate of $21.40 per direct labor hour. Using the production standards set in its standard cost card, Sunbird allocates $1,712 (80 standard direct labor hours allowed × $21.40 per direct labor hour) in fixed manufacturing overhead to each boat produced. (Remember that Sunbird established the $21.40 rate based on an expectation of producing 95 boats and uses the rate to allocate the budgeted fixed costs of $162,640.) Because Sunbird only produced 90 boats, it only allocated $154,080 ($1,712 × 90 boats). In other words, Sunbird underapplied its fixed manufacturing overhead costs by $8,560 ($162,640 − $154,080), which results in an unfavorable volume variance of $8,560. Another way of calculating this volume variance would be to simply multiply the volume difference of five boats by the $1,712 per-boat application rate.

Accounting for Manufacturing Overhead Variances. The four manufacturing overhead variances we've described in the expanded materials section of this chapter all combine together to form the total over- or underapplied manufacturing overhead in the organization. At the end of the current year, Sunbird's manufacturing overhead account appears as shown below:

Manufacturing Overhead

(Actual costs)		(Applied costs)	
Indirect materials	9,373	57,600	applied variable costs
Indirect labor	42,710	154,080	applied fixed costs
Utilities	8,199		
Property taxes	4,015		
Insurance	2,986		
Depreciation—plant	65,533		
Supervisors' salaries	83,490		
	216,306	211,680	
Balance (underapplied)	4,626		

In a normal cost system, we would close out the underapplied overhead directly to Cost of Goods Sold with the following journal entry:

Cost of Goods Sold	4,626	
Manufacturing Overhead		4,626
To close the balance in Manufacturing Overhead and adjust		
the balance in Cost of Goods Sold up to the actual amount.		

However, since Sunbird uses a standard cost system, it recognizes variances in its accounting system and then uses those variances to adjust standard costs and revenues to actual costs and revenues for the income statement. Consistent with the accounting for variances we've done in this chapter, Sunbird will use the underapplied overhead to recognize the four manufacturing overhead variances as shown below:

Variable Overhead Spending Variance	3,546	
Volume Variance	8,560	
Variable Overhead Efficiency Variance		864
Fixed Overhead Budget Variance		6,616
Manufacturing Overhead		4,626
To close the balance in Manufacturing Overhead and recognize		
the manufacturing overhead variances.		

These overhead variances are subsequently closed to Cost of Goods Sold, which will result in an adjustment that increases Cost of Goods Sold by $4,626.

STOP & THINK

As you have worked through the accounting for manufacturing overhead variances, do you see that applied manufacturing overhead is the same number as standard overhead allowed for actual output? A rule of thumb to use in accounting for overhead variances is that when overhead is underapplied, the total of the four overhead variances will be unfavorable (and vice versa). What kind of adjustment to Cost of Goods Sold is required when manufacturing overhead is underapplied? When manufacturing overhead is overapplied? Do you see why managers and accountants think of underapplied overhead as unfavorable and overapplied overhead as favorable?

TO SUMMARIZE: The process of reporting and controlling fixed manufacturing overhead costs is unique among product costs due to the fact that the other product costs are considered to be variable. As a result, the fixed manufacturing overhead budget variance is a fairly straightforward calculation that is essentially measuring the difference between the original budget amount and what was actually spent for fixed manufacturing overhead. Like the variable manufacturing overhead spending variance, the fixed manufacturing overhead budget variance can be further scrutinized by breaking it down into its individual cost components. On the other hand, the volume variance, which is associated with fixed manufacturing overhead, doesn't really report at all on how fixed manufacturing overhead costs are being used. Instead, the volume variance is an output measure that reports on the difference between expected production volume and actual production volume. The standard (predetermined) fixed overhead rate is used to translate the difference in production output units into a dollar number that can be entered into the standard cost accounting system. The volume variance can then be combined with the fixed manufacturing overhead budget variance and the variable manufacturing overhead spending and efficiency variances to account for over- or underapplied overhead.

review of learning objectives

1 Explain why control is such an important activity in the management process. Today, information about how efficiently and effectively an organization is operating is easily accessible worldwide. For a company to survive in this information age, it must deliver the highest-quality products to its customers at the least possible price in the shortest amount of time. The only way an organization can continue to improve on these dimensions is to control well its performance on key processes and products and to identify areas for improvement. This need for continuous improvement makes management control more important than ever before.

2 Describe the responsibility accounting concept and identify the three types of organizational control units. Most companies are divided into segments with responsibilities assigned to segment managers. These segments may be defined in terms of product line, geographic area, or function, for example. In a centralized organization, top management makes most of the important operating decisions; in a decentralized organization, decision-making authority is delegated to lower-level managers as well. The current trend is toward decentralization because it usually results in better, more informed decisions.

With responsibility accounting, managers are held accountable for the costs, revenues, or assets over which they have control. The three types of responsibility centers are cost, profit, and investment. Cost centers are usually found at relatively low levels in the organization, and the managers are held accountable for the costs they incur. Profit and investment centers are found at higher levels, and the managers are held accountable for the profits or the return on investments in assets they generate.

3 Describe standard costing and the basic variance analysis model. Traditionally, performance has been evaluated in cost centers using standard costs. A standard cost system involves setting standard (predetermined) costs that serve as a benchmark for judging what actual costs should be. Standard costs are usually expressed as the per-unit cost of materials, labor, and manufacturing overhead and are used by managers for planning, implementing, and controlling decisions. Standard costs are developed on the basis of careful analysis using the experience of many types of staff, including engineers, supervisors, accountants, purchasing agents, and others. Standard costs have a price component and a quantity component. A comparison of actual and standard costs usually results in two variances: a price (rate) variance and a quantity (usage) variance. In a process referred to as management by exception, significant variances alert management to specific problem areas that require corrective action.

A standard cost system is designed to accumulate actual costs, to compare actual and standard costs to identify variances, and to report operating results (including variances) to management for review and for corrective action when significant variances occur. Manufacturing firms make extensive use of standard costing systems, although these kinds of accounting systems are being increasingly used by service and merchandising organizations as well. While standard cost systems have specific advantages and disadvantages, many organizations have found that the control and insight provided by these systems are worth the effort and investment.

4 **Use materials and labor cost variance analysis to explain how performance is controlled in cost centers.** Materials variances are usually called price variances and quantity variances. The materials price variance reflects the extent to which the actual price varies from the standard price for the actual quantity of materials purchased or used. The materials quantity variance measures the extent to which the quantity of materials used varies from the standard quantity allowed for the achieved level of production. Labor variances are called rate variances and efficiency variances. The labor rate variance is the difference between the actual and the standard labor rates multiplied by the actual hours worked. The labor efficiency variance is the difference between actual and standard hours multiplied by the standard wage rate. Unfavorable variances are recorded in the standard cost system with debit accounting entries, while favorable variances are recorded with credit accounting entries.

5 **Use revenue variance analysis to explain how performance is controlled in profit centers.** Profit center managers are responsible for revenues as well as costs. The best measure of performance in a profit center is a segment-margin income statement, which distinguishes between indirect and direct costs and reports a segment margin that is controllable by segment managers. In profit centers, costs are analyzed in the same way they are in cost centers. Revenues are analyzed by calculating sales price and sales volume variances. The sales volume variance is further broken down into market share and industry volume variances.

6 **Use ROI and residual income analysis to explain how performance is controlled in investment centers.** Investment centers are usually found at higher levels in an organization than profit centers. The managers of investment centers are responsible for costs, revenues, and assets. Commonly used measures of investment center performance are return on investment (ROI) and residual income. ROI is calculated by dividing net income by total assets. An investment center can improve its ROI by (1) decreasing its costs to increase its operating performance ratio, (2) decreasing its assets to increase its asset turnover ratio, or (3) increasing revenue with a corresponding increase in income or segment margin. Residual income is the amount of segment margin an investment center is able to earn above a certain minimum rate of return on assets. The problem with both ROI and residual income is that they tend to encourage managers to make decisions that increase short-run profits but may diminish profits in the long run.

7 **Compute and interpret variable overhead cost variances.** Using an appropriate cost driver, standard costs are computed for each variable overhead item to determine a standard variable overhead rate that is used in applying variable manufacturing overhead to each unit of product. The variable overhead variances may be divided into spending and efficiency variances. The spending variance measures the difference between the costs actually incurred and the amount that should have been incurred at the attained level of activity. The efficiency variance, however, doesn't report on how variable overhead costs were used; rather, this variance reports on the efficient or inefficient use of the underlying activity basis. Hence, if direct labor hours are used to apply variable manufacturing overhead, then the variable manufacturing overhead efficiency variance effectively provides the same information as the direct labor efficiency variance.

8 **Compute and interpret fixed overhead cost variances.** The variances related to fixed manufacturing overhead can be divided into a budget variance and a volume variance. Because fixed manufacturing overhead represents the fixed production costs in the organization, the variance analysis process is different from the variance analysis done for direct materials, direct labor, and variable manufacturing overhead. The fixed manufacturing overhead budget variance is simply the difference between budgeted fixed costs and actual fixed costs. On the other hand, the volume variance is a measure of the difference between expected and actual production output. The number of production units that represent this difference is multiplied by the standard fixed manufacturing overhead per unit to compute the volume variance. By converting the volume variance into a dollar-measured number, this variance can then be combined with the other three overhead variances to account for over- or underapplied manufacturing overhead.

key terms & concepts

review problems

Materials, Labor, and Revenue Variances

The standard cost sheet for Kendra Box Company shows the following unit costs for direct materials and direct labor for each box made:

Direct materials (4 board feet of lumber @ $2)	$ 8
Direct labor (2 standard hours @ $6)	12
Total standard materials and labor costs per box	$20

During the month of October, 83,000 board feet of lumber were used to produce 20,000 boxes, and the following actual costs were incurred:

Lumber purchased (100,000 board feet @ $2.20)	$220,000
Direct labor (39,600 hours @ $6.05)	239,580

The standard selling price per box is $52. The overall market for the box industry is expected to be 420,000 boxes per month. Kendra's expected share of this market is 12%. Actual revenue results for October are as follows:

Actual revenue (47,355 boxes sold at $53 per box)	$2,509,815
Total boxes sold in the box industry during October	430,500 boxes

Required:
Compute the materials, labor, and revenue variances.

Solution
Materials Variances
The price variance is computed when the lumber is purchased, and the quantity variance is computed when the lumber is used.

(continued)

Materials price variance:

Purchase price per board foot for 100,000 feet	$ 2.20	
Standard price per board foot	(2.00)	
Difference	$ 0.20	U
Feet of lumber purchased	×100,000	
Total price variance	$ 20,000	U

Materials quantity variance:

Actual lumber used	83,000	feet
Standard lumber required (20,000 boxes × 4 feet)	(80,000)	feet
Difference	3,000	feet U
Standard cost per board foot	× $2.00	
Total quantity variance	$ 6,000	U

Labor Variances

The labor rate and labor efficiency variances are both based on direct labor hours used; thus, they are computed at the same point in time.

Labor rate variance:

Actual rate	$ 6.05	
Standard rate	(6.00)	
Difference	$ 0.05	U
Actual direct labor hours used	×39,600	
Total labor rate variance	$ 1,980	U

Labor efficiency variance:

Actual direct labor hours	39,600	
Standard direct labor hours	40,000	
Difference	400	F
Standard direct labor rate	× $6.00	
Total labor efficiency variance	$ 2,400	F

Revenue Variances

Sales price variance:

Actual price	$ 53.00	
Standard price	(52.00)	
Difference	$ 1.00	F
Actual quantity of boxes sold	× 47,355	
Total sales price variance	$ 47,355	F

Sales volume variance:

Actual quantity of boxes sold	47,355	boxes
Expected (budgeted) quantity*	50,400	boxes
Difference	3,045	boxes U
Standard price	× $52.00	
Total sales volume variance	$158,340	U

*Expected quantity = Expected total market × Expected market share

Market share variance:

Total actual market × actual market share × standard price (430,500 × 11% × $52)**	$2,462,460	
Total actual market × expected market share × standard price (430,500 × 12% × $52)	2,686,320	
Total market share variance	$ 223,860	U

**Alternative calculation: Actual quantity sold × Standard price

Industry volume variance:

Total actual market × expected market share × standard price (430,500 × 12% × $52)	$2,686,320	
Total expected market × expected market share × standard price (420,000 × 12% × $52)***	2,620,800	
Total industry volume variance	$ 65,520	F

***Alternative calculation: Expected quantity sold × Standard price

eXpanded ▲ ▲ *Material*

Variable and Fixed Manufacturing Overhead Variances

Use the information given in the previous problem, plus the following information, to address issues associated with Kendra Box Company's manufacturing overhead variances.

The company's budget shows the following monthly variable manufacturing overhead costs at several production levels:

	Percent of Standard Capacity		
	80%	90%	100%
Expected number of boxes	20,000	22,500	25,000
Expected direct labor hours	40,000	45,000	50,000
Variable manufacturing overhead costs	$80,000	$90,000	$100,000
Fixed manufacturing overhead costs	$125,000	$125,000	$125,000

The company normally produces at 100% of capacity and uses this production level to establish its predetermined manufacturing overhead rates. The following actual information for October is available:

Variable manufacturing overhead	$83,000
Fixed manufacturing overhead	$133,000
Production	20,000 boxes

Required:
1. Compute the variable manufacturing overhead cost rate (a) per box and (b) per direct labor hour assuming Kendra Box Company produces at normal capacity.
2. Compute the variable manufacturing overhead spending and efficiency variances for October assuming that Kendra produces at normal capacity and that variable manufacturing overhead costs vary with direct labor hours.
3. Compute the fixed manufacturing overhead cost rate (a) per box and (b) per direct labor hour.
4. Compute the fixed manufacturing overhead budget and volume variances for October using direct labor hours to establish the predetermined overhead rate.

Solution
1. Variable Manufacturing Overhead Cost Rates

		Rate per Box	Rate per Hour
Flexible budget at normal capacity:			
Boxes produced per month	25,000		
Labor hours per month	50,000		
Variable manufacturing overhead costs	$100,000	$4	$2

2. Variable Manufacturing Overhead Variances
The following diagram shows the computation of the variable overhead spending and efficiency variances:

(continued)

	AH × SR Actual hours of input × Standard rate	**SHA × SR** Standard hours allowed for actual output × Standard rate
Actual amount spent		
$83,000	39,600 hours × $2.00 = $79,200	40,000 hours × $2.00 = $80,000

Variable overhead spending variance
$83,000 − $79,200 = $3,800 U

Variable overhead efficiency variance*
$2.00 × (40,000 hours − 39,000 hours) = $800 F

*Be sure to compare this calculation to the labor efficiency variance calculated earlier for Kendra Box Company. Do you see how similar these calculations are? Both are based on the efficiency in labor hour usage.

3. Fixed Manufacturing Overhead Cost Rates

		Rate per Box	Rate per Hour
Flexible budget at normal capacity:			
Boxes produced per month	25,000		
Labor hours per month	50,000		
Fixed manufacturing overhead costs	$125,000	$5	$2.50

4. Fixed Manufacturing Overhead Variances
The following diagram shows the computation of the fixed overhead budget and volume variances:

	Budgeted amount (used to establish the predetermined allocation rate)	**SHA × SR** Standard hours allowed for actual output × Standard rate
Actual amount spent		
$133,000	$125,000; $125,000 ÷ 50,000 hours = $2.50 per hour	40,000 hours × $2.50 = $100,000

Fixed overhead budget variance
$133,000 − $125,000 = $8,000 U

Volume variance**
$2.50 × (50,000 hours − 40,000 hours) = $25,000 U

**Alternative calculation: Rate per box × (Expected production − Actual production) or $5 × (25,000 boxes − 20,000 boxes) = $25,000 U

d iscussion questions

1. Why is evaluating personnel and divisions so important to a business, especially in today's economy?
2. Why is it practically impossible for a large firm to be completely centralized, that is, to have top management making all operating decisions?
3. Why is a system of responsibility accounting necessary in most businesses?
4. What are some important behavioral factors that must be considered when responsibilities are assigned to managers?
5. Why are most performance reports called exception reports?
6. What is the difference between a cost center and a profit center? Between a profit center and an investment center?
7. What is a standard cost?

8. What is the purpose of a standard cost system?
9. Who is responsible for the development of the standards to be used in a standard cost system?
10. What is a variance from standard?
11. What is the relationship of a standard cost system to the principle of management by exception?
12. What are the steps in establishing and operating a standard cost system?
13. Why are two variances, rather than one, used to measure and control materials and labor costs?
14. Who is usually responsible for each of the following variances?
    a. Direct materials price variance
    b. Direct materials quantity variance
    c. Direct labor rate variance
    d. Direct labor efficiency variance
15. What are the major advantages and disadvantages of a standard cost system?
16. If a profit center has a net loss, does that always mean it is not making a contribution to the company as a whole?
17. What are the variances used to analyze revenues in profit and investment centers?
18. What is the major disadvantage of using ROI to evaluate the performance of investment centers?

19. What is the major advantage of using residual income to evaluate the performance of investment centers?

20. What are the two steps in developing a management system for use in controlling variable manufacturing overhead?
21. What is a variable manufacturing overhead spending variance, and what does it indicate about variable manufacturing overhead costs?
22. What is a variable manufacturing overhead efficiency variance, and how does it relate to the labor efficiency variance?
23. What does the fixed manufacturing overhead budget variance measure?
24. What does the volume variance measure, and how is this variance different from the other cost variances studied in this chapter?

p r a c t i c e   e x e r c i s e s

Practice 20-1

Changes in the Business Environment
Which one of the following statements is *incorrect*?

a. Globalization has greatly affected business over the past few years.
b. Certain market investors have gained a large amount of power in determining what happens at the companies in which they invest.
c. New technology has made information more expensive.
d. The fast pace of business requires managers to have better information and perform more timely evaluations of personnel and divisions.

Practice 20-2

Centralization versus Decentralization
Which one of the following statements is *not* an advantage of decentralization?

a. Segment managers usually have more information regarding matters within their segments than do managers at higher levels.
b. Segment managers' decisions are always consistent with the overall objectives of the firm.
c. Managers can be evaluated more easily because their responsibilities are more clearly defined.
d. Higher-level management has more time to consider strategic goals when daily decision making is distributed throughout the organization.
e. Segment managers can spot problems and react more quickly than can managers at higher levels.

Practice 20-3

Responsibility Accounting
The company is producing an exception report. One division had $45,000 in budgeted costs, but it actually spent $47,500. How would this variance appear on the exception report?

Practice 20-4

Responsibility Centers

Which one of the following is *not* an example of a responsibility center in an organization?

a. Profit center
b. Asset center
c. Cost center
d. Investment center

Practice 20-5

Standard Cost Card

Using the following standard quantities and standard rates, prepare a standard cost card to determine the total standard cost per unit.

	Standard Quantity	Standard Price or Rate
Direct materials	4 pounds	$ 1.25
Direct labor	2.5 hours	15.00
Variable manufacturing overhead	2.5 hours	1.70
Fixed manufacturing overhead	2.5 hours	0.50

Practice 20-6

Materials Price Variance

The company purchased 4,000 pounds of raw materials at $3.75 per pound. The company's standard cost per pound is $3.60. Calculate the materials price variance for this purchase.

Practice 20-7

Accounting for Materials Price Variances

Refer to the data in Practice 20-6. Make the necessary journal entry to record the cash purchase of the raw materials inventory at standard cost.

Practice 20-8

Materials Quantity Variance

The company used 5,500 board feet of raw materials with a standard cost of $6.00 per board foot to make 400 tables. The company's standard is 14 board feet per table. Calculate the company's materials quantity variance.

Practice 20-9

Accounting for Materials Quantity Variance

Refer to the data in Practice 20-8. Make the necessary journal entry to record the transfer of these raw materials into work-in-process inventory.

Practice 20-10

Labor Rate Variance

Using the following information, compute the labor rate variance.

Number of nightstands produced	150
Actual hours used to produce nightstands	720
Actual labor rate per hour	$15.30
Standard labor rate per hour	$15.00
Standard labor hours per nightstand	5

Practice 20-11

Labor Efficiency Variance

Refer to the data in Practice 20-10. Compute the labor efficiency variance.

Practice 20-12

Accounting for Labor Variances

Refer to the data in Practices 20-10 and 20-11. Make the necessary journal entry to record direct labor at the standard rates.

Practice 20-13

Segment-Margin Income Statement

The company reports the following costs and revenues for one of its segments:

Net sales revenue	$910,000
Cost of goods sold	520,000
Selling and administrative costs	130,000
Advertising cost	94,000
Insurance cost	78,000

Of these costs, cost of goods sold and selling and administrative costs are variable, advertising is a direct fixed cost, and insurance is an indirect fixed cost. Using this information, prepare a segment-margin income statement for this segment.

Practice 20-14

Segment-Margin Ratio

Refer to the data in Practice 20-13. Compute the segment-margin ratio.

Practice 20-15

Revenue Variances

Which one of the following is *not* an example of a revenue variance?

a. Sales price variance
b. Spending variance
c. Industry volume variance
d. Market share variance
e. Sales volume variance

Practice 20-16

Computing Revenue Variances

The company sells one product, which is called Product A. Actual and expected sales data for the most recent year are as follows:

	Company Sales	Sales Price	Total Market	Percent of Market
Actual	500 units	$15	2,500 units	20.0%
Expected	600	13	2,400	25.0

Using these data, compute the following:

1. Sales price variance
2. Sales volume variance
3. Market share variance
4. Industry volume variance

Practice 20-17

Accounting for Revenue Variances

Refer to the data in Practice 20-16. Use the revenue control account to make the single necessary journal entry to record the revenue variances for the period.

Practice 20-18

Return on Investment

The company's profit margin is 8%, and its asset turnover is 4.2. Compute the company's return on investment (ROI).

Practice 20-19

Residual Income

The company had $360,000 in total assets and $94,000 in net income this year, and the company requires at least a 12% return on assets. Compute the company's residual income.

Practice 20-20

Variable Manufacturing Overhead Spending Variance
Using the following data, compute the variable manufacturing overhead spending variance.

Number of nightstands produced	150
Actual hours used to produce nightstands	720
Total actual variable overhead costs incurred	$8,352
Standard variable overhead rate per direct labor hour	$11.00
Standard labor hours per nightstand	5

Practice 20-21

Variable Manufacturing Overhead Efficiency Variance
Refer to the data in Practice 20-20. Compute the variable manufacturing overhead efficiency variance.

Practice 20-22

Fixed Manufacturing Overhead Budget and Volume Variances
The company spent $60,000 on fixed manufacturing overhead during the year. As of the beginning of the year, the company had budgeted to spend $57,000 on fixed manufacturing overhead and to work 1,000 direct labor hours (based on the production of 500 units at two direct labor hours per unit). The actual number of units produced during the year was 400. Fixed manufacturing overhead is applied to production based on direct labor hours. Compute (1) the fixed manufacturing overhead budget variance, (2) the fixed manufacturing overhead volume variance, and (3) the total amount of under- or overapplied fixed manufacturing overhead.

Practice 20-23

Accounting for Manufacturing Overhead Variances
The company has the following manufacturing overhead variances.

Variable manufacturing overhead spending variance	$ 300 F
Variable manufacturing overhead efficiency variance	425 U
Fixed manufacturing overhead budget variance	1,000 U
Fixed manufacturing overhead volume variance	740 F

Make the journal entry necessary to recognize these variances.

exercises

Exercise 20-1

Responsibility Accounting Reports
Lorlily Company is an agricultural supply firm. The management of the company is decentralized, with division managers heading the two operating divisions: Machinery and Seed/Fertilizer. Within each division, the sales are split between the two states of Indiana and Illinois.

The following data are applicable to revenue in 2006:

	Budget	Actual
Machinery—Indiana	$800,000	$750,000
Seed/Fertilizer—Illinois	500,000	580,000
Seed/Fertilizer—Indiana	400,000	530,000
Machinery—Illinois	350,000	250,000

1. Prepare a responsibility accounting report for the head of the Machinery division. For each of the two geographic areas (Indiana and Illinois), show whether the variance between budgeted and actual machinery revenue is favorable or unfavorable.
2. Prepare a responsibility accounting report for the head of the entire company. The company head wants to see only the overall results for each of the two operating divisions (Machinery and Seed/Fertilizer); a detailed breakdown by geographic area is not requested.

Exercise 20-2

Materials Price Variance

Hogan Manufacturing Company has just adopted a standard cost system. You have been asked to analyze the materials purchases and usage for the month of August to determine the materials price variance to be recorded at the end of the month. During August, 5,000 gallons of a chemical were purchased at $3.20 per gallon. Only 4,200 gallons were put into production. The standard price per gallon is $3.15. Compute the following variances:

1. The materials price variance if the chemical is carried in inventory at standard price (i.e., the price variance is accounted for at the time of purchase).
2. The materials price variance if the chemical is carried in inventory at actual price and is charged to Work-in-Process Inventory at the standard price (i.e., the price variance is accounted for at the time of use in production).

Exercise 20-3

Materials Price and Quantity Variances—Journal Entries

Genesis Enterprises produces one product—MX4. The following information relating to raw materials is available for the month of March:

Beginning direct materials inventory	1,500 pounds @ $3.10 per unit
Purchases made during the month	11,000 pounds @ $3.10 per unit
Direct materials placed in production	11,750 pounds

The standard materials usage for one unit of MX4 is 2 pounds with a standard price per pound of $3. Genesis produced 6,000 units of Product MX4 during the month.

1. Compute the materials price and quantity variances for Genesis assuming the materials price variance is computed at the time of purchase.
2. Provide the journal entries required to record:
   a. The purchase of direct materials and the materials price variance.
   b. Placing the direct materials in production and the materials quantity variance.

Exercise 20-4

Direct Materials Purchased and Used

Mary Clarke is concerned about her performance as a recently employed purchasing agent. The accounting department has provided her with the following data for the month of August:

Units produced	2,000
Materials used	1,078 tons
Materials purchased	1,400 tons at $43 per ton

The standard materials usage set by management for one unit of product is half a ton of materials per unit, at $45 per ton. Her performance report shows the following variances:

Used (1,078 tons − 1,000 tons standard) × $45 per ton	$3,510 U
Purchased ($45 per ton standard − $43 per ton actual) × 1,400 tons	2,800 F

If you were Mary Clarke, how would you explain this report?

Exercise 20-5

Analyzing Materials Cost

Mr. Rogers, the production manager, has received a report showing a $16,500 unfavorable total materials variance (materials price variance plus materials quantity variance). He knows that production used 10,000 pounds less than the budgeted amount of direct materials allowed for actual output. Mr. Rogers also knows that the standard price for direct materials was determined to be 80 cents per pound.

What was the actual cost of direct materials used during the period if the budgeted amount allowed was estimated to be 500,000 pounds?

Exercise 20-6

Materials Price and Quantity Variances

Daniel Smith, production manager, has just received a report stating that the total materials variance (materials price variance plus materials quantity variance) for last month was $6,710 unfavorable. However, he is not certain whether the production foremen are overdrawing from inventory or the purchasing department has been unable to acquire materials at reasonable prices. The information he needs is contained in the following report:

Standard production	125,000 units
Actual production	122,000 units
Standard materials per unit	1.5 pounds
Materials used in March	193,000 pounds
Standard price for materials	$1.25 per pound
Actual price for materials	$1.22 per pound

1. Compute the materials price and quantity variances for the month. (*Note:* Mr. Smith's company computes the materials price variance at the time that materials are issued to production.)
2. **Interpretive Question:** What was the cause of the unfavorable variance, and what recommendation would you make to Mr. Smith?

Exercise 20-7

Materials Price and Quantity Variances—Journal Entries

Starship Enterprises produces and sells calibrators. The company began the period with the following inventory of raw material:

200 units at $5.50 per unit (the materials price variance is taken at the time of purchase)

A standard of four units of material for each calibrator produced has been established. During the period, Starship purchased an additional 1,500 units of material at a total cost of $8,220. The dollar amount of materials transferred to Work-in-Process Inventory during the period was $8,800. At the end of the period, Starship had an ending materials inventory of 50 units.

1. Provide the journal entry required to record the materials price variance.
2. Provide the journal entry required to record the materials quantity variance.

Exercise 20-8

Labor Rate and Efficiency Variances

To produce one unit of Product CD requires eight hours of labor at a standard cost per hour of $11.00. During the month of September, 5,000 units were produced. Actual hours and costs for the month are as follows:

Actual direct labor hours	38,400
Actual direct labor costs	$428,160

1. Compute the actual cost per hour of direct labor for the month of September.
2. Compute the labor rate variance.
3. Compute the labor efficiency variance.

Exercise 20-9

Responsibility for Labor Costs

Raymond Stone, a recent business school graduate, has taken a job with Farben Corporation as production manager. His job is to see that production is efficient. After his first month, he is given this memo.

Performance Report

Raymond Stone: $32,000 Unfavorable

The following data are also known for Raymond Stone's first month:

Units produced . . . . 750 units
Direct labor used . . . . 7,600 hours at $20
Standard direct labor hours per unit . . . . 10 hours at $16

1. What justification would you give if you were in Raymond Stone's position, keeping in mind that he is not responsible for hiring, firing, and wage rates? These decisions are handled by the personnel department.
2. What might be theoretically wrong with a conclusion that Raymond Stone is not at all responsible for labor rates?

Exercise 20-10

Labor Variances

During the year, Thompson Plastics was in negotiation with the local union over wages. A settlement was finally reached, and the average wage per hour was increased to $32.80. Production fell to 145,000 units, and 220,000 hours were incurred. Standard production has been set at 150,000 units; 1.5 hours of labor were expected to produce one unit at a standard labor cost of $48.75 per unit. Actual labor cost for the period was $7,216,000.

1. Calculate the labor variances at Thompson Plastics.
2. Prepare the journal entry to enter labor costs in Work-in-Process Inventory and set up the rate and efficiency variances for labor.
3. **Interpretive Question:** Are these variances significant in light of the new wage agreement?

Exercise 20-11

Employee Morale and Production Efficiency

Crest Fabrics is a nonunion textile firm. Employee morale and production efficiency have dropped in the last few weeks, causing management some concern. Further, quality control problems have resulted in a 10% increase in rejects in the last two weeks. The following information may help management identify the causes of current problems:

Employee Production Efficiency Report
(in percentages)

Employee	Wk 14	Wk 15	Wk 16	Wk 17	Wk 18	Wk 19	Wk 20
Baker	96	100	86	93	91	89	85
Johnson	101	97	89	90	93	91	87
Becker	105	109	93	96	95	92	90
Howard	99	98	88	93	97	94	88
Kettle	92	93	81	85	90	91	90

Additional information:

a. Standards for measuring worker efficiency were raised at the start of week 16.
b. Crest Fabrics changed its source of supply of materials in week 15.

1. From the production efficiency report, can you identify trends in the efficiency of individual workers? Which employees might have low morale?
2. **Interpretive Question:** What clues to the causes of the diminishing efficiency and quality can you draw from the information given?

Exercise 20-12

Labor Variances
Compute the missing amounts.

Total labor variance (efficiency plus rate variances)	$ 47,500 U
Labor efficiency variance	42,000 U
Actual labor hours incurred	110,000
Units produced	50,000
Standard hours allowed per unit	2
Total actual labor costs	$467,500
Standard labor hours allowed for output	(a)
Actual labor cost per hour	(b)
Actual labor cost per unit	(c)
Standard labor cost per hour	(d)
Labor rate variance	(e)
Standard labor cost per unit	(f)

Exercise 20-13

Segment-Margin Income Statements
Professional Management, Inc., is a company that sponsors seminars for executives. It has two profit centers, or divisions: a time-management group and a money-management group. Financial information for the two divisions for the year just ended follows:

	Time Management	Money Management
Revenue	$842,000	$965,000
Mailing costs	48,000	102,000
Printing costs	146,000	98,000
Hotel rental costs	425,000	501,000
Travel expenses	72,000	60,000
Advertising costs	108,000	106,000

Of these costs, printing and advertising are direct fixed costs, whereas mailing, hotel rental, and travel are variable costs. Using this information, prepare segment-margin income statements for the two divisions. Include in your statements the computation for contribution margin.

Exercise 20-14

Spreadsheet

Evaluating Performance with Segment and Contribution Margins
Sunshine Center's three profit centers had the following operating data during 2006:

	South	North	East
Revenue (at $21.50 per unit)	$322,500	$215,000	$430,000
Fixed costs:			
Costs unique to the division	131,150	64,500	150,500
Costs allocated by corporate headquarters	45,150	30,100	60,200
Variable costs per unit	13	14	10

Sunshine's management is concerned because the company is losing money. They ask you to:

1. Calculate each profit center's contribution and segment margins, and overall company profits.
2. Determine, on the basis of these calculations, which center(s), if any, should be discontinued. (Assume that the 2006 performance is indicative of all future years. Ignore all nonfinancial factors.)

Exercise 20-15

Measuring Performance Using Segment and Contribution Margins

El Pico Company has two divisions: Maya and Aztec. During 2006, they had the following operating data:

	Maya Division	Aztec Division
Revenue	$100,000	$120,000
Fixed costs:		
Costs unique to the division	50,000	45,000
Costs allocated by corporate headquarters	11,000	10,000
Variable costs per unit	4	4
Unit sales price of division's product	10	8

1. Compute each division's contribution and segment margins, and the contribution each makes to overall company profits.
2. **Interpretive Question:** Based on only the financial information given, should either division be discontinued? Why?

Exercise 20-16

Spreadsheet

Revenue Variances

Fabulous Fragrances makes two products: lotion and shampoo. Actual and expected revenue data for the two products are as follows:

Actual Data			
	Units Sold	Sales Price	Total Actual Market
Lotion	2,400 bottles	$12.00	30,000 bottles
Shampoo	4,800 bottles	7.50	50,000 bottles

Expected Data			
	Units Sold	Sales Price	Expected Market Share
Lotion	3,000 bottles	$11.00	12%
Shampoo	5,600 bottles	8.00	10%

1. Using the above data, compute the sales price and sales volume variances for lotion and shampoo for Fabulous Fragrances.
2. Using the above data, compute the market share and industry volume variances for both lotion and shampoo.

Exercise 20-17

Revenue Variances

Telling Time is a watch retailer. It sells two types of watches: digital and analog. The results for the third quarter for Telling Time are as follows:

	Digital	Analog
Expected sales in units	400	500
Expected sales price	$50	$75
Expected percent of market	12.5%	12.5%
Actual sales in units	375	530
Actual total sales revenue	$19,500	$38,955
Actual total market volume	2,500	5,000

(continued)

1. Calculate the sales price variance, the sales volume variance, the market share variance, and the industry volume variance for digital watches.
2. Calculate the sales price variance, the sales volume variance, the market share variance, and the industry volume variance for analog watches.

Exercise 20-18

Return on Investment

Compute the missing data, items (a) through (i), in the following table:

	Division X	Division Y	Division Z
Revenue	$600,000	$500,000	(g)
Net income	$30,000	$25,000	(h)
Total assets	(a)	$100,000	$200,000
Operating performance ratio	(b)	(d)	10%
Asset turnover ratio	(c)	(e)	4 times
ROI	12%	(f)	(i)

Exercise 20-19

Return on Investment

During 2006, the East and West divisions of Granger Company reported the following:

	East Division	West Division
ROI	12%	24%
Operating performance ratio	3%	4%
Revenue	$72,000	$90,000
Total assets	$18,000	$15,000

1. What was each division's asset turnover ratio in 2006?
2. What operating performance ratio would each division need in order to generate an ROI of 25%?

Exercise 20-20

Measuring Performance: Residual Income and ROI

McCormick Corporation measures the performance of its divisions by using the residual income approach, with a minimum accepted rate of return of 16%. In 2006, the printing division, which has total assets of $250,000, generated a net income of $55,000, or 8% of sales. The operating results are expected to be the same in 2007. In early 2007, the printing division receives a proposal for a $50,000 investment that would generate an additional $10,000 of income per year.

1. Should the manager of the printing division make the investment?
2. Would your answer to part (1) be different if McCormick Corporation used the ROI approach to evaluate the performance of its various divisions? Why or why not?

Exercise 20-21

Measuring Performance: Residual Income and ROI

An investment center of Southwick Corporation made three investment proposals. Details of the proposals follow.

	Proposals		
	1	2	3
Required investment	$80,000	$50,000	$65,000
Annual return	13,000	9,000	9,500

Southwick Corporation uses the residual income method to evaluate all investment proposals. Its minimum rate of return is 15%.

1. As president of Southwick Corporation, which of the investments, if any, would you make? Why?
2. Assuming that Southwick Corporation uses the ROI approach to evaluate investment proposals, which investments, if any, would you make? (Southwick Corporation's current return on assets is 20%.)

Exercise 20-22

Variable and Fixed Manufacturing Overhead Variances
Lauder Company manufactures one product. The standard capacity is 20,000 units per month. Manufacturing overhead costs are budgeted and applied on the basis of two machine hours per unit. At standard capacity, the monthly variable overhead budget is $500,000 and the monthly fixed overhead budget is $900,000. During February, 18,000 units of product were actually manufactured, $460,000 of variable manufacturing overhead was incurred, and $975,000 of fixed manufacturing overhead was incurred. Actual machine hours were 35,000.

1. Compute the variable manufacturing overhead spending and efficiency variances.
2. Compute the fixed manufacturing budget and volume variances.

Exercise 20-23

Manufacturing Overhead Variances
Rollins Manufacturing Company estimates variable manufacturing overhead for the month of November to be $80,000. Fixed manufacturing overhead is estimated to be $195,000. All manufacturing overhead is estimated and applied on the basis of 10,000 direct labor hours. At standard production output capacity, each unit of finished product requires two direct labor hours to complete. During November, 4,900 units of finished product were produced. Actual variable and fixed manufacturing overhead costs incurred were $77,500 and $203,000, respectively. Actual direct labor hours during the month were 9,850.

1. Compute the total amount of manufacturing overhead applied during November.
2. Compute the amount of under- or overapplied overhead for the month.
3. Compute the variable manufacturing overhead spending and efficiency variances.
4. Compute the fixed manufacturing budget and volume variances.

problems

Problem 20-1

Responsibility Accounting Reports
Ryhan Company is a multinational computer services firm. The management of the company is decentralized, with division managers heading the following three divisions: Europe, Asia, and the Americas. Within each division, the three sources of revenue are software sales, service contracts, and consulting fees.

The following data are applicable to revenue in 2006:

(continued)

	Budget	Actual
Europe—software sales	$200,000	$230,000
Asia—software sales	200,000	130,000
Americas—software sales	350,000	420,000
Europe—service contracts	120,000	90,000
Asia—service contracts	70,000	80,000
Americas—service contracts	250,000	190,000
Europe—consulting fees	40,000	90,000
Asia—consulting fees	50,000	35,000
Americas—consulting fees	100,000	60,000

Required:

1. Prepare a responsibility accounting report for the head of the Europe division. For each of the three revenue sources (software sales, service contracts, and consulting fees), show whether the variance between budget and actual is favorable or unfavorable.

2. Prepare a responsibility accounting report for the head of the entire company. The company head wants to see only the overall results for each of the three geographic divisions (budget versus actual); a detailed breakdown by revenue source is not requested.

Problem 20-2

Spreadsheet

Materials and Labor Variances

The standard cost data for Madison Machinery Company show the following costs for producing one of its machines:

Direct materials	400 pounds at $8 = $3,200
Direct labor	150 hours at $15 = $2,250

During April, four machines were built, with actual total costs as follows:

Materials purchased	2,000 pounds at $8.20 = $16,400
Materials used	1,700 pounds
Direct labor incurred	625 hours at $14.80 = $9,250

Required:

1. Compute the following variances:
   a. Materials price variance (raw materials inventory is carried at standard cost)
   b. Materials quantity variance
   c. Labor rate variance
   d. Labor efficiency variance
2. Record the standard materials and labor costs in Work-in-Process Inventory, and enter the variances in appropriate journal entries.

Problem 20-3

Materials and Labor Variances

Mayhem Manufacturing provides the following standard cost data for one of its products:

Direct materials	12 feet at $2.50 per foot
Direct labor	3 hours at $9.50 per hour

During the month of February, the following actual cost data were accumulated:

Materials purchased	94,000 feet at $2.40 per foot
Materials used	92,650 feet
Direct labor incurred	21,750 hours at a total cost of $215,500
Units produced	7,530 units

Required:
Compute the following variances:

1. Materials price variance (this variance is computed at the time of purchase)
2. Materials quantity variance
3. Labor rate variance
4. Labor efficiency variance

Problem 20-4

Materials and Labor Variances

Actual materials	2,000 tons
Actual hours used	1,500 hours
Standard materials for output (tons)	(a)
Standard hours for output	(b)
Actual cost per ton of material	(c)
Standard cost per ton of material	$ 4
Actual cost per direct labor hour	$ 4
Standard cost per direct labor hour	(d)
Total direct labor variance*	$1,625 U
Total direct materials variance**	$ 400 F
Direct materials price variance	(e)
Direct materials quantity variance	$ 0
Direct labor rate variance	$ 750 U
Direct labor efficiency variance	(f)

*Total direct labor variance = Labor rate variance + Labor efficiency variance

**Total direct materials variance = Materials price variance + Materials usage variance (Materials price variance is computed at the time of use in production.)

Required:
Compute the missing amounts.

Problem 20-5

Materials and Labor Variances

Sports Manufacturing, Inc., produces and sells footballs. The standard cost for materials and labor for one regulation-size football is as follows:

Direct materials	2 feet of leather at $5.50 per foot
Direct labor	1/2 hour at $9.00 per hour

During the period, Sports Manufacturing recorded a materials price variance of $100 U and a materials quantity variance of $380 F. In addition, the company recorded a labor rate variance and a labor efficiency variance of $1,200 U and $450 U, respectively. Seven thousand footballs were produced during the period, and the materials inventory did not change during the period.

Required:
1. Compute the actual costs for materials and labor during the period.
2. Provide the journal entries to record the materials price and quantity variances. (*Hint:* The amount of materials purchased and used is the same.)
3. Provide the journal entries to record the labor rate and efficiency variances.

Problem 20-6

Materials and Labor Variances

The following information was taken from the records of Liberty Manufacturing Company for the month of July:

(continued)

Materials (actual):

Purchases of material A:	1,300 pounds × $5.25
Purchases of material B:	750 pounds × $2.50
Used 900 pounds of material A	
Used 525 pounds of material B	

Direct labor (actual):

Manufacturing Division:	1,050 hours × $8.90
Assembly Division:	450 hours × $4.50

Standard cost per unit:

Material A: 2 pounds × $5.20 per pound	$10.40
Material B: 1 pound × $2.60 per pound	2.60
Direct labor—manufacturing: 2 hours × $8.50	17.00
Direct labor—assembly: 1 hour × $4.60	4.60
Standard cost per unit	$34.60

Units produced: 500

Required:
1. Calculate the materials price and quantity variances, assuming that the materials price variance is recognized at the time of purchase.
2. Calculate the labor rate and labor efficiency variances.
3. **Interpretive Question:** What is the advantage, if any, of calculating the materials price variance at the time of purchase rather than at the time of use in production?

Problem 20-7

Materials and Labor Variance Analysis
Cooke Manufacturing Company produces high-quality men's pajamas for several large retail stores. The standard cost card for each dozen pairs of pajamas is as follows:

Direct materials, 30 yards at $0.80	$24
Direct labor, 4 hours at $5.00	20
Manufacturing overhead:	
Variable cost: 4 direct labor hours at $2.00	8
Fixed cost: 30% of direct labor cost	6
Total product cost per dozen pairs	$58

During the month of September, the company filled three orders of pajamas at the following costs:

Order	Number of Dozens	Yards Used	Labor Hours
8	400	12,200	1,500
9	900	26,750	3,750
10	500	15,450	2,140
	1,800	54,400	7,390

The following additional information involving materials and labor was supplied by the accounting department:

a. Purchases of materials during the month amounted to 60,000 yards at $0.82 per yard.
b. Total direct labor cost for the month was $37,689.

Required:
1. Compute the materials price variance for September. (Materials are carried in Direct Materials Inventory at standard.)
2. Compute the materials quantity variance for September.
3. Compute the labor rate and labor efficiency variances for September.

Problem 20-8

Determining How Variances Are Computed

Helon Company uses a standard cost system in its accounting for the manufacturing costs of its only product. The standard cost information for materials and labor is as follows:

Direct materials: 5 pounds at $7 .... $35
Direct labor: 3 hours at $8 24

During April of its first year of operation, the company completed 2,300 units and had the following materials and labor variances:

Materials price variance .... $1,400 F
Materials quantity variance .... 2,100 F
Labor rate variance .... 2,115 U
Labor efficiency variance .... 1,200 U

There was no Work-in-Process Inventory at the beginning or end of April.

Required:
Compute the following amounts:

1. The amount of materials and labor debited to Work-in-Process Inventory during April.
2. The pounds of materials used in production.
3. The actual hours of labor used in production.
4. The actual labor rate per hour.

Problem 20-9

Evaluation of Profit Centers—Segment Margin

Della Brown is the manager of one of the stores in the nationwide EatRite supermarket chain. The following information has been gathered about the performance of Della's store in the most recent quarter:

Operating Departments	Revenue	Contribution-Margin Ratio
Groceries	$600,000	20%
Fresh produce	200,000	40%
Dry goods	500,000	35%
Fixed costs controllable by:		
Manager of grocery department	$ 50,000	
Manager of fresh produce department	70,000	
Manager of dry goods department	80,000	
Store manager	100,000	
Corporate headquarters	100,000	
Total	$400,000	

Required:
Prepare a segment-margin income statement for corporate headquarters' use in evaluating the store manager, Della Brown, and which Della can use to evaluate the managers of the three departments within the store.

Problem 20-10

Evaluation of Profit Centers—Segment Margin

Derrald Pearl Company has two divisions, Computer Consulting and Construction. During the most recent year, the two divisions had the following operating data:

(continued)

Spreadsheet

	Computer Consulting	Construction
Revenue	$600,000	$250,000
Contribution-margin percentage	45%	15%
Fixed costs controllable by division managers	$200,000	$30,000
Fixed costs allocated by corporate headquarters	$100,000	$100,000

Required:
1. Prepare a segment-margin income statement for Derrald Pearl Company. Include three columns—one for the company total and one for each of the two divisions.
2. Based on the segment-margin income statement prepared in part (1), what would happen to overall company profits if the Construction Division were to be discontinued?
3. Should either of the divisions be discontinued? Explain.

Problem 20-11

Revenue Variances
Menendez Company is a merchandiser that sells three products: Product X, Product Y, and Product Z. The following are the actual and expected (standard) data for the three products:

		Actual Data	
	Units	**Sales Price**	**Total Actual Market**
Product X	530	$5.00	2,500 units
Product Y	760	4.00	10,000
Product Z	660	7.00	2,500

		Standard Data	
	Units	**Sales Price**	**Total Market Share**
Product X	500	$6.00	25%
Product Y	900	3.00	10
Product Z	600	5.00	20

Required:
1. Compute the sales price variance, the sales volume variance, the market share variance, and the industry volume variance for Product X.
2. Compute the sales price variance, the sales volume variance, the market share variance, and the industry volume variance for Product Y.
3. Compute the sales price variance, the sales volume variance, the market share variance, and the industry volume variance for Product Z.

Problem 20-12

Revenue Variances
Family Friendly Photography has just finished its first year of business. It specializes in group portraits, though the company also handles individual portraits. Revenue is determined per photo shooting. Family Friendly Photography has divided prices into three different groups: groups of 15 or more, groups of 2 to 15, and individuals. The following information is for its first year of operation:

	Number of Photo Shoots	Price per Photo Shoot	Total Actual Market
Groups of 15+	330	$280.00	1,875 shoots
Groups of 2–15	475	180.00	2,500
Individuals	175	105.00	3,125

At the first of the year, Family Friendly Photography created a budget of expectations for the first year of business. Following are the expectations for the first year of business:

	Number of Photo Shoots	Price per Photo Shoot	Total Market Share
Groups of 15+	300	$275.00	20%
Groups of 2–15	450	200.00	15
Individuals	200	115.00	8

Required:

1. Compute the sales price variance and the sales volume variance for each of the three groups listed above.
2. Compute the market share variance and the industry volume variance for each of the three groups listed above.

Problem 20-13

ROI and Contribution-Margin Analysis

Macro Data Corporation's three divisions had the following operating data during 2006:

	Fax Machine	Calculator	Computer
Revenue	$100,000	$150,000	$200,000
Variable costs	50,000	90,000	135,000
Fixed costs	45,000	56,000	53,000
Total assets	50,000	38,000	120,000

Required:

1. Compute the contribution margin for each division.
2. Compute the segment margin for each division (assume that all fixed costs are direct to each division).
3. Compute the ROI for each division.
4. Which division had the highest operating performance ratio?
5. **Interpretive Question:** Which division had the best performance in 2006? Why?

Problem 20-14

ROI

Frank's Fixtures has two divisions: the Plumbing Division and the Electrical Division. Following are their operating data for 2006:

	Plumbing Division	Electrical Division
Revenue	$150,000	$180,000
Net income	15,000	16,200
Total assets	75,000	72,000
Stockholders' equity	36,000	20,800
Long-term debt	34,500	26,000

(continued)

Required:
1. Calculate the ROI for each division.
2. **Interpretive Question:** On the basis of this return, which division appears to have the better performance? Why?

Problem 20-15

ROI

The following information for 2006 applies to the two sales divisions of Ward Enterprises:

	Division A	Division B
Total inventory	$33,333	$37,500
Operating performance ratio	12%	16%
Net income	$12,000	$10,000

Required:
1. Calculate each division's revenue.
2. Calculate each division's asset turnover ratio assuming that controllable assets include inventory only.
3. **Interpretive Question:** Which division had the better performance for the period? Why?

Problem 20-16

ROI and Residual Income

Pacific Corporation has a number of autonomous divisions. Its real estate division has recently reviewed a number of investment proposals.

a. A new office building would cost $450,000 and would generate yearly net income of $80,000.

b. A computer system would cost $350,000 and would reduce bookkeeping and clerical costs by $50,000 annually.

c. A new apartment house would cost $900,000 and would generate yearly net income of $150,000.

The real estate division currently has total assets of $1.8 million and net income of $350,000.

Required:
1. Assuming that the performance of the manager of the real estate division is evaluated on the basis of the division's ROI, evaluate each of the independent proposals, and determine whether it should be accepted or rejected.
2. Assuming that the manager's performance is evaluated on a residual income basis, determine whether each of the proposals should be accepted or rejected. (The division's minimum accepted rate of return is 15%.)

Problem 20-17

ROI and Residual Income

Albertson Furniture Company is a retailer of home furnishings. It currently has stores in three cities—San Francisco, Los Angeles, and Phoenix. Operating data for the three stores in 2006 were as follows:

	San Francisco	Los Angeles	Phoenix
Revenue	$1,500,000	$1,900,000	$1,800,000
Variable costs	900,000	1,200,000	1,200,000
Fixed costs	300,000	350,000	250,000
Total assets	1,800,000	2,500,000	1,300,000

Required:

1. Compute the segment margin for each store.
2. Compute the operating performance ratio for each store.
3. Compute the asset turnover for each store.
4. Compute the ROI for each store.
5. Compute the residual income for each store. (The minimum rates of return for the stores are San Francisco, 15%; Los Angeles, 13%; and Phoenix, 18%.)

Problem 20-18

ROI and Residual Income

	Division W	Division X	Division Y	Division Z
Revenue	$180,000	$750,000	$ (i)	$950,000
Net income	$ (a)	$175,000	$ (j)	$ (m)
Total assets	$153,000	$ (e)	$400,000	$ (n)
Operating performance ratio	17%	(f)	9%	(o)
Asset turnover ratio	(b)	0.75 time	(k)	3.0 times
ROI	(c)	(g)	(l)	18%
Minimum accepted rate of return	15%	(h)	16%	14%
Residual income	$ (d)	$ 15,000	$ 16,000	$ (p)

Required:
Compute the missing data, labeled (a) through (p).

Problem 20-19

Measuring Performance: Residual Income and ROI
The gaming division of Nevada Corporation had income of $550,000 and total assets of $3 million in 2006. The figures are expected to be similar in 2007. The manager of the gaming division has an opportunity to purchase some new gambling machines for $250,000. He concludes that the new machines would increase annual net income by $44,000.

Required:

1. Calculate the current ROI and the expected return on the proposed investment.
2. Calculate the gaming division's current residual income and the expected residual income on the proposed investment. (Assume that the division's minimum accepted rate of return is 17%.)
3. Should the new machines be purchased:
   a. If the division uses the ROI method?
   b. If the division uses the residual income method?

Problem 20-20

ROI and Residual Income
The manager of the manufacturing division of Minolta Company is evaluated on a residual income basis. He is in the process of evaluating three investment proposals.

a. Pay $500,000 for a new machine that will increase production substantially. This will result in an increased income of $80,000 annually.
b. Pay $350,000 for a new machine that will reduce labor costs by $70,000 annually.
c. Pay $800,000 for a new machine that will increase annual net income by $115,000.

The manufacturing division currently has total assets of $1.2 million and net income of $200,000. Its minimum accepted rate of return is 15%.

Required:

1. Evaluate the three investment proposals independently, and determine which should be accepted.
2. Assuming that the division manager is evaluated on the basis of the division's ROI, determine whether each of the proposals should be accepted or rejected.

Problem 20-21

Manufacturing Overhead Variances

Engraph Manufacturing Company uses standard direct labor hours as a basis for charging manufacturing overhead to Work-in-Process Inventory. The following data were taken from the records:

Data for August:

Actual variable manufacturing overhead	$217,000
Actual fixed manufacturing overhead	$265,700
Actual units produced	8,000
Actual direct labor hours	33,000

Annual budget data:

Budgeted fixed manufacturing overhead	$3,304,800
Budgeted variable manufacturing overhead cost	$2,611,200
Budgeted direct labor hours	408,000
Budgeted units of production	102,000

Required:

1. Compute the annual variable manufacturing overhead rate and annual fixed manufacturing overhead rate to be used to apply overhead to Work-in-Process Inventory.
2. Determine the variable overhead spending variance and the variable overhead efficiency variance for August.
3. Determine the fixed overhead budget variance and the volume variance for August.
4. Prepare the journal entry to transfer standard variable and fixed overhead costs to Work-in-Process Inventory.

Problem 20-22

Variable Manufacturing Overhead Variances

Grover Glove Company attempts to control manufacturing overhead costs through the use of a flexible budget. Standards are set by studying historical overhead cost data, which are shown here. Actual total overhead costs for each month of the second quarter are also shown.

Standard variable overhead: $2.20 per direct labor hour

Months	Actual Direct Labor Hours	Actual Variable Overhead Costs	Standard Hours Allowed
April	76,000	$155,500	74,500
May	57,750	130,000	55,000
June	63,500	150,000	65,000

Required:

1. Compute the variable overhead spending variance and the variable overhead efficiency variance for each month.
2. **Interpretive Question:** Give several reasons why the variable overhead spending variances might be unfavorable.

Problem 20-23

Fixed Manufacturing Overhead Variances

Standard and actual cost data for Willey Corporation for the first three quarters of the year are shown below:

Standards:

Machine hours per unit produced	5.0 machine hours
Units produced per quarter	25,000 units
Fixed manufacturing overhead per quarter	$325,000

	Actual Direct Machine Hours	Actual Fixed Overhead Costs	Actual Number of Units Produced
First quarter	126,000	$321,000	25,500
Second quarter	120,000	330,000	23,000
Third quarter	124,000	324,500	26,500

Required:
1. Compute the fixed overhead budget variance for each quarter.
2. Compute the volume variance for each quarter.
3. **Interpretive Question:** At the end of the third quarter, the production manager at Willey Corporation believes that favorable volume variance in the third quarter means that he has more money to spend in production. Explain to the production manager what the volume variance represents and why it does not indicate that there is more money to spend in production.

Problem 20-24

Variable Manufacturing Overhead Spending and Efficiency Variances
The following production information is available for Porter Corporation:

Budgeted production	150,000 units
Actual production	145,000 units
Actual variable manufacturing overhead	$175,000
Variable manufacturing overhead applied	$0.80 per machine hour
Actual fixed manufacturing overhead	$88,500
Budgeted fixed manufacturing overhead	$90,000
Actual machine hours	220,000 hours
Standard machine hours per unit produced	1.5 machine hours

Required:
1. Calculate the following variances for Porter Corporation:
   a. Variable manufacturing overhead spending variance
   b. Variable manufacturing overhead efficiency variance
   c. Fixed manufacturing overhead budget variance
   d. Volume variance
2. **Interpretive Question:** Explain how the spending variance and the efficiency variance are used to control overhead costs.
3. Identify cost drivers other than machine hours that might be better measures of spending and efficient use of variable manufacturing overhead costs.
4. Can machine hours be considered a good cost driver for fixed manufacturing overhead costs?

 iscussion cases

Case 20-1

Continuous Improvement Needed
One evening after a strenuous day at the office, Janis Walker, president of Western Mills, Inc., a leading textile manufacturing firm, was out jogging to help relieve the tensions of that day's work. While jogging, she focused her thinking on the firm's commercial carpeting division. The major cus-

tomers of the division are companies that are building new office buildings, hotels, and motels and need quality carpet in their buildings. The carpet division is doing quite well, but Walker has a nagging feeling that the division could be doing better. She decided to discuss the performance of the division with the division manager. When she arrived home after jogging, Walker called the division manager and arranged a meeting for the next day.

(continued)

At the meeting, Walker asked the division manager how long it took to deliver an order to the building site after production started. The manager's answer was 17 days. Walker then asked what the industry average was for delivery. The answer was 15 days. Walker wanted to know why Western Mills took longer than competitors to meet order requirements. The manager answered that its product was of a higher quality, so customers were willing to wait longer for the order to be filled. With this information in hand and without hesitation, Walker said, "I will give you six months to reduce the delivery time to 10 days! You study the problem and tell me what resources you need to meet this 10-day delivery goal. I want a report from you as soon as possible."

1. Assuming that the division already has a standard cost system, what limitations of that system resulted in two more days of delivery time than its competitors?
2. Assuming this company has a standard cost system, what changes is the division manager likely to make in order to meet the president's 10-day delivery mandate?

Case 20-2

What Are My Costs Anyway?

You have recently been promoted to be the manager of the camera division of a large corporation. Your most profitable product is an instant camera that takes pictures and then develops them immediately. Historically, the pictures taken by the camera were of a poor quality, but due to large investments in research and new breakthroughs in technology, the instantly developed pictures are of increasingly higher quality. You have just received your segment financial statements for the period, which report the following:

Revenue	$81,000,000
Cost of products sold	40,000,000
Gross margin	$41,000,000

On the basis of this performance you are due to receive a $300,000 bonus. The top executives of the company are ecstatic about your performance because you have increased quality, reduced defects, and dramatically increased the productivity of your segment. Having studied management accounting, however, you know that the manufacturing costs are not the only ones that add value to your products. In fact, in your heart, you believe that were it not for the fact that you've pushed very hard this last year for more research and development, aggressive marketing, and good customer service subsequent to sales, your segment would not be nearly so profitable. Yet, these costs are tracked in other departments and are not your responsibility.

As a manager who is benefiting from traditional performance evaluation methods, you wonder whether you should inform management that they are actually giving you a bonus that is too high. Apparently, you are the only one in your company that is aware that these other value-adding costs should be included in your performance evaluation. What should you do? Do you let well enough alone, or should you go to management and let them know that you are probably being overpaid?

 j **udgment calls**

Judgment 20-1

You Decide: Which is more conducive to a successful organization: a centralized or decentralized company?

With the improvements in technology and communication, many companies are able to decentralize their operations and still work effectively. Many segment managers have been given the responsibility to make decisions and react quickly to problems for their respective department without consulting upper management. Although the trend has been towards decentralization for some time, is this the best solution for today's companies? Many people believe that by decentralizing operations, the overall goals and objectives of the company are forgotten. What one segment manager does for his or her department may not be in the best interest of the company as a whole.

Judgment 20-2

You Decide: Can a company make a conscious decision and set the prices of its products, or does the supply and demand of the market automatically dictate the price?

You were talking to your good friend in the economics department about companies and their pricing strategies. You mentioned a number of models used in accounting, such as variance analysis and ROI, and how these accounting models are helping companies accurately price their products, leading to better financial results. However, your friend disagreed. He believes that all the analysis in the world won't help a company price its products because that is left to the consumer. He said, "The consumer dictates what prices you will charge. It is the law of supply and demand. If you have a product that people want but it is priced too high, they won't buy it!"

Competency Enhancement Opportunities

▶ **Analyzing Real Company Information**
▶ **International Case**
▶ **Ethics Case**
▶ **Writing Assignment**

▶ **The Debate**
▶ **Internet Search**

The following additional assignments provide opportunities for students to develop critical thinking, ethical perspectives, oral and written communication skills, experience with electronic research, and teamwork through group and business activities.

▶ *Analyzing Real Company Information*

Analyzing 20-1 (Microsoft)

In the 2002 Form 10-K for MICROSOFT, you will find Segment Information in Note #20 in the Notes to the Financial Statements. That note is shown below:

	Desktop and Enterprise Software and Services	Consumer Software, Services, and Devices	Consumer Commerce Investments	Other	Reconciling Amounts	Consolidated
Notes to Financial Statements continued (in millions)						
Segment Information						
Year Ended June 30						
2000						
Revenue	$20,410	$ 1,654	$ 182	$691	$ 19	$22,956
Operating income (loss)	13,210	(1,090)	(60)	86	(1,140)	11,006
2001						
Revenue	$22,720	$ 1,961	$ 522	$652	$ (652)	$25,203
Operating income (loss)	14,261	(1,666)	(222)	97	(750)	11,720
2002						
Revenue	$23,786	$ 3,531	$ 245	$537	$ 266	$28,365
Operating income (loss)	14,671	(1,778)	23	59	(1,065)	11,910

1. As you can see, Microsoft has four different segments: Desktop and Enterprise Software and Services; Consumer Software, Services, and Devices; Consumer Commerce Investments; and Other (that is, all other segments combined). How do you think Microsoft primarily evaluates these segments—as cost centers, as profit centers, or as investment centers?
2. Compute the margin (operating income/revenue) for the four divisions for 2000, 2001, and 2002. Which segment is the most profitable? Which is growing the fastest in terms of revenues?

Analyzing 20-2 (Petersen Pottery)

Just outside Elkins, West Virginia, Clive Petersen has been making ceramic bathroom fixtures (sinks, toilets, and bathtubs) since 1960. Petersen's fixtures had become known over the years for their distinctive customer features, their high quality, and their long life. PETERSEN POTTERY started out as a two-man operation. By 1980 it had grown to 20 master potters. By this time, Clive Petersen felt that he had expanded to a point that he needed to institute a formal accounting control system. The insistence of his banker that he get a "real" management accounting system in place was also compelling. As a result, Petersen hired a formally trained management accountant who began working with his most experienced master potters to design cost standards. After some research, Petersen's accountant arrived at the following cost standards for a toilet (note that manufacturing overhead is allocated based on direct labor hours):

Direct materials:
Raw clay	25 lbs. × $0.95 per lb. =	$23.75
Glazing mix	5 lbs. × $0.75 per lb. =	3.75

Direct labor:
Molding	1.0 hr. × $15.00 per hour =	15.00
Glazing	0.5 hr. × $15.00 per hour =	7.50
Variable manufacturing overhead	1.5 hrs. × $3.00 per hour =	4.50
Fixed manufacturing overhead*	2.0 hrs. × $4.00 per hour =	8.00
Total per fixture		$62.50

*Based on budgeted production of 1,200 toilets.

After six months of operations, Petersen was disturbed over the lack of attention paid to the standards by his potters. He felt that the potters were just too set in their ways to adhere to the new system. Many of the potters told Petersen that the new system was "confusing" and didn't help them in their work. In reviewing the June production results, the following actual costs were noted in connection with manufacturing 1,145 toilets:

Materials used:
Raw clay	28,900 lbs. @ $0.92 per lb.
Glazing mix	5,900 lbs. @ $0.78 per lb.

Direct labor:
Molding	1,200 hrs. @ $15.25 per hour (average)
Glazing	600 hrs. @ $15.00 per hour (average)
Actual variable manufacturing overhead	$5,120
Actual fixed manufacturing overhead	$9,700

1. Compute all cost variances for the month of June.
2. What suggestions do you have for Mr. Petersen regarding his new standard cost system?

Source: Adapted from J. K. Shank, "Petersen Pottery" case, *Cases in Cost Management: A Strategic Emphasis* (Cincinnati: South-Western, 1996).

International

International Case

Target Costing in Japan

Japan is always a good place for useful insight on innovative management accounting practice and technique. From early on, the Japanese recognized that the most efficient way to keep costs down was to *design* them out of their products, not to reduce them after the products entered production. This realization reflects a fundamental reality of cost management in Japan; the majority of a product's costs (as much as 90 to 95% according to some experts) are "designed in." Consequently, effective cost control programs in a Japanese business typically focus heavily on the design process for a particular product. This is done primarily using a concept known as target costing, as well as value engineering (VE). Target costing is used to determine what the market is willing to pay for a product. Using the target market price (i.e., the price required to win the customer's business), the manager then subtracts the target profit to arrive at the target cost. After the target cost is determined, VE then is used to design the product in order to achieve the prespecified targeted level of costs. Thus, target costing manages costs by effectively designing into the products and processes the required costs in order to achieve the desired profit.

What do you think is the effect of target costing and VE on the use of variances? Specifically, will materials usage variances and labor efficiency variances be more or less important to a firm that strictly uses target costing and VE versus a traditional firm that is more focused on controlling daily production processes?

▶ *Ethics Case*

Cool Air, Inc.

Jack Lear, an internal auditor for Cool Air, Inc., met with Paul Marsh, the manager of the cost accounting department, to discuss a concern about a possible "glitch" in the standard cost system. Jack explained that he had been reviewing the employee time cards in the company division where air-conditioning units and refrigerators were assembled. The time cards reflected how much employee time was devoted to the assembly of air-conditioning units and how much time applied to refrigerators. Jack's concern was that the hours actually charged for each of these operations always seemed to be right on target with the standard labor times for each air-conditioning unit and each refrigerator unit assembled; yet Jack had been told a number of times by employees in the assembly department that the standard hours for assembling air-conditioning units were too low. The employees felt that they could not meet these standards without "fudging" their time cards or sacrificing some quality work in the assembly process. Since company policy emphasized product quality, Jack suspected that time sheets were being modified by shifting hours worked on air-conditioning units to the time sheets for assembling refrigerators.

Paul Marsh, the cost manager, thought for a minute about what Jack was telling him and then made an interesting observation. He said that he had been concerned about the fact that the company's prices for its air-conditioning units were generally lower than its competitors' prices for the same size and quality of units, whereas its prices for refrigerators were generally higher than those of its competitors. He wondered if the company's pricing structure, which was tied to its standard costs, was out of line with competition. This position was reinforced when Paul and Jack looked at the company's sales of each of these products. Over the past year or so, the company had gained market share in air-conditioner sales and had lost market share in refrigerators! Based on this information, Paul asked Jack to do some "detective" work on the time cards in the assembly division and report back his findings.

A few days later, Jack reported that he had found convincing evidence that the foremen in the assembly division had been in collusion to "doctor" employee time sheets in order to more closely meet the time standards for both air-conditioner and refrigerator assembly.

1. Who are the stakeholders affected by the "doctoring" of time sheets?
2. What are the ethical issues in this situation?
3. What should Paul do?

▶ *Writing Assignment*

Qualitative Variance Analysis

With the push for continuous improvement, stable standards may become a thing of the past. As companies strive for and achieve zero defects and no waste, variances quantifiable in terms of dollars become more and more difficult to obtain. To determine variances from a standard, firms are now turning their attention to qualitative measures such as the number of customer complaints or the number of machine setups. In a one- to two-page paper, identify three standards that might be used in a manufacturing environment and three standards that might be used in a service environment that cannot be readily quantifiable in dollars. Discuss how each of those standards would be measured, as well as how variances from those standards would be measured.

▶ *The Debate*

When Might a Favorable Variance Turn "Bad"?

Consider the labor efficiency variance. As you now understand after working through this chapter, a labor efficiency variance occurs when the hours actually used are more or less than the standard hours allowed based on actual production output. Assume that a team of internal auditors was able to complete a particular auditing project in one of the company's divisions in fewer hours than originally expected. Does this team have a favorable labor efficiency variance? More importantly, assuming there is a favorable labor efficiency variance, is this a good or a bad thing?

Divide your group into two teams and prepare a two-minute defense of your team's assigned position.

- One team represents "Favorable labor efficiency variance—GOOD!" Answer the following questions in your discussion. (1) Is measuring the difference between auditing hours *originally* budgeted and the actual hours used the proper way to measure a labor efficiency variance? (2) Your team should take the position that favorable labor efficiencies are a *good* result in this operation. What positive aspects concerning the audit team's work are indicated by a favorable labor efficiency variance?
- The other team represents "Favorable labor efficiency variance—BAD!" Answer the following in your discussion. (1) Respond to Team 1's report on whether measuring the difference between auditing hours *originally* budgeted and the actual hours used is the proper way to measure a labor efficiency variance. If you disagree, provide a correct response. (2) Your team should take the position that favorable labor efficiencies may *not* be a good result in this operation. What negative aspects concerning the audit team's work could be indicated by a favorable labor efficiency variance?

▶ *Internet Search*

Motivating Employees to Be More Productive

In addition to evaluating employees, as was discussed in this chapter, it is also important to motivate employees and managers by providing appropriate incentives. Many companies provide consulting services to organizations to help them create winning incentives for their employees. For an example of the kinds of services that are offered and some examples of incentives that seemed to work, go to **http://www.goalmanager.com**. Sometimes Web addresses change, so if this address does not work, access the Web site for this textbook (**http://albrecht.swlearning .com**) for an updated link. Once you've gained access to the site, look over some of the success stories and answer the following questions:

1. Describe one employee motivation success story described at this Web site.
2. What was the key to motivating employees in that organization?

Gonzales Company makes compact discs, which it sells to music companies. The following data are available for the company:

Expected sales in units:	
January	1,200 discs
February	1,400 discs
March	1,800 discs
Selling price	$10.00 per disc
Beginning accounts receivable balance, January 1	$4,000.00
Desired finished goods inventory, March 31	380 discs
Beginning finished goods inventory, January 1	300 discs*
Beginning direct materials inventory, January 1	400 ounces*
Desired direct materials inventory, March 31	600 ounces
Standard direct materials needed per disc	4 ounces
Standard direct labor time per finished product	10 minutes
Standard direct materials cost per ounce	$0.50
Standard direct labor cost per hour	$18.00

*The beginning inventory numbers for January were based on the best estimate of January sales in December. The expectations changed in January, and the new expected sales numbers should be used to estimate beginning inventory on hand for February and March.

Additional information:

- Of a month's sales, 60% is collected by month-end; the remaining 40% is collected the following month.
- The desired finished goods inventory each month is 20% of the next month's sales.
- The desired direct materials inventory every month is 10% of next month's production needs.

Required:
1. Using the standard costs for making the discs, prepare the following:
   a. Sales forecasts for January, February, and March (in dollars).
   b. Cash collections budgets for January, February, and March (in dollars). Assume that all sales are on credit.
   c. Production budgets for January, February, and March (in units).
   d. Direct materials usage budgets for January, February, and March (in ounces).
   e. Direct materials purchases budgets for January, February, and March (in ounces).
   f. Direct labor budgets for January, February, and March (in dollars).
2. Assume that actual usage of direct materials to make the discs was 4½ ounces at a cost of $0.60 per ounce. Compute the materials price and quantity variances for each month.
3. Assume that actual labor costs to make the discs were 12 minutes of labor at a cost of $19 per hour. Compute labor rate and efficiency variances for each month.
4. Assuming again that Gonzales is able to make the discs at the standard costs, how much will profits increase if it raises its price to $12 per disc in January, February, and March? Assume total fixed costs of $5,000 per month.
5. Assuming again that Gonzales is able to make the discs at its standard costs, if sales decrease by 300 discs during the three months at the increased price of $12 per disc, should Gonzales raise its price?

chapter

21

Managing Inventory and Service Costs

After studying this chapter, you should be able to:

Learning Objectives

1 Identify the different types of inventory in manufacturing, service, and merchandising organizations and understand how these inventory costs are reflected on the income statement and balance sheet.

2 Analyze the levels of raw materials, work-in-process, and finished goods inventories in a manufacturing organization.

3 Understand how merchants manage inventory in their organizations.

4 Measure profitability and personnel utilization in a service organization.

5 Describe how the concept of just-in-time (JIT) inventory systems is used to improve cost, quality, and timely performance in organizations.

eXpanded *Material*

6 Calculate and interpret holding costs in merchandising and service businesses.

7 Use classic quantitative tools in inventory management (economic order quantity, reorder point, and safety stock).

Sam Walton didn't invent discount retailing, but the company he founded, WAL-MART, is now the undisputed giant in the field.[1] Sam Walton started his career in retailing at a J.C. PENNEY store in Des Moines, Iowa. Sam was a good salesperson, though he disliked the bookkeeping that went along with the job: "[I] couldn't stand to leave a new customer waiting while I fiddled with paperwork on a sale I'd already made."

After World War II, Sam borrowed $20,000 from his father-in-law and bought a variety store in Newport, Arkansas. By 1962, Sam Walton had built a chain of 16 variety stores located in Missouri, Arkansas, and Kansas. By this time, however, Walton had become convinced that there were big opportunities in opening discount retail locations in the smaller U.S. towns and cities that were being overlooked by the traditional retailers such as SEARS. Walton pitched his idea to a couple of retail chains, but he couldn't generate any interest. He finally had to fund the start-up of his first discount store with his own money, putting up 95% of the financing, with another 3% coming from his skeptical brother Bud and 2% from the person he hired to manage the store. On July 2, 1962, this first Wal-Mart opened its doors. Today, Wal-Mart Stores, Inc. is the world's largest retailer ($218 billion in sales in 2002), employing approximately 1.3 million people in more than 4,300 stores. Each week, more than 100 million customers visit Wal-Mart stores worldwide.

FYI:

Two other well-known discount retailers also began operations in 1962: KMART and TARGET.

Providing the management accounting information necessary to effectively control this massive merchandising organization is no easy task. Providing merchandise at the right time, to the right place, and at the right price is how a retailer "wins" customers. Sound simple? Consider that at any given moment, a typical Wal-Mart discount store has more than 70,000 different items of inventory in stock. Every one of these items must be identified, ordered, inventoried, and replenished—all the while keeping an eye on costs. (Inventory costs at a typical Supercenter are even tougher to manage because these stores also carry more than 20,000 grocery items, many of them perishable.) The crucial idea behind discount retailing is that lower prices will lead to a large enough increase in sales volume to make up for the fact that a smaller profit is made on each inventory item. As the discount retailing industry has expanded and become more competitive, Wal-Mart has had to be ever more aggressive in cutting its profit margins in order to keep its prices low. To illustrate, in 1980 Wal-Mart's gross profit percentage was 27%; in 2003, the percentage had dropped to 22%. For a company wrestling with tightening margins, inventory control is a crucial part of operations. Wal-Mart leased its first computer, an IBM 360, in 1969 in order to track the inventory flow at its new distribution center in Bentonville, Arkansas. Ever since, Wal-Mart has been a leader in using information technology to monitor and manage its inventory.

Today, Wal-Mart is a leader in implementing electronic data interchange (EDI), which involves the electronic transfer of invoices, purchase orders, and shipping notices, thus speeding up the communication between Wal-Mart and its suppliers. One important tool in Wal-Mart's EDI system is small handheld computers that link by radio frequency to in-store terminals. The next time you're in a Wal-Mart store, watch to see if you can spot an employee using one of these handheld computers to manage inventory on the shelves. These devices provide the critical link between Wal-Mart's suppliers and customers. With this technology, Wal-Mart management is able to get faster and more accurate information to plan, control, and evaluate every aspect of inventory management. This leads to better cost control and better merchandise and service.

In addition to the use of handheld computers, Wal-Mart's "Retail Link" system now gives vendors access to Wal-Mart's own store-by-store sales information and inventory levels in real time, so that the vendors themselves can know when to make additional product shipments to specific Wal-Mart locations. The information partnership between Wal-Mart and PROCTER & GAMBLE, dating back to 1987, is legendary as an example of a buyer and a seller exchanging detailed transaction data in order to improve the operating efficiency of both companies. As a result of its leadership in technology, Wal-Mart is able to generate management accounting information that provides truly competitive cost, quality, and time information.

FYI:

In its 2003 financial statements, Procter & Gamble (P&G) disclosed that Wal-Mart is its single largest customer, accounting for 18% of P&G's sales in 2003.

1 Information from Sandra S. Vance and Roy V. Scott, *Wal-Mart: A History of Sam Walton's Retail Phenomenon* (New York: Twayne Publishers, 1994); Sam Walton and John Huey, *Sam Walton: Made in America* (New York: Doubleday, 1992); Wal-Mart Stores, Inc., **http://www.walmart.com**, accessed September 25, 2003.

Some companies, such as COCA-COLA and NIKE, have become successful through convincing potential customers that their soft drinks or sports shoes are superior to all others. Hence, we talk of the marketing genius of Coca-Cola and Nike, not their cost management techniques. In contrast, WAL-MART does not offer unique products; to a large extent, Wal-Mart sells the same products sold by every other discount retailer in the world. Wal-Mart attracts us with its low prices, and consistent low prices are possible only in an organization that meticulously and relentlessly controls its inventory costs. In this chapter, we will introduce techniques used to manage inventory in manufacturing organizations, service organizations, and merchandising organizations (like Wal-Mart).

Inventory in Organizations

1 Identify the different types of inventory in manufacturing, service, and merchandising organizations and understand how these inventory costs are reflected in the income statement and balance sheet.

In an earlier chapter on product cost flows, we discussed the ways in which costs flow from one activity to the next in manufacturing, merchandising, and service organizations. These cost flow patterns are summarized in Exhibit 1. You can see in this exhibit that product costs first appear on the balance sheet in the form of inventory, and then flow onto the income statement as cost of goods or services sold (an expense account). Recall that the extended production process characteristic of both manufacturing and service firms means that those organizations have significant levels of work-in-process inventory—goods or services that have not yet been completed but have already resulted in work being done and costs being incurred. In addition, note that both manufacturing and merchandising firms maintain significant inventories of goods that are ready for sale (finished goods or merchandise inventory). On the other hand, it is typically not in the nature of a service business to have finished goods inventory. As soon as the service (e.g., the accountant's audit, the doctor's office visit, the trucking company's transportation contract) has been completed and moves out of the work-in-process services account

Exhibit 1: Cost Flows in Manufacturing, Service, and Merchandising Organizations (sometimes known as the unbilled services account), it is delivered to the final customer, and the product cost[2] is transferred to the cost of services sold expense account.

Exhibit 2 compares the income statements for three fictitious firms. The exhibit also presents selected balance sheet accounts. Carefully examine this exhibit to be sure you understand how the activities and inventories of manufacturing, service, and merchandising organizations are reported in the financial statements.

Exhibit 2: Financial Statement Comparison: Manufacturing, Service, and Merchandising Firms

Income Statements for Different Types of Firms
For the Year Ended December 31, 2006

	Manufacturing Firm	Service Firm	Merchandising Firm
	Mason Tool Company	Brown Engineering, Inc.	Smith Office Supply, Inc.
Sales revenue	$4,000,000	$5,000,000	$2,500,000
Cost of goods sold/Cost of services:			
Cost of goods manufactured/Cost of services:			
Beginning raw materials/supplies inventory	$ 24,000	$ 230	
+ Purchases of materials/supplies	1,153,000	11,400	
Total raw materials/supplies available	$1,177,000	$ 11,630	
– Ending raw materials/supplies inventory	(25,000)	(180)	
Raw materials/supplies used in production	$1,152,000	$ 11,450	
+ Direct labor	445,000	1,890,000	
+ Applied manufacturing/service overhead	1,003,000	798,000	
Total manufacturing/service costs	$2,600,000	$2,699,450	
+ Beginning work-in-process inventory/services	24,000	75,000	
– Ending work-in-process inventory/services	(19,000)	(83,000)	
Cost of goods manufactured/Cost of services	$2,605,000	$2,691,450	
Merchandise purchases			$1,713,000
+ Beginning finished goods/merchandise inventory	24,000		37,000
– Ending finished goods/merchandise inventory	(47,000)		(36,000)
Cost of goods sold/Cost of services	$2,582,000		$1,714,000
+Underapplied manufacturing/service overhead	307,000	22,100	
Adjusted cost of goods sold/Cost of services	$2,889,000	$2,713,550	
Gross margin	$1,111,000	$2,286,450	$ 786,000
Selling and administrative expenses:			
Selling expenses	$ 256,000	$ 367,000	$ 406,000
Administrative expenses	474,000	1,003,000	188,000
Total selling and administrative expenses	$ 730,000	$1,370,000	$ 594,000
Operating income	$ 381,000	$ 916,450	$ 192,000

Selected Balance Sheet Information
December 31, 2006

Accounts receivable	$74,000	$63,000	$ 3,900
Raw materials inventory	25,000		
Work-in-process inventory/services	19,000	83,000	
Finished goods/Merchandise inventory	47,000		36,000
Supplies inventory	750	180	450
Accounts payable	28,000	16,000	48,000

2 We use the term "product cost" to refer to both the cost of goods in manufacturing and merchandising organizations and to the cost of services in service organizations.

As you can see, each income statement in Exhibit 2 follows a typical income statement format:

Sales revenue	$XXX,XXX
Costs of goods sold	(XX,XXX)
Gross margin	$XXX,XXX
Selling and administrative expenses	(X,XXX)
Operating income	$XXX,XXX

Remember that the calculation for cost of goods sold for a manufacturing company (and for a service company) comes from the cost of goods manufactured schedule.[3] This schedule is also included in Exhibit 2 and follows the format below:

Beginning raw materials inventory	$ XXX	
Add: Raw materials purchased	X,XXX	
Total raw materials available	$X,XXX	
Less: Ending raw materials inventory	(XXX)	
Raw materials used in production		$ X,XXX
Direct labor		X,XXX
Applied manufacturing overhead		X,XXX
Total manufacturing costs		$XX,XXX
Add: Beginning work-in-process inventory		XXX
Less: Ending work-in-process inventory		(XXX)
Cost of goods manufactured		$XX,XXX

You should note two important items in Mason Tool's cost of goods manufacturing calculation versus the similar calculation for Brown Engineering. First of all, notice that Brown is using a rather insignificant amount of supplies ($11,450) to create its service product, especially when compared with Mason Tool, which is using a very significant amount of raw materials ($1,152,000) to create its tools. This difference underscores the fact that some supplies are often used in the process of creating and delivering a service product, but these costs are typically not a significant component of cost of services. Secondly, when calculating cost of services (analogous to cost of goods sold), note that Brown Engineering does not hold finished service products for later sale to its customers. Again, the very nature of a service business determines that a completed service is delivered to the customer almost instantly. In contrast, Brown Engineering does have significant work-in-process "inventory," representing the costs of engineering contracts that have not yet been completed.

Smith Office Supply does not create the products it sells. As a result, Smith has no work-in-process inventory, and the cost of goods sold calculation only requires that Smith adjust the total amount of merchandise it purchased in 2006 by the change in its merchandise inventory account.

Balance sheet information for the three companies is presented at the bottom of Exhibit 2. As you can see, all three firms have accounts receivable, supplies inventory, and accounts payable accounts. Because Brown uses supplies directly in providing engineering services to its clients, this account is used in the calculation of cost of services. On the other hand, cost of supplies for Mason Tool and Smith Office Supply is included in the overhead and administrative expenses accounts. In addition, you can see that Mason Tool has three inventory accounts; Smith Office Supply has one inventory account to record the costs of goods until the goods are sold to customers. Brown does not have a raw materials inventory, finished goods inventory, or merchandise inventory account (though supplies inventory is analogous to raw materials inventory for many service firms). However, its work-in-process services account acts much like Mason Tool's work-in-process inventory account and is similarly used to adjust the cost of services account in Brown's income statement.

---

3 If necessary, be sure to review the earlier chapter on product cost flows, particularly Exhibit 3 on page 877 and Exhibit 5 on page 886.

Exhibit 1 reviews how product costs and inventory flow through manufacturing, merchandising, and service organizations, and Exhibit 2 illustrates how these different types of inventory are reflected in the income statement and the balance sheet. In the remainder of this chapter, we will discuss how companies can use this information to manage inventory. The extended production process of a manufacturing or service firm requires careful scrutiny of costs at each important stage of the process. For a merchandising company, cost management focuses on acquiring the right amount of inventory for the right price.

> **TO SUMMARIZE:** Both manufacturing and service organizations must manage substantial production processes; an important managerial accounting function in these organizations is tracing the flow of costs through the various stages of production. Both manufacturing and merchandising organizations traditionally maintain significant levels of inventory ready for sale to customers. These differences among manufacturing, merchandising, and service organizations are reflected in differences in their income statements and balance sheets.

Analyzing Inventory Levels

2 Analyze the levels of raw materials, work-in-process, and finished goods inventories in a manufacturing organization.

In the income statement and balance sheet figures reported in Exhibit 2 for Mason Tool Company, cost of goods sold was determined to be $2,889,000 (after the adjustment for underapplied manufacturing overhead). This is a summary number that is used in the financial statements and is the number that the company's auditors will work hard to attest for the company's published financial statements. However, because it is a summary number, it is not useful for detailed internal decision making. To be useful, management may want to analyze product costs on a product-by-product basis, a period-by-period basis, and a department-by-department basis. By breaking costs down by product, period, and department, management can determine which departments and products are performing well and which are performing poorly. Further, because product costs are used to measure inventory values on the balance sheet, these costs can be used to determine how effectively Mason Tool Company manages its investments in inventory. Exhibit 3 reports the monthly ending balances for the three inventories necessary to produce its products: raw materials, work-in-process, and finished goods. These inventories represent significant investments necessary to support Mason Tool Company's production processes.[4]

Mason maintains a raw materials inventory in order to ensure that there are materials always available for use in production. This flow of materials is represented by the cost of materials used (i.e., the materials transferred onto the factory floor). The work-in-process inventory is important to maintaining a constant flow of production through the factory and into the finished goods warehouse. This "flow" is represented by the cost of goods manufactured (i.e., the completed goods transferred off of the factory floor). Finally, the finished goods inventory is necessary to be sure that products are always available for sale to customers. The flow of product costs to customers is represented by the cost of goods sold.

The top panel of Exhibit 3 reports product cost and inventory ending balance data for table saws at Mason Tool Company (we'll assume that table saws are this company's only product). These data are listed by month, and the total values for the year tie back to the income statement data in Exhibit 2. As you review these data, try to put yourself in the shoes of the Mason Tool Company production manager. Ask yourself this question: how effectively is the company using inventory to support its purchasing, production, and sales processes? It is difficult to answer this question based solely on the data reported in the top panel of Exhibit 3.

---

4 The need to maintain inventory in order to support key business processes such as production and sales is challenged by an important new management concept known as just-in-time inventory systems or JIT. We discuss JIT later in this chapter.

Exhibit 3: Mason Tool Company Inventory Report

Monthly Table Saw Inventory and Cost Data													
(numbers are reported in thousands)													
	Jan.	**Feb.**	**March**	**April**	**May**	**June**	**July**	**Aug.**	**Sept.**	**Oct.**	**Nov.**	**Dec.**	**Balance**
Raw materials inventory	$ 25	$ 20	$ 28	$ 24	$ 24	$ 22	$ 20	$ 21	$ 22	$ 23	$ 27	$ 25	$ 25
Work-in-process inventory	19	20	18	17	21	20	21	23	18	19	21	19	19
Finished goods inventory	48	46	48	46	42	40	41	47	46	48	49	47	47
	Jan.	**Feb.**	**March**	**April**	**May**	**June**	**July**	**Aug.**	**Sept.**	**Oct.**	**Nov.**	**Dec.**	**Total**
Cost of raw materials used	$ 77	$ 86	$ 86	$ 92	$102	$119	$116	$113	$ 94	$ 87	$ 80	$100	$1,152
Cost of goods manufactured	196	195	201	215	226	245	248	234	222	211	207	205	2,605
Cost of goods sold*	195	190	212	223	230	227	247	236	221	198	208	195	2,582

*Because cost of goods sold is usually adjusted only once per year (at the end of the year), these monthly cost of goods sold numbers are unadjusted for over- or underapplied overhead.

Monthly Table Saw Inventory Performance Measures											
	Feb.	**March**	**April**	**May**	**June**	**July**	**Aug.**	**Sept.**	**Oct.**	**Nov.**	**Dec.**
Raw materials inventory turnover	3.8	3.6	3.5	4.3	5.2	5.5	5.5	4.4	3.9	3.2	3.8
Work-in-process inventory turnover	10.0	10.6	12.3	11.9	12.0	12.1	10.6	10.8	11.4	10.4	10.3
Finished goods inventory turnover	4.0	4.5	4.7	5.2	5.5	6.1	5.4	4.8	4.2	4.3	4.1
	Feb.	**March**	**April**	**May**	**June**	**July**	**Aug.**	**Sept.**	**Oct.**	**Nov.**	**Dec.**
Days in raw materials inventory	7.8	8.4	8.5	7.1	5.8	5.4	5.4	6.9	7.8	9.4	7.8
Days in work-in-process inventory	3.0	2.8	2.4	2.5	2.5	2.5	2.8	2.8	2.6	2.9	2.9
Days in finished goods inventory	7.4	6.7	6.3	5.7	5.4	4.9	5.6	6.3	7.1	7.0	7.4

inventory turnover The number of times the inventory in the organization "turns over" during a period of time. It is often easier to think of inventory turnover as the number of times a dollar invested in inventory generates output. Output for raw materials inventory is measured by the cost of raw materials used in production. Output for work-in-process inventory is measured by cost of goods manufactured. Output for finished goods (or merchandise) inventory is measured by cost of goods sold. Inventory turnover is computed as total output for the period divided by average inventory level.

days in inventory Average number of days of use provided by the level of inventory maintained by the organization. This definition is closely related to the "inventory turnover" concept. Days in inventory is computed as number of days in the period being assessed divided by the inventory turnover. (See related definition and computation for inventory turnover.)

By combining inventory data with its related cost flow data, management is able to create a report that helps it control how effectively raw materials, work-in-process, and finished goods inventories are being used. Two measures used to evaluate a company's inventory management practices are **inventory turnover** and **days in inventory**. Exhibit 4 illustrates the computations of inventory turnover and days in inventory in February for table saws at Mason Tool Company.

The inventory turnover measure is based on the following formula:

$$\frac{\text{Cost flow for the period}}{\text{Average inventory level*}} = \text{Inventory turnover}$$

*where the average inventory level is generally measured as:

$$\frac{\text{Beginning inventory} + \text{Ending inventory}}{2} = \text{Average inventory level}$$

This turnover measure indicates how many times during the period the organization completely replenished or replaced the inventory, given the rate at which costs are flowing through the production process. For example, Exhibit 3 reports that Mason's cost of raw materials used during February was $86,000. As shown in Exhibit 4, Mason's average raw materials inventory level for February was approximately $22,500 [($25,000 + $20,000) ÷ 2], which means that its raw materials inventory "turned over" or was replaced 3.8 times during the month. Inventory turnover measures the intensity with which Mason is managing its raw materials inventory—low inventory turnover indicates lots of idle

Caution

Days in inventory is a function of the time period used to compute the production costs used in the related inventory turnover measure. Therefore, if the cost of raw materials used (or cost of goods manufactured or cost of goods sold) is for a six-month period, then the days in raw materials inventory (or days in work-in-process inventory or days in finished goods inventory) should be computed using the numbers of days in a six-month period. The organization generally sets a policy on numbers of days to use. For example, it may choose to consistently use 30 days in a month, 90 days in a quarter, 180 days in a half year, and 360 days in a year.

inventory lying around the raw materials warehouse whereas high inventory turnover indicates extremely active management with little excess inventory.

The days in inventory measure provides an alternative measure of the inventory turnover concept. The computation of this measure is as follows:

$$\frac{\text{Number of days in the reporting period}}{\text{Inventory turnover}} = \text{Days in inventory}$$

For example, Exhibit 3 reports that Mason's cost of goods manufactured (which "flows" out of the work-in-process inventory account) during February was $195,000. Using the inventory turnover formula shown above, Mason's work-in-process inventory turnover for the month is 10.0, meaning that inventory was replaced 10 times in February. If we assume that on average there are 30 days in a month,[5] then Mason maintained approximately three days' worth of work-in-process inventory in February to support the production process. The fewer numbers of days in work-in-process inventory, the more streamlined the production process; a long, complex manufacturing process (such as the construction of a ship) could have more than a year's worth of production costs tied up in unfinished inventory.

Mason Tool Company's performance in terms of how well it efficiently uses finished goods inventory is indicated by the fact that this inventory turned over

Exhibit 4: Analysis of the Levels of Raw Materials, Work-in-Process, and Finished Goods Inventories

Raw Materials Inventory—February

Cost of raw materials used during February	$86,000
Beginning raw materials inventory in February*	$25,000
Ending raw materials inventory in February	$20,000
Average inventory balance during the month	$22,500
Raw materials inventory turnover (cost flow ÷ average inventory)	3.8
Days in raw materials inventory (30 days ÷ inventory turnover)[†]	7.8 days

Work-in-Process Inventory—February

Cost of goods manufactured during February	$195,000
Beginning work-in-process inventory in February*	$19,000
Ending work-in-process inventory in February	$20,000
Average inventory balance during the month	$19,500
Work-in-process inventory turnover (cost flow ÷ average inventory)	10.0
Days in work-in-process inventory (30 days ÷ inventory turnover)[†]	3.0 days

Finished Goods Inventory—February

Cost of goods sold during February	$190,000
Beginning finished goods inventory in February*	$48,000
Ending finished goods inventory in February	$46,000
Average inventory balance during the month	$47,000
Finished goods inventory turnover (cost flow ÷ average inventory)	4.0
Days in finished goods inventory (30 days ÷ inventory turnover)[†]	7.4 days

*Equal to the ending inventory level in January.
[†]<u>Don't</u> round the turnover ratio when computing days in inventory.

5 Although there are 28 (occasionally 29) days in the month of February, we use an average of 30 days per month in this textbook for all monthly days in inventory calculations. This is a standard number of days per month used by many organizations for similar calculations.

4.0 times during February. Alternatively, Mason reports 7.4 days in finished goods inventory for February. This means that Mason is able to sell its entire inventory of table saws to customers approximately every 7.4 days.

Mason Tool Company's inventory turnover and days in inventory computations for the remainder of 2006 are reported in the bottom panel of Exhibit 3. Take a moment to scan these numbers. Do you see any patterns across time in the way that Mason Tool Company is able

business environment

That's a Lot of Inventory! During your last trip to the grocery store, did you count the number of types of product on the shelves? How many different stock keeping units (SKUs) or product items would you estimate your local grocery store uses to monitor its inventory activity? 1,000? 10,000? 100,000? Keeping track of the catalog and inventory of SKUs is made easier by technology. Managers need detailed information to help keep the shelves fully stocked without having too much invested in inventory.

In 1883, when Arthur and Howard Hannaford opened their fruit and vegetable stand in Portland, Maine, life was just a bit slower. Now HANNAFORD BROS. is a supermarket chain operating 116 supermarkets and three distribution centers located throughout Maine, New Hampshire, Vermont, New York, and Massachusetts under the names of SHOP 'N SAVE and HANNAFORD FOOD AND DRUG SUPERSTORES with an average store size of about 48,000 square feet per store. Just like every business, the grocery business is competitive; traditionally thin margins make every penny count. Store managers are under a lot of pressure to control inventory and costs and generate as much revenue as possible.

The company's information philosophy is expressed by Bill Homa, chief information officer of Hannaford, "If we can provide managers with the information they need to reduce their out-of-stocks, we can help them increase their sales." The company used to distribute daily printed merchandising reports to its stores via FEDERAL EXPRESS. Given the number of stores involved, this procedure cost Hannaford several hundred thousand dollars each year.

In order to provide managers with the inventory information they need to effectively operate their stores, Hannaford and

CISCO developed an inventory SKU system to manage its perishable dated products to reduce costs and increase sales. This system alerts managers to early indications of inventory problems, improving their ability to make strategic merchandising and buying decisions. The system also hosts merchandising reports that are updated daily and centralizes decision-support information for corporate planners and store managers.

The Hannaford inventory SKU system eliminates the need for daily printed merchandising reports, which were costing the company hundreds of thousands of dollars in annual express delivery charges. It also gives managers Web-based access to daily merchandising reports and affords them the means to examine sales by item or by category. Thanks to the system, they are able to control "shrink" (the loss associated with products that are outdated, damaged, or stolen), look at weekly variances in sales and labor, and centralize all of this information so that corporate planners can make timely decisions based on updated knowledge of chain-wide trends.

"In the past, we printed new reports every day and shipped them out to the stores. Now store and department managers can use Web browsers to search the online reports and immediately pull off the information they need. And by eliminating paper reports, we're also saving several hundred thousand dollars in annual FedEx charges."

—Bill Homa, chief information officer, Hannaford Bros.

In 1999, Hannaford announced its merger with DELHAIZE AMERICA; allowing Hannaford Bros. Co. to operate as a separate business while being part of a $14 billion company with 1,400 stores from Maine to Florida.

Sources: http://www.cisco.com, "Hannaford Bros. Enables Managers;" **http://www.hannaford.com**, "About Us" content page, accessed August 18, 2003.

to manage its three types of inventory? Look closely at the days in inventory numbers. You should see that Mason is able to reduce its days in finished goods inventory during the summer months by approximately two days (from more than seven days to a little more than five days). This suggests that Mason is experiencing more sales of its table saws in the summer. While Mason may or may not be able to control this seasonal cycle, it does need to anticipate these surges in market demand and plan its production process accordingly. The fact that Mason is basically holding its days in work-in-process inventory consistent at between approximately 2.5 and 3 days indicates that it is working hard to adjust its production outflow to the market demand for its table saws. One inventory problem that Mason likely needs to address is the way it controls its raw materials inventory. This inventory level fluctuates from about 5.5 days in the summer to about 8 days during the winter. Perhaps Mason needs to more aggressively tailor its volume of raw material purchases to coincide with production and sales.

STOP & THINK

It appears in Exhibit 3 that the inventory performance measures are missing for January. Is it possible to compute these measures using the data provided? What data would you need to analyze how well Mason Tool Company managed its three inventory levels during January?

As we finish this section on managing inventory levels, it is important to point out that comparing performance across periods of time is only one way that these two measures can be used to control inventory. Management may also want to compare the inventory levels of different products across the organization, or may want to "benchmark" the performance of its products with those of other companies. Further, in addition to assessing production cost and inventory levels, managers are just as interested in indicators of product and production quality. We'll address some of these quality issues in the next chapter.

TO SUMMARIZE: Cost of goods sold is a summary number that is audited and used in the financial statements, but it is not very useful for managers to use when assessing how well the company controls inventory costs and inventory levels. Two management accounting tools can be used to support good management control of levels of raw materials, work-in-process, and finished goods inventories. These two measures are inventory turnover and days in inventory. Inventory turnover is a measure of the intensity with which the organization is using its inventory. Higher turnover numbers indicate a more efficient use of inventory. The days sales in inventory measure reports the average number of days of inventory use. A lower number of days indicates a more efficient use of inventory.

Managing Cost Information

3 Understand how merchants manage inventory in their organizations.

As discussed in the preceding section, cost data can be used in a manufacturing firm to evaluate the appropriateness of the levels of raw materials, work-in-process, and finished goods inventories. Merchants, or managers of merchandising organizations, are particularly conscious of inventory levels currently in the retail store or in the distribution center. Managing this inventory takes careful and detailed planning. The detail in these plans results from merchants having *many* different types of inventory items, each with its own particular supplier source and targeted customer. Merchants must also be very careful in planning their inventory levels because having either too little or too much inventory can involve critical issues. These issues are listed in Exhibit 5. If accountants are aware of these issues, they can help their organizations avoid a variety of unnecessary out-of-pocket costs or opportunity costs.

Carrying Too Much Inventory

Having inventory is certainly necessary for most merchants if they expect to do business with their customers. However, accumulating as much inventory as possible is *not* the purpose of merchandising (or manufacturing) companies. Good business management entails having the right assets at the right place in the right time and in the right quantity (always a challenging

Exhibit 5: Inventory Management Issues

Carrying Too Much Inventory	Carrying Too Little Inventory
• Increased overhead costs	• Increased risk of lost sales
• Increased financial holding costs	• Increased ordering costs
• Increased risk of loss of market value	• Increased risk of supplier price increases
• Decreased inventory flexibility	• Increased exposure to nondelivery
• Increased inventory shrinkage	• Decreased bulk order discounts

holding costs The financial opportunity costs that result from investing money in an asset such as inventory. Whatever income the money could generate in an alternative investment is the holding cost of the current investment.

inventory shrinkage The disorder, spoilage, and theft that result when a company chooses to maintain inventory on site, resulting in additional out-of-pocket costs to replace inventory.

FYI:

In 1999, FRUIT OF THE LOOM reported that it experienced inventory shrinkage totaling $70.4 million. This represented a 25% increase in shrinkage compared to the prior year. Fruit of the Loom attributed the shrinkage increase to expansion of its network of contractors (factories where its clothing items are produced).

FYI:

How important is the Christmas buying season for a toy merchant? The 2002 annual report for TOYS "R" US, INC., reports that approximately 43% of its sales occur in the months of November, December, and January.

endeavor!). Later in this chapter, we'll introduce you to the concept of just-in-time (JIT) inventory management, which emphasizes the fact that too much inventory creates a lot of management problems. Managers of merchandising organizations are particularly sensitive to this fact. First of all, clearly many out-of-pocket costs are involved in having inventory on site, including costs of storage, security, and record keeping. What may not be as clear is the financial opportunity cost (sometimes called the **holding cost**) of the inventory investment. Every dollar that is invested in inventory cannot be used in alternative business investments, such as expanding another part of the business or simply investing in the stock market or in a bank savings account. Whatever money we *could* make by investing the money elsewhere is the holding cost of the current inventory investment. Accountants measure and report holding costs all the time. We will demonstrate the calculation of holding costs in the expanded material section of this chapter.

Increased overhead costs and holding costs are not the only issues involved in carrying too much inventory. The more inventory a merchant elects to carry, the more risk the merchant faces that the inventory will decrease in market value before it can be sold (of course, inventory may unexpectedly increase in market value as well). In addition, when a merchant invests in a lot of one type of inventory, it becomes difficult to shift to another inventory type that customers may suddenly want to buy. Finally, every merchant understands the tough reality that inventories "shrink" over time. **Inventory shrinkage** happens in a lot of ways. The type of shrinkage we hear about most often is theft (either by customers or employees). However, when inventory is being moved, stacked, stored, retrieved, and rotated, things get broken, parts get lost, and items become mislabeled. Liquid and gas stocks spill or evaporate. Cloth material becomes soiled. Grocery items spoil or become stale. As inventory is piled up around the store or distribution center, this disorder, spoilage, and theft are revealed every time the company takes an annual inventory count, resulting in additional out-of-pockets costs to replace the inventory.

Carrying Too Little Inventory

Clearly, having too much inventory is a poor use of resources. However, poor planning that results in not having enough inventory on hand can also be a source of trouble. It is obvious to most managers and owners that potential sales are lost when customers are turned away because of a lack of inventory. Accountants can support good inventory management when they are able to quantify these opportunity costs for decision makers. As can be seen in Exhibit 5, however, an organization that has inadequate inventory levels also incurs other costs. For example, initiating an order with a wholesaler or manufacturer for the delivery of goods often requires a number of business processes, including counting inventory, preparing purchase orders, receiving and inspecting shipments of goods, and initiating payments for purchases. Most merchants have to initiate and pay for each of these steps every time they purchase inventory. Merchants that maintain low inventory levels by buying in smaller quantities will generally have to make more purchases, and pay for additional employee time, to replenish their stock.

Prices for most types of inventory increase with time. Some items are particularly susceptible to sudden price increases. Have you ever awakened to hear the morning newscast report that automobile gasoline prices have suddenly surged? When you go out to your car and discover the gas tank nearly empty, don't you wish you had filled the tank yesterday? One reason some merchants purchase large amounts of inventory is to temporarily protect themselves from sudden increases in prices. Companies without similar foresight will experience greater out-of-pocket expenses if prices do increase. Companies that keep very low levels of inventory are most likely to have to pay for every price increase. In addition, these same companies are much more dependent on their suppliers to *always* meet their delivery commitments. If a supplier is late in making promised shipments or delivers inventory that is damaged or of the wrong type, the merchant may miss making sales to some customers. Finally, merchants that regularly purchase large levels of inventory often enjoy price discounts from their suppliers. Merchants making smaller purchases should be aware of the opportunity cost related to missing these potential bulk purchase discounts.

Example of Inventory Management Costs

We'll use the fictitious example of two large retailers of children's toys, Kids N Toys, Inc., and Child's Delight, Inc., to explore the issues and costs involved in inventory management for merchandising organizations. As you might expect, the Christmas buying season is a big deal for a toy retailer. Management and buyers for these companies study trend reports and catalogs all year in order to properly plan their investments for December. Both companies have limited resources that can be invested in inventory for the holiday season. Given the necessary **lead time**, as well as the size of the investment, these decisions are absolutely critical to both companies. Once December has arrived, it becomes very difficult to make many adjustments to preplanned inventory types and levels.

A wholesaler of children's dolls has announced the availability of a new doll for Christmas this year, the Burzee Doll. Based on the manufacturer's reputation, as well as the fact that the manufacturer of the doll intends to do a lot of promotional advertising, the wholesaler is confident that the Burzee Doll will sell very well this year. To help make planning decisions, each retailer has its management accountants prepare some forecasts on potential revenues and costs related to the issues listed in Exhibit 5. Based on the projections of its accountants, Kids N Toys, Inc., decides to invest very heavily in the Burzee Doll and orders 50,000 dolls for delivery on November 1. Because of the size of its order, the wholesaler offers Kids N Toys a discount of $2 per doll. On the other hand, the accountants' projections of revenues and costs at Child's Delight, Inc., are not as optimistic. As a result, Child's Delight orders only 5,000 dolls and pays the full wholesale price of $12 per doll. Both retailers follow the manufacturer's recommendation to set the customer price at $30 per doll.

Exhibit 6 outlines all the Burzee Doll events that take place during the holiday season, as well as the resulting revenues and costs for the two companies. As it turns out, the Burzee Dolls are a real hit during the holiday buying season. Child's Delight keeps running out of inventory and must reorder dolls three times during the season. As you can see in Exhibit 6, each time Child's Delight reorders dolls, it is not hard for the accountants to note the amount of inventory shrinkage. Occasionally, dolls are stolen, misplaced, or destroyed in the process of moving, sorting, and stacking. On the other hand, Kids N Toys has lots of dolls spread out all over the store, making it difficult to know much about shrinkage without taking a very expensive inventory count. The accountants at Kids N Toys elect to wait until all the inventory is sold before measuring inventory shrinkage.

lead time Generally, the time interval between initiating a request and finally fulfilling the request.

STOP & THINK

These two companies begin the holiday season with very different levels of inventory in Burzee Dolls. With its very large inventory investment, what additional inventory costs are now a factor for Kids N Toys? What additional inventory costs is Child's Delight susceptible to with its relatively small inventory investment?

Exhibit 6: Management Events in the Burzee Doll Inventory

Date	Event	Kids N Toys, Inc.	Child's Delight, Inc.
Nov. 1	Retailers establish the Burzee Doll inventory.	Company buys 50,000 dolls at $10 per doll. Customer price is set at $30.	Company buys 5,000 dolls at $12 per doll. Customer price is set at $30.
30	Sales on the doll start increasing.	Company has sold 7,500 dolls.	Company has sold 4,950 dolls and is out of stock. Reorders another 5,000 dolls at $12 per doll.
Dec. 10	Sales on the doll are really strong.	Company has sold another 12,000 dolls.	Company has sold another 4,970 dolls and is out of stock again. Reorders another 5,000 dolls at $15 per doll (supplier has increased price).
20	Sales on the doll continue to be very strong.	Company has sold another 15,000 dolls.	Company has sold another 4,990 dolls and is out of stock again. Reorders another 5,000 dolls at $15 per doll.
31	Sales have nearly halted in the last few days.	Company has sold another 7,000 dolls.	Company has sold another 4,940 dolls and is out of stock again. Chooses not to reorder.
Jan. 15	Sales are nearly nonexistent.	Company has sold another 500 dolls and now puts dolls on sale at cost ($10).	Out of Burzee Doll business.
30	Sales pick up a little.	Company has sold another 2,000 dolls and now sells the remaining 4,400 usable dolls to a small merchant for $3 per doll.	Out of Burzee Doll business.
31	Evaluate inventory shrinkage.	Sold a total of 48,400 units indicating that 1,600 units were lost due to shrinkage.	Sold a total of 19,850 units indicating that 150 units were lost due to shrinkage.

By the end of December, Child's Delight has sold all of its dolls and elects not to place a fifth order. On the other hand, Kids N Toys still has a large number of dolls remaining. Since the buying craze for Burzee Dolls appears to be finished, Kids N Toys puts the dolls on sale at cost ($10 per doll) in mid-January. At the end of January, the store liquidates the remaining 4,400 dolls to another retailer at $3 per doll.

The Gross Margin Report

When all Burzee Doll sales are totaled, Kids N Toys sold 48,400 dolls (indicating inventory shrinkage over the last three months of 1,600 dolls); Child's Delight sold 19,850 dolls (indicating inventory shrinkage of 150 dolls). Which of the two retailers did better with the Burzee Dolls? Exhibit 7 provides a gross margin report based on what each company spent on inventory purchases and received in inventory sales. When you look at the gross margin of $793,200 for Kids N Toys, it appears that this company did a much better job selling Burzee Dolls than its competitor, Child's Delight, based on its gross margin of only $325,500.

Return on Inventory Investment

The gross margin numbers presented in Exhibit 7 suggest that Kids N Toys outperformed Child's Delight. However, if you had money to invest in these companies, you might actually like Child's Delight's retail work on Burzee Dolls better than the work done by Kids N Toys.

Exhibit 7: Gross Margin Report on the Burzee Doll Inventory

	Kids N Toys, Inc.		Child's Delight, Inc.	
	42,000 units × $30	$1,260,000		
	2,000 units × $10	20,000		
	4,400 units × $3	13,200		
Sales revenue		$1,293,200	19,850 units × $30	$ 595,500
			10,000 units × $12	
Cost of purchases	50,000 units × $10	(500,000)	10,000 units × $15	(270,000)
Gross margin		$ 793,200		$ 325,500

Think about the average size of the inventory investment that each company maintained. Kids N Toys initially spent $500,000 to acquire 50,000 dolls. By the end of January, this inventory had been fully liquidated back into cash. Hence, Kids N Toys had quite a bit of cash tied up in Burzee Doll inventory! On average, how much cash did it have invested in this inventory during its selling period? On November 1, Kids N Toys had $500,000 in Burzee Doll inventory. On January 30, it had no Burzee Doll inventory. On average, Kids N Toys had about a $250,000 investment in inventory during its three-month selling period ($500,000 ÷ 2).[6]

STOP & THINK

Is there anything wrong with using the gross margin analysis presented in Exhibit 7 to evaluate management performance in these two companies? What costs may be missing?

How does Kids N Toys' average inventory investment compare to its competitor's investment? Rather than one large inventory purchase at the beginning of November, Child's Delight made four smaller investments as needed during November and December. The average inventory purchase amount was $67,500 [($60,000 + $60,000 + $75,000 + $75,000) ÷ 4]. On December 31, it had no Burzee Doll inventory. On average, then, Child's Delight had only about a $33,750 investment in inventory during its two-month selling period ($67,500 ÷ 2).

Obviously, the difference between the two companies' gross margins reported in Exhibit 7 is dramatic. However, the difference in Kids N Toys' average inventory investment of $250,000 versus the $33,750 average inventory investment at Child's Delight is also impressive. Remember from the introductory chapter that the executives in the early days at DUPONT COMPANY recognized that it is just as important to manage the money outflow for asset investment as it is to manage the money inflow from profits. This is the logic underlying Pierre du Pont and Donaldson Brown's ROI (return on investment) formula. Remember that the ROI formula has two parts (if you need a review, see the previous chapter on monitoring performance in cost, profit, and investment centers):

$$\frac{\text{Profit margin}}{\text{(Profit ÷ Revenue)}} \times \frac{\text{Asset turnover}}{\text{(Revenue ÷ Total assets)}} = \text{ROI}$$

Based on ROI, which of these two companies has created the most revenue for each dollar invested in its Burzee Doll inventory asset? Answering this question is really a function of the "asset turnover" section of the ROI formula. Notice, however, that rather than *total* revenue and *total* assets, we are focusing only on Burzee Doll revenue and the value of the Burzee Doll

6 Be careful with this calculation! The fact that Kids N Toys held its doll inventory for three months (or two months, or four months) does not change the fact that average inventory for the company is $250,000. The formal calculation here is (Beginning balance + Ending balance) ÷ 2. Instead of having no inventory, what if Kids N Toys still had $50,000 worth of Burzee Dolls on January 31? The average inventory investment would then be $275,000 [($500,000 + $50,000) ÷ 2]. You might also note that a more accurate measure of average inventory for Kids N Toys could involve assessing inventory levels on a month-by-month basis (we use an approach similar to this when we compute average inventory for Child's Delight, Inc.). However, unless otherwise indicated, this textbook will use the traditional (Beg+End)/2 formula to calculate average inventory.

inventory asset. This fact really doesn't present a problem. Rather than measuring how much total revenue is generated per dollar of total assets, we will simply measure *how much specific revenue is generated per dollar of a specific inventory item.* Hence, how many sales dollars does Kids N Toys generate for each dollar invested in its Burzee Doll inventory compared to Child's Delight?

$$\text{Kids N Toys: Revenue} \div \text{Average inventory}$$
$$\$1,293,200 \div \$250,000 = \$5.17$$

$$\text{Child's Delight: Revenue} \div \text{Average inventory}$$
$$\$595,500 \div \$33,750 = \$17.64$$

Note that organizations have a limited amount of resources to invest. Using the ROI formula, DuPont Company was able to wisely manage the task of maximizing the value of its investments by knowing where in the massive organization to invest its resources. Looking at the calculations above, you can see that Child's Delight made the better use of limited purchasing dollars to manage the Burzee Doll inventory in order to create sales revenue.[7]

Combining the gross margin per sales dollar with the number of sales dollars generated per dollar of inventory yields the following return on inventory investment calculations for Kids N Toys and Child's Delight:

$$(\text{Gross margin} \div \text{Revenue}) \times (\text{Revenue} \div \text{Inventory}) = \text{Return on inventory investment}$$

$$\text{Kids N Toys: } (\$793,200 \div \$1,293,200) \times (\$1,293,200 \div \$250,000) = 317\%$$

$$\text{Child's Delight: } (\$325,500 \div \$595,500) \times (\$595,500 \div \$33,750) = 964\%$$

These numbers suggest that although Child's Delight generated a lower gross margin, it actually performed better than Kids N Toys because of superior inventory management. By the way, these numbers (317% and 964%) probably seem high to you. Don't confuse these numbers with the classic ROI results you'd expect to see in most companies. (We've been careful to not refer to these calculations as ROI calculations.) These numbers *are* high because we have focused on the utilization of just one asset—inventory. In order to sell Burzee Dolls, each merchandiser must also invest in buildings, store shelving and displays, cash registers, and so forth. When we add all of these assets to the inventory, *then* we can calculate the traditional ROI measure. However, these calculations on Burzee Doll inventory usage give a strong indication that, regardless of what the overall ROI of each company is, it appears that Child's Delight has been more effective at managing its acquisition and sales of Burzee Dolls.

The day-to-day effort to manage the Burzee Doll inventory involves many other important issues (as listed in Exhibit 5). Even the inventory measures above do not provide Kids N Toys and Child's Delight management with the data necessary to address all issues as they *plan* for future inventory investments and *control* and *evaluate* the current inventory acquisition and selling process. This is where good management accounting can provide real value in management's effort to improve a merchandising operation. Exhibit 8 provides a management accounting view of the two companies' retail work with the Burzee Doll line of operations. Study both Exhibit 8 and Exhibit 5 for a moment. What information in Exhibit 8 could help a manager trying to work with some of the issues described in Exhibit 5?

---

7 As you can see, we're essentially adjusting the inventory turnover measure here by dividing the retail value of revenue by the wholesale value (or purchase cost) of inventory, and we're very careful to label this new calculation "inventory turnover." As illustrated in the preceding section, inventory turnover is traditionally measured using cost of goods sold rather than sales or revenue. Conceptually, comparing a wholesale number (inventory) to a wholesale number (cost of goods sold) makes more sense than comparing a wholesale number to a retail (sales revenue) number. However, as long as a consistent approach is used, the insights gained are the same. Further, the "revenue ÷ average inventory" calculation allows us to combine inventory turnover and profit margin in our analysis of these two retailers. As you can see, management accounting sometimes must adjust in order to suit the needs of the current decision-making situation.

Exhibit 8: Management Accounting Report on the Burzee Doll Inventory

In addition to cost of purchases, note the following additional inventory costs:

- Average inventory overhead costs are $1.10 per unit per month.
- Average costs to initiate and receive a purchase order are $1,250 per event.

	Kids N Toys, Inc.		Child's Delight, Inc.	
Expected revenue	50,000 units × $30 standard price	$1,500,000	20,000 units × $30 standard price	$600,000
Shrinkage loss	1,600 units × $30	(48,000)	150 units × $30	(4,500)
Market loss	2,000 units × ($30 − $10) +			
	4,400 units × ($30 − $3)	(158,800)		(0)
Actual revenue		$1,293,200		$595,500
Purchase costs	50,000 units × $10 standard cost	(500,000)	20,000 units × $10 standard cost	(200,000)
Lost discount		(0)	20,000 units × $2 lost discount	(40,000)
Price increase		(0)	10,000 units × $3 price increase	(30,000)
Gross margin		$ 793,200		$325,500
Overhead costs	50,000 units ÷ 2 = 25,000 average		5,000 units ÷ 2 = 2,500 average	
	inventory level × $1.10 × 3 months	(82,500)	inventory level × $1.10 × 2 months	(5,500)
Order costs	1 order × $1,250	(1,250)	4 orders × $1,250	(5,000)
Net operating profit		$ 709,450		$315,000

The Management Accounting Report on Kids N Toys' Net Operating Profit

net operating profit The difference between normal business sales and normal business expenses.

As you can see in Exhibit 8, we are identifying some additional out-of-pocket costs on the Burzee Doll operation for each company. Note that the gross margin for each company is the same as that calculated in the gross margin report in Exhibit 7. However, we're approaching the calculation of gross margin differently, as well as identifying some other relevant costs to calculate **net operating profit** for each company. Net operating profit is useful in measuring the performance of these operations. Much more important, though, are the insights gained in the management accounting numbers used to calculate gross margin and net operating profit. These numbers, presented in Exhibit 8, are extremely useful for planning, controlling, and evaluating the Burzee Doll retail operations.

Let's work with Kids N Toys first. This company originally purchased 50,000 units with the intent of selling all of them for $30. Why didn't it then have $1.5 million in revenue? This question cannot be answered using the gross margin report in Exhibit 7, but the answer is obvious in the management accounting report in Exhibit 8. Somehow, 1,600 dolls that Kids N Toys planned to sell were broken, misplaced, or stolen. Based on an intended $30 selling price, this cost the company $48,000 in lost revenue. In addition, the market demand changed while Kids N Toys still had dolls to sell. As a result, the store had to sell some dolls for prices lower than the planned $30. Specifically, Kids N Toys reduced expected revenue by $40,000 when it sold 2,000 dolls for $10, and reduced expected revenue by another $118,800 when it sold 4,400 dolls for $3. This loss of market value is a risk that Kids N Toys management should consider when planning for next year's purchases. Further, management should also evaluate the information on inventory shrinkage to better control the inventory operation.

Caution

Note that shrinkage loss and market loss are based on expected selling prices, not purchase costs.

We mentioned briefly the concept of activity-based costing (ABC) in an earlier chapter on product cost flows. We'll spend a lot of time on the ABC concept in the next chapter. Briefly, ABC is an approach to tracking the relationship between activities and costs that is generally used to better allocate manufacturing overhead costs to products. This concept can also be used to analyze overhead costs in merchandising organizations. Managing the Burzee Doll inventory

STOP & THINK

Both Kids N Toys and Child's Delight are investment centers. If you studied the previous chapter on monitoring performance in cost, profit, and investment centers, you should realize that Exhibit 8 is providing a report on *variances*. Think carefully about some of the items being reported in Exhibit 8 and see if you can identify which variances are being described here.

requires some overhead costs. In this example, let's assume an ABC analysis reveals that the cost for storage, security, and other supervisory activities works out to be about $1.10 per doll per month. In addition, the effort to count inventory and prepare the purchase order, as well as to receive and pay for the inventory, requires about $1,250 in administrative costs each time inventory is purchased. In a standard income statement, only the direct cost of inventory purchases would be used to measure gross margin. Those overhead and purchasing costs related to managing the Burzee Doll inventory are typically combined with all other administrative costs to form Selling and Administrative Expenses on the income statement. However, the management accounting report in Exhibit 8 has specifically identified and related these costs to the Burzee Doll inventory line (this is the goal of the ABC concept). This information allows management to see exactly how the Burzee Doll product line is contributing to Kids N Toys' overall net operating profit. Further, management can evaluate how having a lot of inventory leads to higher overhead costs. On the other hand, though, purchasing all these dolls at once saved Kids N Toys additional purchasing costs.

The Management Accounting Report on Child's Delight's Net Operating Profit

Now let's evaluate operations at Child's Delight using the management accounting report in Exhibit 8. During November and December, Child's Delight purchased a total of 20,000 units with the intent of selling all of them for $30. Similar to Kids N Toys, the difference between expected revenue and actual revenue is explained by the inventory shrinkage of 150 units. Compared to Kids N Toys, why does Child's Delight have a much lower percentage of dolls being broken, misplaced, or stolen? It seems reasonable to expect that Child's Delight found it much easier to maintain and keep track of its much smaller level of inventory. Can this shrinkage be further reduced? Child's Delight should carefully consider this question as it plans for the next buying season.

As noted in Exhibit 5, keeping the inventory levels low helps protect the organization against certain types of costs and risks. However, this can be a challenging balance because other costs occur as a result of low inventory levels; Child's Delight incurred three of these costs. First, because Child's Delight made small inventory purchases, bulk discounts were unavailable to the company. The effect of losing these discounts, $40,000, was to pay $2 more per doll (20,000 dolls × $2). Second, each time Child's Delight ran out of inventory and had to reorder, it had to pay the current market rate. Given the high popularity of Burzee Dolls during the holiday buying spree, it is not surprising that the manufacturer raised the price. This cost was passed through the distributor to Child's Delight, which had to pay an additional $3 per doll for its last two shipments. Overall, this resulted in an additional $30,000 in cost (10,000 dolls × $3). Finally, each purchase event at Child's Delight adds to the management activities that must take place. If we assume that both companies have similar inventory acquisition activities, then Child's Delight must have $5,000 in purchase order costs (4 purchases × $1,250 activity costs). Again, though, low inventory levels have their advantage. Because Child's Delight orders only 5,000 dolls at a time, its inventory will range from 0 to 5,000 dolls. On average, it will generally have 2,500 dolls on hand. Based on an average monthly overhead cost of $1.10 per doll, selling Burzee Dolls led to relatively low overhead costs of $5,500 (again, assuming similar ABC costs for storage, security, and other supervisory activities for Child's Delight and Kids N Toys). Clearly, Child's Delight management should pay attention to all these numbers as it evaluates this year's operations and make plans for next year.

STOP & THINK

What other major costs might Child's Delight have had that are not being considered in this anaylsis?

Remember that the format and content of *financial accounting* reports are standardized in order to allow external users to compare reports from many different companies. In contrast, the format and content of internal *management accounting* reports differ across organizations because each organization customizes the reports to fit specific needs. Hence, the format of the management accounting report in Exhibit 8 is not regulated by anyone! The accountants for one particular retailer will customize the report to best support their own management processes of planning, controlling, and evaluating. The cost calculations displayed in Exhibit 8 are used by many, but not all, organizations in the merchandising industry. In this case, we saw that a simple comparison of gross margins does not necessarily indicate which company (Kids N Toys with a gross margin of $793,200 or Child's Delight with a gross margin of $325,500) made better decisions. By including information on inventory management, we concluded that Child's Delight had more successfully combined the activities of profitable sales with efficient use of its inventory assets. The more detailed profit analysis contained in Exhibit 8 enabled us to look more closely at the specific factors affecting the net operating profit of Kids N Toys and Child's Delight.

TO SUMMARIZE: Because wholesalers and retailers generally do not have to deal with raw materials or work in process, the process of accounting for inventory in a merchandising business is not nearly as complicated as it is in a manufacturing business. However, *managing* inventory costs is both complicated and critical for a merchant. Having too much inventory creates unnecessary overhead costs, financial holding costs, costs due to loss of market value, and costs due to inventory shrinkage. Not having enough inventory may result in unnecessary ordering costs and loss of bulk order discounts, as well as opportunity costs due to lost sales and increased supplier prices. While measuring some of these costs presents a challenge to accountants, the information is very important to the processes of planning, controlling, and evaluating gross margins and net operating profits for individual product lines.

Managing Service Organizations

4 Measure profitability and personnel utilization in a service organization.

As discussed earlier in the chapter on product cost flows, service organizations have many characteristics in common with manufacturing organizations. Both types of organizations engage in a substantial production process before delivering the final product to the customer. In a manufacturing organization, this production process involves people assembling materials using equipment located in factories. In a service organization, materials are of much smaller importance, and the production process focuses on people delivering a service within an infrastructure of tangible assets (hotels, delivery trucks, barbershops, doctors' offices, etc.). In some service organizations, such as airline service, the focus is on the tangible asset infrastructure—while the pilots, flight attendants, and ticket agents are important, most of our interest centers around the reliability of the planes and the baggage handling equipment. In other service organizations, such as legal services, the focus is on person-to-person delivery of customized service—we don't really care how nice the attorney's office is, as long as the attorney gives us good legal counsel. In this section, controlling product costs will be discussed in the context of a service organization.

Characteristics of a Service Organization

Service organizations can be broadly categorized into three basic types: professional services, service shops, and mass services.[8] A professional services organization is associated with people providing a highly customized service process. For example, a good family doctor tailors the treatment to the specific patient, after developing a personal rapport with the patient and carefully extracting a thorough case history. At the other end of the continuum, a mass service organization provides a standardized product with little emphasis on the person delivering the product. For example, MCDONALD'S has developed its fast-food business around the delivery of standard-quality food in a predictable atmosphere; we are pleased when the person serving us is competent and cheerful, but we are primarily interested in the taste of the food and

8 See Lin Fitzgerald, Robert Johnson, Stan Brignall, Rhian Silvestro, and Christopher Voss, *Performance Measurement in Service Businesses* (London: CIMA, 1991).

© 2003 Getty Images

A family doctor clinic is categorized as a professional services organization because the doctor provides a highly customized service—treatment is tailored to individual patients.

the cleanliness of the restrooms. A service shop is somewhere between a professional service and a mass service. For example, in a large-scale laser eye surgery clinic, there is more emphasis on standardization and on the equipment itself than one finds in a family doctor clinic. Also, in a high-end sit-down restaurant, the taste of the food is still important, but the quality of the personal service is at least as important.

The different characteristics of professional services, service shops, and mass services are summarized in Exhibit 9. Professional services are those services that emphasize person-to-person delivery, that focus on the process of service delivery rather than the creation of some final, tangible product, and that are highly customized. Mass services are those services that rely on equipment more than people in delivering the service, that result in the customer taking away a tangible product, and that do little, if any, tailoring to individual customer needs. Service shops provide a mixture of the three dimensions of people/equipment, process/product, and high/low customization.

Cost Management in a Service Organization

As we saw earlier in the chapter in our discussion of cost management in manufacturing and merchandising organizations, it is important for an organization to evaluate the magnitude of its costs and the degree to which it is efficiently utilizing its resources. We looked at cost and profitability measures, as well as at indicators of inventory management (such as inventory turnover). The same two concepts—evaluation of profitability and efficiency—will be used in developing cost management tools for service organizations.

For a manufacturing organization, key resources used in the production process are raw materials, machine hours, factory space, and labor. For a merchandising organization, the management of the level of inventory is crucial to the efficient use of the organization's resources. For a service organization, the management of materials inventories, building space, and equipment usage is also important. However, to emphasize the importance of people in service organizations, our illustration in this chapter will focus on how a service organization can measure the degree to which it is efficiently using its people.

Exhibit 9: Characteristics of Service Organizations

Illustration: Cost Management in an Audit Firm

A large audit firm is a good example of a professional services organization. An "audit" firm is composed of CPA (certified public accountant) professionals who provide specialized accounting, tax, and information systems consulting; and conduct audits of financial statements. The illustration in this section is for the hypothetical audit firm of LeviForrester. This illustration will center on the audit services offered in one large regional office of the firm. The office employs approximately 200 professionals and another 100 support staff. We will examine the costs associated with the professionals in the office. The costs of the support staff, as well as the training, recruiting, marketing, and technical analysis costs charged to the regional office by the national headquarters of LeviForrester, are also very important to the overall profitability of the regional office. However, assigning these support costs and national charges to specific jobs is quite difficult. The task of identifying cost drivers, common costs, and other concepts important to the proper treatment of these indirect support costs will be undertaken in the next chapter where we discuss activity-based costing. For the example in this chapter, we will restrict our attention to personnel costs that can be directly traced to specific client engagements.

The regional office of LeviForrester employs five types of professionals, as listed below.

	Average Years of Service with the Firm	Number of Professionals in the Office
Partner	More than 12 years	10
Senior manager	9 to 12 years	15
Manager	6 to 8 years	20
Senior	3 to 5 years	50
Staff	1 to 2 years	100

The partners exercise overall oversight of the audit practice. They review and approve the supporting documents (in electronic form) for each audit. They also seek to build the business by finding new clients. One of the 10 partners is designated the "managing partner" and is responsible for running the office and setting the strategic direction for the practice in that area. The senior managers and the managers are the professionals who are the primary interface between the audit firm and the clients. These managers keep the client informed about the progress of the audit and also supervise the other members of the audit team (the seniors and staff). The seniors spend much of their time at the clients' offices supervising and performing the actual work of the audit. The staff accountants do the bulk of the routine work of the audit.

Partners are expected to spend about half of their time working on specific client jobs during the year. This works out to be 1,000 hours out of the potential 2,000 working hours (50 weeks × 40 hours per week) during the year. At other times, partners are cultivating new client relationships and making proposals in order to get new client engagements. Senior managers and managers are expected to spend 75% of their time working on specific client engagements; seniors and staff are expected to spend all of their time working on specific client engagements. In fact, an important responsibility within the audit firm is the planning of the demands of various audit engagements to make sure that all of the seniors and the staff are always scheduled for specific engagements and are not sitting around the main office because of "unassigned" time.

These expectations about how much of a professional's time is to be spent in serving specific clients are used to develop billing rates and job cost charges. The computation of these billing rates that are used for job cost charges is shown in Exhibit 10. The job cost charges are

Exhibit 10: Billing Rates and Job Cost Charges for LeviForrester

	Annual Compensation	Expected Billable Hours	Compensation Cost per Billable Hour	Client Billing Rate per Billable Hour
Partner	$400,000	1,000	$400	$500
Senior manager	130,000	1,500	87	300
Manager	100,000	1,500	67	225
Senior	50,000	2,000	25	150
Staff	40,000	2,000	20	100

computed as a professional's total annual compensation divided by the number of client hours to be worked (i.e., billable hours) during a year. For example, the average annual compensation of partners at LeviForrester is $400,000, and each partner is expected to work on specific client engagements for 1,000 hours during a year. Thus, the partner compensation cost assigned to a job is $400 per hour ($400,000 ÷ 1,000 hours). These job cost charges are used by LeviForrester to compute the professional labor cost associated with each audit engagement.

The billing rates are used in computing how much is to be charged to a client for an audit engagement. The billing rate for professional services should be large enough to cover both the professional's compensation and general administrative costs such as secretarial support, computers, supplies, travel, and so forth. As you can imagine, the determination of the billing rates in Exhibit 10 is an extremely important element in LeviForrester's success. Billing rates that are too high will drive away potential customers, whereas billing rates that are too low will lead to low profitability and, perhaps, the inability to appropriately compensate the professionals.

On October 5, the managing partner for the regional office of LeviForrester received the profitability report contained in Exhibit 11. The report is generated in early October because LeviForrester's fiscal year ends on September 30. (It is impossible for LeviForrester to analyze its own business operations at the end of the normal calendar year because January is the busiest month of the year for audit firms as they perform audit work for their clients with December 31 year-ends.) The managing partner used the data in the profitability report to compute profit percentage from personnel (PPP), which is the fundamental measure of profitability used by LeviForrester. The overall PPP for this regional office is computed as follows:

$$\text{PPP} = (\text{Revenue} - \text{Personnel compensation cost}) \div \text{Revenue}$$
$$= (\$60,975,000 - \$14,450,000) \div \$60,975,000$$
$$= 76.3\%$$

Exhibit 11: Profitability Report for LeviForrester Regional Office

	Number of Professionals	Actual Billable Hours	Billing Rate	Total Revenue	Total Compensation Cost
Partners	10	8,200	$500	$ 4,100,000	$ 4,000,000
Senior managers ..	15	20,000	300	6,000,000	1,950,000
Managers	20	35,000	225	7,875,000	2,000,000
Seniors	50	120,000	150	18,000,000	2,500,000
Staff	100	250,000	100	25,000,000	4,000,000
Total				$60,975,000	$14,450,000

The managing partner is quite pleased with this report because the firm-wide goal for PPP is just 73.0%. As the various regional offices within LeviForrester are evaluated, each region's PPP is used to allocate a firm-wide bonus pool—the employees in regions with PPP in excess of 73.0% can expect to receive higher-than-average year-end bonuses.

The managing partner also received the personnel utilization report contained in Exhibit 12. The report contains personnel utilization rates (PUR) for each category of professionals within the firm. The contents of this report are somewhat disturbing. The managing partner sees that the partners in the office spent only 82.0% of the time that they should have on specific client engagements. Senior managers are also working with clients at less than desirable levels (88.9%). On the other hand, the hours billed by other managers, as well as seniors and staff accountants, were well in excess of 100% of the expected amount. This personnel utilization pattern suggests at least two potential future problems. First, existing clients may become concerned that the LeviForrester partners and senior managers are not spending as much time with them as they had anticipated. The clients may feel that the LeviForrester partners are now spending too much time finding new clients and not enough time attending to the needs of the existing clients. Second, the high utilization rates for the managers, seniors, and staff are a warning sign that these key professionals may be working too many hours. Hiring and training new professionals is an expensive process, and LeviForrester does not want to overwork its young professionals, resulting in abnormally high employee turnover.

The two specific measures—PPP and PUR—used to describe service process management at LeviForrester are intended only as illustrations; measures with these specific names are not in use in any real professional services firm. However, measures similar to these are very commonly used in service organizations. These two measures are representative of a broad class of measures that indicate the performance of service organizations on two important dimensions—profitability and personnel utilization. These two performance indicators connect directly with similar concepts used to manage inventory assets in manufacturing and merchandising organizations.

Exhibit 12: Personnel Utilization Report for LeviForrester

	Actual Billable	Budgeted Billable	Utilization Rate
Partners	8,200	10,000	82.0%
Senior managers	20,000	22,500	88.9%
Managers	35,000	30,000	116.7%
Seniors	120,000	100,000	120.0%
Staff	250,000	200,000	125.0%

TO SUMMARIZE: Three broad types of service organizations are professional services, service shops, and mass services. The dimensions on which these types of organizations differ are people/equipment, process/product, and high/low customization. As with manufacturing and merchandising organizations, it is important to measure both profitability and resource utilization in a service organization. In a professional services firm, profitability is measured by comparing the service revenues with the compensation costs associated with the professionals. It is also important to monitor the degree to which the professionals are appropriately utilized within the firm.

Just-in-Time

5 Describe how the concept of just-in-time (JIT) inventory systems is used to improve cost, quality, and timely performance in organizations.

Remember in the introductory management chapter that we described briefly the history of management accounting, and that management accounting has evolved as a result of competition. When one company or industry (or, in the new global economy, country) develops a better management accounting technique or measure, it then competes more strongly in the marketplace. Eventually, the success of the innovator puts pressure on other organizations to adopt the same or a similar approach to their own management accounting systems. This was exactly the situation when U.S. companies began adjusting their management teams and management accounting systems to focus on quality and timeliness. In the 1980s, American manufacturers faced an assault from Japanese companies such as TOYOTA and NEC. These Japanese companies had mastered quality and inventory control, as well as speedier ways to get products to market. Western CEOs studied the competition, deconstructed what made it so good, adopted the better features of their rivals, and changed their management systems. Since then, this new management focus on controlling the cost, quality, and timeliness of inventory has had an impact on management accounting and has spread into U.S. merchandising and service industries, as well as into industries in other countries around the world.

JIT Inventory Systems

just-in-time (JIT) A management philosophy that emphasizes removing all waste of effort, time, and inventory costs from the organization. One obvious result of JIT is the reduction or removal of needless inventory in a production system.

The effort of management to compete on measures of time and to make improvements involving time is captured in the concept of **just-in-time (JIT)** management processes. To understand JIT, you need to first understand how JIT is used to manage inventory, including raw materials inventory, work-in-process inventory, and finished goods inventory. Let's talk for a moment about inventory. What is the purpose of inventory in a manufacturing plant? This may seem obvious. In the past, manufacturers stockpiled inventories in order to avoid shutdowns or slowdowns and to meet customer needs if suppliers were late or if production or delivery was slow. Occasionally (sometimes more than occasionally!), suppliers deliver raw materials that contain some defects, or the production process ruins some work-in-process, or a customer returns an unacceptable product. How do we deal with these unexpected surprises? Again the answer has been to "have a little extra on hand" so that bad parts or products can be replaced without having to interrupt the manufacturing process. Not surprisingly, production managers can get a little nervous when inventory levels get too low.

Because of concerns about risks due to scheduling and quality problems, companies establish policies to keep inventory levels at or above some minimal level. This minimum level of inventory is usually called a "safety stock" (which we will discuss later in the expanded material section of this chapter). However, several years ago some cagey accountants and business owners in Japan created a new competitive view of inventory management. They (like everyone else) realized that maintaining these inventories can be very expensive because of warehousing costs, interest costs incurred to finance inventory, and the opportunity cost of money tied up in stockpiled inventory. The real insight these Japanese business professionals had was that inventories are really only "buffers" that mask inefficient operations or product quality problems. Eliminate these timing and quality problems, and you no longer need the inventory buffers. By concentrating on improving product quality and timely deliveries, many Japanese companies became much more efficient and profitable at the same time that inventories were kept to a minimum or even eliminated. The emerging inventory systems that allow for the elimination of inventory stockpiles, inefficiency, and waste are referred to as just-in-time inventory systems. The competitive value of these new management systems eventually caught on and came to America.

JIT began as a management tool for manufacturing. So, when first learning about JIT, it's probably best to think of it in this context. In a manufacturing setting, JIT is a process by which only enough materials to satisfy immediate production are shipped to the job site. When JIT is functioning perfectly, companies take delivery from suppliers only as raw materials are needed

The Japanese Focus on Inventory Henry Ford, the famous automotive production industrialist, lifted the FORD MOTOR COMPANY to great success during the early and mid-1900s by achieving tremendous cost efficiencies in producing cars. He believed in long production runs where low-skilled workers could build the same car part over and over again. As a result, high manufacturing costs per automobile plummeted, and he was able to offer cars to the public at extremely competitive prices. However, this production approach required high levels of raw materials, work-in-process, and finished goods inventories.

Meanwhile, across the ocean in Japan, Taiichi Ohno, an industrial scientist, and Eliji Toyoda, an executive vice president at TOYOTA MOTOR CORPORATION (and the son of the founder of Toyota), were experimenting with a different approach to large-scale production. While other Toyota executives thought that Toyoda's ideas were impractical, in 1949, in a machine shop in Koromo, Eliji Toyoda began experimenting with a new production control approach using the concepts of a just-in-time (JIT) inventory system. By 1953, the Koromo machine shop had a fully implemented *Kanban* system, which was based on the concept that supplies should be "pulled" through the production process as they are needed. (*Kanban* is essentially a signaling system that pulls parts forward through the production system.) Interestingly, Toyoda copied this idea from the sales methods of U.S. supermarkets. He was able to demonstrate that *Kanban* eliminated waste due to the overproduction of parts, reduced or eliminated the need for buffer inventories in the plant, and dramatically reduced production defects. In 1963, top management decided on the full application of *Kanban* as a means of transforming the production control system. Cost accountants were charged with developing and maintaining performance measures that tracked defects, excess inventory, and throughput time. Eliji Toyoda became chairman of Toyota in 1983. The rest, as they say, is history.

Source: M. Udagawa, "The Development of Production Management at the Toyota Motor Corporation," *Business History*, 1995, pp. 107–120.

for production and complete all inventory started during the day. In addition, inventory is completed only as it is ordered by customers and can be shipped immediately. As the name implies, materials are delivered "just in time" for production, and goods are manufactured "just in time" to meet customers' needs. As described earlier, JIT inventory systems started in Japan and have now been adopted successfully by a number of U.S. organizations. The results of JIT implementation are often dramatic. For example, one AT&T shop realized 54% improvement in quality yield, a 12-fold decrease in manufacturing time, an 88% reduction in scrap and rework, and a 95% increase in on-time deliveries.[9]

JIT and Value-Added Activities

Benefits such as those experienced by AT&T occur because companies that have adopted JIT have been able to avoid buildups of parts and materials and still ensure a smooth and orderly flow of goods to customers. JIT-based environments manage the flow of goods using a "pull" process. Essentially, this means that the final assembly stage for a product sends a signal (a *Kanban*; see the Business Environment on The Japanese Focus on Inventory) to the preceding workstation indicating what parts and materials will be needed during the next few hours.

9 F. B. Green, F. Amenkhienan, and G. Johnson, "Performance Measures and JIT," *Management Accounting*, February 1991, pp. 50–54.

value-added activities Necessary activities in a production or service process that customers identify as valuable and for which they are willing to pay.

non-value-added activities Unnecessary activities in a production or service process that customers typically do not see or care about and for which they are unwilling to pay.

The preceding workstation then sends similar signals all the way back through the manufacturing cycle, ensuring an orderly flow of products. Thus, the demand at the final assembly stage "pulls" the inventory through the production process only as it is needed. Using this system, nothing is produced unless customers demand it. At all stages, inventories are eliminated or reduced to the lowest possible level. Obviously, then, progress toward successful implementation of JIT is inventory-related. Inventory reduction is not the primary purpose of JIT, but it generally is a consequence of JIT efforts to eliminate waste. The goal is to add value to the product or service and reduce or eliminate activities that do not. To be specific, **value-added activities** are essentially defined as those activities for which the customer is willing to pay. On the other hand, **non-value-added activities** are those for which the customer is not willing to pay. For example, clients in a law office are not interested in paying for the time spent running the payroll, organizing the file room, or computing billable hours. These are non-value-added activities. However, these clients should be willing to pay for court time and consultation time. These are clearly value-added activities that the law firm should emphasize. Under JIT, waste is considered to be anything other than the minimum amount of equipment, materials, parts, space, and workers' time that is essential to add desired value to a product. This results in careful management of time spent on value-added activities such as machining and assembly operations (for a manufacturer) and customer service and contact activities (for a service firm). More importantly, the JIT focus on eliminating waste emphasizes removing as much as possible the time spent on non-value-added activities such as setup work, materials handling, and inspection.

JIT and Time

It is important to understand that JIT encourages accountants to emphasize providing time-based performance measures to management. Critical success factors for many JIT manufacturing, service, and merchandising firms include improving timeliness of customer delivery and increasing the product or service provider's flexibility in handling customers' needs. Exhibit 13 provides a sample of appropriate performance measures that support these factors of success, which are particularly important in today's dynamic, customer-oriented environment.

TO SUMMARIZE: Fundamentally, just-in-time (JIT) is an inventory management method that focuses on removing all waste from a production or service process. Originally a Japanese management system, JIT has made a significant impact on the way manufacturing, service, and merchandising companies in the United States and other nations are managed. JIT has a strong emphasis on costs and quality. However, JIT adds an important third dimension to the management process—management of timeliness and flexibility. In a manufacturing setting, demand at the final assembly stage "pulls" the inventory through the production process only as it is needed. Using this system, nothing is produced until customers demand it.

The main goal of JIT is to add value to the product or service and to reduce or eliminate activities that do not. By focusing on removing non-value-added activities and managing time spent on value-added activities, inventories and costs are reduced, while quality and timeliness are improved. Timeliness issues include emphasis on reducing customer delivery times and increasing flexibility within the production, service, or merchandising process.

Exhibit 13: Time-Based Performance Measures in a JIT Firm

Customer Delivery Success Factor (On-time delivery to customers can be affected by suppliers, product design time, and the production process and distribution time.)		**Provider Flexibility Success Factor** (Manufacturing, service, and merchandising flexibility includes the ability to respond quickly to changes in customer demand and product design changes.)	
Measure	**Computation Method**	**Measure**	**Computation Method**
Customer on-time delivery	Number of on-time deliveries divided by total deliveries. Goal: higher	Lead time for new product introduction	Amount of time from idea to readiness for sale. Goal: lower
Supplier on-time delivery	Number of on-time deliveries divided by total deliveries. Goal: higher	Parts and product availability	Number of times a part or product is unavailable when requested. Goal: lower
Design cycle time	Amount of time from initial idea to readied plans. Goal: lower	Number of common parts	Number of parts in a product design common to other products. Goal: higher
Number of contract changes	Number of times a contract is changed. Goal: lower	Inventory level	Average level of inventory. Goal: lower
Schedule attainment	Number of unchanged schedules divided by total schedules. Goal: lower	Capacity utilization	Percentage of process capacity used in current operations. Goal: higher
Lead time	Amount of time from customer's initial request to final product or service delivery. Goal: lower	Downtime	Amount of time a manufacturing or service process was unavailable. Goal: lower
Setup time*	Amount of time required to set up a production run. Goal: lower	Setup time*	Amount of time required to set up a production run. Goal: lower
Throughput time*	Amount of time from beginning of production or service process until process conclusion. Goal: lower	Throughput time*	Amount of time from beginning of production or service process until process conclusion. Goal: lower

*Note that some performance measures are important to both customer delivery and flexibility success factors.

Source: Adapted from J. A. Hendricks, "Performance Measures for a JIT Manufacturer," *Management Accounting*, January 1994, pp. 26–30.

eXpanded *Material*

As mentioned earlier in the chapter, an important element of cost management is the evaluation of whether an organization is utilizing its resources efficiently. In the expanded material section of this chapter, you will learn further details about inventory management. In particular, the expanded material discusses ways to determine the appropriate level of inventory that should be maintained by an organization.

Opportunity Costs in Managing Inventory and Work-in-Process Services

6 Calculate and interpret holding costs in merchandising and service businesses.

Let's return to our Burzee Doll example to discuss opportunity costs involved in managing inventory. As discussed in the introductory management chapter, there are many types of costs involved in managing an organization. All the costs that we discussed in the management accounting report for Kids N Toys and Child's Delight involved out-of-pocket costs (see Exhibit 8). However, there are several cost issues listed in Exhibit 5 that we did not include in the earlier analysis for these two companies. For example, inventory flexibility involves potential opportunity costs related to investing in a lot of inventory. Kids N Toys tied up a lot of money in securing 50,000 Burzee Dolls for the Christmas season—a shopping season that is particularly critical for retailers in the United States. Kids N Toys may have been fortunate that the Burzee Doll line sold as well as it did. If fickle shopper tastes had turned instead to another toy, it would have been difficult for Kids N Toys to shift this part of its inventory investment out of Burzee Dolls and into an alternative item in time to take advantage of the Christmas shopping rush. Kids N Toys may not have had any real problems in this area, but it needs to pay attention to this issue in planning for next year.

Child's Delight was also exposed to some opportunity costs. For example, because it kept its inventory of Burzee Dolls much lower than its competitor, Child's Delight was much more at risk of losing sales due to problems with supplier delivery and other logistics beyond its control. We'll assume in this case that all its deliveries were on time and without problems. However, another opportunity cost that Child's Delight was clearly not so fortunate in avoiding was lost sales due to lack of inventory. During the same period of time that Child's Delight sold its 19,850 dolls, Kids N Toys sold 41,500 dolls (see Exhibit 6 on page 1162). If these retailers were at all similar in terms of competitive factors such as location and advertising, then it appears certain that Child's Delight could have sold more dolls *if* it had had more dolls! How many more dolls could have been sold? Frankly, this is a very difficult number to measure—even for a good accountant. You won't see it measured on any of the management accounting reports in this chapter. That does not at all imply that this number is less important than the others. There is a lot of discussion (and disagreement) on how to measure this number. The important thing is to somehow make decision makers aware of this cost. However, there is so much disagreement in practice as to how to specifically calculate this number that it is best in a textbook such as this to simply make you aware of this particular opportunity cost issue.

Holding Costs and Economic Profit in Merchandising Organizations

Another opportunity cost that both companies in our example experienced is financial holding costs. Financial holding costs are very well defined in practice. We'll use this cost to calculate for these two merchants a third income number called **economic profit**. As we calculated before, during the three-month period of November, December, and January, Kids N Toys had an average of $250,000 invested in Burzee Doll inventory. (See page 1163 if you need help remembering how to calculate average inventory levels.) This money could alternatively have been earning money in a financial investment, or it could have been used to pay off loans or retire stock that Kids N Toys currently has outstanding. Every business has a **cost of capital** that relates to its cost of using money. In fact, you likely have your own individual cost of capital. Do you have any loans? What is the average interest rate on those loans? Let's assume it is 15%. Hopefully, you understand that as long as you have loans, every dollar you use for anything besides paying down your loan(s) costs you 15%. This 15% rate is your cost of capital. To be specific, for every dollar you spend buying a new stereo system, your loan(s) will increase by $0.15 at the end of the year. Hence, buying the stereo had better be worth this implicit financial holding cost. Even if you don't have any loans, you probably (hopefully!) have a savings account. Your cost of capital would then be the interest rate on your investment in the savings account. Let's assume you get a 4% return on your account. In this case, for every dollar you delay putting into the account (such as money spent on your new stereo), at the end of the year, your account will be $0.04 less than it could have been. Obviously, this cost information is important to all decisions involving the investment of limited resources. The formula to calculate a financial holding cost is the same approach traditionally used to calculate interest costs. We'll assume that the cost of capital for both Kids N Toys and Child's Delight is 20%. The financial holding cost of the average Burzee Doll inventory investment for Kids N Toys can be calculated in the following manner:

economic profit The difference between net operating profit and holding costs of inventory and other asset investments. Note that generally accepted accounting principles (GAAP) do not formally recognize opportunity costs such as holding costs.

cost of capital The weighted-average cost of a firm's debt and equity capital equals the rate of return that a company must earn in order to satisfy the demands of its owners and creditors.

$$\text{Financial holding cost} = \text{Average investment} \times \text{Annual rate} \times \text{Number of years}$$
$$\$250{,}000 \times 20\% \times 3/12 \text{ year} = \$12{,}500$$

The financial holding cost for Child's Delight can also be calculated. Remember, we calculated earlier that Child's Delight had a much lower average investment in inventory. In addition, this company's investment in Burzee Dolls lasted for only two months—November and December. As a result, its financial holding cost was much lower than Kids N Toys and is calculated as follows:

$$\$33{,}750 \times 20\% \times 2/12 \text{ year} = \$1{,}125$$

The financial holding cost is as much a cost of being in the business of selling Burzee Dolls as any other cost we calculated and listed earlier in Exhibit 8. Most accountants recognize that measuring financial holding costs is important to managing the economic well-being of the organization. Hence, in Exhibit 14 we have expanded the original management accounting report on the Burzee Doll inventory to include financial holding costs in order to calculate the organization's economic profit.

Before we leave this example and move on to discuss holding costs in service organizations, take one more opportunity to compare the gross margin report in Exhibit 7 and the management accounting report in Exhibit 14. These two merchandising reports would look basically the same regardless of whether Child's Delight and Kids N Toys were retailers or wholesalers of toys. You should now have a pretty clear understanding of how dramatically management

Exhibit 14: Expanded Management Accounting Report on the Burzee Doll Inventory

In addition to cost of purchases, note the following additional inventory costs:

- Average inventory overhead costs are $1.10 per unit per month.
- Average costs to initiate and receive a purchase order are $1,250 per event.
- Average costs of capital are 20%.

	Kids N Toys, Inc.		Child's Delight, Inc.	
Expected revenue	50,000 units × $30 standard price	$1,500,000	20,000 units × $30 standard price	$ 600,000
Shrinkage loss	1,600 units × $30	(48,000)	150 units × $30	(4,500)
Market loss	2,000 units × ($30 − $10) + 4,400 units × ($30 − $3)	(158,800)		(0)
Actual revenue		$1,293,200		$ 595,500
Purchase costs	50,000 units × $10 standard cost	(500,000)	20,000 units × $10 standard cost	(200,000)
Lost discount		(0)	20,000 units × $2 lost discount	(40,000)
Price increase		(0)	10,000 units × $3 price increase	(30,000)
Gross margin		$ 793,200		$ 325,500
Overhead costs	50,000 units ÷ 2 = 25,000 average inventory level × $1.10 × 3 months	(82,500)	5,000 units ÷ 2 = 2,500 average inventory level × $1.10 × 2 months	(5,500)
Order costs	1 order × $1,250	(1,250)	4 orders × $1,250	(5,000)
Net operating profit		$ 709,450		$ 315,000
Holding costs	$500,000 in purchases ÷ 2 = $250,000 average inventory investment × 20% × 3/12 year	(12,500)	($60,000 + $60,000 + $75,000 + $75,000) ÷ 4 = $67,500 average purchase ÷ 2 = $33,750 average inventory investment × 20% × 2/12 year	(1,125)
Economic profit		$ 696,950		$ 313,875

segment Any part of an organization requiring separate reports for evaluation by management.

Economic Value Added (EVA™) A commercialized performance measurement system that emphasizes the incremental profits an organization creates over and above the profit required to cover the costs of capital.

accounting can differ from financial accounting in analyzing results of merchandising organizations. It is also important to point out that the reports in Exhibits 7 and 14 are both **segment** reports that are specific to inventory lines in these companies. A complete net operating profit analysis of all operations at either company should obviously include revenues and costs that are specific to all other inventory lines and overhead costs that are common across the organization (for example, the salaries for company executives). A complete economic profit analysis (sometimes called an **Economic Value Added** or **EVA™** analysis) would include a "holding cost" on all assets belonging to the company (cash, investments, equipment, buildings, land, etc.).

Service Organizations and Holding Costs

Something you should realize about GAAP and the service industry is that there typically has not been nearly as much emphasis on measuring and reporting work-in-process costs as compared to the manufacturing industry. However, it is important that the accountants support the management process by reporting on the costs and processes involved in work-in-process services. Think about the economic facts of work-in-process services for a moment. What do these costs represent? They represent significant investments in services provided to a client that typically have yet to provide any kind of a return in terms of cash receipts. Work in process is obviously necessary in many service companies. However, service companies cannot allow work-in-process services to build up in their organizations without restraint. Otherwise, resources are tied up that could otherwise be used to provide additional salable services. These opportunity costs eventually reduce profits in the company. Doesn't this sound a lot like the same risk of holding costs we described for merchandising companies earlier in this section? Accountants can and should measure holding costs on large service projects. Such measures provide decision makers with the insight to assess the effects of not properly planning and controlling large service projects. For example, consider a large accounting firm that is planning an audit which is expected to take three months to complete. Suppose that by the end of the three months, this large accounting firm has invested $400,000 in supplies, labor, and overhead for the audit project. Because most service companies have outstanding debts that are accruing interest costs or investment opportunities that have a measurable rate of return, these companies will incur a cost of capital just like merchants and manufacturers. If the accounting firm's cost of capital is 20%, the holding costs on this project are:

Average investment during the three-month period—($0 + $400,000) ÷ 2 = $200,000
Holding cost—$200,000 × 20% × 3/12 month = $10,000

What if the accounting firm has not completed the audit at the end of three months? At this point, it appears that the audit will require another month and another $40,000 in costs to complete. What are the additional holding costs of this extra month?

Average investment during the fourth month—($400,000 + $440,000) ÷ 2 = $420,000
Additional holding cost—$420,000 × 20% × 1/12 month = $7,000[10]

FYI:

A study on cost accounting in the service industry reported that 65% of service companies have significant levels of work in process at the end of their reporting periods.

Computing and understanding these cost data provide a lot of incentive for the audit manager to complete the job and collect fees as quickly as possible. In providing these data, the accountant is supporting good planning and control of work in process in the audit service process.

---

10 Note that ($440,000 ÷ 2) × 20% × (4/12) < $10,000 + $7,000. This is because the costs on this audit contract are building much faster in the first three months ($400,000 in three months) than in the last month ($40,000 in one month). Similarly, using $400,000 ÷ 2 assumes that the $400,000 in costs is growing evenly over the three-month period ($133,333 per month). A more accurate method of computing the total holding costs for the four-month period would involve calculating and summing the holding costs for each individual month.

TO SUMMARIZE: Both merchandising and service firms often experience several types of opportunity costs, such as lost sales due to not having enough inventory or delays in completing work in process for customers. These costs are extremely difficult to measure. One important category of opportunity costs that accountants can measure is financial holding costs, which is a measure of the costs of having money tied up in inventory (for merchants) or in work-in-process services (for service companies). Measuring holding costs requires that the company's cost of capital first be identified. The holding cost formula is Average investment in inventory or Work-in-process services × Annual rate × Number of years. Financial holding costs can be deducted from net operating profit to measure economic profit for a particular product line.

Quantitative Inventory Management Methods

7 Use classic quantitative tools in inventory management (economic order quantity, reorder point, and safety stock).

We have spent a lot of time in this chapter discussing the many types of costs involved in managing inventory for merchants (once again, refer to Exhibit 5 to see a list of these issues). Generally, service companies do not carry significant levels of inventory and do not need to pay as much attention to inventory management costs. However, many manufacturing companies carry significant inventory levels of raw materials, work in process, and finished goods. These companies need to pay attention to issues involved in managing costs of carrying too much versus too little inventory. The primary question here is, "How much inventory should a company have?" This section will describe some quantitative methods that can be useful to accountants working to answer this question. We will use the example of a merchandising company to illustrate these methods; however, these inventory management calculations are equally applicable to manufacturing companies.

economic order quantity (EOQ) A specific calculation used to determine the most cost-effective size of a purchase order. The EOQ balances the costs of placing an order against the costs of carrying inventory in the organization.

Economic Order Quantity

It is a significant challenge to balance the costs of carrying too much inventory against the costs of carrying too little inventory. Determining how much inventory a company should have involves two important issues: (1) knowing *how much* inventory to order and (2) knowing *when* to place the inventory order. One well-known method used to handle the first issue is the **economic order quantity (EOQ)**. In calculating the optimal size of an inventory order, the EOQ attempts to balance the costs of carrying inventory (e.g., overhead costs, holding costs, risk of lost market values, shrinkage, etc.) against the costs involved in purchasing inventory.

> ⚠️ **Caution**
>
> It is important that you understand that the purchase costs used to calculate the EOQ are *not* the inventory purchase prices, but the overhead costs involved in handling a purchase order (e.g., preparing purchase orders, receiving and inspecting shipments, initiating payment for purchases, etc.).

We'll return once more to the Burzee Doll example to demonstrate how to balance carrying costs and purchasing costs to calculate EOQ. First, we need to determine a cost per doll that includes all the costs of carrying Burzee Dolls during the two-month holiday buying season (November and December). Look back at Exhibit 14. Carrying costs should include the cost due to shrinkage loss, cost due to market loss, overhead costs, and holding costs. You should realize that combining all these carrying costs into a single cost per unit requires a great deal of analysis and intuition on the part of the accountant. However, let's assume that carrying costs are approximately $5 per doll. In addition, purchase order costs are $1,250 per order. Finally, we'll assume that a merchant can sell as many as 40,000 dolls during the holiday buying season. Exhibit 15 demonstrates one method of calculating EOQ using a cost schedule approach. As you can see, as the order quantity gets higher, the average inventory level in the store increases, and total carrying costs increase; in addition, the total purchase orders for the buying season are reduced, resulting in lower total ordering costs. By calculating the total of both carrying and ordering costs, the accountant can get a general idea of the optimal (i.e., economic) order quantity. According to the numbers in Exhibit 15, it appears that the store should request approximately 4,500 dolls for each of its nine orders during the buying season.

Exhibit 15: Calculating EOQ Using a Cost Schedule

Base data:

- Total market demand for dolls for the period: 40,000 dolls
- Average carrying cost per doll for the period: $5
- Average overhead costs per purchase order: $1,250

Order Quantity	1,500	2,250	3,000	3,750	4,500	5,250	6,000	6,750
	÷ 2	÷ 2	÷ 2	÷ 2	÷ 2	÷ 2	÷ 2	÷ 2
Average inventory level	750	1,125	1,500	1,875	2,250	2,625	3,000	3,375
× Carrying cost	$ 5	$ 5	$ 5	$ 5	$ 5	$ 5	$ 5	$ 5
Total Carrying Costs	**$ 3,750**	**$ 5,625**	**$ 7,500**	**$ 9,375**	**$11,250**	**$13,125**	**$15,000**	**$16,875**
Total demand	40,000	40,000	40,000	40,000	40,000	40,000	40,000	40,000
÷ Order quantity	1,500	2,250	3,000	3,750	4,500	5,250	6,000	6,750
Number of orders (rounded up)	27	18	14	11	9	8	7	6
× Costs per order	$ 1,250	$ 1,250	$ 1,250	$ 1,250	$ 1,250	$ 1,250	$ 1,250	$ 1,250
Total Ordering Costs	**$33,750**	**$22,500**	**$17,500**	**$13,750**	**$11,250**	**$10,000**	**$ 8,750**	**$ 7,500**
Total Costs	**$37,500**	**$28,125**	**$25,000**	**$23,125**	**$22,500**	**$23,125**	**$23,750**	**$24,375**

STOP & THINK

Think about EOQ and the relationship between the costs of carrying inventory versus the costs involved in purchasing inventory. As costs of carrying inventory increase, should the organization increase or decrease the size of its purchase orders? As costs of purchasing inventory increase, should the organization increase or decrease the size of its purchase orders?

There is an alternative, and more precise, approach to calculating the EOQ using a formula (derived by calculus). Without working through the calculus derivation, the EOQ formula is:

$$EOQ = \sqrt{\frac{2QP}{C}}$$

Q = The market demand in units for the period
P = The overhead cost of placing one order
C = The total carrying cost for one unit for the period

By inserting our Burzee Doll data into the EOQ formula, we can calculate the precise EOQ as follows:

$$EOQ = \sqrt{\frac{2(40,000)(\$1,250)}{\$5}} = \sqrt{\frac{\$100,000,000}{\$5}} = \sqrt{20,000,000} = 4,472 \text{ dolls}$$

Now that we have the EOQ, we can calculate the following exact costs:

Total carrying costs = 4,472 ÷ 2 = 2,236 average inventory × $5 = $11,180
Total ordering costs = 40,000 ÷ 4,472 = 9 orders × $1,250 = $11,250
Total inventory management costs = $11,180 + $11,250 = $22,430

Using the EOQ formula is much faster and more precise than working through an EOQ cost schedule. With the EOQ, we can resolve the first of two important issues involved in determining how much inventory a company should have—knowing *how much* inventory to order. Now we will turn our attention to the second issue—knowing *when* to place the inventory order.

Reorder Point and Safety Stock

Knowing *when* to place the inventory order involves the reorder point and the desired safety stock. Assume for a moment that you are the manager of the Kids N Toys store. Now that you have calculated the EOQ, you need to know exactly when to place your order. You don't want to reorder Burzee Dolls too soon, or you'll end up with more inventory on hand than you need.

This will result in unnecessary overhead costs, holding costs, and possibly increased inventory shrinkage. On the other hand, if you wait until you're nearly out of dolls before you place the order, you'll probably run out of inventory before the next shipment arrives. This will result in lost sales—a serious opportunity cost. Walking through your store, you watch the levels of dolls on your shelves and in your storeroom decline as customers make purchases. In terms of level of Burzee Doll inventory, at what point do you place your next order? Essentially, you need to calculate a **reorder point**. The calculation is quite simple:

reorder point The point at which the inventory level in the organization drops low enough to trigger a new purchase order.

$$\text{Reorder point} = \text{Average lead time in days} \times \text{Average daily sales}$$

Lead time, in this case, is the time between when store management initiates a purchase order and when the inventory is finally delivered and ready for sale. Lead time for Burzee Dolls would include the time it takes for Kids N Toys to process any necessary paperwork to initiate the purchase order, for the distributor to process the purchase order and deliver the goods, and for Kids N Toys to receive and prepare the dolls for aisle display. Let's assume that lead time for the Burzee Doll is three days. Further, Kids N Toys sells, on average, 800 dolls per day. The reorder point calculation is:

$$\text{Reorder point} = 3 \text{ days} \times 800 \text{ dolls} = 2,400 \text{ dolls}$$

When the inventory falls to 2,400 dolls, you need to initiate a new purchase order. By the time the order arrives, the store should be selling its last doll.

At this point, a couple of things about this reorder point number may be bothering you. One possible problem is that the reorder point calculation is assuming a perfect world. In other words, the reorder point calculation shown assumes that sales are *always* 800 dolls per day and that the lead time is *always* three days. A sudden surge in customer demand or any problems in order processing or shipping could result in empty shelves. As manager for Kids N Toys, you may think you should build a little cushion into your reorder point calculation to allow for any unexpected problems. This is the purpose of **safety stock**. The calculation of the amount of safety stock has two parts: (1) to handle possible problems in the reorder process and (2) to handle an unexpected spike in sales demand. Let's assume that problems in the reorder process could result in a maximum lead time of four days. Further, as many as 875 dolls could sell in one day. The safety stock calculation would be as follows:

safety stock The minimal level of inventory required to insure against the organization running out of inventory in the case of unforeseen problems in receiving its next purchase order.

Maximum lead time	4 days	
Average lead time in days	3 days	
Surplus	1 day	
Average expected sales per day	× 800 dolls	
Safety stock for reorder problem		800 dolls
Maximum expected sales per day	875 dolls	
Average expected sales per day	800 dolls	
Surplus	75 dolls	
Maximum lead time	× 4 days	
Safety stock for demand changes		300 dolls
Total safety stock		1,100 dolls

Based on these numbers, Kids N Toys will always want to keep at least 1,100 dolls on hand to handle unexpected situations involving either its suppliers or its customers. Hence, this safety stock number should be added to the original reorder point calculation, resulting in a new reorder point calculation that includes a cushion for safety stock:

$$\text{Reorder point with safety stock} = (\text{Average lead time in days} \times \text{Average daily sales})$$
$$+ \text{ Safety stock}$$
$$= (3 \text{ days} \times 800 \text{ dolls}) + 1,100 \text{ dolls} = 3,500 \text{ dolls}$$

Caution

Perhaps you've heard of the saying "Garbage in, garbage out!" The quality of these three quantitative inventory management models (like all decision models and systems in business) is only as good as the quality of the information that is used in the calculations. Before using the EOQ, reorder point, or safety stock calculations, the accountant needs to be sure that all costs and risks of carrying and ordering inventory are understood. Current JIT thinking suggests that accountants in the past may have severely understated the costs of carrying inventory, resulting in unnecessarily large inventory orders and high levels of inventory in the organization.

You've likely noticed that the reorder point calculation that includes safety stock can be directly calculated as:

Reorder point with safety stock = Maximum lead time in days
$\qquad$ × Maximum daily sales
$\qquad$ = 4 days × 875 dolls
$\qquad$ = 3,500 dolls

Combining these two calculations into one simple calculation is acceptable, assuming that management is not interested in knowing the specific level for safety stock. Usually, though, store management wants to know when sales are eating into the safety stock. Such a situation signals that special attention is needed to ensure that the store does not run out of stock and miss some customer sales. Exhibit 16 graphically depicts these relationships.

TO SUMMARIZE: Balancing costs of carrying too much inventory against the costs of carrying too little inventory is a significant challenge for accountants in both merchandising and manufacturing organizations. The economic order quantity, reorder point, and safety stock calculations can help. Exhibit 16 graphically summarizes the relationship between EOQ, reorder points, and safety stock inventory levels. Consider Exhibit 16 in light of the inventory management issues in Exhibit 5. The EOQ model is a useful tool for managing carrying costs (e.g., overhead costs, holding costs, losses due to decreased market value, and the cost of inventory shrinkage). The EOQ model balances these carrying costs against ordering costs. In addition, the EOQ should be combined with intelligent calculations of reorder points and safety stock in order to guard against excessive risk of lost sales due to delivery problems and fluctuating market demand.

Exhibit 16: Graphical Display of EOQ, Reorder Points, and Safety Stock Inventory Levels

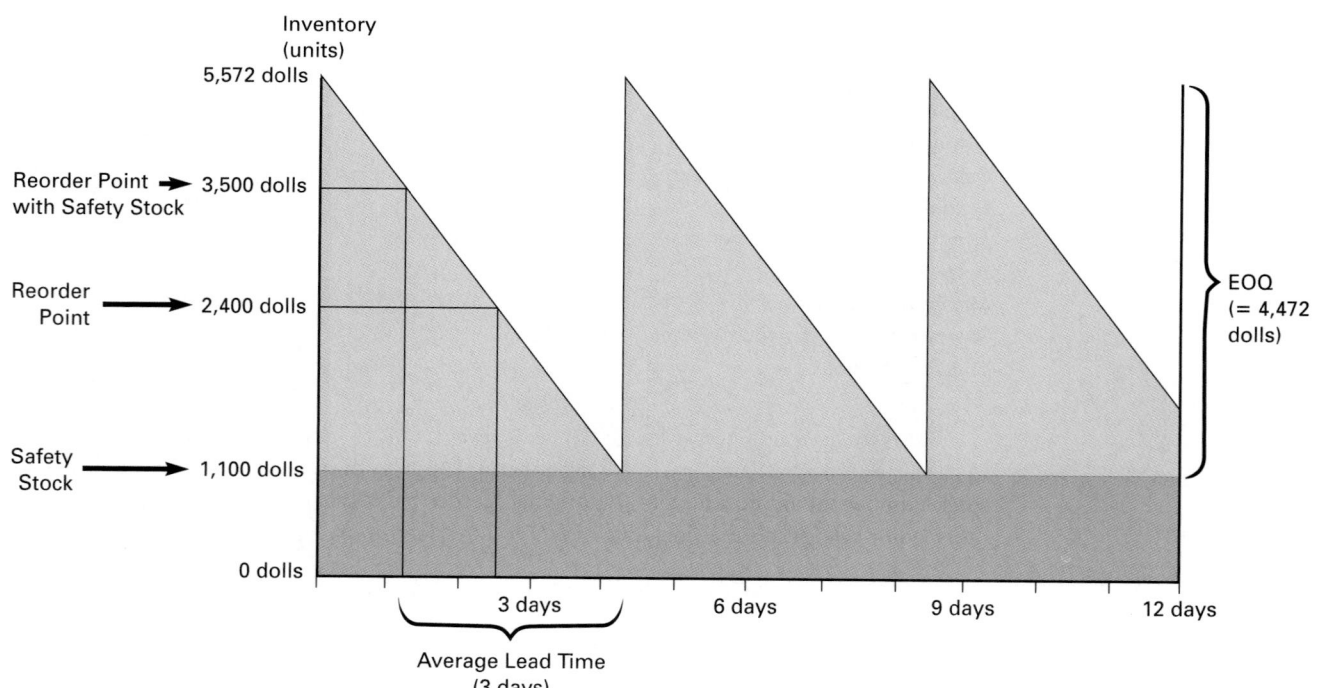

review of learning objectives

1 **Identify the different types of inventory in manufacturing, service, and merchandising organizations and understand how these inventory costs are reflected in the income statement and balance sheet.** Both manufacturing and service organizations maintain substantial production processes. As a result, both types of organizations report work-in-process inventory in the balance sheet. In addition, the computation of cost of goods sold can be quite complex for these types of organizations because the computation involves combining information about materials, labor, and overhead costs. The computation of cost of goods sold in a merchandising organization is relatively simple because inventory is purchased in its final form and substantial additional costs are generally not incurred in getting it ready to sell. Both manufacturing and merchandising organizations maintain significant levels of ending inventory that are reported in the balance sheet.

2 **Analyze the levels of raw materials, work-in-process, and finished goods inventories in a manufacturing organization.** Inventory turnover measures can be used to evaluate effective use of raw materials, work-in-process, and finished goods inventories. The average level of raw materials inventory is used to support the cost of materials used during the period. Work-in-process inventory is used to support the cost of goods manufactured. Finished goods inventory is used to support the cost of goods sold during the period. Two measures of inventory management performance are used to report on and control inventory levels: inventory turnover and days in inventory.

3 **Understand how merchants manage inventory in their organizations.** Because merchants basically purchase inventory in a finished state, the process of accounting for inventory in a merchandising business is not nearly as complicated as it is in a manufacturing business. However, there are a number of important issues associated with managing the inventory in order to maximize sales and minimize a variety of inventory costs. For example, having too much inventory creates unnecessary overhead costs, financial holding costs, costs due to loss of market value, and costs due to inventory shrinkage. Not having enough inventory may result in unnecessary ordering costs and loss of bulk order discounts, as well as opportunity costs due to lost sales and increased supplier prices. Measuring these costs allows management accountants to prepare detailed cost reports that support effective management of gross margins and net operating profits for individual product lines.

4 **Measure profitability and personnel utilization in a service organization.** Like a manufacturing organization, a service organization involves a substantial process before delivering a final product to the customer. Three types of service organizations are professional services, service shops, and mass services. Professional service firms emphasize people-to-people service over automation, the delivery of a process rather than a final tangible product, and high customization. A mass service organization emphasizes the standardized, automated delivery of a tangible product. Service organizations, similar to manufacturing and merchandising organizations, must measure profitability and resource utilization. A professional services firm uses profitability measures based on a comparison of revenues to the compensation cost of the professionals. This textbook reports this performance using a measure called profit percentage from personnel (PPP). Personnel utilization can be measured by comparing the number of billable hours actually worked to the number that was expected. This measure is referred to in this textbook as personnel utilization rates (PUR).

5 **Describe how the concept of just-in-time (JIT) inventory systems is used to improve cost, quality, and timely performance in organizations.** Just-in-time (JIT) has become an important tool for managing manufacturing, service, and merchandising companies across the world. In a manufacturing setting, demand at the final assembly stage "pulls" the inventory through the production process only as it is needed. Using this system, nothing is produced until customers demand it. JIT puts a strong emphasis on costs and quality. However, JIT also focuses on management of timeliness and flexibility. The main goal of JIT is to add value to the product or service and reduce or eliminate activities that do not. By focusing on removing non-value-added activities and reducing time spent on value-added activities, inventories and other costs are reduced, while quality and timeliness are improved.

eXpanded *Material*

6 **Calculate and interpret holding costs in merchandising and service businesses.** Although opportunity costs can be extremely difficult to measure, one important type of opportunity cost that accountants can measure is financial holding costs. Financial holding costs measure the costs of having money tied up in inventory (for merchants) or tied up in work-in-process services (for service companies). Measuring holding costs requires that the company's cost of capital first be identified. The holding cost formula is Average investment in inventory or work-in-process services × Annual rate × Number of years. Financial holding costs can be deducted from net operating profit to measure economic profit for a particular product line. Measuring economic profit for an entire company is sometimes called Economic Value Added (EVA™).

7 **Use classic quantitative tools in inventory management (economic order quantity, reorder point, and safety stock).** Both merchandising and manufacturing orga-

nizations have significant investments in inventory costs. Accountants can balance the costs of carrying too much inventory against the costs of carrying too little inventory by calculating the economic order quantity (EOQ), reorder point, and safety stock. The EOQ model is a useful tool for managing carrying costs (e.g., overhead costs, holding costs, losses due to decreased market value, and the costs of inventory shrinkage). The EOQ model balances these carrying costs against ordering costs. The EOQ is combined with reorder point and safety stock calculations in order to guard against excessive risk of lost sales due to delivery problems and fluctuating market demand.

k ey terms & concepts

days in inventory, 1156
holding costs, 1160
inventory shrinkage, 1160
inventory turnover, 1156
just-in-time (JIT), 1172
lead time, 1161
net operating profit, 1165
non-value-added activities, 1174

value-added activities, 1174

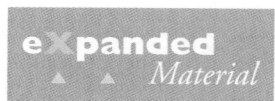

cost of capital, 1176
economic order quantity (EOQ), 1179

economic profit, 1176
Economic Value Added (EVA™), 1178
reorder point, 1181
safety stock, 1181
segment, 1178

r eview problem

Inventory Performance Measures

Part 1

Sparky Manufacturing, Inc. manufactures cell phones. A comprehensive income statement and a partial balance sheet for Sparky Manufacturing, Inc. follow:

Income Statement

Sales revenues	$2,640,000
Cost of goods sold/Cost of goods manufactured:	
Cost of goods manufactured:	
Beginning raw materials	$ 23,300
+ Purchases of materials	950,000
Total raw materials available	$ 973,300
− Ending raw materials	(20,000)
Raw materials used	$ 953,300
+ Direct labor	380,000
+ Applied manufacturing overhead	120,000
Total manufacturing costs	$1,453,300

Total manufacturing costs	$1,453,300
+ Beginning work-in-process inventory	12,400
− Ending work-in-process inventory	(15,200)
Cost of goods manufactured	$1,450,500
+ Beginning finished goods inventory	40,700
− Ending finished goods inventory	(37,600)
Cost of goods sold	$1,453,600
− Overapplied manufacturing overhead	(12,000)
Adjusted cost of goods sold	$1,441,600
Gross margin	$1,198,400
Selling and general administrative expenses:	
Selling expenses	$ 128,000
Administrative expenses	237,000
Total selling and general administrative expenses	$ 365,000
Net operating income	$ 833,400

Selected Balance Sheet Information

Accounts receivable	$59,200
Raw materials inventory	20,000
Work-in-process inventory	15,200
Finished goods inventory	37,600
Supplies inventory	600
Accounts payable	22,400

Required:

Use Sparky Manufacturing, Inc.'s income statement and partial balance sheet to answer the following question.

1. Compute the turnover ratio and days in inventory ratio for all three inventories (use 365 days in a year).

Part 2

Toadstool Wireless is a cell phone retailer that purchases its cell phones from Sparky Manufacturing, Inc. To support sales in the months April through June, Toadstool Wireless bought 890 phones in one order that were received in multiple shipments. Of those 890 phones, 815 were sold at the suggested retail price of $250. The other 75 cell phones were lost due to poor controls in the shipping process. The average cost to initiate and receive each purchase order was $550 per order. Toadstool Wireless expected to pay $110 per phone but due to unexpected tariffs that affected some of Sparky's competitors, the cost per phone was raised to $125. Overhead costs for the three months were initially expected to be $60,000, but were actually only $49,000.

Required:

2. Create a management accounting report that helps management to understand the impact of these changes on net operating profit.
3. Compute the return on inventory investment for Toadstool Wireless.
4. Assume that the company's cost of capital is 12%. Compute the holding costs and economic profit for the company.

Solution
Part 1

1. **Raw materials inventory turnover:**
$953,300 ÷ [($23,300 + $20,000) ÷ 2] = 44.0 times
Raw materials days in inventory: 365 ÷ 44.0 = 8.3 days
Work-in-process inventory turnover:
$1,450,500 ÷ [($12,400 + $15,200) ÷ 2] = 105.1 times
Work-in-process days in inventory: 365 days ÷ 105.1 = 3.5 days
Finished goods inventory turnover:
$1,441,600 ÷ [($40,700 + $37,600) ÷ 2] = 36.8 times
Finished goods days in inventory: 365 days ÷ 36.8 = 9.9 days

Part 2

2.

Expected revenue	$250 × 890 units	$222,500
Shrinkage loss	$250 × 75 units	(18,750)
Actual revenue		$203,750
Expected product costs	$110 × 890 units	(97,900)
Cost increase	$15 × 890 units	(13,350)
Gross margin		$ 92,500
Expected overhead costs		(60,000)
Decrease in overhead costs	$60,000 − $49,000	11,000
Order costs	$550 × 3 orders	(1,650)
Net operating profit		$ 41,850

3. **Return on inventory investment:**
($97,900 + $13,350) ÷ 2 = $55,625 average inventory level
$92,500 ÷ $55,625 = 166.3%

4. **Holding costs:** $55,625 × 12% × 3/12 = $1,669*
Economic profit: $23,100 − $1,669 = $21,431

*Rounded.

discussion questions

1. What similarities are there in the inventories of a manufacturing and a merchandising organization? What are the differences?
2. What similarities are there in the inventories of a manufacturing and a service organization? What are the differences?
3. How does the work-in-process inventory in a manufacturing organization differ from that in a service organization?
4. What is represented by total cost of goods manufactured?
5. Why is the total cost of goods sold number of limited usefulness for detailed internal decision making?
6. What amount is compared to the level of raw materials inventory in computing a useful measure of raw materials inventory turnover? Of work-in-process inventory turnover? Of finished goods inventory turnover?
7. Name three problems associated with carrying too much inventory.
8. Name three problems associated with carrying too little inventory.
9. What is inventory shrinkage? Name three things that can cause inventory shrinkage.
10. What can a company do to evaluate the management of its inventory investment?
11. What are the three basic types of service organizations?
12. The different types of service organizations vary in the emphasis they place on three dimensions. What are these three dimensions?
13. The same two concepts that underlie cost management in manufacturing and merchandising organizations are also used in developing cost management tools for service organizations. What are these two concepts?

14. How did the concept of just-in-time (JIT) change most companies' view that maintaining a minimum level of inventory was desirable? Use the measures of cost, quality, and time as you prepare your answer.

15. "The purpose of just-in-time (JIT) is to reduce inventory." Do you agree or disagree? Explain.

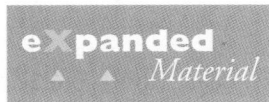

16. What causes holding costs to exist? How is it that holding costs exist in the service industry, which typically does not have inventories?

17. What are the advantages of purchasing inventory in large quantities? What are the advantages of purchasing it in small quantities?

18. What are carrying costs in the denominator of the economic order quantity (EOQ) formula? How do large carrying costs affect the economic order quantity?

19. Explain the reasoning behind the reorder point formula, Reorder point = Lead time × Average daily sales. How does safety stock fit into the reorder point concept?

p ractice exercises

Practice 21-1

Inventory Turnover

Using the following *annual* information, calculate inventory turnover for (1) raw materials inventory, (2) work-in-process inventory, and (3) finished goods inventory.

Cost of raw materials used	$100,000
Ending raw materials inventory	20,000
Ending work-in-process inventory	50,000
Cost of goods sold	250,000
Beginning finished goods inventory	60,000
Cost of goods manufactured	200,000
Beginning work-in-process inventory	40,000
Beginning raw materials inventory	15,000
Ending finished goods inventory	70,000

Practice 21-2

Days in Inventory

Refer to the data in Practice 21-1. Compute the number of days in inventory for (1) raw materials inventory, (2) work-in-process inventory, and (3) finished goods inventory. (Assume 365 days in the year.)

Practice 21-3

Carrying Too Much Inventory versus Carrying Too Little Inventory
Which one of the following statements is *false*?

a. Companies that carry too much inventory face increased overhead costs.
b. Companies that carry too little inventory face increased bulk order discounts.
c. Companies that carry too little inventory face increased exposure of suppliers not delivering inventory on time.
d. Companies that carry too much inventory face increased inventory shrinkage.
e. Companies that carry too much inventory face increased financial holding costs.

Practice 21-4

Gross Margin Comparison
Which of the following companies performed better during the period based on gross margin alone?

(continued)

	Company A	Company B
Beginning total assets	$ 183,000	$ 92,000
Ending total assets	192,000	95,000
Cost of goods sold	1,360,000	420,000
Revenue	1,840,000	870,000

Practice 21-5

Return on Investment Comparison

Refer to the data in Practice 21-4. Based on DuPont's return on investment (ROI) formula, which company performed better during the period?

Practice 21-6

Reports and Decision Making

Which one of the following reports provides management with the most valuable information related to sales of products?

a. Master budget
b. Management accounting report
c. Gross margin report
d. Balance sheet

Practice 21-7

Cost Management in Service Organizations

Which one of the following statements is *false*?

a. Service firms place no emphasis on the cost of materials.
b. Cost management in service organizations measures how efficiently the company uses its people.
c. Professional service organizations implement a high degree of customization.
d. Mass service firms place more emphasis on equipment than on people.

Practice 21-8

Measuring Profitability in Service Organizations

The company is a service organization and has the following numbers of professionals:

	Number of Individuals	Client Billable Hours Expected to Be Worked per Year	Billing Rate per Hour
Class A	5	1,500	$200
Class B	10	2,000	100
Class C	20	2,000	60

During the most recent year, the class A professionals billed a total of 7,000 hours, the class B professionals billed a total of 17,000 hours, and the class C professionals billed a total of 30,000 hours. The 5 class A professionals were paid a total of $1,000,000, the 10 class B professionals were paid a total of $1,500,000, and the 20 class C professionals were paid a total of $1,000,000. The company measures its profitability with the following ratio:

$$(\text{Revenue} - \text{Personnel compensation cost}) \div \text{Revenue}$$

Given the data above, compute the value of this ratio (known as the profit percentage from personnel, or PPP).

Practice 21-9

Measuring Personnel Utilization in Service Organizations

Refer to the data in Practice 21-8. For each class of professional, compute the total actual billable hours during the year as a percentage of total expected billable hours.

Practice 21-10

Just-in-Time Inventory

Which one of the following statements is *false*?

a. Carrying large amounts of inventory can be very costly for a company.
b. JIT environments are usually "push" systems.
c. JIT inventory systems started in Japan.
d. JIT emphasizes reduction of non-value-added activities.
e. Under a JIT system, accountants are encouraged to provide time-based performance measures to management.

Practice 21-11

Opportunity Costs

Which one of the following statements is *false*?

a. Economic profit is less than or equal to net operating profit.
b. A company that has a high quantity of one type of inventory may incur opportunity costs related to other inventory items in lower quantity.
c. Both service and manufacturing firms often experience opportunity costs.
d. Opportunity costs include a number of out-of-pocket costs.
e. Opportunity costs are difficult to measure.

Practice 21-12

Financial Holding Costs

The company had an average of $160,000 worth of a certain product in inventory from September 1 to December 31. If the company's cost of capital is 16%, what is the financial holding cost of this inventory?

Practice 21-13

Economic Order Quantity

Using the following data, compute the company's economic order quantity.

Total units demanded annually	150,000
Cost to place one order	$3,200
Total carrying cost for one unit for the year	$4

Practice 21-14

Reorder Point

The company sells 130 units daily; each time the company orders more units, it takes the supplier four days to deliver the inventory. What is the company's reorder point (in number of units)?

Practice 21-15

Safety Stock

Refer to the data in Practice 21-14. The supplier may take five days to deliver the inventory if any unexpected event occurs, and the daily demand for inventory may also spike to 160 units. Compute the amount of safety stock the company should keep on hand in case both of these events should happen.

Practice 21-16

Reorder Point and Safety Stock

Refer to the data in Practice 21-14. If the company never wants inventory to drop below 200 units, what is the company's reorder point (in number of units)?

e xercises

Exercise 21-1

Spreadsheet

Inventory Turnover in a Manufacturing Company

The following information is the end of year data for Pecos Yo Company:

Raw materials purchased during the year	$203,000
Beginning raw materials inventory	20,000
Ending raw materials inventory	25,000
Applied manufacturing overhead	350,000
Direct labor costs	100,000
Beginning work-in-process inventory	64,000
Ending work-in-process inventory	60,000
Beginning finished goods inventory	37,000
Ending finished goods inventory	40,000

Compute the following:

1. Inventory turnover for raw materials inventory.
2. Days in raw materials inventory. Assume 360 days in a year.
3. Inventory turnover for work-in-process inventory.
4. Days in work-in-process inventory. Assume 360 days in a year.
5. Inventory turnover for finished goods inventory.
6. Days in finished goods inventory. Assume 360 days in a year.

Exercise 21-2

Inventory Turnover in a Merchandising Company

Beanie Company is a merchandising company. Beanie had the following financial data for the years 2005 and 2006:

	2006	2005
Revenues	$200,000	$180,000
Cost of goods sold	110,000	109,000
Gross margin	$ 90,000	$ 71,000
Inventory	$ 40,000	$ 50,000

1. Calculate Beanie Company's turnover for inventory for 2006 and explain what it means.
2. Calculate Beanie Company's days in inventory for 2006, assuming 365 days in a year, and explain what it means.

Exercise 21-3

Inventory Turnover in a Merchandising Company

Both Dave and Kelly own auto parts stores. The following information is available for 2005 and 2006:

	Dave	Kelly
Cost of goods sold:		
2005	$150,000	$300,000
2006	130,000	350,000
Ending inventory:		
2005	75,000	225,000
2006	55,000	255,000

1. Calculate each company's turnover for inventory for 2006.
2. Calculate each company's days in inventory for 2006 (assume 365 days in a year).
2. Which owner manages inventory better? Explain your answer.

Exercise 21-4

Analyzing a Management Accounting Report

You have just finished preparing the management accounting report for your division. You show the following report to your division president, Karen, and tell her that you are very pleased with the performance of your division.

Division Management Accounting Report	
Expected revenue	$1,200,000
Shrinkage loss	(38,400)
Market loss	(127,040)
Actual revenue	$1,034,560
Expected purchase costs	(400,000)
Lost discount	(38,000)
Gross margin	$ 596,560
Overhead costs	(66,000)
Order costs	(1,000)
Net operating profit	$ 529,560

After reviewing the report, Karen does not understand what some of the costs are and why they are in the report. Respond to her questions listed below.

1. What does the $38,400 shrinkage signify?
2. What does it mean to have a $127,040 market loss?
3. Just because we didn't take advantage of a discount on a purchase, why is this a cost when there was no outflow of dollars directly related to the discount?

Exercise 21-5

Analysis of Return on Inventory Investment

Plaids & Stripes and Audrey's Apparel are clothes retailers. August and September are busy months for these two stores because many people are buying new clothes for the start of school. This year these stores expect the largest demand to be in children's clothing. The following information has been given for both stores' children's departments during the months of August and September:

	Plaids & Stripes	Audrey's Apparel
Revenue	$565,000	$1,115,000
Gross margin	296,100	527,300
Average investment in inventory	29,000	165,000

Using the above information, answer the following questions about Plaids & Stripes and Audrey's Apparel.

1. Using the information given, which store generated the most total profit from inventory sales?
2. Calculate the return on inventory investment for both stores' children's departments. (Use both the profit margin and inventory turnover ratios.)
3. Using the calculations from part (2), which store actually manages its inventory more effectively? Explain your answer.

Exercise 21-6

Profitability in a Service Organization

Lorien Company is an engineering firm composed of five engineers. It is expected that each engineer will work 2,000 hours during a year on client jobs. The following additional information has been given for each of the five engineers:

(continued)

	Annual Compensation	Billing Rate per Engineering Hour	Actual Billable Hours
Penny	$270,000	$300	1,900
Jacob	250,000	250	1,900
Mandy	230,000	225	1,800
Edwin	200,000	200	1,800
Jackie	180,000	175	1,800

1. Calculate each engineer's profit percentage from personnel (PPP).
2. Calculate the profit percentage from personnel (PPP) for the entire firm.
3. Which engineer is bringing the most value to the company?

Exercise 21-7

Spreadsheet

Personnel Utilization in a Service Organization

Magily Company is a mathematical model consulting firm. Magily's services are sought by oil exploration companies for interpreting seismic data, by NASA for deciphering signals from deep space probes, and by Wall Street derivatives speculators who want to predict the weather in order to know whether to buy or sell soybean futures. Magily maintains the following mathematician staff:

	Number of Individuals	Client Billable Hours Expected to Be Worked per Year
Full mathematician consultants	5	700
Associate mathematician consultants	10	2,100
Assistant mathematician consultants	40	2,600

During the most recent year, full mathematician consultants worked a total of 3,000 hours; associate mathematician consultants worked a total of 25,000 hours; and assistant mathematician consultants worked a total of 140,000 hours. Compute personnel utilization ratios for each class of mathematician.

Exercise 21-8

Value-Added and Non-Value-Added Activities

Below is a list of activities performed by the Ibapah Bijou, a movie theater. Indicate whether each activity is a value-added activity (VA) or a non-value-added activity (NVA).

a. Redesigning the staff uniforms.
b. Cooking popcorn.
c. Counting the ticket stubs at night to make sure no one got in free.
d. Servicing the quadraphonic speaker system.
e. Paying for the rights to show the next movie starring Julia Roberts.
f. Paying a management fee for the employee pension fund.
g. Renting a storage facility to store the excess inventory of candy, uncooked popcorn, and soft drinks.
h. Paying the accounts payable.
i. Cleaning the white movie screens.
j. Scrubbing the theater floor to remove the sticky residue of spilled soft drinks.

Exercise 21-9

Financial Holding Costs

On January 1, 2006, Owen Corporation has $350,000 in inventory. On May 1, 2006, Owen's inventory is at $400,000. Owen's cost of capital is 13%. What were Owen's financial holding costs for January through April?

Exercise 21-10

Financial Holding Costs

Brady Company sells imported goods made in India. One product it sells is a wooden music box. The music boxes cost Brady $65, and Brady charges its customers a price of $250. Brady's cost of capital is 12%. On average, an entire year elapses between the time Brady pays for a music box and the time Brady collects the cash from the sale of the music box. What are Brady's annual financial holding costs per unit for the wooden music boxes?

Exercise 21-11

Economic Order Quantity

Pace Retailers' best-selling item is its reinforced bicycle tires. Pace sells 4,745 of these tires each year. It costs approximately $200 for Pace to place a purchase order, and it costs on average about $2.50 per tire per year for inventory overhead costs. The retail price of the tires is $12.50. What is the economic order quantity of tires Pace should order at one time?

Exercise 21-12

Reorder Point

Refer to Exercise 21-11. Suppose the lead time to receive a purchase order of reinforced bicycle tires is 13 days. To ensure adequate inventories at all times, Pace maintains a safety stock of 80 tires. Assuming Pace sells the 4,745 bicycle tires uniformly over the 365 days of the year, what is Pace's reorder point?

Exercise 21-13

$\mathcal{S}$preadsheet

Economic Order Quantity

For the past three years, Hawkeye Army Surplus Store has had excessive inventory holding costs. Management believes the excessive costs are due to the large inventory purchase orders the company places. The company hires a consultant, Brad Miles, to analyze the problem and suggest a solution. Information about two products, combat boots and backpacks, is as follows:

	Combat Boots	Backpacks
Annual market demand	20,000 pairs	5,000 packs
Cost per unit	$20	$55
Annual carrying cost per unit	$7	$16
Ordering cost	$500	$500

In order to balance the cost of placing a purchase order against the overhead cost of controlling inventory, how many pairs of combat boots should Brad suggest Hawkeye purchase at a time? How many backpacks?

Exercise 21-14

Reorder Point

Avery Grocery Store is the only grocery store in Rayville, a small town populated mostly by college students. Students have been complaining lately because Avery always runs out of macaroni and cheese, the students' favorite food. Avery management decides it needs to calculate a more suitable reorder point. Information about the macaroni and cheese is as follows:

(continued)

Average daily sales	500 boxes
Average lead time to receive an order	5 days
Avery's cost per unit	$0.30
Price charged to customers	$0.75

1. What should be the reorder point if Avery does not want to maintain any safety stock?
2. What should be the reorder point if Avery wants to maintain a safety stock of 1,000 boxes of macaroni and cheese?

p roblems

Problem 21-1

Inventory Turnover in a Manufacturing Company

The following information is for Bun MaScare Company:

Beginning raw materials inventory	$ 25,000
Raw materials purchased	110,000
Ending raw materials inventory	15,000
Manufacturing overhead (actual)	300,000
Beginning work-in-process inventory	50,000
Ending work-in-process inventory	40,000
Direct labor costs	90,000
Beginning finished goods inventory	200,000
Ending finished goods inventory	270,000
Overapplied manufacturing overhead	15,000

Required:
Compute the following (assume 365 days in a year):

1. Inventory turnover for raw materials inventory.
2. Days' supply of raw materials inventory.
3. Inventory turnover for work-in-process inventory.
4. Days of manufacturing represented by work-in-process inventory.
5. Inventory turnover for finished goods inventory.
6. Days' sales in finished goods inventory.
7. **Interpretive Question:** What conclusions can you draw from your inventory turnover calculations?

Problem 21-2

*S*preadsheet

Management Accounting Reports in a Merchandising Company

Ride EZ and Happy Trails are mountain bike retailers. This season a new bike, the Coaster, was introduced in the market. It was believed that the Coaster would be the most popular mountain bike sold during the season. Both companies sold the bike at the suggested retail price. At the end of each month during the season (May through September), store managers made notes of how many bikes were sold or purchased during the month. The following is a list of these notes:

Date	Ride EZ	Happy Trails
May 1	30 bikes purchased	150 bikes purchased
May 31	27 bikes sold, out of stock; 30 more bikes are purchased	30 bikes sold

June 30	29 bikes sold, out of stock; 30 more bikes are purchased	35 bikes sold
July 31	28 bikes sold, out of stock; 30 more bikes are purchased	37 bikes sold
Aug. 31	24 bikes sold	24 bikes sold
Sept. 30	4 bikes sold at cost; out of stock, no bikes purchased	13 bikes sold at cost; out of stock, no bikes purchased

The following information is also known:

- Suggested retail price is $600.
- The manufacturer sells the Coaster for a normal price of $275.
- Discounts of $25 off the normal price are given on purchases of 100 bikes or more.
- Average overhead costs used to purchase and initiate a purchase order for both retailers are $450 per event.
- Purchases are always made on the last day of the month.
- On June 15, the manufacturer raised the price of the Coaster to $290.
- Average inventory overhead costs for both retailers are $15 per unit per month.
- Both Ride EZ and Happy Trails account for inventory using FIFO.

Required:

Prepare a management accounting report for both Ride EZ and Happy Trails using the information given in the problem.

Problem 21-3

Personnel Utilization in a Service Business

Columbus & Hercules offers the following annual estimates (based on a 50-week work year) regarding the salaries and estimated hours associated with the professionals employed by the firm:

Position	Total Estimated Salaries	Total Estimated Billable Hours
Partners (2 × $100,000)	$200,000	4,400
Managers (3 × $70,000)	210,000	6,600
Seniors (6 × $50,000)	300,000	13,200
Staff accountants (10 × $25,000)	250,000	22,000

During February, Managers 1 and 2 were assigned three staff accountants each; Manager 3 was assigned four staff accountants. At the end of February, the following staff utilization report was generated:

Staff Working for:	Budgeted Billable Hours	Actual Billable Hours
Manager 1	528	690
Manager 2	528	530
Manager 3	704	630
Total	1,760	1,850

Required:

Use the staff utilization numbers to evaluate the staff usage practices by the three managers.

Problem 21-4

Profitability and Personnel Utilization in a Service Company

Diggy Company specializes in caring for the pets of the rich and famous. Diggy gives personal care to each and every pet, and its professional animal "consultants" are on call 24 hours per day. Some details about Diggy's business are given below.

	Number of Individuals	Client Billable Hours Expected to Be Worked per Year	Annual Compensation	Billing Rate
Partners	5	500	$500,000	$400
Consultants	40	2,500	35,000	250

During the most recent year, the five partners billed a total of 3,000 hours, and the 40 consultants billed a total of 56,000 hours.

Required:
1. Compute personnel utilization ratios for each of the two classes of professionals within the firm.
2. Compute the firm's profit percentage from personnel (PPP).
3. Compute the PPP for each of the two classes of professionals within the firm.
4. **Interpretive Question:** Speculate on why the 40 consultants worked the number of billable hours that they did.

Problem 21-5

JIT Inventory

The president of Penman Corporation, John Burton, has asked you, the company's controller, to advise him on whether Penman should develop a just-in-time (JIT) inventory system. Your research concludes that there is a high cost associated with inventory storage facilities; that inventories use a large portion of the company's cash flow; and that because of the nature of the inventory, there is a significant amount of shrinkage. Research also shows that neither of Penman's two competitors uses a JIT inventory system. Most of Penman's employees are trained to do only one job and belong to a local union. The union is strong and, in the past, has opposed major production changes. The union believes major changes will result in the loss of union employees' jobs. Your research indicates that Penman's major production item (a fairly new product in the market) should continue to have strong sales growth.

Required:
1. Using the information provided, advise John Burton to either continue the present system or work to develop a JIT inventory system.
2. Assume John decides to develop an inventory management system. He plans to evaluate the system after one year. List at least four possible performance measures John could use to evaluate the effectiveness of the system. Describe what information these measures would provide John.

Problem 21-6

Economic Profit

Larsen Company has two divisions. The following is information about these two divisions over the past six months:

	Division L	Division M
Net operating profit	$390,000	$400,000
Average investment	$35,000	$200,000
Annual cost of capital	12%	18%

Required:

1. Use the above information to calculate the economic profit for the two divisions.
2. **Interpretive Question:** The division manager for Division M asks you why it is appropriate to include holding costs in the calculation of economic profit. Since holding costs are not included in the audited income statements that are reported by the company to its shareholders, then why would it be appropriate to use this cost in the internal reports that are used to evaluate managers and divisions? How would you respond?

Problem 21-7

Inventory Management

Watersports, Inc., sells high-performance water skis. Because its sales are seasonal, Watersports calculates and uses different reorder points for summer and winter months. The following information is available:

	April–October	November–March
Lead time (days)	3	7
Total customer demand for the period	1,600	400

The water skis cost $150 each, and Watersports sells them to its customers for $300. Watersports' supplier charges $500 for each order placed. Watersports incurs an *annual* carrying cost of $17 per set of skis. Watersports has noticed in the past that sometimes the deliveries can be up to two days later than average and that the customer demand can be as much as 1,800 skis during April through October and 500 skis during the rest of the year.

Required:

1. Calculate the appropriate economic order quantities for the two seasons.
2. Calculate the safety stock for the two seasons that are necessary to accommodate potential delays in inventory deliveries and potential spikes in sales demand.
3. Calculate reorder point (with safety stock) for the two seasons.
4. **Interpretive Question:** What are the value and the cost of having safety stock?

discussion cases

Case 21-1

Buying Inventory for the Holiday Selling Season

Ryan Baird owns a small retail shop. Historically, her annual sales have been about $250,000, with 60% of that coming in the holiday selling season of November and December. This year on a buying trip to southern China, Ryan discovered an item that she is certain will be in huge demand. The item is a mechanical cricket powered by a photovoltaic cell—the cricket automatically silences at night when it gets dark and then starts chirping in the morning when the sun's rays hit it. Ryan can buy the crickets from her Guangdong supplier for $1.00 each; she plans to sell them for $9.95 each.

Ryan is trying to decide how many of the crickets she should order. If she orders 30,000 or more, she can get a volume discount and pay just $0.80 each. However, she does not have room to store that many crickets, and she will have to rent storage space for $3,000 per month (three-month minimum). Also, the Guangdong supplier will only accept cash, and, because Ryan does not have very good credit, she will have to pay 17% annual interest on any money she borrows. She expects any loan to be outstanding for about two months.

Ryan has come to you for advice about whether she should buy a large quantity of crickets or play it safe and order just 10,000. What advice would you give her?

Case 21-2

Financial Holding Costs

You work in the accounting department of Cox Company. You are having a debate with one of your co-workers about holding costs. Your co-worker insists that holding costs should not be considered in making decisions because they do not involve any cash flows. He believes that cash flows are all that the business really cares about. How do you respond to him?

judgment calls

Judgment 21-1

You Decide: Can inventory management tools, such as turnover and days in inventory, be used in a service company that doesn't have significant levels of tangible inventory? Why is it important to manage costs in a service organization?

You have just been hired as an accountant for a large law firm. Your first project is to look at some financial information and determine why net income is declining. The senior partner tells you that total revenues for the company have increased each of the last five years. As a result, a proposal to substantially increase salaries for senior associates is being strongly considered. "A number of partners are preparing to retire, and we need to retain our best associates for future partnership," he said. "No one else in the company has done any research as to why net income has gone down, so we are excited to see what you come up with!" How should you perform the analysis?

Judgment 21-2

You Decide: Can a just-in-time inventory system help companies minimize inventory costs, or is JIT too expensive and cumbersome to implement?

Lately, you have heard a lot of talk about just-in-time inventory systems and how they help companies, like WAL-MART, keep track of inventory. You know that a JIT system can help track and keep inventory costs at a minimum, but is JIT really a viable option for all companies? For example, your neighbor works at a local automobile repair shop and he is always complaining about not having the right parts on hand, which causes him to get behind on his work. He can frequently be heard saying, "We always seem to run out of parts at the wrong time. Jan does a good job at trying to keep inventory in stock, but sometimes that job can get too big. Something else needs to be done or we are going to start losing customers!" How large does a company have to be and how much inventory must it have before JIT makes sense?

<u>C</u>ompetency <u>E</u>nhancement <u>O</u>pportunities

▶ **Analyzing Real Company Information**
▶ **International Case**
▶ **Ethics Case**
▶ **Writing Assignment**

▶ **The Debate**
▶ **Internet Search**

The following additional assignments provide opportunities for students to develop critical thinking, ethical perspectives, oral and written communication skills, experience with electronic research, and teamwork through group and business activities.

▷ *Analyzing Real Company Information*

Analyzing 21-1 (Microsoft)

1. For the year ended June 30, 2002, MICROSOFT's total cost of revenue was $5.191 billion. Can you compute Microsoft's total manufacturing costs for the year? Cost of goods manufactured for the year? Explain.

2. As of June 30, 2002, Microsoft reported the following about the number of its employees:

Employees engaged in research and development	20,800
Employees in sales and marketing	23,500
Employees in administration	4,000
Other employees	2,200
Total	50,500

Refer to Microsoft's income statement in Appendix A and compute the following:

a. Total revenue per employee.
b. Total R&D cost per R&D employee.
c. Total sales and marketing cost per sales and marketing employee.
d. Total administrative cost per administrative employee.

Analyzing 21-2 (Wal-Mart)

1. Through its Retail Link™ system, WAL-MART gives its suppliers access to detailed sales information "store by store, item by item, day by day." What advantages are there to Wal-Mart in sharing this kind of detailed data with suppliers? What disadvantages?

2. Wal-Mart reports (in its 2003 10-K report filed with the Securities and Exchange Commission) that 83% of the goods sold in Wal-Mart stores and Supercenters are first shipped to one of Wal-Mart's 84 regional distribution centers and then shipped to the individual stores. On the other hand, SAM'S CLUBS receive 63% of their goods directly from the supplier. Why is there a difference in the distribution procedure for these two groups of stores?

3. In recent years, SAM'S Clubs sales, as a percentage of total Wal-Mart sales, have decreased, from 15% of sales in fiscal 2000 to 13% of sales in fiscal 2003. What impact do you think this change in sales mix has had on Wal-Mart's overall gross margin percentage? Explain.

International

▶ *International Case*

Deloitte & Touche

DELOITTE & TOUCHE is one of the largest professional services firms in the world. In 2003, the company reported revenues of $15.1 billion generated from its various business units—accounting, assurance and advisory, tax, legal, and management, financial and human capital consulting. Deloitte & Touche has 698 offices in 144 countries, and it employs almost 120,000 people.

1. What does Deloitte & Touche sell?
2. Deloitte & Touche has an office in Quito, Ecuador. What type of company operating in Ecuador would hire Deloitte & Touche instead of a local Ecuadorian professional services firm?
3. Review the chapter discussion of cost information for service companies. What costs would be important to Deloitte & Touche in deciding how much to bid on a consulting contract for a potential new client?

▶ *Ethics Case*

Performance Evaluation: The Illusion of Objectivity?

You are a store manager for a large, regional department store chain. You have been asked by company headquarters to submit an evaluation of the performance of two of your assistant managers. The company is considering promoting one of them to be the manager of another store in the chain.

One of the assistant managers heads the Electronics Department in your store. She is a long-time friend of yours and you would like her to get the promotion. The other candidate heads the Home and Garden Department; she is a good assistant manager but you just don't know her well. You decide to recommend your friend, the head of the Electronics Department, for the promotion.

In order to support your recommendation with objective evidence, you include the following departmental profit numbers for the most recent year:

	Electronics	Home and Garden
Sales	$500,000	$300,000
Net profit	$100,000	$40,000
Profit percentage	20%	13%

On this basis, arguing that the Electronics Department has generated higher sales, higher net profit, and a higher profit margin percentage, you recommend that the promotion be given to your friend. However, you are a little troubled by the following two additional pieces of information:

1. The average value of inventory held in the Electronics Department at any given time is $1.2 million. The comparable number for the Home and Garden Department is $250,000.
2. The profit percentage in the Electronics Department has been fairly stable over the last five years. On the other hand, the profit percentage in the Home and Garden Department is at a 10-year high; the increase coincides with the hiring of the current head of the Home and Garden Department.

Is it ethical for you to recommend the promotion for your friend, the head of the Electronics Department? How should you use the numerical evidence in support of your recommendation?

▶ *Writing Assignment*

Consultant's Report for a Small-Town Supermarket

You have been hired as a financial consultant by a small-town supermarket. The supermarket is considering building a new, larger store and requests your expertise in evaluating the feasibility of the project. You know that the construction of the store will cost $3 million. You also know that the average gross margin percentage in supermarkets is 27%.

Draft a one-page memo to the owner of the supermarket requesting additional cost information to be used in your analysis. The store owner is a clever businessperson but has no experience in using quantitative data in making decisions. Therefore, your memo must be very specific in identifying the information that you will need to perform a useful analysis.

▶ *The Debate*

Overutilization of Young Professionals

As seen in this chapter, an important dimension of performance for a manufacturing, merchandising, or service organization is the efficient utilization of resources. The more intensively resources are used, the greater a company's return on investment. However, when talking about a service organization, this "resource" is often the time of young professionals who are just starting their careers. Competitive pressures on companies can translate into 70- and 80-hour work weeks for college graduates in the first few years of their careers. These work pressures make it difficult for young professionals to develop their lives outside work.

Divide your group into two teams and prepare a two-minute oral presentation supporting the following views.

- One team supports "Work/Life Balance." This group believes that young professionals should not be viewed as "resources" to be utilized but as human beings to be respected.
- The other team supports "Survival of the Fittest." This group believes that it is a dog-eat-dog world out there, and that those young professionals who can't stand the long hours should get out of the way of those who can.

▶ *Internet Search*

Toyota Motor Corporation

Go to TOYOTA's North America Web site at **http://www.toyota.com**. Sometimes Web addresses change, so if this Toyota address doesn't work, access the Web site for this textbook (**http://albrecht.swlearning.com**) for an updated link to Toyota. Once you have gained access to Toyota's Web site, answer the following questions:

1. Access Toyota's Operations section (you can find it within the "About Toyota" menu selection). Find the timeline for Toyota's sales and service. When did Toyota begin selling in North America? When did Toyota begin manufacturing cars in North America?
2. Next, move to Toyota's corporate Web site in Japan at **http://www.toyota.co.jp** and learn about how the just-in-time (JIT) concept works at Toyota. You can do this by finding a news release dated October 9, 2003, titled "The Essence of TPS (the Toyota Production System)." In this article, Teruyuki Minoura, former CEO of Toyota Motor Manufacturing North America, talks about his experiences with TPS, which represents how his company implements a JIT management system. Minoura describes nine concepts that capture the concept of JIT. What are these concepts? (*Hint:* They're listed as subtopic headings in his presentation.)

c hapter

22

Activity-Based Costing and Quality Management

Learning Objectives

After studying this chapter, you should be able to:

1 Explain the fundamentals of activity-based costing (ABC) and activity-based management (ABM).

2 Describe total quality management (TQM) and costs of quality (COQ).

3 Compute the opportunity cost of lost sales.

You most likely wouldn't want to be in Harry Stonecipher's shoes anytime in the next few years; then again, maybe you would.[1] Stonecipher is the recently named President and CEO of BOEING COMPANY, the largest manufacturer of commercial airplanes in the world. If you have ever flown on a commercial jet, odds are you were in one of Stonecipher's (or one of his predecessor's) products. In fact, a Boeing airplane is taking off somewhere in the world every 3.5 seconds. And in the next 24 hours, three million passengers will board 42,300 flights on Boeing jetliners, which will carry them to nearly every country on earth! With its $16.3 billion merger with MC-DONNELL DOUGLAS in 2000, Boeing commanded approximately two-thirds of the $65 billion global market for commercial planes with 100 seats or more. Further, just prior to the McDonnell Douglas merger, Boeing completed a $3.1 billion acquisition of the defense and space operations of ROCKWELL INTERNATIONAL, making Boeing the largest builder of military aircraft in the world, as well as the number one supplier of goods and services to both the Pentagon and NASA. Boeing is basically sitting in the catbird seat. So, why might you hesitate to take Condit's job right now if it were offered to you?

Recent world events have walloped the airline industry. Terrorism, regional conflict, the SARS epidemic, and a sluggish economy have taken their toll on the airlines with a number of airlines filing for bankruptcy protection in the past few years. However, behind the turmoil, Boeing is facing an even more dangerous force: AIRBUS INDUSTRIE is emerging as the world's leading maker of commercial airplanes. The recent economic downturn has forced Boeing's customers to be more cost-conscious, leading to major pricing battles with Boeing's last remaining major competitor.

Airbus, based in Toulouse, France, has been successful against Boeing. By mid-June 2003, Airbus had won 64% of 2003's airplane orders—161 versus 92 for Boeing, including firm orders and memoranda of understanding. But in total value, where it counts the most, Airbus' share is 76% of 2003's orders, with list prices totaling about $26.7 billion versus only $8.2 billion for Boeing. If this lead holds up, it would be the third year in a row Airbus won not only more orders but also more of the lucrative widebody aircraft products. Airbus CEO Noel Forgeard says, "Airbus is taking the lead in a market [that] was considered the home ground of our competitor [that is, Boeing]." Airbus enjoys several key advantages in widebodied aircraft. Its intermediate-size A330 has essentially killed off the Boeing 767 with its greater fuel efficiency and longer flying range. Another plus is Airbus' uniform cockpit design, which gives airlines greater scheduling flexibility as pilots shift easily from one plane model to another.

So, how will Boeing compete? Boeing is counting on successful development of the 7E7. This superefficient plane, which could enter service in 2008, is critical to Boeing's future. "This is a big deal for us," says Michael Bair, a Boeing vice president who oversees the 7E7 program. "If we don't get it right, it influences our future in the business."

At first glance, it seems a good time for Boeing to launch a fuel-sipping jet. Carriers, battered by the falloff in travel, are desperate to cut costs. Boeing believes it could sell 2,500 7E7s in the next 20 years. However, to build the plane, Boeing must reengineer its production. It needs to overcome technical hurdles, including building a plane designed for both short and long hauls that can carry between 220 and 250 passengers while consuming significantly less fuel than planes of similar size now flying. The 7E7 would also be the first commercial aircraft built mostly of composites—carbon-reinforced materials stronger and lighter than the aluminum used in most jetliners. In addition, Boeing aims to assemble each 7E7 in three days, compared with the 20 or so it takes to weld and rivet a 767. Boeing would do so by relying on key suppliers to deliver completed plane sections, meaning fewer workers would be required to actually assemble the 7E7. None of this will come cheap. Development costs could reach $8 billion over five years.

Building this plane requires a radical departure from Boeing's current production practices. Yet the company's history on making such shifts isn't reassuring. In 1997, in another effort to cut costs, Boeing ramped up production too quickly based on unrealistic assumptions. As a result, it lost control of the entire production system, forcing the shutdown of two assembly lines for 30 days. Boeing missed hundreds of airplane deliveries, and the fiasco cost the company more than $2 billion during the biggest boom in commercial airplane history. If you were to take a walking tour of Boeing's 747, 767, and 777 plant in Everett, Washington, you would understand how important (and how difficult) it is for Boeing to control its production process. The cavernous plant in Everett is monstrous, able to house 74 football fields. Planes are

1 Information from "Boeing Is Choking On Airbus' Fumes," *Business Week*, June 30, 2003, p. 50; Boeing Company's home page at **http://www.boeing.com**; "Will this Idea Really Fly?" *Business Week*, June 30, 2003, p. 34.

everywhere in various stages of completion, and *a lot of mechanics* are running around with nothing more complicated than a set of hand tools turning out four massive jets per month, each priced at about $170 million. Each jet is tailor-made to the desires of each customer. The company has always prided itself on giving customers *exactly* what they want. This customization doesn't end with engine specifications and landing systems. It includes choice of paint colors (e.g., if you want white, Boeing offers nearly 110 shades to choose from) and location in the cockpit where the pilot's clipboard will be placed. These are not simple adjustments. Every alteration, even a seemingly minor one such as moving the location of an emergency flashlight holder, consumes thousands of hours of engineering time, requires hundreds of pages of detailed drawings, and costs hundreds of thousands, if not millions, of dollars to execute. Boeing is constantly evaluating and reengineering processes, information systems, and management procedures involved in the manufacturing of its products. It works to better manage costs by reducing and streamlining activities in the production process, as well as reducing parts and work-in-process inventories in order to significantly increase stockturns. It is focused on correcting problems with receiving shipments of parts on time from suppliers and getting completed planes out the door on time to customers. And all these changes must be accomplished without diminishing the absolute quality that is expected of aircraft technology that carries satellites into space, carries military weapons into

battle, and (most importantly) carries three million people daily—a number that exceeds the world's population over a six-year period!

Introducing the 7E7 into the Boeing production system will not be easy. John Leahy, Airbus' chief of global sales, said this about the 7E7, "Dreamliner—a salesman's dream and an engineer's nightmare." Boeing will be working hard to prove Airbus wrong. Success would bring restored credibility and renewed market leadership. Some analysts view the battle between Boeing and Airbus as the "dogfight of the century." So the future certainly does look very exciting, as well as uncertain, for Harry Stonecipher. What do you think? Still want to trade places with him?

Caution

Just because the science of product costing was first developed over 100 years ago, don't assume that there are no new issues today. Business is now more complicated and competitive than ever before. Management accounting systems are expected today to provide cost and performance measures that are more accurate, more relevant, and more strategically focused than ever before!

f there is one thing that is constant in the history of business (and, for that matter, history at large), it is change. A hundred years ago, the executives and management accountants of successful companies such as CARNEGIE STEEL and DUPONT created cost accounting and performance measurement systems that were so new and unique at the time that the decision makers in these companies were able to plan, control, and evaluate critical business processes better than most of their competition. However, these management accounting practices are now well understood and serve as a minimum expectation of most organizations desiring to remain competitive and viable in today's business environment. New management accounting theories and techniques are being developed constantly and tested in the laboratory of the current international market economy. Some of these

new ideas are gaining a lot of attention, and you need to be aware of them. This chapter will introduce two important topics that have had a significant impact in the last 10 or 20 years on the types of information that many management accounting systems are now providing to the management process in an effort to keep organizations competitive. These topics are activity-based costing (ABC) and costs of quality (COQ). In the last chapter of this book where we discuss continuous improvement in management accounting we will introduce a new model of strategic performance measurement that has come into the spotlight in just the last six or seven years. This new innovation, called the balanced scorecard, is getting a lot of attention and may be the next significant step in the innovation of management accounting.

Activity-Based Costing

❚ Explain the fundamentals of activity-based costing (ABC) and activity-based management (ABM).

In the late 1800s, Andrew Carnegie competed very strongly in the steel market with an almost fanatical emphasis on product cost information. Since then, product costing has been a primary purpose of management accounting. Manufacturing processes of today don't look at all like the manufacturing processes of the late 1800s, however. Advances in technology, combined with increasingly intense global competition, have resulted in manufacturing systems that are very complex compared to their predecessors. Because the companies that best understand their costs generally compete well in the economy, product costing has also undergone some important changes that we will consider in this chapter. It is important, though, to remember that the economy has shifted dramatically since the days of Andrew Carnegie. Service companies, such as transportation, consulting, and financial institutions, are the dominant force in today's economy. As you know from your study of the chapter on product cost flows, the service provided by these companies to their clients is a "product" that requires a product costing system very similar to that of manufacturing companies. In fact, service companies are some of the heaviest users of the management accounting techniques discussed in this chapter.

activity-based costing (ABC) A method of attributing costs to products based on first assigning costs of resources to activities and then costs of activities to products.

One major development in product costing is **activity-based costing (ABC)**. Basically, ABC identifies and uses a number of critical activities within the organization to measure product costs. For many types of manufacturing and service companies, ABC is a more accurate product costing system than the traditional product costing systems introduced in the product cost flows chapter. However, ABC requires more time and expense to administer than traditional costing systems.

Product Costing Review

Consider, for example, a small ice cream shop that is owned and managed by one person. Lucas, the owner, hires college students to run the daily operations of preparing and selling his various ice cream desserts. Lucas must decide how to properly price his ice cream desserts. One of his employees, Sally, who just completed her first economics class, tells him to simply "charge whatever the market will bear." Yet this advice provides Lucas only with a price ceiling. Obviously, he cannot charge more than his customers will pay. However, in response to important matters of profitability such as competition and market share, Lucas wonders about his price floor—how low can he go? The obvious answer is that he cannot price below cost (except on occasion). But this begs the elemental question: What does it cost Lucas to make each of his ice cream desserts? Frankly, despite being in the ice cream business for several years, Lucas is not sure.

In relatively "simple" operations like Lucas's ice cream shop, as well as in complex operations such as an airplane manufacturer or a large law firm, product costing is a critical management issue. Today, cost accountants are paid rather well to answer the question, "What does it cost to make a product and prepare it to sell?" In working with Lucas and his ice cream shop, the classic approach to this question is to apply the traditional product cost models that we studied in the chapter on product cost flows. Essentially, for a manufacturing organization, this model states that:

Cost of product = Direct materials + Direct labor + Manufacturing overhead

conversion costs The costs of converting raw materials to finished products; include direct labor and manufacturing overhead costs.

prime costs The direct costs that are "primarily seen" in the product (i.e., direct materials and direct labor).

To calculate the direct materials cost of a banana split, for example, Lucas needs simply to determine the cost of materials directly involved in making a banana split; in other words, the cost of ingredients. The process of converting these "raw" materials into a banana split (the conversion process) requires direct labor and overhead costs, known together as **conversion costs**. Direct labor is simply the hourly wage Lucas pays his employees to physically assemble the ingredients of each dessert sold. Clearly, because each type of dessert requires different ingredients and different amounts of time to create, each will have a different set of direct materials and direct labor costs. Direct materials and direct labor, the **prime costs**, are obvious components in the ice cream dessert production process. Prime costs are easily understood and, typically, can be directly traced and assigned to each type of product produced.

The second cost of the conversion process, overhead, is a little more difficult to understand and directly trace to the dessert production operation. Typically, in a "manufacturing" company like Lucas's shop, manufacturing overhead costs are thought of as "manufacturing support costs." In order to produce banana splits and other desserts, Lucas must have several other components in place besides ice cream and an ice cream scooper. Lights, heat, and other utilities must be present in the kitchen area. Equipment, such as blenders and freezers, must be purchased and maintained. Indirect materials, such as cleaning supplies and light bulbs, must be provided. Likely, Lucas will have other personnel on the payroll besides the counter help. A shop manager and a nightly cleanup crew add additional production costs in the form of indirect labor. All these costs are necessary for Lucas to produce his wares; hence, all are included in manufacturing overhead. As you understand after studying previous chapters, manufacturing overhead is, in essence, a catchall category. In other words, the total cost of a product or service is the cost of everything necessary to produce the product or service. In the case of a manufacturing company, after identifying direct materials and direct labor costs, any remaining product costs are manufacturing overhead costs.

Direct materials, direct labor, and manufacturing overhead do not comprise the total set of costs in Lucas's ice cream shop. Traditionally, product costs are defined as only those costs necessary to actually produce the product. There are other nonproduction costs in Lucas's ice cream shop. These include selling costs, such as costs of advertising the shop and maintaining an area for customers to enjoy their ice cream. Administrative expenses, such as office expenses and Lucas's own salary, are also costs that must be planned and controlled. Because these selling and general administrative costs are not directly connected to any aspect of the production process, they are typically not included in the product cost category. Nonetheless, these are still essential costs. If Lucas does not invest in selling and administrative activities, soon there will be no production. Costs related to selling and administration come under the heading of "period costs." In contrast to product costs, which are incurred as products are produced, period costs seem to be strictly related to the passage of "periods" of time.

Hence, we can summarize all these costs (originally defined in the chapter where we introduced management accounting) as follows:

- *Direct materials:* The cost of the materials that actually become part of the product.
- *Direct labor:* Wages paid to those who physically work to assemble direct materials into the finished product.
- *Manufacturing overhead:* All costs required to produce a product *other than* direct materials and direct labor.
- *Product costs:* Direct materials + Direct labor + Manufacturing overhead.
- *Period costs:* All costs in the company *other than* the product costs; usually include selling and administrative costs.

Hopefully, this quick discussion of Lucas's ice cream shop is simply a review of what you already understand about product costing. At this point, you may feel that it should be a simple task to track the total costs Lucas spends on direct materials, direct labor, and manufacturing overhead in order to answer his question, "What does it cost to make a dessert?" Frankly, tracking Lucas's *total* product costs in his shop is a fairly simple task. However, the key issue for Lucas (and all other product and service managers) is to break those total product costs down for *each type* of product being created. For an ice cream shop that makes and sells many types of desserts, the product cost question becomes much more difficult to answer. It is precisely this question that accountants and managers have been struggling to answer for the last several decades.

SeatJoy, Inc., Is in Trouble!

Consumers are better informed and more demanding than ever before. In addition, competition is increasing as industries are deregulated, technology improves, and national barriers to worldwide competition are removed. The bottom line in this business environment is that margins on goods and services are becoming increasingly tighter. In terms of the ROI model, because most companies cannot sell their goods and services for more money, they need to sell more of their products faster (i.e., increase turnover) in order to remain profitable. What does this mean to an organization that sells a large variety of goods or services? Basically, it means that the organization could be losing money on some of its products and not even realize what is happening. In addition, it may choose to stop providing a particular product based on the false assumption that the product is a money loser. We can better demonstrate this point with an example that we will use for the remainder of this section.

Exhibit 1 displays the 2005 operating results for SeatJoy, Inc. (a fictitious company in the business of making high-quality leather desk chairs). As you can see, SeatJoy has three lines of reclining desk chairs. The Cushman model is its "bread and butter" product. This is the original chair that SeatJoy introduced in 1992 when the company started business. Shortly thereafter, SeatJoy introduced a similar chair that included a swing-out leg rest when the chair reclined. SeatJoy called this chair the Cushman II. More recently (2003), SeatJoy came out with

Exhibit 1: SeatJoy, Inc.: 2005 Operating Results

Manufacturing Overhead Cost Analysis

Annual manufacturing overhead	$18,240,000
Total annual direct labor hours	÷ 456,000
Manufacturing overhead rate per direct labor hour	$40

Labor Cost Analysis

	Cushman	Cushman II	Luxor	Total
Direct labor hours per product	10.0 hours	15.0 hours	12.5 hours	
Annual sales volume	× 18,000 chairs	× 14,400 chairs	× 4,800 chairs	
Total annual direct labor hours	180,000 hours	216,000 hours	60,000 hours	456,000 hours
Wage rate per hour	× $20	× $20	× $20	× $20
Total annual direct labor costs	$3,600,000	$4,320,000	$1,200,000	$9,120,000

Individual Unit Analysis

	Cushman	Cushman II	Luxor
Sales price	$1,000	$ 1,500	$ 3,000
Direct materials per product	$ (335)	$ (650)	$(1,395)
Direct labor per product	(200)	(300)	(250)
Manufacturing overhead per product	(400)	(600)	(500)
Total cost per product	$ (935)	$(1,550)	$(2,145)
Margin per product	$ 65	$ (50)	$ 855
Margin percent	6.5%	(3.3)%	28.5%

Total Annual Results

	Cushman	Cushman II	Luxor	Total
Sales revenue	$ 18,000,000	$ 21,600,000	$ 14,400,000	$ 54,000,000
Total direct materials	$ (6,030,000)	$ (9,360,000)	$ (6,696,000)	$(22,086,000)
Total direct labor	(3,600,000)	(4,320,000)	(1,200,000)	(9,120,000)
Total manufacturing overhead	(7,200,000)	(8,640,000)	(2,400,000)	(18,240,000)
Total product costs	$(16,830,000)	$(22,320,000)	$(10,296,000)	$(49,446,000)
Total margin	$ 1,170,000	$ (720,000)	$ 4,104,000	$ 4,554,000
Selling and administrative expenses				(4,000,000)
Operating profit				$ 554,000

a premium chair made from exotic leathers called the Luxor. Compared to the Cushman lines, the Luxor production process requires closer supervision, as well as more specialized production equipment.

SeatJoy follows a traditional approach of applying manufacturing overhead to products using an overhead application rate based on direct labor hours. The computation of the 2005 overhead rate is shown first in Exhibit 1. Now take a moment to look through all the numbers in SeatJoy's 2005 operating results. Based on an analysis of 2005 results, it appears that the Cushman II line is dragging down company profits. After evaluating these numbers, the management team decides to drop the Cushman II product line. As a result, some suppliers are notified that SeatJoy will be reducing or canceling orders for certain raw materials. Further, one supervisor and the entire Cushman II labor crew are laid off. These are difficult decisions, but management feels strongly that SeatJoy should not absorb in 2006 another $720,000 reduction in operating profit (the total loss on the Cushman II line in 2005). SeatJoy is now in a position to realize a significant jump in operating profit in 2006. Or is it?

STOP & THINK

What do you think is the source of the problem with operations at SeatJoy, Inc.? Should SeatJoy now drop the Cushman product line? Why or why not?

As the accountant prepares and provides the first few monthly profit reports in 2006, it is obvious that there are problems in the operations of the remaining two product lines, particularly in the Cushman line. By the end of the year, when the annual operating results are put together (Exhibit 2), the debacle is confirmed. SeatJoy is in serious trouble! What happened? Sales of both the Cushman and the Luxor product did not change from 2005 results. Further, labor and materials costs per product stayed consistent with 2005 costs, and total manufacturing overhead decreased in 2006. Why didn't company profits improve as management expected after making the decision to drop the Cushman II product line? It looks as if SeatJoy should now consider dropping the Cushman product line in order to save the company.

Comparing the operations reports for 2005 and 2006 should reveal a significant problem. Take a second look at the manufacturing overhead numbers at the top of each exhibit, particularly the overhead rate per direct labor hour. Yes, manufacturing overhead costs did decrease in 2006, as expected since some costs were saved by dropping the Cushman II product. However, these costs did not drop nearly as much as the direct labor hours, resulting in a sharp increase in the overhead application rate per direct labor hour ($40 in 2005 versus nearly $50 in 2006). When the management team decided to drop the Cushman II line, why didn't manufacturing overhead costs decrease as much as expected? Obviously, the current manufacturing overhead application system based on direct labor hours does not provide very accurate insight on cost behavior, particularly in decision-making situations that have strategic implications like adding or dropping a major product line. When management made the decision to drop the Cushman II line, it failed to consider two very important issues:

cross-subsidization A distortion of costs that occurs when costs of one product are erroneously assigned to another product.

common costs Manufacturing overhead costs, such as executive salaries or property taxes, that cannot be attributed to products. Costs of facility support activities are common costs.

Hierarchical Product Cost Model A method of categorizing costs based on types of activities. Activity types include unit-level activities, batch-level activities, product line activities, and facility support activities.

- First, if the allocation system based on direct labor hours is improper, then it is possible that the Cushman II product line was actually subsidizing some manufacturing overhead costs that should have been assigned to one or both of the other products (a problem called product cost **cross-subsidization**). When a poor cost accounting system allows cross-subsidization of product costs, then the management process of planning, controlling, and evaluating is severely compromised.
- Second, some manufacturing overhead costs (known as **common costs**) simply do not relate directly to any particular product line. Examples of these common costs include executive salaries, rent or property taxes on administrative buildings, and general liability insurance. Common costs cannot be allocated meaningfully to products without potentially creating confusion as the organization works to manage its costs effectively.

ABC-based accounting systems are designed to avoid problems related to cross-subsidization effects and common costs allocations by categorizing and assigning manufacturing overhead costs based on the Hierarchical Product Cost Model. Essentially, the **Hierarchical Product Cost Model** provides management accountants with a method for categorizing costs according to the types of activities those costs support. One important benefit of ABC and the Hierarchical Product Cost Model is the way these tools affect our view of variable and fixed costs (more on this in the next section of this chapter).

Exhibit 2: SeatJoy, Inc.: 2006 Operating Results

Manufacturing Overhead Cost Analysis

Annual manufacturing overhead	$11,920,000
Total annual direct labor hours	÷ 240,000
Manufacturing overhead rate per direct labor hour	$49.67 (rounded) (*Note:* All computations below are based on rounding the overhead rate to the nearest penny.)

Labor Cost Analysis

	Cushman	Luxor	Total
Direct labor hours per product	10.0 hours	12.5 hours	
Annual sales volume	× 18,000 chairs	× 4,800 chairs	
Total annual direct labor hours	180,000 hours	60,000 hours	240,000 hours
Wage rate per hour	× $20	× $20	× $20
Total annual direct labor costs	$3,600,000	$1,200,000	$4,800,000

Individual Unit Analysis

	Cushman	Luxor
Sales price	$ 1,000.00	$ 3,000.00
Direct materials per product	$ (335.00)	$(1,395.00)
Direct labor per product	(200.00)	(250.00)
Manufacturing overhead per product	(496.70)	(620.88)
Total cost per product	$(1,031.70)	$(2,265.88)
Margin per product	$ (31.70)	$ 734.12
Margin percent	(3.2)%	24.5%

Total Annual Results

	Cushman	Luxor	Total
Sales revenue	$ 18,000,000	$ 14,400,000	$ 32,400,000
Total direct materials	$ (6,030,000)	$ (6,696,000)	$(12,726,000)
Total direct labor	(3,600,000)	(1,200,000)	(4,800,000)
Total manufacturing overhead	(8,940,600)	(2,980,224)	(11,920,824)
Total product costs	$(18,570,600)	$(10,876,224)	$(29,446,824)
Total margin	$ (570,600)	$ 3,523,776	$ 2,953,176
Selling and administrative expenses			(4,000,000)
Operating loss			$ (1,046,824)

The ABC Hierarchical Product Cost Model

In the first chapter where we introduced management accounting, we provided some very simple definitions of fixed and variable costs. Later in the cost-volume-profit chapter, we spent considerable time describing how much variety there actually is in fixed and variable costs. The important thing to understand in this chapter is that, in practice, very few costs can be definitely categorized as fixed or variable with respect to a single type of activity in the organization, such as direct labor hours, machine hours, or units produced. In fact, every organization has many different kinds of activities, each of which directly affects certain costs. Stated differently, *given enough time and with respect to a particular activity, most costs in the organization can be considered variable.* This is really quite an important concept in the theory of ABC. Before you can predict a cost behavior (which is necessary before you can begin managing the cost), you need to identify the activity that actually drives the cost in question.

Let's return to the situation at SeatJoy, Inc. As you now know, the traditional approach SeatJoy is using to assign manufacturing overhead costs to its products appears to be causing problems. This approach is demonstrated in Exhibit 3. As you can see, SeatJoy simply sums together all manufacturing overhead costs within the organization and assigns those costs to products based on a single activity, direct labor hours. However, consider the variety of costs that are being combined into a single pool of costs. The purpose of a manufacturing overhead allocation rate (in this case, based on direct labor hours) is to *meaningfully* allocate costs to products in a manner that relates to the behavior of the costs. Think about property taxes on the production facility for a moment. Do these costs adjust at all based on changes in total direct labor hours within the organization? Of course not! Neither do the costs of insuring these facilities against damage and liability claims. Perhaps engineering costs and supervision costs, as well as costs to set up a production run and perform quality checks on the output, are related to direct labor hours, but the relationship is not very strong. There likely are other activities in the SeatJoy organization that relate more closely to increases and decreases in these costs than direct labor hours. Identifying these activities is the intent of the Hierarchical Product Cost Model.

Look back at Exhibit 1 for a moment. How does SeatJoy determine how many direct labor hours are used in the plant? As you can see in the second table (labeled "Labor Cost Analysis"), annual labor hours for each product line are really just a function of how many chairs SeatJoy intends to produce and sell. Allocating manufacturing overhead on the basis of the number of direct labor hours per chair is essentially the same thing as allocating manufacturing overhead on the basis of the number of chairs produced. How much of manufacturing overhead costs will be assigned to the Luxor product line? Well, that really depends on how many units SeatJoy will produce in this product line (which then determines how many direct labor hours will be

Exhibit 3: Traditional (Unit-Based) Costing at SeatJoy, Inc.

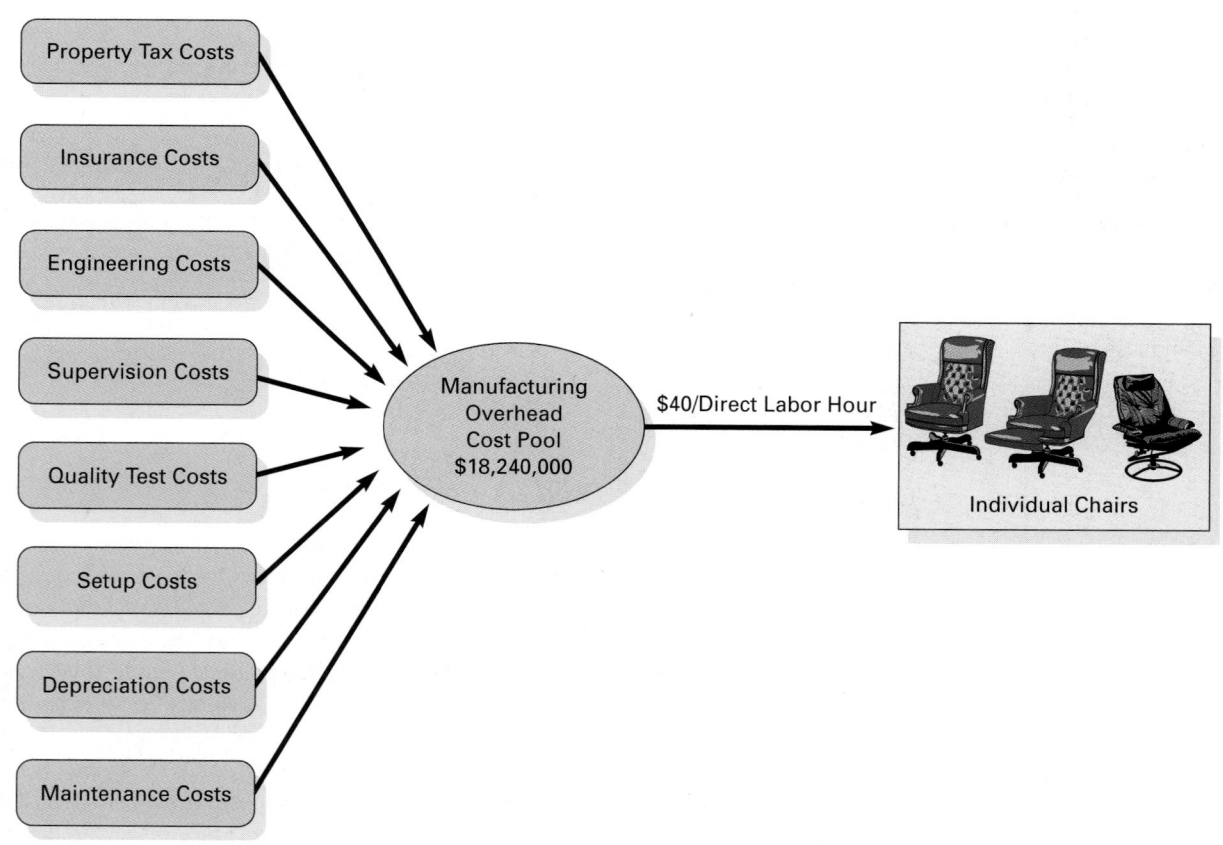

unit-based costing (UBC)
The traditional method of allocating manufacturing overhead using an approach that is essentially based on the number of units produced.

STOP & THINK

We have stated that the overhead allocation rate per direct labor hour for SeatJoy is really just a rate per chair (i.e., unit). Hence, we call this a UBC allocation system. Look at Exhibit 1. What is the manufacturing overhead allocation rate per chair (i.e., per unit)?

⚠ Caution

Don't get the idea from the SeatJoy example that UBC is always a "bad" cost allocation method. On the contrary, UBC is a very good cost allocation method for manufacturing and service organizations with overhead that essentially does change based on the number of units of goods and services produced. Further, compared to ABC, UBC is typically easier and less costly. However, if UBC is causing reported product costs to be distorted, then the management process in the organization can be seriously affected.

cost driver A factor that determines an activity cost. An activity can have more than one cost driver.

used). Because the allocated manufacturing overhead is really a function of the number of units produced, we call this method of allocating manufacturing overhead costs **unit-based costing (UBC)**. Think back to the chapter on product cost flows. Isn't this the basic approach we used in that chapter to allocate overhead in both manufacturing and service companies? UBC is a very traditional cost accounting method used in many types of organizations, and it is the cost allocation approach currently used by the SeatJoy organization in this example. UBC is a good method of cost allocation *in the right context*. However, a UBC approach usually creates problems in an organization with multiple products and services. Cost distortions can develop that make both strategic and short-term planning decisions difficult. The distortions are the result of using an oversimplified information system to represent the complex realities of modern business processes.

You have probably noticed by now that allocating manufacturing overhead costs to products is a two-stage process. First, we gather all the manufacturing overhead costs into a common pool of costs. Second, we allocate these costs to products based on an (hopefully) appropriate allocation rate. This rather simple UBC two-stage allocation process is characterized by the following relationship:

Costs ⟹ **Production Department(s)** ⟹ Products

You can see this relationship demonstrated in Exhibit 3. All the support costs related to the production department at SeatJoy are gathered into a single cost pool. The costs are then allocated to individual chairs using a UBC rate based on direct labor hours.

The two-stage UBC relationship seems to say that products consume costs in production departments. However, that is not true. Costs are consumed by activities. And activities are necessary to create and deliver products and services. Based on this fact, the activity-based costing (ABC) method of allocating manufacturing overhead costs (which is also accomplished in two stages) makes a rather subtle change to the UBC relationship. The ABC two-stage allocation process is characterized by the following relationship:

Costs ⟹ **Activities** ⟹ Products

In the ABC relationship, costs are first attributed to activities. Then, each activity is studied to determine its relationship to the product, and product costs are determined based on these activities. Using this relationship allows the management accountant to refine the categorization of costs as either variable or fixed. The UBC approach, with its focus on production units, strictly defines variable costs as those that proportionally shift when an additional unit is produced. This approach probably works well with direct labor, direct materials, and *some* overhead costs. All other remaining costs are then considered fixed and allocated to units using a unit-based driver such as direct labor hours.

However, in today's complex manufacturing and service environments, production costs are determined by many types of activities, not by the production of single units. An activity that affects a particular cost is called a **cost driver** for that cost. Given the right cost drivers and enough time, most costs are variable. For instance, many costs in a manufacturing organization are variable based on the number of and type of *batches* produced or the number of and the characteristics of *product lines* within the company's product mix. Conversely, these costs are fixed based on the number of units produced. Nearly every cost has at least one cost driver (an activity). Effectively managing costs of providing a product means that *activities, not products, must be managed*. The bottom line is that the traditional management accounting approach to product costs, which states that

Individual cost of product = Direct materials + Direct labor + Manufacturing overhead,

may not be the best perspective of production costs when making planning decisions such as the one facing SeatJoy. Notice, though, that this is the approach used by SeatJoy's management

© 2003 Michael Rosenfeld/Getty Images

accountants to analyze individual unit costs and total annual operating results in Exhibit 1. ABC recommends a different view of production costs based on production activities. Using the Hierarchical Product Cost Model, we can see that production costs are a function of many types of activities. As shown in Exhibit 4, there are four categories of activities that result in production costs. Rather than focusing on the cost for an individual product, the Hierarchical Product Cost Model recognizes that an organization's total production costs are a function of these four categories of activities. As a result, these categories need to be well understood in order to manage the costs related to production. We need to spend some time discussing these four types of activities in order to better assess the situation at SeatJoy, Inc. We'll start at the top with unit-level activities and work our way down.

An activity that affects a particular production cost is called a cost driver. Given the right cost drivers, most costs are variable. Many costs in a manufacturing organization, such as a pharmaceutical factory, are variable based on the number of and type of batches produced.

unit-level activities Activities that take place each time a unit of product is produced.

Unit-Level Activities

In the Hierarchical Product Cost Model, activities that are performed each time a unit of a product or service is produced are classified together and called **unit-level activities**. Think about the SeatJoy production setting. Obviously, direct materials are released and direct labor is used each time a chair is produced. Perhaps many of the production processes are automated, minimizing the amount of direct labor involved in the production of a single chair. Nevertheless, each chair produced increases the amount of operating time on the machinery. Operating SeatJoy's assembly, sewing, and packing equipment generates machine maintenance activities. If SeatJoy uses the unit-based depreciation method on its machinery, then depreciation charges occur as chairs are produced. Energy costs required to run the production machinery are also directly tied to the number of hours the machines are operated. Costs related to all these activities are categorized as unit-based costs. Note that in the traditional UBC approach, all costs are treated as if they took place at the unit level. Direct materials and direct labor are attributed to each unit produced. Additionally, all manufacturing overhead is allocated to each unit produced. In the ABC approach, direct materials, direct labor, and *some types* of manufactur-

Exhibit 4: Hierarchical Product Cost Model

Total Production Costs

Costs of Products

Unit-Level Activities

Batch-Level Activities

Product Line Activities

Common Costs

Facility Support Activities

ing overhead are handled at the unit level. Traditionally, these costs are considered to be the variable costs of production. The remaining manufacturing overhead costs are traditionally considered fixed. In ABC, however, these fixed manufacturing costs are related to batch-level, product line, or facility support activities. It is really this categorization, illustrated in Exhibit 5, that makes ABC quite different from UBC.

Let's assume that the accountants at SeatJoy determine that $3,420,000 of the $18,240,000 in annual manufacturing overhead costs is related to unit-level activities. SeatJoy can continue to use direct labor hours to allocate these costs to chairs. Based on 456,000 annual direct labor hours, this works out to $7.50 per direct labor hour ($3,420,000 ÷ 456,000 hours). As a result, a Cushman II chair is allocated $112.50 in manufacturing overhead for unit-level activities (based on 15 direct labor hours per Cushman II chair).

As you can see in Exhibit 5, ABC takes a hard look at manufacturing overhead costs historically considered fixed. Remember that ABC is based on the premise that, once the proper cost driver is identified, most costs can be managed as variable costs. In terms of both the traditional UBC approach and the more modern ABC approach, unit-level costs are variable. As a product unit is produced or a service is performed, unit-level costs increase. Traditional management accounting using UBC then maintains that all other costs are fixed. Frankly, if we're talking about using individual units of the product as a cost driver, then these costs are fixed. However, the ABC Hierarchical Product Cost Model looks for other activities, required by the production process, that make many (though not all) fixed costs act variable. The result is the categorization of batch-level and product line activities and their related costs.

Batch-Level Activities

Let's consider batch costs. Many production runs flow in batches. An automotive production line builds a particular line of cars until market orders are met. Then the current production line is changed over to produce a different car. A steel mill or a flour mill mixes different components into customized batches, then packages the output to meet customer specifications. These attempts to individually satisfy customer demands result in the need for batch setups on the production line. During setup, production must pause while employees recalibrate or install different machines. The new batch often requires a different mix of raw materials. Ordering, paying for, and moving raw materials into production position entail time and expense. Often some inspection takes place, such as testing the first item of the batch run, to ensure that

Exhibit 5: Relationship between Unit-Based Costs and Activity-Based Costs in a Manufacturing Organization

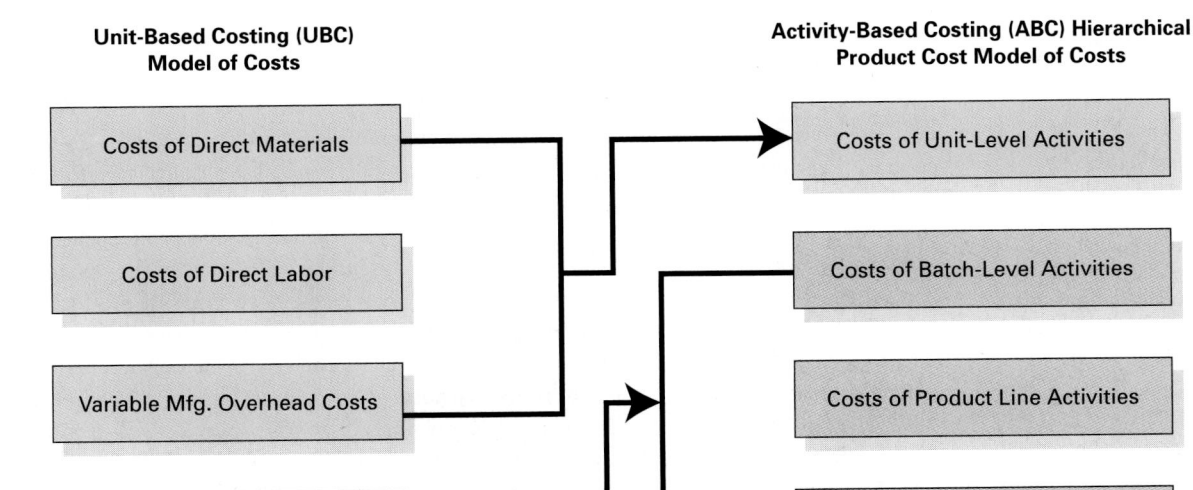

batch-level activities Activities that take place in order to support a batch or production run, regardless of the size.

the configuration and quality of the product are acceptable. These activities that are necessary each time products or services are processed as a batch are known as **batch-level activities**.

Batch-level activities are more common in service firms where there is a lot of customization of the product for customers. A public accounting firm undertakes a lot of setup activities before work can begin on an audit, tax, or consulting job. A trucking company must perform many activities related to setting up a contract and organizing pickup and delivery details before transportation work can begin for a customer. A radio station that sells advertising often does a lot of design work before it can begin running a customer's advertising spot.

Regardless of the size of the batch (1 or 10,000 units, miles, or broadcasts), batch activities must take place, and batch-related costs must be spent. Each organization must evaluate its production operation to determine if and what activities take place to support a batch run. Then, the individual costs of each of these activities are determined. In line with the two-stage cost attribution process of ABC, once costs are assigned to activity cost pools, then batches that require a particular activity are assigned the attending costs. Examples of batch activities at a manufacturing company like SeatJoy include:

- number of setups,
- setup hours,
- movements of materials,
- orders for nonstocked items,
- purchase orders,
- number of inspections, and
- inspection hours.

By tracking batch costs in this manner, much product cost cross-subsidization is avoided. Batch costs can then be averaged across the number of units in the batch (if desired). Units in small batches will then be required to carry a larger burden of these costs. Units in larger batches will experience favorable economies of scale. The cost information system begins reflecting what most managers and supervisors already know: poor scheduling leading to unnecessary production setups results in wasted resources. With this information available, managers can make better-informed decisions concerning the trade-off of large, cost-efficient batches versus production flexibility and low inventory levels that accompany smaller batch runs. Later we will work through some calculations that demonstrate the negative impact that product cost cross-subsidization can have on decisions.

Product Line Activities

product line activities Activities that take place in order to support a product line, regardless of the number of batches or individual units actually produced. Costs of product line activities are also known as capability costs.

Henry Ford infamously said that his customers were welcome to have their Model T car in any color they wanted, so long as it was black! That position has obviously changed at FORD MOTOR COMPANY, as well as at many other companies. Products, including the huge airplanes produced at BOEING, are often customized to satisfy rather small pockets of customers. This leads to the third level of activities in the Hierarchical Product Cost Model—product line activities. **Product line activities** are required to supply a particular product type to the market. These activities are constant regardless of the number of units or batches produced. The number of product line activities is tied to the diversity of the company's product mix and the individual complexity of each product, both of which are important issues in the organization's strategy. Most organizations want to produce more than one or two types of products or services. Otherwise, they are at risk of going out of business should the demand for their particular product or service suddenly drop. Hence, to diversify the risk of market fluctuations and satisfy a myriad of demanding and informed customers, companies must develop and provide a diverse set of products. Organizations with many types of goods or services will require many more product line activities than organizations that produce only a few types of goods or services. This results in increased overhead costs related to product line activities.

Management must be constantly aware of the costs of activities necessary to support an expanding product mix. As with batch activities, management must intelligently trade off the value of a large product mix against the cost of providing a variety of products. There are great opportunities for product cost savings through evaluating the inefficient use of resources by both batch-level and product line activities. Product lines that experience such cost savings should then be able to compete in the market at reduced prices. Sources of product line activities in a manufacturing firm like SeatJoy might include:

- engineering departments where product design changes in a product or production process take place,
- warehouses where materials necessary to each product line are stored and managed,
- supervisors who are dedicated to managing a particular product line,
- purchasing departments that initiate purchase orders, and
- receiving and shipping docks that receive raw materials and ship finished products.

In service organizations like a public accounting firm, a transportation company, or a bank, product line activities might include:

- in-house training resources required to provide specific audit, tax, or consulting services,
- safety specialists who manage transportation of hazardous material, and
- loan officers dedicated to home mortgages versus commercial lending.

capability costs Costs necessary to have the capability to produce a particular product or to provide a particular service. Capability costs are also known as the costs of product line activities.

facility support activities Activities necessary to have a facility in place in order to participate in the development and production of products or services. However, these activities are not related to any particular line of products or services. Costs of facility support activities are often called common costs.

Only when the organization decides to permanently eliminate the product from its product mix can product line activities and their related costs be removed. Costs of product line activities are also referred to as **capability costs**—costs necessary to the capability of providing a particular product or service to the market.

Facility Support Activities

Up to this point we have discussed the top three layers of activities in the Hierarchical Product Cost Model: unit-level, batch-level, and product line (see Exhibit 4). The final level of activities in the Hierarchical Product Cost Model is facility support activities. Essentially, **facility support activities** are those activities that must be in place before development and production of any product or service can begin. Most of these activities are administrative in nature. Facility support activities are the source of the true common costs in the production facility. No single product or product line is responsible for the creation of these costs. Facility support activities are necessary for a business to create any products or services. Examples of facility support costs for a company like SeatJoy include:

- property taxes,
- plant security,
- landscaping,
- accounting, and
- salaries of the general administration (e.g., the vice president of manufacturing) and support staff.

The extent of facility support activities is unrelated to production volume or diversity. Therefore, it is impossible to sensibly relate these costs to the production of any particular product or product line. In the ABC model, there is no intervening activity that can connect costs of facility-sustaining activities to the products. Any assignment of these costs to products is doomed to be arbitrary. Therefore, the ABC approach is to *not* allocate these costs to products.[2] Allocating these costs simply distorts management's view of the relevant costs to be considered when strategically managing a product or product line.

Costs of facility support activities should be pooled together and kept separate from the other product costs. Only the costs of activities at the unit, batch, and product line levels are

---

2 Actually, the idea that allocating common costs cannot be done sensibly does not belong solely to ABC theory. The traditional theory of responsibility accounting also supports not allocating the costs of facility support activities to products.

relevant to the production and management of a particular product line. For this reason, costs of facility support activities are part of the total production costs, but they should not be included in the costs and analysis of any specific line of products. Separating the costs of facility support activities from specific product costs is illustrated in the Hierarchical Product Cost Model in Exhibit 4.

Exhibit 6 illustrates how the two-stage ABC model is blended with the Hierarchical Product Cost Model. As you can see, the total manufacturing overhead costs shown in Exhibit 3 have been split into four separate cost pools based on how the costs relate to types of activities. The manufacturing overhead allocation rates per direct labor hour, per batch run, and per product line are discussed in the next section.

Resolving Cost Distortions

Poor management accounting can create tremendous problems within an organization, particularly when the competition starts driving down market prices. As profit margins are reduced in a competitive market, it becomes increasingly more important for a manufacturing, merchandising, or service firm to accurately identify its product costs. The Boeing Company situation described at the beginning of this chapter is a classic example of an organization that produces many types of complex products in an environment with lots of batch-level and product line activities. Competition is pressuring Boeing to reduce its prices, requiring that Harry Stonecipher and the other executives and managers at Boeing fully understand all production

Exhibit 6: Activity-Based Costing at SeatJoy, Inc.*

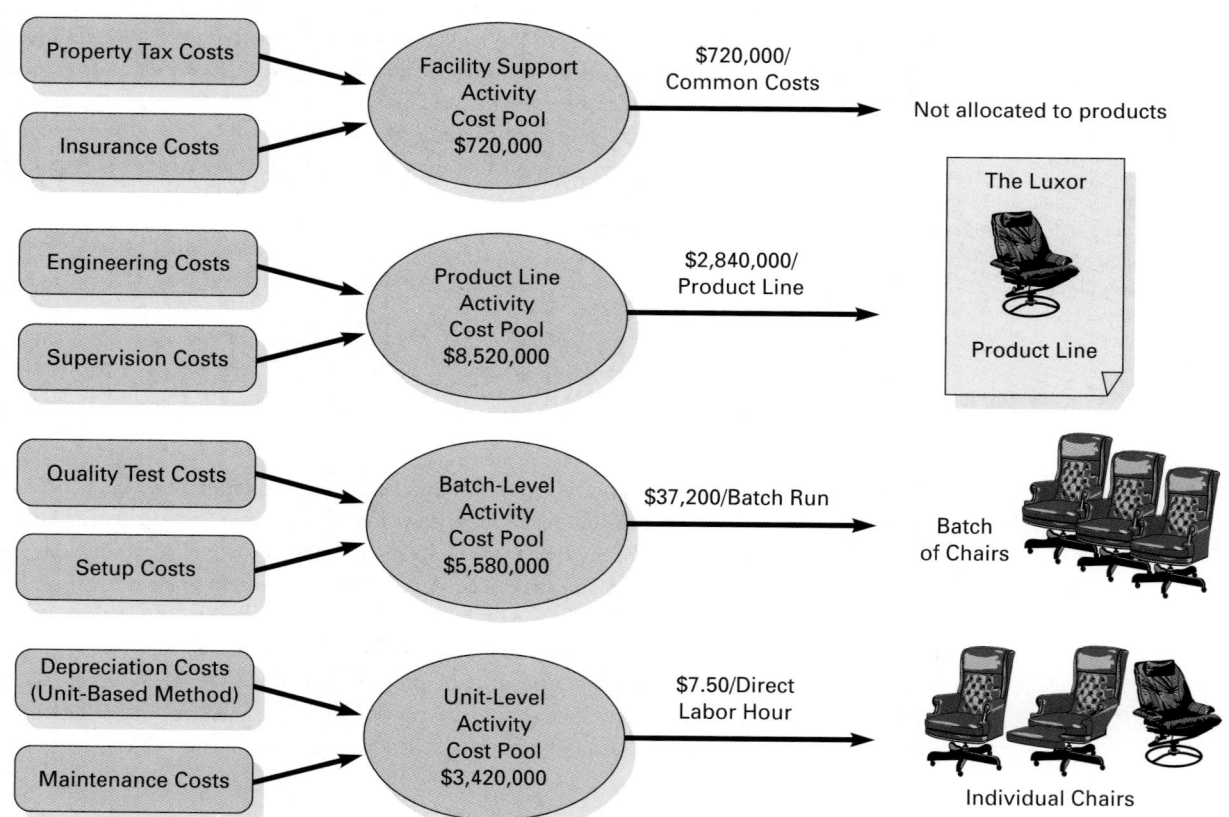

*Calculation of ABC allocation rates is demonstrated in Exhibit 7.

costs *and* how these costs relate to the aircraft they are manufacturing. There is little room for error. To the extent that management accountants provide poor data because of inappropriate cost allocation methods, Boeing will be susceptible to cost distortions such as cross-subsidization and inappropriate allocation of common costs. Each of these cost distortions can lead to decisions that reduce, rather than enhance, the organization's competitive strength.

Product Cost Cross-Subsidization

Let's return to SeatJoy, Inc. The production supervisors at SeatJoy have organized the production process by producing one batch run of each product each week. Typically, production workers spend Monday mornings setting up equipment to produce Cushman chairs. Once everything is set, some chairs are produced and evaluated for quality assurance. With the inspectors' OK, the production process begins, and company employees work until enough chairs are produced to fill all orders placed that week. Sometime Tuesday afternoon or Wednesday morning, they switch to producing Cushman II chairs, and all the setup and quality assurance activities again take place. Hopefully, by Friday morning SeatJoy can begin setting up the production equipment to make Luxor chairs. As you can see in Exhibit 3, SeatJoy has specific costs related to performing setup and quality test activities. Currently, SeatJoy combines these costs with all other manufacturing costs in order to establish its manufacturing overhead allocation rate. However, because the weekly batch run of Luxor chairs is much smaller than the weekly batch run of either Cushman or Cushman II chairs, some of the batch costs related to producing Luxor chairs are being subsidized by the other two products.

With a little additional data, we can compute the size of the product cost cross-subsidization taking place at SeatJoy. Of the $18,240,000 in 2005 manufacturing overhead costs, SeatJoy's cost accountant determines that $5,580,000 is related to batch-level activities. SeatJoy works 50 weeks a year and produces one batch of each product weekly, which works out to 150 total batches each year (50 weeks × 1 batch per week × 3 product lines). As a result, SeatJoy should establish a manufacturing overhead allocation rate of $37,200 *per batch* ($5,580,000 ÷ 150 batches). The average cost *per chair* for batch-level activities at SeatJoy is computed as follows.[3]

Manufacturing Overhead Allocation Using Batch-Level Activities

$5,580,000 ÷ 150 batches = $37,200 Manufacturing Overhead Costs per Batch

	Cushman	Cushman II	Luxor
Annual sales volume in chairs	18,000	14,400	4,800
Annual number of batches	÷ 50	÷ 50	÷ 50
Average batch size in chairs	360	288	96
Overhead costs per batch	$37,200	$37,200	$37,200
Average batch size in chairs	÷ 360	÷ 288	÷ 96
Average batch costs per chair	$103.33	$129.17	$387.50

How do these costs per chair compare when we allocate the $5,580,000 based on direct labor hours? Total direct labor hours for 2005, as well as the average number of direct labor hours per chair, are provided in Exhibit 1. The UBC allocation is computed on the next page.

---

[3] It is critical to remember that we are computing *average* costs per chair here. Hence, because these are batch-level activities, SeatJoy *cannot* change these costs by changing the number of chairs produced. The cost driver for these costs is batches, not units (i.e., individual chairs).

Manufacturing Overhead Allocation Using Unit-Level Activities

$5,580,000 ÷ 456,000 hours = $12.24 Manufacturing Overhead Costs per Direct Labor Hour (rounded)

	Cushman	Cushman II	Luxor
Manufacturing overhead costs per direct labor hour	$ 12.24	$ 12.24	$ 12.24
Direct labor hours per product	× 10.0	× 15.0	× 12.5
Average batch costs per chair	$122.40	$183.60	$153.00

Caution

Be sure to bear in mind that the $5,580,000 in manufacturing overhead costs that we're analyzing here are SeatJoy's 2005 overhead costs related to batch-level activities. We've already determined that $3,420,000 of SeatJoy's overhead costs are related to unit-level activities. The remaining $9,240,000 in overhead costs ($18,240,000 − $3,420,000 − $5,580,000) are related either to product-line activities or to facility support activities.

Look carefully at the difference in the calculations when using batches versus direct labor hours as the cost driver. If these manufacturing overhead costs are truly consumed by batch-level activities, then the first set of calculations is more accurate than the second set. However, in Exhibits 1 and 2, SeatJoy is allocating manufacturing overhead costs using direct labor hours. As a result, Luxor chairs are receiving only *some* of the $387.50 average batch-level overhead costs per chair that this product is actually creating. The rest of these costs are being inappropriately allocated to the Cushman and Cushman II products. In other words, Luxor's batch-level product costs are being *cross-subsidized* by the Cushman and Cushman II product lines. The result of this product cost cross-subsidization is that Cushman and Cushman II products will look less profitable than they really are; and conversely, Luxor chairs will look more profitable than they should.

Just like the product cost cross-subsidization that resulted from using direct labor hours to allocate costs of batch-level activities, SeatJoy is also likely cross-subsidizing costs of product line activities. Of the $18,240,000 in 2005 manufacturing overhead costs at SeatJoy, it is determined that $8,520,000 is related to product line activities. Assuming that each product line consumes about the same level of product line activities (e.g., engineering support, purchasing effort, safety training, etc.), each product line should receive $2,840,000 of these costs ($8,520,000 ÷ 3 product lines).[4] The average cost per chair for these manufacturing overhead costs is computed as follows:

Product Line Manufacturing Overhead Allocation Using Product Line Activities

$8,520,000 ÷ 3 lines = $2,840,000 Manufacturing Overhead Costs per Product Line

	Cushman	Cushman II	Luxor
Manufacturing overhead costs per product line	$2,840,000	$2,840,000	$2,840,000
Annual sales volume in chairs	÷ 18,000	÷ 14,400	÷ 4,800
Average product line costs per chair	$ 157.78	$ 197.22	$ 591.67

How do these costs per chair compare when we allocate the $8,520,000 based on direct labor hours? Again, total direct labor hours for 2005, as well as the average number of direct labor hours per chair, are provided in Exhibit 1. The UBC allocation is computed on the next page.

---

4 To simply divide the costs of product line activities evenly across the three product lines is a relatively straightforward approach to assigning these overhead costs. You'll recall that we used essentially this same approach when assigning the costs of batch-level activities in SeatJoy's ABC system. Another approach is to determine the total costs of each product line activity (as well as each unit- and batch-level activity) and then assign those costs based on how much of that activity is consumed by each product line. Many of the exercises and problems at the end of this chapter use that approach.

Product Line Manufacturing Overhead Allocation Using Unit-Level Activities

$8,520,000 ÷ 456,000 hours = $18.68 Manufacturing Overhead Costs per Direct Labor Hour (rounded)

	Cushman	Cushman II	Luxor
Manufacturing overhead costs per direct labor hour	$ 18.68	$ 18.68	$ 18.68
Direct labor hours per product	× 10.0	× 15.0	× 12.5
Average product line costs per chair	$186.80	$280.20	$233.50

business environment

ABC Provides Legal Defense for Major Chain of Retail Gasoline Service Centers* State and federal laws have been enacted against predatory pricing, which is the selling of products below cost as a deliberate action to drive out the competition. Alternatively, a product may *appear* to be priced below cost because of the use of unrealistic, unit-based traditional costing systems, which results in the appearance of predatory pricing where it does not exist.

This occurred in a case brought under the Motor Fuel Marketing Practices Act of Florida.

The lawsuit was brought against a major chain of retail gasoline service centers, alleging that the chain was selling regular-grade gasoline below cost, as defined under state statutes. The plaintiff's expert witness used a unit-based approach to assign the gasoline service center's average monthly costs to the three grades of gasoline: regular (87 octane), plus (89 octane), and premium (91 octane). When these monthly costs were added to the purchase costs of the gasoline, this approach supported the allegation.

The defendant's original expert witness used a simple average-cost approach to assign the average monthly gasoline service center costs equally to the three grades of gasoline, which supported the defendant's position. The judge in the case made a preliminary ruling that rejected the defendant's analy-

sis and accepted the plaintiff's. The judge issued an injunction prohibiting the defendant from selling regular gasoline below cost as determined in the plaintiff's analysis.

The defendant then engaged an accounting professor as an additional expert witness to review the cost assignment process and make his own recommendation. The expert witness used activity-based costing (ABC) as a third approach to cost assignment. The professor prepared activity cost pools based on labor, kiosk, and gas dispensing to better distribute the costs to the activities performed by the gasoline service centers.

Based on the ABC analysis, the cost per gallon sold actually fell in between the amounts derived from the plaintiff's unit-based approach and the defendant's equal split of labor and overhead costs. In essence, the ABC approach split the difference between the costs per gallon sold obtained from the two extreme approaches. In addition, the ABC analysis better reflected the activities driving the cost of business for the gasoline service centers. After this analysis, the case was settled, and the injunction against the gasoline retailer was lifted.

*The name of the gasoline chain is not disclosed.

Source: Thomas L. Barton and John B. MacArthur, "Activity-Based Costing and Predatory Pricing: The Case of the Petroleum Retail Industry," *Management Accounting Quarterly*, Spring 2003.

As you can see, there is a significant difference in the average costs per chair based on allocating these manufacturing overhead costs using product lines rather than direct labor hours. If these manufacturing overhead costs are truly determined by product line activities, then the first set of calculations is more accurate than the second set. However, since SeatJoy is allocating manufacturing overhead costs using direct labor hours, Luxor chairs are receiving only *some* of the $591.67 product line manufacturing overhead costs. Just like the previous situation involving batch-level activities, some of the product line manufacturing overhead costs belonging to Luxor products are being inappropriately allocated to the Cushman and Cushman II products. Luxor product costs are being *cross-subsidized* by the Cushman and Cushman II product lines in the case of manufacturing overhead costs related to both batch-level and product line activities.

By understanding that batch and product line activities act as cost drivers, costs previously considered to be fixed (which are then allocated using a simple measure like direct labor hours) are actually variable with respect to these types of activities. Products that require these activities should be assigned the burden of these costs. As you can see, product cost cross-subsidization occurs when unit-level cost drivers such as direct labor costs are used to allocate costs of batch-level and product line activities.

Allocating Common Costs and the Death Spiral

Suppose, for example, that it is a company's practice to allocate a share of the cost of property taxes to each product. Neither the product manager nor the production line supervisor has any control over this cost (other than to argue vehemently in management meetings for a smaller share of this cost). When the company is trying to manage the cost effectiveness and customer satisfaction of product lines, this cost allocation only makes the management process more unclear. The product line is not responsible for creating activities that lead to property taxes, so these costs should not be combined with costs of unit-level, batch-level, and product line activities in determining product costs.

Some individuals argue that allocating facility support costs is useful because these activities result in very real costs and must be "covered" by product revenues if the company is to be profitable. It is true that these costs are real. Management needs to be constantly aware of these costs and should be constantly working to ensure that all facility support activities are cost effective. However, consider a simple example. Suppose that a company's annual property taxes are $100,000 and are allocated evenly across four products (Products A, B, C, and D). The product cost information system indicates that the Product D line is generating a $10,000 loss. After several unsuccessful attempts to make the product more profitable, it is discontinued. However, property taxes remain unchanged and are now allocated evenly over the remaining three product lines. Thus, where the three remaining product lines were each previously receiving $25,000 in allocated common costs ($100,000 ÷ 4 product lines), now each receives $33,333 ($100,000 ÷ 3 product lines). Suppose that, with the new allocation, Product C turns unprofitable. Should management now consider discontinuing Product C?

It is doubtful that anyone would be fooled into making the mistake of discontinuing Product C in the simple example above. Hopefully, few would have originally discontinued Product D either. Such imprudent decisions result in a classic case of "death spiral." Essentially, a **death spiral** begins when a company does not fully understand its costs and then attempts to reduce costs by cutting products or other business segments that in fact do not create the costs in question. This results in the remaining costs being reallocated over fewer product lines. So, although the Product D line may be displaying a $10,000 loss, once the unavoidable $25,000 allocation is removed, it is clear that the Product D line is actually contributing $15,000 to help "cover" the $100,000 tax cost and provide overall profit for the company. Removing this product from the company only results in other products having to carry an even larger burden of facility support costs. Continuing to drop products in such a manner will leave the company with $100,000 in property taxes and no revenue-generating products.

Given this simple example, you might expect few to fall into a death spiral trap. However, most large-scale organizations are much more complex than this example. For example, the situation at Boeing Company involves many activities and much cost complexity. It would be

death spiral A series of management decisions based on bad information that results in reducing or removing activities or segments from the organization that are actually profitable.

quite easy to become confused about cost relationships in such a setting. There are several cases of companies falling into this trap and seriously damaging their competitive position before realizing what was happening.

The situation at SeatJoy certainly looks like the beginning of a death spiral. As demonstrated earlier, the accountants are allocating costs of batch-level and product line activities to the Cushman and Cushman II product lines that should belong to the Luxor product line. When SeatJoy management elects to drop the Cushman II product line, the Luxor manufacturing overhead costs being subsidized by the Cushman II line are reallocated to the remaining products. The result is that the Cushman product now looks as if it is unprofitable. Remember, though, that the Cushman line is subsidizing some Luxor costs. In addition, some common costs (i.e., costs of facility support activities) are being allocated to all three products. As demonstrated in Exhibit 6, property tax and insurance costs are facility support costs that really shouldn't be allocated to any of the products. Dropping the Cushman II product line results only in a reallocation of these common costs. This reallocation also contributes to the Cushman product becoming unprofitable in 2006 as shown in Exhibit 2. Of the $18,240,000 in manufacturing overhead at SeatJoy, $720,000 is facility support costs. The average facility support cost per chair as allocated by the traditional manufacturing overhead allocation system is computed below.

Facility Support Manufacturing Overhead Allocation Using Unit-Level Activities

$720,000 ÷ 456,000 hours = $1.58 Manufacturing Overhead Costs per Direct Labor Hour (rounded)

	Cushman	Cushman II	Luxor
Manufacturing overhead costs per direct labor hour	$ 1.58	$ 1.58	$ 1.58
Direct labor hours per product	× 10.0	× 15.0	× 12.5
Average facility support costs per chair	$15.80	$23.70	$19.75

As you can see, the UBC allocation approach assigns $23.70 per chair in common costs to the Cushman II product line. These costs, if removed from the 2005 operating results in Exhibit 1, would go a long way toward reversing what appears to be a loss in this product line. In fact, as you might suspect, once we have corrected accounting problems related to product cost cross-subsidization, removing these common costs should demonstrate that the Cushman II is not an unprofitable product line. Exhibit 7 combines all the ABC allocations we've discussed into a new view of the 2005 operating results. With this information, SeatJoy management should clearly see that dropping the Cushman II product line is not a good decision and will drive overall SeatJoy operations into a loss situation in the year 2006. With the information shown in Exhibit 7, managers at SeatJoy can understand that to improve profits, they must focus on better controlling existing costs rather than making plans to drop any specific line of products.

Activity-Based Management (ABM)

By identifying and classifying activities according to the Hierarchical Product Cost Model, we have seen how SeatJoy is then able to intelligently assign activity costs to products. This is the ABC (activity-based costing) process and is an important tool in managing the costs and quality of *products*. Managers can also use these data to begin the process of improving the costs and quality of *activities*. Remember that ABC is basically a two-stage process. The first stage of ABC involves tracing the flow of resources (and their costs) to activities. The result of the first stage of ABC is activity cost pools. Exhibit 6 illustrates activity cost pools for SeatJoy, Inc. It looks like a simple process to establish activity cost pools for an organization, right? Actually, this work can be both difficult and time-consuming. Allocating costs using UBC can often be done simply by using available records (such as payroll sheets or production reports)

Exhibit 7: SeatJoy, Inc.: ABC Analysis of 2005 Operating Results

	Unit-Level	Batch-Level	Product Line	Facility-Support
Activity cost pools	$3,420,000	$5,580,000	$8,520,000	$720,000
Cushman activity units	180,000 hours	50 batches	1 product line	
Cushman II activity units	216,000 hours	50 batches	1 product line	
Luxor activity units	60,000 hours	50 batches	1 product line	
Total activity units	456,000 hours	150 batches	3 product lines	1 facility
Cost per activity (cost pools ÷ total activity)	$7.50	$37,200	$2,840,000	$720,000
	per direct labor hour	per batch	per product line	in common costs

Labor Cost Analysis

	Cushman	Cushman II	Luxor	Total
Labor hours per product	10.0 hours	15.0 hours	12.5 hours	
Annual sales volume	× 18,000 chairs	× 14,400 chairs	× 4,800 chairs	
Total annual direct labor hours	180,000 hours	216,000 hours	60,000 hours	456,000 hours
Wage rate per hour	× $20	× $20	× $20	× $20
Total annual direct labor costs	$3,600,000	$4,320,000	$1,200,000	$9,120,000

Total Annual Results

	Cushman	Cushman II	Luxor	Total
Sales revenue	$ 18,000,000	$ 21,600,000	$ 14,400,000	$ 54,000,000
Total direct materials	$ (6,030,000)	$ (9,360,000)	$ (6,696,000)	$(22,086,000)
Total direct labor	(3,600,000)	(4,320,000)	(1,200,000)	(9,120,000)
Unit-level overhead	(1,350,000)	(1,620,000)	(450,000)	(3,420,000)
Batch-level overhead	(1,860,000)	(1,860,000)	(1,860,000)	(5,580,000)
Product line overhead	(2,840,000)	(2,840,000)	(2,840,000)	(8,520,000)
Total product-related costs	$(15,680,000)	$(20,000,000)	$(13,046,000)	$(48,726,000)
Total product margin	$ 2,320,000	$ 1,600,000	$ 1,354,000	$ 5,274,000
Facility support overhead				(720,000)
Selling and administrative expenses				(4,000,000)
Operating profit				$ 554,000

Individual Unit Analysis

	Cushman	Cushman II	Luxor
Sales price	$1,000.00	$ 1,500.00	$ 3,000.00
Direct materials per product	$ (335.00)	$ (650.00)	$(1,395.00)
Direct labor per product	(200.00)	(300.00)	(250.00)
Average unit-level OH per product	(75.00)	(112.50)	(93.75)
Average batch-level OH per product	(103.33)	(129.17)	(387.50)
Average product line OH per product	(157.78)	(197.22)	(591.67)
Total cost per product	$ (871.11)	$(1,388.89)	$(2,717.92)
Margin per product	$ 128.89	$ 111.11	$ 282.08
Margin percent	12.9%	7.4%	9.4%

to identify the number of direct labor hours or number of chairs produced. All manufacturing overhead costs are then averaged across the total number of hours or units. On the other hand, to find out how costs *really* flow (i.e., to trace costs to activities), the accountant must leave the office and go out on the production floor or into the service area. Interacting with those involved (department managers, line supervisors, etc.) is the only way to gather accurate insight about how activities affect costs.

The second stage of ABC is assigning to products the costs now pooled (or organized) by activities. In the work of tracing resources to activity cost pools, much of the insight necessary to establish the second ABC stage is also developed. Typically, a budgeted cost is established for each activity. The expected use of the activity is also determined (e.g., number of direct labor hours for unit-level activities, number of batches for batch-level activities, number of product lines for product line activities). Similar to the traditional manufacturing overhead allocation rate, an activity cost allocation rate is established and used to transfer costs as an activity is actually employed.

For example, think of the activity "purchasing" for a merchandising company. The accountants and managers using ABC must determine what costs are required to purchase inventory for the company. The total cost of purchasing activities, as well as the number of expected purchase orders, is budgeted for the year. Using this information, costs per purchase order are set. Then, each time a purchase order is initiated, the costs are assigned to the product requiring a purchase order. Most merchants purchase inventory in large lots, or batches. If this is the case, then costs of purchase orders are related to batch-level activities. Hence, using ABC, the accountants and managers may be able to demonstrate and understand clearly that it is batches of products that must carry (and cover) the costs of purchasing. If the company wants to know the average purchasing costs of a particular inventory item, this is simply a function of the number of product units in each batch of products purchased.

ABC does not provide all the information a company needs to *manage* the costs of purchasing, however. Other things besides number of purchase orders requested may be driving the costs of purchasing activities. Further, the merchant also needs to manage the performance (i.e., the quality and timeliness) of its purchasing activities. With ABC, our focus is on activities. However, effectively tracing costs to products is a separate issue from managing the activity process. In order for the accountant to provide useful information for managing activities within the organization, we need to expand our ABC model as shown below.

Assume that for our purchasing activity example, the ABC team finds that the number of line items in the purchase order and the amount of lead time provided for the purchase order are important drivers of the costs of this activity. In managing costs, it is important that this set of cost drivers be related to the purchasing activity. To better control costs, management needs to concentrate on controlling needlessly high levels of the cost drivers.[5]

In addition, activity *performance* measures should be established. The drive to improve the overall company so that it can better compete within its market means that every critical activity in the organization, not just those directly affecting customers, must be continuously improved. Every activity has a customer—either inside or outside the company. Performance measures used to evaluate the quality of purchasing might include the amount of time required to complete an order (i.e., lead time) and the level of errors in filling an order. The effort to become a world-class merchandiser (or manufacturer or service provider) requires a company

---

5 Often the measure used to assign activity costs to products is also included in the total set of activity cost drivers used to evaluate and control activity costs. However, an activity pool's set of cost drivers and the allocation rate used to assign its cost to products do not have to be the same.

to clearly identify its strategy and then intelligently build performance measures that support achieving its strategic goals.

Identifying and using multiple cost drivers and performance measures to manage an activity is called **activity-based management (ABM)**. As you can see in the previous diagram, ABM expands the basic ABC model by separating the task of product costing using activity-based relationships (Costs → Activities → Products) from the task of directly managing activities in order to achieve cost efficiencies and to enhance quality in business processes (Activity Cost Drivers → Activities ← Performance Measures). Using ABM, opportunities for cost efficiencies are created by separately tracking multiple cost drivers for each critical activity. Using these performance measures to manage important activities contributes to the effort to continuously improve the organization. As you can see, managing activity cost drivers and performance measures for a particular activity is a management task that is actually exclusive of the processes of tracking a single cost driver that allocates the activity's costs to products. Exhibit 8 illustrates the application of ABM for two activities at SeatJoy.

activity-based management (ABM) The identification and use of cost drivers and performance measures to manage the costs, quality, and timeliness of activities.

Exhibit 8: Activity-Based Management at SeatJoy, Inc.

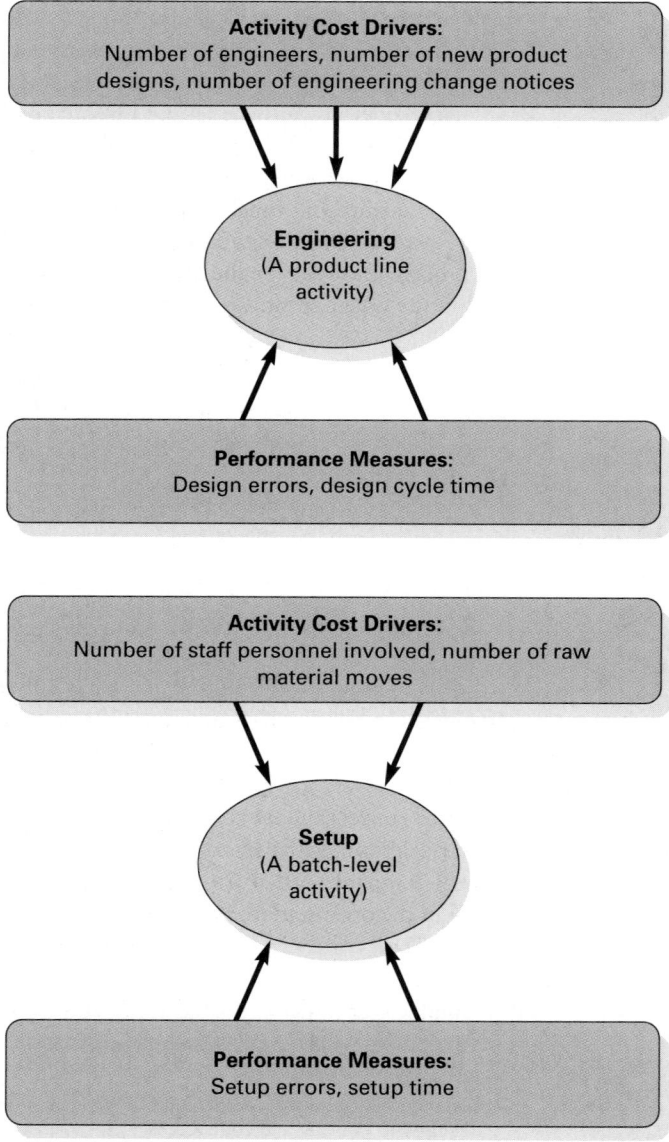

T O   S U M M A R I Z E : Traditional product cost models generally focus on allocating overhead costs based on some measure that is a function of the number of products being produced or the amount of service being provided in the organization. This approach, called unit-based costing (UBC), works well in fairly simple settings with little diversity in the types of products or services offered to customers. In contrast, activity-based costing (ABC) recognizes that activities are the causes of costs. By understanding how activities relate to products, a company with a diverse set of products and processes, such as Boeing Company, can more intelligently allocate manufacturing overhead costs to products.

Activities can be categorized across four levels: unit-level activities, batch-level activities, product line activities, and facility support activities. Generally, variable manufacturing overhead, such as machine maintenance or energy costs to run production equipment, is a function of the number of units produced. Setup costs, materials purchase orders, and route planning are examples of costs traditionally considered fixed that actually are variable in relation to the number of batch runs within the organization. Overhead costs that are a function of product line activities are generally related to engineering, supervision, and warehousing. In contrast to unit-level, batch-level, and product line activities, costs of facility support activities cannot sensibly be connected to any particular product line. Examples of these activities include property taxes, plant security, landscaping, accounting, and executive administration.

Once costs have been pooled together according to the proper activity level (the first stage of ABC), new overhead allocation rates can then be created to separately allocate costs of unit-level, batch-level, and product line activities to product lines (the second stage of ABC). Costs of facility support activities are classified as common costs and should *not* be allocated to individual product lines; otherwise, product costs are distorted. If costs of batch-level and product line activities are allocated using UBC, then cost distortions called product cost cross-subsidization can also take place as one product is erroneously allocated another product's cost in the accounting system. Product cost distortions can lead to a series of management decisions called a death spiral. Managers inadvertently involved in a death spiral will make a decision to drop what is actually a profitable product or service line based on UBC data that erroneously suggest this product or service is unprofitable. Once one product line is dropped, the reallocation of overhead to the remaining products may result in another product looking unprofitable, thereby continuing the spiral.

Once the organization has developed an accurate ABC system, it can turn its attention toward improving activities that support its competitive strategy. The crucial information to be developed for important activities in the organization includes the following:

- A set of activity cost drivers that provides the greatest influence on the activity cost pool. These cost drivers become the focus of effort in controlling the activity cost pool.
- A set of performance measures used to evaluate the quality and timeliness of the activity.

This information is used to expand the ABC model in order to perform activity-based management (ABM).

Total Quality Management

2 Describe total quality management (TQM) and costs of quality (COQ).

We ended the last section on ABC by introducing the important concept that tracking and effectively allocating activity costs is not sufficient for managing activities. In today's highly competitive global markets, managing both the cost *and the performance* of activities is critical to the success of most organizations. This fact supports the importance of ABM to the management process of planning, controlling, and evaluating activities within the organization. Since

total quality management (TQM) A management philosophy focused on increasing profitability by improving the quality of products and processes and increasing customer satisfaction, while promoting the well-being and growth of employees.

the early 1980s, an important management model known as **total quality management (TQM)** has had significant impacts on modern management accounting. TQM is a management philosophy focused on increasing profitability by improving the quality of products and processes and increasing customer satisfaction while promoting the well-being and growth of the employees of the organization. Most managers, if asked, would say that their company seeks to improve quality, increase customer satisfaction, and take care of its employees. Implementing TQM, however, requires more than just endorsing the importance of quality in the company. An organization that has truly implemented TQM exhibits two defining characteristics. First, quality and continuous improvement are emphasized above all else within the organization. The premise here is one of priority. A company focused on TQM manages itself with the assumption that if product quality is high, customers will be satisfied and employees will be happy, and *then* profits can be expected. This contrasts with the assumption that the company cannot focus on quality until it is performing well financially. Second, TQM in the organization is the result of continuously planning, controlling, and evaluating improvement using specific measures. It is in this second assumption that accounting systems built to perform ABM can interface well with TQM. By tracking costs and performance related to TQM activities, accounting can be used to support this critical trend in business management.

TQM Comes to the United States

W. Edward Deming is widely credited with leading the quality revolution in Japan that started in the 1950s. Ironically, Deming received little attention as a consultant to U.S. companies prior to 1950. In contrast, at this same time Japan began to heed his advice on controlling processes, improving systems, and empowering workers. Soon, Deming moved to Japan where he remained for approximately 30 years. In honor of his work, Japan established the national Deming Prize to annually honor companies making significant improvements in the TQM process.

During the 1980s, concerns about American competitiveness spurred many U.S. companies to take a new interest in quality. Several companies invited Deming, then in his eighties, back to the United States to challenge the "old way" of thinking about costs and quality. A hundred years ago Andrew Carnegie essentially built an empire in the steel industry with the following motto: "Watch the costs and the profits will take care of themselves." Deming essentially revised this phrase to "Watch the *quality* and the profits will take care of themselves." The effect he and his colleagues have had on the way organizations work and compete is profound. Deming passed away in December 1993 at the age of 93.

TQM and Management Accounting

statistical process control (SPC) A statistical technique for identifying and measuring the quality status of a process by evaluating its output to determine if serious problems exist in the process.

Perhaps you've heard the term *statistical process control.* **Statistical process control (SPC)** is a technical tool that provides users with the ability to study, control, and improve processes of all types. Using statistical probability analysis, SPC provides management with the ability to know whether the errors in a production or service process are a signal that a serious problem exists in the process. Deming refined this early engineering tool and placed it squarely in the center of his TQM theory of management. Basically, Deming recognized that variation is a regular fact of life. No matter how carefully the fry cook at your local MCDONALD'S prepares a set of hamburgers, each one will be slightly different from the others. This is a natural fact of variation. Frankly, it's probably not very important to you as a consumer that every McDonald's hamburger you purchase is *exactly* like every other hamburger made that day in that store. However, if you're in the business of manufacturing or purchasing baseballs to be used in major league games throughout the summer, you're probably quite interested in consistent product quality. If you're in the business of manufacturing or purchasing surgical scalpels, computer chips, or rocket boosters for the U.S. Space Shuttle Program, then consistent product quality may be even more important.

SPC is having a large effect on management accounting in many organizations today. An accountant usually doesn't need to perform statistical analysis and probability procedures in order to participate in the TQM effort. SPC work is typically the responsibility of engineers and statisticians. Nevertheless, using SPC to support TQM in a company involves a lot of cost management issues. It costs money to create low-variation, high-quality products and services. It costs money to inspect and measure processes in order to know when problems exist. On the other hand, Deming and others have taught us that it costs a great deal of money to allow high-variation, low-quality products and services to exist in our organizations. Tracking and managing these costs is an important part of the TQM effort and is often the responsibility of accountants.

Costs of Quality (COQ)

Let's use baseball manufacturing to help understand exactly how management accounting works with SPC to measure and report quality costs. You may be interested to learn that, although

network exercises

National Institute of Standards and Technology (NIST)

The NATIONAL INSTITUTE OF STAN-DARDS AND TECHNOLOGY (NIST) sponsors a site for the Malcolm Baldrige National Quality Award program at **http://www .quality.nist.gov**. This site will keep you up to date on the latest quality award winners, quality programs for students, presidential speeches on "Baldrige" quality, and descriptive portfolios of the award winners. Check out this site to answer these fundamental questions.

Net Work:

1. Who was Malcolm Baldrige?
2. Why is the award named after him?

FYI:

A Rawlings baseball doesn't last long in a major league game (average life is about six game minutes), but it has to be as perfect as possible. When a professional pitcher throws a ball toward home plate at nearly 100 miles per hour, the slightest blemish in stitching, size, or weight can be the difference between a strike and a home run, the difference between winning a pennant and having a disappointing season.

costs of quality (COQ)
Costs spent to achieve high quality of products and services, as well as costs spent when products fail to have high quality. The four types of costs of quality are prevention costs, appraisal costs, internal failure costs, and external failure costs.

China produces 80% of the world's baseballs, every single baseball pitched in the major leagues is made in a Costa Rican factory owned by RAWLINGS SPORTING GOODS COMPANY. A Rawlings baseball begins life as a "pill," a small sphere of cork and rubber enclosed in a rubber shell. The pill is tightly wound with three different layers of wool yarn, and then finished with a winding of cotton/polyester yarn. This "core" is then coated with a latex adhesive. Over this gooey, hard lump, must be sewn an extremely tight-fitting jacket of leather using exactly 216 raised stitches. Sewing on the cover is a major effort. No one has been able to successfully create a machine that can automatically stitch the cover on a professional baseball. Hence, Rawlings employs about 1,000 baseball sewing experts. In its factory, top sewing pros can sew four to six baseballs an hour, achieving perfect string tension by feel. A wooden press rolls the seams flat, and finished balls are stored in a dehumidifying room that shrinks the covers tight and protects the balls from tropical humidity that might make them bloat illegally. Baseballs are carefully inspected at the Rawlings plant before being packed for shipping. A baseball that turns out too skinny, too hefty, or otherwise off-spec is "blemmed." It's stamped "blem" for blemish and sold as a practice ball.[6]

To be used in the major leagues, a Rawlings baseball should weigh approximately 5.12 ounces and be 9.12 inches in circumference. As we pointed out, however, regardless of how hard the Rawlings Sporting Goods Company works to make sure its sewers are consistently producing baseballs of the perfect weight and size, variation occurs.[7] For the Rawlings plant, the important thing is to distinguish simple random variations in baseball weight and size that occasionally occur in a well-controlled production environment from systematic variations that occur more often when a poorly trained sewer is working or when low-quality leather is being used. Consider the following hypothetical example. Rawlings has determined upper and lower control limits for a baseball. Specifically, baseballs must weigh between 5 and 5.25 ounces and have a circumference between 9 and 9.25 inches. Exhibit 9 shows an SPC chart of measurements of daily baseball weights at Rawlings. As you can see, some of these measurements are outside the control limits, indicating that there are potentially serious quality problems in the factory. Although getting the production process back in control will require some management effort, the problem cannot go on unchecked. Blemmed baseballs cost Rawlings money because the balls cannot be sold at game prices. Worse, though, is the cost to Rawlings' reputation. If Major League Baseball switches to another supplier because of inconsistent quality at Rawlings, the long-term opportunity costs to Rawlings could be devastating.

Before Rawlings' production managers can begin working on a potential quality problem on the production floor, the management accountants need to answer a couple of important questions: "What is it costing Rawlings when it produces blemmed baseballs? What will it cost to get the production process back within control limits?" These questions are the initial step in identifying an important set of costs called "costs of quality." **Costs of quality (COQ)** are costs spent to achieve TQM, as well as costs spent when products and processes fail to have high quality. Once activities that relate to quality in the organization have been identified, the accountant must be able to track the costs of those activities in order to measure COQ. Joseph M. Juran, another American quality guru who, like Deming, was enormously influential in the Japanese quality movement, originally identified COQ as an important accounting concept. Eventually, Juran also returned from Japan to the United States with his COQ theories to guide notable companies such as TEXAS INSTRUMENTS, DUPONT, and XEROX.

---

6 Hannah Holmes, "The Skinny on Sewing Up Baseballs," at **http://www.discovery.com**.

7 *Note:* This example uses fictitious production standards and results in the setting of an actual company. Data used to illustrate quality concepts in this text should not be construed as actual production standards and results for the Rawlings Sporting Goods Company.

Exhibit 9: Rawlings Baseball Production: Statistical Process Control (SPC) Chart of Daily Operating Results

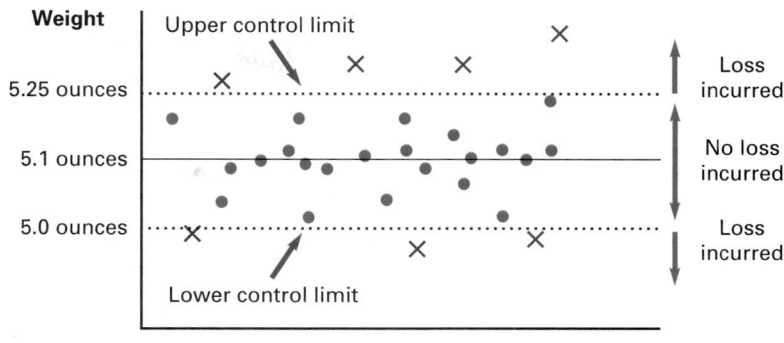

● = Ball weight within control limits with some random variation (no correction required).

✕ = Ball weight outside control limits (correction to production system required).

He understood that organizations need to balance costs of achieving quality against the costs of poor quality. Most importantly, he specifically defined four types of quality costs that form the COQ model: prevention costs, appraisal costs, internal failure costs, and external failure costs.

Prevention Costs

Prevention costs are costs incurred to ensure that tasks are performed correctly the first time and that the product or service meets customer requirements. Examples of prevention costs include costs of process or product design, employee training, education of suppliers, preventive maintenance, and other quality improvement meetings and projects. In the case of Rawlings Sporting Goods, the quality of its baseballs is highly dependent on the quality of its raw materials and on the expertise of those who stitch on the leather covers. This company will likely spend a lot of money working with its suppliers and training its employees to build a quality product.

Appraisal Costs

Appraisal costs are the amounts spent on inspection, testing, and sampling of raw materials, work in process, and finished goods and services. They include overhead expenses for quality inspectors, costs to adjust measuring and test equipment, and costs of associated supplies and materials. Rawlings performs extensive inspections to gather data similar to that shown in Exhibit 9. These inspections require individuals to invest time using special equipment to evaluate each ball for size, weight, color, stitching, etc. Both appraisal and prevention costs can be viewed as investments in the process of providing quality baseballs to Major League Baseball.

Internal Failure Costs

Juran categorizes all the scrap and rework costs that are incurred to dispose of or fix defective products *before* they are shipped to the customer as **internal failure costs**. Costs of downtime or reduced yield due to production of defective parts or services are also included in this cost category. For example, if a Rawlings employee spends 10 minutes sewing a baseball, only to have the cover suddenly rip because of poor-quality leather, the company has lost money due to both the scrapped leather and the wages paid for 10 minutes of sewing a useless ball. In addition, all the materials and labor time spent previously winding, coating, and fitting the ball before the stitching work started are lost and become part of the internal failure costs. Clearly, Rawlings wants to be able to reduce scrap and sell more baseballs. Investments in prevention and appraisal work should reduce internal failure costs in the organization.

prevention costs Costs of quality that specifically relate to the effort to ensure that processes are performed correctly the first time and that products and services meet customers' expectations.

appraisal costs Costs of quality that specifically relate to the effort of inspecting, testing, and sampling activities performed in order to identify and remove low-quality products and services from the system.

FYI:

Rawlings baseballs are selected at random from each shipment to Major League Baseball and shot from an air cannon at a speed of 85 feet per second at a wall made of northern white ash (the wood used to make bats). Each tested ball must bounce back at between 0.514 and 0.578 of its original speed to be suitably lively for Major League Baseball.

internal failure costs Costs of quality that specifically relate to the expenses that occur when low-quality products and services fail before production and delivery to customers.

external failure costs Costs of quality that specifically relate to the costs that occur when low-quality products and services fail after production and delivery to customers.

FYI:

Most experts agree that losses on gross sales due to poor quality range from 20% to 30%. However, most executives underestimate these losses because they consider only the most obvious costs, such as scrap and rework, to be the costs of low quality.

Source: K. G. Rust, "Measuring the Costs of Quality," *Management Accounting*, August 1995, pp. 33–37.

External Failure Costs

Internal failure costs are very expensive. Nevertheless, Rawlings would *much* rather experience an internal failure than an external failure (defined as failure after the product has been delivered to the customers). **External failure costs** are generally the highest costs of a poor-quality process. Some examples are the costs of processing complaints, customer returns, warranty claims, product recalls, field service, and product liability. The most serious type of external failure cost likely results from unhappy customers; because bad news travels fast, defects found by a customer can cause the firm to lose both market share and future profits. In fact, a FORD MOTOR COMPANY survey indicates that a dissatisfied customer tells, on average, six other people. Sometimes the bad news can travel even faster. If a cover of a Rawlings baseball is pulled loose by a pitcher in the act of throwing a knuckleball during a game, the ball is immediately removed from the game. Obviously, more than six people instantly know about the product failure. Worse, though, is when product failure leads to news announcements and discussion in the media. In the last few years, you may recall some famous examples of publicized product failure involving software with bugs, unsafe tires on vehicles, and medicine or medical procedures with unexpected side effects.

Juran originally related all four of these COQ categories back to Deming's SPC model. He taught that if companies really understood the extent of failure costs, they would be willing to invest more in appraisal and prevention costs to keep more of their products performing within established control limits. Accountants should track these costs so that they can better manage the important relationship between costs of low-quality products and costs required to create high-quality products. This is an important relationship to manage. Obviously, high quality saves the company a lot of money as both internal and external product failures are reduced. On the other hand, high quality likely requires large investments in appraisal and prevention costs. Even though TQM requires that managers focus first on quality and then on profits, managers still need to understand how their commitment to TQM affects the company's bottom line (i.e., its profits). The dollar amounts involved in COQ are often quite large. Accountants add important competitive value to the organization when they are able to provide this important cost information. Hence, the ABC/ABM accounting system should identify appraisal and prevention activities, track the cost drivers of these activities, and establish performance measures that relate to reductions in failure costs and activities as a result of appraisal and prevention activities.

COQ Example

Let's return to our example involving the production of baseballs at Rawlings Sporting Goods Company. Rawlings has invested expensive time and equipment to inspect all baseballs represented on the graph in Exhibit 9. As you can see, there are a few baseballs whose individual weights are outside the control limits. Balls failing the test are marked "blems" and sold very cheaply as practice balls. Other balls are not even usable as practice balls and must be scrapped. (Remember that weight is not the only quality criterion at Rawlings. The company is inspecting and scrapping balls for size, stitching, and color problems as well.) In addition to the balls failing the SPC tests, as displayed in Exhibit 9, Rawlings may also occasionally deal with complaints from merchants, athletes, and other organizations involving balls that fail in "the field." Because of the company's high commitment to customer satisfaction, it incurs significant costs in handling these calls, providing replacement balls, and investigating the cause of the product failure back at the factory. To counter these problems, Rawlings is considering making a large investment in its inspection equipment and in better training for its factory workers. Additionally, it is considering a new supplier for some of its raw materials (there are significant costs involved in establishing the new supplier relationship). Rawlings has a difficult planning decision to make that will likely require an intelligent evaluation of the trade-offs across all its quality costs. Rawlings will invest in an increasing level of appraisal and prevention costs in order to increase the percentage of baseballs that conform to all control limits. As the quality of baseballs increases, failure costs decrease dramatically. However, achieving perfect quality requires higher and higher prevention and appraisal costs. Balancing the decreasing costs of product failure with the increasing costs of high quality requires combining *all* costs in order to compute total COQ. The idea is to find the quality level where total COQ is minimized. As an example, look at the fictitious cost numbers in the following table. As the percentage of baseballs that comply with all control limits (color, weight, diameter, etc.) increases, total appraisal and prevention costs increase. On the other hand, as the percentage of baseballs that comply with all control limits decreases, total failure costs increase. Rawlings needs to balance these costs by focusing on the appropriate level of quality in its production process. As you can see by inspecting the numbers presented, all quality costs are minimized in this example at 94% conformance where total COQ equals $2,237,155.

% of balls within all control limits	84%	86%	88%	90%	92%	94%	96%	98%	100%
Total appraisal & prevention costs	$ 100,037	$ 122,554	$ 156,347	$ 211,347	$ 311,850	$ 530,663	$1,164,270	$4,214,198	$44,172,984
Total failure costs	52,100,456	7,927,472	3,713,274	2,549,005	2,018,342	1,706,492	1,495,145	1,338,798	1,216,244
Total costs of quality (COQ)	$52,200,493	$8,050,026	$3,869,621	$2,760,352	$2,330,192	$2,237,155	$2,659,415	$5,552,996	$45,389,228

Locating COQ in the Accounting Records

It is important to see that tracking COQ within traditional accounting records can be challenging. Essentially, if the accountant desires to provide COQ data, most of these data are generally buried in the accounting records. As we discussed in previous chapters, many organizations traditionally categorize product costs as direct materials, direct labor, and overhead; and they categorize period costs as selling or general administrative. Quality costs used in the COQ model are typically spread throughout these traditional categories as shown below.

Prevention Costs		Appraisal Costs		Internal Failure Costs		External Failure Costs	
Cost Type	**Where Found**	**Cost Type**	**Where Found**	**Cost Type**	**Where Found**	**Cost Type**	**Where Found**
Process or product design	General administrative	Quality inspectors	Overhead	Scrap	Direct materials	Processing complaints & returns	Selling
Employee training	Overhead	Purchasing test equipment	Overhead (depreciation)	Rework	Direct labor	Product recalls	Selling or general administrative
Educating suppliers	General administrative	Adjusting test equipment	Overhead	Downtime	Direct labor and overhead or general administrative	Product liability	General administrative
Preventive maintenance	Overhead	Special supplies and materials	Overhead	Reduced yield	Direct materials and direct labor	Lost sales	Not found in the accounting system

Companies using a traditional cost accounting system may have some difficulty separating quality costs from other costs. However, companies using an ABC system should have already identified activities related to many of these quality processes. Often, it is much easier to implement a COQ accounting system in an organization that uses ABC. Note that lost sales (one type of failure costs) are *not* found in the accounting system. Lost sales are an opportunity cost, and opportunity costs are typically not tracked within most accounting systems. Nevertheless, these are extremely important costs for the accountant to measure and provide to decision makers trying to plan, control, and evaluate the quality process in the organization. Lately, there has been some progress in the effort to track these important opportunity costs. Measuring the costs of lost sales is discussed in the expanded material section of this chapter.

TO SUMMARIZE: W. Edward Deming was extremely influential in helping companies understand that quality is an important competitive necessity in business. One of the main TQM (total quality management) tools he prescribed was SPC (statistical process control). Companies use SPC to identify an acceptable range of variation in their products and services. When the variation in the product or service exceeds the control limits established by the firm, then managers begin working to increase the quality of the production process.

A contemporary of Deming, Joseph M. Juran, developed a new categorization of costs called COQ (costs of quality) that can be used to manage decision making based on SPC. Keeping products or services in conformance with control limits requires investing in two types of quality costs: prevention costs (such as good product design and employee training) and appraisal costs (such as inspection and testing). When the production process starts creating variation outside the control limits, two types of quality costs result: internal failure costs (such as scrap and employee downtime) and external failure costs (such as handling complaints and product recalls). Perhaps the most important external failure costs are the opportunity costs of lost sales.

The COQ information that accountants provide managers should illustrate how decreasing failure costs may be offset by increasing prevention and appraisal costs. The level of quality conformance in a production process should be at the point where total quality costs are minimized. Identifying quality costs can be a challenge because these costs are generally intermingled across all the product and period costs within many organizations' accounting systems. Of all the quality costs identified in the COQ model (i.e., appraisal, prevention, internal failure, and external failure costs), the external failure costs are most difficult to measure because these costs include the opportunity costs of lost sales due to customer dissatisfaction.

The focus of this chapter is to introduce you to some of the "cutting-edge" issues in management accounting today. The topics in this chapter are organized around the strategic imperatives of costs (e.g., activity-based costing or ABC) and quality (e.g., total quality management or TQM). Remember that management accounting is not dictated by some regulatory agency. Management accounting practice is determined by competition and the strategic needs of each organization. Accounting tools such as ABC and COQ essentially focus on new ways of measuring and reporting costs. These costs are often recorded somehow in the traditional accounting system. In this expanded section, we will explore a *very* new way of thinking about and reporting the opportunity costs of lost sales. The interesting thing about measuring the costs of lost sales is that this is a measure of costs that is rarely recorded anywhere within the traditional accounting system.

Measuring Costs of Lost Sales

3 Compute the opportunity cost of lost sales.

Want to set a manager's teeth on edge? If you're in manufacturing, show the manager a pile of scrapped work-in-process inventory due to low-quality materials or mistakes made in the production process. If you're in merchandising, show the manager a pile of merchandise that can't be sold due to low-quality materials, poor design, or damage during shipping. These piles represent wasted costs and opportunities and translate into lost profits. The accountant using COQ in a manufacturing or merchandising organization will report these costs as internal failure costs. However, identifying internal failure costs within service companies is more challenging. Where are the piles of scrapped inventory in a service company? Actually, there is often no distinction between internal failures and external failures for a service company such as an airline, a law firm, or a bank. Baggage is misplaced, a client's phone calls are not returned, or deposits are recorded in the wrong account. Internal processes have failed at these service companies, and external customers are *immediately* affected. Instead of scrapped inventory that can't be sold, service companies identify their own kind of scrap heap: customers who will not come back. Frankly, all three types of companies (service firms, merchants, and manufacturers) experience lost opportunities due to disgruntled customers. Perhaps the most significant impact of the TQM revolution across businesses is an increasing determination to make sure the customers' experience with the company is exemplary. (Hopefully, you've personally had a positive experience with a company determined to "delight the customer.")

As we discussed earlier, disappointed customers can lead to a number of external failure costs, including costs of processing complaints, customer returns, warranty claims, product recalls, field service, and product liability. Many of these costs don't apply to service companies. As a result, these companies naturally focus on the effect of losing the goodwill of their customers, which in turn leads to loss of future sales. However, the risk to manufacturers and merchants is that they will focus too much on external failure costs that are easy to measure and will fail to fully appreciate the opportunity cost of lost sales (which is more the focus of service companies).

Robust Quality

If the accountant is somehow able to identify and measure the cost of lost sales, then managers can use this information in better planning, controlling, and evaluating the process of delivering the products that customers want. What kinds of products do customers want? Let's return to our earlier discussion about baseball manufacturing. Think about Randy Johnson pitching for the Arizona Diamondbacks. Does he care if a RAWLINGS baseball appropriately weighs between 5 and 5.25 ounces and has a circumference between 9 and 9.25 inches? Actually, no. What Randy Johnson cares about is that the baseball, when pitched, will perform as he intends—that it will have the desired curve, fade, slide, drop, or heat. Referring back to the SPC chart in Exhibit 9, a ball that weighs between 5 and 5.25 ounces and has a circumference between 9 and 9.25 inches is determined to have no defects because it is within MLB (Major League Baseball) limits. However, one-tenth of an ounce is pretty important to a professional baseball pitcher trying to throw a split-fingered fastball. Hence, we might expect that Randy Johnson's pitching performance will improve and be more consistent as Rawlings works to reduce variation in the weight and size of baseballs—even if the variation is within the limits imposed by Major League Baseball.

robust quality The capability of a product to perform according to customer expectations regardless of surroundings and circumstances.

The effort to reduce all variation is related to the concept of robust quality. **Robust quality** essentially means that the product will perform for the customer under all kinds of circumstances. In other words, you and I really don't care if the stereo, shirt, or sports car we buy was manufactured within some set of control limits or specifications. For us, the proof of a product's quality is in its performance when it is rapped, overloaded, stretched, or soaked. We all prefer stereos that continue to power up (even after a lightning storm has sent electrical surges throughout our neighborhood); we all prefer clothes that don't tear (even when a small child yanks on the sleeve to get our attention); we all prefer cars designed to steer safely and predictably (even on roads that are wet or full of potholes). We say these products are robust. They gain steadfast customer loyalty.

In the mid-1980s, FORD MOTOR COMPANY had a valuable experience with the importance of robust quality.[8] At that time, Ford owned 25% of MAZDA and asked the Japanese company to help build some of the transmissions for a car Ford was selling in the United States. Both Ford and Mazda built their transmissions using the same specifications. Yet, after the cars with Ford-built transmissions had been on the road for a while, they began developing much higher warranty costs and more customer complaints about noise than the cars with Mazda-built transmissions. As a result, Ford engineers disassembled and inspected transmissions made by both companies. They were astounded at the comparison. The Ford transmissions were all built within the range of engineering specifications, but the Mazda transmissions displayed absolutely no variability from the target measures. The Ford transmissions that were breaking down were those shipped with components built quite close to (but still within) the manufacturing control limits. Because the Mazda plant was working hard to reduce all variance—even variance within the acceptable control limits—its transmissions had lower production, scrap, rework, and warranty costs.

Taguchi's Quality Loss Function

Taguchi quality loss function A method developed by Genichi Taguchi for estimating the actual size of all external failure costs, particularly the opportunity costs of lost customer sales that result from dissatisfied customers.

Genichi Taguchi is a very famous Japanese quality expert who made an important adaptation to SPC charts that allows management accountants to actually measure the external failure costs of lost customers. Since its introduction in the 1980s, many U.S. companies have used Taguchi's famous quality loss function. Essentially, the **Taguchi quality loss function** is a method of relating the amount of variation in a product to external failure costs due to dissatisfied customers. Managers and accountants who use the Taguchi quality loss function recognize that shipping a product that barely satisfies the corporate standard gains you virtually nothing over shipping a product that fails. Translation: There is a lot more difference between baseballs that weigh 5.12 ounces versus 5.24 ounces (both balls are within MLB tolerance specifications) than there is between baseballs weighing 5.24 ounces versus 5.26 ounces (only one ball is within tolerance specifications). Nevertheless, using the upper and lower limit controls displayed in Exhibit 9 would have Rawlings feeling just as confident shipping a baseball to the National League weighing 5.24 ounces as shipping a baseball weighing 5.12 ounces. Can you see why this might create a performance problem for Rawlings' customers? The Taguchi motto is: "Don't just try to stay within specifications, get on target!" Every time Rawlings ships a baseball that is more or less than the perfect size and weight, robust quality is reduced, and the likelihood increases that the ball will not perform in the field as expected. The result of being off target is dissatisfied customers, and dissatisfied customers talk to other customers, which can significantly reduce future sales.

The quality loss, as defined by Taguchi, is all the costs of external failure (including costs of lost customer sales). A simple formulation of Taguchi's loss function looks a bit like Einstein's theory of relativity formula (remember $E = MC^2$?). Using Taguchi's formula, the cost of external failures is computed as follows:

$$L = CD^2$$

where L = total external quality loss due to external failures
C = internal costs required to fix the problem and get the product back on target
D = distance from the target measured in standard units

FYI:

A recent study of the performance of Rawlings baseballs notes that even balls within Major League Baseball specifications (i.e., weigh between 5.0 and 5.25 ounces) can have approximately a 10% performance difference. In other words, the study showed that balls at the lightest and liveliest end of the tolerance specifications would typically travel 49.1 feet farther on a 400-foot hit than the heavier balls. That's within Major League Baseball's own specifications and could mean the difference between a lazy fly ball and a home run.

Source: J. Kaat, "Baseball's New Baseball," *Popular Mechanics*, October 13, 2000.

---

8 G. Taguchi and D. Clausing, "Robust Quality," *Harvard Business Review*, January–February 1990, pp. 65–75.

If your geometry skills are reasonably fresh, you might note that this formula is a quadratic function (because of the D^2 term). If it has been a while since your last geometry class, you just need to note that quality loss increases very quickly as the distance between the product and the target increases. The implication here is that if management decides not to incur the voluntary expenses of reducing variation, it involuntarily incurs several times that amount in the form of warranty costs, lost sales due to customer ill will, and so forth. One important idea behind Taguchi's quality loss function is that it disagrees with the traditional notion of quality control limits. Look back at the SPC chart in Exhibit 9. This chart indicates that there is no loss as long as baseballs weigh between 5.0 and 5.25 ounces. Since the SPC chart is reporting that very few balls being shipped to the major leagues are outside the weight specifications, the data suggest that probably little loss is being incurred. But how much is Rawlings potentially losing in external failure costs, and how much could be saved if Rawlings reduced weight variation in baseballs? This is difficult to know precisely. Remember that Rawlings is trying to manufacture baseballs that weigh exactly 5.12 ounces. Let's assume that it would cost $10,000 in prevention and appraisal costs to reduce average variation at Rawlings by each 0.01 ounce. Therefore, if baseballs varied on average only 0.01 ounce from the target of 5.12 ounces (i.e., from 5.11 to 5.13), then it would require only $10,000 to correct the problem and get the production system exactly on the 5.12 ounce target. According to the Taguchi quality loss function, Rawlings would then save approximately $10,000 in external failure costs by making this reduction. It looks like an even trade-off between costs and cost savings, doesn't it? Remember, though, that Rawlings would also save some internal failure costs as well (waste, scrap, downtime, etc.). Now look at the chart of numbers below. As you can see, it will cost Rawlings more to get the baseball weight on target as the distance between the target weight and the actual weights increases. However, the opportunity loss (i.e., external failure costs) is much larger as the variation (i.e., the distance from target) increases. Hence, the Taguchi quality loss function really emphasizes the importance of reducing variation in order to increase robust quality within products and services.

Cost per 0.01 ounce unit to correct	$10,000	$10,000	$10,000	$10,000	$10,000	$10,000
Average distance from target	×1 unit	×2 units	×3 units	×4 units	×5 units	×6 units
Total cost to correct	$10,000	$20,000	$30,000	$40,000	$50,000	$60,000
Cost per 0.01 ounce unit to correct (C)	$10,000	$10,000	$10,000	$10,000	$10,000	$10,000
Distance squared (D^2)	×1 unit	×4 units	×9 units	×16 units	×25 units	×36 units
Total quality loss (L)	$10,000	$40,000	$90,000	$160,000	$250,000	$360,000

Obviously, Taguchi's quality loss measures are not very precise and objective. He is making general *approximations* about how quality problems affect all companies. Some companies may experience more or less loss due to quality problems than Taguchi suggests. Nevertheless, the importance of the quality loss function is to use the management accounting system to provide a valuable *signal* to managers about the importance of continuously improving the quality of their goods and services. Measuring deviations from specifications has always been the job of engineers. However, by taking those deviations and translating them into costs, the accountant is able to draw a lot of attention to the problem.

Is Quality Free?

Before we finish our discussion on quality, you need to know that there is some disagreement in the profession on how to measure quality costs. In fact, you may have even noticed a discrepancy in the section you just read. Remember that in a previous section in this chapter we discussed the importance of identifying the proper level of quality in the organization by offsetting prevention and appraisal costs against internal and external failure costs in order to minimize total costs of quality (COQ). It appears, therefore, that COQ trade-offs will typically justify a level of quality that is less than 100% conformance to all control limits. On the other hand, our discussion in this section of measuring the costs of lost sales using the Taguchi quality loss function seems to indicate that "quality is free!" In other words, when one understands the *full extent* of external failure costs, the minimal quality cost trade-off point is very close to or exceeds 100% conformance. Hence, using the Taguchi quality loss function, companies should spend whatever it takes to have absolute quality and customer satisfaction. Remember that this is the essence of TQM—that quality is emphasized above all else, including costs. Not everyone feels this strongly about TQM. Some managers and accountants disagree with a "field of dreams" approach to managing quality costs (i.e., "if you build *perfect* quality, profits will come"). You should pay attention to this current debate, as there is good logic on both sides. The real test of this concept is in the competitive marketplace. In any event, management accounting systems should be structured to measure COQ, including the cost of lost sales, in order to add competitive value to the organization's TQM efforts.

TO SUMMARIZE: The Taguchi quality loss function attempts to measure external failure costs using a formula where L (quality loss) $= C$ (cost to correct) $\times D^2$ (distance from target). The quality loss function is not a precise measure of external failure costs, but it provides an approximate signal of the significant opportunity costs organizations experience when less-than-perfect goods and services are provided to customers. Using the quality loss function, accountants can provide important insight to help their companies better compete in the marketplace. Some TQM advocates suggest that organizations should strive for 100% quality conformance. These individuals defend this position by suggesting that most organizations underestimate failure costs as a product or service process moves away from 100% quality conformance. Nevertheless, there is currently an active debate on the issue of whether perfect quality is too costly to achieve.

---

review of learning objectives

Explain the fundamentals of activity-based costing (ABC) and activity-based management (ABM). Unit-based costing (UBC) systems generally allocate all manufacturing overhead costs based on some measure related to the number of products being produced or the amount of service being provided in the organization (e.g., direct labor hours). In settings with little diversity in the types of products or services offered to customers, UBC may be an appropriate tool. On the other hand, activity-based costing (ABC) recognizes that activities are the causes of costs. Activities can be categorized across four levels: unit-level activities, batch-level activities, product line activities, and facility support activities. Generally, variable overhead such as machine maintenance or energy costs to run production equipment is a function of the number of units produced. Setup costs, materials purchase orders, and route planning are examples of costs traditionally considered fixed that actually are variable in relation to the number of batch runs within the organization. Overhead costs that are a function of product line activities are generally related to engineering, supervision, and warehousing. Once activity cost pools have been created, costs of unit-level, batch-level, and product line activities can be assigned to

products. If costs of batch-level and product line activities are allocated using UBC, then some products may be inappropriately assigned costs that actually belong to another product. This particular cost distortion is referred to as product cost cross-subsidization.

Costs of facility support activities (e.g., property taxes, plant security, landscaping, accounting, and executive administration) cannot be sensibly connected to any particular product line. These costs (also known as common costs) should *not* be allocated to individual product lines. Otherwise, product costs are distorted, which can lead to a series of management decisions called a death spiral. Managers inadvertently involved in a death spiral will make a decision to drop a product or service line based on UBC data that erroneously suggest that these products or services are unprofitable.

The point of ABC is to appropriately *assign* costs to products. However, ABC does not really provide useful information for managing activities. To *manage* costs of activities, a set of activity cost drivers that provides the greatest influence on the activity cost pool is identified. To manage activity performance, a set of quality- and time-based measures is also created and related to each critical activity in the organization. The process of managing activities using cost drivers and performance measures is called activity-based management (ABM). ABC and ABM combine to form the following model of activities:

Activity Cost Drivers
↓
Costs → **Activities** → Products
↑
Performance Measures

2 **Describe total quality management (TQM) and costs of quality (COQ).** Total quality management (TQM) is a philosophy in which (1) product and process quality is emphasized over profits and (2) quality must be measured in order to be realized. Using SPC (statistical process control), W. Edward Deming became one of the pioneers of TQM in both Japan and America. SPC establishes control limits. When the variation in the product or service exceeds the control limits established by the firm, then managers begin work to increase the quality of the production process. Joseph M. Juran expanded the process of SPC in order to manage four specific types of costs of quality (COQ). Prevention and appraisal costs are viewed as investments in the process of keeping products and services within established control limits. When the production process starts creating variation outside the control limits, internal failure costs (such as scrap and employee downtime) and external failure costs (such as handling complaints and product recalls) occur. If increasing preven-

tion and appraisal costs offset decreasing failure costs, then management accountants should help companies understand how to minimize total quality costs. Identifying quality costs can be a challenge, however, because these costs are generally intermingled across both product and period costs within most organizations' accounting systems. Costs of lost sales due to customer dissatisfaction are important opportunity costs, yet they are particularly difficult to measure.

3 **Compute the opportunity cost of lost sales.** The Taguchi quality loss function provides a means of approximately measuring the impact of *all* external failure costs on the company's costs—including the opportunity costs of lost sales due to customer dissatisfaction. The Taguchi quality loss function measures these costs using a formula where L (quality loss) $= C$ (cost to correct) $\times D^2$ (distance from target). Using this formula, accountants can provide an important signal of the significant opportunity costs organizations experience when less-than-perfect goods and services are provided to customers. Currently, in light of the likely size of cost of external failure, there is some debate on whether prevention and appraisal costs can ever increase enough to justify having less-than-perfect conformance to control limits (i.e., perfect quality).

k **ey terms & concepts**

r **eview problem**

ABC versus Conventional Product Costing

Willett Company makes two types of products: Product A and Product B. The company's management accountants accumulated the following production cost information for 2006:

	Product A	Product B	Total
Production volume (units)	1,000	500	
Number of engineering changes per product line	4	8	
Total cost of engineering changes			$12,000
Direct labor hours per unit	3	2	
Direct materials cost per unit	$5	$7	
Direct labor cost per hour	$6	$12	

Required:

Assume Product A sells for $42 each and Product B sells for $50 each. Assume also that engineering changes are the only manufacturing overhead cost Willett Company incurs. If all products are sold, what is the gross margin of each product assuming the following:

1. Engineering change costs are allocated on the basis of direct labor hours.
2. Engineering change costs are allocated on the basis of the number of engineering changes made.

Solution

1. Allocation on the Basis of Direct Labor Hours

	Product A (1,000 units)	Product B (500 units)
Sales	$42,000 (1,000 × $42)	$25,000 (500 × $50)
Cost of goods sold:		
Direct materials	$ 5,000 (1,000 × $5)	$ 3,500 (500 × $7)
Direct labor	18,000 (1,000 × 3 hrs. × $6)	12,000 (500 × 2 hrs. × $12)
Manufacturing overhead . .	9,000 (1,000 × 3 hrs. × $3*)	3,000 (500 × 2 hrs. × $3*)
Total cost of goods sold . . .	$32,000	$18,500
Gross margin	$10,000	$ 6,500

*Overhead allocation per direct labor hour:

$$\frac{\$12,000 \text{ total costs}}{4,000 \text{ total direct labor hours}} = \$3 \text{ per direct labor hour}$$

Product A (1,000 × 3 hrs.) =	3,000
Product B (500 × 2 hrs.) =	1,000
Total	4,000 direct labor hours

2. Allocation on the Basis of Engineering Changes

Sales	$42,000	$25,000
Cost of goods sold:		
Direct materials	$ 5,000	$ 3,500
Direct labor	18,000	12,000
Manufacturing overhead	4,000*	8,000*
Total cost of goods sold	$27,000	$23,500
Gross margin	$15,000	$ 1,500

*Overhead allocation per engineering change:

Cost per change: $\dfrac{\$12,000}{12} = \$1,000$ per change

Overhead allocations per product:

Product A: 4 changes × $1,000 per change =	$ 4,000
Product B: 8 changes × $1,000 per change =	8,000
Total	$12,000

d iscussion questions

1. What is the lowest price that a company should charge its customers?
2. What is the difference between a product cost and a period cost?
3. Traditionally, what basis has been used to allocate manufacturing overhead costs to products?
4. What type of incorrect decision can be made if a cost accounting system allows cross-subsidization of product costs?
5. "Given enough time, every cost is fixed." Do you agree or disagree? Explain.
6. In what context does a unit-based costing (UBC) system cause problems?
7. Under a Hierarchical Product Cost Model, what are the four classifications of production costs?
8. Give three examples of batch-level activities.
9. In general, which type of fast-food outlet would have higher overhead costs: an outlet selling hamburgers, pizza, and chicken or an outlet selling only hamburgers? Explain.
10. Give three examples of facility support costs.
11. How can the allocation of common costs potentially cause a death spiral?

12. ABC (activity-based costing) uses activity allocation rates in product costing. How are activity cost drivers used in ABM (activity-based management)?
13. In what way do Edward Deming's ideas of total quality management (TQM) change Andrew Carnegie's slogan, "Watch the costs and the profits will take care of themselves"?
14. Briefly describe the four types of costs in costs of quality (COQ).

15. Why are external failure costs generally the highest of the costs of quality (COQ)?
16. Describe the concept of robust quality.
17. According to the Taguchi quality loss function, what happens to the total loss due to external failure as a product's quality gets further from target specifications?

p ractice exercises

Practice 22-1

Product Costing Terminology
Which one of the following statements is *false*?

a. Conversion costs include direct labor and manufacturing overhead costs.
b. Prime costs include direct materials and direct labor.
c. Period costs are all costs other than the product costs.
d. The production supervisor's salary is included in direct labor costs.
e. Product costs include direct labor, direct material, and manufacturing overhead.

Practice 22-2

Overhead Allocation Problem in the SeatJoy Example
Which one of the following statements is *true* with respect to the SeatJoy example described in the text of this chapter?

a. The original process costing system ignored the impact of spoiled goods on the calculation of equivalent units.
b. The original materials warehouse requisition system did include adequate controls to ensure separation of duties.
c. The original manufacturing overhead application system based on direct labor hours did not provide accurate insight on cost behavior.
d. The original prime cost application system overstated cost of goods sold during times of inflation.

Practice 22-3

Overhead Allocation Problems
Which one of the following statements is *false*?

a. Common manufacturing costs should *not* be allocated over each division.
b. Common manufacturing costs include direct labor and direct materials.
c. Cross-subsidization results from incorrect application of manufacturing overhead costs.
d. Cross-subsidization effects are addressed by ABC accounting systems.

Practice 22-4

Characteristics of Traditional Unit-Based Costing
Which one of the following statements is *false* with respect to traditional unit-based costing?

a. Unit-based costing is a good method of cost allocation in the right context.
b. Unit-based costing is widely used by many companies.
c. Unit-based costing essentially allocates overhead costs based on the number of units produced.
d. Unit-based costing usually works well in a company with multiple products and services.

Practice 22-5

Difference between Unit-Based Costing and Activity-Based Costing
Which one of the following statements best summarizes the difference between unit-based costing (UBC) and activity-based costing (ABC)?

a. With UBC, costs are first allocated to departments; with ABC, costs are first allocated to activities.
b. With UBC, costs are first allocated to activities; with ABC, costs are first allocated to departments.
c. With UBC, costs are first allocated to departments; with ABC, costs are first allocated to products.
d. With UBC, costs are first allocated to products; with ABC, costs are first allocated to departments.

Practice 22-6

ABC Hierarchical Product Cost Model
Which one of the following is *not* one of the types of activities in the Hierarchical Product Cost Model?

a. Facility support activities
b. Batch-level activities
c. Unit-level activities
d. Product line activities
e. Manufacturing application activities

Practice 22-7

Unit-Based Costing
The company expects to produce 500,000 units of its only product. Using the unit-based costing approach and the following manufacturing overhead costs for the year, compute the manufacturing overhead allocation rate.

Electricity	$ 48,000
Depreciation	140,000
Engineering	60,000
Quality testing	173,000
Property tax	53,000
Supervisors' salaries	210,000
Maintenance	110,000

Practice 22-8

Unit-Level Activities
The company has determined that $1,029,600 of its total manufacturing overhead costs related to unit-level activities such as electricity costs for running the manufacturing equipment and equipment maintenance costs. The company allocates these costs over the individual units of

production based on machine hours. Using the following expected machine hours for the company's three divisions that all make the same product, (1) determine the manufacturing overhead rate per machine hour and (2) allocate the manufacturing overhead to each division.

Division A	20,000 hours
Division B	40,000
Division C	50,000

Practice 22-9

Batch-Level Activities

Which one of the following would *not* be an example of a batch activity for a manufacturing firm?

a. Purchase orders
b. Production manager's salary
c. Number of setups
d. Number of inspections

Practice 22-10

Product Line Activities

Which one of the following is *not* an example of a product line activity?

a. Orders for nonstocked items
b. Costs related to specialized materials warehouses
c. Production process design activities
d. Training activities for specific types of consulting services

Practice 22-11

Facility Support Activities

Which one of the following is *not* an example of a facility support activity?

a. Manufacturing vice president's salary
b. Property taxes
c. Accounting
d. Production supervisor's salary
e. Plant security

Practice 22-12

Resolving Cost Distortions

Which one of the following statements is *false*?

a. Cross-subsidization can cause a manager to evaluate products incorrectly.
b. Cross-subsidization is a common problem caused by activity-based costing.
c. The death spiral begins when a company cuts products that do not create the costs in question.
d. Allocating common costs can begin the death spiral.

Practice 22-13

Overhead Costs and Dropping a Product Line

The company manufactures three products. Profit computations for these three products for the most recent year are as follows:

	Product X	Product Y	Product Z	Total
Sales	$ 300,000	$ 700,000	$ 800,000	$ 1,800,000
Direct materials	(70,000)	(150,000)	(200,000)	(420,000)
Direct labor	(50,000)	(200,000)	(250,000)	(500,000)
Manufacturing overhead	(100,000)	(400,000)	(500,000)	(1,000,000)
Profit	$ 80,000	$ (50,000)	$(150,000)	$ (120,000)

(continued)

The company traditionally allocates manufacturing overhead based on the level of direct labor cost—$2 of manufacturing overhead are allocated for each $1 of direct labor cost. However, of the company's $1,000,000 in manufacturing overhead costs, $700,000 is directly related to the number of product batches produced during the year. The number of batches of the three products for the year was as follows: Product X, 20 batches; Product Y, 30 batches; Product Z, 50 batches. The remaining $300,000 in overhead is for facility support (property taxes, security costs, general administration, and so forth).

As you can see, the total company loss is $120,000. In an effort to reduce or eliminate this loss, the company has decided to drop Product Z. What would total company profit (or loss) have been in the most recent year if Product Z had been dropped at the beginning of the year?

Practice 22-14

Unit-Level, Batch-Level, Product Line, and Facility Support Costs

The company has determined that its total manufacturing overhead cost of $900,000 is a mixture of unit-level, batch-level, product line, and facility support costs. The company has assembled the following information concerning the manufacturing overhead costs, the annual number of units produced, production batches, and number of product lines in each division.

	Total Overhead Costs	Division A	Division B
Unit-level overhead	$210,000	7,500 units	13,500 units
Batch-level overhead	280,000	50 batches	90 batches
Product line overhead	210,000	10 lines	18 lines
Facility support overhead	200,000	—	—
Total	$900,000		

Compute how much total overhead cost would remain if Division A were eliminated.

Practice 22-15

Activity-Based Management

Which one of the following is a correct flow of information in activity-based management?

a. Activities → Costs → Products
b. Activity Cost Drivers → Performance Measures → Activities
c. Activity Cost Drivers → Activities → Performance Measures
d. Activity Cost Drivers → Activities → Performance Measures
e. Products → Activities → Costs

Practice 22-16

Total Quality Management

Which one of the following statements is *false*?

a. Total quality management is simply a general endorsement of quality in a company.
b. W. Edward Deming led the quality revolution in Japan during the 1950s.
c. Total quality management shifted some of the companies' focus from costs to quality.
d. Statistical process control can help management know whether a process has serious problems.

Practice 22-17

Costs of Quality

Which one of the following is *not* a type of costs of quality?

a. Appraisal costs
b. Adaptive costs
c. Internal failure costs
d. Prevention costs
e. External failure costs

Practice 22-18

Taguchi's Quality Loss Function

The cost required to fix a product defect and get that product on target would cost the company $500. Currently, the product is three standard units from the target specifications. Using Taguchi's quality loss function, compute the total quality loss due to external failures.

e xercises

Exercise 22-1

Product Costing Review

Mad Dog Enterprises manufactures computer game control devices such as joysticks and steering wheels. Following is a list of the costs incurred by Mad Dog in 2006:

Wages paid to assembly workers	$100,000
Cost of plastic used in making devices	25,000
Insurance on factory building	12,000
Salary of factory supervisor	57,000
Interest on money borrowed to finance operations	34,000
Wages paid to factory maintenance workers	61,000
Cost of computer/controller boards installed in devices	38,000
Advertising costs	127,000
Cost of electricity used in factory	46,000

Compute the total cost for each of the following categories:

1. Direct materials
2. Direct labor
3. Manufacturing overhead
4. Period costs

Exercise 22-2

Importance of Manufacturing Overhead Allocation

The percentages of product costs comprised by direct materials, direct labor, and manufacturing overhead for three companies are as follows:

	Company A	Company B	Company C
Direct materials	7%	21%	42%
Direct labor	13	42	49
Manufacturing overhead	80	37	9
	100%	100%	100%

Based on this information, which of these three companies would probably improve its product costing accuracy most by converting to activity-based costing (ABC)? Explain your answer.

Exercise 22-3

Product Cost Hierarchy

For the following list of costs, indicate by the appropriate letter which category of activities each cost applies to: unit level (U), batch level (B), product line (P), or facility support (F):

(continued)

a. Machine fine-tuning adjustment cost (required after the production of each unit)
b. Salary of vice president of finance
c. Machine inspection cost (required after the completion of each day's production)
d. Cost of the external audit firm
e. Direct labor
f. Product testing cost (performed at the start of each day's production)
g. Direct materials
h. Factory security cost
i. Machine straight-line depreciation cost (Generally, machines are dedicated to producing a particular type of product.)
j. Warehousing cost (Each type of product has its own warehouse.)
k. Employee training cost (Training is generally specific to different types of products.)

Exercise 22-4

Spreadsheet

Identifying Cross-Subsidization

Cottrell Company manufactures three products. Gross margin computations for these three products for 2006 are given below.

	Product A	Product B	Product C
Sales	$ 300,000	$ 500,000	$ 600,000
Direct materials	(50,000)	(250,000)	(200,000)
Direct labor	(150,000)	(50,000)	(100,000)
Manufacturing overhead*	(225,000)	(75,000)	(150,000)
Gross margin	$(125,000)	$ 125,000	$ 150,000

*Manufacturing overhead is allocated to production based on the amount of direct labor cost.

Cottrell has reexamined the factors that cause its manufacturing overhead costs and has discovered that the annual amount of manufacturing overhead is more closely related to the number of product batches produced during the year than it is to direct labor costs. The number of batches of the three products for 2006 was as follows: Product A, 10 batches; Product B, 60 batches; Product C, 30 batches.

1. Prepare gross margin calculations for Cottrell's three products assuming that manufacturing overhead is allocated based on the number of batches.
2. Under the direct labor cost method of manufacturing overhead allocation, one of Cottrell's products received a cross-subsidization from the others. Which product received the subsidization, and what was the amount of the subsidization?

Exercise 22-5

Identifying Cross-Subsidization

Halsey, Inc. manufactures two types of baby car seats: standard and deluxe. Information for the year 2006 has been given as follows.

	Standard	Deluxe
Sales price	$50	$80
Units produced and sold	23,400	9,750
Direct materials cost	$195,000	$130,000
Direct labor cost per hour	$10	$10
Direct labor hours	35,100	42,900
Purchase orders	100	25

Manufacturing overhead for the year totals $650,000. Halsey allocates manufacturing overhead by direct labor hour.

1. Prepare gross margin calculations for each product line using direct labor hours as an allocation base.
2. Management has determined that a more correct method of allocating manufacturing overhead is by the number of purchase orders. Prepare new gross margin calculations for management using purchase orders as the allocation base.
3. Assuming that allocating manufacturing overhead by purchase orders is more correct, did one of the product lines receive a cross-subsidization? If so, how much was the cross-subsidization?

Exercise 22-6

Spreadsheet

Allocating Batch-Level and Product Line Manufacturing Overhead Costs

Giles Company has two divisions. Gross margin computations for these two divisions for 2006 are as follows:

	Standard Products	Custom Products
Sales	$1,200,000	$1,800,000
Direct materials	(200,000)	(300,000)
Direct labor	(600,000)	(600,000)
Manufacturing overhead*	(500,000)	(500,000)
Gross margin	$ (100,000)	$ 400,000

*Manufacturing overhead is allocated to production based on the amount of direct labor cost.

Giles has determined that its total manufacturing overhead cost of $1,000,000 is a mixture of batch-level costs and product line costs. Giles has assembled the following information concerning the manufacturing overhead costs, the annual number of production batches in each division, and the number of product lines in each division:

	Total Mfg. Overhead Costs	Standard Products	Custom Products
Batch-level manufacturing overhead	$ 600,000	15 batches	60 batches
Product line manufacturing overhead	400,000	10 lines	30 lines
	$1,000,000		

1. Prepare gross margin calculations for Giles' two divisions assuming that manufacturing overhead is allocated based on the number of batches and number of product lines.
2. Under the direct labor cost method of manufacturing overhead allocation, which division received a cross-subsidization, and what was the amount of the cross-subsidization?

Exercise 22-7

Allocating Batch-Level and Product Line Manufacturing Overhead Costs

Sundance Skis Company is preparing its end-of-year gross margin computations. Sundance Skis manufactures three types of products: skis, snowboards, and snow skates. The following information, as of the end of the year, is available for these products.

(continued)

	Skis	Snowboards	Snow Skates
Total sales revenue	$1,250,000	$1,500,000	$750,000
Units produced	4,500	3,750	6,750
Direct materials	$(625,000)	$(500,000)	$(125,000)
Direct labor	$(125,000)	$(250,000)	$(375,000)
Number of setups	9	18	3
Number of product styles	5	7	3

Total manufacturing overhead is $1,125,000, with $506,250 related to batch-level activities and $618,750 related to product line activities.

1. In the past, Sundance Skis has allocated manufacturing overhead based on the number of units produced. Prepare gross margin calculations for Sundance Skis' three divisions allocating manufacturing overhead according to the number of units produced.
2. After investigation, management at Sundance Skis determined that a more accurate allocation of manufacturing overhead would be to assign these costs using batch-level and product line activities. Prepare gross margin calculations for Sundance Skis' three divisions by assigning manufacturing overhead using batch-level and product line activities. Assume that the number of setups is the activity allocation basis for assigning costs of batch-level activities and that the number of product styles is the allocation base for assigning costs of product line activities.

Exercise 22-8

Common Costs and the Death Spiral
Blaine Avenue Company manufactures three products. Gross margin computations for these three products for 2006 are as follows:

	Product X	**Product Y**	**Product Z**
Sales	$800,000	$ 700,000	$ 600,000
Direct materials	(50,000)	(150,000)	(200,000)
Direct labor	(50,000)	(200,000)	(250,000)
Manufacturing overhead*	(80,000)	(320,000)	(400,000)
Gross margin	$620,000	$ 30,000	$(250,000)

*Manufacturing overhead is allocated to production based on the amount of direct labor cost.

Blaine Avenue has reexamined the activities that relate to its manufacturing overhead costs and has discovered that $500,000 of the annual amount of manufacturing overhead is directly related to the number of product batches produced during the year. The number of batches of the three products for 2006 was as follows: Product X, 100 batches; Product Y, 100 batches; Product Z, 50 batches. The remaining $300,000 in overhead is for facility support (property taxes, security costs, general administration, etc.) and does not vary at all with the level of activity.

1. Prepare gross margin calculations for Blaine Avenue's three products assuming that manufacturing overhead is allocated based on the number of batches. Also, show a "total" column. Facility support costs are not to be allocated to any of the products, but are to be subtracted in the "total" column in the computation of total company operating profit.
2. Using the gross margin numbers prepared under the direct labor cost method of manufacturing overhead allocation, Blaine Avenue's board of directors has tentatively decided to discontinue the Z product line. Assume that this was done at the beginning of 2006. What would have happened to total company operating profit for the year? Explain.

Exercise 22-9

Common Costs and the Death Spiral

Wilken Sandwich Shop maintains three separate menus for breakfast, lunch, and dinner. Gross margin computations for the three menu lines for 2006 are as follows:

	Breakfast	**Lunch**	**Dinner**
Sales	$ 880,000	$1,015,000	$ 720,000
Direct materials	(260,000)	(217,500)	(175,000)
Direct labor	(325,000)	(290,000)	(155,000)
Overhead*	(528,000)	(264,000)	(264,000)
Gross margin	$(233,000)	$ 243,500	$ 126,000

*Overhead is allocated to the menu lines based on the number of customers served each day. In 2006, 4,000 breakfast customers, 2,000 lunch customers, and 2,000 dinner customers were served.

Management at Wilken has tentatively decided to stop serving breakfast in its restaurants because of poor financial performance. Before doing so, they have reexamined the costs of all three menu lines in order to verify that they are correct. Management determined that direct materials and direct labor costs are correct. However, using an activity-based costing approach, they discovered that $408,000 of overhead costs are related to facility support activities and the rest of the overhead ($648,000) is related to the kitchen setup activities required to prepare the menu line each day (a batch-level activity). They determined that a good cost allocation base for batch-level kitchen activities is number of setups per business day. Wilken was open for business 360 days in 2006. The number of daily setup activities for each menu line is as follows:

Breakfast	10
Lunch	15
Dinner	5

1. Since management has tentatively decided to stop serving breakfast, they have asked to see gross margin calculations for the lunch and dinner menus. Assuming the breakfast menu was dropped at the beginning of 2006, prepare gross margin calculations for the lunch and dinner menu lines assuming overhead is allocated based on the number of customers served. Be sure to show a "total" column.
2. Prepare gross margin calculations for Wilken's three menu lines assuming that overhead is assigned using activity-based costing. Facility support costs are not to be allocated to any of the menu lines, but are to be subtracted in the "total" column in the computation of total company operating profit.
3. Using the gross margin numbers prepared in parts (1) and (2), what would have happened to total company operating profit for the year 2006 if Wilken would have dropped its breakfast menu at the beginning of the year? Explain.

Exercise 22-10

Costs of Quality

Some of the costs in the list below are costs of quality. For each cost, indicate by the appropriate letter what type of cost it is: prevention cost (P), appraisal cost (A), internal failure cost (I), external failure cost (E), or not a cost of quality (N/A).

a. Cost of raw materials used in discarded, defective products
b. Salary of the president of the company
c. Cost to purchase product testing equipment
d. Lawsuit costs stemming from the sale of defective products
e. Cost to repair defective products before shipment

(continued)

 f. Employee quality training costs

 g. Employee downtime caused by production halts to repair defective products

 h. Cost of sampling raw materials to ensure quality

 i. Customer warranty costs

 j. Property taxes

 k. Cost of lost reputation (i.e., lost sales)

 l. Cost to help suppliers improve their product shipping procedures

 m. Interest cost on short-term loans

 n. Production process design costs

Exercise 22-11

Costs of Quality

Sara's Stylish Suppers prepares food for wholesale to gourmet restaurants. Quality is very important to consumers of gourmet food. Following is a list of costs that Sara incurred during 2006:

Wages paid during downtime to fix machinery	$ 50,000
Cost of spoiled raw materials (cheese, meat, etc.)	85,000
Training cost for new food handlers	12,000
Wages paid to food samplers	15,000
Lawsuits for severe food poisoning	134,000
Cost of refrigerator used to keep food fresh	75,000
Wages paid to quality inspectors	21,000
Wages paid to chefs who create new gourmet dishes	97,000
Wages paid for redoing poor quality food (found before delivery)	46,000

In addition, Sara's accountants estimated approximately $100,000 in lost sales due to restaurant managers who are unhappy with Sara's products and service.

 Compute the total cost for each of the following categories:

1. Prevention costs

2. Appraisal costs

3. Internal failure costs

4. External failure costs

Exercise 22-12

Optimal Level of Costs of Quality

Beki Browne is planning to open her own homebuilding company. Beki is trying to decide whether to provide low-quality homes, average-quality homes, or high-quality homes. Beki has analyzed the costs of quality related to building homes and has developed the following analysis of the costs of quality:

- *Prevention costs:* The best way to ensure the quality of a home is to hire good subcontractors and use quality materials. Of course, high-quality subcontractors and materials cost more.

- *Appraisal costs:* To improve the quality of the homes, Beki can hire independent verifiers to determine whether the home is adequately livable and "up to code."

- *Internal failure costs:* Sometimes a defect in the home is found just before the home is to be sold. In such a case, Beki must require the subcontractors to spend extra time fixing the home.

- *External failure costs:* If a home containing lots of defects is sold, the bad reputation created will hurt potential future sales. To counteract this effect, Beki must spend more on advertising.

Beki has gathered the following numerical information about the costs of quality in relation to building homes:

	Low Quality	Average Quality	High Quality
Prevention costs:			
Hours spent building home	1,400 hours	1,600 hours	1,800 hours
Subcontractor salary rate	$35/hour	$45/hour	$55/hour
Materials cost per home	$50,000	$60,000	$70,000
Appraisal costs:			
Verifier hours spent on home	4 hours	10 hours	20 hours
Verifier salary rate	$20/hour	$20/hour	$20/hour
Internal failure costs:			
Hours spent fixing home	350 hours	175 hours	15 hours
Subcontractor salary rate	$35/hour	$45/hour	$55/hour
Materials cost for repairs	$10,000	$7,000	$3,000
External failure costs:			
Cost of advertising	$40,000	$10,000	$2,000

Which type of home—low-, average-, or high-quality—should Beki build in order to minimize her total costs of quality? Show your calculations.

Exercise 22-13

$Spreadsheet$

Taguchi Quality Loss Function

Cooley Lane Company manufactures computer disk drives. Occasionally, a defective disk drive (one that spins at the wrong revolutions per minute) is shipped to a customer. Cooley Lane's policy is to fix the drive for free when it is returned by a complaining customer. Cooley Lane has a standardized statistical defect measure whereby each defective drive is given a score of 0 through 5 to indicate how bad it is, with 5 being the worst. A perfect drive receives a score of 0. The direct material and direct labor cost to fix a defective drive is only $25.

The manager in charge of product quality has recently been reading about the Taguchi quality loss function, and she thinks that Cooley Lane is underestimating the external failure costs associated with a defective disk drive. She thinks that Cooley Lane should consider increasing the amount it spends on prevention and appraisal in order to reduce the number of defective drives returned by customers. In the past month, 15 drives have been returned by customers. The drives had the following standardized defect scores:

Standardized Defect Score	Number of Defective Drives
1	2
2	1
3	1
4	4
5	7

Using the Taguchi quality loss function, estimate the dollar value of the quality loss associated with the external failure of these defective drives.

Exercise 22-14

Taguchi Quality Loss Function

Tenille's Toyshack is an online toy store. Customers can log on to the Internet to see Tenille's selection of toys and to make purchases. Tenille's shipping policy is that it will ship any order within 24 hours after the purchase is made. After a purchase has been made, Tenille prepares the purchase order and sends an email notification to all customers as soon as the purchase has been shipped. Tenille provides a $20 store credit if the purchase is not shipped within 24 hours after purchase. Following is information on the purchases that were not shipped within 24 hours of being purchased during the past quarter, listed in order of the number of days the order was actually late.

Number of Purchases Not Shipped in 24 Hours	Number of Days Late
4	6
8	5
15	4
9	3
22	2
31	1
89	

Using the above information and the Taguchi quality loss function, estimate the dollar value of the quality loss associated with the external failure of Tenille's shipping methods.

p roblems

Problem 22-1

Identifying Cross-Subsidization

Rockwell Company has three operating divisions. Gross margin computations for these three divisions for 2006 are given below.

	Division M	Division N	Division O
Sales	$ 600,000	$ 400,000	$ 300,000
Direct materials	(100,000)	(200,000)	(80,000)
Direct labor	(300,000)	(60,000)	(140,000)
Manufacturing overhead*	(210,000)	(42,000)	(98,000)
Gross margin	$ (10,000)	$ 98,000	$ (18,000)

*Manufacturing overhead is allocated to production based on the amount of direct labor cost.

Rockwell has determined that its total manufacturing overhead cost of $350,000 is a mixture of batch-level costs and product line costs. Rockwell has assembled the following information concerning the overhead costs, the annual number of production batches in each division, and the number of product lines in each division:

	Total Mfg. Overhead Costs	Division M	Division N	Division O
Batch-level overhead	$200,000	20 batches	80 batches	100 batches
Product line overhead	150,000	10 lines	30 lines	40 lines
	$350,000			

Required:

1. Prepare gross margin calculations for Rockwell's three divisions assuming that manufacturing overhead is allocated based on the number of batches and the number of product lines.
2. Under the direct labor cost method of manufacturing overhead allocation, one or more of Rockwell's divisions received a cross-subsidization from one or more of the others. Which division(s) received subsidizations, and what was the amount of the subsidizations?
3. After preparing the gross margin calculations in part (1), what advice do you have for Rockwell concerning whether it should shut down any of its three divisions? Is this the same advice that would come from looking at the original gross margin calculations using manufacturing overhead allocated according to direct labor cost? Why is there a difference?

Problem 22-2

Allocating Unit-Level, Batch-Level, and Product Line Manufacturing Overhead Costs

Solar Salt Company has two divisions. Gross margin computations for these two divisions for 2006 are given below.

	Agricultural Products	Retail Products
Sales	$1,600,000	$ 900,000
Direct materials	(100,000)	(50,000)
Direct labor	(900,000)	(500,000)
Manufacturing overhead*	(450,000)	(250,000)
Gross margin	$ 150,000	$ 100,000

*Manufacturing overhead is allocated to production based on the amount of direct labor cost.

Solar Salt has determined that its total manufacturing overhead cost of $700,000 is a mixture of unit-level costs, batch-level costs, and product line costs. Solar Salt has assembled the following information concerning the manufacturing overhead costs, the annual number of units produced, production batches, and number of product lines in each division:

	Total Mfg. Overhead Costs	Agricultural Products	Retail Products
Unit-level overhead	$210,000	13,500 units	7,500 units
Batch-level overhead	280,000	90 batches	50 batches
Product line overhead	210,000	18 lines	10 lines
	$700,000		

(continued)

Required:

1. Prepare gross margin calculations for Solar Salt's two divisions assuming that manufacturing overhead is allocated based on the number of units, number of batches, and number of product lines.
2. Comment on the comparison between the original overhead allocation done using direct labor cost and the manufacturing overhead allocation done in part (1).
3. Repeat part (1), assuming the following information concerning the number of units, batches, and product lines in each division.

	Total Mfg. Overhead Costs	Agricultural Products	Retail Products
Unit-level overhead	$210,000	13,500 units	7,500 units
Batch-level overhead	280,000	50 batches	90 batches
Product line overhead	210,000	10 lines	18 lines
	$700,000		

Problem 22-3

Spreadsheet

Identifying and Using Volume-Based and Activity-Based Cost Allocation Rates

Rane Company produces electronic fish finders. It makes two different fish finders: the standard model, which is produced in bulk and sells for $150, and the deluxe model, which comes in various configurations and sells for $300. Rane's engineering and design overhead cost for 2006 is $60,000. The following information relates to production in 2006:

Number of different machine setups needed for a standard model production run	4
Number of different machine setups needed for a deluxe model production run	11
Number of standard fish finders produced	22,000
Number of deluxe fish finders produced	8,000
Number of engineering design changes needed on the standard model	6
Number of engineering design changes needed on the deluxe model	2
Average batch size per production run for standard model	400
Average batch size per production run for deluxe model	200

Required:

1. Determine the engineering and design costs to be assigned to standard and deluxe fish finders using the following allocation methods:
   a. Number of units produced
   b. Number of setups required
   c. Number of engineering design changes needed
2. Which allocation method do you believe is more equitable?

Problem 22-4

Common Costs and the Death Spiral

Ashlyn Company manufactures three products. Gross margin computations for these three products for 2006 are as follows:

	Widgets	**Gidgets**	**Zidgets**
Sales	$ 600,000	$ 525,000	$ 450,000
Direct materials	(112,500)	(37,500)	(150,000)
Direct labor	(37,500)	(150,000)	(187,500)
Manufacturing overhead*	(60,000)	(240,000)	(300,000)
Gross margin	$ 390,000	$ 97,500	$(187,500)

*Manufacturing overhead is allocated to production based on the amount of direct labor cost.

Ashlyn has reexamined the factors that cause its manufacturing overhead costs and has discovered that $225,000 of the annual amount of manufacturing overhead is directly related to the number of product batches produced during the year. The number of batches of the three products for 2006 was as follows: Widgets, 225 batches; Gidgets, 150 batches; Zidgets, 75 batches. The remaining $375,000 in manufacturing overhead is for facility support (property taxes, security costs, general administration, etc.) and does not vary at all with levels of manufacturing activity in the company.

Required:

1. Assume that the Zidget product was eliminated at the start of the year. Estimate what the gross margin for the remaining two products would have been. Use the direct labor cost method of overhead allocation.
2. Now, assume that both the Gidget and Zidget products were eliminated at the start of the year. Estimate what the gross margin for the remaining product, Widgets, would have been. (Note that no manufacturing overhead allocation computation is needed because there is only one product.)
3. In light of your answers in parts (1) and (2), what problems can arise when facility support manufacturing overhead costs are allocated?
4. Prepare gross margin calculations for Ashlyn's three products assuming that manufacturing overhead is allocated based on the number of batches. Also, show a "total" column. Facility support costs are not to be allocated to any of the products, but are to be subtracted in the "total" column in the computation of total company operating profit.

Problem 22-5

Manufacturing Overhead Allocation Using Activity-Based Costing

The following information is given for Greenbaum Manufacturing Company:

	Product A	**Product B**	**Product C**	**Product D**
Units produced	3,000	3,450	2,875	2,400
Direct materials cost	$135,000	$169,050	$149,500	$103,200
Direct labor cost	$75,000	$124,200	$117,875	$93,600

Manufacturing Overhead	**Mfg. Overhead Costs**	**Relevant Activities**
Engineering	$209,950	Engineering changes
Quality control	129,500	Number of setups
Maintenance	41,065	Maintenance hours worked in each area of production
Manufacturing support	93,800	Production volume (units produced)

(continued)

Activities	Product A	Product B	Product C	Product D
Engineering changes	300	150	275	125
Number of setups	12	5	9	11
Maintenance hours worked in each area of production ...	45	49	56	41
Production volume	3,000	3,450	2,875	2,400

Required:
1. Determine the ABC allocation rate for each activity (i.e., each manufacturing overhead cost pool).
2. Determine the manufacturing overhead cost for each product.
3. If Products A, B, C, and D sell for $130, $125, $156, and $166, respectively, determine the gross margin for Greenbaum's four products. Assume all units are sold.

Problem 22-6

Manufacturing Overhead Allocation Using Activity-Based Costing

Rick's Crane Company manufactures three different crane engines with 50 horsepower (hp), 60 horsepower, and 70 horsepower engines, respectively. Relevant information for each engine is provided as follows:

	50 hp Total	50 hp Per Unit	60 hp Total	60 hp Per Unit	70 hp Total	70 hp Per Unit
Units produced	2,500		2,000		1,500	
Direct materials cost	$425,000	$170	$370,000	$185	$360,000	$240
Direct labor cost	$595,000	$238	$510,000	$255	$472,500	$315
Sales price		$450		$540		$630
Purchases per year	44		52		54	
Number of machine setups per year ..	60		68		80	
Engineering change orders per year ..	72		84		100	

Total manufacturing overhead cost pools:

Engineering	$102,400
Quality control	88,400
Purchasing costs	49,200
Machine maintenance costs	81,000
Total costs	$321,000

Required:
1. Determine the gross margin for each product allocating manufacturing overhead costs on the basis of production volume (units produced).
2. Identify appropriate allocation bases for each of the four pools of manufacturing overhead costs.
3. Determine the ABC allocation rates for each of the four cost pools suggested in part (2).
4. Using the allocation bases suggested in part (2), determine manufacturing overhead costs per product.
5. a. Determine the gross margin per product using the manufacturing overhead costs determined in part (4).
   b. **Interpretive Question:** Which of the methods (unit-based costing or activity-based costing) is the better method to allocate the manufacturing overhead costs?

Problem 22-7

Manufacturing Overhead Allocation with Multiple Products

Schmidt Electronics produces two products: CD105 and HD210. Relevant costing information for each product is as follows:

Per Unit	CD105	HD210
Direct materials	$10.50	$17.25
Direct labor	$10.00	$15.00
Direct labor hours per unit	1	2
Total number of machine setups	400	200
Units produced	6,000	7,000

Manufacturing overhead costs and associated ABC allocation bases are as follows:

	Mfg. Overhead Costs	Allocation Bases
Product inspection	$30,000	Units produced
Materials management	48,000	Number of machine setups
Manufacturing support	16,000	Product lines

Required:

1. If manufacturing overhead is allocated on the basis of direct labor hours, compute the cost per unit for CD105 and HD210.
2. Determine the allocation rate per activity for each ABC allocation basis.
3. Determine the manufacturing overhead cost for each product using your answer to part (2).
4. Using your answer to part (3), compute the cost per unit for CD105 and HD210.
5. Compare your answers to part (1) and part (4). Why the difference in costs?

Problem 22-8

Activity-Based Costing and Gross Margin Calculations

Stafford Manufacturing, Inc., produces two different products. Product 1 sells for $950 each, and Product 2 sells for $700 each. Estimated annual production and sales for Product 1 and Product 2 are 2,100 units and 2,900 units, respectively. Direct materials are $350 for Product 1 and $200 for Product 2. Direct labor costs are $300 for Product 1 and $310 for Product 2. Stafford purchases materials for Product 1 every month and for Product 2 every two months. On average, Stafford performs 10 setups each month for Product 1 production and 8 setups each month for Product 2 production. The following are manufacturing overhead costs incurred by Stafford Manufacturing:

Quality control	$150,000
Purchasing costs	74,880
Miscellaneous manufacturing overhead	62,640

Required:

1. Assuming that the allocation bases for the three manufacturing overhead costs are production volume for quality control, number of purchases for purchasing costs, and number of setups for miscellaneous manufacturing overhead, calculate the cost per unit of each allocation basis.
2. Determine total manufacturing overhead costs for each product.
3. Determine the gross margin percent for Stafford Manufacturing for each product it produces.

Problem 22-9

Allocation of Manufacturing Overhead with Multiple Products

Geddy, Inc., is a manufacturing firm that manufactures two types of boat engines. The Type A engine is designed for a specific type of cruise ship. Because of a long-term commitment with

(continued)

a cruise company, Type A engines need no modifications. Type B engines are designed for slightly smaller cruise ships. Because the Type B engine is designed for several different models of cruise ships and the mounting hardware is different for each, retooling is regularly required. Costs for the two types of engines are presented here:

	Type A Engine (200 Units Produced)		Type B Engine (90 Units Produced)	
	Total	**Per Unit**	**Total**	**Per Unit**
Direct materials cost	$176,000,000	$880,000	$70,200,000	$780,000
Direct labor cost	147,000,000	735,000	60,300,000	670,000
Manufacturing overhead costs:				
Engineering costs			$144,000,000	
Quality control			38,880,000	
Utilities and maintenance			1,305,000	

Required:

1. Determine the amount of manufacturing overhead to be assigned to each unit of activity assuming the following ABC information:

    Manufacturing Overhead Cost
    *   Engineering costs
    *   Quality control
    *   Utilities and maintenance

    Allocation Bases
    *   Engineering change orders per unit
    *   Machine setups per unit
    *   Production volume

    Type A Engines
    *   0 engineering change orders per unit
    *   9 machine setups per unit
    *   200 units produced

    Type B Engines
    *   8 engineering change orders per unit
    *   16 machine setups per unit
    *   90 units produced

2. Determine the amount of manufacturing overhead to be assigned to each type of engine.
3. Compute the gross margin on Type A and Type B engines assuming selling prices of $2,000,000 and $2,300,000, respectively.

Problem 22-10

Allocation of Manufacturing Overhead with Multiple Products

Macey Sprinkling Company produces two types of pipe: (1) lawn sprinkler pipe and (2) building sprinkler pipe. Relevant information for the production of the two types of pipe for 2006 is as follows:

	Lawn Sprinkler Pipe	**Building Sprinkler Pipe**
Feet produced	325,000	150,000
Prime costs	$243,750	$123,000
Manufacturing overhead costs:		
Utilities	$ 75,000	$ 40,000
Support staff	63,000	35,750
Quality control	8,000	4,060
Purchasing	19,200	10,250

Macey allocates utilities and support staff costs on the basis of production volume, quality control costs on the basis of number of machine setups required, and purchasing department costs on the basis of number of purchase orders. During 2006, volume of these various activities per *product line* was:

	Lawn Sprinkler Pipe	Building Sprinkler Pipe
Production volume	325,000 feet	150,000 feet
Machine setups	12	24
Purchase orders	1	30

Required:

1. Determine the cost per unit for each cost driver.
2. Determine the amount of manufacturing overhead to be assigned to the two types of sprinkler pipe.
3. Determine the total cost for each type of pipe produced for the year.

Problem 22-11

Costs of Quality

DeeAnn Martinez is preparing to open her own CPA firm. DeeAnn is a smart businessperson and wants to maximize her profits. She has not yet decided whether to run a low-quality CPA firm (basically offering to sign the financial statements of anyone who will pay her fee), an average CPA firm, or a premium-quality CPA firm (competing head-to-head with the large international accounting firms such as PRICEWATERHOUSE COOPERS).

DeeAnn has analyzed the costs of quality related to operating a CPA firm and has developed the following analysis:

- *Prevention costs:* The best way to ensure the quality of the audit is to increase the quality of the staff hired and to increase the time that the staff spends on each audit. DeeAnn realizes that hiring higher-quality staff will cost more.
- *Appraisal costs:* DeeAnn plans to inspect the work of the staff auditors by having audit managers review the work. The average salary rate for an audit manager (including all fringe benefits) is $50 per hour.
- *Internal failure costs:* Sometimes the audit team will do such a poor job that one of DeeAnn's audit partners will have to personally supervise the completion of the audit work. The average salary rate for an audit partner is $100 per hour.
- *External failure costs:* If investors or creditors rely on financial statements that later prove to be false, the audit firm that approved those financial statements will probably be sued. Of course, the frequency of being sued, and the cost of each lawsuit, will be higher if DeeAnn decides to provide low-quality audits.

DeeAnn has gathered the following numerical information about the costs of quality in relation to operating a CPA firm:

	Low Quality	Average Quality	Premium Quality
Prevention costs:			
Staff hours spent on audit	10 hours	30 hours	100 hours
Staff salary rate	$20/hour	$25/hour	$35/hour
Appraisal costs:			
Manager review of audit work	1 hour	5 hours	20 hours
Internal failure costs:			
Frequency of bad audits	1 in 3	1 in 10	1 in 50
Partner time to fix bad audit	10 hours	5 hours	3 hours
External failure costs:			
Frequency of lawsuits	1 in 5	1 in 40	1 in 100
Expected loss on each lawsuit	$200,000	$100,000	$100,000

(continued)

Required:
1. Assume that the revenue from each audit is the same no matter what the quality of the audit. Therefore, in order to maximize her profits, DeeAnn must minimize the expected cost of each audit. Which type of audit firm—low quality, average quality, or premium quality—should DeeAnn operate in order to maximize her expected profit per audit? Show your calculations.
2. Comment on whether the assumption about revenue made in part (1) seems appropriate.

Problem 22-12

Taguchi Quality Loss Function

TAC Computers is a nationwide distributor of personal computers for home and business use. Its main sales channels are the Internet and telephone sales. Customers either call in to TAC's customer sales center or log on to TAC's Web site to place orders for custom-made computers. One of TAC's distinguishing marketing strategies is its three-year 24 × 7 customer support call center. All TAC customers have the ability to call the customer support center 24 hours a day, seven days a week to receive technical assistance with their machine. TAC prides itself on the high quality of service in this call center. Every customer call is immediately followed with either an e-mail or a postcard survey that asks the customer to provide feedback on the experience and answer the following questions:

1. Was your concern or question thoroughly resolved by the TAC technician?
2. Did the TAC technician handle your call with courtesy and professionalism?

Technicians' performance on the first question is referred to as the "error rate." Performance on the second question is referred to as the "care rate." The customer support call center management team uses performance on the error rate and care rate to manage operations and determine additional training needed by individual call center technicians. Performance on these two measures has been quite good for TAC. The TAC standard for each technician is to have no more than 1% complaints per month on the first question and no more than 0.5% complaints per month on the second question (a full-time technician handles 600 calls per month on average). Management feels that 99% quality on error and 99.5% quality on care is an excellent performance level for this industry.

Currently, few technicians need additional training each month. However, if a technician's error rate exceeds 1% of any month's call volume, that technician goes through a skills verification test to identify areas of weakness in handling specific technical issues, then undergoes some customized training. The cost of running a technician through this analysis and training process is estimated to be about $600. In the event that a technician's care rate exceeds 0.5% of a month's call volume, a manager is assigned to observe the technician in order to identify specific problems in working with customers. Then the technician works through a specialized training program based on the manager's assessment. The average cost of running a technician through this process is about $900.

As the controller for TAC Computers, you've been reading lately about the opportunity costs of low quality, and you're concerned that management of the customer support call center may not recognize the significant cost of lost sales that result when the company's reputation is hurt by technician error or lack of care for the customer.

Required:
1. Assuming that the Taguchi quality loss function is approximately accurate in measuring TAC's quality loss due to the external failure of handling customer calls, calculate the opportunity cost of lost sales when a technician's error rate hits 1%. Calculate the opportunity cost of lost sales when a technician's care rate hits 0.5%.

2. Explain to the management team of the customer support call center how they should interpret and use these Taguchi calculations to improve the operations in their center.

Problem 22-13

Taguchi Quality Loss Function

NorseLabs is a manufacturer of helium-neon (HeNe) lasers used in research. In order to have the maximum amount of energy produced, HeNe lasers must have certain proportions of helium and neon gases. The combination should be 15% helium and 85% neon. There can be an error of $\pm 0.5\%$ of either gas without noticeable energy loss. HeNe lasers must perform within this specification range before they can be approved for delivery to customers.

Each HeNe laser is sold for $600. NorseLabs offers a limited warranty on each HeNe laser sold. If a laser is not performing properly, NorseLabs exchanges the malfunctioning laser for a new laser at a cost to the consumer of 40% of the new laser. The old laser is then refurbished and re-sold. Refurbishing a laser costs NorseLabs $350. A refurbished laser can be resold for $450.

In the past month, NorseLabs has had to exchange and replace 15 lasers. NorseLabs' engineers estimate that these 15 lasers had the average error of approximately $\pm 0.3\%$ from the 15% target ratio in helium and 85% target ratio for neon, which is within the company's established control limits. The controller at NorseLabs, Ronda, has been learning about the high costs of external failure and the Taguchi quality loss function. She is concerned that NorseLabs is underestimating the cost of replacing defective lasers.

Required:

1. Use the Taguchi quality loss function to approximate NorseLabs' quality loss due to external failure of the 15 defective lasers during the past month. Assume that error distance in the gas ratio is measured in 0.01% units. Hence, the 15 returned lasers are measuring 30 units (0.3% ÷ 0.01%) from the targeted gas combination ratio.
2. Help Ronda explain to management at NorseLabs how they should interpret and use the Taguchi calculations [from part (1)] to improve the operations at NorseLabs.
3. Assume management at NorseLabs has decided to improve the process in which gas is measured in its lasers before being sold to a consumer. Management wants to reach a balance between prevention costs, appraisal costs, internal failure costs, and external failure costs. Management determines that this balance should be reached if the Taguchi calculation each month does not exceed $104,000. Assume that NorseLabs sells 100 lasers on average each month. Using the Taguchi quality loss function, determine the maximum average distance from its gas combination target that NorseLabs can have and still remain below a $104,000 external failure cost.

discussion cases

Case 22-1

Stott Knife Company

Stott Knife Company produces three models of kitchen knives: Dicer, Slicer, and CutsAll. Sales and costing information for the three models are as follows:

	Dicer	Slicer	CutsAll
Selling price per unit	$35	$65	$80
Units produced	26,000	16,000	12,000
Direct materials cost	$410,000	$215,000	$125,000
Direct labor cost	$110,000	$45,000	$35,000

In the past, manufacturing overhead has been allocated based on number of units produced. Manufacturing overhead for the period is $810,000, and the predetermined overhead rate is $15 per unit produced.

Based on this information, management has determined that the Dicer is barely breaking even. Because the market for knives is quite competitive, the price for each model is set by the market—not by management. Thus, increasing the price charged for products is not an option. As a result, management is considering discontinuing the Dicer. Before making a final decision, management has come to you for advice. You collect the following information regarding manufacturing overhead:

(continued)

Manufacturing Overhead	Manufacturing Overhead Costs	Allocation Bases
Engineering	$125,000	Engineering changes
Quality control	375,000	Number of units produced
Manufacturing support	310,000	Number of setups
Total overhead	$810,000	

Allocation Bases	Dicer	Slicer	CutsAll
Engineering changes	2	7	6
Number of units produced . .	26,000	16,000	12,000
Number of setups	28	77	65

Determine the gross profit for each model under the current manufacturing overhead allocation scheme. Determine the manufacturing overhead cost for each model using the information relating to activities. Determine the gross profit for each model using the ABC allocated manufacturing overhead. What recommendation would you make to management regarding its decision to discontinue the Dicer?

Case 22-2

Costs of Quality (Starving Sailor Restaurant)

You are the leader of a group of investors that is planning to open a nationwide chain of seafood restaurants that you will call "Starving Sailor Restaurant." You are preparing for a strategy meeting that will be held tomorrow. The investor group is considering two strategies for how the restaurant chain will be operated. One strategy, which you have titled "Classy," proposes to market the restaurant chain as the quality leader among seafood restaurants. The restaurants will be located in good neighborhoods, will offer choice seafood selections, and will have an excellent cleanup crew. Each restaurant will also have a trained manager on site during business hours to handle customer complaints in addition to a national troubleshooting team that will promptly fly to any location to investigate consistent patterns in customer complaints received via a toll-free complaint hotline.

You have titled the other strategy "Tight Budget." The restaurants will be located wherever cheap real estate can be found, will be staffed with the lowest-cost labor possible, and will focus on offering low-cost food. There will be no mechanism for receiving customer complaints, and the store manager will not be trained in customer satisfaction.

A significant portion of the investor group advocates the "Tight Budget" strategy, arguing that it offers the lowest operating costs and, therefore, the highest profit. You are worried that these investors may not have thought carefully about all the costs associated with this strategy. Using the costs of quality (COQ) categories, outline some of the major costs that will differ between these two restaurant strategies.

 j u d g m e n t   c a l l s

Judgment 22-1

You Decide: Does cost information provide help in running a business, or is it only useful within the bounds of an accounting system?

Your friends in the MBA program at your university seem to think that cost information in a company is helpful but that it is rarely used in the decision-making process within a company. One friend said, "You have to know how to work with people and manage what they do on a day-to-day basis. Cost information has its place and time, but is often not relevant. The executives in upper management have more important things to consider in running a business than the cost of products and services!" Do you agree or disagree?

Judgment 22-2

You Decide: Does total quality management help a company revamp and improve its business operations, or is it too much of an administrative burden that takes away from the company's primary goals?

Over the last 20 years, there have been many new developments in the area of total quality management. Companies strive to increase profitability by improving their products and processes. However, you are still a bit skeptical. At your current place of employment, your boss has heard about TQM and tries to meet at least every six weeks to talk about what is being done in implementing TQM and what could be improved. You don't see any benefits from the meetings. Nothing that is brought up in the meetings is ever implemented. It just seems to be an opportunity to meet with your friends and have a free lunch. Are you wasting your time?

▶ **Analyzing Real Company Information**   ▶ **The Debate**
▶ **International Case**   ▶ **Internet Search**
▶ **Ethics Case**
▶ **Writing Assignment**

The following additional assignments provide opportunities for students to develop critical thinking, ethical perspectives, oral and written communication skills, experience with electronic research, and teamwork through group and business activities.

▷ *Analyzing Real Company Information*

Analyzing 22-I (Microsoft)

MICROSOFT, like most other companies, is continually striving to appropriately allocate costs and to increase the quality of its products. We have studied Microsoft's financial statements in past chapters. Now it is time to think beyond the numbers and examine other factors that might affect a firm's performance. Use your knowledge of Microsoft and your understanding of the computer software industry to answer the following questions:

1. What types of overhead costs might Microsoft incur that would be associated with its software products? Identify several cost drivers that Microsoft might consider in allocating overhead using the ABC method of overhead allocation.
2. What sort of product quality issues might Microsoft face associated with its software? List the various costs of quality associated with a faulty software product.

Analyzing 22-2 (Deluxe Corporation)

DELUXE CORPORATION (DELUXE) is the world's largest printer of checks as well as a provider of electronic products and services to financial institutions and retail companies. The company produces more of the nearly 42.5 billion checks written by American consumers and businesses annually than any other check printer. In fact, Deluxe printed enough checks in 2001 that if lined up end to end would stretch to the moon and back. The company serves nearly 1.8 million small businesses annually and provides 2 million products—each with personalized information, most within two days of receiving the order, with 98% order accuracy. Revenues in 2002 were $1.28 billion, with operating income of $214 million. Deluxe was recently ranked by *Fortune* magazine as the 936th largest U.S. company.

Although Deluxe has been profitable in all but one year since it was founded in 1915, market shifts in 1997 from paper-based to electronic transactions were causing margins to erode and revenues to decline in Deluxe's core checkprinting business. These competitive pressures brought about many changes at Deluxe in regards to management and strategy. The centerpiece of all these changes to its management process was a new measure called Deluxe value added (DVA). DVA measures the incremental profits of customers and customer segments after the costs of capital assets required to support these customers are covered. This focus on the profitability of customers was a significant change in view from the company's previous focus on the profitability of its check products.

Measurement of DVA at Deluxe requires accurate cost information. However, at the time that Deluxe adopted DVA, Deluxe's costing system was used primarily to value its check inventory for financial statement purposes. Hence, in 1997 the company decided to implement an activity-based costing (ABC) system to measure the costs of specific customers. A comprehensive project structure was put into place in order to design and implement the new ABC system. An executive sponsor provided focus, resources, and leadership and reviewed performance. A steering committee approved the project plan, established priorities, and approved ongoing progress and results. Two project managers were responsible for quality control, problem resolution, leadership, and training. Field teams consisting of full- and part-time members were responsible for executing the work plan.

A multi-phased project was initiated with a timeline of six months. The plan included forming project teams, analyzing activities and linking costs to customers, analyzing customer profitability, and building a sustainable ABC information system that could be updated on a regular basis as activities and customers changed.

Answer the following questions:

1. Deluxe implemented ABC over a time period of six months. Does this time period seem too short, too long, or just right? Explain your answer.
2. Upon implementing ABC, Deluxe involved teams and groups from various departments within the company. Why do you think it was important for Deluxe to involve so many employees in its implementation of ABC?
3. Is Deluxe's approach to implementation likely to increase or decrease management's use of ABC information for decision making? Explain your answer.

Source: Adapted from P. B. B. Turney, "Deluxe Corporation: Activity-Based Costing," University of Virginia Darden School Foundation (1999).

▶ *International Case*

International

Deming in Japan
As noted in this chapter, the ideas of W. Edward Deming received little attention in the United States in the late 1940s and early 1950s. Deming then moved to Japan where his ideas were accepted and implemented almost immediately. The result was that industries in Japan, such as automobile production, quickly developed a reputation for producing quality products. In the 1980s, the United States found itself trying to catch up to the Japanese in the race for quality products. Can you speculate as to why Deming's ideas were not readily accepted in the United States, yet were quickly adopted in Japan? To answer this question, you may need to recall your world history during the 1940s.

▶ *Ethics Case*

Minuteman Enterprises
You are the controller for Minuteman Enterprises, a manufacturer of rocket booster engines and various aerospace products. Though there are many commercial customers for most of the company's products, the federal government is the only buyer of your rocket booster engines. Because you are the only provider for the engines, the government has agreed to buy these engines at a price equal to your cost plus a 10% markup.

As the controller, you have recently been studying the accuracy of your product costs. Traditionally, manufacturing overhead has been allocated on the basis of direct labor hours. Using this method, rocket boosters have borne a high percentage of manufacturing overhead because they take many more direct labor hours than do the other products.

You have just been presented an analysis by one of your staff members that shows that direct labor hours is not a very relevant base for allocating manufacturing overhead costs.

Rather, she has made a very convincing case that manufacturing overhead should be allocated using activity-based costing with multiple cost drivers. Using her suggested approach, however, you discover that the rocket boosters bear a much smaller portion of manufacturing overhead costs, and therefore, the total cost of the boosters is considerably less than the amount you had been using to determine the price charged to the government.

You know that her calculations using ABC are likely more accurate than the current cost allocation method and that the commercial products should bear a larger amount of manufacturing overhead costs. Yet, you also know that by using ABC and the more accurate cost drivers, your profits from both the boosters and the commercial products will be reduced.

1. What should you do?
2. Is it ethical to continue to allocate manufacturing overhead costs on the basis of direct labor hours?
3. Would it be ethical to use direct labor hours if that were the basis used by other government contractors?
4. If you decide to switch to ABC, should you inform the government that you have overcharged it and return the excess profits?

Writing Assignment

Advantages and Disadvantages of ABC
Your boss recently attended a conference where activity-based costing was discussed. She is intrigued by the ABC concept and wonders if the company is appropriately costing its products. Your company produces and sells four different styles of briefcases. The production process differs for each briefcase, as different features require different equipment. She returns from the conference and asks you to summarize the advantages and disadvantages of ABC. Your assignment is to write a two-page memo addressing these issues.

The Debate

ABC or Bust!
As the text indicates, activity-based costing has received much attention from businesses around the world. Yet some firms still resist adopting an ABC system, and others have adopted ABC and then reverted to their more traditional costing systems. Divide your group into two teams and prepare five-minute presentations defending the following positions:

- Team One is "In Support of ABC." Your team's task is to identify the benefits of using an activity-based product costing system. Briefly explain the advantages that a company will realize if it adopts ABC.
- Team Two is "In Support of Tradition." Your team's task is to identify the benefits of using a more traditional product costing system based on, for example, direct labor hours. Explain the advantages of a traditional system that cause many firms to still choose it over ABC.

Internet Search

The W. Edwards Deming Institute
The home page for the W. EDWARDS DEMING INSTITUTE can be found at **http://www.deming .org.** Go to this Web site to learn more about the Deming Institute and the Deming Prize and

answer the following questions. Sometimes Web addresses change, so if this address does not work, access the Web site for this textbook (**http://albrecht.swlearning.com**) for an updated link.

1. When was the Deming Institute founded, where is it headquartered, and what is its purpose?
2. What is the history of the Deming Prize?
3. What organization won the 2002 Deming Quality Control Award for Operations Business Units?

Part

8

Evaluation

c h a p t e r

23

Making Decisions Using Relevant Information

After studying this chapter, you should be able to:

Learning Objectives

1 Explain how evaluation leads to planning and why products and processes must be continuously evaluated.

2 Understand why benchmarking is so important and how it is conducted.

3 Understand the concepts of sunk costs and differential costs and revenues, and be able to identify those costs and revenues that are relevant to making product and process decisions.

4 Identify several examples of product and process evaluation decisions, and be able to analyze and select the best alternative for each example.

e×panded *Material*

5 Understand the theory of constraints and how focusing on scarce resources can direct activities in manufacturing companies.

chapter 23

Consider the following three scenarios:

- You are the general manager of a professional basketball team. You have decided to keep a player on your team who has a multi-year, multi-million dollar salary contract even though the player is not playing well. To make room for this fading star, you cut a young, promising, inexpensive player. You make this decision because of the high committed cost of the veteran player who will have to be paid whether or not he is cut. You also instruct the coach to give the veteran player more time on the court to justify the high salary he is being paid.

- You and your companion have driven halfway to a mountain resort. Responding to a reduced-rate advertisement, you have previously made a nonrefundable $100 deposit to spend the weekend at the resort, which is at an elevation of 10,000 feet. Both you and your companion are starting to get headaches and are feeling nauseous; you suspect this is because of mild altitude sickness. Your companion says it's too bad that you have already paid for the room because you both would much rather spend the time at home; however, you can't afford to waste $100. You agree.

- You are a theater aficionado and have traveled to New York City for the express purpose of watching as many Broadway plays as possible. On your first night in town, you realize upon arrival at the theater that you've lost your ticket which cost $100. You check in your wallet, and you do have another $100 with which you can replace the ticket. Instead, you decide to go back to your hotel and watch TV because you believe that while the play is worth seeing for $100, it is not worth seeing for $200.

In each of these cases, you are making irrational decisions because you are not recognizing past costs as sunk costs. No matter how much a player is being paid, it is the future performance you should be interested in as long as you can afford to pay the young, promising player. The past contract that was signed with the veteran player is irrelevant. Similarly, the $100 you and your companion spent to reserve the weekend at the resort is irrelevant. The $100 is a sunk cost, and you should do what will benefit you the most in the future. Similarly, in the Broadway play example, the lost ticket and the $100 you paid for it are irrelevant. The new cost of seeing the play is $100, not $200, and to sit around in your hotel room watching TV because you bought and lost a ticket is irrational.

t was Kenny Rogers who sang, "You gotta know when to hold 'em and know when to fold 'em..." A singing accountant would add, "Once you fold 'em, forget 'em." In each of the three opening scenarios, you should have "folded" or "forgotten" the past costs and not considered them in the decision process. When individuals don't understand the relevance or irrelevance of various costs in decision making, they make bad decisions. It doesn't matter whether you are an individual making a decision to spend the weekend in a resort, or a business making a major, multi-million dollar decision.

In this chapter, we will consider several types of business decisions that are routinely made by business managers. If you become skilled in differentiating between differential costs, sunk costs, opportunity costs, and costs that don't change as a result of future actions, you will be a much better business decision maker.

Evaluating Products and Processes

1   Explain how evaluation leads to planning and why products and processes must be continuously evaluated.

Before we discuss decision making, it is important that we review the three functions of planning, controlling, and evaluating. It is these three functions that lead to decision making of the type we will be discussing in this chapter. Thus far in this book, we have discussed the planning and controlling functions. You have learned that planning involves long-run planning, including strategic planning and capital budgeting, and short-run planning, including production prioritizing and operational budgeting. You have learned that controlling involves tracking actual performance in terms of costs, quality, and timeliness measures. These tracked measures (costs, quality, and timeliness) are then used in the evaluating process to compare against budgets previously prepared. Evaluating involves analyzing results, providing feedback to managers and other employees, rewarding performance, and identifying problems. One specific type of evaluation focuses on products and processes. As you learned in the introductory chapter on management accounting, managers need to assess the performance of their products or services, as well as the processes that are in place to create those products or services. In this chapter, we focus on evaluating and making decisions to improve products, services, and processes.

Evaluation brings us back to the point where we started—planning. Information gained through the evaluation process is used for planning during the following period. When managers are evaluating last period's performance, they are also probably making planning decisions that will affect, and hopefully improve, performance in the next period. This planning, controlling, and evaluating cycle is diagrammed below.

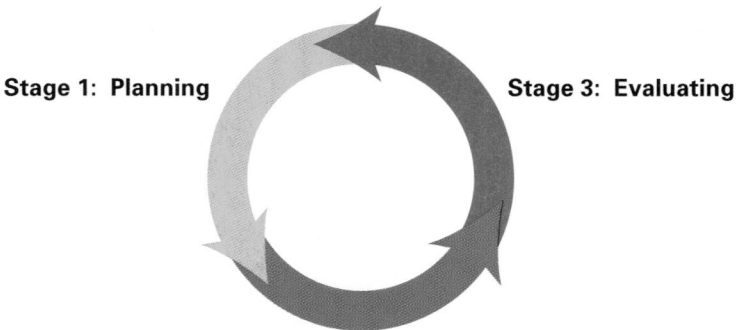

Stage 1: Planning **Stage 3: Evaluating**

Stage 2: Controlling

The evaluation of products, services, and processes leads to decisions that will affect future operations, including whether to enter or exit a market for a particular service or product, whether to make or buy a component, whether to sell a product before or after additional processing, and what prices to charge for services and products.

The evaluation decisions we will discuss in this chapter can have a significant impact on the profitability, quality, and timeliness of the products of an organization for several periods and so must be considered very carefully. In a manufacturing company, for example, evaluation can help a company decide whether to accept a special order, whether to make or buy manufacturing components, whether to build or sell plants, and how to best use limited raw materials in the manufacturing process. In a merchandising company, evaluation can lead to decisions about how to use limited store shelves and whether to open a new store. In a service company, evaluation can help the company decide whether to hire a particular specialist or contract that service to another firm, how to use scarce labor resources, and whether to merge with another company. In a governmental unit, evaluation can affect decisions about whether to collect garbage at the curb or at the house site, whether to hire an in-house lawyer or contract out all legal services, and whether to develop a water system or buy water from a nearby community. In a dot.com company, evaluation could lead to decisions about how to price banner ads, whether to charge an access or user fee, or whether to add or drop existing lines.

At the evaluation stage, companies can make decisions to help them improve their competitive positions. After evaluating its employee health costs, JOHNSON & JOHNSON, the company that makes healthcare, hygiene and pharmaceutical products you are so familiar with, initiated an employee wellness (preventative) program that has saved the company an average of $8.5 million per year since it was put in place. (See the Business Environment on the Web.)

Why Evaluation Is So Important

Today, we live in an age when information is transmitted worldwide almost instantaneously, and change is occurring faster than ever before. With accurate and timely information so readily available, it is absolutely critical that companies produce the highest-quality products at the lowest possible price and faster than anyone else. If a U.S. automobile manufacturer produces a car that is more expensive or of lower quality than cars made in Japan or Germany, for example, U.S. consumers will buy foreign automobiles because information about the Japanese and German cars is readily available to U.S. car buyers. Likewise, if a U.S. automobile company can buy higher-quality tires at a lower price from a Korean tire manufacturer than it can from a U.S. tire manufacturer, it will buy Korean tires because information about the foreign tires is easily accessible.

This increased availability of up-to-date information and the ease with which products and services can be acquired internationally have made it critically important for companies to operate as efficiently and effectively as possible. Because it is so important to be a high-performing, or "world-class," company, organizations are placing more and more emphasis on evaluating their performance and continuously improving. Managers recognize that, in this information age, it is "survival of the fittest" and that only the best-performing companies will be able to compete in the long run.

Companies can be poor performers for several reasons. Some companies do not perform well because they fail to develop appropriate corporate strategies or goals or because they lack vision (planning). Some companies do not perform well because their evaluation methods are poor or do not fit their organizational structures and, therefore, fail to accurately assess how well they are doing. Perhaps most commonly, some companies do not perform well because they fail to execute their strategies and planned actions.

In this chapter, we will discuss several ways companies organize and set goals and then evaluate their performance against those goals. As was the case with product cost determination discussed in the chapter on cost-volume-profit analysis, performance evaluation has been the subject of considerable research in the past few years and has undergone significant changes. Much emphasis has been placed on developing evaluation systems that align performance evaluation with an organization's strategic plan and objectives and that focus on customer and employee needs. Historically, many performance measures have been backward looking and have tended to report results too late to allow corrective action to be taken. New evaluation systems link daily activities with measures that help organizations guide decisions and actions.

Obviously, to effectively evaluate performance, organizations must have goals, objectives, or benchmarks against which to assess their performance. Most organizations establish these goals and benchmarks through a process called strategic planning, which we have already discussed.

FYI:

Much of the continuous improvement literature had its origin in Japan with Japanese companies. As a result, even in U.S. management accounting literature, you will frequently encounter the Japanese term kaizen, which means "continuous improvement." Continuous improvement can take the form of continuous reductions in product defects, delivery time, material waste, inventory size, setup time, and so on. Under continuous improvement programs, one of the major responsibilities of managers and workers is to reduce total costs by continuous improvement in both monetary and nonmonetary standards.

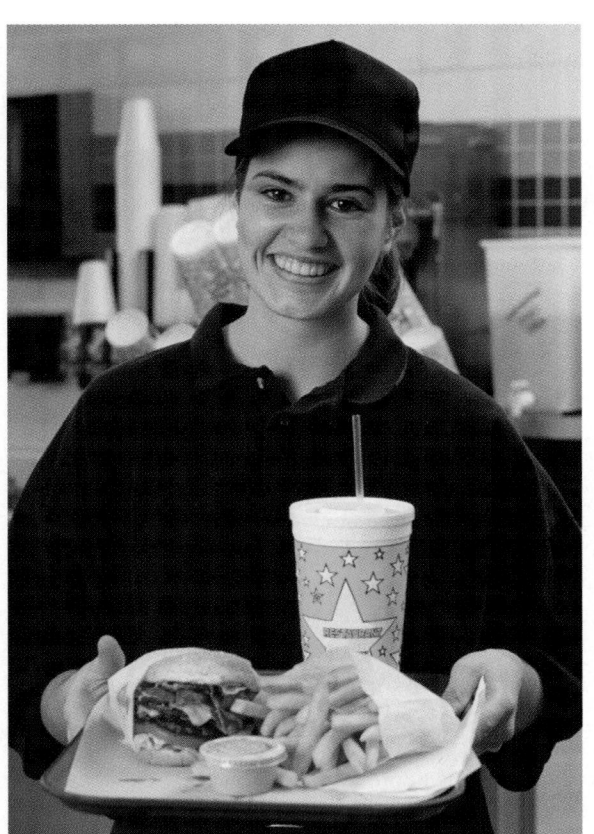

© 2003 Getty Images

Fast-food managers can be evaluated on the kind of service provided to customers. Thus, it is important that employees offer fast service with a smile.

Quality and Time Standards

In evaluating performance, it is important to focus on both monetary and nonmonetary measures. For example, one well-known fast-food chain's managers are evaluated not only on the profitability of their unit, but also on such quality standards as cleanliness and the kind of service provided to customers. In another company, some managers receive more points for developing new technologies and making innovations than for keeping costs in line. At another company, production employees are rewarded on how much they can reduce the delivery time of products to customers. Other nonmonetary measures of performance include creating good employee morale and maintaining equipment in good running order.

For an evaluation system to be successful, the criteria by which products and processes are evaluated should be well defined, objective, and measurable. Usually, qualitative criteria are much harder to evaluate than objective cost measures and resulting variances, but that does not diminish their importance. In fact, quality and time standards are often as important to a firm's success as financial results. Those companies that can deliver the highest-quality products quickest and at the most competitive price will usually be the most successful. Some companies have even developed "best supplier" awards to recognize those suppliers that deliver products at the lowest price, with the highest quality and with the fewest late orders. Criteria used in making these awards usually include such elements as cost reductions, delivery improvement (frequency as well as timeliness), and percentage of defects.

In evaluating quality and time considerations, quality is usually defined as the total features and characteristics of a product or service that bear on its ability to satisfy stated or implied needs. Generally, as a final measure, quality must be viewed from a customer perspective as determined by acceptance in the marketplace. One writer has suggested that quality includes the following eight dimensions:[1]

1. *Performance*—a product's primary operating characteristic. Examples are automobile acceleration and a television set's picture clarity.
2. *Features*—supplements to a product's basic functioning characteristics, such as power windows on a car.
3. *Reliability*—a probability of not malfunctioning during a specified period.
4. *Conformance*—the degree to which a product's design and operating characteristics meet established standards.
5. *Durability*—a measure of product life.
6. *Serviceability*—the speed and ease of repair.
7. *Aesthetics*—how a product looks, feels, tastes, and smells.
8. *Perceived quality*—as seen by a customer.

As an example of how management might apply these quality components to a specific product, consider an automobile tire. Its quality may be measured by tread-wear rate, handling, traction, impact on gas mileage, noise levels, resistance to punctures, and appearance. As another example, the tax service of a CPA may be measured by timely completion of tax returns, tax savings, number of audits or letters from the IRS, suggestions made for future investment opportunities, fees charged, and personal attention given.

This discussion of quality suggests that performance evaluation must be viewed more broadly and from a different perspective than it has been in the past. Controlling costs is still essential, but the emphasis should also be on quality and improvement in processes, products, and services. As we discussed previously, some people argue that the competitive advantage of some Japanese companies is the direct result of acceptance of this quality philosophy, attributed to W. Edwards Deming. The Deming chain reaction is depicted in Exhibit 1.

STOP & THINK

What do you think researchers mean when they say that current evaluation methods do not give enough consideration to intangible capabilities and focus too much on financial returns?

With a broader perspective, managers can seek ways to measure all aspects of company performance. The emphasis should be on the critical activities of the company. The goal is to identify and concentrate on those activities that add the most value to products or services.

In addition to quality, performance evaluation now often considers the time it takes to get a product to the marketplace. By using technology and re-engineering processes, most companies today can deliver goods to customers faster than ever before.

The challenge is to integrate cost, quality, and speed considerations into evaluation systems effectively. The objectives of zero defects, continuous improvement, decreasing manufacturing and delivery time, and meeting customer expectations of quality are admirable. Developing and effectively implementing performance measures that help achieve these objectives is not an easy task, but it is certainly worthy of management's effort. In the end, those organizations that develop the most appropriate performance measures and provide the necessary encouragement and motivation for employees to achieve the organization's objectives will be the most successful.

---

1 David A. Garvin, "Competing on the Eight Dimensions of Quality," *Harvard Business Review* 65 (November–December 1987): pp. 101–109.

Exhibit 1: Deming Chain Reaction

TO SUMMARIZE: In an age when information is inexpensive and readily available, it is important that companies offer the highest-quality products at the lowest possible price and faster than their competitors. Because quality, speed, and price are so important, it is critical that organizations establish good evaluation methods and continuously improve. A company cannot improve its performance until it knows how it is doing. Evaluation helps an organization plan better and control its operations more effectively. In addition to cost considerations, nonmonetary measures should be used in evaluating performance.

To be effective, these criteria must be well defined, objective, and measurable. New approaches to performance evaluation include quality and time considerations. The new approaches are required because all aspects of a company's performance need to be monitored. In the final analysis, those organizations that can deliver the highest-quality products to their customers at the lowest prices and in the shortest amount of time will be the most successful. Significant challenges exist in implementing new performance evaluation approaches.

Benchmarking

2 Understand why benchmarking is so important and how it is conducted.

benchmarking A performance evaluation process used by companies to target areas for improvement by comparing the company's financial and operating performance against the performance of other companies or by comparing the performance of internal departments against each other.

In recent years, there has been an evaluation revolution. Several new evaluation methods have been developed. In this chapter, we will describe only one—benchmarking. One other (the balanced scorecard) will be discussed in the next chapter.

Benchmarking involves comparing a company's financial and operating performance against a competitor's performance or comparing the performance of various internal departments against each other. The benchmarking process usually consists of four steps. Step 1 is to analyze the company's practices, procedures, and performance in a given process and to set forth goals and objectives for improving them. Analysis of the company's practices and procedures is crucial because the practices of other firms will not prove very revealing unless a company has determined its own strengths and weaknesses.

Step 2 involves the selection of a benchmark (or benchmarks). These benchmarks can be departments within a company or competing companies that optimally perform the process under analysis. This step is critical because selection of the wrong benchmarks can result in identifying inappropriate procedures and unrealistic goals for a firm.

In step 3, detailed information on the benchmarks' practices and procedures for that process is collected and shared. Although collecting such data on competing companies may prove difficult, various sources offer benchmark data, and companies are often willing to share information with each other.

In step 4, a company must carefully analyze the data collected in step 3 to determine which of the policies and procedures used by benchmarked companies can best be employed.

Internal versus External Comparisons

The standards of comparison used for benchmarking can be based on the performance of departments or divisions within the same company or appropriate departments from other companies. When using internal units as benchmarks, a company can begin by identifying its best-performing units and then analyze their strategies and practices for performance. Once the approaches have been determined and quantified, less effective departments are encouraged to adopt the practices of the more successful units.

A drawback to internal comparisons alone, however, is that they may foster complacency and may not afford a realistic picture of a unit's potential within the industry. Internal comparisons are often of limited value because a company may be unable to recognize its own shortcomings and faults. Also, although one department within a company may outperform other departments substantially, that fact is not indicative of its performance relative to the industry as a whole. In essence, the department may be outperforming other units within the company, but still be falling short of the performance yields found in other similar companies. For example, it is easy to assume that a growth rate of 4% a year is satisfactory; yet, if outside competitors are realizing growth rates of 8%, there is clearly great room for improvement.

A second approach to benchmarking is to compare a company against top competitors. Most experts believe that this approach is the most relevant point of comparison for both services and products. As mentioned above, a major stumbling block is that obtaining the necessary data for an effective comparison may be difficult. Nevertheless, this type of analysis, peer group benchmarking, is beneficial because it not only allows a company to compare itself to another company with a similar set of attributes, but it may also afford a more invigorating view of what is possible within the industry. Thus, to the extent that key result measurement ratios of individual companies can be compared with averages of a select group of companies with generally similar attributes, peer group examinations can be quite revealing.

A third form of benchmarking is to compare a company with the "best-in-class." This approach entails comparing a company with top-performing firms sharing comparable functions or philosophies, although they may not be in the same industry. The advantage of this type of cross-industry comparison is that practices and procedures followed in other industries may prove very beneficial, even though they have not been used previously in the same industry. Best-in-class comparisons can bring new ideas, new thoughts, and even new concepts. On the downside, however, the introduction of new concepts is somewhat speculative. There is risk whenever a company adapts a new concept or procedure. Because a process performs well in one industry does not necessarily mean it can be carried over effectively to a different industry. This limitation has to be considered before implementing any new ideas.

Benchmarking can yield great benefits in the education of executives and the realized performance improvements of operations. In addition, benchmarking can be used to determine strategic areas of opportunity. In general, it is the application of what is learned in benchmarking that delivers the impressive results so often noted.

The benefits of benchmarking are realized when companies employ recommendations and embark on a change process leading to marked improvements in productivity, costs, and revenues. The following are examples of how companies improved their results through benchmarking:

- GLAXO WELLCOME (now part of GLAXOSMITHKLINE) had over 80 toll-free telephone numbers, over half of which failed to ring anywhere. By eliminating all but one telephone number, Glaxo greatly reduced customer frustration and confusion.
- IBM CANADA suffered a substantial drop in customer satisfaction. In response, the company measured itself against various models to come up with the "Best of the Breed" (BoB) competitors in each of its market segments. Eleven basic processes were reevaluated. The company set some performance improvement targets as high as 200%. Two levels of

authority were dropped, and the corporate culture was redirected toward taking risks and being responsive to customers.

- NORWEST (now part of WELLS FARGO) embarked on a benchmarking campaign and was able to quantify the following benefits:
  - Sales brochure consolidation: $430,000 in savings.
  - Customer and direct mail consolidation: $1 million in savings.
  - Opportunity lending: $20 million in added growth.
  - Teller referrals: up 15%, 33% of which results in additional sales.
  - Use of sales road maps: sales increase up to 102%.
  - Use of partner letters: 150% increase in commercial sales.
  - Performance coaching: 5.08 products per new customer.
- MARRIOTT improved its guest check-in service process 500% by benchmarking the patient admittance process used by hospital emergency rooms.
- SOUTHWEST AIRLINES saved millions of dollars a year and was able to put more aircraft in the air while reducing the number on the ground by benchmarking Indy 500 pit crews.
- XEROX dramatically improved its warehouse order-picking process by benchmarking L.L. BEAN, a catalog order company.
- KPMG borrowed the concept of a supermarket's express checkout to start an express line in its word-processing pools. The change enabled teams with minor document changes to go through an expedited process, which was of great value to the word-processing department and solved a long-standing problem of work assignments.[2]

TO SUMMARIZE: Several new performance measures have been developed in recent years. In this chapter, we discuss one—benchmarking. Benchmarking is the process of comparing a unit's performance with other units either within or outside the company. Benchmarking can result in marked improvements in productivity, costs, and revenue.

Differential Costs, Sunk Costs, and Decision Making

3 Understand the concepts of sunk costs and differential costs and revenues, and be able to identify those costs and revenues that are relevant to making product and process decisions.

sunk costs Costs, such as depreciation, that are past costs and do not change as the result of a future decision.

differential costs Future costs that change as a result of a decision.

opportunity cost The maximum available contribution to profit foregone (or passed up) by using limited resources for a particular purpose.

One of the major reasons companies benchmark and evaluate products and processes is so they can make informed decisions about future actions. In order to make good decisions, however, organizations must understand the nature of their costs and how those costs will change in the future based on actions taken. Earlier in this text and in the opening scenario to this chapter, you were introduced to cost concepts that are critical for making future decisions. To help you remember these cost concepts, consider the following definitions of three cost terms:

- **Sunk cost:** A cost that has already been incurred and that cannot be avoided, regardless of what a manager decides to do. These costs are always the same, no matter what alternatives are being considered and are, therefore, always irrelevant to a decision.
- **Differential cost:** A cost that differs between alternatives. These costs are sometimes referred to as avoidable or incremental costs. Because differential costs differ between alternatives, they are always relevant for decision making. Differential costs can be eliminated in whole or in part by choosing one alternative over another.
- **Opportunity cost:** The maximum available contribution to profit foregone (or passed up) by using limited resources for a particular purpose.

---

2 These examples were taken from "Benefits and Values of Benchmarking," Best Practices, LLC, 6320 Quadrangle Drive, Suite 200, Chapel Hill, NC 27514.

Evaluation of products and processes usually leads to consideration of alternative courses of action. For example, the evaluation of a particular product may lead a company to believe that it must expand capacity, outsource production, or even drop the product in favor of an alternative product. It may also result in the company deciding to buy a competitor. In the rest of this chapter, we provide examples of how products and processes are evaluated to make better decisions. These concepts are probably best understood by examining examples of decisions to change, add, or drop products or processes. Before you can understand how evaluation can lead to better product and process decisions, however, a framework is necessary. In building a framework, we will focus mostly on costs and revenues. Do not forget, however, that the evaluation of timeliness and quality must be considered as well. In making decisions about products and processes, the costs and revenues that are different for, and hence relevant to, various alternative courses of action must be identified. You must be able to distinguish among sunk costs, opportunity costs, future costs that don't change, and differential costs.

To illustrate, assume that you own Speedy Print Shop. A customer wants you to print 500 copies of a one-page flyer immediately. To price the job, you need to know what it will cost. Exhibit 2 includes both an incorrect and a correct analysis of the available cost data. The left column (the incorrect analysis) includes all costs; the right column (the correct analysis) includes only the differential costs. We will explain each cost and how to determine whether the cost is relevant to the pricing decision.

1. *Paper.* The cost of the paper for the printing job is differential because it is a future expenditure that must be made as a result of the decision to accept the order. In a sense, therefore, it is a cost that changes as a result of the decision. If we do not accept the order, we do not need to purchase the paper. Note also that paper is a variable cost—its total cost increases proportionately to the size of the order.

2. *Printing labor.* Accepting the order will require a future expenditure for additional labor to operate the press. This again obviously represents a change from the existing situation—without the order, we would not incur the cost of labor. Also, this example illustrates another important point about measuring future costs. Since this rush order will have to be printed during overtime hours, the appropriate labor rate is time and a half. (Given a normal hourly rate of $16, the labor rate for this job would be $24.) It is easy to overlook this and assume that the normal labor cost per hour ($16) applies. The differential cost of $24 per hour that will be incurred as a result of the decision, however, is the appropriate cost to use. Like paper, printing labor is a variable cost that increases in total proportionately to the size of the order.

network **exercises**

Kinko's

The activities of Speedy Print Shop in this illustration mirror the real-life business of KINKO'S. Kinko's started in 1970 with one copy machine near a U.S. college campus and now has over 900 branches in at least nine different countries. Access Kinko's Web site at **http://www.kinkos.com**.

Net Work:

1. Near which college campus was Kinko's first opened?

2. In which countries does Kinko's now operate?

Exhibit 2: Speedy Print Shop Rush Order Analysis

	Incorrect Analysis (all costs)	Correct Analysis (differential costs)
Variable costs:		
Paper (500 at 10¢)	$ 50	$ 50
Printing labor (5 hours at $16; 5 hours at $24) . . .	80	120
Fixed costs:		
Printing plates	100	100
Printing press depreciation (5 hours at $10)	50	
Manager's salary (5 hours at $20)	100	
Totals	$380	$270

Caution

In this particular case, the issue of whether or not the depreciation is a differential cost is a subtle one. If an asset, such as a building, wears out over time, independent of the level of its use, then its depreciation is irrelevant to a decision of whether or not to use the building. However, if an asset, such as a machine, wears out with the level of its use, then perhaps its depreciation is a differential cost when deciding whether to use the machine or not.

3. *Printing plates.* New printing plates must be prepared for this order, so it is a future expenditure that changes as a result of the decision to accept the order. The important point here is that printing plates are a fixed cost (you can print as many copies as you want from the same set of plates), but the cost is still differential because it is an additional expenditure for this order. A common but incorrect assumption is that only variable costs are relevant and that fixed costs do not have to be taken into account. This is not the case. All future costs that change as a result of accepting the order, whether fixed or variable, are differential.

4. *Printing press depreciation.* This is not a differential cost because it is not a future cost (depreciation is an allocation of a past cost), and it does not change as a result of the decision to accept the order. Costs such as depreciation, which are past costs and do not change, are sunk costs. No decision can change past, or sunk, costs; they are never relevant to a decision.

5. *Manager's salary.* Although the manager's salary is a future cost (we will be paying for future services), it will be paid whether or not the order is accepted. Consequently, the manager's salary is not a differential cost; it does not change as a result of the decision to accept this order. The manager's salary is not a sunk cost because it will be paid in the future, but it is a cost that will not change as a result of whether or not the printing job is accepted.

The differential costs for this rush order total $270. This means that in pricing the job, Speedy Print Shop will be losing money unless it charges at least this much. Similarly, if Speedy Print Shop declines the job at an offered price of $300 because that price is less than the incorrectly calculated differential cost of $380, the company will experience an opportunity cost (loss) of $30 ($300 − $270).

Speaking of opportunity costs, Speedy Print Shop must also carefully consider any other opportunity costs associated with accepting this order. If Speedy Print Shop accepts this order, it may not be able to accept another order that already exists or one that might arrive tomorrow. The lost contribution to profit from not being able to accept alternative jobs is an opportunity cost that must be considered. Obviously, if there is plenty of printing capacity available to accept all jobs that are received, opportunity costs are zero.

To further illustrate the role of differential and sunk costs in making a product or process decision, we assume that Dixon Wholesale Company is thinking of purchasing a delivery truck with an estimated useful life of five years. Following are the costs of acquiring and operating a truck:

Original cost	$20,000

Variable costs per mile:

Gasoline and oil	$ 0.50	
Repairs and maintenance	0.06	
Tires	0.04	
Total variable costs per mile		$ 0.60

Fixed costs per year:

Insurance	$1,000	
Licenses	220	
Depreciation expense ($20,000 ÷ 5 years)	4,000	
Total fixed costs per year		$ 5,220

These variable and fixed operating costs are incurred each year the truck is used. However, they are not all differential costs; they are not all relevant to every decision made about the truck. For the following decisions, we identify the differential costs, the sunk costs, and the reason for the classifications.

Decision 1

Should the truck be purchased? Whether to purchase the truck is really a capital budgeting decision, a topic we discussed in the chapter on capital investment decisions. But the decision is based on differential (future) costs to be incurred if the truck is purchased.

- **Differential costs:** All variable costs (60 cents per mile driven); all fixed costs except depreciation (which is already included in the purchase cost); and the purchase cost ($20,000).
- **Sunk costs:** None.
- **Comment:** All costs except depreciation are differential costs because the truck has not yet been purchased; all costs can be avoided by an alternative decision.

Decision 2

Let's now jump forward in time two years. The truck has now been owned and used for two years, but it has not been licensed or insured for the current (third) year. Should it be licensed and insured, or should some other means of transportation be used? (Assume for now that the truck will not be sold, even if not used.)

- **Differential costs:** All variable costs (60 cents per mile driven) and some fixed costs (insurance, $1,000; licenses, $220).
- **Sunk costs:** Remaining book value of the truck ($12,000 at the beginning of the year).
- **Comment:** As soon as the truck is purchased, its cost becomes a sunk cost. During its estimated life, its remaining book value is a sunk cost if we assume, for simplicity, that the truck has no resale value. The company must absorb the cost of the truck either by using the truck (and depreciating its cost each year) or by writing off the entire cost. All costs except depreciation and the remaining book value are, therefore, differential costs.

Decision 3

The truck has been owned and used for two years and has been licensed and insured for the current (third) year. Should the truck be used for transporting inventory this year? Should other means be arranged?

- **Differential costs:** All variable costs (60 cents per mile driven) and no fixed costs.
- **Sunk costs:** Insurance ($1,000); licenses ($220); remaining book value ($12,000 at the beginning of the year).
- **Comment:** If insurance and license fees are not refundable, these are sunk costs, as is the remaining book value.

Analysis of the costs that are relevant in making these three decisions should help you understand how differential costs are determined. As you can see, variable costs are *usually* differential; fixed costs are *sometimes* differential; and past costs are *never* differential.

Total Costs versus Differential Costs

In trying to improve performance, managers usually prefer to use the differential-cost approach; that is, they disregard sunk costs and other costs that are the same for each alternative being considered. This approach highlights costs that make a difference, takes less time, and reduces the chance of error in the calculation (fewer numbers reduce the chances for mistakes). In some cases, however, a manager may want to review the **total cost** to ensure that some relevant costs are not overlooked.

total cost The total variable and fixed costs incurred in making a product or providing a service.

To illustrate this total-cost approach, we will assume that Dixon Wholesale Company has another decision to make about its truck.

Decision 4

The truck has been owned for four years, but it has not yet been licensed or insured for the current (fifth) year. Should the truck be used for the last year of its economic life, or should it be traded for a new truck that will be driven five years?

Pertinent information is presented in the following table:

	Old Truck	New Truck
Original cost	$20,000	$25,000
Current book value	4,000	
Current resale value	3,400	
Resale value at end of year	0	20,000
Variable operating costs	$0.60 per mile	$0.54 per mile
Annual fixed costs:		
Insurance	$ 1,000	$ 1,100
Licenses	220	220
Depreciation expense	4,000	5,000
Estimated mileage per year	50,000 miles	50,000 miles

On the basis of this information, the total cost of operating the old truck and the total cost of operating a new truck are shown in Exhibit 3.

Note that the total cost of operating the old truck includes the yearly $4,000 depreciation expense. If the new truck is bought, the $4,000 book value of the old truck must still be written off. Thus, the $4,000 is a sunk cost and is the same under both alternatives, so it is not relevant to the decision at hand. The current resale value of the old truck, however, is a reduction in cost that will occur only if the new truck is purchased.

Two observations should be made about the total-cost approach to analyzing alternatives. First, it highlights the more attractive alternative in terms of cost only. In our example, the data appear to favor buying a new truck. However, this requires an investment of additional funds, which forces consideration of other factors. Because these factors were covered in the chapter on capital investment decisions, we have tried to keep our example simple by assuming a fair market value of $20,000 for the new truck at the end of one year. This means that the new truck's annual depreciation expense of $5,000 is equal to the difference between its original cost and its resale value after one year. Had the drop in value been greater than the depreciation expense, the excess would have been an additional cost of using the new truck during its first year.

Second, the total-cost approach is time-consuming because it involves differential costs as well as costs that are the same for all alternatives under consideration. With the differential-cost

Exhibit 3: Total-Cost Analysis for the Current Year: Keeping the Old Truck versus Selling It and Buying a New Truck*

Total Costs	Old Truck	Difference	New Truck
Variable costs:			
$0.60 × 50,000 miles	$30,000		
$0.54 × 50,000 miles			$27,000
Fixed costs:			
Insurance	1,000		1,100
Licenses	220		220
Depreciation expense	4,000		5,000
Book value of old truck to be written off			4,000
Resale value of old truck	0		(3,400)
Total cost	$35,220		$33,920
Difference		$1,300	

*Be aware that in order to emphasize the total-cost and differential-cost approaches, this analysis ignores the time value of money and related income tax effects, which we discussed in the chapter on capital investment decisions.

approach, only costs that are different need to be accumulated and analyzed. Thus, the costs of licensing both trucks and the $4,000 book value of the old truck to be depreciated or written off would not be considered. Exhibit 4 provides a list of the differential costs taken from Exhibit 3.

Although the differential-cost approach accumulates comparative costs and revenues that are different from those of the total-cost approach, it does not alter the relative attractiveness of the alternatives. Both the total and the differential analyses show a savings of $1,300 if the new truck is purchased. Thus, the acquisition of the new truck should bring future benefits to the company.

It should be noted that in both the total analysis and the differential analysis, the resale value of the old truck was treated as a negative cost. Instead, it could have been treated as a differential revenue from which the differential costs had been subtracted. It should also be noted that since both methods of analysis provide the same answer, it is likely that a firm will use the differential analysis method to save time in the collection and analysis of data. The total-cost method will likely be used only when there is considerable uncertainty about whether all differential costs and revenues have been accounted for in the differential-cost approach.

Qualitative Considerations

As has been the case with all management accounting decisions discussed in this book, the effect of product or process decisions on the time and quality with which products or services can be delivered must be considered. In deciding whether to accept the rush print job, for example, Speedy Print Shop must consider the possibility that while accepting the job might lead to additional business, it could affect the quality of printing services to other customers. Likewise, if accepting the rush print job will slow down service to other customers, accepting the job may not be a good decision, no matter how financially attractive it seems to be.

In making a final decision, the cost and qualitative factors may lead you to the same conclusion. If they do not, you must decide what to do to enhance your company's overall profitability in the future. You might decide, for example, to accept the rush print job for an amount near or even below your differential cost to ensure that you get the order and establish a relationship with the customer.

Exhibit 4: Differential-Cost and Revenue Analysis for the Current Year: Operating the Old Truck versus Selling It and Buying a New Truck

Differential Costs and Revenues	Old Truck	New Truck	Difference
Variable costs	$30,000	$27,000	$ 3,000
Insurance	1,000	1,100	(100)
Depreciation expense		5,000	(5,000)
Resale value of old truck	0	(3,400)	3,400
Total differential costs and revenues	$31,000	$29,700	$ 1,300

TO SUMMARIZE: Differential costs are the future costs that change as a result of a decision. Differential costs and revenues are those costs and revenues that are relevant to decisions. Sunk costs are never relevant because they are past costs that cannot be changed. Care must be exercised when estimating future costs because past cost relationships may not continue into the future. Some future costs may not be differential because they do not change as a result of a decision. Both variable and fixed costs may be differential.

There are two approaches to analyzing alternatives: total cost and differential cost. With the total-cost approach, all costs (including sunk costs) are accumulated. The differential-cost approach excludes sunk costs and all common costs, dealing only with costs that are different for the alternatives being considered. Once the quantitative analysis has been completed, qualitative factors must be considered.

Examples of Product and Process Evaluation Decisions

4 Identify several examples of product and process evaluation decisions, and be able to analyze and select the best alternative for each example.

The concepts of differential, sunk, and opportunity costs apply to all evaluation decisions covered in this and the next chapter. In the remainder of this chapter, we will apply differential costing to several examples of short-term product and process evaluation decisions. We will consider five separate examples: (1) accepting or rejecting special orders, (2) making or buying products, (3) exiting or entering a market, (4) determining at what stage of production to sell products, and (5) selecting the best use of a scarce resource. We will also consider the impact of differential, opportunity, and sunk costs on setting selling prices for products.

STOP & THINK

In addition to the specific examples covered in this chapter, identify two other types of decisions that organizations make that would involve evaluating products and/or processes.

special order An order that may be priced below the normal selling price in order to utilize excess capacity and thereby contribute to company profits.

Accepting or Rejecting Special Orders

A **special order** is an order that may be priced below the normal price in order to utilize excess capacity, thus contributing to company profits. We will look at special orders from the perspective of the seller. (A special order from the perspective of the buyer is really a make or buy decision that will be covered later in this chapter.) PRICELINE.COM is a company that specializes in "special orders." That is, this online service specializes in matching customers who insist on paying less than standard market prices with companies that have excess capacity to sell. In a sense, Priceline.com is a special order matchmaker.

Special orders can involve products or services. For example, in manufacturing companies, the special order might involve buying or selling parts on a one-time basis to or from other companies because of a sudden surge in demand. Another example is the one-time outsourcing of the preparation of quarterly payroll tax reports to a local CPA firm. When parts are involved, both the buying and selling companies are manufacturing firms. When a service (such as payroll accounting) is involved, the buyer may be a manufacturing, merchandising, or service company, but the provider is always a service company.

Special Orders—The Seller's Decision

If a seller can sell its products or services profitably at market prices, the decision is an easy one—provide the product or the service. After all, that is the purpose of being in business. Where the difficulty comes is in deciding whether to reduce the normal price of a product or service in order to obtain a special order. Typical situations involving a possible price reduction when idle capacity exists are as follows:

1. A manufacturer sells products under its own brand name, as well as to retail chain stores for sale under the chain's in-store generic brand name.
2. A firm, such as a building contractor or an equipment manufacturer, sells its products or services in a competitive bidding situation.
3. A firm sells a product under distress conditions, for instance, when there has been a sharp decline in demand for its products because of a new product offered by a competitor.
4. A product has significant sales potential with a foreign distributor, whose market demands lower prices than those in the United States.
5. A provider of a product or service has extra capacity and has the opportunity to sign a large contract, at a lower-than-normal price, that would consume the excess capacity.

In each of these situations, we assume that a firm has available capacity that can be utilized to fill the special order. The relevant costs for this decision are the additional, or incremental, costs necessary to produce and deliver the special order. Management must therefore know the incremental costs. This information will indicate the lowest price at which the special order will begin to contribute to the firm's profits.

To illustrate, we will assume that Kent Electronics, which usually sells business calculators for a wholesale price of $29, receives an order from a large department store chain for 10,000 calculators at a price of $23 each. The requested calculators are to be sold under the store's brand name. Kent currently has excess capacity that could be used in producing enough calculators to fill the order. Should the company accept the order?

The answer to this question does not, of course, depend on cost and price factors alone. An obvious consideration, for example, would be whether the order would result in a significant loss of sales of the company's own brand of calculators. Let's assume that this is not a problem.

If the accounting department presents the data on a total-cost basis, the manager might erroneously reject the order. It appears from the schedule on the following page that the firm would have a loss if it accepted the special order:

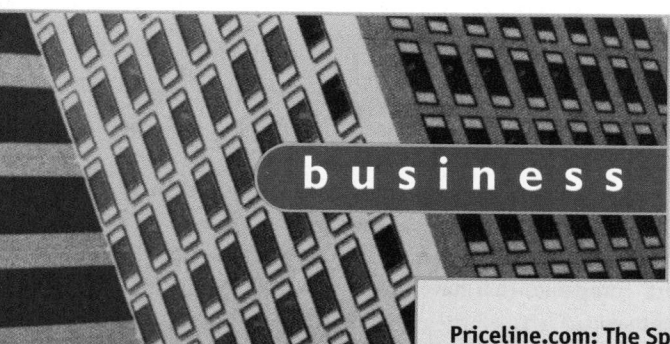

business environment

Priceline.com: The Special Order Matchmaker What began as an outlet to "name-your-price" for airline travel has exploded to include car rentals and purchases, hotel bookings, grocery sales, mortgages, and yard sales. PRICELINE.COM's best sellers are airline tickets. In a recent week, for example, Priceline sold about 80,000 airline tickets. The reason Priceline is so successful is that it offers a tremendous twofold value proposition to its customers. The buyer is able to buy things at a substantial discount below the retail price (or below the price line, hence the name of the company). Savings motivate buyers. Sellers, however, are equally motivated in the Priceline system. The reason for this is that sellers can generate incremental sales of their products by selling below retail prices (special orders) without staining their brand name with a "discount" image. In a sense, Priceline shields the sellers' brands so that the sellers can continue to capture more of the market below their own retail prices. Because of the value Priceline offers to both buyers and sellers, in its first 20 months, the company grew 5% a week.

As an example, consider the travel services Priceline offers. The airline tickets offered by Priceline are strictly for leisure travelers. "Fly any time of the day on any airline" is not the company's business proposition and never was. Instead, Priceline offers cheap air tickets to leisure travelers with flexibility in their travel plans. Priceline's attraction is that instead of driving or staying at home, consumers can now afford to fly. Because airlines have a lot of empty seats, it is a win-win situation for both buyers and sellers.

In essence, Priceline has allowed companies in the travel industry to utilize their excess capacity. Priceline allows an airline, a hotel, or a rental car company to capture incremental sales without publicly discounting its product. If a company publicly discounts its product on the Internet, all buyers see the discounted price and customers who paid the regular price become disgruntled. Priceline solves a very big problem by allowing the seller to privately discount its product and dynamically set prices as a way to clear excess capacity. Is Priceline's model good for selling all products? Probably not. However, any market with excess capacity that attracts buyers who are willing to be flexible on some critical dimension is ideal for the Priceline system.

Source: Information obtained from **http://www .priceline.com/pricelineASPOurCompany/html/ presssayings.htm** (Accessed on November 29, 2003).

Special Order for Calculators—Total-Cost Approach

Sales price		$ 23
Manufacturing costs:		
Direct materials	$ 8	
Direct labor	4	
Manufacturing overhead	14	
Total manufacturing costs		26
Loss per unit		$ (3)
Number of units in order		×10,000
Expected loss exclusive of selling and administrative expenses		$(30,000)

It is not unusual for managers to base decisions on total-cost information because the data are readily available, having been collected in order to prepare financial statements and income tax returns. Unfortunately, such information may lead management to the wrong conclusion—in this case, to reject the order.

The only differential costs, however, are those future costs that change if the order is accepted. These include the variable product costs as well as the direct fixed costs. Fixed costs that are incurred regardless of whether the order is accepted should not be considered. The following analysis, prepared on a differential-cost basis, shows that Kent Electronics should accept the order.

Special Order for Calculators—Differential-Cost Approach

Sales price		$ 23
Variable and differential fixed costs:		
Direct materials	$8	
Direct labor	4	
Variable manufacturing overhead costs	5	
Differential fixed overhead costs	3	
Variable selling and administrative expenses	1	
Total variable and differential fixed costs		21
Remaining margin to cover fixed costs and provide a profit		$ 2
Number of units in order		×10,000
Expected contribution to fixed costs and profit		$ 20,000

These data assume that additional fixed costs of $3 per unit will be incurred if the order is accepted. If no additional fixed costs would be incurred, the margin would increase to $5. The analysis clearly suggests that, from a financial point of view, management should accept the order. This approach identifies not only the differential costs but also a price floor (the total variable and differential fixed costs of $21) below which management should probably not accept an order. As long as the price exceeds total variable and differential fixed costs, the firm will increase its profits by accepting the order. This analysis assumes that the company has no better alternative uses for its excess capacity and that special sales by the chain will have no adverse effect on Kent's normal sales. But what if regular customers hear about this special order and insist on lower prices, thus disrupting the normal pricing structure? Or, what if filling the special order will have an adverse effect on the quality of current products or the speed with which products can be offered to regular customers? These and other qualitative factors must also be considered.

A manager must also consider whether acceptance of such an order would be a violation of the Robinson-Patman Act. This legislation, enacted in 1936, prohibits firms from quoting different prices to competing customers for the same goods unless differences in price can be attributed to differences in cost. In the case of Kent Electronics, the sale is probably legal because the calculators are to be sold under the store's brand name, and the department store will assume all advertising costs.

The differential-cost approach to pricing can also be used in explaining why theater tickets are less expensive for matinees than for evening performances and why it is cheaper to make telephone calls at night and on weekends than on weekdays. If there is excess capacity that can be used to provide a service or make a product that will generate more revenue than the differential cost of providing the service or making the product, the firm will increase its profits by the amount of the margin remaining after deducting differential costs. As explained in a Business Environment included earlier in the chapter, this is exactly the rationale for the existence of PRICELINE.COM.

A few words of caution are in order when making these special order decisions. First, in some situations, there may also be some additional fixed costs that are relevant to the pricing decision. Second, a company must not accept too many orders that barely cover variable costs, or it will not be able to cover all its fixed costs. Third, using all extra capacity to fill a special order at a lower-than-normal price may prevent a company from being able to accept additional work at higher prices in the future; this is an example of an opportunity cost. Fourth, accepting a special order may force a company to cut corners with normal customers, resulting in lower-quality products or services to those customers or decreasing the speed at which other customers are served.

Making or Buying Products

In the previous section, we looked at special orders from the perspective of the seller. Whenever there is a special order, there is also a buyer. Many times, when a buyer has placed a special order, that buyer has made a decision to purchase rather than make the purchased product or service. Other times, the buyer may be a company that does not have the capacity to make the product or service and is placing the special order in the belief that the product or service can be purchased at less than market prices because the seller has excess capacity. If a buyer cannot make the product or service, the only decision is whether or not to buy. Differential-cost analysis doesn't help in making that decision. Rather, questions such as "can we afford to make the purchase," "do we need to make the purchase," and "where should we make the purchase" drive the purchase decision. Where differential-cost analysis makes a difference is when companies are making tradeoffs between making or buying products or services.

Many companies outsource virtually everything. For example, a food packaging plant might outsource to an employment agency the task of hiring, firing, training, and paying its production line employees. The plant might also outsource its custodial and bookkeeping services to local providers of those services. The plant might even outsource key management tasks by asking a consulting or professional services firm to provide a top-level manager to run the plant. As another example, many Internet businesses are "virtual outsourcers." They take orders from customers and relay those orders to manufacturers, which, in turn, ship the products directly to the customers. In contrast, other organizations make or provide most of their products and services internally. In the following section, we describe the factors companies must consider when deciding whether to buy products and services from outsiders or to produce these products and services themselves.

Making or Buying Manufactured Parts

Companies, such as automobile manufacturers, must decide which products and services they will produce and offer internally and which ones they will outsource or buy from outsiders. With respect to manufactured products, if a product consists of a number of parts, management must decide for each component whether to produce it or purchase it from an outside supplier. Over time, and based on a consideration of the relevant quantitative and qualitative factors, management develops a long-term policy regarding the use of its facilities to produce components for its products.

The fact that a long-term policy about make versus buy has been established by a particular company does not mean that the issue is permanently closed. In fact, management should always be reconsidering its decisions and looking for new ways to save money, improve quality, or speed up manufacturing and delivery processes. If a firm has idle facilities, for example, management may wish to find a use for those facilities. One possibility is to manufacture components that are normally purchased. Whether this decision is wise depends not only on cost considerations but also on a number of qualitative factors, such as the likely effect on the regular source of supply, the company's ability to produce a high-quality component, speed of delivery, and management's interest in keeping workers on the payroll. Thus, even though a firm has a long-term policy of purchasing some components and producing others, certain situations may require decisions that alter that policy.

Assuming that the qualitative factors favor the use of idle facilities to produce the part, what costs are relevant to a make-or-buy decision? In general, the purchase cost and all other costs that can be avoided if the part is manufactured are differential costs. Any cost that will be incurred regardless of whether the part is purchased or manufactured is not a differential cost and is irrelevant.

To illustrate how the differential costs in such a decision are identified, assume that Ritter Manufacturing Company has excess capacity that could be used in producing wheel bearings. The accounting department has compiled the following projected total-cost figures for producing the bearings.

	Cost per Unit	Costs for 1,000 Units
Direct materials	$ 3.00	$ 3,000
Direct labor	8.00	8,000
Variable manufacturing overhead	4.00	4,000
Fixed manufacturing overhead, direct	2.50	2,500
Fixed manufacturing overhead, indirect	5.00	5,000*
Total costs	$22.50	$22,500

*Total indirect fixed costs are the same under both alternatives.

The company has been buying this bearing from a regular supplier in 1,000-unit quantities at a price of $19 per unit. Should Ritter continue to buy or start making the bearings? To answer this question, management must identify the differential costs of each alternative, taking into account any additional resources that may be needed, as well as alternative uses for the currently idle facilities. Two possible situations are presented here.

Situation 1

The currently idle facilities have no alternative uses. If the idle facilities do not have any practical alternative use, the opportunity cost is zero. With no opportunity cost, the differential costs would be the costs strictly associated with manufacturing (direct labor, direct materials, and so on).

The costs of the two alternatives can be presented on a total-cost or a differential-cost basis, as shown in Exhibit 5. Although each analysis produces different total costs, both demonstrate that the firm would save $1,500 per 1,000 units ($1.50 per unit) by making the component rather than buying it. The company's final decision would depend, of course, on whether there were negative qualitative factors that would, in the opinion of management, more than offset the $1.50 unit-cost advantage of making the part.

Situation 2

The idle facilities can be rented for $4,000 if they are not used to manufacture bearings. Management estimates that, if the facilities are used for manufacturing, 1,000 wheel bearings could be manufactured during this time.

In this case, the opportunity cost of producing the bearings is $4,000, or an average cost of $4 per unit ($4,000 ÷ 1,000 units). This opportunity cost is an important consideration in the firm's decision whether to buy or make the part, as shown in Exhibit 6. When the opportunity cost is considered, the cost of producing the part is $2,500 more than the cost of buying it. Unless there are quality, time, or other qualitative factors that override this cost, Ritter should buy the bearing and rent the idle facilities. Remember, the essence of the make-or-buy problem is management's desire to achieve the best utilization of existing facilities in the short term.

Because opportunity costs do not represent actual transactions, they are not recorded in the accounts. Yet they are always significant in the decision-making process because each situation has at least two alternatives. Thus, opportunity costs provide a good illustration of why a manager cannot rely solely on the data collected for external financial reports.

FYI:

To see exactly how significant opportunity costs are, consider the following question: What is the largest cost borne by New York City in maintaining Central Park? The answer is not the cost of maintenance employees or equipment. Instead, the largest cost is the opportunity cost of the tens of billions of dollars the city could get by selling the land to real estate developers.

Exhibit 5: Analyses of the Costs of Using Idle Facilities (Situation 1)

	Total-Cost Analysis (per 1,000 Units)		Differential-Cost Analysis (per 1,000 Units)	
	Buy	**Make**	**Buy**	**Make**
Purchase cost	$19,000		$19,000	
Direct materials		$ 3,000		$ 3,000
Direct labor		8,000		8,000
Variable manufacturing overhead		4,000		4,000
Fixed manufacturing overhead:				
Direct		2,500		2,500
Indirect	5,000	5,000		
Total cost	$24,000	$22,500	$19,000	$17,500
Difference		$1,500		$1,500

Exhibit 6: The Effect of an Opportunity Cost on Analyses (Situation 2)

	Total-Cost Analysis (per 1,000 Units)		Differential-Cost Analysis (per 1,000 Units)	
	Buy	**Make**	**Buy**	**Make**
Purchase cost	$19,000		$19,000	
Direct materials		$ 3,000		$ 3,000
Direct labor		8,000		8,000
Variable manufacturing overhead		4,000		4,000
Fixed manufacturing overhead:				
Direct		2,500		2,500
Indirect	5,000	5,000		
Opportunity cost, rental		4,000		4,000
Total cost	$24,000	$26,500	$19,000	$21,500
Difference		$2,500		$2,500

Purchasing Services or Providing Them Internally

In recent years, companies have not only outsourced product parts, but more and more they are also outsourcing services such as cafeteria service, garbage removal, payroll accounting, legal services, and even basic accounting. In deciding whether to acquire services or provide them internally, companies go through the same kind of analysis as if they were buying products. That is, they consider the differential costs of each alternative, as well as qualitative factors, such as the quality of the service, whether space exists to house the service, whether services can be delivered on a timely basis, and management's interest in keeping workers on the payroll. Assuming management believes it can acquire high-quality services both within and outside the company, what costs are relevant to the purchase-or-provide decisions? Costs that will be incurred regardless of whether the service is purchased or provided internally are not differential costs and are irrelevant to the decision.

To illustrate how the differential costs are identified, assume that Ritter Manufacturing Company is considering outsourcing its payroll function. The following annual cost information relating to payroll accounting is available.

FYI:

In the 1990s and early 2000s, major CPA firms became professional service firms that offered all kinds of new services. One of the fasting-growing services that was offered by CPA firms was internal audit services for major corporations. However, with the plethora of financial statement frauds in companies such as ENRON and WORLD-COM, Congress passed the Sarbanes-Oxley Act that, among other things, prohibited CPA firms from being both the external auditor and the internal auditor. ARTHUR ANDERSEN, which went out of business after the Enron debacle, for example, was both the internal and external auditor for Enron. However, CPA firms can still perform internal audit services as long as they are not the external auditor of the same company.

Costs of Payroll Accounting Department	
Salaries of payroll accounting employees	$2,600,000
Training costs	100,000
Depreciation on payroll accounting offices	50,000
Utilities for payroll accounting offices	40,000
Computers, software, and supplies	150,000
Other variable costs	75,000
Total costs of payroll accounting	$3,015,000

A CPA firm has offered to perform the payroll accounting services for $3,100,000 per year. You have determined that if payroll accounting services were contracted out to the CPA firm, the space currently used by the payroll department could be used by the purchasing department, which is currently occupying rented space in a nearby city. The rent paid for offices used by the purchasing department is $10,000 per month.

Should Ritter continue to have its own payroll department, or should it outsource its payroll accounting function to a CPA firm? From a strictly financial point of view, Ritter should not outsource, as shown below.

Cost of outsourcing:

CPA firm cost		$3,100,000
Rent saved by relocating purchasing department		
($10,000 per month × 12 months)		(120,000)
Net cost of outsourcing		$2,980,000

Cost of maintaining payroll department:

Total cost of payroll department		$3,015,000
Less: Nondifferential costs (incurred under either alternative)		
Depreciation expense	$50,000	
Utilities	40,000	
Total nondifferential costs		(90,000)
Differential cost of maintaining payroll department		$2,925,000
Excess cost incurred by outsourcing payroll accounting		$ 55,000

Of course, the one-year cost analysis is really an incomplete analysis. In making the decision, management must determine what the future costs of each alternative will be. If, for example, management can lock into a five-year commitment of $3,100,000 annually and it believes costs of keeping the payroll department will rise $100,000 per year, from a cost perspective, the company may want to outsource even though the cost is higher in the current year.

Caution

Be careful to consider all differential costs and revenues in making evaluation decisions and to exclude the nondifferential costs. For example, in this payroll accounting example, if depreciation and utilities (which will be incurred whether or not payroll accounting services are outsourced) are considered, an incorrect decision will be made.

In addition to costs, management must consider many other factors. For example, will the CPA firm provide payroll services of the same or higher quality as those provided by the internal accountants? Quality of services is very important in an area like payroll accounting, where it is difficult for management to judge whether the company is getting value for its money. Management would also want to consider other factors: (1) Will the CPA firm be able to provide the services in the long run? (2) Can the company use the displaced payroll accounting employees in other positions, or is the company willing to lay off employees? (3) Will outsourcing the payroll accounting services affect the cost of other services received by the company? (4) If payroll accounting was used as an accounting trainee development area (as it is in many companies), are there other efficient and effective ways to train future company accountants?

TO SUMMARIZE: Managers must often decide whether a special order should be accepted (from the seller's perspective) or placed (from the buyer's perspective). A special order is a one-time order that is not considered part of the company's normal ongoing business. Considering finances only, from the seller's perspective, the special order should be accepted if the seller has excess capacity and if the differential costs of providing the special order are less than the differential revenues that will be generated from the special order.

Differential-cost analysis is only helpful in considering special orders from the buyer's perspective when the buyer has an option to either make or buy the product or service. In choosing whether to make or buy a component or service, management must compare the differential costs of making the part or providing the service (including the opportunity costs of alternative uses of the facilities) with the cost of purchasing (outsourcing) the part or service. Qualitative factors must also be considered in special order decisions because they may be significant enough to reverse a decision based only on quantitative considerations.

Exiting or Entering a Market

The decision of whether to exit or enter a market is usually based on careful evaluation, although companies seem to be buying and selling businesses quite often these days. We will first consider the decision of whether to exit a market and then the decision of whether to enter a market.

Exiting a Market

When a segment (product or line of products) is losing money, management must decide whether to drop it. In the Web support material to this textbook, we provide an example of Philips, a company that decided to exit the semiconductor business. Such decisions are particularly difficult because the differential costs are not easy to identify, and this can lead to analyses based on invalid assumptions, as the following example demonstrates.

To illustrate, assume that Augusta Retail Company is thinking of closing one of its stores. The question of the store's continuing viability arose because of the July financial results for the company's three stores (amounts are in thousands):

	Store 1	Store 2	Store 3	Total
Sales revenue	$250,000	$90,000	$60,000	$400,000
Cost of goods sold	170,000	40,000	30,000	240,000
Gross margin	$ 80,000	$50,000	$30,000	$160,000
Operating expenses	55,000	30,000	35,000	120,000
Net income (or loss)	$ 25,000	$20,000	$ (5,000)	$ 40,000

If Store 3 is closed, it would seem reasonable to assume that Augusta Retail Company's profits will increase by $5 million, as shown here.

	Store 1	Store 2	Total
Sales revenue	$250,000	$90,000	$340,000
Cost of goods sold	170,000	40,000	210,000
Gross margin	$ 80,000	$50,000	$130,000
Operating expenses	55,000	30,000	85,000
Net income	$ 25,000	$20,000	$ 45,000

This analysis is based on three assumptions:

1. That all costs shown are differential and therefore relevant to the decision. In other words, there are no joint costs (costs that are common to two or more stores).
2. That the sales of the other stores will not be affected by dropping Store 3.
3. That no qualitative factors have a bearing on the decision.

Before closing Store 3, the company's general manager should check the validity of these assumptions. For simplicity, suppose that the second and third assumptions are valid, and that only the first assumption needs verification. First, the accounting department must separate the total costs of each store into variable costs, direct fixed costs, and indirect (or unavoidable) fixed costs. With this new information, the accounting department might prepare the following modified report for July (amounts are in thousands).

	Store 1	Store 2	Store 3	Total
Sales revenue	$250,000	$90,000	$60,000	$400,000
Variable costs	190,000	50,000	40,000	280,000
Contribution margin	$ 60,000	$40,000	$20,000	$120,000
Direct fixed costs	20,000	15,000	18,000	53,000
Segment margin	$ 40,000	$25,000	$ 2,000	$ 67,000
Indirect fixed costs (not allocated)				27,000
Net income				$ 40,000

The manager can use this modified report to determine whether Store 3 made a positive contribution toward covering the indirect (unavoidable) fixed costs. In looking at this modified report, the manager would immediately see that the segment margin for Store 3 is a positive $2 million. This means that Store 3 is contributing $2 million to the company's overall profit. Thus, if Store 3 is dropped, profits will decrease by $2 million unless another store with greater profit potential is added or Store 3 can be sold to another company. To illustrate the potential decline in profits if Store 3 is dropped, the manager might ask the accounting department to prepare a report to indicate what the company's July financial results would show without Store 3. This pro-forma report would show the following information (amounts are in thousands):

	Store 1	Store 2	Total
Sales revenue	$250,000	$90,000	$340,000
Variable costs	190,000	50,000	240,000
Contribution margin	$ 60,000	$40,000	$100,000
Direct fixed costs	20,000	15,000	35,000
Segment margin	$ 40,000	$25,000	$ 65,000
Indirect fixed costs (not allocated)			27,000
Net income			$ 38,000

Although the original report suggested that profits would increase by $5 million if Store 3 were dropped, total profits would actually decrease by $2 million ($40 million − $38 million). The reason is that Store 3 is generating revenues that are $2 million greater than differential costs (variable costs and avoidable fixed costs). This analysis suggests that Store 3 should not be dropped, unless it can be replaced by another store or business that will contribute more than $2 million to cover unavoidable indirect fixed costs. (Obviously, we have not considered any sales price Augusta could receive from selling Store 3. Any money received from selling Store 3 would need to be weighed against the $2 million annual contribution Store 3 is making toward covering indirect costs.)

Entering a Market

The considerations involved in deciding whether to enter a market are quite similar to those when deciding whether or not to exit a market. From a financial perspective, if adding a product line (segment) will contribute to the income of a firm, it is generally a good decision. The contribution can come in several forms. First, entering a new market can reduce the current cost of doing business. For example, assume that Augusta is considering purchasing a wholesale distribution company that will allow the company to buy directly from manufacturers, rather than from other wholesalers, when acquiring merchandise for its stores. Even if the new wholesale company is not profitable on its own, if it could reduce Augusta's costs enough so that overall profits are higher, the decision to buy might be a good one. Buying a new company or entering a new market could increase overall company profits by having the new segment cover some of the indirect fixed costs now being borne entirely by existing businesses. From a financial perspective, the important point to consider is whether total profits will be higher or lower after the purchase.

In addition to the financial considerations, organizations consider the effects on quality and time to deliver products to customers when deciding whether to enter a market. For example, suppose a small company has superior-quality products, manufacturing knowledge, or other attributes that could enhance the quality of the organization's products. Would it be wise to buy this smaller company even if the purchase doesn't increase overall short-term profits? Probably so. Or, what if a company occupies a strategic location for serving an organization's customers and buying the company would allow the organization to deliver its products more quickly to customers? Would buying the strategically located company be a good decision even if short-term overall profits aren't increased? Again, probably so. Both purchases would allow the organization to serve its customers better by increasing quality and decreasing delivery time. Hopefully, the result of both purchases would be a larger market share and higher profits in the long run. Unfortunately, it is hard to quantify by how much quality and/or delivery time must improve before a purchase is a good one. Because quality and time decisions are subjective, we will focus on the short-term financial considerations in deciding whether to enter a market. You should realize, however, that quality and time considerations are very important, and in considering some purchases, they may be the overriding factors that outweigh short-term financial considerations.

To illustrate entering a new market, assume that Augusta Retail Company now has only two stores. Further, assume that it is considering purchasing the wholesale company just discussed. The following data are available for Augusta Retail Company prior to making the purchase (amounts are in thousands):

	Store 1	Store 2	Total
Sales revenue	$250,000	$90,000	$340,000
Cost of goods sold	170,000	40,000	210,000
Other variable costs	20,000	10,000	30,000
Contribution margin	$ 60,000	$40,000	$100,000
Direct fixed costs	20,000	15,000	35,000
Segment margin	$ 40,000	$25,000	$ 65,000
Indirect fixed costs (not allocated)			27,000
Net income			$ 38,000

As these data show, Augusta currently makes a net income of $38 million. Now, assume that Augusta can purchase a wholesale company that will allow Augusta to buy directly from manufacturers, thus decreasing its cost of goods sold by 30%. However, the wholesale company is currently losing $10 million per year. Should Augusta buy the wholesale company? The following analysis shows that, from a financial perspective, buying the wholesale company would be a good decision (again, amounts are in thousands).

Effect on Current Stores

	Store 1 Before	Store 1 After	Store 2 Before	Store 2 After	Total (before and after purchase) Before	Total (before and after purchase) After	Wholesale Company	Total (including wholesale company)
Sales revenue	$250,000	$250,000	$90,000	$90,000	$340,000	$340,000	$110,000	$450,000
Cost of goods sold	170,000	119,000[1]	40,000	28,000[2]	210,000	147,000	70,000	217,000
Other variable costs	20,000	20,000	10,000	10,000	30,000	30,000	15,000	45,000
Contribution margin	$ 60,000	$111,000	$40,000	$52,000	$100,000	$163,000	$ 25,000	$188,000
Direct fixed costs	20,000	20,000	15,000	15,000	35,000	35,000	35,000	70,000
Segment margin	$ 40,000	$ 91,000	$25,000	$37,000	$ 65,000	$128,000	$ (10,000)	$118,000
Indirect fixed costs (not allocated)					27,000	27,000	—	27,000
Net income					$ 38,000	$101,000	$ (10,000)	$ 91,000

[1]$170,000 − (0.3 × $170,000) = $119,000.
[2]$40,000 − (0.3 × $40,000) = $28,000.

This analysis shows that even though the wholesale company is losing $10 million per year, purchasing the wholesale company will increase overall company profits by $53 million ($91 million − $38 million). Of course, this elaborate analysis really wasn't necessary since many costs (other variable costs, direct fixed costs, and indirect fixed costs) stayed the same. In fact, the only differential costs were the decrease in cost of goods sold (facilitated by being able to buy directly from manufacturers instead of wholesalers) and the $10 million loss the wholesale company incurs. Focusing only on the differential costs, you can see that the net income of the company would be increased by $53 million upon buying the wholesale company (numbers are in thousands).

Differential Costs of Deciding to Enter a Market

Decrease in cost of goods sold of Store 1	$ 51,000
Decrease in cost of goods sold of Store 2	12,000
Loss incurred by wholesaler	(10,000)
Increase in income from buying wholesaler	$ 53,000

This analysis suggests that, from a financial perspective, the wholesale company should be purchased. The decreases in cost of goods sold that will result in Store 1 and Store 2 more than compensate for the losses currently being incurred by the wholesaler.

TO SUMMARIZE: In deciding whether to exit or enter a market, the effect on profits, quality, and speed of delivery should be considered. When focusing on the financial aspects of exiting or entering a market, only the differential costs and revenues need be considered. A product or line of products should not be dropped unless it does not make a contribution toward covering indirect fixed costs. An alternative product or line of products can be added that will contribute more toward covering unavoidable indirect fixed costs. A segment should be added if it increases overall company profits. The increase in overall company profits can come from reduced costs in existing segments or from the profitable margin of the acquired segment.

Determining at What Stage of Production to Sell Products

joint manufacturing process When one material input is used to produce more than one product.

In some companies, all the products evolve out of a **joint manufacturing process**, meaning that one material input is used to produce more than one product. Gasoline, oil, and kerosene, for example, are all produced from refining crude oil; various cuts of beef are provided from butchering a steer; and different qualities and types of lumber are available from processing timber. In all these cases, the products are produced simultaneously and are not individually identifiable until the split-off point in the process. When this is the case, management must decide whether a particular product from the joint manufacturing process should be sold as is at the split-off point, or processed further at additional cost, with the expectation of obtaining a higher price.

In choosing the best time to stop processing a product, management basically compares the additional costs that would be incurred from further processing with the additional revenues. If the incremental revenues are greater than the incremental costs, net income is increased, and additional processing is worthwhile (unless qualitative factors dictate otherwise). If the incremental revenues are less than the incremental costs, the product should probably be sold without further processing. The costs that a firm incurs before the point at which the different products are separated for further processing or immediate sale are called **joint product costs**. These costs are incurred whether the separate products are sold at the point of separation or after further processing. Thus, they are not relevant to a choice between the two alternatives.

joint product costs The costs that a firm incurs before the point at which the different products are separated for further processing or immediate sale.

To illustrate the decision-making process related to further processing, we will assume that Armaco Oil Company derives two products, jet fuel and reformate, from crude oil. Although crude oil cannot be sold independently, both jet fuel and reformate can be, either at the point of separation or after further processing. Further processing jet fuel results in a petrochemical product called xylene, while further processing of reformate results in a petrochemical called toluene. The cost of refining 375,000 gallons of crude oil up to the point of separation is $300,000. Crude oil is then separated into 200,000 gallons of jet fuel and 150,000 gallons of reformate. The remaining 25,000 gallons are lost in the process of refining. The selling prices of jet fuel and reformate at the point of separation, the costs of processing further, and the selling prices after this further processing are estimated by the accounting department to be as follows:

	Gallons	Net Selling Price per Gallon at Separation	Additional Processing Costs	Net Selling Price of Xylene and Tolulene per Gallon After Processing
Jet fuel	200,000	$1.20	$80,000	$1.70 (xylene)
Reformate	150,000	1.00	90,000	1.50 (tolulene)

To help management decide whether to sell jet fuel or reformate at the point of separation or to process them further, the following analysis can be prepared.

Product: Jet Fuel/Xylene

Sales revenue after further processing (200,000 gallons @ $1.70)	$340,000
Sales revenue at point of separation (200,000 gallons @ $1.20)	240,000
Additional revenue from further processing	$100,000
Additional processing costs	80,000
Additional profit from further processing	$ 20,000

Product: Reformate/Tolulene

Sales revenue after further processing (150,000 gallons @ $1.50)	$225,000
Sales revenue at point of separation (150,000 gallons @ $1.00)	150,000
Additional revenue from further processing	$ 75,000
Additional processing costs	90,000
Additional loss from further processing	$ (15,000)

This analysis shows that further processing of jet fuel into xylene will contribute an additional $20,000 to net income because the additional revenues generated exceed the additional processing costs by $20,000. On the other hand, further processing of reformate into tolulene will reduce net income by $15,000 because the additional processing costs are greater than the additional revenues by that amount. Therefore, reformate should be sold at the point of separation.

A total-cost approach to analyzing this decision is shown in Exhibit 7. Selling both products after further processing increases net income by $5,000, but the best choice is to sell reformate at the point of separation and to process jet fuel into xylene before it is sold. The worst choice is to sell jet fuel at the point of separation and further process reformate, resulting in only $75,000 of profit. Note that the joint processing costs were not considered in the earlier analysis of the individual products since they are not differential costs but are the same for each alternative. In the later analysis of the alternative treatments of jet fuel and reformate, however, the joint costs are included simply to illustrate the total-cost approach. But they are not really necessary because the difference in net income is the same whether or not the $300,000 of joint costs are included.

In deciding whether to sell products at the point of separation or after further processing, management must also consider qualitative factors. For example, management will need to consider quality and time issues, as well as the hiring or firing of employees and customers' demands for particular products.

Exhibit 7: A Comparison of Alternatives: Selling at Point of Separation or After Further Processing

	Sell Both Products at Separation	Sell Both Products After Further Processing	Sell Reformate at Separation and Process Jet Fuel Further	Sell Jet Fuel at Separation and Process Reformate Further
Sales revenue:				
Jet fuel/Xylene	$240,000	$340,000	$340,000	$240,000
Reformate/Tolulene	150,000	225,000	150,000	225,000
Total sales revenue	$390,000	$565,000	$490,000	$465,000
Joint product costs	$300,000	$300,000	$300,000	$300,000
Further processing costs	0	170,000	80,000	90,000
Total costs	$300,000	$470,000	$380,000	$390,000
Net income	$ 90,000	$ 95,000	$110,000	$ 75,000

TO SUMMARIZE: In some industries, a number of end products are produced from a single raw material input. Two or more products that are produced from a common input are known as joint products. Joint costs are the costs that are incurred up to the point where the products can be sold as separate products. Differential-cost analysis can help determine whether joint products should be sold at the point where they become recognized as separate products or processed further. It will always be profitable to continue processing a joint product after the split-off point as long as the incremental revenue from the extra processing exceeds the incremental processing costs incurred after the split-off point. Joint costs that have been incurred up to the point of split-off are always irrelevant to the additional processing decision.

Selecting the Best Use of a Scarce Resource

Organizations are often faced with the decision of how to best use scarce resources. In a manufacturing company, the scarce resource might be limited raw materials or limited production capacity. For a retail merchandising firm, such as WAL-MART, the scarce resource might be limited shelf space. For a service firm, the scarce resource might be the limited expertise of the trained professionals. We will illustrate the concept of scarce resources using limited shelf space for a retail merchandising firm.

When a retail merchandising firm sells more than one product and store shelves are inadequate to display all products equally, management has to decide to which products the store should allocate shelf space and how much space should be allocated to each product. With limited shelf space, stocking one product means that another product cannot be stocked or will have to be stocked on a more limited basis. In deciding which products to stock, management needs to know which products and how much of each product to stock in order to maximize net income. A retail store will normally maximize net income by stocking those products that contribute the most toward covering fixed costs and providing profit in relation to the "critical resource factor," in this case, shelf space. The **critical resource factor** is the resource that limits operating capacity by its availability. For example, in a manufacturing company, if machine hours are the most critical resource, a company should concentrate on the product for which revenues exceed variable costs by the highest margin per machine hour. Other critical resources in manufacturing companies might include labor hours, floor space, or special raw materials. Because shelf space is the critical resource factor for our retail store example, from a financial point of view, management should stock those products for which revenues exceed variable costs by the highest margin per square foot of shelf space.

critical resource factor The resource that limits operating capacity by its availability.

To illustrate, we assume that Bolten Retail Company stocks potato chips and cookies. Let's further assume that its capacity, at least in the short term, is limited by the availability of only 20 square feet of shelf space for these two products. The revenue and cost data for one package each of potato chips and cookies are:

	Potato Chips	Cookies
Selling price	$3.10	$3.50
Variable costs	2.48	3.15
Contribution margin per unit	$0.62	$0.35
Percentage contribution margin (contribution margin ÷ selling price) . .	20%	10%

On the basis of this limited information, it would appear that potato chips are more profitable than cookies. The sale of one bag of potato chips will contribute $0.62 toward fixed costs, whereas the sale of one package of cookies will contribute only $0.35.

Before Bolten can decide whether or not to emphasize potato chips, however, management must consider the extent to which each product uses the critical resource, limited shelf space. If a bag of potato chips takes up twice as much space as a package of cookies (two bags of potato chips occupy one square foot of shelf space, while four packages of cookies can occupy the same one square foot of shelf space), the sale of cookies will make a greater total contribution to profits than the sale of potato chips, as shown by the following calculations:[3]

	Potato Chips	Cookies
Contribution margin per unit	$0.62	$0.35
Packages per square foot	× 2	× 4
Contribution margin per square foot of shelf space	$1.24	$1.40

3 We are assuming that the company can sell all the potato chips and cookies it stocks. If it can't, or if one product sells faster than the other, rate of turnover must be considered.

Even though potato chips have a higher contribution margin per unit of product ($0.62 versus $0.35), cookies have a higher contribution margin per square foot of shelf space ($1.40 versus $1.24), which is the critical resource. The management of Bolten Retail Company should stock cookies rather than potato chips, assuming that the company's only critical resource is shelf space.

However, if the demand for cookies is limited and Bolten never has potato chips for sale, will customers start shopping at other stores? In that case, Bolten should stock as many cookies as it can sell and use the balance of the critical resource for stocking potato chips. To illustrate, we assume that the market demand for cookies is 1,800 packages per month or an average of 60 per day.

Because it takes only 15 square feet of shelf space (60 packages ÷ 4 packages per square foot) to store one day's worth of cookies, 5 square feet of shelf space are available to stock potato chips. This means that 10 bags of potato chips can be stocked. Assuming all 10 bags are sold during each day, the combined sales of cookies and potato chips will contribute $27.20 to cover fixed costs and provide a profit, as shown below.

STOP & THINK

Why do you think that most grocery stores allocate more space to breakfast cereals than to most other products?

	Daily Contribution Margin
Packages sold:	
Potato chips (10 bags × $0.62 per bag)	$ 6.20
Cookies (60 packages × $0.35 per package)	21.00
Total	$27.20

This analysis shows that from a financial perspective, the best use of the 20 square feet of shelf space is to use 15 square feet for cookies and 5 square feet for potato chips. Because demand for cookies is limited, only a $21 daily contribution margin can be earned by selling cookies. The other 5 feet of shelf space should be used to stock potato chips. Obviously, nonfinancial factors, such as customer satisfaction, would also have to be considered in making the final decision of how much of each product to stock.

The foregoing analysis dealt with only two constraints: store shelf space and product demand. If a firm is further limited by other factors (such as the ability to buy certain amounts of particular products), management generally has to use the quantitative techniques of linear programming or simulation to help decide how many of each product to produce and/or sell. You can learn about this technique in advanced accounting or business management courses. Regardless of the number of constraints, though, the essence of the decision is to achieve the best short-term utilization of available resources.

In the expanded material section of this chapter, you will find a discussion of the theory of constraints, a philosophical approach to focusing on "constraints" as a way to allocate limited resources and improve management processes.

Caution

It is essential to carefully and accurately identify the scarce resource and the quantity of the scarce resource consumed by each product. For example, in the store shelf space decision, if you don't carefully calculate the amount of space needed for cookies and potato chips and instead look only at the contribution margin per unit, an incorrect decision will be made. It is only when you consider the contribution margin per square foot of shelf space that the correct decision is made.

TO SUMMARIZE: In deciding how to make the best use of critical resource factors, management should choose the item that provides the greatest contribution margin per unit of the most critical resource.

Setting Selling Prices

Some people argue that a discussion of setting prices in a book such as this is a waste of time because the market sets the price and there is nothing management can do to affect prices. Others argue that, especially in some markets, management does set prices or at least influence prices. In this section, we assume that management can influence prices and discuss those factors management should consider.

Pricing a product is partly a matter of guesswork because managers rarely know with any precision how price affects demand (e.g., how many more units could be sold if the price were to be lowered by a certain amount). In addition, other factors, such as advertising and packaging, affect the sale of a product.

The pricing process is further complicated by the fact that there are several broad categories of pricing decisions and the same cost information is not appropriate for all of them. Earlier, we considered the pricing of special orders. In this section, we cover the pricing of normal products. Other pricing categories, including the pricing of new products, are covered in advanced accounting and marketing texts.

Normal Pricing of Products

In deciding whether to accept special orders, we stated that the price must be high enough to cover variable and incremental fixed costs. The price normally charged for a product or service, however, must be high enough to cover all costs (including production, selling, and administrative costs) and still provide a reasonable return on the owners' investments. Therefore, all costs (variable, as well as a fair share of fixed costs) are relevant to the pricing decision. In some cases, however, the final price may be set somewhat above or below the price suggested by total cost plus a reasonable return. This occurs when pricing decisions are based primarily on supply and demand, competition, and other market factors. For example, textbook prices are strictly competitive. Whether it costs $250,000 or $500,000 to produce a textbook, the price of the book has to be close to that of the nearest competitors.

In supplying cost data to aid management in normal pricing decisions, accountants may use a functional approach, summarizing costs by function (manufacturing, selling, or administrative), or a contribution approach, classifying costs by behavior (fixed or variable). To illustrate the two approaches, we assume that Kent Electronics (from the calculator example earlier in the chapter) is pricing a desk calculator. The relevant costs for each approach are as follows:

Functional Cost Approach

Direct materials	$ 6
Direct labor	8
Manufacturing overhead (200% × direct labor cost)	16
Total manufacturing cost	$30
Markup to cover selling and administrative expenses and provide	
a reasonable return on investment (0.40 × selling price)	20
Estimated normal selling price	$50

Contribution Approach

Direct materials	$ 6
Direct labor	8
Variable manufacturing overhead	7
Variable selling and administrative overhead expenses	4
Total variable costs	$25
Markup to cover fixed costs and provide a reasonable	
return on investment (0.50 × selling price)	25
Estimated normal selling price	$50

The markups calculated here are based on the selling price because marketing people generally use this approach. How do we calculate the markup as a percentage of the selling price before that price is known? If the markup is to be 40% of the selling price, as in our first example, the total manufacturing cost must be 60% of the selling price. So we simply divide the manufacturing cost by 60% to get the selling price ($30 ÷ 0.60 = $50). Then, the selling price minus the manufacturing cost is the markup ($50 − $30 = $20).

If a functional cost approach is used, the markup must be large enough to cover all selling and administrative costs and provide a reasonable return on investment. If a contribution approach is used, the markup must be large enough to cover all fixed costs and generate a reasonable return on investment.

> **TO SUMMARIZE:** For normal pricing of products, management should consider all costs, not just differential costs (as was the case with pricing special orders). The markups applied must be high enough to cover all costs and expenses and provide a reasonable return on investment.

eXpanded *Material*

Thus far in this chapter, we have discussed how and why organizations evaluate products and processes, including the concepts of benchmarking and differential costs and revenues. We have also provided several examples of evaluation decisions, such as whether to accept special orders, whether to outsource or provide services and products internally, whether to continue or discontinue existing product lines or expand into new product lines or geographic regions, whether to sell or continue processing products developed from joint manufacturing processes, how best to use critical resources, and how to set selling prices. We have also explained how to make product and process evaluation decisions by focusing on differential costs and revenues. In this expanded section, we discuss another approach to making product and process evaluation decisions—the theory of constraints. This approach or philosophy, which has gained in popularity in recent years, was developed during the 1980s and involves making production decisions by focusing on bottleneck resources. The theory of constraints advocates that only constraint resources should operate at full capacity.

Theory of Constraints

5 Understand the theory of constraints and how focusing on scarce resources can direct activities in manufacturing companies.

theory of constraints (TOC) A management philosophy that focuses on constraint resources and holds that they should operate at full capacity.

To compete against global rivals in the early 1980s, managers from a variety of industries worked hard to revitalize their manufacturing practices. During this period, a manufacturing philosophy called the **theory of constraints (TOC)** or optimized production technology (OPT) received considerable attention. TOC was popularized by Eliyahu Goldratt, an Israeli physicist, in his book *The Goal.* Goldratt claimed that by scheduling production by focusing on bottleneck resources, a firm could develop and maintain a manufacturing-based competitive advantage over other firms. The premise of TOC is that only constraint resources should operate at full capacity. That is, a facility can produce a finished product no faster than the constraint resource can process the materials that go into the product. The constraint resource acts as the "drum," setting the production pace for the entire operation. Once material has been processed on the constraint resource, it should not sit idle but should be kept moving until shipped to the customer. By following a few basic rules, each of which focuses management's attention on the firm's constraint resource, managers can use TOC to maximize the throughput (amount of product produced in available facilities) of their production facility. The result is that the firm is better able to meet its customers' needs.

Constraint management can improve a company's competitive position by helping it better schedule and utilize its productive resources. When the constraint resource becomes the focal point, nonconstraint operations will operate below capacity, facilitating several positive outcomes. For example, nonconstraint resources no longer produce excess work-in-process (WIP) inventory; shop floor clutter and confusion are thereby reduced, production quality is improved, preventive maintenance activities are enhanced, and more time is available for employee training. By identifying the constraint resource and using it as the reference point for decision making, management can alter the very nature of key assumptions regarding product costing, performance measurement, product and process design, and make-versus-buy decisions. In general, the theory holds that more accurate assumptions lead to better decisions and enhanced competitiveness.

Employing TOC requires five basic steps:

1. *Understand the system's constraints.* The constraint may be a manufacturing process, a delivery process, or any other aspect of the process from taking delivery of raw materials to making sure finished products are sold and delivered.
2. *Decide how to exploit the system's constraints.* Production and pricing decisions should be based on the throughput yield per unit of constraint resource.
3. *Subordinate everything else to keeping the constraint resource operating at optimal capacity.* All nonconstraint activities should be coordinated with the constraint resource. This often requires a dramatic shift in managerial mindset, including allowing workers and machinery to sit idle or perform other, unrelated activities when not needed.
4. *Elevate the constraint.* By focusing on the constraint, it may be possible to offload some work to nonbottlenecks by acquiring more equipment or outsourcing some bottleneck work.
5. *If a constraint has been broken, go back to step 1.* Do not allow nonaction or inertia to cause a system constraint. Bottlenecks can, and will, shift around within an organization. Not properly identifying the relevant and current constraint can lead to a return of process inefficiencies and confused management policies.

Examples of companies that have adopted TOC are plentiful in the literature. For example, before employing TOC, a privately held metal tool manufacturing company used the ratio of indirect to direct labor hours as its key performance measure. Focusing on this measure caused the company to develop a "keep the workers busy at all costs" attitude, resulting in piles of excess WIP inventory, production inefficiencies, and a poorly focused pricing strategy. Under TOC, nonconstrained resources are allowed to sit idle, and the company uses this idle time to cross-train employees. As another example, a packing company struggled for a period of time with employees at nonbottlenecks who tried to stay busy by releasing WIP too early to the bottleneck operation. By implementing new, TOC-consistent performance measures, the company was able to eliminate buildups of WIP inventory and become more efficient.

As a simple example of the TOC, assume that Wilton Company requires five processes to make treadmills. The first process involves purchasing materials such as metal, rubber, and electronic components. There is no constraint on the amount of any of these materials that can be purchased. The second process involves manufacturing the various components of the treadmills. The equipment and personnel available to manufacture the components can produce parts for 20 treadmills per hour. The third process involves painting the various components. Painting equipment and personnel can process 18 treadmills per hour. The fourth process involves assembling the finished parts into completed treadmills. Assembly requires specially manufactured equipment that can process only 15 treadmills per hour. Finally, the fifth process, testing, has unlimited capacity because it involves labor only and additional workers can be hired. The following diagram shows the manufacturing processes and their capacities.

| Acquisition of Raw Materials (unlimited capacity) | → | Manufacture of Components (20 treadmills per hour) | → | Painting of Components (18 treadmills per hour) | → | Assembling Treadmills (15 treadmills per hour) | → | Testing of Treadmills (unlimited capacity) |

As you can see, if each process operated at full capacity, every hour the components for two treadmills would be produced that painting couldn't process, and three treadmills would be painted that couldn't be assembled. WIP inventory would accumulate in both the third and fourth processes, making production less efficient.

By focusing on the constraint resource—assembling in this case—the company might choose to purchase another specialized assembly machine, outsource some assembly, use the extra time in manufacturing components and painting to complete other jobs or cross-train, or even have some of the idle employees help out in testing treadmills. By focusing on constraint resources, management will know exactly where the bottlenecks are and can take action to fix the problem. Of course, if the constraint resource—assembly—is allowing the company to meet customer demands for treadmills, management may choose to undertake promotional campaigns or add additional products that can be made using excess capacity in component manufacturing and painting.

> **TO SUMMARIZE:** TOC is a management philosophy that focuses management's attention on the bottlenecks or constraint resources. Other measures can result in excess WIP inventory or other inefficiencies. TOC helps management understand the kinds of decisions that will make the firm more productive.

review of learning objectives

1 Explain how evaluation leads to planning and why products and processes must be continuously evaluated. Evaluation is designed to improve the efficiency and cost-effectiveness of existing operations related to products and operating processes. Such decisions usually are in the form of corrective actions regarding machinery efficiency, reduction of waste, efficient task performance, and overcoming bottlenecks. Evaluation takes place regularly, often daily, weekly, or monthly. Sometimes evaluation leads to strategic decisions that deal with changes in the product or the processes. These decisions might be related to the type or quality of the company's products, fundamental changes in the production process, changing suppliers or types of raw materials, or changing the product distribution system.

2 Understand why benchmarking is so important and how it is conducted. Benchmarking involves comparing a company's financial and operating performance against a competitor's performance or comparing the performance of various internal departments against each other. It consists of four steps: (1) analyzing the company's practices, procedures, and performance in a given process; (2) selecting a benchmark or benchmarks; (3) gathering information on the benchmark's practices and procedures; and (4) analyzing the data collected in step 3 to determine which policies and procedures used by the benchmarked companies can best be employed.

3 Understand the concept of differential costs and revenues, and be able to identify those costs and revenues that are relevant to making product and process decisions. Making product and process decisions involves a consideration of sunk costs, opportunity costs, and differential costs and revenues. Differential costs are future costs that will change as a result of the decision and therefore are the relevant costs in determining whether the decision to change should be made. Differential costs may be variable, fixed, or both. Past costs that do not change as a result of a decision are not relevant to the decision and are called sunk costs.

4 Identify several examples of product and process evaluation decisions, and be able to analyze and select the best alternative for each example. Examples of product and process decisions are (1) accepting or rejecting special orders, (2) making or buying products, (3) exiting or entering a market, (4) determining at what stage of production to sell products, and (5) selecting the best use of a scarce resource. In choosing whether to make or buy a component or service, management must compare the differential costs of making the part or providing the service (including the opportunity cost of alternative uses of the facilities or labor) with the cost of purchasing the part or service. In deciding whether or not to accept a special order in situations where there is excess capacity, the price should be high enough to provide a positive contribution toward covering normal fixed costs and increasing profit. A product or product line should not be dropped or a market exited unless that unit does not make a positive contribution toward covering indirect fixed costs. An alternative product or line of products can be added that will contribute more toward covering unavoidable indirect costs. A market should be entered only if it contributes to the overall profitability of the firm. It will always be profitable to continue processing a joint product after the split-off point as long as the incremental revenue from the extra processing exceeds the incremental processing costs incurred after the split-off point. Joint costs that have been incurred up to the point of split-off are always irrelevant to the decision. In deciding

how to use a scarce resource, management should choose the item that provides the greatest contribution margin per unit of the most critical resource. A product should be processed further if the additional revenues from further processing will exceed the additional costs of further processing. For normal pricing, management should consider all costs, not just differential costs.

5 Understand the theory of constraints and how focusing on scarce resources can direct activities in manufacturing companies. The theory of constraints (TOC) suggests that management should focus on the few "constraints" that are found in any management setting. The premise of TOC is that only constraint resources should operate at full capacity and that a facility can produce a finished product no faster than the constraint resource can process the materials that go into the product.

key terms & concepts

benchmarking, 1271
critical resource factor, 1293
differential costs, 1273
joint manufacturing process, 1291
joint product costs, 1291

opportunity cost, 1273
special order, 1279
sunk costs, 1273
total cost, 1276

theory of constraints (TOC), 1296

review problem

Whether to Make or Buy a Part

Schill Manufacturing Company makes lawn mowers. It has been buying a component from a regular supplier for $11.50 per unit. Because Schill recently has been operating at less than full capacity, the president is considering whether to make the part rather than purchase it. The estimated total cost of making the part under the company's costing system is $14.40, computed as follows:

Direct materials	$ 3.20
Direct labor	5.60
Manufacturing overhead (100% of direct labor cost)	5.60
Estimated total cost to make	$14.40

Variable manufacturing overhead costs are estimated to be 40% of direct labor cost. Fixed manufacturing costs that are not differential are 60% of direct labor cost.

Required:
Decide whether Schill should make or buy the component.

Solution

Differential-Cost Analysis

	Cost to Make	Cost to Buy
Purchase price		$11.50
Direct materials	$ 3.20	
Direct labor	5.60	
Variable manufacturing overhead (40% of direct labor cost)	2.24	
Differential cost to make the part	$11.04	
Differential cost to buy the part		$11.50
Cost savings by making the part	$ 0.46	

Total-Cost Analysis

	Cost to Make	Cost to Buy
Purchase price		$11.50
Direct materials	$ 3.20	
Direct labor	5.60	
Variable manufacturing overhead (40% of direct labor cost)	2.24	
Fixed manufacturing overhead	3.36	3.36
Total cost to make	$14.40	
Total cost to buy		$14.86
Cost savings by making the part	$ 0.46	

Calculations:
$5.60 × 0.40 = $2.24 variable manufacturing overhead
$5.60 × 0.60 = $3.36 fixed manufacturing overhead

Unless qualitative factors override the cost estimate, Schill should make the part rather than purchase it. The decision will be the same whether the calculation is based on differential costs only or on total costs. Note that the fixed manufacturing overhead cost applies to both making and buying the part under the total-cost analysis because these costs will be incurred whichever alternative is selected.

d iscussion questions

1. Why is it so important to continuously evaluate products and processes?
2. Many accounting systems are designed to collect financial information for the purpose of preparing financial statements. What problem does this create for an accountant who is asked to compile relevant data for use by managers to make product and process decisions? Explain.
3. What is a differential cost? Give an example of how differential costs are used by managers making product and process decisions.

4. Distinguish between variable costs and differential costs. Why is the distinction important?

5. Can a fixed cost be relevant to a decision? Explain.

6. What is a sunk cost? Why are sunk costs irrelevant in product and process decision making?

7. In deciding whether to replace an old asset with a new one, which of the following are differential revenues and costs?
   a. Cost of the new equipment
   b. Resale value of the old equipment
   c. Resale value of the new equipment
   d. Book value of the old equipment
   e. Operating costs of the new equipment

8. Distinguish between the total-cost approach and the differential-cost approach to analyzing data for product and process decisions.

9. What is the major limitation in using the total-cost approach to analyze data for product and process decisions?

10. Why must business decisions be based on qualitative as well as quantitative information? Explain.

11. Explain what costs are generally relevant to make-or-buy decisions.

12. Explain why opportunity costs are not included in the accounting records.

13. What is the significance of idle capacity in determining the price of a special order?

14. If total manufacturing costs, including fixed manufacturing overhead, are larger than the price offered by a purchaser for a special order, the order should not be accepted because the profits of the company will be adversely affected. Do you agree? Explain. (Ignore qualitative factors.)

15. In deciding whether to exit or enter a market, what factors should be considered?

16. When should a segment (product, product line, division, etc.) be dropped? When should a segment be added?

17. Why is the contribution margin per unit of a critical resource more important than the contribution margin per unit of product in deciding which products to produce and sell?

18. What determines whether a product should be sold at the point of separation from a joint process or after further processing? (Assume that a decision is to be based solely on quantitative information.)

19. Why does employing the TOC in manufacturing processes lead to less WIP inventory?

20. Proponents argue that the TOC helps management make better use of production resources and better decisions about whether or not to outsource and how to use employees effectively. Explain why this is so.

practice exercises

Practice 23-1

Evaluating Products and Processes

Which one of the following statements is *true*?

a. A company should be careful to completely separate the planning and evaluating functions.
b. Globalization has reduced the need for companies to operate efficiently and effectively.
c. Some companies do not perform well because they fail to develop appropriate corporate strategies.
d. Most methods of performance evaluation are the same now as they were 40 years ago.

Practice 23-2

Quality Dimensions

Which of the following is *not* one of the dimensions of quality mentioned in the chapter?

a. Reliability
b. Changeability
c. Serviceability
d. Durability
e. Perceived quality

Practice 23-3

Benchmarking

Which one of the following is *not* an example of effective benchmarking?

a. Comparing the company to other companies in the industry that have recently declared bankruptcy

(continued)

    b. Comparing less effective departments against the best-performing departments within the same organization

    c. Comparing the company against top competitors

    d. Comparing the company against the "best-in-class" both from within and outside of the company's industry

Practice 23-4

Differential Costs, Sunk Costs, and Opportunity Costs

Which one of the following statements is *false*?

a. A sunk cost is one that has already been incurred.

b. Differential costs can be eliminated in whole or in part by choosing one alternative over another.

c. Opportunity cost is the amount of profit given up by choosing one alternative over another.

d. A differential cost is one that cannot be avoided.

Practice 23-5

Sunk Costs

Which one of the following would be considered a sunk cost?

a. Variable cost of materials to build a new product

b. Additional insurance for a new product line

c. The total amount paid to purchase investment securities last year; the securities have recently declined in value by 50%

d. Expected annual maintenance costs for new equipment

Practice 23-6

Differential Costs and Decision Making

Using the following cost data, decide which alternative the company should pursue with respect to buying and operating a new piece of equipment. Use the differential-cost approach.

	Alternative A	Alternative B
Cost of new equipment	$23,300	$25,000
Licensing fee to operate equipment	1,200	800
Resale value of old equipment	500	500
Expected fixed operating costs	400	120
Original cost of old equipment	20,000	20,000

Practice 23-7

Total-Cost Approach

Refer to the data in Practice 23-6. Repeat your analysis using the total-cost approach.

Practice 23-8

Special Order Pricing

The company is deciding whether to accept a special order. The company's costs for the most recent year were as follows:

Total variable costs	$3,200,000
Total fixed costs	1,300,000

The company produced 100,000 units in the most recent year. What is the minimum price per unit at which the company should accept the special order (ignoring any qualitative factors)?

Practice 23-9

Special Orders—The Seller's Decision

At the end of a very mild winter, the company has enough raw materials to produce 1,000 coats, and the materials can be used only for coats. The material is very sensitive and will not be usable if it is not used immediately. The company does not expect to be able to receive the full sales price of $120 per coat, and the company needs production storage space to make room for the raw materials for its summer clothes inventory production. The company has received a special order from one of its customers for 1,000 coats at $70 per coat. The cost of making one coat (assuming a production run of 1,000 coats) is as follows:

Direct materials	$25 per coat
Direct labor	$40 per coat
Manufacturing overhead	$20 per coat

For the manufacturing overhead, $15 per coat relates to fixed overhead, primarily wages paid to special technicians who repair the equipment used to make the coats. These technicians are hired from an outside company and will not be hired if the coats are not made. Should the company accept the special order?

Practice 23-10

Making or Buying Manufactured Parts

The company currently makes a part used in the production of its best-selling product. The company has the option to buy this same part from a supplier for $34 per part. The company uses 750 of these parts each period and has the following cost data for producing these 750 parts:

	Cost per Unit
Direct labor	$12
Direct materials	7
Variable manufacturing overhead	8
Fixed manufacturing overhead, direct*	4
Fixed manufacturing overhead, indirect*	6

*Based on 750 units per period. If the parts are purchased from the supplier, the direct fixed manufacturing overhead costs can be avoided.

Should the company buy the 750 parts per period from the supplier or continue to make them?

Practice 23-11

Exiting a Market

Using the following information, decide whether the company should close any of its stores:

	Store 1	Store 2	Store 3
Sales revenue	$1,000,000	$1,200,000	$800,000
Variable costs	550,000	610,000	450,000
Direct fixed costs	200,000	310,000	305,000
Indirect fixed costs	70,000	70,000	70,000

Practice 23-12

Entering a Market

Refer to the data in Practice 23-11. The company's main customer is considering whether to merge with the company (and its three stores). If the merger takes place, the efficiencies associated with combining the stores with their main customer will cause variable costs at each of the three stores to decline by 25%. However, the merger will increase overall fixed costs by $300,000. Should the merger take place?

Practice 23-13

Additional Processing

Panaca Pork Products produces and sells ham, bacon, and sausage. For years, Panaca has sold only one version of its three products. However, Panaca is now considering selling "premium" versions of each of its products. The following information is available:

(continued)

	Number of Pounds Produced	Selling Price per Pound for Regular Product	Additional Processing Costs	Selling Price per Pound for Premium Product
Ham	1,000,000	$1.00	$120,000	$1.20
Bacon	400,000	0.90	90,000	1.10
Sausage	600,000	1.10	200,000	1.40

Before any additional processing costs, the total production cost for the 2,000,000 combined pounds of ham, bacon, and sausage is $1,400,000. Which, if any, of the three products (ham, bacon, and sausage) should Panaca sell as a premium product?

Practice 23-14

Contribution Margin Percentage

Using the following information, compute the contribution margin percentage for each product.

	Product A	Product B
Selling price	$380	$140
Variable costs	235	75

Practice 23-15

Critical Resource Factor

Refer to the data in Practice 23-14. Product A requires three units of the company's critical resource, while Product B requires only two units. Compute the contribution margin per unit of critical resource to determine which product the company should emphasize in its marketing campaign.

Practice 23-16

Setting Selling Prices: Contribution Approach

The company prices its products using a 40% markup on total variable cost to cover fixed costs and to provide a reasonable return on investment. Using the following data and the contribution approach to pricing products, estimate the normal selling price. *Note:* The markup will end up being 40% of the selling price.

	Cost per Unit
Direct materials	$10
Direct labor	17
Variable manufacturing overhead	13
Variable selling and administrative expenses	8

Fixed manufacturing overhead totals $80,000 per year. Fixed selling and administrative expenses are $55,000 per year. The average number of units sold per year is 5,000.

Practice 23-17

Setting Selling Prices: Functional Cost Approach

Refer to Practice 23-16. Assume that the company prices its products using a 30% markup on total manufacturing cost to cover selling and administrative expenses and to provide a reasonable return on investment. Using the following data and the functional cost approach to pricing products, estimate the normal selling price. *Note:* The markup will end up being 30% of the selling price.

Practice 23-18

Theory of Constraints
Which one of the following statements is *false*?

a. The process that is the company's constraint will always remain the company's constraint.
b. The constrained resource of an organization sets the pace for the whole operation.
c. Eliyahu Goldratt popularized the theory of constraints in his book, *The Goal*.
d. A company should focus much of its production efforts on exploiting the system's constraint.

Practice 23-19

Identifying the Constraint
The following chain of events represents the production process of the company. Which process is the constraint?

a. Acquisition of raw materials—200 units per hour
b. Cutting—35 units per hour
c. Shaping—65 units per hour
d. Sanding—50 units per hour
e. Assembling—30 units per hour
f. Delivering—150 units per hour

e x e r c i s e s

Exercise 23-1

Classifying Decisions
Indicate whether each of the following activities appears to be mostly related to planning, controlling, or evaluating:

1. Operational budgeting
2. Production prioritizing
3. Providing feedback to managers
4. Tracking performance
5. Strategic planning
6. Rewarding performance
7. Capital budgeting
8. Comparing costs, quality, and timeliness against previously prepared budgets
9. Analyzing results
10. Identification of problems

Exercise 23-2

Relevant Costs
Gilliland Company provides maid services for local hotels. Last year the firm acquired a cleaning machine for $50,000. The firm expected to use the machine for five years. However, this year a new, more efficient machine has been introduced on the market. The accountant for Gilliland has determined that the annual total operating costs for the old machine are $120,000. The annual operating costs for the new machine would be $100,000, and the purchase price is $65,000. The president of Gilliland feels the company should not buy the new machine. He points out that the operating costs of $100,000 and the purchase price of $65,000 for the new machine, plus the original cost of the old machine of $50,000, are greater than the operating costs of the old machine.

1. Do you agree with the president?
2. What type of cost is the $50,000 purchase price of the old machine?

Exercise 23-3

Qualitative Factors

Sturdy Chair Company manufactures wooden chairs. In producing the chairs, a great deal of scrap wood is created. The company currently uses the wood as fuel in a factory furnace. However, it has the opportunity to send the scrap wood to a subcontractor, who would turn it into pressed board to be used to produce small end tables as a new product of Sturdy Chair.

Identify any qualitative factors that Sturdy Chair Company might want to consider in deciding how to use the scrap wood.

Exercise 23-4

Special Order Pricing

You are the controller for Tippets Watch Company. The company has excess watches, which it has not been able to market through its own distribution outlets. To utilize the excess capacity, the president is negotiating with a large department store chain to sell Tippets watches. He has asked you to estimate the minimum selling price below which Tippets should not accept an order from the retail chain. Cost information per watch is:

Direct materials	$16
Direct labor	10
Manufacturing overhead:	
Variable	6
Fixed	4
Selling and administrative expenses:	
Variable	2
Fixed	6

The fixed costs are the same whether or not the order is accepted.

1. What is the minimum selling price the company should accept based solely on cost information (not considering qualitative factors)?
2. Assume that the president agrees to sell 20,000 watches at a price of $38 per watch. What would be the expected increase in profit?

Exercise 23-5

Make-or-Buy Decisions

Nelson Car Audio needs 500 amplifiers to complete this month's car stereo shipment. If Nelson Car Audio buys rather than makes the amplifiers, some of the facilities still cannot be used in another manufacturing activity. Twenty-five percent of the fixed manufacturing overhead costs are indirect and will still be incurred regardless of which decision is made. The per-unit costs of making and buying the amplifiers are:

Cost to make the amplifier:	
Direct materials	$ 25
Direct labor	50
Variable manufacturing overhead	35
Fixed manufacturing overhead	40
	$150
Cost to buy the amplifier from another company	$144

Identify the differential costs of making the amplifier as a basis for deciding whether to make or buy it.

Exercise 23-6

Spreadsheet

Make-or-Buy Decisions

Miller Manufacturing builds and markets personal computers for home and small business use. The company has been approached by an outside supplier offering to provide monitors to the company for $65 each. The company's marketing director negotiated the deal personally and is thrilled about how much cheaper it will be to purchase the monitors from outside. Producing the following cost data, the manager proudly proclaims, "Look, a $9 per-unit savings!"

	Per Unit	15,000 Units per Year
Direct materials	$28	$ 420,000
Direct labor	10	150,000
Variable manufacturing overhead	3	45,000
Fixed manufacturing overhead, direct	6	90,000
Fixed manufacturing overhead, indirect	27	405,000
Total cost	$74	$1,110,000

1. Assuming zero opportunity costs, should the company accept the outside offer?
2. If the monitors are purchased from outside, Miller can produce an alternative product that will contribute $250,000 per year toward covering indirect fixed overhead. Will this affect your decision in part (1)?

Exercise 23-7

Make-or-Buy Decisions

Tricia Company has been manufacturing 9,000 units of part Y for its products. The unit cost for the part is as follows:

Direct materials	$ 9
Direct labor	24
Variable manufacturing overhead	12
Fixed manufacturing overhead	18
Total	$63

A supplier has offered to sell 9,000 units of part Y to Tricia for $54 each. If the part is purchased, Tricia can use its facilities to manufacture another product, which would generate a contribution margin of $12,000. Seventy-five percent of the fixed manufacturing overhead costs are indirect and will still be incurred even if the part is purchased.

Compute the net differential cost in deciding whether to make or buy the part.

Exercise 23-8

Purchasing Services from Outside

Dr. Anderson, a local dentist, is considering reducing his office staff and outsourcing the management of his accounts receivable. Currently, he has an office manager and two part-time workers on his staff. One part-time employee spends almost 100% of her time sending out billing notices and following up on collections. Even then, Dr. Anderson is able to collect on only about 80% of the receivables. A collection agency wants Dr. Anderson's business. It will handle all billing and collection details for a monthly fee of $1,500. The agency believes it can deliver a 90% collection of receivables. Another firm, We Collect, Inc., has approached Anderson with a proposal that would shift all accounts receivable risk to We Collect, Inc. Anderson would receive 85% of all receivables automatically. Additional information follows:

Anderson's average yearly accounts receivable	$400,000
Anderson's average annual bad debt expense	80,000
Part-time accounts receivable employee salary	12,000

Which of the following alternatives should Anderson pursue concerning his accounts receivable?

1. Maintain status quo (part-time employee handling accounts receivable).
2. Outsource to collection agency.
3. Outsource to We Collect, Inc.

Exercise 23-9

Joint Costs and Further Processing

Pure Paint Company has been known for years for its two excellent interior wall paints: Nice & Smooth and Rich & Thick. The company has discovered that by processing Rich & Thick further it could produce a slightly different paint.

Nice & Smooth and Rich & Thick are produced jointly at a cost of $160,000, which is allocated equally between them. If Rich & Thick were processed further, its selling price would increase by $2.25 per unit, and the additional cost per unit would be $1.80.

1. On the basis of the information given (and disregarding qualitative factors), should the company process Rich & Thick further? Do you have enough information to make a recommendation? Explain.
2. **Interpretive Question:** Is the joint cost of $160,000 relevant to this discussion? Why or why not?

Exercise 23-10

Sell Now or Process Further

Colorado Company uses a joint process to manufacture Products R, S, and T. Each product can be sold at the point of separation, or it can be processed further. All additional processing costs are directly traceable to each product that is processed further. Joint production costs for the year are $140,000 and are allocated to Products R, S, and T on the basis of their sales values at the point of separation. The pertinent data accumulated by the accounting department for these products are:

Product	Units	Sales Value at Separation	Allocation of Joint Costs	Sales Value and Additional Costs of Processing Further	
				Sales Value	Additional Costs
R	18,000	$150,000	$70,000	$190,000	$24,000
S	20,000	120,000	56,000	150,000	40,000
T	10,000	30,000	14,000	60,000	25,000

1. Which products should Colorado Company process further (after separation) in order to maximize its profits? Show computations.
2. Explain why you did or did not use the allocated joint costs in deciding which of the products to process further.

Exercise 23-11

Spreadsheet

Discontinuing a Product Line

Swanton Company currently sells three products: desk calendars, pen sets, and paper-clip holders. The company is thinking of discontinuing the production and sales of paper-clip holders. However, because many customers buy the products as a set, Swanton estimates that the sales of the other two products will decrease by 20% if the paper-clip holders are discontinued.

Current data on each of the three products are provided below.

	Desk Calendars	Pen Sets	Paper-Clip Holders	Total
Units	40,000	20,000	12,000	
Sales revenue	$280,000	$240,000	$24,000	$544,000
Variable costs	160,000	160,000	26,000	346,000
Direct fixed costs	40,000	20,000	5,000	65,000
Indirect fixed costs	30,000	40,000	6,000	76,000

1. What is the segment margin of the paper-clip holders?

2. **Interpretive Question:** Would you recommend dropping the paper-clip holder product line? Why or why not?

Exercise 23-12

Adding a New Product

Cuda, Inc. is thinking about adding a new product line. Marketing surveys indicate that sales of the new product would be 100,000 units. Each unit sells for $8. Direct variable costs would be $5.60 per unit, direct fixed costs would be $60,000, and $45,000 represents the company's indirect fixed costs. The company does not expect the new product to affect the sales of its other products.

Should Cuda, Inc. add the new product? Why or why not?

Exercise 23-13

Contribution Margin per Unit of a Critical Resource

Haws Electronics produces two products, CD players and clock radios. Both products are extremely popular, and the company can sell as many of either product as it can produce. Haws Electronics can produce only a limited number of products, however, because only 12,000 direct labor hours are available due to the isolated location of the community. It takes four hours of direct labor to produce a CD player and three hours to produce a clock radio. The selling price of a CD player is $68, and the variable costs are $40. The selling price of a clock radio is $52, with variable costs of $28.

Which product should Haws Electronics produce if its direct labor hours are limited?

Exercise 23-14

Critical Resource Constraints

Whiz Kids manufactures two computer games. Far Out is a quiz game about astronomy, and Dynamite is a mystery game. The company has a limited supply of skilled labor and has been able to obtain only a limited number of "chips," a necessary part in the production process. Information on each product is as follows:

	Far Out	Dynamite
Contribution margin per unit	$ 4	$ 3
Units produced per hour	2	3
Units produced per 100 chips	80	60

Anticipated sales exceed capacity for both products.
Total labor hours available: 9,000 hours
Total chips available: 30,000 chips

1. Identify the critical resource constraint under which Whiz Kids must operate.
2. Which product should be produced?

Exercise 23-15

Pricing Regular Products

Medical Care, Inc., is considering what price to charge for Sparkle, a toothpaste that is sold in its leased store at a hospital. The accountant has been asked to prepare an estimated normal selling price based on the costs that Medical Care incurs in making the product in a factory it operates. Costs of producing one tube of Sparkle are 20 cents for direct materials, 10 cents for direct labor, 20 cents for variable manufacturing overhead, and 10 cents for variable selling and administrative costs. Total direct fixed costs are $10,000. The company estimates that a markup of 40% of the selling price is necessary to cover the fixed costs and provide a reasonable return on investment.

1. Calculate the estimated normal selling price.
2. Would you recommend that the company obtain any other information before establishing a sales price?

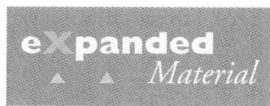

Exercise 23-16

Theory of Constraints

Rudyard Company makes replacement engines for jet aircraft. Making the engines involves four processes: (1) purchasing materials, (2) assembling the engines, (3) testing the engines, and (4) delivering the completed engines to customers. Although each of these processes is critical, delivery to customers is very difficult because of the weight of the engine, the sensitivity of the calibration, and the stabilization required for shipment. Rudyard has no problem purchasing component parts for the engines. Upon order, suppliers can deliver needed parts in any quantity within one day. Assembling engines, however, requires highly skilled employees. The company has three employees who can each assemble one engine every three days. Testing also requires highly skilled engineers who use simulators made to the company's specifications. Right now, Rudyard has two simulators, each of which can test one engine every four days. Currently, there is only one trucking company that can deliver the engines to customers and ensure that they will be treated with the necessary care. The trucking company can haul three engines per truck, but given the location of customers, it can deliver only 15 engines per month.

1. What is the constraint resource in this company?
2. How many engines should Rudyard be making per month?
3. How much excess time is available in the other processes?
4. How would you suggest the company use its excess resources?

p roblems

Problem 23-1

Special Order Pricing

Midwest Company manufactures portable radios. Shop Smart, a large retail merchandiser, wants to buy 200,000 radios from Midwest Company for $12 each. The radio would carry Shop Smart's name and would be sold in its stores.

Midwest Company normally sells 420,000 radios per year at $16 each; its production capacity is 540,000 units per year. Cost information for the radios is as follows:

Production costs:	
Variable production costs	$7
Fixed manufacturing overhead ($2,100,000 ÷ 420,000 units)	5
Selling and administrative expenses:	
Variable	1
Fixed ($420,000 ÷ 420,000 units)	1

The $1 variable selling and administrative expenses would not be applicable to the radios ordered by Shop Smart because that is a single large order. Shop Smart has indicated that the company is not interested in signing a contract for less than 200,000 radios. Total fixed costs will not change regardless of whether the Shop Smart order is accepted.

Required:

1. Identify any opportunity costs that Midwest Company should consider when making the decision.
2. Determine whether Midwest Company should accept Shop Smart's offer.
3. **Interpretive Question:** What qualitative factors might be relevant to this decision?

Problem 23-2

Make-or-Buy Decisions

Logan Company manufactures several toy products. One is a large plastic truck, which requires a plastic truck body, two metal axles, and four rubber wheels. Logan currently manufactures and assembles all the parts.

Another toy company has offered to sell the parts to Logan at $1.70 per truck if 20,000 or more parts are purchased each year, and at $2 per truck if less than 20,000 parts are purchased. Logan is considering this offer. The space used in producing the parts could be used for a new toy, which is scheduled to begin production next year. If Logan continues to produce the parts for the plastic truck, the company will have to lease space from another company in an adjacent building to produce the new toy. The rent would be $8,000 per year.

Other information related to the truck is:

	Produce Parts	Assemble Truck	Total
Direct materials	$1.10	$0.20	$1.30
Direct labor	0.30	0.20	0.50
Variable manufacturing overhead	0.20	0.15	0.35
Fixed manufacturing overhead	0.20	0.40	0.60
Total manufacturing costs	$1.80	$0.95	$2.75

The marketing department has estimated that sales for the plastic truck will be approximately 16,000 units per year for the next three years. The fixed manufacturing overhead is indirect and will still be incurred regardless of which decision is made.

Required:

1. Describe Logan Company's two alternatives for this decision.
2. What costs are relevant to the decision?
3. Which alternative should Logan Company select?
4. What would be the best decision had Logan not planned to produce the new toy?
5. **Interpretive Question:** What are some of the qualitative factors that Logan Company might consider in making the decision?

Problem 23-3

Choosing between Two Machines

Bruce's Bakery is thinking of making its own Danishes. Two machines, A and B, are being considered for purchase. The company now purchases the Danishes from an outside supplier for 20 cents each. The cost information for producing the Danishes would be:

	Machine A	Machine B
Variable costs per Danish	$0.16	$0.14
Annual fixed costs	$3,500	$5,000
Initial cost of machine	$10,000	$24,000
Salvage value at end of five years	$0	$8,000
Estimated life of machine	5 years	5 years

Required:

1. At a sales volume of 275,000 Danishes per year, which of these alternatives is best—buying the Danishes, using machine A, or using machine B? (Ignore the time value of money, and assume straight-line depreciation.)
2. At what level of production would you be indifferent between machine A and machine B? Which machine is preferable if production exceeds this volume?

Problem 23-4

Purchasing Services from Outside

Northeast Reinsurance Company is growing rapidly. As it has grown, it has added legal staff to provide for its legal services. One of the principals of the company is an attorney who has provided oversight over the growing legal department. However, she is now too busy to continue this "legal counsel" role. She suggests that the senior company attorney become an officer of the company and be given the title "legal counsel and secretary." Another of the principals is good friends with an attorney at a prestigious regional law firm. That law firm has offered to provide Northeast with legal services for an annual retainer of $500,000 plus an average billing rate of $100 per hour for all work done over 5,000 hours per year. It is expected that legal work, whether done inside or outside the company, will require about 6,000 hours this coming year and will probably increase by 10% a year thereafter. The current company legal staff may be able to handle the work load for two years before it will have to hire another attorney (at an expected salary and benefit package of $100,000). Other variable costs are expected to increase by 5% a year.

Additional information follows:

	Current Costs of Internal Legal Department
Salaries and benefits of legal staff	$350,000
Travel costs	80,000
Required continuing education costs	10,000
Legal support costs (library, computers, software, supplies, etc.)	100,000
Other variable costs	25,000
Allocated office overhead (depreciation, utilities, etc.)	40,000
Total costs of legal department	$605,000

Required:

1. What are the relevant costs for Northeast to consider in making this decision?
2. From a financial standpoint, should Northeast continue to use its own legal department for legal services or outsource this function to the regional law firm?
3. What other factors might Northeast consider in making this decision?

Problem 23-5

𝒮preadsheet

Unifying Concepts: Make-or-Buy Decisions (Differential Costs and Opportunity Costs)

Snow Corporation manufactures freezers for residential use. The company is planning to produce a new freezer suitable for apartments. These smaller freezers require a component that Snow Corporation can either make or buy from a subcontractor. The subcontractor will sell the part for $46. The costs for making 12,000 units of the part are as follows:

Direct materials	$20 per unit
Direct labor	$15 per unit
Variable manufacturing overhead	$10 per unit
Fixed manufacturing overhead	$40,000*

*The $40,000 fixed manufacturing overhead includes $24,000 of indirect fixed costs allocated to the part and $16,000 for a production manager.

If the part is produced, Snow Corporation will use an idle machine it already owns. If the part is bought, the company plans to rent the machine and the factory space to another company for $8,000 and $14,000 a year, respectively.

Snow expects that, if the part is produced, the company will be able to schedule production so that no warehouse space will be needed. However, if the part is bought, Snow will need to use warehouse space, for which it will have to pay $2,000 a year in rent.

Required:

1. Identify any opportunity costs relevant to the decision to make or buy the component.
2. Determine the differential costs of making the product.
3. Determine the differential costs of buying the product.
4. **Interpretive Question:** Would you recommend that Snow make or buy the component? Why?

Problem 23-6

Processing Past the Point of Separation

Style Company manufactures three items, S1, S2, and S3, which are used in the production of fabrics. Each item can be sold at the point that all three are separated from the joint production process, or they can be processed further. Presently, S1 and S2 are processed past the point of separation. The joint cost of producing the three items to the point of separation is $450,000. The costs past the point of separation are variable and can be traced to each product. The $450,000 joint costs are allocated to each product equally.

The following information is available:

	Number of Units Produced	Selling Price per Unit at Point of Separation	Additional Processing Costs	Selling Price per Unit After Processing
S1	100,000	$10	$120,000	$12
S2	40,000	9	90,000	11
S3	60,000	11	?	13

Required:

1. Should S1 and S2 be processed after the separation point?
2. What maximum additional processing costs could be incurred to process S3 further and still leave a profit?

Problem 23-7

Dropping a Product Line

Bryce Baseballs manufactures baseballs, baseball bats, and baseball gloves. The company is thinking of dropping baseball gloves as a product line. The following report was prepared by the accounting department:

	Baseballs	Baseball Bats	Baseball Gloves	Total
Sales revenues	$ 240,000	$105,000	$ 25,000	$ 370,000
Variable costs	(185,000)	(70,000)	(12,000)	(267,000)
Contribution margin	$ 55,000	$ 35,000	$ 13,000	$ 103,000
Direct fixed costs	(20,000)	(10,000)	(13,500)	(43,500)
Segment margin	$ 35,000	$ 25,000	$ (500)	$ 59,500
Indirect fixed costs	(17,500)	(10,000)	(2,500)	(30,000)
Net income	$ 17,500	$ 15,000	$ (3,000)	$ 29,500

Required:

1. Should the baseball glove line be dropped? Why or why not?
2. **Interpretive Question:** What qualitative factors should be considered in deciding whether to drop the baseball glove line?

Problem 23-8

Adding and Dropping Product Lines

Park Manufacturing Company has been producing three products: W, X, and Y. Now that the plant has been shifted to an assembly-line operation, a fourth product, Z, has been added. Each product has its own assembly-line operation, producing 10,000 units. Total indirect fixed costs of $48,000 are divided proportionately, based on the space allocated to each assembly line. Other pertinent information is given below.

	W	X	Y	Z
Selling price per unit	$6.00	$5.00	$5.40	$3.00
Variable cost per unit	$4.00	$3.60	$3.60	$2.60
Number of square feet	1,600	1,200	1,100	900

Required:
1. Prepare a schedule that shows net income for each product line.
2. Would total company income increase if product Z were dropped? Why or why not?
3. **Interpretive Question:** If you could double the production of W, X, or Y in place of having Z, which would you choose? Why?

Problem 23-9

Shutting Down or Continuing Operations

End Trail Campground is open year-round. However, 80% of its revenues are generated from May through October. Because only 20% of the revenues are generated from November to April, the campground is considering closing during those months. The yearly revenues and cost information expected by End Trail for next year if the campground does not close are:

Camping fees	$1,800,000
Variable costs	990,000
Fixed costs ($40,000 per month)	480,000

The cost to close the campground at the end of October would be $20,000, and the cost to reopen in May would be $50,000. If the campground is closed, the total fixed costs are only $25,000 per month, rather than the $40,000 per month when the campground is open.

Required:
Determine whether End Trail Campground should close from November to April or remain open for the entire year.

Problem 23-10

Determining Production with a Critical Resource Limitation

Clarity Corporation produces three sizes of television sets: 10-inch screen, 19-inch screen, and 24-inch screen. The revenues and costs per unit for each size are as follows:

	Screen Size		
	10-inch	19-inch	24-inch
Selling price	$195	$325	$450
Variable costs:			
Direct materials	$ 55	$100	$126
Direct labor	80	120	180
Variable manufacturing overhead	40	60	90
Total variable costs	$175	$280	$396
Contribution margin	$ 20	$ 45	$ 54
Units ordered for next week	200	150	75

The company has a constraint on the amount of skilled labor available to produce television sets. Direct labor employees are paid $8 per hour. The total amount of labor time available for next week's production is 2,700 hours.

Required:
Given the units ordered for next week, which size or sizes of television sets should be produced and sold to maximize the company's profit?

Problem 23-11

Determining Production with a Critical Resource Limitation
A company is examining two of its products, X-121 and Y-707. The following information is being reviewed:

	X-121	Y-707
Unit selling price	$28.50	$21.00
Materials required per unit	$3.00	$1.50
Direct labor required per unit	$2.50	$1.25
Variable manufacturing overhead per unit	$0.50	$1.00
Production time per unit (in hours)	1.5	1

Required:
1. Which item should the company manufacture if there is no constraint on hours of production?
2. If full production capacity is 1,500 hours, and if the company can sell all the units it makes, which item should it manufacture? Why?

Problem 23-12

Spreadsheet

Contribution Margin per Unit of a Critical Resource
Dresser, Inc., manufactures three super-sports-hero dolls: Super Dunk, Pete Tulip, and Zonk. Production, however, is limited by the skilled labor necessary to produce these unique dolls. Data on each of the dolls are as follows:

	Super Dunk	Pete Tulip	Zonk
Contribution margin per doll	$6	$4	$5
Dolls produced per hour	20	28	25
Expected total market volume (units)	20,000	9,000	100,000

Total skilled labor hours available: 4,500 hours.

Required:
Assuming that there are no relevant qualitative factors, how many dolls of each type should Dresser produce?

Problem 23-13

Unifying Concepts: Production and Advertising
Cole Company manufactures only two products—a battery charger and a testing machine for automobile engines. An average of 30,000 chargers and 50,000 testers are sold each year. This year, the company can afford only $60,000 for advertising the products, which is just enough to advertise one product effectively. The marketing manager expects that the sales of chargers will increase by 20% if they are advertised and that the sales of testers will increase by 10% if they are advertised.

The following information about the two products has been provided by the accountant:

(continued)

	Charger	Tester
Selling price per unit	$70	$90
Variable cost per unit	$30	$40
Fixed cost per unit	$30	$40
Production time per unit (in hours)	2	4

Required:
1. If Cole had an unlimited number of labor hours, would you recommend that it advertise either of its products? If yes, which one and why?
2. Assume that Cole has a capacity of 260,000 labor hours. Should Cole still advertise? If so, which product should it advertise?

Problem 23-14

Normal Selling Price

Chojna Lighting Supply manufactures desktop and ceiling-mounted light fixtures. The company is seeking to come up with a reasonable price for its desktop executive model. Production costs for each unit follow:

Direct materials	$7 per unit
Direct labor	1.5 hour per unit
Direct labor rate	$4 per hour
Variable manufacturing overhead	$3 per labor hour
Variable selling and administrative costs	$2 per unit
Fixed overhead (direct)	$3 per unit
Markup of selling price to cover indirect overhead and expected profit	40%

Required:
Calculate the estimated normal selling price.

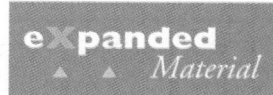

Problem 23-15

Theory of Constraints

Dalton Enterprises makes several products, including microwave ovens, dishwashers, and vacuum cleaners. Each manufacturing process requires several production processes. Right now, the company has large amounts of money tied up in work-in-process inventory at various locations throughout the company. Although Dalton has tried to eliminate this inventory, each month the inventory seems to increase. In addition, the company has a salary incentive system that pays production employees bonuses if they meet budgeted production quotas. The bonuses pay increasingly higher amounts for each unit that is produced in excess of the quota. In recent years, employees have been receiving large production bonuses under the incentive plan, so management knows that the employees are working hard and being productive. These higher bonuses, combined with the money tied up in work-in-process inventory, are creating a cash flow problem for the company.

You have been hired to help the company fix its cash flow problems. You have just attended a conference on the theory of constraints.

Required:
Explain how you could apply what you have learned to help the company with its problems.

discussion cases

Case 23-1

Buying from Inside or Outside the Company

E & B Company has two divisions, processing and finishing. The Finishing Division has been purchasing certain products from the Processing Division at a price of $80 per unit. (A unit consists of 100 yards of material.) The Processing Division has announced that, starting next month, it will raise its price to $100 per unit. As the manager of the Finishing Division, you object to this price and have indicated that you are planning to purchase these units of material from outside suppliers at a price of $85 per unit. You have asked the accounting department to furnish cost data to help you understand why the Processing Division's price has to be raised to $100 per unit. Following is the information supplied about the Processing Division's operations:

Units produced for Finishing Division	2,000
Variable production costs per unit	$60
Indirect fixed costs allocated to the Processing Division	$50,000
Normal profit per unit in Processing Division	$15

If the Finishing Division buys from outside suppliers, the facilities used by the Processing Division to manufacture these units for the Finishing Division will remain idle.

Answer the following questions:

1. If the Processing Division is successful in imposing the $100 price and the Finishing Division elects to buy from outside suppliers, what impact does this action have on the overall profit of E & B Company?
2. Explain why the variable production costs, the fixed costs, and the normal profit are, or are not, each relevant to this decision. (You are not being asked to discuss whether the $100 price is an appropriate price or whether the division managers should be allowed to maintain an autonomous posture in this decision.)
3. What additional factors should E & B Company's top management consider in resolving this matter?

Case 23-2

Sunk Costs

Sam Love owns and manages a small but growing service business. In fact, this year has been so good that Sam is moving his office to a larger, more centrally located site. In an effort to save on moving costs, Sam employs his brother Dan (who owns a large truck) to haul his office furniture and equipment. Unfortunately, Dan doesn't properly secure the rear door of the truck, and one of Sam's two copy machines winds up in a million pieces in the middle of the highway. As the two brothers survey the damage, Sam's office manager approaches and says, "Well, look on the bright side, the machine was half depreciated."

Should Sam take comfort from this statement? Explain your answer.

Case 23-3

Why Most Companies Want to Benchmark

Everyone wants to benchmark these days. Assume you are the dean of a business school with a highly successful MBA program. You have enjoyed increasing numbers of highly qualified applicants, recruiters love your students, and both *Business Week* and *U.S. News and World Report* have ranked you in the top 10 business schools in the United States. You have just been contacted by the deans of two other business schools, whose MBA programs rank well below yours. They would like to spend a couple of days at your school benchmarking against your admissions, advising, placement, and other services, as well as studying your curriculum, faculty development processes, and other ingredients of your success. You would like to help them but are not sure you want to reveal why you have been so successful. If you don't expose your secrets of success, however, their visits would largely be a waste of time. What should you do? Should you welcome your competitors with open arms, or should you refuse to allow them to benchmark against you? Or, should you allow them to come but hide your best secrets from them?

judgment calls

Judgment 23-1

You Decide: Should a company benchmark its financial performance against competitors, or does such benchmarking create tunnel vision with respect to a company's growth and achievement of goals?

Over the years, it has become very common for companies to benchmark or compare themselves to others in the same industry or market. Are companies similar enough that benchmarking is useful, or is it a waste of time? In addition, do you really believe that competitors will share confidential information with each other?

Judgment 23-2

You Decide: Which is more important to a company's overall success and profitability: quantitative or qualitative factors?

Often a company is judged based on the strength of financial indicators, such as sales revenue, net income, or earnings per share. However, many of these measures fail to incorporate intangible items, such as delivery time, quality control, and customer service. In a management accounting field setting, which factors are most important?

Competency Enhancement Opportunities

▶ **Analyzing Real Company Information**
▶ **International Case**
▶ **Ethics Case**
▶ **Writing Assignment**

▶ **The Debate**
▶ **Internet Search**

The following additional assignments provide opportunities for students to develop critical thinking, ethical perspectives, oral and written communication skills, experience with electronic research, and teamwork through group and business activities.

▶ *Analyzing Real Company Information*

Analyzing 23-1 (Microsoft)

Go to the Form 10-K for MICROSOFT provided in Appendix A at the back of this textbook. Read through the report to determine how many segments of business exist within Microsoft. What approach does Microsoft appear to use in identifying operating segments within the company at large?

Analyzing 23-2 (Main Line Pictures, Inc. versus Kim Basinger)

Hollywood produces a lot of entertainment, including accounting entertainment! In early 1993, the Superior Court of the State of California (Los Angeles County) heard a litigation suit filed by MAIN LINE PICTURES, INC., against the actress Kim Basinger for breach of contract. At issue was Basinger's decision to withdraw from a film project after making a verbal commitment to appear in it. The film, released in September 1993, was *Boxing Helena*. Didn't see it? That was the point of Main Line's lawsuit: the studio claimed a lot of people didn't see *Boxing Helena* because the actress who replaced Basinger (Sherilyn Fenn) did not have nearly the same box office appeal.

Main Line claimed damages due to an incremental difference in revenues and costs, which led to actual profits being less than expected, all due to not having Basinger in the film. An expert economist and an expert in film finance were called to testify regarding the appropriate size of the incremental revenue and cost differences. Hence, the case essentially became an accounting argument.

Main Line's lawyers argued that their client lost between $5.1 million and $9.7 million as a result of Basinger's withdrawal. The $5.1 million loss calculation is shown below (all amounts are in millions).

Minimum Damages, Plaintiff			
	With Basinger	Without Basinger	Difference
Foreign presales	$ 7.60	$ 2.70	$ 4.90
Domestic presales	3.00		3.00
Total revenue	$10.60	$ 2.70	$ 7.90
Production costs	(7.60)	(4.80)	(2.80)
Profit (loss)	$ 3.00	$(2.10)	$ 5.10

To understand the numbers above, you need to know a couple of things about revenues and costs in the movie business and this film in particular.

- It is extremely difficult to predict what a film will actually earn when released. There are *plenty* of examples of big budget films that did poorly at the box office, as well as inexpensive, independent films that have done very well. Hence, presale revenue (guaranteed minimum payments by a film distributor to the film producer) is the only sure revenue the producer can bank on when budgeting costs of making the film. If the film does well, then the distributor and producer share in the profits.
- After Basinger dropped out of the film, one of Main Line's partners loaned $1.7 million to the project, to be repaid out of domestic revenues.
- Often the producer will contract to share profits from presales, as well as incremental profits, with key actors. Basinger was to be paid a guaranteed $1 million to star in the film. In addition, she, her proposed co-star Ed Harris, and writer/director Jennifer Lynch were to be paid a total of 20.5% of the producer's net profits. On the other hand, Sherilyn Fenn and her co-star, Julian Sands, each received only a $100,000 guaranteed salary.
- After Basinger dropped from the film project, the producer made some changes to scale back production costs by $1.9 million.
- Often a movie project has many investing partners. Main Line had a partnership with Philippe Caland, who was, essentially, to receive 50% of net profits (after participation payments to the actors and writer), up to a maximum of $2 million.
- After withdrawing from *Boxing Helena*, Basinger received $3 million from a separate producer to star in *Final Analysis*.

Do you agree with the numbers presented above by the plaintiff? Consider all the information provided above and adjust the incremental profit analysis if needed. Be sure to defend your decision to use or not use each piece of information provided.

Source: Adapted from T. L. Barton, W. G. Shenkir, and B. C. Marinas, "Main Line vs. Basinger: A Case in Relevant Costs and Incremental Analysis," *Issues in Accounting Education*, Spring 1996, pp. 163–174.

International

▷ *International Case*

Ameripill Company

Located in Bartow, Alabama, the Pharmaceutical Division of AMERIPILL COMPANY ranks among the top 15 drug companies in the world. The European Unit of the Pharmaceutical Division is divided into three markets: United Kingdom (U.K.), Germany, and France. Actual and budgeted operating reports for two recent years are presented below for these three markets.

	United Kingdom		Germany		France	
	Year 2 Budget	Year 1 Actual	Year 2 Budget	Year 1 Actual	Year 2 Budget	Year 1 Actual
Sales	$49,960	$48,080	$156,840	$137,440	$108,720	$102,560
Cost of sales	(21,982)	(21,155)	(65,872)	(57,995)	(53,414)	(50,254)
Direct expenses	(14,658)	(14,512)	(50,286)	(46,603)	(31,529)	(29,742)
Other income/expenses	(1,499)	(1,155)	(300)	(210)	(946)	(1,026)
Responsibility earnings	$11,821	$11,258	$ 40,382	$ 32,632	$ 22,831	$ 21,538
Interest income/expense*	(358)	(241)	(1,312)	(939)	(1,033)	(1,047)
Exchange gain/loss**	(142)	(338)	(150)	(210)	(272)	(286)
Division charges***	(1,629)	(1,640)	(4,700)	(4,123)	(3,262)	(3,077)
Earnings before taxes	$ 9,692	$ 9,039	$ 34,220	$ 27,360	$ 18,264	$ 17,128
Segment assets	$84,500	$88,860	$ 73,760	$ 72,900	$ 74,220	$ 73,460
Earnings before taxes	19.4%	18.8%	21.8%	19.9%	16.8%	16.7%
Return on assets	11.5%	10.2%	46.4%	37.5%	24.6%	23.3%

*Based on locally incurred debt.

**Based on the average Year 1 exchange rate with the United States.

***Fixed charge negotiated annually between the Bartow Division and the market subsidiary.

1. Analyze these reports carefully. Assuming that Ameripill requires a minimum ROA of 12%, should the company consider dropping the U.K. market?

2. Ameripill currently has a problem with one of the drugs sold in France. In the French market, Saincoeur is a highly successful treatment for heart-attack victims. (It is also sold under other names in all of Ameripill's markets.) Because of regulatory pressure in France, Saincoeur is being sold at a much lower price in France than in Germany or the United Kingdom. Despite the price ceiling, Saincoeur is a profitable product (barely) in France. However, word of the lower price is creating a lot of pressure in the neighboring markets to reduce the prices to a level similar to that of the French market. Saincoeur is a very profitable product in both Germany and the United Kingdom. How do these facts affect your previous decision regarding the U.K. market in part (1)?

Source: Adapted from S. F. Haka, B. A. Lamberton, and H. M. Sollenberger, "International Subsidiary Performance Evaluation: The Case of the Ameripill Company," *Issues in Accounting Education*, Spring 1994, pp. 168–190.

▷ *Ethics Case*

Play World, Inc.

Roger Smith, the controller of Play World, Inc., a toy company, has just completed an analysis of a make-or-buy decision with respect to a particular part for one of the new toys the company is planning to manufacture. The result of the analysis clearly shows that the company should buy the part from one of the three available suppliers (based on written price quotations received from those suppliers within the past few weeks). Based on this analysis, Smith and the division manager, Kate Pfirman, agreed to proceed with placing an order. They issued instructions to the purchasing department indicating that the order should be placed for a price not higher than $3.40 per part. A few days later, Smith received a phone call from the purchasing department indicating that all three suppliers had raised their price to $4.00 per unit. It was a normal business practice to raise prices after written quotations had been issued.

It was immediately clear to Smith that it would be disadvantageous to his company to buy the part at the higher price. He discussed the new information with Pfirman, and they agreed to proceed with manufacturing plans to make the part internally. Smith thought it was rather strange that all three suppliers had raised their price to the same amount, but felt there was nothing he could do about it.

A few days later, Smith's secretary, Lynn Berry, asked if she could have a private conversation with him. Berry was obviously upset, so Smith asked her to come into his office and shut the door. Berry told him she was good friends with the secretary for the president of one of the suppliers from which Play World had planned to buy the part for the new toy. Berry's friend had casually mentioned that her boss had been on the phone with the other suppliers and they had agreed to raise the price for certain parts they were manufacturing to specified dollar amounts. Berry said she was reluctant to tell Smith because she didn't want her friend to get in trouble for revealing confidential information outside her company. For Smith, this information was the missing piece that explained why the price for the part had been raised to $4.00 by all three companies. Smith thanked Berry for the information and told her not to worry; he would keep the information to himself but would give some thought to what he would eventually do with what she had told him.

1. Who are the parties that are affected by this bid-rigging scheme?
2. What should Smith do with the information he received from Berry (keep in mind his responsibilities to the accounting profession, to his company, and to Berry)?

▶ Writing Assignment

Airline Ticket Prices
If you have ever shopped for airline tickets, you are aware of the tremendous diversity in ticket prices for the same flight, even for those who sit in the same section (first-class, coach, etc.). Much of the difference is based on two factors: (1) when you bought your ticket and (2) whether you plan to stay over a Saturday night.

Write a one- to two-page paper describing why airline companies have so many different ticket prices. Also, why do you think it is important to the airline that clients fly back from their business trips on Sunday instead of Saturday?

▶ The Debate

Total Costs versus Differential Costs
As discussed in this chapter, a management accountant can choose whether to present information using total costs or differential (e.g., incremental) costs. Divide your group into two teams. Each group will defend cost analysis for relevant decision making using either total costs or differential costs.

- One team represents "Total Costs." Present the advantages of using total costs for decision making. What are the disadvantages of using differential costs?

(continued)

- The other team represents "Differential Costs." Present the advantages of using differential costs for decision making. What are the disadvantages of using total costs?

▶ *Internet Search*

Benchmarking in Europe

Early in the chapter, we discussed the concept of benchmarking, a new evaluation method that has been used extensively in recent years. We discussed benchmarking in the context of one company comparing its financial and operating performance against a competitor's performance or comparing the performance of various internal departments against each other. However, benchmarking is a concept that can be used in any type of organization or even for yourself. Take the EUROPEAN COMMISSION, for example. Since the mid-1990s, the commission has undertaken a number of benchmarking initiatives so that member countries can compare best practices at three levels: country and business environment, company or enterprise, and industry or sector. The European Commission discusses its benchmark initiatives at the following Web site: **http://www.benchmarking-in-europe.com**. (Sometimes Web addresses change, so if this address does not work, access the Web site for this textbook, **http://albrecht.swlearning.com**, for an updated link.) Go to this site and answer the following questions:

1. List the four basic steps in benchmarking it identifies.
2. Identify the objective of enterprise policy benchmarking.
3. What method has been used to benchmark in the area of enterprise policy?

Continuous Improvement in Management Accounting

After studying this chapter, you should be able to:

1 Explain the fundamentals of building a balanced scorecard.

2 Anticipate that both management accounting and financial accounting are poised for important changes.

Learning Objectives

It has been said, "knowledge is power!" The ability to compete effectively in the economy has always been a function of the knowledge and abilities that a company can pull together and emphasize in the process of creating new products, making good decisions, and implementing effective processes. Throughout this text, we have generally classified organizations as manufacturers, merchandisers, or service providers. However, in this new age, more and more successful companies really can't be classified into *one* of these three categories. We've often used MICROSOFT as an example company in this textbook. What kind of company is Microsoft? Does this company manufacture products? Does it distribute merchandise? Does it sell services? Actually, Microsoft does all three things, but that still doesn't adequately describe this company. Microsoft is one of the key citizens in what might be called a "New Economy" that runs more on intangible assets, such as intellectual property, than tangibles such as plants, equipment, and distribution channels. A lot of these New Economy companies have comparatively few tangible assets, and yet they are obviously considered to be very valuable by the stock market. What this tells you is that traditional accounting models aren't capturing the value. Accounting, in other words, may no longer deliver accountability for many organizations.

For example, Bill Gates and Microsoft are continually hiring many of the world's smartest scientists and creating a giant research laboratory. Their goal is to determine the future of computing. As this effort goes forward, the value of Microsoft as a company rises and falls based on progress and problems in its research and development processes. To support Microsoft's quest to develop new products and technologies, 20,800 of its 50,500 full-time employees work in product development and research. One very interesting process to watch at Microsoft is the internal conflict regarding its flagship Windows product and a rising new software called ".Net"—a platform for XML Web services that allows applications to communicate and to share data over the Internet, regardless of operating system or programming language. Putting an accurate value on the Windows technology at Microsoft is difficult, but no one can question that much of the market value of Microsoft, one of the most important companies in the world today, is based on Windows—a proprietary technology that Microsoft guards very carefully.

However, .Net technology may be the biggest threat to the future of Windows that Microsoft has ever seen. It's ironic, then, that .Net is Microsoft's own technology. When the .Net strategy was launched, Chairman and Chief Software Architect Bill Gates said .Net was a "bet-the-company thing." Initially, Gates committed half of Microsoft's $4 billion budget to .Net breakthroughs. June 2003 marked the third anniversary of the unveiling of .Net and although Microsoft is committed to the vision of .Net, its success has been guarded. Neil Charney, director of Microsoft's Platform Strategy Group, said this about .Net, "If you look back from where we were three years ago, it's been incredible progress. But is there more work to do? Absolutely."

In the midst of all this effort and diverging opinions, the economic value of Microsoft is changing, though traditional accounting has no effective way of measuring or helping to manage these very real changes in the company's critical intangible assets. Only the future will reveal how Microsoft's bottom line will be affected by the efforts of its research teams and the strategic decisions of its executives. One thing is certain, however, traditional performance evaluation systems will struggle very hard to place a value on these kinds of changes.

Sources: A. Webber, "New Math for a New Economy," *Fast Company* (January–February 2000); J. Greene, "Microsoft's Big Bet," *Business Week* (October 30, 2000); Microsoft 2002 Annual Report; P. Galli, ".Net: 3 Years of the 'Vision' Thing," *eWeek* (July 7, 2003), Vol. 20, Issue 27, pp. 26–27.

Competitive pressures in the marketplace require that companies continually look for ways to improve their information systems in order to obtain better insights into how to operate their businesses more effectively and more efficiently. Management accounting, being at the core of business information systems, is always evolving. Managers want management accounting information that supports the strategy of the company. They do not want the information limited to financial measures of performance only. Quality and time measures of performance in customer service (e.g., timely deliveries), internal business processes (e.g., production defects), and growth in the organization (e.g., employee education levels) are becoming more important all the time. As a result, we are at the intersection of new directions in accounting. It's time we take a brief look at the future of management accounting.

You are now in the last chapter of this textbook. You've spent a lot of time studying many details concerning the process of creating and using accounting to add value to an organization. We've established that the management process involves planning, controlling, and evaluating business activities in order to compete well on issues involving cost, quality, and time. We've also discussed managing these concerns across three different types of firms: manufacturing, merchandising, and service. We understand that the accountant must customize a great variety of information sources to fit the specific strategic and operating needs of decision makers. The effort to "manage" this management accounting process may cause you to feel a bit overwhelmed. Of all the information that is possible (and we've presented in this text only a subset of a growing list of possibilities), what information is best for a particular company? Does a model exist that helps accountants and managers identify specific performance measures critical to surviving and thriving in the fast-paced, highly competitive, worldwide economy of the twenty-first century? More importantly, how does management accounting continue to improve performance measures in pace with innovations in products and processes and changes in markets and competition? Actually, there's been a lot of discussion recently among managers and management accountants on this very question. One approach to answering this question is gaining attention in many companies. The approach is called the "Balanced Scorecard," and no education on management accounting is really complete without some awareness of this approach. We'll spend most of this chapter illustrating this new performance measurement model and how it could affect the nature of both management accounting and financial accounting.[1]

The Value of Intangible Assets

The beginning of this chapter discussed the challenges that Microsoft faces in managing a very large organization that is focused essentially on building and selling "knowledge." In other words, the value of Microsoft is not its buildings or inventory, but the capability of its people; and the value of its products is not the software package that you buy, but in the capability of that software to solve problems. These intangible "knowledge" assets are very expensive both to acquire and to develop. And they're extremely difficult to manage. When a drug passes its clinical tests, huge value is created—but there's no transaction. Nothing changes hands. Nobody buys anything, and nobody sells anything. As a result, accounting, by tradition, does not measure or report this kind of information to managers (or investors). When software passes a beta-test, it suddenly becomes valuable—but there's no transaction, so there's no reporting. Or think about how value is destroyed: when a large, older company is late in figuring out how to enter the world of e-commerce, huge value is destroyed—but there's no transaction, and the company continues to be reported by accountants to its managers as doing well. Traditional measures of performance may ignore intangible corporate capabilities that can often lead to higher long-term returns than plant and equipment assets. In short, technology has created far more data than ever before. But what we all need—and what accounting now needs to work on—is the transformation of data into valuable information and knowledge that applies to the unique needs of specific organizations.

---

1 The Balanced Scorecard Model was first presented in a series of articles in the *Harvard Business Review* by Robert S. Kaplan and David P. Norton: "The Balanced Scorecard—Measures That Drive Performance" (January–February 1992); "Putting the Balanced Scorecard to Work" (September–October 1993); "Using the Balanced Scorecard as a Strategic Management System" (January–February 1996). The most complete discussion on this theory is found in Kaplan and Norton's *The Balanced Scorecard: Translating Strategy into Action* (Boston, MA: Harvard Business School Press, 1996) and *The Strategy-Focused Organization: How Balanced Scorecard Companies Thrive in the New Business Environment* (Boston, MA: Harvard Business School Press, 2001).

Let's Take a Flight!

Imagine that a friend of yours is getting her airplane pilot's license and has invited you to sit in the passenger seat of the airplane during her next pilot's lesson. Your friend has not been taking flying lessons very long. However, as you listen to her enthusiastic description of past lessons as the two of you drive out to the airfield the next afternoon, you begin to really look forward to the experience. After parking the car and walking to the Cessna plane that waits on the tarmac, your friend introduces you to the flight instructor, and the three of you climb into the plane. Soon after you take your seat and buckle the seatbelt, your friend revs the engine and the small plane surges forward. The instructor is sitting next to your friend, providing advice and guidance as the plane taxis down the runway gathering speed for takeoff. Suddenly, as you peer over the shoulders of the instructor and your friend in front of you, you notice with some concern that the small plane's instrument panel is noticeably bare of the assortment of instruments, dials, gauges, and controls that are typically part of an airplane's cockpit. In fact, there appears to be only one gauge on the whole panel. Trying to make your question sound casual, you ask about the barren panel and the sole gauge. The instructor looks back over his shoulder to tell you that the gauge measures airspeed. The plane is nearing the end of the runway and is just about to lift off. After swallowing once or twice, you brave more questions about direction, altitude, fuel, temperature, and thrust. Aren't these items also important in flying a plane? Don't most planes have gauges to provide feedback to the pilot on details other than simply airspeed? The instructor agrees but indicates that your friend is currently concentrating on airspeed in her flying lessons. Once she excels at managing airspeed, perhaps the airspeed gauge will be switched for an altimeter, and she can then concentrate on managing altitude. The instructor tells you that he feels it's important to not make the pilot concentrate on too many things at the same time. You notice that your friend is concentrating very hard on the airspeed gauge as the plane noses up and lifts off from the ground. You swallow hard and tighten your seatbelt until it is very snug around your waist. For some reason, you're suddenly imagining about a hundred others places you'd rather be than sitting in this plane.

Flying an airplane is a complicated process. To do it successfully requires that the pilot process a lot of information about various performance aspects of both the equipment and the environment. Managing a company is certainly no less complicated. A lot has to happen at once in order for a company to perform well in its competitive environment as the demands of products, customers, and regulatory agencies change constantly. One of a management accountant's most important functions is to identify and implement **performance measures** that are focused on key strategic and operating plans established by management. These performance measures then become the primary means of controlling and evaluating business processes in the organization. What is the best performance measure for an accountant to provide for an organization? Frankly, there is no one best performance measure.

performance measures A general term used to describe all measures designed to capture information about performance related to a particular activity or process.

The Balanced Scorecard

❙ Explain the fundamentals of building a balanced scorecard.

Balanced Scorecard A new management model designed to link together performance measures for financial, customer, internal process, and learning/growth perspectives that are unique to an organization's particular strategy.

Previous chapters and sections in this textbook have typically focused on subsets of management accounting issues such as merchandising, cost measurement, or the evaluating process. However, in this chapter we are not going to focus the discussion on any particular type of firm, strategic imperative, or management process. Instead, we present a *framework* that a management accountant can use to work with any of these issues. That framework is the Balanced Scorecard.

The **Balanced Scorecard** is a process to manage a set of performance measures that support directly the unique strategy an organization is trying to establish and follow. Exhibit 1 presents the framework of the Balanced Scorecard. The strategic performance measures that a company develops for itself are largely determined by how the organization answers the four basic questions listed in Exhibit 1. The answers to these questions then determine the man-

Exhibit 1: The Balanced Scorecard Framework

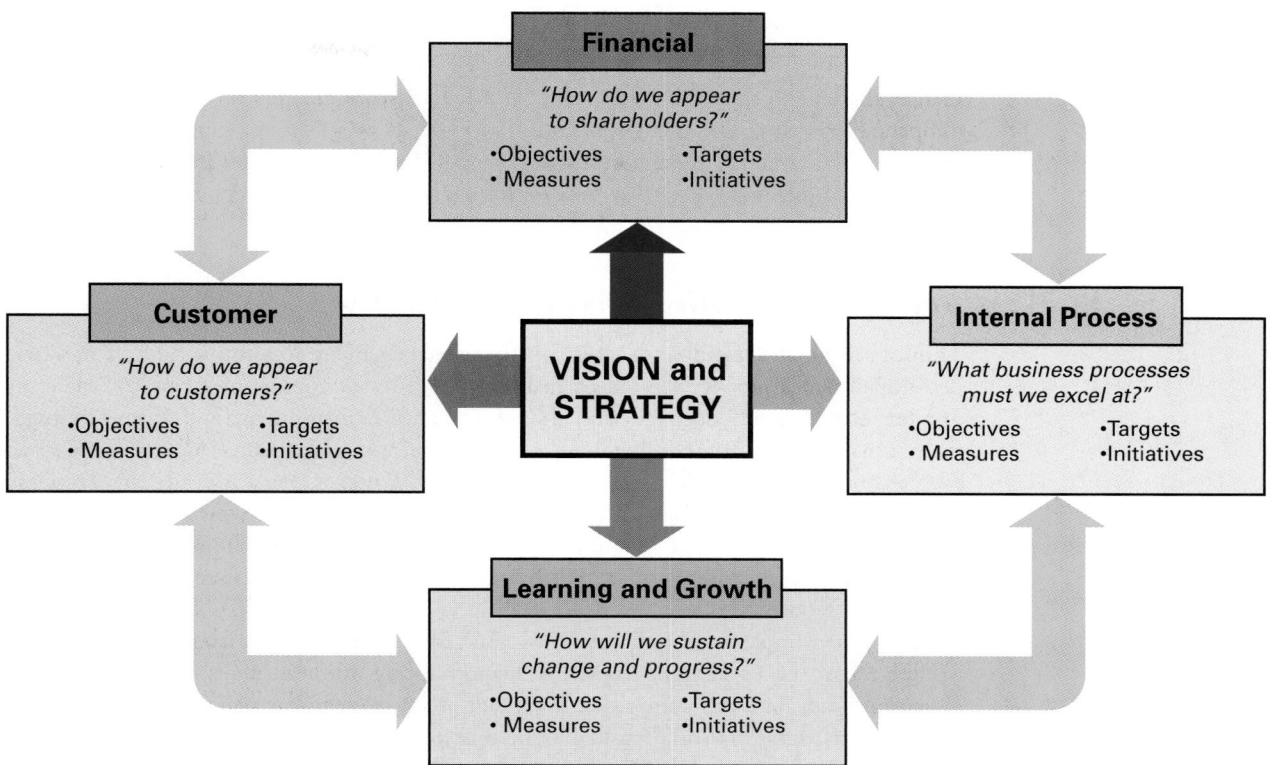

agement *objectives* for the organization, the *measures* that support those objectives, the immediate and long-term *targets* or goals for those measures, and what *initiatives* need to be put into place to begin working toward the targets. The entire balanced scorecard process is driven by the organization's overall vision or strategy.

At first glance, the Balanced Scorecard may not seem to be a very new idea. Shouldn't all performance measures support the organization's strategy? Hasn't management accounting always been focused on supporting the objectives of managers and executives to create a profitable company? Actually, although the purpose of management accounting is to establish performance measures that add value to the organization, too often these measures have been limited to periodic reports composed solely of financial measures. Advances in computer systems technology today allow more information, more variety in information, and more timely information to be created and reported than ever before. The existence of better information capabilities provides an opportunity for accountants, working in conjunction with system technologists and organization executives, to significantly expand the definition of management accounting. As you study this chapter, you need to understand that the Balanced Scorecard is really a guiding theory of management, rather than an exact formula or blueprint that can be automatically implemented in any organization to improve its management processes. Once created, each organization's own balanced scorecard is a direct view of its strategy, its plans, and its management processes. The idea that a balanced scorecard is extremely personal for each organization is captured in the following comment made by an executive as his division completed work on its first balanced scorecard:

> In the past, if you had lost my strategic planning document on an airplane and a competitor found it, I would have been angry, but I would have gotten over it. In reality, it wouldn't have been that big a loss. Or if I had left my monthly operating review somewhere and a competitor obtained a copy,

I would have been upset, but, again, it wouldn't have been that big a deal. This balanced scorecard, however, communicates my strategy so well that a competitor seeing this would be able to block the strategy and cause it to become ineffective.[2]

Hence, there is no such thing as a *standard* balanced scorecard that any organization can use to operate successfully in its environment. Therefore, as we use example performance measures throughout the chapter to describe the Balanced Scorecard theory, you should remember that each organization must design its own performance measures that support its own particular strategy.

Adding Value with Performance Measures

Think back on the last nine chapters involving management accounting and all the various performance measures we've studied involving cost, quality, and time. Frankly, there are a number of problems associated with the performance evaluation methods currently used in many organizations. Some individuals argue that current performance measurement systems even encourage waste, inefficiency, and poor quality. For example, a measure that emphasizes purchase price may encourage the purchasing department to increase the purchase quantity to get a lower price but might ignore quality and speed of delivery. The results may be excess inventory, increased storage and other carrying costs, and failure to use suppliers with the best quality and service.

Another example may be allocating overhead costs based on direct labor hours. Direct labor is often a cost that is small in relation to manufacturing overhead items, which are becoming more significant for many companies. The result of any overemphasis on direct labor as a mechanism for managing overhead costs may be missed opportunities for cost control since major overhead activities are not *directly* planned, controlled, and evaluated by management.

If machine utilization is the performance measure being emphasized, a supervisor may run a machine in excess of daily production requirements to maximize the performance measure. This may result in excess inventory or production that is not needed. Similarly, if the performance measure is focused solely on the number of units produced, poor-quality goods or inventory that is not desired by customers may be produced. A specific example from the former Soviet Union illustrates this point. Oil drillers, in competition with one another, received recognition and compensation based on the number of meters drilled. The award-winning team recognized by *Pravda* (Russia's leading newspaper) drilled meter upon meter but never struck oil. It seems that the first 100 meters of drilling do not require as much effort and expense as the second, third, fourth, and so on. The winning team drilled dry hole after dry hole. And the depth of these wells never exceeded 100 meters.

Some prominent researchers believe that performance evaluation systems used in the United States are quite ineffective and have contributed to a decline in America's competitiveness. One major problem that these researchers identify with traditional performance evaluation methods is the limited focus of these methods. To be specific, they argue that current evaluation methods, which mostly focus on financial returns, are not designed to cope with such intangible corporate capabilities as an excellent workforce, research and development, and knowledge assets. They argue that we have moved from a manufacturing society to an information society and that performance evaluation systems have not kept pace. This argument certainly seems to have merit when considering the competitive position of MICROSOFT described at the beginning of this chapter. Are Microsoft's real assets appropriately displayed on a balance sheet that focuses on inventory, equipment, and buildings? Does it make sense to evaluate performance at Microsoft based on controlling costs of materials, labor, and manufacturing overhead? Microsoft, like many other companies, needs a performance measurement system that is customized to fit its particular strategy.

2 R. S. Kaplan and D. P. Norton, *The Balanced Scorecard: Translating Strategy into Action* (Boston, MA: Harvard Business School Press, 1996), p. 148.

Every company ultimately must perform well financially in order to survive. Even not-for-profit organizations must be able to consistently pay their bills, including payrolls and loans, in order to survive over time. Other companies must consistently show profits, build equity, and provide a return to stockholders. The DUPONT COMPANY made a lot of money by carefully tracking financial measures that contributed to consistent ROI and ROE performance. Remember, however, that successful management accounting methods are eventually copied by other organizations. Hence, strictly using ROI to manage an organization does not provide a competitive edge in today's economy. Organizations must continuously improve their management information processes in order to continue to compete. Traditional financial measures are now being vigorously supplemented in three new areas: customer service, internal process improvement, and learning and growth throughout the organization.

FYI:

In harmony with the idea of an instrument panel on an airplane, some companies prefer to refer to their strategic measurement systems as dashboards rather than scoreboards.

Customers

The first key to strong financial performance is customer satisfaction. When companies understand what their customers value and what services and products they are willing to pay for, then these companies can design customer-focused performance measures that lead to growth in market share, increased revenues, and long-term profits. There are two types of customer performance measures: leading measures and outcome measures. **Leading measures** focus on fulfilling customer expectations regarding cost, quality, and time factors. **Outcome measures** determine if the improvements in leading measures result in more satisfied, loyal customers. Therefore, it is important that there be a clear link between the company's efforts to provide low-cost, high-quality, timely products and services and customer response to these efforts as demonstrated by increased market share and customer profitability (i.e., the company is able to earn sufficient profits by serving its customers). Exhibit 2 provides measures of customer-focused performance.

leading measures Measures that, if successfully implemented, will support desired performance in other business activities. Note that some leading measures can also serve as outcome measures.

outcome measures Measures of desired outcome performance in activities critical to an organization's strategic goals. Note that some outcome measures are also leading measures to support desired performance in other business activities.

Leading Measures of Customer Satisfaction

We have discussed cost, quality, and time measures throughout the last nine chapters of this textbook. Naturally, most customers desire low-cost products and services. However, customer satisfaction is the result of the right combination of cost, quality, and time. As customers, we are willing to balance our demands for these three objectives. For example, when you mail a

---

Exhibit 2: Performance Measures of Customer Satisfaction

Leading Performance Measures			
Cost	**Quality**	**Time**	
		Reliable Delivery	**Fastest Delivery**
• Purchase cost to customer	• Returns by customers	• Percentage of on-time deliveries	• Average response time for service call
• Delivery cost to customer	• Quality rankings by other agencies	• Number of production interruptions	• Time to complete contract
• Setup cost to customer	• Customer survey response		• Production cycle time
• Maintenance and repair cost to customer			

Outcome Performance Measures		
Customer Retention	**Customer Acquisition**	**Market Share**
• Retention rates	• Acquisition rates	• Percent of total number of customers
• Number of defecting customers	• Number of new customers	• Percent of total dollars spent by customers
• Costs to retain customers	• Costs to recruit customers	• Percent of total units sold to customers

Balanced Scorecard and the Government The DEFENSE LOGISTICS AGENCY (DLA) was founded in 1961 to provide worldwide logistics support to U.S. Armed Forces. Logistics support includes fuels, food, clothing, medical and industrial supplies, land weapons systems support, and aviation supplies. The DLA has annual sales of over $29 billion and employs 28,000 people in all 50 states and in 27 countries.

The DLA is run like a business—its services and material are purchased by the Armed Forces. However, it was at one time an enterprise without a "management plan." The DLA was reactive in its approach to customer requests, divided into silos by product, and very decentralized. The DLA at that time was about "filling an order, not about supporting the customer," according to retired Admiral Ray Archer, vice commander of the DLA. At the same time, customers were not obligated to buy from the DLA and would use external vendors if items were out of stock or unavailable—making customer support an important issue.

The DLA and its leadership needed to restructure for change. The DLA was inwardly focused. The organization lacked a common vision and had no management process to guide it through the strategic transformation into an enterprise that was customer focused. In the effort to make this significant change, a balanced scorecard was adopted in the spring of 2000. The DLA believed this was the right tool to address the transformation. The new DLA balanced scorecard provided the strategies and initiatives that supported a corporate vision and allowed the DLA to:

- describe the enterprise,
- define its customers and stakeholders,
- define the value it provided to them,
- identify its internal strengths and weaknesses, and
- put a plan in place for change.

The DLA used its balanced scorecard to define its strategy, restructure the organization, and focus on customers as well as target the internal capabilities (processes and people) needed to deliver its promise—"Right Item, Right Time, Right Place, Right Price, Every Time . . . Best Value Solution for America's Warfighter."

The bottom line results are beginning to come in. In 2002, the DLA achieved $130 million in savings while processing $2.2 billion more in requisitions for its customers.

Source: Taken from the site **http://www.bscol.com/training/success/dla**, accessed August 15, 2003.

package across the nation, you are probably very comfortable making a trade-off decision. The U.S. POSTAL SERVICE, like other package delivery companies, provides various delivery schedules (overnight, two days, three to five days), as well as some options regarding quality of service (contents insurance and registered delivery); each mailing option carries an appropriate price. When you select what mailing method to use, you've effectively communicated what *you* believe at that time to be the value-added services provided by the U.S. Postal Service—and you're willing to pay for those services.

Most companies have spent a great deal of effort understanding how their customers perceive value in terms of timeliness, quality, and price. For many companies, customers are more concerned with reliability than with the fastest delivery. This is particularly true in a JIT environment. TOYOTA demands deliveries from its suppliers to assembly plants within a one-hour time window. Early arrivals of parts are as unacceptable as late deliveries. Hence, observers have sometimes witnessed delivery trucks driving around and around a Toyota assembly plant until it is time to deliver their goods. If you think about it, this is not really strange behavior. Have you ever scheduled a telephone repairperson to come to your home during the day? Your definition of "on time" is probably not sometime between 9:00 A.M. and 3:00 P.M., is it? Further, given a 1:00 P.M. appointment, you probably would not be particularly pleased at the repairperson's effort to "delight the customer" by arriving two hours early. Performance measures regarding reliability versus fastest delivery of goods or services depend on both the strategy of the company and the demands of its customers. A few examples of these types of measures are

© 2003 Getty Images

When you buy a car, the purchase price represents only part of the total cost of car ownership. You must also consider such costs as maintenance, repairs, and gas. In an effort to account for all costs incurred throughout the entire life of a product, some companies use life cycle costing.

life cycle costing The process of measuring all costs involved in creating, producing, and using a product or service. Life cycle costing is not limited to costs incurred by the organization measuring these costs but also includes all costs incurred by the suppliers and the customers of the product or service.

market share The percentage share one company receives of the total sales revenue in the economy for a particular product or service.

Caution

Research indicates that adequate scores on customer satisfaction surveys are not sufficient to create the kind of loyalty that results in high customer retention rates. Companies that cannot consistently *delight* their customers on the most valued performance factors will lose business.

Source: M. C. H. Yeung, L. C. Ging, and C. T. Ennew, "Customer Satisfaction and Profitability: A Reappraisal of the Nature of the Relationship," *Journal of Targeting, Measurement and Analysis for Marketing,* 2002 (Vol. 11, Issue 1), pp. 24–33.

provided in Exhibit 2. You can look back at Exhibit 13 on page 1175 in the chapter on managing inventory for more examples of time-based performance measures.

As you remember from the chapter on activity-based costing, total quality management (TQM) has been firmly rooted in the United States since the 1980s. Commitment to quality is now generally assumed for most products and services—it is a competitive necessity. Companies not committed to the total quality effort will typically struggle to survive. Hence, organizations must pay careful attention to what quality factors are important to their customers and then build measures that accurately track performance of these quality factors.

As mentioned earlier, customers compare timeliness and quality factors with price to evaluate the real value of a product or service. Many companies realize, however, that the purchase price of their product often does not represent the total cost to their customer. If you own a car, you may be painfully aware of this fact. The purchase price of your car is only part of its total cost. Maintenance, repairs, gas mileage, and insurance also combine with the original purchase price to determine the total cost of owning your car. Perhaps you wish you had spent a little more (or less) when purchasing your car in order to better balance the subsequent costs of owning your car. In an effort to account for costs that are an essential part of the total value of a product, some firms are turning to a concept known as life cycle costing. Essentially, **life cycle costing** is a method of costing that focuses on all costs that will be incurred throughout the entire life of a product. The life cycle approach to costing helps to ensure that no costs are omitted when evaluating performance and value. Hence, when evaluating customer satisfaction, an organization also needs to measure performance of its product or service in terms of *all* its costs for its customers. These cost measures are listed as leading performance measures in Exhibit 2.

Outcome Measures of Customer Satisfaction

An organization's focus on customers must be twofold. First, the company works to measure up to customer expectations regarding cost, quality, and time. Then the company must determine if its efforts are being rewarded with increased market share and customer profitability. **Market share** is the proportion of industry sales of a particular product or service that is controlled by a specific firm. Companies increase their market share in two ways: retaining current customers and acquiring new customers. Clearly, companies that cannot service their current customers better than competitors will be hard-pressed to maintain market share. Absolute customer satisfaction is key in this regard. Interestingly, when management accountants ignore expected future cash flows over a customer's life, they miss reporting the real cost (the opportunity cost) of losing customers. Exhibit 3 reports a past study showing how much profit a customer generates over time in four different industries. The implication of this study continues to be true today. As you can see, customer profitability over time really takes off *if* the company can retain its customers' loyalty. This increased profitability over time is the result of increased purchases or higher account balances, reduced operating costs, and profits from referrals. Hence, customer retention rates are very important outcome measures that result from good performance of leading measures related to customers' overall costs, quality of product, and timeliness of delivery.

Once the company has established leading measures that result in high customer retention, it can turn its attention to acquiring new customers in order to grow its market share. Obviously, there is a strong relationship between loyal customers who speak enthusiastically about the company's product and the company's ability to win new customers. As a result, many companies identify customer loyalty as the best way to acquire new customers. In addition, companies also spend a great deal of effort and resources recruiting new customers. Hence, tracking performance in customer acquisition is a strategy of growth in market

Exhibit 3: How Much Profit an Average Customer Generates over Time

Industry	Year 1	Year 2	Year 3	Year 4	Year 5
Credit cards	$ 30	$ 42	$ 44	$ 49	$ 55
Industrial laundry	144	166	192	222	256
Industrial distribution	45	99	121	144	168
Auto servicing	25	35	70	88	88

Source: Adapted from F. F. Reichheld and W. E. Sasser, "Zero Defections: Quality Comes to Services," Harvard Business Review (September–October 1990), pp. 105–112.

share. It is important to understand that there are many ways to successfully maintain and increase market share through customer retention and acquisition. However, retaining and recruiting customers *profitably* is important to strong financial performance. Hence, companies must track the costs spent recruiting new customers, as well as the costs spent retaining current customers. Using activity-based costing (ABC) to track the costs of activities necessary to recruit and retain customers can provide a company with the necessary information to identify desirable customers and to make important decisions to drop certain unprofitable customers. Management accountants who provide outcome measures of their companies' efforts to profitably grow market share can add competitive value to the management process. These customer outcome measures are listed in Exhibit 2.

Internal Processes

Effective management accounting that is built around the Balanced Scorecard can help organizations better understand how satisfying customers (using leading performance measures) relates to growth in customer profitability (using outcome measures). The next issue to be resolved is what processes within the organization must take place in order to satisfy the customer completely? Most of your work in the last nine chapters has focused on building performance measures to support the manager's efforts to plan, control, and evaluate processes within the company. However, building performance measures that effectively support the goal of customer satisfaction requires that the management accountant first understand that there are three types of processes that must be in place in order to take care of the customer: innovation processes, operations processes, and service-after-sale processes. Examples of performance measures for management of internal processes are provided in Exhibit 4.

Innovation Process Measures

We've talked very little in this textbook about planning, controlling, and evaluating the *innovation process,* which involves identifying new products and services, and then creating and bringing those products to market. The reason for this is that most of the management accounting effort has historically been focused on the operations process, which involves building goods or providing services that already exist. For example, accountants spend a great deal of effort developing budgets of operations, then measuring variances from standard costs of direct materials, direct labor, and manufacturing overhead. We focused on this particular management process in earlier chapters on operational budgeting and monitoring performance. However, the innovation process of identifying and creating new products is where much of a company's competitive edge is created. This is why Microsoft spends so much money hiring some of the best minds in the software industry—to ensure that it will continue to create new products that

Exhibit 4: Performance Measures of Internal Processes

	Innovation Processes	**Operations Processes**	**Service-after-Sale Processes**
Cost measures	• R&D costs per new product • Payback on R&D costs	• Unit-level costs • Batch-level costs • Product line costs	• Costs per service incidence • Costs of replacement parts
Quality measures	• Number of modifications required per design • Percentage of sales from new products	• Defects-per-million opportunities (six sigma) • Errors in customer service	• Customer requests handled on first call • Satisfaction survey responses
Time measures	• Lead time (from idea to working model) • Design cycle time	• Lead time (from order to delivery) • Production cycle time	• Lead time (from request to fulfillment) • Repair cycle time

network exercises

J.D. Power and Associates

J.D. POWER AND ASSOCIATES, head-quartered in Los Angeles, has achieved international recognition for its marketing information and consulting in the areas of consumer opinion and customer satisfaction. You may be familiar with the annual customer satisfaction awards this company provides in the automobile industry. In the last few years, J.D. Power and Associates has branched out into the financial, telecommunications, and travel service industries. Go to its home page at **http://www.jdpower.com** and research the awards for the most recent year.

Net Work:

1. What automotive brand had the highest customer satisfaction with dealer service?

2. What auto insurance provider ranked highest in customer satisfaction?

3. What long-distance telephone company had the highest customer satisfaction?

4. What rental car agency had the highest customer satisfaction?

retain and recruit customers. As we move further into the new century, many businesses are spending more in their research, design, and development processes than they do to support their production and operating processes. Microsoft is a great example of this trend. If you look at its income statements for 2000 through 2002, you will see that this company often spends more money on research and development of new products than it spends providing current goods and services to its current customers. These data are provided below.

	2000	**2001**	**2002**
Cost of revenue	$3,002 million	$3,455 million	$5,191 million
Research and development	$3,772 million	$4,379 million	$4,307 million

Admittedly, many companies do not spend the kind of money on the innovation process that Microsoft does. Nevertheless, the resources invested in the innovation process for most companies are significant. It's important to the ultimate financial success of the organization that the critical effort to identify and develop new products and services is effectively managed. At some point, the money invested in the research and development (R&D) effort must provide financial returns. However, an R&D project can require a very long payback period. Many organizations begin significant R&D projects expecting that financial returns will not be realized for many years. Sometimes basic research is done in organizations with no clear idea of what profitable product or service may eventually result. Occasionally, some of our society's most useful innovations have resulted from these kinds of R&D investments. On the other hand, with this strategy it is possible that a lot of resources and energy will be needlessly spent in the innovation process, which means that the strategic imperatives of cost, quality, and time still apply here. Given the size of the investments made, it is important that organizations develop measures to evaluate the costs of their innovation processes. In addition, organizations should assess the effectiveness (e.g., the quality) of innovation work.

Finally, without proper controls, R&D work is at risk of simply taking too long. You're likely familiar with the old adage that "time is money." Clearly, any project that requires time extensions will cost more to complete. You'll remember from the activity-based costing chapter that additional costs due to time overruns will also include increased holding costs. However, in the case of R&D, "time is opportunity!" The market is always moving. Organizations that take longer than their competitors to complete the research and development of new products or services may quickly find themselves seriously disadvantaged in the marketplace. Hence, organizations that manage well their innovation processes will compete well in the marketplace. Performance measures that support the management of the innovation process will typically be custom-built for each organization based on its strategic intent and on the particular nature of its R&D work. Exhibit 4 provides examples of cost, quality, and time-based measures for the innovation process.

business environment

The Balanced Scorecard— Code Red! The job of managing a hospital is extremely difficult! On the one end, you must deal with doctors who oppose any monetary label on patient care, and on the other end you must make financial decisions that will keep the hospital operational. Some of these decisions can be agonizing, leaving you to wonder where you draw the line. For example, do you make the questionably unethical decision of turning away needy patients because of money? These were the very problems facing Dr. Jon Meliones, chief medical director of DUKE CHILDREN'S HOSPITAL in Durham, North Carolina, in the mid-1990s.

The hospital was $11 million in the red. Critical programs were being canceled, the number of patient beds was being reduced, and the quality of patient care was in a miserable state. Dr. Meliones, faced with the disastrous state of the hospital, came across the Balanced Scorecard strategy and instantly decided that applying the principles from the Balanced Scorecard was the solution. Upon learning that the Balanced Scorecard dealt with finance, customer service, learning and growth, and internal processes, Dr. Meliones saw this model as a perfect fit for his hospital. Not only did it deal with the financial administration of running a hospital, but it also took into consideration the very real needs of the patients and doctors who receive and provide the care.

"We wanted everyone—from accountants to physicians to therapists—focusing on a common goal, not individual goals," explained Meliones. "We needed to become a strategy-focused organization if our balanced scorecard was to succeed and, in turn, if the hospital was to succeed." The balanced scorecard effort at Duke Children's Hospital involved distributing daily "report cards" to all hospital employees to ensure they understood where they stood within the strategic goals of the hospital. These report cards empowered the hospital staff to find creative ways to reduce costs, increase the quality of patient care, and help hospital administrators see more than just the bottom line. For example, physicians received information pertaining to their own patient loads, such as average length of stay and average cost per patient. They could then evaluate the results themselves and determine where to cut costs rather than having to follow a mandate issued by someone in management who doesn't understand the medical issues involved in these kinds of decisions.

Not only did these report cards allow doctors and other medical staff to evaluate where they could cut costs, but it also empowered them to look for other ways to improve quality of care. For example, a chief complaint of patients' parents was not being able to identify their child's primary caregiver. So a secretary decided that as patients were admitted, labels with the names of each one's primary doctor and nurse would be placed on their doors. "Prior to this simple solution, only 42% of parents could identify their child's doctor," said Meliones. "But as soon as we began labeling, that number rose to 99%. The balanced scorecard began turning everyone into a chief strategy officer of some sort."

As a result of the cooperative effort between management and medical staff to implement a balanced scorecard, Duke Children's Hospital has gone from $11 million in the red to $4 million in the black, an incredible turnaround!

Source: SAS Institute, Inc., News and Events, "Life in the Balance: Duke Children's Hospital," **http://www .sas.com/news/success/dukehosp.html**, accessed March 5, 2001.

Operations Process Measures

Operations processes involve all of the activities directly related to the sale of goods or services to customers, including receipt of customer orders, creation of products, and delivery of products. Ever since Francis Cabot Lowell established his cotton mill in Waltham, Massachusetts, in 1814 and created the "Waltham system" of accounting to track manufacturing costs, accountants have focused on adding value to the operations processes by measuring cost, quality, and time performance. In the effort to support operations processes, many valuable accounting methods have been developed. As a result, several of the previous chapters have focused on helping you understand these methods. Though management accounting for operations processes has been in place for a long time, new methods continue to evolve in an effort to create information that has competitive value.

The concepts of activity-based costing (ABC) and the Hierarchical Production Model (discussed in the activity-based costing chapter) represent some of the important cost measures created recently to fulfill competitive needs for organizations. An example of a quality measure for manufacturing processes that strongly impacts performance in the marketplace is "six sigma quality." One of the famous measures of quality, six sigma quality is now becoming an important operations management tool for many types of merchandising and service firms. Sigma[3] is a statistical measure of variation in a product or process and is used in statistical process control (SPC) charts to evaluate upper and lower control limits (see the ABC chapter for a review of SPC charts). Sigma measures also provide insight about probabilities. Specifically, when the incidence of a single error in the product or service process occurs at a distance of six sigma from the target value, then the probability that the process itself has quality problems is very low. To be precise (without getting into all the statistics involved), an operation process is said to have **six sigma quality** when defects in the process are occurring at the low rate of 3.4 defects per million opportunities—now that's a high-quality process! Other measures of cost, quality, and time that have competitive value continue to be developed and refined. Exhibit 4 provides some measures that exemplify the continuous improvements we now see in cost, quality, and time measures to support operations processes.

six sigma quality A measure of quality based on statistical analysis. Products or services with six sigma quality have no more than 3.4 defects per million opportunities (e.g., parts or events).

Service-after-Sale Process Measures

Service-after-sale processes are of two types. One type of service-after-sale process involves the billing and collection of payments from customers. The other type involves the organization's commitment to warranty its product, including efforts to repair or replace products and provide post-sale support and guidance in the use of the product. If you've ever purchased a personal computer, you have likely had some experience with technical support to help you resolve a computer problem or simply to figure out how to better use your new computer. Depending on your experience with your computer merchant's technical support (or, for that matter, the post-sale support of any other product or service you've purchased), you probably have strong positive or negative feelings about the quality and timeliness of the support you received, and about the company itself! Do organizations create a competitive edge when they provide quality, timely post-sale support while controlling the costs of that support? You bet! Is it important to effectively control the process of billing and collecting payments from customers? If you remember our extensive discussion of holding costs in an earlier chapter on managing inventory, you know that companies can spend a lot of time and resources creating customer invoices and then following up to ensure prompt collection. Poor management of service-after-sale processes can result in many opportunity costs. Hence, management accountants also pay attention to management of these processes using effective performance measures, some examples of which are provided in Exhibit 4.

FYI:

LANDS' END is a garment mail-order merchant that exemplifies the growing trend of excellent service-after-sale to customers. Despite being a very large company (during peak seasons, close to 1,100 phone lines handle over 100,000 calls per day), it has established a strong reputation for customer service. Lands' End offers one of the simplest guarantees in the industry—"GUARANTEED. PERIOD.®" This means letting the customer return the product at any time, for any reason. As an example of the extent of its guarantee, customers who need additional buttons, have lost a belt, or need a piece of luggage repaired can receive all these services at any time after purchase, free of charge. Even if a child loses a mitten from Lands' End during the same season it was purchased, the "Lost Mitten Club" will replace it at half the price of a pair, and Lands' End will pick up the costs of shipping.

---

3 Sigma is the name of the Latin symbol σ and is used to represent a statistical measure more commonly known as "standard deviation."

Learning and Growth

Perhaps the most interesting example of continuous improvement in management accounting is found in the very recent trend for accountants to help management teams better understand the process of building learning and growth within the organization. In order to survive and thrive in this competitive economy, an organization must continue to learn and grow. Or, to be more specific, the organization's employees, system, and structure must learn, grow, and change in order to continuously build and improve internal processes and satisfy customers. Certainly, the demand of customers today is well described by the question, "What have you done for me lately?" Without learning and growth, internal processes stop improving, customers grow restless and defect, and financial performance stagnates. However, many might react rather strongly to the trend to create performance measures on learning and growth by challenging whether this kind of work is really management accounting at all! How does one measure learning and growth? Frankly, it's not a well-developed accounting discipline. However, because development in this area is rather slight, there is much opportunity for management accountants to create significant competitive value for their organizations by working to build good measures. Don't forget the lesson learned from Donaldson Brown and the DuPont ROI formula in the first chapter where we introduced management accounting. Accountants who are able to provide information useful to plan, control, and evaluate critical business processes, regardless of the initial difficulty of the effort, will add the most value to their organization. By dividing this effort into leading measures and outcome measures (somewhat similar to the effort of managing an organization's work with its customers), the Balanced Scorecard Model suggests some interesting possibilities for measuring performance in the learning and growth effort. Exhibit 5 illustrates some example measures that can be used for managing learning and growth performance.

Leading Measures of Learning and Growth

The ultimate result of building learning and growth in the organization is based on developing employee productivity. Employee productivity then leads to internal process improvements. Related to employee productivity is employee retention and employee satisfaction. These three issues form the desired outcome measures of learning and growth. Therefore, the organization should track performance in the productivity, retention rates, and satisfaction of its employees. However, managing improvements in these important outcome measures requires that management accountants identify the factors that result in high employee productivity, retention, and satisfaction. These factors form *leading* measures in learning and growth: employee capabilities, information system capabilities, and organizational structure capabilities.

Improvements in employee capabilities should lead to improvements in employee productivity. However, improving employee productivity does not necessarily mean that employees are satisfied with their work situation and are committed to staying with the company. If investments in employee capabilities are expected to result in higher satisfaction and retention rates among employees, then companies should also expect to see positive improvements in internal processes, customer care, and financial performance. Measures here can focus on the level of qualifications and certifications among employees, as well as investments made by the company in employee training and education.

In this information age, the strength of a company's information system structure is critical to employee productivity. To build an excellent organization, employees need relevant, accurate, and timely information on the effects of their efforts to improve processes, satisfy customers, and strengthen financial performance within the organization. In addition to information systems, modern technology continues to provide significant opportunities for directly improving

network **exercises**

Metrus Group

Balanced scorecards are often implemented with the help of an outside consultant. METRUS GROUP is an organization whose employees are experts in balanced scorecards and performance measurement strategies. Access the Web site at **http://www.metrus.com**. Then select the "Products and Services" tab, and then "Strategic Performance Measurement." In the first sentence of this Web page, Metrus indicates the importance of focusing attention on the critical few *performance measures* that drive success.

Net Work:

1. According to Metrus, what are the key measures that drive company success?

2. What is the key to creating successful balanced scorecards?

Caution

Remember that management accounting is not a precisely defined discipline. Individual companies adapt good management accounting principles to fit specific information needs to plan, control, and evaluate their unique organizations. No where is this more true than with the Balanced Scorecard, particularly when it comes to measures of an organization's performance on learning and growth. Every organization will have a *very* specific view of what it means for that organization to learn and grow. Therefore, remember that Exhibit 5, as well as other exhibits in this chapter listing balanced scorecard measures, is an example of what some companies might choose to measure when developing an effective balanced scorecard. No two companies' scorecards are alike!

Exhibit 5: Performance Measures of Learning and Growth

	Leading Performance Measures		
	Employee Capabilities	**Information Systems Capabilities**	**Organizational Structure Capabilities**
Cost measures	• On-site training expense per employee • Off-site education expense per employee	• Total costs invested in computer systems within the organization • Systems R&D expense per total systems expense	• Costs invested in assessing and building new communication structures • Costs invested in activities to align goals within the company
Quality measures	• Number of new certifications or degrees • Percentage of employees participating in education activities	• System capability compared to competitor systems • Percentage of employees with access to personal computer	• Assessment of effective communication • Assessment of effective teamwork • Assessment of goal alignment
Time measures	• Average yearly training or education hours per employee • Time required to complete a training module	• Average life cycle time of personal computers (e.g., how often are machines upgraded?) • Time required to complete a system upgrade	• Amount of time spent in teamwork versus individual work • Average time to disseminate information or to receive employee feedback

	Outcome Performance Measures	
Employee Retention	**Employee Satisfaction**	**Employee Productivity**
• Employee turnover rate • Average employee years with company • Number of female managers • Average age of employees	• Survey of employee satisfaction • Percentage of employees having leadership opportunities • Management positions filled by inside versus outside recruits	• Output per employee • Billable hours per consultant • New ideas or patents per employee • Recognition of employees by customers

various business processes in all kinds of organizations. Performance measures on information systems and other types of technologies can focus on the quality of systems, accessibility to systems, and investments in systems.

Poorly run organizations can quickly damage employee satisfaction, as well as create confusion that limits employee productivity. Factors that define a well-run organization include effective communication; alignment of goals (i.e., everyone understands and is working toward the same goals); integration of team efforts across departments; and clearly defined planning, controlling, and evaluating processes. Measuring performance and capability in organizational structures is likely the most undefined and challenging "next step" for management accountants today. Nevertheless, this is important work. Organizations usually work very hard to create effective communication channels, to obtain buy-in from employees on company goals, to form an environment where people will work together, and to establish good management processes. Surveys of employees' perspectives are one good way to measure performance on the drive to create good organizational structure.

Outcome Measures of Learning and Growth

Examples of leading and outcome measures of learning and growth are provided in Exhibit 5. As accountants track these measures, it is critical that good performance in employee capabilities, information system capabilities, and organizational structure capabilities results in improvements in employee satisfaction, retention, and productivity. Obviously, then, management

Market value for a company is computed as the number of shares of stock outstanding multiplied by the average price per share. Essentially, market value measures how much money stockholders believe the company is worth. MICROSOFT's stock price as of June 30, 2002, was $54.70 per share. Based on 5,359,000,000 common shares outstanding at the end of its 2002 fiscal year (ending June 30), this works out to a market value of over $293 billion! However, if you look at Microsoft's 2002 balance sheet (again, dated June 30), you'll see that its net assets (total assets minus total liabilities) are valued at just over $52 billion. Why the huge difference?

leading indicators Measures that indicate the potential success of future business activities. Leading indicators are related to the concept "leading measures."

lagging indicators Measures that indicate the success of past business activities. Lagging indicators are related to the concept "outcome measures."

accountants can (and should) test the relationship between leading measures and outcome measures by evaluating satisfaction of employees using surveys; reporting on resignation trends within the company; and measuring employees' productivity in terms of volume, quality, and timeliness of output. When investments in employee education programs or improvements in information systems fail to improve employee outcome measures, then management accountants should provide useful information to better manage these critical processes. Otherwise, there is likely to be little improvement in internal processes, customer satisfaction, and (finally) financial performance. Are you getting the sense that linking together all performance measures within the organization may be a critical aspect of developing a balanced scorecard? If so, then you are on track with the final concept that we discuss in the next section.

Linking It All Together

So far in this chapter, and, for that matter, throughout this entire textbook, we have been discussing *a lot* of different performance measures! Do management accountants really need to track *all* these data in order to effectively support the management processes within their companies? Clearly, the answer is no. Too much information is often as harmful as too little. Managers and organizations can become overloaded with information. The key is to clearly identify the vision and strategy a company chooses to pursue, and then establish a set of performance measures that supports progress toward specific company goals. Thus far in this chapter, we have learned that a balanced scorecard approach recognizes that management of a company requires information on financial, customer, internal process, and learning and growth activities. Further, performance measures of these activities are not limited to financial measures, but should include nonfinancial measures as well (e.g., quality and time-based measures). Perhaps the most important aspect of a balanced scorecard approach is that all measures must *link together* to eventually support the ultimate financial goals of a company.[4] Good performances on activities that do not directly or indirectly contribute to the ultimate goals the organization has established are obviously a waste of resources. Nevertheless, pointless investments in non-value-added activities probably occur in many organizations. Distinguishing non-value-added activities from value-added activities and identifying which performance measures successfully contribute to helping the company accomplish its strategic goals are the ideas behind linkages within a balanced scorecard.

To illustrate the importance of clearly linking performance measures in a balanced scorecard, look at Exhibit 6. It should be clear that the ability to achieve target financial goals such as a positive ROI (return on investment) or ROE (return on equity) is closely linked to success on customer outcome measures (customer retention, customer acquisition, and market share). However, a company can increase its market share and still experience declining ROI because the type of customers it is serving, or the way it is serving its customers, does not lead to positive profits for the company. This is the concept of leading versus lagging indicators. **Leading indicators** are measures of performance that, if accomplished, should lead to a desired result. Measures of performance on the desired results are the **lagging indicators**. A company may desire positive ROI. However, the company does not really "manage" ROI directly; instead, it manages performance that *leads* to positive ROI. Hence, it is important that the company has clearly determined that there is a strong relationship between its leading and lagging indicators. In other words, a company may determine that high rates of customer acquisition should lead to improvements in its overall ROI. Nevertheless, if the company actually does acquire a lot of new customers but does not experience improved ROI performance, it likely needs to spend some time better identifying exactly what the real leading indicators are for improved profits in its industry.

4 The ultimate goals of an organization do not need to be financial profits in order to apply the Balanced Scorecard Model. For example, not-for-profit organizations (such as governments or charities) will likely emphasize service to constituents or clients as their ultimate strategic goals.

Exhibit 6: Performance Measurement Linkages in a Balanced Scorecard

As you can see in Exhibit 6, cause-and-effect relationships between leading and lagging in-dicators should exist throughout a company's balanced scorecard. Customer outcome measures are leading indicators for financial measures. If the company identifies the cost, quality, and time factors that customers care about, then improved performance in these activities will lead to good outcomes in customer retention, acquisition, and market share. Similarly, effective in-novation, operations, and service-after-sale processes should lead to improved performance in customer leading measures. Continuous improvements in these internal processes are then linked to learning and growth outcome measures (i.e., employee retention, satisfaction, and produc-tivity), which are linked to investments in leading measures of employee, information systems, and organizational structure capabilities. Exhibit 6 illustrates that most performance measures serve as both leading and lagging indicators. When an accountant builds a performance mea-surement system based on this perspective, it should be clear that financial performance is no more important than performance related to internal processes or learning and growth effort. This is the concept of "balance" in a balanced scorecard.

To illustrate this idea of linkages, suppose that a company has identified that repeat and expanded sales to current customers (e.g., the result of customer retention) is the most impor-tant factor leading to improved ROI. Next, customer loyalty is assured by continuous im-provement in product design, coupled with short lead times on customer orders. Finally, improving the process of product design and delivery requires committed and well-educated employees working with state-of-the-art computer systems in an organization with clear com-munication channels. These cause-and-effect relationships form the company's strategy. By building a balanced scorecard that focuses on this particular set of performance measures, a management accountant is able to clearly support the company strategy. Accountants do not *traditionally* perform this kind of work. However, according to a survey, eighty percent of large American companies want to change their performance measurement systems to better support competitive company strategies.[5] Traditional financial measures such as net income or ROI are really "after the fact." The fact that a company is reporting either positive or negative profits is the result of *past* performance with customers, internal processes, and learning and growth efforts. Can an ROI measure be used to predict future performance? As illustrated in Exhibit 6, financial measures are the ultimate lagging indicators of a successful strategy. Managing an organization's strategy requires insight on leading performance measures. What we see from this reality is that the Balanced Scorecard is really a management system. Management accountants who want to add value to the organization must build and support effective management systems.

An Example Scorecard

Exhibit 7 shows the balanced scorecard for a small company (between 100 and 1,000 employees) in the biotechnology industry. This scorecard is in an ever-constant state of evaluation and redesign as the company works to better understand the right strategy and the right performance measures to use in implementing its strategy to succeed in its particular market. Take a moment to examine this scorecard. Can you recognize the objectives this company has identified as important to its strategy? Can you identify linkages between its performance measures?

You might note that the financial goals and measures for this firm are rather basic. The majority of companies in most industries are working to build return on equity, earnings per share, and market share. However, this biotechnology company has determined that it needs to be particularly aggressive in revenue growth in its top line (i.e., best selling) products.

The customer goals are divided into leading and outcome measures. The company has linked early customer payment, product performance, and customer satisfaction as important to its percent of sales from new products and percent of sales taking place early in the buying season. Further, growth in new products should provide future top line products. Getting customers to buy early in the season also seems to be important to building market share and profitability.

Innovation is likely the most important factor in internal processes for a research-intensive firm. This is especially so in the biotechnology industry. Accordingly, you can see that there are a number of measures encouraging successful efforts in innovation processes, which should support customer and financial goals for this company. Additionally, this firm also emphasizes keeping product costs and inventory levels low in order to further support the effort to improve return on equity and earnings per share. Finally, providing accurate invoices should encourage customers to pay early.

FYI:

No company would actually track as many measures as are being listed in Exhibits 2, 4, and 5. Like the example company in Exhibit 7, most organizations will limit their balanced scorecard to between three and six measures in each of the four categories of financial, customer satisfaction, internal processes, and learning and growth.

At the foundation of this company's business are its investments in learning and growth. It is making substantial investments in training and desires to continually train as many employees as possible. In addition, it is also focusing on teamwork efforts. The expectation is that these leading measures of learning and growth will link to improved employee retention and satisfaction, as well as support internal processes and customer service.

As you consider this scorecard, you may feel that some measures and linkages among measures may be missing. You are probably right! Nevertheless, in contrast to being solely focused on short-term financial performance, the management accountants in this company are on their way to creating a performance measurement system that truly incorporates the entire strategy of their company. Studying this scorecard should make it clear to you that good performance measures can capture a unique strategy for a specific firm.

5 B. Birchard, "Making It Count," *CFO* (October 1995), pp. 42–48.

Exhibit 7: Sample Balanced Scorecard

Scorecard for a Biotechnology Firm

Strategic Objectives	Performance Measures
Financial Perspective	
• Growth	• Percent increase in revenue of top line products
• Profitability	• Return on equity; earnings per share
• Industry leadership	• Market share
Customer Perspective Outcome:	
• New products	• Percent of sales from new products
• Early purchase of seasonal products	• Percent of sales recorded by early purchase date
Leading:	
• Early payment	• Percent of customers who pay early
• Product quality	• Product performance vs. industry quality standards
• Customer satisfaction	• Customer satisfaction surveys
Internal Processes Perspective Service-after-Sale:	
• Accurate invoices	• Percent of error-free invoices
Operations:	
• Low-cost producer	• Unit cost vs. competitors
• Reduce inventory	• Inventory as percent of sales
Innovation:	
• New products	• Number of actual introductions vs. target
• New active ingredients	• Number of new ingredients identified by research program
• Proprietary positions	• Number of patents that create exclusive marketing rights
Learning and Growth Perspective Outcome:	
• Employee retention	• Average employee years with company
• Employee satisfaction	• Employee satisfaction surveys
Leading:	
• Employee capabilities	• Training costs invested per employee; percent of employees participating annually in training
• Organizational structure capabilities	• Average weekly hours in teamwork settings; survey of effective teamwork

Source: Adapted from C. W. Chow, K. M. Haddad, and J. E. Williamson, "Applying the Balanced Scorecard to Small Companies," *Management Accounting* (August 1997), Institute of Management Accountants, Montvale, NJ, pp. 21–27.

There Is No "Quick Approach"

The Balanced Scorecard approach to performance measurement recognizes that every organization is unique. This is not the only tool available for organizations that desire to better manage strategy, information, and performance; but it is currently one of the most well-known. Hopefully, as you conclude your work with this textbook, it is clear that a manufacturing company will not manage itself the same as a merchandising or service company. Further, even companies competing within the same industry will each have different sets of goals, objectives, and strategies to attain a specific mission. The process of building a balanced scorecard takes time and effort. The management accountant must have a clear knowledge of both financial and management accounting concepts. Then the organization's specific strategy must be clearly

The Malcolm Baldrige National Quality Award (described earlier in the activity-based costing chapter) is given to companies that have demonstrated excellence in quality management. Since 1988, fifty-one companies have received the Baldrige Award. However, high quality has not always translated into strong financial performance. Many early winners of the Baldrige Award struggled financially after winning the award. For example, FEDEX lost $1.5 billion on its European operation, the WALLACE COMPANY declared bankruptcy, and many RITZ-CARLTON hotels have lost money or become insolvent since winning the award. Furthermore, GM, IBM, KODAK, and WESTINGHOUSE each had Baldrige Award-winning divisions, yet each sustained substantial overall corporate losses that led to the replacement of their chairmen.

On the other hand, the Baldrige Award winners as a group have generally performed quite well in the stock market. The NIST (National Institute of Standards and Technology), the sponsoring agency for the Baldrige Award, has tracked a fictitious stock fund made up of publicly-traded U.S. companies that received the Malcolm Baldrige National Quality Award between 1992 and 2001. The NIST hypothetically "invests" $1,000 into each of the Baldrige company winners and tracks the performance of this stock fund against the Standard & Poor's (S&P) 500 stock index. (The S&P 500 index is generally regarded as an indicator of the overall performance of the entire stock market.) In nearly every year since 1995 when the NIST began the research project, the Baldrige Index has outperformed the S&P 500 by a significant margin. Only in 2003 did the Baldrige Index return a value less than the S&P 500.

Overall, Baldrige winners seem to be financially successful companies. Yet some individual winners of this quality award subsequently fail to deliver award-winning financial results. One possible explanation for the failure can be explained by an important underlying principle of the Balanced Scorecard—the importance of linking performance in strategic focus of a company to financial performance. It may be that failure to invest in quality measures that translate (i.e., *link*) to desired performance financial measures is the reason that some Baldrige Award companies have struggled financially.

Sources: D. Benson and M. Swain, "A Study of the Impact of TQM on the Financial Performance of Firms," *Academy of Accounting and Financial Studies Journal* (Vol. 3, No. 1, 1999), pp. 145–159; Baldrige Stock Studies at **http://baldrige.nist.gov/Stock_Studies.htm**, accessed September 1, 2003.

and specifically defined in terms of cause-and-effect relationships (i.e., linkages) for its particular industry. What cost, quality, and time issues are important to compete successfully within a particular market? An organization cannot expect to be financially rewarded for world-class performance in response time to customer repair requests unless that type of response time is truly valued by its customers. Finally, measures must be developed, tested, and implemented into clear reporting systems that support effective planning, controlling, and evaluating procedures.

Management accountants can easily build elegant looking but irrelevant performance measurement systems. There are examples of this in far too many organizations. The best example of this bad situation is when accounting is determined to be a non-value-added activity in an organization, and managers simply ignore accounting data as they work on their own to build the company. One of the authors of this textbook is reminded of an experience of having dinner with a plant manager who had established his plant as the most successful division within the company. When asked how the plant controller's work figured into the division's successful implementation of cutting-edge management principles such as JIT and TQM, the plant manager smiled grimly and indicated that the controller really had only two jobs in the organization. First, the controller was responsible for handling all requests from the external auditors. Second, the controller was simply to "stay out of his way!" He felt that the controller (the chief accountant in the organization) provided no information useful to him in his efforts to implement and execute strategy. Clearly, both the controller and the plant manager were missing important opportunities. The division was making significant investments in its accounting system without receiving any competitive benefits. The controller's reports were irrelevant to the core activities of the organization. How long would it be before one of the competitors in this division's market could effectively use management accounting to better implement its own strategy and seize the market?

Good management accounting requires that both managers and accountants work together to create information systems and performance measures that add value—that support the organization's unique strategy. This kind of work is not easy, nor is it done quickly. Management accountants must clearly understand the nature of critical business processes in the organization, as well as how managers and executives intend to strategically plan, control, and evaluate those processes. Linkages between activities must be tested. If performance in one activity does not lead to desired outcomes in customer service or financial performance, then relationships need to be reexamined. This is exciting work! The history of business in America has clearly

business environment

Wendy's Balanced Scorecard
WENDY'S INTERNATIONAL, INC., one of the leading fast-food chains in the world with over 8,400 restaurants worldwide, realizes the importance of using nonfinancial performance measures in a balanced scorecard. After adopting a balanced scorecard in 2000, Wendy's was recently inducted into the Hall of Fame of the Balanced Scorecard Collaborative.

When the company began using the scorecard approach, its market capitalization was $2.3 billion; now it is $4 billion. John Barker, vice president over investor relations and financial communications for Wendy's and part of Wendy's strategic planning team, says, "Our stock has been up 73% since we started the balanced scorecard approach in our strategic planning process."

The company's balanced scorecard includes performance measures that track intangibles, such as employee turnover and customer satisfaction. Since implementing its balanced scorecard, Wendy's has reduced employee turnover to 140% per year, while the fast-food industry's employee turnover remains at 230% per year. With lower employee turnover, the company has enjoyed increased profitability and efficiency. To measure customer satisfaction, Wendy's surveys its customers across the nation on certain characteristics of the fast-food industry to find

out how Wendy's ranks among its competitors. Recently, customers rated Wendy's as number 1 in 46 of the 58 characteristics of quality.

"We look at the measures quarterly, annually, and then every three years. You can't move the needle in a quarter or even in half a year," says Barker. "We set goals for three years and then track them. At the beginning of the process, people were skeptical and didn't believe in it. Now we believe in it and live by it every single day." Barker continues, "If you only look at financial measures, what's happening is that you are waiting until you are off course to find out that you have to do something to get back on course. Intangible measures are predictors of the future and will help you see those things to prevent you from getting off course."

Wendy's focus on nonfinancial performance measures has helped the company realize financial targets as well. Since adopting its balanced scorecard in 2000, the company has experienced a 29% growth in profitability; and from March 2000 to August 2003, the company's stock price almost doubled. Wendy's will continue to see long-term growth, as long as it continues to achieve its balanced scorecard objectives.

Sources: "How Wendy's Tracks Value of Intangibles in Its Balanced Scorecard Menu," *Financial Analysis, Planning & Reporting* (August 2002), pp. 1 and 13–14; Balanced Scorecard Collaborative, **http://www.bscol.com/bscol/hof/members/**, accessed August 23, 2003.

demonstrated that successful organizations are willing to spend the necessary creative energy to really understand how the work they do adds value to the marketplace. The spirit of continuous improvement that is now prevalent throughout our economy requires that management accounting continue to identify and support opportunities to improve the cost, quality, and timeliness of the information it provides.

TO SUMMARIZE: The Balanced Scorecard is an important management tool that explicitly supports strategy by integrating performance measures of financial, customer, internal process, and learning and growth activities within an organization. Both financial and nonfinancial measures are used throughout this new management model. A balanced scorecard, once created, is unique to each organization. The process of building a balanced scorecard requires that management accountants work closely with managers, executives, and information technologists in order to clearly understand how measures link together to eventually support successful financial results for the company. This idea of linkages across performance measures is critical to a successful balanced scorecard. Financial performance is linked to customer outcome measures of customer retention, customer acquisition, and market share.

These customer outcome measures in turn are linked to leading measures on customer service involving cost, quality, and time. Supporting customer service are the internal processes that take place within an organization. These internal processes include innovation processes (identifying and creating new products), operations processes (obtaining customer orders and producing and delivering products), and service-after-sale processes (handling warranties and providing support to customers). In order to continually improve its internal processes, an organization must emphasize its employees by measuring outcome performance on employee retention, satisfaction, and productivity. Finally, these employee outcome measures are linked to important investments in the capabilities of employees, information systems, and organizational structure.

Accounting for Tomorrow

2 Anticipate that both management accounting and financial accounting are poised for important changes.

"There is a bulldozer of change coming. You can either be part of the bulldozer, or you can be part of the road."[6] The Balanced Scorecard is one important example of continuous improvement that is characteristic of a competitive world economy that is always growing and changing. Managers and accountants in many organizations are creating new performance measurement systems that support dramatic improvements in products, processes, and people. These professionals understand that measures should focus on monitoring *all* critical activities in an organization in order to anticipate and prepare for future decisions, rather than simply report the financial effects of past decisions.

In this atmosphere of healthy competition and change, you can expect that new models and methods of management accounting will continue to be developed. Financial accounting is moving in this direction as well. Investors, creditors, and regulators are putting a lot of pressure on companies to make public more relevant and more timely information than is now contained in annual reports prepared using the financial accounting model first developed by Italian merchants in the 1300–1400s. The American Institute of Certified Public Accountants (AICPA) has commissioned special committees to study these demands for additional public data about companies and to propose new models of financial accounting. Robert Elliott, chairman of the AICPA in 2000/2001, is one of many leaders in industry who believe that accounting will continue to grow and mature as the global economy and technology grow. He describes the professional practice of a "new finance" that "encompasses hard-core management accounting topics such as cost management, discount rates, and capacity management; manufacturing issues including just-in-time production, distribution channel management, and competitive intelligence; and softer topics like benchmarking, performance measurement, and managing change."

6 Frank Ogden, "Navigating in Cyberspace," MacFarland, Walter, and Ross, 1995.

He says the new finance is "less about accounting and more about becoming strategic advisors and decision makers in our companies."[7]

Exhibit 8 illustrates one way to view the current direction of change that is necessary for accounting in today's marketplace. As you can see, the pressure on accounting to change is threefold. First, financial accounting is being pressured to provide *nonfinancial* data in public reports. Second, preparation of financial accounting reports has always focused on making reports objective, consistent, and reliable. However, users of financial accounting reports want these reports to emphasize more the *relevance* of information to important investing, lending, and regulatory decisions for individual companies. Finally, in an age when the Internet allows users to access and analyze huge amounts of data almost instantaneously, there is increased demand by decision makers trying to evaluate a company based on financial accounting to be able to access information *systems* throughout the year, rather than having to wait one to three months after the year-end for the company to release an annual report document; or, in the case of internal management accounting reports, having to wait days or weeks for cost, quality, and time analysis reports to be completed and delivered to management. It's difficult to predict how these demands will eventually affect the financial accounting reports provided by thousands of companies like Microsoft. However, it's not difficult to predict that changes are coming. This is a very exciting time to be preparing to enter the world of business. Regardless of whether you intend to actually work as an accountant, it is clear that accounting will dramatically impact the way you work. By understanding the concepts of financial and management accounting, as well as the great potential for continuous improvement in these areas, you will be better prepared to use accounting to personally add value to your organization.

Exhibit 8: The Future of Financial Accounting in Public Reports

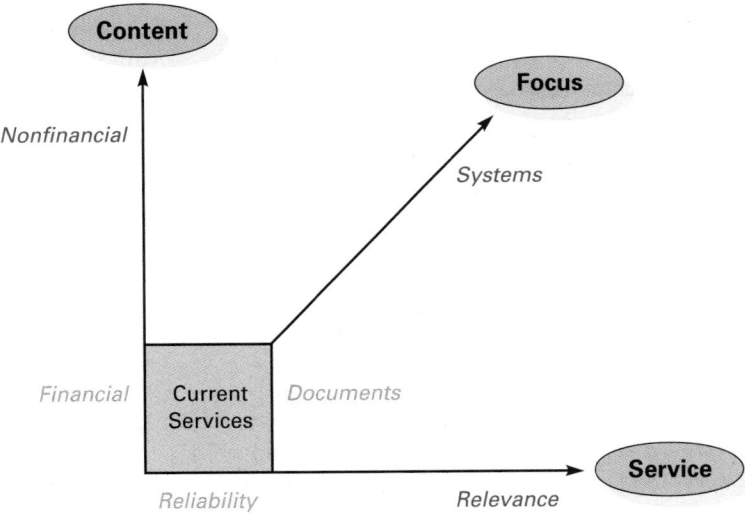

Source: From a 1996 presentation by Robert K. Elliott, Chairperson of the AICPA Special Committee on Assurance Services.

7 P. Fleming, "Steering a Course for the Future," *Journal of Accountancy* (November 1999), pp. 35–38.

review of learning objectives

1 Explain the fundamentals of building a balanced scorecard. Competition requires that companies continually improve their performance measures in order to add value to the products and services they provide within their industries. Nonfinancial measures are growing in importance in today's marketplace as companies work to build better management systems. The Balanced Scorecard is being heralded as an important new management model that explicitly supports a successful strategy by integrating performance measures of financial, customer, internal process, and learning and growth activities within an organization. Management accountants must work closely with managers, executives, and information technologists in order to build a balanced scorecard that is unique to their own organization. One of the most important aspects of a successful scorecard is *linking* all performance measures either directly or indirectly to desired financial performance. The Balanced Scorecard approach to these linkages is to connect financial performance directly to customer outcome measures of customer retention, customer acquisition, and market share. These customer outcome measures in turn are linked to leading measures on customer service involving cost, quality, and time. Internal processes taking place within an organization that support value-added services expected by customers are then identified. These internal processes include innovation processes (identifying and creating new products), operations processes (obtaining customer orders and producing and delivering products), and service-after-sale processes (handling warranties and providing support to customers). Positive employee outcome performance in terms of employee retention, satisfaction, and productivity is necessary in order to support continual improvement of internal processes. Employee outcome measures on retention, satisfaction, and productivity are linked to important investments in the capabilities of employees, information systems, and organizational structure.

2 Anticipate that both management accounting and financial accounting are poised for important changes. This textbook has covered a lot of territory in an effort to introduce you to the world of accounting. You should understand that management accounting has always been a function of competitive need. In other words, the desire to compete well in the marketplace drives companies to develop better methods of management accounting. Hence, as you would expect, today's competitive markets continue to put pressure on both management and financial accounting to make some fundamental changes. The AICPA (American Institute of Certified Public Accountants) has commissioned special committees to investigate these trends. The pressure on accounting to grow and change involves three essential areas: (1) the need to include nonfinancial measures in public accounting reports; (2) the need to better emphasize relevant, rather than just reliable, data; and (3) the need to allow continual access to data systems rather than periodic report documents. Accountants, as well as other business professionals, who can anticipate these needs will be best positioned to add value to their organizations throughout the future.

key terms & concepts

review problem

Applying the Balanced Scorecard to a School District

Knowlton School District is currently developing a balanced scorecard to be used by all the schools in the district (K-12). At a meeting with all of the principals in the Knowlton School District, the following objectives were created for each of the five categories shown on the next page. (Note that balanced scorecard categories can and should be adjusted to suit the specific needs of the organization.)

1. *Student Achievement*
   Objectives:
   - Student mastery of curriculum
   - Nationally competitive students
2. *Customer Satisfaction*
   Objectives:
   - Safe and enriching school environment
   - Parent satisfaction
   - Community involvement
3. *Instructional and Administrative Processes*
   Objectives:
   - Effective instruction
   - Safe and efficient transportation
   - Well-maintained facilities
4. *Staff Learning and Growth*
   Objectives:
   - Competent staff
   - Staff satisfaction
5. *Financial Performance*
   Objective:
   - Sound fiscal management

Required:
For each of these objectives, provide one measure of performance that the school district could use.

Solution*
There are many different measures that could be used. Here are some possible measures.

Goal Area	Objective	Measure
1. Student Achievement	Student mastery of curriculum	• Proficiency tests in various subjects • Retention rates • Drop-out rates
	Nationally competitive students	• SAT scores • AP Exam scores • Enrollments in college-credit courses
2. Customer Satisfaction	Safe and enriching school environment	• Absenteeism and tardy rates • Participation in extracurricular activities • Perception of safety (student surveys)
	Parent satisfaction	• Scores on parent surveys • Number of parent complaints
	Community involvement	• Total volunteer hours • Dollars donated • Number of business partners
3. Instructional and Administrative Processes	Effective instruction	• Percent of students in summer school • Percent of teachers certified in special programs • Percent of teachers using technology
	Safe and efficient transportation	• Accidents per million miles • On-time bus delivery
	Well-maintained facilities	• Accidents per student days • Scores on inspection reports • Level of backlogged maintenance reports

(continued)

Goal Area	Objective	Measure
4. Staff Learning and Growth	Competent staff	• Percentage of teachers with 7+ years of experience • Percentage of teachers with advanced degrees • Percentage of board-certified teachers
	Staff satisfaction	• Absenteeism rates • Percentage of teachers retiring early • Scores on teacher surveys
5. Financial Performance	Sound fiscal management	• Revenue variances of actual to budget • Expense variances of actual to budget • Fund balances

*This balanced scorecard is adapted from the actual balanced scorecard for the Fulton County School System in Georgia and can be viewed at **http://www.fulton.k12.ga.us/bsc200203.pdf**, accessed September 1, 2003.

d iscussion questions

1. Why is it unwise for a company to focus on only one performance measure while ignoring other performance measures?

2. Why do you think performance measures vary from company to company?

3. Why do you think there has been such a revolution in the way companies think about and measure their performance in recent years?

4. What is one way that traditional performance measurement systems, which have historically been tied to financial reporting, may be dysfunctional?

5. Why do you think some researchers argue that traditional performance measures are partly responsible for a decline in America's competitiveness?

6. Describe the two classifications of customer performance measures.

7. What are the key ingredients of customer satisfaction?

8. Why doesn't the purchase price of a product equal the product's total cost to customers?

9. What are the two issues involved in managing a company's market share of its products?

10. What are the three types of processes that should be in place to effectively support customer satisfaction?

11. How can companies plan, control, and evaluate their innovation processes?

12. Is it possible for a company to spend more money on the innovation process than on providing goods and services to current customers?

13. What are the three leading measures of learning and growth in an organization?

14. What are some of the factors of effective organizational structures discussed in this chapter?

15. Why do you think the market value of many companies (as measured by per-share stock price times the number of shares outstanding) is greater than the book value of the net assets (as measured by total assets minus total liabilities) listed on the balance sheets of those companies?

16. How do companies go about managing directly their return on investment (ROI)?

17. Pressure to provide better information to support the competitive needs of today's marketplace is resulting in fundamental changes in the accounting information that is being provided to managers, investors, and creditors. Identify the three primary areas of change.

practice exercises

Practice 24-1

The Balanced Scorecard
Which one of the following statements is *false*?

a. Companies that use the Balanced Scorecard do not need to focus on financial performance.
b. The Balanced Scorecard is not an exact formula that can be automatically implemented in any organization.
c. Companies using the Balanced Scorecard should implement performance measures that support the organization's goals.
d. Lower-level managers tend to pattern their efforts after the performance measures that upper-level management has implemented.

Practice 24-2

Customer Satisfaction
Which one of the following statements is *false*?

a. Leading measures focus on fulfilling customer expectations.
b. Outcome measures focus on whether improvements in leading measures result in more satisfied customers.
c. A decreasing market share is a good indication of high customer satisfaction.
d. Companies that are not committed to quality products usually do not last long.

Practice 24-3

Internal Processes
Which one of the following statements is *false*?

a. One type of operations process is the organization's commitment to warranty its product.
b. Research and development projects can require a very long payback period.
c. An operation process that has six sigma quality allows for only 3.4 defects per million opportunities.
d. One type of service-after-sale process is billing and collection of payments from customers.

Practice 24-4

Learning and Growth
Which one of the following statements is *false*?

a. The ultimate result of building learning and growth in an organization is based on developing employee productivity.
b. Poorly run organizations often have low employee morale.
c. Outcome performance measures, such as output per employee, can be used to estimate how well the leading performance measures, such as training hours per employee, add value to the organization.
d. Learning and growth measurement is a well-developed accounting discipline.

Practice 24-5

Linking It All Together
Which one of the following statements is *false*?

a. All measures of the Balanced Scorecard must link together to eventually support the ultimate financial goals of a company.
b. No company will use every single performance measure available.
c. Lagging measures indicate the potential success of future business activities.
d. Too much information is often as harmful as too little information.

Practice 24-6

Performance Measurement Linkages
Which one of the following represents the correct cause-and-effect sequence of leading and lagging measures in an organization?

(continued)

a. Learning and Growth → Internal Processes → Customer → Financial
b. Financial → Learning and Growth → Internal Processes → Customer
c. Customer → Internal Processes → Learning and Growth → Financial
d. Internal Processes → Financial → Learning and Growth → Customer

Practice 24-7

Implementing a Balanced Scorecard
Which one of the following statements is *true*?

a. The same Balanced Scorecard can be implemented at all organizations for maximum success.
b. Management accountants may build performance measurement systems that are irrelevant to the needs of the business.
c. A correctly implemented Balanced Scorecard usually fails to add value to the organization.
d. Two companies that have different performance measures will not be able to compete against each other.

Practice 24-8

Accounting for Tomorrow
The accounting industry is currently facing pressure in each of the following areas *except*:

a. The need to better emphasize relevant, rather than just reliable, data.
b. The need to include nonfinancial measures in public accounting reports.
c. The need to grow at a faster rate than the other industries to keep up with business demands.
d. The need to allow continual access to data systems rather than periodic report documents.

e xercises

Exercise 24-1

Customer Satisfaction Performance Measures
The following are possible performance measures of customer satisfaction:

1. Purchase cost to customer
2. Customer defection rate
3. Returns by customers
4. Number of new customers
5. Time to complete contract
6. Percent of total units sold
7. Customer survey response
8. Costs to recruit customers

Identify which of these measures are most likely to be considered leading measures and which are outcome performance measures. Also, if they are leading performance measures, identify whether they relate to cost, quality, or time. If they are outcome performance measures, identify whether they relate to customer retention, customer acquisition, or market share.

Exercise 24-2

Internal Processes Performance Measures
The following are possible performance measures of internal processes:

1. Cost of replacement parts
2. Lead time (order to delivery)
3. Lead time (idea to working model)
4. Payback on R&D costs
5. Percentage of sales from new products
6. Unit-level costs
7. Defects per million
8. Repair cycle time

Identify the type of performance measure (cost, quality, or time) and the related process (innovation, operations, or service-after-sale) for each of these measures.

Exercise 24-3

Performance Measures of Learning and Growth
The following are performance measures of learning and growth:

1. Number of new certifications or degrees
2. Average life cycle time of personal computers
3. Assessment of effective communication
4. Employee turnover rate
5. Output per employee
6. Average yearly training or education hours per employee
7. Survey of employee satisfaction
8. Amount of time spent in teamwork versus individual work

Identify which of these learning and growth measures are leading performance measures and which are outcome performance measures. Also, if they are leading performance measures, identify whether they would be classified as cost, quality, or time measures and whether they relate to employee, information system, or organizational structure capabilities. If they are outcome performance measures, identify whether they relate to employee retention, employee satisfaction, or employee productivity.

Exercise 24-4

Balanced Scorecard Linkages
The following are examples of performance measures in a balanced scorecard:

1. ROI
2. Percentage of employees having leadership opportunities
3. Repair cycle time
4. Quality rankings by other agencies
5. ROE
6. Design cycle time
7. Six sigma
8. Systems R&D expense per total systems expense

Classify each of the above performance measures using the categories in Exhibit 6. For each measure, identify the type of lagging measure to which it links.

Exercise 24-5

Classifying Balanced Scorecard Elements
Listed below are a number of scorecard measures for a manufacturing company:

a. Number of new customers
b. Percentage of customers who place multiple orders
c. Percentage of on-time deliveries
d. Number of worker accidents
e. Number of customer complaints about products
f. Number of employees who attend training seminars
g. Percentage of product defects
h. Percentage of back-ordered products
i. Customer satisfaction, as measured through periodic surveys
j. Unit product cost
k. Percentage of revenues from new products
l. Earnings per share
m. Gross margin on products
n. Employee turnover
o. Costs to retain customers
p. Amount of time spent in teamwork

(continued)

Classify each performance measure according to the following:

1. *Perspective:* financial, customer, internal processes, or learning and growth
2. *Focus:* cost, quality, time, or overall financial (*Note:* Some measures may have more than one focus.)
3. *Relationship:* leading or outcome (*Note:* As the measure relates to other measures within its own perspective.)

Exercise 24-6

Balanced Scorecard and Incentives

Recall from the chapter the discussion of the oil drillers from the former Soviet Union who won a production competition based on the number of meters drilled. Those drillers determined that the first 100 meters of drilling were the easiest, so they simply drilled dry wells that never exceeded 100 meters in depth. Naturally, management would be upset when the drillers' tactics were exposed. After all, management's objective was to drill wells and find oil.

1. Can you suggest to management an incentive system that would have prevented such behavior and would instead encourage the desired behavior?
2. Do you consider what the drillers did to be wrong or smart?

Exercise 24-7

Thinking about the Balanced Scorecard

Albert Einstein once commented that "sometimes what can be counted doesn't count, and what can't be counted is what really counts." A business executive stated, "The first indication we don't know what we are doing is a preoccupation with numbers." How do you think these two statements relate to the Balanced Scorecard approach to performance measurement?

Exercise 24-8

Applying the Balanced Scorecard to a Bank*

You have just been hired as the CFO of Bridger Bank, a small community bank in your town. Management is currently in the process of creating a balanced scorecard management system. You have been given the following list of performance measures.

a. Return on equity
b. Sales calls to potential customers
c. Thank you calls or cards to existing customers
d. Lending income
e. Number of new customers
f. Referrals (a referral is when one employee suggests that a customer see another employee for more information about a bank product)
g. Cross-sells (selling multiple products to one customer when the customer comes in for only one product)
h. Employee training hours
i. Nonlending income
j. Employee turnover
k. Customer satisfaction
l. New products introduced
m. Employee satisfaction
n. Customer retention

1. Classify these measures as learning and growth measures, internal processes, customer measures, and financial measures by grouping the measures in a column for each respective category.
2. After classifying the measures in columns, draw arrows from the leading measures to the lagging measures. (*Hint:* Some measures may be both a leading and lagging measure, and some measures may be a leading or a lagging measure for more than one other measure.)

*This exercise is adapted from T. Albright, S. Davis, and A. Hibbets, "Tri-Cities Community Bank: A Balanced Scorecard Case," *Strategic Finance* (October 2001), pp. 54–59.

problems

Problem 24-1

Applying the Balanced Scorecard to Manufacturing

Martin, Inc., manufactures pleasure and fishing boats. Management's goals and objectives for the company are:

1. *Goal:* To maintain strong financial health.
   Objectives:
   - Maintain sufficient cash balances to assure liquidity and solvency
   - Achieve continued growth in sales and profits
   - Provide a good return to investors
   - Increase market share
2. *Goal:* To provide excellent customer service.
   Objectives:
   - Provide boats that meet customer needs
   - Meet customer needs on a timely basis
   - Exceed customer quality standards
3. *Goal:* To be the industry leader in product innovations.
   Objectives:
   - Bring new boats and features to the market before competitors
   - Increase efficiency and productivity faster than competitors

Required:
For each of these objectives, provide one measure of performance the company could use.

Problem 24-2

Applying the Balanced Scorecard to a Small Business

You are an optometrist with your own practice. For the past 20 years, you have focused almost exclusively on profitability of your practice as your sole performance measure. In fact, you have been quite profitable. However, during the past two years, a number of new, low-cost, commercial optometric offices including LENSCRAFTERS, WAL-MART, SHOPKO, and even KMART have opened in your practice area. As a result, your profitability has decreased to the point where you are barely breaking even. Because of your concern for your practice, you have asked a business consultant what you should do.

She has told you that your single-minded focus on profitability is no different than that of your new commercial competitors and has convinced you that these competitors will be more successful than you in making profits because they have lower cost structures than you do. She has suggested that you read her recently published book on the Balanced Scorecard measurement system and respond to the following questions:

Required:
1. Are your current success measures mostly financial, internal processes, learning and growth, or customer focused?
2. Has your focus been on financial, quality, or time measures, or on an appropriate balance of the three?
3. Thinking about your performance perspective (financial, customer, internal processes, and learning and growth), how could you distinguish yourself from the commercial optometrists and create value for your customers?
4. Are there ways you should change your focus regarding cost, quality, and time measures?

Problem 24-3

Applying the Balanced Scorecard to an Internet Company

OnRamp, Inc., is a technology company that provides connections for Internet service providers (ISPs) to the information highway. If U.S. WEST and other long-distance companies that own fiber optic cable are the information highway, OnRamp, Inc., views itself as the on- and off-ramps that provide access to the highway for ISPs, such as EARTHLINK, INC., and their customers. Two years ago, OnRamp, Inc., had an initial public offering (IPO) where it raised $500 million in operating capital. With that money, it built a new office building and developed much of the infrastructure needed to serve as the on- and off-ramp market leader. The company gets its revenue from charging ISPs a small user fee for each customer connected to the information highway. In its prospectus for the IPO, OnRamp, Inc., stated that its only critical performance measure of success was the number of users that it served. It stated that if, in two years, it serviced 2 million individual users, then it would consider itself to be successful. Now, two years later, there are 5 million individual customer accounts within OnRamp's system. Unfortunately, however, OnRamp, Inc., is still losing considerable amounts of money and is experiencing serious complaints about delayed Internet access and server problems.

Required:
1. What do you think about OnRamp, Inc.'s "number of ISP customers" performance measure?
2. If, in fact, OnRamp, Inc., measures its success solely on the basis of number of individual ISP customers, what important performance measures is it ignoring?

Problem 24-4

Applying the Balanced Scorecard to a University
The dean of your business school has determined that there are four major drivers of success for her business school. Those success drivers are having outstanding (1) faculty, (2) students, (3) curricula, and (4) alumni and recruiter support.

Required:
Based on these drivers of success, develop a balanced scorecard performance system that the dean could use to evaluate the operations of her school. Be specific and indicate the purpose of each measure. Make sure that you clearly include both leading and outcome measures in your balanced scorecard.

Problem 24-5

Applying the Balanced Scorecard to a Church
As an accountant and active member of a local church, you have been asked by your pastor to help him develop a balanced scorecard measurement system for the church. He is seriously interested in continuous improvement and believes that by identifying and monitoring the right performance measurements, the church will be more successful. In discussions with the pastor, you have determined that the scorecard should focus on the following four areas:

- Increase in learning and commitment of members
- Size of congregation and membership
- Respect in the community
- Amount of financial contributions

Required:
Develop a performance measurement system for these four areas that includes both leading and outcome measures that could be used by the pastor and his church to grow and measure the success of his ecumenical efforts.

d iscussion cases

Case 24-1

Strategy for Developing a Balanced Scorecard

A company is interested in developing a balanced scorecard approach to evaluating and enhancing its performance. It is looking at two ways of accomplishing the task. The first is for top management to develop the scorecard approach and impose it on managers throughout the organization. The second is to involve managers, customers, and other stakeholders in a grass-roots approach to determine what cost, quality, and time factors should be measured. Which of the two approaches would you recommend to the company?

Case 24-2

How Soon Can You Make Us a Balanced Scorecard?

You are currently the controller for a large manufacturing company. The president of the company calls you to his office and states the following: "I just went to a round-table discussion with presidents of other companies, and they told me that the most important development they had made in their companies was to implement balanced scorecards. I want you to drop whatever you are doing this week and develop a balanced scorecard for our company." You are vaguely aware of the concept of Balanced Scorecards from your reading, but you aren't too sure what they are all about. As you begin to think about your upcoming task, you discover that your com-

pany does not have a strategic plan or mission statement. Is the task given you by the president one that can be accomplished in a week or accomplished at all? What is the effect of not having a strategic plan or mission statement on the development of a balanced scorecard for the company?

Case 24-3

Get Those Business School Ratings Up!

You are the dean of the business school at North Central University. You have recently gone through a strategic planning process involving representatives from all your stakeholder groups (students, staff, faculty, recruiters, alumni, administration, etc.). The result is a newly refined strategic plan, including a mission statement, underlying values, specific objectives and strategies, and assessment outcomes (performance measurements). One of your objectives is to increase the ranking of your business school by *Business News*, a magazine that annually ranks business programs in your region. Given your understanding of the Balanced Scorecard approach and the material covered in this textbook, answer the following questions.

1. Even though it takes longer, is it wise to involve various stakeholders in developing your strategic plan? Why or why not?
2. What are some likely strategies that might be implemented to increase your business school ranking? Explain.

j udgment calls

Judgment 24-1

You Decide: By encouraging employees to work harder and to increase quality, are companies lowering overall costs, or are they increasing waste and inefficiency of materials?

You have just been hired to work as a part-time accountant for a small, local flower shop. Jim, the manager, feels the costs of doing business (purchasing flowers, vases, etc.) are getting too high, and he has asked you to find a solution to this problem. The shop employs two full-time workers and one part-time worker. Jim's philosophy is if you use the highest quality, you will increase business through customer loyalty. However, you have found out that Jim has given the employees permission to use whatever means necessary to ensure the

flower arrangements and bouquets are made of the highest quality, even if it means wasting a lot of materials to create the best flower products possible.

Judgment 24-2

You Decide: Should the Balanced Scorecard concept be a "one-size fits all," or is the Balanced Scorecard more effective when it is catered to and created with an individual company in mind?

You have been introduced to the idea of a balanced scorecard through your classes in business school. At a recent family gathering, you began talking to your Uncle Richard about what you have learned. He has been president of a regional furniture store for the last 10 years and has tried to implement the Balanced Scorecard in his company, but with no success. Your uncle says, "I had a college buddy e-mail me his company's scorecard as an example. He works in the real estate industry and said that it has changed the way they do business. We tried to implement his scorecard in our business, but it just didn't make sense. It might work for some companies, but it sure doesn't work for mine!"

Competency Enhancement Opportunities

▶ **Analyzing Real Company Information**   ▶ **The Debate**
▶ **International Case**   ▶ **Internet Search**
▶ **Ethics Case**
▶ **Writing Assignment**

The following additional assignments provide opportunities for students to develop critical thinking, ethical perspectives, oral and written communication skills, experience with electronic research, and teamwork through group and business activities.

▶ Analyzing Real Company Information

Analyzing 24-1 (Futura Industries)
Remember the last time you walked through a grocery store? Did you notice all of the shelves holding the food? If you are like most people, you probably did not pay much attention to the shelves except to take the food off of them. The aluminum parts that make up the shelves in a grocery store (and other stores) are part of a product family known as aluminum extrusions. Many aluminum extrusions are manufactured by a company in Clearfield, Utah, called FUTURA INDUSTRIES. While Futura's products are not very exciting, they are pretty important. Hence, the management process at Futura is as important as it is at any other type of company, and Futura Industries has a very interesting balanced scorecard. Futura Industries began in the 1930s producing a product called colfonite. During the late 1940s, it started producing aluminum extrusions. By 1979, the Seattle, Washington-based company had moved its entire company to Clearfield, Utah. Futura's current president, Susan Johnson, has chosen to pursue her company's mission (Extraordinary Value through Extrusions) by careful alignment of the company's measures and tactics. She and the rest of the management staff at Futura have developed a balanced scorecard that has proven to be very successful in helping the company to grow.
Strategy of Futura:

> Futura strives to insure financial growth and prosperity by developing customer intimacy, providing flawless new products, and identifying new opportunities in products and processes. In addition, it emphasizes speed and quality in operations, planning and delivery accuracy, and continual reduction of costs. Futura is also focused on working to improve its competencies, providing a safe, challenging, and enjoyable workforce, and hiring people who have its same values.

The following is an alphabetical list of Futura's balanced scorecard measures along with a definition of each measure.

Balanced Scorecard Measure	Definition
Accuracy of price quotes	Number of correct price quotes ÷ total price quotes issued
Average job certification levels	Total sum of job certification levels ÷ total employees
Birthday review	Score based on yearly review on date of employee's birthday
Cash return on total assets	Cash flow ÷ total assets
Cost of plant scrap	Dollar value of scrapped material
Cost of rework	Dollar value of rework before sale
Customer complaints	Number of complaints ÷ total number of customers
Customer satisfaction	Periodic customer surveys
Dollar value of products packaged per person	Total dollar value of product packed ÷ number of employees working
Employees with one year or more turnover ratio	Number of employees employed for one year or more ÷ total number of employees
Income growth	(Current year's income − previous year's income) ÷ previous year's income
Leadership survey	Yearly survey score of employees
Leadership turnover	Number of new employees in leadership positions ÷ total number of employees in leadership positions
Margins on new products and standard products	Gross profit margin on new products and on standard products
On-time deliveries	Number of on-time deliveries ÷ total deliveries
Percent of market in commercial retailing	Number of commercial retail customers ÷ total number of customers
Percent of market in original equipment manufacturers (OEM)	Number of OEM customers ÷ total number of OEM customers
Percent of sales from new products	Sales revenue from new products ÷ total sales revenue
Pounds of products packaged per person	Number of pounds packed ÷ number of employees working
Product returns	Number of items returned
Total company employee turnover	Number of new employees ÷ total number of employees
Total finished goods turnover	Total cost of finished goods sold during year ÷ average finished goods inventory
Total inventory turnover	Total cost of goods sold during the year ÷ average inventory
Total production cost per direct labor hour	Total cost of production ÷ total direct labor hours

Classify Futura's balanced scorecard measures into the four Balanced Scorecard categories: financial measures, customer measures, internal process measures, and learning and growth measures. Use Futura's strategy to help you determine how to classify each measure.

▶ *International Case*

A Balanced Scorecard in Russia

This chapter has discussed the need for companies to focus on more than just the numbers. Additional factors must be considered in addition to financial results. Thus, the concept of the Balanced Scorecard. Consider the case of a country where the economy is not as sophisticated as in the United States—Russia. Inflation runs rampant, shortages prevail, organized crime rules. How could a balanced scorecard approach help a company that finds itself in this situation? Or could it? Can you suggest areas from the balanced scorecard perspective that a company in Russia might emphasize?

▶ *Ethics Case*

"Family" Business

Martin Beemer is the purchasing manager for the police department in a large metropolitan city. The city has 13,000 police officers. The city currently purchases police uniforms from three different manufacturers, one of which is SunKing, International (a Korean company). Martin recently agreed (in private) with SunKing's vice president to give SunKing increased business if SunKing would hire his daughter as a "ghost" salesperson in the United States at a salary of $350,000 per year.

1. Do you believe the actions of Martin and SunKing are unethical? Fraudulent?
2. What internal process performance measures could the city have had in place in the purchasing department that could have revealed the kickback arrangement?

▶ *Writing Assignment*

More Than Just the Numbers

You have found in your study of accounting that accountants generally focus on the numbers. Their job is to summarize financial results and provide information for decision makers. In this chapter, you have read about additional measures that are critical to a company's success: items like customer loyalty and satisfaction and employee productivity. Your assignment is to prepare a one- to two-page memo summarizing the following points:

1. Select an internal process measure, like research and development, and map out how the careful monitoring of that process will eventually show up in a financial measure like ROI.
2. Are accountants the best people to collect information on items such as customer satisfaction and customer loyalty? If not, who in a business would be best suited to collect this type of information?

▶ *The Debate*

Quantitative vs. Qualitative

The concept of the Balanced Scorecard suggests that instead of focusing on the financial aspects of business decisions, a company should manage such items as customer satisfaction, employee growth, and total quality, and the profits will follow. Divide your group into two teams. Each team should prepare a five-minute presentation addressing the following issues:

- One team supports "quantitative" measures. Defend the position that a company should manage by the numbers. The DuPonts and the Carnegies achieved the success they did because they focused on costs and profits. Provide reasons in support of your assigned position.

- The other team supports "qualitative" measures. Defend the position that a company's management should examine more than just the financial statement numbers. Other important information must be managed if a company is to be successful. In your presentation, identify some of that "other important information."

▷ *Internet Search*

Balanced Scorecard Collaborative

The home page for the Balanced Scorecard Collaborative (BSCol) can be found at **http://www .bscol.com**. Go to this Web site to learn more about the Balanced Scorecard Collaborative and answer the questions below. Sometimes Web addresses change, so if this address does not work, access the Web site for this textbook (**http://albrecht.swlearning.com**) for an updated link.

1. What is the purpose or mission of the Balanced Scorecard Collaborative?
2. The BSCol recognizes companies that have successfully implemented the Balanced Scorecard in its Hall of Fame. What are the nomination/selection criteria to be recognized as a BSC Hall of Fame member?

Microsoft Corporation

FORM 10-K

For The Fiscal Year Ended June 30, 2002

INDEX

Access the Microsoft Annual Report at **http://www.microsoft.com**.

United States Securities and Exchange Commission
Washington, D.C. 20549

FORM 10-K

☒ ANNUAL REPORT PURSUANT TO SECTION 13 OR 15(d) OF THE SECURITIES EXCHANGE ACT OF 1934
FOR THE FISCAL YEAR ENDED JUNE 30, 2002

☐ TRANSITION REPORT PURSUANT TO SECTION 13 OR 15(d) OF THE SECURITIES EXCHANGE ACT OF 1934
FOR THE TRANSITION PERIOD FROM _____ TO _____

COMMISSION FILE NUMBER 0-14278

MICROSOFT CORPORATION

WASHINGTON	91-1144442
(STATE OF INCORPORATION)	(I.R.S. ID)

ONE MICROSOFT WAY, REDMOND, WASHINGTON 98052-6399

(425) 882-8080

Securities registered pursuant to Section 12(b) of the Act:
NONE

Securities registered pursuant to Section 12(g) of the Act:
COMMON STOCK

Indicate by check mark whether the registrant (1) has filed all reports required to be filed by Section 13 or 15(d) of the Securities Exchange Act of 1934 during the preceding 12 months (or for such shorter period that the registrant was required to file such reports), and (2) has been subject to such filing requirements for the past 90 days. YES ☒ NO ☐

Indicate by check mark if disclosure of delinquent filers pursuant to Item 405 of Regulation S-K is not contained herein, and will not be contained, to the best of registrant's knowledge, in definitive proxy or information statements incorporated by reference in Part III of this Form 10-K or any amendment to this Form 10-K. ☐

The aggregate market value of common stock held by non-affiliates of the registrant as of July 31, 2002 was $215,553,343,213.

The number of shares outstanding of the registrant's common stock as of July 31, 2002 was 5,378,746,853.

DOCUMENTS INCORPORATED BY REFERENCE

Portions of the definitive Proxy Statement to be delivered to shareholders in connection with the Annual Meeting of Shareholders to be held November 5, 2002 are incorporated by reference into Part III.

PART I

ITEM 1. BUSINESS

GENERAL

Microsoft Corporation (the "Company" or "Microsoft") was founded as a partnership in 1975 and incorporated in 1981. Microsoft's mission is to enable people and businesses throughout the world to realize their full potential, and the Company's vision is empowering people through great software—any time, any place, and on any device. Microsoft develops, manufactures, licenses, and supports a wide range of software products for a multitude of computing devices. Microsoft software products include scalable operating systems for servers, personal computers (PCs), and intelligent devices; server applications for client/server environments; information worker productivity applications; business solutions applications; and software development tools. During fiscal 2002, Microsoft launched Xbox, the Company's next-generation video game system. The Company's online efforts include the MSN network of Internet products and services and alliances with companies involved with broadband access and various forms of digital interactivity. Microsoft licenses consumer software programs; sells hardware devices; provides consulting services; and trains and certifies system integrators and developers.

Microsoft also researches and develops advanced technologies for future software products. A significant portion of the Company's focus is on Microsoft's .NET architecture. Using common industry standards based on XML, a universal language for describing and exchanging data, the Company's goal is to enable seamless sharing of information across many platforms and programming languages, and over the Internet, with XML Web services. In addition, Microsoft has embarked on a long-term initiative called Trustworthy Computing, which aims to bring an enhanced level of security, privacy, reliability, and business integrity to computer systems.

PRODUCTS

During fiscal 2002, Microsoft had four operating segments based on its product and service offerings: Desktop and Enterprise Software and Services; Consumer Software, Services, and Devices; Consumer Commerce Investments; and Other. See Note 20 of the Notes to Financial Statements for financial information regarding segment reporting.

DESKTOP AND ENTERPRISE SOFTWARE AND SERVICES

Desktop and Enterprise Software and Services includes Desktop Applications; Desktop Platforms; and Enterprise Software and Services. For segment reporting purposes, Desktop Applications includes revenue from Microsoft Office; Microsoft Project; Visio; client access licenses (CALs) for Windows NT Server and Windows 2000 Server, Exchange, and BackOffice; Microsoft Great Plains; and bCentral. Desktop Platforms includes revenue from Windows XP Professional and Home; Windows 2000 Professional; Windows NT Workstation; Windows Millennium Edition; Windows 98; and other desktop operating systems. Enterprise Software and Services includes Server Platforms; Server Applications; Developer Tools and Services; and Enterprise Services.

DESKTOP APPLICATIONS

Microsoft Office. Microsoft Office is a software product featuring commonly used desktop functionality. The product is based upon a document-centric concept, with common commands and extensive use of cross-application capabilities. Microsoft Office is available in several versions for the Windows and Macintosh operating systems. Microsoft Office XP, the latest Microsoft Office release, helps users complete common business tasks, including word processing, electronic mail (e-mail), presentations, and data management, with features like smart tags, task panes, integrated e-mail, document recovery, and send for review. The various versions of Microsoft Office include the word processor Microsoft Word, Microsoft Excel spreadsheet, Microsoft Outlook personal information management and e-mail communication client, Microsoft PowerPoint presentation graphics program, and may include Microsoft Access database management application, Microsoft FrontPage Web site creation and management tool, and Microsoft Publisher business desktop publishing program. Most of these applications are also licensed separately.

Other Desktop Application Products. The Company also offers other stand-alone desktop application products. Microsoft Project is a project management program for scheduling, organizing, and analyzing tasks, deadlines, and resources. Visio is a diagramming program that helps people visualize and communicate ideas, information, and systems.

Client Access Licenses. A client access license gives its holder the legal right to access a computer running a Microsoft server product and the services supported by the server using a client computer.

Microsoft Great Plains. Microsoft Great Plains offers a range of integrated business and accounting products, including Dynamics, Solomon, and eEnterprise. Dynamics provides Internet-ready accounting and business management capabilities for small- to mid-sized companies. Solomon offers a full range of e-business and accounting applications for small- to mid-sized companies. eEnterprise supports mid-sized to larger companies by providing a collaborative environment for information management and sharing.

bCentral. Microsoft's small businesses portal, bCentral, includes Site Manager, a Web site management and hosting service which empowers small businesses to easily create and manage their own Web sites, while allowing for higher-end editing in Microsoft FrontPage, and LinkExchange, which provides services to small businesses and Web site owners to increase their online traffic and sales with free advertising banner ads on their site in exchange for placing ads on other network sites.

DESKTOP PLATFORMS

Windows XP. Microsoft launched Windows XP in October 2001. Windows XP extends the personal computing experience by uniting PCs, devices, and services, while enhancing reliability, security, and performance. Windows XP Home Edition is designed for individuals or families and includes experiences for digital photo, music, video, home networking, and communications. Windows XP Professional includes all the features of Home Edition, plus remote access, security, performance, manageability, and multilingual features to help users improve productivity and connectivity.

Windows 2000 Professional. The successor to Windows NT Workstation, Windows 2000 Professional operating system combines features to create a mainstream operating system for desktop and notebook computing in all organizations. Windows 2000 Professional contains the enhanced business features of Windows 98 such as Plug and Play, easy-to-use user interface, and power management and integrates the strengths of Windows NT Workstation including standards-based security, manageability, and reliability.

Windows NT Workstation. A fully integrated, multitasking 32-bit PC operating system, Windows NT Workstation provides improved security features, robustness, and portability. Windows NT Workstation combines the Windows 98 operating system interface and usability features with the reliability and security of Windows NT for the business environment.

Windows Millennium Edition. Windows Millennium Edition (Me) operating system is designed specifically for home users, including capabilities to manage digital photos and music, work with video, create a home network, and communicate with other consumers.

Windows 98. The successor to Windows 95, Windows 98 is a personal computer operating system that provides a Web-oriented user interface and better system performance along with easier system diagnostics and maintenance. Windows 98 supports graphics, sound, and multimedia technologies and provides the ability to easily add and remove peripheral devices and support for Universal Serial Bus (USB).

ENTERPRISE SOFTWARE AND SERVICES

Windows 2000 Server, Advanced Server, and Datacenter Server. Windows 2000 Server is a multipurpose network operating system for businesses of all sizes. Windows 2000 Advanced Server operating system is ideal for e-commerce and line-of-business applications and provides enhanced performance and scalability through symmetric multiprocessing (SMP) and extended memory support. Windows Datacenter Server operating system is built for large-scale line-of-business and enterprise backend usage and supports server consolidation and enhanced scalability.

Microsoft .NET Enterprise Servers. Microsoft .NET Enterprise Servers include Microsoft SQL Server, Exchange Server, Application Center, BizTalk Server, Commerce Server, Content Management Server, Host Integration Server, Internet Security and Acceleration Server, Microsoft Operations Manager, Mobile Information Server, and SharePoint Portal Server.

<u>SQL Server</u> is a comprehensive data management and analysis platform that enables rapid delivery, dependable performance and secure operation of connected applications.

<u>Exchange Server</u> is a messaging and collaboration server that provides e-mail, group scheduling, task management, contact management and document routing capabilities.

<u>Application Center</u> is Microsoft's deployment and management tool for high-availability Web applications built on the Microsoft Windows 2000 operating system.

<u>BizTalk Server</u> enables companies to rapidly build and deploy integrated business processes within their organizations and with partners.

<u>Commerce Server</u> provides a comprehensive set of features for building scalable, user-centric, business-to-consumer, and business-to-business e-commerce sites.

<u>Content Management Server</u> is the enterprise Web content management system that enables companies to quickly and efficiently build, deploy, and maintain highly dynamic Internet, intranet, and extranet Web sites.

<u>Host Integration Server</u> extends Microsoft Windows applications to other systems by providing application, data, and network integration.

<u>Internet Security and Acceleration Server</u> provides secure, fast, and manageable Internet connectivity. It integrates an extensible, multilayer enterprise firewall and a scalable high-performance Web cache.

<u>Microsoft Operations Manager</u> delivers enterprise-class solutions for operations management of Windows 2000, the Microsoft Active Directory service, and other component services in Windows 2000, as well as other Microsoft .NET Enterprise Server applications such as Exchange and SQL Server.

<u>Mobile Information Server</u> mobile-enables the enterprise, extending the reach of Microsoft .NET Enterprise applications, enterprise data, and intranet content to the mobile user.

<u>SharePoint Portal Server</u> extends the capabilities of Microsoft Windows and Microsoft Office by offering information workers a powerful new way to easily organize, find, and share information. It combines the ability to easily create corporate Web portals with document management, content searching, and team collaboration features.

Other Servers. Small Business Server is the flexible network solution designed to help businesses with up to 50 computers. Systems Management Server helps centrally manage the distributed environment with integrated features, including hardware inventory, software inventory and metering, software distribution and installation, and remote troubleshooting tools.

Developer Tools and Services. Software development tools and computer languages allow software developers to write programs in a particular computer language and translate programs into a binary machine-readable set of commands that activate and instruct various hardware devices. The Company develops and markets a number of software development environments and language compilers. In February 2002, Microsoft launched Visual Studio .NET, a comprehensive tool for rapidly building and deploying XML Web services and applications. Visual Studio .NET provides software developers with powerful tools to rapidly design broad-reach Web applications for any device and any platform, and to build powerful Windows applications. Microsoft Visual C++ is the Company's development system for Windows-based application development. Microsoft Visual C# offers beginning and intermediate developers with C++ or Java experience a modern language and robust development environment for creating XML Web services and Microsoft .NET-based applications for Windows and the Web. The Microsoft Visual Basic development system provides easy access to a wide variety of data sources by integrating the Microsoft Access database engine and the ability to take advantage of investments in commercial applications. The Microsoft Visual InterDev development system includes integrated, team-based development tools for building Web-based applications based on HTML, Script, and components written in any language. Developers can subscribe to the Microsoft Developer Network (MSDN) information service and receive periodic updates via CD-ROMs, magazines, and several online information services. In addition, Microsoft receives certification fees through the Microsoft Certified Professional (MCP) program, a program that provides credentials for those who have demonstrated in-depth knowledge of at least one Microsoft product.

Enterprise Services. Microsoft Enterprise Services assist organizations with every stage of technology planning, building, deployment, and support. Specializing in IT solutions for the enterprise, Microsoft offers a full range of consulting services for advance technology requirements, including custom solutions services, enterprise application planning, architecture and design services, and proof-of-concept services. The Company provides product support services aligned to customer segments, partner segments, and communities.

CONSUMER SOFTWARE, SERVICES, AND DEVICES

Consumer Software, Services, and Devices includes Xbox video game system, MSN Internet Access, MSN Network Services, PC and Online Games, Learning and Productivity Software, Mobility, and Embedded Systems.

Xbox. Microsoft Xbox, released in fiscal 2002, is Microsoft's next-generation video game console system that delivers high quality graphics and audio gameplay experiences. For information on Xbox manufacturing, see "Manufacturing" below. Games for the Xbox are developed by Microsoft Game Studios, such as Halo and Project Gotham Racing, and by third-party game development partners, such as Tecmo's Dead or Alive 3. Xbox Live, an online service available to owners of Xbox systems, is expected to be launched in the second quarter of fiscal 2003 and will allow online game play among users of online-enabled Xbox games.

MSN Internet Access. MSN Internet access is Microsoft's service for accessing the Web and experiencing a wide range of rich online services and content. MSN Internet access subscribers can access their account from multiple sources, including a computer, television, Internet appliances, and Personal Data Assistants.

MSN Network Services. The MSN network provides services, content and advertising on the Internet, encompassing MSN Search, Messenger, eShop, Hotmail, Money, and Music, as well as other services and content. MSN Search makes Web searches more useful by providing users with the most relevant results for the most popular search queries on the Web. MSN Messenger is a free Internet messaging service that enables users to see when others are online and exchange instant messages with them. MSN eShop is a one-stop online shopping resource. MSN Hotmail is the world's leading free Web-based e-mail service. MSN Money is a complete online personal financial service that combines finance tools and content from Microsoft with exclusive investment news and analysis from CNBC. MSN Music provides consumers with one place online to find old favorites, as well as discover new music, and delivers a high quality listening experience.

PC and Online Games. The Company offers a line of entertainment products from classic software games to online games, simulations, sport products, and strategy games. Microsoft Flight Simulator is a popular aircraft flight simulation product. Other games include Age of Empires, Dungeon Siege, MechWarrior, Microsoft Links, Train Simulator, Zoo Tycoon, and other action and sports titles. Zone.com is a gaming community on the Internet allowing multiplayer gaming competitions of Microsoft's popular CD-ROM games and classic card, board, and puzzle games.

Learning and Productivity Software. Learning titles include Microsoft Encarta Reference Library, a complete research and reference source with a multimedia encyclopedia database with interactive information, an interactive world atlas with three-dimensional maps, a world English dictionary, Encarta Africana, Researcher, and an online version with monthly updates. Titles for children include a series of products based on the popular children's book and television series, Scholastic's The Magic School Bus. Microsoft's productivity offerings include Microsoft Works, an integrated software program that contains basic word processing, spreadsheet, and database capabilities that allows the easy exchange of information from one tool to another. Microsoft Picture It! brand of products includes Picture It! Photo, with photo editing tools and wizards to easily capture, correct and create photos, and Picture It! Publishing, used to create greeting cards and other print and Web based products. Microsoft Money offers leading tools and resources to conduct a wide range of financial activities. The

Part I
Item 1

Works Suite provides a comprehensive collection of software, including Microsoft Works, Microsoft Word, Microsoft Money, Microsoft Encarta encyclopedia, Microsoft Picture It! Photo, and Microsoft Streets & Trips.

Mobility and Embedded Systems. Microsoft develops a number of software platforms for mobile computing. Products such as Pocket PC, Pocket PC Phone Edition, and Microsoft Windows Powered Smartphone are designed to enable a variety of mobile scenarios. Microsoft's embedded offerings include two embedded operating systems, Microsoft Windows CE and Microsoft Windows NT Embedded, as well as device specific solutions. Microsoft Windows CE, a robust real-time embedded operating system, is targeted at mobile 32-bit devices. Microsoft Windows NT Embedded, based on the desktop and server versions of Microsoft's operating systems, is targeted at higher-end embedded products and devices. Both embedded operating systems offer integrated tool sets to enable embedded system developers to quickly create sophisticated embedded device and application solutions. Microsoft Mobile Information Server is a scalable and reliable mobile applications server that provides enterprise customers and mobile operators with a rich platform for extending .NET Enterprise application and securely delivering real-time, wireless data to mobile devices.

CONSUMER COMMERCE INVESTMENTS

Consumer Commerce Investments include the HomeAdvisor online real estate service and the CarPoint online automotive service.

HomeAdvisor online real estate service. The HomeAdvisor online real estate service is a complete guide to the home-buying process and provides comprehensive tools for finding homes and loans on the Internet. The service includes customized search features, worksheets and calculators, and editorial content and home-buying advice.

CarPoint online automotive service. The CarPoint online automotive service is the leading online automotive marketplace, visited by more than 7 million consumers each month. With details on more than 10,000 car models and 100,000 used vehicles, users can research and compare cars of virtually every make and model, identify local dealers, and receive instructions for post-purchase service and maintenance.

Expedia, Inc. Expedia was included in the Consumer Commerce Investments segment until Microsoft sold its interest in Expedia to USA Networks, Inc. in February 2002. Expedia, Inc. operates Expedia.com, a leading online travel service. Expedia.com provides air, car, and hotel booking, vacation package and cruise offerings, destination information, and mapping.

OTHER

Hardware. The Hardware Group develops and markets several PC accessories including the Microsoft IntelliMouse family of hand-held pointing devices using the IntelliEye optical technology. Hardware also markets several types of keyboards including the Microsoft Natural Keyboard, an ergonomically designed keyboard, the Internet Keyboard featuring two USB ports and Internet hot keys, and a new Wireless Desktop product including wireless keyboard and mouse. Also included in the Hardware Group's portfolio of devices are SideWinder game controllers and force feedback joysticks with realistic performance technology to use with PC games.

Microsoft Press. Microsoft Press offers comprehensive learning and training resources to help new users, power users, and professionals get the most from Microsoft technology through books, CDs, self-paced training kits, and videos that are created to accommodate different learning styles and preferences. Microsoft Press books are authored by professional and technical writers, both by Microsoft employees and independent authors.

SEGMENT REPORTING

In fiscal 2003, the Company will begin reporting the following operating segments: Client; Information Worker; MSN; Home and Entertainment; CE Mobility; Server and Tools; and Business Solutions. These changes are designed to provide a comprehensive end-to-end financial view of Microsoft's key businesses; promote better alignment of strategies and objectives between development, sales, marketing, and services organizations; provide for more timely and rational allocation of development, sales, and marketing resources within businesses; and focus strategic planning efforts on key objectives and initiatives and give business owners more autonomy in detailed planning.

EQUITY METHOD INVESTMENTS

The Company has entered into joint venture arrangements to take advantage of creative talent and content from other organizations. For example, Microsoft owns 50 percent of MSNBC Cable L.L.C., a 24-hour cable news and information channel, and 50 percent of MSNBC Interactive News L.L.C., an interactive online news service. National Broadcasting Company (NBC) owns the remaining 50 percent of these two joint ventures.

PRODUCT DEVELOPMENT

During fiscal years 2000, 2001, and 2002, research and development expense was $3.77 billion, $4.38 billion, and $4.31 billion, respectively. Those amounts represented 16.4%, 17.3%, and 15.2%, respectively, of revenue in each of those years. In accordance with Statement of Financial Accounting Standards (SFAS) 142, *Goodwill and Other Intangible Assets,* the amortization of goodwill was discontinued in fiscal 2002. The amount of goodwill amortization included in research and development expense in fiscal years 2000 and 2001 was $232 million and $272 million, respectively. The Company plans to continue significant expenditures for research and product development.

Most of the Company's software products are developed internally. The Company also purchases technology, licenses intellectual property rights, and oversees third-party development and localization of certain products. Internal development allows Microsoft to maintain closer technical control over its products and gives the Company the freedom to designate which modifications and enhancements are most important and when they should be implemented. Microsoft works on devising innovative solutions to computer science problems, such as making computers easier to use, designing software for the next generation of hardware, improving the software design process, and investigating the mathematical underpinnings of computer science. The Company has created a substantial body of proprietary development tools and has evolved development methodologies for creating and enhancing its products. These tools and methodologies are also designed to simplify a product's portability among different operating systems, microprocessors, or computing devices. Product documentation is generally created internally. The Company strives to become informed at the earliest possible time about changing usage patterns and hardware advances that may affect software design. Before releasing new software platforms, Microsoft provides to software vendors a range of development, training, testing resources, and guidelines for developing applications.

The software industry is characterized by rapid technological change, which requires constant attention to computing technology trends, shifting consumer demand, and rapid product innovation. The pace of change is accelerating as the computing needs of our customers move beyond the PC toward intelligent devices and appliances, such as the Tablet PC. Tablet PCs extend the power of laptop computers running Windows XP with enhanced capabilities such as handwriting and speech input.

The Company believes that making its products trustworthy is critical to their success and has launched a company-wide effort called Trustworthy Computing. Trustworthy Computing has four pillars: reliability, security, privacy, and business integrity. Reliability means that a computer system is dependable, is available when needed, and performs as expected and at appropriate levels. Security means that a system is resilient to attack, and that the confidentiality, integrity and availability of both the system and its data are protected. Privacy means that individuals have the ability to control data about themselves and that those using such data faithfully adhere to fair information principles. Business integrity, in this context, is about being responsible to customers and helping them find appropriate solutions for their business issues, addressing problems with products or services, and being open in interactions with customers. While the Company is continuing to invest significantly in delivering new capabilities that customers ask for, Microsoft is making security improvements a high priority.

Microsoft .NET is Microsoft's platform for XML Web services. XML Web services allow applications to communicate and share data over the Internet or an intranet, regardless of operating system or programming language. The Microsoft .NET platform includes a comprehensive family of products, built on XML and other Internet industry standards, which provide for each aspect of developing, managing, using, and experiencing XML Web services. There are five areas where Microsoft is building the .NET platform today: Tools, Servers, XML Web Services, Clients, and .NET Experiences. In the Tools area, Visual Studio .NET and the Microsoft .NET framework supply a complete solution for developers to build, deploy, and run XML Web services. They maximize the performance, reliability, and security of XML Web services. The .NET Enterprise Servers, including the Windows 2000 Server family, make up Microsoft .NET's server infrastructure for deploying, managing, and orchestrating XML Web services. Designed with mission-critical performance in mind, they provide enterprises with the agility they need to integrate their systems, applications, and partners through XML Web services, and the flexibility to adapt to changing business requirements. Clients are PCs, laptops, workstations, phones, handheld computers, Tablet PCs, game consoles, and other smart devices. These smart devices use software that supports XML Web services, which enable users to access their data regardless of the location, type, and number of clients used. Smart clients and devices leverage XML Web services to create .NET experiences that allow users to access information across the Internet and from stand-alone applications in an integrated way.

To best serve the needs of users around the world, Microsoft "localizes" many of its products to reflect local languages and conventions and to improve the quality and usability of the product in international markets. Localizing a product might require modifying the user interface, altering dialog boxes, and translating text. In Japanese versions, for example, all user messages and documentation are in Japanese with monetary references in the Japanese yen. Various Microsoft products have been localized into more than 30 languages.

MANUFACTURING

Microsoft contracts out most of its manufacturing activities to third parties. Outside manufacturers produce the Xbox, various retail software packaged products, and hardware. There are other custom manufacturers Microsoft could use in the event outsourced manufacturing becomes unavailable from current vendors. The Company generally has multiple sources for raw materials, supplies, and components and is often able to acquire component parts and materials on a volume discount basis. The graphics processing unit (GPU) for the Xbox was custom designed and is produced by NVIDIA Corporation. Quality control tests are performed on purchased parts, CD-ROMs, and other products.

OPERATIONS

The Company has regional operations centers in Ireland, Singapore, and the Greater Seattle area. The regional centers support all operations, including information processing, vendor management and logistics by geographical regions. The regional center in Dublin, Ireland supports the European, African, and Middle East regions, the center in Singapore supports the Asia Pacific region, and the center in the Greater Seattle area supports North and South America. Microsoft Licensing, Inc. (MSLI), a wholly-owned subsidiary in Reno, Nevada, manages the Company's original equipment manufacturer (OEM) and certain organizational licensing operations.

DISTRIBUTION, SALES AND MARKETING

Microsoft distributes its products primarily through the following channels: OEM; volume licensing; online services and products; and distributors and retailers. In fiscal 2002, Microsoft had three major geographic sales and marketing regions: the South Pacific and Americas Region; the Europe, Middle East, and Africa Region; and the Asia Region. Beginning with fiscal 2003, the Company's geographic sales and marketing organization was modified to remove the South Pacific region from the Americas organization, and combine it with Asia. Sales of volume licenses and packaged software products via these channels are primarily to distributors and resellers.

OEM. Microsoft operating systems are licensed primarily to OEMs under agreements that grant the OEMs the right to distribute copies of the Company's products with their computing devices, principally PCs. The Company also markets and licenses certain server operating systems, desktop applications, hardware devices, and consumer software programs to OEMs under similar arrangements. In almost all cases, the products are distributed under Microsoft trademarks. The Company has OEM agreements covering one or more of its products with virtually all of the major PC OEMs, including Acer, Actebis, Dell, eMachines, Fujitsu, Fujitsu Siemens Computers, Gateway, HP, IBM, NEC, Samsung, Sony, and Toshiba. A substantial amount of OEM business is also conducted with system builders, which are low-volume customized PC vendors.

Volume Licensing. The Microsoft Enterprise Agreement program is a licensing program designed to provide a flexible licensing and service solution tailored to customers making a long-term licensing commitment. The agreements are designed to simplify license administration, payment terms, and the contract process. The Microsoft Select program offers flexible software acquisition, licensing, and maintenance options specially customized to meet the needs of large multinational organizations. Marketing efforts and fulfillment are generally coordinated with large account resellers. The Microsoft Open program is a licensing program that is targeted for small- and medium-sized organizations. It is available through the reseller channel and offers discounts based on initial purchase volumes. The Microsoft Enterprise Agreement and Software Assurance under the Select and Open programs provide customers the right to install any new release of products covered in the licensing agreement during the term of their coverage.

Network Service Providers. Microsoft Network Service Providers (NSP) work with a variety of companies worldwide to help them develop and deploy end-to-end network solutions based on Microsoft platforms. NSPs focus on key network service industries including telecommunications and wireless companies and hosts.

Online Services and Products. Microsoft distributes online content and services through MSN Access, MSN Network Services, bCentral small business portal, and other online services. MSN Access delivers simple, personalized Internet access, useful content, services and tools using MSN Internet Explorer. MSN Network Services delivers advertising and other services including online search, shopping, and messaging capabilities to Internet users. bCentral provides the tools and expertise for small-business owners to build, market and manage their businesses online. Other services delivered online include MSDN subscription content and updates, periodic product updates, and online technical and practice readiness resources to support Microsoft partners in developing and selling Microsoft products and solutions.

Distributors and Resellers. The Company distributes products in the finished goods channels primarily to independent non-exclusive distributors and resellers. Distributors and resellers include Ingram Micro, Tech Data, Level 3 Communications, SOFTBANK, Software House International, ASAP Software Express, and Happinet Corporation. Microsoft has a network of field sales representatives and field support personnel who solicit orders from distributors and resellers and provide product training and sales support.

CUSTOMERS

The Company's customers include individual consumers, small- and medium-sized organizations, enterprises, educational institutions, Internet Service Providers (ISPs), application developers, and OEMs. Consumers and organizations obtain Microsoft products primarily through resellers and OEMs, which include certain Microsoft products with their computing devices. No single customer accounted for 10% or more of revenue in 2000, 2001, or 2002.

COMPETITION

The software business is intensely competitive and subject to rapid technological change. As the company pursues its largest strategic initiative, Microsoft .NET, the Company could experience more intense competition during the transition from the traditional core businesses to its new products based on the .NET architecture. The Company continues to face movement from PC-based applications to server-based applications or Web-based application hosting services, from proprietary software to open source software such as the Linux operating system, and from PCs to Internet-based devices. A number of Microsoft's most significant competitors, including IBM, Sun Microsystems, Oracle, and AOL-Time Warner, are collaborating with one another on various initiatives directed at competing with Microsoft. These initiatives relate in part to efforts to move software from individual PCs to centrally managed servers, which would present significant challenges to the Company's historical business model. Other competitive collaborative efforts include the development of new platform technologies that are intended to replicate much of the value of Microsoft Windows operating systems. New computing form factors, including non-PC information devices, are gaining popularity and competing with PCs running Microsoft's software products.

Microsoft faces formidable competition in these new areas and in all areas of its current business activities. The rapid pace of technological change, particularly in the area of Internet platforms and services, continually creates new opportunities for existing competitors and start-ups and can quickly render existing technologies less valuable. Global software piracy—the unlawful copying and distribution of Microsoft's copyrighted software products—deprives the Company of large amounts of revenue on an annual basis.

The Company's competitive position may be adversely affected in the future by one or more of the factors described in this section, particularly in view of the fast pace of technological change in the computing industry.

DESKTOP AND ENTERPRISE SOFTWARE AND SERVICES

The Company's competitors include many software application vendors, such as IBM, Oracle, Apple, Sun Microsystems, Corel, Qualcomm, and local application developers in Europe and Asia. IBM and Corel have large installed bases with their spreadsheet and word processor products, respectively, and both have aggressive pricing strategies. Also, IBM and Apple preinstall certain of their application software products on various models of their PCs, competing directly with Microsoft's desktop application software. Sun Microsystems' Star Office is aggressively priced. Additionally, Web-based application hosting services provide an alternative to PC-based applications such as Microsoft Office.

Microsoft's PC and server operating system products face substantial competition from a wide variety of companies. Competitors such as IBM, Apple Computer, Sun Microsystems, and others are vertically integrated in both software development and hardware manufacturing and have developed operating systems that they preinstall on their own computers. Many of these operating system software products are also licensed to third-party OEMs for preinstallation on their computers. Microsoft's operating system products compete with UNIX-based operating systems from a wide range of companies, including IBM, Hewlett-Packard, Sun Microsystems, and others. Variants of UNIX run on a wide variety of computer platforms and have gained increasing acceptance as desktop operating systems. The Linux open source operating system has gained increasing acceptance as well. Several computer manufacturers preinstall Linux on PC servers and many leading software developers have written applications that run on Linux. Microsoft Windows operating systems also face competition from alternative platforms such as those based on Internet browsing software and Java technology promoted by AOL-Time Warner and Sun Microsystems.

The Company competes in the business of providing enterprise-wide computing solutions with several competitors who enjoy a larger share of sales and larger installed bases. Many companies offer operating system software for mainframes and midrange computers, including IBM, HP, and Sun Microsystems. Since legacy business systems are typically support-intensive, these competitors also offer substantial support services. Software developers that provide competing server applications for PC-based distributed client/server environments include Oracle, IBM, Computer Associates, Sybase, and Informix. There are also several software vendors who offer connectivity servers. As mentioned above, there are numerous companies and organizations that offer Internet and intranet server software, which compete against the Company's business systems. Additionally, IBM has a large installed base of Lotus Notes and cc:Mail, both of which compete with the Company's collaboration and e-mail products.

The Company's developer products compete against offerings from BEA Systems, Borland, IBM, Macromedia, Oracle, Sun Microsystems, Sybase, and other companies.

CONSUMER SOFTWARE, SERVICES, AND DEVICES

Microsoft's online services network, MSN, faces formidable competition from AOL-Time Warner, Yahoo!, and a vast array of Web sites and portals that offer content of all types and e-mail, instant messaging, calendaring, chat, and search and shopping services, among other things.

Xbox competes head-to-head against game systems from Nintendo and Sony, both of which have a large established base of game system users. Game developers like Activision, Capcom, Electronic Arts, Sega, Tecmo, and THQ, to name a few, are both partners and competitors.

Microsoft faces many competitors in the mobile devices space, including Palm, Symbian, Nokia, and Openwave. The embedded operating system market is highly fragmented with many competitive offerings. Key competitors include Wind River and versions of embeddable Linux from commercial Linux vendors such as Red Hat, Lineo, and MontaVista.

CONSUMER COMMERCE INVESTMENTS

Microsoft faces many competitors in the online real estate and online automotive service spaces, including Homestore, AOL's House and Home channel, Autobytel, AOL autos, and Yahoo! autos.

OTHER

PC input devices face substantial competition from computer manufacturers, since computers are typically sold with a keyboard and mouse, and other manufacturers of these devices. Microsoft Press competes in the retail book and eLearning markets with publishers that also create content on Microsoft technologies. A few of the retail competitors are Pearson, WROX, Sybex, and Wiley. The major eLearning competitors are Smartforce and NetG.

EMPLOYEES

As of June 30, 2002, the Company employed approximately 50,500 people on a full-time basis, 34,600 in the United States and 15,900 internationally. Of the total, 20,800 were in product research and development, 23,500 in sales, marketing, and support, 2,200 in manufacturing and distribution, and 4,000 in finance and administration. Microsoft's success is highly dependent on its ability to attract and retain qualified employees. Competition for employees is intense in the software industry. To date, the Company believes it has been successful in its efforts to recruit qualified employees, but there is no assurance that it will continue to be as successful in the future. None of the Company's employees are subject to collective bargaining agreements. The Company believes relations with its employees are excellent.

ITEM 2.   PROPERTIES

The Company's corporate offices consist of approximately 8.4 million square feet of office building space located in King County, Washington, of which 5.7 million square feet of corporate campus space situated on slightly more than 300 acres of land is owned and approximately 2.7 million square feet is leased. The Company is constructing three buildings with approximately 392,000 square feet of space that will be occupied in the Fall of 2003. To accommodate expansion needs the Company purchased approximately 38 acres, and has an option to purchase approximately 112 additional acres, of land in Issaquah, Washington, which can accommodate 2.95 million square feet of additional office space. The Company leases many sites domestically totaling approximately 3.0 million square feet of office building space.

   The Company leases many sites internationally totaling approximately 4.1 million square feet, including the Company's European Operations Center and localization division which leases a 382,000 square-foot campus in Dublin, Ireland, a 45,000 square-foot disk duplication facility in Humacao, Puerto Rico and a 36,000 square-foot facility in Singapore for the Company's Asia Pacific Operations Center. Leased office building space includes the following locations: Tokyo, Japan 343,000 square feet; Unterschleissheim, Germany 253,000 square feet; United Kingdom campus 242,000 square feet; Les Ulis, France 229,000 square feet; and Beijing, China 115,000 square feet.

   The Company's facilities are fully used for current operations of all segments and suitable additional space is available to accommodate expansion needs.

ITEM 3.   LEGAL PROCEEDINGS

See Note 19—Contingencies of the Notes to Financial Statements (Item 8) for information regarding legal proceedings.

ITEM 4.   SUBMISSION OF MATTERS TO A VOTE OF SECURITY HOLDERS

No matters were submitted to a vote of security holders during the fourth quarter of fiscal 2002.

Part I
Item 4

EXECUTIVE OFFICERS OF THE REGISTRANT

The executive officers of Microsoft as of July 31, 2002 were as follows:

Name	Age	Position with the Company
William H. Gates, III	46	Chairman of the Board; Chief Software Architect
Steven A. Ballmer	46	Chief Executive Officer
James E. Allchin	50	Group Vice President, Platforms Group
Orlando Ayala	46	Group Vice President, Worldwide Sales, Marketing, and Services Group
Robert J. (Robbie) Bach	40	Senior Vice President, Games Division
Douglas J. Burgum	46	Senior Vice President, Business Solutions
David W. Cole	40	Senior Vice President, MSN and Personal Services Group
John G. Connors	43	Senior Vice President; Chief Financial Officer
Jean-Philippe Courtois	41	Senior Vice President; President, Microsoft Europe, Middle East, and Africa
Jon Stephan DeVaan	41	Senior Vice President, TV Division
Richard P. Emerson	40	Senior Vice President, Corporate Development and Strategy
Paul Flessner	43	Senior Vice President, .NET Enterprise Servers
Kevin R. Johnson	41	Senior Vice President, Microsoft Americas
Robert L. Muglia	42	Senior Vice President, Enterprise Storage Division
Craig J. Mundie	53	Senior Vice President; Chief Technical Officer, Advanced Strategies and Policy
Jeffrey S. Raikes	44	Group Vice President, Productivity and Business Services
Richard F. Rashid	50	Senior Vice President, Research
Eric D. Rudder	35	Senior Vice President, Developer and Platform Evangelism
Steven J. Sinofsky	36	Senior Vice President, Office
Bradford L. Smith	43	Senior Vice President and General Counsel
Brian Valentine	42	Senior Vice President, Windows
David Vaskevitch	49	Senior Vice President; Chief Technical Officer, Business Platform
Deborah N. Willingham	46	Senior Vice President, Human Resources

Mr. Gates co-founded Microsoft in 1975 and served as its Chief Executive Officer from the time the original partnership was incorporated in 1981 until January 2000, when he resigned as Chief Executive Officer and assumed the position of Chief Software Architect. Mr. Gates has served as Chairman of the Board since the Company's incorporation.

Mr. Ballmer was named Chief Executive Officer and a director of the Company in January 2000. He served as President from July 1998 to February 2001. Previously, he had served as Executive Vice President, Sales and Support since February 1992. He joined Microsoft in 1980.

Mr. Allchin was named Group Vice President, Platforms Group in December 1999. He had been Senior Vice President, Platforms since March 1999. He was previously Senior Vice President, Personal and Business Systems since February 1996. Mr. Allchin joined Microsoft in 1990.

Mr. Ayala was named Group Vice President, Worldwide Sales, Marketing, and Services Group in August 2000. He had been Senior Vice President, South Pacific and Americas since February 1998, and before holding that position, was Vice President of the developing markets of Africa, India, the Mediterranean and Middle East, Latin America, Southeast Asia and the South Pacific. He joined Microsoft in 1991 as Senior Director of the Latin America Region.

Mr. Bach was named Senior Vice President, Games Division in March 2000. He had been Vice President, Home and Retail since March 1999. Before holding that position, he had been Vice President, Learning, Entertainment and Productivity since 1996. Mr. Bach joined Microsoft in 1988.

Mr. Burgum joined the Company upon Microsoft's acquisition of Great Plains Software, Inc. in April 2001. Mr. Burgum became Great Plains' first outside investor in March 1983. He was named President of Great Plains in 1984 and subsequently named Chairman and Chief Executive Officer.

Mr. Cole was named Senior Vice President, MSN and Personal Services Group in November 2001. Before holding that position, he had been Senior Vice President, Services Platform Division since August 2000. He had been Senior Vice President, Consumer Services since December 1999 and Vice President, Consumer Windows since March 1999. Previously, he was Vice President, Web Client and Consumer Experience and Vice President, Internet Client and Collaboration. Mr. Cole joined Microsoft in 1986.

Mr. Connors was named Senior Vice President and Chief Financial Officer in December 1999. He had been Vice President, Enterprise since March 1999. Mr. Connors had been Vice President, Information Technology, and Chief Information Officer since July 1996. He joined Microsoft in 1989.

Mr. Courtois was named Senior Vice President and President, Microsoft Europe, Middle East, and Africa in July 2000. He had been Vice President, Customer Marketing since July 1998. Before holding that position, he had been Vice President of Microsoft Europe since 1997 and General Manager for Microsoft France since 1994. Mr. Courtois joined Microsoft in 1984.

Mr. DeVaan was named Senior Vice President, TV Division in December 1999. He had been Senior Vice President, Consumer and Commerce since September 1999. Mr. DeVaan had been Vice President, Consumer and Commerce since March 1999. He had been Vice President, Desktop Applications since 1995. Mr. DeVaan joined Microsoft in 1985.

Mr. Emerson joined Microsoft in November 2000 as Senior Vice President, Corporate Development and Strategy. Prior to joining Microsoft, he was Managing Director and co-head of Technology and Telecommunications Advisory Services at international investment bank Lazard Freres & Co. LLC. He spent 12 years in San Francisco and New York with Lazard and Morgan Stanley, specializing in advising clients in the technology and telecommunications sectors on mergers, acquisitions, and strategic partnerships.

Mr. Flessner was named Senior Vice President, .NET Enterprise Servers in December 1999. He had been Vice President, Database and Data Access. Since joining the Company, Mr. Flessner's primary responsibilities have been the development of Microsoft's database business. He joined Microsoft in 1994.

Mr. Johnson was named Senior Vice President, Microsoft Americas in February 2002. He had been Senior Vice President, U.S. Sales, Marketing, and Services since August 2001, and before that, Vice President, U.S. Sales, Marketing and Services. Mr. Johnson was named Vice President, Product Support Services in July 1998. He joined Microsoft in 1992.

Mr. Muglia was named Senior Vice President, Enterprise Storage Division in November 2001. Before holding that position, he had been Group Vice President, Personal Services Group since August 2000. He had been Group Vice President, Business Productivity since December 1999. He was named Senior Vice President, Business Productivity in March 1999 and was named Senior Vice President, Applications and Tools in February 1998. He had been Vice President, Server Applications since 1997. He joined Microsoft in 1988.

Mr. Mundie was named Senior Vice President and Chief Technical Officer, Advanced Strategies and Policy in August 2001. He was named Senior Vice President, Consumer Platforms in February 1996. He joined Microsoft as General Manager, Advanced Consumer Technology in 1992.

Mr. Raikes was named Group Vice President, Productivity and Business Services in August 2000. He had been Group Vice President, Sales and Support since July 1998. Before holding that position, he had been Group Vice President, Sales and Marketing since July 1996. Mr. Raikes joined Microsoft in 1981.

Mr. Rashid was named Senior Vice President, Research in May 2000. He had been Vice President, Research since July 1994. He joined Microsoft in 1991.

Mr. Rudder was named Senior Vice President, Developer and Platform Evangelism in October 2001. He had been Vice President, Technical Strategy. Mr. Rudder joined Microsoft in 1988 and has worked in several areas, including networking, operating systems and developer tools, where he previously served as General Manager for the Visual Studio development system.

Mr. Sinofsky was named Senior Vice President, Office in December 1999. He had been Vice President, Office since December 1998. Mr. Sinofsky joined the Office team in 1994, increasing his responsibility with each subsequent release of the desktop suite. He joined Microsoft in 1989.

Mr. Smith was named Senior Vice President and General Counsel in November 2001. He had been Deputy General Counsel for Worldwide Sales and previously was responsible for managing the Company's European Law and Corporate Affairs Group, based in Paris. He joined Microsoft in 1993.

Mr. Valentine was named Senior Vice President, Windows in December 1999. He had been Vice President, Business and Enterprise since March 1999. He had been Vice President, Windows since December 1998. Before managing the Windows group, Mr. Valentine managed the server applications division and had been responsible for the Exchange product unit. He joined Microsoft in 1987.

Mr. Vaskevitch was named Senior Vice President and Chief Technical Officer, Business Platform in August 2001. He was named Senior Vice President, Business Applications in March 2000. He had been Senior Vice President, Developer since December 1999. Before holding that position, he had been Vice President, Distributed Applications Platform. He joined Microsoft in 1986.

Ms. Willingham was named Senior Vice President, Human Resources in February 2001. She had been Vice President, Human Resources since April 2000. Ms. Willingham had been Vice President, Business and Enterprise Division Marketing and was responsible for Windows operating system client and server marketing strategy and training, as well as for providing centralized marketing services for the Consumer Windows Marketing and Streaming Media Marketing teams. She joined Microsoft in 1993.

PART II

ITEM 5. MARKET FOR REGISTRANT'S COMMON STOCK AND RELATED STOCKHOLDER MATTERS

The Company's common stock is traded on The Nasdaq Stock Market under the symbol MSFT. On June 30, 2002, there were 117,730 registered holders of record of the Company's common stock. The Company has not paid cash dividends on its common stock. The high and low common stock prices per share were as follows:

Quarter Ended	Sept. 30	Dec. 31	Mar. 31	June 30	Year
Fiscal 2001					
Common stock price per share:					
High	$ 82.00	$ 70.88	$ 64.69	$ 73.68	$ 82.00
Low	60.31	41.50	43.38	51.94	41.50
Fiscal 2002					
Common stock price per share:					
High	$ **72.57**	$ **69.49**	$ **69.86**	$ **60.38**	$ **72.57**
Low	**49.71**	**51.79**	**57.99**	**48.62**	**48.62**

ITEM 6. SELECTED FINANCIAL DATA

FINANCIAL HIGHLIGHTS

In millions, except earnings per share

Year Ended June 30	1998	1999	2000	2001[1]	2002[2]
Revenue	$ 15,262	$ 19,747	$ 22,956	$ 25,296	$ **28,365**
Operating income	6,585	10,010	11,006	11,720	**11,910**
Income before accounting change	4,490	7,785	9,421	7,721	**7,829**
Net income	4,490	7,785	9,421	7,346	**7,829**
Diluted earnings per share before accounting change	0.84	1.42	1.70	1.38	**1.41**
Diluted earnings per share	0.84	1.42	1.70	1.32	**1.41**
Cash and short-term investments	13,927	17,236	23,798	31,600	**38,652**
Total assets	22,357	38,321	51,694	58,830	**67,646**
Stockholders' equity	16,627	28,438	41,368	47,289	**52,180**

(1) Fiscal year 2001 includes an unfavorable cumulative effect of accounting change of $375 million or $0.06 per diluted share, reflecting the adoption of SFAS No. 133, and $4.80 billion (pre-tax) in impairments of certain investments, primarily cable and telecommunication investments.

(2) Fiscal year 2002 includes $4.32 billion (pre-tax) in impairments of certain investments, primarily related to the Company's AT&T investment and further declines in the fair values of European cable and telecommunications holdings, and a $1.25 billion (pre-tax) gain on the sale of Expedia, Inc.

ITEM 7. MANAGEMENT'S DISCUSSION AND ANALYSIS
OF RESULTS OF OPERATIONS AND FINANCIAL CONDITION

RESULTS OF OPERATIONS FOR 2000, 2001, AND 2002

Management's Discussion and Analysis contains statements that are forward-looking. These statements are based on current expectations and assumptions that are subject to risks and uncertainties. Actual results could differ materially because of factors discussed in "Issues and Uncertainties."

REVENUE

The Company's revenue growth rate was 16% in fiscal 2000, 10% in fiscal 2001, and 12% in fiscal 2002. Revenue growth in fiscal 2002 was led by the addition of Xbox video game system revenue and the strong penetration of Microsoft Windows XP Professional and Home operating systems. Revenue growth in fiscal 2001 was driven primarily by licensing of Microsoft Windows 2000 Professional, Microsoft SQL Server, and the other .NET Enterprise Servers. Revenue growth in fiscal 2000 was driven by strong licensing of Microsoft Windows NT Workstation, Windows 2000 Professional, Windows NT Server, Windows 2000 Server, Microsoft Office 2000, and SQL Server.

Microsoft continued to see a mix shift to volume licensing programs. On October 1, 2001, Microsoft launched Licensing 6.0 to simplify and improve its volume licensing programs, including a simplified approach to software upgrades. One feature of Licensing 6.0 is Software Assurance which gives customers the right to install any new release of products covered in the licensing agreement during the term of their coverage. The success of Microsoft's new volume licensing programs will continue to affect the mix of multi-year licensing agreements with a resulting impact on the timing of revenue recognition. In addition, the timing and extent of a recovery in consumer and corporate spending on PCs and information technology (IT) will be factors affecting revenue growth.

PRODUCT REVENUE

In fiscal 2002, Microsoft had four segments: Desktop and Enterprise Software and Services; Consumer Software, Services, and Devices; Consumer Commerce Investments; and Other. The revenue figures in this Management's Discussion and Analysis (MD&A) differ from those reported in the Company's Segment Information appearing in Note 20 of the Notes to Financial Statements. The revenue figures in the Segment Information represent amounts reported internally for management reporting, while the revenue figures in the MD&A reflect revenue recognized in accordance with generally accepted accounting principles. On July 1, 2002, Microsoft revised its product segments and will begin reporting the new segments in fiscal 2003.

Desktop and Enterprise Software and Services. Desktop and Enterprise Software and Services revenue was $20.40 billion, $22.41 billion, and $24.01 billion in 2000, 2001, and 2002. Desktop and Enterprise Software and Services includes Desktop Applications; Desktop Platforms; and Enterprise Software and Services.

Desktop Applications revenue was $9.30 billion, $9.54 billion, and $9.60 billion in 2000, 2001, and 2002. Desktop Applications includes revenue from Microsoft Office; Microsoft Project; Visio; client access licenses (CALs) for Windows NT Server and Windows 2000 Server, Exchange, and BackOffice; Microsoft Great Plains; and bCentral. In fiscal 2002, Office licensing revenue declined during the year due to a strong mix shift to multi-year annuity licensing agreements, which deferred revenue recognition to future years, and a decrease in consumer purchases in the Asia region, most notably Japan, partially offset by strong OEM licensing. Revenue from client access licenses grew 3% in fiscal 2002 and revenue from Great Plains contributed to the growth in Desktop Applications. In fiscal 2001, revenue from client access licenses increased 14% reflecting strong licensing growth of Windows NT Server and Windows 2000 Server CALs. Office revenue growth was flat during fiscal 2001. In fiscal 2000, revenue growth from Microsoft Office integrated suites, including the Premium, Professional, Small Business, and Standard Editions was very solid.

Desktop Platforms revenue was $7.02 billion, $8.04 billion, and $9.30 billion in 2000, 2001, and 2002. Desktop Platforms includes revenue from Windows XP Professional and Home, Windows 2000 Professional, Windows NT Workstation, Windows Me, Windows 98, and other desktop operating systems. In fiscal 2002, the growth in Desktop Platforms revenue reflected strong multi-year licensing revenue growth and a continued mix shift to the higher priced Windows 2000 and Windows XP Professional operating system through OEMs, despite a decline in reported OEM unit shipments. Fiscal 2001 revenue growth reflected the strong adoption of Windows 2000 Professional, partially offset by flat revenue growth from Windows Me and Windows 98 operating systems, reflecting the slowdown in consumer PC shipments and a higher mix of Windows 2000 Professional and Windows NT Workstation. In fiscal 2000, Desktop Platforms revenue growth was modest due to soft demand for business PCs during most of the year; a slowdown in shipments in anticipation of the post mid-year availability of Windows 2000 operating systems; and, as expected, a longer business migration cycle for the newest Windows operating system offerings. The rate of growth in PC shipments and the mix of Windows 2000 and Windows XP Professional as a percentage of all 32-bit operating systems will continue to impact revenue growth in the future.

Enterprise Software and Services revenue was $4.08 billion, $4.83 billion, and $5.11 billion in 2000, 2001, and 2002. Enterprise Software and Services includes Server Platforms, Server Applications, Developer Tools and Services, and Enterprise Services. In fiscal 2002, Server Applications, including Microsoft SQL Server and .NET Enterprise Servers, increased 10% compared to fiscal 2001. Server Platform revenue, which includes Windows 2000 Server and Windows NT Server operating systems, increased 10% versus fiscal 2001 driven by a modest overall increase in Windows-based server shipments and increased deployment of Windows 2000 Server. Enterprise Services revenue, representing consulting and product support services, was up 17% compared to fiscal 2001, while revenue from Developer Tools and Services was down 19% from fiscal 2001. In fiscal 2001, Server Applications revenue increased 31% versus the prior year as a result of the continued adoption of Microsoft's .NET Enterprise Server offerings. Enterprise Services revenue in fiscal 2001, was up 34% compared to fiscal 2000 and Server Platforms increased 10% while revenue from Developer Tools and Services was flat. In fiscal 2000, Server Platforms revenue growth was particularly strong led by increased adoption by customers of Windows NT Server and Windows 2000 Server. Revenue from Server Applications grew strongly in fiscal 2000, largely due to the strong success of SQL Server 7.0, while Software Developer Tools and Services revenue declined, due to increased suite licensing versus stand-alone licenses, and the lack of a release upgrade of the Visual Studio development system.

Consumer Software, Services, and Devices. Consumer Software, Services, and Devices revenue was $1.63 billion, $1.95 billion, and $3.59 billion in 2000, 2001, and 2002. Consumer Software, Services, and Devices includes the Xbox video game system; MSN Internet access; MSN network service; PC and online games; learning and productivity software; mobility; and embedded systems. The majority of the revenue growth from fiscal 2001 stemmed from sales of the Xbox video game system released in fiscal 2002. MSN Internet access revenue increased as a result of both a higher subscriber base and higher average revenue per subscriber due to a reduction in promotional subscriber programs. Revenue from MSN network services increased despite a declining Internet advertising market. Revenue from embedded systems in fiscal 2002 grew nicely, however learning and productivity software revenue and PC and online games declined compared to fiscal 2001. In fiscal 2001, revenue from MSN network services grew strongly despite a decline in the online advertising market. MSN Internet access revenue also grew solidly from fiscal 2000 as a result of an increased subscriber base, partially offset by a decline in the average revenue per subscriber due to a larger mix of subscribers contracted under rebate programs. Revenue from embedded systems grew strongly from the prior year, while learning and productivity software revenue and PC and online games revenue declined, reflecting softness in the overall consumer market. In fiscal 2000, online revenue growth was very strong and reflected higher subscriber totals, offset by lower net prices for Internet access subscriptions compared to the prior year. Additionally, strong sales of entertainment software in fiscal 2000 produced robust revenue growth in PC and online games.

Consumer Commerce Investments. Consumer Commerce Investments revenue was $182 million, $299 million, and $242 million in 2000, 2001, and 2002. Consumer Commerce Investments include Expedia, Inc., the HomeAdvisor online real estate service, and the CarPoint online automotive service. The decline in revenue compared to fiscal 2001 reflects the sale of Microsoft's majority ownership of Expedia, Inc. to USA Networks, Inc. on February 4, 2002. Acquisitions of Travelscape.com and VacationSpot.com by Expedia, Inc., and increased product offerings from Expedia led to the strong revenue growth in fiscal 2001. The increased overall reach of all properties led to the strong revenue growth in fiscal 2000.

Other. Other revenue, which primarily includes Hardware and Microsoft Press, was $754 million, $630 million, and $530 million in 2000, 2001, and 2002. In fiscal 2002, continued declines in the IT book and consumer market led to a decline in Microsoft Press and Hardware sales. Lower sales of gaming devices and other hardware peripherals as a result of weakness in the consumer market caused the decline in revenue in fiscal 2001. Continued success of the Company's new hardware device offerings led to revenue growth in fiscal 2000.

DISTRIBUTION CHANNELS

Microsoft distributes its products primarily through the following channels: OEM; volume licensing; online services and products; and distributors and retailers. OEM channel revenue represents license fees from original equipment manufacturers who preinstall Microsoft products, primarily on PCs. Microsoft has three major geographic sales and marketing regions: the South Pacific and Americas Region; the Europe, Middle East, and Africa Region; and the Asia Region. Sales of volume licenses and packaged software products via these channels are primarily to distributors and resellers.

OEM revenue was $7.01 billion in 2000, $7.86 billion in 2001, and $9.00 billion in 2002. In fiscal 2002, reported licenses declined compared to fiscal 2001. However, a strong increase in the mix of the higher priced Windows 2000 and Windows XP Professional licenses, and healthy growth in direct and system builder OEMs licenses, led to higher average revenue per license and contributed to the overall OEM revenue growth over fiscal 2001. In fiscal 2001, while total licenses were also impacted by a slowdown in PC shipments, the mix of the higher priced Windows 2000 Professional and Windows NT Workstation increased substantially resulting in higher average revenue per license. A relatively low growth rate in fiscal 2000 was due to lower business PC shipment growth combined with post mid-year availability of Windows 2000 Professional. Average earned revenue per license also declined in fiscal 2000 compared to the prior year, due in part to a mix shift to the lower-priced Windows 98 operating system reflecting the softness in demand for business PCs and lower prices on operating systems licensed through certain OEM channel sectors.

South Pacific and Americas Region revenue was $8.33 billion, $9.52 billion, and $11.41 billion in 2000, 2001, and 2002. In fiscal 2002, the majority of the revenue growth was driven by sales of the Xbox video game system released during the year, as well as strong Windows XP Professional licensing, MSN subscription revenue, and revenue from Microsoft Great Plains. In fiscal 2001, revenue growth was led by strong licensing of Windows 2000 Professional and the family of .NET Enterprise Servers, particularly SQL Server 2000 and Exchange 2000 Server. Revenue from Enterprise services and MSN subscription and services also grew strongly in fiscal 2001. In fiscal 2000, Office 2000 integrated suites, Windows 2000 Server, online revenue, and SQL Server sales were the primary drivers of the revenue growth. Strong retail sales of hardware devices and consumer software also contributed to the growth over the prior year.

Europe, Middle East, and Africa Region revenue was $5.02 billion, $4.86 billion, and $5.13 billion in 2000, 2001, and 2002. In fiscal 2002, the majority of the growth was a result of strong multi-year licensing revenue of Windows XP Home and Professional operating systems and Enterprise Software, as well as the addition of Xbox video game system revenue in the second half of the year. In fiscal 2001, weakening local currencies negatively impacted translated revenue compared to the prior year, while revenue from Windows 2000 Professional and the .NET Enterprise Server family of products was very healthy. In fiscal 2000, retail sales of Windows operating systems and

Office licensing produced moderate growth in the region. Growth from SQL Server licensing, new hardware device offerings, and entertainment software was especially strong.

Asia Region revenue was $2.60 billion in 2000, $3.06 billion in 2001, and $2.83 billion in 2002. In fiscal 2002, Asia region revenue declined most notably due to lower consumer PC shipments, which hampered revenue from localized versions of Microsoft Office 2000 and Microsoft Office XP, especially the Office Personal Edition. Xbox video game system sales partially offset the decline in Office revenue. In fiscal 2001, the region's growth rate reflected strong revenue from localized versions of Microsoft Office 2000 and Microsoft Office XP, especially the Office Personal Edition. This growth was also attributable to Windows 2000 Professional and .NET Server applications licensing. In fiscal 2000, the region's growth rate reflected strong performance resulting from improved local economic conditions. Revenue growth was also influenced by robust growth of localized versions of Microsoft Office 2000, especially the Office Personal Edition sold in Japan, Windows platform and server licensing, and strong adoption of SQL Server.

The Company's operating results are affected by foreign exchange rates. Approximately 30%, 27%, and 25% of the Company's revenue was collected in foreign currencies during 2000, 2001, and 2002. Since a portion of local currency revenue is hedged and much of the Company's international manufacturing costs and operating expenses are also incurred in local currencies, the impact of exchange rates is partially mitigated.

OPERATING EXPENSES

Cost of Revenue.   Cost of revenue as a percent of revenue was 13.1% in 2000, 13.7% in 2001, and 18.3% in 2002. Cost of revenue in fiscal 2002 increased primarily due to costs related to Xbox. In fiscal 2001, higher support and service costs associated with the MSN Internet access and MSN network services were partially offset by the lower relative costs associated with organizational licensing and the drop in the mix of packaged product versus the prior year. Cost of revenue in fiscal 2000 reflected lower costs associated with WebTV Networks' operations, partially offset by the growth in hardware peripherals costs.

Research and Development.   The discontinuation of goodwill amortization in fiscal 2002 in accordance with Statement of Financial Accounting Standards (SFAS) 142, *Goodwill and Other Intangible Assets,* offset the growth in headcount and development costs. In fiscal 2001, the increase in R&D expense was the result of higher headcount-related costs and investments in new product initiatives. The increase in fiscal 2000 was driven primarily by higher headcount-related costs. Prospectively, increased headcount and increased spending in Server Platforms, Home & Entertainment, Business Solutions and CE are currently expected to be significant factors affecting future research and development expense growth.

Sales and Marketing.   Sales and marketing expense as a percentage of revenue was 18.0% in 2000, 19.3% in 2001, and 19.1% in 2002. In fiscal 2002, sales and marketing expense as a percentage of revenue decreased due to lower relative MSN customer acquisition marketing and the large relative increase associated with the onset of Xbox video game system revenue. In fiscal 2001, sales and marketing expenses as a percentage of revenue increased due to higher relative headcount-related costs, higher marketing and sales expenses associated with MSN, the Microsoft Agility advertising campaign, and other new sales initiatives. In fiscal 2000, sales and marketing expenses as a percentage of revenue increased due to higher relative marketing costs associated with new product releases and online marketing. Microsoft expects that it will increase spending on Information Worker, Server Platforms, and Business Solutions sales forces and Windows Client, MSN and Home & Entertainment marketing.

General and Administrative.   General and administrative expenses in fiscal 2002 increased due to a charge of approximately $660 million for estimated expenses related to the Company's consumer class action lawsuits and higher legal fees. In fiscal 2001, general and administrative costs decreased due to a charge related to the settlement of the lawsuit with Caldera, Inc. recorded in fiscal 2000. Excluding this charge in fiscal 2000, general and administrative expenses in fiscal 2001 increased from the prior year due to higher headcount-related costs and legal fees. For fiscal 2000, besides the settlement of the lawsuit, general and administrative expenses also reflected increased legal fees and certain employee stock option-related expenses.

NON-OPERATING ITEMS, INVESTMENT INCOME/(LOSS), AND INCOME TAXES

Losses on equity investees and other consists of Microsoft's share of income or loss from investments accounted for using the equity method, and income or loss attributable to minority interests. The decrease in losses on equity investees and other in fiscal 2002 was attributed to the divestiture of certain equity investments in fiscal 2002. The increase in losses on equity investees and other in fiscal 2001 reflects an increase in the number of such investments during the year. In fiscal 2000 losses on equity investees and other decreased reflecting smaller losses from the MSNBC entities.

Part II
Item 7

The Company recorded net investment income/(loss) in each year as follows:

In millions

Year Ended June 30		2000		2001		2002
Dividends	$	363	$	377	$	**357**
Interest		1,231		1,808		**1,762**
Net recognized gains/(losses) on investments:						
Net gains on the sales of investments		1,780		3,175		**2,379**
Other-than-temporary impairments		(29)		(4,804)		**(4,323)**
Net unrealized losses attributable to derivative instruments		(19)		(592)		**(480)**
Net recognized gains/(losses) on investments		1,732		(2,221)		**(2,424)**
Investment income/(loss)	$	3,326	$	(36)	$	**(305)**

In fiscal 2002, other-than-temporary impairments primarily related to the Company's investment in AT&T and other cable and telecommunication investments. Net gains on the sales of investments included a $1.25 billion gain on the sale of the Company's share of Expedia. Interest and dividend income decreased $66 million from fiscal 2001 as a result of lower interest rates and dividend income.

In fiscal 2001, other-than-temporary impairments primarily related to cable and telecommunication investments. Net gains from the sales of investments in fiscal 2001 included a gain from Microsoft's investment in Titus Communications (which was merged with Jupiter Telecommunications) and the closing of the sale of Transpoint to CheckFree Holdings Corp. Interest and dividend income increased $591 million from fiscal 2000, reflecting a larger investment portfolio. In fiscal year 2000, investment income increased primarily as a result of a larger investment portfolio generated by cash from operations coupled with realized gains from the sale of securities.

At June 30, 2002, unrealized losses on Equity and Other Investments of $623 million were deemed to be temporary in nature. The following, among other factors, could result in some investments being deemed other-than-temporarily impaired in future periods: changes in the duration and extent to which the fair value is less than cost; the financial health of and business outlook for the investee, including industry and sector performance, changes in technology, and operational and financing cash flow factors; and the Company's intent and ability to hold the investment.

in connection with the definitive agreement to combine AT&T Broadband with Comcast in a new company to be called AT&T Comcast Corporation, Microsoft has agreed to exchange its AT&T 5% convertible preferred debt securities for approximately 115 million shares of AT&T Comcast Corporation. It is expected that the transaction will close by December 31, 2002. While it is possible that Microsoft could incur a loss on this exchange transaction up to the carrying value of the AT&T debt securities, management believes that the ultimate loss, if any, will be significantly less. As management is unable to predict whether there will be a gain or loss on the exchange, no loss has been recorded related to this contingent exchange transaction as of June 30, 2002.

The Company's effective tax rate for fiscal 2002 was 32%. The effective tax rate for fiscal 2001 and fiscal 2000 was 33% and 34%, respectively. The decrease in the effective tax rate is due primarily to lower taxes on foreign earnings.

ACCOUNTING CHANGES

Effective July 1, 2001, Microsoft adopted SFAS 141, *Business Combinations,* and SFAS 142, *Goodwill and Other Intangible Assets.* SFAS 141 requires business combinations to be accounted for using the purchase method of accounting. It also specifies the types of acquired intangible assets that are required to be recognized and reported separate from goodwill. SFAS 142 requires that goodwill and certain intangibles no longer be amortized, but instead tested for impairment at least annually. There was no impairment of goodwill upon adoption of SFAS 142. Goodwill amortization (on a pre-tax basis) was $234 million in fiscal 2000 and $311 million in fiscal 2001.

Effective July 1, 2000, Microsoft adopted SFAS 133, *Accounting for Derivative Instruments and Hedging Activities,* which establishes accounting and reporting standards for derivative instruments, including certain derivative instruments embedded in other contracts and for hedging activities. The adoption of SFAS 133 resulted in a cumulative pre-tax reduction to income of $560 million ($375 million after-tax) and a cumulative pre-tax reduction to other comprehensive income (OCI) of $112 million ($75 million after-tax). The reduction to income was mostly attributable to a loss of approximately $300 million reclassified from OCI for the time value of options and a loss of approximately $250 million reclassified from OCI for derivatives not designated as hedging instruments. The reduction to OCI was mostly attributable to losses of approximately $670 million on cash flow hedges offset by the reclassifications out of OCI of the approximately $300 million loss for the time value of options and the approximately $250 million loss for derivative instruments not designated as hedging instruments.

FINANCIAL CONDITION

The Company's cash and short-term investment portfolio totaled $38.65 billion at June 30, 2002. The portfolio consists primarily of fixed-income securities, diversified among industries and individual issuers. Microsoft's investments are generally liquid and investment grade. The portfolio is invested predominantly in U.S. dollar denominated securities, but also includes foreign currency positions in order to diversify financial risk. The portfolio is primarily invested in short-term securities to minimize interest rate risk and facilitate rapid deployment for immediate cash needs.

Cash flow from operations was $14.51 billion for fiscal 2002, an increase of $1.09 billion from fiscal 2001. The increase reflects strong growth in unearned revenue. Cash used for financing was $4.57 billion in fiscal 2002, a decrease of $1.01 billion from the prior year. The decrease reflects the repurchase of put warrants in the prior year. The Company repurchased 122.8 million shares of common stock under its share repurchase program in fiscal 2002, compared to 89.0 million shares repurchased in the prior year. In addition, 5.1 million shares of common stock were acquired in fiscal 2002 under a structured stock repurchase transaction. The Company entered into the structured stock repurchase transaction in fiscal 2001, giving it the right to acquire 5.1 million of its shares in exchange for an up-front net payment of $264 million. Cash used for investing was $10.85 billion in fiscal 2002, an increase of $2.11 billion from fiscal 2001.

Cash flow from operations was $13.42 billion in fiscal 2001, an increase of $2.00 billion from the prior year. The increase was primarily attributable to the growth in revenue and other changes in working capital, partially offset by the decrease in the stock option income tax benefit, reflecting decreased stock option exercises by employees. Cash used for financing was $5.59 billion in fiscal 2001, an increase of $3.39 billion from the prior year. The increase primarily reflects the repurchase of put warrants in fiscal 2001, compared to the sale of put warrants in the prior fiscal year, as well as an increase in common stock repurchased. All outstanding put warrants were either retired or exercised during fiscal 2001. During fiscal 2001, the Company repurchased 89.0 million shares. Cash used for investing was $8.73 billion in fiscal 2001, a decrease of $658 million from the prior year. In fiscal 2000, cash flow from operations was $11.43 billion, a decrease of $720 million from the prior year, reflecting working capital changes partially offset by the increase in the stock option income tax benefit. Cash used for financing was $2.19 billion in fiscal 2000, an increase of $1.33 billion from the prior year, reflecting an increase in common stock repurchased versus the prior year. During fiscal 2000, the Company repurchased 55.2 million shares. Cash used for investing was $9.39 billion in fiscal 2000, a decrease of $808 million from the prior year.

Microsoft has no material long-term debt. Stockholders' equity at June 30, 2002 was $52.18 billion. Microsoft will continue to invest in sales, marketing, and product support infrastructure. Additionally, research and development activities will include investments in existing and advanced areas of technology, including using cash to acquire technology. Additions to property and equipment will continue, including new facilities and computer systems for R&D, sales and marketing, support, and administrative staff. Commitments for constructing new buildings were $111 million on June 30, 2002. The Company has not engaged in any transactions or arrangements with unconsolidated entities or other persons that are reasonably likely to affect materially liquidity or the availability of or requirements for capital resources. Since fiscal 1990, Microsoft has repurchased 982 million common shares while 2.23 billion shares were issued under the Company's employee stock option and purchase plans. The Company's convertible preferred stock matured on December 15, 1999. Each preferred share was converted into 1.1273 common shares.

Management believes existing cash and short-term investments together with funds generated from operations should be sufficient to meet operating requirements. The Company's cash and short-term investments are available for strategic investments, mergers and acquisitions, other potential large-scale needs and to fund the share repurchase program. Microsoft has not paid cash dividends on its common stock.

SUBSEQUENT EVENT

On July 11, 2002, Microsoft acquired Navision a/s as a result of the successful close of a tender offer. Microsoft purchased Navision's shares for approximately $1.45 billion in stock and cash. Navision is a provider of integrated business software solutions for small and medium-sized companies.

APPLICATION OF CRITICAL ACCOUNTING POLICIES

Microsoft's financial statements and accompanying notes are prepared in accordance with generally accepted accounting principles in the United States. Preparing financial statements requires management to make estimates and assumptions that affect the reported amounts of assets, liabilities, revenue, and expenses. These estimates and assumptions are affected by management's application of accounting policies. Critical accounting policies for Microsoft include revenue recognition, impairment of investment securities, accounting for research and development costs, accounting for legal contingencies, and accounting for income taxes.

Microsoft accounts for the licensing of software in accordance with American Institute of Certified Public Accountants (AICPA) Statement of Position (SOP) 97-2, *Software Revenue Recognition.* The application of SOP 97-2 requires judgment, including whether a software arrangement includes multiple elements, and if so, whether vendor-specific objective evidence (VSOE) of fair value exists for those elements. End users receive certain elements of the Company's products over a period of time. These elements include browser technologies updates and technical support, the fair value of which is recognized over the product's estimated life cycle. Changes to the elements in a software arrangement, the ability to identify VSOE for those elements, the fair value of the respective elements, and changes to a product's estimated life cycle could materially impact the amount of earned and unearned revenue. Judgment is also required to assess whether future releases of certain software represent new products or upgrades and enhancements to existing products.

SFAS 115, *Accounting for Certain Investments in Debt and Equity Securities,* and Securities and Exchange Commission (SEC) Staff Accounting Bulletin (SAB) 59, *Accounting for Noncurrent Marketable Equity Securities,* provide guidance on determining when an investment is other-than-temporarily impaired, which also requires judgment. In making this judgment, Microsoft evaluates, among other factors, the duration and extent to which the fair value of an investment is less than its cost; the financial health of and business outlook for the investee, including factors such as industry and sector performance, changes in technology, and operational and financing cash flow; and the Company's intent and ability to hold the investment.

Microsoft accounts for research and development costs in accordance with several accounting pronouncements, including SFAS 2, *Accounting for Research and Development Costs,* and SFAS 86, *Accounting for the Costs of Computer Software to be Sold, Leased, or Other-*

wise Marketed. SFAS 86 specifies that costs incurred internally in creating a computer software product should be charged to expense when incurred as research and development until technological feasibility has been established for the product. Once technological feasibility is established, all software costs should be capitalized until the product is available for general release to customers. Judgment is required in determining when the technological feasibility of a product is established. Microsoft has determined that technological feasibility for its products is reached shortly before the products are released to manufacturing. Costs incurred after technological feasibility is established are not material, and accordingly, the Company expenses all research and development costs when incurred.

Microsoft is subject to various legal proceedings and claims, the outcomes of which are subject to significant uncertainty. SFAS 5, *Accounting for Contingencies,* requires that an estimated loss from a loss contingency should be accrued by a charge to income if it is probable that an asset has been impaired or a liability has been incurred and the amount of the loss can be reasonably estimated. Disclosure of a contingency is required if there is at least a reasonable possibility that a loss has been incurred. The Company evaluates, among other factors, the degree of probability of an unfavorable outcome and the ability to make a reasonable estimate of the amount of loss. Changes in these factors could materially impact the Company's financial position or its results of operations.

SFAS 109, *Accounting for Income Taxes,* establishes financial accounting and reporting standards for the effect of income taxes. The objectives of accounting for income taxes are to recognize the amount of taxes payable or refundable for the current year and deferred tax liabilities and assets for the future tax consequences of events that have been recognized in an entity's financial statements or tax returns. Judgment is required in assessing the future tax consequences of events that have been recognized in the Company's financial statements or tax returns. Fluctuations in the actual outcome of these future tax consequences could materially impact the Company's financial position or its results of operations.

ISSUES AND UNCERTAINTIES

The following issues and uncertainties, among others, should be considered in evaluating the Company's financial outlook.

Challenges to the Company's Business Model. Since its inception, the Company's business model has been based upon customers agreeing to pay a fee to license software developed and distributed by Microsoft. Under this commercial software development ("CSD") model, software developers bear the costs of converting original ideas into software products through investments in research and development, offsetting these costs with the revenues received from the distribution of their products. The Company believes that the CSD model has had substantial benefits for users of software, allowing them to rely on the expertise of the Company and other software developers that have powerful incentives to develop innovative software that is useful, reliable and compatible with other software and hardware. In recent years, there has been a growing challenge to the CSD model, often referred to as the Open Source movement. Under the Open Source model, software is produced by global "communities" of programmers, and the resulting software and the intellectual property contained therein is licensed to end users at little or no cost. The Company believes that there are significant problems with the Open Source model, the principal drawback being that no single entity is responsible for the Open Source software, and thus users have no recourse if a product does not work properly or at all. Further, without the market incentives associated with the CSD model, the Company believes that the vigorous innovation and growth of the software industry over the last 25 years would not have occurred. Nonetheless, the popularization of the Open Source movement continues to pose a significant challenge to the Company's business model, including recent efforts by proponents of the Open Source model to convince governments worldwide to mandate the use of Open Source software in their purchase and deployment of software products. To the extent the Open Source model gains increasing market acceptance, sales of the Company's products may decline, the Company may have to reduce the prices it charges for its products, and revenues and operating margins may consequently decline.

New Products and Services. The Company has made significant investments in research and development for new products, services and technologies, including Microsoft .NET, Xbox, business applications, MSN, mobile and wireless technologies, and television. Significant revenue from these investments may not be achieved for a number of years, if at all. Moreover, these products and services may never be profitable, and even if they are profitable, operating margins for these businesses are not expected to be as high as the margins historically experienced in our Desktop and Enterprise Software and Services businesses.

Declines in Demand for Software. If overall market demand for PCs, servers and other computing devices declines significantly, and consumer and corporate spending for such products declines, Microsoft's revenue growth will be adversely affected. Additionally, the Company's revenues would be unfavorably impacted if customers reduce their purchases of new software products or upgrades to existing products if such new offerings are not perceived to add significant new functionality or other value to prospective purchasers.

Product Development Schedule. The development of software products is a complex and time-consuming process. New products and enhancements to existing products can require long development and testing periods. Significant delays in new product releases or significant problems in creating new products could negatively impact the Company's revenues.

International Operations. Microsoft develops and sells products throughout the world. The prices of the Company's products in countries outside of the United States are generally higher than the Company's prices in the United States because of the cost incurred in localizing software for non-U.S. markets. The costs of producing and selling the Company's products in these countries also are higher. Pressure to globalize Microsoft's pricing structure might require that the Company reduce the sales price of its software in other countries, even though the costs of the software continue to be higher than in the United States. Unfavorable changes in trade protection laws, policies and measures, and other regulatory requirements affecting trade and investment; unexpected changes in regulatory requirements for software; social, political, labor, or economic conditions in a specific country or region, including foreign exchange rates; difficulties in staffing and managing foreign operations; and potential adverse foreign tax consequences, among other factors, could also have a negative effect on the Company's business and results of operations outside of the United States.

Intellectual Property Rights. Microsoft diligently defends its intellectual property rights, but unlicensed copying and use of software represents a loss of revenue to the Company. While this adversely affects U.S. revenue, revenue loss is even more significant outside the United States, particularly in countries where laws are less protective of intellectual property rights. Throughout the world, Microsoft actively educates consumers on the benefits of licensing genuine products and educates lawmakers on the advantages of a business climate where intellectual property rights are protected. However, continued efforts may not affect revenue positively and further deterioration in compliance with existing legal protections or reductions in the legal protection for intellectual property rights of software developers could adversely affect revenue.

Taxation of Extraterritorial Income. In August 2001, a World Trade Organization ("WTO") dispute panel determined that the extraterritorial tax ("ETI") provisions of the FSC Repeal and Extraterritorial Income Exclusion Act of 2000 constitute an export subsidy prohibited by the WTO Agreement on Subsidies and Countervailing Measures Agreement. The U.S. government appealed the panel's decision and lost its appeal. On January 29, 2002, the WTO Dispute Settlement Body adopted the Appellate Body report. President Bush has stated the U.S. will bring its tax laws into compliance with the WTO ruling, but the Administration and Congress have not decided on a solution for this issue. In July 2002, Representative Bill Thomas, Chairman of the House Ways and Means Committee, introduced the American Competitiveness and Corporate Accountability Act of 2002. If enacted, that bill would repeal the ETI regime and introduce broad-based international reform. The proposed reforms would not materially affect the Company. On August 30, 2002, a WTO arbitration panel determined that the European Union may impose up to $4.04 billion per year in countermeasures if the U.S. rules are not brought into compliance. The WTO decision does not repeal the ETI tax benefit and it does not require the European Union to impose trade sanctions, so it is not possible to predict what impact the WTO decision will have on future results pending final resolution of these matters. If the ETI exclusion is repealed and replacement legislation is not enacted, the loss of tax benefit to the Company could be significant.

Litigation. As discussed in Note 19—Contingencies of the Notes to Financial Statements, the Company is subject to a variety of claims and lawsuits. While the Company believes that none of the litigation matters in which the Company is currently involved will have a material adverse impact on the Company's financial position or results of operations, it is possible that one or more of these matters could be resolved in a manner that would ultimately have a material adverse impact on the business of the Company, and could negatively impact its revenues and operating margins.

ITEM 7A. QUANTITATIVE AND QUALITATIVE DISCLOSURES ABOUT MARKET RISK

The Company is exposed to foreign currency, interest rate, and equity price risks. A portion of these risks is hedged, but fluctuations could impact the Company's results of operations and financial position. The Company hedges the exposure of accounts receivable and a portion of anticipated revenue to foreign currency fluctuations, primarily with option contracts. The Company monitors its foreign currency exposures daily to maximize the overall effectiveness of its foreign currency hedge positions. Principal currencies hedged include the Euro, Japanese yen, British pound, and Canadian dollar. Fixed income securities are subject to interest rate risk. The portfolio is diversified and consists primarily of investment grade securities to minimize credit risk. The Company routinely uses options to hedge its exposure to interest rate risk in the event of a catastrophic increase in interest rates. Many securities held in the Company's equity and other investments portfolio are subject to price risk. The Company uses options to hedge its price risk on certain highly volatile equity securities.

The Company uses a value-at-risk (VAR) model to estimate and quantify its market risks. VAR is the expected loss, for a given confidence level, in fair value of the Company's portfolio due to adverse market movements over a defined time horizon. The VAR model is not intended to represent actual losses in fair value, but is used as a risk estimation and management tool. The model used for currencies and equities is geometric Brownian motion, which allow incorporation of optionality of these exposures. For interest rates, the mean reverting geometric Brownian motion is used to reflect the principle that fixed-income securities prices over time revert to maturity value.

Value-at-risk is calculated by, first, simulating 10,000 market price paths over 20 days for equities, interest rates and foreign exchange rates, taking into account historical correlations among the different rates and prices. Each resulting unique set of equities prices, interest rates, and foreign exchange rates is applied to substantially all individual holdings to re-price each holding. The 250th worst performance (out of 10,000) represents the value-at-risk over 20 days at the 97.5th percentile. Several risk factors are not captured in the model, including liquidity risk, operational risk, credit risk, and legal risk.

A substantial amount of the Company's equity portfolio is held for strategic purposes. The Company attempts to hedge the value of these securities through the use of derivative contracts such as collars. The Company has incurred substantial impairment charges related to certain of these securities in fiscal 2002 and fiscal 2001. Such impairment charges have been incurred primarily for strategic equity holdings that the Company has not been able to hedge. The VAR amounts disclosed below are not necessarily reflective of potential accounting losses, as they are used as a risk management tool and reflect an estimate of potential reductions in fair value of the Company's portfolio. Losses in fair value over a 20-day holding period can exceed the reported VAR by significant amounts and can also accumulate over a longer time horizon than the 20-day holding period used in the VAR analysis.

The VAR numbers are shown separately for interest rate, currency, and equity risks. These VAR numbers include the underlying portfolio positions and related hedges. Historical data is used to estimate VAR. Given reliance on historical data, VAR is most effective in estimating risk exposures in markets in which there are no fundamental changes or shifts in market conditions. An inherent limitation in VAR is that the distribution of past changes in market risk factors may not produce accurate predictions of future market risk.

The following table sets forth the VAR calculations for substantially all of the Company's positions:

In millions

Risk Categories	As of June 30,		Year ended June 30, 2002		
	2001	2002	Average	High	Low
Interest rates	$ 363	$ 472	$ 435	$ 535	$ 333
Currency rates	58	310	162	310	58
Equity prices	520	602	584	757	488

The total VAR for the combined risk categories is $908 million at June 30, 2002 and $759 million at June 30, 2001. The total VAR is 34% less at June 30, 2002 and 19% less at June, 30 2001 than the sum of the separate risk categories for each of those years in the above table, due to the diversification benefit of the combination of risks. The reasons for the change in risk in portfolios include: larger investment portfolio size, higher foreign exchange exposure due to stronger non-U.S. currencies, and asset allocation shifts.

ITEM 8. FINANCIAL STATEMENTS AND SUPPLEMENTARY DATA

INCOME STATEMENTS

In millions, except earnings per share

Year Ended June 30	2000	2001	2002
Revenue	$ 22,956	$ 25,296	$ 28,365
Operating expenses:			
Cost of revenue	3,002	3,455	5,191
Research and development	3,772	4,379	4,307
Sales and marketing	4,126	4,885	5,407
General and administrative	1,050	857	1,550
Total operating expenses	11,950	13,576	16,455
Operating income	11,006	11,720	11,910
Losses on equity investees and other	(57)	(159)	(92)
Investment income/(loss)	3,326	(36)	(305)
Income before income taxes	14,275	11,525	11,513
Provision for income taxes	4,854	3,804	3,684
Income before accounting change	9,421	7,721	7,829
Cumulative effect of accounting change (net of income taxes of $185)	–	(375)	–
Net income	$ 9,421	$ 7,346	$ 7,829
Basic earnings per share:			
Before accounting change	$ 1.81	$ 1.45	$ 1.45
Cumulative effect of accounting change	–	(0.07)	–
	$ 1.81	$ 1.38	$ 1.45
Diluted earnings per share:			
Before accounting change	$ 1.70	$ 1.38	$ 1.41
Cumulative effect of accounting change	–	(0.06)	–
	$ 1.70	$ 1.32	$ 1.41
Weighted average shares outstanding:			
Basic	5,189	5,341	5,406
Diluted	5,536	5,574	5,553

See accompanying notes.

BALANCE SHEETS

In millions

June 30		2001		2002
Assets				
Current assets:				
Cash and equivalents	$	3,922	$	**3,016**
Short-term investments		27,678		**35,636**
Total cash and short-term investments		31,600		**38,652**
Accounts receivable, net		3,671		**5,129**
Inventories		83		**673**
Deferred income taxes		1,522		**2,112**
Other		2,334		**2,010**
Total current assets		39,210		**48,576**
Property and equipment, net		2,309		**2,268**
Equity and other investments		14,361		**14,191**
Goodwill		1,511		**1,426**
Intangible assets, net		401		**243**
Other long-term assets		1,038		**942**
Total assets	$	58,830	$	**67,646**
Liabilities and stockholders' equity				
Current liabilities:				
Accounts payable	$	1,188	$	**1,208**
Accrued compensation		742		**1,145**
Income taxes		1,468		**2,022**
Short-term unearned revenue		4,395		**5,920**
Other		1,461		**2,449**
Total current liabilities		9,254		**12,744**
Long-term unearned revenue		1,219		**1,823**
Deferred income taxes		409		**398**
Other long-term liabilities		659		**501**
Commitments and contingencies				
Stockholders' equity:				
Common stock and paid-in capital—shares authorized 12,000;				
Shares issued and outstanding 5,383 and 5,359		28,390		**31,647**
Retained earnings, including accumulated other comprehensive income of $587 and $583		18,899		**20,533**
Total stockholders' equity		47,289		**52,180**
Total liabilities and stockholders' equity	$	58,830	$	**67,646**

See accompanying notes.

CASH FLOWS STATEMENTS

In millions

Year Ended June 30		2000		2001		2002
Operations						
Net income	$	9,421	$	7,346	$	**7,829**
Cumulative effect of accounting change, net of tax		–		375		**–**
Depreciation, amortization, and other noncash items		1,250		1,536		**1,084**
Net recognized (gains)/losses on investments		(1,732)		2,221		**2,424**
Stock option income tax benefits		5,535		2,066		**1,596**
Deferred income taxes		(425)		(420)		**(416)**
Unearned revenue		6,177		6,970		**11,152**
Recognition of unearned revenue		(5,600)		(6,369)		**(8,929)**
Accounts receivable		(944)		(418)		**(1,623)**
Other current assets		(775)		(482)		**(264)**
Other long-term assets		(864)		(330)		**(9)**
Other current liabilities		(992)		774		**1,449**
Other long-term liabilities		375		153		**216**
Net cash from operations		11,426		13,422		**14,509**
Financing						
Common stock issued		2,245		1,620		**1,497**
Common stock repurchased		(4,896)		(6,074)		**(6,069)**
Sales/(repurchases) of put warrants		472		(1,367)		**–**
Preferred stock dividends		(13)		–		**–**
Other, net		–		235		**–**
Net cash used for financing		(2,192)		(5,586)		**(4,572)**
Investing						
Additions to property and equipment		(879)		(1,103)		**(770)**
Purchases of investments		(42,290)		(66,346)		**(89,386)**
Maturities of investments		4,025		5,867		**8,654**
Sales of investments		29,752		52,848		**70,657**
Net cash used for investing		(9,392)		(8,734)		**(10,845)**
Net change in cash and equivalents		(158)		(898)		**(908)**
Effect of exchange rates on cash and equivalents		29		(26)		**2**
Cash and equivalents, beginning of year		4,975		4,846		**3,922**
Cash and equivalents, end of year	$	4,846	$	3,922	$	**3,016**

See accompanying notes.

STOCKHOLDERS' EQUITY STATEMENTS

In millions

Year Ended June 30	2000	2001	2002
Convertible preferred stock			
Balance, beginning of year	$ 980	$ –	$ –
Conversion of preferred to common stock	(980)	–	–
Balance, end of year	–	–	–
Common stock and paid-in capital			
Balance, beginning of year	13,844	23,195	**28,390**
Common stock issued	3,554	5,154	**1,801**
Common stock repurchased	(210)	(394)	**(676)**
Sales/(repurchases) of put warrants	472	(1,367)	–
Stock option income tax benefits	5,535	2,066	**1,596**
Other, net	–	(264)	**536**
Balance, end of year	23,195	28,390	**31,647**
Retained earnings			
Balance, beginning of year	13,614	18,173	**18,899**
Net income	9,421	7,346	**7,829**
Other comprehensive income:			
Cumulative effect of accounting change	–	(75)	–
Net gains/(losses) on derivative instruments	–	634	**(91)**
Net unrealized investment gains/(losses)	(283)	(1,460)	**5**
Translation adjustments and other	23	(39)	**82**
Comprehensive income	9,161	6,406	**7,825**
Preferred stock dividends	(13)	–	–
Immaterial pooling of interests	97	–	–
Common stock repurchased	(4,686)	(5,680)	**(6,191)**
Balance, end of year	18,173	18,899	**20,533**
Total stockholders' equity	$ 41,368	$ 47,289	$ **52,180**

See accompanying notes.

NOTES TO FINANCIAL STATEMENTS

NOTE 1   ACCOUNTING POLICIES

ACCOUNTING PRINCIPLES

The financial statements and accompanying notes are prepared in accordance with accounting principles generally accepted in the United States of America.

PRINCIPLES OF CONSOLIDATION

The financial statements include the accounts of Microsoft Corporation and its subsidiaries (Microsoft). Intercompany transactions and balances have been eliminated. Equity investments in which Microsoft owns at least 20% of the voting securities are accounted for using the equity method, except for investments in which the Company is not able to exercise significant influence over the investee, in which case, the cost method of accounting is used. Issuances of shares by a subsidiary are accounted for as capital transactions.

ESTIMATES AND ASSUMPTIONS

Preparing financial statements requires management to make estimates and assumptions that affect the reported amounts of assets, liabilities, revenue, and expenses. Examples include estimates of loss contingencies and product life cycles, and assumptions such as the elements comprising a software arrangement, including the distinction between upgrades/enhancements and new products; when the Company reaches technological feasibility for its products; the potential outcome of the future tax consequences of events that have been recognized in the Company's financial statements or tax returns; and determining when investment impairments are other-than-temporary. Actual results and outcomes may differ from these estimates and assumptions.

FOREIGN CURRENCIES

Assets and liabilities recorded in foreign currencies are translated at the exchange rate on the balance sheet date. Translation adjustments resulting from this process are charged or credited to other comprehensive income (OCI). Revenue and expenses are translated at average rates of exchange prevailing during the year.

REVENUE RECOGNITION

Microsoft accounts for the licensing of software in accordance with American Institute of Certified Public Accountants (AICPA) Statement of Position (SOP) 97-2, *Software Revenue Recognition*. The Company recognizes revenue when (i) persuasive evidence of an arrangement exists; (ii) delivery has occurred or services have been rendered; (iii) the sales price is fixed or determinable; and (iv) collectibility is reasonably assured. For software arrangements with multiple elements, revenue is recognized dependent upon whether vendor-specific objective evidence (VSOE) of fair value exists for each of the elements. When VSOE does not exist for all the elements of a software arrangement and the only undelivered element is postcontract customer support (PCS), the entire licensing fee is recognized ratably over the contract period. Revenue attributable to undelivered elements, including technical support and Internet browser technologies, is based on the average sales price of those elements when sold separately, and is recognized ratably on a straight-line basis over the product's life cycle. PCS and subscription revenue is recognized ratably over the contract period.

Revenue from products licensed to original equipment manufacturers (OEMs) is based on the licensing agreement with an OEM and has historically been recognized when OEMs ship licensed products to their customers. Licensing provisions were modified with the introduction of Windows XP in 2002 and revenue for certain products is recorded upon shipment of the product to OEMs. The effect of this change in licensing provisions was not material. Revenue from packaged product sales to distributors and resellers is usually recorded when related products are shipped. However, when the revenue recognition criteria required for distributor and reseller arrangements are not met, revenue is recognized as payments are received. Revenue related to the Company's Xbox game console is recognized upon shipment of the product to retailers. Online advertising revenue is recognized as advertisements are displayed. Costs related to insignificant obligations, which include telephone support for certain products, are accrued. Provisions are recorded for estimated returns, concessions, and bad debts.

COST OF REVENUE

Cost of revenue includes direct costs to manufacture and distribute product and direct costs to provide online services, consulting, product support, and training and certification of system integrators.

RESEARCH AND DEVELOPMENT

Technological feasibility for Microsoft's software products is reached shortly before the products are released to manufacturing. Costs incurred after technological feasibility is established are not material, and accordingly, the Company expenses all research and development costs when incurred.

ADVERTISING COSTS

Advertising costs are expensed as incurred. Advertising expense was $1.23 billion in 2000, $1.36 billion in 2001, and $1.27 billion in 2002.

INCOME TAXES

Income tax expense includes U.S. and international income taxes, plus the provision for U.S. taxes on undistributed earnings of international subsidiaries not deemed to be permanently invested. Certain items of income and expense are not reported in tax returns and financial statements in the same year. The tax effect of this difference is reported as deferred income taxes.

FINANCIAL INSTRUMENTS

The Company considers all liquid interest-earning investments with a maturity of three months or less at the date of purchase to be cash equivalents. Short-term investments generally mature between three months and six years from the purchase date. Investments with maturities beyond one year may be classified as short-term based on their highly liquid nature and because such marketable securities represent the investment of cash that is available for current operations. All cash and short-term investments are classified as available for sale and are recorded at market value using the specific identification method; unrealized gains and losses are reflected in OCI.

Equity and other investments include debt and equity instruments. Debt securities and publicly traded equity securities are classified as available for sale and are recorded at market using the specific identification method. Unrealized gains and losses (excluding other-than-temporary impairments) are reflected in OCI. All other investments, excluding those accounted for using the equity method, are recorded at cost.

Microsoft lends certain fixed income and equity securities to enhance investment income. Collateral and/or security interest is determined based upon the underlying security and the creditworthiness of the borrower. The fair value of collateral that Microsoft is permitted to sell or repledge was $499 million at both June 30, 2001 and 2002.

Investments are considered to be impaired when a decline in fair value is judged to be other-than-temporary. The Company employs a systematic methodology that considers available evidence in evaluating potential impairment of its investments. In the event that the cost of an investment exceeds its fair value, the Company evaluates, among other factors, the duration and extent to which the fair value is less than cost; the financial health of and business outlook for the investee, including industry and sector performance, changes in technology, and operational and financing cash flow factors; and the Company's intent and ability to hold the investment. Once a decline in fair value is determined to be other-than-temporary, an impairment charge is recorded and a new cost basis in the investment is established. In 2001, the Company recognized $4.80 billion in impairments of certain investments, primarily in the cable and telecommunication industries. In 2002, Microsoft recognized $4.32 billion in impairments of certain investments, primarily related to further declines in the fair values of U.S. and European cable and telecommunications holdings.

The Company uses derivative instruments to manage exposures to foreign currency, security price, and interest rate risks. The Company's objectives for holding derivatives are to minimize these risks using the most effective methods to eliminate or reduce the impact of these exposures.

Foreign Currency Risk. Certain forecasted transactions and assets are exposed to foreign currency risk. The Company monitors its foreign currency exposures daily to maximize the overall effectiveness of its foreign currency hedge positions. Principal currencies hedged include the Euro, Japanese yen, British pound, and Canadian dollar. Options used to hedge a portion of forecasted international revenue for up to three years in the future are designated as cash flow hedging instruments. Options and forwards not designated as hedging instruments under SFAS 133 are also used to hedge the impact of the variability in exchange rates on accounts receivable and collections denominated in certain foreign currencies.

Securities Price Risk. Strategic equity investments are subject to market price risk. From time to time, the Company uses and designates options to hedge fair values and cash flows on certain equity securities. The security, or forecasted sale thereof, selected for hedging is determined by market conditions, up-front costs, and other relevant factors. Once established, the hedges are not dynamically managed or traded, and are generally not removed until maturity.

Interest Rate Risk. Fixed-income securities are subject to interest rate risk. The fixed-income portfolio is diversified and consists primarily of investment grade securities to minimize credit risk. The Company routinely uses options, not designated as hedging instruments, to hedge its exposure to interest rate risk in the event of a catastrophic increase in interest rates.

Other Derivatives. In addition, the Company may invest in warrants to purchase securities of other companies as a strategic investment. Warrants that can be net share settled are deemed derivative financial instruments and are not designated as hedging instruments.

For options designated either as fair value or cash flow hedges, changes in the time value are excluded from the assessment of hedge effectiveness.

ALLOWANCE FOR DOUBTFUL ACCOUNTS

The allowance for doubtful accounts reflects management's best estimate of probable losses inherent in the account receivable balance. Management determines the allowance based on known troubled accounts, historical experience, and other currently available evidence. Activity in the allowance for doubtful accounts is as follows:

In millions

Year Ended June 30	Balance at Beginning of Period	Charged to Costs and Expenses	Write-offs and Other	Balance at End of Period
2002	$ 174	$ 192	$ 157	$ 209
2001	186	157	169	174
2000	204	77	95	186

INVENTORIES

Inventories are stated at the lower of cost or market, using the average cost method. Cost includes materials, labor, and manufacturing overhead related to the purchase and production of inventories.

PROPERTY AND EQUIPMENT

Property and equipment is stated at cost and depreciated using the straight-line method over the shorter of the estimated life of the asset or the lease term, ranging from one to 15 years. Computer software developed or obtained for internal use is depreciated using the straight-line method over the estimated useful life of the software, generally not in excess of three years.

GOODWILL

Beginning in fiscal 2002 with the adoption of SFAS 142, *Goodwill and Other Intangible Assets,* goodwill is no longer amortized, but instead tested for impairment at least annually. Prior to fiscal 2002, goodwill was amortized using the straight-line method over its estimated period of benefit.

INTANGIBLE ASSETS

Intangible assets are amortized using the straight-line method over their estimated period of benefit, ranging from three to seven years. The Company periodically evaluates the recoverability of intangible assets and takes into account events or circumstances that warrant revised estimates of useful lives or that indicate that an impairment exists. All of Microsoft's intangible assets are subject to amortization.

RECLASSIFICATIONS

Certain reclassifications have been made for consistent presentation.

NOTE 2   ACCOUNTING CHANGES

Effective July 1, 2000, the Company adopted SFAS 133, *Accounting for Derivative Instruments and Hedging Activities,* which establishes accounting and reporting standards for derivative instruments, including certain derivative instruments embedded in other contracts and for hedging activities. The adoption of SFAS 133 on July 1, 2000, resulted in a cumulative pre-tax reduction to income of $560 million ($375 million after-tax) and a cumulative pre-tax reduction to OCI of $112 million ($75 million after-tax). The reduction to income was mostly attributable to a loss of approximately $300 million reclassified from OCI for the time value of options and a loss of approximately $250 million reclassified from OCI for derivatives not designated as hedging instruments. The reduction to OCI was mostly attributable to losses of approximately $670 million on cash flow hedges offset by reclassifications out of OCI of the approximately $300 million loss for the time value of options and the approximately $250 million loss for derivative instruments not designated as hedging instruments. The net derivative losses included in OCI as of July 1, 2000 were reclassified into earnings during the twelve months ended June 30, 2001. The change in accounting from the adoption of SFAS 133 did not materially affect net income in 2001.

Effective July 1, 2001, Microsoft adopted SFAS 141, *Business Combinations,* and SFAS 142, *Goodwill and Other Intangible Assets.* SFAS 141 requires business combinations initiated after June 30, 2001 to be accounted for using the purchase method of accounting. It also specifies the types of acquired intangible assets that are required to be recognized and reported separate from goodwill. SFAS 142 requires that goodwill and certain intangibles no longer be amortized, but instead tested for impairment at least annually. There was no impairment of goodwill upon adoption of SFAS 142.

Net income and earnings per share for fiscal 2000 and fiscal 2001 adjusted to exclude amortization expense (net of taxes) is as follows:

In millions, except earnings per share

Year Ended June 30		2000		2001
Net income:				
Reported net income	$	9,421	$	7,346
Goodwill amortization		203		252
Equity method goodwill amortization		1		26
Adjusted net income	$	9,625	$	7,624
Basic earnings per share:				
Reported basic earnings per share	$	1.81	$	1.38
Goodwill amortization		0.04		0.05
Equity method goodwill amortization		–		–
Adjusted basic earnings per share	$	1.85	$	1.43
Diluted earnings per share:				
Reported diluted earnings per share	$	1.70	$	1.32
Goodwill amortization		0.04		0.05
Equity method goodwill amortization		–		–
Adjusted diluted earnings per share	$	1.74	$	1.37

NOTE 3   UNEARNED REVENUE

A portion of Microsoft's revenue under volume licensing programs is earned ratably over the period of the license agreement. Also, revenue attributable to undelivered elements, including technical support and Internet browser technologies, is based on the average sales price of those elements when sold separately, and is recognized ratably on a straight-line basis over the product's life cycle. The percentage of revenue recognized ratably for undelivered elements ranges from approximately 20% to 25% for Windows XP Home, approximately 10% to 15% for Windows XP Professional, and approximately 10% to 15% for desktop applications, depending on the terms and conditions of the license and prices of the elements. Product life cycles are currently estimated at three years for Windows operating systems and 18 months for desktop applications.

The components of unearned revenue were as follows:

In millions

June 30	2001	2002
Volume licensing programs	$ 1,922	$ 4,158
Undelivered elements	2,818	2,830
Other	874	755
Unearned revenue	$ 5,614	$ 7,743

Unearned revenue by product was as follows:

In millions

June 30	2001	2002
Desktop Applications	$ 2,189	$ 3,489
Desktop Platforms	2,586	3,198
Enterprise Software and Services	391	791
Desktop and Enterprise Software and Services	5,166	7,478
Consumer Software, Services, and Devices, and Other	448	265
Unearned revenue	$ 5,614	$ 7,743

Of the $7.74 billion of unearned revenue at June 30, 2002, $2.28 billion is expected to be recognized in the first quarter of fiscal 2003, $1.64 billion in the second quarter of fiscal 2003, $1.18 billion in the third quarter of fiscal 2003, $817 million in the fourth quarter of fiscal 2003, and $1.82 billion thereafter.

NOTE 4   CASH AND SHORT-TERM INVESTMENTS

In millions

June 30, 2001	Cost Basis	Unrealized Gains	Unrealized Losses	Recorded Basis
Cash and equivalents:				
Cash	$ 1,145	$ –	$ –	$ 1,145
Commercial paper	894	–	–	894
Certificates of deposit	286	–	–	286
U.S. government and agency securities	400	–	–	400
Corporate notes and bonds	1,130	–	–	1,130
Municipal securities	67	–	–	67
Cash and equivalents	3,922	–	–	3,922
Short-term investments:				
Commercial paper	635	3	–	638
U.S. government and agency securities	7,355	9	(42)	7,322
Corporate notes and bonds	17,256	214	(149)	17,321
Municipal securities	1,662	41	–	1,703
Certificates of deposit	694	–	–	694
Short-term investments	27,602	267	(191)	27,678
Cash and short-term investments	$ 31,524	$ 267	$ (191)	$ 31,600

In millions

June 30, 2002	Cost Basis	Unrealized Gains	Unrealized Losses	Recorded Basis
Cash and equivalents:				
Cash	$ 1,114	$ –	$ –	$ 1,114
Commercial paper	260	–	–	260
Certificates of deposit	31	–	–	31
Money market mutual funds	714	–	–	714
Corporate notes and bonds	560	–	–	560
Municipal securities	337	–	–	337
Cash and equivalents	3,016	–	–	3,016
Short-term investments:				
Commercial paper	552	–	–	552
U.S. government and agency securities	10,726	114	(13)	10,827
Corporate notes and bonds	18,822	255	(241)	18,836
Municipal securities	4,462	86	–	4,548
Certificates of deposit	873	–	–	873
Short-term investments	35,435	455	(254)	35,636
Cash and short-term investments	$ 38,451	$ 455	$ (254)	$ 38,652

Realized gains and (losses) from cash and short-term investments were $80 million and $(226) million in 2000, $541 million and $(369) million in 2001, and $816 million and $(558) million in 2002.

NOTE 5   INVENTORIES

In millions

June 30		2001		2002
Finished goods	$	78	$	**505**
Raw materials and work in process		5		**168**
Inventories	$	83	$	**673**

NOTE 6   PROPERTY AND EQUIPMENT

In millions

June 30		2001		2002
Land	$	185	$	**197**
Buildings		1,584		**1,701**
Computer equipment and software		2,292		**2,621**
Other		1,214		**1,372**
Property and equipment – at cost		5,275		**5,891**
Accumulated depreciation		(2,966)		**(3,623)**
Property and equipment – net	$	2,309	$	**2,268**

During 2000, 2001, and 2002, depreciation expense, of which the majority related to computer equipment, was $668 million, $764 million, and $820 million.

NOTE 7   EQUITY AND OTHER INVESTMENTS

In millions

June 30, 2001		Cost Basis		Unrealized Gains		Unrealized Losses		Recorded Basis
Debt securities recorded at market, maturing:								
Within one year	$	500	$	–	$	–	$	500
Between 2 and 10 years		643		12		(3)		652
Between 10 and 15 years		513		–		(9)		504
Beyond 15 years		4,754		–		(829)		3,925
Debt securities recorded at market		6,410		12		(841)		5,581
Common stock and warrants		5,555		2,030		(285)		7,300
Preferred stock		881		–		–		881
Other investments		599		–		–		599
Equity and other investments	$	13,445	$	2,042	$	(1,126)	$	14,361

Part II
Item 8

In millions

June 30, 2002	Cost Basis	Unrealized Gains	Unrealized Losses	Recorded Basis
Debt securities recorded at market, maturing:				
Within one year	$ 485	$ 26	$ –	$ 511
Between 2 and 10 years	893	46	(4)	935
Between 10 and 15 years	541	19	(2)	558
Beyond 15 years	3,036	–	–	3,036
Debt securities recorded at market	4,955	91	(6)	5,040
Common stock and warrants	6,930	1,287	(617)	7,600
Preferred stock	1,382	–	–	1,382
Other investments	169	–	–	169
Equity and other investments	$ 13,436	$ 1,378	$ (623)	$ 14,191

Debt securities include corporate and government notes and bonds and derivative securities. Debt securities maturing beyond 15 years are composed entirely of AT&T 5% convertible preferred debt with a contractual maturity of 30 years. The debt is convertible at the Company's option into AT&T common stock on or after December 1, 2000, or may be redeemed by AT&T upon satisfaction of certain conditions on or after June 1, 2002. In connection with the definitive agreement to combine AT&T Broadband with Comcast in a new company to be called AT&T Comcast Corporation, Microsoft has agreed to exchange its AT&T 5% convertible preferred debt securities for approximately 115 million shares of AT&T Comcast Corporation. It is expected that the transaction will close by December 31, 2002. While it is possible that Microsoft could incur a loss on this exchange transaction up to the carrying value of the AT&T debt securities, management believes that the ultimate loss, if any, will be significantly less. As management is unable to predict whether there will be a gain or loss on the exchange, no loss has been recorded related to this contingent exchange transaction as of June 30, 2002.

Equity securities that are restricted for more than one year or not publicly traded are recorded at cost. At June 30, 2001 the estimated fair value of these investments in excess of their recorded basis was $161 million. At June 30, 2002 the recorded basis of these investments in excess of their estimated fair value was $34 million. This excess of cost over estimated fair value was deemed temporary in nature. The estimate of fair value is based on publicly available market information or other estimates determined by management. Realized gains and (losses) from equity and other investments (excluding impairments discussed previously) were $1.94 billion and $(10) million in 2000, $3.03 billion and $(23) million in 2001, and $2.24 billion and $(121) million in 2002.

NOTE 8 GOODWILL

During fiscal 2002, goodwill was reduced by $85 million, principally in connection with Microsoft's exchange of all of its 33.7 million shares and warrants of Expedia, Inc. to USA Networks, Inc. No goodwill was acquired or impaired during fiscal 2002. As of June 30, 2002, Desktop and Enterprise Software and Services goodwill was $1.1 billion, Consumer Software, Services, and Devices goodwill was $258 million, and Consumer Commerce Investments goodwill was $72 million.

NOTE 9 INTANGIBLE ASSETS

During fiscal 2002, changes in intangible assets primarily relates to the Company's acquisition of $25 million in patents and licenses and $27 million in existing technology, which will be amortized over approximately 3 years. No significant residual value is estimated for these intangible assets. Intangible assets amortization expense was $202 million for fiscal 2001 and $194 million for fiscal 2002. The components of intangible assets were as follows:

In millions

June 30	2001		2002	
	Gross Carrying Amount	Accumulated Amortization	Gross Carrying Amount	Accumulated Amortization
Patents and licenses	$ 407	$ (177)	$ 421	$ (290)
Existing technology	157	(27)	172	(71)
Trademarks, tradenames and other	83	(42)	15	(4)
Intangible assets	$ 647	$ (246)	$ 608	$ (365)

Amortization expense for the net carrying amount of intangible assets at June 30, 2002 is estimated to be $115 million in fiscal 2003, $90 million in fiscal 2004, $36 million in fiscal 2005, and $2 million in fiscal 2006.

NOTE 10   DERIVATIVES

For fiscal 2001, investment income included a net unrealized loss of $592 million, comprised of a $214 million gain for changes in the time value of options for fair value hedges, $211 million loss for changes in the time value of options for cash flow hedges, and $595 million loss for changes in the fair value of derivative instruments not designated as hedging instruments. For fiscal 2002, investment income included a net unrealized loss of $480 million, comprised of a $30 million gain for changes in the time value of options for fair value hedges, $331 million loss for changes in the time value of options for cash flow hedges, and $179 million net loss for changes in the fair value of derivative instruments not designated as hedging instruments.

Derivative gains and losses included in OCI are reclassified into earnings at the time forecasted revenue or the sale of an equity investment is recognized. During fiscal 2001, $214 million of derivative gains were reclassified to revenue and $416 million of derivative losses were reclassified to investment income/(loss). During fiscal 2002, $234 million of derivative gains were reclassified to revenue and $10 million of derivative losses were reclassified to investment income/(loss). The derivative losses reclassified to investment income/(loss) were offset by gains on the item being hedged. The Company estimates that $63 million of net derivative gains included in other comprehensive income will be reclassified into earnings within the next twelve months.

For instruments designated as hedges, hedge ineffectiveness, determined in accordance with SFAS 133, had no impact on earnings for the fiscal 2001 and 2002. No fair value hedges or cash flow hedges were derecognized or discontinued for fiscal 2001 and 2002.

NOTE 11   INVESTMENT INCOME/(LOSS)

The components of investment income/(loss) are as follows:

In millions

Year Ended June 30		2000		2001		2002
Dividends	$	363	$	377	$	357
Interest		1,231		1,808		1,762
Net recognized gains/(losses) on investments:						
Net gains on the sales of investments		1,780		3,175		2,379
Other-than-temporary impairments		(29)		(4,804)		(4,323)
Net unrealized losses attributable to derivative instruments		(19)		(592)		(480)
Net recognized gains/(losses) on investments		1,732		(2,221)		(2,424)
Investment income/(loss)	$	3,326	$	(36)	$	(305)

NOTE 12   INCOME TAXES

The provision for income taxes consisted of:

In millions

Year Ended June 30		2000		2001		2002
Current taxes:						
U.S. and state	$	4,744	$	3,243	$	3,644
International		535		514		575
Current taxes		5,279		3,757		4,219
Deferred taxes		(425)		47		(535)
Provision for income taxes	$	4,854	$	3,804	$	3,684

U.S. and international components of income before income taxes were:

In millions

Year Ended June 30		2000		2001		2002
U.S.	$	11,860	$	9,189	$	8,920
International		2,415		2,336		2,593
Income before income taxes	$	14,275	$	11,525	$	11,513

In 2000, the effective tax rate was 34.0%, and included the effect of a 2.5% reduction from the U.S. statutory rate for tax credits and a 1.5% increase for other items. In 2001, the effective tax rate was 33.0%, and included the effect of a 3.1% reduction from the U.S. statutory rate for tax credits and a 1.1% increase for other items. The effective tax rate in 2002 was 32.0%, and included the effect of a 2.4% reduction from the U.S. statutory rate for the extraterritorial income exclusion tax benefit and a 0.6% reduction for other items.

Deferred income taxes were:

In millions

June 30	2001	2002
Deferred income tax assets:		
Revenue items	$ 1,469	$ **2,261**
Expense items	691	**945**
Impaired investments	1,070	**2,016**
Deferred income tax assets	$ 3,230	$ **5,222**
Deferred income tax liabilities:		
Unrealized gain on investments	$ (395)	$ **(887)**
International earnings	(1,667)	**(1,818)**
Other	(55)	**(803)**
Deferred income tax liabilities	$ (2,117)	$ **(3,508)**

Microsoft has not provided for U.S. deferred income taxes or foreign withholding taxes on $780 million of its undistributed earnings for certain non-U.S. subsidiaries, all of which relate to fiscal 2002 earnings, since these earnings are intended to be reinvested indefinitely.

On September 15, 2000, the U.S. Tax Court issued an adverse ruling with respect to Microsoft's claim that the Internal Revenue Service (IRS) incorrectly assessed taxes for 1990 and 1991. The Company has filed an appeal with the Ninth Circuit Court of Appeals on this matter. Income taxes, except for items related to the 1990 and 1991 assessments, have been settled with the IRS for all years through 1996. The IRS is examining the Company's 1997 through 1999 U.S. income tax returns. Management believes any adjustments which may be required will not be material to the financial statements. Income taxes paid were $800 million in 2000, $1.3 billion in 2001, and $1.9 billion in 2002.

NOTE 13 STOCKHOLDERS' EQUITY

Shares of common stock outstanding were as follows:

In millions

Year Ended June 30	2000	2001	2002
Balance, beginning of year	5,109	5,283	**5,383**
Issued	229	189	**104**
Repurchased	(55)	(89)	**(128)**
Balance, end of year	5,283	5,383	**5,359**

The Company repurchases its common shares in the open market to provide shares for issuance to employees under stock option and stock purchase plans. In 2002, the Company acquired 5.1 million of its shares as a result of a structured stock repurchase transaction entered into in 2001, which gave it the right to acquire such shares in exchange for an up-front net payment of $264 million. To enhance its stock repurchase program, Microsoft has sold put warrants to independent third parties. These put warrants entitled the holders to sell shares of Microsoft common stock to the Company on certain dates at specified prices. In the third quarter of fiscal 2001, the Company issued 2.8 million shares to settle a portion of the outstanding put warrants. At June 30, 2001 and 2002, there were no outstanding put warrants.

During 1996, Microsoft issued 12.5 million shares of 2.75% convertible exchangeable principal-protected preferred stock. The Company's convertible preferred stock matured on December 15, 1999. Each preferred share was converted into 1.1273 common shares.

NOTE 14   OTHER COMPREHENSIVE INCOME

In millions

Year Ended June 30	2000	2001	2002
Cumulative effect of accounting change, net of tax effect of $(37)	$ –	$ (75)	$ –
Net gains/(losses) on derivative instruments:			
Unrealized gains, net of tax effect of $246 in 2001 and $30 in 2002	–	499	55
Reclassification adjustment for (gains)/losses included in net income, net of tax effect of $67 in 2001 and $(79) in 2002	–	135	(146)
Net gains/(losses) on derivative instruments	–	634	(91)
Net unrealized investment gains/(losses):			
Unrealized holding gains/(losses), net of tax effect of $248 in 2000, $(351) in 2001, and $(955) in 2002	531	(1,200)	(1,774)
Reclassification adjustment for (gains)/losses included in net income, net of tax effect of $(420) in 2000, $(128) in 2001, and $958 in 2002	(814)	(260)	1,779
Net unrealized investment gains/(losses)	(283)	(1,460)	5
Translation adjustments and other	23	(39)	82
Other comprehensive income/(loss)	$ (260)	$ (940)	$ (4)

The components of accumulated other comprehensive income were:

In millions

June 30	2001	2002
Net gains on derivative instruments	$ 177	$ 86
Net unrealized investment gains	598	603
Translation adjustments and other	(188)	(106)
Accumulated other comprehensive income	$ 587	$ 583

NOTE 15   EMPLOYEE STOCK AND SAVINGS PLANS

EMPLOYEE STOCK PURCHASE PLAN

The Company has an employee stock purchase plan for all eligible employees. Under the plan, shares of the Company's common stock may be purchased at six-month intervals at 85% of the lower of the fair market value on the first or the last day of each six-month period. Employees may purchase shares having a value not exceeding 15% of their gross compensation during an offering period. During 2000, 2001, and 2002, employees purchased 2.5 million, 5.7 million, and 5.4 million shares at average prices of $72.38, $36.87, and $50.52 per share. At June 30, 2002, 56.8 million shares were reserved for future issuance.

SAVINGS PLAN

The Company has a savings plan, which qualifies under Section 401(k) of the Internal Revenue Code. Participating employees may contribute up to 25% of their pretax salary, but not more than statutory limits. The Company contributes fifty cents for each dollar a participant contributes, with a maximum contribution of 3% of a participant's earnings. Matching contributions were $47 million, $63 million, and $77 million in 2000, 2001, and 2002.

STOCK OPTION PLANS

The Company has stock option plans for directors, officers, and employees, which provide for nonqualified and incentive stock options. Options granted prior to 1995 generally vest over four and one-half years and expire 10 years from the date of grant. Options granted between 1995 and 2001 generally vest over four and one-half years and expire seven years from the date of grant, while certain options vest either over four and one-half years or over seven and one-half years and expire after 10 years. Options granted during 2002 vest over four and one-half years and expire 10 years from the date of grant. At June 30, 2002, options for 371 million shares were vested and 543 million shares were available for future grants under the plans.

Stock options outstanding were as follows:

In millions, except per share amounts

| | | Price per Share | |
	Shares	Range	Weighted Average
Balance, June 30, 1999	766	$ 0.56 – $ 83.28	$ 23.87
Granted	304	65.56 – 119.13	79.87
Exercised	(198)	0.56 – 82.94	9.54
Canceled	(40)	4.63 – 116.56	36.50
Balance, June 30, 2000	832	0.56 – 119.13	41.23
Granted	224	41.50 – 80.00	60.84
Exercised	(123)	0.59 – 85.81	11.13
Canceled	(35)	13.83 – 119.13	63.57
Balance, June 30, 2001	898	0.56 – 119.13	49.54
Granted	41	48.62 – 72.57	62.50
Exercised	(99)	1.02 – 69.81	12.82
Canceled	(38)	1.15 – 116.56	68.67
Balance, June 30, 2002	802	0.79 – 119.13	53.75

For various price ranges, weighted average characteristics of outstanding stock options at June 30, 2002 were as follows:

In millions, except per share amounts

| | Outstanding Options | | | Exercisable Options | |
Range of Exercise Prices	Shares	Remaining Life (Years)	Weighted Average Price	Shares	Weighted Average Price
$ 0.79 – $ 5.97	36	1.6	$ 4.83	35	$ 4.82
5.98 – 13.62	44	0.5	11.19	42	11.18
13.63 – 29.80	90	2.0	15.02	84	14.97
29.81 – 43.62	73	2.7	32.19	66	32.09
43.63 – 60.00	191	6.9	55.81	41	54.03
60.01 – 69.50	146	6.4	66.24	35	66.53
69.51 – 83.28	80	5.1	71.17	21	71.84
83.29 – 119.13	142	4.2	89.87	47	89.29

The Company follows Accounting Principles Board Opinion 25, *Accounting for Stock Issued to Employees,* to account for stock option and employee stock purchase plans. An alternative method of accounting for stock options is SFAS 123, *Accounting for Stock-Based Compensation.* Employee stock options are valued at grant date using the Black-Scholes valuation model, and this compensation cost is recognized ratably over the vesting period.

Had compensation cost for the Company's stock option and employee stock purchase plans been determined as prescribed by SFAS 123, pro forma income statements for 2000, 2001, and 2002 would have been as follows:

In millions, except per share amounts

Year Ended June 30	2000		2001		2002	
	Reported	Pro Forma	Reported	Pro Forma	Reported	Pro Forma
Revenue	$ 22,956	$ 22,956	$ 25,296	$ 25,296	$ 28,365	$ 28,365
Operating expenses:						
Cost of revenue	3,002	3,277	3,455	3,775	5,191	5,699
Research and development	3,772	4,814	4,379	6,106	4,307	6,299
Sales and marketing	4,126	4,468	4,885	5,888	5,407	6,252
General and administrative	1,050	1,284	857	1,184	1,550	1,843
Total operating expenses	11,950	13,843	13,576	16,953	16,455	20,093
Operating income	11,006	9,113	11,720	8,343	11,910	8,272
Losses on equity investees and other	(57)	(57)	(159)	(159)	(92)	(92)
Investment income/(loss)	3,326	3,326	(36)	(36)	(305)	(305)
Income before income taxes	14,275	12,382	11,525	8,148	11,513	7,875
Provision for income taxes	4,854	4,210	3,804	2,689	3,684	2,520
Income before accounting change	9,421	8,172	7,721	5,459	7,829	5,355
Cumulative effect of accounting change	–	–	(375)	(375)	–	–
Net income	$ 9,421	$ 8,172	$ 7,346	$ 5,084	$ 7,829	$ 5,355
Basic earnings per share	$ 1.81	$ 1.57	$ 1.38	$ 0.95	$ 1.45	$ 0.99
Diluted earnings per share	$ 1.70	$ 1.48	$ 1.32	$ 0.91	$ 1.41	$ 0.98

The weighted average Black-Scholes value of options granted under the stock option plans during 2000, 2001, and 2002 was $36.67, $29.31, and $31.57. Value was estimated using a weighted average expected life of 6.2 years in 2000, 6.4 years in 2001, and 7.0 years in 2002, no dividends, volatility of .33 in 2000, .39 in 2001, and .39 in 2002, and risk-free interest rates of 6.2%, 5.3%, and 5.4% in 2000, 2001, and 2002.

NOTE 16 EARNINGS PER SHARE

Basic earnings per share is computed on the basis of the weighted average number of common shares outstanding. Diluted earnings per share is computed on the basis of the weighted average number of common shares outstanding plus the effect of outstanding preferred shares using the "if-converted" method, outstanding put warrants using the "reverse treasury stock" method, and outstanding stock options using the "treasury stock" method.

The components of basic and diluted earnings per share were as follows:

In millions, except per share amounts

Year Ended June 30	2000	2001	2002
Income before accounting change	$ 9,421	$ 7,721	$ 7,829
Preferred stock dividends	13	–	–
Net income available for common shareholders	$ 9,408	$ 7,721	$ 7,829
Weighted average outstanding shares of common stock	5,189	5,341	5,406
Dilutive effect of:			
Put warrants	2	21	–
Preferred stock	7	–	–
Employee stock options	338	212	147
Common stock and common stock equivalents	5,536	5,574	5,553
Earnings per share before accounting change:			
Basic	$ 1.81	$ 1.45	$ 1.45
Diluted	$ 1.70	$ 1.38	$ 1.41

For the years ended June 30, 2000, 2001 and 2002, 45 million, 351 million, and 373 million shares attributable to outstanding stock options were excluded from the calculation of diluted earnings per share because the effect was antidilutive.

NOTE 17 OPERATIONAL TRANSACTIONS

In January 2000, the Company acquired Visio Corporation in a transaction that was accounted for as a pooling of interests. Microsoft issued 14 million shares valued at approximately $1.5 billion in the exchange for the outstanding stock of Visio. Visio's assets and liabilities, which were nominal, are included with those of Microsoft as of the merger. Operating results for Visio from periods prior to the merger were not material to the combined results of the two companies. Accordingly, the financial statements for such periods have not been restated.

In April 2001, the Company acquired Great Plains Software, Inc. for approximately $1.1 billion in stock. Great Plains is a leading supplier of mid-market business applications. The acquisition was accounted for by the purchase method and operating results for Great Plains subsequent to the date of acquisition are included with those of Microsoft. The pro forma impact of Great Plains' operating results prior to the date of acquisition was not material.

NOTE 18 COMMITMENTS

The Company has operating leases for most U.S. and international sales and support offices and certain equipment. Rental expense for operating leases was $201 million, $281 million, and $318 million in 2000, 2001, and 2002. Future minimum rental commitments under noncancellable leases, in millions of dollars, are: 2003, $260; 2004, $219; 2005, $197; 2006, $170; 2007, $135; and thereafter, $302. Microsoft has committed $111 million for constructing new buildings. In addition, the Company has guaranteed $536 million in debt of its equity investees.

NOTE 19 CONTINGENCIES

The Company is a defendant in *U.S. v. Microsoft*, a lawsuit filed by the Antitrust Division of the U.S. Department of Justice (DOJ) and a group of eighteen state Attorneys General alleging violations of the Sherman Act and various state antitrust laws. After the trial, the District Court entered Findings of Fact and Conclusions of Law stating that Microsoft had violated Sections 1 and 2 of the Sherman Act and various state antitrust laws. A Judgment was entered on June 7, 2000 ordering, among other things, the breakup of Microsoft into two companies.

The Judgment was stayed pending an appeal. On June 28, 2001, the U.S. Court of Appeals for the District of Columbia Circuit affirmed in part, reversed in part, and vacated the Judgment in its entirety and remanded the case to the District Court for a new trial on one Section 1 claim and for entry of a new judgment consistent with its ruling. In its ruling, the Court of Appeals substantially narrowed the bases of liability found by the District Court, but affirmed some of the District Court's conclusions that Microsoft had violated Section 2. On October 12, 2001, the trial court held a status conference and entered orders requiring the parties to engage in settlement discussions until November 2, 2001. Microsoft entered into a settlement with the United States on November 2, 2001. Nine states (New York, Ohio, Illinois, Kentucky, Louisiana, Maryland, Michigan, North Carolina and Wisconsin) agreed to settle on substantially the same terms on November 6, 2001. A hearing on the settlement was held by the Court on March 6, 2002. The Court will now decide whether to approve the settlement as being in the public interest. Nine states and the District of Columbia continue to litigate the remedies phase of *U.S. v. Microsoft*. The non-settling states are seeking imposition of a remedy that would impose much broader restrictions on Microsoft's business than the proposed settlement with the DOJ and nine other states. The Court conducted an evidentiary hearing related to the non-settling states' proposed remedies from March 18 to June 19, 2002. A decision is anticipated later in calendar 2002.

In other ongoing investigations, the DOJ and several state Attorneys General have requested information from Microsoft concerning various issues. In addition, the European Commission has instituted proceedings in which it alleges that Microsoft has failed to disclose information that Microsoft competitors claim they need to interoperate fully with Windows 2000 clients and servers and has engaged in discriminatory licensing of such technology, as well as improper bundling of multimedia playback technology in the Windows operating system. The remedies sought, though not fully defined, include mandatory disclosure of Microsoft Windows operating system technology and imposition of fines. Microsoft denies the European Commission's allegations and intends to contest the proceedings vigorously.

A large number of overcharge class action lawsuits have been initiated against Microsoft in various state and Federal courts. These cases allege that Microsoft has competed unfairly and unlawfully monopolized alleged markets for operating systems and certain software applications and seek to recover alleged overcharges that the complaints contend Microsoft charged for these products. Microsoft believes the claims are without merit and is vigorously defending the cases. To date, Microsoft has won dismissals of all claims for damages by indirect purchasers under Federal law and in 17 separate state court proceedings, of which seven have been affirmed and one has been reversed. Claims on behalf of foreign purchasers have also been dismissed. Appeals of several of these rulings are still pending. No trials or other proceedings have been held concerning any liability issues. Courts in several states have ruled that these cases may proceed as class actions, while two courts have denied class certification status to the claims in that state proceeding and another has ruled that no class action is available for claims in that state. In fiscal 2002, the Company recorded a contingent liability of approximately $660 million representing management's estimate of the costs of resolving the contingency. Management's contingent liability estimate is based upon a proposed settlement between Microsoft and lead counsel for the Federal plaintiffs. While the proposed settlement was not approved by the District Court, management believes that the proposal represents the best estimate of the costs of resolving the contingency based on currently available information. The Company intends to continue vigorously defending these lawsuits.

Netscape Communications Inc., a subsidiary of AOL-Time Warner Inc., filed suit against Microsoft on January 22, 2002 in Federal court in the District of Columbia, alleging violations of antitrust and unfair competition laws and other tort claims relating to Netscape and its Navigator browser. The complaint includes claims of unlawful monopolization or attempted monopolization of alleged markets for operating systems and Web browsers, illegal tying of operating systems and browsers, and tortuous interference with Netscape's business relations. Netscape seeks injunctive relief, unquantified treble damages and its fees and costs. Microsoft denies these allegations and will vigorously defend this action. The case has been transferred for pretrial purposes to the District Court in Baltimore, Maryland and is being coordinated with the overcharge class actions described above.

Be Incorporated, a former software development company whose assets were acquired by Palm Incorporated in August 2001, filed suit against Microsoft on February 18, 2002 in Federal court in San Francisco, alleging violations of Federal and state antitrust and unfair competition laws and other tort claims. Be alleges that Microsoft's license agreements with computer manufacturers, pricing policies, and business practices interfered with Be's relationships with computer manufacturers and discouraged them from adopting Be's own operating system for their products. Be is seeking unquantified treble and punitive damages for its alleged injuries along with its fees and costs. Microsoft denies these allegations and will vigorously defend this action. The case has been transferred for pretrial purposes to the District Court in Baltimore, Maryland and is being coordinated with the overcharge class actions described above.

On March 8, 2002, Sun Microsystems, Inc. filed suit against Microsoft alleging violations of Federal and state antitrust and unfair competition laws as well as claims under the Federal Copyright Act. Sun seeks injunctive relief and unspecified treble damages along with its fees and costs. Microsoft denies these allegations and will vigorously defend this action. The case has been transferred for pretrial purposes to the District Court in Baltimore, Maryland and is being coordinated with the overcharge class actions described above.

On June 3, 2002, Microsoft and the Securities and Exchange Commission entered into an administrative settlement resolving a nonpublic investigation of certain of Microsoft's accounting and record keeping practices during fiscal years 1995 through 1998 (SEC File No. 3-10789). The settlement provides that Microsoft will not violate securities regulations that require companies to make accurate filings and maintain sufficient records and controls. The settlement has no impact on the Company's financial results.

The Company is also subject to a variety of other claims and suits that arise from time to time in the ordinary course of its business.

Management currently believes that resolving all of these matters will not have a material adverse impact on the Company's financial position or its results of operations.

Part II
Item 8

NOTE 20   SEGMENT INFORMATION

In millions

Year Ended June 30	Desktop and Enterprise Software and Services		Consumer Software, Services, and Devices		Consumer Commerce Investments		Other		Reconciling Amounts		Consolidated	
2000												
Revenue	$	20,410	$	1,654	$	182	$	691	$	19	$	22,956
Operating income/(loss)		13,210		(1,090)		(60)		86		(1,140)		11,006
2001												
Revenue	$	22,720	$	1,961	$	522	$	652	$	(559)	$	25,296
Operating income/(loss)		14,261		(1,666)		(222)		97		(750)		11,720
2002												
Revenue	$	**23,786**	$	**3,531**	$	**245**	$	**537**	$	**266**	$	**28,365**
Operating income/(loss)		**14,671**		**(1,778)**		**23**		**59**		**(1,065)**		**11,910**

Desktop and Enterprise Software and Services Revenue:

In millions

Year Ended June 30		2000		2001		2002
Desktop Applications	$	9,013	$	9,580	$	**9,327**
Desktop Platforms		7,383		8,265		**9,276**
Desktop Software		16,396		17,845		**18,603**
Enterprise Software and Services		4,014		4,875		**5,183**
Total Desktop and Enterprise Software and Services	$	20,410	$	22,720	$	**23,786**

In fiscal 2002, Microsoft had four segments: Desktop and Enterprise Software and Services; Consumer Software, Services, and Devices; Consumer Commerce Investments; and Other. Desktop and Enterprise Software and Services operating segment includes Desktop Applications, Desktop Platforms, and Enterprise Software and Services. Desktop Applications include Microsoft Office; Microsoft Project; Visio; client access licenses for Windows NT Server and Windows 2000 Server, Exchange, and BackOffice; Microsoft Great Plains; and bCentral. Desktop Platforms include Windows XP Professional and Home, Windows 2000 Professional, Windows NT Workstation, Windows Millennium Edition (Windows Me), Windows 98, and other desktop operating systems. Enterprise Software and Services includes Server Platforms; Server Applications; developer tools and services; and Enterprise services. Consumer Software, Services, and Devices operating segment includes Xbox video game system, MSN Internet access, MSN network services, PC and online games, learning and productivity software, mobility, and embedded systems. Consumer Commerce Investments operating segment includes Expedia, Inc., the HomeAdvisor online real estate service, and the CarPoint online automotive service. Other primarily includes Hardware and Microsoft Press.

Segment information is presented in accordance with SFAS 131, *Disclosures about Segments of an Enterprise and Related Information.* This standard is based on a management approach, which requires segmentation based upon the Company's internal organization and disclosure of revenue and operating income based upon internal accounting methods. The Company's financial reporting systems present various data for management to run the business, including internal profit and loss statements (P&Ls) prepared on a basis not consistent with U.S. generally accepted accounting principles. Assets are not allocated to segments for internal reporting presentations.

Reconciling items for revenue include certain elements of unearned revenue and the treatment of certain channel inventory amounts and estimates. In addition to the reconciling items for revenue, reconciling items for operating income/(loss) include general and administrative expenses ($1.05 billion in 2000, $857 million in 2001, and $1.55 billion in 2002), certain research expenses ($141 million in 2000, $154 million in 2001, and $166 million in 2002), and other corporate level adjustments. The internal P&Ls use accelerated methods of depreciation and amortization. Additionally, losses on equity investees and minority interests are classified in operating income for internal reporting presentations.

Part II
Item 8

Revenue attributable to U.S. operations includes shipments to customers in the United States, licensing to OEMs and certain multinational organizations, and exports of finished goods, primarily to Asia, Latin America, and Canada. Revenue from U.S. operations totaled $15.7 billion, $17.8 billion, and $20.9 billion in 2000, 2001, and 2002. Revenue from outside the United States, excluding licensing to OEMs and certain multinational organizations and U.S. exports, totaled $7.3 billion, $7.5 billion, and $7.5 billion in 2000, 2001, and 2002. No single customer accounted for 10% or more of revenue in 2000, 2001, or 2002.

Long-lived assets (principally property and equipment) totaled $2.2 billion and $2.0 billion in the United States in 2001 and 2002 and $154 million and $220 million in other countries in 2001 and 2002.

NOTE 21   SUBSEQUENT EVENT

On July 11, 2002, Microsoft acquired Navision a/s as a result of the successful close of a tender offer. Microsoft purchased Navision's shares for approximately $1.45 billion in stock and cash. Navision is a provider of integrated business software solutions for small and medium-sized companies. The purchase price allocation is currently being developed for this acquisition.

QUARTERLY INFORMATION

In millions, except per share amounts (unaudited)

Quarter Ended		Sept. 30		Dec. 31		Mar. 31		June 30		Year
Fiscal 2000										
Revenue	$	5,384	$	6,112	$	5,656	$	5,804	$	22,956
Gross profit		4,672		5,356		4,904		5,022		19,954
Net income		2,191		2,436		2,385		2,409		9,421
Basic earnings per share		0.43		0.47		0.46		0.46		1.81
Diluted earnings per share		0.40		0.44		0.43		0.44		1.70
Fiscal 2001										
Revenue	$	5,766	$	6,550	$	6,403	$	6,577	$	25,296
Gross profit		4,941		5,686		5,504		5,710		21,841
Net income		2,206[1]		2,624		2,451		65[2]		7,346
Basic earnings per share		0.42[1]		0.49		0.46		0.01		1.38
Diluted earnings per share		0.40[1]		0.47		0.44		0.01		1.32
Fiscal 2002										
Revenue	$	6,126	$	7,741	$	7,245	$	7,253	$	28,365
Gross profit		5,242		6,197		5,850		5,885		23,174
Net income		1,283[3]		2,283		2,738[4]		1,525[5]		7,829
Basic earnings per share		0.24		0.42		0.51		0.28		1.45
Diluted earnings per share		0.23		0.41		0.49		0.28		1.41

(1) Includes an unfavorable cumulative effect of accounting change of $375 million or $0.07 per basic share and $0.06 per diluted share, reflecting the adoption of SFAS No. 133.
(2) Includes $3.92 billion (pre-tax) in impairments of certain investments.
(3) Includes $1.82 billion (pre-tax) in impairments of certain investments.
(4) Includes $1.25 billion (pre-tax) gain on the sale of Expedia, Inc. and $1.19 billion (pre-tax) in impairments of certain investments.
(5) Includes $1.19 billion (pre-tax) in impairments of certain investments.

INDEPENDENT AUDITORS' REPORT

To the Board of Directors and Stockholders of Microsoft Corporation:

We have audited the accompanying consolidated balance sheets of Microsoft Corporation and subsidiaries (the Company) as of June 30, 2001 and 2002, and the related consolidated statements of income, cash flows, and stockholders' equity for each of the three years in the period ended June 30, 2002. These financial statements are the responsibility of the Company's management. Our responsibility is to express an opinion on these financial statements based on our audits.

We conducted our audits in accordance with auditing standards generally accepted in the United States of America. Those standards require that we plan and perform the audit to obtain reasonable assurance about whether the financial statements are free of material misstatement. An audit includes examining, on a test basis, evidence supporting the amounts and disclosures in the financial statements. An audit also includes assessing the accounting principles used and significant estimates made by management, as well as evaluating the overall financial statement presentation. We believe that our audits provide a reasonable basis for our opinion.

In our opinion, such consolidated financial statements present fairly, in all material respects, the financial position of Microsoft Corporation and subsidiaries as of June 30, 2001 and 2002, and the results of their operations and their cash flows for each of the three years in the period ended June 30, 2002 in conformity with accounting principles generally accepted in the United States of America.

As described in Note 2 to the financial statements, the Company adopted Statement of Financial Accounting Standards No. 133, *Accounting for Derivative Instruments and Hedging Activities*, effective July 1, 2000, and Statement of Financial Accounting Standards No. 142, *Goodwill and Other Intangible Assets*, effective July 1, 2001.

/S/   DELOITTE & TOUCHE LLP

Deloitte & Touche LLP
Seattle, Washington
July 18, 2002

ITEM 9.   CHANGES IN AND DISAGREEMENTS WITH ACCOUNTANTS
ON ACCOUNTING AND FINANCIAL DISCLOSURES

None.

PART III

ITEM 10. DIRECTORS OF THE REGISTRANT

Information with respect to Directors may be found under the caption "Election of Directors and Management Information" of the Company's Proxy Statement for the Annual Meeting of Shareholders to be held November 5, 2002 (the "Proxy Statement"). Such information is incorporated herein by reference.

ITEM 11. EXECUTIVE COMPENSATION

The information in the Proxy Statement set forth under the captions "Information Regarding Executive Officer Compensation" and "Information Regarding the Board and its Committees" is incorporated herein by reference.

ITEM 12. SECURITY OWNERSHIP OF CERTAIN BENEFICIAL OWNERS AND MANAGEMENT AND RELATED STOCKHOLDER MATTERS

EQUITY COMPENSATION PLAN INFORMATION

In millions, except per share amounts

June 30, 2002 Plan category	(a) Number of securities to be issued upon exercise of outstanding options, warrants and rights	(b) Weighted-average exercise price of outstanding options, warrants and rights	(c) Number of securities remaining available for future issuance under equity compensation plans (excluding securities reflected in column (a))
Equity compensation plans approved by security holders	802	$ 53.75	600
Equity compensation plans not approved by security holders	–	–	–
Total	802	$ 53.75	600

The information set forth under the caption "Information Regarding Beneficial Ownership of Principal Shareholders, Directors, and Management" of the Proxy Statement is incorporated herein by reference.

ITEM 13. CERTAIN RELATIONSHIPS AND RELATED TRANSACTIONS

The information set forth under the captions "Certain Relationships and Related Transactions" of the Proxy Statement is incorporated herein by reference.

PART IV

ITEM 14.   EXHIBITS, FINANCIAL STATEMENT SCHEDULES, AND REPORTS ON FORM 8-K

(a) Financial Statements and Schedules

The financial statements are set forth under Item 8 of this report on Form 10-K. Financial statement schedules have been omitted since they are either not required, not applicable, or the information is otherwise included.

(b) Reports on Form 8-K

The Company filed no reports on Form 8-K during the quarter ended June 30, 2002.

(c) Exhibit Listing

Exhibit Number	Description
3.1	Restated Articles of Incorporation of Microsoft Corporation (1)
3.2	Bylaws of Microsoft Corporation
10.1	Microsoft Corporation 2001 Stock Plan (2)
10.2	Microsoft Corporation 1991 Stock Option Plan (3)
10.3	Microsoft Corporation 1981 Stock Option Plan (4)
10.4	Microsoft Corporation 1999 Stock Option Plan for Non-Employee Directors (5)
10.5	Microsoft Corporation Stock Option Plan for Consultants and Advisors
10.6	Microsoft Corporation 1997 Employee Stock Purchase Plan (6)
10.7	Microsoft Corporation Savings Plus Plan (7)
10.8	Trust Agreement dated June 1, 1993 between Microsoft Corporation and First Interstate Bank of Washington
10.9	Form of Indemnification Agreement
10.10	Resignation Agreement between Richard Belluzzo and Microsoft Corporation
21.	Subsidiaries of Registrant
23.	Independent Auditors' Consent
99.1	Certification Pursuant to 18 U.S.C. Section 1350, as Adopted Pursuant to Section 906 of the Sarbanes-Oxley Act of 2002
99.2	Certification Pursuant to 18 U.S.C. Section 1350, as Adopted Pursuant to Section 906 of the Sarbanes-Oxley Act of 2002

(1) Incorporated by reference to Annual Report on Form 10-K For The Fiscal Year Ended June 30, 1999.

(2) Incorporated by reference to Registration Statement 333-52-852 on Form S-8.

(3) Incorporated by reference to Annual Report on Form 10-K For The Fiscal Year Ended June 30, 1997.

(4) Incorporated by reference to Registration Statement 33-37623 on Form S-8.

(5) Incorporated by reference to Registration Statement 333-91755 on Form S-8.

(6) Incorporated by reference to Annual Report on Form 10-K For The Fiscal Year Ended June 30, 2001.

(7) Incorporated by reference to Annual Report on Form 10-K For The Fiscal Year Ended June 30, 2000.

SIGNATURES

Pursuant to the requirements of Section 13 or 15(d) of the Securities Exchange Act of 1934, the Registrant has duly caused this report to be signed on its behalf by the undersigned; thereunto duly authorized, in the City of Redmond, State of Washington, on September 5, 2002.

MICROSOFT CORPORATION

By /s/ JOHN G. CONNORS

John G. Connors
Senior Vice President; Chief Financial Officer

Pursuant to the requirements of the Securities Exchange Act of 1934, this report has been signed below by the following persons on behalf of Registrant and in the capacities indicated on September 5, 2002.

Signature	Title
/s/ WILLIAM H. GATES, III William H. Gates, III	Chairman of the Board of Directors and Chief Software Architect
/s/ STEVEN A. BALLMER Steven A. Ballmer	Chief Executive Officer
/s/ JAMES I. CASH, JR. James I. Cash, Jr.	Director
/s/ RAYMOND V. GILMARTIN Raymond V. Gilmartin	Director
/s/ ANN MCLAUGHLIN KOROLOGOS Ann McLaughlin Korologos	Director
/s/ DAVID F. MARQUARDT David F. Marquardt	Director
/s/ WM. G. REED, JR. Wm. G. Reed, Jr.	Director
/s/ JON A. SHIRLEY Jon A. Shirley	Director
/s/ JOHN G. CONNORS John G. Connors	Senior Vice President; Chief Financial Officer (Principal Financial and Accounting Officer)

CERTIFICATIONS

I, Steven A. Ballmer, certify that:

1. I have reviewed this annual report on Form 10-K of Microsoft Corporation;

2. Based on my knowledge, this annual report does not contain any untrue statement of a material fact or omit to state a material fact necessary to make the statements made, in light of the circumstances under which such statements were made, not misleading with respect to the period covered by this annual report; and

3. Based on my knowledge, the financial statements, and other financial information included in this annual report, fairly present in all material respects the financial condition, results of operations and cash flows of the registrant as of, and for, the periods presented in this annual report.

Date: September 5, 2002

/s/ STEVEN A. BALLMER
Steven A. Ballmer
Chief Executive Officer

I, John G. Connors, certify that:

1. I have reviewed this annual report on Form 10-K of Microsoft Corporation;

2. Based on my knowledge, this annual report does not contain any untrue statement of a material fact or omit to state a material fact necessary to make the statements made, in light of the circumstances under which such statements were made, not misleading with respect to the period covered by this annual report; and

3. Based on my knowledge, the financial statements, and other financial information included in this annual report, fairly present in all material respects the financial condition, results of operations and cash flows of the registrant as of, and for, the periods presented in this annual report.

Date: September 5, 2002

/s/ JOHN G. CONNORS
John G. Connors
Chief Financial Officer

WORLDWIDE MARKETING LOCATIONS*

WWW.MICROSOFT.COM/WORLDWIDE/

Argentina	www.microsoft.com/argentina/	Lebanon	www.microsoft.com/middleeast/
Australia	www.microsoft.com/australia/	Luxembourg	www.microsoft.com/Belux/
Austria	www.microsoft.at/	Malaysia	www.microsoft.com/malaysia/
Belgium	www.microsoft.com/Belux/	Mauritius	www.microsoft.com/africa/ioi/
Bolivia	www.microsoft.com/bolivia/	Mexico	www.microsoft.com/mexico/
Brazil	www.microsoft.com/brasil/	Morocco	www.microsoft.com/northafrica/Morocco/
Bulgaria	www.microsoft.com/bulgaria/	Namibia	www.microsoft.com/africa/southern/
Canada	www.microsoft.com/canada/	Netherlands	www.microsoft.com/netherlands/
Chile	www.microsoft.com/chile/	New Zealand	www.microsoft.com/nz/
China	www.microsoft.com/china/	Nigeria	www.microsoft.com/africa/nigeria/
Colombia	www.microsoft.com/colombia/	Norway	www.microsoft.com/norge/
Costa Rica	www.microsoft.com/costarica/	Pakistan	www.microsoft.com/asia/asiapacific/
Cote d'Ivoire	www.microsoft.com/africa/	Panama	www.microsoft.com/panama/
Croatia	www.microsoft.com/Croatia/	Peru	www.microsoft.com/peru/
Czech Republic	www.microsoft.com/cze/	Philippines	www.microsoft.com/philippines/
Denmark	www.microsoft.com/danmark/	Poland	www.microsoft.com/poland/
Dominican Republic	www.microsoft.com/dominicana/	Portugal	www.microsoft.com/portugal/
Ecuador	www.microsoft.com/ecuador/	Puerto Rico	www.microsoft.com/puertorico/
Egypt	www.microsoft.com/egypt/	Romania	www.microsoft.com/romania/
El Salvador	www.microsoft.com/elsalvador/	Russia	www.microsoft.com/rus/
Finland	www.microsoft.com/finland/	Saudi Arabia	www.microsoft.com/saudi/
France	www.microsoft.com/France/	Singapore	www.microsoft.com/singapore/
Germany	www.microsoft.com/germany/	Slovakia	www.microsoft.com/slovakia/
Greece	www.microsoft.com/hellas/	Slovenia	www.microsoft.com/slovenija/
Guatemala	www.microsoft.com/guatemala/	South Africa	www.microsoft.com/southafrica/
Hong Kong	www.microsoft.com/hk/	Spain	www.microsoft.com/spain/
Hungary	www.microsoft.com/hun/	Sweden	www.microsoft.com/sverige/
India	www.microsoft.com/india/	Switzerland	www.microsoft.com/switzerland/
Indonesia	www.microsoft.com/indonesia/	Taiwan	www.microsoft.com/taiwan/
Ireland	www.microsoft.com/ireland/	Thailand	www.microsoft.com/thailand/
Israel	www.microsoft.com/israel/	Tunisia	www.microsoft.com/northafrica/tunisia/
Italy	www.microsoft.com/italy/	Turkey	www.microsoft.com/turkiye/
Jamaica	www.microsoft.com/westindies/jamaica/	Ukraine	www.microsoft.com/rus/
Japan	www.microsoft.com/japan/	United Arab Emirates	www.microsoft.com/middleeast/
Jordan	www.microsoft.com/middleeast/	United Kingdom	www.microsoft.com/uk/
Kenya	www.microsoft.com/africa/east/	Uruguay	www.microsoft.com/uruguay/
Korea	www.microsoft.com/korea/	Venezuela	www.microsoft.com/venezuela/
Kuwait	www.microsoft.com/middleeast/	Vietnam	www.microsoft.com/vietnam/
Latvia	www.microsoft.com/latvija/		

* For a complete list of subsidiaries, joint ventures, and other legal entities, See the Exhibits to the Company's Form 10-K as Filed with the Securities and Exchange Commission

DIRECTORS AND OFFICERS OF MICROSOFT CORPORATION

DIRECTORS

William H. Gates, III
Chairman;
Chief Software Architect,
Microsoft Corporation

Steven A. Ballmer
Chief Executive Officer,
Microsoft Corporation

James I. Cash Jr.
James E. Robison Professor,
Harvard Business School;
Chairman, Harvard Business
School Publishing

Raymond V. Gilmartin
Chairman; President;
Chief Executive Officer,
Merck & Co., Inc.

Ann McLaughlin Korologos
Chairman Emeritus,
The Aspen Institute;
Senior Advisor, Benedetto,
Gartland & Co., Inc.

David F. Marquardt
General Partner,
August Capital

Wm. G. Reed Jr.
Chairman (retired),
Simpson Investment
Company

Jon A. Shirley
President;
Chief Operating
Officer (retired),
Microsoft Corporation

EXECUTIVE OFFICERS

William H. Gates, III
Chairman of the Board;
Chief Software Architect

Steven A. Ballmer
Chief Executive Officer

James E. Allchin
Group Vice President,
Platforms Group

Orlando Ayala
Group Vice President,
Worldwide Sales, Marketing,
and Services Group

Robert J. (Robbie) Bach
Senior Vice President,
Games Division

Douglas J. Burgum
Senior Vice President,
Business Solutions

David W. Cole
Senior Vice President,
MSN and Personal Services

John G. Connors
Senior Vice President;
Chief Financial Officer

Jean-Philippe Courtois
President, Europe,
Middle East & Africa

Jon Stephan DeVaan
Senior Vice President;
TV Division

Richard P. Emerson
Senior Vice President,
Corporate Development
and Strategy

Paul Flessner
Senior Vice President,
.NET Enterprise Servers

Robert J. (Bob) Herbold
Executive Vice President,
Chief Operating Officer
(Retired)

Kevin R. Johnson
Senior Vice President,
Microsoft Americas

Robert L. Muglia
Senior Vice President,
Enterprise Storage Division

Craig J. Mundie
Senior Vice President and
Chief Technology Officer,
Advanced Strategies
and Policy

Jeffrey S. Raikes
Group Vice President,
Productivity and
Business Services

Richard F. Rashid
Senior Vice President,
Research

Eric D. Rudder
Senior Vice President,
Developer and Platform
Evangelism

Steven J. Sinofsky
Senior Vice President,
Office

Bradford L. Smith
Senior Vice President
and General Counsel

Brian Valentine
Senior Vice President,
Windows

David Vaskevitch
Senior Vice President;
Chief Technical Officer,
Business Platforms

Deborah N. Willingham
Senior Vice President,
Human Resources

DIRECTORS AND OFFICERS OF MICROSOFT CORPORATION

OFFICERS

Brian E. Arbogast
Corporate Vice President,
.NET Core Services
Platform

Deborah A. Black
Corporate Vice President,
Platforms

Scott M. Boggs
Corporate Vice President,
Corporate Controller

Richard I. (Dick) Brass
Corporate Vice President,
Technology Development

Lisa E. Brummel
Corporate Vice President,
Home and Entertainment
Division

Thomas L. (Tom) Button
Corporate Vice President,
Developer Marketing and
Enterprise Tools

Brent Callinicos
Corporate Vice President,
Treasurer

Juha C. Christensen
Corporate Vice President,
Mobility Marketing

Rodrigo Costa
Corporate Vice President,
Original Equipment
Manufacturers

Kurt D. DelBene
Corporate Vice President,
Authoring & Collaborative
Services

Richard R. (Rick) Devenuti
Corporate Vice President,
Chief Information Officer

Gerri T. Elliott
Corporate Vice President,
Industry Solutions Group

Joseph E. Eschbach
Corporate Vice President,
Information Worker, Product
Mgmt Group

Edward (Ed) Fries
Corporate Vice President,
Game Content

Susumu (Sam) Furukawa
Vice President,
Advanced Strategy
& Policy, Japan

Grant N. W. George
Corporate Vice President,
Office Test and Operations

Ralf Harteneck
Corporate Vice President,
Communications and
Meeting Services

Kathleen C. Hebert
Corporate Vice President

Blake J. Irving
Corporate Vice President,
MSN Communications

Bruce A. Jaffe
Corporate Vice President,
MSN Business
Development

Theodore C. (Ted) Johnson
Corporate Vice President,
Business Tools

**Christopher R.
(Chris) Jones**
Corporate Vice President,
Windows Client

Norman B. Judah
Corporate Vice President,
Business Development

Richard J. (Rich) Kaplan
Corporate Vice President,
Content Delivery and
Development Group

Jawad Khaki
Corporate Vice President,
Windows Networking and
Communications

Pieter C. Knook
Corporate Vice President,
Network Service Providers
& Mobility Devices

Mitch L. Koch
Corporate Vice President,
Worldwide Retail Sales
& Marketing, Home &
Entertainment Division

**Theodore G. (Ted)
Kummert**
Corporate Vice President,
Subscription Software

Michel Lacombe
Chairman, Europe,
Middle East & Africa

Bruce A. Leak
Corporate Vice President

Kai-Fu Lee
Corporate Vice President,
Natural Interactive
Services Division

Andrew P. Lees
Corporate Vice President,
US Marketing & Sales

Lewis Levin
Corporate Vice President,
Business Intelligence
Applications

Dan'l Lewin
Corporate Vice President,
.NET Business
Development

Moshe Lichtman
Corporate Vice President,
MSTV

Dr. Daniel T. Ling
Corporate Vice President,
Research

Alexandra W. Loeb
Corporate Vice President,
Tablet PC

Gordon J. Mangione
Corporate Vice President,
SQL Server

**Michelle J. (Mich)
Mathews**
Corporate Vice President,
Marketing

Richard J. McAniff
Corporate Vice President,
Data and Developer
Services

Yusuf I. Mehdi
Corporate Vice President,
MSN

Lori J. Moore Ross
Corporate Vice President,
Product Support Services

Satya Nadella
Corporate Vice President,
Business Solutions
Applications

Michael L. (Mike) Nash
Corporate Vice President,
Security

Yuval Neeman
Corporate Vice President,
Enterprise Storage Division

William C. (Bill) Norman
Corporate Vice President,
Worldwide Operations

Umberto Paolucci
Corporate Vice President,
Europe, Middle East &
Africa, Corporate and
Government Strategy

Sanjay Parthasarathy
Corporate Vice President,
.NET Strategy

Peter D. Pathe
Corporate Vice President,
Structured Document
Services

William (Will) Poole
Corporate Vice President,
New Media Platforms
Division

Michael C. Rawding
Corporate Vice President,
Asia Pacific & Japan

Tami Reller
Corporate Vice President,
Business Solution

Peter Rinearson
Corporate Vice President,
Information Worker New
Markets

Stephen A. (Steve) Schiro
Corporate Vice President,
Retail Sales, South Pacific
& Americas Region,
Home & Entertainment
Division

Robert T. Short
Corporate Vice President,
Windows Core Technology

Michael J. (Mike) Sinneck
Corporate Vice President,
Worldwide Service

Rex C. Smith
Corporate Vice President,
MSN Operations

Mary E. Snapp
Vice President,
Deputy General Counsel,
Product Development
and Marketing

S. Somasegar
Corporate Vice President,
Windows Engineering
Solutions and Services

Lindsay Sparks
Corporate Vice President,
Worldwide Small &
Medium Business Group

Charles G. V. Stevens
Corporate Vice President,
Enterprise Storage Division

Kirill Tatarinov
Corporate Vice President,
Windows Systems
Management

David M. Thompson
Corporate Vice President,
Windows Server
Product Group

Michael J. Toutonghi
Corporate Vice President,
eHome

Jodi A. Uecker-Rust
Corporate Vice President,
Business Solutions Sales,
Marketing, and Services

William L. (Bill) Veghte
Corporate Vice President,
Windows Server Group

Bernard Vergnes
Chairman Emeritus,
Europe, Middle East
& Africa

Hank P. Vigil
Corporate Vice President,
Consumer Strategy and
Partnerships

Ben Waldman
Corporate Vice President

Rogers A. Weed
Corporate Vice President,
Windows Product
Management

a

account An accounting record in which the results of transactions are accumulated; shows increases, decreases, and a balance.

accounting A system for providing quantitative, financial information about economic entities that is useful for making sound economic decisions. Accounting is often called the "language of business" because it provides the means of recording and communicating business activities and the results of those activities.

accounting cycle The procedure for analyzing, recording, summarizing, and reporting the transactions of a business.

accounting equation An algebraic equation that expresses the relationship between assets (resources), liabilities (obligations), and owners' equity (net assets, or the residual interest in a business after all liabilities have been met): Assets = Liabilities + Owners' Equity.

accounting model The basic accounting assumptions, concepts, principles, and procedures that determine the manner of recording, measuring, and reporting a company's transactions.

accounting system The procedures and processes used by a business to analyze transactions, handle routine bookkeeping tasks, and structure information so it can be used to evaluate the performance and health of the business.

accounts receivable A current asset representing money due for services performed or merchandise sold on credit.

accounts receivable turnover A measure used to indicate how fast a company collects its receivables; computed by dividing sales by average accounts receivable.

accrual-basis accounting A system of accounting in which revenues and expenses are recorded as they are earned and incurred, not necessarily when cash is received or paid.

accumulated other comprehensive income Certain market-related gains and losses that are not included in the computation of net income; for example, foreign currency translation adjustments and unrealized gains or losses on investments.

activity-based costing (ABC) A method of attributing costs to products based on first assigning costs of resources to activities and then costs of activities to products or other cost objects.

activity-based management (ABM) The identification and use of costs drivers and performance measures to manage the costs, quality, and timeliness of activities.

adjusting entries Entries required at the end of each accounting period to recognize, on an accrual basis, revenues and expenses for the period and to report proper amounts for asset, liability, and owners' equity accounts.

aging accounts receivable The process of categorizing each account receivable by the number of days it has been outstanding.

allowance for bad debts A contra account, deducted from Accounts Receivable, that shows the estimated losses from uncollectible accounts.

allowance method The recording of estimated losses due to uncollectible accounts as expenses during the period in which the sales occurred.

American Institute of Certified Public Accountants (AICPA) The national organization of CPAs in the United States.

amortization The process of cost allocation that assigns the original cost of an intangible asset to the periods benefited.

annual report A document that summarizes the results of operations and financial status of a company for the past year and outlines plans for the future.

annuity A series of equal amounts to be received or paid at the end of equal time intervals.

appraisal costs Costs of quality that specifically relate to the effort of inspecting, testing, and sampling activities performed in order to identify and remove low-quality products and services from the system.

arm's-length transactions Business dealings between independent and rational parties who are looking out for their own interests.

articulation The interrelationships among the financial statements.

asset turnover A measure of company efficiency, computed by dividing sales by total assets.

asset turnover ratio An overall measure of how effectively assets are used during a period; computed by dividing revenue by average total assets.

assets Economic resources that are owned or controlled by a company.

assets-to-equity ratio A measure of the number of dollars of assets a company is able to acquire using each dollar of equity; calculated by dividing assets by equity.

audit committee Members of a company's board of directors who are responsible for dealing with the external and internal auditors.

audit report A report issued by an independent CPA that expresses an opinion about whether the financial statements fairly present a company's financial position, operating results, and cash flows in accordance with generally accepted accounting principles.

available-for-sale securities Debt and equity securities not classified as trading, held-to-maturity, or equity method securities.

average collection period A measure of the average number of days it takes to collect a credit sale; computed by dividing 365 days by the accounts receivable turnover.

average cost An inventory cost flow assumption whereby cost of goods sold and the cost of ending inventory are determined by using an average cost of all merchandise available for sale during the period.

bad debt An uncollectible account receivable.

bad debt expense An account that represents the portion of the current period's credit sales that are estimated to be uncollectible.

balance sheet (statement of financial position) The financial statement that reports a company's assets, liabilities, and owners' equity at a particular date.

Balanced Scorecard A new management model designed to link together performance measurers for financial, customer, internal process, and learning/growth perspectives that are unique to an organization's particular strategy.

bank reconciliation The process of systematically comparing the cash balance as reported by the bank with the cash balance on the company's books and explaining any differences.

basic earnings per share An earnings per share figure that divides net income by the number of shares of stock outstanding.

basket purchase The purchase of two or more assets acquired together at a single price.

batch-level activities Activities that take place in order to support a batch or production run, regardless of the size.

benchmarking A performance evaluation process used by companies to target areas for improvement by comparing the company's financial and operating performance against the performance of other companies or by comparing the performance of internal departments against each other.

board of directors Individuals elected by the stockholders to govern a corporation.

bond A contract between a borrower and a lender in which the borrower promises to pay a specified rate of interest for each period the bond is outstanding and repay the principal at the maturity date.

bond carrying value The face value of bonds minus the unamortized discount or plus the unamortized premium.

bond discount The difference between the face value and the sales price when bonds are sold below their face value.

bond indenture A contract between a bond issuer and a bond purchaser that specifies the terms of a bond.

bond maturity date The date at which a bond principal or face amount becomes payable.

bond premium The difference between the face value and the sales price when bonds are sold above their face value.

bonus Additional compensation, beyond the regular compensation, that is paid to employees if certain objectives are achieved.

book value The value of a company as measured by the amount of owners' equity; that is, assets less liabilities.

bookkeeping The preservation of a systematic, quantitative record of an activity.

break-even point The amount of sales at which total costs of the number of units sold equal total revenues; the point at which there is no profit or loss.

budget A quantitative expression of a plan of action that shows how a firm or an organization will acquire and use resources over some specified period of time.

budget committee A management group responsible for establishing budgeting policy and for coordinating the preparation of budgets.

budgetary slack The process of inflating a department's budget request for resource inputs (e.g., materials, labor, time, etc.) or deflating the department's budget commitment to output (products, services, etc.) so that the department manager can more easily achieve the budget.

budgeted product cost sheet A schedule of all of the product costs (i.e., the costs of direct materials, direct labor, and manufacturing overhead) used to create a single product.

budgeted service cost sheet A schedule of all of the service costs (i.e., the costs of supplies, wages and salaries, and overhead) used to provide a single service event.

business An organization operated with the objective of making a profit from the sale of goods or services.

business documents Records of transactions used as the basis for recording accounting entries; include invoices, check stubs, receipts, and similar business papers.

calendar year An entity's reporting year, covering 12 months and ending on December 31.

callable bonds Bonds for which the issuer reserves the right to pay the obligation before its maturity date.

capability costs Costs necessary to have the capability to produce a particular product or to provide a particular service. Capability costs are also known as the costs of product line activities.

capital The total amount of money or other resources owned or used to acquire future income or benefits.

capital budgeting Systematic planning for long-term investments in operating assets.

capital lease A leasing transaction that is recorded as a purchase by the lessee.

capital rationing Allocating limited resources among ranked acceptable investments.

capital stock The portion of a corporation's owners' equity contributed by owners in exchange for the shares of stock.

capitalized interest Interest that is recorded as part of the cost of a self-constructed asset.

cash Coins, currency, money orders, checks, and funds on deposit with financial institutions; the most liquid of assets.

cash budget A schedule of expected cash receipts and disbursements during the budget period.

cash dividend A cash distribution of earnings to stockholders.

cash equivalents Short-term, highly liquid investments that can easily be converted into cash.

cash flow adequacy ratio Cash from operations divided by expenditures for fixed asset additions and acquisitions of new businesses.

cash flow-to-net income ratio A ratio that reflects the extent to which accrual accounting assumptions and adjustments have been included in computing net income.

cash inflows Any current or expected revenues or savings directly associated with an investment.

cash outflows The initial cost and other expected outlays associated with an investment.

cash-basis accounting A system of accounting in which transactions are recorded and revenues and expenses are recognized only when cash is received or paid.

ceiling The maximum market amount at which inventory can be carried on the books; equal to net realizable value.

centralized company An organization in which top management makes most of the major decisions for the entire company rather than delegating decisions to managers at lower levels.

certified public accountant (CPA) A special designation given to an accountant who has passed a national uniform examination and has met other certifying requirements.

channel The distribution line that a product travels from the original manufacturer to the eventual end-user customer. The channel is typically composed of a manufacturer, a wholesaler, a retailer, and the end-user customer.

chart of accounts A systematic listing of all accounts used by a company.

classified balance sheet A balance sheet in which assets and liabilities are subdivided into current and long-term categories.

closing entries Entries that reduce all nominal, or temporary, accounts to a zero balance at the end of each accounting period, transferring their preclosing balances to a permanent balance sheet account.

common costs Manufacturing overhead costs, such as executive salaries or property taxes, that cannot be attributed to products. Costs of facility support activities are common costs.

common stock The most frequently issued class of stock; usually, it provides a voting right but is secondary to preferred stock in dividend and liquidation rights.

common-size financial statements Financial statements achieved by dividing all financial statement numbers by total sales for the year.

comparative financial statements Financial statements in which data for two or more years are shown together.

compound journal entry A journal entry that involves more than one debit or more than one credit or both.

compounding period The period of time for which interest is computed.

comprehensive income A measure of the overall change in a company's wealth during a period; consists of net income plus changes in wealth resulting from changes in investment values and exchange rates.

conglomerates A company comprised of a number of divisions with those divisions often operating in different industries.

consignment An arrangement whereby merchandise owned by one party, the consignor, is sold by another party, the consignee, usually on a commission basis.

consolidated financial statements Statements that report the combined operating results, financial position, and cash flows of two or more legally separate but affiliated companies as if they were one economic entity.

contingency Circumstances involving potential losses or gains that will not be resolved until some future event occurs.

contra account An account that is offset or deducted from another account.

contributed capital The portion of owners' equity contributed by investors (the owners) in exchange for shares of stock.

contribution margin The difference between total sales and variable costs; the portion of sales revenue available to cover fixed costs and provide a profit.

contribution margin ratio The percentage of net sales revenue left after variable costs are deducted; the contribution margin divided by net sales revenue.

control activities (procedures) Policies and procedures used by management to meet their objectives; generally divided into adequate segregation of duties, proper procedures for authorization of transactions and activities, adequate documents and records, physical control over assets and records, and independent checks on performance.

control environment The actions, policies, and procedures that reflect the overall attitudes of top management, the directors, and the owners about control and its importance to the entity.

controlling Implementing management plans and identifying how plans compare with actual performance.

conversion costs The costs of converting raw materials to finished products; include direct labor and manufacturing overhead costs.

convertible bonds Bonds that can be traded for, or converted to, other securities after a specified period of time.

convertible preferred stock Preferred stock that can be converted to common stock at a specified conversion rate.

corporation A legal entity chartered by a state; ownership is represented by transferable shares of stock.

cost behavior The way a cost is affected by changes in activity levels.

cost center An organizational unit in which a manager has control over and is held accountable for cost performance.

cost driver A factor that determines an activity cost. An activity can have more than one cost driver.

cost of capital The average cost of a firm's debt and equity capital; equals the rate of return that a company must earn in order to satisfy the demands of its owners and creditors.

cost of goods available for sale The cost of all merchandise available for sale during the period; equal to the sum of beginning inventory and net purchases.

Cost of Goods Manufactured schedule A schedule supporting the income statement that summarizes the total cost of goods manufactured and transferred out of the work-in-process inventory account during a period. These costs include direct materials, direct labor, and applied manufacturing overhead.

cost of goods sold The expenses incurred to purchase or manufacture the merchandise sold during a period.

cost principle The idea that transactions are recorded at their historical costs or exchange prices at the transaction date.

costs of quality (COQ) Costs spent to achieve high quality of products and services, as well as costs spent when products fail to have high quality. The four types of costs of quality are prevention costs, appraisal costs, internal failure costs, and external failure costs.

cost-volume-profit (C-V-P) analysis Techniques for determining how changes in revenues, costs, and level of activity affect the profitability of an organization.

coupon bonds Unregistered bonds for which owners receive periodic interest payments by clipping a coupon from the bond and sending it to the issuer as evidence of ownership.

credit An entry on the right side of a T-account.

critical resource factor The resource that limits operating capacity by its availability.

cross-subsidization A distortion of costs that occurs when costs of one product are erroneously assigned to another product.

cumulative-dividend preference The right of preferred stockholders to receive current dividends plus all dividends in arrears before common stockholders receive any dividends.

current assets Cash and other assets that can be easily converted to cash within a year.

current liabilities Liabilities expected to be satisfied within a year or the current operating cycle, whichever is longer.

current ratio A measure of the liquidity of a business; equal to current assets divided by current liabilities.

current-dividend preference The right of preferred stockholders to receive current dividends before common stockholders receive dividends.

curvilinear costs Variable costs that do not vary in direct proportion to changes in activity level but vary at decreasing or increasing rates due to economies of scale, productivity changes, and so on.

cycle time The total time a product spends moving through a particular process or cycle within the organization, such as the product design cycle, the production cycle, or the order and delivery cycle.

date of record The date selected by a corporation's board of directors on which the stockholders of record are identified as those who will receive dividends.

days in inventory Average number of days of use provided by the level of inventory maintained by the organization. This definition is closely related to the "inventory turnover" concept. Days in inventory is computed as number of days in the period being assessed divided by the inventory turnover. (See related definition and computation for *inventory turnover*.)

death spiral A series of management decisions based on bad information that results in reducing or removing activities or segments from the organization that are actually profitable.

debentures (unsecured bonds) Bonds for which no collateral has been pledged.

debit An entry on the left side of a T-account.

debt ratio A measure of leverage, computed by dividing total liabilities by total assets.

debt securities Financial instruments issued by a company that carry with them a promise of interest payments and the repayment of principal.

debt-to-equity ratio The number of dollars of borrowed funds for every dollar invested by owners; computed as total liabilities divided by total stockholders' equity.

decentralized company An organization in which managers at all levels have the authority to make decisions concerning the operations for which they are responsible.

declaration date The date on which a corporation's board of directors formally decides to pay a dividend to stockholders.

declining-balance depreciation method An accelerated depreciation method in which an asset's book

value is multiplied by a constant depreciation rate (such as double the straight-line percentage, in the case of double-declining-balance).

defined benefit plan A pension plan under which the employer defines the amount that retiring employees will receive and contributes enough to the pension fund to pay that amount.

defined contribution plan A pension plan under which the employer contributes a defined amount to the pension fund; after retirement, the employees receive the amount contributed plus whatever it has earned.

depletion The process of cost allocation that assigns the original cost of a natural resource to the periods benefited.

depreciation The process of cost allocation that assigns the original cost of plant and equipment to the periods benefited.

differential costs Future costs that change as a result of a decision; also called incremental or relevant costs.

diluted earnings per share An earnings per share figure that considers the effect on net income and shares outstanding of events that will likely occur in the future, such as the exercising of favorable stock options.

direct costs Costs that are specifically traceable to a unit of business or segment being analyzed.

direct labor Wages that are paid to those who physically work on direct materials to transform them into a finished product and are traceable to specific products.

direct labor budget A schedule of direct labor requirements for the budget period.

direct materials Materials that become part of the product and are traceable to it.

direct materials budget A schedule of direct materials to be used during the budget period and direct materials to be purchased during that period.

direct method A method of reporting net cash flows from operations that shows the major classes of cash receipts and payments for a period of time.

direct write-off method The recording of actual losses from uncollectible accounts as expenses during the period in which accounts receivable are determined to be uncollectible.

discounted cash flow methods Capital budgeting techniques that take into account the time value of money by comparing discounted cash flows.

disposable income Income left after withholdings and fixed expenses have been subtracted from gross salary; the amount left to cover variable expenditures.

dividend payment date The date on which a corporation pays dividends to its stockholders.

dividend payout ratio A measure of the percentage of earnings paid out in dividends; computed by dividing cash dividends by net income.

dividends Distributions to the owners (stockholders) of a corporation.

dividends in arrears Missed dividends for past years that preferred stockholders have a right to receive under the cumulative-dividend preference if and when dividends are declared.

double-entry accounting A system of recording transactions in a way that maintains the equality of the accounting equation.

DuPont framework A systematic approach for breaking down return on equity into three ratios: return on sales, asset turnover, and assets-to-equity ratio.

earnings (loss) per share (EPS) The amount of net income (earnings) related to each share of stock; computed by dividing net income by the number of shares of stock outstanding during the period.

economic order quantity (EOQ) A specific calculation used to determine the most cost-effective size of a purchase order. The EOQ balances the cost of placing an order against the costs of carrying inventory in the organization.

economic profit The difference between net operating profit and holding costs of inventory and other asset investments. Note that generally accepted accounting principles (GAAP) do not formally recognize opportunity costs such as holding costs.

Economic Value Analysis (EVA™) A commercialized performance measurement system that emphasizes the incremental profits an organization creates over and above the profit required to cover the costs of capital.

effective-interest amortization A method of systematically writing off a bond premium or discount that takes into consideration the time value of money and results in an equal interest rate being used for amortization for each period.

employee stock options Rights given to employees to purchase shares of stock of a company at a predetermined price.

entity An organizational unit (a person, partnership, or corporation) for which accounting records are kept and about which accounting reports are prepared.

environmental liabilities Obligations incurred because of damage done to the environment.

equity method A method used to account for an investment in the stock of another company when significant influence can be imposed (presumed to exist when 20 to 50% of the outstanding voting stock is owned).

equity securities (stock) Shares of ownership in a corporation that can change significantly in value and that provide for a return to investors in the form of dividends.

equivalent units of production A method used in a process costing system to measure the production output during a period. Equivalent units of production essentially measures the "work done" by the center or department in terms of units of output.

estimated manufacturing overhead Budgeted manufacturing overhead costs that are used to establish the predetermined overhead rate.

evaluating Analyzing results, rewarding performance, and identifying problems.

exception reports Reports that highlight variances from, or exceptions to, the budget.

expenses Costs incurred in the normal course of business to generate revenues.

external auditors Independent CPAs who are retained by organizations to perform audits of financial statements.

external failure costs Costs of quality that specifically relate to the costs that occur when low-quality products and services fail after production and delivery to customers.

extraordinary items Nonoperating gains and losses that are unusual in nature, infrequent in occurrence, and material in amount.

facility support activities Activities necessary to have a facility in place in order to participate in the development and production of products or services. However, these activities are not related to any particular line of products or services. Costs of facility support activities are often called common costs.

FIFO (first in, first out) An inventory cost flow assumption whereby the first goods purchased are assumed to be the first goods sold so that the ending inventory consists of the most recently purchased goods.

financial accounting The area of accounting concerned with reporting financial information to interested external parties.

Financial Accounting Standards Board (FASB) The private organization responsible for establishing the standards for financial accounting and reporting in the United States.

financial ratios Relationships between financial statement amounts.

financial statement analysis The examination of both the relationships among financial statement numbers and the trends in those numbers over time.

financial statements Reports such as the balance sheet, income statement, and statement of cash flows, which summarize the financial status and results of operations of a business entity.

financing activities Activities whereby cash is obtained from or repaid to owners and creditors.

finished goods Manufactured products ready for sale.

finished goods inventory Inventory that has completed the production process and is ready for sale to customers.

fiscal year An entity's reporting year, covering a 12-month accounting period.

fixed asset turnover The number of dollars in sales generated by each dollar of fixed assets; computed as sales divided by property, plant, and equipment.

fixed costs Costs that remain constant in total, regardless of activity level, at least over a certain range of activity.

fixed manufacturing overhead budget variance The difference between actual fixed manufacturing overhead incurred and the standard (or budgeted) fixed manufacturing overhead established at the beginning of the reporting period.

flexible budget A quantified plan that projects revenues and costs for varying levels of activity.

floor The minimum market amount at which inventory can be carried on the books; equal to net realizable value minus a normal profit.

FOB (free-on-board) destination A business term meaning that the seller of merchandise bears the shipping costs and maintains ownership until the merchandise is delivered to the buyer.

FOB (free-on-board) shipping point A business term meaning that the buyer of merchandise bears the shipping costs and acquires ownership at the point of shipment.

Foreign Corrupt Practices Act (FCPA) Legislation requiring any company that has publicly traded stock to maintain records that accurately and fairly represent the company's transactions; additionally, requires any publicly traded company to have an adequate system of internal accounting controls.

foreign currency transaction A sale in which the price is denominated in a currency other than the currency of the seller's home country.

franchise An entity that has been licensed to sell the product of a manufacturer or to offer a particular service in a given area.

GAAP oval A diagram that represents the flexibility a manager has, within GAAP, to report one earnings number from among many possibilities based on different methods and assumptions.

gains (losses) Money made or lost on activities outside the normal operation of a company.

generally accepted accounting principles (GAAP) Authoritative guidelines that define accounting practice at a particular time.

generally accepted auditing standards (GAAS) Auditing standards developed by the AICPA.

goal congruence The selection of goals for responsibility centers that are consistent, or congruent, with those of the company as a whole.

going concern assumption The idea that an accounting entity will have a continuing existence for the foreseeable future.

goodwill An intangible asset that exists when a business is valued at more than the fair market value of its net assets, usually due to strategic location, reputation, good customer relations, or similar factors; equal to the excess of the purchase price over the fair market value of the net assets purchased.

gross margin method A procedure for estimating the amount of ending inventory; the historical relationship of cost of goods sold to sales revenue is used in computing ending inventory.

gross profit (gross margin) The excess of net sales revenue over the cost of goods sold.

gross sales Total recorded sales before deducting any sales discounts or sales returns and allowances.

held-to-maturity security A debt security purchased by an investor with the intent of holding the security until it matures.

Hierarchical Product Cost Model A method of categorizing costs based on types of activities. Activity types include unit-level activities, batch-level activities, product line activities, and facility support activities.

high-low method A method of segregating the fixed and variable components of a mixed cost by analyzing the costs at the highest and the lowest activity levels within a relevant range.

historical cost The dollar amount originally exchanged in an arms'-length transaction; an amount assumed to reflect the fair market value of an item at the transaction date.

holding costs The financial opportunity costs that result from investing money in an asset such as inventory. Whatever income the money could generate in an alternative investment is the holding costs of the current investment.

hurdle rate The minimum rate of return that an investment must provide in order to be acceptable.

impairment A decline in the value of a long-term operating asset.

income smoothing The practice of carefully timing the recognition of revenues and expenses to even out the amount of reported earnings from one year to the next.

income statement (statement of earnings) The financial statement that repots the amount of net income earned by a company during a period.

independent checks Procedures for continual internal verification of other controls.

indirect costs Costs normally incurred for the benefit of several segments within the organization; sometimes called common costs or joint costs. **1-17**

indirect labor Labor that is necessary to a manufacturing or service business but is not directly related to the actual production of the manufactured or service product.

indirect materials Materials that are necessary to a manufacturing or service business but are not directly included in or are not a significant part of the actual product.

indirect method A method of reporting net cash flows from operations that involves converting accrual-basis net income to a cash basis.

industry volume variance The part of the sales volume variance that accounts for the impact on sales revenue of an actual total market size that is different from the expected size.

intangible assets Long-lived assets without physical substance that are used in business, such as licenses, patents, franchises, and goodwill.

interest The payment (cost) for the use of money.

internal auditors An independent group of experts (in controls, accounting, and operations) who monitor operating results and financial records, evaluate internal controls, assist with increasing the efficiency and effectiveness of operations, and detect fraud.

internal control structure Safeguards in the form of policies and procedures established to provide management with reasonable assurance that the objectives of an entity will be achieved.

internal earnings targets Financial goals established within a company.

internal failure costs Costs of quality that specifically relate to the expenses that occur when low-quality products and services fail before production and delivery to customers.

internal rate of return The "true" discount rate that will produce a net present value of zero when applied to the cash flows of investment inventory goods held for resale.

internal rate of return method A capital budgeting technique that uses discounted cash flows to find the "true" discount rate of an investment; this true rate produces a net present value of zero.

Internal Revenue Service (IRS) A government agency that prescribes the rules and regulations that govern the collection of tax revenues in the United States.

International Accounting Standards Board (IASB) The committee formed in 1973 to develop world-wide accounting standards.

interpolation A method of determining the internal rate of return when the factor for that rate lies between the factors given in the present value table.

inventory Goods held for resale.

inventory shrinkage The amount of inventory that is lost, stolen, or spoiled during a period; determined by comparing perpetual inventory records to the physical count of inventory.

inventory turnover The number of times the inventory in the organization "turns over" during a period of time. It is also often easier to think of inventory turnover as the number of times a dollar invested in inventory generates output. Output for raw materials inventory is measured by the cost of raw materials used in production. Output for work-in-process inventory is measured by cost of goods manufactured. Output for finished goods (or merchandise) inventory is measured by cost or goods sold. Inventory turnover is computed as total output for the period divided by average inventory value.

investing activities Activities associated with buying and selling long-term assets.

investment center An organizational unit in which a manager has control over and is held accountable for cost, revenue, and asset performance.

job order costing A method of product costing whereby each job, product, or batch of products is costed separately.

joint manufacturing process When one material input is used to produce more than one product.

joint product costs The costs that a firm incurs before the point at which the different products are separated for further processing or immediate sale.

journal An accounting record in which transactions are first entered; provides a chronological record of all business activities.

journal entry A recording of a transaction where debits equal credits; usually includes a date and an explanation of the transaction.

journalizing Recording transactions in a journal.

junk bonds Bonds issued by companies in weak financial condition with large amounts of debt already outstanding; these bonds yield high rates of return because of high risk.

just-in-time (JIT) A management philosophy that emphasizes removing all waste of effort, time, and inventory costs from the organization. One obvious result of JIT is the reduction or removal of needless inventory in a production process.

labor efficiency variance The extent to which the actual labor used varies from the standard quantity; computed by multiplying the difference between the actual quantity of labor used and the standard quantity of labor allowed by the standard rate.

labor rate variance The extent to which the actual labor rate varies from the standard rate for the quantity of labor used; computed by multiplying the difference between the actual rate and the standard rate by the quantity of labor used.

lagging indicators Measures that indicate the success of past business activities. Lagging indicators are related to the concept "outcome measures."

lead time Generally, the time interval between initiating a request and finally fulfilling the request.

leading indicators Measures that indicate the potential success of future business activities. Leading indicators are related to the concept "leading measures."

leading measures Measures that, if successfully implemented, will support desired performance in other business activities. Note that some leading measures can also serve as outcome measures.

lease A contract that specifies the terms under which the owner of an asset (the lessor) agrees to transfer the right to use the asset to another party (the lessee).

least squares method A method of segregating the fixed and variable portions of a mixed cost; the regression line, a line of averages, is statistically fitted through all cost points.

least-cost decision A decision to undertake the project with the smallest negative net present value.

ledger A book of accounts in which data from transactions recorded in journals are posted and thereby summarized.

lessee The party that is granted the right to use property under the terms of a lease.

lessor The owner of property that is leased (rented) to another party.

leverage Borrowing that allows a company to purchase more assets than its stockholders are able to pay for through their own investment.

liabilities Obligations to pay cash, transfer other assets, or provide services to someone else.

life cycle costing The process of measuring all costs involved in creating, producing, and using a product or service. Life cycle costing is not limited to costs incurred by the organization measuring these costs but also includes all costs incurred by the suppliers and the customers of the product or service.

LIFO (last in, first out) An inventory cost flow assumption whereby the last goods purchased are assumed to be the first goods sold so that the ending inventory consists of the first goods purchased.

limited liability The legal protection given stockholders whereby they are responsible for the debts and obligations of a corporation only to the extent of their capital contributions.

line of credit An arrangement whereby a bank agrees to loan an amount of money (up to a certain limit) on demand for short periods of time, usually less than a year.

liquidity A company's ability to pay its debts in the short run.

logistics The management process involved in obtaining, managing, and transporting inventory and other assets in organizations.

long-term assets Assets that a company needs in order to operate its business over an extended period of time.

long-term liabilities Debts or other obligations that will not be paid within one year.

long-term operating assets Assets expected to be held and used over the course of several years to facilitate operating activities.

lower-of-cost-or-market (LCM) rule A basis for valuing inventory at the lower of original cost or current market value.

management accounting The area of accounting concerned with providing internal financial reports to assist management in making decisions.

management by exception The strategy of focusing attention on significant deviations from a standard.

manufacturing organizations Organizations that focus on using labor and/or machinery to convert raw materials into marketable products.

manufacturing overhead All costs incurred in the manufacturing process other than direct materials and direct labor.

manufacturing overhead budget A schedule of production costs other than those for direct labor and direct materials.

manufacturing overhead rate The rate at which manufacturing overhead is assigned to products; equals estimated manufacturing overhead for the period divided by the number of units of the activity base being used.

Market Adjustment—Trading Securities An account used to track the difference between the historical cost and the market value of a company's portfolio of trading securities.

market rate (effective rate or yield rate) of interest The actual interest rate earned or paid on a bond investment.

market share The percentage share one company receives of the total sales revenue in the economy for a particular product or service.

market share variance The part of the sales volume variance that accounts for the difference between the actual market share of each product sold and the expected market share of each product sold.

market value The value of a company as measured by the number of shares of stock outstanding multiplied by the current market price of the stock; the current value of a business.

master budget A network of many separate schedules and budgets that together constitute the overall operating and financing plan for the coming period.

matching principle The concept that all costs and expenses incurred in generating revenues must be recognized in the same reporting period as the related revenues.

materials price variance The extent to which the actual price varies from the standard price for the quantity of materials purchased or used; computed by multiplying the difference between the actual and standard prices by the quantity purchased or used.

materials quantity variance The extent to which the actual quantity of materials varies from the standard quantity; computed by multiplying the difference between the actual quantity of materials used and the standard quantity of materials allowed by the standard price.

merchandising organizations Organizations that focus on procuring tangible products, then distributing them to customers. These customers may include individuals or other business organizations such as manufacturing organizations.

minority interest The amount of equity investment made by outside shareholders to consolidated subsidiaries that are not 100% owned by the parent.

mixed costs Costs that contain both variable and fixed cost components.

monetary measurement The idea that money, as the common medium of exchange, is the accounting unit of measurement, and that only economic activities measurable in monetary terms are included in the accounting model.

mortgage amortization schedule A schedule that shows the breakdown between interest and principal for each payment over the life of a mortgage.

mortgage payable A written promise to pay a stated amount of money at one or more specified future dates; a mortgage is secured by the pledging of certain assets, usually real estate, as collateral.

natural resources Assets that are physically consumed or waste away, such as oil, minerals, gravel, and timber.

net assets The owners' equity of a business; equal to total assets minus total liabilities.

net income (net loss) An overall measure of the performance of a company; equal to revenues minus expenses for the period.

net operating profit The difference between normal business sales and normal business expenses.

net present value The difference between the present values of an investment's expected cash inflows and outflows.

net present value method A capital budgeting technique that uses discounted cash flows to compare the present values of an investment's expected cash inflows and outflows.

net purchases The net cost of inventory purchased during a period, after adding the cost of freight in and subtracting returns and discounts.

net realizable value The selling price of an item less reasonable selling costs.

net realizable value of accounts receivable The net amount that would be received if all receivables considered collectible were collected; equal to total accounts receivable less the allowance for bad debts.

net sales Gross sales less sales discounts and sales returns and allowances.

nominal accounts Accounts that are closed to a zero balance at the end of each accounting period; temporary accounts generally appearing on the income statement.

noncash items Items included in the determination of net income on an accrual basis that do not affect cash; for example, depreciation and amortization.

noncash transactions Investing and financing activities that do not affect cash; if significant, they are disclosed below the statement of cash flows or in the notes to the financial statements.

nonprofit organization An entity without a profit objective, oriented toward providing services efficiently and effectively.

non-value-added activities Unnecessary activities in a production or service process that customers typically do not see or care about and for which they are unwilling to pay.

notes to the financial statements Explanatory information considered an integral part of the financial statements.

NSF (not sufficient funds) check A check that is not honored by a bank because of insufficient cash in the check writer's account.

number of days' purchases in accounts payable A measure of how well operating cash flow is being managed; computed by dividing total inventory purchases by average accounts payable and then dividing 365 days by the result.

number of days' sales in inventory An alternative measure of how well inventory is being managed; computed by dividing 365 days by the inventory turnover ratio.

operating activities Activities that are part of the day-to-day business of a company.

operating lease A simple rental agreement.

operating leverage The extent to which fixed costs are part of a company's cost structure; the higher the proportion of fixed costs to variable costs, the faster income increases or decreases with changes in sales volume.

operational budgeting Managerial planning decisions regarding current operations and those of the immediate future (typically one year or less) that are characterized by regularity and frequency.

opportunity costs The benefits lost or forfeited as a result of selecting one alternative course of action over another.

organizational structure Lines of authority and responsibility.

other revenues and expenses Items incurred or earned from activities that are outside of, or peripheral to, the normal operations of a firm.

outcome measures Measures of desired outcome performance in activities critical to an organization's strategic goals. Note that some outcome measures are also leading measures to support desired performance in other business activities.

out-of-pocket costs Costs that require an outlay of cash or other resources.

overapplied manufacturing overhead The excess of applied manufacturing overhead (based on a predetermined application rate) over the actual manufacturing overhead costs for a period.

owners' equity The ownership interest in the net assets of an entity; equals total assets minus total liabilities.

par value A nominal value assigned to and printed on the face of each share of a corporation's stock.

participative budgeting A bottom-up approach to budgeting where each division manager prepares a budget request for his or her segment.

partnership An association of two or more individuals or organizations to carry on economic activity.

patent An exclusive right granted for 20 years by the federal government to manufacture and sell an invention.

payback method A capital budgeting technique that determines the amount of time it takes the net cash inflows of an investment to repay the investment cost.

pension An agreement between an employer and employees that provides for benefits upon retirement.

performance measures A general term used to describe all measures designed to capture information about performance related to a particular activity or process.

period costs Costs not directly related to a product, service, or asset. These costs are charged as expenses to the income statement in the period in which they are incurred.

periodic inventory system A system of accounting for inventory in which cost of goods sold is determined and inventory is adjusted at the end of the accounting period, not when merchandise is purchased or sold.

perpetual inventory system A system of accounting for inventory in which detailed records of the number of units and the cost of each purchase and sales transaction are prepared throughout the accounting period.

per-unit contribution margin The excess of the sales price of one unit over its variable costs.

physical safeguards Physical precautions used to protect assets and records, such as locks on doors, fireproof vaults, password verification, and security guards.

planning Outlining the activities that need to be performed for an organization to achieve its objectives.

post-closing trial balance A listing of all real account balances after the closing process has been completed; provides a means of testing whether total debits equal total credits for all real accounts prior to beginning a new accounting cycle.

postemployment benefits Benefits paid to employees who have been laid off or terminated.

posting The process of transforming amounts from the journal to the ledger.

predetermined overhead rate A rate at which estimated manufacturing overhead costs are assigned to products throughout the year; equals total estimated manufacturing overhead costs divided by a suitable allocation base, such as number of units produced, direct labor hours, direct materials used, or direct labor costs.

preferred stock A class of stock that usually provides dividend and liquidation preferences over common stock.

prepaid expenses Payments made in advance for items normally charged to expense.

present value of $1 The value today of $1 to be received or paid at some future date, given a specified interest rate.

present value of an annuity The value today of a series of equally spaced, equal-amount payments to be made or received in the future given a specified interest rate.

prevention costs Costs of quality that specifically relate to the effort to ensure that processes are performed correctly the first time and that products and services meet customers' expectations.

price-earnings ratio A measure of growth potential, earnings stability, and management capabilities; computed by dividing market value of a company by net income.

primary financial statements The balance sheet, income statement, and statement of cash flows, used by external groups to assess a company's economic standing.

prime costs The direct costs that are "primarily seen" in the product (i.e., direct materials and direct labor).

principal (face value or maturity value) The amount that will be paid on a bond at the maturity date.

prior-period adjustments Adjustments made directly to Retained Earnings in order to correct errors in the financial statements of prior periods.

process costing A method of product costing whereby costs are accumulated by process or work centers and averaged over all products manufactured in a center or department during a particular production period. There are two methods of process costing: The FIFO method separately tracks the costs of beginning work-in-process units and the costs of units started in the current production period. The weighted-average method (not discussed in this text) averages together the costs of beginning work-in-process units and the costs of units started in the current production period.

product costs Costs associated with products or services offered.

product line activities Activities that take place in order to support a product line, regardless of the number of batches or individual units actually produced. Costs of product line activities are also known as capability costs.

production budget A schedule of production requirements for the budget period.

production cost report A document that compiles all the costs of a manufacturing center for a particular production period. The information on this report is used to control and evaluate production costs, as well as transfer costs and units of output from one manufacturing center to another.

production prioritizing Management's continual evaluation of the profitability of the various product lines and divisions within an organization so that products or divisions that are performing below expectations can be analyzed to identify problems and potential solutions.

profit center An organizational unit in which a manager has control over and is held accountable for both cost and revenue performance.

profit graph A graph that shows how profits vary with changes in volume.

profit margin (operating performance) ratio An overall measure of the profitability of operations during a period; computed by dividing net income by revenue.

profitability index The present value of net cash inflows divided by the cost of an investment.

property, plant, and equipment Tangible, long-lived assets acquired for use in business operations; include land, buildings, machinery, equipment, and furniture.

proprietorship A business owned by one person.

prospectus A report provided to potential investors that represents a company's financial statements and explains its business plan, sources of financing, and significant risks.

Public Company Accounting Oversight Board (PCAOB) Board of five fulltime members established by the Sarbanes-Oxley Act to oversee the accounting and auditing profession.

purchases budget A schedule of projected purchases over the budget period.

ranking The ordering of acceptable investment alternatives from most to least desirable.

raw materials Materials purchased for use in manufacturing products.

raw materials inventory The inventory of raw materials that have not yet begun the production process.

real accounts Accounts that are not closed to a zero balance at the end of each accounting period; permanent accounts appearing on the balance sheet.

realized gains and losses Gains and losses resulting from the sale of securities in an arm's-length transaction.

receivables Claims for money, goods, or services.

registered bonds Bonds for which the names and addresses of the bondholders are kept on file by the issuing company.

regression line On a scattergraph, the straight line that most closely expresses the relationship between the variables.

relevant range The range of operating level, or volume of activity, over which the relationship between total costs (variable plus fixed) and activity level is approximately linear.

reorder point The point at which the inventory level in the organization drops low enough to trigger a new purchase order.

residual income The amount of net income earned above a specified minimum rate of return on assets; used to evaluate investment centers.

responsibility accounting A system of evaluating performance; managers are held accountable for the costs, revenues, assets, or other elements over which they have control.

responsibility center An organizational unit in which a manager has control over and is held accountable for performance.

retailers Second-tier merchants who typically purchase products from wholesalers to distribute to end-user customers. Many large retailers, however, often bypass wholesalers to purchase products directly from the original manufacturers.

retained earnings The amount of accumulated earnings of the business that have not been distributed to owners.

return on equity A measure of the amount of profit earned per dollar of investment, computed by dividing net income by equity.

return on investment (ROI) A measure of operating performance and efficiency in utilizing assets; computed in its simplest form by dividing net income by average total assets. This measure is also known as ROA (return on assets).

return on sales A measure of the amount of profit earned per dollar of sales, computed by dividing net income by sales.

return on sales revenue A measure of operating performance; computed by dividing net income by total sales revenue. Similar to profit margin.

revenue Increase in a company's resources from the sale of goods or services.

revenue budget A service entity's budget that identifies how much revenue (and often cash) will be generated during a period.

revenue recognition The process of recording revenue in the accounting records; occurs after (1) the work has been substantially completed and (2) cash collection is reasonably assured.

revenue recognition principle The idea that revenues should be recorded when (1) the earnings process has been substantially completed and (2) cash has either been collected or collectibility is reasonably assured.

robust quality The capability of a product to perform according to customer expectations regardless of surroundings and circumstances.

safety stock The minimal level of inventory required to ensure against the organization running out of inventory in the case of unforeseen problems in receiving its next purchase order.

sales budget A schedule of projected sales over the budget period.

sales discount A reduction in the selling price that is allowed if payment is received within a specified period.

sales mix The relative proportion of total units sold (or total sales dollars) that is represented by each of a company's products.

sales price variance The difference between the actual price and expected or standard price multiplied by the actual quantity sold; measures that part of the variance between expected and actual sales revenue that is due to differences between expected and actual prices of goods.

sales returns and allowances A contra-revenue account in which the return of, or allowance for reduction in the price of, merchandise previously sold is recorded.

sales tax payable Money collected from customers for sales taxes that must be remitted to local governments and other taxing authorities.

sales volume variance The difference between the actual quantity and the expected quantity sold multiplied by the expected or standard price; measures that part of the variance between expected and actual sales revenue that is due to the difference between expected and actual volume of goods sold.

salvage value The amount expected to be received when an asset is sold at the end of its useful life.

Sarbanes-Oxley Act A law passed by Congress in 2002 that gives the SEC significant oversight responsibility and control over companies issuing financial statements and their external auditors. The Act creates a Public Company Accounting Oversight Board with broad powers and authority to regulate the public accounting profession.

scattergraph (visual-fit) method A method of segregating the fixed and variable components of a mixed cost by plotting on a graph total costs at several activity levels and drawing a regression line through the points.

screening Determining whether a capital investment meets a minimum standard of financial acceptability.

secured bonds Bonds for which assets have been pledged in order to guarantee repayment.

Securities and Exchange Commission (SEC) The government body responsible for regulating the financial reporting practices of most publicly owned corporations in connection with the buying and selling of stocks and bonds.

segment Any part of an organization requiring separate reports for evaluation by management.

segment margins The difference between segment revenue and direct segment costs; a measure of the segment's contribution to cover indirect fixed costs and provide profits.

segment-margin income statement An income statement that identifies costs directly chargeable to a segment and further divides them into variable and fixed cost behavior patterns.

segment-margin ratios The segment margin divided by the segment's net sales revenue; a measure of the efficiency of the segment's operating performance and, therefore, of its profitability.

segregation of duties A strategy to provide an internal check on performance through separation of authorization of transactions from custody of related assets, separation of operational responsibilities from record-keeping responsibilities, and separation of custody of assets from accounting personnel.

selling and administrative expense budget A schedule of all nonproduction spending expected to occur during the budget period.

sensitivity analysis A method of assessing the reasonableness of a decision that was based upon estimates; involves calculating how far reality can differ from an estimate without invalidating the decision.

separate entity concept The idea that the activities of an entity are to be separated from those of the individual owners.

serial bonds Bonds that mature in a series of installments as specified future dates.

service organizations Organizations that focus on delivery of marketable services, such as legal advice or education, to individuals or other organizations.

service overhead budget The budget, prepared by service entities, that identifies projected costs associated with providing the service.

six sigma quality A measure of quality based on statistical analysis. Products or services with six sigma quality have no more than 3.4 defects per million opportunities (e.g., parts or events).

Social Security (FICA) taxes Federal Insurance Distributions Act taxes imposed on the employee and the employer; used mainly to provide retirement benefits.

special order An order that may be priced below the normal selling price in order to utilize excess capacity and thereby contribute to company profits.

specific identification A method of valuing inventory and determining cost of goods sold whereby the actual costs of specific inventory items are assigned to them.

standard cost cards An itemization of the components of a product's standard cost.

standard cost system A cost-accumulation system in which standard costs are used as product costs instead of actual costs. The standard costs are then adjusted to actual costs when financial reports are created. This adjustment creates variances that are reported to management.

stated rate of interest The rate of interest printed on the bond.

statement of cash flows The financial statement that shows an entity's cash inflows (receipts) and outflows (payments) during a period of time.

statement of comprehensive income A statement outlining the changes in accumulated comprehensive income that arose during the period.

statement of retained earnings A report that shows the changes in the retained earnings account during a period of time.

statement of stockholders' equity A financial statement that reports all changes in stockholders' equity.

static budget A quantified plan that projects revenues and costs for only one level of activity.

statistical process control (SPC) A statistical technique for identifying and measuring the quality status of a process by evaluating its output to determine if serious problems exist in the process.

stepped costs Costs that change in total in a stair-step fashion (in large amounts) with changes in volume of activity.

stock dividend A pro rata distribution of additional shares of stock to stockholders.

stock split The replacement of outstanding shares of stock with a greater number of new shares.

stockholders (shareholders) The owners of a corporation.

stockholders' equity The owners' equity section of a corporate balance sheet.

straight-line amortization A method of systematically writing off a bond discount or premium in equal amounts each period until maturity.

straight-line depreciation method The depreciation method in which the cost of an asset is allocated equally over the periods of an asset's estimated useful life.

strategic planning Broad, long-range planning usually conducted by top management.

sum-of-the years' digits (SYD) depreciation method The accelerated depreciation method in which a constant balance (cost minus salvage value) is multiplied by a declining depreciation rate.

sunk costs Costs, such as depreciation, that are past costs and do not change as a result of a future decision.

supplies budget The budget, prepared by service entities, that identifies projected supplies expenses over the budget period.

T-account A simplified depiction of an account in the form of a letter T.

Taguchi quality loss function A method developed by Genichi Taguchi for estimating the actual size of all external failure costs, particularly the opportunity costs of lost customer sales that result from dissatisfied customers.

target income A profit level desired by management.

term bonds Bonds that mature in one single sum at a specified future date.

theory of constraints (TOC) A management philosophy that focuses on constraint resources and holds that they should operate at full capacity.

time value of money The concept that a dollar received now is worth more than a dollar received far in the future.

time-period concept The idea that the life of a business is divided into distinct and relatively short time periods so that accounting information can be timely.

times interest earned A measure of a borrower's ability to make required interest payments; computed as income before interest and taxes divided by annual interest expense.

total cost The total variable and fixed costs incurred in making a product or providing a service.

total quality management (TQM) A management philosophy focused on increasing profitability by improving the quality of products and processes and increasing customer satisfaction, while promoting the well-being and growth of employees.

trading securities Debt and equity securities purchased with the intent of selling them should the need for cash arise or to realize short-term gains.

transactions Exchange of goods or services between entities (whether individuals, businesses, or other organizations), as well as other events having an economic impact on a business.

treasury stock Issued stock that has subsequently been reacquired by the corporation.

trial balance A listing of all account balances; provides a means of testing whether total debits equal total credits for all accounts.

unadjusted rate of return method A capital budgeting technique in which a rate of return is calculated by dividing the increase in the average annual net income a project will generate by the initial investment cost.

underapplied manufacturing overhead The excess of actual manufacturing overhead costs over the applied overhead costs for a period (based on a predetermined application rate).

unearned revenues Cash amounts received before they have been earned.

unit-based costing (UBC) The traditional method of allocating manufacturing overhead using an approach that is essentially based on the number of units produced.

unit-level activities Activities that take place each time a unit of product is produced.

units-of-production method The depreciation method in which the cost of an asset is allocated to each period on the basis of the productive output or use of the asset during the period.

unrealized gains and losses Gains and losses resulting from changes in the value of securities that are still being held.

unrecorded liabilities Expenses incurred during a period that have not been recorded by the end of that period.

unrecorded receivables Revenues earned during a period that have not been recorded by the end of that period.

value-added activities Necessary activities in a production or service process that customers identify as valuable and for which they are willing to pay.

variable cost rate The change in cost divided by the change in activity; the slope of the regression line.

variable costs Costs that change in total in direct proportion to changes in activity level.

variable manufacturing overhead efficiency variance The difference between the standard variable manufacturing overhead for the actual activity level and standard variable manufacturing overhead for the standard activity level allowed. This variance effectively measures the efficiency of the underlying activity used to assign variable manufacturing overhead costs; it does not measure the efficiency of how variable manufacturing overhead costs are used.

variable manufacturing overhead spending variance The difference between actual variable manufacturing overhead incurred and the amount that should have been incurred based on the actual activity used to assign overhead costs to production.

variance Any deviation from standard.

venture capital firm A company that provides needed cash to companies in return for an ownership interest.

volume variance The difference between actual production output and the expected (or budgeted) production output established at the beginning of the reporting period. This difference is then converted into a dollar number by multiplying it by the standard fixed manufacturing overhead costs per unit.

wages and salaries budget The budget, prepared by service entities, that identifies projected labor costs involved directly in providing the service over the budget period.

wholesalers Top-tier merchants who typically deal directly with the original manufacturers to distribute products to retailers.

work in process Partially completed units in production.

work sheet A tool used by accountants to facilitate the preparation of financial statements.

work-in-process inventory Inventory that is partly completed in the production process, but not yet ready for sale to customers.

zero-coupon bonds Bonds issued with no promise of interest payments; only a single payment will be made.

CHAPTER 1

Not Applicable

CHAPTER 2

Exercises

2-2	(c) Owners' equity = $32,000
2-4	Revenues = $91,500
2-6	12/31/06 Owners' equity = $313,000
2-8	Income taxes = $73,380
2-10	(1) Net income = $380,000
2-12	EPS = $9.07
2-14	(b) OA
2-16	N/A
2-18	N/A

Problems

2-2	(1) Total assets = $17,525
2-4	(1) Net income for 2006 = $21,000
2-6	(5) Net income = $74,750
2-8	Net increase in cash = $30,000
2-10	(1) Net income = $22,270
2-12	(2) Total assets = $463,650

CHAPTER 3

Exercises

3-2	N/A
3-4	(2) OE—R
3-6	(3) Credit to Cash = $49,100
3-8	7/14 Debit to Insurance Expense = $7,500
3-10	(1) Debit to Compensation Expense = $105,000
3-12	N/A
3-14	Retained Earnings = $48,000
3-16	(3) Revenues for 2006 = $120,000

Problems

3-2	(2) Cash balance = $96,700
3-4	(2) Cost of goods sold balance = $25,000
3-6	(3) Net loss = ($300)
3-8	Total debits = $647,000
3-10	(4) EPS = $1.84

CHAPTER 4

Exercises

4-2	(1) (b) Net income = $13,640
4-4	(2) Unrecorded receivable
4-6	(4) Debit to Cash = $1,900
4-8	(1) Debit to Unearned Subscription Revenue = $1,400
4-10	(5) Debit to Programming Expense = $800
4-12	(4) No entry
4-14	(1) $6,000
4-16	N/A
4-18	N/A
4-20	(2) Retained Earnings = $97,400
4-22	(1) Credit to Unearned Rent Revenue = $3,250

Problems

4-2	(d) Credit to Rent Revenue = $48,600
4-4	(1) Wages expense = $30,000
4-6	N/A
4-8	(1) Credit to Retained Earnings = $31,300
4-10	(1) Total assets = $820,000
4-12	(2) Ending Cash balance = $33,000

CHAPTER 5

Exercises

5-2	(f) Total liabilities = $120,000
5-4	2006 Income tax expense as percentage of sales = 5.6%
5-6	2006 Total assets as percentage of sales = 23.6%
5-8	(1) Cost of goods sold = $127,500
5-10	2006 Return on sales = 5.0%
5-12	Question's ROE = 8.2%
5-14	Profit margin = 58%
5-16	Retail jewelry stores' return on assets = 7.6%
5-18	2006 Cash flow-to-net income ratio = 0.80

Problems

5-2	(1) Current ratio = 1.93
5-4	(1) 2006 Operating income as percentage of sales = 6%
5-6	(1) 2006 Total assets as a percentage of sales = 40.0%
5-8	(2) 2006 Asset turnover = 2.50
5-10	(1) (b) 2006 Debt ratio = 38.6%

CHAPTER 6

Exercises

6-2	Total assets = $7,801,300
6-4	N/A
6-6	N/A
6-8	N/A
6-10	N/A
6-12	N/A
6-14	N/A

*Note: Check figures are provided for even-numbered exercises and problems, where applicable.

CHAPTER 7

Exercises

7-2   N/A
7-4   N/A
7-6   6/30 Debit to Sales Discounts = $400
7-8   (1) Bad debt expense = $7,000
7-10   (2) Ending Accounts Receivable = $1,340,000
7-12   (3) Net Accounts Receivable = $149,010
7-14   2006 Debit to Bad Debt Expense = $70,000
7-16   (1) Boulder, Inc. average collection period for Year 3 = 118 days
7-18   N/A
7-20   (2) Debit to Estimated Liability for Service = $890
7-22   (2) Debit to Miscellaneous Expenses = $50
7-24   (1) 2.5 billion Vietnamese dong

Problems

7-2   N/A
7-4   N/A
7-6   (2) (a) Net sales = $1,713,000
7-8   (2) Debit to Bad Debt Expense = $63,500
7-10   (2) Debit to Bad Debt Expense = $46,000
7-12   N/A
7-14   (1) Suspected stolen = $28,453

CHAPTER 8

Exercises

8-2   6/30 Debit to Sales Returns = $16,000
8-4   Debit to Inventory Shrinkage = $28,000
8-6   Debit to Cost of Goods Sold = $244,000
8-8   Carter Co. Cost of Goods Sold = $43,100
8-10   Credit to Inventory = $12.25
8-12   (2) LIFO
8-14   (b) Ending inventory LIFO = $55,000
8-16   (1) 96 days
8-18   1(a) $24,000
8-20   (1) Oak = $3,000
8-22   Gross margin = $31,955

Problems

8-2   N/A
8-4   (10) Gross margin = $675
8-6   (2) Ending inventory LIFO = $39,140
8-8   (1) Net purchases = $79,600
8-10   (1) 2006 Correct gross margin = $14,700
8-12   (1) (a) Gross margin = $9,336

CHAPTER 9

Exercises

9-2   (2) Credit to Bonus Payable = $27,030
9-4   N/A
9-6   (2) Pension Expense = $40,000
9-8   (2) Debit to Property Tax Expense = $7,650
9-10   (2) Income Tax Expense = $200,000
9-12   N/A
9-14   Gross margin = $124,938

Problems

9-2   (2) Cash paid to employees = $15,193
9-4   (1) Pension expense = $554
9-6   (3) 2006 Deferred tax liability = $0
9-8   (10) Net sales revenue = $35,000

CHAPTER 10

Exercises

10-2   (1) Debit to Machine = $28,213
10-4   (1) Credit to Cash = $230,000
10-6   Building = $654,800
10-8   (1) (b) 2006 Depreciation expense = $3,450
10-10 (1) Credit to Cash = $47,100
10-12 Credit to Land = $160,000
10-14 (1) Credit to Gain on Sale of Machine = $5,000
10-16 (2) Credit to Patents = $12,500
10-18 (1) Fixed asset turnover = 2.05
10-20 (1) Total cost = $12,350
10-22 (2) 2006 = $8,613
10-24 (4) Credit to Accumulated Depletion, Coal Mine = $100,000

Problems

10-2   N/A
10-4   (3) 1/2 Debit to Leased Computer = $238,820
10-6   (2) Alternative B = $42,150 per year
10-8   (2) Debit to Equipment = $45,000
10-10 (1) Credit to Cash = $114,000
10-12 (3) Debit to Depletion Expense = $230,000
10-14 Debit to Goodwill = $30,000
10-16 (1) Fixed asset turnover = 3.08
10-18 (3) Depreciation = $50,400
10-20 (2) 2006 Depreciation expense = $5,911
10-22 (3) Uranium book value = $24,000

CHAPTER 11

Exercises

11-2 (4) $10,997
11-4 (1) Payment = $75,481
11-6 12/31/06 Credit to Cash = $1,250
11-8 (2) Total interest paid = $17,071
11-10 (2) Debit to Rent Expense = $4,141
11-12 Total issuance price = $79,512
11-14 (3) 3/1 Debit to Bond Interest Expense = $4,200
11-16 (1) Debt ratio = 55.6%
11-18 (1) (b) Debit to Premium on Bonds = $100
11-20 (4) Bonds Payable Carrying Value = $51,772

Problems

11-2 (2) (a) $32,210
11-4 1/1/06 Debit to Interest Payable = $1,295
11-6 (2) 12/31/06 Debit to Interest Expense = $3,496
11-8 (2) Debit to Leased Starship = $270,262
11-10 (4) 10/1/09 Credit to Gain on Bond Retirement = $5,000
11-12 Total current liabilities = $153,800
11-14 (1) Current ratio = 1.6
11-16 (2) (a) Credit to Discount on Bonds = $135
11-18 (1) Debit to Cash = $463,500
11-20 (2) Total interest expense = $24,759
11-22 (2) Total discount amortization = $8,844
11-24 (1) Issuance price on bonds = $467,664

CHAPTER 12

Exercises

12-2 (2) Retained earnings = $130,150
12-4 (c) Credit to Dividends Payable = $76,720
12-6 (e) Credit to Dividends Payable = $79,800
12-8 (3) $1.69 per share
12-10 (2) Total dividends paid = $172,485
12-12 (2) $8.43 per share
12-14 Comprehensive income = $12,300
12-16 (c) Debit to Retained Earnings = $750,000
12-18 (2) Retained earnings = $144,000
12-20 Retained earnings, 12/31/06 = $78,000

Problems

12-2 (2) Total contributed capital = $1,802,200
12-4 (2) Total stockholders' equity = $398,175
12-6 (3) Total preferred stock dividends = $64,000
12-8 (1) (a) Dividend payout ratio = 0.40

12-10 (1) (c) $9,000
12-12 (2) Total contributed capital = $791,500
12-14 (2) Total stockholders' equity = $395,800
12-16 (3) Decrease = $37.6 million
12-18 (2) Total dividends = $170,000
12-20 (2) Total contributed capital = $196,200

CHAPTER 13

Exercises

13-2 12/31 Credit to Unrealized Gain on Trading Securities—Income = $1,560
13-4 12/31/06 Debit to Unrealized Increase/Decrease in Value of Available-for-Sale Securities—Equity = $27,500
13-6 Debit to Investment in Trading Securities = $20,500
13-8 Debit to Market Adjustment—Available-for-Sale Securities = $100
13-10 Credit to Cash = $35,620
13-12 (2) Total present value = $113,592
13-14 (1) 12/31 Debit to Bond Interest Receivable = $1,500
13-16 Total amount of amortization = $3,285
13-18 (2) Credit to Dividend Revenue = $3,000
13-20 (1) Minority interest = $375

Problems

13-2 (1) Unrealized gain/loss for 2005 = $207,000 gain
13-4 8/9 Debit to Realized Loss on Sale of Trading Securities = $28,000
13-6 12/31/06 Credit to Market Adjustment—Available-for-Sale Securities = $1,680
13-8 (3) Debit to Realized Loss on Sale of Available-for-Sale Securities = $3,000
13-10 (2) 12/31 Credit to Market Adjustment—Available-for-Sale Securities = $15,000
13-12 (1) 10/1/06 Credit to Investment in Held-to-Maturity Securities = $109.88
13-14 (2) Total interest revenue = $10,123
13-16 (2) 12/31/06 Credit to Investment in Equity Method Securities to record dividends from Essem = $15,000
13-18 (1) (a) 12/1/05 Credit to Dividend Revenue = $8,000
13-20 (2) Balance sheet—Investment in equity method securities = $645,450

CHAPTER 14

Exercises

14-2 N/A
14-4 (1) (d) Credit to Interest Revenue = $1,500
14-6 (1) Cash collected from customers = $223,000
14-8 Net cash flows provided by operating activities = $59,150
14-10 Net cash flows provided by operating activities = $161,600
14-12 Net cash flows provided by operating activities = $241,800
14-14 Net cash flows provided by operating activities = $116,000
14-16 Net cash flows used in investing activities = ($60,000)
14-18 N/A

Problems

14-2 (2) Net increase in cash = $22,300
14-4 (1) Net cash flows provided by operating activities = $13,000
14-6 (1) Net cash flows from operations = $24,540
14-8 Net income = $95,000
14-10 (1) Cash from operating activities = $707
14-12 (1) Cash paid for taxes = $8,400

CHAPTER 15

Exercises

15-2 N/A
15-4 N/A
15-6 N/A
15-8 N/A
15-10 200 baby chairs
15-12 (1) 113,696 gallons (rounded up)
15-14 (1) Variable costs = $11.80 per bat
15-16 (1) Segment profit for RX-5 = $18,840
15-18 (1) Segment profit = $4,350,000

CHAPTER 16

Exercises

16-2 (1) $2,000 per boat
16-4 (2) $2.50 per unit
16-6 (1) Total variable costs = $22,500 at 750,000 copies
16-8 (1) Profit = $17
16-10 (1) Contribution margin = $360,000
16-12 (1) (b) 15,000 units
16-14 (3) Approximate answers (based on graph) fixed costs $15,000; variable costs $12,000; profits $3,000
16-16 N/A
16-18 (2) Profit = $267,000
16-20 (1) Variable cost per unit = $1.39
16-22 (1) Break-even point in units = 20,000

Problems

16-2 (1) Variable cost = $4 per unit
16-4 (1) Profit = $36,900
16-6 (3) 7,560 units
16-8 (1) Contribution margin ratio = 25%
16-10 (1) (e) Total variable costs per unit = $12.50
16-12 (2) Break-even sales = $93,771
16-14 (1) Profit = $310,000
16-16 Fixed cost = $70,966.36
16-18 (1) Break-even point in sales dollars = $432,000

CHAPTER 17

Exercises

17-2 (1) Predetermined manufacturing overhead rate = $5
17-4 (1) (c) Predetermined overhead rate = $1.30/hr for 2005 and $1.29/hr for 2006
17-6 N/A
17-8 (2) Overhead is underapplied by $2,750
17-10 (2) Total manufacturing overhead in Job #402X = $5,654
17-12 (1) Total manufacturing costs = $193,000
17-14 (1) Overhead rate = $81.82 per direct labor hour
17-16 (1) (b) 2005: $3,000 per moving job; 2006: = $3,871 per moving job (rounded)
17-18 (1) Overhead rate = $41.33 per consulting hour
17-20 (1) Equivalent units of production: 610 for materials costs; 582 for conversion costs

Problems

17-2 N/A
17-4 (1) Predetermined overhead rate = $4 per direct labor hour
17-6 (2) Manufacturing overhead charged to Job #29 = $7,191
17-8 (1) (c) Total cost per chair = $190.10
17-10 Total manufacturing costs = $594,500
17-12 (1) (b) Cost of goods manufactured = $700,000
17-14 N/A

17-16 N/A

17-18 (3) Total costs transferred out = $108,760

17-20 Cost of ending work-in-process = $19,180

CHAPTER 18

Exercises

18-2 (1) Present value = $293,372 (rounded)

18-4 Unadjusted rate of return = 22.5%

18-6 Net present value of fire safety expert = $86,024 (rounded)

18-8 Cost of capital = 16.7%

18-10 (1) Present value of future cash inflow (20 years) = $599,189 (rounded)

18-12 N/A

18-14 N/A

18-16 Investment A's Profitability index = 1.05

Problems

18-2 Net present value = $12,060 (rounded)

18-4 (1) Internal rate of return = 10.55% (rounded)

18-6 Internal rate of return is approximately 18%

18-8 Net present value of Alternative A (Buy) = $(35,102) (rounded)

18-10 (1) Net present value to rent = $308,174 (rounded)

18-12 (2) Net present value = $380

18-14 (1) Net present value and profitability index of Project A: $4,000 and 1.20

18-16 (1) Payback period = 5.2 years

18-18 (1) Net present value at 12% cost of capital = $(7,523)

CHAPTER 19

Exercises

19-2 (1) Salary available for savings = $551

19-4 First quarter budgeted production: CD player = 149; MP3 player = 103

19-6 Total cost of materials used = $15,050

19-8 Total direct labor cost in February = $4,120

19-10 Q1 payments for production overhead = $4,300

19-12 (2) Total revenue = $313,200

19-14 Required financing = $10,430

19-16 Net income = $110,550

19-18 Net increase in cash = $440

19-20 (2) Budgeted wage expense = $169,650

Problems

19-2 (2) 34 months (rounded)

19-4 (2) Third Quarter Collections = $172,500

19-6 Total direct materials purchase = $4,028

19-8 (1) Chocolate almond bars total unit cost = $15.83

19-10 (4) Total MOH costs = $5,577

19-12 (1) Total revenue = $1,655,900

19-14 December excess cash = $87,000

19-16 (2) Total assets = $3,900,000

19-18 Net cash provided by operating activities = $82,300

19-20 (1) Expected annual income for 20 enrollees = $19,500

CHAPTER 20

Exercises

20-2 (1) Materials price variance = $250 U

20-4 N/A

20-6 (1) Materials quantity variance = $12,500 U

20-8 (2) Labor rate variance = $5,760 U

20-10 (1) Labor efficiency variance = $81,250 U

20-12 (d) Standard labor cost per hour = $4.20

20-14 (1) North segment margin = $10,500

20-16 (2) Shampoo industry volume variance = $4,800 U

20-18 (f) 25%

20-20 (1) Residual income of new investment = $2,000

20-22 (2) Volume variance = $90,000 U

Problems

20-2 (1) (c) Labor rate variance = $125 F

20-4 (e) $400 F

20-6 (1) Material B quantity variance = $65 U

20-8 (2) Pounds of material actually used = 11,200 lbs.

20-10 (1) Total net loss = $(122,500)

20-12 (2) Individuals market share variance = $8,625 U

20-14 (1) Electrical division ROI = 22.5%

20-16 (2) Total residual income with the new investment = $95,000

20-18 (p) $12,667

20-20 (2) Total ROI with the new investment = 15.8%

20-22 (1) June variable overhead efficiency variance = $3,300 F

20-24 (1) (a) Variable overhead spending variance = $1,000 F

CHAPTER 21

Exercises

21-2 (1) Inventory turnover = 2.44
21-4 N/A
21-6 (1) Penny's PPP = 52.6%
21-8 N/A
21-10 Annual financial holding costs = $7.80 per unit per year
21-12 Reorder point = 249 tires
21-14 (1) Reorder point = 2,500 boxes

Problems

21-2 Ride EZ net operation profit = $29,135
21-4 (2) Profitability percentage = 74.3%
21-6 (1) Division L economic profit = $387,900

CHAPTER 22

Exercises

22-2 N/A
22-4 (1) Product B gross margin = $(70,000)
22-6 (1) Standard gross margin = $180,000
22-8 (1) Product Z gross margin = $50,000
22-10 N/A
22-12 High Quality: Total expected cost of quality = $175,225
22-14 Total external failure quality loss = $15,700

Problems

22-2 (1) Agriculture gross margin = $150,000
22-4 (2) Gross margin = $(37,500)
22-6 (4) Total manufacturing overhead costs allocated to 70 hp engines = $111,962
22-8 (3) Product 1 gross margin percent = 24.2%
22-10 (3) Total manufacturing overhead costs allocated to Building Pipe = $227,040
22-12 (1) Total external failure quality loss = $21,600

CHAPTER 23

Exercises

23-2 (1) Total relevant costs of the new machine = $465,000
23-4 (1) Total variable costs = $34
23-6 (1) Cost difference between making or buying = $270,000
23-8 Expected benefit of Alternative 2 = $342,000
23-10 (1) Loss of S is processed further = $(10,000)
23-12 Product line contribution = $180,000
23-14 (2) Maximum production of Dynamite = 18,000 units
23-16 (2) Rudyard should produce 10 engines per month

Problems

23-2 (3) The total cost to buy is $1,600 lower than the total cost to make
23-4 (2) Total relevant costs to keep the internal legal department = $565,000
23-6 (1) Advantage of further processing S1 = $80,000
23-8 (2) Total net income without Product Z = $4,000
23-10 Contribution margin per direct labor hour for 24-inch screens = $2.40 per hour
23-12 Hours spent to produce Super Dunks = 500
23-14 Markup = $15.00

CHAPTER 24
Not Applicable

a

j